THE NEW GROVE
DICTIONARY OF MUSIC AND MUSICIANS®

Volume One

The New GROVE Dictionary

of Music and Musicians®

EDITED BY

Stanley Sadie

1

A to Bacilly

GROVE

MACMILLAN PUBLISHERS LIMITED, LONDON
GROVE'S DICTIONARIES OF MUSIC INC., NEW YORK, NY
MACMILLAN PUBLISHERS (CHINA) LIMITED, HONG KONG

© Macmillan Publishers Limited 1980

First Edition of *A Dictionary of Music and Musicians*, planned and edited by SIR GEORGE GROVE, DCL, in
four volumes, with an Appendix edited by J. A. Fuller Maitland, and an Index by Mrs Edmond
Wodehouse, 1878, 1880, 1883, 1890.
Reprinted 1890, 1900

Second Edition, edited by J. A. FULLER MAITLAND, in five volumes, 1904–10

Third Edition, edited by H. C. COLLES, in five volumes, 1927

Fourth Edition, edited by H. C. COLLES, in five volumes, with Supplementary Volume, 1940

Fifth Edition, edited by ERIC BLOM, in nine volumes, 1954; with Supplementary Volume, 1961
Reprinted 1961, 1973, 1975

American Supplement, edited by WALDO SELDEN PRATT, in one volume, 1920
Reprinted with new material, 1928; many later reprints

The New Grove Dictionary of Music and Musicians,®
edited by STANLEY SADIE, in twenty volumes, 1980

The New Grove and *The New Grove Dictionary of Music and Musicians* are registered trademarks
in the United States of Macmillan Publishers Limited, London.

Macmillan Publishers Limited, London and its associated companies are the proprietors of the trademarks
Grove's, *The New Grove*, and *The New Grove Dictionary of Music and Musicians* throughout the world.

First published 1980 in hardback edition.
Reprinted with minor corrections, 1981, 1984, 1985, 1986, 1987, 1988, 1989, 1990, 1991, 1992, 1993, 1994, 1995.
Reprinted 1995 in paperback edition.

Published by Macmillan Publishers Limited, London. Both editions are distributed outside the United
Kingdom and Europe by Macmillan Publishers (China) Limited, Hong Kong, a member of the Macmillan
Publishers Group, and by its appointed agents. In the United States of America and Canada, Macmillan
Publishers (China) Limited, Hong Kong have appointed Grove's Dictionaries of Music Inc., New York,
NY, as sole distributor.

Text keyboarded, corrected, page-made-up and filmset by
Richard Clay (The Chaucer Press) Ltd, Bungay, Suffolk, England

Illustrations originated by Fletcher & Son Ltd, Norwich, England

Music examples processed by Halstan & Co. Ltd, Amersham, England

Printed and bound in the United States of America by R. R. Donnelley & Co., Crawfordsville, Indiana

British Library Cataloguing in Publication Data

The New Grove dictionary of music and
musicians.®
 1. Music-Directories
 2. Sadie, Stanley
780'.3 ML100

ISBN 0–333–23111–2 (hardback)
ISBN 1–56159–174–2 (paperback)

Library of Congress Cataloging in Publication Data
Main entry under title:

The New Grove dictionary of music and musicians.®
Includes bibliographies.
1. Music-Dictionaries.
2. Music-Bio-bibiography.
I. Grove, George, Sir, 1820–1900.
II. Sadie, Stanley.
ML100.N48 780'.3   79-26207

ISBN 0–333–23111–2 (hardback)
ISBN 0–56159–174–2 (paperback)

Contents

PREFACE   vii

INTRODUCTION   xi

ACKNOWLEDGMENTS   xxi

PREFACE TO THE FIRST EDITION   xxvii

GENERAL ABBREVIATIONS   xxix

BIBLIOGRAPHICAL ABBREVIATIONS   xxxiii

LIBRARY SIGLA   xxxvi

A NOTE ON THE USE OF THE DICTIONARY   liv

THE DICTIONARY, VOLUME ONE:

A – Bacilly   1

ILLUSTRATION ACKNOWLEDGMENTS   888

Preface

THE 'NEW' GROVE. When, in 1969, my colleagues and I began to lay our plans, we thought of the work we were preparing as the sixth edition of the dictionary first prepared by Sir George Grove in the 1870s and 1880s. As time and work went on, however, it became clear that we were producing not a new edition but a new dictionary. In his Preface to the fifth edition, my eminent predecessor Eric Blom wrote of his hopes that it would 'continue showing the personality of its founder', and added that 'Much of the old "Grove" . . . remains'. I would echo his hopes. But little of the old dictionary can now stand. The world – certainly the world of musicology – has changed more, and more fundamentally, in the 25 years that separate *Grove 5* from the new dictionary than it did in the 75 years from 1879 (when the first complete volume of the first edition appeared) to 1954. A very much smaller proportion of material – under three per cent – has been retained from earlier editions than was retained in any preceding edition; any such material has been re-edited and, where appropriate, equipped with new bibliographies and work-lists.

We have tried to ensure that something of the fine humane traditions of the earlier editions of *Grove* are to be seen in our pages. Intelligent critical and evaluative writing still have a place in musical lexicography, especially in a work designed to serve a wide range of users. But in many ways this dictionary is different in kind from earlier editions. It belongs to an era in which musicological studies have greatly developed, not only in Europe but particularly in the United States and other countries where European traditions have taken root, as well as in numerous 'third world' countries, eager to preserve and study their own musical heritage. It belongs to an era that sets wider boundaries to music as a human activity, and even within the traditional boundaries has seen the development of new attitudes, increasingly scientific and objective in character, to its study – as is reflected in the existence and the nature of such reference works as *MGG* (*Die Musik in Geschichte und Gegenwart*) and *RISM* (*Répertoire international des sources musicales*; *International Inventory of Musical Sources*). The effects of this will be seen not only in the dictionary's extent, and the space it devotes to substantial bibliographies and informative work-lists, but also in its approach to such topics as the sources of early music and their evaluation, the bibliography of music, the significance of social forces and their bearing on tradition and its nature, and in general in the wider spread of cultures it attempts to embrace in its discussion of many aspects of the art and the materials of music. The net of contributors has been cast much more widely in the pursuit of breadth, authority and excellence: whereas in the fifth edition British contributors outnumbered others by more than five to two, here they make up about one fifth of the total number.

All this, and much more, was bound to affect the shape, the character and the philosophy of the dictionary. To call it the sixth edition of *Grove's Dictionary* would have been misleading, and – although it may cause problems for future editors – 'The New Grove' seemed to be the most accurate title it could bear.

CONTENTS, SCOPE. To quote Eric Blom again: 'Grove aims at being encyclopedic and universal'. *The New Grove*, one might say, is even more universal than its predecessors, for the musical universe has expanded. It seeks to discuss everything that can be reckoned to bear on music in history and on present-day musical life.

Although its changes are principally in other areas, the dictionary's first task, traditionally, is to treat of the people who have written music; more than half the entries are on composers, from ancient and even mythological times to the present. The criteria for the inclusion of a composer vary from period to period. For example, virtually every known medieval composer is entered; and a composer of the Renaissance will have an entry if a set of his works was published, if five or more of his works survive in printed anthologies or a substantial number in manuscript, or if he is known by a smaller number of works but in addition useful biographical information is available about him. *Grove* cannot include every known composer of the past; it is a critically organized repository of historically significant information, not a directory (that role is served by other kinds of reference work). In more recent times, the criteria have necessarily to be more closely linked with critical judgment. Previous editions of *Grove* have tended to emphasize the 19th century, or, to put it more exactly, have tended to retain the bias towards the 19th century that is implicit in the updating of a dictionary dating from that era. Now, in the late 20th century, the 19th must take its place as part of musical history, with consequently different emphases, rather than appear as part of the recent past on which the dust has still to settle. A dictionary that runs to many successive editions, even of increasing size, cannot be cumulative; each generation must reassess it according to its own particular requirements. Specialists working on 19th-century music can always consult earlier editions, which anyway are closer to their sources.

Other persons entered in the dictionary fall into five broad categories. First, performers: from the past, those who sang or played in the first (or important early) performances of major works, those who had particular influence on composers or styles of composition, and those whose names appear frequently in contemporary source material; from the present, those of outstanding attainment – again I should stress that *Grove* is not a directory and that entries are accorded only to those of international reputation or of specially important national achievement. This category includes leading and influential figures in the worlds of jazz and popular music. A second category consists of scholars, writers on music, theorists and administrators; these are included according to the depth and the influence of their work. A third category comprises people eminent in other arts whose work was in some way important to music and musicians. Clearly librettists merit entry in a substantial musical dictionary; so, too, do authors who did not write directly for musical setting but whose works often inspired musicians and affected the nature of their works. Entries will also be found on certain dancers, designers, theatre producers (directors), men of letters, philosophers, scientists and others whose contributions entitle them to a place in a work dealing with musical history. Fourth, patrons (sometimes families of patrons) are entered where they exercised a significant influence on musical composition or performance. Fifth, people concerned in the business of music – in its printing and its publishing, and in the making of musical instruments – are entered, according to their importance; such entries are often on firms rather than families or individuals.

In line with the traditions of the dictionary, the terminology of music is fully treated. Foreign-language words in occasional use and carrying only their literal dictionary meaning are not generally included. There are comprehensive historical entries on musical genres and forms. Early liturgies, Eastern and Western, are discussed. The instruments of music are extensively treated. Entries will be found on many non-Western instruments, especially those of considerable historical or organological importance, or of wide cultural distribution; those specific to particular cultures may be discussed primarily in the entry on the culture itself (see also Introduction, §10, below). There are entries on many cities and towns with significant musical traditions, in Europe, America and other parts of the world. Numerous institutions – orchestras, choirs, societies, colleges etc – have individual entries, but those within cities and towns that are entered in the dictionary in their own right are normally discussed within the appropriate city entry (indicated by a cross-reference if necessary) since they represent a part of that city's musical life.

There are substantial articles on many topics new to *Grove*, ranging widely – for example, Aesthetics, Analysis, Computers, Electronic music, Ethnomusicology, Historiography, Iconography, Performing Practice, Popular music, Psychology, Sociology and Theory; while others on more traditional topics (like Counterpoint, Expression, Harmony, Melody, Mode and Musicology) are treated much more broadly, or 'conceptually', than hitherto, with a wider cultural perspective. There are extensive articles on acoustical topics. The entries on bibliographical and reference material – for example Dictionaries and Encyclopedias, Editions, Libraries and Periodicals – are much more comprehensive than in earlier editions and are supported by extensive lists.

The treatment of bibliographies is discussed in the Introduction, §8, but one particular departure should be mentioned here: the inclusion of a series of extended bibliographies on early music. Some of these are arranged by country (England, France, Germany, Italy, Netherlands, and Spain and Portugal), others by medium or genre (Organum and Discant, Keyboard music etc). These are additional to the bibliographies attached to individual articles on such topics. Another major departure in the coverage of early music is represented by the group of articles on sources, of which that on Sources, MS is particularly extensive in its descriptive coverage of Western manuscript source material before 1600.

The biggest departure, however, lies in the dictionary's treatment of non-Western and folk music, far more extensive and more methodical than anything of the kind attempted before. There are entries on the music of virtually every country in the world. So that this material be readily accessible, it is organized for the most part within entries under the names of individual countries. Modern political boundaries do not, of course, always correspond to cultural ones; articles thus often have to be linked by cross-reference, and in some significant cases individual cultural groups are separately treated (again, such entries are indicated by cross-references in the entries on the countries concerned). The treatment of individual national folk music traditions under the collective rubric 'Folk music', preferred in *Grove 5*, has been abandoned. Many entries on countries are however divided between 'art music' and 'folk music'. In some cases such division is admittedly simplistic, and occasionally the content of these sections may overlap; nonetheless, this treatment is the most practicable one, both from the user's point of view, to facilitate reference, and from an editorial or organizational one. Besides the entries on countries' folk music traditions, there is a series of 'overview' entries designed to give a broader picture of the musical traditions of entire continental areas under such headings as Africa, East Asia, Europe and Latin America. Terms used in articles on non-Western and folk music are indexed in Appendix A, a substantial new feature of the dictionary (see Introduction, §10).

Grove, by long tradition, is the standard multi-volume musical reference work for the English-speaking world. It is a fully international dictionary. But it is proper if in some respects it reflects the tastes and the preferences of the English-speaking countries, for example by admitting marginal figures from those countries who might have been excluded had they come from elsewhere. The dictionary must serve the needs of the public by which it will primarily be used. Particular efforts have however been made to do justice to the composers and other musicians of certain areas often neglected in *Grove* and in other large-scale reference works of the past, notably the smaller countries of eastern Europe, Spain and Portugal, and Latin America.

The dictionary is written by almost 2500 people, and it no doubt embodies many contradictions. Contradictions on matters of interpretation are not of course unwelcome; it is part of a dictionary's role to represent a variety of standpoints. Contradictions of fact, however, are anathema. Every effort has been made to compare articles and, where discrepancies have been found, to establish which statements are true and which false. This has involved much checking by our editorial staff of primary sources, and prolific correspondence between the editorial office and contributors. The results have not always been conclusive. (For example, the contributors concerned are not in full agreement that the year in which Veracini first played in front of Tartini is the same as the year in which Tartini first heard Veracini; in both entries attention is drawn to the discrepancy of opinion.) Users of the dictionary are asked to write to the editorial office, c/o Macmillan, Little Essex Street, London WC2R 3LF, to notify us of errors or omissions so that they may be recorded and set right in the future.

The ensuing introduction is designed to explicate the editorial procedures of the dictionary for the benefit of the reader.

STANLEY SADIE
London, 1979

Introduction

1. Alphabetization systems. 2. Usages. 3. Authors. 4. Article headings. 5. Article structure. 6. Cross-references. 7. Transliteration. 8. Bibliographies. 9. Work-lists etc. 10. Appendixes.

1. ALPHABETIZATION SYSTEMS. In entry headings – fully explained in §4 below – of more than one word, the words are alphabetized as if continuous, ignoring spaces, hyphens, apostrophes, accents, modifications and diacritical marks; German *ä, ö* and *ü* are read as *a, o* and *u*, not as *ae, oe* and *ue*. These rules apply up to the first mark of punctuation, then again thereafter if that mark is a comma; where the entire headings are identical but for an accent or the like, the unaccented word is placed first. Parenthesized letters and words, and square-bracketed matter, are ignored in alphabetization. Some of these points are illustrated by the following (partly hypothetical) sequence of headings:

Alpaerts, Flor	**Alsted, (Carl) Wilhelm**
Alpaerts [Allpaerts], Jef	**Alt, in**
Alphorn	**Alta (i)**
Al-Rāzī, Abu	**Alta (ii)**
Al-Rāzī, Fakhr al-Du	**Altacuria**
Al rovescio	**Altacuria(-Benedictus), Carolus**
Alsbach	**Altacuria, Johannes**
Al segno	**Altargesang**
Al-Shīrazī	**Altenburg, Johann Ernst**
Al'shvang, Arnol'd Alexandrovich	**Ältenburg, Karl**
Alsina, Carlos Roqué	**Altenburg, Michael**
Alsted, Johann Heinrich	**Ältenburg, Michael**

All list material arranged alphabetically in the dictionary follows these principles. Normally the definite or indefinite article is included in the alphabetization.

As a very general principle, we have tried to place each entry where the majority of users of the dictionary will expect to find it. Common sense and established usage are important factors.

Medieval names of the form 'A de B' are normally entered under the given name (A) rather than the name of the locality (B). 'St' is alphabetized as 'Saint', and the prefixes 'Mac', 'Mc' and 'M'' as 'Mac'. Unless there are reasons that dictate otherwise, names incorporating prefixes in the Romance languages are alphabetized under the prefix when it includes the definite article: thus, for French names, those beginning 'L'', 'La' and 'Le' are placed under L and 'Du' under D, but those beginning 'De' are placed under the following word (as are many beginning 'D'', though here established usage demands that some be under D). The reader of the dictionary who looks in the wrong place will be led to the right one by a cross-reference.

2. USAGES. In the editing of this dictionary every effort has been made towards consistency in presentation. Usages in such matters as italicization and capitaliza-

tion will become evident (as far as that is necessary) to readers of the dictionary and do not need explanation here. It should however be said that orthography in general follows British practices, except that wherever possible original sources are followed, for example for titles and quoted matter. Obsolete and foreign letter-forms are normally replaced by their modern equivalents, and usage is standardized for such terms as Kapellmeister (Capell Meister etc), Kantor (Cantor), *cappella* (*capella*) and the like. Capital letters are used in the traditional way in English-language titles, and also for words applied in a specialized sense (e.g. 'Classical' for Viennese music of the Haydn–Mozart–Beethoven era); their use is kept to a minimum in languages other than English. The first objective, here and elsewhere, is clarity.

Abbreviations are confined to those listed on pp.xxix–xxxv (pp.vii–xiii in subsequent volumes).

Some of the particular editorial usages in the dictionary are explained below:

Anglo-American vocabulary. In its authorship and its editing, this dictionary is as much American as British. But its traditions are primarily British, and it accordingly preserves British terminological usage. This affects note names, where semibreves, minims, crotchets and quavers are preferred to whole-, half-, quarter- and eighth-notes etc; note is preferred to tone (except in certain acoustical and non-Western contexts); auxiliary note to neighbour (or neighbor) tone; conjunct to stepwise; bar to measure; part-writing to voice-leading; etc. (Cross-references will be found directing the reader to the British equivalent of any American term that might be expected to have its own entry.) Similarly, the principal violinist in an orchestra is referred to as the leader rather than the concertmaster, and to 'lead' an orchestra means to sit at the first violin desk, not to conduct or direct it. Readers should note that the terms 'professor' and 'faculty' have different meanings in British usage and American.

The Bible. The numbering of psalms follows the Revised Standard Version unless otherwise indicated.

Dates. Following lexicographical convention, dates are given in new style, according to the Gregorian calendar, including those for Russia (which changed to new style only in 1917) and other countries that changed in modern times, except that British dates are given according to the Julian calendar up to the change in 1752. Absolute consistency cannot be guaranteed for certain German and Italian 17th-century dates; usage varied and it is sometimes impossible to tell which calendar is applicable. Anyone needing old-style Russian dates should subtract 13 days for the 20th century, 12 for the 19th, 11 for the 18th etc.

Methods of citing dates that are approximate or conjectural are outlined in §4 below. Here it should be mentioned that when a period is expressed in the form '*c*1630–48' the dates 1630 and 1648 are both approximate, whereas the form '*c*1630–1648' means that only the first is.

Pitch notation. The system used is a modified version of Helmholtz's: middle C is c', with octaves above as c'', c''' etc and octaves below as c, C, C', C'' etc. Octaves are reckoned from C upwards. Italic type is used for specific pitches; pitch-classes are given in roman capital letters. (A different method is followed in a small number of specialized, technical articles; in such cases the exceptional usage is explained.)

Place names. These represent a particularly intractable, and sensitive, issue. For present-day cities, the usage of *The Times Atlas of the World* (London, 5/1975, rev. edn. 1977) is followed, except for those cities where there is a traditional and universally applied English name that differs from the local one (e.g. Vienna, Rome, Munich). Where a city's name has changed in the course of history, an attempt has been made to call it by the name current at the time under discussion, identifying it by its modern name on its initial appearance in an entry if that seems to be necessary or helpful (e.g. 'Pressburg [now Bratislava]'); occasionally common sense demands a little flexibility in the application of this rule. In a few cases we have attempted to anticipate history, or at least custom: what was once Cambodia and then the Khmer Republic is referred to as Kampuchea (correct at the time of going to press, though its historical music may correctly be, and is, referred to as 'Cambodian'); and we have used the name Zimbabwe for the country called, during the period of the dictionary's preparation, Rhodesia.

Weights and measures. To conform with international practice, and with the declared policy of the British and United States governments, metric units are used in this dictionary (except of course in quoted matter). Metricization has in the event proceeded more slowly than was planned, more slowly even than the preparation of the dictionary; and we can only ask the indulgence of readers who are disconcerted to read that (say) Cambridge is 90 km from London.

3. AUTHORS. The names of authors appear, in the form chosen by authors themselves, beneath the article to which they apply. Where authorship is joint or multiple, this is indicated, showing (by reference to the numbered sections of the article) which author is responsible for which sections. Where two or more names appear, separated only by a comma, the entire authorship is joint, or the contributions are fused to a degree where it would be impractical to show how responsibility was divided.

Unsigned articles are of two main kinds: those that are too short for acknowledgment to be appropriate, and those that are contributed by a group of editors working collectively. In a few cases an article is left unsigned because the contributor, for reasons connected with political conditions in his own country, cannot appear as author of material published in the West. Signatures of the form

JOHN SMITH/MARY BROWN

indicate that an article originally by John Smith (normally it will be an article from *Grove 5*) has been revised and updated by Mary Brown;

JOHN SMITH/R

signifies editorial revision and updating. A signature of the form

JOHN SMITH (with MARY BROWN)

means that John Smith is the principal author but Mary Brown contributed material that the author or the editors of the dictionary felt was appropriate for acknowledgment.

4. ARTICLE HEADINGS. Articles on persons begin with their name and place and date of birth and death, followed by a statement of nationality and description, thus:

Smith, John (*b* London, 1 Jan 1800; *d* Manchester, 31 Dec 1870). English composer.

Where dates of baptism (but not birth) or burial (but not death) are known, they are given and specified as such. If the year but not the month or day of birth is known, the parenthesis would appear:

(*b* London, 1800; *d* Manchester, 31 Dec 1870).

According to the state of knowledge, the date of birth could be given with less precision, for example, '1800–05', '*c*1800' (around that year), or '?1800' (to imply conjecture). The question mark is placed close to the statement it qualifies; where it is spaced, it qualifies the series of statements that follows:

> (*b* ?London, 1 Jan 1800 . . .) – born conjecturally in London
> (*b* London, ?Jan 1800 . . .) – born London in 1800, conjecturally January
> (*b* London, ?1800 . . .) – born London, conjecturally 1800
> (*b* ? London, 1800 . . .) – born conjecturally in London, conjecturally in 1800
> (*b* London, 1 Jan ?1800 . . .) – born London, on 1 January, conjecturally 1800
> (*b* London, 1 ?Jan 1800 . . .) – born London, on the first day of a month, conjecturally January, in 1800.

Where a birthdate cannot be conjectured, *fl* (*floruit* – 'he flourished') dates may be given, e.g. '*fl* 1825', '*fl* 1820–35', '*fl* early 19th century' etc. Where nothing is known, nothing is stated. For example,

> (*d* Manchester, 31 Dec 1870)

means that nothing is known of the subject's birth. Any other forms used in such contexts are self-explanatory.

The opening statement gives the subject's nationality as it might be most generally and fairly understood. It may not take account of naturalization, or birth, or ancestry. One cannot very well say 'American conductor of German birth and Hungarian descent': if the subject is normally reckoned as American he will be so described; his American domicile or naturalization and his Hungarian descent will be referred to in the text, and his German birth will be clear from the initial parenthesis. Sometimes, where a double affiliation seems of especial importance, it will be noted: 'American conductor of German birth', or 'German conductor, naturalized American'. The word or words of description outline the subject's musical significance – essentially the reason for his being entered in the dictionary. A composer who engages in other activities will not normally be described as (for example) 'composer, conductor, writer on music, teacher and pianist'.

Parentheses and brackets in name headings have specific meanings:

> **Smith, John (Robert)** – full name 'John Robert Smith'; 'Robert' not normally used
> **Smith, John R(obert)** – full name 'John Robert Smith', normally used in the form 'John R. Smith'
> **Smith** [Smythe], **John** – the name 'Smith' sometimes takes the form 'Smythe'
> **Smith, John** [Johannes] – the name 'John' sometimes takes the form 'Johannes' (certain obvious alternatives, such as the German Carl/Karl, may not be noted)
> **Smith, John** [Schmidt, Johann] – the entire name sometimes takes the form 'Johann Schmidt'
> **Smith, John** [Brown, Thomas] – 'John Smith' is the pseudonym under which Thomas Brown is generally known; or John Smith used the pseudonym Thomas Brown (this will be made clear in the text)
> **Smith, Buster** [John] – 'Buster Smith' is the name under which John Smith is generally known
> **Smith** [née Brown], **Mary** – 'Smith' is Mary Brown's married name, under which she is generally known
> **Smith** [Brown], **Mary** – Mary Smith has the married name or pseudonym Brown; or Mary Brown is generally known under the name Smith (this will be made clear in the text).

Names of titled persons are normally shown thus:

> **Smith**, Sir **John**
> **Smith, John,** 5th Earl of Sussex

but

> **Sussex,** 5th Earl of [Smith, John]

would imply that John Smith, 5th Earl of Sussex, was normally referred to by his title, as Earl of Sussex or Lord Sussex.

5. ARTICLE STRUCTURE. The longer article texts in the dictionary are divided into sections for easier reference. The most usual division is into sections numbered with arabic numerals and with headings in large and small capitals (e.g. 1. LIFE, 2. WORKS); this method is used in many entries on composers. Sections of this kind may be subdivided into smaller ones, headed by parenthesized small roman numerals and with headings in italic. Occasionally other forms of subdivision are needed. Where a long entry consists of two or more substantial sections (for example 'Art music' and 'Folk music' in an entry on a country), these sections are numbered with capital roman numerals and the headings are printed in bold italic type. The following illustrates all three levels of the hierarchy, as well as the lists of 'contents' which are designed to guide the reader to the material he is seeking:

Ruritania. Country in southern Europe.

I. Art music. II. Folk music.

I. Art music
1. Up to 1600: (i) The Middle Ages (ii) 1450–1600. 2. 1600–1848.
3. Since 1848.

1. UP TO 1600.
(*i*) *The Middle Ages.* The earliest reports . . .

'Family' articles, indexed under the family surname, are used when three or more members of a family merit entries. Each entered member is numbered, thus:

Smith. English family of composers.
(1) John Smith (*b* . . . [etc]
(2) Robert Smith (*b* . . . [etc]
(3) Mary Smith (*b* . . . [etc].

The relationships between them are defined, where they are known. Entries on family firms, of publishers or instrument makers, are not necessarily numbered. If two people – whether or not members of the same family, and irrespective of whether or not they have individual entries – bear the same name (which for this purpose means the same name as far as the bold-type title is concerned), that name will always be followed by a parenthesized small roman numeral, chronologically determined (e.g. John Smith (ii); he will normally be referred to in this form throughout the dictionary). It will be understood that, for example, John Smith (i) and (ii) could be members of Smith (i) family, John Smith (iii) and (v) members of Smith (ii) family, and John Smith (iv) not a member of a family at all as far as this dictionary is concerned.

In a very few cases – notably that perennial thorn in the lexicographer's side, the Costas – we have for simplicity's sake allowed ourselves to use a family entry format for a group (Costa (ii)) of whose mutual relationships, if any, we have not the slightest idea. So that each one can readily be found, we have also placed a cross-reference under each individual name: a departure from normal procedure, as people entered within a family entry do not have separate bold-type entries of their own.

6. CROSS-REFERENCES. Cross-references in the dictionary are distinguished by the use of small capitals, with a large capital for the initial letter of the entry referred to, for example:

see LA RUE, PIERRE DE.

If the reference is in running prose it will take the form

he was a pupil of PIERRE DE LA RUE.

All cross-references give the title of the article referred to in exactly the wording in which it appears, in bold type (but excluding parenthesized matter), at the head of the entry. The word 'see' is always italicized in a cross-reference to another entry in the dictionary; where it is printed in roman type the reference is to a different part of the same entry or to another publication.

Cross-references are of two basic kinds. First, there are those 'cross-reference' entries that direct the reader to where he can find the entry he is seeking, thus:

De la Rue, Pierre. *See* LA RUE, PIERRE DE.

Such a cross-reference entry may embody a translation:

Clavecin (Fr.). HARPSICHORD.

This last form indicates that 'clavecin' means 'harpsichord', not simply that the 'clavecin' is discussed in the entry 'Harpsichord'. Plain 'see' references are given only where definition is superfluous, for example

Stage design. *See* OPERA, §VIII.

Many short cross-references of this type include, for the benefit of the reader who does not require fuller information (or to distinguish usages of a term), a brief definition, thus:

Academy of Music. New York theatre opened in 1854; *see* NEW YORK, §2.

Many cross-references of these kinds lead to two or more other entries. Simple cross-references have been included in abundance to help the reader who first looks under a different orthography or formulation.

The other type of cross-reference is that within articles. Some will be found at the ends of short articles, or at the ends of sections, directing the reader to another entry where further information relevant to the subject he is reading about may be found; these may, as appropriate, embody such formulae as '*see also*' or 'for a fuller discussion *see*'. Many further cross-references will be found in running text; but none is provided to titles (names, places, genres etc) that would be understood to have *Grove* entries unless there is particular material to which attention needs to be drawn. The intention has been to direct the reader to places where he can, but might not have expected to, find further information on the topic he has looked up. Thus the article 'Opera' does not contain cross-references to the entries on Verdi or Wagner, although those of course contain material relevant to the history of opera; it does however carry cross-references to entries on other related forms (for example 'Ballad opera' and 'Zarzuela') which are separately considered, and to entries on non-Western countries which contain discussion of musico-dramatic genres akin to opera.

Where an illustration, table or music example is relevant to more than one entry, that will be indicated by cross-reference.

7. TRANSLITERATION. The text of the dictionary is printed in roman script, transliterated by systems chosen according to the requirements appropriate to different languages; in some cases an academic transliteration has been followed, permitting re-transliteration into the original, in others a phonetic one. The transliteration system for Cyrillic scripts (including Bulgarian [Bulg.], Serbian [Serb.] and Ukrainian [Ukr.]) is as follows:

Cyrillic	Roman	Cyrillic	Roman	Cyrillic	Roman
а	a	й	y	х	kh; Serb. h
б	b	к	k	ц	ts; Serb. c
в	v	л	l	ч	ch; Serb. č
г	g[1];Ukr. h/g	м	m	ш	sh; Serb. š
д	d	н	n	щ	shch; Bulg. sht
е	e/ye[2]	о	o	ъ	—[4]; Bulg. a
ё	yo/o[3]	п	p	ы	ï
є	ye	р	r	ь	—[4]; Bulg. a
ж	zh; Serb. ž	с	s	э	e
з	z	т	t	ю	yu
і	i	у	u	я	ya
и	i; Ukr. y	ф	f		

[1] in genitive termination, v
[2] ye, after ъ, ь and vowels
[3] o, after ж, ч, ш and щ
[4] medially ', in bibliographical contexts

Bulgarian: ж– a; ѣ– ee/ay; ай (final) – y.
Serbian: ђ– dj; љ– lj; њ– nj; ћ– ć; џ– dž; ј– j.

Common usage, and common sense, demand that certain exceptions be made. Place names such as Moscow and Kiev are given in their standard forms. Prokofiev and (with some reluctance) Tchaikovsky are spelt in their normal Western ways; so are Tcherepnin (the spelling still followed by the family), Koussevitzky (the spelling still followed by the Foundation) and Cui, a name of Western origins. But several popular transliterations that do not originate in English – usually they come from French or German, and are apt for pronunciation in those languages – have been avoided: thus Balanchin, Dyagilev, Glier, Metner, Rakhmaninov, not Balanchine, Diaghilev or Diaghileff, Glière, Medtner, Rachmaninov or Rachmaninoff. The specified exceptions apart, strict transliteration is used in bibliographical contexts, and (for example when a Russian-language item is cited for a non-Russian composer – this applies commonly to music in the other Soviet republics) orthography in a bibliography may often differ from that in the text of the article to which it belongs.

Modified letter forms in roman script (ł, đ etc) are of course used as needed. The special letter forms sometimes used in representing African languages are replaced by their roman equivalents.

In the romanization of ancient Greek, familiar English forms (sometimes latinized ones for proper names) are used where they exist. Different systems are used for ancient Greek and modern, and for ancient Hebrew and modern.

We are indebted for advice on the transliteration of non-Western languages to many individual contributors and to linguistic authorities (notably those at the School of Oriental and African Studies, University of London). Dr V. Nersessian has advised us over Armenian. The systems used for two particularly complex geographical–cultural regions, India and Indonesia, are outlined at the beginnings of the articles under those headings; for the Indonesian system we are indebted to Dr Merle Ricklefs for his help. The system for Burmese is that devised by John Okell (*A Guide to the Romanization of Burmese*, 1971). The new system for Chinese was devised too late for use in the dictionary.

8. BIBLIOGRAPHIES. Most articles in the dictionary are followed by bibliographies, which in general have been supplied by authors. In the fifth edition, these were intended rather as lists for further reading than as acknowledgments of sources;

here however bibliographies normally include studies on which authors have drawn as well as recommended reading. Bibliographies are not, except in a small number of special cases, intended to represent complete lists of the literature on the topic. Writings that are trivial, ephemeral or inaccurate, in particular, are normally excluded; so, unless a particular historiographical interest attaches to it, is work that has been superseded. General histories of music (or of specific periods etc) are not generally cited unless they contain material of special importance on the topic in question.

Bibliographies are chronologically arranged; items are listed in order of first publication (chronologically within categories for a bibliography that is categorized, as most longer ones are). Items published in the same year are listed alphabetically by author, or, for the same author, by title. At the head, however, are listed certain standard works of reference for which abbreviations are used, in alphabetical order of abbreviation. In some longer articles, bibliographies may be situated at the end of each section, according to convenience of use.

The procedures of citation are broadly speaking self-evident, but it may nevertheless be helpful to outline here the main principles (the reader is also referred to the list of bibliographical abbreviations, p.xxxiii in this volume, p.xi in later volumes, and especially its prefatory note). For books that have appeared in several editions, only the first and the most recent are cited, unless there is particular reason to note intermediate editions – for example because one was revised or translated, or one has been photographically reprinted (denoted by *R*). Thus while '1950, 4/1957' would be a common form of citation, '1950, 2/1951/*R*1978, rev. 3/1955, 4/1958' would also be possible, to signify that the second edition was reprinted and the third substantially revised. English translations are normally noted; for items in less familiar languages, translations into other western European languages may also be listed. Title-page breaks or punctuation are represented by a colon. Publication places are normally given only for first publication. In certain specialized bibliographical contexts publishers are named, in the form 'London: Smith, 1950'. Multi-volume books are not noted as such, but (unless they are through-paginated) page references to them include the volume number, in lower-case roman numerals. Lower-case roman numerals, throughout the dictionary, denote volume numbers, as for periodicals: 'xiv (1950), 123' indicates that the cited article begins on page 123 of volume xiv, published in 1950. Periodicals reckoned by issue rather than volume are expressed in arabic numerals. For periodicals that are not through-paginated by volume, the issue number within the volume is indicated after an oblique stroke (e.g. xiv/3). For long articles, of 30 or more pages, a terminal page number is given. Dissertations, doctoral or otherwise, are noted as 'diss.' and the institution is named, with the submission date. If the dissertation is published, the citation may refer only to the published volume; in a full citation, the place and date of publication follow, thus: '(diss., U. of Vienna, 1927; Leipzig, 1930)'.

Lists of writings, found in entries on scholars, critics etc, are organized according to the same principles. Such lists are as a rule selective, the selection being designed to be representative and to show the range and importance of the subject's work. Unpublished writings, apart from dissertations, are included only if of special significance (where they are, a location is named); the same applies to non-musical writings. Items listed as 'ed.:' are edited by the subject (where they include articles by him, these may be noted as '[incl. . . .]'); items listed as 'ed. J. Smith:' represent works by the subject edited, usually posthumously, by J. Smith. The 'Editions' section in articles of this kind normally includes only scholarly or historically important editions of music. Fuller lists of the subject's writings, as well as autobiographical works and Festschriften devoted to him, may be noted in the bibliography.

Contributors were asked, late in 1976, to send material to supplement bibliographies, and to continue sending such material, for filing towards future editions if it could not be used in the present one. Some contributors did so; others left updating to be done by the editorial staff, who continued during the late stages of the dictionary's preparation to add citations of important new bibliography items. In some cases this may have resulted in an article text's apparently taking no account of facts or opinions cited in the attached bibliography; but it was nevertheless felt that it would be useful to draw readers' attention to significant recent literature.

9. WORK-LISTS. Work-lists are designed not only to show a composer's output (or, for a lesser composer, to outline it), but also to serve as a starting-point for its study. While it would be beyond the scope of a general musical dictionary to be a comprehensive directory of sources – a function served by *RISM* for a large part of the repertory – an attempt has been made to include basic publication information and, in the case of manuscript material, a location. This publication information consists, for earlier music, of place and date of first publication (later printings are referred to only if of particular significance), or, for more recent music, the name of a composer's principal publishers. Any parenthesized date in a work-list is a date of publication. Locations of manuscript material are normally given by means of a *RISM* library sigillum (those used in the dictionary are listed on pp.xxxvi–lii in this volume, pp.xiv–xxx in other volumes; they are always printed in italics); shelf and even folio numbers may be given in cases of special difficulty. National sigla stand until contradicted: thus in a list '*F-Pn, V*; *I-Bc*' the *V* stands for *F-V*. This applies from item to item; a reader seeing an isolated library sigillum should look back to discover the national sigillum that applies. Anthologies listed in *RISM* B/I/1 (*Recueils imprimés*) are referred to by the numbering system used there (e.g. 1615[17]; square brackets in *RISM* are not included). Manuscript locations are not generally supplied when material is published, nor when such information is given in a good library edition (which will be cited; see below) or in an established catalogue. Sometimes only sources supplementary to those given elsewhere are named. Manuscript sources are listed in alphabetical order of national sigla, and within them of library sigla; citations are not evaluative unless stated.

Work-lists are normally categorized, by genre, function or medium, and items are listed chronologically within categories. Where dates are not known, items are listed alphabetically by title. Numbers from established listings are given. Title-page wording is normally used, with capitalization following the general rules of the dictionary; roman numerals may be used to reproduce original wording, but otherwise arabic numerals are preferred, except where their contiguity to opus numbers might cause confusion. (Thus '6 Sonatas', '6 sonates', 'VI sonate', 'op.2 Six Sonatas' etc represent publications under those titles; '6 sonatas' represents a collective listing.) Short titles only are given, with sufficient information for unambiguous identification. For a vocal work, a parenthesized name denotes the text author (his initial is given only on his first appearance in each list, unless its omission introduces an ambiguity); for dramatic works, a parenthesized arabic numeral following the title denotes the number of acts. Where a key is named, it precedes the details of instrumentation; capital letters denote major keys, lower-case minor. Alternative instrumentation is denoted by an oblique stroke (/) or, in complex cases, by an oblique stroke and parentheses: 'Qt, A (pf, fl/ob, cl, bn)/(pf, str trio)'. For voices, symbols separated by commas denote soloists and those printed continuously represent a choral group; thus 'S, A, Bar, SATB' stands for solo soprano, alto and baritone with a chorus of soprano, alto, tenor and bass. Information may be given in less specific form: '3 solo vv, 4vv' means that the work is for three soloists and four-part chorus; for English verse anthems this is notated '3/4vv'. Unless parenthesized (when it is the date of publication), a date following details of a work is the date of composition or, for a dramatic work, the date of first performance. Where quotation marks are included in the title of a mass (e.g. Missa 'Da pacem'), the quoted matter identifies the cantus firmus or parody model.

Editions that include a substantial number of works are cited at the heads of work-lists (or sections of them); often they are assigned a sigillum, appended in square brackets, which is noted, with volume and sometimes page numbers if appropriate, against each item included in them. In such citations, composers' names are indicated in standardized form for ease of reference (e.g. *L. van Beethoven: Werke* rather than *Ludwig van Beethovens Werke*). Smaller editions, and editions of individual works or groups of works in modern anthologies or collections, are cited alongside the particular entry (such citations may refer to a work listed in the bibliography of the article, e.g. 'ed. in Smith (1950)'). Individual items in a work-list may be referred, by a sigillum derived from an original publication date, or from *RISM* B/I/1, to a list of publications above.

Where lost works are listed, the source of information about them is normally cited. 'Inc.', following a title, means that the work is incomplete; following a source citation, it means that the source is.

Any abbreviation found in a work-list and not in the abbreviation list at the beginning of each volume is explained at the head of the list (or of the section of the list) concerned.

10. APPENDIXES. Attention should be drawn to the appendixes to the dictionary, to be found at the back of vol.20. One is a list of contributors, with (for living ones) their last known place of work or residence. The other is an index of the terms used in articles on folk music and non-Western music. This originated as a tool for members of the staff engaged on the editing of articles in these areas; when it became very extensive, it was decided that its publication, as an index, might be useful to scholars. Its scope and its limitations should be understood. It lists terms relating to musical forms and genres, repertories, instruments, ensembles, theory, musicians and musical events, performing practices, song texts, music drama and dances, as well as other miscellaneous topics; a brief identification of each term is supplied and the reader is referred to the article or articles in which the term is mentioned (also to illustrations and music examples, and to other related entries in the appendix). It should be stressed that it is not a guide to world musical terminology but simply an index to the terms used in (and the orthography of) this dictionary.

S.S.

Acknowledgments

The writing and editing of this dictionary represents a large corporate effort on the part of a great number of people, including nearly 2500 contributors and more than 100 editors, consultants and administrative staff. Here I can name and thank only a selection, and apologize to those who cannot be mentioned individually. These include the numerous contributors who have provided help beyond the normal obligations of scholarly collaboration, for example by drawing our attention to facts, publications and indeed potential authors that we might otherwise have overlooked, by warning us of possible sources of error, and in countless other ways. Many besides contributors – scholars, students, librarians, people working in other disciplines than music, and simply music lovers – have provided generous help towards the greater accuracy of the dictionary.

EDITORIAL STAFF. In the dictionary's editorial organization, I must first acknowledge, and express my gratitude for, the work of three senior colleagues (all of them are members of the advisory board, named in full on p.iv, who in the early planning stages gave us the benefit of their experience). These three are Nigel Fortune, the senior text editor and area editor for 17th-century music, on whose clear, careful, detailed editorial work we have all much depended; Ian D. Bent, principal consulting editor as well as area editor for medieval music, notation, and a number of general or 'conceptual' topics, whose wide-ranging approach to music and ways of thinking about it substantially influenced the treatment of many subjects; and Lewis Lockwood, American consulting editor, who contributed much advice and in particular helped us to enlist large numbers of American contributors.

The executive committee, listed on p.iv, includes the scholars who, as 'area editors', played the vital role of planning the coverage of individual subject areas within the dictionary. Some were concerned only with initial planning, some with the more detailed editorial criticism of contributions. A few dealt with both. In this category fall – besides Ian Bent and Nigel Fortune – Howard Mayer Brown, who dealt with instruments, their use and their manufacture; John Warrack, who covered the 19th century; and Gerard Béhague, who had charge of Latin American material. Those who planned specific areas are: Paul Doe, James Haar and Peter le Huray (Renaissance composers); Peter Evans and Jeremy Noble, with Paul Griffiths (20th-century music, chiefly European); H. Wiley Hitchcock (American music), with John Beckwith (Canada); Mantle Hood (non-Western and folk music), with Peter Cooke; Alec Hyatt King, with John Tyrrell (20th-century writers on music); Kenneth Levy, with Geoffrey Chew (ancient and early Christian music); Hugh Macdonald, with Adele Poindexter Evidon (national and local music history); Diana McVeagh (20th-century performers); Edward Olleson (late 18th-century composers); and Michael Tilmouth, with Charles Warren (musical forms and genres). Entries on acoustical topics were planned with the help of Charles Taylor. All such planning was done in close consultation with the central editorial office, at the door of which the blame for shortcomings should be laid.

In 1895 Hubert Parry said, in an address in honour of Sir George Grove:

> It makes me often smile inwardly when I recall the jolly time he and I had together some 20 years ago, when I had the privilege and good fortune to work with him as a sort of sub-editor on his well-known Dictionary of Music. We had some uncommonly dreary and tiresome work to do. If you could have seen the state in which some of the articles were sent in you would wonder how they were ever got into shape. I remember we not only had to recast the details of the language of many of them, but to turn the articles inside out and upside down, to put the end at the beginning and the middle at the end, and to cut out whole paragraphs of rigmarole, till we were driven nearly distracted.

Times have changed; but a century after Grove there was still some 'dreary and tiresome work' to be done, and 'jolly times' to be enjoyed. Those responsible for seeing copy through from submission to print were: for early and medieval music, Geoffrey Chew, David Fallows and David Hiley, with Michael Wood; Renaissance and 17th-century composers, Stanley Boorman, Iain Fenlon and Nigel Fortune, with M. Elizabeth C. Bartlet, Margaret Grant, Anne Lindsey Kirwan, Judith Nagley, Rosemary Roberts and David Scott; for 18th- and 19th-century composers, the Editor, John Warrack (assisted by David Charlton) and Bradford Robinson, with Graydon Beeks, Bruce Carr, Jeffrey Cooper, Peggy Daub, William Drabkin, Richard Evidon, Dennis Libby, Geoffrey Norris, Deane Root and John Tyrrell; for 20th-century material, Paul Griffiths. I should particularly mention the valuable contributions of Elizabeth Bartlet and Bradford Robinson on the treatment of work-lists.

Articles on national and local music history were supervised by Adele Poindexter Evidon, with Timothy Roberts; those on instruments by Mark Lindley, with Carolyn Bryant (assisted by Robert E. Sheldon), William Conner, Barbara Fenton, David Scott and Ian Woodfield. Articles on forms and genres were supervised by Charles Warren, with Suzanne Cusick and Shirley Warren; those on terminology regarding performance by David Fallows; those on theoretical topics by William Drabkin and Ian Bent. Articles on non-Western and folk music were edited by Peter Cooke, with Lucy Durán, Doris Dyen, Helen Myers and Lilija Zobens, assisted by Alison Geldard. Entries on bibliographical topics and sources were supervised by Ian Bent and Stanley Boorman, with Elizabeth Bartlet, William Conner, David Fallows, David Hiley, Judith McBeath, Bradford Robinson and Julie Woodward. Paul Griffiths, with Mark Lindley, supervised articles on acoustical topics. Diana McVeagh supervised entries on performers, Noël Goodwin and Max Loppert having charge of particular areas, with Alison Latham, Helen Simpson and Barry Millington; entries on jazz and popular music were supervised by Bradford Robinson and Deane Root. Articles on 20th-century writers on music were dealt with by John Tyrrell, with Rosemary Wise. Many of the editors named above assisted in a variety of subject areas, as also did Malcolm Boyd. Thomas Walker contributed many valuable ideas; I should also mention the special combination of administrative, editorial and bibliographical skills provided by John Tyrrell.

The team of copy supervisors was headed by the invaluable Alison Latham and Judith Nagley, with Ruth Thackeray, Rosemary Roberts, Bonnie Jacobson and Caroline Ewans. The eagle-eyed Paulène Oliver Fallows was first principal proof reader, later joined by Caroline Coverdale and many of the foregoing. Our team of young scholars working (daily, over several years) on checking and on bibliographical queries at the British Library and elsewhere in London, headed principally by Duncan Chisholm, should be mentioned. We have enjoyed the cooperation of translators too many to enumerate, but I would particularly note Mary Whittall's work on several major articles in German.

The chief illustrations editor was Elisabeth Agate, a great asset to the organization (working with Christine Morley, Claire Cockburn, Sara Cunningham, Audrey Twine and others); maps and technical drawings have mainly been prepared by Constance and Brian Dear, and diagrammatic-typographical illustrations by Oxford Illustrators. Music examples were edited by Damian Cranmer and prepared by Halstan.

The administration of the Grove office during ten years has been a formidable task, involving the management of a large staff, the punctual performance of numerous routine tasks critical to the accuracy of the dictionary, and the maintenance of contacts with contributors, translators, printers and many other people and organizations. This was done initially, with exemplary efficiency and good humour, by Lynda MacGregor. She was succeeded by Caroline Coverdale, under whose sure administrative grasp the shift of emphasis from people to numbers, from the problems of contributors to those of computers, was smoothly negotiated; and finally the administration was in the hands of Māra Ezerkalns, whose understanding and control of the complexities of the computer procedures have been remarkable.

CONSULTANTS, ADVISERS ETC. This category is difficult to circumscribe. Many contributors have acted as unofficial consultants; and much consultancy work has been done by members of the Grove organization already named or listed on p.v. Here I shall refer to those who have given substantial help in specific subject areas.

We have had particular help in the coverage of non-Western and folk music from authorities on the music of various regions. Besides three members of the executive committee – Gerard Béhague (Latin America), Harold S. Powers (South Asia) and Klaus Wachsmann (instruments) – these are Anthony King (Africa), Barbara Krader (USSR and eastern Europe), Colin Mackerras (China), William P. Malm (Japan), Barbara Smith (Pacific Islands) and Owen Wright (Middle East).

I should like next to list those scholars and writers who have helped us towards a well-balanced and well-informed treatment of the music of their own country (or, in a few cases, the country on whose music they have worked). In most cases they have generously expended time and energy on drawing up lists of possible entries or scrutinizing our own draft lists, trimming them, supplementing them, bringing them up to date, reshaping them in fact to bring them into line with the realities of critical and historical evaluation. These contributions were primarily in the fields of 20th-century composition, performance and musical scholarship.

Australia: Andrew McCredie. *Austria:* Rudolf Klein. *Belgium:* Godelieve Spiessens. *Bulgaria:* Lada Brashovanova, Rosalia Bix. *Czechoslovakia:* Alena Němcová, Josef Bek, Oldřich Pukl. *Canada:* John Beckwith, Helmut Kallmann, Keith MacMillan. *Denmark:* John Bergsagel. *Finland:* Erkki Salmenhaara, Alec Crowe. *France:* François Lesure, André Boucourechliev, Christiane Spieth-Weissenbacher, Frank Dobbins. *Germany:* Ludwig Finscher, Wilfried Brennecke, Hans-Heinrich Eggebrecht, Wolfram Schwinger, Dieter Härtwig, Horst Seeger. *Greece:* George S. Leotsakos. *Hungary:* Ferenc Bónis. Istvan Kecskeméti, Desző Legány, Peter Pál Varnai. *Iceland:* Amanda Burt. *Israel:* William Y. Elias. *Italy:* Pierluigi Petrobelli, Carolyn M. Gianturco. *Japan:* Masakata Kanazawa, Shigeo Kishibe. *Netherlands:* Eduard

Reeser, Ellinor Bijvoet, Klooster de Leur. *New Zealand:* Frederick Page, J. M. Thomson. *Norway:* Kari Michelsen. *Philippines:* Lucrecia Kasilag. *Poland:* Teresa Chylińska, Elżbieta Dziębowska, Kornel Michałowski, Bogusław Schäffer, Zygmunt M. Szweykowski. *Portugal:* Robert Stevenson. *Romania:* Viorel Cosma, Romeo Ghircoiașiu. *Spain:* José López-Calo, Jack Sage, Robert Stevenson. *Sweden:* Hans Åstrand, Ingmar Bengtsson. *Switzerland:* Jürg Stenzl. *USSR:* Genrikh Orlov, Boris Schwarz, Yuri Keldïsh, Grigory Shneerson, I. M. Yampol'sky. *USA:* Martin Bernheimer, David Hamilton, Patrick J. Smith, Michael Steinberg. *Yugoslavia:* Bojan Bujić, Stana Djurić-Klajn.

Several people (some already named) have given of their expertise with such special generosity that it would be proper for me to list them separately. These include Robert Stevenson, the inexhaustible author of more entries than any other two contributors together, who has done much to make us (and indeed the rest of the world) aware of the size and the importance of Spanish, Portuguese and Latin American musical traditions; Pierluigi Petrobelli, whose energy, enthusiasm and knowledge have come to our rescue on numerous Italian topics, and others besides; Neal Zaslaw, who not only worked energetically on our behalf himself but also enlisted the help of Cornell University graduate seminars to help with the coverage of French 18th-century music; Eric Sams, who helped unstintingly in many areas of his special expertise, including the updating of the work of his friend the late Maurice Brown on Schubert; and Frank Dobbins, always ready to assist in matters to do with early French music. Desmond Shawe-Taylor, Harold Rosenthal and Rodolfo Celletti have given much help over entries on singers. Max Harrison gave advice on jazz entries.

Lastly, I would like to thank a number of individual contributors and others to whom we are specially grateful, for one reason or another – for example because they have contributed copiously, have carried out particularly irksome or arduous assignments, have taken on long articles at short notice, have guided us to illustrative matter, or have simply given us generous help or advice. These are numerous, but I should name especially the following: Derek Adlam; James R. Anthony; Anthony C. Baines; Philip Bate; Deben Bhattacharya; John Blacking; Joachim Braun; Barry S. Brook; Alexandr Buchner; Sydney Robinson Charles; Zofia Chechlińska; Carl Dahlhaus; Cyril Ehrlich; John Emerson; Georg Feder; Imogen Fellinger; Kurt von Fischer; David Fuller; Ann Griffiths; Charles Hamm; Don Harrán; Peter Hurford; Owen Jander; Gaynor Jones; Michael Kassler; Israel Katz; Michael Kennedy; Donald W. Krummel; Robert Layton; George Leotsakos; Frederic Lieberman; Richard Macnutt; Ramona Matthews; Paula Morgan; Grant O'Brien; Manoug Parikian; Alexander Ringer; Michael Rose; Howard Schott; Boris Schwarz; Watkins Shaw; László Somfai; Susan Thiemann Sommer; Eileen Southern; John Stevens; Nicholas Temperley; Peter Ward Jones; John C. G. Waterhouse; Stanley Webb; Christoph Wolff; and many more, to whom I apologize for not naming them separately.

LIBRARIANS, CURATORS, PUBLISHERS ETC. Many people and organizations outside the dictionary have provided generous help to us and our contributors. First I should thank the numerous librarians who have offered facilities to those working for the dictionary. In particular we are grateful to the authorities of several libraries in London: the British Library and its music staff, headed by O. W. Neighbour; to the University of London music library, under Anthea Baird, which provided working facilities to members of our staff over a long period; and to the Central Music Library, Westminster, and the Intelligence Department of *The Times*. Many European librarians responded helpfully to our requests for information towards making our 'Libraries' entry as accurate and comprehensive as possible. Many others, and many curators of museums or archives, have been specially helpful in the provision of illustrative matter. Among these I would mention Barry S. Brook (RIdIM and RCMI, City University of New York); Oliver Davies, Nathalie Mc-Cance, Watkins Shaw and Elizabeth Wells (Royal College of Music, London); Rudolf Elvers (Staatsbibliothek Preussischer Kulturbesitz, Berlin), Jean Jenkins and W. K. Ridley (Horniman Museum, London); Karl-Heinz Köhler (Deutsche Staatsbibliothek, Berlin); J. H. van der Meer (Germanisches Nationalmuseum, Nuremberg); Nicolas Meeùs (Conservatoire Royal de Musique, Musée Instrumental, Brussels); Hedwig Mitringer (Gesellschaft der Musikfreunde, Vienna); Robert Münster (Bayerische Staatsbibliothek, Munich); Karl Oriwohl (Staatliches Institut für Musikforschung Preussischer Kulturbesitz, Berlin); Habib H. Touma (International Institute for Comparative Music Studies and Documentation, Berlin); Kurt Wegerer (Kunsthistorisches Museum, Sammlung Alter Musikinstrumente, Vienna); Nicole Wild (Bibliothèque et Musée de l'Opéra, Paris); and Vivian Liff and George Stuart of the Stuart-Liff Collection. We have enjoyed the cooperation of several Music Information Centres and similar organizations, such as CeBeDeM (Belgium), the Stichting Donemus (Netherlands) and the Svenskt Musikhistoriskt Arkiv (Sweden). The British Institute of Recorded Sound, in the person of Eric Hughes, supplied most of our citations of discographies for entries on performers. We have enjoyed cordial and helpful relations with the editorial offices of other large-scale music reference works, especially *Die Musik in Geschichte und Gegenwart* and *Sohlmans Musiklexikon*. We are particularly grateful to our colleagues in the office of Bärenreiter-Verlag, Kassel, for permitting us to draw on a number of articles (about 150, the majority of them on minor German musicians) from *Die Musik in Geschichte und Gegenwart*. Usually they are substantially modified, in line with our rather different requirements, and of course updated; wherever possible we worked with the original author to produce a new version. Such articles are noted, at the foot, as 'based on *MGG*, [volume and page number]'; any articles used in essentially the same form as in *MGG* are noted as 'reprinted from *MGG* . . .'. Certain passages in our article 'Africa' are based on material in the equivalent article, by the same author, in *Dizionario Ricordi della Musica e dei Musicisti* (by permission of G. Ricordi & C.S.p.A. Milan); and the parts of the Sachs–Hornbostel classification reproduced in the dictionary, especially in the article 'Instruments, classification of', are based on the original, which first appeared in *Zeitschrift für Ethnologie*, 1914 (published by Albert Limbach Verlag, Brunswick), and was first published in English in the *Galpin Society Journal*, xiv (1961). A portion of the material supplied by Gerard Béhague for the entry on Latin America is, by permission of Prentice-Hall, based on his contribution to *Folk and Traditional Music of the Western Continents*, edited by Bruno Nettl (Englewood Cliffs, 1973, pp.179–206 and 214–32).

Acknowledgments to the copyright-holders of illustrations will be found at the end of each volume, and to those of music examples at the end of vol.20.

*

On a personal note, I would like to pay special tribute to my first wife, Adèle Sadie, for her patience and her hard work on behalf of the dictionary, the completion of which she did not live to see; also to my assistants, from Elisabeth Agate in the early days of the organization, to Helen Simpson, Kate Harney and Jacqueline Kohn. I am grateful to *The Times* (particularly the Editor, William Rees-Mogg, and the Arts Editor, John Higgins) for enabling me to act as Editor. Lastly I would acknowledge the role of the publishers, Macmillan, who, through the concern and enthusiasm of the Rt Hon. Harold Macmillan and Nicholas Byam Shaw (Managing Director), continued to support the enterprise in difficult times, permitted me total editorial freedom and imposed no unwonted restrictions, budgetary or spatial; I am grateful too to Nicolas J. Barker, who in 1969–70 initiated work on the dictionary, and especially to Richard Garnett, whose dogged determination was critical in carrying it through.

S.S.

Preface to the First Edition

BY SIR GEORGE GROVE

THIS work is intended to supply a great and long acknowledged want. A growing demand has arisen in this country and the United States for information on all matters directly and indirectly connected with Music, owing to the great spread of concerts, musical publications, private practice, and interest in the subject, and to the immense improvement in the general position of music which has taken place since the commencement of the present century. Music is now performed, studied, and listened to by a much larger number of persons, and in a more serious spirit, than was the case at any previous period of our history. It is rapidly becoming an essential branch of education; the newest works of continental musicians are eagerly welcomed here very soon after their appearance abroad, and a strong desire is felt by a large, important, and increasing section of the public to know something of the structure and peculiarities of the music which they hear and play, of the nature and history of the instruments on which it is performed, of the biographies and characteristics of its composers – in a word, of all such particulars as may throw light on the rise, progress, and present condition of an art which is at once so prominent and so eminently progressive.

This desire it is the object of the Dictionary of Music and Musicians to meet. It is designed for the use of Professional musicians and Amateurs alike. It contains definitions of Musical Terms; explanations of the forms in which Musical Works are constructed and of the methods by which they are elaborated, as well as of the origin, structure, and successive modifications of Instruments; histories and descriptions of Societies and Institutions; notices of the composition, production, and contents of important works; lists of the principal published collections; biographies of representative composers, singers, players, and patrons of music – all the points, in short, immediate and remote, on which those interested in the Art, and alive to its many and far-reaching associations, can desire to be informed.

The limit of the history has been fixed at A.D. 1450, as the most remote date to which the rise of modern music can be carried back. Thus mere archaeology has been avoided, while the connection between the mediæval systems and the wonderful modern art to which they gave rise has been insisted on and brought out wherever possible. While the subjects have been treated thoroughly and in a manner not unworthy the attention of the professional musician, the style has been anxiously divested of technicality, and the musical illustrations have been taken, in most cases, from classical works likely to be familiar to the amateur, or within his reach.

The articles are based as far as possible on independent sources, and on the actual research of the writers, and it is hoped that in many cases fresh subjects have been treated, new and interesting information given, and some ancient mistakes corrected. As instances of the kind of subjects embraced and the general mode of treatment adopted, reference may be made to the larger biographies – especially that of Haydn, which is crowded with new facts; to the articles on Auber, Berlioz, Bodenschatz, Bull, Cristofori, David, Farinelli, Finck, Froberger, Galitzin, Gibbons, Hasse; on Additional Accompaniments, Agrémens, Arpeggio, Arrangement, Fingering, Form, and Harmony; on Académie de Musique, Bachgesellschaft, Breitkopf and Härtel, Bassoon, Carmagnole, Choral Symphony, Conservatoire, Concerts, Concert Spirituel, Copyright, Drum, English Opera, Fidelio, Grand Prix de Rome, Handel and Haydn Society, Handel Festivals and Commemorations, Harpsichord, Harmonica, Hexachord, and many others. The engraved illustrations have been specially prepared for the work and will speak for themselves.

In an English dictionary it has been thought right to treat English music and musicians with special care, and to give their biographies and achievements with some minuteness of detail. On this point thanks are due to Colonel Joseph Lemuel Chester for much accurate information which it would have been almost impossible to obtain elsewhere, and which he has afforded in every case with the greatest kindness and promptitude.

Every means has been taken to procure an adequate treatment of the various topics and to bring the information down as near as possible to the day of publication. Notwithstanding the Editor's desire, however, omissions and errors have occurred. These will be rectified in an Appendix on the publication of the final volume.

The limits of the work have necessarily excluded disquisitions on Acoustics, Anatomy, Mechanics, and other branches of science connected with the main subject, which though highly important are not absolutely requisite in a book concerned with practical music. In the case of Acoustics, sufficient references are given to the best works to enable the student to pursue the enquiry for himself, outside the Dictionary. Similarly all investigations into the music of barbarous nations have been avoided, unless they have some direct bearing on European music.

The Editor gladly takes this early opportunity to express his deep obligations to the writers of the various articles. Their names are in themselves a guarantee for the value of their contributions; but the lively interest which they have shown in the work and the care they have taken in the preparation of their articles, often involving much time, and laborious, disinterested research, demand his warm acknowledgment.

28 BEDFORD STREET,
COVENT GARDEN, LONDON,
April 1, 1879.

General Abbreviations

A	alto, contralto [voice]
a	alto [instrument]
AB	see BA
ABC	American Broadcasting Company; Australian Broadcasting Commission
Abt.	Abteilung [section]
acc.	accompaniment, accompanied by
AD	anno Domini
add, addl	additional
add, addn	addition
ad lib	ad libitum
Ag	Agnus Dei
all	alleluia
AM	see MA
a.m.	ante meridiem [before noon]
amp	amplified
AMS	American Musicological Society
Anh.	Anhang [appendix]
anon.	anonymous(ly)
ant	antiphon
appx	appendix
arr.	arrangement, arranged by/for
ASCAP	American Society of Composers, Authors and Publishers
attrib.	attribution, attributed to
Aug	August
aut.	autumn
B	bass [voice]
B	Brainard catalogue [Tartini]
b	bass [instrument]
b	born
BA	Bachelor of Arts
Bar	baritone [voice]
bar	baritone [instrument]
BBC	British Broadcasting Corporation
BC	British Columbia (Canada)
BC	before Christ
bc	basso continuo
Bd.	Band [volume]
Berks.	Berkshire (GB)
Berwicks.	Berwickshire (GB)
bk	book
BLitt	Bachelor of Letters/Literature
BM	British Museum
BMI	Broadcast Music Inc. (USA)
BMus	Bachelor of Music
bn	bassoon
Bros.	Brothers
Bs	Benedictus

Bte	Benedicite
Bucks.	Buckinghamshire (GB)
Bulg.	Bulgarian
BVM	Blessed Virgin Mary
BWV	Bach-Werke-Verzeichnis [Schmieder, catalogue of J. S. Bach's works]
c	circa [about]
Calif.	California (USA)
CanD	Cantate Domino
carn.	Carnival
CBC	Canadian Broadcasting Corporation
CBE	Commander of the Order of the British Empire
CBS	Columbia Broadcasting System (USA)
CBSO	City of Birmingham Symphony Orchestra
CeBeDeM	Centre Belge de Documentation Musicale
cel	celesta
CEMA	Council for the Encouragement of Music and the Arts [now the Arts Council of Great Britain]
cf	confer [compare]
c.f.	cantus firmus
CH	Companion of Honour
chap.	chapter
Chin.	Chinese
chit	chitarrone
Cie	Compagnie
cimb	cimbalom
cl	clarinet
clvd	clavichord
cm	centimetre(s)
CNRS	Centre National de la Recherche Scientifique (F)
Co.	Company; County
Cod.	Codex
col.	column
coll.	collected by
collab.	in collaboration with
comm	communion
conc.	concerto
cond.	conductor, conducted by
Conn.	Connecticut (USA)
cont	continuo
Corp.	Corporation
c.p.s.	cycles per second
Cr	Credo, Creed
CSc	Candidate of Historical Sciences
Ct	countertenor
Cz.	Czech

D	Deutsch catalogue [Schubert]; Dounias catalogue [Tartini]	GmbH	Gesellschaft mit beschränkter Haftung [limited-liability company]
d.	denarius, denarii [penny, pence]	govt.	government [district in USSR]
d	died	grad	gradual
Dan.	Danish	GSM	Guildhall School of Music and Drama, London
db	double bass		
DBE	Dame Commander of the Order of the British Empire	gui	guitar
dbn	double bassoon		
DC	District of Columbia (USA)	H	Hoboken catalogue [Haydn]; Helm catalogue [C. P. E. Bach]
Dec	December		
ded.	dedication, dedicated to	Hants.	Hampshire (GB)
DeM	Deus misereatur	Heb.	Hebrew
Dept	Department	Herts.	Hertfordshire (GB)
Derbys.	Derbyshire (GB)	HMS	His/Her Majesty's Ship
dir.	director, directed by	HMV	His Master's Voice
diss.	dissertation	hn	horn
DLitt	Doctor of Letters/Literature	Hon.	Honorary; Honourable
DMus	Doctor of Music	hpd	harpsichord
DPhil	Doctor of Philosophy	HRH	His/Her Royal Highness
DSc	Doctor of Science/Historical Sciences	Hung.	Hungarian
		Hunts.	Huntingdonshire (GB)
		Hz	Hertz [c.p.s.]
ed.	editor, edited (by)		
edn.	edition	IAML	International Association of Music Libraries
e.g.	exempli gratia [for example]		
elec	electric, electronic	ibid	ibidem [in the same place]
EMI	Electrical and Musical Industries	i.e.	id est [that is]
Eng.	English	IFMC	International Folk Music Council
eng hn	english horn	Ill.	Illinois (USA)
ens	ensemble	IMS	International Musicological Society
esp.	especially	Inc.	Incorporated
etc	et cetera [and so on]	inc.	incomplete
ex., exx.	example, examples	incl.	includes, including
		Ind.	Indiana (USA)
		inst	instrument, instrumental
f, ff	following page, following pages	int	introit
f., ff.	folio, folios	IPEM	Institute for Psycho-acoustics and Electronic Music, Brussels
f	forte		
facs.	facsimile	ISCM	International Society for Contemporary Music
fasc.	fascicle		
Feb	February	ISM	Incorporated Society of Musicians (GB)
ff	fortissimo	ISME	International Society of Music Educators
fff	fortississimo	It.	Italian
fig.	figure [illustration]		
fl	flute	Jan	January
fl	floruit [he/she flourished]	Jap.	Japanese
fp	fortepiano	*Jb*	Jahrbuch [yearbook]
Fr.	French	Jg.	Jahrgang [year of publication/volume]
frag.	fragment	jr	junior
FRAM	Fellow of the Royal Academy of Music, London	Jub	Jubilate
FRCM	Fellow of the Royal College of Music, London		
FRCO	Fellow of the Royal College of Organists, London	K	Kirkpatrick catalogue [D. Scarlatti]; Köchel catalogue [Mozart; no. after / is from 6th edn.]
FRS	Fellow of the Royal Society, London		
		kbd	keyboard
		KBE	Knight Commander of the Order of the British Empire
Gael.	Gaelic		
Ger.	German	KCVO	Knight Commander of the Royal Victorian Order
Gk.	Greek		
Gl	Gloria	kHz	kilohertz
Glam.	Glamorgan (GB)	km	kilometre(s)
glock	glockenspiel	Ky	Kyrie
Glos., Gloucs.	Gloucestershire (GB)	Ky.	Kentucky (USA)

£	libra, librae [pound, pounds sterling]	Oct	October
L	Longo catalogue [D. Scarlatti]	off	offertory
Lancs.	Lancashire (GB)	OM	Order of Merit
Lat.	Latin	Ont.	Ontario (Canada)
Leics.	Leicestershire (GB)	op., opp.	opus, opera
lib	libretto	op cit	opere citato [in the work cited]
Lincs.	Lincolnshire (GB)	opt.	optional
lit	litany	orch	orchestra, orchestral
LittD	Doctor of Letters/Literature	orchd	orchestrated (by)
LlB	Bachelor of Laws	org	organ
LlD	Doctor of Laws	orig.	original(ly)
LP	long-playing record	ORTF	Office de Radiodiffusion-Télévision Française
LPO	London Philharmonic Orchestra		
LSO	London Symphony Orchestra	OUP	Oxford University Press
Ltd	Limited	ov.	overture
M.	Monsieur	P	Pincherle catalogue [Vivaldi]
MA	Master of Arts	p.	pars (1p. = *prima pars*, etc)
Mag	Magnificat	p., pp.	page, pages
mand	mandolin	*p*	piano
mar	marimba	p.a.	per annum
Mass.	Massachusetts (USA)	PC	number of chanson in A. Pillet and H. Carstens: *Bibliographie der Troubadours* (Halle, 1933)
MBE	Member of the Order of the British Empire		
Mez	mezzo-soprano	Penn.	Pennsylvania (USA)
mf	mezzo-forte	perc	percussion
mic	microphone	perf.	performance, performed (by)
Mich.	Michigan (USA)	pf	piano
Minn.	Minnesota (USA)	PhD	Doctor of Philosophy
Mlle	Mademoiselle	pic	piccolo
mm	millimetre(s)	pl.	plate; plural
Mme	Madame	p.m.	post meridiem [after noon]
MMus	Master of Music	PO	Philharmonic Orchestra
mod	modulator	Pol.	Polish
Mon.	Monmouthshire (GB)	Port.	Portuguese
movt	movement	posth.	posthumous(ly)
MP	Member of Parliament (GB)	POW	prisoner of war
mp	mezzo-piano	*pp*	pianissimo
MS	manuscript	*ppp*	pianississimo
MSc	Master of Science(s)	pr.	printed
Mt	Mount	PRO	Public Record Office, London
MusB, MusBac	Bachelor of Music	prol	prologue
		PRS	Performing Right Society (GB)
MusD, MusDoc	Doctor of Music	Ps	Psalm
		ps	psalm
MusM	Master of Music	pseud.	pseudonym
		pt.	part
		ptbk	partbook
NBC	National Broadcasting Company (USA)	pubd	published
n.d.	no date of publication	pubn	publication
NJ	New Jersey (USA)		
no.	number		
Nor.	Norwegian	qnt	quintet
Northants.	Northamptonshire (GB)	qt	quartet
Notts.	Nottinghamshire (GB)		
Nov	November		
n.p.	no place of publication	R	[in signature] editorial revision
nr.	near	R.	number of chanson in G. Raynaud: *Bibliographie des chansonniers français des XIIIe et XIVe siècles* (Paris, 1884) and H. Spanke: *G. Raynauds Bibliographie des altfranzösischen Liedes* (Leiden, 1955)
NSW	New South Wales (Australia)		
Nunc	Nunc dimittis		
NY	New York State (USA)		
		R	response
		R	Ryom catalogue [Vivaldi]
ob	oboe	*R*	photographic reprint
obbl	obbligato	*r*	recto
OBE	Officer of the Order of the British Empire		

RAF	Royal Air Force	T	tenor [voice]
RAI	Radio Audizioni Italiane	t	tenor [instrument]
RAM	Royal Academy of Music, London	TeD	Te Deum
RCA	Radio Corporation of America	Tenn.	Tennessee (USA)
RCM	Royal College of Music, London	timp	timpani
re	response	tpt	trumpet
rec	recorder	Tr	treble [voice]
recit	recitative	tr	tract; treble [instrument]
red.	reduction, reduced for	trans.	translation, translated by
repr.	reprinted	transcr.	transcription, transcribed by/for
Rev.	Reverend	trbn	trombone
rev.	revision, revised (by/for)		
RIdIM	Répertoire International d'Iconographie Musicale	U.	University
RILM	Répertoire International de Littérature Musicale	UHF	ultra-high frequency
		UK	United Kingdom of Great Britain and Northern Ireland
RISM	Répertoire International des Sources Musicales	unacc.	unaccompanied
RMCM	Royal Manchester College of Music	unattrib.	unattributed
RNCM	Royal Northern College of Music, Manchester	UNESCO	United Nations Educational, Scientific and Cultural Organization
RO	Radio Orchestra	unperf.	unperformed
Rom.	Romanian	unpubd	unpublished
RPO	Royal Philharmonic Orchestra (GB)	US	United States [adjective]
RSFSR	Russian Soviet Federated Socialist Republic	USA	United States of America
		USSR	Union of Soviet Socialist Republics
RSO	Radio Symphony Orchestra		
Rt Hon.	Right Honourable		
RTE	Radio Telefís Eireann (Ireland)	V	versicle
Russ.	Russian	v, vv	voice, voices
RV	Ryom catalogue [Vivaldi]	v., vv.	verse, verses
		v	verso
		va	viola
S	San, Santa, Santo, São [Saint]; soprano [voice]	vc	cello
		vcle	versicle
S.	south, southern	VEB	Volkseigener Betrieb [people's own industry]
$	dollars		
s	soprano [instrument]	Ven	Venite
s.	solidus, solidi [shilling, shillings]	VHF	very high frequency
SACEM	Société d'Auteurs, Compositeurs et Editeurs de Musique (F)	vib	vibraphone
		viz	videlicet [namely]
San	Sanctus	vle	violone
Sask.	Saskatchewan (Canada)	vn	violin
sax	saxophone	vol.	volume
Sept	September		
seq	sequence		
ser.	series	W.	west, western
sf, sfz	sforzando, sforzato	Warwicks.	Warwickshire (GB)
sing.	singular	Wilts.	Wiltshire (GB)
SJ	Societas Jesu (Society of Jesus)	wint.	winter
SO	Symphony Orchestra	Wisc.	Wisconsin (USA)
SPNM	Society for the Promotion of New Music (GB)	WoO, woo	Werke ohne Opuszahl [works without opus number]
spr.	spring	Worcs.	Worcestershire (GB)
SS	Saints	WQ	Wotquenne catalogue [C. P. E. Bach]
Ss	Santissima, Santissimo	ww	woodwind
SSR	Soviet Socialist Republic		
St	Saint, Sint, Szent		
Staffs.	Staffordshire (GB)		
Ste	Sainte	xyl	xylophone
str	string(s)		
sum.	summer		
Sup	superius	Yorks.	Yorkshire (GB)
suppl.	supplement, supplementary		
Swed.	Swedish		
sym.	symphony, symphonic		
synth	synthesizer	z	Zimmerman catalogue [Purcell]

Bibliographical Abbreviations

All bibliographical abbreviations used in this dictionary are listed below, following the typography used in the text of the dictionary. Broadly, *italic* type is used for periodicals and for reference works; roman type is used for anthologies, series etc (titles of individual volumes are italicized).

Full bibliographical information is not normally supplied in the list below if it is available elsewhere in the dictionary. Its availability is indicated as follows: D – in the article 'Dictionaries and encyclopedias of music'; E – in the article 'Editions, historical'; and P – in the list forming §III of the article 'Periodicals' (in this case the number in that list of the periodical concerned is added, in brackets). For other items, in particular national (non-musical) biographical dictionaries, basic bibliographical information is given here; and in some cases extra information is supplied to clarify the abbreviation used.

Festschriften and congress reports are not, in general, covered in this list. Although Festschrift titles are usually shortened in the dictionary, sufficient information is always given for unambiguous identification (dedicatee; occasion, if the same person is dedicatee of more than one Festschrift; place and date of publication; and where the dedicatee has an entry the editor's name may be found); for fuller information on musical Festschriften up to 1967 see W. Gerboth: *An Index to Musical Festschriften and Similar Publications* (New York, 1969). The only congress report series listed below are those of the international and the German musicological associations; for others cited in the dictionary, sufficient information is always given for identification (society or topic; place; date of occurrence); full information may be found in J. Tyrrell and R. Wise: *A Guide to International Congress Reports in Music, 1900–1975* (London, 1979).

AcM	*Acta musicologica* P [Intl 5]
ADB	*Allgemeine deutsche Biographie* (Leipzig, 1875–1912)
AM	*Antiphonale monasticum pro diurnis horis* (Paris, Tournai and Rome, 1934)
AMe (AMeS)	*Algemene muziekencyclopedie* (and suppl.) D
AMf	*Archiv für Musikforschung* P [D776]
AMI	L'arte musicale in Italia E
AMP	Antiquitates musicae in Polonia E
AMw	*Archiv für Musikwissenschaft* P [D552]
AMZ	*Allgemeine musikalische Zeitung* P [D32, 154, 170]
AMz	*Allgemeine Musik-Zeitung* P [D203]
AnM	*Anuario musical* P [E91]
AnMc	*Analecta musicologica* (some vols. in series Studien zur italienisch-deutschen Musikgeschichte), Veröffentlichungen der Musikabteilung des Deutschen historischen Instituts in Rom (Cologne, 1963–)
AnnM	*Annales musicologiques* P [F638]
AntMI	Antiquae musicae italicae E
AR	*Antiphonale sacrosanctae romanae ecclesiae pro diurnis horis* (Paris, Tournai and Rome, 1949)
AS	*Antiphonale sarisburiense*, ed. W. H. Frere (London, 1901–25/R1967)
Baker 5, 6	*Baker's Biographical Dictionary of Musicians* (5/1958 and 1971 suppl., 6/1978) D
BAMS	*Bulletin of the American Musicological Society* P [US540]
BeJb	*Beethoven-Jahrbuch* [1953–] P [D925]
BJb	*Bach-Jahrbuch* P [D434]
BMB	Biblioteca musica bononiensis E
BMw	*Beiträge zur Musikwissenschaft* P [D1013]
BNB	*Biographie nationale [belge]* (Brussels, 1866–)
BordasD	*Dictionnaire de la musique* (Paris: Bordas, 1970–76) D
Bouwsteenen: JVNM	*Bouwsteenen: jaarboek der Vereeniging voor Nederlandsche muziekgeschiedenis* P [NL20]
BrownI	H. M. Brown: *Instrumental Music Printed before 1600: a Bibliography* (Cambridge, Mass., 2/1967)
BSIM	*Bulletin français de la S[ociété] I[nternationale de] M[usique]* [previously *Le Mercure musical*; also other titles] P [F364]

BUCEM	*British Union-catalogue of Early Music*, ed. E. Schnapper (London, 1957)
BurneyH	C. Burney: *A General History of Music from the Earliest Ages to the Present* (London, 1776–89) [p. nos. refer to edn. of 1935/R1957]
BWQ	*Brass and Woodwind Quarterly* P [US756]
CaM	Catalogus musicus E
CEKM	Corpus of Early Keyboard Music E
CEMF	Corpus of Early Music in Facsimile E
CHM	*Collectanea historiae musicae* (in series Biblioteca historiae musicae cultores) (Florence, 1953–)
CM	Le choeur des muses E
CMc	*Current Musicology* P [US747]
CMI	I classici musicali italiani E
CMM	Corpus mensurabilis musicae E
CMz	*Cercetări de muzicologie* P [R29]
CS	E. de Coussemaker: *Scriptorum de musica medii aevi nova series* (Paris, 1864–76/R1963)
ČSHS	*Československý hudebni slovnik* D
CSM	Corpus scriptorum de musica E
CSPD	*Calendar of State Papers (Domestic)* (London, 1856–1972)
Cw	Das Chorwerk E
DAB	*Dictionary of American Biography* (New York, 1928–)
DAM	*Dansk aarbog for musikforskning* P [DK88]
DBF	*Dictionnaire de biographie française* (Paris, 1933–)
DBI	*Dizionario biografico degli italiani* (Rome, 1960–)
DBL	*Dansk biografisk leksikon* (Copenhagen, 1887–1905, 2/1933–)
DBP	*Dicionário biográfico de musicos portuguezes* D
DČHP	*Dějiny české hudby v příkladech* E
DDT	Denkmäler deutscher Tonkunst E
DHM	Documenta historicae musicae E
DJbM	*Deutsches Jahrbuch der Musikwissenschaft* P [D980]
DM	Documenta musicologica E
DNB	*Dictionary of National Biography* (London, 1885–1901, suppls.)
DTB	Denkmäler der Tonkunst in Bayern E
DTÖ	Denkmäler der Tonkunst in Österreich E

EDM	Das Erbe deutscher Musik E	JbMP	Jahrbuch der Musikbibliothek Peters P [D336]
EECM	Early English Church Music E	JEFDSS	The Journal of the English Folk Dance and Song Society P [GB341]
EIT	Ezhegodnik imperatorskikh teatrov P [USSR17]		
EitnerQ	R. Eitner: Biographisch-bibliographisches Quellen-Lexikon D	JFSS	Journal of the Folk-song Society P [GB183]
		JIFMC	Journal of the International Folk Music Council P [Intl 10]
EitnerS	R. Eitner: Bibliographie der Musik-Sammelwerke des XVI. und XVII. Jahrhunderts (Berlin, 1877)	JMT	Journal of Music Theory P [US683]
EKM	English (later Early) Keyboard Music E	JRBM	Journal of Renaissance and Baroque Music P [US590]
EL	The English Lute-songs		
EM	The English Madrigalists E	JRME	Journal of Research in Music Education P [US665]
EM	Ethnomusicology P [US664]	JVNM	see Bouwsteenen: JVNM P [NL20]
EMDC	Encyclopédie de la musique et dictionnaire du Conservatoire D		
EMN	Exempla musica neerlandica E	KJb	Kirchenmusikalisches Jahrbuch P [D284]
EMS	The English Madrigal School E	KM	Kwartalnik muzyczny P [PL35, 64]
ES	Enciclopedia dello spettacolo D		
ESLS	The English School of Lutenist-songwriters E		
		LaborD	Diccionario de la música Labor D
FAM	Fontes artis musicae P [Intl 16]	LaMusicaD	La musica: dizionario D
FasquelleE	Encyclopédie de la musique (Paris: Fasquelle, 1958–61) D	LaMusicaE	La musica: enciclopedia storica D
		LM	Lucrări de muzicologie P [R27]
FCVR	Florilège du concert vocal de la renaissance E	LSJ	The Lute Society Journal P [GB487]
FétisB	F.-J. Fétis: Biographie universelle des musiciens (2/1860–65) (and suppl.) D	LU	Liber usualis missae et officii pro dominicis et festis duplicibus cum cantu gregoriano (Solesmes, 1896; many later edns., incl. Tournai, 1963)
(FétisBS)			
GerberL	R. Gerber: Historisch-biographisches Lexikon der Tonkünstler D		
		MA	The Musical Antiquary P [GB240]
GerberNL	R. Gerber: Neues historisch-biographisches Lexikon der Tonkünstler D	MAB	Musica antiqua bohemica E
		MAM	Musik alter Meister E
GfMKB	Gesellschaft für Musikforschung Kongressbericht [1950–]	MAP	Musica antiqua polonica E
		MAS	[publications of the British] Musical Antiquarian Society E
GMB	Geschichte der Musik in Beispielen, ed. A. Schering (Leipzig, 1931) E		
		MB	Musica britannica E
GR	Graduale sacrosanctae romanae ecclesiae (Tournai, 1938)	MC	Musica da camera E
		MD	Musica disciplina P [US590]
Grove 1(–5)	G. Grove, ed.: A Dictionary of Music and Musicians, 2nd–5th edns. as Grove's Dictionary of Music and Musicians D	ME	Muzikal'naya entsiklopediya D
		MEM	Mestres de l'escolania de Montserrat E
		Mf	Die Musikforschung P [D839]
Grove 6	The New Grove Dictionary of Music and Musicians D	MGG	Die Musik in Geschichte und Gegenwart D
		MH	Musica hispana E
GS	Graduale sarisburiense, ed. W. H. Frere (London, 1894/R1967)	MJb	Mozart-Jahrbuch des Zentralinstituts für Mozartforschung [1950–] P [A254]
GS	M. Gerbert: Scriptores ecclesiastici de musica sacra (St Blasien, 1784/R1963)	ML	Music and Letters P [GB280]
		MLMI	Monumenta lyrica medii aevi italica E
GSJ	The Galpin Society Journal P [GB415]	MM	Modern Music P [US488]
		MMA	Miscellanea musicologica [Australia] P [AUS19]
		MMB	Monumenta musicae byzantinae E
HAM	Historical Anthology of Music, ed. A. T. Davison and W. Apel, i (Cambridge, Mass., 1946, rev. 2/1949); ii (Cambridge, Mass., 1950) E	MMBel	Monumenta musicae belgicae E
		MMC	Miscellanea musicologica [Czechoslovakia] P [CS191]
		MME	Monumentos de la música española E
HawkinsH	J. Hawkins: A General History of the Science and Practice of Music (London, 1776) [p. nos. refer to edn. of 1853/R1963]	MMFTR	Monuments de la musique française au temps de la renaissance E
		MMg	Monatshefte für Musikgeschichte P [D188]
HJb	Händel-Jahrbuch P [D712, 968]	MMI	Monumenti di musica italiana E
HM	Hortus musicus E	MMN	Monumenta musicae neerlandicae E
HMT	Handwörterbuch der musikalischen Terminologie D	MMP	Monumenta musicae in Polonia E
HMw	Handbuch der Musikwissenschaft, ed. E. Bücken (Potsdam, 1927–) [monograph series]	MMR	The Monthly Musical Record P [GB75]
		MMRF	Les maîtres musiciens de la renaissance française E
HMYB	Hinrichsen's Musical Year Book P [GB381]		
HPM	Harvard Publications in Music E	MMS	Monumenta musicae svecicae E
HR	Hudební revue P [CS80]	MO	Musical Opinion P [GB90]
HRo	Hudební rozhledy P [CS176]	MQ	The Musical Quarterly P [US447]
HV	Hudební věda P [CS204]	MR	The Music Review P [GB376]
		MRM	Monuments of Renaissance Music E
		MRS	Musiche rinascimentali siciliane E
IIM	Izvestiya na Instituta za muzīka P [BG14]	MS	Muzikal'nïy sovremennik P [USSR37]
IMa	Instituta et monumenta E	MSD	Musicological Studies and Documents, ed. A. Carapetyan (Rome, 1951–)
IMi	Istituzioni e monumenti dell'arte musicale italiana E		
		MT	The Musical Times P [GB33]
IMSCR	International Musicological Society Congress Report [1930–]	MVH	Musica viva historica E
		MVSSP	Musiche vocali strumentali sacre e profane E
IMusSCR	International Musical Society Congress Report [1906–11]	Mw	Das Musikwerk E
		MZ	Muzikološki zbornik P [YU37]
IRASM	International Review of the Aesthetics and Sociology of Music P [Intl 32]		
IRMO	S. L. Ginzburg: Istoriya russkoy muzïki v notnïkh obraztsakh D	NA	Note d'archivio per la storia musicale P [I186]
		NBJb	Neues Beethoven-Jahrbuch P [D636]
IRMAS	The International Review of Music Aesthetics and Sociology P [Intl 32]	NBL	Norsk biografisk leksikon (Oslo, 1921–)
		NDB	Neue deutsche Biographie (Berlin, 1953–)
IZ	Instrumentenbau-Zeitschrift P [D806]	NM	Nagels Musikarchiv E
		NNBW	Nieuw Nederlandsch biografisch woordenboek (Leiden, 1911–37)
JAMS	Journal of the American Musicological Society P [US613]	NÖB	Neue österreichische Biographie (Vienna, 1923)

NOHM   *The New Oxford History of Music*, ed. E. Wellesz, J. A. Westrup and G. Abraham (London, 1954–)

NRMI   *Nuova rivista musicale italiana*   P [I 282]

NZM   *Neue Zeitschrift für Musik*   P [D75, 1088]

OHM   *The Oxford History of Music*, ed. W. H. Hadow (Oxford, 1901–5, enlarged 2/1929–38)

OM   *Opus musicum*   P [CS222]

ÖMz   *Österreichische Musikzeitschrift*   P [A233]

PalMus   Paléographie musicale (Solesmes, 1889–) [see entry SOLESMES]

PAMS   *Papers of the American Musicological Society*   P [US543]

PÄMw   Publikationen älterer praktischer und theoretischer Musikwerke   E

PBC   Publicaciones del departamento de música de la Biblioteca de Catalunya   E

PG   *Patrologiae cursus completus*, ii: Series graeca, ed. J.-P. Migne (Paris, 1857–1912)

PGfM   Publikationen der Gesellschaft für Musikforschung   E

PIISM   Pubblicazioni dell'Istituto italiano per la storia della musica   E

PL   *Patrologiae cursus completus*, i: Series latina, ed. J.-P. Migne (Paris, 1844–64)

PM   Portugaliae musica   E

PMA   *Proceedings of the Musical Association*   P [GB80]

PMFC   Polyphonic Music of the Fourteenth Century   E

PNM   *Perspectives of New Music*   P [US724]

PRM   *Polski rocznik muzykologiczny*   P [PL85]

PRMA   *Proceedings of the Royal Musical Association*   P [GB80]

PSB   *Polskich słownik biograficzny* (Kraków, 1935)

PSFM   Publications de la Société française de musicologie   E

Quaderni della RaM   *Quaderni della Rassegna musicale*   P [I 272]

Rad JAZU   *Rad Jugoslavenske akademije znanosti i umjetnosti* (Zagreb, 1867–)

RaM   *La rassegna musicale*   P [I 197]

RBM   *Revue belge de musicologie*   P [B126]

RdM   *Revue de musicologie*   P [F462]

ReM   *La revue musicale* [1920–]   P [F475]

RHCM   *Revue d'histoire et de critique musicales* [1901]; *La revue musicale* [1902–10]   P [F320]

RicordiE   *Enciclopedia della musica* (Milan: Ricordi, 1963–4)   D

RiemannL 12   *Riemann Musik Lexikon* (12/1959–75)   D

RIM   *Rivista italiana di musicologia*   P [I 280]

RISM   *Répertoire international des sources musicales* [see entry under this title]

RMARC   R[oyal] M[usical] A[ssociation] *Research Chronicle*   P [GB496]

RMFC   *Recherches sur la musique française classique*   P [F677]

RMG   *Russkaya muzïkal'naya gazeta*   P [USSR19]

RMI   *Rivista musicale italiana*   P [I 84]

RMS   Renaissance Manuscript Studies   E

RN   *Renaissance News*   P [see US590]

RRMBE   Recent Researches in the Music of the Baroque Era   E

RRMR   Recent Researches in the Music of the Renaissance   E

SartoriB   C. Sartori: *Bibliografia della musica strumentale italiana stampata in Italia fino al 1700* (Florence, 1952–68)

SBL   *Svenska biografiskt leksikon* (Stockholm, 1918–)

SchmidlD (SchmidlDS)   C. Schmidl: *Dizionario dei musicisti* (and suppl.)   D

SCMA   Smith College Music Archives   E

SeegerL   H. Seeger: *Musiklexikon*   D

SEM   [University of California] Series of Early Music   E

SH   *Slovenská hudba*   P [CS192]

SIMG   *Sammelbände der Internationalen Musik-Gesellschaft*   P [Intl 2]

SM   *Studia musicologica Academiae scientiarum hungaricae*   P [H49]

SMA   *Studies in Music* [Australia]   P [AUS20]

SMd   Schweizerische Musikdenkmäler   E

SML   *Schweizer Musiker Lexikon*   D

SMM   Summa musicae medii aevi   E

SMN   *Studia musicologica norvegica*   P [N45]

SMP   *Słownik muzyków polskich*   D

SMw   *Studien zur Musikwissenschaft*   P [D536]

SMz   *Schweizerische Musikzeitung/Revue musicale suisse*   P [CH4]

SOB   Süddeutsche Orgelmeister des Barock   E

SovM   *Sovetskaya muzïka*   P [USSR66]

STMf   *Svensk tidskrift för musikforskning*   P [S46]

TCM   Tudor Church Music   E

TM   Thesauri musici   E

TVNM   *Tijdschrift van de Vereniging voor Nederlandse muziekgeschiedenis*   P [NL26]

UVNM   Uitgaven der Vereniging voor Nederlandse muziekgeschiedenis   E

VMPH   Veröffentlichungen der Musik-Bibliothek Paul Hirsch   E

VMw   *Vierteljahrsschrift für Musikwissenschaft*   P [D282]

VogelB   E. Vogel: *Bibliothek der gedruckten weltlichen Vocalmusik Italiens, aus den Jahren 1500 bis 1700* (Berlin, 1892); rev., enlarged, by A. Einstein (Hildesheim, 1962); further addns in *AnMc*, nos.4, 5, 9 and 12; further rev. by F. Lesure and C. Sartori as *Bibliografia della musica italiana vocale profana pubblicata dal 1500 al 1700* (?Geneva, 1978)

WaltherML   J. G. Walther: *Musicalisches Lexicon oder Musicalische Bibliothec*   D

WDMP   Wydawnictwo dawnej muzyki polskiej   E

WE   Wellesley Edition   E

WECIS   Wellesley Edition Cantata Index Series   E

YIFMC   *Yearbook of the International Folk Music Council*   P [Intl 31]

ZfM   *Zeitschrift für Musik*   P [D75]

ZHMP   Zrodła do historii muzyki polskiej   E

ZI   *Zeitschrift für Instrumentenbau*   P [D249]

ZIMG   *Zeitschrift der Internationalen Musik-Gesellschaft*   P [Intl3]

ZL   *Zenei lexikon*   D

ZMw   *Zeitschrift für Musikwissenschaft*   P [D556]

Library Sigla

The system of library sigla in this dictionary follows that used in its publications (Series A) by Répertoire International des Sources Musicales, Kassel, by permission. Below are listed the sigla to be found; a few of them are additional to those in the published RISM lists, but have been established in consultation with the RISM organization. Some original RISM sigla that have now been changed are retained here.

In the dictionary, sigla are always printed in *italic*. In any listing of sources a national sigillum applies without repetition until it is contradicted. For German sigla, the intermediate *brd* and *ddr* are excluded; the list below shows in which part of Germany or Berlin each library is located.

Within each national list, entries are alphabetized by sigillum, first by capital letters (showing the city or town) and then by lower-case ones (showing the institution or collection).

A: AUSTRIA

Ee	Eisenstadt, Esterházy-Archiv
Eh	——, Haydn Museum
Ek	——, Stadtpfarrkirche
F	Fiecht, Benediktinerordensstift St Georgenberg
Gd	Graz, Diözesan Archiv
Gk	——, Hochschule für Musik und Darstellende Kunst
Gl	——, Steiermärkische Landesbibliothek am Joanneum
Gmi	——, Musikwissenschaftliches Institut der Universität
Gu	——, Universitätsbibliothek
GÖ	Furth bei Göttweig, Benediktinerstift
GÜ	Güssing, Franziskaner Kloster
H	Herzogenburg, Chorherrenstift
HE	Heiligenkreuz, Zisterzienserstift
Ik	Innsbruck, Konservatorium
Imf	——, Museum Ferdinandeum
Imi	——, Musikwissenschaftliches Institut der Universität
Iu	——, Universitätsbibliothek
Iw	——, Prämonstratenser-Chorherrenstift Wilten
KN	Klosterneuburg, Augustiner-Chorherrenstift
KR	Kremsmünster, Benediktinerstift
L	Lilienfeld, Zisterzienser-Stift
LA	Lambach, Benediktinerstift
LEx	Leoben, Pfarrbibliothek St Xaver
LIm	Linz, Oberösterreichisches Landesarchiv
LIs	——, Bundesstaatliche Studienbibliothek
M	Melk an der Donau, Benediktinerstift
MB	Michaelbeuern, Benediktinerabtei
MÖ	Mödling, Pfarrkirche St Othmar
MZ	Mariazell, Benediktiner-Priorat
N	Neuburg, Pfarrarchiv
NS	Neustift, Pfarrarchiv
R	Rein, Zisterzienserstift
Sca	Salzburg, Museum Carolino Augusteum
Sd	——, Dom-Musikarchiv
Sk	——, Kapitelbibliothek
Sm	——, Internationale Stiftung Mozarteum
Smi	——, Musikwissenschaftliches Institut der Universität
Sn	——, Nonnberg, Benediktiner-Frauenstift
Ssp	——, St Peter Benediktiner-Erzabtei
SB	Schlierbach, Stift
SCH	Schlägl, Prämonstratenser-Stift
SE	Seckau, Benediktinerabtei
SEI	Seitenstetten, Benediktinerstift
SF	St Florian, Augustiner-Chorherrenstift
SH	Solbad Hall, Franziskaner-Kloster
SL	St Lambrecht, Benediktiner-Abtei
SP	St Pölten, Diözesanarchiv
SPL	St Paul, Stift
ST	Stams, Zisterzienserstift
STE	Steyr, Stadtpfarrarchiv
TU	Tulln, Pfarrkirche St Stephan
Wd	Vienna, Stephansdom
Wdo	——, Zentralarchiv des Deutschen Ordens
Wdtö	——, Gesellschaft zur Herausgabe von Denkmälern der Tonkunst in Österreich
Wgm	——, Gesellschaft der Musikfreunde
Wh	——, Pfarrarchiv Hernals
Whb	——, Hauptverband des Österreichischen Buchhandels
Wk	——, Pfarrkirche St Karl Borromäus
Wkann	——, Hans Kann, private collection
Wkh	——, Kirche am Hof
Wkm	——, Kunsthistorisches Museum
Wl	——, Archiv für Niederösterreich (Landesarchiv)
Wm	——, Minoritenkonvent
Wmg	——, Pfarre, Maria am Gestade
Wmi	——, Musikwissenschaftliches Institut der Universität
Wmk	——, Akademie für Musik und Darstellende Kunst
Wn	——, Österreichische Nationalbibliothek, Musiksammlung
Wögm	——, Österreichische Gesellschaft für Musik
Wp	——, Musikarchiv, Piaristenkirche Maria Treu
Wph	——, Wiener Philharmoniker, Archiv und Bibliothek
Wps	——, Priesterseminar
Ws	——, Schottenstift
Wsa	——, Stadtarchiv
Wsp	——, St Peter, Musikarchiv
Wst	——, Stadtbibliothek, Musiksammlung
Wu	——, Universitätsbibliothek
Ww	——, Pfarrarchiv Währing
Wweinmann	——, Alexander Weinmann, private collection
Wwessely	——, Othmar Wessely, private collection
WAY	Waydhofen an der Ybbs, Pfarre
WE	Wels, Stift
WIL	Wilhering, Zisterzienserstift
Z	Zwettl, Zisterzienserstift

B: BELGIUM

Aa	Antwerp, Stadsarchief
Aac	——, Archief en Museum voor het Vlaamse Culturleven
Ac	——, Koninklijk Vlaams Muziekconservatorium
Ak	——, Onze-Lieve-Vrouwkathedraal
Amp	——, Museum Plantijn–Moretus
Apersoons	——, Guido Persoons, private collection
As	——, Stadsbibliotheek
Asa	——, Kerkbestuur St-Andries
Asj	——, Collegiale en Parochiale Kerk St-Jacob
Averwilt	——, F. Verwilt, private collection
AN	Anderlecht, St-Guiden Kerk
Ba	Brussels, Archives de la Ville
Bc	——, Conservatoire Royal de Musique
Bcdm	——, Centre Belge de Documentation Musicale [CeBeDeM]
Bg	——, Eglise de Ste Gudule
Bi	——, Institut de Psycho-acoustique et de Musique Electronique

Br	——, Bibliothèque Royale Albert 1er/Koninklijke Bibliotheek Albert I
Brtb	——, Radiodiffusion-Télévision Belge
Bsp	——, Société Philharmonique
BRc	Bruges, Stedelijk Muziekconservatorium
D	Diest, St Sulpitiuskerk
Gar	Ghent [Gent, Gand], Stadsarchief
Gc	——, Koninklijk Muziekconservatorium
Gcd	——, Culturele Dienst Province Ost Vlaanderen
Geb	——, St Baafsarchief med Bibliotheek Van Damme
Gu	——, Rijksuniversiteit, Centrale Bibliotheek
K	Kortrijk, St Martinskerk
Lc	Liège, Conservatoire Royal de Musique
Lu	——, Université de Liège
Llc	Lier, Conservatoire
Llg	——, St Gummaruskerk
LV	Louvain, Dominikanenklooster
LVu	——, Université de Louvain
M	Mons, Conservatoire Royal de Musique
MA	Morlanwelz-Mariemont, Musée de Mariemont
MEa	Mechelen, Archief en Stadsbibliotheek
MEs	——, Stedelijke Openbare Bibliotheek
OU	Oudenaarde, Parochiale Kerk
Tc	Tournai, Chapitre de la Cathédrale
Tv	——, Bibliothèque de la Ville
TI	Tienen, St Germanuskerk
Z	Zoutleeuw, St Leonarduskerk

BR: BRAZIL

Rem	Rio de Janeiro, Escola de Música, Universidade Federal do Rio de Janeiro
Rn	——, Biblioteca Nacional

C: CANADA

E	Edmonton, University of Alberta
Fc	Fredericton, Christ Church Cathedral
Ku	Kingston, Queens University, Douglas Library
Lu	London, University of Western Ontario, Lawson Memorial Library
Mc	Montreal, Conservatoire de Musique et d'Art Dramatique
Mfisher	——, Sidney T. Fisher, private collection [in *Tu*]
Mm	——, McGill University, Faculty and Conservatorium of Music and Redpath Libraries
On	Ottawa, National Library of Canada
Qc	Quebec, Cathédrale de la Sainte-Trinité
Qul	——, Université Laval
SAu	Sackville, Mt Allison University
SJm	St John, New Brunswick Museum
Tb	Toronto, Canadian Broadcasting Corporation
Tm	——, Royal Ontario Museum
Tolnick	——, Harvey J. Olnick, private collection
Tp	——, Toronto Public Library, Music Branch
Tu	——, University of Toronto, Faculty of Music
Vu	Vancouver, University of British Columbia Library, Fine Arts Division
W	Winnipeg, University of Manitoba

CH: SWITZERLAND

A	Aarau, Aargauische Kantonsbibliothek
AShoboken	Ascona, Anthony van Hoboken, private collection
Bchristen	Basle, Werner Christen, private collection
Bm	——, Musikakademie der Stadt
Bmi	——, Musikwissenschaftliches Institut der Universität
Bu	——, Öffentliche Bibliothek der Universität, Musiksammlung
BA	Baden, Historisches Museum (Landvogtei-Schloss)
BEk	Berne, Konservatorium
BEl	——, Schweizerische Landesbibliothek
BEms	——, Musikwissenschaftliches Seminar der Universität
BEsu	——, Stadt- und Universitätsbibliothek; Bürgerbibliothek
BI	Biel, Stadtbibliothek
C	Chur, Kantonsbibliothek Graubünden
D	Disentis, Stift
E	Einsiedeln, Benediktinerkloster
EN	Engelberg, Stift
Fcu	Fribourg, Bibliothèque Cantonale et Universitaire
Ff	——, Franziskaner-Kloster
Fk	——, Kapuziner-Kloster
Fsn	——, Kapitel St Nikolaus
FF	Frauenfeld, Thurgauische Kantonsbibliothek
Gamoudruz	Geneva, Emile Amoudruz, private collection
Gc	——, Conservatoire de Musique
Gpu	——, Bibliothèque Publique et Universitaire

GLtschudi	Glarus, A. Tschudi, private collection
Lmg	Lucerne, Allgemeine Musikalische Gesellschaft
Ls	——, Stiftsarchiv St Leodegar
Lz	——, Zentralbibliothek
LAc	Lausanne, Conservatoire de Musique
LAcu	——, Bibliothèque Cantonale et Universitaire
LU	Lugano, Biblioteca Cantonale
Mbernegg	Maienfeld, Sprecher von Bernegg, private collection
MO	Morges, Bibliothèque de la Ville
MÜ	Müstair, Frauenkloster
N	Neuchâtel, Bibliothèque Publique
R	Rheinfelden, Christkatholisches Pfarramt
S	Sion, Bibliothèque Cantonale du Valais
Sa	——, Staatsarchiv
Sk	——, Kathedrale
SA	Sarnen, Bibliothek des Kollegiums
SAf	——, Frauenkloster
SCH	Schwyz, Kantonsbibliothek
SGs	St Gall, Stiftsbibliothek
SGv	——, Stadtbibliothek
SH	Schaffhausen, Stadtbibliothek
SM	St Maurice, Bibliothèque de l'Abbaye
SO	Solothurn, Zentralbibliothek, Musiksammlung
TH	Thun, Stadtbibliothek
W	Winterthur, Stadtbibliothek
Wpeer	——, Peer private collection
Zi	Zurich, Israelitische Kulturgemeinde
Zjacobi	——, Erwin R. Jacobi, private collection
Zk	——, Konservatorium und Musikhochschule
Zma	——, Schweizerisches Musik-Archiv
Zms	——, Musikwissenschaftliches Seminar der Universität
Zp	——, Pestalozzianum
Zz	——, Zentralbibliothek
ZG	Zug, Stadtbibliothek
ZO	Zofingen, Stadtbibliothek
ZU	Zuoz, Gemeindearchiv

CO: COLOMBIA

B	Bogotá, Catedral

CS: CZECHOSLOVAKIA

Bb	Brno, Klášter Milosrdných Bratří [in *Bm*]
Bm	——, Ústav Dějin Hudby Moravského Musea, Hudebněhistorické Oddělení
Bu	——, Státní Vědecká Knihovna, Universitní Knihovna
BA	Bakov nad Jizerou, pobočka Státní Archívu v Mladé Boleslavi
BEL	Bělá pod Bezdězem, Městské Muzeum
BER	Beroun, Okresní Archív
BRa	Bratislava, Okresní Archív
BRe	——, Evanjelícka a. v. Cirkevná Knižnica
BRhs	——, Knižnica Hudobného Seminara Filosofickej Fakulty University Komenského
BRnm	——, Slovenské Národné Muzeum, Hudobné Oddělenie
BRsa	——, Štátny Ústredný Archív Slovenskej Socialistickej Republiky
BRsav	——, Slovenská Akadémia Vied
BRu	——, Univerzitná Knižnica
BREsi	Březnice, Děkanský Kostel Sv Ignáce
BSk	Banská Štiavnica, Farský Rímsko-Katolícky Kostol, Archív Chóru
CH	Cheb, Okresní Archív
CHOd	Choceň, Děkanský Úřad
CHOm	——, Městské Muzeum
H	Hronov, Muzeum Aloise Jiráska
HK	Hradec Králové, Muzeum
HOm	Hořice, Vlastivědné Muzeum
J	Jur pri Bratislave, Okresní Archív, Bratislava-Vidick
JIa	Jindřichův Hradec, Státní Archív
JIm	——, Vlastivědné Muzeum
K	Český Krumlov, Pracoviště Státního Archívu Třeboň, Hudební Sbírka
KL	Klatovy, Okresní Archív
KO	Košice, Městsky Archív
KOL	Kolín, Děkanský Chrám
KRa	Kroměříž, Státní Zámek a Zahrady, Historicko-Umělecké Fondy, Hudební Archív
KRA	Králíky, Děkanský Úřad
KRE	Kremnica, Městsky Archív
KU	Kutná Hora, Qblastní Muzeum
KVd	Karlovy Vary, Děkanský Úřad
KVso	——, Karlovarský Symfonický Orchestr
L	Levoča, Rímsko-Katolícky Farský Kostol
LIa	Česká Lípa, Okresní Archív

LIT	Litoměřice, Státní Archív
LO	Loukov, Farní Úřad
Mms	Martin, Matica Slovenská, Oddělenie Hudobných Pamiatok
Mnm	——, Slovenské Národné Múzeum, Archív
MB	Mladá Boleslav, Okresní Archív
ME	Mělník, Okresní Archív
MH	Mnichovo Hradiště, Vlastivědné Muzeum
N	Nítra, Státní Archív
ND	Nové Dvory, Farní Úřad
NM	Nové Mesto nad Váhom, Rímsko-Katolický Farský Kostol
OLa	Olomouc, Státní Oblastní Archív v Opava
OLu	——, Státní Vědecká Knihovna, Universitní Knihovna
OP	Opava, Slezské Muzeum
OS	Ostrava, Československý Rozhlas, Hudební Archív
OSE	Osek, Klášter
Pa	Prague, Státní Ústřední Archív
Pak	——, Archív Metropolitní Kapituly
Pdobrovského	——, Knihovna Josefa Dobrovského
Ph	——, Československá Církev Holešovice
Pis	——, Československo Hudební Informační Středisko
Pk	——, Archív Státní Konservatoře v Praze
Pnm	——, Národní Muzeum, Hudební Oddělení
Pp	——, Archív Pražského Hradu
Ppp	——, Památník Národního Písemnictví na Strahově
Pr	——, Československý Rozhlas, Hudební Archív Různá Provenience
Pra	——, Rodinní Archív Karla Kovařovice
Ps	——, Strahovská Knihovna [in *Ppp*]
Psf	——, Kostel Sv Franciscus
Psj	——, Kostel Sv Jakuba
Pu	——, Státní Knihovna ČSSR, Universitní Knihovna
PLa	Plzeň, Městsky Archív
PLm	——, Západočeské Muzeum
PLA	Plasy, Okresní Archív
POa	Poděbrady, pobočka Státní Archívu Nymburk
POm	——, Helichovo Muzeum
PR	Příbram, Okresný Muzeum
PRE	Prešov, Rímsko-Katolický Farský Kostol
RA	Rakovník, Státní Archív
RAJ	Rajhrad, Klášter [in *Bm*]
RO	Rokycany, Okresný Muzeum
ROZ	Rožnava, Biskupski Archív
RY	Rychnov, Muzeum Orlická
Sk	Spišská Kapitula, Katedrálny Rímsko-Katolický Kostol, Knižnica Spišskej Kapituly
SNV	Spišská Nová Ves, Rímsko-Katolický Farský Kostol
SO	Sokolov, Státní Archív
TC	Třebíč, Městsky Archív
TN	Trenčín, Okresní Archív
TR	Trnava, Dóm Sv Mikuláša
TRB	Třebenice, Klášter
TRE	Třebôň, Státní Archív
TU	Turnov, Okresný Muzeum
VE	Velenice, Farní Úřad
VM	Vysoké Mýto, Okresný Muzeum
ZA	Zámrsk, Státní Archív

CU: CUBA

Hn	Havana, Biblioteca Nacional
Hse	——, Biblioteca de la Sociedad Económica de Amigos del País

D: GERMANY

Aa	Augsburg, BRD, Kantoreiarchiv St Annen
Af	——, Bibliothek der Fuggerschen Domänenkanzlei
Ahk	——, Dominikanerkloster Heilig-Kreuz
As	——, Staats- und Stadtbibliothek
Asa	——, Stadtarchiv
AAd	Aachen, BRD, Bischöfliche Diözesanbibliothek
AAg	——, Kaiser Karl-Gymnasium, Lehrerbibliothek
AAm	——, Domarchiv
AAst	——, Stadtbibliothek
AB	Amorbach, BRD, Fürstlich Leiningische Bibliothek, private collection
ABG	Annaberg-Buchholz, DDR, Pfarramt, Kirchenbibliothek
ABGa	——, Kantoreiarchiv St Annen
AD	Adolfseck bei Fulda, BRD, Schloss Fasanerie, Bibliothek der Kurhessischen Hausstiftung
ALa	Altenburg, DDR, Landesarchiv (Historisches Staatsarchiv)
ALs	——, Stadtarchiv
ALt	——, Bibliothek des Landestheaters
AM	Amberg, BRD, Staatliche Provinzialbibliothek
AN	Ansbach, BRD, Regierungsbibliothek
AÖ	Altötting, BRD, Kapuziner-Kloster St Konrad
ARk	Arnstadt, DDR, Kirchenbibliothek
ARsk	——, Stadt- und Kreisbibliothek
ARsm	——, Schlossmuseum
ASh	Aschaffenburg, BRD, Hofbibliothek
ASm	——, Stadtbücherei
ASsb	——, Stiftsbibliothek
B	Berlin, Staatsbibliothek Preussischer Kulturbesitz [W]
Ba	——, Amerika-Gedenkbibliothek (Berliner Zentralbibliothek) [W]; Deutsche Akademie der Künste [E]
Bch	——, Musikbücherei Charlottenburg [W]
Bdhm	——, Deutsche Hochschule für Musik Hanns Eisler [E]
Bds	——, Deutsche Staatsbibliothek (formerly Königliche Bibliothek; Preussische Staatsbibliothek; Öffentliche Wissenschaftliche Bibliothek), Musikabteilung [E]
Bdso	——, Deutsche Staatsoper [E]
Be	——, Institut für Musikerziehung der Humboldt-Universität [E]
Bgk	——, Streit'sche Stiftung [in *Bs*] [E]
Bhbk	——, Staatliche Hochschule für Bildende Kunst [W]
Bhesse	——, A. Hesse, private collection [E]
Bhm	——, Staatliche Hochschule für Musik und Darstellende Kunst [W]
Bim	——, Staatliches Institut für Musikforschung Preussischer Kulturbesitz [W]
Bk	——, Staatliche Museen Preussischer Kulturbesitz [W]
Bko	——, Komische Oper [E]
Blk	——, Bezirks-Lehrerbibliothek Kreuzberg [W]
Bm	——, Marienkirche [E]
Bmb	——, Internationale Musikbibliothek, Verband Deutscher Komponisten und Musikwissenschaftler [E]
Bmi	——, Musikwissenschaftliches Institut der Freien Universität [W]; Musikwissenschaftliches Institut der Humboldt-Universität [E]
Bmm	——, Märkisches Museum [E]
Bn	——, Nikolaikirche [E]
Bp	——, Pädagogisches Zentrum [W]
Br	——, Deutscher Demokratischer Rundfunk, Notenarchiv [E]
Bs	——, Berliner Stadtbibliothek [E]
Bst	——, Stadtbücherei, Hauptstelle Berlin-Wilmersdorf [W]
Btu	——, Universitätsbibliothek der Technischen Universität [W]
Btum	——, Lehrstuhl für Musikgeschichte der Technischen Universität [W]
Bu	——, Universitätsbibliothek der Freien Universität [W]
Buh	——, Universitätsbibliothek der Humboldt-Universität [E]
BAa	Bamberg, BRD, Staatsarchiv
BAf	——, Franziskaner-Kloster
BAs	——, Staatsbibliothek
BAL	Ballenstedt, DDR, Stadtbibliothek
BAR	Bartenstein, BRD, Fürst zu Hohenlohe-Bartensteinsches Archiv, private collection
BAUd	Bautzen, DDR, Domstift und Bischöfliches Ordinariat
BAUk	——, Stadt- und Kreisbibliothek
BB	Benediktbeuren, BRD, Pfarrkirche
BD	Brandenburg an der Havel, DDR, Domstift
BDH	Bad Homburg von der Höhe, BRD, Stadtbibliothek
BE	Berleburg, BRD, Fürstlich Sayn-Wittgenstein-Berleburgsche Bibliothek, private collection
BEU	Beuron, BRD, Benediktiner-Erzabtei
BEV	Bevensen, BRD, Superintendantur, Ephoratsbibliothek und Bibliothek Sursen
BFa	Burgsteinfurt, BRD, Gymnasium Arnoldinum
BFb	——, Fürstlich Bentheimsche Bibliothek [in *MÜu*]
BG	Beuerberg über Wolfratshausen, BRD, Pfarramt, Stiftskirche
BGD	Berchtesgaden, BRD, Katholisches Pfarramt
BH	Bayreuth, BRD, Stadtbücherei
BI	Bielefeld, BRD, Städtisches Ratsgymnasium
BIB	Bibra, DDR, Pfarrarchiv
BIR	Birstein über Wächtersbach, BRD, Fürst von Ysenburgisches Archiv und Schlossbibliothek, private collection

BIT	Bitterfeld, DDR, Kreismuseum
BK	Bernkastel-Kues, BRD, Cusanusstift
BKÖ	Bad Köstritz, DDR, Pfarrarchiv
BMek	Bremen, BRD, Bücherei der Bremer Evangelischen Kirche
BMs	——, Staats- und Universitätsbibliothek
BNba	Bonn, BRD, Beethoven-Haus und Beethoven-Archiv
BNek	——, Gemeindeverband der Evangelischen Kirche
BNms	——, Musikwissenschaftliches Seminar der Universität
BNu	——, Universitätsbibliothek
BO	——, Bollstedt, Pfarramt
BOCHb	Bochum, BRD, Bergbaumuseum
BOCHmi	——, Musikwissenschaftliches Institut der Ruhr-Universität
BOCHs	——, Stadtbibliothek, Musikbücherei
BORp	Borna, DDR, Pfarrkirche
BS	Brunswick, BRD, Stadtarchiv und Stadtbibliothek
BTH	Barth, DDR, Kirchenbibliothek
BÜ	Büdingen, BRD, Fürstlich Ysenburg- und Büdingisches Archiv und Schlossbibliothek
BW	Burgwindheim über Bamberg, BRD, Katholisches Pfarramt
Cl	Coburg, BRD, Landesbibliothek
Cm	——, Moritzkirche
Cv	——, Kunstsammlung der Veste Coburg
CA	Castell, BRD, Fürstlich Castell'sche Bibliothek
CD	Crottendorf, DDR, Kantoreiarchiv
CR	Crimmitschau, DDR, Stadtkirche St Laurentius
CZ	Clausthal-Zellerfeld, BRD, Kirchenbibliothek
CZu	——, Universitätsbibliothek
Dhm	Dresden, DDR, Hochschule für Musik Carl Maria von Weber
Dkh	——. Katholische Hofkirche
Dl	——, Bibliothek und Museum Löbau [in *Dlb*]
Dla	——, Staatsarchiv
Dlb	——, Sächsische Landesbibliothek
Dmb	——, Musikbibliothek
Ds	——, Staatstheater
DB	Dettelbach über Kitzingen, BRD, Franziskanerkloster
DEl	Dessau, DDR, Universitäts- und Landesbibliothek
DEs	——, Stadtarchiv, Rathaus
DI	Dillingen an der Donau, BRD, Kreis- und Studienbibliothek
DIp	——, Bischöfliches Priesterseminar
DIN	Dinkelsbühl, BRD, Katholisches Pfarramt St Georg
DIP	Dippoldiswalde, DDR, Evangelisch-Lutherisches Pfarramt
DL	Delitzsch, DDR, Museum und Bibliothek
DM	Dortmund, BRD, Stadt- und Landesbibliothek
DO	Donaueschingen, BRD, Fürstlich Fürstenbergische Hofbibliothek, private collection
DÖ	Döbeln, DDR, Pfarrbibliothek St Nikolai
DÖF	Döffingen über Bölingen, BRD, Pfarrbibliothek
DS	Darmstadt, BRD, Hessische Landes- und Hochschulbibliothek
DSim	——, Internationales Musikinstitut
DSk	——, Kirchenleitung der Evangelischen Kirche in Hessen und Nassau
DT	Detmold, BRD, Lippische Landesbibliothek
DÜgg	Düsseldorf, BRD, Staatliches Görres-Gymnasium
DÜha	——, Hauptstaatsarchiv
DÜk	——, Goethe-Museum
DÜl	——, Landes- und Stadtbibliothek
DÜmb	——, Stadtbüchereien, Musikbücherei
DÜR	Düren, BRD, Stadtbücherei, Leopold-Hoesch-Museum
Ek	Eichstätt, BRD, Kapuzinerkloster
Es	——, Staats- und Seminarbibliothek
Ew	——, Benediktinerinnen-Abtei St Walburg
EB	Ebrach, BRD, Katholisches Pfarramt
EBS	Ebstorf, BRD, Kloster
EF	Erfurt, DDR, Wissenschaftliche Bibliothek der Stadt
EFd	——, Dombibliothek
EFs	——, Stadt- und Bezirksbibliothek
EIa	Eisenach, DDR, Stadtarchiv
EIb	——, Bachhaus und Bachmuseum
EIl	——, Landeskirchenrat
EIHp	Eichtersheim, BRD, Pfarrbibliothek
EL	Eisleben, DDR, Andreas-Bibliothek
EM	Emden, BRD, Grosse Kirche
EMM	Emmerich, BRD, Staatliches Gymnasium
EN	Engelberg, BRD, Franziskanerkloster
ERms	Erlangen, BRD, Musikwissenschaftliches Seminar der Universität
ERu	——, Universitätsbibliothek
ES	Essen, BRD, Musikbücherei der Stadtbücherei
EU	Eutin, BRD, Kreisbibliothek
F	Frankfurt am Main, BRD, Stadt- und Universitätsbibliothek
Fkm	——, Museum für Kunsthandwerk
Fmi	——, Musikwissenschaftliches Institut der Johann Wolfgang von Goethe-Universität
Fsg	——, Philosophisch-Theologische Hochschule St Georgen
Fsm	——, Bibliothek für Neuere Sprachen und Musik
FBa	Freiberg, DDR, Stadtarchiv
FBb	——, Bergakademie, Bücherei
FBo	——, Geschwister-Scholl-Oberschule, Historische Bibliothek
FBsk	——, Stadt- und Kreisbibliothek
FF	Frankfurt an der Oder, DDR, Stadt- und Bezirksbibliothek
FG	Freyburg, DDR, Pfarrarchiv
FLa	Flensburg, BRD, Stadtarchiv
FLs	——, Staatliches Gymnasium
FRcb	Freiburg im Breisgau, BRD, Collegium Borromaeum
FRms	——, Musikwissenschaftliches Seminar der Universität
FRu	——, Universitätsbibliothek
FRIs	Friedberg, BRD, Stadtbibliothek
FRIts	——, Theologisches Seminar der Evangelischen Kirche in Hessen und Nassau
FS	Freising, BRD, Dombibliothek
FUf	Fulda, BRD, Kloster Frauenberg
FUl	——, Hessische Landesbibliothek
FUp	——, Bischöfliches Priesterseminar, Bibliothek der Philosophisch-Theologischen Hochschule
Ga	Göttingen, BRD, Staatliches Archivlager
Gb	——, Johann Sebastian Bach-Institut
Gms	——, Musikwissenschaftliches Seminar der Universität
Gs	——, Niedersächsische Staats- und Universitätsbibliothek
GA	Gaussig bei Bautzen, DDR, Schlossbibliothek
GAH	Gandersheim, BRD, Stiftsbibliothek
GAM	Gau-Algesheim, BRD, Stadtarchiv
GAR	Gars am Inn, BRD, Philosophisch-Theologische Ordenhochschule der Redemptoristen
GBB	Grossbrembach, DDR, Pfarrarchiv
GBR	Grossbreitenbach bei Arnstadt, DDR, Pfarrbibliothek
GD	Gaesdonck über Goch, BRD, Collegium Augustinianum
GE	Gelenau, DDR, Pfarrarchiv
GERk	Gera, DDR, Kirchenarchiv
GERs	——, Stadtmuseum
GERsb	——, Stadt- und Bezirksbibliothek
GEY	Geyer, DDR, Kirchenbibliothek
GF	Grossfahrer, DDR, Pfarrarchiv Starcklof-Eschenberger
GHk	Geithain, DDR, Evangelisch-Lutherisches Pfarramt
GHNa	Grossenhain, DDR, Archiv
GHNk	——, Kirche
GI	Giessen, BRD, Justus Liebig-Universität
GL	Goslar, BRD, Marktkirchenbibliothek
GLA	Glashütte, DDR, Pfarrarchiv
GM	Grimma, DDR, Göschenhaus, Johannes Sturm, private collection
GMl	——, Landesschule
GO	Gotha, DDR, Evangelisch-Lutherische Stadtkirchengemeinde
GOa	——, Augustinerkirche
GOg	——, Gymnasium
GOl	——, Forschungsbibliothek [former Landesbibliothek]
GOs	——, Stadtarchiv
GOsk	——, Stadt- und Kreisbibliothek
GÖp	Görlitz, DDR, Evangelischer Parochialverband
GÖs	——, Stadtbibliothek
GÖsp	——, Pfarramt St Peter
GOL	Goldbach bei Gotha, DDR, Pfarrarchiv
GRim	Greifswald, DDR, Institut für Musikwissenschaft
GRk	——, Konsistorialbibliothek
GRu	——, Ernst-Moritz-Arndt-Universität
GRÜ	Grünhain, DDR, Pfarramt
GÜ	Güstrow, DDR, Heimatmuseum
GZ	Greiz, DDR, Stadt- und Kreisbibliothek
GZbk	——, Staatliche Bücher- und Kupferstichsammlung

GZmb	——, Städtische Musikbibliothek
GZsa	——, Historisches Staatsarchiv
Ha	Hamburg, BRD, Staatsarchiv
Hch	——, Gymnasium Christianeum
Hhm	——, Harburg, Helmsmuseum
Hj	——, Gelehrtenschule des Johanneum
Hkm	——, Kunstgewerbemuseum
Hmb	——, Musikbücherei der Hamburger Öffentlichen Bücherhallen
Hmg	——, Museum für Hamburgische Geschichte
Hmi	——, Musikwissenschaftliches Institut der Universität
Hs	——, Staats- und Universitätsbibliothek
Hsa	——, Senatsarchiv
Hth	——, Universität, Theatersammlung
HAf	Halle an der Saale, DDR, Hauptbibliothek und Archiv der Franckeschen Stiftungen [in *HAu*]
HAh	——, Händel-Haus
HAmi	——, Institut für Musikwissenschaft der Martin-Luther-Universität
HAmk	——, Marienbibliothek
HAs	——, Stadt- und Bezirksbibliothek
HAu	——, Universitäts- und Landesbibliothek Sachsen-Anhalt
HAI	Hainichen, DDR, Heimatmuseum
HB	Heilbronn, BRD, Stadtarchiv
HCHs	Hechingen, BRD, Stiftskirche
HD	Hermsdorf, DDR, Pfarrarchiv
HEk	Heidelberg, BRD, Evangelisches Kirchenmusikalisches Institut
HEms	——, Musikwissenschaftliches Seminar der Universität
HEu	——, Universitätsbibliothek
HER	Herrnhut, DDR, Archiv der Brüder-Unität
HEY	Heynitz, DDR, Pfarrbibliothek
HG	Havelberg, DDR, Museum
HHa	Hildburghausen, DDR, Stadtarchiv
HIb	Hildesheim, BRD, Beverin'sche Bibliothek
HIm	——, St Michaelskirche
HIp	——, Bischöfliches Priesterseminar
HL	Haltenbergstetten, BRD, Schloss über Niederstetten, Fürst zu Hohenlohe-Jagstberg'sche Bibliothek, private collection
HLN	Hameln, BRD, Stadtbücherei des Schiller-Gymnasiums
HN	Herborn, BRD, Evangelisches Theologisches Seminar
HO	Hof an der Saale, BRD, Jean Paul-Gymnasium
HOr	——, Stadtarchiv, Ratsbibliothek
HOE	Hohenstein-Ernstthal, DDR, Kantoreiarchiv der Christophorikirche
HOG	Hofgeismar, BRD, Predigerseminar
HOR	Horst, BRD, Evangelisch-Lutherisches Pfarramt
HR	Harburg über Donauwörth, BRD, Fürstlich Oettingen-Wallerstein'sche Bibliothek, private collection
HSj	Helmstedt, BRD, Juleum
HSk	——, Kantorat zu St Stephani [in *W*]
HSm	——, Kloster Marienberg
HSwandersleb	——, Bibliothek Pastor Wandersleb
HTa	Halberstadt, DDR, Stadtarchiv
HTd	——, Dombibliothek
HTg	——, Gleimhaus
HVh	Hanover, BRD, Staatliche Hochschule für Musik und Theater
HVk	——, Arbeitsstelle für Gottesdienst und Kirchenmusik der Evangelisch-Lutherischen Landeskirche
HVl	——, Niedersächsische Landesbibliothek
HVs	——, Stadtbibliothek
HVsa	——, Staatsarchiv
HVth	——, Technische Hochschule
HX	Höxter, BRD, Kirchenbibliothek St Nikolaus
Iek	Isny, BRD, Evangelische Kirche St Nikolai
Iq	——, Fürstlich Quadt'sche Bibliothek, private collection
ILk	Ilmenau, DDR, Kirchenbibliothek
ILs	——, Stadtarchiv
IN	Indersdorf über Dachau, BRD, Katholisches Pfarramt
Jmb	Jena, DDR, Ernst Abbe-Bücherei, Musikbücherei
Jmi	——, Musikwissenschaftliches Institut der Friedrich-Schiller-Universität
Ju	——, Universitätsbibliothek der Friedrich-Schiller-Universität
JA	Jahnsdorf bei Stollberg, DDR, Pfarrarchiv
JE	Jever, BRD, Marien-Gymnasium
Kdma	Kassel, BRD, Deutsches Musikgeschichtliches Archiv
Kl	——, Murhardsche Bibliothek der Stadt und Landesbibliothek
Km	——, Musikakademie
Ksp	——, Louis-Spohr-Gedenk- und Forschungsstätte
KA	Karlsruhe, BRD, Badische Landesbibliothek
KAsp	——, Pfarramt St Peter
KAu	——, Universitätsbibliothek
KAL	Kaldenkirchen, BRD, Pfarrbibliothek
KARj	Karl-Marx-Stadt, DDR, Jacobi-Kirche
KARr	——, Ratsarchiv
KARs	——, Stadt- und Bezirksbibliothek
KBs	Koblenz, BRD, Stadtbibliothek
KBEk	Koblenz-Ehrenbreitstein, BRD, Provinzialat der Kapuziner
KFm	Kaufbeuren, BRD, Stadtpfarrkirche St Martin
KFs	——, Stadtbücherei
KII	Kiel, BRD, Schleswig-Holsteinische Landesbibliothek
KImi	——, Musikwissenschaftliches Institut der Christian-Albrecht Universität
KIu	——, Universitätsbibliothek
KIN	Kindelbrück, DDR, Pfarrarchiv, Evangelisches Pfarramt
KMk	Kamenz, DDR, Evangelisch-Lutherische Hauptkirche
KMl	——, Lessingmuseum
KMs	——, Stadtarchiv
KNd	Cologne, BRD, Erzbischöfliche Diözesan- und Dombibliothek
KNh	——, Staatliche Hochschule für Musik
KNhi	——, Joseph Haydn-Institut
KNmi	——, Musikwissenschaftliches Institut der Universität
KNu	——, Universitäts- und Stadtbibliothek
KÖ	Köthen, DDR, Heimatmuseum
KPk	Kempten, BRD, Kirchenbibliothek, Evangelisch-Lutherisches Pfarramt St Mang
KPs	——, Stadtbücherei
KPsl	——, Stadtpfarrkirche St Lorenz
KR	Kleinröhrsdorf über Bischofswerda, DDR, Pfarrkirchenbibliothek
KT	Klingenthal, DDR, Kirchenbibliothek
KU	Kulmbach, BRD, Stadtarchiv
KZa	Konstanz, BRD, Stadtarchiv
KZr	——, Rosgarten-Museum
KZs	——, Städtische Wessenberg-Bibliothek
Lm	Lüneburg, BRD, Michaelisschule
Lr	——, Ratsbücherei
LA	Landshut, BRD, Historischer Verein für Niederbayern
LAU	Laubach, BRD, Gräflich Solms-Laubach'sche Bibliothek
LB	Langenburg, BRD, Fürstlich Hohenlohe-Langenburg'sche Schlossbibliothek, private collection
LCH	Lich, BRD, Fürstlich Solms-Lich'sche Bibliothek, private collection
LEb	Leipzig, DDR, Bach-Archiv
LEbh	——, Breitkopf & Härtel, Verlagsarchiv
LEdh	——, Deutsche Bücherei, Musikaliensammlung
LEm	——, Musikbibliothek der Stadt
LEmh	——, Hochschule für Musik
LEmi	——, Musikwissenschaftliches Institut der Karl-Marx-Universität
LEsm	——, Museum für Geschichte der Stadt
LEt	——, Thomasschule
LEu	——, Universitätsbibliothek der Karl-Marx-Universität
LFN	Laufen an der Salzach, BRD, Stiftsarchiv
LHD	Langhennersdorf über Freiberg, DDR, Pfarramt
LI	Lindau, BRD, Stadtbibliothek
LIM	Limbach am Main, BRD, Pfarramt
LL	Langula über Mühlhausen, DDR, Pfarramt
LM	Leitheim über Donauwörth, BRD, Schlossbibliothek Freiherr von Tucher
LO	Loccum über Wunstorf, BRD, Klosterbibliothek
LÖ	Lössnitz, DDR, Pfarrarchiv
LR	Lahr, BRD, Lehrerbibliothek des Scheffel-Gymnasiums
LST	Lichtenstein, DDR, Kantoreiarchiv von St Laurentius
LÜd	Lübeck, BRD, Distler Archiv
LÜh	——, Bibliothek der Hansestadt
LUC	Luckau, DDR, Nikolaikirche
Ma	Munich, BRD, Franziskanerkloster St Anna
Mb	——, Benediktinerabtei St Bonifaz
Mbm	——, Metropolitankapitel
Mbn	——, Bayerisches Nationalmuseum
Mbs	——, Bayerische Staatsbibliothek

Mcg	——, Georgianum, Herzogliches Priesterseminar
Mdm	——, Deutsches Museum
Mh	——, Staatliche Hochschule für Musik
Ml	——, Evangelisch-Lutherisches Landeskirchenamt
Mmb	——, Städtische Musikbibliothek
Mms	——, Musikwissenschaftliches Seminar der Universität
Msl	——, Süddeutsche Lehrerbücherei
Mth	——, Theatermuseum der Clara-Ziegler-Stiftung
Mu	——, Universitätsbibliothek
Mwg	——, Wilhelms-Gymnasium, Lehrerbibliothek
MAk	Magdeburg, DDR, Kulturhistorisches Museum, Klosterbibliothek
MAkon	——, Konsistorialbibliothek
MAl	——, Landeshauptarchiv
MAs	——, Stadt- und Bezirksbibliothek
MB	Marbach an der Neckar, BRD, Schiller-National-museum
MBG	Miltenberg am Main, BRD, Franziskanerkloster
MCH	Maria Laach über Andernach, BRD, Benediktiner-abtei
ME	Meissen, DDR, Stadt- und Kreisbibliothek
MEIk	Meiningen, DDR, Evangelisch-Lutherische Kirchengemeinde
MEIl	——, Staatsarchiv
MEIo	——, Opernarchiv
MEIr	——, Staatliche Museen mit Reger-Archiv
MEL	Meldorf, BRD, Joachimsche Bibliothek, Dithmarsches Landesmuseum
MERa	Merseburg, DDR, Domstift
MERr	——, Regierungsbibliothek
MERs	——, Stadt- und Kreisbibliothek
MERz	——, Deutsches Zentral-Archiv, Historische Abteilung
MFL	Münstereifel, BRD, St Michael-Gymnasium
MGmi	Marburg an der Lahn, BRD, Musikwissenschaftliches Institut der Philipps-Universität
MGs	——, Staatsarchiv und Archivschule
MGu	——, Universitätsbibliothek der Philipps-Universität
MH	Mannheim, BRD, Wissenschaftliche Stadtbibliothek und Universitätsbibliothek
MHrm	——, Reiss-Museum
MHR	Mülheim, BRD, Stadtbibliothek
MI	Michelstadt, BRD, Evangelisches Pfarramt West
MK	Markneukirchen, DDR, Gewerbemuseum
MLHb	Mühlhausen, DDR, Blasiuskirche
MLHr	——, Ratsarchiv im Stadtarchiv
MMm	Memmingen, BRD, Evangelisch-Lutherisches Pfarramt St Martin
MMs	——, Stadtbibliothek
MÖ	Mölln, BRD, Evangelisch-Lutherische Kirchengemeinde St Nikolai
MOSp	Mosbach, BRD, Pfarrbibliothek
MR	Marienberg, DDR, Kirchenbibliothek
MS	Münsterschwarzach über Kitzingen am Main, BRD, Abtei
MT	Metten über Deggendorf, BRD, Abtei
MÜd	Münster, BRD, Bischöfliches Diözesanarchiv
MÜms	——, Musikwissenschaftliches Seminar der Universität
MÜp	——, Bischöfliches Priesterseminar und Santini-Sammlung
MÜrt	——, Seminar für Reformierte Theologie
MÜs	——, Santini-Bibliothek [in *MÜp*]
MÜsa	——, Staatsarchiv
MÜu	——, Universitätsbibliothek
MÜG	Mügeln, DDR, Pfarrarchiv
MWR	Marienweiher über Kulmbach, BRD, Franziskanerkloster
MZfederhofer	Mainz, BRD, Hellmut Federhofer, private collection
MZgm	——, Gutenberg-Museum
MZgottron	——, Adam Gottron, private collection
MZmi	——, Musikwissenschaftliches Institut der Universität
MZp	——, Bischöfliches Priesterseminar
MZs	——, Stadtbibliothek und Stadtarchiv
MZsch	——, Musikverlag B. Schotts Söhne
MZu	——, Universitätsbibliothek der Johannes-Gutenberg-Universität
Ngm	Nuremberg, BRD, Germanisches National-Museum
Nla	——, Landeskirchliches Archiv
Nst	——, Stadtbibliothek
NA	Neustadt an der Orla, DDR, Pfarrarchiv
NAUs	Naumburg, DDR, Stadtarchiv
NAUw	——, Wenzelskirche
NBsb	Neuburg an der Donau, BRD, Staatliche Bibliothek
NBss	——, Studienseminar
NEhz	Neuenstein, BRD, Hohenlohe-Zentral-Archiv
NEschumm	——, Karl Schumm, private collection
NERk	Neuenrade, BRD, Kirchenbibliothek
NEZp	Neckarelz, BRD, Pfarrbibliothek
NGp	Neckargemünd, BRD, Pfarrarchiv
NIw	Nieheim über Bad Driburg, BRD, Weberhaus
NL	Nördlingen, BRD, Stadtarchiv, Stadtbibliothek und Volksbücherei
NLk	——, Kirchenbibliothek St Georg
NM	Neumünster, BRD, Schleswig-Holsteinische Musiksammlung der Stadt [in *KIl*]
NO	Nordhausen, DDR, Humboldt-Oberschule
NS	Neustadt an der Aisch, BRD, Evangelische Kirchenbibliothek
NSg	——, Gymnasialbibliothek
NT	Neumarkt-St Veit, BRD, Pfarrkirche
NW	Neustadt an der Weinstrasse, BRD, Heimatmuseum
OB	Ottobeuren, BRD, Benediktiner-Abtei
OF	Offenbach am Main, BRD, Verlagsarchiv André
OH	Oberfrankenhain, DDR, Pfarrarchiv
OLl	Oldenburg, BRD, Landesbibliothek
OLns	——, Niedersächsisches Staatsarchiv
OLH	Olbernhau, DDR, Pfarrarchiv
ORB	Oranienbaum, DDR, Landesarchiv–Historisches Staatsarchiv
OS	Oschatz, DDR, Ephoralbibliothek
OSa	Osnabrück, BRD, Niedersächsisches Staatsarchiv
OSm	——, Städtisches Museum
Pg	Passau, BRD, Gymnasialbibliothek
Pk	——, Bischöfliches Klerikalseminar
Po	——, Bischöfliches Ordinariat
Ps	——, Staatliche Bibliothek
PA	Paderborn, BRD, Erzbischöfliche Akademische Bibliothek
PI	Pirna, DDR, Stadtarchiv
POh	Potsdam, DDR, Pädagogische Hochschule
PR	Pretzschendorf über Dippoldiswalde, DDR, Pfarrarchiv
PU	Pulsnitz, DDR, Nikolaikirche
PW	Pesterwitz bei Dresden, DDR, Pfarrarchiv
Q	Quedlinburg, DDR, Stadt- und Kreisbibliothek
QUh	Querfurt, DDR, Heimatmuseum
QUk	——, Stadtkirche
Rim	Regensburg, BRD, Institut für Musikforschung [in *Ru*]
Rp	——, Bischöfliche Zentralbibliothek
Rs	——, Staatliche Bibliothek
Rtt	——, Fürstlich Thurn und Taxis'sche Hofbibliothek, private collection
Ru	——, Universitätsbibliothek
RAd	Ratzeburg, BRD, Domarchiv
RB	Rothenburg ob der Tauber, BRD, Stadtarchiv und Rats- und Konsistorialbibliothek
RE	Reutberg bei Schaftlach, BRD, Franziskanerinnen-Kloster
REU	Reuden, DDR, Pfarrarchiv
RH	Rheda, BRD, Fürst zu Bentheim-Tecklenburgische Bibliothek [in *MH* and *MÜu*]
RIE	Riesa, DDR, Heimatmuseum
RL	Reutlingen, BRD, Stadtbücherei
RMmarr	Ramesloh über Winsen, BRD, G. Marr, private collection
ROmi	Rostock, DDR, Institut für Musikwissenschaft der Universität
ROs	——, Stadt- und Bezirksbibliothek
ROu	——, Universitätsbibliothek
RÖ	Röhrsdorf über Meissen, DDR, Pfarrbibliothek
RÖM	Römhild, DDR, Pfarrarchiv
ROT	Rotenburg, BRD, Predigerseminar
ROTTd	Rottenburg an der Neckar, BRD, Diözesanbibliothek
ROTTp	——, Bischöfliches Priesterseminar
RT	Rastatt, BRD, Friedrich-Wilhelm-Gymnasium
RUh	Rudolstadt, DDR, Hofkapellarchiv
RUl	——, Staatsarchiv
RÜ	Rüdenhausen über Kitzingen, BRD, Fürst Castell-Rüdenhausen Bibliothek
Seo	Stuttgart, BRD, Bibliothek und Archiv des Evangelischen Oberkirchenrats
Sh	——, Staatliche Hochschule für Musik und Darstellende Kunst
Sl	——, Württembergische Landesbibliothek
SAh	Saalfeld, DDR, Heimatmuseum
SAAmi	Saarbrücken, BRD, Musikwissenschaftliches Institut der Universität

SAAu	——, Universitätsbibliothek
SBg	Straubing, BRD, Johannes Turmair-Gymnasium
SBj	——, Kirchenbibliothek St Jakob
SBk	——, Karmeliter-Kloster
SCHhv	Schwäbisch Hall, BRD, Historischer Verein für Württembergisch-Franken
SCHm	——, Archiv der St Michaelskirche
SCHr	——, Ratsbibliothek im Stadtarchiv
SCHEY	Scheyern über Pfaffenhofen, BRD, Benediktinerabtei
SCHM	Schmölln, DDR, Archiv der Stadtkirche
SCHMl	Schmiedeberg bei Dresden, DDR, Pfarramt
SCHWherold	Schwabach, BRD, Herold collection
SCHWk	——, Kirchenbibliothek
SDF	Schlehdorf, BRD, Katholische Pfarrkirche
SF	Schweinfurt-Oberndorf, BRD, Kirchen- und Pfarrbibliothek des Evangelisch-Lutherischen Pfarramts
SFsj	——, Pfarramt St Johannis, Sakristei-Bibliothek
SGh	Schleusingen, DDR, Heimatmuseum
SHk	Sondershausen, DDR, Stadtkirche
SHs	——, Stadt- und Kreisbibliothek
SHsk	——, Schlosskirche
SI	Sigmaringen, BRD, Fürstlich Hohenzollernsche Hofbibliothek, private collection
SLk	Salzwedel, DDR, Katharinenkirche
SLm	——, J. F. Danneil-Museum
SLmk	——, Marienkirche
SNed	Schmalkalden, DDR, Evangelisches Dekanat
SNh	——, Heimatmuseum Schloss Wilhelmsburg
SO	Soest, BRD, Stadtbibliothek im Stadtarchiv
SÖNp	Schönau bei Heidelberg, BRD, Pfarrbibliothek
SPlb	Speyer, BRD, Pfälzische Landesbibliothek, Musikabteilung
SPlk	——, Bibliothek des Protestantischen Landeskirchenrats der Pfalz
SPF	Schulpforta, DDR, Heimoberschule
SSa	Stralsund, DDR, Bibliothek des Stadtarchivs
ST	Stade, BRD, Predigerbibliothek [in *ROT*]
STO	Stolberg, DDR, Bibliothek
SUa	Sulzenbrücken, DDR, Pfarrarchiv
SUH	Suhl, DDR, Stadt- und Bezirksbibliothek Martin Andersen Nexö
SWl	Schwerin, DDR, Wissenschaftliche Allgemeinbibliothek [former Mecklenburgische Landesbibliothek]
SWs	——, Stadt- und Bezirksbibliothek, Musikabteilung
SWsk	——, Schlosskirchenchor
SWth	——, Mecklenburgisches Staatstheater
SZ	Schleiz, DDR, Bibliothek
Tes	Tübingen, BRD, Evangelisches Stift
Tl	——, Schwäbisches Landesmusikarchiv [in *Tmi*]
Tmi	——, Musikwissenschaftliches Institut der Eberhard-Karls-Universität
Tu	——, Universitätsbibliothek
Tw	——, Bibliothek des Wilhelmstiftes
TAB	Tabarz, DDR, Pfarrarchiv, Evangelisch-Lutherisches Pfarramt
TEG	Tegernsee, BRD, Pfarrkirche, Katholisches Pfarramt
TEI	Teisendorf, BRD, Katholisches Pfarramt
TH	Themar, DDR, Pfarramt
TIT	Tittmoning, BRD, Kollegiatstift
TO	Torgau, DDR, Johann-Walter-Kantorei
TOek	——, Evangelische Kirchengemeinde
TOs	——, Stadtarchiv
TRb	Trier, BRD, Bistumarchiv und Dombibliothek
TRp	——, Priesterseminar
TRs	——, Stadtbibliothek
Us	Ulm, BRD, Stadtbibliothek
Usch	——, Von Schermar'sche Familienstiftung
UDa	Udestedt über Erfurt, DDR, Pfarrarchiv, Evangelisch-Lutherisches Pfarramt
V	Villingen, BRD, Städtische Sammlung
VI	Viernau, DDR, Pfarramt
W	Wolfenbüttel, BRD, Herzog August Bibliothek
Wa	——, Niedersächsisches Staatsarchiv
WA	Waldheim, DDR, Stadtkirche St Nikolai
WAB	Waldenburg, DDR, Kirchenmusikalische Bibliothek von St Bartholomäus
WB	Weissenburg, BRD, Stadtbibliothek
WBB	Walberg, BRD, Albertus-Magnus-Akademie, Bibliothek St Albert
WD	Wiesentheid, BRD, Musiksammlung des Grafen von Schönborn-Wiesentheid, private collection
WE	Weiden, BRD, Pfannenstiel'sche Bibliothek, Evangelisch-Lutherisches Pfarramt
WEH	Weierhof, BRD, Mennonitische Forschungsstelle
WEL	Weltenburg, BRD, Benediktinerkloster
WER	Wernigerode, DDR, Heimatmuseum, Harzbücherei
WERk	Wertheim am Main, BRD, Evangelisches Pfarramt
WERl	——, Fürstlich Löwenstein'sche Bibliothek, private collection
WEY	Weyarn, BRD, Pfarrkirche [in *FS*]
WF	Weissenfels, DDR, Heimatmuseum
WFg	——, Heinrich-Schütz-Gedenkstätte
WGk	Wittenberg, DDR, Stadtkirche
WGl	——, Reformationsgeschichtliches Museum, Lutherhalle
WGp	——, Evangelisches Predigerseminar
WH	Windsheim, BRD, Stadtbibliothek
WIl	Wiesbaden, BRD, Hessische Landesbibliothek
WILd	Wilster, BRD, Stadtarchiv (Doos'sche Bibliothek)
WL	Wuppertal, BRD, Wissenschaftliche Stadtbibliothek
WM	Wismar, DDR, Stadtarchiv
WO	Worms, BRD, Stadtbibliothek
WRdn	Weimar, DDR, Deutsches Nationaltheater
WRgm	——, Goethe-National-Museum
WRgs	——, Goethe–Schiller-Archiv und Franz-Liszt-Museum
WRh	——, Franz-Liszt-Hochschule
WRhk	——, Herderkirche
WRiv	——, Institut für Volksmusikforschung
WRl	——, Landeshauptarchiv
WRs	——, Stadtbücherei, Musikbücherei
WRtl	——, Thüringische Landesbibliothek, Musiksammlung
WRz	——, Zentralbibliothek der Deutschen Klassik
WS	Wasserburg am Inn, BRD, Chorarchiv St Jakob, Pfarramt
WÜms	Würzburg, BRD, Musikwissenschaftliches Seminar der Universität
WÜsa	——, Stadtarchiv
WÜu	——, Universitätsbibliothek
X	Xanten, BRD, Stifts- und Pfarrbibliothek
Z	Zwickau, DDR, Ratsschulbibliothek
Zmk	——, Domkantorei der Marienkirche
Zsch	——, Robert-Schumann-Haus
ZE	Zerbst, DDR, Stadtarchiv
ZEo	——, Bücherei der Erweiterten Oberschule
ZGh	Zörbig, DDR, Heimatmuseum
ZGsj	——, Pfarramt St Jacobi
ZI	Zittau, DDR, Stadt- und Kreisbibliothek
ZIa	——, Stadtarchiv
ZL	Zeil, BRD, Fürstlich Waldburg-Zeil'sches Archiv, private collection
ZW	Zweibrücken, BRD, Bibliotheca Bipontina, Wissenschaftliche Bibliothek am Herzog-Wolfgang-Gymnasium
ZZ	Zeitz, DDR, Heimatmuseum
ZZs	——, Stiftsbibliothek

DK: DENMARK

A	Århus, Statsbiblioteket
Dschoenbaum	Dragør, Camillo Schoenbaum, private collection
Hfog	Hellerup, Dan Fog, private collection
Kc	Copenhagen, Carl Claudius Musikhistoriske Samling
Kh	——, Københavns Kommunes Hovedbiblioteket
Kk	——, Det Kongelige Bibliotek
Kmk	——, Det Kongelige Danske Musikkonservatorium
Km(m)	——, Musikhistorisk Museum
Ks	——, Samfundet til Udgivelse af Dansk Musik
Kt	——, Teaterhistorisk Museum
Ku	——, Universitetsbiblioteket 1. Afdeling
Kv	——, Københavns Universitet, Musikvidenskabeligt Institut
Ol	Odense, Landsarkivet for Fyen, Karen Brahes Bibliotek
Ou	——, Universitetsbibliotek
Rk	Ribe, Stifts- og Katedralskoles Bibliotek
Sa	Sorø, Sorø Akademis Bibliotek

E: SPAIN

Ac	Ávila, Catedral
Asa	——, Monasterio de S Ana (Real Monasterio de Encarnación)
Ast	——, Monasterio del S Tomás, Archivo de la Iglesia
AL	Alquezar, Colegiata
ALB	Albarracín, Colegiata
AS	Astorga, Catedral
Ba	Barcelona, Real Academia de Ciencias y Artes
Bac	——, Corona de Aragón

Bc	——, Biblioteca de Cataluña
Bca	——, Catedral
Bcapdevila	——, Felipe Capdevila Rovira, private collection
Bcm	——, Conservatorio Superior Municipal de Música
Bih	——, Instituto Municipal de Historia (formerly Archivo Histórico de la Ciudad)
Bim	——, Instituto Español de Musicología
Bit	——, Instituto del Teatro (formerly Museo del Arte Escénico)
Boc	——, Biblioteca Orfeó Catalá
Bsm	——, S María del Mar
Bu	——, Biblioteca del Universidad
BA	Badajoz, Catedral
BUa	Burgos, Catedral
BUlh	——, Monasterio de Las Huelgas
BUm	——, Museo Arqueológico
BUp	——, Biblioteca Provincial
BUse	——, Parroquia de S Esteban
C	Córdoba, Catedral
CA	Calahorra, Catedral
CAL	Calatayud, Colegiata de S María
CAR	Cardona, Archivo Comunal
CU	Cuenca, Catedral
CUi	——, Instituto de Música Religiosa
CZ	Cádiz, Archivo Capitular
E	El Escorial, Real Monasterio de S Loren:
G	Gerona, Biblioteca Catedralicia
Gm	——, Museo Diocesano
Gp	——, Biblioteca Pública
Gs	——, Seminario Gerundense
GRc	Granada, Catedral
GRcr	——, Capilla Real
GU	Guadalupe, Real Monasterio de S María
H	Huesca, Catedral
J	Jaca, Catedral
JA	Jaén, Catedral
LPA	Las Palmas, Catedral de Canarias
La	León, Catedral
Lc	——, Colegiata de S Isidoro
Lp	——, Biblioteca Pública Provincial
LEc	Lérida, Catedral
LEm	——, Museo Diocesano
Ma	Madrid, Real Academia de Bellas Artes de S Fernando
Mah	——, Archivo Histórico Nacional (Real Academia de la Historia)
Mam	——, Biblioteca Musical Circulante
Mat	——, Museo-Archivo Teatral
Mc	——, Conservatorio Superior de Música
Mca	——, Casa de Alba, private collection
Mcns	——, Congregación de Nuestra Señora
Mic	——, Instituto de Cultura Hispánica, Sección de Música
Mit	——, Ministerio de Información y Turismo
Mlg	——, Fundación Lazaro Galdiano
Mm	——, Biblioteca Municipal
Mmc	——, Casa Ducal de Medinaceli, Bartolomé March Servera, private collection
Mn	——, Biblioteca Nacional
Mp	——, Palacio Real
Mpm	——, Patronato Marcelino Menéndez y Pelayo del Consejo Superior de Investigaciones Científicas
Mrt	——, Radio Nacional de España-Televisión
Msa	——, Sociedad General de Autores de España
Msi	——, Ciudad Universitaria, Facultad de Filosofía y Letras, Biblioteca de S Isidoro
MA	Málaga, Catedral
MO	Montserrat, Monasterio de S María
MON	Mondoñedo, Catedral
OL	Olot, Biblioteca Popular
OR	Orense, Catedral
ORI	Orihuela, Catedral
OS	Osma, Catedral
OV	Oviedo, Catedral Metropolitana
P	Plasencia, Catedral
PAc	Palma de Mallorca, Catedral
PAp	——, Biblioteca Provincial
PAMc	Pamplona, Catedral
PAMm	——, Museo Sarasate
PAS	Pastrana, Iglesia Parroquial
RO	Roncesvalles, Monasterio de S María
Sc	Seville, Catedral
Sco	——, Biblioteca Capitular Colombina [in *Sc*]
SA	Salamanca, Catedral
SAcalo	——, José López-Calo, private collection
SAu	——, Universidad Pontificia, Biblioteca Universitaria

SAuf	——, Universidad Pontificia, Facultad de Filosofía y Letras
SAN	Santander, Biblioteca de Menéndez y Pelayo
SC	Santiago de Compostela, Catedral
SCu	——, Biblioteca Universitaria
SD	Santo Domingo de la Calzada, Archivo
SE	Segovia, Catedral
SEG	Segorbe, Catedral
SI	Silos, Monasterio Benedictino (Abadía) de S Domingo
SIG	Sigüenza, Catedral
SIM	Simancas, Archivo General
SO	Soria, Biblioteca Pública
Tc	Toledo, Archivo Capitular
Tp	——, Biblioteca Pública Provincial y Museo de la Santa Cruz
TAc	Tarragona, Catedral
TAp	——, Biblioteca Pública
TO	Tortosa, Catedral
TU	Tudela, Colegiata (formerly Catedral) de S María
TZ	Tarazona, Catedral
U (also *SU*)	Seo de Urgel, Catedral
V	Valladolid, Catedral
Vp	——, Parroquia de Santiago
VAa	Valencia, Archivo, Biblioteca y Museos Municipales
VAc	——, Catedral
VAcm	——, Conservatorio Superior de Música
VAcp	——, Colegio y Seminario del Corpus Christi del Patriarca
VAim	——, Instituto Valenciano de Musicología
VAu	——, Biblioteca Universitaria
VI	Vich, Museo Episcopal
VIT	Vitoria, Catedral
Zac	Saragossa, Archivo de Música del Cabildo
Zcc	——, Colegio Calasanci
Zfm	——, Facultad de Medicina
Zp	——, Biblioteca Pública
Zs	——, Biblioteca Capitular de la Seo
Zsc	——, Seminario de S Carlos
Zu	——, Biblioteca Universitaria
Zvp	——, Iglesia Metropolitana [in *Zac*]
ZA	Zamora, Catedral

EIRE: IRELAND

C	Cork, University College
Da	Dublin, Royal Irish Academy
Dam	——, Royal Irish Academy of Music
Dcb	——, Chester Beatty Library
Dcc	——, Christ Church Cathedral
Dm	——, Marsh's Library
Dmh	——, Mercer's Hospital
Dn	——, National Library and Museum of Ireland
Dpc	——, St Patrick's Cathedral
Dtc	——, Trinity College
Duc	——, University College

ET: EGYPT

S	Mt Sinai

F: FRANCE

A	Avignon, Bibliothèque Municipale, Musée Calvet
Aa	——, Archives Départementales de Vaucluse
AB	Abbeville, Bibliothèque Municipale
AG	Agen, Archives Départementales de Lot-et-Garonne
AI	Albi, Bibliothèque Municipale
AIXc	Aix-en-Provence, Conservatoire
AIXm	——, Bibliothèque Municipale, Bibliothèque Méjanes
AIXmc	——, Maîtrise de la Cathédrale
AL	Alençon, Bibliothèque Municipale
AM	Amiens, Bibliothèque Municipale
AN	Angers, Bibliothèque Municipale
ANG	Angoulême, Bibliothèque Municipale
ANN	Annecy, Bibliothèque Municipale
APT	Apt, Cathédrale Ste Anne
AR	Arles, Bibliothèque Municipale
AS	Arras, Bibliothèque Municipale
ASO	Asnières-sur-Oise, François Lang, private collection
AU	Auxerre, Bibliothèque Municipale
AUT	Autun, Bibliothèque Municipale
AV	Avallon, Société d'Etudes d'Avallon
AVR	Avranches, Bibliothèque Municipale
B	Besançon, Bibliothèque Municipale
Ba	——, Bibliothèque de l'Archevêché
Be	——, Ecole Nationale de Musique
BD	Bar-le-Duc, Bibliothèque Municipale
BE	Beauvais, Bibliothèque Municipale
BER	Bernay, Bibliothèque Municipale

BG	Bourg-en-Bresse, Bibliothèque Municipale et Musée de l'Ain
BL	Blois, Bibliothèque Municipale
BO	Bordeaux, Bibliothèque Municipale
BOI	Boisguillaume, Musée Boieldieu
BOU	Bourbourg, Bibliothèque Municipale
BR	Brest, Bibliothèque Municipale
BS	Bourges, Bibliothèque Municipale
BSM	Boulogne-sur-Mer, Bibliothèque Municipale
C	Carpentras, Bibliothèque Inguimbertine et Musée de Carpentras
CA	Cambrai, Bibliothèque Municipale
CAc	——, Cathédrale
CAD	Cadouin, Bibliothèque de l'Abbaye
CAH	Cahors, Bibliothèque Municipale
CAL	Calais, Bibliothèque Municipale
CC	Carcassonne, Bibliothèque Municipale
CF	Clermont-Ferrand, Bibliothèque Municipale et Universitaire, Section Centrale et Section Lettres
CH	Chantilly, Musée Condé
CHA	Châteauroux, Bibliothèque Municipale
CHE	Cherbourg, Bibliothèque et Archives Municipales
CHM	Chambéry, Bibliothèque Municipale
CHR	Chartres, Bibliothèque Municipale
CN	Caen, Bibliothèque Municipale
CNc	——, Conservatoire National de Musique
CO	Colmar, Bibliothèque Municipale
COs	——, Consistoire de l'Eglise de la Confession d'Augsbourg à Colmar
COUm	Coutances, Bibliothèque Municipale
COUs	——, Grand Séminaire
CSM	Châlons-sur-Marne, Bibliothèque Municipale
CV	Charleville, Bibliothèque Municipale
Dc	Dijon, Bibliothèque du Conservatoire
Dm	——, Bibliothèque Municipale (Bibliothèque Publique)
DI	Dieppe, Bibliothèque Municipale
DO	Dôle, Bibliothèque Municipale
DOU	Douai, Bibliothèque Municipale
E	Epinal, Bibliothèque Municipale
EP	Epernay, Bibliothèque Municipale
EV	Evreux, Bibliothèque Municipale
F	Foix, Bibliothèque Municipale
G	Grenoble, Bibliothèque Municipale
Ge	——, Ecole Régionale de Musique, de Danse et d'Art Dramatique
GAP	Gap, Archives Départementales des Hautes-Alpes
H	Hyères, Bibliothèque Municipale
Lc	Lille, Conservatoire
Lfc	——, Facultés Catholiques
Lm	——, Bibliothèque Municipale
LA	Laon, Bibliothèque Municipale
LB	Libourne, Bibliothèque Municipale
LG	Limoges, Bibliothèque Municipale
LH	Le Havre, Bibliothèque Municipale
LM	Le Mans, Bibliothèque Municipale
LO	Louviers, Bibliothèque Municipale
LP	Le Puy-en-Velay, Bibliothèque Municipale
LR	La Rochelle, Bibliothèque Municipale
LV	Laval, Bibliothèque Municipale
LYc	Lyons, Conservatoire National de Musique
LYm	——, Bibliothèque Municipale
Mc	Marseilles, Conservatoire de Musique et de Déclamation
Mm	——, Bibliothèque Municipale
MAC	Mâcon, Bibliothèque Municipale
MD	Montbéliard, Bibliothèque Municipale
MEL	Melun, Bibliothèque Municipale
MH	Mulhouse, Bibliothèque Municipale
MIL	Millau, Bibliothèque Municipale
MIR	Mirecourt, Bibliothèque Municipale
ML	Moulins, Bibliothèque Municipale
MLN	Montluçon, Bibliothèque Municipale
MO	Montpellier, Faculté de Médecine de l'Université
MOv	——, Bibliothèque de la Ville et du Musée Fabre
MON	Montauban, Bibliothèque Municipale
MZ	Metz, Bibliothèque Municipale
Nd	Nantes, Bibliothèque du Musée Dobrée
Ne	——, Ecole Nationale de Musique, d'Art Dramatique et de Danse
Nm	——, Bibliothèque Municipale
NAc	Nancy, Conservatoire
NAm	——, Bibliothèque Municipale
NAR	Narbonne, Bibliothèque Municipale
NI	Nice, Bibliothèque Municipale
NIc	——, Conservatoire de Musique

NO	Noyon, Bibliothèque Municipale
NS	Nîmes, Bibliothèque Municipale
NT	Niort, Bibliothèque Municipale
O	Orleans, Bibliothèque Municipale
Pa	Paris, Bibliothèque de l'Arsenal
Pal	——, American Library in Paris
Pbf	——, Centre de Documentation Benjamin Franklin
Pc	——, Conservatoire National de Musique [in *Pn*]
Pcf	——, Comédie-Française, Bibliothèque
Pcrs	——, Centre National de la Recherche Scientifique
Pe	——, Schola Cantorum (Ecole Supérieure de Musique, Danse et Art Dramatique)
Pgérard	——, Yves Gérard, private collection
Pi	——, Bibliothèque de l'Institut
Pim	——, Institut de Musicologie de l'Université, Bibliothèque Pierre Aubry
Pis	——, Institut Supérieur de Musique Liturgique
Pm	——, Bibliothèque Mazarine
Pma	——, Musée Nationales Art et Traditions Populaires
Pmeyer	——, André Meyer, private collection
Pmg	——, Musée Guimet
Pmh	——, Musée de l'Homme
Pn	——, Bibliothèque Nationale
Po	——, Bibliothèque–Musée de l'Opéra
Pphon	——, Phonothèque Nationale, Bibliothèque et Musée
Ppincherle	——, Marc Pincherle, private collection [dispersed 1975]
Ppo	——, Bibliothèque Polonaise de Paris
Prothschild	——, Germaine, Baronne Edouard de Rothschild, private collection
Prt	——, Office de Radiodiffusion-Télévision Française
Psc	——, Société des Auteurs et Compositeurs Dramatiques
Pse	——, Société des Auteurs, Compositeurs et Editeurs de Musique
Psg	——, Bibliothèque Ste Geneviève
Pshp	——, Bibliothèque de la Société d'Histoire du Protestantisme
Psi	——, Séminaire Israélite de France
Pthibault	——, Geneviève Thibault, private collection
PAU	Pau, Bibliothèque Municipale
PE	Périgueux, Bibliothèque Municipale
PO	Poitiers, Bibliothèque Municipale
POu	——, Faculté des Lettres de l'Université de Poitiers, Section de Musicologie
Rc	Rouen, Conservatoire
R(m)	——, Bibliothèque Municipale
RE	Rennes, Bibliothèque Municipale
RO	Roanne, Bibliothèque Municipale
RSc	Rheims, Bibliothèque de la Cathédrale
Sc	Strasbourg, Conservatoire
Sg(sc)	——, Grand Séminaire (Séminaire Catholique)
Sim	——, Institut de Musicologie de l'Université
Sm	——, Archives et Bibliothèque Municipale
Sn	——, Bibliothèque Nationale et Universitaire
Ssa	——, Société des Amis des Arts de Strasbourg
Ssp	——, Séminaire Protestant
SA	Salins, Bibliothèque Municipale
SAU	Saumur, Bibliothèque Municipale
SCL	St-Claude, Bibliothèque Municipale
SDE	St-Denis, Bibliothèque Municipale
SDI	St-Dié, Bibliothèque Municipale
SE	Sens, Bibliothèque Municipale
SEL	Sélestat, Bibliothèque Municipale
SERRANT	Serrant, Château
SO	Solesmes, Abbaye St-Pierre
SOI	Soissons, Bibliothèque Municipale
SQ	St-Quentin, Bibliothèque Municipale
T	Troyes, Bibliothèque Municipale
TH	Thiers, Bibliothèque Municipale
TLc	Toulouse, Conservatoire
TLd	——, Musée Dupuy
TLm	——, Bibliothèque Municipale
TO	Tours, Bibliothèque Municipale
TOgs	——, Grand Séminaire
TOul	——, Bibliothèque Universitaire, Section Lettres
TOur	——, Centre d'Etudes Supérieures de la Renaissance
TOU	Toulon, Ecole Nationale de Musique
TOUm	——, Bibliothèque Municipale
TOUs	——, Société des Amis du Vieux Toulon
TU	Tulle, Bibliothèque Municipale
V	Versailles, Bibliothèque Municipale
VA	Vannes, Bibliothèque Municipale
VAL	Valenciennes, Bibliothèque Municipale
VE	Vesoul, Bibliothèque Municipale
VN	Verdun, Bibliothèque Municipale

GB: GREAT BRITAIN

A	Aberdeen, University Library, King's College
AB	Aberystwyth, National Library of Wales
AM	Ampleforth, Abbey and College Library, St Lawrence Abbey
Bp	Birmingham, Public Libraries
Bu	——, University of Birmingham, Barber Institute of Fine Arts
BA	Bath, Municipal Library
BEas	Bedford, Bedfordshire Archaeological Society
BEcr	——, Bedfordshire County Record Office
BEp	——, Public Library Music Department
BENcoke	Bentley (Hants.), Gerald Coke, private collection
BEV	Beverley, East Yorkshire County Record Office
BO	Bournemouth, Central Library
BRb	Bristol, Baptist College Library
BRp	——, Public Libraries, Central Library
BRu	——, University of Bristol Library
Ccc	Cambridge, Corpus Christi College
Cchc	——, Christ's College
Cclc	——, Clare College
Cfm	——, Fitzwilliam Museum
Cgc	——, Gonville and Caius College
Cjc	——, St John's College
Cjec	——, Jesus College
Ckc	——, Rowe Music Library, King's College
Cmc	——, Magdalene College
Cp	——, Peterhouse
Cpc	——, Pembroke College
Cpl	——, Pendlebury Library of Music
Ctc	——, Trinity College
Cu	——, University Library
Cumc	——, University Music Club
Cus	——, Cambridge Union Society
CA	Canterbury, Cathedral
CAR	Carlisle, Cathedral
CDp	Cardiff, Public Libraries, Central Library
CDu	——, University College of South Wales and Monmouthshire
CF	Chelmsford, Essex County Record Office
CH	Chichester, Diocesan Record Office
CHc	——, Cathedral
DRc	Durham, Cathedral
DRu	——, University Library
DU	Dundee, Public Libraries
En	Edinburgh, National Library of Scotland
Enc	——, New College Library
Ep	——, Public Library, Central Public Library
Er	——, Reid Music Library of the University of Edinburgh
Es	——, Signet Library
Eu	——, University Library
EL	Ely, Cathedral
EXc	Exeter, Cathedral
EXcl	——, Central Library
EXed	——, East Devon Area Record Office
EXu	——, University Library
Ge	Glasgow, Euing Music Library
Gm	——, Mitchell Library
Gsma	——, Scottish Music Archive
Gtc	——, Trinity College
Gu	——, University Library
GL	Gloucester, Cathedral
H	Hereford, Cathedral
HAdolmetsch	Haslemere, Carl Dolmetsch, private collection
Lam	London, Royal Academy of Music
Lbbc	——, British Broadcasting Corporation
Lbc	——, British Council
Lbm	——, British Library, Reference Division (formerly British Museum) (= *Lbl*)
Lcm	——, Royal College of Music
Lco	——, Royal College of Organists
Lcs	——, Vaughan Williams Memorial Library (Cecil Sharp Library)
Ldc	——, Dulwich College
Lgc	——, Gresham College (Guildhall Library)
Lkc	——, University of London, King's College
Llp	——, Lambeth Palace
Lmic	——, British Music Information Centre
Lmp	——, Marylebone Public Library
Lpro	——, Public Record Office
Lsc	——, Sion College
Lsm	——, Royal Society of Musicians of Great Britain
Lsp	——, St Paul's Cathedral
Ltc	——, Trinity College of Music
Lu	——, University of London, Music Library
Lva	——, Victoria and Albert Museum
Lwa	——, Westminster Abbey
Lwcm	——, Westminster Central Music Library
LA	Lancaster, District Central Library
LAu	——, University Library
LEbc	Leeds, University of Leeds, Brotherton Collection
LEc	——, Leeds Public Libraries, Music Department, Central Library
LF	Lichfield, Cathedral
LI	Lincoln, Cathedral
LVp	Liverpool, Public Libraries, Central Library
LVu	——, University Music Department
Mch	Manchester, Chetham's Library
Mcm	——, Royal Northern College of Music
Mp	——, Central Public Library, Henry Watson Music Library
Mr	——, John Rylands University Library, Deansgate Branch
Mrothwell	——, Evelyn Rothwell, private collection
Mu	——, John Rylands University Library
NO	Nottingham, University Library
NW	Norwich, Central Library
NWr	——, Norfolk and Norwich Record Office
Ob	Oxford, Bodleian Library
Obc	——, Brasenose College
Och	——, Christ Church
Ojc	——, St John's College
Olc	——, Lincoln College
Omc	——, Magdalen College
Onc	——, New College
Ooc	——, Oriel College
Oqc	——, Queen's College
Ouf	——, University, Faculty of Music
Oumc	——, University Music Club and Union
P	Perth, Sandeman Music Library
R	Reading, University, Music Library
RI	Ripon, Cathedral
RO	Rochester, Cathedral
SA	St Andrews, University Library
SB	Salisbury, Cathedral
SH	Sherborne, Sherborne School Library
SHR	Shrewsbury, Shropshire County Record Office
SOp	Southampton, Public Library
SR	Studley Royal, Fountains Abbey MS 23 [in *LEc*]
STb	Stratford-on-Avon, Shakespeare's Birthplace Trust
STm	——, Shakespeare Memorial Library
T	Tenbury, St Michael's College [Toulouse–Philidor collection now largely in *F-Pn*, *V*]
W	Wells, Cathedral
WB	Wimborne, Minster
WC	Winchester, Chapter Library
WCc	——, Winchester College
WI	Wigan, Public Library
WO	Worcester, Cathedral
WRch	Windsor, St George's Chapter Library
WRec	——, Eton College
Y	York, Minster
Yi	——, Borthwick Institute of Historical Research

GR: GREECE

Ae	Athens, Ethnike Biblioteke tes Hellados
AT	Mt Athos, Koutloumousi Monastery
ATSch	——, Chilandari Monastery
ATSdionision	——, Dionision Monastery
ATSgreat lavra	——, Monastery of the Great Lavra
ATSiviron	——, Iviron Monastery
ATSserbian	——, Serbian Monastery
ATSvatopedi	——, Vatopedi Monastery
LA	Lavra
P	Patmos

H: HUNGARY

Ba	Budapest, Magyar Tudományos Akadémia Régi Könyvek Tára és Kézirattár
Ba(mi)	——, Magyar Tudományos Akadémia Zenetudományi Intézet Könyvtára
Bb	——, Bartók Béla Zeneművészeti Szakközépiskola Könyvtára
Bev	——, Evangélikus Országos Könyvtár
Bf	——, Belvárosi Föplébániatemplom Kottatára
Bj	——, Józsefvárosi Evangélikus Egyházközség Kottatára
Bl	——, Liszt Ferenc Zeneművészeti Főiskola Könyvtára
Bm	——, Budavári Nagyboldogasszony Templom Kottatára

Bn	——, Országos Széchényi Könyvtára
Bo	——, Állami Operaház
Bp	——, Piarista Gimnázium Könyvtára
Br	——, Ráday Gyűjtemény, Könyvtár és Levéltár
Bs	——, Központi Szeminóriumi Könyvtár
Bst	——, Szent István Bazilika Kottatára
Bu	——, Egyetemi Könyvtár
BA	Bártfa, church of St Aegidius [in *Bn*]
CSg	Csurgó, Csokonai Vitéz Mihály Gimnázium Könyv- tára
DR	Debrecen, Tiszántúli Református Egyházkerület Nagykönyvtára
DRm	——, Déri Múzeum
DRu	——, Kossuth Lajos Tudományegyetem Könyvtára
Ea	Esztergom, Komárom Megyei Levéltár
Efko	——, Főszékesegyházi Kottatár
Efkö	——, Főszékesegyházi Könyvtár
Em	——, Keresztény Múzeum Könyvtára
EG	Eger, Főegyházmegyei Könyvtár
EGb	——, Bazilika Kottatára
Gc	Győr, Püspöki Papnevelő Intézet Könyvtára
Gk	——, Székesegyházi Kottatár
Gm	——, Xántus János Múzeum
Gz	——, Zeneművészeti Szakközépiskola Könyvtára
GGn	Gyöngyös, Országos Széchényi Könyvtár, Bajza József Müemlékkönyvtár
GYm	Gyula, Múzeum
KE	Keszthely, Országos Széchényi Könyvtár Helikon Könyvtára
KI	Kiskunhalas, Református Egyházközség Könyvtára
KŐ	Kőszeg, Plébániatemplom Kottatára
KŐm	——, Jurisich Múzeum
MOp	Mosonmagyaróvár, 1. sz Plébániatemplom Kotta- tára
NY	Nyiregyháza, Református Városi Egyházközség Könyvtára
P	Pécs, Székesegyházi Kottatár
PA	Pápa, Dunántuli Református Egyházkerület Könyv- tára
PH	Pannonhalma, Szent Benedekrend Központi Főkönyvtára
Se	Sopron, Evangélikus Egyházközség Könyvtára
Sg	——, Berzsenyi Dániel Gimnázium Könyvtára
Sl	——, Liszt Ferenc Múzeum
Sp	——, Szentlélekről és Szent Mihályról Nevezett Városplébánia Kottatára
Sst	——, Storno Gyűjtemény
SA	Sárospatak, Tiszáninneni Református Egyházkerület Nagykönyvtára
SD	Szekszárd, Balogh Ádám Megyei Múzeum
SFk	Székesfehérvár, Püspöki Könyvtár
SFm	——, István Király Múzeum
SFs	——, Székesegyházi Kottatár
SG	Szeged, Somogyi Könyvtár
SGm	——, Móra Ferenc Múzeum
SGu	——, Szegedi Orvostudományi Egyetem Könyvtára
SY	Szombathely, Püspöki Könyvtár
SYb	——, Berzsenyi Dániel Megyei Könyvtár
SYm	——, Smidt Múzeum
T	Tata, Plébániatemplom Kottatára
V	Vác, Székesegyházi Kottatár
VE	Veszprém, Püspöki Könyvtár
VEs	——, Székesegyházi Kottatár

I: ITALY

Ac	Assisi, Biblioteca Comunale
Ad	——, Cattedrale S Rufino
Af	——, S Francesco
AC	Acicatena, Biblioteca Comunale
AG	Agrigento, Biblioteca Lucchesiana
AGI	Agira, Biblioteca Comunale
AGN	Agnone, Biblioteca Emidiana
AL	Albenga, Cattedrale
ALEa	Alessandria, Archivio di Stato
ALEi	——, Istituto Musicale Antonio Vivaldi
AN	Ancona, Biblioteca Comunale
ANcap	——, Biblioteca Capitolare
ANd	——, Archivio della Cappella del Duomo
AO	Aosta, Seminario Maggiore
AP	Ascoli Picena, Biblioteca Comunale
AQ	Aquileia, Archivio della Basilica
ARc	Arezzo, Biblioteca Consorziale
ARd	——, Duomo
ASc(d)	Asti, Archivio Capitolare (Duomo)
ASi	——, Istituto Musicale Giuseppe Verdi
ASs	——, Seminario Vescovile

AT	Atri, Museo della Basilica Cattedrale, Biblioteca Capitolare
Baf	Bologna, Accademia Filarmonica
Bam	——, Biblioteca della Casa di Risparmio (Biblioteca Ambrosini)
Bas	——, Archivio di Stato
Bc	——, Civico Museo Bibliografico Musicale
Bca	——, Biblioteca Comunale dell'Arciginnasio
Bl	——, Conservatorio di Musica G. B. Martini
Bof	——, Oratorio dei Filippini
Bpm	——, Facoltà di Magistero dell'Università degli Studi, Scuola di Perfezionamento in Musicologia
Bsd	——, Convento di S Domenico
Bsf	——, Convento di S Francesco
Bsm	——, Biblioteca Conventuale S Maria dei Servi
Bsp	——, Basilica di S Petronio
Bu	——, Biblioteca Universitaria
BAca	Bari, Biblioteca Capitolare
BAcp	——, Conservatorio di Musica Nicola Piccinni
BAgiovine	——, Alfredo Giovine, private collection
BAn	——, Biblioteca Nazionale Sagarriga Visconti-Volpi
BAR	Barletta, Biblioteca Comunale Sabino Loffredo
BDG	Bassano del Grappa, Biblioteca Civica
BE	Belluno, Biblioteca del Seminario
BEc	——, Biblioteca Civica
BGc	Bergamo, Biblioteca Civica Angelo Mai
BGi	——, Civico Istituto Musicale Gaetano Donizetti
BI	Bitonto, Biblioteca Comunale Vitale Giordano
BRa	Brescia, Ateneo di Scienze, Lettere ed Arti
BRd	——, Duomo
BRi	——, Istituto Musicale A. Venturi
BRp	——, Archivio di S Maria della Pace
BRq	——, Biblioteca Civica Queriniana
BRs	——, Seminario Vescovile
BRsg	——, S Giovanni Evangelista (Cappella del Ss Sacra- mento)
BRsmg	——, Madonna delle Grazie
BRss	——, S Salvatore
BRE	Bressanone, Seminario Vescovile Vicentinum
BRI	Brindisi, Biblioteca Pubblica Arcivescovile Annibale de Leo
BV	Benevento, Archivio Capitolare
BVa	——, Archivio di Stato
BVam	——, Biblioteca e Archivio Storico Provinciale Antonio Mellusi
BVT	Borgo Val di Toro, Biblioteca Comunale Manara
BZa	Bolzano, Archivio di Stato
BZc	——, Conservatorio di Musica Claudio Monteverdi
BZd	——, Duomo
BZf	——, Biblioteca dei Minori Francescani
BZtoggenburg	——, Count Toggenburg, private collection
CAc	Cagliari, Biblioteca Comunale
CAcon	——, Conservatorio di Musica Giovanni Pierluigi da Palestrina
CAsm	——, Cattedrale S Maria
CAu	——, Biblioteca Universitaria
CAP	Capua, Museo Provinciale Campano
CARcc	Castell'Arquato, Chiesa Collegiata
CARc(p)	——, Archivio Capitolare (Archivio Parrochiale)
CATa	Catania, Archivio di Stato
CATc	——, Biblioteche Riunite Civica e Antonio Ursino Recupero
CATm	——, Museo Belliniano
CATss	——, Società di Storia Patria per la Sicilia Orientale
CC	Città di Castello, Duomo
CCc	——, Biblioteca Comunale
CDA	Codogna, Biblioteca Civica Popolare L. Ricca
CEb(sm)	Cesena, Badia S Maria del Monte
CEc	——, Biblioteca Comunale Malatestiana
CEN	Cento, S Biagio
CF	Cividale del Friuli, Archivio Capitolare
CFm	——, Museo Archeologico Nazionale
CHR	Chieri, Facoltà Teologica dei Gesuiti
CHT	Chieta, Biblioteca Provinciale Angelo Camillo de Meis
CHV	Chiavenna, Biblioteca Capitolare Laurenziana
CLE	Corleone, Biblioteca Comunale Francesco Benti- vegna
CLO	Corlono, Chiesa della Reggia Ducale
CMac	Casale Monferrato, Archivio Capitolare
CMbc	——, Biblioteca Civica
CMs	——, Seminario Vescovile
CMI	Camogli, Biblioteca Comunale Nicolo Cueno
CMO	Camerino, Biblioteca Valentiniana e Comunale
COc	Como, Biblioteca Comunale
COd	——, Duomo

CORc	Correggio, Biblioteca Comunale
COS	Cosenza, Biblioteca Civica
CPa	Carpi, Archivio Paolo Guaitoli della Commissione di Storia Patria de Carpi
CPc	——, Biblioteca Comunale
CR	Cremona, Biblioteca Statale
CRd	——, Duomo
CRE	Crema, Biblioteca Comunale
CREi	——, Istituto Musicale L. Folcioni
CT	Cortona, Biblioteca Comunale e dell'Accademia Etrusca
CZorizio	Cazzago S Martino, Orizio private collection
DO	Domodossola, Biblioteca e Archivio dei Rosminiani di Monte Calvaro
E	Enna, Biblioteca Comunale
Fa	Florence, Ss Annunziata
Faq	——, Pius XII Institute, Graduate School of Fine Arts, Aquinas Library
Fas	——, Archivio di Stato
Fc	——, Conservatorio di Musica Luigi Cherubini
Fd	——, Duomo
Ffabbri	——, M. Fabbri, private collection
Fl	——, Biblioteca Medicea-Laurenziana
Fm	——, Biblioteca Marucelliana
Fn	——, Biblioteca Nazionale Centrale
Folschki	——, Olschki private collection
Fr	——, Biblioteca Riccardiana e Moreniana
Fs	——, Seminario Arcivescovile Maggiore
Fsa	——, Biblioteca Domenicana, Chiesa S Maria Novella
Fsm	——, Convento S Marco
Fu	——, Università degli Studi, Facoltà di Lettere e Filosofia
FA	Fabriano, Biblioteca Comunale
FAd	——, Duomo
FAN	Fano, Biblioteca Comunale Federiciana
FBR	Fossombrone, Biblioteca Civica Passionei
FEbonfigliuoli	Ferrara, Bonfigliuoli private collection
FEc	——, Biblioteca Comunale Ariostea
FEd	——, Duomo
FEmichelini	——, Bruto Michelini, private collection
FELc	Feltre, Biblioteca Comunale
FELd	——, Duomo
FELm	——, Museo Civico
FEM	Finale Emilia, Biblioteca Comunale
FERc	Fermo, Biblioteca Comunale
FERd	——, Duomo
FERl	——, Liceo Musicale Girolamo Frescobaldi
FERmichelini	——, Bruno Michelini, private collection
FOc	Forlì, Biblioteca Comunale Aurelio Saffi
FOd	——, Duomo
FOG	Foggia, Biblioteca Provinciale
FOLc	Foligno, Biblioteca Comunale
FOLd	——, Duomo
FOSc	Fossano, Biblioteca Civica
FZac(d)	Faenza, Archivio Capitolare (Duomo)
FZc	——, Biblioteca Comunale
FZsavini	——, Ino Savini, private collection
Gc	Genoa, Biblioteca Civica Berio
Gf	——, Biblioteca Franzoniana
Ggrasso	——, Lorenzina Grasso, private collection
Gi(l)	——, Conservatorio di Musica Nicolò Paganini
Gim	——, Istituto Mazziniano
Gsc	——, S Caterina
Gsmb	——, S Maria della Castagna
Gsmd	——, S Maria di Castello, Biblioteca dei Domenicani
Gu	——, Biblioteca Universitaria
GA	Ganna, Badia Benedittina
GE	Gemona, Duomo
GN	Giulianova, Biblioteca Comunale Vincenzo Bindi
GO	Gorizia, Seminario Teologico Centrale
GR	Grottaferrata, Badia Greca
GUA	Guastalla, Biblioteca Municipale Maldotti
GUBsp	Gubbio, Biblioteca Comunale Sperelliana
I	Imola, Biblioteca Comunale
IE	Iesi, Archivio Comunale
IV	Ivrea, Biblioteca Capitolare
La	Lucca, Archivio di Stato
Lc	——, Biblioteca Capitolare Feliniana
Lg	——, Biblioteca Statale
Li	——, Istituto Musicale Luigi Boccherini
Ls	——, Seminario Vescovile
LA	L'Aquila, Biblioteca Provinciale Salvatore Tommasi
LE	Lecce, Biblioteca Provinciale Nicola Bernardini
LI	Livorno, Biblioteca Comunale Labronica Francesco Domenico Guerrazzi
LOc	Lodi, Biblioteca Capitolare
LOcl	——, Biblioteca Comunale Laudense
LT	Loreto, Archivio Storico della Cappella Lauretana
LU	Lugo, Biblioteca Comunale Fabrizio Trisi
Ma	Milan, Biblioteca Ambrosiana
Malfieri	——, Trecani degli Alfieri, private collection
Mb	——, Biblioteca Nazionale Braidense
Mc	——, Conservatorio di Musica Giuseppe Verdi
Mca	——, Archivio della Curia Arcivescovile
Mcap(d)	——, Cappella Musicale del Duomo
Mcom	——, Biblioteca Comunale
Md	——, Archivio della Cappella Musicale del Duomo
Mdonà	——, Mariangelo Donà, private collection
Mr	——, Archivio Storico Ricordi (Casa Editrice)
Ms	——, Biblioteca Teatrale Livia Simoni
Msartori	——, Claudio Sartori, private collection
Mt	——, Biblioteca Trivulziana
Mvidusso	——, Carlo Vidusso, private collection
MAa	Mantua, Archivio di Stato
MAad	——, Archivio Storico Diocesano
MAav	——, Accademia Virgiliana di Scienze, Lettere ed Arti
MAc	——, Biblioteca Comunale
MAi	——, Istituto Musicale Lucio Campiani
MAp	——, Duomo S Pietro
MAs	——, Seminario Vescovile
MAC	Macerata, Biblioteca Comunale Mozzi-Borgetti
MACa	——, Archivio di Stato
MC	Monte Cassino, Biblioteca dell'Abbazia
ME	Messina, Biblioteca Universitaria
MEmeli	——, Alfonso Meli, private collection
MEnicotra	——, Arturo Nicotra, private collection
MEs	——, Biblioteca Painiana del Seminario Arcivescovile
MFc	Molfetta, Biblioteca Comunale Giovanni Panunzio
MFsr	——, Pontificio Seminario Regionale Pio XI
MFsv	——, Seminario Vescovile
MOa	Modena, Accademia Nazionale di Scienze, Lettere ed Arti
MOd	——, Duomo
MOdep	——, Deputazione di Storia Patria per le Antiche Province Modenesi
MOe	——, Biblioteca Estense
MOf	——, Archivio Ferni
MOl	——, Liceo Musicale Orazio Vecchi
MOs	——, Archivio di Stato
MTventuri	Montecatini-Terme, Antonio Venturi, private collection
MV	Montevergine, Biblioteca del Santuario
MZ	Monza, Insigne Basilica di S Giovanni Battista
MZc	——, Biblioteca Civica
Na	Naples, Archivio di Stato
Nc	——, Conservatorio di Musica S Pietro a Majella
Nf	——, Biblioteca Oratoriana dei Filippini
Nlp	——, Biblioteca Lucchesi-Palli [in *Nn*]
Nn	——, Biblioteca Nazionale Vittorio Emanuele III
Ns	——, Seminario Arcivescovile
Nsn	——, Società Napoletana di Storia Patria
Nu	——, Biblioteca Universitaria
NO	Novacello, Biblioteca dell'Abbazia
NON	Nonantola, Seminario Abbaziale
NOVc	Novara, Biblioteca Civica
NOVd	——, Archivio Musicale Classico del Duomo
NOVg	——, Archivio e Biblioteca di S Gaudenzio
NOVi	——, Civico Istituto Musicale Brera
NOVsg	——, Archivio Musicale di S Gaudenzio
NT	Noto, Biblioteca Comunale
Oc	Orvieto, Biblioteca Comunale Luigi Fumi
Od	——, Biblioteca dell'Opera del Duomo
OR	Oristano, Seminario Arcivescovile
ORT	Ortona, Biblioteca Comunale
OS	Ostiglia, Biblioteca Musicale Greggiati
OSI	Osimo, Biblioteca Comunale
Pbonelli	Padua, E. Bonelli, private collection
Pc	——, Biblioteca Capitolare
Pca	——, Biblioteca Antoniana, Basilica del Santo
Pci	——, Museo Civico, Biblioteca Civica e Archivio Comunale
Pi(l)	——, Istituto Musicale Cesare Pollini
Ppapafava	——, Novello Papafava dei Carreresi, private collection
Ps	——, Seminario Vescovile
Pu	——, Biblioteca Universitaria
PAac	Parma, Archivio Capitolare
PAas	——, Archivio di Stato
PAc	——, Conservatorio di Musica Arrigo Boito
PAi	——, Istituto di Studi Verdiani
PAsg	——, S Giovanni Evangelista
PAst	——, Madonna della Steccata

Sigla	Library
PAt	—, Teatro Regio
PAL	Palestrina, Biblioteca Comunale Fantoniana
PAVc	Pavia, S Maria del Carmine
PAVi	—, Civico Istituto Musicale Franco Vittadini
PAVs	—, Seminario Vescovile
PAVsm	—, S Michele
PAVsp	—, S Pietro in Ciel d'Oro
PAVu	—, Biblioteca Universitaria
PCa	Piacenza, Collegio Alberoni
PCc	—, Biblioteca Comunale Passerini Landi
PCcon	—, Conservatorio di Musica G. Nicolini
PCd	—, Duomo
PCsa	—, Biblioteca e Archivio Capitolare di S Antonino
PCsm	—, S Maria di Campagna
PEc	Perugia, Biblioteca Comunale Augusta
PEd	—, Cattedrale
PEl	—, Conservatorio di Musica Francesco Morlacchi
PEsp	—, S Pietro
PEA	Pescia, Biblioteca Comunale Carlo Magnani
PESc	Pesaro, Conservatorio di Musica Gioacchino Rossini
PEScerasa	—, Amadeo Cerasa, private collection [now *VTcerasa*]
PESd	—, Duomo
PESo	—, Biblioteca Oliveriana
PIa	Pisa, Archivio di Stato
PIarc	—, Biblioteca Arcivescovile Cardinale Pietro Maffi
PIc	—, Museo Nazionale di S Matteo
PIca	—, Biblioteca Cateriniana
PIcc	—, Archivio e Biblioteca Certosa di Calci
PIp	—, Archivio Musicale dell'Opera della Primaziale
PIr	—, Biblioteca Raffaelli
PIraffaelli	—, Raffaelli private collection
PIs	—, Fondo Simoneschi
PIst	—, Chiesa dei Cavalieri di S Stefano
PIN	Pinerolo, Biblioteca Comunale Camillo Allinudi
PLa	Palermo, Archivio di Stato
PLcom	—, Biblioteca Comunale
PLcon	—, Conservatorio Vincenzo Bellini
PLd	—, Duomo
PLi	—, Istituto di Storia della Musica, Facoltà di Lettere, Università degli Studi
PLm	—, Teatro Massimo
PLn	—, Biblioteca Nazionale
PLpagano	—, Roberto Pagano, private collection
PLs	—, Baron Pietro Emanuele Sgadari di Lo Monaco, private collection [in Casa di Lavoro e Preghiera Padre Massini]
PLsd	—, Archivio Storico Diocesano
PO	Potenza, Biblioteca Provinciale
POa	—, Archivio di Stato
POd	—, Duomo
PR	Prato, Duomo
PS	Pistoia, Cattedrale
PSc	—, Biblioteca Comunale Forteguerriana
Ra	Rome, Biblioteca Angelica
Rac	—, Accademia di Francia
Raf	—, Accademia Filarmonica Romana
Ras	—, Archivio di Stato
Rc	—, Biblioteca Casanatense
Rcg	—, Curia Generalizia dei Padri Gesuiti; Pontificio Collegio Germano-Ungarico
Rchristoff	—, Boris Christoff, private collection
Rcns	—, Archivio della Chiesa Nazionale Spagnuola
Rco	—, Congregazione dell'Oratorio
Rcsg	—, Oratorio di S Girolamo della Cantà
Rdi	—, Discoteca di Stato
Rdp	—, Archivio Doria-Pamphili, private collection
Rf	—, Archivio dei Filippini
Rgiazotto	—, Remo Giazotto, private collection
Ria	—, Istituto Nazionale di Archeologia e Storia dell'Arte
Rif	—, Istituto di Fisiologia dell'Università
Rig	—, Istituto Storico Germanico
Rims	—, Pontificio Istituto di Musica Sacra
Rla	—, Biblioteca Lancisiana
Rli	—, Accademia Nazionale dei Lincei e Corsiniana
Rlib	—, Basilica Liberiana
Rn	—, Biblioteca Nazionale Centrale Vittorio Emanuele III
Rp	—, Biblioteca Pasqualini [in *Rsc*]
Rps	—, Pio Sodalizio de Piceni
Rsc	—, Conservatorio di Musica S Cecilia
Rsg	—, S Giovanni in Laterano
Rsgf	—, Arciconfraternità di S Giovanni dei Fiorentini
Rslf	—, S Luigi de' Francesi
Rsm	—, Archivio Capitolare di S Maria Maggiore [in *Rvat*]
Rsmm	—, S Maria di Monserrato
Rsmt	—, S Maria in Trastevere
Rsp	—, Santo Spirito in Sassia
Rss	—, S Sabina (Venerabile Convento)
Rv	—, Biblioteca Vallicelliana
Rvat	—, Biblioteca Apostolica Vaticana
RA	Ravenna, Duomo
RAc	—, Biblioteca Comunale Classense
RAs	—, Seminario Arcivescovile dei Ss Angeli Custodi
REas	Reggio Emilia, Archivio di Stato
REc	—, Archivio e Biblioteca Capitolare del Duomo
REd	—, Archivio Capitolare del Duomo
REm	—, Biblioteca Municipale
REsp	—, Archivio Capitolare di S Prospero
RIM	Rimini, Biblioteca Civica Gambalunga
RO	Rosate, S Stefano
RVE	Rovereto, Biblioteca Civica Girolamo Tartarotti
RVI	Rovigo, Accademia dei Concordi
Sac	Siena, Accademia Musicale Chigiana
Sas	—, Archivio di Stato
Sc	—, Biblioteca Comunale degli Intronati
Sd	—, Archivio Musicale dell'Opera del Duomo
Smo	—, Biblioteca annessa al Monumento Nazionale di Monte Oliveti Maggiore
SA	Savona, Biblioteca Civica Anton Giulio Barrili
SAL	Saluzzo, Archivio del Duomo
SAS	Sassari, Biblioteca Universitaria
SDF	San Daniele del Friuli, Biblioteca Civica Guarneriana
SE	Senigallia, Biblioteca Comunale Antonelliana
SI	Siracusa, Biblioteca Comunale
SML	Santa Margherita Ligure, Biblioteca Comunale Francesco Domenico Costa
SO	Sant'Oreste, Collegiata di S Lorenzo
SON	Sondrio, Biblioteca Civica Pio Rajna
SPc	Spoleto, Biblioteca Comunale
SPd	—, Duomo
SPE	Spello, Collegiata S Maria Maggiore
ST	Stresa, Biblioteca Rosminiana
SUsb	Subiaco, Biblioteca S Benedetto
SUss	—, Monumenta Nazionale dell'Abbazia di S Scolastica
Ta	Turin, Archivio di Stato
Tb	—, Convento di Benevagienna
Tci	—, Biblioteca Civica Musicale Andrea della Corte
Tco	—, Conservatorio Statale di Musica Giuseppe Verdi
Td	—, Duomo
Tf	—, Accademia Filarmonica
Ti	—, Istituto Salesiano Valsalice
Tmc	—, Museo Civico
Tn	—, Biblioteca Nazionale Universitaria
Tr	—, Biblioteca Reale
Trt	—, Archivio Musicale Radiotelevisione Italiana
TE	Terni, Istituto Musicale G. Briccialdi
TEc	—, Biblioteca Comunale
TI	Termini-Imerese, Biblioteca Liciniana
TLP	Torre del Lago Puccini, Museo di Casa Puccini
TOD	Todi, Biblioteca Comunale Lorenzo Feoni
TOL	Tolentino, Biblioteca Comunale Filelfica
TRa	Trent, Archivio di Stato
TRc	—, Biblioteca Comunale
TRmd	—, Museo Diocesano
TRmn	—, Museo Nazionale
TRmr	—, Museo del Risorgimento
TRE	Tremezzo, Count Gian Ludovico Sola-Cabiati, private collection
TRN	Trani, Biblioteca Comunale G. Bovio
TRP	Trapani, Biblioteca Fardelliana
TSci(com)	Trieste, Biblioteca Civica
TScm	—, Civici Musei di Storia ed Arte
TScon	—, Conservatorio di Musica G. Tartini
TSmt	—, Civico Museo Teatrale di Fondazione Carlo Schmidl
TSsc	—, Fondazione Giovanni Scaramangà de Altomonte
TSsg	—, Archivio della Cappella della Cattedrale S Giusto
TVca(d)	Treviso, Biblioteca Capitolare (Duomo)
TVco	—, Biblioteca Comunale
Us	Urbino, Cappella del Sacramento (Duomo)
Usf	—, S Francesco [in *Uu*]
Uu	—, Biblioteca Universitaria
UD	Udine, Duomo
UDa	—, Archivio di Stato

UDc	——, Biblioteca Comunale Vincenzo Joppi
UDi	——, Istituto Musicale Jacopo Tomadini
URBc	Urbania, Biblioteca Comunale
URBcap	——, Biblioteca Capitolare (Duomo)
Vas	Venice, Archivio di Stato
Vc	——, Conservatorio di Musica Benedetto Marcello
Vcg	——, Biblioteca Casa di Goldoni
Vgc	——, Biblioteca e Istituto della Fondazione Giorgio Cini
Vlevi	——, Fondazione Ugo Levi
Vmarcello	——, Andrighetti Marcello, private collection
Vmc	——, Museo Civico Correr
Vnm	——, Biblioteca Nazionale Marciana
Vqs	——, Accademia Querini-Stampalia
Vs	——, Seminario Patriarcale
Vsf	——, Conventuale di S Francesco
Vsm	——, Procuratoria di S Marco
Vsmc	——, S Maria della Consolazione detta Della Fava
Vt	——, Teatro la Fenice
VAa	Varese, Archivio Prepositurale di S Vittore
VAc	——, Biblioteca Civica
VCc	Vercelli, Biblioteca Civica
VCd	——, Duomo (Biblioteca Capitolare)
VCs	——, Seminario Vescovile
VD	Viadana, Biblioteca Civica
VEaf	Verona, Società Accademia Filarmonica
VEas	——, Archivio di Stato
VEc	——, Biblioteca Civica
VEcap	——, Biblioteca Capitolare (Cattedrale)
VEs	——, Seminario Vescovile
VEsg	——, S Giorgio in Braida
VG	Voghera, Collegiata di S Lorenzo
VIb	Vicenza, Biblioteca Civica Bertoliana
VId	——, Duomo
VImc	——, Museo Civico
VImr	——, Museo del Risorgimento
VIs	——, Seminario Vescovile
VIGsa	Vigévano, Duomo S Ambrogio
VIGsi	——, S Ignazio
VIM	Vimercate, S Stefano
VO	Volterra, Biblioteca Guarnacci
VTc	Viterbo, Biblioteca Comunale degli Ardenti
VTcarosi	——, Attilio Carosi, private collection
VTcerasa	——, Amadeo Cerasa, private collection
VTp	——, Biblioteca Pio XII, Pontificio Seminario Regionale
VTs	——, Seminario Diocesano
VTM	Ventimiglia, Civica Biblioteca Aprosiana

IL: ISRAEL

J	Jerusalem, Jewish National and University Library
Jp	——, Patriarchal Library
S	Mt Sinai
SS	St Sabas, Monastery

IS: ICELAND

Rn	Reykjavik, National Library

J: JAPAN

Tm	Tokyo, Musashino Ongaku Daigaku
Tma(Tmc)	——, Bibliotheca Musashino Academia Musicae
Tn	——, Nanki Music Library, Ohki private collection

N: NORWAY

Bo	Bergen, Offentlige Bibliotek
Bu	——, Universitetsbiblioteket
Oic	Oslo, Norwegian Music Information Centre
Oim	——, Institutt for Musikkvitenskap, Universitet
Ok	——, Musik-Konservatoriet
Onk	——, Norsk Komponistforening
Or	——, Norsk Rikskringkastings
Ou	——, Universitetsbiblioteket
Oum	——, Universitetsbiblioteket, Norsk Musiksamling
T	Trondheim, Kongelige Norske Videnskabers Selskab
Tmi	——, Musikkvitenskapelig Institutt

NL: THE NETHERLANDS

Ad	Amsterdam, Stichting Donemus
At	——, Toonkunst-Bibliotheek
Au	——, Universiteitsbibliotheek
Avnm	——, Bibliotheek der Vereniging voor Nederlandse Muziekgeschiedenis [in *At*]
AN	Amerongen, Archief van het Kasteel der Graven Bentinck, private collection
BI	Bilthoven, Stichting Gaudeamus
D	Deventer, Stads- of Athenaeumbibliotheek
DHa	The Hague, Koninklijk Huisarchief
DHgm	——, Gemeentemuseum
DHk	——, Koninklijke Bibliotheek
DHmw	——, Rijksmuseum
G	Groningen, Universiteitsbibliotheek
Hs	Haarlem, Stadsbibliotheek
HIr	Hilversum, Radio Nederland
L	Leiden, Gemeentearchief
Lml	——, Museum Lakenhal
Lt	——, Bibliotheca Thysiana [in *Lu*]
Lu	——, Bibliotheek der Rijksuniversiteit
Lw	——, Bibliothèque Wallonne
LE	Leeuwarden, Provinciale Bibliotheek van Friesland
R	Rotterdam, Gemeentebibliotheek
'sH	's-Hertogenbosch, Archief van de Illustre Lieve Vrouwe Broederschap
Uim	Utrecht, Instituut voor Muziekwetenschap der Rijksuniversiteit
Usg	——, St Gregorius Vereniging, Bibliotheek [in *Uim*]
Uu	——, Bibliotheek der Rijksuniversiteit

NZ: NEW ZEALAND

Ap	Auckland, Public Library
Au	——, University Library
Dp	Dunedin, Public Library
Wt	Wellington, Alexander Turnbull Library

P: PORTUGAL

AN	Angra do Heroismo, Biblioteca Pública e Arquivo Distrital
AR	Arouca, Museu Regional de Arte Sacra do Mosteiro de Arouca
AV	Aveiro, Museu de Aveiro, Mosteiro de Jesus
BA	Barreiro, Biblioteca Municipal
BRp	Braga, Biblioteca Pública e Arquivo Distrital
BRs	——, Sé de Braga
C	Coimbra, Biblioteca Geral da Universidade
Cm	——, Biblioteca Municipal
Cmn	——, Museu Nacional de Machado de Castro
Cs	——, Sé Nova
Cug	——, Biblioteca Geral da Universidade
Cul	——, Faculdade de Letras da Universidade
CA	Cascais, Museu-Biblioteca Condes de Castro Guimarães
Em	Elvas, Biblioteca Púbia Hortênsia
EVc	Évora, Arquivo da Sé
EVp	——, Biblioteca Pública e Arquivo Distrital
F	Figuera da Foz, Biblioteca Pública Municipal Pedro Fernandes Tomás
G	Guimarães, Arquivo Municipal Alfredo Pimenta
La	Lisbon, Palácio Nacional da Ajuda
Laa	——, Academia de Amadores de Musica (Conservatorio Municipal)
Lac	——, Academia das Ciências
Lan	——, Arquivo Nacional de Torre do Tombo
Lc	——, Conservatorio Nacional
Lcg	——, Fundação Calouste Gulbenkian
Lf	——, Fábrica da Sé Patriarcal
Lif	——, Instituto de Franca
Ln	——, Biblioteca Nacional
Lr	——, Emissora Nacional de Radiodifusão
Ls	——, Sociedade de Escritores e Compositores Portugueses
Lt	——, Teatro Nacional de S Carlos
LA	Lamego, Biblioteca da Sé
LE	Leiria, Biblioteca Erudita e Arquivo Distrital (Biblioteca Pública)
Mp	Mafra, Palácio Nacional
Pa	Oporto, Ateneu Comercial
Pc	——, Conservatorio de Musica
Pcom	——, Biblioteca Comunale
Peh	——, Museu de Etnografia e Historia
Pf	——, Clube Fenianos Portuenses
Pm	——, Biblioteca Pública Municipal
PD	Ponta Delgada, Biblioteca Pública e Arquivo Distrital
PL	Ponte de Lima, Arquivo da Misericórdia
PO	Portalegre, Arquivo da Sé
Va	Viseu, Arquivo Distrital
Vm	——, Museu Grão Vasco
Vs	——, Arquivo da Sé
VV	Vila Viçosa, Casa da Bragança, Museu-Biblioteca

PL: POLAND

B	Bydgoszcz, Biblioteka Miejska
BA	Barczew, Archiwum Kościoła Parafialnego
Cb	Cieszyn, Biblioteka Śląska, Oddział Cieszyn
Cp	——, Biblioteka Tschammera w Kościele Ewange- lickim
CZp	Częstochowa, Klasztor OO. Paulinów na Jasnej Górze
GD	Gdańsk, Biblioteka Polskiej Akademii Nauk
GNd	Gniezno, Archiwum Archidiecezjalne
GR	Grodzisk, Klasztor OO. Cystersów
Kc	Kraków, Biblioteka Czartoryskich
Kcz	——, Biblioteka Czapskich
Kd	——, Klasztor OO. Dominikanów
Kj	——, Biblioteka Jagiellońska
Kk	——, Kapituła Metropolitalna
Kp	——, Biblioteka Polskiej Akademii Nauk
Kpa	——, Archiwum Państwowe
Kz	——, Biblioteka Czartoryskich
KA	Katowice, Biblioteka Śląska
KO	Kórnik, Polska Akademia Nauk, Biblioteka Kórnicka
Lk	Lublin, Biblioteka Katolickiego Uniwersytetu
Lw	——, Biblioteka Wojewódzka i Miejska im. H. Łopacińskiego
ŁA	Łańcut, Muzeum
ŁO	Łowicz, Biblioteka Seminarium
MO	Mogiła, Klasztor OO. Cystersów
OB	Obra, Klasztor OO. Cystersów
Pa	Poznań, Biblioteka Archidiecezjalna
Pr	——, Miejska Biblioteka Publiczna im. Edwarda Raczyńskiego
Pu	——, Biblioteka Uniwersytecka
PE	Pelplin, Biblioteka Seminarium Duchownego
PŁp	Płock, Biblioteka Towarzystwa Naukowego
R	Raków, Archiwum Kościelne
SA	Sandomierz, Seminarium Duchownego
SZ	Szalowa, Archiwum Parafialne
Tu	Toruń, Biblioteka Uniwersytecka
TA	Tarnów, Archiwum Archidiecezjalne
Wm	Warszawa, Biblioteka Muzeum Narodowego
Wn	——, Biblioteka Narodowa
Wp	——, Biblioteka Publiczna
Ws	——, Biblioteka Synodalna Ewangelicka
Wtm	——, Biblioteka Warszawskiego Towarzystwa Muzycznego
Wu	——, Biblioteka Uniwersytecka
WL	Wilanów, Biblioteka, Oddział Muzeum Narodowego Warszawy
WRol	Wrocław, Biblioteka Ossolineum Leopoldiensis
WRu	——, Biblioteka Uniwersytecka

R: ROMANIA

Ab	Aiud, Biblioteca Documentară Bethlen
Ba	Bucharest, Biblioteca Academiei Republicii Socia- liste România
Bc	——, Biblioteca Centrală de Stat
BRm	Braşov, Biblioteca Municipală
Sb	Sibiu, Muzeul Brukenthal
TMt.	Tîrgu Mureş, Biblioteca Documentară Teleki

S: SWEDEN

A	Arvika, Folkliga Musikskolan
E	Enköping, Samrealskolans Arkiv
ES	Eskilstuna, Stadsbiblioteket
Gem	Göteborg, Etnografiska Museet
Ghl	——, Hvitfeldtska Högre Allmänna Läroverket
Gu	——, Universitetsbiblioteket (formerly Stadsbiblio- teket)
GÄ	Gävle, Vasaskolans Bibliotek
Hfryklund	Hälsingborg, D. Daniel Fryklund, private collection [in *Skma*]
Hs	——, Stadsbiblioteket
J	Jönköping, Per Brahegymnasiet
K	Kalmar, Stifts- och Gymnasiebiblioteket
KA	Karlstad, Stadsbiblioteket
KAT	Katrineholm, Stadsbiblioteket
KH	Karlshamn, Museums Bibliotek
L	Lund, Universitetsbiblioteket
Lbarnekow	——, Barnekow private collection
LB	Leufsta Bruk, De Geer private collection
LI	Linköping, Stifts- och Landsbiblioteket
M	Malmö, Stadsbiblioteket
N	Norrköping, Stadsbiblioteket
Ö	Örebro, Karolinska Skolans Bibliotek
ÖS	Östersund, Jämtlands Läns Bibliotek
Sdt	Stockholm, Drottningholms Teatermuseum

Sic	——, Stims Informationscentral för Svensk Musik
Sk	——, Kungliga Biblioteket
Skma	——, Kungliga Musikaliska Akademiens Bibliotek
Sm	——, Musikmuseet
Smf	——, Stiftelsen Musikkulturens Främjande
Sn	——, Nordiska Museet
Ssr	——, Sveriges Radio
St	——, Kungliga Teaterns Bibliotek
SK	Skara, Stifts- och Landsbiblioteket
STd	Strängnäs, Domkyrkobiblioteket
STr	——, Roggebiblioteket
Uifm	Uppsala, Institutionen för Musikforskning vid Upp- sala Universitetet
Uu	——, Universitetsbiblioteket
V	Västerås, Stadsbiblioteket
Vll	Visby, Landsarkivet
VIs	——, Stadsbiblioteket
VX	Växjö, Landsbiblioteket

SF: FINLAND

A	Turku [Åbo], Sibelius Museum Musikvetenskapliga Institutionen vid Åbo Akademi, Bibliotek & Arkiv
Aa	——, Åbo Akademis, Bibliotek
Hko	Helsinki, Helsingin Kaupunginorkester
Hmt	——, Musiikin Tiedotuskeskus
Hr	——, Oy Yleisradio AB, Nuotisto
Hs	——, Sibelius-Akatemian Kirjasto
Hy	——, Helsingin Yliopiston Kirjasto
Hyf	——, Helsingin Yliopiston Kirjasto, Department of Finnish Music
TA	Tampere, Tampereen Yliopiston Kansanperinteen Laitos

US: UNITED STATES OF AMERICA

AA	Ann Arbor, University of Michigan Music Library
AB	Albany, New York State Library
AL	Allentown (Penn.), Muhlenberg College, John A. W. Haas Library
AM	Amherst (Mass.), Amherst College, Robert Frost Building
ATu	Atlanta (Georgia), Emory University Library
AU	Aurora (NY), Wells College Library
AUS	Austin, University of Texas
Ba	Boston, Athenaeum Library
Bbs	——, Bostonian Society
Bc	——, New England Conservatory of Music
Bco	——, American Congregational Society, Congre- gational Library
Bfa	——, Fine Arts Museum
Bge	——, School of Fine Arts, General Education Library
Bh	——, Harvard Musical Association
Bhh	——, Handel and Haydn Society
Bhs	——, Massachusetts Historical Society
Bl	——, Grand Lodge of Masons in Massachusetts, A. F. and A. M. Library
Bm	——, University, Mugar Memorial Library
Bp	——, Public Library, Music Department
Bth	——, University, School of Theology
BAep	Baltimore, Enoch Pratt Free Library, Fine Arts and Music Department
BAhs	——, Maryland Historical Society
BApi	——, City Library, Peabody Institute
BAu	——, Johns Hopkins University Libraries
BAw	——, Walters Art Gallery
BAT	Baton Rouge, Louisiana State University Library
BE	Berkeley, University of California, Music Library
BER	Berea (Ohio), Baldwin-Wallace College, Ritter Lib- rary of the Conservatory
BETm	Bethlehem (Penn.), Archives of the Moravian Church in Bethlehem
BETu	——, Lehigh University, Lucy Packer Lindeman Memorial Library
BG	Bangor (Maine), Public Library
BK	Brunswick (Maine), Bowdoin College, Department of Music
BLl	Bloomington, Indiana University, Lilly Library
BLu	——, Indiana University, School of Music Library
BO	Boulder, University of Colorado Music Library
BRc	Brooklyn, Brooklyn College Music Library
BRp	——, Public Library
BU	Buffalo, Buffalo and Erie County Public Library
Charding	Chicago, W. N. H. Harding, private collection [in *GB-Ob*]
Chs	——, Chicago Historical Society Library
Cn	——, Newberry Library

Cu	——, University Music Library
CA	Cambridge, Harvard University Music Libraries
CAR	Carlisle (Penn.), Dickinson College
CDhs	Concord, New Hampshire Historical Society
CDs	——, New Hampshire State Library
CG	Coral Gables (Florida), University of Miami Music Library
CHua	Charlottesville, University of Virginia, Alderman Library
CHum	——, University of Virginia Music Library
CHH	Chapel Hill, University of North Carolina Music Library
CIhc	Cincinnati, Hebrew Union College
CIu	——, University of Cincinnati College-Conservatory of Music
CLm	Cleveland, Museum of Art, Cantatorium
CLp	——, Public Library, Fine Arts Department
CLwr	——, Western Reserve University, Freiberger Library and Music House Library
COu	Columbus, Ohio State University Music Library
CR	Cedar Rapids, Iowa Masonic Library
Dp	Detroit, Public Library, Music and Performing Arts Department
DB	Dearborn (Mich.), Henry Ford Museum and Greenfield Village
DE	Denver (Colorado), Public Library, Art and Music Division
DM	Durham (North Carolina), Duke University Libraries
DN	Denton, North Texas State University Music Library
DO	Dover (New Hampshire), Public Library
Eg	Evanston (Ill.), Garrett Theological Seminary
Eu	——, Northwestern University, Music Library
ECstarr	Eastchester (NY), Saul Starr, private collection
EXd	Exeter (New Hampshire), Phillips Exeter Academy, Davis Library
EXp	——, Public Library
FW	Fort Worth, Southwest Baptist Theological Seminary
G	Gainesville, University of Florida Library, Rare Book Collection
GA	Gambier (Ohio), Kenyon College Divinity School, Colburn Library
GB	Gettysburg, Lutheran Theological Seminary
GR	Granville (Ohio), Denison University Library
GRE	Greenville (Delaware), Eleutherian Mills Historical Library
Hhs	Hartford, Connecticut Historical Society Library
Hm	——, Case Memorial Library, Hartford Seminary Foundation
Hp	——, Public Library, Art and Music Department
Hs	——, Connecticut State Library
Hw	——, Trinity College, Watkinson Library
HA	Hanover (New Hampshire), Dartmouth College, Baker Library
HB	Harrisonburg (Virginia), Eastern Mennonite College, Menno Simons Historical Library and Archives
HG	Harrisburg, Pennsylvania State Library
HO	Hopkinton, New Hampshire Antiquarian Society
HU	Huntingdon (Penn.), Juniata College, L. A. Beechly Library
I	Ithaca (NY), Cornell University Music Library
IO	Iowa, University of Iowa Music Library
K	Kent (Ohio), Kent State University Library
Lu	Lawrence, University of Kansas Libraries
LAu	Los Angeles, University of California, Walter H. Rubsamen Music Library
LAuc	——, University of California, William Andrews Clark Memorial Library
LAusc	——, University of Southern California School of Music
LB	Lewisburg (Penn.), Bucknell University, Ellen Clark Bertrand Library
LChs	Lancaster (Penn.), Lancaster County Historical Society
LCm	——, Lancaster Mennonite Historical Library and Archives
LCts	——, Theological Seminary of the United Church of Christ
LEX	Lexington, University of Kentucky, Margaret I. King Library
LOs	Louisville (Ky.), Southern Baptist Theological Seminary, James P. Boyce Centennial Library
LOu	——, University, School of Music Library
LU	Lincoln University (Penn.), Vail Memorial Library
M	Milwaukee, Public Library, Art and Music Department
MI	Middletown (Conn.), Wesleyan University, Olin Memorial Library
MORduncan	Morgantown, Richard E. Duncan, private collection
MSp	Minneapolis, Public Library
MSu	——, University of Minnesota Music Library
MV	Mt Vernon (Virginia), Mt Vernon Ladies Association of the Union Collection
Nf	Northampton (Mass.), Forbes Library
Nsc	——, Smith College, Werner Josten Music Library
NAZ	Nazareth (Penn.), Moravian Historical Society
NBs	New Brunswick, Theological Seminary, Gardner A. Sage Library
NBu	——, Rutgers University Library
NEm	Newark (NJ), Newark Museum
NEp	——, Public Library
NH	New Haven, Yale University, School of Music Library
NORts	New Orleans, Theological Seminary
NORtu	——, Tulane University, Howard Tilton Memorial Library
NP	Newburyport (Mass.), Public Library
NYcc	New York, City College Library, Music Library
NYcu	——, Columbia University Music Library
NYfo	——, Fordham University Library
NYfuld	——, James J. Fuld, private collection
NYgo	——, University, Gould Memorial Library
NYgr	——, Grolier Club
NYhc	——, Hunter College Library
NYhs	——, New York Historical Society
NYhsa	——, Hispanic Society of America
NYj	——, Juilliard School of Music
NYlateiner	——, Jacob Lateiner, private collection
NYma	——, Mannes College of Music, Clara Damrosch Mannes Memorial Library
NYmc	——, City Museum, Theatre and Music Department
NYmm	——, Metropolitan Museum of Art, Thomas J. Watson Library
NYp	——, Public Library at Lincoln Center, Library and Museum of the Performing Arts
NYpm	——, Pierpont Morgan Library
NYq	——, Queens College of the City University, Paul Klapper Library, Music Library
NYts	——, Union Theological Seminary
OA	Oakland (Calif.), Public Library
OAm	——, Mills College, Margaret Prall Music Library
OB	Oberlin, Oberlin College Conservatory of Music
Pc	Pittsburgh, Carnegie Library
Pfinney	——, Theodore M. Finney, private collection [in *Pu*]
Ps	——, Theological Seminary, Clifford E. Barbour Library
Pu	——, University of Pittsburgh, Theodore Finney Music Library
PD	Portland, Maine Historical Society
PER	Perryville (Missouri), St Mary's Seminary
PHbo	Philadelphia, St Charles Borromeo Theological Seminary
PHbs	——, William Bacon Stevens Library
PHchs	——, American Catholic Historical Society of Philadelphia
PHci	——, Curtis Institute of Music
PHem	——, Eric Mandell Collection of Jewish Music
PHf	——, Free Library of Philadelphia
PHhs	——, Historical Society of Pennsylvania
PHkm	——, Lutheran Theological Seminary
PHlc	——, Library Company of Philadelphia
PHma	——, Musical Academy
PHphs	——, Presbyterian Historical Society
PHps	——, American Philosophical Society
PHr	——, Philip H. and A. S. W. Rosenbach Foundation
PHtr	——, Trinity Lutheran Church of Germantown
PHts	——, Westminster Theological Seminary
PHu	——, University of Pennsylvania, Otto E. Albrecht Music Library
PIlevy	Pikesville (Maryland), Lester S. Levy, private collection
PL	Portland (Oregon), Library Association of Portland, Music Department
PO	Poughkeepsie, Vassar College, George Sherman Dickinson Music Library
PRs	Princeton, Theological Seminary
PRu	——, University, Harvey S. Firestone Memorial Library

PROhs	Providence, Rhode Island Historical Society
PROu	——, Brown University Libraries
R	——, Rochester, University, Eastman School of Music, Sibley Music Library
RI	Richmond, Virginia State Library
Sp	Seattle, Public Library
Su	——, University of Washington Music Library
SA	Salem (Mass.), Essex Institute, James Duncan Phillips Library
SB	Santa Barbara, University of California, Library
SFp	San Francisco, Public Library, Fine Arts Department, Music Division
SFs	——, Sutro Library
SFsc	——, San Francisco State College Library, Frank V. de Bellis Collection
SHE	Sherman (Texas), Austin College, Arthur Hopkins Library
SLc	St Louis, Concordia Seminary
SLf	——, Fontbonne College
SLkrohn	——, Ernst C. Krohn, private collection
SLug	——, Washington University, Gaylord Music Library
SLC	Salt Lake City, University of Utah Library
SM	San Marino (Calif.), Henry E. Huntington Library and Art Gallery
SPmoldenhauer	Spokane (Washington), Hans Moldenhauer, private collection
STu	Stanford, University, Division of Humanities and Social Sciences, Music Library
SW	Swarthmore (Penn.), Swarthmore College Library
SY	Syracuse, University Music Library and George Arents Research Library
Tm	Toledo, Toledo Museum of Art
TA	Tallahassee, Florida State University, Robert Manning Strozier Library
U	Urbana, University of Illinois Music Library
Ufraenkel	——, Fraenkel collection
UP	University Park, Pennsylvania State University Library
Wc	Washington, DC, Library of Congress, Music Division
Wca	——, Cathedral
Wcu	——, Catholic University of America Music Library
Wgu	——, Georgetown University Libraries
Ws	——, Folger Shakespeare Libraries
Wsc	——, Scottish Rite Masons, Supreme Council
Wsi	——, Smithsonian Institution, Music Library
WA	Watertown (Mass.), Perkins School for the Blind
WC	Waco (Texas), Baylor University Music Library
WE	Wellesley (Mass.), Wellesley College Library
WELhartzler	Wellman (Iowa), J. D. Hartzler, private collection
WGc	Williamsburg (Virginia), College of William and Mary
WGw	——, Colonial Williamsburg Research Department, historical collection
WI	Williamstown (Mass.), Williams College, Chapin Library
WM	Waltham (Mass.), Brandeis University Library, Music Library, Goldfarb Library
WOa	Worcester (Mass.), American Antiquarian Society
WS	Winston-Salem (North Carolina), Moravian Music Foundation

USSR: UNION OF SOVIET SOCIALIST REPUBLICS

J	Jelgava, Muzei
Kan	Kiev, Tsentral'naya Naukova Biblioteka, Akademiya Nauk URSR
Kk	——, Biblioteka Gosudarstvennoy Konservatoriy imeni P. I. Chaykovskovo
KA	Kaliningrad, Oblastnaya Biblioteka
KAg	——, Gosudarstvennaya Biblioteka
KAu	——, Universitetskaya Biblioteka

KI	Kishinev, Biblioteka Gosudarstvennoy Konservatoriy imeni G. Muzichesku
Lan	Leningrad, Biblioteka Akademii Nauk SSSR
Lia	——, Gosudarstvennïy Tsentral'nïy Istoricheskïy Arkhiv
Lil	——, Institut Russkoy Literaturï
Lit	——, Leningradsky Gosudarstvennïy Institut Teatra, Muzïki i Kinematografii
Lk	——, Biblioteka Leningradskoy Gosudarstvennoy Konservatoriy imeni N. A. Rimskovo-Korsakova
Lph	——, Muzïkal'naya Biblioteka Leningradskoy Gosudarstvennoy Filarmonii
Lsc	——, Gosudarstvennaya Ordena Trudovovo Krasnovo Znameni Publichnaya Biblioteka imeni M. E. Saltïkova-Shchedrina
Lt	——, Leningradskiy Gosudarstvennïy Teatral'nïy Muzey
Ltob	——, Tsentral'naya Muzïkal'naya Biblioteka Gosudarstvennovo Akademicheskovo Teatra Operï i Baleta imeni S. M. Kirova
LV	L'vov, Biblioteka Gosudarstvennoy Konservatoriy imeni N. V. Lysenko
Mcl	Moscow, Gosudarstvennïy Tsentral'nïy Literaturnïy Arkhiv
Mcm	——, Gosudarstvennïy Tsentral'nïy Muzey Muzïkal'noy Kul'turï imeni M. I. Glinki
Mk	——, Gosudarstvennaya Konservatoriya imeni P. I. Chaykovskovo, Nauchnaya Muzïkal'naya Biblioteka imeni S. I. Taneyeva
Ml	——, Gosudarstvennaya Ordena Lenina Biblioteka SSSR imeni V. I. Lenina
Mm	——, Gosudarstvennïyi Istoricheskïyi Muzei
Mt	——, Gosudarstvennïyi Teatral'nïyi Muzei imeni A. Bakhrushina
MI	Minsk, Biblioteka Belorusskoy Gosudarstvennoy Konservatoriy
O	Odessa, Biblioteka Gosudarstvennoy Konservatoriy imeni A. V. Nezhdanovoy
R	Riga, Biblioteka Gosudarstvennoy Konservatoriy Latviyskoy imeni J. Vitola
TAu	Tartu, Universitetskaya Biblioteka
TAL	Tallinn, Biblioteka Gosudarstvennoy Konservatoriy
TB	Tbilisi, Biblioteka Gosudarstvennoy Konservatoriy imeni V. Saradzhisvili
V	Vilnius, Biblioteka Gosudarstvennoy Konservatoriy Litovskoy SSR

YU: YUGOSLAVIA

Bn	Belgrade, Narodna Biblioteka N. R. Srbije
Dsd	Dubrovnik, Knjižnica Samostana Dominikanaca
Dsmb	——, Franjevački Samostan Mala Braća
La	Ljubljana, Knjižnica Akademije za Glasbo
Lf	——, Knjižnica Frančiškanska Samostana
Ls	——, Škofijski Arhiv in Biblioteka
Lsa	——, Slovenska Akademija Znanosti in Umjetnosti
Lsk	——, Arhiv Stolnega Kora
Lu	——, Narodna in Univerzitetna Knjižnica
MAk	Maribor, Glazbeni Arhiv Katedrale
MAs	——, Knjižnica Škofijskega Arhiva
NM	Novo Mesto, Knjižnica Frančiškanskega Samostana
NMc	——, Glazbeni Arhiv Katedrale
O	Ohrid, Narodno Museum
Sk	Split, Glazbeni Arhiv Katedrale
Ssf	——, Knjižnica Samostana Sv Frane
Za	Zagreb, Jugoslavenska Akademija Znanosti i Umjetnosti
Zda	——, Državni Arhiv
Zha	——, Hrvatski Glazbeni Zavod
Zk	——, Glazbeni Arhiv Katedrale
Zs	——, Glazbeni Arhiv Bogoslovnog Sjemeništa
Zu	——, Nacionalna i Sveučilišna Biblioteka

Volume One

A – Bacilly

A Note on the Use of the Dictionary

This note is intended as a short guide to the basic procedures and organization of the dictionary. A fuller account will be found in the Introduction, vol.1, pp.xi–xx.

Abbreviations in general use in the dictionary are listed on pp.vii–x; bibliographical ones (periodicals, reference works, editions etc) are listed on pp.xi–xiii.

Alphabetization of headings is based on the principle that words are read continuously, ignoring spaces, hyphens, accents, bracketed matter etc, up to the first comma; the same principle applies thereafter. 'Mc' and 'M'' are listed as 'Mac', 'St' as 'Saint'.

Bibliographies are arranged chronologically (within section, where divided), in order of year of first publication, and alphabetically by author within years.

Cross-references are shown in small capitals, with a large capital at the beginning of the first word of the entry referred to. Thus 'The instrument is related to the BASS TUBA' would mean that the entry referred to is not '**Bass tuba**' but '**Tuba, bass**'.

Work-lists are normally arranged chronologically (within section, where divided). Italic symbols used in them (like *D-Dlb* or *GB-Lbm*) refer to the libraries holding sources, and are explained on pp. xiv–xxx; each national sigillum stands until contradicted.

A

A (i) (It.: 'with'). A preposition found particularly in 16th- and 17th-century editions of polyphonic music where works are described as being *a due* (*a* 2), *a tre* (*a* 3), *a dieci* (*a* 10), etc, meaning in two, three or ten voices respectively. Many prints had it with an accent (*à* 2, etc), but in modern Italian *à* is a variant form of *ha* ('he has') so is perhaps better avoided in this context wherever possible. It is the current French form, however, and is found particularly in French orchestral scores, *à 2* (*à deux*) meaning the same as the Italian A DUE. As one of the commonest words in the Italian language, *a* occurs in many compound tempo and expression marks and has different meanings that may be found in any Italian dictionary. It appears before a vowel as *ad* and contracts with the definite article as *al*, *allo*, *ai*, *agli*, *alla* and *alle*.

DAVID FALLOWS

A (ii). *See* PITCH NAMES.

A (iii). Abbreviation for *accelerando*, used particularly by Elgar; *see* LARGAMENTE.

Aachen (Fr. Aix-la-Chapelle). City in the Federal Republic of Germany. The cathedral and its music were the creation of Charlemagne (742–814), who made the town the northern capital of the Holy Roman Empire; the Holy Roman emperors were crowned there from 813 to 1531. The city was occupied by France in 1794 and formally annexed in 1801; after the Congress of Vienna (1814–15) it became part of Prussia. It was severely damaged in World War II.

Aachen was the political, religious and cultural centre of Charlemagne's empire, and the Hofkirche was constructed according to his own plans. The Aachen Cathedral choir dates from his founding of the Schola Palatina, whose teachers (including Alcuin from 782) were among the most distinguished scholars of the age. Alcuin described the school in a poem, mentioning a singing teacher named Sulpicius. For Charlemagne the idea of a politically united empire was closely linked with the establishment of a uniform liturgy, set to uniform music; his reforms in this direction led to the burning of all books connected with the Ambrosian rite in order to ensure adherence to the Gregorian style. As early as 774 he sent monks to Rome to study the teaching of such chant, and in 790 Pope Hadrian responded to repeated requests from Charlemagne and sent two trained singers to the north with copies of the antiphonary. Organ music was also cultivated; in the early 9th century an Arab organ was sent to Charlemagne by Caliph Harun-al-Rashid and installed in the Hofkirche, while on the emperor's instructions a second organ was built for the cathedral.

The history of bellfounding in the city began with the early 9th-century founder Tancho (mentioned in the *Gesta Karoli*) and reached its peak in the 16th century in the work of the von Trier family. The growth of the cult of Charlemagne (still commemorated in an annual feast) gave rise to a characteristic Aachen chant repertory, including the rhymed office *Regali natus* and the sequence *Urbs aquensis*. The city came to rival Rome and Santiago de Compostela as a place of pilgrimage in the Middle Ages; the shrine was visited every seven years from about 1238, which further enriched the city's liturgy and music. Popular music and pilgrims' songs were stimulated, and wind music was played from tower galleries, with the participation of the town musicians from 1344. The coronation liturgy set a precedent for the organization of church music, and the 30 coronations that took place there between 936 and 1531 were attended by a fine choir.

In the 16th century Aachen Cathedral was an important centre of polyphony, especially of the style then developing in the Low Countries. Johannes Mangon, working at Aachen in the 1570s, transcribed a comprehensive collection of the music performed there in three choirbooks (1570–75; in *D-AAm*); apart from Mangon's own works, they include those of Chastelain, Claux, Clemens non Papa, Cleve, Crecquillon, Episcopius, Lassus, Maillard, Simon Moreau, Ponta and Rivulo. In 1632 the chronicler Johannes Noppius recorded that there were more musicians around the cathedral 'than there was standing room; and in case anyone should marvel at the beautiful music and splendid ceremonies of this church then let him know that it is just as fitting here as it is *in sede regia*'. In 1707 J. L. Blanche founded a choir school.

During the 18th century the city's cultural life benefited from the presence of visitors attracted by the sulphur springs, the most notable being Handel, who came to recover from his nervous collapse in 1737 and is reputed to have expressed his gratitude by playing the organ in the Abbey Church. The cathedral orchestra, documented from the 17th century, occasionally gave performances in collaboration with the traditional city Harmoniemusik. The Städtisches Orchester was founded in 1852, the first in the Rhineland. As early as 1835 Anton Schindler directed performances in the city and, on feast days, in the cathedral. The city participated in the Niederrheinisches Musikfest from 1825, when it gave the second performance of Beethoven's Ninth Symphony (after its Vienna première) to mark the opening of the Neues Theater. Lortzing, Burgmüller and Franck all began their musical careers in the expanding musical life of 19th-century Aachen, and since Lortzing's time the Aachen opera stage has been a springboard for young talent.

The puritanical Cecilian Movement was fostered in the city, particularly by the Stiftskapellmeister Franz Nekes (d 1914). The Gregoriushaus, a church music school, was founded by the cathedral Kapellmeister Heinrich Böckeler (d 1894); it trains organists to be sent to Ireland and the USA. The cathedral choir built up an international reputation under the Kapellmeister T. B. Rehmann (d 1963) and made many tours in France, Spain, Italy and Austria. After a long period of inactivity the cathedral choir school was re-established in 1972 as a private institution of the cathedral chapter. The musical reputation of the city in the 20th century is indicated by the distinguished succession of general music directors and conductors including Busch (1912–19), Peter Raabe (1920–33), Karajan (1934–42), Sawallisch (1953–8) and Wolfgang Trommer (from 1962).

BIBLIOGRAPHY

P. à Beeck: *Aquisgranum* (Aachen, 1620)
J. Noppius: *Aacher Chronik* (Cologne, 1632)
K. F. Meyer: *Aachensche Geschichten* (Mülheim, 1781)
F. Haagen: *Geschichte Aachens* (Aachen, 1873–4)
Zeitschrift des Aachener Geschichtsvereins (1879–1972)
H. Böckeler: *Kurze Geschichte der Singschulen* (Aachen, 1890)
K. G. Fellerer: *Orgel und Orgelmusik* (Augsburg, 1929)
H. Schiffers: *Aachener Heiligtumsfahrt* (Aachen, 1937)
T. B. Rehmann: 'Aachen', *MGG*
B. Poll: *150 Jahre Aachener Musikleben* (Aachen, 1954)
R. Pohl: *Die Messen des Johannes Mangon* (Aachen, 1960)
B. Poll: *Geschichte Aachens in Daten* (Aachen, 1960)
U. Wagner: *Franz Nekes* (Cologne, 1969)

RUDOLF POHL

Aagesen, Truid [Sistinus, Theodoricus] (*fl* 1593–1615). Danish composer and organist. He was appointed organist of Vor Frue Kirke (now the cathedral), Copenhagen, on 23 June 1593 after having 'pursued and learnt his art during a long period both in Germany and Italy'. He received a number of preferments, such as in 1603 the free residence formerly set aside for the palace preacher. He was also on at least two occasions sent on commissions for the king, once to Prague. He published under his latinized name Theodoricus Sistinus a set of secular *Cantiones* for three voices (Hamburg, 1608; ed. in Dania sonans, ii, 1966), his only known music. The publication is dedicated to King Christian IV of Denmark, and it may be assumed that it won his approval, for during the years 1609–11 he received payments from the royal treasury in addition to his salary as organist, perhaps for teaching at the court. As early as 1604 he was suspected of being 'in the pope's pay', and he seems to have made no attempt to disguise his Catholicism, for a few years later association with him was used as evidence in a complaint of 'Jesuitism' against a student named Udby. In 1611 he lost his royal subsidy, and in 1613, after the publication of the king's letter stating that men of the popish religion should be driven out of Denmark, his position became untenable. On 15 September 1613, the question was raised in the governing body of Copenhagen University, by whom Vor Frue Kirke was administered, whether 'Truid, organist, who let it be publicly known that he was

popishly inclined', should be allowed to continue as organist. The decision was against him and he was immediately informed of his dismissal. He appears, however, to have received his salary until 1 July 1615, when his successor Johan Meincke (or Meineken) took office. His movements thereafter are unknown, but later references to lands as having been in his possession suggest that he was indeed exiled from Denmark.

BIBLIOGRAPHY

A. Hammerich: *Musikken ved Christian den Fjerdes Hof* (Copenhagen, 1892)
E. Abrahamsen: 'Aagesen, Truid', *DBL*

JOHN BERGSAGEL

Aanes. The ENĒCHĒMA of the third plagal (or barys) mode in the Byzantine modal system.

Aarhus. *See* ÅRHUS.

Aaron [Aron], **Pietro** (*b* Florence, *c*1480; *d* probably in Bergamo, *c*1550). Italian theorist and composer. He himself used both spellings of his name. He claimed close association in Florence with Josquin, Obrecht, Isaac and Agricola, but nothing is known of his life before his residence from about 1515 to 1522 in Imola, where he was *cantor* at the cathedral. Here he published his first treatise, *De institutione harmonica*, which embroiled him in a controversy with Gaffurius; GIOVANNI SPATARO in his *Errori di Franchino Gafurio* (1521) took Aaron's part. About 1522 he entered the household of Sebastiano Michiel, Grand Prior in Venice of the Order of St John of Jerusalem; by 1525 he was Michiel's *maestro da casa*. In Venice he associated with prominent musicians such as Adrian Willaert and continued to correspond with Spataro. In 1536 he took the habit of the Cross Bearers and entered the monastery of S Leonardo at Bergamo; he probably left Venice because of Michiel's death. His last surviving letter from Bergamo is dated 1540. He was still a Cross Bearer in 1545 according to *Lucidario*, and he may still have been alive when *Compendiolo* was published, probably in 1549 or 1550.

Of his treatises, *De institutione harmonica* and *Toscanello* are the most comprehensive and systematic. The former, written in Italian but translated into Latin for publication, includes more detail on fundamental matters and is a valuable complement to the better known *Toscanello*. The latter is probably the best general treatise of its generation, invaluable for its clear and progressive discussions of musical practice, particularly counterpoint. It was popular enough to be reprinted as late as 1562. The *Trattato* contains the earliest thorough and explicit discussion of mode in polyphonic music; its supplement continues an exposition of chromatic solmization. The *Lucidario* is a random compilation of observations on all aspects of music theory, many of them highly valuable, whereas the *Compendiolo* is a brief introductory treatise of no great significance. Aaron's correspondence, particularly with Spataro, is very interesting as a sample of the informal discussions of theory between 16th-century musicians. These letters mention many of Aaron's compositions, but the frottola, *Io non posso piu durare*, published in 1505 is the only known work that may be his.

Aaron wrote extensively about practice, scarcely ever touching on speculative theory. His ideas are derived from earlier writers, notably Tinctoris, Gaffurius and

Spataro, but he frequently extended or modified tradition, for example in the *Trattato*, where the system of eight modes is applied to polyphony. For each mode he cited as examples numerous compositions by the most eminent composers, demonstrating his respect for their authority. His explanations of counterpoint are the best of those in the generation before Zarlino. He was the first to report the shift from successive to simultaneous composition, a change which is reflected in the *Toscanello*'s extensive tables of chords in four voices. His early descriptions of four-voice cadences and rudimentary imitation are also notable. Aaron was progressive in his preference for notating all accidentals; his discussions of this topic, especially in the *Toscanello*'s supplement, are of great interest. His practical orientation led him to give in *Toscanello* the earliest description of a mean-tone temperament, though elsewhere he held to Pythagorean tuning as a theoretical standard. His preference for publication in Italian rather than Latin is further evidence of his practical attitude; he was among the first to defy the learned prejudice against the vernacular. He sympathetically reported the practice of his time in detail and his treatises are possibly the most valuable of his generation.

For his contribution to modal theory *see* MODE, §III, 3.

WRITINGS

Libri tres de institutione harmonica (Bologna, 1516/*R*1971)
Thoscanello de la musica (Venice, 1523/*R*1969; rev. with suppl. as *Toscanello in musica*, 1529/*R*1969, 1539/*R*1971, 1562; Eng. trans. collating all edns., 1970)
Trattato della natura et cognitione di tutti gli tuoni di canto figurato (Venice, 1525/*R*1966; Eng. trans. of chaps.1–7 in O. Strunk: *Source Readings in Music History*, New York, 1950); suppl., without title-page or indication of author (Venice, 1531)
Lucidario in musica (Venice, 1545/*R*1969) [bk 4 incorporates the supplement to the *Trattato*]
Compendiolo di molti dubbi (Milan, after 1545/*R*1971)
'Delli principij di tuti li tono [sic] secondo mi Pietro Aaron', *GB-Lbm*, MS bound in printed book K.1.g.10 [not autograph]
Correspondence in *I-Rvat* Vat.Lat.5318, *F-Pn* Ital.1110, *D-Bds* Mus.ms.autogr.theor.1 [Most of Aaron's correspondence is collected in Bergquist, 1964]

BIBLIOGRAPHY
H. Riemann: *Geschichte der Musiktheorie im IX.–XIX. Jahrhundert* (Berlin, 2/1921/*R*1961; partial Eng. trans. 1962)
K. Jeppesen: 'Eine musiktheoretische Korrespondenz des früheren Cinquecento', *AcM*, xiii (1941), 3–39
P. Bergquist: *The Theoretical Writings of Pietro Aaron* (diss., Columbia U., 1964)
——: 'Mode and Polyphony around 1500: Theory and Practice', *Music Forum*, i (1967), 99–161

PETER BERGQUIST

Aaron Scotus (*b* ?Scotland, late 10th century; *d* Cologne, 18 Nov 1052). ?Scottish Benedictine abbot and music theorist. The date of his death (the 14th day before the calends of December 1052) is known from Hartzheim, who had access to local documents now lost. He was abbot of St Martin at Cologne (Cologne like Laon and Liège attracted many Irish and Scots from the 9th century onwards) and at the same time (1042–52) abbot of St Pantaleon: double tenure was not uncommon.

Aaron decreed, presumably after a visit to Rome, that his monks should sing the new Office of St Gregory the Great recently composed by Pope Leo IX (1049–54), instead of the Common of Confessors previously used; it is difficult, however, to identify this Office among surviving Offices of St Gregory (Analecta hymnica medii aevi, v, p.184; H. Latil, *Rassegna gregoriana*, ii, 1903, pp.115ff, according to *I-MC* 542; H. M. Bannister, *Rassegna gregoriana*, ii, 1903, pp.181ff, according

to *I-Rvat* lat.4749). According to Hartzheim, Aaron wrote a chronicle and a musical treatise, *De utilitate cantus vocalis*. Both are lost, as is a second musical treatise, *De modo cantandi et psallendi*, which, Hartzheim claimed, survived in manuscript at St Martin in Cologne in the early 18th century. This treatise must have been very similar to *Instituta patrum de modo psallendi sive cantandi* (*GS*, i, 5–8, edited from *CH-SGs* 556, pp.365ff), which deals with singing, in general and in relation to asceticism. Trithemius attempted to identify this treatise with Aaron's third musical treatise, *De regulis tonorum et symphoniarum*, but it is likely that the latter dealt in a more technical manner with the Gregorian psalm tones and with consonances (*symphoniae*).

BIBLIOGRAPHY
J. Trithemius: *Annalium hirsaugensium opus nunquam hactenus editum . . . e manuscripto bibliothecae sancti Galli publicae luci datum*, i (St Gall, 1690), 196
J. Hartzheim: *Bibliotheca coloniensis in qua vita et libri typo vulgati et manuscripti recensentur omnium archidioeceseos coloniensis* (Cologne, 1747), 1
H. G. Farmer: *A History of Music in Scotland* (London, 1947/*R*1970), 57f

MICHEL HUGLO

Abaco, Evaristo Felice dall'. *See* DALL'ABACO, EVARISTO FELICE.

Abaelard [Abailard], Peter. *See* ABELARD, PETER.

Abatessa [Abadessa, Abbatessa, Badessa], **Giovanni Battista** (*b* Bitonto, nr. Bari; *d* after 1652). Italian composer and guitarist. He is known by four books of pieces for five-course Baroque guitar. They consist mainly of simple *battute* (strummed) accompaniments to popular songs and dances of the early 17th century such as the passacaglia, ciaccona, folia, Ruggiero and aria di Fiorenza. The accompaniments are set down in the alphabet system of chord notation devised by Girolamo Montesardo in which letters of the alphabet designate fingering positions for various major and minor chords. Each of Abatessa's books contains instructions concerning the interpretation of the alphabet tablature, the fingering of the chords and the tuning of the guitar; the 1652 book also explains how to tune the guitar with the harp, presumably for the simultaneous playing of continuo parts. The collections of 1627 and 1652 give instructions regarding the execution of certain kinds of strums such as the *trillo* and *repicco*, while the book of 1635 and the undated *Ghirlanda di varii fiori* contain a table of correspondences between alphabet chords in different positions. The 1635 collection contains five villanellas for one to three voices and continuo. Others are found in the 1652 book, with, however, only the words and the accompanimental chords for guitar notated.

WORKS

Corona di vaghi fiori overo Nuova intavolatura di chitarra alla spagnuola (Venice, 1627)
Cespuglio di varii fiori overo Intavolatura di chitarra alla spagnuola (Orvieto, 1635)
Intessitura di varii fiori overo Intavolatura di chitarra alla spagnuola (Rome and Lucca, 1652)
Ghirlanda di varii fiori overo Intavolatura di chitarra alla spagnuola (Milan, n.d.)

BIBLIOGRAPHY
W. Kirkendale: *L'aria di Fiorenza id est Il Ballo del Gran Duca* (Florence, 1972), 23, 42, 65, 77ff

ROBERT STRIZICH

Abbà Cornaglia, Pietro (*b* Alessandria, 20 March 1851; *d* Alessandria, 2 May 1894). Italian organist and composer. From 1868 to 1871 he attended the Milan Conservatory, studying the piano with Antonio Angeleri and composition with Lauro Rossi and Mazzucato. His graduation exercise, the cantata *Caino e Abele*, won the first prize. He toured abroad as a concert pianist, but from 1880 until his death was organist at the cathedral in Alessandria, where he also founded a school of composition, singing and piano. He composed three operas, *Isabella Spinola* (Milan, 1877), *Maria di Warden* (Venice, 1884) and *Una partita a scacchi* (Pavia, 1892), the latter based on Giuseppe Giacosa's popular comedy. In these works, which did not have much success, Abbà Cornaglia remained uninfluenced by the innovatory tendencies of the 'Scapigliatura' and of Catalani and by the new *verismo* school; instead he gave evidence, especially in *Una partita a scacchi* (vocal score: Milan, 1892), of a tasteful eclecticism and excellent craftsmanship in a traditional vein. He also composed sacred music, chamber music, songs and organ pieces and wrote two books, *Sulla introduzione del canto popolare in tutte le masse di comunità, e specialmente nella scuola* (Alessandria, 1880) and *Impressioni d'un viaggio in Germania* (Alessandria, 1881).

BIBLIOGRAPHY
G. Rossi: 'Pietro Abbà-Cornaglia', *Rivista di storia, arte, e archeologia per la Provincia de Alessandria*, xli (1932), 677
G. Pistarino: 'Abbà Cornaglia, Pietro', *DBI*
GIOVANNI CARLI BALLOLA

Abbado, Claudio (*b* Milan, 26 June 1933). Italian conductor. Son of the violinist and teacher Michelangelo Abbado, and brother of the composer and pianist Marcello Abbado, he learnt the piano with his father, and at the Milan Conservatory until 1955, and then studied conducting under Swarowsky at the Vienna Academy of Music. He won the 1958 Koussevitsky Competition, after which he conducted at provincial concerts and opera houses in Italy, and taught at the Parma Conservatory. After winning the 1963 Mitropoulos Prize, which gave him a five-month attachment to the New York PO, he rapidly became known as an orchestral and opera conductor. He appeared at the 1965 Salzburg Festival, where he conducted the première of Giacomo Manzoni's *Atomtod*. He made his British début with the Hallé Orchestra at Manchester in 1965, and his Covent Garden début in 1968 with *Don Carlos* – the first Verdi opera he conducted. In 1969 he became resident conductor (musical director from 1971) of La Scala, where he helped to raise standards and to broaden the repertory of operas and concerts. His performances there have included Berg's *Wozzeck*, combined with productions of Büchner's play, as well as fine performances of *Simon Boccanegra*, *Aida*, *Un ballo in maschera* and other works from the Italian repertory. His concerts with the La Scala orchestra have included works by Mahler, Bruckner, Schoenberg, Nono, Berio, Stockhausen, Ligeti and Penderecki. In 1971 he was appointed principal conductor of the Vienna PO, and in 1972 he agreed to restrict his appearances in Britain to those with the LSO, with which he had worked since 1966 and which he conducted during its visit to the 1973 Salzburg Festival (the first by a British orchestra). He was appointed principal conductor of the LSO from 1979. His recordings include the symphonies of Brahms, each with a different orchestra, Nono's *Como una ola de fuerza y luz*, written for him and Maurizio

Pollini, and notable performances of Berg's Altenberg songs, *Lulu* Suite and Three Orchestral Pieces. At his best Abbado conducts his wide repertory with impressive rhythmic firmness, well-sustained tension and an ear for vivid detail. From time to time his conducting of orchestral works has been criticized for lack of subtlety and for a tendency to concentrate on the beauty of the moment at the expense of structure. But during the Scala company's memorable visit to Covent Garden in 1976 he won public and critical acclaim, particularly in *Simon Boccanegra*, for the balance between pit and stage, for his integration of detail and subtlety of colour and above all for the broad Verdian line.

ROBERT PHILIP

Abbate, Carlo (*b* Genoa, *c*1600; *d* after 1640). Italian theorist. A Franciscan, he was chaplain and musician to Cardinal Franz von Dietrichstein, Prince-Bishop of Olomouc and governor of Moravia. Before 1629 he probably taught music at the seminary at St Oslowan and from 1629 at the newly established Loretan seminary at Nikolsburg (now Mikulov), the cardinal's principal residence. He returned to Italy in 1632. His treatise *Regulae contrapuncti excerptae ex operibus Zerlini et aliorum ad breviorem tyronum instructionem accommodate* (St Oslowan, 1629/*R*1976), which in spite of its Latin title and dedicatory letter is written in Italian, was conceived as a textbook of counterpoint for his seminarians. It is an entirely unoriginal and conservative compendium of the most elementary rules concerning the use of consonances and dissonances, derived, according to the title, 'from the works of Zarlino and others'.

BIBLIOGRAPHY
ČSHS; *EitnerQ*
E. Bohn: *Die musikalischen Handschriften des 16. und 17. Jahrhunderts in der Stadtbibliothek zu Breslau* (Breslau, 1890/*R*1970)
G. Sántha, ed.: *Epistulae ad S. Iosephum Calasanctium ex Europa Centrali 1625–1648* (Rome, 1969)
J. Sehnal: 'Hudba na dvoře olomouckých biskupů od 13. do poloviny 17. stol.' [Music at the courts of the bishops of Olomouc from the 13th century to the middle of the 17th], *Časopis vlastivědné společnosti muzejní v Olomouci* (1970), 73
J. Košulič: 'Mikulov a počátky barokní hudby na Moravě' [Mikulov and the beginnings of Baroque music in Moravia], *Jižní Morava*, ix (1973), 122
KAROL BERGER

Abbatessa, Giovanni Battista. *See* ABATESSA, GIOVANNI BATTISTA.

Abbatini, Antonio Maria (*b* Città di Castello, 1609 or 1610; *d* Città di Castello, 1677 or *c*1679). Italian composer, teacher and music scholar. He may have been educated by his uncle Lorenzo. According to Baini he was a pupil of the Nanino brothers in Rome, where his brother Guidubaldo, a painter, collaborated with Bernini. He was certainly there from the 1620s: he appears to have been *maestro di cappella* of the Seminario Romano for a short time, possibly in 1626, and he held a similar post at St John Lateran from July 1626 to May 1628. In 1629 he returned to Città di Castello where he married in October 1631. He was *maestro di cappella* of Orvieto Cathedral in 1633, but in the following year was again in Rome, possibly as *maestro di cappella* at the Gesù. He appears to have returned to Città di Castello again in 1636, but by 1640 he was back in Rome; he was *maestro di cappella* of S Maria Maggiore (until 5 January 1646), S Lorenzo a Damaso (1646–9), S Maria Maggiore (28 Sept 1649 to January 1657) and S Luigi dei Francesi (1657–67).

From March to October 1667 he was *maestro di cappella* of the Santa Casa at Loreto, and from March 1672 again of S Maria Maggiore. In 1663, 1666 and 1669 he was also *guardiano* of the Congregazione e Accademia di S Cecilia in Rome. He returned to Città di Castello in 1677. His autobiography (*I-Rvat* Chigi L. VI. 191, ff.217–22) provides the only evidence to support the date of birth proposed above; most reference works give 1595–9.

Abbatini's most important work is the comic opera *Dal male il bene*, which was first performed at the Palazzo Barberini, Rome, in 1653, on the marriage of Maffeo Barberini, Prince of Palestrina, and Olimpia Giustiniani. Based on a comedy by Calderón, it largely avoids the moral atmosphere of much early Roman opera and is a landmark in the early history of *opera buffa*. Abbatini made extensive use of rapid secco recitative, and the ensembles of solo characters that conclude Acts 1 and 3 (Act 2 is by Marco Marazzoli) are among the earliest known examples of the ensemble finale. His only earlier dramatic work was *Il pianto di Rodomonte* (1633), a dramatic cantata for four characters, dedicated to the Accademia degl'Assorditi of Orvieto. An extended lament consisting of nine sections for solo voice (two sopranos, tenor and bass) and a concluding *madrigale spirituale* for two sopranos, bass and continuo, it reflects the vogue for laments created by Monteverdi's 'Lamento d'Arianna'.

It is not certain how much church music Abbatini composed or published. The books of masses (1638–50) listed below as doubtful are (with the possible exception of the first one) probably not by him, because his *Sesto libro di sacre canzoni* (1653) was, as he says in the preface, his first publication for 15 years. Some of the 'lost' psalms and motets may also be spurious: together with the *sacre canzoni*, of which there were evidently six books, they would give a total of 15 books of church music (apart from the 16-part mass of 1627), all published before 1638. Since, however, the *Quinto libro di sacre canzoni*, which appeared in 1638, is only op.9, it would appear that six of these 'lost' books are spurious. One cannot be sure of this, though, for some of Abbatini's works (e.g. *Il terzo libro di sacre canzoni*) appear to have been published without opus numbers. Despite these uncertainties, the above-mentioned mass and the two antiphons, one for 12 basses, the other for 12 tenors, indicate that he was an exponent of the massive polychoral style cultivated in Counter-Reformation Rome. His *sacre canzoni*, on the other hand, are in the smaller concertato style: *Jubilate, cantate psalmum*, from his *Sesto libro*, is a fine piece for three sopranos and organ, embracing trios in triple and common time and solos in recitative and aria styles.

In the 15 years between opp.9 and 10 Abbatini helped to prepare a new edition of the Gregorian hymns (begun in 1634), assisted Kircher in the compilation of his *Musurgia universalis* and contributed to several sacred anthologies, and between 1663 and 1668 he gave 14 lectures on music to academies held at his own house. His pupils included G. P. Colonna, Domenico dal Pane and possibly J. P. Krieger and Cesti (whose relations with Vienna may explain why Abbatini's *Ione* was apparently first performed there). He was described in 1681 as the 'dottissimo teorico già Antonio Maria Abbatini', which indicates that he was highly regarded as a theorist and had not been dead long.

WORKS
(*printed works published in Rome unless otherwise stated*)

DRAMATIC

Il pianto di Rodomonte, cantata, 4vv, bc (Orvieto, 1633/*R*1971)
Dal male il bene (G. Rospigliosi), opera, Rome, Palazzo Barberini, 1653, collab. M. Marazzoli, *I-Bc*, *Rvat*; extracts ed. in Goldschmidt, 325ff; 1 aria ed. in GMB, 258
Ione (A. Draghi), opera, Vienna, Hoftheater, 1664 (according to Pirrotta), or Rome, 1666, *A-Wn*
La comica del cielo, overo La Baltasara (Rospigliosi), opera, Rome, Palazzo Rospigliosi, 1668, *I-Rvat*; 1 aria ed. in Alte Meister des Bel Canto, i (Leipzig, *c*1915), 24

SACRED

Missa, 16vv (1627)
Il terzo libro di sacre canzoni, 2–6vv (Orvieto, 1634)
Il quinto libro di sacre canzoni, 2–5vv, op.9 (1638)
Il sesto libro di sacre canzoni, 2–5vv, op.10 (1653)
[2] Antifone a 12 bassi e 12 tenori . . . cantate in S. Maria sopra Minerva . . . l'anno 1661 (1677)

Motets, 1643[1], 1643[2], 1645[2], 1649[2], 1649[3], 1650[1], 1656[2]
Gaude felix, antiphon, 1v, insts; Pie pater Dominice, sequence: mentioned in *MGG*

ed.: Inni della chiesa in canto gregoriano (1644)

Inveni David, offertory, 4vv, *I-Bc*

SECULAR

In che da il cercar, aria, 1v, bc, *I-Bc*
Amante dubioso, sonnet, 1v, bc, 1662, *MOe*
Ahi, di man de la ragione, cantata, 1v, bc, *MOe*

DOUBTFUL WORKS
(*now lost; mentioned in Baini, FétisB, LaMusicaD*)

Masses, 3 vols., 4–16vv (1638–50)
Psalms, 4 vols., 4–16vv (1630–35)
Motets, 5 vols., 2–5vv, bc (1635–8)
Madrigali . . . senza basso continuo, cited in Berardi

Antiphons, 24vv; masses, psalms, motets, responses, 4–8vv: *I-Rsg*, *Rsm*; S Lorenzo a Damaso, Rome; Gesù, Rome

WRITINGS
[14] Discorsi o lezioni accademiche (MS, *I-Bc*, 1663–8)

BIBLIOGRAPHY
FétisB; *LaMusicaD*
A. Berardi: *Ragionamenti musicali* (Bologna, 1681), 135
G. Baini: *Memorie storico-critiche della vita e delle opere di Giovanni Pierluigi da Palestrina* (Rome, 1828/*R*1966), ii, 38, 477
A. Ademollo: *I teatri di Roma nel secolo XVII* (Rome, 1888/*R*1969), 98ff
H. Goldschmidt: *Studien zur Geschichte der italienischen Oper im 17. Jahrhundert*, i (Leipzig, 1901/*R*1967), 103ff, 325ff
H. Kretzschmar: *Geschichte der Oper* (Leipzig, 1919), 105f
E. Wellesz: 'Die Opern und Oratorien in Wien von 1660–1708', *SMw*, vi (1919), 34
V. Raeli: *Da V. Ugolini ad O. Benevoli nella cappella della Basilica liberiana (1603–46)* (Rome, 1920)
G. Tebaldini: *L'archivio musicale della Cappella lauretana* (Loreto, 1921)
F. Coradini: *Antonio Maria Abbatini e Lorenzo Abbatini: notizie biografiche* (Arezzo, 1922)
R. Haas: *Die Musik des Barocks* (Potsdam, 1928), 60, 70, 72, 78, 150
M. Fuchs: *Die Entwicklung des Finales in der italienischen Opera buffa vor Mozart* (diss., U. of Vienna, 1932)
R. Casimiri: ' "Disciplina musicae" e "mastri di capella" dopo il Concilio di Trento nei maggiori istituti ecclesiastici di Roma: Seminario romano – Collegio germanico – Collegio inglese (sec. XVI–XVII)', *NA*, xv (1938), 56f
D. J. Grout: *A Short History of Opera* (New York, 1947, rev. 2/1965), 74
N. Pirrotta: 'Abbatini, Antonio Maria', *ES*
'Abbatini, Antonio Maria', *DBI*
W. C. Holmes: 'Comedy – Opera – Comic Opera', *AnMc*, no.5 (1968), 101ff
M. K. Murata: *Operas for the Papal Court with Texts by Giulio Rospigliosi* (diss., U. of Chicago, 1975)

COLIN TIMMS

Abbellimenti (It.: 'embellishments'). A term applied both to improvised and to notated embellishments, and both to free ornamentation and to specific ORNAMENTS.

ROBERT DONINGTON

Abbey, John (York) (*b* Whilton, Northants., 22 Dec 1785; *d* Versailles, 19 Feb 1859). English organ builder. In his youth he was employed in the factory of Davis, and subsequently in that of Russell. In 1826 Abbey went to Paris, on the invitation of Sébastien Erard, to work on an organ Erard had designed, which he sent to the Exhibition of the Productions of National Industry in 1827, and also to build an organ for the convent of the Légion d'honneur, at St Denis. He also built an organ to Erard's design for the chapel of the Tuileries in Paris, which was destroyed in the Revolution of 1830.

Having established himself as an organ builder in Paris, Abbey became extensively employed in the construction, renovation and enlargement of organs in France and elsewhere. He built choir organs for accompanying voices for the cathedrals of Rheims, Nantes, Versailles and Evreux, and for the churches of St Eustache, St Nicolas-des-Champs, St Elisabeth, St Médard, St Etienne-du-Mont and St Thomas Aquinas in Paris; and large organs for the cathedrals of La Rochelle, Rennes, Viviers, Tulle, Châlons-sur-Marne, Bayeux and Amiens, and for churches, convents and chapels at St Denis, Orleans, Caen, Châlons and Versailles. He also repaired and enlarged many organs in France and built a number for South America. In 1831 Abbey was employed, at the instance of Meyerbeer (who had introduced the instrument into the score of *Robert le diable*), to build an organ for the Paris Opéra; the instrument continued to be used there until it was destroyed, with the theatre, by fire in 1873. Abbey was the first who introduced into French organs the English mechanism and the bellows invented by Cumming. His example was speedily followed by the French builders. Two of his sons, Edwin and John Abbey, carried on the business of organ building at Versailles after his death.

BIBLIOGRAPHY

J. W. Hinton: *Organ Construction* (London, 1900, rev., enlarged 3/1910)

W. L. Sumner: 'John Abbey: Organ Builder', *The Organ*, xxix (1949–50), 122

——: *The Organ* (London, 1952, rev., enlarged 4/1973)

W. H. HUSK/R

Abbiati, Franco (*b* Verdello, 14 Sept 1898). Italian music critic. He took a diploma in composition at the Turin Conservatory (1929) and studied musicology with Cesari. His career as a critic has been centred in Milan; after working on *Secolo sera* (1928–34), he succeeded Cesari at *Corriera della sera*, remaining there until his retirement (1973). In 1949 he founded the monthly journal *La scala*, which he edited until its closure in 1963; he was particularly interested in opera, especially its authentic performance. Abbiati also published a history of music in five volumes (1939–46), which he later updated and revised in four volumes (1967–8; an abridged one-volume edition appeared in 1955 and was updated in 1971). This was well received, although (being the work of a single author) it was inevitably incomplete; the comments in the second edition on 20th-century composers, notably Italian composers of Abbiati's own generation, are especially valuable as a contemporary response. His four-volume work

on *Verdi* (1959) contains many letters not previously published.

WRITINGS

ed.: *Gaetano Cesari: scritti inediti* (Milan, 1937)

Storia della musica (Milan, 1939–46, rev. 2/1967–8; abridged 1955, rev. 2/1971)

Giuseppe Verdi (Milan, 1959)

Alti e bassi del Simon Boccanegra (Verona, 1973)

CAROLYN M. GIANTURCO

Abbott, Emma (*b* Chicago, 9 Dec 1850; *d* Salt Lake City, 5 Jan 1891). American soprano. She studied first with her father, a singer and music teacher, and later in New York with Achille Errani. In 1872 she went to Europe, studying further with Sangiovanni in Milan and Mathilde Marchesi, François Wartel and Delle Sedie in Paris. She made her operatic début in London on 2 May 1876 and in New York on 8 February 1877, singing Maria in Donizetti's *La fille du régiment* on both occasions in Italian. In 1878 she formed her own opera 'company' (three singers, a pianist and a cornettist) and married its manager, Eugene Wetherell (*d* 1889). Her favourite role was said to be Marguerite in *Faust*.

BIBLIOGRAPHY

S. E. Martin: *The Life and Professional Career of Emma Abbott* (Minneapolis, 1891)

O. Thompson: *The American Singer* (New York, 1937), 127ff

H. WILEY HITCHCOCK

Abbrederis, Matthäus (*b* Rankweil, Vorarlberg, baptized 17 April 1652; *d* after 1725). Austrian organ builder. He was the outstanding master in the upper Rhine valley south of Lake Constance before and after 1700. Stylistically his roots were still firmly in the Baroque of the 17th century, and he remained uninfluenced by the south German late Baroque of the 18th century. His organ for the monastery church of Pfäfers, Switzerland (1693–4), survives unaltered. He also built instruments at other places in Switzerland: Thal (1690), Fischingen (1690), St Luzi, Chur (1712; now at Mon, canton of Graubünden), Sargans (1717), and Maienfeld (1725).

BIBLIOGRAPHY

F. Jakob: 'Die Abbrederisorgel im Psallierchor der ehemaligen Stiftskirche Pfäfers', *Terra plana*, viii (1973), 35

W. Lippuner: *Leben und Werk von Matthäus Abbrederis* (in preparation)

FRIEDRICH JAKOB

Abbreviations. As used in the notation of music, abbreviations fall into two main categories: modifications of normal note shapes, signs etc; and verbal instructions that replace fully written-out music. Abbreviations are far more common in manuscript than in printed music.

Modified note shapes and other non-verbal signs usually represent repetitions of passages of music, varying in length from a single note to a large part of a movement. Other abbreviations of this type avoid such clumsy features of notation as leger lines. See exx.1–11.

Abbreviated verbal instructions are sometimes used in a score when instruments play in unison in orchestral music: the lines belonging to one instrument may be left blank in the score, the notes being replaced by an instruction such as *coi violini* ('with the violins') or *col basso* ('with the bass'). This often occurs when, for instance, first and second violins play in unison, the seconds having *unisono* or *col primo* in the score. Where two parts are written on one staff in the score (e.g. first and second flutes), the sign *a 2* denotes that they play in

Ex.1 Dots over a note denote its repetition

Ex.2 Bar joining notes indicates rate of oscillation, note head indicates duration of oscillation (Ger. *Brillenbässe*)

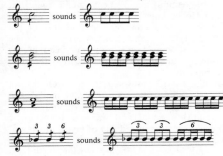

Ex.3 Slash indicates repetition, number of slashes indicates rate of repetition, note head indicates duration of repetition

Ex.4 As exx.2 and 3, but slashes are independent of note stems

Ex.5 Some archaic ways of denoting oscillation are often confused with types shown in ex.3

Ex.6 Other archaic forms

Ex.7 Slash, usually with a dot on either side, or two slashes, to denote repetition of part of a bar, a whole bar or two bars

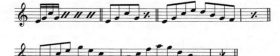

Ex.8
(a) Repetition from the beginning of a movement

(b) Repetition from a later point necessitates another double bar

Ex.9 Avoidance of leger lines

Ex.10 In clarinet music, *chalumeau* has occasionally been used to avoid leger lines

Ex.11 Harp glissandos are usually notated in abbreviated form

Up in 3 beats

unison; *1, a 1* or *solo* denotes that only the first plays. In a string part, however, *a 2, a 3* (etc) may occasionally be used to denote that the section is divided into two, three (etc) groups; the word *divisi* is a more common way of indicating this. *Come sopra* ('as above') is used in manuscript scores when a considerable part of a composition is repeated without alteration, a .corresponding number of bars being left vacant. *Bis* is used to indicate a passage to be performed twice over. Dots indicating a repeat are also a form of abbreviation.

For the commonest abbreviated instructions for expression, dynamics etc, see individual entries; *see also* TEMPO AND EXPRESSION MARKS. Verbal abbreviations used in this dictionary are listed in the front of each volume.

BIBLIOGRAPHY
L. Farrenc: *Traité des abréviations* (Paris, 1897)
J. Wolf: *Handbuch der Notationskunde* (Leipzig, 1913–19/R1963)

'Abd al-Mu'min ibn Yūsuf ibn Fākhir al-Urmawī. See ṢAFĪ AL-DĪN.

'Abd al-Qādir [ibn Ghaybī al-Ḥāfiẓ al-Marāghī] (*b* Maragh; *d* Herat, 1435). Arab instrumentalist, singer, composer and theorist. He first rose to prominence in Baghdad, in the service of the Jalā'irid rulers of Iraq and Azerbaijan, al-Ḥusayn (1374–82) and Aḥmad (1382–1410), and became chief court singer under the latter. After the conquest of Baghdad by Tīmūr (1393), most of his career was spent in Samarkand at the courts of Tīmūr and of his successors al–Khalīl (1404–9) and Shāhrukh (1409–47). He was one of the most important and influential theorists of the Systematist school.

In addition to a commentary on the *Kitāb al-adwār* ('Book of cycles') by Ṣafī al-Dīn, the first Systematist theorist, and a work entitled *Kanz al-alḥān* ('Treasury of melodies'), which is said to have contained notations of some of his compositions but has not survived, 'Abd al-Qādir wrote two general theoretical works covering essentially the same ground, the *Jāmi' al-alḥān* ('Compendium of melodies'), completed in 1405, and the slighter *Maqāṣid al-alḥān* ('Purports of melodies'), probably dating from 1418. Although both thoughtful and highly competent, these works do not show much originality on the theoretical side, being essentially restatements and amplification of the theory elaborated by Ṣafī al Dīn.

The information 'Abd al-Qādir provided about certain aspects of musical practice, however, is rather more extensive than that in most other works of the Systematist school. Apart from details on such matters as lute tunings and playing techniques, he gave extensive lists of the rhythmic cycles and melodic modes used in his day, indicating a new group of 24 modes alongside the traditional 12 and six. Perhaps even more illuminating, especially in view of the sketchy treatment of them in most earlier works, are his discussions of instruments and forms. He listed and partly described many string and wind instruments, including several from outside art music. His account of forms deals with the four-movement suite or *nawba* (and with his own innovation of a fifth movement), shows the variety of types of form used, and has an analysis of one example.

WRITINGS
Jāmi' al-alḥān [Compendium of melodies] (MS, *GB-Ob* Marsh 282; Nūr-i 'Osmānīya Bibliotek, Istanbul, 3644)
Maqāṣid al-alḥān [Purports of melodies] (MS, *GB-Ob* Ouseley 264, 385); ed. T. Bīnish (Tehran, 1966)

Sharḥ al-adwār [Commentary on the *Kitāb al-adwār*] (MS, Nūr-i 'Osmānīya Bibliotek, Istanbul, 3651)

BIBLIOGRAPHY
R. G. Kiesewetter: *Die Musik der Araber* (Leipzig, 1842), 13, 21, 32ff, 56, 88
J. P. N. Land: 'Tonschriftversuche und Melodieproben aus dem muhammedanischen Mittelalter', *VMw*, ii (1886), 347
''Abd al-Kādir', *The Encyclopaedia of Islam* (Leiden and London, 1913–38, rev. 2/1960–)
H. G. Farmer: ''Abdalqādir ibn Ġaibī on Instruments of Music', *Oriens*, xv (1962), 242

O. WRIGHT

Abdel-Rahim [Rehim], **Gamal** (*b* Cairo, 25 Nov 1924). Egyptian composer. His father performed classical Arab music with his own ensemble and invented a quarter-tone flute. This musical background had a deep influence on the young Abdel-Rahim, and he studied the piano with Hickmann and Tiegermann in Cairo. He read history at Cairo University (BA 1945), decided to give his attention to music, and obtained a government scholarship for study in Germany. After a period under Georgiadis in Heidelberg (1950–52) he studied with Genzmer (composition) and Picht-Axenfeld (piano) at the Freiburg Hochschule für Musik (1952–7). Back in Egypt he worked as a composer and teacher at the newly founded (1959) Cairo Conservatory, where he was eventually appointed professor and head of the composition department. In 1973 he received the state prize for composition.

Abdel-Rahim's work shows a long search for an individual style fusing essentially oriental modal and rhythmic features with modern Western techniques. His melodies are always modal, and intervals characteristic of Arab music – the augmented 2nd of *higaz*, the diminished 4th of *saba* – are prevalent, also conditioning his harmonies and linear polyphonic writing, while his rhythm combines traditional irregular patterns (groups of five, seven etc) with 'variable metres'. His use of sonata form (see the Violin Sonata) displays some novel details, stimulated by eastern improvisation, as a means of contrast in the second subject. He belongs to the second generation of Egyptian nationalist composers, and his nationalism is rather subtle: his melodies are usually 'recreations' of folk music rather than direct quotations, except in some variation sets.

WORKS
(*selective list*)
Orch: Suite, 1961; Sym. Variations, 1967; Isis, sym. poem, 1972; Fl Conc., 1972–4; Osiris, suite, perc, harp, chamber orch, 1974
Choral: Erwachen (S. Abdel Sabour), cantata, Bar, chorus, orch, 1966; Cantata [on melody by M. Osman], chorus, orch, 1973; The Sinai Epic, chorus, orch, 1974; folksong arrs.
Inst: Free Variations on an Egyptian Folktune, pf, 1956; Sonata, vn, pf, 1959; An die arabischen Gefallenen, pf, 1973; Heroic Dance, fl, harp, 1974
Music for the cinema, radio and television

Principal publisher: Doblinger

SAMHA EL KHOLY

Abdel-Wahab, Muhammed (*b* Cairo, 1910). Egyptian composer and singer. As a child he had a remarkable musical memory, and at the age of seven he joined a drama troupe to sing during intervals. In 1920 he began studies of traditional Arab music at the Arabic Music Club (now the Institute of Arabic Music), and he also studied Western music for a time at the Bergrün School in Cairo. He then embarked on a dual career as a singer–composer; possessing a fine baritone voice, he achieved great popularity, and he also won fame for his improvisations on the lute. His acquaintance with the poet Ahmed Shawky helped him socially, and his settings of Shawky are classics of the genre. Chosen by Darwish to perform in his operetta *Al barouka* (or *La mascotte*), Abdel-Wahab some years later completed Darwish's posthumous *Cleopatra*, though he composed no original music for the theatre. He has, however, played in many musical films, performing his own songs. Among the awards he has received are the Order of Merit and the State Prize for the Arts.

Abdel-Wahab has been responsible for far-reaching changes in the course of Egyptian music. Throughout his career he has sought new ways to enrich traditional music. His achievements in this have been much debated: conservatives considered his music eclectic, while the public acclaimed him as the star of Egyptian song. He represents the generation of transition, the generation which first came into close contact with Western music through recordings. In his particular case the result has been the superimposition of a mixture of Western features on a foundation of oriental monody. The process of adaptation was long, involving the introduction of European instruments (cello, double bass etc; and later jazz and pop instruments) into the oriental ensemble; the use of Western and Latin American dance rhythms, eventually to the neglect of traditional complex patterns; an ascendancy of the major–minor system over Arab modes; the quotation in some songs of melodies from Western classics; and simple harmonization (his close associate in this and in orchestration was, until his death in 1969, André Ryder). The compromise effected by Abdel-Wahab is quite distinctive; most of the younger song composers have been influenced by him, and he has perhaps helped prepare the way for nationalist composers of the generation of Abdel-Rahim.

SAMHA EL KHOLY

Abdias. Alternative name of Obadiah the Proselyte; *see* JEWISH MUSIC, §I, 2(iv).

Abdon, Bonifacio (*b* Santa Cruz, Manila, 14 May 1876; *d* Manila, 23 April 1944). Filipino composer, conductor and violin teacher. At an early age he studied solfège, composition, conducting and the violin with Ladislao Bonus. He played the violin with the Rizal Orchestra in his youth, and in 1910 he founded the Oriental Orchestra; in the early 1920s he conducted many zarzuelas and operas. He was the moving spirit behind the Manila Chamber Music Society, of which he became director in 1921. A well-known violin teacher, he also excelled as a nationalist composer. Among his works are the zarzuelas *Ang sampaguita* ('The sampaguita flower'), *Anak ng dagat* ('Son of the river'), *Luha't dugo* ('Tears and blood'), *Ang masamang kaugalian* ('The bad traits'), *Delinquente* and *Declaracion de amor*. Other compositions include a cantata, *O! dios sa kalangitan* ('O God in Heaven'), *Ibong adarna* ('The adarna bird') (a coloratura song) and *Kundiman* (1920), a set of popular love-songs, in which he brought dignity and vitality to the genre.

BIBLIOGRAPHY
R. C. Bañas: *The Music and Theater of the Filipino People* (Manila, 1924)
E. A. Manuel: *Dictionary of Philippine Biography*, ii (Quezon City, 1970)

LUCRECIA R. KASILAG

Abdullah ibn Buhaina. See BLAKEY, ART.

Abe, Kōmei (*b* Hiroshima, 1 Sept 1911). Japanese composer. He studied the cello with Werkmeister at the Tokyo Music School, graduating in 1933; he stayed there for three years to study composition with Pringsheim and conducting with Rosenstock. In 1935 he joined the Nippon Gendai Sakkyokuka Renmei and quickly established a reputation for his chamber music. With Hirao and Takada he organized the ensemble Chijin Kai in 1948. He became professor and dean of the music department at the Kyoto Municipal College of Arts and was chairman of the Japanese Society for Contemporary Music (1960–63). Most of his pieces adopt the forms and genres of the classic German tradition.

WORKS
(*selective list*)
Orch: Theme and Variations, 1935; Vc Conc., 1937; Pastoral, pf, orch, 1945; 2 syms., 1957, 1960; Serenade, 1963; Sinfonietta, 1964
Chamber: 9 str qts, 1934, 1937, 1939, 1941, 1946, 1948, 1950, 1952, 1955; 2 sonatas, fl, pf, 1940, 1949; Cl Qnt, 1942; Divertimento, a sax, pf, 1951; Divertimento, 9 insts, 1954; Sextet, fl, cl, pf qt, 1964
Principal publisher: Ongaku-no-Tomo Sha

MASAKATA KANAZAWA

Abeille, (Johann Christian) Ludwig (*b* Bayreuth, 20 Feb 1761; *d* Stuttgart, 2 March 1838). German composer, pianist and organist. He studied at Stuttgart, where in 1782 he became a member of the private band of the Duke of Württemberg. On Zumsteeg's death in 1802 he succeeded him as Konzertmeister, and by 1815 he held the position of organist at court and director of the official music. In 1832, having completed 50 years' service with the court, he was given a gold medal and a pension.

Most of Abeille's compositions date from the first 30 years of his service at Stuttgart. Besides two sonatas for keyboard with accompanying violin (1783), his published instrumental works include sonatas and other pieces for both piano solo and piano duet, a piano trio, a piano concerto and a concerto for piano duet, which was favourably mentioned by Gerber (*Neues Lexikon*). But Abeille was best known for his vocal music; several collections of his songs were published including the *Vermischte Gedichte von Hübner* (1788, 1791), *Zwei Hirten-Lieder aus Florians Estelle von Schwan* (1795) and *Acht Lieder mit Begleitung des Pianoforte* (1805). He also contributed songs to volumes of the *Musikalischer Potpourri* which appeared in Stuttgart in 1790–91. These songs are notable for their stylistic simplicity and their melodic distinction. His setting of Jacobi's *Aschermittwoch Lied* for four voices and piano (1798) was popular in its day, as were his two Singspiels, *Amor und Psyche* (four acts, Stuttgart, 1800) and *Peter und Aennchen* (one act, Stuttgart, 1809). Both were published in vocal score.

C. F. POHL/JOHN D. DRAKE

Abeille, Pierre-César (*b* Salon-de-Provence, baptized 24 Feb 1674; *d* after 1733). French composer. He was the son of Jean Abeille, a royal notary, and may have been a choirboy at the collegiate church of St Laurent in Salon-de-Provence. From 1699 to 1700 he was *maître de chapelle* of the primate's church of St Trophime, Arles; from 31 March 1713 until 17 October 1713, when he was succeeded by François Pétouille, he was *vicaire de choeur* and *maître de musique* at the royal parish church of St Germain-l'Auxerrois in Paris. No further details of his life are known.

His most important compositions were two volumes

of the Psalms of David translated into French by Antoine Godeau, Bishop of Vence, dedicated to Mme de Maintenon and intended for the use of the young ladies at St Cyr. The 150 psalms are set with considerable skill and variety: the earlier ones are short and simple, but the later ones, in three parts alternating with *airs*, duets and ritornellos, become progressively more elaborate and require instrumental accompaniment (violin, flute, oboe or viol), often treated in concertante style with the voice parts. The second volume in particular shows balance and imagination, harmonic subtlety, descriptive episodes and expressive declamation of the words. Several verses are written as passacaglias; there are two chaconnes in Psalm lxxxviii. Abeille's settings are much superior to similar ones by Lemaire, Gobert and Oudot.

WORKS

Les psaumes de David en françois, 2 vols., *F-Pc*
Miserere, chorus 5vv, 4 insts, bc, Bordeaux, 29 June 1733, *Pn*
Actéon (cantate burlesque), 1v, vn/ob, c1700, *Pn*
Airs pubd in 18th-century anthologies, 1706–18

BIBLIOGRAPHY

EitnerQ
F. Raugel: 'La maîtrise et les orgues de la primatiale Saint-Trophime d'Arles', *RMFC*, ii (1961–2), 99, esp. 106
——: 'A travers l'inédit', *RMFC*, iii (1963), 223
M. Bert: 'La musique à la maison royale Saint-Louis de Saint-Cyr', ii, *RMFC*, v (1965), 91, esp. 109

GUY BOURLIGUEUX

Abejo, Rosalina (*b* Tagoloan, Oriental Misamis, 13 July 1922). Filipina composer and conductor. She studied music at Lourdes College, the piano at St Scholastica's College and composition at the Philippine Women's University (MM 1957). Later she attended the Labunski School of Composition in Ohio, the Eastman School and the Catholic University of America, Washington, DC. She is a nun of the Order of the Virgin Mary, teaching music theory and composition, and conducting fund-raising concerts. In addition she has travelled widely to take part in international music conferences. Among the honours she has received are the Republic Culture Heritage Award (1967) and the Philippines' Independence Day Award (1973). She has produced over 300 compositions and some published music text-books. Her style is marked by neo-classical and impressionist features, with quartal harmonies, added-note chords, pentatonic and modal scales.

WORKS

(*selective list*)

Orch: Vespers in a Convent Garden, sym. suite, 1956; 13 Variations, 2 pf, orch, 1964; Valle de los caidos, rhapsody, 1964; Sym. 'The Trilogy of Man', 1971; Sym. 'Guerilla', 1972
Choral: Advent Cantata, 1957; The Conversion of King Humabon, cantata, 1967; Redemption Oratorio, 1969; masses, other pieces
Solo vocal: Pamuhatbuhat [Faith healing], Bar, wind, native perc, str, 1973; Larawan ng Isang Babae [Woman's portrait], S, orch; Buhay [Life], S, orch; sacred songs
Inst: 3 str qts, 1949–54; Academic Festival Qt, 1966; Pf Qnt, 1966; Octet, wind, str, 1970; Maranaw Trail, 2 mar, pf, perc, 1971; Octet, brass, perc, 1972

LUCRECIA R. KASILAG

Abel. German family of musicians. They originated from middle and north Germany and were noted chiefly as viola da gamba players, violinists and composers; some members of the family were painters and landscape gardeners. The spelling 'Abell' is often found, especially among the earlier members of the family, but there is no known relationship to the English composer John Abell (1650–1724). Nor has any relationship been established between them and a musical family of the same name originating in Löwenberg (Mark) and active

in Grosswoltersdorf and Berlin, of whom the first musician was Georg Friedrich Abel (1755–1835); see J. Zachau: 'Die Abel aus Löwenberg (Mark) und ihr musikalisches Erbgut', *Familie und Volk*, v (1952), p. 154.

The earliest known musician of the family was Heinrich Othmar Abel (*b* c1580; *d* after 1630), who is said to have served as town musician in Magdeburg and Brunswick about 1600; for religious reasons he went to Bremen, where he received the freedom of the city in 1615, and from about 1630 he was a musician at Schloss Hünnefeld near Osnabrück. His son Ernst Abel (*b* Bremen, c1610; *d* Bremen, 1680), a keyboard player, was a member of the chapel at Hanover from 1636 and a musician at the Celle court, 1650–56; from 1662 to his death he was a Bremen town musician.

(1) Clamor Heinrich Abel (*b* Hünnefeld, 1634; *d* Bremen, 25 July 1696). Composer, organist and viola da gamba player, son of Ernst Abel. He served at Celle (1662–4) and then at Hanover, where he was court organist and viol player until 1685; possibly he then returned to Celle. His final appointment, in 1694, was as a town musician in Bremen. As a composer he is known for his collection of suites, *Erstlinge musikalischer Blumen*, consisting of 59 pieces: allemandes, courantes, sarabandes, sonatinas and preludes, as well as a 'Sonata battaglia', for four instruments and continuo (three parts, Frankfurt, 1674, 1675, 1677).

(2) Christian Ferdinand Abel (*b* Hanover, c1683; *d* Cöthen, 1737). Viola da gamba player and violinist, youngest son of (1) Clamor Heinrich Abel. As a young man he served with the troops of Charles XII of Sweden, then occupying north Germany and Bremen. He may have served at the Celle court before moving with his elder brother, the landscape gardener Johann Christoph, to join the establishment of Prince Leopold I of Anhalt-Cöthen about 1715. Christian Ferdinand was listed as chamber violinist and viol player when J. S. Bach was appointed Kapellmeister there in 1717; the two were soon good friends, and Bach stood as godfather to Abel's first daughter (*b* 6 Jan 1720). Spitta supposed that Bach had written the six cello suites for Abel, but there is no indication that Abel played the cello, and the Cöthen chapel had a competent and highly paid cellist in Christian Bernhard Linike. Prince Leopold had a particular affection for the gamba, and it is likely that Bach provided the three sonatas for gamba and harpsichord for Abel to teach to the prince. Although Abel's fortunes rose on Bach's departure in 1723, Leopold's death in 1728 brought on the decline of the chapel; Abel was eventually dismissed, and he is said to have died in poverty. Of his six children, the eldest son (3) Leopold August and (4) Carl Friedrich continued the family's musical inheritance.

(3) Leopold August Abel (*b* Cöthen, 24 March 1718; *d* Ludwigslust, 25 Aug 1794). Composer and violinist, eldest son of (2) Christian Ferdinand Abel. He was a pupil of Franz Benda in Dresden (1735) and worked as a violinist in the court orchestras at Brunswick (1745) and Sonderhausen (1757–65). He was next appointed Konzertmeister in the orchestra at Brandenburg-Schwedt (1766), then with Benda in Berlin, and he was finally a first violinist in the chapel of the Prince of Mecklenburg-Schwerin in Ludwigslust from 1770. His compositions include a Symphony in D (1776; *D-SWl*, under 'Leba') and violin 'arpeggien' (*A-Wgm*). His two sons, August Christian Andreas (1751–1834) and Friedrich Ludwig Aemilius (*b* 1770), were both violinists at Ludwigslust; the latter's grandson Ludwig (1835–95) was a violinist in Basle from 1865, and from 1867 at Munich, where he taught at the conservatory, composed for the violin and published a violin method (1875).

(4) Carl [Karl] **Friedrich Abel** (*b* Cöthen, 22 Dec 1723; *d* London, 20 June 1787). Composer and viola da gamba player, son of (2) Christian Ferdinand Abel. He was no doubt a pupil of his father, especially for the gamba; but on his father's death in 1737 Carl Friedrich may have turned to the former relationship with the Bach family and gone to Leipzig to study, as Burney, who knew Abel, stated. By 1743 Abel was a gamba player in the court orchestra under Hasse in Dresden; the connection with the Bachs was maintained – W. F. Bach was an organist there until 1746, and J. S. Bach had held an appointment as court composer from 1736. Abel left Dresden in 1757–8 during the destruction of the city by Frederick the Great. He then travelled, visiting the house of Goethe's family in Frankfurt and probably the musical centres of Mannheim and Paris. He had already begun to compose in Dresden; the Breitkopf catalogue of 1761 advertises solo and trio sonatas and concertos, all with the flute, and describes Abel as a chamber musician to the King of Poland.

During the 1758–9 season Abel went to London, the city where he was to spend most of his remaining years. His first public concert there was on 5 April 1759 (a few days before Handel's death). Abel demonstrated his versatility by performing on the gamba, the harpsichord, and Sir Edward Walpole's newly invented pentachord, as well as being the composer of most of the music. Over the next five years Abel increased his reputation in London through his own annual concerts and through his direction of the concerts of other artists. In 1760 he was granted a royal privilege for the publication of his music in London; while publishing his early works there on his own account, he ensured his Continental reputation by selling his op.1 to Hummel and his opp.2 and 3 to Breitkopf. The association with J. C. Bach began late in 1763, and the first sign of their joint efforts was a concert on 29 February 1764; thus the relationship of the Bach and Abel families continued. Both men were appointed chamber musicians to Queen Charlotte in about 1764, posts they held to their deaths; both were also friends to the Mozarts during their visit to London (1764–5) and served as mentors to the young Wolfgang. Abel's Symphony in E♭ op.7 no.6 was copied by Mozart and was long regarded as Mozart's work (formerly K18).

The association between Abel and Bach led to the establishment of the Bach–Abel concert series. This annual series of 10–15 concerts began on 23 January 1765 and continued up to 9 May 1781. They began as part of Mrs Cornelys's entertainments at Carlisle House, Soho Square, and moved in 1768 to Almack's Great Room, King Street, St James's. Their success encouraged Bach and Abel to enter into partnership with G. A. Gallini, a retired dancer and brother-in-law of Lord Abingdon, to build their own concert room in Hanover Square in 1774. 1775, when that hall opened, marks the zenith of the Bach–Abel concerts, for in addition to their series they offered 11 oratorio evenings at which each presented new works in the sinfonia concertante form and played solo concertos.

The opening of the Pantheon concerts in 1774 gave rise to an element of competition that doomed the complacent Bach–Abel series. The decline was most marked after 1778, when Gallini introduced a rival series at the Hanover Square rooms on another night. Bach's death at the beginning of 1782 might have ended the faltering enterprise, but Abel managed to continue the concerts under his own name for the rest of the season. Strangely, Bach's widow declined Abel's public offer of assistance. Possibly the relationship between Bach and Abel had by then become no more than a business matter; after sharing a home for many years, they had found separate residences in 1771, and unlike his flamboyant partner, Abel seems to have led a quiet and well-ordered life.

Abel's contribution to the Bach–Abel concerts included the direction on alternate evenings. The concerts introduced to London many musicians from the Continent, and while Bach's influence can be seen in the choice of singers, many of the instrumentalists had known Abel at Dresden or his brother at Ludwigslust. Abel seems to have visited Paris with some regularity in the 1770s and 1780s; he was said to be teaching the gamba to a *fermier-général* there, and it was probably he who introduced the several performers from Paris featured at the concerts. The directors also supplied most of the music that was given; much of it must appear among Abel's published symphonies, concertos, quartets and trios. Those and his keyboard sonatas designed for the amateur were published from 1765 by Robert Bremner, who thereafter issued the first editions of almost all Abel's works and reissued those that had been printed before that date. At this time Abel was also active, and highly regarded, as a performer on the viola da gamba, and at most concerts he displayed his talents in a solo or concerto. The concerts Bach and Abel gave at court (for example one for the Prince of Wales's fifth birthday on 12 August 1767) were in a sense an offshoot of their series; their influence is also seen in the number of individual benefit concerts that they were asked to direct both in London and in nearby cities during the summer. The programmes of these events serve as a good guide to the music played at the Bach–Abel series, the programmes of which are not extant.

At the end of the 1782 season Abel left London to visit his homeland. He saw his brother in Ludwigslust and probably his younger brother Ernst Heinrich (who was to claim Abel's possessions after his death) in Hamburg. He also spent some time at the court of Friedrich Wilhelm, Crown Prince of Prussia, at Potsdam; Abel had dedicated his op.15 quartets to the prince in 1780, and now he so impressed with his gamba playing that he received 100 louis d'ors and a gold snuff-box. The manuscripts of five of his symphonies were (until 1943) in the Berlin Stadtsschlossbibliothek, which suggests that he composed them for the prince, possibly on this visit. An advertisement in Cramer's *Magazin der Musik* (25 February 1783) shows that manuscript copies of his sonatas and quartets for the gamba were in circulation.

From the beginning of 1785 until his death Abel was again active at the Hanover Square rooms. He was billed as principal composer and viol player to the Grand Professional Concerts (the successors to the Abel concerts of 1782 that maintained much the same personnel as the Bach–Abel series), but is unlikely to

Carl Friedrich Abel: portrait (before 1777) by Thomas Gainsborough in the Henry E. Huntington Library and Art Gallery, San Marino, California

have contributed much music: his last three sets of works had been published in London during his absence. His last concert appearance was as a gamba virtuoso in a benefit for Mrs Billington, the daughter of Bach's pupil Mrs Weichsell, on 21 May 1787.

That final concert represents an act of generosity typical of the warm-hearted Abel, who often gave concerts for the needy and helped to introduce young performers. The most famous among those whose careers he furthered are the cellists John Crosdill and James Cervetto, for whom Abel provided a showy duet in 1778. With the violinist Wilhelm Cramer and the oboist J. C. Fischer, they formed the core of the Bach–Abel troupe for many years. Cramer's son, the pianist Johann Baptist, later publicly acknowledged Abel as one of his composition teachers, but it seems that Abel had no other famous pupils for either composition or the gamba. His generosity was equalled by the strength of his attachment to his friends, among whom was the painter Thomas Gainsborough; the friendship resulted in an exchange of music and paintings – Gainsborough's magnificent portrait of Abel with his gamba (see illustration) was exhibited at the Royal Academy in 1777 and is now at the Huntington Library, San Marino, California (other portraits of Abel include one by Robineau in the royal collection and an anonymous painting in the Music School at Oxford). Abel appears to have had a particular fondness for art and artists, for in addition to his collection of Gainsboroughs he cultivated the friendship of the designers and engravers Bartolozzi and Cipriani. He was also good friends with the Mannheim violinist Wilhelm Cramer, and the two shared an apartment before Cramer's second marriage, from 1776 to about 1779. It was at this time that Abel first showed signs of the illness that was to kill him; it was apparently brought on by rich living and in particular by an over-indulgence in drink, but it seems impossible to link this with any tragedy in his life (as has been suggested). Up to the time of his death Abel maintained a highly respected position in London society, at court, in the homes of the nobility, in fashionable circles, and among his fellow musicians; the several obituaries were unanimously laudatory.

Abel's reputation as a performer is closely connected with the viola da gamba. He also played the harpsichord well, but references to his performance on the french horn are the result of his admiration for a keyboard sonata by Ferdinand Horn which he must have played either on the harpsichord or in an arrangement for solo viol. The gamba was by this time approaching the end of its history; Abel's obituary in the *Morning Post* of 22 June 1787 remarked that 'his favourite instrument was not in general use, and would probably die with him'. It still had players in amateur circles; and in his last ten years Abel experienced in London the professional competition of Andreas Lidl. His playing on the gamba may have been slightly influenced by the possibilities of the cello; the only direct evidence of his style comes from the gamba obbligato to an aria from *Sifari*, performed with Guarducci on 5 March 1767, which consists of an expressive cantabile in the upper register with few chords. The several pieces for solo gamba now in the New York Public Library exploit the instrument's resources more fully and in virtuoso fashion, especially in the rich adagios and in one fugue; these works may have been written for a pupil rather than for Abel's own performance. Most of the rest of the surviving literature

was obviously intended for amateurs, which perhaps implies that Abel's own performances were usually improvised; Burney wrote: 'I have heard him modulate in private on his six-stringed base with such practical readiness and depth of science, as astonished the late Lord Kelly and Bach, as much as myself'. Abel was especially praised for his refinement of taste and his depth of feeling in adagios. He did not emphasize technical display in his performances; Burney commented that the 'most pleasing, yet learned modulation; the richest harmony; and the most elegant and polished melody were all expressed with ... feeling, taste and science', and that his manner of playing an adagio soon became a model for string players.

Abel was primarily a composer of instrumental music; his few vocal pieces are relatively unimportant. The symphonies, sonatas and gamba pieces form the largest groups among his output. Abel's style underwent little change; although he eventually came to write bass lines free of the plodding continuo style, the texture of two parallel melodic voices with a supporting bass, derived from the trio sonata, can be found in most of his trios and in many of his quartets and symphonies. Most of his works are in three movements, the remainder in two.

Abel's music is generally genial, energetic and light-hearted. He rarely used minor keys, and there is little trace of deeper emotion or *Sturm und Drang*, although his harmonic style is exceptionally rich and expressive. His melodies are often markedly instrumental in character, with broken chords, syncopation and appoggiaturas as common features; but he had a penchant for phrases of unusual lengths, and some of his music is refreshingly free from the two- and four-bar unit so common in the pre-Classical period. The slow movements usually have elegant, lyrical, highly ornamented melodies of considerable breadth; his finales are commonly in dance rhythm, often minuets (sometimes with variations but rarely with trios) or rondos. The result is a refined, urbane version of the Mannheim style with perhaps an Italian influence evident in the more vocal melodies and lighter moods. Burney remarked that his 'invention was not unbounded, and his exquisite taste and deep science prevented the admission of whatever was not highly polished'; he commented on a certain languor, and praised his harmony and 'selection of sounds' as models of perfection.

WORKS

All printed works published in London unless otherwise stated; numbering in left-hand column is that of Knape (1971).

Edition: *K. F. Abel: Kompositionen*, ed. W. Knape (Cuxhaven, 1958–74) [K]

ORCHESTRAL

1–6	VI symphonies à 4 parties, 2 vn, va, bc, op.1 (Amsterdam, *c*1759); K i
7–12	Six Overtures in 8 parts, op.4 (1762); K ii
45a	Ov., D, to T. A. Arne, Love in a Village (comic opera, I. Bickerstaffe), London, Covent Garden, 8 Dec 1762, pubd in Abel, Arne and Smith's Six Favourite Overtures (1763); K viii
45b	Ov., B♭, to S. Arnold, The Summer's Tale (comic opera, R. Cumberland), London, Covent Garden, 6 Dec 1765 (1766); K viii
44	The Periodical Overture in 8 Parts, no.16 (1766); K viii
13–18	Six Simphonies, op.7 (1767); K iii
19–24	Six Simphonies, op.10 (1773); K iv
53–8	Six Concerts, hpd/pf, insts, op.11 (1774); K x
25–30	Six Overtures in 8 Parts, op.14 (1778); K v
42	Simphonie concertante à plusieurs instruments obligés, libro I, vn, ob, vc (Berlin, 1781); ? perf. 1775; K viii
31–6	Six Overtures, op.17 (1783); K vi
46–50	5 fl concs., C, e, D, C, G, before 1759, *D-LEm*; K ix
51	Fl Conc., C, before 1759, *KA*; K ix

52	Vc Conc., B♭, before 1759, *B*; K ix
43	Sinfonia concertante, D, vn, ob, vc, 1783, *Bds*; K viii
37–41	5 syms., C, B♭, E♭, B♭, D, after 1783, formerly *Bds*, destroyed; K vii
59	Fl Conc., G, after 1783, *Dlb*; K x
60	Vc Conc., C, after 1783, *Bds*; K x suppl.

CHAMBER

111–16	Six Sonatas, hpd, vn/fl, vc, op.2 (1760); K xv
80–85	Six Sonatas, vn/fl, vn, hpd, op.3 (1761); K xiii
117–22	Six Sonatas, hpd, vn/fl, vc, op.5 (1764); K xv
123–8	Sei Sonate, fl, bc, op.6 (1765); K xv
61–6	Six Quartettos, 2 vn, va, vc obbl, op.8 (1769); K xi
86–91	Six Sonatas, vn, vc, bc, op.9 (1772); K xiii
67–72	A Second Sett of Six Quartettos, op.12 (1775); K xi–xii
225–6	2 quartets in Six Quartettos . . . by Messrs. Bach, Abel and Giardini, fl, vn, va, bc; 2 vn, va, bc (1776); K xvi
129–34	Six Sonatas, hpd/pf, vn, op.13 (1777); K xvi
102–3	2 trios in Six Sonatas, by Messrs. Bach, Abel and Kammell, 2 vn, vc (1777); K xiv
73–8	Six Quatuors, 2 vn, va, vc obligés, op.15 (1780); K xii
92–7	Six Trios, vn, va, vc, op.16 (1783); K xiv
98–101	Quatre trios, 2 for 2 fl, bc, 2 for fl, vn, bc, op.16 (Berlin, 1783); K xiv
135–40	Six Sonatas, hpd/pf, vn, op.18 (1784); K xvi
228	Duetto, 2 vc (after 1787), perf. 1778; K xvi
104–10	7 sonatas, G, D, G, F, c, G, G, 2 fl, bc, no.106 also for fl, vn, bc, *c*1765, *D-B*; K xvi
213–16	4 minuets from Entradas and Minuetts for the Balls at Court, C, D, G, G, kbd red., 1765–9, *GB-Lbm*; K xvi
217–23	7 regimental marches, F, F, F, F, F, B♭, F, kbd red., ? 1765–9, *Lbm*; K xvi
110a–f	VI sonates à 3, D, G, C, B♭, C, C, fl, vn, bc, ?before 1780, *S-Uu* (doubtful authenticity); K xv
147	Sonata, G, vc, bc, after 1783, *D-Bds*; K xvi
148	Sonata, A, vc, bc, after 1783, *Bds*; K xvi

VIOLA DA GAMBA

141–6	6 Easy Sonattas, hpd/(va da gamba/vn/fl, bc) (Amsterdam, 1771); K xvi
152–85	[34] Sonatas, va da gamba, some with bc, ?*c*1760, *GB-Lbm*; K xvi
186–212	27 pieces, va da gamba, *c*1770, *US-NYp*; K xvi
227	Quatuor, G, fl, vn, va da gamba, vc, no.4, after 1783, MS owned privately, copy in *D-B*; K xvi
149	Sonata, G, va da gamba, bc, after 1783, *Bds*; K xvi
150	Sonata, e, va da gamba, bc, after 1783, *Bds*; K xvi

VOCAL

—	Frena le belle lagrime (aria), S, va da gamba obbl, in Sifari (pasticcio), London, King's Theatre, 5 March 1767, other music by B. Galuppi and J. C. Bach, pubd in The Favourite Songs in the Opera Sifari (1767)
—	Where can we run (air), T, in kbd red., from Tom Jones (comic opera, J. Reed, after H. Fielding), London, Covent Garden, 14 Jan 1769 (1769)
231	Dolly's eyes are so bright (catch), 3vv, *c*1765–70, *GB-Lbm* Add.31463; K xvi

(5) Johann Leopold Abel (*b* Ludwigslust, 24 July 1795; *d* London, 1871). Pianist and composer, grandson of (3) Leopold August Abel. He was brought up by his father, August Christian Andreas Abel, to emulate his great-uncle (4) Carl Friedrich Abel. An attempted tour as a child prodigy, during which he played the piano and violin and later the cello, was a failure. After some success teaching music in German courts, his health failed and he left his homeland in 1819 to travel and regain his strength. He first visited his elder brother, a musician in Savannah, Georgia, and then sailed for England, arriving in London in 1820, in time to meet J. B. Cramer as he was publishing his tribute to Carl Friedrich Abel. Johann Leopold stayed in London, married Luise Hopkins, and published several songs and piano pieces.

BIBLIOGRAPHY

BurneyH

C. L. Junker: *Zwanzig Componisten: eine Skizze* (Berne, 1776), 1
Gentleman's Magazine, lvii (London, 1787), 549
J. B. Cramer, ed.: *The Late C. F. Abel's Adagios in Score* (London, 1820)
C. F. Pohl: *Mozart und Haydn in London* (Vienna, 1867/*R*1970)
C. S. Terry: *John Christian Bach* (London, 1929, rev. 2/1967)

W. Knape: *Die Sinfonien von Karl Friedrich Abel* (diss., U. of Leipzig, 1934)
S. M. Helm: *Carl F. Abel, Symphonist: a Biographical, Stylistic and Bibliographical Study* (diss., U. of Michigan, 1953)
W. Knape: 'Karl Friedrich Abel – ein zu Unrecht vergessener Zeitgenosse Mozarts: zur geplanten Neuausgabe einiger seiner Sinfonien', *Musik und Gesellschaft*, viii (1957), 144
G. Beechey: 'Carl Friedrich Abel's Six Symphonies Op. 14', *ML*, li (1970), 279
W. Knape: *Bibliographisch-thematisches Verzeichnis der Kompositionen von Karl Friedrich Abel* (Cuxhaven, 1971)
——: *Karl Friedrich Abel: Leben und Werk eines frühklassischen Komponisten* (Bremen, 1973)
M. Charters: 'Abel in London', *MT*, cxiv (1973), 1224
——: *The Bach–Abel Concerts* (diss., U. of London, 1978)

WALTER KNAPE, MURRAY R. CHARTERS

Abelard, Peter [Petrus Abailardus, Abaelard, Abailard] (*b* Le Pallet, nr. Nantes, 1079; *d* St-Marcel, nr. Chalonsur-Saône, 21 April 1142). French philosopher, poet and musician of Breton origin. After studying philosophy in Paris, he taught dialectic at the cathedral school. His love affair with Heloise, the young niece of Canon Fulbert, brought him fame as a musician. However, after they had secretly married in 1118 Fulbert had Abelard castrated. Heloise became a nun and he became a monk at St Denis. His highly original scholastic method and his restless and blunt nature aroused opposition to his teaching; principal among his opponents was Bernard of Clairvaux. After condemnation by the Council of Sens in 1140, Abelard found support from Peter the Venerable, Abbot of Cluny.

Abelard's songs are few beside his numerous theological writings. Heloise's testimony suggests that his love-songs must have been important from both a literary and a musical point of view. In a later letter (probably revised by Abelard) she declared that he had 'the gift of poetry and the gift of song'; he 'composed quite a number of metrical and rhythmic love-songs. The great charm and sweetness in language and music, and a soft attractiveness of the melody obliged even the unlettered'. These songs, presumably in Latin, have all been lost: they have not been identified among the anonymous repertory.

Some time after 1130 Abelard composed a hymnbook for Heloise, who was by that time abbess of the convent of the Paraclete. While Bernard of Clairvaux was having a hymnal composed for the Cistercians from the traditional material, Abelard was creating one which was totally new and homogeneous in style. He grouped the hymns by metre, and thus managed with only a few melodies. The hymnbook was not widely used and only one of the melodies has survived: that of the hymn for Saturday, *O quanta qualia*, which owes its wider distribution to the Cistercians. It is in the Dorian mode and in *AAB* form, yet it is shaped in a single long melodic arch. The verse is iambic, but the placing of melismas is as irregular as usual in hymns of the period.

The planctus, written after 1130, mark the climax of Abelard's poetical and musical work: they are six laments based on biblical themes: the lament of Dinah for herself and Sichem, of Jacob over his sons, of the virgins of Israel over Jeptha's daughter, of Israel over Samson, of David over Abner, and of David over Saul and Jonathan. They are conservative in use of rhyme, often employing only assonance, and yet in rhythm and musical structure they show a highly original style. Formally these songs are linked with the intermediate sequence form (*see* SEQUENCE (i)) by their rhymed lines and parallel strophes. Abelard extended this parallelism by three- and fourfold repetition. Internal rhyme and musical repetition are used to make smaller phrase-units within a line. (*See also* PLANCTUS.) The form was imitated in the French LAI, partly by means of direct contrafactum: thus the *Lai des pucelles*, a French love-song from the end of the 13th century, adopted the verse structure and melody of Abelard's *Planctus virginum*.

All six planctus survive with staffless neumes (in *I-Rvat* Reg.lat.288, ff.63*v*–64*v*). Planctus VI is the only one to have survived also in square notation (in *GB-Ob* Bodley 79, ff.53*v*–56); it is in the Mixolydian mode, and yet the first and last strophes are Hypomixolydian. Because of this the song has the unusual range of *d* to *g'*. Certain sections are set syllabically; these are terse and climactic, and have the character almost of recitative. Other sections are set with extensive melisma. The musical form was imitated in Godefroy de Breteuil's Marian lament *Planctus ante nescia* (included in the *Carmina burana*).

The planctus survive only in sources from the late 12th and 13th centuries, and show the influence of later musical taste. Their notation gives no suggestion of modal rhythm, and nothing is otherwise known about how or under what circumstances they were performed.

WORKS

Text editions: *Petri Abaelardi opera*, ed. V. Cousin (Paris, 1849–59/*R*1970)

PL, clxxviii

Lateinische Hymnendichter des Mittelalters: erste Folge, ed. G. M. Dreves, Analecta hymnica, xlvii (Leipzig, 1905), 142–232 [complete edn. of poetry]

HYMN

O quanta qualia, ed. in Monumenta monodica medii aevi, i (Kassel, 1956), no.590

PLANCTUS

Ad festas choreas celibes (Planctus virginum Israel super filia Jepte Galadite) [contrafactum: 'Lai des pucelles', Coraigeus sui des geus k'amors viaut]; ed. G. Vecchi: *Pietro Abelardo: i 'planctus': introduzione, testo critico, trascrizioni musicali*, Collezione di testi e manuali, xxxv (Modena, 1951), i

Dolorum solatium (Planctus David super Saul et Jonatha), ed. in Weinrich (1969) and Dronke; text ed. in Weinrich (1968)

BIBLIOGRAPHY

W. Meyer: *Gesammelte Abhandlungen zur mittellateinischen Rhythmik*, i (Berlin, 1905)

F. Laurenzi: *Le poesie ritmiche di Pietro Abelardo* (Rome, 1911)

J. G. Sikes: *Peter Abailard* (Cambridge, 1932)

E. Gilson: *Héloise et Abélard* (Paris, 1938, 2/1955; Eng. trans., 1955)

A. Machabey: 'Les planctus d'Abélard: remarques sur le rythme musical du XII. siècle', *Romania*, lxxxii (1961), 71

J. Maillard: *Evolution et esthétique du lai lyrique* (Paris, 1961)

W. von den Steinen: 'Die Planctus Abaelards – Jephthas Tochter', *Mittellateinisches Jb*, iv (1967), 122

L. Weinrich: 'Dolorum solatium: Text und Musik von Abaelards Planctus David', *Mittellateinisches Jb*, v (1968), 59

——: 'Peter Abaelard as Musician', *MQ*, lv (1969), 295, 464

P. Dronke: 'Peter Abelard: "Planctus" and Satire', *Poetic Individuality in the Middle Ages: New Departures in Poetry 1000–1150* (Oxford, 1970), 114–49, 202

LORENZ WEINRICH

Abelardo, Nicanor (*b* San Miguel, Bulacan, 7 Feb 1893; *d* Manila, 21 March 1934). Filipino composer, conductor and teacher. As a child he had violin lessons from his father, and in 1901 he wrote his first composition, *Ang unang buko* ('The first fruit'), a waltz. He was sent to study at the Liceo de Manila and he learnt to play the piano, but at the same time he had to take various jobs to support himself and his family. In 1916 he entered the Conservatory of the University of the Philippines, and in the next year he composed a march, *U. P. Beloved*, which won first prize in an open competition. He studied with Carreon (singing), Silos (bandurria), Abdon (violin) and Estella (piano); he received a

teacher's certificate at the conservatory in 1921, and in 1923 he pursued postgraduate studies there. The Piano Concerto, which he wrote for these later courses, was the first concerto written by a Filipino. From the same period are *Nasaan ka irog* ('Where are you beloved') and *Mutya ng Pasig* ('Muse of Pasig river'), examples of his work in developing the *kundiman* (love-song) into an art song form. Even before graduating he had begun to teach at the University of the Philippines, encouraged by his teachers Harrison and Schofield. But in 1925 he came into controversy with the conservatory director, Lippay, when he took charge of the Santa Ana cabaret orchestra. Among the awards he received in the following years were two first prizes at the Philippine Carnival Contest of 1931. In that year he went to the USA under a fellowship from the University of the Philippines, and in 1932 he took the MM at the Chicago Musical College. These were his most productive years, which saw the composition of several important works, among them the polytonal suite *Panoramas* and the concert overture *Cinderella*, with which he won the La Violette Scholarship. He returned to the Philippines in 1932 and rejoined the university staff. At his sudden death he left incomplete a symphony and an opera, *Florante at Laura*. His contribution to Philippine music lies not only in his abundant and profound output (he wrote over 150 works), but also in his work as a brilliant teacher of theory and composition. He published a number of treatises and scholarly essays.

WORKS
(*selective list*)

Orch: Academic Ov., 1921; Mountain Suite, 1921; Pf Conc., b♭, 1923; Valse élégante, sym. band, 1931; Cinderella, ov., 1931; Sinfonietta, 1931

Inst: Cavatina, vn, 1921; Nocturne no.1, pf, 1921; Romanza, vc, 1921; Pf Sonata, C, 1921; Str Qt no.1, F, 1921; Capriccio español, vn, 1923; Fantasie-impromptu, pf, 1923; Fifes and Castagnets, fl, pf, 1931; Naughty Nymph, fl, pf, 1931; Panoramas, fl, cel, pf, vn, va, 1931; Sonata, vn, pf, 1931; Sonata, str qt, 1931; A Visayan Caprice, pf trio, 1932–4

Kundiman: Nasaan ka irog, 1923; Kundiman ng Luha, 1924; Magbalik ka Hirang, 1925; Pahimakas, p1925; Bituing marikit, 1926; Mutya ng Pasig, 1926; Himutok, 1929; Sa iyong kandungan, 1932–4

Other vocal works: Ave Maria, S, vn, 1921; Ang aking bayan, 1v, pf, 1923; Kung hindi man, 1v, pf trio, 1923; Health Service Hymn, 1924; Canto del viajero (J. Rizal), 1v, pf, 1925; National Heroes Day Hymn, 1928; Salve regina mater, S, Bar, vc, pf, 1932–4

Principal publisher: Sixta Naguiat Abelardo [songs]

BIBLIOGRAPHY

R. C. Bañas: *The Music and Theater of the Filipino People* (Manila, 1924)

E. A. Manuel: *Dictionary of Philippine Biography*, i (Manila, 1955)

LUCRECIA R. KASILAG

Abell, John (i) (*b* Aberdeenshire, 1653; *d* ?Cambridge, after 1716). Scottish composer, countertenor and lutenist. His name occurs first in 1679, when he was admitted 'extraordinary' then 'in ordinary' to the Chapel Royal. From about the same time he was listed among the musicians of the King's Private Music as one of the lutes and voices and also as a violinist. Between 1679 and 1688 he received a total of £740 'bounty money' for undisclosed services to the king while travelling abroad, ostensibly to study. Evelyn recorded (27 January 1682):

After supper came in the famous Trebble, Mr Abel, newly return'd from *Italy*, & indeed I never heard a more excellent voice, one would have sworne it had been a Womans it was so high, & so well & skillfully manag'd.

He graduated MusB at Cambridge in 1684. His marriage to Lady Frances Knollys on 29 December 1685 caused something of a scandal, and he left the country after the revolution in 1688, his sympathies being strongly Catholic. He travelled widely on the Continent, visiting France, Germany, Italy, the Low Countries and Poland. There are many anecdotes referring to this period of his life. Hawkins quoted the following:

Upon his arrival at Warsaw, the king having notice of it, sent for him to his court. Abell made some slight excuse to evade going, but upon being told that he had everything to fear from the king's resentment, he made an apology, and received a command to attend the king next day. Upon his arrival at the palace, he was seated in a chair in the middle of a spacious hall, and immediately drawn up to a great height; presently the king with his attendants appeared in a gallery opposite to him, and at the same instant a number of wild bears were turned in; the king bade him then choose whether he would sing or be let down among the bears; Abell chose the former, and declared afterwards that he never sang so well in his life.

In January 1699 he was granted a licence to return to England: it was reported that he had been offered £500 a year to sing in opera in London. Congreve wrote on 10 December 1700:

Abell is here: has a cold at present, and is always whimsicall, so that when he will sing or not upon the stage are things very disputable, but he certainly sings beyond all creatures upon earth, and I have heard him very often both abroad and since he came over.

He went to Ireland in the household of the viceroy, the Duke of Ormonde, in 1703, but returned to London the following year. Up to 1716 he appeared occasionally in concerts and on the stage and in 1703 wrote an ode for Queen Anne's birthday, *Hark, Britain, hark.* Mattheson stated that he possessed some secret that preserved the purity of his voice into old age. He published in London *A Collection of Songs, in Several Languages* (1701, in the copy of which in *GB-Lbm* are further biographical details), *A Collection of Songs, in English* (1701) and *A Choice Collection of Italian Ayres* (1703), but he is remembered as a singer rather than as a composer. His songs were influenced by the Italian style but are short-winded and hardly rise above the trivial.

BIBLIOGRAPHY

HawkinsH
J. Mattheson: *Der vollkommene Capellmeister* (Hamburg, 1739), 95
H. G. Farmer: 'John Abell', *HMYB*, vii (1952), 445
E. S. de Beer, ed.: *The Diary of John Evelyn* (London, 1955)
R. McGuinness: 'An 18th-century Entertainment', *Soundings*, iii (1973), 66
I. Spink: *English Song: Dowland to Purcell* (London, 1974), 257f

IAN SPINK

Abell, John (ii). English music publisher who with WILLIAM RANDALL (ii) succeeded to the firm of Walsh.

Abello de Torices, Benito. *See* BELLO DE TORICES, BENITO.

Abendmusik (Ger.). The name given to a particular type of concert held in the Marienkirche, Lübeck, during the 17th and 18th centuries. The exact origins of the Abendmusiken were already obscure in the mid-18th century, but they began as organ recitals, probably during Franz Tunder's tenure as organist (1641–67), perhaps even earlier. The original purpose may have been to entertain businessmen who assembled in the Marienkirche to await the opening of the stock exchange at noon on Thursdays. However, Tunder already referred to them as 'Abendspiele' in 1646. It is also possible that the Lübeck businessmen who financed them were imitating the municipally sponsored organ recitals in the Netherlands, where Reformed church doctrine prohibited the use of the organ during church services.

Tunder's musical offerings later included vocal and instrumental soloists, but Buxtehude, who succeeded him, added orchestra and chorus, necessitating the building of four extra balconies in 1669 to accommodate 40 performers. He also changed the time from a weekday to 4 p.m. on the last two Sundays of Trinity and the second, third and fourth Sundays of Advent, a schedule which was maintained throughout the 18th century. Although as late as 1700 Buxtehude presented programmes of assorted choral and solo vocal music, he had much earlier introduced oratorios at these concerts. A libretto for his 1678 oratorio *Die Hochzeit des Lammes* survives (published in Pirro); it is in two parts, presumably performed on two successive Sundays. Two Buxtehude oratorios advertised for publication in 1684, *Himmlische Seelenlust auf Erden* and *Das Allerschröcklichste und Allererfreulichste* were each in five parts. Under Buxtehude's successors, Johann Christian Schieferdecker (1679–1732), Johann Paul Kunzen (1696–1756), his son Adolf Karl Kunzen (1720–81) and Johann Wilhelm Cornelius von Königslöw (1745–1833), it became standard practice for the organist to compose and present each year a new oratorio in five parts, extending over all five Sundays. The subjects were mainly taken from the Old Testament (*see* ORATORIO, §7).

Only two oratorios survive that are known to have been performed at the Lübeck Abendmusiken: Adolf Kunzen's *Moses in seinem Eifer gegen die Abgötterey in den Wüsten* (in *D-Bds*) and *Absalon* (in *D-LÜh*). *Das jüngste Gericht,* published by Willy Maxton as a work of Buxtehude (Kassel, 1939), is anonymous in the manuscript source, and Martin Geck has cast doubt upon it as an authentic Buxtehude oratorio. Before World War II manuscripts of numerous other oratorios by Adolf Kunzen and von Königslöw were still extant at Lübeck; they are discussed by Stahl but were lost during the war. They contained chorale settings in addition to the more usual components: recitative, arias and choruses, both dramatic and contemplative.

The Abendmusik concerts were financed mainly by the business community; individual donors were rewarded with a printed libretto and a good seat, but admission to the church was free, and disorderly conduct during the performances was often a problem. In 1752 Johann Kunzen instituted the practice of charging admission to the dress rehearsals that were held on Fridays in the spacious stock-exchange hall, and in time these performances became the more important ones. The free Sunday performances in the Marienkirche were abolished in 1800, and ten years later the Lübeck Abendmusiken ceased entirely as a result of the Napoleonic Wars. The term has since come into general use for concerts in churches anywhere.

BIBLIOGRAPHY

A. Pirro: *Dietrich Buxtehude* (Paris, 1913)
W. Stahl: *Die Lübecker Abendmusiken im 17. und 18. Jahrhundert* (Lübeck, 1937)
O. Söhngen: 'Die Lübecker Abendmusiken als kirchengeschichtliches und theologisches Problem', *Musik und Kirche*, xxvii (1957), 181
M. Geck: 'Die Authentizität des Vokalwerks Dietrich Buxtehudes in quellenkritischer Sicht', *Mf*, xiv (1961), 393; xvi (1963), 175
G. Karstädt: *Die 'extraordinairen' Abendmusiken Dietrich Buxtehudes: Untersuchungen zur Aufführungspraxis in der Marienkirche zu Lübeck; mit den Textbüchern des 'Castrum Doloris' und 'Templum Honoris' in Faksimile-Neudruck* (Lübeck, 1962)
W. Maxton: 'Die Authentizität des "Jüngsten Gerichts" von Dietrich Buxtehude', *Mf*, xv (1962), 382
H. E. Smither: *A History of the Oratorio*, ii: *The Oratorio in the Baroque Era: Protestant Germany and England* (Chapel Hill, 1977)

KERALA JOHNSON SNYDER

Abendroth, Hermann (*b* Frankfurt am Main, 19 Jan 1883; *d* Jena, 29 May 1956). German conductor. He studied at Munich under Ludwig Thuille, Felix Mottl and Anna Langenhan-Hirzel (a pupil of Leschetizky). His first post was as conductor of the amateur Orchestral Society of Munich (1903–4), after which he moved to Lübeck, first as conductor of the Society of Friends of Music, and later also as chief conductor at the Städtische Oper (1907–11). He then became music director at Essen (1911–14), after which he went to Cologne as director of the conservatory in succession to Fritz Steinbach, becoming general music director there in 1918. He began making gramophone records in the 1920s, and his tours abroad included frequent concerts with the LSO (from their 1926–7 season to 1937). After 20 years in Cologne he was appointed to succeed Walter as conductor of the Leipzig Gewandhaus Orchestra, where he remained until 1945. He conducted at the Bayreuth Festival (1943–4), and after World War II he became conductor of the Weimar SO; he was the first German conductor to be invited to the USSR after the war. His reputation was based on the German and Viennese orchestral repertory, especially Mozart, Beethoven, Brahms and Bruckner, in which he was respected for his faithfulness to the composer's score and for his warmth of expression, as well as for his ability to encourage high orchestral standards.

ROBERT PHILIP

Aber, Adolf (*b* Apolda, Thuringia, 28 Jan 1893; *d* London, 21 May 1960). German musicologist and editor. He was a pupil of Kretzschmar, Friedlaender and Wolf at the Academy of Music, Berlin, where he took his doctorate in 1919 with a dissertation on the musical aspects of Luther's Reformation and further developments of music at the German courts down to the mid-17th century. He acted as assistant to Kretzschmar for a time, until in 1919 he settled in Leipzig, where he became the chief music critic of the *Leipziger neueste Nachrichten* (at that time the most important German newspaper outside Berlin) and, in 1927, a partner in the music publishing firm of Friedrich Hofmeister. In 1933 he left Germany, and in 1936 joined the board of directors of Novello & Co. in London. In this position he was able both to enrich Novello's own catalogue by adding to it works by German composers such as Scheidt, Schicht and Kuhnau, and to increase the general availability in England of editions put out by German publishing houses. His own editions include tutors for cornet and saxophone, 16 volumes of studies for wind instruments and collections of German folk dances.

WRITINGS

'Das musikalische Studienheft des Wittenberger Studenten Georg Donat *c*1543', *SIMG*, xv (1913–14), 68–98
'Studien zu J. S. Bachs Klavierkonzerten', *BJb*, x (1913), 5
Die Pflege der Musik unter den Wettinern und wettinischen Ernestinern, von den Anfängen bis zur Auflösung der Weimarer Hofkapelle 1662 (diss., U. of Berlin, 1919; Bückeburg, 1921)
Handbuch der Musikliteratur (Leipzig, 1922)
Die Musikinstrumente und ihre Sprache (Berlin, 1924)
Die Musik im Schauspiel (Leipzig, 1926)
'Die Musik im griechischen Drama', *Die Musik*, xviii (1926), 495
'Die Musik in der Tagespresse', *Die Musik*, xxi (1929), 865
'Hugo Wolf's Posthumous Works', *MR*, ii (1941), 190

ERIC BLOM/MALCOLM TURNER

Aber, Johann (*fl* Milan, 1765–83). Italian composer and flautist of German descent. In 1765 he was flautist in Sammartini's orchestra for a concert in honour of Archduke Leopold. He was flautist in the La Scala orchestra in 1779, flute teacher at the Collegio Longone, and one of the 84 musicians whose names appear on the act of foundation, dated 26 March 1783, of the Pio Istituto dei Professori di Musica. His music, all in manuscript (in *I-Gi*(*l*) and *Mc*), consists of three flute concertos and a considerable amount of chamber music, including duets, sonatas, trios and quartets for various combinations of instruments, always with flute. These display good craftsmanship but a rather simple style, which shows some influence of Mozart.

BIBLIOGRAPHY

P. Cambiasi: *Il Teatro alla Scala* (Milan, 1881)
G. Barblan: 'La musica strumentale e cameristica a Milano dalla seconda metà del '500 alla fine del '700', *Storia di Milano*, xvi (1962), 652
A. Zecca Laterza: 'Aber, Johann', *MGG* [with detailed list of works]

SERGIO MARTINOTTI

Aberdeen. City in Scotland. It has enjoyed several periods of musical distinction; from 1662 to 1720 John Forbes, printer to the town council, was Scotland's only notable music publisher, and during the 1760s and 1770s John Gregory, James Beattie and Alexander Gerard, all professors at King's and Marischal colleges, were the leading British writers on musical aesthetics. From about 1890 to 1930 Aberdeen was the centre of Scots fiddle playing and folksong collecting, and the King's College library houses 90 volumes of Gavin Greig's folksong notes. During the 20th century Aberdeen's most distinguished native musicians have been the operatic soprano Mary Garden, the folksinger Jeannie Robertson and the composer Martin Dalby.

Aberdeen's earliest-known musical institutions are the St Nicholas and St Machar song schools, which were in existence by the beginning of the 16th century. As church schools they survived the Reformation and continued to teach singing, theory and instrumental playing until about 1750, when they were eclipsed by the Enlightenment and by new standards of international professionalism. In 1748 the Aberdeen Musical Society was formed to give weekly aristocratic concerts of Italian Baroque music, which continued until 1801; the composer Robert Mackintosh led the society's orchestra from 1784 to 1787. Meanwhile St Paul's Episcopal Chapel, opened in 1722, held services with Anglican cathedral choral music and organ music, both new phenomena for post-Reformation Scotland. St Paul's organists included the composers Andrew Tait (to 1774), Robert Barber (1774–83) and John Ross (1783–1836).

Around 1800 there was a collapse of upper-class interest in music, but after 30 years a more popular musical awareness showed itself in two Aberdeen Music Festivals (1828 and 1834). There followed the foundation of the Haydn Society (1840) and Euterpean Society (1845), both amateur orchestral bodies, the Aberdeen Harmonic Choir (1847), Aberdeen Choral Society (1849), and the University Choral and Orchestral Society (1870). The Music Hall, still the city's main concert venue, was built in 1859. The Scottish Orchestra (now the Scottish National Orchestra) has visited Aberdeen regularly from Glasgow since its foundation in 1891; more recently, regular visits have been made by Scottish Opera (Glasgow) and the Scottish Baroque Ensemble (Edinburgh). Aberdeen still has no professional performing ensemble of its own, but in addition to much enthusiastic amateur music-making, a weekly concert series is held at the Art Gallery. The university music department, founded just after World War II, has a sizable postgraduate school.

BIBLIOGRAPHY
H. G. Farmer: *Music Making in the Olden Days* (London, 1950)

DAVID JOHNSON

Abert, Anna Amalie (*b* Halle an der Saale, 19 Sept 1906). German musicologist, daughter of Hermann Abert. She studied musicology with Abert, Blume and Sachs as well as history with F. Meinecke and philosophy with E. Spranger at the University of Berlin and took her doctorate there with a dissertation on Schütz's *Cantiones sacrae* in 1934. She then became an assistant lecturer at the musicology institute at the University of Kiel, where she completed her *Habilitation* in 1943 with a work on Monteverdi and music drama. In 1950 she became *ausserplanmässiger Professor* at the University of Kiel and in 1962 research fellow and professor. From 1949 to 1958 she was an editor of *MGG* and since 1964 she has been a member of the Zentralinstitut für Mozartforschung. Since 1971 she has lived in retirement in Kiel. Her main field of research is opera, on whose history from Monteverdi to Richard Strauss she has written a number of valuable studies; in these she deals especially with sources, librettos and opera aesthetics and with the basic problem of the relationship of speech and music.

WRITINGS
Die stilistischen Voraussetzungen der 'Cantiones sacrae' von Heinrich Schütz (diss., U. of Berlin, 1934; *Kieler Beiträge zur Musikwissenschaft*, ii, Wolfenbüttel and Berlin, 1935)
'Das Nachleben des Minnesangs im liturgischen Spiel', *Mf* i (1948), 95
'Schauspiel und Opernlibretto im italienischen Barock', *Mf*, ii (1949), 133
'Der Geschmackswandel auf der Opernbühne, am Alkestis-Stoff dargestellt', *Mf*, vi (1953), 214
Claudio Monteverdi und das musikalische Drama (Lippstadt, 1954)
Christoph Willibald Gluck (Zurich, 1960)
'Liszt, Wagner und die Beziehungen zwischen Musik und Literatur im 19. Jahrhundert', *IMSCR, viii New York 1961*, i, 314
'Rhythmus und Klang in Schuberts Streichquintett', *Festschrift Karl Gustav Fellerer* (Regensburg, 1962), 1
'Stefan Zweigs Bedeutung für das Alterswerk von Richard Strauss', *Festschrift Friedrich Blume* (Kassel, 1963), 7
'Stilistischer Befund und Quellenlage: zu Mozarts Lambacher Sinfonie KV Anh. 221 = 45a', *Festschrift Hans Engel* (Kassel, 1964), 43
'Methoden der Mozartforschung', *MJb 1964*, 22
'Monteverdi e lo sviluppo dell'opera', *RIM*, i (1966), 207
'Webers "Euryanthe" und Spohrs "Jessonda" als grosse Opern', *Festschrift für Walter Wiora* (Kassel, 1967), 435
'Die Opernästhetik Claudio Monteverdis', *Congresso internazionale sul tema Claudio Monteverdi e il suo tempo: Verona, Mantova e Cremona 1968*, 35
'Die Barockoper: ein Bericht über die Forschung seit 1945', *AcM*, xli (1969), 121
'Über Textentwürfe Verdis', *Beiträge zur Geschichte der Oper* (Regensburg, 1969), 131
Die Opern Mozarts (Wolfenbüttel, 1970; Eng. version in *NOHM*, vii, 1973)
'Tasso, Guarini e l'opera', *NRMI*, iv (1970), 827
'Darstellung des Gebets in der Oper', *Triviale Zonen in der religiösen Kunst des 19. Jahrhunderts* (Frankfurt, 1971), 148
Richard Strauss: die Opern (Velber, 1972)
'Leidenschaftsausbrüche zwischen Rezitativ und Arie', *3° congresso internazionale di studi verdiani: Milano 1972*, 56
'Verdi und Wagner', *AnMc*, no.11 (1972), 1
'Opera in Italy and the Holy Roman Empire', *NOHM*, vii (London, 1973), 1–172
'Richard Strauss' Anteil an seinen Operntexten', *Musicae scientiae collectanea: Festschrift Karl Gustav Fellerer* (Cologne, 1973), 1
'Richard Strauss und das Erbe Wagners', *Mf*, xxvii (1974), 165
'Die Oper zwischen Barock und Romantik', *AcM*, xlix (1977), 137
Numerous articles for *MGG* including 'Libretto' and 'Oper'
Articles in *MJb*

EDITIONS
M. Franck: *Fünf Hohelied-Motetten*, Cw, xxiv (1933)
C. Demantius: *Vier deutsche Motetten*, Cw, xxxix (1936, 2/1954)

with L. Finscher: *C. W. Gluck: Orfeo ed Euridice*, Sämtliche Werke, i/1 (Kassel and Basle, 1963)
W. A. Mozart: *Sinfonie in G ('Neue Lambacher Sinfonie')*, NM, ccxvii (2/1967)

BIBLIOGRAPHY
K. Hortschansky, ed.: *Opernstudien: Anna Amalie Abert zum 65. Geburtstag* (Tutzing, 1975) [incl. F. Blume: 'Anna Amalie Abert', 9, and bibliography, 227]

HANS HEINRICH EGGEBRECHT

Abert, Hermann (*b* Stuttgart, 25 March 1871; *d* Stuttgart, 13 Aug 1927). German musicologist. His father was court Kapellmeister at Stuttgart and composed operas, seven symphonies and other works. From 1890 to 1895 Abert studied classics and then music in Berlin under H. Bellermann, Fleischer and Friedlaender. He took the doctorate at Berlin in 1897 with a dissertation on Greek music, and in 1902 he completed his *Habilitation* at the University of Halle with a work on the aesthetic bases of medieval melody. He was appointed honorary professor in 1909 and reader in 1911. In 1920 he was appointed professor at the University of Leipzig (succeeding Riemann) and in 1923 he became professor at Berlin University (succeeding Kretzschmar). In 1925 he was elected an ordinary member of the Prussian Academy of Sciences at Berlin – the first musicologist to have earned this distinction.

Abert was one of the leading German musicologists of his generation, and he did much to increase regard for his subject among followers of more traditional university disciplines. His numerous distinguished pupils include his daughter Anna Amalie, Blume, Fellerer, Gerber and Vetter. His early approach was consistently based on the humanitarian ideals of classical antiquity, in studies of the effect of music on man and of the way in which social patterns and cultural ideals were expressed in the music of various epochs. He later turned towards dramatic music, particularly research into the history of opera. He was not interested in the purely archival and theoretical aspects of musicology. In his later years he frequently returned to the music of Greek antiquity with studies that eventually led him to specific problems of musical aesthetics in ancient times, the Middle Ages and his own time. His interest in 19th-century and contemporary music, shown in studies of Beethoven, Schumann, the Romantic era and Meyerbeer, led him to confront specific problems of opera. Exemplary editions of important operatic works, his editorship of the *Gluck-Jahrbuch* (1913–18) and many monographs (from 1905, and including *Niccolò Jomelli als Opernkomponist*, 1908) preceded his great Mozart biography (1919–21), which, although it made use of new research methods, was still in the tradition of the great 19th-century musical biographies of Jahn, Chrysander and Spitta. Abert modestly called his work the fifth edition of Jahn's biography, but it is in almost every respect an entirely independent work. He presented Mozart in his full stature and in lively, human terms, at the same time revealing in imposing breadth the sources of the various aspects of Mozart's art. Although Mozart scholarship since Abert's time has advanced in the field of source study and in terms of detailed insight and general understanding, this monumental biography is still one of the great standard works of music literature.

WRITINGS
Die Lehre vom Ethos in der griechischen Musik (diss., U. of Berlin, 1897; Leipzig, 1899/R1968)

'Der neue Aristoxenosfund von Oxyrhynchus', *SIMG*, i (1899–1900), 333

Die ästhetischen Grundsätze der mittelalterlichen Melodiebildung (Habilitationsschrift, U. of Halle, 1902; Halle, 1902)

'Zu Casiodor', *SIMG*, iii (1902–3), 439

Robert Schumann (Berlin, 1903, 4/1920)

Die Musikanschauung des Mittelalters und ihre Grundlagen (Halle, 1905/R1964)

'Ein neuer musikalischer Papyrusfund', *ZIMG*, viii (1906–7), 79

Geschichte der Robert-Franz-Singakademie zu Halle (1833–1908) (Halle, 1908)

'J. G. Noverre und sein Einfluss auf die dramatische Ballettkomposition', *JbMP 1908*, 29

Niccolò Jomelli als Opernkomponist (Halle, 1908)

'Antike Musikerlegenden', *Festschrift . . . Rochus Freiherrn von Liliencron* (Leipzig, 1910), 1

'Piccini als Buffokomponist', *JbMP 1913*, 29

'Glucks italienische Opern bis zum "Orfeo" ', *Gluck-Jb*, ii (1915), 1

Johann Joseph Abert, 1832–1915: sein Leben und seine Werke (Leipzig, 1916)

'Der neue griechische Papyrus mit Musiknoten', *AMw*, i (1918), 313

'Giacomo Meyerbeer', *JbMP 1918*, 37

'Paisiellos Buffokunst', *AMw*, i (1918), 402

'J. C. Bachs italienische Opern', *ZMw*, i (1919–20), 313

W. A. Mozart (Leipzig, 1919–21, 3/1955–66) [enlarged 5th edn. of O. Jahn: *W. A. Mozart*, Leipzig, 1856–9] [essay on *Don Giovanni*, Eng. trans., 1976]

'Joseph Haydns Klaviersonaten', *ZMw*, ii (1919–20), 553: iii (1920–21), 535

Goethe und die Musik (Engelhorn, 1922)

'Wort und Ton in der Musik des 18. Jahrhunderts', *AMw*, v (1923), 31

'Geistlich und Weltlich in der Musik', *Zeitschrift für Ästhetik und allgemeine Kunstwissenschaft*, xx (1925), 397

'Kunst, Kunstwissenschaft und Kunstkritik', *Die Musik*, xvi (1923), 1

'Zu Beethovens Persönlichkeit und Kunst', *JbMP 1925*, 9

'Tonart und Thema in Bachs Instrumentalfugen', *Festschrift Peter Wagner* (Leipzig, 1926), 1

ed. F. Blume: *Gesammelte Schriften und Vorträge* (Halle, 1929/R1968)

EDITIONS

N. Jommelli: *Fetonte*, DDT, xxxii, xxxiii (1907/R1958)

Ausgewählte Ballette Stuttgarter Meister, DDT, xliii, xliv (1913/R1958)

C. W. von Gluck: *Le nozze d'Ercole e d'Ebe*, DTB, xxvi, Jg.xiv/2 (1914); *Orfeo ed Euridice*, DTÖ, xliva, Jg.xxi/4 (1914/R1959)

B. Pallavicino: *La Gerusalemme liberata*, DDT, lv (1916/R1958)

BIBLIOGRAPHY

J. S. Handschin: 'Hermann Abert', *SMz*, lxvii (1927), 320

——: 'Hermann Abert', *Neue Zürcher Zeitung* (23 Aug 1927)

H. Moser: 'Hermann Abert', *ZMw*, x (1927–8), 1

R. Gerber: 'Hermann Abert', *Die Musik*, xx (1927), 50

W. Vetter: 'Hermann Abert zum Gedächtnis', *JbMP 1927*, 9

F. Blume, ed.: *Gedenkschrift für Hermann Abert von seinen Schülern* (Halle, 1928) [incl. complete list of publications]

K. G. Fellerer: 'Hermann Abert', *Jahresberichte über die Fortschritte der klassischen Altertumswissenschaften*, lvi (1930), no.228, p.1

Traditionen und Aufgaben der Hallischen Musikwissenschaft (U. of Halle and Wittenberg, 1963) [incl. W. Rackwitz: 'Dokumente zu den Anfängen des Instituts für Musikwissenschaft der Martin-Luther-Universität Halle-Wittenberg', and M. Vetter: 'Die Gründung und die Begründer des Hallischen musikalischen Seminars']

H. A. Brockhaus: *Hermann Aberts Konzeption der musikalischen Historiographie* (Habilitationsschrift, Humboldt U. of Berlin, 1966)

A. A. Abert: 'Hermann Aberts Weg zur Musikwissenschaft', *Musa mens musici: im Gedenken an Walther Vetter* (Leipzig, 1969), 9 [also in *DJbM*, ix (1964), 7]

LOTHAR HOFFMANN-ERBRECHT

Abgesetzte Docke (Ger.). DOGLEG JACK.

Abgestossen [gestossen, abgesondert, tockiret] (Ger.). A term in violin playing whose general meaning is 'pushed away' or 'separated'. It is found in 18th-century German sources (e.g. Leopold Mozart, Quantz). In this general sense *abgestossen* is synonymous with STACCATO in its 18th-century meaning. As a rule, *abgestossen* is indicated by dots or vertical strokes over or under the individual (unslurred) notes concerned, and is generally used in moderate to fast tempos. At these tempos, the player normally makes the 'separation' (*abgestossen*) by halving the duration of sound indicated by the written notes – for instance, a crotchet becomes a quaver followed by a quaver rest. The bow is normally kept on the string for *abgestossen*. (In slow to moderate tempos, a controlled, lifted, off-string stroke is indicated by *absetzen* or *aufheben*.)

DAVID D. BOYDEN

Abingdon, 4th Earl of [Bertie, Willoughby] (*b* Gainsborough, 16 Jan 1740; *d* Rycote, 26 Sept 1799). English music patron and composer. He was educated at Westminster and Oxford. He was brought into close contact with J. C. Bach and C. F. Abel through his brother-in-law Giovanni Gallini, who was concerned in the organization of the Bach–Abel subscription concerts. Latterly Abingdon provided a substantial proportion of the funds. After Bach's death, when the scheme was known as the Professional Concerts, he attempted to persuade Haydn to visit London and direct them.

Abingdon's incentive to compose may have come through his friendship with Haydn, with whom he was very friendly during his visits to England, as can be seen from the many references to him in Haydn's diary. Haydn composed the piano or harp accompaniments to Abingdon's *Twelve Sentimental Catches and Glees, for Three Voices* (*c*1795; reprinted with German words by Breitkopf & Härtel, *c*1906), and there are traces of his influence in Abingdon's own music. He urged Haydn to set *The Invocation of Neptune* translated by Needham from Seldon's *Mare Clausum*, but only two numbers were completed. He gave the manuscript to his publisher, the flute player Monzani, from whom it passed to the British Museum (Add.9284). His most extensive composition is *A Representation of the Execution of Mary Queen of Scots in Seven Views: the Music Composed for and adapted to each View*. Dedicated 'To those female Philosophers, Members of the Blue Stocking Club', it attempts to unite the sister arts of music, poetry and painting in a single work which would be 'thus to the *Outward* Senses as well as to the *Inward* Sense Conveyed'. The music is well written but lacks the power to express the drama of Queen Mary's final hours. A second work of a similarly descriptive nature, to which is attached, as an *impresa*, an engraved picture of the revelation of St John by J. F. Rigaud, is *A Selection of Twelve Psalms and Hymns* scored for chorus, oboes, clarinets, horns, bassoons and timpani. As a songwriter he is distinguished more for his radical choice of words – he was a friend and follower of John Wilkes – than for the music.

Abingdon was a keen amateur flautist and Abel composed, at his request, *Four Trios: two for Two Flutes and a Bass* op.16. J. C. Bach dedicated to Lady Abingdon his *Four Sonatas and two Duetts for the Pianoforte or Harpsicord with Accompaniments* op.15 in 1779.

WORKS

(all printed works published in London)

12 Country Dances and 3 Capriccios . . . with 3 Minuets, 2 fl, b (1787), minuets also with 2 vn, hns

6 Songs and a Duet, 1–2vv, 2 fl, 2 vn, b, hpd/pf (1788)

A Representation of the Execution of Mary Queen of Scots in 7 Views, chorus, orch (1790)

A Selection of 12 Psalms and Hymns, chorus, orch (1793)

12 Sentimental Catches and Glees, 3vv, with pf/harp acc. by J. Haydn (*c*1795)

21 Vocal Pieces, pf acc. (1797)

Mentre dormi, 2vv, str (1798)

6 of the Last Vocal Pieces composed by the late Willoughby, Earl of Abingdon, 1v, pf (?1800)

Collection of [18] Sentimental Catches, 3vv, MS in S. Towneley's private collection, Burnley, Lancs.

Numerous songs, 1 hymn, 1 dance, pubd singly

1 bk of divertimentos; 12 songs; 2 catches; various hymns and marches: all unpubd, presumably extant

BIBLIOGRAPHY
S. L. Lee: 'Bertie, Willoughby, 4th Earl of Abingdon', *DNB*
G. E. C[okayne]: *The Complete Peerage* (London, 1887–98, rev., enlarged 2/1910)
H. C. R. Landon: *The Collected Correspondence and London Notebooks of Joseph Haydn* (London, 1959)

SIMON TOWNELEY

Abingdon, Henry. *See* ABYNDON, HENRY.

Abondante [Abundante, dal Pestrino], **Giulio** [Julio] (*fl* 1546–87). Italian lutenist and composer. 'Pestrin' is Venetian dialect for 'mill' or 'dairy', and may indicate his family's occupation and Venetian origins. He published at least five volumes of solo lute music of which only three are extant. A book of lute music by 'Pestrin', now lost, is listed in Vincenti's catalogue of 1591; this may also have been by Abondante. Because of the different forms of Abondante's name and the 41 years that elapsed between the publication of the first and fifth books, Eitner believed that 'Julio Abondante', composer of the first two books and 'Giulio Abundante, detto dal Pestrino' or 'Giulio dal Pestrino', composer of the fifth book, were different musicians. Tagliavini, however, considered them the same person. In the dedications of his *I nomi antichi e moderni delle provincie* (Venice, 1567) Orazio Toscanella mentioned a Giulio del Pietrino, 'lutenist without equal', who was one of several musicians active in Antonio Zantini's house at Venice; the group included Girolamo Parabosco, Annibale Padovano, Claudio Merulo and Donato.

The three lutebooks are representative of the various kinds of instrumental music prevalent at the time. The first is devoted to dance music and includes 21 galliards, four passamezzos, two pavans and five miscellaneous pieces. The second contains five fantasias and 21 intabulations of vocal pieces, including motets, madrigals, *napolitane* and chansons by Willaert, Rore, Arcadelt, Janequin, Nicola Vicentino, Leonardo Barré, Nollet and Payen. The fifth book comprises 13 fantasias, 12 paduanas, three passamezzos and a *bergamasca*. The intabulations of vocal music are fairly literal transcriptions, sparingly embellished with stereotyped figures. In some of the dances the chordal structure is enlivened by continuous passage-work.

WORKS
(for lute; published in Venice)

Intabolatura . . . sopra el lauto de ogni sorte de balli . . . libro primo (1546; repr. 1563 as Intabolatura di liuto . . . libro primo); 1563 reprint ed. in Lefkoff; 7 pieces ed. in Moe
Intabolatura di lautto, libro secondo madrigali . . . canzoni franzese, mottetti, recercari di fantasia, napolitane, intabulati & accomodati per sonar di lautto (1548¹²); 4 ed. in Chilesotti, 1901–2 and 1902
Il quinto libro de tabolatura da liuto . . . nella qual si contiene fantasie diverse, pass'e mezi & padoane (1587); paduana ed. E. E. Lowinsky, *Tonality and Atonality in Sixteenth Century Music* (Berkeley and Los Angeles, 1961)
Intavolatura di liuto del Pestrin, lib. 7 (n.d.), lost (? by Abondante)

BIBLIOGRAPHY
R. Eitner: 'Giulio Abondante's Lautenbücher', *MMg*, viii (1876), 119
O. Chilesotti: 'Il Pater noster di Adriano Willaert', *SIMG*, iii (1901–2), 468
——: 'Note circa alcuni liutisti italiani della prima metà del cinquecento', *RMI*, ix (1902), 246
L. H. Moe: *Dance Music in Printed Italian Lute Tablature from 1507 to 1611* (diss., Harvard U., 1956) [incl. thematic index of bk.i and of the dances of bk.v]
G. Lefkoff: *Five Sixteenth-century Venetian Lute Books* (Washington, DC, 1960)
L. F. Tagliavini: 'Abondante, Giulio', *DBI*

HENRY SYBRANDY

Aboriginal music. *See* AUSTRALIA, §II.

Abos [Abosso, Avos, Avosso], **Girolamo** (*b* La Valetta, 16 Nov 1715; *d* Naples, Oct 1760). Maltese composer of Spanish descent. The 1729 *conto* book of the Neapolitan conservatory Poveri di Gesù Cristo contains an entry for a student called 'Maltese maggiore'. It may be assumed that it refers to Girolamo Abos, who as a child had been brought to Naples for his musical training. His principal teachers therefore would have been Francesco Durante and Gerolimo Ferraro (not Leonardo Leo), who were the *maestri* of the conservatory at that time. Abos's first major work was an *opera buffa*, Le due zingare simili, staged at the Teatro Nuovo in Naples in 1742. In the same year he replaced Alfonso Caggi as *secondo maestro* of the conservatory Poveri di Gesù Cristo, where Francesco Feo was then *maestro*. Abos lost his post in 1743, when the institution closed to be converted into a seminary. In 1742 he also assisted the aging Ignazio Prota at the conservatory S Onofrio a Capuana, and succeeded him as a *maestro* (1748–60). Among his students were Giovanni Paisiello and the alto castrato Giuseppe Aprile. From 1754 until 1759 he also served as *secondo maestro* of the Conservatorio della Pietà dei Turchini, where his successor was Pasquale Cafaro.

Abos was a respected composer of *opere buffe* and *serie*, which were performed in Italy and beyond, but with varying degrees of success. In 1756 his *Tito Manlio* (Naples, 1751) was presented in London. Walsh printed its 'favourite airs', but Burney commented that 'none were favoured by the public'. However, even after Abos's death, arias from his works appeared in comic opera pasticcios in London (*Love in a Village*, 1763; *The Maid of the Mill*, 1765). That he was the *maestro al cembalo* for the London performance of *Tito Manlio* is often stated but has not been established. In his church music Abos followed the example of Durante, striving for a synthesis of the homophonic concerto and operatic styles with the traditions of sacred vocal polyphony. In older literature (e.g. Villarosa, 1840), biographical information about Girolamo Abos was confused with that on the composer Giuseppe Avossa, and mistaken attributions of their works exist among manuscript copies.

WORKS
OPERAS

Le due zingare simili (opera buffa, A. Palomba), Naples, Teatro Nuovo, spring 1742
Le furberie di Spilletto (commedia), Florence, Teatro Cocomero, spring 1744
La serva padrona (opera buffa, A. Federico), Naples, 1744
La moglie gelosa (commedia), Naples, Teatro dei Fiorentini, 1745
Artaserse (opera seria, Metastasio), Venice, Teatro Grimani, 1746
Pelopida (opera seria, G. Roccaforte), Rome, Teatro Torre Argentina, spring 1747; arias, *F-Pc*, *GB-Lbm*
Alessandro nelle Indie (opera seria, Metastasio), Ancona, Teatro La Fenice, sum. 1747; arias, *F-Pc*
Arianna e Teseo (opera seria, P. Pariati), Rome, Teatro delle Dame, spring 1748; arias, *Pc*
Adriano in Siria (opera seria, Metastasio), Rome, Teatro Torre Argentina, 1750
Tito Manlio (opera seria, ?Roccaforte), Naples, Teatro S Carlo, 30 May 1751; score, *A-Wn*
Erifile (opera seria), Rome, spring 1752; arias, *GB-Lbm*
Lucio Vero o sia Il vologeso (opera seria, Zeno), Naples, Teatro S Carlo, 18 Dec 1752
Medo (opera seria, C. I. Frugoni), Turin, Teatro Regio
?Andromeda (opera seria), *A-Wn*
Songs incl. in the following pasticcios: Armida placata (Migliavam), Vienna, 1750, *A-Wn*; Creso, London, 1758; Love in a Village, London, 1763; The Maid of the Mill, London, 1765

SACRED MUSIC
(all with insts)
Mass, 4vv, 1760; mass, 2 choruses, *D-MÜs*, *I-Nc*; Kyrie et Gloria, *F-Pc*, *I-Nc*; Magnificat, 4vv, *A-Wn*; Litaniae de BVM, 2vv, *Wn*; Lezione terza del Giovedì Santo
Stabat mater, 3vv, 1750, *A-Wn*, *D-MÜs*; Veni Creator Spiritus, ?autograph, *I-Nf*
Dixit Dominus, 5vv, ?autograph; 2 Tantum ergo, 1v, 2vv; 2 cantatas: *Nc*

INSTRUMENTAL MUSIC
Sinfonia, 2 vn, bc, *Mc*

DOUBTFUL WORKS
Juravit Dominus, 5vv; Veni sponsa Christi, 4vv: *Nc*

BIBLIOGRAPHY
C. A. de Rosa, Marchese di Villarosa: *Memorie di compositori di musica del regno di Napoli* (Naples, 1840) [Abos and Avossa are confused]
S. di Giacomo: *I quattro antichi conservatorii di musica a Napoli* (Palermo, 1924)
K. G. Fellerer: *Der Palestrinastil und seine Bedeutung in der vokalen Kirchenmusik des achtzehnten Jahrhunderts* (Augsburg, 1929/*R*1972)
U. Rolandi: *Musica e musicisti in Malta* (Livorno, 1932)
A. Loewenberg: *Annals of Opera, 1597–1940* (Cambridge, 1943, rev. 2/1955)

HANNS-BERTOLD DIETZ

Abraham, Gerald (Ernest Heal) (*b* Newport, Isle of Wight, 9 March 1904). English musicologist. Apart from having piano lessons as a boy, musically he is entirely self-taught. His formal education was completed in Portsmouth in preparation for a career in the navy, but he was obliged to abandon this plan owing to ill-health. During a period of recuperation he was able to put some of his self-acquired musical knowledge into practice by making orchestrations, arrangements and some attempts at original composition for the garrison band on the Isle of Wight. A year spent in Cologne resulted in his first major contribution to musical literature, a study of Borodin, which was begun in 1924 and published in 1927; this book (which he has since disowned) immediately established him as an expert in the field of Russian music. He spent the next eight years as a freelance writer, contributing to a wide variety of publications, notably *Music & Letters*, the *Musical Times*, the *Radio Times* and the *Musical Standard*; he also edited the last-named for the publisher William Reeves. Many of his articles of this period were devoted to detailed analysis of different aspects of Russian music – especially opera – for which purpose he learnt the language. Two important collections of these essays were published by Reeves under the titles *Studies in Russian Music* and *On Russian Music*. Abraham's work in the Russian field also brought him into close contact with his colleague M. D. Calvocoressi, with whom he collaborated on *Masters of Russian Music*; after Calvocoressi's death in 1944, he completed and edited his unfinished study of Musorgsky for the Master Musicians series. The pre-war book which best illustrates the unusually wide-ranging and penetrating quality of his musical analysis is *A Hundred Years of Music*, which covers the century from 1830.

In 1935 Abraham began a long association with the BBC when he became an assistant editor of the *Radio Times*. This led to a period as deputy editor of *The Listener* from 1939 to 1942, when he was appointed director of the gramophone department, an appointment made doubly important during the war by the BBC's severely reduced facilities for broadcasting live music. After a short period during which he helped to launch the Third Programme he left the BBC in 1947 to become the first professor of music at Liverpool University. He edited the *Monthly Musical Record* from 1945 to 1960 and continued to be music editor of *The Listener* until 1962, the year in which he took up his final appointment with the BBC as assistant controller of music. On leaving this post in 1967, he spent a year as a deputy music critic on the *Daily Telegraph* before becoming visiting professor for a year at the University of California at Berkeley, where he delivered the Ernest Bloch lectures (published under the title of *The Tradition of Western Music*). Since 1969 he has devoted himself to writing and editing. In the latter capacity he has been active as secretary of the editorial board of the *New Oxford History of Music* (he is editor of its supplement, *The History of Music in Sound*) and as a member of the editorial committee of *Musica Britannica*. He is also chairman of the editorial board of *Grove 6* and was president of the Royal Musical Association from 1969 to 1974. He is an honorary DMus of Durham University (1961), honorary Doctor of Fine Arts of the University of California (1969) and a Fellow of the British Academy (1972); he was made a CBE in 1974.

Because of his early championing of Russian music Abraham is usually associated particularly with this field. Thanks, however, to a combination of deep musical learning, an inquiring mind and an unusual facility for mastering languages, Abraham has acquired wide-ranging sympathies with which few British musicologists can compete. Although he is primarily a specialist in the 19th century, his writings and editorial work show him to be equally at home with such diverse subjects as medieval music, Handel, Polish music, Sibelius and Bartók. His reconstructions of the postulated string quartet movement original of Wagner's *Siegfried Idyll* (1947) and the last two movements of Schubert's 'Unfinished' Symphony (1971) further display a characteristic, closely reasoned ingenuity. No one volume demonstrates the range of his sympathies and his complete and intimate knowledge of a chosen area better than *Slavonic and Romantic Music*. These essays show all the essential hallmarks of his particular qualities as a musicologist – his broad terms of reference, detailed knowledge of not only his subject but also its wider musical (and indeed its wider cultural) background, his ability to select the right kind of characteristic detail to draw a more generalized conclusion and his detective-like delight in uncovering new facts or exposing past errors. To all this he brings an engaging freshness and enthusiasm that are well served by an unpretentious, lucid command of language.

WRITINGS
'Burns and the Scottish Folksong', *ML*, iv (1923), 71
'The Influence of Berlioz on Richard Wagner', *ML*, v (1924), 239
'The Leitmotif since Wagner', *ML*, vi (1925), 175
Borodin: the Composer and his Music (London, 1927, 2/1935/*R*)
Nietzsche (London, 1933)
This Modern Stuff (London, 1933, 3/1955)
'Handel's Clavier Music', *ML*, xvi (1935), 278
Studies in Russian Music (London, 1935, 2/1969)
Tolstoy (London, 1935)
Dostoevsky (London, 1936)
with M. D. Calvocoressi: *Masters of Russian Music* (London, 1936)
A Hundred Years of Music (London, 1938, rev. 4/1974)
Chopin's Musical Style (London, 1939)
On Russian Music (London, 1939)
Beethoven's Second-period Quartets (London, 1942)
Eight Soviet Composers (London, 1943)
Tchaikovsky (London, 1944)
Rimsky-Korsakov (London, 1945)
ed.: *Tchaikovsky: a Symposium* (London, 1945) [incl. 'Operas and Incidental Music', 124–83; 'Religious and other Choral Music', 230]

'Wagner's String Quartet: an Essay in Musical Speculation', *MT*, lxxxvi (1945), 233
'Gustav Holst', *British Music of our Time*, ed. A. L. Bacharach (Harmondsworth, 1946), 44
ed.: M. D. Calvocoressi: *Mussorgsky* (London, 1946, rev. 2/1974)
ed.: *Schubert: a Symposium* (London, 1946, 2/1952)
ed.: *Sibelius: a Symposium* (London, 1947, 2/1952) [incl. 'The Symphonies', 14]
ed.: *Grieg: a Symposium* (London, 1948, 2/1952) [incl. 'The Piano Concerto', 26]
'Modern Research on Schumann', *PRMA*, lxxv (1948–9), 65
Design in Music (London, 1949)
ed.: *Schumann: a Symposium* (London, 1952) [incl. 'The Dramatic Music', 260]
'Passion Music in the Fifteenth and Sixteenth Centuries', *MMR*, lxxxiii (1953), 208, 235
ed.: *Handel: a Symposium* (London, 1954) [incl. 'Some Points of Style', 262]
'Passion Music from Schütz to Bach', *MMR*, lxxxiv (1954), 115, 152, 175
'Ernest Newman (1868–1959): a Great Music Critic', *The Listener* (23 July 1959), 153
ed., with A. Hughes: *Ars Nova and the Renaissance: 1300–1540*, *NOHM*, iii (London, 1960)
'Czechoslovakia', 'Poland', 'Russia', *A History of Song*, ed. D. Stevens (London, 1960), 181, 323, 338–75
'Slavonic Music and the Western World', *PRMA*, lxxxvii (1960–61), 45
'Bartók and England', *SM*, v (1963), 339
'Rimsky-Korsakov as Self-critic', *Festschrift Friedrich Blume* (Kassel, 1963), 16
'The Operas of Serov', *Essays Presented to Egon Wellesz* (Oxford, 1966), 171
'Creating a Musical Tradition', *Journal of the Royal Society for the Encouragement of Arts*, cxv (1967), 417
'Musical Scholarship in the Twentieth Century', *SMA*, i (1967), 1
'Pskovityanka: the Original Version of Rimsky-Korsakov's First Opera', *MQ*, liv (1968), 58
Slavonic and Romantic Music (London, 1968) [collected essays]
ed.: *The Age of Humanism: 1540–1630*, *NOHM*, iv (1968) [incl., with H. Coates: 'The Perfection of the *A Cappella* Style', 312–71]
'V. V. Stasov: Man and Critic', in V. V. Stasov: *Selected Essays on Music* (London, 1968), 1
'A Lost Wagner Aria', *MT*, cx (1969), 927
'Verbal Inspiration in Dvořák's Instrumental Music', *SM*, xi (1969), 27
'Finishing the Unfinished', *MT*, xii (1971), 547
'Satire and Symbolism in "The Golden Cockerel" ', *ML*, lii (1971), 46
'Heine, Queuille, and "William Ratcliff" ', *Musicae scientiae collectanea: Festschrift Karl Gustav Fellerer* (Cologne, 1973), 12
'Opera in Spain', *NOHM*, vii (1973), 281
'The Apogee and Decline of Romanticism: 1890–1914', 'The Reaction against Romanticism: 1890–1914', 'Music in the Soviet Union', *NOHM*, x (1974), 1–79, 80–144, 639–700
The Tradition of Western Music (London, 1974)
'Arab Melodies in Rimsky-Korsakov and Borodin', *ML*, lvi (1975), 313
'Musicology's Language Curtain', *MT*, cxvi (1975), 788
'The Early Development of Opera in Poland', *Essays on Opera and English Music in Honour of Sir Jack Westrup* (Oxford, 1975), 148
ed.: *Romanticism (1830–1890)*, *NOHM*, ix (in preparation)
'Balakirev, Mily Alexeyevich', 'Borodin, Alexander Porfir'yevich', §§1–3, 'Musorgsky, Modest Petrovich', 'Rimsky-Korsakov, Nikolay Andreyevich', 'Schumann, Robert', 'Union of Soviet Socialist Republics' §IX, 1(i–iii), *Grove 6*

BIBLIOGRAPHY
Editor [J. A. Westrup] and others: 'A Birthday Greeting to Gerald Abraham', *ML*, lv (1974), 131

DAVID LLOYD-JONES

Abraham, Lars Ulrich (*b* Pförten, Lower Lusatia, 25 April 1922). German musicologist and teacher. After his army service (1941–6), he studied musicology and theory at the Musikhochschule in Weimar under Münnich and Moser (1948–50) and musicology under Gerstenberg, Adrio and Reinhard at the Free University of Berlin (1951–4) with art history as a subsidiary subject. He took his doctorate in Berlin in 1960 with a dissertation on the figured bass in Praetorius's works. From 1951 to 1961 he was organist at the Johannes-Kirche and taught theory at the John Petersen Conservatory in Berlin-Zehlendorf; he then became assistant lecturer in music at the Kant-Hochschule in Brunswick (1961–5) and lecturer in music at the Pädagogische Hochschule in Münster (1965–9). Since 1969 he has been professor in musicology and education at the Staatliche Hochschule für Musik in Freiburg and held a teaching post at the university. In his writings and as a teacher he has rid music education of antiquated ideas without merely replacing them by new clichés.

WRITINGS
Der Generalbass im Schaffen des M. Praetorius und seine harmonischen Voraussetzungen (diss., Free U. of Berlin, 1960; *Berliner Studien zur Musikwissenschaft*, iii, Berlin, 1961)
Harmonielehre (Cologne, 1965–9)
'Musiktheoretische Unterweisung an einem Lehrerseminar nach 1850', *Beiträge zur Musiktheorie des 19. Jahrhunderts*, ed. M. Vogel (Regensburg, 1966), 233
with H. Segler: *Musik als Schulfach* (Brunswick, 1966)
'Über Trivialität in protestantischen Kirchenliedmelodien des 19. Jahrhunderts', *Studien zur Trivialmusik des 19. Jahrhunderts*, ed. C. Dahlhaus (Regensburg, 1967), 83
'Das politische Moment im unpolitischen Lied', *Das Politische im Lied*, ed. H. Grosse (Bonn, 1967), 80
Einführung in die Notenschrift (Cologne, 1969)
ed.: *Erich Doflein Festschrift* (Mainz, 1972)
with C. Dahlhaus: *Melodielehre* (Cologne, 1972)

HANS HEINRICH EGGEBRECHT

Abraham, Paul [Ábrahám, Pál] (*b* Apatin, Hungary, 2 Nov 1892; *d* Hamburg, 9 May 1960). Hungarian composer. He studied at the Budapest Academy of Music (1910–16) and began as a composer of serious orchestral and chamber music, a cello concerto being performed by the Budapest PO and a string quartet at the 1922 Salzburg Festival. In 1927, however, he was appointed conductor at the Budapest Operetta Theatre, where he was called upon to write numbers for various operettas. He was invited to work in Germany, and achieved a great success with his first complete operetta, *Viktoria und ihr Husar* (Vienna, 23 December 1930), a work making use of jazz and the dance styles of the time. His success continued with his score for the film *Die Privatsekretärin* (1931) and the operettas *Die Blume von Hawaii* (Leipzig, 24 July 1931) and *Ball im Savoy* (Berlin, 23 December 1932). However, the rise of Hitler forced him to leave Germany, at first for Vienna where the operettas *Märchen im Grand-Hotel* (1934), *Dschainah* (1935) and *Roxy und ihr Wunderteam* (1937) failed to establish themselves. On the outbreak of war he fled to Cuba, where he eked out a living as a pianist, and later moved to New York. In February 1946 he was committed to hospital after a mental breakdown, but in May 1956 he returned to Europe to live in Hamburg.

ANDREW LAMB

Abrahamsen, Erik (Schack Olufsen) (*b* Brande, Jutland, 9 April 1893; *d* Copenhagen, 17 Feb 1949). Danish musicologist. After studying at the Royal Danish Conservatory of Music (1910–13), where he graduated as an organist, he was organist and choirmaster at the Luther Church (1914–24) and head of the music division of the Copenhagen Royal Library (1916–21). As a student he attended Hammerich's lectures in music history at Copenhagen University (there was no degree course in music history until 1915) and in 1917 he became the first MA in musicology in Denmark, graduating with a thesis on the transition from Catholic to Protestant liturgy in Denmark in the 16th and 17th centuries. During his years at the Royal Library he began to study its large collection of Latin liturgical fragments on the basis of which he tried to reconstruct the Danish medieval liturgy and to provide a demonstration of Peter Wagner's theory of the two traditions, Roman and Germanic, of Gregorian chant. He submitted this as a doctoral dissertation to the university in 1921, but when Hammerich retired (1922) and no successor was appointed Abrahamsen submitted it instead to Wagner at the University of Fribourg, where he was awarded the doctorate in 1923. In 1924 he was appointed senior lecturer in music at the University of Copenhagen and subsequently became the first Danish professor of musicology (1926), with responsibility for organizing and directing the study of music in the university and for establishing the musicology institute, which led him to take an active interest in music education at the broadest level. He gained first-hand experience of its problems by teaching music in St Jørgens Gymnasium (1928–43), was a frequent and popular broadcaster on music on Danish radio, and was music critic of the *Nationaltidende* (1934–9) and the *Berlingske tidende* (1939–49). His later books all represent varied attempts to convey elementary musical information and an explanation of music's place in society to the general reader, while also discussing important problems for the professional music teacher. He maintained his earlier scholarly interests by collaborating in the preparation of the valuable editions *En klosterbog fra middelalderens slutning* (1933) and *Niels Jespersøns Gradual 1573* (1935) and of the melodies to *Danmarks gamle folkeviser* (1935–).

WRITINGS
Liturgisk musik i den danske Kirke efter Reformationen (Copenhagen, 1919)
Eléments romans et allemands dans le chant grégorien et la chanson populaire (diss., U. of Fribourg, 1923; Copenhagen, 1923)
Tonekunsten (Copenhagen, 1927)
Musik og samfund (Copenhagen, 1941)
Hvem er musikalsk? (Copenhagen, 1943)

BIBLIOGRAPHY
J. P. Larsen: 'Erik Abrahamsen', *Festskrift udgivet af Københavns Universitet* (Copenhagen, 1949), 178
JOHN BERGSAGEL

Abrahan. *See* EBRAN.

Abrams, Harriett (*b* c1758; *d* c1822). English soprano and composer of Jewish descent. She made her début in October 1775 in *May Day*, a piece designed for her by Garrick with music by her teacher Thomas Arne. However, she had limited success as a stage personality and in 1780 she left Drury Lane to become a principal singer at fashionable London concerts. She appeared in the Handel Commemoration concerts in 1784, when Burney praised the sweetness and taste of her singing, in some of the Antient Music concerts and in seasons organized by Rauzzini and Salomon. By the 1790s she confined her appearances to exclusive concerts in the houses of the nobility, such as the Ladies' Concerts she organized at Lord Vernon's, and to her annual benefits, where in 1792, 1794 and 1795 Haydn presided at the piano. She published two sets of Italian and English canzonets, a collection of Scottish songs harmonized for two and three voices and a number of ballads, one of which, *Crazy Jane*, enjoyed a considerable vogue in 1799–1800. In 1803 she dedicated a collection of her songs to the queen.

Her younger sister Theodosia (c1765–after 1834), whose voice Mount-Edgcumbe described as the most beautiful contralto he ever heard, appeared with her from 1783. Another sister, Eliza (c1772–c1830), sang and played the piano at Harriett's concerts from 1792 and William Abrams appeared as a viola player. A Miss G. Abrams sang on stage with Harriett between 1778 and 1780.

BIBLIOGRAPHY
C. Burney: *Account of the Musical Performances. . .in Commemoration of Handel* (London, 1785)
Earl of Mount-Edgcumbe: *Musical Reminiscences of an Old Amateur* (London, 1824, 4/1834)
W. T. Parke: *Musical Memoirs* (London, 1830)
OLIVE BALDWIN, THELMA WILSON

Abran. *See* EBRAN.

Ábrányi, Kornél (*b* Szentgyörgyábrány, 15 Oct 1822; *d* Budapest, 20 Dec 1903). Hungarian writer on music, composer and pianist. He came from the wealthy Eördögh family; the name means 'devil' and his father changed it to Ábrányi, the name of their estate. In the early 1840s he gave concerts in Hungarian towns, and in 1846 left for Vienna to take piano lessons with Joseph Fischhof. There is no reliable evidence that he was ever a student of Chopin in Paris. From 1847 he lived in Pest, in the 1850s as a piano teacher, and studied composition with Mosonyi, together with whom he became a devoted follower of Liszt and Wagner. He was one of the founders of the first Hungarian music periodical, the *Zenészeti lapok*, in 1860, and as its editor until 1876 he led an important campaign for an original Hungarian musical idiom and for the improvement of musical life and education. To promote these aims he founded and directed (1867–88) the National Association of Choral Societies, played an important part in the establishment of the Budapest Academy of Music (1875) under Liszt's and Erkel's direction, and did much to increase and strengthen Liszt's connections with Hungary. As assistant professor at the academy (until 1888), he was the first to teach harmony, the aesthetics of music and, with Robert Volkmann, composition, and to publish textbooks of harmony (1874, enlarged 2/1881), aesthetics (1877) and the general history of music (1885).

Ábrányi won great fame for his books on 19th-century Hungarian music which, in spite of their occasional errors of fact, are among the richest sources for the study of this particular subject. They are the first biographies of Mosonyi (1872) and of Erkel (1895), the history of 25 years of the National Association of Choral Societies (1892; continued, 1898), *Életemből és emlékeimből* ('From my life and memories', 1897), *Képek a múlt és jelenből* ('Pictures from past and present', 1899), and *A magyar zene a 19. században* ('Hungarian music in the 19th century', 1900). He was very active as a music critic, and as a composer was prolific but less important (he wrote piano works, songs and choruses). Liszt transcribed his five Hungarian folksongs for piano (1873), and composed the 19th Hungarian Rhapsody (1885) on Ábrányi's *Csárdás nobles*. Of Liszt's letters to him, 11 were published by La Mara (*Franz Liszts Briefe*, ii) and 31 by M. Prahács (*Franz Liszt: Briefe aus ungarischen Sammlungen, 1835–1886*, Budapest, 1966).

DEZSŐ LEGÁNY

Abravanel, Maurice (de) (*b* Thessaloniki, 6 Jan 1903). American conductor of Spanish–Portuguese Sephardic descent. He worked towards a medical degree at Lausanne but, on Busoni's recommendation, went to Berlin to study with Weill. Starting in Zwickau, he conducted at various German theatres, including those in Berlin, until Hitler came to power. He conducted ballet in Paris and opera in Australia until 1936 when, on the recommendation of Walter and Furtwängler, he was engaged by the Metropolitan Opera, taking charge during the next two years of repertory as diverse as *Lohengrin* and *Lakmé*, *Tannhäuser* and *Les contes d'Hoffmann*. A victim of internal politics, he moved to Broadway, conducting Weill's *Knickerbocker Holiday*, and becoming known during the next decade as a specialist in the work of his former teacher, some of whose premières he had conducted during his Paris days.

In 1947 the opportunity came to return full time to serious music. The year before, the Utah SO had been organized on a permanent and professional basis. Again on Walter's recommendation, Abravanel was engaged as conductor. His achievement and that of the Utah SO are musically valuable, and they have made many recordings of especial interest. The situation is even more notable sociologically: Utah is one of the poorest states, with no tradition of philanthropy towards the arts, yet under Abravanel's leadership it has become the state with the highest rate of concert attendance. Abravanel has conducted the local premières of such works as Mozart's 'Jupiter' Symphony, Bach's *St Matthew Passion*, and several of the Beethoven and Brahms symphonies.

BIBLIOGRAPHY
P. Hart: *Orpheus in the New World* (New York, 1973)
MICHAEL STEINBERG

Abreu, Antonio [el Portugués] (*b* c1750; *d* c1820). Guitarist, Portuguese or of Portuguese descent, resident in Salamanca. He provided the rules and music to his guitar method, *Escuela para tocar con perfección la guitarra de cinco y seis órdenes con reglas generales de mano izquierda y derecha*. P. F. Victor Prieto discovered Abreu's MS and published it under the original title in Salamanca in 1799 with supplementary material concerning the origins of the guitar and a historical view of the aesthetics of music. Abreu's method offers a systematic approach to pedagogy, and is one of the first to treat the guitar having six double courses. It also discusses guitar accompaniment in the orchestra and, of special note, describes in detail the preparation of right hand fingernails.

BIBLIOGRAPHY
B. Saldoni: *Diccionario biográfico-bibliográfico de efimerides de músicos españoles* (Madrid, 1881)
D. Prat: *Diccionario biográfico, bibliográfico, histórico, crítico de guitarristas, guitarreros* (Buenos Aires, 1933)
H. Anglès and J. Subirá: *Catálogo musical de la Biblioteca nacional de Madrid* (Barcelona, 1951)
RONALD C. PURCELL

Abreu, Eduardo. Brazilian guitarist, brother of SERGIO ABREU.

Abreu (Rebello), Sergio (*b* Rio de Janeiro, 5 June 1948). Brazilian guitarist. He and his brother Eduardo (*b* Rio de Janeiro, 19 Sept 1949) studied with their grandfather, Antonio Rebello, and from 1960 with the Argentinian guitarist and lutenist Adolfina Raitzin Távora, a disciple of Segovia. The brothers formed a duo and made their début in Brazil in 1963, then gave further recitals in Latin America. They made an impressive European début in London in 1968 and the next year gave the première of Santórsola's Double Guitar

Concerto, dedicated to them, with the London Bach Orchestra at the Queen Elizabeth Hall, London. In 1970 they gave the first British performance of Castelnuovo-Tedesco's Double Guitar Concerto, and made their North American début at Carnegie Hall. They have toured in Europe, the USA and Australia. Both brothers possess techniques of a high standard, which, combined with an almost uncanny coordination in articulation, phrasing and tone production, puts them in the forefront of guitar duettists. At most of their recitals each brother gives a selection of solo pieces.

PETER SENSIER

Absatz (Ger.). Term, first used by H. C. Koch, denoting an opening phrase; *see* ANALYSIS, §II, 2.

Absetzen (Ger.). As a musical term, *absetzen* has two meanings: (1) to separate one note from another, i.e. to play staccato, and (2) to transcribe vocal music into tablature for some solo instrument, for example lute or organ. In the 18th century Quantz described staccato playing in general as *abgesetzet*, but he also used the term more specifically to mean lifted, off-string bow strokes on the violin. For a discussion of this usage, see David D. Boyden: *The History of Violin Playing from its Origins to 1761* (London, 1965), pp.412f. In its second meaning the term was in general use from the 16th to the 18th centuries. For example, the title-page of Elias Nicolaus Ammerbach's *Ein new kunstlich Tabulaturbuch* (Nuremberg, 1575) states that the collection includes motets and German lieder 'auff die Orgel unnd Instrument abgesetzt'.

Absil, Jean (*b* Bon-Secours, Hainaut, 23 Oct 1893; *d* Uccle, Brussels, 2 Feb 1974). Belgian composer. He studied the organ, the piano and harmony with Alphonse Oeyen, organist of Bon-Secours. He continued his studies at the Ecole St Grégoire, Tournai, where he gave his first organ recital in 1912. In 1913 he entered the Brussels Conservatory to study the organ with Desmet, the piano with R. Moulaert and harmony with Lunssens. He took a first prize for organ and harmony in 1916 and, after a year's further work under Du Bois, another for counterpoint and fugue. Abandoning the idea of a career as an organist, he went to Gilson for composition lessons (1920–22). In 1921 his First Symphony won the Agniez Prize; in 1922 he took the second Belgian Prix de Rome with the cantata *La guerre* and was appointed director of the Etterbeek Music School. From 1930 he taught practical harmony at the Brussels Conservatory, where he was made professor in 1936. In 1934 he won the Rubens Prize and stayed for a time in Paris. Then with Dotremont and Leirens he founded the *Revue internationale de musique* (1938); in the same year the Piano Concerto, composed for the Ysaÿe Competition, brought him to international notice. For some time he was president of the Belgian section of the ISCM. He was appointed professor of fugue at the Brussels Conservatory and at the Chapelle Musicale Reine Elisabeth in 1939, retiring in 1959. In 1955 he was elected to the Belgian Royal Academy, and in 1964 he received the Prix Quinquennial of the Belgian government.

Absil's conservatory training introduced him to no music later than Franck, and with Gilson he studied only the orchestration of Wagner, Strauss and the Russian nationalists. It was at the concerts given in

Brussels by the Pro Arte Quartet that he came to know the work of Milhaud, Hindemith and Schoenberg, and he attended rehearsals in order to penetrate their scores more deeply. He dedicated his op.9 choruses (1932) to Berg, who sent a warm letter of thanks, and during his Paris stay he met Milhaud, Honegger, Ibert and Schmitt, with whom he struck up a friendship. In imitation of the Parisian Concerts Triton, he collaborated with Chevreuille, Poot, Souris and other young Belgian composers in founding the La Sirène series for performing new music in Brussels and abroad. Faced with public incomprehension Absil published his *Postulats de la musique contemporaine* (Huy, 1937), a brief essay with a preface by Milhaud. In it Absil claimed that the distinction between consonance and dissonance is meaningless and that polytonality has existed since the Middle Ages, *The Rite of Spring* being its first full expression. He considered atonality to be less readily acceptable in Latin or Nordic countries than in central Europe.

In his earliest works Absil was clearly under the influence of his teachers: the *Rhapsodie flamande*, for example, is in the Gilson tradition. With *La mort de Tintagiles*, however, he sought a more individual manner, but his style was formed in the chamber music that he wrote after 1934. This style is essentially polyphonic and polymodal, with different modes used in each work, although there is a predilection for intervals of an augmented 4th and a diminished octave. Changes in metre and irrational divisions are frequent; sometimes there are superimpositions of triple and binary metres, or of differently divided gruppettos, so producing characteristically vigorous effects. Often cast in variation or other conventional forms, Absil's music has great structural clarity. An evolution took place after 1938 when he attempted to make his work more accessible, but without removing its distinctiveness. From drama and ruggedness his music turned to settled charm. He followed Bartók, whose work he much admired, in studying, from 1943, the peasant music of Romania and other countries, and several of his works use folk or folk-like themes. But in 1963 Absil appeared to stop making concessions to public taste and devoted his efforts almost exclusively to instrumental music.

WORKS

ORCHESTRAL

Sym. no.1, d, op.1, 1920; La mort de Tintagiles, op.3, 1923–6; Rhapsodie flamande, op.4, 1928; Berceuse, vc, orch, 1932; Vn Conc. no.1, op.11, 1933; Petite suite, op.20, 1935; Sym. no.2, op.25, 1936; Pf Conc. no.1, op.30, 1937; Rhapsody no.2, op.34, 1938; Andante symphonique, 1939; Vc Concertino, op.42, 1940; Serenade, op.44, 1940; Variations symphoniques, op.50, 1942; Va Conc., op.54, 1942; Rhapsodie roumaine, op.56, vn, orch, 1943; Sym. no.3, op.57, 1943

Conc. grosso, op.60, wind qnt, str, 1944; Jeanne d'Arc, op.65, 1945; Rites, op.79, band, 1952; Rhapsodie brésilienne, op.81, 1953; Mythologie, op.84, 1954; Croquis sportifs, op.85, band, 1954; Divertimento, op.86, sax qt, orch, 1955; Introduction et valses, op.89, 1956; Légendes d'après Dvořák, op.91, band, 1956; Suite d'après le folklore roumain, op.92, 1956; Suite bucolique, op.95, str, 1957; Fantaisie concertante, op.99, vn, orch, 1958; Rhapsodie bulgare, op.104, 1960; 2 danses rituelles, op.105, 1960

Triptyque, op.106, 1960; Fantaisie-humoresque, op.113, cl, str, 1962; Fanfares, op.118, brass band, 1963; Rhapsody no.6, op.120, hn, orch, 1963; Concertino, op.122, va, str, 1964; Vn Conc. no.2, op.124, 1964; Nymphes et faunes, op.130, band, 1966; Pf Conc. no.2, op.131, 1967; Allegro brillante, op.133, pf, orch, 1967; Sym. no.4, op.142, 1969; Sym. no.5, op.148, 1970; Fantaisie-caprice, op.152, a sax, str, 1971; Gui Conc., op. 155, 1971; Ballade, op.156, a sax, pf, orch, 1971; Déités, op.160, 1972; Pf Conc. no.3, op.162, 1973

CHAMBER

Str Qt no.1, op.5, 1929; Pf Trio, op.7, 1931; Str Qt no.2, op.13, 1934; Wind Qnt, op.16, 1934; Str Trio no.1, op.17, 1935; Str Qt no.3, op.19, 1935; Fantaisie rhapsodique, op.21, 4 vc, 1936; Qt no.2, op.28, 4 vc, 1937; Sax Qt, op.31, 1937; Pf Qt, op.33, 1938; 3 pièces en quatuor, op.35, sax qt, 1938; Concert à 5, op.38, fl, str trio, harp, 1939; Str Trio no.2, op.39, 1939; Fantaisie, op.40, pf qt, 1939; Str Qt no.4, op.47, 1941; Suite, op.51, vc, pf, 1942; Sicilienne, fl, harp, 1950; 3 contes, op.76, tpt, pf, 1951

Suite, op.78, trbn, pf, 1952; Suite sur des thèmes populaires roumains, op.90, sax qt, 1956; Silhouettes, op.97, fl, pf, 1958; Burlesque, op.100, ob, pf, 1958; Sonate en duo, op.112, vn, va, 1962; Sonata, op.115, a sax, pf, 1963; Qt, op.132, 4 cl, 1967; Croquis pour un carnaval, op.137, 4 cl, harp, 1968; 5 Pièces, op.138, cl/a sax, pf, 1968; Suite no.2, op.141, vc, pf, 1968; Suite mystique, op.145, 4 fl, 1969; Sonata, op.146, vn, pf, 1970; Suite, op.149, tpt, pf, 1970; Esquisses, op.154, ww qt, 1971; Pf Trio no.2, op.158, 1972; Images stellaires, op.161, vn, vc, 1972

INSTRUMENTAL

Pf: 3 Impromptus, op.10, 1932; Sonatina, op.27, 1937; 3 Pièces, op.32, right hand, 1938; 3 marines, op.36, 1939; Sonatina no.2 (Suite pastorale), op.37, 1939; Bagatelles, op.61, 1944; Grande suite, op.62, 1944; Hommage à Schumann, op.67, 1946; Esquisses sur les 7 péchés capitaux, op.83, 1954; Variations, op.93, 1956; Echecs, op.96, 1957; Danse rustique, 1958; Passacaglia in memoriam Alban Berg, op.101, 1959; Rhapsody no.5, op.102, 2 pf, 1959; Danses bulgares, op.103, 1959; 30 études préparatoires à la polyphonie, op.107, 1961; Du rythme à l'expression, op.108, 1961; Grande suite no.2 'Hommage à Chopin', op.110, 1962; Sonatina, op.125, 1965; Humoresques, op.126, 1965; Ballade, op.129, left hand, 1966; Asymétries, op.136, 2 pf, 1968; Alternances, op.140, 1968; Féeries, op.153, 1971; Poésie et vélocité, op.157, 1972

Gui: 10 Pièces, op.111, 1962; Suite, op.114, 1963; 3 Pièces, op.119, 2 gui, 1963; Pièces caractéristiques, op.123, 1964; Suite, op.135, 2 gui, 1967; Contrastes, op.143, 2 gui, 1969; Sur un paravent chinois, op.147, 1970; 4 Pièces, op.150, 1970; Petit bestiaire, op.151, 1970; 10 Pièces, op.159, 1972

Other: Chaconne, op.69, vn, 1949; 3 Pièces, op.121, bandoneon, 1964; Etude, drum, 1964; 3 Pièces, op.127, org, 1965; Sonata, op.134, vn, 1967; Entrée solennelle pour un Te Deum, org, 1968

CHORAL

La guerre, op.2 (cantata, V. Gilles), 1922; 3 choeurs, op.6 (H. Malteste, I. Gilkin, E. Verhaeren), female 3vv, pf, 1930; 3 poèmes, op.9 (A. Cantillon), 4vv, 1932; 3 choeurs, op.14 (P. Reboux, Cantillon, Verhaeren), 4vv, 1934; 3 choeurs, op.15 (Fort), children 2vv, orch, 1934; 3 choeurs, op.18 (A. Séché, F. de Grammont, Fort), children, orch, 1935; 3 choeurs, op.24 (F. Bataille, P. Brohée, anon.), female 3vv, pf, 1936; Alcools, op.43 (Apollinaire), 4vv, 1940; Philatélie, op.46 (cantata, T. Braun), 1940

Les bénédictions, op.48 (cantata, Braun), 1941; 4 chansons de bonne humeur, op.49 (Klingsor), female 2vv, orch, 1942; Les chants du mort, op.55 (cantata, Rom. trad.), 1943; Bestiaire, op.58 (Apollinaire), chorus 4vv, 1944; Printemps, op.59 (Carême), children, orch, 1944; Zoo, op.63 (J. Sasse), chorus 4vv, 1944; Thrène pour le vendredi-saint, op.66 (cantata, E. de Sadeleer), 1945; L'album à colorier, op.68 (cantata, Sadeleer), 1948; Le zodiaque, op.70 (Braun), chorus, orch, 1949

Le cirque volant, op.82 (cantata, Sadeleer), 1953; Colindas, op.87 (Rom. trad.), female 3vv, 1955; Chansons plaisantes, op.88 (Rom. trad.), children 2vv, orch, 1955; Chansons plaisantes, op.94 (Fr., etc. trad.), children 2vv, orch, 1956; 6 poèmes, op.109 (Carême), children 3vv, 1961; Petites polyphonies, op.128, chorus 2vv, orch, 1966; A cloche-pied, op.139 (Carême), children, orch, 1968; Le chant de l'école, op.144, children, 1969

VOCAL

3 mélodies (Moréas, Gilkin), Mez/Bar, pf, 1927; 3 mélodies, op.8 (Brohée, Cantillon), T, pf, 1932; 5 mélodies, op.12 (Maeterlinck, Valéry, Hugo), Mez, str qt, 1933; 4 poèmes (Maeterlinck), 3 for Mez/Bar, pf, 1 for S/T, pf, 1933; Nostalgie d'Arabella, op.22 (M. Beerblock), A, a sax, pf, perc, 1936; Batterie, op.29 (Cocteau), S/T, pf, 1937; Berceuse (Morgenstern), 1v, pf, 1938; 3 poèmes, op.45 (Klingsor), Mez/Bar, orch, 1938–40; Enfantines, op.52 (M. Ley), Mez/Bar, pf, 1942; 2 poèmes, op.53 (Jammes), S/T, pf, 1942

Chanson de 4 sous (Fort), Mez/Bar, pf, 1942; Phantasmes, op.72 (Michaux, L. Hughe, Beerblock [incl. op.22]), A, a sax, pf, perc, 1950; Rêves, op.80 (R. Lyr), 1v, pf, 1952; Heure de grâce, op.98 (Carême), S/T, pf, 1958; 3 vocalises, op.116, Mez/Bar, pf, 1963; Cache-cache, op.117 (Carême, E. Vollène), Mez/Bar, pf, 1963

INCIDENTAL MUSIC

Peau d'âne, op.26 (H. Ghéon), 1937; Ulysse et les sirènes, op.41 (J. Bruyr), 1939; Fansou ou le chapeau chinois, op.64 (Franc-Nohain), 1944; Le miracle de Pan, op.71 (R. Lyr), 1949; Pierre Breughel l'ancien, op.73 (Lyr), 1950; Epouvantail, op.74 (E. de Sadeleer), 1950; Les voix de la mer, op.75 (Lyr), 1951; Les météores, op.77 (Lyr), 1951

Principal publishers: Berben, Bosworth, CeBeDeM, Chester, Eschig, Lemoine, Schott (Brussels), Universal
MSS in *B-Bcdm*

BIBLIOGRAPHY
Catalogue des oeuvres de compositeurs belges: Jean Absil (Brussels, 1957) [CeBeDeM publication]
R. Wangermée: *La musique belge contemporaine* (Brussels, 1959)
Music in Belgium (Brussels, 1964) [CeBeDeM publication]
R. de Guide: *Jean Absil* (Tournai, 1965)

HENRI VANHULST

Absolute music. The term 'absolute music' denotes not so much an agreed idea as an aesthetic problem. The expression is of German origin, first appearing in the writings of Romantic philosophers and critics such as J. L. Tieck, J. G. Herder, W. H. Wackenroder, Jean Paul Richter and E. T. A. Hoffmann. It features in the controversies of the 19th century – for example, in Hanslick's spirited defence of *absolute Tonkunst* against the *Gesamtkunstwerk* of Wagner – and also in the abstractions of 20th-century musical aesthetics. It names an ideal of musical purity, an ideal from which music has been held to depart in a variety of ways; for example, by being subordinated to words (as in song), to drama (as in opera), to some representational meaning (as in programme music), or even to the vague requirements of emotional expression. Indeed, it has been more usual to give a negative than a positive definition of the absolute in music. The best way to speak of a thing that claims to be 'absolute' is to say what it is not.

It is not word-setting. Songs, liturgical music and opera are all denied the status of absolute music. For in word-setting music is thought to depart from the ideal of purity by lending itself to independent methods of expression. The music has to be understood at least partly in terms of its contribution to the verbal sense. It follows that absolute music must at least be instrumental music (and the human voice may sometimes act as an instrument, as in certain works of Debussy, Delius and Holst). Liszt and Wagner insisted that the absence of words from music did not entail the absence of meaning. Liszt's *Programm-Musik* and Wagner's *Gesamtkunstwerk* both arose from the view that all music was essentially meaningful and no music could be considered more absolute than any other. This view gives rise to a further negative definition of the 'absolute' in music: it is music that has no external reference. So the imitation of nature in music is a departure from an absolute ideal; Vivaldi's concertos the 'Four Seasons' are less absolute than the *Art of Fugue*. The symphonic poem is also tainted with impurity, as is every other form of PROGRAMME MUSIC.

The yearning for the absolute is not yet satisfied. Having removed representation from the ideal of music, critics have sought to remove expression as well. No music can be absolute if it seeks to be understood in terms of an extra-musical meaning, whether the meaning lies in a reference to external objects or in expression of the human mind. Absolute music is now made wholly autonomous. Its raison d'être lies entirely within itself; it must be understood as an abstract structure bearing only accidental relations to the movement of the human soul. Liszt and Wagner claimed that there could be no absolute music in that sense; it is possible that even Hanslick might have agreed with them.

It is at this point that the concept of absolute music becomes unclear. Certainly it no longer corresponds to what Richter and Hoffmann had in mind. Both writers considered the purity of music – its quality as an 'absolute' art – to reside in the nature of its expressive powers and not in their total absence. For Richter music was absolute in that it expressed a presentiment of the divine in nature; for Hoffmann it became absolute through the attempt to express the infinite in the only form that renders the infinite intelligible to human feeling. To borrow the terminology of Hegel: music is absolute because it expresses the Absolute. (On that view, liturgical music is the most absolute of all.)

The notion of the 'absolute' in music has thus become inseparably entangled with the problem of musical expression. Is all music expressive, only some or none at all? The answer to that question will determine the usage of the term 'absolute' in criticism. To define the term negatively leads at once to an intractable philosophical problem. A positive definition has therefore been sought.

An analogy may be drawn with mathematics. Pure mathematics can be defined negatively: it is mathematics which is not applied. But that is shallow; for what is applied mathematics if not the application of an independent and autonomous structure of thought? One should therefore define pure mathematics in terms of the methods and structures by which it is understood. Similarly, it might be argued that music is absolute when it is not applied, or when it is not subjected to any purpose independent of its own autonomous movement. Absolute music must be understood as pure form, according to canons that are internal to itself. Unfortunately, such a positive definition of the term raises another philosophical problem: what is meant by 'understanding music'? And can there be a form of art which is understood in terms that are wholly internal to itself?

Attempts by the advocates of absolute music to answer those questions have centred on two ideas: objectivity and structure. Their arguments have been presented in this century most forcefully by the Austrian theorist Heinrich Schenker and by Stravinsky. Music becomes absolute by being an 'objective' art, and it acquires objectivity through its structure. To say of music that it is objective is to say that it is understood as an object in itself, without recourse to any semantic meaning, external purpose or subjective idea. It becomes objective through producing appropriate patterns and forms. These forms satisfy us because we have an understanding of the structural relations which they exemplify. The relations are grasped by the ear in an intuitive act of apprehension, but the satisfaction that springs therefrom is akin to the satisfaction derived from the pursuit of mathematics. It is not a satisfaction that is open to everyone. Like mathematics it depends on understanding, and understanding can be induced only by the establishment of a proper musical culture.

It is such a conception of the absolute in music that has figured most largely in modern discussions. It is in the minds of those who deny that music can be absolute, as of those who insist that it must be. It has inspired the reaction against Romanticism, and sought exemplification in the works of Hindemith, Stravinsky and the followers of Schoenberg. Indeed, the invention of 12-note composition seemed to many to reveal that music was essentially a structural art, and that all the traditional effects of music could be renewed just so long as the new 'language' imitated the complexity of the classical forms. (Schoenberg did not share the enthusiasm of his disciples for such a theory; for him music had been, and remained, an essentially expressive medium.)

It should be noted that 'absolute' music, so defined, means more than 'abstract' music. There are other abstract arts, including architecture and some forms of painting. To call them abstract is to say that they are not representational. It is not to imply that they are to be understood by reference to no external purpose and no subjective state of mind. An abstract painting does not have to lack expression. Yet 'absolute' music is an ideal that will not allow even that measure of impurity.

As an ideal it certainly existed before the Teutonic jargon of its name. Boethius and Tinctoris gave early expression to it, and even Zarlino was under the influence of its charm. Paradoxically, however, the rise of instrumental music and the development of Classical forms saw the temporary disappearance of the absolute ideal. Only after Herder and his followers had introduced the word, and Wagner (through his opposition to it) the concept, did the ideal once more find expression in serious aesthetic theories.

The advocacy of absolute music has brought with it a view of musical understanding that is as questionable as anything written by Liszt in defence of the symphonic poem. It is of course absurd to suppose that one understands Smetana's *Vltava* primarily by understanding what it 'means'. For that seems to imply that the grasp of melody, development, harmony and musical relations are all subordinate to a message that could have been expressed as well in words. But so too is it absurd to suppose that one has understood a Bach fugue when one has a grasp of all the structural relations that exist among its parts. The understanding listener is not a computer. The logic of Bach's fugues must be heard: it is understood in experience and not in thought. And why should not the musical experience embrace pleasure, feeling and evocation just as much as pure structured sound? Hearing the chorus 'Sind Blitze sind Donner' from the *St Matthew Passion* may provide a renewed sense of the significance of the *Art of Fugue*, and that sense may originate in a recognition of the emotional energy that underlies all Bach's fugal writing. Clearly, however 'absolute' a piece of music may be, it can retain our interest only if there is something more to understanding it than an appreciation of mere patterns of sound.

BIBLIOGRAPHY

E. Hanslick: *Vom Musikalisch-Schönen* (Leipzig, 1854/R1965, 16/1966; Eng. trans., 1891/R1974)
H. Riemann: *Die Elemente der musikalischen Ästhetik* (Berlin and Stuttgart, 1900)
F. Busoni: *Entwurf einer neuen Ästhetik der Tonkunst* (Trieste, 1907, 2/1910/R1974; Eng. trans., 1911); Eng. trans. repr. in *Three Classics in the Aesthetics of Music* (New York, 1962)
M. Griveau: 'Le sens et l'expression de la musique', *IMusSCR, iv London 1911*, 238
A. Schoenberg: *Harmonielehre* (Vienna, 1911; Eng. trans., 1947)
A. Wellek: 'Gefühl und Kunst', *Neue psychologische Studien*, xiv (1939), 1
I. Stravinsky: *Poétique musicale* (Cambridge, Mass., 1942; Eng. trans., 1947)
W. Wiora: 'Absolute Musik', *MGG*
N. Cazden: 'Realism in Abstract Music', *ML*, xxxvi (1955), 17
A. Sychra: 'Die Einheit von "absoluter" Musik und Programmusik', *BMw*, i/3 (1959), 2
H. J. Moser: 'Der Geltungsbereich der absoluten Musik', *Musica*, xiii (1959), 697
P. H. Lang: 'Objectivity and Constructionism in Vocal Music of the 15th and 16th Centuries', *Natalicia musicologica Knud Jeppesen* (Copenhagen, 1962), 115
W. Wiora: 'Zwischen absoluter und Programmusik', *Festschrift Friedrich Blume* (Kassel, 1963), 381

ROGER SCRUTON

Absolute pitch [perfect pitch]. The ability to name the pitch of a note without reference to any previously sounded one (recognition), or to sing a named note without reference to a previously sounded one (recall); recognition is generally found to be easier than recall. 'Absolute tonality' is the ability to name the key of a chord or harmonic passage without previously heard reference notes. The faculty is experienced subjectively as different keys having, as it were, distinctive flavours or colours that are instantaneously recognized and never confused. The absolute recognition of the single note may carry with it an implicit tonality. But the drawing of equivalences or similarities between modalities (between keys and visual colours, for instance, as in synaesthesia) is entirely personal and idiosyncratic however self-consistent it may be, so that efforts to establish a glossary of correspondence between them by consensus are misguided and fruitless. However, a gramophone turntable running too fast and presenting the 'Jupiter' Symphony in C♯ causes a sensory distress to the absolute pitch musician analogous to seeing purple grass or tasting salt chocolate, since the key of the adjacent semitone is so far removed in key relationship; it may add to the confusion that by the compromise of equal temperament the key note and fourth degree of C major sound like the leading note and third degree of C♯. Similarly for the absolute pitch musician the excitement of adventurous modulations is very much an immediate sensory pleasure as well as an intellectual and aesthetic one.

With 'relative pitch' (i.e. knowing the pitch of a reference note, for instance orchestral *a'*, and using it as a fixed point for calculating other notes or tonalities), however rapidly it operates, pleasure in adventurous modulation is predominantly aesthetic and intellectual, without the sensory element. For the possessor of only relative pitch a more complicated process is involved than that of the instantaneous absolute recognition of the single note; it is likely that the incoming stimulus must be retained in short-term memory storage while the image of the reference note is recalled and compared, the interval between the two identified, and then translated from an interval code to a name of note code. This analysis lends point to Teplov's criterion for absolute pitch being not accuracy but speed of recognition.

'Absolute pitch' is almost a misnomer, for around 440 Hz for *a'* there is not a single frequency but a narrow band of them that are acceptable to the absolute pitch musician before the note begins to sound like *b♭'* or *g♯'*; this latitude is necessary for the tolerance of changes in instrumental pitch due to atmospheric conditions. The acceptability of such small changes occurring over time may be a manifestation of adaptation level (see Helson). Helson's theory seeks to explain time–error effects in sensation by suggesting that present perception of the intensity or scale value of a stimulus is affected by the immediately previous stimulation's having left a residue that determines the present state of the nervous system, so that over time the baseline, as it were, of perception has adapted. In some experiments an average error of much larger intervals, even a major 3rd, has been the criterion of accuracy used, but to accept even a semitone seems to ignore the important factor of key relationships mentioned above, by which a miss is as good as a mile. The degree of acceptability, however, varies with the individual: the famous story of the seven-year-old Mozart remarking that his friend Schachter's violin was tuned 'half a quarter-tone flatter than mine here' shows not only absolute pitch but also phenomenal pitch discrimination and memory.

Standard pitch has varied considerably through history (*see* PITCH), and a listener with absolute pitch would now be disorientated to hear a C major Mozart work in the pitch of Mozart's day. But although that indicates that the convention has altered it is not a problem to any explanation of absolute pitch; for the fact that works written in the same key often resemble each other in mood shows that the composer, at whatever epoch, also had a self-consistent association of mood and key-colour (in earlier periods it may have been linked with temperament systems; *see* TEMPERAMENTS). This consistency of association probably enters into the whole cognitive structure by which the possessor of absolute pitch operates, his notion of a specific key-colour having no doubt been built up or enhanced by these resemblances. The composer's dependence on instrumental timbre also enters into it: for instance, Bach's use of the D major trumpet and his consequent casting of his jubilant music in D major, and the open-string basis of differences of resonance between keys, are both factors underlying the perception of key-colour that would be shared by an 18th-century composer and his modern audience, whatever their respective standard pitch levels might be.

A preponderance of the earlier views of psychologists was that absolute pitch was 'an inborn predisposition which manifests itself during childhood and is strikingly immediate and spontaneous' (Seashore, 1940; for reviews see Neu and Bachem). But there is little evidence that it can be attributed to the genetic good luck of specially sensitive ears. Any evidence correlating absolute pitch with musical families argues equally for environmental as for hereditary influence, and a recent survey has shown that 87% of a group of specially gifted concert performers had absolute pitch while none of their siblings or antecedents did. Sergeant found no superiority in hearing acuity with absolute pitch subjects, rather the reverse, and little correlation between possession of absolute pitch and a history of music in previous generations. Thus, although timbre plays a part in its acquisition, since many people begin by having absolute pitch only for a familiar instrument, the superior reception of upper partials (given a richer timbre) by an ear of exceptional acuity does not seem to be a determining factor.

If innate endowment plays a negligible part, then absolute pitch may be attributable to environmental good luck in being provided with verbal labels when attention to sensory experience is uppermost, before the habit of ignoring sound quality has been thoroughly learnt. If names 'red', 'green' and 'blue' are learnt at the age of two or three for wavelengths on the electromagnetic spectrum, why not names 'C', 'E' and 'G' for sound-frequencies? The American linguistics scholar B. L. Whorf thought that visual colour discrimination depends on the availability of names but, in the case of pitch, parents and teachers are seldom equipped to provide them. Sergeant's questionnaire survey shows a correlation between absolute pitch and the age at which formal musical education began. Of those professional musicians whose training began between the ages of two and four, 92·6% had absolute pitch, the percentage steadily diminishing until of those starting between 12 and 14 only 6% had it, and thereafter nil. It must be noted however that his sample was limited to 34% of the members of the Incorporated Society of Musicians of England; more data from a wider sample are needed. Siegel (1974) demonstrated the influence of possession of verbal labels on recognition memory for pitch: testing musicians with and without absolute pitch, using comparison stimuli that varied by either a tenth or three-quarters of a semitone from the standard stimuli, she found no difference in performance or rate of forgetting between the two groups of subjects when the stimulus difference was a tenth of a semitone; but with stimulus differences of three-quarters of a semitone the absolute pitch musicians performed significantly better than the controls.

The general picture is of the growth of absolute pitch from the child's own action, principally vocalizing, and of its spreading from familiarity with the first instrument played and even the first keys. Teplov reported a correlation between a child's absolute pitch accuracy with specific notes and the incidence of those notes in his current repertory. In general, notes within the child's own voice range are better learnt; for adults too, low-pitched notes are harder to identify than middle or upper register ones, although the former are richer in upper partials within the limit of the ear's receptivity. Research on Soviet child development reports the teaching in stages of absolute pitch: pitching voice to note; naming on the basis of this singing sensation; and putting a name to the imagined sensation – a procedure that follows the sequence of Bruner's cognitive development stages of 'enactive' and 'iconic' representation and suggests that the ease of its acquisition depends on its being established before concentration on 'symbolic' cognition removes the focus of attention away from sensory experience. Such attempts to teach absolute pitch to adults as achieved some limited success also gave the learner an active role with immediate feedback of results (Wyatt). Teplov saw absolute tonality as a stage on the way to acquiring absolute pitch since all those with absolute pitch have absolute tonality but not vice versa. Sergeant's finding that those in his sample whose lessons started before the age of eight had absolute pitch, whereas later starters had absolute tonality, supports that view. Abraham's view that absolute tonality is easier than absolute pitch merely because there is more chance of identifying one note if three or four are given disregards the increased richness in timbre in the combined upper partials of all component notes of the chord, if indeed timbre is an operative factor.

However, the role of timbre and transients in absolute pitch judgments is puzzling. Sergeant's experiment comparing performance on normal tones (containing both timbre and transients), reversed tones (no initial transients) and pure tones (neither timbre nor transients) found a superior score for normal tones but equally inferior for reversed and pure tones, suggesting that transients have an important role in recognition. But reversed tones, which give a mirror image of the fluctuations of upper partials, may have introduced an unconscious unfamiliarity factor, and tones with initial transients removed might have been a better test. This author found no difference in scores of adult absolute pitch subjects between transient–non-transient, vibrato–

non-vibrato and complex–pure-tone presentations. The importance of transients may be only that they had served as tags of familiar instruments in the original laying down of a memory store for pitch.

However, the so-called Chroma Theory of Absolute Pitch, which emphasizes timbre, has had its adherents (Abraham, Seashore, 1919, Ogden, Riker). It arose from the observation that the tones of some instruments are identified more accurately than those of others, and holds that the differences in strength of upper partials (which distinguish the timbre of various instruments) must play a part in the individual's absolute pitch judgments. Thus it implies a hereditary factor of sensitive ears and a learning one in the original familiarity with a particular instrument. Apart from the objections to hereditary factors already mentioned, there is the implication in chroma theory that, for particular overtone patterns of each instrument to determine judgments, they must be constant over its frequency range. But, at least for the piano, overtones do not show decay rates to be consistent over the whole range (Sabine, Fletcher and others), and with the violin their respective strengths even for the same tone vary with the intensity with which it is played (Knox). Furthermore, vibrato incessantly alters the relative intensity of overtones, as sonograph recordings show (Fletcher). Sergeant's finding of equally inferior performance for reversed and pure tones reflects the fact that neither exists in nature nor much in music, and that therefore either sensory receptivity to, or familiarity with, timbre could play a part; but their precise roles are not yet clear.

However they may have influenced its acquisition, both sensory receptivity and learning affect the subsequent variations in reliability of absolute pitch. Once established, it is affected by learning and emotional factors (lack of practice or test nerves) and by health, fluctuating with influenza, fatigue and even (as does hearing acuity) with pregnancy. In middle age there are consistent reports of a rise of a semitone in experienced pitch, making the sharp keys sound flat and the flat ones sharp, like a disturbing disorientation of reversed colours. This may be an aging phenomenon in the general population, caused by a loss of elasticity in the basilar membrane, but only people possessing long-established verbal labels to pitch levels are equipped to report it. Those researchers who think that timbre plays an important part could argue that the loss of higher-frequency receptivity with age involves a corresponding loss in timbre where fewer overtones are received for middle and upper register notes.

Arguments that absolute pitch is of doubtful value to a musician (particularly one engaged in transposition) strike one as if a majority of colour-blind people were to tell a minority of normally sighted ones that, even if they wished to be painters, colour vision is more trouble than it is worth. In fact it is less surprising that the few possess it than that the many are without it. The faculty may have been suppressed since infancy through the lack of instruction or the practice of transposition, and the fact that it is difficult to acquire in adulthood might be no more surprising than, say, the difficulties in learning to read after a critical age has been passed. Although absolute pitch is not essential to understanding the syntax of music, it is a sensory and aesthetic life-enhancer.

BIBLIOGRAPHY

O. Abraham: 'Das absolute Tonbewusstsein', *SIMG*, iii (1901–2), 1
C. Seashore: *The Psychology of Musical Talent* (New York, 1919)
R. Ogden: *Hearing* (New York, 1924)
C. Seashore: 'Psychology of Music, 26: Acquired Pitch vs Absolute Pitch', *Music Educators Journal*, xxvi/6 (1940), 18
R. Wyatt: 'Improvability of Pitch Discrimination', *Psychological Monographs*, lviii (1945), 1–58
B. Riker: 'The Ability to Judge Pitch', *Journal of Experimental Psychology*, xxxvi (1946), 331
D. Neu: 'A Critical Review of the Literature on Absolute Pitch', *Psychological Bulletin*, xliv (1947), 249
A. Bachem: 'Absolute Pitch', *Journal of the Acoustical Society of America*, xxvii (1955), 1180
H. Sabine: 'Decay Characteristics of Piano Tones', *Journal of the Acoustical Society of America*, xxxii (1960), 1493
B. Teplov: *Problemi individualnikh raelichin* (Moscow, 1961; Fr. trans., 1966)
H. Fletcher, E. Blackham and R. Stratton: 'Quality of Piano Tones', *Journal of the Acoustical Society of America*, xxxiv (1962), 749
C. C. Knox: *The Orchestral Violin Tone* (diss., Indiana U., 1962)
H. Helson: *Adaptation-level Theory* (New York, 1964)
J. Bruner: *Studies in Cognitive Growth* (New York, 1966)
B. Fred: Review of C. Knox: *The Orchestral Violin Tone, Council for Research in Musical Education Bulletin*, ix (1967), 81
D. Sergeant: *Pitch Perception and Absolute Pitch* (diss., U. of Reading, 1969)
J. Siegel: 'Sensory and Verbal Coding Strategies in Subjects with Absolute Pitch', *Journal of Experimental Psychology*, ciii (1974), 37

NATASHA SPENDER

Abstrich (Ger.: 'down-bow'). In string playing *Abstrich* and *Aufstrich* denote 'down-bow' and 'up-bow', respectively. *See* BOW, §II, 2(ii).

Abt, Franz Wilhelm (*b* Eilenburg, 22 Dec 1819; *d* Wiesbaden, 31 March 1885). German composer. His father, a clergyman and an enthusiastic pianist, gave him his first instruction in music; he then went to Leipzig to study theology and music at the university and the Thomasschule. There he made friends with Lortzing, Mendelssohn and Schumann. On the death of his father (1837), he decided to concentrate entirely on music. Though engaged in Bernburg (1841) as Kapellmeister, he soon left for Zurich, distinguishing himself there as an outstanding and immensely popular choirmaster. He was appointed director of nearly all of its numerous choral societies in succession, often winning prizes for them. In 1852, he moved to the Court Theatre in Brunswick, becoming its chief Kapellmeister in 1855. Faithful to his first love, choral conducting, he developed an international reputation and was invited to conduct in many capital cities of Europe. A spectacular reception awaited him on his tour of the USA (1872). Overworked and in poor health, he retired to Wiesbaden in 1882.

Abt's works run to more than 600 opus numbers comprising over 3000 individual items. Vocal music was his main interest, especially male choral music, whose impoverished repertory he strove to enrich. His style is popular, his melodies simple and fresh, with a pleasing and varied accompaniment, so that some—like *Wenn die Schwalben heimwärts ziehn* and *Die stille Wasserrose*—are easily mistaken for genuine folksong.

His son Alfred (*b* Brunswick, 25 May 1855; *d* Geneva, 29 April 1878) was a Kapellmeister in Rudolstadt, Kiel and Rostock.

WORKS
(*selective list*)

Operas: Des Königs Scharfschütz, 1873; Die Hauptprobe, Reisebekanntschaften, both male vv
Many choral works with orch, incl. All-Deutschland, op.201; Schlachtlied, op.223
Song cycles, chorus, pf acc.: Ein Sängertag, op.85; Die Kirmes, op.101; Frühlingsfeier, male vv, op.181; Rotkäppchen, 2 solo vv, female chorus, pf, op.526; Ein eidgenössisches Sängerfest

Numerous partsongs, mostly 4 male vv, including Vineta, op.163 no.3; Waldandacht, op.175 no.2; Die stille Wasserrose, op.192 no.2; Mir träumte von einem Königskind, op.276 no.4

Solo songs, pf acc.: Wenn die Schwalben heimwärts ziehn, c1850; Agathe, op.39 no.1; Gute Nacht, du mein herziges Kind, op.137 no.2; Es hat nicht sollen sein, op.213 no.2

Children's songs, 2–3vv

Many early works for pf, chiefly salon pieces

BIBLIOGRAPHY

Anon.: *Verzeichnis Sämtlicher Lieder und Gesänge von Franz Abt* (Leipzig, n.d.)

H. Weber: 'Franz Abt der anmuthsvolle Liedercomponist' *Neujahrsblatt der Allgemeine Musikgesellschaft in Zürich*, lxxiv (1886), 1

R. August: 'Zum 100. Geburtstag von Franz Abt am 22 Dez. 1919', *Neue Musikzeitung*, xli (1920), 93

B. Rost: *Vom Meister des volkstümlichen deutschen Liedes, Franz Abt* (Chemnitz, 1924)

EDWARD F. KRAVITT

Abu al-Faraj 'Alī ibn al-Ḥusayn. See AL-IṢFAHĀNĪ.

Abu al-Faraj Muhammad ibn Isḥāq al-Warrāq al-Baghdādi. See IBN AL-NADĪM.

Abū l-Ṣalt Umayya [Ibn 'Abd al-'Azīz ibn Abī l-Ṣalt] (*b* Denia, Spain, 1068; *d* Mahdia, Tunisia, 30 Oct 1134). Arab scientist, philosopher and music theorist. According to Ibn Khallikān, he 'possessed great knowledge in the various branches of general literature . . . was adept in philosophy . . . and was highly skilled in the sciences of the ancients' (i.e. the Greeks). According to Ibn Abī Uṣaybi'a, he not only excelled in musical theory, but was also a lutenist. Although none of his works survives, his *Risāla fī l-mūsīqī* ('Treatise on music') may have been known in Hebrew: Profiat Duran quoted from it in his *Ma'aseh ephod* ('Story of the priestly garment', 1403). His influence as a composer on north African music must have been considerable.

BIBLIOGRAPHY

Ibn Khallikān: *Biographical Dictionary* (Paris and London, 1843–71)

M. Steinschneider: *Jewish Literature* (London, 1857), 337

C. Brockelmann: *Geschichte der arabischen Litteratur*, i (Weimar and Berlin, 1898–1902, 2/1943), 486f

H. G. Farmer: *The Sources of Arabian Music* (Bearsden, 1940, rev. 2/1965), 44

based on *MGG* (i, 69) by permission of Bärenreiter

H. G. FARMER

Abū Naṣr Muḥammad ibn Muḥammad ibn Ṭarkhān. See AL-FĀRĀBĪ.

Abundante, Giulio. See ABONDANTE, GIULIO.

Abū Yūsuf Ya'qūb ibn Isḥāq. See AL-KINDĪ.

Abwāq (Arabic). Plural of BŪQ.

Abyndon, Henry (*b* c1420; *d* 1497). English church musician. He was noted as a fine singer and skilful organist. After service in the household of Humphrey, Duke of Gloucester (until 1447), and as a lay clerk of Eton College (1447–51), where he was one of the four clerks specially responsible for singing polyphony in the college chapel, he became a clerk of the Chapel Royal in 1451, and Master of the Choristers there from 1455 to 1478. His duties included teaching the boys to play the organ, and to sing plainsong and improvised polyphony; also it seems probable that he, in collaboration with e.g. the composer John Browne (clerk of the Chapel Royal from 1463 to after 1470), was instrumental in the introduction about this time of the use of boys' voices in composed polyphony. The grant to him in 1464 of a Cambridge MusB reflects his eminence in the musical profession – he is the earliest known recipient of this degree – while the patronage of Bishop Bekynton brought him valuable sinecures in the diocese of Bath and Wells.

BIBLIOGRAPHY

L. Bradner and C. A. Lynch, eds.: *The Latin Epigrams of Thomas More* (Chicago, 1953), 68f

A. B. Emden: *A Biographical Register of the University of Cambridge to 1500* (Cambridge, 1963), 1f

ROGER BOWERS

Abyssinian rite, music of the. See ETHIOPIAN RITE, MUSIC OF THE.

Abzug (from Ger. *abziehen*: 'to draw off', 'to divert'). (1) In the 16th and 17th centuries, a SCORDATURA tuning, especially on the lute. Several 16th-century anthologies of lute music (for example, those edited by Hans Neusidler in 1536 and 1540) require the bottom course of the lute to be lowered a whole step for some compositions; the lute is then said to be 'im Abzug' (Fr. *luth à corde avalée*). Thus, by extension, *Abzug* came to mean an open string added beneath the stopped strings; Praetorius (*De organographia*, 1619, pl. xvi) labelled the 'theorboed lute' a 'Laute mit Abzügen'.

(2) According to C. P. E. Bach, Marpurg and Quantz in the 18th century, an *Abzug* is a decrescendo into the principal note from a long appoggiatura. Georg Simon Löhlein (*Clavier-Schule*, 1765 and later) said 'Abzug' is synonymous with 'Schneller', that is, a trill with one repercussion starting and ending with the main note, the ornament called 'inverted mordent' by some writers. For these meanings of the term see F. Neumann: *Ornamentation in Baroque and Post-Baroque Music* (Princeton, 1978).

(3) Organ builders have occasionally used the term to refer to a rank of pipes forming part of a mixture or other compound stop that is detached and used as an independent stop.

HOWARD MAYER BROWN

Académie Royale de Musique. Parisian institution, founded in 1672 for the performance of opera, and identical with the Paris Opéra, see PARIS, §§III, 3; IV, 3; VI, 3; VII.

Academy (Fr. *académie*; Ger. *Akademie*; It. *accademia*). A term derived from the name of a Greek mythological character, Academus, denoting the grove in Athens where Plato taught and later a school on Cicero's estate at Tusculum. It took on fresh significance in Italy during the Renaissance: it was revived and its references extended when the zeal for classical style and tradition gave rise to the establishment of an Accademia Platonica in Florence in 1470. Supported by the dominant Medicis this association of intellectual aristocrats, initially led by Marsilio Ficino, and which came to an end soon after Lorenzo's death in 1492, stimulated the formation of similar groups in Rome and Naples. These bodies functioned according to the wishes of their membership, with a tendency to depart from purely classical studies to consider the condition of Italian literature, drama, music and philosophy within a broad framework.

By the middle of the 16th century there were some 200 academies of one sort or another in different Italian towns. As music became increasingly important as part of a courtly education, and underwent rapid technical development, its significance became more notable. In Verona an Accademia Filarmonica was founded in 1547 with a Netherlands musician, Nasco, to supervise certain of its functions. In 1564 an Accademia 'alla Vittoria' (founded 1556) united with the Filarmonica, and before long the new body was giving public concerts. By the end of the century, although the broad concept of an academy as an institution for the study of scientific as well as humanistic themes was maintained, the promotion of music and the encouragement of its study had become matters of absorbing concern. Some academies were specialized even within the province of music; of five at one time active in Ferrara three were devoted primarily to the cultivation of church music. The promotion of music drama and (in the first half of the 17th century) plays with musical *intermedi* came from members of groups that were effectively academies even though otherwise named, notably of such works as Peri's *Euridice* (1600), Monteverdi's *Orfeo* (1607) and Cesti's *L'Argia* (1670), produced respectively in Florence, Mantua and Siena.

While Italy provided the model for the academy during the Renaissance, the need for associations of similar kind was appreciated elsewhere in Europe. In Paris, Baïf (who was born in Venice) and Courville established an Académie de Poésie et de Musique in 1570, particularly concerned with the establishment of new musical styles through the study of poetry (notably *vers mesuré*); after that there was a proliferation of regional bodies concerned with these arts caused by competition between interested public bodies, nobility and bourgeoisie. The Académie Française, whose main aim was (and remains) the protection of the language, was founded by Cardinal Richelieu in 1635. In 1669 the Académie d'Opéra was established by Perrin, Cambert and the Marquis de Sourdéac, under the protection of the king. The first work performed under its aegis was Cambert's *Pomone*. It was short-lived, Perrin relinquishing his privilege to Lully who opened the Académie Royale de Musique in 1672. This underwent many transformations and suffered many vicissitudes but has nominally survived, as the Paris Opéra, to carry responsibility for opera (later also ballet) in its many forms.

In England the functions of an academy were performed at court, at the Inns of Court, the universities and schools such as Eton and Westminster, in all of which drama, literature and music were nurtured within the principles of the 'new learning'. In Germany numerous bodies, modelled on the Florentine Accademia della Crusca, came into being after the foundation of the Fruchtbringende Gesellschaft in Weimar in 1617. On the purely musical side various societies of the genus COLLEGIUM MUSICUM upheld the ideals of the academy.

The significance of the term 'academy' within musical terminology was secured by the celebrated Roman Accademia Arcadia (founded 1690), in which Corelli was prominent and with which Handel was associated, and the Bolognese Accademia de' Floridi and the Accademia Filarmonica, established respectively in 1615 and 1666 by Banchieri and the nobleman Vincenzo Maria Carrati. The Accademia Filarmonica in due course became a regular musical society, but membership was a privilege accorded only after due scrutiny of credentials. The severe test imposed on candidates for admission, which Mozart passed at the age of 14, is described in a letter from Leopold Mozart to his wife (20 October 1770) and attested by the academy's surviving documents (*I-Bc*).

The enthusiasm of members of the English aristocracy (notably the Earl of Burlington) and their desire after making the 'Grand Tour' to civilize their fellow countrymen by taking Italian culture to England led to the setting up of a Royal Academy of Music in 1719 under royal patronage. Planned also as a business enterprise, it aimed to promote Italian opera and in particular the operas of Handel. It collapsed in 1728, and though the attempt to revive it in 1729 was short-lived it was essentially the progenitor of regular international opera in London. In 1726 a number of knowledgeable music-lovers including Henry Needler, a civil servant, and Bernard Gates, Master of the Children of the Chapel Royal, founded an Academy of Vocal Music to promote the scientific study of music. In 1731 the organization was disrupted by a dispute and Greene, organist of St Paul's Cathedral, withdrew to set up another academy; the original academy was taken in hand by one of the founder-members, Pepusch, who considered making it into a school of music. Its activities continued until 1792. It was only later that the term 'academy' came to signify a music-teaching institution, with Burney's plan to reconstitute the Foundling Hospital in London after the manner of a conservatory; not until the opening of the Royal Academy of Music in 1823 were his hopes realized.

Academies of various kinds sprang up in different European centres, and mostly were transformed into concert societies. There was, for example, an Academia Philharmonicorum founded in 1701 in Laibach (now Ljubljana, Yugoslavia) by J. B. Höffer, after the manner of an earlier Academia Operosorum; by the end of the century it had become a Philharmonic Society. During the Classical period the term was often used simply to denote a concert with aristocratic support. A more precise application of the term brought back a formal scholastic meaning. The commercial college in Hamburg was named 'Handelsakademie' ('Academy of commerce'); it has fortuitous musical significance in that C. P. E. Bach organized concerts there. In German universities 'academic concerts' derived their title from the older Actus Academicus Musicorum, and the connection between these and musicological enterprise was made evident by J. N. Forkel in performances he organized at Göttingen from 1779. The term 'Akademie' was often used in 18th-century Germany synonymously with 'concert'. The tradition of the Actus Academicus is recalled in the *Cantata Academica Carmen Basiliense* (1960) composed by Britten for the 500th anniversary of the founding of Basle University.

A desire to study and to perform choral music of former times as well as more recent works inspired the formation of such bodies as the Berlin Singakademie (1791), the Bremen Singakademie (1815), the Akademie für Kirchenmusik (Berlin, 1822) and the Robert-Franz-Singakademie (Halle, 1833). Schools of music with the title of 'academy', other than that in London, were established in many places, including Berlin, Munich, Vienna, Rome, Philadelphia, Glasgow, Dublin and New York. Other uses of the term are represented by the New York Academy of Music (1852), an opera-promoting organization, the Akademie der Tonkunst (Munich, 1874) and the Musikalische Akademie (Cologne, 1886), which were concerned with concert-giving, and the Academy of Music (1877) in Halifax,

Nova Scotia, a concert hall. In recent times the term has been applied to specialist ensembles such as the London chamber orchestra, the Academy of St Martin-in-the-Fields.

BIBLIOGRAPHY
[M. A. C. Lichtenstein]: *Zur Geschichte der Singakademie in Berlin* (Berlin, 1843)
P. Alfieri: *Accademia di Santa Cecilia di Roma* (Rome, 1845)
H. Abert: *Geschichte der Robert-Franz-Singakademie zu Halle* (Halle, 1908)
[E. Wollong]: *Historisches Musikfest in Rudolstadt . . . 24. und 25. September 1921, veranstaltet von der Leitung der 'Deutschen Musikabende' und der Städtischen Singakademie* (Rudolstadt and Berlin, 1921)
Festschrift zum 50 jährigen Bestehen der Akademie der Tonkunst in München, 1874–1924 (Munich, 1924)
M. Maylender: *Storia delle Accademie d'Italia* (Bologna, 1926–30)
U. Baldoni: *Un' accademia musicale estense in Finale Emilia* (Ferrara, 1930)
T. Lockemann: 'Die Anfänge des Jenaer akademischen Konzerts', *Festschrift Armin Tille zum 60. Geburtstag* (Weimar, 1930)
N. Morini: *La reale Accademia Filarmonica di Bologna* (Bologna, 1930)
G. Turrini: *L'Accademia Filarmonica di Verona dalla Fondazione (Maggio 1543) al 1600 e il suo patrimonio musicale* (Verona, 1941)
F. Yates: *The French Academies in the Sixteenth Century* (London, 1947)
H. Burton: 'French Provincial Academies', *ML*, xxxvii (1956), 260
H. Engel: *Musik und Gesellschaft* (Berlin, 1960), 231ff
The Letters of Marsilio Ficino, i (London, 1975) [ed. by members of the Language Department of the School of Economic Science, London]
E. Strainchamps: 'New Light on the *Accademia degli Elevati* of Florence', *MQ*, lxii (1976), 507
PERCY M. YOUNG

Academy of Ancient Music (i). London society, probably founded in 1710; *see* LONDON, §VI, 4(i).

Academy of Ancient Music (ii). English ensemble, founded in 1973 by CHRISTOPHER HOGWOOD for the performance of 17th- and 18th-century music on instruments of the time (or reconstructions of such instruments). Based in London, it performs and records as a chamber group or as a small orchestra, and covers a repertory from Locke and Purcell through Vivaldi and Arne to J. C. Bach and Mozart.

Academy of Music. New York theatre opened in 1854; *see* NEW YORK, §2.

Academy of St Martin-in-the-Fields. London orchestra founded in 1959 by Neville Marriner; *see* LONDON, §VI, 2(ii).

Academy of Vocal Music. London society of aristocratic amateurs founded in 1726 in 'an attempt to restore ancient church music'; *see* LONDON, §VI, 4(i).

Acaen. *See* CAEN, ARNOLD.

A cappella [alla cappella] (It.: 'in the style of the church [chapel]'). Normally, choral music sung without instrumental accompaniment. It is thought that the term derives from the practice of not using instruments to accompany voices in the Sistine Chapel; hence it originally referred only to sacred choral music. But since the 19th century *a cappella* has achieved a broader meaning, and can also be used for secular music. From a historical point of view the term can be misleading, for much 16th-century music, previously thought to have been sung unaccompanied, could indeed have been accompanied by an organ or other instruments doubling the voice parts. Yet the term, referring particularly to the music of Palestrina and his contemporaries, survives in common usage and is often specifically used to describe Palestrina's style of composition.

The spelling *capella* is occasionally found; Giovanni Gabrieli marked sections for chorus alone 'capella', and J. J. Fux (*Gradus ad Parnassum*, 1725) referred to 'Stilus à Capella'.

See also CHAPEL.

WILLIAM C. HOLMES

A capriccio. *See* CAPRICCIO, A.

Accademia Monteverdiana. An organization founded in 1961 by Denis Stevens, then professor of music at Columbia University, New York. It prepares scholarly and practical editions of medieval, Renaissance and Baroque music; it is also a performing body, with a base in London, and is active at European festivals (including the Promenade Concerts). The Accademia has made several records, including a 'History of Music' series and others of little-known music, vocal and instrumental, of historical significance.

Accademico Bizzarro Capriccioso (*fl* 1620–23). Italian composer. He is known only by the name that he assumed in the Accademia dei Capricciosi. He was a pupil of Massimiliano Fredutii, *maestro di musica* at Fano Cathedral. He dedicated his op.1 to Fredutii and included a short instrumental piece by Fredutii in his op.2; each volume also includes one piece by Girolamo Avanzolini. Il Bizzarro's secular works, which are chiefly for two voices and continuo, are lively settings of light-hearted texts; some include short ballettos for two violins and continuo.

WORKS
Trastulli estivi concertati . . ., 2–4vv, bc, libro primo, op.1 (Venice, 1620)
Il secondo libro de trastulli estivi concertati, 2–4vv, bc, op.2 (Venice, 1621)
Motetti . . . concertati . . ., 5vv, bc, libro primo, op.3 (Venice, 1623)
ELEANOR SELFRIDGE-FIELD

Accardo, Salvatore (*b* Turin, 26 Sept 1941). Italian violinist and conductor. He studied the violin with Luigi d'Ambrosio at the Naples Conservatory, obtained his diploma in 1956, and took a postgraduate course with Yvonne Astruc at the Accademia Chigiana, Siena. He won the international competitions at Vercelli (1955) and Geneva (1956), and in 1958 both the Italian radio Spring Trophy and the Paganini International Violin Prize at Genoa. He toured throughout Europe and North and South America and soon became one of the best known and most admired Italian violinists of his generation. An instinctive player with an easy, agile and brilliant technique, he is an all-round musician with a repertory ranging from Vivaldi and Bach to contemporary composers; he is considered a fine interpreter of Paganini (whose 24 capriccios and six concertos he has recorded). He has developed an interest in chamber music and is one of the organizers of the ensemble music week held at Naples each year; in addition he plays with the Italian Chamber Orchestra, which he also conducts, and with various instrumentalists. He teaches at the Accademia Chigiana, Siena.

BIBLIOGRAPHY
J. Creighton: *Discopaedia of the Violin, 1889–1971* (Toronto, 1974)
C. Kolbert: 'Touch of Gold', *Records and Recording*, xx/10 (1977), 20
PIERO RATTALINO

Accelerando (It.: 'hastening', 'quickening'; gerund of *accelerare*). A direction to increase the speed of a musical performance, often over a fairly long passage. It is usually abbreviated to *accel.*, and is in practice much rarer than its contrary, *rallentando*. Koch (*Musikalisches Lexikon*, 1802), translating it as *eilend*, drew attention to terms he considered more common at the time, *il tempo crescendo* and *poco a poco il tempo va crescendo*.

For bibliography *see* TEMPO AND EXPRESSION MARKS.

Accelli, Cesare. *See* ACELLI, CESARE.

Accent. The prominence given by a more or less sudden and conspicuous increase of volume, or by a slight lengthening of the duration, or by a minute preceding silence of articulation, or by any combination of these means. On instruments capable of immediate dynamic nuance, including the voice and most strings, wind and percussion, an increase of volume is always the chief element in this prominence, commonly at the start (with a more assertive effect), but alternatively just after the start (with a more insinuating effect, for which one specific term is SFORZANDO). On instruments not capable of much if any immediate dynamic nuance, such as harpsichords and organs, the desired prominence can be given, and an effect of dynamic accentuation simulated, by a duration lengthened slightly at the expense of what follows, particularly if there is also a silence of articulation at the expense of what precedes; and these two means are also usually elements added to dynamic accentuation.

A term (partially acclimatized as English usage) for the prominence caused by slight lengthening is 'agogic' accent. This derives from *Agogik*, the German term coined from the Greek *agōgē* (in the sense of rhythmic movement) by H. Riemann in his *Musikalische Dynamik und Agogik* (Leipzig, 1884). A term appropriate to the prominence caused by a preceding silence of articulation might be 'articulation' accent. There are also technical and artistic distinctions between 'weight' accents, 'pressure' accents and 'speed' accents produced by the bow on stringed instruments, and on other instruments by comparable variations of method.

For the French and German use of the term, *see* ORNAMENTS.

ROBERT DONINGTON

Accentuation. That aspect of musical execution and expression which, whether by stress (quality) or duration (quantity), contributes (together with PHRASING, ARTICULATION, DYNAMICS etc) shape and meaning to a succession of notes, and which, if words are present, has the further responsibility of conforming as exactly and expressively as possible to the natural accent of those words.

Musical accentuation will characteristically rise to and fall away from the point of prominence at the peak note, which is often also the highest note, of a phrase; at the moment of greatest dissonance, whether unprepared or prepared, including the dissonant moment of a suspension when the moving part strikes the sustained part(s); at moments of verbal stress (if words are present); and at emphatic moments in rhythmic patterns, and especially when these are typical of a dance or have been established as a deliberate OSTINATO. But on the other hand, the mere implication of an 'accented beat' or 'downbeat' in the metre is not necessarily to be rendered literally by an ACCENT. On the contrary, true musical accentuation frequently introduces a kind of counterpoint of rhythms between the regular accents which the metre schematically implies (so that they are subliminally present in the listener's expectations), and the far from regular accents which the performer actually makes (so that the listener distinctly hears them). This is a situation comparable to that found in all but the simplest poetry; and it is for the performer to bring it out both subtly and clearly in his interpretation of the music, as a good reader will in declaiming poetry.

ROBERT DONINGTON

Accentus (Lat.). A term used in the 16th century (e.g. Ornithoparchus, *Musicae activae micrologus*, 1517) for the simple forms of plainchant based on recitation tones as used in the EPISTLE, GOSPEL, prayers etc; for a general survey of such forms, *see* INFLECTION. *Accentus* forms are contrasted with *concentus* forms, or with the more developed forms such as antiphons or responsories.

Acciaccatura (It.; Fr. *pincé étouffé*; Ger. *Zusammenschlag*). A 'crushed note', consisting of an accessory note adjacent to the main note (commonly a semitone below), sounded at the same time as the main note and released as soon as struck. It is normally notated like an appoggiatura but with a stroke through a quaver stem. *See* ORNAMENTS, §II, 8.

Acciaiuoli, Filippo (*b* Rome, 1637; *d* Rome, 8 Feb 1700). Italian theatre manager, machine designer, poet and ?composer. He came of an old and wealthy Florentine family and as a young man travelled throughout Europe, visited the Middle East and north Africa and even reached the coast of America. He was a Knight of Malta and enjoyed a thorough education at the Seminario Romano, afterwards specializing in mathematics. In January 1657 he was admitted to the Florentine Accademia degli Immobili and danced with other members of the nobility in the intermezzos to Cavalli's *Ipermestra* in June 1658. By the end of 1667 he was again in Rome, where in February 1668 his libretto *Girello* was performed at the Palazzo Colonna with Jacopo Melani's music. *Girello* burlesques certain conventions of the *dramma per musica*, relies heavily on low comedy (noted with displeasure by some contemporaries: see Ademollo) and adopts several characters from the *commedia dell'arte*. It has also been interpreted as a 'political satire directed against absolutism' (Weaver, 1971). The following Carnival his *L'empio punito*, the first operatic treatment of essential elements of the Don Juan story, was staged with music by Alessandro Melani. Acciaiuoli provided only the framework of the play; the verse was set by G. F. Apolloni, who may have done the same for *Girello*, for which he certainly wrote the prologue. From 1670 to early 1672 Acciaiuoli administered, with considerable difficulty, D'Alibert's Teatro Tordinona.

Acciaiuoli was best known to his contemporaries as an inventor of machines and a designer of intermezzos, 'infinite capricciose trasformazioni' (Crescimbeni) which he displayed primarily at the Roman theatres Tordinona and Capranica. There he was in the circle of Queen Christina of Sweden and was a close friend of Cardinal Flavio Chigi and from 1690 a member of the Arcadian Academy with the name Irenio Amasiano. He also maintained relations with the Medici family in Florence, where in May 1684 he presented a comedy for marionettes of his own design. In 1689 he contributed to *Il greco in Troia* (libretto by M. Noris; performed for the marriage of Grand Duke Ferdinando III) a Trojan horse so complicated that he had to be called from Rome to operate it. His reputation as a producer of puppet operas is probably exaggerated; in particular his supposed authorship of several such dramas for Venice (1680–82), based on a performance there of *Girello*, is unproven and in some cases even demonstrably false. According to Rofeatico (quoting Crescimbeni), he wrote words and music for *Chi è cagion del suo mal pianga se stesso* (Rome, 1682; 'poesia d'Ovidio e musica d'Orfeo'); any other activity as a composer is doubtful.

BIBLIOGRAPHY

G. M. Crescimbeni: *Comentarii all'istoria della volgar poesia*, i (Rome, 1702), 211
M. Rofeatico [pseud. of M. G. Morei]: 'Filippo Acciaiuoli', *Notizie istoriche degli Arcadi morti*, ed. G. M. Crescimbeni, i (Rome, 1720), 357
A. Ademollo: *I teatri di Roma nel secolo decimosettimo* (Rome, 1888/R1969)
——: *La storia del 'Girello'* (Milan, 1890)
F. Fuà: *L'opera di Filippo Acciaiuoli* (Fossombrone, 1921)
A. Cametti: *Il teatro di Tordinona poi di Apollo* (Tivoli, 1938)
R. L. Weaver: *Florentine Comic Opera of the Seventeenth Century* (diss., U. of North Carolina, 1958)
C. Rotondi: 'Acciaiuoli, Filippo', *DBI*
G. Macchia: *Vita, avventure e morte di Don Giovanni* (Bari, 1966) [incl. edn. of *L'empio punito*]
J. M. Minniear: *Marionette Opera: its History and Literature* (diss., North Texas State U., 1971)
R. L. Weaver: '*Il Girello*, a 17th-century Burlesque Opera', *Quadrivium*, xii/2 (1971), 141
M. Murata: 'Il carnevale a Roma sotto Clemente IX Rospigliosi', *RIM*, xii (1977), 83

THOMAS WALKER

Accidental. A sign placed, in modern practice, before a note, which alters its previously understood pitch by one or two semitones. The sharp (♯; Fr. *dièse*; Ger. *Kreuz*; It. *diesis*) raises a note by one semitone; the double sharp (𝄪; Fr. *double dièse*; Ger. *Doppelkreuz*; It. *doppio diesis*) raises it by two semitones. The flat (♭; Fr. *bémol*; Ger. *Be*; It. *bemolle*) lowers a note by one semitone; the double flat (♭♭; Fr. *double bémol*; Ger. *Doppel-Be*; It. *doppio bemolle*) lowers it by two semitones. The natural (♮; Fr. *bécarre*; Ger. *Auflösungszeichen* or *Quadrat*; It. *bequadro*) cancels a previous sharp or flat. A double sharp is changed to a single sharp by writing ♮♯ or occasionally ♯, a double flat to a single flat by ♮♭ or occasionally ♭.

For a discussion of the addition of accidentals to early music *see* Musica ficta; *see also* Editing and Solmization.

1. Early use. 2. Accidentals and solmization. 3. Use from the 17th century.

1. EARLY USE. The ♭ sign on the one hand and the ♮ or ♯ signs on the other originate in the forms suggested by Guido of Arezzo for the two possible pitches of the note B: *rotundum* ('round b'; also *b molle*: 'soft b') and *quadratum* ('square b'; also *b durum*: 'hard b'), representing modern B♭ and B♮ respectively (see Table 1). The two shapes appear in *Aliae regulae* (*GS*, ii, 36) and in *Micrologus* (chap.2: *CSM*, iv, 1955, p.93), both treatises dating from about 1030. Guido was not the first to suggest different shapes for the two notes B. The process whereby the notes of plainchant melodies became more or less permanently associated with the letter names that most of them still retain seems to have been completed by the end of the millennium (*see* Nota-

TION, §III, 1(vi)). Although it would have been possible to eliminate the need for one of the two forms of B by notating melodies using B♭ a 4th lower or a 5th higher, or conversely by notating melodies using B♮ a 5th lower or a 4th higher, this was never systematically done. Many melodies included both notes; and the alphabetization may originally have assumed two notes E and two notes F as well (see Jacobsthal, 1897, on the fate of these and the use of transposition to accommodate them.) A notable early witness to the alphabetization of chant is the celebrated tonary of St Bénigne, Dijon, written by 1031 (*F-MO* H159; facs. in PalMus, viii, 1904): this employs an alphabet from 'a' to 'p'; for the two notes B the letters 'i' and '*i*' are used. A copy of the tonary of Odorannus de Sens, made in Sens just before Odorannus's death in 1046 (*I-Rvat* Reg.577), uses an inverted letter b, i.e. q, for B♮. (For other systems and the decisions of medieval musicians regarding the tonality of chants with accidentals see M. Huglo: *Les tonaires*, 1971.)

TABLE 1

(*i*)	♭♭	modern double flat
(*ii*)	♭	modern flat
(*iii*)	♭	*b* rotundum ('round')
(*iv*)	♭♮	*b* quadratum ('square')
(*v*)	♮	modern natural
(*vi*)	♯	modern sharp
(*vii*)	※	*b* iacente ('recumbent')
(*viii*)	×	modern double sharp

Recognition of the two notes B therefore precedes Guido's work on notation; and although the shapes and nomenclature that he suggested have become standard they are not purely the outcome of his hexachord theory and solmization technique, with which they are usually connected.

Apart from a few exceptional uses of other letters and/or unorthodox use of the coloured line system in early chant manuscripts (see Smits van Waesberghe, 1951, p.43), the ♭ sign and the ♮ or ♯ or *quadratum* signs were used for lowering or raising a note by a semitone on any degree of the scale. This is not to imply that every note could be both lowered and raised, and in practice it was always one or the other (e.g. C could not be lowered nor E raised) until the chromatic madrigals and fantasias of the late 16th century, when, for example, both G♭ and G♯, D♭ and D♯ might appear in the same piece. This meant that ♮ before E after a series of appearances of E♭ restored E♮, or in a piece with E♭ signature indicated a temporary E♮, but before F meant the modern F♯.

The choice of the *quadratum*, ♮ or ♯ signs for these purposes depended on the scribe's training or the printer's custom. The form ♮ for the *quadratum* is found as early as the 12th century, and ♯ in the 13th. The B *iacente* sign ('recumbent B': see Table 1 (*vii*)) gained ascendancy in the second half of the late 15th century, the ♯ regaining supremacy in the 18th, by which time the ♮ was restricted to a cancelling function. German printers of the 16th century used the letter 'h' for the *quadratum*, and this passed into common German currency, which has B for B♭ and H for B♮.

The term *molle* has persisted in the French and Italian names for B♭; and *molle* and *durum* survive in the German terms for minor and major keys: *moll* (with flat or minor 3rd) and *dur* (with sharp or major 3rd). The application of the term *diesis* (Gk.) to the ♯ sign is a 14th-century development: the term has quite different origins (*see* DIESIS (ii)).

2. ACCIDENTALS AND SOLMIZATION. In Guido's *Micrologus* hexachord theory is at an early stage of formation: at first only transposition of the series C–D–E–F–G–A up a 5th was discussed, and not until the 12th century was the distinction between the *hexachordum naturale* (C–D–E–F–G–A), the *hexachordum molle* (literally 'hexachord with the soft-cornered B': F–G–A–B♭–C–D) and the *hexachordum durum* ('hexachord with the sharp-cornered B': G–A–B♮–C–D–E) regularly made (see Smits van Waesberghe, 1969, p.116).

The hexachord system and its solmization (fitting the syllables *ut–re–mi–fa–sol–la* to the hexachord, always understanding a semitone between *mi* and *fa*) facilitated the memorization of the position of semitones in a plainchant melody, and in the case of B♭ and B♮ helped to avoid the need to think of a note which, written on the staff, had two possible meanings. Most music in the Middle Ages and Renaissance was performed from memory, and its intervallic structure was learnt not as a series of visual signs on a page but in terms of hexachord constructions and solmization syllables. This affected the attitude to written music of even the most accomplished solo performers who could sight-read their parts (but whose training would have been dominated by solmization from their earliest years). A proper skill in solmization obviated the need for a use of accidentals as explicit as in modern practice: once the performer had decided that a passage belonged to certain hexachords, its intervallic structure was determined; thus only the accidentals necessary to ensure the correct choice of hexachord and thus the correct solmization, needed to be entered in a copy of the music. They were often written several notes in advance of the one they affected most directly: in terms of solmization they affected all the notes of that passage. Reconstruction of the decisions in solmization likely to have been made by performers of medieval and Renaissance polyphony is a prerequisite of editing and performing the music.

The use of ♭ as a prefacing signature at the beginning of a staff (or even, in the absence of any other letter, as a clef in early English sources: *see* CLEF) is found in the earliest manuscripts using the staff (11th–12th centuries). A two-flat signature appears in the conductus *Hac in die rege nato* (*I-Fl* 29.1, f.332*r*) in both voices for six whole systems (f.333*r*); the piece begins and ends without signature. Such signatures affected the interval structure of the whole piece (or a long section of a piece), but the intervals were as liable to modification in detail as a piece without signature. Much early polyphony relied on the interval of the 5th for most of its structurally important harmonies; this meant that the voices of, for example, a two-part composition might very frequently be in a relationship parallel to that of the *hexachordum naturale* (with next highest note B♭) to the *hexachordum durum* (with B♮). Consequently pieces with one more flat in the signature of the lower part(s) than that of the upper part(s) are not rare in the 13th century and became very common in the 14th.

3. USE FROM THE 17TH CENTURY. The introduction of bar-lines to mark off regular metric periods in music (as opposed to bar-lines that merely help to coordinate voices of polyphony notated in score, which are of no metrical significance) is found in German organ tablature of the 15th century, and in printed music of the late 1520s. But not until the end of the 17th century were bar-lines generally understood to terminate the effect of accidentals. By this time too the influence of modal theory on the use of signatures had waned. Discrepancies to be found in early 18th-century music between modal and the modern tonal practice chiefly occur in pieces written in the modern 'minor keys', but notated in Dorian (*d–d'* without signature) or transposed Dorian modes (one flat less than modern practice). Such pieces are Bach's 'Dorian' Toccata and Fugue (BWV538) and, from the *Clavierübung*, iii, BWV680, 681–2 (one extra sharp), 683–5 and 689. The modern forms of double flat and double sharp were also accepted generally by the 18th century.

The restriction of the efficacy of an accidental to the note immediately succeeding it was first suggested and practised by composers of chromatic madrigals at the end of the 16th century (e.g. Lassus, Ruffo etc: see Kroyer, p.81). The difficulties caused by strongly chromatic and atonal music became critical at the end of the 19th century. While Schoenberg, in many works from the last movement of the Second String Quartet op.10 (1907–8), prefaced every note with an accidental (♯, ♭ or ♮) which was to apply to one note only, van Dieren (*Six Sketches*, 1910–11) and Busoni (*Sonatina seconda*, 1912) used ♯ and ♭ but not ♮, again to affect only the note they immediately preceded.

BIBLIOGRAPHY
G. Jacobsthal: *Die chromatische Alteration im liturgischen Gesang der abendländischen Kirche* (Berlin, 1897/*R*1970)
T. Kroyer: *Die Anfänge der Chromatik im italienischen Madrigal des XVI. Jahrhunderts* (Leipzig, 1902/*R*1968)
J. Wolf: *Handbuch der Notationskunde* (Leipzig, 1913–19)
W. Apel: *The Notation of Polyphonic Music, 900–1600* (Cambridge, Mass., 1942, 5/1953)
J. Smits van Waesberghe: 'The Musical Notation of Guido of Arezzo', *MD*, v (1951), 15–53 [Eng. trans. of pp.47–85 of *De musico paedagogico et theoretico Guidone Aretino*, 1953]
——: *Musikerziehung*, Musikgeschichte in Bildern, iii/3 (Leipzig, 1969)
H. Besseler and P. Gülke: *Schriftbild der mehrstimmigen Musik*, Musikgeschichte in Bildern, iii/5 (Leipzig, 1972)
L. East: 'Busoni and van Dieren', *Soundings*, v (1975), 44
B. Stäblein: *Schriftbild der einstimmigen Musik*, Musikgeschichte in Bildern, iii/4 (Leipzig, 1975)

DAVID HILEY

Acclamation (Lat. *acclamatio, adclamatio, conclamatio, vox* etc; Gk. *euphēmia, euphēmēsis, polychronion, polychronisma*). A formula pronounced or sung corporately by a group, expressing a common sentiment, and normally referring to a specific person or object. Acclamations are an important part of all Christian liturgies, and also developed independently as expressions of the public recognition of spiritual and temporal dignitaries, both in eastern and western Christendom. They were widely used in the ancient world.

In ancient Rome *acclamationes*, sometimes rehearsed, were shouted at triumphs, theatres etc; they served to ratify senatorial decisions, since much juridical authority attached to them, and were used at imperial elections. Such acclamations as 'Axios!' ('Worthy!'), became customary in the Christian Church at the election of bishops; they are first attested in the 3rd century (cf *Revelation* iv.11). They were used also at ordinations, ecclesiastical councils (from Chalcedon,

451) and coronations, and they may represent a conversion to Christian use of the Roman senatorial acclamations.

From these acclamations there developed complex litany-like public acclamations of dignitaries: in the Carolingian empire the LAUDES REGIAE, and in the Byzantine empire comparable panegyric salutations termed *euphēmiai* and *polychronia* or *polychronismata* (the latter were acclamations wishing longevity to the emperor and took their name from the word 'polychronion' ('long-lasting') with which they began). A distinction was drawn between *polychronia*, meaning imperial acclamations, and *euphēmēseis*, or acclamations of church dignitaries, but this distinction was dropped after the fall of the empire in 1453. Acclamations, some involving instrumental music, were performed at many occasions. According to the *De caeremoniis* of Constantine VII Porphyrogennetus (912–59), imperial acclamations were performed by two choirs of kraktai drawn from the court officials, and acclamations of ecclesiastics by choirs of psaltai drawn from the clergy. Melodies for the Byzantine acclamations survive only from the late empire, and then only for the imperial acclamations, but these may be considerably older than the sources in which they are first found.

Simpler acclamations occur in many liturgies. The early church adopted some from the synagogue, such as 'Hosanna', AMEN and ALLELUIA. Since early times the canon of the Eucharist has begun with a liturgical salutation ('Dominus vobiscum') and acclamation ('Et cum spiritu tuo'). Another common acclamation is the 'Deo gratias', biblical in origin and used as a rallying cry in the 4th century by the Christians against the 'Deo laudes' of the Donatists; it is the response to the announcement 'Lumen Christi' at the New Fire ceremonies of the Easter Vigil, and appears also in the liturgy following lessons, as a response to the admonition 'Benedicamus Domino' (incorporated in the 10th century into the Latin Mass). The KYRIE ELEISON is an important acclamation.

All such acclamations are properly congregational, and their melodies are therefore generally simple; in the 20th century increased stress has been laid on this aspect, and liturgical acclamations have been introduced in the Roman rite (especially since the institution of the feast of Christ the King in 1925; *see* ORDO CANTUS MISSAE) and some Anglican rites. Nevertheless, even the simplest acclamations have at times been relegated to the *schola*. 'Deo gratias' exists in polyphonic settings since the Middle Ages; even the acclamations from the beginning of the Mass canon were set in a simple four-voice chordal harmonization of the chant tone and printed by Pierre Certon in his *Missarum musicalium quatuor vocum* of 1540.

BIBLIOGRAPHY

P. Wagner: *Geschichte der Messe*, i (Leipzig, 1913/R1972), 248f

M. Righetti: *Manuale di storia liturgica*, i (Milan, 1944, 3/1964), 208ff

E. Wellesz: *A History of Byzantine Music and Hymnography* (Oxford, 1949, 2/1962), 98ff

T. Klauser: 'Akklamation', *Reallexikon für Antike und Christentum*, i (Stuttgart, 1950), 216

M. Fuhrmann: 'Acclamatio', *Der kleine Pauly*, i, ed. K. Ziegler and W. Sontheimer (Stuttgart, 1964), 30

K. Levy: 'Three Byzantine Acclamations', *Studies in Music History: Essays for Oliver Strunk* (Princeton, 1968), 43

GEOFFREY CHEW

Accollatura (It.). SYSTEM (i).

Accoluthus, Jan (*fl* 1673). Polish theologian. He was minister of the Protestant church of St Elisabeth, Breslau (now Wrocław). He published *Doskonały kancjonał polski* ('Perfect Polish hymnbook') (Brieg, 1673). It contains 647 pieces, some of which had been published earlier, especially in the great Toruń (Thorn) hymnbook of PIOTR ARTOMIUS. The collection contributed significantly to the continuing tradition and development of Polish religious song in Silesia.

BIBLIOGRAPHY

SMP

E. Oloff: *Polnische Liedergeschichte* (Danzig, 1744)

MIROSŁAW PERZ

Accompagnando. *See* ACCOMPAGNATO.

Accompagnato (It.: 'accompanied'; past participle of *accompagnare*). Short for *recitativo accompagnato*, i.e. RECITATIVE accompanied by the orchestra. Handel used the term both in the strict sense of recitative, where the accompaniment allows the singer freedom, e.g. 'O notte' in *Amadigi*, and as a description of what would more correctly be described as arioso, where a regular tempo is implied, e.g. 'For behold, darkness shall cover the earth' in *Messiah*. The appearance of the word 'accompagnato' where a tempo mark would be expected is therefore also an indication that the pulse may be irregular. The gerund *accompagnando* ('accompanying') is sometimes used to denote the subsidiary nature of a part in, for instance, Stravinsky's Symphonies of Wind Instruments.

See also TEMPO AND EXPRESSION MARKS.

JACK WESTRUP, DAVID FALLOWS

Accompanied keyboard music. A term used to describe fully written-out keyboard music (as opposed to the realization of a figured bass) to which one or more instrumental parts are added, subordinate to, or on an equal basis with, the keyboard part. In the case of 19th- and 20th-century chamber music with piano – violin and piano sonatas, piano trios etc – the question of whether a given work belongs in the category of accompanied keyboard music or not is really one of intent and balance. In the original titles of the majority of such works in the 19th century, the piano is named first, and Mendelssohn and even Brahms spoke of a violinist 'accompanying' in a sonata with piano, even though the two instruments might be treated as equally as their natures permitted. In the 20th century we have so accustomed ourselves to regarding the piano as an accompanying instrument that the opposite possibility has ceased to occur to players, impresarios, reviewers and recording engineers, with the result that performances of accompanied keyboard music of the Classical and early Romantic periods, where the piano usually has the leading role, are seriously distorted.

Whatever the balance between the piano and other parts in such music, its ancestry in the 18th-century keyboard music 'with accompaniments' is not in doubt, nor is there any doubt that it is only very indirectly related to Baroque chamber music with continuo accompaniment, which died with the 18th century. It is a common error to attribute the appearance of the sonata for keyboard and violin – the kind, for example, that Mozart wrote – to a dissatisfaction on the part of composers with the unpredictable nature of an accompaniment improvised over a figured bass, or to a decline in the art of thoroughbass itself. There was no cross-over, no publication of realizations of continuo parts, no rewriting of sonatas with continuo accompaniment. Instead, the accompanied keyboard sonata and the sonata with continuo existed side by side for half a century, even issued sometimes from the pen of the same composer, each genre with its own conventions of form and style, the former a new one, growing steadily in popularity, the latter an increasingly unfashionable survival from a great era of the past.

The connection between accompanied keyboard music and the tradition of Baroque chamber music is traceable through the sonatas that J. S. Bach wrote for harpsichord with violin, flute or viola da gamba while at Cöthen. There can be little doubt that the trio textures in these works, like those in the organ sonatas, hark back in some cases to the model of the old trio sonata, in others to the double concerto; they were not newly invented, their roots are in the past. But they also lead on into the future through the accompanied sonatas of C. P. E. Bach, possibly Schaffrath, possibly Giardini and others, by paths as yet uninvestigated. The connection between the trio sonata and the sonata with obbligato harpsichord is more immediately obvious in Telemann's *Six concerts et six suites* (1734), of which the *concerts* could be performed either way.

There is another line of development, however, which, though it ultimately joins the German one, originated around 1734 in France with the *Pièces de clavecin en sonates avec accompagnement de violon* by J.-J. Cassanéa de Mondonville. This work, far from being an outgrowth of the continuo sonata, was created as a new kind of sonata: the composer tells us so himself. (For though the idea of accompanying harpsichord music with a violin was not entirely new in France, this Franco-Italian fusion of keyboard and string styles was.) His next work, a set of violin sonatas with continuo, shows that he did not think of his new invention as a replacement for the older type, and his next after that further shows that the *Pièces de clavecin en sonates* were the fruit of a continuing interest in ways of accompanying harpsichord music: the player was to accompany himself by singing, or if he had no voice, he could have a violinist play that part. But here the composer was equivocal about what was or was not accompaniment: he said that for want of either voice or violin, 'the *accompaniment* may take the place of the piece'. Neither of these experiments was modelled on the trio sonata; in both the keyboard writing is free and idiomatic with a pronounced element of virtuosity.

Mondonville's first idea instantly became popular, but as a new addition to the world of chamber music, not as a replacement for the continuo sonata. His imitators, Dupuits and Rameau in 1741, Boismortier in 1742, Clément in 1743, Guillemain in 1745, Luc Marchand in 1748 and Corrette in 1750, continued to experiment with textures and accompaniments, now veering towards the trio sonata, now towards the *pièce de clavecin*. In the 1750s and 1760s, with the beginning of the German influx into Paris and the stylistic upheavals of the mid-century, the accompanied sonata became increasingly international, and the preferred form of keyboard music. Instrumental accompaniments spread to other forms – variations, arrangements from operas, programme pieces, etc – and were even added to works which were never intended to be thus embellished. For a time, the line separating this kind of music from the keyboard concerto wavered and faded as the latter term was applied to works in CONCERTO style or form with only one or a few accompanying instruments. But with this vast proliferation of accompanied keyboard music at the expense of the solo repertory, there occurred at the same time a paradoxical atrophy of the instrumental parts, which reached its extreme in the 1770s. Accompaniments by melody instruments were nothing more than sustained harmony notes or doublings of the melody; very often they were marked AD LIBITUM, and sometimes they were not supplied at all, the accompanist being expected to read the right-hand melody over the shoulder of the harpsichordist. C. P. E. Bach, who began with true trio textures like his father's, shared in this decline (e.g. WQ89 no.3). The earliest sonatas by Mozart are of this type.

Then, still in the 1770s, life began to flow back into the accompaniments, and as the Classical style became enriched with a new kind of contrapuntal vitality, the accompanied sonata took on the character of a 'partnership of equals'. Yet the old habits persisted; sonatas and trios continued to be listed 'for the piano with accompaniments', and the idea of the pianist as accompanist for other instruments remained foreign to the thinking of composers.

BIBLIOGRAPHY

E. Reeser: *De klaviersonate met vioolbegeleiding* (Rotterdam, 1939)
W. Newman: 'Concerning the Accompanied Clavier Sonata', *MQ*, xxxiii (1947), 327
D. Fuller: 'Accompanied Keyboard Music', *MQ*, lx (1974), 222
DAVID FULLER

Accompaniment (Ger. *Begleitung*). In the most general sense, the subordinate parts of any musical texture made up of strands of differing importance. A folksinger's listeners clap their hands in accompaniment to his song; a church organist keeps his congregation to the pitch and tempo with his accompaniment; the left hand provides the accompaniment to the right in a piano rag; when one part of a Schoenberg string quartet momentarily carries the symbol for *Hauptstimme*, the other parts are an accompaniment, though they may take their turns as *Hauptstimmen* later on. The meaning of the term 'accompaniment' is variable and not subject to rigorous definition. The counter-subject of a Bach fugue 'accompanies' the subject, but in principle all the voices are equal and the counter-subject may well be more prominent than the subject. In one sense, the added parts of a cantus firmus composition are an 'accompaniment', yet the pre-existing tune may be so stretched out and buried as to become less a melody than a kind of Schenkerian *Urlinie*. One might even postulate layers of accompanimental function, as for the CONTINUO accompaniment of the orchestral accompaniment of an opera.

To discuss accompaniment in all of its ramifications would be to write a history of music. What is worse, it would involve one in futile hair-splitting at every turn. Are the instrumental parts of a 14th-century chanson an 'accompaniment'? Does Wagner's orchestra 'accompany' his singers? The purpose of this article is partly to direct the reader to other articles dealing with special kinds of accompaniment or with topics that include considerations of accompaniment. The focus of attention here is on accompaniment by the chordal instruments – those capable of playing part-music: keyboard instruments, lute, guitar, harp, and so forth – and on the accompaniment of the keyboard by melody instruments.

There is much vocal part-music for which no written

accompaniment has been provided by the composer. If the aim is historical authenticity, practical considerations apart, we may put the question: 'were accompaniments added, and if so, how and when?' A full discussion of these questions would raise issues such as the '*a cappella* ideal', and in any case we do not have enough information to allow us to formulate rules. Still, there is evidence that 16th-century church music was sometimes accompanied on the organ, though little evidence to tell us whether the composers thought it desirable; and there is increasingly abundant and reliable evidence that as the 17th century wore on into the 18th unaccompanied singing became an even greater rarity.

The introduction of melody instruments to double or substitute for the parts of a vocal ensemble was probably the simplest way of accompanying when there was no score and everyone performed from partbooks; in church music, however, this practice impinged on questions of liturgical propriety (*see* ORCHESTRATION). In the absence of a score, keyboard players of the 16th century had the options of playing directly from a group of partbooks – an accomplishment sometimes required of organists of the time – of making their own 'short score' from the partbooks, or else of playing as well as they could from the bass part (*see* KEYBOARD MUSIC, §I). The organ accompaniments to Victoria's volume of masses (Madrid, 1600) furnish examples of the 'short score', and the last option led ultimately to the thoroughbass of the Baroque era.

The subject of accompaniment in the 16th century and early 17th is inseparable from those of improvisation, transcription ('intabulation' of vocal polyphony), the development of thoroughbass and the history of all the forms of music where accompaniment is found: the lute ayre, consort music and the verse anthem, the Italian madrigal, dramatic music, and so on. Two works will illustrate the complex interrelations of vocal polyphony and instrumental accompaniment at this time. In Luzzaschi's *Madrigali per cantare e sonare* (published in Rome in 1601, but probably composed in the 1580s), one to three voices are accompanied by a keyboard part which appears to be an intabulation of the 'other voices', but which was in fact conceived from the beginning in its present form; Monteverdi's *Lamento d'Arianna* (1608) was first an operatic solo with continuo accompaniment and then, in a reversal of a process that must have been familiar in the late Renaissance, was expanded by the composer into five-part polyphony and published in his sixth book of madrigals (1614).

For the rest of the 17th century and all of the 18th, the art of accompaniment was identical with that of thoroughbass in all but a few areas of music: solo song, English consort music with a keyboard part written out (Coprario, Jenkins, W. Lawes), ACCOMPANIED KEYBOARD MUSIC, and organ accompaniments to hymns and chants (*see* KEYBOARD MUSIC, §§I–II). Lute and guitar accompaniments to songs in the 17th century, especially in France and England, were fully written out in tablature, reaching a high level of sensitivity and refinement; and in the later 18th century, figured bass song accompaniments gradually gave way to keyboard (or harp) accompaniments that were fully written out, the earliest important collection being C. P. E. Bach's *Gellerts geistliche Oden und Lieder* of 1758.

Owing to its great flexibility and economy, the piano has been the overwhelmingly preferred instrument for accompanying a singer since the end of the 18th century,

except in church (*see* KEYBOARD MUSIC, §III). In the 20th century, the art of accompanying has been elevated to the level of a professional speciality by many first-class pianists, some of whom have written about their art. The history of the development of the art song from the 18th century to the 20th is to a large degree a history of piano accompaniment – of the growing and changing contribution of the piano part to the total effect and expression of the song. The reader is referred to articles on the song and its composers for further discussion.

BIBLIOGRAPHY

BrownI
F. Bridge: *Organ Accompaniment of the Choral Service* (London, 1885)
W. H. Cummings: 'Organ Accompaniments in England in the Sixteenth and Seventeenth Centuries', *PMA*, xxvi (1899–1900), 193
C. W. Pearce: *The Organist's Directory to the Accompaniment of the Divine Service* (London, 1906)
A. M. Richardson: *Modern Organ Accompaniment* (London, 1907)
O. Kinkeldey: *Orgel und Klavier in der Musik des 16. Jahrhunderts* (Leipzig, 1910/R1968)
A. Lindo: *The Art of Accompanying* (New York, 1916)
E. Evans: *How to Accompany at the Piano* (London, 1917)
G. Adler: 'Das obligate Akkompagnement der Wiener klassischen Schule', *Kongressbericht: Leipzig 1925*, 35
F. T. Arnold: *The Art of Accompaniment from a Thorough-bass* (Oxford, 1931/R1965)
G. Moore: *The Unashamed Accompanist* (London, 1944)
C. V. Bos: *The Well-tempered Accompanist* (Bryn Mawr, 1949)
G. Moore: *Singer and Accompanist* (New York, 1954)
R. Stuber: *Die Klavierbegleitung im Liede von Haydn, Mozart, und Beethoven: eine Stilstudie* (Biel, 1958)
W. S. Newman: *The Sonata in the Classic Era* (Chapel Hill, 1963, rev. 2/1972)
K. Adler: *The Art of Accompanying and Coaching* (Minneapolis, 1965)
P. Cranmer: *The Technique of Accompaniment* (London, 1970)

See also ADDITIONAL ACCOMPANIMENTS; HARPSICHORD; OBBLIGATO.
DAVID FULLER

Accorambani, Agostino. *See* ACCORIMBONI, AGOSTINO.

Accord (Fr.). (1) Being in tune.
(2) A CHORD.
(3) The tuning of an instrument. *See also* ACCORDATURA and SCORDATURA.

Accordatura (It.). A general term for the tuning of an instrument, especially string instruments. Accordatura is often used in the sense of the 'usual' tuning as opposed to a special or exceptional tuning. For the latter, *see* SCORDATURA.

Accordion (Fr., *accordéon*; Ger., *Akkordeon, Handharmonika, Klavier-Harmonika, Ziehharmonika*; It., *armonica a manticino, fisarmonica*; Russ., *bayan*). A portable instrument of the reed organ family consisting of a treble keyboard (with piano keys or buttons) and casework, connected by bellows to the bass casing and button keyboard. The player 'puts on' the instrument by means of its shoulder-straps; the right hand plays the treble keyboard and the left hand plays the bass keyboard buttons while controlling the bellows movement. The instrument's working parts are shown in fig.1.

The sound is produced by free reeds, made of highly tempered steel. The reed tongues are riveted to an aluminium alloy reed plate containing two slots of the same size as the reeds, one reed being set on each side of the plate and a leather or plastic valve attached on the opposite side to each reed. A set of reed plates corresponding to the range of the keyboard is affixed in order on a wooden reed block which aligns with the holes in the palette board and three or four of these blocks are fitted in the treble casing. The treble keyboard is at-

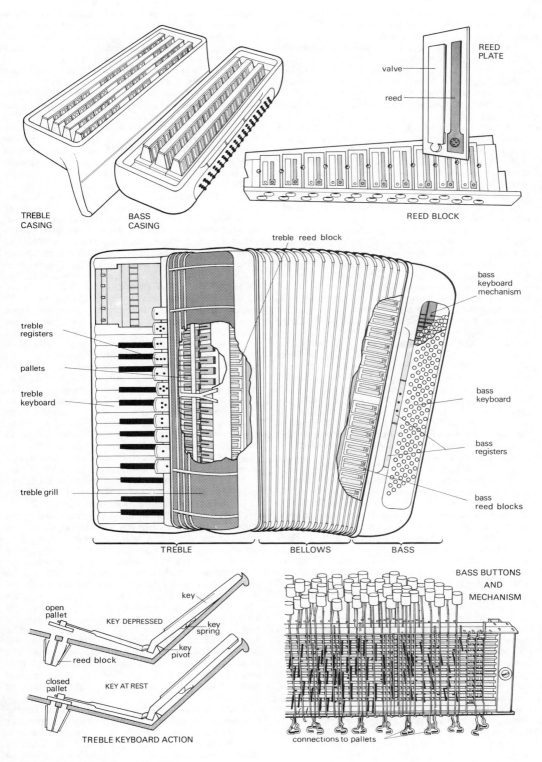

REED PLATE

valve

reed

TREBLE CASING

BASS CASING

REED BLOCK

treble reed block

bass keyboard mechanism

treble registers

pallets

treble keyboard

bass keyboard

bass registers

treble grill

bass reed blocks

TREBLE

BELLOWS

BASS

key

open pallet

KEY DEPRESSED

key spring

key pivot

reed block

closed pallet

KEY AT REST

TREBLE KEYBOARD ACTION

BASS BUTTONS AND MECHANISM

connections to pallets

1. The working parts of an accordion

tached at a right angle to the casing. The reed blocks and the slide mechanism of the register switches are on the bellows side of the palette board.

The depression of a treble key raises the palette, and allows air to pass through the reed block to actuate the reed; the air-flow is created by the inward or outward movement of the bellows. The palette action is covered by the treble grill, a fretted metal cover lined with gauze. The fundamental tone of the accordion is that produced by a single reed at normal (8′) pitch over the entire range of the keyboard (f to a'''). Button-key models have a range of almost six octaves. Register switches add either one or two similar sets of reeds slightly off-tuned to create a vibrato akin to the 'voix céleste' of the organ. A suboctave set of reeds (16′) is also provided, together with a superoctave set (4′), and the register switches allow varying combinations of these sets to be sounded simultaneously giving a variety of tone colours.

The bellows are built up from strong manilla cardboard, folded and pleated with soft leather gussets inset in each inner corner and shaped metal protectors on each outside corner, secured by calico strips along each fold. Wooden frames connect each end to the casings; soft leather or plastic washers keep the instrument airtight. Internal locks or external straps are provided to keep the bellows closed when not in use.

The bass casing is also divided by a palette board, the bellows side of which contains the bass reed blocks and the bass register slide mechanism. The bass palettes are fitted on the outer side of the palette board. They are attached to the complicated system of rods and levers which connect the buttons of the bass keyboard on the front of the casing to the appropriate palettes. This lower section is covered by the bass board, in which gauze-covered holes allow the passage of both air and sound. A bass hand-strap is fitted over the full length of the bass board and an air-release valve button provided to enable the bellows to close silently when desired. The organization of the reed work on the bass side is quite different from that of the treble. Four or five sets of reeds, fixed to three or more reed blocks, are provided, each set covering a chromatic range of one semitone short of the octave. The lowest set sounds from C or E, and each succeeding set is tuned one octave higher, covering a range of four or five octaves.

The usual 120-button Stradella ('fixed bass') keyboard consists of two rows of bass notes, the fundamental and counterbass rows, which are arranged in 5ths, the counterbass row being a major 3rd above the fundamental bass. The remaining buttons consist of four rows of chord buttons (major, minor, dominant 7th and diminished triads respectively). With full coupling the bass notes sound in five octaves simultaneously, and chord buttons sound in the three upper octaves only, though this can be modified by use of the bass registers. This type of keyboard is designed to provide effective accompaniments, bearing in mind that the movement of the left hand is restricted by the bass hand-strap and the need to control the bellows movements. Because of the limited pitch range, melodic use of the bass buttons is restricted, and the chords produced by the chord buttons always sound in one fixed position. The musical limitations of this type of keyboard have been overcome by the provision of an extra manual of buttons in three rows arranged chromatically, producing single or octave-coupled notes over a range of five octaves, and called the

'bassetti', 'baritone' or 'freebass' manual. On other models, the addition of a converter switch alters the chord button rows of the Stradella keyboard to a similar five-octave chromatic range of single notes which can be used to perform correctly pitched melodies and all types of chord combinations in any inversion. Some models have only this 'freebass' keyboard.

In addition to the standard instrument, accordions are also made in smaller sizes with more limited ranges on both keyboards. Some diatonic accordions are still in use, particularly in folk music, and include the melodeon, the British chromatic instrument, and the continental club model in which the treble keyboard produces different notes on inward and outward movement of the bellows.

The introduction of the Chinese *sheng* into Europe in 1777 by Père Amiot stimulated the use of the free reed principle in the construction of organs and other instruments like Haeckel's 'Physharmonica' (Vienna, 1818). Christian Friedrich Ludwig Buschmann (1805–64) constructed his mouthblown 'Aura' in 1821 and developed it by adding a button keyboard and hand-operated bellows which he patented as the 'Handaeoline' in the same year. This latter instrument was further developed by Cyrillus Demian (1772–1847) in Vienna by the addition of accompanying chords which he patented in 1829 under the name of 'Accordion'. From 1830, the manufacture of this type of instrument was taken up by Charles Buffet (Belgium), Napoleon Fourneaux and M. Busson (France) and produced in quantity. Made in rosewood with inlays of ivory and mother-of-pearl, having ten to 12 treble keys and two bass buttons, these diatonic instruments were made in various keys with brass reed work giving a weak but mellow tone. By 1859, Busson had introduced the organ accordion (accordéon-orgue, flutina or harmonieflûte) having a small three-octave piano keyboard and push-action bellows giving uniform tone, rather similar to the contemporary seraphine or harmonium. The use of uniform tone, probably derived from Wheatstone's concertina or aeola of 1844, and the provision of steel reeds in the early commerical production by such firms as Hohner (Trossingen, 1857), Soprani (Castelfidardo, 1872) and Dallapé (Stradella, 1876) led to the instrument's increasing popularity, and stimulated by the players' demands, the chromatic instrument with uniform tone became standard. By the beginning of the 20th century, the bass keyboard had gradually been developed to provide accompaniments in all keys, but the instrument remained essentially an instrument of the people, heard in cafés, dance halls and music halls all over the world. A music school for accordion teachers was established in Trossingen in 1931; it became an official state academy in 1948 under the principalship of Hugo Herrmann (1896–1967), whose *Sieben neue Spielmusiken* of 1927 was the first original composition of musical importance for the solo accordion. The British College of Accordionists was founded in 1936 and its syllabus of examinations has proved a vital factor in the musical development of the accordion in this country.

A large repertory of educational music exists for the instrument. Sonatas, concertos and other concert works have been composed for it by Robert Russell Bennett, Ivor Beynon, Paul Creston, David Diamond, Roy Harris, Hugo Herrmann, Alan Hovhaness, Wolfgang Jacobi, Paul Pisk, G. Romani, William Grant Still,

Virgil Thomson, Herman Zilcher and others. Several major composers of the 20th century have used the instrument: for example, Berg (*Wozzeck*), Paul Dessau (*The Trial of Lucullus*), Prokofiev (*Cantata for the 20th Anniversary of the October Revolution* op.74), Seiber (Introduction and Allegro for cello and accordion), Roberto Gerhard (various works).

BIBLIOGRAPHY
L. Peguri and J. Mag: *Du bouge . . . au Conservatoire* (Paris, 1950)
A. Roth: *Geschichte der Harmonika Volksmusikinstrumente* (Essen, 1954)
T. Charuhas: *The Accordion* (New York, 1955)
H. Herrmann: *Einführung in die Komposition für Akkordeon* (Trossingen, 1955)
A. Fett: *Dreissig Jahre Neue Musik für Akkordeon* (Trossingen, 1957)
P. Monichon: *Petite histoire de l'accordéon* (Paris, 1958)
A. Baines, ed.: *Musical Instruments through the Ages* (London, 1961)
A. Mirek: *Spravochnik po garmonikam* [Tutor for the accordion] (Moscow, 1968)
B. Kjelstrøm: *Dragspel: om kett kaert och misskaent instrument* (Stockholm, 1976)

G. ROMANI, IVOR BEYNON

Accordo (It.). CHORD.

Accorimboni [Accoramboni, Accorimbeni, Accorrimboni], **Agostino** (*b* Rome, 28 Aug 1739; *d* Rome, 13 Aug 1818). Italian composer. Breitkopf's 1785–7 catalogue records his name as Agosti, and this led both Gerber and Eitner to list him also under that name. A. Fuchs recorded his dates of birth and death, and his studies with Rinaldo di Capua, on the title-page of a *Recordare virgo* by Accorimboni; in his memoirs the abbot Lucantonio Benedetti noted that Accorimboni's opera *Il marchese di Castelverde* drew a large crowd of noblemen 'because the composer also belonged to the patrician class'. Between 1768 and 1785 he wrote several operas, all but one of them comic, and he is also known to have composed an oratorio and several religious pieces. His *Il regno delle Amazzoni* (1783) enjoyed particular success, and Martinotti mentioned a cantata composed for the return of Pope Pius VII which led to an appointment (apparently refused) to the Württemberg court.

WORKS
(music lost unless otherwise indicated)

STAGE
Le scaltre contadine di Montegelato (farsetta, 2, A. Gatto), Rome, Tordinona, 2 Jan 1768
Le contadine astute (farsetta, 2, T. Mariani), Rome, Tordinona, 8 Jan 1770
L'amante nel sacco (farsetta, 2, G. Mancinelli), Rome, Tordinona, 2 Jan 1772
Le finte zingarelle (farsetta, 2, G. B. Lorenzi), Rome, Tordinona, 31 Jan 1774
Nitteti (heroic opera, 3, Metastasio), Florence, Pallacorda, carn. 1777
Il finto cavaliere (farsetta, 2), Rome, Pace, carn. 1777; also known as Das Herbstabentheuer
L'amor artigiano (intermezzo, 2, Goldoni), Rome, Tordinona, 7 Jan 1778
Le virtuose bizzarre (intermezzo, 2), Rome, Tordinona, 29 Dec 1778
Il marchese di Castelverde (comic opera, 3), Rome, Delle Dame, carn. 1779
Il podestà di Tufo antico, o sia Il tutore burlato (farsetta, 1, F. Ballani), Rome, Valle, summer 1780
Lo schiavo fortunato, o sia La marchesina fedele (intermezzo, 2), Rome, Pace, carn. 1783
Il regno delle Amazzoni (comic opera, 2, G. Petrosellini), Parma, Ducale, 27 Dec 1783; 2 arias, *I-PAc*
Il governatore delle Isole Canarie (intermezzo, 2, C. Mazzolà), Rome, ˈ Valle, carn. 1785

OTHER WORKS
Giuseppe riconosciuto (oratorio), Rome, 1757
Veni sponsa Christi, 4vv, org; Ave Maria, 2 S, B, org: both *D-MÜs*; Recordare virgo, S, B, org, *D-Bds*; other sacred works

Se mi lasci, infido, aria, in Journal d'ariettes italiennes (Paris, 1786); Fate largo, signori, aria, *I-Bc*, *GB-T*
Symphony, D, *I-Rdp*, ? opera ov.

BIBLIOGRAPHY
EitnerQ; *GerberL*; *GerberNL*
C. Gervasoni: *Nuova teoria di musica dall'odierna prattica* (Parma, 1812), 78
D. Silvagni: *La corte e la società romana nei secoli xviii e xix*, ii (Florence, 2/1883), 150
A. Pironti: 'Accorimboni, Agostino', *DBI*
F. Lippmann: 'Die Sinfonien-Manuskripte der Bibliothek Doria-Pamphilj in Rom', *AnMc*, v (1968), 204
S. Martinotti: 'Accorimboni, Agostino', *MGG*

MICHAEL F. ROBINSON

Acelli [Accelli], **Cesare** (*fl* late 16th century). Italian composer. Only five compositions by him are known, all of them madrigals: for five voices in *RISM* 1586[9] and 1588[14]; for four voices in 1588[18]; and for three voices in 1588[20].

HARRY B. LINCOLN

Aceves y Lozano, Rafael (*b* La Granja de S Ildefonso, Segovia, 20 March 1837; *d* Madrid, 21 Feb 1876). Spanish composer. From 1853 he studied at the Madrid Conservatory, where his teacher of composition was Emilio Arrieta. In 1858, at the end of his course, he won the first prize for piano and in 1863 the gold medal for composition. As a composer, he was influenced by Arrieta towards the zarzuela. His zarzuelas were well received in his time, particularly *Sensitiva* (1870), although his fame has now been eclipsed by that of his contemporaries Barbieri and Gaztambide. *El testamento azul* was written in collaboration with Barbieri and Oudrid, and *El trono de Escocia* with Fernández Caballero. For an opera competition in 1869, he composed, in collaboration with A. Llanos, *El puñal de misericordia*, which was awarded a prize. He also wrote some religious music, most notably a *Stabat mater*.

BIBLIOGRAPHY
'Aceves y Lozano (Rafael)', *Enciclopedia universal ilustrada europeo-americana* (Barcelona, 1907)

JOSÉ LÓPEZ-CALO

Achaemenid Kingdom, music of the. *See* PERSIA.

Achenbach, Max. *See* ALVARY, MAX.

Achron, Joseph (*b* Lozdzieje, Poland, 13 May 1886; *d* Hollywood, Calif., 29 April 1943). American violinist and composer of Lithuanian birth. He began the study of the violin with his father at the age of five, and first performed in public three years later in Warsaw. At the St Petersburg Conservatory, from which he graduated in 1904, he studied violin with Auer and composition with Lyadov. In 1913 he went to Russia, becoming head of the violin and chamber music departments at the Conservatory of Kharkov, and served in the Russian Army between 1916 and 1918. In the years after World War I he toured extensively as a concert artist in Europe, the Near East and Russia. He was appointed head of the violin master class and chamber music department at the Leningrad Artists' Union. In 1925 he emigrated to the USA and settled in New York, where he taught violin at the Westchester Conservatory. He performed his Violin Concerto no.1 with the Boston Symphony Orchestra in 1927. His Golem Suite, also written during this period, was chosen by the ISCM for performance in Venice in 1932; its opening section is recapitulated in exact retrograde to symbolize the downfall of the monster. In 1934 he moved to Hollywood, where he composed music for films and continued his career as concert violinist. He performed his second violin concerto with the Los Angeles Philharmonic Orchestra in 1936 and his third (commissioned by Heifetz) with the same orchestra in 1939. Atonality and polytonality are among the techniques used in his later works.

WORKS
(selective list)

ORCHESTRAL

Hebrew Melody, op.33, vn, orch, 1911; Hazen, op.34, vc, orch, 1912; 2 Hebrew Pieces, op.35, 1913; Dance Improvisation, op.37, c1913; Shar, op.42, dance, cl, orch, 1917; 2 Pastels, op.44, vn, orch, 1917 The Fiddle's Soul, op.50, 1920; Vn Concerto no.1, op.60, 1925; Konzertanten-Kapelle, op.64, vn, orch, 1928
Golem, suite, chamber orch, 1932; Dance Ov., 1932; Little Dance Fantasy, 1933; Vn Concerto no.2, op.68, 1933; Vn Concerto no.3, op.72, 1937

CHORAL

Epitaph [in memory of Skryabin], op.38, 4vv, orch, 1915; Salome's Dance, op.61, mixed vv, pf, perc, 1925 (1966); Evening Service of the Sabbath, op.67, Bar, 4vv, org, 1932

CHAMBER AND INSTRUMENTAL

1ère suite en style ancien, op.21, vn, pf, c1914 (1923); Chromatic Str Qt, op.26, c1915; Vn Sonata no.1, op.29, c1915; Symphonic Variations and Sonata on a Palestinian Theme, op.39, pf, c1916; Suite bizarre, op.41, vn, pf, c1917; Vn Sonata no.2, op.45, c1917 Children's Suite, op.57, cl, str qt, pf, c1925; Elegy, op.62, str qt, 1927; 4 Improvisations, op.65, str qt, 1927; Golem, vc, tpt, hn, pf, 1931; Sinfonietta, op.71, str qt, 1935

MISCELLANEOUS

Spring Night, ballet music for a short film, 1935; incidental music for the stage; songs; pf works; pieces for pf, vn; vn transcriptions

Principal publishers: C. Fischer, Boosey & Hawkes (New York), Bloch Publishing Co., Israeli Music Publications

PEGGY GLANVILLE-HICKS

Achté, Aïno. See ACKTÉ, AÏNO.

Achtel-Note (Ger.). QUAVER (eighth-note); *Fusel* is also used. *See also* NOTE VALUES.

Acker, Dieter (*b* Sibiu, Romania, 3 Nov 1940). German composer and teacher. He began his studies in piano and organ in Sibiu in 1950, remaining there until 1958. From 1958 to 1964 he studied at the Cluj School of Music (composition under S. Toduta), and on the completion of his studies he was offered an appointment at the school to teach theory. He gave this up in 1972 for a position at the Düsseldorf Conservatory. In 1972 he was appointed to teach music theory and composition at the Munich Musikhochschule. Acker's early compositions, written in Romania, are freely atonal or serial, but he has incorporated new techniques into his work since about 1969. He became known internationally through his prizewinning composition *Prager Frühling*, and between 1970 and 1972 he received three more prizes in West Germany.

WORKS
(selective list)

Prager Frühling, str qt, 1966; texturae I, orch, 1970; Myriaden I, org, perc, 1971; Marginalien, vc, 1972; texturae II, chamber orch, 1972; Attituden für 3 × 2, 2 cl, 2 bn, 2 hn, 1973; Figuren/Figures, vn, 1973; Myriaden II, org, 1973; Stigmen, va, vc, pf, 1968–73; Tiraden I, cl,1973; Tiraden II, cl, db, str, 1974; Duo, fl, vc, 1975; pf works

Principal publishers: Musicala, Gerig

BIBLIOGRAPHY
R. Lück, ed.: *Neue deutsche Klaviermusik* (Cologne, 1974)

RUDOLF LÜCK

Ackere, Jules E(mile) van (*b* Heule, 8 Feb 1914). Belgian musicologist and cultural historian. In 1939 he obtained a degree in Romance philology at Ghent University, at the same time completing his musical studies at the Ghent Royal Conservatory. He then taught French at secondary schools in Tienen, Mechelen and Antwerp until 1959, when he was appointed professor in Italian language and literature at the Catholic University of Antwerp (UFSIA). His numerous essays on music and Italian culture are based on a sound technical and historical knowledge and are written in a particularly fluent and lyrical style. As a musicologist he has shown special interest in the French impressionists. He has also composed chamber music and some songs.

WRITINGS
Eeuwige muziek: een inwijding in de meesterwerken der orkestliteratuur (Antwerp, 1944, rev. 5/1960)
Inwijding in de meesterwerken van het klavier (Antwerp, 1944, rev. 4/1966)
De intieme vormen der muziek: de kamermuziek en het lied (Antwerp, 1946, rev. 3/1967)
Dichterschap en levensvlam bij Keats en Baudelaire (Kortrijk, 1947), 189
Claude Debussy (Antwerp, 1949)
Pelléas et Mélisande (Brussels, 1952)
Igor Stravinsky (Antwerp, 1954)
Muziek van onze eeuw, 1900–1950 (Antwerp, 1954)
Maurice Ravel (Brussels, 1957)
Schubert en de romantiek (Antwerp, 1963)
Gabriele d'Annunzio (Bruges, 1966)
L'âge d'or de la musique française (1870–1950) (Paris and Brussels, 1966)
Luigi Pirandello (Bruges, 1968)
Renaissance, Barok en Rococo in Europa (Brussels, 1969)
Levensstijl en schoonheidsdrift in de italiaanse Renaissance (Louvain, 1972)

BIBLIOGRAPHY
Archief en Museum voor vlaams cultuurleven (Antwerp), dossier A 1859
M. Boereboom: 'Een vlaams essayist: Jules van Ackere', *Boekengids*, xxxix (1961), 201
VWS-Cahiers: bibliotheek van de westvlaamse letteren, xi (1968), 1, 10

GODELIEVE SPIESSENS

Ackermann, Otto (*b* Bucharest, 18 Oct 1909; *d* Wabern, nr. Berne, 9 March 1960). Swiss conductor. After studying at the Royal Academy in Bucharest and the Berlin Hochschule für Musik, Ackermann became Kapellmeister at the Düsseldorf Opera House, and in 1932 chief Kapellmeister and opera producer at the German Theatre in Brno. He was chief Kapellmeister at the Municipal Theatre of Berne (1935–47); from 1949 to 1955 he worked in the Zurich Opera House. In 1955 he became director of music at the Cologne Opera House; during this period he gave guest performances with the Vienna Staatsoper, and in opera houses in Monaco and Italy. In 1958 he returned to the Zurich Opera but soon became seriously ill. Ackermann was internationally renowned as an opera conductor, and was a particularly sympathetic interpreter of Johann Strauss's operettas and Mozart's operas.

BIBLIOGRAPHY
W. Reich: 'Otto Ackermann†', *SMz*, c (1960), 194

JÜRG STENZL

Ackeroyde, Samuel. See AKEROYDE, SAMUEL.

Ackley, A(lfred) H(enry) (*b* Bradford Co., Penn., 21 Jan 1887; *d* Whittier, Calif., 3 July 1960). American composer and editor of gospel hymns and choruses, associated with Homer A. Rodeheaver. See GOSPEL MUSIC, §I.

Ackley, B(entley) D(eforrest) (*b* Bradford Co., Penn., 27 Sept 1872; *d* Winona Lake, Indiana, 3 Sept 1958).

American composer of gospel hymns and songs, brother of A. H. Ackley. *See* GOSPEL MUSIC, §I.

Ackté [Achté], **Aïno** (*b* Helsinki, 23 April 1876; *d* Nummela, 8 Aug 1944). Finnish soprano. She studied first with her mother, a principal soprano of the Helsinki Opera, and then at the Paris Conservatoire, first appearing at the Opéra, on 8 October 1897, as Gounod's Marguerite. Her success there and in other European cities led to her engagement in the 1903–4 season at the Metropolitan, where she sang Gounod's Juliet, Micaela and Eva; the last role she repeated, with Elsa, Elisabeth and Senta, in Van Dyck's 1907 German Opera Season at Covent Garden. She was widely praised as Salome in the first English performances (1910) of Strauss's opera, under Beecham; according to Ernest Newman, she 'acted and sang with unflagging spirit and striking characterisation', and she was further commended for performing the Dance of the Seven Veils herself. The later part of her career was spent largely in Finland. She helped to found the Finnish Opera in 1911, and for one year (1938–9) was its director. She wrote the libretto for Aarre Merikanto's opera *Juha*. A cultivated musician as well as a striking personality, she was the dedicatee of Sibelius's *Luonnotar*. Her few and rare gramophone records show the flexibility of her strong, dramatic voice.

WRITINGS
Minnen och fantasier (Stockholm, 1916)
Muistojeni kirja [The book of my recollections] (Helsinki, 1925)
Taiteeni taipaleelta [My life as an artist] (Helsinki, 1935)

BIBLIOGRAPHY
C. L. Bruun: 'Aino Ackté', *Record News* (Toronto), v (1960), 183 [with discography]   J. B. STEANE

Acosta, Afonso [Alfonso] **Vaz de.** *See* COSTA (i).

Acourt, Johannes. *See* HAUCOURT, JOHANNES.

Acoustic [acoustical]. A term, meaning 'not electric', used in this special sense to designate a recording cut with a stylus activated directly (through a diaphragm) by sound waves rather than by electronic impulses, or, as in 'acoustic guitar', an instrument not amplified electronically. It was first applied to recordings in the early 1930s (electric recordings were first made in 1925), and to instruments in the mid-1960s, in response to the widespread use in commercial folk and pop music of electric guitars and other electronically amplified instruments. Used of a room, it indicates that room's acoustical characteristics.   BRUCE CARR

Acoustics. A term that can embrace all aspects of the science of sound and hearing, but is here treated in two specific senses, that of room acoustics, considered only with reference to the performance of music, and that of sound-source acoustics, limited to various classes of musical instruments and the voice. For other acoustical matters *see* HEARING and SOUND; for the history of the subject *see* PHYSICS OF MUSIC.

I. Room acoustics. II. String instruments. III. Keyboard string instruments. IV. Wind instruments. V. The voice.

I. Room acoustics

1. Introduction. 2. Reflection. 3. Resonance, reverberation and absorption. 4. Insulation against noise. 5. Radio and television studios. 6. Introduction to the history of acoustics. 7. Classical times. 8. Medieval times. 9. Renaissance and Baroque periods. 10. 18th and 19th centuries. 11. The science of acoustics.

1. INTRODUCTION. A room that has good acoustics is one in which it is possible to hear each sound clearly in all parts of the room; or, in other words, a room in which the sound is adequately loud and evenly distributed. In addition, it is normally required that the quality of sound being listened to in the room should match the type of sound being produced by the source. Room acoustics are relied on in some cases to sustain the sound in the room after the original source has stopped producing it, thus masking unevenNesses in the ensemble, while in other cases sound too much sustained would mask the clarity of individual instruments or small groups. Acoustical problems are further complicated if opera is to be performed, for here every syllable is expected to be clearly heard and understood, and therefore only moderate sustained sound is desirable, yet the large ensemble demands sustained sound. Although scientific study permits a certain degree of accuracy in acoustical design, great difficulty is still experienced in determining the correct specification of the acoustics that ought to be provided.

2. REFLECTION. Sound travels across a room in the form of vibrations in the air. Inevitably the amount of energy is diminished as the sound waves spread across the room, which means that there is a limit to the distance an average sound will travel without becoming faint. For increased loudness one normally relies on reflections from walls, ceiling and floor to augment the direct sound arriving at the ears.

Sound can conveniently be thought of as spreading out from its source along straight paths and, like light, casting a shadow when it meets an obstruction (fig.1*a*). But the nature of this shadow depends on the relationship between two quantities, the wavelength and the dimension of the obstruction. The waves 'bend' at the edges of the obstruction, so that if the wavelength of a sound is large compared with the width of the obstruction, practically no shadow is formed (fig.1*b*). This condition is easily achieved with low-pitched sounds and the objects or screens in a normal room.

Sounds can be focussed to a point by concave reflectors, in the same way as a headlight beam is focussed, or spread out by convex reflectors so that their effect is diminished (fig.2*a* and *b*). Because the wavelengths of sounds are so much longer than those of light, the sizes of the reflectors needed to perform these tasks are quite large. For middle C an adequate size would be about 1·2 m.

Similarly, sound can be reflected by a plane wall in just the way light is reflected by a plane mirror. There is an 'image' formed behind the wall, which acts as the imaginary source for all sound reflected from the wall. As with light, the angle of incidence is equal to the angle of reflection (fig.2*c*). Very small reflectors do not work effectively for fundamental sounds, and reflectors for even the higher instrumental sounds need to be relatively wide; for the lowest notes reflectors more than 6 m wide are necessary.

If there is too much reflection in a room the acoustic may be loud and harsh, and the endless reflections produce booming effects. Or concave reflectors may focus sounds so that some areas of the room receive little or none. Examples are the use of a curved wall behind an orchestra, which produces 'sound foci' in parts of the audience (see fig.3*a*), and the use of a hard domed surface on the ceiling of a ballroom; in fig.3*b* the

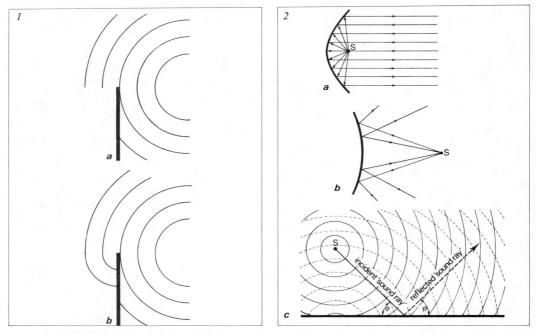

1. (a) *The creation of an acoustic shadow by an obstruction in the path of a sound wave; (b) the absence of an acoustic shadow behind an obstruction when the sound wave is of low frequency (i.e. of a wavelength large relative to the size of the obstruction)*

2. (a) *Reflections from a parabola; (b) reflections from a convex surface; (c) reflections from a plane surface (after Parkin and Humphreys)*

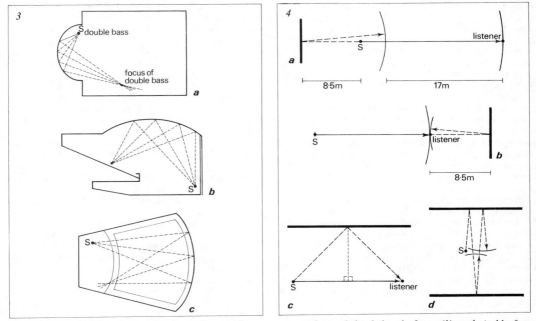

3. (a) *Undesirable foci from an orchestra created by a concave reflector behind the platform; (b) undesirable focus created on a balcony by a concave ceiling; (c) undesirable focus created in a seating plan by a concave rear wall*

4. *Creation of an echo by (a) a reflector more than 8·5 m behind the source of sound; (b) a reflector more than 8·5 m behind the listener; (c) a difference in sound paths of more than 17 m; (d) flutter echo produced by sound reflected from two parallel surfaces*

curved ceiling of the section produces the maximum focussing effect and by corollary the maximum area of diminished sound, sometimes known as a 'dead spot'. A further example is that of the curved rear wall in an auditorium, which may concentrate sound back on the source or on the people in the front rows (see fig.3c).

Echo is one of the most serious problems introduced by reflections. Fortunately it occurs only when there is a pronounced audible gap between the direct sound and the first reflection (or between two reflections), lasting more than 0·05 seconds. Ability to hear echoes varies with the individual, but this time interval can be perceived by most people, and has therefore to be avoided. The distances travelled by the two sound paths would have to differ by 17 m before this time interval would occur. This means that any reflector behind the source or behind the listener and more than 8·5 m away is potentially likely to produce an echo (fig.4a and b). Reflectors in side walls or ceilings can generally be further away before they produce echoes, as the difference in length between direct and reflected sound paths is less than in the former case.

A complicated echo occurs when two reflective walls, or a reflective floor and ceiling, are exactly parallel and opposite each other. The difference in paths of travel of the sounds necessary to produce the echo is then formed again and again, resulting in a multiple or 'flutter' echo (fig.4d). This is particularly disturbing to the person producing the sound, but may also be heard by members of the audience. For this reason it is normal practice to ensure that reflectors are not exactly parallel; the deviations from the true parallel need not be so much that they are seen.

Two of the problems in room acoustics may be solved with the aid of properly designed reflecting surfaces. The first is the transmission of sound from the front to the back of the room so that it may be heard with reasonable loudness (yet without introducing any artificial coloration, as would almost inevitably happen with electronic amplification). The second is the problem of uneven distribution of sound, which is dealt with by 'diffusion', with the aim of producing a 'diffuse sound field'.

(i) *Transmission and the design of reflectors.* The transmission of sound from the front to the back of a room is normally aided by specially designed reflecting surfaces. As an example, consider a recital room of small size, with a flat floor, fairly low ceiling, and a raised podium for the performer. It is shown in fig.5a before the reflectors are designed, in fig.5b after reflectors on walls and ceilings have been calculated, and in fig.5c after additional angled reflectors have been added to strengthen the sound. The remaining surfaces are not useful areas for strengthening the loudness of the sound, and indeed may be dangerous if they are left as flat reflectors, introducing echoes or sounds that are too prolonged. For this reason the remaining areas of wall and ceiling are usually treated as absorbent or diffusing surfaces (see below).

In larger rooms the shape of the walls, of the ceilings, and even of the floor, may be determined by acoustic needs. Shaping the floor is usually thought necessary when the audience numbers more than 100, and desirable even when it is only 50. The audience seats are raised on tiers so that sound can travel unobstructed to the ears, passing over the heads of the people in front; this compensates to some extent for the greater distance

sound has to travel. As an added improvement the musicians may also be raised on tiers so that they are unobstructed by performers in front. It is an old adage among designers that 'if one can see well one can hear well'. Fig.6c shows a floor shape thus determined, and fig.6d shows the plan of the seating so that the entire audience has a clear view of the whole source of sound. Three sources are shown (S, S_1, S_2), together with their images (I, I_1, I_2) produced by reflection from the various reflecting surfaces, the images being constructed here geometrically.

Electronic amplification may be used when reflection is insufficient to produce a suitable volume, but the concomitant coloration and distortion have tended to discourage its use except in the special case of electronic music or when quiet instruments (e.g. harpsichord, guitar) are required to sound well in a large hall.

(ii) *Reflectors as diffusing surfaces.* Any rough surface will scatter sound waves, and hence 'diffuse' the sound

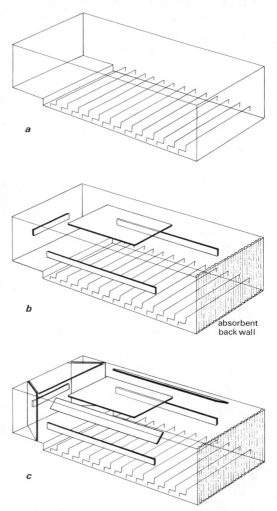

a

b

absorbent
back wall

c

5. *A small room (a) without reflectors, (b) with reflecting areas calculated on walls and ceiling, (c) with the addition of angled reflectors*

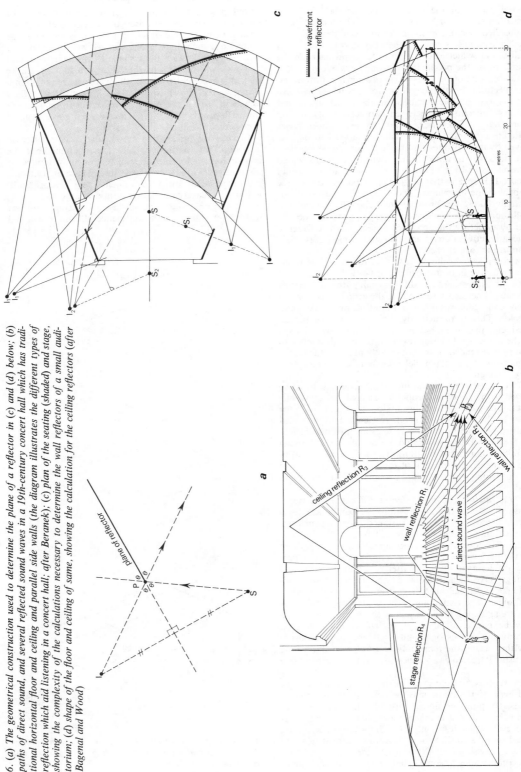

6. (a) The geometrical construction used to determine the plane of a reflector in (c) and (d) below; (b) paths of direct sound, and several reflected sound waves in a 19th-century concert hall which has traditional horizontal floor and ceiling and parallel side walls (the diagram illustrates the different types of reflection which aid listening in a concert hall; after Beranek); (c) plan of the seating (shaded) and stage, showing the complexity of the calculations necessary to determine the wall reflectors of a small auditorium; (d) shape of the floor and ceiling of same, showing the calculation for the ceiling reflectors (after Bagenal and Wood)

field. Unless the roughness is pronounced, however, the sounds affected will be limited to those at the extreme upper end of the frequency scale. In order to affect sounds over the whole of the frequency range the roughness of the wall has to be of the order of at least 0·75 m and generally it is designed even larger. In the design of diffusing surfaces curved surfaces are often favoured, whether in concave sections, in convex sections, or undulating (fig.7). Research has suggested that diffusing surfaces made up of rectangular parallelepipeds are equally efficient, but diffusion can also be achieved in quite a different way, by alternating small areas of absorbing and reflecting materials.

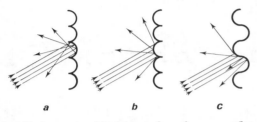

a   b   c

7. *Diffusion produced by (a) a surface of concave reflectors of small radius, (b) a similar surface of convex reflectors, (c) a similar undulating surface*

It is an ideal in acoustics to produce a 'diffuse sound field', so that the sounds reaching the audience are coming from every direction at equal strength. This ideal is never attained, but its approximation is important in producing predictable acoustical behaviour in a room.

3. RESONANCE, REVERBERATION AND ABSORPTION. The property of sympathetic vibration is encountered in its direct form in room acoustics in the rattling of window panes, light shades and movable panels in the presence of very loud sounds, such as may occasionally be produced by a full organ. The value of resonance in sound absorption is discussed below.

Volume resonance occurs when standing waves are created by correspondences between the wavelengths of a fundamental sound and the dimensions of the room, and may result in uneven distribution of sound. This effect is at its worst in small rooms and becomes decreasingly serious in large volumes, where the dimensions are so great that they exceed the fundamental wavelengths of the lowest audible sounds, although the resonances of overtones can still be heard.

A sound that is prolonged by multiple reflections around walls, floor and ceiling is said to have reverberated. The time of reverberation can be used as a simple yardstick to compare the capacities of different rooms for prolonging sound but for the yardstick to be practically serviceable, all the variables have to be specified. These include the frequency at which the reverberation is tested, and the range of loudness over which the time of reverberation is measured. Thus, for practical purposes, the 'reverberation time' is defined as the time taken for the sound in a room to die from 60 decibels to inaudibility (fig.8). It is customary to compare the reverberation times of rooms at a frequency of 512 Hz (i.e. c′), but for fuller comparisons reverberation time at 128, 512, 1024, 2048 and 4096 Hz are all used, to provide a composite picture of the prolonging char-

acteristics of each room throughout the spectrum of fundamental sounds.

Reverberation is determined by the ability of sounds to bounce around a room for some time, that is, by the number and area of reflecting surfaces. A larger room naturally has sounds travelling for a longer period and the reverberation is more prolonged, though it can be reduced by replacing reflecting surfaces with absorbing ones. Analyses have been made of the acoustic characteristics of many concert halls throughout the world that are thought to have 'good' acoustics so that they may be compared and a synthesis of the optimum acoustic characteristics determined. The reverberation characteristics are summed up in the graph in fig.9. Using this it is possible to compare the reverberation of a projected room (calculated in advance by means of a standard formula) with the accepted aggregate norm.

Audience size affects reverberation markedly. A full audience often represents 30% of the absorption provided in a room. In an endeavour to reduce the effect of this inevitably variable function, the seating is often designed to provide a maximum of absorption when empty; it is covered with softly padded fibrous material, and the underneath surfaces perforated. But this is only a partial solution to the problem of varying audience size, for at middle frequencies the absorption of the seat is little more than half the absorption provided when a person is sitting in it.

The absorbing surfaces in a room vary in efficiency with the pitch of the sounds reaching them. High frequencies are normally absorbed by fibrous materials – woollen curtains or carpets, or specially designed surfaces incorporating fibrous materials. Sometimes cheap wood fibre blankets are placed behind perforated surfaces to achieve the same end. Glass fibre or slag wool blankets may also be used in this way, or wood fibre may be pressed into boards or tiles ('acoustic tiles') that are drilled or otherwise roughened to allow sound to penetrate into the material. Low frequencies are absorbed by using the capacity of resonant surface materials to absorb energy. Such a surface material begins to resonate when its natural frequency is close to that of the sounds reaching it, and in doing so it takes energy from the sound waves. After reflecting from the resonating surface, the sound waves have lost a good deal of their loudness. Resonant surfaces of this type usually depend partly on a trapped air space behind them; in other words, they are rather like sounding boxes, which, though never activated by enough sound energy to produce audible sounds, continue to resonate whenever small amounts of energy impinge on them. The resonating surface is usually wood or some flexible panel material.

An invention applying this resonating principle to absorb low-frequency sounds is the Helmholtz resonator, which uses the principle of sympathetic vibration of an organ pipe or an open bottle. A container, generally made of concrete or asbestos cement, is fixed behind the ceiling or walls, and connected to the room only by a small opening, or 'neck' (fig.10a). Helmholtz resonators are more frequency selective than resonant panels, and a series of them are used to correct specific peaks in the low-frequency spectrum. For this purpose holes are often left in some surfaces in a room when it is being built, enabling Helmholtz resonators to be inserted to correct unevenness in the acoustic spectrum, should that be necessary when the room is completed.

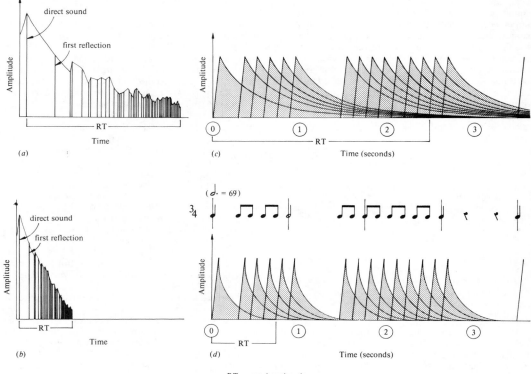

8. Sound waves, including all direct and reflected sound waves together as they are heard in a room of (a) long and (b) short reverberation time (RT); (c) effect of a long reverberation time (approximately 2·5 seconds) in the blurring of consecutive sounds in the opening bars of Beethoven's Eighth Symphony; (d) increased clarity achieved in the same passage when played in a room with a short reverberation time (approximately 0·75 seconds)

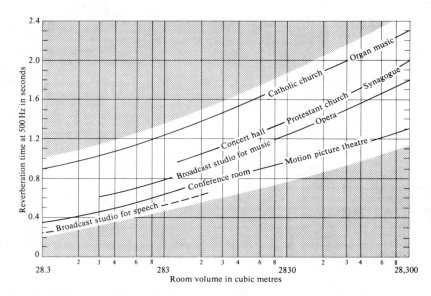

9. Optimum reverberation times of rooms according to volume and use (after Beranek)

The Helmholtz resonator principle has been used in the design of a special panelled surface that combines the advantages of all three types of absorbent discussed above, absorbing sound over a wide frequency range. The Helmholtz resonator panel surface, or perforated resonating panel, has a dense surface material (compressed hardboard or asbestos cement) perforated with holes usually 3 mm in diameter spaced approximately 25 cm apart; to the volume behind it each perforation acts as the neck of a single Helmholtz resonator (fig.10b). The frictional resistance of each hole is often increased by gluing hessian across the back of the board. Whether this is provided or not, a layer of fibrous material (slag wool or glass wool, usually 2·5 cm in thickness) behind the holes provides considerable frictional resistance and absorbs resonant vibrations as they are set up in the air space and the panel. An important factor is the size of the air space (i.e. the distance between the panel and the wall behind it); this is approximately 13 cm ideally, and the absorption reduces in efficiency as it is decreased.

Another absorbing surface, which has the advantage of improved appearance though it is less efficient, is the strip panel resonator (fig.10c). This is made by fastening narrow strips of wood side by side, leaving small air gaps between them that act as the necks of individual Helmholtz resonators, although these operate only in one dimension of the surface (i.e. at right angles to the direction of the strips). The important dimensions here are those of the width of the strips (not much more than 2·5 cm), the width of the gaps between them, which should be between one fifth and one tenth of the width of the strips, and the depth of the air space, optimally 13 cm as above. Hessian and porous materials are fixed as with perforated resonating panels. The final appearance of the wood strips may be varied considerably; they may be shaped, patterned, painted or varnished without affecting the acoustic absorbent properties of the surface. Also, using the same Helmholtz resonating surface principle, many other absorbent devices are possible. A valuable derivative is the suspended absorbent cone, made of perforated hardboard or asbestos cement, which may be hung in rooms in which the walls and ceiling are difficult to render absorbent.

Besides absorption provided by the walls, floor, ceiling and furnishings of a room, and by the audience, reverberation is also affected by the absorption of the air in the room; in particular, high frequencies are absorbed if they travel considerable distances through air. But the effect of such absorption is only really noticeable in buildings with dry air.

Because of selective absorption, and, even more, the effects of standing waves near the walls and corners of a room, the quality of sound and the spectrum of reverberation may vary markedly from one part of a room to another. Although they may be anticipated and corrected to some extent, variations of this sort are difficult to eliminate altogether and may become quite serious in small rooms. Similarly, coloration of the acoustics in small rooms is frequency distortion that appears to be due to interference in the reverberation, so that the latter is no longer heard as prolongation of the separate sounds. It impairs the quality of speech or music unless removed by careful design or treatment.

Great pains have to be taken in small rooms to create the diffuse sound field necessary for good acoustics, by scattering the absorbing surfaces so that they alternate

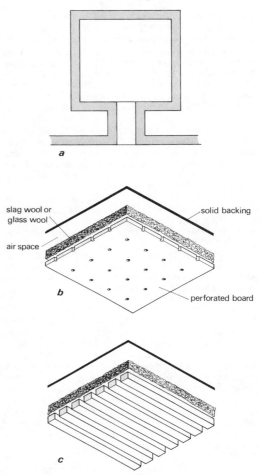

slag wool or glass wool

solid backing

air space

perforated board

10. (a) Section through a Helmholtz resonator; (b) axonometric section through a Helmholtz resonator panel; (c) axonometric section through a strip panel resonator

with reflecting surfaces in relatively small areas, and by the provision of broken, concave or convex diffusing surfaces. Two spaces connected to each other by an opening, such as the stage tower volume connected to an auditorium by the proscenium opening, may produce curious acoustical affects. One volume, the stage tower, is frequently less absorbently treated than the other, the audience volume; the reverberation in the stage tower will then be audible from many of the house seats after the reverberation in the auditorium has died away. This fault can be eliminated by correct design and adequate acoustical treatment.

Reverberation can be measured in completed rooms by a number of methods using physical recording equipment, or by the subjective tests of trained observers. In models it can be measured reasonably accurately, provided care is taken to duplicate materials and surfaces at a smaller scale, or to make allowances for their omission. The patterns of wave distribution may be studied by the use of wave patterns on the surface of water when model sections of the room are placed in test tanks, or by spectrum photographs of the behaviour of sound inside a model placed in a smoke chamber.

In severe cases of lack of reverberation, artificial reverberation may be introduced by distributing loud-speakers around the walls, floors and ceiling of a room, and relaying suitably delayed recorded sounds through them into the room. A specially devised tape recorder is used which allows delays of a fraction of a second to be achieved between recording and replay. While the result achieved is often a great improvement if too small a room is being used for orchestral, choral or organ music, its use tends to be confined to recording and broadcasting studios, because of the resistance of per-formers and audiences to artificial alterations of the natural sound in live performance.

At the Royal Festival Hall, London, unexpected defi-ciencies were found in the frequency spectrum of sound as a result of excessive absorption at certain frequencies. To correct this, artificial resonance was introduced by placing loudspeakers in resonant cavities closely resembling Helmholtz resonators, designed to resonate at the deficient frequencies, and activated by specially placed microphones. In this way the reverberation at many frequencies was increased without audible artifi-ciality or coloration of sound.

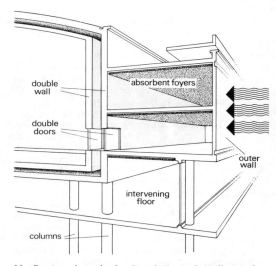

11. Section through the Royal Festival Hall, London, showing the methods of sound insulation (after Parkin and Humphreys)

4. INSULATION AGAINST NOISE. The acoustics of a room are seriously affected by external sound penetration. Ideally, external sound should be eliminated, but this is often both difficult and expensive, especially as it involves sealing windows and doors, which in turn necessitates air-conditioning the room. An alternative approach is to accept that there must be a certain amount of sound penetration into the room from out-side, and to determine the 'tolerable' noise level within the room. Fortunately, sounds inside the room are cap-able of masking disturbing noises from outside, but it is clear that for optimum room acoustics no expense should be spared in reducing the penetration of unwanted noise. This is achieved by dealing with both of the two quite different kinds of noise penetration encountered under typical conditions. The first is noise reaching the room through the air, whether from inside or outside the building, usually called 'air-borne sound'. The second is sound generated in the solid material of the building, or in the ground or solid material of neigh-bouring buildings, known as 'impact sound'. Of these two, the latter is by far the more difficult to cope with, and treatment of impact sound normally automatically deals with most of the problems of air-borne noise.

Impact sound ranges from the noise of water falling in drainage pipes to slamming doors, footsteps, and the vibration of passing trains or buses. Internally all the floors of the building are usually designed to 'float' on insulating pads, so that impact noises are not carried into the structure. Alternatively, the floor material itself becomes the insulator, being soft and resilient, and thick enough to absorb vibrations; materials like thick cork or pile carpeting can be used in this way. Slamming doors and plumbing and drainage noises are either eliminated by careful design, or kept from the structure by thor-ough insulation. External vibration travelling through the ground and then up into the building through the foundations is much more difficult to deal with. Thick fibrous or rubber pads (when compressed remaining 15 cm thick, or even thicker) may be placed under the

foundations to provide some improvement. In the case of the Royal Festival Hall, the whole auditorium was raised three storeys above the ground on tall slender columns that are thought to attenuate some of the solid-borne vibrations within their height (see fig.11).

Air-borne noise ranges from sounds made by tele-phones and instruments playing in other parts of the building to chiming clocks, traffic noises and aero-planes. In order to insulate the auditorium from all these noises it is often found best to surround it with two completely separate skins of construction supported on separate foundations at ground level (see fig.11); it is thus difficult for any vibrations set up in the outer skin to pass into the inner skin, which serves as the envelope of the room. This insulation is effective only if the gap between the two skins is at least 30 cm, and its effec-tiveness is sometimes slightly improved by introducing into the gap a fibrous insulating material, such as fibreglass blanket. The points of weakness in such a design are clearly the windows and doors; windows may be sealed, but this is not possible for doors so a 'sound trap' in the form of a small sound absorbent lobby must be provided. Doors and windows have to be of thick material to improve their sound insulation, and the double skin principle is usually introduced in the glass of the windows, with a wide air gap between (ideally 40 cm). As a final precaution the whole of the auditorium volume is surrounded by a blanket of other rooms and foyers, all treated with absorbent surfaces so that sounds passing through them are absorbed before reaching the auditorium, as in fig.11. Even with all these precautions, complete sound insulation is never achieved, and the principle of masking referred to above has to be relied on to disguise loud external noise and air-conditioning hum. A large audience usually provides a natural mask-ing level of between 20 and 30 decibels.

5. RADIO AND TELEVISION STUDIOS. The acoustics of radio and television studios follow the same general principles as normal room acoustics, with more rigid

standards necessitated by: the special problems of recording and transmitting sounds via microphones; the double reverberation problem introduced by having one reverberation in the room of broadcast or recording and another in the receiving room; and the outside noise, which has an even more serious effect on broadcast than on live sound.

Reverberation becomes a major concern in studio acoustics because too much of it reduces the definition and clarity of broadcast sound. On the other hand, elimination of reverberation would weaken the 'character' of the sound, and is, of course, inconceivable for the performance of music in ensemble. Of particular importance is the variation of acoustic behaviour in different parts of the room, which must be avoided if several microphones are to be used at the same time. For these reasons the reverberation is reduced but not eliminated, and great pains are taken to achieve even diffusion of sound.

The commonest type of studio in a radio broadcasting centre is the small announcing studio with a listening room alongside equipped for control, editing or playback. Of domestic room size, such studios provide spoken programmes of all kinds, and from them drama and music programmes are announced and monitored. A broadcasting centre has larger studios for drama, as well as a range of studios of different sizes for the performance of music; the largest are comparable in size with concert halls.

Stereophonic transmission does not greatly alter the acoustic requirements of studios, and as a rule the same studios are used, with different microphone placings. However, noise interference must be guarded against even more stringently, and precautions taken to avoid strong reflections altering the apparent position of a sound source; the latter usually involves increasing the areas of absorption at microphone level.

The design of small studios is affected by their tendency to add colorations to the sound; these disappear if the studio is made larger. A great deal has been learnt about the acoustic correction of this and other defects in small rooms (see Gilford). Briefly, this is done in two ways: by improving diffusion, ensuring that all walls, the floor and the ceiling have approximately the same absorption; and by careful measurement of the dimensions of a rectangular room so that prominent standing waves are not separated from each other by intervals of 20 Hz or more.

Since all the available evidence suggests that the radio audience prefers music with the same balance and character as under live conditions, experiments with microphone placing have gradually ceased in favour of a placing that duplicates the ears of a single listener in the body of a reasonably sized concert room, and at a distance that produces a good blend and a natural reverberation. It has been found that the ratio of intensity of reverberant sound to direct sound should be approximately 5 : 8, and that the absence of an audience can be compensated for by moving the microphone closer to the source than it would be under normal conditions. With these assumptions, broadcast studios for music generally have the same design problems and solutions as concert halls. Care has to be taken to achieve adequate diffusion by using irregularities to scatter the wavefronts during reflection, and to avoid masking the bass by allowing too long a bass reverberation relative to middle and upper frequency reverberation.

Predominant bass is sometimes avoided by placing special absorbers near loud brass and percussion instruments.

6. INTRODUCTION TO THE HISTORY OF ACOUSTICS. Although a good deal was known about the propagation of sounds and the acoustics of musical instruments from ancient Greek times onwards, the acoustics of rooms was imperfectly understood until well into the 20th century, and many traditional concepts and remedies are now known to have been false. Acoustic designs were empirical, successful in the evolution of efficient shapes but permitting the growth of a good deal of mystique where 'resonance' and 'absorption' were concerned. A particular misconception was the nature of resonance in room acoustics; it was thought that the principle of the sounding box of a lute or lyre could be transferred to architectural design, not taking into account the large amounts of mechanical energy needed if such 'resonant chambers' were to operate as amplifiers and enrichers of sound, energy far in excess of any that could be transmitted by the travel of sound through air. The result was that in many cases the 'resonant chambers' acted instead as absorbers of lower frequency sounds, quite the opposite of the intended function. Equally fallacious were many of the attempts to absorb sound; it was thought by some designers until quite recently that any material soft to the touch would absorb sound energy, whereas many resilient materials are in fact poor absorbers (e.g. cork and rubber). Wires suspended around a room above head height were used to absorb excess sound energy, although they are now known to have had negligible effect because of their small cross-sectional area. And the properties of wood panelling and large volumes of air as absorbers of sound energy were not generally known. Viewed with hindsight, therefore, the acoustics of the rooms for which much great music and opera was written must be expected to vary a great deal from what would now be considered satisfactory conditions. Nevertheless, the acoustics in those rooms that were considered excellent in earlier periods often approximate closely to those that would now be chosen for the performance of the same music. This is becoming clearer as famous churches and music rooms undergo thorough testing with recently developed techniques.

7. CLASSICAL TIMES. Before classical times there are only the vaguest references to buildings designed to allow music or speech to be clearly heard (e.g. royal courtyards for audiences or theatre in India were to be 'built so that each sound [svara] and letter [aksara] should be audible', Manasara, xxxiv, 506).

The basis of the modern science of acoustics was formulated in Greece by the Pythagoreans in the 6th century BC; Aristotle and his followers, the Peripatetics, continued its development as an empirical science. Aristoxemus of Tarentum (4th century BC), whom Horace called 'musicum idemque philosophus', examined the study of musical sounds from a physical–acoustical point of view, going beyond the origin and propagation of sound to consider the problems of perception by the human ear. The work concerning acoustics of Vitruvius (1st century BC), the Roman writer on architecture, is largely based on Aristoxemus's writings (see below).

Greater understanding of acoustics at the beginning of the 5th century BC is exemplifed in the design of the first of the great Greek theatres, that of Dionysos at Athens (c498 BC), and its successor the theatre at Syracuse (475 BC). The seats were arranged in curved rows round the circular orchestra, which provided a large horizontal reflecting surface to transmit sounds made by the chorus and by actors on the raised platform that served as a stage behind. Further high frequency reflections were provided by the scenes, painted on skins, which are thought to have served as backdrop and wings to the stage. Because of the shape of the seating the furthest distance between the stage and the back row was only about 30 m. The propagation of sound to the audience was aided by the megaphone effect of the masks worn by the actors; besides providing facial expressions of nobility, anger or mirth, these masks improved the mechanical coupling between the vibrations within the actors' heads and the surrounding air, thus enabling more of the available vocal energy to emerge in the form of sound waves and directing it towards the audience. A notable feature of later masks was the large

notably at Catania and Magnesia, theatres became more exaggerated in shape, with side walls converging not to the orchestra but to the stage. In the 4th century BC this trend was reversed with the erection of the great semicircular theatre at Epidaurus (see fig.13a). The increased length of the seating area brought more of the audience close to the stage and thus improved the acoustics, especially as less of the sound could escape at the sides of the orchestra, and consequently more was retained in the volume of the auditorium. On the other hand, the direction in which the actors were facing became of greater importance, and the height of the stage building was increased and made of stone to provide more reflection from behind and improve the distribution of the sound. In the following centuries the older theatres were enlarged, both by extending seating at the sides and by building more seats beyond the back rows to emulate and surpass Epidaurus. Eventually the distance from the stage to the rear seats became 70 m at Syracuse and as much as 100 m at

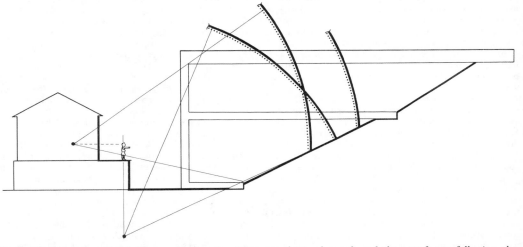

12. Section through a Greek theatre showing the direct wavefront of sound, and the wavefronts following close behind reflected from the orchestra floor and the skēnē (after Bagenal and Wood)

opening of the mouth, which concealed megaphone-shaped cavities within the lips. Cassiodorus (51st epistle) remarked that the actors' voices were so strengthened by 'concavities' that it was difficult to believe they could issue from the chest of a man. Acoustical devices were used in the design of the theatre to enhance vocal effects. For example, the space under the wooden stage platform, open to the audience and partly enclosed by removable wooden panels, appears to have been intended to act as a kind of resonant chamber. A similar but smaller volume in the middle of the orchestra housed an altar that was raised for thymelic spectacles but also played an acoustical role when the chorus chose to call down into it. It is thought that the narrowness of the stage was necessary to prevent the actors stepping so far back that the orchestra floor ceased to function as the main reflector, or so far forward that the backdrop lost its reinforcing effect on the higher frequencies (see fig.12).

Later developments in the shape of theatres are all thought to have been due to attempts at improving the acoustics. In the second half of the 5th century BC,

Athens. The stages had to be increased in height and further framed to contain the sound.

In the late Hellenistic drama the chorus assumed a reduced role, while action and scenery grew in importance; the stage was enlarged and began to encroach on the orchestra, so that it no longer formed a complete circle. This was the model for the Roman theatre (fig.13b), in which the stage building was for the first time completely joined to the seating. Thus the whole building became one compact form, with a very high skēnē carrying a large slanting roof over the stage, which deflected sound towards the audience. The stage could now become much deeper, since the reflecting properties of the back wall were not of such importance for the clarity of speech. Similarly, a gallery was built over the back seats to deflect sound back to them. There were even examples of parabolic ceiling reflectors, apparently for directing the sound more accurately back into the auditorium (e.g. the theatre at Orange, AD 1st century).

In De architectura (1st century BC) Vitruvius discussed both the fundamental principles of acoustics and their application to the design of theatres (bk v,

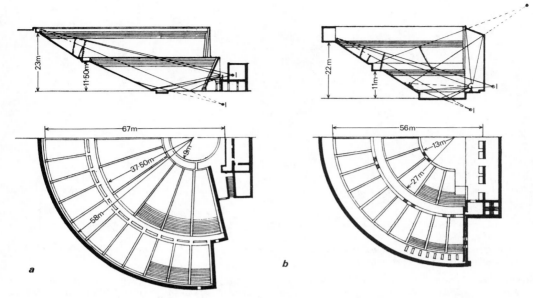

13. Greek and Roman theatres compared: (a) Greek theatre at Epidaurus (c340 BC); (b) Roman theatre at Aspendus (AD 1st century) (after Bagenal and Wood)

chaps. 3–8). In chapter 5 he referred for the first time to acoustic vases (*echea*):

Now in accordance with these researches bronze vases should be made in mathematical proportions [to each other], taking into account the size of the theatre: and they should be designed so that when they are excited they sound a series of notes at intervals of a fourth, fifth, and so on up to 2 octaves.

Then cubicles should be built among the auditorium seats on the basis of music theory, and the vases placed in them in such a way that they are not in contact with any of the upright stonework, and have a free space around and above; they should be placed upside-down, with wedges not less than [15 cm] high under them, on the side facing the stage. And in line with these cubicles openings should be left [in] the slabs of the lower rows, [0·62 m] wide and [0·15 m] deep.

The method of marking out the positions in which the jars are to be placed is as follows. If the theatre is not very large, a horizontal line should be marked out, halfway up the slope [of the auditorium], and 13 vaulted cubicles built, with 12 equal intervals between them: then the sounding jars as described above are placed in them [see fig. 14].

So by this arrangement, the voice, radiating from the stage as from a centre, spreads itself around [the auditorium]: and, by exciting resonance in particular vases, produces an increased clarity and a series of notes which harmonize with itself.

Chapter 5 elucidates how such a system of acoustic vases might be extended in a larger theatre, with three horizontal rows of cubicles, one for the *harmonia*, a second for the chromatic and a third for the diatonic (fig.15).

The term for 'clarity', 'claritas', is probably an equivalent for the Greek term 'lamprotēo', defined by Aristotle in *De audibilis*, implying, besides distinctness, loudness and purity; and the context almost certainly implies a singing rather than a speaking voice. The function of the vases would have been to make some sounds louder than others, and to make them purer by stressing their fundamentals and suppressing their harmonics or overtones. The 'series of notes which harmonize' with the voice seems to refer to the fact that each vase would resonate and then re-radiate sound after the voice had ceased singing its fundamental note, so that if the concordant scale were sung, a number of the vases might be heard sounding together. In this way a kind of

I	nētē hyper bolaiōn
II	nētē die zeugmenōn
III	paramesē
IV	nētē synhēmmenōn
V	mesē
VI	hypatē mesōn
in media	hypatē hypatōn

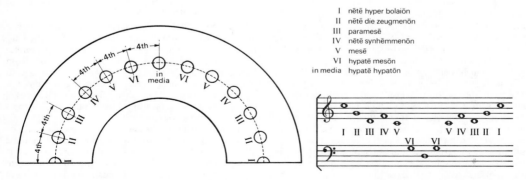

14. Plan of a Roman theatre, according to Vitruvius, showing the disposition of acoustic vases he recommended, and with pitches (with Roman names) to which they should be tuned (after Landels)

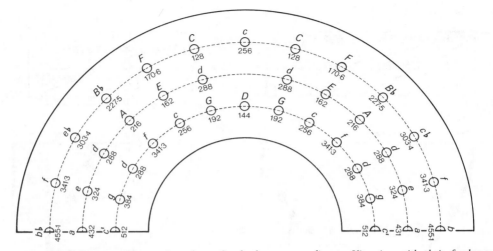

15. *Arrangement of the acoustic vases in a large Greek theatre according to Vitruvius, with their fundamental resonances indicated in Hz next to their pitches*

artificial reverberation time (estimated as 0·2–0·5 seconds) of particular quality would be produced in an open-air theatre that otherwise had none.

Although some modern scientists (e.g. Knudsen) have dismissed the efficacy of such acoustic vases, others (e.g. Brüel) have attempted to duplicate their behaviour by direct experiment. As Vitruvius's original diagrams illustrating the size and shape of the bronze vases were lost in late antiquity, these experimental vases were made in a wine beaker shape of hard-burnt baked clay and with wider mouths than would be necessary to absorb low frequencies. The experiments showed that they enhanced reverberation at the resonant frequency, although they were not tested in an open-air theatre. There is a clear need here for further practical research. That resonance can be used to augment reverberation is confirmed by acoustical theory (see Gilford, p.155) although the amount of augmentation is limited. No remains of bronze resonators from antiquity have survived, which is scarcely surprising, since throughout the Middle Ages and the Renaissance ancient bronze was melted down for metal.

12 pairs of compartments corresponding to those described by Vitruvius have been found in the supporting wall of the uppermost row of seats of the Greek theatre at Aizani in Phrygia, eight in the podium of the Roman theatre at Nicopolis, and seven in the Greek theatre at Scythopolis in Syria. There are 20 niches in the upper part of the Greek theatre of Gerasa in Jordan; at Ierapetra and Gortyn in Crete the theatres have 13 niches each; and at Lyktos, also in Crete, there are three rows of 13 niches each (see fig.16, Müller and Belli).

Vitruvius was at some pains to explain why acoustic vases were not used in the theatres of Rome built in his day. He said it was because of their wooden construction. Singers who wished to sound a loud note could direct their voices towards the scene doors (*valvae*) and 'receive help' from them; when the theatre was to be built of solid materials, such as stone or concrete, which do not resonate, then it should be equipped with the sounding jars described. According to Vitruvius there were many examples of theatres that used them in Greek cities and in the provincial towns. The theatre of Corinth was cited as a classic example; when Lucius Mummius sacked the town (146 BC) he carried off the bronze jars as part of his spoil, and dedicated them at the temple of Luna in Rome, where Vitruvius had seen three of them. Finally, Vitruvius mentioned that 'many clever architects who have built theatres in small cities, from the want of others have made use of earthen vessels, yielding the proper tones, and have introduced them with considerable advantage'.

Besides bringing a reverberant response into the Greek theatre, it is possible that the acoustic jars helped an unaccompanied singer to keep to proper pitch for long periods. The vases resonating in various parts of the auditorium may also have served to disguise inferior musicianship by giving emphasis to musically important pitches. At the beginning of some early editions of Terence there is a short treatise in which the commentator, whose name is unknown, spoke of brass vases. He assigned to them the same use as Vitruvius, and then added:

I hear that there exists to this day something very like them, in some ancient temples, which have been preserved in their integrity down to our time. At the lower and upper parts of the roof are to be seen holes distributed on both sides, and corresponding diametrically with each other. In these holes are set vases of brass, the opening of which is smaller than the body, and is turned outwards, without projecting. The voices of those who sing in the temple, reverberating in these vases, grow more distinct and harmonious.

8. MEDIEVAL TIMES. With medieval acoustics one can turn from speculation about acoustic vases to the consideration of their tangible effects, for many examples survive in church buildings throughout Europe, from Russia to Britain (see Harrison); terms for them exist in most European languages. Although little modern research has been done on their effectiveness it appears that earthenware jars were used both as absorbers (see Brüel) and as resonators.

The methods of use of medieval acoustic jars may be roughly summarized as follows: (*a*) Areas of spaced jars in two or three rows inserted in the stone walls of the interior above ground level, usually about 2·5 m from the floor, with their mouths opening inwards to the nave or choir (e.g. Fairwell, near Lichfield). According to Viollet le Duc, in his *Dictionaire*, many examples in

France are placed near angles in the walls. (*b*) A single or double row of jars inserted in the stone walls just below the ceiling, trusses or vault, often extending down the full length of both side walls (e.g. Leeds Church, near Maidstone, Kent – 48 or 52 vases). (*c*) Jars inserted at regular intervals across the stone barrel vaulting of the choir (e.g. St Martin, Angers; Bjeresjoe, Sweden – about 45 in five rows; and Montréale, France, according to Viollet le Duc). (*d*) Jars inserted in the sleeper walls below the choir stalls or in pits or cavities (e.g. St Peter Mancroft, Norwich – 40 jars; Fountains Abbey, York – seven jars). These are often separated from the volume of the church by the wooden flooring (e.g. St Peter-Mountergate, Norwich – 16 jars) but in other cases a gap is left so that the jars are acoustically coupled to the air in the church (Church of the Cordeliers, Amiens).

The jars used were either specially manufactured (e.g. Leeds, Kent – about 50 jars with their bottoms perforated; and Luppitt, Devon – about six jars flattened on one side; fig.17), or else jars of ordinary domestic type, greatly varying in shape. Most of the jars were between 20 cm and 30 cm in length, and probably resonated at fundamental frequencies of between 90 and 350 Hz. They were 13–15 cm wide at the mouth; the mouths of the wider jars were often reduced in aperture by being placed behind perforated stone or wooden screens (Denford, Northamptonshire; and St Mary Tower, Ipswich) or partly plugged with a wooden block (see fig.18), but a number of vases appear never to have

had any such constriction of the opening. The former seem to have been intended to act as absorbing resonators to reduce echoes in corners or in the vaults, the latter as resonators to enhance or assist sound. Some of the unconstricted vases in Scandinavia had peat or ashes in them, and it has been thought that they were intended to absorb sound by damping instead of re-radiating resonant sounds. It should be noted that many of the medieval vases were cemented into the masonry, and not placed loose in an air cavity like the Greek vases described by Vitruvius. This would not have prevented them acting as resonators, but it may have reduced their efficacy.

Archaeologists have frequently been sceptical about the function of these vases in spite of the existence of records testifying that they have been known as 'acoustic' or 'sound vases' since medieval times; they have often been considered relic vases, or their purpose was thought to be the drying of walls to protect fresco paintings, or they were assumed to have some structural purpose. However, such sources as the Metz Chronicle (1432) establish their function clearly: 'il fit et ordonnoit de mettre les pots au cuer de l'église et pensant qu'il y fesoit milleur chanter et que il ly resonneroit plus fort'. Acoustic jars are therefore a valuable indication of the attitude of medieval designers to acoustics. At least some of the vases were clearly intended to add resonance and amplification to speech and music, although the Chronicler commented, after recording the Metz example: 'je ne seay si on chante miez que on ne fasoit'.

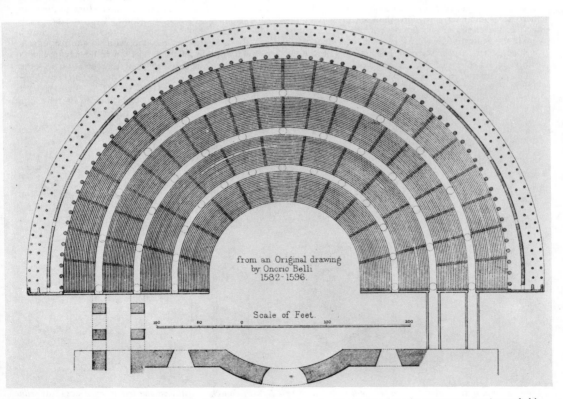

16. *Plan of the theatre at Lyktos, Crete, showing the three rows each with 13 chambers for acoustic vases* (*recorded by Belli, c1580; from Hills*)

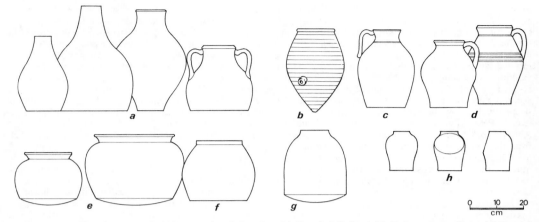

17. *Some examples of acoustic vases from medieval churches:* (a) *Youghal, Ireland,* (b) *St Laurent-en-Caux,* (c) *Fry,* (d) *St Peter-Mountergate, Norwich,* (e) *St Olave's, Chichester,* (f) *Denford,* (g) *Leeds, Kent,* (h) *Luppitt (after Hills)*

Vitruvius was certainly the source from which the medieval use of these vases originated. Harrison cited 12 copies of his works known to have existed in England during the Middle Ages, and there were many copies available elsewhere in Europe. They appear to have been used throughout the medieval period and up to the 17th century. In a satire by Claude Pithoys, published in 1662 at St Leger, Luxembourg, he reproved the clergy for negligence of their duties: 'Of 50 singing men that the public maintain in such a house, there are sometimes not more than six present at the service; the choirs are so fitted with jars in the vaults and in the walls that six voices there make as much noise as 40 elsewhere'. Little scientific research has been done on the actual effects of the vases in these churches.

The reverberation times of some important medieval churches have been carefully tested, and this has led to a better understanding of their acoustical characteristics.

S Paolo fuori le Mura, Rome (AD 386), an example of a large early Christian basilica with double aisles, an open trussed roof and a transverse *bema* at the east end (see fig. 19), has a reverberation time at mid-frequency of 9·1 seconds in the nave. The walls and columns have hard smooth surfaces, leading to close acoustical coupling of all parts of the building, so that it functions to some extent as a single air volume. Nevertheless, some absorption is provided by the depth of the aisles, which scatter the sound so that it does not return to the nave; for this reason there is no echoing from the side walls. The acoustic result is a sustained sound in the church, but also a relatively clear one, with no confusion, echo or fluctuation in intensity. The low frequency reverberation is more pronounced than reverberation at other frequencies, though the decrease to the higher-pitched sounds is a gradual one (R. S. and H. K. Shankland). It is likely that in its original form, before its rebuilding

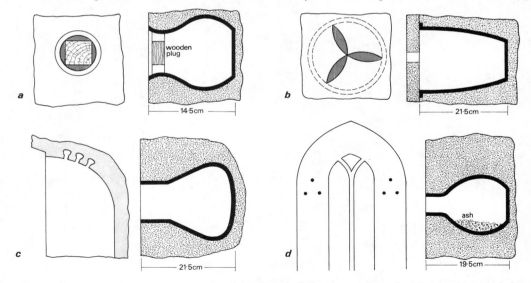

18. *Cross-sections of acoustic vases found in Swedish and Danish churches, with, on the left in each case,* (a) *front appearance in wall with block of wood inserted to constrict mouth of jar,* (b) *front appearance of pierced stone cover,* (c) *cross-section, to a small scale, showing positions in vault,* (d) *front appearance of positions in wall (after Brüel)*

after a fire, the diffusion caused by ornament and fluting would have improved the acoustics even further.

S Paolo is an exceptionally large church subdivided by screens of columns, and some of its special acoustical quality is due to its size. Other large basilicas with similar screens that have been tested, such as S Maria Maggiore (AD 352), have been found to have even better acoustics, with shorter reverberation times, providing almost ideal listening conditions for choral and organ music when full. S Maria Maggiore has only single aisles, but there are chapels beyond the side walls, and a chancel arch separating the apse from the nave. The large volume is therefore broken up into a number of separate volumes coupled together, with the surrounding volumes absorbing sounds made in the nave. The measured reverberation times are 4·9 seconds when empty and 2·5 seconds when full (R. S. and H. K. Shankland). It must be expected that smaller basilicas did not achieve the same degree of separation between the volumes of nave, aisles, *bema* and chapels, and therefore the reverberation times were longer, and the acoustics less satisfactory.

With the arrival of the Romanesque style the height of the nave was increased, and stone vaulted ceilings were introduced to protect the interiors against fire. These ceilings increased reflections and reduced diffusion, leading to a significant change in acoustic quality; not merely was the reverberation time lengthened, but the focussing effect of the ceilings brought fluctuations in the reverberant sound, with a resultant decline in clarity. Sounds appeared to pile on top of one another to produce an effect of surging confusion. Gothic cathedrals suffered from the same kind of unruly acoustics, but conditions were often better in large buildings, where the great height of the ceilings reduced the interference of sounds reflected from them. Tests in Durham, Canterbury, Salisbury and York cathedrals have shown that they all have remarkably similar acoustics, the reverberation times falling from an average of 8 seconds at low frequencies to 5·5 seconds at midfrequencies, and continuing to decline as high frequencies are reached. All have volumes of more than 30,000 m³; in such conditions the presence or absence of the congregation has little effect on the acoustic quality (Purkis).

There seems no doubt that long reverberation times were thought to enhance both music and prayer. Writing in 1535, Francesco Giorgi of Venice recommended that a new church should 'have all the chapels and the choir vaulted, because the word or song of the priest echoes better from the vault than it would from rafters'. But an increased concern with clarity of speech during the sermon led architects as early as the 13th century to omit aisles and transepts altogether, and design churches with single volumes (e.g. S Francesco, Assisi; S Caterina, Barcelona). Even so, it was found that the reverberation continued to be pronounced until the vaults had been lowered and the ceiling flattened. The final improvement was replacing the stone ceiling with a wooden one, which absorbed the predominant low frequency reverberation, and covering the surface of the ceiling with elaborate decoration of small ribs or coffering, which greatly reduced the fluctuation of sound by increasing uniform diffusion. Giorgi mentioned both these effects in making his recommendations of 1535. 'In the nave of the church, where there will be sermons, I recommend a ceiling (so that the voice of the preacher

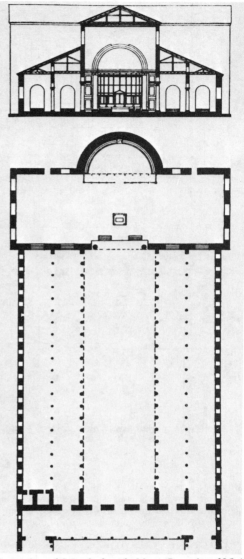

19. *Basilica of S Paolo fuori le Mura, Rome* (AD 386) in *plan and section*

may not escape nor re-echo from the vaults). I should like to have it coffered with as many squares as possible . . . they will be very convenient for preaching: this the experts know and experience will prove it'.

Spacious Gothic churches, such as thosse of Holland and Germany built without transepts and with nave and aisles of equal height, often have excellent acoustics. On the other hand, late polyphonic music was frequently written to exploit the peculiar acoustics of the older churches. St Mark's in Venice had two organs and two choirs by the 15th century; the two choirs, with the accompanying organs, were placed facing one another in the tribunes, halfway up the height of the choir, from which position the unusual acoustical effects of the cathedral could be used without too long an initial delay in reflections from the ceilings. The choral and instrumen-

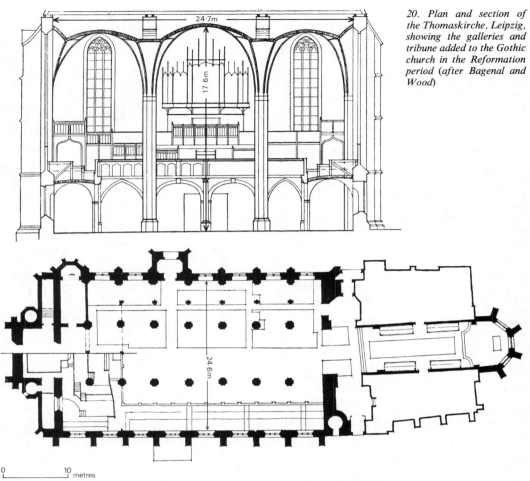

20. *Plan and section of the Thomaskirche, Leipzig, showing the galleries and tribune added to the Gothic church in the Reformation period (after Bagenal and Wood)*

24·7m

17·6m

24·6m

0   10
|_____| metres

tal groups were gradually multiplied, until as many as four choirs and four organs, with instrumental accompaniment, provided the means for achieving a unique kind of polyphonic vocal and instrumental music.

9. RENAISSANCE AND BAROQUE PERIODS. Reformation church builders laid great emphasis on acoustic clarity, which suited sermons but necessitated adjustments in church music. Luther arranged his congregation around the sides of his churches, and later Gothic churches were altered by the Protestants to enable similar focussed seating arrangements; an example is the Thomaskirche, Leipzig, to which galleries and tribunes were added, with an especially wide organ loft gallery at the west end used by Bach for the choir and orchestra (see fig.20). As the vaults of this spacious Gothic church were low (8 m), the introduction of the galleries created shallow volumes with short paths of reflection. The reverberation time was quite short when the church was crowded (1·6 seconds), with excellent diffusion and absorption of low frequencies due to wooden panelling and carving; at the same time the high frequencies were bright and clear (Beranek).

St Peter's in Rome has a remarkably short reverberation time, caused by the combination of its exceptional

size and its complex internal structure; in effect the basilica is five large churches interconnected and acoustically coupled, each damped by the air spaces leading into the others (R. S. and H. K. Shankland). Thus sound travels from the nave into the side spaces, where it undergoes extensive multiple reflection and delay before returning in a markedly attenuated form. The result is a reverberation time in the nave of 5 seconds at mid-frequencies when a large congregation is present.

During the Counter-Reformation one of the main aims was the design of churches in which every word of the service might be clearly heard. Vignola, the architect of the Gesù in Rome, was instructed to design the church with a nave as wide and short as possible, and without aisles, clearly with the intention of improving the acoustics. This was a quality that does not seem particularly to have concerned the Church of England, for Wren's St Paul's Cathedral in London has pronounced reverberation due to its relatively long low vaults and high central dome, and the fact that the nave, choir and dome do not function as acoustically separate volumes. When nearly empty the reverberation time is approximately 12 seconds at mid-frequencies, but it improves steadily as the congregation size increases, until it is 6·5 seconds at maximum capacity (Purkis).

The earliest Renaissance theatres maintained the forms, and therefore presumably some of the acoustic qualities, of the classical Greek and Roman theatres as described by Vitruvius; examples include Serlio's Vicenza theatre (1539), and Palladio's Teatro Olimpico, Vicenza (1588). An orchestra was added to the latter, seated on either side of the proscenium between the actors and the audience, but it apparently played only an occasional accompaniment or interlude. The extensive use of wood in the construction of these theatres, the use of elaborate decoration, and in particular the addition of wooden coffered ceilings, must have ensured good diffusion with brilliant high frequencies and rather dulled low frequencies. Allowing for the dense crowding of audiences which was common, the reverberation times must have been very short.

In the earliest operas, music was subordinated to the clarity of the text. It is known that in the first public performance of Peri's *Euridice* (1600) the orchestra was placed behind the scenes. Cavalieri's instructions for the performance of his *Rappresentatione di Anima, et di Corpo* in the same year were explicit. It was to be given in a theatre or a hall containing not more than 1000 spectators; the orchestra was to be situated behind the scene and be 'adapted to the needs of each performance', the latter presumably referring to acoustic conditions as well as other exigencies.

The masques held in the banqueting hall of Whitehall Palace early in the 17th century used musicians seated on either side of the stage at the front; this position appears to have been a common one, necessitated partly by the fact that the flat floor area between the stage and the raised seats of the audience was used for dance. There is a design for a masque house by Inigo Jones that has the same arrangement with the orchestra partly screened (see fig.21). The Duke's Theatre in Dorset Garden, London (1671), designed by Wren, had a music balcony above Grinling Gibbons's stage front, proscenium balconies over the stage doors, and galleries for the audience.

The first theatres to be built with ranges of boxes one above the other, the Venetian theatres of S Cassiano and SS Giovanni e Paolo (1637–8), were characterized by the crowding of a lay audience into the flat floor area in front of the stage. Boxes were sometimes reserved for the use of musicians on either side of the stage, these boxes being called 'proscenium boxes' or 'trumpet loges'. Often an area in front of the stage was enclosed for the use of other members of the orchestra, later increased in size to become the orchestra pit. Such theatres had surprisingly good acoustics. They were small, with closely packed audiences, were largely made of wood and had flat ceilings. The sound had only a short distance to travel to the audience, and there was little risk of echo because of the large areas of absorption provided by the audience and the boxes. Sound reflected from balcony fronts and ceiling was scattered by decorated surfaces to aid in achieving uniform diffusion. The reverberation time was short, and low frequencies were absorbed by the wooden construction, which reflected high frequencies to preserve brilliance.

Even the great opera houses of the 18th century retained these qualities. The original La Scala in Milan (1778) had about 2300 seats, packed closely together, many with a view of only two thirds of the stage area because of the horseshoe shape of the six tiers of boxes (see fig.22). The openings of boxes were relatively small,

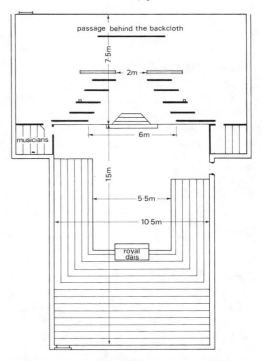

21. *Design for a masque house after the plan by Inigo Jones in GB-Lbm Lansdowne 1171*

1·4 m square, which meant that a greater reflecting surface than usual remained in the box fronts. The acoustics were good for all members of the audience, except those at the rear of the boxes; sound was loud and clear, warm in tone and brilliant. The reverberation time at mid-frequencies was about 1·25 seconds (Beranek). But it must be remembered that the acoustic quality of the voices fell off markedly if the singers retreated from the forestage into the volume of the scenery behind the proscenium arch.

The literature of acoustics begins with the theatrical treatises of the 17th century. Carini Motta's study of the design of theatres and stages (1676) mentions the importance of the ceiling as a sound reflector, and recommends that it and the supporting structure should be of wood. Motta believed that rooms used for performances in private palaces should have the same kind of construction.

10. 18TH AND 19TH CENTURIES. In 18th-century theatres ingenious methods were often resorted to in order to improve the acoustics. In the theatre in Turin (1740) the architect attempted to overcome the lack of balance between a large chorus and a small string orchestra by constructing a hard-surfaced semicylindrical resonant chamber running the full length of the orchestra pit below the wooden floor (see fig.23). The dish shape was clearly meant to act as a reflector of sound back to the orchestra, while the floor and volume of air acted together in resonance. The device was often copied, sometimes, apparently, with grilles opening into the orchestra pit from the resonant chamber. In other cases, as at Turin, there were two tubes connecting the ends of the resonant trough with the

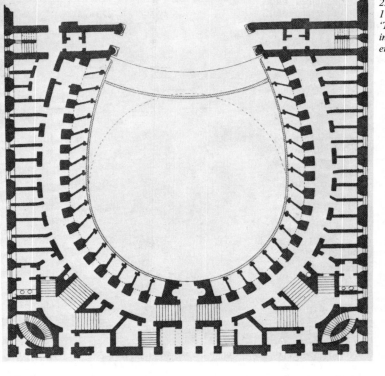

22. *Plan (left) of La Scala, Milan, 1778, from George Saunders, 'Treatise on Theatres' (1790), and interior view of the opera house: engraving by Cherbuin after Sidoli*

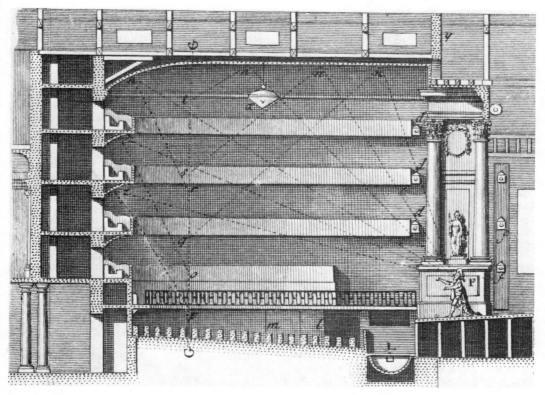

23. *Section of the Teatro di Torino (1740) as slightly amended in Pierre Patté, 'Essai sur l'architecture théâtrale'* (1782)

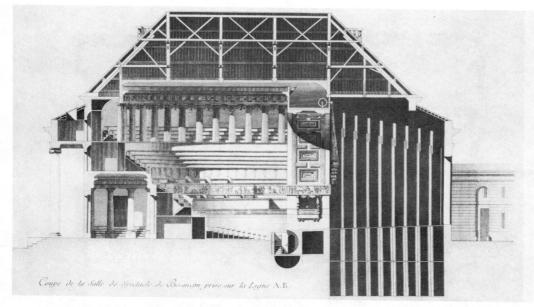

Coupe de la Salle de spectacle de Besançon, prise sur la Ligne A.B.

24. *Section of the Théâtre de Besançon, Paris, by Ledoux, 1778: from M. H. Raval, 'L'architecture considérée sous le rapport de l'art'* (1804)

25. Holywell Music Room, Oxford

front of the stage so that the orchestral sound could be heard better by performers and audience. Patté in his *Essai sur l'architecture théâtrale* (1782), stated that the Turin theatre had good acoustics, and attributed this to the housing of the orchestra. The volume of sound from the orchestra was considered so strong in its largely enclosed space that it could activate the floor and the volume of air underneath to cause an amplifying resonance.

The success of these features led to further experiments with shaped sections of masonry. In the Teatro Nuovo in Parma the entire parterre of the theatre was built over an enormous masonry saucer, shallow and semi-elliptical in section, with sound passages entering it from the orchestra pit. It is not clear whether grilles were set into the parterre floor allowing sound to pass into the audience without obstruction by the floor. In the

Teatro d'Argentina, Rome (1732), the acoustic problems of an extremely large house, with six tiers of boxes, are said to have been satisfactorily solved using another original device. Here the problems introduced by the size of the theatre were compounded by the elimination of the forestage, which meant that singers' voices on the stage could not be clearly heard. The design of the theatre was modified after its opening by the introduction of a channel of water under the parterre running from the stage to the back of the theatre; it appears that sound was reflected from the surface of the water inside a vaulted brick enclosure and thus travelled under the parterre whence it emerged through grilles in the floor.

In his project for the Théâtre de Besançon, Paris (1778), Ledoux proposed both a semi-cylindrical resonant chamber under the orchestra pit floor, and a semi-cylindrical stone dish reflector behind the orchestra (see fig.24). This must have had an extraordinary focussing effect on the players themselves, but the result was judged successful, as is proved by the repetition of the same device in other theatres, such as Covent Garden, London (1809). Another part of the theatre considered of great importance for its acoustic effect was the ceiling of the auditorium. Writers continued to recommend that it should be made of wood (Algarotti, 1762, for 'a full, sonorous and agreeable sound'). The ceiling in the Turin theatre had in addition a 'resonating' chamber above it, but here its only effect could have been to increase the absorption of low frequencies. The Bordeaux theatre (1773), which was generally considered to have excellent acoustics, was, like all 18th-century theatres, very compact; the maximum distance from the stage to the boxes was only 19·5 m.

Rooms specifically built for the public performance of music without acting or stage presentation began to appear in the 18th century. The oldest music room still in use in Europe is that at Holywell, Oxford, opened in 1748 (see fig.25) and designed to satisfy a demand for

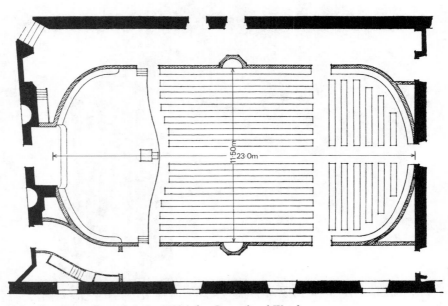

26. *Plan of the Altes Gewandhaus, Leipzig, 1780 (after Bagenal and Wood)*

oratorio and choral works. Before the addition of a curtain to one of the side walls (in 1959) the hall, seating 300, must have had a relatively long reverberation time; the present value is 1·5 seconds at mid-frequencies (Beranek). That composers of this period considered the reverberation time of theatres and opera houses too short is indicated by, for example, Handel's remark on hearing on one occasion that his theatre would be half empty: 'Never mind, the music will sound the better'.

The precise music of the Classical period, particularly, required a predominance of direct over reflected sound. Mozart wrote, after a performance of *Die Zauberflöte* in 1791: 'You have no idea how charming the music sounds when you hear it from a box close to the orchestra – it sounds much better than from the gallery'. This implies that a narrow rectangular hall, such as was often used at this time for concerts, enhanced the music better than a wide hall, in which the direct sound was submerged by the reflected sound. The narrow Redoutensaal in the Royal Palace of Vienna, in which a good deal of Haydn's, Mozart's and Beethoven's music was first performed, is estimated to have had a reverberation time of about 1·4 seconds at mid-frequencies with a full audience of 400. The much admired Altes Gewandhaus (1780) in Leipzig (see fig. 26), also a narrow rectangular hall, accommodated the same audience and had a reverberation time of only 1·3 seconds (Beranek). This building, in which Mendelssohn held his concerts from 1835 to 1846, was entirely constructed of wood, securely jointed, which lent the hall the quality of an immense musical instrument.

The development of the orchestra in the early years of the 19th century seems to have given rise to the desire for more sustained reverberation. When the first large halls were constructed specifically for concerts, in the middle of the century, they had longer reverberation times and a lower ratio of direct to reflected sounds. The old Boston Music Hall (1863) had a reverberation time

at mid-frequencies of over 1·8 seconds with an audience of 2400; the Grosser Musikvereinssaal (1870) in Vienna had a reverberation time of 2 seconds with an audience of over 2000.

Wagner wished the architects of the Bayreuth Festspielhaus (1876) to create a building that would enhance the orchestral sound but still permit the work to be intelligible. At length the reverberation time of 1·6 seconds at mid-frequencies was arrived at, with a full audience of 1800. An important development was the complete sinking of the orchestra pit so that the musicians could no longer distract the audience by their movements (see fig.27). A carefully shaped orchestra chamber projects the sound, but at the same time blends the orchestral tones so that instruments cannot be heard individually. The steeply raked, fan-shaped parterre permits clear vision of the stage and ensures minimum shading of direct sound from the singers by the heads of the audience in front. Also, the paired columns along the sides of the seating towards the stage act as acoustic reflectors, diffusing the sound effectively.

Not all concert halls were acoustically satisfactory. The Royal Albert Hall (1871) in London was regarded as disastrous from its opening when 'The Prince of Wales' ... welcoming address ... in many parts ... could be heard twice, a curious echo bringing a repetition of one sentence as the next was begun'. Of immense size, 90,000 m³, and an awkward shape, elliptical in plan with a huge dome, the Albert Hall seats 5000 people. The reverberation time must have exceeded 3 seconds when it was opened, and it remains 2·5 seconds after extensive correction (see fig.28). Such a hall only begins to function satisfactorily when orchestral and choral forces are large. Nevertheless the visually unifying shape of the Albert Hall is preferred by many performers and listeners to the more acoustically desirable rectangular shape of other famous concert halls.

The undoubted acoustic success of the Paris Opéra's

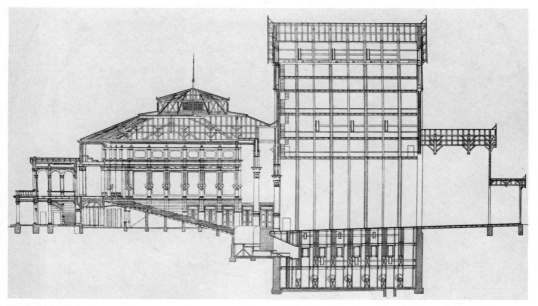

27. Section of the Bayreuth opera house from Sachs and Woodrow, 'Modern Opera Houses and Theatres', i (1896)

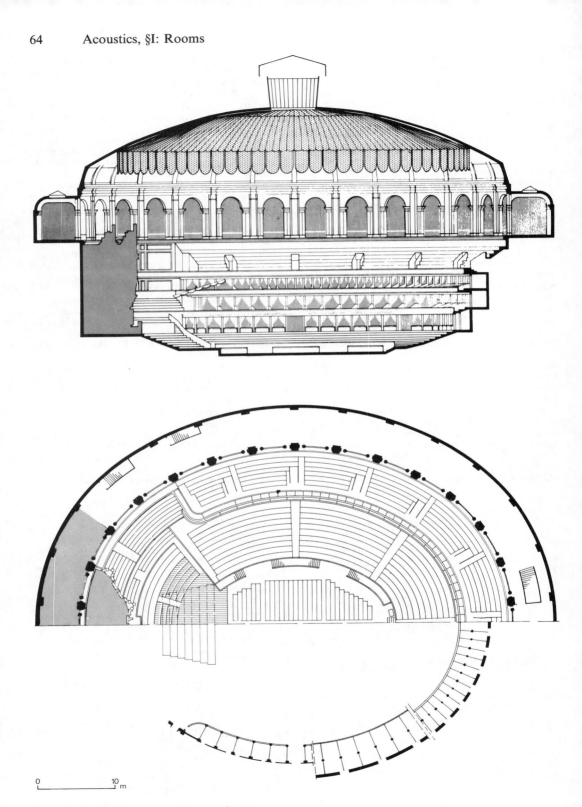

28. *Plan and section of the Royal Albert Hall, London, 1871 (after Beranek)*

building (1869–75) was shrugged off by the architect, Charles Garnier:

I gave myself great pains to master this bizarre science [of acoustics] but ... nowhere did I find a positive rule to guide me; on the contrary, nothing but contradictory statements.... I must explain that I have adopted no principle, that my plan has been based on no theory, and that I leave success or failure to chance alone ... like the acrobat who closes his eyes and clings to the ropes of an ascending balloon.

11. THE SCIENCE OF ACOUSTICS. The science of acoustics received its name from Sauveur, its first noted exponent, who discovered and studied overtones at the beginning of the 18th century. His work was further developed by Euler, who devised a system of binary logarithms to facilitate musical calculations. Ernst Chladni's *Akustik* (1802) contained his studies of the vibration of strings, rods and plates by means of sand figures and his discovery of the modal lines. Charles Delezenne (1776–1866) applied calculus to the solution of acoustic problems, and Félix Savart (1791–1840) made investigations into resonance, especially in string instruments. D. B. Reid of Edinburgh published in 1835 his 'On the Construction of Public Buildings in Reference to the Communication of Sound' (*Transactions of the British Association*). It shows an accurate application of recent discoveries in physics to room acoustics, and contains the earliest clear recognition of reverberation.

Hermann von Helmholtz (1821–94) laid the foundations for much modern physical and physiological research in acoustics. Rudolf Koenig (1832–1901) manufactured instruments for the study of acoustics and conducted extensive research. Others who followed closely behind were John Tyndall (*Sound*, 1867), Lord Rayleigh (*Theory of Sound*, 1877–8) and Carl Stumpf (*Psychology of Tone*, 1883–90). Stumpf's insistence that the scientific system of music theory depended on the psychological interpretation of acoustic data opened a new discipline and many new avenues for research.

W. C. Sabine pioneered the study of applied acoustics in buildings in the period 1895–1915, publishing his results in a series of important papers. Sound decay was analysed in detail and the prediction of reverberation time in rectangular rooms by calculation was made possible. The impedance method of specifying acoustical materials was developed, and a wide variety of acoustical materials began to be manufactured. At the Bell Telephone Laboratories, Harvey Fletcher studied loudness and masking in the 1920s and 1930s, and developed new, more accurate techniques of acoustic analysis and measurement. Other research laboratories, especially those in California, England and Germany, contributed to rapid advances in scientific acoustics.

The first large-scale experiment in the application of the new scientific understanding of acoustics to room design came with the building of the Salle Pleyel in Paris (1927), which seated 3000; it was a 'notorious disappointment' (Beranek). The whole shape of the hall, in plan and section, was designed to send sound to the audience (see fig.29). Sound diffusion was poor and uneven, and reverberation short. The result was a room in which a large audience could enjoy recitals and chamber music, but in which orchestral music lacked body and colour. In addition, the seats in the front and middle of the parterre received their first reflections from the ceiling, high at this point, with too long a delay after the direct sound, resulting in the loss of any sense of intimacy (Knudsen).

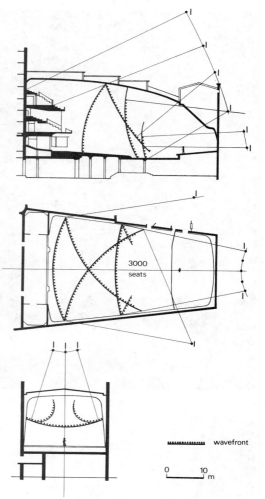

29. *Plan and section of the Salle Pleyel, Paris, 1927, showing the waves from various surfaces and the theoretical positions of the images* (*I*) *from which they originate* (*after Bagenal and Wood*)

After the disappointment of the Salle Pleyel, no major attempt to apply the new scientific knowledge of acoustics to design was made until the building of the Royal Festival Hall in 1948–51 (*see* LONDON, fig.30). Great care was taken to avoid external and internal noise interference (see fig.11); the entire auditorium was raised high in the air and a double construction used to isolate the interior. In this respect the hall was an important and successful experiment. The interior was designed along principles not dissimilar from those of the Salle Pleyel, and with some of the latter's defects. In particular, concentrating the first reflections at the audience by reflectors over almost the whole ceiling means that a large proportion of the sound energy is absorbed in a much shorter time than the reverberation time of the hall. The effect is to make reverberation much less evident than it is in the older concert halls because it is relatively less loud, and so the hall seems 'dry', especially in loud ensemble passages.

30. *Tanglewood Music Shed, Lenox, Massachusetts*

31. *Beethovenhalle, Bonn: a continuous diffusing ceiling is made up of various semispherical and pyramidal shapes*

32. Maltings Concert Hall, Snape

Later advances in acoustics have therefore concentrated on finding methods of increasing the amplitude and the length of reverberation while maintaining a high level of direct and first-reflection sound to all the seats. One solution is that adopted with success in the Tanglewood Music Shed in Lenox, Massachusetts (1959; fig.30); a pattern of suspended ceiling panels reflects a proportion of the sound to the audience from quite a short distance above the orchestra, while the spaces between allow the rest of the sound to travel into the volume above, where it is diffused before returning as prolonged reverberation. A defect of this technique is that sounds of short wavelength are almost completely reflected by the panels, whereas sounds of long wavelength pass almost completely around them, giving an imbalance in first reflections and a further imbalance in reverberation. Such problems led to the initial failure of one of the major concert halls to be built in the 1960s, Philharmonic Hall at the Lincoln Center in New York (1961).

Other recent concert halls have concentrated on relating the volume carefully to the type of music for which the hall is built, achieving ceilings that give a maximum of diffusion of sound and providing only a few reflectors of direct sound close to the orchestra. The result has been a considerable increase in the reverberation time; the Maltings at Snape, Suffolk (1967; fig. 32), for example, has a reverberation time of 2·25 seconds at midfrequencies, whereas the Royal Festival Hall, with a volume nearly three times as large, has a reverberation time of only 1·47 seconds. This is in accordance with research that has suggested that a listener's acoustical impression of a hall depends on the first reflections heard after the direct sound. If the reflections follow closely (within 0·01 seconds) he has an impression of 'intimacy'. It is in this way that one registers 'acoustical space'; it is therefore important to reinforce sound using reflectors near the source. The longer reverberation provides fullness of tone and gives the performer a sense of 'response' from the room. In addition, new concert halls, such as the De Doelen Hall in Rotterdam, have more

uniform reverberation, and the balance between low and high frequencies is carefully maintained. It seems likely that acoustical criteria may lead in the future to the replacement of general-purpose concert halls by those designed specifically for particular types and styles of music.

BIBLIOGRAPHY
O. Belli: 'History of Candia', in E. Falkener: *Museum of Classical Antiquities* (London, 1854)
G. M. Hills: 'Earthenware Pots (Built into Churches) which have been called Acoustic Vases', *Transactions of the Royal Institute of British Architects* (1882), 65
A. Müller: *Lehrbuch der Griechischen Bühnenalterthümer*, ii (Freiburg, 1886), 46
H. Bagenal and A. Wood: *Planning for Good Acoustics* (London, 1931)
V. O. Knudsen: *Architectural Acoustics* (New York, 1932)
P. V. Brüel: 'Panel Absorbants of the Helmholtz type', *First Summer Symposium of the Acoustics Group: Papers on Resonant Absorbers* (London, 1947)
F. Giorgi: 'Memorandum for S. Francesco della Vigna', in R. Wittkower: *Architectural Principles in the Age of Humanism* (London, 1949)
P. H. Parkin and H. R. Humphreys: *Acoustics, Noise and Buildings* (London, 1958, 3/1969)
L. L. Beranek: *Music, Acoustics and Architecture* (New York, 1962)
H. J. Purkis: 'The Reverberation Times of some English Cathedrals', *Bulletin of the Institute of Physics and the Physical Society* (1963), no.14, p.8.
G. R. Jones, T. I. Hempstock, K. A. Mulholland and M. A. Stott: *Teach yourself Acoustics* (London, 1966)
J. G. Landels: 'Assisted Resonance in Ancient Theatres', *Greece and Rome*, xiv (1967), 80
K. Harrison: 'Vitruvius and Acoustic Jars in England during the Middle Ages', *Transactions of the Ancient Monuments Society*, xv (1967–8), 49
R. Taylor: *Noise* (London, 1970)
R. S. and H. K. Shankland: 'Acoustics of St Peter's and Patriarchal Basilicas in Rome', *Journal of the Acoustical Society of America*, 1 (1971), 2
C. Gilford: *Acoustics for Radio and Television Studios* (London, 1972)
A. H. Benade: *Fundamentals of Musical Acoustics* (New York, 1976)

II. String instruments

1. Foundations. 2. Bowing. 3. The mute and vibrato. 4. Differences between viols and violins. 5. Violins: development, string tension and varnish. 6. The plucked string. 7. Current research.

1. FOUNDATIONS. The acoustic centre of any string instrument is the string. Its action under the fingers and the bow, its responsiveness, and even the problems it forces the player to solve are major factors in establishing the musical identity of a family of instruments. The essence of the bowed string families (violins and viols) and of the plucked strings (guitars and lutes) is in each case a set of strings mounted on a wooden box containing an almost enclosed air space. Some energy from the vibrations of the strings is communicated through the bridge to the box and air space, in which are set up corresponding vibrations. The loudness and nature of the sound, putting aside the acoustics of the room and the skill of the player, depend on the transfer of vibration from the strings to sounding box to air.

The sounding box, or body, of a string instrument is like a bell in one important respect. When it is tapped or struck lightly a multitude of notes, covering many octaves, is set into vibration, though of course this is more obvious with the bell than with the sounding box. The luthier is deeply concerned with the frequencies of these 'tap tones', or resonances, and with the patterns of their amplitudes over the surface of the instrument; the old masters were certainly aware of these facts, even though they tested them with their hands and ears rather than electronically. The body of a good instrument, therefore, has to be tuned to the frequency range in which it is to be used, the many resonances being

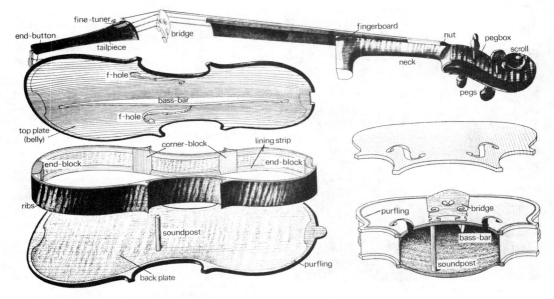

33. Exploded diagram of a viola (after Hutchins, 1962)

suitably spaced within that range. A superb one must also have the best possible distribution of activity over its surface. The combination of the vibrating string as generator, providing a wide range of harmonics, and the sounding box as resonator, responding selectively according to its pattern of resonances, is the basis of a string instrument.

A vibrating string by itself produces almost no sound for two reasons: it is so thin that almost no air is disturbed; and two diametrically opposite sides of the string are so close together that though the air on one side is compressed at a given moment and on the other rarefied, the two effects are so close that they arrive at the listener almost exactly together, thus cancelling each other. In order to avoid cancellation, one vibration must arrive earlier than the other by a substantial fraction of its vibration period.

The design of a musical sounding board or instrument box must circumvent these pitfalls. In the piano, the single soundboard is effective because its dimensions exceed, or at least are not negligible by comparison with, the wavelengths of the pitches throughout much of its compass. The upper and lower sides radiate with sufficient independence that their radiations do not cancel each other, even though the two surfaces of the single board move in identical patterns and to the same degree. When a single soundboard is smaller than the wavelengths of sounds coming from it, the radiations from the two sides tend to cancel each other when heard from a distance. This is why the bowed and plucked string instruments use a box in which the two surfaces possess different patterns and amplitudes of vibration which support each other within an important range of frequencies. Unlike the single soundboard, the top and back, under favourable conditions, can move inward or outward at a given moment so that almost the entire surface of an instrument cooperates to change the volume of displaced air, thus acting as a 'Nullstrahler' or 'simple source', at least in the lower frequency range (see Cremer, 1971).

In bowed string instruments this volume change in the body, so important to the sounds in the lower octaves, is made possible by the asymmetrical interior arrangement of the soundpost and bass-bar (see fig.33). When the bow is pulled across the string parallel to the top of the instrument, a rocking motion is set up in the bridge so that the forces that the two feet of the bridge exert downward are in 'push–pull' relationship with one pressing down and the other up in opposite phase. If the box had complete bilateral symmetry there would be no volume change, for the motion of one foot would completely offset the effect of the other. As it is, however, the soundpost beneath the right foot of the bridge (as the violinist sees it), firmly coupling the top to the more rigid back, tends to immobilize the right foot, while at the same time enhancing the motion of the left foot (see Schelleng, 1971), so causing important changes in the bodies of violins and viols to occur in step with the left bridge foot. This creation of asymmetry is the chief acoustical function of the soundpost, called in French 'l'âme'; its position, shape, wood quality and fitting can be highly critical to the performance of an instrument.

The bass-bar, running the length of the top plate approximately under the string of lowest tuning, tends to keep the vibrations of the upper and lower areas of the top plate in step with the left foot of the bridge. It is glued in such a way as to lend static strength to the thin wood of the top plate, which together with the soundpost, must support a downward force from the strings of 7–9 kg in the violin itself. The final shaping of the bass-bar is one of the most critical tasks in the proper thinning, or 'tuning', of the top plate (see Hutchins: 'Progress Report', 1973).

The soundholes, f-shaped in the violin family, and C-shaped or flame-shaped in the viol family, have two chief acoustical purposes: first to reduce the stiffness of the floor on which the bridge stands; and second to form a Helmholtz resonator. The rocking motion of the bridge, in addition to being affected by the bass-bar and sound-post, is limited by the stiffness of the wood between the soundholes (see Minnaert and Vlam, and Reinicke). In the violin family the thickness and width of the wood between the upper ends of the holes is particularly important. This reduction in stiffness provides a suitably tapered transition between the bridge and radiating areas of the top plate (see Hutchins, 1962, and Schelleng, 1963). The second function of the soundholes is to strengthen the sound in the lowest octave of the instrument. They are not simply openings to 'let the sound out of the box' generally over the frequency range; together with the walls of the box, the sound-holes, or ports, form a Helmholtz resonator. The frequency of the Helmholtz resonance depends on the volume of air enclosed and the equivalent area of the soundholes, as well as on the flexibility or compliance of the walls. Savart reported in 1819 an effect often over-looked, that the insertion of the soundpost causes an increase in the frequency of both the air and the wood vibrations of the violin. In both viol and violin families this Helmholtz resonance is usually the lowest fundamental resonance in the spectrum of the instrument. Reinforcement of sounds below this comes from the effect of strong resonances higher up. For example, the strong resonance characteristically near a' in the violin acts as the second harmonic reinforcing a on the G string (see Hutchins: 'Instrumentation and Methods for Violin Testing', 1973).

Some unknown inventor discovered the usefulness of holes in the bodies of string instruments long before the invention of the somewhat similar 'reflex bass' of loud-speakers. The air in and about the ports swings rapidly in and out against the compression and rarefaction of the air within, thus providing the mass and stiffness necessary to a simple harmonic vibrator. Within a considerable range about the frequency of resonance,

radiation due to the motion of air in the soundholes reinforces that arising directly at the outside surface of the box. According to simple acoustic theory this enhancement becomes zero at half an octave below resonance, a theoretical justification for the common practice in violin making of placing the Helmholtz air resonance of the violin near C♯–D on the G string (see Hutchins, 1962, and Schelleng, 1963).

Fig.34a, which shows the distribution and intensity of sounds produced by an excellent violin when the force exerted by the bow on the bridge is simulated electronically, using a sine-wave sweeping from 20 Hz to 20,000 Hz, illustrates the abundance of resonances encountered (see Meyer). The peak near 275 Hz is the Helmholtz air resonance already described. The others, with possible exceptions, are resonances in the wood. Fig. 34b shows a 'loudness curve' made by bowing each semitone for an octave on each string as loudly as possible and measuring the intensity levels in decibels with a sound-level meter. Note that there is a resonance near g (196 Hz) not found with a sine-wave input. This occurs because the resonance peak near g represents not a fundamental but a 'subharmonic' (see Hutchins, Hopping and Saunders, 1960), which is strong in the wide-band input from the bowed string where the resonance at 392 Hz acts as the second partial, reinforcing the lower octave.

2. BOWING. When a bow is drawn across the string, the string appears to widen in a smooth ribbon of a lenticular shape; but this is an optical illusion. To a first approximation, the string under the bow takes the form of a sharply bent straight line, a phenomenon noted by Helmholtz. A slow-motion camera would show this bend, or discontinuity, moving around the lenticular path extending between the ends of the string as in fig.35. The 'stick–slip' action of the bow on the string, though somewhat similar to the chattering of a piece of chalk on a blackboard or the squeaking of a chair leg across the floor, is more complicated. As the discontinuity, or kink, moving from nut to bridge, passes the bow it dislodges the string from the hair to which it has been clinging and reverses the string's motion. When the discontinuity returns from the bridge it restores the forward motion of the string, which again sticks to the hairs. The bow is thus freed from the string not as a result of the gradual increase in stress between the rosined hair and the rosined string, but because the kink has arrived to set it loose. During the time of sticking, motion is in one direction followed by a quick snap back in the other on release, thus giving the saw-tooth wave-form of fig.36. If the motion of fig.36a is produced by a down-bow, the entire pattern will be reversed by an up-bow as in fig.36b. A vivid experiment to illustrate the change in direction as the kink moves around the lenticular path is shown in fig.37.

Under the repetitive action of the bow the many partials, all simultaneously present, are kept in simple multiple relationship to the fundamental frequency even though the string may have a little stiffness. Stiffness in a string causes the partials to be somewhat higher in frequency than harmonic partials would be. In present-day strings the amount of stiffness is of little consequence, but when gut was the only material available for the heavier strings it was largely stiffness that made the G string of the violin family unsatisfactory. Metal and gut strings differ in tone quality when played open

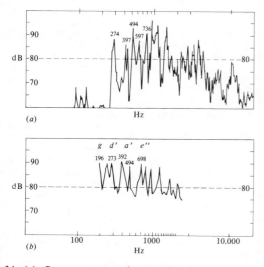

34. (a) Response curve showing the distribution and intensity of sounds produced by a violin when the force exerted on the bridge is simulated electronically; (b) loudness curve obtained on the same violin by bowing each semitone for an octave on each string as loudly as possible

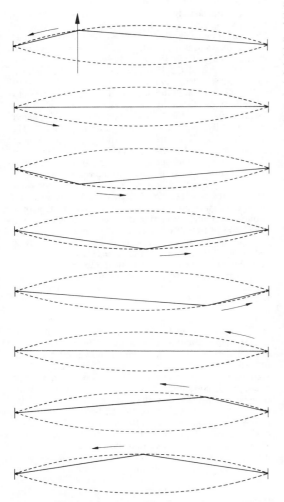

35. *Shapes taken by a bowed string at a series of discrete points in time (solid lines) as the kink created at the point of bowing travels to the fixed end of the string and back once in every vibration, causing the optical illusion of a lenticular curve (dotted lines) (after Schelleng, 1974)*

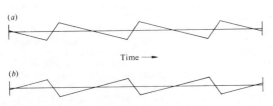

36. *Saw-tooth waveforms of string displacement produced by the alternate sticking and release of the rosined string by the rosined bow hair (a) when bowed with a down-bow, (b) with an up-bow*

string because the relative absence of internal friction in metal permits greater response at higher harmonics. This difference is reduced in the fingered string by the soft, inelastic nature of the fingertip. The rubber dampers used with metal strings help to control this effect. Also, the higher harmonics are reduced by the practice of making wound metal strings with a core of several thin wires, sometimes braided, covered with two or three layers of wrapping.

It may not be obvious to some players that the bowed string is tolerant to a wide range of bow 'pressures' (technically 'bow force'), and that this is indeed a condition without which playing would be all but impossible. For any given bow velocity and location with respect to the bridge there is a minimum and a maximum tolerable pressure. Below the minimum the friction between hair and string becomes insufficient for proper sticking. Above the maximum it is too great to allow the string to detach itself when it should. In the first case the fundamental vibration gives place to a higher mode (at first to the octave); in the second a simple periodic vibration gives way to one of raucous irregularity. Fig.38 illustrates the different domains of bowing for one particular case. Within the area labelled 'normal', as pressure increases from minimum to maximum the content of higher harmonics increases with corresponding changes in tone-colour. If Helmholtz's approximation (see above) were strictly true, tone quality would be independent of location and pressure of the bow and, relative to usual experience, would be considered brilliant because of the strong harmonic content of the sawtooth wave of fig.36a. Reduction of pressure lengthens the duration of slipping (to as much as doubling that indicated by Helmholtz) and smoothes the corners of fig.36a, thus reducing high harmonics. This decrease is most noticeable when the bow is furthest from the bridge and pressure is near the minimum, that is, when one plays *sul tasto*. A similar increase in brilliance occurs as the bow approaches the bridge. Increase in velocity (bow speed) with corresponding increase in pressure is the common way of increasing loudness without change in tone-colour. Within limits, loudness is affected by any one of these parameters alone (velocity, position, pressure). Normally the player must have all three of these in mind in order to produce the proper combination of volume and tone quality. For further information on the acoustics of bowing, see Cremer (1972–3) and Schelleng (1973, 1974).

Bowed string instruments frequently display a disconcerting phenomenon known as the 'wolf' note, a narrow range of frequency within which response tends to stutter in a raucous manner (see Schelleng, 1963, and Firth and Buchanan). In most cases this occurs at or very near the frequency of the most prominent resonance of the body of the instrument, at which the wood is moving vigorously. The wolf occurs at this frequency because the bridge is unable to provide a solid enough support for the vibrations, particularly of the heavier lower strings. Among members of the violin family, the viola and cello are most subject to this difficulty, which occurs in the viola around *f–f♯* on the G and C strings, and on the cello around *E* on the G and C strings. The heavier the string the more prominent the wolf. The usual cure is to attach a mass such as the commercial wolf-eliminator (a blob of plasticene will do) to the string between the bridge and tailpiece so that this portion of the string has the same frequency of natural

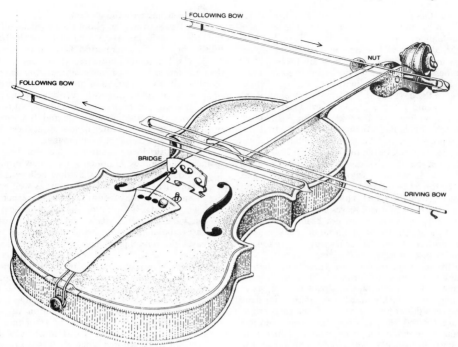

37. *'Following bow' experiment to demonstrate the action of a bowed string: a light (following) bow is suspended at its heavy end, with the point resting on a string near the bridge; a second (driving) bow sets the string in motion, and after a short period of slipping the suspended bow begins to follow in the same direction as the driving bow, thus indicating the direction of string motion during the longer interval of each vibration (when the suspended bow is placed at the opposite end of the string it moves in the opposite direction from the driving bow) (after Schelleng, 1974)*

vibration as that of the wolf. To do this the bridge should be made relatively immobile by attaching to it a heavy mute or weight, and the mass and position of the eliminator adjusted until the frequency of the wolf is matched, as judged by plucking the string lightly and listening.

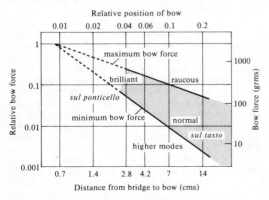

38. *Graph indicating the normal playing range for a bowed string instrument at constant bow velocity; the maximum and minimum bow force tend towards equality when the bow is very close to the bridge and diverge when it is further away (after Schelleng, 1974)*

3. THE MUTE AND VIBRATO. The mute, which consists merely of a suitable mass attached to the top of the bridge, changes both the volume and quality of the sound. Its tendency to immobilize the top of the bridge increases with frequency, so that higher tones are reduced and timbre becomes softer and less brilliant; the loudness of sound is correspondingly reduced. The low partial notes of the instrument are not greatly affected, but the loudness of the low notes is indirectly reduced by virtue of the 'residue effect'. According to this, the subjective sensation of fundamental pitch produced by the higher harmonics is somewhat reduced.

Of vibrato, much has been written from a musical point of view. Here only the physical characteristics will be considered, namely the changes in frequency level (recognized by the ear as pitch changes), intensity level (loudness), and variations in harmonic structure of the sound. The changes in pitch as the finger moves back and forth on the string are quite familiar. This motion causes all the harmonics to have the same rate of pitch variation as the vibrato rate, typically four to six per second. The intensity level of each harmonic also varies at this rate, but is different for each harmonic, some having a high intensity level and some a very low. Also, for some of the harmonics the intensity level is increasing, while at the same time it is decreasing for others. These variations cause the aurally pleasing changes in the quality of the sound of notes played with vibrato. For further details see Fletcher and Sanders.

4. DIFFERENCES BETWEEN VIOLS AND VIOLINS. So far the common features of bowed instruments, both viol and violin families, have been considered. Turning to the differences: although viols and violins both have arched top plates made of spruce, with the grain following the longer dimension, the tops of viols tend to have somewhat higher archings and slightly thinner wood than violins. Since the days of the highly arched violins of the Amati family and Jacobus Stainer, there seems to have developed a preference for the flatter archings and more powerful tone of violins similar to those of Stradivari and Giuseppi Guarneri. All these early masters carefully matched the arch of the top to the arch of the back of a violin. On the other hand, viols traditionally have a thin flat back of beautiful wood, usually curly maple. This is reinforced at several places with fairly heavy cross braces, including one on which the soundpost rests. Thus the back of a viol serves as a support for the soundpost, but traditionally has not been 'tuned' as in the case of the violin. In the violin family back and top plates are both tuned, the frequencies of the tap tone or 'ring mode' (see Hutchins: 'Progress Report', 1973) differing by not more than two or three semitones, as Savart discovered in 1830. Instead of the four strings characteristic of the violin family, viols have five, six or more strings, more slackly tuned than violin strings and supported on a flatter heavier bridge. Often their fingerboards are crossed by gut frets, and their tailpieces heavier and more rigidly supported than in violins. Thus viols have less brilliance, power and dynamic range than violins.

5. VIOLINS: DEVELOPMENT, STRING TENSION AND VARNISH. Few changes were made in the structure of classical violins until the early 19th century, when there was a demand for increased power. To achieve this violin makers lengthened the neck by slightly more than a centimetre and increased its angle to the plane of the violin body, while at the same time enlarging the bassbar to provide appropriate stiffness and support. The resultant increase in string tension and the more acute angle of the strings at the bridge provided greater force from the strings through the bridge to the top of the violin. These changes gave the desired increase in power and dynamic range in modern violins. The thin-wooded, highly arched instruments apparently have not responded as well to these changes as those having thicker wood and flatter archings. With the increase of interest in early music many of the former are now being restored to their original condition to play the chamber music for which they were intended.

In spite of their frail structure, the instruments of the violin family are able to withstand the large tension of the strings; that in the violin is around 25 kg weight and that in the cello over 45 kg weight. In the violin this tension exerts a downward force through the bridge on the top plate of 7–9 kg weight, and on the cello there is a correspondingly larger force. In any given case the string tension is determined uniquely by the length, mass and frequency of the vibrating section of the string, and is independent of other factors. If a gut string and one of steel have the same mass per unit length, the tensions will be identical. The idea that a steel string is inherently harder on an instrument than a gut one is true only to the extent that heavier strings are used, or that the instrument is left unused with strings up to pitch for long periods during which changes in moisture in the body tend to increase the tension.

Much has been written about the beneficial effects on tone of the early varnishes, particularly of the beautiful finishes of the 'Cremona period' used on violins around 1800. Until recently, however, there has been little documentation based on physical measurements of the changes in the violin sound or in the vibrating properties of spruce and maple caused by various coatings. These coatings are of two basic types: the undercoat (sealer or filler) applied to the clear wood; and the varnish or protective coating of greater or lesser thickness depending on the methods of the violin maker.

There is little documentation of the acoustical effects of the undercoatings, although work is now in progress. Many violin makers report that they believe this is an important element in tone production as well as in the preservation of the wood. However, experimental evidence provides information on the acoustical effects of the varnish itself. Meinel found that 'varnishing increases the damping ... and that a hard varnish increases the damping at higher frequencies less than does a soft varnish'. Schelleng's measurements (1968) show that there is a decrease of motion in radiating plates, more or less uniformly throughout the spectrum, of about 1 dB due to added impedance of the varnish layer. Also, the increase in damping, as well as loss from internal friction caused by the addition of varnish, superposes additional reductions at resonance peaks. This reduction can amount to as much as 4 dB, an amount not to be ignored when 5 dB (see Lottermoser and Meyer) can be the measure of difference between an instrument of extraordinary power and one that is too weak.

In addition to overall changes, tests show that the spruce wood of the violin top and the maple used in the back respond differently to the coatings, especially with respect to cross-grain stiffness and damping. This means that the careful tuning of the plates, especially the top with the bass-bar, is altered markedly by the addition of filler and varnish. Violin makers are accustomed to compensating as far as possible for this effect, but many of them report that a violin 'in the white' sounds better than after it is varnished. Evidence indicates that the 'secret of varnish' may well be a method of providing adequate protection and acceptable appearance with the least possible material.

6. THE PLUCKED STRING. When the string is plucked, the pull of the finger creates a kink, or discontinuity, that divides the string into two straight sections. On release, a dynamic condition is set up in which two discontinuities travel in opposite directions, one towards the bridge and one towards the nut. These are identical to the modes of motion described for the up-bow and down-bow action in the bowed string. Since they are now both present at the same time, however, the wave shape of the force exerted on the bridge is radically different from that of the bowed string. In the bowed string, the Helmholtz approximation indicates a sawtooth wave in which reversal is instantaneous regardless of the position of the bow on the string (fig.39a). This differs from fig.36a, which shows displacement at the bow where the shape of the curve depends on bow position. With the plucked string, on the other hand, the force at the bridge has a rectangular shape that depends entirely on the point of plucking. If plucking occurs at the middle of the string, the shape is that of a square

wave with a minimal content of the higher overtones (fig.39b). If the pluck is near the bridge or nut, a sharp rectangular wave is produced which is exceedingly rich in high-frequency components (fig.39c). Thus a wider range of timbre is possible by changing the point of plucking than by changing the point of bowing. The actual change, however, is less than expected on ideal assumptions, because, in plucking, the high-frequency components die out more rapidly than in bowing, where they are maintained by the repetitive stick–slip action.

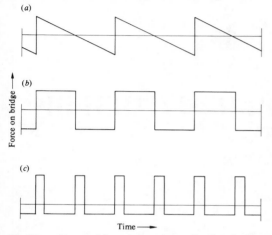

39. Wave shapes of force (not to be confused with those of displacement shown in fig.35) of a vibrating string on the bridge: (a) a bowed string, (b) a string plucked at its centre, (c) a string plucked near the bridge

Another important difference between bowing and plucking is that in the first case the phenomenon is periodic, so that overtones are kept in a strictly harmonic relationship to the fundamental. With plucking, on the other hand, any stiffness in the string – and this is important in the guitar and lute – makes the higher overtones sharper than integral multiples of the fundamental. As in the piano, this lends a highly desirable and characteristic colour to the tone of plucked string instruments. Since a plucked string instrument is designed to resonate at a single impact or pluck, a long ring, or decay time, is of prime importance. For this reason, a wood such as rosewood, which characteristically has a long ring, or low damping, is usually preferred for the back and sides of the guitar, with spruce for the top. The use of large, thin, flat plates in guitar construction also helps enhance the amplitude as well as duration and quality of the sounds produced.

7. CURRENT RESEARCH. It is apparent that, in respect to quantitative analysis and the predetermining of the effects of structure, wind instruments possess two important advantages over strings: their shapes are amenable to simpler mathematical description, and the resonating material, air, is homogeneous, with the same elasticity in all directions. By contrast, the shapes of string instruments, while a delight to the connoisseur, are forbidding to the mathematician, and the resonating material, wood, is neither homogeneous nor isotropic, and cannot be standardized. This uncertain property of wood is not a serious difficulty in woodwind instruments because their massive walls do not share vitally in the resonance

of the instrument. The result has been that designers of wind instruments have had the possibility, which they have brilliantly used, of forecasting the effects of changes in design, while the scientific luthier has been far more dependent on a series of steps in carving the plates of his instruments, each step guided by the best means at his disposal.

Since the mid-1950s eight instruments of the violin family, one at each half octave from the tuning of the double bass to an octave above the violin, have been developed through an effective combination of mathematics, acoustical theory and testing, and skilled violin making (see Hutchins, 1962 and 1967, and Hutchins and Bram). Designed to project the resonance characteristics of the violin into seven other tone ranges, these instruments (see fig.40) provide consistent quality of string tone covering the musical range and bring to fruition a concept of Praetorius. These same techniques are being applied to the construction of fine-sounding conventional violins, violas, cellos and basses.

Thus it is by improvement in methods of test and a coordination of skills and knowledge that a significant advance is being realized in the art and science of making string instruments.

BIBLIOGRAPHY

M. Praetorius: *Syntagma musicum*, ii (Wolfenbüttel, 1618, 2/1619/R1958), 26

F. Savart: *L'institut*, viii/67–71 (1840)

M. G. J. Minnaert and C. C. Vlam: 'The Vibrations of the Violin Bridge', *Physica*, iv (1937), 361

W. Lottermoser and J. Meyer: 'Akustische Prufung der Klangqualität von Geigen', *IZ*, xii (1957), 42

H. F. Meinel: 'Regarding the Sound Quality of Violins and a Scientific Basis for Violin Construction', *Journal of the Acoustical Society of America*, xxix (1957), 817

C. M. Hutchins, A. S. Hopping and F. A. Saunders: 'Subharmonics and Plate Tap Tones in Violin Acoustics', *Journal of the Acoustical Society of America*, xxxii (1960), 1443

C. M. Hutchins: 'The Physics of Violins', *Scientific American* (1962), Nov, 78

J. C. Schelleng: 'The Violin as a Circuit', *Journal of the Acoustical Society of America*, xxxv (1963), 326

H. Fletcher and L. C. Sanders: 'Quality of Violin Vibrato Tones', *Journal of the Acoustical Society of America*, xli (1967), 1534

C. M. Hutchins: 'Founding a Family of Fiddles', *Physics Today*, xx (1967), 23

J. C. Schelleng: 'Acoustical Effects of Violin Varnish', *Journal of the Acoustical Society of America*, xliv (1968), 1175

L. Cremer: 'Die Geige aus Sicht des Physikers', *Nachrichten der Akademie der Wissenschaften in Göttingen*, ii, Mathematisch-Physikalische Klasse (1971), 12

J. C. Schelleng: 'The Action of the Soundpost', *Catgut Acoustical Society Newsletter*, no.16 (1971), 11

L. Cremer: 'The Influence of "Bow Pressure" on the Movement of the Bowed String', *Catgut Acoustical Society Newsletter*, no.18 (1972), 13; no.19 (1973), 21

E. Jansson: 'On the Acoustics of the Violin', *IMSCR*, xi Copenhagen 1972, 462

I. M. Firth and J. M. Buchanan: 'The Wolf in the Cello', *Journal of the Acoustical Society of America*, liii (1973), 457

C. M. Hutchins: 'Instrumentation and Methods for Violin Testing', *Journal of the Audio Engineering Society*, xxi (1973), 563

——: 'Progress Report on a Method of Checking Eigenmodes of Free Violin Plates during Instrument Construction', *Catgut Acoustical Society Newsletter*, no.19 (1973), 17

C. M. Hutchins and M. Bram: 'The Bowed Strings – Yesterday, Today, and Tomorrow', *Music Educators Journal* (1973), Nov, 20

W. Reinicke: 'Übertragungseigenschaften des Streichinstrumentenstegs', *Catgut Acoustical Society Newsletter*, no.19 (1973), 26

J. C. Schelleng: 'The Bowed String and the Player', *Journal of the Acoustical Society of America*, liii (1973), 26

——: 'The Physics of the Bowed String', *Scientific American* (1974), Jan, 87

J. Meyer: 'An Acoustical Method of Violin Testing', *Catgut Acoustical Society Newsletter*, no.23 (1975), 2

C. M. Hutchins, ed.: *Musical Acoustics* (Stroudsburg, 1975–6) [incl. reprs. of almost all articles above]

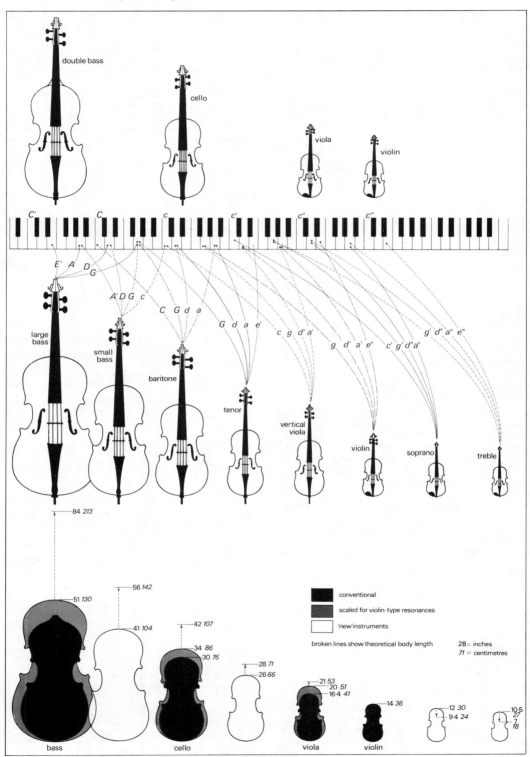

40. *An acoustically matched set of instruments of the violin family*

III. Keyboard string instruments

1. Foundations. 2. Clavichord. 3. Harpsichord. 4. Piano.

1. FOUNDATIONS. Keyboard string instruments are distinguished by key-operated mechanical devices which are used initially to shock the strings into free vibration, and finally to damp these free vibrations. Differences in the shape, size, material and function of these percussive and damping devices create most of the characteristic variations at the beginnings and ends of the notes. These differences also influence the timbre while the strings are vibrating freely, because the initial shock determines the waveform of the ensuing vibrations. There are other acoustical factors, such as the stiffness of the strings, the wrapping of the bass strings, the gradual damping of tone at the string supports, the number of strings per key, the acoustical properties of the structure supporting the strings and, in some cases, the effect of passive sympathetic strings.

The clavichord, harpsichord and piano all have systems of individually tuned strings lying approximately in a plane. Each string is under tension between a hitch-pin, secured in the string-supporting structure, and a tuning-pin which during tuning is screwed into and out of a wooden pinblock. Between these two pins and generally near each of them the string bears against a point of sliding contact. The distance between the two intermediate contact points defines the length of the tuned vibrating string segment. Each string can vibrate freely at a series of frequencies which would be a harmonic series if the string were perfectly flexible. Because wire strings have some stiffness (remotely resembling a bar) the series of natural frequencies for string vibration is slightly, but audibly, inharmonic. Research has shown that this minute degree of inharmonicity is an important characteristic of the timbre. The inharmonicity also causes the optimum tuning of the instrument scale to be slightly stretched (flat on low notes, sharp on high notes) from the strictly mathematical scale of 2:1 octaves.

In keyboard string instruments the playing-key action causes a dynamic string excitation event. Some impact sound occurs immediately at the point of impact, and more comes through the string vibration system soon after. This is the 'cause' sound. The nature of both the impact and of the resulting string excitation differs for each of the three major types of instrument, but in each case the shape of at least a portion of the tuned string segment is suddenly and momentarily changed. This string shape change is the pulse wave which travels up and down the string between the two contact points after the event occurs. This is the 'effect' sound.

The pulse wave is partially reflected back and forth repeatedly at the string contact points, causing the string vibration and the resulting note to sustain. However, some of the stored wave energy is removed during each reflection, eventually causing the note to die away. This vibratory energy, removed at the end of each round trip of the wave, vibrates the supporting structure, particularly the soundboard from which most of the note enters the air. Only a small part of the sound reaches the air directly from the motion of the strings. The string typically vibrates at many frequencies simultaneously. Because these frequencies lie almost in a harmonic series, the listener hears the combination as a single note having a pitch corresponding to the lowest frequency in the series. The relative amount of sound produced at each frequency within the complex tone largely determines the timbre during the 'effect' portion of the tone. This depends on the shape of the pulse given to the string at impact, the response of the contact point of the supporting structure at each frequency of string vibration and the efficiency of the structure at each frequency in the transformation of vibration into sound.

In Table 1 the structural and mechanical differences between the three major types of keyboard string instrument are shown; the acoustical effects are explained below. For diagrams of the mechanisms described below, see articles on individual instruments.

2. CLAVICHORD. The clavichord is typically a rectangular box with the keyboard occupying the left two-thirds of the long side. The strings are stretched in a horizontal plane from hitch-pins near the left end to tuning-pins near the right end. In the right end there is a very small horizontal soundboard supporting a bridge (sometimes segmented) which provides one of the downbearing contact points for each string. The longer bass strings are closest to the keyboard; the shorter treble strings are near the rear. Each playing key is pivoted on a balance-rail, and the key is guided by a rear pin which rides up and down in a vertical slot. The unique mechanical feature of the clavichord action is the tangent, a wedge-shaped piece of iron or brass borne upon the rear key extension. As the key is depressed, the tangent rises and strikes the string directly, remaining in contact with the string until the key is released. The tangent thus serves two functions: its impact creates the string excitation without the aid of any intermediate action mechanism; and it provides the second downbearing contact point for its associated string, thus defining the length of the vibrating string segment and controlling its pitch frequency. In other words, the striking point and the termination point of the tuned segment are the same.

In many clavichords the same string is used for several notes that would seldom be played in combination (e.g. C and C♯), by positioning the tangents at different points along the same string. Such instruments are known as fretted clavichords. Some others employ individual strings for greater musical versatility and better tuning.

The sustained contact between the key-borne tangent and the struck string gives the clavichordist a 'Bebung' tonal effect not obtainable with other keyboard string instruments. When the player varies the key force periodically (after striking) the string tension fluctuates, producing a pitch vibrato.

Between the tangent strike points and the hitch-pins there are strips of cloth interwoven among the strings. They quickly damp string vibrations to the left of the strike point where the string segment would not be properly tuned. They also damp the entire string vibration when the tangent contact with the string is released, making a separate damper action unnecessary.

Clavichords have several inherent acoustical advantages and disadvantages. The metal edge striking at the string termination excites a complete frequency series. The pulse shape sharpens with harder blows, giving dynamic range in brilliance. However, both the maximum tangent velocity and the area of the soundboard are so small that the clavichord is limited in output. The direct connection through the key from the player's finger to the string permits 'Bebung' vibrato, but it also provides mechanical damping which shortens note duration.

TABLE 1: Comparison of typical acoustical factors in keyboard string instruments

Factor		Clavichord	Harpsichord	Piano
STRINGS:	number per key	1 or less	1 per footage	2/3
	material	brass/steel	brass/steel	steel
	diameter, stiffness	smaller	smaller	larger
	tension	low	medium	high
	bass wrapping	—	fine gauge	heavier gauge
STRUCTURE:	string terminations	tangent, bridge	bridge, bridge	cast iron, bridge
	soundboard size	small	small to medium	medium to large
	structure material	wood	wood	metal and wood
	structure mass	light	medium	heavy
EXCITATION:	mode	strike–hold	pluck	strike–rebound
	exciter material	metal	quill, leather	felt
	exciter shape	edge	tapered	curved
	exciter size	small	small	large to medium
DAMPING:	mode	threaded through strings	jack weight/spring	damper head
	damper material	cloth	felt/cloth	felt
	damper shape	strip	flat	V/flat
	damper size	continuous	small	large

3. HARPSICHORD. Members of the harpsichord family have one of three orientations for the usually horizontally stretched strings. In the small, rectangular virginals the strings run crosswise as in the clavichord; in the small, wing-shaped spinet the strings extend obliquely from tuning-pins just behind the keyboard to hitch-pins in a row curving away to the right of the keyboard; and in the large harpsichord the strings extend directly away from the keyboard. This shape difference and the additional long bass strings make the harpsichord a larger instrument. Larger soundboards can provide greater tonal efficiency and fuller timbre.

In all three the strings are excited by the upward plucking action of a quill or plectrum which engages with, then releases the string. The plectrum projects from the central tongue portion of a narrow vertical jack which slides within guides, and is supported on the rear of the pivoted playing key. In large harpsichords there are two or more sets of strings and two or more manuals of keys. Thus different plectra borne by the same key can simultaneously pluck strings related by octave in the different string sets. The same string can also be plucked at different points along its length by plectra from different manuals. The closer the plectrum is to the string termination, the stronger are the higher, brighter partials of note. The farther away, the stronger are the lower partials. Plectra may be quill, leather, wood, metal or plastic. The harder materials and the sharpest edges give the brightest timbre.

The most important acoustical difference between harpsichords and other keyboard string instruments is the plucking initiation of notes. The smallness and the sharpness of the plectrum edge, and the suddenness of string release as the plectrum passes on, produce a string waveform with ample high-pitched partials, giving the characteristic brilliance of harpsichord tone. In contrast with clavichord action, the string exciter leaves the string immediately and cannot absorb string vibration and so shorten note duration. The return of the plectrum on release of the playing key often produces a weak second excitation of the string. This stroke is minimized by the curved shape of the plectrum underside and by the pivoting of the returning jack tongue. Although the resulting sound is a subtle characteristic of harpsichord tone, it happens so immediately before the jack-borne damper reaches the string that it sounds like part of the damping action.

4. PIANO. The first Cristofori piano was a harpsichord with the string-plucking action replaced by an upstriking hammer action with escapement. This freed the leather-covered hammer before impact, allowing it to strike the string and bounce back, in contrast with the tangent action of the clavichord. The hammer action gave both *piano* and *forte* levels with fully controlled gradations in between, introducing the era of keyboard dynamic expression. This instrument was the predecessor of the grand piano. The piano hammers were larger and more rounded than the previous tangents and plectra, imparting a larger, rounder pulse shape to the strings. This gave more power in the low partials and less in the higher ones, making piano tone fuller than that of the harpsichord. Hammer sizes and shapes were smaller and more pointed for high notes, where brilliance is needed.

Later a smaller piano was developed by combining a simple, upstriking hammer action with a string vibration system similar to that of the virginals. Because it was small, this piano was acoustically weak but considerably louder than the virginals. Many different action mechanisms were invented for this popular instrument, the predecessor of the rectangular or 'square' piano.

The substitution of hammers for plectra allowed multiple coplanar unison strings for each note, which had not been feasible in harpsichords. This increased tonal loudness and produced other advantages described below. Forward-striking hammer actions were developed for vertical piano string systems, requiring less floor space than horizontal pianos. Cast iron plates to support string forces and steel piano wire of higher tensile limits permitted larger wire diameters and higher-tension strings increasing tonal power and brilliance. Compressed felt replaced leather hammer covering, softening the tone and increasing hammer control and durability. Crossing bass strings over tenor strings reduced piano size, and more oblique cross stringing and drop actions led to the small vertical piano.

Multiple strings for each individual note contribute significantly to the distinctiveness of piano tone, adding a choral effect to each tone because of slight differences in string tuning. Research has shown that slight detuning of unison strings (less than 0.1%) is aurally preferred to mathematically exact tuning; experienced piano tuners typically leave this tuning margin. Immediately after piano hammer impact the multiple strings vibrate in close synchronism. At this time the rate of power transfer to the bridge and soundboard is maximal, causing rapid tone diminution initially. Later the strings gradually become asynchronous because their frequencies are slightly different, and the note dies away more slowly. This characteristic dual decay rate in well-tuned pianos lets successive notes stand out clearly over recently played, sustained notes, and this has influenced the development of composition for the piano. The vibrations of struck strings travel along the piano bridge to other strings, which can vibrate sympathetically when the sustaining pedal lifts the dampers, producing a stronger choral effect. In grand pianos the soft pedal moves the action transversely, reducing the number of strings the hammer strikes.

Except in the treble range, each piano note contains many partials, with the strongest lying between 100 and 1000 Hz. Hammer-string impact sound, which spreads throughout the pitch range, is an important characteristic of piano tone but is noticed only in the treble, where the partials are too sparsely spaced to conceal it.

Standard zero-beat procedures used by piano tuners for tuning octaves produce a stretched scale. Upper notes are higher and lower notes lower than strict equal temperament by about a third of a semitone at each extreme, an effect resulting from slight inharmonicity of the partials of string tone. Research has shown that pianists and listeners prefer the piano scale stretched this way, and attempts to synthesize true piano tone from a strictly harmonic series of partials have had limited success.

BIBLIOGRAPHY

Trendelenburg, Thienhaus and Franz: 'Zur Klangwirkung von Klavichord, Cembalo und Flügel', *Akustische Zeitschrift*, vi (1940)

D. Martin: 'Decay Rates of Piano Tones', *Journal of the Acoustical Society of America*, xix (1947), 535

R. Kirk: 'Tuning Preferences for Piano Unison Groups', *Journal of the Acoustical Society of America*, xxxi (1959), 1644

D. Martin and W. Ward: 'Subjective Evaluation of Musical Scale Temperament in Pianos', *Journal of the Acoustical Society of America*, xxxiii (1961), 582

IV. Wind instruments

1. Introduction. 2. Modes of oscillation of an air column. 3. Maintenance of oscillation. 4. Brass instruments. 5. Reed instruments. 6. Flute. 7. Wind instrument tone-colour.

1. INTRODUCTION. Every wind instrument consists of a long and carefully shaped duct coupled to an airflow control system that converts the steady wind supply from the player's lungs, or from the wind chest of a pipe organ, into oscillations of the instrument's air column. The mechanism for controlling the airflow can be the reed of a clarinet or bassoon, the vibrating lips of a trumpet player, or the less easily visualized steering of a jet of air from the flautist's lips as it travels across the embouchure hole. In each of these the flow control device sends puffs of air in a regularly varying sequence into the instrument's mouthpiece to keep the air column oscillating in its longitudinal vibratory motion. The nature and timing of these puffs are in turn controlled by acoustical variations taking place within the mouthpiece, these being a manifestation of the air column's own oscillations. In order to make this two-part oscillating system useful for musical purposes, the performer must be able to select one or another of the possible sounds that it can generate. A bugler who plays the

notes of a call is making such a selection, as is a woodwind player who uses a single fingering to sound notes in the bottom and second registers of his instrument. A musician is able to fill in the remaining gaps left in the musical scale by transforming the original air column of his instrument into a longer or shorter one. These will give alternative sets of sounds from which he can choose according to his needs. In brass instruments, changes in air column length are produced by the addition of various lengths of tubing in the middle of the air column, as exemplified by the slide of a trombone or the valve loops of a french horn. In woodwind instruments these length changes are accomplished by opening a greater or lesser number of tone holes arranged to pierce the air column wall at various points along it.

To be successful the design of a wind instrument must achieve several relationships between the air column and its flow control device: the two must be able to work together to permit the prompt and stable production of each one of the various notes in the scale, and these must be under good control by the player; the pitches of these notes must lie close to those belonging to the musical scale; and the tone-colour of the generated sounds must conform to aesthetic standards, which may vary from period to period and from nation to nation. The nature of these relationships and the way they may be attained is briefly outlined below.

2. MODES OF OSCILLATION OF AN AIR COLUMN. The sloshing of water in a length of rain gutter is made up of oscillatory motions which provide some insight into analogous motions that take place in the air column of a wind instrument. Fig.41 shows a water-filled trough and the first three modes of oscillatory motion that are possible within it; these modes are those having the lowest frequencies of oscillation. Observation of the motion of the water in such a trough makes it quickly apparent that the vertical motion of the water level is very different from the water's back and forth flowing motion: points of small horizontal motion lie at points of maximum vertical motion; conversely, the vertical

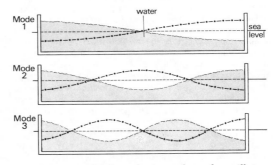

41. *Diagram showing three modes of oscillatory motion possible within a water-filled trough*

motion displays its nodes at those points where the horizontal motion is large. To summarize, every mode of water oscillation has two interlaced aspects: a vertical and a horizontal motion. These motions are inextricably coupled to one another by the fact that the only way to change the water level at some point is to have water flowing towards or away from it.

This longitudinal sloshing motion of water is directly analogous to the oscillatory flow of air back and forth along the bore of a musical instrument. The vertical motion of the water (a consequence of a localized inflow or outflow of water) is the cognate of the rise and fall of air pressure at some point within the duct; obviously such changes in air pressure arise from the flow of air. Because woodwind reeds and brass players' lips are ultimately controlled by pressure variations acting on them within the mouthpiece, and also because eardrums respond directly to the acoustic pressure variations exerted on them by the surrounding air, it is generally convenient to describe the behaviour of air columns in terms of the pressure aspect of their vibrations rather than the flow or displacement aspect, which is more useful when one is dealing with the vibrating strings of violins and pianos.

Every air column, regardless of its shape and the way in which its ends are terminated, has its own characteristic collection of sloshing modes; each of these modes has its own pattern of flow and pressure and its own frequency of oscillation. Air columns of different shapes not only have different frequencies for their various modes of oscillation but also different ratios between them. It is a straightforward (though sometimes tedious) business to calculate the frequencies of an air column regardless of its shape, or, conversely, to calculate the shape needed to give a specified set of frequencies. As shown in §3 below, there are only a very few basic air column shapes that can be coupled to a flow control device in order to make a useful note generator. It is a fortunate circumstance that these same shapes are also compatible with the requirements for proper tuning.

3. MAINTENANCE OF OSCILLATION. A water analogue to a musical instrument can help one to visualize the way a flow control device maintains a steady oscillation. Fig.42 shows a device that could be called a water trumpet, in which a water supply valve is arranged to open or close progressively in response to the rise and fall of the water level at the shallow end of a tapering channel containing water. The end at which the valve is located is analogous to the mouthpiece end of a trumpet, and the valve itself replaces the player's lips. A water valve arranged to open and close in this manner acts as a flow controller worked by variations in water height as it maintains oscillations in the duct. In a similar way, the single and double reeds of orchestral woodwind instruments and the lips of brass players function as flow controllers of the pressure-operated type, in that they open and close under the predominating influence of acoustic pressure oscillations within the mouthpiece cavity of the instrument. The generic name 'reed-valve' will be used for all these pressure-operated controllers, including those associated with brass instruments.

It was pointed out in §2 above that any acoustic disturbance has a pattern of flows intertwined with a corresponding pattern of pressure variations. If attention is directed to the flow variations, they should suggest the possibility of another kind of controller that operates by the flow aspect rather than the pressure aspect of the disturbance within the mouthpiece; this other type is found in the flute family.

In 1877 Helmholtz presented the simple theory of the maintenance of oscillation by means of a reed-valve, showing that such oscillations tend to occur at one or other of the natural frequencies of the air column to which the reed-valve is attached (see also Backus). Wilhelm Weber had already in 1830 elucidated the influence of the reed's own elasticity on these natural frequencies (see Bouasse). It remained for Bouasse in the late 1920s to recognize that under certain conditions several modes of air column oscillation can act simultaneously on the reed-valve to facilitate the maintenance of a note. Since 1957 the implications of Bouasse's observations have been worked out and given practical application (see Worman, and Benade, 1973).

The nature of the collaborative effect of several resonances can be summarized in the following terms. The various characteristic air column modes influence one another via the shared excitatory airflow. The valve must therefore come to terms with the oscillatory preferences of these modes to produce a self-consistent oscillation that includes several harmonically related frequency components in setting up what is known as a 'regime of oscillation'. The name is chosen deliberately to draw attention to what can metaphorically be considered as political negotiations taking place between the air column's own set of vibrational tendencies and those of the reed-valve, with the alliances changing as varying musical conditions give dominance to different members of the regime. Oscillation is particularly favoured when the air column has two or more natural frequencies arranged to coincide with the partials of the note being produced.

4. BRASS INSTRUMENTS. The vibration of a brass player's lips is controlled by the oscillatory pressure present in the mouthpiece: this pressure is an aspect of the air column's own oscillation. It is convenient to characterize the air column itself with the help of measurements carried out with an electronically operated pump (a special type of miniature loudspeaker) that produces a sinusoidally varying flow of air in and out of the mouthpiece cavity at any desired frequency. A 'tiny microphone placed inside the mouthpiece measures the amplitude of the resulting pressure variations. This microphone gives the desired air column response information, which can be displayed on a graph as a function of the pump driving frequency (see Benade, 1973). Such a graph will be called a 'pressure response curve'; formally it is known to acousticians as an input impedance curve. Fig.43 shows an example of such a curve for a modern B♭ trumpet; its general nature is typical of the pressure response curves of all brass instruments. Each of the peaks on this curve indicates a large pressure variation within the mouthpiece cavity, and each peak corresponds to excitation at the frequency of one of the sloshing modes of the air column. The fourth peak of this curve, for example, corresponds to the mode sketched in fig.42.

As an illustration of the usefulness of a pressure response curve, consider what fig.43 shows for the playing of the written note c'. The figure indicates that a regime of oscillation is set up for this note involving response peaks 2, 4, 6 and 8 of the air column, which collaborate with the player's lips to generate a steady oscillation containing many harmonically related partials. The lowest four of these partials get their major sustenance from the peaks named. When the trumpeter plays very softly, peak 2 dominates the oscillation and, because it is not very tall (i.e. the given excitation produces only a mild oscillation in this mode), the note is not well stabilized. As the musician plays louder the other peaks become influential and the note is steadier and better defined. The regime of oscillation for the

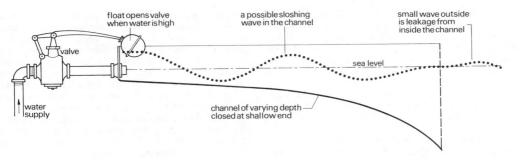

float opens valve
when water is high

a possible sloshing
wave in the channel

small wave outside
is leakage from
inside the channel

valve

sea level

water
supply

channel of varying depth —
closed at shallow end

42. 'Water trumpet' in which the movement of water, controlled by a valve, parallels that of air in a wind instrument controlled by lips or reed

written note g' is dominated by peak 3 with the cooperation of peaks 6 and 9. Since peak 3 is taller than peak 2, at *pianissimo* playing levels g' will be steadier than c'. During a crescendo the tall sixth peak enters the regime for g' and greatly stabilizes the oscillation, which gains some help also from peak 9. These are the acoustical reasons why g' is one of the easiest notes to play on a trumpet.

Further examination of fig.43 shows why the notes become increasingly hard to play as one moves up the scale. For example, g'' is still fairly easy to play softly because it is fed by the tall sixth peak; but during a crescendo it becomes progressively more 'stuffy', because the increasing dissipation of acoustic energy via the generation of higher partials in the note is inadequately offset by the contributions made by the small 12th peak. The note c''' is difficult at all levels, since it is sustained only by the eighth peak, which is not particularly tall and which, moreover, has no assisting peak in the neighbourhood of its second harmonic (near 1864 Hz).

In every case described above, the tuning of each note is determined not only by the resonance peak closest to the nominal frequency of the note, but also by any other peaks that lie at whole-number multiples of this frequency. If errors in the shape of the air column lead to resonance peaks that are not exactly in harmonic relationship, not only is the steadiness and clarity of the note spoiled by the less than perfect cooperation at *forte* levels, but also the player must compensate for pitch shifts that take place during crescendos and diminuendos as the misplaced resonances gain or lose their votes in the regime. The fact that misplaced resonances lead to changes of playing pitch during a crescendo provides the basis for an extremely sensitive technique for the adjustment of the proportions of brass instruments. An instrument whose resonances have been aligned to meet the requirements of maximum cooperation also has improved intonation, since the whole-number relationships between the resonances that promote good response, steady tone and pitch stability during a crescendo are precisely the same as those that underlie the just intervals that provide the guideposts for formal music.

It has already been shown that the positions of the various resonance peaks are crucial to the proper speech of a wind instrument, and there have been hints that their frequencies may systematically be adjusted by suitable modifications of the air column shape. For example, if a mouthpiece is to work properly on any given brass instrument, there is a certain critical relationship that must be maintained between its total volume (cup plus backbore) and its 'popping frequency', which is the frequency of the sound made by slapping the rim closed against the heel of the hand. Similar adjustments can be made at the other end of the instrument. The skilled horn player develops great sensitivity in moving his hand as he goes from note to note. The placement of his hand in the bell ekes out the last bit of perfection in the alignment of the resonances of his instrument. On other brass instruments it is left to the maker to carry out similar but fixed adjustments of the bells.

In an air column's resonance curve, the positions and alignment of the peaks are important, but so also are their heights. For example, the mouthpiece of a brass instrument has an acoustical duty beyond the simple one of helping to achieve suitable frequency relationships between the peaks: it is responsible also for the increased height of the middle four or five peaks relative to their low- and high-frequency neighbours, the maximum peak height lying roughly in the region of the mouthpiece popping frequency itself. Without this area of added height in the response peaks, even a perfectly aligned brass instrument tends to be difficult to play.

The bell also plays an important role in influencing the height of the resonance peaks, in that it causes the disappearance of the peaks above a certain frequency, determined by its rate of flare. The presence of the horn player's hand in the bell raises the frequency above which there are no resonances, which allows the pres-

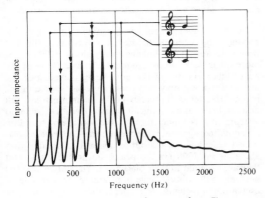

Input impedance

0   500   1000   1500   2000   2500
Frequency (Hz)

43. *Pressure response curve for a modern B♭ trumpet sounding the notes c' or g'*

sure response curve to have half a dozen additional resonance peaks. If these additional peaks are properly aligned, they will join with the other peaks to stabilize various regimes of oscillation and will also raise the upper limit of the player's range. Much of the confusion surrounding the phenomenon of handstopping is resolved when proper account is taken not only of the fact that moving the hand rearranges the peaks which collaborate in producing the note, but also of the fact that handstopping makes additional peaks available to the collaboration.

This discussion of brass instruments will be concluded with a description of the musically useful air column shapes, and how these shapes are affected when valve loops are used to alter their length. Acoustical theory dictates that there are only two simple air column shapes whose natural frequencies provide the complete harmonic series required for proper cooperation with the player's lips. One of these basic shapes is the simple cone complete nearly to the apex, while the other one has the widely flaring shape of a nearly complete rectangular hyperbola. The standing wave patterns for the sloshing modes within both types of air column have the general nature sketched in fig.42. The internodal distances along the air columns are not uniform, nor are they alike in the two types. Neither of these basic air columns is directly useful for brass instruments, in part because the unaided resonance peaks are not sufficiently tall to command the player's lips adequately. Once a mouthpiece is provided so that sufficient height for the mid-frequency peaks is assured, the two basic shapes must be modified to restore the correct resonance frequencies, making their shapes more similar. The trumpet, trombone and french horn are descendants of the hyperbolic prototype, whereas the flugelhorn, alto and baritone horns and many tubas are all of the conical type. There is no meaningful acoustical categorization that can be based on the percentage of cylindrical tubing used in the air column, nor on the shape of the mouthpiece cup. All kinds of intermediate shapes are possible by suitable proportioning of the mouthpiece and bell.

Turning to the effect of inserting pieces of tubing into the middle of an air column as a means for transposing the available playing pitches to a lower range, it is at once apparent that the addition of such tubing reduces the taper of the air column and so alters the relative positions of its response peaks. In particular, the lower-frequency peaks are shifted downwards to a greater extent than are the upper ones. If the instrument played properly before the addition of tubing, it will not do so after a major addition is made. However, for transpositions of no more than three or four semitones the system can be made to work quite acceptably. Tuning errors produced by using combinations of valve loops are not as serious as is commonly believed, because of the presence of inter-mode cooperations, and also because the addition of tubing changes the shape of the air column.

5. REED INSTRUMENTS. It was shown in §4 above that a conical air column is able to set up regimes of oscillation in conjunction with a brass instrument mouthpiece. Reed woodwind instruments are also based on this air column shape: the oboe, the saxophone and the bassoon are familiar examples. In such instruments the apical segment of the prototypical cone is replaced by a reed cavity (or mouthpiece) with a staple, neck or bocal, while the lower, large end of the active bore extends down to the first of a row of open tone holes. It is important to recognize that the presence of closed tone holes on the bore significantly alters its acoustical behaviour.

Fig.44 shows the pressure response curves measured on an oboe for the air columns (including staple and reed cavity) used in playing the low-register notes b', f' and b (the curves for intermediate notes follow the trend implied in the figure). These curves are closely similar to those found for notes having similar fingering on the other conical woodwind instruments.

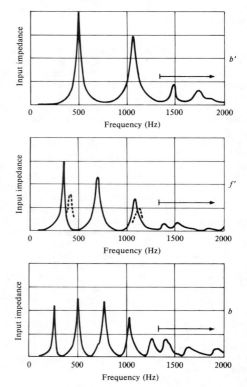

44. *Pressure response curves measured on an oboe for the air columns used in sounding the notes b', f' and b*

In reed instruments each low-register note is produced by a regime of oscillation involving the first (lowest-frequency) resonance peak, along with one or more other peaks whose frequencies match those of the next higher partials of the note being played. For the note b' there are only two peaks that participate in the regime, the higher-frequency peaks being much less tall besides being inharmonically positioned. On a good instrument f' is a much more stable note, being based on a negotiated agreement between three accurately positioned resonance peaks. Once again it is notable that above about 1300 Hz the peaks are not very tall, and they are irregular in their placement. The note b near the bottom of the oboe's scale is produced by a regime of oscillation involving four accurately harmonic and fairly tall peaks, with one less tall peak whose position is a little below the frequency of the tone's fifth partial. The size, spacing and chimney length of the tone holes determine the frequency above which the air column resonance peaks become less tall and more irregular in their position. The behaviour is reminiscent of the manner in which the bell of a brass instrument puts an upper limit on the number of resonance peaks. This explains why the bell of a woodwind instrument (even that of an english horn) can be replaced by an extension of the main bore, if this is provided with a suitably designed set of additional tone holes.

The second register of a conical woodwind instrument's playing range is produced by regimes of oscillation involving response peak 2, along with peak 4 if it exists. The question arises as to how the reed can be persuaded to operate in such a regime. As a general principle, when one plays *pianissimo* on a reed instrument, oscillation is favoured at the frequency of the tallest air column response peak, and intermode cooperative effects are relatively unimportant. Fig.44 shows that the fingerings for *b'* and *f'* give air columns that favour low-register playing under these conditions, whereas *pianissimo* playing using the *b* fingering favours sound production an octave higher at *b'* because of the deficient height of the first peak (a deficiency characteristic of all nearly complete conical air columns). The tendency of the lowest notes to jump an octave in soft playing plagues every saxophonist, and also causes problems of harshness and instability for the player of double-reed instruments. When the *b* fingering is used to play loudly, the reed prefers the low-register regime, based on all four peaks, to the two-part regime, based on peaks 2 and 4. The different behaviour of the regimes under loud and soft playing conditions explains the functioning of the register hole of a woodwind instrument. This hole must produce two changes: it must cause peak 1 to become less tall than peak 2 in order to assure second-register playing at a *pianissimo* level; and it must shift the frequency of peak 1, giving it an inharmonic relationship with the other peaks (an inharmonicity chosen to produce the maximum possible disruption of any cooperative effects) in order to assure second-register playing at the *forte* level. The dotted curves in the middle segment of fig.44 show how opening a register hole alters the heights and positions of peaks 1 and 3 for the *f'* fingering, leaving peak 2 unscathed and ready to produce the note *f''* at all dynamic levels.

As in the case of brass instrument mouthpieces, there is a fixed relationship between the proportions of the air column of a conical instrument and the reed cavity and neck or bocal with which it can function. The active volume of the reed cavity (under playing conditions) with that of the associated tube must closely approximate the volume of the missing apical segment of the basic cone. Furthermore, the playing frequency of the reed with its cavity and neck must (when sounded using a normal embouchure) agree with that of a doubly open cylindrical pipe whose length is that of the missing part of the cone. Systematic methods are available for the mutual adjustment of the air column, tone holes, reed cavity and neck of conical woodwind instruments. These can be as helpful in the fitting of a proper reed to an ancient instrument as they are in the construction of a modern one. The best instruments of all eras show great consistency with the principles outlined above.

The clarinet family (which uses a basically cylindrical air column) has properties remarkably similar to those of the conical woodwind instruments described above. The fingering used to produce the clarinettist's *e'* is analogous to that used for *b'* on the oboe. Once again it gives an air column with only two response peaks, while the lower notes of the scale are played using air columns with an increasing number of active peaks, exactly as before. The replacement of the conical air column by a cylindrical one has the effect of shifting the natural frequency ratios from the 1 : 2 : 3 etc, harmonic series to a sequence of the type 1 : 3 : 5 etc, made up of the odd members of a harmonic series. This has two noteworthy musical consequences. First the clarinet has an enormously large and easily controlled dynamic range in the low register. As one goes from *pianissimo* playing (peak 1 alone being active) to a *mezzopiano* level, the nascent second harmonic partial in the note occurs at a dip in the resonance curve, preventing a tendency for an abrupt growth of tone which would otherwise result from its entry into the regime of oscillation (e.g. as tends to happen on the saxophone). Harder blowing progressively brings in the influence of the third harmonic partial as it cooperates now with response peak 2. The successive entry of cooperative and anticooperative influences as the odd and even partials become important is what makes a crescendo so easily manageable on a clarinet. The second consequence is that the notes of the clarinet's second register sound a 12th above the corresponding low-register notes, rather than an octave above as among the conical instruments.

6. FLUTE. As remarked in §2 above the airstream from a flute player's lips is steered alternately into and out of the instrument's embouchure hole under the influence of the flow aspect of the air column's oscillation. It is worthwhile to maintain the analogy with the reed instruments by referring to the controlled airstream informally as an 'air-reed', to distinguish it from the aerodynamicist's 'edge tone', with whose action it is often confused. It will suffice to note that an air-reed sets up regimes of oscillation in conjunction with the dips rather than the peaks of the air column response curves. Apart from this the behaviour is strictly analogous to that of reed instruments.

There are three basic shapes of air column that provide adequate cooperation with an air-reed by giving harmonically related response dips: the cylindrical pipe, the contracting cone and the expanding cone. Only the first two shapes are in common use. Certain subtleties of the cooperative action of an air-reed require a contraction of the bore near the blowing end as compared with the trend of the main bore. Thus a cylindrical tube requires a contracted headjoint, as exemplified by the Boehm flute, while the Baroque flute has its conical taper contracted into a cylinder in the headjoint. In both cases the volume of the small cavity existing between the cork and the embouchure hole can be adjusted to match the proportions of the hole itself to the rest of the instrument and to its player.

7. WIND INSTRUMENT TONE-COLOUR. There are four significant influences on the tone-colour of a wind instrument. First, varying the profile of the reed tip and the mouthpiece tip on single-reed instruments changes the relation between the shapes of the puffs of air that come through the reed and the acoustic stimulus (in the mouthpiece) that controls them, thus causing modifications in the strengths of the generated partials. Similar behaviour is observed in brass instruments, flutes and

organ pipes. Second, the number of cooperating peaks in the regime of oscillation and their height directly influence the strengths of the partials of a note generated within the instrument. Partials that are directly sustained by the cooperating peaks have strengths roughly proportional to the height of the peaks. The higher partials, lying at frequencies where the peaks are irregular or nonexistent, are weak because they are by-products of the main oscillation. Third, the transmission of sound out of an instrument into the room via the bell of a brass instrument or via the set of open woodwind tone holes also affects the tone-colour. This transmission is small for the lower partials of the internally generated note, rising steadily to a maximum value at the frequency at which the resonance peaks disappear. The resulting 'treble boost', characteristic of the emission process, partially offsets the progressively weaker generation of the higher partials. One hears the aggregate result of both effects. Experiment shows that a rise of only 2–3% in the frequency beyond which there are no resonance peaks makes an easily perceived brightening of the tone-colour on any wind instrument. Fourth, misalignments in the resonances will make many changes in the whole sound, but such misalignments are not normally acceptable because of the accompanying deterioration in the responsiveness of the instrument.

BIBLIOGRAPHY

H. von Helmholtz: *Die Lehre von der Tonempfindungen* (Brunswick, 1863, 4/1877; Eng. trans., 1875/R1954 as *On the Sensations of Tone*)
H. Bouasse: *Instruments à vent* (Paris, 1929–30)
A. Benade: 'On the Mathematical Theory of Woodwind Finger Holes', *Journal of the Acoustical Society of America*, xxxii (1960), 1591
J. Backus: 'Small-Vibration Theory of the Clarinet', *Journal of the Acoustical Society of America*, xxxv (1963), 305
A. Benade and J. French: 'Analysis of the Flute Head Joint', *Journal of the Acoustical Society of America*, xxxvii (1965), 679
J. Coltman: 'The Sounding Mechanism of the Flute', *Journal of the Acoustical Society of America*, xliv (1968), 983
C. Nederveen: *Acoustical Aspects of Woodwind Instruments* (Amsterdam, 1969)
W. Worman: *Self-sustained Nonlinear Oscillations of Medium Amplitude in Clarinetlike Systems* (diss., Case Western Reserve U., Cleveland, Ohio, 1971)
K. Wogram: *Ein Beitrag zur Ermittlung der Stimmung von Blechbläsinstrumenten* (diss., Technical U. of Brunswick, 1972)
A. Benade: 'The Physics of Brasses', *Scientific American* (1973), July, 24
N. Fletcher: 'Nonlinear Interactions in Organ Flue Pipes', *Journal of the Acoustical Society of America*, lvi (1974), 645
E. Jansson and A. Benade: 'On Plane and Spherical Waves in Horns of Nonuniform Flare', *Acustica*, xxxi (1974), 79, 185
A. Benade: *Fundamentals of Musical Acoustics* (New York, 1976)

V. The voice

1. Introduction. 2. Air pressure supply. 3. Oscillator. 4. Resonator. 5. Peculiarities in singing.

1. INTRODUCTION. The voice organ can be regarded as a wind instrument consisting of an air pressure supply driving an oscillator, the output signal of which is fed into a resonator from which the sound is radiated to the air outside the instrument (see fig.45). The air pressure supply is the respiratory system (i.e. the lungs and the respiratory muscles). In the case of voiced sounds, the oscillator is the set of vocal folds (or cords); they convert the airstream from the lungs into a complex sound built up by a great number of harmonic partials. For voiceless sounds the oscillator is a narrow slit through which the airstream is forced; the laminar airstream is then converted into a turbulent airstream which generates noise. The sound generated by the oscillator is called the 'voice source'. It propagates through the resonator constituted by the cavities separating the oscillator from the free air outside the instrument. In resonators the ability to transmit sound varies considerably with the frequency of the transmitted sound. At certain frequencies (i.e. the resonance frequencies), this ability reaches maximum. Thus in the case of the voice, those voice source partials that lie closest to a resonance are radiated with higher amplitudes than other partials. In this way the spectral form of the radiated sound mirrors the properties of the resonator. The resonances and the resonance frequencies of the vocal tract are called 'formants' and 'formant frequencies' respectively.

2. AIR PRESSURE SUPPLY. In singing, the air pressure seems to be much more carefully regulated than in normal speech, by a skilled control of the inspiratory and expiratory muscles (see Bouhuys, Proctor and Mead). The air pressure provided by the respiratory system in singing varies with pitch and vocal effort, generally between 5 and 40 cm of water (see Rubin, LeCover and Vennard). The resulting air flow depends also on the glottal conditions. Air flow rates of 5–20 litres a minute have been observed in singers. These air pressure and air flow ranges do not appear to deviate appreciably from values observed in untrained speakers.

3. OSCILLATOR.

(i) *Voiced sounds.* The vocal folds orginate at the angle of the thyroid cartilage, course horizontally backwards and are inserted into each of the arytenoid cartilages. By adduction (i.e. drawing these cartilages towards each other), the slit between the folds, called the 'glottis', is narrowed, and an airstream can set the folds into vibration. A vibration cycle can be described as follows. When the glottis is slightly open an airstream from the lungs can pass through it. This airstream generates a negative pressure along the edges of the folds owing to the Bernoulli effect. The sucking effect of this negative pressure along with the elasticity and other mechanical properties of the folds closes the glottis again. Then the air pressure difference across the glottis throws the folds apart, thus starting the next vibratory cycle. The frequency of the vibration is determined by the transglottal air pressure difference and the mechanical properties of the folds. A high pressure difference or tense and thin vocal folds, or both, give a high frequency; converse states give a low frequency. The mechanical properties of the folds are regulated by a series of muscles that vary the length and thickness of the folds by manipulating the positions of the laryngal cartilages. Thus these muscles are used to regulate the vibration frequency. As the vibration frequency determines the pitch perceived, these muscles are often referred to as the 'pitch regulating muscles'. An increase of the subglottal pressure raises the amplitude of the sound produced, and at the same time increases the vibration frequency and so the pitch. Thus, in order to perform a crescendo at constant pitch a singer has to raise the subglottal pressure and simultaneously compensate for the pitch increase by adjusting the pitch-regulating muscles (see Hirano, Vennard and Ohala).

By vibrating, the vocal folds repeatedly interrupt the airstream from the respiratory system. Thus they act as a valve oscillating between open and closed positions: the result is a chopped airstream corresponding to a complex note, the fundamental frequency of which is

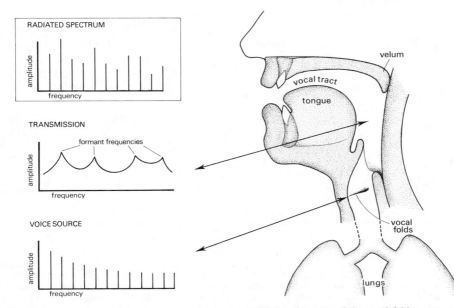

45. *Schematic representation of the generation of voiced sounds: the vibrations of the vocal folds generate a complex tone, the voice source, which has a uniform spectrum envelope fall; voice source partials with frequencies corresponding to formant frequencies (such as the 2nd and 5th partials in the figure) are radiated with higher amplitudes than others*

equal to the vibrating frequency of the folds. The glottal opening is schematically shown as a function of time in fig.46. The horizontal portion of the curve corresponds to the closed phase of the glottal vibration cycle, and the triangular portion is the open phase. As the folds generally open more slowly than they close, the triangular part of the curve is asymmetrical in the figure. In trained voices the closed phase is often observed to be of longer duration than in untrained voices. Also, the vibration pattern appears to vary considerably less with pitch and vocal intensity in trained voices than in untrained ones.

The sound generated by the chopped transglottal airstream is built up by a great number of harmonic partials whose amplitudes generally decrease monotonically with frequency by roughly 12 dB per octave. It is noteworthy that this holds as an approximation for all voiced sounds. The highest partial of measurable amplitude in the source spectrum is

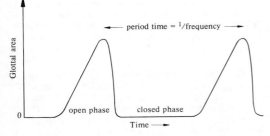

46. *Diagram showing how the glottal opening area varies with time in voiced sounds (the pitch perceived corresponds with the fundamental frequency, which is the inverse period time)*

generally found to be between 4 and 6 kHz. This means that a tone with a fundamental frequency of 100 Hz may contain between 40 and 60 partials of appreciable amplitude. However, the amplitudes of the source spectrum partials vary with pitch and vocal intensity, particularly in untrained voices. In trained male singers the spectrum fall has been observed to vary with respect to the relative amplitudes of the partials with a frequency lower than 1 kHz, approximately, the slope below that frequency being somewhat more than 12 dB per octave at weak vocal intensity and in low-pitched notes (see Sundberg, 1973).

(*ii*) *Voiceless sounds*. The sound source in this case is noise generated by a turbulent airstream. The narrow slit required for the noise generation can be formed at various places along the vocal tract, the lowest position being at the glottis itself, which can be kept wide enough to prevent the folds from vibrating and narrow enough to make the airstream turbulent. This is the oscillator used in the 'h' sound. Another place used in some languages is the velar region, which can be constricted by the tongue hump. The resulting sound is used as the voice source in the German 'ach' sound. In most remaining unvoiced sounds the tongue tip constricts the vocal tract in the palatal, alveolar or dental region as in the initial phonemes of 'sheep', 'cheap' and 'sip'. In the 'f' sound the upper incisors and the lower lip provide the slit.

4. RESONATOR. The frequencies of the formants depend on the shape of the resonator. In the case of non-nasalized sounds the resonator consists of the pharynx and mouth cavities. In vowels these cavities constitute a tube resonator which may be regarded as closed at the glottal end and open at the lip end. The average vocal tract length for males is generally considered to be 17·5

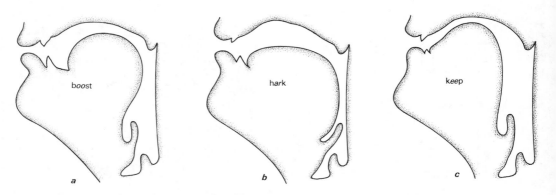

47. *Tracings from x-ray pictures of the midsagittal contours of the vocal tract for the vowels indicated*

cm. A tube of that length and having a uniform cross-sectional area would display a series of resonances falling close to the odd multiples of 500 Hz, but as the cross-sectional area of the vocal tract is not uniform, the formants deviate from these frequencies. The vocal tract shape is determined by the positions of the articulators (i.e. the lips, the jaw, the tongue, the velum and the larynx). The positions of these articulators are continuously varied in singing and in speech, so that the formants are tuned to various target frequencies. Thus each sound corresponds to a certain pattern of articulator positions.

The dependence of the formant frequencies on the articulatory configuration is rather complex. Only a few factors have the same type of effect on all formant frequencies; for instance, all formants drop in frequency more or less when the vocal tract length is increased by protrusion of the lips or lowering of the larynx or both, and when the lip opening area is decreased. Moreover, certain formants are more dependent on the position of a specific articulator than are others. The first is particularly sensitive to the jaw opening: the wider the jaw opening, the higher the first formant frequency. The frequencies of the second and third formants are especially sensitive to the position of the tongue body and tongue tip respectively. The highest frequencies of the second formant (2–3 kHz) are obtained when the tongue body constricts the vocal tract in the palatal region, as in the front vowel of 'keep'. The lowest values of the third formant (around 1500 Hz) are associated with a tongue tip lifted in a retroflex direction. Fig.47 provides examples of articulatory configurations associated with some vowels.

These guidelines apply to oral sounds; in nasalized sounds the dependence of the formants on the articulator positioning becomes considerably more complex. The nasal tract introduces minima in the sound transfer of the resonator at several frequencies. The acoustical effect of nasalization varies between vowels, but a general feature is that the lowest partials are emphasized .

For both oral and nasalized sounds the two lowest formant frequencies are generally decisive in the vowel quality perceived. Frequencies typical of male speakers are given in fig.48. Females have shorter vocal tracts and therefore higher formant frequencies. On average

for vowels, the three lowest formant frequencies of female voices are 12, 17 and 18% higher, respectively, than those of male voices. Children, having still shorter vocal tracts, possess formant frequencies that are 35–40% higher than those of males (see Fant).

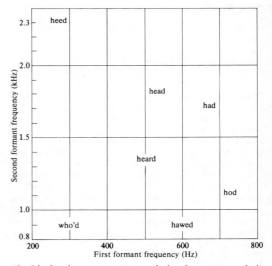

48. *Idealized representations of the frequencies of the two lowest formant frequencies for American-English vowels spoken by men according to measurements by G. E. Peterson and H. L. Barney: 'Control Methods used in the study of Vowels', 'Journal of the Acoustical Society of America', xxiv (1952), 175*

The amplitudes of the partials emitted from the lip opening depend on the sound transfer ability of the vocal tract. This ability depends not only on the partials' frequency distance from the closest formant, but also on the frequency distance between formants. Thus a halving of the frequency distance between two adjacent formants increases the sound transfer ability by 6 dB at the formant frequencies and by 12 dB midway between the formant frequencies. Another factor important to the amplitudes of the radiated partials is the sound radiation

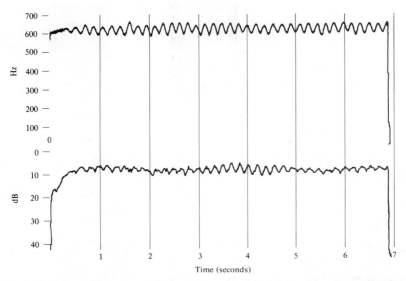

49. *Variations in the fundamental frequency in Hz (upper curve) and in the overall amplitude in dB (lower curve) in a vowel sung by a female singer (note that a rise in frequency is not necessarily accompanied by a rise in amplitude)*

properties of the lip opening, which boosts the entire spectrum envelope by 6 dB per octave. For this reason, the amplitudes of all spectrum partials increase with the pitch even when there is no change in vocal effort.

5. PECULIARITIES IN SINGING. Basically the voice organ seems to be used in the same way in singing as in speech. In both cases the sound produced is entirely determined by the properties of the sound source and the vocal tract resonances. In other words, there seems to be no reason to assume that in non-nasalized vowels the resonators outside the vocal tract, such as the maxillary sinuses or the lungs, contribute to the acoustic output to any appreciable extent. In singing, however, the possibilities inherent in the normal voice organ are used in quite special ways.

(*i*) *Vibrato.* One of the typical peculiarities of opera and concert singing is vibrato. Its acoustical correlate is an undulation of the frequencies and amplitudes of the partials (see fig.49). The undulation is almost sinusoidal and has a rate of 5–7 Hz in good voices; the rate is quite constant for a given singer, and the magnitude of the frequency excursions is of the order of ± 50 cents. Vibrato increases in regularity as voice training proceeds (see Bjørklund). The frequency and amplitude undulations are synchronous, but not always in phase, the phase relationship presumably depending on the frequency difference between the strongest spectrum partial and the nearest formant. For instance, if the partial is slightly lower in frequency than the formant, an increase in frequency will cause the amplitude to increase, and thus frequency and amplitude will vary in phase. Clearly, the opposite will occur if the partial is slightly higher than the formant frequency.

The physiological origin of vibrato is not well under-

stood. It has been found that vibrato rate can be altered if the auditory feedback is delayed (i.e. if the singer hears his own voice over headphones with a slight time delay). This suggests that the auditory system may be involved (see Deutsch and Clarkson). Measurements of the electrical muscle signals, or 'EMG measurements', in laryngal muscles often reveal undulations in the registered signals which are synchronous with the frequency variations (see Vennard, Hirano, Ohala and Fritzell). This suggests that the laryngal muscles take part in the generation of vibrato. Possibly as a consequence of this, the transglottal air flow varies with the frequency variations, and the resulting vibrato notes tend to consume more air than vibrato-free notes (see Large and Iwata). However, on the basis of available data it seems impossible to exclude the subglottal pressure as the vibrato-generating mechanism. In some singers the variations in the muscle activity affect the larynx height and even other parts of the voice organ. Pitch seems to be perceived with comparable accuracy regardless of the presence of vibrato for a single note. The perceived pitch agrees within a few cents with the pitch of a vibrato-free note with a fundamental frequency equal to the average frequency of the vibrato note (see Sundberg, 1972).

(*ii*) *Register.* The term 'register' is used for a group of notes that sound similarly and are felt to be produced in the same way. There are a great number of conflicting nomenclatures and definitions in common use, and the lack of objective knowledge is apparent. In untrained voices in particular a change from one register to another may be accompanied by a sudden jump in pitch and a marked shift in tone quality. Such phenomena are referred to as 'register breaks'; a typical example is the contrast between the normal voice and the falsetto in males (similar observations can often be made in females within the fourth octave, i.e. 262–523 Hz). It is frequently assumed that the physiological origin of register is confined to the voice source. According to some experts, a difference between the falsetto and the normal voice in males is that the vocal folds never reach full contact with each other during the vibration cycle in falsetto. Transitions between registers have been found to be accompanied by changes in the EMG signals from laryngal muscles, and by changes in transglottal air flow. There is reasonable agreement on the importance of the laryngal muscles to registers, though a purely acoustical interaction between the glottal oscillator and the resonator has been advanced as an alternative explanation. Definite acoustical correlates of register differences have been established in some cases. For instance, the 'heavy' register in male and female voices has been reported typically to contain stronger high partials than the 'light' register. It seems that the 'light' register is equivalent to falsetto and 'head voice' in male and female voices respectively.

(iii) *Voice categories.* Male and female voices differ significantly in their formant frequencies as well as pitch range, and this factor seems also to be significant in differentiating tenors, baritones and basses. Thus when singing the same pitch, voices of these types can be distinguished by their vowel formant frequencies. In most vowels a bass is likely to show the lowest formant frequencies and a tenor the highest; and all formants, not only the two lowest, are relevant. The formant frequency differences between male and female voices resemble closely those observed between bass and tenor voices, which suggests that the dimensions of the resonating system are of major importance (see Cleveland).

(iv) *Singing formant.* The 'singing formant', or the 'singer's formant', belongs to the characteristics of male opera and concert singing. It corresponds acoustically to a high spectrum envelope peak which is present in all vowels and generally centred at a frequency of 2·5–3·5 kHz. In vocal pedagogy it is often referred to as 'singing in the mask', 'focussing' etc. The singing formant is generated by the introduction of an extra formant closely related to the larynx tube. If the pharynx is wide enough, the larynx tube can act as a separate resonator, the resonance frequency of which is quite unaffected by the rest of the vocal tract; it may be tuned to a frequency lying between those of the third and fourth formants in normal speech. The condition of a widening of the pharynx seems to be met when the larynx is lowered, a gesture occurring typically in male professional singing. At high pitches the demands on a wide pharynx are increased, and extreme lowering of the larynx is frequently observed when males sing high-pitched notes (see Shipp and Izdebski). In such cases the term 'covering' is used. The widening of the pharynx and the lowering of the larynx affect the frequencies not only of the higher formants, but also those of the lower formants. As an acoustical consequence of these articulatory gestures, the frequency of the second formant drops in front vowels. This alters the vowel quality to some extent, so that, for instance, the vowel in 'sheep' is 'coloured' towards the German 'ü' sound.

The perceptual function of the 'singing formant' seems to be to make the voice easier to hear above a loud orchestral accompaniment (see Sundberg, 1974). It has also been suggested that it helps the singer make himself heard in large auditoria (see Winckel).

(v) *Female high-pitched singing.* The general rule is that a given pattern of formant frequencies is confined to a given vowel, and these formant frequencies are maintained regardless of the fundamental frequency in singing. However, this seems to hold only when the fundamental is not above the first formant frequency, as it may be in the singing of tenors, altos and sopranos. In these cases the principle seems to be that the first formant is tuned to a frequency close to that of the fundamental. That partial is the strongest in the source spectrum, and if it coincides with the first formant frequency it will be emitted with the highest possible amplitude. The result then is that a note is produced with maximum loudness and minimum vocal effort. According to observations received from female singers, the tuning of the first formant frequency is achieved by adjusting the jaw, opening or retracting the corners of the mouth, or both. The formant frequencies determine the vowel quality, as mentioned, and the abnormal values of the first formant frequency alter the vowel quality. However, the disadvantage is small, because in high-pitched singing the vowel quality cannot be maintained even with correct formant frequencies, owing to the great frequency distance between the partials in relation to the number of formants (see Sundberg, 1975).

(vi) *Tibetan Choomi chant.* If a partial and a formant agree in frequency, this partial will be emitted with the highest possible amplitude, other things being equal. Such partials will then dominate others in the radiated spectrum, and will be perceptible as individual pitches within the total spectrum. This situation has been suggested in explanation of the Tibetan Choomi chant, where one singer produces a constant drone together with sequences of high-pitched whistling notes. The fundamental frequency of the drone is generally found to lie between 100 and 150 Hz, and the dominating whistling notes are often chosen from between the sixth and the 13th partials. The singer tunes a formant, presumably the second, to the frequency of a partial, thus emphasizing that partial. By tuning the formant to the frequency of different partials in succession, they can be made discernible as individual pitches, and the singer can play melodies. The sound quality gives the impression of a nasal articulation, possibly serving the purpose of reducing the amplitudes of the partials near the first formant. The basic technique is well-known and not difficult to learn, but the great prominence of the dominating partials seems to be a speciality of the Tibetans. The drone has been assumed to be produced by a special vocal fold operation in which each second vibration cycle does not give a complete glottal closure, so reducing the pitch by an octave (see Smith, Stevens and Tomkinson, and Walcott).

BIBLIOGRAPHY

G. E. Peterson and H. L. Barney: 'Control Methods used in the Study of Vowels', *Journal of the Acoustical Society of America*, xxiv (1952), 175
F. Winckel: 'Physikalische Kriterien für objektive Stimmbeurteilung', *Folia phoniatrica*, v (1953), 232
J. A. Deutsch and J. K. Clarkson: 'Nature of the Vibrato and the Control Loop in Singing', *Nature*, clxxxiii (1959), 167
A. Bjørklund: 'Analyses of Soprano Voices', *Journal of the Acoustical Society of America*, xxxiii (1961), 575
A. Bouhuys, D. F. Proctor and J. Mead: 'Kinetic Aspects of Singing', *Journal of Applied Physiology*, xxi (1966), 483

H. J. Rubin, M. LeCover and W. Vennard: 'Vocal Intensity, Subglottic Pressure and Air Flow Relationships in Singers', *Folia phoniatrica*, xix (1967), 393

H. Smith, K. N. Stevens and R. S. Tomkinson: 'On an Unusual Mode of Chanting by Certain Tibetan Lamas', *Journal of the Acoustical Society of America*, xli (1967), 1262

M. Hirano, W. Vennard and J. Ohala: 'Regulation of Register, Pitch and Intensity of Voice', *Folia phoniatrica*, xxii (1970), 1

W. Vennard, M. Hirano, J. Ohala and B. Fritzell: 'A Series of Four Electromyographic Studies', *National Association of Teachers of Singing Bulletin*, xxvii/1–4 (1970–71)

J. Large and S. Iwata: 'Aerodynamic Study of Vibrato and Voluntary "Straight Tone" Pairs in Singing', *Folia phoniatrica*, xxiii (1971), 50

J. Large: 'Towards an Integrated Physiologic-acoustic Theory of Vocal Registers', *National Association of Teachers of Singing Bulletin*, xxviii/3 (1972), 18

J. Sundberg: 'Pitch of Synthetic Sung Vowels', *Speech Transmission Laboratory Quarterly Progress and Status Report* (1972), no.1, p.32

G. Fant: *Speech Sounds and Features* (Cambridge, Mass., and London, 1973)

J. Sundberg: 'The Source Spectrum in Professional Singing', *Folia phoniatrica*, xxv (1973), 71

——: 'Articulatory Interpretation of the "Singing Formant" ', *Journal of the Acoustical Society of America*, lv (1974), 838

R. Walcott: 'The Chöömij of Mongolia: a Spectral Analysis of Overtone Singing', *Selected Reports*, ii/1 (1974), 55

T. Shipp and K. Izdebski: 'Vocal Frequency and Vertical Larynx Positioning by Singers and Nonsingers', *Journal of the Acoustical Society of America*, lviii (1975), 1104

J. Sundberg: 'Formant Technique in a Professional Female Singer', *Acustica*, xxxii (1975), 89

T. Cleveland: *The Acoustic Properties of Voice Timbre Types and their Importance in the Determination of Voice Classification in Male Singers* (diss., U. of Southern California, 1976)

RONALD LEWCOCK (I), JOHN C. SCHELLENG, CARLEEN M. HUTCHINS (II), DANIEL W. MARTIN (III), ARTHUR H. BENADE (IV), JOHAN SUNDBERG (V)

Act (Fr. *acte*; Ger. *Aufzug*; It. *atto*). One of the main divisions of a drama, opera or ballet, usually completing a definite part of the action and often having a climax of its own. Although ancient Greek drama was not divided thus except by the periodic intervention of the chorus, and the division into acts of the plays of Roman authors such as Plautus is the work of later hands, Horace (*Epistle to the Pisos*) recommended five acts as the proper manner of dividing a play. In attempting to recreate the ancient drama this structure was adopted in early operas and was usually preserved in serious French opera of the 17th and 18th centuries even when the three-act form had become established in other types of opera. Rousseau (*Dictionnaire de musique*, 1767) insisted that the unities of time and place should be observed in each act even in the 'genre merveilleux'. But there were already many exceptions (e.g. Rameau's *Hippolyte et Aricie*, 1733, in which the fifth act embraces two tableaux), and the development of stage techniques that afforded ways of presenting transformation scenes, together with the relaxation of the unities and the more fluid requirements in the representation of time and place in Romantic opera, meant that Rousseau's principles were soon discarded. From the late 18th century, operas were written in anything from one to five acts and, particularly in works for the popular theatre, little attempt was made to observe the unities of time and place (e.g. Mozart's *Die Zauberflöte* has two acts and a total of 13 scenes, most of which have different settings). Wagner's ideal music drama was to consist of three acts. He regularly adopted this division in his mature works, but other composers and librettists have remained unconvinced of the need for so restrictive a practice.

Most oratorios are divided into parts rather than acts, but Handel, whose works in this genre were conceived in theatrical terms, used the latter expression. It was also employed in England during the 18th and early 19th centuries for the various subdivisions of a concert.

MICHAEL TILMOUTH

Action (Fr. *méchanique*; Ger. *Mechanik*, *Mechanismus*; It. *meccanica*). (1) The mechanism by means of which the strings or pipes of a keyboard instrument are sounded when a key is depressed.

(2) The mechanism by means of which the pedals of a harp change the pitches of its strings.

EDWIN M. RIPIN

Action musicale (Fr.). A translation of Wagner's 'Handlung für Musik', his designation of the *Lohengrin* libretto, used by French Wagnerians (e.g. d'Indy, on the title-pages of his *Fervaal* and *L'étranger*) to suggest something more elevated than a mere opera.

ANDREW PORTER

Act music. Music specially written for the celebration of the Act at Oxford in the late 17th and early 18th centuries. The Act, held originally in July, was a traditional function at which candidates for degrees gave public evidence of their fitness. In 1669 it was held for the first time in the newly opened Sheldonian Theatre and was incorporated in the ceremony of the Encaenia (the commemoration of founders and benefactors). Act music, as opposed to works composed for degrees in music, dates from that year. Composers who contributed music for the occasion included Locke and Blow. The Act ceased to be held after 1733, but the Encaenia survived. In addition to its function as a commemoration it is now the occasion for the conferment of honorary degrees and the recitation of excerpts from prize compositions (prose and verse) in Latin, Greek and English. The only music performed is an organ recital before the ceremony.

JACK WESTRUP

Acton, Carlo [Charles] (*b* Naples, 25 Aug 1829; *d* Portici, nr. Naples, 2 Feb 1909). Italian composer and pianist. He studied the piano and composition in his native town, where he spent his entire life. His prolific output of fluently written, light and brilliant pieces (more than 400 works) won great success with the conventional middle class in Naples, which was culturally behind the times and inclined towards the flimsy, often frivolous genre of salon pieces: Acton's works became an indispensable part of the piano repertory of all daughters 'of good family' in Bourbon Naples. An amiable figure but of little distinction, he had no following of his own as a teacher, unlike his Neapolitan colleagues Costantino Palumbo and Alfonso Rendano.

WORKS

Operettas, incl. Una cena in convitto (farce, Acton)
Sacred works, incl. Le ultime sette parole di Nostro Signore sulla croce, 3vv, org; Oratio S Bernardi memorare, chorus; O sacrum convivium, 2 solo vv, chorus; Prima della SS Comunione, chorus; Resurrexit, female vv; Tantum ergo, 3vv
Partsongs; solo songs
Numerous instrumental pieces: vc, pf; 1–2 mand, pf; pf 4 hands; pf solo; org/harmonium

BIBLIOGRAPHY
G. Pannain: *Ottocento musicale italiano* (Milan, 1952)
FRANCESCO BUSSI

Act tune. Term used in England mainly in the 17th and 18th centuries for a piece of music played between the acts of an opera or play. Until the 18th century the curtain was not normally dropped during the course of a play except for special scene effects, and the end of each act was marked by music. During the 17th century each play usually had its own act music, though this was rarely relevant to the action. The music provided consisted of not only the four act tunes proper but also the First Music, Second Music and Overture performed before the play. Purcell wrote such sets for about 11 plays, giving each a variety of key and mood rare in those of his contemporaries. In the early 18th century, English theatres began to offer more lavish entertainment between the acts and special act tunes ceased to be composed, though only in the early 20th century was the practice of providing some diversion between the acts finally abandoned. *See also* ENTR'ACTE and ZWISCHENSPIEL.

BIBLIOGRAPHY

M. Summers: *The Restoration Theatre* (London, 1934), chaps.4–5
J. S. Manifold: *The Music in English Drama from Shakespeare to Purcell* (London, 1956), chap.2
A. M. Laurie: *Purcell's Stage Works* (diss., U. of Cambridge, 1963), chap.4

MARGARET LAURIE

Actus musicus. Term used from the mid-17th century to the early 18th in Protestant Germany, particularly in the areas of Saxony and Thuringia, for sacred dramatic compositions based on biblical stories. The *actus musicus* is similar in function and general structure to the Lutheran *historia*, that is, both were performed within the context of the liturgy and both are musical and textual elaborations of a biblical story. The *actus musicus* differs from the *historia* in its greater use of non-biblical interpolations and its greater emphasis on the dramatic element. While both genres are important as antecedents of the oratorio of Protestant Germany, the *actus musicus* is related more closely to the oratorio and less closely to the liturgy than is the *historia*.

See ORATORIO, §7.

BIBLIOGRAPHY

B. Baselt: 'Actus musicus', *MGG*
——: 'Actus musicus und Historie um 1700 in Mitteldeutschland', *Hallesche Beiträge zur Musikwissenschaft*, viii (1968), 77–103

HOWARD E. SMITHER

Acuff, Roy (Claxton) (*b* Maynardville, Tenn., 15 Sept 1903). American country-music singer, guitarist, songwriter and publisher. He organized his first band in 1932, became a medicine-show performer, and by 1936 had performed on radio stations in Knoxville with at least three bands (the Tennessee Crackerjacks, the Crazy Tennesseeans and the Smoky Mountain Boys). He joined the 'Grand Ole Opry' radio programme in 1938, and through such songs as *Wabash cannon ball* and *The great speckled bird* became the most popular country singer of the World War II era. His intense, wailing style, suggestive of the Southern fundamentalist country churches, was atypical at a time when jazzy, swing styles were gaining ground in country music. Acuff's personal popularity did much to make the 'Grand Ole Opry' the leading country radio and stage show, and his publishing firm, Acuff–Rose (founded in 1942 with Fred Rose), helped establish Nashville as a country-music centre.

BIBLIOGRAPHY

E. Schlappi: *Roy Acuff and his Smoky Mountain Boys Discography* (Cheswold, Delaware, 1966)
B. C. Malone: *Country Music, USA* (Austin, 1968)
E. Schlappi: 'Roy Acuff', *Stars of Country Music*, ed. B. C. Malone and J. McCulloh (Urbana, Ill., 1975), 179

BILL C. MALONE

Adagietto (It., diminutive of *adagio*, but current only in musical contexts). As a tempo designation it suggests something more lighthearted than ADAGIO. But its most famous use is in Mahler's Fifth Symphony, where the fourth movement, for strings and harp, has the title Adagietto and the tempo designation *sehr langsam*; there it is used to mean a relatively brief slow movement with a relatively light texture.

See also TEMPO AND EXPRESSION MARKS, §3.

DAVID FALLOWS

Adagio (It.: 'at ease', 'leisurely', also found as *ad agio*). A tempo designation whose meaning has changed substantially over the years. Early forms of the word in musical scores include *adaggio* (Monteverdi, 1610; Cavalli, *L'Elena*, 1659) and *adasio* (Frescobaldi, 1635; Erasmus Kindermann, 1639). In the 18th and 19th centuries it was often abbreviated to *ad°* and *adag°*.

Praetorius (*Syntagma musicum*, iii, 2/1619) equated it with *largo* and *lento*, translating all three *langsam*; in the preface to his *Sonnata's of III Parts* (London, 1683) Purcell said that it and *grave* 'import nothing but a very slow movement'. Monteverdi seems to have used the word in this sense in the six-voice *Magnificat* of his 1610 collection where he gave the organist the instruction 'Et si suona Adaggio, perchè li soprano cantano di croma' ('play slowly because the sopranos sing quavers'). Banchieri was probably the first to use it specifically as a tempo designation, rather than just part of an elaborate explanatory sentence, in 'La battaglia' from *L'organo suonarino* (1611). For him, as for many other early users of *adagio*, including Domenico Mazzocchi (1626, 1638) and Carlo Farina (1627), it was the slowest tempo.

But it is likely that Frescobaldi meant *adagio* in its literal sense of 'at ease' or even 'as you wish', both in the prefaces to his two 1615 volumes and in the music of his 1635 *Fiori musicali*: the musical context suggests that a freer, less metrical style of playing was expected for the sections so marked. And something of the kind was also implied by Brossard (*Dictionaire*, 1703), who translated it 'comfortable, at one's ease, without hurrying', but added that it usually meant 'slowly, dragging the beat a little'.

The ambiguity of the word lies in its position as one of the first words in music to mean 'slow' and its equally widely accepted position as the second of the five main degrees of movement in music (as described, for instance, by Rousseau, 1768), lying between *largo*, the slowest, and *andante*: Rousseau (article 'Mouvement') translated *adagio* as *modéré*. Throughout the 18th century there was an unvoiced disagreement among the theorists as to whether *adagio*, *largo* or *grave* was the slowest tempo; in his own copy (now in *GB-Lbm*) of Grassineau's *Musical Dictionary* (1740), Burney corrected the definition of *adagio* as 'the slowest of any except *grave*' to 'the slowest of any'.

But by the 19th century *adagio* was generally agreed to be the slowest tempo, while *largo* was used to suggest something more grand and *grave* became more serious but was rarely slower as well. Only *adagissimo* (or *adagiosissimo*) was slower: it had been used by J. S. Bach at the end of his D minor Toccata and of the chorale prelude *O Mensch bewein*; and it replaced the earlier *adagio adagio*, which appears in works by Martino Pesenti (1639, 1647) and was equated with *largo* by Brossard (1703), who translated it as *très lentement* (although he translated *largo* as *fort lentement*).

Adagio was also used as a noun, perhaps more frequently than any other tempo designation except *allegro*. It meant any slow movement: Bruckner, for instance, gave it as the title for the slow movement in most of his symphonies, but gave something else entirely as the tempo designation (*sehr feierlich, sehr langsam*, etc); and Haydn, in the autograph of Symphony no.96, wrote at the end of the first movement *segue adagio* though the next movement is in fact marked *andante*.

Also in the same sense, it meant for Baroque composers any slow movement that would normally be embellished. Quantz (*Versuch*, 1752) devoted an entire chapter to the subject 'Von der Art das Adagio zu spielen', and included the comment:

The *adagio* may be viewed in two ways with respect to the manner in which it should be played and embellished; that is, it may be viewed in accordance with the French or the Italian style. The first requires a clean and sustained execution of the air, and embellishment with the essential graces, such as appoggiaturas, whole and half-shakes, mordents, turns, *battemens, flattemens*, etc., but no extensive passage-work or significant addition of extempore embellishments. . . . In the second manner, that is, the Italian, extensive artificial graces that accord with the harmony are introduced in the *adagio* in addition to the little French embellishments. . . . If the plain air of this example is played with the addition of only the essential graces already frequently named, we have another illustration of the French manner of playing. You will also notice, however, that this manner is inadequate for an *adagio* composed in this fashion.

But modes change, and Leopold Mozart (1756) had the following to say:

Some people think they are bringing something wonderful to the world when they thoroughly distort an *adagio cantabile* and turn a single note into a few dozen. These music-butchers thereby manifest their poor judgment and tremble when they must hold out a long note or play even a few notes cantabile without mixing in their accustomed, nonsensical and laughable doodling [*fick fack*].

A similar feeling is expressed more ironically in J. Riepel's *Grundregeln zur Tonordnung* (1755, chap.2, p.110):

Pupil: Now tell me quickly whether a little piece like this can be used any more or not at all?
Teacher: Why not? Just write the word 'Solo' on top and mark it *adagio*. A violinist will decorate it with embellishments; in fact it will be a thousand times preferable to him than if a composer should cobble together a solo for him without understanding the violin.

As late as 1802, Koch in his *Musikalisches Lexikon* (article 'Manieren') implied that the practice was still common by expressing the opinion that adagios were embellished only to cover up the weaknesses of a performer who was not able to sustain a line so slowly. But already in 1789 Burney could write in the third volume of his *History*:

It was formerly more easy to compose than to play an Adagio, which generally consisted of a few notes that were left to the taste and abilities of the performer; but as the composer seldom found his ideas fulfilled by the player, adagios are now more *chantant* and interesting in themselves, and the performer is less put to the torture for embellishments.

For bibliography *see* Tempo and expression marks.
DAVID FALLOWS

Adagissimo. *See* Adagio.

Adalbert of Prague [Vojtěch; Wojciech] (*b* ?Libice, Bohemia, *c*956; *d* nr. Danzig, 23 April 997). Czech saint, bishop, missionary and martyr. He belonged to the powerful Slavník family, and was baptized Vojtěch, taking the name Adalbert at his confirmation. He was educated at Magdeburg, and consecrated Bishop of Prague in 983. Owing to opposition he twice resigned the see and travelled to Rome, returning each time to Prague. In Italy he became a Benedictine (989) and visited Monte Cassino; he founded the first Benedictine houses in Bohemia (Březnov, 993) and Poland (Międzyrzec, *c*996). He was canonized in 999 and venerated particularly in Bohemia, Poland and Hungary; for a list of Offices, hymns and sequences connected with his cult see Morawski.

The early biographies (edited in *Monumenta Germaniae historica: scriptores*, iv and xv/2) offer no conclusive evidence that Adalbert was a musician. He has been credited, nevertheless, with the earliest vernacular religious songs of both Bohemia (*Hospodine, pomiluj ny*) and Poland (*Bogurodzica*). Both songs are invocations ending with 'Kyrie eleison' or an equivalent and were sung at state occasions in the late Middle Ages; the ascriptions are doubtful. An *Exposicio cantici sancti Adalberti* (dated 1397) by a monk of Březnov (often but uncertainly attributed to John of Holešov) contains the earliest surviving version of the melody of *Hospodine, pomiluj ny*, claimed to be more authentic than other contemporary versions and attributed to Adalbert, the founder. The text also survives in a version of 1380. Earlier references to the singing of Kyries may signify the use of this particular song, as may also a 13th-century reference to a 'hymnus a sancto Adalberto editus'. The earliest known version of *Bogurodzica* dates from 1407; its text contains Bohemian expressions but resembles other early Polish vernacular material in that respect. Feicht has suggested that the melody dates from the 13th century. It was ascribed to Adalbert by the 16th century.

BIBLIOGRAPHY
H. G. Voigt: *Adalbert von Prag* (Berlin, 1898)
Z. Nejedlý: *Zpěv předhusitský* [Pre-Hussite song], Dějiny husitského zpěvu, i (Prague, 1954), 42, 45, 312, 319ff
H. Feicht: 'Polskie średniowiecze' [The Polish Middle Ages] *Kultura staropolska*, ed. Z. Szweykowski (Kraków, 1957), 39, 144
J. Morawski: 'Adalbertus', *MGG*

GEOFFREY CHEW

Adalid y Gurréa, Marcial del (*b* La Coruña, 24 Aug 1826; *d* Lóngora, nr. La Coruña, 16 Oct 1881). Spanish composer. He studied the piano with Moscheles in London from 1844 to 1849, and possibly also had lessons from Chopin in Paris. On his return to Spain he first lived in Madrid, where some of his compositions were performed, and then at his palace of Lóngora, where he dedicated himself wholly to composition. The influence of Moscheles and, particularly, Chopin was decisive throughout his creative life. He composed one opera, *Inese e Bianca*, which, in spite of his efforts, was never staged. More important are his piano works and songs, the latter clearly influenced by lieder. In his *Cantares nuevos y viejos de Galicia* (1877) he united the folklore of his native province with the technique and spirit of Romantic piano music. His works for piano solo are equally Romantic in technique.

BIBLIOGRAPHY
R. A. de Santiago: *Marcial del Adalid: sintesis biográfica* (La Coruña, 1965)

JOSÉ LÓPEZ-CALO

Adam (*fl* 1420–30). ?French composer. Known only from three rondeaux (in *Gb-Ob* Can.misc.213), he has been tentatively identified as either Adam Fabri, a clerk at Notre-Dame in 1415, or Adam Maigret, first chaplain to Charles VI of France in 1422; it seems much less likely that he was the Erasmus Adam mentioned in a motet (in *I-AO*) on the death of Emperor Albert. All three works are for three voices, and in each only the upper voice, generally the most lively, is supplied with text. Imitation is used in the opening of *A temps vendra*.

WORKS

Edition: *Early Fifteenth-century Music*, ed. G. Reaney, CMM, xi/2 (1959) [R]

A temps vendra, 3vv, R
Au grief hermitage, 3vv, R
Tout a coup, 3vv, R

BIBLIOGRAPHY

J., J. F. R. and C. Stainer, eds.: *Dufay and his Contemporaries* (London, 1898/R)

A. Pirro: *La musique à Paris sous le règne de Charles VI (1380–1422)* (Paris, 1930).

TOM R. WARD

Adam, Adolphe (Charles) (*b* Paris, 24 July 1803; *d* Paris, 3 May 1856). French composer. He composed more than 80 stage works, some of which, especially those written for the Paris Opéra-Comique, obtained considerable and lasting success.

1. LIFE. His father (Jean) Louis Adam (*b* Muttersholtz, Bas-Rhin, 3 Dec 1758; *d* Paris, 8 April 1848) was a pianist, composer and teacher; he taught the piano at the Paris Conservatoire from 1797 to 1842 (his pupils included Frédéric Kalkbrenner and Ferdinand Hérold), composed several keyboard sonatas (many with violin accompaniment) as well as lighter works, and wrote a *Méthode, ou Principe général du doigté pour le forté-piano* and a *Méthode du piano du Conservatoire* that was translated into German and Italian. Adolphe was not encouraged by his father to become a musician, but, influenced by his friendship with Hérold (12 years his senior), he decided at an early age that he wished to compose, and to compose, specifically, theatre music. He first studied the piano with Henry Lemoine, and at 17 entered the Conservatoire, where he studied the organ with Benoist, counterpoint with Reicha and composition with Boieldieu, the chief architect of his musical development. By the age of 20 he was already contributing songs to the Paris vaudeville theatres; he played in the orchestra at the Gymnase, later becoming chorus master there. In 1824 he entered the competition for the Prix de Rome, gaining an honourable mention, and again in 1825, when he won a *second prix*; of more practical use was the opportunity to help Boieldieu with the preparation of *La dame blanche*, produced at the Opéra-Comique on 10 December 1825. Adam's transcriptions for the piano on themes from the opera were published by Janet & Cotelle; on the proceeds he toured the Netherlands, Germany and Switzerland in summer 1826 with a friend.

Museums and the beauties of nature did not appeal much to Adam, and the most fruitful event of his trip was a meeting, in Geneva, with Eugène Scribe. Adam had already written music for a one-act vaudeville by Scribe (and Mazères), *L'oncle d'Amérique*, given at the Gymnase on 14 March 1826; now he obtained from the librettist the text of a one-act comic opera, *Le mal du pays, ou La batelière de Brientz*, which was produced at the Gymnase on 28 December 1827. Just over a year later, on 9 February 1829, *Pierre et Catherine*, his first work to be accepted by the Opéra-Comique, was given in a double bill with Auber's *La fiancée* and achieved over 80 performances.

Adam's next piece for the Opéra-Comique, the three-act *Danilowa*, was successfully produced in April 1830, but its run was interrupted by the July Revolution. Meanwhile he continued to write vaudevilles and pasticcios for the Gymnase and the Nouveautés, where his first ballet, the pantomime *La chatte blanche*, composed in collaboration with Casimir Gide, was presented on 26 July. After the Revolution theatrical conditions became difficult in Paris, and Adam went to London, where his brother-in-law, Pierre François Laporte, was manager of the King's Theatre. In 1832 Laporte leased the Theatre Royal, Covent Garden, and on 1 October, as an afterpiece to *The Merchant of Venice*, he presented *His First Campaign*, a 'military spectacle' with music by Adam, which featured the 12-year-old Elizabeth Poole as a drummer boy. *The Dark Diamond*, a historical melodrama in three acts, which followed on 5 November, failed to repeat the success of *His First Campaign*. Adam returned to Paris for the première of Hérold's *Le pré aux clercs* (15 December), and went back briefly to London early in 1833, when his ballet *Faust* was presented by Laporte at the King's Theatre.

Adam then achieved one of his greatest popular successes; *Le chalet*, a one-act *opéra comique* with text, based on Goethe's *Jery und Bätely*, by Scribe and Mélesville, was first produced on 25 September 1834 and reached its 1000th performance at the Opéra-Comique in 1873. Boieldieu, who died 13 days after the première, was present at his pupil's triumph. After considering, but in the end turning down, a text by Planard, *L'éclair* (later set by Halévy), Adam accepted a libretto from de Leuven and Brunswick provisionally entitled *Une voix*. He also composed a ballet, *La fille du Danube*, for Marie Taglioni, which was performed at the Paris Opéra – Adam's first work for that venue – on 21 September 1836. Meanwhile *Une voix*, by now called *Le postillon de Lonjumeau*, was already in rehearsal at the Opéra-Comique, where its successful première took place on 13 October, with the tenor Jean-Baptiste Chollet (who also created the title roles of Auber's *Fra diavolo* and Hérold's *Zampa*) as the postilion Chapelou.

Another ballet, *Les mohicans*, for the Opéra, and four more works for the Opéra-Comique followed in quick succession, then in September 1839 Adam left Paris for St Petersburg. *La fille du Danube* was given immediately after his arrival, then his new ballet for Taglioni, *L'écumeur de mer*, was danced before the imperial court on 21 February 1840. Four days later *Le brasseur de Preston*, first heard in Paris in 1838 and dedicated to Tsar Nicholas I, was performed by the German opera company in St Petersburg with Adam conducting. Adam left Russia at the end of March, stopping on the way back to Paris at Berlin, where he wrote and presented an opera-ballet, *Die Hamadryaden*, at the Court Opera (28 April 1840).

Adam's next important work was the composition by which he is now best known – the ballet *Giselle*. He completed the music in three weeks (it had taken Théophile Gautier and his collaborator Saint-Georges three days to write the scenario, based on a legend recounted by Heine in his book *De l'Allemagne*) and *Giselle*, with Carlotta Grisi dancing the title role, began its triumphant career at the Opéra on 28 June 1841. Adam then reorchestrated Grétry's *Richard Coeur-de-lion*, revived for King Louis Philippe at Fontainebleau with its original sets, which survived at the theatre. He also completed the score to *Lambert Simnel*, an opera left unfinished by Hippolyte Monpou. Adam's first 'grand opera', *Richard en Palestine*, was produced at the Opéra in 1844, arousing little interest.

Adolphe Adam: engraving by E. Champollion from Arthur Pougin's 'Adolphe Adam: sa vie, sa carrière, ses mémoires artistiques' (1876)

That same year, having quarrelled with Basset, the new director of the Opéra-Comique, who vowed never to perform a work by Adam at his theatre, the composer found his main source of income removed. He made plans to open a third opera house in Paris, to be called the Opéra-National. A large amount of money – 250,000 francs down payment on the theatre, 200,000 francs for repairs and alterations and 100,000 francs, of which Adam had already paid half out of his own pocket, for the licence to perform new works – was required, and after some difficulty borrowed. The Opéra-National opened on 15 November 1847 with Aimé Maillart's *Gastibelza*, preceded by *Les premiers pas*, a prologue with music by Adam, Auber, Carafa and Halévy. For a few months the theatre flourished, then in February 1848 revolution again broke out in Paris, and on 26 March the Opéra-National closed down.

Adam was completely ruined. He owed 70,000 francs and when his 89-year-old father died in April, he could not pay the funeral expenses. Assigning all his royalties to pay off the debt, he turned to journalism as a means of earning some money and contributed reviews and articles to *Le constitutionnel* and the *Assemblée nationale*. He also became a professor of composition at the Conservatoire, a post he held until his death. Meanwhile Basset had left the Opéra-Comique and Adam was able to re-enter his spiritual home. In July 1850 one of his best works, the opera *Giralda, ou La nouvelle*

Psyché (with a text by Scribe, originally intended for Auber) was produced there, with an unknown soprano, Marie Félix Miolan, in the title role: as Miolan-Carvalho she was to be Gounod's first Marguerite, Mireille and Juliette, all at the Théâtre-Lyrique, the successor to the ill-fated Opéra-National. Adam wrote the very successful *Si j'étais roi* for the Théâtre-Lyrique, where it was performed with two different casts on 4–5 September 1852. That year no fewer than six new works of his were produced, and by the end of it his debts were finally cleared.

During the remaining three years of his life Adam composed- as prolifically as ever; he arranged Donizetti's *Betly* (on the same subject as his own opera *Le chalet*) for the Opéra (27 December 1853); one of his finest ballets, *Le corsaire*, was presented there on 23 January 1856, after a year's preparation. His final dramatic work, the charming one-act operetta *Les pantins de Violette*, was produced at the Bouffes-Parisiens, where it shared the bill with Offenbach's *Le thé de Polichinelle*, on 29 April 1856. Four nights later Adam died in his sleep.

2. WORKS. Adam was a prolific composer who wrote music with extreme facility, but a large amount of his huge output is of purely ephemeral interest; this includes innumerable piano arrangements, transcriptions and potpourris of favourite operatic arias, the many light songs and ballads, the popular numbers contributed to vaudevilles and comic operas during his apprentice years, even some of the theatre music written in his maturity; but there remain several operas and ballets that are not merely delightful examples of their kind, but are also scores full of genuine inspiration. *Le chalet*, his first significant success, incorporates the music from *Ariane à Naxos*, the cantata written for the 1825 Prix de Rome competition, but the opera is distinguished by its freshness of invention, as indeed are all his best works.

If *Le chalet* was Adam's most popular opera in France throughout the 19th century, *Le postillon de Lonjumeau* outdistanced it in other European countries, particularly in Germany, where every tenor who could boast the necessary top notes indefatigably performed the title role. But *Le postillon* is more than a vocal showpiece; Madelaine is as well characterized as Chapelou, and the various duets between them, first as young bride and bridegroom, later as 'Madame Latour' and 'Saint Phar' the famous tenor, are aptly differentiated. Above all, the score is imbued with a sense of theatre, the inborn gift that Adam brought so abundantly to all his stage works, even the weakest. In *Le brasseur de Preston* (1838), *Le roi d'Yvetot* (1842) and *Le roi des halles* (1853) Adam and his librettists de Leuven and Brunswick attempted, with only partial success, to repeat the formula of *Le postillon*. The most stylish, tuneful and accomplished of his later operas are *Giralda* and *Si j'étais roi*, the overtures to both pieces being particularly graceful and charming.

Adam found ballet music even easier and more rewarding to compose than operas – 'On ne travail plus, on s'amuse', he observed; and his ballet scores have a stylistic unity not always found in his operatic works. *Giselle* owes its vividly flourishing existence after 135 years as much to the music as to the subject. Adam, lucky in his interpreters – Taglioni, Grisi, Leroux, Cerrito – gave them eminently danceable music, and *La jolie fille de Gand, La filleule des fées* and *Le corsaire* have scores, if not plots, of similar quality to that of *Giselle*. Adam's religious music, on the other hand, is a paler reflection of his theatre music. His journalism, which he continued even when it was no longer a financial necessity, is lively and readable, while his judgments on contemporary composers – Meyerbeer and Verdi for example – are fair and open-minded; Berlioz, he admitted, he could neither understand nor appreciate.

WORKS
(all printed works published in Paris unless otherwise stated)

OPERAS
All first performed in Paris unless otherwise stated. Works performed at the Gymnase, Vaudeville and Nouveautés are mainly vaudevilles; the remaining works are all *opéras comiques* unless otherwise stated.

GY – *Gymnase*	OC – *Opéra-Comique*
VA – *Vaudeville*	TL – *Théâtre-Lyrique*
NO – *Nouveautés*	

vs – *vocal score*

Pierre et Marie, ou Le soldat ménétrier (1), GY, 22 Jan 1824
Le baiser au porteur (1), GY, 9 June 1824
Le bal champêtre (1), GY, 21 Oct 1824
La haine d'une femme (1), GY, 14 Dec 1824
L'exilé (2), VA, 9 July 1825
La dame jaune (1, Carmouche and Mazères), VA, 7 March 1826
L'oncle d'Amérique (1, Scribe and Mazères), VA, 14 March 1826
L'anonyme (2, Jouslin de la Salle, Dupeuty and Villeneuve), VA, 29 May 1826
Le hussard de Felsheim (3, Dupeuty, Villeneuve and Saint-Hilaire), VA, 9 March 1827
L'héritière et l'orpheline (2, Anne and Henry), VA, 12 May 1827
Perkins Warbeck (2, Théaulon, Brazier and Carmouche), GY, 15 May 1827
Mon ami Pierre (1, Dartois), NO, 8 Sept 1827
Monsieur Botte (3, Dupeuty and Villeneuve), NO, 15 Nov 1827
Le Caleb de Walter Scott (1, Dartois and Planard), NO, 12 Dec 1827
Le mal du pays, ou La batelière de Brientz (1, Scribe and Mélesville), GY, 28 Dec 1827, vs (?1828)
Lidda, ou La jeune servante (1, Anne), NO, 16 Jan 1828
La reine de seize ans (2, Bayard), GY, 30 Jan 1828
Le barbier châtelain, ou La loterie de Francfort (3, Anne and Théaulon), NO, 7 Feb 1828
Les comédiens par testament (1, Picard and Laffite), NO, 14 April 1828
Les trois cantons, ou La Confédération suisse (3, Villeneuve and Dupeuty), VA, 16 June 1828
Valentine, ou La chute des feuilles (2, Saint-Hilaire and Villeneuve), NO, 2 Oct 1828
Le clé (3, Leroi and Hyppolyte), VA, 5 Nov 1828
Le jeune propriétaire et le vieux fermier (3, Dartois), NO, 6 Feb 1829
Pierre et Catherine (2, J. H. Vernoy de Saint-Georges), OC, 9 Feb 1829 (?1829)
Isaure (3), NO, 1 Oct 1829
Henri V et ses compagnons (pasticcio, 3), NO, 27 Feb 1830
Danilowa (3, J. B. Vial and P. Duport), OC, 23 April 1830 (?1830)
Rafaël (pasticcio, 3), NO, 26 April 1830
Trois jours en une heure (1, Gabriel [J. J. G. de Lurieu] and Masson), OC, 21 Aug 1830, collab. Romagnesi
Les trois Catherine (3), NO, 26 July 1830, collab. C. Gide
Joséphine, ou Le retour de Wagram (1, Gabriel and Delaboullaye), OC, 2 Dec 1830 (?1830)
Le morceau d'ensemble (1, Carmouche and F. de Courcy), OC, 7 March 1831 (?1831)
Le grand prix, ou Le voyage à frais communs (3, Gabriel and Masson), OC, 9 July 1831 (?1831)
Casimir, ou Le premier tête-à-tête (2), NO, 1 Dec 1831
His First Campaign (military spectacle, 2), London, Covent Garden, 1 Oct 1832
The Dark Diamond (historical melodrama, 3), London, Covent Garden, 5 Nov 1832
Le proscrit, ou Le tribunal invisible (3, Carmouche and Saintine), OC, 18 Sept 1833 (?1833)
Une bonne fortune (1, Féréol [L. Second] and Edouard), OC, 28 Jan 1834 (1834)
Le chalet (1, Scribe and A. H. J. Mélesville), OC, 25 Sept 1834 (1834)
La marquise (1, Saint-Georges and A. de Leuven), OC, 28 Feb 1835 (1835)
Micheline, ou L'heure d'esprit (1, Saint-Hilaire, Masson and Villeneuve), OC, 29 June 1835 (1835)

Le postillon de Lonjumeau (3, de Leuven and Brunswick [L. L. Lhérie]), OC, 13 Oct 1836 (?1836)
Le fidèle berger (3, Scribe and Saint-Georges), OC, 6 Jan 1838 (1838)
Le brasseur de Preston (3, de Leuven and Brunswick), OC, 31 Oct 1838 (1838)
Régine, ou Les deux nuits (2, Scribe), OC, 17 Jan 1839 (?1839)
La reine d'un jour (3, Scribe and Saint-Georges), OC, 19 Sept 1839 (?1839)
La rose de Péronne (3, de Leuven and A. P. d'Ennery), OC, 12 Dec 1840
La main de fer, ou Le mariage secret (3, Scribe and Leuven), OC, 26 Oct 1841, vs (?1841)
Le roi d'Yvetot (3, de Leuven and Brunswick), OC, 13 Oct 1842 (1842)
Lambert Simnel (3, Scribe and Mélesville), OC, 14 Sept 1843 [completion of work begun by H. Monpou]
Cagliostro (3, Scribe and Saint-Georges), OC, 10 Feb 1844 (?1844)
Richard en Palestine (opera, 3, P. Foucher), Opéra, 7 Oct 1844, vs (?1844)
La bouquetière (opera, 1, H. Lucas), Opéra, 31 May 1847, vs (?1847)
Les premiers pas (prologue, 1, Vaëz and Royer), Opéra-National, 15 Nov 1847, collab. Auber, Carafa and Halévy
Le toréador, ou L'accord parfait (2, T. Sauvage), OC, 18 May 1849 (?1849)
Le Fanal (opera, 2, Saint-Georges), Opéra, 24 Dec 1849, vs (?1849)
Giralda, ou La nouvelle Psyché (3, Scribe), OC, 20 July 1850 (?1850)
La poupée de Nuremberg (1, de Leuven and A. de Beauplan), Opéra-National, 21 Feb 1852 (1852)
Le farfadet (1, F. A. E. de Planard), OC, 19 March 1852, (vs (1852)
Si j'étais roi (3, Ennery and J. Brésil), TL, 4 Sept 1852 (?1852)
La faridondaine (drama with songs, 5, Dupeuty and Bourget), Port-St Martin, 30 Dec 1852 collab. de Groot
Le sourd, ou L'auberge pleine (3, Langlé and de Leuven, after P. J. B. Choudard Desforges), OC, 2 Feb 1853, vs (?1853)
Le roi des halles (3, de Leuven and Brunswick), TL, 11 April 1853, vs (?1853)
Le bijou perdu (3, de Leuven and P. A. A. P. Desforges), TL, 6 Oct 1853, vs (?1854)
Le muletier de Tolède (3, Ennery and Clairville), TL, 16 Dec 1854, vs (1854)
À Clichy (1, Ennery and E. Grangé), TL, 24 Dec 1854, vs (c1855)
Le houzard de Berchini (2, Rosier), OC, 17 Oct 1855, vs (1855)
Falstaff (1, Saint-Georges and de Leuven, after Shakespeare), TL, 18 Jan 1856, vs (1856)
Mam'zelle Geneviève (2, Brunswick and Beauplan), TL, 24 March 1856
Les pantins de Violette (operetta, 1, L. Battu), Bouffes-Parisiens, 29 April 1856, vs (?1856)

Many excerpts, arrs. pubd separately

BALLETS
(all first performed in Paris unless otherwise stated)
La chatte blanche, Nouveautés, 26 July 1830, collab. C. Gide
Faust (3, Deshayes), London, King's Theatre, 16 Feb 1833
La fille du Danube (2, Taglioni and Desmares), Opéra, 21 Sept 1836
Les mohicans (2, Guerra), Opéra, 5 July 1837
L'écumeur de mer (2), St Petersburg, 21 Feb 1840
Die Hamadryaden (opera-ballet, 2, Colombey), Berlin, Court Opera, 28 April 1840
Giselle, ou Les Wilis (2, Gautier, Saint-Georges and Coralli), Opéra, 28 June 1841, arr. pf (1841), full score (London, 1948)
La jolie fille de Gand (3, Saint-Georges and Albert), Opéra, 22 June 1842
Le diable à quatre (2, de Leuven and Mazillier), Opéra, 11 Aug 1843, 10 nos. arr. pf (London, 1846)
The Marble Maiden (3, Saint-Georges and Albert), London, Drury Lane, 27 Sept 1845
Grisélidis, ou Les cinq sens (3, Dumanoir and Mazillier), Opéra, 16 Feb 1848, arr. pf (London, 1848)
La filleule des fées (3, Saint-Georges and Perrot), Opéra, 8 Oct 1840 collab. C. de Saint-Julien,
Orfa (2, Trianon and Mazillier), Opéra, 29 Dec 1852 (c1860)
Le corsaire (2, Saint-Georges and Mazillier), Opéra, 23 Jan 1856

Many excerpts and arrs. pubd separately

OTHER STAGE WORKS
Les nations (cantata, Banville), Paris, Opéra, 6 Aug 1851
La fête des arts (cantata, Méry), Paris, Opéra-Comique, 16 Nov 1852, vocal score (?1853)
Victoire (cantata, Carré), Paris, Opéra-Comique and Théâtre-Lyrique, 13 Sept 1855 (1855)
Cantata (Pacini), Paris, Opéra, 17 March 1856

OTHER WORKS
Sacred: Messe solennelle, 4 solo vv, chorus, perf. 1837 (1837); Mass, 3vv, collab. Saint-Julien; Messe de Ste Cécile, solo vv, chorus, orch, perf. 1850 (c1855); Messe de l'orphéon, 4 male vv, orch, perf. 1851

(?n.d.) [collab. Halévy, Clapisson, A. Thomas]; Mois de Marie de St Philippe, 8 motets, 1–2vv, org acc (?c1855); Domine salvum, 3 solo vv, chorus, org acc.; Hymne à la vierge, solo vv, org acc. ad lib (c1860); Noël, solo v (London, 1858); O salutaris, 2vv (Paris, c1900); O salutaris, vv, org, orch (?n.d.); others

Secular choral: Agnès Sorel (Viellard), cantata, 1824; Ariane.à Naxos (Vinaty), cantata, 1825; Les métiers, 4 male vv; Les enfants de Paris, 4 male vv, unacc., 1848 (?n.d.); La garde mobile, 4 male vv, orch, 1848; La marche républicaine, 4 male vv, orch, 1848 (n.d.); La muette, 4 male vv, unacc.

Many vocal duos, songs, romances, ballads (some in collections)

Grande sonate, pf, vn, vc, op.12 (?n.d.)

Pf: c200 light works, incl. potpourris and fantasias on operatic airs or melodies, arrs., transcrs.

Works for harmonium; harmonium, pf; org; org, pf

ARRANGEMENTS AND REORCHESTRATIONS

Grétry: Richard Coeur-de-lion, Zémire et Azore; Monsigny: Félix, Aline, Le déserteur; Dalayrac: Gulistan; Solié: Le diable à quatre; Nicolo: Cendrillon; Donizetti: Betly [recits]

WRITINGS

Souvenirs d'un musicien ... précédés de notes biographiques (Paris, 1857, many later edns.)

Derniers souvenirs d'un musicien (Paris, 1859, many later edns.)

BIBLIOGRAPHY

J. Lardin: Zémire et Azor par Grétry: quelques questions à propos de la nouvelle falsification de cet opéra (Paris, 1846)

——: Adrien François Boieldieu: Adolph Adam: Biographien (Kassel, 1855)

F. Halévy: Notice sur la vie et les ouvrages de M. Adolphe Adam (Paris, 1859); repr. as 'Adolphe Adam' in Halévy: Souvenirs et portraits (Paris, 1861)

P. Scudo: Critique et littérature musicales, ii (Paris, 1859)

F. Clément and P. Larousse: Dictionnaire lyrique, ou Histoire des opéras (Paris, 1867–9, enlarged 3/1905/R1969, ed. A. Pougin)

F. Clément: Les musiciens célèbres depuis le seizième siècle jusqu'à nos jours (Paris, 1868, rev., enlarged 4/1887)

E. de Mirecourt: Adolphe Adam (Paris, 1868)

A. Pougin: Adolphe Adam: sa vie, sa carrière, ses mémoires artistiques (Paris, 1876)

C. W. Beaumont: The Ballet Called Giselle (London, 1944)

H. Searle: Ballet Music: an Introduction (London, 1958, rev., enlarged 2/1973)

I. Guest: The Romantic Ballet in Paris (London, 1966)

ELIZABETH FORBES

Adam, Jean. See ADAM, JOHANN.

Ádám, Jenő (b Szigetszentmiklós, 12 Dec 1896). Hungarian composer, conductor and teacher. From 1911 until 1915 he received instruction in organ playing and theory at the Budapest teacher-training college. Then, as a prisoner of war (1916–20), he organized and conducted a men's choir and an orchestra in Russia. He studied composition at the Budapest Academy of Music under Kodály (1920–25) and conducting in Weingartner's master class in Basle (1933–5). He conducted the orchestra (1929–39) and the choir (1929–54) of the Budapest Academy where he also taught Hungarian folk music, choral conducting and methodology from 1939 to 1959, and where he directed the singing department from 1942 to 1957.

Ádám began his career as a conductor in Budapest in 1929 with a performance of Haydn's The Seasons. From 1929 until 1933 he was deputy conductor of the Budapest Choral and Orchestral Society. With the male choir Budai Dalárda, which he directed from 1933 until 1942, he made concert tours of Yugoslavia, Italy, Germany and Scandinavia. Also, in 1935–6 he was conductor of the Budapest Palestrina Choir. He conducted the first performance in Budapest of Purcell's Dido and Aeneas (1941), and he was a champion of Handel's music in Hungary. From 1935, together with Kodály, he worked on a reform of music teaching in lower and middle schools; the tangible results of this work are their joint singing textbooks. In order to popu-larize serious music and old Hungarian folk music, he gave several hundred lectures on radio and television, at home and abroad. He was the originator of the programme 'Fifteen Minutes of Folksong' on Hungarian radio. In 1955 he received the title Merited Artist of the Hungarian People's Republic and in 1957 the Kossuth Prize.

As a composer Ádám gradually freed himself from the stylistic influence of his teacher Kodály and developed his own specifically Hungarian lyrical-romantic musical language. He was one of the first to use Hungarian folktunes in symphonic and stage works, in some ways anticipating Kodály.

WORKS
(selective list)

Stage: Magyar karácsony [Hungarian Christmas] (opera, 1, K. Tüdős), 1930, Budapest, Royal Opera, 22 Dec 1931; Mária Veronika (mystery, 2, A. Rékai, after M. Bethlen), 1934–5, Budapest, Royal Opera, 27 Oct 1938

Vocal orch: Lacrima sonata (I. Balogh, S. Boross, Ady), Bar, orch, 1928; Ember az úton [Man on the road] (liturgy, Rékai), S, A, T, B, chorus, orch, 1944–5; 35 magyar népdal [35 Hungarian folksongs], 1v, gypsy ens, 1951–2; Két szál pünkösdrózsa [Two peonies] (Hung. trad.), Mez, Bar, chorus, orch, 1951; Toborzó [Verbunkos] (L. Amadé), Bar, male chorus, orch, 1952; Arany János dalai [Arany's songs] (Arany, Petőfi, Amadé, F. Kölesey), S, Bar, chorus, orch, 1957; Tulipán [Tulip] (Hung. trad.), S, Bar, chorus, orch, 1963; Ábel siratása [Lament for Abel] (liturgy), A, B, chorus, orch, 1966; Dankó Pista dalai (A. Békefy, G. Gárdonyi, T. Péterfy, L. Pósa, Z. Thury), S, A, T, B, chorus, orch, 1967

Unacc. choral: Adventi ének [Advent song], 1929; Falu végén kurta kocsma [At the end of the village] (Petőfi), male vv (1938); Psalm xlvi, 4vv (1942); 3 Canons (Petőfi, D. Berzsenyi, S. Endrődi) (1948); Jelige [Motto] (F. Kazinczy), male vv (1958); many folksong arrs.

Inst: Dominica, suite, orch, 1926; 2 str qts, 1925, 1931; Sonata, vc, pf, 1926

Many folksong arrs, for 1v, pf

Principal publishers: Editio Musica, Magyar Kórus

WRITINGS

A skálától a szimfóniáig [From the scale to the symphony] (Budapest, 1943)

with Z. Kodály: Szó-mi (Budapest, 1943–6) [singing textbooks for elementary schools]

Módszeres énektanítás a relatív szolmizáció alapján [Systematic singing teaching based on the tonic solfa] (Budapest, 1944)

with Z. Kodály: Énekeskönyv [Singing book] (Budapest, 1948–58) [series for elementary schools]

A muzsikáról [On music] (Budapest, 1954, 2/1954)

BIBLIOGRAPHY

'Mária Veronika, Ádám Jenő dalműve az Operaházban', A zene, xx (1938)

'Élő magyar zeneszerzők: Ádám Jenő' [Living Hungarian composers: Ádám], A zene, xxv (1943)

Z. Kodály: Visszatekintés [Retrospection] (Budapest, 1964)

FERENC BÓNIS

Adam, Johann [Jean] (b c1705; d Dresden, 13 Nov 1779). German composer. He was a Jagdpfeifer at the Dresden court, 1733–6, then until his death a violist in the Dresden Hofkapelle. He was also 'ballet-compositeur' of the court opera (from c1740), and composer and director of music for the elector's French theatre (1763–9). According to Burney and Fürstenau he added ballet music to operas by J. A. Hasse and made an adaptation of Rameau's Zoroastre (Dresden, 1752); the documents of the Hofkapelle in the Dresden State Archives indicate that he also composed new pieces for various opéras comiques, and in 1756 he published a Recueil d'airs à danser executés sur le Théâtre du Roi à Dresde, arranged for harpsichord. The concertos and chamber works listed under 'Adam' in the Breitkopf catalogues may also be attributed to him. Few of his compositions are extant; apart from his arrangements of works by other composers, the Sächsische Landesbibliothek in Dresden contains only a concerto in G for flute and strings by him.

BIBLIOGRAPHY

GerberL

C. Burney: *The Present State of Music in Germany, the Netherlands and United Provinces* (London, 1773, 2/1775); ed. P. Scholes as *Dr. Burney's Musical Tours* (London, 1959)

M. Fürstenau: *Zur Geschichte der Musik und des Theaters am Hofe zu Dresden*, ii (Dresden, 1862/R1971), 226f, 269

B. S. Brook, ed.: *The Breitkopf Thematic Catalogue, 1762–1787* (New York, 1966)

O. Landmann: *Quellenstudien zum italienischen Intermezzo comico per musica und zu seiner Geschichte in Dresden* (diss., U. of Rostock, 1972)

ORTRUN LANDMANN

Adam, Play of [Jeu d'Adam; Mystère d'Adam]. An anonymous 12th-century play of the Fall of Man; it was originally entitled *Ordo representationis Ade* and was written in Norman French with elaborate Latin stage-directions and rubrics for the singing of Latin responsories. In the manuscript (*F-TO* 927) the Adam and Eve scene is followed by one of Cain and Abel and a Prophet play.

See also MEDIEVAL DRAMA, §III, 2(ii).

JOHN STEVENS

Adam, Theo (*b* Dresden, 1 Aug 1926). German bass-baritone. As a boy he was a member of the Dresdener Kreuzchor, and he studied in the city and at Weimar before making his début at the Dresden Staatsoper in 1949. He joined the Berlin Staatsoper in 1952. That year he made his début in a small role at Bayreuth, graduating to King Henry in 1954 and to Wotan in 1963; his later roles there have included the Dutchman, Amfortas and Hans Sachs. At the Salzburg Festival he has been heard as Ochs (1969) and Wozzeck (1972), and at the Vienna Staatsoper he sang the title role in a new production of *Don Giovanni* in 1972. Also in Vienna he sang a memorable Pizarro in the Beethoven bicentenary production of *Fidelio* at the Theater an der Wien in 1970, conducted by Bernstein. His other roles include King Philip, King Mark and La Roche (*Capriccio*). He made his débuts at Covent Garden as Wotan in 1967 and at the Metropolitan Opera as Hans Sachs in 1963. Adam is also a notable Bach singer and a fine Elijah. He has recorded most of his Wagner and several other roles. All his interpretations display an understanding of dramatic situation allied to an intelligently used, if not always totally ingratiating, voice. Since Hotter's retirement he has been one of the leading Wotans of his day, and his Sachs, Amfortas, Dutchman and Pizarro are all considerable readings.

ALAN BLYTH

Adamberger, (Josef) Valentin (*b* Munich, 6 July 1743; *d* Vienna, 24 Aug 1804). German tenor and singing teacher. He studied under Valesi in Italy where he sang from 1762 under the name of Adamonti. In 1772 he was engaged in Munich, and in 1777 in London, appearing at the King's Theatre in Sacchini's *Creso*. In 1780 he went to Vienna, where he became a firm favourite; Joseph II described him as 'our incomparable Adamberger'. In the Gluck revivals of 1781 he appeared as Orestes in *Iphigénie en Tauride*, Admetus in *Alceste* and Orpheus in *Orfeo ed Euridice*; in 1785 a performance of *Die Pilgrime von Mekka* was given for his benefit.

Adamberger's greatest claim to fame was as Mozart's

leading German tenor. He created the roles of Belmonte in *Die Entführung aus dem Serail* (16 July 1782) and Herr Vogelsang in *Der Schauspieldirektor* (7 February 1786). Other works which Mozart wrote for Adamberger were 'Per pietà, non ricercate' K420 (intended for Anfossi's *Il curioso indiscreto*), *Misero! o sogno!* K431/425b, *Davidde penitente* K469 and *Die Maurerfreude* K471. He also sang in Mozart's rescored version of Handel's *Messiah* on 7 April 1789. It is clear from Mozart's correspondence that the men were friends and that Mozart thought well of Adamberger's singing (see his letters of 26 September 1781 and 21 May 1785).

On the dissolution of the German company in Vienna in 1789 Adamberger joined the Italian company, retiring in 1793; but he remained with the Hofkapelle and became eminent as a singing teacher. The playwright Gebler wrote that Adamberger 'combined great art with a beautiful voice' (letter to Nicolai, 31 October 1780). Other contemporaries also stressed his musicianship but drew attention to a nasal quality at the top of his voice and his somewhat stiff deportment on stage.

BIBLIOGRAPHY

O. Michtner: *Das alte Burgtheater als Opernbühne* (Vienna, 1970)

CHRISTOPHER RAEBURN

Adam de Givenchi [Givenci, Gevanche, Gievenci] (*fl* 1230–68). Trouvère. His name implies that he was born in the village of Givenchy (Pas de Calais). His activity centred around Arras where he seems to have come in contact with Simon d'Authie, Pierre de Corbie, Guillaume le Vinier and Jehan Bretel. His name appears first in two charters dated May and July 1230 where he is given the title of clerk to the Bishop of Arras. In 1232 an act of procedure named him among the official household and as agent for the same bishop. In 1243 he is listed as priest and chaplain to the bishop and in 1245 as 'doyen de Lens'. Eight surviving poems are commonly attributed to Adam including two jeux-partis in which he is partnered by Jehan Bretel and Guillaume le Vinier. The latter, *Amis Guillaume, ainc si sage ne vi*, has survived with several melodies. Only four other songs have surviving melodies of which two are *chansons avec des refrains*; one of them, *Pour li servir*, is completely notated while the other, *Assés plus*, lacks music for the refrains. All the songs are in an *AAB* form with simple melodies.

WORKS

(all in F-Pn fr.844)

Amis Guillaume, ainc si sage ne vi, R.1085, *Pn* fr.12615, *A* 139, *I-Rvat* Reg.1490

Assés plus que d'estre amés, R.912, *F-Pn* fr.12615

Mar vi loial voloir et jalousie, R.1164

Pour li servir en bone foi, R.1660, *Pn* fr.12615

Si com fortune d'amour, R.1947, *Pn* fr.12615

BIBLIOGRAPHY

A. Jeanroy, L. Brandin and P. Aubry: *Lais et descorts français du XIIIe siècle*, Mélanges de musicologie critique, iii (Paris, 1901), 18ff

E. Ulrix: 'Les chansons du trouvère artésien Adam de Givenci', *Mélanges Camille de Borman* (Liège, 1919), 499

A. Jeanroy, ed.: *Le chansonnier d'Arras* (Paris, 1925) [facs. edn.]

A. Långfors, A. Jeanroy and L. Brandin: *Recueil général des jeux-partis français* (Paris, 1926), pp.xxxvi, xxxvii, 333

J. and L. Beck, eds.: *Le manuscrit du roi: fonds français 844 de la Bibliothèque nationale*, Corpus cantilenarum medii aevi, 1st ser., ii (Philadelphia, 1938) [facs. edn.]

R. Dragonetti: *La technique poétique dans la chanson courtoise* (Bruges, 1960), 336, 370, 652f

For further bibliography *see* TROUBADOURS, TROUVÈRES.

IAN R. PARKER

Adam de la Bassée (*d* 1286). ?French poet and priest. He was a canon and priest of the collegiate church of St Pierre in Lille, near Arras. About 1280, he wrote a metrical and rhymed paraphrase of the famous poem, *Anticlaudianus*, by the 12th-century doctor, philosopher and poet ALAIN DE LILLE. Its plot concerns Nature's formation of a perfect man to be imbued with the Arts and Virtues, and an ascent to heaven, on which journey the music of the spheres is heard, to request a soul from God. Adam named his new work *Ludus super Anticlaudianum*. It survives today in one MS (*F-Lm* 316), thought to be partly autograph. Adam's work retains the plot, the moral and the didactic character of the original, but the forbidding allegory and encyclopedic tone is modified in favour of a simpler style and language so that the work, although in Latin, is almost like a *roman*. Emphasizing a more entertaining but still serious purpose, Adam inserts within the work 38 musical pieces with sacred or semi-sacred texts; 36 are monophonic songs and the remaining two are polyphonic compositions. 20 of these are contrafacta modelled on earlier compositions whose titles are in most cases mentioned in the rubrics. They consist of hymns, sequences, a responsory, an alleluia, a processional antiphon, trouvère songs, dances (a lai-*notula* and a rondeau), a pastourelle and a polyphonic motet. Of the other 18 pieces, one is a two-part Agnus in conductus style. Altogether, the pieces in the *Ludus* form a kind of anthology in which almost every contemporary sacred and secular style is represented.

The insertions are not made arbitrarily but mostly fall into two large sections where the choice of form or style seems to emphasize the action of the poem. In the first section, whose poetry consists of supplications to and praises of the saints, Christ and the Virgin, Adam used contrafacta of secular songs, of hymns and of some unspecified items which have the character of antiphons. Here there is a resemblance to a canonical Office. Later, the newly-formed man whose creation is the subject of the poem is endowed with gifts by the Arts and Virtues and finally receives the soul brought from heaven to make him perfect. The series of offerings followed by the descent of the Spirit is symbolized in music by the choice of certain items from the Mass, namely the responsory (analogous to the gradual), alleluia, sequence and finally the motet, which is based on a plainsong for Pentecost.

The musical insertions thus have an unusually clear and demonstrable symbolic meaning.

The sources of the contrafacta are either popular and widely distributed compositions of the century, such as songs by Roi Thibaut de Navarre and Henri de Brabant and ecclesiastical tunes such as the sequence *Letabundus*, or are of local importance, like the chants to St Peter and St Elizabeth. Two contrafacta should be singled out: the motet, *O quam sollempnis*/Tenor *Amor*, based on *Et quant iou remir son cors*/Tenor *Amor*, is known in a large number of MSS including *I-Fn* 29.1 (F); the *notula* is one of the few examples of this form, which Johannes de Grocheo mentioned in *De musica* (*c*1300). The notation of the *Ludus* is that of contemporary plainsong or of the secular chansonniers.

Adam de la Bassée possibly influenced ADAM DE LA HALLE, who worked in Arras up to 1283 and wrote his *Jeu de Robin et Marion* after this date, thus after the *Ludus*. The slight clues suggesting such influence have not yet been investigated. The effect of Adam on the authors of *romans*, many of whom lived in the area of Lille and Arras, is, however, more probable. The *Ludus*, as a comprehensive musical anthology, may have been a direct predecessor of the *Roman de Fauvel* (1316), a similar anthology with other shared characteristics.

EDITIONS
Analecta hymnica, xlviii, ed. G. M. Dreves and C. Blume (Leipzig, 1905/*R*1967), 298ff [texts of musical items only]
Ludus super Anticlaudianum, ed. P. Bayart (Tourcoing, 1930) [complete edition of text; includes facsimiles and old-fashioned transcriptions of the musical folios]

BIBLIOGRAPHY
Andrew Hughes: 'The "Ludus super Anticlaudianum" of Adam de la Bassée', *JAMS*, xxiii (1970), 1

ANDREW HUGHES

Adam de la Halle [Adan de la Hale, Adan le Bossu, Adan le Boscu d'Arras, Adan d'Arras] (*b* Arras, 1245–50; *d* Naples, ?1285–8, or ?England, after 1306). French trouvère poet and composer. His musical and literary works encompass virtually every genre current in the late 13th century. He is one of the few medieval musicians to be credited with both monophonic and polyphonic music.

1. LIFE. Apart from his own works, there is little other documentary evidence for a biography of Adam de la Halle. It seems certain that he was born in Arras, as his name sometimes appears as Adam d'Arras, or, in one source, Adam le Boscu d'Arras – forms that were probably used when he was a student in Paris. Tax records show that there was a 'Maison d'Adam d'Arras' there in 1282, although it is unlikely that he was living in it at that time. The most common form of his name is Adan le Bossu (the hunchback), a name which his family apparently adopted to distinguish themselves from the other 'Hale' families in Arras. In the *Roi de Secile* Adam protested that, although he was called 'the hunchback', he was not that at all ('On m'apèle Bochu, mais je ne le sui mie'). The origin of this unusual name is not known, but it may be that some member of the family was indeed a hunchback, and the name thereafter remained.

In the *Jeu d'Adam ou de la feuillie*, it is stated that Adam's wife's name was Maroie and that his father was a Maistre Henri de la Hale. In the *Nécrologe de la Confrérie des jongleurs et de bourgeois d'Arras* there is a Maistre Henri Bochu, whose death was recorded in 1290. In 1282, the death of the wife of Henri de la Hale is likewise recorded. The same *Nécrologe* lists two persons who may have been Adam's wife: in 1274, a Maroie li Hallee is mentioned, and in 1287 Maroie Hale. It would be difficult to choose between these two, although Adam, in the *Jeu d'Adam* apparently written about 1276 (see Cartier, 1971), referred to his wife as still living.

The frequently repeated accounts of Adam's early schooling in Vaucelles and his exile to Douai are based on faulty interpretations of two lines of the *Jeu d'Adam* and of four lines of Baude Fastoul's *congé* respectively. He probably studied in Paris: he is often described in the sources as 'maistre', and in the *Jeu d'Adam* he expressed the desire to return to his studies in Paris. The jeux-partis with other trouvères of Arras indicate that he was a member of the local *pui*. The jeux-partis with Jehan Bretel (*d* 1272) provide the only reliable date from Adam's early life; they were most likely written after his return from Paris which was probably in about 1270. (In *Adan, a moi respondés*, Jehan Bretel referred

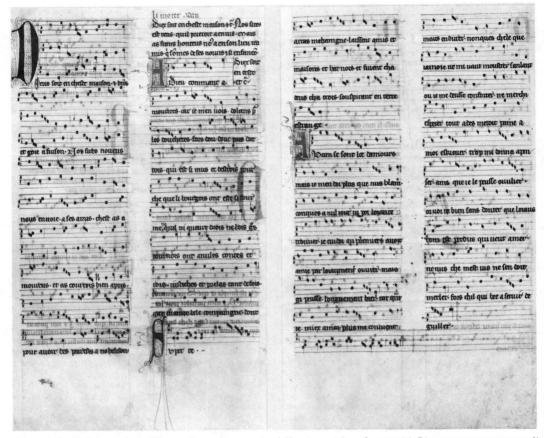

Adam de la Halle's rondeau 'Dieus soit en cheste maison' (3vv in score) and motet 'A Dieu commant amouretes'/ 'Aucun se sont loe d'amours'/'Super te' (F-Pn fr.25566, ff.34v–35)

to Adam as 'bien letrés', thus strengthening the impression that his studies took place before the jeux-partis were written.) His marriage to Maroie must have occurred shortly after this date (see Cartier).

He probably did not remain in Arras for long as both the *Jeu d'Adam* and his *congé* (written c1276–7) are 'farewells'. When he expressed the desire in the *Jeu d'Adam* to return to Paris his departure is not pictured as imminent; in his *congé*, however, departure is imminent, although Paris is no longer mentioned. His destination after the *congé* was more likely Italy, where he served Robert II, Count of Artois. Robert made several trips to Italy on behalf of his uncle Charles of Anjou beginning in 1274. In 1283, Robert travelled to Italy again to aid his uncle in his war against the Sicilians. In Italy, Adam entered the service of Charles of Anjou, the subject of the fragmentary *chanson de geste*, *Le roi de Secile*. During this period the *Jeu de Robin et de Marion* was also composed.

After the death of Charles of Anjou in 1285, two contradictory pieces of evidence concern Adam's further activities and his death. In what is presented as a posthumous tribute written in 1288 by Adam's nephew Jehanes Mados, Adam's departure from Arras and his death are recorded ('ses oncles Adans li Boscus ... laissa Arras, ce fu folie, car il est cremus et amés. Quant

il morut, ce fu pitiés': *F-Pn* fr.375, f.119v; a person named Mados is mentioned in the *Jeu d'Adam* as well, but it is uncertain whether the two are identical or even related). If this account is reliable, Adam would have been about 50 years old at the time of his death, and his father would have survived him by two to five years. However, an English source from the year 1306 lists a 'maistre Adam le Boscu' among the minstrels engaged for the coronation of Edward II in 1307 (see Gégou). This raises the possibility that Adam did not die in Naples as apparently reported by his nephew. Both the unusual name 'Boscu' and the appellation 'maistre' are distinctive, though it may be that the English Bossu was a younger member of the same family (? Adam's son). If this is the composer, his death would have occurred after 1306, when he would have been about 60 years old.

2. WORKS. Adam wrote in a wide variety of genres. In addition to the monophonic chansons, the jeux-partis, the shorter rondeaux and the three plays with musical inserts, he wrote one of the three extant *congés* by Artesian poets (the others are by Baude Fastel and Jehan Bodel) and the incomplete epic poem *Le roi de Secile*. Some critics have even doubted that his poetry could all be the work of a single man. His works comprise not only the continuation of the courtly lyric but

also the even older tradition of the *chanson de geste* alongside the modern, bourgeois elements in the *Jeu d'Adam* and in *Robin et Marion*. The *Jeu d'Adam* has provoked the greatest interest both in the earlier and the more recent Adam criticism; it has been characterized as 'the fusion of courtly lyric, allegory and social criticism ... a tour de force without parallel in any literature, with the exception of such non-dramatic works as the *Canterbury Tales* of Chaucer, the *Decameron*, *Don Quixote* or *Gargantua* and *Pantagruel*' (Cartier, p.181). It is all of these things, and in addition has the distinctly modern characteristics of being autobiographical (Adam himself appears in the play) and strongly individualistic.

His works survive in over two dozen manuscripts, one of which (*F-Pn* fr.25566) is virtually a complete edition arranged by genres. In this source the chansons are entered first, followed by the jeux-partis ('parture'), the rondeaux, the motets and finally the dramatic and narrative works. No other source is so complete, but several contain both monophonic and polyphonic works. The motets are transmitted in the principal motet collections of the late 13th century. (See Wilkins for sources of all the musical works.)

Of the 54 monophonic works listed below, 18 are jeux-partis. In 16 of these, Jehan Bretel is the partner, which means that they were written no later than 1272. Since the melody of the jeu-parti was presumably composed by the 'questioner' who sings the first strophe, very few of these can be considered musical works of Adam, who is the 'respondent' in 13 cases. It may be, however, that the early encounter with Bretel was an important influence on the younger man's melodic style in the chansons. Compare, for instance, the melody for *Adan, a moi respondés* in ex.1 with the melody which

Ex.1 *F-AS* 657 (olim 139) f. 150*v*

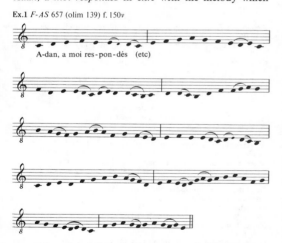

A-dan, a moi res-pon-dés   (etc)

served for two of Adam's chansons, ex.2. Without postulating any direct relationship between these two works, or even suggesting which was written earlier, there are, nevertheless, similarities that cannot be overlooked. The pieces are virtually identical in range and share a basically 'C major' tonality; both remain in the lower part of the range for the first four phrases, and rise later. The two melodies have few identical turns of phrase, but the 3rds C–E and E–G are important in both. While Bretel's melody is diffuse and loosely organized, however, Adam's is formally clear and melodi-

cally sophisticated. The initial repeated pair of phrases is not conceived as a clearly contrasted pair, but as open and closed variants of the same phrase. The second of these appears, again slightly varied, as a musical refrain in the last line. In addition, both the penultimate and antepenultimate phrases recall the cadences found in the first two lines. Similar melodies are found in other jeux-partis and in the chanson *De cuer pensieu*.

Ex.2 *Ibid* f. 135

He - las il n'est mais nus qui aint   (etc)

Ex.3 *Ibid* f. 134

Il ne muet pas de sens ce-lui qui plaint (etc)

While the melody shown in ex.2 gives a distinctly modern – or at least uncourtly – impression, other chansons seem closer to the older tradition. *Il ne muet pas de sens celui qui plaint* may represent this tradition (ex.3). Its characteristic combination of falling and rising motion in the first two phrases recalls the oldest and most central tradition of French monophonic song (e.g. Bernart de Ventadorn's *Be m'an perdut lai enves Ventadorn* and the Chastelain de Couci's *Quant li rossignol iolis*). Adam's style tends to exhibit the major tonality, the clear arrangement of the cadences and the formal sophistication already noted in ex.2 in which the last two lines are an exact complement of the first two without being a literal reprise, and the middle lines reflect the contour of the first lines in reverse, at the same time presenting a complete contrast in their cadences both to what precedes and to what follows.

The rondeaux are both interesting and important as early indications of the secular direction which polyphonic music was to take in the 14th century. Although labelled 'Li rondel' in the sources, only 14 of the 16 are actually rondeaux in the later, 'fixed' sense. This is entirely appropriate to the 13th century's understanding of the term 'rondeau' (*see* RONDEAU (i)), which was applied more or less universally to refrain songs which are 'round' by virtue of an initial refrain that recurs periodically. The exceptions to the standard rondeau form are *Fines amouretes ai*, a virelai, and *Dieus soit*, a ballade with an initial refrain. These pieces are set polyphonically in note-against-note style. The scoring in the sources always has the principal melody in the middle voice, even though at times this voice may actually be the lowest sounding part. Adam occasionally introduced variety into the strict rondeau form by varying the added voices when the form demands a repetition in the principal melody. Thus in *Je muir*, a standard eight-line rondeau, the following scheme results:

added voices: *ABcAcdAB*
melody: *ABaAabAB*

In *Dieus soit* a kind of variety is achieved by exchanging the added voices.

Five motets are attributed to Adam with some certainty and six others have been attributed to him by modern editors because they quote material found in the genuine works. All the authentic motets are based on plainchant tenors, two of which are among the most widely used tenors in the 13th century (*Omnes* and [*In*] *seculum*). These pieces are basically conservative and include refrains from other works of Adam. The remaining motets contrast strikingly with the authentic ones in that four are based on French secular tenors, one of which (*He, resvelle toi, Robin*) also occurs in the *Jeu de Robin et de Marion*. As in the first group, refrains, primarily from the polyphonic rondeaux, are quoted in almost every one of these motets. In general, their style is slightly later than that of the authentic ones. The quoted material in them is the only evidence for Adam's authorship, and it is equally likely that other composers could have quoted Adam's songs. In the case of *Dame bele*, however, the interdependence of motet and rondeau goes somewhat deeper, extending to the melodic construction of the tenor and the triplum. This raises the possibility that the rondeau may have been based on the motet, in which case it would be entirely unnecessary to assume that Adam is the composer of the latter.

Of the three dramatic works containing music only *Robin et Marion* uses music extensively. While it shares with the later *opéra comique* the combination of sung and spoken parts, it is more closely related to the narrative *pastourelle* than to later examples of *opéra comique*. Indeed, the early opera did grow at least in part from the same pastoral tradition, but Adam's early precedent was not taken up by the next generation, and thus remains an isolated phenomenon.

It has been argued that much of the music of *Robin et Marion* is not original, but was simply culled from current popular song. Certainly, most of the melodies seem to be of a popular cast, but Adam composed similar melodies for his polyphonic rondeaux. Only the fact that some of the melodies from *Robin et Marion* do occur elsewhere might suggest that they are borrowed, whatever their source.

Adam de la Halle occupies a unique, though somewhat paradoxical, position in the history of music. The largest part of his musical composition was devoted to the monophonic chanson. This labels him as a composer of the past, a masterly representative of a dying tradition. But he is one of a small number of 13th-century composers who wrote both monophonic chansons and motets. The musical style of the rondeaux is basically conservative, but the idea of polyphonic settings of secular texts and melodies outside the motet tradition does point to the immediate future. It is in the dramatic works that Adam shows himself to be distinctly progressive and, indeed, far ahead of his time. *Robin et Marion* and the *Jeu d'Adam* both set precedents in different ways, but neither was to exercise any direct influence on the generations immediately following. The fact that he

directed most of his creative energy into genres which were either on the wane, such as the monophonic chanson, or into the secular drama with music, whose full development lay far in the future, is an accident of history, and not a critical comment on his importance as an author and composer. This accident means, however, that, for the music historian, Adam remains essentially a man of the past. The opinion of the literary critics seems to apply also to his music: he was a versatile and fertile creator in all of the secular genres of the 13th century.

WORKS

Editions: *Oeuvres complètes du trouvère Adam de la Halle: poésies et musique*, ed. E. de Coussemaker (Paris, 1872/*R*1965) [complete poetry edn. with most of the music] [C]

Polyphonies du 13e siècle, ed. Y. Rokseth (Paris, 1936–9) [R]

Adam de la Halle: Le jeu de Robin et Marion, ed. F. Gennrich, Musikwissenschaftliche Studienbibliothek, xx (Langen, 1962) [G]

The Lyric Works of Adam de la Hale, ed. N. Wilkins, CMM, xliv (1967) [complete music edn.] [W]

JEUX-PARTIS
(all monophonic)

Adan, a moi respondés, R.950 (with Jehan Bretel); W 33, C 152

Adan, amis, je vous dis une fois, R.1833 (with Jehan Bretel); W 37, C 169

Adan, amis, mout savés bien vo roi, R.1675 (with Jehan Bretel); W 38, C 172

Adan, d'amours vous demant, R.331 (with Jehan Bretel); W 31, C 141

Adan, du quel cuidiés vous, R.2049 (with Jehan Bretel; no music); W 45

Adan, li qués doit mieus trouver merci, R.1066 (with Jehan Bretel); W 42, C 189

Adan, mout fu Aristotes sachans, R.277 (with Jehan Bretel); W 36, C 165

Adan, qui aroit amée, R.494 (with Jehan Bretel); W 34, C 157

Adan, se vous amiés bien loiaument, R.703 (with Jehan Bretel); W 33, C 148

Adan, si soit que ma feme amés tant, R.359 (with Jehan Bretel); W 41, C 184

Adan, s'il estoit ainsi, R.1026 (with Jehan Bretel); W 30, C 133

Adan, vauriés vous manoir, R.1798 (with Jehan Bretel; 3 melodies); W 30, C 137

Adan, vous devés savoir, R.1817 (with Jehan Bretel); W 35, C 161

Assignés ci, Grieviler, jugement, R.690 (with Jehan de Grievilier); W 42, C 193

Avoir cuidai, engané le marchié, R.1094 (with Jehan Bretel); W 43, C 197

Compains, Jehan, un gieus vous vueil partir, R.1443 (with Jehan Bretel); W 40, C 181

Sire, assés sage vous voi, R.1679 (no music); W 44

Sire Jehan, ainc ne fustes partis, R.1584 (with Jehan Bretel); W 32, C 145

CHANSONS
(all monophonic)

Amours m'ont si doucement, R.658; W 14, C 59

Amours ne me vient oir, R.1438; W 26, C 119

Au repairier de la douce contree, R.500; W 13, C 55

Dame, vos hom vous estrine, R.1383; W 20, C 88

D'amourous cuer voel vueil chanter, R.833; W 3, C 3

De chanter ai volenté curieuse, R.1018; W 14, C 62

De cuer pensieu et desirant, R.336; W 27, C 122

De tant con plus aproisme mon pais, R.1577 (no music); W 27, C 126

Dous est li maus qui met le gent en voie, R.1771; W 25, C 114

Glorieuse vierge Marie, R.1180; W 24, C 106

Grant deduit a la douce savoureuse vie, R.1237; W 28

Helas, ils n'est mais nus qui n'aint, R.148 (contrafactum of next song); W 6, C 24

Helas, ils n'est mais nus qui aint, R.149 (contrafactum of preceding song); W 6, C 20

Il ne muet pas de sens celui qui plaint, R.152; W 5, C 16

Je n'ai autre retenance, R.248; W 4, C 11

Je ne chant pas reveleus de merci, R.1060; W 18, C 81

Je senc en moi l'amour renouveler, R.888; W 8, C 31

Li dous maus me renouvelle, R.612; W 10, C 39

Li jolis maus que je sent ne doit mie, R.1186; W 3, C 7

Li maus d'amer me plaist mieus a sentir, R.1454; W 9, C 35

Ma douce dame et amours, R.2025; W 15, C 65

Merci, Amours, de la douce doulour, R.1973; W 11, C 47

Merveille es quel talent j'ai, R.52; W 16, C 73

Mout plus se paine amours de moi esprendre, R.632; W 20, C 92

On demande mout souvent qu'est amours, R.2024; W 12, C 51

On me defent que mon cuer pas ne croie, R.1711; W 7, C 28

Onkes nus hom ne fu pris, R.1599; W 29
Or voi je bien qu'il souvient, R.1247; W 22, C 99
Pour ce se je n'ai esté, R.432; W 21, C 96
Pour quoi se plaint d'Amours nus, R.2128; W 10, C 42
Puisque je sui l'amoureuse loi, R.1661 [model for: 'Puisque je sui l'amoureuse loi', R.1661a; Guillaume de Bethune, 'Puisque je sui l'amoureuse loi', R.1662]; W 23, C 102
Qui a droit veut Amours servir, R.1458; W 16, C 69
Qui n'a pucele ou dame amée, R.495; W 28, C 127
Sans espoir d'avoir, R.2038; W 17, C 77
Se li maus qu'Amours envoie, R.1715; W 24, C 110
Tant me plaist vivre en amoureus dangier, R.1273, W 19, C 84

'RONDEAUX'
(all 3vv)

A Dieu commant amouretes, W 52, C 215, G 46
A jointes mains vous proi, W 56, C 223, G 50
Amours, et ma dame aussi, W 54, C 220, G 49
Bonne amourete, W 57, C 229, G 53
Dame, or sui trais, W 54, C 218, G 48
Dieus soit en cheste maison (ballade), W 58, C 232, G 54
Diex, comment porroie, W 56, C 226, G 51
Fines amouretes ai (virelai), W 51, C 211, G 45
Fi, maris, de vostre amour, W 53, C 217, G 47
Hareu, li maus d'amer, W 51, C 210, G 44
Hé, Diex, quant verai, W 56, C 225, G 51
Je muir, je muir, d'amourete, W 49, C 207, G 43
Li dous regars de me dame (two different settings), W 50, C 209, C 428, G 44
Or est Baiars en la pasture, W 55, C 221, G 49
Tant con je vivrai, W 58, C 230, G 53
Trop desir a veoir, W 57, C 228, G 52

MOTETS
(all 3vv)

A Dieu commant amouretes/Aucun se sont loé d'amours/Super te, W 60, C 239, R 103 (quotes the refrain, words and music of the rondeau 'A Dieu commant' in the triplum)
De ma dame vient/Diex, comment porroie/Omnes, W 62, C 246, R 138 (quotes the refrain, with the music transposed, of the rondeau 'Diex, comment porroie' in the duplum; a refrain from 'Le jeu de la feuillie' is quoted in the same voice)
Entre Adan et Hanikiel/Chiès bien séans/Aptatur, W 65, C 259, R 92
J'ai adès d'amours chanté/Omnes, W 69, C 271
J'os bien a m'amie parler/Je n'os a m'amie aler/Seculum, W 68, C 266

(authorship uncertain)
Bien met amours son pooir/Dame, alegies ma grevance/A Paris, W 76, R 165 (quotes the refrain, words and music, of rondeau 'Hé, Diex, quant verai')
Dame bele e avenant/Fi, mari, de vostre amour/Nus n'iert ja jolis s'il n'aime, W 72, C 421 (quotes the refrain, words and music, of rondeau 'Fi, maris, de vostre amour' to which tenor and triplum are also related musically)
En mai, quant rosier sont flouri/L'autre jour, par un matin/He, resvelle toi Robin, W 74, R 116 (tenor is a rondeau which appears in the 'Jeu de Robin et de Marion')
Mout me fu grief li departir/Robin m'aime, Robin m'a/Portare, W 73, C 423, R 108 (duplum is a pastourelle which also appears in the 'Jeu de Robin et de Marion')
Se je sui liés et chantans/Jolietement/Omnes, W 80, R 214 (end of triplum quotes beginning of duplum of motet 'Entre Adan/Chiès bien séans/Aptatur')
Theoteca Virgo geratica/Las, pour quoi l'eslonge tant/Qui prandroit, W 78, R 188 (quotes refrain, words and music, of rondeau 'Hé, Diex, quant verai')

MISCELLANEOUS
Le jeu d'Adam ou de la feuillie, C 295 (contains one brief refrain)
Le jeu de Robin et de Marion, C 345, G
Le jeu du pelerin, C 413 (contains two brief refrains)

BIBLIOGRAPHY
H. Guy: Essai sur la vie et les oeuvres littéraires du trouvère Adan de la Hale (Paris, 1898)
J. Chailley: 'La nature musicale du Jeu de Robin et Marion', Mélanges . . . G. Cohen (Paris, 1950), 111
F. Gennrich: 'Adam de la Halle', MGG
A. Adler: Sens et composition du Jeu de la Feuillée (Ann Arbor, 1957)
R. Dragonetti: La technique poétique des trouvères dans la chanson courtoise (Bruges, 1960)
G. Reaney: 'The Development of the Rondeau, Virelai and Ballade Forms from Adam de la Halle to Guillaume de Machaut', Festschrift Karl Gustav Fellerer zum sechzigsten Geburtstag (Regensburg, 1962), 421
F. Gégou: 'Adam le Bossu était-il mort en 1288 ?', Romania, lxxxvi (1965), 111
P. Ruelle: Les congés d'Arras (Brussels, 1965)
P. Zumthor: 'Entre deux esthétiques: Adam de la Halle', Mélanges . . . J. Frappier (Paris, 1970)
N. R. Cartier: Le bossu désenchanté (Geneva, 1971)
J. H. Marshall, ed.: The Chansons of Adam de la Halle (Manchester, 1971)
R. Barth-Wehrenalp: 'Der "Trouvère" Adan de la Hale – ein französischer Meistersinger', IMSCR, xi Copenhagen 1972, 250
J. Stevens: '"La grande chanson courtoise": the Songs of Adam de la Halle', PRMA, ci (1974–5), 11
——: 'The Manuscript Presentation of the Chansons of Adam de la Halle', Source Materials and the Interpretation of Music: a Memorial Volume to Thurston Dart (in preparation)

ROBERT FALCK

Adami da Bolsena, Andrea ['Il Bolsena'] (b Bolsena, 30 Nov 1663; d Rome, 22 July 1742). Italian singer, writer and composer. After early study at Montefiascone he was sent to Rome and at the precocious age of 15 was admitted as a soprano to the Sistine Chapel. He was a castrato of obviously unusual talent, but the remarkable success of his career also owed much to the fact that he enjoyed the protection of Cardinal Pietro Ottoboni – the most influential Roman music patron of the day – in whose palace he served as musician-in-residence from 1689 to 1699. In 1690 he became a member of the Arcadia – the foremost musico-literary academy in Rome – where he was dubbed 'Caricle Piseo'. Aided by Ottoboni's patronage he became maestro di cappella of the Sistine Chapel, an office that he held from 1700 to 1714. He had already entered the priesthood and during his period of office at the Vatican was granted a sinecure as archpriest at S Maria Maggiore, Rome.

Adami's importance rests on his Osservazioni per ben regolare il coro dei cantori della Cappella pontificia (Rome, 1711). This treatise, while interesting for its avowed purpose as a description of the functions of the papal choir, is most valuable for its numerous biographies of leading musicians associated with the Vatican establishment such as Palestrina, Gregorio Allegri and G. M. Nanino. He also wrote on non-musical subjects. Paradoxically he seems to have written no sacred music at all. His only known compositions are a few secular cantatas, a genre in which he earned a considerable reputation as a singer (one chronicler reported his affecting performance, at a musical occasion promoted by Ottoboni, of a cantata by Stradella); only two survive (in GB-Lbm Add.34055). Several volumes of cantatas by other composers survive from his private library, all bearing a coat-of-arms created specially for him; these handsome volumes (now in Cfm, Lbm, US-NH), as well as two portraits painted by notable Roman artists (see MGG), give substance to the contemporary description of him as 'ricchissimo e fortunatissimo'.

BIBLIOGRAPHY
E. Celani: 'I cantori della Cappella pontificia nei secoli XVI–XVII', RMI, xvi (1909), 69
H. J. Marx: 'Die Musik am Hofe Pietro Kardinal Ottobonis unter Arcangelo Corelli', AnMc, v (1968), 162
——: 'Adami, Andrea', MGG

OWEN JANDER

Adamis, Michael (b Piraeus, 19 May 1929). Greek composer and musicologist. In addition to his theological studies at Athens University, from which he graduated in 1954, he studied at the Athens, Piraeus and Hellenic conservatories (1947–59), receiving diplomas in neo-Byzantine music, harmony, counterpoint and fugue and composition (under Yannis A. Papaioannou). At Brandeis University (1962–5) he continued advanced studies in composition and Byzantine music palaeography, and became an associate of the electronic music studio. He founded the Greek Royal Palace Boys' Choir in 1950, and directed it until 1967; in 1958 he established the Athens Chamber Choir. Between 1961 and 1963 he taught neo-Byzantine music at Holy Cross Theological Academy, Boston, Massachusetts. In 1966 he became special secretary to the Greek section of the ISCM, and in 1968 he was appointed head of the music department and choral director at Pierce College, Athens. He was made a member of the council of the Association of Greek Composers in 1971.

Adamis's career as a composer began in the late 1950s, when he wrote some instrumental pieces employing dodecaphonic and 'tonally centred' techniques. After his period at Brandeis University he worked more particularly with electronic media, often turning to Byzantine chant for his source material, as in *Apocalypsis–ékti sfragida*, *Génesis* and *Miroloi*. Fundamental to his style is a strictly horizontal conception of melos: his involvement with medieval and neo-Byzantine monody has greatly influenced his method of employing new techniques within old forms (e.g. the *Byzantine Passion*, the *Anastasimi Ode* and *The Fiery Furnace*). He is a prolific composer, and his works, in a wide diversity of genres, have met with enthusiasm abroad as well as in Greece.

WORKS
(selective list)

Vocal: Fones (Cavafy), chorus, 1959; Apocalypsis–ékti sfragida [Apocalypse 6th seal], 5 vocal ens, narrator, 2 2-track tapes, 1967; Vyzantina Pathi [Byzantine Passion], 6 solo vv, 4 choruses, bells, talanda, simandra, 1967; Génesis, 3 choruses, narrator, tape, 1968; Miroloi, 2 psaltes, isokrates, chorus, perc, tape, 1970–73; Tetelestai, psaltis, chorus, chimes, tape, 1971; Iketirion, 2 narrators, 30 female vv, perc, 1971; Kratima, psaltis, ob, tuba, tape, 1971; Orestis, Bar, tape, 1972; Photonymon, psaltis, chorus, talanda, simandra, 1973
Inst: Liturgikon Conc., ob, cl, bn, str orch, 1955; 2 Pieces, vn, pf, 1958; Suite in ritmo antico, pf, 1959; Sinfonietta, chamber orch, 1961; 3 Pieces, db, pf, 1962; Anakyklisis, fl, ob, cel, va, vc, 1964; Pro-optiki, fl, pic, perc, 1965; Epitymbio, pf, 1965
Tape: Minyrismos, 1966; Iphigenia in Aulis, 1970; Metallika glypta, 1972

Principal publishers: Adamis, Modern

WRITINGS

Review of O. Strunk: *Specimina notationum antiquiorum*, MMB, vii (1966), *Epetiris Etairias Byzantinon Spoudon*, xxv (1966), 443
'Catalogue of Byzantine Musical Manuscripts in Zante', *Epetiris Etairias Byzantinon Spoudon*, xxv (1966), 313–65
'Neotropi melodiki kataskeni' [New ways of melodic construction], *Epoches*, xl (1966), 154
'An Example of Polyphony in Byzantine Music of the Late Middle Ages', *IMSCR, xi Copenhagen 1972*
'A Reference to the Chanting in the East and the West', *Studies in Eastern Chant*, iv (1974)

DIMITRI CONOMOS

Adam of St Victor (*d* St Victor, Paris, 1177 or 1192). Writer of *prosae* (texts, not melodies), active at the Abbey of St Victor, a house of Augustinian canons regular, in Paris. He was a student of Hugh of St Victor (*d* 1141) and a contemporary of Richard of St Victor (*d* 1173). The *prosae* attributed to him are in the style most representative of the later Middle Ages. This style is characterized by a theological mysticism current in 12th-century monasticism, especially at St Victor; by a highly developed use of verbal symbolism and poetic imagery; and by a very refined control of word-accent and sonority. In this style the *prosae* is no longer 'prose', but verse, its module a group of eight syllables, accented alternately: *Écce dies triumphális*. These modules are most often combined in threes, the third slightly

changed (8 + 8 + 7) to produce the long phrases characteristic of sequence melodies:

Écce díes triumphális/Gáude túrma spiritális/spiritáli gáudio;

Occasional variations in the accentual pattern, the length of the module, or the combination of these recall the frequent freedom and irregularity of the sequence.

The melodies to which these texts were sung were by this time highly formularized, and – because of the modular construction of the texts – phrases of melody could be transferred from one version and from one melody to another.

The number of *prosae* attributed to Adam varies; the prosaria associated with the abbey, and specifically with Adam, contain many that are not his, and attributions have to be made on purely stylistic grounds. Lists given are by P. Aubry and E. Misset, in *Les proses d'Adam de St. Victor* (Paris, 1900), and by F. Wellner, in *Adam von St. Victor: sämtliche Sequenzen* (Vienna, 1937). See also *Analecta hymnica*, liv, where substantial doubts are raised about some attributions, especially that of *Laudes crucis*. See SEQUENCE (i) and PROSA.

RICHARD L. CROCKER

Adamonti. See ADAMBERGER, VALENTIN.

Adams, Charles R. (*b* Charlestown, Mass., 9 Feb 1834; *d* West Harwich, Mass., 4 July 1900). American tenor. He studied singing in Boston and in 1856 was soloist in the Handel and Haydn Society's performance of *The Creation*. In 1861 he made concert and opera appearances in the West Indies and Holland. He studied in Vienna with Carlo Barbieri, was engaged for three years by the Berlin Royal Opera, then for nine (1867–76), except for one year, as principal tenor of the Vienna Imperial Opera. He also sang at La Scala and Covent Garden. In 1877 he returned to the USA and during the 1877–8 season sang the title role in the first American production of Wagner's *Rienzi*. From 1879 he lived in Boston as a successful singing teacher; Melba and Eames were among his pupils.

BIBLIOGRAPHY
F. L. Gwinner Cole: 'Adams, Charles R.', *DAB*
O. Thompson: *The American Singer* (New York, 1937), 85ff

H. WILEY HITCHCOCK

Adams, James B. (*fl* 1770–1820). English composer. From his extant published works (the first appeared in 1770, the last in 1820), it can be seen that Adams was a competent purveyor of small-scale vocal and instrumental works in the manner of Haigh, Osmond or Reeve. His music shows an awareness of changing styles: the early songs and canzonets accompanied either by harpsichord or orchestra with obbligato instrument are in the manner of Arne, giving way to a symphonic style like that of J. C. Bach or Hook in the three sonatas of op.4 (for piano or harpsichord with violin or flute accompaniment); his late sonata for piano duet shows some grasp of larger forms, and *The Nightingale*, a canzonet in the vein of Haydn or Pinto, has subtle use of the pedal in the onomatopoeic piano writing. Adams also wrote a treatise, *A Familiar Introduction to the First Principles of Music* (London, n.d.).

ROBIN LANGLEY

Adams, Nathan (*b* Dunstable, New Hampshire, 21 Aug 1783; *d* Milford, New Hampshire, 16 March 1864).

American brass instrument maker. He invented a valve with movable tongues or flaps within the windway. A trumpet in F by Adams with three such valves is displayed on board the *USS Constitution*; it dates from about 1830. A similar instrument, unsigned, with three primitive rotary valves, is in the Essig Collection, Warrensburg, Missouri. Adams is listed as a musical instrument maker in the New York City Directory for 1824. For the next four years he was bandmaster on the *USS Constitution*. In about 1828 he settled in Lowell, Massachusetts, continuing there as a music instrument maker until 1835. The latter part of his life was spent as a machinist and repairman in Provincetown, Massachusetts. He was the composer of at least one published song, *The Ruins of Troy*, written while on board the *Constitution*.

BIBLIOGRAPHY

Contributions of the Old Residents' Historical Association, Lowell, Massachusetts, v (Lowell, 1894)

R. E. Eliason: 'Early American Valves for Brass Instruments', *GSJ*, xxiii (1970), 86

ROBERT E. ELIASON

Adams, Suzanne (*b* Cambridge, Mass., 28 Nov 1872; *d* London, 5 Feb 1953). American soprano. She studied with Marchesi and Bouhy in Paris and made her début at the Paris Opéra in 1895 as Juliet, a role which, together with Marguerite in *Faust*, she seems to have studied with Gounod, who greatly admired her brilliant yet flexible tone and fine vocal method. She sang at Covent Garden (1898–1904), where she created Hero in Stanford's *Much Ado About Nothing*; she was also a member of the Metropolitan Opera (1896–1903). Her repertory included Eurydice, Donna Elvira, Micaela and Marguerite de Valois. As an oratorio singer she earned distinction in England and the USA, and her singing of the soprano in *Messiah* at Carnegie Hall in 1904 was described as the finest heard in New York since Tietjens sang it there. She married the cellist Leo Stein, whose death in 1904 led to her early retirement from the stage. She then taught singing in London.

BIBLIOGRAPHY

J. Freestone: 'Suzanne Adams', *Gramophone*, xxxi (1953), 361 [with discography]

HERMAN KLEIN/HAROLD ROSENTHAL

Adams, Thomas (i) (*d* London, 1620). English bookseller and publisher. He was established in London from 1591 and financed several significant musical publications, including John Dowland's *Third and Last Booke of Songes or Aires*, printed by Peter Short in 1603, and Robert Dowland's *Musicall Banquet*, printed by Thomas Snodham in 1610. He also had the right to reprint several other titles, but this was disputed by William Barley. Between 1611 and 1620 he traded at 'the Bell in St. Paul's churchyard'. He is thought to have published Orlando Gibbons's *Fantazies of III Parts* (*c*1620), which bears the imprint 'London. At the Bell in St. Pauls churchyard'.

BIBLIOGRAPHY

C. Humphries and W. C. Smith: *Music Publishing in the British Isles* (London, 1954, rev. 2/1970)

MIRIAM MILLER

Adams, Thomas (ii) (*b* London, 5 Sept 1785; *d* London, 15 Sept 1858). English organist and composer. At 11 years of age he began to study music under Thomas Busby. He became organist at Carlisle Chapel, Lambeth (1802), at St Paul's, Deptford (1814), and at St George's, Camberwell (1824). On his appointment to the newly rebuilt church of St Dunstan-in-the-West, Fleet Street (1833), he retained the Camberwell post, and he continued to hold both until his death. He was one of the most prominent organists of his time, and gave many performances of a kind that would now be termed 'recitals'. He was much in demand at the openings of newly built organs, and from 1817 onwards he supervised and often took part in the periodic evening performances on the monstrous 'Apollonicon'.

Adams was a master of the developing art of imitating orchestral effects on the organ. A typical recital of his, at the opening of the new Exeter Hall organ on 23 January 1840, consisted of one fugue by Bach (from the '48'), three extemporizations, and 12 arrangements of orchestral, vocal and choral music. But, more unusually for his time, he was equally at home in what was called the 'strict' style of organ music, predominantly contrapuntal, and making sectional use of contrasting ranks of pipes based on diapason tone. How uncommon this had become may be judged from one of his obituarists: 'In his use of the organ, Mr Adams seems to have regarded it chiefly as a means of displaying his own peculiar style of composition and powers of execution'. His compositions do indeed show a most remarkable divergence from the general musical style of the time. Even in his early sets of piano variations he used an unusually dense texture, strongly marked harmonic progressions, and examples of strict canon and other learned devices. In his organ voluntaries, in which a fugue was always the principal movement, he pursued contrapuntal logic with the ruthlessness of Clementi. Like Beethoven and other 19th-century admirers of Bach, he could match the intensity but not the spontaneity of Bach's fugues. His most ambitious works are generally called 'organ pieces' rather than 'voluntaries', and are in several contrasting movements including at least one fugue and one slower movement with an ornate melody played on a solo stop.

Adams carefully indicated registration in his organ music, and extracted great variety from the English organ of his day. Samuel Wesley mentioned Adams's 'great skill and ability in the management of the Pedals', but this must have been merely relative, for there are only one or two rudimentary pedal passages in all his music. Best told how Adams 'regaled himself by serving up one or two of Bach's "48", adding a droning pedal when his bunions were propitious'.

The statement in *Grove 5* that Adams 'published . . . many vocal pieces, consisting of short anthems, hymns and sacred songs' confuses him with another Thomas Adams, who was organist of St Alban's, Holborn, in the later 19th century.

WORKS

(all printed works published in London)

Org: 6 Fugues, org/pf (1820); 6 Voluntaries (*c*1820); 12 Voluntaries (*c*1824); Grand Organ Piece (*c*1824); 6 Pieces (*c*1825); 3 Pieces (*c*1835); 90 Interludes (1837)

Instrumental: Grand March and Quick Step, wind band (*c*1808); 6 sets of variations, pf (1810–18); Melross Abbey, divertimento, pf (*c*1815); 6 Little Airs, pf (*c*1820)

Vocal: satirical harmonization of 'Old 100th' psalm tune, *MT*, xl (1899), 604; 5 songs; 1 hymn; 1 anthem, *GB-Lcm*

BIBLIOGRAPHY

GB-Lbm Add.27593, p.54 (Wesley); Add.34693; Add.35027, f.8

Musical World, xiii (1840), 73; xxxvi (1858), 682

'The Organ Recital', *MT*, xl (1899), 600

O. A. Mansfield: 'W. T. Best', *MQ*, iv (1918), 211

N. Temperley: *Instrumental Music in England 1800–1850* (diss., U. of Cambridge, 1959), 302ff

NICHOLAS TEMPERLEY

Adam von Fulda (*b* Fulda, *c*1445; *d* Wittenberg, 1505). German composer and theorist. Until about 1490 he was at the Benedictine monastery of Vormbach, near Passau, but he had to leave it when he married. In 1490 he entered the service of Frederick the Wise of Saxony, working first as a singer, then as a historiographer (from 1492), finally becoming Kapellmeister by 1498. In 1502 he was appointed professor of music at the newly founded University of Wittenberg. Between 1503 and 1504 he wrote his chronicle of Saxon history undertaken at Frederick's suggestion in 1492, and after Adam's death (of the plague) in 1505, it was completed by Johannes Trithemius, Abbot of Würzburg.

In 1490, while still at Vormbach, Adam finished his famous treatise *De musica* (*GS*, iii, 329). The manuscript was burned in 1870 but the text had already been printed by Gerbert in 1784. In it he noted that Dufay's music extended Guido's musical system by three degrees, and upheld Busnois as a model to be emulated. Adam inveighed against minstrels ('ioculatores') and artless folksingers ('laici vulgares'), for, he said, they had no knowledge of the art of music-making. He was the first theorist to distinguish between vocal and instrumental music in the modern sense. He also wrote some religious verses which were published by Wolff Cyclopius in 1512 as *Ein sehr andechtig christenlich Buchlein* with eight woodcuts by Lukas Cranach (facs. repr. Berlin, 1914).

Adam belonged to the early generation of German composers that includes Heinrich Finck. Most of his music consists of settings (usually for four voices) of a chorale melody or secular lied. His sacred music comprises a mass, a *Magnificat*, seven hymns, two antiphons and a respond. The structure of the hymns, with a canon in the upper voices, is often somewhat clumsy. The hymn *Nuntius celso*, with a canon in the superius and tenor, has a second text, the sequence Psallite, underlaid to the vagans (bass) part voice. Two manuscripts in the monastery of St Gall name Adam as the composer of three secular songs for four voices published anonymously by Arnt von Aich in his *LXXV. hubscher Lieder* (*RISM* 1519⁵). *Ach hülf mich leid* was widely known: Glarean published it in his *Dodekachordon* with the Latin text *O vera lux*, and the melody was often used, for example in Poland and Switzerland in the organ tablatures of Lublin and Hör. Schöffer printed the melody with a sacred version of the text in his *Liederbuch* (*RISM* 1513²) and from 1529 to 1673 it was to be found in protestant sacred songbooks.

WORKS

Mass, Magnificat *D-Bds*, ed. in *KJb*, xvii (1902), Ehmann
7 hymns, 2 antiphons, respond, *LEu*, ed. in EDM, 1st ser., xxxii–xxxiii (1956–60)
3 songs, 1519⁵, ed. E. Bernoulli and H. J. Moser, *Liederbuch des Arnt von Aich* (Kassel, 1930)

BIBLIOGRAPHY

H. J. Moser: 'Leben und Lieder des Adam von Fulda', *Jb der Staatlichen Akademie für Kirchen- und Schulmusik*, i (1929), 7
W. Ehmann: *Adam von Fulda als Vertreter der ersten deutschen Komponistengeneration* (Berlin, 1936)
W. Gurlitt: 'Die Kompositionslehre des deutschen 16. und 17. Jahrhunderts', *GfMKB, Bamberg 1953*, 103
C. Petzsch: 'Die rhythmische Struktur der Liedtenores des Adam von Fulda', *AMw*, xv (1958), 143
——: 'Glareans lateinische Textparodie zum Ach hülff mich leid des Adam von Fulda', *Mf*, xi (1958), 483

KLAUS WOLFGANG NIEMÖLLER

Adán, Vicente (*b* Algemesí, province of Valencia; *fl* 1775–87). Spanish composer and theorist. According to early biographers he was organist at the Madrid royal chapel and the Convento de los Desamparados. He is best known for a small treatise, *Documentos para instrucción de músicos y aficionados que intentan saber el arte de la composición* (Madrid, 1786), whose stated purpose was to compensate for the lack of teaching materials on secular music in Spain. Quite elementary, it consists mostly of examples of counterpoint and free composition, and also gives the instrumental ranges. It was attacked in a satirical *Carta laudatoria a don Vicente Adán* (Madrid, 1786), to which Adán replied in *Respuesta gratulatoria de la carta laudatoria* (Madrid, 1787). Various 18th-century publishers' lists and bibliographies indicate that many volumes of his compositions were printed in Madrid in the 1780s. Most of these were for the psaltery, which experienced a strong revival in the 18th century, although it had been known in Spain since the Moorish occupation. Adán's compositions for this instrument include preludes, sonatas, divertimentos and fandangos as well as an instruction book; there is also evidence that he published organ works and vocal music, both sacred and secular. None of these other publications are extant, although one untitled piece of his for psaltery is in *E-Mn* M.2249.

BIBLIOGRAPHY

J. Ruiz de Lihory: *La música en Valencia: diccionario biográfico y crítico* (Valencia, 1903)
R. Mitjana y Gordón: 'La musique en Espagne', *EMDC*, I/iv (1920), 2119, 2191
H. Anglès and J. Subirá: *Catálogo musical de la Biblioteca nacional de Madrid*, i (Barcelona, 1946); iii (Barcelona, 1951)
J. Subirá: *Historia de la música española e hispanoamericana* (Barcelona, 1953), 589
J. Moll: 'Una bibliografía musical periódica de fines del siglo XVIII', *AnM*, xxiv (1969), 247
F. J. León Tello: *La teoría española de la música en los siglos XVII y XVIII* (Madrid, 1974)

ALMONTE HOWELL

Adasio. See ADAGIO.

Adaskin, Murray (*b* Toronto, 28 March 1906). Canadian composer. He studied the violin with Luigi von Kunits, Kathleen Parlow and William Primrose, and was a member of the Toronto SO (1926–36). Composition studies began in 1944 with John Weinzweig in Toronto and continued with Charles Jones and Darius Milhaud. In 1952 he became head of the department of music, University of Saskatchewan, Saskatoon, and in 1966 was appointed composer-in-residence, retiring in 1972. He was a member of the Canada Council (1966–9). Numerous CBC commissions include the *Algonquin Symphony* (1957–8), *Rondino* for nine instruments (1961) and an opera, *Grant, Warden of the Plains* (1967). The National Arts Centre Orchestra commissioned *Diversion for Orchestra* for its inaugural concert, 7 October 1969.

The opening theme of the *Serenade Concertante* (1954), with its whimsical 'knocking' motif and explicit tonal underpinning, is typical of the lyrical amplitude in many of Murray Adaskin's works. This work also exemplifies Adaskin's concern with craft: everything is clearly audible in an ingenious contrapuntal texture, and the form articulates recapitulations that avoid any obvious symmetry. Still governed by the bar-line, the rhythms in Adaskin's music are energetic, extrovert and, in their irregular groupings and revolving or repeated chord patterns, reminiscent of Stravinsky. More recent orchestral works incorporate materials from Canadian folklore and evoke the country's vast space and vanishing folk cultures. Examples are *Qalala and Nilaula of the North* (1969), *There is my People Sleeping* (1970) and *Nootka Ritual* (1974). Their elegiac strain is complementary to the basic characteristic of his music as a whole, its celebratory optimism.

WILLIAM AIDE

Added sixth chord (Fr. *sixte ajouté*). In functional harmony a subdominant chord with an added major 6th above the bass (e.g. *f–a–c′–d′* in C major, *f–ab–c′–d′* in C minor); it can also be derived as the first inversion of a 7th chord built on the supertonic. The ambivalent construction of the added 6th chord engenders an ambivalence in the way it resolves, as Rameau observed in the *Génération harmonique* (1737). For if the chord is viewed as an embellished subdominant triad, the added 6th must resolve upwards to the 3rd of the tonic (ex.1*a*); whereas if it is interpreted as an inversion of II′, the added 6th is itself the root of the chord and remains stationary in a resolution to the dominant (ex.1*b*).

Ex.1

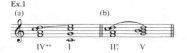

Adderley, Cannonball [Julian Edwin] (*b* Tampa, Florida, 15 Sept 1928; *d* Gary, Ind., 8 Aug 1975). Black American jazz alto saxophonist. After studying at the US Naval School of Music he entered Oscar Pettiford's band (1955), briefly led his own group with his brother Nat Adderley as trumpeter (1956), and worked for Miles Davis in 1958, recording on Davis's influential album *Kind of Blue*. From 1959 he led a popular and remarkably stable sextet, again with Nat Adderley, at times joined by Yusef Lateef or Charles Lloyd (flute and saxophone) to form a sextet. Adderley early rose to prominence as a possible successor to Charlie Parker, but the promise remained largely unfulfilled. His style, which derived from the bop idiom and at times looked back to gospel singing and the playing of Benny Carter, was largely unaffected by the innovations of the free jazz movement; but in the early 1970s he incorporated modal harmonies, more complex metric patterns and an electronic rhythm section into his group. His best recordings are those dominated by other musicians, particularly Davis.

BIBLIOGRAPHY
I. Gitler: 'Cannonball Adderley', *Jazz*, ii (1959), sum., 197; aut., 289
J. Adderley: 'The Education of a Combo Leader', *Jazz Panorama*, ed. M. Williams (New York, 1962), 258
J. Grunnet Jepsen: *Jazz Records 1942–65*, i (Holte, 1966), 10ff
A. Morgan: 'Cannonball Adderley', *Jazz on Record*, ed. A. McCarthy (London, 1968), 1

Addinsell, Richard (*b* London, 13 Jan 1904; *d* London, 14 Nov 1977). English composer. After a short course of study at the RCM he studied abroad (1929–32), chiefly in Berlin and Vienna, and in 1933 he visited the USA where he wrote film music for Hollywood. In 1941 he began a collaboration as composer and accompanist with Joyce Grenfell, writing *I'm going to see you today* and other music for most of her one-woman shows. He wrote almost exclusively for the theatre, radio and the cinema. Among his better known film scores are *Fire over England* (1937), *Goodbye Mr Chips*

(1939), *Blithe Spirit* (1945), *The Prince and the Showgirl* (1957), *A Tale of Two Cities* (1958), *Greengage Summer* (1961), *The Roman Spring of Mrs Stone* (1961) and *The Waltz of the Toreadors* (1962), but his most popular work is the *Warsaw Concerto*, a one-movement piano concerto in the style of Rakhmaninov used in *Dangerous Moonlight* (1941). Addinsell's principal publishers are Chappell and Keith Prowse.

CHRISTOPHER PALMER

Addison, Adele (*b* New York, 24 July 1925). American soprano. Her vocal and musical abilities won her scholarships to Westminster Choir College, Princeton, and the Berkshire Music School, Tanglewood, where she studied with Boris Goldovsky. She made her recital début at Boston in 1948 and, after further coaching with Povla Frijsh in New York, appeared at Town Hall in 1952. This established her reputation as an intelligent musician and led to engagements with most American orchestras, and the New England and New York City Opera Companies. In 1962 she sang in the inaugural concert at Lincoln Center. The silvery timbre of her voice, her agility and distinguished musicianship all made her an ideal performer of Baroque music, as her recordings of Bach (*St Matthew Passion*) and Handel (Ode to St Cecilia) attest. These qualities also made her an admired exponent of contemporary music – she gave the first performances of Poulenc's *Gloria* (1959) and Foss's *Time Cycle* (1961), among many other works.

RICHARD BERNAS

Addison, John (i) (*b* London, *c*1766; *d* London, 30 Jan 1844). English double bass player and composer. He was the son of a mechanic, at an early age displayed a taste for music and learnt to play several instruments. Having, about 1793, married Miss Willems, a niece of F. C. Reinhold, and herself a fine singer, he decided to become a professional musician. Soon after her marriage Mrs Addison made a successful appearance at Vauxhall Gardens, where her husband was a cellist. Addison then went with his wife to Liverpool, performing on the cello, and subsequently on the double bass, to which instrument he afterwards confined himself professionally. From Liverpool they went to Dublin, where Addison soon became director of the amateur orchestra of a private theatre and, having to arrange the music, improved himself in composition. In 1796 they returned to London, where on 17 September Mrs Addison appeared at Covent Garden Theatre as Rosetta in *Love in a Village*, and afterwards performed other characters. In 1797 they went to Bath, where she studied under Rauzzini. After a three-year engagement at Dublin they proceeded to Manchester, where Addison was induced to abandon the musical profession and embark on cotton manufacture. But he was unsuccessful, and soon returned to music. After a spell in the provinces he returned to London, shared with Michael Kelly the management of his music business and produced most of his own theatrical music. He was also engaged at the Italian Opera and the Antient and Vocal Concerts as a double bass player.

WORKS
(*selective list*)

THEATRICAL
(*all first performed and published in London; all libs in MS at US-SM*)
The Sleeping Beauty (play, L. St G. Skeffington), Drury Lane, 6 Dec 1805, vocal score (1805)

Maids and Bachelors, or My Heart for Yours (comedy, Skeffington), Covent Garden, 6 June 1806

False Alarms, or My Cousin (comic opera, J. Kenney), Drury Lane, 12 Jan 1807, collab. J. Braham, M. P. King, lib (1807)

The Russian Imposter, or The Siege of Smolensko (opera, H. Siddons, S. J. Arnold), Lyceum, 22 July 1809, vocal score (1809)

My Aunt (operatic farce, Arnold), Lyceum, 1 Aug 1815, lib (1815)

Bobinet the Bandit, or The Forest of Monte-Scarpini (musical entertainment), Covent Garden, 4 Dec 1815, vocal score (c1815)

Two Words, or The Silent not Dumb! (play, Arnold), Lyceum, 2 Sept 1816, vocal score (1816)

Free and Easy (comic opera, Arnold), Lyceum, 16 Sept 1816, vocal score (1816)

My Uncle (operetta, S. Beazley), Lyceum, 23 June 1817, vocal score (1817)

Songs for insertion in other works, incl. Shield's Robin Hood (revived at Drury Lane, 1813) and Bishop and Attwood's For England Ho! (Covent Garden, 1813)

OTHER WORKS

6 Sonatas or Duets, 2 vn/rec, op.1 (London, 1772)

Pieces in A Collection of Psalms and Hymns for . . . Parish Churches (Cambridge, 1790)

Elijah Raising the Widow's Son (sacred musical drama), Drury Lane Lenten Oratorios, 3 March 1815, lost, adapted from music of P. Winter

Songs of Almack's, melodies by H. Bishop and Addison, symphonies and accompaniments by Addison (London, 1831)

Singing Practically Treated, in a Series of Instructions (London, 1836)

BIBLIOGRAPHY

W. B. Squire: 'Addison, John', DNB

W. H. HUSK/ALFRED LOEWENBERG

Addison, John (ii) (b Chobham, 16 March 1920). English composer. He studied at the RCM with Jacob (composition), Goossens (oboe) and Thurston (clarinet). His first major work was the Woodwind Sextet (1949) – performed at the 1951 ISCM Festival – which shows a particular aptitude for wind writing. Addison is best known for his incidental scores: he wrote the music for several Royal Court Theatre productions and has been successful as a composer for films. In this medium he has favoured small ensembles, associating solo instruments with specific characters as demonstrated by his use of the oboe in The Girl with Green Eyes (1964) and of the harpsichord in Tom Jones (1963) and Sleuth (1973). Other notable films are Pool of London (1951), Reach for the Sky (1956), A Taste of Honey (1961), The Honey Pot (1967) and The Charge of the Light Brigade (1968). Addison also wrote the ballet Carte blanche (1953); his music is published by Oxford University Press.

BIBLIOGRAPHY

C. Palmer: 'British Composers for the Screen: Ron Goodwin and John Addison', Performing Right (1971), Nov, 20

CHRISTOPHER PALMER

Addison, Joseph (b Milston, Wilts., 1 May 1672; d Kensington, London, 17 June 1719). English public servant and man of letters. After some years as a Fellow of Magdalen College, Oxford, he went abroad in 1699, returning to England in February 1704. In July 1705 he was appointed Under-Secretary of State. While abroad he had taken an interest in opera, and he viewed with disapprobation the growing popularity of Italian opera on the English stage, feeling that England should instead develop an operatic style of its own. To encourage this he set himself to write an opera text that, while it observed Italian conventions, would be essentially English in feeling. This libretto, Rosamond, has elegance and humour and some differentiation of character. It was set by Thomas Clayton and first performed on 4 March 1707 but failed dismally owing to the poor quality of the music – a crippling blow to the prospects

of opera in English. A later setting by Arne was fairly successful in the 1730s.

In 1709 Addison was appointed secretary to Lord Wharton, Lieutenant of Ireland, but political changes caused him to fall from office in 1710. During the ensuing period of political inactivity he devoted much of his time to the Spectator (1711–12), the earlier numbers of which include several critical essays on opera. On the death of Queen Anne in 1714, he was again called into political service and rose by 1717 to the rank of Secretary of State.

BIBLIOGRAPHY

P. Smithers: The Life of Joseph Addison (Oxford, 1954)

MARGARET LAURIE

Additional accompaniments. The addition of extra instruments to the scores of 17th- and 18th-century works for voices with instrumental accompaniment, with or without modifications of the original scoring. Bach and Handel have in the past been the chief victims of this practice, which has no historical or aesthetic justification.

The earliest attempt to 'improve' Handel's orchestration seems to have been made at the Handel Commemoration in London in 1784, when the monster orchestra included a double bassoon, 12 horns and six trombones. In 1786 Johann Adam Hiller (1728–1804) provided additional accompaniments for a performance of Messiah in Berlin. Mozart, at the invitation of Baron van Swieten, wrote accompaniments for Handel's Acis and Galatea (1788), Messiah (1789), Alexander's Feast (1790) and Ode for St Cecilia's Day (1790). His purpose was not to replace the keyboard continuo, since in several places a harpsichord is still needed, but to create the characteristic sound of the orchestra of his time. His versions were published after his death and acquired wide currency, though strong objections were voiced in the early 19th century. Mendelssohn, who in his youth had written additional accompaniments for Handel's 'Dettingen' Te Deum and Acis and Galatea, became one of the objectors and refused to write accompaniments for Israel in Egypt.

In the course of the 19th century, various additions were made to Mozart's texts, so that what were known as 'Mozart's additional accompaniments' decreasingly represented his original intentions. Ignaz Franz von Mosel (1772–1844) not only wrote accompaniments for several of Handel's oratorios but altered the text by transferring pieces from one work to another. In the course of the 19th century a number of musicians, more or less eminent, continued the tradition of writing additional accompaniments for Handel's works, the need for which was kept alive by performances given by large choirs. The practice continued in the 20th century, though with increasing opposition from those who, like Tomášek in 1846, felt that 'Handel's work cannot endure the introduction of the garish sound-effects of our present era'.

The first to revise Bach's orchestration was Christian Friedrich Gottlieb Schwencke (1767–1822), who produced versions of the Magnificat and the Mass in B minor, in addition to Handel's Messiah and Alexander's Feast. The most industrious worker in this field was Robert Franz (1815–92), who wrote accompaniments for the St Matthew Passion, the Christmas Oratorio and other works, including several cantatas. Bach, however, soon won a respect denied to Handel, and additional accompaniments to his works dropped out of use. In the 20th century additional accompaniments have been written for operas by Monteverdi and Cavalli, on the unfounded assumption that the scores left by these composers are merely incomplete outlines.

JACK WESTRUP

Adelaide. Australian city, capital of South Australia. The original settlement in 1836 was made under the idealistic Wakefield scheme of subsidized migration, and never became a convict settlement. Later the presence of German Lutheran migrants resulted in the predominance of choral music, fostered by numerous Liedertafel as well as by English-style 19th-century choral societies, several of which are still active. During its early years, because of its isolation and small population, Adelaide did not receive as many visits from touring artists as Melbourne and Sydney. Local music societies were formed, the most notable being the Adelaide Choral Society (1844–59), whose activities culminated in a Handel centenary festival. The conductor Carl Linger was the most influential resident musician in the mid-19th century.

Even in this remote centre of Western culture, opera has played a large part in musical entertainment. The first opera production was Auber's *Masaniello* in 1840, 12 years after its Paris première. As early as 1865 the touring Bianchi Italian Opera Company produced a season of over three months; the repertory included *Norma*, *Lucia di Lammermoor*, *Il trovatore*, *La traviata* and *Rigoletto*. Also notable were the productions of *Aida*, *Carmen* and *Lohengrin* in 1879 by the Melbourne entrepreneur William Saurin Lyster. Operas are now performed at the Adelaide Festival, by the touring Australian Opera Company (*see* SYDNEY) and by the local Intimate Opera Company.

The first South Australian Orchestra was formed by E. Harold Davies in 1921. In 1936 the Australian Broadcasting Commission (ABC) established a permanent studio orchestra of 17 players, which made possible the formation of the Adelaide SO and the inauguration of a series of celebrity orchestral concerts; the orchestra became the South Australian SO in 1949, with 55 players under Henry Krips, and inaugurated a series of subscription concerts. Free open-air Sunday concerts attract crowds of up to 35,000; there are regular tours of country centres and concerts for schools and youth audiences. The orchestra reverted to its original name (Adelaide SO) in 1975. Chamber music concerts are presented on a subscription basis by the ABC and by MUSICA VIVA AUSTRALIA, with foreign and local performers.

Notable choral societies have included the Adelaide Liedertafel, the Glee Club, the Orpheus Society, the Bach Choir and the Philharmonic Society. The Adelaide Singers, disbanded in 1976, were the best-known small group in Australia; they were employed by the ABC and were the only choir in Australia working on a full-time basis throughout the year in festival, radio and concert work. The Adelaide Festival of Arts, a biennial festival of music, opera, drama and ballet, first held in 1960, was largely a result of the initiative of John Bishop, then professor of music and director of the Elder Conservatorium; it features local musical organizations.

In 1883 Cecil Sharp and Immanuel Reimann founded the Adelaide College of Music, which in 1898 merged with the newly formed Elder Conservatorium. In the same period music became a recognized subject at Adelaide University and the chair of music was endowed in 1897 by Thomas Elder. The two institutions are affiliated. The members of the University of Adelaide Wind Quintet encouraged Australian composition by inviting distinguished composers to give courses there, including Henk Badings, Peter Maxwell Davies and Bernard Rands. The Flinders Street Music School is developing rapidly, and a lectureship has been established at Flinders University.

For bibliography *see* AUSTRALIA.

ANN CARR-BOYD

Adelaide Singers. Australian choir. In 1936–7, to provide choral music for light programmes and concerts, the Australian Broadcasting Commission established full-time choirs in each state. Of these, the Adelaide Singers was by far the longest-lived (it disbanded in 1976), and achieved a national reputation through consistently high standards. Conducted by William Cade, it was first known as the ABC Adelaide Wireless Chorus, becoming the ABC Adelaide Singers in 1945. Under the direction of Norman Chinner it established its reputation. Its later conductors were Juan Azeldegui, Patrick Thomas (conductor of many recordings) and James Christiansen. Many of Australia's leading concert singers belonged at one time to the choir, which also performed under distinguished visiting conductors; it was notable for its accompanied choral work and *a cappella* singing in music of all periods. Among its records of Australian works are Alfred Hill's *A Symphony of Life*, William G. James's *Australian Christmas Carols* and Nigel Butterley's *In the Head the Fire* (Italia Prize, 1966).

ANN CARR-BOYD

Adelaide Wind Quintet. Australian ensemble. It was founded in 1964 by professors at the University of Adelaide's Elder Conservatorium of Music, an important centre for wind instrument teaching in Australia. The members are Zdeněk Bruderhans (flute), Jiří Tancibudek (oboe), David Shephard (clarinet), Thomas Wightman (bassoon) and Patrick Brislan (horn). Bruderhans and Tancibudek are graduates of the Prague Conservatory and Academy of Music, and have toured extensively as soloists, as well as holding positions in European orchestras. Wightman played in the London SO and the Philharmonia; he was an original member of the quintet formed by the horn player Dennis Brain. Brislan was a member of three Australian state orchestras, and a founder-member of the New Sydney Woodwind Quintet in 1965. Shephard studied at the RCM, London; in Australia he was principal clarinettist of the Queensland SO. In 1969, in association with Musica Viva Australia, the quintet undertook its first international tour, and since then it has played in 15 countries. Musica Viva Australia also organized many of the quintet's appearances in Australia, including 'outback' and interstate tours. It has also given lecture recitals and master classes for schools and universities. Its repertory is wide, from Baroque to contemporary music, and includes music for smaller combinations within the group and unaccompanied solos. The group has commissioned works from several leading Australian composers, among them Dreyfus, Meale, Sculthorpe, Butterley and Werder.

ANN CARR-BOYD

Adelboldus (*d* 1024). Bishop of Utrecht under Emperor Henry II. The proximity of two short treatises on the division of the monochord to Adelboldus's treatise on geometry, *De crassitudine sphaerae*, in a 12th-century manuscript from Tegernsee (*D-Mbs* Clm.18914) prompted Gerbert to attribute them to Adelboldus in his *Scriptores* (*GS*, i, 303–12). Other considerations such as calligraphy and foliation, however, refute these attributions, and the works (both depending heavily on Boethius) must now be considered anonymous.

BIBLIOGRAPHY
H. Schmid: 'Zur sogenannten *Musica Adelboldi Traiectensis*', *AcM*, xxvii (1956), 69
A. Thijm: 'Adelbold', *ADB*

CECIL ADKINS

Adelburg, August (*b* Pera, Turkey, 1 Nov 1830; *d* Vienna, 20 Oct 1873). Violinist and composer of Croatian and Italian descent. In his childhood he lived in Constantinople, where his father was in the Austrian diplomatic service; his mother was the Contessa Franchini. From the age of 12 he studied in Vienna, and against his father's will chose an artistic career as a student of Mayseder (violin, 1850–54) and Hoffmann (composition). After 1855 he had a career as an excellent violinist in various cities including Prague, Leipzig and (in 1858) Paris; he married in Pest in 1859. Nevertheless, he always remained close to the spirit of the orient, as is manifested in his literary works (e.g. *Oriental Music*). Among his 120 works there were operas composed to his own librettos, including the spectacular but short-lived *Zrinyi* (Pest, 1868), *Martinuzzi* (Buda, 1870), choral works (a mass, 1858; a *Te Deum*, 1864), the overture *Wallenstein* (Leipzig, 1867), violin concertos, five string quartets (1863–4), sonatas, *L'école de la vélocité* and songs. In his pamphlet *Entgegnung* (Pest, 1859), he attacked Liszt's book on the gypsy origin of Hungarian music. Later he also tried his hand at painting (Vienna exhibition, 1871).

DEZSŐ LEGÁNY

Adell, Arthur (Gotthard) (*b* Örtomta, 25 March 1894; *d* Uppsala, 24 Nov 1962). Swedish theologian and writer on church music. He studied theology at Uppsala University and after his ordination in 1919 held several clerical appointments including that of pastor at Lund; from 1938 he was parish priest of Söderköping. In 1926 he founded the *Tidskrift för kyrkomusik och svenskt gudstjänstliv* (renamed *Svenskt gudstjänstliv* in 1942) and in 1941 the associated society Laurentius Petri Sällskapet; he directed both until his death. In addition to his interest in church music, Adell played an important part in the movement for liturgical reform in Sweden from the 1920s. The services he devised with his fellow clergyman Knut Peters, though never officially adopted, were widely influential. He was awarded an honorary doctorate by the University of Uppsala in 1952.

WRITINGS
ed.: *Nya Testamentet på svenska 1526* (Lund, 1936)
Den svenska kyrkohandboken (Lund, 1938)
ed., with K. Peters: *Evangelisk tidegärd* (Lund, 1938)
ed.: *Musikhandskrifter från Högs och Bjuråkers kyrkor* (Lund, 1941)
ed., with K. Peters: *Den svenska tidegärden* (Lund, 1944, 2/1952)
ed., with K. Peters: *Det svenska antifonalet* (Lund, 1949 and 1959)
I guds rika hus (Stockholm, 1954)
ed. R. Holte: *Gregorianik*, i (Lund, 1963)

MALCOLM TURNER

Adelphi Theatre. London theatre opened in 1806 and known as Sans Pareil until 1819; see LONDON, §IV, 3.

Adelung, Jakob. See ADLUNG, JAKOB.

Ademollo, Alessandro (Felice) (*b* Florence, 20 Nov 1826; *d* Florence, 22 June 1891). Italian scholar. According to some sources he died in Rome on 26 June 1891. From 1845 he wrote political articles for Florentine journals as a liberal moderate. In 1860 he became *consigliere* of the Corte dei Conti (State Audit Board) and moved with the central government to Rome after it became part of the kingdom of Italy in 1870. He carried out research into many aspects of Italian cultural history, particularly of the 17th and 18th centuries, publishing the results from about 1875 in a series of books and numerous articles in Italian periodicals, particularly the *Opinione* and *Fanfulla della Domenica* of Rome. Ademollo was a careful and thorough scholar, and much of his work, particularly that on theatrical history, actors and singers, one of his specialities, is of great value, presenting archival material available nowhere else, much of it still undigested by music historians.

WRITINGS
Il carnevale di Roma nei secoli XVII e XVIII (Rome, 1883, rev. 2/1883)
I primi fasti della musica italiana a Parigi (1645–1662) (Milan, 1884)
I Basile alla corte di Mantova (1603–1628) (Genoa, 1885)
La bell'Adriana ed altre virtuose del suo tempo alla corte di Mantova (Città di Castello, 1888)
Un avventuriere francese in Italia nella seconda metà del settecento (Bergamo, 1891) [biography of Ange Goudar, incl. list of Ademollo's writings up to 1890]

BIBLIOGRAPHY
A. d'Addario: 'Ademollo, Alessandro Felice', *DBI*

DENNIS LIBBY

Adeney, Richard (Gilford) (*b* London, 25 Jan 1920). English flautist. In 1937 he entered the RCM, and in 1938 he made his orchestral début in the *St Matthew Passion* under Vaughan Williams. He joined the LPO in 1941 and remained as principal flute until 1950, returning for a further nine years from 1960. He was a founder-member of the Melos Ensemble and played for many years with the English Chamber Orchestra. He has toured extensively abroad. Adeney is noted for the delicacy and refinement of his playing, which, in spite of his basically English training, has much affinity with the French school in style and tone. He was for long devoted to the wood flute with a thinned head but later changed to a specially made cadmium–silver alloy instrument.

PHILIP BATE

Adgate, Andrew (*b* Norwich, Conn., 22 March 1762; *d* Philadelphia, 30 Sept 1793). American singing teacher and compiler. In 1783 he assisted Andrew Law in a Philadelphia singing school. By 1785 he had opened his own Free School for vocal music, later reorganizing it as the Uranian Academy. Adgate conducted many concerts during the mid-1780s, most notably a 'Grand Concert' on 4 May 1786, at which works by Handel, James Lyon, William Billings, William Tuckey and others were performed by 230 choristers and an orchestra of 50. Adgate published an instruction manual, the *Rudiments of Music*, in 1788; the next year he compiled the *Philadelphia Harmony*, a tune book made up of popular American and European sacred music. Published in one volume, the two items ran through nine editions in Philadelphia by 1807.

BIBLIOGRAPHY

O. G. Sonneck: *Early Concert-life in America* (Leipzig, 1907/*R*1949), 103ff

C. Rourke: *The Roots of American Culture* (New York, 1942), 172ff

R. Crawford: *Andrew Law, American Psalmodist* (Evanston, 1968), 62ff

See also PSALMODY (ii), §II.

RICHARD CRAWFORD

Adlam, Derek (Leslie) (*b* Kingston-on-Thames, 30 May 1938). English maker of fortepianos, clavichords and harpsichords. He was educated at the Guildhall School of Music, London, where he specialized in keyboard instruments, studying the piano with Frank Laffitte, the harpsichord with Celia Bizony and the organ with Harold Dexter. After some years as a music teacher, during which he also undertook some restorations of early keyboard instruments, he became curator of the Colt Clavier Collection, Bethersden, Kent (1963–73). While continuing to teach and perform, Adlam studied the craft of instrument building at the Feldberg workshop in Sevenoaks. After further years of restoration experience he began producing new instruments in 1971, and in November that year formed a partnership with the pianist and collector Richard Burnett. The Adlam–Burnett restoration and production workshops are in the grounds of Finchcocks, a large 18th-century house in Goudhurst, Kent, which contains an extensive collection of antique keyboard instruments. Adlam–Burnett's own production is modelled closely on historical prototypes. While it includes reproductions of Flemish and French harpsichords, increasing emphasis is being placed on the 18th-century piano and clavichord, instruments that have not enjoyed so extensive a revival as the harpsichord. Adlam has contributed on the subject of harpsichord restoration to *Early Music* (iv, 1976, p.255).

HOWARD SCHOTT

Adler, Guido (*b* Eibenschütz [now Ivančice], Moravia, 1 Nov 1855; *d* Vienna, 15 Feb 1941). Austrian musicologist. After the death of his father, the family settled in 1864 in Vienna, where Adler entered the Akademisches Gymnasium. In 1868 he began his studies in theory and composition with Bruckner and Dessoff at the conservatory, but his original intention was to prepare for a legal career, for which purpose he studied law at the University of Vienna (JurD 1878). While at the university Adler gave a series of lectures on Wagner's *Ring* (1875–6) which he later published as a book, and together with Felix Mottl founded the Akademischer Wagnerverein. After serving briefly on the Vienna Handelsgericht Adler decided to take up music history, in which his interest had been aroused by the writings of Ambros, Jahn, Spitta and Chrysander. He attended Hanslick's lectures at the university, taking his doctorate in 1880 with a dissertation on music up to 1660; in 1882 he completed his *Habilitation* with a work on the history of harmony. In the same year he represented Austria at the International Congress for Liturgy at Arezzo. With Spitta and Chrysander, Adler founded the *Vierteljahrsschrift für Musikwissenschaft* (1884) and a year later became professor of music history in Prague. In 1888 he submitted to the Austrian government a *Denkschrift* advocating the publication of a Monumenta Historiae Musices. This project was to become the Denkmäler der Tonkunst in Österreich series, of which Adler was gen-

eral editor from 1894 to 1938. He was instrumental in getting the Austrian government to acquire the Trent Codices, selections of which he published in DTÖ, and from 1913 to 1938 he edited the *Beihefte der DTÖ* (*Studien zur Musikwissenschaft*), to which he and his pupils made substantial contributions. In 1892 Adler organized the music section of the International Music and Theatre Exhibition in Vienna, writing the catalogue and introducing Smetana's *The Bartered Bride* to an international public. His work for the exhibition revealed his gift for organizing large-scale festivals in conjunction with musicological congresses, and he later similarly organized the Vienna centenary festivals of Haydn (1909) and Beethoven (1927). The formation of the IMS in 1927 was largely due to his initiative.

In 1898 Adler succeeded Hanslick at the University of Vienna, where he founded the Musikwissenschaftliches Institut, the model for musicological institutes elsewhere. Adler's lectures attracted a wide circle of students from all Europe, many of whom were later to achieve fame as composers (Webern, Wellesz, Pisk, Grosz and Weigl) or as musicologists (Orel, Haas, Fischer, Geiringer, Ficker, Kurth, Jeppesen, Smijers and Jachimecki). Adler took great interest in Vienna's musical life and was seen frequently at concerts and the opera. He enjoyed an intimate friendship with Mahler, on whom he published a book, and when in 1912 a cello concerto by G. M. Monn (1717–50) was published in DTÖ, Adler entrusted the realization of the continuo part to Schoenberg.

Modern musicology owes a great debt to Adler. As early as 1885, in a pioneering essay, he laid down the chief principles of the new discipline and was the first to emphasize the importance of style criticism in music research – ideas which he put into practice at his institute. Though he concentrated his own studies on the music history of Austria, notably the Viennese Classics, the systematic investigation of the musical style of other periods and countries was an outstanding feature of Adler's 'Vienna School'. This was amply demonstrated in his editorship of the *Handbuch der Musikgeschichte*, the work of an international body of scholars, to which he contributed the chapter on Viennese Classicism.

See also ANALYSIS, §II, 5.

WRITINGS

Die historischen Grundclassen der christlich-abendländischen Musik bis 1600 (diss., U. of Vienna, 1880; *AMZ*, xv (1880), 689, 705, 721, 737)

Studie zur Geschichte der Harmonie (Habilitationsschrift, U. of Vienna, 1882; Vienna, 1881)

'Umfang, Methode und Ziel der Musikwissenschaft', *VMw*, i (1885), 5

'Die Wiederholung und Nachahmung in der Mehrstimmigkeit', *VMw*, ii (1886), 271

rev.: *Verzeichnis der musikalischen Autographen von Ludwig van Beethoven im Besitze von A. Artaria* (Vienna, 1890)

Richard Wagner: Vorlesungen (Leipzig, 1904)

'Über Heterophonie', *JbMP 1908*

Joseph Haydn (Vienna and Leipzig, 1909)

Der Stil in der Musik (Leipzig, 1911, 2/1929)

Gustav Mahler (Vienna, 1916)

Methode der Musikgeschichte (Leipzig, 1919)

'Periodisierung der Musikgeschichte', 'Die Wiener klassische Schule', 'Die Moderne: Allgemeines', *Handbuch der Musikgeschichte*, ed. G. Adler (Frankfurt, 1924, rev. 2/1930/*R*1961)

'Das obbligate Akkompagnement der Wiener klassischen Schule', *Kongressbericht: Leipzig 1925*, 35

'Haydn, Mozart, Beethoven', *Almanach der Deutschen Musikbücherei* (Regensburg, 1926)

'Beethoven's Charakter', *Almanach der Deutschen Musikbücherei* (Regensburg, 1927)

'Schubert and the Viennese Classical School', *MQ*, xiv (1928), 473

'Haydn and the Viennese Classical School', *MQ*, xviii (1932), 191

'Johannes Brahms: Wirken, Wesen und Stellung', *SMw*, xx (1933), 6

EDITIONS

M. A. Cesti: Il pomo d'oro, DTÖ, vi, Jg.iii/2 (1896/*R*); ix, Jg.iv/2 (1897/*R*)
G. Muffat: Componimenti musicali per il cembalo, DTÖ, vii, Jg.iii/3 (1896/*R*); *12 Toccaten und 72 Versett für Orgel und Klavier*, DTÖ, lviii, Jg.xxix/2 (1922/*R*)
J. T. Froberger: Orgel- und Klavierwerke I–III, DTÖ, viii, Jg.iv/1 (1897/*R*); xiii, Jg.vi/2 (1899/*R*); xxi, Jg.x/2 (1903/*R*)
H. Biber: Acht Violinsonaten, DTÖ, xi, Jg.v/2 (1898/*R*)
with O. Koller: *Trienter Codices I–III*, DTÖ, xiv–xv, Jg.vii (1900/*R*); xxii, Jg.xi/1 (1904/*R*); xxxviii, Jg.xix/1 (1912/*R* [with F. Schegar and M. Loew]
J. J. Fux: Mehrfach besetzte Instrumentalwerke, DTÖ, xix, Jg.ix/2 (1902/*R*)
O. Benevoli: Festmesse und Hymnus, DTÖ, xx, Jg.x/1 (1903/*R*)
A. Draghi: Kirchenwerke: zwei Messen, eine Sequenz, zwei Hymnen, DTÖ, xlvi, Jg.xxiii/1 (1916/*R*)
Messen für Soli, Chor und Orchester in dem letzten Viertel des 17. Jahrhunderts, DTÖ, xlix, Jg.xxv/1 (1918/*R*)
Drei Requiem für Soli, Chor und Orchester aus dem 17. Jahrhundert, DTÖ, lix, Jg.xxx/1 (1923/*R*)

BIBLIOGRAPHY

W. Fischer: 'Guido Adlers *Methode der Musikgeschichte*', *ZMw*, vii (1924–5), 500
Studien zur Musikgeschichte: Festschrift für Guido Adler (Vienna, 1930)
G. Adler: *Wollen und Wirken: aus dem Leben eines Musikhistorikers* (Vienna, 1935) [autobiography]
M. Carner: 'A Pioneer of Musicology: Guido Adler', *Of Men and Music* (London, 1944), 14
R. von Ficker: 'Guido Adler und die Wiener Schule', *ÖMz*, i (1946)
R. Heinz: 'Guido Adlers Musikhistorik als historisches Dokument', *Die Ausbreitung der Historismus über der Musik*, ed. W. Wiora (Regensburg, 1969), 209
E. R. Reilly: *Gustav Mahler and Guido Adler* (Vienna, 1978)

MOSCO CARNER

Adler, György (*b* Győr, 1789; *d* Buda, 1867). Hungarian composer. From 1811 he was a church musician in Győr. In 1839 he became *regens chori* of the church of St Matthew in Buda, a post he held until his death. His daughter Adél was the wife of Ferenc Erkel. Adler wrote a quantity of vocal and chamber music, much of which was published in his lifetime: a set of variations and a polonaise for string quartet; a violin sonata; various piano works, including a sonatina, an 'easy and agreeable' fantasia, a set of variations, and a rondo on a theme from Rossini's *La Cenerentola*; *Libera me Domine* (his only published sacred work); a birthday cantata for Prince Ernst of Schwarzenberg; and a number of lieder (including a setting of Heine's *An Sie*); and Hungarian songs to texts by Pál Kovács, János Garay, József Bajza and Sándor Kisfaludy.

Adler, Israel (*b* Berlin, 17 Jan 1925). Israeli musicologist of German birth. He settled in Palestine in 1937, and studied music at the Paris Conservatoire (1949–53) and under Corbin at the Ecole Pratique des Hautes Etudes (diploma 1961). He then attended the musicology institute at the Sorbonne, where he studied with Chailley and in 1963 took a doctorat de 3ème cycle with a dissertation on learned musical practice in several Jewish communities in 17th- and 18th-century Europe. Concurrently he was head of the Hebraica-Judaica section at the Bibliothèque Nationale (1950–63). He returned to Israel to become the director of the music department and national sound archives at the Jewish National and Hebrew University library in Jerusalem (1963–9), and was subsequently director of the library (1969–71). In 1964 he founded the Jewish music research centre at the Hebrew University and was its director (1964–9 and from 1971); he was appointed

senior lecturer at Tel-Aviv University (1970), senior lecturer (1973) and head of the musicology department (1974–7) at the Hebrew University, Jerusalem. His main area of research is Jewish music, particularly medieval and Renaissance sources, and the period until the emancipation of the Jews in Europe. In 1967 he became president of the Israel Musicological Society. He has edited *Yuval: Studies of the Jewish Music Research Centre* since its inception in 1968. In 1974 he became a vice-president of IAML, and is on the research committee of RISM.

WRITINGS

'Musique juive', *FasquelleD*
Le livre hébraïque: incunables, publications israéliennes (Paris, 1962)
La pratique musicale savante dans quelques communautés juives en Europe aux XVIIe et XVIIIe siècles (diss., U. of Paris, 1963; Paris, 1966)
'Zimrat pùrim', *Kiriat Sefer*, xxxix (1964), 419
'Les chants synagogaux, notés au XIIe siècle (ca. 1103–1150) par Abdias, le prosélyte normand', *RdM*, li. (1965), 19–51; abridged in *Ariel* (1966), no.15, p.27
'Une source hébraïque de 1602 relative à la musica reservata?', *FAM*, xvi (1966), 9
'Report on Israeli Activities in the Field of Traditional Music', *Creating a Wider Interest in Traditional Music: Berlin 1967*, 177
'The Rise of Art Music in the Italian Ghetto', *Jewish Medieval and Renaissance Studies*, ed. A. Altman (Cambridge, Mass., 1967), 321–64
'Histoire de la musique religieuse juive', *Encyclopédie des musiques sacrées*, i, ed. J. Porte (1968), 469
'Les mensurations du tuyaux d'orgue dans le ms. Héb. 1037 de la Bibliothèque nationale de Paris', *AcM*, xl (1968), 43
'Le traité anonyme du manuscrit hébreu 1037 de la Bibliothèque nationale de Paris', *Yuval*, i (1968), 1–47
'Abraham Levi dall' Arpa', *Tatzlil*, ix (1969), 105
'Fragment hébraïque d'un traité attribué à Marchetto de Padoue', *Yuval*, ii (1971), 1
Musical Life and Traditions of the Portuguese Jewish Community of Amsterdam (Jerusalem, 1974)
ed.: *Hebrew Writings concerning Music in Manuscripts and Printed Books*, RISM, B/IX/2 (1975)
with J. Cohen: *Catalogue of the A. Z. Idelsohn Archives at the Jewish National and University Library* (Jerusalem, 1976)

WILLIAM Y. ELIAS

Adler, Kurt Herbert (*b* Vienna, 2 April 1905). American conductor and opera director of Austrian birth. He was educated at the Musikakademie and university in Vienna, and made his début in 1925 as a conductor for the Max Reinhardt theatre, then conducted at the Volksoper and opera houses in Germany, Italy and Czechoslovakia. He assisted Toscanini in Salzburg (1936) and went to the USA in 1938 for an engagement with the Chicago Opera. He joined the staff of the San Francisco Opera in 1943, initially as chorus master, becoming artistic director in 1953, and general director three years later. Although he occasionally conducts, most of his time is devoted to administrative duties. During his regime the San Francisco Opera has become increasingly adventurous in repertory, the engagement of unproven talent, and the implementation of modern staging techniques. He has organized subsidiary organizations in San Francisco to stage experimental works, to perform in schools and other unconventional locales, and to train young singers. His work has received citations from the governments of Italy, Germany, Austria and Russia.

MARTIN BERNHEIMER

Adler, Larry [Lawrence] (*b* Baltimore, 10 Feb 1914). American harmonica player. He is acknowledged as the first harmonica player to achieve recognition and acceptance in classical musical circles and to have elevated the instrument to concert status. His ability has been recognized by such composers as Vaughan Williams, Milhaud, Gordon Jacob and Malcolm Arnold, all of whom have written orchestral works with Adler as soloist. He has toured extensively and broadcast frequently on radio and television in many countries, and has taken a keen interest in all aspects of teaching the instrument. Adler has written scores for a number of films, including *Genevieve*.

IVOR BEYNON

Adler, Marx vom. *See* DALL'AQUILA, MARCO.

Adler, Peter Herman (*b* Jablonec, 2 Dec 1899). American conductor of Czech birth. After studying composition and conducting with Alexander von Zemlinsky at the Prague Conservatory, he became music director of the Bremen Staatsoper (1929–32) and the State Philharmonia of Kiev (1933–6), and also appeared as guest conductor throughout Europe. He left for the USA in 1939 and made his début with the New York PO in 1940, after which he toured in the USA. From 1949 to 1959 he was music and artistic director of the NBC Opera Company, sharing artistic responsibility with Toscanini, who was then conductor of the NBC SO. After Toscanini's death Adler became musical director of the Baltimore SO (1959–68). In 1969 he became music and artistic director of WNET (National Educational Television). His Metropolitan Opera début was in 1972. Adler was a pioneer director of television opera in the USA, and commissioned many operas for television, among them Menotti's *Amahl and the Night Visitors* and *Maria Golovin* (of which he conducted the première at the 1958 Brussels World Fair), dello Joio's *St Joan* and Martinů's *The Marriage* (all at NBC); and Pasatieri's *The Trial of Mary Lincoln* and Henze's *La cubana* at NET.

ELLIOTT W. GALKIN

Adler, Richard (*b* New York, 3 Aug 1921). American songwriter. He was the son of the concert pianist Clarence Adler and was largely self-taught in music; after studying at the University of North Carolina (AB 1943) and serving in the navy (1943–6) he began writing songs. From 1950 he collaborated with Jerry Ross (Jerrold Rosenberg) (*b* Bronx, 9 March 1926; *d* New York, 11 Nov 1955); their first success was *Rags to Riches* and their first work for Broadway was four songs in the revue *Almanac* (1953). In 1954 they were acclaimed for their first musical *The Pajama Game* (after R. Bissell's *7½ cents*, partly staged by Jerome Robbins; filmed 1957); its songs (e.g. 'Hey there' and 'Hernando's Hideaway') were mostly well integrated with the plot and used American speech idioms. Adler and Ross followed this with *Damn Yankees* (1955; filmed 1958), one of the first musical comedy versions of the Faust story, from which the songs 'Heart' and 'Whatever Lola Wants' became famous. After Ross's death Adler wrote words and music for 'Everybody Loves a Lover' (1958), television musicals, advertising jingles and two unsuccessful musicals – *Kwamina* (1961) and *A Mother's Kisses* (1968). He was also an arts consultant to the White House (1965–9) and has produced several Broadway shows.

BIBLIOGRAPHY
D. Ewen: *Popular American Composers* (New York, 1962; suppl. 1972)

Adler, Samuel (*b* Mannheim, 4 March 1928). American composer, conductor and teacher of German origin. He moved to the USA in 1939 and studied composition with Herbert Fromm (1943–7), with Norden at Boston University (1946–8, BM) and with Piston, Thompson and Hindemith at Harvard University (1948–50, MA). In addition, he attended courses at Tanglewood (1949, 1950) under Copland for composition and Koussevitzky for conducting. In 1950 he joined the US Army and organized the Seventh Army SO, which he conducted in more than 75 concerts in Germany and Austria; he was awarded the Medal of Honor for his musical services. Subsequently he conducted concerts and operas in Europe and the USA. He was appointed professor of composition at North Texas State University in 1958, and in 1966 he joined the staff of the Eastman School, eventually becoming professor and chairman of composition. He has received many commissions and awards, including grants from the Rockefeller and Ford foundations.

WORKS
(selective list)

Operas: The Outcasts of Poker Flat, 1959; The Wrestler, 1971; The Lodge of Shadows, 1973

Orch: Sym. no.1, 1953; Sym. no.2, 1957; Sym. no.3 'Diptych', wind, 1960; Requiescat in pace, 1963; Sym. no.4 'Geometrics', 1967; Conc., wind, perc, 1968; Org Conc., 1970; Conc. for Orch, 1971; Sym. no.5 'We are the Echoes', Mez, orch, 1975; Concertino no.2, str, 1976; several other works

Vocal: Shir chadash, synagogue service, 1960; The Vision of Isaiah, cantata, B, chorus, orch, 1962; B'sharaay t'filah, synagogue service, 1963; Shiru ladonay, synagogue service, 1965; The Binding, oratorio, 1967; From Out of Bondage, cantata, solo vv, chorus, brass qnt, perc, org, 1968; A Whole Bunch of Fun, cantata, Mez/Bar, 3 choruses, orch, 1969; We Believe, ecumenical mass, vv, 8 insts, 1974; Of Saints and Sinners, song cycle, Mez/Bar, pf, 1976; It is to God I shall sing, vv, org, 1977; many other sacred and secular works

Inst: Sonata, hn, pf, 1948; Sonata no.2, vn, pf, 1956; Toccata, Recitation and Postlude, org, 1959; Sonata breve, pf, 1963; Str Qt no.4, 1963; Str Qt no.3, rev. 1964; Pf Trio, 1964; Sonata no.3, vn, pf, 1965; Sonata, vc, 1966; Str Qt no.5, 1969; Gradus, pf studies, 1969; 4 Dialogues, euphonium, mar, 1974; Str Qt no.6, Mez/Bar, str qt, 1975; Canto IX, perc, 1976; many other solo and ens pieces

Numerous works for children, arrs.

Principal publishers: Boosey & Hawkes, Fischer, Mills, Oxford University Press, Peters, Presser

WRITINGS

Anthology for the Teaching of Choral Conducting (New York, 1971)
Numerous articles in *American Choral Review*, *American Music Teacher* and *Music Educators Journal*

JERALD C. GRAUE

Adlgasser, Anton Cajetan (*b* Inzell, Upper Bavaria, 1 Oct 1729; *d* Salzburg, 22 Dec 1777). German composer and organist. In 1744 he was a chorister at the choir school of the Salzburg court chapel. He studied the organ and violin, and may have learnt composition with Johann Ernst Eberlin. While a student he sang and acted in many school plays produced chiefly at the university. He became court and cathedral organist in 1750, after Eberlin's promotion to the post of Hofkapellmeister. In 1752 he married Eberlin's daughter, Maria Josepha; his second marriage was to Maria Barbara Schwab (1756) and following her death he married the court singer Maria Anna Fesemayr (1769). All three weddings were witnessed by Leopold Mozart, whose account of the Salzburg musical establishment (in Marpurg's *Historisch-kritische Beyträge*, iii, 1757) described Adlgasser's duties as including the accompaniment of court chamber music on the harpsichord. The archbishop, who was fond of Italian opera, was apparently pleased with Adlgasser's services and sent him to Italy for a year's study, 1764–5.

After 1760 Adlgasser was organist at both the cathedral and the Trinity church in Salzburg; he also gave keyboard lessons at the choir school. His death, while playing for Vespers at the cathedral, is described in detail by Leopold Mozart (letter of 22 December 1777). He was succeeded as cathedral organist by W. A. Mozart, and Michael Haydn took on his duties at the Trinity church.

As a composer Adlgasser represents the transitional period from south German and Austrian late Baroque style to the Classicism found in the young Mozart's works. Although he composed keyboard and other instrumental music, his vocal writing, both sacred and secular, had greater significance at the time. His liturgical music continued to be performed in Salzburg well into the 19th century, but his other vocal works soon disappeared from the repertory. They include an Italian opera, oratorios, several Singspiels and other German dramatic works (Schuldramen, Finalkomödien) performed at the Salzburg Benedictine University. Adlgasser collaborated with Michael Haydn and Mozart in the oratorio Die Schuldigkeit des ersten Gebotes (1767), of which only Mozart's music for Act 1 survives. Of his stage works, several consist of musical dramas within spoken plays, sometimes with additional insertions of comic scenes. His liturgical compositions include works in the modern (Italian, soloistic) and 'strict' or contrapuntal styles. Mozart praised Adlgasser and Michael Haydn as 'excellent masters of counterpoint' (letter to Padre Martini, 4 September 1776); both composers had studied Eberlin's sacred works, especially those in contrapuntal style.

WORKS

For detailed list with thematic index see Rainer (1963), summarized in Rainer (1962–3).

ORATORIOS

(all performed in Salzburg; MSS mainly in A-Ssp)

Christus am Ölberg, 31 March 1754; Die wirkende Gnade Gottes oder David in der Busse, April 1756; Esther, ?1761; Ochus regnans oder Samuel und Heli, 1763; Bela Hungariae Princeps oder David und Jonathas, 11 June 1763; Amysis oder Jechonias und Evilmerodach, 30 Aug 1765; Iphigenia mactata oder Chalcis expugnata, 1765; Mercurius oder Pietas in Deum, 1772; Amyntas, frag.

Lost: Via viri in adolescentia, 1762; Israel et Albertus, 1762; Hannibal, Capuanae urbis hospes, 1767; Die Schuldigkeit des ersten Gebotes, pt.3, collab. W. A. Mozart, M. Haydn; Abraham und Isaak, 1768; Kampf der Busse und Bekehrung, 1768; Philemon und Baucis (Der Besuch Jupiters), 1768; Clementia Theodosii, 1768; Kaiser Constantin I. Feldzug und Sieg, pt.1, 1769, collab. Scheicher, M. Haydn; Synnorix et Camna, 1769; Die gereinigte Magdalena, 1770; Der laue Christ, 1771; Pietas in hospitem, 1772

OTHER WORKS

La Nitteti (opera, Metastasio), 1766, music lost

Sacred: 8 masses, 2 Requiem, 6 Tantum ergo, Stabat mater, 23 offertories, 15 litanies, 17 Marian antiphons and motets, 2 Ave maris stella, Vespers, responsory, 13 sacred arias: MSS mainly A-Sd, Ssp, Sn, KR, 2 ed. in DTÖ, lxxx, Jg.xliii/1 (1936/R)

Other vocal: Der Mensch, die Schwachheit und die Gnade, cantata, 1745, Sn; Dedicatio et sinfonia, cantata, ?1772, Ssp; Aria; Qt; Lied

Inst: 9 syms., incl. 2 doubtful, complete edn. in DTÖ (in preparation); 2 kbd concs. (see also MJb 1968–70, 347); 2 kbd sonatas, in Oeuvres mélées, v, viii (Nuremberg, 1759–63); 3 movts, hpd; Praeambulum, org; 103 versetti, org; ed. J. F. Doppelbauer (Altötting, 1966)

THEORETICAL WORKS

Fundamenta compositionis (MS, D-Mbs)

Partitur fundament (MS, A-Sca)

Partiturfundament von berühmten Auctoren H. Cajetan Adlgasser und H. Michael Heyden (MS, Ssp)

BIBLIOGRAPHY

S. Keller: 'Biographische Mitteilungen über A. C. Adlgasser', MMg, v (1873), 42

C. Schneider: 'Zur Lebensgeschichte des Salzburger Komponisten A. C. Adlgasser', Salzburger Museumsblätter, iv (1925)

——: 'Die Oratorien und Schuldramen A. C. Adlgassers', SMw, xviii (1931), 36–75

C. A. Rosenthal: 'The Salzburg Church Music of Mozart and his Predecessors', MQ, xviii (1932), 559

C. Schneider: Geschichte der Musik in Salzburg (Salzburg, 1935)

C. A. Rosenthal: 'Salzburg Influences in Mozart's Church Music', BAMS, viii (1945), 3

W. Rainer: 'Verzeichnis der Werke A. C. Adlgassers', MJb 1962–3, 280

——: Das Instrumentalwerk A. C. Adlgassers (diss., U. of Innsbruck, 1963; extracts in Mitteilungen der Gesellschaft für Salzburger Landeskunde, cv, 1965, 205–37)

M. H. Schmid: Mozart und die Salzburger Tradition (Tutzing, 1976)

REINHARD G. PAULY

Ad libitum (Lat.: 'at the pleasure' [of the performer]). Used in titles, particularly in the later 18th century, to indicate that one or more instruments may be left out, e.g. Tapray: Simphonie concertante pour le clavecin et le piano-forte avec orchestre ad libitum (c1782), and in scores, as a direction to the player to improvise or ornament. Handel's Organ Concertos op.7 furnish several examples: embellishment of a written line (no.2, Overture), elaboration of a fermata (same movement), continuation of a solo passage (no.1, first movement), improvisation of an adagio on a harmonic skeleton (no.5), and improvisation of a whole movement ex nihilo (no.2). The term is also sometimes used to indicate that the performer may depart from strict tempo.

DAVID FULLER

Adlung [Adelung], Jakob (b Bindersleben, nr. Erfurt, 14 Jan 1699; d Erfurt, 5 July 1762). German organist and scholar. His father, David, was a teacher and organist, and his mother was Dorothea Elisabetha, born Meuerin, from Tondorf. Adlung recorded vividly his own life in the 'Vorrede', part ii of Musica mechanica organoedi (1768). His earliest musical training came from his father who, in 1711, sent his son to Erfurt to the St Andreas lower school. In 1713 he matriculated at the Erfurt Gymnasium, while living in the home of Christian Reichardt who taught him the organ and expanded his general musical knowledge. In 1723 he went to the university at Jena, where he pursued a wide range of subjects including philosophy, philology and theology. At the same time he studied the organ with Johann Nikolaus Bach. A friendship developed with Johann Gottfried Walther in Weimar, which enabled Adlung to borrow theoretical works on music. This enthusiasm for music theory led him while in Jena to write several books on the subject, most of which were later lost in a fire that destroyed his home in 1736. He graduated in 1726 and, although planning to become a teacher there, he was recalled to Erfurt in 1727 to become the successor to Johann Heinrich Buttstedt who until his death had been organist at the Prediger church. Adlung retained this position for the rest of his life. In 1732 he married Elisabeth Ritter, daughter of the mayor of Gross-Wanzleben near Magdeburg. Adlung was a professor of languages at the Erfurt Gymnasium and also taught numerous organ students (he accounts for 218 keyboard pupils and 284 language pupils between 1728 and 1762). He also mastered the craft of building keyboard instruments, completing 16 in his lifetime.

Adlung belongs to a distinguished group of scholar-musicians of the mid-18th century who wrote invaluable, comprehensive studies of their art. Together with Mattheson, Mizler and Walther, to name three of the most important, Adlung possessed enormous erudition in the theory and aesthetics of music. His publications, *Musica mechanica organoedi* and *Anleitung zu der musikalischen Gelahrtheit*, are major sources about the German Baroque in music. The former, not published until six years after Adlung's death (although he said that it was written as early as 1726), is a unique compilation of data about organs in Germany, their construction and tonal characteristics. Adlung prepared in effect an organ builder's encyclopedia, with details about the case, wind chamber, pipes and registers, and lengthy discussions regarding tuning and temperament, as well as methods of testing new instruments. Not the least significant are his detailed descriptions of more than 80 German organs.

In *Anleitung zu der musikalischen Gelahrtheit* Adlung organized a vast collection of information for both the scholar and amateur. He recorded all the sources of knowledge known to him about such a variety of theoretical and practical subjects as: the history of music, music and mathematics (including problems of tuning), the history of the organ, organ registration, organ construction and building costs, descriptions of other musical instruments, the art of singing, thoroughbass, the chorale (including a significant description of various kinds of organ chorale preludes), the art of improvisation, the Italian tablature and the art of composition. This accumulation of factual data and the variety of Adlung's own practical observations have as yet to be fully assimilated in modern research. As the testimony of a learned musician this work offers a dramatic example of the accomplishment of German musical scholarship in the mid-18th century.

WRITINGS

Vollständige Anweisung zum Generalbasse; Anweisung zur italienischen Tabulatur; Anweisung zur Fantasie und zu den Fugen (all written between 1723 and 1727, lost when Adlung's home was destroyed by fire in 1736)
ed. J. L. Albrecht: *Musica mechanica organoedi* (Berlin, 1768/*R*1961); ed. C. Mahrenholz (Kassel, 1931)
Anleitung zu der musikalischen Gelahrtheit (Erfurt, 1758/*R*1953, 2/1783)
ed. J. L. Albrecht: *Musikalisches Siebengestirn. Das ist: Sieben zu der edlen Tonkunst gehörige Fragen* (Berlin, 1768)

GEORGE J. BUELOW

Admetus de Aureliana (*fl* c1300–10). French theorist. He came from Orleans and is known only by a group of quotations in Robert de Handlo's treatise of 1326 (*CS*, i, 397). He used a ternary mensuration of semibreves with separate symbols for *minimae* and *minoratae*, mentioning a regional practice of cantors of 'Navernia' (? Nevers or Navarre).

See also FRANCE: BIBLIOGRAPHY OF MUSIC TO 1600 and THEORY, THEORISTS.

GORDON A. ANDERSON

Adni, Daniel (*b* Haifa, 6 Dec 1951). Israeli pianist. At the age of 12 he gave his first public recital, in Haifa. In 1968 he was heard by, among others, Menuhin, Arrau and Curzon, who helped promote a year's study at the Paris Conservatoire under Perlemuter; in June 1970 he participated in Anda's Zurich master classes. His London début recital (Wigmore Hall, 1970) won high praise; his Festival Hall début (September 1971) was under Klemperer. Adni's gifts are obvious and abundant: tone always luminous, phrasing shapely, projection gently fastidious. His command of the more forceful keyboard sonorities tends to lack muscle. He gave the first performance outside Britain of Goehr's Piano Concerto (Berlin, May 1973); his recordings include

complete sets of Mendelssohn's *Lieder ohne Wörte* and Grieg's *Lyric Pieces*.

MAX LOPPERT

Ad Nonam (Lat.). NONE.

Adolf, R. Name under which ADOLF RZEPKO performed.

Adolfati, Andrea (*b* Venice, 1721 or 1722; *d* Padua, 28 Oct 1760). Italian composer. After studying with Galuppi, he became *maestro di cappella* of S Maria della Salute in Venice. In 1745 he left this post to serve the Modenese court where his *La pace fra la virtù e la bellezza* was performed the following year. Adolfati provided recitatives, choruses and six arias for Hasse's *Lo starnuto d'Ercole* (P. G. Martelli) which, according to Allacci, was performed with puppets (*bambocci*) at the Venetian palace of Angelo Labia in 1745. A printed libretto indicates that it was staged conventionally at the Teatro S Girolamo, Venice, during the carnival of 1746. From 1748 until early 1760 Adolfati was director of music at the Annunziata church in Genoa; then he moved to Padua, where he succeeded Rampini as *maestro di cappella* on 30 May.

Adolfati was not highly regarded by Metastasio, who heard his setting of *La clemenza di Tito* in 1753 and who wrote to him in 1755 and 1757. Although Adolfati's style is in general conventional, he composed an aria in 5/4 time and, as a youth, even attempted to use 7/4.

WORKS

OPERAS
(*music lost unless otherwise indicated*)

Artaserse (Metastasio), Verona, Teatro Filarmonico, carn. 1741
La pace fra la virtù e la bellezza (divertimento da camera, Liberati, after Metastasio), Modena, Teatro Ducale, 1 Jan 1746; *I-MOe*
Didone abbandonata (Metastasio), Venice, Teatro S Girolamo, carn. 1747
Arianna (P. Pariati), Genoa, Teatro Falcone, wint. 1750
Adriano in Siria (Metastasio), Genoa, Teatro Falcone, aut. 1751
La gloria e il piacere (festa da ballo), Genoa, Teatro Falcone, carn. 1751
Vologeso (after Zeno: Lucio Vero), Genoa, Teatro Falcone, carn. 1752
Ipermestra (Metastasio), Modena, Teatro Rangoni, carn. 1752
La clemenza di Tito (Metastasio), Vienna, Burgtheater, 15 Oct 1753; *A-Wn*
Sesostri re d'Egitto (Zeno), Genoa, Teatro Falcone, carn. 1755; *I-Gi(l)*

OTHER
Miserere, 4vv, insts, *D-Dkh*
Nisi Dominus, lv, bc; Laudate, 4vv; In exitu, 5vv, insts: all *F-Pn*
Domine ne in furore, 4vv, insts, *D-MÜs*
6 cantatas, S, str, *I-Gi(l)*: Gia la notte s'avvicina (Metastasio); Filen, cruda Fileno; Perdono amata Nice (Metastasio); Cortesi amanti; Ingratissimo Tirsi; No, non turbati, o Nice (Metastasio)
6 sonate, 2 vn, 2 fl, 2 hn, bn, b, op.1 (Paris, n.d.), also pubd in Amsterdam
Sinfonia, F, ov., D, *I-Gi(l)*

BIBLIOGRAPHY

EitnerQ; FétisB; GerberL; SchmidlD
L. Allacci: *Drammaturgia* (Venice, enlarged 2/1755/*R*1961)
F. Caffi: *Storia della musica sacra nella già cappella ducale di San Marco in Venezia dal 1318 al 1797*, i (Venice, 1854, repr. 1931), 403
R. Giazotto: *La musica a Genova* (Genoa, 1951)
B. Brunelli, ed.: *P. Metastasio: Tutte le opere*, iii (Milan, 1951–4)
G. Piamonte: 'Adolfati', *DBI*
K. G. Fellerer: 'Thematische Verzeichnisse der fürstbischöflichen Freisingischen Hofmusik von 1796', *Festschrift Otto Erich Deutsch* (Kassel, 1963), 229
S. Pintacuda: *Genova, Biblioteca dell'Istituto musicale 'N. Paganini': catalogo* (Milan, 1966), 13, 69ff

SVEN HANSELL

Adolfson, Adolf Gustaw. *See* SONNENFELD, ADOLF GUSTAW.

Adorno, Theodor W(iesengrund) (*b* Frankfurt am Main, 11 Sept 1903; *d* Visp, Switzerland, 6 Aug 1969). German social philosopher, sociologist of music and composer. Adorno made a precocious reputation as a music critic, and edited *Anbruch* from 1928 to 1931. He studied composition under Alban Berg. Torn between music and philosophy, he chose a career in the latter, but was ejected from his position as *Privatdozent* at Frankfurt by the Nazis. He emigrated to Oxford in 1934, and in 1938 followed Max Horkheimer's expatriated Institut für Sozialforschung to New York, where he became musical director of the Princeton Radio Research Project. By this time he had consolidated a position as a leading apologist for modern music and a critic of popular culture. In 1940 he went with the institute to Los Angeles, where he advised Thomas Mann on the musical aspects of *Doktor Faustus*. In 1949 he returned to Frankfurt with the repatriated institute, succeeding Horkheimer as director, and was appointed to Frankfurt University, becoming professor in 1956.

Adorno's development of the concept of 'negative dialectic' made him a leader of left-wing social thought in post-war Germany, where his fame is primarily that of a social philosopher. As a musicologist, he harnessed Freudian and Marxist ideologies to the service of avant-garde music, which he enlisted in the cause of the free individual repressed by the 'managed societies' of east and west alike. Serious music must nowadays be difficult and disagreeable, for charm and pleasure have become means to make men into docile consumers. Not only popular music, but the use made of serious music by the 'culture industry', which he was the first to name and anatomize, encourage regression to an infantile condition.

As the conscience of the leftist avant garde, Adorno conducted devastating polemics against musical amateurism, against serial composers who relapse into formalism, against non-serial composers who evade the duty of difficulty, and against the Stalinist demand that communists be optimists. His advocates claim that the success of these campaigns has transformed the whole climate of musical opinion since 1950. His opponents contend that his intolerance of anything simple reflected mere personal élitism, that his championing of Schoenberg (for which he received the Schoenberg Medal in 1954) expressed a rationalized nostalgia for his schooldays, and that he sacrificed theoretical solidity to literary style.

WRITINGS
Philosophie der neuen Musik (Tübingen, 1949, 3/1967; Eng. trans., 1973)
Versuch über Wagner (Berlin, 1952, 2/1964)
Prismen: Kulturkritik und Gesellschaft (Frankfurt, 1955, 3/1969; Eng. trans., 1967)
Dissonanzen: Musik in der verwalteten Welt (Göttingen, 1956; enlarged 3/1963)
Klangfiguren: musikalische Schriften I (Berlin, 1959)
Mahler: eine musikalische Physiognomik (Frankfurt, 1960, 2/1963)
Einleitung in die Musiksoziologie: Zwölf theoretische Vorlesungen (Frankfurt, 1962, 2/1968; Eng. trans., 1976)
Der getreue Korrepetitor: Lehrschriften zur musikalischen Praxis (Frankfurt, 1963)
Quasi una fantasia: musikalische Schriften II (Frankfurt, 1963)
Moments musicaux: neu gedruckte Aufsätze 1928 bis 1962 (Frankfurt, 1964)
Ohne Leitbild: Parva aesthetica (Frankfurt, 1967, 2/1968)
Berg: der Meister des kleinsten Uebergangs (Vienna, 1968)
Impromptus: zweite Folge neu gedruckter musikalischer Aufsätze (Frankfurt, 1968)
Gesammelte Schriften (Frankfurt, 1971–) [20 vols. scheduled]

BIBLIOGRAPHY
K. Oppens and others: *Ueber Theodor W. Adorno* (Frankfurt, 1968)
T. Kneif: 'Der Bürger als Revolutionär', *Melos*, xxxvi (1969), 372
R. Stephan: 'Theodor W. Adorno (1903–1969)', *Mf*, xxii (1969), 269
A. Silbermann: 'Theodor W. Adornos kunstsoziologische Vermächtnis', *Kölner Zeitschrift für Soziologie und Sozialpsychologie*, xxi (1969), 712
H. Schweppenhaüser, ed.: *Theodor W. Adorno zum Gedächtnis* (Frankfurt, 1971) [contains an extensive though incomplete bibliography of Adorno's writings by K. Schultz]
Zeitschrift für Musik Theorie, iv/1 (1973) [Adorno issue]
O. Söhngen: *Erneuerte Kirchenmusik: eine Steitschrift* (Göttingen, 1975)
W. Gramer: *Musik und Verstehen: eine Studie zur Musikästhetik Theodor W. Adorno* (Mainz, 1976)
O. Kolleritsch, ed.: *Theodor W. Adorno und die Musik*, Studien zur Wertungsforschung, xii (Graz, 1968)

F. E. SPARSHOTT

Ad Primam (Lat.). PRIME.

Adriaenssen [Adriaensen, Adriansen, Adriensen, Hadrianus, Hadrianius], **Emanuel** (*b* Antwerp, *c*1554; *d* Antwerp, buried 27 Feb 1604). South Netherlands lutenist, teacher and composer. He went to Rome to study in 1574, a visit that probably accounts for the Italian elements in his publications. He was a Protestant, but after the fall of Antwerp in 1585 he was compelled for political reasons to embrace the Catholic faith. With his brother Gysbrecht he opened a school for lutenists at Antwerp, but in 1587 they came into conflict with the musicians' guild because neither of them was a member; later, however, Emanuel must have qualified as a freeman of the guild, for he occasionally assumed the title of master. He was appointed captain of the citizens' watch, which brought him a regular income, and in 1595 he took part in the relief of the nearby town of Lier, which had been occupied by the Dutch. He moved in the highest circles in Antwerp, and the principal families doubtless admired his virtuosity as a lutenist and engaged him to perform. His publications brought him wider fame, and they were to be found in the libraries of many prominent people, among them Constantijn Huygens, King John IV of Portugal and Cardinal Mazarin. He was mentioned by Adrian Denss (1594), Robert Dowland (1610), G. L. Fuhrmann (1615), J.-B. Besard (1617), W. C. Printz (1690) and J. G. Baron (1727) as a leading composer of lute music, but his music inclines to an excess of ornamentation, a feature alien to the pure lute style, and for this reason he cannot quite rank with the greatest of his Italian, French and English contemporaries. As a teacher, however, he is in the front rank, both because of the unique intabulation tables that he published and because he was the founder of an Antwerp lute school that probably included Denss, Gregorio Huet and Joachim van den Hove.

Adriaenssen published *Pratum musicum longe amoenissimum, cuius spatiosissimo, eoque iucundissimo ambitu comprehenduntur. . .omnia ad testudinis tabulaturam fideliter redacta . . . opus novum* (Antwerp, 1584[12], rev. 2/1600[18], *editio nova priori locupletior*) and *Novum pratum musicum. . .selectissimi diversorum autorum et idiomatum madrigales, cantiones, et moduli . . . opus plane novum, nec hactenus editum* (Antwerp, 1592[22]/R1977; music from all three ed. in MMBel, x, 1966, and in Spiessens, 1974–6). Each of these three books is in French lute tablature and consists of five fantasias, some 50 vocal pieces and some 30 dances. The fantasias, which are all original pieces, are small-scale embryonic fugues; the counterpoint is neat, and they are forward-looking, almost Baroque, in style and form. The intabulations of vocal music are for the most part virtuoso lute arrangements of madrigals, chansons and motets by 28 prominent Netherlands, French and Italian composers of the 16th century; there are also a number of anonymous *napolitane* and French *airs* of popular origin, set in a simpler manner. To each intabulation two or more vocal parts are added in mensural notation; these pieces can thus be performed vocally or instrumentally or both. The dances are virtuoso variations on anonymous tunes, especially passamezzos, galliards, allemandes, courantes, voltas and branles. The *Novum pratum musicum* is particularly interesting for its instructions (printed in Latin) on methods of intabulating polyphonic music: they include tables in which mensural notation is shown alongside the corresponding tablature signs.

BIBLIOGRAPHY

A. Goovaerts: *Histoire et bibliographie de la typographie musicale dans les Pays-Bas* (Antwerp, 1880/R1963), nos.293, 319f, 370

J. P. N. Land: *Het luitboek van Thysius* (Amsterdam, 1889), 14, 261, 321, 360

P. Hamburger: 'Die Fantasien in Emanuel Adriansens Pratum musicum (1600)', *ZMw*, xii (1929–30), 148

F. Noske: 'Remarques sur les luthistes des Pays-Bas (1580–1620)', *Le luth et sa musique: CNRS Neuilly-sur-Seine 1957*, 179

G. Spiessens: 'Adriaenssen, Emanuel', *Nationaal Biografisch Woordenboek*, i (Brussels, 1964)

——: 'Emmanuel Adriaenssen et son Pratum Musicum', *AcM*, xxxvi (1964), 142

——: Introduction to MMBel, x (1966)

——: 'Adriaenssen, (Emanuel)', *BNB*

C. MacClintock: 'Two Lute Intabulations of Wert's "Cara la vita" ', *Essays in Musicology: a Birthday Offering to Willi Apel* (Bloomington, Ind., 1968), 93

J. Myers: 'Performance Practice Indications in Emanuel Adriansen's Lute Ensemble Music', *Journal of the Lute Society of America*, ii (1969), 18

G. Spiessens: *Leven en werk van de Antwerpse luitcomponist Emanuel Adriaenssen (ca. 1554–1604)* (Brussels, 1974–6)

GODELIEVE SPIESSENS

Adriani, Francesco (*b* S Severino, nr. Ancona, 1539; *d* Rome, 16 Aug 1575). Italian composer. It is uncertain when he went to Rome, but he is listed among the members of the Sistine Chapel from 17 July 1572 until 1573, when he succeeded François Roussel as *maestro di cappella* at St John Lateran, a post he retained until his death. As a composer he can be judged only from two madrigals in anthologies published in 1568, since only the bass parts of his own madrigal books remain.

WORKS
(all published in Venice)

Il primo libro de [33] madrigali, 6vv (1568)
Il primo libro de [30] madrigali, 5vv (1570)
Il secondo libro de [31] madrigali, 5vv (1570)
1 madrigal, 5vv, in 1568¹²; 1 madrigal, 5vv, in 1568¹⁶

BIBLIOGRAPHY

E. Celani: 'I cantori della cappella pontificia nei secoli XVI–XVIII', *RMI*, xiv (1907), 758

PATRICIA ANN MYERS

Adrien [Andrien *l'aîné*; La Neuville], **Martin Joseph** (*b* Liège, 26 May 1767; *d* Paris, 19 Nov 1822). South Netherlands bass, teacher and composer. He learnt music as a chorister at Liège Cathedral and later at the Ecole Royal de Chant in Paris. He appeared as a singer at the Concert Spirituel in 1781 and made his début at the Opéra on 20 June 1785. From 1804 he no longer appeared on the stage but was made a *chef de chant*. In March 1822 he succeeded Laîné as professor of lyric declamation at the Ecole Royale de Musique but died eight months later. An advocate of the old French

system of declamation, he was said to have had a harsh voice and a bad method of singing, but he had merit as an actor.

During the Revolution Adrien composed a number of topical choral works, including an *Invocation à l'Etre suprême* (Delaporte) and a *Hymne à la victoire sur l'évacuation du territoire* (Lacombe), both published in 1794, and a *chanson, Aux martyrs de la liberté*, in the same year. According to Fétis he also wrote music for *Elodie, ou La vierge du monastère*, a melodrama by V. Ducange produced at the Théâtre de l'Ambigu-Comique on 10 January 1822. Five collections of songs were published but it is not certain whether they are all by Martin Joseph or by one of his two brothers. One, J. Adrien (*c*1768–*c*1824), was chorus master at the Théâtre Feydeau in 1794; the other, Ferdinand (*c*1770–*c*1830), was a singing teacher in Paris and, from 1798 to 1800, *chef de chant* at the Opéra before Martin Joseph. One of the brothers may have written the opera *Le fou ou La Révolution*, produced at the Antwerp opera on 3 December 1829.

BIBLIOGRAPHY

FétisB

C. Pierre: *Hymnes et chansons de la Révolution* (Paris, 1904), 104, 940

MARIE-LOUISE PEREYRA/JOHN LADE

Adriensen, Emanuel. *See* ADRIAENSSEN, EMANUEL.

Adrio, Adam (*b* Essen, 4 April 1901; *d* Schlüchtern, 18 Sept 1973). German musicologist. In addition to German studies and philosophy he studied musicology with Abert, Schering and Blume at the Free University, Berlin (1923–5, 1927–31); in 1934 he took the doctorate at Berlin with a dissertation on the beginnings of the sacred concerto. He held posts as assistant lecturer in the music history department at Berlin University (1932–45), lecturer in church music and musical liturgy at the Protestant theology faculty (1935–43), lecturer in music history at the Berlin School of Church Music (1935–43, 1946–50) and lecturer at the Hochschule für Musikerziehung und Kirchenmusik (1942–3). In 1949 he completed his *Habilitation* in musicology at the Free University, Berlin; he was appointed reader in 1951 and professor of musicology in 1953; he retired in 1967. Adrio's field of study was the history of Protestant church music of the 16th and 17th centuries as well as that of more recent times. He wrote some 50 articles for *MGG* and was editor of the *Berliner Studien zur Musikwissenschaft* (from 1959) and the new complete works of Schein (from 1963).

WRITINGS

Die Anfänge des geistlichen Konzerts (diss., Free U. of Berlin, 1934; Berlin, 1935)

'Die Matthäus-Passion von J. G. Kühnhausen (Celle um 1700)', *Festschrift Arnold Schering* (Berlin, 1937), 24

'Wirkungen Goethes im Berliner Musikleben seiner Zeit', *Goethe in Berlin*, ed. F. Moser (Berlin, 1949), 67

'Heinrich Schütz und Italien', *Bekenntnis zu Heinrich Schütz* (Kassel, 1954), 55

'Dietrich Buxtehudes Kunst in den musikalischen Bestrebungen seiner Zeit', *Musik und Kirche*, xxviii (1958), 1

ed., with F. Blume, W. Blankenburg, L. Finscher and G. Feder: *Geschichte der evangelischen Kirchenmusik* (Kassel, 2/1965; Eng. trans., enlarged,1974 as *Protestant Church Music: a History*) [incl. 'Erneuerung und Wiederbelebung' [20th century], 273–340]

'Tradition und Modernität im musikalischen Schaffen der Schütz-Zeit', *Sagittarius*, i (1966), 43

Essays on the history of church music in Festschrifts for Osthoff (1961), Fellerer (1962, 1973), Blume (1963), Vötterle (1968) and Mahrenholz (1970)

EDITIONS
J. H. Schein: Sechs deutsche Motetten, Cw, xii (1931)
J. H. Schein and C. Demantius: Der 116. Psalm, Cw, xxxvi (1935)
J. G. Kühnhausen: Matthäus-Passion, Cw, 1 (1938)
Die Fuge I, Mw, xix (1960)
S. Scheidt: Geistliche Konzerte, Teil II, Gesamtausgabe, ix (Hamburg, 1960); *Teil III*, ibid, x–xi (Hamburg, 1964)
J. H. Schein: Israelsbrünnlein, 1629, Neue Ausgabe sämtlicher Werke (Kassel, 1963); *Cantional oder Gesangbuch Augsburgischer Konfession 1627 und 1645*, ibid, ii/1–2 (Kassel, 1965–7); *Diletti pastorali. Hirtenlust, 1624*, ibid, viii (Kassel, 1969)
H. Hartmann: Vier deutsche Motetten, Cw, xcviii (1965)

BIBLIOGRAPHY
A. Forchert: 'A. Adrio (1901–1973)', *Mf*, xxvii (1974), 1
                                    HANS HEINRICH EGGEBRECHT

Ad Sextam (Lat.). SEXT.

Adson, John (*b* late 16th century; *d* London, 1640). English instrumentalist and composer. He was in the service of the Duke of Lorraine from 1604 to 1608. He became a London wait in 1614 and eventually joined the English court band in 1625. By 1633 he was described as 'musician in ordinary' for the king's wind instruments and played the flute, cornett and recorder at the Blackfriars theatre. He organized the 'loud' music in Shirley's masque *The Triumph of Peace* (first performed on 3 February 1634). As both a wait and court musician, divided loyalties caused him to become involved in a dispute with Nicholas Lanier over whether his fellow players in the king's band or his former colleagues at Blackfriars should play in the subsequent performance. Later in 1634 he was appointed music teacher to Charles I. At the time of his death he was receiving a stipend of £46 p.a.

He composed *Courtly Masquing Ayres* (London, 1611, 2/1622) comprising 31 pieces, of which 21 are five-part and ten six-part. Three of the five-part works are described as 'for sackbuts and cornets' (these works may derive from music originally intended for a masque). 'Framed only for instruments; of which kind, these are the first that have ever been printed', as the title-page runs, the contents employ a free dance-form in three parts with a final section in triple time; in this way the collection resembles those made by contemporary English composers working in Germany (e.g. Brade and Simpson). Their principal charm lies in the use of attractive melodic motifs. One piece from the collection has been edited in *Jacobean Consort Music*, MB, ix (1955, 2/1966); other modern editions have also been published of some of the pieces.

BIBLIOGRAPHY
J. P. Cutts: 'Jacobean Masque and Stage Music', *ML*, xxxv (1954), 185
M. Lefkowitz: 'The Longleat Papers of Bulstrode Whitelocke', *JAMS*, xviii (1965), 42
A. J. Sabol: 'New Documents on Shirley's Masque "The Triumph of Peace"', *ML*, xlvii (1966), 10
                                    NORMAN JOSEPHS

Ad Tertiam (Lat.). TERCE.

A due (It.: 'with two'). An instruction found in scores (also as *a 2, à 2*) where two parts are written on one staff to say that they should be played either in unison (*all'unisono*) or separately (*divisi*). The ambiguity is resolved by the context. *A due* is also used in descriptions of polyphonic works to denote 'in two voices'; *see* A (i).

Aegidius de Zamora. *See* EGIDIUS DE ZAMORA.

Aelred of Rievaulx [Ethelred] (*b c*1109; *d* York, 1166). English saint, theologian and historian. A pupil of St Bernard, and a liturgical purist, Aelred was tutor to Henry, son of David I, at the court of Scotland, and later (1146) abbot of the Cistercian abbey of Rievaulx in Yorkshire. Music forms only a small part of his writings: a *De abusu musices* attributed to him by van der Straeten (*Grove 5*) cannot be identified as his, but chapter xxiii of the second book of *Speculum caritatis* deals with the same topic. Complaining about the use of instruments (*organa*) and bells in church, about the thundering of wind instruments, about *infractio* and *confractio* of the voice, Aelred objected chiefly to certain musical techniques, apparently hocketing and sustained-note polyphony: 'This voice sings afterwards, that one below, another above, another divides and cuts into the middle of certain notes. A note is sung rapidly, then broken, then thrust against another note, then drawn out in extended sound ... Sometimes you may see a man with an open mouth, not to sing but as it were to expire by shutting in his breath, and with a ridiculous interception of his voice to threaten silence'.

Aelred's statements closely resemble those of his contemporary John of Salisbury, and provide some evidence of the cultivation of complex polyphony in 12th-century England.

BIBLIOGRAPHY
GS, i, 26
M. Gerbert: *De cantu et musica sacra* (St Blasien, 1774/*R*1968), ii, 93, 96, 100, 126, 145
H. E. Wooldridge: *OHM*, i/1 (1901, rev. 2/1929), 290
A. Hoste and C. H. Talbot, eds.: *Aelredi Rievallensis opera omnia Corpus christianorum, Continuatio mediaevalis*, i (Turnhout, 1971), i, 97–9
For further bibliography *see* ENGLAND: BIBLIOGRAPHY OF MUSIC TO 1600.
                                    ANDREW HUGHES

Aelyau. *See* TAMBOURINE.

Aeolian. The name given by Glarean in the *Dodecachordon* (1547) to denote the authentic mode on A, which uses the diatonic octave species *a–a'*, divided at *e'* and composed of a first species of 5th (tone–tone–semitone–tone) plus a second species of 4th (semitone–tone–tone), thus *a–b–c'–d'–e' + e'–f'–g'–a'*. With this octave species identical to that of the natural minor scale on A, the Aeolian mode, together with its plagal counterpart, the HYPOAEOLIAN, most closely resembles the descending melodic minor scale. In the MINOR mode of tonal music the dominant lies a 5th above the tonic, or principal scale degree, and the sixth degree is characteristically a semitone above the dominant; for this reason scholars in the last three centuries have tended to think of the minor mode of tonal music as a lineal descendant of Glarean's Aeolian scale. In fact the minor tonalities of tonal music are of heterogeneous origins. Even the key of A minor is indirectly but closely related historically to the old transposed modes 1 and 2 with finals on *a*, and it is at least as nearly descended from polyphonic mode 3 (*e–e'* with strong cadences at *a* and *c'*) and polyphonic psalm tone 3 (*e–e'* with final at *a*) as it is from Glarean's Aeolian (*see* MODE, §III, 5). Other minor tonalities also have multiple historical evolutions, if not always so complex, and the old D modes (Dorian and Hypodorian), with their *cantus mollis* (one-flat) and *cantus fictus* (two-flat) forms on *g* and *c* respectively, are historically more nearly in the direct line of ancestry of the minor tonalities than Glarean's Aeolian–Hypoaeolian group and its Italian and French imitators.

HAROLD S. POWERS

Aeolian American Corporation. American firm of instrument makers. It was formed in 1932 when the American Piano Corporation (the successor of the AMERICAN PIANO CO.) merged with the AEOLIAN CO. Its name was changed to the AEOLIAN CORPORATION in 1959.

Aeolian Co. American firm of player piano manufacturers. It was founded by William B. Tremaine, who had begun as a piano builder with Tremaine Brothers. He formed the Mechanical Orguinette Co. in New York (1878) and the Aeolian Organ & Music Co. (by 1888) to manufacture automatic organs and perforated music rolls. His son Harry C. Tremaine sensed the possibility of a larger market and directed the company in an extensive advertising campaign that resulted in the sale of millions of player pianos during the first three decades of the 20th century. In 1913 the company introduced the Duo-Art Reproducing Piano, a sophisticated mechanism (fitted in quality pianos) that made it possible to record and reproduce through paper rolls the slightest nuances of dynamics, tempo and phrasing; a number of leading pianists of that time were recorded in this way.

In 1903 (with a capital of 10 million dollars) Tremaine formed the Aeolian, Weber Piano & Pianola Co., of which the Aeolian Co. formed a significant part; the first successful American piano trust, the parent company eventually controlled such other firms as the Chilton Piano Co., Choralian Co. of Germany and Austria, Mason & Hamlin, Orchestrelle Co. of Great Britain, Pianola Company Proprietary Ltd of Australia, George Steck & Co., Stroud Piano Co., Styvesant Piano Co., Technola, Universal Music Co., Vocalian Organ Co., Votey Organ Co., Weber Piano Co. and Wheelock Piano Co. Noted for its development and aggressive marketing of various mechanical instruments, the Aeolian Co. manufactured the Aeriole, Aeolian Orchestrelle Pianola, Metrostyle Pianola and Aeolian pipe organs. The firm's offices were in New York, where it maintained the Aeolian Concert Hall. In 1932 the company merged with the American Piano Corporation to form the Aeolian American Corporation.

CYNTHIA ADAMS HOOVER

Aeolian Corporation. American piano corporation. It was formed as the result of two mergers, the first of which, on 1 September 1932, between the AEOLIAN CO. and the American Piano Corporation (formerly the AMERICAN PIANO CO.), created the Aeolian American Corporation. In May 1959 the assets of the corporation were purchased by Winter & Co. The parent company changed its name to the Aeolian Corporation on 12 June 1964; it retained the name Aeolian American Corporation for the East Rochester division until April 1971 when it was changed to the Aeolian American Division of the Aeolian Corporation.

The corporation acquired the assets (including trademarks, plans and factories) of many formerly independent American piano companies. Its instruments are made in three cities under the following trade names: Mason & Risch (Toronto); Mason & Hamlin; Chickering; Wm. Knabe & Co. (East Rochester, New York); Cable; Winter; Hardman, Peck; Kranich & Bach; J. & C. Fischer; George Steck; Vose & Sons; Henry F. Miller; Ivers & Pond; Melodigrand; Duo-Art; Musette; and Pianola Player Piano (Memphis, Tennessee).

CYNTHIA ADAMS HOOVER

Aeolian Hall. London concert hall opened in 1904; *see* LONDON, §VI, 5(iv).

Aeolian harp (Fr. *harpe d'Eole*, *harpe éolienne*; Ger. *Äolsharfe*, *Windharfe*; It. *arpa eolia*, *arpa d'Eolo*). A string instrument sounded by natural wind, interesting as much for its symbolic significance as for its musical importance.

1. Structure. 2. Acoustics. 3. History. 4. Literature.

1. STRUCTURE. Normally four to 12 (though sometimes 24 or 48) strings 'of catgut or brass wire, equal in length, unequal in thickness' (*Magasin pittoresque*, 1845) are stretched over one or two hardwood bridges of triangular cross-section, mounted on a thin pine, maple or mahogany box of variable shape – measuring 75–200 cm (normally 85–110 cm) long, 11–35 cm (normally 12–26 cm) wide and 5–17 cm (normally 5–9 cm) deep. The ends of this soundbox may be of beech, for insertion of iron hitch-pins or wooden tuning-pegs. Most instruments have some device such as a slit draught for concentrating the wind on the strings.

Six variants of this structure exist: (1) A rectangular soundbox with a single horizontal row of strings, the most popular model in England, and, until 1803, in Germany; also the simplest type.

(2) A more practical variant developed only in England, with the strings on an inclined fingerboard over which a lid was mounted, whose horizontal top allowed the wind to blow over the strings where the incline was lowest and funnel up the inclined soundboard to the highest point at the back of the instrument (see figs.1 and 2). This structure ideally fitted sash windows, being mounted on the sill with the frame brought down on top of the lid to hold the instrument in place.

(3) A vertically strung soundbox with wind-funnelling 'wings' used throughout western Europe since its inception by Kircher in 1650 at Rome.

(4) A further development of the vertically strung model (see fig. 3) with double banks of strings, one on each side of the instrument (always in the same plane as the wind direction), used by Steudal (from 1803) and J. C. Dietz in Germany.

(5) A model on which the strings were mounted on a semicircular soundbox (so that at least one or two strings would present themselves at the correct angle, whatever the wind direction), developed apparently by the Swiss.

(6) An apparently popular variant in France of this semicircular model consisting of a triangular soundbox mounted with strings on two or three faces.

2. ACOUSTICS. The exact means by which aeolian tones are generated is still not fully understood. Kircher in 1650, noticing that several notes may be heard from one string, suggested that the string was to the wind as a prism to light, separating component sounds from the single energy source. His colleague Bartoli poured scorn

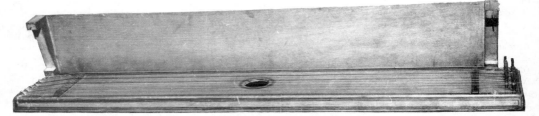

1. Aeolian harp with 12 strings, English, early 19th century, shown with lid in raised position (E. R. Mickleburgh Collection, Bristol)

2. The same, with lid in position

on this theory in *Del suono de' tremori e dell'udito* (Rome, 1679). Since then, no exact theory has been propounded. The Abbot Gattoni of Milan in 1783 and H. C. Koch 18 years later experimented with various string metals, and examined the conditions under which aeolian tones were produced. Their findings were quantified by Pellisov in 1822, but V. Strouhal of Würzburg established by empirical experiment that the frequency of any one aeolian tone was not dependent on the material or length of the string, but was equal to the product of the airstream speed some way from the string and a constant (normally 0·185, known as the Strouhal number), divided by the string diameter. But Strouhal's theory depended on the string vibrating in the same plane as the airstream, whereas Rayleigh, characteristically examining through a home-made telescope a string stretched under his chimney, claimed the string vibrated across the airstream. Further researches by E. G. Richardson and more recently in 1956 by Etkin and others in the USA have only feebly penetrated the problem. Present theory suggests that it is the eddies creating a vortex pattern behind the string, like the small whirlpools visible when a stick is held in flowing water, which make the aeolian tone, which may occasionally be of the same pitch as the string's natural frequency, thus causing it to vibrate. An exact solution of the creation of these vortices and their resultant pattern, termed 'Kármán Street' (after von Kármán, 1912), appears to be beyond the capability of present mathematical techniques.

3. HISTORY. Legends from 800 BC (Homer) onwards describe how Hermes invented the lyre by letting the wind blow over dried sinews in a tortoise carapace; in later legends, such as that of David's harp, God-sent wind blows upon and sounds an already invented instrument. Like David, St Dunstan (*d* 988) also had his harp sounded by God; it played the anthem *Gaudent in*

coelis, and all nearby marvelled (W. Stubbs, *Memorials of St Dunstan*, London, 1874). Only later and for different reasons was he convicted of sorcery.

Although G. Porta's *Magia naturalis* (Rome, 1540) made reference to aeolian phenomena, the harp's technological development began with Kircher's rediscovery of the Aeolian harp (*Musurgia universalis*, 1652; and *Phonurgia nova*). He called them 'musical autophones'. J. J. Hofmann's *Lexicon universale* (Basle, 1677) appears to be the first source employing the aeolian adjective to describe the wind harp: he called it *Aeolium instrumentum*, and quoted Kircher about its construction and sound effect.

A visit to Kircher's museum inspired an article in the newly founded Breslau University's *Sammlung von Natur* of 1726, but the harp did not become fashionable until the 1780s. Then the accumulation of Alexander Pope's *Commentary of Eusthasius*, James Thomson's aeolian poetry of the 1740s, and the report on the structure of the Aeolian harp in a letter from 'A.Z.' in the *Gentleman's Magazine* (1754) culminated in an article 'On the Eolian Harp' in W. Jones's *Physiological Disquisitions* (London, 1781). On announcing that he was 'prepared to dispose of them at a reasonable price to such gentlemen as take a pleasure in this agreeable class of experiments', Jones and London instrument makers such as Longman & Broderip, Hintz, and Silber & Fleming set a trend that was to prevail in England until at least the announcement of 48-string instruments in Metzler's catalogue of 1884, and Burkardt and Doebler's 1862 Manchester patent of 'Improvements in the Aeolian Harp'.

But whereas in England the Aeolian harp's place, like that of woman, was apparently in the home, on the Continent it was usual to place instruments in grottos, gardens, summer-houses or inhabited châteaux (such as in Pierrefonds, Oise, in 1830), or uninhabited châteaux (like Baden-Baden in 1853) or even strung between the spires of two churches (by Abbot Gattoni of Milan in 1783). Kastner commented that 'Harps that maintain themselves in decent state in the garden have long been sought after' (*La harpe d'Eole*, p.83). Only the *Neue Berliner Musikzeitung* (28 June 1854) recommended the Aeolian harp for public parks as well as aristocratic gardens.

Europe's reaction to England's enthusiasm was consequently varied. France cared little for the instrument (though Clementi expressed some interest in those developed by Pleyel) except in the Alsace district, where Kastner, Frost, Echel, Gaïb and Roth developed a number of ingenious vertical models. The Italian Gattoni outdid everyone with his 'armonica meterologica' which

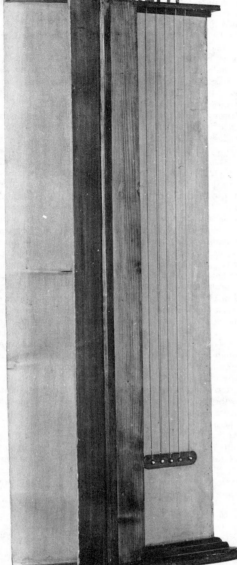

3. Vertical aeolian harp, with five strings on each side, by Nicolas Eugen Simoutre, Basle, 1870–85 (Historisches Museum, Basle)

contained some interesting notes. After the review of this work in the *Allgemeine musikalische Zeitung* (1801) there were further journal articles over the next 50 years, and a lengthy study in H. C. Koch's *Musikalische-Lexicon* (Frankfurt, 1801). The only full study was Kastner's *La harpe d'Eole*, which added an opera as an appendix for good measure.

The harp's sufficient epitaph, until the recent revival in England and the USA, was Troyte's gift of an instrument, with the appropriate 'Enigma' variation painted on one side, to Elgar in 1904. It typified the Aeolian harp's European history as one not so much of increasingly sophisticated technology as of individuals working in self-styled directions: rarely taking much notice of each other's efforts, but often using Kircher as a working basis.

Outside Europe, idiophonic Aeolian harps have been observed in Ethiopia (Begamder tribe), Java, China (*fêng chêng, yao p'ien* and *yao ch'in* kites, shaped like fish or dragons – noted even by Kircher in 1650 – flown each spring, the Chinese words meaning 'abundance' and 'water fertility' respectively), and Guyana, where the Macoosis and Warrau tribes use the leafstalk of the Itah palm (*mauritia flexuosa*) stuck in the ground or on house tops.

4. LITERATURE. Poetry about the Aeolian harp began in England in the 1740s, with James Thomson in his 1748 *Castle of Indolence* hymning 'Wild-warbling Nature all above the reach of Art'. 50 years later the poet Robert Bloomfield was writing in much the same vein, and it took Coleridge in his *The Eolian Harp* (1795) and *Dejection* (1802) to think less of the Aeolian harp as the man-made medium through which Nature speaks to Man than as the tragic reflection of his own life-experience, an 'Actor, perfect in all tragic sounds!'. Goethe and Mörike (*An eine Äolsharfe*, 1867), and Thoreau and Melville in the USA, preferred this inter-pretation, bearing out M. Abrams's statement that 'Not until the nineteenth century did the wind-harp become an analogy for the poetic mind as well as a subject for poetic description' (*The Mirror and the Lamp*, New York, 1953, p.51). But with the decline of the harp itself, the imagery changed to mockery, culminating in a derisive reference in R. L. Stevenson's *The Beach of Falesà* (1892), such that 'The music of the spheres died of shame' (Bonner, iii, p.90).

BIBLIOGRAPHY

R. Bloomfield: *Nature's Music* (London, 1801) [reprinted by Bonner]
G. Kastner: *La harpe d'Eole* (Paris, 1856)
G. Grigson: *The Harp of Aeolus, and Other Essays* (London, 1947)
B. Etkin, G. K. Korbacher and R. T. Keefe: 'Acoustic Radiation from a Stationary Cylinder in a Fluid Stream', *Journal of the Acoustical Society of America*, xxix (1957), 30
S. Bonner and M. G. Davies, eds.: *Aeolian Harp* (Duxford, Harlow and Halesowen, 1968–74)

STEPHEN BONNER

sounded whenever the Milan weather was about to change (*Opusculi scelti, Milan*, 1785, p.298). The only country besides England to show any lasting interest was Germany: two articles in the *Göttingen Taschenkalendar* of 1789 and 1792 were followed by another by Quandt in the *Lausizische Monatsschrift* for 1795, and J. F. H. von Dalberg's fairy tale *Die Äol-sharfe: ein allegorischer Traum* (Erfurt, 1801), which

Aeolian Quartet. British string quartet. Since its incep-tion in 1927 it has had 11 different second violinists but only two cellists, John Moore until 1956 and then Derek Simpson. The first violist, Lawrence Leonard, was succeeded in 1932 by Watson Forbes, who remained with the quartet for 32 years until Margaret Major took his place at the beginning of 1965. Originally the group was called the Stratton Quartet, the leader being George Stratton and the second violin William Manuel. The present name was adopted when

Max Salpeter became leader on Stratton's retirement in 1944. Subsequent leaders were Alfred Cave (1946–52) and Sydney Humphreys (1952–70). From 1970 the members have been Emanuel Hurwitz, Raymond Keenlyside, Margaret Major and Derek Simpson, who have established a new period of stability in the quartet's history. A recording of all Haydn's string quartets, in a new edition prepared by H. C. Robbins Landon and Reginald Barrett-Ayres, was completed in 1976. In 1975 they broadcast on television on successive evenings all Beethoven's late quartets. Tours abroad include annual visits to various European countries, and to the Americas, Australia and New Guinea, the Caribbean, Canada, Israel and the Lebanon. They coach and teach at summer schools, notably at Monterosso, north Italy.

The quartet has close connections with several British universities, in particular with Newcastle upon Tyne where they give an annual week of concerts, and where they were awarded honorary MA degrees in 1970. They play on instruments with contrasting qualities: Hurwitz uses a violin by the Amati brothers which was also played by a former leader of the quartet, Cave; Keenlyside plays a violin by Pietro Guarneri, Major has an Amati brothers viola; and Simpson's cello was made by Andrea Guarneri. Their aim is not so much to make the quartet sound like a single, vibrant instrument as to separate and clarify the individual strands within the texture. This gives their performances a distinct and exciting character, and can throw new light on a frequently heard work. Their Haydn performances in particular have been welcomed for their avoidance of an over-polished, courtly style.

S. M. NELSON

Aeolian-Skinner Organ Co. American organ building firm. It was founded in 1901 by Ernest M(artin) Skinner (*b* Clarion, Penn., 15 Jan 1866; *d* Duxbury, Mass., 27 Oct 1961) who began as an apprentice with George H. Ryder of Reading, Massachusetts. He was later employed by Hutchings of Boston as a draughtsman and, later, foreman. Soon after beginning his own business in South Boston he began to obtain important contracts, one of the earliest of which was for an organ for the Cathedral of St John the Divine, New York (1910). While still with Hutchings, Skinner developed his version of the so-called 'Pitman' windchest, which is still used extensively in electro-pneumatic action organs. Much of his reputation derived from his success in developing organ stops imitating orchestral instruments during the period when orchestrally orientated organ literature was in vogue. By 1920 the firm's rapid growth made necessary its acquisition of the Steere Organ Co. of Springfield, Massachusetts.

In 1927 G. Donald Harrison (*b* Huddersfield, 21 April 1889; *d* New York, 14 June 1956) entered the firm. He had previously worked as a patent attorney and as engineer with the Willis Organ Co., of which he ultimately became a director.

In 1932 the Skinner firm merged with the Aeolian Co., founded in the 1890s by C. M. Tremaine & Brothers, which had made its reputation building organs for private houses and self-playing mechanisms. In 1933 a reorganization occurred in which Harrison became technical director and Skinner's activities were curtailed. In the same year Skinner, after increasing disagreement with Harrison over tonal matters, began a new company in Methuen, Massachusetts, managed by his son, Richmond, although he appears to have maintained a contractual connection with Aeolian-Skinner until 1936. Skinner's new venture was undistinguished and small in scope, and after World War II it was sold to Carl Bassett who subsequently moved it to Florida, still under the Skinner name. In 1970 the company was purchased by John Bolten and Roy E. H. Carlson and moved to Newburyport, Massachusetts, where it now operates as a supplier to the trade of Pitman chests.

During the 1930s the Aeolian-Skinner Co. continued to rise in popularity, and in 1940 Harrison became president, succeeding Arthur Hudson Marks (1874–1939), a wealthy businessman who had held a financial interest in the company since 1916, and later became the principal owner. Under Harrison the firm became a leader in the trend away from orchestral tonal practices and towards a more classical sound. On Harrison's death, Joseph S. Whiteford, a lawyer and majority stockholder, became president. Although he had some experience of organ building, he did not possess Skinner's or Harrison's background, and under him a slow decline began. In the early 1960s he withdrew his interest, and Donald M. Gillett, the head voicer, became president. In 1968 Robert L. Sipe, who for ten years had been building organs in Dallas, joined the company and in 1970 became vice-president and tonal director. A year earlier the firm had moved to new premises in Randolph, Massachusetts. The move did not improve the firm's financial standing, which continued to worsen in spite of drastic cutbacks. Nevertheless, in 1970 Aeolian-Skinner built its first mechanical-action organ for Zumbro Lutheran Church, Rochester, Minnesota. However, by 1972 the firm was forced to leave its new quarters and reorganize. Gillett left to become tonal director for M. P. Möller, Sipe returned to Texas and his own business, and Emil David Knutson, chairman of the board, became president.

At the peak of its career Aeolian-Skinner built many organs for notable churches, halls and colleges, including Grace Cathedral, San Francisco (1934), Symphony Hall, Boston (1950), the Mother Church, Boston (1952), Riverside Church, New York (1955) and Lincoln Center, New York (1962)

BIBLIOGRAPHY

E. M. Skinner: *The Modern Organ* (New York, 1917)

'A Memoir of Ernest M. Skinner', *The Diapason*, xlvii (1956)

BARBARA OWEN

Aeolina. An ORGAN STOP.

Aeoliphone. *See* WIND MACHINE.

Aeolodicon. A keyboard instrument on the free-reed principle; *see* HARMONIUM.

Aerophon. *See* AEROPHOR.

Aerophone. General term for musical instruments that produce their sound by using the air itself as the primary vibrating agent. Aerophones form one of the four main classes of instruments (along with idiophones, membranophones and chordophones – to which a fifth, electrophones, has recently been added) in the system of classification devised by C. Sachs and E. M. von Hornbostel and published by them in *Zeitschrift für*

Ethnologie in 1914 (Eng. trans. in *GSJ*, xiv, 1961, p.3). Their system, the one most commonly used today, is based on Victor Mahillon's division of instruments according to the nature of the vibrating bodies, which he devised for his catalogue of the instruments in the Royal Conservatory in Brussels. Aerophones are subdivided according to whether the vibrating air is unconfined by the instrument ('free aerophones' as in the bull-roarer, the blade of grass, the pop gun or the motor horn) or is enclosed within a tube (the wind instrument proper). The latter subdivision comprises 'air reeds' (that is, so-called 'edge instruments' like flutes, with or without ducts), cane reeds (double or single) and 'lip reeds' (trumpets and horns, with or without extra devices to alter the pitch). Each category may be further subdivided according to the more detailed characteristics of an instrument. To each category Sachs and Hornbostel gave a number derived from the Dewey decimal library classification system.

See also INSTRUMENTS, CLASSIFICATION OF.

HOWARD MAYER BROWN

Aerophor [Aerophon]. A device invented by the German flautist Bernhard Samuel *c*1912. By means of a tube with a mouthpiece, it provides players of wind instruments with air from bellows operated by the foot and thus enables them to sustain notes indefinitely as on the organ. Although Richard Strauss called for it in his *Alpensinfonie* and *Festliches Praeludium*, it has never found general acceptance.

Aertssens [Aertsen], **Hendrik** (*b* Antwerp, baptized 22 May 1586; *d* Antwerp, buried 14 April 1658). Flemish printer. He issued his first publication in 1613 and in 1640 his son Hendrik Aertssens (ii) (*b* Antwerp, baptized 17 April 1622; *d* Brussels, 30 Sept 1663) joined his father's firm. They were well known for their publications of sacred vernacular songs, particularly *Het paradys der gheestelycke en kerckelycke lof-sanghen* which was reprinted five times. Hendrik Aertssens (iii) (*b* Antwerp, baptized 27 Dec 1661; *d* Antwerp, 16 July 1741) also became a printer, obtaining his patent in 1686. By clever scheming he managed to establish a virtual monopoly of music publishing for the Flemish region; however, his publications, mostly reprints and mainly of Italian music, were criticized by contemporaries, including Sir John Hawkins, for their poor typography.

BIBLIOGRAPHY

HawkinsH
E. vander Straeten: *La musique aux Pays-Bas avant le XIXe siècle*, v, vii (Brussels 1880–85/*R*1969)
A. Goovaerts: *Histoire et bibliographie de la typographie musicale dans les anciens Pays-Bas* (Antwerp, 1880/*R*1963)
P. Genard: 'De drukker Hendrik Aertssens de Jongere en de veiling zijner boeken in 1662', *Bulletin Maatschappij Antwerpsche bibliophileen*, ii (1882–6), 87
D. F. Scheurleer: *Nederlandsche liedboeken* (The Hague, 1912–23)
F. T. Arnold: 'A Corelli Forgery?', *PMA*, xlvii (1922–3), 93
R. Vannes: *Dictionnaire des musiciens (compositeurs)* (Brussels, 1947), 261
B. Huys: *Catalogue des imprimés musicaux des XVe, XVIe et XVIIe siècles* (Brussels, 1965)

GODELIEVE SPIESSENS

Aeschbacher, Adrian (*b* Langenthal, 10 May 1912). Swiss pianist. Until he was 17 he was taught the piano by his father, the choral conductor Carl Aeschbacher (1886–1944); after that he studied with Emil Frey and Volkmar Andreae at the Zurich Conservatory and finally in Berlin with Schnabel. In 1934 he began an international concert career which, after the war, took him outside Europe. His repertory is based on Classical and Romantic music, but he has championed many contemporary piano works by Swiss composers such as Schoeck, Honegger and Sutermeister. In 1965 Aeschbacher started a series of master classes at the Saarbrücken Academy of Music. He made many recordings.

BIBLIOGRAPHY

SML
H. Lindlar: 'Aeschbacher, Adrian', *MGG*

JÜRG STENZL

Aeschbacher, Niklaus (*b* Trogen, canton of Appenzell, 30 April 1917). Swiss conductor, pianist and composer. After studying at the Zurich Conservatory and the Berlin Hochschule für Musik, he was répétiteur at theatres in Zittau and Brunswick. In 1942 he was appointed conductor at the Berne Stadttheater, becoming its musical director in 1949. Aeschbacher was principal conductor of the Japanese Radio SO (1954–6) and director of music in Kiel (1959–65) and then at the Detmold Landestheater. He has also made a reputation as a pianist and as a composer in a classicist style of broadened tonality. Among his main works are the radio opera *Die roten Schuhe* (1943), the ballet *Chalanda Mars* (1940), orchestral suites and studies, a Divertimento for seven woodwind, instrumental pieces and songs.

FRITZ MUGGLER

Aeschylus [Aischylos] (*b* Eleusis [now Elevsina], 525 BC; *d* Gela [now Terranuova], Sicily, 456 BC). Greek tragic poet. He wrote about 80 dramas, tragedies and satyr plays, of which eight, all tragedies, have survived. Probably the earliest was the *Persians* (472 BC), which celebrated the Greek victory over vast invading forces led by Xerxes; set at the Persian court, the play is one long lament. With one exception (the singing of a paean by the Greeks, l.393), the references to music emphasize the tone of mourning: 'there resounds a song unlike that of victory' (*kelados ou paiōnios*, l.605). The hymns of the Persians are directed to the dead (ll.619f, 625), and their singing is a cry of pain (l.1043, *iuze melos*). In the remarkably extended sequence of strophic lyrics with which the play closes (ll.852–1076) the chorus speak of the lamentation of a Mariandynian mourner (l.939). The scholiast on this line referred to a saying about playing on Mariandynian auloi, famous for the playing of dirges, in the Iastian (Ionian, later Hypophrygian) mode; the resulting problem of modal ethos remains unresolved.

The *Seven against Thebes* (467 BC) chronicles the doomed attackers at the city's seven gates and the deaths of two brothers in civil war; hence the women must sing a 'loathsome paean' (l.870), a paradoxical phrase.

In the *Suppliant Maidens* (*Hiketides*, ?463 BC) the daughters of Danaus, who have taken refuge in Argos from insistent suitors, form the chorus. Distraught, they speak of themselves (l.69; cf scholium on *Persians*, l.939) as 'fond of grieving in Ionian patterns of melody', high-pitched songs suited to lamentation (ll.112ff), and of Ares as 'without dance, without lyre' (l.681, *achoron, akitharin*). Once assured of protection, they sing hopefully of a blessed Argos, a place of singers before the altars and of 'song that loves the lyre' (ll.694–7).

The *Oresteia* (458 BC), the only extant trilogy, contains more references: there is a notable long interchange (*kommos*) between the chorus and the frenzied Cassandra in the *Agamemnon*, and the following plays contain two choral passages: the savage invocation of the dead Agamemnon and the 'binding hymn' (*desmios hymnos*) of the Erinyes, who as benevolent powers are escorted from the stage in a joyous closing processional. The references are always appropriate in mood to their dramatic context and Aeschylus's chief concern in making them was to establish a contrast or paradox. The celebrated refrain of the opening chorus of the *Agamemnon* is an example: 'Sing sorrow, sorrow: but good win out in the end' (ll.121, 159, trans. Lattimore; on *ailinon*, *see* LINUS). The songs mentioned in the trilogy are almost all sorrowful or give way to laments, until the downward movement is reversed and the *Eumenides* ends with the triumphant singing of the processional.

Throughout the *Oresteia* auloi are unmentioned; the lyre is noted only as having no part in the real or imagined hymn of the Erinyes (*Agamemnon*, l.990, *akitharin*; *Eumenides*, ll.332f, *aphormingtos*). There are repeated mentions, however, of the ritual forms of song, paean, dirge, *nomos* and hymn; these are not mere repetitions, but enriched and made individual by their contexts.

The treatment of music elsewhere in Aeschylus's work corresponds to that in the *Oresteia*. None of the basic terms for the reed pipes or the lyre (aulos, kithara, lyra, phorminx), occurs, and when any of them appears in a compound term or in a phrase, the usual effect is paradoxical or ironical; *philophorminx* (*Suppliant Maidens*, l.697, noted above) is an exception.

Nothing is definitely known about performing practice of music in Aeschylus's plays (*see* EURIPIDES).

See also ARISTOPHANES and GREECE, §I.

BIBLIOGRAPHY

H. W. Smyth, ed. and trans.: *Aeschylus: Tragedies*, i (London and Cambridge, Mass., 1922, 8/1973)
——: *Aeschylus: Tragedies*, ii (London and Cambridge, Mass., 1926, 7/1971; suppl. by H. Lloyd-Jones, 1956)
E. T. Owen: *The Harmony of Aeschylus* (Toronto, 1952)
E. Moutsopoulos: 'Une philosophie de la musique chez Eschyle', *Revue des études grecques*, lxxii (1959), 18–56
J. A. Haldane: 'Musical Themes and Imagery in Aeschylus', *Journal of Hellenic Studies*, lxxxv (1965), 33
W. D. Anderson: *Ethos and Education in Greek Music* (Cambridge, Mass., 1966, 2/1968), 54, 59ff
M. Pintacuda: *La musica nella tragedia greca* (Cefalù, 1978), 83–125

WARREN ANDERSON

Aesthetics of music. The philosophy of the meaning and value of music.

1. Definition. 2. Kinds of writing. 3. Chief topics. 4 Hellenic and Hellenistic thought. 5. Early Christian thought. 6. Medieval thought. 7. Renaissance thought. 8. Baroque thought. 9. Rationalism. 10. Enlightenment. 11. Romanticism. 12. Idealism. 13. Composition and performance. 14. Formalism. 15. Musicological aesthetics. 16. Marxism. 17. The problem of tonality. 18. Neo-formalism. 19. Neo-expressionism. 20. Vanguardism. 21. Aesthetics and logic. 22. Aesthetics in other civilizations. 23. The present and future of musical aesthetics.

1. DEFINITION. The term 'aesthetics of music' normally designates attempts to explain what music means: the difference between what is and what is not music, the place of music in human life and its relevance to an understanding of human nature and history, the fundamental principles of the interpretation and appreciation of music, the nature and ground of excellence and greatness in music, the relation of music to the rest of the fine arts and to other related practices, and the place or places of music in the system of reality. Aesthetics in this sense is to be distinguished from the psychology and sociology of musical composition, performance and listening; from the history and natural history of musical practice; from the physics of sound and the physiology of the ear; from the analysis and description of particular works and traditions in music; and from all other empirical inquiries, even though fruitful discussions of questions in aesthetics may in practice be inseparable from some such inquiry. The word 'aesthetics' is also often used more broadly, to include all the intellectual enterprises we have just ruled out; and more narrowly, to apply only to attempts to establish a rational basis for enjoyment and evaluation.

The scope of the present article is for the most part confined to what has been thought and said about music in the tradition of Western civilization; but it includes some suggestions as to how that tradition might be enriched by contributions from elsewhere.

2. KINDS OF WRITING. The best contributions to the aesthetics of music are not all to be found in writings expressly devoted to that subject. Some are enshrined in systematic philosophies and histories of art in general, or of education or culture. Much of the most creative work is produced by musicians and their allies in the course of promoting or attacking novelties of musical practice. Much is produced by analysts of music to justify their analytic procedures, by critics buttressing their critiques, and by historians explaining why what happened had to happen. Yet more is produced, incidentally or even unawares, by analysts, critics and historians in the ordinary course of their work. Much has been produced by cultivated literati, explaining their own experiences to themselves or narrating the adventures of their souls among masterpieces. Some has even been written by serious students who have taken the aesthetics of music for their theme.

The literature of the aesthetics of music is somewhat less rich than that of the other arts. There are three related reasons for this. First, the technical complexities of the production and notation of music have diverted to practicalities and to the codification of styles much energy that might have been bestowed on more general speculations, and lay writers often allow themselves to be intimidated by these technicalities. Second, writers on the other arts have found it easy to be eloquent on the relation between works of art and the realities they represent and embody, and it has been doubted whether such relations are important in music. And third, humane studies were long dominated by an intellectualism that assigned a lowly place to the supposedly emotional art of music, which appeared to be a mere ornament of the culture whose more vital structures could be articulated by literary and pictorial means. At least the first of these reasons remains operative today, and modern theorizing about music rises above the arcane and the nugatory less often than does comparable writing about the visual arts.

3. CHIEF TOPICS. Theoretically, the fundamental question for an aesthetics of music must be the nature of the musical work itself. Is it essentially an object of a certain sort, an achieved reality which, once made, may

be understood and enjoyed for whatever it is; or a partial manifestation of some cosmic force or principle, through which the forces of the world may be understood or even controlled; or is it rather a sample of a means of communication among men? If we gave the first answer, we would locate the main task of aesthetics in the proper description and classification of musical entities: the musically significant properties of sounds, and the formally significant principles of their arrangement and combination. If we preferred the second answer, the main question would become one of what cosmic principles are shown, how they are shown, and how they are known to be shown. The favourite candidates are mathematical laws, because of the mathematical describability of musical scales and structures, and some sort of life force, because of the dynamism of musical events. If we like the third answer best, the main questions will turn on how music communicates what. Since language conveys thoughts, it is usual to agree that music conveys feelings, and to debate about what feelings of whom are affected in what ways: does music express what is already felt, arouse new feelings, alter their character, distract one from them, or unite men in them? More subtly and profoundly, it is debated whether the musical language of feeling is natural or conventional, and whether musical effects penetrate to deep layers of the character or merely modify transitory passions.

In practice, the last of the three answers has prevailed, to the extent that musical aesthetics has been dominated by a single theme: the nature and import of that powerful yet indeterminate emotional impact that music has or is thought to have. Even those theorists who denounce such effects as distracting from the true comprehension of music tend to spend much energy on the denunciation and on explaining the alleged phenomena away. When aesthetics turns aside from this question, as in the Middle Ages and to some extent in very recent years, it may be a sign that the music of the aestheticians has become detached from what is vital in the musical life of the people at large.

In considering musical values, the three possible views of the nature of the musical work tend to simplify themselves into a posing of alternatives. Are musical values 'autonomous', grounded in the music itself, or 'heteronomous', based on something else? This is an ambiguous question. One version asks whether musical beauty is natural in the sense that it lies in such properties as an instructed ear can discern in the music itself, or derivative in the sense that it lies in the relation between the music and something else – usually assumed to be something the music represents or imitates or expresses. The other version asks whether the value of music lies in its beauty at all, whether that beauty be original or derived, rather than in the effects it may have on composers, performers and listeners.

Until a few decades ago, the problem of the true nature of music was often discussed in the guise of an inquiry into the origin of music. Was it a gift from the gods to mankind, a casual product of idleness, outgrowth of a natural urge to self-expression, or testimony to a universal formal inquisitiveness in man? Different conjectures as to how music began reflected unargued convictions as to whether music is fundamentally mysterious or rational, trivial or vital, emotive or cognitive, natural or conventional. The question seemed

open because music fills no such obvious communicative need as may serve to explain why men speak and draw. More recently, these alternative convictions have shown up in diverse accounts of music history: from what beginning to what end, by steady evolution or by dialectical reversal, by necessity or by chance, independently or as an inseparable part of history at large.

The criss-crossing of such questions and themes as the foregoing makes up the substance of musical aesthetics.

Since all the positions mooted above have been argued by intelligent men, all must be theoretically tenable and applicable to at least a substantial amount of available music. This fact suggests that music is not all of a piece. Many aestheticians suggest that there are two or more arts of music, which proceed on divergent principles, though it is usual to single out some one of these as the only true art. In particular, the tendency of an esoteric music for music-lovers to hive itself off from an exoteric music for the masses repeatedly leads some to assert that the 'true' music must be so difficult an art that listeners, like performers, need arduous training, and others to denounce such estericism as a perversion of 'true' music, which must speak directly to the uninstructed and uncorrupted heart. But perhaps we must in any case admit that there are many musics; for there is certainly such a thing as musical expertise, and it is surely true of any expertise that among those who wield it someone will be found to put it to any use to which it can possibly be put. The attitude taken to this last problem of the diversity of music will depend, even more obviously than the others we mentioned, on general views about art and life that reach far beyond the domain of music and its aesthetics.

4. HELLENIC AND HELLENISTIC THOUGHT. The commonest positions in the aesthetics of music are borrowed and developed from classical antiquity. Greek musical practice being inaccessible, the theories related to it have been freely adapted to the practice of whatever day it might be – a licence less available to those who similarly exploited classical writings on less fugitive arts. The language of musical aesthetics has thus often suggested a certain remoteness from what was actually going on.

Although 'music' (*mousikē*) is a Greek word, classical Greece did not use it to mean what we call music. It had no word for that. Etymologically, the word means 'the business of the Muses', who were goddesses of poetic inspiration. As a body of practice, the 'music' of classical Greece extended to cover all imaginative uses of language and dance, and as an object of theoretical study 'music' was largely the study of scale-construction and tuning systems. But this divergence between Greek conceptualization and our own dwindled away in Hellenistic times.

Among the debris of ancient thought we may distinguish at least six views about the nature and significance of music.

The first view is assigned to the thinkers, mostly anonymous, associated with the name of Pythagoras (6th century BC), traditionally the first to take note of the relevance of certain small-number ratios to the intervals recognized as consonant and invariant in the music of the day. By the 5th century BC the Pythagoreans were speculating that similar ratios should be discoverable everywhere in the world. That music embodies numerical principles and somehow answers to the laws of nature seems already to have been accepted everywhere from China to Babylon; the Pythagorean contribution was to make this hitherto mysterious relationship amenable to rational inquiry. The ratios found in musical intervals were sought in the distances of planets, in the compositions of stuffs, in the souls of good men, and in everything that contributed to cosmic order. Musical structures should thus have analogues in the human mind and in the world at large, and their felt but ineffable meaningfulness should be explicable by those analogies. Music is important as the only field in which these ratios have been discovered rather than merely postulated. But the mathematicians of the 4th century BC borrow the name 'music' for the branch of their study devoted to the theory of proportions, and the specifically audible varieties and manifestations of such proportions become theoretically accidental. The doctrine that music is or ought to be an 'abstract' system of relationships statable in a set of equations has haunted musical aesthetics ever since, though the habit of linking music to astronomy by a supposed 'music of the spheres' died with Kepler (1619).

The second Greek view of music adapted the Pythagorean notions to fit the view (popular then as now) that national music expresses national character, or *ethos*. Damon of Athens seems to have done the adapting in the middle of the 5th century BC (cf Lasserre, 1954). National styles or 'modes' are construed as essentially scale systems, whose intervals are generated by ratios characteristic of the personality types and behaviour patterns of their users: Dorians, Phrygians and the like. Damon thought of music as primarily a means of moral indoctrination. Plato, from whom these ideas descend to modern times, cut them loose from their mathematical underpinnings: his *Republic* (c380BC) merely postulates a series of causal connections, as follows. The specific mental characteristics that assign a person to a given sort find expression in corresponding patterns of thinking; these patterns achieve utterance in characteristic forms of poetical speech, and such formal speech evokes a fitting melodic and rhythmical accompaniment. To hear, and especially to perform, the resulting music will tend to re-create the originating mental characteristics, so that the student performer becomes the same sort of person as his composer–teacher. The charms of music are thus the same as those exerted by an attractive personality, except that music is expressive through and through whereas the excellence of a man may require him to be inexpressively reticent. In this Platonic version of the *ethos* theory, the expressiveness of music reflects that of an actual or possible poetic text. This answers to the Greek practice of teaching gentlemen to accompany themselves on plucked strings, leaving wind instruments and bravura generally to low-born professionals. The verbalizing version of *ethos* theory has the advantage over the mathematicizing version that it calls for no cosmological commitments; on the other hand, this modesty leaves it with no hidden resources to counter empirical rebuttals.

A third view of music, which has also proved perennial, is implicit in the histories of music that survive from the first centuries of our era. Like the analogous histories of other arts, these sources take a technical view of music: its history is the progressive mastery of more and more elaborate instruments, performing techniques and sound patterns. Music is seen as exploring the possibilities of a self-contained world of sound. However, this view of culture history is modified by an assumption derived from Aristotle's cosmology and reinforced by cultural nostalgia for the classical age of Greece. The world of sound, like the world at large, is not infinite; the possibilities to be explored are not endless; and the fruitful development of the art of music was completed long ago at a period defined by that completion as classical. This complication of the progressivist view of music has also been revived from time to time, with the idealized classical age suitably updated; but its revivers are mostly musical revolutionaries who modify the theory by claiming that new worlds of music can be substituted for the old, so that new explorations can proceed – even if, as conservatives will protest, the new worlds cannot sustain human life. In its extreme form, this last modification becomes the claim that every serious musical work is or should be a self-contained musical universe.

The ancient progressivist theories of music history, whether or not they held that progress must end somewhere, ran counter to a deep-seated belief in social degeneration, which assigned the 'golden age' to a technically primitive past. When these tendencies collide, we have a view of music history in which musicians continually press for innovations which statesmen and moralists untiringly resist. Plato, writing as a moralist, reinterpreted the conflict between reactionary and progressive musicians as one between two kinds of music: one, the true music, rationally based and logically developed, exemplifies the structural principles of all reality, including the human mind; the other music, impressionistic and fantasticated, merely imitates the sounds of nature and the passing show of temporary feelings. Variants of this contrast, which despite its incoherence is deeply rooted in Plato's general metaphysic, keep reappearing in the history of aesthetics, most recently in T. W. Adorno's pitting of the severities of dodecaphony against the confectionery of the culture industry. The contrast has been strikingly reflected in recent decades in debates over the proprieties of interpretation: a music whose vocation is subtly to mould the perceptible surface of sound is a performer's art for which composers merely provide the material, but if music is to unfold profound tonal structures it must be elaborated in the study and its performer must reveal only such treasures as the composer has buried for him.

The reason why the underlying view of music history whose vicissitudes we have traced gives rise to such continued controversy is that it starts by equating the progress of music with the elaboration of its means, rather than with the exploration of deep structures. Even the intonational researches whereby the Greek theorists finally excogitated a unified system, within which the originally incommensurable tribal modes could each appear as a possible variant, were represented as a mere development of new possibilities of modulation rather than as an investigation of the nature of modality as such.

A less tendentious account of the division within music that the ancient histories of music sought to explicate is adumbrated in Aristotle's *Politics* (c330BC): there are two musics because there are two uses for music. Rituals and festivals call for an exciting and ecstatic music, demanding virtuosity of its performers and moving its audience to a salubrious frenzy. A gentleman needs a different sort of music to play for his recreation, as one of the amenities of everyday life. 'What passion cannot Music raise and quell?' Dryden was to ask. But not all music has the raising and quelling of passion as its function.

A fourth view of music was sketched by Aristoxenus (c300BC), a student of Aristotle. He refuted the Pythagorean numerology and the *ethos* theory that was built on it by pointing out that the ratios generating harmonies are inaudible, and music is concerned with the audible. What can be heard is sounds in relation. The ear certainly needs the aid of memory and mind, but the contribution of memory is to make protracted structures perceptible, and the intellect is called on, not to intuit any underlying reality, whether cosmic or psychic, but to grasp the mutual relations of notes within the system of a scale. Music is thus a self-contained phenomenological system, and the significant form of any work is not derived from its relation to any other reality but is identical with the principle of its own organization. Why men should make such things and delight in them Aristoxenus does not say, but no Aristotelian need ask: any refined exercise of mind and senses is inherently delightful, for man is by nature hungry for information. Aristoxenus concedes that such audible constructions may acquire by association an ethical significance, but this is adventitious.

Aristoxenus's embryonic formalism strikes a responsive chord today, but was little noted in antiquity. To Ptolemy in the 2nd century AD he was only the bellwether of one of the two extremist schools of musical theory, the latter-day Pythagoreans being the other. Ear and reason are judges of harmony, says Ptolemy, the ear establishing the facts and the reason divining their explanation. Musical theorists, like astronomers, must lay bare the design that unifies the phenomena, thus showing that the real is not irrational. He complained that the Aristoxenians trust the ear alone and forego theoretical explanation, while the Pythagoreans trust reason at the cost of observational accuracy. The philosophy of music is thus shown to involve difficulties of principle that are still central in 20th-century philosophy of science.

A fifth view of music was current among the followers of Epicurus, represented by Lucretius in the 1st century BC, for whom music was nothing but a source of innocent pleasure, natural in the sense that it represents a complex use of man's natural endowments: 'Every creature has a sense of the purposes for which he can use his own powers'. Such elaborations, discovered by accident and developed by experience, afford relaxation, distraction in distress, and an outlet for excess energy. No further explanation of musical delight is possible or necessary, and the pretensions of highfalutin theories are merely absurd. The Epicurean tradition did not survive the triumph of Christianity, but such Philistine mutterings remain a permanent possibility for aesthetics, one that is congenial to most of us some of the time, and to some of us most of the time.

A sixth, sceptical view goes beyond the Epicureans by agreeing that music is a diversion but denying that it is natural. Musical practice is conventional through and through: it may have effects on the character, but only because it is believed to have them. In fact, the Sceptics denied that music could be an object of knowledge, since it is constituted by the relations between notes, which themselves have no reality; and what is unreal cannot be known. This ontological scepticism, known to us from the work of Sextus Empiricus (3rd century AD), was to find when less crudely stated a permanent place in musical aesthetics.

The last four of these ancient traditions, the ones that flourished after the Greek cities lost their independence, allow music no social or civic significance. When an art claims autonomy, it may be a sign that it accepts a peripheral place in the culture of its day.

5. EARLY CHRISTIAN THOUGHT. The Stoics had slighted music as irrelevant to the life of reason, and the Church Fathers followed them in finding it irrelevant to salvation. Yet music played an important part in the liturgy. This generated some tension. In fact, we find St Augustine (4th century) torn between three attitudes to music: exaltation of musical principles as embodying principles of cosmic order; ascetic aversion from musicmaking as carnal; and a recognition of jubilation and congregational song as respectively expressing inexpressible ecstasy and promoting congregational brotherhood. Being a rhetorician and not a musician by training, he thought of the numerical side of music as embodied in poetic metres rather than in music proper, but the other two attitudes left him agonizing: it is as if a man were seduced by worship.

Medieval musical aesthetics, while preserving the Augustinian attitudes, resembles medieval philosophy of culture generally in basing itself on the attempt by Boethius (6th century) to consolidate the consensus of classical philosophy, whose three-tiered metaphysical and epistemic structures readily adapted themselves to the notion of a triune God. Boethius thought of music as a branch of mathematics, unlike other branches in that its proper manifestations are perceptible and affective as well as intelligible. There are three musics: *musica mundana*, cosmic music, the 'harmony' or order of the universe; *musica humana*, human music, the order of the virtuous and healthy soul and body; and *musica instrumentalis*, music in use, the audible music men make. This framework haunts musical thought for a millennium. Its significance lies in its Neoplatonic and Christian implications. Man, according to Neoplatonism, can and should associate himself with the higher, intelligible level of reality, but turns in his weakness to the lower, sensuous level. Now, the human voice is not an artefact, but a direct embodiment of intelligence: in a sense, it belongs to *musica humana*. Stoics like Epictetus had taught that man attunes himself with the eternal Mind by an intellectual 'song' of praise: that is, by philosophy. Christian writers – using, like St John Chrysostom (c400AD), the homely analogy of work-songs that ease men's necessary toil – had adapted this rhetoric to a literal advocacy of psalmody, audible praise facilitating mental praise of a personal God. This complex of thought now gives rise to a new version of the old dichotomy between two musics: a low, sensual, instrumental, secular music is contrasted with an exalted, intellectual, vocal, sacred music. This dichotomy is reinforced by another Boethian doctrine, that the artist, in this case the musicologist who understands practice, is better than the mere practitioner, in this case the player or singer who uncomprehendingly follows the guidance of his training or his instrument – 'It is the definition of a beast, that he does what he does not understand', as Guido of Arezzo (c1030) unkindly remarked of singers.

6. MEDIEVAL THOUGHT. Boethius, by treating music as a mathematical science, gave it a high place in the life of the mind (higher than rhetoric, for instance), but cut it off from secular song and dance. This sealed the fate of musical aesthetics in the early Middle Ages. The art of music became a rational mystery underlying practice, and medieval theorists tended to be preoccupied with ways of calculating and representing musical ratios. Since these ratios are exemplified everywhere in the cosmic economy, allegorical interpretations of all sorts abound, without any one of them being much developed or emphasized. However, in the 9th century the philosopher Eriugena used the fact that the cosmic order is one of simultaneous complexity to explain the peculiar value of polyphony. For the first time, musical harmony was equated with the internal relationships of an audible object.

The drive towards polyphony and polyrhythm is one of the factors·that led to the development of a graphic, mensural notation, without which such complex music could scarcely be learnt and certainly could not be transmitted throughout the newly cosmopolitan and bookish culture of the 11th century and after. The introduction of such a notation, as systematized by Franco of Cologne around 1216, is not itself a contribution to aesthetics but transforms aesthetics by radically changing the nature of the art. It facilitates complexities of a wholly new order; it liberates musical time immediately from the tyranny of the syllable, and ultimately from any expressiveness based on words; it enables·the composer to be an intellectual working at his desk, rather than a performing musician; and finally, as Nelson Goodman and Thurston Dart have emphasized in different ways, it lends emphasis and authority to those aspects of music that it records, so that a composition comes to be defined by its score. Thus the abandonment of conventional notation by the advanced composers of our day has left some musicians feeling as if the solid ground of their art had vanished from under their feet.

The notation evolved for the sacred music of the Middle Ages had not only to record musical facts but also to disclose them as rational. Hence abstruse controversies arose about the nature of perfect and imperfect numbers, and the metaphysical superiority of triple (trinitarian) over duple (manichean) relations. But by the early 14th century a more sophisticated and subtle logic led in aesthetics, as in philosophy at large, to a rejection of the equation between rationality and structural simplicity. The new mood appeared in a passing remark of Jehan de Murs (1319): 'What can be sung can be written down'. The reactionary Jacques de Liège (c1330) attacked the 'new art' as lascivious, incoherent and above all irrational: if three is admittedly the perfect number, why admit imperfections? But he was too late.

Medieval aesthetics in general rests on the ancient theory of beauty as that which gives immediate pleasure when perceived, rather than on any theory of art. Allegorical explanations are introduced only when the literal level is exhausted: it may be true that polyphony mirrors the universe, but beauty must be experienced before it is explained, and the fundamental fact is that

counterpoint sounds well. This position allows of little theoretical development; but Roger Bacon, among others, drew the conclusion that the most beautiful work would be one that pleased all the senses at once, and in which music formed only one component (De Bruyne, 1947).

7. RENAISSANCE THOUGHT. A versatile mathematical intelligence does not demand simple forms, but adapts itself to the complexities of the real. The advances of late medieval logic thus prepare the way for the conclusion that mathematical considerations have no essential bearing on music. In the later 15th century, the view of music as that branch of mathematics which pertains to sounds tends to give way to a humanist view of music as a sonorous art, to which mathematics is relevant only as calculating or explaining means to musical ends otherwise determined. Johannes de Grocheo had already made the essential point around 1300, urging that the mathematical *science* of music is not the same as the *art* of music, which is the application of such theory to singing. This art is not a branch of mathematics, and neither *musica mundana* nor *musica humana* has any place in it. His cool Aristotelian pragmatism made little headway in that age of numerological hermeticism. But Tinctoris in the late 15th century, and yet more clearly Glarean in 1547, remodelled the theory of music on the basis of its actual history, practice and effects. They thought of music primarily as a form of human activity rather than as a closed science or a model of the cosmos; and the conventional ethical associations of old and new modes received less attention than the actual effects that genius and discipline may achieve. Tinctoris (c1473–4), enumerating and classifying the effects claimed for music, was content to cite authorities; but a century later writers like John Case (1586) put flesh on his bones. Such humanism comes the more readily because no myth claims divine origin for polyphony. God may have taught Adam to sing His praise, and Jubal to play upon instruments, as J. A. Scheibe still maintained in 1754; but counterpoint was invented by men in historical times.

Glarean already sensed a crisis in music, a tension between polyphonic skill and melodic feeling, between art and nature. Zarlino in 1558 attempted a synthesis involving a subtle humanization of the ancient *ethos* theory. Of all musical effects, he says, the ear is judge. But the ear finds a fundamental contrast between the feeling-tone of joyful major and mournful minor triads. Instead of finding metaphysical reasons why each mode should reflect a different type of character or feeling, he appeals to experience to testify to a correlation of harmonies with feeling within a single harmonic scheme. Then, instead of saying with Plato that the harmony and rhythm of a piece should be determined by those actually inherent in the accompanied words and their meanings, he demands that harmony and rhythm be those perceived as suiting the general feeling-tone of the subject matter of the words.

While thus adapting ancient proprieties to a modernized and humanized form in which they have remained so familiar as to seem obvious, Zarlino introduced another fateful concept of a quite different tendency. Just as a poem may have a subject, such as the fall of Troy, so does a musical composition have a subject – but this is a musical subject, a theme, a series of sounds. Music is about music. It is thus at once autonomous, through its melodic organization, and heteronomous, through its harmonic and rhythmic affectivity.

Zarlino's professional Venetian compromise between ancient theory and modern practice was soon challenged by the mainly amateur circle formed at Florence around Giovanni de' Bardi, whose chief theorist was Zarlino's pupil Vincenzo Galilei (1581). They pointed out that the Greek humanism that was now the acknowledged ideal had rested on the practice of a monodic and heteronomous music in which a singing line traced and induced a flow of emotion: the gentleman troubadour, long ignored or disparaged by theorists, came into his own now that gentlemen were writing the books. Polyphonic music cannot raise and quell passions, because the effects of simultaneous melodies must cancel out. To emulate the fabled effects of Greek music at Alexandrian feasts, arcane and autonomous pattern-making must be replaced by the expressive voice of a natural man. And what is expressed is merely sentiment and speech, not (as in Plato's fantasy) character and thought. Significantly, this polemic is launched in the name of Boethius's second level against his third; the revival of Neoplatonism might have encouraged the opposition to take the yet higher ground of Boethius's first level, but the unfashionableness of logic and mathematics seems to have discouraged them from doing so.

Zarlino (1588) found the obvious reply to the Florentine arguments: music is music, it is not rhetoric. But that was the point at issue: rhetoric was the cornerstone of a courtly education, musicians' music was work for monks and lackeys. The debate continued and, *sotto voce*, continues yet; but, as the 17th century saw, it was rather unnecessary, since the Venetians had in mind a public and ceremonious music, and the Florentines envisaged a music for a more private use.

8. BAROQUE THOUGHT. Towards 1700, the controversies between old and new musics settled down to a squabble of gentlemen over their amusements. The favoured contrast was that between stiff French correctness and supple Italian invention. The divergent styles found different rationales. Le Cerf de la Viéville (1704) claimed for the French party that the accepted rules formulated the established requirements of good taste and stood for reason and method as against the vagaries of fancy and passion. Raguenet (1702) maintained that the Italians, trained to music from the cradle, could dispense with rules because their underlying principles had become second nature. If they took risks, it was because they had developed a sense for when something risky would come off. The arguments on both sides are closely analogous to those used at the time in controversies over painting and literature. Both parties occupy the lowest ground of sentimental humanism: hedonism and a courtly ambience are assumed, and the rules appealed to turn out to be no more than recipes for a rational enjoyment.

If humanistic thought can find for music a deeper significance than that of mere amusement, it must be through its working on human passion. Here an issue had been left unsettled between Venice and Florence: how does music most fitly express feeling? Through the 17th century and after, three modes were mooted. Music may follow the inflections of a voice speaking in passion – a device practically abandoned at Florence soon after it was first tried, but still theoretically entertained by Grétry 200 years later; it may echo the sense

of a text word by word, as a man who gestures while he speaks – Rosseter (1601) thought it vulgar to do so, Morley (1597) thought it absurd to do otherwise; or it may convey the general tone of its text. All three modes were defended around 1600, and confused (as by Richard Hooker in 1617) with the very different doctrine of *ethos* according to which music mirrors not passion but character. But what if there is no text to accompany? The rise of a purely instrumental music that is more than an accompaniment for dancing seems to call for compositional principles that are purely structural, but how can these be used without sacrificing humanistic meaning? 'Sonata, what do you want of me?' asked Fontenelle (Rousseau, 1753).

Answers to this newly pressing problem were sought from the art of rhetoric. There were three good reasons for this. First, it afforded the only actual model for the articulation of temporally extended forms on a large scale; second, it formed the basis of genteel education; and third, of most direct relevance, the ancient treatises on rhetoric had as their avowed aim the systematic analysis of the passions and the means of working on them, so that J. J. Quantz (1752) could say that 'The orator and the musician have, at bottom, the same aim'.

Rhetoric was actually used in two ways. First, theorists of the Baroque age tried to describe musical forms and figures by making various figurative uses of terminology derived from the articulations and ornamentations of discourse. These systems, never stabilized, died out as our special vocabulary for describing musical forms gradually made its way. And second, musical theorists tried to adapt directly to music the programme for a scientific rhetoric first enunciated in Plato's *Phaedrus* (*c*375BC): an analysis of human passions and the ways to arouse them. These attempts leaned heavily on Descartes' treatise on the passions (1649), which argued that the most complex emotions could be shown to result from the mechanical combination of a few simple psychological components by a strict causal necessity. Such writers as Johann Mattheson (1739) offer elaborate analyses of the emotions along these lines, with detailed specifications of the corresponding musical devices. The resulting emotive packages are mediated by dance forms, since in a dance a complete musical complex, often with ethnic and hence ethical connotations, is already wedded to gesture and thus as it were integrated into a way of life. On examination, the mediation proves somewhat programmatic: the musical specifications could be at best sketchily correlated with the analyses of the passions, since only a few simple musical variables had an emotive significance that could be specified. In theory, that would not detract from a Cartesian analysis, which actually called for the reduction of complexities to combinations of a few simple forms; but in practice the Cartesian programme has rather limited application, and the more elaborate versions of the 'theory of affections' were eventually abandoned.

Such theories of emotive meaning admit an important ambiguity: are the feelings in question to be worked on or only to be symbolized? The more sophisticated authors write as if the primary function of the emotive meaning were to make the music intelligible. A work of art has to be unified as well as articulated, and Mattheson's requirement that each piece confine itself to a single emotion suggests that at least part of what is at stake is the use of a consistent *manner* as a unifying principle. But the question was not clearly posed, and evocation of the represented passion was not ruled out. What was excluded was the demand that the composer be imbued with the feeling he expresses or imparts. This exclusion showed that music was being assimilated to rhetoric and not to poetry: traditionally, the poet is inspired by the feeling he arouses, while the orator must keep cool to control his audience.

To the extent that the doctrine of affections pertains to the meaning rather than to the effects of music, its intellectual affinities are not with the Cartesian 'hydraulics of the animal spirits' already alluded to, but with the later contention of such Enlightenment sages as Holbach and Hume that it is the function of reason to articulate and thus to civilize the passions.

We have noted the demand that each piece be dominated by a single mood. Such a demand envisages the composer as master of various styles. The notion of style is imported into musical theory in the 17th century from its original home in rhetoric, which required of the orator the ability to speak in diverse literary manners and to suit diverse occasions. The Baroque age found this notion useful when coping with the survival of contrapuntal church music alongside a basically monodic secular music. No longer are there rival musics: the accomplished musician knows how to write church music, theatre music or chamber music, in a diversity of national manners.

9. RATIONALISM. It was not only through the doctrine of affections that Descartes left his mark on the aesthetics of music. He (1656) and his friend Mersenne (1636–7) both attempted once more the impossible task of rationalizing the mathematical basis of harmony. More important was Rameau's (1722) successful interpretation of harmony itself as a system on the Cartesian plan, reducing the bewildering variety of possible chords to the simple system of triads and their inversions. The modern notion of harmony, already implicit in Zarlino, thus suddenly acquires an intelligible basis and occupies the centre of musical thought. As the notion of the 'position' of a chord suggests, music comes to be envisaged as occupying a 'space' with vertical (chordal) and horizontal (cadential) dimensions. The Baroque vocabulary borrowed from rhetoric does not fit this way of thinking about music, and it becomes easier to think of it in formal, even in architectural, terms.

Rameau himself points out the more immediate significance of his theories. The squabbles of italophile and francophile cliques and cabals over operatic styles and persons, which through most of the 18th century retained the interest of the lay public, mostly concerned the style of vocal melody. They were therefore trivial in comparison with the issue of principle between the theories and practices that put melody first and those that put harmony first. Melody tends to be interpreted heteronomously, in terms of what it expresses; in giving harmony priority over melody Rameau lays new foundations for the autonomy of music, at the same time making it easier for instrumental music to take up a central position that it had never before occupied and from which it has yet to be evicted.

Rameau's revolutionary move coincides with, and purports to incorporate, a more fundamental discovery. This is Joseph Sauveur's almost single-handed development of the science of acoustics, making sounds into objects susceptible of systematic investigation and description. The scepticism of Sextus Empiricus is finally refuted, and from now on music can be slowly, subtly and profoundly transformed into an art of sound. Meanwhile, Rameau fastens on the overtone series, already identified by Mersenne but now explicated by Sauveur, as affording a natural basis for the harmonic relations he is expounding. Musical structures are thus founded on nature – not the nature of the heavens, or of the soul, or of the eternal objects of mathematics, but the nature of sound itself.

In seeking a basis in nature for the structures he explored, Rameau was typical of his age. The reference to 'nature', which might be most variously conceived, is one aspect of a convergence between the criticism of music and that of the other arts that continued throughout the 18th century. The notion of the 'fine arts' had been conceived when palaces became museums in the 16th century; its gradual emergence reflects the dominance of monarchic courts making symbolic use of acquisition and display. Like other cultural movements of the epoch, this conceptual unification of the fine arts had to be validated by an appeal to classical antiquity, and the only rationalization to be found there was the concept of 'arts of imitation' implicit in Plato's *Republic* and explicit in his *Epinomis* (c350BC). Music, then, like other arts, must imitate what is not art; and what is not art is nature. But the nature of what? The growing separation of composer and performer from their public meant that the honorific answer of the ancient *ethos* theory, that music directly shows and moulds character, would no longer do; and the difficulty of finding any other laudatory answer threatened to relegate music to the last place in the pecking order of the arts. Among the early systematizers of the arts, Dubos (1719) held that music imitates the voice, and gives pleasure through the style of that imitation. Batteux (1746), arguing that all the arts exist to portray an idealized nature, seems to have been the first to think of music as a language of the heart that is natural because it precedes all conventions.

Rameau's breathtaking proposal of a Cartesian science of music did not fit into these systematizations of the arts, and seemed politically objectionable at a time when progressive thinkers were exalting the natural voice of the natural man (cf Diderot, 1821). Its impact, though in the long run decisive, was therefore delayed.

10. ENLIGHTENMENT. Batteux's description of music as the language of the heart, itself a sentimental blurring of the contemporary doctrine of affections, was developed by Jean-Jacques Rousseau (1781) into a popular and durable theory about the origin and nature of language. The first human speech must have been a chant that expressed thought and feeling together; developed languages confine themselves to communicating thought, leaving to music, in its original form of song, the task of expressing feeling. Such expression is indeed the true function of all art. And since Rousseau equated nature with human nature, and this with the naively passionate side of man as opposed to the artificial 'rationality' his schooling imposes on him, music 'imitates nature' more than any other art does. But only melody is thus vindicated. Harmony and counterpoint, gothic and barbarous inventions designed merely to produce a volume of agreeable sound, fall altogether below the level of art.

The compilers of the *Encyclopédie*, the foundation of progressive thought in the later 18th century, followed Rousseau in deriving beauty from 'nature' interpreted as simplicity and truth but did not agree on the consequences for music. D'Alembert (1751) disparaged music in a way that had become traditional, for the poverty of its representational resources. Diderot (1751), however, set music highest among the arts; not for Rousseau's reasons, but because musical relationships are perceived directly and not mediated through interpretation of content, so that music gives imagination more freedom.

Diderot's appeal to imagination invokes an alternative tradition in aesthetics, according to which the fine arts are not exercises in imitation that call for rationalized skill but sources of 'pleasures of the imagination' open to the free play of creative genius. To this school, dominant in British aesthetics throughout the 18th century, not the poem but the landscape garden, in which artifice merges with the infinite, is the paradigm of art. It is this view of art and music that romanticism was to develop. Meanwhile Kant (1790), systematizer of the Enlightenment and synthesizer of British and German aesthetics, acknowledged both conflicting evaluations of music: of all arts it is the least rational and the most delightful, a language of feeling that contrives to be universal in scope only by forswearing all cognitive meaning, so that it can never be integrated into the truly human life of reason.

Such odious comparisons between the arts were not universal. G. E. Lessing (1766) pointed out that different arts used such heterogeneous means that it was pointless to compare them. Music, deployed through time, must relate to other realms of experience than do those arts whose works are extended in space and presented all at once; how can they be thought to compete? And J. G. Herder (1800) denounced all attempts to set up hierarchies of the arts, especially that of Kant.

11. ROMANTICISM. The late 18th-century revolutions were made in the name of human nature, but their effect was to replace nature by history: Man makes himself by making his culture. In the spirit of this new age, prepared by the growing selfconsciousness of Baroque art, encyclopedic surveys in the old manner of Kircher (1650) yielded to histories of practice like those of Hawkins (1776), La Borde (1780) and Forkel (1788–1801) as the preferred form for massive writing on music. At first, the obsolete music thus recalled to mind figures merely as the outgrown infancy of the art. But the new public of the post-revolutionary age finds all serious music mysterious, and the mystery of old music only slightly deeper. This is the viewpoint of literary romanticism.

The Enlightenment had taught that music's vocation was to express feelings too intimate for words. Now intimacy is equated with depth, depth with vagueness, and vagueness with mystery. This line of thought is first clearly expressed in 1797 by the young W. H. Wackenroder, spokesman for a generation to whom 'reason' suggested 'terror'. In Wackenroder's view, the non-conceptual character of musical language, recently expounded by Kant, frees it from mundane associations and makes it the sole expression of those feelings whereby alone we penetrate the secrets of earth and heaven – much like the 'jubilation' of which Augustine had spoken. All music thus reconciles the human and the divine, but especially the church music of Palestrina and his contemporaries; for Wackenroder's circle, ignorant of its formal principles, believed it to be vague and hence found it to be glamorous. Wackenroder's rhapsodizing style permanently lowered the acceptable tone for serious writing on music. For the first time, cultivated men avowed a principled preference for obsolete music over that of their own day, and conceived an unfocussed rapture to be a proper aesthetic response, thinking of musical techniques not as rational means of construction and expression but as occult mysteries.

Wackenroder's hysterically mystical view of music eventually invaded the writings of musicians themselves, notably of Liszt. A partial explanation of this is that general aesthetics was coming to be dominated by the notions of genius and 'organic' form, so that all set forms became suspect. The old problem of how to organize a large-scale musical structure thus reappeared in an acute form. Some form of programme or other heteronomous organization was necessary, and a succession of vague and nameless moods issuing in an ecstasy offered the best prospect of reconciling musical independence with the required dimensions.

The growth of the foregoing ideas in the early 19th century goes with the exaltation of the artist as spiritual hero. As early as 1813, E. T. A. Hoffmann recognized in Beethoven the paradigm of such a visionary revolutionary, and the figure of Beethoven came to dominate the artistic imagination of the century. The old theme of music's sway over the passions now took a special form: it became the musician's domination of his public. Wagner (1850) made strategic use of this theme, taking the choral finale of Beethoven's Ninth Symphony as evidence that pure music is not enough: it must be absorbed into a 'total' art form, dominated by drama and responsive to communal need rather than individual taste or ambition, in which the unity of artist and public would celebrate and accelerate a new social dynamism, and the split between word and music, between head and heart, would be healed at last.

Robert Schumann (1854) cut the romantic notion of genius loose from its mystagogic accompaniments and set it to work in a body of critical journalism expressly designed to raise the level of musical understanding among the new class of cultured bourgeoisie. The sole standard of judgment is genius (as opposed to talent): original, unforced, authentic expression, avoiding all that is contrived or conventional, and without reference to any preconceived formal proprieties. Schumann explained the import of such expression in terms of poetic and humanistic values, but the means of expression are soberly discussed with close attention to technique. He added nothing new to aesthetic theory, and as a composer-litterateur lacked the verve and dexterity of Berlioz (1852), but his openness to new forms of expression and the balance he achieved between technical and humanistic considerations set an abiding standard for later critics.

12. IDEALISM. G. W. F. Hegel's posthumously published lectures on aesthetics (1835) united the romantic association of music with infinity to Kant's double evaluation of music in a majestic and widely influential system that related the arts to each other and to the spiritual development of mankind. Two arts, maturing at different epochs, represent apogees of art: Greek sculpture, the perfect and perfectly clear wedding of sensuous matter to intelligible form, is really the highest point of art; but music, flowering around 1800, represents an etherealization in which matter is totally absorbed by form. This does not mean that instrumental music is

to be construed formalistically, for then it would be unworthy of the name of art; rather, its resolution of tensions presents the articulation of temporal experience and hence of consciousness itself. Music, then, is a higher spiritual manifestation than sculpture, but at the cost of abandoning the balanced perfection proper to art. Art has become obsolete, its functions assumed by more intellectualized forms of spiritual life.

A similar antithesis among the arts, but without its temporal implications, was articulated by Schopenhauer (1819). His metaphysics describes a world with two basic components, a system of eternal Ideas and an undifferentiated Will. The arts other than music symbolize the Ideas, but music alone reveals the Will, which is the more fundamental of the two. Schopenhauer thus assigned to music a deeper cognitive meaning than any other serious thinker.

The maverick classicist Friedrich Nietzsche (1872), consciously adapting Schopenhauer, went back to Aristotle to find within music itself a dichotomy corresponding to that which Schopenhauer had thought separated music from other arts: there is an Apollonian art that invites contemplation, and a Dionysian art that compels involvement and drives to frenzy. Nietzsche's dichotomy has remained very popular among the more literary aestheticians.

Music was the only art in which the 19th century could claim to excel. Modern European music seemed unique among the world's musics, and unique among the manifestations of its age. The pre-eminence of music was explained later in the century by a revision of Hegel's ideas in a purely aesthetic sense. In Walter Pater's words (1894), 'All art aspires to the condition of music', in the precise sense that in music content and form are one. Music is unlike other arts in that it produces its own material: the pitches and timbres of its sounds, and the fixity of the intervals between them, form a system not modelled on nature, the artificiality of which becomes yet more obvious as the increasing use of equal temperament signals the abandonment of the age-old search for a 'just intonation' based on natural principles. It is significant in this connection that whereas optics deals with visibilia of all sorts indifferently, the main concern of acoustics has always been musical sound as a relatively isolated system. Musical form is not imposed on a recalcitrant matter, for a musical subject is itself a musical phrase, whereas pictures are made from subjects and stuffs whose inert resistance remains partly unassimilated in the completed work. The notion, derived from music, that the only true work of art is one in which content and matter are totally assimilated by form, became a key theme in the aesthetics of B. Croce (1902) and R. G. Collingwood (1938), and has remained a dominant strain in the aesthetics of this century, especially in Italy where Croce's influence was immense.

13. COMPOSITION AND PERFORMANCE. The Crocean aesthetic raises with especial acuteness the problem of musical interpretation. For Croce, the audience must strive to intuit just what the artist expressed; and our increasing recognition of the diversity of past styles of realization, together with the arrival in the concert hall of a new kind of scholarly virtuoso, leaves us wondering whether the performer's task is that of a mere executant or of a fellow creator, and just how (in the latter case) the fellowship in creation is to be understood. This issue, exacerbated by the unprecedented specificity of modern scores in matters of expression and the like, has been hotly debated among such Italian aestheticians as A. Parente (1966) and S. Pugliatti (1940), but the best-known vindication of the performer's freedom is that of G. Brelet (1951). Music, she insists, exists only as and while it is performed, so that even the composer's version of his own work is complete only in his internal realization of it in this or that specific incarnation.

Whether musical creation is construed primarily as a composer's or a performer's art tends to depend on whether one thinks of a musical work as an incorporeal artefact, a thing made once and for all, or as a contribution to communication among men. In its most general form, the problem of musical interpretation is but one aspect of the general problem of hermeneutics, which has increasingly preoccupied the philosophical aesthetics of recent decades. How is one to explain the 'meaning' of a monument that was produced to satisfy the concerns of one age, survives to meet the different needs of a later age, and yet through it all remains in some sense the same work? There are no short and easy answers.

14. FORMALISM. The duality that Nietzsche discerned in music was already outlined and put to polemical use by Eduard Hanslick (1854), the first effective writer against romanticism. The romantics were amateur litterateurs, or chose (like Schumann) to write as if they were; Hanslick assumed the stance of a scholarly critic, bringing a musicological approach to bear for the first time on newspaper reviewing. In his theoretical work, he says that the music of the Schopenhauerian Will, that expresses and arouses feeling, is unmusical and sub-artistic. Music becomes art only when the feeling it expresses is indeterminate. The romantics had seen that, but failed to note that the feeling in artistic music was indeterminate because it was irrelevant to the import of the music, which lay entirely in the form it articulated. Musical structures are autonomous, to be apprehended and not swooned at. Moreover, the forms of music, and hence its beauty also, are *sui generis*, rather than manifesting a spiritual life that (as the romantics supposed) resists any ultimate differentiation. In developing this theme, which exactly reverses Hegel's evaluation of formal and expressive principles, Hanslick was applying the general aesthetics of J. F. Herbart (1808). Herbart had argued that the value of art lies in its formal relations and not in its expressiveness, and that the critic's proper business is with the unique set of formal principles that each art has at its disposal. Hanslick's development of this theme has won acceptance as the classic statement of one of the permanently possible positions in the aesthetics of music, though a more penetrating and versatile analysis of the unique nature of musical form is to be found among the prolixities of Edmund Gurney's *The Power of Sound* (1880).

Hanslick's formalism has had a distinguished following in France. J. Combarieu (1907) defined music as the art of thinking in sounds, an autonomous activity that cannot express statable meanings but whose products are inherently meaningful; a similar view was expressed by that self-appointed Frenchman Igor Stravinsky (1942). A more systematic but less exclusive formalism was extended to all the arts by the neo-Thomist Etienne Gilson (1964).

15. MUSICOLOGICAL AESTHETICS. Since the middle of

the 19th century, the aesthetics of music has been increasingly overshadowed by empirical studies of acoustics and of the psychology of musical perception and of hearing generally, and by investigations of the history and anthropology of musical systems and practices. Beginning with F. J. Fétis (1835–44), the old-style histories that sought to explain and justify present practice as the fruit of past progress are replaced, as in political history, by a scientific historiography whose ideal is to establish, in Leopold von Ranke's famous phrase, 'the way it actually happened'. Some theorists argue that all these researches, collectively dubbed 'musicology', facilitate and demand the replacement of an obsolete philosophical and literary aesthetics by an up-to-date scientific aesthetics; others retort that the data compiled have done little for aesthetics proper, since the facts still require interpretation, and factual erudition and theoretical sophistication seldom go hand in hand.

One can hardly explain music without knowing what music and its affines are and have been, and there is nowadays no excuse for ignoring the diversity of musical styles, practices and contexts, or for confusing musical ideology with scientific fact. But the demand, apparently first made by F. Chrysander (1863), that musical aesthetics become the preserve of musicologists, has questionable implications. To say that aesthetics is to be derived from musicology but is not itself musicology is to suppose that values are to be determined by past practice: whatever was, is right. Again, to accept a disjunction between learned musicians and ignorant public and then to claim that the pipers should call the tune is to make music once more the mystery that some would have made it in the Middle Ages. There is a tendency, which has no parallel in the other arts, for musical aesthetics to become, not merely a professional aesthetics, but a trade aesthetics. More subtly, since music exists while it is performed, the massive revival of past works and the accompanying recreation of the appropriate practices has established the whole history of music in a simultaneous present: the future of music lies ever deeper in its past. The musicological viewpoint is that of the performer as opposed to the creator, and a claim by musicology to hegemony over music and its aesthetics may threaten the vitality of the art.

If the musicologist may be a dangerous master for the aesthetician, he remains an invaluable colleague. In practice, aesthetics suffers from too little musicology rather than too much. C. Sachs (e.g. 1946) and W. Wiora (1961) have sought to extract the underlying principles from the totality of the world's music; but C. Lalo's attempted synthesis of 1908, though cranky and long obsolete, may be the last work to counterbalance amplitude of information with an adequate theoretical power.

16. MARXISM. Marxist theory regards the postulated objectivity of musicological historiography as bourgeois mystification. Though the development of music conforms superficially to its own historical logic, it is like the other arts in that its history ultimately reflects the changes in economic relationships that determine the course of all events. The artist's mission is to discern the as yet hidden tensions that will carry the class struggle in his society on to its next phase: he is the prophet of revolution. Marxists agree on this, but argue among themselves about whether the growth of an art has some

limited independence or must be explained directly in economic terms, and about whether artists retain their visionary function after a political party has assumed responsibility for the future, or must now show only what the commissar has seen.

Karl Marx and Friedrich Engels, in outlining the foregoing theory of the history and function of art, left music alone, confining their attention to arts whose descriptive content made the prophetic function easier to demonstrate; and the subsequent debates of Marxist aesthetics have mostly concerned arts other than music. Most later Marxist aesthetics of music have taken the form of historical explication and criticism, both of music itself and of musical aesthetics. Since Marxists see the basic types of social and economic order as very few, the range of explanatory categories at their disposal for writing such histories may strike the unsympathetic reader as very narrow. But a sufficient reply to this objection could be that the fundamental types of music – or of anything else, for that matter – are indeed extraordinarily few, and that it is the triumph of Marxism that it at once reveals and explains this paucity. In any case, it may be that the most solid contribution of Marxism to the aesthetics of music has lain in its provision of an alternative history of human progress, in music as in other fields: a history in which spiritual achievement figures as part of the world's work. Marxist principles have found less scope in discussions of the import of living music, in which they tend to reduce to the conviction that bourgeois music is commercial or esoteric, and hence a device for lulling the proletariat and concealing the impotence of the bourgeoisie, whereas proletarian music affirms and proclaims solidarity for chorus and orchestra. In the last assertion, the influence of Wagner is more discernible than that of Marx.

The general thesis (Fischer, 1959) that good music reflects a rising class and bad music reflects an oppressive or vestigial class, while the best music of all will reflect the full humanity of a classless society, is plainly a recrudescence of the ancient *ethos* theory. It yields a historical aesthetic that satisfies for two reasons: it is simple, and it is clearly relevant to matters of unquestionable importance. But its applications must rest on the sense of congruence of their expositor. It is a basic tenet of Marxism that, since every such expositor is historically situated, his vision is strictly relative to his situation: to someone differently placed, his interpretations must at first seem no better than arbitrary manipulations. A methodology is needed to overcome this crippling relativity, and in the field of music the development of such a 'sociology of knowledge' has been seriously hampered by a historical accident. A Marxist reading of history seems to demand that European music between 1848 and 1917, when bourgeois culture was in its death-throes, should have been utterly corrupt (Zoltai, 1970); but since the rise of Stalin the official Soviet view, which for a long time set the pace for Marxists everywhere, has in effect taken the music of just that age as its model. A way around the resulting impasse was found by T. W. Adorno (1949, 1956): a difficult, progressive music represents the forces of human progress and resistance against the commercialism of the west and the bureaucratization of the east. But in developing this theme Adorno was driven back from Marx to Hegel: he effectively abandoned historical materialism by assigning to the *materia musica*, the resources available to the musical mind, the place that Marx and Engels had reserved for the means and conditions of material production.

17. THE PROBLEM OF TONALITY. Although musical methods have changed constantly, the harmonic system of the late 19th century seemed to have evolved from that of Aristoxenus and even Pythagoras by steps so natural that neither origin nor outcome stood in need of fundamental justification. When in doubt, one appealed to the overtone series. Musicians could even continue unselfconsciously to ascribe an emotional connotation to this or that scale in the equal-tempered system, as though such scales were somehow the counterparts of the old church modes, and those in turn of the tribal musics of 5th-century Greece. As a result, the alleged depletion of the resources of the entire tonal system, and the rise of musics that repudiate it, have raised unprecedented doubts about how any musical system works. For instance, whether the dodecaphonic system is a legitimate heir of the harmonic tradition or a rejection of it depends on what one thinks the basis of the original system was; and this proves to be controversial. Schoenberg (1911, 1954) claims continuity, on the ground that concinnity is a function of familiarity, so that the contrast between concord and discord is self-liquidating; writers influenced by Schenker (1906) argue the contrary, urging that both that contrast and the function of tonic centres are somehow guaranteed by nature. The difference is radical. Those who think of tonality as natural tend to regard a musical work as a dynamic system, developing through time by accumulation and release of tension in a sort of systole and diastole. Those who think of tonality as one of an infinity of possible musical systems tend to regard such distinctions as those between simultaneous and successive, forward and backward, up and down, as of secondary import, and a musical work as a system of relationships to be contemplated. To the former school, a discord is defined by its instability, by the fact that it calls for a certain consequent; the latter school defines a discord, as Tinctoris had in 1477, by its quality as a disagreeable or unacceptable combination.

Was the tonal system workable for any deeper reason than that it was familiar to the ear? And if so, what description of its procedures will account for its workability? One can no longer be sure. Today's history-conscious composer is at a loss to proceed, whether within the tonal tradition or against it, for there is no agreement as to what requirements a workable musical system must fulfil. Schoenberg (1950) and Stravinsky can appeal only to their industry, passion and integrity as warrant that their work has satisfied whatever the unknown requirements may be.

18. NEO-FORMALISM. Recent decades have seen a variety of attempts to establish the basic principles of musical structures, answering to different ideas about what music is and leading to divergent evaluations of musical works.

One approach, taking music as the art of temporal creation, describes the 'virtual' time established by musical progressions and relates it to the actual succession of events, to the human experience of duration, and to the prospective and restrospective aspects of consciousness. The most elaborate development of this approach is that of G. Brelet (1949).

A second approach, regarding music as communi-cation from player to hearer, explicates it in terms of the mathematical theory of information. Since musicians are not literally encoding anything in the sense required by that theory, such key terms as 'redundancy' and 'message' become mere metaphors; but this does not make the theory inapplicable. In particular, the concept of redundancy has been found useful in giving precision to the concept of style (Youngblood, 1958).

A more radical formalism recapitulates the ancient reduction of music to mathematics by seeking to generalize such basic musical terms as 'note' and 'interval', with the aim of extending the concept of music to include all possible structures that bear appropriate formal analogy to what the world has hitherto recognized as music.

An equally pure formalism with a different thrust is that of Nelson Goodman's general theory of symbol systems (1968), meant to fit all possible arts and languages. Goodman gives the concept of notation a precision it never had before, and reveals with disconcerting clarity its implications for the ideal relation between score and performance. His system assumes that a score functions as a definition of what a work is, rather than as a set of instructions for making music; and the moral may be that it is unwise to assume that.

A more complex account of musical meaning has been elaborated by W. Coker (1972), who argues that any musical work must be intrinsically meaningful both as an organized sign complex and as an interpersonal gesture. Current researches begin to show that systems of meaning are much more various and complex than anyone had recognized, and Coker's work may represent a preliminary acknowledgment that all this variety and complexity may be realized within music.

19. NEO-EXPRESSIONISM. Most leading aestheticians of the English-speaking world accept the view that musical systems rely on the generation and release of tensions. They have tried to formulate the rather old-fashioned view that music is the language of feeling in ways that will somehow respect musical autonomy and tie in with the requirements of formal analysis. S. K. Langer (1942, 1953) argued that music neither voices nor arouses actual feelings, but has stress-patterns isomorphic with those of the flow of emotion, and it is this isomorphism that makes music meaningful. Her influential theory was developed from that of the Neo-Kantian Ernst Cassirer (1923–31), and forms part of a general theory of art and culture. A generalized version of the theory has been put forward by Terence McLaughlin (1970), according to whom the isomorphism holds between the musical pattern of tensions and resolutions and patterns of brain activity set up by all sorts of mental and bodily events, a synthesis of which the music accordingly evokes. His conclusions essentially recapitulate those of Ogden, Richards and Wood (1922).

A more thorough synthesis of form and feeling was effected by L. B. Meyer (1956), who interpreted styles as culturally conditioned systems of expectations and derived musical meaning from the arousal, frustration and eventual fulfilment of these expectations. His general account of musical process marries Schenker's method of analysis to a notion of aesthetic experience that had been developed by John Dewey (1934) without specific reference to music.

The most extreme version of the thesis that music is a language of feeling is that argued by Deryck Cooke (1959), whose demonstration that tonal music at least used such a language, of which he provides a glossary, has proved easier to deride than to ignore.

20. VANGUARDISM. Tape recorders make it easy to combine and reproduce natural sounds, and electronic synthesizers theoretically make it possible to produce any conceivable combination of any conceivable sounds. New possibilities for the artistic use of sound thus proliferate, and call into question the definition of 'music'. Should that term, with the associated range of our sympathies and practices, now be extended to any art that combines sounds otherwise than in speech? Or should we restrict it to arts that organize sounds in ways analogous to the traditional ones? Or should we even define music without reference to sound, as whatever may be structured by a given type of order? Many answers are offered, but there seems to be no decisive reason for preferring one answer over the others; the problem remains the great unmet challenge to contemporary aesthetics of music.

One extreme position is that of John Cage (1961), perhaps the most widely influential theorist of the avant garde. In effect, Cage exploits the contrast between the continuing solidity and vitality of musical institutions of instruction and performance, and the new uncertainty about what music to make with them. What is all that apparatus for? Cage's writings suggest a number of alternative or complementary answers. One line, followed by others as well, has been to isolate the ritual or ceremonious from the sonorous aspect of musical performances, and to present in the guise of music works that consist of silent pieces of musical ceremony (bowing to the audience, opening and closing the piano lid), of civil ceremony (the performers shaking each other by the hand), or even of the musician's establishing the musicality of the occasion by his mute presence on the platform. A second line, the converse of the first, isolates the sound of music from the ceremony: a composer is identified as a mere tyrant, imposing his own ideas about what should be heard on listeners who have minds and ears of their own. According to this strain in Cage's thought, all organized music is evil because it represents the hybristic affirmation of the human will in opposition to nature, making us listen to men instead of to sounds. Instead of manipulating sounds, we ought to give ourselves up to whatever sounds chance may offer. A third line followed by Cage asserts that 'everything we do is music'. The sense in which this is so is not made explicit, but what seems to be implied is that music, as a form of play that is serious though purposeless, is an affirmation of life itself, and is to be identified as an attitude that anyone may take to anything at any time.

On the whole, Cage's preferred stance has been that of a Zen Savonarola, denouncing all art as blasphemous. Despite the difficulty of extracting a coherent position from his writings, his sallies have yet to be met with a subtlety and wit approaching his own, and his failure to be consistent has not prevented him from being influential.

Cage remains committed to music in some sense, but it is hard to discern what he is committed to, and for what reasons. Among those who have retained a commitment to music-making in something like the traditional sense, but in full awareness of the openness of the contemporary scene and without preferring the conservatory to the laboratory, a key position is held by Pierre Schaeffer. Schaeffer was among the first to recognize the significance for composition of contemporary recording techniques, and formulated (1952) the idea of *musique concrète*: instead of proceeding, as conventional or 'abstract' music does, from the idea of a musical form to its realization in sound, 'concrete' music takes an existing sound and manipulates it into significant form. But what principles should such shaping follow? The difficulty of determining how to answer that question, and the concomitant practical difficulties of composing concrete music, revealed to Schaeffer that music is a subject about which man knows little, and drove him to investigate how musics are possible. The result of his researches is an unprecedentedly elaborated analysis (1966) of all actual and possible determinants of musical experience, an analysis that serves rather to reveal the limitations of extant musical systems than to suggest possibilities for the music of the future.

A more direct approach to the problems of composing in an unstructured situation has been taken by Karlheinz Stockhausen, who has acted as bellwether for the advanced musicians of Europe since the second world war. Our musical situation at mid-century, he has argued (1963–71), is like that of postwar Germany: 'The cities are razed', we must rebuild music from the ground up. Total freedom from tradition demands and facilitates total control: any principle may be used to organize a musical work, but coherence demands that the same formative idea be applied to every variable aspect of the work, including the distribution of sound-sources in space. Stockhausen's insistence that a new age calls for new methods and materials and new habits of mind represents an application to music of the attitudes and arguments developed by painters and architects between 1910 and 1920, and adumbrated for music at that time by Ferruccio Busoni. His contribution to vanguard thought, unlike those of Cage and Schaeffer, has not taken the form of a body of theory whose interest survives abstraction from his practice as composer and analyst of music.

In considering advanced movements in the arts, it is useful to differentiate five sorts of thinker. One sort, exemplified by Harry Partch's exploration of the possibilities of just intonation (1949), seeks to reform the principles of an art. A second seeks to extend its boundaries. A third seeks to eliminate the art as a distinguishable entity, in favour of Art conceived in some more general way. A fourth attacks art itself, as blasphemous or unnatural or uncivilized. And a fifth is practising a variant of the art of theatre, the purported theoretical pronouncements being uttered because they sound well. A practitioner of any of the first three kinds of discourse may be assigned to the avant garde, provided that he subscribes to two principles: that there is at any time one direction in which art (or a particular art) is going, and that he is leading the procession.

21. AESTHETICS AND LOGIC. The aesthetics of music does not grow in a cultural vacuum. As Fubini (1964) observed, the extent to which the aesthetics of music is independent of general aesthetics is itself a problem for musical aesthetics – but also for general aesthetics.

Among the more striking relationships is that between trends in musical aesthetics and developments in logic. For instance, Plato's relation of musical forms to personality structures reflects a general tendency to place logical questions in the context of self-criticism. Again, the 13th century emphasized a formal logic, concerned with principles of analysis and validation rather than the procedures of the mind at work; and such was its aesthetics of music. When Renaissance humanism reversed this emphasis, replacing mathematics and formal logic by literary culture and rhetoric, a new musical aesthetics concerned itself with the proprieties of courtly song. In the late 17th century, Descartes' new analytical methods were exemplified both by the doctrine of affections and by Rameau's studies of harmony. The later 18th and 19th centuries turned logic into a study, half analytical and half historical, of how complex forms unfold from simple origins, and the musical aesthetics of the age was marked by an unprecedented interest in what the effects of music actually are and how they are generated. Later in the 19th century formal logic was rediscovered, formal analysis recovered a depth and subtlety long lost, and musical aesthetics turned to a renewed and more searching investigation of the principles of actual and possible scales and systems (e.g. Busoni, 1907). This analytic interest in logic soon became a full-blown conventionalism, and a few decades later such advanced thinkers as Pierre Boulez (1966) developed theories of music as the invention and exploration of conventional schemata. A conventionalist logic begets its own repudiation in favour of exoticism and irrationalism, and some recent aesthetics of music shows a similar transition from mathematics to mysticism.

A satirical observer might discern in recent aestheticians a tendency to succumb to the paralogisms current in their homelands. Boulez exemplifies the pseudo-Cartesian 'logic' of the *lycée*, which 'rigorously' applies a single simple procedure to all subject matters indiscriminately, regardless of its appropriateness. T. W. Adorno (1949) follows the post-Hegelian 'He who says A must say B' of Germany, insisting that music must follow whatever direction is suggested by its last move, whether that is where it wants to go or not. L. B. Meyer, true to his technological culture, interprets musical processes in the light of models devised to describe the behaviour of the most advanced machinery. And the Anglo-Canadian writer of this article, imperfectly inspired by J. S. Mill, follows his native practice of muddling through, in its local variant: muddling through provincially.

22. AESTHETICS IN OTHER CIVILIZATIONS. European music has developed in directions that set it apart from the other musics of the world, and the reflections of other civilizations on their musics have seemed less relevant to its traditions than has, for instance, the Chinese theory of painting to our visual arts. For that reason they have been left out of account here. But two examples may serve to illustrate how our traditions might have been enriched from these alien sources.

The concept of *rasa*, the central term in Indian poetics, is sadly missed in the west. It stands for a sort of relish that remains purely aesthetic while firmly related to one of a limited number of domains of human sensibility, and might have served better than our own concept of expression as a counterpoise to technique.

Western theorists often write as though the sole alternative to analytic pedantry were a sentimental subjectivity, for no better reason than that the term 'expression' seems to them to carry that suggestion; and 'taste' has connotations of aestheticism and dilettantism that seem to contrast it alike with technical knowledge and with true feeling. *Rasa* seems to stand for a better frame of mind.

In the other great civilization of the orient, traditional Chinese thought assigned music an important place in the great system of equipoises that was understood to pervade the cosmos, the social order and the human mind, in a way that seems to articulate more systematically the attitude to which Pythagoreanism gave mathematical expression in the west. The ancient Chinese seem to have made a conceptual distinction in this connection that bears analogy to the distinction Boethius made among his three levels: there is 'ceremony', observances on earth that mirror and encourage order in heaven; there is 'music', the harmonious manifestation of internal order; and there is mere 'notes', sounds sung or played with no further purpose than to give pleasure. 'The theory of music and ceremonies embraces the whole nature of man', says the *Yueh Chih*.

23. THE PRESENT AND FUTURE OF MUSICAL AESTHETICS. Aesthetics traffics in interpretation, not information. Its problems are therefore perennial. Progress lies not in solving them, but in using new knowledge to illuminate them, and prevalent doctrine changes when interests change rather than when errors are corrected. Where aesthetics stands now, and whither it is heading, may sufficiently appear from the preceding survey. But some more general remarks may provide a fitting conclusion.

Disarray in aesthetics of music reflects disorder in musical practice. Music, whatever else it is, must in the first instance be a set of human practices, and the basic task of aesthetics must be to find principles that will make those practices intelligible. Consequently, a revolution or crisis in music (as in any art) precipitates a comparable trauma in its aesthetics. When practice becomes incoherent it can have no principles to elucidate, so that the aesthetician must either select some body of practice that seems explicable or confine himself to charting the bounds of chaos. To do the former risks arbitrariness, to do the latter risks an incoherence comparable to that surveyed.

Any disorder in today's music touches neither popular music nor serious performance, which flourish and prosper, but serious composition. The composer's problem lies in the profound gulf (unparalleled in any other art) that divides him from popular practice, in the lack of an adequate public, and in the absence of a firm tradition to support his procedures. He is faced with the absurd demand for absolute originality in the name of abstract principle, and the word 'serious' as applied to his art acquires an ironic ring.

Aesthetics cannot help the composer, but reflection on the first two aspects of his predicament suggests the need for a more comprehensive theory of musical values and practices. As the 17th century recognized the legitimacy of different musics for chamber, church and theatre, tomorrow's aesthetician might chart a world in which Darmstadt, Nashville and Huddersfield have each their appointed place. If he insists that no music without a large audience should be deemed serious (cf Pleasants,

1969), or that nothing that fails to challenge the understanding should be called 'music', he might still think seriously about the social functions, the aesthetic values and the relations to other practices of what he thus depreciates. Few living aestheticians other than W. H. Mellers (1967) have achieved such detachment.

The third aspect of the composer's problem calls for continued inquiry into the theoretical constraints on the practicability of musical systems. This is the old topic of the relation between natural and conventional beauty. Current practice suggests that some musical interest may be taken in anything, so that anything may pass for music with some audience on some occasion in some sense. Does that show that any arbitrary convention could form the basis for a generally accepted musical practice? If not, are the limits on the viability of systems such as to suggest a single ideal system, or are they conditions that could be equally well fulfilled in many ways? And, if many systems may be equally workable, what are the limits on their co-existence in a single society? These questions have been courageously attempted, as by L. B. Meyer (1967), but they call for that combination of musicological erudition with theoretical stringency that is so hard to come by.

The psychology of hearing raises a question related to the last. Since Sauveur, we have habitually justified our musical practices by appealing to the natural harmonies implicit in the overtone system: good sound means good vibrations. But this will not do, for what we hear is by no means what the experimenter's instruments record (cf Winckel, 1960). The facts are clear, but it is by no means clear what their implications are for theory or practice. What are the natural limits to audible order? It is a tantalizing problem on the boundaries of philosophy and psychology.

A final problem arises not within music but on its borders. The edges of the arts are becoming blurred. Can and should we continue to think of music as an art distinct from all others, or should we once more face the prospect that, as Roger Bacon and Wagner suggested in their different ways, the future of music lies within some more comprehensive form of aesthetic activity? It is a problem on the frontiers of philosophy and sociology, for it may be that music as we have known it is proper to a phase of civilization that is passing away.

BIBLIOGRAPHY

Titles marked with an asterisk (*) are directly concerned, as a whole or in large part, with aesthetics.

GENERAL REFERENCE
* R. Schäfke: *Geschichte der Musikästhetik in Umrissen* (Berlin, 1934)
W. D. Allen: *Philosophies of Music History* (New York, 1939, 2/1962)
P. H. Lang: *Music in Western Civilization* (New York, 1941)
* O. Strunk, ed.: *Source Readings in Music History* (New York, 1950) [= *StrunkSR*]
* J. Portnoy: *The Philosopher and Music* (New York, 1954)
* H. H. Dräger and A. Wellek: 'Musik-Ästhetik', *MGG*
* E. Fubini: *L'estetica musicale dal settecento a oggi* (Turin, 1964, 2/1968)
* D. Zoltai: *Ethos und Affekt* (Budapest, 1970)

HELLENIC AND HELLENISTIC
H. S. Macran, trans.: *The Harmonics of Aristoxenus* (Oxford, 1902)
I. Düring, trans.: *Ptolemaios und Porphyrios über die Musik* (Göteborg, 1934)
E. Barker, trans.: *The Politics of Aristotle* (Oxford, 1946)
C. Bailey, trans.: *T. Lucreti Cari De rerum natura* (Oxford, 1947)
R. G. Bury, trans.: *The Works of Sextus Empiricus*, iv (London, 1949)
* F. Lasserre, ed.: *Plutarque de la musique* (Olten, 1954)
* A. J. Neubecker: *Die Bewertung der Musik bei Stoikern und Epikureern* (Berlin, 1956)
E. Hamilton and H. Cairns, eds.: *Collected Dialogues of Plato* (New York, 1961)

* W. D. Anderson: *Ethos and Education in Greek Music* (Cambridge, Mass., 1966)

EARLY CHRISTIAN AND MEDIEVAL
Augustine: *Confessions*, in *PL*, xxxii (Eng. trans., 1942)
——: *De musica*, in *PL*, xxxii (Eng. trans., 1947)
——: *In psalmum XCIX enarratio*, in *PL*, xxxvii (Eng. trans., 1888)
Joannes Chrysostomus: *In psalmum XLI commentarius*, in *PG*, 1v (Fr. trans., 1868; part trans. in *StrunkSR*)
Boethius: *De institutione musica*, in *PL*, lxiii (Eng. trans. C. M. Bowra, diss., George Peabody College, 1967; part trans. in *StrunkSR*)
Joannes Scotus Eriugena [John Scotus Erigena]: *De divisione naturae*, in *PL*, cxxi
Guido Aretinus [Guido of Arezzo]: *Regulae rhythmicae*, in *GS*, ii, 25
Franco de Colonia: *Ars cantus mensurabilis*, in *CS*, i, 117 (part trans. in *StrunkSR*)
Jacobus Leodiensis [Jacques de Liège]: *Speculum musicae*, vii, in *CS*, ii, 383 and CSM, iii/1–7 (1955–) (part trans. in *StrunkSR*)
Johannes de Grocheo: *De musica*, ed. E. Rohloff, with Ger. trans. as *Der Musiktraktat des Johannes de Grocheo* (Leipzig, 1943) (Eng. trans., ed. A. Seay: *Concerning Music: De musica*, 1967)
Joannes de Muris [Jehan des Murs]: *Ars novae musicae*, in *GS*, iii, 255 (part trans. in *StrunkSR*)
J. Tinctoris: *Conspectus effectuum musices* (*c*1473), in *CS*, iv, 191
——: *Liber de arte contrapuncti* (1477), in *CS*, iv, 76 (Eng. trans., 1961)
H. Riemann: *Geschichte der Musiktheorie im IX.-XIX. Jahrhundert* (Leipzig, 1898, 2/1920; part Eng. trans., 1962)
* H. Abert: *Die Musikanschauung des Mittelalters und ihre Grundlagen* (Halle, 1905)
* E. de Bruyne: *L'esthétique du moyen âge* (Louvain, 1947; Eng. trans., 1969)

RENAISSANCE AND BAROQUE
H. Glarean: *Dodecachordon* (Basle, 1547/R1966; Eng. trans., 1965)
G. Zarlino: *Le istitutioni harmoniche* (Venice, 1558, 4/1589/R1966; pt. iii, Eng. trans., 1968; part trans. in *StrunkSR*)
——: *Sopplimenti musicali* (Venice, 1588/R1966)
* V. Galilei: *Dialogo della musica antica et della moderna* (Florence, 1581/R part trans. in *StrunkSR*)
* J. Case: *The Praise of Musicke* (London, 1586)
T. Morley: *A Plaine and Easie Introduction to Practicall Musicke* (London, 1597/R1937); ed. R. A. Harman (London, 1952/R1963)
P. Rosseter: *Book of Ayres* (London, 1601/R1970)
R. Hooker: *Of the Lawes of Ecclesiasticall Politie* (London, 1617)
J. Kepler: *De harmonice mundi* (Augsburg, 1619; part trans. in *HawkinsH*, 618)
R. Descartes: *Les passions de l'âme* (Amsterdam, 1649; Eng. trans., 2/1931)
A. Kircher: *Musurgia universalis* (Rome, 1650; part trans. in *HawkinsH*, 35, 97, 101, 637, 639)
* F. Raguenet: *Parallèle des italiens et des francais en ce qui regarde la musique et les opéras* (Paris, 1702; Eng. trans. 1709/R1967; trans. in *StrunkSR*)
* J.-L. Le Cerf de la Viéville: *Comparaison de la musique italienne et de la musique françoise* (Brussels, 1704–6; part trans. in *StrunkSR*)
J. Mattheson: *Das neu-eröffnete Orchester* (Hamburg, 1713)
——: *Der vollkommene Capellmeister* (Hamburg, 1739/R1954)
J. J. Quantz: *Versuch einer Anweisung die Flöte traversière zu spielen* (Berlin, 1752, 3/1789/R1953; Eng. trans., 1966 as *On Playing the Flute*)
C. P. E. Bach: *Versuch über die wahre Art das Clavier zu spielen* (Berlin, 1753, 4/1787; Eng. trans., 1949)
J. A. Scheibe: *Abhandlung vom Ursprung und Alter der Musik* (Altona, 1754)
* M. C. Boyd: *Elizabethan Music and Music Criticism* (Philadelphia, 1940, 2/1962)
* M. F. Bukofzer: *Music in the Baroque Era* (New York, 1947)
* H. Lenneberg: 'Johann Mattheson on Affect and Rhetoric in Music', *JMT*, ii (1958), 47–84, 193–236
* E. Bodky: *The Interpretation of Bach's Keyboard Works* (Cambridge, Mass., 1960)
F. Blume: *Renaissance and Baroque Music* (New York, 1968) [trans. of *MGG* articles]

RATIONALISM AND ENLIGHTENMENT
* M. Mersenne: *Harmonie universelle* (Paris, 1636/R1963; Eng. trans., 1957)
* R. Descartes: *Musicae compendium* (Utrecht, 1650/R1967; 2/1656; Eng. trans., 1961)
* J.-B. Dubos: *Réflexions critiques sur la poésie et sur la peinture* (Paris, 1719; Eng. trans., 1748)
* J. P. Rameau: *Traité de l'harmonie réduite à son principe naturel* (Paris, 1722/R1967; Eng. trans., 1971; part trans. in *StrunkSR*)
* C. Batteux: *Les beaux-arts reduits à un même principe* (Paris, 1746)
D. Diderot: *Lettre sur les sourds et les muets* (Paris, 1751)
J. LeR. d'Alembert: 'Discours preliminaire des éditeurs', *Encyclopédie*, i (Paris, 1751; Eng. trans., 1963)

*C. Avison: *Essay on Musical Expression* (London, 1752, enlarged 3/1775)

J.-J. Rousseau: *Lettre sur la musique française* (Paris, 1753)

*G. E. Lessing: *Laoköon* (Berlin, 1766; Eng. trans., 1959)

*J. Beattie: 'On Poetry and Music as they Affect the Mind', *Essays* (Edinburgh, 1776)

J.-J. Rousseau: 'Essai sur l'origine des langues' (1754), *Traités sur la musique* (Geneva, 1781; Eng. trans., 1966)

A. E. M. Grétry: *Mémoires, ou essais sur la musique* (Paris, 1789, enlarged 3/1797; part trans. in *StrunkSR*)

*I. Kant: *Kritik der Urteilskraft* (Berlin, 1790; Eng. trans., 1952)

*J. G. Herder: *Kalligone* (Leipzig, 1800)

D. Diderot: *Le neveu de Rameau* (Paris, 1821; Eng. trans., 1964)

*H. Scherchen: *Vom Wesen der Musik* (Winterthur, 1946; Eng. trans., 1950), chap. 'Joseph Sauveur', 29

P. O. Kristeller: 'The Modern System of the Arts', *Journal of the History of Ideas*, xii (1951), 496–527; xiii (1952), 17–46

ROMANTICISM AND IDEALISM

Hawkins H

*J.-B. La Borde: *Essai sur la musique ancienne et moderne* (Paris, 1780/R1972)

J. N. Forkel: *Allgemeine Geschichte der Musik* (Leipzig, 1788–1801)

*W. H. Wackenroder: *Herzensergiessungen eines kunstliebenden Klosterbruders* (Berlin, 1797; part trans. in *StrunkSR*)

E. T. A. Hoffmann: 'Beethovens Instrumentalmusik' (1813), *Fantasiestücke in Callot's Manier* (Bamberg, 1819; part trans. in *StrunkSR*)

A. Schopenhauer: *Die Welt als Wille und Vorstellung* (Leipzig, 1819, enlarged 3/1859; Eng. trans., 2/1958)

*G. W. F. Hegel: *Vorlesungen über die Ästhetik* (Berlin, 1835, 2/1842; Eng. trans., 1920)

*R. Wagner: *Das Kunstwerk der Zukunft* (Leipzig, 1850; Eng. trans., 1892)

*R. Wagner: *Oper und Drama* (Leipzig, 1852; Eng. trans., 1893)

H. Berlioz: *Les soirées de l'orchestre* (Paris, 1852; Eng. trans., 1956)

R. A. Schumann: *Gesammelte Schriften über Musik und Musiker* (Leipzig, 1854; Eng. trans., 1891)

*F. Nietzsche: *Die Gebürt der Tragödie* (Leipzig, 1872; Eng. trans., 1967)

F. Liszt: 'Berlioz und seine Haroldsymphonie', *NZM*, xliii (1855/R), 25, 37, 49, 77, 89; *Gesammelte Schriften*, ed. L. Ramann (Leipzig, 1880–83), iv, 1–102; (part trans. in *StrunkSR*)

W. Pater: *The Renaissance* (London, 5/1894), chap. 'The School of Giorgione'

*B. Croce: *Estetica come scienza dell' espressione e linguistica generale* (Milan, 1902, 4/1912; Eng. trans., 2/1922)

*R. G. Collingwood: *The Principles of Art* (Oxford, 1938)

*A. Einstein: *Music in the Romantic Era* (New York, 1947)

F. Blume: *Classic and Romantic Music* (New York, 1972 [trans. of *MGG* articles)

COMPOSITION AND PERFORMANCE

*S. Pugliatti: *L'interpretazione musicale* (Messina, 1940)

*G. Brelet: *L'interpretation créatrice* (Paris, 1951)

R. T. Dart: *The Interpretation of Music* (London, 1954, 4/1967)

*A. Parente and others: 'Note e commenti', *La rassegna musicale*, ed. L. Pestalozza (Milan, 1966), 485

*R. Leibowitz: *Le compositeur et son double* (Paris, 1971)

FORMALISM

J. F. Herbart: *Allgemeine praktische Philosophie* (Göttingen, 1808)

*E. Hanslick: *Vom Musikalisch-Schönen* (Leipzig, 1854, 7/1885; Eng. trans., 1957)

*E. Gurney: *The Power of Sound* (London, 1880/R1966)

*J. Combarieu: *La musique, ses lois, son évolution* (Paris, 1907; Eng. trans., 1910)

*I. Stravinsky: *Poétique musicale sous forme de six leçons* (Cambridge, Mass., 1942; Eng. trans., 1947)

*G. Brelet: *Le temps musicale* (Paris, 1949)

*E. Gilson: *Matières et formes* (Paris, 1964; Eng. trans., 1966)

MUSICOLOGICAL AESTHETICS

FétisB

F. Chrysander: 'Vorwort und Einleitung', *Jb für musikalische Wissenschaft*, i (1863), 9–16

H. L. F. Helmholtz: *Lehre der Tonempfindungen als psychologische Grundlage für die Theorie der Musik* (Brunswick, 1863; Eng. trans., 6/1913)

*C. Lalo: *Eléments d'une esthétique musicale scientifique* (Paris, 1908, 2/1939)

*C. Sachs: *The Commonwealth of Art* (New York, 1946)

A. Daniélou: *Traité de musicologie comparée* (Paris, 1959)

W. Wiora: *Die vier Zeitalter der Musik* (Stuttgart, 1961; Eng. trans., 1965)

MARXISM

*K. Marx and F. Engels: *Literature and Art* (New York, 1947)

*T. W. Adorno: *Philosophie der neuen Musik* (Tübingen, 1949, 3/1967; Eng. trans., 1973)

——: *Dissonanzen* (Göttingen, 1956, 2/1958)

*E. Fischer: *Von der Notwendigkeit der Kunst* (Dresden, 1959; Eng. trans., 1963)

*G. Lukács: *Ästhetik* (Neuwied am Rhein, 1963)

THE PROBLEM OF TONALITY

H. Schenker: *Harmonielehre* (Vienna, 1906; Eng. trans., 1954)

*A. Schoenberg: *Harmonielehre* (Vienna, 1911; Eng. trans., abridged, 1948)

——: *Style and Idea* (New York, 1950)

——: *Structural Functions of Harmony* (New York, 1954)

*V. Zuckerkandl: *Sound and Symbol: Music and the External World* (New York, 1956)

R. Reti: *Tonality, Atonality, Pantonality* (London, 1958)

NEO-FORMALISM AND NEO-EXPRESSIONISM

*C. K. Ogden, I. A. Richards and J. Wood: *The Foundations of Aesthetics* (London, 1922)

E. Cassirer: *Philosophie der symbolischen Formen* (Berlin, 1923–31; Eng. trans., 1953–7)

*J. Dewey: *Art as Experience* (New York, 1934)

*S. K. Langer: *Philosophy in a New Key* (Cambridge, Mass., 1942)

*——: *Feeling and Form* (New York, 1953)

*L. B. Meyer: *Emotion and Meaning in Music* (Chicago, 1956)

*A. A. Moles: *Théorie de l'information et perception esthétique* (Paris, 1958; Eng. trans., 1966)

J. E. Youngblood: 'Style as Information', *JMT*, ii (1958), 24

*D. Cooke: *The Language of Music* (Oxford, 1959)

*G. Epperson: *The Musical Symbol* (Ames, Iowa, 1967)

*N. Goodman: *Languages of Art* (Indianapolis, 1968)

*T. McLaughlin: *Music and Communication* (London, 1970)

*W. Coker: *Music and Meaning* (New York, 1972)

VANGUARDISM AND THE PRESENT AND FUTURE

*F. Busoni: *Entwurf einer neuen Ästhetik der Tonkunst* (Trieste, 1907; Eng. trans. in C. Debussy and others, *Three Classics in the Aesthetics of Music*, New York, 1962)

H. Partch: *Genesis of a Music* (Madison, 1949)

*P. Schaeffer: *A la recherche d'une musique concrète* (Paris, 1952)

F. Winckel: *Phänomene des musikalischen Hörens* (Berlin, 1960; Eng. trans., 1967)

*J. Cage: *Silence* (Middletown, Conn., 1961, 2/1966)

*K. Stockhausen: *Tecte* (Cologne, 1963–71)

*P. Boulez: *Penser la musique d'aujourd'hui* (Paris, 1963; Eng. trans., 1971 as *Boulez on Music Today*)

——: *Relevés d'apprenti* (Paris, 1966; Eng. trans., 1968)

W. H. Mellers: *Caliban Reborn* (New York, 1967)

*P. Schaeffer: *Traité des objets musicaux* (Paris, 1966)

*L. B. Meyer: *Music, the Arts, and Ideas* (Chicago, 1967)

*H. Pleasants: *Serious Music and All That Jazz* (London, 1969)

*R. M. Schafer: *The New Soundscape* (Scarborough, Canada, 1969)

OTHER CIVILIZATIONS

J. Legge, trans.: 'Yo Kī or the Record of Music', *The Sacred Books of the East*, ed. F. M. Müller (Oxford, 1885), xxviii, 92

J. L. Masson and M. V. Patwardhan: *Aesthetic Rapture* (Poona, 1970)

MISCELLANEOUS

*M. P. G. de Chabanon: *Observations sur la musique et principalement sur la métaphysique de l'art* (Paris, 1779, 2/1785)

*S. Kierkegaard: *Enten-eller* (Copenhagen, 1843; Eng. trans., 1944)

*G. Dyson: *The Progress of Music* (London, 1932)

*A. Einstein: *Greatness in Music* (New York, 1941)

*H. Leichtentritt: *Music, History, and Ideas* (Cambridge, Mass., 1938)

*R. Sessions: *The Musical Experience of Composer, Performer, Listener* (Princeton, 1950)

*A. Copland: *Music and Imagination* (Cambridge, Mass., 1952)

*H. J. Moser: *Musikästhetik* (Berlin, 1953)

*K. Huber: *Musikästhetik* (Ettal, 1954)

*E. Ansermet: *Les fondements de la musique dans la conscience humaine* (Neuchâtel, 1961)

*C. Chavez: *Musical Thought* (Cambridge, Mass., 1961)

F. E. SPARSHOTT

Aetheria. *See* EGERIA.

Aevia [Aeuia]. A technical pseudo-word formed from the vowels of 'Alleluia' and used in medieval service books as an abbreviation in the same manner as EVOVAE. Steinmeyer has shown that the abbreviation of biblical words and phrases through the use of the vowels alone was not unusual even as early as the second half of the 11th century. *Aevia* and *Evovae*, however, are in a special category since both sprang from a musical rather than a purely scribal necessity, i.e. to show singers the exact underlay of syllables; *Aevia* appears to have been used less frequently than *Evovae*.

Unless little space was available, scribes preparing pages for musical notation generally preferred to write the word 'alleluia' in full. For simple settings, they might use one of the normal scribal abbreviations, such as 'allā'. However, of all the forms of abbreviation *Aevia* was the only one that could show with precision the correct underlay of the text in a florid musical setting.

BIBLIOGRAPHY

E. Steinmeyer: 'Beiträge zur Entstehungsgeschichte des Clm.18140', *Festschrift seiner kgl.Hoheit dem Prinzregenten Luitpold von Bayern zum 80.Geburtstage dargebracht* (Erlangen, 1901), 30

B. Bischoff: 'Paläographie', *Deutsche Philologie im Aufriss*, ed. W. Stammler, i (Berlin, 1952), 379–446

H. Walther: *Carmina medii aevi posterioris latina*, ii/2 (Göttingen, 1964), 325, ex.10943a

WILLIAM S. ROCKSTRO/MARY BERRY

Afanas'yev, Nikolay Yakovlevich (*b* Tobol'sk, 12 Jan 1821; *d* St Petersburg, 3 June 1898). Russian violinist and composer. He received his musical education from his father, the violinist Yakov Ivanovich Afanas'yev, an illegitimate son of the writer and poet Prince Ivan Dolgorukov. In 1836 he made his début as a violinist in Moscow, and two years later was appointed leader of the Bol'shoy Theatre Orchestra. He resigned in 1841 to become conductor of the serf orchestra maintained by the wealthy landowner I. D. Shepelyov at Vïksa, near St Petersburg. In 1846 he decided to pursue a career as a solo violinist and toured the major provincial cities of Russia, settling in St Petersburg in 1851. There he made occasional appearances as a soloist, and also led the orchestra of the Italian opera, sometimes deputizing for the regular conductor. In 1853 he became a piano teacher at the Smol'nïy Institute and relinquished his orchestral post. He visited western Europe in 1857, performing with some success in Germany, France, England, Switzerland and Italy.

On his return to Russia, Afanas'yev decided to devote himself to composition. He was a prolific composer, at his best in small-scale works; in these there is less evidence of the uneven quality of his technical skill, the result of his very informal musical education. His chamber music was well received: his string quartet *Volga* (*c*1860) was awarded a prize by the Russian Musical Society in 1861. His operas, however, met with little success: *Ammalet-bek* was performed at the Mariinsky Theatre in 1870, but has not been revived. *Sten'ka Razin* was rejected by the censor, and *Kuznets Vakula* ('Vakula the smith'), composed for the competition which was won by Tchaikovsky in rather suspicious circumstances (1875), was never performed. Other operas, as well as several orchestral works, remain in manuscript. Many of Afanas'yev's more attractive pieces reflect his interest in Russian folk music, making effective use of folksong and rhythms associated with folk dances. In 1866 he published a popular anthology of folksongs arranged for four-part choir. He drew on his experiences as a touring musician to present a fascinating survey of the musical life in mid-19th-century Russia in his memoirs (1890). In 1896 he was made an honorary member of the Russian Musical Society.

WORKS
(all unpublished, unless otherwise stated; MSS in USSR-Lk)

VOCAL

Ammalet-bek (opera, 4, A. F. Weltmann, after A. A. Bestushev-Marlinsky), St Petersburg, 23 Nov 1870
Kuznets Vakula [Vakula the smith] (opera, after Gogol), 1875
Taras Bul'ba (opera, after Gogol)
Sten'ka Razin (opera)
5 other operas
Pir Petra Velikovo [The feast of Peter the Great], cantata, 1860; choral music; songs, incl. a set of children's songs

INSTRUMENTAL

Orch: 6 syms.; 9 vn concs.; Vc Conc., C, *c*1840–50, ed. (Moscow, 1949); Adagio et rondo, D, vn, orch; Variations brillants, G, vn, orch, op.17; Nocturno, E, vn, orch; Ptichka [The little bird], E, vn, orch; Fantaisie et variations brillants, E, vn, orch, op.26; other concs.
Vn, pf: Sonata, a-A (St Petersburg, *c*1860); Fantaisie et variations sur des motifs russes, d, op.25; Morceaux de salon: Barcarolle, Nocturne, Romance sans paroles, Soirée d'automne, Rencontre, Elégie, Aveu, Tarantelle, Barcarolle; Variations brillants sur de thème tirolien, G; other pieces
Other chamber: Novosel'ye [Housewarming], double qt; Le souvenir, double qt; Str Sextet; 2 str qnts, incl. Italia, F; Souvenir d'Italie, F, pf qnt; 12 str qts, incl. Volga (Leipzig, 1866); Contredance, 2 vn, vc, db; trios; sonatas

FOLKSONG EDITIONS

64 *russkiye narodnïye pesni* [64 Russian folksongs] (St Petersburg, 1866)

WRITINGS

Rukovodstvo k obucheniyu v narodnïkh shkolakh peniyu [A guide to teaching in national singing schools] (St Petersburg, 1866)

BIBLIOGRAPHY
ME

A. Ulïbïshev: 'Russkiy skripach N. Ya. Afanas'yev', *Severnaya pchela* (9 Nov 1850)
Ts. Kyui [C. Cui]: 'Muzïkal'nïye zametki: Volga, kvartet g. Afanas'yev' [Afanas'yev's Volga quartet], *Sanktpeterburgskiye vedomosti* (19 Nov 1871)
N. Ya. Afanas'yev: 'Vospominaniya' [Reminiscences], *Istoricheskiy vestnik*, xli (1890), 23, 255
Obituary, *RMG* (1898), 659
A. G.: 'Skripichnïye p'yesï N. Afanas'yeva' [Afanas'yev's violin pieces], *SovM* (1950), no.8, p.101
I. M. Yampol'sky: *Russkoye skripichnoye iskusstvo: ocherki i materialï* [The art of the violin in Russia: essays and materials] (Moscow, 1951)
L. Ginzburg: *Istoriya violonchel'novo iskusstva* [The history of the art of the cello], ii (Moscow, 1957)
N. Shelkov: 'Nikolay Afanas'yev', *Muzïkal'naya zhizn'* (1962), no.10, p.17

JENNIFER SPENCER

Afat (*fl c*1440). ?Italian composer. He may have been active in Brescia where a Sanctus (now in *I-Bc* 2216) attributed to him was copied. This work, the only one said to have been composed by him, is for three voices, all of which have the complete text.

BIBLIOGRAPHY

F. A. Gallo: *Il codice musicale 2216 della Biblioteca universitaria di Bologna* (Bologna, 1970)

TOM R. WARD

Affections, doctrine of the (Ger. *Affektenlehre*). In its German form, a term first employed extensively by German musicologists, beginning with Kretzschmar, Goldschmidt and Schering, to describe in Baroque music an aesthetic concept originally derived from Greek and Latin doctrines of rhetoric and oratory. Just as, according to ancient writers such as Aristotle, Cicero and Quintilian, orators employed the rhetorical means to control and direct the emotions of their audiences, so, in the language of classical rhetoric manuals and also Baroque music treatises, must the speaker (i.e. the composer) move the 'affections' (i.e. emotions) of the listener. It was from this rhetorical terminology that music theorists, beginning in the late 16th century, but especially during the 17th and 18th centuries, borrowed the terminology along with many other analogies between rhetoric and music. The affections, then, were rationalized emotional states or passions. After 1600 composers generally sought to express in their vocal music such affections as were related to the texts, for example sadness, anger, hate, joy, love and jealousy. During the 17th and early 18th centuries this meant that most compositions (or, in the case of longer works, individual sections or movements) expressed only a single affection. Composers in general sought a rational unity that was imposed on all the elements of a work by its affection. No single 'doctrine' of the affections was, however, established by the theorists of the Baroque period. But beginning with Mersenne and Kircher in the mid-17th century, many theorists, among them Werckmeister, Printz, Mattheson, Marpurg, Scheibe and Quantz, gave over large parts of their treatises to categorizing and describing types of affection as well as the affective connotations of scales, dance movements, rhythms, instruments, forms and styles.

The so-called DOCTRINE OF MUSICAL FIGURES was closely related to the compositional craft required for the establishing of affections in Baroque music. *See also* RHETORIC AND MUSIC, §4.

GEORGE J. BUELOW

Affectueusement. *See* AFFETTUOSO.

Affekt. *See* AFFECTIONS, DOCTRINE OF THE.

Affektenlehre (Ger.). AFFECTIONS, DOCTRINE OF THE.

Affetto. *See* AFFECTIONS, DOCTRINE OF THE.

Affettuoso (It.; 'affectionate', 'loving'). A word used in musical scores to indicate an affectionate or affect-conscious style of performance, used as a qualification to tempo designations, as a tempo (and mood) designation in its own right, and as a mark of expression. Other related forms include *con affetto*, the noun *affetto*, the adverb *affettuosamente* (all three mentioned in Brossard's *Dictionaire* of 1703), *affetti* (Marini), the French cognate and equivalent *affectueusement* and the commonly encountered misspelling *affetuoso*. Brossard also mentioned the superlative forms *affettuoso affettuoso* and *affettuosissimo*, translating them *fort tendrement*.

As might be imagined, the various forms appear often in 17th-century discussions of music, and indeed of the other arts: Caccini (*Le nuove musiche*, 1601/2) mentioned *esclamazione affettuosa*; Frescobaldi (preface to *Toccate e partite*, 1615) stated that the runs should be taken *men velocemente et affettuoso*; F. Rognoni (1620) mentioned a violin bowing he called *lireggiare affettuoso*; and Monteverdi directed that the lament in his *Lamento della ninfa* (1638) should be performed in 'tempo dell'affetto del animo e non quello de la mano', which presumably implies a fluid and variable beat. But its actual appearances in musical sources are scarce before the 18th century: François Couperin (using *affecteuesement*) and Gottlieb Muffat were among the earliest in a series of composers who favoured it as a tempo and expression mark for their slow movements. The theorists were almost unanimous in placing it between *adagio* and *andante* as an independent tempo designation; and as a qualification it appeared most often with *largo*, *adagio* and *larghetto*. Perhaps the most famous use of *affettuoso* is in the second movement of

the Fifth Brandenburg Concerto: the formality and delicacy of that movement should be sufficient to explain why the word went out of fashion in the 19th century.

For bibliography *see* TEMPO AND EXPRESSION MARKS.

DAVID FALLOWS

Affilard, Michel l'. *See* L'AFFILARD, MICHEL.

Affinalis [confinalis] (Lat.). In medieval theory, the FINAL of a transposed mode. Commonly, *a* was the *affinalis* of the Dorian or Hypodorian mode transposed up a 5th and the Phrygian or Hypophrygian mode transposed up a 4th; *b* was the *affinalis* only of the Hypophrygian mode transposed up a 5th; and *c'* was the *affinalis* only of the Hypolydian mode transposed up a 5th.

Affonso, Alvaro. *See* AFONSO, ALVARO.

Affrettando (It.: 'hurrying', 'quickening'; gerund of *affrettare*). An instruction to increase the tempo, with the implication of increased nervous energy. The distinction between *affrettando* and *accelerando* or *stringendo* is largely academic but is suggested by Verdi's marking at the end of the 'Lux aeterna' in his Requiem over some woodwind arpeggiated semiquaver figuration, *dolciss. con calma senza affrettare* (in the manuscript, though the published score contains the incorrect reading *affretare*), 'very sweetly, calm and without any hurry'. The past participle *affrettato* ('hurried') is also found and indicates the arrival of a faster tempo, which then remains steady. Both forms occur primarily in Italian music of the later 19th and early 20th centuries.

See also TEMPO AND EXPRESSION MARKS.

DAVID FALLOWS

Afghanistan. Republic in Central Asia.

1. Ethnic and geographic distribution. 2. Social background. 3. Musical instruments. 4. The Pashtuns. 5. The Baluch. 6. The Herat oasis. 7. The Hazaras. 8. The Turkmens. 9. Uzbek and Tajik music of Turkestan. 10. Tajiks of Badakhshan. 11. Nuristanis and Pamir peoples. 12. Other minority groups.

1. ETHNIC AND GEOGRAPHIC DISTRIBUTION. Afghanistan is situated at the juncture of three major cultural areas: Central Asia, the Near East and India. Each has exercised pervading influence in Afghanistan at various points in history. In its ethnic origin, language and topography, Afghanistan is more clearly related to Central Asia and the Near East than to India. The present-day boundaries of Afghanistan (fixed *c*1895) enclose extensions of the Iranian Plateau to the west and south, the Turkestani steppe-desert to the north and the foothill boundary region of India to the east. All of these areas surround the great central massif of the 1100-km Hindu Kush–Koh-i-Baba–Paropamisus mountain chain, which links up with the Pamirs in the far north-east.

Afghanistan's peoples reflect this mixed background. The majority of the population is Iranian, grouped mainly into Pashtuns (or Pathans), some 50% of the total, who speak a western Iranian language, and Tajiks, perhaps 30% of the total, the term 'Tajik' being used for a great variety of Persian speakers of different origin and dialects. The Baluch of the south-west also speak an Iranian language, as do the Pamir, small groups of peoples who speak highly archaic Iranian tongues. The Hazaras of central Afghanistan, a large group, speak Persian. Their origin is not clear, but they have a markedly Turco-Mongol appearance.

After the Iranians, Turkic peoples are the next most important. This group includes mainly the Uzbeks and Turkmens (together perhaps 10% of the total), with small groups of Kazakhs and Kirghiz. Numerous small, isolated and distinctive populations abound in Afghanistan. Of these only the Nuristanis (formerly Kafirs) will be discussed; their languages belong to an extremely old branch of the Indo-Iranian family, and they have preserved a unique musical heritage from pre-Islamic times (i.e. before 1895).

Clearly it is difficult to generalize about such a varied land, save for the fact that nearly every Afghan professes the Islamic faith. The following discussion of general characteristics only provides guidelines, as specifics of the music culture vary considerably even from village to village.

2. SOCIAL BACKGROUND. In Afghan life there is a clear distinction of musical roles by sex. In most cases women do not play or even handle musical instruments except for the tambourine and the jew's harp (the latter is also played by children). Men, on the other hand, master a great variety of lutes and fiddles, and generally shun the women's instruments. Outside the small group of professional women singers (urban and radio), there is scarcely any public feminine performance; women sing primarily at domestic festivities such as weddings.

Traditionally, a negative attitude towards the performing arts has been fostered by religious and state authorities. This widespread bias against performance is not uniform in application and is now beginning to change, but it has left its mark on village and urban musical life. Individuals may hide their interest in music and dance to appear 'respectable', or local authorities may censor public performances. In its extreme form this leads to tight controls over music, while at the other end of the spectrum, particularly among nomads, there may be a considerable amount of unrestricted music-making. Criticism of dance is especially keen, as both male and female dancing is often associated with potential or actual moral laxity. Dancing-boys have long been a feature of Afghan entertainment.

Closely related to this complex of attitudes is the fact that music has a low social status. The position of any large body of musicians is, inescapably, the bottom of the social scale. This is particularly true of the barber-musicians, who form the main group of professionals in many districts and whose joint craft is hereditary. Gypsy musicians also belong to this group of lowly performers.

Music seems to a considerable extent to be linked to youth, and it is often deemed unseemly for older people (other than known professionals) to perform in public. Professionals are selected on the basis of talent rather than ambition: a teenage villager who displays talent will be encouraged by a critical audience to continue his efforts, and if his promise and personality augur well for a successful career, he will gradually take on the attributes of the professional musician. The bulk of musicians other than the hereditary performers mentioned above are produced through this process. Even the most successful virtuoso, though highly professional in skills, repertory and earning power, may cling to the title of *showqi* ('amateur'). In this way the non-hereditary performer dissociates himself from the lowly status of musician through class origin.

The term *showqi* connects music to a large complex of extra-musical attitudes and practices which reflect on the role of the performing arts. Basically the term implies an individual's predilection for a particularly absorbing hobby, which may include such diverse pastimes as gun-collecting, kite-flying or partridge-fighting. The unifying factor is the element of deep involvement in the chosen *showqi* pastime. While many such occupations do not have negative overtones, certain others such as gambling, drugs, music and dance evoke censorious reactions among observers if carried to excess. Individuals highly addicted to drugs or music may be called *diwana* ('mad'), or *majnun*, the name of the love-maddened hero of Near Eastern tales.

Despite this rather bleak picture of the musical life of Afghanistan, music nevertheless has a definite value for participants and spectators. Music is recognized as being able to create a good mood, and as being indispensable in the celebration of major occasions such as holidays, weddings and circumcisions. In the home, women and young people take advantage of such festivities to express themselves musically, while for adult males a trip to the local market town provides an opportunity for teahouse relaxation and entertainment by professional performers in some regions.

In general, the emergence of the radio since c1950 as a powerful disseminator of music has noticeably relaxed the traditional restrictions on music. Radio has created a gradual improvement of the musician's status, higher pay for his work if associated with the radio, and simply a much greater occurrence of music in any given place. Thus, while formerly a musician of purely local fame may have been slighted in his home area, now as a nationally famous singer he is sought after and well paid. Whereas in 1950 music was limited to a handful of professionals, occasional amateurs and poor-quality 78 rpm records of Indian popular music, the broadcasts of Radio Afghanistan in the 1970s reach even the farthest districts of the Hindu Kush. Unquestionably this has led to a homogenization of musical taste, since nomad shepherds and wealthy town dwellers listen to the same broadcasts, and to that extent radio has played an important role in the unification of national musical standards. At the same time, the introduction in 1972 of increased programming in local languages may serve to strengthen regional traditions as well.

To summarize, there are two kinds of musical attitudes and repertories in Afghanistan: the traditional structure, which tends to reflect purely local interest and keep music within recognized, acceptable boundaries; and the newer system propagated through the radio, which acknowledges music celebrities, international musical influence and a considerable amount of artistic freedom (in the western sense).

3. MUSICAL INSTRUMENTS. Even the most casual observer of Afghan music is struck by the great proliferation of lutes, both plucked and bowed (mainly long-necked), with a baffling variety of names, shapes, sizes and ethnic affiliations. These can be grouped geographically, according to whether they are found mainly in Afghanistan or are widespread in neighbouring countries as well; or ethnically, according to whether they are unique to one group or common to several.

Several types of lute are confined to Afghanistan. Among these are the *robab* (fig.1), a short-necked fretted lute said to be the forerunner of the Indian *sarod* and

1. Dhol (drum), tanbur and robab (lutes)

2. Dambura (lute)

3. Sarinda (fiddle)

played predominantly by Pashtuns; the *tanbur* (fig.1), a long-necked fretted lute with resonating (drone) strings beside the melodic strings (also predominantly Pashtun, though less so than the *robab*); and the *dambura* (fig.2) of the north, a long-necked, two-string fretless lute played largely by Uzbeks and Tajiks but adopted by numerous other ethnic groups (see ex.1).

Ex.1 Tajik *felak* tune for *dambura*, north-east region; rec. and transcr.

The types of lute most clearly linked to neighbouring countries include the Uzbek and Turkmen *dutar* (long-necked, two-string, fretted), the Pamir *robab* (six-string) and Kazakh *dömbra*, also played in Soviet Central Asia; the Herati *dutar*, also played in Iranian Khorasan; and the bowed Pashtun and Baluch *sarinda* (or *saroz*, fig.3), related to the North Indian *sarinda*.

The Nuristani (Kafir) *vaj* (fig.4), or *waji*, deserves special attention. This is an arched harp, apparently the only survivor in the region of an instrument with a wide distribution 2000 years ago, according to ancient carvings and paintings. The harp traditions nearest to Nuristan are those of South India and Burma to the east, the Transcaucasus to the west and the Ob River valley to the north-east.

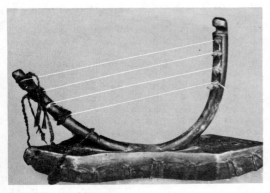

4. Vaj (harp) of Nuristan

Flutes occur in a wide variety of types. Long open end-blown flutes are played by the Turkmens (*tüidük*) and some Nuristanis, as well as by Pashtuns and Baluch (*nal, nai*). Flutes can be found among some Hazaras (Bamian area), in Kohistan (north of Kabul) and

Badakhshan (north-east). Single-reed pipes are represented only by the Turkmen *dili-tüidük*, whereas double-reed pipes of the general Near Eastern variety (*surnai*) are played by most of the major peoples. The only horn, the long *karnai* of the Uzbeks, seems to have died out recently.

Four basic types of drum are used. A large tambourine (*doira, daria, daf*) is widespread as a women's instrument, whereas the vase-shaped single-headed *zirbaghali* ('under the arm') is mainly played by men. Both are clearly of Near Eastern provenance. The two-headed *dhol* seems to be related chiefly to the Indian drum of the same name, and on the whole is limited to Pashtuns. The North Indian *tablā-bāyā* set of drums is rather restricted in use, except in radio music. Idiophones are principally represented by the popular metal jew's harp (Persian *chang*, Uzbek *changko'uz*) and, in the north, by the small finger cymbals used by singers to mark the beat (Persian *zang, tal*; Uzbek *tüsak*). A pair of stone castanets, *qairaq*, is rarely found today. Northern lutenists often use the *zang-i kaftar* ('dove bells'), a set of small metal crotals tied around the right hand, to accentuate rhythmic patterns.

There are also several widely used children's instruments, including zoomorphic whistles (*ushpulak*), ratchets (*ghergheranak*) and toy drums. The *ghergheranak* consists of a two-headed drum with attached beaters on strings, a type of instrument that is also used as a toy in the Far East.

4. THE PASHTUNS. The Pashtuns (Pathans in British literature) are divided into two fairly equal large groups, from the politico-geographic and dialectic points of view: those on the Afghan side, who mainly speak the 'soft' (Pashto) dialect; and those on the Pakistani side, whose dialect (Pakhto) is 'hard'. The cultural centre of the former group is generally considered to be the Afghan city of Kandahar; that of the latter, the Pakistani town of Peshawar. Within and overlapping these simplified categories are large tribal confederations, subdivided into sub-confederations, tribes, sub-tribes and clans reflecting shifting alliances and creating a highly complex set of affiliations.

Folklore and music are a principal unifying element of the diverse Pashtun groups. Epics and tales abound in the camps of nomadic Pashtuns. They may concern the distant, semi-legendary past, as in the widespread epic about Adam Khan and his beloved Durkhana, or may be concerned with recent historical events, as in the extensive body of stories about the Anglo-Afghan wars. One of the tests of the true Pashtun is his ability to learn and extemporize stories and verses commemorating the group's heroes.

The Pashtuns of Afghanistan accompany their song and dance with several instruments: the *dhol* and *surnai* (fig.5), which are essential to the many versions of the *attan* round-dance, male or female, the *sarinda* and the *robab*. Urban Pashtuns and those influenced by radio music also play the *tanbur* and the *armonia* (harmonium).

A basic folksong genre common to nearly all Pashtuns is the *landai*. It has best been defined by S. Shpoon as a 'non-rhymed two-lined catalectic verse with five anapestic paeon feet, two in the first line and three in the second, ending in *ma* or *na*'. As is the case with another brief poetic form, the Japanese *haiku*, the *landai* depends on the opening section to set a scene or a mood

5. Two dhols (drums) and surnai (oboes)

which is then consolidated, often with a 'punch line' in the concluding section. Here are two *landais* on common topics, love and war, transcribed and translated by Shpoon:

Orrai de yakh kavel keter kerr
Pe meni rraghle salaamat ghwarre guloona.

You spent all summer in cool Kabul;
You return in the fall and want your flower intact?

Ke pe maiwand ke shaaid ne shwe
Khudaaygo laalaya be nangi la de saatina.

Young love, if you do not fall in the battle of Maiwand,
By God, someone is saving you for a token of shame.

As these two texts demonstrate, most *landai* (Shpoon's estimate: 80%) are apparently composed by women, yet they are frequently sung by men, a musical phenomenon not encountered among other ethnic groups of Afghanistan. *Landais* are sung to a handful of stock melodies, which, unlike the texts themselves, may vary from one Pashto-speaking region to another. (A typical *landai* tune is shown in ex.2.) In a *landai* performance a group of the couplets, usually on a given topic, is strung together by the singer, whose skill may be judged by his artistic ability to select poems.

Ex.2 Pashtun *landai* tune, south-west region; rec. and transcr. M. Slobin

While the *landai* is performed throughout Afghanistan, other Pashtun songs are regional in distribution. Thus, for example, in the Laghman area east of Kabul a school of regional poets flourishes whose fame is almost entirely local. Urban Pashtuns, particularly those of Kabul, have long adopted Persian in addition to Pashto and have added the repertory of Persian poetry and songs to their own. This is apparent in the music of Radio Afghanistan. Although it is partly based on Pashtun folk poetry (e.g. the *landai*), it is primarily dedicated to Persian language and song forms, which however are to a great extent created and performed by Pashtun musicians.

Of all the ethnic groups of Afghanistan, Pashtuns are the people who have been most influenced by the musical culture of North India and Pakistan. Groups of amateur musicians in Kabul study Hindustani *ragas* and may even spend time in Pakistan studying with master musicians. The overwhelming majority of performers on Indian instruments (*tablā*, sitar, etc) in Afghanistan is Pashtun in origin, and many Pashtun singers have learnt the Urdu language and its neighbour, Hindi, so that they can learn the songs of Indian and Pakistani films.

5. THE BALUCH. The Baluch live in contiguous regions of Afghanistan, Pakistan and Iran, and there is also a small population in Soviet Turkmenia. In much of their territory they are closely associated with Pashtuns and have adopted some Pashtun folk customs. Baluchi song has been described most extensively by Dames (1907), who also cited three principal musical instruments: the open end-blown *nar* flute (akin to the Pashtun *nal*), the *saroz* fiddle and a four-string lute, the *dambiro*. Identification of the *dambiro* with present-day lutes in the area is difficult. The Baluch observed by Dames considered singing beneath their dignity and would hire a caste-like professional group of musicians called *doms* to perform songs composed by the Baluch. 19th-century travellers described a similar custom among some Pashtuns. The name and a description of the author was recited before a poem was sung. Even today Baluchi flute pieces are associated with certain stories. The chief forms were ballads, sung to the accompaniment of the *dambiro*, about the internecine Baluch wars of the 15th and 16th centuries; and short love songs (*dastangah*) played by the Baluch themselves on the flute. Among both Afghan and Iranian Baluch the flute can produce solo two-part music; the player holds a low fundamental hum while fingering a high-pitched tune. This technique can be found in parts of eastern Europe and Central

Asia. Vocal lines often begin tensely at a high pitch and gradually descend to middle range in parlando-rubato style.

6. THE HERAT OASIS. The oasis of Herat lies near the Iranian border in an area traditionally considered to be culturally part of eastern Iran (Khorasan). Herati customs and dialect are the closest of any region of Afghanistan to those of Iran. In music, links with Persia are also clear. The most important instrument, the *dutar*, is similar in construction to the neighbouring Khorasani *dutar*, though since the 1950s the number of strings on the Herati lute has increased from two to up to 15, including several sympathetic vibrating strings (like the Afghan *tanbur*). Herati singing style parallels that of Khorasan in its extended introductory passages in free rhythm with melismatic melody, followed by tunes of regular rhythm accompanied by a drum.

Herat was renowned for its musical culture under the Timurids in the 15th century. Particularly under the last ruler of the dynasty, Husain-i Baiqara (a contemporary of Lorenzo de' Medici), Herat enjoyed an extraordinary literary and musical flowering, guided by the great Persian poet and music theorist Jami and by the Turco-Persian author and statesman Mir Alisher Navai (*d* 1501).

7. THE HAZARAS. The Hazaras, who number perhaps 1,000,000, live mostly in the folds of the massive Koh-i-Baba and Hindu Kush ranges of central Afghanistan. Hazara music is predominantly vocal; the *dambura* lute is occasionally used as an accompanying instrument. The *chang* (jew's harp) is played only by women, as elsewhere in Afghanistan and Central Asia. Women, men and children have separate repertories which include various genres, but according to Sakata the Hazara recognize only two classes of songs as music: lullabies (female) and love songs (male). The latter may be termed *bait*, referring to the text, or simply *ishqi* (from *ishq*, 'love'), referring to the topic. Children's songs are named for associated sounds and movements. *Peshpuk* is a song in which children bounce up and down while squatting, chanting '*peshpuk*', and *kardugak* is a style in which children singing nursery rhymes hit their throats with their fingertips to produce a wide vibrato.

Hazara men's songs, like those of many areas of Afghanistan, consist of short quatrains, possibly related, strung together (*charbaiti* or simply *bait*). Song texts are basically syllabic, so that the melodic line tends to be shaped around words, following a combination of everyday speech stress and poetic metre. However, as the same melody is used for successive verses, the tune tends to predominate over the rhythm of the text. Sakata gave the following example of a Hazara quatrain as typical:

Ma qorban-a shawom ai duriala

Tanagak shishta-i zeri nihala
Tanagak shisht-i aena ba dastat

Sharara medehat chashma-e mastat

May I be sacrificed to you 'O Sublime Pearl'
You sit alone under a sapling
You sit with a mirror in your hand
Your eyes sparkle intoxicatingly.

Lullabies, on the other hand, are most often cast in octosyllabic couplets.

Hazara music is most often heard at domestic festivities; there is little public music because there are very few urban centres with teahouses. The main occasions for music-making are weddings, Afghan independence celebrations (*jeshen*) and major Muslim holidays. As in other parts of Afghanistan, knowledge of many songs and the ability to play a string instrument add greatly to a performer's reputation and to demands for his performances.

The western neighbours of the Hazara are several small groups of people often known collectively as the Char Aimaq ('four tribes'), the Firozkohi, Taimani, Jamshidi and Teimuri. Little is known about their music, but the scanty available sources show that their manner of voice production is similar to that of the Hazara; however, it is distinguished by the occasional use of a technique approaching yodelling.

8. THE TURKMENS. The Turkmens, who number perhaps a quarter- to a half-million, live mostly in a narrow strip of land extending some 50 miles south from the Soviet border. Though Turkmens have lived on Afghan soil for a long time the majority arrived between 1917 and 1940 from Soviet Turkmenia. They generally live in villages clustered about a local market town, and maintain their own culture.

The three main Turkmen instruments are the *tüidük*, a long end-blown flute related both to Near Eastern *nai* flutes and Central Asian flutes; the *dili-tüidük*, a small single-reed pipe; and the *dutar*, a lute similar in structure to the Uzbek *dutar* but considerably smaller. Unlike their compatriots in Turkmenia, Afghan Turkmens rarely play the *ghichak*, a spike fiddle related to the Persian *kamancha*.

Turkmens play music at festivities but also for general entertainment during long winter nights. The *buzkashi* matches, strenuous horsemanship contests that take place in winter, also provide occasions for music. Although many Turkmens are amateur musicians, outstanding performers are honoured by a title, *bakhshi*, which is then always affixed to their name (e.g. Akhmadbakhshi, a leading dutarist). The same word (of Chinese origin) means 'epic reciter' among Uzbeks and 'shaman' among Kirghiz, Kazakhs and some northern Afghans.

Dutar music is especially beloved by Turkmens. It may be based on well-known songs or may consist of instrumental improvisations. One of the common forms is based on a well-defined tonic (often the open-string pitches) to which the player returns after extensive departures from different levels above the tonic. Thus, a piece may have a section beginning a 5th above the tonic

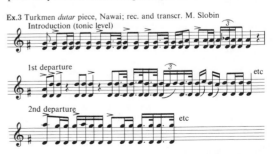

Ex.3 Turkmen *dutar* piece, Nawai; rec. and transcr. M. Slobin

returning to the tonic, then a section starting an octave above the tonic, etc (see ex.3). Considerable skill is then displayed in delaying the return to the tonic or embellishing important notes in the tonal structure. *Dutar* pieces may be in strict rhythm or may consist of a subtle blending of free-rhythm and legato passages.

Turkmen song is also highly distinctive. After a long instrumental introduction, the singer begins with an extremely intense, high-pitched passage in parlando-rubato, after which the melody gradually descends. The songs are strophic, and at the close of stanzas the singer may make use of a variety of uniquely Turkmen ornaments often based on short, repeated guttural tones. Songs are classified according to whether they are widespread and have texts by well-known poets (*khalqi*) or are the performer's own private compositions (*uzduridan*).

Afghan Turkmens have three basic dances: a male pastoral round-dance with shepherd's staffs, a solo female dance and a female round-dance. The latter two are performed only at weddings.

9. UZBEK AND TAJIK MUSIC OF TURKESTAN. Uzbek music can be treated in two categories: Afghan Uzbek folk style, which constitutes the majority of Uzbek music; and immigrant (Transoxanian) classical Bukharan style. The two are differentiated by their instruments, repertory and audience.

The Bukharan style is restricted to immigrant circles in principal towns (though it has recently begun to be broadcast over Radio Afghanistan) and relies on traditions brought from cities such as Samarkand and Bukhara (*see* UNION OF SOVIET SOCIALIST REPUBLICS, §XI). The main instrument used is the Uzbek *dutar*. In the Andkhoi area silk strings are still used for the *dutar*, a tradition largely abandoned in Uzbekistan. The town of Andkhoi is considered the centre of the classical style and still boasts the largest number of its exponents.

The Afghan Uzbek folk style, on the other hand, is strictly local in origin and does not occur in Uzbekistan. Whereas music in the classical style is largely performed in private homes, the Afghan Uzbek musical styles are mainly heard in public teahouses or at large parties. The principal instrument of this traditon is the *dambura*, an unfretted two-string lute most closely related to the *dombra* of southern Uzbekistan and to the *dambura* or *dumbrak* of Afghan Badakhshan and Soviet Tajikistan. Another instrument often played is the *ghichak*, a two-string spike fiddle with a tin-can resonator. It differs markedly from the Transoxanian *ghichak*, a relative of the Persian *kamancha*. The tin-can *ghichak* is widely used by mountain Tajiks and perhaps originated with them.

The standard Uzbek teahouse ensemble consists of two singers, seated cross-legged face to face with a *dambura* player between them. The singers mark time with a pair of small finger cymbals and alternately sing quatrains in which they compete in wit, often using members of the audience as targets for satire. This practice is reminiscent of the singing contests that are common throughout Central Asia and Mongolia.

The purely instrumental tunes of the Afghan Uzbeks are usually associated with dance. They consist of repeated strings of small melodic motifs, with very slight variations of rhythm, pitch and accentuation setting off the repetitions. The *dambura* player guides the dancer, the variations indicating different stances, gestures or tempo.

In the home women may play the tambourine and sing secular narratives (see ex.4). Often a single tale has two versions, told from the differing points of view of male and female. The topics may be old Near Eastern love stories (e.g. that of Yusuf and Zulaikha) or local themes based on historical occurrences (such as the tale of Baijura, a boy who died in a sudden flood and landslide while tending sheep south of Andkhoi). Afghan Uzbeks also have a large repertory of religious song, usually sung on major Muslim holidays such as Mohammed's birthday or the end of Ramadan.

Ex.4 *Zibājān*, Uzbek women's tale; rec. and transcr. M. Slobin

Zi-bā-jān ow-li sal-di pas pas qi—ni

Gul i — ki-bān ya e-kan bir das gi-na

Gul-i-dan is-kei-di-san te-kan-e-bār

La-bi-dan u-pai-di-sam chār-xā-le bār

The Tajiks of Turkestan are closely associated with the Uzbeks and have contributed much towards a joint musical culture, which contains elements from both ethnic groups. As already said, the *ghichak* fiddle is probably of Tajik origin, while the *dambura*, the most widespread instrument, is made mostly by Tajiks in the area near Samangan (south-eastern Turkestan) and seems to be a combination of Uzbek and Tajik lute types. The musicians of Tashqurghan (or Khulm), a town near the juncture of major Uzbek and Tajik populations, have been particularly important in the creation of a shared music culture. Tashqurghan has traditionally produced a large number of wandering minstrels who are bilingual in Uzbek and Persian (the language of the Tajiks) and who have composed and disseminated the bulk of the repertory common to modern Turkestan. Singers sometimes alternate quatrains in Uzbek and Persian or intersperse lines or even single words from one language into the other throughout their performance. There is an interesting instrumental form which also reflects this mixture of cultures: it consists of a string of tunes of diverse origin played on the *dambura*, sometimes with *ghichak*. The melodies are taken from four basic sources: Radio Afghanistan, Indian films, local Uzbek and local Tajik music, all of which may be combined in a single piece.

The creation of a distinctive Turkestani style has influenced the music of minority groups in the area. Teahouse music is often performed by Turkmens in towns such as Aqcha and Andkhoi, and northern Pashtuns can be heard playing Uzbek-Tajik pieces. Turkestani music and musical instruments have also spread to the Hazaras of central Afghanistan and as far southeast into Pashtun territory as Ghazni and Jalalabad.

10. TAJIKS OF BADAKHSHAN. Badakhshan lies at the juncture of the Hindu Kush and Pamir mountain ranges in a rugged, isolated region of Central Asia. The music and culture of the Tajiks in this area on both sides of the present Soviet-Afghan border is nearly identical. The distinctive mountain Tajik style has influenced the music of the Pamir peoples to the east and that of Turkestan

(through the intervening area of Kataghan) to the west.

The principal musical instruments of Badakhshan are the *dambura* (called *dumbrak* in Soviet territory), a lute which differs from its Turkestani counterpart mainly in having a neck and body in one piece rather than two, and the *tula*, a wooden flute which tapers towards the bottom finger-holes and is marked by incised bands. Apart from the *ghichak* fiddle described above, the other instruments are the ubiquitous *chang* (metal jew's harp) and the *daf* (tambourine), both primarily women's instruments.

The predominant genre of Badakhshani music is the *felak* ('firmament', 'fate'). *Felaks* can be solo songs, accompanied songs or solo instrumental pieces; the unifying factor is the basic style, which consists of free rhythm or a 2 + 2 + 3 metre, an extremely narrow range (often as little as four adjacent semitones), and extreme prolongation of the tonic, which often occurs at the end of the melodic line. In the vocal *felak*, the quality of the voice tends to be rasping and strained. There is little sub-regional variation of this general pattern, which is surprising in view of the extreme ruggedness and poor transport of the region. Stylistic traits are shared by performers from Keshm in the south-west, the Wakhan in the far east and Darwaz in the extreme north of Badakhshan. Ex.1 shows the basic sections of a typical solo *dambura felak*.

The Badakhshan-Tajikistan area has a particularly interesting repertory of masked dances and folk dramas. Dances often mimic animal activities and gestures, and dramas treat everyday domestic scenes in a satirical manner. The activities of local *maskharabaz* comedians closely parallel those of the Uzbek *qiziqchi* in various parts of Uzbekistan.

11. NURISTANIS AND PAMIR PEOPLES. In the north-east there are two distinctive groups of peoples living in mountain refuge areas and speaking extremely archaic languages. The small, isolated populations (numbering some hundreds) of Pamir peoples (Shughnis, Wakhis, Yidgha-Munjis, Sanglechi-Ishkashmis) speak languages related to ancient Persian. The Nuristanis speak several languages that date from the period before the Indic and Iranian groups split off from the Indo-European language family.

Pamir music has been influenced by that of the neighbouring mountain Tajiks of Badakhshan, but retains some unique characteristics, for example the remarkable *robab*, a heavy long-necked lute marked by wide spurs protruding from the belly and a thick leather lid attached with nails. This instrument is perhaps related to nearby Himalayan lutes such as the Nepalese *damyan*. The Pamir peoples live on both sides of the River Panj (the Afghan-Soviet border), and similar styles can be heard on both banks.

Nuristani music in the isolated mountain valleys south of Badakhshan (Waigal, Peich, etc) is remarkable both for its instruments and for its styles. In addition to the rare *vaj*, or *waji*, an arched harp with no nearby counterpart, Nuristanis also play a small leather-covered fiddle and a short end-blown flute. Stylistically, traditional (pre-Islamic, i.e. pre-1895) Nuristani music is in part based on a complex stratification of vocal and instrumental lines. A piece may begin with an ostinato figure on the harp underlying two soloists, who are later joined by a chorus holding an interval of a 2nd and, finally, by syncopated hand-clapping (ex.5). This use of

vocal polyphony is particularly interesting, as it is absent from the traditional music cultures of Afghanistan and Central Asia.

Ex.5 Nuristani song with harp, north-east region

Melodies constructed over an ostinato figure also occur in pieces for two solo flutes. Here the lower flute may maintain a repeated figure with some melodic and rhythmic variation, while the upper flute has its own motive which revolves mainly round only two notes with occasional reference to a third note. This results in a rhythmically complex stratification similar to that of the larger harp and chorus repertory. Such instrumental counterpoint, like the vocal polyphony, is not found anywhere else in Afghanistan or Central Asia.

12. OTHER MINORITY GROUPS. A small number of people in eastern Afghanistan speak Pushai, a North Indian language. From the small amount of available documentation, it appears that they often use various types of call-response and antiphonal singing. One of these types involves the overlapping of the last few syllables of a line by two singers as they alternate in solo song; in another, a chorus joins in for a refrain as the soloist ends his phrase. These singing styles are fairly

rare in Afghanistan, though further research is needed to clarify what might constitute a distinctive Pushai music culture.

Another small population with its own musical traditions is that of the Kazakhs, located in a few important cities (Mazar-i Sharif, Kunduz, Kabul, Herat). The Kazakhs are for the most part immigrants from Soviet Kazakhstan. To a considerable extent they have retained their traditional music, and this is true even of the generation born in Afghanistan. The only musical instrument they have kept is the *dömbra*, a two-string fretted lute, on which they play the programmatic pieces of their homeland. In most cases the story behind the piece has been forgotten.

BIBLIOGRAPHY

M. L. Dames: *Popular Poetry of the Baloches* (London, 1907)
V. M. Belyayev: *Afganskaya narodnaya muzïka* (Moscow, 1960)
H. L. Sakata: *Music of the Hazarajat* (diss., U. of Seattle, 1968)
S. Shpoon: 'Paxto Folklore and the Landey', *Afghanistan*, xx/4 (1968), 40
F. Hoerburger: *Volksmusik in Afghanistan nebst einem Exkurs über Qor'an Rezitation und Thora-Kantillation in Kabul* (Regensburg, 1969)
M. Slobin: 'Persian Folksong Texts from Afghan Badakhshan', *Iranian Studies*, iii (1970), 91
——: 'Rhythmic Aspects of the Tajik *maqam*', *EM*, xv (1971), 100
P. and M. Centlivres and M. Slobin: 'A Muslim Shaman of Afghan Turkestan', *Ethnology*, x (1971), 160
F. Hoerburger: 'Langhalslauten in Afghanistan', *Asian Music*, vi (1975), 28
M. Slobin: *Music in the Culture of Northern Afghanistan* (Tucson, Arizona, 1976)
Asian Music, viii/1 (1976) [Afghanistan issue]

MARK SLOBIN

Afochê. *See* CABACA.

Afonso [Affonso], **Alvaro** (*fl* 1435–45). Portuguese court musician. Afonso V (ruled 1438–81) sent him to England in 1439 to obtain the ceremonial in use at the court of Henry VI, to serve as a model for the Portuguese court. According to Vieira, this document, entitled *Forma siue ordinaçõ capelle illustrissimi e xtianissimi prinsipis Henrici sexti Regis Anglie et ffrancie ac dni hibernie, descripta Serenissimo Principi Alfonso Regi Portugalie Illustri, per humile servitore su[o], Wili' u Say, Decanû, capelle supradicta*, still existed in Évora Public Library in the late 19th century. It described various liturgical ceremonies, principally those for the coronation of the king and queen and for royal exequies. The plainsong for some antiphons and the Requiem were appended. Perhaps he is identifiable with the Alvaro who compiled an office dedicated to Afonso V for his victory over the Moors in North Africa in 1471. The MS, which still existed in the 18th century and was partly described by Barbosa Machado, was entitled *Vesperae, Matutinum, & Laudes cum antiphonis, & figuris musicis de inclyta, ac miraculosa victoria in Africa*. The musical portion was said to have been in plainsong. This identification, however, remains unproven.

BIBLIOGRAPHY

DBP, i, 2ff, 25f
D. Barbosa Machado: *Bibliotheca Lusitana* (Lisbon, 1741–59/*R*1965–7), iv, 10
S. Viterbo: *Subsidios para a historia da musica em Portugal* (Coimbra, 1932), 3ff

ALBERT T. LUPER

Afranio degli Albonesi. Italian 16th-century cleric who invented the PHAGOTUS.

Afrêm. *See* EPHREM SYRUS.

Africa. It is customary in the Western world for people to use the term 'African music' as if it were a single clearly identifiable phenomenon. Yet when one considers the size of the continent (the second largest in the world), the enormous differences in climate and terrain producing contrasting ways of life across the land mass, and, above all, its extreme multilingualism (more than 1000 different languages have been identified), one should not be surprised at the diversity of music and the difficulty of isolating distinctly African features common to the whole continent. Besides, the study of its music did not proceed everywhere with equal thoroughness, insight or purpose. Thus an overview of music in Africa can be no more than a selection of opinions mainly from African and Western published sources.

For fuller discussion *see* entries on individual countries.

1. History. 2. North Africa. 3. Sub-Saharan Africa. 4. Society and musical form. 5. Instruments. 6. Emotional and aesthetic content. 7. The 20th century.

1. HISTORY. African musicology began with the invention of the recording machine, which partly compensates for the absence of a written musical tradition (with the notable exception of the ancient notation of the Ethiopian church; *see* ETHIOPIAN RITE, MUSIC OF THE). Apart from a few sporadic recordings the first important collections of cylinders date from the first decade of the 20th century; an example is the collection made in 1905 by Pater F. Witte in Togo. But, in spite of the enormous development of recording since then, much of the music of Africa remains unknown, not only to outsiders but also to Africans themselves. One of the difficulties in assessing the phenomena of African music in Western terms arises from the impossibility of developing any depth of historical perspective. Beyond the range of living memories what has been discovered consists of no more than a musical instrument here or there, or a picture in which people or instruments are shown in a musical or social setting. For a view into the distant past one must turn to the prehistorian and the archaeologist. The prehistorian, dealing with a span of half a million years beginning with the rise of man as a toolmaker, possibly in east Africa, has nothing of interest to report to musicologists until the invention of the bow some 30,000 to 15,000 years ago. The bow was perhaps the first tool to make use of stored energy, but not necessarily for the sole purpose of shooting an arrow. There is evidence which suggests that the bow is just as likely to have been used for the production of sound (*see* MUSICAL BOW). Evidence of the existence of the shooting bow at this early date comes from north Africa.

The earliest known reference to African music from classical antiquity also concerns north Africa. Commenting on loud cries uttered in Hellenic sacred rites, Herodotus observed: 'the Libyan women are greatly given to such cries, and utter them sweetly' (Bates). Such informative references are unfortunately rare in ancient Greek literature. Contributions from archaeological studies in other areas have been less frustrating, and ancient Egypt especially has yielded a comparatively rich harvest. A rock engraving of a blind harpist found in a tomb at Saqqâra, dating from about the 18th century BC, is an example.

With the exploration of Africa, which began sporadically in the Middle Ages and expanded vigorously with the rise of Portuguese seamanship in the 15th century, came historical records. Travellers' reports, European and Arab, from both east and west coasts occasionally mention music, and show, for instance, that the uniquely African LAMELLAPHONE (known to ethnologists as *sansa*, to others as *mbira*, and to some Western writers as thumb piano or hand piano) existed in southern Africa in its fully developed form in 1586 (Kirby, 1934), and that by the time of Vasco da Gama's exploration of the southern tip of Africa the STOPPED FLUTE ENSEMBLE featured prominently in dances (Kirby, 1933). In 1620 Michael Praetorius pictured African instruments in his *Theatrum instrumentorum*. 16th- and 17th-century Nigerian bronze castings depicting instruments and musicians, and several bells and rattles in bronze and ivory, have also survived (see Dark and Hill, in Wachsmann, 1971).

If one wishes to speculate beyond prehistory, two factors could be taken into account: first, the homogeneity of culture during the Stone Ages in Africa; and, second, the slow development of culture, which gives an impression almost of immobility in time. This slow development characterizes especially the earliest phases: it made it possible for one technique – the manufacture of certain tools – to persist with hardly any change for 20,000 years. There is a strong temptation to speculate that what has been true of tools may also have been true of music, and it was this aspect of development together with a general tendency to explore evolutionary hypotheses that stimulated and justified collecting and research work during the late 19th century and the early 20th. This interest was furthermore fed by a growing interest in non-Western sounds. From the 1930s onwards, however, major contributions from African scholars have greatly changed the picture. At first these scholars were trained in Western musicology, getting their vocabulary, concepts and approaches from Europe and the USA, but with the establishment of training centres in Africa more distinctly African approaches could develop. The intense interest in archaeology and the recording of oral history in Africa support these developments.

2. NORTH AFRICA. The southern edge of the Sahara is generally regarded as the dividing line between north Africa and the rest of the continent ('Afrique blanche' versus 'Afrique noire' in traditional French terminology). Despite the diversity of the area, two elements are common to almost the whole of north Africa: most of its inhabitants speak Afro-Asiatic languages (in Greenberg's terminology), and Arab culture has had a profound impact there. Even Tiersot, one of the first French musicologists to take an interest in African music (one result of African participation in the World Exhibition in Paris, 1889), adopted the customary division between 'les Arabes' and 'les Nègres'. In predynastic times this region must have possessed a broad common heritage of culture that stretched from the Red Sea to the Atlantic.

Features like the stick dances can be quoted in support of a similar claim: at the time of the New Kingdom (1567–1085 BC) it was reported that the Libyan mercenaries practised war dances with gently curved percussion sticks, and similar sticks are used in the 20th century to the south-east of this region at the Nile-Congo watershed, among the Amba and Metu peoples. In the western part of this area music is characterized by the institution of the professional singer and poet. A typical disc (Rouget: 'Musique maure') illustrates the use of the Mauritanian *ardīn* (a 10- to 16-string harp), exclusively played by women; the use of the four-string plucked and bowed lutes; and the metallic buzzing of jingling devices suspended from the instrument, rattled by the woman as she drums with bare hands on the sound-skin of her harp. The disc also demonstrates a vocal vibrato produced by a male singer with extreme effort accompanied by an almost convulsive movement of head and throat.

Among the Tuareg (*see* TUAREG MUSIC) the *amzad* (monochord bowed fiddle), now almost extinct, was played by women of the aristocracy; Tuareg herdsmen still play the flute. In one recording a flautist illustrated the events of a cattle raid (UNESCO disc, AI.56.ii). Black inhabitants of the Sahara accompany their dancing with iron clappers. The Berber-speaking populations, for instance in Morocco, have melodies of an archaic pentatonic pattern and a type of rhythm that puzzled some scholars because of its resemblance to Chinese music (Schneider, 1960; *see* BERBER MUSIC).

North Africa has always been exposed to influences from the east and the north. Phoenicians, Romans, Vandals, Byzantines and Turks all made contact, but there is no evidence that their music left much trace. One can, however, gain at least an impression of the impact of Arab and Persian art. In its purest form it is found in the towns along the shore of the Mediterranean (*see* ARAB MUSIC; IRAN); an Arab proverb claims that 'Tunis invents; Oran gives the classic form; Algiers adds the final polish' (Wellesz). Béla Bartók (1920) saw the distinctive qualities of Arab folk music with the eyes of a sensitive Western musician. He described as the two main features of Arab folk music the use of percussion instruments as accompaniment to almost every tune and the tonal relationship – which differed from place to place, from singer to singer, and from instrument to instrument. He noted the complexity of the rhythm, identified different types of syncopation unknown in the eastern European folksong with which he was familiar, and drew attention to a form of multiple rhythm that, as he said, was caused by the simultaneous performance of two melodic phrases of equal length but with rhythmically divergent patterns. Regarding the manner of vocal performance he mentioned the gurgling, vibrating quality of song whose notes he transcribed as trills, but whose timbre, he said, could not be captured by notation. That Arab folk music had also been influenced by Arab art music is illustrated by his reference to the simplified folk forms of the *nawba* suite, which in its purer form consists of a series of alternating instrumental and vocal improvisations in contrasting moods and is based on rhythmic and melodic formulas. At first sight his description could apply to music in Africa generally, and there are frequent references in the literature to Arab elements in non-Arab music – in many cases without conclusive evidence.

The traveller James Bruce wrote in 1774 of 'the terrible, loud, and hoarse tone of these trumpets in Abyssinia; played on the march, or before the enemy appear in fight it had the effect upon the soldiers of transporting them absolutely to fury and madness' (Burney). It is also likely that the north African usage of trumpets and drums influenced the trumpet ensembles of black Africa proper, where they are mostly employed as regalia instruments. The monochord fiddle, already mentioned in connection with the Tuareg, also spread in the trail of Islam and even beyond its reach. In a recording from the Djerma of Niger the player imitates the sounds of a hunt on his instrument (A. Schaeffner:

'African Music from French Colonies'). In Uganda the fiddle is most popular, although introduced as late as 1907, and in spite of its nasal tone, which is alien to the instrumental sounds of this area.

Of the music of the Senegalese countries, placed between Mauritania and the Sahara in the north and the region of black music proper in the south, Rouget (1960) gave an informed summary under the heading, for want of a better term, 'Soudanese'. Here, too, as in Arab folk music, the forced voice production, the prevalence of the head register in both sexes and solo performance are noted, and stress is placed on the extreme rarity of polyphony and the paucity of instruments. The existence side by side of pentatonic scales and heptatonic scales with fairly consistent semitones is mentioned.

Summarizing the characteristics of the music of the Maghrib, Schaeffner (1946) observed that 'all oriental music, from the Maghreb (and even Spain) to India is based upon patterns of pure arabesque, apparently endless in spite of its internal interruptions'.

For a discussion of the Arab music cultures in the north part of the continent, see NORTH AFRICA.

3. SUB-SAHARAN AFRICA.

(i) General patterns. Schaeffner wrote that the music of 'Black Africa differs from that of the Maghreb by a tendency to repeat, by the rigidity of these repetitions, by the relative brevity of the phrases, by an apparent disinclination to use variations, and by the ease with which polyphonic constructions are brought about'. In the following paragraphs the term 'black' is used in this sense. Schaeffner also referred to the virtuosity of black rhythm, comparable in his view only to that of Arab, Hindu and Malay music, but unique in its 'earthiness' and its physical nature. As Bartók commented on the remarkable multiple rhythms of Arab folk music in north Africa, so Jones (1954) claimed as a cardinal principle in black music south of the Sahara that 'there is practically always a clash of rhythm'. Several theories on this subject have been put forward; Merriam's summary ('African Music', 1959, p.65) provides an excellent short cut to comparing them:

Ward notes one drum playing a basically unvarying beat; Hornbostel sees the organization in terms of motor behaviour, which is the opposite of the Western concept. Waterman postulates the concept of the metronome sense; and Jones makes the point of lack of coincidence of the main beats. While these specific details remain to be worked out, the consensus about the use of multiple meter is so strong as to remain unquestioned as the basis for African rhythm.

Ekwueme (pp.34f) applied Schenker's theories to the phenomenon of rhythm in African music. He demonstrated that form is merely rhythm in the long span, and that the rhythm of African music is built on three distinguishable structural levels. The background material is a skeleton of the structure which gives us the form of the music often reducable to the antiphonal 'call and response' or 'call and refrain' pattern; the middle-ground contains rhythm motifs such as the standard patterns and other delimiters on which the music is based, while decorative motifs such as are employed by the master drummer are merely foreground material which do not significantly affect the structure of the music.

Mental organization in the perception of rhythm was discussed particularly by Brandel. She felt that however complex the acoustic evidence the listener still had the choice of whether he wished to hear one dominant line or an intricate assemblage of opposing patterns. She quoted J. H. Nketia as saying that 'in theory all the drummers (and not only the master drummer) are supposed to hear all the parts simultaneously, but that in practice they probably hear only their own parts'. Bran-

del was here discussing both simultaneous (vertical) hemiola and hemiola in sequence: it is a feature that has attracted the attention of other scholars, including Nketia, and its importance is underlined by Nketia's remark that certain passages in Western music sounded African, particularly the music of Brahms, but that just when he thought the composer was going to make something of it he went and spoiled it (Merriam, 'Characteristics of African Music', 1959, p.19). Merriam furthermore found a uniquely African trait in the music's percussiveness. He stated that this was not a matter of rhythmic organization or feeling, and was presumably thinking of two acoustic characteristics found in much African music-making, namely the placing of the volume peak of a note at its beginning, and the subsequent rapid fading (found mainly in drumming and plucking). Non-percussive sounds would be those of bowed and wind instruments, provided the players made them in such a way that a comparatively gentle attack at the beginning of each note was followed by sustained sound that was manipulated even while the sound was fading – a technique employed, for instance, on Chinese zithers. Merriam suggested that in Africa vocal music too was percussive, but Herzog rightly pointed out that 'American Indian singing was even more percussive in attack than African'; in making this comparison one should remember that it has become increasingly obvious that the 'selection of what are dominant characteristics of a particular style of music depended largely on the background of the listener who did the selecting, and it usually involved comparison with other styles known to him' (Herzog and Nketia, in Merriam: 'Characteristics', 1959, p.19).

Whether the music is percussive or not, musicians show their preference and their skills when they play on the African lamellaphone. Its music draws attention just as much to tunefulness and melodic quality, especially noticeable in multiple-tune structures, as to percussion and rhythm. Jaap Kunst wisely recommended the more general term 'multipart music' rather than terms with more special meanings like 'harmony' and 'polyphony'. Jones (1959, p.217), supported mainly by experience in Zambia, looked upon harmony in Africa as evidence of a stage in the growth of harmony analogous to strict organum in which the parallel motion of the parts was still unaffected by considerations of form or tonality.

A casual survey of the literature might give the impression that African music is homogeneous in the extreme. Jones, for instance, wrote (1959, p.199): 'The music of the Western Sudanic-speaking Ewe people is one and the same music as that of the Bantu-speaking Lala tribe in North Rhodesia'. But some scholars are less intent on finding uniformity. That cultural differences exist in music is extremely likely if one recalls the culture areas and provinces that Herskovits (Bascom and Herskovits, 1959, p.37) and Baumann, Thurnwald and Westermann have described. Attempts at differentiation have been made with a measure of success (for example Rouget, 1960; Merriam, 1959). Two main divisions of sub-Saharan Africa are recommended: west Africa, and east and southern Africa; the music of the Khoisan-speaking and Pygmy peoples requires separate discussion.

(ii) West Africa. The region includes Liberia and the Guinea coast, a little north of the Equator, which it follows almost to the Nile. It includes the Republic of the Congo, reaches south into Angola and then extends east where on some cultural maps it touches the Indian Ocean. This area embraces the cultures of the primeval forest and of the matrilinear Bantu, which Baumann (Baumann, Thurnwald and Westermann, p.41) bracketed together under the name of 'westafrikanische Kultur', and its instruments include the slit-drum (mainly used as a signalling instrument), log xylophone, notched flute, nose flute and globular flute. Found in the same area, but belonging to a later stratum (Hornbostel's 'fifth cultural area'), is the gourd xylophone (Hornbostel, 1934).

Rouget (1960) subdivided the region into three music culture areas: first that of Guinean music proper, further to the west of the Gulf of Guinea from Liberia to the coastal regions of the Ivory Coast; second, that of the Bight of Benin; and third, the remaining area, which embraces the black region not only of southern Africa but of Nigeria, the Cameroons, Gabon, Zaïre and Angola. According to Rouget the first differs from the other two by the special place in its use of the interval of the 3rd in multipart music, both vocal and instrumental. Rouget also observed that, unexpectedly, the music of the Malagasy Republic is comparable in this. Of the second group Rouget wrote that where the song deals with sacred subjects it is largely homophonic and that the melodic construction is comparatively long and highly elaborate. In the third group he found that the general features of black music were clearly marked. As such he listed the 'natural' treatment of the voice, the tendency to use the low register, the spontaneous manner in which music is 'made', the mixed nature of the choirs, the predominantly pentatonic tonal structures, the skill in using large ensembles of instruments and voices resulting in differentiations of timbre and, of course, the frequent rendering of choral music in polyphonic textures. The first and second groups share the general features of black music with the third to a lesser extent, apart from those special features ascribed to them.

Rouget also mentioned a fourth group which briefly could be described as those musical cultures represented by isolated splinters to the north of his west African region. Across the breadth of Africa south of the Sahara there is an ethnographically fragmented borderland of considerable depth, a 'marginal region' (Herskovits) into which linguists place the 'Bantu line'. Its complex nature, which may be understood from a linguistic map, makes great demands on the musicologist's alertness and knowledge; one could say of its music what Herskovits said of its culture, namely that 'it manifests the characteristics of the neighbouring areas, which are present in diluted form, and none of these, even in new combinations, are sharp enough to yield distinct configurations'.

In a musical map by Jones (1959) the interval of the 3rd is shown to be limited mainly to the west African area. It occurs in a number of different forms, of which the most important are parallel 3rds and broken 3rds. An instrumental example may be heard in a recording made by Pepper from Gabon, in which the tuning process on a harp gradually moves from tuning to prelude and then to the song itself, and shows both techniques in the same performance. For Merriam ('African Music', 1959, p.79) the west coast is different from other areas because of its emphasis on percussion instruments and especially for its use of 'hot' rhythm (see Waterman).

(*iii*) *East and southern Africa*. The main musical feature of this area is the exalted social position awarded to the drum, particularly the east African variety of kettledrum. North of the Equator the sultans and kings use it extensively as symbol of their status and power; the farther north this practice is studied, the more likely it is that links will be found with Ethiopian and possibly Arab traditions. Yet, whatever their origins, the beliefs surrounding these drums may not all be derived from the Islamic influence of the Arabs. Jones (1959, p.217) found that the music of the drums in Africa does not differ in essentials, but it is generally agreed that it is less contrived in the east. In Uganda drum batteries often consist of four instruments, including one that to a Western ear sounds like a metronomic or regulative beat, but for a native listener is fully integrated into the texture of the music. In Buganda the clans tap out catch phrases on a drum that carry verbal meaning and proclaim the clan's identity.

It seems almost to be an axiom of the economy of musical devices in Africa, at least to the foreign observer, that the preference for an elaborate polyphony goes hand in hand with moderation in rhythmical variety, and vice versa. Thus it is not surprising that, in a region where rhythm plays a comparatively modest part, other excellent musical qualities should dominate. Schneider (1937) summed these up as the tendency to develop the choral texture more extensively, to bring out the rich potential variation of the interplay between leader and chorus, to show distinct tonality in the melodic structure and to evolve polyphonic form.

Blacking (1959) has suggested that the Venda use a definite 'harmonic' progression in duets on globular flutes. In Teso and Alur in Uganda it has been noted that the simultaneous performance of two different notes on an instrument occurs in a set sequence, which may be dictated as much by the physical pattern of the playing motion as by an experience of 'harmony'. It was found that this occurred among people who otherwise showed little inclination towards simultaneously performed notes. The texture of instrumental music in Buganda does not facilitate the experience of harmony arising from simultaneously sounded notes; on the harp, for instance, the strings are manipulated in such a way that, except for the octave, no interval is ever struck simultaneously: the notes of two complementary tunes interlock 'like the fingers of folded hands'. Wachsmann (1950, 1967) studied the tuning technique of xylophonists and harpists in Buganda; they apply a set procedure that reveals a tendency towards intervals of equal size, but the question of whether this is a temperament, a scale, or something else must still be left unanswered. Evidence of set tuning procedures that pay equal attention to consistency within restricted acoustic limits is rare, particularly evidence that would give an indication of the patterns in the minds of the musicians (see Tracey). The Lugbara of Uganda, for instance, seem to be less interested in well-defined intervals, although they name the five strings of the lyre using the different status terms of women. Kirby (1949) found in the musical bows of the South African Bantu and their neighbours that the harmonic technique of these instruments always followed three principles: 'The overtones are either performed simultaneously, or exploited singly in the construction of melody, or in conjunction with their fundamentals used to create a simple form of multipart music'.

Influences from external sources have often been

suspected. That contact in the 9th century existed with the Far East has been borne out by documents. Several centuries later Indian merchant princes are found to have set up trading settlements along the east coast of Africa. Regalia trumpets and drums preserved, for instance, by the Vumba at the extreme south-east corner of Kenya add to the evidence of the closeness of the contact with the Muscat Arabs. Earlier contacts with southern Arabia are assumed to have taken place by way of Ethiopia and, of course, the Arab slave trade has penetrated deeply into the interior. Indonesian contacts may well have survived in some musical phenomena, and not only in the form of xylophones, their tunings and playing techniques, but extreme caution is advisable here, especially in the dating of such contacts. For a description of similar problems in the Malagasy Republic see Sachs (1938).

(iv) *Khoisan and Pygmy areas.* East and southern Africa, as here defined, includes the Khoisan-speaking peoples, of whose music traces appear to have survived in other African cultures (*see* BUSHMAN MUSIC); but the relationship of these peoples with non-Khoisan peoples is by no means clear. Their music has to be considered separately, along with that of the Pygmies (*see* PYGMY MUSIC), although the Pgymies do not live in the east African region as termed above. Rouget and Grimaud showed the similarities between Pygmy and Khoisan music: both peoples yodel and use wordless vocal polyphony. However, Grimaud confessed that, as the investigation progressed, she became also aware of the differences between them. Rouget added that yodelling was also known elsewhere: e.g. among the Zezuru of Rhodesia, the Bayaka of Zaïre and the Niabua of the Ivory Coast. Grimaud listed the following features, in addition to the yodel, of this Pygmy–Khoisan polyphony: vocal timbre integrated with the character of the motif, so that different choral parts are distinguished by their timbre; the relatively wide range of the voice; the frequent development of the voice by disjunct intervals and pseudo-arpeggios, particularly among the Khoisan-speaking peoples; the use of imitation, augmentation, contraction and extension of intervals; repetition in echo and ornamental counterpoint; the use of tritonic, tetratonic and more often pentatonic patterns; and rhythmical counterpoint above an ostinato.

4. SOCIETY AND MUSICAL FORM. Many observers have been struck by the spontaneity, vitality and wealth of African music-making. These qualities are largely attributable to the closeness between the arts (music included) and the utilitarian in everyday life. The fusion of music with life may be seen more clearly in some situations than in others. At an African festival, for instance, burlesques, farces, skits, processions, dialogues and narrative forms are rendered on some topical theme during the general music-making. On such occasions the ordinary rules affecting slander are suspended and 'actors' exploit the situation in drawing attention to current irregularities in the society. All this goes on within the context of music; in Africa dramatic forms are musical. Certain aspects of African festivals are ritual in the sense that they are concerned with religion and magic and the rites of passage, and are restricted to a small inner circle of mediums, officiants and devotees. In these situations music serves as the line of communication with the spirit world from where forces come and possess the mediums. Through them the wishes of the spirit world are revealed, sometimes with clues to current problems and directions of procedure in the conduct of human affairs in the world of the living. Music here directly serves the ends for which religion exists. Festivals in Africa also provide occasions for presenting afresh to society the focal point of authority and social hierarchy. Chiefs, sub-chiefs, priests, high priests and mediums appear at some stage in full regalia, each group accompanied and identified by a frequently specific type of music or instruments.

Song texts draw both on political events, such as wars, the genealogies of rulers and the development of clan structures, and on topical events in living memory. The historical references are mostly highly allusive and the key to this understanding is jealously guarded by professional musicians. (Rouget, in Wachsmann, 1971, analysed in great depth the various levels of historical allusion in Dahomey song texts.) By far the largest part of the African musical repertory is text-based with poetic (song) structures lying at the core of musical forms: this applies even to much apparently purely instrumental music. Leaving aside the much vaunted skill of sending verbal messages by drum etc (see, for example, Carrington), some seemingly abstract multipart xylophone performance (for instance among the Lobi; see Strumpf) is, in fact, extensive dialogue, easily rendered in speech by the player if asked to do so. Since tone is important in so many African languages it follows that verbal pitch contours are likely to be important factors in the creation of melodies. Blacking (1967), Rycroft, Morris and others have concerned themselves with these relationships, some finding that the extent to which words control pitch varies considerably. It was one of the chief complaints against the missionary liturgies that they were insensitive to these values. This complaint became one of the starting-points for music research and composition by African musicians and students who wished to focus on the essence of their musical traditions.

Like music everywhere else in the world, African music depends on some kind of interaction or transaction between musicians as much as between hands and voice, or, in the case of the solo singer-instrumentalist, voice and instrument ('transaction' is perhaps the more suitable term; see J. Dewey and A. F. Bentley: *Knowing and the Known*, Boston, Mass., 1949). For musicologists the emphasis is on transaction between voices, the structural parts and other sounds: for social anthropologists the interaction in the music is postulated to be generated by, or be reflected, or at least be defined by social organization. Certain forms of polyrhythms expressed for Blacking (1973, p.30) 'concepts of individuality in community, and of social, temporal and spatial balance'. Even melodic counterpoint can be interpreted in the same way: thus in Bushman music (according to England, 1970):

The interchanging of melodic phrases is a common method of music making . . . and it is a principle . . . that epitomizes the Bushman way in general: it clearly reflects the Bushman desire to remain independent [of other voices] and at the same time he is contributing vitally to the community life [the musical complex].

It is not surprising that in a continent that is said to attach so much value to community, the interplay between individuals becomes re-enacted in the characteristic (and virtually ubiquitous) leader-chorus form. Schneider (1937) produced a survey of its musical dimensions which has not been bettered. Rycroft,

examining Nguni vocal polyphony, used circular notational models (see fig.1) which not only isolated clearly
the different divisions of basic patterns between soloist
and chorus but also demonstrated a cyclical type of
structure. In contrasting such structures, Wachsmann
(1956, p.8) asked: 'Is it too fantastic to suggest that the
songs of the Sebei [specifically those associated with
circumcision] are so dominated by short choral interjections because the tribe is so loosely organized, and that
the autocratic rule of the chiefs [in Buganda] is reflected in the large share which falls to the soloist in
their songs?'. Since the mid-20th century such ideas have
become fashionable, tending to become dominant theory
in the attempt to explain African musical structures: but
in the absence of a music history they must remain mere
conjectures.

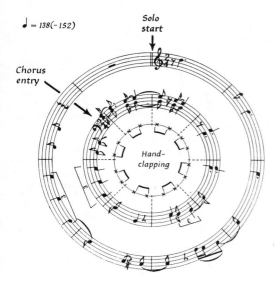

1. Circular notational model of a Xhosa wedding song
'Wo, luphelile, mntakabawo!' ('Alas! it has ended, O
child of our father') (Rycroft, 1967, p.99)

The repertory of transaction is further enriched by a
number of hocket-like structures; the simple hocket
(where each performer inserts his single note at
appropriate points) could be seen as the purest expression of transaction. But there are other hocket forms
which invite analogy with social hierarchy: Nketia's
survey of hocket (1962) includes an example of a trumpet
set which consists of a single high-pitched solo trumpet
sounding speech patterns as the leader, a group of trumpets performing in simple hocket and a second group
performing blocks of simultaneous sounds. Geographically trumpet hocket largely coincides with the distribution of kingship which, according to Oliver and Fage
(p.44), spread during the Meroitic or post-Meroitic
period from the upper Nile valley westwards across the
southern edge of the Sahara to the mouth of the Senegal,
eastwards to the Red Sea, and southwards down the
central highland spine of black Africa to Zimbabwe.
Hocket in various forms is exhibited in ensembles of
'reed flutes' (see STOPPED FLUTE ENSEMBLE) whose distribution to some extent overlaps that of trumpet ensembles, but is mostly concentrated along the line of the

Great Rift Valley from the Venda heartland in South
Africa to the highland region of Ethiopia.

If to the layman rhythm as heard in drumming is the
most important feature of African music, this view is
now regarded by African musicians as a Western overstatement. The drum itself is a melodic instrument just
as 'melodic' instruments are often played percussively;
an understanding of the close relationship between
speech and music is stressed now that there is a more
widespread knowledge of African languages. Leopold
Senghor and Klaus Wachsmann, however, have both
drawn attention to what has been labelled the 'double
phenomenon': much music seems to be conceived at two
levels or in two currents representing both a contrast
and a syndesis of the two disparate elements – speech-
borne melody and pure rhythm. Thus hand-clapping can
go along with singing – not simply a time marker but
also a contrasting timbre. There are many more complex examples: a 'quartet' of drums traditionally accompanied the 'sextet' of flutes playing vocally derived
melodies in the royal flute ensemble of the former kingdom of Buganda; similarly the playing of harps and
other chordophones is frequently accompanied by percussive rhythms beaten out on percussion troughs (in
the case of Padhola harp music) and on the body of the
harp itself (in the case of the *ardīn* of Mauritania).
Where the harpist sings and plays alone without assistance from other instruments or musicians, his singing
versus the harp pattern is a realization of such a 'double
phenomenon'. Leopold Senghor, the Senegalese states-
man-philosopher, attempted to explain this 'double
phenomenon' when discussing poetry, adding 'But its
essential rhythm is not that of speech but of the percussion instruments that accompany the human voice, or
rather those instruments that mark the basic rhythm.
We have here a kind of polyrhythm, a kind of counterpoint'. Such a 'counterpoint' (and contrast of timbres)
between what is essentially melody-borne speech-
rhythm on the one hand and pure rhythm on the other
was seen by Senghor not as two elements in conflict but
as 'a dynamic symbiosis of complementary parts', and he
added: 'it is in this that culture consists' – a comment
which further emphasizes the deep relationship between
musical structure and culture (see Reed and Wade,
pp.88ff).

At the beginning of the 20th century the interest in
scales and intervals dominated Western thinking and
not surprisingly continues in Western music teaching.
Africa posed many problems, and interval patterns may
well be accounted for by different principles: consonance, as for instance in musical bow music, according
to Kirby (1949), or distance, for example in the pen-
equidistant tunings of Wachsmann (1967). Regarding
the latter, the evidence shows that instrumental tunings
do not represent merely instrumental patterns but are
observed also by vocalists. Not every musical performance depends on perfectly tuned octaves, yet the
octave is frequent and musicians take pains in producing
it. Rouget's recordings from Dahomey have given a
clear insight into microtonal practices (1961). Gradual
pitch shifts occur in many African cultures, not because
of the incompetence of the singers but as an element of
style.

5. INSTRUMENTS. Many different types of instrument are
used in Africa, but what needs to be stressed above all is
the bond between instruments and language. Nketia

(1964, p.11) put it thus:

Because oral literature is based on the spoken word or sung word, it can also be conveyed through musical instruments capable of imitating speech: instruments such as bells or gongs, horns or trumpets and flutes. In some places such as north-west Ghana the xylophone may be used for a similar purpose.

Many instruments, such as the *masenqo* and *endingidi* fiddles of Ethiopia and Uganda respectively, appear even to imitate vocal timbre; others with similar timbres are used in alternation with the shouted eulogies of a praise singer, as in the case of the *algaita* (shawm) of the Hausa of northern Nigeria. The voice and the instrument frequently imitate each other, borrowing from and supplementing each other; thus in harp playing the singer-player may add rhythmic vocables during what is essentially an instrumental interlude (*see* HARPS, AFRICAN).

Little can be added to Hornbostel's magnificent pan-African instrument distribution survey of the 1930s, although parts of the map have been filled out in copious and meticulous detail by scholars such as Boone and Laurenty, who surveyed the musical instruments of what is now Zaïre, and others such as Kirby (1934) and Wachsmann (1953). Distribution maps pose many problems for Africanists, but also corroborate the theories of historians and ethnologists, illustrating migrations and acculturation processes and helping to identify the complex culture clusters of parts of Africa. Such surveys have yet to take into account statistics such as density of occurrence. For instance, it is misleading to say that panpipes and lyres are known in Uganda without adding the qualification that panpipes are limited to one family in one clan in one Soga village, whereas an informed guess of the number of bowl lyres in Buganda would be more than 100 and in Busoga the number must once have been considerably larger. The importance of statistics is illustrated, for instance, by Jaap Kunst's estimation that in Bali there was one gamelan for every 250 inhabitants – a clear measure of the importance of gamelan playing (*Music in Java*, 1973, p.244).

6. EMOTIONAL AND AESTHETIC CONTENT. A number of writers, mainly African, have provided clues to an understanding of this large but under-researched area. If the views that follow differ, they are not necessarily irreconcilable; rather they reflect the diversity of contexts and peoples of this vast continent.

J. H. Nketia, in discussing artistic values, found he could isolate concepts and their realization in sound by analysing the music by itself in terms of structure, instrumentation, singing style etc and discuss them with Western colleagues. But the more he talked to people in the West the more he became convinced that he and they did not always listen to the same things in African music, new or old (Nketia, 1966). He instanced the way a Westerner might listen to Akan two-part singing in parallel 3rds, suggesting that Western musicians would instinctively be interested in the vertical relationships, whereas Akan musicians would follow the horizontal flow of the two lines as if they were equals, giving scant regard for their intervallic relationship. Elsewhere, however, he has maintained that judgments about music in general will also apply to African music. He has also pointed to the importance of creative verbal ability in music-making: 'the musician is not only a performer of music but also a creator of words', a poet who links music and poetry by taking his cues from the intonation of words (1968, pp.143ff).

Zahan (p.58), reporting on the Bambara verbalized aesthetic, provided further evidence that 'the word' lies at the very centre of African aesthetics. The Bambara compare 'the word' to the crested (crowned) crane, a bird remarkable for its striking appearance, its double cry (the only creature known to the Bambara that inflects its voice) and its mating dance: the appearance, the cry and the dance make the crested crane the bird of the word ('la parole') because in Bambara thinking these three notions are co-relative. The appearance is 'a word' ('une parole') in the static sense, the dance (or the rhythm) is the unfolding of the word ('verbe'). Bambara tradition alludes in many different contexts to these three features of the crested crane. Thompson's study of aesthetic values among the Yoruba of Nigeria showed that the role of the word is not expressed solely in such symbolism as that of the Bambara. He found an extensive vocabulary which enabled Yoruba to converse about the arts and apply explicit canons of art criticism not only to sculpture but also to dance.

The east African writer Okot p'Bitek (who studied social anthropology at Oxford) in warning colleagues of the pitfalls of a new trend in Africa – the presentation of traditional dance and music in the theatre – stressed the social and psychological dimensions of music, which cannot be disregarded without destroying the music altogether (see Kakoma, Moore and p'Bitek). For him musical taste is a matter not only of what one hears but of what one believes: thus a funeral dance of the Acooli (Uganda), taken out of context and performed, for example, on stage, becomes an empty shell. A Westerner might not apply such an aesthetic judgment to Bach's *St Matthew Passion* performed in a 20th-century concert hall but, for p'Bitek, African music proper must be wedded to its proper social-psychological context. His poem *Song of Lawino: Let no-one uproot the pumpkin in the old homestead* (Nairobi, 1966) illustrates on almost every page how music and dance enshrine deep emotional and conceptual values in Acooli society.

De Ganay (p.239), reporting the words of a Sara musician (of the central Shari region, Chad), provided vivid evidence of the physical excitement of music and of the differing responses of listener and performer. The sound of a xylophone 'singing in several voices' excited a 'feeling of joy, of contentment, which most often is further enhanced by the pleasure of watching a virtuoso skilfully wielding his beaters'. In a cycle of excitement the listener's hair alternately rose on end and fell again, but when the pleasure was most intense contemplation ceased and 'he arises, for the desire to dance has become irresistible. The musician on the other hand, must not abandon himself to the contentment engendered by the music. . . . The pleasure which he experiences will only give more ardour and skill to his playing if he knows how to stay entirely master of his sensations, of his thoughts'; if not, 'distracted, he will go wrong, play badly or too loudly, sometimes even breaking his instrument'. The Sara musician is here acknowledging a physical dimension to aesthetics where body is not divorced from mind as is traditionally the case in Western aesthetic criticism. On the contrary, he recognizes that music reaches out to touch him and move him physically.

Early conditioning and child-rearing are considered to be of particular importance in musical education. The way African children are reared during their earliest days (up to two years, until they are weaned) predisposes them to tactile interpretation of sense impressions. This period is spent mostly on the mother's hips or back, feeling her muscular movements in everyday life and dance before seeing them, and feeling as well as hearing the vibrations of her voice in speech and song. With his hands, legs and face or ears in almost continuous touch with her skin, he makes his earliest sensory-motor adaptation. The use of physical contact with another person to feel the other's rhythm persists into adult life and is exploited in teaching situations where, for example, an Ashanti (Ghana) teacher of drumming may tap out appropriate rhythms on the bare shoulders of the apprentice. Senghor, in his essay on the psychology of the black African (1962), wrestled with musical problems in terms that embrace both aesthetics and physiology: he concluded that when music or other aesthetic creations are observed reaching out to the roots of one's body, this is not simply 'sensuality': 'Sensitory receptivity is really at work here'. African spirituality has its roots in sensuousness, in physiological response.

St Augustine (4th century), who was a native of north Africa, possibly of Berber extraction, was troubled by this sensuousness, recording in his *Confessions*, 'It is no good that the mind should be enervated by this bodily pleasure' and 'whenever it happens that I am more moved by the singing, than by the thing sung, I admit I have grievously sinned' (Sheed, pp.194f). He used the imagery of artistic mastery of song displayed before an exacting connoisseur-patron as a parable for the state of grace in which a Christian should praise his God. It contrasts with the thinking of Senghor and the Sara musician. Their views have, from the 1960s, found support in African universities, where the desire to Africanize the curriculum has crystallized into a demand that music be taught as a sensuous experience and not just as a rational technique. For Frantz Fanon, a black writer who although born in Martinique considered himself Algerian, these were side issues. Like other revolutionaries he argued (in the words of Keita Mamadi, head of the Guinean delegation to the Pan-African Festival of Culture held in Algiers, 1969) that culture should be 'an arm of economic and social liberation' (Pace) and that music should fulfil whatever role society demands of it.

The findings of several European scholars have in common the association of song-making with troubled minds. Wiegräbe found few 'happy' songs among the Ewe; Deborah Bertonoff stated 'in Ghana the source of dance is sorrow'; and Dampierre found similar evidence in Nzakara poetry. Gourlay, in his research into Karimojong music (Uganda), explained this recurrent theme (p.512): 'The "traumatic event" which unconsciously sparks off much individual composition and produces themes of deprivation and danger . . . leads *through performance* to a conscious association of music with happiness'.

7. THE 20TH CENTURY. Not all 20th-century Africans make and enjoy music in the traditional way: increasing numbers born, bred and living in urban centres possess not all the basic skills or concepts of their country. Their music and concepts are new, being often produced by external influences. Some of Africa's contacts with the outside world have been long and close. The possibility of oriental influence cannot be ruled out: certain links between African and Indonesian music have long been suspected by scholars, and along the east African coast the development of a new hybrid form of popular music known as Ta-Arab music demonstrates the blending of elements from African music and that of Arab settlers and traders. But in the 20th century the influences of the West have been paramount. It is noteworthy that even freedom movements have not rejected Western culture: most of the background music in the film *Vencermos* ('We will succeed') – which was provided by soldiers of the Mozambique Liberation Front – and the music of other political songs of central Africa are in a Western melodic idiom with European-derived harmony, or are even adaptations of Western popular songs.

The clearest and strongest external influences on African musicians are to be seen in the mid-20th-century pop music of southern and west Africa. In southern Africa what is often described as 'Afro-jazz' has dominated night clubs and other types of entertainment in various forms (*see* KWELA). From the Congo area the rumba and *kriki* dance genres show how heavy the Latin American influence has been (*see* CONGOLESE MUSIC). Both styles are widely enjoyed elsewhere in Africa, as is west African HIGHLIFE. Some of these genres are being absorbed into newly developing musico-dramatic forms. All these popular styles feature a blend of Western and African elements, deriving specific tone-colour from their use of Western instruments. The appeal of Afro-American, Caribbean and Latin American music which became accessible through gramophone records and later through sound film, radio and television can clearly be seen in the growth of this new music. Furthermore, the prevailing general acceptability of Western values, fostered by Western education, prepared African musicians to be receptive towards these influences, and the spread of a money economy and conditions of urbanization supported the trend.

The concept of cultured music is as difficult to apply in Africa as its connotations are arguable in the West. Concurrently with the growth of popular music, and probably preceding it, a genre of music developed that was created by those African musicians who had had formal training in techniques of Western art music: this too had become available in African urban centres. In Ghana, for instance, amateurs were taking part-time courses run on a private basis. As early as the 1920s many schools also offered musical instruction on an extra-curricular basis. Achimota School, built later that decade, had a music school with a hall and practising rooms and eventually developed a small symphony orchestra that played European classical music. In other countries, too, facilities have become available, although they are fewer in number. Music diplomas and degrees from Western academies and universities are no longer rare. Many of these composers are competent performers on Western instruments and capable vocalists, and their compositions have satisfied Western academic requirements. The aim of post-school training has been to compose in the Western styles initially and then to experiment with African melodies and rhythms; the product is, as in Western art music, addressed to 'listening' audiences. The careers of four prominent west African composers, Ephraim Amu and J. H. Nketia of Ghana, and Fela Sowande and Akin Euba of Nigeria, must suffice as examples.

Modern composers of Africa have applied their talents in more than one direction. The church has provided opportunities as well as inspiration: examples include the organ pieces of Fela Sowande, and Kyagambiddwa's creation of an Oratorio in the Luganda language and in a Ganda musical idiom for the Roman Catholic liturgy. The stage has provided another source of inspiration: in west Africa theatrical genres have been dominated by popular and amateur musicians, and in Nigeria the new Yoruba folk opera is popular. In Uganda Solomon Mbabi-Katana's efforts indicate that the serious 'trained' musician is determined to add this area to his domain.

During the 1960s composers gradually returned to African musical elements and the exploitation of African instrumental resources. Composers strive towards African-derived music, yet address themselves frequently to a listening audience rather than a dancing or otherwise visibly participating audience. The 'listening' audience, however, is itself one of many genuinely African traditions.

BIBLIOGRAPHY

GENERAL

BurneyH

J. Tiersot: *Musiques pittoresques* (Paris, 1889)
P. F. Witte: 'Lieder und Gesänge der Ehwe Neger', *Anthropos*, i (1906), 69, 194
O. Bates: *The Eastern Lybians* (London, 1914), 154f, fig.63
B. Bartók: 'Die Volksmusik der Araber von Biskra und Umgebung', *ZMw*, ii (1919–20), 489, 494
T. A. Dixon: 'The Regalia of the Wa-Vumba', *Man*, xxi (1921), 33
H. Baumann, R. Thurnwald and D. Westermann: *Völkerkunde von Afrika* (Essen, 1940), 41, 73
A. Schaeffner: 'La musique d'Afrique noire', *La musique dès origines à nos jours*, ed. N. Dufourq (Paris, 1946; rev. and enlarged 3/1959), 460
P. R. Kirby: 'Bantu', *MGG*
H. Tracey: *Chopi Musicians: their Music, Poetry and Instruments* (London, 1948)
S. Lagerkrantz: *Contributions to the Ethnography of Africa* (Lund, 1950)
G. Rouget: 'Musique maure', MH54–4 [disc notes]
J. Gray: 'The Wadebuli and the Wadiba', *Tanganyika Notes and Records*, xxvi (1954), 22
M. H. Alimen: *Préhistoire de l'Afrique* (Paris, 1955; Eng. trans., 1957), 442
J. H. Greenberg: *Studies in African Linguistic Classification* (New Haven, 1955)
A. Schaeffner: 'African Music from French Colonies', Columbia SL 205 [disc notes]
E. Wellesz, ed.: *The History of Music in Sound*, i: *Ancient and Oriental Music* (London, 1957), 37
G. S. P. Freeman-Grenville: 'Some Recent Archaeological Work on the Tanganyika Coast', *Man*, lviii (1958), 106
A. P. Merriam: 'African Music', *Continuity and Change in African Cultures*, ed. W. R. Bascom and M. J. Herskovits (Chicago, 1959), 65, 76
——: 'Characteristics of African Music', *JIFMC*, xi (1959), 13
J. H. Greenberg: 'Africa as a Linguistic Area', *Continuity and Change in African Cultures*, ed. W. R. Bascom and M. J. Herskovits (Chicago, 1959), 15
G. Rouget: 'La musique d'Afrique noire', *Histoire de la musique*, i, ed. Roland-Manuel (Paris, 1960), 215
M. Schneider: 'Nochmals Asiatische Parallelen zur Berbermusik', *Ethnologica*, new ser., ii (1960), 433
R. Oliver and J. D. Fage: *A Short History of Africa* (London, 1962), 44
J. H. Nketia: 'The Techniques of African Oral Literature', *Proceedings of the Ghana Academy*, ii (1964), 11
L. J. P. Gaskin: *A Select Bibliography of Music in Africa* (London, 1965)
A. P. Merriam: *African Music on L.P.: an Annotated Discography* (Evanston, Ill., 1970)
H. Pepper: 'Anthologie de la vie africaine', 320/C/128 3B [disc notes]
K. P. Wachsmann: 'Ethnomusicology in Africa', *The African Experience*, i, ed. J. N. Paden and E. W. Soja (Evanston, Ill., 1970), 128
K. P. Wachsmann, ed.: *Essays on Music and History in Africa* (Evanston, Ill., 1971) [incl. P. J. C. Dark and M. Hill: 'Musical Instruments on Benin Plaques', 65; G. Rouget: 'Court Songs and Traditional History in the Ancient Kingdoms of Porto-Novo and Abomey', 27]
J. Blacking: *How Musical is Man?* (Seattle and London, 1973)

K. P. Wachsmann: 'African Music', *Musica indigena: einheimische Musik und ihre mögliche Verwendung in Liturgie und Verkündigung: Musikethnologisches Symposion: Rom 1975*, 36
L. E. N. Ekwueme: 'Structural Levels of Rhythm and Form in African Music with Particular Reference to the West Coast', *African Music*, v/4 (1975–6), 27
S. Arom: 'Situation de la musique dans quelques pays d'Afrique centrale et occidentale', *AcM*, xlviii (1976), 2

ANALYTICAL STUDIES

M. Schneider: 'Über die Verbreitung afrikanischer Chorformen', *Zeitschrift für Ethnologie*, lxix (1937), 78
R. A. Waterman: ' "Hot Rhythm" in Negro Music', *JAMS*, i/1 (1948), 3
K. P. Wachsmann: 'An Equal-stepped Tuning in a Ganda Harp', *Nature*, clxv (1950), 40
A. M. Jones: 'African Rhythm', *Africa*, xxiv (1954), 27
K. P. Wachsmann: 'The Transplantation of Folk Music from One Social Environment to Another', *JIFMC*, vi (1954), 41
——: *Folk Musicians in Uganda*, Uganda Museum Occasional Paper, ii (Kampala, 1956), 8
J. Blacking: 'Problems of Pitch, Pattern and Harmony in the Ocarina Music of the Venda', *African Music*, ii/2 (1959), 15
R. Brandel: 'The African Hemiola Style', *EM*, iii (1959), 106
A. M. Jones: *Studies in African Music* (Oxford, 1959), 199, 217, 230
G. Rouget: 'Un chromatisme africain', *L'homme*, i/3 (1961), 32 [with disc, Musée de l'Homme ID 17/3]
J. H. Nketia: 'The Hocket Technique in African Music', *JIFMC*, xiv (1962), 44
J. Blacking: *Venda Children's Songs: a Study in Ethnomusicological Analysis* (Johannesburg, 1967), 193
N. M. England: 'Bushman Counterpoint', *JIFMC*, xix (1967), 59
D. Rycroft: 'Nguni Vocal Polyphony', *JIFMC*, xix (1967), 88
K. P. Wachsmann: 'Pen-equidistance and Accurate Pitch: a Problem from the Source of the Nile', *Festschrift für Walter Wiora* (Kassel, 1967), 583
Y. Grimaud and G. Rouget: 'Notes on the Music of the Bushmen compared to that of the Babinga Pygmies', Peabody Museum, Harvard, LD 9 [disc notes]

INSTRUMENTS

E. M. von Hornbostel: 'The Ethnology of African Sound Instruments', *Africa*, vi/2 (1933), 129, 284; vii/1 (1934), 277
P. R. Kirby: 'The Reed Flute Ensembles of South Africa', *Journal of the Royal Anthropological Institute*, lxiii (1933), 313
——: *The Musical Instruments of the Native Races of South Africa* (London, 1934/R1953), 47
C. Sachs: 'Les instruments de musique de Madagascar', *Travaux et mémoires de l'Institut d'ethnologie*, xxviii (1938), 70
J. F. Carrington: *Talking Drums of Africa* (London, 1949)
O. Boone: *Les tambours du Congo Belge et du Ruanda-Urundi* (Tervuren, 1951)
K. P. Wachsmann: 'The Sound Instruments', in M. Trowell and K. P. Wachsmann: *Tribal Crafts of Uganda* (London, 1953), 321, 407
J. S. Laurenty: *Les cordophones du Congo Belge et du Ruanda-Urundi* (Tervuren, 1960)
——: *Les sanza du Congo* (Tervuren, 1962)
M. Strumpf: *Ghanaian Xylophone Studies* (Legon, 1970), 10

EMOTIONAL, AESTHETIC AND TEXTUAL CONTENT

S. de Ganay: 'Le xylophone chez les Sara du Moyen Chari', *Journal de la Société des africanistes*, xii (1942), 239
F. J. Sheed, trans.: *The Confessions of St. Augustine* (London, 1944)
P. Wiegräbe: 'Ewelieder', *Afrika und Übersee*, xxxvii (1953), 99
D. Bertonoff: *Dance towards the Earth* (Tel Aviv, 1963)
E. de Dampierre, ed.: *Poètes nzakara* (Paris, 1963)
L. S. Senghor: 'Negritude: zur Psychologie des Negro Afrikaners', *Neue Rundschau*, lxxiv (1963), 539 [trans. of 'De la négritude: psychologie du Negro Africain', *Diogènes*, xxxvii (1962)]
D. Zahan: *La dialectique du verbe chez les Bambara* (Paris, 1963)
G. W. Kakoma, G. Moore and O. p'Bitek, eds.: *Conference on African Traditional Music: Kampala 1964*, 45
H. F. Morris: *The Heroic Recitations of the Bahima of Ankole* (London, 1964)
J. Reed and C. Wade, eds.: *Léopold Senghor: Prose and Poetry* (London, 1965)
J. H. Nketia: 'Artistic Values in African Music', *Composer*, xix (1966), 16
——: 'Discussant's Comments', to K. P. Wachsmann: 'Ethnomusicology in African Studies: the Next Twenty Years', *Expanding Horizons in African Studies: 20th Anniversary Conference: Evanston 1968*, 143
F. R. Thompson: 'Aesthetics in Traditional Africa', *Art News*, ix (1968), 44
E. Pace: 'Militant Africa turns back on Négritude', *The Times* (30 July 1969)

K. Gourlay: *Studies in Karimojong Musical Culture* (diss., U. of East Africa at Makerere, 1971), 512
KLAUS WACHSMANN, PETER COOKE

African Music Forum. A congress instituted in 1970 by the INTERNATIONAL MUSIC COUNCIL.

African Music Society. South African association founded in 1947 by Hugh Tracey and Winifred Hoernlé. Its principal objective is to encourage research in African folk and popular music, and to publish or assist in publishing original work on this and allied arts, such as drama and dance. It is affiliated to the INTERNATIONAL FOLK MUSIC COUNCIL.

The society places emphasis on the importance of recordings to document the range and character of African indigenous music, much of which is extremely localized due to barriers of distance and language, and through dependence on oral tradition. It also encourages the dissemination of musical styles through education and radio programmes.

In 1953 Tracey founded the International Library of African Music at Roodepoort, Transvaal, to provide a headquarters for the society and a centre for the collection of data for publication. Since then several thousand recordings have been issued: two series of L.P. discs, 'Sound of Africa' and 'Music of Africa', contain music from over 130 language groups in central and southern Africa.

The society published an annual newsletter from 1948 to 1953 which was replaced by an annual journal, *African Music* (1954–), containing articles by musicologists and experts in other fields of African culture, in English and, occasionally, French. Other publications of the society have been *Lalela Zulu* (1948), a collection of Zulu lyrics by Tracey; *The Icila Dance – Old Style* (1952) by A. M. Jones and L. Kombe; *African Dances of the Witwatersrand Gold Mines* (1952) by Tracey; and *African Music Codification and Textbook Project* (1969), by G. Kubik, Tracey and Andrew Tracey. The society arranges occasional lectures on aspects of African musical life and encourages displays of dancing and drama.

HUGH TRACEY

Afro-American music. See LATIN AMERICA, §III; UNITED STATES OF AMERICA, §II, 2(iii), 7; CANADA, §II, 4.

Afro-Cuban jazz. A jazz style that arose in the late 1940s, primarily in the work of the trumpeter and band-leader Dizzy Gillespie. Although a Latin American influence is discernible in jazz from its earliest beginnings and in the 1930s appeared openly in the work of Mario Bauza (trumpeter with Cab Calloway) and Juan Tizol (trombonist with Duke Ellington), Afro-Cuban jazz became a clearly defined style and acquired an international following only when Gillespie (who was at first influenced by Bauza) began to collaborate with the outstanding Cuban percussionist and composer Chano Pozo (Luciana Pozo y Gonzales) (1915–48) from 1946. The next year Gillespie with his big band recorded several notable examples – *Manteca*, *Algo bueno* (*Woody'n you*) and George Russell's *Cubano Be/Cubano Bop* – all of which featured Pozo's playing of the conga drum and combined Latin American rhythms with the bop idiom. Other examples have appeared in the work of Gillespie and many other jazz musicians, though not sufficiently to establish Afro-Cuban jazz as an independent genre.

See also SALSA.

GUNTHER SCHULLER

Afterpiece. An English opera or pantomime, usually about an hour long, designed for performance following a play or other theatrical work, in the 18th century; a notable example is Arne's *Thomas and Sally* (1760). *See* OPERA, §V, 1.

Afzelius, Arvid August (*b* Hornborga, Västergötland, 6 May 1785; *d* Enköping, 25 Sept 1871). Swedish pastor and folksong collector. After studying theology he took a clerical post in Stockholm from 1809 to 1820, and from 1820 was pastor in Enköping. In 1811 he became a member of the Götiska Förbundet and was deeply involved in the collecting of early folk tales, poems and melodies. He was an amateur flautist, but had little training in music; his friends helped him notate the melodies he heard.

Afzelius was the first to notate and publish the folksong *Näckens polska*, which he heard sung by a peasant girl in Småland in 1810, and to which he later wrote the poem *Djupt i havet*; the melody and text were printed in the journal *Iduna* in 1812. He collaborated with Erik Gustaf Geijer in the three-volume collection, *Svenska folkvisor* (1814–17), and supplied a number of melodies for Olof Åhlström's anthology, *Traditioner af swenska folk-dansar* (1814–15). He also edited a collection of folk poems for *Afsked af swenska folksharpan* (1848), whose melodies were arranged by Erik Drake, and wrote a memoir of Åhlström (1867).

BIBLIOGRAPHY
W. Samuelsson: 'Arvid August Afzelius och de svenska folkvisorna', *Läsning för svenska folket*, new ser., xxx (1919), 317
C.-A. Moberg: 'Från kämpevisa till locklåt', *STMf*, xxxiii (1951), 5–52
KATHLEEN DALE/AXEL HELMER

Agatea, Mario (*b* between 1623 and 1628; *d* Bologna, 1699, before 28 Jan). Italian singer, composer and instrument maker. He was an Augustinian monk who was employed from about 1649 as a soprano at the Este court at Modena. During much of the later part of his career, however, he was resident at Bologna. On 13 November 1660 he was appointed to the choir of S Petronio there, with a stipend of 50 lire a month; he was discharged on 24 April 1662 but rejoined on 25 July 1663. In October 1665 he returned to Modena, where he succeeded Marco Uccellini as choirmaster of the cathedral. He vacated this post in November 1673 and by early 1674 was again living at Bologna, where in 1685 he was made a member of the Accademia Filarmonica. A letter that he wrote to the Duke of Modena in 1689 from the monastery of S Biagio, Bologna, shows that he had not severed his connections with the Este court during his years in Bologna; in the letter he requested the duke to grant him a pension in view of his old age and failing eyesight. In 1692 he wrote twice more to the duke: on 13 January to say that he had become totally blind and on 13 May to say that he had been transferred, on his doctors' advice, from S Biagio to the monastery of S Maria della Misericordia outside Bologna. His death is recorded in the *Registro di bolletta della corte* of Modena for 28 January 1699, where his age is given as 'about 75', which would suggest that he was born about 1623–5; an inscription to an engraved portrait of him dating from 1676, however, gives his age as 48, which would point to a birth date of 1627 or 1628. During his lifetime he seems to have been better known as a singer than as a composer. He is described in the *Atti capitolari* (f.87) of Modena Cathedral as 'a soprano singer of uncommon excellence'; in 1666 (not 1664 as Roncaglia stated) Cazzati dedicated a motet to him, describing him as a 'renowned musician'. A letter to G. P. Colonna reveals that he was also a maker of keyboard instruments. Most of his few surviving vocal compositions are secular, though several are moral in tone. Roncaglia considered him a competent composer with a gift for melodic writing.

WORKS

Venite celeres, 1v, bc, 1670[1]
I pianti d'un core, canzonetta, 1v, bc, 1670[3]

Cantatas, 1v, bc: Calco appena il suol col piede; Chi non sa che sia tormento; Fido esempio d'amore; Frangi l'arco; Mentre l'ombra bambina; Poiche la vera fede; Vanti pur il dio Cupido: *I-MOe* Mus.F.1366 and Mus.G.2
Per baciar volto si vago, aria, 1v, bc, *MOe* Mus.G.250 [Amor fammi goder, aria with vc obbligato in this MS, wrongly attrib. Agatea; see Roncaglia]

WRITINGS

8 letters to the Duke of Modena, *MOs*
5 letters to G. P. Colonna, *Bc*

BIBLIOGRAPHY

EitnerQ; *SchmidlD*
I-Bc U/12
Decreta Congregationis, vi (MS, *I-Bsp*, 1650–73), ff.119v, 133, 147v, 149, 154
E. Colombani: *Catalogo della collezione d'autografi lasciata alla R. Accademia filarmonica di Bologna dall'accademico M. Masseangeli* (Bologna, 1896/R1969), 4
S. L. Astengo: *Musici agostiniani anteriori al sec. XIX* (Florence, 1929), 15ff
G. Roncaglia: *La cappella musicale del duomo di Modena* (Florence, 1957), 127ff
L. F. Tagliavini: 'Agatea, Mario', *DBI*

JOHN WHENHAM

Agazzari, Agostino (*b* Siena, 2 Dec 1578; *d* Siena, ?10 April 1640). Italian composer and organist. He was the author of an influential early treatise on thoroughbass.

1. LIFE. On the title-pages of his first two publications Agazzari is called a 'Sienese nobleman', but nothing further is known about his origins or early years. It has been doubted that Agazzari went to Germany and worked at the court of the Emperor Matthias; but this is related in an early and generally reliable source (Pitoni), and it is chronologically possible if Matthias were rather the future emperor at the time of Agazzari's stay. From March 1602 to October 1603 Agazzari was *maestro di cappella* of the German College in Rome, with its adjoining church of S Apollinare. Pitoni stated that Agazzari were 'introduced the manner of the concerto which he had learned in passing from Father Ludovico Viadana'. This could have been by personal acquaintance or through a study of Viadana's *Cento concerti ecclesiastici* (Venice, 1602). No other evidence connects Agazzari personally with Viadana.

In 1606 Agazzari was *maestro di cappella* of another Jesuit institution in Rome, the Roman Seminary. His pastoral opera *Eumelio* was performed there in the same year. He relates in the preface that he had been asked to set this play to music one month before carnival time; he therefore composed the music in two weeks, and it was also learnt and rehearsed in two weeks. From 1606 onwards Agazzari is named 'Armonico Intronato' in his publications: it appears that in that year he was made a member of the famous Accademia degli Intronati at

Siena (the added title 'Armonico' shows that he was being honoured as a musician). From the dedications in his publications it is apparent that he returned to Siena in 1607, and he remained there except for a visit to Venice in 1613. Payments to him as organist of the Siena Cathedral are recorded for 1613–14, and according to Pitoni he was *maestro di cappella* there until his death. His date of death as given by Fétis has not been substantiated; but certainly his last publication dates from 1640.

2. WORKS. As a church musician Agazzari had occasion to write mainly sacred compositions. The largest number of his works are motets, written at all stages of his career and for various numbers of voices. The majority are for two or three voices and continuo, but they range from solo motets to eight-part works, with continuo accompaniment. His other sacred works – masses, psalms, litanies – are also accompanied by continuo. This was a very modern feature, coming at the start of his career. As early as 1603 he published a volume of motets with a separate partbook called 'Bassus ad organum et Musica instrumenta'. In 1605 an earlier collection of 1602 was reprinted with a separate organ part. Although this organ part largely duplicates the lowest vocal part it is nevertheless a required part for a continuo instrument. Agazzari's madrigals, on the other hand, are for three, five or six voices without basso continuo. His first publications, in 1596 and 1600, were madrigals, and his other books of madrigals are not much later.

Eumelio, Agazzari's one theatrical work, was published with the sub-title '*dramma pastorale*'. It was intended, as he said in his preface, for the private entertainment of the students in the Roman Seminary; and it is of a suitable size and character. The text concerns the boy Eumelio who is enticed away from his simple pastoral life by the Vices, then rescued from the Underworld and returned to Arcadia by Apollo and Mercury. A Prologue sung by Poetry is followed by three short acts. The music is predominantly for solo voice and continuo, and it consists mainly of recitatives and strophic arias. But the choruses of Vices and shepherds are also important, especially at the ends of acts. *Eumelio* is closer to Cavalieri's *Rappresentatione di Anima, et di Corpo* (Rome, 1600) than to Peri's *Euridice* (Florence, 1600). Agazzari's choruses, like Cavalieri's, are prominent and varied in style, and the solo writing is also similar. Both *Eumelio* and *La rappresentatione* were written partly for moral purposes, and both were first performed in religious institutions.

Agazzari became best known for his treatise *Del sonare sopra 'l basso con tutti li stromenti e dell'uso loro nel conserto*, one of the earliest treatises on thoroughbass to be published. It was recommended in August 1607, even before it was published, by Adriano Banchieri in the preface to his *Ecclesiastiche sinfonie* (Venice, 1607), and was included in the three reprints (1608–13) of Agazzari's *Sacrarum cantionum . . . Liber II* (1607). A version of it was included in Banchieri's *Conclusioni nel suono dell'organo* (Bologna, 1609), and it was used extensively, with careful acknowledgment, by Michael Praetorius in his *Syntagma musicum*, iii (Wolfenbüttel, 1618, 2/1619). In his sixth chapter, on thoroughbass, Praetorius gave long quotations from Agazzari, occasionally in the original Italian, more often in German translation, and he also paraphrased Agazzari in some places and included his one example of a realized bass (Strunk in his translation realized two others).

In his treatise, Agazzari began by distinguishing between instruments 'like a foundation' and instruments 'like an ornament'. Included in the first group are organ, harpsichord, lute, theorbo and harp; in the second group lute, theorbo and harp again, bass lira, cittern, spinet, guitar, violin and pandora. While these two groups have different functions, the players in both must be able to improvise upon a bass. Indeed the players of instruments 'like an ornament' must have a knowledge of counterpoint so that they can 'compose new parts upon the bass, and new and varied passages and counterpoints'. Agazzari described musical styles suitable for individual instruments, and how to play in ensemble. He gave instructions for playing from an unfigured bass and explained why it was necessary in modern music to be able to play from a bass. His treatise is short, practical and very lively in style, and it accomplishes exactly what is promised in the title. It is not surprising that this excellent little treatise found immediate and continued success.

WORKS

DRAMATIC

Eumelio, dramma pastorale (3, T. de Cupis, Tirletti), Rome (Venice, 1606)

SACRED

Sacrarum cantionum, 5–8vv, liber primus (Rome, 1602)
Sacrae laudes, 4–8vv, bc (org), insts, liber secundus (Rome, 1603)
Sacrarum cantionum, 5–8vv, bc (org), liber tertius (Rome, 1603)
Sacrae cantiones, 2–3vv, bc (org), liber quartus (Rome, 1606, 2/1606); as Motetti, libro quarto (Milan, 1606)
Sacrarum cantionum, 2–5vv, bc (org), liber II, op.5 (Milan, 1607, 2/1608 with Del sonare sopra 'l basso con tutti li stromenti, 4/1613)
Cantiones, motectae vulgo appellatae, 4–8vv, insts (Frankfurt am Main, 1607); selections from 1602 and 1603 publications
Psalmi sex, 3–4vv, bc (org), op.12 (Venice, 1609)
Psalmi ac magnificat, 5vv, org, op.13 (Venice, 1611)
Sertum roseum ex plantis Hiericho, 1–4vv, bc (org), op.14 (Venice, 1611)
Psalmorum ac magnificat, 8vv, op.15 (Venice, 1611)
Dialogici concentus, 6–8vv, bc (org), op.16 (Venice, 1613)
Missae quattuor tam organis, 4–8vv, bc (org), op.17 (Venice, 1614)
Sacrae cantiones, 1–4 vv, bc (org), op.18 (Venice, 1615)
Stille soavi di celeste aurora, 3–5vv, bc, op.19 (Venice, 1620)
Eucaristicum melos, 1–5vv, bc (org), op.20 (Rome, 1625)
Litaniae beatissimae virginis, 4–8vv, bc (org), op.21 (Rome, 1639)
Musicum encomium, 2–5vv, bc (org) (Rome, 1640)

SECULAR

Il primo libro de madrigali, 6vv (Venice, 1596)
Il primo libro de madrigali, 5–8vv (Venice, 1600)
Il secondo libro de madrigali, 5vv (Venice, 1606)
Il primo libro de madrigaletti, 3vv (Venice, 1607)
Il secondo libro de madrigaletti, 3vv (Venice, 1607)

WRITINGS

Del sonare sopra 'l basso con tutti li stromenti e dell' uso loro nel conserto (Siena, 1607; 2/1608 in Sacrarum cantionum); repr. in Kinkeldey (1910), 216ff; facs. edns. (Milan, 1933; Bologna, 1969); Eng. trans. in Strunk (1950), 424ff
La musica ecclesiastica dove si contiene la vera diffinitione della musica come scienza, non piu veduta, e sua nobiltà (Siena, 1638)

BIBLIOGRAPHY

G. O. Pitoni: Notitia de contrapuntisti e de compositori di musica (MS, I-Rvat C.G., I/2, c1725), 732ff
A. W. Ambros: Geschichte der Musik, iv (Leipzig, 1878, rev. 3/1909 by H. Leichtentritt)
O. Kinkeldey: Orgel und Klavier in der Musik des 16. Jahrhunderts (Leipzig, 1910/R1968)
M. Schneider: Die Anfänge des Basso continuo und seiner Bezifferung (Leipzig, 1918/R1971)
F. Arnold: The Art of Accompaniment from a Thorough-bass (London, 1931/R1965)
A. Adrio: Die Anfänge des geistlichen Konzerts (Berlin, 1935)
——: 'Agazzari, Agostino', MGG
O. Strunk: Source Readings in Music History (New York, 1950/R)
N. Pirrotta: 'Agazzari, Agostino', ES
G. Barblan: 'Contributo a una biografia critica di Agostino Agazzari', CHM, ii (1957), 33–63
G. Rose: 'Agazzari and the Improvising Orchestra', JAMS, xviii (1965), 382
T. D. Culley: Jesuits and Music, i. A Study of the Musicians connected with the German College in Rome during the 17th Century and of their Activities in Northern Europe (Rome, 1970)
M. F. Johnson: 'Agazzari's Eumelio, a "dramma pastorale" ', MQ, lvii (1971), 491
——: Agostino Agazzari (1578–1640): the Motets for One to Four Voices (diss., Tulane U., 1972)

GLORIA ROSE

Agende (Ger.: 'liturgy', 'ritual'). In the German Protestant rites, the name for the entire ritual of the service. The term, derived from the Latin agenda ('to be done'), occurs as early as the second Synod of Carthage (390) and was later used for liturgical books setting out the ordering of the divine service. At the time of the Reformation it was replaced by the term rituale in the Roman rite, but it was retained in the Protestant Church as a synonym of Kirchenordnung, for example in the title Agenda, das ist Kyrchenordnung, wie sich die Pfarrer und Seelsorger in iren Ampten und Diensten halten sollen (1540).

See also LUTHER, MARTIN, §2.

Aggere, Antonius de (fl early 16th century). Flemish theorist. According to the explicit at the end of his treatise he was magister (i.e. teacher of Gregorian chant) at St Martin's, Ghent. The treatise, Formulae octo tonorum secundum Guidonem (Guido of Arezzo), is dated 8 November 1503 and is found in a composite manuscript (B-Gu 421), which also contains treatises by Guido of Arezzo, Jehan des Murs, Hugo von Reutlingen and Tinctoris. Aggere was probably also the author of the treatise immediately preceding, Ars intonandi secundum regulas ab institutoribus musicae traditas. Both treatises deal with Gregorian chant and performing practice based on practical experience. The first discusses psalm tone formulae and the second the intoning of chant by the cantor and the schola cantorum. (See R. Eitner, MMg, v, 1873, p.63.)

HEINRICH HÜSCHEN

Aggházy, Károly (b Pest, 30 Oct 1855; d Budapest, 8 Oct 1918). Hungarian composer and pianist. He studied at the National Conservatory in Pest (1867–70), at the Vienna Conservatory (1870–73) and at the Academy of Music in Budapest (1875–8), where he was a pupil of Liszt (piano) and Volkmann (composition). With A. Juhász and I. Lépessy, he won the Liszt Scholarship in two successive years, and at the final examination he made a great impression with his Andante and Scherzo for orchestra (op.1). He and Jenő Hubay established a reputation as a concert duo from the end of 1878 in Paris, which they consolidated the following summer in Austria and during the autumn on an extended tour through Hungary. Their first joint composition, Puszta-Klänge, for violin and piano (op.7), dates from that time. Between 1880 and 1881 they appeared many times in Paris, London (June–August 1880) and Brussels; concluding their concert tours in Algiers (May 1881), they returned to Hungary, where Aggházy became a professor of the piano at the National Conservatory while Hubay was appointed (February 1882) to the professorship vacated by Wieniawski in Brussels. This put an end to Aggházy's concert activities: thereafter he seldom appeared in public as a pianist, and then only as an accompanist or in chamber music. For a short time he edited a musical periodical, but he turned more and more to composition and teaching. From 1883 to 1889 he was a professor at the Stern and Kullak Conservatories in Berlin, and then returned to the National Conservatory in Budapest.

Agghàzy was not a prolific composer, but in the best of his piano music his attempts to unite a genuinely Hungarian idiom, under a French influence, with some stylistic features of the Baroque, represents a transition from Liszt to the new Hungarian music of the early 20th century, in so far as this was possible within the limits of Agghàzy's talent and the possibilities of the post-Romantic era. Of about 170 compositions, most of them short, more than 140 were published. He composed two operas, some incidental music, four orchestral works, a cantata, *Ràkóczi* (1905), 18 choral works, 34 songs, some chamber music (e.g. his String Quartet op.25) and more than 100 piano works, among them *Poèmes hongroises* (op.13), *Moments caractéristiques* (op.16), *Suite hongroise* (op.19, four hands), *Ländlerstimmungen* (op.22), *Trois pièces* (op.33), *Vier Klavierstücke* (op.41) and *Soirées hongroises* (i–iii).

DEZSŐ LEGÁNY

Agincourt, François d'. *See* DAGINCOUR, FRANÇOIS.

Agio, ad. *See* ADAGIO.

Agist, Dietmar de. *See* DIETMAR VON AIST.

Agitato (It.: 'agitated', 'restless'; past participle of *agitare*, to agitate, excite, urge forward). A tempo (and mood) designation found particularly as a qualification of *allegro* or *presto*: Verdi's *Otello* opens *allegro agitato*. It was little used before the 19th century, though Koch (*Musikalisches Lexikon*, 1802) gave it a substantial article, noting its use as an independent designation and as a qualification; he also drew attention to its occasionally being wrongly understood to denote an increase in tempo.

For bibliography *see* TEMPO AND EXPRESSION MARKS.

DAVID FALLOWS

Aglié, Count **Filippo** [Philippe] **d'** (*b* 1604; *d* Turin, 19 July 1667). Italian diplomat, courtier, poet, choreographer and composer. He began a brilliant political and artistic career in the service of Cardinal Maurizio of Savoy. About 1630 he entered the household of Duke Carlo Emanuele I of Savoy, on whose death in 1637 he became chief counsellor and favourite of the Duchess Cristina, accumulating honours and fortune. Except for an enforced sojourn in Paris from 1640 to 1644 his official duties kept him more at the Savoy court where he wrote or conceived more than 30 ballets, plays with music, water festivals and carousels to celebrate significant political alliances and Cristina's birthdays. His first work, *Bacco trionfante dell'India e caccia pastorale*, dates from 1624, his last, *La perla peregrina*, from 1660.

Variety, ingenuity and spectacle characterize all d'Aglié's works, which also include elegant and witty allusions to court personalities (*Il Gridelino*, 1652) or to specific tastes (*Il tabacco*, 1650) as well as using mythological themes to praise political achievements (*Hercole expugnator*, 1635). In greatly expanding the role of choreography, he seems to have been influenced by French practice and can thus be compared with ISAAC DE BENSERADE. He also provided more opportunities for musical development. In works such as

L'educatione d'Achille (1650) solos alternated with duets and massed choirs. While sustained solo vocal roles are rare, ensembles of instruments and voices were frequently used for melodramatic effects, and they were sometimes given interesting representational roles (as in the musical and choreographic dispute that accompanies the entry of King Tugine in *La perla peregrina*, 1660). D'Aglié composed some of the music himself; the music for four of his works is in *I-Tn* 9m.11.83–6.

BIBLIOGRAPHY
A. Solerti: 'Feste musicali alla corte di Savoia nella prima metà del secolo XVII', *RMI*, xi (1904), 675–724
G. Tani: 'Le comte d'Aglié et le ballet de cour en Italie', *Les fêtes de la Renaissance I: CNRS Abbaye de Royaumont 1955*, 227
M. Viale Ferrero: *Feste delle Madame reali di Savoia* (Turin, 1965)
M. M. McGowan: 'Les fêtes de cour en Savoie: l'oeuvre de Philippe d'Aglié', *Revue d'histoire du théâtre*, iii (1970), 183–241
MARGARET M. McGOWAN

Aglio, Bartolomeo dall'. *See* DALL'AGLIO, BARTOLOMEO.

Aglione, Alessandro (*fl* 1599–1621). Italian composer. He was a monk who is described on title-pages as 'of Spoltore, Abruzzo'. Apart from eight motets in *RISM* 1627[2] all his music is either lost or incomplete. Into the latter category fall *Canzonette spirituali* for three voices (Venice, 1599) and *Il quinto libro dei motetti a 1–4 voci con una messa e vespero* (Venice, 1621). His lost music is known to have included *Giardino di spirituali concenti a 2–4 voci con alcuni motetti a voce sola* op.4a (Venice, 1618).

Agnanino, Spirito. *See* ANAGUINO, SPIRITO.

Agneletti, Giovanni Battista (*fl* 1656–73). Italian composer. He is known only by a volume of sacred music for solo voice and continuo, *Sacri canti et hinni . . . parte de'quali con sinfonie ad libitum, et parte puonno servire interamente per sonate* (Venice, 1673), and by two arias for one voice and continuo in *RISM* 1656[4].

Agnelli, Lorenzo (*b* 25 March 1610; *d* 1674). Italian composer. The title-page of his *Salmi e Messa* (Venice, 1637), describes him as an Olivetan monk who worked in Bologna. This publication includes vesper psalms and a mass, all for four voices and organ continuo, and places Agnelli among the many north Italian composers of unambitious liturgical music at this period. Although he still used outdated *falsobordone* chanting in some psalm settings, others are interesting because of the structural devices aimed at unifying long pieces: one has a straightforward chaconne in the continuo part, another is based on a complex variation scheme in the bass in the manner of some of Monteverdi's later psalms. Melodious solos are offset by tuttis with imaginative harmonies. The mass is bound together by a recurring motif in the voice parts, an unusual formal device at this time, and has interesting and varied melodic lines with much syllabic writing. The volume also includes some motets, and Agnelli published his *Secondo libro di mottetti* in Venice in the following year.

BIBLIOGRAPHY
J. L. A. Roche: *North Italian Liturgical Music in the Early 17th Century* (diss., U. of Cambridge, 1968)
JEROME ROCHE

Agnelli [Agnello], **Salvatore** (*b* Palermo, 1817; *d* Marseilles, 1874). Italian composer. At the age of eight he entered the Palermo Conservatory and in 1830 that of Naples, where he studied until 1834 under Furno, Zingarelli and Donizetti. Donizetti supported his theatrical début in 1837 at the Teatro del Fondo with the *opera buffa I due pedanti*. Agnelli followed this first success with nine other comic operas, performed in Naples and Palermo between 1838 and 1842. In 1846 he moved to Marseilles, where he tried his hand at *opera seria* with *La jacquerie* (1849) and *Léonore de Médicis* (1855) and composed three ballets. He also produced some sacred music and a cantata in honour of Napoleon I, performed with three orchestras in the Jardin des Tuileries in 1856. In 1872 he visited Naples, hoping in vain to arrange a performance there of his opera *Cromwell*. Agnelli was an imitator of Donizetti and Mercadante without great distinction.

BIBLIOGRAPHY

FétisB
F. Florimo: 'Salvatore Agnelli', *Cenno storico sulla scuola musicale di Napoli*, ii (Naples, 1871), 2152 [incl. list of works in *I-Nc*]
R. Bonvicini: 'Agnelli, Salvatore', *DBI*

GIOVANNI CARLI BALLOLA

Agnes, Play of Saint. An anonymous Provençal saints' play, found in a single 14th-century manuscript (*I-Rvat* Chigi C.V.151); it contains some 20 sung passages.

For further information and bibliography see MEDIEVAL DRAMA, §III, 2 (ii), esp. Monaci (1880), Jeanroy (1931) and Hoepffner (1950).
JOHN STEVENS

Agnesi, Maria Teresa (*b* Milan, 17 Oct 1720; *d* Milan, 19 Jan 1795). Italian composer, harpsichordist, singer and librettist. As a girl she performed in her home while her older sister Maria Gaetana (later a distinguished mathematician) lectured and debated in Latin. De Brosses, who heard them on 16 July 1739 and was highly impressed, reported that Maria Teresa performed harpsichord pieces by Rameau and both sang and played compositions of her own invention. Her first theatrical work, *Il ristoro d'Arcadia*, was successfully presented in Milan's ducal theatre in 1747. At about this time she dedicated collections of her own arias and instrumental pieces to the rulers of Saxony and Austria; according to Simonetti the Empress Maria Theresia sang from a collection of arias that Agnesi had given her. She married Pier Antonio Pinottini on 13 June 1752 but had no children. Her next opera, *Ciro in Armenia*, produced at the ducal theatre in 1753, used her own libretto. In 1766 her *Insubria consolata* was performed in Milan to honour the engagement of Beatrice d'Este and the Archduke Ferdinand. Her portrait hangs in the theatre museum of La Scala; other portraits are reproduced in the encyclopedia *Storia di Milano* (vols. xii, xiv).

WORKS

Il ristoro d'Arcadia (cantata pastorale, G. Riviera), Milan, Teatro Ducale, 1747; ?identical to La gara del genio germanico col genio d'Italia, Milan, 20 May 1747
Ciro in Armenia (dramma serio, 3, Agnesi), Milan, Teatro Ducale, 26 Dec 1753; *I-Mc* (acts 2–3 only)
Sofonisba (dramma eroico, 3, G. F. Zanetti), Naples, 1765; *A-Wgm*, *Wn*
Insubria consolata (componimento drammatico, 2, ?Agnesi), Milan, Teatro Ducale, 1766
Nitocri (dramma serio, 3, A. Zeno), Venice, 1771
Ulisse in Campania (serenata, 2, ?Agnesi), *I-Nc*
Il re pastore (dramma serio, 3, Metastasio), *A-Wn*

12 arie, with insts, *D-Dlb*; Airs divers, 1v, harp, formerly *A-Wn*; 2 kbd concertos, *Wgm*, *B-Bc*; sonata, hpd, *D-KA*; 2 fantasie, 1 allegro, *B*
Numerous arias, lost; 2 kbd concertos, 2 kbd sonatas, cited in Breitkopf catalogues

BIBLIOGRAPHY

G. M. Mazzuchelli: *Gli scrittori d'Italia*, i (Brescia, 1753), 198f
C. de Brosses: *Lettres historiques et critiques sur l'Italie* (Paris, 1798–9; It. trans., 1957)
L. Anzoletti: *Maria Gaetana Agnesi* (Milan, 1900)
G. Seregni: 'La cultura Milanese nel settecento', *Storia di Milano*, xii (1959), 567–640
G. Barblan: 'Il teatro musicale in Milano: il settecento', *Storia di Milano*, xii (1959), 965–96
B. S. Brook, ed: *The Breitkopf Thematic Catalogues, 1762–87* (New York, 1966)
S. Simonetti: 'Agnesi', *MGG*

SVEN HANSELL

Agnus Dei. Acclamation of the Latin Mass, sung between the Fraction and the communion antiphon. Since the text does not change from day to day (except for the Mass for the Dead), the Agnus Dei is counted as part of the Ordinary of the Mass. Many chant settings were made between the 11th and 16th centuries; some of the most widely used were included in the *Liber usualis*.

Apart from the Credo, the Agnus Dei is the most recent of the acclamations of the Latin Mass, and in some respects the least firmly entrenched. It seems to have been added to the Mass as a *confractorium* (or chant to accompany the breaking of the bread) late in the 7th century, perhaps by Pope Sergius I. The text itself is from *John* i.29: 'Behold the Lamb of God; behold him who taketh away the sins of the world.'; but the specific association of the sacrificial lamb with Christ in the Eucharist and on the altar seems to be characteristic of Syrian practice of the early centuries. In any case, the direct address to the Son, found here as well as in 'Christe eleison' and in the christological portion of the Gloria in excelsis, contrasts with the Roman habit of addressing only God the Father in prayers of the Mass. Other rites, however (Ambrosian, Visigothic), had other *confractoria*.

As long as loaves of leavened bread were used, the breaking of it occupied an appreciable space of time, during which the petition, 'O Lamb of God, that takest away the sins of the world, have mercy upon us', was repeated an indefinite number of times (*Ordo romanus I/III*), presumably either antiphonally or with the people responding with the last phrase. With the substitution of small units of unleavened bread, the Fraction occupied only a moment, and the Agnus Dei, after a period of uncertain transition, took on other functions: it was most often associated either with the Kiss of Peace, or with the administration of Communion immediately following. During this same period (10th–12th centuries) the number of petitions gradually established itself at three, and 'dona nobis pacem' was substituted for the third 'miserere nobis', having the same number of syllables and pattern of accents.

The period of liturgical transition happens to coincide with that in which the medieval repertory of Agnus Dei chants, together with their tropes, came into being. Many questions regarding musical practice in this period have still to be settled on the basis of the early documents, especially the tropers. For example, while the latter usually indicate the dovetailing of tropes and Agnus Dei by the cue for 'miserere (nobis)' variously abbreviated, they often omit reference to one or more repetitions of Agnus Dei altogether. Common opinion, and perhaps common sense, ascribes this omission to mere abbreviation, and assumes that the 'standard' text of Agnus Dei remains intact, the tropes being added to it (but in ways not yet made clear). Given the instability of the Agnus Dei at that time, however, and given its open-ended litany-like nature earlier, it seems at least possible that the tropers faithfully preserve an actual practice, one in which one or more of the invocations 'Agnus dei, qui tollis peccata mundi', was actually replaced by a trope, only the 'miserere nobis' remaining as a response – a practice analogous to some Kyrie 'tropes'.

In any case, the picture presented by the MS sources for the Agnus Dei chants sometimes does not support the impression given by the *Liber usualis* of a carefully moulded threefold arch form with contrasting middle section. The second and third acclamations may vary in different sources, or be missing entirely, which (together with the hints in the tropers) suggests that a continuing ad libitum repetition might have been practised well into the later Middle Ages. It is true that the three-fold form is most often *ABA* (tabulation in Schildbach), but the form *AAA* is frequently found too, to which may be added variants such as *AA¹A*, in which the 'miserere nobis' often remains constant, pointing again to a litany response.

The most popular melodies are generally well represented in the repertory in the *Liber usualis* (but it must be studied only in conjunction with Schildbach's catalogue). Agnus Dei II, IX, XV, XVI and XVII best represent popular medieval practice from the 11th century on; III, IV and VI, while relatively early, are more characteristic of German than of French sources. As with the Kyrie and Gloria, the simple melody XVIII, usually presumed the earliest, has an unconvincing MS representation; but it may still reflect an early tradition, mainly because the same melody is found also in the Agnus Dei in the received chant for the Litany of the Saints (Stäblein). In any case, it has little to do with the more elaborate, antiphon-like melodies represented by Agnus Dei II. The high degree of moulding within the construction of any single acclamation in Agnus Dei IX or III seems indigenous to chant styles of the 11th century and after, when beautifully shaped phrases tended to prevail over other aspects of composition.

BIBLIOGRAPHY

J. A. Jungmann: *Missarum sollemnia* (Vienna, 1948, 5/1962; Eng. trans., 1951)

M. Schildbach: *Das einstimmige Agnus Dei und seine handschriftliche Überlieferung vom 10. bis zum 16. Jahrhundert* (diss., U. of Erlangen, 1967)

RICHARD L. CROCKER

Agobard of Lyons (*b* Spain, 769; *d* Lyons, 840). Frankish archbishop. He occupied the see of Lyons (816–35) and composed an *Epistola de correctione antiphonarii* which was influential within the chant tradition. *See* ANTIPHONER, §3(iii).

Agōgē (Gk.). In antiquity, a term variously signifying tempo or style, or the course of a melody; *see* ETHOS, §9, and LASUS OF HERMIONE.

Agogic. A qualification of EXPRESSION and particularly of ACCENTUATION and ACCENT. The qualification is concerned with variations of duration rather than of dynamic level.

ROBERT DONINGTON

Agōn (Gk.: 'contest'). In ancient Greece, a competitive public festival such as the Olympian or PYTHIAN GAMES, held at fixed intervals, or a contest within such a festival. The contests might be athletic, musical and dramatic; the more important festivals attracted their public from long distances. The term has been revived in its primary sense, 'contest', as the title of a ballet (1954–7) by Stravinsky.

GEOFFREY CHEW

Agosti, Guido (*b* Forlì, 11 Aug 1901). Italian pianist and composer. He studied the piano under Mugellini, Ivaldi and Busoni at the Bologna Conservatory, graduating in 1914, and composition privately with Benvenuti; at the University of Bologna he took a degree in literature. He made his début in 1908, but his adult career began in Italy and the USA in 1921, later extending to many other countries where he performed with some of the most distinguished conductors and instrumentalists, among them Vecsey, Pierre Fournier and the Budapest Quartet. His repertory is wide, but he is particularly renowned for his playing of Beethoven and Debussy and in his earlier days he was a noted interpreter of Skryabin. His playing style is based on a closely analytical approach to the musical text. Also of great importance has been his teaching at the conservatories of Venice (1933–40) and Rome (1941–5), the Accademia di S Cecilia, Rome, where he also taught chamber music, the Accademia Chigiana, Siena (from 1947), the Franz Liszt Hochschule, Weimar (from 1963), and at the Sibelius Academy, Helsinki (from 1970). He has composed music for voice and piano, and for piano solo, edited works by G. B. Martini, Beethoven and Chopin, and published a booklet *Osservazioni intorno alla tecnica pianistica* (Siena, 1943).

PIERO RATTALINO

Agostinho da Cruz. *See* CRUZ, AGOSTINHO DA.

Agostini, Agostino (*b* ?Ferrara; *d* Ferrara, 20 Sept 1569). Italian composer and singer; he was a relation (probably uncle) of Lodovico Agostini. He served as a singer at the ducal court of Ferrara between 1540 and 1545, and then as a beneficed priest and canon at Ferrara Cathedral. In 1563 Pendaglia described him as a priest, singer and practising doctor, and according to Scalabrini he was rector of S Salvatore, Ferrara. His known works comprise two four-voice madrigals published in Lodovico Agostini's *Musica . . . libro secondo de madrigali* (*RISM* 1572⁷), and two pieces to Latin texts, for six and seven voices respectively, in Lodovico's *Canones, et echo* (*RISM* 1572¹³).

BIBLIOGRAPHY

B. Pendaglia: *Quattro canti* (Ferrara, 1563), 30

G. A. Scalabrini: *Riassunto di spese di sacrestia del Duomo di Ferrara* (MS, *I-FEc*), 198

For further bibliography *see* AGOSTINI, LODOVICO.

Agostini, Lodovico (*b* Ferrara, 1534; *d* Ferrara, 20 Sept 1590). Italian composer and singer; he was a relation (probably nephew) of Agostino Agostini. He came from a family with strong musical traditions, and from an early age studied for a musical and religious career. He became a priest. The appearance of his first known piece in Barré's *Il terzo libro delle muse* (Rome, 1562⁷) suggests that he received his early training in Rome. According to Cavicchi (in *MGG*), he was associated from 1572 with the *cappella* of Ferrara Cathedral, where older members of his family had also worked; in 1578 his name first appeared in the payment records of the court of Duke Alfonso II d'Este at Ferrara, in whose service he remained until his death. During the 1580s he served as an informal composition tutor to Duke

Guglielmo Gonzaga. He was associated with many notable poets, among them Tasso and Guarini, and with members of the highest aristocracy. He pursued a distinguished religious career which culminated in his being created a Monsignore and an apostolic prothonotary. He composed no liturgical music, but his writings on religious subjects, *Sermoni alla Santissima . . . Communione* (Ferrara, 1589), were extremely popular and were reprinted many times up to 1701. He was buried in S Spirito, Ferrara.

The variety of styles in Agostini's writing exemplifies the rich musical life at the court of Alfonso II. The pieces in the early *Musica . . . sopra le rime bizarre*, dedicated to the poet, Andrea Calmo, are stylistically close to villottas; the texts abound in dialect jokes, puns and satirical parodies of well-known authors. A similar penchant for the startling, the amusing and the witty informs the *Enigmi musicali* and *L'echo, et enigmi musicali. Il nuovo echo* is full of chromatic curiosities, and contains brief instrumental passages; it is possible that some early collections of short instrumental pieces, such as those by Salamone Rossi, may have been intended as ritornello-like passages for insertion in vocal music. The third book of six-voice madrigals exploits the virtuoso singing style associated in its early stages with the *concerto di donne* ('Ladies of Ferrara'); the book may be the first complete publication to reflect the repertory of that ensemble. It contains madrigals dedicated to the singers Laura Peverara and Anna Guarini, and to Luzzaschi, as well as one piece 'sopra il lauro secco' and another praising virtuoso singing in general. His last publication, *Le lagrime del peccatore*, is a set of spiritual madrigals based on texts by Tansillo.

WORKS
(published in Venice, unless otherwise stated)

Musica . . . sopra le rime bizarre di M. Andrea Calmo, & altri autori, 4vv (Milan, 1567)
Musica . . . il primo libro de madrigali, 5vv (1570)
Enigmi musicali . . . il primo libro, 6vv, con dialoghi, 7, 8, 10vv (1571)
Musica . . . libro secondo de madrigali, 4vv (1572[7])
Canones, et echo, eiusdem dialogi, liber primus, 6vv (1572[13])
Canzoni alla napolitana . . . libro primo, 5vv (1574); ed. in MMI, 2nd ser., i (1963)
L'echo, et enigmi musicali . . . libro secondo, 6vv (1581[5])
Madrigali . . . libro terzo, 6vv (Ferrara, 1582)
Il nuovo echo . . . libro terzo, 5vv, op.10 (Ferrara, 1583)
Le lagrime del peccatore . . . libro quarto, 6vv, op.12 (1586)

3 madrigals, 4, 5vv, 1562[7], 1586[10], 1591[9]
4 madrigals, 5vv, *I-MOe* (c1580)

BIBLIOGRAPHY
B. Pendaglia: *Quattro canti* (Ferrara, 1563), 30
A. Superbi: *Apparato degli uomini illustri di Ferrara*, iii (Ferrara, 1620), 130
M. A. Guarini: *Compendio historico delle chiese di Ferrara* (Ferrara, 1621)
A. Libanori: *Ferrara d'oro imbrunito*, iii (Ferrara, 1674), 191, 312
F. Borsetti: *Historia almi Ferrariae gymnasii* (Ferrara, 1735)
G. A. Scalabrini: *Riassunto di spese di sacrestia del Duomo di Ferrara* (MS, *I-FEc*), 198
L. N. Cittadella: *Notizie relative a Ferrara* (Ferrara, 1864), 717
A. Bertolotti: *Musici alla corte dei Gonzaga in Mantova dal secolo XV al XVIII* (Milan, 1890/R1969), 61
T. Kroyer: *Die Anfänge der Chromatik im italienischen Madrigal des 16. Jahrhunderts* (Leipzig, 1902/R1968)
W. Weyler: 'Documenten betreffende de musiekkapel aan het hof van Ferrara', *Bulletin de l'Institut Historique Belge de Rome*, xx (1939), 81
A. Einstein: *The Italian Madrigal* (Princeton, 1949/R1971), 769, 855
W. Boetticher: *Orlando Lasso und seine Zeit* (Kassel, 1958), 59, 82, 88, 98, 164, 310, 409, 693
A. Cavicchi: 'Lettere di musicisti ferraresi: Lodovico Agostini (1534–1590)', *Ferrara viva*, iv (1962), 185
A. Cavicchi and R. Nielsen: Introduction to MMI, 2nd ser., i (1963), 7
A. Newcomb: *The musica secreta of Ferrara in the 1580's* (diss., Princeton U., 1970), 167, 213f, 221
A. Cavicchi: 'Agostini, Lodovico', *MGG*

IAIN FENLON

Agostini, Paolo (*b* Vallerano, nr. Viterbo, *c*1583; *d* Rome, 3 Oct 1629). Italian composer and organist. At the age of eight, at the choir school at S Luigi dei Francesi, Rome, he became a pupil of Nanino, whose daughter he later married. He completed his musical studies in 1607, and his first appointment was as organist and *maestro di cappella* of S Maria del Ruscello, Vallerano. He later returned to Rome to become organist at S Maria in Trastevere. He then worked simultaneously as vice-*maestro di cappella* there and as *maestro di cappella* of Ss Trinità dei Pellegrini. From 1619 he was vice-*maestro* of S Lorenzo in Damaso. On 17 February 1626 he succeeded Vincenzo Ugolini as *maestro di cappella* of the Cappella Giulia at St Peter's and held the position until his death.

Agostini's output consists entirely of church music. He was a highly skilled contrapuntist. The five books of masses published in 1627 are written in strict contrapuntal style. In his *Saggio fondamentale pratico di contrappunto* (ii, 1775, 295ff) Padre Martini printed, as a model of canonic writing, the Agnus Dei of the Hexachord Mass in the first book, which is constructed on three canons. The second Agnus Dei of the five-part *Missa 'Si bona suscepimus'* in the third book bears further witness to Agostini's outstanding mastery of the technique of strict canon; by the addition of a sixth part, which forms a canon with the bass, this section of the work can be sung in 14 different ways. The rhythmic structure of Agostini's motets is related to both the vocal polyphony of the late 16th century and the concerted style of the early 17th. Rich modulations, sonorities that are often rather restrained but at the same time very colourful, and a telling use of chromaticism are the characteristics of his style. The three-part *Salmi della madonna* is another notable collection, which includes, in addition to the psalms for the Marian Vespers, the five antiphons for the second Vespers and numerous motets. *Cantate Domino* is a typical Roman solo motet of the early decades of the 17th century; the melodic writing is reminiscent of the late 16th-century polyphonic style, but the embellishments, periodic and sequential organization of the melody, and contrasts effected by frequent change of metre are attributes of the new style. Agostini was one of the outstanding exponents of Roman polychoral music, and his works for four, six and eight choirs attracted great attention in Rome (see Liberati).

WORKS
Salmi della madonna, Magnificat, Ave maris stella, antifone, motetti, lib.1, 1–3vv, bc (Rome, 1619)
Liber secundus missarum, 4vv (n.p.), 1626)
Spartitura delle messe del primo libro, 4, 5vv (Rome, 1627)
Spartitura del secondo libro delle messe e motetti, 4vv (Rome, 1627)
Partitura del terzo libro della messa sine nomine, con 2 Resurrexit, 4vv (Rome, 1627)
Libro quatro delle messe in spartitura (Rome, 1627)
Spartitura della messa et motetto Benedicam Dominum ad canones, 4vv (Rome, 1627)
Partitura delle messe et motetti con 40 esempi di contrappunti, 4, 5vv (Rome, 1627)
Missarum liber posthumus (Rome, 1630)
Works in 1618[3], 1623[13], 1625[1], 1643[1]
Masses, motets, etc, *D-B, Mbs, MÜs, Rp, GB-T, I-Bsp, PAc, Rli*

BIBLIOGRAPHY
A. Liberati: *Lettera scritta . . . in risposta ad una del sig. Ovidio Persapegi* (Rome, 1685), 27
A. Cametti: 'La scuola dei "pueri cantus" di S Luigi dei Francesi in Roma e i suoi principali allievi (1591–1623)', *RMI*, xxii (1915), 595f, 618

S. Simonetti: 'Agostini, Paolo', *DBI*

KLAUS FISCHER

Agostini [Augustini], Pietro Simone [Piersimone] (*b* Forlì, *c*1635; *d* Parma, 1 Oct 1680). Italian composer. According to Giuseppe Pitoni in his manuscript *Notitia de contrapuntisti e de compositori di musica* (MS, *I-Rvat*, C. G., I/1-2, *c*1725), he led a swash-buckling and notorious life and had 'a natural inclination to impropriety and baseness'. As a young man he was expelled from his native city because of his involvement in a murder. He went to Ferrara, where he received his basic musical training from Mazzaferrata. Then he abruptly took up a military career and for serving in Crete in the war against the Turks was made a Knight of the Golden Spur. His earliest datable pieces are the new prologue and several arias and dances that he wrote for a performance of *Il Tolomeo* in Venice in 1658. In 1660 he competed unsuccessfully for the post of *maestro di cappella* at Urbino Cathedral.

Apparently by 1664 Agostini had arrived in Genoa. According to Pitoni he once attended a Vespers service there and was so harsh in his criticism of the music that he was invited to compose a service of his own for the same church, which he did with a success that added notably to his local reputation. In Genoa too he was commissioned to write at least two works for the Teatro Falcone (*Eliogabalo* and *La costanza di Rosmonda*, both 1670). It was probably because of his successes there that he was invited to compose operas for the Teatro Ducale in Milan, since the governor of Milan, Paolo Spinola Doria, was a member of important patrician families of Genoa. Not long afterwards, however, Agostini was banned from Genoa because of his involvement with a nun.

Agostini next went to Rome. His first patron there was Cardinal Flavio Chigi, for whom he composed a highly successful opera, *Gl'inganni innocenti* (first performed at the Villa Chigi, Ariccia, in 1673 and produced in Bologna and Milan). He also composed for the Oratorio del Ss Crocifisso. Through the patronage of Cardinal Giovanni Battista Pamphili he obtained the prestigious post of director of music at S Agnese in the Piazza Navona. Among the young musicians who studied with him in Rome was Giovanni Lorenzo Lulier. In 1675, complaining of ill-health and blaming it on the bad air in Rome, he began to seek employment elsewhere; furthermore, from 1676, when Innocent XI became pope, the future for opera composers in Rome became much less promising. In 1679 he accepted an invitation to become *maestro di cappella* at the court of Ranuccio Farnese II, Duke of Parma, but shortly after arriving there he died suddenly.

Most of Agostini's dramatic works are known to us only through their librettos. His few surviving sacred works are conservative and lacking in flair. His most inspired music occurs in his secular cantatas, most of which he wrote probably during his late years in Rome. With good reason Tosi (*Opinioni de' cantori*, Bologna, 1723/R; Eng. trans., 1742, 2/1743/R1969) mentioned him alongside Stradella as a particular master of the cantata during its early maturity. The two composers were closely linked in the minds of their contemporaries: they had similarly adventurous careers, worked in several of the same cities and enjoyed the patronage of the same families, and not surprisingly three large man-uscripts (in *I-Bc*, *I-Nc* and *A-Wn*) are important sources

of cantatas by both of them.

WORKS

(all lost unless otherwise stated)

Il Tolomeo, Venice, 1658
La regina Floridea (opera), Milan, Ducale, ?1669, collab. Rossi and Busca; perf. 1688 as Floridea, Venice, SS Apostoli, 1688
Ippolita, reina delle Amazoni (opera, C. M. Maggi), Milan, Ducale, 1670, collab. Busca and P. A. Ziani, *I-Nc*
Eliogabalo (musical drama, A. Aureli), Genoa, Falcone, 28 Jan 1670
La costanza di Rosmonda (melodramma, Aureli), Genoa, Falcone, 1670 (see Giazotto)
Gl'inganni innocenti, ovvero L'Adalinda (favola drammatica, G. F. Apolloni), Ariccia [nr. Rome], for the Accademici Sfaccendati, 1673; rev. Bologna, 1675; rev. with new arias, Milan, Ducale, 1679; *I-MOe*
Il ratto delle Sabine (dramma, G. F. Bussani), Venice, S. Giovanni Grisostomo, Dec 1680, *Bc*, *Vnm*
Il 1° e il 2° miracolo di S Antonio, oratorio, 4 solo vv, chorus, insts, Modena, 1687, *MOe*
*c*30 secular cantatas in *A-Wn*, *B-Bc*, *D-Dlb*, *Kl*, *Mbs*, *MÜs*, *F-Pc*, *GB-Cfm*, *Lbm*, *Lgc*, *Och*, *I-Bc*, *Fc*, Baron Krauss Collection, Fiesole, *Mc*, *MOe*, *Nc*, *Rc*, *Rn*, *Rvat*; full listing in WECIS, x (1976)

Sacred works in *A-Wn*, *D-Bds*, *I-Af*, *Bc*, *Bsp*

BIBLIOGRAPHY

B. Ligi: 'La cappella musicale del duomo d'Urbino', *NA*, ii (1925), 113
N. Pelicelli: 'Musicisti in Parma nel sec. XVII', *NA*, ix (1932), 243
H. C. Wolff: *Die venezianische Oper in der zweiten Hälfte des 17. Jahrhunderts: eine historisch-soziologische Untersuchung* (Berlin, 1937)
R. Giazotto: *La musica a Genova* (Genoa, 1951)
S. T. Worsthorne: *Venetian Opera in the Seventeenth Century* (Oxford, 1954/R1968), 77
A. Liess: 'Materialien zur römischen Musikgeschichte des Seicento', *AcM*, xxix (1957), 153

OWEN JANDER

Agram (Ger.). ZAGREB.

Agrell, Johan Joachim (*b* Löth, Östergötland, 1 Feb 1701; *d* Nuremberg, 19 Jan 1765). Swedish composer, violinist and harpsichordist. His father was a priest. He went to school in Linköping and studied at Uppsala University from 1721 to 1722 or 1723, where he probably played in the university orchestra, then led by the *director musices* Eric Burman. Agrell may have been a pupil of J. H. Roman, who returned to Sweden from England in 1721. Early biographers said that Prince Maximilian of Hesse heard Agrell's violin playing in 1723 and called him to Kassel. Firm evidence of Agrell's activity there is found from 1734, when F. Chelleri was Kapellmeister. He was still working in Kassel between 1737 and 1742, when Count Wilhelm VIII was in power; the court long owed him payment for service, as well as 'ale and food money', for the years 1743 to 1746. During his time at Kassel Agrell is reported to have made several journeys, visiting England, France, Italy and elsewhere.

Uncertain economic circumstances seem to have driven Agrell to seek the post of Kapellmeister in Nuremberg, a post which he obtained in 1746 (succeeding M. Zeitler); he combined this with duties as *director musices*, leader of the town musicians and holder of the position of 'chief wedding and funeral inviter', which gave him the right to compose music for weddings and other festivities. One of his duties was to direct music in the town's main churches, in particular the Frauenkirche. Of his work in the *Musikalische Kirchen-Andachten* only the text survives. On 3 September 1749 Agrell married the daughter of an organist, the singer Margaretha Förtsch (*d* 1752).

Practically none of Agrell's output dates from his youth in Sweden. It may be mentioned as a curiosity that one of his polonaises (from a collection printed in 1746) survived as a reel in the tradition of Swedish fiddlers throughout the 19th century. Whether Agrell had been influenced by Swedish folk music is uncertain. Another sign of contact with his homeland is the dedication to Adolf Fredrik of Holstein-Gottorp, successor to the Swedish throne, of his *Sei sonate per il cembalo solo* (1748), in which he referred to his 'dear homeland, Sweden', and remarked that 'fate had so far forced him to live abroad'; perhaps he cherished a hope of being called home to serve as a musician to the Swedish court.

Agrell's works divide into two categories: the vocal music, occasional and commissioned, much appreciated in his day, but now lost; and his many instrumental works for 'Kenner und Liebhaber' (connoisseurs and amateurs), most of which were published during Agrell's lifetime, sometimes on their own, sometimes in anthologies. Among the most important instrumental works are his symphonies, chiefly from the period 1720–50, which (like the work of his compatriot, Roman) constitute an interesting early experiment in this genre with the beginnings of thematic contrast, and his numerous harpsichord concertos from the 1750s and 1760s. There are also a number of concertos for other solo instruments, as well as for harpsichord and a melody instrument, chamber music and works for solo harpsichord. No thorough study of Agrell's style and its development has yet been made. He was evidently influenced from many directions, at first by Chelleri and Roman, among others, later by the more up-to-date Italian composers of his time and by German music of the milieu in which he worked. He had a sound technique, and was fluent in the new forms of his time. His style has clear *galant* tendencies, but even if Agrell (as one might suppose) harboured aesthetic ideals like those of Mattheson, he was not really a gifted melodist, a fact which occasioned Schubart's oft-cited judgment (*Ästhetik der Tonkunst*, Vienna, 1806): 'A true artist, but a cold nature'. Nevertheless his works provide several indications of sensitivity, not least in his slow movements, and the affinities between the music of Agrell and that of Bach's sons would be worth examination.

WORKS

(all printed works published in Nuremberg unless otherwise stated)

6 sinfonie (D, C, A, Bb, G, F), 2 vn, va, hpd/vc, with hns, tpts, obs, recs, fl ad lib, op.1 (1746), nos.1, 2 with timp [nos.1, 4 in *D-RUl*; no.4 in *S-Uu*]

6 sonate (B, G, F, e, D, g), hpd, op.2 (1748), also incl. ariettes, polonaises and minuets [no.3 as concerto, *F-Pn*]

[3] Sonates (A, Bb, G), hpd (?1751–2), also incl. ariettes, polonaises and minuets

3 concerti (F, D, A), hpd, 2 vn, va, vc, op.3 (1751) [no.3 in *D-MÜu*]

[3] Sonate (G, E, –), vn, hpd/vc (1752), no.3 pubd singly and lost

3 concerti (A, b, G), hpd, fl/vn, 2 vn, va, vc, op.4 (1753)

4 concerti (Bb, D, A, D), hpd, 2 vn, va, vc (1755–61), also for hpd solo; no.1 without vc; all pubd singly, nos.2, 3 lost

6 Sonatas (G, C, G, G, G), 2 fl/vn, bc, op.3 (London, c1757)

[2] Sonata a due, fl/vn, hpd (1762–5), both pubd singly and lost

A Collection of Easy Genteel Lessons, hpd, bk 2 (London, c1767), incl. one Vivaldi concerto arr. hpd

Pièce(s) in Collection recréative de pièces, hpd, fl/vn, premier couple (1746), lost; 1 sonata each in 6 Sonatas or Duets, 2 fl/vn, op.2 (London, 1751), Oeuvres mélées, hpd, partie 1re, lxxi (1755), 20 sonate, hpd, op.2 (Paris, 1760); ?1 piece in Pièces choisies, hpd, bk 1 (Amsterdam, c1760); pieces in A Collection of Lessons . . . by sigr. Jozzi, hpd, bks 1–3 (London, 1761–4), and A Collection of Lessons . . . by sigr. Kunzen, hpd (London, 1762); 1 [?3] concerto(s) in 6 Concertos . . . by Sigr. Graun, hpd/org, op.2 (London, 1762)

4 symphonies (A, F, Bb, D), *B-Bc*; 9 symphonies (D, F, F, D, G, D, E, G, E), Sonata, capriccio and polonaise, hpd, *D-DS*; sonata (A), hpd, vn obbl, c1743, *Mbs*; 2 symphonies (Eb, Bb), 2 concertos (A, F),

hpd, 2 vn, va, b, and 1 concerto (F), fl, 2 vn, va, b, *MÜu*; 3 symphonies (D, E, E), *Rtt*; 4 symphonies (D, Bb, D, D), *RUl*; concerto (F), *F-Pc*; symphony (A), *GB-Lbm*; 4 symphonies (D, F, F, Bb), *S-Uu*; concerto (D), vn, 2 vn, va, b, *US-Wc*

Lost works, all cited in Breitkopf catalogues: 6 sinfonie [3] a 4 und [3] a 6 voci; partita no.1 in 6 partite da diversi autori, 2 hn, 2 vn, va, b; Sinfonia a 4 (Bb); 2 concerti, vn, 2 vn, va, b; 12 concertos, hpd, 2 vn, va, b [no.2 (G), attrib. Graun, *GB-Lbm*; no.1 also as symphony (E), *D-DS*; no.3 (D) lost concerto no.2 (1755)]; Concerto, hpd, 2 vn, bc; 6 sonate, bn, bc; solo (A), hpd [also in A Collection of Lessons, bk 2]; solo (G), vn, bc

Many compositions for official celebrations of the City of Nuremberg, including 5 serenades, and for the Frauenkirche and Marienkirche, including the Musikalische Kirchen-Andachten, are lost

WRITINGS

Anleitung zur Composition (MS)
Tabellen für den Generalbass und die Tonsetzkunst (MS)

BIBLIOGRAPHY

FétisB

J. Mattheson: *Grundlage einer Ehren-Pforte* (Hamburg, 1740); ed. M. Schneider (Berlin, 1910/R1969)

A. Abrahamsson Hülphers: *Historisk Afhandling om Musik och Instrumenter* (Västerås, 1773/R1969)

J. C. Mainberger: *Leichen- und Hochzeit-Musiken und diesfallsige Differenzen betreffend. Anno 1804* (MS, *D-Nst*)

K. Valentin: 'Johan Agrell', *Svensk Musiktidning*, xxx (Stockholm, 1911), 25

P. Lindfors: 'En studie över Johan Agrells liv och musikaliska stil', *STMf*, xix (1937), 99

S. Walin: *Beiträge zur Geschichte der schwedischen Sinfonik* (Stockholm, 1941)

C. Engelbrecht: 'Die Hofkapelle des Landgrafen Carl von Hessen-Cassel', *Zeitschrift des Verein für hessliche Geschichte und Landeskunde*, lxviii (Kassel, 1957)

H. Heussner: 'Agrell, Johan Joachim', *MGG*

B. S. Brook, ed.: *The Breitkopf Thematic Catalogue, 1762–1787* (New York, 1966)

INGMAR BENGTSSON

Agréments (Fr.). EMBELLISHMENT. The word is used both by itself and in the terms *agréments du chant* ('embellishments of the melody') and *agréments de musique* ('embellishments of music'). The alternative spelling 'agrémens' is now obsolete.

Agresta, Agostino (*b* ?Naples, *c*1575–85; *d* after 1617). Italian composer. He may have supported himself much as did his elder brother Giovanni Antonio, who in 1598 was teaching singing to the children of the Prince of Roccella, Fabrizio Carafa. Cerreto mentioned both brothers as excellent composers in *Della prattica musica* (1601), but only works by Agostino have survived. He published a book of six-part madrigals (Naples, 1617); there are also single five-part madrigals by him in *RISM* 1606[5] and 1609[16] and in Macedonio di Mutio's second book of five-part madrigals (1606). Between 1600 and 1630 Naples was the most important centre for the composition and printing of the increasingly outmoded polyphonic madrigal without continuo. During this period the only books of six-part madrigals published there were Agresta's and a posthumous collection by Gesualdo (1626); Agresta's reveals what the style of Gesualdo's incompletely preserved book may have been. Like many of his Neapolitan contemporaries influenced by Gesualdo's virtuoso madrigals, Agresta occasionally surpassed him in the degree of contrast between slow chromatic *durezze e ligature* and diatonic, scalar points of imitation in quavers and semiquavers. While the former are less striking and cogent, the latter are usually longer and more lively and intricate than Gesualdo's. A third of all points of imitation in the book combine two different motifs setting the same text, and about two thirds have paired voices in 3rds, 6ths and 10ths, a common feature of the late Neapolitan madrigal. The last madrigal in the book, *Io penso e nèl pensiero*, is an intellectual challenge to virtuoso singers; each voice has its own series of such proportions as 2:3, 10:1, 1:10, 3:2 and ₵.

BIBLIOGRAPHY

Anon.: 'Napoli musicale alla fine del cinquecento: gli stipendii dei maestri', *Napoli nobilissima*, new ser., iii (1922), 151

G. Watkins: *Gesualdo: the Man and his Music* (London, 1973), 228, 223

KEITH A. LARSON

Agricola, Alexander (*b* ?1446; *d* Valladolid, late Aug 1506). Franco-Netherlands composer active in Italy, France and the Low Countries. He was renowned for his masses, motets, chansons and instrumental works. Some biographical information can be gleaned from the commemorative poem, *Epitaphion Alexandri Agricolae symphonistae regis Castiliae*, in which he is called a Belgian ('Belgam') who was brought to Spain by King Philip of Castile, and died at the age of 60 in the same year (1506) as his master.

The earliest chapel or court records of the composer are Italian and refer to him as Alessandro Alemanno, Alexander de Alemanna or Alessandro d'Allemagna. One very early document of 1456 from the Aragonese archives at Naples lists a singer, Alessandro Alemanno, probably not the composer. Milanese archives of the early 1570s, on the other hand, contain genuine accounts of Agricola's career. From 1471 to 1474 he was a highly esteemed singer and composer to Galeazzo Maria Sforza, Duke of Milan. In 1474 he probably sought a new post: on 23 March the duke dictated a letter recommending 'Alessandro d'Allemagno nostro famiglio et musico' to Lorenzo de' Medici. A safe conduct authorizing him to travel to the Low Countries followed ten weeks later. Finally on 7 July 1474 Agricola wrote from Florence to the Duke of Milan, but made no mention of a new position.

Two years later he was in Cambrai; according to a financial statement of 4 March 1476, the cathedral paid him four livres. The text of the statement suggests that Agricola was a *petit vicaire*, a title usually indicating a singer of the canonical hours. The organist 'Alexander' in the city of Utrecht mentioned in a document of 1477 cannot be identified with Agricola with any certainty. Apart from the name, the only evidence is a remark in *Epitaphion Alexandri Agricolae* that Agricola was 'renowned of voice and hand'.

Nothing is known of the posts Agricola held in the next 16 years (1476–91); but he spent the last part of this period at the French royal chapel. By 1491 he had left France without the king's permission, and made his way to Florence via Mantua. On 1 October 1491 Agricola's name was inscribed as a singer at Florence Cathedral, where he remained until the last days of April 1492. His departure from Florence was followed almost immediately by the arrival of a letter dated 25 April from Charles VIII of France to Piero de' Medici with an urgent request that Agricola be returned to France. By that time the composer was approaching or had arrived at the Aragonese court in Naples where he was received by its ruler Ferrante I. Pressure for Agricola's return to the French royal chapel was exerted by an emissary of Charles as well as Piero de' Medici in a letter of 13 May 1492. In a communication of 13 June Ferrante wrote to Charles that Agricola had been dismissed and was on his way back to France. Agricola

remained at the French chapel until at least 4 September 1493, the date when Ferrante finally terminated negotiations (possibly secret) with the composer for a permanent position at Naples.

Nothing is known of Agricola's activities from 1493 until February 1500, when he entered the service of Philip the Handsome, Duke of Burgundy and King of Castile (1478–1506). Probably he remained at the French court until the death of Charles in 1498.

From the beginning of his service at the Burgundian court until his death in 1506, Agricola's name appears regularly on most chapel lists. He accompanied the duke on trips through Luxembourg, France and Spain. During the first trip to Spain (4 November 1501–8 November 1503) Agricola travelled through France where he had spent his earlier years. His reputation as a singer and composer was then so high that the chronicler of the tour complimented a French singer with the accolade 'second Alexander'. Another trip to Spain followed about three years later, during which, according to *Epitaphion Alexandri Agricolae* and court records, the composer died of plague at the age of 60. A musician of the same name employed at Mantua from 1520 to 1523 cannot be the master, although he may have been a relative (perhaps a son).

None of Agricola's works can be dated precisely. Only in the case of the secular motet *Transit Anna timor* can a date of composition be conjectured. The text refers to the King Louis' recovery from a serious illness of either 1503 or 1505. The short phrases and greater use of imitation indicate a stylistic shift from the irregular contrapuntal lines and casual imitation of his earlier works. *Nobis Sancte Spiritus*, written in pervading imitation and surviving in only one late source, is probably also a late work. Otherwise a chronology of Agricola's compositions on stylistic grounds is difficult because most of his works display uniform features.

Although Agricola spent many years in Italy, few of his compositions are word-orientated. His style is probably closest to that of Ockeghem, with whom he was associated at the royal chapel. Both men favoured a rhythmically rich, melismatic flow of counterpoint. But whereas Ockeghem often rejected such integrating devices as repetition, sequence and imitation, Agricola tended to use them. He adopted the long, rhythmically complex lines of the older master, but constructed them of short, decorative motifs linked with frequent yet unobtrusive cadences. Of all the Franco-Netherlands composers who came to Italy at the end of the 15th century, Agricola seems to have been least influenced by Italianate concepts of formal clarity and melodic cohesion. In these respects he remained closer to the 'Gothic' manner which other northerners left behind when they crossed the Alps.

WORKS

Edition: *A. Agricola: Opera omnia*, ed. E. R. Lerner, CMM, xxii/1–5 (1961–70) [L]

MASSES AND MASS MOVEMENTS

Missa 'In myne zin', 4vv, L i, 105 (c.f. from his own chanson, In minen zin)

Missa 'Je ne demande', 4vv, L i, 34 (c.f. from Busnois' chanson)

Missa 'Le serviteur', 4vv, L i, 1 (c.f. from chanson by ?Dufay)

Missa 'Malheur me bat', 4vv, L i, 66 (c.f. from chanson by ?Ockeghem)

Missa Paschalis, 4vv, L ii, 1 (cantus firmi: German versions of Ky I, Gl I, San XVII, Ag XXII, cf *Graduale pataviense*, Vienna, 1511, ff.184v–185r, 194v)

Missa primi toni, 4vv, L ii, 23

Missa secundi toni, 4vv, L ii, 47

Missa sine nomine, 4vv, L ii, 78 (c.f. in Cr: Cr I)

Credo, Sanctus, 3vv, L ii, 125

Credo, 4vv, L ii, 94 (c.f. from chanson, Je ne vis oncques, by Dufay or Binchois)
Credo, 4vv, L ii, 103 (c.f. from chanson, Je ne vis oncques, by Dufay or Binchois)
Credo vilayge, 4vv, L ii, 114 (c.f.: Cr I)

HYMNS, LAMENTATIONS, MAGNIFICAT SETTINGS

A solis ortus cardine, 4vv, L iii, 17 (hymn; c.f. German version of plainsong, cf Monumenti monodica medii aevi, i, Kassel and Basle (1956), 219)
Ave maris stella, 4vv, L iii, 20 (Marian hymn; c.f. German version of plainsong, cf. *I-MOe* α.X.1.11, f.7*v*)
Lamentations, 3vv, L iii, 1 (c.f. plainsong)
Lamentations, 4vv, L iii, 8 (c.f. plainsong)
Magnificat primi toni, 4vv, L iii, 23, 34 (c.f. plainsong; 2 versions: one long, one short)
Magnificat secundi toni, 4vv, L iii, 41 (c.f. plainsong)
Magnificat octavi toni, 4vv, L iii, 51 (c.f. plainsong)

MOTETS

Amice ad quid venisti [= Dictes moy toutes], 3vv, L iv, 64 (text from Matthew xxvi)
Arce sedet Bacchus, 2vv, L iv, 65 (probably a contrafactum from a lost mass; c.f. T of Caron's chanson, Le despourveu infortuné)
Ave domina sancta Maria, 4vv, L iv, 1 (to BVM)
Ave pulcherrima regina, 4vv, L iv, 3 (Marian text set to a German tune, see Schmitz)
Ave que sublimaris [= Comme femme], 3vv, L iv, 60
Da pacem, 3vv, L iv, 47 (prayer for peace; c.f. plainsong)
Ergo sancti martyres, 4vv, L iv, 28
Nobis Sancte Spiritus, 4vv, L iv, 36 (text: 1st verse, hymn sung at Horae canonicae de Spiritu Sancto)
O crux ave, 4vv, L iv, 38 (text: 6th verse, hymn, Vexilla regis; c.f. plainsong)
O quam glorifica, 3vv, L iv, 48 (text: 1st stanza Marian hymn; c.f. plainsong)
O virens virginum, 4vv, L iv, 5 (to BVM)
Regina coeli, 4vv, L iv, 7 (Marian ant; c.f. German version of plainsong, cf *Antiffanarium*, Augsburg, 1495)
Salve regina, 4vv, L iv, 10 (Marian ant.; c.f. plainsong, cf *Sacerdotale*, Venice, 1564, f.291*v*)
Salve regina, 4vv, L iv, 20 (Marian ant.; cantus firmi: same version of plainsong as above, T of Frye's motet, Ave regina coelorum)
Sancte Philippe appostole [= Ergo sancti martyres], 4vv, L iv, 32
Si dedero, 3vv, L iv, 50 (text: verse of the respond In pace in idipsum; c.f. plainsong, cf *AS*, p.150)
Transit Anna timor, 4vv, L iv, 41 (thanksgiving for Louis XII's recovery from illness)
Virgo sub ethereis [= Comme femme], 3vv, L iv, 62

MOTET-CHANSONS

Belles sur toutes/Tota pulchra es, 3vv, L iv, 52 (rondeau quatrain in S, T; c.f. plainsong in B)
L'heure est venue/Circumdederunt me, 3vv, L iv, 54 (virelai in S, T; text of B int for Septuagesima Sunday)
Revenez tous regretz/Quis det ut veniat, 4vv, L iv, 58 (rondeau cinquaine in S, A, T; text of B verse of respond Nonne cognoscit)

SECULAR VOCAL

Adieu m'amour, 3vv, L v, 43
Adieu m'amour, 3vv, L v, 44
A la mignonne de fortune, 3vv, L v, 3 (bergerette)
Allez mon cueur, 3vv, L v, 19 (rondeau quatrain)
Allez, regretz, 3vv, L v, 20 (rondeau cinquain; T from Hayne van Ghizeghem's chanson)
Amor che sospirar, 3vv, L v, 66 (strophic song)
Ay je rien fet, 3vv, L v, 45 (quatrain)
C'est mal cherche, 3vv, L v, 22 (rondeau cinquain; 4th voice ad lib)
C'est trop sur, 3vv, L v, 23 (rondeau quatrain)
C'est ung bon bruit, 3vv, L v, 46
Crions nouel, 3vv, L v, 54 (text lost)
D . . ., 3vv, L v, 55 (text lost)
Dictes moy toutes, 3vv, L v, 24 (rondeau quatrain)
Donne, noi siam dell'olio facitori (L. de' Medici), ?3vv (strophic carnival song; only 5 extant)
En actendant, 3vv, L v, 26 (rondeau cinquain)
En dispitant, 3vv, L v, 56 (text lost)
En m'en venant, 3vv, L v, 27 (rondeau quatrain)
Et qui la dira, 3vv, L v, 48 (chanson à refrain on a popular tune, cf *F-Pn* f.fr.9346)
Fortuna desperata, 6vv, L v, 68 (strophic song; based on a 3-voice anon. chanson, ed. A. Smijers, *Josquin Desprez: Missen*, Werken, i/4, fasc.13, Leipzig (1929), 105)
Gentil galans, 3vv, L v, 57 (text lost)
Guarde vostre visage, 3vv, L v, 58 (text lost)
Il me fauldra maudire, 3vv, L v, 59 (text lost)
Il n'est vivant, 3vv, L v, 5 (bergerette)
In minen zin, 3vv, L v, 63 (sets popular Flemish melody)
J'ay beau huer, 3vv, L v, 28 (rondeau quatrain)

Je n'ay dueil, 4vv, L v, 7 (bergerette; related to a motif in B of Ockeghem's chanson)
Je ne puis plus, 3vv, L v, 60 (text lost)
Je ne suis point, 3vv, L v, 30 (rondeau cinquain)
Mauldicte soit, 3vv, L v, 49 (chanson huitaine)
Mijn alderliefste moeschkin, 3vv, L v, 65
Oublier veul, 3vv, L v, 60 (text lost)
Par ung jour de matinee, 3vv, L v, 50 (?chanson sixaine)
Pour voz plaisirs, 3vv, L v, 31 (rondeau quatrain)
Princesse de toute beaulte, 3vv, L v, 62 (text lost)
Royne des flours, 3vv, L v, 11 (bergerette on tune in *Pn* f.fr.9346)
Se je fais bien, 3vv, L v, 35 (rondeau quatrain)
Se je vous eslonge, 3vv, L v, 13 (bergerette)
Se mieulx ne vient d'amours, 3vv, L v, 32 (rondeau cinquain)
Serviteur soye, 3vv, L v, 15 (bergerette)
Si conge prens, 3vv, L v, 1 (ballade on tune in *Pn* f.fr.12744)
S'il vous plaist, 3vv, L v, 36 (rondeau quatrain)
Si vous voullez, 3vv, L v, 17 (bergerette)
Soit loing, 3vv, L v, 37 (rondeau quatrain)
Sonnes muses melodieusement, 3vv, L v, 51
Va t'en, regret, 3vv, L v, 39 (rondeau cinquain)
Vostre bouche dist, 3vv, L v, 53 (quatrain)
Vostre hault bruit, 3vv, L v, 41 (rondeau cinquain)

INSTRUMENTAL

Amours, amours, 3vv, L v, 71 (c.f. T of Hayne van Ghizeghem's rondeau)
Cecus non judicat de coloribus, 3vv, L v, 102
Comme femme, 4vv, L v, 72 (arr. of T of rondeau by ?Binchois)
Comme femme, 3vv, L v, 75 (arr. of T of rondeau by ?Binchois)
Comme femme, 2vv, L v, 76 (arr. of T of rondeau by ?Binchois)
De tous biens plaine, 4vv, L v, 78 (arr. of T of Hayne van Ghizeghem's rondeau)
De tous biens plaine, 3vv, L v, 79 (arr. of T of Hayne's rondeau)
De tous biens plaine, 3vv, L v, 81 (arr. of T of Hayne's rondeau)
De tous biens plaine, 3vv, L v, 82 (arr. of T of Hayne's rondeau)
De tous biens plaine, 3vv, L v, 83 (arr. of T of Hayne's rondeau)
D'ung aultre amer, 4vv, L v, 85 (arr. of T of Ockeghem's rondeau)
D'ung aultre amer, 4vv, L v, 86 (arr. of T of Ockeghem's rondeau)
D'ung aultre amer, 3vv, L v, 87 (arr. of T of Ockeghem's rondeau)
D'ung aultre amer, 3vv, L v, 88 (arr. of T of Ockeghem's rondeau)
[Duo], 2vv, L v, 112 (upper voice by Agricola, lower voice by Ghiselin)
Gaudeamus omnes, 2vv, L v, 106 (c.f. plainsong int.)
Jam fulsit, 4vv, L v, 113
L'homme banni, 3vv, L v, 89
O Venus bant, 3vv, L v, 97 (arr. of popular tune)
O Venus bant, 3vv, L v, 98 (arr. of popular tune)
Pater meus agricola est, 3vv, L v, 107
Pourquoy tant/Pour quelque paine, 3vv, L v, 91 (arr. of 2 lines of an anon. 3-voice chanson, see Plamenac)
Tandernaken, 3vv, L v, 99 (arr. of popular tune)
Tout a par moy, 4vv, L, v, 92 (arr. of T of Frye's rondeau)
Tout a par moy, 3vv, L v. 95 (arr. of T of Frye's rondeau)

DOUBTFUL WORKS

Missa sine nomine, 3vv (attrib. Agricola in *E-SE* and Aulen in *D-LEm*, *Rp*, *PL-WRu*; by Aulen)
Credo Tmeisken, 4vv (in some sources incl. in the Missa Paschalis, but in *A-Wn* 1783 attrib. Isaac; probably by Isaac)
Magnificat quarti toni, 4vv, L iii, 60, 71 (c.f. plainsong; 2 versions: the long attrib. Josquin Desprez; the short attrib. Pierre de La Rue, Agricola)
Magnificat quarti toni, 4vv, L iii, 77, 88 (c.f. plainsong; 2 versions: the long attrib. Brumel, the short attrib. Agricola)
Que vous madame/In pace in idipsum, 3vv, L v, 128 (c.f. plainsong respond in B; attrib. Josquin Desprez more often)
Ha qu'il m'ennuye, 3vv, L v, 116 (bergerette; also attrib. Fresneau)
J'ars du desir, 3vv, L v, 118 (rondeau attrib. Agricola, but questionable on stylistic grounds)
La saison en est, 3vv, L v, 119 (rondeau; attrib. Compère more often)
Les grans regretz, 3vv, L, v, 120 (rondeau attrib. Hayne van Ghizeghem more often)
Notres assovemen, 3vv, L v, 122 (text lost; also attrib. Fresneau)
De tous beins plaine, 3vv, L v, 123 (inst; c.f. from Hayne's chanson; also attrib. Bourdon)
Fors seullement, 4vv, L v, 124 (inst; c.f. from chanson by ?Ockeghem; also attrib. Brumel)
Helas madame, que feraige, 3vv, L v, 125 (inst; ?c.f. from Caron's chanson; also attrib. 'P')

BIBLIOGRAPHY

H. Kinzel: *Der deutsche Musiker Alexander Agricola in seinen weltlichen Werken* (diss., U. of Prague, 1934)
A. Schmitz: 'Ein schlesisches Cantionale aus dem 15. Jahrhundert', *AMf*, i (1936), 393
P. Müller: *Alexander Agricola: seine Missa In minen zin: chansonale Grundlagen und Analyse* (diss., U. of Marburg, 1939)

D. Plamenac: 'A Postcript to Vol. II of the "Collected Works" of Johannes Ockeghem', *JAMS*, ii (1950), 37

E. R. Lerner: *The Sacred Music of Alexander Agricola* (diss., Yale U., 1958)

——: 'The "German" Works of Alexander Agricola', *MQ*, xlvi (1960), 56

M. Picker: 'A Letter of Charles VIII of France concerning Alexander Agricola', *Aspects of Medieval and Renaissance Music: a Birthday Offering to Gustav Reese* (New York, 1966), 655

A. W. Atlas: 'Alexander Agricola and Ferrante I of Naples', *JAMS*, xxx (1977), 313

EDWARD R. LERNER

Agricola [née Molteni], **Benedetta Emilia** (*b* Modena, 1722; *d* Berlin, 1780). Soprano, wife of JOHANN FRIED-RICH AGRICOLA. She was the first of the three leading ladies (the other two were Giovanna Astrua and Elisabeth Schmeling Mara) at the Berlin Opera under Frederick the Great. A pupil of Porpora, Hasse and Salimbeni, she made her début in 1743, during the first season of Frederick's new opera house, as prima donna in C. H. Graun's *Cesare e Cleopatra*. The arrival of Astrua in 1748 forced her to take second place, but strengthened her impulse towards oratorio: thus, for example, she sang the leading solo soprano part in Graun's *Tod Jesu* at its première in 1755.

In 1772 Burney (*Present State of Music in Germany*) wrote of her singing: 'she is now near fifty years of age, and yet sings songs of *bravura*, with amazing rapidity . . . her compass extends from A in the base, to D in *alt*, and she has a most perfect shake and intonation'. When her husband died in 1774 she was dismissed in spite of Princess Anna Amalia's intercession on her behalf; she died in obscurity.

EUGENE HELM

Agricola, Georg Ludwig (*b* Grossfurra, Thuringia, 25 Oct 1643; *d* Gotha, 20 Feb 1676). German composer and writer. After initially going to school in his native town he was sent in 1656 to Eisenach for three years. There he attended the town school, the staff of which included Theodor Schuchardt, a highly respected teacher of music and Latin. From 1659 to 1662 Agricola studied for his school-leaving examination at the Gymnasium of Gotha; the headmaster there was Andreas Reyher, who was the co-author of the *Gothaer Schulmethodus*, an educational work which set an example for the teaching of music too. In 1662–3 Agricola studied philosophy at Leipzig University and from 1663 to 1668 theology and philosophy at Wittenberg, where he was awarded a master's degree by the faculty of philosophy. His four recorded scholarly essays dating from this period are lost. He had begun to learn the fundamentals of music during his school years, and he may also have been a pupil of the Kantor of the Thomaskirche, Leipzig, Sebastian Knüpfer. He continued his musical training at Wittenberg, completing the study of composition under the guidance of Italian musicians resident there. Returning to his native Thuringia he was able to turn his musical abilities to good use in the Kapelle of the Schwarzburg-Sondershausen court until in 1670 Duke Ernst the Pious of Saxe-Gotha appointed him his court Kapellmeister at Gotha in succession to W. C. Briegel. He held this post very successfully until his death. Very little of his music has survived. His three lost volumes of *Musicalische Nebenstunden* comprised sonatas, preludes, allemandes, courantes and ballettos. His extant vocal works show the influence of Schütz and the tradition of the Saxon Kantors, who, in the early history of

the Lutheran cantata, used forms which gained currency in central Germany.

WORKS

(all printed works lost; all published in Gotha unless otherwise stated)

Musicalische Nebenstunden, Sonaten, Praeludien, Allemanden, etc, 2 vn, 2 viols, bc (Mühlhausen, 1670)

Musicalische Nebenstunden ander Theil (1671)

Ander und dritter Theil Sonaten, Praeludien . . . auf französischer Art (1675)

Buss- und Communionlieder, 5–12vv (1675)

Deutsche geistliche Madrigale, 2–6vv (1675)

5 motets, 3–8vv, 3–8 insts, bc, *D-B, Bds, GOl, S-Uu*

7 motets, 1–18vv, 2–7 insts, lost

BIBLIOGRAPHY

FétisB; *GerberNL*; *WaltherML*

P. Spitta: 'Leichensermone auf Musiker des 16. und 17. Jahrhunderts', *MMg*, iii (1871), 35

S. Kümmerle: *Enzyklopädie der evangelischen Kirchenmusik*, i (Gütersloh, 1888)

A. Schering: *Musikgeschichte Leipzigs*, ii (Leipzig, 1926), 331

A. Fett: *Musikgeschichte der Stadt Gotha, von den Anfängen bis zum Tode G. H. Stölzels (1749)* (diss., U. of Freiburg, 1952), 117f, 200f

W. Braun: 'Theodor Schuchardt und die Eisenacher Musikkultur im 17. Jahrhundert', *AMw*, xv (1958), 291

W. Reich: *Die deutschen Leichenpredigten des 17. Jahrhunderts als musikgeschichtliche Quelle* (diss., U. of Leipzig, 1962)

F. Krummacher: *Die Überlieferung der Choralbearbeitung in der frühen evangelischen Kantate* (Berlin, 1965)

H. Engel: *Musik in Thüringen* (Cologne and Graz, 1966), 44f

KARL-ERNST BERGUNDER

Agricola [Noricus], **Johannes** (*b* Nuremberg, *c*1560–70; *d* ?Erfurt, after 1601). German composer. In 1601, when he published a collection of motets, Agricola was teaching at the Gymnasium Augustinianum at Erfurt; he can scarcely be identified with the Christianus Johannes Agricola who was a discantist in the Kapelle at Weimar in 1594. The surname 'Noricus', used on the title-page and in the dedication, meant 'born at Nuremberg', and a Johannes Agricola baptized on 29 November 1564 at St Sebald's Church at Nuremberg could be the composer. Yet another Johann Agricola, Kantor at St Bartholomäus, Frankfurt, in 1591, who died in 1605, was probably not the composer.

As a composer Agricola is known only by *Motetae novae pro praecipuis in anno festis* (Nuremberg, 1601), dedicated to the Erfurt senate; the bass partbook addresses the same dedication to the Mühlhausen senate, so possibly the collection appeared in at least two editions. The preface is a humanistic essay about the importance of music from ancient times to the 16th century. The 26 motets, for four to six, eight and twelve voices, are settings in a freely imitative style characterized by fluent counterpoint. The exact scansion of the Latin texts, which include some on secular subjects, is evidence of Agricola's humanistic education and profession.

LINI HÜBSCH-PFLEGER

Agricola, Johann Friedrich (*b* Dobitschen, Saxe-Altenburg, 4 Jan 1720; *d* Berlin, 2 Dec 1774). German musicographer, composer, organist, singing master and conductor. His father occupied an important post as government agent and jurist in Dobitschen. Burney, who visited the Agricolas in 1772, reported that Johann Friedrich's mother, born Maria Magdalena Manke, 'was a near relation of the late Mr Handel, and in correspondence with him till the time of his death'; but later Handel research has failed to substantiate this claim.

Agricola began his study of music as a young child. From 1738 to 1741 he was a student at the University of Leipzig, and was also a pupil of J. S. Bach. He heard

Hasse's operas in Dresden. In 1741 he moved to Berlin, became a pupil of Quantz, made the acquaintance of C. P. E. Bach, C. H. Graun and their contemporaries, and embarked on a musical career of remarkable versatility. He was profoundly influenced by music criticism and theoretical speculation in Berlin, and his work as a musicographer has proved to be his most lasting accomplishment. In 1749 he published, under the pseudonym 'Flavio Amicio Olibrio', two pamphlets on French and Italian taste, taking the part of Italian music against F. W. Marpurg's advocacy of French music. As a former pupil of J. S. Bach, he was able to collaborate with C. P. E. Bach in writing the obituary that appeared in Mizler's *Musikalische Bibliothek* in 1754 and became a central source for subsequent biographies of Bach. He published Tosi's *Opinioni de' cantori antichi e moderni* in German translation in 1757, adding notes and comments which have caused the translation to be regarded as a landmark in the teaching of singing. As well as arbitrating the debate that began in 1760 between Marpurg and G. A. Sorge, he corresponded with Padre Martini and the dramatist Lessing and assisted in the preparation for publication of Jacob Adlung's *Musica mechanica organoedi* (1768), drawing particularly on what he had learnt about the construction of organs and other keyboard instruments from Bach. In his contribution to the 1769 and 1771 volumes of Friedrich Nicolai's *Allgemeine deutsche Bibliothek* he displayed his inability to appreciate the significance of Gluck's 'reform' operas. His study of melody (1771) remains one of the important writings about a neglected subject; and his biographical sketch of Graun (1773), like his participation in the Bach obituary, served as a point of departure for later writers on the subject.

Agricola's career as a thoroughly Italianized composer of opera was fostered and then blighted by the patronage of Frederick the Great. His first intermezzo, *Il filosofo convinto in amore*, was performed with much success at Potsdam in 1750, and Frederick appointed him a court composer in 1751. But in the same year he married Benedetta Emilia Molteni, one of the singers of the opera, against the king's rule that the singers must remain single. Frederick punished the pair by reducing their joint salary to 1000 thalers, whereas Molteni's single salary had been 1500 thalers. When Graun, Frederick's chief opera composer, died in 1759, Agricola was appointed musical director of the Opera without the title of Kapellmeister, and his output as a composer in that genre began to decline. Within a few years his operas were little more than pallid imitations of Graun's. In October 1767, after hearing the rehearsals of Agricola's *Amor e Psiche*, Frederick wrote to his attendant Pöllnitz: 'You will tell Agricola that he must change all of Coli's arias – they are worthless – as well as those of Romani, along with the recitatives, which are deplorable from one end to the other'. An effort of 1772 entitled *Oreste e Pilade*, ordered by Frederick as entertainment for a visit by the Queen of Sweden and the Duchess of Brunswick, proved to be so far from what Frederick wanted that the entire opera had to be rewritten and retitled *I greci in Tauride*.

As a performer-teacher, and in aspects of composition not so zealously supervised by his royal patron, Agricola fared better. He sang the tenor part in the première of Graun's *Tod Jesu* in 1755, continued as a distinguished singing teacher throughout his career and

carried on the Bach tradition of organ playing; in 1772 Burney wrote that he was 'regarded as the best organ-player in Berlin, and the best singing master in Germany'. His keyboard compositions show him to have been a fine craftsman in the Bach tradition who nevertheless joined the trend towards *Empfindsamkeit* or even, in some cases, towards sentimentality; and his songs are competent products of the so-called 'First Berlin School' of song composition, perhaps rather dry, but ranking high in craftsmanship and good taste.

WORKS

OPERAS

Il filosofo convinto in amore (intermezzo), Potsdam, 1750, *D-Dlb*
La ricamatrice divenuta dama (intermezzo), Berlin, 1 Nov 1751, lost
Cleofide (3, Metastasio), Berlin, carn. 1754, *B*
La nobiltà delusa (dramma giocoso), 1754, *?ROmi*
Il tempio d'amore (festa teatrale, Tagliazucchi, after Frederick II), Charlottenburg, 30 Sept 1755, *?DS*
Triumphlied bei der Rückkehr Friedrichs II (cantata), 1763, *B*
Achille in Sciro (opera seria), 16 Sept 1765, *B*
Amor e Psiche (Landi), Oct 1767, lost
Les voeux de Berlin (cantata), Aug 1770, *B*
Il re pastore (?Villati), Sept/Oct ?1770, lost
Oreste e Pilade (Landi), early 1772, rewritten as I greci in Tauride, Potsdam, March 1772: both lost

Incidental music to Semiramis (Voltaire)

OTHER WORKS

Ov., *B-Bc*
12 oratorios and sacred cantatas, *D-B*, incl.: Ps. xxi (Ger. trans. Cramer), 4vv, orch, 1757 (Berlin, 1759); Trauerkantate, 1757; Die Auferstehung des Erlösers, 1758; Auferstehung und Himmelfahrt (Ramler); Lobet den Herrn; Die mit Tränen säen; Kündlich gross ist das gottselige Geheimnis, 4vv, orch; Gelobet sei Gott; Singet fröhlich Gotte, 4/4vv, insts; Ein Kind ist uns geboren; Ein schnelles Brausen; Mag, 5vv, orch, bc
Other cantatas, lost
Numerous songs and odes in collections, incl.: Birnstiel's Oden mit Melodien, i (Berlin, 1753); Marpurg's Historisch-kritisch Beyträge, i (Berlin, 1755/*R*1970); Marpurg's Neue Lieder (Berlin, 1756); Marpurg's Raccolta delle più nuove composizioni (Leipzig, 1756–7); Berlinische Oden und Lieder, i–ii (Leipzig, 1756–9); Geistliche, moralische und weltliche Oden (Berlin, 1758); Musikalisches Allerley (Berlin, 1761); Auserlesene Oden zum singen beym Clavier, ii (Berlin, 1764); Lieder der Deutschen mit Melodien, i–iv (Berlin, 1767–8); 1 ed. M. Friedlaender, *Das deutsche Lied im 18. Jahrhundert* (Stuttgart, 1902/*R*1962)
Some sonatas and descriptive pieces, kbd, incl. sonata, F, in Musikalisches Mancherley, iii (Berlin, 1762); 1 ed., Hermann: *Lehrmeister und Schüler Joh. Seb. Bachs* (Leipzig, 1935)
Choral preludes, org, *D-B*

WRITINGS

Schreiben eines reisenden Liebhabers (Berlin, 1749)
Schreiben an Herrn . . . (Berlin, 1749)
with C. P. E. Bach: 'Nekrolog [J. S. Bach]', *Musikalische Bibliothek*, iv (Leipzig, 1754)
Anleitung zur Singekunst (Berlin, 1757; trans. with additions of P. F. Tosi's *Opinioni de' cantori antichi e moderni*, 1723) [facs. edn. of both ed. E. R. Jacobi (Celle, 1966)]
with J. Adlung: *Musica mechanica organoedi* (Berlin, 1768)
Articles in C. F. Nicolai's *Allgemeine deutsche Bibliothek* (Berlin, Kiel and Stettin, 1766–96)
'Beleuchtung der Frage von dem Vorzuge der Melodie vor der Harmonie', *Magazin der Musik*, ii (1786) [begun in 1771]
'Lebensbeschreibung des Kapellmeisters Graun', in Graun's *Duetti, Terzetti* (Berlin, 1773), ed. J. P. Kirnberger

BIBLIOGRAPHY

BurneyH; EitnerQ
C. Burney: *The Present State of Music in Germany, the Netherlands and the United Provinces* (London, 1773, 2/1775); ed. P. Scholes as *Dr. Burney's Musical Tours* (London, 1959)
C. C. Rolle: *Neue Wahrnehmungen zur Aufnahme und weitern Ausbreitung der Musik* (Berlin, 1784)
L. Schneider: *Geschichte der Oper und des königlichen Opernhauses in Berlin* (Berlin, 1852)
H. Goldschmidt: *Die italienische Gesangsmethode* (Breslau, 1890, 2/1892)
C. H. Mennicke: *Hasse und die Brüder Graun als Symphoniker* (Leipzig, 1906)
H. Wucherpfennig: *J. Fr. Agricola* (diss., U. of Berlin, 1922) [incl. some letters]
H. Löffler: 'Die Schüler J. S. Bachs', *BJb*, xl (1953), 5

E. E. Helm: *Music at the Court of Frederick the Great* (Norman, Oklahoma, 1960)

A. Dürr: 'Zur Chronologie der Handschriften J.Chr. Altnikols und J. Fr. Agricolas', *BJb*, lvi (1970), 44

EUGENE HELM

Agricola, Johann Paul (*b* Hilpoltstein, nr. Nuremberg, 1638 or 1639; *d* Neuburg an der Donau, buried 3 May 1697). German composer, organist and musician. He was educated at the Jesuit Gymnasium of St Salvator, Augsburg. In 1660 he wrote the music for a play performed there. On 23 October of the same year he matriculated at the University of Ingolstadt, where he read theology. In 1663 he became a chamber musician and court organist at Neuburg an der Donau to Count Palatine Philipp Wilhelm, who was renowned for his patronage and understanding of the arts. The court Kapellmeister was G. B. Mocchi, who had been a pupil of Carissimi and who in 1675 renounced in Agricola's favour a prebend that Pope Alexander VII had granted him in 1655. Agricola was required to compose a number of large-scale works for weddings in the count's family. When the count's eldest son, Johann Wilhelm, married the Archduchess Maria Anna, sister of the Emperor Leopold I, in 1679, two operas and a pastoral by him, and another work, *Freudens-Triumph* (with an equestrian ballet), that was probably by him, were performed; the music is all lost. On the occasion of the wedding of Princess Maria Sophia Elisabeth and King Pedro II of Portugal, which was celebrated lavishly in 1687 at Heidelberg with a performance of Sebastiano Moratelli's opera *La gemma Ceraunia*, Agricola received two ornamental goblets and a present of money 'for his many and varied labours over the comedy and other matters' (no music that he may have written on this occasion can be identified). In the summer of 1689 Philipp Wilhelm commissioned him to set for the impending wedding by proxy of his daughter Maria Anna to King Carlos II of Spain three cantatas to texts by the court poet G. M. Rapparini. In a letter to the prince-elector on 14 July 1689, Philipp Wilhelm described in detail the plan and contents of these works, which again are lost. Records relating to Agricola's funeral state that he was 58 when he died. With the regrettable loss of all of his stage music his only surviving works are three motets, which show the influence of the Augsburg school of J. M. Gletle; from catalogues compiled at Ansbach and Freising it appears that other sacred works by him are lost.

WORKS

STAGE WORKS

(all lost; librettos D-Mbs)

Streit der Schönheit und der Tugend, opera, Neuburg, 1679

Freudens-Triumph des Parnassus, Neuburg, 13 Feb 1679 [with equestrian ballet; probably by Agricola]

Die beneidete, jedoch nicht beleidigte Liebe, abgebildet in einem poetischen Sinngedichte von dem Schäfer Damon und der Nymphe Melisse, pastoral, Neuburg, Carnival 1679

Die gesuchte, verlorene, und endlich wiedergefundene Freiheit in der Begebnis zweier Sicilianischer Princessinnen Salibene und Rosimene, opera, Neuburg, 1679

Cardio-Sophia . . . das ist Hertzen Schuel, school play, Augsburg, St Salvator Gymnasium, 6 and 9 Sept 1660

3 motets: Accede o anima; Laudate pueri; Secundum magnam misericordiam, *D-Bds*

Other sacred works, now lost, listed in J. J. Pez: Catalogus Musicalium (Freising, 1710)

BIBLIOGRAPHY

F. Walter: *Geschichte des Theaters und der Musik am kurpfälzischen Hof* (Leipzig, 1898)

A. Einstein: 'Italienische Musiker am Hofe der Neuburger Wittelsbacher, 1614–1716', *SIMG*, ix (1907–8), 336–424

C. Sachs: 'Die Ansbacher Hofkapelle unter Markgraf Johann Friedrich (1672 bis 1686)', *SIMG*, xi (1909–10), 1

LINI HÜBSCH-PFLEGER

Agricola [Sore], **Martin** (*b* Schwiebus, 6 Jan 1486; *d* Magdeburg, 10 June 1556). German music theorist, teacher and composer. He claimed to be the son of a peasant and self-taught in music. In 1519–20 he went to Magdeburg where he taught music both privately and at one of the parish schools. He became choirmaster of the town's Protestant Lateinschule either in 1525 when it was founded or after its expansion in 1527, remaining there for the rest of his life. Between 1527 and 1541 he enjoyed free board and lodging with the Magdeburg town councillor Heinrich Alemann, an enthusiastic music lover. Agricola was also a friend of the Wittenberg music printer Georg Rhau.

Agricola was an enthusiastic follower of Luther and one of the first Protestant school musicians in Germany. His early texts on music, written in German, addressed not only the pupils of the Lateinschule but also every amateur musician and music lover in Germany. In his later treatises on music he yielded, not without resistance, to the demands of the humanists for the use of Latin as the language of instruction. A number of his translations of technical terms from Latin into German are still used today. His compositions show sound technical ability. Josquin's influence can be seen in his motets, which are often in several sections and have texts from the psalms, the Gospels or the scriptures. He modelled the hymns, generally to texts by Aurelius Prudentius and Georg Fabricius, on the humanist odes. *Ein Sangbuchlein aller Sontags Evangelien* containing two- and three-voice German Protestant songs arranged according to the church calendar is the oldest collection of its kind. The *Instrumentische Gesenge*, a posthumous collection of 54 three- and four-part instrumental pieces with canons in the upper parts and freely contrapuntal lower parts, is one of the most important sources of information about the art of the early German instrumentalists.

WORKS

THEORETICAL

Ein kurtz deudsche Musica (Wittenberg, 1528, 3/1533/*R*1969 as *Musica choralis deudsch*); abridged Lat. version as *Rudimenta musices* (Wittenberg, 1539/*R*1966); the latter in abridged Ger. version as 'Eine kurtze deutsche Leyen Musica', preface to Ein Sangbuchlein aller Sontags Evangelien (Magdeburg, 1541)

Musica instrumentalis deudsch (Wittenberg, 1529/*R*1969, enlarged 5/1545)

Musica figuralis deudsch, with suppl. 'Büchlein von den Proportionibus' (Wittenberg, 1532/*R*1969)

Scholia in musicam planam Venceslai Philomatis, with suppl. 'Libellus de octo tonorum regularium compositione' (n.p., 1538) [commentary on Philomates's *Musicorum libri quatuor*, Wittenberg, 5/1534]

Quaestiones vulgatiores in musicum (Magdeburg, 1543)

Musicae ex prioribus editis musicis excerpta (Magdeburg, 1547) [extracts from earlier writings]

'Duo libri musices', preface to Instrumentische Gesenge (Wittenberg, 1561)

VOCAL

Ein Sangbuchlein aller Sontags Evangelien (Wittenberg, 1541)

Instrumentische Gesenge (Wittenberg, 1561), ed. H. Funck (Wolfenbüttel, 1933)

Magnificat tertii toni, *D-LEu* Thomaskirche 49–50

18 motets, Melodiae scholasticae (Wittenberg, 1557), 1567[1], *Dlb* Grimma LI A 272–4, *LEu* Thomaskirche 49–50, *Z* 1, 1; 73, 12; 2 ed. B. Engelke, *Magdeburger Geschichtsblätter* (1913)

10 hymns, 1552[1]

4 sacred songs, 1544[21], *HB* XI–XV, suppl., *Rp* A.R.95, AR 940–42; 3 ed. in DDT, xxxiv (1908/*R*)

BIBLIOGRAPHY

E. Praetorius: *Die Mensuraltheorie des Franchinus Gafurius* (Leipzig, 1905)

J. Wolf: *Handbuch der Notationskunde* (Leipzig, 1913–19/*R*1963)

G. Schünemann: *Geschichte der deutschen Schulmusik* (Leipzig, 1928)

H. Funck: *Martin Agricola: ein frühprotestantischer Schulmusiker* (Wolfenbüttel, 1933)

E. Valentin: 'Musikgeschichte Magdeburgs', *Magdeburger Geschichtsblätter* (Magdeburg, 1933–4)

H. Funck: 'Zur Komponistenfrage und Überlieferung des einzigen mehrstimmigen Spottgesangs auf das Augsburger Interim', *ZMw*, xvi (1934), 92

HEINRICH HÜSCHEN

Agricola, Rudolph (*b* Groningen, 1443; *d* Heidelberg, 28 Oct 1485). German humanist and philosopher who was also active as a musician. His early studies took place in Groningen, but in the late 1460s he travelled to Italy for further humanistic training. In 1468 he was at the University of Pavia, where he studied jurisprudence for several years. Later he transferred to Ferrara, where he studied Greek at the *Studio* and in 1476 delivered a Latin oration for the opening of the academic year in the presence of Duke Ercole I d'Este of Ferrara. This oration praised Duke Ercole's musical abilities with more than rhetorical flattery; Ercole was remarkably interested in music, and Agricola was formally engaged in December 1476 as organist of the ducal chapel, one of the largest and most opulent in Europe. Agricola's appointment is confirmed by archival records and by his letters (see Allen); in a letter written at Easter 1476 he stated that he was serving as ducal organist at a stipend of five ducats a month and 'hopes for six'. He served until 1477. His ability as a musician was noted by his biographers and by the German theorist Luscinius (1515).

Agricola is regarded as one of the most important figures in the transmission to northern Europe of Italian humanism. His interest in music and his practical musical ability distinguish him from many of his contemporary humanistic scholars and mark a turning point in the relationship between this broad intellectual movement and music. He was later strongly influential in the development of philosophy and education in Germany, and was greatly admired by Erasmus and Melanchthon.

BIBLIOGRAPHY

E. vander Straeten: *La musique aux Pays-Bas avant le XIXᵉ siècle* (Brussels, 1867–88/*R*1969), vi, 123f

P. S. Allen: 'The Letters of Rudolph Agricola', *English Historical Review*, xxi (1906), 302

W. Woodward: *Education in the Age of the Renaissance* (London, 1906)

E. Garin: 'Guarino Veronese e la cultura a Ferrara', *Ritratti di Umanisti* (Florence, 1967), 69–106

L. Lockwood: 'Music at Ferrara in the Period of Ercole I d'Este', *Studi musicali*, i/1 (1972), 101–31

LEWIS LOCKWOOD

Agricola, Wolfgang Christoph (*b* 1600–10; *d* c1659). German composer, organist and public official. It is possible that he is the same person as the Christoph Bauer who entered the University of Würzburg in 1625. From 1632 to 1642 he was at Neustadt an der Saale, from 1642 to 1644 at Bodenlauben and Ebenhausen and from 1645 to 1659 at Münnerstadt. In each place he was town clerk and notary; at Neustadt he was organist as well, and at the last three, which are near Würzburg, he was also an official of the Archbishop of Würzburg. He may have been a pupil of the Würzburg court composer Heinrich Pfendner, on works by whom he based eight eight-part masses (1647). His *Geistliches Waldvöglein* is a large collection of sacred songs in four parts, artless settings of popular, simple, often clumsy

verses, in which, however, 'the beginnings of the *Singmesse*' (see Ursprung) are discernible.

WORKS

(all published in Würzburg)

Fasciculus musicalis . . . liber 1, 2vv (1637)

Fasciculus musicalis octo missarum super octo cantionibus Henrici Pfendneri, 8vv (1647)

Fasciculus musicalis variarum cantionum, 2–4, 6, 8vv (1648)

Geistliches Waldvöglein, 4vv (2/1664)

Keusche Meer-Fräulein, 1v, bc (1718)

BIBLIOGRAPHY

O. Ursprung: *Die katholische Kirchenmusik* (Potsdam, 1931), 225

M. Sack: *Leben und Werk Heinrich Pfendners: ein Beitrag zur süddeutschen Musikgeschichte im frühen 17. Jahrhundert* (diss., Free U. of Berlin, 1954), 215ff

HANS-CHRISTIAN MÜLLER

Agthe, Albrecht Wilhelm Johann (*b* Ballenstedt, 13 July 1790; *d* Berlin, 8 Oct 1873). German pianist, music teacher and composer, son of Carl Christian Agthe. He received his musical education from Ebeling in Magdeburg and Seebach in Klosterbergen before studying composition and counterpoint with M. G. Fischer in Erfurt. In 1810 he settled in Leipzig as a music teacher and second violinist in the Gewandhaus Orchestra, and there published his first compositions. He founded a music academy in Dresden with C. Kräger in 1823 which was publicly endorsed by Carl Maria von Weber; J. B. Logier's methods of keyboard instruction were used there. In the next decade he set up similar institutes in Posen (1826), where Theodore and Adolf Kullak were his pupils, in Breslau (1831) and finally in Berlin (1832). He was forced to retire in 1845 because of weak eyesight. His compositions include at least nine opus numbers for piano (some with other instruments) and two manuscript songs in the Stiftung Preussischer Kulturbesitz, Berlin.

BIBLIOGRAPHY

C. F. von Ledebur: *Tonkünstler-Lexicon Berlin's* (Berlin, 1861/*R*1965) [with list of works]

G. Faulhaber: 'Agthe, Albrecht Wilhelm Johann', *MGG*

DIETER HÄRTWIG

Agthe, Carl Christian (*b* Hettstedt, 16 June 1762; *d* Ballenstedt, 27 Nov 1797). German organist, harpsichordist and composer, father of Albrecht Wilhelm Johann Agthe. He first learnt music with his grandfather Johann Michael Agthe, Kantor at the Rathsschule, and his great-uncle Andreas Agthe, a local organist; he later continued his musical studies as a choirboy and as a member of the local Stadtpfeiffe. From 1776 to 1782 he was director of music with the Hündelberg theatrical company in Reval, where he composed his first Singspiels. He then moved to Ballenstedt to join the court orchestra of Prince Friedrich Albrecht of Anhalt-Bernburg as an organist and harpsichordist. There he became known as one of the best organists of his time and, after further studies with F. W. Rust, as an active composer of Singspiels, songs and instrumental pieces. His best-known work is a setting of Kotzebue's *Der Spiegelritter* (1795), which was first performed by an amateur society in Ballenstedt and several times revived. Agthe himself undertook the publication of his only extant published works – two volumes of songs and a set of three easy keyboard sonatas.

WORKS

STAGE

(music lost)

Singspiels: Martin Velten, Reval, 1778; Aconcius und Cydippe (after Ovid), Reval, ?1780; Das Milchmädchen, Reval, ?1780; Erwin und Elmire (Goethe), Ballenstedt, c1785; Der Spiegelritter (3, A. von Kotzebue), Ballenstedt, 1795

Others: Philemon und Baucis (divertissement), mentioned in Reichard; Die weissen Inseln, pubd lib in *D-BAL*

VOCAL

Mehala, die Tochter Jephta, musical drama, 4vv, chorus, orch, *US-Wc*
Lieder eines leichten und fliessenden Gesangs, 1v, kbd (Ballenstedt and Dessau, 1782)
Der Morgen, Mittag, Abend und Nacht (Sander), songs, S, kbd (Ballenstedt and Dessau, 1784)
Empor erhebe dich Gesang, cantata, 1v, chorus, *D-GBR*
6 songs, 1v, pf, *USSR-KAu*

INSTRUMENTAL

Orch: 11 syms., *D-B*; sym., *W*; fl conc., *B*; conc., vn, hpd, orch, *B*; 14 dances, *Bds*
Kbd: 3 leichte Sonaten, hpd/pf (Ballenstedt and Leipzig, 1790); 3 fugues, org, *B*

BIBLIOGRAPHY

GerberL; *GerberNL*
H. A. O. Reichard, ed.: *Theater-Kalender 1793* (Gotha, 1793), 107
G. Schilling, ed.: *Encyclopädie der gesammten musikalischen Wissenschaften oder Universal-Lexikon der Tonkunst* (Stuttgart, 1835–42/*R*1973)
G. Faulhaber: 'Agthe, Carl Christian', *MGG*

DIETER HÄRTWIG

Aguado (y Garcia), Dionysio (*b* Madrid, 8 April 1784; *d* Madrid, 29 Dec 1849). Spanish guitar virtuoso and composer. 'Padre Basilio' of Madrid, possibly Miguel Garcia, gave him his first instruction in the guitar, an instrument for which tablature notation wass still used in Spain. In about 1800 Aguado, like Fernando Sor, was influenced by the Italian Federico Moretti and adopted the conventional staff notation for the guitar; thereafter both Spaniards published their music in the improved manner championed by Moretti, distinguishing the musical parts by the direction of note stems, use of rests, etc. Aguado's artistic career unfolded slowly, owing to the Napoleonic invasion of Spain and its aftermath. He retreated to the village of Fuenlabrada in 1803, teaching and perfecting his technique there until 1824, the year his mother died; his *Colección de estudios para guitarra* appeared in Madrid in 1820. He moved to Paris in 1825 (while Sor was in Russia) and immediately gained an enviable reputation as a virtuoso and teacher; a revised version of his *Escuela de guitarra* (Madrid, 1825) was translated into French as *Méthode complète pour la guitare* and published in Paris towards 1830. The last ten years of Aguado's life were allegedly spent in Madrid, where he revised his method and devoted himself to teaching.

In the years before his final departure from Paris (1838), Aguado was in close collaboration with Sor. They gave many concerts together, and Sor dedicated a duet op.41, *Les deux amis*, to his younger colleague. They did not agree on right-hand technique in guitar playing; Aguado recommended the use of fingernails in plucking the strings for the sake of clarity, while Sor advocated using the flesh of the fingertips for a mellower and more powerful tone. But despite their differences, they greatly admired one another, Sor gallantly 'excusing' Aguado's fingernail technique on account of the latter's superb musicianship and skilled execution.

A complete catalogue of Aguado's compositions is not available. According to Prat, he wrote several dozen studies, rondos, dances and fantasias. His guitar method was extremely popular in the 19th century, and was republished frequently. He is also known for the invention of the *tripedisono*, which supported the guitar away from the performer's body.

BIBLIOGRAPHY

'Aguado', *Encyclopédie pittoresque de la musique*, ed. I. A. Ledhuy and H. Bertini (Paris, 1835)
D. Prat: 'Aguado', *Diccionario biografico de guitarristas* (Buenos Aires, 1934)
E. Pujol: *El dilema del sonido en la guitarra* (Buenos Aires, 1960)
P. Cox: *The Evolution of Playing Techniques of the Six-stringed Classic Guitar as seen through Teaching Method Books from ca. 1780–ca. 1850* (diss., Indiana U., in preparation)

THOMAS F. HECK

Aguiari [Agujari], **Lucrezia** ['La Basterdina', 'La Bastardella'] (*b* Ferrara, 1743; *d* Parma, 18 May 1783). Italian soprano. Traditions explaining her curious nickname describe her variously as a foundling raised by Leopoldo Aguiari, his natural daughter or that of Marchese Bentivoglio, while her pronounced limp was supposedly the result of having been partly eaten in infancy by a dog or hog. Her early studies in Ferrara with Brizio Petrucci, *maestro di cappella* at the cathedral, and then with Abbé Lambertini revealed her exceptional talents. After her opera début (Florence, 1764) and initial successes (Padua, Verona, 1765; Genoa, Lucca, Parma, 1766) she settled in Parma, where she met the composers Mysliveček, with whom she had an affair, and Giuseppe Colla, the newly appointed *maestro*. On 1 January 1768 the court at Parma appointed her *virtuosa di camera*. From then until her retirement she was one of Europe's most sought-after sopranos.

In May 1768 Aguiari sang at Naples in Paisiello's *festa teatrale* for the wedding of the king and Maria Carolina. Paisiello, reportedly out of spite, composed for her two extremely difficult arias, which, however, she carried off triumphantly. At Parma in summer 1769, after singing in Gluck's *Le feste d'Apollo* commemorating the same wedding, she began her nearly exclusive devotion to the works of Colla, whose pastorale *Licido e Mopso* she also sang then. Their association took them to Venice for his *Vologeso* (spring 1770) and Genoa for his *L'eroe cinese* (summer 1771). At Turin (Carnival 1772 and 1773), Parma (August 1773) and Milan (Carnival 1774) she always sang at least one work by Colla. After a visit to Paris (July 1774) and Turin (1775) she sang from 1775 to 1777 at the Pantheon concerts in London, where Colla was with her, at least in 1775 (in spring 1776 she went with him to Pavia). She then appeared for two more years in Italy (Florence, autumn 1778, Carnival 1779; Venice, Carnival 1780) before leaving the stage. By 1780 she and Colla were married. She died of tuberculosis and not, as rumoured, of slow poisoning by jealous rivals.

Aguiari's voice was an object of wonder to her contemporaries, especially her range of three and a half octaves and her facility in executing the most difficult passage-work. 'I could not believe that she was able to reach C sopra acuto' wrote Leopold Mozart on 24 March 1770, 'but my ears convinced me'. In a postscript Wolfgang seconded this testimony, noting some bravura passages she had sung. Burney called her 'a truly wonderful performer. The lower part of her voice was full, round, of an excellent quality and its compass . . . beyond any one who had then [been] heard . . . . Her shake was open and perfect, . . . her execution marked and rapid; and her style of singing . . . grand and majestic'. According to Fanny Burney, Aguiari's voice 'has a mellowness, a sweetness, that are quite vanquishing . . . . She has the highest taste, with an expression the most pathetic'. As an actress, wrote Sara Goudar, Aguiari 'depicts on the stage any character whatsoever with the greatest realism. She is comparable to Raphael, in that she is outstanding as much in the expression of the music as in the harmony of her singing'.

BIBLIOGRAPHY

BurneyH
S. Goudar: *Remarques sur la musique et la danse* (Venice, 1773; It. trans., n.d.), 30
Lord Mount-Edgcumbe: *Musical Reminiscences* (London, 4/1834/ R1972)
F. D'Arblay: *Memoirs of Doctor Burney*, ii (London, 1832), 21ff, 42
Castil-Blaze: *L'opéra italien de 1548 à 1856* (Paris, 1856), 159ff, 209ff, 213
J. Harris [Earl of Malmesbury], ed.: *A Series of Letters of the First Earl of Malmesbury, his Family and Friends from 1745 to 1820*, i (London, 1870), 297
E. Greppi and A. Giulini, eds.: *Carteggio di Pietro e di Alessandro Verri*, vi (Milan, 1923), 83, 183, 185
N. Pelicelli: 'Musicisti in Parma nel sec. XVIII', *NA*, xi (1934), 239–81, esp. 280
E. Anderson, ed.: *The Letters of Mozart and his Family* (London, 1938, 2/1966), i, 120ff; ii, 663f
R. Giazotto: *La musica a Genova nella vita pubblica e privata dal XIII al XVIII secolo* (Genoa, 1951), 201, 233f
R. Nielsen: 'Aguiari, Lucrezia', *DBI*

KATHLEEN KUZMICK HANSELL

Aguilar, Antonia Maria. *See* GIRELLI, ANTONIA MARIA.

Aguilar, Gaspar de (*fl* 1st half of the 16th century). Spanish music theorist. He wrote a treatise *Arte de principios de canto llano* (published between 1530 and 1537); it is a conventional work following traditional lines, limited to purely technical aspects of liturgical chant. He regarded the B♭ as a necessary accidental for chant based on F to avoid the melodic tritone, gave rules for the use of *plicae*, categorized intervals according to their effect on the senses, and rejected the Pythagorean classification. Aguilar seems to have been familiar with the writings of his contemporaries, citing Espinosa and Tover among Spaniards, Burzio, Fogliano and Gaffurius among Italians. His quotations are more accurate than most writers' and add considerably to the merit of the work.

BIBLIOGRAPHY

R. Stevenson: *Spanish Music in the Age of Columbus* (The Hague, 1960)
F. J. León Tello: *Estudios de historia de la teoría musical* (Madrid, 1962)

F. J. LEÓN TELLO

Aguilera de Heredia, Sebastián (*b* ?Saragossa, *c*1565; *d* Saragossa, 16 Dec 1627). Spanish composer and organist. When, in some copies of his *Canticum Beatissimae Virginis deiparae Mariae* (published 1618), Aguilera de Heredia called himself 'Caesaraugustano presbytero' ('Saragossan priest') he was probably referring to his birthplace. In 1585 he was appointed organist at Huesca Cathedral and remained there until, on 29 September 1603, he became 'priest and master organist' at the Cathedral of La Seo, Saragossa. By 20 January 1604 he was exempted, because of his eminence, from service at canonical hours except on solemn feasts. Repeatedly over the years the cathedral organ was repaired according to his specifications. In recognition of his *Canticum Beatissimae Virginis deiparae Mariae*, he received gifts from La Seo (100 libras) and Huesca Cathedral (150 reales). In December 1620 he used his influence to ensure the appointment as assistant organist of his pupil José Ximénez, who succeeded him as organist after his death.

Aguilera wrote exclusively for the church, in his organ works as well as his vocal music. His organ works are on the one hand within the traditions established in Spain by Cabezón and Santa Maria, while on the other they include enough that was new to prompt the developments found in the work of men such as Cabanilles, Correa de Arauxo, Rodrigues Coelho and Ximénez. His tientos (sometimes called 'obra', *medio registro*, etc) are of several types. For three of them he was the first Iberian composer to use – if not the device itself – the term *falsas* to denote compositions in slow tempo with almost continuous use of dissonance, unexpected harmonic progressions, false relations, affective melodic intervals and the like. Five monothematic tientos constitute another group. A single theme may either be used in each of several sections accompanied by differing contrapuntal figuration as in the contemporary fantasia, or it may itself be transformed in a series of sections set off by changes of metre. Historically perhaps the most significant of Aguilera's organ pieces are those employing *medio registro* technique, common in Spain, whereby each half of the keyboard is capable of independent registration. Contrapuntal development of a theme is here secondary to the highlighting of one hand as a solo – always, with Aguilera, the left hand. This means that a phrase of two to four bars recurs systematically with successive transpositions to the dominant or subdominant. Figuration is continuous and often virtuosic, but animation never degenerates into superficial brilliance. Four other compositions are based on hymn melodies popular in Spain. Two settings of *Salve regina* employing only the first four notes of the plainsong are extended contrapuntal works analogous to fugally elaborated chorales. The other two settings, in which the traditional Spanish *Pange lingua* melody is treated as a cantus firmus, were apparently intended to accompany singing of the hymn. Rhythmic vitality and variety are conspicuous features of these pieces, especially when they take the form of repeated asymmetrical patterns such as the two shown in ex.1.

Ex. 1

Aguilera was famous for his widely used *Canticum Beatissimae Virginis deiparae Mariae*, a collection of 36 settings of the *Magnificat* – an exceptionally large number for one composer. It consists mainly of four cycles, each containing eight settings, one for each tone; the cycles are for five, six, eight and four voices respectively. Polyphonically composed verses alternate with the chant. Each verse of each five-part work has a canon at an interval corresponding to the number of the tone (canon at the unison for 1st tone, at the second for 2nd tone and so on). Aguilera treated plainsong recitation tones as cantus firmi and occasionally made effective use of sharp dissonances and false relations. The remaining four works are complete settings of the canticle for double chorus in the grand manner of the late works of Victoria. Except that there are no continuo parts, these settings, in which polyphony is skilfully contrasted with massive homophonic sections featuring vigorous speech rhythms, show the direction in which Spanish polychoral music was moving.

WORKS

Editions: *Spanish Organ Masters after Antonio de Cabezón*, ed.
W. Apel, CEKM, xiv (1971) [S]
Antología de organistas españoles del siglo XVII, i–iv, ed.
H. Anglés (Barcelona, 1965–8) [A]
S. Aguilera de Heredia: Choral Works, ed. B. Hudson, CMM,
lxxi (1975)

CHORAL

Canticum Beatissimae Virginis deiparae Mariae (Saragossa, 1618), 36
Magnificat, 1 in each of the 8 tones, for 4, 5, 6, 8vv, 1 each in tones 1,
3, 6, 8 for 8vv (double chorus)
De profundis (Ps cxxix), dubious authenticity

ORGAN

Pange lingua a tres sobre vajo, S no.10, A iii, no.2
Salbe de lleno, 1. tono, S no.11
Salbe de 1. tono por delasolre, S no.12, A ii, no.2
Tiento de 4. tono de falsas, S no.13, A iii, no.4
Tiento de 4. tono de falsas, S no.14, A i, no.2
Falsas de 6. tono, S no.15, A iv, no.11
Obra de 1. tono, S no.16, A i, no.4
Obra de 1. tono, S no.17, A i, no.3
Tiento de 4. tono, S no.18, A ii, no.1
Obra de 8. tono per gesolreut, S no.19
Tiento de 8. tono por delasolre, S no.20, A iii, no.5
Obra de 8. tono alto. Ensalada, S no.21, A iv, no.17
Vajo, 1. tono, S no.22, A iii, no.3
Vajo de 1. tono, S no.23, A iv, no.1
Registo baixo de 2. tom, S no.24
Dos vajos de 8. tono, S no.25, A ii, no.3
Pange lingua, S no.26, A i, no.1

ANON. WORKS ATTRIB. AGUILERA

Tiento lleno, 1. tono, A iii, no.6
Tiento lleno, 5. tono, A iii, no.11
Tiento lleno, 6. tono, A iii, no.13
Tiento lleno, 7. tono, A iii, no.14
Tiento lleno, 8. tono, A iii, no.15
Tiento de batalla, 8. tono, A iv, no.14

BIBLIOGRAPHY

G. Frotscher: *Geschichte des Orgel-Spiels und der Orgel-Komposition*
(Berlin, 1936, 2/1959)
S. Kastner: *Contribución al estudio de la música española y portuguesa*
(Lisbon, 1941)
W. Apel: 'Spanish Organ Music of the early 17th Century', *JAMS*, xv
(1962), 174
L. Siemens Hernández: 'La Seo de Zaragoza, destacada escuela de
órgano en el siglo XVII', pt. i, *AnM*, xxi (1966), 147
W. Apel: *Geschichte der Orgel- und Klaviermusik bis 1700* (Kassel,
1967; Eng. trans., rev. 1972)

BARTON HUDSON

Aguinaldo. A generic term used in Venezuela for both
religious and secular Christmas songs, including the
villancico, *alabanza*, *romance*, *décima*, *estribillo* and
canto de adoración. Melodies are usually in 2/4 or 6/8
metre. Syncopated melodies and vocal harmonizations
in either parallel 3rds or contrapuntal style are common. Percussion ensembles featuring the *pandareta*
(tambourine), *tambora criolla* (drum), *charrasca*
(scraper), *chineco* (rattle) and the *furruco* (friction drum)
are characteristic, as are string instruments such as the
guitar, *cinco* (small five-string guitar), *tiple* (small 12-
string guitar) and, especially, the *cuatro* (small four-
string guitar).

WILLIAM GRADANTE

Aguirre, Julián (*b* Buenos Aires, 28 Jan 1868; *d* Buenos
Aires, 13 Aug 1924). Argentinian composer and pianist.
He attended the Madrid Conservatory (1882–6), studying composition with Arrieta, harmony with Aranguren
and fugue with Cató, and taking first prizes for piano,
harmony and counterpoint. While in Spain he impressed
Albéniz with his playing, and when he returned to
Argentina in 1886 he made a reputation as a pianist. He
gave concerts in the interior of the country, staying for a
year in Rosario, and then settled in Buenos Aires, where
he played a significant part in the musical life of the city.
As a composer he followed the national style initiated

by Williams, using Creole melodies, particularly *tristes*,
in numerous songs. These established him as one of the
most highly esteemed Argentinian composers of his
generation. He was secretary and harmony professor at
the conservatories founded by Gutiérrez and Williams;
and he helped to create the music section of the Buenos
Aires Athenaeum (1892) and the Argentine Music
School (1916). His compositions are in the main small-
scale instrumental and vocal pieces, of which the choral
works gave a new impetus to Argentinian youth choirs.
Juan José Castro, Ansermet and other conductors
arranged his instrumental pieces for orchestra.

WORKS
(*selective list*)

Choral for 4vv: La clase, Emblema, Madrigal, Matinal, Pasional
Songs for 1v, pf: Berceuse, Canciones argentinas, Caminito, Chansons
pour elle, Huella, Jardins, La lune est transie, Las mañanitas, El nido
ausente, Rosas orientales, La rose, Ton image
Vn, pf: Balada, Berceuse, Nocturno, Rapsodia argentina, Sonata
Pf: Aires nacionales, 4 vols.; La danza de Belkis, Gato, Huella, Idilio,
Intimas nos.1–2, Mazurca española, Romanza, Sonata

BIBLIOGRAPHY

J. F. Giacobbe: *Julián Aguirre* (Buenos Aires, n.d.)
Special number, *ARS* (Buenos Aires, 1949)

SUSANA SALGADO

Agus, Giuseppe (*b* c1725; *d* c1800). Italian composer.
He probably arrived in England about 1750. He was
soon in demand as a composer of ballet music for the
Italian opera, and by 1758 works by him were included
in Hasse's *Opera Dances*. The eighth volume of that
anthology is entirely by him, and between 1768 and
1788 he published no fewer than seven other books of
opera dances. In addition to publishing collections of
vocal and instrumental music, Agus edited *Six
Favourite Overtures in 8 Parts* (London, 1762) containing works by Cocchi, Galuppi, Jomelli and Graun. His
sonatas and trios are fluent essays in the Tartini idiom,
with judicious use of double stopping. But public taste
was best suited by his flair for brief but tuneful dance
movements in a variety of styles, the tambourin being
especially favoured.

WORKS
(*all published in London*)

OPERA DANCES

Pieces in The Comic Tunes . . . to the Celebrated Dances . . . Compos'd
by sigr. Hasse, vi–vii (1758–9)
The Comic Tunes to All the late Opera Dances . . . Compos'd by Sigr
Agus, viii (1761)
The Allemands danced at the King's Theatre (c 1767)
Opera Dances, fl, vn, hpd, i–v (c1768–c1788)
The Ballet Champêtre, a comic dance, pf (1775)

OTHER WORKS

op.
1   Sonate, vn, b (c1750); as 6 Solos (1751)
2   6 Solos, vn, hpd (1751)
3   6 Trii, 2 vn, vc (?1764)
4   6 Notturnos, 2 vn, vc obbl (1770)
[5] 12 Duets, 2vv, hpd (1772)
6   6 Sonatas (c1775); 2 for vn, tr viol, vc; 2 for 2 vn, bc; 2 for fl, vn,
     bc
9   6 Italian Duetts, 2vv, pf (c1795)
opp.7, 8 unknown
Was ever poor fellow, air, 1v/fl/vn, hpd, in Love in a Village (1763)

BIBLIOGRAPHY

L. de La Laurencie: *L'école française de violon de Lully à Viotti* (Paris,
1922–4/*R*1971)
J. A. Parkinson: 'Who was Agus?', *MT*, cxiv (1973), 693

JOHN A. PARKINSON

Agus, Joseph (*b* 1749; *d* Paris, 1798). Italian violinist
and composer, probably son of Giuseppe Agus. Having
studied the violin under Nardini in Italy 'Agus jr' first
appeared in London on 26 February 1773 at the Hay-

market. In 1778 Blundell published his duets for two violins.

On 19 March 1778 he was found guilty at Kingston assizes of attempted rape upon his godchild, Elizabeth Weichsell, aged 11. In view of her later notoriety (as ELIZABETH BILLINGTON) some doubt must be cast upon the veracity of the child's testimony which secured Agus's conviction despite his protestations of innocence. As a result of this scandal he emigrated to France. He was appointed *maître de solfège* at the Paris Conservatoire in 1795, where he received a grant of 3000 livres from the National Council. He contributed to the collection of solfeggi issued under the Conservatoire's auspices. Two collections of catches and glees arranged for instruments were published in England, and a set of trios in Paris, where Barbieri impudently republished his violin duets as Boccherini's op.37.

Many errors in earlier editions of *Grove* and other dictionaries are due to Fétis, who misnamed Agus 'Henri' and confused him with his father.

BIBLIOGRAPHY

FétisB

J. Ridgeway, ed.: *Memoirs of Mrs Billington from her Birth* (London, 1792)

C. Pierre: *Conservatoire de musique documents historiques* (Paris, 1900)

L. de La Laurencie: *L'école française de violon de Lully à Viotti* (Paris, 1922–4/R1971)

J. A. Parkinson: 'Who was Agus?', *MT*, cxiv (1973), 693

JOHN A. PARKINSON

Ágústsson, Herbert H. (*b* Mürzzuschlag, 8 Aug 1926). Icelandic horn player, teacher and composer of Austrian birth. He completed studies in Graz under Mixa and Michl in 1944 and was then first horn of the Graz PO for seven years. In 1952 he moved to Iceland, where he has been active as first horn of the Iceland SO, besides teaching and conducting choirs. As a composer he has taken some interest in 12-note methods while favouring sacred music in an abstract style.

WORKS
(selective list)

Orch: Shades of Colour, op.17, 1965; Conc. breve, op.19, 1970; Veränderungen, 1972; Sinfonietta, wind, 1973

Vocal: Prelude and 3 Psalms, B, orch, 1966; Psalms in the Atomic Age, Mez, fl, ob, pf, vc, 1968; Athvarf, S, orch, 1974; Music funebre (Bible, M. Johannesson), S, A, T, B, chorus, orch, 1975

Inst: Struktura, fl, pf, 1967

BIBLIOGRAPHY

A. Burt: *Iceland's Twentieth-century Composers and a Listing of their Works* (Fairfax, Virginia, in preparation)

AMANDA M. BURT

Ahern, David (Anthony) (*b* Sydney, 2 Nov 1947). Australian composer. He studied theory at the New South Wales State Conservatorium of Music and composition privately with Richard Meale and Nigel Butterley. He attended master classes given by Stockhausen in Cologne and Darmstadt in 1968, and in 1969 worked as Stockhausen's assistant in Cologne; during this period he also worked with Cornelius Cardew in London. He had considerable success with his first orchestral work, *After Mallarmé* (1966), in which the influences of Boulez, Stockhausen and Penderecki are effectively absorbed. Since then he has sought new directions. In 1971 he formed a group called Teletopa to perform both compositions and intuitive improvisations of a kind related to the activities of Stockhausen, Cardew and others. This has involved the use of conventional and unconventional musical instruments with varied electronic manipulation in a kind of 'musical theatre'. His *Cinemusic* (1972) shows an extension of this process with the interaction of live performers and film.

WORKS

4 orch works, incl. After Mallarmé, 1966; Ned Kelly Music, 1967

7 works for various solo insts and chamber groups

Journal, radiophonic, 1968–9

Stereo/Mono, wind soloists, loudspeaker feedback, 1971

Cinemusic, various insts and film, 1972

Principal publisher: Universal

BIBLIOGRAPHY

A. McCredie: *A Catalogue of 46 Australian Composers and Selected Works* (Canberra, 1969), 1

D. Ahern and B. Low: 'Interview with Teletopa', *Music Now*, ii (1972), 18

J. Murdoch: *Australia's Contemporary Composers* (Melbourne and Sydney, 1972), 1ff

DAVID SYMONS

Ahle, Johann Georg (*b* Mühlhausen, baptized 12 June 1651; *d* Mühlhausen, 2 Dec 1706). German composer, theorist, organist and poet, son of Johann Rudolf Ahle. He no doubt received his musical education from his father, whom he succeeded at the age of 23 as organist of St Blasius, Mühlhausen. Like his father he held the post until his death, and he was succeeded by the young Bach. Again like his father, he was elected to the town council. He was described on the title-page of his *Sapphisches Ehrenlied* (1680) as a bachelor of law, but it is not known where he studied. His education may well have included training in literary composition, for he distinguished himself as a poet and was crowned poet laureate by the Emperor Leopold I in 1680. His music, some of which is lost, is almost totally unknown. Much of it is scattered through his series of anecdotal novels named after the Muses which themselves deserve closer study. He clearly followed his father in his interest in writing songs, both sacred and secular, and his style in them seems to be even more popular and folklike. He also composed music for the church and for occasions such as weddings, anniversaries, celebrations of political events and ceremonies honouring distinguished visitors to Mühlhausen. Among his theoretical writings is his enlarged and copiously annotated edition of his father's singing manual. Here, as in his own treatises, among which the four *Musikalische Gespräche* are conspicuous, he displayed a comprehensiveness of musical knowledge and a richness of documentation of various theoretical facts that point to an education in the theory and history of music as thorough as that of such notable writers as Printz and Werckmeister (the latter was a personal friend of his). The *Musikalische Gespräche*, although written as fanciful dialogues between friends and the author (writing as 'Helianus', an anagram of 'Ahlenius') as they enjoy the pleasures of nature during the four seasons, are invaluable documents for the history of music theory. The *Frühlings-Gespräche* and *Herbst-Gespräche* consider consonance and dissonance, the *Sommer-Gespräche* treats of cadences, musical-rhetorical figures and the modes, and the *Winter-Gespräche* of intervals and further about the modes.

WORKS
(all printed works published in Mühlhausen)

SACRED

Neues Zehn geistlicher Andachten, 1, 2vv, 1–4 insts, bc (1671), ?lost; 1 melody in J. Zahn, *Die Melodien der deutschen evangelischen Kirchenlieder* (Gütersloh, 1888/R1963)

Ach! Ach! ihr Augen, Ach! in Der Gläubigen . . . Adel und Würde . . . bey Beerdigung des . . . Johann Rudolph Ahlen, 11 July 1673, a 5 (1673)

Nun danket alle Gott, denen . . . Bürgermeistern . . . des neuen Rats . . . Mitgliedern, 4vv, chorus 7vv, 5 insts, bc (1675), ?lost
Göttliche Friedensverheissung: Ach, wenn wird in unsern Landen . . . mit singenden und klingenden Stimmen ausgezieret, 8 Jan 1679, 4vv, 5 insts, bc (1679)
3 neue . . . Behtlieder . . . an den Drei Einigen Gott um gnädige Beschirmung für der . . . sich einschleichenden grausamen Pest, 4vv, bc (1681)
Sing- und Klingestücklein: Wohl dem, der ein tugendsam Weib hat, wedding motet, 20 June 1681, 1v, 3 insts, bc (1681)
Psalm xci: Wer gnädig wird beschützet, occasional work, 9 Jan 1682, 4vv, 5 insts, bc (1682)
Veni Sancte Spiritus, 5vv, chorus 5vv, 5 insts, bc, D-Bds

SECULAR

Instrumentalische Frühlingsmusik, 2 vols. (1675–6), ?lost
Freudenlied . . . wegen des neugeborenen Erzherzoglichen Prinzen . . . Dank- Lob- und Freudenfeste (1678), ?lost
Sapphisches Ehrenlied . . . Georg Neumarken, 17 Aug 1680 (1680), ?lost; for fuller title see MGG

NOVELS

(only those including music)

Unstrutische Clio oder Musicalischer Mayenlust, i (1676), 1 ed. in Winterfeld; ii as Unstrutische Calliope (1677); iii as Unstrutische Erato (1677), 1 ed. in Winterfeld and in J. Zahn, Die Melodien der deutschen evangelischen Kirchenlieder (Gütersloh, 1888/R1963); iv as Unstrutische Euterpe (1678)
Unstrutische Melpomene, begreiffend XII. neue . . . Beht- Buss- und Sterbelieder, 4vv (1678)
Unstrutische Polyhymnia, XII . . . Fest- Lob- und Danklieder, 4vv (1678), ?lost; 1 ed. in Winterfeld and in J. Zahn, Die Melodien der deutschen evangelischen Kirchenlieder (Gütersloh, 1888/R1963)
Unstrutische Urania, XII . . . geistliche Lenzen- und Liebeslieder, 4vv (1679), ?lost
Unstrutische Thalia, XX . . . Geigenspiele, a 4 (1679), ?lost
Anmutiges Zehn . . . Violdigambenspiele, a 4 (1681), ?lost
Unstruhtischer Apollo begreiffend X. sonderbahre Fest- Lob- Dank- und Freudenlieder (1681); 1 ed. in Winterfeld
Unstrutische Terpsichore (n.d.), see Walther

WRITINGS

(all published in Mühlhausen)

Johan Georg Ahlens musikalisches Frühlings-Gespräche, darinnen fürnehmlich vom grund- und kunstmässigen Komponiren gehandelt wird (1695)
Johan Georg Ahlens musikalisches Sommer-Gespräche (1697)
Johan Georg Ahlens musikalisches Herbst-Gespräche (1699)
Johan Georg Ahlens musikalisches Winter-Gespräche (1701)
Johan Georg Ahlens Unstruhtinne, oder musikalische Gartenlust, welcher beigefügt sind allerhand ergetz- und nützliche Anmerkungen (1687)
Kurze doch deutliche Anleitung zu der lieblich- und löblichen Singekunst . . . mit . . . nöthigen Anmerkungen . . . zum Drukke befördert durch des seeligen Verfassers Sohn Johann Georg Ahlen (1690; enlarged 2/1704) [enlarged edn. of J. R. Ahle: Brevis et perspicua introductio]

BIBLIOGRAPHY

WaltherML
C. von Winterfeld: Der evangelische Kirchengesang, ii (Leipzig, 1845/R1966)
H. Kretzschmar: Geschichte des neuen deutschen Liedes (Leipzig, 1911/R1966)
Z. V. D. Sevier: The Theoretical Works and Music of Johann Georg Ahle (diss., U. of North Carolina, 1974)

GEORGE J. BUELOW

Ahle, Johann Rudolf (b Mühlhausen, 24 Dec 1625; d Mühlhausen, 9 July 1673). German composer, organist, writer on music and poet, father of Johann Georg Ahle. He was a prolific composer of popular sacred music, notably songs, in central Germany during the generation before Bach was born there.

1. LIFE. The date of Ahle's birth derives from a report published in the Neues Mühlhäusisches Wochenblatt (1798, no.31; see Wolf). He was educated first at the local Gymnasium and then, from about 1643, at the Gymnasium at Göttingen. In the spring of 1645 he entered Erfurt University as a student of theology. Nothing is known of his musical training, though in 1646, while enrolled at the university, he was appointed

Kantor at the elementary school and church of St Andreas, Erfurt, and at this period he became well known for his ability as an organist. He returned to Mühlhausen to marry in 1650, but only at the end of 1654 does he seem to have obtained his first and only position as a musician there, as organist of St Blasius. In addition to this post, in which his fame grew throughout Thuringia and in which his son succeeded him after his death, he held several municipal offices, belonged to the town council and in the year of his death was elected mayor.

2. WORKS. Except for his collection of dances of 1650, Ahle's large output of music consists entirely of sacred vocal works. On the whole it is interesting not because it is original but because it is typical of the music written for the Protestant Church in Thuringia and Saxony during the third quarter of the 17th century. Moreover, since Ahle and his son were the immediate predecessors of the young Bach, who as his first employment held the same position as they did at St Blasius, the state of music under them provides at least a few clues to some of the early influences on Bach's style. Ahle was probably influenced by Michael Altenburg and especially by Hammerschmidt, who, though belonging to the generation of Schütz, wrote simpler and more popular church music: certainly the tendency towards popularization characterizes almost all of Ahle's output. His music exhibits the variety of forms and styles characteristic of the combined heritage of 16th-century German Protestant music, especially chorales, and the infusion in the 17th century of Italian innovations from composers such as the Gabrielis and Monteverdi. There is considerable emphasis on the technique of the vocal concerto, in which the continuo supplies the foundation for the free, dramatic vocal writing for one or more solo voices, up to 24 (as in the 1665 volume). Ahle often added ritornellos and postludes for small instrumental combinations, which in the concerto style are also integrated within the vocal writing, imitating or emphatically underscoring it. Many of his vocal concertos are on a small scale, but he could create an impressive dramatic structure on a large scale, for example the noble Misericordias Domini: Ich will singen von der Genade des Herren ewiglich from the 1665 volume (in DDT, v). It is basically a concerto for two voices, with two violins, founded on an ostinato consisting of a rising C major scale, and he built on these foundations a set of variations of ever-increasing musical drama and fine variety that can bear comparison with the chaconne variations found in Bach's church cantatas. Some works by Ahle are based on varied forms of chorale melodies, though more frequently he retained only the chorale text in his concertos. His monodies and dialogues (as in the 1648 book) continue, like those of Hammerschmidt, the Italian-influenced tradition of such pieces that Schütz developed with such memorable results. Many of his dialogues are settings of the type of over-dramatic, rather stereotyped Baroque expression of antithesis found in two obviously contrasted poetic thoughts – for example the words of Mary Magdalene and Jesus at the tomb (set by Ahle in the second work in DDT, v) – such as is later found in Bach's cantata duets.

Ahle is best remembered for his large corpus of sacred songs (Arien) for one to four voices with ritornellos, which, as he directed, can be performed 'with or without the basso continuo'. The texts are either from the Bible or by such well-known poets as Johann Franck, Martin Opitz and Johann Rist and authors from Mühlhausen – Johann Vockerodt (Ahle's predecessor at St Blasius), Ludwig Starck and Ahle himself. These simple, chorale-like tunes were not originally meant for congregational singing but could be performed either by soloists, chorus, or a solo singer with instrumental accompaniment. They were a successful outcome of Ahle's intention to revitalize sacred music. Many of the tunes were incorporated into the Mühlhausen hymnbook in the 18th century, and at least three of them, *Morgenglanz der Ewigkeit*, the well-known *Liebster Jesu, wir sind hier* and *Es ist genug*, are still used in Protestant services; the last has had a long musical life (see Geiringer), including new versions by Bach and Brahms, and was most recently used by Berg (in his Violin Concerto). Ahle also wrote a method for teaching singing to children in the schools of Mühlhausen, of which his son later brought out a revised and greatly expanded edition.

WORKS

Editions: J. R. Ahle: *Ausgewählte Gesangswerke mit und ohne Begleitung von Instrumenten*, ed. J. Wolf, DDT, v (1901/R) [W]
    C. von Winterfeld: *Der evangelische Kirchengesang*, ii (Leipzig, 1845/R1966) [Wi]

SACRED VOCAL
(published in Mühlhausen unless otherwise stated)

Harmonias protopaideumata in quibus monadum seu uniciniorum sacrorum decas prima (Erfurt, 1647)
Himmel-süsse Jesus-Freude . . . auss dem Jubilo B. Bernhardi, durch schöne Concertlein und liebliche Arien [2vv], nechst dem Basso Continuo cum Textu . . . nach Belieben ohne Fundament (Erfurt, 1648)
Erster Theil geistlicher Dialogen deren etliche aus denen . . . Sonn- und Fest Tags Evangelien, theils aber aus anderen Orthern heiliger Schrifft, zusammen getragen, 2–4 and more vv, bc (Erfurt, 1648); 2 in W
Fried- Freud- und Jubel-Geschrey Christo Jesu [Singet dem Herrn ein neues Lied], 15–24 and more vv, bc (Erfurt, 1650), ?lost
Neu-gepflanzter thüringischer Lustgarten, in welchen XXVI. neue geistliche musicalische Gewächse . . . auf unterschiedliche Arten . . . versetzet, 3–10 and more vv and insts, some with bc (1657), 6 in W; Ander Theil (30 works), 1–10 and more vv and insts, bc (1658), 4 in W, 1 in Wi; Neu-gepflantzten . . . Lustgartens Nebengang (10 works), 3–10 and more vv and insts, bc (1663), 1 in W; Dritter und letzter Theil (10 works), 3–20 and more vv and insts, bc (1665), 3 in W
Erstes Zehn neuer geistlicher Arien [1–4vv] mit oder ohne Fundament, sampt beygefügten Ritornellen auff 4 Violen nach Belieben zu brauchen (1660), 2 in W; Anderes Zehn, 1–4 and more vv, 4 str, bc (ad lib) (1660), 4 in W; Drittes Zehn, 1–6 and more vv, str, bc (ad lib) (1662), 3 in W, 1 in Wi; Vierdtes Zehn, 1–5 and more vv, str, some with bc (1662), 1 in W, 2 in Wi
Neue geistliche auf die hohen Festtage durchs gantze Jahr gerichtete Andachten . . . sampt beygefügten Ritornellen . . . nach Belieben zu brauchen, 1–4, 8vv, 4 viols, bc (ad lib) (1662), 9 in W
Neue geistliche Chorstücke . . . in einem leichten Stylo abgefasset, 5–8vv, bc (ad lib) (1663–4); 1 in W
Neue geistliche auf die Sontage durchs gantze Jahr gerichtete Andachten . . . sampt beygefügten Ritornellen . . . nach Belieben zu brauchen, 1–4 and more vv, 3 viols, bc (ad lib) (1664); 5 in W, 1 in Wi
Verlangter Liebster, aus dem 3. Cap. des Salomonischen Hochliedes, 2vv, 2 vn, bc (1664)
Musikalische Frühlings-Lust . . . 12 neue geistliche Concertlein, 1–3 and more vv, bc (1666); 2 in W
Neuverfassete Chor-Music, in welcher XIV geistliche Moteten enthalten . . . in einem leichten und anmutigen stylo gesetzet, 5–10vv, bc, op.13 (1668); 2 in W
Neue geistliche Communion und Haupt Fest-Andachten, 1–4 and more vv, 2–5 insts, bc, op.14 (1668); 1 in W
Letzter Traur- und Ehren-Dienst . . . dem Laurentio Helmsdorffen [Siehe, der Gerechte kömt umb], a 6 (1669)
Anmuthiges Zehn neuer geistlicher Arien, 1–4 and more vv, 2–5 insts, bc, op.15 (1669), ?lost
Psalmus CXXXVIII: Confitebor tibi Domine, 3vv, chorus, 5 insts, bc (n.p., n.d.), 9 pr. ptbks with MS title-page, *D-Bds*

INSTRUMENTAL
Dreyfaches Zehn allerhand newer Sinfonien, Paduanen, Balleten,

Alemanden, Mascharaden, Arien, Intraden, Courenten und Sarabanden, 3–5 insts (Erfurt, 1650), inc.
64 works, org, mentioned in *MGG*

WRITINGS
Compendium musices pro tenellis (Erfurt, 1648), lost
Brevis et perspicua introductio in artem musicam, das ist Eine kurze Anleitung zu der lieblichen Singkunst mit etlichen Fugen und den gebräuchlichsten terminis musicis vermehret (Mühlhausen, 1673) [probably 2nd edn. of *Compendium*, see *MGG* and Wolf]; ed. J. G. Ahle as *Kurze doch deutliche Anleitung zu der lieblich- und loblichen Singekunst mit . . . nöthigen Anmerkungen . . . zum Drukke befördert durch des seeligen Verfassers Sohn Johann Georg Ahlen* (Mühlhausen, 1690, enlarged 2/1704)

BIBLIOGRAPHY
WaltherML
C. von Winterfeld: *Der evangelische Kirchengesang*, ii (Leipzig, 1845/R1966) [incl. edns.]
J. Wolf: 'Johann Rudolph Ahle: eine bio-bibliographische Skizze', *SIMG*, ii (1900–01), 393
H. Kretzschmar: *Geschichte des neuen deutschen Liedes* (Leipzig, 1911/R1966)
E. Noack: 'Die Bibliothek der Michaeliskirche zu Erfurt', *AMw*, vii (1924–5), 65
F. Blume: *Die evangelische Kirchenmusik*, HMw, x (1931, rev. 2/1965 as *Geschichte der evangelischen Kirchenmusik*, Eng. trans., enlarged, 1974, as *Protestant Church Music: a History*)
K. Geiringer: '*Es ist genug, so nimm Herr meinen Geist*: 300 Years in the History of a Protestant Funeral Song', *The Commonwealth of Music, in Honor of Curt Sachs* (New York, 1965), 283
J. P. Johnson: *An Analysis and Edition of Selected Sacred Choral Works of Johann Rudolf Ahle* (diss., Southern Baptist Theological Seminary, 1969)

GEORGE J. BUELOW

Ahlefeldt, Countess **Maria Theresia** (*b* Regensburg, 28 Feb 1755; *d* Prague, 4 Nov 1823). German composer, writer and pianist. The daughter of Prince Alexander Ferdinand of Thurn and Taxis, she spent her early years at her father's court in Regensburg. In 1780 she married the Danish diplomat Count Ferdinand Ahlefeldt. In the following decade they lived at the court of the last Margrave of Ansbach, Karl Alexander, where she belonged to the circle of Lady Elizabeth Craven (later margravine) and was active in musical and literary spheres. In 1791, after the dissolution of the Ansbach court, the Countess Ahlefeldt moved to Denmark with her husband, who was superintendent of the royal theatre in Copenhagen from 1792 to 1794. There, as in Ansbach, she came to public notice as a composer, having particular success with the four-act opera-ballet *Telemak på Calypsos Øe* (1792) for which she composed orchestral numbers throughout and vocal numbers in Act 2. Based on a libretto by Vincenzo Galeotti, the renowned Italian ballet master, it ran for 37 performances until 1813 in Copenhagen alone. The work is rooted in the period of *galanterie* and sensibility, but owes something to operetta and in places shows expressive qualities and a Classical shape reminiscent of Gluck. In this, as in her other works (few of which have survived), it is apparent that her natural wealth of feeling exceeded her technical abilities. She was also 'highly thought of and well known as a sensitive virtuoso pianist' (Schilling).

WORKS
Telemak på Calypsos Øe (opera-ballet, 4, V. Galeotti), Copenhagen, Royal Theatre, 28 Dec 1792; vocal score (Copenhagen, 1794); score, 1805, *DK-Kk*
Incidental music for Vaeddemalet (P. H. Haste), 1793, lost
Other vocal: L'harmonie, cantata, 2 S, B, orch, 1792, vocal score *D-Dlb*; Romance de Nina, S, 2 vn, 2 hn, b, score *Dlb*; Klage, 1v, fl, kbd, in I. F. Zehelein: *Vermischte Gedichte* (Bayreuth, c1788)
Inst: sym., F, *Rtt*; sym., D, *Rtt*, also attrib. Pokorny

Lib ? and music to La folie, ou Quel conte! (comic opera, 2), music lost, lib in E. Craven: *Nouveau théâtre*, ed. E. Asimont, i (Anspach, 1789)

BIBLIOGRAPHY

EitnerQ

G. Schilling: *Encyclopädie der gesammten musikalischen Wissenschaften oder Universal-Lexikon der Tonkunst* (Stuttgart, 1835–42/*R*1973)

J. M. Barbour: 'Pokorny und der "Schacht-Katalog"': ein Beitrag zur Geschichte der fürstlichen Hofmusik', *Beiträge zur Kunst- und Kulturpflege im Hause Thurn und Taxis* (Kallmünz, 1963), 269

U. Härtwig: 'Ahlefeldt, Maria Theresia Gräfin', *MGG*

DIETER HÄRTWIG

Ahlersmeyer, Matthieu (*b* Cologne, 29 June 1896). German baritone. He studied with Karl Niemann in Cologne and made his début at Mönchengladbach in 1929 as Wolfram. He sang at the Kroll Opera, Berlin, 1930–31, at the Hamburg Staatsoper, 1931–4 and 1946–61, and at the Dresden Staatsoper, 1934–44, where he created the role of the Barber in Strauss's *Die schweigsame Frau*. In 1939 he created the title role in Egk's *Peer Gynt* at the Berlin Staatsoper. He appeared at Covent Garden in 1936 with the Dresden Staatsoper as Don Giovanni and Count Almaviva, and at the Edinburgh Festival with the Hamburg Opera in 1952 as Hindemith's Mathis. In 1947 he shared the title role in von Einem's *Dantons Tod* with Paul Schoeffler at the Salzburg Festival.

HAROLD ROSENTHAL

Ahlgrimm, Isolde (*b* Vienna, 31 July 1914). Austrian harpsichordist. She played the piano in public while still a child. After completing her musical education at the academy (now the Hochschule) in Vienna, where she was a pupil of Viktor Ebenstein, Franz Schmidt and Emil von Sauer, she changed to the harpsichord and early piano in 1935, teaching herself technique and style from 17th- and 18th-century treatises. Since then she has made numerous concert tours of Europe and the USA. Her large repertory includes the complete keyboard music of Bach, which she has often performed as a cycle of 12 recitals and has recorded. She is also a noted exponent of Austrian harpsichord music, especially the works of Johann Fux. Richard Strauss wrote a suite from Capriccio for her (1944). Ahlgrimm joined the teaching staff of the Vienna Hochschule in 1945, where she was appointed reader in 1969 and professor in 1975. She has taught there continuously, except during 1958–62 when she was professor at the Salzburg Mozarteum. In 1975 she was awarded the Austrian Gold Medal.

WRITINGS

'Unter dem Zeichen des Bogens', *ÖMz*, xix (1964), 151

'Die Rhetorik in der Barockmusik', *Musica*, xxii/6 (1968), 447 [enlarged and trans. in 'De retoriek in de Barokmuziek', *De praestant*, xviii (1969), no.3, p.57; no.4, p.92; xix (1970), no.1, p.1

'Cornelius Heinrich Dretzel, der Autor des J. S. Bach zugeschriebenen Klavierwerkes BWV 897', *BJb*, lv (1969), 67

'Das vielgestaltige Arpeggio', *ÖMz*, xxviii (1973), 574

HOWARD SCHOTT

Ahlström, Jacob Niclas (*b* Visby, 5 June 1805; *d* Stockholm, 4 May 1857). Swedish composer, conductor and organist. He studied music at the University of Uppsala and became the musical director of E. V. Djurström's theatre company in 1828. From 1832 to 1842 he was a teacher at the Gymnasium in Västerås and the city's cathedral organist. He then moved to Stockholm, where he was a conductor of various theatre orchestras, for which he composed the music for about 100 productions, often in collaboration with August Blanche. His only full-length opera, *Alfred den store* ('Alfred the Great'), based on a text of Theodor Körner, was written

in 1848 but never performed; another opera, *Abu Hassan*, was not finished. His other compositions include about 300 entr'actes, a vocal symphony, some orchestral works, a piano concerto and solo piano pieces. He also edited collections of Swedish and Nordic folksongs and folkdances and compiled a pocket dictionary of music (*Musikalisk fickordbok*, Stockholm, 1843).

BIBLIOGRAPHY

F. A. Dahlgren: *Anteckningar om Stockholms theatrar* (Stockholm, 1866)

A. Blanche: *Minnesbilder* (Stockholm, 1873)

J. M. Rosén: *Några minnesblad* (Stockholm, 1877)

E. Sundström: 'Jacob Niclas Ahlström: biografisk skiss', *STMf*, xxi (1939), 143

AXEL HELMER

Åhlström, Olof (*b* Åletorp, Vårdinge, 14 Aug 1756; *d* Stockholm, 11 Aug 1835). Swedish composer and music publisher. After taking lessons from the organist of his own parish he entered the newly founded Academy of Music in Stockholm in 1772 as one of its first pupils, his principal teacher being F. Zellbell the younger. In 1777 he became organist at the Marian church in Stockholm, and in 1786 at Jacobskyrka; he retained the latter post until his death. In 1792 he was elected a member of the Academy of Music, where he was director of education from 1803 to 1805. From 1780 to 1824 he also held various governmental posts. He was granted a royal privilege as printer of music from 1788 to 1823, and for a long time he was the only music publisher in Sweden, though from 1818 his privilege was gradually reduced. Åhlström published compositions by native and foreign composers, as well as his musical journals *Musikaliskt tidsfördrif* (1789–1834) and *Skaldestycken satte i musik* (1790–1823). He also printed C. M. Bellman's *Fredmans epistlar och sånger* (1790–95). As a composer he was most highly esteemed for his songs, over 200 of which were published in his journals.

WORKS

(first performed and published in Stockholm; MSS mostly in S-Skma)

Frigga (1-act opera, C. G. af Leopold), 1787

Incidental music: Den bedragne Bachan [Bachus cheated] (comedy, 1, Gustav III), 1789; Eremiten (comedy, 3, Eurén, after Kotzebue), 1798; Tanddoctorn [The dentist] (comedy, 3, C. G. Nordforss), 1800

2 cantatas; over 200 songs; 7 sonatas, vn, pf, opp.1–2 (1783–4); 3 sonatas, pf, op.3 (1786), 3 sonatinas, pf, op.4 (1786), 3 other sonatas, 6 sets of variations, pf, in Musikaliskt tidsfördrif (1792–1820)

Choralbok (1832)

WRITINGS

(all published in Stockholm)

Några underrättelser . . . för begynnare uti klavér spelning [Some lessons for beginners on the piano], i–ii (1803–19)

with A. Afzelius: *Traditioner af svenska folkdansar* (1814–15)

BIBLIOGRAPHY

A. Afzelius: *Tonsiaren Olof Åhlströms minne* (Stockholm, 1867)

T. Norlind: 'Olof Åhlström och sällskapsvisan på Anna Maria Lenngrens tid', *STMf*, viii (1926), 1–64

A. Wiberg: 'Olof Åhlströms musiktryckeri', *STMf*, xxxi (1949), 83–136

AXEL HELMER

Aho, Kalevi (*b* Forssa, 3 March 1949). Finnish composer. He studied at the Sibelius Academy, Helsinki, and under Blacher in Berlin (1971–2). His music is entirely in large-scale symphonic forms employing classical polyphony; the orchestration suggests Shostakovich, while Mahler is another influence, as in the waltz quotation of the First Symphony. In 1973 he received the Leonie Sonning Prize.

WORKS

3 str qts, 1967, 1970, 1971; 4 syms., 1969, 1970, (Sinfonia concertante), 1971–3, 1972–3; Sonata, vn, 1973

MSS in *SF-Hmt*

BIBLIOGRAPHY

E. Salmenhaara: 'Uusi suomalainen sinfonikko' [A new Finnish symphonist], *Musiikki* (1971), no.1, p.30

K. Aho: article in *Miten sävellykseni ovat syntyneet*, ed. E. H. Salmenhaara (Helsinki, 1976), 9

ERKKI SALMENHAARA

Ahrend & Brunzema. German firm of organ builders. Jürgen Ahrend (*b* Göttingen, 28 April 1930) and Gerhard Brunzema (*b* Emden, 6 July 1927) served their apprenticeship together and then worked as colleagues before setting up their own workshop at Leer (East Friesland) in 1954. They followed the precedents of historical organ-building practice (with some compromises), and made a special study of the surviving examples of north German organ builders' work in the Netherlands, from which they adopted many important features in such matters as tone quality and touch. In the 1960s they carried out detailed research on historic organs and on organs of their own, based on Brunzema's technical studies at Brunswick. The workshop became well known not only for new organs – such as those at Zorgvlietkerk, Scheveningen, near The Hague (1959; three manuals, 26 stops), St Martini, Bremen (1962; three manuals, 33 stops), Cantate Domino, Frankfurt am Main (1970; three manuals, 32 stops), University of Oregon, Eugene (1972; four manuals, 38 stops), and the Church of the Reconciliation, Taizé (1974; three manuals, 28 stops) – but also for the restoration of valuable historic organs, including those at Marienhafe, East Friesland (1713/1969; two manuals, 20 stops), Schluderns, Churburg (1559/1969; one manual, seven stops), and the Franciscan court church, Innsbruck (1555–61/1970; two manuals, 15 stops). In 1962 Ahrend and Brunzema received the craftsmanship prize of Lower Saxony. On 2 January 1972 the partners separated, but the workshop at Leer continued under the name of Jürgen Ahrend Orgelbau. In April 1972 Gerhard Brunzema joined the firm of Casavant at St Hyacinthe, Quebec, as tonal director.

BIBLIOGRAPHY

U. Pape: 'Jürgen Ahrend and Gerhard Brunzema', *Organ Yearbook*, iii (1972), 24

HANS KLOTZ

Ahrens, Joseph (Johannes Clemens) (*b* Sommersell, Westphalia, 17 April 1904). German composer and organist. He studied under Schnippering at Büren and Volbach at Münster; his first training in choral music was undertaken at the Benedictine abbeys of Gerleve and Beuron. In 1925 he enrolled in the Staatliche Akademie für Kirchen- und Schulmusik in Berlin, where he completed his formal education under Sittard, Middelschulte and Seiffert. Having already been appointed professor for improvisation and organ playing at the Berlin Institut, he was made lecturer at the Berlin Akademie in 1928. In 1934 he was appointed organist of St Hedwig, Berlin. This appointment was followed by a professorship in Catholic church music at the Berlin Hochschule für Musik, as well as a nomination to the Orgelsachverständigen des Bistums Berlin. A member of the academic senate of the Berlin Hochschule in 1945, he was deputy director of the institution (1954–8) and chairman of the keyboard department. After 1955

he also headed the department of church music and served as president of the examination board for church musicians. His numerous honours include the Arts Prize of the City of Berlin (1955), knighthood in the Gregorian Order (1965) and the silver pontifical medal, awarded while he was at Villa Massimo, Rome (1968). In 1963 he was elected to the Berlin Academy of Arts.

WORKS
(selective list)

Org: Partita 'Zu Bethlehem geboren', 1929; Toccata eroica, 1932; Ricercare, a, 1934; Partita 'Christ ist erstanden', 1935; Partita 'Pange lingua', 1935; Partita 'Regina coeli', 1937; Partita 'Jesu, meine Freude', 1942; Toccata and Fugue, e, 1942; Partita 'Veni creator Spiritus', 1947; Partita 'Lobe den Herren', 1947; Partita 'Verleih uns Frieden', 1947; Triptychon über BACH, 1949; Das heilige Jahr, 3 vols., 1948–50; Cantiones gregorianae, 3 vols., 1957; Trilogia sacra, 1959–60; Die Verwandlungen, 3 vols., 1963–5; Fantasie und Ricercare über ein Thema von Joannis Cabanilles, 1967; 5 Liesen, 1969; Canticum organi, 1972

Choral: Missa gotica, 1948; Missa hymnica, 1948; Matthäus-Passion, 4–8vv, 1950; Das Weihnachtsevangelium nach Lukas 'Sei uns willkommen, Herre Christ', 4–12vv, 1952; Johannes-Passion, 1961; Missa dodekaphonica, 1966; 14 motets

Principal publishers: Böhm, Schott, Willy Müller

BIBLIOGRAPHY

W. David: 'Das Orgelschaffen von Joseph Ahrens', *Musik und Altar*, i–ii (1948–9), 61

R. Walter: 'Joseph Ahrens: der Schöpfer eines neuen Orgelstils', *Musik und Altar*, i–ii (1948–9), 63

——: 'Joseph Ahrens: "Das heilige Jahr" ', *Musik und Altar*, v (1952), 159; 191

T.-M. Langner: 'Das heilige Jahr', *Melos*, xix (1952), 354

W. Koch: 'Chormusik als Gotteslob: zum Chorschaffen von Joseph Ahrens', *Musik und Altar*, vi (1953), 10

——: *Joseph Ahrens zum 50. Geburtstag* (Berlin, 1954)

R. Walter: 'Der Kirchenmusiker Joseph Ahrens', *Zeitschrift für Kirchenmusik*, lxxiv (1954), 203

O. Riemer: 'Musik der Verkündigen: Zum Schaffen von Joseph Ahrens', *Musica*, xi (1957), 396

G. Berger: 'Zu den "Cantiones gregorianae" von Joseph Ahrens', *Musik und Altar*, xiii (1960), 34

J. Schell: 'Joseph Ahrens zum 60. Geburtstag: Weg, Werk und Bedeutung', *Katholische Kirchenmusik*, lxxxix (1964), 78

W. Brune: 'Missa dodekaphonica von Joseph Ahrens', *Musica sacra*, xxxviii (1968), 114

JOHN MORGAN

Ahrens, Sieglinde (*b* Berlin, 19 Feb 1936). German composer and organist. She had her first music lessons from her father, Joseph Ahrens, with whom she continued organ studies at the Berlin Hochschule für Musik, where her composition teacher was Blacher. In 1947 she made her début, and from then until 1957 she played at the Salvatorkirche, Berlin. Subsequently she studied with Milhaud and Messiaen at the Paris Conservatoire. She has made concert tours in Germany, France and the Netherlands, winning numerous awards. In 1962 she was appointed to teach organ playing at the Folkwang-Hochschule, Essen, and in 1964 she received the Förderungspreis of the North Rhine-Westphalia arts prize. Her compositions include Three Pieces, a Fantasia and a Suite for organ, a Sonata for violin and organ, Five Pieces for string trio and Three Songs for bass and organ.

JOHN MORGAN

Ahronovich, Yury [Georgy] (*b* Leningrad, 13 May 1932). Israeli conductor of Soviet birth. He entered the Leningrad Central School of Music in 1939 until his studies were interrupted by the war, during which he remained in Leningrad; he resumed his studies there in 1945, principally as a violinist, and went on to the Leningrad Conservatory. Later he studied conducting with Natan Rakhlin and Kurt Sanderling, and in 1956 was appointed conductor of the Saratov PO; he also taught at the conservatory there and conducted his first operas. The next year he became conductor at Yaroslav, remaining there until his appointment as chief conductor of the Moscow RSO in 1964; his guest engagements included appearances with the Bol'shoy Ballet.

Ahronovich left the USSR in 1972, made his home in Israel and became an Israeli citizen. After concerts with the Israel PO he began touring, appearing in London with the RPO and with the New York PO in the USA. He made his operatic début in the West with *Otello* at Cologne, where he was appointed conductor of the Gürzenich Concerts from 1975 (the possibility of his also becoming musical director of the Cologne Opera was discussed). He first appeared at Covent Garden in 1974, conducting Musorgsky's *Boris Godunov*, when he was warmly praised for a combination of exhilarating spirit with clarity of musical purpose, qualities he also brought to Prokofiev's *Romeo and Juliet* on a guest engagement with the Royal Ballet the next year.

BIBLIOGRAPHY
A. Blyth: 'The Law of Yury Ahronovitch', *The Times* (23 July 1975)
NOËL GOODWIN

Aibl. German firm of music publishers. The lithographer Joseph Aibl (*b* Munich, 1802; *d* Munich, 1834), a pupil of Theobald Boehm, worked from 1819 to 1825 in Berne as a musician and later as a lithographer with a music dealer. In 1825 he founded a business that published music and dealt in instruments in Munich; after his death it was continued by his widow and from 1837 by the merchant Eduard Spitzweg (*b* Munich, 1811; *d* Munich, 1884), a brother of the painter Carl Spitzweg. Under the directorship of Eduard's son Eugen Spitzweg (*b* Munich, 1840; *d* Munich, 1914) the publishing house was sold in 1904 to Universal Edition. Composers represented by the firm included Peter Cornelius (i), Rheinberger, Alexander Ritter, Theobald Boehm, Bülow, Reger and Richard Strauss.

BIBLIOGRAPHY
A. Ott: 'Richard Strauss und sein Verlegerfreund Eugen Spitzweg', *Musik und Verlag: Karl Vötterle zum 65. Geburtstag* (Kassel, 1968), 466
K. Ventzke: 'Zur Frühgeschichte des Musikverlages Joseph Aibl in München', *Mf*, xxv (1972), 316
KARL VENTZKE

Aiblinger, Johann Kaspar (*b* Wasserburg, Bavaria, 23 Feb 1779; *d* Munich, 6 May 1867). German composer. He received his first introduction to music at the Benedictine Abbey at Tegernsee. Later he attended the Gymnasium in Munich, at the same time having lessons in composition from Joseph Schlett, and subsequently studied philosophy and theology in Landshut. He then went to Italy as a pupil of Simon Mayr: he studied in Vicenza (1804–11), Venice and Milan. In 1819 he returned to Munich, where he became Kapellmeister of the Italian Opera House. In 1823 he was appointed assistant conductor at the Royal National Theatre, and became court Kapellmeister there in 1826. In 1833 he was sent by King Ludwig I to Italy to collect old music. After retiring from the opera house he worked at the Allerheiligen-Hofkirche in Munich with the provost, Michael Hauber, and with Caspar Ett, in the revival of church music. He retired in 1864.

Although his opera *Rodrigo und Chimene* is flawed by its libretto and the lack of unity in its style (a medley of Italian and French operatic conventions), Aiblinger was an outstanding composer of classical sacred music. His *Marienlieder* are notable for their folklike charac-

ter. He was poorly equipped for dramatic music, but his numerous religious works (of which several have been published) are distinguished by their balanced symphonic style and skilful construction.

WORKS
(selective list)

Many MSS, some autograph, are in St Kajetan, Munich, all of sacred music

Operas: La burla fortunata ossia I due prigionieri, Venice, 1811; Rodrigo und Chimene (2, J. Sendtner, after Corneille: Le Cid), Munich, Königliches Hoftheater, 1821; several arias for operas of other composers

Ballets (all first perf. in Milan): La spada di Kennet, 1818; I titani, 1819; Bianca, 1819

Sacred choral: over 30 masses, a cappella and with pf, orch acc., some female vv; *c*30 vesper psalms, 20 offertories; 4 litanies, 3 requiems, TeD, 2 Ave regina; Salve regina; Veni Sancte Spiritus; Stabat mater; hymns, incl. Hymnus de conceptione Beatae Mariae Virginis (MS *I-Rvat*); psalm settings, incl. Parafrasi del Salmo 60 (MS *I-Mc*)

Marienlieder (G. Görres), 1–3 female vv; 6 sacred songs, 1v, kbd

BIBLIOGRAPHY
EitnerQ
P. Hötzl: *Zum Gedächtnis Aiblingers* (Munich, 1867)
L. Schiedermair: 'Aus Aiblingers italienischem Briefwechsel', *KJb*, xxiv (1911), 71; repr. in *Musica sacra*, xlvi (1913), 84
B. Wallner: 'Zum 50. Todestag Aiblingers', *Musica sacra*, I (1917), 72
H. Kier: *Raphael Georg Kiesewetter (1773–1850), Wegbereiter des musikalischen Historismus* (Regensburg, 1968), 205f
SIEGFRIED GMEINWIESER

Aich, Arnt von (*b* ?Aachen; *d* Cologne, *c*1528–30). German printer. He came into possession of the Lupus Press in Cologne through marriage to its owner, Ida Grutter, and began publishing in 1512 or 1513. He brought out some 35 works on a variety of subjects before his death. The business was continued by his widow and son-in-law, Laurenz von der Mülen, until his son Johann von Aich was old enough to take it over. Under the latter's direction some 35 more books were issued from the Lupus Press, the last of them dated 1557.

Arnt von Aich's main output consists of religious writings, a few of which exhibit Protestant sympathies and may have been printed illegally. In music his fame rests on a single collection, *LXXV hubscher Lieder*, printed by means of woodblocks. Although like many of Arnt von Aich's publications it is not dated, the repertory indicates an early date (probably between 1512 and 1520). No composers are named in the collection; some of the songs have been identified as the work of Hofhaimer, Isaac, Rener and Grefinger – all of whom were active in southern Germany and Austria. Since they had no connection with Cologne, Moser suggested that the collection may represent a reprint of an earlier Augsburg edition now lost. The repertory itself can most readily be linked to the court of the Augsburg Bishop, Friedrich II of Zollern (*d* 1505), whose setting of *Fried gib mir Herr* concludes the collection. Many of the composers and even some of these works are also found in the song collections published by Oeglin and Schoeffer.

MUSIC PUBLICATIONS
LXXV hubscher Lieder myt Discant, Alt, Bas, und Tenor (Cologne, 1512–20); ed. E. Bernoulli and H. J. Moser, *Das Liederbuch des Arnt von Aich* (Kassel, 1930)
Hertzich Ernst in gesanges wyss gair leiflich zo hoeren (Cologne, *c*1529)

BIBLIOGRAPHY
H. J. Moser: *Paul Hofhaimer* (Stuttgart, 1929, rev. 2/1966)
——: Foreword to *Das Liederbuch des Arnt von Aich* (Kassel, 1930)
G. Domel and G. Könitzer: 'Arnd von Aich und Nachkommen . . .', *Gutenberg-Jb* (1936), 119
K. Gudewill: 'Aich, Arnt von', MGG

J. Benzing: 'Die Drucke der Lupuspresse zu Köln (Arnd und Johann von Aich)', *Archiv für Geschichte des Buchwesens*, i (1958), 365 [with list of publications]

MARIE LOUISE GÖLLNER

Aichinger, Gregor (*b* Regensburg, 1564–5; *d* Augsburg, 20–21 Jan 1628). German composer and organist. He ranks with Hans Leo Hassler among the most important and prolific composers in southern Germany in the late 16th and early 17th centuries.

1. LIFE. Aichinger's birthdate is derived from the inscription on his tombstone in the cloister of Augsburg Cathedral; his age at his death is given as 63. He was still at Regensburg in 1576, and in 1577 he presented a composition to the Bavarian court at Munich and was paid for it. Although the Munich court chapel under Lassus often recruited choirboys from Regensburg, there is no conclusive evidence that Aichinger was a member. On 2 November 1578 he enrolled at the University of Ingolstadt, which had become a stronghold of Jesuit influence. Among his fellow students was Jakob Fugger (ii), a member of one of the most prominent families in southern Germany (*see* FUGGER), and he formed a lifelong friendship with him. He probably continued his musical training at Ingolstadt (perhaps under the organist Hans Pruckhman). In 1584 he was appointed official organist to Jakob Fugger (i), uncle of his student friend, and in this position he provided music for the Fugger household and presided over the organ that his employer had donated to St Ulrich, Augsburg. He evidently held the organist's position until his death, since his successor, Elias Fabricius, is first mentioned in the church records in 1628.

Some time between 1584 and 1588 Aichinger travelled to Venice, where, sponsored by Jakob Fugger (i), he became one of the first German pupils of Giovanni Gabrieli; the first fruits of his study are contained in his *Sacrae cantiones* (1590), dedicated to his patron. Matriculation records at the University of Siena show that he enrolled there on 15 November 1586. Having visited Rome, he returned to Germany, and on 21 July 1588 he again enrolled at the University of Ingolstadt. His published music from this period includes several individual pieces written for special occasions in the Fugger family; the *Sacrae cantiones* of 1595, for example, contains an eight-part Latin choral dialogue composed for the younger Jakob's ordination at Augsburg in 1592. In 1598 the elder Jakob Fugger died; Heinrich von Knöringen, who later may have been primarily responsible for Aichinger's decision to enter the priesthood, was consecrated prince-bishop in Augsburg Cathedral; and Aichinger made a second journey to Italy, arriving in Rome before December. He enrolled at the University of Perugia in 1599, returned to Rome in 1600 and was in Venice by December. In Rome he gained the favour of Marquard von Schwenden (canon at Salzburg, Augsburg and Passau), to whom he later dedicated his *Virginalia* (1607). According to the foreword to this work, the Roman publisher, Simone Verovio, provided him with the texts; it was probably through Verovio and his publications that he became acquainted with the Roman spiritual canzonetta, the style of which influenced many of his works after 1600.

From the time of his return to Augsburg – probably early in 1601 – until his death, Aichinger lived under the aegis of the church. He discussed a benefice with Augsburg Cathedral chapter in January 1600, while still in Italy, and he was awarded the benefice of S Maria Magdalena, which included the position of *vicarius chori*. He probably took holy orders in Italy, though he may have been ordained only after receiving the benefice, for not until 1603 did he begin to prefix his name in his publications with the words 'Reverendus Dominus'. By then he had already renounced secular music, a fact noted in the foreword to his *Odaria lectissima* (1601), and in the preface to the *Divinae laudes* (1602) he had referred to the dedication of his life to God. He later held additional benefices, including a canonry of the college of St Gertraud, Augsburg. The seriousness with which he took his ecclesiastical calling is shown by his publication of a book of pious meditations, *Thymiama sacerdotale* (1618). He continued to compose prolifically, and he still maintained a close association with members of the Fugger family: he dedicated his *Solennia augustissimi corporis Christi* (1606) to the Sodalitas Corporis Christi, a Catholic organization of which he was a member and whose founder was Marcus Fugger; and he composed his *Teutsche Gesenglein* (1609) while staying at Johann Fugger's castle at Babenhausen. The funeral of Emperor Rudolph II in Augsburg Cathedral in March 1612 probably occasioned the writing of Aichinger's *Officium pro defunctis*; copied into a large choirbook in about 1613, this work later appeared in print with an added continuo part. About 50 books from his personal library are known to exist: volumes of Italian music and works on religion, philosophy, history, geography and medicine indicate the wide range of his interests. The epitaph on his tombstone praises him as 'a man wonderfully pleasing beyond his piety, his expert knowledge of music and the elegance and ease of his manners'.

2. WORKS. The differing styles apparent in Aichinger's music reflect his background and training. Although he used modern idioms derived from Italian models, he nevertheless remained true to his German heritage in tempering his music with conservatism; indeed, much of his output consists of works for three, four and five voices in the traditional polyphonic style of earlier composers such as Lassus. The influence of Giovanni Gabrieli is evident not only in his early polychoral works for large ensembles but also in his later vocal concertos; these contain numerous sections that appear to be reductions of polychoral textures to their essential outer voices, the rest being supplied by the organ.

The contents of Aichinger's *Sacrae cantiones* (1590) are consistent with those of the publications of some of Gabrieli's other pupils, including Latin polychoral motets and Italian madrigals; the second and third books of *Sacrae cantiones* (1595 and 1597) also include some polychoral music. His *Cantiones ecclesiasticae* (1607), containing mostly Latin motets and *Magnificat* settings for three voices and basso continuo, clearly shows the influence of Viadana. This collection was not only the first significant German publication of music with thoroughbass, but also included the first treatise printed in Germany on thoroughbass notation and performance. After 1607 Aichinger included a continuo part in most of his published collections; vocal concertos featuring an essentially independent continuo part are printed in his *Cantiones* (1609), *Encomium verbo incarnato* (1617), *Quercus dodonaea* (1619), *Corolla eucharistica* (1621) and *Flores musici* (1626). Although Aichinger was one of the first to introduce Viadana's concerto style into Germany, he wrote no solo vocal concertos. A significant number of his works use light textures and dance-like rhythms typical of the Roman canzonetta; most of these are settings of metrical texts, both with and without basso continuo.

WORKS

Editions: *Musica divina*, 1st ser., ii–iv, ed. K. Proske (Regensburg, 1854–62) [P]
    G. Aichinger: Ausgewählte Werke, ed. T. Kroyer, DTB, xviii, Jg.x/1 (Leipzig, 1909/*R*) [K]

Sacrae cantiones, 4–6, 8, 10vv (Venice, 1590); incl. 6 It. madrigals; 1 motet in P, 9 motets in K
Liber secundus sacrarum cantionum, 4–6vv . . . missa, & Magnificat, nec non dialogi aliquot, 8, 10vv, 3 ricercares a 4 (Venice, 1595); pubd singly and with above vol. (Venice, 1594), lost, cited in 17th-century catalogue; 6 motets from 1595 edn. in K
Liber sacrarum cantionum, 5–8vv (Nuremberg, 1597)
Tricinia Mariana: antiphonae, hymni, Magnificat, litaniae, laudes BVM, 3, 4vv (Innsbruck, 1598); 8 in P
Odaria lectissima, 3, 4vv (Augsburg, 1600), lost, cited in 17th-century catalogue; 2/1601, enlarged 4/1611)
Divinae laudes, 3vv (Augsburg, 1602)
Liturgica sive sacra officia, ad omnes dies festos magnae Dei matris, 4, 5vv (Augsburg, 1603); 4 in P
Vespertinum virginis canticum sive Magnificat, 5vv (Augsburg, 1603)
Ghirlanda di canzonette spirituali, 3vv (Augsburg, 1603)
Lacrimae D. virginis et Ioannis in Christum a cruce depositum, 5, 6vv (Augsburg, 1604, altered 2/1604); K
Psalmus 1, Miserere mei Deus, 8–12vv (Munich, 1605)
Solennia augustissimi corporis Christi, 5vv (Augsburg, 1606); 1 in K
Vulnera Christi, a D. Bernardo salutata, 3, 4vv (Dillingen, 1606)
Fasciculus sacrarum harmoniarum, 4vv, 3 ricercares a 4 (Dillingen, 1606); 3 in P
Cantiones ecclesiasticae, 3vv, bc, 4vv, 1 canzona a 2, bc (Dillingen, 1607); 2 in P; ed. W. E. Hettrick, RRMBE, xiii (1972)
Virginalia: laudes aeternae Virginis Mariae, 5vv (Dillingen, 1607)
Divinarum laudum . . . pars II, 3vv (Dillingen, 1608)
Sacra Dei laudes sub officio divino concinendae, 5–8vv (Dillingen, 1609)
Altera pars huius operis, cantiones nimirum, 2–4vv, bc, 5 canzoni a 4, 5 (Dillingen, 1609); 1 repr. in 1622[2] ed. in Hettrick
Teutsche Gesenglein: auss dem Psalter dess H. Propheten Davids, 3vv (Dillingen, 1609)
Liber secundus sacrarum harmoniarum super L. Psalmum Miserere mei Deus, 4–6vv (Dillingen, 1612), lost, cited in 17th-century catalogue
Zwey Klaglieder vom Tod und letzten Gericht, 4vv (Dillingen, 1613)
Officium pro defunctis, 4, 5vv, bc (Augsburg, 1615); lost; MS copy *D-As*
Triplex liturgiarum fasciculus, 4–6vv, bc (Augsburg, 1616)
Officium angeli custodis à S. Romana Ecclesia, 4vv, bc (Dillingen, 1617); 1 in P, 1 in K
Encomium verbo incarnato, 4vv, bc (Ingolstadt, 1617); 2 in P, 1 ed. in Hettrick
Quercus dodonaea, 3, 4vv, bc (Augsburg, 1619); 1 ed. in Hettrick
Corolla eucharistica, 2, 3vv, bc (Augsburg, 1621); 1 ed. in Hettrick
Flores musici ad mensam Ss convivii, 5, 6vv, bc (Augsburg, 1626[6])
Other vocal pieces, some intabulated: 1585[37], 1590[5], 1596[2], 1597[13], 1598[2], 1600[2], 1600[6], 1604[7], 1605[1], 1607[6], 1607[29], 1609[28], 1613[1], 1613[2], 1616[2], 1617[24], 1621[2], 1622[2], 1623[2], 1624[1], 1626[2], 1627[1], 1627[2], 1629[1]
Other vocal pieces, some intabulated, *D-As, BS, Mbs, Rp, Rtt*

BIBLIOGRAPHY

A. Sandberger: 'Bemerkungen zur Biographie Hans Leo Hasslers und seiner Brüder, sowie zur Musikgeschichte der Städte Nürnberg und Augsburg im 16. und zu Anfang des 17. Jahrhunderts': introduction to *Werke Hans Leo Hasslers*, DTB, viii, Jg.v/1 (1904/*R*), p.xi–cxii
T. Kroyer: 'Gregor Aichingers Leben und Werke: mit neuen Beiträgen zur Musikgeschichte Ingolstadts und Augsburgs': introduction to DTB, xviii, Jg.x/1 (1909/*R*), pp. ix–cxxix
——: 'Zu Aichingers Fraktur-Kontrapunkten', *Caecilienvereinsorgan*, xlvi (1911), 221
——: 'Gregor Aichinger als Politiker', *Festschrift Peter Wagner* (Leipzig, 1926), 128
E. F. Schmid: 'Hans Leo Hassler und seine Brüder: neue Nachrichten zu ihrer Lebensgeschichte', *Zeitschrift des Historischen Vereins für Schwaben*, liv (1941), 60–212
——: 'Aichinger, Gregor', *MGG*
——: 'Gregor Aichinger', *Lebensbilder aus dem bayerischen Schwaben*, i (1952), 246–76
R. Schaal: 'Zur Musikpflege im Kollegiatstift St. Moritz zu Augsburg', *Mf*, vii (1954), 1
A. Layer: *Musik und Musiker der Fuggerzeit: Begleitheft zur Ausstellung der Stadt Augsburg* (Augsburg, 1959)
——: 'Augsburger Musikkultur der Renaissance', *Musik in der Reichsstadt Augsburg*, ed. L. Wegele (Augsburg, 1965), 43–102
W. E. Hettrick: *The Thorough-bass in the Works of Gregor Aichinger (1564–1628)* (diss., U. of Michigan, 1968) [incl. edns.]

WILLIAM E. HETTRICK

Aiguino da Brescia, Illuminato (*b* ?Orzivecchi or Orzinuovi, nr. Brescia, *c*1520; *fl* 1562–81). Italian theorist and Franciscan friar. He was influenced by his teacher Aaron, by Spataro and by Marchetto da Padova. His *La illuminata de tutti i tuoni di canto fermo* (Venice, 1562) expounds a modal theory applicable to plainchant: a mode is a form of diatonic octave divided into segments of 5th and 4th; corresponding authentic and plagal modes comprise the same segments but in reverse order, and the order of steps within the segments is also reversed. There are eight regular modes (authentic and plagal) with finals on *d*, *e*, *f* and *g*, and six irregular modes with finals on *a*, *b* and *c′*. The treatise is largely devoted to modal identification of chants with an ambitus smaller or greater than an octave, or which use more than one mode. Identification is based primarily on the predominance of the segments of a single mode within a chant, and only secondarily on the final and ambitus. *Il tesoro illuminato di tutti i tuoni di canto figurato* (Venice, 1581) expands this modal theory to accommodate polyphony. A specific affective character is ascribed to each mode, and composers are urged to choose the principal and secondary modes of a composition according to the sentiments expressed in the text. One voice should observe the principal mode more strictly than the others in order to indicate the mode of the composition. Cadences are constructed on the final and 5th of the principal mode, although intermediate cadences on the final and 5th of secondary modes are admissible.

BIBLIOGRAPHY

FétisB
J. Mattheson: *Exemplarische Organisten-Probe im Artikel vom General-Bass* (Hamburg, 1719), 70f
J. N. Forkel: *Allgemeine Litteratur der Musik* (Leipzig, 1792/*R*1962), 298
G. Gaspari: *Catalogo della Biblioteca del Liceo Musicale di Bologna*, i (Bologna, 1890/*R*1961), 189
G. Treccani degli Alfieri: *Storia di Brescia* (Brescia, 1961)
H. Atteln: 'Aiguino, Illuminato', *MGG*

KAROL BERGER

Aikin, Jesse B. (*fl* Philadelphia, 1846–93). American composer and tune book compiler (*see* SHAPE-NOTE HYMNODY, §§3–4). His *Christian Minstrel* (Philadelphia, 1846) introduced the seven-shape system which eventually prevailed throughout the USA; the collection reached its 171st edition by 1873. Other song collections by him in seven-shape notation include *The Juvenile Minstrel* (Philadelphia, 1847), *Harmonia ecclesiae* (Philadelphia, 1853), *The Sabbath-school Minstrel* (Philadelphia, ?1870), *The Imperial Harmony* (with H. Main and C. Allen; New York and Chicago, 1876) and *The True Principles of the Science of Music with a Rare Collection of a few of the Best Tunes* (Philadelphia, 1891).

BIBLIOGRAPHY

P. G. Hammond: *A Study of the 'Christian Minstrel' (1846) by Jesse B. Aikin* (diss., Southern Baptist Theological Seminary, 1969)

HARRY ESKEW

Aim, Vojtěch Bořivoj (*b* Rovne, Bohemia, 13 April 1886; *d* Prague, 10 Sept 1972). Czech composer and choirmaster. He studied both at the Charles University and at the Prague Conservatory under Vitězslav Novák.

He was a director, and then an inspector of music schools, and in the early days of Czechoslovak Radio he contributed music programmes for children. Later he was appointed a professor at the Prague Conservatory; but his chief importance was as a fine choirmaster, principally of the Typografia male choir, which achieved high standards under his leadership, and made tours of Germany, Austria, Switzerland, Russia and Hungary.

WORKS
(selective list)

The Centaurs, chorus, 1924; Svět a hmota [World and matter], male chorus, 1937; Revolution of the Machines, chorus, 1938; Cantata for Double Chorus, 1939; Znící svět [Resounding World], 1939; Through the Festive Gateway of May Days, chorus, 1945; Cradle Song, chorus, 1947; Night of Stars, chorus, 1949; To the Sons of Mellantrich, male chorus, n.d.; Long Live Dresden, male chorus, n.d.
Ecce homo (Aim, anon. Czech, Arab), song cycle in 10 parts, 1944–6
Piano works, chamber music, educational pieces

Principal publisher: Hudební matice

BIBLIOGRAPHY
Sborník k 70, narozeninám (Prague, 1956)

JOSEF PLAVEC

Aimeric de Peguilhan (*b* c1175; *d* c1230). Provençal troubadour. According to his *vida*, he was the son of a Toulouse cloth merchant (Peguilhan is a village in the Haute Garonne, near St Gaudens). He was apparently a wanderer who was received at many courts in southern France, Spain and northern Italy. Raimon V of Toulouse may have been his first patron, while others may have included Guilhem de Bergadan, Gaston VI of Béarn, Bernard IV of Comminges, Pedro II of Aragon, Alfonso VIII of Castile, Guillaume IV of Montferrat, Marquis Guilhem of Malaspina and Azzo VI of Este, together with his sister Beatrice. Aimeric's poetry, which includes chansons, sirventes, *chansons de croisade*, tensos, planhs and partimens, was admired and cited by such writers as Matfre Ermengaut, Jaufré de Foixa, Berenguier de Noia, and by Dante (in *De vulgari eloquentia*). Modern evaluations vary widely, some considering the poet to be of great distinction, while others view him as technically competent though neither profound nor original.

Among the more than 50 surviving poems attributable to Aimeric, only six survive with music. Four of these have isometric, decasyllabic strophes. Only one melody, *En Amor*, is cast in bar form. This is a setting, curiously, of a strophe whose first four lines have the same masculine rhyme while the last four have a related feminine rhyme. Literal repetition of phrases is not present in other works, although *Per solatz* does embody a varied repeat of the fifth phrase. However, Aimeric occasionally presented a melodic outline in multiple guise by regrouping various notes and adding or omitting embellishments; motivic play is also a factor in formal design. All melodies except the two settings of *Qui la vi* use authentic modes, *Atressi·m* and *En greu pantais* employing the seldom-used finals *e* and *B* respectively. The melodies tend to begin in the upper register (*En greu pantais* opening a 9th above the final) and to introduce the final cadentially only in the latter half of the strophe. Most are relatively florid, and none displays clear elements of rhythmic symmetry. *Qui la vi*, considered a descort by some and a chanson by others, is built of extremely lengthy, tripartite strophes. The setting in *F-Pn* fr.22543 has the repetition structure characteristic of the lai, but gives music for the first strophe only. That in the Manuscrit du Roi (*F-Pn* 844) is a late addition in mensural notation, which presents new textual material and treats the four strophes in through-composed fashion.

WORKS

Edition: *Der musikalische Nachlass der Troubadours*, ed. F. Gennrich, SMM, iii, iv, xv (1958–65) [G]

Atressi·m pren com fai al jogador, PC 10.12, G iii, 177
Cel que s'irais ni guerrej' ab amor, PC 10.15, G iii, 178
En Amor trop alques en que m refraing, PC 10.25, G iii, 179; ed. in Gennrich, p.58, and *MGG*
En greu pantais m'a tengut longamen, PC 10.27, G iii, 180; ed. in Anglès, p.400
Per solatz d'autrui chan soven, PC 10.41, G iii, 181
Qui la vi, en ditz, PC 10.45, G iii, 182

BIBLIOGRAPHY

H. Anglès: *La mùsica a Catalunya fins al segle XIII* (Barcelona, 1935)
W. P. Shephard and F. M. Chambers: *The Poems of Aimeric de Peguillan* (Evanston, 1950)
F. Gennrich: *Lo Gai Saber*, Musikwissenschaftliche Studien-Bibliothek, xviii–xix (Darmstadt, 1959)

For further bibliography *see* TROUBADOURS, TROUVÈRES.

THEODORE KARP

Aimon, (Pamphile Léopold) François (*b* L'Isle, nr. Avignon, 4 Oct 1779; *d* Paris, 2 Feb 1866). French cellist, conductor and composer. He became conductor at the theatre of Marseilles when he was 17, at the Théâtre du Gymnase-Dramatique in Paris in 1821 and at the Théâtre-Français for a few years from the retirement of Baudron in 1822. His opera *Les jeux floraux* was performed in 1818, and the song *Michel et Christine* (1821) was very popular. His later years he devoted to teaching.

WORKS
(selective list)

Les jeux floraux (3 acts, J. N. Bouilly), Paris, Opéra, 16 Nov 1818, *F-Po*
Ov. and choruses for a reduction of Favart and Duni's La fée Urgèle (1 act, Favart), Paris, Gymnase-Dramatique, 6 Jan 1821
Les sybarites, ou Les francmaçons de Florence (3 acts, Castil-Blaze) (Paris, 1831), collab. 5 others
5 other operas, now lost, mentioned in *FétisB*
2 bn concertos; Concertino, vc; Récréation, 2 vc, hn, pf; Solo, cl, pf/str qt (Lyons, n.d.); 21 str qts; 1 str qnt; 1 qt with pf; several trios, 3 vn; duos, 2 vn; duos, vn, gui: all (Paris, n.d.) unless otherwise indicated.

WRITINGS

Connaissances préliminaires de l'harmonie (Paris, 1813)
Etude élémentaire de l'harmonie, ou nouvelle méthode pour apprendre ... à connaître tous les accords et leurs principales résolutions, ouvrage agréé par Grétry (Paris, n.d.)
Sphere harmonique, tableau des accords (Paris, 1827)
Abécédaire musicale, principes élémentaires à l'usage des élèves (Paris, 1831)

BIBLIOGRAPHY

G. d'Orgeval: 'Aimon (Léopold-Pamphile-François)', *DBF*

BRUCE CARR

Ainsworth, Henry (*b* Swanton Morley, Norfolk, 1570; *d* Amsterdam, ?1622–3). English minister and biblical scholar. He was expatriated as a 'Brownist' in 1593 and settled in Amsterdam, where he became 'teacher' of a church in 1596; together with its pastor, he founded an Independent church, eventually becoming minister of it himself. He was the author of a number of religious tracts, annotations and translations of scripture, including *The Book of Psalmes: Englished both in Prose and Metre. With Annotations* (Amsterdam, 1612, 5/1644). This psalter, which included 39 monophonic psalm tunes, 'most taken from our former Englished psalms [and also] the gravest and easiest of the French and Dutch', was used by the Pilgrim settlers of the Plymouth Colony in 1620, thereby beginning the history of psalmody in New England. By the late 17th century, however, it was no longer in use there, having been replaced by the Bay Psalm Book and other psalters.

See PSALMODY (ii).

WRITINGS

Two Treatises (Edinburgh, 1789) [preceded by an account of Ainsworth's life and writings]

BIBLIOGRAPHY

Anon.: *Work of John Robinson, Pastor of the Pilgrim Fathers* (London, 1851)

W. E. A. Axon and E. Axon: *Henry Ainsworth, the Puritan Commentator* (Manchester, 1889)

W. S. Pratt: *The Music of the Pilgrims* (Boston, 1921)

H. WILEY HITCHCOCK

Aiodos (Gk.). A term used by HOMER in the *Odyssey* to denote a bard.

Aiolle, Francesco dell'. *See* LAYOLLE, FRANCESCO DE.

Aiolli, Alamanno. *See* LAYOLLE, ALAMANNE DE.

Aiolli, Francesco dell'. *See* LAYOLLE, FRANCESCO DE.

Air [ayre]. A term apparently originating in England and France in the 16th century and frequently used rather loosely as synonymous with 'tune' or 'song'.

1. The term 'air'. 2. The English 'ayre'.

1. THE TERM 'AIR'. At first the word was used especially of lighter pieces. Morley, for example, in his *Plaine and Easie Introduction to Practicall Musicke* (1597) applied it to all the secular vocal forms of his day except the madrigal, which was the most serious of them. Moreover, it was consistently used in England from the same year for published volumes of lute-songs, several of which, however, are serious. Here the spelling 'ayre' was often preferred. After the decline of the lute 'ayre', towards the mid-17th century, the form 'air' was often used again in its more general sense. By the 18th century it clearly denoted a simple, unpretentious song, quite different from the Italian or Italianate aria, which in both operas and cantatas was often a complex, highly developed form.

English writers sometimes used the word 'air' in another, somewhat different way, apparently denoting not a tune itself but the aesthetic quality of a piece of music that might be summed up as inevitable rightness – perfection, even – in which the various elements, especially melody and harmony, complement and enhance one another. This usage is doubtless not unconnected with two of the many everyday meanings of an unusually versatile word: general bearing, manner or outward appearance; and atmosphere or aura investing a person or object. The word 'aria' was sometimes used in a similar way (see Pirrotta, 1968, and ARIA, §1). Roger North wrote much about this aspect of air, notably in *An Essay of Musicall Ayre* (c1715; annotated excerpts in Wilson), whose title-page shows that it is concerned 'cheifly to shew the foundations of Melody joyned with Harmony, whereby may be discovered the Native genius of good Musick'. In the 12th edition (1694) of John Playford's *An Introduction to the Skill of Musick*, Purcell wrote of a music example that he had improved from earlier editions that it 'carries more Air and Form' in it.

Just as in England the word 'ayre' has been used of a particular kind of song, so in France a variant of *air* was used in a comparable way: for some 80 years from 1571 the term AIR DE COUR was regularly used for solo lute-songs and ensemble songs, again comprising light and serious pieces. Another specific term, AIR À BOIRE, subsequently came into being to denote lighter songs. By this time – the 1670s – the more serious type was

generally called simply *air*. From now on, into the 18th century, the *air*, frequently qualified by an epithet – for instance *air tendre* – was one of the most important elements of stage works and cantatas. Although used of unpretentious pieces it was applied too to serious, more extended monologues comparable in effect to arias in Italian works; an example is 'O jour affreux' in Act 3 scene i of Rameau's *Dardanus* (1739).

Some of the *airs* in French operas are accompanied by dancing, and several of them are purely instrumental (*airs de danse*). These highlight the fact that from at least the early 17th century the word 'air' was widely applied to instrumental as well as to vocal pieces. (At first the instrumental air in England was, like the vocal, spelt 'ayre' in many sources.) Like many of their vocal counterparts, such pieces tend to be of the lighter type, and some are dance-like – witness the *Courtly Masquing Ayres* (1621) of John Adson. But the term is generally used for simple pieces which, like vocal airs, are of a predominantly melodic cast and can indeed be seen as instrumental songs. They are not usually dance-like, and the inclusion of such a piece in a suite may have been prompted by a desire on the composer's part to offer contrast to the surrounding pieces in specific dance rhythms. Locke's *Little Consort* can plausibly be seen to consist of ten suites all with the sequence pavan–air–courante–saraband, and airs figure prominently in comparable ways in all his other consort sets except the duos for bass viols. There are several instrumental airs by Purcell, notably in the stage works, and there are keyboard transcriptions of a few of them. The many melodic airs in suites by later Baroque composers include one of the most celebrated movements by Bach – the air in the Suite no.3 in D BWV1068 – and one of Handel's too (the so-called 'Harmonious Blacksmith' in Suite no.5 in E). Some airs at this period are faster and generally in bourrée rhythm.

Finally the word 'air' is used of a signal, or more often a march, of clairons, and fifes or oboes, to which a drum batterie is usually attached; *see* SONNERIE.

2. THE ENGLISH 'AYRE'. The vogue of the English lute ayre began in 1597 when Dowland published his *First Booke of Songes or Ayres*. This collection was highly successful and went through four more editions between 1600 and 1613 (more than any other English printed volume of that time). Dowland went on to publish three more collections of lute ayres, and other composers followed suit, notably Campion, Rosseter, Danyel, Jones, Pilkington and Alfonso Ferrabosco (ii). Dowland's *First Booke* established the format for these songbooks: they were of large folio size, and composers tended to favour publishing multiples of seven songs, 21 being a common number. As well as the parts for solo voice and lute (the latter in tablature notation,) composers generally provided an optional part for bass viol, and often extra vocal parts as well, for alto, tenor and bass. Thus the ayres could be performed as solo songs with instrumental accompaniment, or as partsongs for several voices; or if desired, the extra vocal parts could be performed on instruments. Such flexibility in performance was characteristic of the time; moreover, at a time when music publishing in England was still in its infancy, and rather uncertain financially, it was an obvious advantage to provide music that could be adapted to suit the differing tastes and musical resources of amateur musicans. When extra parts were provided they

were printed facing in different directions so that several performers seated round a table could read from a single copy.

The immediate English antecedents of the lute ayre were the partsong and the consort song. Although the surviving repertory of partsongs is not large there is sufficient evidence to show that before the vogue of the madrigal and lute ayre in England there was a strong partsong tradition, examples of which can be seen in keyboard arrangements of mid-century partsongs in the Mulliner Book (MB, i) and in Whythorne's *Songs for Three, Fower, and Five Voyces* of 1571. Like the lute ayres these are generally strophic (i.e. the same music is repeated for every stanza), and the musical style covers a wide spectrum from simple harmonized tunes to quite elaborate contrapuntal compositions. The simpler partsongs in particular, like the anonymous *I smile to see how you devise* or Richard Edwards's *When griping griefs* (both in the Mulliner Book) are the forerunners of many 'light ayres' by Campion, Rosseter and Ford. In such pieces as these, with their straightforward melodies and chordal texture, the accompaniment can be provided equally well by voices or by a chord-playing instrument, and so it is not surprising that there are arrangements of some of these partsongs for voice and lute.

The other type of music just mentioned as being an important forerunner of the lute ayre, the consort song, was normally composed for solo voice accompanied by four viols. A substantial repertory of consort songs survives from the mid-16th century onwards by composers such as Richard Farrant, Robert Parsons and Byrd, and these provided a model for the more extended and contrapuntal lute ayres composed by Dowland, Cavendish and Danyel. Consort songs were also sometimes arranged for voice and lute, thus providing a direct link between the two media.

In addition to these English antecedents it seems clear that the French chanson, or *air de cour* as the lighter type came to be known, influenced the development of the English ayre. French chansons appear in two of the very few music books printed in England before 1588: the *Recueil du mellange d'Orlande de Lassus* (1570) and Adrian Le Roy's *Briefe and Plaine Instruction* (1574). Moreover, Dowland had ample opportunity to become acquainted with this music during his sojourn in France in the early 1580s: an interesting sidelight on this is the fact that the music of the song ascribed to 'Tesseir' in the anthology *A Musicall Banquet* (1610), compiled by Dowland's son Robert, first appeared in Guillaume Tessier's *Premier livre d'airs* in 1582, that is, while John Dowland was in France. The Tessiers seem to have had other English connections, for in 1597 – the same year as Dowland's *First Booke* – Charles Tessier's *Premier livre de chansons et aires de court* was published in London by East. Several general parallels can be drawn between the French *air de cour* and the English ayre – strophic setting, a predilection for light homophonic textures, and the provision of alternative arrangements for solo voice and lute or vocal ensemble (though, in the French case, not within the same volume) – and it seems likely that some of the impetus for the English movement, and indeed for the term 'ayre', came from its French counterpart.

Finally, in considering the various factors that fused to give rise to the English lute ayre it should not be forgotten that the songbooks were important sources of lyric verse and were evidently valued as such, judging by the number of lutenist lyrics which found their way into printed and manuscript collections of poetry. From a literary point of view the songbooks of Dowland and his circle can be seen as a continuation of the sequence of Tudor poetical miscellanies that began with *The Court of Venus* (*c*1537) and included Tottel's *Songes and Sonettes* (1557), *A Handefull of Pleasant Delites* (1566), *The Paradyse of Daynty Devices* (1576) and *A Gorgious Gallery of Gallant Inventions* (1578). All these contain at least a proportion of poems that were evidently 'verse for song' and for which in some instances musical settings survive. Just as these volumes have been described as 'songbooks without music', so the lutenist's folios may be considered as 'poetical miscellanies with music'. The title of Jones's last songbook, *The Muses Gardin for Delights*, recalls the flowery titles of some of the earlier miscellanies.

The ayres of the lutenists cover a wide stylistic spectrum from extended contrapuntal compositions to short harmonized tunes. The former extreme is represented at its best by some of Dowland's ayres, such as the three magnificent songs with obbligato viol parts in his *Pilgrimes Solace* (1612). In these the influence of the consort song is particularly evident, the expressive phrases of the vocal line, punctuated by rests, being supported by a continuous polyphonic accompanying texture. Other composers who wrote in this vein were Cavendish, Morley and Danyel. Dowland frequently used touches of chromaticism to heighten the expression, but the most extreme of the lutenists in this respect was Danyel, notably in *Can doleful notes*. In ayres like these, especially where strophic form is abandoned in favour of new music for each stanza (or where just one stanza is set), the composer often paid close attention to details in the text, and the result is reminiscent of the work of the madrigalists; but more generally, the lutenists were content to express the general mood of the lyric rather than to depict the details.

At the other extreme is the 'light ayre' advocated by Campion. Campion is notable among the lutenists as having been a poet as well as a composer, and the lyrics he set to music are all generally taken to be his own work. He was the only songwriter to express in print any views on the subject of word-setting in songs, and the prefaces to his own songbooks and the one that he shared with Rosseter are also interesting. As a poet he was naturally concerned that the music should not obscure the words, and for this reason he insisted that complicated polyphony had no place in the ayre, which should be short, simple and 'well seasoned' like an epigram (he himself wrote Latin epigrams). He also ridiculed madrigalian word-painting. In ayres like *Shall I come, sweet love, to thee* and *When to her lute Corinna sings* he achieved a refined and eloquent simplicity, as did his friend (and possibly teacher) Rosseter in ayres like *What then is love but mourning*. One of Campion's ayres, *Come let us sound with melody*, reflects his interest in reviving classical prosody. The poem is written in Sapphic metre, and the melody matches the long and short syllables with minims and crotchets respectively, like the *musique mesurée* of some French chanson composers.

In between the two extremes represented by the contrapuntal ayres of Dowland and Danyel and the light ayres of Campion there is a great variety of styles. One genre specially cultivated by Dowland was the dance ayre, i.e. a song written in the form and style of a dance such as the pavan or galliard. The most famous of all his ayres, *Flow, my tears*, is a vocal pavan. Many instrumental versions of it survive entitled *Lachrimae*, and it seems certain that in this and some other instances the work was first composed as an instrumental piece and words added later. Some ayres by Jones and Cavendish reflect the influence of the canzonet and ballett. Cavendish's single volume, like that of Greaves, contains madrigals as well as ayres, and some of the items printed as ayres (e.g. *Say, shepherds, say*) are really canzonets or madrigals with the lower vocal parts intabulated for lute.

The most important stylistic development during the vogue of the lute ayre was the rise of the declamatory style. Once again Dowland led the way; he had visited Italy in 1595 and was almost certainly acquainted with the work of Caccini and other Italian monodists. In *Come, heavy sleep* (1597) and *Sorrow, stay* (1600) he used declamation momentarily for special expressive effect, but in later songs, such as *Tell me, true love* and *Welcome, black night* (1612), it is much more pervasive. Some of these later declamatory songs were written for masques, and it seems that in England as in Italy the new style was associated with theatrical entertainment. Another composer whose airs show this tendency was Alfonso Ferrabosco (ii), who collaborated with Ben Jonson in a number of masques; others are Coprario, Mason and Earsden.

The last lutenist to publish a printed songbook was John Attey in 1622, only 25 years after Dowland had inaugurated the movement. But in addition to the printed songbooks there are a number of manuscript collections, such as *GB-Lbm* Add.15117, 15118, 24665 and 29481 and manuscripts at *Ob*, *Och*, *Cke* and *US-NYp*. Some of the ayres in these sources are elaborately embellished, sometimes apparently just for embellishment's sake, but sometimes to heighten the expression, after the fashion of the Italian monodists. In many cases they are provided only with an unfigured bass accompaniment, but they are essentially the same as the lute ayres, and in fact many printed lute ayres reappear in manuscripts with only a bass accompaniment. Nevertheless the provision of a simple bass accompaniment which could be realized on any chord-playing instrument was a sign of a decline in the prestige of the lute itself. In the manuscripts one finds the work of a younger generation of songwriters – men like Nicholas Lanier (ii), Robert Johnson (ii), John Wilson and William and Henry Lawes; in fact, these manuscripts afford the clearest evidence that the ayre did not die with Attey's songbook of 1622 but continued to evolve with undiminished vitality.

BIBLIOGRAPHY

ESLS, 1st and 2nd ser., i–xxxii, ed. E. H. Fellowes (London, 1920–32, rev., enlarged T. Dart as EL, 1959–)
E. H. Fellowes: *English Madrigal Verse* (Oxford, 1920, rev., enlarged 3/1967 by F. W. Sternfeld and D. Greer)
P. Warlock and P. Wilson: *English Ayres* (London, 1922–5, enlarged 2/1927–31/R1964)
P. Warlock: *The English Ayre* (London, 1926)
G. Bontoux: *La chanson en Angleterre au temps d'Elisabeth* (Oxford, 1936)
M. C. Boyd: *Elizabethan Music and Musical Criticism* (Philadelphia, 1940, 2/1962)
B. Pattison: *Music and Poetry of the English Renaissance* (London, 1948, 2/1970)
C. M. Ing: *Elizabethan Lyrics: a Study in the Development of English Metres* (London, 1951)
J. P. Cutts: 'A Bodleian Song Book: Don.C.57', *ML*, xxxiv (1953), 192
Musique et poésie au XVᵉ siécle: CNRS Paris 1953
N. Greenberg, W. H. Auden and C. Kallman: *An Elizabethan Song Book* (Garden City, NY, 1955/R1968)
J. P. Cutts: 'Seventeenth-century Lyrics: Oxford, Bodleian MS Mus.b.1', *MD*, x (1956), 142–209
——: 'Early Seventeenth-century Lyrics at St. Michael's College', *ML*, xxxvii (1956), 321
V. Duckles: 'Florid Embellishment in English Song of the late 16th and 17th Centuries', *AnnM*, v (1957), 329
La luth et sa musique: CNRS Neuilly-sur-Seine 1957
I. Spink: *English Declamatory Ayres from between c1620 and 1660* (diss., U. of Birmingham, 1958)
J. P. Cutts: *La musique de scène de la troupe de Shakespeare* (Paris, 1959)
——: 'Seventeenth century Songs and Lyrics in Edinburgh University Library Music MS Dc.1.69', *MD*, xiii (1959), 169–94
——: *Seventeenth Century Songs and Lyrics* (Columbia, Missouri, 1959) [from MSS]
——: ' "Mris Elizabeth Davenant 1624": Christ Church MS Mus. 87', *Review of English Studies*, new ser., x (1959), 26
A. J. Sabol: *Songs and Dances for the Stuart Masque* (Providence, Rhode Island, 1959)
J. Wilson, ed: *Roger North on Music* (London, 1959), 65ff
I. Spink: 'English Cavalier Songs', *PRMA*, lxxxvi (1959–60), 61
J. P. Cutts: ' "Songs unto the Violl and Lute" – Drexel MS 4175', *MD*, xvi (1962), 73
R. J. McGrady: *The English Solo Song from William Byrd to Henry Lawes* (diss., U. of Manchester, 1963)
W. Mellers: *Harmonious Meeting* (London, 1963)
U. Olshausen: *Das lautenbegleitete Sololied in England um 1600* (Frankfurt am Main, 1963)
J. P. Cutts: 'Drexel Manuscript 4041', *MD*, xviii (1964), 151
E. Doughtie: 'Words for Music: Simplicity and Complexity in the Elizabethan Air', *Rice University Studies*, li (1965), 1
F. W. Sternfeld, ed: *English Lute Songs, 1597–1622*, i–ix (Menston, 1967–71) [fasc. reprints]
V. Duckles: 'The English Musical Elegy of the Late Renaissance', *Aspects of Medieval and Renaissance Music: a Birthday Offering to Gustave Reese* (New York, 1966), 134
D. Greer: 'The Partsongs of the English Lutenists', *PRMA*, xciv (1967–8), 97
N. Fortune: 'Solo Song and Cantata', *NOHM*, iv (1968), 194
N. Pirrotta: 'Early Opera and Aria', *New Looks at Italian Opera: Essays in Honor of Donald J. Grout* (Ithaca, NY, 1968), 57f
M. Joiner: 'British Museum add. MS 15117: a Commentary, Index and Bibliography', *RMARC*, vii (1969), 51
E. Doughtie: *Lyrics from English Airs, 1596–1622* (Cambridge, Mass., 1971) [omits Campion's lyrics]
D. Poulton: *John Dowland* (London, 1972)
D. Greer: 'Songbooks 1500–1660', *New Cambridge Bibliography of English Literature*, i (London, 1974), 1337
I. Spink: *English Song: Dowland to Purcell* (London, 1974)
E. H. Jones: ' "To Sing and Play to the Base-violl alone": the Bass Viol in English 17th Century Song', *LSJ*, xvii (1975), 17
F. B. Zimmerman: 'Air: a Catchword for New Concepts in Seventeenth-century English Music Theory', *Studies in Musicology in Honor of Otto E. Albrecht* (Kassel, 1977)

NIGEL FORTUNE (1), DAVID GREER (2)

Air à boire. A French drinking-song. The term was used principally between the second half of the 17th century and the mid-18th century for strophic, syllabic songs whose texts are of a light, frivolous nature in contradistinction to *airs sérieux*, whose texts deal with love, pastoral scenes or political satire. The CHANSON POUR BOIRE was its predecessor; there is no appreciable difference between the two types.

Most *airs à boire* appeared in Paris in prints and MSS for from one to three voices, with accompaniment for lute or continuo. Between 1674 and 1745 over 250 collections, containing several thousand songs, were entitled *Airs sérieux et à boire*. In at least two collections ritornellos are added. In addition some collections, both printed and MS, contain either only *airs à boire* – volumes by Cambert, Sicard and Denis Lefebvre are good examples – or only a few such *airs* among numerous other types of song (Lefebvre's volume is unusual in being for four voices). Prolific composers of *airs à boire* include Brossard, Du Bousset, one of the Du Buisson family, Louis Lemaire, Renier and Sicard. The main publishers were Christophe Ballard (who published several huge series of anthologies) and Boyvin in Paris and Etienne Roger in Amsterdam. *Airs à boire* were so fashionable in the 1690s that a new collection was published every three months. For a representative selection, see *Airs sérieux et à boire à 2 et 3 voix*, ed. F. Robert, Le pupitre, vi (Paris, 1968).

JOHN H. BARON

Airardus Viciliacensis. An obscure figure, Magister Airard of Vézelay (a Benedictine monastery situated along a major pilgrimage route to the shrine of St James at Santiago de Compostela) appears as author of a two-part conductus, *Annua gaudia*, in the 12th-century Calixtine MS (*E-SC*). Whether he was actually a musician or poet is unknown, since the Calixtine attributions are generally acknowledged to be spurious.

SARAH FULLER

Air column. The body of air inside the tube of a wind instrument. When a note is sounded the air column is in a state of longitudinal vibration, i.e. subject to a cyclic succession of local compressions and rarefactions among its component particles. The frequency of these disturbances determines the pitch of the sound heard and is governed mainly by the dimensions of the air column, but also to an extent by the way in which the disturbances are engendered. Frequency is affected by such factors as the temperature and moisture content of the air, frictional effects at the surface of the confining tube or vessel (*see* BORE) and the transfer of energy among its particles without transfer of heat. Departures from certain ideal geometrical forms such as the cylinder or cone, which occur in almost all wind instruments, also affect the frequency characteristics of the air column. When the column is in vibration the periodic disturbances do not terminate abruptly at the ends of the confining tube but extend a short distance into the surrounding air. Thus it is necessary to apply a correction factor when determining its 'effective length' (*see* OVERBLOWING).

PHILIP BATE

Air de cour. The term was used by French composers and publishers from 1571 to the 1650s to designate many secular, strophic songs sung at court. From 1608 until approximately 1632 these were the most important and numerous vocal compositions in France.

Airs de cour were composed either for four or five unaccompanied voices (a few examples are for six and eight voices) or for one voice usually with lute accompaniment. They were written for the entertainment of the king and his courtiers by the finest composers at court, all of whom were excellent singers. Nearly all *airs* were published first by the royal printers Le Roy & Ballard, later by Ballard alone, often in series of collections appearing over a number of years. From 1608 a number of *airs* in these collections were taken from the year's most successful *ballets de cour*.

In the preface to the first collection of *airs de cour*, *Livre d'air de cours miz sur le luth par Adrian Le Roy* (1571), Le Roy stated that he was presenting a light, simple type of song known previously as VAUDEVILLE (or *voix de ville*). The collection contains 22 solo *airs* with lute accompaniment. Most of the texts are by Ronsard, but Sillac, Pasquier, Desportes and Baïf are also represented. 13 *airs* are arrangements of four-part

vaudevilles from *Chansons de P. de Ronsard, Ph. Desportes et autres, mises en musique par N. de la Grotte* (Paris, 1570). Le Roy took over intact the original superius voice, which predominates, and adapted the lute part from the other voices. The lute part of three *airs de cour* appears in two versions, one simple, the other ornamented. As in La Grotte's vaudevilles, the *airs* mix metres; there is a steady tactus, but the accents do not occur in a regular musical metre. The influence of *musique mesurée* is often clear. A few *airs* are in the form *AAB*, but most do not fall readily into sections, though motifs recur.

All the *airs de cour* that appeared during the rest of the 16th century were not solo but polyphonic. Collections of *airs* by Didier Le Blanc and Jehan Planson (1582 and 1587 respectively), though not specifically labelled *de cour*, fit into the tradition of such pieces on the basis of their similarity to the *airs de cour* of the next decade. Le Blanc collected 43 short, simple, strophic, mostly homophonic ametrical *airs* for four voices by several composers, and Planson's 38 *airs* are similar. The only difference lies in the strophe form: in Le Blanc's collection it is non-repetitive, in Planson's it is nearly always *ABB*. Another anthology of such pieces appeared in 1595 (*Airs mis en musique à quatre, et cinq, parties: de plusieurs autheurs*), and was followed in 1597 by two collections specifically entitled *airs de cour* by Denis Caignet and Charles Tessier respectively.

The major production of *airs de cour* occurred in the 17th century, mostly during the reign of Louis XIII (1610–43). Although this is when the greatest number of solo *airs de cour* appeared, polyphonic *airs* for four or five voices also abound, primarily in the four volumes edited by Pierre Guédron between 1608 and 1618 and the nine volumes edited by Antoine Boësset between 1617 and 1642. In addition two collections were printed in 1610 and 1613, and others were composed by Macé (1634), Chancy (1635–44), François Richard (1637), Etienne Moulinié (5 vols., 1625–39) and Cambefort (1651–5). Sercy's *Airs et vaudevilles de cour* (1665–6) seem to be isolated late examples.

Between 1608 and 1632 Ballard brought out 15 volumes of *Airs de différent autheurs avec la tablature de luth*, anthologies of solo *airs de cour* accompanied by lute; a number were sufficiently in demand to require second editions. In 1643, the last year of Louis XIII's reign, Ballard published the last book of solo *airs de cour*; here the editor and chief composer, Boësset, stated that all his publications of *airs* had been to amuse and satisfy the king, who had received them with love, the highest recompense. All the lute *airs* are simple, essentially syllabic, strophic and mostly ametrical in metre. The vocal range rarely exceeds an octave. The harmony is tonal and simple. A number are arrangements of polyphonic *airs* from the collections listed above.

The texts, deriving from Italian pastorals, by authors such as Tasso and Guarini, translated by d'Urfé and others, are strictly symmetrical, with rhyming lines of six to 13 syllables and strophes of four to eight lines. Malherbe's concise modern diction and careful rhyme and verse patterns prevail. Despite the Italian sources of the texts, in no case does the music suggest the influence of contemporary Italian madrigals and monody. The composers include, besides Antoine Boësset and Guédron, the court musicians Moulinié, Jean Boyer, Bataille, Jean-Baptiste Boësset, François Richard, Auget, Rigaud, Vincent, Grand-Rue, Le Fegueux and Sauvage, most of whom published their own separate collections of *airs*.

Between 1615 and 1628 Ballard published eight volumes of monophonic *airs de cour* without any accompaniment. All appear unaltered but with accompaniment in the collections of *Airs de différents autheurs avec la tablature de luth*.

Airs drawn from *ballets de cour* seldom differ from the other *airs*. They were usually composed for a soloist accompanied by lute, but in a few cases there are polyphonic ballet *airs* which appear in alternative versions in polyphonic, voice-and-lute and monophonic collections. In many ballets the song served as an introduction to an act or as part of an entrée; in such cases it was sometimes limited to one strophe.

The *airs* were not always performed as written. The alternative versions of the accompaniment of three songs in the 1571 collection attest to an improvisatory ornamentation of the lute part. The voice in solo *airs* can also be ornamented in ways often similar to Italian practice, as discussed by Mersenne: 'Seconde partie de l'art d'embellir la voix' in 'Traitez des consonances', *Harmonie universelle*, ii (Paris, 1637/R), 355ff; B. de Bacilly: *Remarques curieuses sur l'art de bien chanter* (1668; trans. and ed. A. Caswell as *A Commentary upon the Art of Proper Singing*, Brooklyn, 1968, 135fff); and J. Millet: *La belle méthode, ou l'art de bien chanter* (Besançon, 1666/R1973). Bataille stated in the 1608 collection of lute *airs* that he was putting down only the simplest form of the song, no doubt so that less gifted amateurs could enjoy them, the professionals knowing how to apply ornaments.

The popularity of the *air de cour* spread well beyond the borders of Paris and France. Besides the *airs* published by Jean Mangeant in Caen (1608 and 1615), a number appeared in French in Germany in J. B. Besard's *Thesaurus harmonicus* (1603) and in England in Tessier's *Airs de cour* (1597). Translations of French *airs* into English appear in Robert Dowland's *A Musicall Banquet* (1610) and Edward Filmer's *French Court-airs, with their Ditties Englished* (1629). The tunes were frequently copied with totally new, vernacular texts in Holland. In France the *airs* were also borrowed with new, sacred texts in several multi-volume sacred collections: *La pieuse Alouette, Philomèle séraphique* and François Berthod's *Livre d'airs de dévotion*.

After about 1650 the term *air* by itself was frequently used, most notably in 33 volumes of *Airs de différents autheurs à deux parties* (Paris, 1658–88). At the end of that century and in the next, *air* alone became synonymous with an aria in a French opera, while *air sérieux* designated a song similar to the earlier *air de cour* in text and musical structure. There are also *airs à boire* (*see* AIR À BOIRE). The vogue for *airs de cour* was succeeded in the 1630s by that for the CHANSON POUR BOIRE and the *chanson pour danser*.

EDITIONS
L. de La Laurencie, A. Mairy and G. Thibault, eds.: *Chansons au luth et airs de cour français du xvie siècle* (Paris, 1934)
A. Verchaly, ed.: *Airs de cour pour voix et luth (1603–1643)* (Paris, 1961)

BIBLIOGRAPHY
K. J. Levy: 'Chanson', §iv, *MGG*
N. Fortune: 'Solo Song and Cantata', *NOHM*, iv (London, 1968), 185
W. Müller-Blattau: 'Vaudeville, Chanson und Air de cour', *Volks- und Hochkunst in Dichtung und Musik* (Saarbrücken, 1968), 135
A. Cohen: '*L'art de bien chanter* (1666) of Jean Millet', *MQ*, lv (1969), 170
D. L. Royster: *Pierre Guédron and the 'air de cour' 1600–1620* (New Haven, Conn., in preparation)

JOHN H. BARON

Ais (Ger.). A♯; *see* PITCH NAMES.

Aischylos. *See* AESCHYLUS.

Aisis (Ger.). A𝄪; *see* PITCH NAMES.

Aist, Dietmar von. *See* DIETMAR VON AIST.

Aitken, John (*b* Dalkeith, ?1745; *d* Philadelphia, 8 Sept 1831). American metalsmith, music engraver, compiler, publisher and dealer of Scottish birth. He arrived in Philadelphia by 1785, and issued a *Compilation of Litanies and Vespers, Hymns and Anthems* in 1787 (later edn., 1791), the only 18th-century American musical collection for the Roman Catholic Church. In 1797 he brought out the compendious *Scots Musical Museum*, and between 1806 and 1811 was one of Philadelphia's busiest publishers, issuing more than 90 secular songs – including at least one of his own – and several secular collections, as well as more sacred music. Aitken's musical activity seems to have ceased after 1811.

BIBLIOGRAPHY
F. J. Metcalf: *American Writers and Compilers of Sacred Music* (New York, 1925/R1967), 45f
R. J. Wolfe: *Secular Music in America 1801–1825: a Bibliography* (New York, 1964)

RICHARD CRAWFORD

Aitken, Robert (Morris) (*b* Kentville, Nova Scotia, 28 Aug 1939). Canadian flautist and composer. He studied with Nicholas Fiore (in Toronto) and Marcel Moyse; later with Rampal and Gazzelloni. He was principal flautist of the Vancouver SO (1958–9) and of the Toronto SO (1965–70). In 1971 he was a prizewinner of the Concours International de Flûte de Paris. He is a member of the Lyric Arts Trio (soprano, flute, piano) and musical director of New Music Concerts (Toronto) and Music Today (Shaw Festival, Ontario), as well as a soloist whose engagements take him to Europe, North America, Japan and Iceland. Technically adept, he has a pure, intense tone and a finished sense of phrasing. In 1971 he became an associate professor at Toronto University (where he had earlier taken the MM degree). As a composer he has been awarded the Canada Music Citation (1969) and received numerous commissions.

WORKS
Composition, fl, tape, 1962; Hamlet (incidental music, Shakespeare), 4-track tape, 1963; Noesis, 4-track tape, 1964; Conc., 12 insts, orch, 1968; Spectra, 4 ens, 1969; Kebyar, fl, cl, perc, 2 db, tape, 1971; Nekuia, orch, 1971; Lalitá, fl, 2 harps, 2 perc, 3 vc, 1972; Nĩṛa, fl, ob, pf, hpd, vn, va, db, 1974

Principal publishers: Kirby, Ricordi, Salabert

BRUCE MATHER

Aiuola, Francesco dell'. *See* LAYOLLE, FRANCESCO DE.

Aius (Lat., from Gk. *hagios*: 'holy'). A term used in the Gallican rite for the Trisagion; *see* GALLICAN RITE, MUSIC OF THE, §7(iii).

Aix-en-Provence. French city. Strophic songs, 'planchs de St Estève', were chanted from the 9th century for the feast of St Stephen in the former cathedral, Notre Dame de la Seds, but the city suffered for a long time from Saracen invasions and was able to resume any artistic activity of note only from the 11th century. The first known *maître de chapelle* was Pons (Pontius Grammaticus) who 'for 40 years taught the tuneful singing of the Psalms of David' to about 20 churchmen in the second half of the century. The first stone of the cathedral, St Sauveur, was laid in 1060; the building was consecrated in 1103 and in 1115 there were 40 canons and churchmen to sing the Office. No troubadours are known, probably because the princes who owned the town then resided in Barcelona, Toulouse or Aragon rather than in Aix; a palace was built there only in the second half of the 12th century. In the second half of the 13th century the first choir school was established at St Sauveur, with between eight and ten boys. The marriage of Béatrix de Provence and Charles I d'Anjou, who took Adam de la Halle into his service, is the main reason for the Bibliothèque Méjanes in Aix now possessing a fine manuscript of the *Jeu de Robin et de Marion*, with stage directions.

Music flourished during the 15th century: in 1400, 1401 and 1408 Vincent Ferrier, a Spanish Dominican preacher, sang High Mass at St Sauveur using portative organs and the regular singers. The university was founded at the beginning of the century. In 1437 King René had himself installed as canon of the metropolitan church, which probably prompted the inauguration of a large organ in 1470, the completion of the building from 1471 and the organization of plays for Corpus Christi, with processions, interludes, masquerades and cavalcades to the sound of the flageolet and tabor. The king may have composed the tune for the dance of the Queen of Saba, an episode in the procession. At his court the king retained minstrels, musicians and composers of all nationalities. His chapel contained 'the best singers anyone could find', according to Louis XI who, in 1481, was there recruiting them for the Sainte-Chapelle in Paris. In the same year Provence had been attached to France, and in 1539 François I imposed French as the language of royal administration. Henceforth cultivated circles wrote in French but for long after still spoke Provençal, retaining tunes and even composing songs which then became 'traditional'. But the court's style of life was adopted: intense, artistic, festive and amorous. Elsewhere mystery and morality plays and *soties* were still performed. In St Sauveur from 1517 Mass was sung daily, and the choir school of 53 members sang the polyphonic repertory. In 1543 the 'Feast of Fools' was abolished. In 1558 a new Psalter took into account the instructions of the Council of Trent, and in 1620 there was a solemn ceremony for the inauguration of the Roman Office according to the Tridentine reforms. But this did not prevent a performance, as soon as the occasion arose and funds permitted, with double choir, violins, oboes, trumpets, fifes and drums, and even cannon shots in the square, and bell peals with the organ playing the same notes as the bells, which was how a *Te Deum* was performed in 1660 for the entry of Louis XIV. 17th-century *maîtres de chapelle* included Sauveur Intermet (*c*1629), Annibal Gantez (April 1636 to June 1638), François Gal, succeeded by Guillaume Poitevin (1667–93), Jean Gilles (1693–5), Cabassol (1695–8) and Poitevin again (from 1698 until his death in 1706). An early 17th-century manuscript in the Bibliothèque Méjanes, the *Livre des vers du luth* (ed. A. Verchaly, Aix, 1958), reveals a fashionable society fond of courtly airs.

The town was too small to support an opera company and was dependent on Marseilles, Avignon and even Nice. It had visits from travelling Italian and French troupes, and in particular from Gautier's Marseilles troupe in 1695 and 1696. In their college the Jesuits staged tragedies and special ballets, both mythological and didactic. For the performance of orchestral music a group existed in 1701 of 14 musicians including violins, oboes, kettledrums and bass. There were two bands of violins in 1718, and in 1740 a *concert* playing in what is roughly the present Salle Méjanes. From 1756 there was an Academy of Music. Traditional instruments were not abandoned: an advertisement in 1777 announced that 'Monsieur Chateauminois has brought the playing of the flutet or gaboulet (three-holed flageolet) to a peak of perfection that no-one would have thought possible'. But the centralizing influence of Versailles and Paris reduced the musical material available in the town, and the choir school at St Sauveur remained the most lively centre. As early as 1631 Louis XIII had taken one of the choirboys for the Chapel Royal. Most 17th-century *maîtres de chapelle* left Aix, as did André and Joseph Campra, who had been trained in the choir school. Claude Pellegrin, *maître de chapelle* since 1706, left in 1724, though he took up his post again (1731–48) apparently after a lawsuit brought against him by the chapter. After 1758 E. J. Floquet, also trained in the choir school, left for Paris despite the great success he had in Aix as a child prodigy. Nevertheless, because of the number and quality of its singers and instrumentalists, the school was able to devise and perform motets for large chorus and orchestra in the Versailles style. In 1786 the Marquis de Méjanes bequeathed his collection of works, manuscripts and prints to the town. In 1794 the choir school was disbanded, each boy receiving an indemnity; St Sauveur became the Temple of Reason.

Despite the efforts of many individuals, musical life in 19th-century Aix was much reduced through financial difficulties and problems of taste. In 1807 the St Sauveur choir school was started again, with three boys. Félicien David, who began as choirboy, became *maître de chapelle* in 1828–9. In 1835 the school was annexed by the Petit Séminaire. The organ, built in 1743 by Jean-Esprit Isnard, was entirely reconstructed, apart from the case, by Ducroquet in 1854–5; in 1880 Cavaillé-Coll renewed part of the mechanism and altered some of the stops. At the end of the century Abbé Marbot applied himself to restoring the choir school, but this was destroyed in World War I. In 1849 Marius Lapierre, composer and orchestral conductor, organized a solfège course, and in 1856 classes for wind instruments, the violin and the cello were added. This led to the formation of the L. Bruguier–A. Giraud–S. Gautier–L. Pourcel Quartet, the first and last being respectively the violin and the cello professors. In 1884 this school became a national one. Milhaud, who was born in Aix, studied with Bruguier from 1899 until he entered the Paris Conservatoire (1909); he returned to Aix during World War II. From 1896 to 1914, owing to the initiative of Jean de Villeneuve, an Association Musicale organized chamber and choral concerts, mostly using forces from outside Aix. Seats at the annual international summer festival of opera (established 1948) are too costly for most local people so Charles Nugue started a free street festival (Musique dans la Rue) in 1972, and this is also the only organization to promote concerts of contemporary music, including the avant garde, with workshops for performance and improvisation. Each year the Association des Concerts du Conservatoire, directed by Pierre Villette, gives seven Classical and neo-classical concerts, the university music club gives 11 concerts, mostly of Baroque and Classical chamber music, the Jeunesses Musicales gives six performances and the Municipal Theatre presents six musical works for the stage.

BIBLIOGRAPHY

FétisB

E. Marbot: *La maîtrise métropolitaine d'Aix: son histoire* (Aix, 1880)

M. Brenet: 'La musique à la cour du Roi René', *Le ménestrel*, li (1885), 148, 157

E. Marbot: *Les livres choraux de St Sauveur d'Aix* (Paris, 1894)

——: *La liturgie aixoise* (Aix, 1899)

——: *Histoire de Notre-Dame de la Seds d'Aix* (Aix, 1904)

F. Raugel: 'La bibliothèque de la maîtrise de la Cathédrale d'Aix-en-Provence', *IAML* ii *Lüneburg 1950*, 33

C. Aubry: 'La Cathédrale de St Sauveur d'Aix-en-Provence', *Revue l'orgue*, cxliii (1972), 92

MARCEL FRÉMIOT

Aix-la-Chapelle (Fr.). AACHEN.

Ajolle, Francesco dell'. *See* LAYOLLE, FRANCESCO DE.

Akathistos. An anonymous Byzantine KONTAKION, possibly dating from the 6th century, which is chanted in Orthodox churches on the fifth Saturday of Great Lent. It comprises two prooimia and 24 oikoi, each alternate oikos forming an acrostic of the letters of the Greek alphabet. To each of the odd-numbered oikoi is appended a number of salutations to the Virgin. The earliest surviving MSS with complete settings of the akathistos date from the 12th and 13th centuries, and are written in a highly melismatic style (*see* PROOIMION).

DIMITRI CONOMOS

A Kempis. Flemish family of musicians.

(1) Nicolaus a Kempis (*b* c1600; *d* Brussels, buried 11 Aug 1676). Composer and organist. From 1626 he replaced Antoon van den Kerckhoven as organist of Ste Gudule, Brussels, and he was named his successor on 25 November 1627. He was succeeded by his son (3) Joannes Florentius a Kempis between 1670 and 1672. The contents of his four books of *Symphoniae* are among the earliest known sonatas in the Low Countries. They range from solo sonatas with continuo to pieces in six parts; they are scored basically for strings, but the bassoon, cornett and trombone are sometimes called for. They are for the most part unpretentious pieces intended for domestic performance; a few are based on popular melodies.

WORKS

Symphoniae, 1–3 vn (Antwerp, 1644)

Symphoniae, 1–5 insts, adjunctae quatuor, 2vv, 3 insts, liber primus, op.2 (Antwerp, 1647)

Symphoniae, 1–6 insts, op.4 (Antwerp, 1642[sic])

Missae et motetta, 8vv, bc (org) (Antwerp, 1650); lost, sometimes attrib.

(3) J. F. a Kempis, but probably by Nicolaus on grounds of age

(2) Thomas [Petrus] **a Kempis** (*b* Brussels, baptized 2 April 1628; *d* 21 Sept 1688). Organist, second son of (1) Nicolaus a Kempis. He joined the Premonstratensian order and took the name Thomas in place of his baptismal name, Petrus. He contributed to the *Antiphonarium, graduale et processionale Praemonstratense* (Antwerp, 1688).

(3) Joannes Florentius [Jean-Florent] **a Kempis** (*b* Brussels, baptized 1 Aug 1635; *d* after 1711). Organist and composer, fifth son of (1) Nicolaus a Kempis. He

was organist of the Eglise de la Chapelle, Brussels, in 1657 and succeeded his father (with whom he has sometimes been confused) as organist of Ste Gudule between 1670 and 1672. He retired on 5 August 1690, leaving the post to his son Guillelmus. He published *Cantiones natalitiae* for five voices (Antwerp, 1657; inc.). An eight-part *Messe pro defunctis* by him is mentioned in an inventory of music at the royal chapel, Brussels, dated 21 August 1666, and Hawkins reported that Thomas Britton owned a set of 12 sonatas by him for violin with viola da gamba and bass.

BIBLIOGRAPHY

HawkinsH

E. H. Meyer: 'Die Vorherrschaft der Instrumentalmusik im niederländischen Barock', *TVNM*, xv/1 (1936), 56; xv/2 (1937), 65; xv/4 (1939), 264

G. Defever: *Nicolaus a Kempis* (diss., Katholieke U., Louvain, in preparation)

JEAN FERRARD

Åkerberg, (Carl) Erik (Emanuel) (*b* Stockholm, 19 Jan 1860; *d* Stockholm, 20 Jan 1938). Swedish composer, organist and conductor. He attended the Stockholm Conservatory (1882–6), studying counterpoint and composition with J. Dente, and was a pupil of Franck in Paris (1887–8). In Stockholm he was coach at the Royal Opera (1888–90), organist at the synagogue (1890–1928), music teacher at Norrmalm's grammar school (1895–1923) and teacher at Richard Anderssons Musikskola (1897–1909). From 1886 he conducted several choirs, including the Bellmanska Sällskapet, which he also founded (1891–1926), and the Filharmoniska Sällskapet (1900–03). Åkerberg's compositions often approach the style of Swedish folk music, especially the ballads *Kung Svegder* and *Prinsessan och Svennen*. They are technically sound but conventional.

WORKS

(*MSS in S-Skma, Svenska Tonsättares Internationella Musikbyrå*)

Operas: Turandot (4, E. Wallmark), 1906, unperf.; Pinntorpafrun (fairytale opera, 4, A. Sandberg), 1915, excerpts only perf.

Vocal: Kung Svegder, ballad, Bar, orch, 1885; Prinsessan och Svennen (K. A. Melin), solo vv, chorus, orch, 1887; Der Barde, solo v, male chorus, orch, 1895; other choral works, cantatas, songs

Orch: Sym., f, 1885; Concert Ov., c, 1884; Swed. folksong arr., small orch, 1888

Inst: 4 str qts.: A, 1884, F, 1925, f, 1926, A, 1926; 2 pf qnts.: a, 1889, d, 1909; str qnt, g, 1925; Trio, b, pf, vn, vc, 1886; works for pf and vn, org

WRITINGS

Musiklifvet inom Par Bricole 1779–1890 (Stockholm, 1910)

Skrubben nr. 24 (Stockholm, 1923) [documents on founding of Bellmanska Sällskapet]

BIBLIOGRAPHY

H. Lindqvist: 'Erik Åkerberg', *Svensk musiktidning*, xii (1892), 1

T. Norlind: 'Åkerberg, Carl Erik Emanuel', *Allmänt musiklexikon*, ii (Stockholm, 1916, 2/1928)

G. Percy: 'Åkerberg, Carl Erik Emanuel', *Sohlmans musiklexikon*, iv (Stockholm, 1952)

H. Glimstedt: *Tonkonsten* (Stockholm, 1957)

KATHLEEN DALE/AXEL HELMER

Akeroyde [Ackeroyde], **Samuel** (*fl* 1684–1706). English violinist and composer. His name suggests that he was a Yorkshireman. He is listed among the king's musicians between 1687 and 1690, in which year he was in the party that accompanied him to Holland. Thereafter he does not appear in the Lord Chamberlain's records, but he was admitted a wait of the City of London in 1695. In 1700 he contributed a commendatory poem 'To my true Friend, Dr Blow, On His Amphion Anglicus'.

Akeroyde was a prolific and presumably popular composer; his songs, over 100 in number, are competent enough but colourless (fully listed in *MGG*). They are to be found principally in collections from 1684 onwards: *The Theater of Music* (1685–7), *Vinculum societatis* (1687–91), *The Banquet of Musick* (1688–92), *Thesaurus musicus* (1693–6) and *Pills to Purge Melancholy* (1699–1720). He contributed songs to the following plays: D'Urfey's *Commonwealth of Women* (1685), Crowne's *Sir Courtly Nice* (1685), D'Urfey's *The Banditti* (1686), Cheeke's *History of Adolphus* (1691), Southerne's *The Maid's Last Prayer* (1693), D'Urfey's *Don Quixote*, III (1695), Motteux's *Love's a Jest* (1696), D'Urfey's *Massaniello* (1699), Harris's *Love's a Lottery* (1699), D'Urfey's *The Bath* (1701) and *Wonders in the Sun* (1706). Instrumental pieces by him are in *GB-Lbm* Add.35043 and *Ob* Mus.Sch.C.95.

BIBLIOGRAPHY
R. McGuinness: 'An Eighteenth-century Entertainment', *Soundings*, iii (1973), 66

IAN SPINK

Akimenko [Yakimenko], **Fyodor Stepanovich** (*b* Khar'kov, 20 Feb 1876; *d* Paris, 3 Jan 1945). Ukrainian composer, pianist and musicologist. He studied until 1895 with Balakirev at the Imperial Hofkapelle, where he later taught for a time. In 1901 he completed the composition course under Rimsky-Korsakov, Lyadov and Vītols at the St Petersburg Conservatory, and from 1903 to 1906 he lived in Paris. He was then a teacher (from 1915) and professor (1919–23) at the Petrograd Conservatory, returning to Paris in 1929. His compositions, predominantly in miniature forms, were influenced by French impressionism; his musicological work included many articles in the *Russkaya muzïkal'-naya gazeta* (1909–15). He was Stravinsky's first composition teacher.

WORKS
(selective list)

Opera: Feya snegov [The snow fairy], 1914
Orch: Rusalka (after Lermontov), op.4 (1900); Poème lyrique, op.20 (1903); Ange (after Lermontov) (1924); other pieces
Other works: several sets of songs, many pieces for solo inst and pf, many pf pieces, etc

Principal publishers: Belaieff, Bessel, Jurgenson, Leduc, Rouart–Lerolle

BIBLIOGRAPHY
N. Malkov: 'F. S. Akimenko: muzïkal'no-kharakteristicheskiye etyudï', *Ezhegodnik petrogradskikh gosudarstvennïkh teatrov, 1918–19* (1922), nos.9–10
L. Sabaneyeff: *Modern Russian Composers* (London, 1929, 2/1967)
G. Bernandt and I. M. Yampol'sky: *Kto pisal o muzïke* (Moscow, 1971), 20

DETLEF GOJOWY

Akkadia, music of. *See* MESOPOTAMIA.

Akkolade (Ger.). SYSTEM (i).

Akkord (Ger.). CHORD.

Akkordeon (Ger.). ACCORDION.

Akkordzither (Ger.). AUTOHARP.

Akolouthiai. Officially called akolouthiai or 'Orders of Service' but also designated by such names as anthologion, anoixantarion, papadikē, psaltike and mousikon, these handbooks transmit the Byzantine musical art of the 14th and 15th centuries. A new class of musical MS, the akolouthia was presumably edited for the first time about 1300 by JOANNES KOUKOUZELES, a singer and composer in Constantinople and later an Athonite monk at the Great Laura. Within a single volume the akolou-

thia provides a collection of monophonic chants, both Ordinary and Proper, for psalmody in the Byzantine Offices of Vespers and Orthros as well as settings for texts sung in the three liturgies throughout the ecclesiastical year. The immediate antecedents of the akolouthiai were the asmatikon and psaltikon, two kinds of Byzantine music MSS which apparently preserved the chanted repertories from urban rites of Hagia Sophia in Constantinople between the 11th and 13th centuries. Although certain chants from the asmatikon and psaltikon remained in earlier copies of akolouthiai, by the 15th century most of this older repertory had disappeared. This change in usage also reflects a shift in liturgical gravity which had occurred by the end of the 13th century from the imperial rite of Hagia Sophia to practices followed in Byzantine monasteries.

Although such rubrics as 'palaion' or 'archaion' identify an older and anonymous layer of chants in the akolouthiai, the MSS mainly contain newly composed liturgical music by Koukouzeles, his contemporaries and successors. Attribution of chants to specific composers is one feature which distinguishes the akolouthiai from older collections. Generally similar in contents, each copy of the akolouthiai may reflect musical predilections of a certain monastery and even the editorial tastes of a particular scribe. Although akolouthiai transmit the earlier strata of the new musical corpus, scribes were constantly modernizing repertories and bringing them up to date by the deletion of older chants and the substitution of new chants as they were composed. Through this editorial process approximate dates of activity can be established for many Byzantine composers who flourished during the Palaeologan renaissance. Out of more than 100 composers whose chants are preserved in 14th- and 15th-century akolouthiai, those who contributed the greatest number of works to the new repertory include Joannes Glykys, Nikephoros Ethikos, Joannes Koukouzeles, Xenos Koronis, Georgios Kontopetris, Demetrios Dokeianos, Lampadarios (Joannes Klada) and Manuel Chrysaphes. Rubrics which accompany some chants even indicate usage in certain localities through such designations as 'hagiosophitikos' ('of Hagia Sophia'), 'Thessalonikaios' ('of Thessaloniki') or 'hagioretikos' ('of Mount Athos').

Although no fewer than 14 akolouthiai survive from the 14th century, and MSS from the 15th century in more than twice this number, the number of copies continues to grow as MSS are rediscovered in monastery libraries. The number of extant akolouthiai shows a further sharp rise after the fall of Constantinople in the mid-15th century, and this type of MS was still being copied as late as the 18th and early 19th centuries. The oldest dated akolouthia is a paper MS copied in 1336, probably during the lifetime of Koukouzeles, and now in *GR-Ae* 2458. Two other copies, *Ae* 2401 and 2406, are unusually large and rich anthologies which transmit chants composed by various local composers in small Greek towns as well as music sung in the city of Thessaloniki and in certain Athonite monasteries. Both of the MSS were copied in the middle of the 15th century, the latter bearing the date 1453, the very year that the empire fell.

Although most copies of akolouthiai transmit a preliminary PAPADIKĒ or treatise on Byzantine music and notation, the chanted repertories in these MSS fall into three principal liturgical divisions: (1) the evening

Office of Great Vespers; (2) Orthros, the morning Office; and (3) the three liturgies. Major repertories for Great Vespers include chants for certain verses from the prooimiac psalm (Psalm ciii of the Greek Septuagint), from psalms of the first stasis of the first kathisma in the Psalter (Psalms i, ii and iii), and from the kekragarion (Psalms cxl, cxli, cxxix and cxvi). A few akolouthiai even preserve the older and by this time archaic *hesperinos asmatikos* or 'chanted' Vespers, a relic from the urban rite of Constantinople. Chants for Orthros, the morning Office, include antiphons proper to major feasts, prokeimena for the entire week and special feasts, megalynaria and selected verses from the polyeleos psalm (Psalm cxxxv). Most akolouthiai also transmit three settings of the lengthy amomos psalm (Psalm cxviii) composed for several different occasions. For the Byzantine liturgies MSS normally contain the trisagion, the cherubic hymn which accompanies the Great Entrance, and settings of other hymn texts which, according to the occasion, replace the cherubic hymn. Also present are allēlouïaria for great feasts as well as settings catalogued by mode for several texts which serve as communion hymns.

In addition to the transmission of both older (anonymous) and newly composed (attributed) chants in relatively simple and short melodic settings of Greek liturgical texts, the greater portion of an akolouthia is devoted to vast collections of kalophonic settings for most of these same texts. A kalophonic chant generally interlaces two types of text: one or more lines from a Greek liturgical text combined with TERETISMATA. Within those portions of kalophonic chants drawn from psalm texts Byzantine composers have juxtaposed lines and edited verses to suit their own purposes. The musical structure of kalophonic chants appears as a rhapsodic assemblage of melodic fragments which are linked sequentially. Kalophonic settings, especially the enormously prolix kratēmata, display a predilection for series of repeated pitches, a percussive vocal effect often accompanied by rapid changes of pitch level at the distance of a perfect 5th. A special kind of kalophonic chant in the akolouthiai is a 'composite' setting in which a short texted prologos prefaces a kratēma that functions as an effusive coda and can be described as a single long teretism. Although most kalophonic chants are the work of a single composer, 'composite' chants may combine the work of two men. The prologos, for example, may be by one composer, its appended kratēma composed by another. The kalophonic repertory in the akolouthiai leaves little doubt that these chants were written not only for accomplished singers but even for virtuoso soloists. That there were singers who possessed vocal resources to meet such musical demands discloses a phenomenal flowering of Byzantine chant during the late empire.

BIBLIOGRAPHY

O. Strunk: 'The Antiphons of the Oktoechos', *JAMS*, xiii (1960), 50
K. Levy: 'A Hymn for Thursday in Holy Week', *JAMS*, xvi (1963), 127–75
M. Velimirović: 'Byzantine Composers in MS. Athens 2406', *Essays presented to Egon Wellesz* (Oxford, 1966), 7
E. V. Williams: 'The Treatment of Text in the Kalophonic Chanting of Psalm 2', *Studies in Eastern Chant*, ii (London, 1971), 173

For further bibliography *see* BYZANTINE RITE, MUSIC OF THE.
EDWARD V. WILLIAMS

Akses, Necil Kâzım (*b* Instanbul, 6 May 1908). Turkish composer. He is a member of the Turkish Five, a group of outstanding composers who, from the 1930s, promoted a western musical style. Akses first played the violin and then took up the cello at the age of 14. He studied harmony with Cemal Reşit Rey at the Istanbul Municipal Conservatory. In 1926 he left for Vienna where he attended Joseph Marx's harmony, counterpoint and composition classes at the Academy for advanced students. After receiving his diploma in 1931, he went to Prague and studied with Josef Suk and Alois Haba at the Prague State Conservatory. He returned to Turkey in 1934 and was appointed a teacher of composition at the Music Teachers School, becoming its director in 1948. Later he filled official positions: in 1949 he was director general of the Fine Arts Section of the Ministry of Education; in 1954 he was cultural attaché in Berne, and later in Bonn; and in 1958 he was appointed director to the State Opera in Ankara. Some time later he left this position to teach at the Ankara State Conservatory, and at present he is the director general of the Ankara State Opera. Akses's works are few in number, but lengthy and important in reflecting the influence of modern musical movements of central Europe; at the same time he has skilfully incorporated into them melodies adapted from ancient Turkish art music and folk rhythms.

The composer's earliest works are for piano (1930). The most important orchestral work in his symphonic poem, *Ankara kalesi* ('The Ankara fortress') which was completed in 1942 and was performed in Ankara and in Berlin the same year; it was also recorded in Germany. Other noteworthy works are his *Poème* and his Violin Concerto, completed at the beginning of 1972 and performed in Ankara. Akses has written two short operas and music for several plays.

WORKS
(selective list)

2 short operas: Mete, 1933; Bayönder, 1934
Ankara kalesi, sym poem, 1942; Poème, vc, orch, 1946; Ballade, orch, 1950; Vn Concerto, 1972; Scherzo, orch, 1972
Pf Sonata, 1930; 5 Pieces, pf, 1930; Miniatures, 7 pieces, pf, 1936

Principal publishers: Universal, State Conservatory Edition (Ankara)
FARUK YENER

Akutagawa, Yasushi (*b* Tokyo, 12 July 1925). Japanese composer. He studied at the Tokyo Music School with Hashimoto, Shimofusa and Ifukube for composition and with Kaneko for conducting. In 1949, the year of his graduation, he won first prize in the Japanese radio competition, and the next year his Music for Symphonic Orchestra attracted the attention of Thor Johnson, who conducted it more than 200 times in the USA alone. He formed with Dan and Mayuzumi the Sannin no Kai (Group of Three) in 1953, and visited Moscow for the first time in 1954, after which date he returned frequently to the USSR, sometimes appearing as a conductor; he was thus able to develop relations with Shostakovich, Khachaturian, Kabalevsky and other Soviet composers. His work shows a strong kinship with Soviet music, particularly that of Prokofiev, whose scherzo style he has skilfully emulated. He is also a master of modern orchestration, with a special fondness for strings. Other characteristic features of his music include an abundance of ostinatos and an individual kind of orientalism. His opera *Hiroshima no Orfe* ('Orpheus in Hiroshima') won an Anerkennungspreis when it was performed at the Salzburg Opera Festival in 1968. Akutagawa has taken several administrative appointments: assistant chairman of the Japan Federation of Composers (1969), director of the Japanese Society of Rights of Authors and Composers (1971), executive director of the Yamaha Foundation for Music Education (1972) and jury member of the annual competition organized by the Mainichi Press and Japanese radio.

WORKS
(selective list)

Operas: Kurai kagami [Dark mirror], Tokyo, 1960; Hiroshima no Orfe [Orpheus in Hiroshima], Tokyo, Japanese television, 1967

Ballets: Kotei no yume [The dream of the lake], Tokyo, 1950; Shitsuraku-en [Paradise lost], Tokyo, 1951; Kappa, Tokyo, 1951; Kumo no ito [Spider's web], Tokyo, 1968

Orch: Prelude, 1947; Trinita sinfonica, 1948; Music for Sym. Orch, 1950; Triptyque, str, 1953; Sym. no.1, 1954; Divertimento, 1956; Sym. 'Twin Stars', for children, 1957; Ellora Sym., 1958; Music for Str, 1962; Inga [Negative picture], str 1969; Ostinata sinfonica '70, 1970; Rhapsody, 1971

Other works: La danse, suite, pf, 1948; Songs of Papua, S, pf, 1950; Ballata, vn, pf, 1951

Principal publishers: Kawai Gakufu, Ongaku-no-Tomo Sha

WRITINGS

Watashi no ongaku dangi [My musical talks] (Tokyo, 1959)
Ongaku no genjō [The field of music] (Tokyo, 1962)
Ongaku o aisuru hito ni [For music lovers] (Tokyo, 1967)
Ongaku no kiso [The foundations of music] (Tokyo, 1971)

MASAKATA KANAZAWA

Ala, Giovanni Battista (*b* Monza, nr. Milan, *c*1598; *d* Milan, *c*1630). Italian composer and organist. All that is known of his life derives from the title-pages of his publications and from Picinelli. In 1618 he was organist of the collegiate church in Desio and in 1621 of S Maria dei Servi, Milan. He died at the age of 32. Picinelli praised him as an excellent organist and a wonderful ('stupendo') composer. He was an adherent of the monodic and concertato style of among others Monteverdi, whose duet *Sancta Maria* he published for the first time in his *Primo libro di concerti ecclesiastici* (1618).

WORKS

Canzonette e madrigali, 2vv, hpd, chit, other insts, libro I (Milan, 1617); lost, cited in Picinelli

Primo libro di concerti ecclesiastici, 1–4vv, org (Milan, 1618); contains Monteverdi's Sancta Maria

Secondo libro de concerti ecclesiastici, 1–4vv, org, op.3 (Milan, 1621)

L'Armida abbandonata e L'amante occulto: madrigali a 4 e arie a 1 e 2 (Milan, 1625), lost

Magnificat IV. tono a 4 concertato, in 1626[5]

Concerti ecclesiastici, 1–4vv, org, libro IV (Milan, 1628), lost

Iubilemus, 4vv, in *c*1630[5]

Luscinia sacra sive cantiones, 1–4vv, bc, accedit litania nova B. virginis, 5vv (Antwerp, 1633)

Pratum musicum variis cantionum sacrarum flosculis consitum, 1–4vv, bc, quarum aliae decerptae ex libro secundo sacrarum cantionum I. B. Ala da Monza (Antwerp, 1634[2])

Madrigali, 2–4vv, libro V, op.9; lost, cited in Picinelli

BIBLIOGRAPHY

F. Picinelli: *Ateneo de' letterati milanesi* (Milan, 1670), 268f

M. Donà: *La stampa musicale a Milano fino all'anno 1700* (Florence, 1961)

MARIANGELA DONÀ

Alabado [alabanza] (Sp.-American: 'praise'). A hymn of praise for the Eucharist, the Blessed Virgin Mary or other saints. It was brought to the New World at least as early as 1716 by the Franciscans, who continued the Spanish custom of chanting the *alabado*, or *alabanza*, as it is called in Spain, in their missions to Texas and California, as they had done in their monasteries. One of the earliest *alabados* taught to Indian converts is shown in ex.1; this was probably the melody used at all the missionary establishments. The form still survives in some parts of Argentina, Mexico and New Mexico, notably in the rites of the Penitential Brotherhood.

Ex.1

A - la - ba - do y en sal - za - do   Se - a el Di - vi - no

Sa - - - cra - men - to.

BIBLIOGRAPHY

L. T. Shaver: 'Spanish Mission Music', *Proceedings of the Music Teachers' National Association*, xiii (1918), 204

A. B. McGill: 'Old Mission Music', *MQ*, xxiv (1938), 186

J. B. Rael: *The New Mexico Alabado* (Stanford, 1951)

Alabanza. See ALABADO.

Alaigrement. See ALLEGRO.

Alain. French family of musicians.

(1) Jehan (Ariste) Alain (*b* St Germain-en-Laye, 3 Feb 1911; *d* Petit-Puy, nr. Saumur, 20 June 1940). Composer and organist. He was the son of Albert Alain, with whom he had his first organ lessons, and for whom he deputized from 1924 at the church in St Germain-en-Laye. After studying the piano with Augustin Pierson, he entered the Paris Conservatoire in 1927 and remained there for 12 years, taking *premiers prix* in 1934 for harmony and fugue, and for organ in 1939 after a period of study with Dupré. His composition teachers were Dukas and Roger-Ducasse. From 1935 to 1939 he was organist of St Nicolas de Maisons Lafitte, Paris, and in 1936 he won the Prix des Amis de l'Orgue for the Suite.

From 1929 until the end of his life (he was killed in action in World War II) composition was Alain's preoccupation. He produced a handful of charming chamber works and songs, the former including the delightful *Trois mouvements* (1935) for flute and piano. Few of his piano and organ pieces were published during his lifetime. Alain was a brilliant performer on both instruments, and the style of his keyboard music was dictated largely by his inventive skill as an improviser. He wrote a number of short works that are full of original and varied rhythms, harmonies and sonorities, revealing a quickly developing musical personality. The influences of Satie, Debussy and Messiaen can be detected, but Alain's attitude to composition is well expressed in some remarks he jotted in one of his notebooks: 'Music is created to translate the states of the soul at some time, some moment, above all, the evolution of a soul state. Thus mobility is essential. Do not try to translate an individual emotion, even an eternal emotion . . . What matters in music is perhaps less charm than mystery'.

The pictorial impressions and fleeting ideas that passed through Alain's imagination are reflected in the fanciful titles he gave to some of his keyboard pieces. More serious feelings are the concern of such organ works as the *Deuils* and *Luttes*; there is an oriental flavour in the *Deux danses à Agni Yavishta* and much religious fervour in the *Litanies*. The detailed registrations that Alain noted on his organ pieces were worked out in terms of the organ at his home, an instrument whose pedal-board operated in two divisions with 16' and 8' stops on the lower half and stops of higher pitch on the top half. His most individual achievement as an organ composer was in the music of the years 1934–6: *Le jardin suspendu*, the Intermezzo and the two

Fantaisies. Ostinato patterns dominate these works, treated with engaging imagination and resourcefulness.

WORKS
(selective list)

ORGAN

L'oeuvre d'orgue de Jehan Alain, 3 vols. (Paris, 1943, rev. 3/1971):
Vol.i: Suite: Introduction et variations, Scherzo, Choral, 1934–6; 3 danses: Joies, Deuils, Luttes, 1937–9; Aria, 1939
Vol.ii: 2 danses à Agni Yavishta, 1934; Le Jardin suspendu, 1934; Intermezzo, 1935; Prélude et fugue, 1935; Variations sur un thème de Clément Jannequin, 1937; Litanies, 1937
Vol.iii: Berceuse sur deux notes qui cornent, 1929; Ballade en mode phrygien, 1930; Postlude pour l'office de Complies, 1930; Lamento, 1930; Variations sur Lucis creator, 1932; Petite pièce, 1932; Grave, 1932; Premier prélude profane, 1933; Deuxième prélude profane, 1933; Choral cistercian pour un élévation, 1934; Première fantaisie, 1934; Climat, 1934; Deuxième fantaisie, 1936; Monodie, 1938
2 Chorals, 1935
Transcrs. of works by F. Campion

PIANO

L'oeuvre de piano de Jehan Alain, 3 vols. (Paris, 1944): Choral, Etude de sonorité, Un cercle d'argent souple, Heureusement, la bonne fée, Mythologies japonaises, Romance, Nocturne, A♭, Suite facile I, g, Suite facile II, b, Thème varié, Ecce ancilla Domini, Etude, Togo, Lumière qui tombe d'un vasistas, Histoire d'un homme, Prélude, Il pleuvra toute la journée, Etude sur un thème de 4 notes, Petite rapsodie, Dans le rève laissé, Taras Boulba, Encelade leare, other pieces
Suite monodique, 1934

OTHER WORKS

Choral: Cantique en mode phrygien, 4vv, 1932; Complainte de Jean Renaud, 4vv, 1935; Messe grégorienne de mariage, chorus, str qt, 1938; Messe de Requiem, 1938; Messe brève, S, chorus, insts, 1938
Inst: Andante varié, str qnt, 1934; Intermezzo, 2 pf, bn, 1935; 3 mouvements, fl, pf, 1935; Invention, wind, 1937; 3 danses [after org work], orchd 1939–40, completed by R. Gallois-Montbrun
Songs: Laisse les nuages blancs (Jammes), 1v, pf, 1935; Chanson (Kipling), 1v, pf, 1936; Ave Maria, 1v, org, 1937

Principal publisher: Leduc

BIBLIOGRAPHY

B. Gavoty: *La jeune école d'orgue française* (Paris, 1937)
N. Dufourcq: *La musique d'orgue française de Jehan Titelouze à Jehan Alain* (Paris, 1941, 2/1949)
B. Gavoty: *Jehan Alain: musicien français (1911–1940)* (Paris, 1945) [incl. full list of works]
M.-C. Alain: 'L'oeuvre d'orgue de Jehan Alain', *L'organo*, vi (1968), no.2, pp.181–220
G. Beechey: 'The Organ Music of Jehan Alain', *MT*, cxv (1974), 422, 507

(2) Olivier Alain (*b* St Germain-en-Laye, 3 Aug 1918). Composer, pianist and musicologist, brother of (1) Jehan Alain. He learnt to play the organ and piano as a child. Equally drawn to the study of literature, he did not enter the Paris Conservatoire until after graduating from the Sorbonne; at the Conservatoire (1950–51) he was the pupil of Aubin and Messiaen. In addition to his activities as a composer and concert pianist, he has worked as music critic (for *Le Figaro*) and as a teacher of sight-reading, analysis and composition. He has directed the St Germain-en-Laye Conservatory (1950–64) and the Ecole César Franck, Paris (from 1961), and has acted as an inspector of music with special responsibility for the conservatories. His compositions, of notable clarity and harmonic refinement, include many motets, organ works and piano pieces, and also an oratorio, *Chant funèbre sur les morts en montagne* (1950); the principal publishers of his work are Leduc and Schola Cantorum.

WRITINGS

L'harmonie (Paris, 1965)
'Liszt le novateur: essai de recensement', *Génies et réalités: Liszt* (Paris, 1967), 233–69
with H. Schack and M.-C. Alain: *L'oeuvre d'orgue de Jean-Sébastien Bach* (Paris, 1968)
Bach (Paris, 1970)

(3) Marie-Claire Alain (*b* St Germain-en-Laye, 10 Aug 1926). Organist, sister of (1) Jehan Alain. She entered the Paris Conservatoire in 1944, studying with Duruflé for harmony, Plé-Caussade for counterpoint, fugue and musical pedagogics and Dupré for organ. In 1950 she won an organ prize at the Geneva International Competition and gave her first recital at St Merri, Paris. The following year she won the Bach Prize of the Amis de l'Orgue in Paris; she then spent two years studying with Litaize. Her scrupulous attention to the details of articulation and ornamentation, coupled with secure technique and musicianship, has resulted in many authoritative interpretations. She specializes in 17th- and 18th-century music, and her regard for historical authenticity has determined her preference for appropriate mechanical organs: Schnitger or Marcussen for Bach; Clicquot, Gonzalez or Haerpfer-Erman for Couperin and De Grigny. Her numerous recordings include, in addition to French and German Baroque music, the complete works of her brother (1) Jehan Alain, issued with her valuable, informative notes and memoir. She has contributed many scholarly articles to such periodicals as *L'orgue* and *L'organo*, and with Hans Schack and her brother (2) Olivier wrote a brochure to accompany her recording of the complete works of Bach. An honorary doctorate was conferred on her by Colorado State University in 1971.

WRITINGS

'Appunti sulla maniera francese', *L'organo*, v (1964–7), 6
with H. Schack and O. Alain: *L'oeuvre d'orgue de Jean-Sébastien Bach* (Paris, 1968)

BIBLIOGRAPHY

P. Denis: 'Les organistes français d'aujourd'hui: 1 – Marie-Claire Alain', *L'orgue* (1965), no.113, p.26 [interview]
GWILYM BEECHEY (1), BRIGITTE MASSIN (2), BARRY MILLINGTON (3)

Alain de Lille [de L'isle; Alanus de (ab) Insulis] (*b* Lille, 1114–28; *d* Citeaux, 12 July 1202). French philosopher and poet. He was a scholar of such encyclopedic learning that he became known as *Doctor universalis*. He probably taught at the University of Paris from about 1157 to 1170, at Montpellier from about 1171 to 1185, and then possibly again at Paris. He retired as a simple lay brother to Cîteaux, where he died.

Alain was particularly famed in his day for two of his Latin poems, *De planctu naturae* – a satire on human vices – and *Anticlaudianus*, a long and elaborate allegory on the arts and on morals written towards the end of the century, and the basis for his musical importance. In the *Anticlaudianus* the Seven Liberal Arts, daughters of Prudence, are introduced, and each discusses the particular art she represents. Music is the fifth sister, and Alain, following the philosophical emphasis of his time, makes her expound the moral worth of music rather than its practical application. Boethius's threefold classification is combined with contemporary neo-Platonic thought: *musica mundana* controls the changes of the seasons and the times; it conjoins the elements, and it produces the motions and melodies of the heavenly bodies. *Musica humana* builds the members of the human body; it unites the rational and irrational parts of the soul, and it exercises control in blending soul and body. *Musica instrumentalis* is not divided in the Boethian manner (string, wind, percussion) but illustrates the combining of voices in polyphony; it gives sound its quality (enharmonic, diatonic, chromatic), and it makes clear the nature of consonance (diapason, diapente, diatesseron). Alain's musical importance does not end with this work, for in about 1280 Adam de la Bassée wrote an important *Ludus super Anticlaudianum* with many musical interpolations.

BIBLIOGRAPHY

PL, ccx

T. Wright: *Anglo-Latin Satirical Poets and Epigrammists of the 12th Century*, ii (London, 1872)

B. Hauréau: *Mémoire sur la vie et quelques oeuvres d'Alain de Lille* (Paris, 1885)

C. Bäumker: *Handschriftliches zu den Werken des Alanus ab Insulis* (Fulda, 1894)

P. Bayart: *Ludus Adae de Basseia canonici insulensis super Anticlaudianum* (Tourcoing, 1930)

M. Manitius: *Geschichte der lateinischen Literatur des Mittelalters*, iii (Munich, 1931), 794

H. Hüschen: 'Alanus ab Insulis', *MGG*

G. Raynaud de Lage: *Alain de Lille: poète du xiie siècle* (Paris, 1951)

F. J. E. Raby: *A History of Christian-Latin Poetry from the Beginnings to the Close of the Middle Ages* (Oxford, 1953), 297

R. Bossuat: *Alain de Lille: Anticlaudianus* (Paris, 1955)

N. C. Carpenter: *Music in the Medieval and Renaissance Universities* (Norman, Oklahoma, 1958/R1972), 55

D. S. Chamberlain: '*Anticlaudianus*, III. 412–445, and Boethius' *De musica*', *Manuscripta*, xiii (1969), 167

A. Hughes: 'The *Ludus super Anticlaudianum* of Adam de la Bassée', *JAMS*, xxiii (1970), 1

See also FRANCE: BIBLIOGRAPHY OF MUSIC TO 1600 and THEORY, THEORISTS.

GORDON A. ANDERSON

Alaire [Allaire, Alere] (*fl* 1534–49). French composer. According to Fétis, there was a singer called Allaire at Notre-Dame Cathedral in Paris in April 1547. However, the name is not mentioned in Chartier's study of the *maîtrise*. All the surviving music ascribed to Alaire, one mass and eight chansons, was published in Paris by Attaingnant and was apparently not issued elsewhere. It is unlikely, therefore, that he can be identified with either Simon Alard or Jacques Alardy, contemporary Flemish musicians, or with the 'Alardino' whose six-voice madrigal *Passa la nava mia* was printed in Venice (*RISM* 1561¹⁶).

Bien mauldit, in which two of the voices proceed in strict canon, is fairly typical of the contrapuntal style of the post-Josquin generation. The remaining seven chansons resemble those of Sermisy in their alternation of imitative and homophonic passages and clear form.

WORKS

(all 4vv unless otherwise indicated)

Missa 'Sancta et immaculata', 1534² (on Hesdin's motet)

Bien mauldit est l'estat des amoureux, 5vv, 1534¹³; Cruelle mort qui de rien n'est contente, 1534¹³, *F-CA* 125–8, ed. R. van Maldeghem, *Trésor musical*, xvii (Brussels, 1881) with substitute text, De peu de bien; Il n'est douleur qui tant soyt admirable, 1529²⁴; Martin menoit son pourceau au marché (C. Marot), 1534¹⁴

N'aurai-je point de mon mal allégéance, 1534¹³; Pour vous donner parfaict contentement (Margaret of Navarre), 1535⁶; Quant je vous ayme ardentement (Marot), 1538¹⁴; Triste pensif par le pourchas de rigueur, 1534¹³, *CA* 125–8, ed. R. van Maldeghem, *Trésor musical*, xviii (Brussels, 1882)

BIBLIOGRAPHY

FétisB

F.-L. Chartier: *L'ancien chapitre de Notre-Dame de Paris et sa maîtrise* (Paris, 1897/R1971), 78

FRANK DOBBINS

Ala-Könni, (Martti) Erkki [Erik] (*b* Ilmajoki, 2 Feb 1911). Finnish musicologist and folklorist. He studied at Helsinki Conservatory (1929–36) and under A. O. Väisänen at Helsinki University (MA 1942), where he took the doctorate in 1956 with a dissertation on the polska in Finland. His extended fieldwork on folk music and instruments in Finland and Sweden resulted in a collection of over 10,000 melodies (now in Tampere University library). After teaching music at Helsinki Conservatory (1951–7) and lecturing at Helsinki University (1957–62) he held a research grant from the State Humanities Committee (1962–75) and in 1975 became professor of folk research at Tampere University. He has been active in many folk music research organizations.

WRITINGS

Die Polska-Tänze in Finnland (diss., U. of Helsinki, 1956; Helsinki, 1956)

Articles on folk music in *Kytösävel*, iii (1947), *Kyrönmaa*, vii (1950) and *Kalevalaseuran vuosikirja*, xxxiii (1953)

FOLKSONG EDITIONS

Ilmajoen nuottikirja [Tune book from Ilmajoki] (Vammala, 1973)

Jalasjärven nuottikirja [Tune book from Jalasjärvi] (Vammala, 1974)

ERKKI SALMENHAARA

Alalá (Sp.). Genre of Galician (Spanish) song, characterized by the refrain sung at the end of each verse to the vocables 'ay-la-la'. *See* SPAIN, §II, 7 (i).

Alaleona, Domenico (*b* Montegiorgio, Ascoli Piceno, 16 Nov 1881; *d* Montegiorgio, 28 Dec 1928). Italian musicologist, theorist, conductor and composer. He studied at the Liceo di S Cecilia, Rome, where he gained his diploma in 1906 and was from 1916 professor of aesthetics and music history. He also graduated in 1907 from Rome University with a thesis, subsequently expanded into a book, on the Italian oratorio; his scholarly writings in general helped to lay the foundations of modern Italian musicology. As a conductor he specialized in choral music, and in 1926 he founded the Madrigalisti Romani. He also fought hard for the improvement of Italian music education. His most ambitious composition, the opera *Mirra*, is eclectic and often crude, but shows enterprise in the use of a specially constructed 'pentaphonic harmonium', based on a division of the octave into five equal parts (cf Indonesian *slendro*). Various kinds of equal octave division and 12-note chord are discussed in two articles he published in the *Rivista musicale italiana* in 1911. Only rarely, it seems, did such speculations lead him to write wholly satisfactory music, but his harmonic novelties are sometimes poetic and his researches helped to give a pleasantly archaic tinge to some of his vocal works.

WORKS

(selective list)

Vocal: Mirra (opera, after V. Alfieri), 1910–13, Rome, 1920; Requiem, chorus 4vv, 1927; Il cantico di Frate Sole, chorus, org/orch, 1927; many songs, incl. at least 21 settings of G. Pascoli

Inst: 2 sinfoniette italiane; 6 canzoni italiane, str qt; 2 canzoni italiane, str, harp, cel, timp, 1917; pf music

Principal publisher: Ricordi

WRITINGS

Studi su la storia dell'oratorio musicale in Italia (Turin, 1908; 2/1945 as *Storia dell'oratorio musicale in Italia*)

'Le laudi spirituali italiane nei secoli XVI e XVII', *RMI*, xvi (1909), 1–54

'I moderni orizzonti della tecnica musicale', *RMI*, xviii (1911), 382–420

'L'armonia modernissima', *RMI*, xviii (1911), 769–838

'Il rinascimento musicale italiano e Giacomo Carissimi', *Nuova antologia*, cclv (1914), 662

Corso di cultura per musicisti (Rome, 1915); subsequent edns. as *Il libro d'oro del musicista* (Milan, 5/1961)

Several hundred other articles

BIBLIOGRAPHY

E. G. Rovira: 'In attesa della Mirra di Domenico Alaleona', *Musica*, xiv/2 (Rome, 1920), 1

'Il cantico di Frate Sole del maestro D. Alaleona', *Almanacco delle missioni francescani 1928* (Rome, 1928), 3
A. de Angelis: *L'Italia musicale di oggi: dizionario dei musicisti* (Rome, 3/1928), pt.1, 20f [incl. worklist and bibliography]
G. Cardi: *Domenico Alaleona: musicista e musicologo* (Ascoli Piceno, 1957)
'Alaleona, Domenico', *DBI*
J. C. G. Waterhouse: *The Emergence of Modern Italian Music* (*up to 1940*) (diss., U. of Oxford, 1968), 181ff, 584f
JOHN C. G. WATERHOUSE

Alamani, Jo(?hannes). Composer. He was active in the 14th century, and is possibly to be identified with the 'Johan d'Alamanya, juglar del duch Aendrich de Gascunya' mentioned as one of the minstrels of King Peter IV of Aragon in 1351. His only known work is an incomplete three-voice Credo (edn. in CMM, xxix, 94), which is clearly based on the popular discant-style Credo by Sortes (ibid, 89). Possible corroboration of his identity with the minstrel comes from the fact that the Credo survives in a manuscript of which fragments exist in *E-Bc* 971 and *E-G*.

BIBLIOGRAPHY
H. Anglès: 'Cantors und Ministrers in den Diensten der Könige von Katalonien-Aragonien im 14. Jahrhundert', *Kongressbericht: Basel 1924*, 63
——: 'Gacian Reyneau am Königshof zu Barcelona in der Zeit von 139 . . . bis 1429', *Studien zur Musikgeschichte: Festschrift für Guido Adler* (Vienna, 1930), 64
H. Stäblein-Harder: *Fourteenth-century Mass Music in France*, MSD, vii (1962), 61, 148f
H. Harder and B. Stäblein: 'Neue·Fragmente mehrstimmiger Musik aus spanischen Bibliotheken', *Colloquium amicorum: Joseph Schmidt-Görg zum 70. Geburtstag* (Bonn, 1967), 131, pls.xi–xii
GILBERT REANEY

A la mi re. The pitches *a* and *a'* in the HEXACHORD system.

Alamire, Pierre [Petrus; Peter van den Hove] (*b* between *c*1470 and 1475; *d* after 1534). Flemish music scribe. He was active principally at the courts of Margaret of Austria, regent of the Netherlands, and Emperor Charles V, in Mechlin and Brussels. He was one of the three main copyists of a complex of 51 manuscripts of polyphonic music produced there between about 1495 and 1534. The earliest mention of Alamire is a payment to him in the 1496 accounts of the Marian Brotherhood in 's-Hertogenbosch, for having copied one book of masses and portions of a second book, and a book of motets. He may be the Peter van den Hoven listed in a municipal tax list for 1497. By 1503 he was in Antwerp and in that year Philip the Fair, Duke of Burgundy, bought from him 'a large book of music, made up of 26 *cahiers* of parchment, containing several masses and other pieces used in the divine service which is celebrated daily in the domestic chapel of the household of this lord'. Alamire was still living in Antwerp in 1505, but by 1516 had moved to Mechlin.

In 1509 Alamire was attached to the chapel of the Archduke Charles (later Charles V) as 'scribe and keeper of the books'. He retained this position, apparently continuously, for 25 years, producing a large number of manuscripts, undertaking the calligraphy of music and texts personally with only occasional help. He probably also designed the books and engaged workshops for illumination and binderies, to complete them. 40 of those manuscripts have survived, among them some of the largest and most handsomely penned and decorated choirbooks of the time (for illustration *see* JOSQUIN DESPREZ, fig.2), as well as smaller, more modest sets of partbooks. Together these contain a significant portion of the contemporary repertory of Franco-Flemish polyphony, including almost all the works of Pierre de La Rue, and many works by Josquin, Mouton, Févin, Obrecht, Isaac, and lesser composers. Some of the books were made for the chapels of Charles, Margaret, Emperor Maximilian and other members of the Habsburg dynasty, and for highly placed courtiers; others were prepared for presentation by the court to such patrons of music as Frederick the Wise of Saxony, Pope Leo X, Henry VIII, and the Fugger family of Augsburg. While serving the Netherlands court Alamire continued to fulfil private manuscript commissions, notably for the Marian Brotherhoods at Antwerp (1512–16) and 's-Hertogenbosch (1530–31), and he also sold instruments and paintings. Documents calling him a singer, and a four-voice *Tandernack* attributed to him (in *A-Wn* 18810), suggest that he was a practising musician.

Four autograph letters in Latin from Alamire to Henry VIII and Cardinal Wolsey, and a series of letters to them from the English ambassadors at the Netherlands court, show that between 1515 and 1518 Alamire not only supplied music manuscripts and instruments to Henry, but also served the king as a spy against Richard de la Pole, exiled pretender to the English throne. Often aided by another Flemish musician, Hans Nagel, a former sackbut player of Henry's, Alamire gathered political information in Metz, where de la Pole lived, Wittenberg, Frankfurt and France. In June 1516 he went to England to receive instructions from Henry and Wolsey. His service for the king ceased when it was found that he was also a counterspy for de la Pole. Alamire often served as a diplomatic and private courier. In 1519 he was sent to Augsburg and Wittenberg in connection with the election of Emperor Charles V, and between 1517 and 1520 he carried a number of messages and letters from Frederick of Saxony to Margaret of Austria, and from Frederick's secretary, Georg Spalatin, and the Nuremberg humanist Willibald Pirkheimer to Erasmus. The last, humorously describing how Alamire had delivered six old letters to him in August 1519, calls the scribe 'a not unwitty man', a portrait corroborated by Alamire's letters, and epigrams and insults directed at the singers in his manuscripts. By order of Mary of Hungary (Margaret's successor), acting for the emperor, Alamire was pensioned off on 1 January 1534, and his name is no longer in court records after that time.

The other two scribes involved in copying the corpus of manuscripts produced at the Netherlands court have been designated Netherlands court scribes B and C. It is probable that B was Martin Bourgeois, a chaplain in the service of Margaret, Philip the Fair and Charles V from 1498 to 1514, and Alamire's predecessor as principal music scribe. Scribe B is the main copyist of seven manuscripts dating from about 1495 to about 1508. All that is known of Netherlands court scribe C is that he was active at the same time as Alamire and collaborated with him on at least two manuscripts. Three manuscripts, dating from about 1508 to 1523, can be wholly or partly attributed to him.

MANUSCRIPTS
Wholly or partly copied by Alamire: *A-Wn* 4809, 4810, 11778, 15941, 18746, 18825, 18832, 9814 ff.132*r*–152*v*, 11883 (several fascicles), S.M.15496, S.M.15497; Archives of Ste Gudule, Registres 29–30

(covers); *Br* 215–16, 6428, 15075, IV 922; *MEa* choirbook; *D-Ju* 2, 4, 5, 7, 8, 9, 20, 21; *Mbs* 6, 7, 34, F; *E-MA* 766, 773; *GB-Lbm* Roy.8 G VII; *I-Rvat* C.S.34, C.S.36, C.S.160, Pal. lat. 1976–9; *SUsb* 248; *NL-'sH* 72A, 72B, 72C

Wholly or partly copied by scribe B: *A-Wn* 1783; *B-Br* 9126; *D-Ju* 22; *GB-Ob* Ashmole 831; *I-Fc* Basevi 2439, *Rvat* Chigiana C VIII 234, *VEcap* 756

Wholly or partly copied by scribe C: *A-Wn* S.M.15495, S.M.15497 (with Alamire), 18746 (with Alamire); *B-Br* 228; *D-Ju* 3, 12

BIBLIOGRAPHY

J. S. Brewer: *Letters and Papers Foreign and Domestic of the Reign of Henry VIII*, ii (London, 1864)

G. van Doorslaer: 'Calligraphes de musique à Malines au XVIe siècle', *Bulletin du cercle archéologique, littéraire et artistique de Malines*, xxxiii (1928), 91

A. Smijers: 'De illustre Lieve vrouwe broederschap te 's-Hertogenbosch', *TVNM*, xiii/4 (1932), 181–237; xvi/1 (1940), 63–106

K. E. Roediger: *Die geistlichen Musikhandschriften der Universitätsbibliothek Jena* (Jena, 1935)

L. Nowak: 'Die Musikhandschriften aus Fuggerschem Besitz in der Österreichischen Nationalbibliothek', *Die Österreichische Nationalbibliothek: Festschrift ... Josef Bick* (Vienna, 1948), 505

H. J. M. Ebeling: 'Peter Van den Hove Alias Alamire', *Brabantia*, ii (1953), 49

H. Kellman: 'The Origins of the Chigi Codex', *JAMS*, xi (1958), 6

M. Picker: *The Chanson Albums of Marguerite of Austria* (Berkeley, 1965)

H. Kellman: 'Josquin and the Courts of the Netherlands and France: the Evidence of the Sources', *Josquin des Prez: New York 1971*

B. Huys: 'An Unknown Alamire-choirbook ("Occo Codex") Recently Acquired by the Royal Library of Belgium', *TVNM*, xxiv/1 (1974), 1

H. Kellman: *A Census-catalogue of Manuscript Sources of Renaissance Polyphony, 1400–1550*, MSD (in preparation)

HERBERT KELLMAN

Álamo, Lázaro del (*b* El Espinar, nr. Segovia, *c*1530; *d* Mexico City, between 17 March and 19 May 1570). Spanish composer, active in Mexico. He served as a choirboy at Segovia Cathedral from 1542 to 1549, where he was taught by Gerónimo de Espinar (who later taught Victoria at Avila) and from 1544 by the *maestro de capilla* there, Bartolomé de Olaso (*d* 1567). He was employed at Salamanca University by Matheo Arévalo Sedeño, a rich nobleman, who later acted as his sponsor at Mexico City; he became a cathedral singer there on 16 October 1554 and, after being ordained, was appointed *maestro de capilla* on 2 January 1556. For the commemoration services for Charles V held in Mexico City on 29 November 1559 he composed an *alternatim* psalm setting in four parts. His several 'motetes, villancicos y chanzonetas' composed for Corpus Christi and Christmas (many to texts by Juan Bautista Corvera) earned the approval of the Archbishop Alonso de Montúfar, who had him promoted from prebendary to canon on 25 June 1568. Álamo's services to the cathedral include the establishment of a fine library of choral music, the recruitment of Manuel Rodríguez, an outstanding Spanish organist, and the training of choirboys and adult singers there.

BIBLIOGRAPHY

R. Stevenson: 'Lázaro del Álamo, primer compositor europeo en México', *Heterofonia: revista musical bimestral*, ii/12 (1970), May–June, 7, 44

ROBERT STEVENSON

Al-Āmulī [Muḥammad ibn Maḥmūd] (*fl* mid-14th century). Persian encyclopedist and music theorist. His encyclopedia *Nafā'is al-funūn* ('The precious things of the sciences'), written in Persian (1334–41), contains a section on music theory, which later Kiesewetter drew on in his work on Arabian music (1842).

BIBLIOGRAPHY

R. G. Kiesewetter: *Die Musik der Araber* (Leipzig, 1842), viii, 13, 89

C. Rieu: *Catalogue of the Persian MSS in the British Museum* (London, 1879–83), 435f

H. G. FARMER/R

Alanus, Johannes [Jo. Alani] (*d* ? Windsor, 1373). English composer. He is now generally credited with only the isorhythmic motet *Sub Arturo plebs/Fons citharizancium/In omnem terram* and four songs; for the composer of one, or possibly two later pieces in the Old Hall Manuscript, *see* ALEYN. The composer of the motet (ascribed 'Jo. Alani' and containing a reference to 'J. Alani minimus') is normally identified with the Dominus Johannes Aleyn, canon of St George's Chapel, Windsor, who died in 1373: 'unus rotulus de Cantu musico' was bequeathed by the canon to the chapel. He received a prebend at St Paul's Cathedral on 18 December 1361, and in the subsequent years he acquired several others, apparently enjoying special favour from the king who even sent him to Kent (possibly his home) to borrow money.

Alanus's motet appears in *F-CH* 568 and *I-Bc* Q15; the tenor alone is cited in a treatise in *I-Fl* Redi 71 (ed. in Carapetyan). Trowell has convincingly associated it with the Order of the Garter at St George's Chapel, Windsor, founded on St George's Day 1349 when, according to a contemporary chronicler, Edward III 'renewid the Round Table and the name of Arthure', and particularly with the celebrations for the victory at Poitiers (1356) which were mounted on St George's Day 1358, when Edward officially opened the Round Tower to house his Round Table. The triplum text names 14 musicians who were evidently singing on the occasion: Trowell has identified most of them, though some are hidden under extraordinary latinizations (G. de Horarum Fonte is William of Tideswell, Nicolaus de Vade Famelico is Nicholas of Hungerford, etc). The motetus texts refers to many theorists and musicians whose work had led Alanus to compose a piece of such complexity. Some doubt has been expressed as to whether the date 1358 can be correct for a motet in such an advanced style (see Günther, 1961, and Bent). Bent drew attention to its 'classical 15th-century structure, ... three levels of diminution, and rhythmic overlapping between upper voices and tenor in the final section'; she also pointed out that many of the people identified are not mentioned in the sources as being musicians, but merely members of the chapel, which is not necessarily the same thing. But this perhaps dismisses too much as mere coincidence: even if the proposed date must be adjusted a little, it seems more likely that there is still some room for adjustment to received notions of mid-14th-century style or styles.

The four songs ascribed 'Alanus' in the lost Strasbourg manuscript (*F-Sm* 222) may help bridge the stylistic gap between the motet and the mass music of Aleyn. *Mein herze al zit frouwen pflegen* (also with the contrafactum text *O quam pulchra*; ed. in Funck) has a melodic style strongly reminiscent of that in English songs from the early 15th century; and although the virelai *S'en vous por moy* (with that text in *F-Pn* n.a.fr.6771; *Sm* 222 has only the contrafactum text *Lux jocunda*; ed. in Apel) is more complex, the same could be said of it and of *Min frow min frow*. Of the fourth song only an untexted incipit survives.

BIBLIOGRAPHY

H. Rosenberg: *Untersuchungen über die Deutsche Liedweise im 15. Jahrhundert* (Wiesbaden, 1931)

H. Funck, ed.: *Deutsche Lieder des 15. Jahrhunderts aus fremden Quellen*, Cw, xlv (1937), 9f

A. Carapetyan, ed.: *Anonimi notitia del valore delle note del canto misurato*, CSM, v (1957), 57

B. Trowell: 'A Fourteenth-century Ceremonial Motet and its Composer', *AcM*, xxix (1957), 65

——: *Music under the Later Plantagenets* (diss., U. of Cambridge, 1960)

U. Günther: 'Das Wort-Ton-Problem bei Motetten des späten 14. Jahrhunderts', *Festschrift Heinrich Besseler* (Leipzig, 1961), 163

——, ed.: *The Motets of the Manuscripts Chantilly . . . and Modena*, CMM, xxix (1965), pp.l ff [commentary], 49ff [edn.]

F. Ll. Harrison, ed.: *Motets of French Provenance*, PMFC, v (1968), 172ff [edn.], 200, 206, 217, suppl. 20f

W. Apel, ed.: *French Secular Music of the Late Fourteenth Century*, i, CMM, liii/1 (1970), 1

M. Bent: 'The Transmission of English Music 1300–1500: Some Aspects of Repertory and Presentation', *Studien zur Tradition in der Musik: Kurt von Fischer zum 60. Geburtstag* (Munich, 1973), 65, esp. 70ff

DAVID FALLOWS

Alanus de [ab] **Insulis.** See ALAIN DE LILLE.

Alard, (Jean-)Delphin (*b* Bayonne, 8 March 1815; *d* Paris, 22 Feb 1888). French violinist and composer. At the age of ten, he performed Viotti's Concerto no.12 so well that the citizens of Bayonne decided to send him to Paris. There he entered Habeneck's class at the Conservatoire in 1827 and won first prize in 1830. He continued to study composition with François Fétis (1831–3) while serving as a violinist in the Opéra orchestra. In 1831 he made his début as a soloist with the Société des Concerts du Conservatoire, earning the praise of Paganini who was in the audience. Soon Alard became known as an excellent performer. At the memorial concert for Mendelssohn in 1848, he was chosen to perform the composer's recent Violin Concerto. He also became known as a superb chamber music player, particularly with his own string quartet. In 1840 he was appointed a member of the royal orchestra and became solo violinist on Baillot's death in 1842; he assumed a similar post in 1853 with the imperial orchestra.

Alard's most enduring achievement was in his long period (1843–75) as professor at the Paris Conservatoire. Appointed as successor to Baillot, he transmitted the great Italian-French tradition of Viotti to a generation of violinists. His most famous student was Sarasate, a first-prize winner in 1857. Alard's teaching skill is also evident in his excellent *Ecole du violon: méthode complète et progressive* (Paris, 1844), which was translated into several languages, and his numerous studies (among which are 24 caprices in all keys, op.41). His other compositions, including two violin concertos, two *symphonies concertantes* and many opera fantasias, have disappeared from the repertory. His anthology *Maîtres classiques du violon* (Mainz, 1863), valuable for rescuing many older pieces from oblivion, consists of 56 compositions (issued singly) by 18th- and early 19th-century composers; unlike many contemporary editors, Alard was faithful to the originals, merely adding an unpretentious realization of the figured bass. He played until late in life and was last heard at a benefit concert in 1884. Through his father, the famous luthier Vuillaume, he owned some of the most beautiful violins, including the 'Alard' Stradivari and the incomparable 'Messiah' Stradivari.

BIBLIOGRAPHY

FétisB

A. Bachmann: *Les grands violonistes du passé* (Paris, 1913)

E. van der Straeten: *The History of the Violin* (London, 1933)

A. Moser: *Geschichte des Violinspiels* (Berlin, 1923, rev., enlarged 2/1966)

BORIS SCHWARZ

Alard, Lampert (*b* Krempe, 27 Jan 1602; *d* Brunsbüttel, 29 May 1672). German theologian, historian, hellenist, philologist, poet and music theorist. After studying in Krempe and Hamburg he completed his studies at Leipzig University in 1624 and in the same year was crowned poet laureate. Meanwhile in 1621 he had become tutor to the children of a wealthy Leipzig bookseller, Henning Gross. Disappointed at not being made a professor at the university, he became a pastor and from 1630 practised his vocation at Brunsbüttel; he was also assessor to the consistory at nearby Meldorf. He was in contact with the Dutch humanists JOHANNES MEURSIUS and Daniel Heinsius. He devoted only one work to music, *De veterum musica . . .* (Schleusingen, 1636). Its point of view is that of a moralist and erudite humanist, and it contains many references to Greek and Latin texts; it is divided into 29 short chapters. After studying the relationship of music to other sciences, Alard presented some rudiments of Greek theory. There follow ten chapters on the effects of music: when well employed it exorcises evil, demons and madness and inspires virtue and piety. Alard then denounced the corrupt music of his time and censured the intrusion of virtuosity and ornaments into religious music. He devoted the last chapter to the mythological or legendary inventors of musical instruments. In an appendix he included the Greek text of the treatise of MICHAEL PSELLUS with a Latin translation.

BIBLIOGRAPHY

FétisB; *WaltherML*

P. Lichtenthal: *Dizionario e bibliografia della musica* (Milan, 1836)

MONIQUE ESCUDIER

Alardy [Alardi, Alardino, Alard, Alart], **Jacques** [Jacobus] (*b c*1515; *d* Spain, *c*1593). Flemish composer active in Spain. His name appears on lists of singers in the chapel of Charles V in 1524 and 1525. On 1 March 1530, his voice having changed, he was sent to the Low Countries for further education. In the listing of Flemish singers of 1556 he was described as a chaplain. In 1569 he was called chaplain for the prayed (i.e. low) Masses, but in 1572 was designated chaplain for the sung (i.e. high) Masses. In 1569 he assisted the royal organist Michel de Bock in recruiting singers from the Low Countries. He continued in the chapel of Philip II for many years, appearing for the last time in the list of 1593. Several of his works are attributed under his sources to 'Alart', 'Alard' or 'Alardino'; this has led to confusion with Simon Alart (*d* after 1515), a precentor and canon at St Quentin. Simon Alart may be the composer of a madrigal ascribed to 'Alardino' (in *RISM* 1561[16]); the only other work probably by him is a four-voice motet *Dum transisset Sabbatum* (*RISM* 1539[13]) which in reprints, however, is ascribed to 'Jacobus Alard' or 'Jacobus Alart'.

WORKS

Missa, 4vv, *D-As*

Works in 1549[10], 1561[16] (? by Simon Alart), 1562[2]

Dum transisset Sabbatum, 4vv, 1539[13] (probably by Simon Alart)

BIBLIOGRAPHY

P. Becquart: *Musiciens néerlandais à la cour de Madrid: Philippe Rogier et son école* (Brussels, 1967), 6, 22, 228

T. Antonicek: 'Alard, Simon', *MGG*
——: 'Alardy, Jacques', *MGG*

LAVERN J. WAGNER

Alarie, Pierrette (Marguerite) (*b* Montreal, 9 Nov 1921). Canadian soprano. She studied in Montreal with Salvator Issaurel and Jeanne Maubourg and in Philadelphia with Elisabeth Schumann. She made her début in 1940 in Montreal with the Variétés Lyriques, later singing in *La fille du régiment, Il barbiere di Siviglia, La traviata* and *Mireille*. In 1943 she sang Mozart's Barbarina under Beecham. She made her Metropolitan Opera début in 1945 in *Un ballo in maschera* under Bruno Walter after winning the Auditions of the Air. In 1949 she made her début at the Paris Opéra as Olympia in *Les contes d'Hoffmann*, remaining in Paris for several seasons, appearing frequently with the tenor Léopold Simoneau, whom she had married in 1946. Both have given numerous performances in opera, concert, recital, television and recording. At the 1953 Aix-en-Provence festival she sang for the first time *Chanson* and *Romance du comte Olinos*, two concert arias written for her by Egk. She appeared at the 1959 Salzburg Festival in *Die schweigsame Frau*. For some years she taught in Montreal before moving to San Francisco in 1972.

GILLES POTVIN

Alart, Jacobus. *See* ALARDY, JACQUES.

Alart, Simon. French composer, not identifiable with JACQUES ALARDY.

Alauro, Hieronymo. *See* LAURO, HIERONYMO DEL.

Alba (Old Fr. *aube*; Ger. *Tagelied*). Provençal term for a type of troubadour poem in which lovers part at dawn after having spent the night together. In the few poems of this type that survive (nine in Provençal according to Woledge) not only are the words of one or both lovers heard but also (in all except one of them) those of a third person, a watchman, who warns the furtive lovers of the coming of day, and with it the danger of being discovered. Perhaps the most salient feature in all except one of these songs is the occurrence of the word 'alba' (literally 'white of dawn') in a prominent position, usually near or at the end of each stanza.

Although there are few surviving examples, the alba was in its time evidently considered a distinct type of song because it is mentioned as one of the many genres of lyric poetry in *De doctrina de comprendre dictats* (ed. and trans. in Woledge, 379). Furthermore, there are two Old Provençal poems that are more or less parodies of the normal dawn song and in which the word 'alba' occurs in the usual prominent position; but in these, instead of regretting the arrival of dawn, the poet actually looks forward to it because he has had to spend the night alone rather than with his beloved. In the beginning of one of these parodies the author, Uc de la Bacalaria, stated that he was making an alba with a new tune.

The music has survived for only two albas (Giraut de Bornelh, *Reis glorios* and Cadenet, *S'anc fui belha*) so characterization of the musical style is impossible. The sources of the poems indicate that the entire group can be considered as dating from the 12th, 13th and early 14th centuries. It is obvious that they grew out of an older tradition – possibly that including the part-Latin

and part-Provençal *Phebi claro nondum orto* – about which one can only speculate.

The study of dawn poetry edited by Hatto makes clear that the theme of lovers parting at dawn after a furtive nocturnal meeting occurs in literature of various times and various countries; there are some remarkable common elements such as a person or a bird announcing the daybreak and the lovers expressing alternately desires to stay together eternally and fears of being discovered. Nevertheless, nowhere in western Europe is there such a closely connected group of dawn songs as the Provençal alba. The few Old French dawn songs of the same period have only the main theme in common with the Provençal alba; the term 'aube' used in reference to these poems does not occur as a technical term in medieval treatises about Old French poetry, and if it occurs at all in a dawn poem it does so as a mere indication of time rather than as a salient feature as in the alba. Similarly, the German terms 'Tagelied' and 'Tagewîse' occurring in medieval poetry seem to refer more generally to songs and tunes performed by nightwatchmen at daybreak, and in this sense they are probably synonymous with the later term 'Wächterlied'.

BIBLIOGRAPHY
A. Jeanroy: *Les origines de la poésie lyrique en France au moyen âge* (Paris, 1889, 3/1925), 61ff
——: *La poésie lyrique des troubadours* (Paris, 1934), 292ff, 339ff
B. Woledge: 'Old Provençal and Old French', *Eos: an Enquiry into the Theme of Lovers' Meetings and Partings at Dawn in Poetry*, ed. A. T. Hatto (The Hague, 1965), 344–89
A. T. Hatto: 'Medieval German', ibid, 428–72
R. J. Taylor: 'Melodies of Medieval Romance and German Dawn Songs', ibid, 825
P. Dronke: *The Medieval Lyric* (London, 1968), 167ff
For further bibliography *see* TROUBADOURS, TROUVÈRES.

HENDRIK VANDERWERF

Alba, Alonso [Alfonso] **Perez de** (*d* after 1519). Spanish composer. According to Asenjo Barbieri he was chaplain and singer to Queen Isabella in 1491. However, his name first appears in the lists of members of the queen's chapel on 6 February 1501 when 'Alonso Dalva capellán sacristán' is cited at the beginning of the list of permanent chaplains, with a payment of 7000 maravedís for services rendered the previous year. He served there until the queen's death in November 1504. Then he probably served King Ferdinand, or one of the princes, but there are no extant notices until 1512 when Alba's name appears in the prebendary registers of Queen Juana with the title *capellán et sacristán mayor* of Tordesillas Chapel, a position that he held until 1519. After Ferdinand's death this chapel maintained a conservative musical tradition. Alba is not identifiable with the Alonso de Alva (*d* before 6 September 1504) who became *maestro de capilla* of Seville Cathedral on 25 January 1503.

WORKS
(all sacred works in E-TZ 2, 3)

Misa, 3vv, ed. in MME, i (1941), 156; Agnus Dei of Misa 'Rex virginum', 4vv (other movts by Escobar, Peñalosa, Hernandes)
Alleluias: Alleluia, Angelus Domini, 3vv; Alleluia, Ascendo ad Patrem, 3vv; Alleluia, Assumpta est Maria, 3vv; Alleluia, Deus verus, 3vv; Alleluia, Nativitas tua, 3vv; Alleluia, O adoranda Trinitas, 3vv; Alleluia, Vidimus stellam, 4vv
Antiphons: Ave Maria, 3vv; Vidi aquam, 4vv; Vidi aquam, 4vv
Hymns: Beata nobis gaudia, 4vv; Christe, redemptor omnium, 4vv; Tibi Christe, splendor Patris, 4vv; Ut queant laxis, 4vv; Veni Creator Spiritus, 4vv; Vexilla Regis, 4vv
Motets: O felix Maria, 4vv; O sacrum convivium, 4vv; Stabat mater, 3vv; Te ergo quaesumus, 4vv
No me le digáis mal (villancico), 4vv; ed. in MME, x (1951), no.391

BIBLIOGRAPHY

F. Asenjo Barbieri: *Cancionero musical de los siglos XV y XVI* (Madrid, 1890), 19

R. Stevenson: *Spanish Music in the Age of Columbus* (The Hague, 1960), 164ff

J. Sevillano: 'Catálogo musical del Archivo capitular de Tarazona', *AnM*, xvi (1961), 152

JOSÉ M. LLORENS

Al-Baghdādī. *See* ṢAFĪ AL-DĪN.

Albanese [Albanèse, Albaneze], **(Egide-Joseph-Ignace-) Antoine** (*b* Albano Laziale, nr. Rome, 1729; *d* Paris, 1800). French castrato and composer of Italian origin. Educated in Naples, he went to Paris in 1747 and soon found employment in the royal chapel of Louis XV. From 1752 to 1762 he was a prominent soloist in the Concert Spirituel, appearing frequently in performances of Pergolesi's *Stabat mater*. At many of the *concerts spirituels* he performed duos with a pupil, Mlle Hardy (or Hardi). He apparently retired from public performance about 1764–5, and thereafter taught singing and composed solo songs and duos with various combinations of instrumental accompaniment. In 1774 he received a life pension of 2000 livres annually, equivalent to the total income from his royal appointments. His published works include several collections of airs for one or more voices (some in collaboration with Joseph Mongenot or with J.-G. Cardon and all but one published between 1767 and 1781), as well as some chamber music. He also wrote the music for two lyric scenes, *Les adieux d'un soldat* (1778) and *Le soldat français* (1779, a collaboration with Stanislas Champein).

BIBLIOGRAPHY

EitnerQ; *FétisB*; *GerberL*

J.-B. de La Borde: *Essai sur la musique ancienne et moderne* (Paris, 1780/*R*1972), 490

A. Choron and F. Fayolle: *Dictionnaire historique des musiciens* (Paris, 1810–11/*R*1971)

M. Brenet: *Les concerts en France sous l'ancien régime* (Paris, 1900/*R*1969)

A. Loewenberg: 'Albanèse, Egide Joseph Ignace Antoine', *Grove 5*

C. Johansson: *French Music Publishers' Catalogues of the Second Half of the Eighteenth Century* (Stockholm, 1955)

P. Chaillon-Guiomar: 'Albanese, Egide-Joseph-Ignace-Antoine', *MGG*

C. Pierre: *Histoire du Concert spirituel, 1725–1790* (Paris, 1975)

KENNETH LANGEVIN

Albanese, Licia (*b* Bari, 22 July 1913). American soprano of Italian birth. After study with Giuseppina Baldassare-Tedeschi, her career began at the Teatro Lirico, Milan, where in 1934 she was an emergency replacement for an indisposed Cio-cio-san in the second half of *Madama Butterfly*. The same opera, always closely identified with her, occasioned her formal début at Parma (10 December 1935) and her début at the Metropolitan Opera (9 February 1940). In 1937 she participated in the Covent Garden Coronation season, subsequently singing at virtually every important opera house. During her career she made more than 1000 appearances in 48 roles, in the lyric or *lirico spinto* repertory, including Mozart (Donna Anna, Zerlina, Susanna) and French opera (Micaela, Manon, Gounod's Marguérite) as well as the obvious Italian challenges; her speciality was the Puccini heroines. A singer of extraordinary technical skill and emotional intensity, she was the Violetta and Mimì in Toscanini's recorded NBC broadcasts. Active in the movement to save the old Metropolitan Opera House, she never rejoined the company at Lincoln Center. In later years she taught, and sang sporadically in concert and in roles

the Metropolitan had, perhaps wisely, denied her, such as Aida and Santuzza.

BIBLIOGRAPHY

E. Gara and R. Celletti: 'Albanese, Licia', *Le grandi voci* (Rome, 1964) [with opera discography by R. Vegeto]

MARTIN BERNHEIMER

Albani [Lajeunesse], Dame **Emma (Marie Louise Cécile)** (*b* Chambly, nr. Montreal, 1 Nov 1847; *d* London, 3 April 1930). Canadian soprano. Her father was a professor of the harp, piano and organ. She was educated at the Couvent du Sacré-Coeur at Montreal. She gave concerts in some Quebec towns before her family moved to Albany, New York, in 1864; there she became a soloist at St Joseph's Church and the Albany

Emma Albani as Elsa in Wagner's 'Lohengrin'

bishop and others advised Lajeunesse that his daughter should adopt a musical career. She went to Paris in 1868 where she was taught by Duprez. Later she studied with Lamperti at Milan. In 1870 she made her début at Messina as Amina in Bellini's *La sonnambula*, adopting, as suggested by her elocution teacher, the name of Albani, borrowed from an old Italian family. She then sang successfully at Malta and Florence.

On 2 April 1872 she made her London début at Covent Garden as Amina. The beautiful qualities of her voice and the charm of her appearance were at once appreciated. She sang nearly every season there until 1896, in a great variety of parts, notably as Elsa (1875) and Elizabeth (1876) in the first London performances of *Lohengrin* and *Tannhäuser*. In 1878 she married Ernest Gye, who became lessee of Covent Garden on his father's death. Later she was very successful as Eva (*Die Meistersinger*) and Desdemona (she sang in the first Covent Garden and Metropolitan productions of *Otello*). The last and greatest triumph of her stage career was on 26 June 1896, as Isolde to the Tristan and King Marke of Jean and Edouard de Reszke.

Albani was for many years a great favourite at the Handel and provincial festivals and sang in many new works, notably in those of Gounod, Sullivan, Mackenzie, Cowen, Dvořák, Elgar (*The Apostles*), etc and in 1886 in *St Elizabeth* on the occasion of Liszt's farewell visit to England. She also sang in opera and concerts in Paris, Brussels, Germany, the USA, Mexico and Canada, and later on tour in India, Australia and South Africa. Her voice was a rich soprano of remarkably sympathetic quality. The higher registers were of exceptional beauty, and she had perfected the art of singing *mezza voce*.

On 14 October 1911 she gave a farewell concert at the Albert Hall, afterwards devoting herself to teaching the Lamperti method. In June 1925 she was created DBE.

BIBLIOGRAPHY

E. Albani: *Forty Years of Song* (London and Toronto, 1911/R1977)
H. Charbonneau: *L'Albani* (Montreal, 1938)
N. A. Ridley: 'Emma Albani', *Record Collector*, xii (1959), 77 [with discography]

ALEXIS CHITTY/GILLES POTVIN

Albani, Mathias (*b* St Nikolaus in Kaltern, 28 March 1621; *d* Bolzano, 7 Feb 1712). Tyrolean violin maker who worked in Bolzano. Representations of his label are found in many violins, mostly of ordinary 18th-century German manufacture, and it is clear that his name was for a long time misused by unscrupulous dealers. The false labels appear consistently from 1640 onwards, but only towards 1690, when Albani was an old man, did the original labels begin to appear, and they continued until the year of his death. Albani did not marry until 1671, and since after his death both of his sons, Michael and Joseph, made instruments, it is possible that they were partly or almost entirely responsible for much of the work supposed to be by their father. In any case, the Albani influence was strong among Tyrolean makers of the 18th century, and especially on the Jais family of Bolzano, and Mayr and his fellow members of the Salzburg school. Albani in Bolzano, Joannes Tononi in Bologna, and Kaiser and Goffriller in Venice all emerged in north-eastern Italy at the end of the 17th century, but it is not known who taught whom.

Albani's instruments, those with genuine labels, have little if anything in common with those by Stainer, his famous Tyrolean contemporary (born in the same year), nor do they look like the first efforts of a man of over 70. They are quite neatly made on normal A. and H. Amati lines, with a very good orange craquelé varnish of Italian quality. Albani's violins do not quite have the tonal quality or response of a Venetian or a Bolognese instrument. Perhaps this is because the varnish is a shade more brittle, even though it has worn off easily and dissolves as quickly as any.

BIBLIOGRAPHY

W. L. Lütgendorff: *Die Geigen- und Lautenmacher vom Mittelalter bis zur Gegenwart* (Frankfurt am Main, 1904, 3/1922/R1969, 6/1922)
R. Vannes: *Essai d'un dictionnaire universel des luthiers* (Paris, 1932, 2/1951/R1972 as *Dictionnaire universel des luthiers*, suppl. 1959)

CHARLES BEARE

Albania. Republic of south-east Europe.

1. Introduction. 2. South Albania. 3. North Albania. 4. Instrumental music.

1. INTRODUCTION. Until the second half of the 20th century, the entire musical life of Albania was determined by folk music, which is characterized by archaic forms and practices that can provide information on previous stages of musical development in Europe. Few sources are available for scientific investigation as field research projects have not covered the whole country. Ramadan Sokoli's collections and studies, the material from Erich Stockmann's German–Albanian expedition of 1957 (analysed by Doris Stockmann), a Romanian–Albanian expedition and the activities of the Institute of Folklore of the University of Tiranë have contributed considerably to research work.

The Albanians' Indo-European ancestors, part of a Thraco-Illyrian ethnic group, came from the north in the 2nd millennium BC; besides the Greeks they were among the earliest inhabitants of the Balkans. During their eventful history the Albanians came into contact with Greeks, Romans and Slavs; these contacts, and their subjugation by the Turks from the 15th century until 1912, partly shaped their language and culture. In their struggles with foreign peoples the Albanians developed a strong resistance which was essential to the survival of their musical culture; they often escaped assimilation and alien influence by withdrawing to the remote mountain regions. This enforced cultural isolation and the continuation of the peasant way of life have contributed to the preservation of traditional folk music with social functions almost unchanged. During the Turkish occupation forms of popular music with oriental features, particularly instrumental music, developed only in the towns. Even in the 20th century this oriental element contrasts vividly with the rural folk music. The religions of the Albanians and their separate musical traditions (70% Muslim throughout the country, 20% Greek Orthodox in the south and 10% Roman Catholic in the north) did not influence folk music substantially. The most important ethnic groups are the Gegs, living in north Albania, and the Tosks, who live in the south, along with the smaller groups of Labs and Chams; these are separated by musical as well as language dialects.

2. SOUTH ALBANIA. There is a marked difference, particularly in the vocal folk music, between the northern and southern parts of the country, divided by the Shkumbin River. The Gegs have a tradition of monophonic singing whereas the southern peoples have developed many types of part-singing, probably more than any other region of Europe; much of it may belong to the earliest stratum of European vocal polyphony.

Although south Albanian folksongs are mostly performed by a group of singers, solo singing and sometimes strictly monophonic choral singing also occur. The monophonic style seems to be rather rare and random, whereas solo performance is connected with specific genres. Lullabies and most laments are sung solo, both genres belonging to the women's repertory. In a few parts of the country funeral laments are sung by a leader and chorus; partly overlapping yodel-like singing by two soloists occurs very occasionally. Lullabies and laments generally have many archaic features: sequences of text lines not broken into stanzas; short isometric lines in the lullabies (ex.1); heterometric lines of varied length in the laments (ex.2); a tendency for melodies to fall; different forms of portamento; numerous specific sounds for stylized weeping or sighing; and a narrow range or only a few notes within a wider range. The minor 7th is a preferred frame interval in the laments: it is often sung as a melodic interval, especially as a cadential formula (*see* LAMENT).

Ex.1 from lullaby, Cham female voice (Stockmann and Fiedler, 1965)

Ex.2 from funeral lament, Cham female voice (Stockmann and Fiedler, 1965)

Ex.3 Heterophonic singing from love-song, Cham male group (Stockmann and Fiedler, 1965)

The sexes and, to some extent, age groups are separated in group singing, and folk terminology distinguishes the different singing styles: *grarishte* (women's style, *djemurishte* (young men's style) and *pleqërishte* or, more rarely, *lashtërishte* (old men's style); but the repertories do not show substantial differences. Ballads, historical or political songs, lyrical songs (e.g. love-songs), dance- and drinking-songs, satirical and jocular songs belong to the repertories of all groups; only the ritual and ceremonial songs connected with different customs, for example the spring ceremonies of Llazore (Lazarus Day) or the rain ceremonies in early summer, are sung mainly by women and children. The singing style of men differs from that of women mainly in its wider tonal range. Pentatonic or other melodies of less than an octave, for instance those based on the 2nd and 4th degrees, are most usual.

South Albanian group singing can be divided into two main categories: polyphony with a drone and choral songs without a drone. The latter are usually two-part, and belong mainly to a specific type of heterophony which M. Schneider has called 'Variantenheterophonie'. The leader sings the beginning of a line or double line, while the chorus joins in at a point not strictly fixed, which can be nearer or further from the beginning of every musical unit (see ex.3). Another kind of two-part singing without a drone consists of a melody and counter-melody, performed by two soloists or leader and chorus, as in some funeral laments.

Polyphony with a drone shows the following features of vertical and horizontal structure: songs are mostly three-part – two solo parts (melody, counter-melody) with a choral drone; four-part singing, found more rarely and only among the Labs, also consists of two solo parts (melody and counter-melody) but is accompanied by a double drone, one choral and one solo; there is some two-part polyphony with a melody and choral drone. The drone (Albanian *iso*, related to the *ison* of Byzantine church music) is performed in two ways: among the Tosks and Chams it is always sung continu-

ously to the syllable 'e', the singers using staggered breathing; among the Labs it is sometimes rhythmic, being performed to the text of the song. Solo singers, especially young men, characteristically sing with considerable strength and volume. The structure of the solo parts differs considerably according to the different ways of performing the drone, but there is also a great variety of structures within the two drone types, especially in the pedal style widespread among all the ethnic groups. This is due to the differing singing styles of women, young and older men, and also to regional dialects. The most diverse styles offer certain contrasts: expanding melodic lines tend to have a wide range often embellished with melisma and rich ornamentation, extremely or relatively free rhythm and consonant harmonies, found among the Tosks and Chams (ex.4);

Ex.4 Polyphonic singing with choral drone from lyrical song, Tosk male group (Stockmann, 1960)

whereas lively oscillating melodies tend to have a narrow range with no ornamentation, but sharp accents, strict rhythm (often asymmetrical) and harmonic clusters of 2nds and other small intervals (especially around the drone), represented by some styles of the Labs (see ex.5). Between these extremes there is a great variety of singing styles, combining, for instance, rhythmic features of the second type with melodic and harmonic features of the first. The stylistic boundaries between the Labs and the Tosks and Chams are therefore variable.

Ex.5 Polyphonic singing with choral drone from drinking song, Lab male group (Stockmann, 1960)

The same applies to the formal structure of the songs, which ranges from a steady strophic organization of regular musical units, usually corresponding to the verse line (sometimes among the Labs) to a looser arrangement of melodic phrases (or pairs of phrases) of different length, with or without partial repetition (common among Tosks and Chams), or to relatively free sequences of lines (sometimes also among the Labs).

The singers may begin a song or stanza in different succession and may combine to different degrees within it: the solo phrases may be simultaneous, overlapping or strictly alternating, while the chorus may join in at the very beginning, together with the second soloist (who as a rule follows the first), or after the second soloist has performed a characteristic formula. The first soloist occupies mostly the upper tonal range, the second soloist the lower; each makes use of characteristic formulae and singing style. Both melodic parts may be absolutely individual, though never quite independent parts of the whole structure, or, particularly in overlapping or alternating structures, the two solo parts may become similar both in range and in melodic contour. The function of each part in Albanian vocal polyphony with a drone is described in Albanian folk terminology: the first solo part is known as *ia merr* ('takes it', i.e. the voice); the second *ia pret* ('waits for it', or 'cuts it'); the chorus part is known as *iso* or *ia mban* ('holds it') among the Tosks or *ia mbush* ('fills it') among the Labs.

There are three non-Albanian ethnic minorities in south Albania. A small Slavonic group lives near Lakes Ohrid and Prespa; its folk music is closely related to

that of neighbouring Macedonia. In western Albania there is a group of Greeks who share musical characteristics with the Labs and Chams, also showing relations to folk music in Epirus. The folk music of the nomadic Vlachs or Arumuni (originating in Romania), who graze their flocks near the sea during winter and in the Grámmos mountains in summer, resembles that of the Tosks and Chams.

3. NORTH ALBANIA. Vocal folk music of north Albania is predominantly monophonic. The epic tradition of the northernmost part of the country, closely related to the corresponding Slavonic traditions in neighbouring Montenegro, is important in the Gegs' musical culture. *Këngë trimash* (heroic songs) and *këngë kreshnikësh* (short epics) are characterized by a recitative style within a narrow tonal range, normally a 5th (see ex.6); they are usually accompanied by a *lahutë* (one-string fiddle) or *çifteli*, also known as *sharki* (two-string lute). *Këngë kreshnikësh* gradually developed out of the *këngë trimash*, some of which describe events as early as 8th-century battles between the Albanian Illyrians and the Slavs; the former primarily concern conflicts between the Slavs and Turks after 1470. The brothers Muho and Halil are the heroes of the most important cycle of songs and epics which developed in the mid-17th century. These narrative songs continued to recount chiefly the struggles against the oppressors and enemies of the Albanian people, and they continue to play an important role in north Albanian folk music. A favourite example is the ballad of Halil and Hajrije (ex.6), based on an event of the early 19th century. The heroic epics and ballads are performed by men and are sung only exceptionally by professional singers.

Ex.6 from *Halil and Hajrije* ballad, male voice, north Albania (Lloyd, 1968)

The fairly scarce lyrical songs (e.g. love-songs) are also performed solo, the singer accompanying himself on the *çifteli*. Like the epics, these are musically archaic, their most conspicuous feature being a narrow tonal range. The ritual and ceremonial songs (at weddings, seasonal rituals etc), traditionally sung by male or female groups, belong to the same archaic musical style. Singing, usually by women, is often accompanied by the sound of a metal tray (*tepsi*) being spun round on the floor or a low table. Songs of 19th-century urban origin, mostly of lyric character and with a more developed musical structure, have spread to rural areas in only a limited degree, particularly to the country round Tiranë.

The cries called *maje krahe*, by means of which mountain-dwellers communicate over long distances, are also peculiar to the north; they are uttered with great power and volume, and function like the signals made by shepherds' trumpets which, surprisingly, are not found in this region.

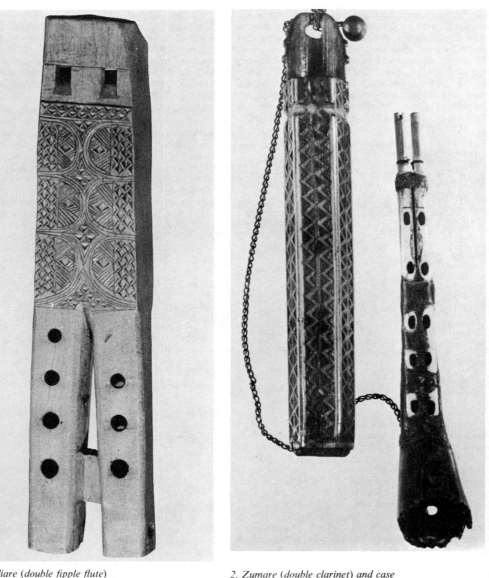

1. Cyla-diare (double fipple flute)   *2. Zumare (double clarinet) and case*

4. INSTRUMENTAL MUSIC. Instrumental folk music is less important than vocal music in Albania; in the south there are even regions where almost none is performed. There is no regional differentiation such as characterizes vocal music, although certain instruments are found only in particular regions.

Folk instruments can be divided into three major groups according to origin, function and social context. Because of Albania's former economic dependence on sheep-rearing, shepherds' instruments are the most important group, consisting mainly of wind instruments. *Fyell* or *kavall* (long end-blown flutes) are fundamental to this group and are considered national instruments; two variants are found throughout the country. The

smaller, 30 to 40 cm long and with six finger-holes, is especially used by the Gegs, whereas the larger, about 60 to 80 cm long, with seven finger-holes and one thumb-hole, is common among the Tosks. The shepherds who play these instruments use a special breathing technique known as the 'oriental' technique, inhaling through the nose and using the cheeks as an air reservoir, which allows them to play without pausing for breath. Their repertory is astonishingly large, a substantial part being closely related to work: almost every part of the work routine, for example when the sheep are driven to water, when they drink, when they are milked or when the cheese is made, has a particular instrumental representation or a characteristic musical motif, to which the shepherds give titles. Animal and other natural sounds are imitated and characteristic forms of movement are illustrated musically. The instrumental pieces have an open musical form marked by a musical motif repeated at various pitches or by several different motifs strung together. The pieces can be extended almost indefinitely through frequent and varied repetition of the short musical formulae and are usually played while the corresponding work is carried out. The flute music serves to keep the animals calm as they move from place to place so that they are easier to herd. Shepherd music also functions partly as a signal.

Fipple flutes with six finger-holes are rare, but the *cyladiare* (double fipple flute, see fig. 1) is used by the Labs and Chams of south-western Albania. The instrument consists of two pipes bored in a block of wood. Four or five finger-holes on the right pipe are used for the melody, three on the left for a variable drone. Small single-reed instruments made from cane or a stalk of corn with idioglott or heteroglott reeds are found throughout the country. The *zumare* (fig.2), a type of double clarinet with a heteroglott reed, is used only by the shepherds of north-western Albania. It consists of two pipes, normally about 20 cm long and made from cane, bones of birds or (more recently) metal; these are bound together with wool and wax, and each has five parallel finger-holes. Both pipes are fitted into a bell of goat or ram's horn. The instrument is also blown by means of the 'oriental' breathing technique. The *gajdë* (bagpipe (fig. 3)) is found along the eastern border of Albania; it consists of a goatskin bag, with a single drone and a six-hole chanter, both with a single reed. Other shepherds' instruments are animal horns, double-reed instruments with a pipe made from bark, and several types of bell for goats and sheep; all are usually made by the shepherds themselves. They belong to the oldest instruments in Albania and are normally used by the shepherds specifically in connection with their work.

The second group of instruments includes some string instruments originating in the Persian–Arab culture, whose main function is to accompany epic and lyrical songs. The *lahutë* (one-string fiddle) is used exclusively by epic singers for accompaniment but is found only in the northernmost part of the country. It is made from one piece of wood and has a skin sound-table. The string is stopped from the side by the fingers or nails because there is no fingerboard on the neck; it is bowed with a strong curved horsehair bow. Throughout the northern and central parts of Albania the Gegs also use a plucked two-string lute known by the original Turkish name *çifteli* to accompany heroic ballads and lyric songs. The instrument has a pear-shaped body made from one piece of wood, a thin wooden soundboard and a long neck with 11 to 13 frets. The two strings, the upper for the melody and the other for a constant drone, are usually tuned a 4th apart. Both instruments are normally made by the singers themselves, who are often semi-professional musicians. The Tosks do not use instruments to accompany songs, except in the towns where the Arab short lute called *ut*, *llaute* or *bozuk* is occasionally used.

The third group contains instruments for dance music, most of them also originating in oriental cultures. Sometimes only one idiophone or membranophone is used to mark the dance rhythm: for instance, the *dajre* or *def* (a round frame drum with a single skin and metal jingles); the *darabuke* (a goblet drum made of potter's

clay, with one skin) near the small town of Kavajë; a pair of wooden spoons or a pair of *zil* (small bronze cymbals) which are clapped together like castanets by the dancers themselves. The traditional instrumental ensemble for the Gegs' dance music in northern and central Albania consists of a *lodrë* (cylindrical double-headed drum) which is beaten with two sticks, and a *surle* (conical double-reed instrument) with eight finger-holes, one of them for the thumb: it is also customarily used for wedding ceremonies. These two instruments are played mostly by gypsy musicians. The combination of the *gajdë* and *dajre* is a rural ensemble very common in the bagpipe region. In rural districts the *çifteli* or *fyell* are also sometimes used to accompany dance.

Urban instrumental ensembles demonstrate the strength of Turkish influence on urban folk music during the Ottoman occupation. In the north the fundamental instrument in the ensemble is always a *saze* (long-necked lute), hence the names *sazet* or *sazexhijtë* for the ensembles. The *saze* has ten strings divided into three courses, tuned a 4th and a tone apart (e.g. C–F–G). Approximately 20 frets on the neck produce a scale with intervals smaller than a semitone. Other instruments in the ensemble in northern towns are usually the *dajre*, sometimes the *çifteli*, and nowadays factory-made instruments like the violin (played vertically on the knees like the *lahutë*) and the clarinet. Instrumental ensembles in the south are composed of the *llaute* (short lute, with the same role as the *saze* in the north), *dajre*, clarinet, accordion and sometimes the violin. Small ensembles of clarinet, accordion and *dajre* without the *llaute* have become popular, especially in

3. Gajdë (bagpipe)

the southern towns and their surroundings. The musicians of all urban ensembles are mostly semi-professional or professional.

BIBLIOGRAPHY

P. Dungu, ed.: *Lyra shqiptare* (Novara, 1940)
G. K. Kujxhija: *Dasëm shkodrane* [Shkodër wedding] (Florence, 1943)
Y. Arbatsky: *Beating the Tupan in the Central Balkans* (Chicago, 1953)
R. Sokoli: *Les danses populaires et les instruments musicaux du peuple albanais* (Tiranë, 1958)
D. and E. Stockmann: 'Die vokale Bordun-Mehrstimmigkeit in Südalbanien', *Ethnomusicologie III: Wégimont V 1960*, 85–135
E. Stockmann: 'Klarinettentypen in Albanien', *JIFMC*, xii (1960), 17
—–: 'Zur Sammlung und Untersuchung albanischer Volksmusik', *AcM*, xxxii (1960), 102
D. Stockmann: 'Zur Vokalmusik der südalbanischen Çamen', *JIFMC*, xv (1963), 38
E. Dheri, M. Daiu and Q. Haxhihasani, eds.: *Këngë popullore* [Folksongs] (Tiranë, 1964)
E. Dheri, M. Daiu and A. Mustaqi, eds.: *Këngë popullore dashurie* [Folk love-songs] (Tiranë, 1965)
R. Sokoli: *Folklori muzikor shqiptar: morfologjia* [Albanian folk music: morphology] (Tiranë, 1965)
D. and E. Stockmann and W. Fiedler: *Gesänge der Çamen*, Albanische Volksmusik, i (Berlin, 1965)
E. Dheri, M. Daiu and A. Mustaqi, eds.: *250 këngë popullore dasme* [250 folk weddings songs] (Tiranë, 1966)
R. Sokoli: *Veglat muzikore të popullit shqiptar* [Musical instruments of the Albanian people] (Tiranë, 1966)
A. L. Lloyd: 'Albanian Folk Song', *Folk Music Journal*, i (1968), 205

DORIS STOCKMANN, ERICH STOCKMANN

Albano, Marcello (*fl* Naples, 1601–16). Italian composer and musician. He was mentioned by Cerreto as one of a number of singers and instrumentalists in Naples. He published two volumes of music at Naples in 1616. The first was *Il primo libro di canzoni, e madrigaletti*, for three and four voices (*RISM* 1616[11]). It includes settings of texts by Rinuccini, Tasso, Marino and Francesco degl'Atti. The canzoni – in fact canzonettas – usually have four-line stanzas and use triple metre occasionally. The tenor parts can be omitted. The five madrigalettos (one of which is by Scipione Dentice) are longer and avoid triple metre but are similar in style to the canzonettas. Albano recommended that lute, harp or harpsichord accompaniment be used, that the tempo be a little rushed and that, whereas intermediate cadences must be sung in strict time, final cadences could be drawn out a little. His other print is *Madrigali* for five voices, which survives incomplete. The poets set include Guarini, Rinuccini and P. Petracci. The madrigals are only slightly chromatic. Their texts are shorter and their textures more imitative than was usual in Neapolitan madrigals of the time. In both prints Albano was occasionally old-fashioned in that he set accented text syllables to high pitches on weak beats and unaccented syllables to low pitches on strong beats.

BIBLIOGRAPHY

S. Cerreto: *Della prattica musica vocale e strumentale* (Naples, 1601/R1969), 154ff, 302

KEITH A. LARSON

Albareda, Marcián (*b* late 16th century; *d* probably Barcelona, mid-17th century). Spanish composer. He was appointed *maestro de capilla* at the Cathedral of La Seo at Urgel on 15 January 1622. In 1626 he followed Juan Pujol in the same capacity at Barcelona Cathedral, where he probably stayed for the remainder of his life. Only a few of Albareda's works survive: masses, motets, villancicos and unaccompanied romances, for four, six and eight voices. They lack Pujol's creative ingenuity and technical brilliance, though Albareda did successfully preserve the Catalonian musical tradition for his successor Vicente Luís Gargallo. This music is all in

MS in *E-Bca*, except the following four pieces, which are in MS at *E-Bc*: *responsión, A la media noche*, 6vv; *Alma, llegad al convite*, 6vv; romance, *Convidando está a su mesa*, 4vv; villancico for the Holy Sacrament, *Hoy deste pan consagrado pienso comer un bocado*, 8vv.

BIBLIOGRAPHY

J. Wolf: *Historia de la música, con un estudio crítico de historia de la música española por Higinio Anglés* (Barcelona, 1943, 3/1949)

BARTON HUDSON

Albéniz, Isaac (Manuel Francisco) (*b* Camprodón, Lérida, 29 May 1860; *d* Cambô-les-Bains, 18 May 1909). Spanish composer and pianist. One of the most important figures in Spain's musical history, Albéniz helped to create a national idiom and an indigenous school of piano music.

1. LIFE. In 1864, at the age of four, he appeared as a pianist at the Teatro Romea in Barcelona, so startling the audience with his performance that some kind of trickery was suspected. In 1865 he took lessons from Narciso Oliveras and in 1867 went with his mother to Paris, where he was praised by Marmontel, professor of piano at the Conservatoire, but was not considered old enough to become a student there. In 1868 he made a concert tour of Catalonia with his father. In 1869, when the family moved to Madrid, Albéniz entered the conservatory, where he studied under Mendizábal, but in 1870 he ran away to the Escorial and then gave concerts in various cities of Castile, being on one occasion robbed of his luggage by bandits. After returning to his father's house, he broke away once more in 1872, giving concerts in Andalusia and embarking in Cádiz as a stowaway for South America. A precarious life in Argentina, Uruguay, Brazil, Cuba, Puerto Rico and the USA led him finally to San Francisco and back to Spain in 1873. In that year he went to Liverpool and London, and then on to Leipzig, where he studied under Jadassohn and Reinecke. (In 1874 his sister Blanca committed suicide, after being refused entry as a singer to the Teatro de la Zarzuela.)

In 1877 Albéniz returned to Madrid, where he was given a scholarship by Count Morphy (a high dignitary under Alfonso XII) to go to Brussels and study composition under Gevaert and the piano under Brassin. His stay in Belgium was episodic, being interrupted by a trip to Cuba and the USA but he won a first prize in 1879 at the conservatory. Immediately after this, he went to Weimar, Prague, Vienna and Budapest, following Liszt, whom he had met on 18 August 1880 and with whom he perfected his piano technique. In 1883, after another journey to South America, he settled in Barcelona. On 23 June 1883 he married Rosina Jordana, and at about this time met Felipe Pedrell, who was to inspire and guide him in the creation of music with truly Spanish roots. In 1885, his son Alfonso was born and in 1889 and 1890 two daughters. In 1885 he moved to Madrid and in 1889 performed in London and Paris, but about 1890 he gave up his concert career. From 1890 to 1893 he lived in London, having first spent some time in Paris studying under Dukas and d'Indy. In 1891 he signed a contract with the London banker Francis Burdett Money-Coutts (Lord Latymer), on the basis of which, in exchange for substantial financial support, he committed himself to setting the latter's librettos to music. The alliance was not very fruitful artistically, since the librettos written by the banker had little appeal for the musical temperament of Albéniz, who turned out rather mediocre works as a result, the only exception being the masterpiece *Pepita Jiménez*, adapted by Money-Coutts from Juan Valera's novel.

In 1893 Albéniz's opera *The Magic Opal*, to a libretto by Arthur Law, was given its first performance at the Lyric Theatre in London. In the same year he moved to Paris, where he had fruitful relationships, both musical and personal, with d'Indy, Fauré, Debussy and Dukas. In 1895 the Teatro del Liceo in Barcelona gave *Henry Clifford* its first performance, and in 1896 *Pepita Jiménez*. Throughout this period he was also an assistant teacher of the piano at the Schola Cantorum in Paris. In 1897 he made two trips to Prague; on the first, he showed his generous nature by paying Breitkopf

Isaac Albéniz

secretly for the publication of Chausson's *Poème*, while the second was for the first performance in Prague of *Pepita Jiménez*. In 1898, a trip to Granada inspired him to write his important piano work *La vega*. In 1900, following the death of his mother, he moved back to Barcelona, but because of severe ill-health (he suffered for years from Bright's disease) and his failure to get his opera *Merlin* performed, he returned to Paris in 1902.

In 1903, following the death of his father, Albéniz went to live near Nice. His last years were spent in work on his masterpiece, the *Suite Iberia* for piano. On 9 May 1906 at the Salle Pleyel in Paris, Blanche Selva played the first book of this work. On 11 September 1907 she gave the first performance of the second book, this time at St Jean de Luz; on 2 January 1908, she played the third at the house of Mme de Polignac in Paris, and on 9 February 1909, the fourth and last at the Société Nationale. In March of the same year, Albéniz moved to Cambô, where his final illness set in. After his death the French government awarded him the Grand Cross of the Légion d'honneur. He left two piano works unfinished, *Navarra* and *Azulejos*. The first was completed by Déodat de Sévérac, the second by Granados.

2. WORKS. Albéniz's works are numerous and varied, the majority being for the piano. His first compositions conform to the taste of the period of his youth and in their virtuosity betray the influence of Liszt. They were turned out quickly and in great numbers. But from the time of Barbieri's publication in 1890 of the *Cancionero de palacio*, and as a result also of his contacts with Pedrell, Albéniz turned more and more to Spanish folk music as the basis for his work. Other influences were the piano literature of the 19th-century salon and impressionist harmony. So far as the latter is concerned, it is important to note that Albéniz was not simply a follower of the French school. His arrival in Paris preceded the first important works of Debussy; he was a friend of the French composers, exchanged ideas with them and himself helped to create the impressionist style. His piano writing directly influenced Debussy and Ravel. The crowning expression of his genius is undoubtedly the *Suite Iberia*, a work distinguished by its extraordinarily complex piano technique, harmony that is free and bold and occasional instrumental effects, in which the piano imitates the guitar or castanets.

As a composer of theatre music, Albéniz did not achieve the same heights as in his piano music, although the opera *Pepita Jiménez* and the zarzuela *San Antonio de la Flórida* are of high quality. The bulk of his work has until recently been little known, because of the extraordinary and nearly exclusive popularity of the *Suite Iberia*. Other piano works, such as *La vega*, the *Suite española*, *Cantos de España* and above all some of the sonatas (no.5 especially) are now recognized as also being of interest. In the orchestral genre Albéniz is known principally through the arrangement by Enrique Fernández-Arbóz of some parts of the *Suite Iberia*, but he produced some interesting orchestral pieces himself, such as *Catalonia*, *Rapsodia española* and a piano concerto.

One of the most important aspects of Albéniz's career was his ability as a pianist. Unfortunately he left no recordings; for evidence of his performing style one must depend on contemporary accounts. From them it appears that he had a very personal piano technique, based partly on intuition and a rare innate facility, partly on the solid mechanism inculcated in him by his teachers. This technique was orientated towards transcendental effects of post-Lisztian virtuosity. His own works exemplify this, and he apparently possessed an inimitable gift for endowing their performance with colour and life by means of a highly personal manner of relating the basic harmonic and dynamic formulae.

Albéniz's works, especially the early ones, are numerous and widely dispersed. They have never been systematized into a complete catalogue, and the gaps in the opus numbers in the following list, which is complete except for pieces of negligible importance, indicate that many are lost or have not yet come to light.

WORKS
(published in Madrid unless otherwise stated)

PIANO SOLO

Pavana capricho, op.12 (1883); Sonata no.1, op.28, scherzo pubd (1883), other movts lost; Suite española, op.47 (1886): Granada, serenata, Cataluña, corranda, Sevilla, sevillanas, Cádiz, canción [=op.181, added *c*1918], Asturias, leyenda [=op.232/1, added *c*1918], Aragón, fantasia [=op.164/1, added *c*1918], Castilla, seguidillas [=op.232/5, added *c*1918], Cuba, capricho; Suite antigua, op.54 (1887); Gavota, Minuetto

Suite antigua no.2, op.64 (1887): Sarabanda, Chacone; 7 estudios en los tonos naturales mayores, op.65 (1887); 6 mazurkas de salón, op.66

(1887): Isabel, Casilda, Aurora, Sofia, Christa, Maria; Sonata no.2 (1887); Sonata no.3, op.68 (1887); Recuerdos de viaje, op.71 (1887): En el mar, barcarola, Leyenda, Alborada, En la alhambra, Puerta de tierra, bolero [also pubd as Andalucia], Rumores de la caleta, malagueña, En la playa

Sonata no.4, op.72 (1887); Suite antigua no.3 (1887); Minuetto, Gavota; Sonata no.5, op.82 (1887); 12 piezas características, op.92 (1888–9): Gavota, Minuetto a Silvia, Barcarola (Ciel sans nuages), Plegaria, Conchita, polka, Pilar, waltz, Zambra, Pavana, Polonesa, Mazurka, Staccato, capricho, Torre bermeja, serenata; 2 mazurkas de salón (1889): Amalia, op.95, Ricordatti, op.96

Suite española no.2 (1889): Zaragoza, Sevilla; Album of Miniatures: Les saisons, op.101 (London, 1892): Le printemps, L'été, L'automne, L'hiver; Sueños, op.101 bis (London, ?1892): Berceuse, Scherzino, Canto de amor; 2 morceaux caractéristiques: Spanish national songs, op.164 (London, 1889): Jota aragonesa, Tango; España: 6 hojas de album, op.165 (London, 1890): Preludio, Tango, Malagueña, Serenata, Capricho catalán, Zortzico

Serenata española, op.181 (London, 1890); Mallorca, barcarola, op.202 (London, 1891); España (Souvenirs), (1896): Preludio, Asturias; Cantos de España, op.232 (1896): Preludio, Oriental, Bajo la palmera, Córdoba, Seguidillas; La vega (Paris, 1897); Suite Iberia, 4 bks: 1 Evocación, El puerto [orchd 1907, unpubd, E-Bc], El Corpus en Sevilla (1906), 2 Rondeña, Almería, Triana (1906), 3 El Albaicín, El polo, Lavapiés (1907), 4 Málaga, Jerez, Eritaña (1908); Navarra, inc., autograph E-Bc, completed by D. de Séverac (1912); Azulejos, inc., completed by Granados (Paris, 1911)

DRAMATIC

Early lost works, mentioned by Guerra y Alarcón: Cuanto más viejo (zarzuela, 1); Catalanes de gracia (zarzuela, 1); El canto de salvación (zarzuela, 2); El Cristo (oratorio)

The Magic Opal (comic opera, 2, A. Law), London, Lyric, 19 Jan 1893; vocal score (London, 1893)

Additional nos. for Millöcker: Poor Jonathan, London, Prince of Wales, 1893

San Antonio de la Flórida (zarzuela, 1, E. Sierra), Madrid, Apolo, 26 Oct 1894; vocal score (Barcelona, ?1894)

Henry Clifford (opera, 3, F. B. Money-Coutts), Barcelona, Liceo, 8 May 1895; vocal score (Barcelona, n.d.)

Pepita Jiménez (lyric comedy, 2, Money-Coutts, after J. Valera), Barcelona, Liceo, 5 Jan 1896; vocal score (Leipzig, 1896)

King Arthur (opera trilogy, Money-Coutts, after Malory): Merlin (3), not perf., vocal score (Paris, 1906), Lancelot, inc., Guinevere, not composed

OTHER WORKS

Orch: Rapsodia cubana, op.66, arr. pf (1887); Rapsodia española, pf, orch, op.70, arr. pf (1887) [orchd by Enescu, 1911]; Pf Conc., a, op.78, arr. 2 pf (?1887); Escenas sinfónicas catalanas, perf. 1889, unpubd; Catalonia, suite populaire, movt 1 perf. 1899 (Paris, 1908), movts 2, 3 inc.

Songs: 6 [It.] baladas (Marquesa de Bolaños) (1887): Barcarola, La lontananza, Una rosa in dono, Il tuo sguardo, Morirò!!!, T'ho riveduta in sogno; [5] Rimas de [G. A.] Bécquer (1889): Besa el aura, Del salón en el ángulo oscuro, Me ha herido recátandose, Cuando sobre el pecho inclinas, De dónde vengo?; To Nellie (Money-Coutts), 6 songs (Paris, 1896): Home, Counsel, May-day song, To Nellie, A Song of Consolation, A Song; 2 Songs (Money-Coutts), 1897, unpubd: The Caterpillar, The Gifts of the Gods; 6 Songs (Money-Coutts), lost except no.2 Will you be mine, 1897, no.3 Separated, 1897, both E-Boc; 2 morceaux de prose de Loti (Saint-Sébastien, 1897): Crépuscule, Tristesse; 4 mélodias (Money-Coutts) (Paris, 1909): In Sickness and Death, Paradise Regained, The Retreat, Amor summa injuria

BIBLIOGRAPHY

A. Guerra y Alarcón: Isaac Albéniz: notas crítico-biográficas (Madrid, 1886); partly repr. in Arteaga y Pereira: Celebridades musicales (Barcelona, 1886)

H. Collet: 'Isaac Albéniz et Joaquim Malats', Revista musical catalana, vi (1909), 377

R. Mitjana: Para música vamos!: estudios sobre el arte musical contemporáneo en España (Valencia, 1909) [incl. essay on Merlin]

F. Pedrell: 'Isaac Albéniz', Revista musical catalana, vi (1909), 182

——: Músicos contemporáneos y de otros tiempos (Paris, 1910)

C. Debussy: 'Concerts Colonne – Société des nouveaux concerts: musique espagnole', B.I.S.M., ix/3 (1913); 46 ed. F. Lesure, Monsieur Croche et autres écrits (Paris, 1971), 244

G. Jean-Aubry: 'Isaac Albéniz (1860–1909)', MT, lviii (1917), 535

J. de Marliave: 'Isaac Albéniz', Etudes musicales (Paris, 1917), 119

H. Klein: 'Albéniz's Opera Pepita Jiménez', MT, lix (1918), 116

P. Gilson: Notes de musique et souvenirs (Brussels, 1924)

H. Collet: Albéniz et Granados (Paris, 1926, 2/1948)

E. Ïstel: 'Isaac Albéniz', MQ, xv (1929), 117–48

A. Salazar: La música contemporánea en España (Madrid, 1930)

R. Moragas: 'Epistolario inédito de Isaac Albéniz', Música, i (1938), 38

A. de las Heras: Vida de Albéniz (Barcelona and Madrid, 1941)

V. Espinos: El maestro Arbos (Espasa Calpe, 1942)

V. Ruiz Albéniz: Isaac Albéniz (Madrid, 1948)

M. Raux Deledicque: Albéniz y su vida inquieta y ardorosa (Buenos Aires, 1950)

A. Sagardía: Isaac Albéniz (Madrid, 1951)

G. Laplane: Albéniz: sa vie, son oeuvre (Paris, 1956) [with list of works]

J. M. Llorens Cisteró: 'Notas inéditas sobre el virtuosismo de Isaac Albéniz y su producción pianística', AnM, xiv (1959), 91

——: 'El "Lied" en la obra musical de Isaac Albéniz', AnM, xv (1960), 123

E. Franco: 'La Suite Iberia di Albéniz', NRMI, vii (1973), 51

TOMÁS MARCO

Albéniz, Mateo (Antonio) Pérez de (*b* Spanish Basque region, *c*1755; *d* San Sebastián, 23 June 1831). Spanish composer and theorist. After serving as *maestro de capilla* in San Sebastián, he took up the same post in Logroño collegiate church during the French invasion (1795). Five years later he returned to San Sebastián as *maestro de capilla* at S María la Redonda, where he remained until 1829. He composed a large number of sacred works, which enjoyed great success throughout northern Spain during his lifetime, in particular masses, Vespers, the Office for the Dead, motets and villancicos, many of which survive in manuscript at the churches which he served. He also wrote some piano music (of which a sonata is edited in J. Nin's *Classiques espagnols du piano*, i, 1925) and a 133-page theoretical work, *Instrucción metódica, especulativa, y práctica, para enseñar á cantar y tañer la música moderna y antigua* (San Sebastián, 1802), which relies on Antonio Soler for an explanation of Renaissance notation. But Albéniz was no blind traditionalist harking back to old styles; he extolled both Haydn and Mozart, and was the first in Spain to print extended examples from them for students to imitate. The operetta *Los enredos de un curioso* sometimes attributed to Albéniz is the work of Carnicer, Saldoni, Francesco Piermarini and Albéniz's son Pedro Albéniz y Basanta.

BIBLIOGRAPHY

M. Soriano Fuertes: Historia de la música española (Madrid and Barcelona, 1859), iv, 253f

A. Palau y Dulcet: Manual del librero hispanoamericano, xiii (1961), 27

ROBERT STEVENSON

Albéniz y Basanta, Pedro (*b* Logroño, 14 April 1795; *d* Madrid, 12 April 1855). Spanish pianist, composer and teacher. He was the son of Mateo Pérez de Albéniz, a keyboard player and composer, and received his first music lessons from his father. Later he went to Paris for further training; he studied piano with Henri Herz and composition with Friedrich Kalkbrenner, and became a friend of Rossini. Upon his return to Spain he was organist at the church of S María in San Sebastián, and later at a church in Logroño. When Queen María Cristina founded the Madrid Conservatory he was appointed a professor, on 17 June 1830, and in 1834 he became organist of the royal chapel. He gave private instruction to Queen Isabel II, and was the first to introduce modern methods of keyboard technique and pedagogy into Spain. Although his compositions are of little interest, and are generally inferior to his father's sonatas, he wrote a *Método completo para piano* (Madrid, 1840), which was the official textbook of the Madrid Conservatory.

BIBLIOGRAPHY

FétisB; LaborD

R. Mitjana y Gordón: 'La musique en Espagne', EMDC, I/iv (1920), 2149, 2285

ANTONIO IGLESIAS

Alber [Alberus], **Erasmus** (*b* Bruchenbrücken, nr. Friedberg, before 1500; *d* Neubrandburg, 5 May 1553). German theologian and hymn writer. Related to the noble house of Reiffenstein, he studied in Mainz about 1517, and in Wittenberg from 1518 to 1520 with Luther, who later became a friend. From 1522 to 1527 he was a schoolmaster in Oberursell and was a minister in Sprendlingen from 1528 to 1539, bringing the Reformation to surrounding districts. There, too, he met academics and printers from Hesse, including Eobanus Hessus, Adam Krafft and Christian Egenolff. Thereafter he appears to have travelled frequently: in 1537 he was in Küstrin, later he visited Wittenberg and other cities, and in 1548 he went to Magdeburg. He was forced to leave in 1551 because of his strong Lutheran views. He was appointed senior minister in Neubrandennburg on 19 October 1552, and died there a few weeks after his arrival in March 1553.

Alber left an extensive corpus of writings including several volumes of fables freely adapted from Aesop, printed between 1534 and 1550, and a German dictionary, *Novum dictionarii genus* (Frankfurt am Main, 1540). In these works he vividly portrayed the traditional music of his country, described instruments, and expressed his opinions on music-making and musical instruction in schools. He was a prolific hymn writer; in 1550 he wanted Egenolff to publish 40 hymns by him, and he must already have made a considerable contribution to the first edition of Egenolff's hymnal of about 1535. To date 23 hymns have been ascribed to Alber including such well-known examples as 'Christe, du bist der helle Tag', 'Ihr lieben Christen, freut euch nun' and 'Wir danken Gott für seine Gab'n'. He wrote or arranged at least some of the melodies, and for others adapted existing tunes as contrafacta.

BIBLIOGRAPHY

C. E. P. Wackernagel: *Das deutsche Kirchenlied von der ältesten Zeit bis zum Anfang des 17. Jahrhunderts*, iii (Leipzig, 1870), 879ff [contains edns.]

W. Braune, ed.: *Erasmus Alberus: Die Fabeln* (Halle, 1892)

E. Körner: *Erasmus Alber* (Leipzig, 1910)

F. Blume: *Die evangelische Kirchenmusik*, HMw, x (1931, rev. 2/1965 as *Geschichte der evangelischen Kirchenmusik*; Eng. trans., enlarged, 1974, as *Protestant Church Music: a History*)

L. Uhl: *Alberus und die Musik: eine volkskundliche Untersuchung* (Giessen, 1937)

K. Ameln and others, eds.: *Handbuch der evangelischen Kirchenmusik*, i/1 (Göttingen, 1941), 259, 477ff, 662f, no.352

W. Lueken: *Lebensbilder der Liederdichter und Melodisten* (Göttingen, 1957)

W. Lipphardt: 'Kontrafakturen weltlicher Lieder in bisher unbekannten Frankfurter Gesangbüchern vor 1569', *Quellenstudien zur Musik: Wolfgang Schmieder zum 70. Geburtstag* (Frankfurt, 1972), 125

HANS-CHRISTIAN MÜLLER

Alberch Vila, Pere [Alberch y Vila, Pere; Albercio Vila, Petro; Vila, Pedro (Alberto)] (*b* Vich, 1517; *d* Barcelona, 16 Nov 1582). Spanish composer. He was organist of Barcelona Cathedral from 1538 and was made a canon in 1559. He was widely respected not only as an organist but also as a composer and organ builder and consultant (or tuner). His nephew, Lluís Ferran Vila, succeeded him as organist, having been appointed his assistant in 1580 at the age of 15 or 16. Alberch Vila composed two volumes of *odas*, neither of which survives complete. The *Odarum* (*quas vulgo madrigales appellamus*) ... *liber primus* (Barcelona, 1561), contains four-voice settings of Castilian, Italian and Catalan lyrics; the second volume comprises five- and six-voice compositions in Castilian and Catalan. Only one partbook of the printed volumes survives, but

two more parts for the second volume exist in manuscript. A five-voice motet, a three-voice Lamentation setting, two *ensaladas* and two keyboard tientos are also extant. The tientos, typical Spanish 16th-century ricercares, are thematically similar; the attractive second one seems the stronger, but the first appears to have omissions and may have suffered from Venegas de Henestrosa's editing. The existence of an alleged *Libro de tientos* (or *Tentos de organo de Petro Villa Doctor*) by Alberch Vila, mentioned by Anglès (MME, ii, 1944, 172) and Brown as forming part of the library of John IV of Portugal, has been disputed by Romeu Figueras (1971). If this book ever existed, it was lost in the Lisbon earthquake of 1755.

WORKS

Odarum spiritualium . . . liber secundus (Barcelona, 1560) (A only; Sup and B in *E-Bc* M.588/2)

Odarum (quas vulgo madrigales appellamus) . . . liber primus (Barcelona, 1561) (A only)

O crux, ave spes unica, 5vv, *Bc* M.587; Lamentation, 3vv, *Boc* M.6

2 ensaladas, 1581[13], *Bc* M.588/1

2 kbd tientos, L. Venegas de Henestrosa, Libro de cifra nueva (Alcalá, 1557), ed. in MME, ii (1944)

BIBLIOGRAPHY

BrownI

Primeira parte do index da livraria de musica do muyto alto, e poderoso Rey Dom João o IV. nosso senhor (Lisbon, 1649/*R*1967); ed. J. de Vasconcellos (Oporto, 1874–6)

J. Romeu Figueras: 'Mateo Flecha el Viejo, la corte literariomusical del duque de Calabria y el Cancionero llamado de Upsala', *AnM*, xiii (1958), 25–101, esp. 50, 93

F. Baldelló: 'Órganos y organeros en Barcelona', *AnM*, xxi (1966), 131, esp. 137

J. Romeu Figueras: 'Notas a la bibliografía del músico Pere Alberch Vila', *AnM*, xxvi (1971), 75

CHARLES JACOBS

Alberdi Recalde, Lope (*b* Gauteriz de Arteaga, Vizcaya, 25 Sept 1869; *d* Barcelona, 19 March 1948). Spanish organ builder. He began his career as an apprentice in the workshops of Aquilino Amezúa in Barcelona in 1885, and was active for more than 50 years. In 1895, on the retirement of Amezúa, Alberdi became director of the firm, and in 1896 the owner. His sons, Antonio and Luis Alberdi Aguirrezábal, assisted him in the workshop, which was the most productive in Spain, building nearly 200 organs (in particular those at the monastery of Montserrat, the Jesuit church in Madrid and the cathedrals of Gerona and Santiago). Alberdi's construction methods were extremely advanced: he incorporated many of the best techniques of the time and invented others. He always used mixed mechanical systems and was especially noted for systems without sliding valves; later he abandoned the troublesome pneumatic machinery and utilized the possibilities of electricity. He always used the best of the various methods and systems available. Organs from his workshop were built for use in South America and the Philippines.

BIBLIOGRAPHY

LaborD

Diccionario de la música ilustrado, i (Barcelona, 1927), 35

R. Puigneau: 'Organos y organeros. Los viejos maestros. Lope Alberdi Recalde', *Tesoro sacro musical* (1963), 65

JOSÉ LÓPEZ-CALO

Albergati (Capacelli), Pirro (*b* Bologna, 20 Sept 1663; *d* Bologna, 22 June 1735). Italian composer. Born of noble parents, Marcantonio Albergati Capacelli and Vittoria Carpegna, he soon took a lively part in Bolognese musical life, and was a friend (and perhaps pupil) of G. A. Perti and Corelli. The dedication of Albergati's op.5 to Leopold I led Eitner to assume that he was in that emperor's service, but this thesis is unsupported. Although Albergati accepted a post as *maestro di cappella* in Puiano in 1728, his chief musical activity besides composition was that of enlightened dilettante and patron of other composers. G. M. Bononcini and Giuseppe Jacchini both dedicated works to him. The Albergati palace in Bologna, according to the chronicles, was the scene of many festive serenatas, academies and cantatas. Albergati was 24 times elected to the governing body of Bologna, the Anziani, between 1682 and 1731. From 1701 to 1708 he served six times as gonfalonier of justice. In 1721, at the age of 68, he married a woman of 21, Elisabetta della Porta of Gubbio; she died only six years later.

Although never a member of the important Accademia Filarmonica, Albergati was a prolific composer, publishing 15 sets of instrumental works, sacred music and cantatas. He also made significant contributions to the Bolognese oratorio, though mostly only the libretto of his works survive, as do those for several theatrical works. Albergati's ties with the Bolognese instrumental school of the late 17th century are evident in the sonatas and dance pieces (especially the sonata for trumpet and strings), though they lack the skill shown by his more famous contemporaries. He was at his best in vocal music: the solo cantatas and oratorios show considerable vocal virtuosity, dramatic vigour and interesting instrumental settings. The mass and psalm settings of op.4 show him firmly rooted in the Bolognese tradition of concerted sacred music established by his contemporaries, G. P. Colonna and Perti. Two of his letters to Perti are extant (in *I-Bc*).

WORKS

ORATORIOS

(music lost unless otherwise stated)

Nabucodonosor, Bologna, S Maria di Galliera, Palm Sunday 1686
Giobbe, Bologna, S Maria di Galliera, 3rd Sunday in Lent 1688
S Orsola, Bologna, S Maria di Galliera, Palm Sunday 1689
L'Iride di pace, o sia il B. Nicolò Albergati, Bologna, S Maria di Galliera, Palm Sunday 1690
Il convito di Baldassare, Bologna, S Maria di Galliera, 1691, score, 1702, *A-Wn*
L'innocenza di S Eufemia, Bologna, S Maria di Galliera, Passion Sunday 1694, score, 1700, *A-Wn*
Il martirio di S Sinibaldo, Bologna, Palazzo Albergati, 13 May 1696
Il ritorno dalla capanna, Bologna, Congregazione di S Gabriele, Christmas 1696
La B. Caterina da Bologna tentata di solitudine, Bologna, Congregazione di S Gabriele, All Saints Day 1697, pubd in op.10
S Eustachio, Bologna, Congregazione di S Gabriele, Palm Sunday 1699, pubd in op.10
Maria Annunciata dall'Angelo, Bologna, Congregazione di S Gabriele, 19 March 1701
S Ottilia, Bologna, Congregazione di S Gabriele, Palm Sunday 1705
Morte di Cristo, Bologna, Arciconfraternità della Morte, Good Friday 1719
Il trionfo della Grazia ovvero la conversione di Maddalena, Bologna, 1729
S Petronio principale protettore di Bologna, Bologna, 1732

OTHER SACRED VOCAL

op.
4   Messa e salmi concertati, 1–4vv, insts (Bologna, 1687); score, *I-Bc*
7   Motetti e antifone della B. Vergine, 1v, bc (Bologna, 1691)
11 Hinno e antifone della B. Vergine, 1v, insts (Bologna, 1715)
12 Motetti con il responsorio di S Antonio di Padoa, 1–3vv, insts (Bologna, 1717)
15 Messa, Litanie della BV, Tantum ergo, etc, 4vv (Venice, 1721)
–   Laudate Dominum, 4vv, *GB-Lbm*
–   Missa, 4vv, insts, org, *F-Sm*

OPERAS AND SERENATAS

(all lost)

Serenata, 2vv, Bologna, public square, 27 Aug 1692
Gli amici (pastorale, P. J. Martelli), Bologna, Malvezzi, Aug 1699
Il principe selvaggio (opera, F. Silvani), Bologna, Formagliari, Jan 1712

OTHER VOCAL

op.
3   Cantate morali, 1v (Bologna, 1685)
6   Cantate da camera, 1v (Bologna, 1687)
9   Cantate spirituali, 1–3vv, insts (Modena, 1702)
10 Cantate et oratorii spirituali, 1–3vv, insts (Bologna, 1714)
13 Corona de pregi di Maria (cantata), 1v (Bologna, 1717)
–   Già ch'Amor così vuole (cantata), in Melpomene coronata da Felsina: cantate musicali . . . date in luce da signori compositori bolognesi, 1v (Bologna, 1685)
–   3 cantatas, A, bc: Cintia appassionata, Io ti lascio, Sfogava un dì sue pene; *I-Bsp*
–   Quella cara pupilletta (cantata), 1v, *I-Pca*

INSTRUMENTAL

op.
1   Balletti, correnti, sarabande e gighe, 1/2 vn, vle (Bologna, 1682)
2   Suonate, 2 vn, org, theorbo/vc (Bologna, 1683)
5   Pletro armonico composto di 10 sonate da camera, 2 vn, bc, vc obbl (Bologna, 1687)
8   Concerti varii da camera a 3, 4 e 5 (Modena, 1702)
14 Caprici vari da camera a 3 (Venice, 1721)
–   Sonata a 5 strumenti con tromba, *I-Bsp*

BIBLIOGRAPHY

A. Ghiselli: *Memorie antiche mss. di Bologna* (MS *I-Bu*)
G. M. Mazzuchelli: *Gli scrittori d'Italia*, i (Brescia, 1753)
G. Fantuzzi: *Notizie degli scrittori bolognesi* (Bologna, 1781–8)
C. Ricci: *I teatri di Bologna nei secoli XVII e XVIII* (Bologna, 1888/*R*1965)
L. Frati: 'Musicisti e cantanti bolognesi del settecento', *RMI*, xxi (1914), 189

ANNE SCHNOEBELEN

Alberghetti [Alberghetto], **Bernardino** (*b* Faenza, probably *c*1600; *d* ?Mantua, after 1649). Italian composer and musician. According to manuscripts of 1622 of the Philippine fathers of Ripatransone, near Ascoli, he was educated for the priesthood there and then went to Rome and finally to Mantua, where he was a canon at the ducal church of S Barbara and a musician in the service of Carlo II, Duke of Mantua and Monferrato. He published at Venice in 1649 *Missarum octo vocum . . . opus primum*, for two four-part choirs.

BIBLIOGRAPHY

EitnerQ
G. Gaspari: *Catalogo della biblioteca del Liceo musicale di Bologna*, ii (Bologna, 1892/*R*1961), 21

based on *MGG* (xv, 96) by permission of Bärenreiter
GIUSEPPE VECCHI

Alberghi, Paolo Tommaso (*b* Faenza, baptized 31 Dec 1716; *d* Faenza, 11 Oct 1785). Italian violinist, composer and teacher. He studied with Tartini, probably between 1728 and 1733, by which date his name appears in the list of musicians at Faenza Cathedral, as third (and last) violinist under the direction of his brother, Don Francesco Alberghi, *maestro di cappella*. In 1742 he was referred to in Faenza chronicles as 'Paolo Alberghi, Professore', and both his virtuosity and his compositions – sonatas and violin concertos – were extravagantly praised. In 1755 he became first violinist and, on his brother's death in 1760, *maestro di cappella* as well; he retained both positions until his death. Alberghi supplemented his small salary from the cathedral by playing for civic festivities and for the two academies of Faenza, and by composing and teaching; among his pupils were Bernardo Campagnoli, Cristoforo Babbi and Giuseppe Sarti. A portrait of Alberghi in the Biblioteca Comunale of Faenza (which, together with the Archivio Capitolare del Duomo, contains much biographical material in manuscript) indicates that he was blind in one eye.

Alberghi was essentially a late Baroque composer. His instrumental works are in Tartini's style. Most of the solo sonatas and trios are in three movements, but there are a few two-movement works and some four-movement trio *sonate da chiesa*. Individual movements are generally monothematic. Alberghi's concertos also follow Tartini's three-movement model: the opening movements are in ritornello form, the slow movements are highly ornate lyric arias for the violin, and concluding movements are often dance-like and *galant* in character and suggest a folksong influence. The violin writing, especially in the concertos, bears out Alberghi's reputation as a virtuoso: he used extensive ornamentation, chains of trills, intricate dotted rhythms, long sequences of figuration built on arpeggios, broken chords and scales, often with patterns that involve rapid string crossing. Later works call for performance in 7th position and long passages in multiple stops, often with two melodies carried simultaneously. In the concertos the solo passages become increasingly elaborate during the course of each movement, culminating in extremely difficult caprices, and usually ending with improvised cadenzas.

In Alberghi's sacred vocal music the phrase structure is asymmetrical and the texture contrapuntal with smoothly flowing lines over a steadily moving continuo part. Some of the works for double chorus, however, are chordal and use the choruses antiphonally. In his later works, the counterpoint becomes more complex, but the style is freer and the melodic lines smoother and increasingly expressive. The influence of contemporary opera is evident throughout Alberghi's music in the vocal style of the melodic lines, the harmonic idiom and the formal structures.

His son Ignazio Alberghi (baptized Faenza, 17 Dec 1758; *d* after *c*1836) was a tenor *di mezzo carattere* and a church composer; he appeared between 1782 and 1812 in most of the major theatres in north Italy and Naples, and seems to have divided his time between Italy and Germany, performing in operas in both countries, serving as *maestro di cappella* at Faenza Cathedral, 1787–96, and for 20 years in the service of the Elector of Saxony in Dresden. A cantata by him dated 1797 survives (in *D-Dlb*).

WORKS

11 Sonatas, vn, b, *US-BE* It.2–15; 17 trios, 2 vn, b, *BE* It.16–32; 23 trios, 2 fl, b, *BE* 805 A–C [12 duplicate trios in *BE* It.16–32]; 20 concertos, vn, *BE* It.33–62, 1051, 1053 [embellished versions of *BE* It.33 and 62 in It.1005:24 and It.993:1, 1005:26]: see Duckles and Elmer

2 sonatas, vn, b, *I-Bc*; 1 sonata, 2 fl, b, *Ps*; 3 concertos, vn [1 duplicates *BE* It.40], Ov. and scene 'Tu restarà mia cara', *US-Wc*

Magnificat, 1780; Mass, 1763; 30 hymn settings; 2 responsories for Holy Week; 1 Gloria; 1 Compieta (cantata for Christmas eve): all *I-FZac(d)*

Faenza liberata dalla peste (componimento drammatico, F. Maccabelli) (oratorio), Faenza, 1769, music lost, lib pubd (Faenza, 1769/*R*1929–30)

Il genio romano e il genio faentino (componimento drammatico, N. Tosetti) (cantata), Faenza, 1767, music lost, lib pubd (Faenza, 1767)

BIBLIOGRAPHY

BurneyH

I. Alberghi: *Diario* (MS, *I-FZc*)
——: *Note sulla famiglia Alberghi* (MS, *FZc*)
V. Lee: *Il settecento in Italia* (Milan, 1882; Eng. trans., 1887)
C. Pasolini-Zanelli: *Giuseppe Sarti, musicista del secolo XVIII* (Faenza, 1883)
C. Rivalta: 'Guiseppe Sarti, l'uomo e l'artista', *Società musicale 'G. Sarti'*, vii (Faenza, 1929), 23
P. Beltrani: 'La bella casa settecentesca di un musico faentino', *Valdilamone*, (1930), 180
D. Beltrani and G. Cornacchia: *Documenti storici intorno alla Beata vergine delle grazie di Faenza* (Faenza, 1931)
D. Beltrani: *Della Compagnia dei battuti servi di S. Maria delle grazie e del Corpo santo di Cristo di Faenza* (Faenza, 1937), 17ff
E. van der Straeten: *The History of the Violin* (London, 1933)

V. Duckles and M. Elmer: *Thematic Catalog of a Manuscript Collection of Eighteenth-century Italian Instrumental Music in the University of California, Berkeley, Music Library* (Berkeley, 1963)
D. Boyden: *The History of Violin Playing from its Origins to 1761* (London, 1965)
P. Petrobelli: *Giuseppe Tartini: le fonti biografiche* (Venice, 1967)

GLORIA EIVE-FELDMAN

Albericus Archiepiscopus Bituricensis [? Alberic of Rheims] (*d* 1141). A celebrated scholar who headed the cathedral school at Rheims from about 1114 to 1136 when he became archbishop of Bourges. One polyphonic piece in the Compostela manuscript (*E-SC*), *Ad superni regis decus*, is attributed to him. Since this piece appears early (late 10th century) in the 'Saint-Martial' repertory as *Noster cetus psallat letus*, the attribution to Alberic would probably apply only to the new text if indeed it is not, like most of the Calixtine attributions, entirely fictitious. (*See* SANTIAGO DE COMPOSTELA.)

SARAH FULLER

Albersheim, Gerhard (Ludwig) (*b* Cologne, 17 Nov 1902). American musicologist and pianist of German origin. After schooling in Cologne he was awarded a music teacher's diploma by the Austrian State Commission in 1930. He studied musicology at the University of Vienna (1933–8), and took his doctorate in 1938 with a dissertation on acoustical psychology. He also studied privately with Schenker. In 1940 he emigrated to the USA, later becoming an American citizen, and was active as a conductor, teacher, accompanist and répétiteur. He held teaching posts at the Los Angeles Conservatory of Music and Art (1947–53) and the University of California at Los Angeles (1953–6) before his appointment in 1956 as professor of music at the California State University at Los Angeles, where he taught until his retirement in 1970 as professor emeritus. He frequently served as accompanist to distinguished singers such as Elisabeth Schumann, Pinza and Fischer-Dieskau, and assisted Lotte Lehmann in her art-song courses. Albersheim was one of the first to write on the importance of the theories of Heinrich Schenker, whose influence is occasionally reflected in his writings. His main studies have been in the areas of acoustics and the psychology of hearing, and their relationships to musical aesthetics.

WRITINGS

'Heinrich Schenker', *Rheinische Theater- und Musikzeitung* (1930) nos.15, 16
Zur Psychologie der Ton- und Klangeigenschaften unter Berücksichtigung der 'Zweikomponenten-Theorie' und der Vokalsystematik (diss., U. of Vienna, 1938; Strasbourg, 1939, rev. 2/1975)
'The Sense of Space in Tonal and Atonal Music', *Journal of Aesthetics and Art Criticism*, xix (1960–61), 17; Ger. orig. in *Musikalische Zeitfragen*, x (1962), 75
'Die Tonstufe', *Mf*, xvi (1963), 139; Eng. trans. in *Philosophy and Phenomenological Research*, xxvi (1965–6), 63
'Mind and Matter in Music', *Journal of Aesthetics and Art Criticism*, xxii (1963–4), 289; Ger. orig. in *SMz*, civ (1964), 218
'Die Rolle der Konvention für das Musikverständnis: Sinn und Sinnlosigkeit in der Musik', *Wissenschaftliche Zeitschrift der Humboldt-Universität zu Berlin: Gesellschafts und Sprachwissenschaftliche Reihe*, xv (1966), 395
'Die Rolle der Enharmonik in der Abendländischen Musik', *Festschrift für Walter Wiora* (Kassel, 1967), 149
'Ludus Atonalis', *Musikerziehung*, xx (1969), 150; Eng. trans. as 'Ludus Atonalis and the Future of Music Education', *Journal of Aesthetic Education*, iv (1970), 117
'Reflexionen über Musikwissenschaft und Soziologie', *IRMAS*, i (1970), 200
'Die Wesensverschiedenheiten von Fugen- und Sonaten-Thema als Beispiel für den Stilunterschied zwischen Barock und Klassik', *GfMKB, Bonn 1970*, 323; also in *Musikerziehung*, xxiv (1971), 109

'Lohnt es sich heute noch, eine Lanze für die Zwölftontechnik zu brechen?: eine Stellungnahme', *Mf*, xxv (1972), 59

'Zusätzliches zum Begriff des musikalischen Sinnes', *IRASM*, iii (1972)

Zur Musikpsychologie (Wilhelmshaven, 1974)

Zur Theorie und Grammatik der Musiksprache (in preparation)

SAUL NOVACK

Albert, Prince Consort [Francis Charles Augustus Albert Emmanuel; Franz Karl August Albert Emanuel, Prince of Saxe-Coburg-Gotha] (*b* Rosenau, Coburg, 26 Aug 1819; *d* London, 14 Dec 1861). German musician, consort of Queen Victoria. Music formed a regular part of his early education and appears prominently in the rigorous programme of study which he drew up for himself at the age of 13. He became proficient in singing, played the piano and organ (Mendelssohn admired his organ playing) and began to compose before he was 18. In 1839 he sang the bass solo in a performance of Beethoven's *Der Preis der Tonkunst* at Dresden. After he married Queen Victoria in 1840 he made his mark on the court's musical life by expanding the private band into a fair-sized orchestra capable of taking part in the first English performances of Schubert's Symphony no. 9, Bach's *St Matthew Passion* and Mendelssohn's *Athalie* and *Oedipus at Colonos*, given either at Windsor Castle or Buckingham Palace under the prince's organization. During his directorship of the Concert of Ancient Music (1846), he introduced much new music and conducted some concerts himself.

As a composer the prince showed a distinct talent in smaller forms; his melodic gifts were not matched by harmonic variety or adventurousness. In general, the music bears the stamp of the German Romantic school; in the later works the clearest influence is Mendelssohn. The prince left some 40 completed songs set to German words, with others in draft apparently dating from the late 1830s. Two songs have cello obligato, and the *Lied des venezianischen Gondoliers* has a charming accompaniment for flute, basset-horn and bassoon. The church music, dating partly from the 1840s, is in vocal score only; his *Te Deum* in C was scored for choir, solo voices and orchestra by Ernst Lampert in 1845. The cantata *Invocazione all'armonia* is perhaps his best large-scale work. An edition of his compositions, by W. G. Cusins and including 30 songs, church music and other pieces, was published in London (?1882/*R*1969).

BIBLIOGRAPHY

C. Grey: *The Early Years of his Royal Highness the Prince Consort* (London, 1867)

T. Martin: *The Life of his Royal Highness the Prince Consort* (London, 1875–80)

Catalogue of the King's Music Library [British Museum], ii–iii (London, 1929) [lists some unpubd music and sketches]

ALEC HYATT KING

Albert, Charles Louis Napoléon d' (*b* Menstetten, nr. Altona, Hamburg, 25 Feb 1809; *d* London, 26 May 1886). French dancing-master and composer, father of Eugen d'Albert. His father was a captain of cavalry in the French army. On his death in 1816 the mother and son emigrated to England, where d'Albert received piano tuition from Kalkbrenner and composition lessons from S. S. Wesley. After a period with the ballet in Paris (with Saint-Georges he wrote the libretto for Adam's ballet-pantomime *La jolie fille de Gand*, 1842) he became ballet-master at the King's Theatre, London, and Covent Garden, but gave up the stage in order to compose and teach. Eventually he settled at Newcastle upon Tyne and married there in 1863. His dance music was very popular, particular favourites being the *Bridal Polka*, *Sweetheart's Waltz*, *Sultan's Polka* and *Edinburgh Quadrille*. He also published *Ballroom Etiquette* (Newcastle upon Tyne, 1835).

A. J. HIPKINS/DAVID CHARLTON

Albert, Eugen [Eugène] **(Francis Charles) d'** (*b* Glasgow, 10 April 1864; *d* Riga, 3 March 1932). German composer and pianist. His antecedents were Italian and included the composers Giuseppe Matteo Alberti (*b* 1685) and Domenico Alberti (*c*1717–1740). Charles d'Albert, Eugen's father, was a pupil of Kalkbrenner and for some time ballet-master at Covent Garden. Eugen never felt himself to be a true Englishman and he inclined increasingly towards Germany; in Paris he was known as 'le petit allemand'. Although occasionally given some instruction by his father, he was essentially a self-taught musician. From 1874 he held a bursary at the New Music School, London, directed by Sullivan, and from 1876 he attracted the attention of Ernst Pauer, a German pianist engaged at the school. Rubinstein also predicted a great future for the youth as a pianist and composer. D'Albert became acquainted with Liszt through Richter, and it was Liszt who determined the course of his artistic development. In addition, Brahms and Hanslick became aware of him at this time. D'Albert married the well-known pianist Teresa Carreño (1853–1917) and made numerous concert tours throughout the world, building and consolidating his reputation until late in life; however, as he became more involved with opera composition in his last years, he paid little attention to piano technique. In his early years as a virtuoso his performances of Beethoven, Liszt and Brahms were considered perfect. He also won considerable respect – together with Busoni and Reger, both of whom he knew – for his Bach playing, despite the fact that his interpretations were wilful. His concert arrangements and transcriptions of Bach have many qualities, but d'Albert's taste in this field was erratic and the pieces have not survived their period: at the time they were valued as stylistically precise realizations.

As a composer for the piano d'Albert was devoted to the character piece. The Suite op.1 is a valuable work in Baroque dance forms, but the Sonata op.10 is huge, and although its final triple fugue displays great skill, it is satisfying neither stylistically nor musically. In contrast, the small, mostly virtuoso, genre pieces have formal charm, an uncommon sound and a pleasing character. A similar lyricism is at the foundation of the three concertos. His string quartets draw on Beethoven and Brahms but as Hanslick, who was kindly disposed to d'Albert, noted, they bear the 'stamp of his personality, the individual physiognomy'. D'Albert's lieder are not of the quality reached by his greatest contemporaries and few of them have remained in the repertory. His efforts were largely put into the stage works. Often with startling virtuosity and naivety d'Albert paid homage to the spirit of the age. Many of the operas are charming and nicely executed, but they suffer from poor texts and did not long survive their creator. Even *Tiefland*, often performed immediately after its première, fell into neglect; yet it is musically superior to the works of Mascagni and Leoncavallo and it has a genuinely dramatic kernel. Lighter works, such as *Die Abreise* or *Flauto solo* (an intermezzo about Frederick the Great), are akin to the comic operas of Wolf-Ferrari.

WORKS
(selective list)

STAGE

Der Rubin (Musikalisches Märchen, d'Albert, after F. Hebbel), Karlsruhe, 12 Oct 1893; Ghismonda (opera, d'Albert, after K. Immermann), Dresden, 28 Nov 1895; Gernot (G. Kastropp), Mannheim, 11 April 1897; Die Abreise (F. von Sporck, after A. von Steigentesch), Frankfurt, 20 Oct 1898; Kain (H. Bulthaupt), Berlin, 17 Feb 1900; Der Improvisator (Kastropp), Berlin, 20 Feb 1902; Tiefland (Musikdrama, R. Lothar, after A. Guimeras: Terra baixa), Prague, 15 Nov 1903; Flauto solo (musical comedy, H. von Wolzogen), Prague, 12 Nov 1905; Tragaldabas (Komische Oper, Lothar), Hamburg, 3 Dec 1907

Izeÿl (Musikdrama, Lothar), Hamburg, 6 Nov 1909; Die verschenkte Frau (Komische Oper, Lothar, R. Batka), Vienna, 6 Feb 1912; Liebesketten (Lothar), Vienna, 12 Nov 1912; Die toten Augen (H. H. Ewers), Dresden, 5 March 1916; Der Stier von Olivera (Batka), Leipzig, 10 May 1918; Revolutionshochzeit (F. Lion), Leipzig, 26 Oct 1919; Scirocco (L. Feld, K. M. von Levetzow), Darmstadt, 18 May 1921; Mareike von Nymwegen (Legendenspiel, H. Alberti), Hamburg, 31 Oct 1923; Der Golem (Musikdrama, Lion), Frankfurt, 14 Nov 1926; Die schwarze Orchidee (opera burlesca, Levetzow), Leipzig, 1 Dec 1928; Mister Wu (Levetzow), Dresden, 29 Sept 1932, completed L. Blech

OTHER WORKS

Vocal: Der Mensch und das Leben, op.14 (O. Ludwig), chorus, 1893; Seejungfräulein, op.15, scena, 1v, orch, 1897; Wie wir die Natur erleben, op.24, S/T, orch, 1903; 2 Lieder, op.25, S/T, orch, 1904; Mittelalterliche Venushymne, op.26, T, male chorus, orch, 1904; An den Genius von Deutschland, op.30, solo vv, chorus, 1904; 58 lieder for 1v, pf in 10 vols.

Orch: Pf Conc., b, op.2, 1884; Sym., F, op.4, 1886; Ov. to Grillparzer: Esther, op.8, 1888; Pf Conc., E, op.12, 1893; Vc Conc., C, op.20, 1899; Aschenputtel, op.33, suite, 1924; Sym. Prelude to Tiefland, op.34, 1924

Inst: Pf Suite, d, op.1, 1883; Str Qt no.1, a, op.7, 1887; Pf Sonata, f♯, op.10, 1893; Str Qt no.2, E♭, op.11, 1893; 4 vols. pf pieces

Principal publisher: Bote & Bock

BIBLIOGRAPHY

E. Hanslick: *Ouvertüre von d'Albert* (Berlin, 1892)
——: *Der Mensch und das Leben* (Berlin, 1896)
J. Korngold: *Deutsches Opernschaffen der Gegenwart* (Leipzig and Vienna, 1921)
E. Istel: *Die moderne Oper vom Tode Richard Wagners bis zur Gegenwart* (Leipzig, 2/1923)
A. Aber: 'Eugen d'Albert "Die schwarze Orchidee"', *Die Musik* (1928–9)
W. Raupp: *Eugen d'Albert: ein Künstler- und Menschenschicksal* (Leipzig, 1930)
H. Heisig: *D'Alberts Opernschaffen* (diss., U. of Leipzig, 1942)

HELMUT WIRTH

Albert, Eugène (*b* Brussels, 1816; *d* Brussels, 1890). Belgian woodwind instrument maker. He was renowned for his superb workmanship, particularly of his clarinets, which are still highly prized by the few players who adhere to the 'simple' system. The model he favoured was evolved by Iwan Müller with Sax's addition of the 'spectacle' or 'brille' vent key on the lower joint. About 1860 Albert added the 'extra' c♯ key (though others claimed priority in that invention), creating what has often been called the 'Albert System'. He not only built special models for individual players but devised some excellent types of bass and contrabass clarinets, quite advanced for their period.

The Albert business began in 1846 and was continued by three of the founder's sons, Jean Baptiste, Jacques (père) and Eugène Joseph. Jacques Lucien, a son of Jacques, conducted an independent business in Brussels which still continues. The London agents for E. Albert instruments were first the celebrated impresario, Jullien, and later S. Arthur Chappell. About 1880 Boosey & Co. began to add woodwind instruments to their manufactures and in that year Albert visited London to instruct some of their workmen. At the Paris Exhibition of 1889 the firm, by then called Albert Frères, was awarded a gold medal for clarinets and saxophones.

PHILIP BATE

Albert, Heinrich (*b* Lobenstein, 8 July 1604; *d* Königsberg, 6 Oct 1651). German composer and poet. His formal musical training began in 1622, when he moved to Dresden and worked for his cousin Schütz. While a law student in Leipzig from 1623 to 1626 he began to compose arias, some of which he later included in his published collections; he was influenced by Schein, then Kantor at the Thomaskirche. He moved to Königsberg in 1626. In 1627 he set out for Warsaw with some Dutch diplomats and was taken prisoner by the Swedes for a year. He was not an altogether innocent bystander in the Thirty Years War, for when he returned in 1628 he was involved with the science of fortification. From December 1630 he seems to have given up his earlier profession, to become a full-time musician in Königsberg for the rest of his life. He became organist at the cathedral and studied with Johann Stobaeus. In 1634 he renewed contact with Schütz in Copenhagen and remained in touch with him.

Albert's main achievement lies in his eight volumes of *Arien*. The 170 songs, sacred and secular, reflect the political and artistic life of Königsberg: they were written for various occasions, such as weddings, funerals, anniversaries and the visits of important persons, as well as for the private enjoyment of friends. The dedications accompanying each song, with specific details of its purpose and a precise date, provide a valuable record of life in Königsberg. The songs show the influence of Schein's *Musica boscareccia*; a few for solo voice and basso continuo are arrangements of arias for two or more voices that were originally published separately. Nearly all are short, strophic and syllabic. A few are more elaborate, with ritornellos and melismas for word-painting, and there is some contrapuntal interest among the songs for several voices. The longest work (ii, no.20) was written in honour of Opitz's visit to Königsberg in 1638: numerous recitative verses alternate with instrumental passages, and it ends with a chorus. The poems, 18 of which are by Albert himself, are fine examples of the work of the Königsberg school; the poet he most frequently set was SIMON DACH, like him a leading figure in the Kürbs-Hütte literary group; other poets whose work he set include Andreas Adersbach, Johann Peter Titz, Robert Roberthin and Christoph Kaldenbach. Albert also set three poems by Opitz, whose reforms were their guiding principles. He based 25 songs on foreign tunes that he admired, mostly from France, Italy and Poland. His songs were extremely popular, and at least 25 of his tunes became chorales.

Mattheson was probably the first to point to the prefaces of the first two volumes as important for the study of basso continuo practice in the early Baroque period. Albert stated that continuo playing should not be 'like hacking cabbage'. He gave nine rules to guide the beginner in the proper realization of a figured bass, which in general should be light in texture – triads without much doubling; at imitative entries triads should not be brought in until all the voices have entered. The prefaces are also important for other suggestions about performance: it is pleasant, he said, if a violin is added for ornamentation, and when the voice part is recitative the words should be sung slowly and clearly without regular accents. In the *Musicalische*

Kürbs-Hütte, he again provided useful material about performance. He presented the songs in score as an aid to the choir director and particularly to the organist, who could learn more easily how to realize a figured bass from this method. He also allowed for ornamentation of the parts as printed.

WORKS

Arien, 8 vols., all pubd in Königsberg: i (1638), ii (1640), iii (1640), iv (1641), v (1642), vi (1645), vii (1648), viii (1650); several songs were pubd separately and reprinted in later anthologies; edn. in DDT, xii–xiii (1903–4/*R*)
Musicalische Kürbs-Hütte, 3vv, bc (Königsberg, 1645)
Further songs in Seladons weltliche Lieder (Frankfurt am Main, 1651), 1651[4], 1653[6], 1656[6] and the Clodius Liederbuch (*D-B* Ger.Oct.231)
4 motets: Gott, sei uns gnädig, 1632; Wohl dem, den du erwählt, 1646; Herr, wer wird wohnen, 1647; So wird dein Licht in Finsternis ausgehen; Te Deum, 1647; *USSR-KA*
*c*50 other works, some lost, including 2 dramatic allegories for which only the texts (S. Dach) survive (Cleomedes, 1635; Prussiarchus, oder Sorbuisa, 1645), *D-B, Kl, USSR-KA*

BIBLIOGRAPHY

H. Osthoff: 'Albert, Heinrich', *MGG*
J. Müller-Blattau: 'H. Albert und das Barocklied', *Deutsche Vierteljahresschrift für Literaturwissenschaft und Geistesgeschichte*, xxv (1951), 401
——: 'Heinrich Albert', *Musik und Kirche*, xxiii (1953), 70
G. Kraft, ed.: *Festschrift zur Ehrung von Heinrich Albert (1604–1651)* (Weimar, 1954)
R. H. Thomas: *Poetry and Song in the German Baroque* (Oxford, 1963)
J. H. Baron: *Foreign Influences on the German Secular Solo Continuo Lied of the Mid-seventeenth Century* (diss., Brandeis U., 1967)
JOHN H. BARON

Albert, Karel (*b* Antwerp, 16 April 1901). Belgian composer. He studied with Marinus de Jong at the Royal Antwerp Conservatory. He was musical adviser and conductor of Het Vlaams Volkstoneel (a travelling Flemish theatre company) from 1924 to 1933, and assistant director with the NIR (Belgian National Broadcasting Service – Flemish Section) in Brussels until 1961. Later his activities were limited to music reviews (*Het toneel*) and composition. He became known for his modern stage music for Vlaams Volkstoneel and Théâtre du Marais. At first his musical style ranked him with the expressionist school, but during World War II he turned to a more traditional, simple and comprehensible style; in 1956 he became influenced by dodecaphony.

WORKS

Dramatic: De toverlantaarn (ballet), 1943, perf. Antwerp Flemish Opera, 1946; Europa ontvoerd (opera buffa), 1950; Het tornooi (ballet), 1953
Incidental music: Marieken van Niemeghen (medieval miracle play), 1924, 1928; Lucifer (Vondel), 1926; Tijl (A. Van de Velde), 1926; Oedipus a Colonus (Sophocles), 1931; Hamlet (Shakespeare), 1933, etc
Orch: 4 symphonies, 1941–65; Anank, ov., 1926; Het beestenspel, 1933; Vlaamse suite, 1947; De nacht, 1958; Sinfonietta, 1969; Mini-symfonie, 1974
Songs: Frédérique (J. Daisne), S/T, pf, 1969; Ik heb de lente ontmoet in de herfst (Daisne), S/T, pf, 1969; Najaar (Daisne), S/T, pf, 1969; Het geuzenplein (M. Bilke), Mez/Bar, pf, 1973; other songs
Pf: Klaverblad, 1969; Wandelingen, 1969; Sonatina no.4, 1973; Een dag uit het leven van Janneke en Mieke, 1975; other pf
Chamber music

Principal publishers: Melodia, Metropolis, Mozart-Edition, De Ring, De Sikhel, Pero
MSS in *B-Brtb*

WRITINGS

Zingen als lezen (n.p., 1927)
De evolutie van de muziek aan de hand van fonoplaten (Brussels, 1947)
Numerous articles

BIBLIOGRAPHY

C. Mertens: *Hedendaagse muziek in België* (Brussels, 1967)
CORNEEL MERTENS

Albertarelli, Francesco (*fl* late 18th century). Italian bass. He was engaged in Vienna from 1788 until 1790 and made his début there as Biscroma in Salieri's *Axur, rè d'Ormus* on 4 April 1788. Three weeks later he appeared as Don Gavino in the première of Paisiello's *La modista raggiratrice*; Count Zinzendorf noted in his diary that he 'performed well'. His main appearances were in *opera buffa*, and he sang the title role in Mozart's *Don Giovanni* at its first Vienna performance (7 May 1788). In June 1788 Anfossi's *Le gelosie fortunate* was given in a version containing pieces by nine different composers; Mozart contributed 'Un bacio di mano' for Albertarelli, which contains material he later used in the first movement of the 'Jupiter' Symphony. Albertarelli appeared at the King's Theatre in London in 1791 and in concerts presented by Salomon in 1792.
CHRISTOPHER RAEBURN

Albertet de Sestaro [Sestairo, Sestarron, Terascon; Albert de Sestaro, Terascon] (*fl* 1210–21). Troubadour. According to his *vida* he was born in the neighbourhood of Gap (Hautes-Alpes), the son of a jongleur called Asar. He was renowned for the originality of his melodies but not for his texts. He remained for many years at the court of Orange but worked also in Italy from 1210 to 1221. He finally returned to Sistaron where he died. Of the 23 songs ascribed to him only two have complete melodies and a further one (*En mon cor*) is partly notated. One of the unnotated songs, the descort *Bel m'es oimais* (PC 16.7a) may have been the model for Colin Muset's strophic lai *Bel m'est li tans* (R.284) but this is also without melody in its single source. Too few complete songs have survived to verify the extent of Albertet's melodic originality. *Mos coratges* is conventional in form but, as recorded in the Ambrosiana manuscript, extremely ornate in style. The surviving portion of *En mon cor* gives the impression of a through-composed form with some *AAB* features. *A! mi no fai chantar* is, however, more complex. Subtle variation conceals an underlying structure of $ABaA^1C^1A^2BaDEF$. Though simple in style it is unusual in its combination of intervals and range of phrases.

WORKS

Edition: *Der musikalische Nachlass der Troubadours*, ed. F. Gennrich, SMM, iii, iv, xv (1958–65) [G]

(*principal sources: F-Pn fr.844, 20050*)

A! mi no fai chantar foilla ni flors, PC 16.5a (= 461.138), G iii, 189
En mon cor ai un' aital encobida, PC 16.14, G iii, 190
Mos coratges m'es camjatz, PC 16.17a, G iii, 191

BIBLIOGRAPHY

A. Kolsen: *Dichtungen der Trobadors* (Halle, 1916–19)
J. Boutière: 'Les poésies du troubadour Albertet', *Studi medievali*, x (1950), 1
J. Boutière and A.-H. Schutz: *Biographies des troubadours* (Toulouse, 1950, rev. 2/1964), 508

For further bibliography *see* TROUBADOURS, TROUVÈRES.
IAN R. PARKER

Alberti, Antonio degli (*b* Florence, *c*1360; *d* Bologna, 1415). Italian poet. He was wealthy and educated, corresponded with FRANCO SACCHETTI and entertained in his sumptuous villa the best minds of the day. He took an active part in politics, holding important offices. About 1400 he was banished from Florence as a traitor and spent his last years in Bologna. Two madrigals survive: *Piovuto m'è dal ciel per grazia manna* and *I' fui già bianc'uccel con piuma d'oro*, the latter set to music by Donato da Firenze.

BIBLIOGRAPHY
A. Bonucci: *Sonetti et canzone del clarissimo Antonio degli Alberti* (Florence, 1863)

W. THOMAS MARROCCO

Alberti, Domenico (*b* Venice, *c*1710; *d* Rome, 1740). Italian composer, harpsichordist and singer. Kast ('Rom', §D, *MGG*) gave his death date as 14 October 1746, presumably after an inscription on his tomb in St Mark's in the Palazzo Veneto. Alberti's claim to historical recognition rests traditionally on his harpsichord sonatas, in which the arpeggiated bass that lent his name a posthumous notoriety is a prominent feature (*see* ALBERTI BASS). In his lifetime, however, Alberti was equally famous as a singer and performer (sometimes as self-accompanist) on the harpsichord. His amateur status was perhaps unfairly seized upon by his detractors, for his reported early training in singing and counterpoint under A. Biffi and A. Lotti, both eminent musicians, does not suggest insufficient grounding; it may, however, account for the restricted quantity and scope of his output. Of his non-musical career little is recorded except that he served the Venetian ambassador as a page on a visit to Spain in 1736, provoking Farinelli's admiration of his singing, and subsequently joined the household of Marquis Molinari in Rome. His harpsichord sonatas are generally believed to date from these last years.

14 complete sonatas out of an estimated total of 36 survive, together with ten isolated movements. Eight sonatas, constituting the so-called op.1, were published by Walsh in 1748 in response to an act of flagrant plagiarism by Alberti's former pupil, the castrato Giuseppe Jozzi (*c*1710–*c*1770), which became a *cause célèbre*. (Jozzi continued the deception after his removal to Amsterdam.) All Alberti's sonatas follow the two-movement scheme popular with contemporary Italian keyboard composers. The two movements are contrasted in character rather than tempo; though both are cast in binary form, that of the first often prefigures sonata form, whereas the second retains the modest proportions and uncomplicated design of a dance movement. Alberti's *galant* idiom, much admired as a novelty in its day, proves an adequate vehicle for musical thought that is facile and short-winded, though not lacking in taste and workmanship.

WORKS

DRAMATIC

Endimione (Metastasio), Venice, 1737
Galatea (Metastasio), Venice, 1737
Olimpiade, Venice, 1739
Various arias in *A-Wn*; *D-Mbs, Bds, Dlb*; *I-Bc* (one, *D-Dlb*, is described as from an opera Temistocle of which no record survives)

KEYBOARD

VIII sonate per cembalo, op.1 (London, 1748); an earlier London edn. giving the composer as G. Jozzi is untraced, but similarly misattrib. edns. (Amsterdam, 1761, *c*1765) survive
Miscellaneous sonatas and movts in: XX sonate per cembalo di vari autori, opp.1, 2 (Paris, *c*1758, 1760); A Collection of Lessons for the Harpsichord . . . Book 1 (London, 1761); The Harpsichord Miscellany . . . Book Second (London, 1763)
MS sonatas in *B-Bc*; *D-B, KA, MÜs, SWl*; *GB-Lbm*; *I-Mc*

BIBLIOGRAPHY
F. Torrefranca: 'Poeti minori del clavicembalo', *RMI*, xvii (1910), 763–821
G. Cucuel: *La Pouplinière et la musique de chambre au XVIIIe siècle* (Paris, 1913)
F. Torrefranca: 'Le origini dello stile Mozartiano', *RMI*, xxviii (1921), 263–308
W. Wörmann: 'Die Klaviersonate Domenico Albertis', *AcM*, xxvii (1955), 84

W. S. Newman: *The Sonata in the Classic Era* (Chapel Hill, 1963, rev. 2/1972)

MICHAEL TALBOT

Alberti, Gasparo [Albertis, Gaspare de; Albertus, Gaspare; Gaspare bergomensis, Gaspar de Padua] (*b* Padua, *c*1480; *d* Bergamo, *c*1560). Italian composer. In 1508 he was a singer at S Maria Maggiore, Bergamo, having gone there from Padua. He spent the greater part of his life in Bergamo, and was last mentioned there in an allusion to his old age in 1560. Further entries in the *Terminationes* of the Basilica state that he was occasionally *maestro di cappella* at S Maria Maggiore, and that he had a certain amount of prestige there. When the famous music theorist Pietro Aaron was admitted to the Paduan monastery of S Leonardo in 1536, he was received by Alberti, who with 22 singers performed Vespers *a cori spezzati*. In 1550 Alberti was released as *maestro di cappella* on account of advancing age, but in 1552 he resumed his duties for a further two years. The chapter granted him financial support in 1560. When he died his manuscripts passed to S Maria Maggiore. Three of these choirbooks are now in the Biblioteca Civica and are the only manuscript sources of Alberti's creative production. In addition, three masses were published in partbooks in Venice in 1549, the first printed volume to be devoted solely to the masses of one Italian composer. He is one of the few musicians of the period to be captured in a first-rate portrait by Giuseppe Belli (see illustration).

Gasparo Alberti: portrait by Giuseppe Belli in the Accademia Carrara di Belle Arti, Bergamo

Alberti's surviving compositions are without exception liturgical polyphonic vocal music. As well as the five masses there are settings of the Lamentations, canticles, *Magnificat* and above all psalms. Stylistically the writing is confined within the limits of Italian *falsobordone* and Flemish polyphony. The psalms, Passions and Lamentations settings adhere most closely to the *falsobordone* tradition, whereas the canticles, *Magnificat* settings and particularly the masses are contrapuntal. The polyphonic settings never attain the profundity of their Flemish prototypes; Alberti seems to have been more concerned with flexible, correctly accented declamation of the words. Most of his works display a strong move towards textual clarity showing that he was influenced by current humanism. This was one of Alberti's chief merits and justifies Jeppesen's opinion that 'Gaspare de Albertis . . . is with Costanzo Festa perhaps the most important personality in Italian music in the epoch just before Palestrina'. Alberti's three settings of the Passions are polyphonic, interpreting all direct speech, even the words of Christ, in a contrapuntal texture. They appear to be the first to be written in this manner and their dramatic effect is exceptionally significant. Two eight-voice *Magnificat* settings dating respectively from 1541 and 1542 are unique in their combination of styles: they display modified double-choir writing (the two choirs never actually sing together) but, instead of being set verse by verse, as was customary in the 15th and 16th centuries, they fall into two parts, obviously influenced by the layout of large-scale motets. Alberti's role in the evolution of writing for double choir seems to have been important and influential. In addition to the two double-choir *Magnificat* settings the choirbook *I-BGc* 1209D contains four-voice psalm verses headed 'chorus secundus': unfortunately the companion manuscript for the first choir is missing, but it is evident that technique and layout correspond fairly exactly to Ruffino d'Assisi's works, which until now have been considered to be the earliest examples of *cori spezzati* (*c*1539–40). It is clear that Alberti played a leading part in the evolution of northern Italian sacred polyphonic vocal music. His keen interest in formal innovations and sonority, coupled with an awareness of humanist approaches to the text, resulted in compositions of considerable interest.

WORKS
Edition: *Italia sacra musica*, ed. K. Jeppesen (Copenhagen, 1962) [J]

Il primo libro delle messe (Venice, 1549): Missa 'Dormend'un giorno', 5vv, J ii; Missa 'Italia mia', 5vv, J i; Missa 'Quaeramus cum pastoribus', 4vv, J iii

Missa de beata virgine, 6vv; Missa Sancto Rocho, 4vv (dated 1524); Passio [St Matthew], 4vv, J iii; 2 Passio [St John], 4vv; 15 Lamentations, 4vv (4 anon.), 1 ed. in J iii; 2 Magnificat, 8vv (dated 1541, 1542); 10 canticles, 4vv; 16 motets, 4–6vv (2 anon.), 3 ed. in J i; 14 psalms, 4vv, inc.; 7 psalms, 8vv, inc.; Litany, 4vv; all in *I-BGc* 1207D–1209D

BIBLIOGRAPHY
G. d'Alessi: 'Precursors of Adriano Willaert in the Practice of Coro spezzato', *JAMS*, v (1952), 187
K. Jeppesen: 'A Forgotten Master of the Early 16th Century: Gaspar de Albertis', *MQ*, xliv (1958), 311
V. Ravizza: 'Frühe Doppelchörigkeit in Bergamo', *Mf*, xxv (1972), 127
——: 'Gasparo Alberti, ein wenig bekannter Komponist und dessen Portrait', *Festschrift Arnold Geering* (Berne, 1972), 63
A. Carver: 'The Psalms of Willaert and his North Italian Contemporaries', *AcM*, xlvii (1975), 270

VIKTOR RAVIZZA

Alberti, Giuseppe Matteo (*b* Bologna, 20 Sept 1685; *d* Bologna, 1751). Italian composer and violinist. He studied the violin first with C. Manzolini and later with P. M. Minelli, and counterpoint with F. Arresti. On the title-page of his op.1 concertos published in 1713 Alberti described himself as a violinist in the orchestra of S Petronio, Bologna, and as a member of the Accademia Filarmonica, although it appears that he was admitted to

the academy only in the following year. These ten concertos were first performed under the composer's direction at the house of Count Orazio Bargellini. In 1721 Alberti was chosen president (*principe*) of the Accademia Filarmonica, a post to which he was re-elected in 1724, 1728, 1733, 1740 and 1746. A set of violin sonatas, op.2, followed in 1721, and a further set of concertos, collectively entitled 'Sinfonie', was issued by Le Cène in 1725 – presumably without the composer's authorization as they are incorrectly designated op.2. (This possibly inadvertent duplication of an opus number led to the renumbering of the violin sonatas as op.3 when published by Walsh shortly afterwards.) From 1734 Alberti deputized for G. A. Perti as *maestro di cappella* of S Domenico, Bologna.

The success enjoyed by Alberti's concertos, particularly in England, doubtless owed much to their clarity of expression, tautness of construction and moderate technical requirements. They were among the first concertos by an Italian composer to show Vivaldi's direct influence, which is seen most clearly in op.1 in the five examples with an obbligato principal violin part. The distinction between ritornello and episode in their outer movements is a notable feature. Similar general qualities characterize the violin sonatas, which remain, however, firmly in the post-Corellian mould.

WORKS
ORCHESTRAL
[10] Concerti per chiesa e per camera op.1 (Bologna, 1713)
XII sinfonie a quattro 'op.2' (Amsterdam, 1725)
Concerto 1 in VI concerti a 5 (Amsterdam, c1718)
Concerto 1 in Harmonia mundi, 2nd Collection (London, 1728)
Miscellaneous orchestral works (concertos, sinfonias, etc) in MS, *A-Wn, D-Dlb, KA, MÜu, F-Pc, GB-Mp, I-Bsp*

CHAMBER
Sonate a violino e basso op.2 (Bologna, 1721)
1 sonata in Corona di dodici fiori armonici . . . a 3 (Bologna, 1706)

VOCAL
Regina Coeli, 8vv, 1714, *I-Baf*
Questo cuor ch'è duro ancora (cantata), A, str, 1719, *I-Baf*
La vergine annunziata (oratorio) (Bologna, 1720)
Canzonets in La ricreazione spirituale (Bologna, 1730)

BIBLIOGRAPHY
C. Ricci: *I teatri di Bologna* (Bologna, 1888)
A. Schering: *Geschichte des Instrumental-Konzerts* (Leipzig, 1905, 2/1927/R1965)
W. S. Newman: *The Sonata in the Baroque Era* (Chapel Hill, 1959, 2/1966)
L. F. Tagliavini: 'Alberti, Giuseppe Matteo', *DBI*
M. Talbot: 'A Thematic Catalogue of the Orchestral Works of Giuseppe Matteo Alberti (1685–1751)', *RMARC*, xiii (1976), 1

MICHAEL TALBOT

Alberti, Innocentio (*b* Treviso, *c*1535; *d* Ferrara, 15 June 1615). North Italian instrumentalist and composer. He came of a family of musicians that had lived in Treviso since the mid-15th century. His father was the town trumpeter; his uncle and brother were musicians in the courts of Ferrara and Munich respectively. He was one of the three young men brought to the newly founded Accademia degli Elevati in Padua in 1557 as music tutors under Francesco Portinaro. His first published madrigals appeared, together with madrigals by Rore, Portinaro and other members of the group around Rore, in Rore's fourth book of madrigals for five voices (*RISM* 1557[23]). In 1560 the Accademia degli Elevati was dissolved and Alberti went to work for the Este court at Ferrara. He remained on the salary rolls there, listed among the instrumentalists as 'Innocentio del cornetto', until the dissolution of the court early in 1598. In 1568 he prepared an MS collection of madrigals for Henry, Earl of Arundel. In an autograph letter of 1607 (in *I-MOs*) Alberti appealed for financial relief to the Duke of Modena; an accompanying letter states that Alberti was 'very poor and, what is worse, old, weak, and unable to earn his way'.

The perusal of a handful of Alberti's madrigals from the 1580s indicates that he was a composer of minor importance, whose style was conservative and serious and whose craftsmanship was above average. The final three books of madrigals for four voices, published in the first decade of the 17th century, are almost certainly collections of madrigals written 10 to 30 years earlier.

WORKS

SACRED
Salmi penitenziali armonizzati, libro primo, 6vv (Ferrara, 1594)
Motetti, libro secondo, 6vv (Ferrara, 1594)

SECULAR
Il primo libro de madrigali, 4vv (Venice, 1603)
Il secondo libro de madrigali, 4vv (Venice, 1604)
Terzo libro de madrigali, 4vv (Venice, 1607)
Further madrigals, 4, 5vv, 1557[23], 1560[20], 1582[5], 1586[10], 1591[9], 1592[14]
22 madrigals, 1568, *GB-Lbm* Roy.App.36–40; 4 madrigals, after 1580, *I-MOe* Mus.F.1358
Canzoni, 5vv, lost; cited in catalogue *FEc*

BIBLIOGRAPHY
A. Einstein: *The Italian Madrigal* (Princeton, 1949/*R*1971)
                                              ANTHONY NEWCOMB

Alberti, Johann Friedrich (*b* Tönning, Schleswig, 11 Jan 1642; *d* Merseburg, 14 June 1710). German composer and organist. A versatile man, he studied theology at Rostock, intending to enter the ministry. Dogged by ill-health he read law instead at Leipzig University, concurrently studying music with Werner Fabricius to such good purpose that Duke Christian I of Saxony appointed him organist at his court and at Merseburg Cathedral. Alberti also studied with Vincenzo Albrici. An apoplectic stroke caused paralysis, which incapacitated him for the last 12 years of his life.

Although Alberti apparently wrote much sacred and keyboard music, unfortunately only four chorale compositions survive (they are in various MSS, mainly in libraries in Berlin, and they have been included in several modern anthologies of organ music such as *Orgelmeister des 17. und 18. Jahrhunderts*, ed. K. Matthaei, Kassel, 1933; *80 Choralvorspiele des 17. und 18. Jahrhunderts*, ed. H. Keller, Leipzig, 1937; and EDM, 1st ser., ix, 1937; for some lost works see Seiffert in *AMw*, ii, 1920, p.371). He was admired by eminent contemporaries, and his surviving music exhibits several remarkable traits; with the ability to conjure up attractive counter-subjects he avoided presenting the chorales in full and never embellished them, and he was an expert contrapuntist.

In both *Herzlich lieb hab' ich dich, O Herr* and *Gelobet seist du* the first chorale line alone is stated in skilful association with two contrasting counter-subjects, giving, particularly in the former, a sense of singular intimacy. The two-movement *Te Deum* consists of a ricercare-like double fugue on the first two chorale lines, followed by another on the first line combined with an animated free counter-subject. The three variations of *O lux beata Trinitas* treat only the first line of the chorale, the second variation being notable for the fourfold repetition of the theme accompanied by its double diminution. The high quality of these works makes regrettable the loss of 12 ricercati by Alberti which, according to Mattheson (*Grundlage einer Ehrenpforte*, 1740), explored every facet of contrapuntal art.

BIBLIOGRAPHY
F. Dietrich: *Geschichte des deutschen Orgelchorals im 17. Jahrhundert* (Kassel, 1932)
W. Apel: *Geschichte der Orgel- und Klaviermusik bis 1700* (Kassel, 1967; Eng. trans., rev. 1972)
                                                    G. B. SHARP

Alberti, Pietro (*fl* 1697–1706). Italian composer, violinist and organist resident in northern Europe. At one time he was in the service of the Prince of Carignan (a small town in the French Ardennes) and in this capacity appeared as a violinist before Louis XIV in 1697. About 1703 he was organist of the monastery at Kranenburg, on the present Dutch–German border. He published *XII suonate a tre, duoi violini e violone col basso per l'organo* op.1 (Amsterdam, 1703); the only surviving set bears his signature, dated 1706. The contents are all church sonatas, and each contains between six and eight movements, all in the same key. They are stolid, old-fashioned, rather uninspired works, competently written for the most part but using only the simplest imitative techniques and frequently becoming homophonic. The part for violone, which for Alberti meant 'cello', is sometimes quite elaborate, creating a genuine four-part texture.

                                               ROBIN BOWMAN

Alberti bass. Left-hand accompaniment figure in keyboard music consisting of broken triads whose notes are played in the order: lowest, highest, middle, highest (see ex.1), and taking its name from Domenico Alberti (*c*1710–1740). Recent research suggests that, obvious as this little figure may seem, Alberti was in fact the first to make frequent use of it. The term ought to be restricted to figures of the shape described and not extended loosely to other types of broken-chord accompaniment.

Ex. 1 Duphly: 'La De Drummond'
Quatrième livre de pièces de clavecin (Paris, 1768)

BIBLIOGRAPHY
G. A. Marco: 'The Alberti Bass before Alberti', *MR*, xx (1959), 93
W. S. Newman: *The Sonata in the Classic Era* (Chapel Hill, 1963), 180ff
                                                DAVID FULLER

Albertini, Giuliano (*fl* 1705–29). Italian alto castrato. He was a Florentine, in the employment of the Cardinal and later the Grand Duchess of Tuscany. He sang in one opera at Venice in 1705, four (including A. Scarlatti's *Teodosio*) at Naples in 1707–9, three (two by Lotti and Handel's *Agrippina*) at Venice in 1709, one each at Bologna in 1711 and Modena in 1716, three at Venice in 1718–19 and one at Rome in 1729. In *Agrippina* he played the freedman Narciso, a part that makes slight demands on range and skill; its compass is *a* to *d''*.

                                                WINTON DEAN

Albertini [Albertino], **Ignazio** (*b* ?Milan, *c*1644; *d* Vienna, 22 Sept 1685). Italian composer and musician.

He is first heard of in a letter of 6 September 1671 in which the Prince-Bishop of Olomouc, Karl Liechtenstein-Kastelkorn, told J. H. Schmelzer that he need not have apologized for some apparent bad behaviour on Albertini's part, since he himself in any case had a good opinion of him. At the time of his death (he was murdered) Albertini was chamber musician in Vienna to the Dowager Empress Eleonora. He himself prepared for publication his printed collection of sonatas and signed the dedication to Leopold I, but it did not appear until seven years after his death (the delay may have been due to the cost of engraving, towards which the emperor had granted a subsidy as early as 1686). The 12 sonatas are in no fixed order of movements. Most of the opening and closing movements are adagios; two sonatas begin with a separate movement marked 'Praeludium' characterized by figuration over a supporting bass. The form of each movement stems as a rule from freely varied development of phrases – usually, but not always, the initial one – which reappear in new guises and thus with a fresh impulse. Larger sections are never repeated literally. In a few of the sonatas there are thematic connections between several (though never between all) movements. One sonata, no.9, is a passacaglia whose theme is presented at the beginning and end as a canon at the 5th and whose formal sections sometimes overlap with the statements of the ostinato theme. Double stopping appears conspicuously in the last sonata, which as a consequence consists entirely of imitative movements.

WORKS

Sonatinae XII [XII sonate], vn, bc (Vienna and Frankfurt am Main, 1692)
Intrada, allemanda, courante, gavotte, sarabande, gigue e finale, a 4, 1683; lost, formerly A-Wn
Sonata hyllaris ex C, a 10, cited in 1699 inventory of the Palace Tovačov (see Racek)

BIBLIOGRAPHY
FétisB; GerberNL
P. Nettl: 'Die Wiener Tanzkomposition in der zweiten Hälfte des siebzehnten Jahrhunderts', SMw, viii (1921), 68, 86, 160, 169
—: 'Weltliche Musik des Stiftes Ossegg (Böhmen) im 17. Jahrhundert', ZMw, iv (1921–2), 352, 356
A. Moser: Geschichte des Violinspiels (Berlin, 1923), 68; (rev., enlarged 2/1966–7), 267
A. Breitenbacher: Hudební archiv kolegiátního kostela sv. Mořice v Kroměříži (Kroměříž, 1928)
J. Racek: 'Inventář hudebnin tovačovského zámku z konce 17. století', Musikologie, i (1938), 49, 66
J. Sehnal: 'Die Musikkapelle des Olmützer Bischofs Karl Liechtenstein-Castelcorn', KJb, li (1967), 112
H. Knaus: Die Musiker im Archivbestand des kaiserlichen Obersthofmeisteramtes (1637–1705), ii (Vienna, 1968), 123, 125, 140
THEOPHIL ANTONICEK

Albertini, Joachim [Gioacchino] (b Pesaro, 1749; d Warsaw, 27 March 1812). Polish composer of Italian birth. The first reference to him as an aria composer and 'young virtuoso' was in the Journal littéraire de Varsovie of 23 April 1777. Later he was conductor at Prince Karol Radziwiłł's residence at Nieśwież, and from 1782 maître de chapelle at King Stanisław August Poniatowski's court in Warsaw. From 1795 he was granted a life pension by Prince Stanisław Poniatowski, the king's nephew. In 1796 he went to Rome, and in autumn 1803 was back in Poland, where he spent the rest of his life.

Albertini is principally known as composer of the three-act opera Don Juan albo Ukarany libertyn ('Don Juan or The rake punished'), believed to have been performed in Warsaw with an Italian text by G. Bertati

in 1780–81; in 1783 it was performed in Polish (translated by Wojciech Bogusławski), and it was later twice revised by Albertini for performances in 1790 and 1803.

WORKS
STAGE
La cacciatrice brillante (intermezzo, G. Mancinelli), Rome, Teatro Tordinona, Feb 1772
Don Juan albo Ukarany libertyn [Don Juan or The rake punished] (opera, G. Bertati, trans. W. Bogusławski), Warsaw, 23 Feb 1783; score (It. text), I-Fc; 2 fragments (It. text), PL-Ła; Pol. lib (Warsaw, 1783)
Circe und Ulisses (opera seria), Hamburg, spring 1785
Virginia (opera seria, L. Romanelli), Rome, Teatro delle Dame, 7 Jan 1786; 1 song (London, c1788)
Scipione africano (opera seria, N. Minato), Rome, 1789
La virgine vestale (opera seria, M. Prunetti), Rome, Teatro delle Dame, carn. 1803; lib pubd
Kapelmajster polski [Polish conductor] (intermezzo, L. A. Dmuszewski), Warsaw, 28 Oct 1808

Many choruses, songs, marches, ballets for insertion in foreign operas in Warsaw, lost

OTHER WORKS
Missa solemnis, d, 28 Aug 1782, PL-BA
Offertorium, Bb, CZp
Cantata on the anniversary of the King's election, 7 Sept 1790, lost
Symphony, c1797, Kd
Septet, 25 April 1806, lost

BIBLIOGRAPHY
SMP
U. Monferrari: Dizionario universale delle opere melodrammatiche (Florence, 1954)
A. Nowak-Romanowicz: Z dziejów polskiej kultury muzycznej [A historical survey of musical culture in Poland], ii (Kraków, 1966)
Z. Raszewski: 'Rondo alla Polacca', Pamiętnik literacki, ii (1970)
ALINA NOWAK-ROMANOWICZ

Albertini, Thomas Anton (b c1660; d Olomouc, 3 Oct 1735). German composer. After 1690 he came to Olomouc from Vienna and entered the services of the Olomouc chapter; in 1693 he became musical director at the cathedral. In 1696 he married Magdalena Cecilie Zindel, daughter of the cathedral organist. Although his salary was raised at the start of his activities in Olomouc, Albertini complained throughout his life of the low pay and waged continual battles with the chapter, which refused to meet his demands and blamed him for the decline of music in the cathedral. In 1708 Albertini requested special leave to perform his compositions before the Emperor Joseph I in Vienna; he overstayed his leave and the chapter gave him notice, which was revoked only after the emperor's direct intervention. In spite of perpetually strained relations with the chapter Albertini remained in his post until his death. He was probably related to the Ignaz Albertini who applied for a musical post in Olomouc as early as 1671. Thomas Albertini's son Reymund (b Olomouc, baptized 23 January 1701) was a musician in the orchestra of Count Rottal in Holešov (c1734–7) and later with Count Leopold Dietrichstein in Brno. All that survive of Albertini's extensive works are two orchestral suites from the year 1694, dedicated to the Bishop of Olomouc, a pastoral sonata for strings, a mass and a Te Deum (A-Wn, CS-Bm, Kr).

BIBLIOGRAPHY
A. Breitenbacher: Hudební archiv kolegiátního kostela sv. Mořice v Kroměříži (Olomouc, 1928), 136
A. Neumann: 'Příspěvky k dějinám hudby a zpěvu při olomoucké katedrále (1614–1780)', Hlídka (1939), 39
J. Sehnal: 'Hudebníci 17. století v matrikách kostela sv. Petra a Pavla v Olomouci', Zprávy Vlastiv. ústavu v Olomouci, cxxiii (1965), 8
JIŘÍ SEHNAL

Albertis, Gaspare de. See ALBERTI, GASPARO.

Albertsen, Per (Hjort) (*b* Trondheim, 27 July 1919). Norwegian composer, organist and teacher. A qualified architect (1943), he studied the organ with Ludvig Nielsen, Arild Sandvold and Per Stenberg, and also had lessons with Tarp in Copenhagen, Ralph Downes in London and Jelinek in Vienna. He worked as an organist in Trondheim (1947–68) and as a lecturer in music at Trondheim University (1968–72) before his appointment as director of the conservatory in the same city (1972). His music shows the influences variously of Palestrina, Haydn, Les Six and Bartók; national elements occur, but they are not striking.

WORKS
(selective list)

Orch: Concertino, op.7, 1948; Sym. Prelude, op.10, 1951; Gunnerussuite, op.11, 1952; Minor suite, op.14, 1955; Presentation, op.20, 1958; Notturno e danza, op.22, 1960; Conc. piccolo, op.23, vn, str, 1961; Conc., op.33, pf, school orch, 1969; Tordenskioldiana, op.39, 1972

Sacred vocal: Cantata, op.15, 1953; Christmas Mass, op.24, 1961; Summer Mass, op.28, 1966; unacc. choral pieces

Secular vocal: Bendik og Årolilja, T, chorus, pf, 1943; Villemann og Magnill, op.8, S, Bar, orch, 1951; Russicola, op.17, school opera, 1956; unacc. choral pieces, songs

Inst: Slåttesonaten, op.4, pf, 1946; Sonata, op.9, cl, pf, 1950

Other music for theatre, radio and school use

Principal publisher: Norske Komponisters Forlag

NIKOLAI PAULSEN

Albertus, Gaspare. *See* ALBERTI, GASPARO.

Albertus cantor (*fl* 1147–*c*1180). French musician, active at Notre Dame, Paris; he may be identifiable with ALBERTUS PARISIENSIS.

Albertus Magnus [Albertus de Bollstadt] (*b* Lauingen, Swabia, ?1193; *d* Cologne, 15 Nov 1280). German theologian and music theorist, canonized in 1931. While studying at Padua he joined the Dominican order (1222–3). He taught principally at the Dominican Studium Generale, Cologne, where Thomas Aquinas was his pupil. Although he did not create the scholastic union of theology and philosophy that Thomas achieved, he brought together the scriptures, the church fathers, earlier medieval scripture exegesis and scholastic writings, as well as much of the newly accessible writings of Aristotle and Arab philosophers. In addition his intense interest in scientific observation and experiment expressed itself in his specifically scientific works, as well as in innumerable remarks elsewhere in his writings. He rejected music of the spheres as 'ridiculous', on the grounds that if it existed it would be more destructive and unbearable than thunder, and that observation showed that the movement of the heavens could not generate sound (*De coelo et mundo*, bk 2; Borgnet, iv, 193). A *Summa de scientia musicali* and a commentary on Boethius's *De musica* are known only from an early 15th-century list.

Albertus wrote that a balance of proportions in music is delightful and a lack of it distasteful: 'there is sweetness in the ear from a minor 6th as [in painting] from much white together with a little red' (*Summa de creaturis*, ii; Borgnet, xxxv, 196). He stated further that just as the beauty of the universe consists in antithesis, so in music 'when rests are interposed in choral singing, it becomes sweeter than continuous sound' (*Summa theologiae*, ii; Borgnet, xxxii, 601). He felt that in worship singing expresses sublime spiritual joy (*Super Isaiam*, chap.5.1, Geyer, xix, 68, and, for example,

Commentarius in psalmos, xlvi.6, Borgnet, xv, 692), while, through his commentary on the *Psalms*, instrumental music stands for mortification. His view of the relationship of music to the different parts of the Mass can be seen in *Liber de sacrificio missae*. In his exposition of Pseudo-Dionysius's *De ecclesiastica hierarchia* (Borgnet, xiv, 652ff) Albertus developed its concepts of the purifying effects of liturgical chant and reading; he maintained that chant acts at three subjective levels, according to the three hierarchical actions – totally purging the energumens, illuminating the baptized to contemplate and participate in the realities of the sacraments, and nourishing the perfect through holy contemplations and 'perfecting' them in God.

The richest source of his musical observations is Albertus's commentary on Aristotle's *Politics* (viii), where his magisterial summaries are glossed with Christian texts. He held that music serves three purposes: game, purification and recreation (chap.6). In recreation, he said, men expect music suited to their tastes, whether good or depraved; here professional musicians, who have to provide a service, can be distinguished from people with real taste, whose interest in music can be 'liberalis et honesta' (chaps.2, 4; cf *Super Lucam*, chap.7. 32). Yet choral singing of music within their powers is an appropriate education for young men provided it does not weaken them for military or political life. Song is a means of expressing heartfelt feelings on special occasions (chap.4; cf *Super Lucam*, chap.7. 32, and *Super IV Sententiarum*, Borgnet, xxix, 633: 'I do not think it matters what melody you have then, because on these occasions it has to be something light'). Here he not only witnessed to an unscripted tradition, but showed that lyricism had a place in medieval popular music, analogous to the more spiritual joy of scripted liturgical chant (but cf Corbin, 80ff). He also recognized that intense joy could be expressed in gesture and music together (chap.3), and quoted Pseudo-Pythagoras's *De tripudio*, which he probably knew from Arab sources. The Dorian mode is stabilizing, he said, the Phrygian disturbing (chap.6). Glossing the term 'raptus' in a Christian sense, he found that sacred music 'shows to men a realm of innocence', and, acting like a medicine, soothes the passions through the pleasure it gives.

BIBLIOGRAPHY

A. Borgnet, ed.: *Albertus Magnus: Opera omnia* (Paris, 1890)
W. Scherer: 'Der selige Albertus Magnus über die Musik', *KJb*, xxiv (1911), 65
S. M. Albert: *Saint Albert the Great* (Oxford, 1948)
B. Geyer, ed.: *Albertus Magnus: Opera omnia* (Cologne, 1951–)
H. Hüschen: 'Albertus Magnus und seine Musikanschauung', *Speculum musicae artis: Festgabe für Heinrich Husmann* (Munich, 1970), 205
——: 'Albertus Magnus', *MGG*
S. Corbin: 'L'apparition du lyrisme dans la monodie médiévale', *Studi musicali*, ii (1973), 73

EDWARD BOOTH

Albertus Parisiensis. Magister Albert of Paris is known from the 12th-century Calixtine MS (*E-SC*) where a two-part piece (to which an alternative, simplified upper voice was later added), *Congaudeant catholici*, is attributed to him, probably spuriously. Whether this Albert may be identified with an *Albertus cantor* active at Notre Dame in Paris from 1147 to *c*1180 is uncertain.

BIBLIOGRAPHY

J. Handschin: 'Zur Geschichte von Notre Dame', *AcM*, iv (1932), 5
SARAH FULLER

Albicastro, Henricus [Weissenburg, Heinrich] (*fl* 1700–06). ?Swiss composer and violinist resident in Holland. The only information about his life is that given by Walther according to which he was Swiss by birth and pursued a military career, serving in the War of the Spanish Succession as a cavalry captain in the army of the allied powers. The designation 'del Biswang' in the dedication of his op.1 serves only to increase the uncertainty about his origins. He is however the 'Johannes Hendrik Weysenbergh, Viennensis' who enrolled as a 'musicus academiae' at the University of Leiden in 1681. He undoubtedly lived for some time in Amsterdam, where nine major collections of instrumental works by him appeared. To judge from these works he must have had a thorough musical training and was certainly no mere soldier nor just the 'musical amateur' that he modestly called himself on the title-page of his op.1. Quantz (in his autobiography published in 1755) stated that in his youth he diligently studied Albicastro's music along with that of Biber and J. J. Walther, thus associating him with two of the leading violinists and violin composers of the age. He must indeed have been a very fine violinist, with a sure command over both the technique of solo playing of the Italians and the double stopping of the Germans. As a composer too he was completely up-to-date. His harmony, often richly chromatic, is sometimes amazingly bold, and his sophisticated fugal and imitative writing is that of an experienced contrapuntist.

WORKS

(all published in Amsterdam c1700 unless otherwise stated)

XII suonate, 2 vn, vc, bc (org), op.1
Sonate, vn, vc/bc, libro I e II, op.2
XII sonates, vn, vle, bc, op.3; 2/Il giardino armonico sacro profano di 12 suonate (Bruges, 1696)
XII suonate, 2 vn, vc, bc (org), op.4
Sonate, vn, bc, op.5; no.4 ed. in Beckmann, ii
Sonate, vn, bc, op.6 o vero parte 2 del op.5
Concerti, 2 vn, alto va, vc, bc (org), op.7; ed. in SMd, i (1955)
Sonate da camera, 2 vn, vc, bc (org), op.8; ed. in SMd, x (1974)
XII sonate, vn, bc (vle), op.9
Coelestes angelici chori, motet, *B-Bc*

BIBLIOGRAPHY

WaltherML

A. Schering: *Geschichte des Instrumental-Konzerts* (Leipzig, 1905, 2/1927/*R*1965)
G. Beckmann: *Das Violinspiel in Deutschland vor 1700*, i (Leipzig, 1918); ii (Berlin and Leipzig, 1921)
A. Moser: 'Zur Genesis der Folies d'Espagne', *AMw*, i (1918–19), 358
——: *Geschichte des Violinspiels* (Berlin, 1923, rev., enlarged 2/1966–7)
J. Zwart: 'Albicastro in Nederland', *De muziek* (March 1928)
E. Refardt: *Historisch-biographisches Musikerlexikon der Schweiz* (Leipzig and Zurich, 1928)
D. D. Boyden: *The History of Violin Playing from its Origins to 1761* (London, 1965)
E. Darbellay: 'Giovanni Henrico Albicastro alias Heinrich Weissenburg', *SMz*, cxvi (1976), 1

MAX ZULAUF

Albin, Roger (*b* Beausoleil, Alpes Maritimes, 30 Sept 1920). French conductor. He studied the cello with Umberto Benedetti, and attended the Paris Conservatoire until the age of 15. He returned there after the war to follow courses in fugue with Noël Gallon, composition with Milhaud and analysis and musical aesthetics with Messiaen. He also studied conducting with Roger Desormière, Carl Schuricht and Hans Rosbaud. He began his career as a cellist, touring and recording both as a soloist and with the pianist Claude Helffer. His career as a conductor started at the Opéra-Comique, where he was chorus master for three years;

he then went to Nancy (director of music at the theatre), Toulouse (Théâtre du Capitole) and finally Strasbourg, where he became conductor of the Strasbourg Radio SO in 1966.

Albin conducts the Classical and Romantic repertories with equal ease, as well as contemporary and avant-garde works. He is a sensitive conductor, and this characteristic is also reflected in his compositions. These include two symphonies, a cello concerto, a suite for cello solo, short pieces for piano, a cantata for soprano and women's choir, and *Sonata, Cantata, Toccata*, a piece written for the Percussions de Strasbourg and performed at the 1972 Marais Festival.

CHRISTIANE SPIETH-WEISSENBACHER

Albini [Albino], **Filippo** (*b* Moncalieri, nr. Turin, probably between 1580 and 1590; *d* 1626 or later). Italian composer and musician. He came of a long-established family whose members had included painters and a royal doctor. He became a musician in the service of the court of Savoy at Turin. In 1619 a number of students destined for careers in music or the church were assigned to his care. During the next few years he deputized for Sigismondo d'India, director of court chamber music who was often absent, as a composer of occasional music for court use which he published in his op.2 of 1623. In that year d'India left the court, but Albini did not succeed him. He soon became instead a musician to Cardinal Maurizio, son of the Duke of Savoy, Carlo Emanuele I. This position, which he held when his op.4 appeared in 1626, probably necessitated his spending most of his time in Rome. His surviving music is contained in two similar volumes: *Musicali concenti* op.2, for one, two and four voices and continuo (Milan, 1623), and *Il secondo libro dei musicali concenti* op.4, for one and two voices and continuo (Rome, 1626). As well as the contents of op.2, some pieces in op.4 were written for court occasions. This volume comprises a few madrigals and sonnet settings and several strophic arias (one a setting of a French text). Some of the latter are quite attractive, but the other music is frequently stiff and overladen with embellishments.

BIBLIOGRAPHY

S. Cordero di Pamparato: 'I musici alla corte di Carlo Emanuele I di Savoia', *Biblioteca della Società storica subalpina*, cxxi (1930), 105
N. Fortune: *Italian Secular Song from 1600 to 1635: the Origins and Development of Accompanied Monody* (diss., U. of Cambridge, 1954), 340
F. Mompellio: *Sigismondo d'India, musicista palermitano* (Milan, 1956), 60
J. Racek: *Stilprobleme der italienischen Monodie* (Prague, 1965), 12, 16, 95, 137, 143, 294

NIGEL FORTUNE

Albinoni, Tomaso Giovanni [Zuane] (*b* Venice, 14 June 1671; *d* Venice, 17 Jan 1751). Italian composer. His father, Antonio Albinoni, was a wealthy paper merchant who owned several shops in Venice and some landed property. Tomaso, the eldest son, learnt the violin and took singing lessons; his teachers are not known (Legrenzi's name has been suggested). Despite his talent he was not tempted on reaching adulthood to seek a post in church or court, preferring to remain a *dilettante* – a man of independent means who delighted himself (and others) through music. As a composer he first had an unsuccessful flirtation with church music. A mass for three unaccompanied male voices is the sole survivor of this episode (the *Magnificat* in G minor ascribed to him is of dubious authenticity); juvenile infelicities abound, yet it clearly shows his penchant for contrapuntal pattern-weaving. In 1694 Albinoni had two successes in fields for which his musical training had probably better prepared him: an opera (*Zenobia, Regina de' Palmireni*) was staged at the Teatro SS Giovanni e Paolo at the beginning of 1694, and his op.1, 12 trio sonatas, was published by Sala. Instrumental ensemble music (sonatas and concertos) and secular vocal music (operas and solo cantatas) were to be his two areas of activity in a remarkably long career as a composer which terminated 47 years later with a prematurely entitled 'oeuvre posthume' (six violin sonatas, c1740) and the opera *Artamene* (1740–41).

It has been suggested that Albinoni briefly served Ferdinando Carlo di Gonzaga, Duke of Mantua, as a chamber musician immediately before 1700, but the only biographical evidence is Albinoni's description of himself on the title-page of his *Sinfonie e concerti a cinque* op.2 (1700) as 'servo' of the duke, the work's dedicatee. Albinoni more probably used the word of an honorary or even merely idealized attachment; he may have met Ferdinando Carlo on one of the duke's frequent visits to the Venetian opera houses. Albinoni's theatrical works soon began to be staged in other Italian cities, the first being *Rodrigo in Algeri* (Naples, 1702). He visited Florence to direct performances, as leader of the orchestra, of a new opera, *Griselda*, in 1703, and may have stayed there for a time, as another opera, *Aminta*, followed later in the year. In 1705 Albinoni married the operatic soprano Margherita Rimondi from Verona (or possibly Salara; she was nicknamed 'La Salarina'). In 1699, when she was about 15, she had appeared in Draghi's *Amor per vita* at S Salvatore, Venice. After her marriage she continued to appear intermittently on the stage (despite bearing and rearing six children) and travelled as far as Munich, where she sang in Torri's *Lucio Vero* in 1720. She died in 1721.

In 1709 Antonio Albinoni died. Under the terms of his will (1705), Tomaso inherited a token share of the family business (one shop), the principal management being left to two younger brothers, who had to give him a third of the revenue. This renunciation of an elder son's normal rights and responsibilities reflects Tomaso's total commitment to music by this date. From c1710 Albinoni styled himself 'musico di violino', as if to emphasize his independence. According to Caffi he ran a flourishing school of singing, but exactly when, and for how long, are not known. He can have derived little income from his family after 1721, when the business was acquired after a lawsuit by an old creditor of his father.

In 1722 Albinoni's career reached its climax. He had just composed a set of 12 concertos – his most imposing to date – and had dedicated them to the Elector of Bavaria, Maximilian Emanuel II. Now he was invited to Munich to superintend performances of his opera *I veri amici* and a smaller stage work *Il trionfo dell'amore*, both in celebration of the marriage of Karl Albert, the Prince-elector, to Maria Amalia, younger daughter of the late Emperor Joseph I (Mattheson received a glowing report of the opera from a member of the audience, who was at pains to establish that the Albinoni present at the festivities was the 'real' one, and not an impostor who had been touring Germany and eventually departed for Sweden). From the 1720s Albinoni's operas were frequently performed outside Italy, though in many

cases they were adapted or supplemented to suit local needs. *Vespetta e Pimpinone*, an intermezzo which had originally appeared with *Astarto* in 1708, was especially popular. However, Albinoni gradually composed fewer new works in both operatic and instrumental fields. He seems to have retired in 1741. His death certificate dated 17 January 1750/51 states that he had been confined to bed for about two years.

Albinoni's association with other musicians was remarkably limited at all times during his career. Antonio Biffi, *primo maestro* at St Mark's, witnessed his marriage, but no prior or subsequent connections are known. A violin sonata dedicated to J. G. Pisendel points to a meeting between the two men in 1716, when Friedrich August, Prince-elector of Saxony, visited Venice. Operatic collaborations, including one with Gasparini for *Engelberta* (1709), were probably mediated by theatre managements. Albinoni did not even pay other composers the compliment of borrowing their musical ideas, though he did borrow from himself in a cunningly inconspicuous fashion. His relationships with a representative section of European nobility, doubtless motivated by thoughts of personal advancement, seem to have been more consequential. Besides those already mentioned one may cite Corelli's patron, Cardinal Pietro Ottoboni (dedicatee of op.1); Ferdinand III, Grand Prince of Tuscany (op.3); Ferdinand's uncle, Cardinal Francesco Maria de' Medici (op.4); Count Christian Heinrich von Watzdorf, the German music lover resident in Rome (op.8); Don José Patiño, a Spanish military commander (op.10). For the name days of Emperor Karl VI and his wife, Elisabeth Christine von Braunschweig-Wolfenbüttel, Albinoni composed the serenata *Il nome glorioso in terra, santificato in cielo* (1724) and a 'componimento pastorale', *Il nascimento dell'aurora* (c1710).

His output was immense. The libretto of his penultimate opera *Candalide* (1734) describes it as his 80th. Only something over 50 'public' operas are known from librettos or the few scores that have survived, but the balance may well have been made up from intermezzos and more intimate stage works for private performance, for which librettos were not published. The solo cantatas total over 40. 79 sonatas for between one and six instruments and continuo composed in church, chamber or mixed styles, 59 concertos and 8 sinfonias (found independently of larger works) are extant. Many attributions to Albinoni in 18th-century sources are doubtful, despite their over-eager endorsement by some scholars and editors in modern times.

Albinoni's reputation has fluctuated, but is probably higher now than at any time since his own age, when his instrumental music was much in demand all over Europe, particularly among amateurs, and was ranked with that of Corelli, Vivaldi and (in France) Mascitti. The solo cantatas were scarcely less popular, though a smaller proportion was published. J. S. Bach, who based four keyboard fugues on subjects taken from Albinoni's op.1 (BWV946, 950, 951, 951a), is known to have used other works as teaching material. J. G. Walther transcribed two concertos from op.2 for organ. Albinoni's earlier instrumental works in particular were reissued and reprinted as much as any in the first three decades of the century; extracts, usually rather mutilated, abound in contemporary instruction manuals for the violin. He was less of an innovator in the field of the string concerto than Quantz thought 50 years later.

Autograph MS of the finale of Albinoni's Violin Sonata in B♭, composed c1716 (D-Dlb)

Passages for solo violin in his concertos play no structural role, which is why they are unpredictable in length or often altogether missing. However, he was probably the first composer to use the three-movement cycle consistently, and may have been influential in popularizing fugal finales which, for his purposes, he took almost ready-made from sonata models. His oboe concertos of op.7 were the first of their kind by an Italian composer to be published. There are interesting parallels to be drawn between Albinoni's treatment of the oboe (or, in half the cases, two oboes) and his treatment of the voice in arias, in respect of both the melodic idiom, which emphasizes conjunct movement in contrast to the arpeggiated manner of his writing for violin, and the use of a motto opening. His sonatas, which (with two exceptions) are in four movements, are conservative in layout.

Some general assessments of Albinoni's music have been harsh: he has been taxed with dryness and a lack of harmonic finesse. In recent investigations he has been charged with an over-addiction to certain formal stereotypes of his own devising (such as the immediate, literal repetition of the opening phrase of a period in a different key as a simple means of modulating) coupled with a lack of receptivity to outside stimuli (except perhaps in the 1710s, when he temporarily came under the Vivaldian spell); and neither of these last points is easy to refute. In compensation, Albinoni possessed remarkable melodic gifts (which kept him in demand as a composer of operas long after the popularity of his contemporaries faded), had a sure judgment of medium, and achieved a classic poise second to none among the neo-Corellians, to whom he is more akin, in many respects, than to his fellow Venetians, Gentili excepted. This equilibrium of form and content is perhaps most perfectly realized in the works of his early maturity such as the ballettos (or chamber sonatas) op.3 and the concertos op.5. In the later works, especially op.10, the same formal stereotypes, devised in the 1700s, prove unsatisfactory when used with a more sophisticated, even *galant*, melodic-harmonic idiom. Some partisans have seemed to exaggerate his skill as a 'pure' as opposed to 'applied' contrapuntist: his fugal and canonic movements, always in quick tempo, are more remarkable for their rhythmic buoyancy than for any contrapuntal ingenuity.

Albinoni's strongest asset is the pronounced individuality of his music, to which the insularity of his life may have contributed. His output may be largely mass-produced, but his ideas are all his own. If the instrumental music seems certain to survive, the same cannot yet be said of his vocal music despite its equal historical importance. The cantatas are rather too formalized for modern tastes and the operas are too inert dramatically. But, considered as absolute music, they reveal no less the hand of a skilled craftsman.

WORKS

OPERAS
(music lost unless otherwise stated)

Edition: *T. G. Albinoni: Gesamtausgabe der Instrumentalmusik*, ed. W. Kolneder (Berg, 1974–)

Zenobia, Regina de' Palmireni (A. Marchi), Venice, 1694; arias, *A-Wn*; as Il vinto trionfante del vincitore, 1717
Il prodigio dell'innocenza (F. M. Gualazzi), Venice, 1695
Zenone, Imperator d'Oriente (Marchi), Venice, 1696
Tigrane, rè d'Armenia (G. C. Corradi), Venice, 1697; arias, *GB-Ob*
Primislao primo, rè di Boemia (Corradi), Venice, 1697
L'ingratitudine castigata (F. Silvani), Venice, 1698
Radamisto (Marchi), Venice, 1698
Diomede punito da Alcide (A. Aureli), Venice, 1700
L'inganno innocente (Silvani), Venice, 1701; as Rodrigo in Algeri, Naples, 1702, add arias by G. B. Stück
L'arte in gara con l'arte (Silvani), Venice, 1702
Griselda (A. Zeno), Florence, 1703; arias, *I-Mc*
Aminta (Zeno), Florence, 1703
Il più fedel tra i vassalli (Silvani), Genoa, 1705
Le prosperità di Elio Sejano (N. Minato), Genoa, 1707
La fede tra gl'inganni (Silvani), Venice, 1707
Astarto (Zeno, P. Pariati), Venice, 1708; aria, *D-SWl*
Vespetta e Pimpinone (Pariati), intermezzo perf. with Astarto; score, *A-Wn, D-MÜs*
Il tradimento tradito (Silvani), Venice, 1709
Engelberta (Zeno, Pariati), Venice, 1709, collab. Gasparini; arias, *D-B*
Ciro (Pariati), Venice, 1710
Il tiranno eroe (V. Cassani), Venice, 1711; score, *B-Bc*
Il Giustino (N. Beregani, rev. Pariati), Bologna, 1711
Alarico, Piacenza, 1712
Le gare generose (A. Zaniboni), Venice, 1712
Lucio Vero (Zeno), Ferrara, 1713
L'amor di figlio non conosciuto (D. Lalli), Venice, 1716; as Die grossmütige Tomyris, Hamburg, 1717
Eumene (Salvi), Venice, 1717
Meleagro (P. A. Bernadoni), Venice, 1718
Cleomene (V. Cassani), Venice, 1718
Gli eccessi della gelosia (Lalli), Venice, 1722; arias, *D-Hs, SWl, GB-Lbm*; as La Mariane, Venice, 1724, with adds by G. Porta
I veri amici (Silvani, Lalli), Munich, 1722; arias, *GB-T*
Eumene (Zeno), Venice, 1723; aria, *GB-Lbm*
Ermengarda (A. M. Luchini), Venice, 1723
Antigono tutore di Filippo, Rè dei macedoni (G. Piazzon), Venice, 1724, collab. G. Porta
Scipione nelle Spagne (Zeno), Venice, 1724
Laodice (A. Schietti), Venice, 1724
Didone abbandonata (Metastasio), Venice, 1725
L'impresario delle Canarie (Metastasio), intermezzo perf. with Didone abbandonata; lib, *I-Rsc*
I rivali generosi (Zeno), Brescia, 1725
Alcina delusa da Ruggero (Marchi), Venice, 1725; as Gli evenimenti di Ruggero, Venice, 1732
La Statira (Zeno, Pariati), Rome, 1726; score, *A-Wn*
Malsazio e Fiametta, intermezzo perf. with La Statira; lib, *I-Vgc*
Il trionfo di Armida (G. Colatelli), Venice, 1726
L'incostanza schernita (Cassani), Venice, 1727; arias, *GB-T*; as L'infedeltà delusa, Vicenza, 1729; as Filandro, Venice, 1729
Le due rivali in amore (Aureli), Venice, 1728
La fortezza al cimento (Silvani), Milan, 1729
Gli stratagemmi amorosi (F. Passerini), Venice, 1730
Elenia (L. Bergalli), Venice, 1730
Il più fedel tra gli amanti (Sorietti), Treviso, 1731
Merope (Zeno), Prague, 1731, music mostly by Albinoni
Ardelinda (B. Vitturi), Venice, 1732
Candalide (Vitturi), Venice, 1734
Artamene (Vitturi), Venice, 1741

Unidentified extracts of Albinoni's works used in the pasticcios Thomyris, London, 1707, and Clotilda, London, 1709

SHORT STAGE WORKS
(music lost unless otherwise stated)

Il nascimento dell'aurora, ?Vienna, c1710; score, *A-Wn*
Il trionfo d'amore (Pariati), Munich, 1722
Il nome glorioso in terra, santificato in cielo (Cassani), Venice, 1724; score, *A-Wn*
Il concilio dei pianeti, Venice, 1729

CHURCH MUSIC

Messa, 3vv, *I-Vnm*
Magnificat, formerly *Dlb*, lost

CANTATAS
(all for S/A, bc)

Là dove il nobil Gian, in *Cantate a 1 e 2 voci* (Amsterdam, c1701)
[12] Cantate, 1v, bc, op.4 (Amsterdam, 1702): Amor, Sorte, Destino; Da l'arco d'un bel ciglio; Del chiaro rio; Riedi a me luce; Lontananza crudel; Filli, chiedi al mio cor; Ove rivoglio il piede; Mi dà pena quando spira; Parti, mi lasci; Son qual Tantalo novello; Poi che al vago seren; Chi non sà quanto inhumano
5 movts from nos.2 and 8 repr. with Eng. texts in The Opera Miscellany (London, c1730)
16 unpubd cantatas in *D-B*; 8 more in *I-Nc*; others in *A-Wgm, B-Bc, D-SHs, GB-Lbm, SA*

ORCHESTRAL

op.
2   [6] Sinfonie e [6] concerti a cinque, 2–3 vn, 2 va, vc, bc (Venice, 1700); extracts from concerto no.6 in Select Preludes and Voluntarys for the Violin (London, 1705); concertos nos.4–5, arr. for org by J. G. Walther, ed. in DDT, xxvi–xxvii (1906/R); sonata no.6 ed. in NM, clxxxix (1956)
5   [12] Concerti a cinque, 3 vn, 2 va, vc, bc (Venice, 1707)
7   [12] Concerti a cinque, 1–2 ob, 2 vn, va, vc, bc (Amsterdam, 1715)
9   [12] Concerti a cinque, 1–2 ob, 2–3 vn, va, vc, bc (Amsterdam, 1722); no.8 ed. F. Giegling (London, 1973)
10 [12] Concerti a cinque, 3 vn, va, vc, bc (Amsterdam, ?1735–6)
Sonata, no.3 of 6 sonates ou concerts 'à' 4, 5, & 6 (Amsterdam, c1708–12), anon. but identical in part to sinfonia in *A-Wn*
Concerto, no.11 in Concerti a cinque (Amsterdam, ?1717–18)
Overture to Croesus, pasticcio, London, 1714, anon. in Six Overtures for Violins (London, c1724), identical to sinfonia in D, *A-Wn, S-Skma*
6 balletti a cinque, 2 vn, 2 va, vc, vle, bc, *A-Wn* and elsewhere
12 balletti a quattro, 2 vn, va, bc, *Wn* and elsewhere
Sonata a 6, tpt, 2 vn, 2 va, vle, bc, *Wn*
Sonata di concerto a 7, tpt, 2 vn, 2 va, vc, vle, bc, *PL-Wu* and elsewhere
Violin concertos, 3 vn, va, vc/vle, bc, *Wn, D-Dlb*
Sinfonias, 2 vn, va, vc, bc, *A-Wn, D-Dlb, S-L, Skma, Uu*

CHAMBER

op.
1   [12] Suonate a tre, 2 vn, vc, hpd (Venice, 1694); no.12 (London, 1704) and in Harmonia Mundi . . . the First Collection (London, 1707); no.3 ed. in NM, xxxiv (1929/R1959); nos.10–12 ed. W. Kolneder (Mainz, 1959)
3   [12] Balletti a tre, 2 vn, vc, hpd (Venice, 1701); numerous extracts in vn tutors; nos.1–3 ed. W. Kolneder (Mainz, 1964)
[4] [6] Sonate da chiesa, vn, vc/bc (Amsterdam, c1709); later edns. as op.4
6   [12] Trattenimenti armonici per camera, vn, vle, hpd (Amsterdam, c1712); nos.1, 11, ed. in NM, ix (1928/R1958)
8   [6] Balletti e [6] Sonate a tre, 2 vn, vc, hpd, con le sue fughe tirate à canone (Amsterdam, 1722)
—   [5] Sonate, vn, bc, . . . e uno suario o capriccio . . . del sig. Tibaldi (Amsterdam, c1717)
—   6 sonates da camera, vn, hpd, op.posth. (Paris, c1740)
[6] Sonate a tre, 2 vn, vc, hpd, *A-Wn*; Vn Sonata, ded. Pisendel, *D-Dlb* (autograph)

DOUBTFUL WORKS

Teseo in Creta, 1725, cited in Reichardt and Schilling, possibly confused with F. Conti's opera of the same name
Magnificat, g, 4vv, insts, *D-Bds*
Concertos nos.3–4 in Harmonia mundi . . . the 2nd Collection (London, 1728)
[6] Sinfonie a quattro, *D-DS*
Concertos, *A-Wn, D-MÜu, GB-Mp, S-L, Uu*; sinfonias, *D-Dlb*; sonatas, *CH-Zz, D-MÜu*

BIBLIOGRAPHY

GerberL; GerberNL
J. Mattheson: *Critica musica*, i (Hamburg, 1722/R1964), 255
J.-B. de La Borde: *Essai sur la musique ancienne et moderne* (Paris, 1780/R1972)
J. F. Reichardt: *Studien für Tonkünstler und Musikfreunde* (Berlin, ·1793), 4
G. Schilling: *Universal-Lexicon der Tonkunst*, i (Stuttgart, 1835), 127
F. Caffi: *Storia della musica teatrale* (MS, *I-Vnm*)
P. Spitta: *Johann Sebastian Bach* (Leipzig, 1873–80, 5/1962; Eng. trans., 1884–99/R1951)
A. Schering: *Geschichte des Instrumental-Konzerts* (Leipzig, 1905, 2/1927/R1965)
E. Schmitz: *Geschichte der weltlichen Solo-Kantate* (Leipzig, 1914, rev. 2/1955)
L. de La Laurencie: *L'école française de violon de Lully à Viotti* (Paris, 1922–4/R1971)
A. Moser: *Geschichte des Violinspiels* (Berlin, 1923, rev. 2/1966)
R. Haas: *Die estensischen Musikalien* (Regensburg, 1927)
R. Giazotto: *Tomaso Albinoni* (Milan, 1945) [contains thematic catalogue]

M. Pincherle: *Antonio Vivaldi et la musique instrumentale* (Paris, 1948)

W. S. Newman: 'The Sonatas of Albinoni and Vivaldi', *JAMS*, v (1952), 99

——: *The Sonata in the Baroque Era* (Chapel Hill, 1959, 2/1966/*R*1972)

A. Hutchings: *The Baroque Concerto* (London, 1961, rev. 3/1973)

M. Talbot: *The Instrumental Music of Tomaso Albinoni* (diss., U. of Cambridge, 1968) [contains thematic catalogue]

——: 'The Concerto Allegro in the Early Eighteenth Century', *ML*, lii (1971), 8, 159

——: 'Albinoni: the Professional Dilettante', *MT*, cxii (1971), 538

I. Mamczarz: *Les intermèdes comiques italiens au XVIIe siècle en France et en Italie* (Paris, 1972)

M. Talbot: 'Vivaldi and Albinoni', *Vivaldi-Informations*, i (1972), 23

——: 'Albinoni's Oboe Concertos', *The Consort*, xxix (1973), 14

J. E. Solie: 'Aria Structure and Ritornello Form in the Music of Albinoni', *MQ*, lxiii (1977), 31

MICHAEL TALBOT

Albinus, Father. A Capuchin monk who provided music for hymns written by PROCOPIUS VON TEMPLIN.

Albisophon. A bass flute invented by Abelardo Albisi in about 1911; *see* FLUTE, §3.

Albonesi, Afranio degli. Italian 16th-century cleric, who invented the PHAGOTUS.

Alboni, Marietta [Maria Anna Marzia] (*b* Città di Castello, 6 March 1826; *d* Ville d'Avray, 23 June 1894). Italian contralto. She studied at the Liceo Musicale, Bologna, with Alessandro Mombelli. Rossini coached her in the principal contralto roles in his operas. With this great advantage, she easily procured an engagement from Merelli, an impresario for several theatres in Germany and Italy. She made her début at Bologna on 3 October 1842 as Climene in Pacini's *Saffo*, and then sang Maffio Orsini in Donizetti's *Lucrezia Borgia*. In the same year she first appeared at La Scala, Milan (30 December), in Rossini's *Le siège de Corinthe*, and later in the season also sang in Marliani's *Ildegonda*, Donizetti's *La favorite*, Salvi's *Lara*, Bellini's *Norma* and Pacini's *L'ebrea*. With equal success she sang in Vienna for the first time in 1843 as Pierotto in Donizetti's *Linda di Chamounix* and spent the winter 1844–5 in St Petersburg, where she sang Pierotto, Maffio Orsini, Gondi in Donizetti's *Maria di Rohan* and Arsace in Rossini's *Semiramide*. During the next two years she toured Germany and eastern Europe, appearing in the title role of Rossini's *Tancredi* in Berlin (1846) and as Anzileto in the first perf㸀mance of Gordigiani's *Consuelo* in Prague (1846). She also sang in Hamburg, Poland, Hungary and Venice. In the spring of 1847 she went to London, and on 6 April she sang Arsace in the performance of *Semiramide* that opened the first season of the Royal Italian Opera at Covent Garden. During the same season, she also sang major roles in four other Rossini operas, in three by Donizetti, as Cherubino and as Don Carlos (the baritone role) in Verdi's *Ernani*. She sang again at Covent Garden in the following season (Urbain in *Les Huguenots*) and at Her Majesty's Theatre in 1849, when her roles included Zerlina, and subsequently there until 1858.

She made her Paris début at the Théâtre-Italien on 2 December 1847, again as Arsace, and then sang the title role of Rossini's *La Cenerentola*. In November 1849 she sang in Brussels and in January 1850 she made a tour through the French provinces, singing in Donizetti's *La fille du régiment*, *La favorite* and Halévy's *La reine de*

Marietta Alboni as Smeaton in Donizetti's 'Anna Bolena': lithograph

Chypre. On her return to Paris she appeared at the Opéra for the first time, as Fidès in Meyerbeer's *Le prophète*; a year later, on 16 May 1851, she sang Zerline in the first performance of Auber's *La corbeille d'oranges* at the Opéra. She next made a tour of Spain and on 26 May 1852 she sailed from Southampton arriving in New York on 15 June, and staying in the USA for nearly a year of successful touring. Later, she married and settled in Paris. She sang a duet from Rossini's *Stabat mater* with Patti at the composer's funeral in 1868. She toured in performances of his *Petite messe solennelle* through France, Belgium and Holland, giving the first of 64 performances on 24 February 1869 in Paris, and singing the work in London in 1871. Her final appearance was at the Théâtre-Italien in April 1872, as Fidalma in Cimarosa's *Il matrimonio segreto*.

Her voice was considered a true contralto, rich and even from *g* to *c'''*, though she also sang several soprano roles, including Anna Bolena, Norina in *Don Pasquale* and Amina in *La sonnambula*. Her singing was thought by some to lack fire; nevertheless, the beauty of her voice and the perfection of her technique made her one of the great representatives of classical Italian bel canto.

BIBLIOGRAPHY

A. Pougin: *Marietta Alboni* (Paris, 1912)

G. Adami: *Tre romanzi dell '800* (Milan, 1943)

F. d'Amico: 'Alboni, Marietta', *ES*
H. Pleasants: *The Great Singers* (London, 1967)

ELIZABETH FORBES

Alborada (Sp.: 'morning song'). An instrumental or vocal composition, or concert, performed at daybreak, often out of doors, to celebrate a traditional festival or honour an individual (*see also* AUBADE). In the 15th century alboradas were played at court 'softly, to waken people pleasantly' (Miguel Lucas de Iranzo, *Cróncia*); an alborada was also performed as the first musical offering to a bride on her wedding morning, a custom which still continues. A marriage alborada from Alto Aragón (printed in A. Martínez Hernández: *Antología musical de cantos populares españoles*, Barcelona, 1930) begins with a *salute* (greeting) in a moderate 3/4 metre and concludes with a *despedida* (farewell) in a quick 2/4 metre. The term also refers to a type of instrumental piece, particularly popular in Galicia; the melody, characterized by unequal groups of bars, is performed by bagpipes and accompanied by a tambourine repeating an invariable rhythm. A similar type common in Valencia, called 'albae', is played on the dulzaina (oboe) and tamboril (small drum) and performed as an *estribillo* in alternation with singing. Ravel's *Alborada del gracioso* from *Miroirs* (1904–5), with its alternating 6/8 and 9/8 metres and brilliant arpeggios, owes some of its characteristics to the folk alborada. Rimsky-Korsakov used the word 'alborada' as the title of the first and third sections of his *Capriccio espagnol* (1887).

BIBLIOGRAPHY
LaborD
G. Chase: *The Music of Spain* (New York, 1941, rev. 2/1959)
A. Livermore: *A Short History of Spanish Music* (London, 1972)

Alboreá [albolea]. Flamenco-style Andalusian gypsy song and dance form. *See* FLAMENCO, Table 1, and EUROPE, §I, 5.

Alborea, Francesco [Franceschello, Francischello] (*b* Naples, 7 March 1691; *d* Vienna, 20 July 1739). Italian cellist. He attended the Conservatorio di Loreto in Naples and was a pupil of Gian Carlo Cailò. In 1725 Quantz heard him in Naples at a concert in honour of Prince Lichtenstein, in which Farinelli sang. In Rome, Francischello (as he was widely known) accompanied Niccolini in a cantata of Alessandro Scarlatti with the composer at the keyboard, and Geminiani remarked on his expressive playing. Berteau was reputed to have given up the viol for the cello after hearing him. In 1726 he was appointed chamber virtuoso to Count Uhlenfeld in Vienna where Franz Benda played trios with him and the count. Benda remarked after hearing him play that his only desire was to imitate on the violin the playing of Francischello on the cello. According to Gerber (but doubted by Fétis) he later went to Genoa where Duport (*b* 1741) went to meet and hear him. His date of death has been surmised (by van der Straeten and others) as about 1771, probably on the basis of Gerber's account. The earlier date is given by Köchel. A portrait by Martin von Meytens (Mytens), court painter at Vienna from 1732, shows him playing his cello; a copy of an engraving by Haid, after Meytens, is reproduced by van der Straeten (vol.i, pl.xxii). A caricature by Pier Leone Ghezzi is in the Codex Ottoboni (*I-Rvat*). No compositions are extant.

BIBLIOGRAPHY
FétisB; *GerberL*
C. Burney: *The Present State of Music in France and Italy* (London, 1771), 135
L. von Köchel: *Die Kaiserliche Hof-Musikkapelle in Wien von 1543–1867* (Vienna, 1869), 70
E. Celani: 'Il primo amore di Pietro Metastasio', *RMI*, xi (1904), 228–64
E. van der Straeten: *History of the Violoncello* (London, 1915/R1971)

MARY CYR

Albrecht. German family of musicians who settled in Russia during the first half of the 19th century.

(1) **Karl (Franzovich) Albrecht** (*b* Posen [now Poznań], 27 Aug 1807; *d* Gatchina, nr. St Petersburg, 8 March 1863). Conductor and composer. He began his musical career in Breslau, where from 1823 he studied harmony and counterpoint with Josef Schnabel. From 1825 he played first violin in the Breslau theatre orchestra, and ten years later took up an appointment as répétiteur in Düsseldorf. At about this time he produced several compositions, including a ballet *Der Berggeist* (in Russian, *Gorniy dukh*, 'The spirit of the mountains', 1825), a mass, three string quartets and a number of vocal pieces. After directing a travelling opera company, he decided to leave Germany and move to Russia, where he was engaged as conductor of the St Petersburg theatre orchestra in 1838. Subsequently he directed the German opera in St Petersburg before becoming director of the Russian opera; there he conducted the first performance of *Ruslan and Lyudmila* (1842). From 1850 he taught music and singing at the orphanage in Gatchina.

(2) **Konstantin Karl** [Karlovich] **Albrecht** (*b* Elberfeld, 4 Oct 1836; *d* Moscow, 26 June 1893). Teacher and administrator, son of (1) Karl Albrecht. From 1854 he was a cellist in the orchestra of the Moscow Bol'shoy Theatre. He was a close friend of Tchaikovsky, who dedicated his Serenade for Strings to him, and of Nikolay Rubinstein, whom he assisted both in the formation of the Russian Musical Society in 1860 and in the foundation of the Moscow Conservatory; there he was an inspector and taught singing and elementary theory (1866–89). He had an enthusiasm for choral music, and founded the Moscow Choral Society in 1878; he also produced a handbook on choral singing. His other important work was a thematic catalogue of Glinka's songs and operas.

WRITINGS
Rudovodstvo k khorovomu peniyu po tsifernoy metode Sheve [A guide to choral singing, using Chevé's number system] (Moscow, 1866, rev. 2/1885)
Tematicheskiy perechen' romansov, pesen i oper M. I. Glinki v khronologicheskom poryadke s oboznacheniyem metronoma [Thematic catalogue of Glinka's ballads, songs and operas in chronological order and with metronome markings] (Moscow, 1891)

BIBLIOGRAPHY
EIT 1892–3, 502, 503

(3) **Eugen Maria** [Evgeny Karlovich] **Albrecht** (*b* St Petersburg, 16 July 1842; *d* St Petersburg, 9 Feb 1894). Instrumentalist, teacher and administrator, son of (1) Karl Albrecht. From 1857 to 1860 he studied at the Leipzig Conservatory, where his principal teachers were Ferdinand David (violin), Moritz Hauptmann (composition) and Karl Brendel (history of music). In 1860 he was appointed violinist in the orchestra of the Italian Opera at St Petersburg and from 1862 to 1887 he played second violin in the quartet of the St Petersburg branch of the Russian Musical Society. He was well known as a music teacher, and taught several

members of the imperial family; his elementary guides to violin and cello playing were published in 1871 and 1872 respectively. He helped to institute the St Petersburg Society for Quartet Music (1872), which was renamed the Society for Chamber Music (1878). He served as librarian of the Central Music Library from 1892, and as inspector of music in the St Petersburg theatres from 1877 until his death. Like his brother, (2) Konstantin Karl Albrecht, he was concerned with problems of music education; this is reflected in several of his writings, and his expertise was officially recognized in 1872, when he was appointed to a committee set up to devise a system of teaching music in military academies. He was president of the St Petersburg Philharmonic Society from 1881 to 1886.

WRITINGS

'O ratsional' nom prepodavanii peniya i muzïki v shkolakh' [On the systematic teaching of singing and music in schools], *Pedagogicheskiy sbornik, izdavayemïy pri glavnom upravlenii voyenno-uchebnïkh zavdeniy*, xi (St Petersburg, 1870)

'Orkestrovïye muzïkantï v Rossii' [Orchestral musicians in Russia], *Golos* (1882), no.146

Obshchiy obzor deyatel'nosti . . . S.-Peterburgskovo filarmonicheskovo obshchestva [A general survey of the activities of the St Petersburg Philharmonic Society] (St Petersburg, 1884)

Proshloye i nastoyashcheye orkestra: ocherk sotsial'novo polozheniya muzïkantov [The orchestra past and present: a survey of the social position of musicians] (St Petersburg, 1886)

Sanktpeterburgskaya konservatoriya [The St Petersburg Conservatory] (St Petersburg, 1891)

Muzïkal'noye obrazovaniye v Evrope i prepodavaniye muzïki v shkolakh [Music education in Europe and the teaching of music in schools] (n.p., n.d.)

FOLKSONG EDITIONS
(all collab. N. Vessel)

Sbornik soldatskikh, kazatskikh i matrosskikh pesen [Collection of soldiers', Cossack and sailors' songs] (St Petersburg, 1875)

Gusel'ki [The swans: a collection of lullabies and other children's songs] (St Petersburg, 1888)

Shkol'nïye pesni [Songs for schools] (St Petersburg, 1879)

BIBLIOGRAPHY
EIT 1893–4, 447

(4) Ludwig (Karlovich) Albrecht (*b* St Petersburg, 27 May 1844; *d* Saratov, 1899). Cellist, son of (1) Karl Albrecht. He studied the cello with Karl Schubert and Karl Davïdov at the St Petersburg Conservatory. After graduating in 1865, he moved to Moscow, where he taught at the Conservatory (1878–89). He composed several cello pieces and wrote a two-volume cello tutor, *Shkola dlya violoncheli* (Moscow, n.d.).

GEOFFREY NORRIS

Albrecht, Alexander (*b* Arad, Romania, 12 Aug 1885; *d* Bratislava, 30 July 1958). Slovak composer, conductor and teacher. At the Budapest Academy he studied the piano with Thomán and Bartók, and composition with Koessler. He held several appointments in Bratislava: he was director of the City Music School and choirmaster and director of the church music society at the cathedral. Although his music derived from the German late Romantic tradition, he wrote in concise forms and for an orchestra reduced to chamber proportions. Often alternating chromatic and diatonic sections, he weakened tonality by emphasizing the augmented 4th, and by using oscillating 7th and 9th chords over a pedal point. Aesthetically he was strongly influenced by movements in pictorial art in the early part of the century.

WORKS
(selective list)

Pf Qnt, 1906; Str Qt, 1919; Šípková ružička [Sleeping beauty], sym. poem, 1919; Marienleben (Rilke), S, chorus, orch, 1923; Sonatina, 11 insts, 1925; Spomienky a túžby [Memories and desires] (T. Wunderlich), orch, 1932; Variations, tpt, pf, 1946; Sym. Variations, tpt, orch, 1947; Noc [Night], vc, pf, 1950; Balada [Ballad], 1v, orch, 1956; many choruses, cantatas and sacred works

Principal publishers: Tischer & Jagenberg, Zierfuss, Slovenské hudobné vydabatel'stvo, Opus

BIBLIOGRAPHY
F. Klinda: *Alexander Albrecht* (Bratislava, 1959)

LADISLAV BURLAS

Albrecht [Albright], Charles (*b* 1759 or 1760; *d* Philadelphia, 28 June 1848). American piano maker of German birth. He was active in Philadelphia as a piano maker by the 1790s. He is not listed in the 1785 city directory but his name appears in tax records, census entries and city directories from 1788 onwards. Described as a 'joiner' until 1793, Albrecht had already begun to make pianos in Philadelphia (a square piano dated 1789 is now owned by the Historical Society of Pennsylvania). From 1793 until 1824 he made instruments at 95 Vine Street, after which he retired. Albrecht made some of the earliest surviving American pianos; his square pianos (four at the Smithsonian Institution) are examples of handsome cabinet work, with a range of five to five and a half octaves (*F*' to *c*''''').

CYNTHIA ADAMS HOOVER

Albrecht, Christian Frederick Ludwig (*b* Hanover, 6 Jan 1788; *d* Philadelphia, March 1843). American piano maker active in Philadelphia. Although some sources cite Christian Albrecht as the son of Charles Albrecht, there is no evidence to support this theory. He emigrated to Philadelphia from Germany on 17 October 1822, but did not join Charles, setting up his own business at a different address (106 St John Street) during the last two years that Charles was still active as a maker (1823–4). From 1830 until 1843 his address was 144 South 3rd Street. On his death, his small business was bequeathed to his wife Maria. His pianos exhibit excellent craftsmanship; his upright and square pianos at the Smithsonian Institution, in empire style, both have six octaves.

CYNTHIA ADAMS HOOVER

Albrecht, Gerd (*b* Essen, 19 July 1935). German conductor, son of Hans Albrecht. He studied conducting under Brückner-Rüggeberg at the Hamburg Musikhochschule, 1955–8, and musicology at the universities of Kiel and Hamburg. He won the international conductors' competitions at Besançon (1957) and Hilversum (1958) and was principal conductor at the Mainz Stadttheater, 1961–3. Albrecht has been Generalmusikdirektor at Lübeck, 1963–6, and Kassel, 1966–72, and principal conductor at the Deutsche Oper, Berlin, from 1972. He was additionally appointed director of the Zurich Tonhalle in 1975, and has appeared as a guest conductor with most leading European orchestras, including the Berlin PO and L'Orchestre de Paris, and as an operatic conductor in Vienna, Munich, Copenhagen and Buenos Aires. His repertory ranges from Classical to contemporary works, and he conducted the first performances of Henze's *Telemanniana* (1967), Fortner's *Elisabeth Tudor* (1972), and works by Huber, Kelemen, Ligeti and Reimann.

RUDOLF LÜCK

Albrecht, Hans (*b* Magdeburg, 31 March 1902; *d* Kiel, 20 Jan 1961). German musicologist. He studied at the Essen Conservatory (1913–21), at the University of Münster and (1921–5) at Berlin under Wolf, Abert, Sachs and von Hornbostel. From 1925 to 1937 he held various teaching posts, organized music festivals in Bremen (1929), Essen (1931) and Aachen (1933), and was active in the Reichsverband Deutscher Tonkünstler und Musiklehrer. After a short period as choral adviser to the Reichsministerium für Volksaufklärung und Propaganda, he joined the Staatliche Institut für Deutsche Musikforschung, Berlin, in 1939, becoming professor there in 1940 and director in 1941. In 1942 he was elected a member of the Senate of the Preussische Akademie der Künste, representing on that body the interests of musicology.

After the war he became director of the Landesinstitut für Musikforschung, Kiel, in 1947, where he remained until his death, becoming professor at the University of Kiel in 1955. He also held the posts of director of the Johann-Sebastian-Bach-Institut, Göttingen (1951–61), and of the Deutsches Musikgeschichtliches Archiv, Kassel (1954–9). In addition he was editor of the periodicals *Die Musikforschung* (1948–60) and *Acta musicologica* (1957–60), and of the series Documenta Musicologica (1951–60), Das Erbe Deutscher Musik (1953–9) and Organum (1950–58).

WRITINGS

Die Aufführungspraxis der italienischen Musik des 14. Jahrhunderts (diss., U. of Berlin, 1925)
'Lupus Hellinck und Johannes Lupi', *AcM*, vi (1934), 54
Caspar Othmayr: Leben und Werk (Habilitationsschrift, U. of Berlin, 1942; Kassel, 1950)
'Die deutschen Psalmen und Kirchengesänge des Jobst von Brandt', *AMf*, vii (1942), 218
'Zwei Quellen zur deutschen Musikgeschichte der Reformationszeit', *Mf*, i (1948), 242–85
'Musik und Dichtkunst im 16. Jahrhundert', *Mf*, viii (1955), 335
'Der neue Grove und die gegenwärtige Lage der Musiklexikographie', *Mf*, viii (1955), 464

EDITIONS

with O. Gombosi: *T. Stoltzer: Sämtliche lateinischen Hymnen und Psalmen*, DDT, lxv (1931)
C. Othmayr: Ausgewählte Werke, EDM, 1st ser., xvi (1941); xxvi (1956)
T. Stoltzer: Ausgewählte Werke, EDM, 1st ser., xxii (1942)
G. Rhau: Enchiridion utriusque musicae practicae, DM, 1st ser., *Druckschriften-Faksimiles*, i (1951)
Zwölf französische Lieder aus Jacques Moderns La parangon des chansons, Cw, lxi (1956)
B. Ducis: Zwei Psalmmotetten, MAM, vi (1957)
B. Ducis: Missa de beata vergine, MAM, xi (1959)
G. Rhau: Symphoniae jucundae (Kassel, 1959)

BIBLIOGRAPHY

A. A. Abert: 'Hans Albrecht zum Gedächtnis', *Mf*, xiv (1961), 129
F. Blume: 'Hans Albrecht', *AcM*, xxxiii (1961), 60 [includes 'Versuch einer Bibliographie']
W. Brennecke: 'In memoriam Hans Albrecht', *RBM*, xv (1961), 3
W. Brennecke and M. Haase, eds.: *Hans Albrecht in memoriam* (Kassel, 1962) [contains list of publications]
B. Wiechens: 'Albrecht, Hans', *Rheinische Musiker*, iv, ed. K. G. Fellerer (Cologne, 1966) [contains an extensive bibliography]
ERIC BLOM/MALCOLM TURNER

Albrecht, Johann Lorenz (*b* Görmar, nr. Mühlhausen, 8 Jan 1732; *d* Mühlhausen, 1773). German writer on music and composer. He was a *magister* of philosophy, an honorary member of the German Society of Altdorf University, and an imperial poet laureate. His writings include an original work on theory, contributions to the current discussions of Rameau's theories which he favoured, and translations and editions of works of others. In addition, he published an important article on the state of music in Mühlhausen, two in defence of

music in the church, and one on the German language. His musical compositions, consisting largely of sacred vocal works for which he composed both text and music, were mostly written for the Marienkirche in Mühlhausen, where he was Kantor and music director. They include a setting of the Passion and a yearly cycle of cantatas (texts published in 1764), as well as two published collections of keyboard and vocal pieces intended for students. Only a sacred song *Herr Gott, dich loben wir* (Berlin, 1768) and the cantata *O Traurigkeit, O Herzeleid* (manuscript in the Brussels Conservatory) are extant.

WRITINGS

ed.: *D. A. Steffanis Sendschreiben* (Mühlhausen, 1760) [rev. and enlarged edn. of A. Steffani: *Quanta certezza habbia da suoi principii la musica*, trans. A. Werckmeister (1699)]
Gründliche Einleitung in die Anfangslehren der Tonkunst: zum Gebrauche musikalischer Lehrstunden . . . nebst . . . einem kurzen Abrisse einer musikalischen Bibliothek (Langensalza, 1761)
Gedanken eines thüringischen Tonkünstler über die Streitigkeit welche der Herr . . . Sorge wider den Herrn . . . Marpurg . . . erreget hat (n.p., 1761)
'Urtheil [in the controversy between Marpurg and Sorge]', *Historisch-kritische Beyträge zur Aufnahme der Musik*, ed. F. Marpurg and others, v (Berlin, 1762), 269
. . . kurze und unpartheyische Nachricht von dem Zustande und der Beschaffenheit der Kirchenmusik in der Oberstädtischen Hauptkirche Beatae Mariae Virginis zu Mühlhausen', *Historisch-kritische Beyträge zur Aufnahme der Musik*, ed. F. Marpurg and others, v (Berlin, 1762), 381
Abhandlung über die Frage, ob die Musik bey dem Gottesdienst zu dulden oder nicht (Berlin, 1764)
Versuch einer Abhandlung von der Ursachen des Hasses, welche einige Menschen gegen die Musik von sich blicken (Frankenhausen, 1765)
ed., with J. F. Agricola: J. J. Adlung: *Musica mechanica organoedi* (Berlin, 1768)
ed.: J. J. Adlung: *Musicalische Siebengestirn* (Berlin, 1768)

BIBLIOGRAPHY

Autobiographical sketch in *Kritische Briefe über die Tonkunst*, ed. F. W. Marpurg, iii (Berlin, 1764), 1ff
H. Serwer: ' "Wiedrigkeit" and "Verdriesslichkeit" in Mühlhausen', *MQ*, 1v (1969), 20
HOWARD SERWER

Albrecht, Otto E(dwin) (*b* Philadelphia, 8 July 1899). American musicologist and music librarian. He studied Romance languages and literature at the University of Pennsylvania, where he received the BA in 1921, the MA in 1925 and the PhD in 1931, and at the University of Copenhagen from 1922 to 1923. He taught both French and music at the University of Pennsylvania from 1923 until 1970, when he retired as emeritus professor of music. From 1937 he was curator of the university library, named the Otto E. Albrecht Music Library on his retirement. He has also held several government positions, serving on the Intergovernmental Committee on Refugees for Bavaria (1945–6), as chief of the publications section for the United States Military Government in Hesse (1947) and in Russia as specialist in musicology for the Department of State (1961).

Albrecht's historical interests include German lieder and music in America to 1860. He has also compiled several important bibliographies, including *A Census of Autograph Music Manuscripts*, an indispensable guide to European MSS in the United States, and the catalogue and MS descriptions of the Mary Flagler Cary Music Collection of the Pierpont Morgan Library, New York. He has twice served as vice-president of the Music Library Association, and from 1954 to 1970 he was treasurer of the AMS. In 1971 he was elected an honorary fellow of the Pierpont Morgan Library.

WRITINGS

ed.: *Four Latin Plays of St. Nicholas from the 12th Century Fleury Playbook* (Philadelphia, 1935)

'18th-century Music in the University Library', *University of Pennsylvania Library Chronicle*, v (1937), 13

'Microfilm Archives and Musicology', *PAMS 1938*, 62

'Francis Hopkinson, Musician, Poet and Patriot', *University of Pennsylvania Library Chronicle*, vi (1938), 3

'Catalogue of Compositions by Anton Rubinstein', in C. D. Bowen: *Free Artist: the Story of Anton and Nicholas Rubinstein* (New York, 1939), 375

'Adventures and Discoveries of a Manuscript Hunter', *MQ*, xxxi (1945), 492

ed., with C. D. Saltonstall and H. C. Smith: *Catalogue of Music for Small Orchestra* (Washington, DC, 1947)

A Census of Autograph Music Manuscripts of European Composers in American Libraries (Philadelphia, 1953)

'Filadelfia', 'Teatro musicale', *ES*

'Philadelphia', *MGG*

'English Pre-romantic Poetry in Settings by German Composers', *Studies in Eighteenth-century Music: a Tribute to Karl Geiringer* (New York and London, 1970), 23

with H. Cahoon and D. Ewing: *The Mary Flagler Cary Music Collection* (New York, 1970)

'Musical Treasures in the Morgan Library', *Notes*, xxviii (1971–2), 643

'Autographs of Viennese Composers in the USA', *Beiträge zur Musikdokumentation: Franz Grasberger zum 60. Geburtstag* (Tutzing, 1975)

Checklist of Early Music and Books on Music in the University of Pennsylvania Libraries (Philadelphia, 1977)

'Collections, private', 'Philadelphia', *Grove 6*

BIBLIOGRAPHY

J. Hill, ed.: *Studies in Musicology in Honor of Otto E. Albrecht* (Kassel, 1977)

PAULA MORGAN

Albrecht & Co. American firm of piano makers active in Philadelphia. In 1863 Charles Albright (Albrecht by 1864) entered into a partnership with Frederick Riekes and Richard T. Schmidt (1864–74), and later with Riekes and Edmund Wolsieffer (1875–6), thereby creating the firm of Albrecht & Co. This firm was owned by Blasius & Sons from 1887 to 1916, the name being continued by Rice-Wuerst until 1920. Although later advertisements for Albrecht & Co. stated that the firm was established in 1789, there is no evidence to support this claim. No relationship between Albrecht & Co., Charles Albrecht and Christian Albrecht has yet been established.

CYNTHIA ADAMS HOOVER

Albrechtsberger, Johann Georg (*b* Klosterneuburg, nr. Vienna, 3 Feb 1736; *d* Vienna, 7 March 1809). Austrian composer, teacher, theorist and organist. From the age of seven he served as a choirboy for the Augustinians in Klosterneuburg, where he learnt the organ and figured bass from the dean, Leopold Pittner. His studies in composition under G. M. Monn (if accurately reported by Albrechtsberger's pupil Johann Fuss) must have taken place during this period. As a student and choirboy at Melk Abbey from 1749 until 1754, he received a thorough training in composition and organ from Marian Gurtler, the *regens chori*, and Joseph Weiss, the abbey's organist. After a year of study at the Jesuit seminary in Vienna he worked as an organist in various provincial localities: Raab (now Győr, Hungary), 1755–7; Maria Taferl, near Melk, 1757–9; and Melk Abbey, 1759–65, where he succeeded his former teacher Weiss. His precise place of employment in 1766 remains unknown, but Melk sources indicate that he left the abbey voluntarily in November 1765 to join his brother Anton in the service of a Baron Neissen in Silesia (perhaps at what is now Nysa, Poland).

Albrechtsberger's activities can be traced from his parents' home in Ebersdorf (near Melk) in 1767 to Vienna, where he married in May the following year. From 1772 he served both as *regens chori* for the church of the Carmelites (later known as St Joseph's) and as organist in the imperial court orchestra. In addition he was appointed assistant to the Kapellmeister Leopold Hofmann at St Stephen's Cathedral in 1791, a position arranged for him by his friend and predecessor Mozart. All of these duties were set aside when he became Kapellmeister following Hofmann's death in 1793. He retained this post – the highest in the empire for a church musician – for the remainder of his life.

Albrechtsberger was a prolific composer of some 284 church compositions, 278 keyboard works and over 193 works for other instruments. His most interesting and original music was composed during his years as a provincial organist before settling permanently in

Johann Georg Albrechtsberger: portrait by an unknown artist, in the Gesellschaft der Musikfreunde, Vienna

Vienna. He cultivated a modern, homophonic idiom in the instrumental works of this period and used unusual instrumentation with special effects such as scordatura and slow movements marked 'con sordino'. The church music is more contrapuntal in conception and occasionally experimental in its treatment of the voices (e.g. alternating solo quartet and chorus, and the use of recitative). Some of his best vocal music is in the early oratorios, several of which belong to the Austrian tradition of Easter *sepolcro*. At Melk he was considered 'a most commendable artist in this genre', although there seems to have been no occasion for him to write oratorios after 1781.

After his imperial appointment in 1772 he became increasingly preoccupied with the composition of fugues – over 240 for instruments in addition to numerous examples in the sacred music. His two-movement *sonate* (slow homophonic, fast fugal), of which he wrote over 120 for various instrumental combinations after 1780, developed out of the Baroque church sonata but were intended for chamber rather than church performance. They had little influence on the already mature sonata form. His approach to Viennese church composition tended, as Weissenbäck noted, towards formal sectionalization or polarization of homophonic and polyphonic textures. In spite of their technical refinements, these late works seem less imaginative than those of his earlier years.

Eye-witness accounts by critics such as Maximilian Stadler, Burney, Nicolai and Pasterwitz leave little doubt that Albrechtsberger was an extraordinarily talented organist. Mozart, the most reliable judge of all, considered his playing the standard by which other organists were to be measured (letter to Constanze, 16 April 1789). Towards the end of his life he was recognized as 'perhaps the greatest organist in the world'.

Nevertheless it was through his teachings and theoretical writings that Albrechtsberger exerted the strongest influence on his contemporaries and succeeding generations of composers. He began attracting students as early as 1757 (Franz Schneider), and by the time of his death he was the most sought-after pedagogue in Europe. Haydn regarded him as 'the best teacher of composition among all present-day Viennese masters' and unhesitatingly sent Beethoven to him for instruction (1794–5). The fugues of Beethoven's last years, particularly op.133, owe much to his teachings. His international reputation as a theorist rested on his extremely popular treatises on composition (1790) and figured bass (c1791). In place of innovatory theoretical concepts these works contained a skilful combination of elements borrowed primarily from Fux and Marpurg. His principal achievement in this area was to formulate 18th-century theory in a language and format which were practical and suitable to the needs of contemporary instruction.

As a champion of the contrapuntal tradition Albrechtsberger occupied a unique position among composers of the Viennese Classical school. His intensive study of polyphonic writing – as shown by music examples in his theoretical works, and by his copies and arrangements – extended from Palestrina to Mozart (K228/515b). He copied most of the fugues in Bach's '48' and collected canons by other north German Protestant composers (Mattheson, C. P. E. Bach, Kirnberger, Marpurg and C. F. C. Fasch). By perpetuating this tradition into the second half of the 18th century, he helped to create the atmosphere in which Baroque polyphony and mid-century homophony fused to form mature Classicism. Unfortunately his own music remained largely unaffected by this stylistic synthesis.

WORKS
(all autograph, H-Bn, unless otherwise stated)

Editions: *J. G. Albrechtsberger: Instrumentalwerke*, ed. O. Kapp, DTÖ xxxiii, Jg.xvi/2 (1909) [K]
　J. G. Albrechtsberger: Instrumentalwerke, ed. F. Brodsky and O. Biba, DM, nos.282–91, 337–8, 408, 432, 654, 657–8 (1968–75) [B]

VOCAL
Oratorios: Oratorium III Christo Kreutz-Erfindung (Metastasio), 1757; Oratorium II, c1760; Oratorium de Passione Domini (Metastasio), Melk, 1762; Oratorium de nativitate Jesu, 1772; Oratorium no.7 Geburth Christi, 1772; Die Pilgrime auf Golgatha (J. F. W. Zachariä), Vienna, Kärntnerthor, 1 April 1781
Cantatas: Sacrificium Jubilaeum (G. Müller), Säusenstein, 18 July 1762, music lost, pubd lib (Krems, 1762); Applausus musicus, Melk, 24 Feb 1763, music lost; Mea dilecta coronato Urbano [Hauer] (H. Teufel), Melk, 15 Aug 1763, music lost, lib A-M; Singgedichte bey der Durchreise der Kaiserlichen. . .Majestäten (B. Schuster), Melk, 21 Jan 1765, autograph, Wn; Hellsteigenter Tag (U. Petrack), Melk, 5 April 1785, music lost, lib M

Latin sacred (1755–1806, mostly for 4vv, insts and/or org): 35 masses, 3 ed. in Österreichische Kirchenmusik, i, viii, xiii (Vienna, 1946–); 3 Requiem; 48 graduals; 42 offertories; 21 psalms; 10 vespers; 38 hymns; 16 Magnificat; 2 Te Deum; 25 Marian antiphons; 5 litanies; 4 introits; Compline; 15 motets; c20 miscellaneous works; principal sources GÖ, KN, KR, M, H-Bn (c160 in autograph); for thematic index see Weissenbäck (1914)

INSTRUMENTAL
Orch: 4 syms., F, C, 1768, D, 1770, D, 1772, 2 ed. in K; Org Conc., 1762, ed. in Musica rinata, i (Budapest, 1964); Trbn Conc., 1769, ed. in Musica rinata, x (Budapest, 1966); 2 concs., jew's harp, mandora, 1770–71; Harp Conc., 1773, ed. in Musica rinata, ii (Budapest, 1964); Kbd Conc., before 1792; Sonata in pieno coro, 1801
5–8 str: 6 sonate, 2 vn, 2 va, b, op.3, 1782, 1787–8, 1 ed. in B; 6 sonate, 3 vn, va, b, op.6, 1783, 1787; sonata, Bb, 3 vn, va, b, op.9b, 1791; 6 sonate, 5 str, op.12, 1794–5, 1 ed. in B; Quintuor, 3 vn, va, b, 1798 (Vienna, c1803), ed. in K; 6 sextuors, 2 vn, 2 va, vc, b, op.13 (Vienna, c1802); 6 sonate, 2 vn, va, vc, b, op.15, A-Wgm; 3 sonate a 2 cori, double str qt, op.17, 1798–9 (Vienna, 1803), 1 ed. in B; 6 sonate, 2 vn, 2 va, b, op.22, 1801–3, 1 ed. in B; 6 qnts, opp.25, 27, cited in Seyfried (1826), lost
Str qt: 4 divertimentos, 1760, 1764, 1 ed. in B; 6 quatuors en fugues, op.1, 1780, as op.2 (Berlin, 1781), 2 ed. in Organum, 3rd ser., lxx–lxxi (Cologne, 1969); 6 quatuors en fugues, op.2, 1782 (Offenbach, ?1835), 1 ed. in B; 6 sonate, op.5, 1786; III quartetti, op.7 (Pressburg, c1781–3), ed. in K; 3 as op.7, 1787; qt, 1790, ed in B; 6 sonate, op.10, 1791–2, 1 ed. in K; Sonata pro festo Paschalis, op.11a, 1792; 6 as op.16, 1798, as op.21 (Vienna, 1803); 3 sonate, op.19, 1799, 1 lost; 6 sonate, op.23, 1805; 6 sonate, op.24, 1806–7; 6 sonate, op.26, 1807 8, Wn; divertimento, attrib. J. Haydn, H III:D3; 18 arrs. of kbd fugues, opp.1, 7, Wn
2–4 str: 8 divertimentos, 3 str, 1756–9, 1767, 1786, 2 ed. in B; 2 partitas, vn, va d'amore, b, c1770, 1772, ed. in Musica rinata, xix (Budapest, 1971); 6 terzetti, 2 vn, b, op.4, 1784, 1 ed. in B; 6 sonate, 2 vn, b, op.8, 1789; 6 terzetti, vn, va, b, op.9a, 1789, 1793 (Offenbach, 1796); 6 sonate, vn, va, b, op.11b, 1794–5, 1 ed. in B; 6 sonate, vn, vc, 1797, Wgm (Leipzig, c1803); 6 sonate, vn, va, vc, b, op.14, 1798–9; 6 sonate, vn, 2 va, b, op.18, 1799; 6 quartetti con fughe per diversi stromenti, op.20, 1800 (Vienna, c1801), 1 ed. in B; 6 sonate, 2 va, 2 vc, op.21, 1801, 1 ed. in B; Sonata alla camera, vn, 2 va, vc, 1802
Other chamber: 2 divertimentos, fl, str, 1761, 1777; 2 concertinos, jew's harp, mandora/kbd, 2 str, b, 1769, 1771, ed. in Musica rinata, xxi–xxii (Budapest, 1974); 4 concertinos, harp, insts, 1772, 1 ed. in Musica rinata, xvii (Budapest, 1970); Partita, fl, va d'amore, vle, 1773; Notturno, concertino, ob, str, 1775–6, ed. in Concertino (Mainz, 1967); Notturno, fl, str, 1777; Qt, kbd, str (Vienna, ?1785); Quintetto, fl, str, 1801; Serenata, 2 ob, cl, hn, bn, 1806

KEYBOARD
(all printed works published in Vienna unless otherwise stated)
Fugues: 12 as op.1, org/hpd (Berlin, 1783), 2 ed. in B; Fuga, C, org/pf, op.4 (c1786); Fuga sopra do, re, mi, fa, sol, la, org/hpd, op.5 (c1789); 6 as op.7, org/hpd (1796); 6 as op.8, org/hpd (1799); 6 fughe colle cadenze, org/pf, op.9 (c1800), 1 ed. in K; 6 as op.10, org/pf (1802), 1 ed. in K; 6 as op.11, org/hpd (1802); Fuga a 4 mani, org/pf (c1808); 27 for org/pf: 6 as op.16 (c1809), 1 ed. in B, 6 as op.17 (1810); 6 as op.18, 1808, A-Wgm, Wst (c1809); 3 as op.21 (1802); 6 as op.29 (n.d.); 1 in 3 Orgelfugen von Kirnberger, Albrechtsberger und Gelineck (c1808)
Other works: 12 préludes et 1 fugue, org/hpd, op.3 (Amsterdam, c1781), fugue (autograph, Wn) and 3 preludes ed. in K and B; 6 fughe e preludie, org/hpd, op.6 (c1787); IIIte Sammlung von [12] Praeludien, 1790, M; 12 Präludien, org/pf, op.12, 6 autograph, Wgm (1802–3), 2 ed. in K and B; 6 préludes et fugues, hpd/pf, op.15 (c1795), 2 ed. in K; 12 neue leichte Präludien, org, 1804, autograph D-Bds, 6 ed. in K and B; Prélude et fugue, pf 4 hands (1805); Sonata, hpd/pf 4 hands, autograph, Wgm; 6 Praeludien, pf (1810); 44 Versetten oder kurze Vorspiele, org/pf (c1812); 50 Versetten und 8 Fugen, org (c1836), ed. R. Walter as Octo toni ecclesiastici per organo (Altötting, 1974), 1 ed. in K; 26 further preludes, fugues and verset collections cited in Fuchs, sources unknown

WRITINGS
(editions in Seyfried, 1826)
Gründliche Anweisung zur Composition . . . mit einem Anhange von der Beschaffenheit und Anwendung aller. . .musikalischen Instrumente (Leipzig, 1790/R1968, enlarged 3/1821; Fr. trans., 1814; Eng. trans., 1844)
Kurzgefasste Methode den Generalbass zu erlernen (Vienna, c1791, enlarged 2/1792; Fr. trans., 1815; Eng. trans., 1815)
Ausweichungen von C-dur und C-moll in die übrigen Dur- und Moll-Töne (MS, D-Bds, 1793) [holograph; incl. *Inganni: Trug Schlüsse, per l'organo o piano-forte* (Vienna, c1806) and *Unterricht über den Gebrauch der verminderten und übermässigen Intervale* (Vienna, c1806)]

Anfangsgründe zur Klavierkunste (MS, *A-Wgm*) [?autograph]; pubd as
    Clavierschule für Anfänger (Vienna, c1800)
*Kurze Regeln des reinsten Satzes als Anhang zu dessen gründlicher
    Anweisung zur Composition* (MS, c1804)
Generalbass- und Harmonielehre (MS, *Wgm*)

BIBLIOGRAPHY

EitnerQ; *GerberL*; *GerberNL*
J. Fuss: 'Über Albrechtsbergers Tod und Trauermarsch auf denselben',
    AMZ, xi (1809), col.445
I. von Seyfried, ed.: *J. G. Albrechtsberger's sämmtliche Schriften über
    Generalbass, Harmonie-Lehre, und Tonsetzkunst* (Vienna, 1826, 2/
    1837/R1975; Fr. trans., 1830; Eng. trans., 1834)
A. Fuchs: *Thematisches Verzeichniss von J. G. Albrechtsbergers sämt-
    lichen Compositionen* (MS, *D-Bds*, 1838)
G. Nottebohm: *Beethoveniana: Aufsätze und Mittheilungen* (Leipzig,
    1872/R1970)
——: *Beethovens Unterricht bei J. Haydn, Albrechtsberger und Salieri*,
    Beethoven's Studien, i (Leipzig, 1873/R1971)
O. Kappelmacher: *Johann Georg Albrechtsberger: sein Leben und seine
    Instrumentalwerke* (diss., U. of Vienna, 1907)
R. Oppel: 'Albrechtsberger als Bindeglied zwischen Bach und
    Beethoven', *NZM*, lxxviii (1911), 316
A. Weissenbäck: 'Thematisches Verzeichnis der Kirchenkompositionen
    von Johann Georg Albrechtsberger', *Jb des Stiftes Klosterneuburg*, vi
    (1914), 1–160
——: 'Johann Georg Albrechtsberger als Kirchenkomponist', *SMw*,
    xiv (1927), 143
G. Uebele: *Johann Georg Albrechtsberger, der Theoretiker* (diss., U. of
    Vienna, 1932)
H. Goos: 'Albrechtsberger, Johann Georg', *MGG*
K. Pfannhauser, ed.: 'Chronologisches Verzeichnis der Literatur über
    Johann Georg Albrechtsberger', appx to *J. G. Albrechtsberger: Messe
    in Es-dur*, Österreichische Kirchenmusik, viii (Vienna, 1951)
A. Schramek-Kirchner: *Johann Georg Albrechtsbergers Fugen-
    kompositionen in seinen Werken für Tasteninstrumente* (diss., U. of
    Vienna, 1954)
U. Thomson: *Voraussetzungen und Artung der österreichischen
    Generalbasslehre zwischen Albrechtsberger und Sechter* (diss., U. of
    Vienna, 1960)
L. Somfai: 'Albrechtsberger-Eigenschriften in der Nationalbibliothek
    Széchényi, Budapest', *SM*, i (1961), 175; iv (1963), 179; ix (1967),
    191–220
W. Kirkendale: 'The "Great Fugue" Op.133: Beethoven's "Art of
    Fugue" ', *AcM*, xxxv (1963), 14
——: *Fuge und Fugato in der Kammermusik des Rokoko und der
    Klassik* (Tutzing, 1966; Eng. trans. in preparation)
R. N. Freeman: *The Practice of Music at Melk Monastery in the
    Eighteenth Century* (diss., U. of California, Los Angeles, 1971)
R. Harpster: *The String Quartets of J. G. Albrechtsberger* (diss., U. of
    Southern California, 1975)
E. Paul: *Johann Georg Albrechtsberger: ein Klosterneuburger Meister
    der Musik und seine Schule* (Klosterneuburg, 1976)
                                                    ROBERT N. FREEMAN

Albrici, Bartolomeo (*b* ?Rome, c1640; *d* ?London, after
1687). Italian keyboard player and composer, brother
of Vincenzo Albrici. He is listed in January 1650 as a
soprano at the Cappella Giulia of St Peter's, Rome. The
same list includes his uncle Alessandro Costantini, an
organist. Still as a boy soprano Bartolomeo travelled
with his father and brother to Lombardy, then to Germany, Flanders and Sweden. All three were employed,
with 13 other Italian musicians, at the Swedish court of
Queen Christina from 30 November 1652 to 1 March
1653; some stayed on until the queen's abdication in
1654. Bartolomeo was then a court organist at Dresden
until 1663. By 1666 at the latest he was in London,
where he worked at the court of Charles II and then in
the chapel of James II. He became well known in
London as a performer and teacher of the harpsichord.
Two of his pieces were printed in the *Scelta di canzonette italiane de piu autori* (London, 1679).

BIBLIOGRAPHY

G. Radiciotti: 'Aggiunte e correzioni ai dizionari biografici dei
    musicisti', *SIMG*, xiv (1912–13), 551
J. A. Westrup: *Purcell* (London, 1937, 3/1975)
——: 'Foreign Musicians in Stuart England', *MQ*, xxvii (1941), 70
T. Norlind: *Från tyska kyrkans-glansdagar* [From the popular age of
    the German church] (Stockholm, 1944–5)
E. Sundström: 'Notiser om drottning Kristinas italienska musiker',
    STMf, xliii (1961), 297
G. Rose: 'Pietro Reggio – a Wandering Musician', *ML*, xlvi (1965),
    207
J. M. Llorens: *Le opere musicali della Cappella Giulia. I. Manoscritti e
    edizioni fino al '700* (Rome, 1971)
                                                           GLORIA ROSE

Albrici [Alberici], **Vincenzo** (*b* Rome, 26 June 1631; *d*
Prague, 8 Aug 1696). Italian composer and keyboard
player, brother of Bartolomeo Albrici. His family,
originally from the province of Ancona, included
several professional musicians: his uncles Fabio and
Alessandro Costantini were composers with important
church positions, and his father Domenico Albrici was
an alto singer who settled in Rome. On 12 May 1641
Vincenzo entered the German College in Rome as a boy
soprano. For the next five years he studied there under
the *maestro di cappella* Carissimi and in 1646 was a
paid organist there. Later he was *maestro di cappella* at
the Chiesa Nuova in Rome. Radiciotti, following a contemporary source, said that he was only 16 at the time, a
credible possibility because musical training at the
German College was outstanding and Albrici's
movements in and shortly after 1647 are otherwise
undocumented; Pitoni put the appointment much later,
between Vincenzo's stays in Germany.

From Rome Domenico Albrici took his sons
Vincenzo and Bartolomeo to Lombardy, then on to
Germany, Flanders and Sweden. Vincenzo was director
of the 15 other Italian musicians employed at the
Swedish court of Queen Christina from 30 November
1652 to 1 March 1653. During the next few years, from
1654 onwards he served in the Dresden court chapel
as a Kapellmeister with Bontempi and Schütz. In
Dresden he befriended the young Kuhnau, who studied
his compositions and his manner of playing. Vincenzo
then joined the train of Queen Christina, possibly at
Rome in 1658, certainly at Stralsund in 1660 and at
Neuburg in 1662. After further service in the Dresden
court chapel in 1662–3 he went to England and worked
at the court of Charles II from 1664 or 1665 to 1667 or
1668. Yet another stay in Dresden, immediately afterwards, was interrupted by a trip to France. When
Vincenzo returned to Dresden in 1676 he was made
director of the Italian musicians at court. But in 1680
Dresden court music was reorganized and all the
Italians dismissed. Vincenzo became organist at
the Thomaskirche, Leipzig, in 1681, and was converted to Protestantism. He soon converted back to
Catholicism and from 1682 until his death was musical
director of St Augustin, Prague.

In view of Albrici's itinerant life it seems likely that
his works survive only in part and haphazardly. The
preponderance of Latin motets may be due chiefly to the
fact that they were copied by the great collector Gustaf
Düben. In any event they are well written, with careful
regard to the text and the total structure. They are
scored for a variety of voices and instruments with
sections for solo voice, vocal ensemble and instruments
alone. Albrici's high ability shows in his cantata *Su
l'arenoso lido*, a long and powerful lament of Dido; its
flexible structure and expressive style are very much in
the vein of his early master Carissimi. Pitoni gave an
interesting report of Albrici's reputation: 'he was a good
composer, but a much more excellent player of organs
and harpsichords, which he managed with great velocity
and with very good taste of a mixture Italian and

ultramontane'. Evidently he learnt from his northern colleagues, while teaching them the styles of his native Italy.

WORKS

Mass, 5vv, insts, bc (org), according to *EitnerQ* in *D-Dkh*; another, 3vv, insts, according to *EitnerQ* in *Dlb*

Te Deum, 2 choruses, insts, according to *EitnerQ* in *A-Wn* and *D-DS*

c40 Latin motets, 3–8vv, insts, according to *EitnerQ* in *Bds*, *Dlb*, *DS*, *S-Uu*

The Lord's Prayer, 5vv, insts, *Uu* [in Swed.]

10 It. solo cantatas, *D-Dlb*, *F-Pn*, *GB-Lbm*, *Och*, *I-Rc*, *Rvat*

Sinfonia, a 6, dated 1654, and sinfonia, a 4, *S-Uu*

Sonata, a 5; ed. in GMB, no.214 (1931)

BIBLIOGRAPHY

EitnerQ; *GerberNL*

G. O. Pitoni: *Notitia de contrapuntisti e de compositori di musica* (MS, *I-Rvat* C.G.1/2, c1725), 691f

J. Mattheson: *Grundlage einer Ehren-Pforte* (Hamburg, 1740); ed. M. Schneider (Berlin, 1910/R1969), 5ff, 153ff

M. Fürstenau: *Zur Geschichte der Musik und des Theaters am Hofe zu Dresden* (Dresden, 1861–2/R1971)

G. Radiciotti: 'Aggiunte e correzioni ai Dizionari biografici dei musicisti', *SIMG*, xiv (1912–13), 551

E. Schmitz: *Geschichte der weltlichen Solokantate* (Leipzig, 1914, rev. 2/1955)

J. A. Westrup: 'Foreign Musicians in Stuart England', *MQ*, xxvii (1941), 70

T. Norlind: *Från tyska kyrkans glansdagar* [From the popular age of the German church] (Stockholm, 1944–5)

E. Sundström: 'Notiser om drottning Kristinas italienska musiker', *STMf*, xliii (1961), 297

C.-A. Moberg: 'Vincenzo Albrici und das Kirchenkonzert', *Natalicia musicologica Knud Jeppesen* (Copenhagen, 1962), 199

——: 'Vincenzo Albrici (1631–1696): eine biographische Skizze mit besonderer Berücksichtigung seiner schwedischen Zeit', *Festschrift Friedrich Blume* (Kassel, 1963), 235

T. D. Culley: *Jesuits and Music, i: a Study of the Musicians Connected with the German College in Rome during the 17th Century and of their Activities in Northern Europe* (Rome, 1970)

GLORIA ROSE

Albright, Charles. *See* ALBRECHT, CHARLES.

Albright, William Hugh (*b* Gary, Indiana, 20 Oct 1944). American composer, organist and pianist. He attended the Juilliard Preparatory Department (1959–62), the University of Michigan (1963–70) and the Paris Conservatoire; his teachers included Finney, Rochberg and Messiaen (composition) and Marilyn Mason (organ). In addition to many commissions, Albright has received numerous honours, including two Koussevitzky Composition Awards, a Fulbright Fellowship, the Queen Marie-José Prize (for his *Organbook* I) and an award from the American Academy of Arts and Letters. In 1970 he was appointed to teach at the University of Michigan where, as associate director of the electronic music studio, he has pursued research in live and electronic modification of acoustic instruments. Although his early organ works reflect the influence of Messiaen in their colourful registration and chromaticism, Albright's later works often combine a complex rhythmic and atonal style with elements of American popular music. Though his works are formally concise, he stresses the value of music as communication and the supremacy in music of intuition, imagination and beauty of sound. Through his modern rag compositions and his performances of classical ragtime, stride piano and boogie-woogie, he has been a principal figure in the revival of interest in Scott Joplin and other ragtime masters. He has given many first performances of organ and piano works by American and European composers.

WORKS

Foils, wind, perc, 1963–4; Frescos, ww qt, 1964; 2 Pieces for Nine Instruments, ens, 1965–6; Caroms, 8 players, 1966; Marginal Worlds, 12 players, 1969–70; Take That, 4 drummers, 1972; Danse Macabre, vn, vc, fl, cl, pf, 1971

Juba, org, 1965; Pianoàgogo, pf, 1965–6; Pneuma, org, 1966; Organbook I, org, 1967; Grand Sonata in Rag, pf, 1968; The Dream Rags, pf, 1970; Organbook II, org, tape, 1971

Tic, soloist, 2 ens, tape, films, 1967; Beulahland Rag, narrator, jazz qt, improvisation ens, tape, films, slides, 1967–9; Alliance, 3 parts, orch, 1967–70; Night Procession, chamber orch, 1972

Principal publishers: Jobert, Elkan-Vogel

BIBLIOGRAPHY

A. G. Fried: 'New York Premières of Two Works on Albright Program', *Music: The AGO and RCCO Magazine*, vi/3 (1972), 30

W. Salisbury: 'William Albright: a Review', *Diapason*, lxiii/4 (1972), 17

E. Hantz: 'An Introduction to the Organ Music of William Albright', *Diapason*, lxiv/6 (1973), 1

DON C. GILLESPIE

Albumleaf (Ger. *Albumblatt*; Fr. *feuille d'album*). A composition originally written in the album of a friend or patron and usually dedicated to him. The style was therefore simple and the dimensions slight. An example is Schubert's Albumblatt in G, D844, written for Anna Hönig. But the form of the albumleaf was undefined, and in time its original purpose was lost sight of: substantial pieces such as Beethoven's *Albumblatt für Elise* were dedicated to friends but no longer written in albums. During the 19th century the albumleaf became merely a convenient title among many others. Sometimes series of such pieces were published as albums: Schumann, besides his Albumblätter, op.124, composed an *Album für die Jugend*, op.68, Tchaikovsky a 'Children's Album', op.39, consisting of 24 pieces, and Anton Rubinstein two separate albums of 12 and 6 pieces respectively. In time such a piece was simply called 'Blatt'; thus Schumann's well-known *Bunte Blätter*, op.99, Reger's *Lose Blätter*, op.13 and *Bunte Blätter*, op.36, lack the prefix 'Album'. A publisher's device, the 'album musicale', consisting of a number of piano solos by different composers, was adopted from early in the 19th century; for example in Vienna (1821), Leipzig (1827) and Paris (1830).

Other Albumblätter are by Busoni (Drei Albumblätter, entitled 'Zürich', 'Rome', 'Berlin'), Dvořák (Three Albumleaves, 1881), Grieg (Albumblade, opps.28 and 47), Liszt (*Album d'un voyageur*; Albumblatt in E), Chopin (Albumblatt in E), Mendelssohn (op.117 in E minor, called 'Lied ohne Worte'), Poulenc (*Feuillets d'album*) and Saint-Saëns (opps.72 and 169). There is an Albumblatt in D, op.19 no.3, by Tchaikovsky and an albumleaf called 'Meditation' by Musorgsky (1880). Wagner wrote several such pieces, and his Album Sonata for Mathilde Wesendonk is a significantly interesting work. At first albumleaves were composed exclusively for piano solo, but Beethoven's 'Ich denke dein', WoO74, is a song with variations and with accompaniment for piano duet; it was written in an album belonging to Josephine Deym and her sister Therese von Brunsvik. Wagner composed an Albumblatt for violin and piano, and Saint-Saëns (op.81) and Florent Schmitt (op.26) wrote similar pieces for piano duet.

MAURICE J. E. BROWN

Albuzio, Giovanni Giacopo [Albutio, Joan Jacomo; Hans Jacob von Mailandt] (*b* Cleves; *fl* Milan, 1536). Lutenist, viola player and skilled composer of German birth. He apparently resided in Milan long enough to acquire the epithet 'from Milan' and to be counted among the foremost musicians and composers of that city. His extant music consists of two lute fantasias which first appeared in Giovanni Antonio Casteliono's *Intabolatura de leuto de diversi autori* (Milan, 1536) and were reprinted in collections of lute music published in Nuremberg, Louvain (both 1552) and Venice (1563). They are characterized by a continuous unfolding of musical ideas within broad phrases that subvert any attempt at a cadence. G. Lefkoff's *Five Sixteenth-century Lute Books* (Washington, 1960) contains transcriptions of Albuzio's two fantasias.

ARTHUR J. NESS

Alcaeus (*b* Lesbos, *c*620 BC; *d* after 580 BC). Lyric poet. The earlier tradition of sung poetry on Lesbos had been choral, religious, impersonal; now choral lyric faced the challenge of monody. In contrast to the impersonality of the earlier poets, Alcaeus wrote as an individual, describing in an intensely personal manner his chequered political fortunes. Many of his poems, however, were amatory or convivial, consisting of drinking-songs and after-dinner verses (*skolia*); the range of subjects even included monodic hymns. His favourite metre was the compact four-line stanza which bears his name, though he also used the sapphic stanza. Like his compatriot and friend Sappho, Alcaeus wrote in the distinctive Aeolic dialect of Lesbos.

References to musical instruments show considerable diversity. He seems to have composed an address to the trumpet (*salpinx*), poeticized as a sounding conch (Edmonds, frag.85). He once mentioned the *pēktis* (Diehl, frag.71), and in two lost poems he evidently used the term 'chelys' (Edmonds, frags.1, l.3; 4, l.9). (For both terms, *see* SAPPHO.) Nevertheless, the string instrument specially associated with Alcaeus, as with Sappho, was the barbiton. He referred to it only once in the extant poetry (Edmonds, frag.70, l.3), using the term 'barmos' for *barbitos*. The barbiton differed from the lyre proper chiefly in having longer, outcurving arms. Since it had a greater string length than either lyre or kithara, it necessarily sounded a lower basic pitch, thereby providing a distinctive accompaniment for Aeolic lyric.

WRITINGS
In *Lyra graeca*, ed. and trans. J. M. Edmonds (London and New York, 1922–7, 2/1928–40)
In *Anthologia lyrica graeca*, ed. E. Diehl (Leipzig, 1925, rev. 3/1940/*R*)
In *Poetarum lesbiorum fragmenta*, ed. E. Lobel and D. L. Page (Oxford, 1955)

BIBLIOGRAPHY
C. M. Bowra: *Greek Lyric Poetry* (Oxford, 1936, rev. 2/1967), 130ff
M. Treu, ed.: *Alkaios* (Munich, 1952, 2/1963)
D. L. Page: *Sappho and Alcaeus* (Oxford, 1955, 4/1970)
D. L. Page, ed.: *Lyrica graeca selecta* (Oxford, 1968), 55–96
G. M. Kirkwood: *Early Greek Monody: the History of a Poetic Type* (London and Ithaca, 1974), 53–99

For further bibliography *see* GREECE, §1.

WARREN ANDERSON

Alcaide, Tomáz (de Aquino Carmelo) (*b* Estremoz, 16 Feb 1901; *d* Lisbon, 9 Nov 1967). Portuguese tenor. He studied in Portugal and in Milan (under Franco Ferrara). His beautiful lyric voice was flexible, with easy high notes and excellent breath control. He was a distinguished actor, careful of minute detail in costume, stage properties and dramatic truth. He sang leading roles in about 30 operas (most frequently *Rigoletto*, *Faust*, *Les pêcheurs de perles*, *Manon*, *La bohème* and *Tosca*), mainly between 1925 and 1940, at La Scala (début 1930), the Paris Opéra, La Monnaie, Brussels, the Vienna Staatsoper, and at the Salzburg Festival. From 1963 he produced for the Portuguese National Opera Company in Lisbon. He wrote his memoirs, *Um cantor no palco e na vida* (Lisbon, 1961).

JOÃO DE FREITAS BRANCO

Alcaraz, Alfonso Flores d'. *See* FLORES, ALFONSO.

Alcarotto [Alcarotti, Algarotti], **Giovanni Francesco** (*b* Novara, *c*1536; *d* 8 May 1596). Italian composer. He spent his early years in Rome. Having taken orders he served at S Stefano, Novara, and S Giovanni Battista, Milan, before going to Como in about 1567 as cathedral organist. After three years he returned to Novara where he served as a canon in the cathedral. In 1587–9 he travelled to the Holy Land; his account of this journey, *Del viaggio in Terra Santa*, includes some description of musical culture.

WORKS
Il primo libro de madrigali, 5, 6vv (Venice, 1567)
Il secondo libro di madrigali, 5, 6vv, con 2 dialoghi, 8vv (Venice, 1569)
Lamentationes Ieremiae, cum responsoriis, antiphonis et cantico Zachariae psalmoque Miserere, 5vv (Milan, 1570)

WRITINGS
Del viaggio in Terra Santa (Novara, 1596)

BIBLIOGRAPHY
M. Longhetti and O. A. Tajetti: *Appunti per una storia musicale di Como I* (Como, 1967)
L. Sante Colonna: 'Alcarotti, Giovanni Francesco', *MGG*

GLENN WATKINS

Alcedo [Alzedo], **José Bernardo** (*b* Lima, 20 Aug 1788; *d* Lima, 28 Dec 1878). Peruvian composer. He received his musical education in the convents of S Agustín and S Domingo of Lima, as was customary during the viceregal period. Thus from the beginning of his career he inclined towards sacred music. In 1821 he took part in a contest for the composition of a national march. Thanks to General San Martín's enthusiasm his work was selected and it soon became the Peruvian national anthem. As a result Alcedo has not suffered the oblivion of some of his contemporaries. A strong supporter of the independence movement, he served in the army as *músico mayor* (1823–8) and was stationed in Chile. There he remained, providing music for Santiago Cathedral (1829–41) and becoming *maestro de capilla* at the cathedral in 1846. On his return to Peru in 1864 he was appointed general director of the army bands.

In his treatise *Filosofía elemental de la música* (Lisbon, 1869) he praised his contemporary musicians and wrote enthusiastically about the folksongs of highland Peru. Alcedo is an important representative of the transitional period from the viceroyalty to the republic, when cultural life was not fundamentally altered. He wrote numerous masses, motets, villancicos and liturgical pieces for all occasions. Some of his religious works were criticized as being 'operatic rhapsodies' because they were sung in Spanish and not in Latin. Alcedo interpreted such a view as an overt opposition to the contemporary style.

BIBLIOGRAPHY
R. Palma: 'La tradición del himno nacional', *Tradiciones peruanas*, iv (Madrid, 1932), 146
E. Pereira Salas: *Los orígenes del arte musical en Chile* (Santiago, 1941), 146ff
R. Barbacci: 'Apuntes para un diccionario biográfico musical peruano', *Fenix: revista de la Biblioteca nacional de Lima*, vi (1949), 415
C. Raygada: *Historia crítica del himno nacional* (Lima, 1954), 15–105
——: 'Guia Musical del Peru', *Fenix: revista de la Biblioteca nacional de Lima*, xii (1956–7), 20

R. Stevenson: 'Homenaje a José Bernardo Alcedo (1788–1878)',
Boletín interamericano de música, lxxx (Washington, 1971), 3
CÉSAR ARRÓSPIDE DE LA FLOR

Alcman (*fl c*630 BC). Lyric poet, possibly a native of
Sardis in Lydia. He spent his entire professional life in
Sparta. This city was then startlingly different from the
grim barracks state that it had been and would again
become: its citizens cultivated art, poetry, music and the
dance with intensity and brilliance. The poet himself
comments on this: 'To play well upon the lyre weighs
evenly with the steel', i.e. military valour (Edmonds,
frag.62).

As the trainer of a choir of girls who sang and danced
at Spartan religious festivals, Alcman wrote maiden-
songs (*partheneia*) which brought him particular fame.
Extensive portions of one of these have survived; the
lines re-create with great immediacy the half-humorous,
half-impassioned rivalry of his young choristers. For
solo performance he composed proöimia, preludes to
the recitation of Homeric poetry (*see* TERPANDER); and
several vivid fragments of amatory verse also survive.
He describes the sleep of nature in a passage remarkable
for its subtly musical gradations of vowel and consonant
(frag.36).

Alcman referred to himself as a professional performer on the kithara, and characterized its clear, sharp
sound (frag.37 82). But he also twice mentioned aulos
playing (frag.79 80), with specific reference to its associations with Asia Minor. In one passage (frag. 143) he
spoke of the many-stringed Asiatic *magadis*. According
to Pseudo-Plutarch (*De musica* xiv = frag.83), he described Apollo himself as playing the aulos; the ascription may be evidence of an early desire for a native
Dorian tradition in which the foreign aulos has gained
acceptance.

BIBLIOGRAPHY

J. M. Edmonds, ed. and trans.: *Lyra graeca*, i (London and Cambridge, Mass., 1922, 5/1963), 44–135
C. M. Bowra: *Greek Lyric Poetry* (Oxford, 1936, rev. 2/1967), 16–73
D. L. Page, ed.: *Alcman: the Partheneion* (Oxford, 1951)
——: *Poetae melici graeci* (Oxford, 1962), 2–91
D. A. Campbell, ed.: *Greek Lyric Poetry* (London and New York, 1967), 18ff, 192ff
D. L. Page, ed.: *Lyrica graeca selecta* (Oxford, 1968), 1ff

For further bibliography, *see* GREECE, §I.

WARREN ANDERSON

Alcock, John (i) (*b* London, 11 April 1715; *d* Lichfield,
23 Feb 1806). English organist and composer, father of
John Alcock (ii). He was a chorister of St Paul's
Cathedral when, in his own words (*GB-Lcm* 1189), he
and Boyce were 'Schoolfellows and Bedfellows' under
Charles King. Afterwards he was apprenticed to John
Stanley. In the early years of the 18th century, growth
in the number of organs in large provincial parish
churches afforded new professional opportunities, and
Alcock is an early example of an organist who reached a
cathedral position through posts in parish churches – in
his case St Andrew's, Plymouth (1737), and St
Laurence, Reading (1742). He was admitted vicar-
choral and organist of Lichfield Cathedral in January
1750. He took the BMus degree at Oxford in 1755 and
the DMus there in 1766. The cathedral documents fail
to make clear exactly when he ceased to be organist, but
this was certainly by September 1765. By the cathedral
statutes, the organist held a place as vicar-choral, which
constituted a freehold, and this Alcock continued to

hold for the rest of his life, living in the cathedral close
and doing duty in the choir. He was organist of Sutton
Coldfield parish church, Warwickshire, from 1761 to
1786 (part of this time while still organist of Lichfield
Cathedral), and of Tamworth parish church from 1766
to 1790. He was also private organist to the Earl of
Donegal.

In the dedication of his Service in E minor in 1753
Alcock stated that sometimes only one priest vicar and
one lay vicar attended the cathedral services, and he also
alluded to ridiculous criticism of his organ accompaniments. In 1758 trouble arose between him and the men
of the choir, who accused him of mockery and of 'splen-
etic tricks upon the organ to expose or confound the
performers'. Alcock's fiery temperament is revealed in
his semi-autobiographical novel, *The Life of Miss Fanny
Brown* (published pseudonymously, under the name of
John Piper, in 1761), in which these events are described. That Alcock considered himself hard done by
as a result of his conditions of work at Lichfield is
abundantly clear from his argumentative preface to his
anthems published in 1771. It is possible that, far away
in the Midlands yet having troubled to take a doctorate
(for what it was then worth), he felt he lacked the status
which his contemporary Boyce and others enjoyed. For
that reason, perhaps, it was a gratification to him when
visiting London in his old age to be invited to join the
Musical Graduates' Meeting established by Samuel
Arnold (whom he helped with his *Cathedral Music*,
1790).

In the course of his work Alcock became impressed
by the 'numberless Mistakes' in manuscript copies of
older cathedral music, and in 1752 he issued a pros-
pectus of a plan for a quarterly publication of a service
engraved in score. He proposed to start with Tallis's
Dorian Mode Service, Byrd's Short Service and
Gibbons's in F (all of which it is interesting to note that
he proposed to transpose up a tone), and working
through to Charles King. Apparently for lack of
response nothing came of this, though Alcock issued his
own Service in E minor as a specimen of the engraving.
When he heard of Greene's proposal to publish an
anthology of cathedral music he presented him with the
materials already gathered. Greene's plan, as is well
known, eventually came to fruition in Boyce's *Cathedral
Music*. Alcock had antiquarian interests, scoring for
himself some of Tallis's and Byrd's Latin church music
and Morley's canzonets and balletts (*Lbm* Add.23624
and *Lcm* 952–3). He once owned the Tregian
anthology, the 'Sambrooke MS' (now *US-NYp* Drexel
4302). It is to him that the story of Byrd's contact with
Philippe de Monte is owed.

Alcock's own music has a good general level of competence in an idiom adhering to that prevailing in his
early manhood. No doubt his instrumental music
derived from Stanley, but without the master's freshness
and vigour. His anthems are in similar mould to those of
Greene, whose general style they share, and in fact in his
aforementioned preface he felt it necessary to anticipate
possible charges of plagiarism from both Croft and
Greene. But only the Service in E minor, of all his
church music, ever attained any currency, and this is too
lacking in character to have survived. As published it is
a slightly revised form of the original composed in
1732. Alcock's output includes several large-scale
anthems with orchestra, including *We will rejoice*,
which he contributed to the Worcester Music Meeting

of 1773. He cultivated the art of catch and canon writing, and won Catch Club prizes in 1770, 1772 and 1778.

In connection with the organ accompaniment to cathedral music, Alcock made some remarks that are worth mentioning. To the anthem *Unto thee have I cried* he supplied an organ part in full (virtually a short score), in order to prevent people, when the vocal bass part rests, from 'keeping a continual Roaring upon the Full-Organ, by striking Chords, or, at least, Octaves, with the Left-hand, to every Note'. And in relation to his E minor Service he said:

As in *Cathedral Music* the usual Method is to play the *Treble* [voice-part] uppermost, I have left out those *Figures* which are of Course expressed in that *Part* . . . they being quite unnecessary . . . [In verses] the *Notes* in the upper *Parts* [are] play'd just as they are wrote, (except when the *Contra-Tenor*, and *Tenor Parts* are uppermost, which are often performed eight Notes above) and not as in *Through Bass*, which is the Reason why I have not *figured* most of the *Verses*.

WORKS
(printed works published in London unless otherwise stated)

SACRED VOCAL

A Morning [Communion] and Evening Service, e, 3–6vv, org, 1732 (1753) [with important ded.]

Six and Twenty Select Anthems . . . a Burial Service . . . and part of . . . the 150th Psalm, 1–8vv, org, 1732–71 (1771 [with preface], 2/ c1775)

Miserere, 4vv, 1756 (Lichfield and London, 1771)

3 anthems, 1778–9, in Six New Anthems, 2–4vv, 2 ob, bn, org (c1790) [remainder by John Alcock (ii)]

Chants and psalm tunes in: Psalmody, a Collection of Psalm Tunes . . . with Several Festival Hymns (Reading, ?1749); Divine Harmony (Birmingham, 1752); The Pious Soul's Heavenly Exercise (1756) [with preface]; The Harmony of Sion (1779, 2/1816); The Harmony of Jerusalem (1801)

Services, *GB-Lsp*, *LF*: Verse Service, Bb, 1771; Third Service, F, 1788; services in C, Eb, a; setting of Commandments, etc

Anthems: Laudate Dominum, double choir, orch, 1754, *LF* [rev. 1771 as We will rejoice]; Blessed is he, vv, orch, 1761, *Ob* [rev. 1776 as O praise the Lord]; The Ways of Sion, double choir, orch, 1766, *Ob* [rev. from verse anthem in Six and Twenty Select Anthems]; Sing unto the Lord, vv, orch, 1776, *LF*; Behold how good, 1785, *LF*; Almighty and everlasting God, 1789, *LF*; Why do the heathen, 1793, *Lcm*; Let every Soul, 1794; Lord, teach us, 1798, *LF*

OTHER WORKS

Six Suite's of Easy Lessons . . . with a Trumpet Piece, hpd (1741, 2/1742)

Twelve English Songs with a Recitativo and Duet out of . . . Rosamond, 1v, fl, bc (1743) [duet acc. vn, bc]

Six Concerto's in Seven Parts [2 fl, 2 ob, bn], 4 vn, va, vc, bc (1750)

Ten Voluntaries, org/hpd, i (1774); 4 ed. in *Tallis to Wesley*, xxiii (1961)

Harmonia Festi, or a Collection of Canons . . . Glees and Catches, mostly 4–5vv (Lichfield, 1791)

Songs, catches, canons, glees and kbd works pubd singly and in contemporary anthologies

Attend, harmonious saint (J. Addison), ode, *Ob* [BMus exercise 1755]; Two constant hearts, wedding ode, 1766, *Ob*; submissions to Noblemen and Gentlemen's Catch Club competitions, 1769–86, *Lbm*, *US-Bp*, *CA*

Numerous works cited in preface to Six and Twenty . . . Anthems, 1771, now lost, incl. most of the opera Rosamond, 6 sonatas, 2 fl/vn, bc, All creatures breathing on the earth, ode, ?1766; various items in White, also lost

ed.: Byrd: Diliges Dominum (1770); Fifty Select Portions from The Singing Psalms [in verse, after Merrick] (Reading, ?1749, 2/1793)

BIBLIOGRAPHY
'Eugenius': 'Biographical Sketch of Dr. Alcock', *Monthly Mirror*, iv (1797), 137

Obituary, *Gentleman's Magazine*, lxxvi (1806), 286, 377

White: *A Catalogue of the . . . Library . . . of the Rev. John Parker* (London, 1813) [incl. details of Alcock's collection]

H. D. Johnstone: 'The Genesis of Boyce's "Cathedral Music" ', *ML*, lvi (1975), 26

P. Marr: 'John Alcock and Fanny Brown', *MT*, cxviii (1977), 118

WATKINS SHAW (with PETER MARR)

Alcock, John (ii) (*b* Plymouth, baptized 28 Jan 1740; *d* Walsall, buried 27 March 1791). English organist and composer, eldest son of John Alcock (i). As a chorister under his father at Lichfield Cathedral, he deputized for him from the age of 12, and from 1758 to 1768 he was organist and master of the song school at Newark. In 1766 father and son both went to Oxford, the former to take the DMus degree and the latter the BMus degree which he gained with a setting of Pope's *Messiah* (in *GB-Ob*). His final appointment, at St Matthew's, Walsall, followed in 1773, not long after his father had opened a new organ there. His published compositions include church music, songs, cantatas, together with convivial and instrumental music (including a duet for two bassoons or cellos). A volume of anecdotes, *The Instructive and Entertaining Companion* (Wolverhampton, 1779; ?unique copy in *US-U*), shows that he had inherited some of his father's literary propensities.

PETER MARR

Alcock, Sir Walter (Galpin) (*b* Edenbridge, 29 Dec 1861; *d* Salisbury, 11 Sept 1947). One of the most able English cathedral organists of his day, Alcock had the unique distinction of having played in Westminster Abbey at the coronation of three English kings: Edward VII, George V and George VI. After studying under Sullivan and Stainer, he was successively organist at the Chapel Royal, assistant to Frederick Bridge at the Abbey, and then organist of Salisbury Cathedral for 30 years (from 1917 until his death). Much in demand as a recitalist, he was one of the famous ABC trio (Alcock, Thalben-Ball and G. D. Cunningham) who jointly opened the BBC concert hall organ in the early 1930s. H. C. Colles wrote of 'his finished technique, cleanness of phrasing and impeccable taste'; and up to the age of 80 he continued to play with the vigour of a man half his age. His 1930 recording of Bach's Fantasia and Fugue in C minor was issued on LP in 1970. He had considerable influence as a teacher at the Royal College of Music and composed a number of organ and choral works, now rarely performed. He received an MVO after the coronation of George V and was knighted in 1933.

STANLEY WEBB

Alcorta, Amancio (*b* Santiago del Estero, 16 Aug 1805; *d* Buenos Aires, 3 May 1862). Argentinian composer. He studied harmony, the violin and the flute under Cambeses at the Colegio de Monserrat, Córdoba. A competent violinist, he met most of the leading composers of the time. He also distinguished himself as a scholar, Latinist and economist: he held important state posts in Argentina. His compositions, of recognized sensitivity, consisted in the main of salon pieces, published in two volumes as *Colección de composiciones para piano* (Paris, 1869–83). In addition he produced a number of songs to his own texts, and some religious works with organ accompaniment. With Alberdi and Esnaola he was one of the pioneers of Argentinian music.

SUSANA SALGADO

Alcuin [(Flaccus) Albinus] (*b* Northumbria, *c*735; *d* Tours, 19 May 804). Scholar, writer and poet. He was a counsellor and cultural adviser to Charlemagne sporadically from *c*780 and permanently from 793. Alcuin was educated at and spent most of his life in York, with at least two journeys to Rome; at the end of his life he was abbot of the prestigious monastery of St Martin in Tours.

There is some reason to believe that he wrote on music. An anonymous 9th-century *vita* relates that at the request of Charlemagne he wrote 'a most useful book on the Holy Trinity, and also on rhetoric, dialectic and music' (Monumenta Germaniae Historica, Scriptores, xv/1, 194), and a work on music by him is listed in a 9th-century library catalogue from Fulda Abbey. There is no way of knowing, however, what the contents of such a work may have been, for it is never cited by subsequent authors; this fact makes its existence extremely doubtful. At any rate, the short work on the church modes (*GS*, i, 26–7) under the title *Musica* has no claim to authenticity. The ascription to Alcuin comes from one MS only, *A-Wn* Cpv 2269, of the 13th century (of which Gerbert used a good 16th-century copy, Cpv 5271) in which it is accompanied by works on arithmetic and astronomy also attributed to Alcuin in this MS but known to be by other authors. There are at least 15 other MS versions of the work on the modes, most of them earlier than the Vienna MS, but none ascribed to Alcuin; nevertheless, the obvious conclusion, that all versions derive from the earliest one, in chapter 8, 'De octo tonis', of Aurelian of Réôme's *Musica disciplina*, may be quite incorrect, since textual analysis indicates the possibility of a common Carolingian ancestor to Aurelian and 'Alcuin'.

It was suggested by Eitner that Alcuin wrote a sequence to St Michael, *Summi regis archangele Michahel*, ascribed to him in *D-TRs* 1285 and in at least three other German MSS of the 11th century. His authorship appears unlikely in view of the usually accepted date for the sequence. Szövérffy gave a list of ten hymn texts by Alcuin, but whether their melodies are Carolingian is another matter.

When the history of Carolingian liturgy has been fully investigated, Alcuin will certainly occupy an important place. He is credited, for example, with introducing the feast of All Saints and the chanting of the creed at Mass into the Frankish (Gallico-Roman) rite.

BIBLIOGRAPHY

EitnerQ

J. Szövérffy: *Die Annalen der lateinischen Hymnendichtung* (Berlin, 1964)

LAWRENCE GUSHEE

Alda [Davies], **Frances (Jeanne)** (*b* Christchurch, 31 May 1883; *d* Venice, 18 Sept 1952). New Zealand soprano. After the death of her parents, she was brought up by her maternal grandparents in Australia. Her first engagements were in light opera at Melbourne. She then went to Paris and studied with Marchesi, who suggested that she adopt the name Alda; she also arranged Alda's début as Manon at the Opéra-Comique in 1904. After successful appearances at the Monnaie in Brussels (1905), Covent Garden (1906) and La Scala (1908), where she met Toscanini and Gatti-Cassazza, she was engaged by the Metropolitan (début, December 1908), where she sang until her retirement in 1930. In 1908 Gatti-Cassazza left La Scala to become director of the Metropolitan; he married Alda in 1910. Her pure, lyrical voice, technically almost faultless, was ideally suited to such roles as Gilda, Violetta, Desdemona, Manon (Massenet), Louise, Mimì and Cio-Cio-San. She created the leading soprano roles in Damrosch's *Cyrano de Bergerac*, Victor Herbert's *Madeleine* and Henry Hadley's *Cleopatra's Night*. She is well represented on record.

BIBLIOGRAPHY

F. Alda: *Men, Women and Tenors* (Boston, 1937)

A. Favia-Artsay: 'Frances Alda', *Record Collector*, vi (1951), 228 [with discography]

ALAN BLYTH

Aldana, José Manuel (*b* Mexico City, 1758; *d* Mexico City, 7 Feb 1810). Mexican violinist and composer. As a boy, he studied at the Mexico City Cathedral Colegio de Infantes, a choir school where Nicolás Gil de la Torre taught him the violin. On 27 January 1775 the cathedral authorities appointed him a violinist in the cathedral orchestra at 200 pesos annually; on 12 January 1784 his yearly salary was raised from 300 to 400 pesos.

In 1786 he was second violinist of the theatre orchestra at the Mexico City Coliseo, a post that conflicted with his cathedral duties to such an extent that on 9 January 1788 the chapter asked him to resign one post or the other. Choosing the Coliseo, he was in the 1790–91 season promoted to leader of the orchestra. In 1808 he headed the Mexico City choir school while still continuing as leader at the Coliseo.

A critic writing in the 18 December 1806 issue of *Diario de México* compared Aldana favourably with Antonio Lolli (*d* 1802) and rated him the best Mexican-born composer of the day. Aldana pioneered in composing devotional music honouring the Mexican protomartyr, San Felipe de Jesús (1575–97, crucified in Nagasaki). His Mass in D does not approach the quality of his Office for the Dead vesper psalms with full orchestra accompaniment.

WORKS

(all MS; at Mexico City cathedral archive, unless otherwise indicated)

Mass, D, Mexico City, National Conservatory of Music [defective copy]

Confitebor, c, Domine ne in furore, c, for Office of the Dead, vv, orch

Dixit, 2vv, orch

Versos, 3 cycles, vv, orch

Verso e himno for S Felipe de Jesús, vocal score

Himno de los santos inocentes, boys' vv, 1790

Boleras nuevas, 2vv, 2 gui, Mexico, S Rosa de S María de Valladolid (Morelia) archive

Minuet de variaciones, kbd, ?1800, facs. in Mayer-Serra (1941), 66f, transcr. in Stevenson (1952)

BIBLIOGRAPHY

Mexico City Cathedral: *Actas capitulares*, lii (1773–4), folio 110

Diario de México, 1v/414 (18 Nov 1806), 332; iv/443 (18 Dec 1806), 440; xii/1601 (18 Feb 1810), 194ff

G. Saldívar: *Historia de la música en México (épocas precortesiana y colonial)* (Mexico City, 1934), 114f

M. Bernal Jiménez: *Morelia colonial* (Mexico City, 1939), 44

O. Mayer-Serra: *Panorama de la música méxicana* (Mexico City, 1941), 66f

R. Stevenson: *Music in Mexico* (New York, 1952, 2/1971), 155ff, 180ff

E. Olavarría y Ferrari: *Reseña histórica del teatro en México 1538–1911* (Mexico City, 1961), i, 44, 71, 162, 164

R. Stevenson: *Renaissance and Baroque Musical Sources in the Americas* (Washington, DC, 1970), 147f, 187

ROBERT STEVENSON

Alday [Aldaye, Aldée]. French family of musicians. Considerable confusion surrounds the members of the Alday family, as several have the same first initial; both *Grove 5* and *RISM* have attributed many of the works of the various Aldays incorrectly. The first known musician in the family, Alday *le père* (first name unknown, *b* Perpignan, 1737), was a violin teacher and composer. According to Fétis's unsupported story, he learnt the mandoline in Italy while secretary to a *grand seigneur*, and was married in Avignon. Choron and Fayolle reported that he settled in Paris as a professor of the mandoline. His sons were (1) François Alday *l'aîné* and (2) Paul Alday *le jeune*.

(1) François Alday [*l'aîné*] (*b* Mahón, Menorca, *c*1761; *d* ?Lyons, after 1835). Violinist, organist, teacher and music director, older son of Alday *père*. The Alday name, presumably referring to François, first appeared in the Parisian press in 1771 after a performance at the Concert Spirituel: 'M. Aldaye fils, âgé d'environ dix ans, a joué sur la mandoline avec autant de rapidité que de précision' (*Mercure de France*, April 1771, ii, 182). He does not appear to have been an outstanding soloist; the name 'Aldée' is listed last in the second violin section of the Concert Spirituel in 1786, and probably refers to him rather than to his brother Paul. In 1797 he was a music teacher and 'premier violon du spectacle' in Lyons. In 1810 he founded the Cercle Harmonique, a concert society comprising the best musicians in that city. As its director, he played an important role in the musical life of Lyons; he encouraged the performance of contemporary music, including the first performance in that city of Beethoven's *Prometheus* overture. From 1823 to at least 1826 he directed private *soirées lyriques*, and as late as 1830 he, or possibly his son (3) Francisque Alday, played a subscription series of five *matinées musicales*. In about 1830 he was the organist at the chapel of the *lycée*. The last contemporary reference to him is in the Lyons *Almanach commercial* of 1835. He is best known for his *Grande méthode pour l'alto* (*c*1827), which includes 25 exercises, ten *leçons élémentaires*, three duos for the violin and viola, and three *Fantasies ou rondeaux*. Ignace Pleyel made several arrangements of his chamber works.

Alday's four sons, including (3) Francisque Alday, were active musically in Lyons: Auguste, probably the eldest, was a violinist (first violinist at the Grand-Théâtre) and violin teacher; Philibert, the third son, played the double bass at the Grand-Théâtre and was a professor of music; Joseph, the youngest, performed on the violin with his father, (3) Francisque and Philibert in March 1818.

WORKS

Geneviève de Brabant (opéra comique, 3, A. J. Leroy de Bacre), Paris, Louvois, 23 Nov 1791, lost
Orch: Concerto à violon principale E♭ (Paris, *c*1785); Concerto de société, G, vn solo, op.16 (Lyons, *c*1815); Va Conc. (Lyons, 1818), lost
Chamber: 9 str qts in 2 sets (Paris, 1799 and later); 6 str qts in 2 sets (Lyons, n.d.); 6 duos, 2 vn, op.21 (Lyons, before 1825), lost; 6 duos, 2 vn (Lyons, before 1825), lost; 3 duos, vn, va, op.23 (Lyons, before 1825)
Solo vn: 6 airs variés, b acc. (Paris, 1782); Polonaise, acc. 2 vn, va, b, op.17 (Lyons, 1820); Un rien avec variations, unacc., op.18 (Lyons, 1820), lost; Rondeau russe, acc. 2 vn, va, b (Lyons, 1825), lost
Pedagogical: Grande méthode pour l'alto (Lyons, *c*1827)

(2) (Jérôme) Paul (Bonaventure) Alday [*le jeune*] (*b* Perpignan ? or Paris, *c*1763; *d* ? Dublin, 1835). Violinist and composer, younger son of Alday *père*. He studied with Viotti in 1785 and between 1783 and 1790 performed no fewer than 25 times at the Concert Spirituel in his own works as well as those by J. A. Fodor, Giornovichi, Mestrino and Viotti. In 1789 he performed a symphonie concertante with 'Vauthy' (Viotti) in Lyons. Fétis placed Alday *le jeune* in England after 1791. His stay in London was apparently short: an account in *Jackson's Oxford Journal* announced that he performed in Oxford in May 1793. In the same year, he married a harpist 'lately arrived from Paris', Adélaïde Rosalie Delatouche (1768 or 1769–1835), in Oxford. He remained there until at least 1796, when he gave a benefit concert. Gerber placed him in Edinburgh in

1806 as a music director and professor of music. According to Carr (*Grove 5*) he went to Dublin in 1809, bought a music business in 1811, opened a music academy in 1812 and was still listed as a professor of the violin as late as 1820. He was a more celebrated violinist than his brother, and his violin concertos enjoyed considerable popularity in both Paris and Berlin; according to Gerber, his fourth violin concerto was performed in Berlin in 1792 and 1797.

WORKS

Orch: 4 vn concs. (Paris, *c*1785–1789); Symphonie concertante, C, 2 solo vn, *c*1788 (Paris, 1800)
Chamber: 1 set of airs variés, vn, ?b (Paris, 1786); 1 set of airs variés, vn, va (Paris, 1787), lost; 1 set of airs variés, vn, b (Paris, 1788); Variations on 'God Save the King', 2 vn (London and Oxford, 1795); 3 Str Qts (London, *c*1795); A Grand Pastoral Overture, pf, vn, vc (?London, *c*1795); 3 Trios, 2 vn, vc (London, n.d.); Duos, 2 vn (Paris, n.d.); Mélanges, 2 vn (Paris, n.d.)

(3) Francisque Alday (*b* Lyons, *c*1800; *d* Lyons, after 1846). Violinist and music director, second son of (1) François Alday. A talented violinist, he performed at the Cercle Harmonique in 1818. He wrote *Vingt-huit études pour le violon* op.4 (Lyons, before 1825) and contributed significantly to the *Grande méthode élémentaire pour le violon dédiée à leur père et composée par les fils Alday* (Lyons, *c*1824), a work which is probably the Aldays' chief contribution to music history: it achieved widespread recognition, and was reprinted throughout the 19th century; as late as 1907 J. M. Bay, professor of violin at the Lyons Conservatory, published in Lyons a *Méthode de violon après la célèbre méthode des fils Alday*. In 1828 and 1830, Francisque Alday played second and first violin, respectively, in the orchestra of the Grand-Théâtre. Like his father, he was influential in the musical life of Lyons, assuming the directorship of its Société Philharmonique in 1836. Contemporary accounts indicate that he was active until at least 1846.

(4) Ferdinand Alday (*b* Lyons, *c*1830; *d* ?Lyons, after 1875). Son, or possibly nephew, of (3) Francisque Alday. The following appearances of the name Alday may refer to Ferdinand: in 1862 an Alday appeared on the list of second violins in the orchestra of the Lyons Grand-Théâtre; in 1872 an 'F. Alday' was professor of the piano at the Lyons Conservatory, a post he gave up between 1875 and 1882; in 1875, an organist named Alday was employed at the Eglise de la Charité.

WORKS

Vocal: Ma mandoline (J.F.D.), vv, org (Paris, 1857); La sylphide (E. Cousineau), vv, pf (Paris, 1858); Noël (J. C. Bert), solo vv, 2 choruses, pf (Paris, 1862); La noce et l'orage, 4vv (Paris, 1865); 2 cantiques, 2, 3vv (Lyons, n.d.); La petite chapelle, 6 motets, 2–3vv, harmonium (Lyons, n.d.)
Inst: Fantaisie brillante, harmonium, op.15 (Paris, 1859); Fantaisie de salon, org, op.16 (Paris, 1860); Adagio, pf, vn, harmonium, op.12 (Paris, 1862); Un conte de fée, pf, op.22 (Paris, 1862); Simple histoire, vn, pf, op.43 (Paris, 1865); Altes und Neues, 7 melodies, vn (London, n.d.)

BIBLIOGRAPHY

FétisB; GerberNL
A. Choron and F. Fayolle: *Dictionnaire historique des musiciens* (Paris, 1810–11/*R*1971)
F. Hainl: *De la musique à Lyon depuis 1713 jusqu'à 1852* (Lyons, 1852)
J. Goizet: *Dictionnaire universel du théâtre en France et du théâtre français* (Paris, 1867)
E. Mathieu de Monter: 'La musique et les musiciens dans les grandes villes de France', *Revue et gazette musicale de Paris*, xlii (1875), 285
M. Reuchsel: *La musique à Lyon* (Lyons, 1903)
P. Holstein: *Le Conservatoire de musique et les salles de concert à Lyon* (Lyons, 1904)
B. Pazdirek and F. Pazdirek: *Universal-Handbuch der Musikliteratur* (Vienna, 1904–10/*R*1967)

A. Sallès: 'Les sociétés de concerts à Lyon au XIXe siècle', *Revue musicale de Lyon*, iv (1906–7), 833

J. H. Mee: *The Oldest Music Room in Europe* (London, 1911)

A. Sallès: *Les premiers essais de concerts populaires à Lyon, 1826–1876* (Paris, 1919)

G. Vuillermoz: *Cent ans d'opéra à Lyon: le centenaire du Grand-Théâtre de Lyon, 1831–1931* (Lyons, 1932)

C. Johansson: *French Music Publishers' Catalogues of the Second Half of the Eighteenth Century* (Stockholm, 1955)

B. S. Brook: *La symphonie française* (Paris, 1962) [incl. detailed bibliography]

B. S. Brook and J. Gribenski: 'Alday', *MGG* [incl. detailed bibliography]

C. Pierre: *Histoire du Concert spirituel 1725–1790* (Paris, 1975)

BARRY S. BROOK, RICHARD VIANO

Alday, Edward. *See* ALLDE, EDWARD.

Aldeburgh Festival. An annual series of opera productions, concerts and related non-musical events, established around Benjamin Britten and based on the small Suffolk coastal town which was his home from 1947 (as well as the historical setting for his opera *Peter Grimes*). The festival was inaugurated in 1948 and takes place each June; its duration has varied from ten days to three weeks. It is organized with support from the Arts Council, local authorities and from numerous private subscriptions and donations.

Britten's taste, imagination and personality helped to give the festival an outstanding and distinctive musical character. His own music forms an important but not preponderant element in the programmes, which regularly include new and recent works by other British composers, and occasionally by foreign composers also. A variety of greater and lesser classics is customarily performed by leading British and foreign artists, many of them personal friends of Britten and his colleagues.

The festival was born from a suggestion by Peter Pears and set out to provide a focus of cultural events in East Anglia. It also secured an outlet for productions by the English Opera Group after this ceased to be associated with the Glyndebourne Festival. The artistic direction was at first nominally carried out by the English Opera Group, which Britten and Pears helped to found. They were individually named as artistic directors of the festival in 1955 and were successively joined by Imogen Holst in 1956, Philip Ledger in 1968, Colin Graham in 1969, Steuart Bedford in 1973 and Mstislav Rostropovich from 1977. Since 1961 the English Chamber Orchestra has been the resident festival ensemble for most operas and concerts.

Even on the larger scale of recent years, the idea of 'concerts by friends' originally envisaged by Pears has continued to be the basis of festival programmes. Its international outlook has been cultivated from strong local roots, which have continued to ensure a certain intimacy of character. The highest professional accomplishment has been supported by an unusual degree of voluntary enthusiasm. From its inception to 1976 the chairman of the festival administration was the Countess of Cranbrook, with Stephen Reiss as festival manager and secretary until 1971, when he resigned and was succeeded by William Servaes. From 1976 the responsibility was vested in a reorganized Aldeburgh Festival–Snape Maltings Foundation.

Britten and Pears regularly performed at the festival, the former often appearing as conductor as well as pianist. They collaborated with a number of visiting foreign composers, including Copland, Henze, Kodály, Lutosławski and Poulenc. Fruitful friendships were estab-

lished in the early years with such artists as Kathleen Ferrier and Dennis Brain; more recently with Julian Bream, Dietrich Fischer-Dieskau and others, and especially with a group of Soviet artists including Mstislav Rostropovich and his wife Galina Vishnevskaya, Sviatoslav Richter and Dmitry Shostakovich (whose Symphony no.14, dedicated to Britten, had its British première at the 1970 festival).

For several years the festival's scope was physically restricted by the available buildings. Even opera productions were confined to the tiny Jubilee Hall, which, after extensions completed in 1960, seats about 350. Besides the parish church at Aldeburgh (where the inaugural concert took place), the festival scheme has at different times been extended to neighbouring churches at Blythburgh, Framlingham and Orford and to Ely Cathedral, as well as to more modest locations at Thorpeness. When a 19th-century malthouse in the nearby village of Snape became available, funds were raised to convert it into a multi-purpose concert hall and open-stage theatrical auditorium seating nearly 800. The Snape Maltings was formally opened by Queen Elizabeth II on 2 June 1967 but was destroyed by fire on the opening night (7 June) of the 1969 festival. In spite of this, only one concert that year had to be cancelled; the others (and even some opera) were accommodated in various of the churches already mentioned. The Maltings was immediately rebuilt, with the help of numerous small donations (£20,000 being subscribed within two months of the fire), and it was reopened in time for the following festival on 5 June 1970. From 1977 its buildings also housed a School of Advanced Musical Studies.

Interior of the Snape Maltings

The exceptionally fine acoustic qualities of the Maltings have encouraged its additional use as a studio for television, radio and gramophone recording, and its availability has enabled festivals to be planned on a larger scale than previously. A modification of festival policy was made in 1972, however, when the duration of the June festival was curtailed in favour of more opera and other events being organized at different times of the year, rather than being concentrated in a single summer period.

For many years the public demand for tickets to festival events has regularly exceeded the supply. Since 1958 students and young people have been assisted by grants from a fund established by Margaret, Princess of Hesse and the Rhine. Awards are given to selected applicants under the age of 25, who need not necessarily be music students but are expected to show evidence of taking an active part in the musical life of the community where they normally live or work. The scheme has served a valuable propagatory function and was supplemented from 1975 by a festival study course enabling those over 25 to attend selected events and lectures.

The following works by Britten were given first performances at the festivals noted: *Saint Nicolas* (1948); *Let's Make an Opera*, incorporating *The Little Sweep* (1949); *Lachrymae* for viola and piano, and a new realization of *The Beggar's Opera* (1950); *Six Metamorphoses after Ovid* for solo oboe (1951); a Variation on 'Sellenger's Round' (1953); *Noye's Fludde* (1957); *Songs from the Chinese* (1958); *A Midsummer Night's Dream* (1960); Cello Sonata (1961); *Curlew River*, and *Nocturnal* for guitar (1964); *Songs and Proverbs of William Blake*, Suite no.1 for Solo Cello and *Gemini Variations* (1965); *The Burning Fiery Furnace* (1966); *The Golden Vanity* and Overture, *The Building of the House* (1967); *The Prodigal Son* and Suite no.2 for Solo Cello (1968); Suite in C for Harp (1969); Canticle IV: *The Journey of the Magi* (1971); *Death in Venice* (1973); String Quartet (1975); Cantata, *Phaedra*, and the first British production of *Paul Bunyan* (1976).

BIBLIOGRAPHY

I. Holst: *Britten* (London, 1966)
'Britten on Aldeburgh and the Future', *Opera*, festival no. (1967), 7 [incl. contributions by J. Cross, M. Harewood, I. Holst, P. Pears]
E. W. White: *Benjamin Britten: his Life and Operas* (London, 1970)
R. Blythe, ed.: *Aldeburgh Anthology* (Aldeburgh and London, 1972)
A. Kendall: *Benjamin Britten* (London, 1973)

NOËL GOODWIN

Aldée. See ALDAY family.

Alder, Cosmas (*b* Baden, Switzerland, *c*1497; *d* Berne, 1553). Swiss composer. He attended the school attached to St Vincent's, Berne, until 1511, and in 1524 became Kantor there. After the Reformation the post was discontinued and Alder held various clerk's positions in Berne that gave him financial security. In 1534 he became a house owner and in 1538 a member of the Great Council. He died of the plague.

Alder left few compositions, but those that remain show that he was a competent minor composer. Of his sacred works the 57 hymns printed in 1553 deserve special mention: they follow the traditional liturgical order while using texts adapted for Protestant congregations by Wolfgang Musculus. He also wrote several Latin motets, two occasional motets (one on the death of Zwingli in 1531) and, more important, a few German motets that were included in the popular dramas of the Bernese writer Hans von Rüte. Alder's motets show the influence not only of his contemporary Senfl, but also of Josquin in their expressiveness: he often used duo sections and interrupted contrapuntal writing with sections of homophony, resulting in a clear formal structure. He tended to emphasize the highest part and liked writing canons. When using a chorale melody as the cantus firmus, as in his hymn settings, he generally presented it in an expressive rhythm rather than in the regular rhythmic values of *contrapunctus fractus* found in the work of Sixt Dietrich and other German composers. Of Alder's polyphonic settings of secular lieder the most noteworthy is *Innsbruck, ich muss dich lassen*. The remainder fall within the normal range of style and quality for Gesellschaftslieder of the second quarter of the 16th century.

WORKS

MOTETS

Hymni sacri numero LVII (Berne, 1553); 1 in 1568[7]

Cum Rex gloriae, 4vv, *D-Z* 73; De profundis, 4vv, *Kl* Mus.4° 24; Floreat Ursine gentis (Musicorum Bernensium catalogus), 4vv, *CH-Bu* F.X 5–9; Inclytus antistes, 4vv, *Bu* F.II 35, ed. in *Zwingliana*, ii (1907), 139 (on Zwingli's death); Nisi Dominus, 4vv, *D-Kl* Mus.4° 24; Veni electa mea, 5vv, *CH-Bu* F.X 5–9

Ach Herr vernimm min kläglich Stimm, 4vv, *Bu* F.IX 32–5, ed. A. Geering, *Psalmen und geistliche Gesänge von Johannes Wannenmacher und Cosmas Alder* (Geneva, 1934) (doubtful); Da Jakob nun das Kleid ansah, 4vv, *Bu* F.X 5–9 (anon. in *PL-WRu* 10; attrib. Senfl in *D-Rp* A.R.891, A.R.940–42, C 93), ed. in DDT, xxxiv (1908/*R*) (Senfl); Wie Joseph in Egyptenland, 4vv, *CH-Bu* F.X 5–9 (doubtful)

SONGS

3 songs, 1536[8], ed. H. J. Moser, *65 deutsche Lieder . . . nach dem Liederbuch von Peter Schöffer und Matthias Apiarius* (Wiesbaden, 1967)
2 songs, *Bu* F.X 5–9, 1 ed. in *IMusSCR*, ii Basle 1906

BIBLIOGRAPHY

A. Fluri: 'Cosmas Alder', *Zwingliana*, ii (1907), 214
H. Dübi: *Cosmas Alder und die Bernische Reformation* (Berne, 1930)
A. Geering: *Die Vokalmusik in der Schweiz zur Zeit der Reformation* (Aarau, 1933), 157ff

MARTIN STAEHELIN

Aldomar, Pedro Juan (*fl* 1506). Spanish composer. A native of Barcelona, he became *maestro de capilla* of Barcelona Cathedral on 19 January 1506. He was inscribed as a singer in the chapel of Ferdinand V on 1 March 1508. Three villancicos by him appear in the Cancionero Musical de Palacio and one in the Cancionero Musical de Barcelona. The most felicitous is the three-voice pastoral dialogue, *¡Ha Pelayo, qué desmayo!*. It opens with a dialogue between the superius and tenor and continues with text in all voices. The simple expressive melody in triple metre is set syllabically in chordal style. A four-part version is found in a collection printed in Venice (*RISM* 1556[30]).

WORKS

En las sierras donde vengo, 3vv, ed. in MME, x (1951), no.252
¡Ha Pelayo, qué desmayo!, 3vv, ed. in MME, v (1947), no.89 (4-voice version in 1556[30])
Di pastorico, pues vienes, 3vv, *E-Bc* 454
Si mi señora m'olvida, 3vv, ed. in MME, x (1951), no.297

BIBLIOGRAPHY

J. Bal y Gay, ed.: *Cancionero de Upsala* (Mexico City, 1944)
R. Stevenson: *Spanish Music in the Age of Columbus* (The Hague, 1960)

ISABEL POPE

Aldovrandin [Aldovrandini], **Giuseppe Antonio Vincenzo.** See ALDROVANDINI, GIUSEPPE ANTONIO VINCENZO.

Aldrich, Henry (*b* Westminster, London, Jan 1648; *d* Oxford, 14 Dec 1710). English divine, scholar, architect, collector of music and composer. After attending Westminster School, Aldrich in 1662 proceeded to a studentship to Christ Church, Oxford, with which his whole career was from that time bound up. He took the degrees of BA and MA in 1666 and 1669. He then received holy orders and was appointed incumbent of Wem, Shropshire, but continued to reside at Christ

Church, of which he became a tutor. In 1681 he was promoted to be a canon of Christ Church and in 1682 proceeded to the degree of DD. He was appointed dean of Christ Church in 1689 and held this office until his death. From 1692 to 1695 he was vice-chancellor of the University of Oxford. By his will he directed that all his personal papers should be destroyed, but he bequeathed his musical library to Christ Church. He is buried in Christ Church Cathedral.

Aldrich was a versatile man of no small attainments. He early distinguished himself in mathematics, which led him to architecture. There is strong reason to believe that at the age of 32 he was responsible for the fine portal to the Old Ashmolean in Oxford. His share in a considerable number of Oxford buildings is not altogether easy to determine, but his most important architectural memorials are the chapel of Trinity College, and Peckwater Quadrangle in Christ Church (the whole matter is fully discussed in Hiscock). Interested too in engraving and printing, he exerted a valuable influence on the university press, and in about 1696 he caused to be engraved three pieces of his own music and Orlando Gibbons's *Behold, thou hast made my days*. His textbook *Artis logicae compendium* continued in use down to the close of the 19th century; and he was one of the editors of Clarendon's *History of the Great Rebellion* (1702–4).

Aldrich's musical activities may be grouped under three headings. Keenly interested in the practice of music, he organized weekly music meetings in his rooms at Christ Church, both before and after his appointment as dean. He was also an important collector and transcriber of music, and his collection forms both the basis and the greater part of the music library now at Christ Church (*see* LIBRARIES). This collection declares his interest in English music of the Elizabethan and early 17th-century periods. Among other things he acquired two fine sets of partbooks of sacred music by Byrd and others (*GB-Och* 979–83; 984–8) besides instrumental parts of string fantasias by Orlando Gibbons and others and printed items such as Morley's *The Triumphes of Oriana* (1601). He was also interested in Italian music, both sacred and secular, and the transcriptions in his collection from Marenzio, Monteverdi, Carissimi, Cesti and others survive as evidence of his enthusiasm. Lastly he was active as a composer. Naturally, in view of his calling, the bulk of his output was in the form of cathedral music. But the sociable side of his musical activities is reflected in a small number of catches, including one with rests thoughtfully provided to enable singers to puff at their pipes (*Good indeed the herb's good weed*) and the attractive, deservedly famous *Hark the bonny Christ Church bells*. He also wrote various items of music for the Oxford 'Act' in different years (*see* ACT MUSIC). Christ Church Mus.1187 contains material for a treatise on music which was for long considered to be wholly Aldrich's work. It is now established, however, that only the account of Greek music is in Aldrich's hand, and the larger part, containing very important details of the structure of musical instruments of the second half of the 17th century, is by James Talbot.

The whole of Aldrich's known sacred music survives at Christ Church, almost all of it in authoritative form in two albums (Mus.16 and 19). It is the work of a conscientious amateur who knew his musical grammar but without particular inspiration. He showed himself familiar with the verse-anthem style of the late 17th

century as well as with the older full anthem. Probably not many of the anthems achieved any currency outside Christ Church, though *God is our hope*, *Out of the deep*, and *O give thanks* were fairly popular, the last two being included in Boyce's anthology. The services are of little interest. That in E minor, never published, contains *Benedicite* instead of *Te Deum*. The Service in G still survives in occasional use at cathedral evensong and, if not specially distinguished, is no disgrace to a distinguished man. It is one of the few settings of the Communion Service of its time to include Sanctus and Gloria.

A number of adaptations of other men's music form a curious feature of Aldrich's work. He not only adapted to English words one or two Latin works of Tallis and Byrd but tinkered with English anthems. He also made adaptations to English words of various Latin compositions by Italian composers. All but one of those by Palestrina are identified in Tudway's anthology (*Lbm* Harl.7338); but apart from the adaptation of a part of *Jephte*, those stated to be derived from Carissimi remain unidentified. The nature of Aldrich's adaptations is not always easy to determine, and Arkwright suggested that one or two works ostensibly by Aldrich may in fact be adaptations.

WORKS
(all in GB-Och unless otherwise stated)

Editions: *Cathedral Music*, ed. W. Boyce (London, 1760–73) [B]
    Cathedral Music, ed. S. Arnold (London, 1790) [A]

SACRED
Morning, Communion and Evening Service, A; A i, 187
Morning, Communion and Evening Service, G; B i, 228
Morning, Communion and Evening Service, e
Morning, Communion and Evening Service, F

Anthems: Behold how good and joyful, inc., *GB-WO*; Comfort ye, my people; Give the king thy judgments; God is our hope, ed. in J. Page, *Harmonia sacra* (London, 1800), i, 50; Have mercy upon me; I am come into my garden; If the Lord himself; I waited patiently; I will exalt thee; I will love thee; O give thanks unto the Lord, B ii, 140; O God, thou art my God; O Lord, grant the queen; O Lord, I have heard; O Lord our governor; O Lord, rebuke me not, *Cu*; O praise the Lord all ye heathen, A i, 294; O sing unto the Lord; Out of the deep, B ii, 135; Praise the Lord, ye servants; Sing unto the Lord, O ye saints; The Lord is king; Unto thee, O Lord; We have a strong city; Who is this that cometh?

Motets: O bone Jesu; Salvator mundi

SECULAR
Instrumental and vocal music for the Oxford Act (including possible adaptations from Carissimi), *Ob*, *Och*
Catches (listed in Day and Murrie)

ADAPTATIONS
(works by English composers)
All people that on earth that do dwell (believed by Aldrich to be by Tallis), A, i, 224
Be not wroth (from Byrd: Civitas sancti tui), *Och*, *US-AUS*
Call to remembrance (from R. Farrant)
Give sentence (from O. Gibbons: Almighty and everlasting God)
Hide not thou thy face (from R. Farrant)
I look for the Lord (from Tallis: Absterge Domine)
I will wash my hands in innocence (from R. White: O how glorious)
Not unto us (from Lord for thy tender mercy sake, believed by Aldrich to be by R. Farrant, and from H. Lawes: Zadok the priest), A i, 290
O Lord, I bow the knees (from W. Mundy)
O Lord, make thy servant (from W. Byrd)
O Lord my God (from Bull: Almighty God, who by the leading of a star), B iii, 165
Thy beauty, O Israel (from Wise), *US-AUS*, B iii, 208

(works by Italian composers)
Behold in heaven; For Zion's sake; Haste thee, O Lord, my God (from Jephte); I am well pleased, *US-AUS*, A iii, 48; O how amiable; O Lord I will praise thee; O pray for the peace of Jerusalem (all from Carissimi)
Hold not thy tongue; My heart is fixed; O God, the king of glory; The eye of the Lord; We have heard with our ears, A i, 276; Why art thou so vexed: *Lbm* Harl.7338 (all from Palestrina)

O Lord God, O God of my salvation, *Lbm* Add.31399 (from Palestrina)

(*unidentified works*)

Behold now, praise the Lord; Give ear, O Lord

DOUBTFUL WORKS

Be thou exalted; Blessed is the man; By the waters of Babylon; God is our refuge: possibly adaptations

Two-part instrumental music in *Och* Mus.90–91 may be by Aldrich

BIBLIOGRAPHY

G. E. P. Arkwright: *Catalogue of Music in the Library of Christ Church, Oxford*, i (Oxford, 1915)

A. Hiff: *Catalogue of Printed Music prior to 1801 in Christ Church, Oxford* (Oxford, 1919)

C. L. Day and E. B. Murrie: *English Song-Books, 1651–1702* (London, 1940)

W. G. Hiscock: *Henry Aldrich of Christ Church, 1648–1710* (Oxford, 1960)

A. H. King: *Some British Collectors of Music* (Cambridge, 1963)

WATKINS SHAW

Aldrich, Putnam C(alder) (*b* Swansea, Mass., 14 July 1904; *d* Cannes, 18 April 1975). American musicologist and harpsichordist. After receiving the BA from Yale University in 1926, Aldrich went to Europe, where he studied the piano with Matthay in London and the harpsichord with Landowska in France. He returned to the USA to take the MA at Harvard in 1936 and the PhD there in 1942, working with Apel and Leichtentritt. From 1936 to 1944 he was director of the Boston Society of Ancient Instruments.

He began his teaching career in 1942 at the University of Texas, where he taught until 1944. He was on the staff of Western Reserve University (1946–8) and Mills College, Oakland, California (1948–50). In 1950 he was appointed professor of music at Stanford University, where he taught until his retirement in 1969.

Aldrich combined his scholarly interests with an active career as a harpsichordist. In particular he wrote on the performing practice of early music and the musical ornamentation of the 17th and 18th centuries. His study of the rhythm of 17th-century Italian monody examines notational problems encountered by present-day performers and editors of this music and furnishes provocative, sometimes controversial solutions.

WRITINGS

'Ornamentation', *Harvard Dictionary of Music*, ed. W.' Apel (Cambridge, Mass., 1944; rev. 2/1969)

Ornamentation in J. S. Bach's Organ Works (New York, 1950, 2/1969)

'Ornement'; 'Ornementation', *Encyclopédie de la Musique* (Paris, 1961), iii, 358

Rhythm in Seventeenth-century Italian Monody (New York, 1966)

'An Approach to the Analysis of Renaissance Music', *MR*, xxx (1969), 1

' "Rhythmic Harmony" as taught by Johann Philipp Kirnberger', *Studies in Eighteenth-century Music: a Tribute to Karl Geiringer* (New York and London, 1970), 37

'Classics of Musical Literature', *Notes*, xxvii (1970–71), 461

PAULA MORGAN

Aldrich, Richard (*b* Providence, Rhode Island, 31 July 1863; *d* Rome, 2 June 1937). American critic. He was educated at Harvard University, where he studied music under J. K. Paine, graduating in 1885. In the same year he became music critic to the *Providence Journal*, after serving his apprenticeship in general journalism. In 1889 he became private secretary to US Senator Dixon, and at the same time held the post of music critic to the *Evening Star*, Washington. In 1891 he relinquished both posts to join the staff of the *New York Tribune*, on which paper he held various editorial posts, particularly that of assistant critic to H. E. Krehbiel, until 1902, when he became music editor of the *New York Times*;

he retired in 1923, remaining on the editorial staff in an advisory capacity.

Throughout his career Aldrich was notable for the breadth of his musical knowledge and the soundness of his judgment; in general he was sympathetic to modern music, though vehemently opposed to extreme trends. As one might expect from a member of the National Institute of Arts and Letters he was distinguished for the excellence of his style and for the wit and urbanity of his writing. He collected an important library of books on music, which he catalogued during the leisure of his later years; it remains intact in the possession of his heirs.

WRITINGS

Guide to Parsifal (New York, 1904)

Guide to the Ring of the Nibelung (New York, 1905)

Musical Discourse (Oxford, 1928)

A Catalogue of Books relating to Music in the Library of Richard Aldrich (New York, 1931)

Concert Life in New York 1902–1923 (New York, 1941)

H. C. COLLES/MALCOLM TURNER

Aldrovandi, Clelia. *See* GATTI-ALDROVANDI, CLELIA.

Aldrovandini [Aldovrandini, Aldrovandin, Aldrovandon, Altrobrandino], **Giuseppe** [Gioseffo] **Antonio Vincenzo** (*b* Bologna, 1672–3; *d* Bologna, 9 Feb 1707). Italian composer. He studied composition and counterpoint with Perti, probably while the latter was *maestro di cappella* of S Pietro, Bologna; in 1695, after at least two of his oratorios had been performed in the city's churches, he became a member of the Accademia Filarmonica, and in 1702 was elected its *principe*. Librettos from 1702 on name him as honorary *maestro di cappella* to the Duke of Mantua, and later he is also called *maestro* of the Accademia del Santo Spirito, Ferrara. Contemporary accounts indicate that he was a man of intemperate habits, which perhaps accounted for his lack of professional preferment and for his habitual poverty despite the recognition of his talent. He died at the age of 34: leaving a waterfront tavern in an intoxicated condition at about 3 a.m., he fell into a canal and was drowned.

Aldrovandini belonged stylistically to the late 17th-century Bolognese school of vocal and instrumental composers, though he possessed a degree of original brilliance that has not yet been fully assessed. His operas were widely performed not only in north Italy but in Naples as well, and his printed works were noted by Walther (*Musicalisches Lexikon*, 1732). Three of his first four operas are important in the history of *opera buffa*, since they point to an early regional development of the genre independent of the Neapolitan school. *Gl'inganni amorosi scoperti in villa* (1696), in Bolognese dialect except for the leading romantic roles, enjoyed great popularity, with numerous revivals as late as 1759, although the first production was suspended by church authorities until some *doubles entendres* had been excised from the text. Dramaturgically the work is more sophisticated than its earliest Neapolitan dialect counterparts, with more clearly planned spacing between recitative passages and set numbers. As in the serious operas of the time, the first two acts end with arias rather than ensembles, although duets and trios appear frequently within acts. In form the arias appear to alternate freely between da capo structures and shorter songs. The music of this work, as well as that of Aldrovandini's other dialect comedy, *Amor torna in s'al so'* (1698), and of *Dafni* (1696), a pastoral comedy, has disappeared, but its style can perhaps be inferred from the comic episodes and intermezzos of the surviving *Cesare in Alessandria* (Naples, 1699). The failure of these comic operas to inspire successors in Bologna until G. M. Buini's time was probably due less to lack of public interest (Goldoni commented on the Bolognese appetite for comedy) than to the severe view of comedy taken by the archiepiscopacy.

A number of Aldrovandini's serious operas were successful enough to be revived outside their cities of origin. He wrote their arias – almost without exception in da capo form – according to the motto principle; the second sections of da capo arias often use the same formal device. Although the serious operas are not formally innovatory their music is of impressive quality. Harmonic schemes are by no means merely stereotyped but are dictated by the expressive turns of the text; vocal melismas are included not just for display but are reserved for emotionally heightened words. In addition Aldrovandini was imaginative in his use of the orchestra. At a time when the continuo provided the standard accompanimental texture to arias he sometimes varied it by specifying 'violone solo'; elsewhere he scored more fully, employing wind and brass as well as strings, not only as accompaniment but also in concertato textures with the voice parts.

WORKS

OPERAS

Gl'inganni amorosi scoperti in villa (L. M. Landi), Bologna, Formagliari, 28 Jan 1696
Dafni (E. Manfredi), Bologna, Malvezzi, 18 Aug 1696
Ottaviano (N. Beregani), Turin, Regio, carn. 1697
Amor torna in s'al so', over se L' nozz dla Checha e d' Bdett (A. M. Monti), Bologna, Formagliari, carn. 1698; with title Amor torna in s'al so', over L' nozz dla Flippa e d' Bdett, Bologna, Marsigli-Rossi, carn. 1733 [the erroneous title Amor torna in 5 al 50 first appeared in L. Allacci: Drammaturgia, Venice, 2/1755]
La fortezza al cimento (F. Silvani), Venice, S Salvatore, Feb 1699
Cesare in Alessandria (F. M. Paglia), Naples, S Bartolomeo, sum. 1699; *F-Pn, I-Nc* [dated 1700, includes intermezzos Mirena e Lesbina and Mirena e Floro], scena buffa and Mirena e Floro in *D-Dlb*
Le due Auguste (P. P. Seta), Bologna, Formagliari, 16 Aug 1700
Semiramide (?G. A. Moniglia), Genoa, del Falcone, carn. 1701; *F-Pn, I-Nc*, scena buffa in *D-Dlb*
Mitridate in Sebastia (G. Maggi), Genoa, del Falcone, aut. 1701, with musical adds by G. Vignola, Naples, S Bartolomeo, 1706; *I-Mc*, arias only in *Nc*
Turno Aricino (S. Stampiglia), Genoa, del Falcone, carn. 1702
Pirro (A. Zeno), Venice, S Angelo, ?carn. 1704
L'odio e l'amore (M. Noris), Naples, S Bartolomeo, 1704; 8 arias in *I-Nc*
L'incoronazione di Dario (?A. del Pò), Naples, S Bartolomeo, carn. 1705; *Mc, Nc*
Il piu fedel tra i vassalli (Silvani, with adds by G. Convò, Stampiglia), Naples, S Bartolomeo, ?spr. 1705
Li tre rivali al soglio (Stampiglia), Bologna, Marsigli-Rossi, 2 Jan 1711

Doubtful works: Il prologo dilucidazione ed epitome del Lodovico Pio, Bologna, 1694; L'orfano, Naples, 1699; Il Trace in catena, Venice, 1704; Muzio Scevola, 1705; Berenice (?pasticcio), Venice, 1705; Amor non vuol rispetti, Cento, Bologna, 1719; Zelida; Perseo

ORATORIOS

S Sigismondo (G.-B. Monti), Bologna, Confraternità de S Sigismondo, 1691
La guerra in cielo (T. Stanzani), Bologna, Arciconfraternità di SS Sebastiano e Rocco, 1691
Giesù nato (G. B. Taroni), Bologna, Congregazione della Madonna in Galliera, 24 Dec 1698
L'Italia humiliata, Bologna, S Martino, 1702
La grazia giubilante (Monti), Bologna, S Sigismondo, Lent 1704
Il doppio martire (M. Vangini), Bologna, SS Sebastiano e Rocco, 20 Jan 1706

OTHER WORKS

(all printed works except anthologies published in Bologna)
Armonia sacra concertata in [10] motetti, 2,3vv, 2 vn, vle/theorbo, bc (org), op.1 (1701)
[10] Cantate, 1v, vn, bc, op.2 (1701)
[10] Concerti sacri, 1v, 2 vn, vle/theorbo, bc (org), op.3 (1703)
[10] Concerti, vn, vc/theorbo, bc, op.4 (1703)
[10] Sonate, 2 vn, vc, bc (org), op.5 (1706)

Motet in 1695[1]; arias in Recueil lyrique d'airs choisis (Paris, 1772) and Musicalisch-italienischer Arien Crantz, ed. J. Steiner (Zurich, 1724)
2 sonatas, vn, vc, in *c*1695[16]; sonatas, a 3, *c*1700[7]

Lamentationes, *D-Bds*; Dixit Dominus, *I-Bc*; Salve regina, *GB-T*
Numerous arias and solo cantatas in *A-Wgm, B-Bc, Br, D-Bds, F-Pn, GB-Cfm, Lbm, I-Bc, Fc, Mc, Nc*; duets in *F-Pn*
3 sonatas, vn, *A-Wn*
According to EitnerQ, other works in *D-Bds, Dkh, Dlb, I-Bc, Bsp*

BIBLIOGRAPHY

EitnerQ
C. Goldoni: *Mémoires*, ii (Paris, 1787), chap.24; ed. G. Ortolani, *Tutte le opere* (Verona, 1935–56), i, 346ff
H. Lavoix: *Histoire de l'instrumentation* (Paris, 1878), 201ff
C. Ricci: *I teatri di Bologna nei secoli xvii e xviii: storia aneddotica* (Bologna, 1888/R1965), esp. 92, 95ff, 376ff, 386, 388f, 398, 428
L. Busi: *Il Padre G. B. Martini, musicista-letterato del secolo xviii* (Bologna, 1891), 130ff
A. Schering: *Geschichte des Oratoriums* (Leipzig, 1911/R1966), 126f
——: *Geschichte des Instrumental-Konzerts* (Leipzig, 1905, 2/1927/R1965), 27ff

JAMES L. JACKMAN

Aldulescu, Radu (*b* Piteasca-Pasărea, 17 Sept 1922). Romanian cellist. He studied the cello with Dimitrie Dinicu at the Bucharest Conservatory, then took advanced lessons in Spain with Cassadó. A successful début on Radio Bucharest in 1941 was followed by membership of the Bucharest PO and Opera House orchestra and by a developing career as a soloist and chamber music player in the Bucharest Trio. He also taught at the Bucharest Conservatory and the Military Lyceum of Music in the same city, 1945–64, and in 1965 joined the RAI SO in Rome and the Rome String Trio. From 1968 he taught at the Paris Conservatoire, and formed a duo with the pianist Yonty Solomon. His tours in Europe, North and South America, Africa and the Middle East confirmed his mastery of varied musical styles, combining freshness of imagination with seriousness of approach. He has made a number of gramophone records.

BIBLIOGRAPHY

V. Cosma: *Interpreți români* (Bucharest, 1977)

VIOREL COSMA

Aleatory. A term applied to music whose composition and/or performance is, to a greater or lesser extent, undetermined by the composer.

1. Introduction. 2. History. 3. Aleatory composition. 4. Mobile form. 5. Indeterminate notation. 6. Graphics. 7. Texts. 8. The role of the performer. 9. The aesthetics of chance.

1. INTRODUCTION. As defined above, the term 'aleatory' ('aleatoric' represents an etymological distortion) applies to all music: it is impossible for a composer to prescribe every aspect in the realization of a composition; even the sound result of a tape playback will depend on such variables as the equipment used and the acoustic conditions. However, it is usual to restrict the term to compositions in which the composer makes a deliberate withdrawal of control, excluding certain established usages which fall within this category: for example, keyboard improvisation, the cadenza, the *ossia*, the *ad libitum*, unmeasured pauses, alternative scorings and the provision of sets of independent pieces (e.g. the Goldberg Variations). It is possible to distinguish three types of aleatory technique, although a given composition may exhibit more than one of them, separately or in combination: (i) the use of random procedures in the generation of fixed compositions (see §3); (ii) the allowance of choice to the performer(s) among formal options stipulated by the composer (see §4); and (iii)

methods of notation which reduce the composer's control over the sounds in a composition (see §§5–7). The liberty offered by these various means can extend from a choice between two dynamic markings to almost unguided improvisation. Some theoretical considerations and practical consequences are outlined in §§8–9.

2. HISTORY. Until the mid-20th century European composers were constantly seeking notational developments that would enable them to determine sounds with greater exactness, an attitude entirely opposed to the aleatory. There were, however, some trivial examples of aleatory music in the 18th century, when schemes were published for generating simple pieces in response to the results of dice throws. These games usually left only one aspect to guided chance: the ordering of bars supplied with the scheme, for instance, or the melody to be placed over a given rhythmic–harmonic pattern. Mozart and Haydn were sometimes claimed as authors, but without any more than commercial justification. One might also consider the art of keyboard improvisation as a precursor of aleatory music, but here the creator and the performer are identical; once an improvisation is published for performance by others, it has to be respected as much as any other printed score. In most aleatory music, on the other hand, the creator provides a score which gives a degree of freedom to any performer. Similarly, other improvised musics, such as jazz and folk traditions, were not initially the most important influences on aleatory music.

The first composer to make a significant use of aleatory features was Ives, whose scores include exhortations to freedom, alternatives of an unprecedentedly important character, and unrealizable notations which silently invite the performer to find his own solution. From the 1930s Cowell followed Ives's lead in such works as the String Quartet no.3 'Mosaic' (1934), which allows the players to assemble the music from fragments provided. He used other 'elastic' (his own word) notations to introduce chance or choice into the performance, occasionally instructing the performers to improvise a certain number of bars or *ad libitum*. His sometime pupil Cage began to use what he called 'chance operations' in composition during the early 1950s, notably in the *Music of Changes* for piano (1951). At first Cage's work had most influence on his immediate associates: Feldman wrote a number of 'graph' pieces, such as the *Intersection* and *Projection* series, in which notes are replaced by boxes, determining pitch only relatively; and Brown abandoned all conventional notation in, for example, *December 1952*, consisting of 31 black rectangles printed on a single sheet.

European composers were more hesitant in taking up aleatory techniques. Such early examples as Stockhausen's *Klavierstück IX* (1956) and Boulez's Piano Sonata no.3 (1956–7) allow the player no more than limited freedom in the ordering of composed sections. By this time Cage had gone much further in abandoning the control exercised by the composer, or even the performer(s), reaching an extreme point in *4′ 33″* (1952), whose only sounds – those of the environment – are quite unpredictable. About 1960 purely verbal scores were introduced by LaMonte Young and others, and the following decade saw the pursuit of aleatory methods to a wide range of ends throughout the world. Composers such as Henze and Lutosławski used aleatory incidents in otherwise determined compositions, while Rzewski, Globokar, Stockhausen and others produced scores that give only a few specifications to stimulate improvisation.

3. ALEATORY COMPOSITION. As here defined, aleatory composition involves the use of random procedures in determining musical aspects that are to be notated; unless other aleatory techniques are also used, the resultant score is no less fixed than a conventional composition. Chance procedures in composition have been most fully and diversely exploited by Cage. In producing the *Music of Changes*, for example, he tossed coins to decide how he should make choices from charts of pitches, durations, intensities and other sound aspects, deriving his chance operations from the 'I Ching', the Chinese book of changes. Similar methods were used in assembling *Williams Mix* for tape (1952) and in notating the parts for 12 radio receivers in *Imaginary Landscape no.4* (1951). (The latter work is inevitably unusual, in that the sounds heard in performance are out of the control of both composer and players, depending on the broadcasts that happen to be received.) Other random techniques employed by Cage include placing notes on imperfections in the music paper (Music for Piano, 1952–6) and using templates drawn from maps of the constellations (*Atlas eclipticalis*, 1961–2). An example of random composing combined with other aleatory features in Cage's *Winter Music* (1957), in which from one to 20 pianists may use any quantity of the chance-composed score.

It is necessary to distinguish aleatory composition from the 'stochastic' composition practised by Xenakis. In such works as *ST/4* for string quartet (1956–62), Xenakis used the assistance of a computer in producing music modelled on stochastic processes, in which events on the smallest scale are indeterminate though the shape of the whole is defined. Thus randomness is introduced as a necessary part of a willed product, and Xenakis retained the right to modify the computer result. Few composers other than Cage have made much use of true aleatory composition.

4. MOBILE FORM. By contrast with Cage and his chance operations in composition, other composers have avoided introducing any randomness into their composing or notation, but have permitted the performer some flexibility in realization by means of the provision of alternative orderings. Sometimes, as in Stockhausen's *Klavierstück XI*, the player is instructed to pick from the alternatives on the spur of the moment; other works, such as Boulez's Piano Sonata no.3, suggest a more considered choice. The sonata is in five parts which may be played in any of several permutations, and each part contains sections which may be variously ordered and/ or omitted. Fig.1 shows the 'Troisième texte', one of the tiniest satellites of Boulez's mobile-form *Structures II* for two pianos (1956–61); note that the ordering of events is to some extent free, and that durations and dynamics are variable. Other notable works of mobile form include Boulez's *Pli selon pli* for soprano and orchestra (1957–62), Stockhausen's *Momente* for soprano, chorus and instruments (1962–4) and Pousseur's 'fantaisie variable genre opéra' *Votre Faust* (1960–67), which draws the audience, too, into the

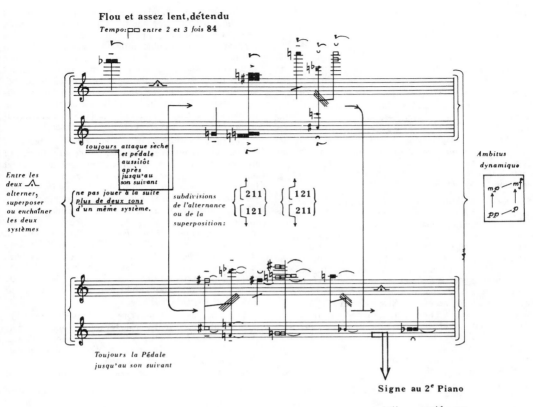

1. 'Troisième texte' from 'Structures II' (1956–61) by Boulez

decision-making. All of these works provide comprehensive rules for the assembling of a performance, whereas when Cage has used formal variability, as in *Winter Music* or the Concert for Piano and Orchestra (1957–8), he has left options as open as possible: any amount of the solo part of the Concert may be omitted, as may any or all of the orchestral parts, and the piece may be performed simultaneously with others by Cage.

5. INDETERMINATE NOTATION. The types of aleatory music so far described use conventional notation to determine sounds, although, in compositions of mobile form, new signs may be necessary to guide the performer(s) in choosing a route. Many composers have introduced new notations which render the sounds themselves indeterminate, frequently by abandoning traditional signs for graphics or texts, each of which is considered below. But it is also possible to use conventional notation in an indeterminate manner. An early example is Stockhausen's *Zeitmasse* (1955–6), whose tempos depend on the physical capacities of the five wind players: the duration of a single breath, or the fastest speed possible.

The composer can also allow flexibility in the interpretation of conventional symbols by giving alternatives

or by specifying sound aspects in only relative terms. Alternative tempos, dynamic degrees and so on have been extensively used by Boulez. Relative notation has often been employed to specify a more or less narrowly defined register rather than a determined pitch, particularly in vocal music. Boulez's *Structures II* contains an analogously imprecise notation of durations (see fig.1), and Boulez has frequently specified a range of tempo rather than a definite figure, so setting limits to a fluctuating rubato.

Greater indeterminacy is introduced, still with conventional notation, when performers are asked to improvise on the basis of given pitches or rhythms, to interpret a given pitch sequence with any rhythm, to interpret a given rhythm with any pitches, and so on. All of these demand invention from the performer, and they have been used by composers as different as Kagel and Lutoslawski.

The most systematic use of newly invented symbolic notations is to be found in Stockhausen's 'process' compositions, which specify how sounds are to be changed or imitated rather than what they are to be. The first of these compositions was *Plus–Minus* (1963), whose title indicates the two principal signs which Stockhausen has introduced for these purposes: the plus sign means that

$$\left[\begin{array}{c} \text{POLY} \\ + \\ + \\ + \\ + \end{array}\middle| \begin{array}{cccc} - & = & = & = \\ & & = & = \end{array}\middle| + (E) = \middle| \begin{array}{c} + \\ + \\ + \end{array} (AKK) + + \begin{array}{c} + \\ + \end{array}\middle| \underset{G}{=} + \underset{+ + +}{-} \overset{\frown}{(BAND)}\right]$$

2. Plus–minus notation in a fragment from Stockhausen's 'Spiral' (1969)

a sound is to be increased in some 'parameter' with respect to some preceding sound (i.e. it may be louder, higher in pitch, longer, more subdivided etc), and the minus sign has the reverse significance. Fig.2 shows this notation in a fragment of *Spiral* for solo performer (1969). The number of plus and/or minus signs in any 'event' indicates the number of parameters to be changed; other signs refer to articulation (e.g. 'POLY' indicates a polyphonic event).

6. GRAPHICS. Graphic notation – which may be distinguished from the preceding by the fact that it signifies, if at all, by analogy instead of by symbol – has been employed to supplement conventional notation where the latter proves inadequate. For example, the 'shape' of a glissando (i.e. the variation of pitch with time) can be shown by a curved line on a staff; though the aleatory character of such notations is an inevitable concomitant rather than a deliberate addition. A more truly aleatory use of graphics occurs in Stockhausen's *Zyklus* for solo percussionist (1959), a compendium of quasi-conventional graphic notation used in conjunction with traditional signs. Fig.3, from Haubenstock-Ramati's *Tableau II* for orchestra (1970), shows some examples of this type of graphic notation.

Alternatively, graphics may be used as a total

replacement for standard symbols, as in Brown's *December 1952*. Logothetis, Cardew (in *Treatise*, 1963–7) and other composers have continued in this direction, raising graphic notation to the level of visual art, but beyond the level of musical intelligibility, since such scores often provide the performer with little or no information as to how the signs are to be interpreted, and the possibilities for sound realization are exceedingly diverse. Fig.4 is an example of enigmatic graphic notation from Cage's *Fontana Mix* (1958), a score consisting of transparent sheets to be superposed.

7. TEXTS. Like graphics of this latter sort, verbal texts can be used to give the performer a very large degree of freedom in determining both form and content. The text may be a straightforward instruction for action – often a far from conventionally musical action, as in Young's *Composition 1960 no.5*, whose principal requirement is 'Turn a butterfly (or any number of butterflies) loose in the performance area'. Other text scores are more inscrutable; Young's *Piano Piece for David Tudor no.3*, for example, consists of the text: 'most of them were very old grasshoppers'. More usually, texts have been used to give a more or less clearly stated basis for ensemble improvisation; notable examples include Rzewski's *Love Songs* (1968) and Stockhausen's *Aus den sieben Tagen* (1968).

8. THE ROLE OF THE PERFORMER. Aleatory music implies a quite new inventive role for the performer, and its evolution has been closely linked with the technical innovations and accomplishments of individuals, such as Tudor or Boulez, and of ensembles.

In some respects, compositions of mobile form

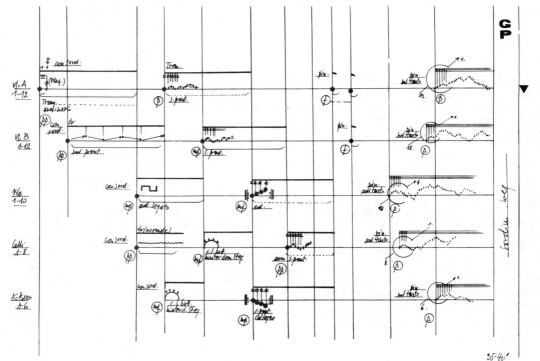

3. Aleatory graphic notation from Haubenstock-Ramati's 'Tableau II' (1970)

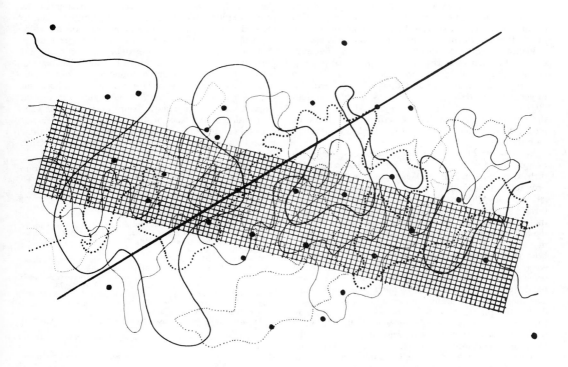

4. Enigmatic graphic notation from Cage's 'Fontana Mix' (1958)

introduce the fewest new problems, since the material can be fully composed. It is significant that the earliest European efforts in this direction – Stockhausen's *Klavierstück XI* and Boulez's Piano Sonata no.3 – are each for a solo player, who is in a position to make spontaneous or rehearsed decisions about the ordering of the music. When more performers are involved and when the composer does not want an anarchic result, either the performers must make all decisions in advance, as in Stockhausen's *Momente*, or else the composer must supply a system of cues and other signals. This was the procedure adopted by Boulez in writing for two pianos (*Structures II*), for chamber ensemble ('. . . *explosante-fixe . . .*') and for orchestra in several works (*Pli selon pli*, *Eclat*, *Domaines*) which expand the conductor's function.

Where the notation, or lack of it, renders the music still more indeterminate, the performer's responsibility becomes weightier. It is often difficult for the composer to make his intentions clear without hampering the player more than he wishes, so aleatory scores have frequently to be understood against the background of a composer's more determinate work or within an implicit cultural milieu; but a performer may choose to take the score out of that background or milieu – as, for example, when the English composer Gavin Bryars made a realization of Stockhausen's *Plus–Minus* with fragments from Schubert's C major String Quintet and a pop song – and so draw attention to the new division of labour between composer and executant.

The common reaction to this problem has been the establishment by composers of performing traditions within their own ensembles, of which the Sonic Arts Union (consisting of the four composers Ashley, Behrman, Lucier and Mumma) and the Stockhausen Ensemble have been prominent. Such groups have been able to develop collective qualities of reaction previously rare outside long-established string quartets, and composers have in turn made use of these group characteristics. Sometimes this has meant that very little has to be specified in the score – Stockhausen's *Aus den sieben Tagen* texts represent an extreme case. Other composers have welcomed the extreme variability with which minimally notated scores may be interpreted, and have made no attempt to form a tradition of performance. Their interest has been, rather, in exciting the players to awareness of their own and their colleagues' potentialities, a position exemplified by Wolff's work.

Some performing ensembles have dispensed even with this unassuming stimulus from a composer, and have engaged in 'free improvisation', though most have continued to play composed music as well. Among the groups which have had some success in this field are Musica Elettronica Viva (Rzewski and others) and New Phonic Art (Globokar and others). It is only at this point that other improvisatory musics have had much direct influence on aleatory practice in Western art music, and some players, among them Michel Portal and Barry Guy, have been able to involve themselves concurrently in jazz and 'free improvisation'.

9. THE AESTHETICS OF CHANCE. The introduction of

chance into a work of art undermines the notion that creation requires, at each moment and on every level, a definite choice on the part of the artist. One implication of Mallarmé's *Un coup de dés*, a work that had a great influence on European aleatory composers, is that each creative decision gives rise to a multiplicity of possible continuations, and in the projected *Livre* he was to provide for alternative continuations to be realized. But in general the Western work of art was, until the mid-20th century, supposed to have an ideal identity, and, in the case of performed arts, a performance might be judged by the extent to which it was held to correspond with that identity.

In the works of most European composers, the operation of aleatory technique does not fundamentally disturb that conception. The composition is still the product of an individual mind, though some aspects are left indefinite; the performer has still to realize the composer's intentions. (One problem in aleatory music is that of whether the performance should communicate the fact of indeterminacy. The flexible features of a work may not be perceived as such if the listener does not hear frequent different performances, still less if the work is heard most usually in a single recording. In some disc issues, such as that of Pousseur's *Votre Faust*, the difficulty has been tackled by having the listener take decisions about operating balance and volume controls during the playing.) And the roots of the aleatory in European music are principally within the European tradition itself. If composers were impressed by the freedom of performance in oriental musics, their reaction was to attempt to establish some equivalent in Western terms. In doing so, they found more immediate stimulus in literary parallels (particularly Mallarmé and Joyce) and in the principle of serialism as it had been developed in Europe up to the mid-1950s. This development had brought about the avoidance of large-scale formal processes, and so the ground was laid for forms in which sections could be moved about without disrupting the whole. In addition, the permutational character of serialism was seen as implying permutable forms. Yet another field of activity within European music which stimulated aleatory innovations was electronic music: first, composers had observed that a sound is partly determinate and partly indeterminate (Boulez was to write of the main parts of his Piano Sonata no.3 as its 'formants'), and second, there was the desire to achieve in instrumental music what had proved obstinately unobtainable in electronic music, namely variability with performance.

Aleatory music in Europe might, in general, be considered as a matter of choice rather than chance, and the most significant choices have usually remained with the composer, whether he exercises them in notating a score or in directing a performance. In either event, the criteria for judging the result as a work of art are barely altered. Even improvisation groups in Europe have customarily retained a traditional regard for achievement, finish and the expression of defined ideas (whether musical or political), although few have succeeded in establishing a code of practice, such as exists in most jazz, within which their improvisations may be understood.

Cage's use of chance was, from the first, more destructive of the traditional notion of a work of art (just as, previously, his 'automatic' procedures had been). Influenced by Zen Buddhism as well as by the musics of the east, his aim was to remove the barrier of his discrimination: any sound was to be admitted, freed to 'be itself'. It was a persistent search for means of avoiding willed choice that led him to investigate procedures that took music out of the control of both composer and performer. Although certain of Cage's associates, notably Brown and Feldman, found a parallel for their ideas in the work of visual artists (Calder's mobiles and Pollock's action paintings, for example), the central Cagean idea was to remove from music any reference to tradition or any trace of subjectivity, and chance, not choice, was the obvious means. This extreme aleatory position was stated at its most exact in Cage's lecture 'Indeterminacy':

Finally I said that the purpose of this purposeless music would be achieved if people learned to listen; that when they listened they might discover that they preferred the sounds of everyday life to the ones they would presently hear in the musical program; that that was alright as far as I was concerned.

BIBLIOGRAPHY

P. Boulez: 'Alea', *Nouvelle revue française* (1957), no.59; repr. in *Relevés d'apprenti* (Paris, 1966), 41; Ger. trans. in *Darmstädter Beiträge zur neuen Musik*, i (1958), 44; Eng. trans. in *PNM*, iii/1 (1964), 42
——: 'Zu meiner III. Sonate', *Darmstädter Beiträge zur neuen Musik*, iii (1960), 27; Eng. trans. in *PNM*, i/2 (1963), 32
K. Stockhausen: 'Musik und Graphik', *Darmstädter Beiträge zur neuen Musik*, iii (1960), 5; repr. in *Texte*, ii (Cologne, 1964), 74
H. R. Zeller: 'Mallarmé und der serielle Denken', *Die Reihe* (1960), no.6, p.5; Eng. trans. in *Die Reihe* (1964), no.6, p.5
J. Cage: *Silence* (Middletown, Conn., 1961)
D. Behrman: 'What Indeterminate Notation Determines', *PNM*, iii/2 (1965), 58
R. Reynolds: 'Indeterminacy: some Considerations', *PNM*, iv/1 (1965), 136
Source (Sacramento, Calif., 1966–) [magazine of short articles on aleatory music, scores and discs]
T. W. Adorno: 'Vers une musique informelle', *Darmstädter Beiträge zur neuen Musik*, x (1966), 9
K. Boehmer: *Zur Theorie der offenen Form in der neuen Musik* (diss., U. of Cologne, 1966; Darmstadt, 1966)
E. Brown: 'On Form', *Darmstädter Beiträge zur neuen Musik*, x (1966), 57; Fr. trans. in *Musique en jeu* (1971), no.3, p.29
K. H. Eschman: *Changing Forms in Modern Music* (Boston, Mass., 1967)
W. Lutosławski: 'O roli elementu przypadku w technice komponowania' [On the role of chance elements in compositional technique], *Res facta*, i (1967), 35
T. H. O'Beirne: '940,369,969,152 Dice-music Trios', *MT*, cix (1968), 911
V. Globokar: 'Réagir . . .', *Musique en jeu* (1970), no.1, p.70
R. Kostelanetz, ed.: *John Cage* (New York, 1970)
L. G. Ratner: '*Ars combinatoria*: Chance and Choice in Eighteenth-century Music', *Studies in Eighteenth-century Music: a Tribute to Karl Geiringer* (New York and London, 1970), 343
D. Charles: 'L'interprète et le hasard', *Musique en jeu* (1971), no.3, p.45
C. Deliège: 'Indétermination et improvisation', *IRASM*, ii/2 (1971), 155–91
G. M. Potter: *The Role of Chance in Contemporary Music* (diss., Indiana U., 1971)
C. Cardew, ed.: *Scratch Music* (London, 1972)
V. Globokar: 'Ils improvisent . . . improvisez . . . improvisons', *Musique en jeu* (1972), no.6, p.13
M. E. Keller: 'Improvisation und Engagement', *Melos*, xl (1973), 198
M. Nyman: *Experimental Music: Cage and Beyond* (London, 1974)
S. A. Hedges: 'Dice Music in the Eighteenth Century', *ML*, lix (1978), 180

PAUL GRIFFITHS

Alectorius, Johannes. *See* GALLICULUS, JOHANNES.

Alegramente. *See* ALLEGRO.

Alegría. Flamenco-style Andalusian gypsy song and dance form. *See* FLAMENCO, Table 1.

Alegría, José Augusto (*b* Évora, 6 Jan 1918). Portuguese musicologist. He studied music at the Évora

Seminary and in Rome at the Pontificio Istituto di Musica Sacra, where he obtained the licentiate in 1951. From 1940 he taught music and conducted the choir at the Évora Seminary; he also taught at the Centro de Estudios Gregorianos, Lisbon, where he succeeded Mario Sampayo as conductor of the Polyphonia, a choir devoted to the interpretation of early music (particularly Portuguese). In 1974 he resigned from both posts. He has contributed to the encyclopedia *Verbo* and to various national journals, and has taken part in many conferences, both national and international. His publications, particularly his transcriptions of Portuguese early music, are noted for their accuracy.

WRITINGS

ed.: *J. Mazza: Diccionario biográfico de músicos portugueses* (Lisbon, 1945) [with preface and notes]
'Fray Manuel Cardoso', Cadernos de repertório coral polyphonia, *série azul* (Lisbon, 1955)
'A música litúrgica e as interferências populares', *Lumen* (Lisbon, 1958)
ed.: *Tractado de canto llano (1533) de Mateus de Aranda*, Rei musicae Portugaliae monumenta (Lisbon, 1962)
'O primeiro colégio de Évora', *Congresso internacional do IV centenário da Universidade de Évora* (Coimbra, 1967)
'Paixão e Glória de Cláudio Monteverdi', *Estudos. italianos em Portugal* (Lisbon, 1967), no.30
A problemática musical das cantigas de Amigo (Lisbon, 1968)
'Diogo Dias Melgaz', Cadernos de repertório coral polyphonia, *série azul* (Lisbon, 1969)
Catálogo do Arquivo das músicas da Sé de Évora (Lisbon, 1973)
História da Escola de música da Sé de Évora (Lisbon, 1973)
Biblioteca Pública de Évora: catálogo dos fundos musicais (Lisbon, 1977)

EDITIONS

M. Cardoso: *Liber primus missarum*, PM, ser.A, v–vi (1962–3); *Livro de vários motetes*, PM, ser.A, xiii (1968); *Liber secundus missarum*, PM, ser.A, xx (1972); *Liber tertius missarum*, PM, ser.A, xxii (1973); *Cantica Beatae Mariae Virginis*, PM, ser.A, xxvi (1974)

JOSÉ LÓPEZ-CALO

Alemana (It.). ALLEMANDE.

Alembert, Jean le Rond d'. *See* D'ALEMBERT, JEAN LE ROND.

'Alenu (Heb.: 'adoration'). A chant of the Jewish liturgy; *see* JEWISH MUSIC, §I, 8.

Aleotti, Raffaella (*b* Ferrara, *c*1570; *d* after 1646). Italian composer and organist, elder sister of Vittoria Aleotti. She was the daughter of Giovanni Battista Aleotti, architect to Alfonso II d'Este, Duke of Ferrara. She studied the harpsichord and composition with Alessandro Milleville and after his death (in 1586) with Ercole Pasquini. When very young she entered the Augustinian convent of S Vito, Ferrara, and took her vows about 1590. In the flourishing musical life of her convent her musical talents found ample room for development, and about 1593 she took over the direction of the main ensemble there, the 'concerto grande'. According to Bottrigari and Artusi the ensemble consisted of 23 singers and instrumentalists, the latter playing the harpsichord, lutes, bass viols, flutes, cornetts and trombones. They also praised the ensemble's high level of accomplishment, and composers such as Wert, Costanzo Porta, Merulo, Luzzaschi, Fontanelli and Gesualdo expressed their admiration for it. It was at its finest under Raffaella Aleotti's direction: in particular the performance given in 1598 in the presence of Pope Clement VIII and the Queen of Spain were admiringly chronicled. The queen tried in vain to persuade Aleotti to return to Spain with her as her personal organist. G. B. Chinelli (in 1637) and Lorenzo Agnelli (in 1638)

dedicated volumes of motets to her. She is known to have been alive in 1646, when she was advanced in years. As a composer she is known only by *Sacrae cantiones . . . liber primus* (Venice, 1593) for five, seven, eight and ten voices. It contains motets for voices and instruments which are among the earliest Italian music in the concertante style: they were doubtless written for the 'concerto grande' at S Vito. Aleotti also wrote secular music, but it is lost.

BIBLIOGRAPHY

Anon.: *Elenco delle monache che furono in S Vito agostiniane* (MS, I-FEc Antolini 56)
E. Bottrigari: *Il desiderio* (Venice, 1594; Eng. trans., MSD, ix, 1962)
G. M. Artusi: *L'Artusi, overo Delle imperfettioni della moderna musica* (Venice, 1600/R1969), 1ff
M. A. Guarini: *Compendio historico delle chiese di Ferrara* (Ferrara, 1621), 376
G. Sardi and A. Faustini: *Libro delle historie ferraresi* (Ferrara, 1646), 89

ADRIANO CAVICCHI

Aleotti, Vittoria (*b* Ferrara, *c*1573; *d* after 1620). Italian composer, younger sister of Raffaella Aleotti. Her father was Giovanni Battista Aleotti, architect to Alfonso II d'Este, Duke of Ferrara. Like her sister she studied with Alessandro Milleville and Ercole Pasquini, and took her vows in the convent of S Vito, Ferrara, where she helped her sister assiduously in the performances of music for voices and instruments. Her reputation as a composer when still very young was such that one of her madrigals for five voices was included in the famous anthology *Il giardino de musici ferraresi* (Venice, 1591[9]) alongside pieces by leading Ferrarese madrigalists. In the same year her father published a collection of four-part madrigals by her – *Ghirlanda de madrigali* (Venice, 1591, one work ed. P. G. Pistone, *Raccolta di musiche corali antiche e moderne*, Turin, 1941) – all to texts by Guarini. The music closely reflects the spirit of the words, no less in the two serene spiritual madrigals than in the 19 secular ones, which evoke an overwhelming, hopeless passion. The combination of spontaneous inspiration, graceful melody and simple counterpoint produces pieces which in their heightened lyricism need not fear comparison with madrigals by better-known composers of the time.

For bibliography *see* ALEOTTI, RAFFAELLA.

ADRIANO CAVICCHI

Alere. *See* ALAIRE.

Alessandra, Caterina. *See* ASSANDRA, CATERINA.

Alessandrescu, Alfred (*b* Bucharest, 2 Aug 1893; *d* Bucharest, 18 Feb 1959). Romanian composer, pianist and conductor. He studied with D. G. Kiriac, A. Castaldi, E. Saegiu and D. Dinicu at the Bucharest Conservatory (1903–11), completing his education with two periods of study in Paris (1913–14, 1923–4), where he studied with d'Indy at the Schola Cantorum and with Paul Vidal at the Conservatoire. A remarkable accompanist, he worked with Enescu, Thibaud, Mainardi, Moodie and others during the period 1919–45. As a conductor he always achieved a soberly balanced performance; he conducted more than 1500 performances at the Romanian Opera in Bucharest (1921–59), where he specialized in the French repertory. In his capacities as conductor of the Bucharest PO (1926–40) and artistic manager of the Radio Bucharest SO (1933–59) he did much to encourage Romanian composers. He was also active as a music critic for

Romanian and French reviews. Much of his compositional work was done during his student years; Debussy was a major influence on his lyrical and evocative style. His major works include three symphonic poems – *Amurg de toamnă* ('Late autumn'; 1910), *Didona* (1911) and *Acteon* (1915) – and some outstanding songs.

VIOREL COSMA

Alessandri, Felice (*b* Rome, 24 Nov 1747; *d* Casinalbo, nr. Modena, 15 Aug 1798). Italian composer. According to Manferrari, he was born at S Damaso, near Modena. He studied in Naples and had his first large work, the oratorio *Il Tobia*, performed in Rome in 1765. Having gained recognition as a harpsichordist and conductor in Turin and in Paris at the Concert Spirituel, he visited Verona and Venice to prepare his first operas, *Ezio* and *Il matrimonio per concorso*, for Carnival 1767. At about this time he married the *buffa* singer Maria Lavinia Guadagni (*b* Lodi, 21 Nov 1735; *d* Padua, *c*1790), sister of the celebrated castrato Gaetano Guadagni; both were employed by the King's Theatre, London, for which Alessandri composed the comic operas *La moglie fedele* and *Il re alla caccia*. Although he must have visited Vienna for the première of his opera *L'argentino* (spring 1768), he was again in London as a harpsichordist in 1770.

Alessandri's career has not been thoroughly investigated. Simonetti stated that he was summoned from Genoa to Dresden in 1773 to direct his *L'amor soldato*, but this opera was probably written by a composer with whom he is sometimes confused: Alessandro Felici. From 1773 until April 1775 he was mainly in Turin, where his operas *Argea*, *La cameriera per amore* and *Alcina e Ruggero* were performed. A *Medonte* (Milan, Carnival 1774) is attributed to Luigi Alessandri in a printed libretto in the Brera library, Milan, but to Felice in the *Gazzetta di Milano* of 28 December 1774. Two comic operas composed for Venetian theatres (not for London as stated by Fétis), received first performances later in 1775: *La sposa persiana* and *La novità*, and another for Lucca, *Sandrina* (not composed with Sacchini as claimed by Gerber).

During the following summer Alessandri was invited by Joseph Legros to share his direction of the Concert Spirituel and to compose for the Concerts des Amateurs in Paris. He lived in Legros' house and served these organizations for two years (1777–8). In December 1778 his opera *Calliroe* was staged at Milan's new Teatro alla Scala; his ballet *Venere in Cipro* was performed there soon after. During the next few years he had other operas staged in various Italian cities, including Padua, where he was highly regarded by the direction of the Teatro Nuovo. In 1783 the nobility of Padua commissioned him to set the cantata *Le virtù rivali* honouring Alvise Mocenigo, the retiring governor.

Hoping for an appointment as composer to the Russian court, Alessandri went to St Petersburg in 1786. As he found only the post of a singing teacher, he moved in autumn 1789 to Berlin where he was named assistant director of the court opera, reportedly at the instigation of the prima donna Luisa Todi. The works he composed were not well received, however. Gerber reported that his first opera, *Il ritorno di Ulysse a Penelope* (January 1790) was generally admired, and yet the composer encountered difficulties with J. F. Reichardt and other colleagues (according to Schneider) and

displeased his patron Friedrich Wilhelm II with his second opera, *L'ouverture du grand opéra italien à Nankin*. His next opera, *Dario* (Carnival 1791), proved a disaster, as did his last effort, a pasticcio entitled *Vasco di Gama* (January 1792). Finally, the king withdrew the *scrittura* for another opera, *Alboino*, and dismissed him (4 July 1792).

Alessandri remarried and returned in autumn 1792 to Italy, where his opera *Virginia* was performed (Venice, 1793). He rejected an offer to compose a *Medea* for the Paris Opéra, but travelled to Vienna and Berlin in 1794 in search of commissions. Later that year his operas *Zemira* and *Armida* received great applause in Padua, and he was named honorary member of the Modenese Accademia dei Filarmonici. His last opera, of unknown title, was given at the Teatro Rangoni, Modena, shortly before his death.

WORKS

SERIOUS OPERAS

Ezio (3, Metastasio), Verona, Filarmonica, carn. 1767; *I-Mc*
Arianna e Teseo (pasticcio), London, King's, 11 Oct 1768
Argea (3, G. Boggio), Turin, Regio, carn. 1773
Creso (3, G. Pizzi), Pavia, Quattro Signori, spr. 1774
Il Medonte re d'Epiro (3, G. de Gamerra), Milan, Ducale, 26 Dec 1774
Alcina e Ruggero (3, V. A. Cigna-Santi), Turin, Regio, carn. 1775
Calliroe (3, M. Verazi), Milan, La Scala, 26 Dec 1778
Adriano in Siria (3, Metastasio), Venice, S Benedetto, 26 Dec 1779
Erifile (3, ? G. B. Neri), Padua, Nuovo, 12 June 1780
Attalo re di Bitinia (3, A. Salvi), Florence, Pergola, Sept 1780; *F-Pn*
Arbace (3, G. Sertor), Rome, Argentina, 29 Dec 1781
Demofoonte (3, Metastasio), Padua, Nuovo, 12 June 1783
Artaserse (3, Metastasio), Naples, S Carlo, 4 Nov 1783
Il ritorno di Ulysse a Penelope (3, A. Filistri), Potsdam, court theatre, 25 Jan 1790; *D-B*
Dario (3, Filistri), Berlin, Königliches, Jan 1791; *B*
Vasco di Gama (pasticcio, 3, Filistri), Berlin, Königliches, 20 Jan 1792
Virginia (3, A. Pepoli), Venice, La Fenice, 26 Dec 1793
Zemira (2, Sertor), Padua, Nuovo, 12 June 1794
Armida (2, G. M. Foppa), Padua, Nuovo, 1 July 1794; autograph *I-Bc*, duets, *PAc*, *Vnm*

COMIC OPERAS

Il matrimonio per concorso (3, G. Martinelli, after Goldoni), Venice, S Moisè, carn. 1767; *A-Wn*
La moglie fedele (2), London, King's, 27 Feb 1768
L'Argentino (2), Vienna, Burg, spr. 1768
Il re alla caccia (3, Goldoni), London, King's, 1 March 1769
La cameriera per amore (2, F. Livigni), Turin, Carignano, aut. 1774
Sandrina, ossia La contadina di corte (2, Goldoni), Lucca, Pubblico, 1775
La novità (2, G. Bertati), Venice, S Moisè, aut. 1775; *I-Mc*
La sposa persiana (3, Goldoni), Venice, S Samuele, aut. 1775; *MOe*, *D-Dlb*
Il vecchio geloso (2, Bertati), Milan, 1 Oct 1781; *I-Bc*, *Fc* [inc.]
La finta principessa, ossia Li due fratelli Pappamosca (2, Livigni), Venice, S Moisè, aut. 1782; *D-DS*, *I-CRg*, ov., aria *Gi(l)*
I puntigli gelosi (2, Livigni), Venice, S Samuele, carn. 1783
L'imbroglio delle tre spose (2, Bertati), Florence, Pergola, spr. 1784
La villanella rapita (2, Bertati), Bologna, Formagliari, aut. 1784
L'ouverture du grand opéra italien à Nankin (La compagnia d'opera à Nanchino) (2, Filistri), Berlin, Kleines, 16 Oct 1790
I sposi burlati (2), Mantua, Nuovo Nazionale, 26 Dec 1798

OTHER WORKS

Cantatas: Il tempio della fama, Milan, 1782; La virtù rivali (2, F. Pimbiolo degli Engelfreddi), Padua, Nuovo, 5 July 1783
Ballets: Venere in Cipro (scenario ?Verazi, choreography G. Canziani), Milan, La Scala, 30 Dec 1779, perf. with Anfossi's Cleopatra; L'enlèvement des Sabines (S. Gallet), Alessandria, Città, Oct 1779, perf. with G. Ferrero's La disfatta di Dario
Oratorios: Il Tobia (2), Rome, 1767, *I-Rf*; Bethulia liberata, Padua, 1781, *Pca*
Inst: 6 sinfonie, 2 vn, va, 2 ob, 2 hn, bc, op.6 (Paris, n.d.); 6 hpd concs., acc. 2 vn, vc (London, n.d.); 6 sonatas, 2 vn, bc (hpd) (London, n.d.); sinfonie, *I-Mc*, *CH-Zz*; Hpd Sonata, D, *I-OS*

BIBLIOGRAPHY

BurneyH; *EitnerQ*; *FétisB*; *GerberNL*
L. Schneider: *Geschichte der Oper und des königlichen Opernhauses in Berlin* (Berlin, 1852)
L. F. Valdrighi: *Felice Alessandri maestro di cappella di Federico Guglielmo II re di Prussia (1790–92)* (Modena, 1896)

R.-A. Mooser: *Annales de la musique et des musiciens en Russie au XVIIIme siècle*, ii (Geneva, 1951)
E. Zanetti: 'Alessandri, Felice', *ES*
U. Manferrari: *Dizionario universale delle opere melodrammatiche*, i (Florence, 1954)
S. Simonetti: 'Alessandri, Felice', *DBI*
——: 'Alessandri, Felice', *MGG*
The London Stage, 1660–1800 (Carbondale, Ill., 1960–68)

SVEN HANSELL

Alessandri, Giulio d' (*b* ?Ferrara; *fl* 1684–96). Italian composer. He possibly served for a time as *maestro di cappella* of Ferrara Cathedral. He was appointed *vice-maestro di cappella* of Milan Cathedral in 1684, shortly after which he competed unsuccessfully for the post of *maestro di cappella*. In the libretto of his oratorio *La Bersabea* (1686) he is described as a canon at S Nazaro in Broglio, Milan. In 1696 he participated, along with 19 other composers, in the pasticcio *L'Etna festivo*. He wrote in a basically homophonic, concerted style. In *La Bersabea* roughly a quarter of the arias are strophic and half are accompanied by other instruments besides continuo. He frequently moved from recitative to aria (marked there) and back to recitative within a single piece. Both parts of the work end with recitative rather than with the usual chorus or ensemble.

WORKS

La Bersabea, oratorio (M. Brugueres), Milan, 1686, *I-MOe*
S Francesca Romana, oratorio, *A-Wn, D-B, Dl*
One of 20 composers to write music for the pasticcio L'Etna festivo: introduttione di ballo (O. d'Arles), Milan, 1696 [music lost]
Duet, holograph, *D-Bds*; Te Deum, 8vv, insts, holograph, *A-Wn*
Te Deum, 8vv, insts, holograph, *A-Wn*

BIBLIOGRAPHY

R. G. Kiesewetter: *Galerie der alten Contrapunctisten* (Vienna, 1847)
C. A. Vianello: *Teatri, spettacoli, musiche a Milano nei secoli scorsi* (Milan, 1941)
H. Kier: *Raphael Georg Kiesewetter (1773–1850): Wegbereiter des musikalischen Historismus* (Regensburg, 1968)

JULIA ANN GRIFFIN

Alessandri & Scattaglia. Italian firm of music and general engravers and publishers, music and print sellers. The firm was active in Venice at the sign of the Beata Vergine della Pace on the Rialto from about 1770 to at least 1803. It was founded by the engravers Innocente Alessandri (*b* Venice, *c*1740), a pupil of Bartolozzi, and Pietro Scattaglia. From about 1770, during the years of publication of their joint magnum opus, *Animali quadrupedi* (Venice, Carlo Palese, 1771–5, illustrated with 200 plates designed, engraved and hand-coloured by themselves), they also worked as engravers and selling agents for the music publisher Luigi Marescalchi; on at least one title-page they are also described as his printers, which may have been another of their regular responsibilities. Together with Marescalchi they were associated in the revival of music publishing in Italy after 70 years of almost total inactivity. The fact that their names appear on almost all title-pages of Marescalchi's Venice editions has often led cataloguers and bibliographers to ascribe to them publications that should properly be regarded as Marescalchi's, resulting in numerous errors in *RISM*, the *British Union Catalogue* and other reference works. It is probable that Alessandri & Scattaglia did not publish an edition of their own until after Marescalchi had closed his Venice business about 1775; even after that date their status is often described merely as selling agent on title-pages of editions whose publishers are not specified (it must, however, be recognized that modern definitions of the respective titles and functions of publisher and distrib-

utor may not be rigidly applicable to the music-publishing trade in late 18th-century Venice).

Of the handful of editions that bear Alessandri & Scattaglia's unquestioned imprint, the outstanding one is the full score of Bertoni's *Orfeo* (*c*1776); it was only the second complete opera to be published in full score in Italy since 1658. A reissue from the same plates, but without an imprint, was published for the opera's revival at the Venice Carnival (1782–3). After about 1785 the firm gradually did less music engraving, but the premises on the Rialto were retained at least until late 1803. Music of every type was sold there, including manuscript copies of numbers from the latest operas, dressed up within decoratively engraved paper wrappers. The majority of publications with which the firm was associated are in oblong format and have ornamental title-pages of uncommon elegance.

BIBLIOGRAPHY

C. Sartori: *Dizionario degli editori musicali italiani* (Florence, 1958), 6, 96f [inaccurate]

RICHARD MACNUTT

Alessandro, Charles-Guillaume. *See* ALEXANDRE, CHARLES-GUILLAUME.

Alessandro [Alessandri], **Gennaro d'** (*fl* 1739–40). Italian composer. In the document recording his appointment as *maestro di coro* at the Ospedale della Pietà, Venice, in 1739 he is called 'Alessandro Gennaro Napolitano', which indicates that he was born or educated or both in the Neapolitan region. Fétis stated that he was born in Naples in 1717, but no confirmation of this is known. He was in service at the Pietà from 21 August 1739 to 13 May 1740 when he was dismissed for lack of diligence. Within that period he was not entirely idle, however, for he presented his opera *Ottone* at the S Giovanni Grisostomo theatre, Venice, during carnival 1740 and his serenata *Il coro delle muse* at the Ospedale on 21 March of the same year in honour of the Electoral Prince of Saxony, Friedrich Christian. Goldoni, who wrote the words of the serenata, said in his memoirs (*Delle commedie di Carlo Goldoni*, Venice, 1761) that he had adapted them to music that Alessandro had written for three preceding cantatas with texts by Goldoni, *La ninfa saggia*, *Gli amanti felici* and *Le quattro stagioni*. It is presumed that these three cantatas were also composed around 1739–40. No information on Alessandro's movements after his dismissal from the Ospedale has come to light.

Little of his music remains. The catalogue of *I-Bc* lists an aria from *Ottone*, 'Se brami la mia morte', while that of *B-Bc* mentions another aria, 'Già per te non sento amore'. L. de La Laurencie recorded six sinfonias by Alessandro in *Inventaire critique du fonds Blancheton de la Bibliothèque du Conservatoire de Paris*, i (Paris, 1930).

MICHAEL F. ROBINSON

Alessandro, Raffaele d' (*b* St Gall, 17 March 1911; *d* Lausanne, 17 March 1959). Swiss composer, pianist and organist. He began his music studies in Zurich in 1932, for the most part teaching himself; from 1934 to 1937 he studied in Paris with Dupré, Paul Roës and Nadia Boulanger, and returned to Switzerland in 1940. Settling in Lausanne, he worked as a concert pianist, composer, music critic and broadcaster. His eclectic style took elements from the varied musical currents of the time, but he retained a basis of sonata form and tonal harmony. He preferred driving rhythms and his writing is complex and compact.

WORKS
(selective list)

Orch: Conc. grosso, op.57, 1946; Pf Conc. no.3, op.70, 1951; Isla persa, op.71, ballet, 1951; Sym. no.2, op.72, 1952–3; Conc., op.75, bn, str, 1956; Tema variato, op.78, 1957; Ob Conc., op.79, 1958

24 Preludes, op.30, pf, 1940; Sonata, op.46, fl, pf, 1942; 12 Etüden, op.66, pf, 1949; Sonata, op.67, ob, pf, 1949; Sonata, op.68a, a fl, pf, 1958; Str Qt no.2, op.73, 1953

Principal publishers: Bote & Bock, Erdmann, Foetisch, Symphonia

BIBLIOGRAPHY
L. Marretta-Schär: *Raffaele d'Alessandro: Leben und Werk* (diss., U. of Berne, 1972)
LUISE MARRETTA-SCHÄR

Alessandro Mantovano (*fl* c1510–?c1530). Italian composer. He may have been the 'Alessandro nostro musico' at the Mantuan court in 1530 (see Bertolotti). 11 frottolas are attributed to him in Antico's third book of frottolas (*RIŞM* 1513[1]; ed. in SCMA, iv, 1941); more expansive than those by Rossino Mantovano, they are typical of a later phase and include higher verse forms such as the madrigal. A reprint of Antico's third book (*RISM* c1517) attributes two more frottolas to him, but in the first edition one of these is ascribed to Cara and the other is anonymous. There is no evidence that he was related to Gian Pietro Mantovano, who may have been the 'Gian Pietro della viola' at the Mantuan court in 1485 (see Bertolotti and Pirrotta). One frottola by Gian Pietro survives, in an intabulation for lute and voice by Bossinensis (*RISM* 1511; ed. B. Disertori, *Le frottole per canto e liuto intabulate da Franciscus Bossinensis*, Milan, 1964).

BIBLIOGRAPHY
A. Bertolotti: *Musici alla corte dei Gonzaga in Mantova dal secolo XV al XVIII* (Milan, 1890/*R*1969)

P. M. Tagmann: *Archivalische Studien zur Musikpflege am Dom von Mantua* (Berne, 1967)

K. Jeppesen: *La frottola* (Århus and Copenhagen, 1968–70), i, 82ff, 106, 118, 128ff; ii, 265ff

N. Pirrotta: *Li due Orfei: da Poliziano a Monteverdi* (Turin, 1969, 2/1975), 127ff

W. Prizer: *Marchetto Cara and the North Italian Frottola* (diss., U. of North Carolina, 1974)
JOAN WESS

Alessandro Padovano (*b* Padua; *fl* 1563). Italian composer. He is known by five motets published in Rinaldo da Montagnana's *Il primo libro di motetti a cinque voci* (*RISM* 1563[5]). It seems likely that Montagnana, who spent his known career in Padua, was Alessandro's teacher.

Alevi, Giuseppe. *See* ALLEVI, GIUSEPPE.

Alexander, Charles McCallom (*b* Meadow, Tenn., 24 Oct 1867; *d* Birmingham, England, 13 Oct 1920). American revivalist and publisher of gospel hymn collections. *See* GOSPEL MUSIC, §I; H. C. Alexander and J. K. Maclean: *Charles M. Alexander* (London, 1920)

Alexander, Haim [Heinz] (*b* Berlin, 9 Aug 1915). Israeli composer and teacher of German birth. In his youth his musical activities were rich and varied: he studied the piano at the Stern Conservatory, sang in the children's choir of the Hochschule für Musik, and composed and improvised in jazz and art styles. This period was cut short by the Nazi persecution in 1934, and in 1936 Alexander moved to Jerusalem at the suggestion of Emil Hauser. There he studied the piano and composition under Irma and Stefan Wolpe and others at the

Palestine Conservatory and Academy of Music, from which he graduated in 1945. Gradually he became well known and respected as a teacher of the piano, theory and composition, and as a composer. The lively Six Israeli Dances (1950), which won an Engel Prize in 1956, are representative in their Israeli modal chromaticism and their rather traditional textures and forms; his choral works, cantatas and some instrumental pieces developed along similar lines. At the same time Alexander was producing a separate body of serial works as a result of the 'musical shock' (his own term) he received in Darmstadt (1958) and elsewhere in Germany (1962 and 1964). The two styles are integrated in *Patterns*, a test piece for the 1973 Rubinstein Piano Competition. Professor of composition at the Jerusalem Academy of Music, he taught improvisation at the Institut Jaques-Dalcroze in Geneva in 1971.

WORKS
(selective list)

Orch: 6 Israeli Dances, 1950; A Journey into the Present, 1971

Chamber: Cl Qnt, 1947; 6 Israeli Dances, vn, pf, 1950; Metamorphoses, vn, 1968; Variations on a Folktune, trbn, pf, 1969

Vocal: Rubayat, Mez/Bar, ens, 1963; 4 cantatas, c20 choral songs, popular songs, folksong arrs.

Pf: 6 Israeli Dances, pf/2 pf, 1950; Suite, 2 pf, 1951; Sonata brevis, 2 pf, 1960; Sound Figures, 1965; Patterns, 1973; D'après un mazurke, 1974; educational works

Principal publishers: Israel Music Institute, Israeli Music Publications, Merkaz Letarbut Ulechinuch

BIBLIOGRAPHY
Y. W. Cohen: *Werden und Entwicklungen der Musik in Israel* (Kassel, 1976) [pt.ii of rev. edn. of M. Brod: *Die Musik Israels*]

W. Y. Elias: *The Music of Israel* (in preparation) [bibliography]
NATHAN MISHORI

Alexander, John (*b* Meridian, Mississippi, c1925). American tenor. After pre-medical studies at Duke University and service with the American Air Force he trained at the Cincinnati Conservatory; his most influential teacher was the baritone Robert Weede. He made his début as Faust with the Cincinnati Opera in 1952, joined the New York City Opera as Alfredo five years later, and the Metropolitan Opera as Ferrando in 1961. Important European engagements found him singing in Korngold's *Die tote Stadt* at the Vienna Volksoper (1967), *La bohème* at the Vienna Staatsoper (1968), and Pollione in *Norma* at Covent Garden (1970). The Bellini opera became one of his specialities, and he has sung it in a single season opposite the three most celebrated Normas of the time: Sutherland, Caballé and Sills. In May 1973 he undertook the title role in the first American performance of the original French version of *Don Carlos*, staged by the Boston Opera. Alexander's value to leading American opera companies rests partly with his remarkable versatility and reliability in an enormous repertory, spanning belcanto at one extreme and such Germanic roles as Bacchus and Walther von Stolzing at the other. Although his acting sometimes lacks ardour and his singing is not invariably notable for dynamic finesse, he makes the most of taste, fervour, stamina, and a voice that commands an exceptionally brilliant ring at the top.
MARTIN BERNHEIMER

Alexander, Meister [Der wilde Alexander] (*fl* 2nd half of the 13th century). Itinerant poet–composer from south Germany. He is not attested in official documents or mentioned in contemporary literature. The only biographical clues are certain allusions in his poetry to historical events between 1287 and 1291 but more recent study shows additional allusions to events from 1247 to 1253. In two manuscripts he is named 'der wilde Alexander', probably because of his unusual style, and in the Jena manuscript he is called 'Meister Alexander'. But the Meistersinger did not regard him as one of the 12 masters.

Alexander was one of the most important Minnesinger and composers of *Sprüche* (*see* SPRUCH) after the time of Walther von der Vogelweide. In the surviving sources he is represented mainly by *Sprüche*, but also by some Minnelieder and one *Leich*. The principal themes of his *Spruch* poetry are admonition and criticism of the times, with reference both to the life of the individual and to religious and political circumstances. The themes of his Minnesang are still those of the chivalrous *hohe Minne*; yet the repertory of motifs in classical Minnesang, with its tendency to idealize, is given new life by his highly personal, adventurous and passionate manner. Alexander's lyric poetry has much of the formal style of classical courtly poetry, but is characterized by his own powerful, dark, allegorical style. The originality and forward-looking form of his melodies reflect his poetic skill. Alexander's musical style is similar to that of classical Minnesang; but at the same time the melodies show a more modern and refined stylistic intent, and some suggest early 14th-century style in their extensive melismas.

WORKS

Text edition: *Deutsche Liederdichter des 13. Jahrhunderts*, ed. C. von Kraus and H. Kuhn (Tübingen, 1952–8), i, 1ff [K]
Music editions: *Gesänge von Frauenlob, Reinmar von Zweter und Alexander*, ed. H. Rietsch, DTÖ, xli, Jg.xx/2 (1913/R) [R]
    Minnesang des 13. Jahrhunderts, ed. H. Kuhn (Tübingen, 1953) [with melodies ed. G. Reichert] [KR]
    Ausgewählte Melodien des Minnesangs, ed. E. Jammers (Tübingen, 1963) [J]
    The Art of the Minnesinger, ed. R. J. Taylor, i (Cardiff, 1968) [T]

Ach owê, daz nâch liebe ergât, K 13, *D-Ju* E1.f.101 [Jenaer Liederhandschrift], *A-Wn* 2701 [Wiener Leichhandschrift]; R, J, T
Ein wunder in der werlde vert, K 2, *Ju*; J, T
Hie vor dô wir kinder wâren, K 12, *Ju*; KR, J, T
Mîn trûreclîchez klagen ('Minneleich'), K 15, *Ju*, *Wn* 2701 (with diverging music); KR 154 (after *Wn*), J (*Ju*), T (*Ju*, *Wn*)
Siôn, trûre, K 10, *Ju* (frag., melody to lines 17–26 missing); KR, J, T

BIBLIOGRAPHY

R. Haller: *Der wilde Alexander* (Würzburg, 1935)
H. Kuhn: *Minnesangs Wende* (Tübingen, 1952, 2/1967), 134ff
R. J. Taylor: *The Art of the Minnesinger*, ii (Cardiff, 1968), 3ff
J. Biehl: *Der wilde Alexander: Untersuchungen zur literarischen Technik eines Autors im 13. Jahrhundert* (diss., U. of Hamburg, 1970)
N. Wagner: 'Die Lebenszeit des wilden Alexander', *Zeitschrift für deutsches Altertum und deutsche Literatur*, civ (1975), 338
For further bibliography *see* MINNESANG and SOURCES, MS.

                    BURKHARD KIPPENBERG

Alexander Brothers. A family firm of wind instrument makers, established in Mainz in the late 18th century. Originally manufacturers of both woodwind and brass instruments, since about 1900 they have restricted their production to the latter, although they still supply all types of instruments. Their German, wide-bore orchestral horns are particularly esteemed.

The business was begun in 1782 by Franz Ambros Alexander (*b* Miltenberg, Lower Saxony, 1753; *d* Mainz, 1 Dec 1802) under privilege of Friedrich Carl Josef, Elector of Erthal. On the death of the founder, his sons Philipp (*b* Mainz, 1787; *d* 1826) and Kaspar Anton (1803–72) took over the management, and the firm was then first known as Alexander Brothers.

Kaspar Anton's two sons Franz Anton (1836–1926) and Georg Philipp (1849–97) continued the business. In the next generation it was again the sons of the younger son who assumed control: Anton (1873–1913) and Philipp (1879–1916). In 1926 ownership of the company passed to Anton's son, Philipp (*b* 1904).

In addition to producing their own standard models, Alexander Brothers have done much research for various theorists and have made special instruments, notably the 'Bach' trumpets of Werner Menke.

                    PHILIP BATE

Alexandra Choir. London choir founded in 1940; *see* LONDON, §VI, 3(ii).

Alexandre [Alessandro], **Charles-Guillaume** (*b* c1735; *d* Paris, late 1787 or early 1788). French composer and violinist. His first names are undoubtedly Charles-Guillaume (given by La Borde, 1780) rather than Claude-Guillaume (from the report of his wife's death in *Annonces*, 14 August 1792). He is first mentioned in *Les spectacles de Paris* as a violinist in the orchestra of the Opéra-Comique from 1753 to 1755. By 1756 he had composed music for at least two *spectacles à machines* at the Théâtre des Tuileries. The *Annonces, affiches et avis divers* of 15 September 1760 referred to him as first violin and *maître de musique* at the music school of Sieur Dubugraire; in the announcement of his *Six trio* op.4 (1762) he is described as the first violin of the Duc d'Aiguillon, a prominent patron in the French capital. Soon afterwards he began to take advantage of the expanding bourgeois musical life in Paris and for almost three decades he made his living as a composer, arranger and violin teacher. Although he is known to have been a violinist, his name does not appear as a soloist nor as a member of any Parisian orchestra after 1755. He is listed as a composer in the *Almanach musical* (1775–9). He must have died shortly before 27 March 1788, when a sale of his personal musical effects was advertised in the *Annonces*.

Most of Alexandre's printed works were arrangements of popular opera *airs*, including 30 quartet arrangements of such works as Gluck's *Alceste*, Grétry's *Richard Coeur-de-Lion* and Dalayrac's *Nina*. These were tailored to the limited performing skills of his market; the announcement of his *Six quatuors* (1778) in the *Annonces* of 28 June 1779 clearly shows their purpose: 'These quartets have a simple and agreeable melody: they will suit all classes of amateurs, who will find enough difficulties in them to exert themselves and enough simple traits to make their execution continually seem brilliant'. Alexandre went further in this field than most of his contemporaries by writing violin concertos based on popular *airs*. Such works enjoyed considerable popular appeal; at the performance of one of these concertos at the Concert Spirituel in 1765, the *Mercure de France* commented: 'Aside from M. Capron's beautiful execution, this concerto gave pleasure from the number of pleasant tunes that were brought together and the art with which they were assembled'. Of his original compositions the opera *Le petit-maître en province* was praised by the *Mercure de France* for being in 'French taste'; but Grimm (*Correspondance littéraire*, October 1765) found the composer 'a fabricator of notes ... without having a single musical idea'. His *Sei sinfonie* op.6, however, are well-constructed pieces demanding a high level of technical proficiency and fusing Italian, Mannheim and French traits.

WORKS
(printed works published in Paris)

STAGE

(first performed in Paris)

Le triomphe de l'amour conjugal (spectacle orné de machines, 5, G. N. Servandoni), Tuileries, 16 March 1755 (1755), lost
La conquêt du Mogol par Thamas Kouli-Kan, Roi de Perse, et son triomphe (spectacle à machines, 5, Servandoni), Tuileries, 4 April 1756 (1756), lost
Georget et Georgette (opéra comique, 1, Harny de Guerville), Foire St-Laurent, 28 July 1761 (1761)
Le tonnelier (opéra comique, 1, N.-M. Audinot, A. F. Quétant), Comédie-Italienne, 16 March 1765, collab. Gossec, Philidor, Schobert, Trial, Ciapalanti, Kohaut (1765)
Le petit-maître en province (comedie, 1, Harny de Guerville), Comédie-Italienne, 7 Oct 1765 (1765)
L'esprit du jour (opéra comique, 1, Harny de Guerville), Comédie-Italienne, 22 Jan 1767, airs pubd in contemporary anthologies
Godefroy de Bouillon (spectacle à machines, Servandoni), Tuileries, cited by La Borde

OTHER WORKS

Inst: 6 trio, op.4 (1762), lost; 6 sinfonie à 8, op.6 (1766), mistakenly attrib. F. Alessandri and G. d'Alessandro; 6 duetto, 2 vn, op.8 (1775); 6 quatuors, str qt (1778), lost; ov., no.5 in 6 overture a più stromenti composta da varri autori (before 1760), probably by A. Bernasconi
Arrs.: Les beaux airs ou Symphonies chantantes, 1ère [–3e] suite (1766); 1er [–6e] concerto d'airs connus à 7 (before 1775); 12 duos d'airs connus, 2 vn, op.1 (1775); [1er–9e] Concert d'airs en quatuor, str qt (1775–6); 1ère [–13e, 15e, 22–3e, 25–9e] suite d'airs d'opéra comiques en quatuor concertants avec l'ouverture, str qt (1775–c1783), nos.5–6, 13, 15, 22–3, 25–9 extant
Motets, lost: Confitemini Domino, perf. Dubugraire's music school, 17 Sept 1760; Paratum cor meum, perf. Concert Spirituel, April 1774; others, MS, formerly in Alexandre's estate

BIBLIOGRAPHY

FétisB; GerberL; GerberNL

L. C. de La Vallière: *Ballets, opéras et autres ouvrages lyriques* (Paris, 1760)
J.-B. de La Borde: *Essai sur la musique ancienne et moderne* (Paris, 1780/R1972), iii, 375
J. Goizet: *Dictionnaire universal des théâtres* (Paris, 1867)
F. Grimm and others: *Correspondance littéraire*, ed. M. Tourneux (Paris, 1877–82), vi, 388f; vii, 222
G. Tholin and A. Bosvieux: *Inventaire sommaire des archives communales antérieures à 1790: supplement à la série II* (Paris, 1884)
M. Brenet: *Les concerts en France sous l'ancien régime* (Paris, 1900/R1969), 352
L. de La Laurencie: *L'école française de violon de Lully à Viotti*, ii (Paris, 1924/R1971), 370
C. Johansson: *French Publisher's Catalogues of the Second Half of the Eighteenth Century* (Stockholm, 1955)
B. S. Brook: *La symphonie française dans la seconde moitié du XVIIIe siècle* (Paris, 1962)

BARRY S. BROOK, RICHARD VIANO

Alexandrov, Alexander Vasil'yevich (*b* St Petersburg, 1 April 1883; *d* Moscow, 8 July 1946). Soviet composer and conductor. He studied with Glazunov and Lyadov at the St Petersburg Conservatory and with Vasilenko at the Moscow Conservatory. From 1918 he taught at the Moscow Conservatory, where he was made head of the choral conducting department in 1925. Choral music gradually became the centre of his attention; most of it was composed for the Soviet Army Song and Dance Ensemble, which he founded in 1928 and which he led to great success in the USSR and abroad. After his death the ensemble was named after him.

Alexandrov's choral songs are of various types: rousing, heroic, lyrical and comic. They are simple in style, always linked with Russian folksong and sometimes show delicate polyphonic writing. *Svyashchennaya voyna* ('A holy war', text by Lebedev-Kumach) was written in the first few days of fighting against German invasion in June 1941 and became something of a musical symbol for the Soviet people in World War II.

Alexandrov's works also include about 60 other songs, about 70 folksong arrangements, operas, instrumental pieces and the national anthem of the USSR.

BIBLIOGRAPHY

D. Kabalevsky: 'O masterstve' [On craftsmanship], *SovM* (1952), no.3, p.21
G. Polyanovsky: *A. V. Alexandrov* (Moscow, 1959)

GALINA GRIGOR'YEVA

Alexandrov, Anatoly Nikolayevich (*b* Moscow, 25 May 1888). Russian composer. He studied with Taneyev and Vasilenko (composition) and Igumnov (piano) at the Moscow Conservatory (1910–16), where from 1923 he was a composition professor. Among his distinctions is the title People's Artist of the USSR. He has composed in most genres, but the piano works are among his best. At first his piano style was influenced by Skryabin, Metner and Rakhmaninov; later he developed an individual manner marked by colour and rich inventiveness. There is a particular delicacy and refinement in his songs, many of which have entered the Soviet repertory, and his operas are lyrical, melodic and expressively direct. He has shown great interest in Russian national musics, making many vocal and piano arrangements. Among his numerous incidental scores, that for Paustovsky's film *Severnaya povest'* ('Northern tale') was notably successful. In general his music is characterized by emotional depth and colourfulness, and by its close links with 19th-century Russian traditions.

WORKS
(selective list)

Operas: Bela (Yu. Stremin, after Lermontov), Moscow, Bol'shoy, 1946; Dikaya Bara [Wild Bara] (S. Severtsev, after B. Němcová), 1957
Orch: Klassicheskaya syuita (1931); Romanticheskaya syuita (1932); Uvertyura na russkiye narodnïye temï [Ov. on Russian folk themes], c1948; Zabavnaya syuita [Comic suite] (1956); Teatral'no-tantseval'naya syuita (1957); Pamyat' serdtsa [Heart's remembrance], sym. poem, 1960; Sym., 1965; Russkiye narodnïye melodii [Russian folk melodies], orch suite, 1970; Pf Conc., 1974
Inst: 4 str qts (1921), (1942), (1942), (1953); 14 pf sonatas; other pf pieces; folksong arrs.
Songs: over 150 songs (Aliger, Baratinsky, Blok, Fet, Pushkin, Tikhonov, Tyutchev, etc); c100 songs for children; folksong arrs.
Incidental music for the theatre, cinema and radio

Principal publishers: Muzgiz, Sovyetskiy kompozitor

BIBLIOGRAPHY

V. Belyayev: *A. N. Alexandrov* (Moscow, 1927)
G. Kreytner: 'Tvorchestvo Anatoliya Alexandrova' [Alexandrov's work], *SovM* (1938), no.7, p.11
A. Khokhlovkina: 'Bela – opera Anatoliya Alexandrova', *SovM* (1946), no.11, p.19
K. Petrova: 'Novïye romansï Anatoliya Alexandrova', *SovM* (1952), no.1, p.94
R. Ledenyov: 'Chistoserdechnoye sluzheniye iskusstvu' [Candid service to art], *Muzïkal'naya zhizn'* (1968), no.11, p.10

GALINA GRIGOR'YEVA

Alexandrov, Boris Alexandrovich (*b* Bologoye, 4 Aug 1905). Russian composer and conductor. He graduated from the Moscow Conservatory under Glier in 1929 and worked as a music director in Moscow clubs (1923–9), music director of the Red Army Theatre (1930–37), lecturer at the Moscow Conservatory (1933–41) and leader of the Soviet Radio Song Ensemble (1942–7). From 1937 to 1946 he was deputy director of the Alexandrov Red Army Song and Dance Ensemble, which was founded by his father, Alexander Vasil'yevich Alexandrov, and, after the latter's death, came under his direction. He received the State Prize (1950) and the title People's Artist of the USSR (1958). In the Two Piano Pieces op.1 (1928) he developed a compositional system synthesizing the principle of the 12-note series (with inversions and permutations) with a harmonic set technique and mirror symmetry. Later works, such as the well-known musical comedy *Svad'ba v Malinovke* ('Wedding in Malinovka'), exploit the tonal harmonies of Ukrainian folk music or exotic pentatonic harmony (as in the Chinese Suite).

WORKS
(selective list)

Musical comedies: Svad'ba v Malinovke [Wedding in Malinovka] (L. Yukhvid), 1937; Sotïy tigr [The 100th tiger] (L. Tarsky, M. Triger), 1939; God spustya [A year later] (V. Tipot), 1940; Devushka iz Barselonï [A girl from Barcelona] (I. Nazarov, A. Sofronov, G. Yaron), 1942; Moya Gyusel (E. Pomeshchik, N. Rozhkov), 1946; 101-ya zhena [The 101st woman] (Tipot, Sh. Dadiana), 1954

Ballets: Levsha [The left-handed man], P. Abolimov, after N. Leskov, 1954; Druzhba yunïkh [Youthful friendship], Abolimov, after A. Butkevich, 1954–5

Vocal orch: Songs from Svad'ba v Malinovke, vv, jazz orch (1941); Molodost' mira [The world's youth], vv, orch (1953); Soldat oktyabrya zashchitayet mir [The October soldier defends peace], oratorio, speaker, solo vv, chorus, orch (1970); Delo Lenina [Lenin's acts], oratorio (1973)

Orch: 2 syms., 1928, 1930; Pf Conc., 1929; Tpt Conc., 1933; Cl Conc., 1936; Chinese Suite, 1953; Ov. (1955); Conc.-Fantasy, pf, folk orch, 1955

Choral: many choruses and songs incl. Pesnya o partii [Party songs], 1956; Slushay [Listen], male vv, 1959; Da zdravstvuyet Kuba [Long live Cuba], 1961; army songs

Inst: 2 p'yesy (2 morceaux), op.1, pf (1928); 2 str qts, 1931; Ww Qt, 1932; Nocturne-Allegro, cl, pf (1947)

Incidental music, film scores, folksong arrs.

Principal publisher: Soviet State Publishing House

BIBLIOGRAPHY

D. Gojowy: 'Zwölftontechnik in Russland', *Melos*, xxxix (1972), 129

DETLEF GOJOWY

Alexandru, Tiberiu (*b* Ilimbav, Sibiu, 14 May 1914). Romanian ethnomusicologist. He studied at the Bucharest Conservatory (1931–6) and became Brăiloiu's closest collaborator, working with him at the folklore archive of the Societatea Compozitorilor Români (1935–8); he continued his research appointment there when the archive was incorporated in the Institutul de Folclor (1949, from 1963 the Institutul de Etnografie şi Folclor), undertaking several field studies and collecting numerous examples of Romanian folksong, some of which have been recorded. He was Brăiloiu's successor in the folklore department of Bucharest Conservatory (1943–8), where he held various posts before becoming professor (1954–9). In 1956 he did research in China and from 1965 to 1967 he was the folklore expert of the Ministry of Culture of the United Arab Republic in Cairo, where he made recordings of Egyptian and Nubian folksong. In his writing on folk music, which is remarkable for its factual precision, he has concentrated on instruments and the work of important individuals. His recordings include the six-disc *Antologia muzicii populare româneşti* (1960–62). In 1957 he became a member, and in 1971 an executive member, of the IFMC. The Romanian Academy awarded him the Ciprian Porumbescu Prize in 1957.

WRITINGS

Muzica populară bănăţeană (Bucharest, 1942)

with others: *Dirijorul de cor* [Choir conducting] (Bucharest, 1955)

Instrumentele muzicale ale poporului român (Bucharest, 1956)

'Tilinca: ein uraltes rumänisches Volksinstrument', *Studia memoriae Bélae Bartók sacra* (Budapest, 1956, 3/1959), 107

'Vioara ca instrument muzical popular', *Revista de folclor*, ii/3 (1957), 29

Béla Bartók despre folclorul românesc (Bucharest, 1958)

'Armonie şi polifonie în cîntecul popular românesc', *Muzica*, ix (1959), no.3, p.14; no.10, p.20; no.12, p.22; x (1960), no.3, p.30; no.9, p.29; no.10, p.19

'The Study of Folk Musical Instruments in the Rumanian People's Republic', *JIFMC*, xii (1960), 13

'Despre meşterii "fluieraşi" din Hodac' [Observations on the master flautists of Hodac], *Studii şi cercetări de etnografie şi artă populară* (Bucharest, 1965), 271–307

'Constantin Brăiloiu (1893–1958)', *Revista de etnografie şi folclor*, xiii (1968), 457

'Les instruments musicaux du folklore égyptien et ceux des pays des Balkans', *XV Kongresa Saveza udruženja folklorista Jugoslavije: Jajce 1968*, 327

'Sensuri şi valori ale etnomuzicologiei româneşti' [The sense and value of Romanian ethnomusicology], *Studii de muzicologie*, vii (1971), 79

'D. Cantemir şi muzica orientală', *Revista de etnografie şi folclor*, xviii (1973), 335

'Die rumänische Panflöte', *Festschrift to Ernst Emsheimer* (Stockholm, 1974), 13

Muzica populară românească (Bucharest, 1975)

'Romania', §II, *Grove 6*

Articles in *MGG*

FOLKSONG EDITIONS

N. Lighezan: *Folclor muzical bănăţean* (Bucharest, 1959)

I. Cocişiu: *Cîntece populare româneşti* (Bucharest, 1960, 3/1966)

BIBLIOGRAPHY

V. Cosma: *Muzicieni români* (Bucharest, 1970)

VIOREL COSMA

Alexanian, Diran (*b* Constantinople, 1881; *d* Chamonix, 27 July 1954). Armenian cellist. He studied with Grützmacher and while a student played chamber music with Brahms and Joachim. At the age of 17 he appeared as the soloist in Strauss's *Don Quixote* with the composer conducting and scored a triumph; he was then invited to play concertos with Nikisch and Mahler. In 1901 he settled in Paris, where Casals saw some of his fingerings and recognized that Alexanian shared his own, then revolutionary, ideas on technique and interpretation. Many years' collaboration followed, leading to the publication in 1922 of their joint treatise *Traité théorique et pratique du violoncelle* and in 1929 of Alexanian's analytical edition of the solo cello suites of Bach. Alexanian was professor of the Casals class at the Ecole Normale de Musique from 1921 to 1937, when he left for the USA. His classes in Paris, Baltimore and New York attracted artists and students from all over the world, and his influence extended far beyond his own pupils (among them Maurice Eisenberg and Antonio Janigro) to such cellists as Feuermann, Cassadó, Piatigorsky and Fournier. He was also a conductor of distinction.

DOROTHY C. PRATT

Alexeyev, K. Pseudonym of KONSTANTIN ALEXEYEVICH KUZNETSOV.

Alexeyev, Konstantin Sergeyevich. See STANISLAVSKY, KONSTANTIN SERGEYEVICH.

Alexeyeva, Ekaterina Nikolayevna (*b* Kiev, 11 Dec 1899). Russian administrator, music historian and singer. She received her vocal training in Moscow: in 1926 she graduated from the Institute of Dramatic Art, in 1929 from the Moscow Conservatory and in 1935 from the School of Advanced Studies in the Arts, where she studied with M. Vladimirova, N. Raysky and A. Dolivo-Sobotnitsky. From 1929 to 1931 she sang at the Bolshoy Theatre in Moscow, and from 1929 to 1936 in concerts with the Moscow Philharmonic and on the radio. In 1936 she was appointed deputy director of the Scientific Research Institute of the Moscow Conservatory, and in 1938 director of the Glinka Central Museum of Musical Culture. During her 35 years' work in this post she accumulated vast collections for the museum, which has become the country's biggest musical archive and research centre, and has organized numerous exhibitions. Based on these collections, Alexeyeva has published a series of valuable articles, in particular on Maria Olenina d'Alheim, mainly in the periodicals *Sovetskaya muzïka* and *Muzïkal'naya zhizn'* but also in the *Bol'shaya sovetskaya entsiklopediya*.

WRITINGS
'M. Olenina d'Al'geym', *SovM* (1960), no.1, p.105
'M. Deysha-Sionitskaya (k 30-letiyu so dnya smerti)' [M. Deysha-Sionitskaya on the 30th anniversary of her death], *SovM* (1962), no.8, p.80
'Yevgeniya Mravina', *SovM* (1964), no.4, p.92
with G. A. Pribegina: *Vospominaniya o Moskovskoy konservatorii* [Reminiscences about the Moscow Conservatory] (Moscow, 1966)
'Priznaniye bol'shovo khudozhnika (k yubileyu M. A. Oleninoy d'Al'geym)' [Tribute to a great artist: on the jubilee of M. A. Olenina d'Algeym], *SovM* (1969), no.10, p.62
with L. Danilevich, T. Lebedeva and B. Yarustovsky: *Muzïka na frontakh Velikoy Otechestvennoy voyni* [Music at the fronts during World War II] [A. wrote the preface and was on the editorial board]

IGOR BELZA

Aleyn (*fl c*1400). English composer. The name is too common to permit a firm identification, though many candidates have been put forward, the most important of whom is the composer of the motet *Sub Arturo plebs*, JOHANNES ALANUS. Aleyn's name appears against a cantilena-style Gloria in the Old Hall MS (no.8). It is in score, homorhythmic but without a cantus firmus, and is notable for its unselfconsciously sprightly word setting. An erased descant setting of Sarum Agnus no.3 (Old Hall MS, no.128) may have borne an ascription to 'W. Aleyn'; if verified, this would invalidate many of the 'identifications', including one with a musical canon of St Paul's Cathedral and (later) of Windsor, John Aleyn, *d* 1373.

For edition and bibliography *see* OLD HALL MS.

MARGARET BENT

Alfano, Franco (*b* Posillipo, Naples, 8 March 1875; *d* San Remo, 27 Oct 1954). Italian composer. After studying the piano privately with Alessandro Longo, and harmony and composition with C. de Nardis and P. Serrao at the Conservatorio di S Pietro a Maiella, Naples, he moved in 1895 to Leipzig, where he completed his composition studies under Jadassohn. In 1896 he went to Berlin and launched himself as a pianist, though he did not continue this activity systematically for long: in later life he appeared in public only as a song accompanist and chamber music player, mainly in his own works. From 1899 until about 1905 he was based in Paris, but travelled as far afield as Russia. He then settled in Milan, moving in 1914 to San Remo, which remained at least his summer home for the rest of his life. From 1916 he taught composition at the Liceo Musicale, Bologna, which he directed from 1918. While there (1920), he helped to found the society Musica Nova, which in some ways paralleled Casella's more important Società Italiana di Musica Moderna. Alfano was appointed director of the Liceo Musicale (later Conservatory) of Turin in 1923, remaining there until 1939. He was then superintendent of the Teatro Massimo, Palermo (1940–42), subsequently becoming for a few months professor of operatic studies at the Conservatorio di S Cecilia, Rome. From 1947 to 1950 he was acting director of the Liceo Musicale, Pesaro.

Although generally known outside Italy only as the composer who completed Puccini's *Turandot*, Alfano was far from being a mere Puccini disciple. It is true that he won his first major success with an opera in the Puccini–Giordano tradition, *Risurrezione*, which had many revivals, reaching its 1000th Italian performance by 1951. But the best of his subsequent operas were much less conformist, and consequently less popular. *L'ombra di Don Giovanni*, though uneven and a bit inchoate, shows an awareness both of the more complex, radical aspects of Debussy and of the Strauss of *Salome* and *Elektra*, without being slavishly imitative of either. The harmonic vocabulary sometimes has coincidental affinities with that of the more troubled music of Bax.

La leggenda di Sakuntala, unquestionably Alfano's most important stage work, fulfilled most of what *L'ombra* had promised. The earlier opera's rather diffuse turbulence is replaced, however, by a poised, luminous though still very complex texture, saturated with the exotic, scented atmosphere of the Indian legends on which the libretto is based. De'Paoli aptly compared the intricate, colourful orchestral fabric to 'certain oriental carpets'. The influence of Debussy remains fundamental; yet the rich harmonic palette is no less individual than in *L'ombra*. Moreover, the lyrical impulse is still recognizably Italian, notably in such highlights as Sakuntala's monologue 'O nuvola' in Act 2, one of Alfano's most inspired passages. The operas after *Sakuntala* show a decline. Alfano seemed to lose the courage of his convictions, and yielded to the temptation to meet the big public half way. As a result these later operas contain much that is conventional and rhetorical, despite an orchestral imagination which remains rich and distinctive. Only a few scenes show marked signs of renewed inspiration, usually now in a picturesque or lighter vein, with Ravel's influence tending to replace Debussy's (see, for instance, the opening ensemble in *L'ultimo lord*, set in a toy-shop). Nevertheless, the last parts of Acts 2 and 4 in the very uneven *Cyrano de Bergerac* show that he was still capable, on occasion, of a truly moving pathos.

Alfano's output of songs is dominated by the four main groups of Tagore settings: chips from his operatic workshop, often profoundly Debussian in conception, yet with personal touches. Although not all equally successful, these songs have rightly retained a firm foothold in the Italian repertory. As an orchestral composer Alfano first came to prominence, shortly before World War I, with the picturesque *Suite romantica* (later renamed *Eliana*) and the sumptuous, long-winded First Symphony, which both, in their different ways, represent transitional stages between the styles of *Risurrezione* and *L'ombra di Don Giovanni*. The war years and the 1920s saw the composition of his most important chamber works, among which the agitated, improvisatory Violin Sonata and the more mellow and contemplative Cello Sonata are outstanding (the former especially in its unrevised first version, for all its heavy-textured prolixity). Both pieces, in their different ways, spring from the same creative roots as *Sakuntala*, and the Cello Sonata is probably his instrumental masterpiece.

By the 1930s, when Alfano returned to 'pure' orchestral composition after an interruption of 20 years, he was showing signs of neo-classical tendencies: the Second Symphony is more succinct and economical in texture than the First, and more diatonic and trenchant in its themes, though it too has moments of padding and leaves one unconvinced that he was a born symphonist. His most successful later instrumental work is the Divertimento, whose bright, kaleidoscopic outer movements represent his neo-classical phase at its best. Taken as a whole, Alfano's achievement, though less than Pizzetti's, Casella's or G. F. Malipiero's, rates near enough to theirs to give some justification to the common Italian practice of mentioning the four men together (with or even without Respighi as a fifth) as the leading Italian composers of their generation.

WORKS
(selective list)
STAGE
Miranda (opera, Alfano, after Fogazzaro), 1896, unperf., unpubd
La fonte di Enschir (opera, Illica), 1898; Breslau, 1898; unpubd
Napoli (ballet), 1900; Paris, 1900; unpubd
Lorenza (ballet), 1901; Paris, 1901; unpubd
Risurrezione (opera, C. Hanau, after Tolstoy), 1902–3; Turin, 1904
Il principe Zilah (opera, Illica), 1907; Genoa, 1909
I cavalieri e la bella (opera, Adami, T. Monicelli), 1910, inc.
L'ombra di Don Giovanni (opera, E. Moschino), 1913; Milan, 1914; rev. as Don Juan de Manara, Florence, 1941
La leggenda di Sakuntala (opera, Alfano, after Kalidasa), 1914–20; Bologna, 1921; orch score destroyed in World War II, reconstructed as Sakuntala, Rome, 1952
Eliana (ballet, R. Pantini) [= Suite romantica]; Rome, 1923
Madonna Imperia (opera, 1, A. Rossato, after Balzac), 1927; Turin, 1927
L'ultimo lord (opera, U. Falena, Rossato), 1930; Naples, 1930
Vesuvius (Hic est illa Napolis) (ballet, V. Viviani) [? after 3 unpubd songs, 1931 or earlier]; San Remo, 1933; rev. concert version, chorus ad lib, orch (1949)
Cyrano de Bergerac (opera, H. Cain, trans. C. Meano, F. Brusa, after Rostand), 1933–5; Rome, 1936
Il dottor Antonio (M. Ghisalberti, after G. Ruffini), begun 1941; Rome, 1949
Completion of G. Puccini: Turandot, 1925; Milan, 1926

INSTRUMENTAL
Orch: Pf Conc., A, c1900, unpubd, lost; other pieces, c1900, unpubd, lost; Suite romantica (Eliana), 1907–9; Sym. no.1, E, 1908–10, rev. [movts 1, 2 and 4 only] (1923), rev. as Sinfonia classica, 1953; Danza e finale di Sakuntala (1923); 2 intermezzi [after middle movts of Str Qts nos.1 and 2], str, 1931; Sym. no.2, C, 1931–2; Divertimento, small orch, pf obbl, 1934; Una danza, 1948
Chamber: Str Qt no.1, 1914–18; Sonata, vn, pf, 1922–3, rev. 1933; Sonata, vc, pf, 1925; Str Qt no.2, 1926; Conc., pf trio, 1929; Pf Qnt, 1936; Giorno per giorno [no.3 of 3 liriche, 1928], arr. vc, pf (1941); Str Qt no.3, 1945; smaller pieces
Pf: mostly early pieces, before 1904

VOCAL
Choral: Himno al libertador Simon Bolivar 1830–1930, unison vv, orch, 1930
Songs: 3 poemi di Rabindranath Tagore, 1918, orchd (1943); 6 liriche di autori diversi, 1919–22; 3 liriche (Tagore), 1928; Nuove liriche tagoriane, 1934, orchd (1943); 3 nuovi poemi (Meano, L. Orsini), 1939; È giunto il nostro ultimo autunno (M. Bona) (1943); 5 nuove liriche tagoriane, 1947; c20 others

Principal publishers: Pizzi, Ricordi, Sonzogno, Suvini Zerboni, Universal

BIBLIOGRAPHY
Gaianus [C. Paglia]: 'Artisti contemporanei: Franco Alfano', Emporium, xlix (Bergamo, 1919), 129
G. M. Gatti: 'Franco Alfano', Musicisti moderni d'Italia e di fuori (Bologna, 1920, 2/1925), 9; Eng. trans., MT, lxii (1921), 158
G. Cesari: 'La leggenda di Sakuntala di Franco Alfano', RMI, xxviii (1921), 666
A. Veretti: 'La leggenda di Sakuntala di Franco Alfano', Pensiero musicale, i (Bologna, 1921), 30
M. Castelnuovo-Tedesco: 'Sakuntala di Franco Alfano', Lo spettatore, i/1 (Rome, 1922), 78
L. Perrachio: 'Franco Alfano', Il pianoforte, iii (Turin, 1922), 11
A. Veretti: 'Profili: Franco Alfano', Pensiero musicale, ii (1922), 144
G. M. Gatti: 'Franco Alfano', MQ, ix (1923), 556
G. Pannain: La leggenda di Sakuntala di F. Alfano (Milan, 1923)
G. Rossi-Doria: 'Franco Alfano', Musikblätter des Anbruch, vii (1925), 402
G. Pannain: 'Sonata per violoncello e pianoforte di Franco Alfano', RMI, xxxiii (1926), 604
F. Brusa: 'Madonna Imperia di Franco Alfano', RMI, xxxiv (1927), 248
G. M. Gatti: 'Franco Alfano', Musikblätter des Anbruch, ix (1927), 293
L. Perrachio: 'Madonna Imperia di Franco Alfano', Musica d'oggi, 1st ser., ix (Milan, 1927), 149
G. M. Gatti: 'Madonna Imperia von Franco Alfano', Melos, vii (1928), 534
A. Lualdi: 'La Sinfonia in mi di F. Alfano al conservatorio', 'La leggenda di Sakuntala di Franco Alfano alla Scala', Serate musicali (Milan, 1928), 54, 90
E. Desderi: 'Franco Alfano', Bollettino bibliografico musicale, vi/6 (Milan, 1931), 5 [incl. list of works]
M. Saint-Cyr: 'Franco Alfano', Rassegna dorica, ii (Rome, 1930–31), 198
L. Perrachio: 'Una seconda sinfonia di Franco Alfano', Rassegna dorica, iv (1932–3), 117
A. Della Corte: Ritratto di Franco Alfano (Turin, 1935) [incl. list of works]
D. de'Paoli: La crisi musicale italiana (Milan, 1939), esp. 63f, 96f, 142ff, 209ff, 303f
H. Amano: Gendai itaria ongaku [Contemporary Italian music] (Tokyo, 1939), 186ff [incl. list of works, 350ff]
Franco Alfano (Milan, 1955) [Ricordi pamphlet]
F. Mompellio: 'Franco Alfano: biografia minima', Ricordiana, new ser., i (Milan, 1955), 2
R. Rossellini: 'Dolce ricordo di Alfano', Polemica musicale (Milan, 1962), 133
J. C. G. Waterhouse: 'Franco Alfano', Ricordiana, xi/4 (London, 1966), 1
——: The Emergence of Modern Italian Music (up to 1940) (diss., U. of Oxford, 1968), esp. 537ff
A. Gentilucci: Guida all'ascolto della musica contemporanea (Milan, 1969), 37ff
G. Vigolo: 'Sakuntala: tramonto in uno specchio', Mille e una sera all'opera e al concerto (Florence, 1971), 139
JOHN C. G. WATERHOUSE

Al-Fārābī [Abū Naṣr Muḥammad ibn Muḥammad ibn Ṭarkhān] (b Wāsij, district of Fārāb, Turkestan; d Syria, 950). Islamic philosopher and writer on music. He lived for some time in Baghdad, and spent his last years mainly in Aleppo, having accepted an invitation from the Ḥamdānid ruler Sayf al-Dawla. He was one of the greatest of Islamic philosophers, and his Kitāb al-mūsīqī al-kabīr ('Great book on music'), the second part of which is lost, remains the most imposing of all Arab works on music. The surviving part consists of an introduction, and three books, each in two sections, and is important not only for its elaborate treatment of theory, largely based on Greek concepts, but also for its material on contemporary practice, contained principally in the sections on instruments and rhythm.

The extensive introduction is of particular interest for its methodology, and presents some of the material to be developed in the first book, the first section of which begins with the physics of sound and goes on to discuss intervals, intervallic relationships and species of tetrachord; both the subject matter and the treatment exerted considerable influence on many later theorists. The second section of the first book deals with octave divisions in the context of the Greater Perfect System, and then, starting with the concept of the chronos prōtos, surveys various rhythmic structures. The second book is concerned with instruments: the first section is devoted to the 'ūd (short-necked lute), with an elaborate discussion of frettings followed by a presentation of different (and for the most part purely notional) string tunings; the second section covers two kinds of ṭunbūr (long-necked lute), wind instruments, the bowed rabāb (described for the first time) and instruments with unstopped strings, such as the harp. The emphasis throughout is on the scales that are or can be produced on these instruments, scales that in some cases differ considerably from each other. The third book contains a further section on the rhythmic cycles, but is concerned principally with song structure and composition (the latter viewed mainly in terms of an abstract survey of note combinations and schematic melodic patterns). The discussion of the rhythmic cycles in the Kitāb al-mūsīqī al-kabīr is rather complex, and two slighter works have survived in which al-Fārābī returned to the subject with a different approach: the *Kitāb al-īqā'āt* ('Book of rhythms') and the *Kitāb iḥṣā' al-īqā'āt* ('Book of the enumeration of rhythms').

Unlike al-Fārābī's purely musical works, his *Kitāb iḥṣā' al-'ulūm* (*De scientiis*), which contains a brief section on music, became known in the West, and was translated in the 12th century by both Gerard of Cremona and John of Seville. The section on music, dealing with general definitions and describing the scope of musical theory, is incorporated (under the title *De divisione musicae secundum Alpharabium*) in the *De musica* of Jerome of Moravia (13th century), and borrowings from it are also to be found in the Pseudo-Aristotelian treatise *De musica* (13th century) and in the *Quatuor principalia musicae*, often ascribed to Simon Tunstede (*d* 1369).

WRITINGS

Kitāb al-mūsīqī al kabīr [Great book on music] (MS, *NL-Lu* 651); ed. G. A. M. Khashaba (Cairo, ?1970); ed. R. d'Erlanger: *La musique arabe*, i (Paris, 1930), 1–306; ii (1935), 1–101
Kitāb iḥṣā' al-'ulūm [Book of the classification of the sciences] (MS, *E-E* 646); ed. A. González Palencia: *Alfarabi catálogo de las ciencias* (Madrid, 1932)

BIBLIOGRAPHY

C. Brockelmann: *Geschichte der arabischen Litteratur*, i (Weimar and Berlin, 1898–1902, 2/1943), 210ff
[H. G. Farmer]: 'Mūsīḳī', *The Encyclopaedia of Islām* (Leiden and London, 1913–38, rev. 2/1960–)
[R. Walzer]: 'Al-Fārābī, *The Encyclopaedia of Islām* (Leiden and London, 1913–38, rev. 2/1960–)
H. G. Farmer: *History of Arabian Music* (London, 1929/R1967), 175f
E. A. Beichert: *Die Wissenschaft der Musik bei Al-Fārābī* (Regensburg, 1931)
H. G. Farmer: *Al-Fārābī's Arabic–Latin Writings on Music* (Glasgow, 1934)
——: *The Sources of Arabian Music* (Bearsden, 1940, rev. 2/1965), 34f
E. Neubauer: 'Die Theorie vom īqā', i: Übersetzung des Kitāb al-Iqā'āt von Abū Naṣr al-Fārābī', *Oriens*, xxi (1968), 196–232
D. M. Randel: 'Al-Fārābī and the Role of Arabic Music Theory in the Latin Middle Ages', *JAMS*, xxix (1976), 173

O. WRIGHT

Alfieri, Pietro (*b* Rome, 29 June 1801; *d* Rome, 12 June 1863). Italian musicologist and composer. He was a Roman priest whose life was entirely directed towards the déliverance of liturgical music from what he saw as the debased theatrical style of contemporary composers and the neglect and incompetence of singers and organists in regard to Gregorian chant and Renaissance music. He contributed most importantly to this goal through his editions, particularly the *Raccolta di musica sacra* (Rome, 1841–6), the seven volumes of which provided the first large modern collection of Palestrina's music. Palestrina was Alfieri's ideal for new church music, which, according to his *Ristabilmento*, should be grave, succinct and suited in expression to the words, which were to be presented clearly and with few repetitions. His own compositions, many of them published at Rome, exemplified, without transcending, these principles.

Alfieri was also a pioneer in Italy in the historical and scientific study of Gregorian chant, which he sought to restore to its original purity, although along lines that now appear somewhat arbitrary and subjective. His early *Saggio* and *Accompagnamento* are practical manuals, designed to improve performance of the chant. In the 1850s he completed an edition of the Roman Gradual, Antiphonal and Hymnal, setting out his methods in the *Précis historique*. He was, however, unable to get his version accepted by the Church or even

published, and the resulting disappointment caused him to lose his mind. According to his friend Fabi Montani, Alfieri's outspoken devotion to his mission was the reason for his failure to receive an important church music post in Rome. He taught Gregorian chant in the Collegio Inglese there and was a member of numerous scholarly societies.

WRITINGS

Saggio storico teorico pratico del canto gregoriano o romano per istruzione degli ecclesiastici (Rome, 1835, 2/1836)
Accompagnamento coll'organo de' toni ecclesiatici (Rome, 1840)
'Ristabilimento del canto e della musica ecclesiastica', *Annali delle scienze religiose*, xvi (1843), 37–96, 161–211, 321 [also circulated in extract]
Précis historique et critique sur la restauration des livres du chant grégorien (Rennes, 1856; It. trans., rev., 1857)

BIBLIOGRAPHY

Catalogo delle opere di musica sacra pubblicate da Monsig. Pietro Alfieri romano cameriere secreto di S.S. Papa Pio IX (Rome, c1864) [catalogue of Alfieri's pubd writings, edns., compositions on sale by his heirs]
F. Fabi Montani: 'Monsignor Pietro Alfieri, maestro compositore di musica', *Il Buonarroti*, 2nd ser., iv (1869), 53
'Alfieri, Pietro', *DBI*

DENNIS LIBBY

Alfiero [Alfieri], **Giuseppe** (*b* Naples, 1630; *d* Naples, 21 Jan 1665). Italian composer. He studied at the Conservatorio dei Poveri di Gesù Cristo from 1642 to 1649 and about 1658 was named *maestro di cappella* of the city of Naples. In 1655 he composed for the Teatro S Bartolomeo *La fedeltà trionfante* (text, G. C. Sorrentino), one of the first operas originally written for Naples. Prota-Giurleo ascribed to him two other dramatic works: *Le magie amorose* (Naples, 1653) and *Il trionfo della pace* (Naples, 1658; text, G. Gastaldo). The former certainly is not by him: it is a renamed version of Cavalli's *La Rosinda*. Alfiero's only surviving work is a hymn to S Maria Egyptiana in *I-Nf*.

BIBLIOGRAPHY

B. Croce: *I teatri di Napoli* (Naples, 1891)
U. Prota-Giurleo: *Francesco Cirillo e l'introduzione del melodramma a Napoli* (Gruma Nevano, 1952)
——: 'Alfiero, Giuseppe', *DBI*

THOMAS WALKER

Al fine (It.: 'to the end'). An indication to return to the start of a piece (especially a da capo aria), but to proceed with the repetition only to the point marked (or intended) as the end.

Alfonso V ('el magnánimo') (*b* 1396; *d* Naples, 27 June 1458). King of Aragon (from 1416) and of Naples (from 1442, as Alfonso I) and patron of music, son of Ferdinand I of Antequera, 'el honesto'. From his earliest years he showed great interest in music: as a prince he already had his own chapel of singers and instrumentalists and he wrote to his father expressing his special pleasure in modern music. As king he followed the example of John I in seeking fine musicians throughout Europe, asking for the 'best singers and tenoristas' in Rome and establishing a permanent choir school for boys. The number of musicians resident at his court rose to 15 and more. Alfonso laid the foundations of what was to be the Spanish school of music from the time of the Catholic Monarchs on: although he had musicians in his chapel from all over Europe, and the sacred repertory there was fundamentally European, it was he who first favoured the Spanish secular polyphonic song. Thus in his courts at Barcelona and Naples, it was primarily Spanish (Castilian) amorous polyphony that was performed.

BIBLIOGRAPHY
H. Anglès: *Scripta musicologica* (Rome, 1975–6), ii, 765, 869–911 (esp. 880ff, 897ff), 913–62, 963–1028

JOSÉ LÓPEZ-CALO

Alfonso, Javier (*b* Madrid, 1 Feb 1904). Spanish pianist and composer. He studied at the Madrid Conservatory and at the Ecole Normale de Musique in Paris, his teachers including Cortot for piano and del Campo and Monteux for composition. As a pianist and lecturer he has toured throughout the world, winning several prizes and also serving on the juries of international competitions. He was partly responsible for introducing Bartók's music into Spain. Later in his career he was appointed professor of piano at the Madrid Conservatory.

WORKS
(*selective list*)

Orch: Concierto-fantasía, pf, orch, 1939; Variaciones sobre un tema castellano, 1948; Suite, gui, orch, 1955; Harp Conc., 1957
Chamber: Pf Trio, 1930; Str Qt, 1948
Pf: Capricho en forma de bolero, 1937; Variaciones, 2 pf, 1942; Preludio y toccata, 1954; Suite 'Homenaje a Albéniz', 1960
Vocal music

Principal publishers: Salabert, Unión Musical Española

GUY BOURLIGUEUX

Alfonso el Sabio [Alfonso X] (*b* Toledo, 23 Nov 1221; *d* Seville, 4 April 1284). Spanish monarch, patron and poet. The son of Ferdinand the Saint, he became King of Castile and León in 1252. 'El Sabio' may be taken as both 'the Wise' and 'the Learned', for Alfonso's works show his conviction that learning begets wisdom. A remarkable patron of the arts, sciences and culture generally, he may have been a poet and a musician. He recognized the importance of Spain's Islamic as well as its Roman and Visigothic heritage, and his court became celebrated as a meeting-place for Christian, Islamic and Jewish scholars and artists. He has long stood accused of sacrificing his family relations and political stability to impractical schemes for liberal reform but, though out of favour with those close to him in his latter years, he fostered notable social, educational and judiciary reforms, encouraged the use of the vernacular in learning and art, and made Spain respected in Europe. In 1254 he founded a chair of music at the University of Salamanca, stipulating 'that there should be a teacher of composition [*órgano*]'. The songs in his *Cantigas de Santa María* probably occupied more of his time than any other of his cultural projects (which include books on history, law, astronomy and games, and poetry); they amply vindicate his statement in the first cantiga that 'composition entails understanding'. A selection of his works appeared in 1922, edited by A. García Solalinde, who, with others, issued a further edition (Madrid, 1930–).

See CANTIGA and SOURCES, MS, §III.

BIBLIOGRAPHY
J. B. Trend: *Alfonso the Sage and other Spanish Essays* (London, 1926)
H. Anglès: *La música de las Cantigas de Santa María del Rey Alfonso el Sabio* (Barcelona, 1943–59)
J. E. Keller: *Alfonso X, El Sabio* (New York, 1967)

JACK SAGE

Alford, Kenneth J. [Ricketts, Frederick Joseph] (*b* Ratcliff, London, 21 Feb 1881; *d* Reigate, 15 May 1945). British composer and bandmaster. He enlisted as a bandboy in the Royal Irish Regiment in September 1895, playing the cornet as well as the piano and the organ, and he was stationed at Limerick before serving in India. From 1904 to 1908 he was a student bandmas-ter at the Royal Military School of Music, Kneller Hall, and in 1908 he was appointed bandmaster of the Argyll and Sutherland Highlanders. Under his pseudonym (Alford being his mother's maiden name) he began composing marches, of which *Colonel Bogey* (1914) remains the best known. Several of his finest marches date from World War I, while *Dunedin* and *Old Panama* commemorate a trip to New Zealand for the South Seas Exhibition. In 1927 Ricketts became director of music for the Royal Marines at Deal, moving to Plymouth in 1930. He was made lieutenant in 1927, captain in 1935 and (after being recalled from retirement in 1940) major in 1942. Further marches were produced during World War II before ill-health forced him to retire finally in April 1944. Alford was one of the very finest of military march composers, his works surpassing those of Sousa and continental bandmasters in their range of expression, which was combined with clear melodic line, often ingenious counter-melodies and, above all, perfectly judged instrumentation. His brother R. R. Ricketts, bandmaster of the Essex Regiment and the Royal Corps of Signals, wrote military music under the name of Leo Stanley, his best known piece being the march *The Contemptibles*.

WORKS
(*all published in London; for orch, band or pf unless otherwise stated*)

Marches: Holyrood (1912), The Vedette (1912), Colonel Bogey (1914), The Great Little Army (1916), On the Quarter Deck (1917), The Middy (1917), The Voice of the Guns (1917), The Vanished Army (1919), The Mad Major (1921), Cavalry of the Clouds (1923), The Thin Red Line (1925), Dunedin (1928), Old Panama (1929), H. M. Jollies (1929), The Standard of St George (1930), By Land and Sea (1941), Army of the Nile (1941), Eagle Squadron (1942)
Other works: Valse Riviera (1910); Thoughts, waltz (1917); Sparks, xyl, with acc. (1923); The Two Imps, 2 xyl/cornet, with acc. (1923); Mac and Mac, 1/2 xyl, with acc. (1928); The Smithy, pastoral fantasia (1933); The Two Dons, 2 xyl, with acc. (1933); The Hunt, rhapsody (descriptive ov.) (1940)
Arr: A Musical Switch, humoresque (1921); The Lightning Switch, fantasia (1924); Colonel Bogey on Parade, march fantasia (1939); Lilliburlero (1942); A Life on the Ocean Wave (1944)

ANDREW LAMB

Alfvén, Hugo (Emil) (*b* Stockholm, 1 May 1872; *d* Falun, 8 May 1960). Swedish composer, conductor and violinist. He attended the Stockholm Conservatory (1887–91) and then took private lessons with Lindegren (composition) and Zetterquist (violin); from 1887 he also studied painting. A violinist in the Hovkapellet (the opera orchestra, 1890–92), he decided in 1892 to make his career in music. From 1904 to 1957 he conducted the Siljan Choir – a group of five church choirs and regional choirs in Dalarna – and he was the director of other choruses, including the Orphei Drängar (1910–47), with whom he made 22 tours throughout most of Europe. In addition he was Director Musices of Uppsala University (1910–39). A Hugo Alfvén-Foundation has been founded in Stockholm.

Alfvén's music is distinguished by orchestral subtlety and by a painterly exploitation of harmony and timbre. His output was almost entirely of programme music, often suggested by the Swedish archipelago; he commented that 'my best ideas have come during my sea-voyages at night, and, in particular, the wild autumns have been my most wonderful times for composition'. A few pieces, often performed, have maintained his reputation: *Midsommarvaka* ('Midsummer vigil'), a picture of the Swedish summer in highly-coloured orchestral splendour, based on Swedish folk music and inspired by a rude peasant wedding; *Festspel*, composed for the inauguration of the Stockholm New Dramatic Theatre in 1908; the 'Elegi' from the suite *Gustav II Adolf*, frequently used as funeral music; 'Vallflickans dans' ('Shepherd-girl's dance') from the ballet-pantomime *Bergakungen*; *Sveriges flagga*, which has become almost a second Swedish national anthem; and *Roslagsvår* ('Spring in Roslag'), which, like *Midsummer Vigil*, soon became generally known in Sweden as a light piece. The choral folksong arrangements also achieved wide popularity.

Alfvén considered his most important works to be the first four symphonies and the oratorio *Herrans bön* ('The Lord's prayer'), the last combining high-Romantic harmony with full contrapuntal artistry, notably in the quadruple fugue of the finale. In the last movement of the Second Symphony the chorale *Jag går mot döden var jag går* comes at the end of a powerful fugue, and the same melody is transformed into a dance of death in the scherzo of the Fifth Symphony. The heliocentric Third Symphony is a work of the south, written in Italy, and the Fourth, composed over a period of 20 years, tells a love story against a symbolic sea- and rockscape background, using a large orchestra, supplemented by two wordless voices, with virtuoso effectiveness. According to Alfvén, *En skärgårdssägen* ('A tale from the archipelago') was a preliminary study for the Fourth Symphony. The first movement of the Symphony no.5, often played separately, is built on a theme which was also used in *Bergakungen* and was, in Alfvén's opinion, 'the least bad thing I have written'.

WORKS
(the numbering is that of Rudén, 1972)

ORCHESTRAL

24 Symphony no.1, f, op.7, 1897
28 Symphony no.2, D, op.11, 1897–8
45 Midsommarvaka [Midsummer vigil] (Svensk rhapsodi no.1), op.19, 1903
49 En skärgårdssägen [A tale from the archipelago], op.20, tone poem, 1904
54 Symphony no.3, E, op.23, 1905
58 Uppsala-rhapsodi (Akademisk festouverture, Svensk rhapsodi no.2), op.24, 1907
59 Festspel, op.25, 1907
62 Drapa [in memoriam King Oscar II], op.27, 1908
66 Bröllopsmarsch [Wedding march], 1909
67 Fest-ouverture, op.26, large military band, 1909
92 Elégie: Vid Emil Sjögrens bår [At Emil Sjögren's funeral], op.38, tone poem, 1918
93 Symphony no.4 'Från havsbandet' [From the outskirts of the archipelago], c, op.39, 1918–19
99 Bergakungen, op.37, ballet-pantomime, 3, 1916–23; orch suite and Vallflickans dans [Shepherd-girl's dance], last arr. vn, pf
105 Hjalmar Brantings sorgmarsch [Hjalmar Branting's funeral march], op.42, wind, 1924
120 Svensk rhapsodi no.3 (Dalarhapsodien), op.47, 1931
121 Gustav II Adolf, op.49 (incidental music, L. Nordström: Vi), 1932; orch suite; Sarabanda, str orch; Bourrée, 3 bn; Menuett, orch; Elegi, small orch
134 Synnöve Solbakken, op.50, suite from film music, pf/orch, 1934
141 Festmarsch till Stockholmsutställningens öppnande, op.41, 1930, reorchd 1936
201 Fest-ouverture, op.52, 1944
202 Mans kvinna, film score, 1944
202a En bygdesaga [A district fairytale], op.53, suite, 1944
204 Singoalla, film score, 1949
209 Symphony no.5, a, op.54, 1942–53
214 Den förlorade sonen [The prodigal son], ballet, 5 scenes, 1957; orch suite
Several folksong arrs.

CHORAL

32 Vid sekelskiftet [At the turn of the century], op.12 (Karlfeldt), S, chorus, orch, 1899
35 Frihetssång [Freedom] (Bishop Thomas), male vv/mixed vv/(unison vv/1v, pf), 1900
Lugn i tron [Rest in truth] (E. J. Stagnelius), male vv, ?1900
39 Herrans bön [The Lord's prayer], op.15 (Stagnelius, after Martyrerna), S, A, Bar, chorus, orch, 1899–1901

40 Här är landet [Here is the country] (W. Nordin), male/mixed vv, ?1901
48 Harrgårstösa i äppelapla [Country-house girl in an apple tree] (G. Fröding), male vv, ?1904
55 Fosterlandspsalm [National hymn] (Runeberg), (1v/chorus, pf)/(unison vv, orch)/orch/military band, 1906
57 Afton [Evening] (D. Fallström), Bar, male vv, ?1907
60 Vårens vandring [The wandering spring] (Fallström), male vv, 1908
61 Marsch (E. G. Geijer), male vv, 1908
71 Gustaf Frödings jordafärd [Gustaf Fröding's funeral], op.29 (V. von Heidenstam), male vv/pf, 1911
— Kvinnornas lösen (Ossiannilsson), unison vv, pf, 1911
76 Unge Herr Sten Sture [The young Sir Sten Sture], op.30 (H. Tigerschiöld), Bar, male vv, orch, 1912
79 Spåmannen [The fortune teller] (incidental music, Heidenstam), chorus, small orch, 1912
80 Uppenbarelsekantat [Revelation cantata], op.31 (Bible), Bar, B, 2 choruses, org, harmonium, harp, cel, str, 1913
83 Kantat vid Baltiska utställningens i Malmö öppnande, op.33 (N. Flensburg), Bar, chorus, orch, 1914
84 Motett, op.34/52 (J. O. Wallin), chorus, org ad lib, 1914
86 Kantat vid Uppsala läns Kungliga Hushållningssällskaps 100-årsjubileum 1915, op.35 (K. Hamilton), chorus, orch, 1915
87 Sveriges flagga (K. G. Ossiannilsson), male vv/1v, pf/mixed vv/small orch, 1916
89 En visa om troheten [A song of loyalty] (E. Brogren), male vv, ?1917
90 Kantat vid Reformationsfesten i Uppsala 1917, op.36 (1695 hymnbook, Karlfeldt), Bar, chorus, orch, 1917
95 Lindagull (B. Gripenberg), (T, male vv)/(T, 2 hn, cel, harp, str)/(1v, pf), 1919
98 Minnessång över Gustav Vasa, op.40 (C. Larsson i By), T, Bar, chorus, org/orch, 1920
102 En visa om Barnens ö på Barnens dag [A song of Children's Island on Children's Day] (C. Granér), children's vv, male vv, 1923
103 Kantat vid Världspostunionens halvsekelsjubileum 1924, op.41 (A. Albert-Henning), Bar, chorus, orch, 1924
106 För Sverige! (I. Lindberg), male vv/(unison vv, military band)/(1v, pf), 1925
109 5 sånger, op.42 (G. Salwén, Geijer, trad., A. Fryxell), male vv, 1923–6
111 Kantat vid Uppsala universitets 450-årsjubileum, op.45 (G. M. Silfverstolpe), A, Bar, chorus, orch, 1927
112 Manhem, op.47 (Geijer), T, male vv, orch, 1928
115 Kantat vid Svenska Röda korsets högtidssammankomst 2 maj 1930, op.46 (A. Albert-Henning), A, chorus, orch, 1930
116 Natt [Night] (G. Alexanderson), Bar, male vv, 1930
117 Barnens bön för fäderneslandet [Children's prayer for the native land] (Z. Topelius), children's 4vv, 1930
125 Gryning vid havet [Dawn over the ocean] (S. Selander), male vv, 1933
126 Min kära [My beloved] (Selander), male vv, 1933
127 Vaggvisa [Lullaby] (E. Blomberg), male vv/mixed vv/1v, pf/cl, gong, str), 1933
128 Julsång [Christmas song] (Nyblom), 1934
134 Synnöve Solbakken (film score, Björnson), S, chorus, orch, 1934
135 Eldsång [Fire song], op.51 (F. Nycander), male vv/mixed vv/mixed vv, pf, 1935
136 Hymn till Sverige (Tigerschiöld), male vv, 1935
137 Kantat vid Sveriges Riksdags 500-års minnesfest 1935 (Selander), Bar, chorus, orch, 1935
138 Psalm (P. Jönsson Rösiö), 1935
143 Papillon (Fjärilen) (Alexanderson), male/mixed vv, 1936
145 Sång till Stockholm (G. Fant), 1v/unison male vv, pf/mixed vv, male vv, 1936
146 Midsommarlåt i Leksand (S. Gabrielsson), 1936–7
153 Kosack-vaggvisa [Cossack lullaby] (Lermontov, trans. J. Brenning), male vv/mixed vv/str orch/pf trio, 1938
156 Stemning(Stimmung,Stämning)(Jacobsen),mixed vv/male vv/str orch, mixed vv ad lib [2 versions], 1938
161 Tattare-Emma [Gipsy Emma] (Jeremias i Tröstlösa [L. Rickson]), male vv, 1938
167 Endräkt – en sång i orostiden 1940 [Concord – a song in the time of solicitude 1940] (A. Grape), (1v/unison vv, pf)/male vv, 1940
173 Berceuse (E. Kléen), (T, male vv)/(1v, 2 hn, str)/(1v, pf), 1940
174 Vårsång, Maj [Spring song, May] (A. Hed), male/mixed vv, 1941
182 I vapen [In arms] (I. Edwall), unison male vv, pf, 1941
183 Taltrasten [The song-thrush] (Hed), (male/mixed vv)/(1v, pf/fl, eng hn, str), 1941
187 Aftonen [Evenings] (H. Sätherberg), (mixed/male vv)/(1v, pf/2 cl, 2 hn, harp/pf, str), 1942
192 Mitt i en blomstermånad [In the midst of a month of flowers] (H. Gullberg), male vv, 1943

196 Nordens länder (H. Dhejne), male/mixed vv, 1943
198 Till SHT (G. Kallstenius), male vv, 1944
205 Champagnevinet (F. M. Franzén), male vv, 1949
211 Roslagsvår [Spring in Roslag] (A. Henrikson), mixed/male vv/pf, 1954
212 Festsång till Arla Coldinu-orden (O. Wahlström), male vv, 1955

16 arrs. of works by other composers
Numerous folksong arrs. for male/mixed vv

CHAMBER AND INSTRUMENTAL

1–8 Early pf pieces, 1884–5, no.8 inc.
9 Romance, fl, pf, 1885
11 Barcarol, vn, pf, 1888
12 Souvenir de Säter, vn, pf, 1888
— Souvenir de Visby, fl, pf, 1890
13 4 Mazurkas, pf, 1890s
14 5 Mazurkas, pf, 1890s
15 Festmarsch, pf, 1890s
19 Triumfmarsch, op.10, pf, 1893
20 Minne från Åsen, Dalarne, pf, 1893
21 Romans, op.3, vn, pf, 1895
23 Sonata, op.1, vn, pf, ?1896
25 Elegi, op.5, hn/vc, org, 1897
26 Drömmeri (Rêverie), pf, ?1898
37 Menuett, op.2, pf, ?1901
38 Sorg (Air mélancolique), op.14, pf, ?1901
42 Serenad, vn, pf, ?1902
43 Serenade på mammas födelsedag [Serenade on mother's birthday], fl, cl, vn, pf, 1902
44 Skärgårdsbilder [Archipelago pictures], op.17, pf, 1901–2
75 Nocturne, pf, 1911
77 Mostellaria (incidental music, Plautus), fl, 1912
80 Andante religioso [from Uppenbarelsekantat, 80], cel, harp, str qt, 1913
94 Margita dansar, waltz, pf, ?1919
206 ?Marsch, ?2 vn, c1950
207 Potpourri över svenska folkvisor och låtar, 3 insts, 1950
213 Roslagspolketta, vn, pf, 1956
Several folksong arrs.

VOCAL

6 Barnatro [Childlike faith] (Topelius), 1v, pf, 1884
10 Visa med pianoaccompagnement (W. Vennberg), ?1887
16 Romans, 1v, ?vn, pf, 1891
17 fugue exercise, S, T, Bar, 1890s
18 Fuga di tono (H. Spegel), S, A, 1890s
21 Vaggvisa [Lullaby] (Runeberg), 1v, pf, ?1896
27 10 sånger, op.4 (J. Alströmer jr, E. Ekgren, Fallström, T. Hedberg, A. Fet trans. H. Wigert-Lundström, T. von Wehl, C. D. af Wirsén, Fjalar [C. L. Östergren], trad.), 1v, pf, 1898; nos.3, 8, 10 [2 versions] orchd, no.8 arr. vc, orch
29 O stode du i kylig blåst [O wert thou in the cauld blast], op.6 (Burns), 1v, pf, ?1899
30 2 lyriska stämningar, op.8 (E. Lundberg), 1v, pf, 1899, no.2 orchd
31 Ur Lyckans visor [From Songs of happiness], op.9 (K.-E. Forsslund), 1v, pf, 1899
33 Klockorna [The bells], op.13 (F. Holmgren), Bar, orch, 1900
41 Trubadurens ande [The minstrel's spirit], op.18 (A. Butenschön), 1v, pf, 1901
50 Marias sånger, op.21 (E. Aarestrup), 1v, pf, 1903–4
51 Bön [Prayer], op.?16 (A. Österling), 1v, pf, 1905
52 Pioner [Peonies], op.22 (Österling), 1v, pf/orch, 1905
53 Minnesskrift [In memoriam] (Österling), 1v, pf, 1905
56 Hos drottning Margareta (Junker Nils sjunger till lutan), op.18 (Fallström), 1v, pf/orch, ?1907
63 7 dikter, op.28 (E. Thiel), 1v, pf, 1908; nos.4–7 orchd, no.4 arr. vn/vc, pf, no.6 arr. vc, orch
65 Julsång [Carol] (E. Evers), 1v, pf/chorus, ?1908
68 Ställ flaggan så jag ser den [Place the flag so that I can see it], op.29 (Fallström), 1v, pf, 1910
72 Stockholms nations sång (O. Thunman), 1v, pf, ?1911
73 Geflüster im Gange (O. J. Bierbaum), 1v/S, T, pf, 1911
74 Hälsningskväde till damerna vid SHT-festen 1911 (Grape), Bar, pf, 1911
78 Julsång [Carol] (O. Levertin), 1v, pf, 1912
81 Kring ditt rika och vågiga hår och andra dikter [About your abundant and wavy hair and other poems], op.32 (Thiel), 1v, pf, 1913
91 Vandrarens julsång [Wanderer's carol] (B. Mörner, Arafi), 1v, pf, ?1917
97 I bruset [In the rush] (Mörner), 1v, pf, 1920
108 En båt med blommor [A boat with flowers], op.44 (Levertin), Bar, orch, 1925
147 Mikaelidagen (trad.), 1v, pf, 1936–7
152 Det unga hemmet [The young home] (Alexanderson), 1v, pf, 1937

162 Vaggsång [Lullaby] (Thunman), 1v, pf/(harp/pf, str), 1939
168 I stilla timmar [In quiet hours] (J. Hemmer), 1v, pf/orch, 1940
203 Saa tag mit hjerte [So take my heart] (T. Ditlevsen), 1v, pf/orch, 1946
208 Sången till Folkare (C. A. Norrgren), Bar, pf/male chorus, pf/ male chorus, 1951
Several folksong arrs. for 1v, pf/orch

Principal publishers: Lundquist, Nordiska musikförlaget, Gehrman
MSS in *S-Smf* and *Uu*

WRITINGS

Femtio år och litet till med Leksands kyrko- och hembygdskör (Leksand, 1939)
Första satsen: ungdomsminnen (Stockholm, 1946) [autobiography]
Tempo furioso: vandringsår (Stockholm, 1948) [autobiography]
I dur och moll: från Uppsala-åren (Stockholm, 1949) [autobiography]
Final (Stockholm, 1952) [autobiography]
Minnen (Stockholm, 1972) [selections from autobiography]

BIBLIOGRAPHY

K. Nyblom: *Hör i Orphei Drängar* (Uppsala, 1928)
——: *O.D.: årsredogörelser*, i–xix (Uppsala, 1929–47)
O.D.-minnen tillägnade Hugo Alfvén (Uppsala, 1942)
S. E. Svensson: *Hugo Alfvén som människa och konstnär* (Uppsala, 1946) [incl. worklist and bibliography]
A. More: 'Hugo Alfvén 85 år', *Dalarnas hembygdsbok* (1957), 113
P. Lindfors: 'Hugo Alfvén', *Studiekamraten* (1960), 109
S. Wilson: 'Hugo Alfvén in memoriam: han var svensk och han var vår', *Musikrevy*, xv (1960), 137
E. Olsson: *Leksands kyrko- och hembygdskör 75 år/Siljansbygdens körförbund 60 år* (Borås, 1965)
P. Lindfors: *Hugo Alfvén berättar* (Stockholm, 1966) [radio interviews]
J. O. Rudén: *Hugo Alfvén: kompositioner/Musical Works: käll- och verkförteckning/Thematic Index* (Stockholm, 1972)
Alfvén issue, *Musikrevy*, xxvii/2 (1972), 49 [incl. essays by B. Berthelson, U.-B. Edberg, D. Hall, L. Hedwall, G. Percy, S. Wilson, C.-G. Åhlén]
Alfvén issue, *Musikkultur*, xxxvi/4 (1972), 5 [incl. essays by A. Hallenberg, S. Karlsson, G. Reimers]
L. Hedwall: *Hugo Alfvén: en svensk tonsättares liv och verk* (Stockholm, 1973)

ROLF HAGLUND

Algaita. The most common name for a type of shawm in the savannah zone of the west African states of Niger and Nigeria, as well as in Chad, the Central African Republic and Cameroon. The instrument is related both organologically and by its name to the Maghribi *ghaiṭa*,

Hausa algaita (shawm) player from Nigeria, 1972

and its appearance in west Africa is first noted in the 18th century. Unlike its counterpart in north Africa, however, which is used for music in a variety of social situations, the *algaita* is almost exclusively associated with the traditional authority of emirs and other rulers, and with their senior officials.

The body of the instrument, consisting of a leather-covered pipe about 30 cm long and a bell end about 10 cm long, is made from a single piece of wood. The mouthpiece is usually made from brass and the double reeds are prepared from suitable stalks of wild grass. The *algaita* has four finger-holes and is held with the left hand farthest from the mouth. The finger-holes are stopped by the index finger of the right hand and the index, second and third fingers of the left hand. The performer uses his cheeks as an air reservoir so that the instrument can be blown continuously without pausing for breath (see illustration).

See also HAUSA MUSIC, NIGERIA, CAMEROON, CHAD, CENTRAL AFRICAN REPUBLIC, BERBER MUSIC, §1.

ANTHONY KING

Algarotti, Francesco (*b* Venice, 11 Dec 1712; *d* Pisa, 3 May 1764). Italian writer on opera, poet and savant. He was well educated at Rome and Bologna, whence he was welcomed into the learned circles of London and Paris. He lived for a time with Voltaire. In 1740 Frederick the Great took him into his personal service and gave him the title of count. From 1742 to 1747 he was also adviser to Augustus III, Elector of Saxony and King of Poland. At both Berlin and Dresden he was actively engaged in operatic productions, arranging and versifying Italian librettos to the taste of his patrons. He returned to Italy in 1753 because of ill-health. His *Saggio sopra l'opera in musica* was written the following year and first published in 1755. It attacks the unruliness prevalent in Italian public theatres, which compared unfavourably with the well-regulated and varied spectacles beginning to emerge at the court theatres of northern Europe. Other contemporary essayists such as Blainville, John Brown, Calzabigi, Krause, Ortes and Durazzo said much the same thing in condemning the dominance of the singers over every other aspect of serious opera in Italy.

The *Saggio* was the best-grounded and most wide-ranging of these critiques, also the one that received the widest diffusion through reprinting and translation. It proposed that all parts of music, including singing, be subordinated to a unifying poetic idea, preferably a remote or exotic tale because the fabulous lent itself most readily to the extreme stylization endemic to the operatic genre. Graun's *Montezuma* for Berlin was held up as a model. Metastasio's librettos were dismissed with faint praise; only two of them, *Didone abbandonata* and *Achille in Sciro*, were mentioned as providing sufficient opportunity for spectacle. An ideal collaboration between poet and musician was achieved by Quinault and Lully. Algarotti concluded the *Saggio* with two examples of the path to be followed: a sketch for an *Enea in Troia*, after Virgil, and a fully-fledged French libretto for an *Iphigénie en Aulide*, after Euripides and Racine. The latter represented a bold departure from the Metastasian canon in the direction of a Greek-like severity and simplicity. It lacked amorous intrigue and confidantes; choruses, ballets and spectacle were integrated into its action. Two years later Diderot

proclaimed the same subject to be the salvation of serious opera, but without mention of Algarotti. A spate of operas more or less indebted to Algarotti's *Iphigénie* followed in the last third of the century, the best-known being Gluck's for Paris, which Algarotti did not live to see. He did witness and to a small extent supervise the reform operas of Traetta and Frugoni for Parma, beginning in 1759, an attempt to wed Rameau's style of *tragédie lyrique* and *opera seria* that was timid by comparison with the thorough-going integration achieved by Gluck in Vienna and Paris. The revolution in taste during the 1750s that saw the Rococo style dethroned found an eloquent voice in the *Saggio*, described by Voltaire as 'the foundation for the reform of the castrato's realm'. The ensuing wave of archaeological neo-classicism is already apparent in Algarotti's work, particularly in his call for large, sparely adorned opera houses, with semicircular halls modelled after ancient arenas. Practical man of the theatre that he was, Algarotti tempered this antique-inspired vision of the future with advice about the materials and dimensions likely to produce the best acoustic, and about the compromises necessary between proscenium stage and arena for maximum sight lines.

BIBLIOGRAPHY

E. Newman: *Gluck and the Opera* (London, 1895), 232ff
C. Malherbe: 'Un précurseur de Gluck: le comte Algarotti', *RHCM*, ii (1902), 369, 414
H. Goldschmidt: 'Die Reform der italienischen Oper des 18. Jahrhunderts und ihre Beziehungen zur musikalischen Aesthetik', *IMusSCR*, iii *Vienna 1909*, 196
I. Treat: *Un cosmopolite italien du XVIIIème siècle: Francesco Algarotti* (Trévoux, 1913)
E. Wellesz: 'Francesco Algarotti und seine Stellung zur Musik', *SIMG*, xv (1913–14), 427
M. Fubini, ed.: *La cultura illuministica in Italia* (Turin, 1957), chap. 'Dall'Arcadia all'illuminismo: Francesco Algarotti'
G. Roncaglia: 'Il Conte Francesco Algarotti e il rinnovamento del melodramma', *Chigiana*, xxi (1964), 63
P. Petrobelli: 'Tartini, Algarotti e la corte di Dresda', *AnMc*, ii (1965), 72
D. Heartz: 'From Garrick to Gluck: the Reform of Theatre and Opera in the Mid-eighteenth Century', *PRMA*, xciv (1967–8), 111
——: 'Operatic Reform at Parma: "Ippolito ed Aricia"', *Atti del convegno sul settecento Parmense nel 2° centenario della morte di C. I. Frugoni* (Parma, 1969), 271

DANIEL HEARTZ

Algarotti, Giovanni Francesco. *See* ALCAROTTO, GIOVANNI FRANCESCO.

Algeria. For discussion of Algerian musical traditions, *see* ARAB MUSIC; BERBER MUSIC; NORTH AFRICA.

Al-Ghazālī [Abū Ḥāmid Muḥammad ibn Muḥammad] (*b* Ṭūs, Persia, 1058; *d* Ṭūs, 1111). Arab Sufi theologian, brother of Majd al-Dīn. After studying in Persia he taught at the Niẓāmiyya University in Baghdad from 1091 to 1095, and from 1106 in Neyshābūr. Between these duties he wrote the four parts of his principal work, *Iḥya' 'ulūm al-dīn* ('Revival of religious sciences'). The first part, on the practice of worship, deals with Koranic recitation (*tilāwa*) and the call to prayer (*adhān*). The second part, on morals and custom, includes a detailed chapter on the extent to which performing and listening to music (*samā'*) should be permitted. Noting that nowhere in the Koran is music expressly forbidden, al-Ghazālī demonstrated with numerous examples that the issue is not one of condemning specific musical forms or instruments, but depends on whether the intention is to arouse or strengthen good or bad qualities through music. He quoted many dogmatic and legal works, and refuted too strict interpretations of verdicts by recognized authorities that were against the practice of music. His liberal attitude to the dervish dance and religiously motivated music seems to have influenced the theory and practice of mosque and monastery music, especially in Turkey. The chapter on music in the *Miftāḥ al-sa'āda* by the Turk Ṭāshkuprī-zādah (Ṭāshköprüzāde) (*d* 1561), for example, is wholly indebted to al-Ghazālī.

WRITINGS

Iḥya' 'ulūm al-dīn [Revival of religious sciences]; ed. in D. B. Macdonald: 'Emotional Religion in Islām as affected by Music and Singing: being a Translation of a Book of the Iḥya' 'ulūm al-dīn of al-Ghazzali with Analysis, Annotation, and Appendices', *Journal of the Royal Asiatic Society* (1901), 195–252, 705–48; (1902), 1; ed. (Cairo, 1928–9)

BIBLIOGRAPHY

C. Brockelmann: *Geschichte der arabischen Litteratur*, i (Weimar and Berlin, 1898–1902, 2/1943), 419ff; suppl. i (Leiden, 1937), 744ff

H. G. Farmer: *The Sources of Arabian Music* (Bearsden, 1940, rev. 2/1965), 40

——: 'The Religious Music of Islam', *Journal of the Royal Asiatic Society* (1965), 60

Ṭāshkuprī-zādah [Aḥmad ibn Muṣṭafā]:*Miftāḥ al-sa'āda wa-miṣbāḥ al-siyāda* [Key to blissfulness and the lantern towards greatness], iii (Cairo, 1968), 285ff

ECKHARD NEUBAUER

Alghisi [Algisi], Paris Francesco (*b* Brescia, 19 June 1666; *d* Brescia, 30 or 29 March 1733). Italian composer and organist. He began musical studies at an early age with Orazio Polaroli (organist of Brescia Cathedral) and spent a short time (*c*1681–3) serving at the court of the Polish king when Polaroli was its *maestro di cappella*. After his return to Brescia, Alghisi entered the order of S Filippo Neri without, however, ceasing to compose secular music. The title-page to his collection of trio sonatas describes him as a member of the Brescian Collegio dei Nobili and of the Accademia Filarmonica of Bologna as well as *maestro di cappella* of the Congregazione dell'Oratorio di S Filippo Neri in Brescia. In the libretto for his oratorio *Il serafino* performed in S Domenico, Bologna, 1703, Alghisi is for the first time cited as the organist of Brescia Cathedral (a position that the libretto for *Il transito* of 1700 does not mention). Although very little of his music is known – no copy of his cantata collection published in Bologna (no later than 1694) is known to modern scholars – Tagliavini reported that a large part of his music was given to the Benedictine abbey of Disentis in Graubünden, Switzerland, and the remainder, including his harpsichord, to the S Filippo Neri congregation in Brescia. A collection of his letters belonged to the 18th-century Brescian scholar Orazio Chiaramonti, who published one of them in his *Idea dell'orazione* (Brescia, 1782). A theoretical work (cited by Eitner) is lost.

The preface to F. G. de Castro's *Trattenimenti armonici* (Bologna, 1695) praises Alghisi as teacher and composer. Towards the end of his life, moreover, he acquired the reputation of a saintly ascetic (Fétis). The claim that another Brescian composer named P. F. Alghisi lived from 1733 to 1767 (*Storia di Brescia*, iii, 268) is false; some of Alghisi's sacred music continued to be performed in Brescia after his death.

WORKS

OPERAS

L'amor di Curzio per la patria (G. C. Corradi), Venice, SS Giovanni e Paolo, wint. 1690

Il trionfo della continenza (Corradi), Venice, SS Giovanni e Paolo, aut. 1691

ORATORIOS

(*librettists unknown*)

Le piaghe sanate da una ferita, Brescia, 1689

La mensa bersagliatrice dell'eresia, Brescia, 1695

Il trionfo della fede, Brescia, 1697

Megera delusa, Brescia, 1698

Il transito del glorioso S Antonio di Padoa, Brescia, church of S Francesco, 20 June 1700

Il disinganno dell'intelletto, Brescia, 24 June 1701

Il serafino nell'amore e cherubino nell'intendere, Bologna, church of S Domenico, 1703

Il trionfo della sapienza, Bologna, church of S Domenico, 1704

Lite in cielo tra la sapienza e la santità per l'incoronazione dell'angelico maestro S Tomaso d'Aquino, Bologna, church of S Domenico, 1705

OTHER WORKS

Sonate da camera, 2 vn, vc/hpd, op.1 (Modena, 1693)

Cantate (Bologna, by 1694), lost, cited by Peroni

Suaves accentus (motet), S, str, org, *D-B*; Divote canzonette, for the Ursuline of Vienna, extant according to Martinotti; various sacred works, extant according to Martinotti

Numerous works, incl. 1 theoretical work, formerly in *CH-D* and *I-Nf*, lost; some cited in Peroni

BIBLIOGRAPHY

EitnerQ; *FétisB*; *GerberL*

O. Chiaramonti: *Idea dell'orazione ed elevazioni a Dio* (Brescia, 1782)

V. Peroni: *Biblioteca bresciana*, i (Brescia, 1818/*R*1968), 27

F. Dalola: *Memorie spettanti alla vita del servo di Dio P. F. Alghisi da Brescia* (Florence, n.d.) [incl. engraved portrait of Alghisi]

C. Ricci: *I teatri di Bologna nei secoli XVII e XVIII* (Bologna, 1888/*R*1965), 393ff

A. Valentini: *I musicisti bresciani ed il Teatro grande* (Brescia, 1894), 3

C. Sartori: *Bibliografia della musica strumentale italiana* (Florence, 1952), 572f, 583f

L. F. Tagliavini: 'Alghisi, Paris Francesco', *DBI*

Storia di Brescia, iii (1964), 179, 268, 925

S. Martinotti: 'Alghisi, Paris Francesco', *MGG*

SVEN HANSELL

Al-Gurgānī. See AL-JURJĀNĪ.

Al-Ḥasan ibn Aḥmad [ibn 'Alī al-Kātib] (*fl* ? late 10th century). Arab writer on music. He was the author of two works, only one of which is extant: *Kamāl adab al-ghinā'* ('The perfection of musical knowledge'), which appears on internal evidence to have been written probably during the late 10th century. On the theoretical side it borrows extensively from al-Fārābī, and also quotes al-Sarakhsī, a pupil of al-Kindī whose works have not survived. Of much greater interest is the material relating to practice, for here al-Ḥasan ibn Aḥmad dealt with a number of aspects little discussed by other writers: particularly valuable are his remarks on comportment (of both performer and audience), voice quality and training, nuances of instrumental and vocal technique, and the modal system.

BIBLIOGRAPHY

A. Shiloah: *La perfection des connaissances musicales: Kitāb kamāl adab al-ghinā'* (Paris, 1972)

O. WRIGHT

Alice Tully Hall. New York concert hall opened in 1969, part of Lincoln Center; *see* NEW YORK, §3.

Aliff. *See* AYLIFF.

'Alī ibn Muḥammad al-Jurjānī. Full name of al-Jurjānī, Arab philosopher and scientist, possibly the author of SHARḤ MAWLĀNĀ MUBĀRAK SHĀH BAR ADWĀR.

Alió y Brea, Francisco (*b* Barcelona, 27 March 1862; *d* Barcelona, 31 March 1908). Spanish composer, folklorist and music critic. He studied composition with Antonio Nicolau and Anselmo Barba and piano with C. G. Vidiella in Barcelona and was music critic for various journals there, including *La renaixensa*,

L'avenç and, from 1905 to 1908, *El poble català*. He published his *Collecció de 6 melodies per a cant i piano* and five *Cansons per cant i piano* (both Barcelona, 1887), which are settings of poems by Angel Guimerá, Francisco Matheu y Fornells, Apeles Mestres and Jacinto Verdaguer. He illustrated the latter volume himself, and some of his work was displayed at an exhibition of the Sociedad de Acuarelistas in Barcelona. A distinguished folklorist as well as a sensitive composer and skilful melodist, he collected Catalan folksongs and published arrangements of 23 of these in *Cansons populars catalanas* (Barcelona, 1891). He used native rhythms and melodies in his songs and piano pieces (among them *Ballet*, *Marxa fantàstica*, *Nota de color* and several barcarolles) and was one of the great initiators of the Catalan music revival while Luis Millet and Amadeo Vives were founding the Orfeó Català (1891).

BIBLIOGRAPHY

A. Elías de Molins: *Diccionario biográfico y bibliográfico de escritores y artistas catalanes del siglo XIX* (*apuntes y datos*), i (Barcelona, 1889)
F. Pedrell: *Diccionario biográfico y bibliográfico de músicos y escritores de música españoles*, i (Barcelona, 1897)
L. Millet: 'Francisco Alió', *Revista musical catalana*, v (June, 1908); repr. as 'Pel nostre ideal', *Recull d'escrits* (Barcelona, 1917)
L. B. Nadal: 'Francisco Alió', *Revista musical catalana*, v (June, 1908)
F. Pedrell: *Lírica nacionalizada: estudios sobre folklore musical* (Paris, n.d.)

JOCELYNE AUBÉ

Aliprandi, Bernardo (*b* ?Milan, *c*1710; *d* Frankfurt am Main, *c*1792). Italian cellist and composer. Although early sources (Eitner, Rudhart) claimed a Milanese origin for Aliprandi, the family has not been definitely traced. One of the numerous Italians who found careers north of the Alps, Aliprandi first appears in the records of the Bavarian court at Munich on 1 October 1731 as a chamber and court musician, with a yearly stipend of 1000 florins. In 1737, when G. Ferrandini vacated the position of composer of chamber music, Aliprandi succeeded him on 22 August; on 11 March 1744 he was promoted to Konzertmeister, with his salary increased to 1200 florins. By 1777 this amount had been reduced to 1105 florins, and in 1778 he retired with a pension of 500 florins. In 1791 he was living in Frankfurt; a petition by his son Bernardo Maria dated May 1793 indicates that he had died by then.

Aliprandi's works for the Bavarian court opera include *Mitridate* (B. Pasqualigo, 1738) and *Semiramide riconosciuta* (Metastasio, 1740); he also wrote a *festa teatrale* for Nymphenburg, *Apollo trà le muse in Parnasso* (Perozzo do Perozzi, 1737) and two works for performance at the Munich College of Jesuits, *Vocatio tertia ad nuptias filii regis* (G. Arnold, 1737) and *De via a caelo* (Neumayr, 1738). The *Iphigenia in Aulide* (Munich, 1739) sometimes attributed to Aliprandi was probably by Giovanni Porta. A piano score of *Mitridate* and a *Stabat mater* of 1749, for soprano, alto and chamber orchestra, survive (*D-Dlb*). 18 sinfonias are listed in the 1753 catalogue of the Munich Hofkapelle. In Münster's judgment Aliprandi's style was conservative, isolated from the newer Italian operatic developments, although the writing in the *Stabat mater* has emotional power.

BIBLIOGRAPHY

FétisB
F. J. Lipowsky: *Baierisches Musik-Lexicon* (Munich, 1811/*R*1971)
M. Rudhart: *Geschichte der Oper am Hofe zu München. Erster Theil: Die italiänischen Oper von 1654–1787* (Freising, 1865), 125f, 131, 166
F. W. Thieme: *Thieme-Becker: allgemeines Lexikon der bildenen Künstler*, i (1907), 291f
R. Münster: 'Aliprandi, Bernardo', *MGG*
R. Schaal: 'Ein un bekanntes Inventar der Münchner Hofkapelle aus dem Jahre 1753', *Convivium musicorum: Festschrift Wolfgang Boetticher* (Berlin, 1974), 309

JAMES L. JACKMAN

Aliprandi, Bernardo [Bernhard] **Maria** (*b* Munich, 5 Feb 1747; *d* Munich, 19 Feb 1801). Italian cellist and composer, son of Bernardo Aliprandi (*c*1710–*c*1792). The young Bernardo probably studied with his father; he played the cello for the Munich court, 1762–5. From 1768 he was the unpaid assistant director of the court orchestra. In 1778 he succeeded his father as court virtuoso; by 1799 he received 400 florins yearly. Lipowsky, who had possibly heard him play, praised his performance. According to Fétis, he published some works for the cello (not, as Gerber and others claimed, for the viola da gamba); none appear to have survived.

For bibliography *see* ALIPRANDI, BERNARDO.

JAMES L. JACKMAN

Aliquot. A mathematical term meaning 'contained in another a certain number of times without leaving any remainder' (*OED*); for example, 2 is an aliquot part of 6. Hence, by extension, the word 'aliquot' is used in music to refer to overtones or harmonics, the frequencies of which are exact multiples of the frequency of the fundamental. Aliquot strings (or aliquot scaling) are sympathetic ones (*see* SYMPATHETIC STRINGS) that vibrate in resonance with those that are struck or bowed; an aliquot piano has additional strings in the upper register that vibrate in sympathy with those struck by the hammers, as in some instruments manufactured by BLÜTHNER. *Aliquotstimmen* is the German term for mutation stops (*see* MUTATION STOP), i.e. organ stops pitched at a 5th, 10th and so on, above the fundamental.

HOWARD MAYER BROWN

Alís, Román (*b* Palma, Majorca, 24 Aug 1931). Spanish composer. He studied at the Barcelona Conservatory with Zamacois, Pich and Toldrá. From 1960 he was active as a pianist in various ensembles for new music, but he soon turned instead to teaching and composition. He took a leading part in the musical life of Seville until 1970, when he moved to Madrid; there he was appointed professor of composition at the conservatory. His early compositions employed 12-note serialism; later his technique became more open and flexible, as shown in the highly complex *Los salmos cosmicos* for chorus and instruments (1968).

WORKS
(*selective list*)

Orch: Sinfonia de cámara, brass, str, 1962; Variaciones breves, 1962; Suite, 1966; Musica para un festival en Sevilla, 1967; Reverberaciones, 1970

Choral with insts: Psalm xxi, chorus, wind, 1963; Misa armónica, 1966; Misa simple, 1967; Los salmos cósmicos, 1970

Chamber: Impresión, vn, pf, 1956; Huacca-china, fl, eng hn, hn, pf, 1957; Musica para 10 insts de viento, 1958; Canciones visnavas, vn, pf, 1960; Espejismos sonoros, ob, str, 1963; Estudios I–II, vn, pf, 1967; Atmosferas, cl, pf, 1968; other pieces

Songs for 1v, pf: Canciones, 1957; Al lado de mi cabaña, 1958; El canto de Lorelei, pf, Rima, 1970

Pf: 4 piezas breves, 1957; Poemas de la baja Andalucía, 1958; Sonata, 1964; Tema con variaciones, 1964; Tocata y fuga sobre un tema gitano, 1968

MANUEL VALLS

Aliseda, Jerónimo de (*b* *c*1548; *d* Granada, 28 June 1591). Spanish composer. He was the son of SANTOS DE ALISEDA. From about 1557 to September 1577 when he was ordained, he was a member of the choir of Granada Cathedral. In the summer of 1580 the chapter accepted him as successor to his father without the customary public competition. As *maestro de capilla* he was required to give board and instruction to the choirboys, to provide daily lessons in polyphony and to compose chanzonetas for important feasts. In 1589 he was relieved of these obligations because of ill-health. He died in poverty, like his father. Aliseda's solemnly expressive motets owe much to those of Morales in structure and style, particularly to the latter's *Emendemus in melius*.

WORKS
(all in E-GRc or GRcr unless otherwise stated)

2 masses, lost
Lamentation: Quomodo sedet sola, 4vv; ed. in López-Calo
4 motets, 5vv: Ad te levavi; Ave Maria; Beatus Franciscus; Domine, ne in ira tua: ed. in López-Calo
Popule meus, 5vv, *Tc*

BIBLIOGRAPHY
J. López-Calo: *La música en la catedral de Granada en el siglo XVI* (Granada, 1963)

ROBERT STEVENSON

Aliseda, Santos de (*d* Granada, 4 July 1580). Spanish composer. He was appointed *maestro de capilla* of Granada Cathedral on 19 November 1557 despite the opposition of his predecessor, Luis de Cózar, who intended his own nephew to succeed him. After an unsuccessful appeal to the archbishop, Cózar was forced to hand over the charge of the choirboys to Aliseda in May 1558. Aliseda had already begun to search for better singers, but was hindered by the poor salaries which the Granada Cathedral chapter offered.

Throughout his 23 years as *maestro de capilla* Aliseda won praise from the chapter for his diligent teaching, his punctuality and particularly for his care of the choirboys. In 1579, in appreciation of his merits, the chapter recommended him to Philip II for a prebend, and on 14 May 1580 voted him a gift of 12 ducats to aid him in his illness.

Aliseda's six-part motet *Similabo eum* shows him to have been a composer of great contrapuntal skill and sophistication. The 16 motets in the Toledo Cathedral archive are untranscribable owing to severe deterioration of the manuscript.

WORKS
Missa 'Ecce vir prudens', 4–6vv, *E-GRc*; ed. in López-Calo
6 motets and 1 lamentation in *GRc*: Filiae Jerusalem, 5vv; Haec est virgo sapiens, 4vv; Misericordiae Domine, 4vv (Lamentation); O doctor optime, 5vv; Pulchra facie, 4vv; Similabo eum, 6vv; Verba mea auribus percipe, 4vv: ed. in López-Calo
16 motets, *Tc*
Laudate Dominum (Ps cxvi), *P-VV*

BIBLIOGRAPHY
M. Joaquim: *Vinte livros de música polifónica do Paço Ducal de Vila Viçosa* (Lisbon, 1953), 90
J. López-Calo: *La música en la catedral de Granada en el siglo XVI* (Granada, 1963)

ROBERT STEVENSON

Al-Iṣfahānī [Abū l-Faraj 'Alī ibn al-Ḥusayn] (*b* Iṣfahān, 897; *d* Baghdad, ?967). Arab man of letters. As a writer on music he belongs to the school of ISḤĀQ AL-MAWṢILĪ, whose *Kitāb al-aghānī al-kabīr* ('Great book of songs') was the main source for al-Iṣfahānī's principal work of the same name, which is said to have taken him 50 years to write. This comprehensive book covers Arab cultural history from pre-Islamic times to the early 'Abbāsids, with emphasis on poetry and music. Its first published edition comprised 21 volumes. Its arrangement follows that of *Al-mi'at al-ṣawt al-*

mukhtāra ('The 100 selected songs') compiled by IBRĀHĪM AL-MAWṢILĪ and others, and accessible in the edition of 'Alī ibn Yaḥyā al-Munajjim (*d* 888), a pupil of Isḥaq al Mawṣilī. The texts of the songs are accompanied by notes on the compositions and their melodic and metrical modes. Each text is followed by the biography of a poet or musician often with an historical excursus; almost 100 musicians and singers from the late 6th century to the 9th are treated in this way. Soon after its completion the book was so renowned that Caliph al-Ḥakam II (961–76) of Córdoba sent al-Iṣfahānī 1000 gold dinars with a request for a copy. It is still the vital source for descriptions of early Arab musical history.

WRITINGS
Kitāb al-aghānī al-kabīr [Great book of songs]; pubd (Cairo, 1868–9, suppl., Leiden, 1887, 2/1905–6, rev. 1927–); part Fr. trans. in Quatremère

BIBLIOGRAPHY
E. M. Quatremère: 'Mémoire sur l'ouvrage intitulé Kitab al-agâni, c'est-à-dire "Recueil de chansons" ', *Journal asiatique*, 2nd ser., xvi (1835), 385–419, 497–545; 3rd ser., vi (1838), 465–526
'Abu l-Faraj al-Iṣbahānī', *The Encyclopaedia of Islam* (Leiden and London, 1913–38, rev. 2/1960–)
H. G. Farmer: *A History of Arabian Music* (London, 1929/R1973), 164f
——: *The Sources of Arabian Music* (Bearsden, 1940, rev. 2/1965), 31f
——: 'The Song Captions in the Kitāb al-aghānī al-kabīr', *Transactions of the Glasgow University Oriental Society*, xv (1955), 1
F. Sezgin: *Geschichte des arabischen Schrifttums*, i (Leiden, 1967), 378ff [with list of writings]
M. Stigelbauer: *Die Sängerinnen am Abbasidenhof um die Zeit des Kalifen al-Mutawakkil* (Vienna, 1975)

ECKHARD NEUBAUER

Alison [Allison, Allinsonne, Allysonn, Aloyson, etc], **Richard** (*fl* 1592–1606). English composer. In his *The Psalmes of David in Meter* (1599) he was described as 'Gent. Practitioner in the Art of Musicke', and as 'living in the Dukes place neere Alde-gate'. In the dedication to Anne Countess of Warwick, Alison wrote of 'your H. husband, sometimes my good Lord and Master'. This would not necessarily imply that he was or had been a servant; he could have been either a page or a gentleman retainer in the earl's household. Beck suggested that Morley may have been referring to Alison when, in his *First Booke of Consort Lessons*, he wrote it was 'set forth at cost and charges of a Gentleman'.

The first of Alison's music to be printed were the harmonizations he contributed to Thomas East's *Whole Booke of Psalmes* in 1592. These, in common with the rest of the collection, have the 'church tunes' in the tenor. Next came his own full-scale work *The Psalmes of David in Meter* (1599), 'The plaine Song beeing the common tunne to be sung and plaide upon the Lute, Orpharyon, Citterne or Bass Violl, Severally or altogether, the singing part to be either for Tenor or Treble to the Instruments, according to the voyce, or for fowre voyces'. Dowland and Sir William Leighton contributed laudatory poems. It was the first published book of vocal music in which this special form of instrumental accompaniment was provided, although it may in practice have been more common than the extant sources would lead us to suppose. The style is mostly simple like that of the psalms he harmonized for East. The underlay is mainly syllabic, and the part-movement not elaborate. With few exceptions the 'church tunes' come from the Sternhold and Hopkins psalter. There are a number of curious discrepancies between the instrumental parts, mostly between those for the lute and cittern.

In the same year Thomas Morley's *First Booke of Consort Lessons* was published. Although the lutebook of the set is missing, reconstruction from closely allied manuscript sources has been possible. Of the pieces in this collection, and in Rosseter's *Lessons for Consort* (as far as can be judged from the surviving parts) Alison's compositions are the most elaborate, and show a careful disposition of the instruments. It seems possible that he may have prepared the pieces for publication himself. Beck believed this to be so, and commented that he 'achieved real orchestration in the modern sense for the first time'.

Alison's last work was *An Howres Recreation in Musicke* (1606), 'apt for instruments and Voyces'. It was dedicated to Sir John Scudamore, 'most honoured Knight, and my worthiest Patrone'. For this collection Alison generally chose poems of a high standard, and his settings move with an unhurried serenity, having something of the same quality that he brought to his harmonizations of the psalms.

WORKS

VOCAL

The Psalms of David in Meter (London, 1599/R1968)
An Howres Recreation in Musicke (London, 1606); ed. E. H. Fellowes, EM, xxxiii (1924, rev. 2/1961)
10 psalm harmonizations in 1592[7]

INSTRUMENTAL

Edition: *The First Book of Consort Lessons collected by Thomas Morley* (London, 1599, rev. 2/1611[21]); ed. S. Beck (New York, 1959) [B]

Allison's Knell, lute, tr viol, fl, b viol, cittern, bandora, B 11
Allmayne, inc., Sampson [formerly Tollemache] MS, R. Spencer's private collection, Woodford Green, Essex (facs. Leeds, 1974), *US-OAm*
De la tromba pavin, lute, tr viol, fl, rec, b viol, cittern, bandora, B 3
Dolorosa Paven, lute, tr viol, rec, fl, b viol, cittern, *Cu* Dd.3.18, ff.46v–47, Dd.5.21, f.7v, Dd.5.20, f.7v; *GB-BEV*, no.11; *US-OAm*, no.11
Galliard to De la tromba, inc., fl, cittern only, in P. Rosseter: Lessons for Consort (London, 1609)
Galliard to the Quadro Pavin, tr viol, fl, b viol, cittern, bandora, B 2
Goe from my window, lute, tr viol, rec/fl, b viol, cittern, bandora, B 12
In Nomine, 5 viols, *GB-Ob* Mus.Sch.D.212–16
Mrs Millicents Paven, lute, fl, cittern, b viol; Millicents Galliard, fl, cittern, inc., in Rosseter
Responce pavin, tr viol, fl, bandora, B 179
The Bachelar's Delight, lute, tr viol, fl, b viol, cittern, bandora, B 24
The Quadro Pavin, tr viol, fl, b viol, cittern, bandora, B 1
In the Walsingham Consort Books (for sources see Edwards, *ML*, lv, 1974): Goe from my window (same setting in B); Mr Allisons almayne; Mr Allisons knell; Mr Allisons sharp pavin; Paven dolorosa; The bachilers delight; The Lady Frances Sidneys almayne; The Lady Frances Sidneys goodmorowe (= De la tromba pavin in B); The Lady Frances Sidneys goodnight (attrib. Bachiler in cittern book); The Quadro galliard (same setting in B); The Quadro Paven (same setting in B); The Spanish measure
Lute solos: Allmaine, *Cu* Dd.2.11, f.75; Galiarde, *Lbm* Hirsch 1353, f.9; 5 pavans, *Lbm* Add.31392, ff.30v–34, Hirsch 1353, f.63v (concordances in *Cu* Dd.2.11, Dd.5.78), 1615[24] [anon. arr.]; Paven doloroasa, *Cu* Dd.2.11, ff.4v–5, Dd.5.78, f.32v; The quadren pavine, *Cu* Dd.4.22, ff.4v–5, ed. D. Lumsden, *An Anthology of English Lute Music* (London, 1954); Gallyard, Goe from my wyndowe, Passamesu pavan and galliard, Premero, divisions on Galliarde W. Bradbery Sir Walter Rawley F. Cutting, Board MS, R. Spencer's private collection, Woodford Green, Essex (facs. Leeds, 1975)
Lute duets: De la trumba, *Lbm* Eg.2046, ff.6v–8; Spanish measures treble with ground, Board MS, R. Spencer's private collection, Woodford Green, Essex (facs. Leeds, 1975); The sharp pavin, *Lbm* Eg.2046, f.12 (concordances in *Lbm* Add.38539, Berkshire County Record Office, Reading, Add.6, *US-Ws* 1610.1)
Fantasia, bandora, *GB-Cu* Dd.2.11, f.28v

BIBLIOGRAPHY

M. Frost: *English and Scottish Psalm Tunes* (London, 1953)
D. Lumsden: *The Sources of English Lute Music, 1540–1620* (diss., U. of Cambridge, 1956–7)
S. Beck: *The First Book of Consort Lessons* (New York, 1959) [incl. important preface]

I. Harwood: 'Rosseter's *Lessons for Consort* of 1609', *LSJ*, vii (1965), 15
L. Nordstrom: 'The Cambridge Consort Books', *Journal of the Lute Society of America*, v (1972), 70–103
W. E. Edwards: *Sources of Elizabethan Consort Music* (diss., U. of Cambridge, 1974)
——: 'The Walsingham Consort Books', *ML*, lv (1974), 209

DIANA POULTON

Al-Jurjānī ['Alī ibn Muḥammad al-Jurjānī] (*b* Tājū, Astarabad, 1339; *d* Shīrāz, 1413). Arab philosopher and scientist, possibly the author of SHARH MAWLĀNĀ MUBĀRAK SHĀH BAR ADWĀR.

Alkaios. *See* ALCAEUS.

Alkan [Morhange], **(Charles-)Valentin** (*b* Paris, 30 Nov 1813; *d* Paris, 29 March 1888). French pianist and composer. His real name was Morhange. He was one of the leading piano virtuosos of the 19th century and one of its most unusual composers, remarkable in both technique and imagination, yet largely ignored by his own and succeeding generations.

1. Life. 2. Alkan as pianist. 3. Works and style.

1. LIFE. Of Jewish parentage, Alkan was the eldest of five brothers, all of whom, with an elder sister as well, became musicians under the assumed name Alkan; Napoléon Alkan, the third brother (1826–1910), taught solfège at the Paris Conservatoire for over 50 years. Valentin Alkan's career at the Conservatoire started brilliantly with a *premier prix* for solfège at the age of seven. When Alkan was nine Cherubini observed that he was 'astonishing for his age' and described his ability on the piano as 'extraordinary'. He won a *premier prix* for piano in 1824, for harmony in 1827 and for organ in 1834. His op.1 was published in 1828, when he was 14. As a child prodigy he enjoyed great success, especially in the salon of the Princesse de la Moskova, although he later admitted feeling eclipsed by the yet greater success of the young Liszt. His teachers were Dourlen for harmony and P.-J. Zimmermann for the piano. Still on the crest of his youthful success he visited London in 1833, according to Fétis, and was 'cheerful, outgoing and confident' (Marmontel).

Alkan soon came under the spell of Chopin, whose close friendship he enjoyed and whose music he much admired. He was friendly too with George Sand and others of their circle. Yet there soon appeared the strain of shyness and misanthropy that was later to become Alkan's dominant characteristic. His life is undocumented for long periods when he withdrew from the concert platform; his publications appeared only at intervals; and he seems more and more to have avoided company. He held no official appointments. From 1829 until 1836 he was a part-time teacher of solfège at the Conservatoire, but he was never a full member of its staff. In 1848, on the death of Zimmermann, there was public controversy as to whether Alkan or Marmontel should succeed to the teaching post at the Conservatoire. The two men fell out when Marmontel was appointed and Alkan remained without public office or honour.

Alkan's concert appearances were rare, and he played more music by other composers than his own works. After 1838 he disappeared from view until 1844 when he gave two concerts for *La France musicale*, followed by two in 1845 in the Salle Erard. By this time he had attracted the attention of leading critics, including Liszt, Schumann and d'Ortigue, and he was definitely regarded as among the principal virtuosos of the day. Yet he again withdrew until 1853, when he gavee two concerts of 'classical and retrospective music'; this was followed by a further gap of 20 years until 1873, when he began the series of 'Petits concerts', giving up to six concerts a year until 1880 in both the Salle Erard and the Salle Pleyel. He continued to play at Erard's twice a week until his death, giving afternoon classes. His most eminent pupil was Elie-Miriam Delaborde (*b* Paris, 8 Feb 1839; *d* Paris, 9 Dec 1913), generally thought to be Alkan's illegitimate son. Like his father, Delaborde favoured the pedal piano and was a composer. But in contrast, his character was extroverted and urbane; he toured widely as a virtuoso, painted a little and knew both Bizet and Manet well.

Valentin Alkan: pastel portrait by Eduard Debufe (private collection)

Alkan's publications were nearly as intermittent as his concerts; there is an uncharted gap in the 1860s, a period of his life of which virtually nothing is known. His works were known, if at all, from publication rather than performance, which perhaps accounts for the obscurity in which they have lain both during and since his lifetime. It is fortunate that so many works, many of them of considerable dimensions, should have been published at all.

Alkan's enigmatic character, clearly reflected in his music, has been well described by Marmontel and de Bertha. He dressed in a severe, old-fashioned, somewhat clerical manner, discouraged visitors and went out rarely. He felt he had lived beyond his time. Niecks described how Alkan became warm-hearted and almost convivial once the outer reserve had been penetrated. He had few friends, though he particularly enjoyed the patronage of Russian aristocratic ladies, 'des dames très parfumées et froufroutantes', as Isidore Philipp described them. He was nervous in public and pathologically worried about his health, even though it was

good. He remained a strict member of the Jewish faith in which he had been brought up, and was widely read in classical and biblical lore. This may account for the story, which seems to have no basis of truth, that he died under a collapsed bookcase; de Bertha's account of his death mentions no such incident.

2. ALKAN AS PIANIST. Accounts of Alkan's playing are in accord on its virtuosity, although he only rarely played his most difficult pieces. He performed the Symphonie from op.39, for example, only once, and never played the complete Concerto (from the same set) or the *Grande sonate* op.33. D'Ortigue in 1844 called his playing 'firm, powerful, brilliant and severe', while the 'Rover of Concerts' (*Revue et gazette musicale*, xii, 1845, 139) said: 'his playing is clear, pure, brilliant, perfectly controlled; but it lacks breadth, passion, poetry or individuality, despite his claim to display these qualities in his music'. He was proud of the strictness and precision of his playing, and was a rigorous user of the metronome. His variations *Le festin d'Esope* are headed 'senza licenza quantunque', and he insisted that Chopin, whom he greatly admired, should be interpreted in a classical manner.

Alkan was particularly noted for his attachment to a wide repertory of historical music and for his promulgation of music, such as the late Beethoven sonatas and Schubert's piano music, not fashionable at the time. He published transcriptions of Bach, Handel, Marcello, Grétry and others, and composed in the 'style ancien' from time to time. He was an ardent champion of the *pédalier* (the pedal piano), for which he wrote some impressive works, especially near the end of his life.

3. WORKS AND STYLE. Most of Alkan's works are for the piano. Of the two early chamber concertos, the second was later arranged by Alkan for solo piano. The orchestral symphony in B minor, described by Léon Kreutzer in 1846, is lost. There are three substantial chamber works and some miscellaneous vocal pieces of no special interest, save the comical march on the death of a parrot for choir and woodwind. His earliest piano compositions are variations and rondos wholly in the fashion of the day, many based on popular operatic melodies, but without true marks of individuality. The characteristic brilliance for which he was soon to be noted appears plainly in the various sets of studies published in 1837 and 1838. In 1844 followed a group of works that display his taste for unusual titles and subject matter, *Le chemin de fer* for example, and the style is noticeably bolder and more original. In the next group the scale is enormously enlarged with the *25 préludes* op.31 in all the major and minor keys (C major appears twice) in 1847 and the *Grande sonate: Les quatre âges* op.33 and the *12 études* in all the major keys op.35 in 1848. The full conception was realized in 1857 with the appearance of his most ambitious work, the *12 études* in all the minor keys, op.39; these comprise a four-movement symphony, a three-movement concerto, a set of variations, an overture and three miscellaneous pieces, some of the movements being of enormous length. Other collections show his fondness for assembling many pieces into one folder, for example the five *Recueils de chants* published between 1857 and about 1873, modelled in part on Mendelssohn's *Lieder ohne Worte*, and the *48 motifs* or *esquisses* published in four books in 1861.

Alkan's originality is evident in nearly all his music,

but he was in debt to both old and new music for elements of his style. His admiration for 18th-century Classics has already been mentioned, and the more formal mannerisms of Bach and Handel are plentiful. He was close in spirit, at least in his early music, to Zimmermann, Henri Bertini, Kalkbrenner and the Parisian virtuoso school of the 1820s. Above all he felt the influence of Chopin, whose ornamental phraseology he adopted, combining it with a different melodic and harmonic style. The extra-musical element and his recurrent boldness have invited comparison with Berlioz (who appears to have shown no interest in Alkan). Schumann made the comparison in 1839, and so did Sorabji, in 1932, when he said that Alkan's *Sonatine* op.61 sounded like Berlioz attempting to compose a Beethoven sonata. But Alkan was altogether more puzzling and impenetrable. His titles are obscure and elliptical, often with a satanic or mocking tone. He revelled in Faustian ideas yet at other times assumed a childish, domestic simplicity. Military motifs and quasi-religious tones, biblical or Hebraic, are also common. Superscriptions and instructions abound.

A surprising aspect of Alkan's style is its technical rigour, for he wrote not as a pianist with a keyboard before him but with the cerebral exactness of someone for whom the notation is more important than the sound. He refused to spell enharmonically and facilitate reading, with the result that at least twice he was compelled to use a notation for a triple sharp; he was scrupulous in his part-writing. The same obstinacy is to be seen in his harmonic writing in which, for example, he used pedal points or ostinatos against theoretically incompatible counterpoints; *Fa* op.38 no.8 makes a special feature of this. His clashing harmony is nearly always the result of one part's refusing to move into line with another and the effect can be very harsh. His playing without rubato was a kindred characteristic; indeed one of the *48 motifs* (no.28) is entitled *Inflexibilité*.

At a period when the piano was undergoing universal exploitation for new and more dazzling sonorities, Alkan made a positive contribution to virtuoso technique. His music can be exacting beyond the capacity of any but the most powerful players in technique, dynamic demands and stamina. It can also be disarmingly simple. He exploited the extreme ends of the keyboard, often in deliberate contrast with the middle range. *Salut cendre du pauvre* op.45 has fine side-drum effects, also found in the powerful Mahlerian *Le tambour bat aux champs* op.50*bis*. *Le grillon* op.60*bis* imitates the chirping of the cricket; *Le chemin de fer*, obviously, imitates a train. Other instruments are imitated, for example the cello in *La voix de l'instrument* op.70 no.4, and a string quartet is evoked with remarkable precision in *Début du quatuor*, no.31 of the *48 motifs*. No.15 of the same set is a *Tutti de concerto dans le genre ancien* in a heavy orchestral manner with a clearly differentiated entry for the 'soloist'. The Concerto in op.39 takes this idea to extreme lengths with the orchestral and solo elements in balance throughout. The fine opening of the Symphonie in the same work has a real orchestral surge.

Alkan's melodic gift was variable, rarely comparable to that of Chopin or Berlioz, and sometimes critically weak. But he was master of a naive style as, for example, in the *maggiore* section of the slow movement of the Symphonie or in *Promenade sur l'eau*, no.6 of *Les mois*

op.74. A piece such as the powerful *Morituri te salutant*, no.21 of the *48 motifs*, achieves its effect entirely without recourse to melody in the normal sense. His interest in unusual metres and rhythmic combinations was keen as can clearly be seen in the second book of impromptus op.32: of the four pieces three are in quintuple time and one is in septuple.

Alkan had unconventional ideas about tonal structure and was not bound by unity of key in his larger forms. As early as 1832, in the first chamber concerto, the first movement begins in A minor and concludes in E major and the last movement ends in C♯ major. The four movements of the *Grande sonate* op.33 not only get progressively slower to illustrate increasing age (the first movement is a scherzo), but are all in different keys. Both the Symphonie and the Concerto in op.39, being parts of a scheme of 12 studies in all the minor keys, have all their movements in different keys. In the second chamber concerto the three movements are continuous, with the third returning to the material of the first. Alkan's structures sometimes run to epic length; the largest is the first movement of the Concerto, which lasts nearly 30 minutes. But many of his pieces are no more than a dozen bars long. One of his favourite devices was the stark juxtaposition of quite different elements, the best example of which is *Héraclite et Démocrite* op.63 no.39.

Alkan's music has been seriously neglected. Pianists have been slow to explore the great range and variety of his music, not all of which is extravagantly difficult to play. But he was greatly valued by Liszt, Busoni and many others, and should eventually take his due place among the most important figures of his time.

WORKS

Editions: *Ch. V. Alkan: oeuvres choisies*, ed. E. Delaborde and I. Philipp (Paris, c1900) [incl. many kbd works]
The Piano Music of Alkan, ed. R. Lewenthal (New York, 1964) [incl. works from 7 op. nos.]
Ch. V. Alkan: oeuvres choisies pour piano, ed. G. Beck, Le pupitre, xvi (Paris, 1969) [incl. 12 works]

(all printed works published in Paris)

VOCAL

Hermann et Ketty (de Pastoret) [Prix de Rome cantata], 1832, unpubd
L'entrée en loge (Gail) [Prix de Rome cantata], 1834, unpubd
Romance du phare d'Eddystone, 1v, pf, 1845, lost
Etz chajjim hi, 2S, T, B, unacc. (1847)
Halelouyoh, S, A, T, B, pf/org (1857)
Marcia funebre sulla morte d'un papagallo, 2S, T, B, 3 ob, bn (1859)
Stances de Millevoye, 2S, A, pf (1859)

ORCHESTRAL

op.	
10	Concerto da camera no.1, a, pf solo, c1832
—	Concerto da camera no.2, c♯, pf solo, before 1834; rev. pf solo
—	Pas redoublé, wind band, 1840, unpubd
—	Symphony, b, 1844, lost

CHAMBER

21	Grand duo concertant, vn, pf (c1840)
30	Piano Trio (1841)
47	Sonate de concert, vc, pf (1857)

KEYBOARD

(for piano unless otherwise stated)

1	Variations on a theme from Steibelt: Orage (1828)
2	Les omnibus, variations (1829)
3	Il était un p'tit homme, rondoletto (1830)
4	Rondo brillant, str qt ad lib (c1833)
5	Rondo, on Rossini: Largo al factotum from Il barbiere di Siviglia (c1833)
12	Rondeau chromatique (1833)
16/4	Variations on Donizetti: Ah segnata é la mia morte from Anna Bolena (1834)
16/5	Variations on Bellini: La tremenda ultrice spada from I Capuleti e i Montecchi (1834)

16/6　Variations quasi fantaisie sur une barcarolle napolitaine (1834)
12　Trois improvisations dans le style brillant (1837)
13　Trois andantes romantiques (1837)
15　Trois morceaux dans le genre pathétique (1837): 1 Aime-moi, 2 Le vent, 3 Morte
16　Tre scherzi (1837)
16　Six morceaux caractéristiques (1838), also as op.8; repubd as nos.1, 4, 5, 7, 8, 12 of Les mois, op.74
17　Finale, pf 4 hands (1838–40)
76　Trois grandes études (c1838): 1 Fantaisie, left hand, 2 Introduction, variations and finale, right hand, 3 Etude à mouvement semblable et perpetuel
—　Jean qui pleure et Jean qui rit [2 fughe da camera] (c1840)
—　Variations à la vielle, on a theme from Donizetti: Elisir d'amore (c1840)
—　Variations on a theme from Donizetti: Ugo conte di Parigi (1842)
22　Nocturne (1844)
23　Saltarelle (1844)
24　Gigue et air de ballet dans le style ancien (1844)
25　Alleluia (1844)
17　Le preux, étude de concert (1844)
26　Variations-fantaisie on themes from Mozart: Don Giovanni, pf 4 hands (1844)
27　Le chemin de fer, étude (1844)
—　Désir (1844)
—　L'amitié, étude (1845), repubd as op.32(1)/2
—　Impromptu, F♯ (c1845)
29　Bourrée d'Auvergne (1846)
26　Marche funèbre (1846)
27　Marche triomphale [originally Marche héroïque] (1846)
26c　Vaghezza, impromptu (1847), repubd as op.32(1)/1
26b　Fantasietta alla moresca (1847), repubd as op.32(1)/3
31　Vingt-cinq préludes, in all major and minor keys, pf/org (1847)
33　Grande sonate: Les quatre âges (1848)
34　Scherzo focoso (1848)
35　Douze études, in all major keys (1848)
32(1)　Quatre impromptus (1848): 1 Vaghezza, 2 L'amitié, 3 Fantasietta alla moresca, 4 La foi [nos.1, 2, 3 also pubd separately]
32(2)　Deuxième recueil d'impromptus, 3 airs à 5 temps et 1 à 7 temps (1849)
—　Pro organo, org, 1850, unpubd
—　Fantasticheria (c1850)
45　Salut, cendre du pauvre!, paraphrase (1856)
37　Trois marches, quasi da cavalleria (1857)
38　Premier recueil de chants (1857)
38　Deuxième recueil de chants (1857)
39　Douze études, in all minor keys (1857): 1 Comme le vent, 2 En rythme molossique, 3 Scherzo diabolico, 4–7 Symphonie, 8–10 Concerto, 11 Ouverture, 12 Le festin d'Esope, variations
40　Trois marches, pf 4 hands (1857)
41　Trois petites fantaisies (1857)
42　Réconciliation, petit caprice (1857)
46　Minuetto alla tedesca (1857)
50　Capriccio alla soldatesca (1859)
51　Trois menuets (1859)
52　Super flumina Babylonis, paraphrase (1859)
53　Quasi-caccia, caprice (1859)
54　Benedictus, pedal pf/pf 3 hands (1859)
55　Une fusée, introduction et impromptu (1859)
—　Petit conte (1859)
—　Petits préludes sur les 8 gammes du plain-chant, org (1859)
57　Nocturnes nos.2, 3 (1859)
60　Deux petites pièces (1859): 1 Ma chère liberté, 2 Ma chère servitude
50bis　Le tambour bat aux champs, esquisse (1859)
60bis　Nocturne no.4, Le grillon (1859)
61　Sonatine (1861)
63　Quarante-huit motifs (esquisses) (1861)
64　Treize prières, org/pedal pf/pf 3 hands (c1870)
65　Troisième recueil de chants (c1870)
66　Onze grands préludes and transcr. of Handel: Messiah, pedal pf/pf 3 hands (c1870)
69　Impromptu sur le choral de Luther, org/pedal pf (c1871)
—　Douze études, pedals only (org/pedal pf) (c1871)
—　Chapeau bas, 2me fantasticheria (c1872)
—　Bombardo-carillon, pedal-board 4 feet/pf 4 hands (c1872)
72　Onze pièces dans le style religieux and transcr. of Handel: Messiah, org/harmonium/pf (c1872)
74　Les mois, 12 morceaux caractéristiques (c1872) [incl. op.16]
75　Toccatina (c1872)
67　Quatrième recueil de chants (c1873)
70　Cinquième recueil de chants (c1873)
—　Douze fugues, pedal pf/org (n.d.)
—　Zorcico, danse ibérienne, ed. G. Beck (1969)
Transcrs. of works by Bach, Beethoven, Gluck, Grétry, Handel, Haydn, Marcello, Meyerbeer, Mozart, Weber etc

BIBLIOGRAPHY

FétisB
F. Liszt: 'Trois morceaux dans le genre pathétique par C.-V. Alkan', *Revue et gazette musicale*, iv (1837), 460
R. Schumann: 'Etuden für Pianoforte: C. V. Alkan, 3 grosse Etuden, op.15', *NZM*, viii (1838), 169
——: 'Ch. Valentin Alkan, 6 charakteristische Stücke, op.16', *NZM*, x (1839), 167
J. d'Ortigue: 'Concerts de la France musicale', *France musicale*, vii (1844), 65
L. Kreutzer: 'Compositions de M. V. Alkan', *Revue et gazette musicale*, xiii (1846), 13
F. J. Fétis: 'Revue critique – C.-V. Alkan', *Revue et gazette musicale*, xiv (1847), 244
H. von Bülow: 'C. V. Alkan, Douze études pour le piano en 2 suites, op.35', *Neue Berliner Musikzeitung*, xi (1857), 273
A. Marmontel: *Les pianistes célèbres* (Paris, 1878, 2/1887)
A. Pougin: 'Nécrologie', *Le ménestrel*, liv (1887–8), 120
A. de Bertha: 'Ch. Valentin Alkan aîné – étude psycho-musicale', *BSIM*, v (1909), 135
T. Bolte: 'Charles Valentin Morhange Alkan: zur 100. Wiederkehr seines Geburtstages', *NZM*, lxxx (1913), 665
F. Niecks: 'More Glimpses of Parisian Pianists of Another Day', *MMR*, xlviii (1918), 4
H. H. Bellamann: 'The Piano Works of C. V. Alkan', *MQ*, x (1924), 251
V. d'Indy: 'Impressions musicales d'enfance et de jeunesse: III Adolescence', *Annales politiques et littéraires*, xcv (15 May 1930)
K. Sorabji: *Around Music* (London, 1932)
S. Sitwell: 'A Note upon Alkan', *Liszt* (London, 1934, rev. 2/1955, 3/1967)
B. van Dieren: *Down among the Dead Men and other Essays* (London, 1935), 12ff
H. Searle: 'A Plea for Alkan', *ML*, xviii (1937), 276
J. Bloch: *Charles-Valentin Alkan* (Indianapolis, 1941)
R. Gorer: 'A Nineteenth-century Romantic', *The Listener*, xxxvi (1946), 688
H. Searle: 'Alkan', *Grove 5*
R. Lewenthal: Introduction to *The Piano Music of Alkan* (New York, 1964)
G. Beck: Preface to *Ch. V. Alkan: oeuvres choisies pour piano*, Le pupitre, xvi (Paris, 1969)
D. Dille: 'L'Allegro barbaro de Bartók', *SM*, xii (1970), 3
R. and M. Sietz, eds: 'Der Nachlass Ferdinand Hillers', *Mitteilungen aus dem Stadtarchiv von Köln*, ed. H. Stehkämper, lix (Cologne, 1970)
R. Smith: 'Charles-Valentin Alkan', *The Listener*, lxxxvi (1971), 25
K. Franke: 'Im Schatten Liszts: Charles Valentin Alkan, Misanthrop unter den Heroen seiner Zeit', *Fonoforum*, iv (1972), 266
H. Macdonald: 'The Death of Alkan', *MT*, cxiv (1973), 25
L. Sitsky: 'Summary Notes for a Study on Alkan', *SMA*, viii (1974), 53–91
D. Hennig: *Charles-Valentin Alkan* (diss., U. of Oxford, 1975)
H. Macdonald: 'The Enigma of Alkan', *MT*, cxvii (1976), 401
R. Smith: *Alkan: the Enigma*, i (London, 1976)

HUGH MACDONALD

Al-Kātib. *See* YŪNUS AL-KĀTIB and AL-ḤASAN IBN AḤMAD.

Al-Kahlīl ibn Aḥmad (*b* Baṣra, *c*718; *d* Baṣra, *c*790). Arab philologist. He is regarded as the father of Arab lexicography and the sciences of prosody and rhythm. His writings on music include *Kitāb al-nagham* ('Book on melodic modes'), *Kitāb al-īqā'* ('Book on rhythm') and perhaps *Kitāb tarākīb al-aṣwāt* ('Book on the combining of notes'). These works are lost, but seem to have been fundamental to the musical teaching of Isḥāq al-Mawṣilī and his school. The immediate sources of al-Khalīl's musical theory are not known. Besides the Arab tradition, with its Syriac-Byzantine and Persian elements, Indian views may have influenced his theory of modal rhythm. He probably had no knowledge of the classical Greek music theorists and no practical knowledge of music; his works on musical theory were judged by scholars such as al-Naẓẓām (*d* 845) and al-Jāḥiẓ (*d* 868) less favourably than his philological writings. His name, like that of Isḥāq al-Mawṣilī, is linked with the view, current in antiquity, that is fundamental to Arab teaching of modal rhythm – that rhythm is a sister discipline to prosody. The revival of this view in the West in medieval times does not preclude its transmission by the Arabs.

BIBLIOGRAPHY

'Al-Khalīl ibn Aḥmad', *The Encyclopaedia of Islam* (Leiden and London, 1913–38, rev. 2/1960–)
O. Rescher: *Abriss der arabischen Litteraturgeschichte*, ii (Stuttgart, 1933), 119ff
H. G. Farmer: *The Sources of Arabian Music* (Bearsden, 1940, rev. 2/1965), 1
A. Codazzi: 'Il trattato dell'arte metrica di Giovanni Leone Africano', *Studi orientalistici G. Levi della Vida*, i (Rome, 1936), 180ff
G. and M. 'Auwad: *Al-Khalīl ibn Aḥmad al-Farāhīdī: ḥayātuh waāthāruh fī l-marāji' al-'arabiyya wa-al-ajnabiyya* [Al-Khalīl ibn Aḥmad al-Farāhīdī: his life and works in Arabic and foreign sources] (Baghdad, 1972)
F. Sezgin: *Geschichte des arabischen Schrifttums*, ii (Leiden, 1975), 613
ECKHARD NEUBAUER

Al-Kindī [Abū Yūsuf Ya'qūb ibn Isḥāq] (*b* ?Kufa, *c*790; *d* Baghdad, *c*874). Arab philosopher and writer on music. He was a figure of great importance in the early development of Islamic philosophy. His father was the governor of Kufa, and he was educated at Basra, a lively intellectual centre at the time. During the reigns of al-Ma'mūn (818–33) and al-Mu'taṣim (833–42) he was attached to the 'Abbāsid court in Baghdad, coming into close contact with the scholars who were beginning to make Greek philosophical works available in Arabic. Known as the 'philosopher of the Arabs', he was a prolific author with wide-ranging interests, and his works include a number of short treatises on music, at least five of which have survived. Reflecting his general receptiveness to both the Aristotelian and the neo-Platonic and Pythagorean traditions, they are eclectic in approach and cover a rather wider range of subjects than many later writings. His analysis of intervals and scales uses Greek concepts such as the Greater Perfect System, but the presentation is in terms of strings and frettings on the indigenous '*ūd* (short-necked lute), a pattern followed by all the other major theorists. (Unlike them, however, he did not regard the lute as a mere adjunct to theoretical demonstration, and he also provided a fairly detailed description of it.) The texts also include an elliptically brief survey of the rhythmic cycles, and a schematic analysis of melodic pattern. In addition al-Kindī dealt at some length with cosmology (an area ignored by most other Arab theorists, with the notable exception of the Ikhwān al-Ṣafā') laying particular emphasis on sets of associations in which number and numerical relationships provide the chief common factors.

WRITINGS

Al-risāla l-kubrā fī al-ta' līf [Grand treatise on composition]; ed. Z. Yūsuf in *Mu'allafāt al-Kindī al-mūsīqiyya* [Al-Kindī's musical works] (Baghdad, 1962)
Mukhtaṣar al-mūsīqī fī ta'līf al-nagham wa-ṣan'at al-'ūd [Summary on music with regard to the composition of melodies and lute making] (MS, *D-B* 5531); ed. Z. Yūsuf (Baghdad, 1962); ed. A. Shiloah: 'Un ancien traité sur le '*ūd* d'Abū Yūsuf al-Kindī', *Israel Oriental Studies*, iv (1974), 179
Risāla fī ajzā' khabariyya fī l-musīqī [Treatise in informative sections on the theory of music] (MS, *D-B* 5503); ed. Z. Yūsuf (Baghdad, 1962)
Risāla fī aluḥūn wal-nagham [Treatise on melodies and notes]; ed. Z. Yūsuf (Baghdad, 1965)
Risāla fī khubr ṣināat al-ta' līf [Treatise concerning inner knowledge of the art of composition] (MS, *GB-Lbm* Oriental 2361); ed. C. Cowl: The Risāla fī ḥubr ta'līf al-'alḥan of Ja'qūb ibn Isḥāq al-Kindī', *The Consort*, xxiii (1966), 129–66, ed. Y. Shawqō (Cairo, 1969)

BIBLIOGRAPHY

'Al-Kindī', *The Encyclopaedia of Islam* (Leiden and London, 1913–38, rev. 2/1960–)
H. G. Farmer: *The Influence of Music: from Arabic Sources* (London, 1926), 12ff
——: *A History of Arabian Music* (London, 1929/*R*1973), 127f
——: *The Sources of Arabian Music* (Bearsden, 1940, rev. 2/1965), 7, 19f
——: *Sa'adyah Gaon on the Influence of Music* (London, 1943), 17ff
O. WRIGHT

Alla breve (It.). In the system of PROPORTIONS of the late Middle Ages and Renaissance, another name for *proportio dupla* (time signature 2/1 or more commonly ¢), where note shapes diminished in relative value in the ratio 2 : 1. The *tactus* thus shifted from its normal place on the semibreve (*alla semibreve*) to the breve. *Alla breve* still retains its connotation of a smaller relative value per note shape in modern practice, and is commonly used for music in a relatively quick tempo, where ¢ indicates two beats to a bar of four crotchets while C indicates four beats.

Alla cappella. *See* A CAPPELLA.

Allacci [Allacius, Allatius], **Leone** [Lione] (*b* Chios, 1588; *d* Rome, 19 Jan 1669). Italian theologian and scholar of Greek origin. He came to Italy as a child and studied philosophy, theology and classics in Rome at the Greek Catholic Collegio di S Atanasio from 1599 to 1610. After a period in Chios he studied medicine at Rome until 1616. Thereafter he was employed in the Vatican Library and was responsible for moving the Biblioteca Palatina from Heidelberg to Rome in 1622–3. In 1661 he succeeded Luca Holstenio as chief curator of the Vatican Library. He wrote extensively on a wide range of subjects including theology, Byzantine studies, classical antiquity and Italian letters. He is significant for the history of music by virtue of his *Drammaturgia . . . divisa in sette indici* (Rome, 1666), a compendious and surprisingly accurate list of dramatic works of all kinds, including opera librettos, published in Italy; it also lists many unpublished works. A second, vastly enlarged and updated edition by Giovanni Cendoni, Apostolo Zeno, Giovanni degli Apostoli and others unnamed (Venice, 1755/*R*1961) adds the names of composers to *drammi per musica* and remains a major work of reference for Italian drama studies, although it must be used with caution. Many of Allacci's manuscripts and his large collection of printed dramas are now in the Vatican Library. A treatise, *De melodiis Graecorum*, searched for in vain by Gerbert, appears not to have existed.

BIBLIOGRAPHY

M. Gerbert: *De cantu et musica sacra*, ii (St Blaise, 1774), 20
D. Musti: 'Allacci, Leone', *DBI*
C. Jacono: *Bibliografia di Leone Allacci (1588–1669)* (Palermo, 1962)
N. Savarese: 'Per una nuova *Drammaturgia* (vicende, problemi, bibliografia)', *Biblioteca teatrale*, iv (1972), 73
THOMAS WALKER

Al-Lādhiqī [Muḥammad ibn 'Abd al-Hamīd] (*fl* late 15th century). Arab theorist. His *Al-risāla al-fathiyya* ('The victory treatise'), dedicated to the Ottoman Sultan Bāyazīd II (1481–1512), is the last significant addition to the Systematist school of theoretical writing derived from Ṣafī al-Dīn. It treats mainly of intervallic relationships, tetrachord, pentachord and octave species, and rhythm; however, in common with several of the later Systematist treatises, it makes no significant theoretical contributions. It is important rather for its information on musical practice, for while it reproduces the definitions of the modes and rhythms given by earlier theorists, it also has extensive lists relating to contemporary usage which give some insight into the various changes and developments taking place during the 14th and 15th centuries.

WRITINGS

Al-risāla al-fatḥiyya fī al-mūsīqī [The victory treatise concerning the theory of music] (MS, *GB-Lbm* Oriental 6629; National Library, Cairo, f.j.7); ed. R. d'Erlanger: *La musique arabe*, iv (Paris, 1939), 257–498

Zayn al-alḥan fī 'ilm ta'līf al-awzān [The adorning of melodies in the composition of the measures] (MS, National Library, Cairo, f.j.350)

BIBLIOGRAPHY

H. G. Farmer: *The Sources of Arabian Music* (Bearsden, 1940, rev. 2/1965), 57

O. WRIGHT

Allaire. *See* ALAIRE.

Alla longa (It.). In the system of PROPORTIONS of the late Middle Ages and Renaissance, another name for *proportio quadrupla* (time signature 4/1), where note shapes diminished in relative value in the ratio 4 : 1. The *tactus* thus shifted from its normal place on the semibreve (*alla semibreve*) to the long.

Alla minima (It.). In the system of PROPORTIONS of the late Middle Ages and Renaissance, another name for *proportio subdupla* (time signature 1/2), where note shapes augmented in relative value in the ratio 1 : 2. The *tactus* thus shifted from its normal place on the semibreve (*alla semibreve*) to the minim.

Allan, Richard van. *See* VAN ALLAN, RICHARD.

Allard, Maurice (*b* Sui-le-Noble, Nord, 25 May 1923). French bassoonist and teacher. A precocious talent, he won a *premier prix* at the Paris Conservatoire at the age of 17. He won a first prize at the Geneva International Competition in 1949 and was appointed to the Paris Opéra the same year. In 1957 he succeeded his teacher Dhérin as professor of bassoon at the Paris Conservatoire, where he maintains the traditions of the French school of playing. He is active as a soloist and has made several notable gramophone recordings. Among the many composers who wrote concertos for him are Marcel Bitsch, Pierre Max Dubois, Jolivet, Rivier, Tisné, Tomasi and Marc Vaubourgoin. The outstanding French bassoonist of his time, he is an energetic champion of the French, as opposed to the German, instrument; in 1975 he founded Les Amis du Basson Français, an organization to defend the interests of the French-system Buffet instrument.

WILLIAM WATERHOUSE

Allargando (It.: 'broadening', 'spreading'; gerund of *allargare*, to spread). An instruction to slow down the tempo and often to develop a fuller and more majestic playing style. But this is not always intended. Verdi, for example, almost invariably accompanied *allargando* with a decrease in texture or volume: thus the very end of the prelude to *La traviata* has the successive markings *allargando*, *diminuendo* and *morendo*. The forms *slargando* and *slargandosi* also appear, with the same meaning.

See also TEMPO AND EXPRESSION MARKS.

DAVID FALLOWS

Alla semibreve (It.). A term used to describe the normal tempo of late medieval and Renaissance music where the *tactus* fell on the semibreve, as opposed to the breve (*alla breve*) or other note shape; *see* PROPORTIONS.

Allatius, Leone [Lione]. *See* ALLACCI, LEONE.

Alla turca. *See* TURCA, ALLA.

Alla zingarese. *See* ZINGARESE, ALLA.

Allde [Alday], **Edward** (*d* 1634). English music printer. He printed a few musical works between 1610 and 1615, only his initials 'E.A.' appearing on certain imprints. He printed Thomas Ravenscroft's *A Briefe Discourse* (1614) and John Amner's *Sacred Hymnes of 3, 4, 5 and 6 parts for Voyces and Vyols* (1615). His address was 'neere Christ-Church' in London. His name appears among a list of printers granted printing monopolies by James I and his successors as 'Edw. Alday, to print sett songs et al' but he apparently made little use of any such privilege.

BIBLIOGRAPHY

E. Arber: *A Transcript of the Register of the Company of Stationers of London* (London, 1875–94)

C. Humphries and W. C. Smith: *Music Publishing in the British Isles* (London, 1954, rev. 2/1970)

MIRIAM MILLER

Alldis, John (*b* London, 10 Aug 1929). English conductor and chorus master. After reading music at Cambridge (as a choral scholar at King's College under Boris Ord) he formed the John Alldis Choir, originally of 16 professional singers. It won immediate success, particularly in modern works: its first concert (London, 1962) included the first performance of Goehr's *A Little Cantata of Proverbs*, and later that year it gave the first performance of Williamson's *Symphony for Voices*. Alldis prepared the choir for its participation in Stravinsky's *Requiem Canticles* under Boulez (first European performance, Edinburgh Festival, 1967) and in Stockhausen's *Mikrophonie II* under the composer (first British performance, London, 1969). From 1968 the choir expanded in numbers as required, in order to take part in various opera recordings under Solti, Leinsdorf and others.

Alldis is equally noted for his direction of amateur choirs. In 1966 he formed the LSO Chorus, mainly from students of the GSM, where he began teaching in 1962. In 1969 he transferred to the London Philharmonic Choir, and in 1972 added to this the directorship of the Danish State Radio Chorus. He himself conducted the London Philharmonic Choir with a section of the LPO in the first performance of Bedford's *Star Clusters, Nebulae, and Places in Devon* (London, 1972).

ARTHUR JACOBS

Allegranti, (Teresa) Maddalena (*b* Venice, 1754; *d* Ireland, after 1801). Italian soprano. She made her début in 1770 in Venice (S Benedetto) and in 1771 went from Florence to Mannheim, possibly on a recommendation by Casanova to the Mannheim court poet, Mattia Verazi. Holzbauer gave her singing lessons, and employed her as second soubrette in the court opera (Court Calendar 1772–5). Her début in the Palatinate was as Angiolina in Florian Gassman's *L'amore artigiano* in May 1772, followed in June by the role of Tancia in Antonio Sacchini's *La contadina in corte*. At a repeat performance of this opera on 9 August Burney gave a glowing report of her. The libretto to Salieri's *Fiera di Venezia*, produced at Mannheim in 1772, calls her 'Virtuosa da Camera'. After 1778 she sang in Venice and Florence, in 1781 in London, making her début there on 11 December in Pasquale Anfossi's *I viaggiatori felici*. On 20 July 1783 she was engaged by Bertholdi at a salary of 1000 ducats as *prima donna buffa* at the Dresden court opera. Mozart heard her there in 1789 and placed her above Ferrarese (letter of 16 April 1789). She returned by way of Venice (1798) to London (on 13 April 1799, singing Carolina in Cimarosa's *Il matrimonio segreto*), where she retired from the stage in 1801. After a few years teaching singing she is said to have retired with her husband, a guards' officer called Harrison, to his home in Ireland. Horace Walpole ranked her success in London in 1781 above that of the dancer Gaetano Vestris, but Parke was critical of her 20 years later. Her portrait was engraved by F. Bartolozzi after Cosway.

BIBLIOGRAPHY
C. Burney: *The Present State of Music in Germany* (London, 1773, 2/1775); ed. P. Scholes as *Dr Burney's Musical Tours* (London, 1959)
A. Choron and F. Fayolle: *Dictionnaire historique des musiciens* (Paris, 1810–11)
W. T. Parke: *Musical Memoirs* (London, 1830)
F. Walter: *Geschichte des Theaters und der Musik am kurpfälzischen Hofe* (Leipzig, 1898/R1968)
E. Anderson, ed.: *The Letters of Mozart and his Family* (London, 1938, rev. 2/1966)
ROLAND WÜRTZ

Allegretto (It., diminutive of *allegro*, but current only in musical contexts). A tempo (and mood) designation, normally indicating something a little less fast, and perhaps a little more lighthearted, than ALLEGRO. But there is some evidence that in Paris around 1800 it was understood to be faster than *allegro*, most specifically in J.-B. Cartier's *L'art du violon* (Paris, 1798) and in Renaudin's *Plexichronomètre* readings (see B. Brook: *La symphonie française*, Paris, 1962, i, 318). It is found occasionally in Vivaldi and Domenico Scarlatti, but hardly at all in their precursors, even though Brossard mentioned the word in his *Dictionaire* of 1703. During the second half of the 18th century it came into special popularity, for the idea of a fastish tempo that should on no account show any sign of hurry was peculiarly appropriate to the *galant* style. Leopold Mozart (1756) said it should be performed 'prettily, frivolously and jokily' ('artig, tändelend und scherzhaft'). When included in graduated lists of tempo marks it was normally placed between *allegro* and *andantino*.

The slow movement of Beethoven's Seventh Symphony is perhaps the most famous example of *allegretto*, and a glimpse of the word's precise nature may result from the attempt to consider how that movement would have been affected if Beethoven had chosen instead to mark it *andantino*. He marked the second movement of his Quartet op.59 no.1 *allegretto vivace e sempre scherzando*, presumably in an attempt to suggest a fast tempo with the minimum of metrical accentuation and a maximum of fluidity.

For bibliography *see* TEMPO AND EXPRESSION MARKS.
DAVID FALLOWS

Allegri, Domenico (*b* Rome, *c*1585; *d* Rome, 5 Sept 1629). Italian composer. He was brought up in Rome. He was a private pupil of G. B. Nanino from April 1594 and a choirboy at S Luigi dei Francesi from October 1595; by February 1596 he was learning to compose. He left S Luigi in January 1602, after his voice had broken, but returned as an alto in December and remained until May 1603. He is next heard of at the collegiate church of S Maria at Spello, where he was *maestro di cappella* from at least June 1608 (possibly from 1606) to January 1609. He then moved back to Rome and was *maestro di cappella* at S Maria in Trastevere from September 1609 to April 1610 and at S Maria Maggiore from then to his death. He was one of the first to write independent instrumental accompaniments in vocal chamber music: his *Modi quos expositis in choris* (Rome, 1617) includes solos and duets with accompaniments for two violins (sometimes muted). A motet by him in *RISM 1634¹* is an attractive example of the Roman style. A volume of motets for two to five voices (Rome, 1638) appears to be lost. Two works attributed to him by Fétis – *Euge serve bone* and *Beatus ille servus* – are by Abbatini, and a 16-part mass mentioned in the same source may be too.

BIBLIOGRAPHY
G. Baini: *Memorie storico-critiche della vita e delle opere di Giovanni Pierluigi da Palestrina* (Rome, 1828/R1966), i, 133, 369
A. Cametti: 'La scuola dei "pueri cantus" di San Luigi dei Francesi in Roma', *RMI*, xxii (1915), 609
V. Raeli: *Da Vincenzo Ugolini ad Orazio Benevoli nella cappella della Basilica liberiana (1603–46)* (Rome, 1920)
A. Cametti: 'L'insegnamento privato della musica alla fine del cinquecento', *RMI*, xxxvii (1930), 74
L. Fausti: 'La cappella musicale della collegiata di S. Maria in Spello', *NA*, x (1933), 136
COLIN TIMMS

Allegri, Gregorio (*b* 1582; *d* Rome, 7 Feb 1652). Italian composer and singer. From 1591 to 1596 he was a boy chorister and then until 1604 a tenor at S Luigi dei Francesi, Rome. From 1600 to 1607 he studied with G. M. Nanino, who gave him a firm grounding in the traditions of Roman counterpoint. After this he was active as a singer and composer at the cathedrals at Fermo (1607–21) and Tivoli, and at least from August 1628 to the end of 1630 he was *maestro di cappella* of Santo Spirito in Sassia, Rome. His principal appointment came after this when he became a singer in the papal choir under Urban VIII. Many of his works, including the famous *Miserere*, were written for this choir and also for that of S Maria in Vallicella (the church where papal singers were customarily buried), and many of them are to be found in the manuscript collections of the two institutions.

Allegri's fame has stemmed largely from his connections with the papal choir, for his surviving printed music consists of a mere three volumes of motets and a number of pieces in anthologies; and his reputation now rests on his *Miserere*, a psalm setting which has traditionally been sung in Holy Week by the papal choir ever since it was written. In its basic form this is a simple *falsobordone* chant in five parts. But it is transformed by the interpolation of ornamented passages for a second, four-part choir of soloists whose highest part reaches a top C, rare at this period. These passages were a closely guarded secret of the papal choir for many years, and only three copies appear to have been made – for the Emperor Leopold I, the King of Portugal and Padre Martini – before 1770, when Burney discovered it; it was through him that the Novello edition, still used, first appeared. Mozart copied it out from memory when he was 14, and both Goethe and Mendelssohn were among the Romantics who enthused over it at a time when Roman polyphony was becoming the subject of attention for the earliest musicologists. Regarded dispassionately it is an interesting, if untypical, example of the practice of ornamentation in the papal choir.

As one would expect from a composer taught by an eminent follower of Palestrina, Allegri wrote his best music in the *a cappella* style without continuo, and his six- and eight-part masses were performed and recopied into the Sistine Chapel manuscripts for at least a century. The six-part *Vidi turbam magnam*, based like others on a motet of his own, is a fine example: it shows that the *stile antico*, far from being insipid, could be the vehicle for superbly controlled sonority and counterpoint, using syncopation to lead to a climax and with a bass line entirely harmonic in function. As in Palestrina's late masses, Allegri's Gloria and Credo are homophonic with contrapuntal decoration, and he occasionally resorted to the madrigalian device of chromatic alteration for harmonic variety.

Along with other Roman composers, however, Allegri responded to the new vogue for small-scale concertato church music already well established in northern Italy, and his published pieces are mostly in a more modern idiom. Clearly this was not the sort of music for the papal choir but for more parochial establishments in Rome such as Santo Spirito in Sassia, for which Allegri sometimes worked, or for a provincial centre such as Fermo, where he was living when they were published. The first book of *Concertini* has not survived, but the second is written in an unambitious post-Viadana idiom, neither melodious in the manner of the best north Italians nor ornamented. Some pieces include dance-like triple-time sections, though with contrapuntal entries. One five-part piece, *Dilectus meus*, is very like a late 16th-century madrigal in style, with delicate textural and rhythmic contrasts. The volume is dedicated to the Duke of Altaemps, who contributed a three-part motet himself.

WORKS

Concertini, 2–5vv, bc, libro I (Rome, 1618), lost
Concertini, 2–5vv, bc, libro II (Rome, 1619[12])
Motecta, 2–6vv (Rome, 1621)
Sinfonia, a 4, ed. A. Kircher, Musurgia universalis (Rome, 1650)
Il salmo Miserere mei Deus, 9vv, *I-Rvat*; ed. in Amann
Missa 'Che fa oggi il mio sole', 5vv; Missa 'Christus resurgens', 8vv; Missa 'In lectulo meo', 8vv; Missa 'Salvatorem exspectamus', 6vv; Missa 'Vidi turbam magnam', 6vv: *Rvat*
2 Lamentationes Jeremiae prophetae, c1640, c1651, *D-Bds*
Te Deum, 8vv, *A-Wn*
Laudate regem, 8vv, *I-Rvat*
Motets in 1618[3], 1619[5], 1621[3], 1623[2], 1625[1], 1626[2], 1626[4], 1639[2]

BIBLIOGRAPHY

L. Virgili: 'La cappella musicale dalla chiesa metropolitana di Fermo', *NA*, vii (1930), 1–69
J. Amann: *Allegris Miserere und die Aufführungspraxis in der Sixtina* (Regensburg, 1935)
A. Allegra: 'La cappella musicale di S Spirito in Saxia di Roma', *NA*, xvii (1940), 28, 31
                                        JEROME ROCHE

Allegri, Lorenzo (*b* c1573; *d* Florence, 15 July 1648). Italian composer and lutenist, possibly of German birth. Cesare Tinghi, the Medici court diarist, called him (in Solerti) 'Lorenzo' or 'Lorenzino todesco del liuto', which has encouraged the notion that he may have been of German origin; but no other contemporary document contains any appellation or remark suggesting this. He entered the ranks of salaried musicians at the Medici court on 15 April (not 11, as has frequently been stated) 1604 as a lutenist at a monthly salary of 12 scudi; in 1636–7 he was referred to as *maestro di liuto*. In due course he was also placed in charge of the pages who played, sang and danced in court entertainments. He continued to serve the court until his death. He seems chiefly to have written instrumental music. Only two

vocal pieces by him are known, *Tu piangi*, a madrigal for solo voice and continuo published in Antonio Brunelli's *Scherzi, arie, canzonette, e madrigali* (Venice, 1614[14]) and a short stage work for one to six voices to a text by Ferdinando Saracinelli beginning 'Spirto del ciel, scendi volando a noi'. The latter was published in his only collection of music, *Primo libro delle musiche* (Venice, 1618). This volume, which is printed in score, otherwise consists of a sinfonia and eight suites of dances for five or six unspecified instruments and continuo (extracts in *Lorenzo Allegri: Ballet Suites for String Orchestra and Basso Continuo*, ed. H. Beck, London, 1967, and in Mw, xxvi, 1964, Eng. trans., 1966). All of the dances can be identified as belonging to entertainments produced at the Medici court between 1608 and 1615, including *La notte d'Amore* (1608), *La serena* (1611, reworked as *Le ninfe di Senna*, 1613), *Alta Maria* (1614), *I Campi Elisi* (1614) and *L'Iride* (1615); each suite consists of dances from a single work. The sinfonia, which opens the book, is divided into a slow first section in duple metre and with dotted rhythms and a faster second section in triple metre and mildly imitative, a scheme that can rightly be regarded as adumbrating the French overture. The suites contain three to seven dances. Each begins with a ballo in duple metre and moderate tempo and continues with such dances as the galliard, corrente, canario, branle and gavotte. Various combinations of them, sometimes interspersed with ritornellos, produce alternations of moderate and fast tempos, balance pairs of moderate duple-metre dances with fast triple-metre pairs or, following Brunelli's principle, provide increasing movement through the course of a suite. The last suite, with its seven movements (five dances and two ritornellos), symmetrical balancing of metres, and acceleration of tempo in successive movements, marks the artistic peak of the book and of the small body of Allegri's surviving works.

BIBLIOGRAPHY

H. Bellermann: 'Lorenzo Allegri', *AMZ*, iv (1869), 220
A. Solerti: *Musica, ballo e drammatica alla corte medicea dal 1600 al 1637* (Florence, 1905/R1968 and 1969), 65, 81, 87, 106
R. Gandolfi: 'La cappella musicale della corte di Toscana (1539–1859)', *RMI*, xvi (1909), 509f
F. Ghisi: 'Ballet Entertainments in Pitti Palace, Florence, 1608–1625', *MQ*, xxxv (1949), 421
H. Beck: 'Lorenzo Allegris "Primo libro delle musiche" 1618', *AMw*, xxii (1965), 99
——: Introduction to *Lorenzo Allegri: Ballet Suites for String Orchestra and Basso Continuo* (London, 1967)
F. Hammond: 'Musicians at the Medici Court in the Mid-seventeenth Century', *AnMc*, no.14 (1974), 158f, 165
                                        EDMOND STRAINCHAMPS

Allegrissimo (It.). See ALLEGRO.

Allegri String Quartet. British string quartet. At its inception in 1953 the members were Eli Goren (first violin), James Barton (second violin), Patrick Ireland (viola) and William Pleeth (cello). James Barton was succeeded by Peter Thomas in 1963, and in 1968 the quartet was re-formed with Hugh Maguire as leader, David Roth, Patrick Ireland and Bruno Schrecker. In 1977 Peter Carter succeeded Maguire as leader, and Prunella Pacey replaced Ireland as viola player. Besides many tours abroad, including visits to Germany, Hong Kong, Ireland, Austria, Spain, north Africa and India, the quartet spends a short period each term at a British university where, under the sponsorship of the Radcliffe Trust, the members give lecture-recitals, workshop sessions and concerts. The trust has also sponsored first performances and some recordings by the quartet of British works including those by Sherlaw Johnson, Maconchy, Sebastian Forbes, Sculthorpe and LeFanu. Britten asked the Allegri Quartet to record his quartets nos.1 and 2, and notable among other recordings are the quartets by Goehr and Bridge. Each member is a soloist in his own right, and Maguire joined the quartet after leading the BBC SO for some years. In 1975 the members of the quartet were awarded MMus degrees by the University of Hull. Their tonal blend is frequently praised, and another notable feature of their performances is the players' ability to convey a sense of their own enjoyment of music-making. With a repertory covering most of the standard works – they performed all Beethoven's quartets at the 1975 Cheltenham Festival – and a wide range of contemporary works, the Allegri Quartet occupies an important position in British music.

S. M. NELSON

Allegro (It.: 'merry', 'cheerful', 'lively'). Probably the most common tempo designation in all music. It was often abbreviated, particularly in the 18th century, to *all*°. Practically all the lists of tempo marks in musical dictionaries and handbooks give *allegro* as the standard moderately fast tempo, though its very ubiquity has led to its use with a variety of different shades of meaning: as early as 1703 Brossard needed to say that it sometimes meant 'quick' and sometimes meant 'moderately fast'. It was used particularly often by those composers who were economical in their use of tempo marks, such as Corelli or Mozart; and the more flamboyant composers have tended to use it for the base of some of their more outrageous designations: *allegro cristiano*, Rossini; *allegro felice*, Walford Davies; *allegro orgoglioso*, Nielsen; *allegro irato, allegro allegro molto più che si può*, Vivaldi (the superlative form *allegro allegro* used here is mentioned by Brossard).

Its earlier musical uses were purely adjectival with absolutely no implication of tempo. Ganassi (*Fontegara*, 1535) used it to characterize a certain trill. Zarlino (1558) noted that singers should follow the sense of the words: 'quando le parole contengono materie allegre, debbono cantare allegramente & con gagliardi movimenti' ('when the words contain cheerful matter, they should sing cheerfully and with vigorous movement'). The same was the case in the early 17th century: Bernardino Bottazzi (1614) gave 'Rules how to make melancholy *canti fermi allegri*'; and in 1650 Giovanni Scipione was still talking about *tempo allegro*. This adjectival use also appears in musical scores, beginning with Andrea Gabrieli's *Fantasia allegra* (1596), continuing through M. Cazzati's tempo designation *allegro e presto* (op.8, 1648) in which *allegro* seems to define the mood and *presto* the tempo, and still common in Handel and Domenico Scarlatti, both of whom used the designation *andante allegro* (but *see* ANDANTE). In 1690 W. C. Printz still translated *allegro* literally into Latin: 'hilaris'.

But as a tempo designation in its own right it was already used by Banchieri in 'La battaglia' (*L'organo suonarino*, 1611) and was shortly afterwards to be used by Jelich, Frescobaldi and Monteverdi. By 1683 *allegro* was common enough for Purcell to use it in his *Sonnata's of III Parts* and to translate it and *vivace* in the preface to that volume as 'a very brisk or fast

movement'. Although the direction *allegro ma non presto* was relatively common there is nothing to suggest that 17th-century composers had any general conception of a difference between *allegro* and *presto*: some used one to the exclusion of the other and others used both interchangeably or even simultaneously (e.g. Marini, op.22, 1655). Curiously enough J. F. B. C. Majer's *Museum musicum* (Schwäbisch Hall, 1732) has no entry for *allegro* but lists *alegramente* and *alaigrement*.

The superlative *allegrissimo* was used as the faster tempo by Jelich (1622) and by both Alessandro and Domenico Scarlatti; although this is not included in the music dictionaries of Brossard (1703) and Rousseau (1768), it appears surprisingly enough in that of Koch (1802).

There is some evidence of a change in the meaning of *allegro* at the end of the 18th century with the increasing use of a large variety of tempo marks. Quantz (*Versuch*, 1752) had warned that 'Whatever speed an Allegro demands it ought never to depart from a controlled and reasonable movement'. And a similarly moderate tempo was also implied in Koch's *Musikalisches Lexikon* (1802):

The performance of *allegro* requires a masculine tone and a rounded, clear articulation of the notes, which in this movement should only be slurred together either when this is explicitly marked or when a prominent cantabile section makes it necessary.

But in the 1802 edition of his *Clavierschule*, D. G. Türk wrote that 'A far more moderate tempo is taken for granted for an Allegro composed 50 years or more ago than that employed for a more recent composition with the same superscription'. And it seems that the idea of an *allegro ma non troppo* was unknown to the early 18th century although it was a particular favourite in the early 19th century.

Yet such considerations can be advanced only tentatively because there were also regional preferences. C. P. E. Bach observed (*Versuch*, i, 1753) that in Berlin *adagio* was 'far slower and *allegro* far faster than elsewhere' (on which see Zaslaw, 1972, p.729); later Spohr noted in his autobiography that in 1820 he had found Parisian allegros 'unreasonably quick'.

As a noun, Allegro can be used to mean any fast movement: Quantz (1752) included a chapter 'Von der Art das Allegro zu spielen'. The term 'sonata-allegro' is used more specifically for the extended and carefully worked-out form characteristic of the first movements of symphonies and sonatas: it was in this sense that Shostakovich declared his difficulty in writing allegros and Schering wrote his article 'Zur Entwicklungsgeschichte des Orchesterallegros' (*Festschrift für Guido Adler*, 1930); *see* SONATA FORM.

For bibliography *see* TEMPO AND EXPRESSION MARKS.

DAVID FALLOWS

Allēlouïarion. In Byzantine hymnody, a modally arranged sequence of melodies set to the chant 'Allelouia', alternating with verses from the Psalms. These are chanted in the liturgy before the reading of the Gospel.

Alleluia [hallelujah] (Heb.: 'praise Yahweh', usually rendered 'praise the Lord' in English Bibles). A popular acclamatory refrain or response, as in Psalm cxiii.1 (one of the so-called Hallel psalms). Traditionally it was the song sung by men and angels, and was used by Christians at a very early date in a wide variety of ways. It featured within both Eastern and Western liturgies from the 4th century at the latest.

I. Latin rite. II. Byzantine rite.

I. Latin rite

1. General description. 2. Before 900. 3. The 10th and 11th centuries. 4. After 1100. 5 Other Western liturgies. 6. Tropes, sequences and polyphony.

1. GENERAL DESCRIPTION. The alleluia is the third chant of the Proper of the Roman Mass and is sung before the reading of the gospel. From Septuagesima Sunday until Good Friday it is replaced by the tract; on the eves of Easter and Pentecost both alleluia and tract are sung; in the period after Easter from the Saturday in Easter week (Sabbato in albis), two alleluias are sung, rather than the gradual and the alleluia as is usual, between the epistle and the gospel.

The alleluia and its repetition enclose a verse, the text of which varies according to the requirements of the liturgy; a tripartite form thus results (alleluia–verse–alleluia). The alleluia itself concludes with a long textless melisma, the so-called JUBILUS, sung on the final vowel of the alleluia. Since the precentor and choir sing in alternation, the alleluia counts as one of the responsorial chants of the Mass.

There are also alleluias without verses; these conform to the ecclesiastical modes and can be added to other chants of both Mass and Office which are in the same mode, particularly those of the Easter period. The alleluia was closely associated with Easter from the outset; antiphons based on alleluias (functioning as refrains), which are sung antiphonally between psalm verses, are found in the Easter liturgy. These alleluias may be set to special melodies or to melodies originally having other texts. This tradition of alleluia singing was known in the synagogue as well as the early church.

The alleluia chant in the Mass does not accompany any liturgical action. This fact lends it a particular importance since it was free to develop musically more than any other category of plainsong melody. Moreover, the nucleus of melodies and verses, only some of which were prescribed for particular festivals, expanded steadily during the Middle Ages; this process can be traced historically and geographically.

2. BEFORE 900. Alleluia verses survive from the 8th century and alleluia melodies from the 10th; but numerous patristic references show that the alleluia was known to all churches, both West and East, from the 4th century at the latest, and was associated with the liturgy, particularly that of the Easter period. A letter of Gregory I (d 604) provides evidence, if it can be trusted, that the alleluia was introduced from Jerusalem into the Roman liturgy in the 4th century. The word itself is a latinization of the Hebrew 'hallelujah'; the association of lessons with psalms in the part of the Roman Mass forming the framework for the alleluia was also found in Jewish religious services.

Literary evidence suggests two early influences on the alleluia, psalmody and extra-liturgical popular song. The link with the psalms is suggested by the existence of the alleluia psalms, and by the structure of the Liturgy of the Word in which the alleluia replaces a psalm between the lessons. In the synagogue, the precentor was answered after each verse of the psalm with a congregational alleluia, a practice which remains in the Roman Mass in the responsorial performance of the alleluia. Moreover, of the oldest verses associated with alleluia melodies known to us, more than half are taken from the Psalter (see Table 1); many of the oldest al-

leluia melodies derive from psalmodic melody. (An outstanding example is the alleluia with the verse *Dies sanctificatus*, both with its usual well-known melody and also with a second melody found in northern France, England, southern Germany and northern Italy. Another example is the *Alleluia, Confitemini Domino quoniam bonus* for Holy Saturday; it lacks a jubilus and has no melodic link with its verse.) Old Roman alleluia verses were sung to psalmodic formulae.

The second influence suggested is that of popular song outside the liturgy. From the 4th century to the 6th exclamations in the form of long textless melismas were sung in fields and vineyards, on ships and during military campaigns; they were called *jubilationes*, or *jubilare sine verbis*. The expression of an ecstatic emotion which could not be put into words was introduced into the alleluia of the Mass in the jubilus. The repetitive forms of many jubilus melodies reflect their popular origin. Thus the alleluia was in the first place a juxtaposition of liturgical psalmody and popular chant.

In the MS sources of the alleluia, however, it is scarcely possible to distinguish these different elements. The six oldest MSS with texts of the Roman Mass are also the oldest with alleluias in the modern sense; in them, each alleluia is already linked with one, two or three verses taken from the psalms. They do not show how the link between alleluia and verse came about, nor whether the verses were remnants of psalms originally sung in their entirety, as is the case with other Mass chants (introit, gradual, tract, offertory and communion). Indeed, there is barely any connection between the 8th-century alleluia and the earlier literary evidence which had spoken only generally of alleluia and psalms. The musical evidence of the oldest alleluia melodies (from the 10th century) is equally inconclusive: although the alleluia is supposed to have been originally unlike plainsong from a musical point of view, and the verse to have derived from plainsong, alleluia and verse are musically similar; the popular and the psalmodic traditions have become fused in them. Only the *Alleluia, Confitemini Domino quoniam bonus* (mentioned above) is an exception and perhaps shows the original musical distinction between alleluia and verse.

Alleluia, Beatus vir qui timet (ex.1) is from the oldest repertory of alleluia melodies; it appears in all six 8th-century sources for the text of the Mass, and in almost all complete MSS with mass chants after 900. It is interesting for its use of the mode on F (rare in plainsong melody) with the movement in 3rds usual in this mode. There are obvious links between alleluia and verse: the first section of the verse ('Beatus vir qui timet Dominum') opens with the alleluia intonation ('Bea-') before making a climax on e', higher than that of the alleluia melody ('-tus vir'); in the second half of this section the jubilus is taken up in a slightly extended form; the two further sections ('in mandatis ejus' and 'cupit nimis') of the tripartite verse melody remain within the ambitus (f to d') of the alleluia. It belongs to a group within the oldest repertory in which the end of the verse does not conform musically with the alleluia or even with the jubilus, but in which the sections of the melody are vaguely similar to one another. These alleluias may be older than those in which repetition is exact. One of them, however, the *Alleluia, Adorabo ad templum* offers a clue to the dating of the older alleluias: the relevant festival of the Dedication of a Church was officially instituted in 608.

Ex.1 Alleluia with verse *Beatus vir qui timet* (*F-Pn* lat.903, 22v, after Monumenta monodica medii aevi, vii, 46)

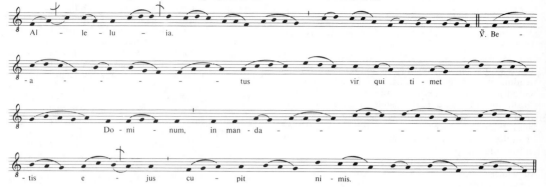

Beatus vir qui timet is one of the alleluia verses which was not prescribed for any specific liturgical occasion, but which could be used freely for a certain class of festival (in this case, the Common of a martyr). From the liturgical point of view, three different groups of alleluia verses can be distinguished even in the oldest repertory. First, there are verses assigned in all the MSS to a specific festival, usually one of the main festivals in the first half of the church year (e.g. for the first four Sundays in Advent, Christmas, Epiphany etc); second, verses assigned to a class of festival (e.g. the Common of a martyr, of a virgin, of a confessor, of several martyrs, of apostles, etc, but also for Easter, Pentecost etc); finally, verses for the series of Sundays after Pentecost. (The varying order of verses in this series is an important factor in relating MSS to one another.)

Beatus vir qui timet is the only verse text found in surviving sources with the melody as it appears in ex.1. Nonetheless, there are many verse melodies in the oldest repertory which were used for the texts of several different verses; an example is the melody originally set to the verse *Dies sanctificatus* which was used for at least eight further texts in the 8th, 9th and 10th centuries, and still more after 1000. Each of the following original verse texts was also replaced with several others: *Dominus dixit* (or *Ostende nobis*), *Justus ut palma*, *Justi epulentur*, *Laetabitur justus* (or *Concussum est mare*), *Adducentur regi* (or *Paratum cor meum*, or *Veni Domine et noli tardare*) and *Benedictus es Domine*. (This is why only about 75 verse melodies survive from the period before 1000 even though there are about 100 surviving verse texts.) An immense number of new alleluias appeared in MSS of the 10th and 11th centuries because of the possibility of substituting new texts for old.

Table 1 represents an attempt to reconstruct the oldest musical repertory of alleluias by linking the oldest verses with the 10th-century melodies associated with them. The verses are taken from the six MSS published by R.-J. Hesbert (*B-Br* 10127–44; *I-MZ* CIX; *F-Pn* lat.12050 and lat.17436; *F-Psg* 111; *CH-Zz* Rh.30); the melodies are drawn from about 120 MSS of the 10th and 11th centuries. There are, nevertheless, ambiguities: some verses are associated after 900 with more than one melody from the oldest repertory, and it is impossible to determine which melody has priority in a given case; some verses are no longer found in sources of the 10th century, and thus no melodies are known for them.

3. THE 10TH AND 11TH CENTURIES. Alleluia melodies are first found in 10th- and 11th-century MSS with neumes. From this time until the close of the Middle Ages virtually all MS sources preserved intact the original nucleus of alleluia texts and melodies. (For the most part this is also the case in the Vatican edition of the chant.) This nucleus, which may be termed Gregorian or Roman in the strict sense, survives in its purest form in MSS from England, northern France, the area around St Gall, Einsiedeln and Reichenau, and northern Italy; the graduals, missals and cantatoria of these areas before 1100 present only isolated verses and melodies which do not belong to the oldest nucleus.

On the other hand, there are many texts and melodies in MSS from southern France and central and southern Italy which cannot be found in the original repertory, and which set themselves apart as belonging to regional traditions. There are more than 400 extant 11th-century alleluia melodies; almost two-thirds of them belong to regional repertories. Most are found in MSS from southern France and southern Italy, the former Roman province of Aquitaine and the duchy of Benevento, which maintained independent liturgical and musical traditions even after the Roman liturgical and plainsong had been introduced. In alleluia melodies the traditions were continued rather in the creation of new melodies than in the preservation of original melodies. This thesis is supported by the connections between the alleluias and the ends of the verses, and by the subdivision of most melodies into sections for the sake of the overall form.

Both Aquitanian and Beneventan neumes were almost diastematic from the beginning; the regional alleluia melodies are, therefore, mostly capable of being transcribed. Ex.2 shows the *Alleluia, Offerentur regi* (a parallel to the Roman *Alleluia, Adducentur regi*), found in four 11th-century Aquitanian MSS. Most of these melodies are in the mode on D, and frequently show remarkably expansive development. The intonation is often complete in itself. In the middle of the verse there is an extensive melisma divided into sections in which the range increases to an octave; at the end of the verse the jubilus is repeated literally. The overall structure is clear: an intonation in the form of a self-contained phrase rising to a climax and then returning to its starting-point, a jubilus rising further to the 5th (*a'*), a verse in almost symmetrical form rising to the octave in the middle, and a literal repetition of the jubilus after the last word of the verse. This structure cannot be characteristic of an archaic melodic tradition.

TABLE 1

LIST OF ROMAN ALLELUIA VERSES IN THE OLDEST REPERTORY

The letters in parentheses refer to the mode of the melody, where known; where a verse text from the original repertory is found with more than one melody, this fact is recorded in parentheses. The incipits indented below entries refer to other verse texts found, from the 10th century, with the same melodies. The table is based on R.-J. Hesbert: *Antiphonale missarum sextuplex* (Brussels, 1935) and K. Schlager: *Thematischer Katalog der ältesten Alleluia-Melodien* (Munich, 1965).

Adducentur regi (E)
    Paratum cor meum
    Veni Domine et noli tardare
Adorabo ad templum (G)
    Posui adjutorium
Attendite popule meus (F)
Beatus vir qui metuit (not found after 900)
Beatus vir qui timet (F)
Benedictus es Domine Deus (G)
Caeli enarrant (found with the melodies of *Domine Deus salutis* and *Exsultate Deo*)
Cantate Domino (D; found with the melodies of *Eduxit Dominus* and *Qui timent Dominum*)
    2nd verse: *Notum fecit*
Concussum est mare (G)
    Levita Laurentius
Confitebor tibi Domine (G)
Confitebuntur caeli (found with the melodies of *Dies sanctificatus*, *Excita Domine* and *Dominus dixit*)
Confitemini Domino et invocate (D)
    2nd verse: *Cantate ei et psallite*
    3rd verse: *Laudamini in nomine*
Confitemini Domino quoniam bonus (G)
Confitemini Domino quoniam bonus (G: second melody)
Crastina die (found with the melodies of *Benedictus es Domine, Dextera Dei, Domine refugium* and *Dominus dixit*)
De profundis clamavi (G)
Deus judex justus (G)
Dextera Dei (E)
Dextera Domini (found after 900 only with a more recent melody)
Dies sanctificatus (D)

    Disposui testamentum
    Hic est discipulus
    Inveni David
    Justi in perpetuum
    Justus non conturbabitur
    Sancti tui Domine benedicent
    Tu es Petrus (2nd verse: *Beatus es Simon Petre*)
    Video caelos
    Vidimus stellam

Diligam te Domine (F)
Dinumerabo eos (G)
Domine Deus meus (D)
Domine Deus salutis (E)
Domine in virtute (F)
Domine refugium (G)
Dominus dixit (G)

    Confiteantur
    Diffusa est gratia
    Dominus in Sina
    Dominus regnavit exsultet
    Haec dies quam fecit
    Lauda anima
    Memento nostri Domine
    Mittat tibi
    Nimis honorati sunt
    Ostende nobis
    Specie tua

Dominus regnavit a ligno (not found after 900)
Dominus regnavit decorem (D)
Elegit (found after 900 with various melodies)
Eduxit Dominus (D)
Excita Domine (E)
    Ascendit Deus
    Emitte spiritum
    Lauda Jerusalem
    Laudate Deum in sanctis
    Laudate Deum omnes angeli
    Qui posuit
Exsultabunt sancti (G)
Exsultate Deo (G)
Fulgebunt justi (D)
Gaudete justi (E)
Gloria et honore (found with the melodies of *Dies sanctificatus*, *Dominus dixit* and *Redemptionem*)
In exitu Israel (D)
In omnem terram (found after 900 with various melodies)
In te Domine speravi (E)
Ipse praeibit (D)
Jubilate Deo omnis terra (E)
Judica Domine (G)
Justi epulentur (D)
Justus ut palma (D)
Laetatus sum (D)
    2nd verse: *Stantes erant*
Laudate Dominum omnes gentes (D)
Laudate Dominum quoniam (not found after 900)
Laudate nomen Domini (not found after 900)
Laudate pueri (E)
    2nd verse: *Sit nomen Domini*
Memento Domine David (F)
Mirabilis Dominus (D)
Multae tribulationes (G)
Omnes gentes (D)
Oththi theos (= *Quoniam Deus*; G)
Pascha nostrum (G)
    2nd verse: *Epulemur in azymis*
    3rd verse: *Non in fermento*
Qui confidunt in Domino (found after 900 with various melodies)
Qui sanat (E)
Qui timent (D)
Quoniam Deus (G)
Redemptionem (D)
Regnavit Dominus super omnes gentes (D)
Sit gloria (not found as first verse after 900)
Spiritus Domini replevit (E)
Surrexit altissimus [Dominus] de sepulchro (D)
Surrexit Dominus vere et apparuit (G)
Te decet hymnus (G)
    2nd verse: *Replebimur*
Te martyrum candidatus (G)
Venite adoremus (not found after 900)
Venite benedicti (G)
Venite exsultemus (G)
    2nd verse: *Praeoccupemus*
    3rd verse: *Hodie si vocem eius*
Vindica Domine (found after 900 with various melodies)

The *Alleluia, Spes nostra* (ex.3) is from southern Italy and found in an MS from the end of the 11th century. Like many of these melodies, it is in the mode on G and is limited in range to a 6th. Owing to the limited range, the melody line proceeds mainly by step, the sections of the melody resemble one another, and there are no pronounced musical caesuras corresponding to the divisions of the text. The association of the melody with the text is, indeed, only loose; the text might conceivably be distributed differently. This type of melody in the mode on G is found also in the central Italian regional repertory in MSS, for example, from Modena, Pistoia and Nonantola; the melodies have a more extended range and thus the tendency towards the strict repetition of sections is more easily discernible in them.

In the 11th century the alleluia repertory was extended in all traditions. The older nucleus, however, remained intact and the new melodies were assigned either to the Common of Saints or to the Proper for the major festivals. In the latter case because they were inserted after the standard melody, it is not clear whether the resulting group of verses were alternatives or whether they were all to be sung. From the outset the repertory was enlarged because so few melodies and verses were available for saints' days; this often resulted

Ex.2 Alleluia with verse *Offerentur regi* (*F-Pn* lat.776, 111, after Monumenta monodica medii aevi, vii, 348

in a repetition of some verses and melodies several times during the course of the year; moreover, the number of festivals was increasing, and churches and monasteries wished to elaborate the celebration of their patronal festivals.

In the 11th century verses multiplied faster than melodies because many new verses were set to older melodies. For this purpose the melodies of the older nucleus were mainly used (some survive with as many as 45 texts from the 11th century) and melodies from the regional repertories only rarely. The reverse process also occurred: some verses are found with as many as nine different melodies (e.g. *Gloria et honore, Justum deduxit Dominus, In omnem terram, Crastina die*). Consequently the situation is confused and cannot be made

to conform to the ordered and clearly defined system of Gregorian chant. The alleluia tradition in its diversity is in fact more like that of tropes and sequences than that of the other Mass and Office chants.

4. AFTER 1100. The alleluia repertory continued to be enlarged throughout the Middle Ages according to the principles established before 1100. New and old verses are found with new and old melodies; the basic nucleus of melodies was still favoured, being used for 400 of the texts added between the 12th and 15th centuries. (The verse texts of the older repertory were preserved too, but often transferred to other melodies.) The melodies frequently found with new texts are those with the following original verses: *Laetabitur justus* (or *Concussum*

Ex.3 Alleluia with verse *Spes nostra* (*I-BVa* VI. 39, 138v, after Monumenta monodica medii, aevi, vii, 462)

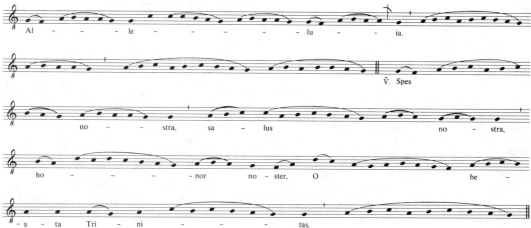

est mare), *Dies sanctificatus*, *Veni sancte spiritus*, *Justus ut palma*, *Domine in virtute tua* and *Dulce lignum*. One melody in the mode on E, known since the 10th century with the verse *Surrexit pastor bonus*, appeared with striking frequency with new texts, particularly in German MSS.

As in the 10th and 11th centuries, most new verses continued to be assigned to saints' days and newly instituted festivals. There are also new verses for the festivals of the Virgin Mary, and many for the festivals of Anne, Barbara, Catherine, Margaret, Martha and Ursula; the former reflect the increasing veneration of Mary from the 12th century, while the latter point to the composition of new offices and later new masses. Most were products of an emotional and personal piety to some extent designed to accommodate the laity. The texts, seldom biblical in origin, are generally freely composed and often begin (like prayers and invocations) with interjections ('Ave', 'Hodie', 'O', 'Salve'). Many are rhymed, paralleling rhymed Offices and hymns. Like the texts, the melodies also reflect their period. The range and melodic intervals used are quite different from those of the early modal melodies. Many of the new melodies are a jumble of heterogeneous elements. This is particularly clear in the verses where syllabic nuclei (such as tropes with rhythmic texts) have been inserted; in these cases there is an immediate juxtaposition of long melismas and syllabic sections, of plainsong and strophic melodies, and of sacred and secular musical styles.

These new melodies are found, moreover, in a new area, southern Germany and (above all) Bohemia, which was a focus of European cultural history about 1400 and about 1500. Until the 11th century, the regional alleluia repertory north of the Alps had consisted only of about 80 melodies (most of which cannot be transcribed since the neumes are not diastematic); but it then grew into a repertory as extensive and as original as the earlier regional repertories of Italy and southern France. The alleluia with the beginning of the verse *O Maria virgo pia* (ex.4), from a 15th-century Tegernsee MS is an example of a late medieval text and melody. Its melody is in the mode on E, with *c* as the prominent lowest note; its range (*c* to *e'*) includes the compasses of both the authentic and the plagal modes on E. The melodic intervals

used include the leap of an octave and several steeply falling series of 3rds. There is direct juxtaposition of melismatic and syllabic styles. The text is characterized by the rhymes, by the invocatory form and by the piling-up of descriptive attributes.

This type of alleluia was often considerably extended by troping; here it is seen in its most striking late form. Such alleluias are found above all in Bohemian song-books (cantionals) of the 14th, 15th and 16th centuries (now in *CS-Pnm* and *Pu*); some of the verses have vernacular texts; some of the melodies (e.g. those with the original verses *Ave benedicta Maria* and *O Maria rubens rosa*) are found in many sources, frequently with different texts.

Even though many late medieval alleluia melodies favoured the modes on E and F and thus tended to include 'triadic' leaps of 3rds which are alien to plainsong, most of them nevertheless retained the framework of plainsong melody. The original repertory was maintained completely unchanged in both melodies and verses; the new melodies, most often re-used for new texts, resemble the original repertory more closely than is illustrated in ex.4. They include the melodies with the original verses *O consolatrix pauperum*, *Felix es sacra virgo Maria* and *Laetamini in Domino*.

5. OTHER WESTERN LITURGIES. Alleluias were sung in all the liturgies which existed at the time when the Roman liturgy was being diffused, or earlier. No definite musical evidence survives except for the Old Roman and Milanese alleluia melodies. The laudes of the Mozarabic (Spanish) and Gallican liturgies each correspond to the Roman alleluia, but the former resembles it more closely. They were sung after the gospel in a responsorial form (alleluia–verse–alleluia) like that of the Roman alleluia. The Gallican alleluia, related in form to the triple alleluia of the Milanese Mass, occurred in the Mass of the Faithful after the chant corresponding to the Roman offertory. These laudes may survive fragmentarily in the so-called *Alleluia francigena* in *I-Bc* Q2, and perhaps also in some of the alleluia melodies in 11th-century southern French tropers and prosers. (*See also* GALLICAN RITE, MUSIC OF THE and MOZARABIC RITE, MUSIC OF THE.)

The ten alleluia melodies of the Milanese (Ambrosian)

Ex.4 Alleluia with verse *O Maria virgo pia* (*D-Mbs* Cgm 716, 106*v*)

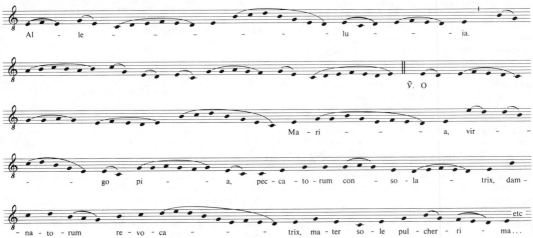

liturgy, still in use today and found in the Ambrosian *Antiphonale missarum*, are at times sung with several different texts. They have two forms of the jubilus, one before and one after the verse (*see also* AMBROSIAN RITE, MUSIC OF THE).

The Old Beneventan Mass formularies contain both Roman and non-Roman alleluia melodies; they survive in the three oldest Beneventan 11th- and 12th-century missals and graduals. The melody probably with the original verse *Pascha nostrum* is the only one in these formularies with several additional texts: it may be an Old Beneventan alleluia melody (*see* BENEVENTAN RITE, MUSIC OF THE).

In the Old Roman liturgy two groups of alleluia melodies must be distinguished. The first group was sung at Mass. It appeared also in the original Roman alleluia repertory; there are differences between the Old Roman and Roman forms of the melodies which correspond to the differences in other categories of chant. The second group was sung at Vespers in Easter week; some were sung with several verses one after another in Latin and Greek.

6. TROPES, SEQUENCES AND POLYPHONY. In Carolingian times the potential in the composition of new texts was rediscovered in the practice of troping. Since the alleluia is a responsorial chant with long melismas in both verse and jubilus, it was natural to add a syllabic text to the melismas to fit the existing verse text in grammar and sense. These new texts were usually added to the whole melody, and were often longer than the existing verse texts: in effect, the alleluia melodies were completely retexted. As early as the 9th century the text *Psalle modulamina* was added in this way to the alleluia verse (in an MS of St Emmeram at Regensburg) *Christus resurgens ex mortuis*.

From the 10th century texts might be added to part or the whole of the jubilus, before or after the verse, or to inner melismas. This became the most common way in which the alleluia was troped; one seldom finds tropes of both text and music. The melodies and verses of the original Gregorian nucleus were favoured for troping in this way. Even in southern Italy (remote from the centre of the practice of troping in the Frankish empire) where the texts of more than 70 melodies were troped in the 11th century, the standard melodies and verses outnumber those of the regional repertory. (*See also* PROSULA.)

The sequences developed from a particular form of alleluia trope. Amalar of Metz referred in Carolingian times to the more extensive jubilus after the verse as a *sequentia*. Notker of St Gall wrote about 880 that texts were added, after the west Frankish pattern, to the long melismas of the *jubilatio*, in order to make the 'very long melodies' easier to memorize. Other factors also contributed to the development of the sequence: the use of the alleluia intonation at the beginning of the sequence, and the performance of the sequence immediately after the alleluia (practices which still survive) recall the solid connections between sequence and alleluia in the 8th and 9th centuries. As early as the 10th century, however, not all sequence melodies began with the intonations of liturgical alleluias; later, sequences with various texts and melodies can be found associated with a single alleluia (*see also* SEQUENCE (i)).

Together with graduals, Matins responsories and settings of the *Benedicamus Domino*, alleluia melodies were, further, used as a basis for a high proportion of

the works in the late 12th-century Notre Dame polyphonic repertory. Only the solo sections of the responsorial chants were set in polyphony; the choral sections remained monophonic.

For fuller descriptions of the musical MSS *see* SOURCES, MS.

II. Byzantine rite

1. The Byzantine allēluïarion. 2. The Byzantine and Roman alleluias.

1. THE BYZANTINE ALLĒLUÏARION. The alleluia takes its place in the Divine Liturgy, the Mass of the Orthodox Church, just before the recitation of the gospel and immediately after the reading from the apostolos (the epistle). The alleluia in fact comprises the singing of the word 'alleluia' followed by two or three psalm verses (stichoi), the latter known collectively as the allēluïarion. The following instructions taken from the 12th–13th-century euchologion *ET/IL-S* 1020 illustrate this:

> PSALTES: Alleluia, a Psalm of David.
> DEACON: Attention
> And the alleluia is sung.
> Psaltes [sings] the allēluïarion.
> People [sing] the alleluia.

The first alleluia is presumably sung by the psaltēs (the soloist peculiar to the Byzantine liturgy), and is then repeated by the people.

Now only the word 'alleluia' is sung, but the liturgical books still contain the psalm verses belonging to the classical period. Of great musicological interest, however, is the medieval form reflected in the euchologion quoted above. In medieval MSS we find a cycle of 59 allēluïaria covering the Church year. They are divided into six modes. (Since the tritos, or F modes, do not occur, only six of the ordinary eight modes are represented.) Unlike the Roman tradition there are only six melodies in the Byzantine rite associated with the word 'alleluia', one for each mode. Thus, for example, all allēluïaria of the first authentic mode have one common alleluia melody.

By way of illustration, the alleluia of the first plagal mode is given in ex.5 as it appears in the early psaltikon *GR-P* 221 (dating from 1177), and the related melody of *Alleluia, Dominus regnavit* as it appears in the Roman gradual. The similarity between the two examples springs to some extent from a direct relationship between the two melodies, and to some extent from the common character of the mode. (See below for the relationship between Byzantine and Roman chant.) Whereas the Roman alleluia continues with the celebrated jubilus ending, the latter is not found in the Byzantine form.

Ex.5

The existence of no more than six short melodies in association with the word 'alleluia' throws the main interest on to the melodies of the allēluïarion – the verses from the Psalter of the biblical canticles which follow. For medieval Byzantine music these are to be found in the psaltikon, the book which belongs to the office of the psaltēs and presents a special genre, perhaps the oldest one, of the psaltikon style (*see* KONTAKION). These verses are divided into two to ten lines. The structure of the line is so stable that the verse (stichos) is without question the Byzantine form most strongly influenced by CENTONIZATION (as defined by Ferretti). The structure is determined by constantly recurring motifs, formulae and cadences.

As an example of a stichos, the first line of the allēluïarion for Christmas Day (Psalm xix, 'The heavens declare the glory of God') is given in ex.6 in two versions: the two main traditions, the so-called 'short' and 'long' psaltikon traditions represented respectively by *I-Rvat* gr.345 and Ashb.64. The modal characteristics stand out clearly. In theory the melodies belong to the 1st authentic mode. In practice the 'short' form may better be described as a 1st plagal melody with a fixed B♭, whereas the 'long' form after its first few notes turns out to be a transposition one degree of the scale higher as compared with its counterpart. The F♯ is particularly remarkable. Consequently the occurrence of the 1st authentic mode in the allēluïarion cycle seems to be a fiction. An analysis reveals only three or four modal groups, a fact which partly explains the weak position of the octoechic system. For the modal system of the psaltikon, *see* KONTAKION.

Ex.6

2. THE BYZANTINE AND ROMAN ALLELUIAS. From both the musicological and liturgical points of view, the Byzantine allēluïarion cycle attracts attention because its relatively late musical evidence may prove that some of the alleluias of the Roman Mass were based on Byzantine models with the so-called Old Roman tradition as an intermediate stage. The cases in point are the alleluias *Dominus regnavit* (ex.5 above), *In te Domine* and *Quoniam Deus magnus*. Ex.7 demonstrates the three stages of the development for the *Alleluia, Quoniam Deus magnus*: (1) the allēluïarion (tetartos mode); (2) the Old Roman version (from *I-Rvat*

lat.5319), in which the original Greek text is transliterated into Latin letters; (3) the equivalent from the ordinary Roman gradual.

Ex.7

This example shows that since the transition from the Byzantine to the Old Roman form and the Gregorian transformation of the Old Roman melody between the 6th and 8th centuries, the melodies have developed according to their own stylistic rules until their codification in 13th and 14th century MSS. Nevertheless, in general the similarities remain.

BIBLIOGRAPHY
LATIN RITE

R.-J. Hesbert: *Antiphonale missarum sextuplex* (Brussels, 1935)

L. Brou: 'L'alleluia dans la liturgie mozarabe', *AnM*, vi (1951), 31

E. Wellesz: 'Gregory the Great's Letter on the Alleluia', *AnnM*, ii (1954), 7

E. Jammers: *Die Anfänge der abendländischen Musik* (Strasbourg, 1955)

H. Husmann: 'Justus ut palma', *RBM*, x (1956), 112

W. Irtenkauf: 'Die Alleluia-Tropierungen der Weingartner Handschriften', *Festschrift zur 900-Jahr-Feier des Klosters Weingarten* (Weingarten, 1956), 345

H. Husmann: 'Zum Grossaufbau der Ambrosianischen Alleluia', *AnM*, xii (1957), 17

——: 'Alleluia, Sequenz und Prosa im alt-spanischen Choral', *Miscelánea en homenaje a Monseñor Higinio Anglés* (Barcelona, 1958–61), 407

E. Jammers: 'Ein spätmittelalterliches Alleluia', *Mf*, xii (1959), 307

E. Werner: *The Sacred Bridge* (London, 1959)

A. Wellnitz: *Die Alleluia-Melodien der Handschrift St. Gallen 359* (diss., U. of Bonn, 1960)

E. Gerson-Kiwi: 'Halleluia and Jubilus in Hebrew-oriental Chant', *Festschrift Heinrich Besseler* (Leipzig, 1961), 43

H. Husmann: 'Studien zur geschichtlichen Stellung der Liturgie Kopenhagens', *DAM*, ii (1962), 3

E. Jammers: *Musik in Byzanz, im päpstlichen Rom und im Frankenreich* (Heidelberg, 1962)

B. Stäblein: 'Das sogenannte aquitanische *Alleluia Dies sanctificatus* und seine Sequenz', *Hans Albrecht in memoriam* (Kassel, 1962), 22

——: 'Der Tropus *Dies sanctificatus* zum Alleluia *Dies sanctificatus*', *SMw*, xxv (1962), 22

W. Wiora: 'Jubilare sine verbis', *In memoriam Jacques Handschin* (Strasbourg, 1962), 39

B. Stäblein: 'Zwei Textierungen des Alleluia *Christus resurgens* in St. Emmeram, Regensburg', *Organicae voces: Festschrift Joseph Smits van Waesberghe* (Amsterdam, 1963), 157

H. Husmann: 'Die Oster- und Pfingstalleluia der Kopenhagener Liturgie und ihre historischen Beziehungen', *DAM*, iv (1964–5), 3

K. Schlager: *Thematischer Katalog der ältesten Alleluia-Melodien aus Handschriften des 10. und 11. Jahrhunderts*, Erlanger Arbeiten zur Musikwissenschaft, ii (Munich, 1965)

——: 'Anmerkungen zu den zweiten Alleluia-Versen', *AMw*, xxiv (1967), 199

——: 'Ein beneventanisches Alleluia und seine Prosula', *Festschrift Bruno Stäblein* (Kassel, 1967), 217

——, ed.: *Alleluia-Melodien I: bis 1100*, Monumenta monodica medii aevi, vii (Kassel, 1968)

L. Treitler: 'On the Structure of the Alleluia Melisma: a Western Tendency in Western Chant', *Studies in Music History: Essays for Oliver Strunk* (Princeton, 1968), 59

A. Burt: *The Alleluias in the Manuscript Paris, Bibliothèque Nationale, lat.903* (diss., Catholic U. of America, 1969)

M. Huglo: 'Les listes alléluiatiques dans les témoins du graduel grégorien', *Speculum musicae artis: Festgabe für Heinrich Husmann* (Munich, 1970), 219

K. Levy: 'The Italian Neophytes' Chants', *JAMS*, xxiii (1970), 181

B. Stäblein: 'Die altrömischen Vespern der Osterwoche', *Die Gesänge des altrömischen Graduale Vat.lat.5319*, Monumenta monodica medii aevi, ii (Kassel, 1970), 84

H. G. Hammer: *Die Allelujagesänge in der Choralüberlieferung der Abtei Altenberg*, Beiträge zur rheinischen Musikgeschichte, lxxvi (Cologne, 1971)

E. Jammers: *Das Alleluia in der Gregorianischen Messe*, Liturgiewissenschaftliche Quellen und Forschungen, lv (Münster, 1973)

BYZANTINE RITE

E. Wellesz: 'Gregory the Great's Letter on the Alleluia', *AnnM*, ii (1954), 7

C. Høeg, ed.: *Contacarium Ashburnhamense*, MMB, *Facsimilia*, iv (1956)

C. Thodberg: *Der byzantinische Alleluiarionzyklus: Studien im kurzen Psaltikonstil*, MMB, *Subsidia*, viii (1966)

KARLHEINZ SCHLAGER (I), CHRISTIAN THODBERG (II)

Alleluiatici. Alleluiatic antiphons; *see* MOZARABIC RITE, MUSIC OF THE, §3 (ii).

Alleluiaticum (Lat.). In the Gallican rite, a term denoting Psalms cxlviii–cl when sung in the liturgy; *see* ANTIPHON, §1, and GALLICAN RITE, MUSIC OF THE, §§8–10.

Allemande [allemand, almain, alman, almond] (Fr.: 'German [dance]'; It. *alemana, allemanda*). One of the most popular of Baroque instrumental dances and a standard movement, along with the courante, sarabande and gigue, of the suite. It originated some time in the early or mid-16th century, appearing under such titles as 'Teutschertanz' or 'Dantz' in Germany and 'bal todesco', 'bal francese' and 'tedesco' in Italy. Originally a moderate duple-metre dance in two or three strains, the allemande came to be one of the most highly stylized of all Baroque dances and by 1732 was likened to a rhetorical 'Proposition, woraus die übrigen Suiten, als die Courante, Sarabande, und Gigue, als Partes fliessen' (*WaltherML*). 30 years later Marpurg (*Clavierstücke*, 1762, ii, 21) referred to the allemande as similar to the prelude, in that it was said to be based on a succession of changing harmonies in an improvisatory style, although he noted that in the allemande dissonances were to be more carefully prepared and resolved.

1. 16th-century allemandes. 2. Allemandes for keyboard and lute. 3. Ensemble allemandes. 4. Late 18th-century 'allemandes'.

1. 16TH-CENTURY ALLEMANDES. The origins of the allemande are obscure. Possibly the dance began as a German variant of the basse danse or HOFTANZ, for the earliest known use of the title 'allemande' occurs in a short dancing manual devoted to the basse danse published in London in 1521 (*Here Followeth the Manner of Dancing Bace Dances after the Use of France and Other Places translated out of French in English by Robert Coplande*, an appendix to Alexander Barclay's *The Introductory to Write and to Pronounce French*, London, 1521, repr. 1937). One of the seven choreographies included by Coplande, without its accompanying music, is entitled *La allemande*. It is a short basse danse, filling only 20 longs instead of the usual 32. This may not be the first appearance of the dance, however. As early as the 1480s two Italian dancing treatises, Guglielmo Ebreo's *De praticha seu arte tripudii* (ed. F. Zambrini in *Scelta di curiosità letterarie*, cxxxi, 1873) and Giovanni Ambrosio's *De pratica seu arte tripudii* (*F-Pn* it.476) referred to one of the four varieties of bassadanza to be derived by imposing proportions on a single tenor, the quadernaria, as 'saltarello tedesco'. (The series is bassadanza, quadernaria, saltarello, piva, with the mensural proportions $\bigcirc$:C:3:2.) It is worth noting that the proportion bassadanza to quadernaria or 'saltarello tedesco', 6:4, is very nearly that of the normal basse danse in Coplande's treatise to the dance he called 'La allemande'.

In the middle of the 16th century, allemandes began to appear both in prints and manuscripts across Europe. French and Netherlands printers seem to have been responsible for the application of the term 'allemande', or 'alemande', to the new dance, for Phalèse (*Carminum testudine liber III*, 1546), Morlaye (*Tabulature de guiterne où sont chansons, gaillardes, pavanes, bransles, allemandes*, 1550), Adrian Le Roy (*Premier livre de tabulature de luth*, 1551), Gervaise (*Troisième livre de danceries*, 1556) and Susato (*Het derck musyck boexken ... bassedansen, ronden, allemaingien, pavanen*, 1551) used that title for pieces called simply 'Tantz' or 'ballo todescho' in contemporary German and Italian sources. Susato's inclusion of both basse danses and allemandes in the title cited above suggests that if the allemande had begun as a kind of bassadanza, by 1551 it was a distinct genre. Most of these early allemandes were grouped together at the end of dance music collections, after the basse danses, pavanes and galliardes, and many were followed by afterdances (with such titles as 'Nachtanz', 'saltarello', 'reprise', 'recoupe') using the same harmonic and melodic material for a faster triple-metre dance.

Only one French choreography with music for the allemande is extant, that given by Arbeau in *Orchésographie* (1588). It is a couple dance, with the man and woman side by side; the dancers proceed in a line of couples from one end of a hall to the other, each turning his partner around in such a way as to reverse the line and go back to the original place. Arbeau called it 'a plain dance of a certain gravity', and claimed that it must be among 'our most ancient dances, for we are descended from the Germans'. The steps are shown in ex.1 with the opening strain of an allemande for lute printed by Le Roy in 1551: step 1 represents the basic unit, repeated over four minims, consisting of three walking steps followed by a *grève*, or raising of the free foot in the air. Occasionally the four minims might be taken up by a step–*grève*–step–*grève* pattern, shown here as step 2. Arbeau mentioned a third 'part' to the allemande, to be danced 'with greater lightness and animation', with little jumps inserted between each step 'as in the courante'; apparently he referred to the third section of the dance itself rather than to a separate after-dance. Afterdances were nearly always in triple metre,

Ex.1 Adrian Le Roy: Almande from *Premier livre de tabulature de luth* (Paris, 1551)

and he specified that one is to continue in duple in this third section. Further, contemporary literary references to the allemande consistently mention 'almayne leaps' (as in Ben Jonson's *The Devil is an Ass* Act 1 scene i: 'And take his almain-leap into a custard'). The music he provided for this third livelier section of the allemande is similar melodically and identical harmonically with that provided for the first strain of the allemande.

A typical 16th-century allemande (ex.2), one of the earliest surviving (*GB-Lbm* Roy.App.75, *c*1548), shows some of the traits that may have encouraged the extensive stylization of the form in the 17th and 18th centuries. The dance is written in ¢ with no syncopation, consists of three repeated strains, each of which is in turn made of repeated motifs, and has a homophonic texture. As in many 16th- and early 17th-century allemandes, the tonality of the second strain of the dance contrasts with that of the first and third strains, and this contrast is often emphasized by the use of shorter

phrases. In ex.2, as in the 'air de allemande' printed with Arbeau's description of the dance, the third strain returns to the original 'key' with a variant of the opening motifs, creating a rounded (*ABA¹*) form. Often the middle section of an allemande stresses the area of a half-cadence (i.e. the modern dominant), although stress on the subdominant and minor supertonic, as well as on the relative major, are equally common. Such a formal scheme, shared by many of the dances called 'Teutschertanz' and 'bal todescho', seems to be one of the chief characteristics of the allemande, for it occurs even in dances of only two strains (the first phrase of the second strain would either hover around a cadence formula in the contrasting 'key' or begin with a cadence in that 'key' and move by sequence back to the original tonal area). This rather early tendency to explore contrasting tonal areas, coupled with the apparently flexible tempo limits and neutral duple metre of the 16th-century allemande, may have predisposed this form, of all the dances emerging from the late Renaissance, to develop into the prelude-like succession of harmonies described by Marpurg.

2. ALLEMANDES FOR KEYBOARD AND LUTE. The English school of virginalists in the early 17th century seem to have been almost as fond of the allemande as of the pavan–galliard, and Mohr has credited them with a significant contribution to the development of the allemande as a form independent of actual dancing. About two dozen 'almans' appear in the Fitzwilliam Virginal Book, rather fewer in other sources like *Parthenia* and the Dublin Virginal Manuscript (*c*1583), as well as in manuscript sources of works by such composers as Byrd and Orlando Gibbons. Roughly half show a rounded tonal and motivic plan like that of ex.2, described above, while half consist of successive unrelated strains, each built in two-bar units and each followed by a 'reprise' or variation displaying some aspect of keyboard virtuosity. In both kinds of allemande, harmonic movement seems to be the main organizing factor, for melodic phrases are often irregular, blurred by the free-voice arpeggiation essential to the sustaining of harmonies on the harpsichord.

Contemporary French composers for both lute and

Ex.2 *Allemana d'Amor, GB-Lbm* Roy. App. 75, f. 44r. The manuscript has key signatures of one flat in the Altus and Tenor parts.

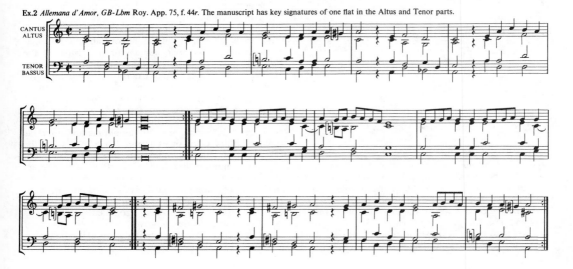

Ex.3 François de Chancy: *Allemande pour luth* from Mersenne:
Harmonie universelle, ii (1637), 88

Ex.5
(a) Froberger: Allemande

(b) J. S. Bach: Allemande from French Suite in B minor

keyboard combined the idiomatic need for arpeggiation (*style brisé*) shared by both instruments with a growing awareness of the contrapuntal possibilities of the newly intricate texture. Ex.3, the beginning of an allemande for lute by François de Chancy (printed by Mersenne in *Harmonie universelle*, 1636), shows an early application of *style brisé* to the French allemande, written in free-voice texture enlivened by motivic play among the parts. The tendency of the allemande to be a vehicle for motivic and harmonic exploration within a binary or rounded binary form continued through the works of Denis Gaultier, Pinel, Nicolas Vallet, Joseph de La Barre, N.-A. Lebègue, J.-H. d'Anglebert, Chambonnières, and Louis and François Couperin (see HAM, nos.216 and 250). Ex.4, from Chambonnières' second set of *Pièces de clavessin* (1670), shows a typical French stylization of the allemande, including a somewhat veiled use of points of imitation at the opening (see brackets in ex.4) and the use of motivic inversion in bars 6 and 7.

Ex.4 Chambonnières: Allemande from *Pièces de clavessin*, ii, 1670

French contributions to the emerging allemande style, which included a wide range of tempo markings, were absorbed by German keyboard composers of the late Baroque period; ex.5 shows the openings of allemandes by Froberger (*c*1681) and J. S. Bach, both revealing a clear interest in the exploitation of motivic play and a pseudo-polyphonic texture. Similar examples can be found in the keyboard allemandes of F. T. Richter, J. C. F. Fischer, Gottlieb Muffat, Pachelbel, J. P.

Krieger, and in the deliberately archaic allemande movement of Mozart's suite for piano K399/385*i* (1782).

3. ENSEMBLE ALLEMANDES. Allemandes for ensemble performance were slower to relinquish the relatively simple texture and clear phrase structure of the Renaissance form. Early 17th-century composers such as H. L. Hassler, Melchior Franck and Scheidt used the allemande to open their groups of dances for ensemble, while Schein continued the older practice of ending groups of dances with an allemande and its *Nachtanz* in the suites of his *Banchetto musicale* (1617). Schein's allemandes, typical of most written by his generation, were nearly all homophonic, written in two or three strains with occasional motivic and tonal links between the first and last sections. The use of imitation in the allemande was not unknown in 17th-century Germany, for a five-voice allemande by William Brade appeared in Hamburg in 1609 (*Neue auserlesene Paduanen, Galliarden*, printed in GMB, no.156), written as a strict four-voice canon over a drone. Nonetheless, German allemandes for ensemble rather than keyboard by composers such as Rosenmüller, J. C. Pezel, R. I. Mayr, Hieronymus Gradenthaler, Esias Reusner and Pachelbel (see examples printed in Mohr) were unaffected by the concern for textual and motivic interest that marked keyboard versions of the dance. Ex.6 shows the beginnings of two allemandes by Pachelbel, one from a keyboard suite and one from a trio sonata, illustrating how differently the texture of the allemande might be treated by a single composer.

English and Italian composers of ensemble music treated the allemande with more contrapuntal imagination than their German contemporaries. Most of the 'alman' movements in the fantasia-suites of William Lawes, John Jenkins and Coprario feature imitative openings in the two main sections, and several have rather long sections in which the two upper parts play in canon (see MB ix, xxi and xxvi). Corelli's use of the allemande in his trio sonatas and some of his concertos is more varied; some are as homophonic and direct as contemporary German examples, while others use the exchange of motifs among parts to suggest imitation. Genuine imitation like that of the English composers remained rare. Corelli's tempo markings for the allemande are among the most diverse encountered, ranging from *largo* and *adagio* to *allegro* and even *presto*. Neither Corelli nor such prominent Italians as Bononcini and Vivaldi, however, were much concerned with introducing the motivic imitation of keyboard allemandes into their ensemble settings.

Ex.6

(a) J. Pachelbel: Allemande from Suite in E

(b) J. Pachelbel: Allemande from Sonata for 2 violins and continuo

4. LATE 18TH-CENTURY 'ALLEMANDES'.

The allemande apparently continued to be performed as a dance throughout the 17th and 18th centuries, for a choreography first published by Raoul Feuillet in 1702, a couple dance in duple metre, appears in several other manuscript and printed sources. Although the Baroque allemande survived in art music as late as Mozart's suite K399/385*i* mentioned above, the title 'allemande' apparently came into use to refer to a new dance in triple metre. Guillaume (1768) pictured the new 'allemande' as a sentimental and tender dance, in which the partners joined hands throughout while turning around each other in various ways (see reproduction in Horst). In 1793, Mozart's German Dances K571, for piano, appeared in Paris under the title 'Allemandes'. A character in Sheridan's *The Rivals* linked the allemande with the cotillon (Act 3 scene v, ll.43–5, Acres: 'these outlandish heathen Allemandes and Cotillons are quite beyond

An 18th-century allemande: engraving, 'Le bal paré' (c1763), by A. J. Duclos after Augustin de St Aubin

me'), suggesting that some sort of CONTREDANSE was meant, perhaps the new waltz-like allemande. Pieces called allemande by the turn of the 19th century, such as Weber's *Douze allemandes* op.4 (1801), are actually examples of the newly popular GERMAN DANCE, a waltz-like form known as early as the 1730s that eventually evolved into a couple dance in the 19th century.

BIBLIOGRAPHY

T. Arbeau: *Orchésographie* (Langres, 1588; Eng. trans., 1925/R1968)
C. Negri: *Le gratie d'amore* (Milan, 1602/R1969, 2/1604 as *Nuove inventioni di balli*)
L. Pécour: *L'allemande dance nouvelle* (Paris, 1702)
Dubois: *Principes d'allemandes* (Paris, 1760)
S. Guillaume: *Almanach dansant, ou Positions et attitudes de l'allemande* (Paris, 1768)
F. M. Böhme: *Geschichte des Tänzes in Deutschland* (Leipzig, 1886)
E. Mohr: *Die Allemande* (Leipzig, 1932)
C. Sachs: *Eine Weltgeschichte des Tanzes* (Berlin, 1933; Eng. trans., 1937/R1963)
L. Horst: *Pre-classic Dance Forms* (New York, 1937/R1968)
A. Anders: *Untersuchungen über die Allemande als Volksliedtyp des 16. Jahrhunderts* (diss., U. of Frankfurt, 1940)
M. Dolmetsch: *Dances of England and France 1450–1600* (London, 1949)
K. H. Taubert: *Höfische Tänze* (Mainz, 1968)

MEREDITH ELLIS LITTLE, SUZANNE G. CUSICK

Allen, Betty (*b* Campbell, Ohio, 1930). Black American mezzo-soprano. Financial hardships resulted in several interruptions of her early studies, but in 1950 she was awarded a private scholarship to the Hartford School of Music. She studied with Sarah Peck Moore, winning a contest which resulted in a scholarship to the Berkshire Music Festival, Tanglewood, where she was chosen by Bernstein to sing the solo in his 'Jeremiah' Symphony. In 1952 she sang in the New York revival of Virgil Thomson's *Four Saints in Three Acts*, and in 1955 she undertook a European tour sponsored by the American State Department. She has earned a considerable reputation as soloist in concerts (notably in Mahler) and recitals, to which the richness and wide emotional range of her large voice are particularly suited. In the 1970s her tone acquired a contralto-like deepening (and a degree of hardening), which can be heard on her recording of *Alexander Nevsky* under Ormandy.

RICHARD BERNAS

Allen, Henry (James) 'Red', jr (*b* Algiers, Louisiana, 7 Jan 1908; *d* New York, 17 April 1967). Black American jazz trumpeter and singer. He received his first musical instruction from his father and soon played in the groups of George Lewis, King Oliver (1927), Fate Marable (1927–9) and others. He won national recognition when he joined Luis Russell's orchestra in New York (1929) and began recording both with that ensemble and on his own. He revealed a style which, like that of most trumpeters of his generation, was indebted to Louis Armstrong's, but which, in its more legato attack and easy asymmetry of phrase, already had an individual character. Between 1933 and 1937, as a member of Fletcher Henderson's orchestra and later the Mills Blue Rhythm Band, Allen set standards for 'big band' trumpet improvisation, and his solos on such Henderson recordings as *King Porter Stomp, Wrappin' it up* and *Down South Camp Meeting* became models for other players undertaking those and similar pieces. After a period as a soloist with Louis Armstrong's orchestra (1937–40) he turned to leading his own small ensembles. He had a long tenure at New York's Metropole club (1954–65), during which he also made several European tours. A series of recordings made for American RCA in the late 1950s illustrates his continued development, particularly in an original treatment of dynamics and register and an imaginative use of rips, smears and other 'vocal' devices.

Henry 'Red' Allen

BIBLIOGRAPHY

M. Williams: 'Some Words for Red Allen', *Metronome* (1961), Oct
D. Ellis: 'Henry (Red) Allen is the most Avant-garde Trumpet Player in New York City', *Down Beat* (28 Jan 1965), 13
W. Balliett: 'The Blues is a Slow Story', *Such Sweet Thunder* (New York, 1966)
M. Williams: 'Henry Red', *Jazz Masters of New Orleans* (New York, 1967)

MARTIN WILLIAMS

Allen, Henry Robinson (*b* Cork, 1809; *d* London, 27 Nov 1876). Irish baritone singer and composer. He was educated at the RAM in London and first attracted public attention by his performance, on 5 Febuary 1842, of Damon in the stage production of Handel's *Acis and Galatea* under Macready at Drury Lane. In the early part of 1846 he was engaged at Drury Lane, where he played, on 3 February, Basilius in Macfarren's *Don Quixote*. Apropos of this part, Chorley considered him, both as singer and actor, as the most complete artist on the English operatic stage.

Allen retired from public life about 1856 and devoted himself to teaching and the composition of ballads, two of which became popular: *The Maid of Athens* and *When we two parted*.

BIBLIOGRAPHY

H. F. Chorley: Review of Macfarren's *Don Quixote*, *The Athenaeum*, cmliv (1 Feb 1846), 156
J. E. Cox: *Musical Recollections of the Last Half-century* (London, 1872), ii, 138f
J. Brown and S. Stratton: *British Musical Biography* (Birmingham, 1897) [mentions 13 songs]

ALEXIS CHITTY/R

Allen, Sir Hugh (Percy) (*b* Reading, 23 Dec 1869; *d* Oxford, 20 Feb 1946). English organist, conductor and musical administrator. He made an early start to a remarkable career by becoming organist of St Saviour's, Reading, in 1880. As a student at Cambridge he plunged into practical music-making, laying the foundation of his justly earned reputation as a conductor of Bach by his performances of the cantatas in his college chapel. Subsequently he held appointments as organist of St Asaph's Cathedral (1897) and Ely Cathedral (1898), where he continued his championship of Bach, and gave performances of the Brahms Requiem. His appointment in 1901 as organist of New College, Oxford, marked the start of 17 years' untiring effort for the development of music in the university. He maintained the chapel choir at a high level, performing music ranging from Palestrina and Schütz to works by modern composers, organized an amateur orchestra, and conducted both the town and university choral societies in a succession of concerts of very high standard, culminating in a four-day Bach Festival in 1914.

In 1908 he was made a Fellow of New College, a post carrying an implied commitment to some definite musical research; but this was not to his liking, and he soon resigned the fellowship rather than give himself to scholarly work. The position of Choragus to the university, however, to which he was appointed in 1909, enabled him to revolutionize the Oxford music examinations and to produce a scheme for the practical training of music students within the university which has had far-reaching results.

Meanwhile, Allen's conducting fame spread beyond the university. In 1907 he became conductor of the London Bach Choir, and in 1913 he was invited to conduct the Bach B minor Mass and other works at the Leeds Festival. Finally, in 1918, he achieved the extraordinary distinction of succeeding, in the same year, Sir Hubert Parry as director of the RCM and Sir Walter Parratt as professor of music at Oxford. He resigned practically all his other commitments, making only rare appearances as a professional conductor – at the London Bach Choir Festival in 1920, at the Leeds Festival in 1925 (the B minor Mass) and 1922 (commemorative performances of some works by Parry, another of the composers whom he particularly championed). He retired from the directorship of the RCM in 1937 but retained the Oxford professorship until his death in 1946, as a result of being run down by a bicycle. It was not in his nature to treat either of these two key positions in British music as a sinecure. At the RCM he remodelled the training, and enlarged and reformed his staff to meet the flood of post-war students and the requirements of a new age. At the university he converted the professorship into a practical directorship, and brought to fruition the reforms he had begun as Choragus.

Allen owed his position less to his musical than to his organizing abilities, and to sheer energy and driving force. Nevertheless, the many honours which came to him in the inter-war years (he was knighted in 1920, created GCVO in 1935 and became Master of the Worshipful Company of Musicians in 1937) testify to a life of service which will give him a secure and important place in the history of British music.

BIBLIOGRAPHY

E. J. Dent: 'Sir Hugh Allen', *Music Bulletin*, v (1923), 6
T. Armstrong: 'Sir Hugh Allen', *MT*, lxxxvii (1946), 73
J. A. Westrup: 'Sir Hugh Allen (1869–1946)', *ML*, xxvii (1946), 65
C. Bailey: *Hugh Percy Allen* (Oxford, 1948)
T. Wood: 'Portrait of H.P.A.', *ML*, xxxi (1950), 290
H. C. COLLES/MALCOLM TURNER

Allen, J(oseph) Lathrop (*b* Holland, Mass., 24 Sept 1815; *d* c1905). American brass instrument maker. About 1850 he designed a very efficient rotary valve, featuring flattened windways, string linkage and enclosed stops. This valve was quite successful in the USA during the second half of the 19th century. Other makers who adopted the Allen valve included B. F. Richardson, D. C. Hall and B. F. Quinby, all of whom had at one time worked with Allen.

Allen began making brass instruments about 1838 in Sturbridge, Massachusetts, a short distance from his birthplace. He moved to Boston in 1842 where his experiments with valved instruments began. From 1846 to 1849 he is known to have worked in Norwich, Connecticut; and in 1852 he returned to Boston. During the 1850s in Boston his flat-windway valve won respect among leading musicians and his instruments received favourable comment at mechanics exhibitions.

From 1864 to 1870 Allen worked in New York City, but after that little is known about him even though he is thought to have lived for another 30 years. There are many instruments with Allen valves in American collections of 19th-century brass instruments. Several instruments signed by Allen are found in the collections of Fred Benkovic, Milwaukee, and the Henry Ford Museum, Dearborn, Michigan.

BIBLIOGRAPHY

R. E. Eliason: 'Early American Valves for Brass Instruments', *GSJ*, xxiii (1970), 86
ROBERT E. ELIASON

Allen, Paul Hastings (*b* Hyde Park, Mass., 28 Nov 1883; *d* Boston, Mass., 28 Sept 1952). American composer. After graduating from Harvard University (AB 1903), he moved to Florence and was an American diplomat in Italy during World War I. He settled in Boston in 1920. Allen was a prolific composer, particularly of operas (of which he wrote 12, mostly to Italian texts) and chamber music (including some 50 sonatas) in a late Romantic style. His *Pilgrim Symphony* of 1910 won the Paderewski Prize.

H. WILEY HITCHCOCK

Allen, Samuel (*b* Cornwall, 1848; *d* c1905). English bowmaker. He worked for W. E. Hill & Sons from about 1880 until 1891. During this time he made many bows marked with the brand of his employers, some of them with exquisitely decorative mountings. He also repaired and modernized old sticks. On leaving Hills he continued to make bows, branding them 'S. Allen'; he made at least one double bass as well. Some players complain that his violin bows are too 'whippy', but strong sticks were apparently not highly regarded by players at that time. He earned his reputation mainly through his cello bows: patterned in most respects after Tourte, they are medium to heavy in weight, of the strongest Pernambuco wood, and in every way ideal for the modern cellist. His sticks are almost always octagonal.

BIBLIOGRAPHY

W. C. Retford: *Bows and Bow Makers* (London, 1964)
CHARLES BEARE

Allen, Thomas (Boaz) (*b* Seaham Harbour, Co. Durham, 10 Sept 1944). English baritone. He studied singing and the organ at the RCM (1964–8) and, after a season in the Glyndebourne chorus, joined the Welsh National Opera, making his début as Rossini's Figaro in 1969. His other roles there included Mozart's Count, Guglielmo, Papageno, Falke, and Billy Budd. In 1971 he made his Covent Garden début as Donald in *Billy Budd*, and he joined the company the following year. At first he sang supporting roles, among them a notably convincing Paolo Albiani (*Simon Boccanegra*, 1973) and a melancholy, sympathetic Schaunard; he soon graduated to Belcore, Rossini's Figaro and Marcello, which he also sang during the Royal Opera's visit to La Scala in 1976. His Glyndebourne début was as Papageno in 1973, and he returned as Mozart's Figaro (1974), Guglielmo (1975) and Don Giovanni (1977). His concert repertory embraces lieder and oratorio, and works by Rameau, Gluck, Berlioz, Vaughan Williams, Tippett and Copland. His vocal range is wide, encompassing Orff's *Carmina burana* and Mozart's Figaro with equal ease; his voice is evenly produced and clearly projected, agile in florid passages and firm in tone. As Valentin (*Faust*, 1974) and as Musgrave's Count (*The Voice of Ariadne*), a role he created at the 1974 Aldeburgh Festival, he shows his ability to generate dramatic tension. He is also a deft comedian.

HELEN SIMPSON

Allende(-Sarón), Pedro Humberto (*b* Santiago, 29 June 1885; *d* Santiago, 17 Aug 1959). Chilean composer and ethnomusicologist. He studied at the Santiago National Conservatory (1899–1908), where he received a diploma in the violin (under Silva) and composition. The Chilean government then sent him to France and Spain for further study (1910–11). On returning to Chile he was elected to the Folklore Society. He travelled again to Europe in 1922 and was one of the founders of the International Academy of Fine Arts in Paris (1923). In 1928 he was appointed professor of composition at the National Conservatory, where he remained until his retirement in 1950, teaching many Chilean composers who later came to international prominence. On another visit to Europe, also in 1928, he served as vice-president of the music section at the First International Congress of the Popular Arts in Prague and was elected to permanent membership of the International Council for the Popular Arts. As a guest of the Spanish government he attended performances of various of his works at the Ibero-American Festival in Barcelona (1929). He was an honorary member of the Kharkov Folklore Society, the Costa Rican Academy of Fine Arts and the Chilean National Association of Composers, and he was the first Chilean composer to receive his country's National Arts Prize (1945).

Allende's work as a composer was complemented by extensive research into the indigenous and popular musics of Chile; he was responsible for issuing the first field recordings of Araucanian Indian music. His mature compositional style showed a keen assimilation and development of French impressionist techniques, applying these to Chilean peasant tunes and rhythms. He produced a number of school songs and hymns commissioned by charitable and educational institutions in Chile.

WORKS
(*selective list*)

Chamber opera for children: La Cenicienta, 1948
Orch: Sym., Bb, 1910; Escenas campesinas, suite, 1913; Conc. sinfonico, vc, orch, 1915; La voz de las calles, sym. poem, 1920; 6 tonadas, str, 1925; 6 tonadas, 2 sets of 3, 1930, 1936; Vn Conc., 1940
Choral: Paisaje chileno (C. Mondaca), chorus, orch, 1913; Oda a España (S. Lillo), Bar, chorus, orch, 1922; Se bueno (Allende), 1923
Chamber: Str Trio, 1920; Str Qt, 1930
Solo vocal: Debajo de un limón verde (M. Jara), S, A, pf, 1915; El encuentro (Mondaca), 2S, pf, 1915; Mientras baja la nieve (Mistral), 1v, pf, 1925; A las nubes (Mistral), 1v, pf, 1925; El surtidor (Mistral), 1v, pf, 1925; La despedida (I. P. Valdes), 2S, A, orch, 1933; La partida, S, orch, 1933; Luna de la media noche (M. M. Moure), S, orch, 1937; En una mañanita (T. A. Ponce), S, orch, 1945
Pf: 12 tonadas, 1918–22; Miniaturas griegas, 1918–29; 9 Studies, 1920–36

Principal publishers: Durand, Instituto de Extensión Musical, Senart

WRITINGS

Conferencias sobre la música (Santiago, 1918)
Metodología original para la enseñanza del canto escolar (Santiago, 1922)
'Chilean Folk Music', *Bulletin of the Pan American Union* (1931), Sept, 917
'La musique populaire chilienne', *Ier congrès international des arts populaires: Prague 1928*, 118

BIBLIOGRAPHY

Revista musical chilena, i/5 (1945) [Allende issue]
A. Leng: 'Pedro Humberto Allende', *Antártica* (1945), Aug, 81
C. Isamitt: 'Anotaciones alrededor de Humberto Allende y su obra', *Boletin latino-americano de música* (1946), April, 237
Composers of the Americas, ii (Washington, DC, 1956), 5

JUAN A. ORREGO-SALAS

Allende-Blin, Juan (*b* Santiago, 24 Feb 1928). Chilean composer. His father, Adolfo Allende, was a composer and critic; his mother, Rebeca Blin, a pianist and teacher. He studied in Santiago with his uncle Pedro Humberto Allende and with Free Focke, and at the National Conservatory with Amengual (composition) and Pizzi (oboe). In 1951 he entered the Detmold Musikakademie, where he studied with Bialas and Thomas, and later he was a pupil of Messiaen at Darmstadt and of Kaufmann in Hamburg. On returning to Chile he was appointed to teach analysis at the National Conservatory (1954–7); he then returned permanently to Germany, where he has worked for the radio stations in Hamburg and Frankfurt. In 1971–2 he collaborated with the builder-designer Herman Markard on an 'Orgelwiese' for the jubilee celebrations of the Essen Folkwang Museum. This outdoor instrument used water-filled acrylic cylinders to produce its aural and visual effects, and Allende-Blin wrote *Open Air and Water Music* for it.

WORKS
(*selective list*)

Ballets: Séquence, 1961, concert version as Distances, fl, vib, harp, perc, 1961; Profils, 1964
Outdoor: Open Air and Water Music, 1971–2
Chamber: Transformationen, perc, 1953; Rencontres, fl, sax, trbn, pf, harp, vn, vc, 1958; Transformationen, wind, perc, cel, pf, 1961; Profils, cl, tpt, trbn, perc, vc, 1964; Les champs magnifiques, cl, pf, db, tape, 1969; Silences interrompus, cl, pf, db, 1970
Org: Transformations, 1952; Sonorités, 1962–4; Sons brisés, 1966–7; Echelons, 1967; Arretages, 1968; Mein blaues Klavier, 1969–70
Vocal: 2 Brecht songs, 1954, 1960

JUAN A. ORREGO-SALAS

Allentando (It.: 'relaxing', 'slackening'). *See* RALLENTANDO and TEMPO AND EXPRESSION MARKS.

Allevi [Allevi Piacenza, Alevi, Allievi, Allevo, Levi, Leva], **Giuseppe** [Gioseppe, Gioseffo, Josefo, Joseffo, Iseppe] (*b* Piacenza or Cremona, 1603 or 1604; *d* Piacenza, 18 July 1670). Italian composer. The date of his death is usually incorrectly given as 1668. Although little is known of his life, it is certain that the invariable addition to his name of the word 'Piacenza' indicates his complete identification with the city where he worked and probably was born (though his inclusion in Giuseppe Bresciani's *La virtù ravivata de cremonesi insigni*, MS, 1665, see Pontiroli, suggests that he may have been born at Cremona). The first evidence of his reputation in musical circles at Piacenza dates from Carnival 1644, when his ballet *Le ninfe del Po*, to a text by Bernardo Morando, was performed in the public square of the Cittadella, which was transformed into a theatre on the occasion of the festivities marking the arrival in Piacenza of Francesco I d'Este, Duke of Modena, and his wife. On the basis of the dates and information derived from Allevi's three collections of sacred music, all previous dictionaries have stated that he was *maestro di cappella* of Piacenza Cathedral from 1654 to 1668. It is clear, however, from the records of the Congregazione del Sacro Cordone at S Francesco, Piacenza, for which he also worked, that he must have taken up this position by 21 May 1652; he remained in it until his death. At his death he also held a prebend at the cathedral. His successor at the Congregazione del Sacro Cordone was appointed in 1670, but the next recorded *maestro* of the cathedral is F. M. Bazzani, who was appointed in 1679. A good deal of the printed music in the archives of Piacenza Cathedral bears his signature and must therefore have belonged to him. His reputation as a musician, especially as a skilled contrapuntist, is attested to by Bresciani. He was a reasonably up-to-date composer, largely of small-scale concertato motets, which are technically assured and display occasional flashes of lively invention, while a certain variety is evident in the dialogue-like writing for the obbligato instruments.

WORKS

Compositioni sacre, 2–4vv, org (Venice, 1654)
Compositioni sacre, 2–4vv, vns, messa de morti da capella, a 4, agiontovi una sequenza et offertorio, 4vv, org, libro secondo (Venice, 1662³)
Terzo libro delle compositioni sacre, 2–4vv, vns, con sonate a 3 [La Tortona, La Morella, La Tonola] e le letanie della beatissima vergine, 4vv, bc (Bologna, 1668)
Magnificat, psalms, 8vv, org, *I-PCd*
Le ninfe del Po, equestrian ballet (B. Morando), Piacenza, Cittadella, 13 March 1644 (lib only)

BIBLIOGRAPHY

EitnerQ; *FétisB*; *RicordiE*; *SchmidlD*
G. Gaspari: *Catalogo della biblioteca del Liceo musicale di Bologna*, ii (Bologna, 1892/*R*1961), 337
F. Bussi: *Panorama musicale piacentino* (Piacenza, 1955), 233
——: *Alcuni maestri di cappella e organisti della cattedrale di Piacenza (sec. XVI–XIX)* (Piacenza, 1956), 7f
G. Pontiroli: 'Notizie di musicisti cremonesi dei sec. XVI e XVII da Giuseppe Bresciani', *Bollettino storico cremonese*, xxii (1961–4), 160, 169
F. Bussi: 'Piacenza', *MGG*
——: *Piacenza, Archivio del duomo: catalogo del fondo musicale* (Milan, 1967), 8, 64, 88, 123
——: *Due importanti fondi musicali piacentini: la Biblioteca-archivio capitolare del duomo e la Biblioteca del conservatorio statale di musica 'Giuseppe Nicolini'* (Piacenza, 1972), 6f, 9
L. Bianconi and T. Walker: 'Dalla *Finta pazza* alla *Veremonda*: storie di Febiarmonici', *RIM*, x (1975), 420
FRANCESCO BUSSI

Allgemeiner Richard-Wagner-Verband. *See* WAGNER SOCIETIES.

Allin, Norman (*b* Ashton-under-Lyne, 19 Nov 1884; *d* Hereford, 27 Oct 1973). English bass. He studied at the Royal Manchester College of Music (1906–10), intend-ing to become a teacher, but after marrying the mezzo-soprano Edith Clegg took up performing. He made his concert début in Manchester and his stage début in 1916 with the Beecham Opera Company at the Aldwych Theatre, London, as the Old Hebrew in *Samson et Dalila*; he later sang Dosifey when *Khovanshchina* was first given in English at Drury Lane. At Covent Garden in 1919 he appeared as Khan Konchak and Boris, and as Gurnemanz won particular praise for the beauty of his singing and the dignity of his acting. In 1922 he became a director and principal bass of the newly formed British National Opera Company, and added Mephistopheles, King Marke, Osmin and Sarastro to his notable roles. He took part in the international seasons from 1926 to 1933, sang Mozart's Bartolo at the first Glyndebourne season in 1934 and then appeared with the Carl Rosa Company from 1942 to 1949. His extensive concert repertory ranged from Purcell to Musorgsky. The leading British bass of his day, he had a voice of comparative rarity, a true, voluminous bass capable of considerable agility and vitality. He was still singing with breadth and power well into his 60s.

BIBLIOGRAPHY

J. B. Richards: 'Norman Allin', *Record Collector*, x (1955), 101 [with discography by J. B. Richards and J. Fryer]
ALAN BLYTH

Allinsonne [Allison], Richard. *See* ALISON, RICHARD.

Allitsen [Bumpus], (Mary) Frances (*b* London, 30 Dec 1848; *d* London, 30 Sept 1912). English composer. She was the daughter of the bookseller John Bumpus and sister of John and Edward Bumpus, the music distributors; 'Allitsen' was a pseudonym. She had a natural gift for melody but 'had no technical knowledge' until she studied at the Guildhall School of Music. She made a late singing début in 1882, but devoted herself largely to composition. Her songs were immensely popular, particularly those in a patriotic vein, and were presented to the public by the leading singers of the day; Hayden Coffin and Clara Butt were her special favourites. Her settings of Heine and her four songs on Chinese poems (1910) from *A Lute of Jade* are on a higher level. She also experimented with other musical forms, including song cycles (*Seven Psychological Studies*, 1906; *Moods and Tenses*, 1905) and dramatic cantatas (*Cleopatra*, 1904, for Clara Butt; *For the Queen*, 1911). *For the Queen*, a full-scale musical drama in two scenes, indicates her growing interest in theatrical presentations. In 1912 her two-act romantic opera *Bindra the Minstrel* was published, but it remained unperformed. The detailed diary of her dealings with music publishers in the last years of her life, with her melancholy personal comments (*GB-Lbm*), provides interesting and useful information about the publishing business.

DUNCAN CHISHOLM

Allorto, Riccardo (*b* Mosso S Maria, Vercelli, 31 Jan 1921). Italian musicologist. He took diplomas in the piano at the Parma Conservatory (1942) and in choral music at the Turin Conservatory (1948), and studied music history with Della Corte at Turin University, where he took an arts degree (1946). He subsequently taught music history in the conservatories of Bolzano (1950–51), Parma (1951–5) and Milan (from 1954); he has edited the journals *Almanacco musicale italiano*

(1954–5), *Ricordiana* (1955–7) and *Musica d'oggi* (1958–63) and been vice-director of *Enciclopedia della musica Ricordi* (1960–64). Music education is one of his major interests; he became director of the series Manuali di Didattica Musicale and Canti nel Mondo (Ricordi) in 1965, and editor of *Educazione musicale* in 1964, and taught music education at the Milan Conservatory (1967–8). He has also been artistic director of Angelicum records (1958–67), of the Angelicum (1959–67) and of La Scala (from 1969). Allorto's *Storia della musica* (10/1969) is one of the histories most frequently used in Italian conservatories; he followed it with other surveys, *Piccola storia della musica* (1959), *Antologia di storia della musica* (1959) and *Antologia sonora della musica italiana* (ten recordings), all responding to a great need in Italian musical education. He has edited vocal and instrumental works by Banchieri, Boccherini (including his *Stabat mater*), Carissimi and Logroscino.

WRITINGS

'Stefano Arteaga e "Le rivoluzioni del teatro musicale italiano" ', *RMI*, lii (1950), 124
'La "Musica ragionata" di Carlo Giovanni Testori', *RMI*, liii (1951), 242
Indici della 'Rassegna musicale' (Rome, 1952)
Storia della musica (Milan, 1955, 10/1969)
'Adriano Banchieri: dalla "Prudenza" alla "Saviezza giovenile" ', *CHM*, ii (1957), 9
with A. Ferrari: *Dizionario di musica* (Milan, 1958)
Le sonate per pianoforte di Muzio Clementi (Florence, 1959)
La musique sacrée à Milan à la moitié du XVIIIᵉ siècle (Paris, 1960)
'Il canto ambrosiano nelle lettere di G. B. Martini e di Charles Burney', *SMw*, xxv (1962), 1
'Fortuna della opere minori di Verdi in Italia nel l'ultimo vertennio', *Iº congresso internazionale di studi verdiani: Venezia 1966*, 242
with V. D'Agostino: *La moderna didattica dell'educazione musicale in Europa* (Milan, 1967)
'Il consumo musicale in Italia', *NRMI*, i (1967), 89, 534, 758; ii (1968), 283
'La formazione del senso ritmico', *Educazione musicale*, iv/4 (1967), 101
'Il Conservatòrio e la formazione professionale', *Rassegna musicale Curci*, xxi/1 (1968), 2
'Il prologo dell'Orfeo: note sulla formazione del recitative monteverdiano', *Congresso internazionale sul tema Claudio Monteverdi e il suo tempo: Venezia, Mantova e Cremona 1968*, 157
Guida all'esame di abilitazione di educazione musicale nella scuola media (Milan, 1969)
'Gli esami di abilitazione all'insegnamento dell'educazione musicale nella scuola media: considerazioni generali', *Educazione musicale*, vi/1 (1969), 19
'I conservatori di musica nel quadro dell'insegnamento della musica in Italia', *Educazione musicale*, vi/2 (1969), 33
'La Legge Corona ha compiuto due anni', *NRMI*, iii (1969), 708
'L'educazione musicale, i nuovi procedimenti didattici e i mezzi di comunicazione di massa', *Educazione musicale*, viii/1 (1971), 1
'Variazioni su un tema ostinato: la riforma dei conservatori di musica', *Educazione musicale*, ix/1 (1972), 1; ix/2 (1972), 37
cd.: *Nuovo dizionario Ricordi della musica e dei musicisti* (Milan, 1976)

CAROLYN M. GIANTURCO

All'ottava [all'8va] (It.: 'at the octave'). An instruction to play an octave above the written pitch if the sign is placed above the notes (sometimes specified as *ottava alta*, or *sopra*); if an octave lower is intended, this is indicated by placing the sign below the notes or by specifying with *ottava bassa* or *sotta*. The duration of the transposition is sometimes shown by a dotted line; and when the notes are again to be played as written, the word 'loco' (Lat.: 'in its place') is sometimes inserted. In orchestral scores, especially manuscripts, *all'8va* is sometimes used as a shorthand signifying that one instrument plays in octaves with another, either above or below. In figured bass, *all'ottava*, like ALL'UNISONO,

instructs that no harmony is to be used, but merely a duplication of the bass line at the octave.

EBENEZER PROUT/DAVID FALLOWS

All'unisono (It.: 'at the unison'). An instruction that any parts thus shown are to be taken as one part, either at the same pitch or (where the range of the voice or instrument implies it) at the octave (or double octave) above or below. In orchestral scores the term is used to show that two or more instruments whose parts are written on the same staff are to play in unison; in the later 19th century the words *a due*, *a tre*, etc, are more often used. In figured bass, *all'unisono* instructs that no harmony is to be used, but merely a duplication of the bass line in as many octaves as desired, whereas *tasto solo* instructs that the bass line is to be played only at the pitch notated; but this distinction is not always strictly observed.

EBENEZER PROUT/ROBERT DONINGTON

'Allūyah [Abū l-Hasan 'Alī ibn 'Abdallāh ibn Sayf] (*b* Medina; *d* between 847 and 861). Arab singer and lutenist. He was a freedman of the house of Umayya, came from a musical family and studied under Ibrāhīm al-Mawṣilī. He was highly regarded at the courts of the Caliphs Hārūn (786–809), al-Amīn (*d* 813) and al-Ma'-mūn (*d* 833). When IBRĀHĪM IBN AL-MAHDĪ and his school introduced the romantic movement 'Allūyah joined him, and as a result of this he and Isḥāq al-Mawṣilī fell into disfavour. In the *'Iqd al-farīd* ('The unique necklace') of Ibn 'Abd Rabbihi (*d* 940) 'Allūyah was censured for introducing foreign notes into Arab music and was held partly responsible for the neglect of the classical Arab art.

BIBLIOGRAPHY

al-Iṣfahānī: *Kitāb al-aghānī al-kabīr* [Great book of songs]; ed. in N. al-Hūrīnī, x (Cairo, 1868–9, 2/1905–6, rev. 1927–), 120ff
H. G. Farmer: *A History of Arabian Music* (London, 1929/*R*1973), 123

based on *MGG* (i, 354) by permission of Bärenreiter

H. G. FARMER

Allwood, Richard. *See* ALWOOD, RICHARD.

Allysonn, Richard. *See* ALISON, RICHARD.

Almain. *See* ALLEMANDE.

Al-Makkī [Abū 'Uthmān Yaḥ yā ibn Marzūq] (*b c*800). Arab editor and singer. His name indicates that he came from Mecca. He was a freedman of the house of Umayya and leader of the players of the Ḥijāz during the Umayyad period. He was known at the court of Caliph al-Mahdī (775–81) and flourished until the era of al-Ma'mūn (813–33). His fame was so great that the Caliph al-Amīn (809–13) awarded him 10,000 silver pieces for giving a lecture to his brother, Prince Ibrāhīm ibn al-Mahdī. Even the famous virtuoso IBRĀHĪM AL-MAWṢILĪ esteemed him as a singer, but his principal fame was as an editor and his *Kitāb fī l-aghānī* ('Book of songs') was the standard collection of songs until his son Aḥmad ibn Yaḥyā al-Makkī (*d* 864), also a noted writer on music, published a revised edition of some 3000 songs. As a complement to the above-mentioned work the elder al-Makkī also published a *Kitāb mujarrad fī l-aghānī* ('Book of songs alone', that is, without any biographical information about the editors, composers, singers etc). Both works were used by later collectors, including AL-IṢFAHĀNĪ.

BIBLIOGRAPHY

H. G. Farmer: *A History of Arabian Music* (London, 1929/*R*1973), 113

——: *The Sources of Arabian Music* (Bearsden, 1940, rev. 2/1965), 15, 18

based on *MGG* (i, 355) by permission of Bärenreiter

H. G. FARMER

Alman. See ALLEMANDE.

Almandoz, Norberto (*b* Astigarraga, Guipúzcoa, 1893; *d* Seville, 7 Dec 1970). Spanish composer and organist. He studied with Eduardo Mocoroa, Beltrán Pagola, Buenaventura Zapirain, Donostia, Otaño and, in Paris, Cools. In 1919 he was appointed *maestro de capilla* at Orense Cathedral and then organist at Seville Cathedral, where he became *maestro de capilla* in 1939. He taught counterpoint and fugue at the Seville Conservatory until 1934, and was made director of that institution in 1936. A remarkable performer and a brilliant improviser, he composed prolifically in a style sometimes tinged by impressionism and sometimes drawing on Basque folk music.

BIBLIOGRAPHY

Obituary, *L'orgue* (1971), no.140, p.201

GUY BOURLIGUEUX

Alma Redemptoris mater (Lat.: 'Sweet mother of the Redeemer'). One of the four Marian antiphons. It is sung at the end of Compline from the first Sunday of Advent to the Purification (2 February). It is now sung as a self-contained item, but originally it preceded and followed the chanting of a psalm or canticle. In the light of recent scholarship, the traditional ascription of the words and music to HERMANNUS CONTRACTUS no longer appears tenable. Of the two melodies in the *Liber usualis*, the more elaborate (p.2) is thought to be the older. This melody, of uncommon beauty and originality, served as the basis for numerous polyphonic compositions during the medieval and Renaissance periods. It appears as the tenor of a number of polytextual motets in the 13th-century Montpellier, Bamberg and Las Huelgas manuscripts. Leonel Power's *Missa super 'Alma Redemptoris mater'* uses the first half of the melody in each of the movements of the mass as a unifying cantus firmus. In Dufay's three-voice setting the melody is embellished in the superius; it is assigned to the alto and bass respectively in settings by Ockeghem and Obrecht. Josquin's two settings show typical contrapuntal ingenuity: in one version the melody is treated in canon between alto and tenor; in the other it is combined in double counterpoint with the *Ave regina* melody. There are also settings by Gombert, Mouton, Palestrina, Victoria, Philips, Aichinger and others.

BIBLIOGRAPHY

G. Reese: *Music in the Middle Ages* (New York, 1940)

——: *Music in the Renaissance* (New York, 1954, rev. 2/1959)

R. Steiner: 'Alma redemptoris mater', *New Catholic Encyclopedia* (New York, 1967)

Al-Mawṣilī. See ISHĀQ AL-MAWṢILĪ and IBRĀHĪM AL-MAWṢILĪ.

Almayne. See ALLEMANDE.

Almeida, Antonio (Jacques) de (*b* Neuilly-sur-Seine, 20 Jan 1928). French conductor. He studied theory and musicology with Ginastera in Argentina, then, in the USA, musicology with Hindemith and conducting with Koussevitzky and Szell. His career started in 1949 in Lisbon and soon became international. He held conducting posts with Portuguese radio in Lisbon (1957–60), the Stuttgart PO (1962–4), and the Paris Opéra (1965–7), and was invited to conduct many of the world's leading orchestras. Appointed principal guest conductor of the Houston SO in 1969, he has since returned there with the same title. His conducting has been admired for its neatness and elegance. He was appointed to the Légion d'honneur in 1976 for his work as music director to Nice.

Almeida's many recordings include Haydn's *L'infedeltà delusa* (in collaboration with H. C. Robbins Landon) and the first recording of Bizet's *Le docteur Miracle*. His work as an editor includes a little-known overture by Bizet, the complete symphonies of Boccherini, and a thematic catalogue of Offenbach's works.

CHRISTIANE SPIETH-WEISSENBACHER

Almeida, Fernando de (*b* Lisbon, *c*1600; *d* Tomar, 21 March 1660). Portuguese composer. He studied with Duarte Lobo. In 1638 he professed as a friar in the Ordem de Cristo at the monastery at Tomar, where he was *mestre de capela*. He was elected visitor of his order in 1656. King John IV had his Holy Week music copied for performance in the royal chapel, and he also owned his 12-part *Missa tertii toni*. None of this music or indeed any other music by him – which included responsories and *Miserere* settings – now survives.

BIBLIOGRAPHY

Primeira parte do index da livraria de musica do muyto alto, e poderoso Rey Dom João o IV. nosso senhor (Lisbon, 1649/*R*1967), 448 [*recte* 452]; ed. J. de Vasconcellos (Oporto, 1874–6)

D. Barbosa Machado: *Bibliotheca lusitana*, ii (Lisbon, 1747), 16

ROBERT STEVENSON

Almeida, Francisco António de (*b c*1702; *d* ?Lisbon, 1755). Portuguese composer. From about 1720 to 1726 a royal stipend enabled him to study at Rome, where his oratorio *Il pentimento di Davidde* was sung in 1722 and his *Giuditta* in 1726. For Carnival production at the royal palace of Ribeira in Lisbon he composed on his return home the operas *La pazienza di Socrate* (1733) and *La Spinalba* (1739), and the serenata *La finta pazza* (1735). He also wrote, to librettos by the local poet Antonio Tedeschi, the serenatas *Le virtù trionfanti* (1738) for performance in the palace of the patriarch of Lisbon, Tomaz Almeida, when named cardinal, and *L'Ippolito* for the Ribeira palace on Queen Maria Bárbara's birthday (4 December 1752).

His sacred music includes an eight-voice mass, an eight-voice *Veni Sancte Spiritus* with organ, and four-voice settings with organ of the *Benedictus*, a Good Friday Lamentation, the *Miserere*, a litany, St Anthony matins, and two motets. His *Beati omnes* in four voices is marked 'concertato' because ripieno voices alternate with the solos, a technique also used in his four-voice sacrament motet *O quam suavis est Domine*: both testify to his genius at catching in soaring contrapuntal lines the expressive qualities of the text. Almeida, whom Trabucco praised for his immediate mastery of the Italian language, not only completely assimilated the characteristic idioms of current Italian church music but also those of the reigning Neapolitan *opera buffa* style. His orchestra was that of Alessandro Scarlatti: paired oboes and horns with strings. For recitative accompaniments he contented himself with a figured bass. The male roles in his one complete opera are assigned not to castratos but to male voices.

WORKS

SACRED VOCAL

Il pentimento di Davidde (oratorio, A. Trabucco), Rome, S Girolamo della Carità, 2nd Sunday in Lent 1722, lost
Giuditta (oratorio), Rome, S Girolamo della Carità, Lent 1726; *D-Bds*
Mass, 8vv; Veni sancte spiritus, 8vv, org; Benedictus; Lamentación para el Viernes Santo; Miserere; litany; St Anthony matins; 2 motets: all in *P-Lf*, unless otherwise stated for 4vv, org
Beati omnes, 4vv; O quam suavis est Domine, 4vv: both in *Em*; Beatus vir, 2vv, insts; Domine ad adiuvandum me festina, 4vv, insts: both formerly in *D-Dlb*

SECULAR VOCAL
(all performed in Lisbon)

La pazienza di Socrate (opera, 3), Ribeira palace, carn. 1733; act iii, *P-La*
La finta pazza (dramma per musica), Ribeira palace, carn. 1735, lost
Le virtù trionfanti (serenta, A. Tedeschi), Cardinal Almeida's palace, 1738, lost
La Spinalba ovvero Il vecchio matto (opera, 3), Ribeira palace, carn. 1739; *P-La*, ed. in PM, ser.B, xii (1969)
L'Ippolito (serenata, Tedeschi), Ribeira palace, 4 Dec 1752

BIBLIOGRAPHY
DBP, i, 13–19; ii, 481f
F. M. Sousa Viterbo: 'Subsídios para a história da música em Portugal', *O instituto*, lxxii (1925), 478
'Zaduzbina Calouste Gulbenkian donosi operu u Rim', *Zvuk*, xc (1968), 670

ROBERT STEVENSON

Almeida, Inácio António de (*b* Guimarães, 18 Feb 1760; *d* Braga, 25 Oct 1825). Portuguese composer. In 1790 he became acting (and on 19 August 1793 titular) *mestre de capela* at Nossa Senhora de Oliveira, Guimarães, the collegiate church in which he was baptized. Vasconcellos's claim that he long served at Braga Cathedral as *mestre de capela* cannot be substantiated from any existing records at the cathedral, which instead give an uninterrupted succession of four others from 1752 to 1831. The sole work credited to him in the cathedral's 1895 music inventory is an orchestrally accompanied *Oficio de difuntos*, now lost. The decline of standards in church music during the early 19th century is illustrated by a trivial set of Christmas Matins for two sopranos, bass and piano (in *P-Ln*), signed by the 'abbade de Penedono', Almeida's ecclesiastical title. Much of his music for Holy Week (including 15 solo Lamentations and two *Miserere* settings) as well as 16 string quartets opp.5–7 survives (*E-Mp*), providing these works have been correctly attributed by the cataloguer.

BIBLIOGRAPHY
DBP
J. de Vasconcellos: *Os músicos portuguezes*, i (Oporto, 1870), 5f
J. G. Marcellán: *Catálogo de música de la Real capilla de palacio* (Madrid, 1936), 17f, 155
Á. Carneiro: *A música em Braga* (Braga, 1959), 41ff, 141

ROBERT STEVENSON

Almeida, Renato (*b* S Antônio de Jesus, Bahia, 6 Dec 1895). Brazilian musicologist and folklorist. After graduating from law school in Rio de Janeiro, he set out to be an author, journalist and critic. His first writings dealt with criticism and philosophy, but he also wrote important works on music, including the well-known *História da música brasileira* (Rio de Janeiro, 1926). The second edition (1942) contains over 150 musical examples and gives a chronological treatment to the art-music tradition as well as a detailed account of Brazilian folk and popular music. This was the standard Brazilian reference book for many years.

From 1947 Almeida turned his attention to folk music and folklore studies. For many years he was a member of the executive board of the International Folk Music Council. He is a founder-member of the Brazilian Academy of Music and chief of the information service of the Brazilian Ministry of Foreign Relations. He was also the first chairman of the Comissão Nacional de Folclore, created in 1947. His chief contribution to the field of folklore and folk music is the theoretical book *A inteligência do folclore* (Rio de Janeiro, 1957). His achievements as the executive director of the Campanha de Defesa do Folclore Brasiliero in the 1960s and as director of the *Revista brasiliera de folclore* have been outstanding.

BIBLIOGRAPHY
Estudos e ensaios folclóricos em homenagem a Renato Almeida (Rio de Janeiro, 1960)

NORMAN FRASER/GERARD BÉHAGUE

Almenraeder, Carl (*b* Ronsdorf [now Wuppertal], 3 Oct 1786; *d* Biebrich, 14 Sept 1843). German bassoonist, inventor and composer. From his early youth he had opportunities of hearing music, as his father played the piano and the flute and gave private lessons to augment the meagre income he earned as a schoolmaster. Carl Almenraeder often attended these lessons, so was a largely self-taught performer on the piano, horn and flute. At 13 he was given an old bassoon which he taught himself to play so well that he could soon undertake the first bassoon part in small orchestral concerts; from fees earned at these he bought a new instrument and eventually became a soloist.

His father's transfer to Cologne in 1808 led to Almenraeder's being busily occupied as a professional bassoonist. Bernard Klein gave him further instruction in the theory of music and persuaded him to devote his career exclusively to the bassoon. In addition to orchestral and church engagements, he was appointed in 1810 to teach the bassoon in the newly founded Cologne School. Two years later he joined the Frankfurt Theatre under Joseph Schmitt, who was then music director. The move to Frankfurt, however, reduced his teaching fees and he endeavoured to augment his income by reed-making. Poverty obliged him to change his lodging frequently, and to make bassoon reeds in an unheated attic. In 1814 he returned to Cologne to become bandmaster of the 3rd Prussian Militia, serving in France, and in 1816 he accepted a similar position with the 34th Line Regiment at Mainz. In 1817 through his friendship with Gottfried Weber, the opera director, he became bassoonist in the Mainz Theatre and resigned his military appointment.

Almenraeder's association with Gottfried Weber was of the greatest importance to his subsequent career and led him to make fundamental improvements in the bassoon. Weber, a ducal court official, was a talented musician and a learned acoustician and theorist, and Almenraeder proved an apt student of Weber's principles. In 1817 he was able to experiment in the instrument factory of B. Schotts Söhne and first published his findings in a *Traité sur le perfectionnement du basson avec deux tableaux* (Mainz, c1819–20), with French and German text, describing his improved 15-key bassoon. In 1820, after Weber's departure from Mainz, Almenraeder was obliged to return to Cologne to teach and perform, and he also established a workshop of his own to make flutes and clarinets in his leisure hours. But· this undermined his health and he gave up his workshop in 1822 on his appointment as first bassoon in the Duke of Nassau's court orchestra at Biebrich and Wiesbaden. He was thus able to continue his researches in Schott's factory and to superintend the making of bassoons according to his design and Weber's principles. His successive improvements were fully described by Weber in *Caecilia*, ii (Mainz, 1825), p.123, and ix (Mainz, 1828), p.128.

Almenraeder remained at Biebrich for the rest of his life, apart from several concert tours, particularly in Holland. In 1829 he published in *Caecilia* an article on the maintenance of bassoon-reeds. In the same year J. A. Heckel, who was 17, arrived in Mainz from Vogtland and entered Schott's factory, where he attracted the attention of Almenraeder, who took him into partnership in 1831. Thus the business of Heckel, still the chief German manufacturer of German bassoons, was founded in Biebrich. In Mainz in 1843 Almenraeder published his *Fagottschule* in German and French, for his 15-key bassoon; this tutor, which includes reed-making instructions, has gone through many editions. At his death he left in manuscript many compositions which have never been published.

WORKS

(all published between 1825 and 1841)

Bassoon Concerto, c (Mainz)
Pot-pourri, bn, orch, op.3 (Mainz)
Variations, vn, va, vc, op.4 (Mainz)
Introduction and Variations, bn, str qt, op.6 (Darmstadt)
Duettinos, 2 bn, op.8 (Mainz)

BIBLIOGRAPHY

FétisB

G. Schilling: *Encyclopädie der gesammten musikalischen Wissenschaften* (Stuttgart, 1835–42/*R*1973)
H. Mendel: *Musikalisches Conversations-Lexikon* (Berlin, 1870)
H. Heyde: 'Carl Almenräders Verdienst um das Fagott', *BMw*, xiv (1972), 225
D. Krickeberg: 'Almenräder, Carl', *MGG*

LYNDESAY G. LANGWILL

Almeri, Giovanni Paolo (*b* Senigallia, 17 Aug 1629; *d* after 1689). Italian composer. In 1654 he was *maestro di camera* to the papal nuncio to Venice, in 1689 canon and *maestro di cappella* of Senigallia Cathedral. He published two volumes of motets for small groups. The first (Venice, 1654) consists of 17 pieces for solo voice and continuo distinguished by expansive melodies. The second, *Motetti sagri* op.2 (Bologna, 1689), consists of pieces for two and three voices and continuo.

BIBLIOGRAPHY

G. Radiciotti: *Teatro, musica e musicisti in Sinigaglia* (Tivoli, 1893), 143f

NIGEL FORTUNE

Almérie. A kind of lute, perhaps one activated by a wheel, invented by the French polymath JEAN LE MAIRE (*c*1581–*c*1650). The word 'almérie' is an anagram of the inventor's name.

Almond. *See* ALLEMANDE.

Almorox, Juan (*fl* 1485–1504). Spanish composer. He was a singer in Ferdinand V's chapel from 1485 until at least 1498, and composed a patriotic song celebrating the Spanish victory over the French at Gaeta in 1504. The Cancionero Musical de Palacio contains three pieces by him: *Gaeta nos es subjecta*, *O dichoso i desdichsdo* and *Porque os vi* (ed. H. Anglès, *La música en la corte de los reyes católicos: Cancionero musical de palacio*, MME, v, x (1947–51), nos.423, 200, 211). In all of them triple metre alternates with duple, and passages for one, two or three voices interrupt the four-voice texture. *Gaeta nos es subjecta* is set in a chordal, hymnlike style. A mass for three voices is in *E-Tz* 3.

BIBLIOGRAPHY

F. Asenjo Barbieri, ed.: *Cancionero musical de los siglos XV y XVI* (Madrid, 1890)
R. Stevenson: *Spanish Music in the Age of Columbus* (The Hague, 1960), 164

ISABEL POPE

Almqvist, Carl Jonas Love (*b* Stockholm, 28 Nov 1793; *d* Bremen, 26 Nov 1866). Swedish author, journalist and composer. After his mother's early death he was educated mainly by his grandfather, the prominent magazine publisher C. C. Gjörwell. In 1815 he graduated from the University of Uppsala and subsequently became a government official and fellow-clerk of the neo-Romantic poet E. J. Stagnelius. At this time Almqvist was greatly influenced by the German poets (Goethe, Tieck, Hoffmann and Schlegel), by Swedenborg and by the Gothic movement: his enthusiasm for old Nordic culture – the so-called 'Alliance of Mannheim' included Almqvist as a member in 1816 – was exceptional for the period. But eventually he abandoned neo-Romanticism, which he found too allegorical, and worked towards a poetry of reality in a wider sense. In 1823–6 he attempted to put Rousseau's philosophy into practice as a subsistence farmer, but he returned to Stockholm and became headmaster of the Nya Elementar-skolan in 1829.

While still a student, Almqvist wrote poetry and philosophy. In 1822 he was forced to destroy the whole edition of *Amorina*, a 'poetical fugue' (a compound of lyrics and drama), because it attacked the doctrine of free will. As a teacher Almqvist wrote books on educational subjects but also novels in *Törnrosens Bok* ('The Book of the Thorn-rose'), which was published in two formats, a duodecimo edition (1832–42) and an imperial edition (1839–49). Gradually his publications became more radical; he pleaded for universal suffrage, humane prison discipline, the emancipation of women and finally, in the short story *Det går an* (1840, Eng. trans. as *Sara Videbeck and the Chapel*, New York, 1919), he recommended free union based on love, without marriage.

Almqvist had taken holy orders in 1837 and was warned by the Chapter for moral crime and finally forced to resign his orders in 1841; he then supported himself as a journalist on the liberal newspaper *Aftonbladet*. In 1851 he was accused of murder by poison and was forced to flee the country. Recently attempts have been made by Jägerskiöld to vindicate him. After living in the USA under pseudonyms, including 'Gustavi', he left for Bremen in 1865, where he died while working on an ambitious study of Swedish metrics.

Almqvist was a master of various literary styles and was well versed in a wide variety of subjects, including music. In his *Monografi* (1844–5), principally a reply in the moral controversy, he developed his view on musical matters (*Om poesi i sak till åtskillnad ifrån poesi i ord*). He described how the beauty of 'Melody' had to give way to the counterpoint of Bach and was defeated by 'Harmony':

Accordingly one realizes that as soon as *the difficult* gains a firm footing and still more when it gets the better of the artist's own discernment as well as that of the public, then the impossible (the easy), that which is the truly *beautiful*, retreats more and more into the background; *Art* itself, in its largest sense, retreats, and *eccentric art* advances.

As a composer Almqvist was admittedly self-taught; he struggled against the enthusiasm for virtuosos and 'the empire of instrumental music' and upheld the right of genius to shape its own rules. The collection of 26 piano pieces *Fria Fantasier* ('Free fantasies', 1847–9), (the publication of which was interrupted by Almqvist's exile) was criticized, perhaps justly, for being too plain. Some of these pieces, however, are unique for their period, being naive in a folklike manner, as are his masterpieces, the unaccompanied songs to his own texts, *Songes* ('Dreams'), which were composed c1830 and intended to be used in *tableaux vivants*. They bear witness to his profoundly original musical gifts. Recent supplementary additions of piano parts by Wilhelm Bauck, Knut Håkanson, Lille Bror Söderlund and others must be regarded as contrary to Almqvist's aesthetic.

WORKS

Editions: *C. Almqvist: Törnrosens bok*, duodecimo edn (Stockholm, 1832–42) [T-d]
    C. Almqvist: Törnrosens bok, imperial edn (Stockholm, 1839–49) [T-i]

(all printed works published in Stockholm)

VOCAL

3, 4vv: Namnsdags-Quäde in *Samlaren*, 1924; Songes nos. 10, 15–16, 19, 22, 23, T-i, i (1839); Songes, nos.4–8, 10–13, 19, 21, 22, 28, 29, 35, 37, 40, 42, 45, 47, T-i, ii (1849); Songes, nos.15, 20, *S-Sm*
2vv: 1 song in T-i, i (1839); Songes, nos.2, 3, 9, 17, 23, 49, T-i, ii (1849)
1v: Tintomaras sång, T-d, iv (1834); 1 song in T-i, i; Songes, nos.1, 14–16, 20, 24–7, 30, 32, 34, 36, 38, 41, 43, 44, 46, 48, T-i, ii (1849)
1v, pf: Songes, nos.18, 31, 50, T-i, ii (1849)

INSTRUMENTAL

Andante grazioso, E♭, str qt, *S-Sm*; Håtuna Saga, kantele, T-i, ii (1849); Niakuns polska, harp, T-i, ii (1849); Sigtuna Saga, harp, T-i, ii (1849)
Pf solo: [26] Fria Fantasier (1847–9) [excerpts in T-i, i (1839)]; Songes, nos.39, 50, T-i, ii (1849); Baldvins Riddare, in *Teater och Musik*, i (1876); other works, *S-Skma*

WRITINGS
(selective list)

Monografi (Jönköping, 1844–5) [incl. *Om poesi i sak till åtskillnad ifrån poesi i ord; R1959]*
Bref till Adolf Fredrik Lindblad från Mendelssohn, Dohrn, Almqvist och andra (Stockholm, 1913)
Collected Works (Stockholm, 1920–38) [prose with some music]

BIBLIOGRAPHY

'C. J. L. Almqvist såsom musiker', *Teater och Musik*, ed. W. Bauck (Stockholm, 1876)
S. Marström, ed.: *Minnen från Törnrostiden*, i–iv (Skara, 1916–33)
A. Nyman: *Musikalisk intelligens* (Lund, 1928)
H. Olsson: *C. J. L. Almqvist till 1836* (Stockholm and Uppsala, 1937)
M. Pergament: *Svenska tonsättare* (Stockholm and Uppsala, 1943)
A. Bergstrand: *Songes, litteraturhistoriska studier i C. J. L. Almqvists diktsamling* (Uppsala, 1953)
L. Hedwall: 'C. J. L. Almqvist och hans Fantasier för piano', *Musikkultur*, xxx (1966), no.5, p.4; no.6, p.8
R. Berg: *C. J. L. Almqvist som journalist* (Uppsala, 1968)
B. Romberg, ed.: *Brev 1803–1866 i urval* (Stockholm, 1968)
S. Jägerskiöld: *Från Jaktslottet till landsflykten* (Helsinki, 1970)

CARL-GUNNAR ÅHLÉN

Al-Munajjim [Yaḥyā ibn 'Alī ibn Yaḥyā ibn Abī Manṣūr] (*b* Baghdad, 856; *d* Baghdad, 912). Arab courtier, poet and writer on music. He was a member of an intellectually distinguished family closely associated with the 'Abbāsid court. His father, 'Alī ibn Yaḥyā al-Munajjām (*d* 888), had been a pupil of Isḥaq al-Mawṣilī, the most celebrated musician of his day, and had written a book about him. The one extant musical treatise by al-Munajjim is of considerable interest; unlike other theoretical works of the 9th and early 10th centuries, it does not attempt to expound Greek ideas but outlines certain basic features of the modal system in terms of the indigenous theory as elaborated by Isḥaq al-Mawṣilī. Despite its brevity and incompleteness, it is a vital source for any study of the modal structure of Arab art music from the 7th to 9th centuries.

WRITINGS

Risāla fī l-mūsīqī [Book about music] (MS, *GB-Lbm* Oriental 2361); ed. M. Bahjah: 'Risāla fī l-mūsīqī', *Majallat al-Majma' al-'ilmī al-irāqī*, i/1 (1955), 113; ed. Z. Yūsuf (Cairo, 1964)

BIBLIOGRAPHY

'Yaḥyā ibn 'Alī', *The Encyclopaedia of Islam* (Leiden and London, 1913–38, rev. 2/1960–)
H. G. Farmer: *A History of Arabian Music* (London, 1929/R1973), 167f
——: *The Sources of Arabian Music* (Bearsden, 1940, rev. 2/1965), 32
C. Sachs: *The Rise of Music in the Ancient World: East and West* (New York, 1943), 280
H. G. Farmer: 'The Song Captions in the Kitāb al-aghānī al-kabīr', *Transactions of the Glasgow University Oriental Society*, xv (1955), 1

O. WRIGHT

Alnaes, Eyvind (*b* Fredrikstad, 29 April 1872; *d* Oslo, 24 Dec 1932). Norwegian composer, conductor and organist. He studied with Peter Lindeman (organ) and Holter (harmony, counterpoint and composition) at the Christiania Music and Organ School (1888–92), and was then a pupil of Reinecke (composition) and Ruthard (piano) at the Leipzig Conservatory (1892–4). Appointments as organist followed in Drammen (1895–1907) and Oslo (1907–32), where he served at the cathedral from 1916. He was one of those responsible for the foundation of the Norsk Komponistforening, of which he was president from 1921 to 1923. As a member of the Koralbokkomiteen (1922–6) he harmonized most of the melodies in the chorale book of the Norwegian Church, and he edited preludes to all of the chorales. He was also president of TONO, the International Music Bureau of the Norwegian Composers' Union (1931), and active as a teacher. Among the awards he received were the King's Gold Medal and the Order of St Olav (1932). Particularly outstanding as a composer of solo and choral songs, he began composing in a distinctly late-Romantic style with complex harmonic ornamentation; some of the later works, however, show a tendency towards an impressionist handling of chords and freer experiment with dissonance. There is little trace in his work of the influence of folk music.

WORKS
(selective list)

Orch: 2 syms., c, 1898, D, 1923; Symfoniske variasjoner, 1909; Pf Conc., 1914
Inst: 2 suites, vn, pf; Suite, 2 vn, pf; Symfonisk marsj, 2 pf; many pf pieces; Norsk pianoskole, 1931
Vocal: many choral pieces, choral folksong arrs., c100 songs
Edn.: *Norges melodier*, ii–iv (Oslo, 1922)

Principal publisher: Norsk Musikforlag

BIBLIOGRAPHY

P. R. Johnsen: '50 aar', *Musikbladet* (1922), 61
J. Arbo: 'Eyvind Alnaes 60 år', *Mandssangen* (1932), 41
Tom: 'Eyvind Alnaes 60 år', *Tonekunst* (1932), 69
J. Arbo: 'Eyvind Alnaes', *Mandssangen* (1933), 1
K. Wilhelmsen: 'Eyvind Alnaes 1872–1932', *Norsk musiktidsskrift* (1972), no.1, p.5; no.2, p.49

PETER ANDREAS KJELDSBERG

Alnar, Hasan Ferit (*b* Istanbul, 11 March 1906). Turkish composer and conductor. He had his first music lessons from his mother. He showed a precocious talent for playing the *qānūn* and at 16 he composed a musical play in traditional Turkish monophonic style. In 1927 he went to Vienna and studied composition with Joseph Marx at the Academy of Music and conducting with Oswald Kabasta. He returned to Turkey in 1932, was appointed conductor to the Istanbul City Theatre Orchestra and taught history of music at the Istanbul Conservatory. In 1936 he became assistant conductor of the Ankara Presidential PO, taught piano at the State Conservatory and was an assistant to Carl Abert at the Ankara State Opera. In 1946 he was appointed conductor of the Presidential PO and held the post until 1952, when he left because of a nervous breakdown, though he continued to teach at the conservatory and to appear as guest conductor in Ankara and with the Vienna SO and the Stuttgart RO. One of the Turkish Five, Alnar showed strong attraction in his works to the rhythmic and melodic patterns of Turkish monophonic music.

WORKS
(selective list)

Romantic Ov., 1932; Préludes et 2 danses, orch, 1935; Vc Conc., 1943; Qánún Conc., 1944; 2 Singspiels; film music

Principal publishers: Ankara State Conservatory, Universal (Vienna)

FARUK YENER

Aloisi, Giovanni Battista (*b* Bologna; *fl* 1628–44). Italian composer. He became a Franciscan friar and a doctor of theology; he was also *maestro di cappella* at the Cathedral of Sacile, near Udine, and later, in 1628, at the Franciscan friary in Bologna. He travelled north in the 1630s, for the dedication of the *Contextus musicarum* (1637) was written in Vienna. His output, entirely of church music, is mostly up to date in style and competently written. The masses of 1628 do, however, contain works in the *stile antico* as well, mellifluous and harmonically unadventurous compared to the music in the then modern manner, which is based more on contrasts. The *Coelestis Parnassus*, published in the same year, includes two motets with violins, which are used in delicate interplay with tenor voices. Aloisi's expressive technique includes chromaticism, used with telling effect in the third setting of *Alma Redemptoris mater* in the *Corona stellarum* and in the motet *Quid mihi est in caelo* from the *Contextus musicarum*. The six-part pieces of the latter collection recall a grander style, using imitative building up of the texture, dramatic pauses and daring counterpoints.

WORKS
(all published in Venice)

Coelestis Parnassus, 2–4vv, bc (1628)
Celeste Palco . . . solo, op.2 (1628)
Harmonicum coelum . . . missae harmonicis, 4vv, bc (org), op.3 (1628)
Contextus musicarum, 2–6vv, bc (org), op.4 (1637)
Corona stellarum 12 antiphonis de Beatae Virginis, 2–4vv, bc (org), op.5 (1637)
Vellus aurem Sacrae Deiparae Virginis litaniis, 4–8vv, bc, op.6 (1640)
3 motets, 1641³, 1643⁷, 1646⁴
Psalm, 1646³

BIBLIOGRAPHY
J. L. A. Roche: *North Italian Liturgical Music in the Early 17th Century* (diss., U. of Cambridge, 1968)
J. Sehnal: 'Hudba na dvoře olomouckých biskupů od 13. do poloviny 17. stol' [Music at the courts of the bishops of Olomouc from the end of the 13th century to the mid-17th], *Časopis vlastivědné společnosti muzejní v Olomouci* (1970), 73

JEROME ROCHE

Alomía Robles, Daniel (*b* Huánuco, 3 Jan 1871; *d* Lima, 17 July 1942). Peruvian ethnomusicologist and composer. When he was 13 he was sent by his mother to Lima, and there in 1887 he began studies of solfège with Cruz Panizo and the piano with Rebagliatti. He studied medicine at the Lima Facultad de S Fernando (1892–4), but in 1896, while on a lengthy visit to the hinterland Campas tribe, he was stimulated by a Franciscan to devote himself to the study of aboriginal music. The Cuban pianist Sebastiana Godoy, whom he married in

1897, helped him to harmonize and arrange the Andean tribal music collected during the numerous journeys throughout Ecuador, Peru and Bolivia that occupied him intermittently until 1917. A lecture-demonstration at S Marcos University, Lima (21 February 1910), brought his Inca researches to national notice; after the issue of 13 discs of his orchestrally accompanied arrangements, he became the best-known Peruvian musician of his time. He spent periods in Havana (1917–22) and the USA (1922–33), and from 1939 to 1941 he directed the fine arts section of the Peruvian Ministry of Education. His oeuvre falls into three categories: 696 notated Andean melodies, 319 harmonizations and 238 original compositions. The last, often of a regional character, include piano pieces, works for vocal and instrumental combinations, three zarzuelas, an opera and an unfinished operetta.

BIBLIOGRAPHY
R. Holzmann: 'Catálogo de las obras de Daniel Alomía Robles', *Boletín de la Biblioteca de la Universidad mayor de San Marcos*, xiii (1943), 25–78
C. Raygada: 'Guía musical del Perú', *Fénix* (1956–7), no.12, p.24

ROBERT STEVENSON

Alonso (*fl* 1500). Spanish composer who may be identifiable with ALONSO DE PLAJA.

Alotin, Yardena (*b* Tel Aviv, 19 Oct 1930). Israeli composer. She studied at the Tel Aviv Music Teachers' College (1948–50) and at the Israel Academy of Music (1950–52), her principal composition teacher being Partos and her piano teacher Vincze-Kraus. Her music is an attempt to recapture the spirit of biblical times in terms of novel compositional technique. A large part of her work consists of youth or educational music, much of it widely performed.

WORKS
(selective list)

Yefei nof, chorus, 1952; Songs of the Stream, S, pf, 1954: Cantata, chorus, 1956; Fugue, str trio, 1957; Al golah dvuyah [A painful exile], Mez, orch, 1958; Str Qt, 1961; Hinei ma tov, chorus, 1967; Sonatina, vn, pf, 1970; songs, chamber music, pf pieces

Principal publishers: Israel Music Institute, Merkaz L'Tarbut

ZVI KEREN

Aloysis. *See* PIÉTON, LOYSET.

Aloyson, Richard. *See* ALISON, RICHARD.

Alpaerts, Flor (*b* Antwerp, 12 Sept 1876; *d* Antwerp, 5 Oct 1954). Belgian composer and conductor. He studied at the Flemish Music School and the Royal Flemish Conservatory at Antwerp under Peter Benoit and Jan Blockx, and conducting under Eduard Keurvels. In 1903 he became professor at the Antwerp Conservatory, and was director of that institution from 1934 to 1941, when he retired. He was also active as an orchestral and operatic conductor, and was a member of the Académie Royale de Belgique.

Alpaerts was one of the outstanding personalities in Flemish musical life, both as conductor and composer; he was also a great teacher and an admirable organizer. As a composer he was, like Paul Gilson and August de Boeck, a typical Flemish representative of the impressionist school. As a conductor he was recognized abroad as well as in Antwerp.

WORKS
DRAMATIC

Shylock (opera, after Shakespeare); Antwerp, Royal Flemish Opera, 22 Nov 1913

Incidental music: Oedipus Rex (Sophocles), 1906; Salome (Wilde), 1907; Die versunkene Glocke (G. Hauptmann), 1907; Cymbeline (Shakespeare), 1938, etc

ORCHESTRAL

Symphonic poems: Psyche, 1899–1901; Herleving, 1904; Cyrus, 1905; Pallieter, 1921–4; Thijl Uilenspiegel, 1927; Symphonic Poem, fl, orch, 1903, rewritten 1940
James Ensor Suite, 1929
Serenade, ww, 1915
Vn concerto, 1948

MISCELLANEOUS

Church music; cantatas; chamber music; 3 Fantasias, pf, 1913, and other pf works; songs

Principal publishers: CeBeDeM, Metropolis

WRITINGS

Muzieklezen en zingen (Antwerp, 1918)

BIBLIOGRAPHY

A. Corbet, ed.: Flor Alpaerts (Antwerp, 1941) [with contributions by C. van den Borren, F. van der Mueren, P. Gilson, J. Jongen, L. Jongen and others]

AUGUST CORBET/CORNEEL MERTENS

Alpaerts, Jef (b Antwerp, 17 July 1904; d Antwerp, 15 Jan 1973). Belgian pianist and conductor, son of Flor Alpaerts. He was educated partly in England during World War I, then studied at the Royal Flemish Conservatory, Antwerp, and later at the Schola Cantorum and Ecole Normale de Musique, Paris, where his teachers were d'Indy, Isidore Philipp and Cortot. In 1936 he became professor at the Antwerp Conservatory, where he taught a course in chamber music until 1969. He formed the Trio Jef Alpaerts (1930), with which he gained a high reputation, and founded, with August Corbet, the Collegium Musicum Antverpiense (1938), a society devoted to the performance of Baroque and earlier music. In 1945 he also formed a Mozart Society and the Association des Concerts Classiques, both with Corbet as musicological adviser, and later the Jury National de Musique and Concerts de Midi, Antwerp. Much admired as a pianist and harpsichordist in European cities, he also toured widely as a conductor, including appearances in New York and Morocco. He wrote Exercices journaliers (Paris, 1929), a manual of piano technique.

AUGUST CORBET/CORNEEL MERTENS

Alphorn [Alpenhorn]. Wooden trumpet of pastoral communities in the Alps. The name is also conveniently used to cover similar instruments of Scandinavia, Russia, the western Slav countries, Hungary, Romania and, up to the last century, some of the highlands of Germany. Szadrowsky's vague reports of alphorns in the Pyrenees and the Scottish highlands are unconfirmed. An alphorn is made of a young fir, lime, poplar etc; a mountainside tree curving upwards from the roots is often chosen, giving an upturned bell. The wood is longitudinally halved by axe or saw and each half is hollowed. The two pieces are reunited under strips of bark or binding of roots or gut. The mouthpiece may be either cut in the wood or made separately. In several areas the folded shape of a trumpet is sometimes imitated. The commonest length of the alphorn is about 185 cm, in which case its range extends to the 5th or 6th harmonic (as quoted by Beethoven at the end of the Pastoral Symphony). Many alphorns are 120 cm in length or less; however, instruments 335 cm long have been known in Switzerland since the 15th century, and specimens up to 520 cm occur in Slovakia. Tunes may then ascend to the 12th harmonic or even higher.

Alphorns are known best as herdsmen's calling

Swiss alphorn

instruments, serving also in some areas to summon to church and formerly to war. They may also be numinous: among the Mari of the USSR the long wooden trumpet is made for the spring festival and afterwards sacrificially burnt or hidden in a sacred place. Overall likeness in making and using alphorns, and their distribution, suggest that they possibly may have originated among post-Celtic peoples of the Migration Era. There is no firm evidence of prior existence; 'cornu alpinus' in Tacitus is less than proof of a wooden trumpet, of which the earliest specimen, from the 9th-century Oseberg ship (Oslo, Vikingskiphuset) supports iconographic suggestions that wooden trumpets of moderate size were used as summoning and military instruments in early medieval northern Europe in addition to their pastoral functions.

BIBLIOGRAPHY

H. Szadrowsky: 'Die Musik und die tonerzeugenden Instrumente der Alpenbewohner', Jahrbuch des Schweitzer Alpenklubs, iv (1867–8), 275

For further bibliography see SWITZERLAND, §II.

ANTHONY C. BAINES

Al-Rāzī, Abū Bakr [Muḥammad ibn Zakariyya; Rhazes] (b Rayy, Aug 865; d Rayy, 27 Oct 925). Arab physician and music theorist. His medical works in Latin and Hebrew were used as textbooks in Europe. He studied music until he was 20, and wrote a Kitāb fī jumal al-mūsīqī ('Book of the summings-up of music').

BIBLIOGRAPHY

C. Brockelmann: Geschichte der arabischen Litteratur, i (Weimar and Berlin, 1898–1902, 2/1943), 233f
'l-Rāzī, Abū Bakr Muḥammad ibn Zakarīyā', The Encyclopaedia of Islam (Leiden and London, 1913–38, rev. 2/1960–)
H. G. Farmer: The Sources of Arabian Music (Bearsden, 1940, rev. 2/1965), 33

H. G. FARMER/R

Al-Rāzī, Fakhr al-Dīn [Abū ʿAbdallāh Muḥammad] (*b* Tehran, 7 Feb 1149; *d* Herat, 1209). Persian philosopher and music theorist. A scholar of prodigious literary output, he studied at Tehran and Maragha. Among his works is an encyclopedia *Jāmiʿ al-ʿulūm* ('Assembling of the sciences') containing a brief section on music. It was originally written in Persian for ʿAlā' al-Dīn Khwārizmshāh in 1178–9.

BIBLIOGRAPHY

C. Brockelmann: *Geschichte der arabischen Litteratur*, i (Weimar and Berlin, 1898–1902, 2/1943), 506f

'Fakhr al-Dīn al-Rāzī', *The Encyclopaedia of Islam* (Leiden and London, 1913–38, rev. 2/1960–)

H. G. Farmer: *The Sources of Arabian Music* (Bearsden, 1940, rev. 2/1965), 45

H. G. FARMER/R

Al rovescio (It.: 'upside down', 'back to front'). A term that can refer either to INVERSION or to RETROGRADE motion. Haydn called the minuet of the Piano Sonata in A HXVI:26 *Minuetto al rovescio*: after the trio the minuet is directed to be played backwards (retrograde motion). In the Serenade for Wind in C minor K388/384a, Mozart called the trio of the minuet *Trio in canone al rovescio*, referring to the fact that the two oboes and the two bassoons are in canon by inversion.

Alsbach. Dutch firm of music publishers. Carl Georg Alsbach (*b* Koblenz, 20 Jan 1830; *d* Rotterdam, 3 Jan 1906) founded the firm in Rotterdam on 15 March 1866 and it became one of the most important music publishing firms in the Low Countries in the first half of the 20th century. In 1898 the business moved to Amsterdam where the founder's son Johann Adam Alsbach (*b* Rotterdam, 12 April 1873; *d* Amsterdam, 20 May 1961) directed it from 1903 until his death, when the firm was taken over by Editions Basart. By purchasing the stock of several publishing houses, including Brix von Wahlberg (1898), Stumpf & Koning (1898), J. W. L. Seyffardt and A. A. Noske, Alsbach became the publishers for the majority of Dutch composers (e.g. J. Röntgen, Diepenbrock, Sigtenhorst Meyer and Badings). From 1910 to 1960 the firm produced the publications of the Vereniging voor Nederlandse Muziekgeschiedenis. It also issued a large number of works concerned with music teaching and practical music-making, both vocal and instrumental. J. A. Alsbach was in addition the joint proprietor of a retail firm in Amsterdam (Alsbach & Doyer).

BIBLIOGRAPHY

M. van Hase: 'Johann Alsbach, Musikverleger in Amsterdam†', *Börsenblatt für den Deutscher Buchhandel*, xvii (Frankfurt, 1961), 1049

A. J. Heuwekemeijer: 'Amsterdamse muziekuitgeverijen vanaf de 18 eew tot heden', *Mededelingenblad van de Vereniging voor nederlandse muziekgeschiedenis* (1967), no.24, p.39

HENRI VANHULST

Al segno (It.: 'to the sign'). An instruction to proceed, on repetition, only to the point at which a sign is placed. It is also used to indicate the duration of some other instruction, for example *sul tasto al segno* (Stravinsky, *Dumbarton Oaks* concerto, second movement).

Al-Shīrāzī. See QUTB AL-DĪN.

Al'shvang, Arnol'd Alexandrovich (*b* Kiev, 1 Oct 1898; *d* Moscow, 28 July 1960). Soviet music historian, pianist and composer. He entered the Kiev Academy of the Russian Musical Society in 1911, but in 1914 he was exiled to the northern Olonets government by tsarist authorities. Returning eventually to Kiev he continued his musical education and worked illegally in courses for workers. At the Kiev Conservatory (reorganized by Glier on the basis of the old academy) he studied composition with Glier and Boleslav Yavorsky, and graduated in 1920 from the piano class, where he had studied under Khodorovsky and Genrikh Neygauz. In the same year he graduated from the Institute of National Economy.

Al'shvang began teaching in public classes on music history in 1919, and in the same year he was appointed head of the Soviet Military Music School in Kiev. From 1923 he taught at the Kiev Conservatory and at the Valery Bryusov Institute of Literature and Fine Arts in Moscow. From 1923 to 1931 he also appeared as a pianist in many towns in the USSR. In 1930 he began to give a course in music history at the Moscow Conservatory, but a serious illness interrupted his teaching work in 1934. However, he continued to publish books and a large number of articles, and until the last days of his life he was involved in a wide range of interests, including the music of Debussy and Ravel, the philosophical problems of Skryabin's music and the music of Russian and contemporary Soviet composers. In 1944 he was awarded the degree of Doctor of Arts in recognition of his services to Soviet musicology. As a composer Al'shvang is known for a symphony (1922), a symphonic poem on Ukrainian folk themes (1927), songs, choral works and piano pieces; all his works have remained in manuscript.

WRITINGS

Klod Debyussi: zhizn' i deyatel'nost', mirovozzreniye i tvorchestvo [Debussy: life and activities, ideology and works] (Moscow, 1935)

'Filosofskiye motivï v tvorchestve Skryabina' [Philosophical motives in Skryabin's works], *SovM* (1935), no.7, p.16; (1936), no.1, p.12

'Sovetskiye shkolï pianizma' [The Soviet schools of piano playing], *SovM* (1938), nos.10–11, p.91; no.12, p.61; (1939), no.3, p.103; no.7, p.44 [on Igumnov, Neygauz, Gol'denveyzer and Nikolayev]

A. N. Skryabin: k 25-letiyu so dnya smerti [On the 25th anniversary of his death] (Moscow, 1940, 2/1945)

Betkhoven (Moscow, 1940, rev. 2/1952, enlarged 3/1963)

'O filosofskoy sisteme Skryabina' [Skryabin's philosophical system], *Aleksandr Nikolayevich Skryabin*, ed. S. Markus (Moscow, 1940), 145

Frantsuzskiy muzïkal'nïy impressionizm: Debyussi, Ravel' [French impressionist music: Debussy and Ravel], Muzïkal'nïy universitet, v (Moscow, 1945)

Sovetskiy simfonizm [The Soviet symphony], Muzïkal'nïy universitet, iv (Moscow, 1945)

Venskiye klassiki: Gaydn, Motsart, Betkhoven [The Viennese Classics: Haydn, Mozart and Beethoven], Muzïkal'nïy universitet, vi (Moscow, 1945)

M. P. Musorgsky (Moscow, 1946)

'Chamber Music', in D. Shostakovich and others: *Russian Symphony: Thoughts about Tchaikovsky* (New York, 1947), 160–92

Iosif Gaydn [Haydn] (Moscow, 1947)

Opït analiza tvorchestva P. I. Chaykovskovo [An attempt to analyse the works of Tchaikovsky] (Moscow, 1951)

'Ekspressionizm v muzïke' [Expressionism in music], *SovM* (1959), no.1, p.59

P. I. Chaykovsky (Moscow, 1959, 2/1967)

'Mesto Skryabina v istorii russkoy muzïki' [Skryabin's place in the history of Russian music], *SovM* (1961), no.1, p.77

Proizvedeniya K. Debyussi i M. Ravelya [The works of Debussy and Ravel] (Moscow, 1963)

ed. A. M. Seslavinskaya: *Izbrannïye sochineniya* [Selected works] (Moscow, 1964–5)

BIBLIOGRAPHY

G. B. Bernandt and I. M. Yampol'sky: *Kto pisal o muzïke* [Writers on music], i (Moscow, 1971) [incl. list of writings]

IGOR BELZA

Alsina, Carlos Roqué (*b* Buenos Aires, 19 Feb 1941). Argentinian composer and pianist. He studied privately with Fuchs (1951–9) and with Kröpfl at the Estudio de Fonologia Musical of the National University in Buenos Aires (1962–4). After a period as assistant conductor at the Teatro Colón (1960–64) he moved to Germany, taking a similar appointment with the Deutsche Oper in 1966. He was a member of the Center of the Creative and Performing Arts at the State University of New York, Buffalo (1966–8), where he taught contemporary piano music in 1967. In 1969 he joined Globokar, Portal and Drouet in the group New Phonic Art, whose performances have included compositions (among them Alsina's *Rendez-vous*) and 'free improvisations'.

Developing from the floridity of the *Klavierstück no.2*, Alsina has been much concerned with the extreme limits of instrumental skill, often with the intention of 'integrating' the timbres of quite different instruments (such as clarinet and cello in *Unity*). In this, his contacts with Berio (from the mid-1960s) and with the other members of New Phonic Art have been influential. He has also approached Kagel in his use of quite unconventional sound-resources and his exploiting of theatrical possibilities latent in musical performance, though these are not always features of his work.

WORKS
(selective list)
Klavierstück (Estudio) no.1, op.3, 1958; Klavierstück (Estudio) no.2, op.6, 1960; Klavierstück no.3, op.8, 1962–5; Wind Qnt, op.9, 1961; 3 Pieces, op.13, str orch, 1964; Funktionen, op.14, fl, cl, bn, tpt, pf, 2 perc, vn, vc, 1965; Consecuenza I, op.17, trbn, 1966; Auftrag, op.18, fl, cl, bn, hn, perc, vn, va, vc, db, 1967; Trio 1967, trbn, perc, vc, 1967; Textes 1967 (theatre piece), S, fl, tpt, trbn, pf, perc, vn, vc, db, 1967; Jeu de cloches, 3 or more insts, tape, 1969; Symptom, op.21, orch, 1969; Klavierstück no.4, op.23, 1969

Rendez-vous, op.24, cl + sax, trbn + alphorn, pf, pf + org + perc, 1970; Überwindung, op.25, 4 insts, orch, 1970; Consecuenza II, op.26, female v, 1971; Schichten, op.27, chamber orch, 1971; Omnipotenz, op.28, 2 insts, chamber orch, 1972; Approach, op.30, pf, perc, orch, 1973; Unity, op.31, cl, vc, 1973; Etude, op.32, zarb, 1973; Fusion, op.33 (ballet), 2 pf, 2 perc, 1974; Themen, perc, 1974; Themen II, 12 str, perc, 1975

Principal publishers: Bote & Bock, Suvini Zerboni

PAUL GRIFFITHS

Alsted [Alstedt, Alstedius], **Johann Heinrich** (*b* Ballersbach, nr. Herborn, March 1588; *d* Weissenburg, 9 Nov 1638). German theologian and music theorist. He taught at Herborn University from 1608 and, after its decline as a result of the Thirty Years War, at Weissenburg, from 1630. JAN ÁMOS KOMENSKÝ was among his pupils. Alsted developed his theological understanding of music on the basis of Calvin's teaching. More liberal than Calvin, he tolerated secular music (both polyphonic and instrumental) alongside strictly regulated church music as long as it was committed to the spiritual purpose of all music. Within the framework of his encyclopedic writings he classified the teaching of music among the mathematical sciences. The significance of his theories lies in their comprehensiveness and their systematic presentation. Like Erycius Puteanus and David Mostart, he favoured seven-syllable solmization series (*ut-re-mi-fa-sol-la-bi* or *bo-ce-di-ga-lo-ma-ni*). In his work on triads he followed Zarlino and Johannes Lippius. From the former he took the mathematical derivation of the triad from the spacing of intervals; from the latter he took the principle that inversions of a chord should be regarded merely as different aspects of the same chord in root position.

WRITINGS
'Elementale musicum', *Elementale mathematicum* (Frankfurt, 1611), 287

'Musica', *Methodus admirandorum mathematicorum*, ix (Herborn, 1613), 439

'Musica sacra', *Triumphus bibliorum sacrorum* (Frankfurt, 1625), 148

'Musica', *Encyclopaedia VII tomis distincta* (Herborn, 1630); also in *Scientiarum omnium encyclopaedia* (Lyons, 1649), 616 (Eng. trans. J. Birchensha: *Templum musicum*, London 1664/R1968)

BIBLIOGRAPHY
I. Schultz: *Studien zur Musikanschauung und Musiklehre Johann Heinrich Alsteds* (diss., U. of Marburg, 1967)

INGO SCHULTZ

Alt, in (from It. *in alto*: 'high'). A term often found in vocal music to denote those notes that lie above the highest line of the treble staff and within the compass *g''* to *f'''*. The notes of the octave above this are said to be *in altissimo*. See PITCH NOTATION.

Alta (i). 15th-century term for the group of two or three shawms and sackbut that constituted one of the standard instrumental ensembles of the period. The word is evidently an abbreviation of *alta musica* (It.), that is, *haute musique* (Fr.) or 'loud music' as opposed to *basse musique*, 'soft music'. The *haut* instruments included shawms, sackbuts, trumpets, drums, and so on, while the *bas* instruments were recorders, viols or fiddles, harps, psalteries, and so on.

In his incompletely surviving treatise, *De inventione et usu musicae* (*c*1485), Johannes Tinctoris described the alta as a standard combination, and explained that the treble and tenor shawms usually played the superius and tenor vocal parts, and the sackbut the contratenor. Many paintings, miniatures and other art works of the 15th and early 16th centuries show the typical alta;

Alta: detail from a painting on the Adimari wedding cassone, Italian, c1450, in the Galleria dell'Accademia, Florence

Besseler, for example, reproduced a representative selection of such pictures in his *Die Musik des Mittelalters und der Renaissance* (Potsdam, 1931–4). Many of these pictorial sources – for instance the well-known *cassone* painting of the Adimari wedding in Florence (see illustration) – include four performers; three play while one evidently rests his lips.

Most towns and courts, and many civic organizations like guilds, regularly employed a small band of minstrels during the 15th century, and surviving contracts make clear that such musicians also formed their own ad hoc groups to secure whatever engagements they could. Presumably their principal instruments were sackbut and shawm, although their training under an apprenticeship system leading to entry into the musicians' guild would have taught them to double on various other instruments as well. Polk's dissertation and his various articles provide the most complete survey to date of the history of these wind bands in Flanders; he also explained how these musicians learned to improvise independent parts over a given melody.

The repertory of the 15th-century alta is not altogether clear; no source reveals precisely which music minstrels performed. In pictures they are almost always shown without music books, but nevertheless they probably did play composed music, motets and chansons and perhaps even mass sections, as well as improvising contrapuntal parts against given song-tunes and dances. At least in courtly milieux, they would most probably have improvised chiefly basses danses. The one composition actually called 'Alta' is a textless piece for three voices by F. de la Torre, in the MS Cancionero de Palacio (*E-Mp* 2–1–5; the piece is printed, among other places, in Barbieri: *Cancionero musical de los siglos XV y XVI*, and in HAM, i, no.102), and may be taken as a typical example of their improvisatory style. It is a polyphonic arrangement of the widely distributed basse danse tenor *La Spagna*, in which the *cantus prius factus* is set out in long notes with a contratenor that moves against it in more or less note-against-note motion, with a highly decorated fast-moving upper part. Since de la Torre's *Alta* probably reflects the standard improvisatory style of the late 15th century, we can use it as model to imagine how the repertory of basses danses, surviving in a number of sources only as monophonic tenors, was realized in actual performance. Heartz, who made use of the extensive modern research into this monophonic repertory, connected the music with its choreography.

In the 16th century cantus firmus dances were replaced by other kinds, improvised or not; the wind bands grew in size to accommodate music in four parts, which by then had become the normal texture; and as the century wore on minstrel bands came more and more to include string instruments. Thus the three-man alta gradually gave way to larger and more varied ensembles. The present-day Catalonian *cobla*, a band that plays dances called 'sardanas', continues to some extent the 15th-century tradition; at least it features a modern version of the shawm, and the principal melody is traditionally played by the tenor member of the family.

BIBLIOGRAPHY

K. Weinmann: *Johannes Tinctoris und sein unbekannter Traktat 'De inventione et usu musicae'* (Regensburg, 1917/R1961)

H. Besseler: 'Katalanische Cobla und Alta-Tanzkapelle', *IMSCR, iv Basle 1949*, 59

A. Baines: 'Fifteenth-century Instruments in Tinctoris's *De inventione et usu musicae*', *GSJ*, iii (1950), 19

H. Besseler: 'Die Entstehung der Posaune', *AcM*, xxii (1950), 7

A. Baines: 'Shawms of the Sardana Coblas', *GSJ*, v (1952), 9

D. Heartz: 'The Basse Dance: its Evolution circa 1450 to 1550', *AnnM*, vi (1958–63), 287–340

K. Polk: *Flemish Wind Bands in the Late Middle Ages: a Study of Improvisatory Instrumental Practices* (diss., U. of California, Berkeley, 1968)

——: 'Wind Bands of Medieval Flemish Cities', *BWQ*, i (1968), 93

——: 'Municipal Wind Music in Flanders in the late Middle Ages', *BWQ*, ii (1969), 1

HOWARD MAYER BROWN

Alta (ii) [alta danza] (Sp.). SALTARELLO.

Altacuria, Johannes. *See* HAUCOURT, JOHANNES.

Altargesang. German term for the sections of the chant of the Mass sung by the celebrant rather than the choir or congregation; also used for the adaptations of Gregorian chant made, using the German language, in the Lutheran church in Germany. *See* LUTHER, MARTIN.

Altenburg, Johann Ernst (*b* Weissenfels, 15 June 1734; *d* Bitterfeld, 14 May 1801). German trumpeter, organist and theorist, son of Johann Caspar Altenburg. He was sworn into apprenticeship by his father at two years of age and was released from his articles as a trumpeter 16 years later. Because of the decline of Baroque social order, however, he was never able to find a position as a trumpeter. He became a secretary to a friend of his father's, a royal Polish stablemaster, then studied the organ and composition with Johann Theodor Römhild in Merseburg until 1757 and (briefly) with Bach's son-in-law, Johann Christoph Altnikol, in Naumburg. In 1757 he joined the French army as a field trumpeter and participated in the Seven Years War, then travelled to various German states, returning to Weissenfels in 1766. In 1767 he found a position as an organist in Landsberg, and in 1769 in the small village of Bitterfeld. He auditioned unsuccessfully for better positions and died embittered and impoverished.

Altenburg is best known for his valuable treatise on the 'heroic and musical trumpeters' and kettledrummers' art', which, though finished in manuscript and offered on a subscription basis by J. A. Hiller as early as 1770, was not published until 1795. It contains important information on the declining position of court and field trumpeters, seen at first hand, and of their tightly knit organization ('Cameradschaft') founded on privileges granted by the Holy Roman Emperors since 1623. His detailed description of the training of pupils shows him to have been a good teacher. His treatise is of lasting value because of its explanation of technical and stylistic matters pertaining to the natural trumpet. The 'secret' of Baroque trumpeters, so fascinating and elusive to modern writers, had little to do with their art of playing in the clarino register – which Altenburg treated in a rather matter-of-fact manner, for example mentioning only in passing the required 'lipping' of the out-of-tune 7th, 11th, 13th and 14th tones of the harmonic series (p.71) – but was rather associated with the repertory of the field trumpeters. Their five 'field pieces' or military signals were handed down by rote from teacher to pupil and were executed with special kinds of tonguing (and 'huffing'). For playing in the clarino register Altenburg exhorted imitation of the human voice and gave examples of unequal tonguing, practised throughout the Renaissance and Baroque periods on all wind instruments.

Altenburg is known to have composed six piano sonatas, published in manuscript by C. G. Thomas (1780) and by Breitkopf (1781). The works for two to seven trumpets included in his treatise are not necessarily of his own authorship; indeed, the fugue in G minor (p.104) was published in H. I. F. Biber's *Sonatae tam aris* (1676).

Altenburg's father, Johann Caspar Altenburg (*b* Alach, nr. Erfurt, 1689; *d* Weissenfels, 1761), presumably a descendant of the 17th-century church musician Michael Altenburg, served as court and chamber trumpeter for three successive dukes of Weissenfels (1711–46) and also performed in many other German courts (1731–3). According to his son's *Versuch*, which includes a full biography of him, he was especially praised for his playing in the high register.

WRITINGS

Lebens-Umstände des Organisten Altenburg (MS, 1769, Archiv des Kirchenkreises, Bitterfeld); ed. in Werner (1931)

Versuch einer Anleitung zur heroisch-musikalischen Trompeter- und Pauker-Kunst (Halle, 1795/R; Eng. trans., 1974)

17 letters to I. Breitkopf, destroyed World War II (copies formerly owned by A. Werner); letter, *D-Bds*, ed. in *MMg*, xxiv (1892), 159

BIBLIOGRAPHY

GerberNL

J. A. Hiller: *Musikalische Nachrichten und Anmerkungen* (Leipzig, 1770), no.51, p.398

A. Werner: 'Die Thüringer Musikerfamilie Altenburg', *SIMG*, vii (1905–6), 119

——: *Musikpflege in Stadt und Kreis Bitterfeld* (Bitterfeld, 1931), 75ff

——: 'Johann Ernst Altenburg, der letzte Vertreter der heroischen Trompeter- und Paukerkunst', *ZMw*, xv (1932–3), 258

D. Altenburg: *Untersuchungen zur Geschichte der Trompete im Zeitalter der Clarinblaskunst 1500–1800*, i (Regensburg, 1973), 38, 143

EDWARD H. TARR

Altenburg, Michael (*b* Alach, nr. Erfurt, 27 May 1584; *d* Erfurt, 12 Feb 1640). German composer, clergyman and schoolmaster. He was sent to school at Erfurt in 1590 and went on to study theology at the university there in 1598, gaining the bachelor's degree in 1599 and the master's degree in 1603. He taught at Erfurt from 1600, beginning at the Reglerschule; from 1601 he was Kantor at St Andreas and from 1607 was also rector of the school connected with it. He abandoned teaching in 1609 and became a pastor: he worked in the parishes of Ilversgehofen and Marbach, near Erfurt, until 1610 and then moved to Tröchtelborn, near Gotha, where he stayed until 1621 and was probably also Kantor. He published most of his music during these years. He was likened to Lassus as an 'Orlandus Thuringiae' and he himself was conscious of living at a time of great musical activity: as he wrote in the preface to his *Intraden* (1620), 'soon there will not be a single village, especially in Thuringia, in which music, both vocal and instrumental, will not flourish in good order with splendour or refinement, according to the resources of the place'.

This happy and musically fertile period in Altenburg's life came to an end when he moved to the Bonifaciuskirche at Sömmerda. His contemporaries continued to 'praise him as a most devout, exemplary and inspired preacher, and his hymns ... are held in high esteem and are frequently sung in the churches of Gross-Sömmer and indeed throughout the whole locality'. The Thirty Years War, however, was bringing suffering to his homeland, and his creativity ceased. His congregation was decimated by plague in 1636; his wife died in 1637, and of their 13 children only three survived him. In 1637 the war drove him back to Erfurt, where he spent the rest of his life, first as deacon, then from 1638 as minister, of St Andreas.

Altenburg's church music was well known and greatly valued in his lifetime, and 17 of his melodies were used in congregational singing. His song *Verzage nicht, du Häuflein klein!*, to a text by Jacob Fabricius, became the marching song of King Gustavus Adolphus of Sweden. He composed vocal concertos for large forces, including trumpets and timpani, in up to 18 parts, but his motet-like pieces and simple but effective chorale-based intradas with their independent instrumental ensembles show that he was also a master of relaxed, madrigalian textures in polyphonic forms. A concern with deeper significance co-exists in his works with a tendency towards simplification of expression and technical requirements: as Blume said 'he can perhaps be called the first popularizer in the Protestant church music of his age'.

WORKS

(all published in Erfurt unless otherwise stated)

Das 53. Capitel des ... Propheten Esaiae, das ist das ... Leiden und Sterben sampt ... Aufferstehung unseres Herrn ... auch der ... Passion-Spruch ... Bernhardi, 6vv (1608)

Adams hochzeitliche Freude ... 6vv, neben dem Symbolo, Fidenti sperata cedunt, 7vv (1613)

Gaudium Christianum, das ist christliche musikalische Freude (6 motets), 5–16vv, 3 tpt, 2 timp (Jena, 1617), lost

Musicalischer Schild und Schirm ... das ist der 55. Psalm, 6vv (1618)

Hochzeitliche musicalische Freude ... darein zugleich ein Choral Stimme beneben 2 Clareten und 1 Trombet gerichtet ist [ad lib] (*Isaiah* lxii), 9 or 12vv (1620)

Erster Theil newer ... zierlicher Intraden ... auf Geigen Lauten Instrumenten und Orgelwerck gerichtet ... darein zugleich eine Choralstimm ... kann mit gesungen werden, 6vv (1620); 3 ed. A. Egidi, *Drei Intraden zu Advent und Weihnacht* (Berlin, 1930); some ed. H. Erdlen and E. Rabsch, *Choral-Intraden* (Leipzig, 1932)

[11] Cantiones de Adventu Domini ac salvatoris nostri Jesu Christi, 5, 6, 8vv (1620)

Erster Theil [15] christlicher ... newer Kirchen und Haussgesänge, so auff alle Festtage und ... zu jederzeit, 5vv (1620)

Der ander Theil [25] christlicher ... newer Kirchen und Haussgesenge von Ostern biss auff das Advent, 5, 6, 8vv (1620)

Der dritte Theil [22] christlicher ... newer Kirchen und Haussgesänge ... durchs gantze Jahr ... 5, 6, 8vv, dessgleichen 2 newe Intraden 10 Voc. zu 2 Choren, der erste auff Geigen, der ander auff Zincken und Posaunen ... oder nur auff das Orgelwerck, darein ein Choral Stimm ... kann gesungen werden (1620–21)

Vierdter Theil der [15] Fest Gesänge ... auff Himmelfahrt, Pfingsten, Trinitatis, 5–9vv (1621)

Musikalische Weynacht- und New Jahrs Zierde, 4–9vv (1621)

Dritter Theil musicalischer Fest Zierde, das ist ... [14] Festgesänge auff Mariae Reinigung, Mariae Verkündigung ... Passion ... Ostern und jederzeit, 5–14vv (1622)

Der cxvi Psalm, 3–5vv, 1623[14]

3 lieder, 1641[4]

Edns. of lieder: 3 in Winterfeld; 17 in Zahn, i–v; 14 in L. Schöberlein: *Schatz des liturgischen Chor- und Gemeindegesangs* (Göttingen, 1865–72/R1928–9)

BIBLIOGRAPHY

EitnerQ

C. von Winterfeld: *Der evangelische Kirchengesang*, ii (Leipzig, 1845/R1966)

A. Auberlen: 'Michael Altenburg, 1584–1640: ein Beitrag zu seiner Biographie', *MMg*, xi (1879), 185

E. Bohn: *Bibliographie der Musik-Druckwerke bis 1700, welche ... zu Breslau aufbewahrt werden* (Berlin, 1883/R1969), 44f

J. Zahn: *Die Melodien der deutschen evangelischen Kirchenlieder* (Gütersloh, 1888–93/R1963), v, vi

L. Meinecke: 'Michael Altenburg: ein Beitrag zur Geschichte der evangelischen Kirchenmusik', *SIMG*, v (1903–4), 1–45

F. Blume: *Die evangelische Kirchenmusik*, HMw, x (1931, rev. 2/1965 as *Geschichte der evangelischen Kirchenmusik*)

B. Kitzig: *Gustav Adolf, Jacobus Fabricius und Michael Altenburg, die drei Urheber des Liedes 'Verzage nicht, du Häuflein klein!'* (Göttingen, 1935)

H. J. Moser: *Heinrich Schütz: sein Leben und Werk* (Kassel, 1936, rev. 2/1954; Eng. trans., 1959)

G. Kraft and R. Schaal: 'Erfurt', *MGG*

K. Ameln: 'Michael Altenburg', *Jb für Liturgik und Hymnologie*, viii (1963), 153

H. Engel: *Musik in Thüringen* (Cologne and Graz, 1966)
W. Schmieder and G. Hartwieg: *Kataloge der Herzog-August-Bibliothek Wolfenbüttel, xii, xiii: Musik alte Drucke bis etwa 1750* (Frankfurt am Main, 1967), 14ff, 844

KARL-ERNST BERGUNDER

Altered chord. In tonal harmony a chord one or more of whose notes is altered chromatically but whose function remains the same. Examples include the NEAPOLITAN SIXTH CHORD and any of the forms of the AUGMENTED SIXTH CHORD.

Alternatim (Lat.: 'alternately'). A term commonly used to describe the manner in which alternate sections of certain liturgical items were performed by distinct and normally dissimilar forces. The practice had its roots in the antiphonal psalmody of the early Western church. One of its first characteristic manifestations was in the performance of responsorial chants (e.g. gradual, alleluia) where the soloists (*cantores*) alternated with the choir (*schola*) (*see* PSALM, §II, and RESPONSORY, §5). In the organum settings of these texts in the Notre Dame repertory, the soloists sang polyphonically the sections normally reserved for the cantor, while the choir sang its sections in plainchant. Some Renaissance settings of responsorial texts show the same alternation of polyphony with plainchant (e.g. the settings of *Audivi media nocte* by Taverner and Tallis).

The practice of *alternatim*, however, was not restricted to liturgical texts that were responsorial in character, nor to the opposition of plainchant to polyphony: psalms, canticles, hymns, sequences and the Ordinary of the Mass were also set in this fashion, one verse alternating with the next; and the alternation of organ with choir, or fauxbourdon with plainchant, rapidly gained currency during the 15th century. The introduction of the organ as a partner in *alternatim* practices (some time in the 14th century; *see* ORGAN MASS) led in particular to a fine body of liturgical organ music in Italy, Spain and France during the 16th and 17th centuries (*see* ORGAN VERSET and ORGAN HYMN). Settings in which polyphony alternated with plainchant became common during the Renaissance: a Kyrie and Gloria by Dufay reveal the penetration of this manner of performance into the Mass Ordinary; but more numerous are the plainchant–polyphonic settings of the *Magnificat*, sequences and hymns. Victoria (1581) and Palestrina (1589) each published important collections of hymn versets in addition to numerous sets for the *Magnificat*; other notable composers of *alternatim Magnificat* settings include Dufay, Fayrfax, Festa, Gombert, Morales and Taverner (*see also* MAGNIFICAT, §2).

In the modern performance of *alternatim* pieces a problem may arise when apparently insufficient versets are furnished by a composer. For instance, Dufay often provided only a single polyphonically worked verset for a particular hymn; in such a case one would have been expected to repeat the same music for succeeding alternate versets. Similarly, in Attaingnant's publication *Magnificat sur les huit tons* (Paris, 1530), six of the eight sets of organ versets for the canticle contain only two versets (a minimum of six is required for the *Magnificat*); here the organist would have been expected to improvise the remainder.

Attention may also be drawn to *alternatim* patterns of greater complexity. The *Caeremoniale parisiense* (1662) describes the following manner of performing the invitatory at Matins (I = invitatory; i = section of invitatory; C = choir; cc = cantors; O = organ): I(cc); I(O); v.1(cc); I(C); v.2(cc); I(O); v.3(cc); I(C); v.4(cc); I(O); v.5(cc); I(C); *Gloria Patri* (cc); i(0); i(cc); i(C). Le Sieur de Moléon referred to another interesting *alternatim* scheme (*Voyages liturgiques*, Paris, 1718, p. 132) which was used for the Mass in Tours Cathedral on the feast of St Martin (12 May):

Le chantre de l'Eglise de S. Martin commence l'Introit, dont l'Orgue et la Musique chantent chacun la moitié. Le chantre des religieux chante le Verset et recommence l'Introit, que les Moines continuent; et le Chantre de l'Eglise le *Gloria Patri*, et reprend l'Introit pour la troisiéme fois, que la Musique poursuit; et ainsi du reste de la Messe qu'on chante à trois choeurs.

Such schemes 'à trois choeurs' were by no means unusual in 17th- and 18th-century France, the organ often being permitted to assume the role of 'La Musique' (i.e. the polyphonic choir).

EDWARD HIGGINBOTTOM

Alternativo (It.). An 18th-century term indicating that pairs of pieces such as a minuet and trio or a pair of gavottes should be played in alternation, that is, the first repeated after the second.

Altflöte (Ger.). Alto flute; *see* FLUTE, §3.

Althorn (i) (Ger.). A brass instrument, usually in E♭, a 5th below the cornet, with bugle-like bore. It is used in

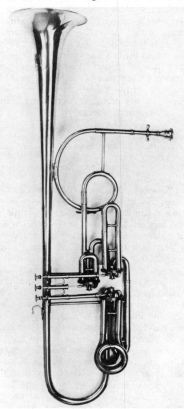

Althorn in C (high pitch) by John Köhler, London, c1840 (Spencer Collection, Brighton Museum)

all brass bands in Germany, Switzerland and eastern Europe to fill the alto register and supply off-beats. It is made in various shapes: 'trumpet-form', with bell to the front; 'tuba-form', upright (see illustration); and 'oval-form', which is the upright oval shápe first seen in instruments of the early 1850s by Červený and is today the favourite form. The circular 'Waldhorn-form' is rarer. The mouthpiece is a deep funnel, wider than that of an orchestral horn. Few details are known of the early althorn, which W. F. Wieprecht was testing in Berlin in 1837 as alternative to an earlier 'Alt-Kornett'. An early upright example by Moritz, Berlin, is in the Städtisches Sammlung, Munich.

In England around 1845 the lists of Distin and other makers and importers give 'Alt Horn' as an instrument pitched a 4th lower in B♭, at first with the form of a clavicor, then of a baritone saxhorn. Contemporary military band journals allot it a solo part, which later in the century was renamed 'B♭ Baritone' and performed on that instrument.

ANTHONY C. BAINES

Althorn (ii) (Ger.). TENOR HORN.

Altieri, Paolo (*b* Naples, 29 Jan 1745; *d* Noto, 17 Oct 1820). Italian composer and music teacher who worked in Noto, a small city in south-eastern Sicily, from 1766 until his death. He was educated in Naples, where he met two wealthy citizens from Noto who invited him to their city. Altieri arrived in 1766, became a music teacher, married and held the position of *maestro di cappella* for all the city's churches.

A collection of Altieri's compositions was given to the Biblioteca Comunale of Noto by a local bishop who had acquired it from a relative of Altieri's: it comprises 449 works, mostly sacred vocal music, but also secular vocal music and instrumental works.

BIBLIOGRAPHY
D. Russo: *Indice alfabetico delle opere e della Raccolta musicale del M.o Paolo Altieri, Biblioteca comunale di Noto* (Noto, 1913)
STEPHEN TOBRINER

Altisent Domenjo, Miguel (*b* Balaguer, 22 Oct 1898; *d* Barcelona, 31 Jan 1975). Spanish scholar of plainchant. He showed an early aptitude for music, and was privately taught. A pupil at the Seo de Urgel seminary, he later entered the Pius Schools order and developed a strong interest in religious music under the influence of Gregorio María Suñol, who taught him Gregorian chant; he subsequently spent long periods at the monastery of Solesmes. In 1936 he became professor of Gregorian chant at the Istituto di Musica Sacra, Milan, which he also directed. After the Spanish Civil War he returned to Spain (1939) and became professor of Gregorian chant at the seminary and later at the conservatory in Barcelona, where he served until his death. Altisent devoted himself to the study of Gregorian chant and its popularization through books, lectures, articles and performance, and was instrumental in the restoration of Ambrosian chant in Milan. His last work, *El canto gregoriano* (Lérida, 1973), sums up his theories concerning the nature of Gregorian chant and its interpretation.

BIBLIOGRAPHY
P. Carceller Galindo: 'In memoriam, P. Miguel Altisent Domenjo', *Tesoro sacro musical* (1975), 23
JOSÉ LÓPEZ-CALO

Altmann, Wilhelm (*b* Adelnau, Posen, 4 April 1862; *d* Hildesheim, 25 March 1951). German musicologist. He received lessons in the violin and music theory from Otto Lüstner while at school in Breslau, and studied medieval history and classical philology at Marburg and Berlin (1882–5). After training as a librarian at the Royal University Library, Breslau, he moved in 1889 to Greifswald University where in addition to his library duties he held the post of lecturer in medieval history and in librarianship from 1893. In 1900 he obtained a post at the Royal Library in Berlin, where he was instrumental in founding the Deutsche Musik Sammlung, and where he finally became director of the music section in 1915 in succession to Albert Kopfermann. He held this position until his retirement in 1927. The energetic cultivation of his dual interests, music and librarianship, both during his professional career and after his retirement to Hildesheim, resulted in the production of an invaluable series of catalogues of published works for various instruments or combinations of instruments.

WRITINGS
Chronik des Berliner Philharmonischen Orchesters (Berlin, 1902)
Heinrich von Herzogenberg (Berlin, 1903)
Richard Wagners Briefen nach Zeitfolge und Inhalt (Leipzig, 1905/R1971)
ed.: *Johannes Brahms: Briefwechsel*, iii (Berlin, 1908), xiv (Berlin, 1920)
Kammermusik Katalog (Leipzig, 1910, 6/1945)
ed.: *Wagners Briefwechsel mit seinen Verlegern* (Leipzig, 1911/R1971)
Max-Reger-Katalog (Berlin, 1917, 2/1926)
Orchester-Literatur-Katalog, i (Leipzig, 1919, enlarged 2/1926/R1972); ii (Leipzig, 1919, 3/1936/R1972)
ed.: *Otto Nicolai: Briefe an seinen Vater* (Regensburg, 1924)
'Die Schaffung einer internationalen Bibliographie der Musikliteratur', *Kongressbericht: Basel 1924*, 51
ed.: *Richard Wagners Briefe: ausgewählt und eingeleitet* (Leipzig, 1925; Eng. trans., 1972)
ed.: *Kurzgefasstes Tonkünstlerlexikon ... begrundet von P. Frank, neubearbeit von ... Wilh. Altmann* (Leipzig, 1926 [=12th edn. of Paul Frank's *Kleines Tonkünstlerlexicon*, 1860], 15/1948–9)
'Über thematische Katalog', *Beethoven-Zentenarfeier: Wien 1927*, 283
Handbuch für Streichquartettspieler (Berlin, 1928–31)
ed.: R. Wagner: *Mein Leben* (Leipzig, 1933)
Handbuch für Klaviertriospieler (Wolfenbüttel, 1934)
Katalog der seit 1861 in den Handel gekommenen theatralischen Musik (Wolfenbüttel, 1935–9)
Handbuch für Klavierquintettspieler (Wolfenbüttel, 1936)
Handbuch für Klavierquartettspieler (Wolfenbüttel, 1937)
ed.: *Carl Maria von Weber: ausgewählte Schriften* (Regensburg, 1937)
with V. Borissowsky: *Literaturverzeichnis für Bratsche und Viola d'Amore* (Wolfenbüttel, 1937)
Verzeichnis von Werken für Klavier vier- und sechs-händig sowie für zwei und mehr Klaviere (Leipzig, 1943)

BIBLIOGRAPHY
W. Krabbe: 'Wilhelm Altmann zum Gedächtnis', *Mf*, iv (1951), 347
ERIC BLOM/MALCOLM TURNER

Altmeyer, Theo [Theodor] **(Daniel)** (*b* Eschweiler, nr. Aachen, 16 March 1931). German tenor. After studying at Cologne he joined the Städtische Oper, Berlin, in 1956, creating the title role in Searle's *Diary of a Madman* in 1958. Two years later he joined the Landestheater at Hanover. In the concert hall he specializes in Bach, particularly the role of the Evangelist in the Passions, which he has sung at festivals throughout Europe; he has also sung in many other

Baroque works and in the sacred repertory generally. He has a clear, well-controlled voice which he uses with great sensitivity, and his natural, expressive articulation of the text has been much praised.

ALAN BLYTH

Altnikol [Altnickol], Johann Christoph (*b* Berna bei Seidenberg, Oberlausitz, baptized 1 Jan 1720; *d* Naumburg, buried 25 July 1759). German organist and composer. He attended the Lauban Lyceum in 1733, and was a singer and assistant organist at S Maria Magdalena, Breslau, from about 1740 until the end of 1743. He then wished to return to Germany and devote himself to 'higher studies' at Leipzig, and as his parents were poor, he asked for a viaticum. He was granted four thalers on 23 January 1744, and on 19 March he matriculated at Leipzig University as a theological student. He soon began to assist Bach, chiefly as a bass, and did so regularly from Michaelmas 1745. In taking on a university student Bach exceeded his authority, but he was always short of basses, for the boys of the Thomasschule often left before their voices had settled. On 16 April 1746 W. F. Bach recommended Altnikol as his successor at Dresden, saying that he had studied the keyboard and composition with his father; but he was disregarded. On 26 April 1747 Altnikol applied to the Leipzig Council for a grant, saying that he had been singing bass for three years (i.e. from April 1744). Burgomaster Stieglitz seized the opportunity to say that the Kantor had no business to make such appointments; but the council agreed to pay 12 thalers (19 May), given proof that Altnikol had actually done the work. Bach certified on 25 May that Altnikol had worked continuously from Michaelmas 1745.

On 8 November 1747 a vacancy for an organist and schoolmaster arose at Niederwiesa (near Greiffenberg, Silesia); on 3 December the son of some local worthy drafted a letter inviting Altnikol to apply. The draft went to another local worthy for approval (no names are given) with a covering letter stating that the writer had known Altnikol at Lauban and Leipzig, and that he was a peaceable and upright man, no great theologian, but a good bass, violinist and organist, who understood composition and had endeared himself to Herr Bach. Subsequent events show that he had also endeared himself to Fräulein Bach. On 1 January 1748 Bach testified that Altnikol was a pupil of whom he need not be ashamed; on 18 January Altnikol was appointed, and he gave satisfaction. He is said to have been a fine organist.

A post at St Wenceslaus, Naumburg, fell vacant in the summer, and on 24 July 1748 Bach recommended Altnikol to the council, who unanimously appointed him on 30 July, before they had even received his formal application. There is a story that the council preferred Bach's candidate to Johann Friedrich Gräbner, who was being put forward by the all-powerful Count Brühl; by rushing the matter, they were able to say that the Count's recommendation came too late. Gräbner nevertheless became Altnikol's successor in 1759.

Altnikol moved in at mid-September, and married Bach's daughter Elisabeth on 20 January 1749. He invited the Naumburg Council to the wedding, thus securing a present of six thalers. A son, Johann Sebastian, was born on 4 October, but was buried on 21 October. On 24 October Altnikol's father died, and a

few months later Bach fell seriously ill. According to Forkel, it was to Altnikol that Bach dictated his last chorale prelude (though the familiar manuscript fragment is not in Altnikol's hand). After Bach's death, Altnikol took in the half-witted son Gottfried Heinrich; he also taught J. G. Müthel, Bach's pupil, until 1751. At the end of 1753 he, like W. F. Bach, competed unsuccessfully for an appointment at St John's, Zittau; and in 1757 he taught the trumpeter J. Ernest Altenburg.

His widow must have stayed at Naumburg for a time, for her brother Gottfried died there in 1763. Later she moved to Leipzig, where both her daughters married, and she herself died on 24 August 1781; she had received an allowance from her stepbrother Emanuel.

In Gerber's day the Breitkopf hire library included a *Magnificat* and various cantatas by Altnikol, all heavily scored, but very few of his works survive. Bach spoke well of them, perhaps for personal reasons; they have in fact attracted little attention. Altnikol is now remembered because he was Bach's son-in-law, and a trustworthy copyist.

WORKS

2 sonatas, 7 dances, kbd, *D-Bds*
Ricercar a 4, *GB-Cfm*
2 Sanctus settings, holograph, 1748, *Bds*
Frohlocket und jauchzet, cantata, *Bds*, according to *EitnerQ*
Motets: Nun danket alle Gott, *Bds*, according to *EitnerQ*; Befiel du deine Wege, ed. in Veröffentlichungen der neuen Bach-Gesellschaft, Jg.xxxv/1 (1934)

BIBLIOGRAPHY

A. Werner: in *BJb* [iii] (1906), 131
A. Arnheim: in *BJb*, ix (1912), 147
C. S. Terry: *The Origin of the Family of Bach Musicians* (London, 1929), table VII
F. Hamann: 'J. Chr. Altnickol in Greiffenberg (Schlesien)', *BJb*, xxxvi (1939), 62
W. Neumann and H.-J. Schulz, eds.: *Bach-Dokumente*, i, ii (Kassel and Leipzig, 1963, 1969)
K. Geiringer: *Johann Sebastian Bach: the culmination of an era* (London, 1967), 103
A. Dürr: 'Zur Chronologie der Handschrift Johann Christoph Altnickols und Johann Friedrich Agricolas', *BJb*, lvi (1970), 44

WALTER EMERY

Alto. (1) The Italian form of ALTUS, a vocal part lying above the tenor. The term first became common in partbooks (especially of secular music) printed in the second half of the 16th century. In the 16th–18th centuries alto parts in sacred music were sung by men: falsettists, high tenors or castratos. Only in the secular repertory were they sung by women. In English usage a distinction is often made between alto and CONTRALTO, the former referring either to a boy alto or (more often) a falsettist, and the latter to a female voice. The distinction is often blurred, however, and even more so in America, where the tradition of FALSETTO singing is less strong. In both countries the term 'alto' is commonly applied to the female voice in choral music. *See also* COUNTERTENOR and HAUTE-CONTRE.

(2) The French and Italian term for the VIOLA, a usage deriving from the instrument's range relative to other members of the violin family.

(3) A term applied as a qualifying adjective to instruments, especially wind (e.g. alto clarinet, alto flute), that are the second highest members of their family. Alto instruments often have a range about a 5th below that of the highest member of the family. The alto recorder (in English usage, the treble) is exceptional in being the representative instrument of its kind.

BIBLIOGRAPHY
W. J. Hough: 'The Historical Significance of the Countertenor', *PMA*, lxiv (1937–8), 1
G. M. Ardran and D. Wulstan: 'The Alto or Countertenor Voice', *ML*, xlviii (1967), 17

HOWARD MAYER BROWN, OWEN JANDER

Alto clarinet. A member of the clarinet family (*see* CLARINET, §1), normally pitched in E♭. It is used chiefly in military bands and wind bands, and is usually built with an upturned metal bell and a curved metal crook; the two-piece body carries mechanism of similar design and layout to that of the soprano clarinet, with two common exceptions. First, because the tone holes are a little large for convenient covering, the instrument is frequently made with tone holes covered by plates instead of directly by the fingers; second, there are commonly two speaker keys, as on the bass clarinet.

The history of the alto clarinet as we now understand it may be said to begin in the early 19th century with the design of instruments of large bore, first in F and later in E♭ for military bands, both in France (those made by Cuvillier and Simiot, for example) and Germany (Grenser and Wiesner). In England, the alto clarinet in F seems to have survived as a non-military instrument of narrower bore, confusingly known as the tenor clarinet.

The alto clarinet has a good full tone, and blends well; unlike the basset-horn, it has no difficulty in balancing other modern instruments. It has been little used in the orchestra, however, and is no longer included in British Army bands, though it is a regular constituent of American concert bands.

NICHOLAS SHACKLETON

Alto flute. A flute pitched in G, a 4th below the concert flute; *see* FLUTE, §3.

Alto horn. American term for a valved brass instrument pitched in E♭ below the cornet and employed in some wind bands; its form is upright, often with the bell turned forward. It is equivalent to the English TENOR HORN.

Altrobrandino, Giuseppe Antonio Vincenzo. *See* ALDROVANDINI, GIUSEPPE ANTONIO VINCENZO.

Altus (Lat.: 'high'). A voice designation that originated in the mid-15th century as an abbreviation of CONTRATENOR ALTUS. In the early 16th century 'altus' and 'contratenor' were used interchangeably as designations for a voice lying below the superius (or cantus) and overlapping, more or less, with the tenor. As inner voices became more clearly stratified in range 'altus' (or 'alto') became the more common term, and during the second half of the 16th century 'contratenor' fell into disuse on the Continent. In England the terms 'contra' and 'countertenor' persisted well into the 17th century, and the latter term is still used.

See also ALTO; CONTRALTO; HAUTE-CONTRE.

OWEN JANDER

Aluredus. *See* AMERUS.

Al-Urmawī. *See* ṢAFĪ AL-DĪN.

Alva, Alonso de (*d* ?Seville, before 6 Sept 1504). Spanish *maestro de capilla* who has sometimes been confused with ALONSO PEREZ DE ALBA.

Alva, Luigi [Alva Talledo, Luis Ernesto] (*b* Lima, 10 April 1927). Peruvian tenor. He studied in Lima with Rosa Morales and later in Milan with Emilio Ghirardini and at La Scala School with Ettore Campogalliani. He spent a year as a cadet in the Peruvian navy. His début was in 1949 in Lima in a zarzuela called *Luisa Fernanda*, and the next year he sang Beppe there in *Pagliacci*. His European début was at the Teatro Nuovo, Milan, in 1954 as Alfredo. He sang Paolino in *Il matrimonio segreto* to open the Piccola Scala in 1955, and in 1956 at La Scala sang Rossini's Almaviva, a role in which his admirable sense of comedy and lack of exaggeration were to win him admiration on many stages. He has sung regularly in Milan (where he appeared in the premières of Chailly's *Una domanda di matrimonio* and Malipiero's *La donna è mobile*), at Covent Garden from 1960 and at the Metropolitan Opera, where he made his début as Fenton in 1964; and he has appeared at the Aix-en-Provence, Salzburg and Glyndebourne festivals. His elegant and refined style are specially suited to Mozart and Rossini.

BIBLIOGRAPHY
G. Gualerzi: 'Alva, Luigi', *Le grandi voci* (Rome, 1964) [with opera discography by R. Vegeto]

HAROLD ROSENTHAL

Alvarado, Diego [Diogo] **de** (*b* c1570; *d* Lisbon, 12 Feb 1643). Basque organist and composer. He had already been in the service of the Spanish crown for some time when on 13 April 1602 he became organist of the royal chapel at Lisbon, with the modest annual salary of 30,000 reis and (from 13 June) three *moios* of wheat. According to his epitaph he was a keyboard player in the royal chapel for 43 years.

His only surviving works are two tientos (*P-La*, in a manuscript appendix to 38-XII-27) which show him to have been a highly skilled composer; the second is a superbly constructed monothematic ricercare and the first a much shorter but highly polished treatment of the Spanish *Pange lingua*, in which a counterpoint to the plainsong serves throughout as a unifying motif. Two motets were in the library of King John IV.

BIBLIOGRAPHY
DBMP
Primeira parte do index da livraria de musica do muyto alto, e poderoso Rey Dom João o IV. nosso senhor (Lisbon, 1649/*R*1967), 455ff, 468ff; ed. J. de Vasconcellos (Oporto, 1874–6)
C. Castello Branco: *O regicida* (Lisbon, 1874), 215
F. M. Sousa Viterbo: 'Subsidios para a historia da musica em Portugal', *O instituto*, lxxiii (1926), 91; lxxxiv (1932), 111
M. S. Kastner, ed.: *Libro de tientos . . . compuesto por Francisco Correa de Arauxo*, MME, xii (1952), 13f, 30, 242f, 262ff
M. A. Machado Santos: *Catálogo de música manuscrita* (Lisbon, 1958), i, 19

ROBERT STEVENSON

Alvarenga, Oneyda (Paoliello de) (*b* Varginha, 6 Dec 1911). Brazilian folklorist and musicologist. At the São Paulo Conservatory of Drama and Music, Mário de Andrade directed her towards the study of Brazilian folk and popular musical traditions; she also studied ethnography and folklore with Dina Lévi-Strauss (1937). Her main areas of activity have been sound archive organization, ethnomusicology and folklore: she organised and directed the Discoteca Pública Municipal de São Paulo from its foundation in 1935 until her retirement in 1968. She is a founder-member of the Brazilian Academy of Music, a member of the Conselho Nacional de Folclore of the Ministry of Education and of the executive committee of the International Association of

Music Libraries, a corresponding member of the International Folk Music Council, and a member of the Conselho de Música Popular Brasileira, do Museu da Imagem e do Som established at Rio de Janeiro. Her publications include editions of the volumes on music in the complete works of Mário de Andrade.

WRITINGS

'Cateretês do sul de Minas Gerais', *Revista do Arquivo municipal*, no.30 (São Paulo, 1937), 31–70

'Pequena contribuição ao estudo das questões de organização discotecária', *Boletín latino-americano de música*, iv (1937), 267

'Comentários a alguns cantos e danças do Brasil', *Revista do Arquivo municipal* (São Paulo, 1941), no.80, pp.209–46

'A discoteca pública municipal', *Revista do Arquivo municipal* (São Paulo, 1942), no.87, pp.7–98

'O movimento de consultas da Discoteca Pública Municipal durante 1941 e 1942', *Revista do Arquivo municipal* (São Paulo, 1943), no.92, p.53

'A influência negra na música brasileira', *Boletín latino-americano de música*, vi (1946), 357–407

'Sonora política', *Revista do Arquivo municipal* (São Paulo, 1946), no.106, pp.7–44

Música popular brasileña (Mexico City, 1947; Port. orig., 1950; It. trans., 1953)

Melodias registradas por meios não-mecânicos (São Paulo, 1948)

Tambor-de-mina e tambor-de-crioulo (São Paulo, 1948)

Xangô (São Paulo, 1948) [record catalogue]

'Bibliografia', *Manual bibliográfico de estudos brasileiros*, ed. R. Borba de Moraes and W. Berrien (Rio de Janeiro, 1949), 299

Catimbó (São Paulo, 1949) [record catalogue]

Babassuê (São Paulo, 1950) [record catalogue]

Catálogo ilustrado do Museu folclórico (São Paulo, 1950)

Discography of Brazilian Folk Music, *International Catalogue of Recorded Music* (London, 1954)

Chegança de Marujos (São Paulo, 1955)

Mario de Andrade: um pouco (Rio de Janeiro, 1974)

Numerous articles in *Revista brasileira de folclore*

EDITIONS

M. de Andrade: *Danças dramáticas do Brasil*, Obras completas de Mario de Andrade, xviii (São Paulo, 1959); *Música de feitiçaria no Brasil*, ibid, xiii (São Paulo, 1963); *Os côcos*, ibid (in preparation); *As melodias do boi e outras peças*, ibid (in preparation)

GERARD BÉHAGUE

Alvares Frouvo, João. *See* FROUVO, JOÃO ÁLVARES.

Álvarez Solar-Quintes, Nicolás (*b* Gijón, Oviedo province, 23 July 1893; *d* Madrid, 9 Aug 1967). Spanish musicologist, folklore specialist and composer. After attending the municipal music schoool at Gijón he took a post in the Archive, Library and Museum Service and qualified as paymaster general of the National Historical Archives and the National Foundation of Historical Archives. For many years he was secretary of the Gijón Philharmonic Society and music and theatre critic of the Gijón newspaper *El comercio*, and a member of the Spanish Institute of Musicology. He published several studies on the history of music at the Spanish court and chapel from Philip II to Charles IV and he left in manuscript an important *Cancionero asturiano*. He also wrote two zarzuelas, five farces, several pieces for piano and numerous Asturian songs which became highly popular, e.g. *El roble*. He also wrote two volumes of poetry (unpublished).

WRITINGS

'Las relaciones de Haydn con la casa de Benavente; nuevos documentos sobre Luigi Boccherini; Manuel García, íntimo', *AnM*, ii (1947), 81

'Nuevas aportaciones a la biografía de Carlos Broschi (Farinelli)', *AnM*, iii (1948), 187

'Documentos sobre la familia de Domenico Scarlatti', *AnM*, iv (1949), 137

'El compositor Francisco Courcelle: nueva documentación para su biografía', *AnM*, vi (1951), 179

'El compositor español José de Nebra († 11-VII-1768): nuevas aportaciones para su biografía', *AnM*, ix (1954), 179

'Músicos de Mariana de Neoburgo y de la Real capilla de Nápoles', *AnM*, xi (1956), 165–94

'Panorama musical desde Felipe III a Carlos II: nuevos documentos sobre ministriles, organistas y Reales capillas flamenca y española de música', *AnM*, xii (1957), 167–200

'Nuevas obras de Sebastián Durón y de Luigi Boccherini, y músicos del Infante Don Luis Antonio de Borbón', *AnM*, xiii (1958), 225–59

'Nuevas facetas de la lírica popular astur', *Boletín del Instituto de estudios asturianos*, xiii (1959), 27; see also 163

'Cantares de trabajo y obreristas en Asturias', *Boletín del Instituto de estudios asturianos*, xiv (1960), 299

'Nuevos documentos sobre ministriles, trompetas, cantorcicos, organistas y capilla real de Felipe II', *Miscelánea en homenaje a Monseñor Higinio Anglés* (Barcelona, 1958–61), 851–88

ed.: *Madrid en el siglo XVI: reales cédulas de Felipe II y adiciones de Felipe III a la escritura fundacional del Monasterio de las Descalzas de Madrid (1556–1601)* (Madrid, 1962)

'La imprenta musical en Madrid en el siglo XVIII', *AnM*, xviii (1963), 161–95

with Y. Gérard: 'La bibliothèque musicale d'un amateur éclairé de Madrid: la Duchesse-Comtesse de Benavente, Duchesse d'Osuna (1752–1834)', *RMFC*, iii (1963), 179

'Contradanzas en el Teatro de los Caños del Peral de Madrid', *AnM*, xx (1965), 75–103

BIBLIOGRAPHY

G. Bourligueux: 'La obra de Don Nicolás Álvarez Solar-Quintes', *Boletín del Instituto de estudios asturianos*, xxi (1967), 256 [with complete list of writings]

GUY BOURLIGUEUX

Alvaro (*fl* 1470–75). Portuguese court musician who may be identifiable with ALVARO AFONSO.

Alvars, Elias Parish. *See* PARISH ALVARS, ELIAS.

Alvary [Achenbach], Max(imilian) (*b* Düsseldorf, 3 May 1856; *d* Grosstabarz, Thuringia, 7 Nov 1898). German tenor. He pursued his singing career over the initial objections of his father, the painter Andreas Achenbach, and studied in Frankfurt with Julius Stockhausen and in Milan with Lamperti. He made his début (1879) in Weimar, under the name of Max Anders, singing the title role of Flotow's *Alessandro Stradella*, and remained at the Weimar Opera until 1885 enjoying the favour of the grand duke. He had great success at the Metropolitan in New York, making his début there on 25 November 1885 singing Don José in German. He was the USA's first Siegfried (in *Siegfried*), his most celebrated role, in 1887; other important roles of his four years at the Metropolitan included Adolar in *Euryanthe* (1887), Loge (1888) and Alvarez in Spontini's *Fernand Cortez* (1888). In 1890 he was engaged by the Munich Hofoper and in 1891 by the Hamburg Stadttheater. He sang Tristan and Tannhäuser at Bayreuth in 1891, and in the following year he made his London début singing Siegfried (in *Siegfried*) at Covent Garden with Mahler conducting. He returned to London in 1893 and 1894 and was heard as Max in *Der Freischütz*, Florestan, Tannhäuser, Lohengrin, Loge, Siegmund and Tristan. In October 1894 he was seriously injured in a fall while rehearsing *Siegfried* at Mannheim and never fully recovered; he retired from the stage in 1897. He was the outstanding Wagnerian tenor of his time for dramatic force and refined interpretation, and the first to break tradition by performing Tristan and the other heroic parts without a beard.

BIBLIOGRAPHY

A. von Mensi-Klarbach: *Alt-Münchner Theater-Erinnerungen* (Munich, 1924), chap. 'Max Alvary'

HAROLD ROSENTHAL

Alva Talledo, Luis Ernesto. *See* ALVA, LUIGI.

Alveri, Giovanni Battista (*b* Bologna, ?1660–70; *d* after 1719). Italian composer and instrumentalist. He was a pupil of G. P. Colonna and is described in his *Cantate a voce sola da camera* op.1 (Bologna, 1687; one ed. H. Riemann: *Ausgewählte Kammer-Kantaten*, Leipzig, [1911]), as a musician in the service of Marquis Guido Rangoni. He also published *Arie italiane amorose e lamentabili* for solo voice and continuo (Antwerp, 1690), and two operas by him (*Il re pastore, overo il Basilio in Arcadia* and *L'Isione*) were performed at the court of Brunswick-Wolfenbüttel in 1691. The libretto of *Il re pastore* describes him as a 'virtuoso' of the duke there and as a member of the Accademia Filarmonica of Bologna. His name appears in a list of instrumentalists who were at Parma Cathedral on 10 August 1719. According to Schmitz his cantatas are mostly fairly conservative in form although not without interesting features. Seven motets by him are in the Staatsbibliothek, Berlin; since his book of 1687 is his op.1, printed volumes of cantatas by him of 1671 and 1678 mentioned by Fétis must be spurious.

BIBLIOGRAPHY

FétisB
E. Schmitz: *Geschichte der weltlichen Solokantate* (Leipzig, 1914, rev. 2/1955)
N. Pelicelli: 'Musicisti in Parma nel secolo XVIII', *NA*, xi (1934), 51
R. Brockpähler: *Handbuch zur Geschichte der Barockoper in Deutschland* (Emsdetten, 1964)
COLIN TIMMS

Alvsleben, Melitta. *See* OTTO, MELITTA.

Alwood [Alwoode, Allwood, Allwoode], **Richard.** English 16th-century composer. At the end of his six-voice Mass '*Praise him praiseworthy*' (ed. in EECM, i, 1963) in the Forrest-Heyther Partbooks (*GB-Ob* Mus. Sch.E.376–81), John Baldwin, who copied the last pages of 381, described him as 'Mr. Alwood, priest'. Alwood's In Nomine in the Mulliner Book (ed. in MB, i, 1951, rev. 2/1954) is based on the same five-note cantus firmus as the mass, and is related to the 'In nomine' of its Sanctus. The Mulliner Book contains four other keyboard pieces by Alwood: a voluntary, two settings of *Clara paschali gaudio* and an untitled piece; two more keyboard In Nomines are in *Lbm* Add.30485. Four of these pieces are edited by M. Glyn, *Early English Organ Music* (London, 1939).

JOHN BERGSAGEL

Alwyn, Kenneth [Wetherell, Kenneth Alwyn] (*b* Croydon, 28 July 1925). English conductor. He gained the Manns Prize for conducting at the RAM and made his début with Sadler's Wells Theatre Ballet in 1952. After four years with that company he joined the Royal Ballet as associate conductor, 1957–61, taking part in their tours of North America and the Far East, where he also gave concerts. A close association with Western Theatre Ballet from 1961 included his appointment as musical director (1967–9) and a number of first performances. He has worked frequently in the commercial theatre and for radio and television, and became a staff conductor of the BBC Concert Orchestra in 1968 and principal conductor of the BBC Northern Ireland Orchestra in 1969.

NOËL GOODWIN

Alwyn, William (*b* Northampton, 7 Nov 1905). English composer, flautist and teacher; also painter and writer. He was educated at Northampton Grammar School, where he showed outstanding promise in both music and painting, and at the RAM (1920–23), of which he later became a Fellow. He has written warmly of his professor of composition, John B. McEwen, from whom he 'learned much about music and philosophy . . . but little about the technique of composition'; he also studied the flute (Ross Scholarship) with Daniel Wood and the piano with Cuthbert Whitemore. However, composition was already his principal interest and for this he was awarded the Sir Michael Costa Scholarship. On the sudden death of his father, Alwyn had to leave the RAM at the age of 18 and start earning his living. For a year he taught in a preparatory school, then played the flute in various theatre orchestras, and in 1926 returned to the RAM to teach composition. He was himself composing vigorously and in 1927 his Five Preludes for orchestra were introduced at a promenade concert by Wood. Two other early landmarks are the Piano Concerto (1930) and a large-scale oratorio to words by Blake, *The Marriage of Heaven and Hell* (1936), on the strength of which Alwyn was awarded the Collard Fellowship (1938–41) in succession to Lambert. In 1939, however, he made a severe re-appraisal of his position: 'I realized that my technique was not to be matched with my great contemporaries, and from then on technical perfection and virtuosity became my main concern'; and he came to consider all his music written before the Flute Divertimento best forgotten.

Alwyn's emphasis on precise workmanship is reflected in all his work, of which the five symphonies, three concerti grossi and other orchestral pieces form the backbone. By nature both an aesthete and an artisan, he thinks deeply about artistic experience – as in the extended essay-poem *Daphne, or the Pursuit of Beauty* (1972) – but is wary of an undue intellectualism in the creative process, particularly when he feels the intellect proceeds in defiance of intelligibility. That he is also concerned with self-renewal is evidenced at each stage in his development. In the 1940s his orientation was broadly neo-classical; a more romantic phase followed, culminating in *Lyra angelica* (1954) and *Autumn Legend* (1955), after which he felt the need to subject his imagination to a new discipline – and a new stimulus. In the Symphony no.3 (1955–6) and in several subsequent works up to and including the String Trio (1962), Alwyn used his own, tonal form of 12-note technique. Although comparable with Schoenberg's method, this was in fact suggested by Indian music: 'A salutary experience', he has written, 'which did nothing but good to my outlook, but I am never content to remain static, and always look for new means of expression while remaining faithful to the artistic "credo" I have expressed in *Daphne*'.

Alwyn's independence is not aggressive, nor is his eclecticism brash or superficial. In the very accomplished String Quartet in D minor (1955) one may sense affinities with Schubert, Ravel, late Beethoven, Dvořák and Walton – in that order, more or less – but the music's purpose is never in doubt. This same aptness is evident in his film music, which includes some of the finest. He wrote his first film score in 1936, became fascinated by 'the rhythmic relationship and interplay of the *spoken* word and music' and learnt a lot about orchestral technique. Of his more than 60 film scores, perhaps the most important are those for *Odd Man Out*, *The Fallen Idol* and the wartime documentaries *Desert Victory*, *Fires were Started* and *World of Plenty*. In 1958 he was made a Fellow of the British Film

Academy. He has also done distinguished work for radio, particularly in collaboration with MacNeice.

In 1955 Alwyn gave up his teaching at the RAM and in 1961 retired to Suffolk to be free to compose when and what he wished. A founder-member of the Composers' Guild of Great Britain, he has three times been its chairman (1949, 1950 and 1954). Intermittently he has felt the need to paint and to write: of special interest is the journal, *Ariel to Miranda*, written while the Symphony no.3 was in progress. A gifted linguist, he is also a connoisseur of painting and at one time possessed an important collection of Pre-Raphaelites. He was made a CBE in 1978.

WORKS
(selective list)

Orch: Conc. grosso no.1, B♭, small orch, 1942; Conc., ob, harp, str, 1944; Scottish Dances, small orch, 1946; Fanfare for a Joyful Occasion, 1948; Sym. no.1, 1949; Conc. grosso no.2, str, 1950; Festival March, 1951; The Magic Island, sym. prelude, 1952; Sym. no.2, 1953; Lyra angelica, harp, str, 1954; Autumn Legend, eng hn, str, 1955; Sym. no.3, 1955–6; Elizabethan Dances, 1957; Sym. no.4, 1959; Derby Day, ov., 1960; Conc. grosso no.3, 1964; Sinfonietta, str, 1970; Sym. no.5 'Hydriotaphia', 1972–3; Sinfonietta, str, 1976

Inst: Divertimento, fl, 1939; Sonata alla toccata, pf, 1942; Str Qt, d, 1955; Fantasy-Waltzes, pf, 1955; Crépuscule, harp, 1955; 12 Preludes, pf, 1957; Str Trio, 1962; Movements, pf, 1963; Sonata, cl, pf, 1963; Moto perpetuo, recs, 1970; Naiades, fantasy-sonata, fl, harp, 1971; Str Qt no.2 'Spring Waters', 1976

Vocal: Slum Song (MacNeice), 1v, pf, 1947; Mirages (song cycle, Alwyn), Bar, pf, 1970; The Libertine (opera, Alwyn), 1965–71; Nocturnes (song cycle, M. Armstrong), 1v, pf, 1973

Principal publishers: Boosey & Hawkes, Lengnick, Oxford University Press

WRITINGS

'Ariel to Miranda', *Adam International Review* (1967), nos.316–18, pp.4–84
An Anthology of Twentieth Century French Poetry (London, 1969) [poems trans. by Alwyn]
Winter in Copenhagen and *Mirages* (Southwold, 1971)
Daphne, or the Pursuit of Beauty (Southwold, 1972)

BIBLIOGRAPHY

H. Keller: 'Film Music: Speech Rhythm', *MT*, xcvi (1955), 486
T. Hold: 'The Music of William Alwyn', *Composer* (1972), no.43, p.22; no.44, p.15

HUGH OTTAWAY

Alyabyev, Alexander Alexandrovich (*b* Tobolsk, Western Siberia, 15 Aug 1787; *d* Moscow, 6 March 1851). Russian composer. Alyabyev's father, the governor of Tobolsk, was a pioneer of local culture; his brother, Vasily, was a poet and playwright. At 14 Alyabyev entered government service and in 1812 enlisted with the army; during the war he participated in the army's entry into Dresden and Paris. He was discharged from the army in 1823.

Alyabyev displayed considerable musical talent at an early age. His first important composition was his String Quartet in E flat major (1815), which shows a gift for instrumental part-writing and melody as well as an effective use of mild chromatic harmonies. It was the first of many chamber works which included two more string quartets, a trio in A minor for piano, violin and cello, a wind quintet in C minor and several unfinished ensemble pieces. Early in the 1820s Alyabyev started to compose for the stage. His comic opera *Lunnaya noch', ili Domovīye* ('The Moonlit Night, or The House Spirits'), with a libretto by P. A. Mukhanov and P. N. Arapov, was produced in 1822, a few months after his vaudeville *Novaya shalost', ili Teatral'noye srazheniye* ('A New Prank, or The Theatrical Battle'), composed in collaboration with Verstovsky and Maurer to Nikolay

Khmelnitsky's text. *Derevensky filosof* ('The Village Philosopher'), his most popular vaudeville, followed the next year. It was at the same time that he wrote his famous song *Solovey* ('The Nightingale') to words by Anton Delvig. Several prima donnas, including Pauline Viardot, Adelina Patti and Marcella Sembrich, incorporated this song into the singing lesson scene in Act 2 of Rossini's *Il barbiere di Siviglia*; it was later also transcribed for piano by Liszt. Alyabyev composed about 170 songs to texts chosen widely from the literary and poetical works of his contemporaries, including Pushkin, Zhukovsky, Lermontov and Ogaryov.

In a card game on 24 February, 1825, Alyabyev allegedly struck one of his guests and the man died some days later. Alyabyev was imprisoned, and, after legal proceedings lasting nearly three years, was found guilty of murder and exiled to his native town in 1828. The evidence was inconclusive, so Tsar Nicholas I was presumably anxious for Alyabyev to be away from the capital for another reason, possibly his connection with the Decembrist movement. Alyabyev continued to compose vaudevilles in prison and during his exile contributed much to local musical life, conducting and organizing concerts. His compositions of this period include a symphony in E minor, inscribed 'Tobolsk, 1830; 30th October', of which only the first movement survives.

In 1831 he was allowed to travel from Tobolsk to the Caucasus to cure an eye complaint. Here he met the Decembrist poet Alexander Bestuzhev-Marlinsky, author of the story on which Alyabyev's opera *Ammalat-bek* was based. While in the south Alyabyev became interested in folk music and in 1834 published a collection devoted entirely to Ukrainian melodies. On medical advice he moved north to Orenburg and arrived in Moscow in 1836, remaining there, with only brief trips away, until his death.

The years in Moscow were successful both professionally and privately: he became established as a composer, particularly of stage music, and in 1840 married Ekaterina Alexandrovna Ofrosimova (née Rimsky-Korsakov). Shortly after his arrival in Moscow he produced incidental music to three plays, his brother Vasily's *Otstupnik, ili Osada Korinfa* ('The Apostate, or The Siege of Corinth') in 1837, Shakespeare's *The Merry Wives of Windsor* and Pushkin's *Rusalka* ('The Water-Nymph'), both in 1838. He also wrote two Shakespearean operas in the 1830s: *Burya* ('The Tempest'), and *Volshebnaya noch'* ('The Enchanted Night'), composed in 1838–9 and based on *A Midsummer Night's Dream*. Alyabyev continued to compose in spite of ill-health, working on the opera *Ribak i rusalka, ili Zloye zel'ye* ('The Fisherman and the Water-Nymph, or The Evil Potion') between 1841 and 1843 and on his last opera, *Ammalat-bek*, from 1842 to 1847.

WORKS
(for a fuller list see Dobrokhotov, 1966)
STAGE

Lunnaya noch', ili Domovīye [The Moonlit Night, or The House Spirits] (Opera, 2, P. A. Mukhanov, P. N. Arapov), 1821–2
Volshebnīy baraban, ili Sledstvīye Volshebnoy fleytï [The Magic Drum, or A Sequel to the Magic Flute] (ballet, 2, F. Bernardelli), 1827
Redkaya naslednitsa, ili Muzh po zaveshchaniyu [The Unusual Heiress, or The Inherited Husband] (incidental music, A. M. Redkin), 1827
Burya [The Tempest] (opera, 3, after Shakespeare), c1835
Otstupnik, ili Osada Korinfa [The Apostate, or The Siege of Corinth] (incidental music, V. A. Alyabyev), 1837
Rusalka [The Water-Nymph] (incidental music, Pushkin), 1838

Vindzorskiye kumushki [The Merry Wives of Windsor] (incidental music, Shakespeare), 1838

Volshebnaya noch' [The Enchanted Night] (opera, 3, A. F. Weltman, after Shakespeare: A Midsummer Night's Dream), 1838–9

Rïbak i rusalka, ili Zloye zel' ye [The Fisherman and the Water-Nymph, or The Evil Potion] (opera, 3), 1841–3, orch interlude (Moscow, 1965)

Ammalet-Bek (opera, 5, A. F. Weltman, after A. A. Bestuzhev-Marlinsky), 1842–7

Edwin i Oscar (opera, 4), sketch only

Music for 19 vaudevilles, many in collaboration with Verstovsky and Scholz; a 'melodrama' to the second part of Pushkin's poem, Kavkazsky plennik (The Prisoner of the Caucasus), 1828; 'dramatic incident' Bezumnaya [The Reckless Girl] (1 act, I. I. Kozlov), 1841; Prospero's aria, Burya [The Tempest] (play, A. A. Shakhovskoy), 1827

OTHER WORKS

3 str qts: E♭, 1815 (Moscow, 1952); G, 1825 (Moscow and Leningrad, 1950); g, 1842, unfinished

Wind Qnt, c, unfinished (Moscow, 1953); Pf Qnt, E♭ (Moscow, 1954); Nocturne, C, hn, 2 vn, va, vc, pf; Pf Trio, a (Moscow, 1950)

Pf Sonata, A♭ in *Russkaya fortepiannaya muzïka s kontsa XVIII do 60-kh gg., XIX veka*, ii (Moscow, 1956), ed. V. A. Natanson and A. A. Nikolayev; Vn Sonata, e

Also sketches for another str qt, an unfinished fl qt; and various sketches and scores for other ensembles

4 symphonies, no.1, G, c1815; no.2, E♭, c1815; no.3, e (1 movement), 1830 (Moscow, 1955); no.4, 1850

11 overtures, and many dances, marches (wind band/sym orch)

Several pieces for solo inst and orch, choral works, c170 songs

Principal publisher: Soviet State Publishing House

Principal MS collection: *USSR-Mcm*

EDITIONS

Golosa ukrainskikh pesen [Ukrainian songs] (Moscow, 1834)

BIBLIOGRAPHY

G. A. Timofeyev: *A. A. Alyabyev: ocherk zhizni i tvorchestva* [Alyabyev: life and works] (Moscow, 1912)

S. S. Popov: 'A. A. Alyabyev: biograficheskv ocherk', *SovM* (1937), no.5, p.71

B. V. Dobrokhotov: 'Alexander Alexandrovich Alyabyev', *SovM* (1951), no.4, p.69

A. Ilyin: 'Alyabyev v Sïbiri', *SovM* (1952), no.8, p.67

B. S. Shteynpress: *A. A. Alyabyev v izgnanii* [Alyabyev in exile] (Moscow, 1959)

B. V. Dobrokhotov: *Alexander Alyabyev* (Moscow, 1966)

GEOFFREY NORRIS

Alyff. See AYLIFF.

Alypius. Greek ?3rd-century writer on music. He was the author of an introduction to music (*Eisagōgē mousikē*), which provides the fullest and most authoritative account extant of ancient Greek musical notation. Recent scholarship has suggested that he was active in the 3rd or 4th century, and the earlier of these two datings is more likely to be correct. The essay portion of his introduction consists of four brief paragraphs. He began by naming harmonics, rhythmics and metrics as the essential ·sciences which constitute music. Harmonics he regarded as the basic division of these three: he first defined it, employing the terms used by Claudius Ptolemy in the 2nd century, and then proposed to divide it into 'the so-called *tonoi* and *tropoi*, 15 in number'. This undertaking occupies the entire remainder of his treatise.

Alypius's *tonoi* or transposition-scales bear the names of the old individual modes (*harmoniai*) which had fallen into disuse many centuries earlier: Lydian, Aeolian, Phrygian, Iastian and Dorian. With each of these five basic scales the corresponding 'hypo-' and 'hyper-' form is given as well. The resulting 15 *tonoi* consist of double octaves in regular tetrachordal sequences, with the provision for añ alternative tetrachord (*synēmmenōn*). Spaced a semitone apart, they cover a range of three octaves and a whole tone; indications of pitch are entirely relative. The scale movement

is ascending, a clear indication that the treatise reflects the practice of the Roman Imperial period.

For each of the 15 scales Alypius gave the names of the notes from the lowest (proslambanomenos) to the highest (nētē hyperbolaiōn), with a description and a presentation of the letters or signs which designated each in the notation. This was a double task, and he clearly distinguished between the two notational sequences thus presented. The question of whether they actually were different, however, continues to be raised; at any rate there is a great difference in appearance. The older form, called 'instrumental' by Alypius, is made up of a mixture of Greek letters and archaic signs, some of which may be based on Oriental prototypes. In this notation the same letter or sign very often reappears in two altered forms, one turned on its side and the other presented as in a mirror image. These represent respectively the sharp and double-sharp form (so to speak) of the basic note, raised by successive quarter-tone intervals. All basic notes are invariably given in the diatonic genus, although the listing of the 15 scales is continued through the chromatic and enharmonic as well. (The manuscript does not include all of these.) The other notation, described by Alypius as 'vocal', is much simpler; it consists chiefly of unaltered forms of the Ionic alphabet, officially established in Athens at the close of the 5th century BC. It has, in addition, some admixture of altered letter forms together with signs. Both notations employ wholesale repetition, with individuating marks. The two systems are shown in ex.1 in Isobel Henderson's presentation.

Ex. 1

The instrumental system is given at the bottom of the diagram; row no.1 represents the diatonic sequence of notes. In the vocal system this order is reversed, so that the diatonic is found in row no.3. The remaining two rows in both systems uniformly designate the sharp or double-sharp quarter-tone relationship to the diatonic notes. It seems probable that the triads of identically shaped but differently placed signs, predominant in the older notation, were originally meant to express the varied positions of the inner notes of the chromatic or enharmonic tetrachord. The tables of Alypius, however, make no distinction between these two genera except in the Lydian; there diagonal strokes have been added to the signs for the chromatic form of the *tonos*. It is noticeable that the placing of the letters of the Ionic alphabet coincides roughly with the range of the Dorian transposition-scale. The central place of the Dorian in Alypius's scheme was demonstrated at the beginning of the present century by Samoïloff, who worked out a theory whereby a template indicated the position of each scale on a basic grid of notes. Curt Sachs argued that the instrumental notation originally represented patterns of fingering and was based upon a pentatonic tuning of the lyre; his claims have not won general acceptance.

Recent scholars, most notably Henderson, have pointed out and sought to explain much that is irregular in the Alypian notational systems; these are unquestionably attended by difficulties. In relating signs to values they display a number of inconsistencies, they appear to have been expanded somewhat arbitrarily from an original range of about two octaves, their vocal and instrumental forms are interchanged confusingly in some papyrus fragments, and although the predominant genus is diatonic, they are built upon the quarter-tone intervals of the enharmonic tetrachord. It must nevertheless be recognized that many of the signs listed by Alypius actually occur in fragments of Greek music as early as the 3rd century BC. Whatever the elements of difficulty and possible artificiality, he has given the most nearly complete description of ancient Greek musical notation which has survived from late antiquity; other, more fragmentary sources of such information only corroborate the essential value of his presentation.

BIBLIOGRAPHY

K. von Jan, ed.: *Musici scriptores graeci* (Leipzig, 1895–9/R1962), 357–406
C. Sachs: 'Die griechische Instrumentalnotenschrift', *ZMw*, vi (1923–4), 289
——: 'Die griechische Gesangsnotenschrift', *ZMw*, vii (1924–5), 1
A. Samoïloff: 'Die Alypiusschen Reihen der altgriechischen Tonbezeichnungen', *AMw*, vi (1924), 383 and pl.1–6
R. P. Winnington-Ingram: 'The Pentatonic Tuning of the Greek Lyre', *Classical Quarterly*, new ser., vi (1956), 173
I. Henderson: 'Ancient Greek Music: the Notations', *NOHM*, i (1957), 358
J. M. Barbour: 'The Principles of Greek Notation', *JAMS*, xiii (1960), 1
E. Pöhlmann: *Griechische Musikfragmente* (Nuremberg, 1960), 5ff
A. Bataille: 'Remarques sur les deux notations mélodiques de l'ancienne musique grecque', *Recherches de papyrologie*, i (1961), 5
J. Chailley: 'Nouvelles remarques sur les deux notations musicales grecques', *Recherches de papyrologie*, iv (1967), 201
J. F. Mountford and R. P. Winnington-Ingram: 'Music', §11, *Oxford Classical Dictionary* (Oxford, 2/1970), 711
E. Pöhlmann, ed.: *Denkmäler altgriechischen Musik* (Nuremberg, 1970), 142ff
WARREN ANDERSON

Alzedo, José Bernardo. *See* ALCEDO, JOSÉ BERNARDO.

Amabile (It.: 'charming', 'gracious'). A performance direction found particularly in the later 18th century and mentioned, for instance, in Koch's *Musikalisches Lexikon* (1802). Beethoven used *con amabilità* ('with charm') as an expression mark at the opening of his op.110 Piano Sonata.

For bibliography *see* TEMPO AND EXPRESSION MARKS.
DAVID FALLOWS

Amabilità, con (It.). *See* AMABILE.

Amadei, Filippo (*fl* 1690–1730). Italian cellist and composer. He has been variously called 'Sigr Pippo' or 'Pipo' (in English documents of the years 1719–21), 'Filippo Mattei' (in Mattheson's *Critica musica*, 1722–3), and 'Pippo Amadio' (in Gerber's *Lexikon* of 1812). He first appeared as an instrumentalist in concerts and religious functions given in Rome under the patronage of Cardinal Pietro Ottoboni between 1690 and 1696. Among his early compositions was the oratorio *Amans delusus* sung in the Roman church of S Marcello on the Friday before Palm Sunday 1699. At the beginning of the 18th century he participated in the cello class of the Società del Centesimo created within the Congregation of S Cecilia, and there is also mention of him as a trumpeter among the musicians of the Campidoglio. Evidence of his activity as composer at this time comes from volume i of Crescimbeni's *Comentarj dell'istoria della volgar poesia* (Rome, 1702) in which he is referred to as a composer of cantatas in the employ of Cardinal Ottoboni. In 1708 his oratorio *L'Abele* was performed in the cardinal's palace in Rome and in 1711 another oratorio, *Santa Cassilda*, was sung at the Chiesa Nuova. *Teodosio il giovane*, his first known opera, was given in the cardinal's palace in 1711 with sets designed by Filippo Juvarra.

For the next seven years nothing is known of his movements, but by early 1719 he was in London where, as Sigr Pippo, he gave several concerts, some of them together with the violinist Giovanni Carbonelli. In 1720 he was a member of the orchestra of the newly founded Royal Academy of Music of which Handel was a musical director. He also served the academy as composer, adding 14 arias to Orlandini's opera *Amore e maestà* which the academy produced under the title of *Arsace* on 1 February 1721. The next academy production (15 April 1721) was *Muzio Scevola*, Act 1 of which was composed by Amadei, Act 2 by G. Bononcini and Act 3 by Handel. Amadei was still in London in 1723, when his name appeared among subscribers to an Italian grammar published by Angelo Maria Cori. But his next moves are uncertain. According to H. J. Marx he returned to Rome to serve Cardinal Ottoboni until 1729. The date and place of his death have not been ascertained.

Little of his music survives. His Act 1 to *Muzio Scevola* and a solo cantata *Il pensiero* (1709; words by Ottoboni) are in the British Museum; other surviving cantatas include *Ove fuggi* (*GB-T*) and *Pastorella sventurata* (*GB-Cfm*).

BIBLIOGRAPHY

C. Petrucci: 'Amadei, Filippo', *DBI*
H. J. Marx: 'Die Musik am Hofe Pietro Kardinal Ottobonis unter Arcangelo Corelli', *AnMc*, v (1968), 104–77
MICHAEL F. ROBINSON

Amadei, Michelangelo (*fl* 1614–15). Italian composer. The title-pages of the two collections of *Motecta* (Venice, 1614–15) do not indicate whether he held a post; as they were printed in Venice he may have worked in northern Italy. They contain motets for one to six voices with organ continuo; it can thus be seen that he adopted the up-to-date concertato style and was also interested in the modern art of the solo motet.
JEROME ROCHE

Amadeus Quartet. English string quartet. It was founded in London in 1947. The members are Norbert Brainin (*b* Vienna, 12 March 1923), Siegmund Nissel (*b* Vienna, 3 Jan 1922), (Hans) Peter Schidlof (*b* Vienna, 9 July 1922) and Martin Lovett (*b* London, 3 March 1927). Its three upper players came to England in 1938–9 and were pupils of Max Rostal in the 1940s. Brainin had earlier studied under Riccardo Odnoposoff and Rosa Hochmann, and briefly in London under Carl Flesch. Lovett had studied under his father and at the RCM (1942–5) under Ivor James; in 1950 he married the violinist Suzanne Rozsa. Schidlof had been a violinist and took up the viola to make the quartet possible. They made a highly successful début at the Wigmore Hall, London, on 10 January 1948, and quickly became established as the leading quartet in Britain. Tours in Europe soon followed, as did appearances at most leading festivals (Edinburgh, Holland, Salzburg etc) and performances in the USA, Canada, South America, Australasia and Japan; in the 1960s and 1970s the quartet toured regularly, in the

Amadeus Quartet: (from left to right) Norbert Brainin, Siegmund Nissel, Peter Schidlof and Martin Lovett

USA and Germany in particular. In 1966–8 they served as resident quartet at the University of York, where in 1968 all the members were awarded honorary doctorates of music. Their other honours include the OBE (1970), the Gross Verdienstkreuz of the German Federal Republic (1973) and the Ehrenkreuz für Kunst und Wissenschaft of Austria (1974). Their performances, in London and in Germany particularly, regularly include complete Beethoven cycles as well as series of Mozart and Schubert. Their repertory is not large, but as well as the standard Classical and Romantic repertory they perform quartets by Bartók, Britten, Tippett and other 20th-century composers. Brainin and Schidlof each appear occasionally as soloists in concertos and have often performed Mozart's Sinfonia concertante K364/320d. All four play early Italian instruments: Brainin a Guarneri del Gesù dated 1734 (once owned by Pierre Rode; he also has the use of the 'Chaconne' Stradivari of 1725), Nissel a Stradivari of 1731, Schidlof a Stradivari of 1701 (the 'Macdonald') and Lovett a Stradivari of 1725 (the 'Vaslin' or 'La belle blonde').

Recognized as probably the leading quartet in Europe, and among the most admired in the world, the Amadeus Quartet's reputation is based, first, on their outstandingly secure and homogeneous technique, with an exceptional command of ensemble, chording and texture, and second on their sensitive and polished interpretative style. They have occasionally been criticized for a manner too sophisticated and too concerned with expressive nicety to be appropriate to certain music, notably that of Haydn or Beethoven; the silky quality of their tone and their use of portamento have also met with adverse comment in certain repertories. But their natural and responsive musicianship, their ability to inflect detail expressively without damage to the music's broader continuity (especially a virtue in their Schubert interpretations), the consistent beauty of their tone and phrasing and their delicate treatment of line and figuration ensure the high and individual quality of their performances. Their grasp of subtle emotional nuance gives them few rivals among interpreters of Mozart. They have made many gramophone records, mainly of Haydn, Mozart and Schubert in their early years, more recently also of Beethoven and Brahms. They have often given works for larger ensembles, usually with Cecil Aronowitz (viola) or William Pleeth (cello), and have played with several distinguished pianists, including Clifford Curzon.

STANLEY SADIE

Amadino, Ricciardo (*fl* Venice, 1572–1621). Italian printer. In February 1572 he witnessed a codicil to the will of Girolamo Scotto. The fact that the will states he was a printer, rather than a bookseller, suggests that he may have worked in Scotto's shop in Venice at the time. In 1583–6 in Venice he printed jointly with GIACOMO VINCENTI more than 76 music books. A few were reprints of popular volumes by Arcadelt, Lassus, Marenzio, Palestrina, and Bernardino Lupacchino and Gioan Maria Tasso, but most were first editions of the works of some 33 composers, of whom the best known are Asola, Bassano, Caimo, Giuseppe Guami, Marenzio, Stivori and Virchi, as well as anthologies. For their printer's mark Vincenti & Amadino used a woodcut of a pine cone, with the motto 'Aeque bonum atque tutum'. When they began to print separately (from 1586) Vincenti kept the pine-cone symbol, while

Amadino adopted a woodcut of an organ, with the motto 'Magis corde quam organo'. The dissolution of the partnership must have been amicable, for afterwards they seem to have shared type and ornamental pieces, and some of their editions have mistakes in common. Moreover, they jointly signed several theological and philosophical books between 1600 and 1609.

Working alone from 1586, Amadino printed vocal and instrumental music in such quantity as to assure him a position among Venice's four leading music printers. His preferred composers were Gastoldi, Banchieri, Monteverdi, Agazzari and Asola; the last, who is mentioned in one of the few dedications signed by Amadino, was doubtless a personal friend. Amadino also printed several theoretical volumes, including the first edition of Bottrigari's *Il desiderio* (1594). Non-musical publications by him are rare; they include two tragedies, *La Eutheria* (1588) and *Cratasiclea* (1591), both by Paolo Bozzi, who was also one of Amadino's composers.

The opening of Orpheus's 'Possente spirto' from Act 3 of Monteverdi's 'Orfeo': the Amadino edition of 1615

Amadino printed several folio editions and a few octavo, but otherwise virtually his whole production was in high quarto format (collated apparently in half-sheets). This reflected the current trend, and indeed his whole musical production mirrors the shifting musical tastes of the time; he printed canzonettas and works for *cori spezzati* as they grew in popularity, along with *falsibordoni*, accompanied solos and duets (including those by Gastoldi, d'India and Rubini), dramatic music (e.g. Monteverdi's *Orfeo* and Domenico Belli's *Orfeo dolente*) and all types of concertato music. Many of his publications were commissioned, either by the composers or by other printer–booksellers, such as Tozzi in Padua, Bozzola in Brescia or Pietro Tini in Milan. But Amadino's own preferences must account for his persistent loyalty to certain composers, such as Asola. After 1617 he printed only one surviving work, appropriately a reprint of Asola's *Officium psalmi et missa defunctorum* (1621). He deserves a place in the front rank of Italian music printers of his time for the sheer volume of his output and for his many first editions and reprints of leading composers' works.

BIBLIOGRAPHY

EitnerQ

C. Sartori: *Dizionario degli editori musicali italiani* (Florence, 1958)

——: 'La famiglia degli editori Scotto', *AcM*, xxxvi (1964), 19

L. G. Clubb: *Italian Plays (1500–1700) in the Folger Library* (Florence, 1968), nos. 186f

O. Mischiati: 'Adriano Banchieri (1568–†1634): profilo biografico e bibliografia dell'opere', *Annuario 1965–70 del Conservatorio G. B. Martini di Bologna*, i (1971), 38–201

THOMAS W. BRIDGES

Amadio, Neville (*b* Sydney, 5 Feb 1912). Australian flautist. A member of a family of well-known musicians, and brother of the clarinettist Clive Amadio, he was trained at the New South Wales State Conservatorium of Music (where he later taught, 1951–61). When only 14 he became principal flautist in the original Sydney SO, then known as Sydney's 2FC Broadcasting Orchestra, and his continued presence helped its woodwind section to achieve a cohesion and brilliance noted by many visiting conductors. He has frequently performed as a concert soloist elsewhere in Australia, and has appeared as associate artist with visiting singers, including Elisabeth Schwarzkopf, Lisa Perli (Dora Labbette), Erna Berger, Rita Streich and Mattiwilda Dobbs. During the visit of the Sydney SO to the Commonwealth Arts Festival in 1965, Amadio gave solo performances in Glasgow, Birmingham and at the Festival Hall, London, as well as in Tokyo.

Amadio has also been prominent in chamber music. He has appeared regularly with Musica Viva Australia since its formation in 1945, and was also a founder-member of both Collegium Musicum, a society formed for giving first performances in Australia, and, with his brother, of Sinfonia da Camera. In 1965 Amadio and other leading players of the Sydney SO formed the New Sydney Woodwind Quintet which has given many concerts in Australia and Asia and has made recordings.

ANN CARR-BOYD

Amadio, Pippo. *See* AMADEI, FILIPPO.

Amadis, Pietro. Pseudonym of MICHAEL ZADORA.

Amadori, Giuseppe (*b* c1670; *d* after 1730). Italian composer; not to be confused with Giovanni Tedeschi, 'detto Amadori' (*d* c1780). Giuseppe Amadori was active in Rome between 1690 and 1709. In 1690 he was in the service of Cardinal Pietro Ottoboni as organist and harpsichordist. His oratorio *Il martirio di S Adriano* was performed in 1702, and in 1707 and 1709 he was active in the Accademie del Disegno. An autograph *Pange lingua* for soprano and continuo and an aria with instrumental accompaniment are in the St Sulpitiuskerk, Diest (according to Eitner); two manuscript arias for soprano and continuo are in the Schlosskirche at Sondershausen and the Giuseppe Verdi Conservatory, Milan. Instrumental movements by him are included in two anthologies published in London, *A second Collection of Toccatas, Vollentarys and Fugues* (1719) and *The Lady's Entertainment* (1708). According to Arteaga, Amadori was highly regarded as a singing teacher; the possibility that Arteaga confused him with Giovanni Amadori cannot be excluded.

BIBLIOGRAPHY

EitnerQ

E. de Arteaga: *Le rivoluzioni del teatro musicale italiano dalle sue origini fino al presente* (Bologna, 1783–5)

HANS JOACHIM MARX

Amalar [Amalherus, Amalarius of Metz or Trier, Amalarius Fortunatus, Symphosius Amalarius] (*b* 'Belgic Gaul', *c*775; *d* ?Metz, *c*850). Writer on plainchant and liturgy, but probably not a monk, although he may have been educated at the monastery of St Martin at Tours during Alcuin's abbacy. Possibly he was Archbishop of Trier between 809 and 814. In 813 Amalar travelled to Constantinople at the behest of Charlemagne, returning the next year, perhaps visiting Rome. He then began his literary activity, probably at Aachen. The first edition of his longest, most widely known and most significant work, the *Liber officialis*, appeared *c*823 and in a second edition *c*830. In 831 Amalar travelled to Rome and on his return stayed at the monastery of Corbie, where he compiled an antiphoner. His extensive commentary on its contents and organization, the *Liber de ordine antiphonarii*, was not completed until at least ten years later. Meanwhile, Amalar had been made administrator of the diocese of Lyons in 835, only to be removed after four years, probably because of his condemnation for heresy by the Council of Quierzy in 838. He is thought to have spent the remaining years of his life at Metz, completing the commentary on the antiphoner, as well as one (now lost) on the gradual.

Amalar's *Liber officialis* is of interest to the historian of plainchant, as is the *Liber de ordine antiphonarii*, which, like much of his work, is replete with comparisons between Frankish and Roman church music, and which contains much on the role of the church singer. In general, many comparisons may be made between Amalar and such writers on music as Aurelian of Réôme and Berno of Reichenau. Nevertheless, Amalar restricted his subject matter almost entirely to repertory, form and ritual, and he used neither musical notation nor the technical musical vocabulary which was developed in the following two or three generations (the latter would in any event have been out of place in a treatment of the liturgy). It is therefore difficult to relate his writings to later sources.

Amalar's lost antiphoner can be partly reconstructed from his other writings and does not appear to have differed greatly from other early sources, when one takes into account the usual variability of Office chants. In one respect, however, it must have been unusual: it often presents two versions of a chant, one Roman and the other Gallican (in many cases perhaps from the Metz use), leaving the choice to the singer. The modern edition of Amalar's liturgical works is exemplary in all respects save perhaps one: the very extensive and indispensable editorial commentary is in Latin.

BIBLIOGRAPHY

J. M. Hanssens, ed.: *Amalarii episcopi opera liturgica omnia*, Studi e testi, cxxxviii–cxl (Rome, 1948–50)

LAWRENCE GUSHEE

Amalia Catharina, Countess of Erbach (*b* Arolsen, 8 Aug 1640; *d* Cuylenburg [now Culemborg], 4 Jan 1697). German poet and composer. She was the daughter of Count Philipp Theodor von Waldeck; her mother was born Countess of Nassau. She appears to have spent her youth at Arolsen, the seat of the Waldeck family. In 1664 she married Count Georg Ludwig von Erbach, and then settled at Michelstadt, near Erbach, Odenwald. She was typical of the numerous princesses of the years around 1700 who inclined to Pietism and gave expression to it in verse. She published *Andächtige Sing-Lust, das ist i. Morgen-, ii. Abend-, iii. Tage-, iv. Beth-, v. Buss-, vi. Klag- und Trost-, vii. Lob- und Dank-, viii. Lehrlieder* (Hildburghausen, 1692). The place of publication is explained by its being the residence of one of her sisters, who was the wife of the Duke Ernst of Saxe-Hildburghausen and to whom she dedicated her book. It is therefore possible that it was written under Middle German influence. Moreover, the Princesses of Reuss and Schwarzburg, who lived nearby, were ardent disciples of Pietism. Amalia Catharina's publication is a collection of songs for household devotion. It contains 67 poems, some of which are provided with melodies with figured bass. This music (which is not given by Zahn) is certainly by Amalia Catharina herself and is an important contribution to the development of the German sacred continuo song.

BIBLIOGRAPHY

G. Simon: *Die Geschichte der Dynasten und Grafen zu Erbach und ihres Landes* (Frankfurt am Main, 1858)

J. Zahn: *Die Melodien der deutschen evangelischen Kirchenlieder*, vi (Gütersloh, 1893/R1963)

WALTER BLANKENBURG

Amance, Paul d'. *See* DAMANCE, PAUL.

Amara [Armaganian], **Lucine** (*b* Hartford, Conn., 1 March 1927). American soprano of Armenian descent. She studied with Stella Eisner-Eyn in San Francisco, where she sang in the opera chorus from 1945 to 1946, when she made her concert début at the San Francisco Memorial Auditorium. In 1948 she won a contest leading to an appearance at the Hollywood Bowl. At the Metropolitan she made her début (in November 1950) as the Heavenly Voice in *Don Carlos*. By her 25th anniversary performance there, in November 1975, as Micaela, she had taken 41 roles, both lyrical and dramatic, in 35 operas, with regular appearances as Leonora (*Il trovatore*), Aida, Cio-cio-san, Mimì, Donna Anna, Pamina, Tatyana, Gluck's Eurydice, Nedda, and Ellen Orford (*Peter Grimes*). Her voice is clear, cool, refined in timbre and production, and used with sure musicianship; a want of dramatic projection has sometimes robbed her portrayals of full impact. She appeared as Ariadne (1954, 1957–8) and Donna Elvira (1955) at Glyndebourne, and as Aida at the Vienna Staatsoper in 1960, and has sung widely in the USA. Her recorded roles include Nedda (twice), Musetta (under Beecham) and Elsa.

ALAN BLYTH

Amat, Joan Carlos [Carles (y) Amat, Joan] (*b* Monistrol de Montserrat, Catalonia, *c*1572; *d* Monistrol de Montserrat, 10 Feb 1642). Spanish physician and writer on the guitar and other subjects. He was the son of Joan Carles and Joana Amat; thus his name was properly Joan Carles y Amat. He was a man of broad interests and wrote not only on guitar playing but also on medicine, arithmetic, astrology and poetry. He collected a book of Catalonian aphorisms which was used in the province's schools until the 19th century. He was named physician to the municipality of Monistrol on 4 January 1618 and retained the post until the 1630s; he served the monastery of Montserrat in the same capacity for many years. After 1637 he was active in public life in Monistrol and was elected mayor on 1 January 1642, but he died, a much loved citizen, a few weeks later.

By the age of seven Amat was accomplished at singing to his own guitar accompaniment. In 1596 he published his brief *Guitarra española de cinco ordenes*, a milestone in the literature on the instrument, of which the earliest surviving copy dates from 1627. Many editions followed, under varying titles, in Spanish and Valencian, the last in 1819. To issues after 1639 is appended a 'Tractat brev' with added explanations in Catalonian and a letter from a certain Fray Leonardo de San Martín of Saragossa which provides much biographical information. The *Guitarra española* is the first treatise to deal with the five-stringed guitar and to teach the *rasgueado* technique – strumming broken chords – in contrast to the traditional *punteado* method of the vihuela and lute. For this purpose Amat devised a system to denote the 12 major and 12 minor chords using numbers which antedated by ten years a similar approach in Italy of Girolamo Montesardo. He also explained an easy method of transposition. His simple, efficient method was to revolutionize guitar playing and prepare the way for the work of Briçeño, Ruiz de Ribayaz and Sanz.

BIBLIOGRAPHY

F. Pedrell: *Catàlech de la Biblioteca musical de la Diputació de Barcelona*, i (Barcelona, 1908)

J. Subirá: 'Amat, Juan Carlos', *MGG*

E. Pujol: 'Significación de Joan Carlos Amat (1572–1642) en la historia de la guitarra', *AnM*, v (1950), 125

M. Hall: 'The "Guitarra española" of Joan Carlos Amat', *Early Music*, vi (1978), 362

BARTON HUDSON

Amateur Concert. London concert organization active during the 1780s; see LONDON, §VI, 1.

Amateur Orchestral Society. London orchestra founded in 1872; it became the Royal Amateur Orchestral Society in 1880. See LONDON, §VI, 2(iii).

Amati. Italian family of violin makers, active in Cremona.

What little is known of Andrea Amati (*b* before 1511; *d* Cremona, before 1580) has been deduced from his few surviving instruments. He is important in that he appears to have originated the form of violin, viola and cello as they are known today; indeed he all but perfected it. The design of each part was carefully thought out, using dividers and compass according to contemporary knowledge of measurement and proportion. There may have been violins before Andrea Amati (as shown for example in the paintings of Gaudenzio Ferrari) but if so, those of Andrea represent a huge step forward. It is this same classical construction that distinguishes instruments of the Cremonese school from almost all made elsewhere, and gives them much of their visual superiority. It may also have an influence on the tone.

Of the few instruments by Andrea that survive – violins of two sizes, large violas (tenors) and large cellos – most have the coat-of-arms of Charles IX of France painted on the back. The earliest is dated 1564 (see fig.1) and the latest 1574, probably quite late in the maker's working life, and the period when Gasparo da Salò was beginning his work in Brescia. Presumably Andrea had been working well before that time since his fame reached the French court, but labelled instruments have not survived to confirm this.

The elegant curves of the outlines of body and scroll of his instruments are matched by those of the arching and soundholes. The work is delicate, the result one of charm to the eye and sweetness to the ear. His violins are lighter in substance than those of later generations, but the golden or golden brown coloured varnish is very much the same as that which followed.

Andrea Amati's two sons were Antonio Amati (*b* Cremona, *c*1540; *d* Cremona) and Girolamo [Hieronymus] Amati (i) (*b* Cremona, 1561; *d* Cremona, 1630). They were named heirs to their father's business in 1580, but eight years later Girolamo bought out Antonio. Nevertheless, in all but a very few instances the productions of the Amati shop until 1630 bore printed labels indicating that the two worked together, and they are commonly known as 'the brothers Amati'. They continued to develop the craft of violin making from where their father had left off, improving the form of the soundhole and in subtle ways giving their instruments more strength. They experimented with different forms of outline and arching, and also with the visual aspect of the edge and purfling, but always retained that special quality of sound and an elegance that delights the eye. One innovation attributed to them, though possibly made by the Brescians a few years earlier, was the contralto viola, the size regarded as more or less ideal today. The larger tenor was commonly played at the time, and the Amatis made many of them. They also made many large size cellos, and both these and the tenors have mostly been reduced for modern playing. After Girolamo's death from the plague which swept the region, the continuance of the dynasty was left in the capable hands of his son, Nicolo.

The influence of the work of the brothers Amati spread far and wide, both in Italy and abroad. They were soon copied, even counterfeited, and were later a source of inspiration in Turin, Venice, Bologna, Milan, Bolzano, Florence and the Netherlands. In England they were much in vogue at the end of the 18th century, the time of Forster and Banks. Since that time, however, the work of Nicolo has generally been more appreciated by violin makers, and the brothers are sometimes underrated by comparison.

Nicolo [Nicolaus] Amati (*b* Cremona, 3 Dec 1596; *d* Cremona, 12 April 1684) was the son of Girolamo Amati. He was the most refined workman of the family, and today its most highly regarded member. His had been the dominant hand in instruments signed by his father and uncle from about 1620, but the takeover on his father's death in 1630 can hardly have been a smooth one, and violins from the next decade are exceedingly rare. The plague which killed Nicolo's parents and two of his sisters had been preceded by two years of famine, devastating the city of Cremona. The same plague killed Maggini in 1632, and apart from a few provincial followers of the Brescian School, Nicolo Amati was suddenly the only violin maker of any consequence in Italy. But for his survival, the craft in Cremona would surely have faded away, long before its

1. Front, side and back views of violin ('Charles IX') by Andrea Amati, Cremona, 1564 (Ashmolean Museum, Oxford)

greatest years. The task of passing it on fell into very capable hands.

By 1640 the violin making momentum had been regained, instruments were once more pouring forth in response to heavy demand, and the census returns show that Nicolo had assistance in his work. Over the years his pupils included Andrea Guarneri, Francesco Rugeri, Giovanni Baptista Rogeri, Giacomo Gennaro and, of course, Antonio Stradivari. In 1645 Nicolo married Lucrezia Pagliari, and their son, Girolamo, took a leading hand in the workshop as soon as he was of age. Jakob Stainer may at some time have been Nicolo's pupil as well.

Most of Nicolo Amati's production seems to have consisted of violins, the proportion of violas and cellos being very small compared with that of his father and uncle. Though, as previously, the violins were of differing dimensions, he favoured a wider model than before, known in modern times as the 'Grand Amati', and these violins are the most sought after. Well curved, long-cornered, and strongly and cleanly purfled they perhaps represent the height of elegance in violin making. The soundholes too have a swing to their design, and the

scrolls are in the best Amati tradition. The varnish leans away from brown and towards golden orange in colour: it must have been quite soft, as the top coat has now usually worn away. Only the arching can be criticized, with a tendency towards what is known as 'scoop' near the edges. This degree of flatness, invariably exaggerated by imitators, causes the flanks of an instrument to be thinner than might be tonally desirable. Nicolo Amati's instruments are appreciated for the noble quality of the sound, combined with ease of response. There is also ample strength to the tone, at least until comparison is made with instruments of Stradivari and Guarneri 'del Gesù'.

By about 1670 Nicolo was less active in the workshop, leaning more and more on the energy of his son. Accordingly the character of the violins changed, and the 'grand pattern' became rarer, though the golden varnish remained. Nicolo's achievement was as much in the impetus he gave to violin making as in the great instruments that he made with his own hands.

Girolamo [Hieronymus] Amati (ii) (*b* Cremona, 26 Feb 1649; *d* Cremona, 21 Feb 1740) was the son of Nicolo Amati. Though he was a fine maker, it is difficult

2. Front, side and back views of violin ('Alard') by Nicolo Amati, Cremona, 1649 (Ashmolean Museum, Oxford)

to be kind about 'Hieronymus II', when comparing him to the other members of his family. The late instruments of Nicolo, many of which Girolamo made unaided, are distinctly less inspiring than the earlier ones, somehow lacking an extra dimension that the father was able to create. He did, however, get rid of any hint of 'scooped' edges, the arching being rather full in the upper and lower flanks. His soundholes, though perfectly pleasant, do not really flow, and the scrolls appear heavy with the fluting left rather flat. After Nicolo's death the varnish lost its golden brightness, becoming a reddish brown and perhaps a little less transparent. It must have been quite clear to Girolamo, as well as to everyone else, that the best maker in Cremona was now Antonio Stradivari. If this was a discouragement, more was at hand from the Casa Guarneri, if not from the Rugeris. At any rate, by 1700 Hieronymus seems to have made few instruments, and only occasional examples are met with from the next ten or fifteen years.

BIBLIOGRAPHY

W. H., A. F. and A. E. Hill: *Antonio Stradivari: his Life and Work* (London, 1902/R1963, 2/1909; Fr. trans., 1907)
W. L. Lütgendorff: *Die Geigen- und Lautenmacher vom Mittelalter bis zur Gegenwart* (Frankfurt am Main, 1904, 3/1922/R1969)
W. H. Hill: *The Violin Makers of the Guarneri Family* (London, 1931)
R. Vannes: *Essai d'un dictionnaire universel des luthiers* (Paris, 1932, 2/1951–9 as *Dictionnaire . . .*)

CHARLES BEARE

Amati, Dom Nicolo (*fl* Bologna, *c*1725–50). Italian violin maker. He is not believed to have had any connection with the Cremonese Amati family.

Amato, Pasquale (*b* Naples, 21 March 1878; *d* Jackson Heights, NY, 12 Aug 1942). Italian baritone. He studied in Naples, and appeared for the first time at the Teatro Bellini there in *La traviata* (1900) and several other operas. Having made his way rapidly in the smaller Italian theatres, he was soon in demand in the larger houses and abroad. In the autumn season of 1904 he appeared successfully at Covent Garden as Amonasro, Rigoletto, Marcello and Escamillo (with Caruso as Don José); but his popularity in London was somewhat overshadowed by that of the newly arrived Sammarco and of Scotti, and he made no further appearances at Covent Garden. In two successive seasons at La Scala (1907 and 1908), Amato sang many leading parts under

Toscanini, including Kurwenal and Golaud (both in Italian). Although this was a period unusually rich in Italian baritones of the first rank, he was soon able to establish himself as an indispensable member of the Metropolitan Opera Company, with whom he made his début (a few days after that of Toscanini) as Germont on 20 November 1908. He remained at the Metropolitan for every season but one until 1921, singing all the principal roles of the Italian repertory besides Valentin, Escamillo and many other parts in French, and Kurwenal and Amfortas in German. He often sang with Caruso, notably in the role of Jack Rance at the première of *La fanciulla del West* in 1910. After his

Pasquale Amato as Escamillo in Bizet's 'Carmen'

retirement from the Metropolitan, he made sporadic appearances with smaller opera companies elsewhere in the USA, and then settled in New York as a singing teacher. On the 25th anniversary of his Metropolitan début he emerged from retirement to sing the same role (Germont) to an audience of 5000 at the New York Hippodrome.

Amato's voice was of splendid quality and extensive range, with brilliant resonance in the upper register; during his New York years he became an exceptionally reliable and complete artist, with impeccable enunciation, classical purity of style and strong dramatic powers. These and other qualities, including pathos and humour, are best shown in a long series of admirable recordings made for Victor (1911–15), among which the *Pagliacci* Prologue, Figaro's 'Largo al factotum', the scene with the courtiers from *Rigoletto*, 'O vecchio cor' from *I due Foscari*, and several duets with Caruso, Gadski and Hempel can be called exemplary.

BIBLIOGRAPHY

P. Kenyon and C. Williams: 'Pasquale Amato', *Record Collector*, xxi (1973), 3 [with discography]

DESMOND SHAWE-TAYLOR

Amato [D'Amato, De Amato, Di Amato], **Vincenzo** (*b* Ciminna, nr. Palermo, 6 Jan 1629; *d* Palermo, 29 July 1670). Italian composer, uncle of Alessandro Scarlatti. His family were connected with the princely houses of Ventimiglia and Gambacurta. His younger brother Paolo, author of *Teatro marmoreo della marina* (1682), was one of Sicily's greatest architects. His sister Eleonora was the mother of Alessandro Scarlatti. Deputizing for the local parish priest, he personally baptized Scarlatti, and together with Marc'Antonio Sportonio he was probably his first teacher. He spent his life at Palermo. Entering the Seminario dei Chierici in adolescence, he obtained a degree in theology and took holy orders. In 1665 he was appointed *maestro di cappella* at the cathedral. He was commissioned by the church of the Carmine Maggiore to compose two Passions (one according to St Matthew, the other according to St John), entirely in recitative, for soprano (Evangelist) and bass (Christ), with continuo. They are not oratorio Passions but liturgical works. Recitative replaces Gregorian chant in the readings of the Gospels for Palm Sunday and Good Friday. There is no music for the other characters; for them the use of cantus firmus tones (or perhaps polyphonic passages, now lost) is implied. The Passions have an unusual history. For nearly three centuries, until a few decades ago, they were continually sung by Sicilian chapel choirs, and there is a report of a performance at Mayenne, near Rennes in France, not long before the Revolution; the *St John Passion* survives in a copy of the late 18th century or early 19th century, and there are late 19th-century copies of both; all seem to be accurate. The recitative is even simpler than Carissimi's but no less concentrated and dramatic and with a few subtle inflections that betray Amato's experience as a polyphonist – brief embellishments on emotive words and melodic and harmonic chromaticisms and expressive dominant 7ths. All of Christ's dignified and austere utterances start with a regular opening figure consisting of one or two rising trochees. The roots of Alessandro Scarlatti's recitative writing can probably be found in these works.

WORKS

Passio secundum Johannem, 2vv, bc, *I-PLcon*, *PLpagano* (adapted and with choral sections for turba by I. Schiavo)
Passio secundum Mattheum, 2vv, bc, *PLpagano* (adapted and with choral sections for turba by I. Schiavo)

Sacri concerti, 2–5vv, con una messa, 3–4vv, libro primo, op.1 (Palermo, 1656), lost
Messa e salmi di vespro e compieta, libro primo, 4, 5vv, op.2 (Palermo, 1656), lost
Isaura, opera, Palermo, 1664, lost (mentioned in Gerber)
L'Aquila, opera, 1666, lost (mentioned in Allacci)
Il martirio di santa Caterina (V. Giattino), oratorio, Palermo, 1669, music lost

BIBLIOGRAPHY

EitnerQ; *FétisB*; *GerberL*; *SchmidlD*; *WaltherML*
Epitaph (MS, *I-PLcom* Qq-H-158, n.VIII)
[Anon.]: Biography of Paolo Amato, introduction to P. Amato: *La nuova prattica di prospettiva* (Palermo, 1714)
A. Mongitore: *Bibliotheca sicula*, ii (Palermo, 1714/*R*1971), 274
L. Allacci: *Drammaturgia* (Venice, enlarged 2/1755/*R*1961), 474
G. Bertini: *Dizionario storico critico degli scrittori di musica e dei più celebri artisti*, i (Palermo, 1814), 28; suppl. (Palermo, 1815), 2
O. Tiby: 'The Polyphonic School in Sicily of the 16th–17th Century', *MD*, v (1951), 203
R. Pagano: 'La vita musicale a Palermo e nella Sicilia del Seicento', *NRMI*, iii (1969), 446ff

O. Tiby: *I polifonisti siciliani del XVI e XVII secolo* (Palermo, 1969), 53, 55, 100

P. E. Carapezza: 'I *duo* della scuola siciliana', introduction to MRS, ii (1971), p.xii [with Eng. trans.]

L. Bianconi: 'Sussidi bibliografici per i musicisti siciliani del cinque e seicento', *RIM*, vii (1972), 17

R. Pagano and L. Bianchi: *Alessandro Scarlatti* (Turin, 1972), 10, 20ff, 27, 51, 256

PAOLO EMILIO CARAPEZZA

Amatucci, Paolo (*b* Loreto, 14 Oct 1868; *d* Pisa, 17 Jan 1935). Italian composer. He studied at the Pesaro Conservatory, obtaining a diploma for composition in 1889. Then for about eight years he lived at Trent, where he worked as an organist and band conductor; for a short time he was organist at the imperial court in Vienna. He returned to Italy in 1898 and settled in Rome, where his family lived. With Lorenzo Perosi and Guerrino Amelli as close collaborators, he prepared the encyclical *Motu proprio* on the reform of sacred music issued by Pius X on 22 November 1903. In 1901 he was appointed *maestro di cappella* at Pisa Cathedral, where he devoted himself entirely to the composition of sacred works until his retirement in May 1934. His manuscripts are held at Pisa Cathedral and the Lucca Musical Institute.

FRANCO BAGGIANI

Ambiela, Miguel de (baptized La Puebla de Albortón, Saragossa, 29 Sept 1666; *d* Toledo, 29 March 1733). Spanish composer. He was successively *maestro de capilla* at Lérida (1686–8), Jaca, El Pilar in Saragossa (1700–07), Descalzas Reales convent at Madrid, and from 22 March 1710 until his death at Toledo Cathedral. He was the last Toledo *maestro de capilla* to leave to the cathedral a large and important choirbook repertory; it consists of eight four-voice masses parodied on his own motets, the eight motets themselves, and three hymns. He published there in 1717 a 20-folio *Disceptacion música y discurso problemático* defending Francisco Valls's use of unprepared dissonance. Latin and vernacular works by him survive in several Spanish collections (*E-Bc, H, Mn, MO, Tc, Zac*). Several of his works were included in a collection copied in Tarragona by Crisóstomo Ripollés in 1704 (formerly *D-B*).

BIBLIOGRAPHY

LaborD

F. Rubio Piqueras: *Música y músicos toledanos* (Toledo, 1923), 54

R. Stevenson: 'The Toledo Manuscript Polyphonic Choirbooks', *FAM*, xx (1973), 92

ROBERT STEVENSON

Ambira. *See* LAMELLAPHONE, §3, and MARIMBA, §1.

Ambitus (Lat.: 'a going around'). Literally the 'course' (*cursus*) of a melodic line, but in the Middle Ages and later usually the range of scale degrees attributed to a given mode, particularly in Gregorian chant, or to the range of a voice, instrument or piece. The higher or lower tessitura of a melody relative to its final note determined whether the mode of the melody was authentic or plagal. Gaffurius and others termed modes perfect when the ambitus was exactly an octave, imperfect when it was less than an octave, and pluperfect when it exceeded an octave. If a melody used notes from both an authentic mode and its plagal, the mode was termed *mixtus*; if it used notes from the authentic or plagal version of another mode the mode was termed *commixtus*.

Synonyms for ambitus used by medieval authors include *cursus* (Johannes Afflighemensis: *GS*, ii, pp.244ff), *medium* (*Speculum musice*: *CS*, ii, p.244) and *processus* (*CS*, ii, p.246). All these were used by Renaissance theorists in the same sense, e.g. *medium* by Tinctoris (*CS*, iv, 18, 27, etc), or *processo* by Pietro Aaron in his *Trattato . . . di . . . tuoni di canto figurato* (chaps.1, 4, etc). The word *modulus* is used for ambitus in the *Questiones in musica* (pp.45ff).

It has recently been recognized that ambitus is a significant aspect of musical style in Gregorian chant: in graduals and offertories, for example, the ambitus of the verse is usually higher than that of the respond. Stäblein has noted that in troped introits the ambitus of the tropes differs from that of the introits.

BIBLIOGRAPHY

P. Aaron: *Trattato della natura e cognizione di tutti gli tuoni di canto figurato* (Venice, 1525)

R. Steglich, ed.: *Die Questiones in musica: ein Choraltraktat* (Leipzig, 1911)

W. Apel: *Gregorian Chant* (Bloomington, Ind., 1958, 3/1966)

B. Stäblein: 'Zum Verständnis des "klassischen" Tropus', *AcM*, xxxv (1963), 84

HAROLD S. POWERS, RICHARD SHERR

Ambleville, Charles d' (*b* Burgundy, late 16th century; *d* Rouen, 6 July 1637). French composer. All that is known of his life is that in 1626 he was *procureur* of the Compagnie de Jésus at Rouen. He left only musical works, from which we may infer that he was director of music of one of the colleges of his order. His *Octonarium sacrum* is a set of five-part verses for the *Magnificat*, using all eight tones; they are fugal and closely resemble similar pieces by Formé. The music that he published two years later, in two complementary volumes for four and six voices respectively, is distinctly modern. It includes works for double choir in a style originating in Italy that had already been adopted in France by several composers, Du Caurroy and Le Jeune, notable among them; each volume also contains several masses and motets for a single choir. The double-choir works are for liturgical use and comprise psalms, motets and hymns. In his preface d'Ambleville states that they may be performed ad lib according to the forces available, e.g. by two groups – one of four soloists, the other a six-part chorus – by a soprano and bass duet from each choir or by a solo soprano, the missing voices being replaced by instruments or, failing them, by organ alone. He normally wrote either in fauxbourdon style (which he also called 'musica simplex') or contrapuntally, including fugal textures ('musica figurata'), which he handled skilfully. Apart from these Latin works he was also, according to Gastoué (p.264), the composer of the music published in 1623 for *Airs sur les hymnes sacrez . . .* to words by Michel Coyssard that had appeared in 1592; the music is old-fashioned for 1623.

WORKS

Airs sur les hymnes sacrez, odes et noëls, 4vv (Paris, 1623); attrib. in Gastoué

Octonarium sacrum, seu canticum BVM, 5vv (Paris, 1634)

Harmonia sacra, seu Vesperae . . . una cum Missa ac litaniis BVM, 6vv (Paris, 1636)

Harmonia sacra, seu Vesperae, 4vv (Paris, 1636)

BIBLIOGRAPHY

A. and A. Backer: *Bibliothèque de la Compagnie de Jésus*, ed. C. Sommervogel, i (Brussels, 1890)

A. Gastoué: *Le cantique populaire en France* (Lyons, 1924)

D. Launay: 'Le motet à double choeur en France dans la première moitié du XVIIème siècle', *RdM*, xl (1957), 173

DENISE LAUNAY

Amboss (Ger.). ANVIL.

Ambrogini Poliziano, Angelo. *See* POLIZIANO, ANGELO.

Ambros, August Wilhelm (*b* Mauth [now Vysoké Myto], 17 Nov 1816; *d* Vienna, 26 June 1876). Austrian music historian, critic, pianist and composer. His mother, sister of the musicologist Kiesewetter, fostered his love of music, painting and architecture; the performance of older music in the Kiesewetter home belonged to Ambros's strongest early impressions. He acquired a musical training, despite his father's objections, through a keen enthusiasm, an exceptional memory and an unbounded capacity for work. A humanistic gymnasium education, a doctorate of law completed in 1839 at Prague University and vast reading, with a youthful predilection for Jean Paul, underlay his later scholarship and influenced his prolix style. Robert Schumann was his spiritual and journalistic model, and as 'Flamin' he associated with enthusiastic young followers, including Hanslick as 'Renatus', in a Bohemian branch of the 'Davidsbund' to fight musical conservatism in Prague. He was more indebted to the concepts and methods of art historians and historians of antiquity, of law and of literature, than to such musical colleagues as Kiesewetter or Fétis.

Ambros's historical perspective was strongly Hegelian, although tempered by an effort to understand historical particulars as discrete events, as well as a unified and progressive cultural vision in the manner of Burckhardt's *Civilization of the Renaissance in Italy*. A qualified respect for A. B. Marx's and F. Brendel's strictly Hegelian writings on music history and aesthetics, an open mind towards the friends and idols of his youth, Berlioz and Liszt, and a benevolent though apprehensive ambivalence towards Wagner and the Gesamtkunstwerk were the bases of his efforts to counter-balance Hanslick's controversial and conservative *Vom Musikalisch-Schönen* (1854) with his own first important publication *Die Grenzen der Musik und Poesie* (1856). The deaths of Mendelssohn and Schumann, disillusionment in the aftermath of the 1848 revolutions, and the growing politicization of European cultural life account for his persistent pessimism about the course of contemporary history.

For years Ambros laboured dutifully through the Austrian civil service, the legacy of his father's insistence on a respectable profession. At the age of 44, he received an unexpected commission from the Leipzig publisher F. E. C. Leuckart to realize his long-standing intention of writing a music history, based on original source studies and worthy of comparison with the far more advanced historiography of other disciplines. Accordingly he undertook extensive archival studies in Austria, south Germany and Italy between 1861 and 1869; he amassed materials and made transcriptions in Venice, Bologna, Florence, Modena, Rome and Naples. His travels in Italy were a turning point in his life, and in 1861 he wrote to his wife from Venice: 'As I survey the fruits of my stay here I cannot help being very well satisfied. I have found what I sought – and more. The impressions which I take with me of Italy give me the intellectual and spiritual dimension I have lacked up to now.' As a devout Catholic and friend of the Abbé Liszt, he gained entrance to Roman society and the blessing of Pius IX, who gave him special privileges to study in the papal archives. The Austrian Royal Imperial Academy of Sciences assisted him financially in his researches.

In 1869 he attained his life's ambition by becoming professor of the history of music and professor of art in Prague, having previously lectured informally at the conservatory and at the art academy. In 1871 he was called to the attorney general's office in Vienna and in 1872 moved to the capital with his wife and seven children, gradually taking on so many activities and posts as to elicit an incredulous comment from Hanslick in his autobiography. He lectured at the Vienna Conservatory and, despite Hanslick's opposition, at the university; he was also the private tutor to the Archduke Rudolf in the history of the arts. He was associated with the Central Commission for the Study and Preservation of Artistic and Historical Monuments and with the Austrian Museum, was president of the St Cecilia Association, drafted a plan for the reorganization of music in Austria's churches and contributed to several foreign journals.

With his *Geschichte der Musik*, which began to appear in 1862, Ambros achieved a place of distinction in the writing of music history as cultural history. He prefaced the publication with provocative ambivalence:

Let us leave open the question whether the development of music, as manifested with vital energy through almost three centuries, when great masters appeared not singly but at once in whole groups and one personality came hard upon the heels of the preceding, may not have come to an end for the time being. It is certain, however, that we are in a position to understand these epochs better and to honour them more justly than has ever been the case before – perhaps just because we ourselves have not been endowed to the same degree with the ability to create and invent significant works of art as were those epochs in which the masters of Italy and Germany gave the world no time to reflect on works of art, when yet more important works appeared and demanded attention even before their predecessors had been completely fathomed. For this reason it is above all the critical, art-philosophical, biographical, and historical orientation of our time which has achieved much that had not been achieved before . . . The work of the aesthetician, of the historian of art, can always retain its rightful place vis à vis the work of art itself.

Throughout his career, Ambros also wrote, in a far-ranging and fanciful style, numerous essays on music, art, literature and contemporary events, which appeared in *Bohemia* (Prague), the *Wiener Allgemeine Musikzeitung*, the *Neue Zeitschrift für Musik*, *Anregungen für Kunst, Leben und Wissenschaft* (Leipzig), *Wiener Zeitung*, *Wiener Abendpost* and *Deutsche Rundschau* (Berlin), among other papers and journals, as well as in book form. They supplement his unfinished magnum opus and are also of considerable significance for 19th-century intellectual history.

Ambros's published compositions (24 opus numbers) were chiefly songs, piano sonatas and character pieces for piano with titles reflecting his Schumannesque orientation such as the *Landschaftsbilder* op.8 (1859), *Kindheitstage* op.9 (1860), *Phantasiestücke* op.14 (1862) and *Musikalische Reisebilder* op.24 (1876). More ambitious than these were his unpublished works, many of them lost, including a *Missa solemnis* (MS now in the Österreichische Nationalbibliothek, Vienna) which was performed several times between 1857 and 1889, two symphonies, overtures to plays by Kleist, Calderón and Shakespeare, a Czech opera *Břetislav a Jitka* and a violin sonata premièred in 1865 by Camillo Sivori and Liszt. The first volume of the history treats music in ancient civilizations, including the Chinese, Indian and Arabic, up to classical Greece and Rome. Volume two spans the period in western music from early Christianity to the evolution of Burgundian polyphony in the late Middle Ages. The third and most important volume explores Netherlands and French music and music theory of the Renaissance, with separate chapters on Josquin and Ockeghem, as well as 15th-century German, English and Italian music. The posthumously issued fourth volume, edited by Nottebohm, embraces Italian subjects from Palestrina to Monteverdi and early opera, from the Counter-Reformation to organists, theorists and teachers of the 17th century.

WRITINGS

Die Grenzen der Musik und Poesie: eine Studie zur Aesthetik der Tonkunst (Prague, 1856/R1976; Eng. trans., 1893)

Das Conservatorium zu Prag: eine Denkschrift bei Gelegenheit der fünfzigjährigen Jubelfeier der Gründung (Prague, 1858)

Der Dom zu Prag (Prague, 1858)

Zur Lehre vom Quintenverbote: eine Studie (Leipzig, 1858)

Culturhistorische Bilder aus dem Musikleben der Gegenwart (Leipzig, 1860, 2/1865)

Der Minne Regel, von Eberhardus Cersne aus Minden, 1404 (Vienna, 1861)

Geschichte der Musik, i (Leipzig, 1862, rev. B. von Sokolowsky 3/1887/R1968); ii (Leipzig, 1864, rev. H. Riemann 3/1891/R1968); iii (Leipzig, !868, rev. O. Kade 2/1893/R1968)

Die Burg Carlstein in Böhmen und ihre Restaurierung (Vienna, 1865)

Bunte Blätter: Skizzen und Studien für Freunde der Musik der bildenden Kunst (Leipzig, 1872, 2/1896); new ser. (Leipzig, 1874, 2/1896)

G. Nottebohm, ed.: *Geschichte der Musik*, iv (Leipzig, 1878, rev. H. Leichentritt 3/1909/R1968)

J. Batka, ed.: *Aus Italien* (Pressburg and Leipzig, 1880) [essays and letters]

Musikalische Nachlasshefte, ii (Pressburg and Leipzig, 1887)

Geschichte der Musik, v (Leipzig, 1882, 3/1911) [collection of 15th- and 16th-century music examples pubd by O. Kade in part from Ambros's transcriptions – 800 of his transcriptions are in *A-Wn*]

BIBLIOGRAPHY

C. von Wurzbach: 'Ambros, August Wilhelm', *Biographisches Lexikon des Kaiserthums Oesterreich* (Vienna, 1855)

R. Eitner: 'August Wilhelm Ambros', *MMg*, ix (1877)

H. Mendel: 'Ambros, August Wilhelm', *Musikalisches Conversationslexikon*, i (Berlin, 1880) [based on autobiographical essay of 1859]

E. Hanslick: *Aus meinem Leben* (Berlin, 1894)

M. Dietz: 'Ambros, August Wilhelm', *ADB*

G. Adler: 'Ambros, August Wilhelm', *NÖB* [Eng. trans. in *MQ*, xvii (1931), 360]

F. Blume: 'Ambros, August Wilhelm', *MGG* [incl. detailed list of compositions]

P. Naegele: *August Wilhelm Ambros: his Historical and Critical Thought* (diss., Princeton U., 1954) [incl. detailed list of Ambros's reviews and articles]

W. Beyer: *Zu einigen Grundproblemen der formalistischen Ästhetik E. Hanslicks und August Wilhelm Ambros* (diss., U. of Prague, 1957); extracts in *MMC*, xiv (1960), 85

M. Očadlik: 'August Wilhelm Ambros na pražké univ.', *Acta Universitatis Carolinae, philosophica et historica*, ii (Prague, 1958)

R. Heinz: *Geschichtsbegriff und Wissenschaftscharakter der Musikwissenschaft in der zweiten Hälfte des neunzehnten Jahrunderts* (Regensburg, 1968)

B. Meier: 'Zur Musikhistoriographie des neunzehnten Jahrhunderts', *Die Ausbreitung des Historismus über die Musik* (Regensburg, 1969)

PHILIPP NAEGELE

Ambros, Vladimír (*b* Prostějov, Moravia, 18 Sept 1890; *d* Prostějov, 12 May 1956). Czech composer and conductor. He studied at the Brno Organ School (1908–10) and was then a pupil of Knorr (composition) and Basserman (conducting) at the Frankfurt Conservatory. Ambros was répétiteur at the Frankfurt Opera (1911–13), conductor of the Carl Rosa company and répétiteur at Covent Garden (1915–18). After returning to Czechoslovakia in 1921 he worked in his home town as a teacher, choirmaster and conductor of the Orchestrální Sdružení, promoting music education throughout the rural areas of Moravia. He was head of the Břeclav School of Music (1926–8) and then returned to Prostějov where from 1945 he devoted his attention to composition. At first influenced by Janáček, as in the opera *Ukradené štěstí* ('Stolen happiness',

1924), Ambros later successfully assimilated Novákian impressionism, notably in the songs *Labutinka* (1934) and *Sbohem a šáteček* ('Farewell and a handkerchief', 1935) and in lyrical, generally intimate chamber pieces such as the String Quartet no.1 (1937). An individual style had already been achieved in the orchestral trilogy *Beskydy* (1928–32) stimulated by the Moravian landscape. In response to the oppressive conditions of 1938 Ambros produced the formally compressed *Symphonietta* (1938), which has a habanera second movement intended as a homage to struggling republican Spain. Ambros continued in this manner during World War II with the song cycle *Nálady z atlanty* (1940) to texts by black writers and the first two symphonies (1941, 1944). In a final period (1945–56) he turned to a socialist realist technique, basing his works on contemporary subjects. Notable pieces from these years are the cantata *Veliký návrat* ('Grand return', 1951), the opera *Maryla* (1951), the *Rolnická suita* ('Peasant suite', 1952), the *May Quartet* (1953) and the Symphony no.3, 'O naší krásné vlasti' ('On our beautiful land', 1946–54), but Ambros was most successful with his miniatures and works for children: the song cycle *Co rok dal* ('What the year gave us', 1953) and the cantata *Maminka* ('Mother', 1956).

BIBLIOGRAPHY

ČSHS

V. Gregor: *Vladimír Ambros* (Prostějov, 1969)

VLADIMÍR HUDEC

Ambrosch, Joseph Karl (*b* Krumau, Bohemia, 6 May 1759; *d* Berlin, 8 Sept 1822). German tenor and composer of lieder, of Czech descent. He studied with J. A. Kozeluch in Prague, and made his vocal début in Bayreuth in 1784. In 1791 he was appointed first tenor of the Berlin Royal Theatre. In collaboration with his Czech countryman Joseph Böheim he edited the collection *Freymaurer Lieder mit Melodien* (1793), adding a number of original pieces to its second edition (1795) and to Böheim's *Auswahl von Maurer-Gesänge* (1798). He retained his position at the Royal Theatre until he was pensioned in 1811, and remained a prominent and respected musical figure in Berlin until his death.

Ambrosch's lied style ranges from simple, strophic, folklike works to more complex pieces with varied strophes. His accompaniments are quite simple, but his vocal lines often have numerous embellishments and a high tessitura. In addition to the works in Böheim's anthologies, he published two volumes of *Deutsche und italienische Lieder mit Variationen* (Berlin, 1796), a set of *Sechs Lieder mit Veränderungen* (Zerbst, 1797) and other lieder in contemporary anthologies and in single-sheet publications. He also made choral arrangements of many of his lieder. His daughter and pupil Wilhelmine Ambrosch Becker (*b* Berlin, 1791) was a pianist and singer in Berlin, and was later appointed first soprano of the Hamburg City Theatre.

BIBLIOGRAPHY

EitnerQ; *GerberNL*

C. von Ledebur: *Tonkünstler-Lexicon Berlin's* (Berlin, 1861/R1965)

W. Bollert: 'Ambrosch, Joseph Karl', *MGG*

RAYMOND A. BARR

Ambrose (*b* Trier [Treves], *c*340; *d* Milan, 397). Saint, bishop and Doctor of the Church. He was the son of the Roman prefect of Gaul, and embarked upon a successful political career, being named consular governor of Liguria and Aemilia in about 370. While yet unbaptized he was elected Bishop of Milan by popular acclaim on 7

December 374. Together with Augustine and Jerome he is acknowledged as one of the three great Latin Church Fathers of the 4th and 5th centuries. He was primarily a public figure, however, unlike Augustine, the philosopher, or Jerome, the scholar; he consolidated the position of the Church against the powerful Arian heresy and the counter-attacks of paganism.

Tradition has assigned to him a musical significance exceeding that of any other early Christian leader; he has been particularly noted for his involvement in the development of Ambrosian or Milanese chant, the authorship of the *Te Deum*, the introduction of hymns and of antiphonal singing into the Latin church, and the composition of a number of hymns.

In the late 19th century, scholars (including Dreves and Morin) rejected the first two achievements as medieval legends, while reaffirming the latter two. These, though still generally accepted by 20th-century music historians, are nevertheless open to serious question. Ambrose's supposed introduction of antiphonal psalmody and of non-Biblical hymnody into the west rests primarily on Augustine's famous passage from the *Confessions* (ix, chap.17), describing a time when the Church at Milan was under severe pressure from the Arians: 'at that time it was instituted that hymns and psalms (*hymni et psalmi*) be sung according to the custom of the east'. Apart from any general question of anecdotal hyperbole, three specific points are noteworthy: Ambrose (though mentioned in the passage) was not specifically named as responsible for the innovation; the term 'hymni' was not common 4th-century usage for non-Biblical song or *psalmi idiotici*; and 'according to the custom of the east' cannot be assumed to mean so-called antiphonal psalmody. The latter term, moreover, is often used carelessly, without a due consideration of its precise relationship to the practice of alternating double choirs.

As regards Ambrose's hymn compositions, it is virtually certain that he wrote at least four, probably six, of those attributed to him. There is, however, no evidence that he composed tunes for them, and Dreves's speculations in this respect, while responsible and convincing to many, are not conclusive.

BIBLIOGRAPHY

G. Dreves: *Aurelius Ambrosius: 'Der Vater des Kirchengesanges'*, Stimmen aus Maria-Laach, suppl.lviii (Freiburg, 1893)
G. Morin: 'Nouvelles recherches sur l'auteur du Te Deum', *Revue bénédictine*, xi (1894), 49
V. Ermoni: 'Ambrose (Saint) hymnographe', *Dictionnaire d'archéologie chrétienne et de liturgie*, ed. F. Cabrol and J. Leclercq, i/1 (Paris, 1924), 1347
F. H. Dudden: *The Life and Times of St Ambrose* (Oxford, 1935)
E. Jammers: 'Rhythmische und tonale Studien zur Musik der Antike und des Mittelalters: II', *AMf*, viii (1943), 30
B. Stäblein: *Hymnen*, Monumenta monodica medii aevi, i (Kassel, 1956)
E. Kähler: *Studien zum Te Deum* (Göttingen, 1958)
H. Leeb: *Die Psalmodie bei Ambrosius*, Wiener Beiträge zur Theologie, xviii (Vienna, 1967)

JAMES W. Mc KINNON

Ambrose, Bert (*b* London, 1897; *d* Leeds, 18 June 1971). English dance band-leader and violinist. He emigrated to the USA where he studied the violin and worked in New York in a cinema orchestra and (from 1917) as musical director of the Club de Vingt (at the Palais Royal). He was invited to lead the band at the Embassy Club, London (1920–27), where he was immensely popular with the highest society, being recalled from a brief spell as musical director of the Clover Gardens, New York (1922), by the Prince of Wales. In 1927 he became musical director of the Mayfair Hotel, where his band was an immediate success, acquiring a recording contract, making a stage appearance at the London Palladium, and broadcasting fortnightly from 1928. The broadcasts and records made Ambrose a national figure. Subsequently he held posts at the Embassy Club (1933–6), the Mayfair Hotel (1936–7, 1939–40), Ciro's Club (1937) and the Café de Paris (1938), and he continued to lead a band, mainly touring the theatres, into the mid-1950s. From 1956 he was a band manager.

BIBLIOGRAPHY
A. McCarthy: *The Dance Band Era* (London, 1971)

Ambrose, John (*fl c*1520–45). English composer. A brief and undistinguished canon (two-in-one) attributed to him is in *GB-Lbm* Roy. App.58. The same source also contains a longer, but still somewhat pedestrian, keyboard work in free-composed fantasia form (it also occurs in *Och* 1034). He may be identifiable with the John Ambrose who became a clerk in the choir of the collegiate church of St Anthony, London (St Anthony's Hospital), in 1522.

ROGER BOWERS

Ambrosian [Milanese] **rite, music of the.** A chant repertory, distinct from Gregorian chant, found at and near Milan. In this repertory there are contrasted musical styles that have coexisted for centuries. Milan was one of the most notable centres of western liturgy, open to outside influences (there are chants of eastern and of Roman origin), but essentially conservative; thus archaic forms of chants, which had changed elsewhere, were preserved. The Milanese predilection for the archaic is found also in the few polyphonic pieces (*discordantes*) for the rite given by Gaffurius: the responsory *De profundis* and the *Litaniae mortuorum*.

1. Independence of the rite. 2. Sources of the rite. 3. Developments documented in the MSS. 4. Musical characteristics and forms.

1. INDEPENDENCE OF THE RITE. Milanese chant is the oldest western repertory of liturgical music to have survived parallel to the Gregorian repertory, and it is only now being undermined owing to the recent liturgical reforms. The independence of the rite was due to the political and ecclesiastical authority commanded by Milan during the Middle Ages, and reinforced by the prestige accruing from the most famous of the bishops of Milan, St AMBROSE, to whom the Milanese liturgy and chant were often attributed. Ambrosian liturgy also influenced neighbouring regions and spread as far as central Europe (Bohemia) and central and southern Italy, although it is confined in modern times to the diocese of Milan and some nearby parishes in such places as Novara and Ticino.

2. SOURCES OF THE RITE. The rite and its chants contain a basic nucleus, apparently of local origin, as well as elements from other areas. The east is one such area. Some of the oriental chants which were borrowed at Milan, probably between the 5th and 7th centuries, were taken over also at Rome and by other western rites. There are also, however, many Milanese chants of oriental origin not found elsewhere in the west: some of the transitoria (the Ambrosian equivalents of the Gregorian communions) and the antiphons, as well as other pieces. (An example is the *post evangelium* antiphon *Coenae tuae mirabili*, which probably originated at Jerusalem.)

Other versions of some of these oriental chants survive in the Byzantine liturgy.

Some of the Milanese chants were borrowed from the Gallican and Mozarabic rites: examples are the transitorium, *Maria et Martha*, and the offerenda (i.e. the equivalent of the Gregorian offertory), *Curvati sunt caeli*. These borrowings are not always unambiguously identifiable, particularly with respect to the music. Most of the borrowed (Milanese) chants – mainly for the Mass – are of Roman origin, and generally only to be distinguished from the Milanese by their texts; the chant melodies were nearly always adapted after borrowing, according to local practice. (This appears clearly, for example, at cadences.) In the past scholars have not always agreed on the origins of certain chants, but it is now thought that of the chants common to Rome and Milan, those in the Ambrosian repertory were borrowed from the Roman repertory rather than vice versa, even though the Milanese melodies have often been subject to less subsequent modification than the melodies in Rome or elsewhere. (An example is *Coenae tuae mirabili* mentioned above.)

3. DEVELOPMENTS DOCUMENTED IN THE MSS. The principal difficulty in the study of Ambrosian chant arises from the late date of the sources. Apart from some early MS fragments written in non-diastematic neumes, the earliest surviving sources date from the 11th and 12th centuries. Nonetheless, as noted above, the Milanese sources can be shown to preserve early forms of chants that have been subject to modification in Gregorian sources, and to preserve chants or parts of chants that have disappeared from the Gregorian repertory. (An example is the gradual, *Tibi Domine*: Milan retained its psalm verse *Confitebor tibi*, which is probably a vestige of a responsorial chant more extensive than any found in Roman sources.) Indeed, there are many instances where the degree to which Gregorian chants have been modified can be shown by comparing them with the corresponding Ambrosian chants.

The earliest Ambrosian chant MSS are the so-called antiphonaries; they contain a mixture of both Mass and Office chants. In later MSS there was a separation of the two repertories. (*See* ANTIPHONER.)

Another development in later Ambrosian MSS is the progressive disappearance of melismas and the more elaborate melodies. The latter were replaced by simpler melodies in the 15th century, and the longer melismas were omitted by the copyists of later MSS.

4. MUSICAL CHARACTERISTICS AND FORMS. In Ambrosian chant, unlike Gregorian, an individual category of chant does not have a well-defined musical style regarded as proper to it. In the lucernaria (chants for Vespers with interesting Mozarabic parallels), for example, some chants are syllabic and follow the psalm formulae; some include single melismas at the ends of musical phrases; a third group is completely melismatic, although in them the basic psalmodic structure is nonetheless recognizable.

Where stylistic distinctions are made, however, they are often sharper than those made in the Gregorian repertory. The simple Office antiphons, for example, show a rigorous application of syllabic treatment (see ex.1). Whereas the syllabic chants are more syllabic than their Gregorian counterparts (even granting some exceptions among the antiphons) the melismatic chants are more melismatic than their Gregorian equivalents. The latter point is clearly demonstrated by the melisma on 'pacem' in ex.2 – a comparison of the Ambrosian and Gregorian versions of the gradual, *Benedictus Dominus*, found in both liturgies.

Another difference between Ambrosian and Gregorian chant lies in the modality of the chants. This is much more vague in Ambrosian chant than it is in Gregorian, and the lack of a well-defined modality is accentuated by a greater variety of intermediate cadence. In this respect, as in the conservatism of the melodic tradition, Ambrosian chant seems to evade well-defined categories and to represent an early stage of the evolution of the chant. There is, however, great uniformity in cadence structure: the most frequent and typical cadence is (with *d* as final) *d–e–f–d–d*, sometimes expanded to *d–e–f–e–d–d*.

Melodically, Ambrosian chant resembles Old Roman and Beneventan chant and differs notably from Gregorian in its predilection for stepwise motion, for sequential structure in melismas (e.g. in responsories, alleluias and offerendae) and for the frequent repetition of melodic motifs within a chant. (See ex.3, *Rex*; the same phenomenon is found in Mozarabic chant.) Ambrosian chant, further, tends to favour leaps of a 4th rather than a 3rd or a 5th.

Some Milanese psalmelli such as *A summo caelo*, *Aedificavit Dominus* and *Assurgentes*, are, like their equivalents the Gregorian graduals, centonate (*see* CENTONIZATION). In all there are a dozen such chants in the A mode; psalmelli in the F mode are rare. In these and many other psalmelli (as also in certain Old Roman and, less often, Gregorian graduals) the same melody is used to end both the respond and the verse.

The jubilus of the Milanese alleluia can appear in two different forms (called *melodiae primae* and *melodiae secundae*); the *melodiae secundae*, to be sung in the repetition of the alleluia after the verse, contain melismas of extraordinary length, corresponding to the *sequentiae* or *melodiae longissimae* north of the Alps. Such melismas may have been added to the alleluias and to the Office responsories *cum infantibus* (so called as a result of performance mainly by boys or young singing men) in the 8th and 9th centuries.

The Milanese offerendae vary greatly in character, but are mostly melismatic, some greatly developed with a use of sequence. Unfortunately only a few complete offerendae survive: they generally appear in MSS with only one verse.

Ex.1 Ambrosian Office antiphons   *I-Rvat* Vat. lat. 12932, f. 15 (early 12th century)

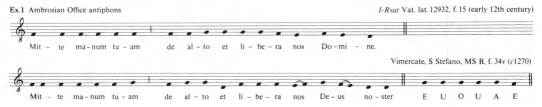

Vimercate, S Stefano, MS B, f. 34v (c1270)

Ex.2 A comparison of the Milanese [MED], Old Roman [ROM] and Gregorian [GREG] versions of the verse *Suscipiant* from the gradual or psalmellus
Benedictus Dominus

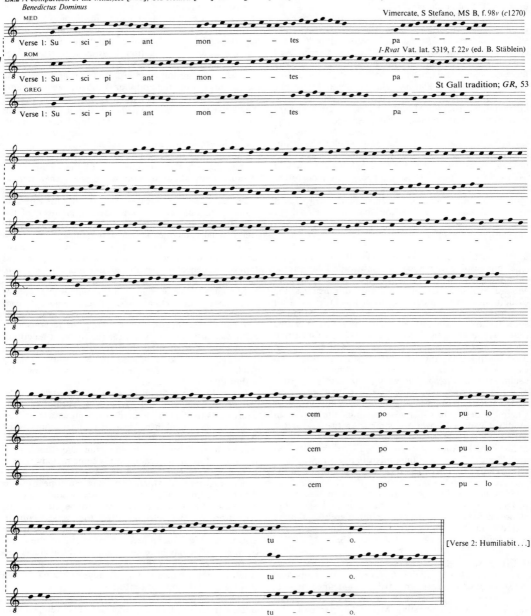

The melismatic chants include the ingressae (equivalent of the Gregorian introits) which lack the psalmodic character of Roman introits or Gallican and Mozarabic antiphons *ad praelegendum*, the Office psallendae, the confractoria (fraction antiphons) and transitoria (communion antiphons). All these chants often contain stereotyped ornaments, found very frequently throughout the repertory, even in essentially syllabic chants. (Ex.4 contains examples of these at para*te* and *viam*.) These characteristic ornaments sometimes occur at the end of melodic sections, as for example in the

transitorium *Te laudamus* (ex.5; cf the psallenda, *O quam beatus Vitus*). This transitorium is characteristic in another respect, i.e. in the literal repetition of a melodic motif; this is found in other Ambrosian pieces and in the old Italic repertory.

Psalmodic patterns, undoubtedly of great antiquity, underlie the Ambrosian recitation tones. In them, the first three syllables of each psalm are set to the intonation, without regard to the accentuation of the text. The tenor (dominant) is always the true tenor of the antiphon: the tenors *e* and *b* were never raised a semitone

Ex.3 Ambrosian responsory *cum infantibus, in baptisterio* (Lodi), showing the repeated use of five melodic fragments (*a, b, c, d, e*)

Vimercate, S Stefano, MS B, f. 43*v* (*c*1270)

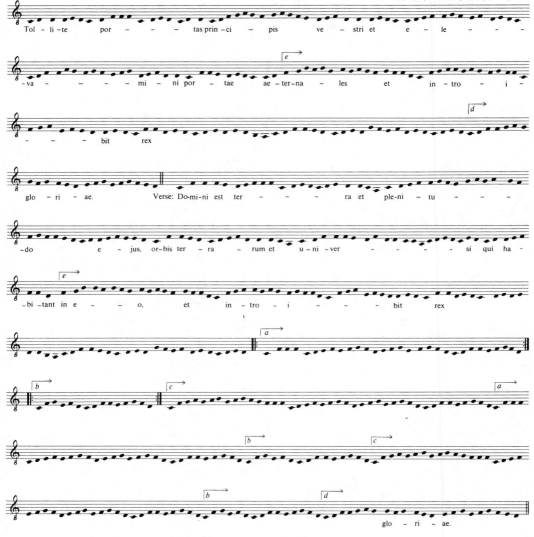

as they were in the Gregorian repertory, and a greater number of dominants is possible for a given final in the Ambrosian repertory than in the Gregorian. (For

Ex.4 Ambrosian ingressa *Vox clamantis*

I-*Rvat* Vat.12932, f. 14 (early 12th century)

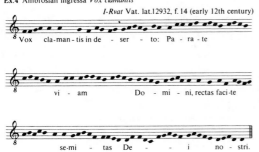

example, the antiphons with *d* as final can have recitation-tone dominants on *a, g, f* or *e*.)

Milanese chant, like the Mozarabic chant, lacked the psalmodic mediation until it was introduced in the 15th or 16th century under Gregorian influence. There are many final cadential formulae (endings, *differentiae*) that are matched in different ways in the MSS to the beginning of the antiphon. Cadences with two accents are unknown in Ambrosian chant, in which there are only three groups of older cadences: cadences with an inflection on the last syllable, syllabic cadences usually beginning on the fourth syllable from the last, and cadences which may have one or more preparatory notes and which are organized with respect to the accented syllable.

See also BENEVENTAN RITE, MUSIC OF THE; GREGORIAN AND OLD ROMAN CHANT; RAVENNA RITE, MUSIC OF THE.

Ex.5 Ambrosian transitorium *Te laudamus*   *I-Rvat* Vat. lat.13156, f. 119*v* (14th century)

Te lau – da – mus Do – mi – ne om – ni – po – tens: qui se – des su – per che – ru – bin et se – ra – phin.
Quem be – ne – di – cunt an – ge – li, arch – an – ge – li: et lau – dant pro – phe – tae et a – po – sto – li.
Te lau – da – mus Do – mi – ne o – ran – do: qui ve – ni – sti pec – ca – ta sol – ven – do.
Te de – pre – ca – mur ma – gnum re – dem – pto – rem: quem Pa – ter mi – sit o – vi – um pa – sto – rem.
Tu es Chri – stus Do – mi – nus sal – va – tor: qui de Ma – ri – a Vir – gi – ne es na – tus.
Hunc sa – cro – san – ctum ca – li – cem su – men – tes: ab om – ni cul – pa li – be – ra nos sem – per.

EDITIONS

M. Magistretti: *Beroldi mediolanensis ecclesiae kalendarium et ordines* (Milan, 1894)

Antiphonarium ambrosianum du Musée Britannique, PalMus, v, vi (1896–1900)

Antiphonarii ambrosiani pars hiemalis, pars aestiva, proprium et commune sanctorum (Milan, 1898)

Antiphonario ambrosiano novissima editio appendix (Milan, 1898)

M. Magistretti: *Manuale ambrosianum ex cod. saec. XI olim in usum Canonicae Vallis Travaliae* (Milan, 1905)

A. M. Ceriani, A. Ratti and M. Magistretti: *Missale ambrosianum duplex* (Milan, 1913)

G. Bas: *Manuale di canto ambrosiano* (Turin, 1929)

E. Garbagnati: *Melodie ambrosiane* (Milan, 1929)

A. Pini: *Cantus liturgici in die Purificationis* (Milan, 1930)

G. M. Suñol: *Antiphonale missarum juxta ritum sanctae ecclesiae mediolanensis* (Rome, 1935)

——: *Canti ambrosiani per il popolo* (Milan, 1936)

——: *Officium et missa pro defunctis cum exequiarum ordine* (Rome, 1936)

——: *Liber vesperalis juxta ritum sanctae ecclesiae mediolanensis* (Rome, 1939) [reviewed in *Archiv für Liturgiewissenschaft*, i (1951), 414]

MS STUDIES

M. Huglo and others, eds.: *Fonti e paleografia del canto ambrosiano*, Archivio ambrosiano, vii (Milan, 1956)

C. Marcora: *Due importanti codici della biblioteca del Capitolo di Gallarate* (Gallarate, 1958)

R. Amiet: 'La tradition manuscrite du missel ambrosien', *Scriptorium*, xiv (1960), 16–60

M. J. Holthaus: *Beneventan Notation in the Vatican Manuscripts* (diss., U. of Southern California, 1961), 101

K. Gamber: *Codices liturgici latini antiquiores* (Fribourg, 1963, rev. 2/1968) [reviewed in *Rivista di storia della chiesa in Italia*, xxiii (1969), 490]

B. Comolli: 'Un codice ambrosiano-monastico della Badia di Ganna', *Rivista della Società storica varesina*, viii (1964), 89

C. Santoro: *I codici medioevali della Biblioteca Trivulziana* (Milan, 1965)

J. Gołos: 'Antyfonarz ambrozjański Biblioteki Jagiellońskiej w Krakowie', *Studia Hieronymo Feicht* (Kraków, 1967), 129

E. Moneta Caglio: 'I corali di S. Nazaro', *La basilica degli Apostoli e Nazaro martire nel culto e nell'arte* (Milan, 1969), 225

P. Ludwig: 'Lamentations notées dans quelques manuscrits bibliques', *Etudes grégoriennes*, xii (1971), 127

G. Tibiletti: 'Antifonario processionale delle Litanie Triduane (manoscritto del 1492)', *Ephemerides liturgicae*, lxxxvii (1973), 145

BIBLIOGRAPHY

C. Perego: *La regola del canto fermo ambrosiano* (Milan, 1622)

T. Nisard: 'Ambrosien, chant', *Dictionnaire liturgique* (Paris, 1854, 2/1860), 115

J. Pothier: *Les mélodies grégoriennes* (Tournai, 1880)

A. Kienle: 'Über ambrosianische Liturgie und ambrosianischen Gesang', *Studien und Mitteilungen des Benediktiner- und Cistercienser-Ordens*, v (Brno, 1884), 346

E. Soullier: 'Causeries sur le plain-chant: Saint Ambroise', *Etudes* (1890), 263

P. Wagner: *Einführung in die gregorianischen Melodien*, i (Leipzig, 1895, 3/1911/R1970; Eng. trans., 1907); iii (Leipzig, 1921/R1970)

P. Cagin: 'Avant-propos sur l'antiphonaire ambrosien', PalMus, v (1896), 1–200

A. Mocquereau: *Notes sur l'influence de l'accent et du cursus toniques latines dans le chant ambrosien* (Milan, 1897)

A. Nasoni: 'Il canto ambrosiano', *Conferenze santambrosiane* (Milan, 1897), 255

F. Tadra: *Kulturní styky Čech s cizinou až do válek husitských* [Cultural contacts of Bohemia with foreign parts up to the Hussite wars] (Prague, 1897), 355

A. Andreoni: *Breve metodo teorico-pratico di canto fermo ambrosiano* (Milan, 1900, 3/1929)

G. Morin: *Les véritables origines du chant grégorien* (Rome, 1904)

A. Gatard: 'Ambrosien (chant)', *Dictionnaire d'archéologie chrétienne et de liturgie* (Paris, 1905)

A. Gastoué: *Les origines du chant romain* (Paris, 1907)

A. Mocquereau: *Le nombre musical grégorien ou rythmique grégorienne* (Rome and Tournai, 1908–27, Eng. trans., 1932)

R. Andoyer: 'L'ancienne liturgie de Bénévent', *Revue du chant grégorien*, xx (1911–12), 176; xxi (1912–13), 14, 44, 81, 112, 144, 169; xxii (1913–14), 8, 41, 80, 106, 141, 170; xxiii (1919–20), 42, 116, 182; xxiv (1920–21), 48, 87

E. Garbagnati: 'Ricerche sull'antica salmodia ambrosiana', *Rassegna gregoriana*, x (1911), 361; *Ambrosius*, iv (1928), 25, 131, 181; v (1929), 33

G. A. Amelli: 'L'epigramma di Paolo Diacono intorno al canto gregoriano ed ambrosiano', *Memorie storiche forojuliesi*, ix (1913), 153

A. Gastoué: *Le graduel et l'antiphonaire romains* (Lyons, 1913)

K. Ott: *Le melodie ambrosiane studiate specialmente in rapporto alle gregoriane* (Rome, 1915)

A. Baumstark: 'Ein frühchristliches Theotokion in mehrsprachlicher Überlieferung', *Oriens christianus*, new ser., ix (1920), 36

E. Bishop: *The Mozarabic and Ambrosian Rites: Four Essays in Comparative Liturgiology* (London, 1924)

J. Huré: *Saint Augustin musicien d'après le De musica* (Paris, 1924)

A. Bernareggi: 'Ciò che certamente la liturgia ambrosiana deve a S. Ambrogio', *Ambrosius*, i (1925), 130; ii (1926), 8, 45, 99, 113; iii (1927), 45, 231

M. Busti: 'Un'antica melodia ambrosiana del Gloria in excelsis', *Ambrosius*, ii (1926), 12

E. Garbagnati: 'Le modulazioni ambrosiane per le orazioni', *Ambrosius*, iii (1927), 13

G. Bas: 'Ambrosiano, canto', *Enciclopedia italiana*, ii (1929), 806

D. Cantù: 'Le modulazioni ambrosiane delle orazioni', *Ambrosius*, v (1929), 202

——: 'Il canto del Dominus vobiscum e le modulazioni ambrosiane delle orazioni', *Ambrosius*, vi (1930), 118

E. Garbagnati: 'Gloria, Credo, Sanctus', *Ambrosius*, vi (1930), 13

——: 'Ancora della modulazione delle orazioni e del Dominus vobiscum nel rito ambrosiano', *Ambrosius*, vi (1930), 152

P. Wagner: 'Ambrosianischer Gesang', *Lexikon für Theologie und Kirche*, i (1930), 345

P. Borella: 'Note storiche circa l'antifona ad crucem alle laudi', *Ambrosius*, vii (1931), 225

D. Cantù: 'Federico Borromeo per il canto liturgico', *Ambrosius*, vii (1931), 345

R.-J. Hesbert: 'La tradition bénéventaine dans la tradition manuscrite', PalMus, xiv (1931), 60–479

P. Borella: 'L'antifona ante crucem', *Ambrosius*, viii (1932), 217

——: 'L'antifona post Evangelium', *Ambrosius*, viii (1932), 97

D. Cantù: 'La modulazione salmodica ambrosiana', *Ambrosius*, viii (1932), 23

G. M. Suñol: 'Il canto liturgico nella tradizione ambrosiana', *Ambrosius*, viii (1932), 254

P. Borella: 'Il Capitulum delle lodi ambrosiano e il Versus ad repetendum romano', *Ambrosius*, ix (1933), 241

E. T. Moneta Caglio: 'Capitulum e Completorium', *Ambrosius*, ix (1933), 191

G. M. Suñol: 'La notazione musicale ambrosiana', *Ambrosius*, ix (1933), 253, 280; x (1934), 43

A. Gastoué: 'Les chants du Credo', *Revue du chant grégorien*, xxxviii (1934), 14

G. M. Suñol: 'Versione critica del canto del Praeconium paschale ambrosiano', *Ambrosius*, x (1934), 77

E. T. Moneta Caglio: 'L'Ingressa', *Ambrosius*, xi (1935), 34

——: 'La Laus angelorum, l'inno mattinale dell'antichità', *Ambrosius*, xi (1935), 209

——: 'Ad te Domine', *Ambrosius*, xii (1936), 207

——: 'Dominus vobiscum', *Ambrosius*, xii (1936), 14

O. Heiming: 'Vorgregorianische römische Offertorien in der mailändischen Liturgie', *Liturgisches Leben*, v (1938), 72 [repr. in *Ambrosius*, xv (1939), 83]

R.-J. Hesbert: 'L'Antiphonale missarum de l'ancien rit bénéventain', *Ephemerides liturgicae*, lii (1938), 28–66, 141; liii (1939), 168; lix (1945), 69; lx (1946), 103–41; lxi (1947), 153–210

B. Neunheuser: 'Orientalisches Reichtum in der mailändischen Liturgie: das Transitorium', *Der christliche Orient in Vergangenheit und Gegenwart*, iii (1938), 45 [repr. in *Ambrosius*, xv (1939), 173]

G. M. Suñol: 'La restaurazione ambrosiana', *Ambrosius*, xiv (1938), 145, 174, 196, 296; xv (1939), 113; xvi (1940), 12, 108

E. T. Moneta Caglio: *Intendere la messa* (Milan, 1939)

R.-J. Hesbert: *Le problème de la transfixion du Christ dans les traditions biblique, patristique, iconographique et musicale* (Tournai, 1940)

G. Reese: *Music in the Middle Ages* (New York, 1940), 104ff

M. Altissent: 'Il "tonus praefationis" ambrosiano', *Ambrosius*, xvii (1941), 23

E. T. Moneta Caglio: 'L'antifona post Evangelium', *Ambrosius*, xvii (1941), 119

B. Kahmann: *Lo stile melodico nel canto ambrosiano* (diss., Pontificio Istituto di Musica Sacra, Rome, 1942)

E. Cattaneo: *Il breviario ambrosiano: note storiche ed illustrative* (Milan, 1943)

G. M. Suñol: 'Contributo del canto ambrosiano allo studio della modalità', *Ambrosius*, xxii (1946), 6

M. Avery: 'The Beneventan Lections for the Vigil of Easter and the Ambrosian Chant banned by Pope Stephen IX at Montecassino', *Studi gregoriani*, i (1947), 433

O. Heiming: 'Inizio o antifona completa prima dei salmi?', *Ambrosius*, xxiii (1947), 108

E. Wellesz: *Eastern Elements in Western Chant*, MMB, *Subsidia*, ii (Oxford, 1947)

M. Altissent: 'L'accompagnamento del canto ambrosiano', *Ambrosius*, xxiv (1948), 31

P. Borella: 'L'Ingressa della messa ambrosiana', *Ambrosius*, xxiv (1948), 83

E. Cattaneo: 'Una scuola ed un trattato di canto nel 1400', *Ambrosius*, xxiv (1948), 106

——: 'Franchino Gaffurio e il canto ambrosiano', *Ambrosius*, xxv (1949), 8

——: 'I canti della frazione e comunione nella liturgia ambrosiana', *Miscellanea liturgica in honorem L. C. Mohlberg*, ii (Rome, 1949), 147

D. Delalande: *Vers la version authentique du graduel grégorien: le graduel des Prêcheurs* (Paris, 1949)

B. Stäblein: 'Alleluia', MGG

G. M. Suñol: 'Ambrosiano, canto', *Enciclopedia cattolica* (1949)

E. Cattaneo: *Note storiche sul canto ambrosiano* (Milan, 1950)

——: 'Rito ambrosiano e liturgia orientale', *Questioni e bibliografia ambrosiane*, ed. P. Borella and others (Milan, 1950), 19

L. Brou: 'L'alleluia dans la liturgie mozarabe: étude liturgico-musicale d'après les manuscrits de chant', *AnM*, vi (1951), 3

E. Griffe: 'Aux origines de la liturgie gallicane', *Bulletin de littérature ecclésiastique*, lii (1951), 17

M. Huglo: 'A proposito di una nuova enciclopedia musicale: le melodie ambrosiane', *Ambrosius*, xxvii (1951), 114

B. Stäblein: 'Credo', MGG

H. Anglès: 'Ambrosian Chant', *NOHM*, ii (London, 1954, 2/1955), 59

E. Cattaneo: 'Il canto ambrosiano', *Storia di Milano*, iv (Milan, 1954), 575

J. Handschin: 'Trope, Sequence and Conductus', *NOHM*, ii (London, 1954, 2/1955), 128

——: 'Vestiges d'un ancien répertoire musical de Haute-Italie', *2. Internationaler Kongress für katholische Kirchenmusik: Wien 1954*, 142

M. Huglo: 'L'invito alla pace nelle antiche liturgie beneventana e ambrosiana', *Ambrosius*, xxx (1954), 158

Z. Nejedlý: 'Zpěv předhusitský' [Pre-Hussite song], *Dějiny husitského zpěvu v Čechách* [The history of Hussite song in Bohemia], i (Prague, 1954), 82

M. Huglo: 'Antifone antiche per la Fractio panis', *Ambrosius*, xxxi (1955), 85

R. Jesson: *Ambrosian Chant: the Music of the Mass* (diss., Indiana U., 1955)

H. Hucke: 'Die gregorianische Gradualweise des 2. Tons und ihre ambrosianischen Parallelen', *AMw*, xiii (1956), 284

J. Pinell: 'Vestigis del lucernari a occident', *Liturgica*, i (1956), 91

B. Stäblein: 'Gloria', 'Graduale (Gesang)', MGG

A. Baumstark: *Nocturna laus: Typen frühchristlicher Vigilienfeier und ihr Fortleben* (Münster, 1957)

M. Huglo: 'L'annuncio pasquale della liturgia ambrosiana', *Ambrosius*, xxxiii (1957), 88

H. Husmann: 'Zum Grossaufbau des ambrosianischen Alleluia', *AnM*, xii (1957), 17

E. T. Moneta Caglio: 'I responsori cum infantibus nella liturgia ambrosiana', *Studi in onore di Mons. C. Castiglioni* (Milan, 1957), 481–578

——: 'Stato attuale delle ricerche concernenti il canto ambrosiano', *3e congrès international de musique sacrée: Paris 1957*, 218

B. Stäblein: 'Hymnus', 'Introitus', 'Italien: A. Mittelalterliche Einstimmigkeit', MGG

H. Husmann: 'Alleluia, Sequenz und Prosa im altspanischen Choral', *Miscellánea en homenaje a Monseñor Higinio Anglés*, i (Barcelona, 1958), 407

R. Jesson: 'Ambrosian Chant', in W. Apel: *Gregorian Chant* (Bloomington, Ind., 1958, 3/1966), 465

E. T. Moneta Caglio: 'Lo stacco espressivo nel canto ambrosiano', *Musica sacra*, lxxxii (1958), 114

M. Huglo: 'Une antienne ambrosienne diffusée hors de Milan', *Ambrosius*, xxxv (1959), 145

A. A. King: *Liturgies of the Past* (London, 1959)

J. Claire: 'L'évolution modale dans les répertoires liturgiques occidentaux', *Revue grégorienne*, xl (1962), 196, 229; xli (1963), 49, 77, 127

E. Jammers: *Musik in Byzanz, im päpstlichen Rom und im Frankenreich: der Choral als Musik der Textaussprache* (Heidelberg, 1962)

B. Stäblein: 'Psalm', MGG

A. Bär: 'Enige kanttekeningen bij het vergelijken der oudromeinse en gregoriaanse introitus- en communiemelodieën en hun ambrosiaanse pendanten' [Some observations on the comparison of the Old Roman and Gregorian introit and communion melodies and their Ambrosian parallels], *Gregoriusblad*, lxxxiv (1963), 11

J. Claire: 'La psalmodie responsoriale antique', *Revue grégorienne*, xli (1963), 8

H. Hucke: 'Responsorium', MGG

K. Levy: 'A Hymn for Thursday in Holy Week', *JAMS*, xvi (1963), 127

B. Stäblein: 'Zur archaischen ambrosianischen (Mailänder) Mehrstimmigkeit', *A Ettore Desderi* (Bologna, 1963), 169

G. B. Baroffio: *Die Offertorien der ambrosianischen Kirche: Vorstudie zur kritischen Ausgabe der mailändischen Gesänge* (Cologne, 1964)

P. Borella: *Il rito ambrosiano* (Brescia, 1964)

G.-M. Oury: 'Psalmum dicere cum alleluia', *Ephemerides liturgicae*, lxxix (1965), 97

P. Borella: 'Il responsorio Tenebrae nel codice 123 dell'Angelica e nella tradizione ambrosiana', *Miscellanea liturgica ... G. Lercaro*, i (Rome, 1966), 597

S. Corbin: 'Il canto ambrosiano', *LaMusicaE*

M. Huglo: 'Relations musicales entre Byzance et l'Occident,' *XIIIth International Congress of Byzantine Studies: Oxford 1966*, 267

R. G. Weakland: 'The Performance of Ambrosian Chant in the Twelfth Century', *Aspects of Medieval and Renaissance Music: a Birthday Offering to Gustave Reese* (New York, 1966), 856

G. B. Baroffio: 'Die mailändische Überlieferung des Offertoriums Sanctificavit', *Festschrift Bruno Stäblein* (Kassel, 1967), 1

P. M. Ernetti: *La musica aquileiese* (Udine, 1967–8) [reviewed in *Rivista liturgica*, lvii (1970), 832]

H. Leeb: *Die Psalmodie bei Ambrosius* (Vienna, 1967)

G.-M. Oury: 'Formulaires anciens pour la Messe de Saint Martin', *Etudes grégoriennes*, vii (1967), 21

R. G. Weakland: 'Milanese Rite, Chants of', *New Catholic Encyclopedia*

N. Ghiglione: *La formula sol-la-si-do-do e le sue varianti nel canto ambrosiano* (diss., Pontificio Istituto Ambrosiano di Musica Sacra, Milan, 1968)

C. A. Miller: 'Gaffurius's *Practica musicae*: Origin and Contents', *MD*, xxii (1968), 105

T. L. Noblitt: 'The Ambrosian *Motetti missales* Repertory', *MD*, xxii (1968), 77

E. T. Moneta Caglio: 'Il canto nel duomo prima della costituzione della Cappella musicale', *Il duomo di Milano: congresso internazionale: Milano 1968*, ii, 3

G. B. Baroffio: 'Benevent', MGG

K. Levy: 'The Italian Neophytes' Chants', *JAMS*, xxiii (1970), 181

E. T. Moneta Caglio: 'Alle origini dello jubilus', *Musica sacra*, 3rd ser., xciv (Bergamo, 1970), 5

B. Stäblein: 'Der altrömische Gesang', *Die Gesänge des altrömischen Graduale Vat.lat.5319*, Monumenta monodica medii aevi, ii (Kassel, 1970), 3–164

T. Bailey: *The Processions of Sarum and the Western Church* (Toronto, 1971)

K. Levy: 'Lux de luce: the Origin of an Italian Sequence', *MQ*, lvii (1971), 40

G. B. Baroffio: 'Die liturgischen Gesänge im Abendland: ambrosianische Liturgie'; 'Die liturgischen Gesänge im Abendland: Liturgie im beneventanischen Raum', *Geschichte der katholischen Kirchenmusik*, i, ed. K. G. Fellerer (Kassel, 1972), 191; 204

——: 'Osservazioni sui versetti degli offertori ambrosiani', *Ricerche storiche sulla chiesa ambrosiana*, iii (1972), 54

M. Huglo: 'Die liturgischen Gesänge im Abendland: altgallikanische Liturgie', *Geschichte der katholischen Kirchenmusik*, i, ed. K. G. Fellerer (Kassel, 1972), 219
J. Hourlier: 'Notes sur l'antiphonie', *Gattungen der Musik in Einzeldarstellungen: Gedenkschrift für Leo Schrade* (Berne and Munich, 1973), 116
M. Curran: *The Hymns and Collects of the Antiphonary of Bangor and the Monastic Office at Bangor: a Study of their Sources and Content* (diss., Pont. Athen. Auselmianum, Rome, 1973–4)
GIACOMO BONIFACIO BAROFFIO

Ambrosian Singers. London choir formed in 1952 by John McCarthy; *see* LONDON, §VI, 3(ii).

Ambrosianum (Lat.). A term used in the Rule of St Benedict for the hymns composed by St AMBROSE; *see also* ANTIPHON, §1; BENEDICTINE MONKS, §2; HYMN, §II.

Ambrosio, Giacomo [Jacovo] **d'**. Italian 18th-century composer and singer; *see* VENTURA, GIUSEPPE.

Ambrosio, Giovanni (*fl* after 1450). Italian dancing-master, who may be identifiable with GUGLIELMO EBREO DA PESARO.

Ambrosio Cremonese. *See* CREMONESE, AMBROSIO.

Ambruys, Honoré d'. *See* D'AMBRUYS, HONORÉ.

Ame (Fr.: 'soul'). A term used to denote the SOUNDPOST of instruments of the violin and viol families. In certain French sources, the bow also is called the 'soul' of the instrument. L'abbé *le fils* wrote in 1761: 'On peut appeler l'archet L'Ame de l'Instrument qu'il touche' ('one can call the bow the soul of the instrument it touches').
DAVID D. BOYDEN

Ameling, Elly [Elisabeth] **(Sara)** (*b* Rotterdam, 8 Feb 1938). Dutch soprano. She studied with several Dutch teachers and later with Pierre Bernac, who encouraged her affinity for French song. After winning the 1956 's-Hertogenbosch and 1958 Geneva competitions, she gave her first recital in Amsterdam in 1961. Since her London (1966) and New York (1968) débuts, she has regularly visited Britain and the USA, as well as touring internationally. Although she has played Ilia in *Idomeneo* (with the Netherlands Opera in 1973, and in Washington, DC, in 1974), her chosen career is in concert and recital. In lieder, particularly Schubert's, her warm, unaffected personality, linguistic accomplishment, interpretative freshness and effortless technique are always apparent; she performs Satie's songs with charm and wit. Her purity of tone, particularly in *pianissimo* passages, and delicate control of vibrato are admirably suited to Handel, to Bach's cantatas and Passions, and to Mozart's opera and concert arias, several of which she has recorded. Baroque and Classical works, Mendelssohn, Wolf, Mahler, Ravel, Stravinsky and Britten are included in her extensive repertory. She performs with several accompanists but has a special rapport with Dalton Baldwin. She was awarded the Edison Prize in 1965 and 1970, and was made a Knight of the Order of Oranje Nassau in 1971.

BIBLIOGRAPHY
A. Blyth: 'Elly Ameling Talks', *Gramophone*, li (1974), 1689
HELEN SIMPSON

Ameln, Konrad (*b* Neuss, Rhineland, 6 July 1899). German musicologist and choir director. He studied musicology with Ludwig at Göttingen University

(1919–21) and subsequently with Gurlitt at Freiburg University, where he received the doctorate in 1924 with a dissertation on the melodies *Innsbruck, ich muss dich lassen* and *Ach Gott, vom Himmel sieh darein*. He was a lecturer at the Bauernhochschule in Rendsburg (1924–5) and at the Volkshochschule in Kassel (1925–6). He then acted as music consultant to the Central Office for General Librarianship in Leipzig (1926–8) and lectured in Protestant church music at the University of Münster (1930–39). After the war he lectured at the Landeskirchenmusikschulen of Hanover (1947–8) and the Rhineland (1949–57).

In the early 1920s Ameln embarked on a fruitful career as a choral and orchestral conductor and director of choral courses. His object was the authentic performance of old music, and this was coupled with considerable editorial work. He edited the journal of the Finkenstein League, *Die Singgemeinde* (1925–33). In 1935 he founded the Lüdenscheider Musikvereinigung, which he ran until 1973, and in 1938 he initiated the Kleine Musikfeste in Lüdenscheid (the 30th was held in 1973). His most important writings on church music are the *Handbuch der deutschen evangelischen Kirchenmusik* which he edited with C. Mahrenholz and others (Göttingen, 1935–), and his hymnological studies, which since 1935 have appeared chiefly in the *Jahrbuch für Liturgik und Hymnologie*, of which he is an editor. He has also made numerous facsimile editions of sacred songs and hymn books. In 1959 he founded the Internationale Arbeitsgemeinschaft für Hymnologie and he is co-editor of *Das deutsche Kirchenlied*, an interdenominational critical collected edition of hymn tunes. He has written extensively on Bach, Handel and Leonhard Lechner.

WRITINGS
Beiträge zur Geschichte der Melodien 'Innsbruck, ich muss dich lassen' und 'Ach Gott, vom Himmel sieh darein' (diss., U. of Freiburg, 1924)
'Die Anfänge der deutschen Passionshistorie', *IMSCR, iv Basle 1949*, 39
'Historische Instrumente in der gegenwärtigen Musikpraxis', *GfMKB, Bamberg 1953*, 96
with H. Schnoor: *Deutsche Musiker: Briefe, Berichte, Urkunden* (Göttingen, 1956)
Leonhard Lechner (Lüdenscheid, 1957)
'Zur Entstehungsgeschichte der Motette "Singet dem Herrn ein neues Lied" von J. S. Bach (BWV 225)', *BJb*, xlviii (1961), 25
'Die Wurzeln des deutschen Kirchenliedes der Reformation', *Kirchenmusik in ökumenischer Schau: 2. Internationaler Kongress für Kirchenmusik: Bern 1962*, 47
The Roots of German Hymnody of the Reformation Era (St Louis, 1964)
'Quem pastores laudavere', *Jb für Liturgik und Hymnologie*, xi (1966), 45–88
'Das handschriftliche Choralbuch des Organisten C. I. Engel vom Jahre 1775', *Jb für Liturgik und Hymnologie*, xii (1967), 171
'Leonhard Lechner in his time', *Cantors at the Crossroads: Essays on Church Music in Honor of Walter E. Buszin* (St Louis, 1967), 75
'Resonet in laudibus', 'Joseph, lieber Joseph, mein', *Jb für Liturgik und Hymnologie*, xv (1970), 52–112
'Lechner, Leonhard', 'Lied', §C, 'Zahn, Johannes', *MGG*
ed., with M. Jenny and W. Lipphardt: *Das deutsche Kirchenlied: kritische Gesamtausgabe der Melodien*, i/1: *Verzeichnis der Drucke*, RISM, B/VIII/1 (1975)
Numerous articles in *Die Singgemeinde* (from 1927), *Musik und Kirche* (from 1931), *Monatsschrift für Gottesdienst und kirchliche Kunst* (from 1938), *Jb für Liturgik und Hymnologie* (from 1955) and in Festschriften for J. Müller-Blattau (1960 and 1966), W. Vötterle (1968), and C. Mahrenholz (1970)

EDITIONS
G. F. Handel: Das Alexander-Fest, Hallische Händel-Ausgabe, i/1 (Kassel, 1957)
L. Lechner: Historia der Passion und Leidens unser einigen Erlösers und Seligmachers Jesu Christi (1593), Werke, xii (Kassel, 1960); *Newe teutsche Lieder mit fünf Stimmen: con alcuni madrigali, 1579*, ibid, v (Kassel, 1970)

J. S. Bach: Motetten, Neue Ausgabe sämtlicher Werke, iii/1 (Kassel, 1965)

Locheimer Liederbuch und Fundamentum organisandi des Conrad Paumann, DM, 2nd ser., Handschriften-Faksimiles (1972) [facs. edn.]

BIBLIOGRAPHY

L. Fischer, ed.: G. Rhau: Newe deutsche geistliche Gesenge [Wittenberg, 1544], iii (Kassel, 1969) [facs. edn.; incl. list of Ameln's publications in honour of his 70th birthday]

G. Schuhmacher, ed.: Traditionen und Reformen in der Kirchenmusik: Festschrift für Konrad Ameln zum 75. Geburtstag (Kassel, 1974) [incl. list of writings, 234]

HANS HEINRICH EGGEBRECHT

Amen (Heb.: 'so be it'; from the root *'mn*, 'to be trustworthy'). Liturgical acclamation used especially as the seal or intensification of a DOXOLOGY or other prayer.

In the Old Testament it generally represents the acclamation of an individual or a group assenting to an affirmation (e.g. a curse, doxology or blessing) of another. It was the people's response to the doxology (*berakhah*) pronounced by priests and Levites in the Temple in the Persian epoch (*Nehemiah* viii.6, *1 Chronicles* xvi.36, etc); later it was replaced in the Temple by a doxological formula, but became an important element in synagogue worship.

In the New Testament, Christ's assertions are sometimes introduced with the word 'amen' (retained in the Latin 'Amen dico vobis', as in the texts of some antiphons). This use of the word did not displace the older usage for Christians.

For the early Christian church, 'amen' was an acclamation chanted unceasingly in the heavenly liturgy (*Revelation* xix.4, etc), and a symbol of Christ, the sure ratifier of God's promises (*2 Corinthians* i.19–20). Hence the word has generally been left untranslated in other languages, epitomizing as it does the act of faith. In the primitive liturgy it was used, as in the synagogue, as a congregational acclamation after a doxology, especially after the eucharistic consecration prayer; it was also used at communion and after blessings. These uses of the amen are found in both eastern and western Christian liturgies. In the western liturgies, 'amen' still invariably concludes the lesser doxology and most prayers; it is used also after the Gloria and Creed of the Mass. At the Reformation Luther added independent amens to other liturgical chants.

During the Middle Ages the amen was relegated to the choir rather than the congregation, and some amen melodies became florid. This process of elaboration continued especially in polyphonic settings of the sections of the Mass Ordinary: from an early date, the amens to the Gloria and Creed were often set separately (e.g. by Machaut, as separate isorhythmic sections). After the time of A. Bertali (1605–69), fugal amens became common, with much repetition of the word 'amen', as for example in the masses of Bach, Mozart and Beethoven and in the amen chorus from Handel's *Messiah*.

Short independent polyphonic amen settings were written by English composers from the 16th century, as a part of the Preces and responses of the Anglican Offices; many others have been written for various liturgical purposes since the Reformation, including the well-known 'Dresden' amen, a setting of a traditional melody by J. G. Naumann (1741–1801), sung at the royal chapel at Dresden and elsewhere in Saxony, and often quoted in the works of later composers (Wagner, in *Parsifal*, Bruckner, Mendelssohn, Stanford). Settings of the amen as a simple IV–I cadence (hence called

'amen cadence') were in the 19th century very often appended to congregational hymns in English-speaking countries; the practice is today increasingly restricted (especially in Anglican churches) to hymns ending with a Trinitarian doxology.

Muslims, like Jews and Christians, use the word as the corroboration of a prayer. It is used especially after the recitation of the first *sūra* ('al-fātiḥa') of the Koran, where it is pronounced by the *imām* and repeated by the congregation.

BIBLIOGRAPHY

L. Ginzberg: 'Amen', Jewish Encyclopedia, i (New York, 1901), 491

F. Cabrol: 'Amen', Dictionnaire d'archéologie chrétienne et de liturgie, ed. F. Cabrol and others, i (Paris, 1907), 1554

M. Righetti: Manuale di storia liturgica, i (Milan, 1944, 3/1964), 210ff

A. Stuiber: 'Amen', Jb für Antike und Christentum, i (1958), 153

J. Pedersen: 'Amīn', The Encyclopaedia of Islām, ed. H. A. R. Gibb and others, i (Leiden, 1960), 436

GEOFFREY CHEW

Amenábar, Juan (*b* Santiago de Chile, 22 June 1922). Chilean composer. Introduced to music by his father, a cellist, he studied theory and the piano at the Catholic Conservatory from 1935 to 1939. After taking courses in civil engineering at the University of Chile (1940–45), he pursued work in composition with Jorge Urrutia Blondel at the National Conservatory (1948–52). He made his first experiments in electronic music when he was planning music programmes for Chilean Radio (1953–6), and in 1956 created the Experimental Sound Workshop at the Catholic University of Santiago. It was there that he produced *Los peces* (1957), a monodic study on the Fibonacci series which is considered the first tape composition made in Latin America. In 1958 he studied electronic music with Meyer-Eppler and collaborated with José Vicente Asuar in proposing the creation of an electronic music studio at the University of Chile. A composer of film music in addition to works in traditional forms, he has been active as a teacher, composer and promoter of electronic music. He has also served as a board member and later as president of the National Association of Composers.

WORKS
(*selective list*)

Choral: Misa litúrgica, male vv, ens, gui obbl., 1964; Sol de septiembre, male vv, ens, perc, 1964; several unacc. works

Inst: 4 diálogos, fl, vn, 1953; Toccata, org, 1955; Cantos de Alicia, A, rec, hpd, 6 str, 1964; Feedback, vn, 1965; Alternativas, pf, 1969; Divertimento Cordovés, perc, ens, tape, 1971

Elec: Los peces, 1957; Klesis (Invitación), 1968; El vigía del personal, 1968; Música continua, 1969; High Key, 1970; Sueño de un niño, 1970; Amacatá, ?1972; Ludus vocalis, ?1972

Principal publisher: Instituto de Extensión Musical (U. of Chile)

BIBLIOGRAPHY

R. Escobar: 'Instituto Chileno-Alemán de Cultura', Revista musical chilena (1970), no.24, p. 107

Composers of the Americas, xvii (Washington, DC, 1971), 15ff

JOHN M. SCHECHTER

Amen cadence. A plagal cadence; *see* CADENCE.

Amendola, Giuseppe (*b* ?Palermo, *c*1750; *d* ? Palermo, 1808). Italian composer. Between 1772 and 1792 he was active in Palermo, where several cantatas by him were performed, including an *Orfeo* to a text by G. Azzoli (Teatro S Cecilia, 1788). In about 1790 the young Nicolò Isouard, destined by his family for a career in commerce, secretly took lessons from Amendola in harmony, 'the classical operas of Leo and Durante, and the duets and trios of Clari'. Amendola's only known opera, the comedy *Il Begliar-Bey di Caramania*, was apparently first performed in Madrid in 1776; it was probably produced in Bologna in 1778 (as *La schiava fedele*), and subsequently achieved notable success in other European capitals. At least until World War II scores were extant at the Paris Conservatoire, the Thurn and Taxis collection in Regensburg, and at the Dresden Landesbibliothek, which also held a rondo for soprano and keyboard.

BIBLIOGRAPHY

FétisB

U. Rolandi: *Musica e musicisti in Malta* (Livorno, 1932), 67f

JAMES L. JACKMAN

Amener (Fr.: 'to lead'). A 17th-century dance in moderate triple metre characterized by six-bar phrases usually grouped into either three-bar units or a four-bar and a two-bar unit. The *amener* is generally considered to have derived from the branle *de Poitou à mener*, in which one couple led the other dancers. Its characteristic phrasing is similar to that of the BRANLE and the early MINUET, and the resemblance to the latter led some writers (Praetorius and, later, Pierre Rameau) to posit a relationship between the two. Examples of music for the *amener* are quite rare, but may be found among the dance music collected by Ecorcheville (*Vingt suites d'orchestre*, Paris, 1906/R1970), the theatrical dances of Alessandro Poglietti, and the suites of Biber and J. C. F. Fischer.

Amengual(-Astaburuaga), René (*b* Santiago, 2 Sept 1911; *d* Santiago, 2 Aug 1954). Chilean composer and pianist. He studied with Allende for composition and Renard for the piano at the Santiago National Conservatory (1923–35), where he then held appointments as coach at the opera department (1935), assistant professor of the piano (1937), professor of analysis (1940) and director (1945). At the same time he taught at the Liceo Manuel de Salas in Santiago. He was secretary-general to the Instituto de Extensión Musical (from 1941), a founder-director of the Escuela Moderna de Música, Santiago (1940) and a member of various arts societies. In 1943 he went to the USA as a guest of the Institute of International Education and in 1953 he was in Europe for the performance of his Wind Sextet at the ISCM Festival. His early compositions show the influences of French music and Chilean folklore; from the late 1940s his work became more expressionist and abstract.

WORKS
(selective list)

Orch: Preludio sinfónico, 1939; Pf Conc., 1941–2; Harp Conc., 1950
Vocal: El vaso (Mistral), S, chamber orch, 1942; many songs and unacc. choral pieces
Chamber: 2 str qts, 1941, 1950; Sonata, vn, pf, 1944; Suite, fl, pf, 1945; Wind Sextet, 1953
Pf: Burlesca, 1932–8; Transparencias, 1938; Introduction and Allegro, 2 pf, 1939; Sonatina, 1939; 2 Short Preludes, 1950

Principal publishers: Instituto de Extensión Musical, G. Schirmer

BIBLIOGRAPHY

J. Orrego-Salas: 'El concierto para arpa y orquesta de René Amengual', *Revista musical chilena* (1950), no.39, p.54
M. Aguilar: 'La evolución estilística en la obra de René Amengual', *Revista musical chilena* (1954), no.46, p.9
V. Salas-Viú: 'La obra de René Amengual del neoclasicismo al expresionismo', *Revista musical chilena* (1964), no.90, p.62

JUAN A. ORREGO-SALAS

Amenreich [Armenreich], **Bernhard** (*b* Heilbronn, 1535–8; *d* in or after 1576). German composer and organist. He studied at Heidelberg in 1553. He spent the first part of his career in Central Franconia, from 1557 as Kantor at Hilpoltstein, from 1560 as organist at

Feuchtwangen, from 1563 as a schoolmaster at Windsheim and from 1565 as a court musician at Ansbach. After again studying at Heidelberg in 1568 he was from 1569 to 1575 Kapellmeister and organist to Landgrave Philipp the Younger of Hesse at Schloss Rheinfels and also organist at St Goar, south of Koblenz. He wrote *Magnificat* settings on the eight tones for organ, a wedding song for Landgrave Philipp in 1569, an autobiographical threnody, *Biss in den Himmel clage ich über Tyrannei* (in *A-Wn*), a four-part piece to words by the Elector Palatine Friedrich III (1576; in *I-Rvat*) and other occasional works.

BIBLIOGRAPHY

G. Pietzsch: *Quellen und Forschungen zur Geschichte der Musik . . . zu Heidelberg bis 1622* (Mainz, 1963)

Amerbach, Bonifacius (*b* Basle, 11 Oct 1495; *d* Basle, 24 or 25 April 1562). Swiss humanist and musician. The youngest son of the printer Johann Amerbach (*c*1440–1513) from Amorbach (Lower Franconia), Bonifacius Amerbach studied at the universities of Basle, Freiburg and Avignon from 1508 to 1523. He first matriculated in the faculty of arts of Basle University, where he would also have heard lectures on *musica speculativa*. In Basle he met the organist Hans Kotter and took music lessons with him which initiated a tablature book, the so-called Amerbach Tablature (*CH-Bu* F.IX.22; ed. in SMd, vi/1, 1967; corrigenda in *Mf*, xxiv, 1971, p.243); with its numerous compositions for organ or clavichord and its *Fundamentum totius artis musicae*, it is one of the most extensive sources from the earlier 16th century. During Amerbach's time in Freiburg, where from 1513 he studied jurisprudence, he was friendly with Sixt Dietrich and Johann Weck, the cathedral organist. He continued his organ studies with Weck. Amerbach is known to have been interested in other instruments, and to have owned more than one clavichord.

The book of tablatures begun by Kotter and continued by Weck contains 55 compositions for organ or clavichord. Almost every instrumental form of the time is represented, from unornamented *intavolatura* to elaborate settings of chorales. It includes preludes and dances by Buchner, Kotter and Weck, and intabulations of vocal models by Isaac, Hofhaimer, Alexander Agricola, Josquin, Dietrich, Moulu and others. The last piece in the manuscript is probably in Amerbach's own hand. Part of his collection of notes (organ and lute tablatures, a book of bass voice parts and a copy of Buchner's *Fundamentum*) was given by his son Basilius Amerbach to Basle, where it is now kept in the university library.

BIBLIOGRAPHY

W. Merian: 'Bonifacius Amerbach und Hans Kotter', *Basler Zeitschrift für Geschichte und Altertumskunde*, xvi (1917), 140–206
A. Hartmann: *Die Amerbachkorrespondenz* (Basle, 1942)
H. J. Marx: 'Der Tabulatur-Codex des Basler Humanisten Bonifacius Amerbach', *Musik und Geschichte: Leo Schrade zum sechzigsten Geburtstag* (Cologne, 1963), 50

HANS JOACHIM MARX

America. See LATIN AMERICA and NORTH AMERICA; *see also* UNITED STATES OF AMERICA and other individual countries.

American Company. Theatre company active in the USA from 1767 to 1774; *see* NEW YORK, §1.

American Composers Alliance. A publishing and service organization in New York, owned and operated by composers and founded in 1938 by Copland, Thomson, Riegger and others to promote the interests of American composers. It reproduces members' scores in the Composers Facsimile Edition, sponsors concerts and radio broadcasts and records contemporary works through Composers Recordings Inc. The ACA official journal, *The Bulletin*, was published to 1965.

RITA H. MEAD

American Conservatory of Music. Conservatory established in Chicago in 1886; *see* CHICAGO, §4.

American Federation of Musicians. A trade union for American and Canadian professional musicians, affiliated with the AFL-CIO (the major confederation of labour unions in the USA). It was founded in 1896 and in 1974 had over 650 local unions with 330,000 members. It negotiates both national and local contracts and enforces employers' observance of working conditions, wage scales and fringe benefits. Local unions have jurisdiction in local areas of employment, but the international union bargains collectively in the fields of network radio and television, recordings and films. The AFM has negotiated a number of pension, welfare and retirement funds for members. Its official journal, published monthly, is the *International Musician*.

RITA H. MEAD

American Guild of Musical Artists. A national labour union, chartered in 1937, and affiliated with the AFL-CIO (the major confederation of labour unions in the USA). It has jurisdiction in the professional fields of opera, ballet, dance, concert, recital and oratorio and operates in the USA, Canada and Central America, negotiating contracts and providing benefits for its members.

RITA H. MEAD

American Guild of Organists. An organization of organists chartered in 1896; its founders included John Knowles Paine and George Whitefield Chadwick. Its membership in 1974 was 16,000 in 300 chapters throughout the USA. In order to encourage consistently high standards, it conducts examinations in practical organ playing, choir training and the theory and general knowledge of music. Successful candidates receive certificates and are designated fellow, associate or choirmaster. The official AGO magazine, *Music*, is published monthly.

RITA H. MEAD

American Institute of Applied Music. New York conservatory founded in 1886, known as the Metropolitan Conservatory until 1891 and the Metropolitan College of Music from then until 1900; *see* NEW YORK, §10.

American Institute of Musicology. Organization founded by Armen Carapetyan in 1944, as the Institute of Renaissance and Baroque Music, principally to publish scholarly editions of the compositions and theoretical sources of early music (primarily those of the Middle Ages and the Renaissance), thus promoting such studies as part of the humanistic disciplines in higher education. Until 1949 a group of eminent scholars formed an advisory board, but it subsequently functioned under the sole direction of Carapetyan. In 1946 its headquarters were moved from Cambridge, Massachusetts, to Rome, and it was renamed. An office was maintained in Cambridge until 1954, and the circulation office was in Dallas, Texas, until 1974 when it was transferred to the firm of Hänssler-Verlag in Stuttgart. Initially the institute engaged in other activities in addition to publishing. A choir was established in 1947 and summer sessions featuring advanced studies in medieval and Renaissance music history were held in 1947 and 1948; both were soon discontinued.

The institute's publications aim at high standards equally of scholarship and of book production. It issues several series: Corpus Mensurabilis Musicae, covering the principal musical sources of the Middle Ages and Renaissance, including collected works and transcriptions of manuscript sources; Corpus Scriptorum de Musica, a series of theoretical treatises published in the original languages; Musicological Studies and Documents, consisting of monographs on various topics of medieval and Renaissance music history, together with source materials not covered by the above series; Corpus of Early Keyboard Music, consisting of keyboard works in modern notation; Renaissance Manuscript Studies; and Miscellanea, covering other studies and sources. The institute's yearbook, *Musica disciplina*, began publication in 1946 as the *Journal of Renaissance and Baroque Music* and was renamed the following year; it is devoted to research studies and inventories of primary sources.

BIBLIOGRAPHY
Ten Years of the American Institute of Musicology, 1945–1955 (Nijmegen, 1955)

PAULA MORGAN

American Music Center (AMC). An organization (with offices in New York) of composers, publishers, institutions, and professional and student musicians. It was founded in 1940 by Marion Bauer, Copland, Howard Hanson, Otto Luening and Quincy Porter to encourage the composition, publication, distribution and performance of contemporary music. In 1975 there were about 875 members, most of them composers. The AMC became the official US information centre for music in 1962; its library contains biographical information on American composers and an extensive collection of scores, most of them unpublished, available to performers and scholars. Other services include sponsoring conferences, preparing radio broadcasts and assisting young composers to meet the expenses of copying parts when they have a guarantee of performance. Its bi-monthly newsletter informs subscribers of competitions, awards and recent recordings and publications.

RITA H. MEAD

American Musicological Society. An organization founded in 1934 to advance scholarly research in the various fields of music; it grew out of the New York Musicological Society (1930–34) and was first named the American Musicological Association. Its founders were George S. Dickinson, Carl Engel, Gustave Reese, Helen Heffron Roberts, Joseph Schillinger, Charles Seeger, Harold Spivacke, Oliver Strunk and Joseph Yasser; its first president was Otto Kinkeldey. The society, with 2600 individual members and 1069 subscribing institutions, holds annual meetings where papers, symposia and concerts are given; members also read papers at meetings of the 15 regional chapters. In addition the society gives awards, provides an employment service and coordinates activities with other music societies and councils. It is a constituent member of the American Council of Learned Societies and its president serves as a delegate in the consultative committee of the International Musicological Society. It participates in *RISM*, *RILM* and an international listing of dissertations in musicology.

Major efforts are directed to publications. Earlier, annual bulletins (1936–47) and papers read at annual meetings (1936–41) were issued; members now receive abstracts of papers and a biannual *Newsletter*. In 1948 the official publication, the *Journal of the American Musicological Society*, was founded; it is published three times a year. Other studies and documents published by the society include Ockeghem's collected works edited by Dragan Plamenac (1966), Dunstable's complete works edited by Manfred Bukofzer, published jointly with Musica Britannica (2/1970), Joseph Kerman's *The Elizabethan Madrigal* (1962), E. R. Reilly's *Quantz and his Versuch* (1971), E. H. Sparks's *The Music of Noel Bauldeweyn* (1972), *Doctoral Dissertations in Musicology* edited by C. D. Adkins in succession to Helen Hewitt (1952, 1957, 1961, 1965, 1971), *A Selective List of Masters' Theses in Musicology* compiled by D. R. de Lerma (1970) and an *International Index of Dissertations* (1977).

BIBLIOGRAPHY
B. S. Brook, ed.: *American Musicological Society, Greater New York Chapter: a Programmatic History 1935–1965* (New York, c1965)
W. J. Mitchell: 'A Hitherto Unknown – or a Recently Discovered . . .', *Musicology and the Computer*, ed. B. Brook (New York, 1970), 1
'Constitution and By-laws', *JAMS*, xxiii (1970), 558
RITA H. MEAD

American Opera Center. A section of the Juilliard School; *see* NEW YORK, §2.

American Opera Society. New York society active from 1951 to 1970; *see* NEW YORK, §2.

American organ. A HARMONIUM with suction bellows.

American Piano Co. American firm of piano manufacturers. Its incorporation in June 1908 consolidated such older American piano firms as Chickering & Sons and Wm. Knabe & Co. with the firms owned by the Foster–Armstrong Co. Foster–Armstrong, founded in Rochester, New York by George G. Foster and W. B. Armstrong in 1894, had bought the Marshall & Wendell Piano Co. of Albany in 1899; after the construction of a new plant in 1906 in East Rochester, New York, it acquired other firms and incorporated with a capital of 12 million dollars.

Formed to market pianos that ranged from concert instruments to mass-produced commercial ones, the American Piano Co. also established a special player department in 1909 and developed a reproducing player mechanism under the name of Ampico, which along with its competitors Welte Mignon and Duo-Art dominated the American market of sophisticated automatic piano mechanisms. In 1922 the Mason & Hamlin Piano Co. became part of the firm, but was sold to the Aeolian Co. in the early 1930s. The American Piano Corporation in 1930 succeeded the American Piano Co., at which time numerous lease commitments on company-owned retail operations were relinquished. On 1 September 1932 the American Piano Corporation merged with its competitor the AEOLIAN CO. to form the Aeolian American Corporation, in an attempt to create a firm which would survive the effects of the Depression, the radio and the phonograph on the piano trade.

CYNTHIA ADAMS HOOVER

American Society of Ancient Instruments. A society founded in Philadelphia in 1929; *see* PHILADELPHIA, §1.

American Society of Composers, Authors and Publishers (ASCAP). *See* COPYRIGHT COLLECTING SOCIETIES, §IV.

American Society of University Composers. An organization serving composers in universities of the USA. It was founded in New York in 1966 by Donald Martino, J. K. Randall, Claudio Spies, Henry Weinberg, Peter Westergaard, Charles Wuorinen and Benjamin Boretz. It works to establish standards for teaching composition, to improve communication within the profession, and to represent its members' interests to the public. In addition to the proceedings of its annual national conference the ASUC publishes a newsletter and the *Journal of Music Scores*, produces a series of recordings and prepares a radio programme for distribution to stations throughout the USA.

RITA H. MEAD

American Symphony Orchestra League (ASOL). A non-profit-making service organization. It was founded in 1942 by Leta G. Snow and Theresa Shier with national headquarters in Vienna, Virginia, and serves as a coordinating, research and educational agency for symphony orchestras, assisting in the formation of new orchestras and encouraging the work of American musicians, conductors and composers. Symphony orchestras, classified according to size of budget, are voting members, while individuals, firms and institutions are non-voting associate members. Besides holding training sessions for orchestra managers and presenting courses for young conductors, the ASOL works actively for financial and legislative support for the performing arts. The Women's Council, an affiliated body established in 1964, organizes fund drives and other community activities for symphony orchestras. The league has published a large number of studies and over 600 monographs, and it also issues a newsletter, *Symphony News*, six times a year. Its Gold Baton Award is presented annually to those making significant contributions to music, and the joint award of ASOL and the American Society of Composers, Authors and Publishers (ASCAP) is given to ASCAP-licensed orchestras for good programming of contemporary music.

BIBLIOGRAPHY
C. Pavlakis: *The American Music Handbook* (New York, 1974)
RITA H. MEAD

Amerus [Aluredus, Annuerus, Aumerus] (*fl* 1271). English theorist active in Italy. He was a clerk and a member of the household of Cardinal Ottobono Fieschi (later Pope Hadrian V), and wrote his *Practica artis musice* in the cardinal's house, perhaps in August 1271 at Viterbo where the cardinal was staying for the conclave. The work is explicitly designed for teaching boys music and includes all the conventional notions of the period concerning *musica plana*. The central part of the work contains the tonary according to the practice of the French and English churches and the Roman curia.

There is a chapter towards the end devoted to the composition of polyphonic music (*cantilene organice*); this chapter may be the first treatise on measured music written in Italy. The simple notes described are the long, breve and semibreve, in a binary relationship (i.e. the long equals two breves and four semibreves). Ligatures are equated to various rhythmic feet, and the greatest value is normally assigned to the last note.

BIBLIOGRAPHY

P. Blanchard: 'Alfred le musicien et Alfred le philosophe', *Rassegna gregoriana*, viii (1909), 419

J. Kromolicki: *Die Practica artis musicae des Amerus und ihre Stellung in der Musiktheorie des Mittelalters* (Berlin, 1909)

F. A. Gallo: *La teoria della notazione in Italia dalla fine del XIII all'inizio del XV secolo* (Bologna, 1966), 13ff

M. Huglo: *Les tonaires: inventaire, analyse, comparaison* (diss., U. of Paris; Paris, 1971), 227ff, 344f

F. A. Gallo: 'Citazioni di teorici medievali nelle lettere di Giovanni del Lago', *Quadrivium*, xiv (1973), 171

C. Ruini, ed.: *Ameri Practica artis musice*, CSM, xxv (1975)

F. ALBERTO GALLO

Amerval, Eloy d'. See ELOY D'AMERVAL.

Ameyden, Christian (*b* Oirschot, Brabant, *c*1534; *d* Rome, 20 Nov 1605). Flemish tenor and composer. After studying with his uncle, who was a singer at Antwerp Cathedral, he went to Rome, and by 1 March 1564 was a tenor in the papal chapel. He was released from this appointment on 31 August 1565, with 13 other musicians. On 10 March 1569 he was appointed a singer in the Pauline chapel, made a canon, and given the prebend recently vacated by the death of Simon Sauvage. Returning to the papal chapel, he became an abbot on 2 January 1572 and a *punctator* (responsible for choir attendances) in 1573. In 1593 and 1594 he was named head of the singers' society, and in 1596 he retired from his singing duties and was pensioned. He is buried in S Maria dell'Anima, Rome. *I-Rvat* 30 contains a five-part mass, *Fontes et omnia*, and manuscript 29 a four-part *Magnificat*. Lassus's third book of madrigals (Rome, 1563) included Ameyden's five-part *Quel dolce suon*.

BIBLIOGRAPHY

E. vander Straeten: *La musique aux Pays-Bas avant le XIXᵉ siècle* (Brussels, 1867–88/R1969), i, 150f; iii, 199; vi, 441ff

——: *Les musiciens néerlandais en Italie du quatorzième au dix-neuvième siècle* (Brussels, 1882), 337, 445ff

F. X. Haberl: 'Giovanni Maria Nanino', *KJb*, vi (1891), 85

LAVERN J. WAGNER

Amfiteatrov [Amfitheatrof], **Massimo** (*b* Paris, 27 Feb 1907). Italian cellist of Russian birth, brother of Daniele Amfitheatrof. He studied in St Petersburg with Louis, in Paris, and with Gilberto Crepax at the Milan Conservatory. He began his career as first cellist with the Turin Radio Orchestra (1936–7) and the Rome Radio Orchestra (1938–47), and taught briefly at the Naples Conservatory (1940–41). From 1947 he began to tour widely as a soloist in other European countries. He appeared in London and at the Edinburgh Festival in 1950 as soloist and leader of the cellos with the Orchestra of La Scala, and in the USA, Australasia, India and South Africa, gaining much admiration for his virtuoso skill and interpretative style. He formed a duo with the pianist Ornella Santoliquido, a trio with the addition of the violinist Arrigo Pelliccia, and the Rome Quartet with the further addition of Luigi Alberto Bianchi (viola).

PIERO RATTALINO

Amfitheatrof [Amfitheatrov], **Daniele (Alexandrovich)** (*b* St Petersburg, 29 Oct 1901). Italian composer and conductor of Russian origin. A grandson of the composer Nikolay Sokolov and a brother of the cellist Massimo Amfiteatrov, he studied under Vītol in St Petersburg and Křička in Prague, but the greater part of his training was undertaken in Rome, where he studied composition with Respighi at the Conservatorio di S Cecilia (diploma 1924) and the organ at the Pontifical Academy of Sacred Music. He was engaged as pianist, organist and chorus assistant at the Augusteo (1924–9), also conducting the orchestra under Molinari's supervision. Thereafter he was artistic director of the Genoa and Trieste radio stations and conductor and manager for Italian radio in Turin; he also conducted elsewhere in Europe. In 1937 he went to the USA as associate conductor of the Minneapolis SO, and in 1939 he settled in Hollywood as a film composer. He moved to New York in the 1950s and then to Venice. Most of Amfitheatrof's works are in a Respighi-like romantic-impressionist style marked by vivid orchestral colouring.

WORKS
(*selective list*)

Choral: Requiem, perf. 1962

Orch: Poema del mare, 1925; Miracolo della rosa, 1927; Panorama americano, 1933; Pf Conc., 1937–46

Film scores: I'll be seeing you, 1945; Song of the South, 1946; The Lost Moment, 1947; Letter from an Unknown Woman, 1948; Salome, 1953; The Mountain, 1956; Major Dundee, 1965

Principal publisher: Ricordi

CHRISTOPHER PALMER

Amicis, Anna Lucia de. See DE AMICIS, ANNA LUCIA.

Ami du clavier, Un (*fl c*1750). Pseudonym of the composer of *Sei concerti a cinque, cembalo concertino, violino primo, violino secondo, alto viola e violoncello, avec quatre fugues pour l'orgue*, of which an incomplete manuscript copy exists in the Bibliothèque Nationale, Paris. In the same library are orchestral and keyboard parts (under two different shelf numbers) of an engraved 'nouvelle édition' (before 1758) of the concertos only. The manuscript, which breaks off before the fugues, is probably a copy of the first edition. Handel's influence is clear, especially in an air with variations inspired by the 'Harmonious Blacksmith', and that of Hasse is likely. There are many oddities, including finales in which the violin takes over completely as the solo instrument while the harpsichordist accompanies from a figured bass.

BIBLIOGRAPHY

H. Gericke: *Der Wiener Musikalienhandel* (Graz, 1960)

A. Devriès: *Edition et commerce de la musique gravée à Paris* (Geneva, 1976)

DAVID FULLER

Amiens. City in northern France. Christianity was introduced in the 4th century, St Firmin being the city's first bishop. The Cathedral of Notre Dame, the largest in France, was built between 1220 and 1270. During the Middle Ages the town's prosperity was based on the cloth trade. By the Treaty of Arras (1435) King Charles VII ceded Amiens to Duke Philip the Good of Burgundy, but Louis XI recaptured the city in 1471 and, except for brief occupations by the Spanish in 1597 and the Germans in 1914 and 1940, the town has remained part of France.

The history of the city's music centres on the cathedral. The first evidence of plainchant dates from after the Norman invasion, when Bishop Gervin (1091–

1102) engaged choirboys and a cantor named Rogerus. Surviving manuscripts include a late 13th-century 'Liber ordinarius' in plainchant and a 14th-century 'Liber organicus' in polyphony. By 1146 a *scola cantorum* was established to train the choristers and the adult *vicarii*. During the 13th century the choir was increased from ten (including four boys) to 16, under a precentor; by the early 16th century the number of boys had increased to ten. In the 18th century the *vicarii* were chosen according to their talent as singers or instrumentalists and apart from the organist, two serpents were engaged (one doubling on bassoon), supplemented by two cellos on feast days. The cathedral musicians included Philippe Caron (1422); Jean Mouton (*Maistre des enffans*, 1500); François Dulot (1514); and Laurent Bonard (1547–53). Vulfran Samin was a chorister at the brotherhood of the Puy-Notre-Dame in 1543–4.

During the 17th century outstanding musicians in the city included Jean de Bournonville (choirmaster 1619–32), his pupil Artus Auxcousteaux, who was born at Amiens (choirmaster, 1633), and Valentin de Bournonville (choirmaster, 1643). The cathedral's strong musical tradition survived until the Revolution, under the direction of E. J. A. Blanchard (1734–99) and others, but subsequently Amiens lost its importance as a musical centre.

BIBLIOGRAPHY
G. Durand: 'Les orgues de la cathédrale d'Amiens', *Tribune de St-Gervais*, ix (1903)
——: 'La musique de la cathédrale d'Amiens avant la Révolution', *Bulletin de la Société des antiquaires de Picardie*, xxix (1922), 362; repr. in *La vie musicale dans les provinces françaises* (Geneva, 1971)
FRANK DOBBINS

Amiot, Jean Joseph Marie (*b* Toulon, 8 Feb 1718; *d* Peking, 8 Oct 1793). French Jesuit missionary. After a classical education, he entered the Society of Jesus as a novice in 1737, taught in Jesuit colleges for ten years, then, on being ordained, requested assignment to the China mission. He arrived in Peking in 1751 and remained there until his death.

Amiot's remarkable output of monographs, translations, dictionaries and voluminous scholarly correspondence includes several extensive works on Chinese music – among the first serious western studies of any non-western music. He first translated the 17th-century book *Ku yüeh ching chuan* ('Commentary on the classic of ancient music') by Li Kuang-ti; although paraphrased by Amiot and others, the translation was never published, and the manuscript was lost. His next work on Chinese music, the *Mémoire sur la musique des Chinois*, was edited for publication by Abbé Pierre Joseph Roussier, a theorist specializing in ancient and foreign music; however, Roussier added lengthy, pedantic notes of little value while deleting many plates, all Chinese characters, and significant portions of the text, thus obscuring the original and impairing its value for future scholars. Other important manuscripts remain unpublished, including a study of contemporary Chinese music practice and a notebook containing 54 tunes transcribed into staff notation.

Amiot was a competent and sincere scholar who attempted to convey Chinese music in a Chinese manner. His work was frequently quoted throughout the 19th century; used with caution it is still a significant source for the state of Chinese music and theory at the end of the 18th century, and for the history of ethnomusicology.

WRITINGS
(*only those relating to music included*)
De la musique moderne des Chinois (MS, *F-Pn* Rés. Vmb 14)
Divertissements chinois, ou Concerts de musique chinoise, les notes chinoises mises sur des lignes à notre manière (MS, 1779, *Pn* chinois Bréquigny 14)
Mémoire sur la musique des Chinois tant anciens que modernes (MS, *Pn*); ed. P. J. Roussier (Paris, 1779/R1973) and in J. Amiot: Mémoires concernant l'histoire, les sciences, les arts, les moeurs, les usages des Chinois, vi (Paris, 1780), 1–254
Concernant la fabrication d'un instrument de musique 'yun-lo', vulgairement appelé 'tam-tam' [letter of 1786 to Bertin, ed. F.-J. Fétis, *Revue musicale*, i (1827), 365]

BIBLIOGRAPHY
P. C. de Rochemonteix: *Joseph Amiot et les derniers survivants de la mission française à Pékin, 1750–1795* (Paris, 1915)
A. Pfister: *Notices biographiques et bibliographiques sur les Jésuites de l'ancienne mission de Chine, 1552–1773* (Shanghai, 1932–4)
A. H. Rowbotham: *Missionary and Mandarin: the Jesuits at the Court of China* (Berkeley, 1942)
Ysia Tchen: *La musique chinoise en France au XVIIIᵉ siècle* (diss., U. of Paris, 1948)
FREDRIC LIEBERMAN

Amir, Nahun (*b* Haifa, 8 Feb 1936). Israeli composer. He studied composition with Ben-Haim at the Rubin Academy, Jerusalem, graduating in 1964. For further study he went to the USA, where he was a pupil of Carter and Sessions, and of Overton at the Juilliard School (MMus 1969). In 1972 he received the PhD from the Jewish Theological Seminary, New York, for work on sacred music, and the next year he was appointed pedagogical counsellor in the theory and composition department of the Rubin Academy at Tel-Aviv University. His compositions bear witness to his twin interests: Jewish music and biblical cantillation, and string instruments.

WORKS
(*selective list*)
3 str qts; Music for Str, 1969; Sonata, vn, 1970; The Penitence Cantata, S, Mez, chorus, chamber orch, 1970; Friday Evening Service, cantor, chorus, org, 1973

Principal publisher: Israel Music Institute

BIBLIOGRAPHY
Y. W. Cohen: *Werden und Entwicklungen der Musik in Israel* (Kassel, 1976) [pt.ii of rev. edn. of M. Brod: *Die Musik Israels*]
W. Y. Elias: *The Music of Israel* (Tel-Aviv, in preparation)
WILLIAM Y. ELIAS

Amiran-Pougatchov, Emanuel (*b* Warsaw, 8 Aug 1909). Israeli composer and teacher of Russian descent. His family returned to Russia when he was four and he began music studies in Moscow at the age of nine. He studied further in Berlin (1922–4), in Jerusalem with Rosovsky (1928–9) and at Trinity College, London, with Bantock and Rowley (1934–5). Together with Kestenberg he founded in 1945 the Tel-Aviv Music Teachers' College, and in 1949 he was appointed chief supervisor of music education at the Ministry of Education and Culture. He has also held several administrative posts in Israeli musical life. Among his works are many incidental scores, notably for productions at the Habima-Israel National Theatre and the Ohel Theatre (1935–55), and some very popular solo and choral songs.

WORKS
(*selective list*)
Orch: Hashomer [The guard], Evel [Mourning], Sym. Movt
Cantatas: Acharei moti [After my death], Nahamu ami [Comfort ye my people]
Chamber and pf pieces
Songs: Ki mitzion [Out of Zion comes the Torah], Mayim, mayim [The wells of salvation], Hagez [Shearing song], Halleluiah, Shechora ani [I am black but comely], Dodi tsach v'adom [My beloved is white and ruddy], *c*400 others

Principal publishers: Education and Culture Centre of the General Federation of Labour Histadrut, Israel Music Institute

BIBLIOGRAPHY

Y. W. Cohen: *Werden und Entwicklungen der Musik in Israel* (Kassel, 1976) [pt.ii of rev. edn. of M. Brod: *Die Musik Israels*]

W. Y. Elias: *The Music of Israel* (in preparation) [bibliography]

WILLIAM Y. ELIAS

Amirov, Fikret (Meshadi Jamil') (*b* Gyandzha [now Kirovabad], 22 Nov 1922). Soviet composer. The son of a famous *tar* player and singer, he studied at the Kirovabad Music College (*tar* class 1938) and then at the Baku College in the composition classes of Burshteyn and Karnitskaya. In 1939 he entered Zeydman's composition class at the Azerbaijan State Conservatory, and he also studied the foundations of Azerbaijani music under Hajibeyov with enthusiasm. His years at the conservatory, marked by active creative work, were interrupted by the war. He was wounded at the front and, being demobilized, returned to his studies, which he completed in 1948, presenting as his diploma work the opera *Ulduz*. Other compositions of this period include his most famous pieces: the symphony *Pamyati Nizami* ('To the memory of Nizam', 1947), *Shchur* and *Kyurd Ovsharï* (1948), both symphonic *mugam*, and the opera *Sevil'* (1953). Throughout his career he has taken a leading part in music administration: he was artistic director of the Kirovabad PO (1942–3) and the Baku PO (1947), director of the Azerbaijani Theatre of Opera and Ballet (1956–9) and secretary to the Azerbaijani Composers' Union. In 1965 he received the title National Artist of the USSR.

Amirov's best orchestral works are the first two symphonic *mugam*, which won him a State Prize in 1949. In them he created a new symphonic genre based structurally on the folk *mugam* form; the majority of the traditional divisions are retained, as is the principle of alternating episodes of a quasi-improvisational type with rhythmically strict passages in song or dance style (for these Amirov used carefully selected folk melodies). The free development inherent in the traditional *mugam* combines naturally with the variational and polyphonic treatment. In 1970 Amirov produced a further symphonic *mugam* showing his mastery of the form, *Gyulistan–Bayatï shirazi*.

Sevil', the first national lyrical-psychological opera, holds a very important place in the operatic art of Azerbaijan. The plot, after Jabarlï's play, concerns the liberation of Azerbaijani women, and the work has met with widespread success by reason of the sharpness of its dramatic conflicts, the delicate musical characterization of its personalities and its decisively national idiom. Vocally the work is dominated by an aria style; indeed, free vocal melody is native to Amirov's talent, and the melodic style of his opera strongly influences its harmony. In general his music combines the traditions of Azerbaijani folk music with those of Russian and European art music. His use of the orchestra is notable above all for its clarity and, at times, picturesqueness.

WORKS
(selective list)

Operas: Ulduz (I. Idayat-zade), 1948; Sevil' (T. Eyubov, after D. Jabarlï), 1953, Baku, 1953

Musical comedies: Pokhititel' serdets [Kidnapper of hearts] (M. Ordubadï), 1943; Radostnaya vest' [Happy news] (M. Ali-zade), 1945, Baku, 1946

Orch: Poema, 1941; Pamyati geroyev Otechestvennoy voynï [To the memory of the heroes of World War II], sym. poem, 1943; Pamyati

Nizami [To the memory of Nizam], sym., str, 1947; Shchur, Kyurd Ovsharï, sym, mugam, 1948; Uzeir Hajibeyov, dedication, unison vns/vcs, pf, orch, 1949; Suite 'Azerbaijan', 1950; Kontsert na arabskiye temï, pf, orch, 1957, collab. E. Nazirova; Azerbaydzhanskoye kaprichchio, 1961; Simfonicheskiye tantsï, 1963; Simfonicheskiye portretï, 1970

Vocal: Gyulistan–Bayatï shirazi, sym. mugam, Mez, timp, chamber orch, 1970

Inst: Pamyati Asafa Zeynallï [To the memory of Asaf Zeynalla], vc/va, pf, 1948; 12 miniatyur, pf, 1955; Syuita na albanskiye temï, 2 pf, 1955, collab. Nazirova

Other works: choral pieces, chamber music, songs, folksong arrs., incidental music, film scores etc

For fuller list see *Soyuz kompozitorov Azerbaydzhana* [Azerbaijani Composers' Union] (Baku, 1965)

BIBLIOGRAPHY

K. Karayev: 'Simfonischeskiye mugamï Fikreta Amirova', *SovM* (1949), no.3, p.40

L. Karagicheva and G. Ismaylova: 'Sevil'', *SovM* (1954), no.4, p.39

G. Ismaylova: *Fikret Amirov* (Baku, 1956)

D. Danilov: *Opera 'Sevil' Fikreta Amirova* (Baku, 1959)

D. Mamedbekov: *Simfonicheskiye mugamï Fikreta Amirova* (Moscow, 1961)

S. Kasimova: 'Narodnïye istoki muzïkal'novo yazïka operï *Sevil'* Amirova' [The folk origins of the musical language of *Sevil'*], *Uchyonïye zapiski Azerbaydzhanskoy gosudarstvennoy konservatorii* (1964), no.1, p.37

D. Mamedbekov: *Fortepiannïy kontsert na arabskiye temï F. Amirova i E. Nazirovoy* (Baku, 1964)

E. Abasova: 'F. Amirov', *Uchyonïye zapiski Azerbaydzhanskoy gosudarstvennoy konservatorii* (1965), no.2, p.30

D. Danilov: *Fikret Amirov* (Baku, 1965)

——: *Simfoniya 'Nizami' Amirova* (Baku, 1966)

YURIY GABAY

Ammerbach, Elias Nikolaus (*b* Naumburg, *c*1530; *d* Leipzig, buried 29 Jan 1597). German organist and keyboard music arranger. In the foreword of his 1571 tablature Ammerbach stated that he had 'from childhood on, even from birth, a singular desire and love, charm and inclination' towards music so that he 'proceeded to eminent masters in foreign lands, to probe, bear, and endure much for it'. He enrolled for half a year at the University of Leipzig in 1548–9. From 1 January 1561 to April 1595 Ammerbach served as organist at the Thomaskirche in Leipzig. The civic records during his long tenure testify to an easygoing attitude (perhaps even resignation) to his financial difficulties and the death of his first two wives. His third wife and five children survived him.

In his first publication Ammerbach introduced what has since been called new German organ tablature in which pitches are expressed in letter notation with rhythm-signs above them. The decoration of vocal pieces when played on instruments, however, is a technique that undoubtedly predates even the earliest known written instrumental music. Ammerbach's first tablature is also the first printed German organ music. 'Instrument' in the title, according to Ammerbach, includes 'positive, regal, virginal, clavichord, clavicembalo, harpsichord and the like'. Ammerbach arranged the contents of this book, *Orgel oder Instrument Tabulatur* (1571), into five progressively more difficult categories. Little or no coloration occurs in the first group of 44 German songs in four voices (see illustration of nos.37 and 38). The composers of many are unknown; some pieces have been borrowed from Le Maistre, Forster, Buchner, Senfl, Isaac and others. A group of 27 dances, several of them paired, follows. These employ repeated chords and a minimum of decoration, except in the passamezzos of the third section, where the varied top voice requires considerable decoration. In the fourth section (12 four-part vocal works) and in the fifth (seven five-part vocal

Two German songs from Ammerbach's 'Orgel oder Instrument Tabulatur', 1571 works) lavish coloration occurs on every line. The sacred and secular vocal models are by Clemens non Papa, Zirler, Senfl (2), Heintz, Hofhaimer, Buchner, Lassus (4), Scandello and Ivo de Vento. The bass range extends to *C*, the treble to *a''*. (In the tablature of 1583 Ammerbach extended the treble to *c'''*.)

Ein new künstlich Tabulaturbuch (1575) includes 40 vocal intabulations and one praeambulum. The 26 sacred works, with one exception, have Latin titles; the remaining secular works have German titles. Identified composers of the sacred repertory include Lassus (10), Clemens non Papa (3), Formellis (2), Meiland (2), Arcadelt, Berchem, Crecquillon, Dressler, Gastritz, Ville Font (1 each). The secular songs were composed by Lassus (7), Scandello (5) and Ivo de Vento (2). Five-part settings outnumber six-part settings, with even fewer four-part settings. These pieces, more than the ones in the first book, come from the popular international repertory. All lines carry profuse ornamentation.

In 1583 Ammerbach revised and expanded his 1571 publication. He added more works with German titles than with French and Italian. Composers new to this edition include Meiland, Regnart, Josquin, Sandrin, Rore, Crecquillon, Godard, Ferrabosco, Berchem and Arcadelt. In the 1583 tablature Ammerbach gave all these songs without coloration; some may in fact have been simplified for students, to whom the work is addressed. The number of dances was substantially increased, since pieces found also in instrumental publications of Gervaise, Le Roy, Phalèse and others were added.

WORKS
Orgel oder Instrument Tabulatur (Leipzig, 1571, 2/1583)
Ein new künstlich Tabulaturbuch (Leipzig, 1575)

BIBLIOGRAPHY
BrownI
W. Merian: *Der Tanz in den deutschen Tabulaturbüchern* (Leipzig, 1927/*R*1968) [incl. four dances by Ammerbach]
C. W. Young: 'Keyboard Music to 1600', *MD*, xvi (1962), 115
E. Kraus, ed.: *Cantantibus organis*, xi (Regensburg, 1963) [incl. four German songs by Ammerbach]
E. L. Boos: *The Keyboard Tablature of Elias Nicolaus Ammerbach* (diss., Indiana U., in preparation)
                                    CLYDE WILLIAM YOUNG

Ammon [Amon], Blasius (*b* Imst, Tyrol, *c*1560; *d* Vienna, between 1 and 21 June 1590). Austrian composer. He may have belonged to a Franconian family who moved to Imst from Bamberg in the mid-16th century. He was a choirboy in the Hofkapelle of Archduke Ferdinand I at Innsbruck and probably attended the choir school there (it was founded in about 1569). According to the first of two dedications in his 1590 motet collection, he later went to Venice for further study, presumably when his voice broke. After he returned (in 1577 or 1578) he was in the employ of the Franciscan order until 1580, when he probably entered the service of Johannes Ruoff, abbot of the Cistercian monastery at Zwettl, north-west of Vienna, to whom he dedicated his 1582 book of introits. He was Kantor at the Cistercian monastery of Heiligkreuz from 1585 to 1587, when he entered the Franciscan monastery in Vienna. He later took his vows at this house and died there during the printing of his 1590 collection.

Ammon was perhaps the first of a number of late 16th- and early 17th-century composers north of the Alps whose work was strongly influenced by Venetian music. His 1582 introits, by their very nature, are in

short sections, and he seems to have been concerned with rich sonority, all five voices being kept busy for most of the time. Chordal writing predominates, enlivened by strong, verbally derived rhythms and syncopations of one voice against the rest. Imitation is usually found only at the beginning of a piece and in the more melismatic codas on such words as 'Alleluia'; it is for the most part shortwinded. The motets of 1590 for four to eight voices are much more varied and make use of the split ensembles so beloved of the Venetians. The three eight-part motets are real double-choir pieces, much in the style of Andrea Gabrieli, with long passages for single choir punctuated by tuttis and close echo effects. Many short passages in the six- and seven-part motets, and even in the five-part *Magi videntes*, are scored for two contrasting groups. The five-part *O vos omnes* is a remarkably expressive piece, in contrast to the fanfares of *Canite tuba*, for instance, and it uses at the outset a remarkable A–G♯–A ostinato that is heightened to E–D♯–E in the soprano part. Ammon seems to have adopted a forward-looking, tonal attitude to leading-notes and to accidentals generally.

WORKS
Edition: *B. Ammon: Kirchenwerke I*, ed. C. Huigens, DTÖ, lxxviii, Jg.xxxviii/1 (1931/*R*) [H]

Liber sacratissimarum quas vulgo introitus appellant cantionum selectissimus, 5vv (Vienna, 1582); H
Missae quatuor . . . quibus unica . . . pro fidelibus defunctis est adiecta, 4vv (Vienna, 1588)
Sacrae cantiones, quas vulgo moteta vocant, quibus adiuncti sunt ecclesiastici hymni de nativitate, resurrectione & ascensione Domini, 4–8vv (Munich, 1590); H
Breves et selectae quaedam motetae, 4–6vv (Munich, 1593)
Introitus dominicales per totum annum, 4vv (Vienna, 1601)
Works (possibly incl. some reprs. from above vols.) in 1603¹, 1609¹, 1627¹, 1628²

Ave Maria, 4vv, *A-Wm* (according to *EitnerQ*)
Vocavit me Dominus, 5vv, *D-Z* (according to *EitnerQ*)
For other MSS and list of concordances see H

BIBLIOGRAPHY
C. Huigens: *Blasius Amon, ca. 1560–1590: ein Beitrag zur Geschichte der Kirchenmusik* (diss., U. of Vienna, 1914)
——: 'Blasius Amon', *SMw*, xviii (1931), 3 [rev. version of part i of preceding]
A. Geering: 'Amon, Blasius', *MGG*
W. Senn: *Musik und Theater am Hof zu Innsbruck* (Innsbruck, 1954), 96ff, 154, 188, 195
                                    ANTHONY F. CARVER

Ammon, Conrad. See PRAETORIUS, CONRAD.

Ammon, Wolfgang (*b* Elsa, nr. Coburg, 26 Jan 1540; *d* Marktbreit, Bavaria, 26 Jan 1589). German clergyman and hymn writer. He matriculated at the University of Wittenberg on 13 October 1561, at the University of Jena in September 1562 and at Wittenberg again in October 1564; he took the MA in 1565. Ordained at Ansbach in 1566, he first went to work at Weidelbach, near Dinkelsbühl, Bavaria, and from 1567 was deacon of the Protestant Spitalkirche at Dinkelsbühl. He lost this post in 1579 because his teaching was out of line with Lutheran christological doctrines, but in the same year he was reinstated as a vicar at Marktbreit. He published *Libri tres odarum ecclesiasticarum, de sacris cantionibus* (Frankfurt am Main, 1578, repr. 1579) which contains 66 German congregational songs, with Latin translations and 64 well-known melodies. *New Gesangbuch teutsch und lateinisch, darinn die fürnembste Psalmen und Gesänge der Kirchen Augsp. Confession* (Frankfurt am Main, 1581, 5/1606) is an edition of it in four books instead of three and with 20 songs added. In supplying Latin translations of the German texts Ammon had the needs of schools in mind, for with the help of his work the Protestant services could be celebrated in Latin by 'pupils and scholars'. Moreover as he pointed out 'foreigners who had a grasp of Latin but no German would have access to the true doctrine and would therefore be better able to unite in a proper understanding of the Christian faith'.

BIBLIOGRAPHY

EitnerQ

C. von Winterfeld: *Der evangelische Kirchengesang*, i (Leipzig, 1843/*R*1966)

J. Zahn: *Die Melodien der deutschen evangelischen Kirchenlieder*, vi (Gütersloh, 1893/*R*1963)

F. Blume: *Die evangelische Kirchenmusik*, HMw, x (1931, rev. 2/1965 as *Geschichte der evangelischen Kirchenmusik*; Eng. trans., enlarged, 1974 as *Protestant Church Music: a History*)

J. Hopfengärtner and M. Simon: *Pfarrerbuch der Reichsstädte Dinkelsbühl, Schweinfurt, Weissenburg in Bayern und Windsheim sowie der Reichsdörfer Gochsheim und Sennfeld*, Kirchengeschichte Bayerns, xxix (Nuremberg, 1962)

AUGUST SCHARNAGL

Ammons, Albert (C.) (*b* Chicago, 1907; *d* Chicago, 2 Dec 1949). Black American jazz pianist. After playing as a soloist and with various bands in Chicago, he formed his own Rhythm Kings sextet in 1934, and with them recorded his version of 'Pine Top' Smith's *Boogie Woogie*, which he called *Boogie Woogie Stomp* (1936). He later became identified with that piano blues style. From 1938 he was active in New York, first in piano trios with Meade 'Lux' Lewis and Pete Johnson, later in a duo with Johnson, with whom he made a series of recordings (1941). Other important solo recordings from this period include *Shout for Joy* (1939) and *Bass goin' Crazy* (1942). In later years his playing declined, but he continued to perform and record, sometimes with his son Gene Ammons as tenor saxophonist.

BIBLIOGRAPHY

W. Russell: 'Boogie Woogie', *Jazzmen*, ed. F. Ramsey and C. Smith (New York, 1939), 183

M. Harrison: 'Boogie Woogie', *Jazz*, ed. N. Hentoff (New York, 1959), 105–137

Y. Bruynoghe: 'Albert Ammons', *Jazz Era: the 40s*, ed. S. Dance (London, 1961), 48

P. Oliver: 'Albert Ammons', *Jazz on Record*, ed. A. McCarthy (London, 1968), 5

MARTIN WILLIAMS

Amner, John (*b* Ely, baptized 24 Aug 1579; *d* Ely, buried 28 July 1641). English composer and organist. He was born into a family which had close connections with the music of Ely Cathedral; a Michael Amner, who was a lay clerk there from 1576 to 1588, was John's uncle, and a Ralph Amner (possibly John's brother) was a lay clerk successively at Ely, Windsor and the Chapel Royal. John himself left Ely to study music at Oxford under the patronage of the Earl of Bath, but returned in 1610 to succeed George Barcroft as *Informator choristarum*. He did not, however, graduate BMus until 1613. Two years later his only publication, *Sacred Hymns of 3, 4, 5 and 6 parts for Voyces and Vyols* appeared. Amner was subsequently ordained to the diaconate, and later appointed *vicarius* (minor canon); so he drew the annual stipends of both organist and prebendary. Throughout his tenure of office (31 years) he continued to compose for the Anglican liturgy. As late as 1640 he graduated MusB of Cambridge. Only two years after his death, choral services were discontinued at Ely.

As a contemporary of Gibbons and Tomkins, Amner occupies an interesting period in the history of provincial cathedral music between the Reformation and the Commonwealth. His early compositions reflect the stylistic patterns of his predecessors at Ely – Tye, White, John Farrant, Fox and Barcroft – clearly favouring a simple syllabic setting of readily intelligible texts. But with the rise of the high-church movement of such men as Laud and Cosin (as well as of his own dean, Henry Cesar, a generous patron of the cathedral's music), he adapted his idiom to that of the more intricate verse-anthem and polyphonic choral styles.

Of Amner's service music, two sets of Preces survive, both for five voices; the first belongs with a festal setting of Psalm lxxxix for Evensong on Christmas Day, while the second was evidently intended for the morning Office, as it is followed by *Venite* in the MSS. The lack of concomitant settings of the responses after the Creed precludes their frequent use today. Of the four settings of the daily canticles, only two survive complete. One is cast in the form of a 'short' service, avoiding repetitions and lengthy elaborations. The other, known as 'Cesar's Service', is a verse setting of great beauty in which the verse sections are allocated to groups of soloists rather than single voices. Of the incomplete settings, the evening canticles are of particular interest: the surviving organ part indicates that the verse sections were disposed among all the different voices, singly as well as in ensemble. The final 'Amen' is identical with the ending of 'O ye little flock', suggesting that the service was in six parts.

Of the shorter four-part anthems, the surviving sources of *O God my King* and *O Lord of whom I do depend* show that they were simple note-against-note settings without contrapuntal points, while *Blessed be the Lord God* is built around short overlapping imitative phrases. *Come let's rejoice*, a madrigalian setting of a paraphrased text from *Venite*, ending with a melismatic 'Alleluia', is of passing interest. *Woe is me* is a simple but effective lament about the exile of the Jews. *Christ rising again* begins as a straightforward homophonic setting of part of the Easter Anthems, but the intensity of the text prompted Amner to expand the original texture by dividing the meane, alto and tenor parts.

Among the five-part anthems, *Lift up your heads* is the most interesting, both in its tonal scheme and in its treatment of the text. Here Amner attempted a rapprochement between the full and the verse styles: of the three sections, the second uses a three-part verse texture to pose the question 'Who is the King of Glory?', and the final section brings in the full choir with the answer 'It is the Lord'. The penitential *Remember not, Lord, our offences* sets a collect from the Litany with unusual poignancy; the opening section makes use of the lower tessituras of the voices as well as chromatic vocal lines. In contrast, *He that descended* sets a joyful Ascensiontide text with great verve, at one point using the voices to imitate trumpet calls, as Byrd had done in *Sing joyfully*. The exuberant *O come hither and hearken*, which follows 'Cesar's Service' in the York Partbooks as 'the anthem to the service', culminates in a joyful homophonic outburst, 'Praised be God which hath not cast out my prayer'. The two seven-part anthems represent Amner's most ambitious choral writing in the full style. They are both settings of laudatory texts, and both feature overlapping imitative phrases of the doubled voices which lend a driving rhythmic inevitability to the rich vocal texture.

The verse anthems show Amner's superb ability to match music with text in an antiphonal context. The two long Christmastide pieces from the *Sacred Hymns*, *O ye little flock* and *Lo how from heav'n*,· skilfully juxtapose verse and full sections. Perhaps Amner's most beautiful anthem is *Consider, all ye passers by*, a setting of a Passiontide text of great fervour for solo countertenor with five-part chorus. *I will sing unto the Lord* features a solo tenor; here the main interest is in the verse sections, where Amner used sequential writing to good effect for the repetitions, especially when triplet movement is introduced for 'my joy shall be in the Lord'. The whole anthem builds up to an impressive climax for the full 'Praise the Lord'. In *My Lord is hence removed* Amner again made use of a tenor soloist, but this time a single verse section leads into the full 'Alleluia'. The only verse anthem to make use of a solo bass is *Glory be to God on high*, which is described in the MSS as 'an anthem for Easter Communion'. In *Hear, O Lord* two solo meanes imitate and complement each other during three verses, while a four-part chorus echoes both music and text of the soloists.

Amner's only extant keyboard piece is unique in that it is the only known set of variations on a metrical psalm tune. The melody appeared in Day's *Certaine Notes*, composed by Tallis for *O Lord in thee is all my trust*. Each of the eight variations bears testimony to the scope of Amner's rhythmic, melodic and contrapuntal invention, as well as to his skill as a performer.

WORKS

Sacred Hymns (London, 1615) [SH]

SACRED

1st Service (TeD, Jub, Ky, Cr, Mag, Nunc), inc., *GB-Cu*
2nd Service ('Cesar's'; Ven, TeD, Jub, Ky, Cr, Mag, Nunc), 4/5vv, *Cp, Cu, DRc, Lbm, Y*
3rd Service ('short'; TeD, Bs, Ky, Cr, Mag, Nunc), 4vv, *Cp, Cu, Lbm, Y*
1st Preces with Psalm lxxxix, 5vv, *Cp*
2nd Preces with Venite, 5vv, *Cp*
Evening Canticles, inc., ?/?6vv, *T*
A stranger here, 6vv, *Cp, Cu, Lbm, Ob, US-NYp, BE*
Away with weak complainings, 3vv, *SH*
Blessed be the Lord God, inc., 4vv, *GB-Cu*
Christ rising again, 4vv, *Lbm, US-NYp*
Come let's rejoice, 4vv, *NYp, GB-Lbm, SH*
Consider, all ye passers by, inc., 1/5vv, *Och, T*
Distressed soul, 4vv, *SH*
Glory be to God on high, 1/4vv, *Cp, Cu, US-NYp*
Hear, O Lord and have merey, 2/4vv, *NYp, GB-Cp, Cu*
He that descended man to be, 5vv, *Lbm, Ob, US-NYp, SH*
How doth the city, 5vv, *GB-Cp, Ob, US-NYp, SH*
I am for peace, inc., *GB-Och, T*
I will sing unto the Lord as long as I live, 1/5vv, *Ckc, Cp, Cû, DRc, Lbm, US-NYp*
I will sing unto the Lord, for He hath triumphed, 5vv, *GB-Lbm, Ob, US-NYp, SH*
Let false surmises perish, 3vv, *SH*
Lift up your heads, inc., *GB-Cp, US-NYp*
Like as the hart, inc., *NYp*
Lo, how from heav'n like stars, 2/6vv, *NYp, GB-Ob, SH*
Lord, I am not high minded, 5vv, *Cp, Cu, Lbm*
Lord in thy wrath reprove me not, inc., *Cu, Lbm, Ob, Och, Ojc, T, US-NYp*
Love we in one consenting, 3vv, *SH*
My Lord is hence removed and laid, 1/6vv, *US-NYp, SH*
My shepherd is the living Lord, inc., *GB-Och, US-NYp*
O come hither and hearken, 5vv, *GB-Cp, Cu, T, Y, US-BE, NYp*
O come thou spirit divinest, 3vv, *SH*
O God my King, inc., 4vv, *GB-Cu*
O Lord of whom I do depend, inc., 4vv, *Cu, US-NYp*
O love beseeming well, 3vv, *SH*
O magnify the Lord our God, inc., *GB-Och, US-NYp*
O sing unto the Lord, 3vv, *GB-Cp, Cu, GL, Lbm, US-NYp*
Out of the deep, 3vv, *GB-Cp*
O worship the Lord, inc., *US-NYp*
O ye little flock, 4/6vv, *NYp, GB-Cp, Cu, Ob, T, SH*
. . . Rejoice, rejoice, fragment of an inc. anthem, *Cu*
Remember not, Lord, our offences, 5vv, *Cp, Cu, Lbm, Ob, T, US-NYp, SH*
St Mary now, 4vv, *NYp, GB-Lbm, SH*
Sing, O heav'ns, 7vv, *Cu, Lbm*
Sweet are the thoughts, 4vv, *Lbm, US-NYp, SH*

The King shall rejoice, inc., *NYp, GB-Och*
Thus sings the heav'nly choir, 5vv, *Ob, SH*
With mournefull musique (elegy for Thomas Hynson), 6vv, *SH*
Woe is me that I am constrained, 4vv, *Cp, US-NYp, SH*

INSTRUMENTAL

Pavan, Galliard, viols, inc., *GB-Lbm*
Variations for keyboard on O Lord in Thee is all my trust, *US-NYp*

BIBLIOGRAPHY

M. C. Boyd: *Elizabethan Music and Musical Criticism* (Philadelphia, 1940, 2/1962), 63, 65, 89
E. H. Fellowes: *English Cathedral Music* (London, 1941, rev. 5/1969)
P. le Huray: *Music and the Reformation in England, 1549–1660* (London, 1967), 128f, 388ff
K. R. Long: *The Music of the English Church* (London, 1971), 185f
R. T. Daniel and P. le Huray: *The Sources of English Church Music 1549–1660*, EECM, suppl.i (1972)

ANTHONY J. GREENING

Amodei, Cataldo (*b* Sciacca, nr. Agrigento, *c*1650; *d* Naples, *c*1695). Italian composer. He went from his native Sicily to Naples to complete his musical education and remained there until his death. He was *maestro del coro* at S Paolo Maggiore and later at the Conservatorio di S Onofrio (1681–8). On 14 September 1687 he was appointed second *maestro di cappella* at the Conservatorio di S Maria di Loreto 'to teach the boys, in the morning, to play and sing'. The governors there described him as 'one of the outstanding personalities of the city', but in 1689 he had to resign 'because of his many commitments', as is stated in the governors' document appointing Alessandro Scarlatti in his place. He dedicated his op.1 to the Emperor Leopold I of Austria.

WORKS

Primo libro de' mottetti, 2–5vv, op.1 (Naples, 1679)
Cantate, libro primo, 1v, op.2 (Naples, 1685)

L'innocenza infetta dal pomo, 1685; Il flagello dell'empietà, 1685; La Susanna, 1686; Il trionfo della purità di Maria, 1687; Il Giosuè vittorioso: oratorios, all performed in Naples, music lost, libs *I-MOe, Nc, Nn, Pci*
La sirena consolata, serenata, Naples, 1692, lost
Cantatas, 3vv, spiritual canzoni, other sacred works, pastorali, duets, 2vv, bc, *Nf*

BIBLIOGRAPHY

LaMusicaD
S. di Giacomo: *I quattro antichi conservatorii di musica di Napoli* (Palermo, 1924–8)
D. Confuorto: *Giornali di Napoli dal MDCLXXIX al MDCIC* (Naples, 1930), ii, 313
R. Pagano and L. Bianchi: *Alessandro Scarlatti* (Turin, 1972), 104f

RENATO BOSSA

Amomos. A setting of Psalm cxviii in the Byzantine service for the dead. The word 'amomos' ('undefiled') appears in the first line of the psalm.

Amon, Blasius. *See* AMMON, BLASIUS.

Amon, Johannes Andreas (*b* Bamberg, 1763; *d* Wallerstein, Bavaria, 29 March 1825). German conductor and composer. He studied singing with Fracasini and the violin with Bäuerle at Bamberg. After his voice broke, he studied the horn with Punto, who took him on concert tours in Germany, France and Austria. From 1781 to 1782 they stayed in Paris, where Amon studied composition with Sacchini. During his subsequent travels, Amon met J. A. Hiller, Reichardt, Hoffmeister, Haydn and Mozart. He continued to tour with Punto until 1789, when he accepted the post of musical director at Heilbronn. Poor health forced him to give up playing the horn, and he concentrated on improving his violin, viola and piano technique. In 1817 he became Kapellmeister to the Prince of Oettingen-Wallerstein, in whose service he remained for the rest of his life.

Amon was an expert conductor and a versatile musician, a good performer on the horn, and later on the violin, viola and piano; he also taught singing and a variety of instruments. His many compositions include duos, trios, quartets, quintets, symphonies, marches, solo sonatas for various instruments and sonatas and variations for piano. He also wrote concertos, two Singspiels, two masses, cantatas, songs and a requiem which was performed at his funeral. Many of his works are unpublished. His eldest son Ernest wrote a set of variations for flute and orchestra.

BIBLIOGRAPHY
FétisB; *RiemannL* 12
Obituary, *AMZ*, xxvii (1825), 365
A. von Dommer: 'Amon, Johannes Andreas', *ADB*
L. Schiedermair: 'Die Blütezeit der Öttingen-Wallerstein'schen Hofkapelle', *SIMG*, ix (1907–8), 116
JEFFRY MARK/GAYNOR G. JONES

Amorevole. *See* AMOROSO.

Amorevoli, Angelo (Maria) (*b* Venice, 16 Sept 1716; *d* Dresden, 15 Nov 1798). Italian tenor. After establishing his reputation in Porpora's operas *Mitridate* and *Siface* (Rome, January–February 1730) and in Hasse's *Dalisa* (Venice, May 1730), he sang in Milan from 1731 until 1735. Between 1736 and 1740 he appeared in ten Neapolitan productions, including Leo's *Achille in Sciro*, which inaugurated the Teatro S Carlo (4 November 1737). Horace Mann heard him in Giuseppe Scarlatti's *Arminio* (Florence, June 1741) and recommended him to Horace Walpole, who reported that *Alexander in Persia*, a pasticcio given its première in London on 31 October 1741, was unsuccessful until Amorevoli joined the cast in mid-November. He then sang in ten other operas and several concerts at the King's Theatre before the end of the 1742–3 season. In 1744–5 he was again in Milan. Except for visits to Vienna (where Metastasio praised his singing in 1748) and Italy (Milan, 1748–9 and 1760–61), he made Dresden his home from 1745 in order to sing Hasse's music. After his retirement from the stage in 1764 he remained at that court as a chamber and church singer. Burney wrote of him: 'Amorevoli was an admirable tenor, I have heard better voices of his pitch; but never, on the stage, more taste and expression'.

BIBLIOGRAPHY
BurneyH; *GerberL*; *SchmidlD*
M. Fürstenau: *Zur Geschichte der Musik und des Theaters am Hofe zu Dresden*, ii (Dresden, 1862/*R*1971)
H. W. Singer: *Allgemeiner Bildniskatalog*, i (Leipzig, 1930/*R*1967) [cites engraving and two drawings of Amorevoli in the Dresden Kupferstichkabinett]
B. Brunelli, ed.: *Tutte le opere di Pietro Metastasio*, iii (Milan, 1951), 352, 605f, 1223, 1240
E. Zanetti: 'Amorevoli, Angelo', *ES*
O. E. Deutsch: *Handel: a Documentary Biography* (London, 1955)
W. S. Lewis, ed.: *The Yale Edition of Horace Walpole's Correspondence: Horace Walpole's Correspondence with Sir Horace Mann*, i–ii (New Haven, 1955)
G. Piamonte: 'Amorevoli, Angelo', *DBI*
P. H. Highfill, K. A. Burnim and E. A. Langhans, eds.: *A Biographical Dictionary of Actors, Actresses, Musicians … in London, 1660–1800*, i (Carbondale, Ill., 1973), 77
SVEN HANSELL

Amoroso (It.: 'loving', 'affectionate', 'amorous'). A performance direction found throughout the 18th century. Rousseau (1768) equated it with the French *tendrement*, with the qualification that *amoroso* had 'plus d'accent, et respire je ne sais pas quoi de moins fade et de plus passionné' ('more emphasis and is perhaps a little less insipid and more impassioned'). Other forms encoun-

tered include *amorevole* (also an adjective) and *con amore*.

For bibliography *see* TEMPO AND EXPRESSION MARKS.
DAVID FALLOWS

Amphion. Ancient Greek mythological figure, son of Zeus and Antiope. When he and his twin brother Zethus built the walls of Thebes (Homer, *Odyssey* xi, ll.260–65), the stones set themselves in place through the power of his lyre (Hesiod, *frag*.96, ed. Evelyn-White). According to Pausanias (ix, 5, 8), Hesiod's near contemporary Eumelus of Corinth called Amphion the first lyre player, taught by Hermes; late sources made further claims typical of the feats credited to Orpheus, Marsyas and other names in the pre-history of Greek music. To Virgil Amphion was simply a pastoral singer (*Eclogues*, ii, ll.23f); Horace mentioned the miraculous power of Amphion's singing (*Odes*, iii, ll.1–3, invocations to Mercury and the lyre).

BIBLIOGRAPHY
G. Wille: *Musica romana* (Amsterdam, 1967), esp. 551ff
WARREN ANDERSON

Amplitude. The maximum amount of disturbance from the equilibrium state in a vibration or wave. *See* SOUND, §5.

Amram, David (Werner) (*b* Philadelphia, 17 Nov 1930). American composer and conductor. As well as playing the piano and the horn, he developed in his youth an interest in jazz, working with Louis Brown and performing in a Dixieland band. In 1948 he entered the Oberlin Conservatory, and a year later he transferred to George Washington University. He played the horn in the National SO and in the Seventh Army SO in Germany. An association with Joseph Papp, producer of the New York Shakespeare Festival, began in 1956 and led to the composition of 18 incidental scores. Amram was composer-in-residence with the New York PO (1966–7), and in 1972 he was appointed conductor of the Brooklyn Philharmonia's youth concerts. His music is romantic, dramatic and colourful, marked by rhythmic and improvisatory characteristics of jazz. He published *Vibrations: the Adventures and Musical Times of David Amram* (New York, 1968).

WORKS
(selective list)
Orch: Autobiography, str, 1959; Shakespearean Conc., ob, hn, str, 1959; The American Bell, 1962; King Lear Variations, wind, 1965; Conc., hn, wind, 1966; Hn Conc., 1969; Bn Conc., 1970; Elegy, vn, orch, 1970; Triple Conc., 5 ww, 5 brass, jazz qnt, 1970
Choral: Friday Evening Service 'Shir l'erer shabat', 1960; By the Rivers of Babylon, S, SSAA, 1964; A Year in our Land (cantata, Baldwin, Dos Passos, Kerouac, Steinbeck, Wolf, Whitman), solo vv, SATB, orch, 1965; Let us Remember (cantata, L. Hughes), 1965
Inst: Sonata, vn, pf, 1960; Discussion, fl, pf, perc, vc, 1960; Dirge and Variations, pf trio, 1962; Str Qt, 1962; 3 Songs for Marlboro, hn, vc, 1962; Sonata, vn, 1964; The Wind and the Rain, va, pf, 1964; Fanfare and Processional, 5 brass, 1966; Wind Qnt, 1968
Incidental music, film scores incl. The Manchurian Candidate, 1962

Principal publisher: Peters

OLIVER DANIEL

'Amr ibn Bāna ['Amr ibn Muḥammad ibn Sulaymān ibn Rāshid] (*b* Baghdad, *c*820; *d* Sāmarrā', 891). Arab musician. His father was a scribe and high state official. Although he learnt music from Isḥāq al-Mawṣilī, a champion of the 'classical school' of Arab music, he turned to the 'romantic school' of Ibrāhīm ibn al-Mahdī and became one of its main representatives. He appeared at the courts of the Caliphs al-Ma'mūn (813–33), al-

Mu'taṣim (833–42) and al-Mutawakkil (847–61), to the last of whom he was a companion (nadīm). He was said to be 'a brilliant singer and a good poet', but is better known through his Kitāb mujarrad al-aghānī ('Book of songs alone') and a Kitāb fī l-aghānī ('Book about songs'); the latter work was severely criticized by al-Iṣfahānī.

BIBLIOGRAPHY

Ibn Khallikān: Biographical Dictionary (Paris and London, 1843–71)
Al-Iṣfahānī: Kitāb al-aghānī al-kabīr [Great book of songs], ed. N. al-Hurīnī (Cairo, 1868–9, 2/1905–6, rev. 1927–), 52ff
H. G. Farmer: The Sources of Arabian Music (Bearsden, 1940, rev. 2/1965), 21

based on MGG (i, 430) by permission of Bärenreiter

H. G. FARMER

AMS. See AMERICAN MUSICOLOGICAL SOCIETY.

Amsterdam. Capital city of the Kingdom of the Netherlands. The musical history of Amsterdam reflects the rapid growth of the city from a fishing village in the late Middle Ages to a leading commercial centre. In the 16th and 17th centuries, as a result of Dutch colonial expansion and of the war against Spain for the independence of the Netherlands, Amsterdam became one of the most important centres of world trade.

1. Religious institutions. 2. Opera. 3. Concert life. 4. Education.

1. RELIGIOUS INSTITUTIONS. Amsterdam's two main churches in the later Middle Ages were the Oude Kerk or Nicolaaskerk (c1300) and the Nieuwe Kerk (early 15th century). Two parish churches, the Nieuwezijdskapel or Sacramentskapel (1347), and the Oudezijdskapel or St Olofskapel (mid-15th century), were also musically important. Although little has survived from the repertory of these churches it appears that polyphony was accepted relatively late (c1500) by both main churches. In the 15th century the visits of the Dukes of Burgundy Philip the Good and Charles the Bold, and later the Emperors Maximilian I and Charles V, brought the Burgundian court chapel to the city, and the citizens probably heard the works of Alexander Agricola, Binchois, La Rue and others. In the 16th century laymen were admitted to the church choirs, and in 1561 both parish schools acquired a songbook printed in Louvain by Pierre Phalèse (i), 200 copies of which were ordered by the city fathers. Amsterdam became Calvinist in 1578, and Latin was no longer used in the parish churches and the 21 monasteries. Organ accompaniment of psalm singing was forbidden until 1680; as a result the organ was used primarily as a solo instrument, especially at the Oude Kerk. Peter Swybbertszoon was organist there from about 1564 to 1573 and was succeeded by his son, J. P. Sweelinck, who served from 1580, at the latest, to 1621, and was a widely influential performer, composer and teacher. He was succeeded in turn by his son Dirck, organist until his death in 1652. The tradition of playing the organ before and after the services and at other times was continued until 1727. Other well-known 17th-century organists included Sybrand van Noordt (ii) and Nicolaas de Koning, and Jacobus Nozeman, who was associated with the Remonstrantse Kerk in the first half of the 18th century. G. J. Vogler played in Amsterdam between 1785 and 1790. Daniel Brachthuyser (d 1832), a later representative of the Amsterdam organ tradition, was renowned for his improvisation and for his carillon playing.

2. OPERA. In 1634 Jan Hermanszoon Krul founded the Amsterdamsche Musijck Kamer, a society where music was to be cultivated in connection with drama; however, the society seems not to have lasted long. In the late 17th century, efforts were made to establish an opera company, and an opera house on the Leidse Gracht was inaugurated in 1680 with a work by P. A. Ziani, Le fatiche d'Ercole per Deianira (first staged at Venice in 1662). A pastoral play, De triompheerende min, written for the Peace of Nijmegen in 1678 by Dirk Buysero with music by Carel Hacquart but apparently never performed, was published in 1680. At the Stadsschouwburg, the city theatre on the Keizersgracht (see fig.1), French operas by Lully and others were performed. For its centenary in 1738 the Stadsschouwburg invited Vivaldi to Amsterdam to give a concert of Italian music.

The popularity of opera grew rapidly in the 18th century; the leading opera composer and conductor in Amsterdam was Bartholomeus Ruloffs. The Stadsschouwburg burnt down in 1772 during a performance of Monsigny's Le déserteur, and a new theatre was opened in the Leidse Plein in 1775. Ruloffs was its musical director and composed operas in the French style to texts by Pieter Pijpers, including Zemire en Azor (1784). Previously the French opera from The Hague had given performances in Amsterdam, but between 1788 and 1855 the city had a permanent French theatre, whose small chorus and orchestra performed works by Grétry, Gluck, Méhul, Rodolphe Kreutzer and others, building up an excellent reputation. In 1781 the French founded the Collège Dramatique et Lyrique for the training of actors and singers. Meanwhile the High German Theatre company, conducted by Carl Joseph Schmidt, performed works by Dittersdorf, Hiller and Mozart, including Don Giovanni in 1793. Jacob Neyts brought Italian and other operas in Dutch translation to the Stadsschouwburg. The general decline of Amsterdam's musical life in the first half of the 19th century inevitably affected the opera; nevertheless the Stadsschouwburg became better equipped during this period. An important event for opera in the city was the foundation of the Wagner-Vereniging by Henri Viotta in 1884. This society mounted a performance of Siegfried in 1893 and subsequently gave a chronological cycle of Wagner's works from Tannhäuser onwards. Viotta, the chief conductor until 1919, also introduced works by Richard Strauss and Humperdinck. Since 1922 the Wagner-Vereniging has performed operas by Debussy, Ravel, Dukas, Gluck, Lully, Pijper and Britten. In 1941 and from 1946 to 1964 the Nederlandse Opera was resident in Amsterdam, and the Nederlandse Opera-stichting subsequently presented occasional opera performances there. The city still did not have its own opera house in the 1970s, although there had been plans for one after World War II.

3. CONCERT LIFE. Amsterdam's prosperity in the 17th century was reflected in the widespread private cultivation of music, for it lacked the support of a court or comparable institution. A collegium musicum existed in Sweelinck's time, and he dedicated some works to it. The Muiderkring was an exclusive circle of leading poets, scientists and connoisseurs in the first half of the 17th century, for whom music making was a favourite occupation. A well-known lutenist in the city was Nicolas Vallet. At the end of the century Hacquart and

Hendrik Anders composed chamber music in addition to works for the stage, and Johannes Schenck was an outstanding viol player and composer. Locatelli was celebrated as a violin virtuoso during his period in Amsterdam (c1730–64), and Conrad Friedrich Hurlebusch worked as a singing and harpsichord teacher there from 1737 onwards. This activity stimulated the growth of music publishing. Estienne Roger's firm, established by 1697, was the most important music publisher in the city; later publishers included H. Constapel, J. J. Hummel, J. Olofsen and J. Covens the younger.

Amsterdam's public concerts date from 1777, when the Felix Meritis Society was founded by Willem Brits. The society, also concerned with commerce and science, had a concert room (seating 600) on the Keizersgracht, and its own orchestra. About 20 concerts were given each season, on Friday nights. The society's concert activities ceased with the foundation of the Concertgebouw in 1888. Concerts were also given on Sundays from 1796 onwards by Eruditio Musica, in the German theatre, with an orchestra of 75 players conducted by Schmidt; later Johann Wilhelm Wilms became its conductor. Eruditio Musica contributed much to the popularity of Mozart in the Netherlands. In 1798 Mozart's sister-in-law Aloysia Lange sang with them, and in 1801 they performed Haydn's *The Creation* in the Nieuwe Kerk. 19th-century concert life was dominated successively by Johannes Bernardus van Bree and Johannes Verhulst. The latter, having studied in Leipzig with Mendelssohn and Schumann, came to

Amsterdam in 1864 and conducted the orchestra of the Felix Meritis Society, the Maatschappij Caecilia and the Toonkunst choir. Although a fine conductor, his conservatism irritated the public; he never performed the works of Berlioz, Liszt, Wagner or the contemporary French school. In 1886 he resigned his positions in Amsterdam.

In 1882 it was decided to build a new concert hall to replace the Oude Parkzaal. The acoustically fine Concertgebouw (fig.2) was built in the Van Baerlestraat and was inaugurated in 1888 with a concert by an ensemble of 700, conducted by Viotta. Later that year the Concertgebouw Orchestra was established, conducted by Willem Kes. When Kes left for Glasgow in 1895 he was succeeded by Willem Mengelberg, who, conducting the orchestra until 1941, built up a world-wide reputation. Festivals of Dutch music were given in 1902 and 1912 in conjunction with the Wagner-Vereniging and the Toonkunst Choir, and Mengelberg directed a Mahler festival in 1920, a French festival in 1922, a Richard Strauss festival in 1924 and the orchestra's golden jubilee celebrations in 1938; he conducted at the 11th ISCM festival, held in Amsterdam in 1933. Among the guest conductors of the orchestra during this period were Richard Strauss, Ravel, Walter, Fritz Busch, Beecham, Boult, Lambert, Monteux and Stravinsky. Eduard van Beinum succeeded Mengelberg in 1941 and was followed in 1961 by Haitink, who shared the appointment with Jochum until 1964, after which he continued alone. Since World War II the Concertgebouw Orchestra has become independent of

1. *Interior of the Amsterdam Stadsschouwburg showing the royal box (centre) during a performance arranged for the official visit of William V of Orange on 1 June 1768: engraving by Simon Fokke*

2. Interior of the Amsterdam Concertgebouw

the building after which it is named, and it is now a state organization.

Choral singing in Amsterdam was stimulated by the foundation of the Maatschappij Caecilia (1841), conducted by Verhulst from 1865 to 1886. The Toonkunst choir, based on the MAATSCHAPPIJ TOT BEVORDERING DER TOONKUNST, which was founded in 1829, gave concerts in the Oude Parksaal and has given annual performances of Bach's *St Matthew Passion* with the Concertgebouw Orchestra on Palm Sunday since 1899. In addition to the Concertgebouw, Amsterdam has a number of other permanent orchestras founded since World War II, including the Amsterdam PO, formerly the Kunstmaandorkest, under Kersjes, and the Netherlands Chamber Orchestra under Szymon Goldberg and David Zinman. Other musical activities in Amsterdam are promoted by the GAUDEAMUS FOUNDATION.

The HOLLAND FESTIVAL, held each summer since 1947, is centred on Amsterdam: concerts are held in the Concertgebouw and various churches, and operas are performed in the Stadsschouwburg. Since World War II Amsterdam has become important in the revival of early music, particularly through the work of Gustav Leonhardt, organist of the Waalse Kerk and professor of the harpsichord at the conservatory.

4. EDUCATION. The Amsterdam Conservatory was founded in 1884 by Daniël de Lange and has been widely influential in Dutch musical life. The Amsterdam Muzieklyceum has also been important as a training institute for musicians. At Amsterdam University (1882) music history has been taught since 1929, originally by Bernet Kempers, for whom a chair was created in 1946. Chairs of musicology have subsequently been occupied by Smits van Waesberghe (1957–71), Noske (from 1968) and Chris Maas (from 1971). Ethnomusicology was introduced in 1936 at the Koloniale Instituut (now the Instituut voor de Tropen) by Jaap Kunst, the specialist in Indonesian music, and from 1970 was taught at the university by Frank Ll. Harrison. The musicological institute of the university

has an important collection of manuscript and printed music, including the former library of the Maatschappij tot Bevordering der Toonkunst.

BIBLIOGRAPHY

D. F. Scheurleer: *Het muziekleven in Amsterdam in de zeventiende eeuw* (The Hague, 1897)
J. W. Enschedé: *30 jaren muziek in Holland (1670–1700)* (Haarlem, 1904)
H. J. Westerling: 'De oudste Amsterdamsche opera', *De Gids* (1919), Aug, 277
D. J. Balfoort: *Het muziekleven in Nederland in de zeventiende en achttiende eeuw* (Amsterdam, 1938)
J. A. Bank: 'Middeleeuwsche kerkmuziek in Amsterdam' [Medieval church music in Amsterdam], *Zeven eeuwen Amsterdam*, ed. A. E. d'Ailly, i (Amsterdam, n.d.), 249
——: *De opera in Nederland* (Amsterdam, 1946)
S. A. M. Bottenheim: 'Muziek te Amsterdam gedurende de achttiende eeuw', *Zeven eeuwen Amsterdam*, ed. A. E. d'Ailly, iv (Amsterdam, n.d.), 173
——: *Geschiedenis van het Concertgebouw* [History of the Concertgebouw] (Amsterdam, 1948)
G. K. Krop: *Concertgebouw orkest in diamant* [The diamond jubilee of the Concertgebouw Orchestra] (Amsterdam, 1949)
E. Reeser: *Een eeuw Nederlandse muziek* [A century of Dutch music] (Amsterdam, 1950)
——: *Music in Holland* (Amsterdam, 1959)
A. J. Heuwekemeijer: 'Amsterdamse muziekuitgeverijen vanaf de 18e eeuw tot heden' [Amsterdam music publishers from the 18th century to the present], *Mededelingenblad vereniging voor nederlandse muziekgeschiedenis* (1967), no.24, p.39
B. Huys: 'An Unknown Alamire-choirbook ('Occo Codex') Recently Acquired by the Royal Library of Belgium: a New Source for the History of Music in Amsterdam', *TVNM*, xxiv/1 (1974), 1
E. A. Klusen: *Johann Wilhelm Wilms und das Amsterdamer Musikleben (1772–1847)* (Buren, 1975)

JAN VAN DER VEEN

Amusia. The inability to comprehend or produce musical sounds. The term has been applied to 'innate' lack of musical aptitude, or to a musical deficit of cultural or environmental origin; strictly it pertains to the effects of brain pathology. The study of amusia, particularly that of previously capable musicians, may illuminate the mechanisms of musical memory and the way in which the complex integration of functions involved in music is organized.

Memory is the dynamic physical record in the nervous system of previous events, and some functions have come to be recognized as associated with particular areas in either of the cortical hemispheres. As aphasia is the deficit from damage to the speech area, so amusia is thought to concern a similar area or system of areas, as yet not clearly defined or identified, though evidence from neurological research and experimental psychology gives strong topographical indications. The association of certain memory traces with points on the cortex has been reported from the electrical stimulation used in open brain surgery, which evokes a recurrence of hitherto irretrievable memories; but it is difficult to assess these correlations, since stimulation may be interrupting widespread neuronal circuits rather than affecting a circumscribed storage point. However, Penfield described the vivid recurrence of musical memories, and sometimes compulsive singing, linked with stimulation of a microscopic point on the temporal lobe. There is a similar difficulty in assessing the significance of functional deficit associated with particular brain pathology; for any higher mental function is an integrated system based on the combined work of a dynamic structure of cortical zones working together, each zone contributing its own factor (Luria, 1966). Where the interplay of perception, memory and action is complex, as in musical performance, the neuronal circuits must integrate the areas of the cortex specific to primary sensory input (auditory, visual and kinaesthetic) with those attenuating or enhancing, registering or excluding it, with the 'association areas' concerned in retrieval from long-term memory storage, and with the motor areas.

The appreciation by a musically educated listener of a work new to him involves the retention of an ephemeral memory trace of the opening themes so that they are recognizable as they recur or are transformed. Experimental psychology distinguishes three stages of the memory process (Waugh and Norman): the sensory or 'echoic' image, which fades in milliseconds and is thought to be a reverberation of the nerve circuits; short-term or primary memory, which can code the rapidly fading sensory trace into more durable form but which is a labile system of limited capacity where information is lost in a few seconds if mental rehearsal is prevented; and long-term memory, which accommodates not only the entire repertory of familiar music but also grammatical comprehension of music (hence musical expectancies) upon which ability to retain a once-heard phrase depends. Long-term durable memory is thought to depend on structural changes in nerve junctions. In spite of the problematic nature of localization of memory storage, there is a broad indication of separate sites for music and for speech in those cases where localized damage has caused amusia without aphasia or vice versa. Dorgeuille, for instance, reported six cases of aphasia without amusia with left-hemisphere lesions and two of right-hemisphere lesions had amusia without aphasia.

The term 'laterality' is used in this context to define the asymmetry between the two cortical hemispheres in types of learning stored. Each hemisphere serves the neural pathways predominantly from the opposite side of the body. But also, at least in most right-handed people, the left hemisphere is concerned with speech and verbal learning, and both clinical and normal evidence seems to indicate a right-hemisphere role in music, though there is not as yet agreement, perhaps because a wide diversity of tests and various aspects of music are discussed.

The ability accurately to locate sources of sounds is a faculty depending on two coordinated ears. This symmetry of auditory function originated before the evolution of the cortex; its survival may be partly due to elements of subcortical analysing mechanisms, akin to those of earlier species, underlying the controlling action of the auditory cortex. But brain laterality in primates and man evolved with the development of cognitive function, particularly language (Geschwind) and, while human ears perform symmetrically in monitoring the environment, in certain types of listening they are influenced by this cortical asymmetry. Further elaboration of interdependent brain systems evolved, functionally distinct from the language area and serving to mediate fine skills such as music. On this view the cortex, through neural pathways descending to the cochlea, influences ear dominance to the degree to which acoustic signals are being analysed linguistically, or according to some other cognitive code.

While there are broad indications of laterality in amusia, the details of the interdependence of musical and other cognitive functions make amusia research difficult to interpret more specifically. Luria (1966) described the three-year-long aphasia of a Russian composer, suffering from severe left-hemisphere lesions, who was unable to distinguish consonants yet wrote his best symphonies during his illness. Milner (1962) gave Seashore's musical tests to patients before and after removing one temporal lobe for the relief of focal epilepsy; she found no musical effects for left-lobe removal, whereas with right-lobe removal timbre and memory tests were affected and all except rhythm deteriorated. Kimura pursued the laterality problem with normal rather than clinical subjects, by testing right-handed nurses, presenting two different tunes simultaneously, one to each ear (the 'dichotic' listening task), then asking subjects to identify both tunes from a set of four played consecutively. Scores were significantly higher for tunes presented to the left ear (transmitting predominantly to the right hemisphere), whereas the presentation of spoken digits instead of melodies yielded a right-ear superiority. Shankweiler used the same dichotic tasks testing patients with temporal lobe removal; he found perception of melody impaired with right lobe removed, perception of digits with left lobectomy. Gordon found no difference between ears for melodies but left-ear superiority for chords, with healthy music students as subjects. He suggested that the equality of ears for melodies indicates bilaterality of the rhythmic function; that seems plausible, and also would account for Milner's results, because speech articulation is also rhythmically based (though the rhythms are regular only in poetic metres).

The trend in amusia research is to distinguish the various factors in the higher mental function of music and search for specific physiological correlates, bearing Luria's caution in mind. Just as speech aphasias can selectively affect receptor or motor function, and there can be 'word blindness' or 'word deafness', so particular musical deficits occur, affecting selectively the ability to sing or to recognize melodies, to read or to write music, to recall recently heard melodies, intervals or rhythms. Botez and Wertheim devised 45 tests to distinguish the various aspects of musical function, whatever the mental or musical level of the patient. Two areas in the right hemisphere, the frontal and temporal lobes, seem to be of particular importance (though all levels from the cochlea to the cortex are involved). In general, frontal lobes seem to be concerned in the structuring of temporal order (though in amusia and laterality studies its relation to rhythm needs to be more sharply defined); and Botez and Wertheim's frontal patient had difficulty with abstracting tunes and repeating time patterns. But frontal lobes are so closely integrated with other structures that assigning to them a particular musical function is extremely problematic, where the tests given are purely musical.

However, rhythmic deficit has also been associated with temporal lobe damage, and Gordon's results raise the question: exactly how are speech rhythms and musical rhythms related? Unlike Milner (1962) and Luria (1966), Dorgeuille presented evidence of the effect of right temporal damage on rhythm. But he also showed cases of 'avocalie' or inability to sing tunes with left temporal lobe damage, and his one case where musical reading and writing were affected was of left temporal lesion, involving the language hemisphere, as in alexia and agraphia. It is quite possible that motor aspects of speaking and singing should be more functionally conglomerate, while storage sites for the verbal language code remain distinct from those for other codes such as music and pattern recognition; indeed Kimura presented evidence of visual and auditory codes other than language being stored in the right hemisphere.

But the problematic nature of the linguistic–non-linguistic distinction constitutes a great difficulty for the interpretation of amusia in terms of laterality. Musicians, for example, particularly those trained in Tonic Sol-fa, may very well have an inbuilt verbal code underlying their perception of melody, however much it has been absorbed into the perceptual process, much as vocalizing underlines the original acquisition of a written linguistic code (Nazarova, 1952; quoted by Luria, 1966). However, it has been demonstrated with recordings of brain electrical activity that 'different neural events occur in the left hemisphere during analysis of linguistic versus nonlinguistic parameters of the *same* acoustical signal' (Wood and others), which suggests that in spite of interactions the distinction is tenable. A case of auditory agnosia (inability to comprehend) has shown an impaired ability to recognize the meaning or identity of the source of non-verbal sounds while comprehension of language remained intact, but there was a distinct superiority in recognizing musical instruments over other non-verbal sounds (Albert and others, 1972). Such isolated cases yield valuable insights, but the sporadic flow of clinical evidence and the wide differences in musical literacy between both patients and normal subjects make further difficulty in distinguishing verbal and musical perceptual systems.

The contribution to musical psychology of this search for physiological correlates may not seem great at present, but it is likely to grow with the increased precision of neurological techniques and the sharpening of the definitions of different musical aptitudes. Indeed, the problem of amusia and laterality is central to musical psychology, for to understand the workings of interacting memory systems more needs to be known about their neural substrates. The evidence in amusia cases correlating deficits in any of these related processes with particular brain structures is of great importance, just as the more extensive knowledge gained from clinical study of language-centres in the brain has illuminated understanding of the integrated components of speaking, listening to and remembering language.

BIBLIOGRAPHY

M. Botez and N. Wertheim: 'Expressive Aphasia and Amusia Following Right Frontal Lesion in a Right-handed Man', *Brain*, lvxxxii (1959), 186

B. Milner: 'Laterality Effects in Audition', *Inter-hemispheric Relations and Cerebral Dominance*, ed. V. Mountcastle (Baltimore, 1962), 177

D. Kimura: 'Left–Right Differences in the Perception of Melodies', *Quarterly Journal of Experimental Psychology*, xvi (1964), 355

A. R. Luria, L. S. Tsvetkova and D. A. Futer: 'Aphasia in a composer', *Journal of Neurological Sciences*, ii (1965), 288

C. Dorgeuille: *L'amusie* (diss., Académie de Paris, 1966)

A. Luria: *Higher Cortical Functions in Man* (London, 1966)

D. Shankweiler: 'Effects of Temporal-lobe Damage on Perception of Dichotically Presented Melodies', *Journal of Comparative and Physiological Psychology*, lxii (1966), 115

H. Gordon: 'Hemispheric Asymmetries in the Perception of Musical Chords', *Cortex*, vi (1970), 387

B. Milner: 'Interhemispheric Differences in the Localization of Psychological Processes in Man', *British Medical Bulletin*, xxvii (1971), 272

C. Wood, W. Goff and R. Day: 'Auditory Evoked Potentials During Perception', *Science*, clxxiii (1971), 1248

M. Albert, R. Sparks, T. von Stockert and D. Sax: 'A Case Study of Auditory Agnosia', *Cortex*, viii (1972), 427

N. Geschwind: 'Language and the Brain', *Scientific American* (1972), April, 76

D. Kimura: 'The Asymmetry of the Human Brain', *Scientific American* (1973), March, 70

G. Assal: 'Wernicke's Asphasia without Amusia in a pianist', *Review of Neurology*, cxxix (1974), 251

T. G. Bever and R. J. Chiarello: 'Cerebral Dominance in Musicians and Nonmusicians', *Science*, clxxxv (1974), 537

M. Critchley and R. A. Henson: *Music and the Brain: Studies in the Neurology of Music* (London, 1976)

NATASHA SPENDER

Amy, Gilbert (*b* Paris, 29 Aug 1936). French composer and conductor.

1. LIFE. Showing early musical gifts, he began piano lessons at the age of six, but in his youth he also took a lively interest in such subjects as literature, architecture and history. In 1954 he took the Baccalauréat and won a national award in philosophy. He then studied at the Paris Conservatoire (1955–60) with Plé-Caussade (counterpoint and fugue), Milhaud (composition), Roget (accompaniment) and Messiaen (analysis), also studying the piano and harmony with Loriod (1956–8). His meeting with Boulez in 1956 was of decisive importance to him as a composer and later as a conductor (he attended Boulez's courses in Basle in 1965). In the late 1950s he wrote his first important compositions, notably the Piano Sonata, which he introduced himself in 1960 at the Darmstadt summer courses, where he had studied from 1958. In 1964 he spent a year in Berlin on a Ford Foundation grant. His career as a conductor had begun in 1962, when he was appointed to an assistant post at the Odéon. Besides this he conducted his own works and those of contemporaries, particularly after he succeeded Boulez as director of the Domaine Musical in 1967; and from the late 1960s he has appeared internationally, conducting both classical and contemporary music. The Domaine Musical was disbanded in 1973, and that year he was appointed musical adviser to the ORTF. He received the prize of the Paris Biennale in 1967 for *Trajectoires* and the Grand Prix de la Promotion Symphonique de la SACEM in 1971.

2. WORKS. The first composition Amy showed to Milhaud at the Conservatoire was *Oeil de fumée* (1955), a set of songs of a subtle facture and melodic grace recalling now and then the first songs of Webern. A more rigorous spirit informs the Variations for four instruments (1956), and this new stage was revealed

more decisively in the *Cantate brève* for soprano and three instruments (1957). Here, through a very supple handling of serialism, text and music are bound together in refined relations that at times indicate the importance of Amy's recent acquaintance with *Le marteau sans maître*. What is most striking in these three works is not only their technical sureness but also the exactness and richness of Amy's approach and, above all, the unusually precocious affirmation of a well-defined aesthetic orientation which has remained, broadly speaking, stable in Amy's production, and within which these pieces already display, beyond inevitable influences, certain constants of his style: clear, effective, polyphonic writing and instrumental finesse.

Between 1957 and 1960 Amy was engaged on the Piano Sonata, whose first movement he spent a long time in reworking on Boulez's advice. The sonata was the culmination of a period of research in areas ranging from generalized serialism to mobile form, and it shows how much Amy's evolution at this period coincided with that of the European serial movement. His rigorous outlook, formed in the strict postwar serial school, is evident here and in the works, often of extreme difficulty and complexity, which followed. While composing the sonata he was also at work on *Mouvements* for 17 instruments (commissioned by Boulez for Darmstadt in 1958 and played at the Domaine Musical the same year), a piece founded on a rich counterpoint of tempos, and *Inventions I–II* (1959–61), which centres on the notion of 'equivalence' and uses its four instruments in a resolutely concertante manner. The orchestral *Antiphonies* (1960–63), which Amy had contemplated since hearing *Gruppen* in 1958, indicates new preoccupations in the domains of sound and of space. Requiring two conductors, the piece is conceived for two principal orchestras and a median 'concertino' group, and the music is, in Amy's words, 'absolutely coordinated, not only in the passages where several tempos are superposed but also in the passages where there is no traditional metre. No "chance", no floating superposition'.

Epigrammes (1961), a short piano piece in mobile form, was a direct continuation from the Piano Sonata, and in turn gave rise to the *Cahiers d'épigrammes* (1964), which can be intercalated between two performances of it. In this context, *Diaphonies* for two identical ensembles each of 12 players (1962) appears a somewhat curious development: luminous and subtle, it already has that breath of poetry which distinguishes Amy's orchestral works from the end of the decade. The succeeding piece for wind sextet, *Alpha-beth* (1963–4), can be regarded as a set of studies on major compositional problems of the moment, some of them pursued further in the mobile-form *Relais* for brass quintet (1967). *Cycle* (1964–6) was written for Les Percussions de Strasbourg with the intention 'to formulate and structure "musically" the different types of sonority and playing that constitute the domain of the percussion'.

Meanwhile Amy had embarked on a sequence of orchestral works with *Triade* (1965), after Michaux's mescalin-stimulated writings, a revised concert version of music he had written for a film of 1963, retaining the strange and gripping form originally dictated by the visual image. *Strophe* for dramatic soprano and orchestra (1964–6), a work of large scope, confirmed in brilliant fashion Amy's 'symphonic' inclinations. Five

lines of Char are 'by turns (Strophe A then B) enunciated, vocalized (Vocalise), torn into shreds of phonemes (Envoi)'; the large orchestra is again divided into two, but without spatial separation and under one conductor, the singer being 'in some sort the axis of this symmetry'. *Trajectoires* (1966) is scored for violin and orchestra but is distant indeed from the conventional concerto, despite its technical difficulty (concerned notably with the use of quarter-tones). Within a strange atmosphere of waking dream, the violin, a solitary and pensive traveller, and the many-faced orchestra develop, little by little, mysterious and changing relationships, brief chance encounters between the 'trajectories' marked out by large groups of brass, pizzicato strings or percussion. *Chant* (1967–9), 'composed with a highly elaborated material of pitches and timbre complexes', was considered by Amy as bringing to an end this group of orchestral pieces, containing as it does 'several "reminiscences" of earlier works, each acting not directly on the structure but rather on the articulation of the different phrases of development'.

Amy had now reached a decisive point in his career: as the subsequent works have demonstrated, he was entering a period of full maturity. In particular, his orchestration, bearing the influence of his growing experience as a conductor, shows from this period an often highly novel sense of colour, at once sumptuous and refined. *Cette étoile enseigne à s'incliner* (1970), the title taken from a picture by Klee, uses men's voices, ten instruments and tape in music of uncharacteristic stability, the predominant deep register creating a solid, sombre climate in accord with the text from Dante. Another vocal work of the same year, *Récitatif, air et variation* for 12 voices, sets out the drama of its own genesis by means of different treatments of the poem: at first informally 'dreamed', then vocalized, expres.ed, and finally uttered, before being phonetically dislocated. With *Jeux* (1970) for one to four oboes (some of which may be recorded) Amy returned to the possibilities of concertante writing, the 'game' consisting notably in realizing certain sections according to established rules. *Jeux et formes* (1970) explores anew 'open or mobile forms' with an ensemble in which the solo oboe plays the role of master of ceremonies.

1972 was marked by Amy's return to the orchestra with *Refrains* and *D'un espace déployé*. The former is a set of five orchestral studies in a form, as the title suggests, with 'repeats', bringing together some of the most typical features of Amy's orchestral writing; the subtitles, such as 'Pour la sonorité des cordes', point to an affinity with Debussy's piano *Etudes*. *D'un espace déployé* is of a quite different conception. As in *Antiphonies* of a decade earlier, the orchestra is divided into two groups, but here unequally: the larger is entrusted with 'big sound blocks', the smaller has a scoring 'more individual, sometimes virtuoso', so that there is some analogy with the disposition in a concerto grosso. But in addition there is a solo soprano, placed in the smaller ensemble, who takes part in the last two movements but intervenes 'formally' only in the short central piece, which uses elements from the brief . . . *D'un désastre obscur* (1971). The basic set of *D'un espace déployé*, G–A–B–D♯–F–F♯–A♯, is clearly announced at the beginning. Amy seems here to have taken a new and large step towards the exploration of extremes of expression (for example, the 'delirium' of the E♭ clarinet in the third movement). This was confirmed in the

Sonata pian'e forte for two female voices and three instrumental groups (1974), in which he ventured into zones previously judged 'dangerous' (the prepared piano, singing into the piano etc), all the while investigating afresh new aspects of mobility.

WORKS

CONCERT

Piece, org, 1954, unpubd
Oeil de fumée (A. Parrot), 5 songs, S, pf, 1955, orchd 1957, unpubd
Variations, 4 insts, 1956, unpubd
Cantate brève (Lorca), S, fl, mar, vib, 1957, unpubd
Mouvements, 17 insts, 1958
Piano Sonata, 1957–60
Inventions I–II, fl, pf + cel, harp, perc, 1959–61
Epigrammes, pf, 1961
Diaphonies, 24 insts, 1962
Antiphonies, 2 orchs, 1960–63
Alpha-beth, fl, ob, cl, b cl, bn, hn, 1963–4
Cahiers d'épigrammes, pf, 1964
Triade, orch, 1965
Cycle, 6 perc, 1964–6
Strophe (Char), S, orch, 1964–6
Trajectoires, vn, orch, 1966
Relais, 2 tpt, 2 trbn, hn, 1967
Chant, orch, 1967–9
Cette étoile enseigne à s'incliner (Dante), male vv, 10 insts, 2-track tape, 1970
Jeux, 1–4 ob, 1970
Jeux et formes, ob, 17 insts, 1970
Récitatif, air et variation (R. Daumal), 12 solo vv, 1970
... D'un désastre obscur (Mallarmé), Mez, cl, 1971
Refrains, orch, 1972
D'un espace déployé (Mallarmé), S, 2 orchs, 1972–3
Sonata pian'e forte (Amy), 2 solo female vv, 3 inst ens, 1974
Seven Sites, 14 insts, 1975

INCIDENTAL MUSIC

Stage plays: Comment s'en débarrasser (Ionesco), 1957; La vie est un songe (Calderón), 1958; Le cadavre encerclé (K. Yacine), 1958; La femme sauvage (Yacine), 1958–63; Biederman et les incendiaires (Frisch), 1960; Oedipe roi (Sophocles), 1961–2; Oedipe à Colone (Sophocles), 1961–2; Le grand cérémonial (Arrabal); La soif et la faim (Ionesco), 1966
Films: Traveling (E. B. Weil), 1962; Images du monde visionnaire (Michaux), 1963; L'alliance (C. de Challonges), 1970

Principal publishers: Heugel, Universal

WRITINGS

'L'espace sonore', *Esprit* (1960), no.1, p.75
'Sur quelques problèmes récents ... et futurs', *Phantomas* (1960), no.15, p.33
'Wagner, Richard', *FasquelleE*
'Musique pour "Misérable miracle" d'Henri Michaux', *Tel quel* (1964), no.17, p.83
'Redécouvrir l'écoute', *Preuves* (1965), no.177, p.29
'Sur Henri Michaux', *L'herne* (1966), no.8, p.194
'Forme et liberté', *Lettres françaises* (28 June 1967)

BIBLIOGRAPHY

M. Faure: 'Entretien avec Gilbert Amy', *Lettres nouvelles* (1961), no.11, p.165
D. Jameux: 'Entretien avec Gilbert Amy', *Musique en jeu* (1971), no.3, p.72
Sillon no.12 (1971), Oct [special issue]
A. Durel: 'Diriger "Carré": débat avec Gilbert Amy', *Musique en jeu* (1974), no.15, p.27
E. Walter: 'Entretien avec Gilbert Amy', *Harmonie* (1975), no.103

BETSY JOLAS

Ana [Anna], **Francesco d'** [Franciscus Venetus; Francesco Varoter, etc] (*b* ?Venice, *c*1460; *d* Venice, late 1502, or 1503, before 6 Feb). Italian composer and organist. He was appointed second organist at St Mark's, Venice, in 1490, having previously been organist at S Leonardo there. He held the position at St Mark's until his death, which must have occurred shortly before 6 February 1503 when he was replaced by Giovanni de Marino and was described as 'recently deceased'. He is therefore not identifiable with Francesco d'Ana of Padua who was appointed organist at Concordia Cathedral on 15 March 1554.

Many of Ana's works are marked only with the initials 'F.V.' in Petrucci's books. In a list of corrections to *Tenori e contrabassi intabulati ... libro primo* (1509) Petrucci named 'F.V.' as Francesco Varoter (Francesco the furrier). On the basis of this, Disertori attributed to Varoter all the other works ascribed to 'F.V.'. However, *Nasce l'aspro mio tormento*, ascribed to 'F.V.' in the 1509 book, was ascribed to 'Fran. Vene. Orga.' in the original source, Petrucci's *Frottole libro secondo* (1505), and it seems more likely that either Petrucci's later alteration was a mistake or Ana was also a furrier.

Ana wrote one motet and 28 frottolas. Two more frottolas may be by him: one that is also ascribed to Tromboncino, and one that is ascribed to 'F.'. He seems to have been one of the earliest of the important frottolists: his music appears in three early manuscripts (*I-MOe* α, F.9,9, compiled in Padua in 1495; *I-Mt* 55; and *GB-Lbm* Eg.3051), all of which seem to predate Petrucci's first printed frottola collection of 1504. After Petrucci's *Tenori e contrabassi intabulati ... libro primo* (1509) no more music by Ana appeared; thus he seems to have played little part in the move towards higher-quality texts in the frottola. However, he set two sonnets, one of which, the first printed sonnet setting, *Quest'è quel loco*, was by Niccolò da Correggio, one of the more literary frottola poets. In both sonnets he set both the first quatrain and the first tercet.

In his *barzellette* Ana generally set only the *riprese* and refrains: only four of his 16 settings provide new music for the stanzas. They are characterized by syllabic text settings and many repeated notes in the melodic lines. The lower voices alternate between non-imitative polyphony and homorhythmic movement with the cantus. *Dal ciel crudo* was still known in 1649 when King John IV of Portugal cited it as an example of an antiquated style. In contrast to the *barzellette*, Ana's 12 *strambotti* have extremely melismatic lines.

Ana's one sacred work, *Passio sacra nostri Redemptoris*, is not a true Passion, but rather a motet in two sections, using selected passages from the Gospels. It is generally homorhythmic and has many fermatas.

WORKS

1 motet, 1506[1]
28 frottolas, 1504[4], 1505[3], 1505[4], 1505[5], 1505[6], 1506[3], 1507[4], 1509[3]
Voi, voi che passate, attrib. 'F.V.' in 1509[3]; attrib. Tromboncino in 1507[3], *US-Cn* Capirola Lutebook: anon. in *GB-Lbm* Eg.3051 (may be by Ana)
Amati cor mio, attrib. 'F.' in *I-MOe* α, F.9,9 (may be by Ana)
Edns. in AMI, i (1897/*R*); R. Schwartz, Publikationen älterer Musik, viii (Leipzig, 1935/*R*); G. Cesari and others, *Le frottole nell'edizione principe di Ottaviano Petrucci* (Cremona, 1954); Einstein; Jeppesen

BIBLIOGRAPHY

A. Einstein: *The Italian Madrigal* (Princeton, 1949/*R*1971)
N. Bridgman: 'La frottola e la transition de frottola au madrigal', *Musique et poésie au XVIe siècle: CNRS Paris 1953*, 63
K. Jeppesen: *La frottola* (Århus and Copenhagen, 1968–70)

WILLIAM F. PRIZER

Anabathmoi. In the Byzantine morning Office, a set of three or four antiphons to the Gradual psalms (verses from Psalms cxix–cxxx and cxxxii). There is a set for each of the eight modes. Although they were compiled in the 8th century, the oldest surviving manuscript copies of the music date from the 10th and 11th centuries and are written in Chartres notation (*GR-LA* gamma 67; *ATSvatopedi*, 1488); *see* NEUMATIC NOTATIONS, §IV.

BIBLIOGRAPHY

O. Strunk: 'The Antiphons of the Oktoechos', *JAMS*, xiii (1960), 50

DIMITRI CONOMOS

Anabolē. A term used in ancient Greece in the period of Pindar for the prelude or introduction to a song but subsequently associated with the melodically extravagant, chromatically inflected solo songs or monodies of which Timotheus of Miletus was the most significant exponent. HANS KOTTER used the term (in Greek) in the early 16th century for a freely constructed keyboard prelude in a tablature (in *CH-Bu*) assembled for the humanist Bonifacius Amerbach (facs. in W. Apel: *The Notation of Polyphonic Music* (Cambridge, Mass., 1953), 29; transcr. in HAM, no.84g).

BIBLIOGRAPHY

W. Merian: *Der Tanz in dem deutsche Tabulaturbüchern* (Leipzig, 1927), 37–75

Y. Rokseth: 'The Instrumental Music of the Middle Ages and Early Sixteenth Century', *NOHM*, iii (1960), 435

O. Tiby: 'La composition anabolique', *Encyclopédie de la Pléiade: Histoire de la musique*, i (Paris, 1960), 419

See also MELANIPPIDES and PROOIMION.

MICHAEL TILMOUTH

Anacker, August Ferdinand (*b* Freiberg, Saxony, 17 Oct 1790; *d* Freiberg, 21 Aug 1854). German Kantor and composer. He studied at the Freiberg Gymnasium, then at the University of Leipzig, where he took the master's degree. He continued his education with Schicht, Riem, Härtel and Friedrich Schneider and lived in Leipzig as a singer, pianist and music teacher. In 1821 he was given a post in Freiberg as the city's music director, becoming the cathedral Kantor and a teacher at the Gymnasium and the teachers' training college; he also founded the Singakademie in 1823 and reorganized the Bergmusikkorps. He visited Beethoven in Vienna and became a champion of his music; he was also a friend of Mendelssohn, Reissiger and Wagner. His most important pupils were Brendel, Finsterbusch and Volkmann.

Anacker anticipated the modern German Kantor who was principally concerned with musical education and artistic competence. His compositions, mainly sacred and secular choral, are distinguished for their modernity and emotional intensity; the oratorio *Bergmannsgruss* (1831–2) was one of the most popular and best-known choral works of the 19th century.

BIBLIOGRAPHY

F. Rassmann: *Pantheon der Tonkünstler* (Quedlinburg and Leipzig, 1831)

A. von Dommer: 'A. F. Anacker', *ADB*

F. Brendel: 'A. F. Anacker', *Gesammelte Aufsätze zur Geschichte und Kritik der neueren Musik* (Leipzig, 1888)

A. Anacker: 'A. F. Anacker bis zu seinem Amtsantritt in Freiberg', *Mitteilungen des Freiberger Altertumsvereins*, lxii (1932), 53

W. Anacker: 'Zwei Briefe von Felix Mendelssohn Bartholdy', *Musik und Gesellschaft*, xxii (1972), 654

WALTER HÜTTEL

Anacreon (*b* Teos, *c*570 BC; *d* 490 or 485 BC). Greek lyric poet. An Ionian by birth and upbringing, he spent his professional life in the service of Polycrates, tyrant of Samos, and later at Athens under the patronage of Peisistratus's son Hipparchus. His poetry reflects the gay, sophisticated atmosphere of the courts where he was musical arbiter; underlying it is the cultural heritage of his native Ionia, especially the distinctive tradition of lighthearted monody.

Although the writings of Anacreon include elegiac and iambic poetry as well as lyric, extant musical references occur only in the lyrics. He spoke of 'the lovely *pēktis*' and 'the 20-string *magadis*' of his homeland (frag.18, ll.2–3; 19, ll.1–2; see Edmonds); he also mentioned auloi with only three finger-holes instead of the usual six (frag.22). Critias, an early 5th-century writer (in Athenaeus, xiii, 600*d*), portrayed the poet himself as an antagonist of the aulos and fond of the barbiton. Anacreon is the first Greek musician of whom credible personal portraits are known, two vase-paintings that come from his own time. Both show him holding the barbiton (*see* ALCAEUS), and a late source (Athenaeus, iv, 175*e*) even credits him with having invented it. Many poems were written in imitation of his style until five centuries or more after his death; these had a literary and musical influence of their own.

BIBLIOGRAPHY

U. von Wilamowitz-Moellendorff: *Sappho und Simonides* (Berlin, 1913), 105f, 114ff

J. M. Edmonds, ed. and trans.: *Lyra graeca*, ii (London and New York, 1924, 5/1964)

C. M. Bowra: *Greek Lyric Poetry* (Oxford, 1936, rev. 2/1967), 268–307

D. L. Page, ed.: *Poetae melici graeci* (Oxford, 1962)

——: *Lyrica graeca selecta* (Oxford, 1968), 147ff

M. L. West, ed.: *Iambi et elegi graeci*, ii (Oxford, 1972), 30f

G. M. Kirkwood: *Early Greek Monody: the History of a Poetic Type*, Cornell Studies in Classical Philology, xxxvii (Ithaca, NY, and London, 1974), 150ff

WARREN ANDERSON

Anacreontic Society (i). London society of aristocratic and wealthy amateur musicians founded in 1766; *see* LONDON, §VI, 4(i).

Anacreontic Society (ii). Orchestra founded in 1814 in BELFAST.

Anacrustic. *See* CRUSTIC, ANACRUSTIC.

Anagnino, Spirito. *See* ANAGUINO, SPIRITO.

Anagnōstēs. A reader in the Orthodox Church. His function is to announce the PROKEIMENON of the day and to chant the appropriate lessons from the Old Testament or the Epistles (*see* EKPHŌNĒSIS).

Anagrammatismos. A kalophonic ('embellished') setting of certain Byzantine stichera used on festal occasions. Only a part of the hymn text is used, and this is preceded and followed by very florid TERETISMATA (*see* STICHĒRON).

Anaguino, Spirito (*fl* 1617–25). Italian composer. His name has sometimes been wrongly spelt 'Anagnino' and 'Agnanino'. He was an Augustinian monk and lived for part of his life in Naples. He published several volumes of music but only two survive (and the second of these is incomplete): *Nova sacra cantica . . . liber secundus*, for one to four voices and continuo (Naples, 1617), and *Sacro convito celeste* op.6, for two to six and eight voices and continuo (Orvieto, 1625).

Analysis. The resolution of a musical structure into relatively simpler constituent elements, and the investigation of the functions of those elements within that structure. In such a process the 'structure' may be part of a work, a work in its entirety, a group or even a repertory of works, in a written or oral tradition. The distinction often drawn between formal analysis and stylistic analysis is a pragmatic one, but is unnecessary in theoretical terms. Both fall within the above definition, since on the one hand any musical complex, no matter how small or large, may be deemed a 'style'; and on the other hand, all the comparative processes that characterize stylistic analysis are inherent in the basic analytical activity of resolving structure into elements.

A more general definition of the term as implied in common parlance might be: that part of the study of music which takes as its starting-point the music itself, rather than external factors.

I. General. II. History. III. Analytical method.

I. General

1. The place of analysis in the study of music. 2. The nature of musical analysis.

1. THE PLACE OF ANALYSIS IN THE STUDY OF MUSIC. The phrase 'musical analysis', taken in a general sense, embraces a large number of diverse activities. Some of these are mutually exclusive: they represent fundamentally different views of the nature of music, music's role in human life, and the role of the human intellect with regard to music. These differences of view render the field of analysis difficult to define within its own boundaries. (Such a definition will be the concern of §2 and of §III, 1 below.) More difficult still, in some ways, is to define where precisely analysis lies within the study of music. Underlying all aspects of analysis as an activity is the fundamental point of contact between mind and musical sound, namely musical perception (*see* PSYCHOLOGY OF MUSIC).

The concerns of analysis as a whole can be said to have much in common on the one hand with those of musical aesthetics and on the other with those of compositional theory. The three regions of study might be thought of as occupying positions along an axis which has at one extreme the placing of music within philosophical schemes and at the other the giving of technical instruction in the craft of composition.

The analyst, like the aesthetician, is in part concerned with the nature of the musical work: with what it is, or embodies, or signifies; with how it has come to be; with its effects or implications; with its relevance to, or value for, its recipients. Where they differ is in the centres of gravity of their studies: the analyst focusses his attention on a musical structure (whether a chord, a phrase, a work, the output of a composer or court etc), and seeks to define its constituent elements and explain how they operate; but the aesthetician focusses on the nature of music *per se* and its place among the arts, in life and reality. That the two supply information to each other is undoubted: the analyst provides a fund of material which the aesthetician may adduce as evidence in forming his conclusions, and the analyst's definition of the specific furnishes a continual monitoring service for the aesthetician's definition of the general; conversely, the aesthetician's insights provide problems for the analyst to solve, condition his approach and method, and ultimately furnish the means of exposing his hidden assumptions. Their activities may overlap so that they often find themselves doing similar things. Nonetheless, they have two essential differences: first, that analysis tends to strive towards the status of a natural science, whereas aesthetics is a branch of philosophy, the significance of this being that it sets up a one-way flow whereby analysis supplies evidence in answer to the empirical questions of aesthetics (and the extent to which it fails to do this effectively is a measure of the scientific achievement of analysis so far); and second, that the analyst's ultimate concern is with the place of a musical structure within the totality of musical structures, whereas the aes-

thetician's is with the place of musical structures within the system of reality. (For further discussion, *see* AESTHETICS OF MUSIC, §§1–3.)

Similarly, the analyst and the theorist of musical composition (*Satztechnik*; *Kompositionslehre*) have a common interest in the laws of musical construction. Many would deny a separation of any kind and would argue that analysis was a subgroup of musical theory. But that is an attitude that springs from particular social and educational conditions. While important contributions have been made to analysis by teachers of composition, others have been made by performers, instrumental teachers, critics and historians. Analysis may serve as a tool for teaching, though it may in that case instruct the performer or the listener at least as often as the composer; but it may equally well be a private activity – a procedure for discovering. Musical analysis is no more implicitly a part of pedagogical theory than is chemical analysis; nor is it implicitly a part of the acquisition of compositional techniques. On the contrary, the statements of musical theorists can form primary material for the analyst's investigations by providing criteria against which relevant music may be examined.

Of greater significance is the fact that analytical procedures can be applied to styles of performance and interpretation as well as to those of composition. But the point at which composition ceases and interpretation begins is rarely incisive. Most Western analysis takes a score as its subject matter and implicitly assumes it to be a finalized presentation of musical ideas. If it is true that the notated form in which a medieval, Renaissance or Baroque work survives is an incomplete record, it is even more to the point that for the analyst of ethnomusicological material recorded on tape a score is only an intermediary device which in no way marks off 'composer' from 'performer'. It provides a coarse communication of the detail recorded on tape, much of which he will have to analyse by ear or with electronic measuring equipment. Analytical techniques can be applied to aurally perceived material, in any tradition (whether ethnomusicology or that of Western performance).

Briefly, then, analysis is concerned with musical structure, however it arises and is recorded, not merely with composition. Moreover, within the subject matter that analysis and compositional theory have in common, the former is by definition concerned with resolution and explanation, so that its reverse procedure – synthesis – is no more than a means of verification; the latter is concerned directly with the generation of music, and analytical method is only a means of discovery. Again, the fields overlap but with essential differences of subject, of aim and of method. (For further discussion, *see* THEORY, THEORISTS and COMPOSITION.)

A rather different relationship exists between musical analysis and musical history. To the historian, analysis may appear as a tool for historical inquiry. He uses it to detect relationships between 'styles', and thus to establish chains of causality which operate along the dimension of time and are anchored in time by verifiable factual information. He may, for example, observe features in common between the styles of two composers (or groups of composers) and inquire by internal analytical methods and external factual ones whether this represents an influence of one upon the other; or, in reverse order, seek common features of style when he knows of factual links. Conversely, he may detect features out of common between pieces normally associated for one reason or another, and proceed to distinguish by comparative analysis distinct traditions or categories. Again, he may use an analytical classification of features as a means of establishing a chronology of events.

In turn, the analyst may view historical method as a tool for analytical inquiry. His subject matter is rather like sections cut through history. When under analysis they are timeless, or 'synchronic'; they embody internal relationships which the analyst seeks to uncover. But factual information, concerning events in time, may for example determine which of several possible structures is the most likely, or explain causally the presence of some element which is incongruous in analytical terms. Comparative analysis of two or more separate phenomena (whether separated chronologically, geographically, socially or intellectually) only really activates the dimension of time – becoming 'diachronic' – when historical information relating the phenomena is correlated with the analytical findings. Historical and analytical inquiry are thus locked together in mutual dependency, with all things in common as to subject matter and with completely complementary methods of working. (For further discussion, see HISTORIOGRAPHY and MUSICOLOGY, §II, 1–2.)

One further proximity needs to be accounted for: that of analysis and criticism. Criticism is inseparable on the one hand from aesthetics and on the other from analysis. Within criticism there has been constant debate as to the extent to which it is a descriptive or a judicial activity. The 'descriptive' critic tries to do either or both of two things: to portray in words his own inner response – to depict his responding feelings – to a piece of music or a performance, or to think his way into the composer's or performer's mind and expound the vision that he then perceives. The 'judicial' critic evaluates what he experiences by certain standards. These standards may at one extreme be dogmatic canons of beauty, of truth or of taste – pre-set values against which everything is tested; or, at the other extreme, values that form during the experience, governed by an underlying belief that a composer or performer must do whatever he is attempting to do in the clearest and most effective way. This last approach suggests the way that most modern musical criticism works: by trying to deduce the artistic conception that lies behind what the critic experiences, and by evaluating the effectiveness with which the conception is realized, not to mention the extent to which the conception itself answers its prior demands (an 'occasion' for a commissioned work, a dramatic starting-point for a stage work, the work itself as presented by the composer for a performance).

In none of the above does criticism differ categorically from analysis: there is a latent debate within analysis as to whether the analyst's function is descriptive or judicial. There is perhaps a difference of degree. In general, analysis is more concerned with describing than with judging. Most analysis arrives ultimately at the point that the judicial critic has reached when he has perceived to his own satisfaction the artistic 'conception', and is about to present judgment. In this sense, analysis goes less far than criticism, and it does so essentially because it aspires to objectivity and considers judgment to be subjective. But this in turn suggests the other difference between analysis and criticism, namely that the latter stresses the intuitive response of the critic, relies upon his wealth of experience, uses his ability to relate present response to prior experience, and takes these two things as data and method, whereas analysis tends to use as its data definable elements: phrase-units, harmonies, dynamic levels, measured time, bowings and tonguings, and other technical phenomena. Again this is a difference only of degree: a critic's response is often highly informed and made in the light of technical knowledge; and the analyst's definable elements (a phrase, a motif etc) are often defined by subjective conditions. To say that analysis consists of technical operations and criticism of human responses is thus an oversimplification, though it helps to contrast the general characters of the two.

Finally, whereas criticism works always through the medium of words (perhaps with music examples and illustrations) analysis may work through graphic display or annotated score, or even through musical sound rather than through words. (See also CRITICISM.)

2. THE NATURE OF MUSICAL ANALYSIS. The primary impulse of analysis is an empirical one: to get to grips with something on its own terms rather than in terms of other things. Its starting-point is a phenomenon itself rather than external factors (such as biographical facts, political events, social conditions, educational methods and all the other factors that make up the environment of that phenomenon). But like all artistic media, music presents a problem, inherent in the nature of its material. Music is not tangible and measurable as is a liquid or a solid for chemical analysis. The subject of a musical analysis has to be determined; whether it is the score itself, or at least the sound-image that the score projects; or the sound-image in the composer's mind at the moment of composition; or an interpretative performance; or the listener's temporal experience of a performance. All these categories are possible subjects for analysis. There is no agreement among analysts that one is more 'correct' than others – only that the score (when available) provides a reference point from which the analyst reaches out towards one sound-image or another.

Analysis is the means of answering directly the question 'How does it work?'. Its central activity is comparison. By comparison it determines the structural elements and discovers the functions of those elements. Comparison is common to all kinds of musical analysis – feature analysis, formal analysis, functional analysis, information-theory analysis, Schenkerian analysis, semiotic analysis, style analysis and so on: comparison of unit with unit, whether within a single work, or between two works, or between the work and an abstract 'model' such as sonata form or arch form. The central analytical act is thus the test for identity. And out of this arises the measurement of amount of difference, or degree of similarity. These two operations serve together to illuminate the three fundamental form-building processes: recurrence, contrast and variation.

This is a highly 'purified' portrayal of analysis, impartial, objective, yielding the answer 'It works this way . . .' rather than 'It works well' or 'It works badly'. In reality the analyst works with the preconceptions of his culture, age and personality. Thus the preoccupation which the 19th century had with the nature of 'genius' led to the phrasing of the initial question not as 'How does it work?' but as 'What makes this great?', and this has remained the initial question for some analytical traditions late in the 20th century. Since the 'scientific', comparative method was predominant over evaluation in such traditions, and since only works of genius possessed the quality of structural coherence, it followed that comparison of a work with an idealized model of structure or process produced a measure of its greatness.

This is only one example of many. The history of musical analysis that follows inevitably recounts the application of intellectual outlooks from successive ages to musical material: the principles of rhetoric, the concepts of organism and evolution, the subconscious mind, monism, probability theory, structuralism and so forth. Ultimately, the very existence of an observer – the scientist, the analyst – pre-empts the possibility of total objectivity. No single method or approach reveals the truth about music above all others, yet each age has felt that it is moving towards the authentic method.

For further discussion of analytical method, and its subdivision into categories, see §III, 1 below.

II. History

1. Early history. 2. 1750–1840: phrase structure and formal model. 3. 1840–1900: organic growth and the teaching of form. 4. Historical awareness in the 19th century. 5. Early 20th century: reduction techniques and personal style. 6. 1920–45: tension-theory and structural layers. 7. 1945–60: linguistics, cybernetics and thematic unity. 8. Analysis since 1960: set theory and computers.

1. EARLY HISTORY. Analysis, as a pursuit in its own right, came to be established only in the late 19th century; its emergence as an approach and method can be traced back to the 1750s. However, it existed as a scholarly tool, albeit an auxiliary one, from the Middle Ages onwards. The precursors of modern analysis can be seen within at least two branches of musical theory: the study of modal systems, and the theory of musical rhetoric. Where, in either of these branches, a theorist cited a piece of music as illustrating a point of technique or structure, only a small amount of discussion was necessary before he was using what would now be called the analytical approach.

In a sense, the classificatory work carried out by the Carolingian clergy in compiling tonaries was analytical: it involved determining the mode of every antiphon in a repertory of chant, and then subclassifying the modal groups according to their variable endings ('psalm tone differences': see TONARY). Such theorists as Wilhelm of Hirsau, Hermannus Contractus and Johannes Afflighemensis in the 11th century cited antiphons with brief modal discussion, as did later theorists such as Marchetto da Padova and Gaffurius. Their discussions were essentially analysis in the service of performance. Renaissance theorists such as Pietro Aaron and Heinrich Glarean discussed the modality of polyphonic compositions by Josquin. (For examples, see MODE, §§II, 2–4; III, 3, 4.)

Such citations of individual works were all concerned with matters of technique and substance. It was only with the development of musical rhetoric that the idea of 'form' entered musical theory. The literature of ancient classical Greek and Roman rhetoric was rediscovered with the finding of Quintilian's *Institutio oratorio* in 1416. But the application of the ideas of classical oratory has been traced back as far as the Notre Dame polyphony of the early 13th century, and its direct impact is clear in late 15th-century music. It was with Listenius (*Musica*, 1537; Eng. trans., 1975) that *musica poetica* – musical rhetoric – was introduced into musical

theory. Dressler (1563–4) alluded to a formal organization of music that would adopt the divisions of an oration into *exordium* ('opening'), *medium* and *finis*. Pietro Pontio (1588) discussed the standards for composing motets, masses, madrigals, psalms and other genres, and similar discussions occur in Cerone (1613), Praetorius (1618), Mattheson (1739) and Scheibe (1737–40).

A plan similar to Dressler's appeared in Burmeister (1606). Burmeister had already proposed (1599, 1601) that musical 'figures' could be treated as analogous to rhetorical figures, and it was he who first set out a full formal analysis of a piece of music. It was Burmeister, too, who gave the first definition of analysis (1606, pp.71f):

Analysis of a composition is the resolution of that composition into a particular mode and a particular species of counterpoint [*antiphonorum genus*], and into its affections or periods. . . . Analysis consists of five parts: 1. Determination of mode; 2. of species of tonality; 3. of counterpoint; 4. Consideration of quality; 5. Resolution of the composition into affections or periods.

He then discussed each of the parts of analysis in detail, and followed this by his analysis of Lassus's five-voice motet *In me transierunt*. He defined the mode as authentic Phrygian, and discussed the total range of the piece and the individual vocal ranges. He defined the tonality as 'diatonic', the species of counterpoint as 'broken' (*fractum*), the quality as *Diazeugmenorum*. Burmeister then proceeded to the fifth stage (pp.73f):

Furthermore, the work can be divided up very comfortably into nine periods, of which the first comprises the *Exordium*, which is elaborated with double ornament, also with regular imitation [*fuga realis*] and with imitation in contrary motion [*Hypallage*]. The seven middle periods make up the *Corpus* of the work (just like . . . the *Confirmatio* in oratory). Of these, the first is ornamented with word-painting [*Hypotyposis*], repetition a 2nd higher [*Climax*] and the repetition of a closing phrase at the beginning of a new section [*Anadiplosis*]; the second similarly, but with repetition also of a phrase at different pitches in different voices [*Anaphora*].

His analysis continues through the seven middle periods and discusses the final section (likening this to the Epilogue in oratory).

Six years later Lippius (1612) discussed rhetoric as the basis of the *forma*, or structure of a composition. Throughout the Renaissance and Baroque periods the principles of rhetoric were prescriptive: they provided routine techniques for the process of composition rather than descriptive techniques for analysis. But they played an important part in the growing awareness of formal structure during these periods, and in particular the function of contrast and the links between contrasted sections, out of which the analytical faculty was eventually to develop. Mattheson (1739) enumerated six parts to a well-developed composition such as an aria (p.236):

Exordium, the introduction and beginning of a melody, in which its purpose and entire intention must be shown, so that the listener is prepared and his attention is aroused. . . .
Narratio is a report or a narration in which the meaning and nature of the discourse is suggested. It is found immediately at the entrance of the voice – or the most important concerted [instrumental] part, and is related to the Exordium . . . by means of a suitable association [with the musical idea found in the Exordium].
Propositio briefly contains the meaning and purpose of the musical speech, and is simple or compound . . . Such propositions have their place immediately after the first phrase of melody, when actually the bass takes the lead and presents the material both briefly and simply. Then the voice begins its *propositio variata*, joins with the bass, and thus creates a compound proposition.
Confirmatio is the artistic strengthening of the proposition and is usually found in melodies by imaginative and unexpected repetitions, by which is not to be understood the normal Reprise. What we mean here are

agreeable vocal passages repeated several times with all kinds of nice changes of decorated additions.

Confutatio is the resolution of objections [i.e. contrasted or opposing musical ideas]. In melody it may be expressed either by tied notes or by the introduction and rejection of passages which appear strange.

Peroratio, finally, is the end or conclusion of our musical oration, and must above all else be especially expressive. And this is not found just in the outcome or continuation of the melody itself, but particularly in the postlude, be it either for the bass line or for a strong accompaniment; whether or not one has heard the Ritornello before. It is customary that the aria concludes with the same material as it began; so that our Exordium also serves as a Peroratio.

Mattheson then went on to apply this sectionalization to an aria by Marcello, complete with discussion and musical examples (pp.237ff), introducing other technical terms as he did so. (*See* RHETORIC AND MUSIC.)

2. 1750–1840: PHRASE STRUCTURE AND FORMAL MODEL. The origins of musical analysis as one now thinks of it lie in early 18th-century philosophy and are linked with the origins of the aesthetic attitude itself. For it was in the 18th century, and particularly with the English philosophers and essayists, that the idea came to the surface of contemplating beauty without self-interest – that is, without motive of personal improvement or utility. This new attitude was termed, by one of its earliest protagonists, Lord Shaftesbury (1671–1713), 'disinterested attention'. It embodied a mode of interest that went no further than the object being contemplated, and was engrossed in the contemplation itself. Leibniz, at about the same time, had evolved a concept of perception as an activity in itself rather than as a processing of sense-impressions. This active concept of perception was important in the work of Alexander Baumgarten (1714–62), who coined the word 'aesthetics'. It was during this period that the notion of 'fine art' as such, divorced from context and social function, arose.

In Shaftesbury's equation of disinterested attention with 'love of truth, proportion, order and symmetry in things without' lies the germ of formal theory as it was developed in Germany during the second half of the 18th century. His declaration that '*the Beautiful, the Fair, the Comely*, were never in the *Matter*, but in the *Art* and *Design*; never in the *Body* it-self, but in the *Form* or *forming Power*' (*Characteristicks of Men, Manners, Opinions, Times*, 1711, ii, 405) drew attention to the outward form as the object of contemplation rather than content. Such an attitude came through in, for example, Kirnberger's *Der allezeit fertige Polonoisen- und Menuettencomponist* (1757), one of a number of publications that laid down a fixed chord scheme for dances, and supplied several motifs for each bar from which one was to be selected by throwing a dice.

However, it was not in the field of analysis or of criticism, as one might expect, that these perceptually-based ideas were fully articulated in music for the first time. It was in composition teaching: in particular in the writings of the theorist H. C. Koch (1749–1816). The most significant aspects of Koch's important work, *Versuch einer Anleitung zur Composition* (1782–93), were the twin subjects of phrase structure and formal model.

Koch's exposition of melodic phrase structure was of the profoundest importance for musical theory, ultimately also for analysis, and it led directly to Riemann's theory of dynamic and agogic. The exposition is in Part ii of the *Versuch* (section 2, subsection 3 'On the construction of melodic sections', and subsection 4 'On the combining of melodic sections, or the construction of

periods'), occupying in all some 500 pages. It follows immediately on a discussion of rhythm and metre, and establishes a hierarchical framework in which two-bar 'segments' or 'incises' (*vollkommene Einschnitte*) combine in pairs to form four-bar 'phrases' (*Sätze*) which in turn combine to make 'periods' (*Perioden*). Koch then laid down rules as to how this framework might be modified without loss of balance. Chapter 3 of subsection 4 contains three studies 'Of the use of melodic extension'. The first is by repetition of all or part of a phrase; here Koch conveyed the idea of function within a phrase rather than melodic material, speaking often of 'the repetition of a bar' when the content of that bar is different on second statement. The second is multiplication of phrases and cadential figures. The third is the highly significant concept whereby a two-bar or four-bar phrase-unit may be embedded within an existing melody. Koch explained with each extension device (*Verlängerungsmittel*) how it could be used without upsetting the general effect of symmetry. Thus for example he stated that 'When a phrase contains one-bar units of which the first is repeated, then the second must also be repeated', because if not 'the unequal handling of these small units stands out as an unpleasant effect' (ii, 63f).

Chapter 3 of subsection 3 describes processes of melodic compression effected by the telescoping of two phrase-units to form a single unit. In this chapter he used a bar-numbering system that shows the bar at the point of telescoping as having two functions. Fig.1 shows the telescoping of two four-bar phrases into a seven-bar period, with the suppressed bar (*Tacterstickung*) marked with a square (ii, 455).

1. From H. C. Koch: '*Versuch einer Anleitung zur Composition*' (*1782–93*), ii, 455

Koch's principle of phrase extension had its forerunner in the *Anfangsgründe zur musikalischen Setzkunst* (1752–68) of Joseph Riepel (1709–82). In his second chapter (Frankfurt, 1755) Riepel had discussed the construction of eight-bar phrases in two four-bar units, designating each according to its type of cadence as *Grundabsatz, Aenderungsabsatz* or *Aenderungscadenz* (pp.36ff). He went on (pp.54ff) to discuss repetition and phrase extension (*Ausdähnung*) and interpolation (*Einschiebsel*). Koch's use of graphic signs can be traced back to Riepel, who used the square, crosses and letters to designate constructional devices. In his fourth chapter (Augsburg, 1765) Riepel considered melodic 'figures' (*Figuren*) not in the rhetorical Baroque sense but as units of formal construction. He presented the first five bars of an aria, marking the four musical figures by brackets and numbers (see fig.2*a*). He then took no.1 and showed how it might be repeated sequentially at the interval of a 3rd (marking the repetition with a double cross; see fig.2*b*), then at the 2nd and the 5th. He then worked a sequential extension of no.2 which continued with no.4 (see fig.2c), and so on (pp.81ff). The examples were still very much in the style of Baroque melodic construction, but Koch described Riepel's work as 'the first ray of light' (ii, 11).

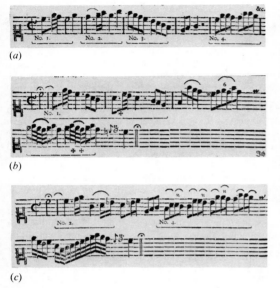

(a)

(b)

(c)

2. From J. Riepel: 'Anfangsgründe zur musikalischen Setzkunst' (1752–68), iv, 81–2

Koch's processes of extension and compression show his concern with symmetry and proportion on the smaller scale. Subsection 4 also presents the construction of compositions in ascending order of magnitude, from 'the combining of melodic sections into periods of the smallest size, or the organization of small compositions' (chap.2; iii, 39–152) involving the combination of four melodic sections 'of which two have a cadence in the home key' (p.57), 'of which one has a cadence in a related key' (p.81), and 'in which only a single closing phrase occurs' (p.111), and the combination of 'more than four sections in small compositions' (p.128) to 'the combination of melodic sections into periods of greater length, or the organization of larger compositions' (chap.4; iii, 231–430). In this way Koch drew all the musical elements of a composition into mutual relationship – for music is 'that art which expresses feelings through the relationships between notes' (i, 4).

It is in these two chapters that the other important aspect of Koch's work comes to the fore: that of the formal model. In this respect he cited as his authority the Swiss aesthetician J. G. Sulzer, in whose Allgemeine Theorie der schönen Künste (1771–4) the idea of 'layout' (Anlage) or model is put forward. Such a model sets down a plan for a work and the most salient features. The artist, following this model, is then to proceed to the 'execution' (Ausführung) or completion of design and finally to the 'elaboration' (Ausarbeitung) of the work in all its details. Accordingly, within the discussion of smaller forms (iii, 39ff) Koch provided the plan and characteristic details of the gavotte, bourrée, polonaise, anglaise, minuet and march, concluding with the chorale

and figured melody. He described, for example, the gavotte as 'a dance piece of lively and pleasant character' much used in theatrical dance. Its features are '(1) an even time signature which is usually in 2/2 and not too fast; (2) that each phrase begins with a two-crotchet upbeat; (3) that it has even-numbered rhythmic units with a detectable phrase division at each second bar; (4) that it comprises two sections, each of eight bars'.

All these models were offered as generative: from them compositions could be created, almost mechanically – 'almost', because Koch held the view that 'living expression' (lebendiger Ausdruck) was essential to the artist ('the poet who abandons expression, image, figure, and becomes a dictionary-user, is in error', i, 6). They form part of an instruction manual which proceeds from harmony to counterpoint and then to melody and form. Yet they are important, too, in the history of analysis, because they separate 'norm' from individuality, implicitly stating what was 'expected' and thereby defining liberty. Moreover, although most of Koch's abundant music examples were specially written for the book (in the contemporary style of Graun, Benda, and early Haydn and Mozart), he appended to his discussion of the combination of four melodic sections a brief analysis (iii, 58ff) of the minuet from Haydn's Divertimento in G (HII:1). The criteria for his analysis are particularly interesting: 'This little minuet', he began, 'has the most complete unity'. He followed the philosophical dictate, transmitted by Sulzer (under 'Einheit'), that 'wholeness ... and beauty consist of diversity bound together in unity'. Sulzer described unity with reference to a clock: 'if only one of its mechanical parts is removed then it is no longer whole [Ganzes] but only a part of something else'. In his analysis Koch identified the first four bars as the 'sole principal idea', repeated to form a closing phrase. The opening of the second half, also repeated as a closing phrase, 'while different from the preceding sections, is actually no less than the self-same phrase used in another way; for it is stated in contrary motion, and by means of a thorough deviation which results from this becomes bound together through greater diversity'.

Not only is the 'model' an important tool for formal analysis, later to be used by Prout, Riemann and Leichtentritt, but also the Sulzerian process of model–execution–elaboration is itself an important concept of artistic creation which later acquired its analytical counterpart in the theory of layers (Schichten). In addition, Koch equipped the composer and analyst with a terminology, derived from grammar and rhetoric, for the description of structure. For him, melody was 'speech in sound' (Tonrede), comprising grammar and punctuation. He sought to establish a 'natural law' of musical utterance (Tonsprache) which he called the 'logic of the phrase'. In this logic the smallest sense-unit, called 'incomplete segment' (unvollkommener Einschnitt), normally occupied one bar, the 'complete segment' (vollkommener Einschnitt, itself divisible into two Cäsuren in Sulzer's definition of Einschnitt) two bars. Such segments combine to form the 'phrase' (Satz), defined as either 'opening phrase' (Absatz) or 'closing phrase' (Schluss-Satz). Phrases form a 'period' (Periode). All three principal words are grammatical constructs: Einschnitt as phrase, Satz as clause, and Periode as sentence, the third of these divisible, according to Koch, into 'subject' (i.e. first four bars, enger Satz) and 'predicate' (latter four bars).

A set of comparable technical terms was established

in French some 30 years later by the Czech composer and theorist Antoine Reicha (1770–1836), a friend of Beethoven, who had produced a treatise in 1803, *Practische Beispiele*, containing models of forms and genres, and who spent the last 28 years of his life as a teacher in Paris. In his *Traité de mélodie* (1814, 2/1832) he used 'dessin' to denote the smallest unit of construction (equivalent to *Einschnitt*), and likened it to an *idée*; two or three *dessins* normally make up a *rythme* (equivalent to *Satz* – Sulzer spoke of *Rhythmus* as being widely used for a subdivision of the period), repetition or multiplication of which (the second of a pair being called the *compagnon*) produces the *période*. A composition made up of several *périodes* is a *coupe*: that of two or three *périodes* is a *petite coupe binaire* or *ternaire*, and that of two or three *parties*, each comprising several *périodes*, is a *grande coupe binaire* or *ternaire*.

The *dessin* is punctuated by a quarter-cadence (*quart de cadence*), the *rythme* by a *demi-cadence*, the *période* by a *trois-quarts de cadence* (if repeated) or by a *cadence parfaite*. Koch's division into grammar and punctuation is mirrored in this view, as is his fundamental concept of hierarchical phrase structure – for Reicha spoke of *la symétrie* (p.9): 'A good melody . . . needs (1) to be divided into equal and like units [*membres* – in German, *Glied* was used in the same generic way]; (2) to have its units forming points of repose [*repos*] of greater or lesser strength which are located at equal distances; that is, symmetrically placed'. He then gave an eight-bar rhythmic scheme (*mouvement*), and said of it:

Symmetry exists because (1) each division is into two bars; (2) after each division there is a repose which separates one from another; (3) all the divisions are equal within the scheme; (4) the points of repose, or cadences, are placed at equal distances – that is, the weaker repose occurs in the second and sixth bar, the stronger in the fourth and eighth: in short, there is in this scheme a regular plan, and it is this alone that fixes the attention.

Rythme implies not rhythmic patterning at the level of

detail but rather control over the number of bars in related units, coordination (p.13). It is thus more an equalizing force than a unit as such, and reveals a sense of rhythm at a higher level, at the level of formal disposition.

Koch's principles of phrase extension and compression also have their equivalents. Reicha said that the four-bar *rythme* was 'commonly called the *Rythme carrée*' (p.21), and that in practice the 'grands maîtres' avoid monotony by using *rythmes* of 2, 3, 5, 6 and 8 bars as well. Thus *rythmes* may be extended by using the device of *écho*, whereby an internal unit is repeated, or compressed by using suppression (*supposition*) of a bar (pp.20ff).

Dessin has much in common with Riepel's *Figur*, and implies melodic character. Like Koch's *Einschnitt* it exists at more than one level. Thus Reicha took the theme of the last movement of Mozart's String Quartet K458, 'The Hunt', divided it into two *membres* (i.e. *rythmes*), each comprising two *dessins* of two bars' duration. Three of the four *dessins* are melodically distinct (his nos.1, 2 and 3), and Reicha broke each of these further into two sub-units, numbering five of them (nos.4–8) and still calling them *dessins*. All this is illustrated in his music example B⁵, of which the first section is shown in fig.3. The theme is represented first as a set of numbered sub-units, and then graphically with brackets and labels. Reicha termed this analytical process *décomposition du thème* (or *motif*) (pp.61f). Moreover he went on, like Riepel, to explore in the next 19 examples which of these two-bar and one-bar *dessins* lend themselves to repetition and sequential restatement.

Perhaps the most striking aspect of Reicha's melody treatise is its citation of so many examples from actual music (he listed the composers in his preface). All these examples are submitted to segmentation and discussion. This in itself represents a significant shift from the compositional to the analytical standpoint – Reicha remarked in the preface to the *Traité de mélodie* that 'It

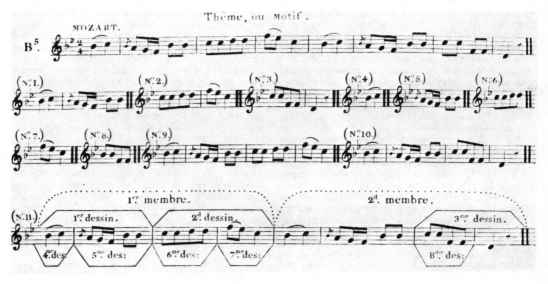

3. From A. Reicha: 'Traité de mélodie' (1814), Planches, 46

(*) Ici, la cadence devrait être interrompue (soit par l'harmonie, soit par la mélodie,) et non parfaite, ce que Piccini n'a point fait; elle devrait être par exemple :

Cette cadence parfaite dans cet air fait qu'on croit que les 5 mesures qui la suivent doivent appartenir à une toute autre Période, tandis qu'elles appartiennent nécessairement à la Période précédente; ces 5 mesures paraissent après cette cadence parfaite tout-à-fait superflues, parce que la 1re partie de cet air serait parfaitement bien terminée avec cette cadence. On ne peut jamais alonger une Période après une cadence parfaite mélodique et harmonique.

4. From A. Reicha: 'Traité de mélodie' (1814), Planches, 34

is with music as with geometry: in the former it is necessary to prove everything by music examples, just as it is with the latter by geometric figures'. Such a shift is emphasized by the inclusion of six extended analyses of works by Haydn (pp.40f and ex.D[4]), Mozart (p.43, E[4]), Cimarosa (pp.43ff, F[4]), Sacchini (pp.45ff, G[4]), Zingarelli (pp.47f, Q[4]) and Piccinni (pp.49ff, R[4]). Each piece is presented as a continuous melodic line annotated with brackets, labels and comments, and a page or two of discussion in the text.

Fig.4 shows the first page of the last of these analyses, with one of Reicha's footnotes. The aria by Piccinni is divided graphically into two *parties* and 16 *rythmes*. These *rythmes* are labelled from *a* to *p*, their lengths are indicated and the types of cadence defined. In the text Reicha said of *rythme f* that it 'ought to be divisible into two equal parts, each of four bars, but it lacks a bar between bars 3 and 4'. It is clear that he was not describing *supposition* here: his 'ought to' implies adverse criticism. In contrast to his purpose in analysing Mozart, Reicha set himself the task of explaining here why a piece which violates the principles of rhythm, which is 'vague, uncertain', in which 'the vocal phrases do not link well together, appear isolated and exhibit no symmetry', should have gained the approbation of 'an enlightened public'. He deduced that there are two aspects to a melody: *rythmé* and *non rythmé*; and that a composition that excels in only one may still have charm. He praised the 'colour' of the piece, its 'sweet, natural and simple harmony', its 'nuances of loud and soft', and its use of instrumental timbre. Finally he suggested that the nature and prosody of the French language may be the cause of rhythmic defect.

Reicha's *Traité de haute composition musicale* (1824–6) is devoted to counterpoint, harmony, canon and fugue. Book 6, however, is a manual of form, and 26 pages of it are taken up with a segmental analysis of the first part of Mozart's overture to *Le nozze di Figaro*, after which Reicha composed additional sections to show ways in which Mozart might have developed its musical ideas (pp.236ff). He then gave analyses of three whole movements. He used structural diagrams in his section on large-scale binary and ternary forms. Fig.5 shows the diagram for the *grande coupe binaire* (ii, 300): punctuation signs are used to denote cadence types, dotted phrase marks to indicate sections (*idée mère* signifies thematic material, and *motif* the principal thematic material).

Between the treatises of Koch and Reicha came a work that gave an unprecedented amount of space and range of thought to analysis. J.-J. de Momigny (1762–1842) in his *Cours complet d'harmonie et de composition* (1803–6) devoted no fewer than 144 pages, including analytical plates, to an analysis of the first movement of Mozart's String Quartet in D minor K421/417b. He provided a double analysis, examining both phrase structure and expressive content. Momigny's phrase-structure analysis is based on the novel rhythmic concept that musical units proceed from upbeat (*levé*) to downbeat (*frappé*) and never vice versa. He termed his smallest sense-unit, made up of two successive notes, upbeat and downbeat, the *cadence* or *proposition musicale*. These two notes are in the relationship of *antécédent* and *conséquent*. In the opening bars of the movement by Mozart (see fig.6), two *cadences mélodiques* pair off in antecedent–consequent relationship to form a *cadence harmonique*, two of these forming a *hémistiche*, two *hémistiches* forming a *vers*, and two *vers* forming a *période*. Momigny's concept does not, however, insist on hierarchy by pairs, and allows for as many as six or eight *vers* to make up a *période* in certain contexts. The *périodes* form further into *reprises* and are designated according to function within their *reprise* as 'de début', 'intermédiaire', 'de verve', 'mélodieuse', or 'complémentaire'. (In other contexts Momigny used other terms from versification also to designate structural units of intermediate size: *distiche*, *strophe* and *stance*.)

In this phrase-structure analysis Momigny laid the basis for a view of music that was to become important at the end of the 19th century: of music as a succession of spans of tension. In his expressive analysis, on the other hand, he was looking back to the *Affektenlehre* of

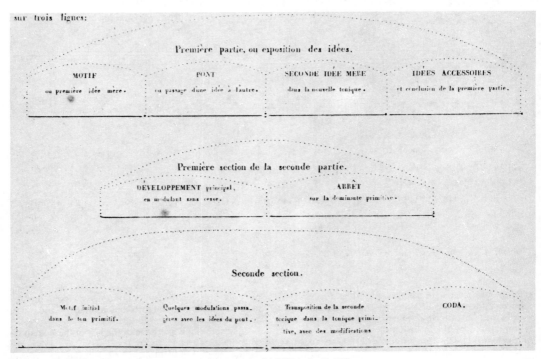

5. From A. Reicha: 'Traité de haute composition musicale' (1824–6), ii, 300

6. From J.-J. de Momigny: 'Cours complet d'harmonie et de composition' (1803–6), iii, 109–10

the 18th century. His method was to determine the *caractère* of the work under analysis, to select a verbal text that had the same character, and to set the text to the principal melodic material of the work so that melodic repetition was mirrored by verbal repetition, fluctuations of musical mood by fluctuations of textual meaning. He constructed a poetic parallel with the music, offering through it an interpretation of both form and content.

The plates for the analysis present the music laid out on ten parallel staves; the top four show the quartet in conventional score, the fifth staff presents the melodic line (and notes printed small here reveal the beginnings of melodic reduction technique) with its *cadences* marked, the sixth and seventh staves provide a harmonic reduction of the texture with harmonic *cadences* marked, the eighth and ninth staves present the principal melodic material with poetic text underlaid (in this case a dramatic scene between Dido and Aeneas, with notes from the first violin assigned to Dido and from the cello assigned to Aeneas, and with simple piano accompaniment, and the tenth staff shows the roots of the prevailing harmony as a fundamental bass (see fig.6).

Extended examples of 'analysation' were given also by J. B. Logier (1777–1846) – the German inventor of the 'Chiroplast' system of piano instruction, who lived most of his life in Ireland – in his *System der Musik-Wissenschaft und der practischen Komposition* (1827). Logier (who, in this title, seems to have coined the term *Musikwissenschaft*) offered analyses (Eng. trans.,

pp.294–320) of a concerto grosso by Corelli and the Adagio of Haydn's Quartet in G op.76 no.1 examined under eight distinct headings: key – time – fundamental basses – modulation and fundamental 7ths – dissonances – passing notes, auxiliary notes and secondary harmony – periods – sections and imitation. The scheme constitutes a wider base for analysis than hitherto, yet has something of the mechanical nature of Burmeister's rhetorical scheme. More interesting were Logier's instructions as to 'How to construct melodies' (Eng. trans., pp.276ff), in which the student proceeds in four stages, first laying down an abstract bass line of three notes (C–G–C) which frames the period and divides it into two half-periods, then constructing a 'fundamental bass' over it, then overlaying this with the 'inverted bass'

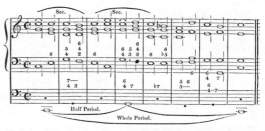

7. From J. B. Logier: 'System der Musik-Wissenschaft und der practischen Composition' (1827; from Eng. trans.), 278

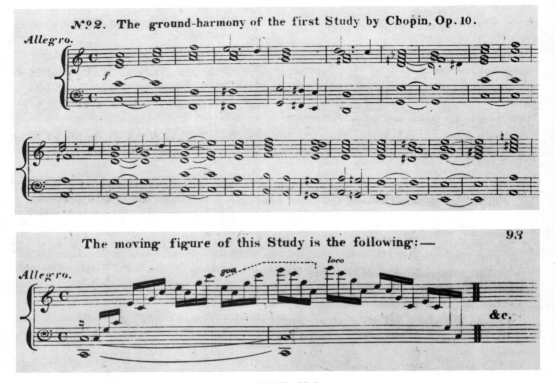

8. From C. Czerny: 'School of Practical Composition' (1849), 92–3

(i.e. the sounding bass line) and finally building a super-structure of melody and inner parts. The result looks graphically not unlike a Schenkerian reduction (see fig.7).

A different type of reduction occurs in Czerny's *School of Practical Composition* (1849). Czerny stripped away the surface figuration ('the moving figure') from several compositions, leaving only the underlying harmonies ('the ground-harmony'), presented in block chords. He did this for Chopin's Etude op.10 no.1 (see fig.8), for the first prelude of Bach's *Das wohltemperirte Clavier*, i, and for the introduction to a sonata by Clementi; he also reduced a study by Cramer to its basic part-writing ('the ground-melody').

Czerny's *School* rests, as does Reicha's *Traité*, on citation of authority. (That is not surprising, since Czerny had previously translated Reicha's *Cours de composition* of 1816 and two *Traités* as *Vollständiges Lehrbuch der musikalischen Komposition*, Vienna, 1832.) All the music examples are attributed (they represent the next generation, of Beethoven, Hummel, Rossini, Méhul etc), and many analyses of whole compositions are included. It was unique in being the first independent manual of form and instrumentation. It took for granted a grounding in harmony and counterpoint, and concerned itself exclusively with the development of ideas and the formation of compositions 'from the most simple Theme to the Grand Symphony, and from the shortest Song to the Opera and Oratorio' (i, p.iii). It is a veritable compendium of musical forms, including exotic dances (such as the bolero, fandango and tarantella and a section on Russian national dances),

vocal forms (such as the *romance*, *preghiera* and ballad), as well as the constituent movements of a sonata, many other forms, and genres such as the quartet, quintet and sextet.

Other theorists of the time concerned with form were J. B. H. Birnbach (1793–1879), whose *Der vollkommene Komponist* was published between 1832 and 1846, but to whom the first use of the phrase 'second theme' is credited in 1827 (Berlin – *Allgemeine musikalische Zeitung*, iv); also J. C. Lobe (1797–1881), whose *Compositionslehre* was published in 1844 and *Lehrbuch der musikalischen Komposition* between 1850 and 1867.

3. 1840–1900: ORGANIC GROWTH AND THE TEACHING OF FORM. Czerny's attitude towards form was highly determinate: 'the composition must ... belong to a species already in existence; consequently, in *this* respect, no originality is, in general, necessary' (i, 1). His understanding of '*form* and *construction*' is itself quite specific (i, 6):

1st [A work's] extent and proper duration.
2ly The requisite modulations, partly into established keys, and partly also into arbitrary and extraneous ones, as well as the places where they are introduced.
3ly The rhythm (the proportion or symmetry) both of the whole, and also of the individual parts and periods of a piece.
4ly The manner in which a principal or an accessory melody is brought in at the proper place, and where it must alternate with such passages as form either a continuation, a moving figure, or a bridge to the following.
5ly The conduct and development of a principal or accessory idea.
6ly The structure and proper succession of the different component parts of the piece, answerable to the species of composition which the author has had in view, as expressed in the title.

There are . . . a tolerable number of different forms in music. These, however, are reducible to a far lesser number of each principal form, as are totally different in their structure from one another.

A. B. Marx (1795–1866), in his *Die Lehre von der musikalischen Komposition* (1837–47), was less procrustean. 'The number of forms is unlimited', he said, and there are ultimately no laws dictating what form a particular composition should take. For Marx, form was 'the way in which the content of a work – the composer's conception, feeling, idea – outwardly acquires shape'. A better term for it, he suggested, might have been 'the externalization of content'. Nonetheless, the student-composer cannot learn composition through inspiration and idea alone. He needs the models of previous composers as an intermediate stage on the road towards free composition. Thus 'it is possible to *derive* certain *principal forms*, and also certain composite or *compound forms* which are made up of these or variations of them; and only by creating these distinctions does it become possible to comprehend and master the immeasurable array of [formal] moulds [*Gestalten*]' (ii, 5). For Marx, 'form' was almost synonymous with 'whole' (*Ganzes*) (ii, 4f):

Every work of art must have its form. For every work of art has of necessity its beginning and its end, hence its extent. It is made up in different ways of sections of different type and number. The generic term for all these features is the *form* of a work of art. . . . There are as many forms as works of art.

Marx acknowledged that there were similarities in form between pieces, but denied strongly that forms were, as a result, 'routines' through which composers worked. Content was not really separable from form. Even so, the very appearance of similarities suggests that 'there must be some rationale underlying these moulds, some concept which is of broader significance, greater strength and longer duration' (ii, 7). Thus Marx denied form as 'convention' and proposed for it an epistemological basis. Forms are patterns abstracted from past practice, rather than conscious guidelines; they represent deep-seated principles of organization which analysis uncovers.

This idea is close to the ideas of A. W. Schlegel (1767–1845) concerning the relationship between art and nature: beneath the consciously moulded work of art must lie an unconsciously moulded work of nature. Nature 'is an intelligence . . . [It should be understood] not as a mass of products but as itself a producing [force]' (*Vorlesungen über schöne Literatur und Kunst*, i, 1801–2). Very much abreast of the Romantic philosophy of his day, Marx believed in the originality of the artist, in genius as a special endowment, in the developing 'idea' as all-important, in rules as existing to be broken. Marx was also influenced by the outlook of the Swiss educationist Heinrich Pestalozzi (1746–1827), who saw the law of man's development as essentially 'organic' – not as a combination of circumstances but as an inner growth process. All processes have a starting-point, they germinate and grow, and at all points are harmonious and whole. At that starting-point Marx placed the *Motiv*, a tiny unit of two or more notes which serves as 'the seed or sprout of the phrase out of which it grows' (i, 27).

Marx's discussion of sonata form (*Sonatenform* – he was probably the first to use that term for the internal scheme of one movement) differs significantly from that of Czerny. Marx offered (ii, 498ff) a page of formal instruction on sonata form in the major key followed by

twice as much indicating ways in which the 'ground-form' may be deviated from, stressing always that the spirit (*Geist*) of the composer may lead him in some other direction, and citing specific cases in Mozart and Beethoven. He pointed only to the unique balance of the key scheme, spelling it out in a highly original fashion, and recommended the composer to keep its advantages carefully in mind.

In 1841–2 Marx engaged in public dispute with G. W. Fink over methods of teaching composition, showing himself fully aware of the philosophical basis of his position (see *Die alte Musiklehre im Streit mit unserer Zeit*, 1841; see also Eicke, 1966). Marx's *Die Lehre von der musikalischen Komposition* went through six editions during his life and eventually underwent revision by Hugo Riemann between 1887 and 1890 (i, rev. 9/1887; ii, rev. 7/1890; iv, rev. 5/1888). An English translation of the fourth edition was issued in 1852. The work was used in theory teaching well into the 20th century, and profoundly influenced generations of musicians. Riemann's own *Katechismus der Kompositionslehre* appeared in 1889, and the bulk of his powerful theory of rhythm in his *Musikalische Dynamik und Agogik* (1884) and *System der musikalischen Rhythmik und Metrik* (1903), and was summarized in the *Vademecum der Phrasierung* (1900; 8/1912 as *Handbuch*).

A forerunner of Riemann had been Moritz Hauptmann (1792–1868), whose work was conditioned by Hegelian philosophy, and who did much to introduce the idea that music theory should be systematic and founded on logical principles. He formulated (1853) a theory of harmony and rhythm based on what he claimed to be universals. His theory of rhythm, like that of Momigny, took a two-element pattern as its basic unit and explained all units comprising more than two elements as intersections of two-element units. In Hegelian terms, a two-element unit was the 'thesis', a three-element unit the 'antithesis' and a four-element unit the 'synthesis' in the metrical system. Hauptmann's basic unit, unlike Momigny's, was made up of downbeat followed by upbeat, and it was Mathis Lussy (1828–1910) who in his study of the anacrusis (1874) took up Momigny's *levé-frappé* pattern and developed the theory further. From this Riemann proceeded to develop a full theory based on the indivisible unit of the *Motiv*. Underlying the theory is the idea of a single unit of energy (*Lebenskraft*) passing through phases of growth, peak and decay. Musical form is constructed of many such units overlapping and interacting to produce extended and compressed spans of energy, these interactions occurring against a 'background' of absolutely regular hierarchically built-up patterns. (For Riemann's method see also §III, 5 below.)

In 1852 E. F. E. Richter produced his manual of musical form and analysis, influenced by Kirnberger and Weber, and in 1853–4 the immensely influential Simon Sechter published his composition treatise. In 1885 Salomon Jadassohn produced volume iia of his composition treatise, entitled 'Forms in musical works of art analysed and graded as a course of study'. In 1887 the American writer A. J. Goodrich published his *Complete Musical Analysis*, and the American teacher Percy Goetschius (1853–1943) produced a succession of books on musical form, of which his *Models of the Principal Musical Forms* (1895) was the first. Between 1893 and 1897 the English theorist Ebenezer Prout

(1835–1909) produced his two volumes *Musical Form* and its sequel *Applied Forms*. He expressed himself indebted to Riemann for the fundamental principles of rhythm, and in particular the study of motifs, and admitted that both volumes had involved intensive study of 'large German treatises'. The first volume proceeds from motif to 'phrase' and 'sentence', and then to simple binary and ternary forms, the second from dance forms to sonata form and vocal music, including a chapter on 'cyclic forms' which deals with the symphonic poem. In 1908 Stewart Macpherson produced his *Form in Music*, which has been the standard manual for English music students for much of the 20th century.

Hugo Leichtentritt (1874–1951) completed his *Musikalische Formenlehre* in 1911, later to become the first part of a more extended study (translated into English in 1951) including chapters on 'Aesthetic ideas as the basis of musical styles and forms' and 'Logic and coherence in music'. It also had detailed analyses of works, notably the 45-page study of Bruckner's Eighth Symphony and the chapter devoted to Schoenberg's piano pieces opp.11 and 19. It was with Prout and Leichtentritt that *Formenlehre* became a branch of the discipline of musical analysis rather than a prescriptive training for composers, and hence entered the field of musicology (see §III, 4 below; *see also* RHYTHM, §§I, 4; II, 13).

4. HISTORICAL AWARENESS IN THE 19TH CENTURY. The use of analysis to serve an interest in musical objects themselves, rather than to supply models for the study of composition, reflected a new spirit of historical awareness which arose with Romanticism. It was not a dispassionate 'scientific' interest in the past as specimens, but a desire to enter into the past, to discover its essence. This spirit (exhibited in Thibault's *Über die Reinheit der Tonkunst*, 1824, concerning music from Palestrina to Handel), in confluence with the Romantic image of 'genius', resulted in a new type of monograph, biographical and historical. Early examples were Baini's study of Palestrina, *Memorie storico-critiche della vita e delle opere di Giovanni Pierluigi da Palestrina* (1828), Winterfeld's of Palestrina (1832) and Giovanni Gabrieli (1834), Ulïbïshev's of Mozart (1843), Jahn's of Mozart (1856–9) and Spitta's of Bach (1873–80).

Even before these, Forkel's *Über Johann Sebastian Bachs Leben, Kunst und Kunstwerke* (1802), while including nothing that could be termed formal analysis as such, contained an extended characterization of Bach's music as a whole – in short, a stylistic analysis. Forkel, like A. B. Marx, was much influenced by the concept of 'organism' in contemporary philosophy and education; to seek the depths of 'Bach's transcendent genius' (Eng. trans., 1920, p.xxix) in the totality of his work rather than in individual compositions was consistent with this – 'The butterfly method, a sip here and there, is of little use' (p.147). Forkel stressed the presence of two indispensable factors in Bach's creative make-up: 'genius and indefatigable application' (p.152). It was an educational as well as a musical embodiment of organism that led Forkel to say that '[genius] enabled him to develop out of a given subject a whole family of related and contrasted themes, of every form and design' (p.87). He declared Bach's mastery of technique; at the same time he tried to define where 'Bach followed a course of his own, upon which the text books of his day were silent' (p.74). To identify genius he took, in chap-

ters 5 and 6 ('Bach the Composer'), five aspects of music: harmony, modulation, melody, rhythm and counterpoint. His method·was to cite a technical context, state the conventional in terms of contemporary theory or practice, and then consider Bach's handling of such a context. He thus had illuminating things to say about Bach's part-writing, his use of passing notes, of pedal points, of remote modulations, his contrapuntal solo melodic writing, his fugal counterpoint and his use of the voice; for example (p.77):

there is a rule that every note raised by an accidental cannot be doubled in the chord, because the raised note must, from its nature, resolve on the note above. If it is doubled, it must rise doubled in both parts and, consequently, form consecutive octaves. Such is the rule. But Bach frequently doubles not only notes accidentally raised elsewhere in the scale but actually the *semitonium modi* or leading-note itself. Yet he avoids consecutive octaves. His finest works yield examples of this.

For Forkel such transgression on Bach's part always produced a more natural, spontaneous or smooth effect than orthodoxy. The link between genius and nature was axiomatic: 'when [Bach] draws his melody from the living wells of inspiration and cuts himself adrift from convention, all is as fresh and new as if it had been written yesterday' (p.83).

Jahn's *W. A. Mozart* was very different from Forkel's Bach biography. It was closer at once to contemporary theory of composition and to critical writing. Its four volumes described a single biographical 'progress'. All material, historical, biographical and analytical, was taken in on the way; there was no separate place for stylistic extrapolation or long-distance perspective. There are many analyses of individual works, often very detailed, sometimes occupying whole chapters. Even when he did draw certain groups of works together for consideration as genres – the early instrumental works, the piano music, the symphonies, and so on – he generalized only on matters of form before dealing with works individually. But in these chapters there are valuable comparative analyses of two or more works. For Jahn 'the genuine impulses of artistic creation proceed from universal and unalterable laws; the artist does but impress his individual stamp upon the composing elements of the work' (Eng. trans., iii, 41). The more technical analyses tend to approach their subject from three points of view: external form, thematic character, and use of instruments or voices. The first of these embodied the 'laws' most strongly, and it was here that Jahn traced the ancestry of individual forms before placing Mozart within the historical continuum. Thus (i, 309):

The rule that the quartet . . . should consist, like the symphony and the sonata, of four fixed movements, was laid down by Joseph Haydn. It was his inexhaustibly fertile invention and his freedom in the treatment of form which nourished and developed the germ of this chamber-music, until it bore the most beautiful blossoms of German music art. Mozart, destined later to surpass in this direction his freely acknowledged example, displays evident tokens of Haydn's influence even in his youth.

Jahn's analyses were not only historical and analytical: they also contained critical comment; thus, of the C minor Mass 'It cannot be said . . . that the instrumental part of this work is as brilliant and full of colour as others composed at the same period; the tone colouring is on the whole monotonous . . . the inflexibility of form has something in it of pedantry' (ii, 396f).

Spitta (1841–94) organized his *Johann Sebastian Bach* in the same single biographical sweep that one finds in Jahn's *Mozart*, giving the same prominence to examination of individual works and particularly extended treatment to large-scale works. There was, however, rather less formal analysis and much more on musical character. Spitta aimed, by description, 'to call up the spirit which alone can give [music] life and soul' (Eng. trans., i, p.viii). Spitta went further and attempted a symbolic interpretation, notably for the B minor Mass: for example (iii, 51):

to represent the essential Unity as clearly as possible, Bach treats the parts in canon on the unison at the beginning of the principal subject each time, not using the canon on the fourth below till the second bar; thus both the Unity and the separate existence of the two Persons are brought out.

There was a second aspect to the growth of historical awareness which in turn contributed to analytical thinking. This was the development of musical text criticism, bringing with it the first of the massive collected editions (see EDITIONS, HISTORICAL and MUSICOLOGY, §II, 3). Whereas Jahn and Spitta both examined only the finished work in their analyses, Forkel's Bach biography contained the seeds of this new element as well as of stylistic classification. Chapter 10, 'Bach's Manuscripts', though only four pages long, pointed to the evidence that variant sources of a given piece might yield of Bach's process of composition – his adjustment of a single note, his drastic cutting down, his continual self-correction. Forkel indeed urged the supplementing of a complete edition of Bach's works by the noting of source variants, an initiative that was eventually taken up in the Bachgesellschaft edition. It was another historical scholar involved with textual criticism and the editing of collected editions, Guido Adler, who about this time, in 1885, published a programme for musicology in which historical and analytical research were fully integrated (see §II, 5 below).

The most influential scholar in this field was Gustav Nottebohm (1817–82), who worked on the collected editions of Beethoven (1862–5) and Mozart (from 1878). In a long series of studies of sketches and other composition materials, published between 1865 and 1890, he tackled the problems of Beethoven's creative processes: how many pieces Beethoven worked on at a time, how he used sketches, drafts and scores, how he worked from single-line draft to full texture, how he conceived and modified formal structure. What Nottebohm came across on the way, namely Beethoven's painful formulation of thematic material, was a living exemplification of the ideas of melodic motif, germ-cell, organic growth, unity – ideas which were rife and had found their way into the theoretical tradition. Here was a way of getting behind the finished text, of showing the composition student how a masterpiece was put together, errors, false starts and all, and at the same time of verifying one's deductive analyses (Ein Skizzenbuch von Beethoven, 1862, p.7):

We can observe the progressive development of a plant, learn about its step-by-step growth. Taking shape by continual transformation, following specified rules as it does so, it constantly brings new things to light. But all that is new is always old. Thus it can successfully be explained in genetic terms. It is different with a piece of music; for this in its outward appearance is tied to the expression of a particular individual, and in its very particularity follows not a natural law, as does the plant, but the laws of the spirit [Geist]. We can consider a piece of music as an entirety and unity, analyse its structure, enjoy its beauty. Its genesis, however, and how it has come about, is concealed from us. The formal completeness with which it appears to us means that all trace has been eradicated of the development that lies behind it. If we view it as an organic structure we are forced to assume that it came into being by organic means and developed from within itself as a unified whole. Now it is true that in the sketchbooks, where everything that is fixed and unalterable in the finished piece is so to speak movable, many a process of birth, of discovery, of shaping, and the like, is laid bare.

One of the first analysts to draw on Nottebohm's findings was George Grove. Each of the analyses in Beethoven and his Nine Symphonies (1896) presented a rounded picture of its subject, with a balance of historical and biographical information, text-critical evidence and formal analysis – both plentifully illustrated with music examples – and critical judgment. Each concluded with a survey of the work's critical reception. Grove adopted a narrative approach for his formal analyses which has since become the stock in trade of descriptive writers on music, by animating the orchestra ('This is prolonged by the wind instruments in a humorous passage') or the piece itself ('after a reference back . . . a new subject appears . . . as harsh and uncompromising as the first subject') or by treating the listeners as visitors ('After this we arrive at a pause'). In another respect, too, Grove differed from the German analysts. He was uninfluenced by the idea of motivic growth. The tangible evidence of how a theme came about was of interest to him, and he was ready to point up similarities between the themes of different composers (e.g. the 'kindred themes' of Brahms, Schubert, Mozart and Beethoven, pp.59f). Similarities were matters of historical influence: 'the links which convey the great Apostolic Succession of Composers from generation to generation'. He recognized resemblance, but refused to construct theories around it: he was down to earth, an empiricist. And in the same spirit he largely eschewed naturalistic descriptions of the music, preferring to cite E. T. A. Hoffmann's imagery, or Schindler's yellow-hammer theory, or Beethoven's alleged 'fate knocking at the door' than to invent his own. For he was at heart a historian: he was interested in the impact of events on Beethoven's creativity, and explored this by drawing together the two strands – music and events – and suggesting the causal connection only with great restraint.

Two writers from the early part of the 19th century whose work is properly classified as musical criticism and who were imbued rather with the spirit of Romantic genius than with historical awareness in what they wrote, but who were nonetheless influential, were E. T. A. Hoffmann and Robert Schumann. Their respective reviews of Beethoven's Fifth Symphony (1810) and Berlioz's Symphonie fantastique (1835) are both classic pieces of critical writing. Schumann's tackles its subject from four distinct points of view: formal construction, style and texture, the poetic 'idea' lying behind the work, and the spirit that governs it. The review ranges itself against critics of the work, examining its structure section by section to show that 'despite its apparent formlessness, there is an inherent correct symmetrical order' (Eng. trans., 1946, p.168); discussing harmonic and modulatory style, melodic and contrapuntal fabric, acknowledging the contravention of many theoretical rules but justifying them by the work's intensity, its 'entirely individual, indestructible energy' (p.172); recounting the work's programme, and arguing that it spurs the listener's imagination to perceive its own further meaning; and finally affirming that the work is 'informed with spirit', though 'not as the masterpiece of a master but as a work outstanding in its originality' (p.182).

In 1887 a writer who rejected both the formal analytical approach and that of naturalistic description, and was at the same time mistrustful of historical information, began publication of a guide to the concert repertory, Führer durch den Konzertsaal. This was Hermann

Kretzschmar. The guide contained many hundreds of analyses that he had written during earlier years for concerts, classified into 'Symphony and Suite', 'Sacred Works' and 'Oratorios and Secular Choral Works', each category arranged in order by date of composition. It spanned nearly 300 years, from Monteverdi to Mahler, including works by French and Russian composers, and was an unprecedented undertaking. Kretzschmar forged his own approach to musical appreciation which saw music as a language, universal in character, with meanings recognizable by those with the necessary aesthetic training (*Satzästhetik*). Such training brought with it an instinctive sense of how a phrase should be performed, a perception of the inner character of the phrase. At the end of this training stood a method of interpretation which Kretzschmar called 'musical HERMENEUTICS', and which he saw as a revitalization of the Baroque doctrine of affects.

In two articles promoting this method (*JbMP 1902, 1905*) Kretzschmar sought to attack the free poetic description of music which many writers of the time indulged in, and to show how his own method was both firmly based on technical criteria and also capable of illuminating whole compositions rather than merely individual passages. At the heart of the method was 'thematic character' as defined by interval and contour. In these terms, the subject of the C major fugue of Bach's *Das wohltemperirte Clavier*, i, has an 'energetic disposition' which 'rests on the motif of the 4th as the principal element of the melodic structure'; but 'with the descending final phrase and the cautious approach to the main motif, the flow of the unmistakable energy which forms the middle section is framed on either side with expressions of melancholy' (*JbMP 1905*, p.282).

5. EARLY 20TH CENTURY: REDUCTION TECHNIQUES AND PERSONAL STYLE. It was observed above (§II, 3) that A. B. Marx, while using the word *Gestalt* for a formal 'mould', regarded 'form' as virtually synonymous with 'whole' (*Ganzes*). He felt, too, that formal 'moulds' were not merely conventions: they represented deep-seated principles of organization in the human mind. It was also observed that with Prout and Leichtentritt the subject of musical form (*Formenlehre*) had entered the realm of analysis instead of being a training in composition. It was at the time of Prout and Leichtentritt that a new branch of psychology was emerging, which laid emphasis on perception rather than on motivation: Gestalt psychology. Research gave an experimental scientific basis to some of the new attitudes towards musical experience. In essence it was concerned with form (in keeping with the views of Hanslick, 1854, and of J. F. Herbart, 1811): it laid stress on the power of the perceiver mentally to organize whatever objects or situations he encounters, and to do so in formal terms rather than in terms of individual components and his previous experience of them. Thus visually, objects which are in close proximity to each other, and objects which are similar in shape or colour, tend to be perceived as a group. Moreover, the perceiving mind seeks the simplest available grouping, looking for basic, complete shapes – for 'continuous wholes'. It looks also for repetition and symmetry, for equal separation in space and time. In short, it tries to place the simplest, most regular, most complete interpretation on the data before it.

Musical sound was used for illustrative purposes by the early Gestalt psychologist Christian von Ehrenfels. He pointed, in 1890, to the fact that a melody does not lose its melodic identity when transposed, despite the change of each note: a melody has a shape which can be heard, recognized and learnt without recognition of its constituent notes, intervals or rhythms. Perception of the shape comes not as a slow process but as a flash of insight; it is like the completion of an electric circuit.

There are three principles which relate to this. 'Closure' is the principle whereby the mind, when presented with a shape that is almost complete but not quite, will complete the shape automatically. 'Phi phenomenon' is the principle whereby the mind, when confronted with two separate occurrences, may link them together and attribute movement from one to the other. 'Prägnanz' is the principle whereby the mind will look for the interpretation of data which yields the most 'pregnant' result – the 'best' interpretation. All these processes can be seen at work in for example perception of a lute transcription of a 16th-century vocal piece, where the original vocal lines are presented only incompletely because of the technical limitations of lute technique; or in a solo violin or cello work by Bach, where several contrapuntal lines are carried, all of them incompletely yet with a general sense of the polyphony.

One final principle is of fundamental importance to music: figure–ground perception. Very often the mind selects from the data before it only certain salient features; these it organizes as a 'pregnant' figure (*Gestalt*), leaving the rest of the data to remain in the field of perception. Ultimately only the figure is passed up from the nervous system (where this organization of sensory experience takes place) to the psychological field where it is 'understood'. The rest of the data remains as the 'ground'. This process is akin to what the musical analyst calls 'reduction', an early example of which is Czerny's stripping away of surface ornament in Chopin, Bach and Clementi to reveal the underlying essential structure (§II, 2 above and fig.8). Significantly, but quite conversely to Gestalt terminology, Czerny called the surface ornament 'the moving figure' and the structure 'the ground-melody' or 'the ground-harmony'.

The first full-scale use of Gestalt procedures was probably Arnold Schering's examination of the 14th-century Italian madrigal (1911–12). In it he introduced the idea of 'disembellishment' (*Dekolorieren*). This involved removing groups of short note values from melodic lines and substituting fewer notes of proportionately longer value to occupy the same amount of time: 'laying bare from within a melismatic passage the simple melodic progression'. Fig.9 shows an example of this (the reduction technique shows elements of 'closure' and 'Phi phenomenon', and is a clear example of figure–ground perception). Schering called what he uncovered 'melodic kernels' (*Melodiekerne*) or 'cells' (*Keime*), both terms being familiar from the organic music theorists of the 19th century. But in fact what he set out to reveal were medieval folksongs, since he believed that the elaborate 14th-century madrigals were really keyboard arrangements of folktunes. Such a theory is not inconceivable: there were keyboard arrangements in the 14th century, and Schering was simply reversing the procedure known as PARAPHRASE whereby a melody, usually a passage of plainsong, was embellished in one voice of a polyphonic composition in the late Middle Ages and Renaissance. The difficulty lay in verifying the results as folksongs, and Schering adopted the interest-

9, 10. From A. Schering: 'Das kolorierte Orgel-madrigal des Trecento', SIMG, xiii (1911–12), 193, 194, 197

9. Johannes de Florentia: 'Nel meço a sei paon'

10(a). Lorenzo da Firenze: 'Ita se n'er'a star'

10(b). Vincenzo da Rimini: 'Ita se n'era a star'

ing confirmatory device of reducing two different madrigals by different composers to the same underlying
melodic progression. The two madrigals had the same
poetic text, and Schering's assertion was that they both
presented elaborated versions of the original folk
melody for these words: see fig.10. Schering's work provided in embryonic form the techniques for both the
melodic evolutionists (Réti, Keller and Walker) and also
the work of Heinrich Schenker in structural harmony.

In 1906 Schenker (1867–1935) had published his
Harmonielehre, the first volume of his highly influential
Neue musikalische Theorien und Phantasien. It contained the seeds of two concepts new to harmonic
theory, which were to underpin Schenker's later analytical procedures: 'compositional unfolding' (*Auskomponierung*) and 'prolongation' (*Prolongation*). He argued
several times in the book, citing passages from Fux,
Beethoven, Chopin, Liszt and Wagner in support, that
arrangements of notes that look on the surface like
chords in their own right are not always essential steps
(*Stufen*) in a harmonic progression, but are often merely
expansions of other essential steps (see especially Eng.
trans., pp.141ff, 155, 212). In this way Schenker established a distinction between 'triads' and 'steps' whereby
not all of the former in a given tonal context rise to the
rank of the latter. Thus he analysed the first 16 bars of
Variation 15 of Beethoven's Diabelli Variations op.120
as comprising five 'steps' (his ex.130/164) – see fig.11.

11. From H. Schenker: 'Harmonielehre' (1906), 206

He began to represent harmonic progressions graphically on two levels (e.g. his ex.173/234), using in one
instance a 'formula' to show short-term triadic movement
over longer-term harmonic steps (p.244), in which I –
V : I – V is shown as numerator and I as denominator.
On the larger scale he saw the key areas to which a
composition modulated as either 'established', in which
case they functioned as 'steps' at a higher level of form, or
'unestablished', in which case they served only to elaborate other key areas. Schenker's harmonic theory represented a shift away from that of Rameau (*Traité de l'har-*

monie, 1722), introducing the psychological notion of
'valuation'; that is, assessment by the hearer of chords
and modulatory key areas in relation to longer-term
pulls of tonality, and interpretation of them as either
fundamental steps or elaborations of such steps. This
valuation was the starting-point for the new way of
hearing music – long-distance listening – for which
Schenker has become so famous.

In *Ein Beitrag zur Ornamentik* (1904) Schenker illustrated by reference to form in a sonata of C. P. E. Bach
the idea of 'group construction' (*Gruppenbildung*) which
was also partly stated in *Harmonielehre* (pp.241ff): the
diversifying of a single tonal unit of structure by thematic and motivic variety, by interior harmonic movement, by variety of rhythmic placing and patterning, and
by contrast of dynamic levels (pp.11ff). Schenker's
scholarly activities – in particular his concern for authenticity in editing and performance, and his respect for
the authority of autograph scores and authorized editions – had led him to this study of ornamentation in C.
P. E. Bach, Haydn, Mozart, Beethoven and others. It
was a significant study for his development as an analyst, too, since he was later to develop a technique of
stripping away layers of ornamentation in the process of
revealing the ultimate structure of a piece. In his so-
called 'Erläuterungsausgabe' of four of Beethoven's last
five piano sonatas (1913–21 – that of op.106 did not
appear because its autograph could not be found; there
is however an unpublished essay on the sonata) he
achieved a balance between the analytical and the textual
sides of his work. In the last volume of the set, on
op.101, he developed the idea of reduction by carrying
it through successive stages. Fig.12 shows the stages
laid out one above the other. Schenker, however, introduced this example with the words 'Here are shown
the lines that Beethoven's imagination followed': he
intended it as a tracing of the creative process step by
step, not as an analysis. Thus he spoke not of 'reduction'
but of the reverse, *Diminution* (i.e. embellishment). The
way in which the notes e′ g♯′–a′–b♭′–a′ g♯′–a′ in the
right hand of bars 1–4 are reduced to (e′)–g♯′–a′ g♯′–a′
and ultimately to g♯′–a′ shows the technique of his later
analyses already formed. Although Schenker's final line
(a) here does not take the form of his eventual *Urlinie*,
and he used only the term *Ton-Urreihe* to describe it, the
term *Urlinie* is used elsewhere in the study.

It was one of the greatest figures of historical musicology, Guido Adler (1855–1941), who attempted
through his book *Der Stil in der Musik* (1911) to
change the nature of historical writing about music by
introducing the notion of style as the central concern of
the historian. As early as 1885 Adler had published a
programme for the future of musicology, placing strong
emphasis on analysis, arguing for its rightful place in
historical inquiry. He set out a series of criteria for the
examination of structure in a work, under general headings such as rhythmic features, tonality, polyphonic
construction, word-setting, treatment of instruments,
and performing practice. In his book Adler criticized his
contemporaries for making history out of a string of
composers' names. What was necessary, he believed, was
the formulation of a terminology adequate for the description of music 'without names to prop it up'. If music
could be described in this way then it would become
possible to compare work with work, and thus to specify
what features works have in common – or rather, in the

12. From H. Schenker:
'Die letzten fünf Sonaten
Beethoven: Sonata A dur
Op.101' (1921), 52–3

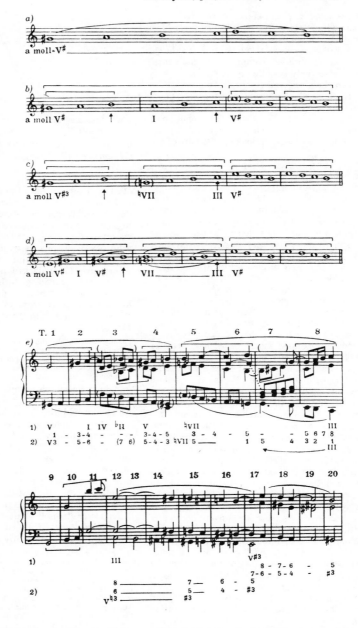

more dynamic terms that Adler used, what features 'link works together'.

Music history was to Adler like a self-weaving textile whose threads, of different colours, thicknesses and strengths, were features of style. Threads might discontinue, change colour, change places or merge. Thus he spoke of 'stylistic direction' (*Stilrichtung*), 'stylistic change' (*Stilwandel*), 'stylistic transfer' (*Stilübertragung*), 'stylistic hybridization' (*Stilkreuzung*), 'stylistic mixing' (*Stilmischung*) (pp.19–48). His view of art was as an organism. Everything in it could be accounted for; nothing occurred by chance (p.13):

The style of an epoch, of a school, of a composer, of a work, does not arise accidentally, as the casual outcome and manifestation of artistic will. It is, on the contrary, based on laws of becoming, of the rise and fall of organic development. Music is an organism, a plurality of single organisms which in their changing relationships and interdependencies form a totality.

Adler sharply criticized what he called the 'hero-cult' – that is, history written in terms only of leading composers: 'the edifice of style is built out of minor figures just as much as major, and all need investigation if the true picture is to appear'. (It is significant that Adler had been the prime mover in the Austrian national series of editions, Denkmäler der Tonkunst in Österreich, of which he was editor from 1894 to 1938; he must have been particularly conscious of the need to place lesser composers in historical perspective.) The task that he set the historian was to observe and apprehend that edifice of style in an essentially scientific manner; for 'style is the centre of the handling and comprehension of art . . . it is the yardstick by which everything in the work of art is measured and judged' (p.5). He placed emphasis on 'apprehension' as the first stage: that is, a recognition of the facts purely as they are, which avoids value judgments and subjective preconceptions on the part of the historian.

Adler offered two methods of approaching this task, and it is here that his work is important for the analyst. One method is that of taking several pieces and examining them to identify what they have in common and how they differ. This is Adler's 'inductive method', by which the historian can perceive the forces that cause an established group of works to hold together; he can discover which works in a random collection are relatively close in style and which more distant; or he can trace links between works composed in chronological succession. The other, the 'deductive method', is to compare a given work with surrounding works, contemporary and preceding, measuring it against them by set criteria and establishing its position within them. Such criteria are the use of motif and theme, rhythm, melody, harmony, notation and so forth. Other criteria concern the function and medium of music: sacred or secular, vocal or instrumental, lyrical or dramatic, courtly, virtuoso etc. Adler's book is far from a manual of stylistic analysis. It does not offer method in detail. It was a laying of foundations for method. Adler sought to establish a 'framework of laws' (*Rahmengesetz*) by which style operates and within which research could proceed.

Adler made a particular study of the Viennese Classical style. Wilhelm Fischer too, his assistant from 1912 to 1928, completed a dissertation on the genesis of that style in 1915. Two other scholars pursued stylistic studies in scholarly fashion at this time, Ernst Bücken (1884–1949) and Paul Mies (1889–1976), notably in their joint article on the foundations, methods and tasks of stylistic research into music (1922–3). Both also worked on Beethoven; indeed, Beethoven became a centre of attention for studies of personal style, with Gál's examination of individual features in the young Beethoven (1916), Becking's of Beethoven's personal style (1921), Mies's of the meaning of the sketches for an understanding of Beethoven's style (1925), Schiedermair's of the young Beethoven (1925), August Halm's of middle-period works (in *Beethoven*, 1926) and Engelsmann's of Beethoven's levels of composition (1931). Other studies of personal style include Danckert's 'Personal types in melodic style' (1931), later enlarged as 'Primal symbols in melodic formation' (1932). Becking was particularly interested in rhythm as a determinant of individuality (1928) and devised a set of graphic devices, known as 'Becking curves', for representing the rhythmic 'national constants' and 'personal constants': fig.13 shows the curves for the 18th-century Italian–German mixture of styles represented by Handel, and for Wagner's early style.

The most distinguished and influential example of stylistic analysis at this time was however Knud Jeppesen's *The Style of Palestrina and the Dissonance*, first prepared as a doctoral dissertation in Danish in

13. From G. Becking: 'Der musikalische Rhythmus als Erkenntnisquelle' (1928), 58, 110

1923, and subsequently translated into German in 1925 and English in 1927. Jeppesen provided in this book the detailed analytical procedure that Adler had left wanting. His choice of 'inductive' or 'deductive' method was conditioned by his general purpose: he saw the need for a history of dissonance treatment. He felt that modern manuals of counterpoint, based on Fux (*Gradus ad Parnassum*, 1725), lacked precisely that historical account, that 'genetic' growth of dissonance treatment, which would illuminate the development of musical style in time and place from the Middle Ages to the late Renaissance and from there to the end of the 18th century (pp.3f):

Passing from an absorbing study of Gregorian music to primitive polyphonic forms, from the style of Palestrina to the commencement of dramatic music, or from Bach's polyphony to the classical art of Vienna, would be the best manner of proceeding for recognizing immediately the essential peculiarities of the new style.

In taking Palestrina as his special study Jeppesen was starting with a 'central' point, and a stable one, from which he could look backwards (since Palestrina's work was a 'vast summary of the musical development of the preceding centuries') and forwards. At the same time he was starting with the best-known phenomenon in the field, and investigating it against a background which was in his terms virtually uncharted. He was therefore driven to the 'inductive' method, with no established criteria and only the possibility of comparing case with case until such criteria began to appear.

Jeppesen himself called this method 'empiric-descriptive', and identified it expressly with Adler's method. He stated it clearly (p.8):

through comparison of variants of homogeneous forms of [the] language [of music] – whether taken from contemporary or from historically separated periods – to indicate and fix common qualities, which with certainty can be supposed to possess the essential accentuations of these forms. The material thus obtained may then serve as a basis upon which to build up the laws of the language, the laws of musical evolution. These, psychologically translated, finally develop into certain regulations and directions of will – the hidden force behind these laws.

Jeppesen in this way extended Adler's inquiry from the surface of music, considered empirically, to the subconscious controls of style, considered psychologically. In so doing he enunciated the motivation for most present-day feature analysis, including computer-assisted analysis (see §II, 8 below). His method of working is indeed particularly well suited to computer operation.

Jeppesen presented first an account of Palestrina's melodic style (pp.48–84) with regard to pitch contour, rhythmic flow and the width and direction of intervals. The preliminary work for this analysis must clearly have been an exhaustive search through every vocal part of Palestrina's entire output (in the Leipzig collected edition of 1862–1903) in order to count and note every interval in relation to its metrical placing. Thus he located and listed for the reader (p.55, note 3) the occurrence of major 6ths and descending minor 6ths as 'dead' intervals (i.e. between two phrases rather than during a phrase: 32 cases in all). The investigation of upward leaps in rhythmic context led to the uncovering of a subconscious law: 'on considering the style with regard to crotchets ... we meet with the astonishing fact, not previously observed, that a rule (almost without an exception) forbids the leap upward from an accentuated crotchet' (p.61). By contrast, Jeppesen listed no fewer than 35 melodic patterns in which a downward leap occurs from an accented crotchet, and charted all the places in which these patterns occur. It is in the much larger second discussion, that of dissonance treatment (pp.84–287), where he defined each dissonance in turn and discussed its degree and manner of use by Palestrina, that Jeppesen entered into historical comparison. Thus for example he considered the use of the 'portamento dissonance' (the anticipation of a note on a weak beat), stating: 'by Palestrina it was most frequently employed immediately before a syncope [i.e. syncopation] and in descending movement ... though the syncope is not an invariable condition' (pp.184f). He then contrasted this limitation with the use by other composers, citing cases in Josquin, Obrecht, Carpentras, Cara and La Rue.

The aspect of Jeppesen's work that makes it scientific is the fact that the analyst is not selecting and summarizing: he is presenting the entire data for each case and adducing laws from it objectively.

6. 1920–45: TENSION-THEORY AND STRUCTURAL LAYERS. One of Adler's pupils was Ernst Kurth. Kurth's ideas were closely allied to those of the Gestalt psychologists, but also used Schopenhauer's concept of the 'Will' and Freud's of the subconscious mind. The Gestalt theorists saw three levels of aural perception: physical perception by the ear, sensory organization in the nervous system, and understanding at the psychological level. Kurth saw three levels of activity in musical creation, which he expounded as part of his theory of melody in the first part of Grundlagen des linearen Kontrapunkts (1917). The first of these levels is the operation of the 'Will' (which in art is unselfish and disinterested) in the form of kinetic energy (Bewegungsenergie); this, a continuous flow, is the living power of music; 'the origin of music ... is the will to move'. The second level is the psychological: the submerged stirrings of the unconscious mind draw on this energy to produce a 'play of tensions' (Spiel von Spannungen), each tug of tension describing an arc of growth and formation (Ur-Formung or Erformung). This play of tensions does not become conscious until the moment that it takes form in musical sound – the third level, the acoustic manifestation (Erscheinungsform). Because these three levels are activated one after the other to produce melody, the resultant line has unity and wholeness. Its shape is conceived before either notes or harmonic implications are brought into play; it is thus a 'closed progression'. This is the essence of Kurth's concept of the 'linear'. He saw it particularly at work in the music of Bach – a texture made up of lines, each of which is powered by kinetic energy and internally unified, and which make harmonic sense together only as a secondary phenomenon. This is what Kurth called

'linear counterpoint'. He evolved a concept of 'linear phase', a unit of growth and decay, quite separate from the conventional idea of 'phrase' in that it did not depend on rhythmic patterning, only on proportion and contour. The motif was such a phase: unified, distinctive, not losing its identity when its pitches, intervals and durations are modified (pp.21ff, 68ff).

Notes forming a melody contain kinetic energy; notes forming a chord contain 'potential energy'. Tonal harmony is a system of internal coherence, carrying the possibility of change, brought about by potential energy. The most powerful tension in this system is that of the leading note. In his second book, on Romantic harmony (1920), Kurth first expounded chromatic alteration as a process of placing the leading note where it would not normally occur. He distinguished between two forces at work in Romantic harmony, creating a polarization: 'constructive' and 'destructive' forces (pp.272ff). It is the cohesive forces of tonality that are constructive, and the dissolving forces of chromaticism that are destructive: alteration, the use of chords of the 7th, 9th etc in place of triads, and the use of chords for coloristic effects.

Kurth had taken Wagner's Tristan, and in particular the many statements of the famous 'Tristan chord', as the central material for his second book; it contains little actual analysis, yet it offered a new perspective for handling the large-scale tonal structure of Wagner's operas, giving insight into long-term tonal relationships despite pervading chromaticism and movement to remote key areas for long periods. The scholar who grasped the problem of form and tonality in Wagner and exposed its 'secret' analytically was Alfred Lorenz. After a doctoral dissertation on form in the Ring (1922) and a study of the Tristan prelude (1922–3) he published the first of his four volumes of Das Geheimnis der Form bei Richard Wagner which were to analyse form in the Ring (1924), Tristan (1926), Meistersinger (1930) and Parsifal (1933).

Lorenz's work was a landmark in the history of analysis. It was the largest-scale piece of sustainedly analytical writing so far. It used graphic and tabular techniques of presentation in a thorough-going way: the 'sine curve' for harmonic movement, the 'projectile curve' for extended formal contour, the graph for modulatory scheme (see fig.14 for the graph representing the whole Ring cycle as a vast unified structure in Db major, with lateral spacing marking 40 pages of score and each horizontal line a major and space a minor key area) and type-set diagrams for more detailed tonal movement (see fig.15 for the diagram of Das Rheingold, which is complementary to fig.14 and shows the opera as an introduction (748 bars) in the dominant of the dominant followed by a massive symmetrical section (3128 bars) in Db pivoting round the relative minor, Bb).

Lorenz's work was the confluence of all the main developments in analysis before his time. It contained ideas from the Gestalt writers; his notion of periodization and symmetry derived from Riemann; his defining of structure drew on traditional Formenlehre; his perception of harmonic movement came from Kurth (to whom he dedicated his Tristan volume). It is also built from a large body of existing writings on Wagner's musical and dramatic structures (especially those by Hostinský, 1877; Grunsky, 1906, 1907; and von Ehrenfels, 1896, 1913) and on his leitmotifs (e.g.

14. From A. O. Lorenz: 'Das Geheimnis der Form bei Richard Wagner', i (1924). 'Der musikalische Aufbau des Bühnenspiels Der Ring des Nibelungen', p.48

Mayrberger, 1881; von Wolzogen, 1876, 1880, 1882), and above all from Wagner's own prose writings.

Lorenz saw formal construction (*Formbildung*) as created out of three primary things: harmony, rhythm and melody. He segmented the entire *Ring* cycle into periods according to key area (pp.23ff). He also analysed the distribution of leitmotifs into formal groupings: repetition forms, arch forms, refrain forms and bar forms. It is in this last area that his main contribution to music theory lies. Lorenz perceived a hierarchical structure in music, the two extremes of which are his *kleine Rhythmik* and *grosse Rhythmik*. The second of these arises out of the first by forms being 'raised to a higher power' (*potenzierte Formen*). By this process, three consecutive passages of music may each be constructed in arch form (*ABA*); the third of them may be a restatement of the first and so create an arch form at a higher level. The process may be traced at more than two levels. He also described the embedding of small-scale units within forms, extending them and changing the balance, and very large-scale forms which contain small-scale forms of different sorts. By analysing formal units in this way, Lorenz sought to uncover the architectonics (*grosse Architektonik*) of very large musical structures.

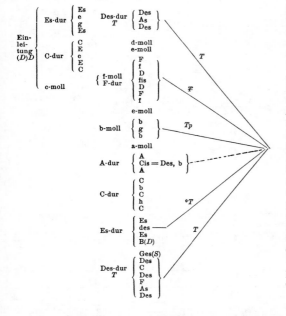

15. From A. O. Lorenz: 'Das Geheimnis der Form bei Richard Wagner', i (1924), 'Der musikalische Aufbau des Bühnenspiels Der Ring des Nibelungen', p.27

A year after Lorenz had issued the first volume of his *Geheimnis der Form*, Schenker produced the first issue of a yearbook, *Das Meisterwerk in der Musik*, which was to run to only three issues (1925, 1926, 1930). It contained ten analytical studies, of works by J. S. Bach, Domenico Scarlatti, Beethoven and Chopin, accompanied by Schenker's new type of graphic analyses, together with a long essay on 'Die Kunst der Improvisation' (itself containing important analyses of keyboard works by C. P. E. Bach and Handel), a polemic 'Weg mit dem Phrasierungsbogen' ('Away with

phrase-marks') and a study-in-progress of the concept of 'fundamental line' (*Urlinie*). This was not the first journal that Schenker had produced: he had published ten issues of *Der Tonwille* between 1921 and 1924, the first two of which had contained preliminary studies of the *Urlinie* idea together with analyses using the so-called *Urlinie-Tafeln* – graphic analyses showing the fundamental line. The most important analytical product of *Der Tonwille* was the study of Beethoven's Symphony no.5, produced in instalments and later issued separately (1925). (The two journals contained material exclusively by Schenker.)

The *Urlinie-Tafel* as developed at this stage was usually a presentation of a piece in full or partly reduced, with normal use of note values and complete with time signature and the original barring (numbered for reference). This was overlaid with auxiliary analytical symbols: horizontal and sloping square brackets over the staff to show the movement of the fundamental line; note heads printed large to indicate structural importance; curved lines like phrasing or bowing marks to indicate important progressions (often also labelled *Quintzug, Quartzug* etc); dotted curves to indicate the longer-term structural retention of a particular pitch (or transfer to another octave) despite intervening pitches; and the fundamental harmonic steps (*Stufen*), symbolized below the staff by roman numerals, with conventional bass figuring to show the overlying harmonies. In some cases Schenker added a parallel staff above the *Urlinie-Tafel*: this carried his reduction of the piece to bare harmonic essentials – already termed *Ursatz* – and partly abandoned the durational significance of note symbols in favour of a valuation whereby greater duration denoted greater structural importance. Fig.16 (*Das Meisterwerk*, i, *Urlinie-Tafeln*, pl.2) illustrates all these features and many others (the *Urlinie-Tafel* showing the Largo from Bach's Violin Sonata no.3 BWV1005 bar-for-bar but in skeletal form): bar 7, and bar 17 a 5th lower, show how the fundamental line ($f''-e''-d'$) moves from the top line of the texture to the bottom and back, and how the last of its notes is not actually sounded but only implied (hence the parentheses). For this particular piece, Schenker chose also to give a three-layer graph (see fig.17) of which the bottom layer is a partly reduced form of the piece, the middle one an intermediate stage of reduction, and the top one a complete reduction corresponding to the upper parallel staff of the *Urlinie-Tafel*. These two graphs are accompanied by 11 pages of closely reasoned text with further music examples.

The main achievements of the yearbook were a long and lucid essay on Mozart's Symphony no.40 in G minor (vol.ii) and the massive analysis of Beethoven's 'Eroica' Symphony (vol.iii). The layers (*Schichten*) are identified as 'foreground', 'middleground' and 'background'; horizontal brackets are abandoned in preference to the beaming together of structural notes, and many other graphic devices are adopted. Such was the sophistication of Schenker's graphs during the last five years of his life that he was able to discard verbal commentary altogether. His *Five Graphic Analyses* (1932) are self-sufficient graphings of works by Bach, Haydn and Chopin. The full range of his terminology is to be found in these graphs. Moreover, the *Ursatz* had by then taken its final form in Schenker's mind as a melodic progression of 3–2–1 extensible to 5–4–3–2–1 or rarely 8–7–6–5–4–3–2–1, over a 'bass arpeggiation'

16. From H. Schenker: 'Das Meisterwerk in der Musik', i (1925), 'Urlinie-Tafeln', pl.2

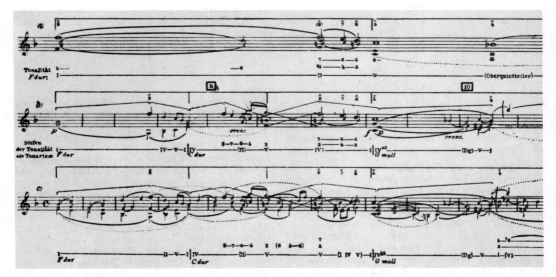

17. From H. Schenker: 'Das Meisterwerk in der Musik', i (1925), 'Urlinie-Tafeln', graph between pp.61 and 62

(*Bassbrechung*) of 1–5–1: the ultimate projection of the major triad into the dimension of time which Schenker saw as lying at the heart of his theory. This meant that the basic structure of any tonal piece of music was diatonic, and all modulations were considered as 'prolongations' of diatonic harmonic steps. The fullest statement of Schenker's approach was his posthumously published *Der freie Satz* (1935), which was incomplete at his death and in which the theories of metre and rhythm and of form were as yet undeveloped. (For Schenker's method see also §III, 2 below.)

Schenker's analytical work was designed primarily for the performer, and his final graphic method led the reader stage by stage from the familiar text of a work through to an understanding of it in its complex totality. His analyses were thus always pedagogical in function.

In his *Unterweisung im Tonsatz* of 1937 the composer Hindemith believed himself to have laid down the basis of a *lingua franca* for modern composition, 'proceeding from the firm foundation of the laws of nature'. Like Schenker, he believed in the force of tonality and the primacy of the triad; but his theory is far more systematically acoustical. To Hindemith, if any one of the notes of the chromatic octave scale be taken, then the other 11 notes can be ranged in descending order of relationship to it. This order he called 'Series 1'. Adopting the principle of inversion (by which, for example, minor 7th = major 2nd), he determined an order for intervals based on combination-tone curves in increasing complexity. This produced 'Series 2', of intervals in descending order of value with respect to a given note. This series acknowledges no point at which consonance ends and dissonance begins. From this Hindemith developed a system of chordal analysis, which first allocates to any chord a root – always present in the chord, unlike the roots of Rameau's harmonic system – and then measures the intensity of that chord. Hindemith classified chords containing three to six notes into separate groups and subgroups in terms of their harmonic intensity. Using these groups, a com-

poser might put together a succession of chords in whatever 'harmonic crescendo and decrescendo' he wished. Such an increase and decrease of intensity he called a 'harmonic fluctuation' (a concept closely related to Kurth's idea of *Spannung*); and he devised a graphic means of demonstrating this beneath the staff (see fig.18, which shows the group and subgroup of each chord as well as the graphic fluctuation). Hindemith proceeded from there to determine harmonic relationships on a larger scale by measuring the progression of prevailing roots, the 'degree-progression', against Series 1.

Although *Unterweisung im Tonsatz* was intended as a constructional tool for composers, and stressed the realms of harmony that Hindemith felt were not adequately covered by conventional harmonic theory, its theories were meant to apply equally to the harmony of the past and thus to function as a means of interpreting and analysing the music of any period. Hindemith himself supplied, at the end of the first volume, a set of analyses of music ranging from plainchant to Schoenberg and his own music. As an analytical method his system is like Schenker's in being based on a theory of melody and harmony with no separate theory of rhythm. It is unlike it in that there are no structural levels: all notes at the surface can be related to the tonal centre, and modulation is an accepted tonal procedure which is not reduced out of existence.

In 1932 another composer, Schoenberg, wrote: 'For nearly 20 years I have been collecting material, ideas and sketches, for an all-inclusive textbook of composi-

18. From P. Hindemith: 'Unterweisung im Tonsatz' (1937; from Eng. trans., 1942), i, 120

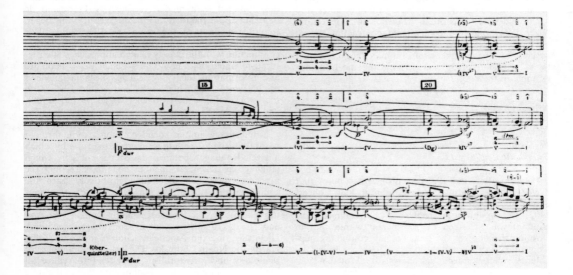

tion'. The project was never completed. Only *Harmonielehre* (1911) and *Models for Beginners in Composition* (1942) were published in his lifetime, and *Structural Functions of Harmony* (1954) shortly after his death. Since then, two sets of notes designed for teaching purposes, both dating from the 1930s, have been assembled and issued: *Preliminary Exercises in Counterpoint* (dating from *c*1936; 1963) and *Fundamentals of Musical Composition* (dating between 1937 and 1948; 1967). The last is a small manual of form. Not at all radical in conception, it sets out definitions of terms in thematic construction before proceeding to small forms, the subsidiary parts of larger forms, rondo forms and the sonata–allegro. The material was intended for composers, but it rests on analytical exemplification and is to some extent a manual of analysis, drawing particularly on examples from Beethoven's piano sonatas.

Schoenberg saw form as implying comprehensibility in two dimensions: as subdivision, which enables the mind to grasp the whole through units; and as logic and coherence, without which such units remain disconnected. It was on questions of coherence that Schoenberg was at his most original. He adhered to the 19th-century view of music as organic. Construction thus begins with the motif, the motif must by its nature be repeated, repetition requires variation. He thus explored rhythmic, intervallic, harmonic and melodic means of variation, subdividing each systematically, then considered variation by addition of ancillary notes and the connecting of different motif forms. All this is demonstrated with analytical examples. In the course of his exposition he supplied the analyst with a valuable set of working definitions for terms such as 'motif', 'phrase', 'antecedent' and 'consequent', 'period', 'sentence' and 'section'. Among the melodic concepts that he introduced was that of 'liquidation', whereby a unit gradually loses its characteristic features until only a residue remains.

The most influential aspect of the book, as it was disseminated through his teaching, is his atomic splitting of the motif into 'element' or 'feature'. The 'element' is often a single interval underlying a pattern of notes, and itself undergoes repetition, transposition, inversion, internal multiplication, enlargement, contraction and all the other processes to which the motif is subject. His reduction of the first theme of Brahms's Symphony no.4 to a succession of 3rds is perhaps the most famous example in the book (see fig.19).

19. From A. Schoenberg: *'Fundamentals of Musical Composition' (1967), 11*

Between 1935 and 1939 the programme notes that Tovey had been writing for the Edinburgh Reid Concert Series since the mid-1910s (though some go back to 1902) were published together in six volumes. The material was arranged by genre, and within that in chronological order, the final volume containing supplementary essays and a glossary. As a whole, the volumes made a substantial analysis book of the 18th- and 19th-century orchestral and choral repertory. To this he added in 1944 a further volume on chamber music (some of whose essays go back to 1900). Later Tovey produced a set of analyses of Beethoven's piano sonatas (1948). These books, and his articles for the *Encyclopaedia Britannica* written between 1906 and 1910, have been the strongest influence on British analytical and critical writing. They are noted for their pungent prose and avoidance of dogma. They are true examples of English empiricism, rejecting the analyst's formal models as 'nonsensical', and equally rejecting the idea of organic unity as '*a priori* fancies'. All such theories were 'fallacies' (1948, pp.298, 3, 8f). Even the terms 'first subject' and 'second subject' were discarded: the latter had 'worked . . . havoc in our notions of sonata form and sonata themes' (1935, p.2); and 'binary' and 'ternary' 'not only miss the essential grounds of classification, but are thoroughly misleading in all that they imply'. He deprecated any terminology that 'assumes a map-like or space-like view of music instead of a time-like view' (1935, pp.10f).

Tovey saw himself as dealing only with the 'facts'. He thus proceeded 'bar-by-bar', 'phrase-by-phrase as a process in time'. He called the method 'précis-writing', and attributed it to Hubert Parry. It is a judicious mixture of descriptive, naturalistic writing and technical information, illustrated with frequent musical examples and allocating letter-symbols to figures and themes. But here again Tovey was critical of others: 'we shall do well to beware of the exclusively subjective methods of criticism . . . which may be but mildly caricatured as consisting in sitting in front of a work of art, feeling our pulses, and noting our symptoms'. Tovey's own method was a blend of the hermeneutic and the formalistic which implicitly stated that there are things in music beyond explanation. (For Tovey's method see also §III, 4 below.)

7. 1945–60: LINGUISTICS, CYBERNETICS AND THEMATIC UNITY. In the years after World War II, two highly influential lines of intellectual thought came to impinge on musical theory. To some extent both were approaches to phenomena – methodologies – rather than fields of study in their own right. The first was linguistics, founded as a modern science by Ferdinand de Saussure about the turn of the 20th century; this began to influence musical theory in the 1930s and 1940s before making a great impact in the 1950s and 1960s in conjunction with the closely related approaches of structuralism and semiology. The second was cybernetics and information theory, which as mechanistic views of the world began life at the end of the 1940s with the work of Norbert Wiener (*Cybernetics*, 1948), and Claude Shannon and Warren Weaver (*The Mathematical Theory of Communication*, 1949).

Linguistics examines social communication through natural language, seeking to uncover the rules by which a given language operates, the deeper rules by which language as a general phenomenon operates, and the processes by which individuals intuitively learn the complex rules of their own language. It took important strides forward with the work of three circles of linguistics scholars: that in Prague, including Roman Jakobson and N. S. Trubetzkoy; that in Copenhagen, including Hjelmslev; and the American scholars including Zellig Harris and Noam Chomsky. The kindred approaches of semiology and structuralism both tend to reduce all kinds of non-linguistic social communication to the state of natural language, semiology by treating all the ways in which human beings signal to each other (by the clothes they wear, the gestures they make, the food they eat, and so on) as 'codes' containing 'messages' which can be encoded and decoded by those familiar with that code, structuralism by seeing all social phenomena as 'wholes' (or 'structures') whose elements are governed by well-defined laws. Semiology has derived much from the mechanistic view of cybernetics, while structuralism (which developed in the 1950s and 1960s with the work of the Belgian anthropologist Claude Lévi-Strauss, the Swiss psychologist Jean Piaget and the French literary critic Roland Barthes) has been constructed on a special field of mathematics known as group theory.

Cybernetics sees all activities, human, animal and machine, in terms of control systems. Thus the nervous system of a human and the electronic system of a computer and the servo system of a complex machine plant are seen as analogous processes, with inputs and outputs, with information feeding back to modify the operation of the system, and so forth. Information theory measures the capacity of systems to receive, process, store and transmit information. Information is thought of as a choice of one message from a set of possible messages; some messages come more frequently than others, thus setting up different probabilities for the arrival of any one message. Information theory reduces any existing range of choices to a network of two-way or 'binary' choices. When a highly probable choice is presented within a message, that choice is said to contain 'low information'; and conversely when an unlikely choice is presented then that choice contains 'high information'. In other words, information is generated by non-confirmation of expectation. Information theory spread rapidly in the early 1950s to fields of application as widely differing as genetics, neuro-physiology, sociology and philosophy, and soon to aesthetics, where it came upon certain difficulties. For in the arts what information theory calls 'redundancy' (namely, confirmation of expectation, non-information) plays a special role in creating form and structure.

The first 15 postwar years also saw a considerable extension of the notion of motivic growth in music, and its reshaping into an analytical theory. In the course of this reshaping, the theory took over elements of Freudian psychology. The Jungian concept of the collective subconscious also figured briefly in analysis in the 1960s.

The first musical contribution in either of the new fields of thought was probably an address to the first International Congress of Phonetic Sciences in Amsterdam as early as 1932 by the musicologist, style analyst and ethnomusicologist Gustav Becking (see §5 above). It was phonology (the science of distinguishing between elements in a stream of vocal linguistic sound and the apprehension of the rules by which these sounds are linked together), as developed by Trubetzkoy, that seemed relevant to music. And in particular it was the scholars of non-Western music, with their rapidly developing scientific approach to their material, by whom the relevance was first seen. Becking, in discussing Serbo-Croat popular epic, pointed to a certain parallel between basic problems in phonology and those in musicology, illustrating this by the different constructions that people of different world cultures place on a given single musical sound. Such people operate within different musical systems, and Becking tried to set up a typology of systems, 'unidimensional', 'bidimensional',

'tridimensional' and 'quadridimensional'. The great linguistics scholar Roman Jakobson took up Becking's point in the same year, stressing that the particular property of music, as of poetry, is that its conventions are wholly phonological in operation, and do not concern etymology or vocabulary. He urged musical analysts to study the model of phonology.

13 years later Milos Weingart explored the analogies between musical and language phrase structure, with reference to Czech, and in 1949 Antonín Sychra examined folksong by means of linguistic method. In 1956, in a volume of essays to Jakobson, George P. Springer provided a comparison of language and music which surveyed the progress of linguistic analysis in music. He discussed the distinction between repetition (i.e. identity) and difference as a binary opposition, and the modification which the idea of variation brings to this, concluding that music (1956, p.510):

is subject to conventional rules of combination and distribution, and *ipso facto*, of probability. . . . Moreover, music turns out to be not only a stochastic process (producing a 'sequence of symbols . . . according to certain probabilities') but the special kind of stochastic process known as the Markov chain (where 'probabilities depend on previous events').

In his first important book (1956) the aesthetician Leonard B. Meyer came close to information theory in his view of styles as culturally conditioned systems of expectations, and of musical meaning as deriving from the arousing, frustrating and fulfilling of such expectations. Meyer was still working within the Gestalt concepts of *Prägnanz* and closure. In the following year, however, he introduced the fundamentals of information theory into his argument and revised his definition of 'meaning' in music. As early as 1956 R. C. Pinkerton and Abraham Moles had produced articles relating information theory, as presented by Shannon and Weaver, to music, and in 1958 and 1959 a spate of material was based on the subject: two basic presentations by David Kraehenbuehl and Edgar Coons, an article by Joseph Youngblood, a monograph by W. Fucks, and an extended book on the broader application of the theory to aesthetic perception by Abraham Moles that devotes a chapter to perception of 'sonic material'. But Meyer, in his redefinition, fashioned three stages of what he called 'embodied meaning': the 'hypothetical meaning' before a sound-pattern has been heard, the 'evident meaning' when the sound-pattern has become a concrete event, which initiates a stage of 'revaluation' comparable with 'feedback' in control systems, and the 'determinate meaning' that arises later in the total experience. Meyer dealt, as Moles had previously done, with the concept of 'noise' whereby information is distorted. The maturity of Meyer's thought is shown in his subsequent essay (1961), which subjected the view of music as information to the actual situation of music frequently reheard. Two of the articles from 1958 appeared in the second issue of a new journal published at the Yale School of Music, the *Journal of Music Theory*, begun in 1957 as a forum for musical theory in a creative spirit rather than as dry academicism; it has regularly found space for detailed analyses, studies in the nature and problems of analysis, and analytical symposia.

During the 15 years just described, a new approach to organic motivic analysis was being forged, which has influenced analytical writing in Britain but has found little sympathy elsewhere in Europe or in the USA. It was first expounded by Rudolph Réti in two books

(1951, 1958), of which the earlier, *The Thematic Process in Music*, is his classic exposition. But before that, Réti, who had lived in Vienna most of his life until emigrating to the USA in the 1930s, had worked intensively on analyses of sonatas by Beethoven between 1944 and 1948 in an attempt to grasp Beethoven's compositional process. These analyses were published, ten years after his death, in 1967. Réti started from the two-dimensional view of formal construction that was implied in Schoenberg's *Fundamentals*: motivic expansion, and division and demarcation. Réti reconciled these two dimensions. His method in itself produces, by reduction of thematic material, a series of 'cells'. Each cell is the extracted contour of a motif, and it comprises usually one, two or three intervals presented without rhythmic values in Réti's music examples. Each cell can undergo transposition and inversion. But Réti saw specific sequences of such cells recurring in each of the movements of a large-scale work and forming what he called a 'thematic pattern'. Such a pattern supplies its own natural thematic grouping which, in Beethoven's work, often takes the place of strict textbook form, and creates a symmetry or unity between movements, which Réti considered a conscious act of composition.

Réti's first book, *The Thematic Process in Music*, extends these ideas, dealing more fully with his architectural concept of thematic evolution and resolution, and also with key relationships, presenting a greater diversity of examples and attempting a historical survey of the thematic process. His second book expounded what he saw as a new kind of tonality 'which does not appear on the surface but is created by the ear singling out hidden relationships between various points of a melodic or contrapuntal web' (p.65). At the heart of his idea was the 'moving tonic'. Réti supplied a wide range of contemporary analytical examples in support of his thesis. (For Réti's method see also §III, 3 below.)

Two years before this last book of Réti, Hans Keller presented the first of a succession of short, pithy articles in which he put forward the principles of 'functional analysis'. 'Functional analysis postulates that contrasts are but different aspects of a single basic idea, a background unity' (1956–7, p.15). Criticizing conventional Toveyan analysis as 'anatomical', and thus concerned with 'dissection', Keller proposed a method that would attempt 'to elucidate the unifying *functions* of the living organism that is a musical work of art' (*MR*, xviii, 1957, 203). He saw his analytical work as the purely objective isolating of background unities, and strongly refuted charges of subjectivity. Unlike Réti's treatment of a single movement, Keller saw the whole musical structure proceeding from a single idea. He added to this view the idea of the 'suppressed background', too obvious to be stated by the composer yet vitally important for the analyst to reconstruct in order that the unity of what followed might be demonstrated. For him, the contrasts on the surface of a piece of music were 'manifest', and the unity that lay behind it was 'latent'. It was precisely the analyst's job to demonstrate that what appeared new was not new at all. This concept of background and foreground was comparable with Schenker's structural layers in that the structure lies at the back, but is totally different in that Schenker's background comprised the *Ursatz* projected, stretched, 'composed out', whereas Keller's background comprised an ever-present idea, a model that contains the common elements of all the work's themes. Keller in 1957 took a

bolder step even than Schenker when the latter abandoned the word for the graph: Keller abandoned word and graph for sound, by preparing an analytical score which demonstrated what he saw as the background unities of Mozart's String Quartet in D minor K421/417b entirely in musical sound. Several such analyses were prepared and broadcast in Britain and on the Continent. (For Keller's method see also §III, 3 below.)

In the later 1950s there were significant developments in the linguistic analysis of music: a brief proposal by Bruno Nettl (1958), and the first contribution by the most influential figure in this field, Nicolas Ruwet, in which he sought to define the aural problems of listening to integral serial music by reference to phonology and the need for a 'margin of error' between the phonemes in a phonemic system (1959).

The trains of thought discussed above had their impact not only on analytical work but also on the work of composers. There is a striking similarity, for example, between the work that phonologists did with phonemes to test the point at which modification converts one phoneme into another and the work that Pierre Schaeffer did with recorded natural sound in the late 1940s and early 1950s in *musique concrète*. Similarly, probability theory came to be used as a means of generating compositions mechanically, for example in the work of Lejaren Hiller (who in 1958 completed a master's dissertation which included the famous *Illiac Suite* for string quartet by Hiller and Isaacson).

Finally, the postwar years were a period of revival for the ideas and teaching of Schenker, with important books by Adele Katz (1945) and Felix Salzer (1952), and with a resurgence of practical analyses along Schenkerian lines (e.g. Forte, 1955). There was a revival, too, of hermeneutic theory in *The Language of Music* by Deryck Cooke (1959), which argued for the materials of music as a quite specific vocabulary of intervallic contours with the connotations of emotional states. These connotations arise not by convention but from the inherent forces of the intervals that make up the contours: forces of tension and direction. The analysis is thus apparently based on natural phenomena, translating a musical expression of psychological states and events (presumably those of the composer) into a verbal expression.

8. ANALYSIS SINCE 1960: SET THEORY AND COMPUTERS.

The output of analytical writing since 1960 has been prodigious, and yet only two significant new factors have been introduced in that time. The first is mathematical set theory, which has its origin in the work of Georg Cantor between 1874 and 1897, and which had already entered the theory of musical composition with the work of Webern before becoming of paramount importance to the serialists of the early 1960s. The second is the use of the digital computer, a device for the rapid processing of information, which was developed during the latter years of World War II and whose use for purposes other than number calculation developed enormously during the 1950s.

The fundamental concept of set theory is that of membership. A 'set' is made up of the 'elements' that are members of that set. The set may contain 'subsets' all of whose elements are members of the set itself. Where several sets exist, certain relationships can apply among them: relationships of equivalence (in which one set can be reduced to another by some simple procedure), intersection (in which sets have certain elements in common), union (in which sets are joined together), complementation (in which sets have no elements in common and together make up all the elements of some larger order, often called the 'universal set'), and so forth. In the realm of atonal music, set theory seemed to offer both a way of increasing the sophistication of the 12-note system and a way of relating pitches systematically that was as highly organized as the tonal system without depending on traditional tonality in any acoustical sense.

The importance of the computer for research in the fine arts, especially for literature and music, is twofold: it can count, and therefore can produce statistics concerning features of style which may lead it to suggest or question authenticity or simply to define a style as an aggregate of 'features'; and it can compare, and thus detect identity and difference (the binary opposition spoken of earlier), and can use such comparison to define the way in which elements are distributed, which of them occur in combination and under what conditions, and which never occur in combination – in short, it can deduce a 'syntax' for the behaviour of the material in a given work or style. There is no essential difference between a human doing these operations by hand and a computer carrying them out electronically, but a computer has the advantages of speed, accuracy and exact memory. It is here that the largest quantity of analytical work has been done in music since 1960, and the very large amount of published material is the more astonishing when one realizes that it is only the tip of an iceberg whose main bulk exists in the form of computer printout, punched cards, and punched or magnetic tape.

One further external factor entered into discourse on music at about this time: the philosophical view of the world known as 'phenomenology'. Phenomenology is a 'science of experience'. It is concerned not with the world as natural object or with mind as a store of knowledge. It deals with the contact between object and mind; it studies consciousness directed towards objects ('intentionality'), and aims to describe the structure of consciousness. The principal work of this type in music is the massive two-volume study by the Swiss conductor and mathematician Ernest Ansermet (1961). Ranging across mathematical, acoustical and philosophical issues, it reaches a study of musical structures that centres on the idea of the 'melodic path' (*chemin mélodique*). Classifying intervals as 'active extrovert', 'active introvert', 'passive extrovert' and 'passive introvert', it tries to give a value to the degree of tension in a melody. The method reckons tension between phrase-units and calculates the total tension for a melody (pp.237ff). Other phenomenological work has been carried out by Batstone (1969) and Pike (1970), but no working method of analysis has yet emerged.

Alongside these new developments there has been a crescendo of activity in linguistic analysis, a slightly diminishing flow of work in information theory, a steady stream of functional analysis, and a continued resurgence of Schenkerian work. A number of independent approaches have resulted, including a study by Albert B. Lord (1960) of Yugoslav epic which proceeds from the concept of oral composition and examines the mechanism by which a singer spontaneously creates or re-creates a song. This mechanism operates through the 'theme' and the 'formula'. The crux of the theory (which originated with the classical scholar Milman Parry: see

The Making of Homeric Verse, 1971) is the capacity of formulae to group into 'systems' which provide the singer with alternatives to match different metrical situations in the poetry that he is creating. This idea, though scarcely applied to music by Lord, has been taken up by Treitler (1974) for the analysis of plainchant.

Aspects of mathematical set theory already existed in the compositional technique of Webern in the 1930s, not to mention Josef Hauer's theory of 'tropes' 20 years earlier still. They also emerge in the writings of Leibowitz, Rufer and Perle. More important is the theory of hexachords presented by Rochberg (1955, 1959), and the statements concerning musical technique made by Boulez (1964, chap.2; 1966, part ii). But the proper formulation of a set theory of music has been the work of Milton Babbitt (1955, 1960, 1961, 1972), Donald Martino, David Lewin and John Rothgeb (*JMT*, iii–v, x, xi). Although Babbitt's work, using particularly the mathematical concept of the group, has dealt with harmony and with the functions of melodic and rhythmic configurations in 12-note music, and also with the interaction of components over longer spans of time, it belongs to the realm of compositional theory rather than analysis. The most significant analytical contribution has been made by Allen Forte (1964, 1965, 1972). Forte has extended the notion of pitch-class set (i.e. a set of pitches irrespective of their octave register) and its relationships to include the association of sets in 'set-complexes' and 'subcomplexes' – a 'complex' being an array of all the sets that are related by inclusion to any one given central set. This additional concept establishes a type of organization which has analogies with tonality. It makes possible the elucidation of tonal coherence in large-scale musical structures and the links between sections of such structures. With this theory Forte has provided analyses of atonal works by Berg, Schoenberg, Stravinsky and Webern.

For Forte, the use of the computer has facilitated the compilation of a roster of such complexes. It has also made possible the analysis of compositions into sets and set-complexes and the formulation of a 'syntax' for these compositions; and this has opened up the possibility too of formulating a syntax for individual styles (*JMT*, 1966). The use of the computer in music goes back at least to 1949, when Bernard Bronson, editor of the melodies of the Childe ballads, analysed range, metre, modality, phrase structure, refrain pattern, melodic outline, anacrusis, cadence and final of folksongs, using data on punched cards. The measuring of such quantities and the production of sets of statistics was the facility most readily available from the computer. 'Languages' for encoding music into a form that a computer could 'read' were rapidly developed, and special compilers (internal programmes that translate the user's simplified way of giving the machine instructions into the computer's own terms) with biases towards the demands of musical material were created in the early 1960s (*see* COMPUTERS AND MUSIC, §§5, 9). An important article by Selleck and Bakeman (1965) explained two strategies for analysing melodic structures: one through probabilities, which derives from information theory, the other through comparing and sorting melodic units, which derives from linguistics.

Two important publishing events occurred at this time. The first was the inception of the journal *Computers and the Humanities* in 1966, which, apart from including material on computers and music, maintains a directory of projects in progress, enabling scholars to be aware of other work in their field and encouraging collaboration. The second was the publication in 1967 of a collection of essays on electronic data processing in music, under the editorship of Harald Heckmann; this presented a cross-section of work, including 'languages' for representing music, strategies of computational analysis, sample analyses and articles raising more general issues. There were discussions of the application of information theory by such writers as Bean (1961), Hiller (1964), Meyer-Eppler (1962), Winckel (1964) and Brincker (1970); but the most significant study of mathematics and music has been Xenakis's treatise *Musiques formelles* (1963). Although his exposition of probabilities, stochastics, Markov chains and the theory of games is intentional, is focussed on the means of production, and resorts to analysis mostly in order to trace the compositional means in works of his own, the framework that he set out places the art of music on a more universal plane, opening it up to investigation according to precise laws. His book (which inherits the theoretical tradition of Messiaen, 1944, and which pours scorn on existing cybernetic and linguistic analyses of music as tending towards 'absurdities and desiccations', as elementary and pseudo-objective) proposes 'a world of sound-masses, vast groups of sound-events, clouds, and galaxies governed by new characteristics such as density, degree of order, and rate of change' in place of traditional 'linear' musical thought, and puts forward a 'distinction in musical architectures of categories between "outside-time", "in-time" and "temporal" ' (see pp.180ff), whereby the elements of a composition outside time are 'mapped' into time. Apart from his discussion of ancient Greek and Byzantine music Xenakis offered only one example of analysis by his methods: a bar and a half of Beethoven's 'Appassionata' Sonata subjected to 'vectorial algebra' – 'a working language which may permit both analyses of the works of the past and new constructions by setting up interacting functions of the components' (pp.163f).

A work that has much in common externally with Xenakis's treatise is Pierre Schaeffer's *Traité des objets musicaux* (1966). This is not a work on musical analysis in any conventional sense, but a dissertation on the sonorous material from which music is made: an attempt to present a full typology of that material, and to discover its general laws. Like Ansermet's phenomenological book referred to earlier, Schaeffer's treatise is underpinned with acoustics and with philosophy (Schaeffer, like Ansermet, brought special technical training to bear on his subject), and is centred on 'l'expérience musicale'; but it is much more tangible in its formulation of a 'solfège des objets musicaux'. This 'solfège' is in practice a system of classification by seven criteria: mass (one of the central notions in Schaeffer's thought), dynamic, harmonic timbre, melodic profile, mass profile, grain and inflection (*allure*).

Xenakis's and Schaeffer's treatises both represent the work of teams of experts: Xenakis's CEMAMu group of mathematicians, electronic engineers, psychologists and philosophers, Schaeffer's comparable team of technicians at the French radio. Both groups work in Paris, as does the even larger team of specialists being built up by Boulez in the Petit-Beaubourg plan: the institute of acoustical-musical researches (IRCAM) which was to have been part of the massive cultural centre on the Les Halles site in Paris. IRCAM is divided into four departments: instrumental and vocal, headed by Vinko Globokar; electronic and electro-acoustical, headed by Luciano Berio; synthetic and analytical, headed by Jean-Claude Risset (in close collaboration with CEMAMu); and of 'mobile unity', headed by Diego Masson. With these organizations the history of analysis perhaps reaches its most esoteric realms. To them should be added the work of analysts and composers at Princeton University; Benjamin Boretz's 'Meta-Variations' articles in the journal *Perspectives of New Music* (of which he is editor, and which was founded at Princeton in 1962 as a forum for musical theory) which do something comparable, by surveying the existing 'models' for music, examining the bases of these models, conceptual, perceptual and theoretical, and moving towards analyses of single works; and the work of Babbitt, Westergaard and others; and the computer work of Robison, Regener, Howe and others – all these activities represent the most highly sophisticated level of thought.

One other institutional group deserves mention within the esoteric realms of analysis: the Groupe de Recherches en Sémiologie Musicale at the University of Montreal, headed by Jean-Jacques Nattiez. The formation of this group, with its series of monographs in musical analysis, came after 15 years of development in the field of musical SEMIOLOGY, of which the backbone was a series of brilliant articles by the professor of linguistics at the University of Paris at Vincennes, Nicolas Ruwet. The most important of these articles was his proposition of an analytical method (1966) which took a simple melody (a 14th-century flagellant song), proceeded to segment it crudely and then to pass the segmentation through a sequence of transformational rules which in effect recognized similarities and equivalences. This yielded a phrase-structure analysis that was a syntax of the melody. The success of this exercise was not so much the quality of the finished analysis as the fact that it had been produced by an exact and verifiable procedure. The article triggered off a dispute among semiologists as to whether in such a mechanized procedure the analysis should begin with musical units of large proportions and work towards a microscopic finished analysis, or begin with a microscopic segmentation and gradually construct the larger formal units by the recognition of equivalents (i.e. phrases with differences of detail which a machine would treat as 'different' but which have the same function in the musical syntax). Ruwet had taken an intermediate course by starting with middle-size units, 'niveau (level) I', refining these by subdividing them ('niveau II'), and then reconstituting 'niveau I' before associating its units to reach a large-scale 'niveau 0'. (For Ruwet's method see also §III, 7 below, and fig.31.) The immediate dispute was won by the second school of thought, and Nattiez produced intensive analyses which proceed from small-scale segmentation (e.g. 'Densité 21.5', 1975; see §III, 7 below and figs.32–4). Other writers on this subject have been Eco (1968: an important general treatise), Arom (1969), Mâche (1970) and Lidov (1975); and semiology has been given generous space in the journal *Musique en jeu* (from 1970). (*See also* STRUCTURALISM AND MUSIC.)

Two further collections of essays on computer applications, published in 1970 (Brook, Lincoln), between them presented a useful picture of the range of activity and current state of development. In the second half of the 1960s important research was in progress, including that by Lindblom and Sundberg which continues the earliest computer applications but at a much higher level (1969). Their work combines concepts of linguistic syntax with probabilities, first analysing simple nursery tunes, producing 'tree-diagrams' (see, for example, fig.32 below) of their structures, and then verifying by synthesizing such melodies according to the syntax deduced.

Techniques of great sophistication were demonstrated by Norbert Böker-Heil at the International Musicological Society conferences in 1972 and 1977, analysing features, defining and differentiating styles. A project has been running since the 1960s at Princeton under the direction of Arthur Mendel and Lewis Lockwood which aims to define the style of Josquin's music. The programme has for example made studies of all the simultaneities (i.e. all the harmonic effects, no matter how incidental) and of suspension formations; it can also compare the variants of a single piece in several sources, determine the filiation between the sources and their comparative authority. In 1972 the journal *Interface* was founded as a specialist forum for computer application, and the journal *Computers and the Humanities* has included much musical material since its inception in 1966.

There has been great interest in style analysis. Richard Crocker produced *A History of Musical Style* (1966), and in 1970 Jan LaRue published his *Guidelines for Style Analysis*. In the latter, LaRue established a 'style-analytical routine' which examines each of the elements of a piece or style in turn at various 'magnifications' (large, middle and small dimensions), and then tries to understand the functions and relationships of those elements. For LaRue the four contributing elements of music are sound, harmony, melody and rhythm, and a fifth 'combining and resultant' element is 'growth'. Growth is subdivided into 'movement' and 'shape'. For the coordination between these elements LaRue introduced the concept of 'concinnity' (for which he quoted Webster: 'the skilful arrangement and mutual adjustment of parts'). LaRue's approach is commonsense and empirical: its use of acronym and simple symmetrical classification, its measurement by direct alternatives ('coloristic–tensional', 'active–stable' etc) and its single-level treatment of music (its three 'dimensions' owe virtually nothing to Schenker's structural layers) all lend it to direct practical analytical work. It controls and channels the analyst's personal judgment rather than by-passing it. It also makes a useful contribution to the graphic representation of musical style: a system of letter- and number-symbols with brackets (deriving from the parsing of language) maps what LaRue called 'shape' in a neat shorthand, and a device termed a 'timeline' enables the analyst to diagram the rhythmic and formal structure of a piece with indications of the fabric. (For LaRue's method see also §III, 6 below.)

In passing, the work of Ernő Lendvai on the music of Bartók should be mentioned, not so much for its theory of a tonal axis system as for its locating of proportion in musical structure. Lendvai sought to demonstrate the presence of the Golden Section and of the Fibonacci series (2, 3, 5, 8, 13, 21, 34 . . .) in Bartók's compositions, and this kind of numerological analysis has been carried out by other scholars, notably by Van Krevel on the masses of Obrecht and by Marianne Henze on the music of Ockeghem.

The work of Réti and Keller was furthered in the 1960s by two books of Alan Walker. In the first of these (1962) he argued for the validity of mirror forms, and introduced the Freudian elements of repression and preconscious association into the theory of motivic unity. Walker's second book, on musical criticism (1966), offers much analytical material, demonstrating above all the 'all-pervading background forces' that operate in musical creation, and furthering the Freudian theory. The book contains a useful exposition of 'historical background', a concept fundamental to Keller's work.

Schenkerian analytical work has continued in great strength, and an occasional publication under the title *Music Forum* was founded by Felix Salzer and William J. Mitchell in 1967 to present extended analyses of which some in each issue would use Schenkerian techniques. The series has particular value because of the attempts made in it to extend Schenker's techniques to music outside the domain for which it was created: to medieval and Renaissance music (Salzer and Bergquist, 1967) and to contemporary music. Among the non-Schenkerian material in *Music Forum* is Lockwood's masterly study of the autograph of Beethoven's Cello Sonata op.69, a rare blend of rigorous historical musicology and analytical method (1970).

There have been many independently minded analytical publications. One such is Donington's Jungian interpretation of Wagner's *Ring* (1963), another is Rosen's perceptive book on *The Classical Style* (1971); Lomax's study of 'cantometrics' (1968) offers a classificatory 'grid' not totally dissimilar to LaRue's, but adapted to the analysis of non-European song. (For Lomax's method see also §III, 6 below.)

Finally, there have been some useful surveys of analysis. Above all, Hermann Beck's *Methoden der Werkanalyse* (1974) is a remarkable systematic account of analytical method from early times to the early 1970s, though with some German-language bias. Diether de la Motte's *Musikalische Analyse* (1968) is a skilful demonstration of different approaches to analysis, each monitored with comments by Carl Dahlhaus. Beck also offers a large bibliography.

III. Analytical method

1. Introduction. 2. Fundamental structure (Schenker). 3. Thematic process (Réti) and functional analysis (Keller). 4. Formal analysis. 5. Phrase-structure analysis (Riemann). 6. Category and feature analysis. 7. Distributional analysis (Ruwet). 8. Information theory.

1. INTRODUCTION. A variety of classifications have been formulated for musical analysis as a whole. There is the widely accepted division into 'stylistic analysis' and 'analysis of the individual work' which was described at the beginning of this article as pragmatic but theoretically unnecessary. There is the threefold classification into 'constructional analysis', 'psychological analysis' and 'analysis of expression' put forward by Erpf in *MGG* (1949–51). This classification does not correspond exactly with, but is roughly equivalent to, Meyer's distinction (1967, pp.42f) between 'formal', 'kinetic-syntactic' and 'referential' views of musical signification. Meyer characterized the 'formal' view as placing central importance upon the 'relationships existing among the structural units that constitute a musical event', as looking for such things as 'symmetry, balance, . . . proportion', and as essentially 'somewhat static'; the

'kinetic-syntactic' as concerned with music as a 'dynamic process', with 'tension and repose, instability and stability, and ambiguity and clarity'; the 'referential' as depicting the 'concepts, actions, and passions of "real", extra-musical experience'. The first tends to centre on the musical structure itself (hence Erpf's 'constructional'), the second on the listener's response (hence 'psychological'), the third on the interaction of the two, on communication.

Roughly equivalent, but again not exactly homologous, is the classification (*see* AESTHETICS OF MUSIC, §3) into 'autonomous' and 'heteronomous' values of music, where the former designates music as to be 'understood and enjoyed for whatever it is', the latter as either 'a partial manifestation of some cosmic force or principle' or 'a means of communication among men'. Dahlhaus (*RiemannL 12*, 1967) made a fourfold distinction: 'formal analysis', which explains the structure of a work 'in terms of functions and relationships between sections and elements';' "energetic" interpretation', which deals in phases of movement or tension spans; and Gestalt analysis, which treats works as wholes; these three make up between them the field of analysis proper, which he distinguished from his fourth category, 'hermeneutics', the interpretation of music in terms of emotional states or external meanings. The first, second and fourth of these correspond broadly with the three categories of Erpf and Meyer, while the third deals with analyses based on the idea of organism. (*See also* FORM.)

The difficulty with these classifications is that their categories are not mutually exclusive. Thus, for example, Riemann is cited always as the prime example of a formal and constructional analyst, and yet Riemann's work rests on a fundamental idea of 'life force' (*Lebenskraft, lebendige Kraft, energisches Anstreben*) which flows through music in phases and is actualized in phrase contours, dynamic gradings, fluctuations of tempo and agogic stress. This idea is closer to the kinetic view of music; it suggests that Riemann's work belongs to two of Meyer's three categories.

A thorough-going typology of musical analysis would probably have to encompass several axes of classification. The analyst's view of the nature and function of music would certainly be one of these. But his approach to the actual substance of music would be a second; his method of operating on the music would be a third; and the medium for presentation of his findings would be a fourth. Then there might be subsidiary axes of, for example, the purpose for which the analysis was carried out, the context in which it was presented, the type of recipient for which it was designed.

Under approaches to the substance of music would be categories such as that a piece of music is (*a*) a 'structure', a closed network of relationships, more than the sum of its parts; (*b*) a concatenation of structural units; (*c*) a field of data in which patterns may be sought; (*d*) a linear process; and (*e*) a string of symbols or emotional values. These five categories embrace the approaches of formal analysts such as Leichtentritt and Tovey, structuralists and semiologists, Schenker, Kurth and Westphal, Riemann, hermeneutics, stylistic analysis and computational analysis, information theory analysis, proportion theory, Réti and functional analysis, and much else. The categories are still not exclusive. For example, (*a*) and (*c*) are not wholly incompatible in that

approach (*c*) may lead to approach (*a*). Then again, two approaches may co-exist at two different levels of construction: perhaps (*a*) or (*b*) for large-scale form and (*d*) for small-scale thematic development.

Under methods of operating would be categories such as (*a*) reduction technique; (*b*) comparison, and recognition of identity, similarity, or common property; (*c*) segmentation into structural units; (*d*) search for rules of syntax; (*e*) counting of features; and (*f*) reading-off and interpretation of expressive elements, imagery, symbolism.

Under media of presentation would be categories such as (*a*) annotated score or reduction or continuity line (see figs.28–9); (*b*) 'exploded' score, bringing related elements together (fig.31); (*c*) list, or 'lexicon' of musical units, probably accompanied by some kind of 'syntax' describing their deployment (see figs.33–4); (*d*) reduction graph, showing up hidden structural relationships (figs.21–2); (*e*) verbal description, using strict formal terminology, imaginative poetic metaphor, suggested programme or symbolic interpretation; (*f*) formulaic restatement of structure in terms of letter- and number-symbols (see §7 below); (*g*) graphic display: contour shapes (fig.18), diagrams (figs.15, 31, 32, 35), graphs (fig.14), visual symbols for specific musical elements (fig.13); (*h*) statistical tables or graphs; and (*i*) sounding score, on tape or disc, or for live performance (see §3 below). Such media can be used together within an analysis, and elements of two or more can be combined.

The types of analysis described below are arranged according to method of operation, beginning with reduction techniques and proceeding through comparative method to different types of segmentation, category measurement and feature counting, syntax formulation and probability measurement. For each type, some description of the underlying aesthetic approach is supplied, and also of the medium of presentation.

2. FUNDAMENTAL STRUCTURE (SCHENKER). Schenker's unique view of a musical composition is that works that are tonal and exhibit mastery are 'projections' in time of a single element: the tonic triad. The projection of this triad comprises two processes, its transformation into a two-part 'fundamental structure' called the URSATZ, and the 'elaboration' (*Auskomponierung*) of the structure by one technique or more of PROLONGATION. The *Ursatz* is made up of a linear descent to the root of the triad – the 'fundamental line' (*Urlinie*) – accompanied by an 'arpeggiation' in the bass (*Bassbrechung*), from the tonic to the dominant and back to the tonic. In the simplest form of

20. *From H. Schenker: 'Neue musikalische Theorien und Phantasien', iii (1935), 'Der freie Satz', p.1*

the *Ursatz* the linear descent begins with the 3rd of the tonic triad, and each note in it is accompanied by one chord in the bass (see fig.20). But this is a highly abstract notion, and in practice the elaboration begins with the structure in an already articulated form, representing the 'background' (*Hintergrund*) of the work. The number of possible forms of the background is theoretically infinite.

The elaboration of a basic contrapuntal design, as a way of viewing composition, emerged early in Schenker's development as a theorist (see §II, 5–6 above), and the method of analysis logically entailed by it was reduction. The concept of projection from a universal starting-point, which came to him only gradually during the last decade of his life, added a new factor to his analytical method: the tracing and highlighting of a structural 'norm', a kind of phasic process. The crucial idea in Schenker's theory is 'the perception of a musical work as a dynamic totality, not as a succession of moments or a juxtaposition of "formal" areas related or contrasted merely by the fact of thematic or harmonic similarity or dissimilarity' (Babbitt, *JAMS*, v, 1952, 262). Its reduction down to a small structural core which embraces the entire composition – the reverse of projection – is thus the crucial analytical operation.

Schenker controlled this reduction by the establishment of three structural layers (*Schichten: see* LAYER). Of these, the 'foreground' contained the elements of the contrapuntal design that are immediately perceptible, eliminating only ornamentation and note repetition from the surface of the work. The 'middleground', which might consist of more than one layer, presented the work without any of its surface detail, and so brought together structural elements that might be widely separated in the foreground. The 'background' presented the basic core, with as little as one melody note and harmonic function representing a theme or section of the work.

In order to present this Schenker devised a graphic notation whereby all the layers except the foreground were set out one above the other. Each of these layers was laid out on a single staff and made use of notational symbols (though with unconventional meaning), slurs, brackets and parentheses. Roman numerals were used for harmonic steps (from I to VII), capped arabic numerals for melodic degrees of the scale (1̂, 2̂, 3̂ etc), ordinary arabic numerals for bar numbers and bass figuring; words and auxiliary symbols were also used. The layers were aligned vertically, so that any element of the composition could be traced upwards to its place in the structural core.

Figs.21–2 show Schenker's analysis of Chopin's Etude in C minor op.10 no.12, as published in *Fünf Urlinie-Tafeln* (1932). The analysis is laid out on no fewer than five staves. The foreground is in this case presented separately, occupying far more lateral space than the other layers and thus not aligned with them (fig.22, showing only bars 1–18). Then three layers are presented in vertical alignment, of which layer 1 corresponds with the background and layers 2 and 3 both with the middleground. Above these the fundamental structure is set out, so that its transformation into background can be observed. The fundamental structure has in fact been broken into two parts: the first two elements of the fundamental structure are presented before the

statement is broken off, recommenced and concluded. This transformation is known as 'interruption', and the point of breaking off is marked by the word '(Teiler)' ('divider' – often indicated by two short vertical lines just above the staff, especially later, when *Teiler* tended to signify small-scale anticipatory interruption). At level 2 this interruption is multiplied to three occurrences.

In layers 2 and 3 of fig.21, void note-heads are used to indicate notes of relatively greater structural importance, black note-heads notes of relatively less. The void note-heads are linked together by large beams, pointing up the fundamental two-part movement of the composition. Black note-heads are linked together by slur marks, which pick out detailed melodic progressions, and these progressions are often labelled verbally (e.g. *Terzug abwärts*, 'conjunct progression down a 3rd', *Sext-Brechung-aufwärts*, 'upwards arpeggiation across a 6th'). They are also linked by beams to void notes. Dotted slur marks indicate not progression but recurrence of a structural note after the intervention of other notes (thus the recurrence of *d″* in the first half of layer 2). Black notes with tails (quaver symbols) are used to point up small-scale events of special interest (such as the auxiliary-note patterns *g′–f♯′–g′* and *c‴–b♮″–c‴* in layer 2).

Spatially the treatment of bars 1–10 is most striking. The fundamental structure first emerges in bar 11, and the preceding three melody notes are considered functionally as an 'ascent' (*Anstieg*) to the first melody note of this structure: they 'open the space' between the tonic note C and the first melodic structural note E♭. Moreover, in layer 3 the first ten bars are compressed into a melodic arpeggio of three notes (*b♮″–d‴–f‴*), the B♮ being interpreted also as a bass note and the harmony being labelled as auxiliary (*Nebennotenharmonie*). This is further compressed into two notes in layer 2, and disappears altogether at layer 1.

The harmonic indications at the bottom of fig.22 show that what is considered as I–IV–V at foreground level becomes entirely I at the middleground. Moreover, Schenker's analytical method completely rejects the conventional idea of modulation: key changes are viewed as harmonic elaborations of diatonic harmonies. Thus the moves to B♭ minor, D♯ minor and C♯ minor and F minor around bar 30 are seen ultimately as prolongations of C minor harmony.

Although Schenker's analytical method was designed, and can be used in its full form, only for tonal music, some of its principles and most of its techniques can be applied to non-tonal music. Salzer (1935, 1952) analysed medieval and Renaissance compositions and 20th-century works, and other applications can be found in *Music Forum*. The concepts of prolongation and directed motion are relevant, as are the graphic devices and the structural layers; but Schenker's norm, the *Ursatz,* has to be discarded.

3. THEMATIC PROCESS (RÉTI) AND FUNCTIONAL ANALYSIS (KELLER). Réti's view of music, overtly expressed in his writings, is as a linear compositional process: the composer starts not with a theoretical scheme but with a motif that has arisen in his mind, which he allows to grow by constant transformation – by transposition, inversion, reiteration, paraphrase, variation. Its growth is evolutionary. In time, he makes a significant modification to the motif or picks up a detail

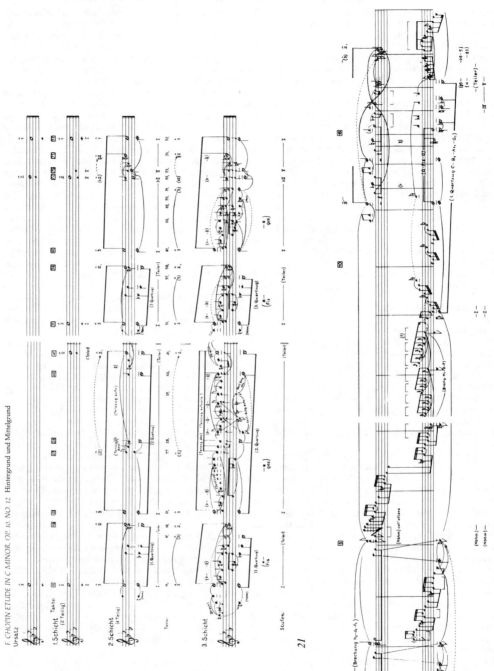

21–2. H. Schenker: 'Fünf Urlinie-Tafeln' (1932; from Eng. trans., 1969), 54–5, 56–7 (21 shows the fundamental structure; 22 shows the foreground 'graph')

from his elaborative material, and this becomes the centre of focus. A work is thus seen as 'a musical improvisation, a true thematic song around a few motifs'. The succession of motifs itself forms a grouping at a higher level, a 'thematic pattern', and this pattern recurs from movement to movement, becoming 'the skeleton of all themes in all movements; it determines the modulations, the figurations and the bridges, and above all, it provides an outline for the overall architecture' (1967, p.94).

Underlying the motivic material of a work are several 'prime cells'. These are small-scale melodic contours comprising two or three intervals and in origin non-rhythmic. Thus the two prime cells of the 'Pathétique' Sonata of Beethoven are as shown in fig.23. Réti arrived

(a piece, as with Schenker, that exhibits mastery) is of unity within diversity: of constant 'latent' presence of a single basic idea, articulated in time as a succession of 'manifest' contradictions.

The diversity of the foreground is meaningless unless it occurs against a background of unity. It is thus the job of analysis to discover the basic idea from which all the foreground material springs. However, this 'idea' has nothing apart from its singularity in common with Schenker's 'fundamental structure'; it is not a structural norm but a small-scale idea, a germ-cell, whose internal elements are reproduced at the surface in close proximity, and which recurs again and again. All the principal thematic material must be brought together, and by reduction the highest common factor within that material

**23–6. From R. Réti:
'Thematic Patterns in Sonatas
of Beethoven' (1967), 17, 19, 23, 91**

at these cells by reduction of all the thematic material of the work to its abiding common elements. He gave them separate functions by designating them 'prime cell' and 'concluding motif' respectively. Fig.24 shows where the cells are located in the opening bars of the first movement. The motifs (still without rhythm) which can be derived from these cells may be set out in a table: fig.25. An entire movement can then be set out, in non-rhythmic form with its melodic shapes grouped to reveal the motif forms, as a 'thematic song' (see fig.26, the slow movement).

Réti's view of music is considerably simpler than Keller's. It is a single process passing from beginning to end, almost like a chain except that some of the links overlap or occur side by side, and except also that certain large patterns recur. Keller's view of music is as a double process: a linear development – argument would be a better word, for Keller's view is that music communicates and that the listener 'understands' it – but one controlled by a single cell-like 'basic idea'. The singularity of the basic idea introduces an element of projection into the compositional process. Keller spoke of musical thought as two-dimensional: that is, as having 'background' and 'foreground'. The background proceeds by the law of identity, the foreground by the law of contradiction. Thus music has the quality, not open to logical thought, that something may both be and not be something. In context, Keller's view of a piece of music

must be isolated. To identify the pervasive, all-embracing idea is the first task of the analyst, but to account for the continuity of the foreground is the second. This involves not only explaining how each manifestation of the basic idea is derived from the original but also why that particular derivation occurs at that point. Analysis elucidates the functions of a piece as if it were a living organism.

As with Réti, the basic idea is usually a melodic outline, a succession of intervals out of time. Its manifestation is thus a rhythmicization. The foreground derivation may involve transposition, inversion, retrogression or 'interversion' (the reordering of the elements of the idea). Keller is, however, less open than is Réti to the criticism of neglecting rhythmic aspects of a structure, for his method recognizes fundamental rhythmic patterns, and thus augmentation and diminution are further types of derivation. Also very important in foreground continuity are the separation of two phrases latently in antecedent–consequent relationship – called 'postponed complementation' by Keller – and the reversing of the order of two such phrases.

Early presentation of functional analysis was by verbal text with music examples. Such examples showed thematic material with labelled motifs and derhythmicized reductions. Soon, however, Keller stated the principle that 'music about music is immeasurably more objective than words about music, because music is absolutely concrete' (*MR*, xix, 1958, 200). He devised a method that involved composing a score, for the same forces as the work under analysis, in which passages of the original are interspersed with aural demonstrations of the links between themes. He claimed for this method the advantages that it avoids the transition between musical and verbal thought, that the through-composition of the analytical score leads along purely musical lines, and that the subjectiveness of verbal description is eliminated. (Unfortunately it has the disadvantage that since the controversial broadcasts in the late 1950s Keller's analytical scores have been completely unavailable.) As to the last of these, a further distinction between the work of Réti and that of Keller is that Réti regarded what he produced not (in the words of his widow) as 'graven in stone, but . . . as creative insights, . . . by which the listener . . . might be stimulated to new discoveries' (1967, p.8), whereas Keller regarded his best analytical work as incapable of being improved. For him, where two functional analyses ('FAs', as he abbreviated them) differ, 'one will be objectively better' (1958, p.199). (For the history of functional analysis see also §II, 7–8 above.)

4. FORMAL ANALYSIS. In §I, 2 above, the three basic form-building processes were proposed as 'recurrence', 'contrast' and 'variation', expressible as *AA*, *AB* and *AA'*. Formal analysis is concerned with the recognition of these three processes and the description of works in terms of them.

During the late 18th century and the 19th, music theorists defined certain structural patterns – not genres or species such as concerto or minuet, but more widely applicable processes of formal construction common to many genres and species, and now often called formal models (see §II, 2–3 above). These are in turn reducible to two fundamental patterns: *AB* and *ABA*, subsumed in German terminology under the single term *Liedform* (first proposed by A. B. Marx, 1837–47) in its 'two-part' (*zweiteiliges*) and 'three-part' (*dreiteiliges*) form, and distinguished in English terminology as BINARY FORM and TERNARY FORM. Broadly speaking, these terms refer to small-scale forms; they apply most directly to instrumental dance movements of the 17th and 18th centuries, and rely on the concept of regular phrase structure with the eight-bar period as the principal unit of construction. Larger-scale formal models are regarded as extensions of one or other of the two fundamental patterns: thus SONATA FORM is the extension of the binary pattern, and RONDO of the ternary.

There is however an additional distinction to be made between two basic processes of extension: that of a succession of formal units, and that of development. The former (in German, *Reihungsform* or *plastische Form*) relies on proportion and symmetry, and is architectural in nature; the latter (*Entwicklungsform* or *logische Form*) on continuity and growth. The rondo, *ABACADA*, extends ternary form by succession; sonata form extends binary form by development. And the two processes are both brought into operation in the so-called sonata rondo: *ABACAB'A*.

There is a further process by which larger forms may be created out of one of the two basic patterns: by the operating of one or both patterns at more than one level of structure (*Potenzierung*, 'exponentiating'). By this means, such structures as *A* (*aba*)–*B* (*cdc*)–*A* (*aba*) are produced. Related to this is the concept of 'cyclic form', whereby movements in recognizable forms are grouped together to form larger units such as the suite and the sonata. (For Lorenz's use of *Potenzierung* see §II, 6 above.)

Manuals of formal analysis vary in the extent to which they see the totality of musical formations, from the Middle Ages onwards and for all vocal and instrumental media, as governed by these fundamental patterns. Many manuals now have separate descriptions of 'the contrapuntal forms' and allow a category of 'free forms'. Nonetheless, the underlying idea of formal analysis is that of the 'model', against which all compositions are set and compared and measured in terms of their conformity to or 'deviation' from the norm. It was against this *a priori* concept that Tovey rebelled so vociferously (1935–9, 1948).

Quite apart from the universality of the basic models, there are many difficulties in determining criteria for their recognition. For some analysts, identity is or nonidentity is determined by thematic character; for others, by key scheme; for others, by length of units. Thus, for Dahlhaus (*RiemannL 12*, 1967), the prime conditions of the two-part *Liedform* |: *A* :||: *B* :| are, first, that the first part ends on a half-close in the tonic or a full-close in a related key, and, second, that the parts are melodically different (or related |: *AX*:||: *AY*:| or |: *AX*:||: *BX*:|). For Scholes (*Oxford Companion to Music*, 'Form') binary form rests on the key scheme |: tonic–dominant (or relative major) :||: dominant (or relative major)–tonic :|, and the absence of 'strong contrast' in thematic material. For Prout, key scheme is not really a determinant at all for binary form, for he allowed |: tonic–tonic: ||: remote key–tonic:|; nor is thematic relationship, for he allowed *AA'BA''* as well as *ABCB*. The basic determinant for Prout is that the form shall constitute 'two complete sentences'. Thus the form |: *A*:||: *BA*:|, which for Dahlhaus is three-part *Liedform*, is for Prout binary form unless the first part is itself a complete binary form, self-contained and rounded.

Tovey (see §II, 6 above) felt a basic antagonism towards the formal analytical approach, and yet his method, which represents the tradition of analysis and descriptive criticism in Britain as a whole, accepted the standard forms and framed its analyses in terms of them. Terms such as 'transition', 'development', 'return', 'recapitulation', 'episode', 'coda' and 'codetta' are part of his normal vocabulary. He disliked 'first subject' and 'second subject' because 'there is no prescribed number of subjects to a movement in sonata form', and substituted 'group' for 'subject', 'which has the merit of not necessarily implying themes at all' (1935, p.2). Thus his analyses of sonata form movements (in 1948) are laid out under subheadings 'First Group', 'Transition', 'Second Group', 'Development' and 'Recapitulation'. Under each subheading there appear bar numbers at the left-hand side of the page, with verbal commentary and music examples (the themes and 'figures' being labelled with letter-symbols). Hence Tovey called his method 'bar-by-bar', and it was the successive aspect of his description that was most important to him, since he saw analysis as tracing the same process in time that the 'naïve listener' experienced.

Tovey's verbal commentary contains technical information on phrase structure ('Eight-bar theme (A); 2 + 2 in sequence, followed by 1 + 1 in sequence'), thematic identity ('New theme (B) rhythmically allied to (a) + (b) [figures of (A)]'), key structure and formal process ('interlocking thrice in self-repetition, and the third time augmenting its last notes to two full bars'). But it also contains metaphor. Thus the scherzo of Beethoven's Fifth Symphony seems 'finished, exhausted, played out' – because the main section that is 'dark, mysterious, and, in part, fierce' has 'suddenly collapsed' after which a trio 'dies away' and the return of the scherzo is 'one of the ghostliest things ever written' (*Beethoven*, 1945, pp.16f). What he did was to 'describe the technical means and the aesthetic effect and invite the reader to contemplate, if not their logical or necessary connection, at all events their simultaneity and likely association' (Kerman, 1975–6, p.798). His method is thus partly hermeneutic, and he achieved it by animation of the orchestra ('A piccolo, a contra-fagotto and a triangle contribute with grotesque poetic aptness') or animation of the work itself ('When this has died wistfully away on an inconclusive chord, the original theme sternly reappears in the windband'), or by treating the commentary as a guided tour ('We are now in the full swing of a perfectly regular recapitulation'). The style is almost that of Schumann at times, and it achieves a humanity, an accessibility and yet a formality which makes it an excellent tool for introducing a listener to a work he is about to hear or a performer to his subject of study.

5. PHRASE-STRUCTURE ANALYSIS (RIEMANN). Riemann's theory of phrase structure rests on the postulate that the pattern weak–strong is the 'sole basis for all musical construction' (1895–1901, i, 132). This fundamental unit is termed the *Motiv*. It is fundamental because it represents a single unit of energy passing from growth to decay by way of a central stress point. It is thus a dynamic trace, a flux, and is far removed from the traditional notion of 'beats' in a 'bar', each beat being separate and having its own 'weight'.

Where two such *Motiv* units occur in succession they form the two elements of a *Motiv* at the next level of structure: the first forming the growth phase, the second the stress point and decay phase. And in turn, two such larger *Motiv* units form a still higher-level *Motiv*, and so on in a hierarchy. The result is a kind of grid, made up of equal units of energy: a grid that is conceptual in the sense that very few pieces of music are made up of equal-length phrases and unvarying tempos, and yet is not as imaginary as, say, the grid of a map because the lines of this grid bear an intrinsic relationship to the topography of the music they concern (but only to the topography: *Motiv* has no connotation of thematic identity in Riemann's theory).

Given this theory, the process of analysis is one of locating the lines of the grid behind the articulated surface of a piece or passage of music. A piece that was totally slavishly aligned to its grid would be made of regular modules, each module comprising eight bars of 2/4 or 3/4 and pairing off into 16-bar, 32-bar, 64-bar and so forth units at higher levels. The eight-bar module is shown for 2/4 in fig.27 (*Zweitaktgruppe* is Riemann's term for a pair of *Motiv* units in weak–strong relationship; *Halbsatz* for a four-bar unit – either antecedent or consequent; *Periode* for an eight-bar module: 1895–1901, i, 163). But in practice music adopts certain 'symmetry-disturbing processes', some of which stretch or compress the grid, others of which temporarily upset the internal relationships without affecting the regularity of the grid itself. Chief among these processes are:

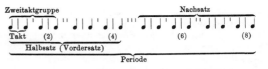

27. From H. Riemann: 'Präludien und Studien' (1895–1901), i, 163

(*a*) Elision: the suppression of the growth phase of a unit (the first element of a *Motiv*, the first *Motiv* of a two-bar group, the first two-bar group of a four-bar half-phrase etc), thus yielding a strong–weak–strong pattern. An example is the minuet of Mozart's G minor String Quintet: fig.28 (1900, 8/1912, p.84).

(*b*) Cadential repetition: restatement of the stress point and decay phase of a unit at any level of structure. A classic example is the introduction to Schubert's Symphony no.9: fig.29 (ibid, p.80). This example contains double repetition, and the doubling of values on the second restatement.

(*c*) Dovetailing: a transfer of function whereby a final stressed unit is converted into an initial unstressed one (i.e. decay is converted into growth phase, for example when the eighth bar of a period becomes the first of a new period.

28–9. From H. Riemann: 'Handbuch der Phrasierung' (1912), 84–5, 80

(*d*) General upbeat: a large-scale upbeat, often occupying only the space of the upbeat to a *Motiv* but functioning as the upbeat to a larger formal unit. (For an example, see GENERALAUFTAKT.)

(*e*) Appended *Motiv*: a subsidiary phrase unit placed immediately after the strong beat of a main phrase unit. It serves to generate a second strong beat where a weak beat would normally occur. (For an example, *see* ANSCHLUSSMOTIV.)

The first three of these processes alter the temporal distance between points on the grid, the last two may alter the impression of such distance but do not necessarily alter the number of intervening beats.

Riemann's own analyses take one of two forms: books of analyses (those of Bach's '48', 1890, and Beethoven's String Quartets, 1903, and Piano Sonatas, 1918–19), or 'phrase-structure editions' (of sonatas of Mozart, Beethoven and Haydn). The latter are editions which use special phrase-marks and signs, as shown in Table 1, and number the bar-functions beneath the staff. The former adopt as their method of presentation the 'continuity line': a single staff which shows all the main thematic material, accompanied by the special signs and numbering used in the editions, and employing also Riemann's system of harmonic symbols (fully explained in his *Handbuch des Generalbass-Spiels*, 4/1917, pp.12ff; for his harmonic theory in general *see* HARMONY, §4.) These books also use conventional terminology when dealing with thematic material and aim at fully rounded 'technical and aesthetic analyses of pieces of music'. Yet it is in his theory of phrase structure, much disputed and now somewhat neglected, that Riemann had most to offer: in the field of metre and rhythm, where analysis has been most deficient, offering a set of criteria for segmentation and at the same time a means of defining the functions of large time spans.

TABLE 1

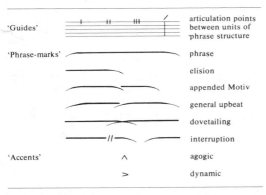

'Guides'		articulation points between units of phrase structure
'Phrase-marks'		phrase
		elision
		appended Motiv
		general upbeat
		dovetailing
		interruption
'Accents'	∧	agogic
	>	dynamic

6. CATEGORY AND FEATURE ANALYSIS. These two types of analysis both take a wider view of musical material than any of the types so far described. In both, structure is only one of the aspects brought under examination. Consequently they are both particularly useful as methods for stylistic analysis, where construction and cohesion are but two of the terms of reference, along with techniques of instrumentation and vocal writing, usages of consonance and dissonance, of metre and rhythm, of texture and such like, which characterize a style or repertory. Usable though both types are for analysis of the single work, they tend to analyse that work synchronically (i.e. out of the continuum of time), treating it as a style rather than as a piece, usually with reference to other pieces in the same style or comparable styles, and present their findings in non-temporal form as tables, statistics, graphs or summarized descriptions.

Category analysis starts with the recognition that music is too complex a phenomenon to be comprehended without some way of breaking down its material into elements – not so much its temporal elements (phrase, motif etc), though these may be part of the 'breaking-down' process, as those facets that are constantly present: the 'parameters'. What the analyst requires is, in LaRue's words, 'a set of categories that are satisfactorily distinct, yet without undue branching and proliferation' (1970, p.10). Each category is then given a scale of measurement, and it is this measuring that is the critical operation in the analysis.

Two fully worked-out systems will serve to illustrate the type: that by LaRue (1970) for style in Western Classical music (designed with the 18th-century instrumental repertory in mind) and that by Lomax (1968) for singing style (hence its name, CANTO-METRICS) in the folk music of world cultures.

In abstract, category analysis establishes a two-dimensional grid, a 'matrix', one dimension comprising categories, the other the scale of measurement. Lomax's 'behavioral grid' is made up of 37 categories and 13 degrees. It operates on a single level. It ultimately locates any singing style somewhere along a spectrum of style whose extremes are 'highly individualized and group-dominating performance' and 'highly cohesive, group-involving performance' (p.16). It can easily be coded for comparative analysis by computer, and the computer will present its results in a graph (pp.75ff). (*See* COMPUTERS AND MUSIC, §11.)

LaRue's system has only five categories (its 'four Contributing Elements' and 'fifth Combining Element') and three degrees (the Aristotelian 'Rule of Three': two extremes and a mean). In practice, however, the system contains hierarchies and is consequently much more complex to operate. The five categories are: Sound, Harmony, Melody, Rhythm, Growth (acronymically known as 'SHMRG'). But sound is subdivided into 'Timbre', 'Dynamics', 'Texture and Fabric'; harmony into 'Color' and 'Tension'; melody into 'Range', 'Motion', 'Patterns' and so on. Each subcategory has its own set of degrees of measurement: thus melodic patterns are measured as Rising, Falling, Level, Waveform, Sawtooth or Undulating (abbreviated R, F, L, W, S or U); and the number of degrees varies from subcategory to subcategory (which is true also of Lomax's degrees, but the variation is built into the system). Moreover, each category is considered at each of three levels of structure (LaRue's 'Dimensions'): Large, Middle, Small. The resultant analytical grid is really three-dimensional, with categories and subcategories as one dimension, the three levels of structure as the second, and the variable degrees of measurement as the third. However, a finished analysis is displayed as a table, with categories as rows and dimensions as columns: each box in the table contains (if anything, i.e. if relevant) a verbal description that does not limit itself to quantification but also supplies information about context and function.

LaRue appended to his analytical system a method of extracting the essential and relevant information from analyses of individual works so that comparative analysis may be performed without drowning in data. It comprises three headings: 'Sources of Shape' (subdivided into articulation, recurrence/development/response/contrast, connection/correlation/concinnity, and conventional forms), 'Sources of Movement' (subdivided into states of change, stability/local activity/directional motion, and types of change, structural/ornamental), and 'Conventional and Innovative Features' (which isolates distinctive features from the stylistic background: LaRue stressed the need for large sampling of any given repertory as a frame of reference from judging distinctiveness).

Feature analysis involves taking not variables (categories) into which values (measurements) are placed, but invariables (features, such as a particular interval or chord or rhythmic unit or dynamic level) to which frequencies of occurrence within a given passage or piece or repertory are assigned after a counting operation. Such invariable features will tend to be small and indivisible, but can be larger units or 'patterns'. This method is of particular application in stylistic analysis, where counts for individual pieces are being compared and correlated for 'affinity'. It is one that views music as a universe of features, and any one style as a clustering of certain of those features in differing frequencies; style is seen as statistical in nature.

Crane and Fiehler, for example (in Lincoln, 1970, chap.15), expound a method (derived from R. Sokal and P. H. A. Sneath: *Principles of Numerical Taxonomy*, 1963) by which affinity can be calculated so as to produce three classes: coefficients of association, coefficients of correlation and coefficients of distance. The last conceives a work's style as a unique point in multidimensional Euclidean space. As Crane and Fiehler say, the result of any of these affinity calculations will be a 'matrix like a mileage-between-cities table, whose columns and rows are headed by the identifications of each work. At the intersection of row i and column j will be entered the affinity between works i and j'. They go on to describe ways in which the clustering of works, the 'mutual relations among a set of works' may be determined and graphically expressed. Fig.30 shows a 'dendrogram' displaying the clustering of 20 chansons from the 15th century: each horizontal line shows the coefficient of distance at which the two works or clusters below it join; the lower the coefficient the greater the affinity.

Mention has already been made of the notion of 'context', in connection with LaRue's category analysis. 'Context-sensitivity' has direct relevance to feature analysis. The statement, about a piece of music, that 'The rising 4th followed by falling minor 3rd occurs 247 times' takes on greater significance when completed by 'with conjunct motion preceding it in all but 30 cases and following it in all cases'; and even more if information about the points in the metrical structure at which the pattern begins and about the three note values involved can be included.

Context-sensitivity (a term used in linguistics) may lead to another concept with wide application outside music: the 'equivalence-class'. Where two (objectively distinct) features have an identical context or set of possible contexts for a given piece or repertory, they may be described as 'functionally equivalent'. The set of all such features that have their contexts exactly in common constitutes an equivalence-class. Context-sensitivity and equivalence are, however, concepts not of feature analysis as such but of syntactical analysis, which deals with the ways in which elements combine and the rules by which they may or may not do so. This type of analysis is considered in the next section.

7. DISTRIBUTIONAL ANALYSIS (RUWET). Distributional analysis views music as a stream of sounding elements governed by rules of 'distribution': that is, of ways in which the elements associate with or complement or mutually exclude each other. Its aim is to state these rules as 'adequately' as possible for any given passage of music, or work or group of works; to formulate, in other words, a syntax for the music. Its method is to break the stream of music into component units (or 'unities' – i.e. units that either cannot be further subdivided or do not need to be because their sub-units never occur independently). It does this by comparing all possible units with all other possible units; when an identity is found, the contexts of the two occurrences are examined for identity. From this comparative analysis emerges a list of all 'distinctive units', an account of the distribution of each, and a grouping into units distributed in identical or related ways; and ultimately a restatement of the stream of music in terms of these units and the laws that govern them.

This method differs from traditional formal analysis in recognizing no standard formal templates. Every analysis thus starts from first principles, striving to avoid preconceptions and to achieve scientific objectivity. The method is used by musical semiologists (such as Ruwet, Nattiez, Lidov and Mâche) and syntactical analysts (such as Forte, Boretz, Sellek and Bakeman). It is carried further by those who, under the linguistic influence of Chomsky, attempt to test their syntax by using it to generate musical utterances in the same style (Lindblom and Sundberg, Laske).

The restatement of the stream of music in terms of units and laws usually employs simple labels made of letters and numbers. A typical example is the labelling system of Ruwet (1966). Units at the middle level of structure that Ruwet called 'niveau I', which repeat and are thus defined, are allocated capital letters from the

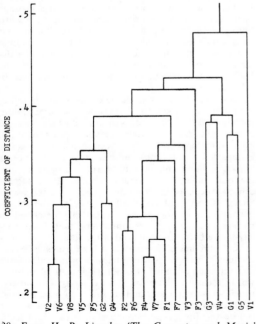

30. *From H. B. Lincoln: 'The Computer and Music'* (1970), 217

31. From N. Ruwet: 'Méthodes d'analyse en musicologie', RBM, xx (1966), 81

beginning of the alphabet; non-repeating material is then allocated capital letters from the end of the alphabet. These produce a string of symbols such as A + B + A + X + B + Y. Units at the smallest level of structure, Ruwet's 'niveau II', are assigned lower-case italic letters, the late letters of the alphabet again being allocated to non-repeating units. The segmentation of middle-level units may reveal relationships between such units. Thus, if A = $a + b$ and X = $a + c$, then it may be possible to rewrite A + X as A + A'. Middle-level units may also be aggregated into high-level units, Ruwet's 'niveau 0', and these latter are assigned arabic numerals in parentheses. Thus A + X + A + Y may become (1).

Using this system of labelling and of rewriting, Ruwet (1972) analysed a troubadour song, *Molt me mervoil* by Guiot de Provins (see fig.31). His initial segmentation at level I produced X (bars 1–4) + B (bars 1–5) + Y (bars 9–28) + B (bars 29–32). On grounds of phrase length, X is then rewritten as A, and Y as C + D + E + F + G. But at level II, C = $z + a$ and G = $z' + a'$, so that G is rewritten as C'. The result so far is: A + B + C + D + E + F + C' + B. Level II now comes into operation:

A = $x + a$	B = $y + b$
C = $z + a$	D = $w + b$
E = $v + a''$	F = ?
C' = $z' + a'$	B = $y + b$

Level 0 now also comes into operation, since by the laws of 'equivalence' the pairs of segments (A + B), (C + D) and (C' + B) are seen as 'manifestations of the same abstract structure', which can be set out as:

$$\left\{ \begin{matrix} x \\ z \end{matrix} \right\} \quad a \qquad \left\{ \begin{matrix} y \\ w \end{matrix} \right\} \quad b$$

This formula indicates that x and z are distributionally interchangeable and that the same applies to y and w. Each pair forms an 'equivalence-class', as discussed in §6 above. The pair (E + F) is more problematic, but Ruwet suggested that E ($v + a''$) is equivalent to the first part of the formula, and F externally (but not internally) equivalent to the latter part. Ruwet did not rewrite the string of symbols, but it would presumably appear as (1) + (1) + (1) + (1), or (1) + (1) + (1)' + (1), or (1) + (1) + (2) + (1), depending upon how one viewed the pair (E + F).

This kind of comparative analysis can be carried out very efficiently by computer, especially when using a computer language designed for 'pattern matching' (a process whereby a string of characters is scanned to see

whether a second string of characters is contained within it) such as SNOBOL or SPITBOL. The highly sophisticated work of Forte (especially 1966) shows the computer used in this way to 'parse' and rewrite the structure of music by Webern.

Nattiez has developed other modes of presentation, including the tree-structure diagram (borrowed from linguistics; see fig.32: '*Densité 21°5*', 1975, p.311, of Brahms's Intermezzo op.119 no.3), the lexicon of items (see fig.33: ibid, p.346, of rhythmic elements in Debussy's *Syrinx*) and the table of distributions (see fig.34: ibid, p.296, of Varèse's *Intégrales*).

See also Computers and music, §9, and Ethnomusicology, §3.

8. INFORMATION THEORY. Information-theory analysis views music as a linear process. The process is governed by a syntax, but the syntax is stated in terms of the probability that any one element will occur next in the line rather than in terms of grammatical laws. Music is treated by analogy with the transmission of a message from sender to receiver, but neither that nor the word 'information' should give the impression that the method deals with meaning and communication in the hermeneutic sense. It deals exclusively with the arousal, satisfaction or frustration of expectation in the receiver. The history of its application to music has been sketched in §II, 7 above.

A message is a chain of discrete sense-units. In music these units are taken to be 'events' in a composition: usually isolated notes, chords or simultaneities. Any one event in the chain arouses a prediction of its following event. If the prediction is confirmed then no information is imparted; if it is 'non-confirmed' then information is imparted. But events in music form into patterns, and the total amount of information contained in a pattern can be calculated by a formula and expressed as an 'index'. Coons and Kraehenbuehl (1958) offered two indices, one of articulateness which they described as measuring 'how neatly the conditions of "unity" and "variety" have been arranged so that the force of neither is dulled', and one of hierarchy, which measures 'how successfully a "variety" of events has been arranged to leave an impression of "unit" ' (p.150). Their method, in other words, measures the phenomena of unity and variety, which are so important in analysis, in an objective and tangible way rather than a subjective and vague way. It can do this for a single structure, or it can do it for a work with respect to the known terms of reference of that work's style.

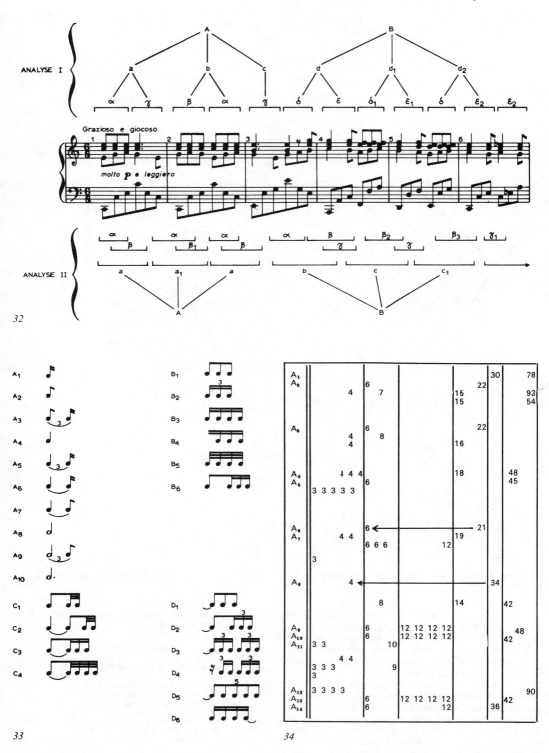

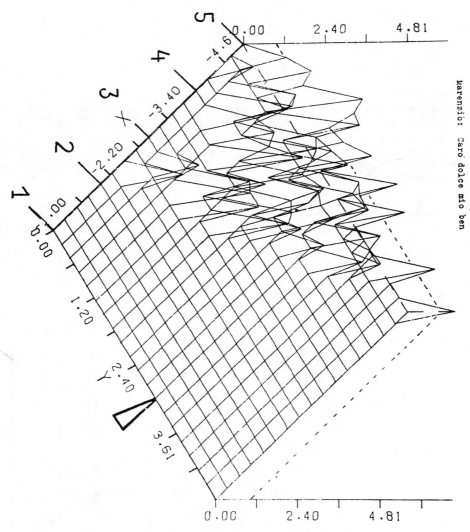

35. *From N. Böker-Heil: 'Musikalische Stilanalyse und Computer: einige grundsätzliche Erwägungen', IMSCR, xi Copenhagen 1972, i, 120*

Artistic 'communication' is, however, different in nature from other forms of communication in that it is not primarily concerned with transmitting maximum information: it is concerned rather with transmitting structure. It therefore requires a certain degree of what information theory calls 'redundancy'.

Information theory analysis generally presents its findings in statistical tables, which can be converted into graphs for easier understanding. Computers lend themselves naturally to the complex calculations which are involved in any but the simplest analysis of this type; and they in turn can produce graphic representations directly by means of a plotter, such as the three-dimensional representations of style in madrigals by

Palestrina, Rore and Marenzio produced by Böker-Heil (1972, pp.117ff; see fig.35).

BIBLIOGRAPHY

G. Dressler: *Praecepta musicae poeticae* (1563–4); ed. B. Engelke: *Geschichte-Blätter für Stadt und Land Magdeburg*, xlix–1 (1914–15), 213–50
P. Pontio: *Ragionamento di musica* (Parma, 1588)
J. Burmeister: *Hypomnematum musicae* (Rostock, 1599)
——: *Musica autoschediastike* (Rostock, 1601)
——: *Musica poetica* (Rostock, 1606/R1955)
J. Lippius: *Synopsis musicae novae* (Strasbourg, 1612)
P. Cerone: *El melopeo y maestro* (Naples, 1613/R)
M. Praetorius: *Syntagma musicum*, iii (Wolfenbüttel, 1618, 2/1619/R1958)
J. A. Scheibe: *Der critische Musikus* (Hamburg, 1737–40, 2/1745)
J. Mattheson: *Der vollkommene Capellmeister* (Hamburg, 1739/R1954)

J. Riepel: *Anfangsgründe zur musikalischen Setzkunst* (Regensburg and elsewhere, 1752–68)

J. G. Sulzer: *Allgemeine Theorie der schönen Künste* (Leipzig, 1771–4) [musical articles by Sulzer, Kirnberger and Schulz]

H. C. Koch: *Versuch einer Anleitung zur Composition* (Leipzig and Rudolstadt, 1782–93/R1969)

A. Reicha: *Practische Beispiele: ein Beitrag zur Geistescultur des Tonsetzers* (Vienna, 1803)

J.-J. de Momigny: *Cours complet d'harmonie et de composition* (Paris, 1803–6)

J. F. Herbart: *Psychologische Bemerkungen zur Tonlehre* (Königsberg, 1811)

A. Reicha: *Traité de mélodie* (Paris, 1814, 2/1832)

——: *Cours de composition musicale* (Paris, 1816)

G. Weber: *Versuch einer geordneten Theorie der Tonsetzkunst* (Mainz, 1817–21, 3/1830–32)

A. Reicha: *Traité de haute composition musicale* (Paris, 1824–6)

J. B. Logier: *System der Musik-Wissenschaft und der praktischen Komposition* (Berlin, 1827; Eng. trans., 1827/R1976 as *A System of the Science of Music and Practical Composition*)

J. B. H. Birnbach: *Der vollkommene Komponist* (Berlin, 1832–46)

A. B. Marx: *Die Lehre von der musikalischen Komposition, praktisch-theoretisch*, i (Leipzig, 1837, rev. 9/1887, 10/1903; Eng. trans., 1852); ii: *Die freie Komposition* (Leipzig, 1837, rev. 7/1890); iii (Leipzig, 1845, 5/1879); iv (Leipzig, 1847, rev. 5/1888; Eng. trans., 1910)

——: *Die alte Musiklehre im Streit mit unserer Zeit* (Leipzig, 1841)

J. C. Lobe: *Compositionslehre* (Weimar, 1844)

C. Czerny: *School of Practical Composition* (London, 1849; Ger. orig., ?1849–50)

J. C. Lobe: *Lehrbuch der musikalischen Komposition* (Leipzig, 1850–67)

E. F. E. Richter: *Die Grundzüge der musikalischen Formen und ihre Analyse* (Leipzig, 1852)

M. Hauptmann: *Die Natur der Harmonik und der Metrik zur Theorie der Musik* (Leipzig, 1853, 2/1873; Eng. trans., 1888)

S. Sechter: *Die Grundsätze der musikalischen Composition* (Leipzig, 1853–4)

E. Hanslick: *Vom Musikalisch-Schönen* (Leipzig, 1854, 7/1885; Eng. trans., 1957 as *The Beautiful in Music*)

A. B. Marx: *Ludwig van Beethoven: Leben und Schaffen* (Berlin, 1859)

H. Riemann: *Über das musikalische Hören* (diss., U. of Göttingen, 1873; Leipzig, 1874; also pubd Leipzig, 1873 as *Musikalische Logik*)

M. Lussy: *Traité de l'expression musicale* (Paris, 1874, 8/1904; Eng. trans., 1885)

H. von Wolzogen: *Thematischer Leitfaden durch die Musik zu Richard Wagners Festspiel 'Der Ring des Nibelungen'* (Leipzig, 1876)

O. Hostinský: *Das Musikalisch-Schöne und das Gesamtkunstwerk vom Standpunkte der formalen Ästhetik* (Leipzig, 1877)

H. Riemann: *Musikalische Syntaxis* (Leipzig, 1877/R1971)

H. von Wolzogen: *Thematischer Leitfaden durch die Musik von Richard Wagners Tristan* (Leipzig, 1880)

C. Mayrberger: 'Die Harmonik Richard Wagners an den Leitmotiven des Vorspiels zu Tristan und Isolde erläutert', *Bayreuther Blätter*, iv (1881), 169

H. von Wolzogen: *Thematischer Leitfaden durch die Musik von Richard Wagners Parsifal* (Leipzig, 1882)

E. von Hagen: *Beiträge zur Einsicht in das Wesen der Wagnerschen Kunst: Gesammelte Aufsätze* (Berlin, 1883)

H. Riemann: *Der Ausdruck in der Musik*, Musikalischer Vorträge, 1 (Leipzig, 1883)

S. Jadassohn: *Musikalische Kompositions-Lehre* (Leipzig, 1883–9)

H. Riemann: *Musikalische Dynamik und Agogik: Lehrbuch der musikalischen Phrasierung* (Hamburg and St Petersburg, 1884)

G. Adler: 'Umfang, Methode und Ziel der Musikwissenschaft', *VMw*, i (1885), 5

T. Helm: *Beethovens Streichquartette: Versuch einer technischen Analyse dieser Werke im Zusammenhange mit ihrem geistigen Gehalt* (Leipzig, 1885, 2/1910)

G. Adler: Die Wiederholung und Nachahmung in der Mehrstimmigkeit', *VMw*, ii (1886), 271

A. J. Goodrich: *Complete Musical Analysis* (Cincinnati, 1887)

H. Kretzschmar: *Führer durch den Konzertsaal*, i (Leipzig, 1887, 7/1932); ii (Leipzig, 1888, 5/1921); iii (Leipzig, 1890, 5/1939)

H. Riemann: *Systematische Modulationslehre als Grundlage der musikalischen Formenlehre* (Hamburg, 1887)

J. Schalk: 'Das Gesetz der Tonalität', *Bayreuther Blätter*, xi (1888), 192, 381; xii (1889), 191; xiii (1890), 65

H. Riemann: *Katechismus der Kompositionslehre (Musikalische Formenlehre)* (Leipzig, 1889, 3/1905 as *Grundriss der Kompositionslehre*; Eng. trans., n.d.)

——: *Handbuch der Fugen-Komposition (Analyse von J. S. Bachs 'Wohltemperiertem Klavier' und 'Kunst der Fuge')* (Leipzig, 1890, 2/1906; Eng. trans., 1925 as *Analysis of J. S. Bach's Wohltemperirtes Clavier (48 Preludes and Fugues)*)

——: *Katechismus der Phrasierung* (Leipzig, 1890)

F. Koegel: 'Der Bau des Tristandramas', *Bayreuther Blätter*, xv (1892), 257

P. Goetschius: *Lessons in Music Form: a Manual of Analysis* (New York, 1893/R1970)

W. H. Hadow: *Studies in Modern Music* (London, 1893–5)

E. Prout: *Musical Form* (London, 1893–7/R1971)

A. Ernst: 'Die Uebereinstimmung der einzelnen Szenen in den Dramen Wagners', *Bayreuther Blätter*, xvii (1894), 234

P. Goetschius: *Models of the Principal Musical Forms* (Boston, Mass., 1895)

E. Prout: *Applied Forms* (London, 1895)

H. Riemann: *Präludien und Studien: Gesammelte Aufsätze zur Ästhetik, Theorie und Geschichte der Musik* (Leipzig, 1895–1901)

C. von Ehrenfels: 'Die musikalische Architektonik', *Bayreuther Blätter*, xix (1896), 257

G. Grove: *Beethoven and his Nine Symphonies* (London, 1896)

H. Riemann: *Vademecum der Phrasierung* (Leipzig, 1900, 8/1912 as *Handbuch der Phrasierung*)

M. Arend: 'Harmonische Analyse des Tristanvorspiels', *Bayreuther Blätter*, xxiv (1901), 160

C. Hynais: *Die Harmonik Richard Wagners in Bezug auf die Fundamentaltheorie Sechters* (Vienna, 1901)

K. Mey: *Musik als tönende Weltidee* (Leipzig, 1901)

C. Capellen: 'Harmonik und Melodik bei R. Wagner', *Bayreuther Blätter*, xxv (1902), 2

H. Kretzschmar: 'Anregungen zur Förderung musikalischer Hermeneutik', *JbMP 1902*, 47; *1905*, 75; also in *Gesammelte Aufsätze aus den Jahrbüchern der Musikbibliothek Peters*, i (Leipzig, 1911), 168; ii (Leipzig, 1911), 280

H. Riemann: *Grosse Kompositionslehre*, i: *Der homophone Satz*; ii: *Der polyphone Satz*; iii: *Der Orchestersatz und der dramatische Gesangstil* (Berlin and Stuttgart, 1902–13)

M. Lussy: *Grammaire de l'exécution musicale: l'anacruse dans la musique moderne* (Paris, 1903)

H. Riemann: *Beethovens Streichquartette* (Berlin, 1903)

——: *System der musikalischen Rhythmik und Metrik* (Leipzig, 1903)

G. Adler: *Wagner-Vorlesungen* (Leipzig, 1904)

H. Schenker: *Ein Beitrag zur Ornamentik* (Vienna, 1904, 2/1908)

K. Grunsky: 'Wagner als Sinfoniker', *Wagner-Jb*, i (1906), 242

H. Schenker: *Harmonielehre* (Berlin and Stuttgart, 1906; Eng. trans., 1954 as *Harmony*)

J.-G. Prod'homme: *Les symphonies de Beethoven* (Paris, 1906)

E. Ergo: 'Über Wagners Melodik und Harmonik', *Bayreuther Blätter*, xxx (1907), 125, 181, 270; xxxi (1908), 33

K. Grunsky: 'Vorspiel und I Akt Tristan und Isolde', *Wagner-Jb*, ii (1907)

R. Mayrhofer: *Psychologie des Klanges und die daraus hervorgehende, theoretisch-praktische Harmonielehre* (Leipzig, 1907)

S. Macpherson: *Form in Music with Special Reference to the Designs of Instrumental Music* (London, 1908; repubd with appx, 1912, rev. 1915)

R. Mayrhofer: *Die organische Harmonielehre* (Berlin, 1908)

A. Schering: 'Die Lehre von der musikalischen Figuren', *KJb*, xxi (1908), 106

P. Coindreau: *Analyse des dix-sept quatuors de Beethoven* (Paris, 1910)

E. Prout: *Analysis of J. S. Bach's Forty-eight Fugues (Das Wohltemperirte Clavier)* (London, 1910)

H. Schenker: *Kontrapunkt I* (Stuttgart and Berlin, 1910); *Kontrapunkt II* (Vienna, 1922)

G. Adler: *Der Stil in der Musik*, i: *Prinzipien und Arten des musikalischen Stils* (Leipzig, 1911, 2/1929) [ii, on style in historical periods, never issued, but see Adler, 1919]

I. Krohn: 'Über die Methode der musikalischen Analyse', *IMusSCR, iv London 1911*, 250

H. Leichtentritt: *Musikalische Formenlehre* (Leipzig, 1911, enlarged 2/1927; Eng. trans., 1951)

A. Schoenberg: *Harmonielehre* (Vienna, 1911; Eng. trans., 1948)

A. Schering: *Musikalische Bildung und Erziehung zum musikalischen Hören* (Leipzig, 1911, 4/1924)

——: 'Das kolorierte Orgelmadrigal des Trecento', *SIMG*, xiii (1911–12), 172

H. Schenker: *Beethoven: Neunte Sinfonie* (Vienna, 1912/R1969)

C. von Ehrenfels: *Richard Wagner und seine Apostaten* (Vienna and Leipzig, 1913)

A. O. Halm: *Die Symphonie Anton Bruckners* (Munich, 1913, 2/1923)

E. Kurth: 'Die Jugendopern Glucks bis Orfeo', *SMw*, i (1913), 193–277

——: *Die Voraussetzungen der theoretischen Harmonik und der tonalen Darstellungssysteme* (Berne, 1913/R1973)

H. Schenker: *Die letzten fünf Sonaten Beethovens* ['Erläuterungsausgaben'] (Vienna 1913–21, 2/1971–2) [i: *Sonata A dur Op.101* (1921); iii: *Sonate As dur Op.109* (1913); iv: *Sonate As dur Op.110* (1914); v: *Sonate C moll Op.111* (1916)]

H. Erpf: *Der Begriff der musikalischen Form* (Stuttgart, 1914)

A. Schering: 'Zur Grundlegung der musikalischen Hermeneutik', *Zeitschrift für Ästhetik und allgemeine Kunstwissenschaft*, ix (1914)

W. Fischer: *Zur Entwicklungsgeschichte des Wiener Klassischen Stils*

(Habilitationsschrift, U. of Vienna, 1915; extracts in *SMw*, iii (1915), 24–84)

H. Gál: 'Die Stileigentümlichkeiten des jungen Beethoven', *SMw*, iv (1916), 58–115

E. Kurth: *Grundlagen des linearen Kontrapunkts: Einführung in Stil und Technik von Bachs melodischer Polyphonie* (Berne, 1917, 5/1956)

——: 'Zur Motivbildung Bachs', *BJb*, xiv (1917), 80–136

R. Lach: 'Der Inhaltsproblem in der Musikästhetik: ein Beitrag der musikalischer Hermeneutik', *Festschrift Hermann Kretzschmar* (Leipzig, 1918/*R*1973), 74

P. Linke: *Grundfragen der Wahrnehmungslehre* (Munich, 1918)

E. Sapir: 'Representative Music', *MQ*, iv (1918), 161

G. Becking: ' "Hören" und "Analysieren" (über Riemanns Beethoven-Analysen)', *ZMw*, i (1918–19), 587

H. Riemann: *Ludwig van Beethovens sämtliche Klavier-Solosonaten: ästhetische und formal-technische Analyse* (Berlin, 1918–19, 4/1920)

G. Adler: *Methode der Musikgeschichte* (Leipzig, 1919) [expansion of Adler, 1911]

E. Kurth: *Romantische Harmonik und ihre Krise in Wagners 'Tristan'* (Berne and Leipzig, 1920/*R*1968, 3/1923)

R. Schlösser: 'Der Stufenweg rechts und das Umrahmungsmotiv', *Bayreuther Blätter*, xliii (1920), 28

S. Anheisser: 'Das Vorspiel zu "Tristan und Isolde" und seine Motivik: ein Beitrag zur Hermeneutik des Musikdramas Wagners', *ZMw*, iii (1920–21), 257–303

G. Becking: *Studien zu Beethovens Personalstil: das Scherzothema* (Leipzig, 1921)

H. Schenker: *Der Tonwille* (Vienna, 1921–4) [in 10 issues]

A. O. Lorenz: *Gedanken und Studien zur musikalischen Formgebung in R. Wagners 'Ring des Nibelungen'* (diss., U. of Frankfurt am Main, 1922)

W. Werker: *Studien über Symmetrie im Bau der Fugen . . . des 'Wohltemperierten Klaviers'* (Leipzig, 1922)

E. Bücken and P. Mies: 'Grundlagen, Methoden und Aufgaben der musikalischen Stilkunde', *ZMw*, v (1922–3), 219

A. O. Lorenz: 'Die formale Gestaltung des Vorspiels zu Tristan und Isolde', *ZMw*, v (1922–3), 546

H. Mersmann: 'Versuch einer Phänomenologie der Musik', *ZMw*, v (1922–3), 226–69

H. Grabner: *Die Funktionstheorie H. Riemanns und ihre Bedeutung für die praktische Analyse* (Munich, 1923, 2/1930)

K. Jeppesen: *Palestrinastil med särligt henblik paa dissonansbehandlingen* (Copenhagen, 1923; Ger. trans., 1925; Eng. trans., 1927, 2/1946/*R*1971 as *The Style of Palestrina and the Dissonance*)

A. Schmitz: *Beethovens 'Zwei Prinzipe'* (Berlin and Bonn, 1923)

R. Steglich: 'Das c-moll-Präludium aus dem ersten Teil des Wohltemperierten Klaviers J. S. Bachs', *BJb*, xx (1923), 1

W. Werker: *Bach-Studien*, ii: *Die Matthäuspassion* (Leipzig, 1923)

G. Becking: 'Über ein dänisches Schul-Liederbuch: über Mitbewegungen und Gestaltanalyse', *ZMw*, vi (1923–4), 100

E. Bücken: 'Der galante Stil: eine Skizze seiner Entwicklung', *ZMw*, vi (1923–4), 418

G. Adler: 'Periodisierung der Musikgeschichte', *Handbuch der Musikgeschichte* (Frankfurt, 1924, rev. 2/1930/*R*1961)

A. Lorenz: 'Betrachtungen über Beethovens Eroica-Skizzen', *ZMw*, vii (1924–5), 409

——: *Das Geheimnis der Form bei Richard Wagner*, i: *Der musikalische Aufbau des Bühnenfestspiels Der Ring des Nibelungen*; ii: *Der musikalische Aufbau von Richard Wagners 'Tristan und Isolde'*; iii: *Der musikalische Aufbau von Richard Wagners 'Die Meistersinger von Nürnberg'*; iv: *Der musikalische Aufbau von Richard Wagners 'Parsifal'* (Berlin, 1924–33/*R*1966)

H. Besseler: 'Grundfragen des musikalischen Hörens', *JbMP 1925*, 35

F. Cassirer: *Beethoven und die Gestalt: ein Kommentar* (Stuttgart, 1925)

W. Engelsmann: 'Die Sonatenform Beethovens: Probleme in der Klaviersonate As-Dur opus 110', *Neue-Musikzeitung*, xlvi (1925), 203, 222

H. Grabner: *Lehrbuch der musikalischen Analyse* (Leipzig, 1925)

E. Kurth: *Bruckner* (Berlin, 1925/*R*1971)

P. Mies: *Die Bedeutung der Skizzen Beethovens zur Erkenntnis seines Stiles* (Leipzig, 1925; Eng. trans., 1929)

C. Pieper: *Musikalische Analyse: eine musikalische Formenlehre in der Form von Musteranalysen klassischer Tonstücke* (Cologne, 1925)

H. Schenker: *Beethoven: Fünfte Sinfonie: eine Darstellung des musikalischen Inhaltes unter fortlaufender Berücks* (Vienna, 1925/*R*1969) [re-issued from *Der Tonwille*, 1921–4]

——: *Das Meisterwerk in der Musik: ein Jahrbuch* (Munich, Vienna and Berlin, 1925–30/*R*1974; Eng. trans. of i, p.61 in *Music Forum*, iv (1976), 141 as 'The Largo of J. S. Bach's Sonata No.3 for Unaccompanied Violin [BWV 1005]'; Eng. trans., p.45 in *JMT*, xii (1968), 164 as 'Organic Structure in Sonata Form', and of ii, p.97 in *Music Forum*, ii (1970), 274 as 'The Sarabande of J. S. Bach's Suite No.3 for Unaccompanied Violoncello (BWV 1009)') [essays and analyses, incl. analyses of Mozart: Symphony in G minor no.40, ii,

pp.105–59 and Beethoven: Symphony no.3 in E♭, iii, pp.25–99]

A. Schering: 'Bach und das Symbol', *BJb*, xxii (1925), 40; xxv (1928), 119

L. Schiedermair: *Der junge Beethoven* (Leipzig, 1925, 3/1951)

A. O. Lorenz: 'Das Finale in Mozarts Meisteropern', *Die Musik*, xix (1927), 621

W. R. Spalding: *Manuel d'analyse musicale* (Paris, 1927)

G. Becking: *Der musikalische Rhythmus als Erkenntnisquelle* (Augsburg, 1928)

A. O. Halm: 'Über den Wert musikalischer Analysen', *Die Musik*, xxi (1928–9), 481

W. Karthaus: 'Die musikalische Analyse', *Die Musik*, xxi (1928–9), 264

W. Danckert: 'Stil als Gesinnung', *Bärenreiter-Jb*, v (1929), 24

R. von Ficker: 'Primäre Klangformen', *JbMP 1929*, 21

A. Schering: 'Musikalische Analyse und Wertidee', *JbMP 1929*, 9

W. Riezler: 'Die Urlinie', *Die Musik*, xxii (1929–30), 502

B. F. Asaf'yev: *Muzїkalnaya forma kak protsess* [Musical form as process] (Moscow, 1930–47, 2/1963 ed. E. Orlova, 3/1971; Cz. trans., 1965; Ger. trans., 1976)

R. Steglich: *Die elementare Dynamik des musikalischen Rhythmus* (Leipzig, 1930)

W. Danckert: *Personal Typen des Melodiestils* (Kassel, 1931, enlarged 2/1932 as *Ursymbole melodischer Gestaltung*: see below)

W. Engelsmann: *Beethovens Kompositionspläne* (Augsburg, 1931)

E. Kurth: *Musikpsychologie* (Berlin, 1931/*R*1969, 2/1947)

E. Schwebsch: *J. S. Bach und die Kunst der Fuge* (Stuttgart, 1931)

K. Westphal: 'Analyse und Interpretation', *Die Musik*, xxiv (1931–2), 5

G. Becking: 'Der musikalische Bau des Montenegrischen Volksepos', *1st International Congress of Phonetic Science: Amsterdam 1932* [*Archives néerlandaises de phonétique expérimentale*, vii–ix (1933)], 144

W. Danckert: *Ursymbole melodischer Gestaltung: Beiträge zur Typologie der personalstile aus sechs Jahrhunderten der abendländischen Musikgeschichte* (Kassel, 1932)

F. Gennrich: *Grundriss einer Formenlehre des mittelalterlichen Liedes als Grundlage einer musikalischen Formenlehre des Liedes* (Halle, 1932/*R*1970)

R. Jakobson: 'Musikwissenschaft und Linguistik', *Prager Presse* (7 Dec 1932); Eng. trans., *Selected Writings*, ii (The Hague, 1971)

G. de Saint-Foix: *Les symphonies de Mozart* (Paris, 1932; Eng. trans., 1946)

H. Schenker: *Fünf Urlinie-Tafeln* (Vienna, 1932; Eng. version with glossary, 1969 as *Five Graphic Analyses*)

J. Yasser: *A Theory of Evolving Tonality* (New York, 1932)

R. Stöhr, H. Gol and A. Orel: *Formenlehre der Musik* (Leipzig, 1933, 2/1954)

W. Danckert: *Beitrag zur Bach-Kritik* (Kassel, 1934)

O. Jonas: *Das Wesen des musikalischen Kunstwerks* (Vienna, 1934, rev. 2/1972 as *Einführung in die Lehre Heinrich Schenkers*)

A. Schering: *Beethoven in neuer Deutung* (Leipzig, 1934)

R. O. Morris: *The Structure of Music: An Outline for Students* (London, 1935)

F. Salzer: *Sinn und Wesen der abendländischen Mehrstimmigkeit* (Vienna, 1935)

H. Schenker: *Der freie Satz* (Vienna, 1935, 2/1935; Eng. trans., T. H. Krueger, diss., U. of Iowa, 1960)

R. von Tobel: *Die Formenwelt der klassischen Instrumentalmusik* (Berne and Leipzig, 1935)

K. Westphal: 'Barockes und Klassisches Formhören', *SMz*, lxxv (1935), 365

——: *Der Begriff der musikalischen Form in der Wiener Klassik* (Leipzig, 1935)

D. F. Tovey: *Essays in Musical Analysis*, i: *Symphonies*; ii: *Symphonies (II), Variations, and Orchestral Polyphony*; iii: *Concertos*; iv: *Illustrative Music*; v: *Vocal Music*; vi: *Supplementary Essays, Glossary, and Index* (London, 1935–9)

P. Bogatyrev: 'La chanson populaire du point de vue fonctionnel', *Travaux du Cercle Linguistique de Prague*, vi (1936), 222

A. Schering: *Beethoven und die Dichtung* (Berlin, 1936)

P. Hindemith: *Unterweisung im Tonsatz* (Mainz, 1937, 2/1940; Eng. trans., 1942 as *The Craft of Musical Composition*)

J.-G. Prod'homme: *Les sonates pour piano de Beethoven* (Paris, 1937)

M. S. Schaeffer: *Harmonic Analysis and Musical Style: Harmonic Causal Factors of Style Recognition in Music; Methods of Analysis* (diss., Western Reserve U., 1937)

H. Mersmann: *Musikhören* (Potsdam and Berlin, 1938, 2/1952)

G. W. Cooper: *An Introduction to the Analysis of Certain Contemporary Harmonic Practices* (diss., Harvard U., 1939)

A. Gabaud: *Guide pratique d'analyse musicale* (Paris, 1940)

A. Schering: *Das Symbol in der Musik* (Leipzig, 1941)

A. Schoenberg: *Models for Beginners in Composition* (Los Angeles, 1942, enlarged 2/1943, rev. L. Stein, 1973)

O. Messiaen: *Technique de mon langage musicale* (Paris, 1944; Eng. trans., 1956)

D. F. Tovey: *Essays in Musical Analysis*, vii: *Chamber Music* (London,

1944)
——: *Musical Articles from the Encyclopaedia Britannica* [14th edn.] (London, 1944)

A. T. Katz: *Challenge to Musical Tradition: a New Concept of Tonality* (London, 1945)

M. Weingart: 'Etude du langage parlé suivi du point de vue musical avec considération particulière du Tchèque', *Travaux du Cercle Linguistique de Copenhague*, i (1945), 172

J. Schillinger: *The Schillinger System of Musical Composition* (New York, 1946)

W. Koch: 'Inhaltliche oder formale Analyse? Zur Krise des musikalischen Hörens', *Musica*, i (1947), 192

M. McMullin: 'The Symbolic Analysis of Music', *MR*, viii (1947), 25

K. von Fischer: *Die Beziehung von Form und Motiv in Beethovens Instrumentalwerken* (Strasbourg and Zurich, 1948, rev. 2/1972)

D. F. Tovey: *A Companion to Beethoven's Pianoforte Sonatas (Bar-to-bar Analysis)* (London, 1948)

M. E. Brockhoff: 'Zur Methodik der musikwissenschaftlichen Analyse', *IMSCR, iv Basel 1949*, 80

B. H. Bronson: 'Mechanical Help in the Study of Folksong', *Journal of American Folklore*, lxii (1949), 81

K. Jeppesen: 'Zur Kritik der Klassischen Harmonielehre', *IMSCR, iv Basel 1949*, 23

M. Mann: 'Schenker's Contribution to Music Theory', *MR*, x (1949), 3

A. Sychra: 'La chanson folkloristique du point de vue sémiologique', *Slovo a slovesnost* (Prague, 1949), 7; repr. in *Musique en jeu*, x (1973), 12

H. Erpf: 'Analyse', *MGG*

H. B. Buys: 'Gestallsymboliek en diminutietechniek', *Mens en melodie*, iv (1950), 321

H. Federhofer: *Beiträge zur musikalischen Gestaltanalyse* (Graz, 1950)

H. Grabner: *Musikalische Werkbetrachtung* (Stuttgart, 1950)

A. Schmitz: *Die Bildlichkeit der wortgebundenen Musik J. S. Bachs* (Mainz, 1950)

A. Schoenberg: *Style and Idea* (New York, 1950; repr. 1975 with additional material as *Style and Idea: Selected Writings of Arnold Schoenberg*, ed. L. Stein)

B. C. Benward: *A Proposal for the Analysis of Motion Factors in Music* (diss., U. of Rochester, 1951)

E. Ratz: *Einführung in die musikalische Formenlehre: über Formprinzipien in den Inventionen und Fugen J. S. Bachs und ihre Bedeutung für die Kompositionstechnik Beethovens* (Vienna, 1951, 3/1968)

R. Réti: *The Thematic Process in Music* (New York, 1951)

F. Salzer: *Structural Hearing* (New York, 1952, 2/1962)

J. N. David: *Die Jupiter-Symphonie: eine Studie über die thematisch-melodischen Zusammenhänge* (Göttingen, 1953, 4/1960)

E. Ratz: *Probleme der musikalischen Formenlehre* (Vienna, 1953)

V. H. Talley: 'A Critique of Musical Analysis', *JAMS*, vi (1953), 87

M. D'Ollone: *Le langage musicale* (Paris and Geneva, 1954)

J. Mainwaring: ' "Gestalt" Psychology', *Grove 5*

A. Schoenberg: *Structural Functions of Harmony* (London, 1954, rev. 2/1969)

M. Babbitt: 'Some Aspects of Twelve-tone Composition', *The Score and IMA Magazine*, xii (1955), 53

A. Forte: *Contemporary Tone-structures* (New York, 1955)

A. A. Reformastky: 'Rech'i mužika v penii' [Musical speech in song], *Voprosï Kul'turï rech'i*, ed. S. I. Ozegov (Moscow, 1955), i, 173

N.-E. Ringbom: *Über die Deutbarkeit der Tonkunst* (Åbo, 1955)

G. Rochberg: *The Hexachord and its Relation to the Twelve-tone Row* (Bryn Mawr, Penn., 1955)

A. Schmitz: 'Figuren, musikalisch-rhetorische', *MGG*

E. H. Alden: *The Role of the Motive in Musical Structure* (diss., U. of North Carolina, 1956)

R. Guldenstein: 'Synthetische Analyse', *SMz*, xcvi (1956), 205

R. L. Jacobs: 'Gestalt Psychologists on Music: a Discussion of the Article on Gestalt Psychology in Grove V', *MR*, xvii (1956), 185

H. Keller: 'KV503: the Unity of Contrasting Themes and Movements', *MR*, xvii (1956), 48, 120

S. Łobaczewska: *Die Analyse des musikalischen Kunstwerks als Problem der Musikwissenschaft* (Vienna, 1956)

L. B. Meyer: *Emotion and Meaning in Music* (Chicago, 1956)

A. A. Moles: 'Informationstheorie der Musik', *Nachrichtentechnische Fachberichte*, iii (1956)

R. C. Pinkerton: 'Information Theory and Melody', *Scientific American*, cxciv (1956), 77

L. G. Ratner: 'Eighteenth-century Theories of Musical Period Structure', *MQ*, xlii (1956), 439

R. Réti: 'The Role of Duothematicism in the Evolution of Sonata Form', *MR*, xvii (1956), 110; Ger. trans., *ÖMz*, xi (1956), 306

G. Springer: 'Language and Music: Parallels and Divergences', *For Roman Jakobson: Essays on . . . his Sixtieth Birthday* (The Hague, 1956), 504–613; Fr. trans., *Musique en jeu*, v (1971), 31

R. Traimer: 'Zum Problem der musikalischen Werkanalyse', *NZM*, cxvii (1956), 621

H. Keller: 'A Slip of Mozart's: its Analytical Significance', *Tempo*, no.42 (1956–7), 2

L. B. Meyer: 'Meaning in Music and Information Theory', *Journal of Aesthetics and Art Criticism*, xv (1956–7), 412; repr. as *Music, the Arts and Ideas* (Chicago, 1967), chap.1

V. Zuckerkandl: *Sound and Symbol*, i: *Music and the External World;* ii: *Man the Musician* (Princeton, 1956–73)

J. N. David: *Die zweistimmigen Inventionen von Johann Sebastian Bach* (Göttingen, 1957)

H. Degen: *Handbuch der Formenlehre* (Regensburg, 1957)

H. Keller: 'Functional Analysis: its pure Application', *MR*, xviii (1957), 202; see also xxi (1960), 73, 237

——: 'Knowing Things Backwards', *Tempo*, no.46 (1957), 14

——: 'The Musical Analysis of Music', *The Listener* (29 Aug 1957)

——: 'Wordless Analysis', *Musical Events*, xii (1957), Dec, 26

J. LaRue: 'A System of Symbols for Formal Analysis', *JAMS*, x (1957), 25; see also xix (1966), 403

A. Palm: *J. J. de Momigny: Leben und Werk* (diss., U. of Tübingen, 1957)

I. Supičic: *La musique expressive* (Paris, 1957)

P. Barford: 'Wordless Functional Analysis', *MMR*, lxxxviii (1958), 44

E. Coons and D. Kraehenbuehl: 'Information as a Measure of Structure in Music', *JMT*, ii (1958), 127–61

H. Federhofer: 'Die Funktionstheorie H. Riemanns und die Schichtenlehre H. Schenkers', *IMSCR, vii Cologne 1958*, 183

R. Francès: *La perception de la musique* (Paris, 1958)

W. Fucks: *Mathematische Analyse der Formalstruktur von Musik* (Cologne and Opladen, 1958)

L. A. Hiller: *On the Use of a High-speed Electronic Digital Computer for Musical Composition* (diss., U. of Illinois, 1958)

G. Kähler: *Studien zur Entstehung der Formenlehre in der Musiktheorie* (diss., U. of Heidelberg, 1958)

H. Keller: 'The Home-coming of Musical Analysis', *MT*, xcix (1958), 657

——: 'Wordless Functional Analysis: the First Year', *MR*, xix (1958), 192

A. A. Moles: *Théorie de l'information et perception esthétique* (Paris, 1958; Eng. trans., 1966)

B. Nettl: 'Some Linguistic Approaches to Musical Analysis', *JIFMC*, x (1958), 37

R. Réti: *Tonality, Atonality, Pantonality: a Study of some Trends in Twentieth Century Music* (London, 1958)

W. H. Reynolds: 'Unity in Music', *JMT*, ii (1958), 97; see also reply by W. Gettel, 240; iii (1959), 140

Roland-Manuel: 'L'analyse musicale: langage, styles et formes', *Précis de musicologie*, ed. J. Chailley (Paris, 1958), 332

J. E. Youngblood: 'Style as Information', *JMT*, ii (1958), 24

D. Kraehenbuehl and E. Coons: 'Information as a Measure of Experience in Music', *Journal of Aesthetics and Art Criticism*, xvii (1958–9), 510

J. Chailley: 'Essai sur les structures mélodiques', *RdM*, xliv (1959), 139–75

D. Cooke: 'In Defence of Functional Analysis', *MT*, c (1959), 456

——: *The Language of Music* (London, 1959/R1962)

H. Eimert: 'Debussy's "Jeux" ', *Die Reihe*, v (1959), 3; Eng. trans., *Die Reihe*, v (1961), 3

A. Forte: 'Schenker's Conception of Musical Structure', *JMT*, v (1959), 1–30

L. A. Hiller and L. M. Isaacson: *Experimental Music: Composition with an Electronic Computer* (New York, 1959)

F. B. Mâche: 'Connaissance des structures sonores', *ReM*, no.244 (1959), 17

W. Meyer-Eppler: *Grundlagen und Anwendungen der Informationstheorie* (Berlin, 1959)

G. Rochberg: 'The Harmonic Tendency of the Hexachord', *JMT*, iii (1959), 208

N. Ruwet: 'Contradictions du langage sériel', *RBM*, xiii (1959), 83; repr. in *Langage, musique, poésie* (Paris, 1972), 23

R. Travis: 'Towards a New Concept of Tonality', *JMT*, iii (1959), 257; see reply by E. Oster, iv (1960), 85

A. Walker: 'Unconscious Motivation in the Composing Process', *MR*, xx (1959), 277

G. Altmann: *Musikalische Formenlehre: Beispiele und Analysen* (Berlin, 1960, 2/1968)

M. Babbitt: 'Twelve-tone Invariants as Compositional Determinants', *MQ*, xlvi (1960), 246; also pubd in *Problems of Modern Music*, ed. P. H. Lang (New York, 1960), 108

E. T. Cone: 'Analysis Today', *MQ*, xlvi (1960), 172

G. W. Cooper and L. B. Meyer: *The Rhythmic Structure of Music* (Chicago, 1960)

F. B. Crane: *A Study of Theoretical Writings on Musical Form to ca. 1460* (diss., U. of Iowa, 1960)

C. Dahlhaus: 'Zur Kritik musiktheoretischer Allgemeinprinzipien', *Musikalische Zeitfragen*, ix (1960), 68

D. N. Ferguson: *Music as Metaphor: the Elements of Expression* (Minneapolis, 1960)

H. Keller: 'The Principles of Composition (I)', *Score*, no.26 (1960), 35
——: 'Wordless Functional Analysis: the Second Year and Beyond', *MR*, xxi (1960), 73, 237
D. Kraehenbuehl and others: 'The Professional Music Theorist – his Habits and Training: a Forum', *JMT*, iv (1960), 62
A. B. Lord: *The Singer of Tales* (Cambridge, Mass., 1960)
Q. R. Nordgren: 'A Measure of Textural Patterns and Strengths', *JMT*, iv (1960), 19
J. Nordmark: 'New Theories of Form and the Problem of Thematic Identities', *JMT*, iv (1960), 210
J. K. Randall: 'Haydn: String Quartet in D Major, op.76, no.5', *MR*, xxii (1960), 94
H. E. Smither: *Theories of Rhythm in the Nineteenth and Twentieth Centuries, with a Contribution to the Theory of Rhythm for the Study of Twentieth-century Music* (diss., Cornell U., 1960)
J. E. Youngblood: *Music and Language: some Related Analytical Techniques* (diss., Indiana U., 1960)
E. Ansermet: *Les fondements de la musique dans la conscience humaine* (Neuchâtel, 1961)
M. Babbitt: 'Set Structure as a Compositional Determinant', *JMT*, v (1961), 72
C. Bean: *Information Theory Applied to the Analysis of a Particular Formal Process in Tonal Music* (diss., U. of Illinois, 1961)
P. Benary: 'Musikalische Werkbetrachtung in metrischer Sicht', *Mf*, xiv (1961), 2
I. Bengtsson: 'On Relationships between Tonal and Rhythmic Structures in Western Multipart Music', *STMf*, xliii (1961), 49
A. Forte: *The Compositional Matrix* (New York, 1961/*R*1974)
H. Goldschmidt: 'Zur Methodologie der musikalischen Analysen', *BMw*, iii/4 (1961), 3
V. L. Kliewer: *The Concept of Organic Unity in Music Criticism and Analysis* (diss., Indiana U., 1961)
L. B. Meyer: 'On Rehearing Music', *JAMS*, xiv (1961), 257; repr. in *Music, the Arts, and Ideas* (Chicago, 1967), chap.3
E. Oster: 'Register and the Large-scale Connection', *JMT*, v (1961), 54
N. Ruwet: 'Fonction de la parole dans la musique vocale', *RBM*, xv (1961), 8; repr. in *Langage, musique, poésie* (Paris, 1972), 41
R. Smith: 'The Sorry Scheme of Things', *MR*, xxii (1961), 212
H. Beck: 'Zur musikalischen Analyse', *GfMKB, Kassel 1962*, 291
J. E. Cohen: 'Information Theory and Music', *Behavioral Science*, vii (1962), 137
G. Geowey and J. Kucaba: *Understanding Musical Form* (Dubuque, 1962)
E. Karkoschka: 'Musik und Semantik', *Melos*, xxxii (1962), 252
W. Kolneder: 'Visuelle und auditive Analyse', *Veröffentlichungen des Instituts für Neue Musik und Musikerziehung Darmstadt*, iii (1962, 2/1965), 57
J. LaRue: 'On Style Analysis', *JMT*, vi (1962), 91
H. Lemacher and H. Schröder: *Formenlehre der Musik* (Cologne, 1962, 2/1968; Eng. trans., 1967)
G. Madell: 'Thematic Unity and the Language of Music', *MR*, xxiii (1962), 30
W. Meyer-Eppler: 'Informationstheoretische Probleme der musikalischen Kommunikationen', *Die Reihe*, viii (1962), 7; Eng. trans., *Die Reihe*, viii (1968), 7
L. Stein: *Structure and Style: the Study and Analysis of Musical Forms* (Evanston, 1962) [see also companion book *Anthology of Musical Forms* (Evanston, 1962)]
A. Walker: *A Study in Musical Analysis* (London, 1962)
P. Westergaard: 'Some Problems in Rhythmic Theory and Analysis', *PNM*, i/1 (1962), 180
H. Federhofer: 'Johann Nepomuk Davids Analysen von Werken Johann Sebastian Bachs', *AMw*, xix–xx (1962–3), 147
A. Palm: 'Mozarts Streichquartett d-Moll, KV 421, in der Interpretation Momignys', *MJb 1962–3*, 256
A. Walker: 'Back to the Couch', *Music and Musicians*, xi/10 (1962–3), 20, 53
W. Bright: 'Language and Music: Areas for Co-operation', *EM*, vii (1963), 26
R. Donington: *Wagner's 'Ring' and its Symbols: the Music and the Myth* (London, 1963, 3/1974)
M. Kassler: 'A Sketch of the Formalized Use of Languages for the Assertion of Music', *PNM*, i/2 (1963), 83
J. W. Mitchell: *A History of Theories of Functional Harmonic Progression* (diss., Indiana U., 1963)
A. Schoenberg: *Preliminary Exercises in Counterpoint*, ed. L. Stein (London, 1963)
Y. Xenakis: *Musiques formelles: nouveaux principes formels de composition musicale* (Paris, 1963; Eng. trans., 1971 as *Formalized Music: Thought and Mathematics in Composition*)
R. Zaripov: *Kibernetika i muzïka* (Moscow, 1963; Eng. trans., *PNM*, vii/2 (1969), 115–54)
K. Stockhausen: *Texte*, ed. D. Schnebel, i: *Texte zur elektronischen und instrumentalen Musik*; ii: *Texte zu eigenen Werken, zur Kunst anderer*; iii: *Texte zur Musik, 1963–70* (Cologne, 1963–71)
P. Boulez: *Penser la musique aujourd'hui* (Paris, 1964; Eng. trans.,

1971)
J. Chailley: *Traité historique d'analyse musicale* (Paris, 1964)
D. N. Ferguson: *Image and Structure in Chamber Music* (Minneapolis, 1964)
A. Forte: 'A Theory of Set-complexes for Music', *JMT*, viii (1964), 136–83; see also discussion, ix (1965), 163, 173
H. Heckmann: 'Neue Methoden der Verarbeitung musikalischer Daten', *Mf*, xvii (1964), 381
H. R. Hensel: *On Paul Hindemith's Fluctuation Theory* (diss., U. of Illinois, 1964)
L. A. Hiller: 'Informationstheorie und Musik', *Darmstädter Beiträge zur neuen Musik*, viii (1964), 7
G. T. Jones: 'Symbols used in Music Analysis: a Progress Report', *Council for Research in Music Education Bulletin*, no.2 (1964), 9; no.16 (1968), 68
R. Kluge: 'Definition der Begriffe Gestalt und Intonation', *BMw*, vi (1964), 85
W. Korte: 'Struktur und Modell als Information in der Musikwissenschaft', *AMw*, xxi (1964), 1
C. Lévi-Strauss: *Le cru et le cuit* (Paris, 1964; Eng. trans., 1970 as *The Raw and the Cooked*), esp. 14–32
M. Philippot: 'Ansermet's Phenomenological Metamorphoses', *PNM*, ii/2 (1964), 129
B. Reimer: 'Information Theory and the Analysis of Musical Meaning', *Council of Research in Music Education Bulletin*, no.2 (1964), 14
G. H. Roller: *The Development of the Methods for Analysis of Musical Compositions and for the Formation of a Symmetrical Twelve-tone Row using the Electronic Digital Computer* (diss., Michigan State U., 1964)
G. Saint-Guirons: 'Quelques aspects de la musique considerée d'un point de vue linguistique (recherche d'une analyse musicale distinctive)', *Etudes de linguistique appliquée*, iii (1964), 12
H. E. Smither: 'The Rhythmic Analysis of 20th-century Music', *JMT*, viii (1964), 54–88
J. Tenney: *Meta (+) Hodos: a Phenomenology of Twentieth Century Musical Materials and an Approach to the Study of Form* (New Orleans, 1964)
R. E. Tyndall: *Musical Form* (Boston, 1964)
F. Winckel: 'Die informationstheoretische Analyse musikalischer Strukturen', *Mf*, xvii (1964), 1
E. Apfel: *Beiträge zu einer Geschichte der Satztechnik von der frühen Motette bis Bach* (Munich, 1964–5)
M. Babbitt: 'The Use of Computers in Musicological Research', *PNM*, iii/2 (1965), 74
H. G. Bertram: *Material–Struktur–Form: Studien zur musikalischen Ordnung bei J. N. David* (Wiesbaden, 1965)
A. Cohen and J. D. White: *Anthology of Music for Analysis* (New York, 1965)
C. Dahlhaus: 'Über das Analysieren neuer Musik: zu Schönbergs Klavierstücken Op.11, 1 und Op.33a: Fortschritt und Rückbildung in der deutschen Musikerziehung', *Vorträge der 6. Bundesschulmusikwoche: Bonn 1965*
C. Deliège: 'La musicologie devant le structuralisme', *L'arc*, no.26 (1965), 45
W. Fucks and J. Lauter: *Exaktwissenschaftliche Musikanalyse* (Cologne and Opladen, 1965)
D. M. Green: *Form in Tonal Music: an Introduction to Analysis* (New York, 1965)
H. Kaufmann: 'Fortschritt und Reaktion in der Lehre Heinrich Schenkers', *NZM*, cxxvi (1965), 5; *Das Orchester*, xiii (1965), 44
R. Klein: 'Vom Sinn der Analyse', *ÖMz*, xx (1965), 37
L. Knopoff: 'Some Technological Advances in Musical Analysis', *SM*, vii (1965), 301
W. Kolneder: 'Zur Geschichte der Analyse musikalischer Kunstwerke', *SMz*, cv (1965), 68
G. Roller: 'Development of a Method for Analysis of Musical Compositions using an Electronic Digital Computer', *JRME*, xii (1965), 249
J. Selleck and R. Bakeman: 'Procedures for the Analysis of Form: two Computer Applications', *JMT*, ix (1965), 281
E. L. Waeltner, ed.: *Meisterwerke der Musik: Werkmonographien zur Musikgeschichte* (Munich, 1965–)
G. Berlind, ed.: *Writings on the Use of Computers in Music* (New York, 1966)
W. Berry: *Form in Music: an Examination of Traditional Techniques of Musical Structure and their Application in Historical and Contemporary Styles* (Englewood Cliffs, 1966)
H. Boatwright and E. Oster: 'Analysis Symposium', *JMT*, x (1966), 18–53
P. Boulez: *Relevés d'apprenti*, ed. P. Thévenin (Paris, 1966; Eng. trans., 1966)
R. Crocker: *A History of Musical Style* (New York, 1966)
C. T. Davie: *Musical Structure and Design* (New York, 1966)
C. Deliège: 'Approche d'une sémantique de la musique', *RBM*, xx (1966), 21
K.-E. Eicke: *Der Streit zwischen Adolph Bernhard Marx und Gottfried

Wilhelm Fink um die Kompositionslehre (Regensburg, 1966)

A. Forte: 'A Program for the Analytic Reading of Scores', *JMT*, x (1966), 330–64

——: 'Computer-implemented Analysis of Musical Structure', *West Virginia University Conference on Computer Applications in Music: Morgantown 1966*, 29

L. Hiller and C. Bean: 'Information Theory Analyses of Four Sonata Expositions', *JMT*, x (1966), 96–137

D. M. Hsu: 'Ernst Kurth and his Concept of Music as Motion', *JMT*, x (1966), 2

Jaarboek I.P.E.M. [Institut voor Psychoakoestiek en Elektronische Muziek, U. of Ghent] (1966–) [incl. analyses of individual works and studies in perception]

R. Kluge: 'Volksliedanalyse und -systematisierung mit Hilfe eines Rechenautomaten', *GfMKB, Leipzig 1966*, 458

J. LaRue: 'Some Computer Aids to Musicology', *GfMKB, Leipzig 1966*, 466

G. Lefkoff: 'Computers and the Study of Musical Style', *West Virginia University Conference on Computer Applications in Music: Morgantown 1966*, 43

M. McLean: 'A New Method of Melodic Interval Analysis as Applied to Maori Chant', *EM*, x (1966), 174

N. Malmendier: *Grundlagen der statistischen Teste und die Möglichkeiten ihrer Anwendung bei der Analyse der Formalstruktur von Werken der Sprache und Musik* (diss., Technische Hochschule, Aachen, 1966)

P. Rummenhöller: 'Die dialektische Theoriebegriff: zur Verwirklichung Hegelschen Denkens in Moritz Hauptmanns Musiktheorie', *GfMKB, Leipzig 1966*, 387

N. Ruwet: 'Méthodes d'analyse en musicologie', *RBM*, xx (1966), 65; repr. in *Langage, musique, poésie* (Paris, 1972)

P. Schaeffer: *Traité des objets musicaux: essai interdisciplines* (Paris, 1966)

W. Thomson: 'The Problem of Music Analysis and Universals', *College Music Symposium*, vi (1966), 89

L. Treitler: 'Music Analysis in an Historical Context', *College Music Symposium*, vi (1966), 75

M. Vetter: *Untersuchungen zu den in der deutschen musikalischen Fachliteratur von 1918 bis 1964 enthaltenen Methoden der musikalischen Werkanalyse* (diss., Institut Greifswald, 1966)

M. Vogel, ed.: *Beiträge zur Musiktheorie des 19. Jahrhunderts* (Regensburg, 1966)

A. Walker: *An Anatomy of Musical Criticism* (London, 1966)

'A Glossary of the Elements of Graphic Analysis', *Music Forum*, i (1967), 260 [of Schenkerian analysis]

P. Barford: 'Urphänomen, Ursatz und Grundgestalt', *MR*, xxviii (1967), 218

I. Bengtsson: 'On Melody-registration and "Mona" ', *Elektronische Datenverarbeitung in der Musikwissenschaft*, ed. H. Heckmann (Regensburg, 1967), 136

P. Bergquist: 'Mode and Polyphony around 1500: Theory and Practice', *Music Forum*, i (1967), 99–161

H. A. Brockhaus: 'Probleme der musikalischen Analyse', *Musik und Gesellschaft*, xvii (1967), 433

P. Carpenter: 'The Musical Object', *CMc* (1967), no.5, pp.56–87

M. W. Cobin: ' "Musicology and the Computer": a Plenary Session at the 1966 Annual Meeting of the American Musicological Society, in New Orleans', *Computers and the Humanities*, i (1967), 131

E. T. Cone: 'Beyond Analysis', *PNM*, vi/1 (1967), 33; see also reply by D. Lewin, vii/2 (1969), 59 and response by Cone, 70

C. Dahlhaus: 'Analyse', *RiemannL 12*

——: 'Gefühlsästhetik und musikalische Formenlehre', *Deutsche Vierteljahrsschrift für Literaturwissenschaft und Geistesgeschichte*, xli (1967), 505

A. Daniélou: *Sémantique musicale (essai de psychologie auditive)* (Paris, 1967)

D. de la Motte: 'Reform der Formenlehre?', *Veröffentlichungen des Instituts für Neue Musik und Musikerziehung Darmstadt*, vii (1967), 30

A. Dommel-Dieny: *L'analyse harmonique en exemples de J. S. Bach à Debussy* (Neuchâtel, 1967)

H. H. Eggebrecht: 'Figuren, musikalisch-rhetorische', *RiemannL 12*

G. Epperson: *The Musical Symbol: a Study of the Philosophic Theory of Music* (Ames, Iowa, 1967)

H. Erpf: *Form und Struktur in der Musik* (Mainz, 1967)

K. G. Fellerer: *Klang und Struktur in der abendlaendischen Musik* (Cologne, 1967)

P. Fontaine: *Basic Formal Structures in Music* (New York, 1967)

A. Forte: 'Music and Computing: the Present Situation', *Proceedings of the Fall Joint Computer Conference: 1967*; also in *Computers and the Humanities*, ii (1967), 2

K. Gabura: *Music Style Analysis by Computer* (diss., U. of Toronto, 1967)

R. Harweg: 'Sprache und Musik', *Poetica*, i (1967), 390, followed by discussion; see also reply 'Noch einmal: Sprache und Musik (Replik)', 556 and discussion, ii (1968), 433; orig. article, Eng.

trans., *Foundations of Language*, iv (1968), 270; Fr. trans., *Musique en jeu*, v (1971), 19

E. Karkoschka: 'Zur musikalischen Form und Formanalyse', *Veröffentlichungen des Instituts für Neue Musik und Musikerziehung Darmstadt*, vii (1967), 40

M. Kassler: *A Trinity of Essays: toward a Theory that is the Twelve-note Class System; toward Development of a Constructive Tonality Theory based on Writing by Heinrich Schenker; toward a Simple Programming Language for Musical Information Retrieval* (diss., Princeton U., 1967)

H. Kirschenbaum: 'Music Analysis by Computer', *Music Educators Journal*, liii (1967), 94

R. Kluge: 'Typ, Funktion, Bedeutung: Bemerkungen zur semantischen Analytik musikalischer Typen', *BMw*, ix (1967), 98

——: 'Zur automatischen quantitativen Bestimmung musikalischer Ähnlichkeit', *IMSCR*, x *Ljubljana 1967*, 450

K. Kropfinger: 'Zur thematischen Funktion der langsamen Einleitung bei Beethoven', *Colloquium amicorum: Joseph Schmidt-Görg* (Bonn, 1967), 197

J. LaRue: 'Two Problems in Musical Analysis: the Computer Lends a Hand', *Computers in Humanistic Research: Readings and Perspectives*, ed. E. A. Bowles (Englewood Cliffs, 1967)

Z. Lissa: 'Hegel und das Problem der Formintegration in der Musik', *Festschrift für Walter Wiora* (Kassel, 1967), 112

G. W. Logemann: 'The Canons in the Musical Offering of J. S. Bach: An Example of Computational Musicology', *Elektronische Datenverarbeitung in der Musikwissenschaft*, ed. H. Heckmann (Regensburg, 1967), 63

L. Mazel': 'Ästhetik und Analyse von Musikwerken', *Kunst und Literatur*, xv (1967), 489

L. B. Meyer: *Music, the Arts and Ideas: Patterns and Predictions in Twentieth-century Culture* (Chicago, 1967)

R. Mix: *Die Entropieabnahme bei Abhängigkeit zwischen mehreren simultanen Informationsquellen und bei Übergang zu Markoff-Ketten höherer Ordnung, untersucht an musikalischen Beispielen* (Cologne and Opladen, 1967)

Music Forum, i (1967), ii (1970), iii (1973) [incl. extended analyses of individual works]

W. Reckziegel: 'Die Notenschrift im Computer dargestellt', *SM*, ix (1967), 395

——: 'Musikanalyse: eine exakte Wissenschaft?', *Elektronische Datenverarbeitung in der Musikwissenschaft*, ed. H. Heckmann (Regensburg, 1967), 203

——: 'Musikanalyse und Wissenschaft', *SM*, ix (1967), 163

——: *Theorien zur Formalanalyse mehrstimmiger Musik* (Cologne and Opladen, 1967)

E. Regener: 'A Multiple-pass Transcription and a System for Music Analysis by Computer', *Elektronische Datenverarbeitung in der Musikwissenschaft*, ed. H. Heckmann (Regensburg, 1967), 89

——: 'Layered Music-theoretic Systems', *PNM*, vi/1 (1967), 52

R. Réti: *Thematic Patterns in Sonatas of Beethoven*, ed. D. Cooke (London, 1967)

T. D. Robinson: '*IML-MIR*: a Data-processing System for the Analysis of Music', *Elektronische Datenverarbeitung in der Musikwissenschaft*, ed. H. Heckmann (Regensburg, 1967), 103

P. Rummenhöller: *Musiktheoretisches Denken im 19. Jahrhundert: Versuch einer Interpretation erkenntnistheoretischer Zeugnisse in der Musiktheorie* (Regensburg, 1967)

N. Ruwet: 'Musicologie et linguistique', *Revue internationale des sciences sociales*, xix (1967), 85

——: 'Quelques remarques sur le role de la répétition dans la syntaxe musicale', *To Honor Roman Jakobson* (The Hague, 1967), 1693

F. Salzer: 'Tonality in Early Medieval Polyphony: towards a History of Tonality', *Music Forum*, i (1967), 35–98

N. Schiødt and B. Svejgaard: 'Application of Computer Techniques to the Analysis of Byzantine Sticherarion Melodies', *Elektronische Datenverarbeitung in der Musikwissenschaft*, ed. H. Heckmann (Regensburg, 1967), 187

A. Schoenberg: *Fundamentals of Musical Composition*, ed. G. Strang and L. Stein (London, 1967)

D. M. Schwejda: *An Investigation of the Analytical Techniques used by Rudolph Réti in the 'Thematic Process in Music'* (diss., Indiana U., 1967)

S. Slatin: *The Theories of Heinrich Schenker in Perspective* (diss., Columbia U., 1967)

I. Spink: *An Historical Approach to Musical Form* (London, 1967)

R. Stephan, ed.: *Neue Wege der musikalischen Analyse: acht Betrachtungen von L. U. Abraham, J. Baur, C. Dahlhaus, H. Kaufmann und R. Stephan*, Veröffentlichungen des Instituts für Neue Musik und Musikerziehung Darmstadt, vi (Berlin, 1967) [two analyses on each of Beethoven: Diabelli Variations; Mahler: Symphony no.4; Schoenberg: Georgelieder; Webern: Bagatelle op.9]

——: *Probleme des musiktheoretischen Unterrichts*, Veröffentlichungen des Instituts für Neue Musik und Musikerziehung Darmstadt, vii (Berlin, 1967) [report of conference, 12–16 April 1966]

——: *Versuche musikalischer Analysen: sieben Beiträge von P. Ben-*

ary, S. Borris, D. de la Motte, H. Enke, H.-P. Raiss und R. Stephan, Veröffentlichungen des Instituts für Neue Musik und Musikerziehung Darmstadt, viii (Berlin, 1967)

W. Stockmeier: *Musikalische Formprinzipien, Formenlehre* (Cologne, 1967)

P. A. Tove, L. Ejdesjö and A. Svärdström: 'Frequency and Time Analysis of Polyphonic Music', *Journal of the Acoustical Society of America*, xli (1967), 1265

V. Tsukkerman: 'Vidï tselostnovo analiza' [Aspects of integrated musical analysis], *SovM* (1967), no.4, p.100

V. Ukmar: 'Stilsko estetska pitanja savremenog muzickog stvaralastav' [The problem of style as interpreted by Stanko Vurnik], *MZ*, iii (1967)

M. H. Wennerstrom: *Parametric Analysis of Contemporary Musical Form* (diss., Indiana U., 1967)

A. Whittall: 'Post-twelve-note Analysis', *PRMA*, xciv (1967–8), 1

P. Barbaud: *La musique, discipline scientifique: introduction élémentaire à l'étude des structures musicales* (Paris, 1968)

E. T. Cone: *Musical Form and Musical Performance* (New York, 1968)

D. de la Motte: *Musikalische Analyse* (Kassel, 1968) [with critical commentary by C. Dahlhaus]

U. Eco: *La struttura assente* (Milan, 1968; Fr. trans., 1972)

R. F. Erickson: 'Musical Analysis and the Computer: a Report on some Current Approaches and the Outlook for the Future', *Computers and the Humanities*, iii (1968), 87

——: 'Musical Analysis and the Computer', *JMT*, xii (1968), 240

M. Hughes, L. Moss and C. Schachter: 'Analysis Symposium: Moments musicals Op.94, Franz Schubert', *JMT*, xii (1968), 184–239; see also xiii (1969), 128, 218

A. Lomax: *Folk Song Style and Culture* (Washington, DC, 1968)

C. B. Nelson: 'Programmed Analyses of Musical Works: an Experimental Evaluation', *Bulletin of the Council for Research in Music Education*, xiv (1968), 11

A. A. Pierce: *The Analysis of Rhythm in Tonal Music* (diss., Brandeis U., 1968)

W. Reckziegel: 'Musik im Datenspeicher', *Mf*, xxi (1968), 427

F. Ritzel: *Die Entwicklung der 'Sonatenform' in musiktheoretischen Schrifttum des 18. und 19. Jahrhunderts* (Wiesbaden, 1968)

J. Rohwer: 'Zur Analyse neuer Musik', *Mf*, xxi (1968), 69

C. Seeger: 'Factorial Analysis of the Song as an Approach to the Formation of a Unitary Field Theory', *JIFMC*, xx (1968), 33

F. J. Smith: 'Vers une phénoménologie du son', *Revue de métaphysique et de morale*, iii (1968), 328

T. Winograd: 'Linguistics and the Computer Analysis of Tonal Harmony', *JMT*, xii (1968), 2–49

J. LaRue: 'Fundamental Considerations in Style Analysis', *Notes*, xxv (1968–9), 447

P. Aldrich: 'An Approach to the Analysis of Renaissance Music', *MR*, xxx (1969), 1

S. Arom: 'Essai d'une notation des monodies à des fins d'analyse', *RdM*, lv (1969), 175

P. Batstone: 'Musical Analysis as Phenomenology', *PNM*, vii/2 (1969), 94

D. Beach: 'A Schenker Bibliography', *JMT*, xiii (1969), 1–37

D. Beach, D. Mintz and R. Palmer: 'Analysis Symposium', *JMT*, xiii (1969), 186–217

M. Bense: *Einführung in die informationstheoretische Ästhetik* (Reinbeck bei Hamburg, 1969)

W. Berger: 'Structuri sonore şi aspectele lor armonice', *Muzica*, xix (1969), no.9, p.10; no.10, p.8

B. Boretz: 'Meta-variations: Studies in the Foundations of Musical Thought (I)', *PNM*, viii/1 (1969), 1–74; 'II: Sketch of a Musical System', viii/2 (1970), 49–111; 'III: Analytic Fallout (I)', xi/1 (1972), 146–223; 'IV: Analytic Fallout (II)', xi/2 (1973), 156–203

H. A. Brockhaus: 'Probleme den Kategoriensystems', *BMw*, xi (1969), 245

G. S. Dickinson: *A Handbook of Style in Music* (New York, 1969)

H. Engel: 'Thematische Satzverbindungen zyklischer Werke bis zur Klassik', *Musa–mens–musici: im Gedenken an Walther Vetter* (Leipzig, 1969), 109

R. F. Erickson: 'A General-purpose System for Computer Aided Musical Studies', *JMT*, xiii (1969), 276

J. L. Hanson: *An Operational Approach to Theory of Rhythm* (diss., Yale U., 1969)

H. Kaufmann: 'Zur Problematik der Werkgestalt in der Musik des 18. Jahrhunderts', *NZM*, cxxx (1969), 290

H. B. Lincoln: 'The Computer and Music Research: Prospects and Problems', *Council for Research in Music Education Bulletin*, xviii (1969), 1

B. Lindblom and J. Sundberg: 'Towards a Generative Theory of Melody', *Speech Transmission Laboratory Quarterly Progress and Status Report*, iv (1969), 53–86

J. Mainka: 'Frühe Analysen zweier Stücke aus dem "Wohltemperierten Klavier" ', *Musa–mens–musici: im Gedenken an Walther Vetter* (Leipzig, 1969), 177 [essays by J. A. P. Schulz, 1773]

R. M. Mason: 'An Encoding Algorithm and Tables for the Digital Analysis of Harmony', *JRME*, xvii (1969), 286, 369

R. P. Morgan: *The Delayed Structural Downbeat and its Effect on the Tonal and Rhythmic Structure of Sonata Form Recapitulation* (diss., Princeton U., 1969)

B. P. Moyer: *Concepts of Musical Form in the Nineteenth Century with Special Reference to A. B. Marx and Sonata Form* (diss., Stanford U., 1969)

F. R. Noske: *Forma formans: een struucturanalytische methode toegepast op de instrumentale muziek van Jan Pieterszoon Sweelinck* (Amsterdam, 1969)

L. Treitler: 'The Present as History', *PNM*, vii/2 (1969), 1–58

G. E. Wittlich: *An Examination of some Set-theoretic Applications in the Analysis of Non-serial Music* (diss., U. of Iowa, 1969)

——: 'Programming a Computer for Music Analysis', *Your Musical Cue*, v (1969), 3

K. H. Wörner: *Die Zeitalter der thematischen Prozess in der Geschichte der Musik* (Regensburg, 1969)

B. Boretz: 'The Construction of a Musical Syntax', *PNM*, ix/1 (1970), 23; ix/2–x/1 (1971), 232–70

J. Brincker: 'Statistical Analysis of Music: An Application of Information Theory', *STMf*, lii (1970), 53

B. S. Brook, ed.: *Musicology and the Computer: Musicology 1966–2000: a Practical Program, Three Symposia* (New York, 1970) [i and iii on analysis and cataloguing; ii on music input languages]

A. C. Chandola: 'Some System of Musical Scales and Linguistic Principles', *Semiotica*, ii (1970), 135

T. Clifton: 'An Application of Goethe's Concept of Steigerung to the Morphology of Diminution', *JMT*, xiv (1970), 165

C. Dahlhaus: 'Analyse und Werturteil, Musikpädagogik', *Forschung und Lehre*, viii, ed. S. Abel-Struth (Mainz, 1970)

——: 'Hermann von Helmholtz und der Wissenschaftscharakter der Musiktheorie', *Über Musiktheorie: Arbeitstagung: Berlin 1970*, 49

H. de la Motte-Haber: 'Typologien musikalischen Verhaltens: ein Überblick', *Musica*, xxiv (1970), 136

R. F. P. Erickson: *Rhythmic Problems and Melodic Structure in Organum purum: a Computer-assisted Study* (diss., Yale U., 1970)

A. Feil: ' "Abmessung und Art" der Einschnitte": Rhythmus in Beethovens Satzbau', *GfMKB, Bonn 1970*, 33

W. Fucks: 'Über formale Struktureigenschaften musikalischer Partituren', *Experimentelle Musik: Raum-Musik, Visuelle Musik*, ed. F. Winckel (Berlin, 1970), 33

G. George: *Tonality and Musical Structure* (New York, 1970)

S. Gilbert: *The Trichord: an Analytical Outlook for Twentieth-century Music* (diss., Yale U., 1970)

F. E. Hansen: 'Musikalsk analyse ved hjaelp af modeller', *STMf*, lii (1970), 50

T. Karp: 'A Test for Melodic Borrowings among Notre Dame "Organa dupla" ', *The Computer and Music*, ed. H. B. Lincoln (Ithaca, NY, 1970), 293

J. LaRue: *Guidelines for Style Analysis* (New York, 1970)

H. B. Lincoln, ed.: *The Computer and Music* (Ithaca and London, 1970), 115–295 [incl. analyses of works, ethnomusicological analyses, and essays in stylistic analysis]

B. Lindblom and J. Sundberg: 'Towards a Generative Theory of Melody', *STMf*, lii (1970), 71

L. Lockwood: 'The Autograph of the First Movement of Beethoven's Sonata for Violoncello and Pianoforte, Opus 69', *Music Forum*, ii (1970), 1–109

D. Loeb: 'Mathematical Aspects of Music', *Music Forum*, ii (1970), 110

H. Meyer: 'Analytische und/oder hermeneutische Werkbetrachtung', *Musica*, xxiv (1970), 346

A. Pike: *A Phenomenological Analysis of Musical Experience and Other Related Essays* (New York, 1970)

H. Pousseur: *Fragments théoriques, i: Sur la musique expérimentale* (Brussels, 1970)

H. G. Rohrer: *Musikalische Stilanalyse auf der Grundlage eines Modelles für Lernprozesse* (Berlin and Munich, 1970)

J. Rohwer: *Die harmonischen Grundlagen der Musik* (Kassel, 1970)

H. Rösing: *Probleme und neue Wege der Analyse von Instrumenten- und Orchesterklängen* (Vienna, 1970)

I. Supičic: 'Matter and Form in Music', *IRASM*, i (1970), 149

W. Thomson: 'Style Analysis: or the Perils of Pigeonholes', *JMT*, xiv (1970), 192

B. Vermazen: 'Information Theory and Musical Value', *Journal of Aesthetics and Art Criticism*, xxix (1970–71), 367

R. A. Beeson: 'Background and Model: a Concept in Musical Analysis', *MR*, xxxii (1971), 349

J. Blacking: 'Deep and Surface Structures in Venda Music', *YIFMC*, iii (1971), 91

——: 'Towards a Theory of Musical Competence', *Man: Anthropological Essays Presented to O.F. Raum* (Cape Town, 1971), 19

N. Böker-Heil: 'DODEK –eine Computerdemonstration', *Zeitschrift für Musiktheorie*, ii (1971), 2

——: 'Ein algebraisches Modell des Durmoll tonalen Systems', *1. Internationalen Kongress für Musiktheorie: Stuttgart 1971*, 64–104

A. Clarkson and E. Laufer: 'Analysis Symposium: Brahms Op.105/1', *JMT*, xv (1971), 2–57

D. Cohen: 'Palestrina Counterpoint: a Musical Expression of Unexcited Speech', *JMT*, xv (1971), 84

R. Court: 'Langage verbale et langages ésthétiques', *Musique en jeu*, ii (1971), 14

T. Kneif: 'Bedeutung, Struktur, Gegenfigur: zur Theorie des musikalischen "Meinens"', *IRASM*, ii (1971), 213

A. J. Komar: *Theory of Suspensions: a Study of Metrical and Pitch Relations in Tonal Music* (Princeton, 1971)

O. E. Laske: 'An Acoulogical Performance Model for Music', *Electronic Music Reports*, no.4 (1971), 31–64

H. Lefebvre: 'Musique et sémiologie', *Musique en jeu*, iv (1971), 52

E. Lendvai: *Béla Bartók: an Analysis of his Music* (London, 1971)

F. B. Mâche: 'Méthodes linguistiques et musicologie', *Musique en jeu*, v (1971), 75

J.-J. Nattiez: 'Lexique des termes linguistique'; 'Bibliographie', *Musique en jeu*, v (1971), 93; 96 [incl. bibliography of musical semiology]

——: 'Situation de la sémiologie musicale', *Musique en jeu*, v (1971), 3

P. Nielsen: *Den musikalske formanalyse fra A. B. Marx' 'Kompositionslehre' til vore dages strukturanalyse* (Copenhagen, 1971)

D. Osmond-Smith: 'Music as Communication: Semiology or Morphology?', *IRASM*, ii (1971), 108

A. Pike: 'The Perceptual Aspects of Motivic Structure in Music', *Journal of Aesthetics and Art Criticism*, xxx (1971–2), 79

L. S. Rappoport, A. Sokhor and Yu. Kholopov, eds.: *Teoreticheskiye problemī musīkal'nïkh form i zhanrov* [Theoretical problems of musical form and genre], i (Moscow, 1971), ii (Moscow, 1972)

C. Rosen: *The Classical Style: Haydn, Mozart, Beethoven* (London, 1971, 2/1972)

J. Rothgeb: 'Design as a Key to Structure in Tonal Music', *JMT*, xv (1971), 230

A. Salop: *Studies on the History of Musical Style* (Detroit, 1971)

I. Supičic: 'Expression and Meaning in Music', *IRASM*, ii (1971), 194

I. Xenakis: *Musique, architecture* (Paris, 1971)

N. Moutard: 'L'articulation en musique', *La linguistique*, vii/2 (1971), 5; viii/1 (1972), 25

B. Alphonce: 'The Invariance Matrix as an Analytical Tool', *IMSCR*, xi *Copenhagen 1972*, i, 228

M. Babbitt: 'Contemporary Music Composition and Music Theory as Contemporary Intellectual History', *Perspectives in Musicology*, ed. B. S. Brook (New York, 1972), 151–84

D. Bartha: 'Liedform-Probleme', *Festskrift Jens Peter Larsen* (Copenhagen, 1972), 317

I. D. Bent: 'Current Methods in Stylistic Analysis', *IMSCR*, xi *Copenhagen 1972*, i, 43

N. Böker-Heil: 'Musikalische Stilanalyse und Computer: einige grundsätzliche Erwägungen', *IMSCR*, xi *Copenhagen 1972*, i, 45, 108

H. A. Brockhaus: 'Bemerkungen zur Verbalisierung des Musikalischen im Prozess der Analyse', *IMSCR*, xi *Copenhagen 1972*, i, 309

J. L. Broeckx and W. Landrieu: 'Comparative Computer Study of Style, Based on Five Liedmelodies', *Interface*, i (1972), 29–92

V. Chenoweth: *Melodic Perception and Analysis: a Manual on Ethnic Melody* (Ukarumpa, Papua, 1972)

L. Crickmore: 'The Musical Gestalt', *MR*, xxxiii (1972), 285

C. Dahlhaus: 'Wagners dramatisch-musikalischer Formbegriff', *AnMc*, no.11 (1972), 290

F. Delalande: 'L'analyse des musiques électro-acoustiques', *Musique en jeu*, viii (1972), 50

H. H. Eggebrecht: 'Zur Methode der musikalischen Analyse', *Erich Doflein Festschrift* (Mainz, 1972), 67

M. Fink: *Music Analysis: an Annotated Bibliography* (Los Alamitos, 1972)

J. Finscher: 'Thesen zu Analyse und Interpretation', *IMSCR*, xi *Copenhagen 1972*, i, 54

A. Forte: 'Sets and Nonsets in Schoenberg's Atonal Music', *PNM*, xi/1 (1972), 43

R. Frisius: 'Musik–Sprache', *Musik und Bildung*, iv (1972), 575

H. Heckmann: *Musikwissenschaft und Computer* (Leipzig, 1972)

J. T. Hutcheson: *Musical Form and Analysis: a Programmed Course* (Boston, Mass., 1972)

O. E. Laske: 'On Musical Strategies with a View to a Generative Theory of Music', *Interface*, i (1972), 111

J.-J. Nattiez: 'Is a Descriptive Semiotics of Music Possible?', *Language Sciences*, no.23 (1972), 1

——: 'La linguistique: voie nouvelle pour l'analyse musicale?', *Cahiers canadiens de musique*, iv (1972), 101; Eng. trans. *IRASM*, iv (1973), 56

H. Pousseur: *Musique, sémantique, société* (Paris, 1972)

P. Rummenhöller: 'Anmerkungen zur musikalischen Analyse', *Zeitschrift für Musiktheorie*, iii/1 (1972), 2

N. Ruwet: *Langage, musique, poésie* (Paris, 1972) [incl. articles on music written 1959–67]

L. Treitler: 'Methods, Style, Analysis', *IMSCR*, xi *Copenhagen 1972*, i, 61

P. Westergaard: 'On the Notion of Style', *IMSCR*, xi *Copenhagen 1972*, i, 71

C. Wolff: 'Toward a Methodology of Dialectic Style Consideration: Preliminary Terminological and Historical Considerations', *IMSCR*, xi *Copenhagen 1972*, i, 74

H. Chiarucci: 'Essai d'analyse structurale d'oeuvres musicales', *Musique en jeu*, xii (1973), 11–44

R. Cooper: 'Propositions pour un modèle transformationnel de description musicale', *Musique en jeu*, x (1973), 70

R. Court: 'Musique, mythe, langage', *Musique en jeu*, xii (1973), 45

A. Forte: *The Structure of Atonal Music* (New Haven and London, 1973)

R. A. Hall: 'La struttura della musica e del linguaggio', *NRMI*, vii (1973), 206

G. Hausswald: *Musikalische Stilkunde* (Wilhelmshaven, 1973)

R. Jackson: 'Music Theory: a Single or Multiple View?', *College Music Symposium*, xiii (1973), 65

G. Jones: *Heinrich Christoph Koch's Description of the Symphony and a Comparison with Selected Symphonies of C. P. E. Bach and Haydn* (diss., U. of Calif., Los Angeles, 1973)

E. Karkoschka: 'Über Exaktheit in Musikanalyse', *Zeitschrift für Musiktheorie*, iv/2 (1973), 3

J. Kramer: 'The Fibonacci Series in Twentieth-century Music', *JMT*, xvii (1973), 111–48

A. Labussière: *Codage des structures rythmo-mélodiques à partir de créations vocales* (Paris, 1973)

O. E. Laske: *Introduction to a Generative Theory of Music* (Utrecht, 1973)

L. B. Meyer: *Explaining Music: Essays and Explorations* (Berkeley, 1973)

C. Miereanu: ' "Textkomposition"–voie zéro de l'écriture musicale', *Musique en jeu*, xiii (1973), 49

J.-J. Nattiez and L. Hirbour-Paquette: 'Analyse musicale et sémiologie: à propos du Prélude de "Pelléas" ', *Musique en jeu*, x (1973), 42

J.-J. Nattiez: 'Analyse musicale et sémiologie: le structuralisme de Lévi-Strauss', *Musique en jeu*, xii (1973), 59

——: 'Linguistics: a New Approach for Musical Analysis?', *IRASM*, iv (1973), 53

——: 'Rencontre avec Lévi-Strauss: le plaisir et la structure', *Musique en jeu*, xii (1973), 3

——: 'Sémiologie et sémiographie musicales', *Musique en jeu*, xiii (1973), 70

——: 'Trois modèles linguistiques pour l'analyse musicale', *Musique en jeu*, x (1973), 3

W. A. Schulz: 'Anmerkung zur Stilanalyse', *Mf*, xxvi (1973), 241

L. J. Solomon: *Symmetry as a Determinant of Musical Composition* (diss., U. of West Virginia, 1973)

C. Dahlhaus: 'Schoenberg and Schenker', *PRMA*, c (1973–4), 209

A. Goehr: 'The Theoretical Writings of Arnold Schoenberg', *PRMA*, c (1973–4), 85

D. W. Beach: 'The Origins of Harmonic Analysis', *JMT*, xviii (1974), 274–307

H. Beck: *Methoden der Werkanalyse in Musikgeschichte und Gegenwart* (Wilhelmshaven, 1974)

T. Fay: 'Context Analysis of Musical Gestures', *JMT*, xvii (1974), 124

A. Forte: 'Theory', *Dictionary of Contemporary Music*, ed. J. Vinton (New York, 1974)

S. E. Gilbert: 'An Introduction to Trichordal Analysis', *JMT*, xviii (1974), 338

G. Hennenberg: *Theorien zur Rhythmik und Metrik*, Mainzer Studien zur Musikwissenschaft, vi (Tutzing, 1974)

S. Keil: 'Zum Begriff "Struktur" in der Musik', *Musica*, xxviii (1974), 324

S. M. Kosta: *A Bibliography of Computer Applications in Music* (Hackensack, 1974)

N. Ruwet: 'Théorie et méthodes dans les études musicales', *Musique en jeu*, xvii (1974), 11

S. W. Smoliar: 'Process Structuring and Music Theory', *JMT*, xviii (1974), 309

R. Travis and A. Forte: 'Analysis Symposium: Webern, Orchestral Pieces (1913) Movement 1 ("bewegt")', *JMT*, xvii (1974), 2–43

L. Treitler: 'Homer and Gregory: the Transmission of Epic Poetry and Plainchant', *MQ*, lx (1974), 333–72

W. Berry: *Structural Functions in Music* (Englewood Cliffs, 1975)

D. Lidov: *On Musical Phrase*, Monographies de sémiologie et d'analyses musicales, i (Montreal, 1975)

B. Lortat-Jacob: 'Quelques problèmes généraux d'analyse musicale', *RdM*, lxi (1975), 3–34

J.-J. Nattiez: *'Densité 21.5' de Varèse: essai d'analyse sémiologique*, Monographies de sémiologie et d'analyses musicales, ii (Montreal, 1975)

——: *Fondements d'une sémiologie de la musique* (Paris, 1975)

J.-M. Vaccaro: 'Proposition d'analyse pour une polyphonie vocale', *RdM*, lxi (1975), 35

A. Whittall: 'Tonality and the Whole-tone Scale in the Music of Debussy', *MR*, xxxvi (1975), 261

J. Kerman: 'Tovey's Beethoven', *American Scholar* (1975–6), Wint., 795

N. K. Baker: 'Heinrich Koch and the Theory of Melody', *JMT*, xx (1976), 1–48

R. D. Cogan and O. Pozzi Escot: *Sonic Design: the Nature of Sound and Music* (Englewood Cliffs, 1976)

U. Eco: *A Theory of Semiotics* (Bloomington, 1976)

J. Jiránek: 'Observations on the Theory and Historical and Contemporary Practice of Musical Analysis', *HV*, xiii (1976), 106

R. P. Morgan: 'Dissonant Prolongation: Theoretical and Compositional Precedents', *JMT*, xx (1976), 49–91

C. Schachter: 'Rhythm and Linear Analysis: a Preliminary Study', *Music Forum*, iv (1976), 281–334

S. W. Smoliar: 'Music Programs: an Approach to Music Theory through Computational Linguistics', *JMT*, xx (1976), 105

G. Stefani: 'Analisi, semiosi, semiotica', *RIM*, xi (1976), 106

M. Yeston: *The Stratification of Musical Rhythm* (New Haven and London, 1976)

E. Narmour: *Beyond Schenkerism: the Need for Alternatives in Musical Analysis* (Chicago, 1977)

M. Yeston, ed.: *Readings in Schenker Analysis and other Approaches* (New Haven, 1977)

IAN D. BENT

Ananeanes. The ENECHEMA of the first authentic mode in the Byzantine modal system.

Ananeotes, Michael. Composer of Byzantine kalophonic chant; *see* GLYKYS, JOANNES.

Anatolia. A region roughly equivalent to Asiatic Turkey. This article covers the period from the earliest surviving evidence in the 6th millennium BC until the Persian invasion of Anatolia in the 6th century BC. Although problems remain, knowledge of this subject has grown appreciably in the 20th century as a result of archaeological finds and the increasing availability of Hittite texts in translation. The instrumentarium was large, and music was widely used. For Anatolian music in later periods, *see* IRAN; HELLENISTIC STATES; ROME, §I; BYZANTINE RITE, MUSIC OF THE; TURKEY.

1. Peoples in early Anatolia. 2. Surviving instruments and iconography: (i) Prehistoric and Hattian period (ii) Hittite Old Kingdom (iii) Hittite Empire (iv) From the fall of the Hittite Empire. 3. Hittite literary evidence.

1. PEOPLES IN EARLY ANATOLIA. Early Anatolian history may be subdivided according to the ascendancy of the following peoples (the dates – all BC – are approximate):

Hattians (the original inhabitants, speaking a non-Indo-European language): 3rd millennium
Hittite Old Kingdom: 20th–15th centuries
Hittite Empire (under a new dynasty, possibly of Hurrian origin): 15th–12th centuries
Phrygians: 12th–7th centuries (ultimately defeated by the Cimmerians, who in turn were defeated by the Lydians)
Lydians and Phrygians: 7th–6th centuries.

2. SURVIVING INSTRUMENTS AND ICONOGRAPHY.
(*i*) *Prehistoric and Hattian period.* In the remarkable drawings of animal dances at Çatal Höyük (6th millennium BC), two of the dancers may be holding a round frame drum (fig.1) and panpipes (see Mellaart, 1966, pl.lxia); these instruments also appear in later sources.

Highly developed Hattian sistra (late 3rd millennium BC), probably used in religious ceremonies, have been found at Horoztepe and at an unknown central Anatolian site (fig.2). Similar instruments were used at Alaca Höyük (see Özgüç and Akok, 1958, p.49). From the same period from Horoztepe come some striking discs; each has a handle ending in an obliquely pierced

boss attached to the centre of the disc (see Özgüç, 1964, fig.5; Özgüç and Akok, 1958, pl.vii, 3, fig.20; Tezcan, 1960, pl.18, 2f). Bronze or copper specimens have been discovered at Alaca Höyük (see Arık, 1937, pl.cclxxvii; Kosay, 1951, p.160) and at Soloi in the south (see Bittel, 1940, figs.15f). Conico-cylindrical bells have been found at Alaca Höyük (Arık, 1937, pl.clxxxvii).

(*ii*) *Hittite Old Kingdom.* A seal impression from Kültepe, of the 20th or 19th century BC, depicts a lyre with its resonator in the form of a bull, like instruments of the 3rd millennium BC in Mesopotamia (*see* MESOPOTAMIA; and T. and N. Özgüç, 1953, pl.lxii, no.702). Another lyre, taller than the two musicians playing it, is depicted on a vase from Inandik (16th century BC; see Duchesne-Guillemin, 1969, p.11).

Three sherds with painted relief decoration, of the first half of the 2nd millennium BC, from Kabaklı (see Bossert, 1952, pl.6), Bitik (see T. Özgüç, 1957, pl.IV*b*) and Alishar Höyük (see von der Osten, 1937, fig.155, c.2623) show musicians with cymbals. The Alishar Höyük sherd also shows the end of the neck of a lute, with two strings hanging from it; another fragment of the Bitik vase (see T. Özgüç, 1957, pl.iva) depicts two men with daggers perhaps performing a sword dance.

(*iii*) *Hittite Empire.* Few representations of instruments date from the Hittite Empire. Three figurines (see Behn, 1954, pl.39, fig.91; Wegner, *MGG*, pl.16, 6) of unknown provenance feature a round drum and two conical wind instruments. The latter (see Aign, 1963, figs.103f) have been regarded as trumpets, but (because of their playing position) may possibly be shawm-type instruments. The classification of an object held by a figure in the Alaca Höyük reliefs as a trumpet is similarly doubtful (see Akurgal, 1962, pl.93; Frankfort, 1970, fig.268); the object resembles a Hittite sword, and some authorities view the figure as a sword-swallower.

A lute player stands with the acrobats and dancers of the Alaca Höyük reliefs (see Behn, 1954, pl.39, fig.90; Bossert, 1942, fig.506; Stauder, 1970, fig.2g; Wegner, 1950, pl.10a; Wegner, *MGG*, fig.1). His waisted instrument is quite unlike the usual small-bodied long-necked lutes of ancient western Asia; the five soundholes in each side of the table (absent in Syrian and Mesopotamian lutes may indicate Egyptian influence. On a sherd from Alishar Höyük (see von der Osten, 1937, fig.154, d.1622) another lute is depicted, but only the end of the neck with its two strings remains.

Harps are absent from Hittite sources, but a Hittite plays a vertical angular harp on an Egyptian figurine from Gurob (see Petrie, 1890, pl.xviii, 38). Round-based lyres are shown on a seal from Mardin (12th century BC; see fig.3) and on one with a similar scene from Tarsus (see Porada, 1956, fig.j).

(*iv*) *From the fall of the Hittite Empire.* A relief from Karatepe (*c*700 BC) shows a procession led by a figure playing divergent double pipes (*see* AULOS), followed by two lyre players and a drummer (see Aign, fig.101; Akurgal, 1962, pl.142; Bossert and Alkım, 1950, pl.xi, 55, pl.xiii, 68; Frankfort, 1970, fig.360). Another relief from Karatepe, of similar date (fig.4), also shows an aulos player, here wearing a *phorbeia*; the pipes are clearly unequal in length. Two drums of unequal size are being beaten; a fourth musician plays a lyre, and they all accompany a dancer.

The three different types of lyre in these reliefs illustrate an admixture of various cultural influences. The

1. *Ritual leopard dance: transcript of a wall painting (6th millennium* BC) *at Catal Höyük*

2. *Hattian bronze sistrum (c2100–2000* BC) *from Horoztepe (Arkeoloji Müzeleri, Ankara)*

4. *Dancer, with musicans playing double auloi (bottom right), lyre (bottom left) and drums: relief (c700* BC) *from Karatepe*

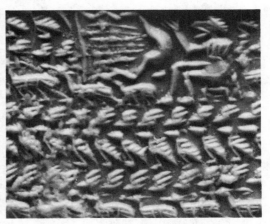

3. *Round-based lyre: detail of a seal (12th century* BC) *from Mardin (British Museum, London)*

second lyre in the procession has a round-based resonator and symmetrical arms; the lyre in the second relief has curved symmetrical arms and a yoke with handles to facilitate tuning. (These lyres are close to Greek or Aegean models.) The remaining Karatepe lyre has a rectangular resonator, asymmetrical arms and an angled yoke. A similar lyre appears in a relief from Zinjirli (see Aign, 1963, fig.112; Behn, 1954, pl.40, fig.92; Bossert,

1942, fig.949; Luschan, 1893–1943, iii, pl.lxii; Wegner, 1950, pl.15b; Wegner, *MGG*, pl.16, 4), but the latter has more strings and a steeper yoke than the Karatepe lyre, and shows little sign of a resonator. The Zinjirli relief has yet another type of lyre, with eyes painted or inlaid in the resonator, and symmetrical arms; its yoke, arms and resonator form a rectangle.

The Zinjirli lyre players are accompanied by two

5. *Map of major Hittite sites*

6. *Musicians with lute (left), aulos and clappers: relief (beginning of the 1st century* BC) *from Carchemish (Arkeoloji Müzeleri, Ankara)*

drummers, and another Zinjirli relief depicts two drummers with one standing on the other's shoulders (Bossert, 1942, fig.950; Frankfort, 1970, fig.356; Luschan, 1893–1943, iii, fig.259*b*). The 9th-century BC reliefs of Zinjirli have several figures in Hittite costume, but these musicians are portrayed as Assyrians; the Zinjirli lutenist (see Bossert, 1942, fig.948; Moortgat, 1932, pl.lxxxi; Luschan, 1893–1943, iii, fig.119, pl.xxxviii*a*; Wegner, *MGG*, pl.15, 1) is dressed differently again, and is shown seated. His long-necked lute has a small spherical resonator without soundholes. Another (damaged) relief from Zinjirli shows part of a set of double pipes (see Przeworski, 1936, pl.x, 6) and several bronze bells (see Luschan, 1893–1943, v, p.106, pl.48).

Musicians dressed similarly to the Zinjirli lutenist appear on three reliefs from Carchemish, a city which retained close links with imperial Hittite culture. A cult meal has a standing lutenist in attendance (see Bossert, 1942, fig.833; Garstang, 1929, fig.35; Moortgat, 1932, pl.lvii; Stauder, 1970, fig.2f; Woolley, 1921, pl.B.30*b*). A scene of accompanied dancing has another standing lutenist, an aulos player and a figure with small clappers (fig.6). The third Carchemish relief (Moortgat, 1932, pl.lxxix; Wegner, *MGG*, pl.16, 7; Woolley, 1921, pl.B.18*b*) has a large drum apparently supported by one figure and beaten by two others, and a horn player.

A fragment from Marash shows the end of the neck of a lute and the feet of its standing player (see Bossert, 1942, fig.808; Garstang, 1929, fig.22; Meyer, 1914, fig.31); another Marash fragment has the head of a double-aulos player (see Behn, 1954, pl.41, fig.93; Przeworski, 1936, pl.x, 2). A relief also from Marash shows a woman with a child in her lap, seated before a table and holding a small, almost rectangular lyre (see Aign, 1963, fig.147; Bossert, 1942, fig.810; Behn, 1954, pl.38, fig.88; Garstang, 1929, fig.19; Meyer, 1914, fig.30; Wegner, *MGG*, pl.15, 2).

A relief from Tell Halaf, showing an elongated lyre played by a bear and a drum played by a lion while other animals dance (see Behn, 1954, pl.41, fig.94; Bossert, 1942, fig.473; Galpin, 1937, pl.viii, 1; Wegner, *MGG*, pl.15, 3), is Hurrian or Aramaic rather than Hittite. The theme has Mesopotamian links. Another relief, possibly from the Gaziantep region, which has been dated *c*700 BC, shows a figure with panpipes (fig.7).

From Mylasa in Caria comes a bronze figurine of a trumpeter, wearing a *phorbeia* and supporting his instrument with his left hand (fig.8); Aign (1963) has dated this bronze in the 8th or 7th century BC. Another 8th-century figurine wears a Phrygian cap and plays a hornpipe (see Rimmer, 1969, pl.viii*c*).

Two 6th-century monuments show Cybele in conjunction with musical instruments. A relief from Altın Taş, near Afyonkarahısar, shows Cybele and Attis on a couch; below them is a procession of musicians (see Bossert, 1942, fig.1107; Buckler and Calder, 1939, pl.65, no.369). The second figure plays divergent double pipes (not the *auloi elymoi* of the Cybelean cult, since they lack a horn bell), and the third plays a single pipe; the first and fourth figures extend their hands in a clapping gesture. The other monument, a statue from Boğazköy (fig.9), shows Cybele accompanied by musicians playing a lyre and parallel double auloi with long double reeds. The pipes player wears a *phorbeia* (see Aign, 1963, fig.140); the lyre has seven strings and is decorated with a duck's head (see Aign, fig.141).

3. HITTITE LITERARY EVIDENCE. A number of the texts from the Hittite capital of Ḫattušas (now Boğazköy) refer to instruments and music. These are from the imperial period, some being copies of earlier texts; none is later than 1200 BC. Instruments are named either with Hittite words or with Sumerian words in place of a Hittite word; as yet, the Sumerian terms cannot certainly be equated with Hittite readings. The term (LÚ) *kinirtalla-* in the texts is another foreign borrowing: *kinir* is related to *kinnari* in a Hurrian text from

7. *Figure with panpipes: relief (c700 BC), possibly from the Gaziantep region (Musée du Louvre, Paris)*

Ugarit (see Wulstan, 1971, p.371) and to the Hebrew *kinnor* (*see* JEWISH MUSIC, §4(iv)), an instrument now identified as the western Semitic lyre and no doubt known to the Hittites even though it does not occur in their iconography.

The Sumerian ideograms that refer to instruments are GIŠ.dINANNA, (GIŠ)ŠÀ.A.TAR, GI.GÍD and (GIŠ)BALAG.DI. Hittite names with the determinative GIŠ ('wood') are *arkammi*, *ḫuḫupal*, *mukar* and *ḫunzinar*. The determinative for copper (URUDU) occurs with *galgalturi*, and that for horn (SI) with *šawatar*. *Šawatar* can be translated with certainty as 'horn'. GI.GÍD (GI = 'long', GÍD = 'reed') has generally been trans-

8. *Trumpeter wearing a phorbeia: bronze figurine (8th or 7th century* BC) *from Mylasa in Caria (British Museum, London)*

9. *Cybele, with musicians playing double auloi and lyre: statue (6th century* BC) *from Boğazköy (Anadólu Medeniyetleri Müzesi, Ankara)*

lated 'flute'; since no flutes are depicted or extant, a better translation would be 'reed pipe'.

The linguistic evidence allows a classification of Hittite instruments into two groups, determined by the verbs indicating the method of sound production: *hazzik-* or *walḫ-* ('strike') and *pariparāi-* ('blow'). Struck instruments include the string instruments; they comprise the group *arkammi, ḫuḫupal, galgalturi,* GIŠ.dINANNA, (GIŠ)ŠÀ.A.TAR, (GIŠ)BALAG.DI. The wind instruments are *šawatar* and GI.GÍD. *Ḫunzinar* occurs with the verb SÌR (*išhamai-*), which means 'sing'. These verbs are used with other instruments: Kümmel (1973) has explained such instances as elliptical formulae to be translated 'sing to the accompaniment of the . . . instrument'.

Descriptive references to instruments are few; the evidence is mostly insufficient to establish correspondences between names and instruments. The *ḫuḫupal*, however, can be identified as a vessel clapper: it was a struck instrument of boxwood or ivory, which might be 'in sets' (see Kronasser, 1963, p.8f), filled with wine (see Alp, 1957, p.7) and tied to the feet (KUB XXV 37 II 26, communicated by O. R. Gurney, 1975). The latter reference recalls the Greek *kroupezion* or *kroupalon* (foot clapper).

The *mukar*, used by a priest to summon the weather-god of Nerik, may be a signalling instrument. Some depicted instruments occur in large (GAL) and small (TUR) varieties; these qualifications exist for the GIŠ.dINANNA, but the possibilities of identification are various, although the decoration of silver possible for the large GIŠ.dINANNA (see Otten, 1958, p.27) recalls the similarly decorated lyre from Ur (see Rimmer, 1969, pl.ii). The association of the small GIŠ.dINANNA with a system of eight modes (see Werner, 1948, p.2) rests on a suspect translation from a text that is insufficiently identified. The GIŠ.dINANNA instruments were regarded as 'holy places' in the temple, and offerings were placed before them.

Priests sang solo or in chorus during the ceremonies, accompanied most often by GIŠ.dINANNA instruments, although these might alternate with other instruments (see Alp, 1940, p.54). The priests may sometimes have sung unaccompanied (see Neu, 1970, p.33). The (LÚ)NAR priest sang in Hattian, Hittite or Hurrian, depending on the ethnic associations of the god being invoked (see Alp, 1940, p.52); tablets found at Ugarit (Ras Shamra) contain Hurrian hymns with neumatic notation (transcriptions in Wulstan, 1971).

The cult of animals is attested in the women of Nerik singing the Song of the Bull (see Haas, 1970, p.63). Other occasions for music were death rituals (see Otten, 1958, p.14) and the king's journey to Nerik (see Haas, 1970, p.271).

BIBLIOGRAPHY

MUSIC AND INSTRUMENTS

F. W. Galpin: *The Music of the Sumerians and their Immediate Successors the Babylonians and the Assyrians* (Cambridge, 1937)

A. Machabey: 'La musique des Hittites', *RdM*, xxiii (1944), 1

E. Werner: 'The Oldest Sources of Octave and Octoechos', *AcM*, xx (1948), 1

M. Wegner: *Die Musikinstrumente des alten Orients* (Münster, 1950)

F. Behn: *Musikleben im Altertum und frühen Mittelalter* (Stuttgart, 1954)

M. Wegner: 'Hethitische Musik', *MGG*

B. Aign: *Die Geschichte der Musikinstrumente des ägäischen Raumes bis um 700 vor Christus* (Frankfurt, 1963)

M. Duchesne-Guillemin: 'La théorie babylonienne des métaboles musicales', *RdM*, lv (1969), 3

J. Rimmer: *Ancient Musical Instruments of Western Asia in the British Museum* (London, 1969)

F. Ellermeier: 'Beiträge zur Frühgeschichte altorientalischer Saiteninstrumente', *Archäologie und altes Testament: Kurt Galling Festschrift* (Tübingen, 1970), 75

H. G. Güterbock: 'Musical Notation in Ugarit', *Revue d'Assyriologie*, lxiv (1970), 44

W. Stauder: 'Die Musik der Sumerer, Babylonier und Assyrer', *Orientalische Musik*, Handbuch der Orientalistik, ed. B. Spuler, Abteilung i, suppl.iv (Leiden, 1970), 171–243

A. D. Kilmer: 'The Discovery of an Ancient Mesopotamian Theory of Music', *Proceedings of the American Philosophical Society*, cxv/2 (1971), 131

D. Wulstan: 'The Earliest Musical Notation', *ML*, lii (1971), 365

A. Spycket: 'La musique instrumentale mesopotamienne', *Journal des savants* (1972), 153–209

H. Turnbull: 'The Origin of the Long-necked Lute', *GSJ*, xxv (1972), 58

H. M. Kümmel: 'Gesang und Gesanglosigkeit in der hethitischen Kultmusik', *Festschrift Heinrich Otten* (Wiesbaden, 1973), 169

ARCHAEOLOGY AND TEXTS

W. M. Flinders Petrie: *Kahun, Gurob and Hawara* (London, 1890)

F. von Luschan: *Ausgrabungen in Sendschirli*, i–v (Berlin, 1893–1943)

E. Meyer: *Reich und Kultur der Chetiter* (Leipzig, 1914)

C. L. Woolley: *Carchemish II* (London, 1921)

A. Götze: *Ḫattušiliš* (Leipzig, 1925)

J. Garstang: *The Hittite Empire* (London, 1929)

A. Moortgat: *Die bildende Kunst des alten Orient und die Bergvölker* (Berlin, 1932)

S. Przeworski: 'Notes d'archéologie syrienne et hittite III: quelques nouveaux monuments de Marash', *Syria*, xvii (1936), 32

R. O. Arık: *Alaca Höyük hafriyatı* [Excavations in Alaca Höyük] (Ankara, 1937)

H. H. von der Osten: *The Alishar Hüyük: Seasons of 1930–32, Part II*, University of Chicago Oriental Institute Publications, xxix (Chicago, 1937)

W. H. Buckler and W. M. Calder, eds.: *Monuments and Documents from Phrygia and Caria*, Monumenta Asiae minoris antiqua, vi (Manchester, 1939)

S. Alp: *Untersuchungen zu den Beamtennamen im hethitischen Festzeremoniell*, Sammlung orientalistischer Arbeiten, v (Leipzig, 1940)

K. Bittel: 'Der Depotfund von Soloi-Pompeiopolis', *Zeitschrift für Assyriologie*, new ser., xii (1940), 183

H. Otten: 'Ein Bestattungsritual hethitischer Könige', *Zeitschrift für Assyriologie*, new ser., xii (1940), 206

H. P. T. Bossert: *Altanatolien* (Berlin, 1942)

E. Laroche: 'Teššub, Hebat et leur cour', *Journal of Cuneiform Studies*, ii (1948), 113

S. Alp: 'Die soziale Klasse der Nam.Ra-Leute und ihre hethitische Bezeichnung', *Jb für kleinasiatische Forschung*, i (1950), 113

H. P. T. Bossert, U. B. Alkım and others: *Karatepe kazıları: birinci önrapor* [Excavations at Karatepe: first preliminary report] (Ankara, 1950)

H. G. Güterbock: 'The Song of Ullikummi', *Journal of Cuneiform Studies*, v (1951), 135; vi (1952), 8

H. Koşay: *Alacahöyük kazısı 1937–1939: les fouilles d'Alacahöyük* (Ankara, 1951)

H. P. T. Bossert: 'Kleine Mitteilungen', *Jb für kleinasiatische Forschung*, ii (1952–3), 106

T. and N. Özgüç: *Ausgrabungen in Kültepe* (Ankara, 1953)

K. Bittel: 'Eine hethitische Reliefvase aus Kappadokien', *Festschrift für Carl Weickert* (Berlin, 1955), 23

E. Porada: 'A Lyre Player from Tarsus and his Relations', *The Aegean and the Near East: Studies Presented to Hetty Goldman* (Locust Valley, NY, 1956), 185

S. Alp: 'Zu den Körperteilnamen im Hethitischen', *Anatolia*, ii (1957), 1–48

T. Özgüç: 'The Bitnik Vase', *Anatolia*, ii (1957), 57

K. Bittel and others: 'Vorläufiger Bericht über die Ausgrabungen in Boğazköy im Jahre 1957', *Mitteilungen der deutschen Orient-Gesellschaft zu Berlin*, xci (1958), 1

H. Otten: *Hethitische Totenrituale* (Berlin, 1958)

T. Özgüç and M. Akok: *Horoztepe: an Early Bronze Age Cemetery and Settlement* (Ankara, 1958)

P. Oliver: 'Art of the Ancient Near East: the Second Millennium B.C.', *Bulletin of the Metropolitan Museum of Art*, new ser., xviii (1959–60), 253

H. P. T. Bossert: 'Unveröffentlichte hethitische Skulpturen', *Orientalia*, new ser., xxix (1960), 104

R. Temizer: 'Un bas-relief de Cybèle découvert à Ankara', *Anatolia*, v (1960), 183

B. Tezcan: 'New Finds from Horoztepe', *Anatolia*, v (1960), 29

E. Akurgal: *The Art of the Hittites* (London, 1962)

G. M. A. Hanfmann: 'A "Hittite" Priest from Ephesus', *American Journal of Archaeology*, lxvi (1962), 1

J. Mellaart: 'Excavations at Çatal Hüyük', *Anatolian Studies*, xii (1962), 41

H. Kronasser: 'Die Umsiedlung der schwarzen Gottheit', *Sitzungsberichte der Österreichische Akademie der Wissenschaften, phil.-hist. Klasse*, ccxli/3 (1963), 1

T. Özgüç: 'New Finds from Horoztepe', *Anatolia*, viii (1964), 1

O. R. Gurney: *The Hittites* (Harmondsworth, 1966)

J. Mellaart: 'Excavations at Çatal Hüyük 1965: 4th Preliminary Report', *Anatolian Studies*, xvi (1966), 165

H. Frankfort: *The Art and Architecture of the Ancient Orient* (Harmondsworth, 1970)

V. Haas: *Der Kult von Nerik: ein Beitrag zur hethitischen Religionsgeschichte* (Rome, 1970)

E. and H. Klingel: *Die Hethiter und ihre Nachbarn* (Leipzig, 1970)

E. Neu: *Ein althethitisches Gewitterritual*, Studien zu den Boğazköy-Texten, xii (Wiesbaden, 1970)

H. Otten: *Ein hethitisches Festritual*, Studien zu den Boğazköy-Texten, xiii (Wiesbaden, 1971)

HARVEY TURNBULL

Anavathmoi. *See* ANABATHMOI.

Ančerl, Karel (*b* Tučapy, Bohemia, 11 April 1908; *d* Toronto, 3 July 1973). Czech conductor. He studied composition and conducting at the Prague Conservatory and then was assistant conductor to Hermann Scherchen in Alois Hába's opera *The Mother* at Munich in 1931. He became a member of Scherchen's conducting class in Strasbourg, and later also studied with Talich in Prague. His career as conductor for the theatre and for Prague radio (1933–9) was interrupted by the Nazi occupation of Czechoslovakia. He was sent to concentration camps and was the only member of his family to survive. He returned to conduct the Czech RO (1947–50) and the Czech PO (1950–68). He received a Czechoslovakian State Prize in 1958 and was named National Artist in 1966. Ančerl's speciality in Czech music and in modern music had been demonstrated before the war at ISCM festivals in Amsterdam (1933), Prague (1935), Barcelona (1936) and Paris (1937). After the war he toured more widely, conducting orchestras in Belgium and Holland (1947), the USSR (1948) and elsewhere, and taking the Czech PO to various countries of Europe (including England in 1956 and 1962) and to Australia, New Zealand, Japan, China and India in 1959. He returned to England from 1967 as guest conductor with the LPO and later with other orchestras. In 1969 he succeeded Ozawa as music director of the Toronto SO; this appointment marked his decisive separation from the political pressures of musical life in Czechoslovakia. He never achieved the eminence of his younger contemporary, Rafael Kubelík, but he became after Kubelík the best known of his generation of Czech conductors; he made many gramophone records in a repertory ranging from Mozart to Stravinsky. The direct, lyrical and profoundly enjoyable qualities of his conducting were praised when he first

Karel Ančerl

appeared in London, and his work continued to be characterized by a warm though not ostentatious appeal.

BIBLIOGRAPHY
K. Sřom: *Karel Ančerl* (Prague and Bratislava, 1968)

ARTHUR JACOBS

Anche (Fr.: 'reed'). The French term for the prepared reed of a wind instrument, as distinct from *roseau* meaning 'reed' in a general or botanical sense. (The latter word is used by the reed growers and is extended by French suppliers to cover cut and split sections of the plant stem up to the actual stage of shaping.) The plural, *anches*, is also used in French organ registration to designate the reeds.

PHILIP BATE

Anchieta, Juan de (*b* ?Urrestilla, nr. Azpeitia, 1462; *d* Azpeitia, 30 July 1523). Spanish composer. He was the second son of Martín García de Anchieta and Urtayzaga de Loyola (an aunt of Ignatius Loyola) and may have studied at Salamanca University, where the music professor from 1481 to 1522 was Diego de Fermoselle, the elder brother of Juan del Encina. After his appointment on 6 February 1489 as a singer in Queen Isabella's court chapel at an annual salary of 20,000 maravedís Anchieta travelled constantly, for Isabella often moved her court (15 times between 1491 and 1503).

Anchieta's salary was raised to 30,000 maravedís on 30 August 1493. Two years later Isabella named him *maestro de capilla* to her 17-year-old son Don Juan (1478–97). His excellent services to the young prince prompted the queen to reward him with several ecclesiastical preferments. After her death in 1504 Anchieta was transferred with other members of the Castilian royal household to the service of her daughter Joanna, whose consort was Philip the Fair; in their entourage he visited Flanders, and from January to April 1506 he was in the south of England during the return voyage to Spain. The court's singers on this journey also included Pierre de La Rue, Alexander Agricola and Marbriano de Orto.

From 1507 to 1516 Anchieta earned 45,000 maravedís annually as 'Queen Joanna's chaplain and singer'. A bitter family feud erupted on 20 February 1515, when the two younger Loyola brothers assaulted Anchieta during a visit to his home; Ignatius attempted to flee but was caught and briefly imprisoned at Pamplona. In 1499 Anchieta had been appointed an absentee benefice-holder at Villarino, in the diocese of Salamanca, and a year later rector of the parish church of S Sebastián de Soreasu in Azpeitia; he was made Abbot of Arbos in 1518. That year his nephew García de Anchieta was named his successor as rector of S Sebastián de Soreasu, but was assassinated shortly afterwards.

On 15 August 1519 Charles V issued a declaration that the 57-year-old Anchieta was too old for further service at court, but confirmed the annual salary of 45,000 maravedís that he had received until 1516. A court payment record of 23 October 1520 described Anchieta as 'ill in his house at Azpeitia'. In April 1521 he secured a papal rescript permitting him to transfer the income from his Villarino benefice to a new foundation of Franciscan sisters in Azpeitia; the sisters made him their business manager and promised him a privileged burial place in their convent church. Anchieta signed his will on 19 February 1522; contrary to his wishes, he was buried at S Sebastián de Soreasu, which set off a dispute that lasted for 12 years.

Anchieta's earliest extant composition is the four-part *romance En memoria d'Alixandre* written in the summer of 1489. His *Missa 'Ea iudios a enfardelar'*, written in 1492 but now lost, was mentioned by Francisco de Salinas, who quoted the popular song on which it was based. The piece that seems to have remained popular longest is *Dos ánades*, a spirited three-voice villancico that Francisco de Quevedo (*Cuento de cuentos*, 1626) described as still frequently sung, though old-fashioned. Cervantes paid tribute to the same work in his comic tale *La ilustre fregona* (1614).

Anchieta's works lack the variety and ingenuity of device found in those of Peñalosa, his greatest Spanish contemporary. Designed for large choirs rather than for highly trained small ensembles, Anchieta's music confirms Bermudo's description of Spanish style in *Libro primero de la declaración de instrumentos* (1549) as graceful and sonorous. Even when quoting a tune such as *L'homme armé*, found in the tenor of the Agnus Dei of his *Missa [quarti toni]*, he never invested it with any of the learned devices dear to Peñalosa and to the Flemish composers whom Anchieta had met in his travels and whose music he surely knew. He used imitation but never in a recondite way, nor at intervals other than the unison, octave, 4th or 5th; he was interested not in puzzles but in sound.

Anchieta's quotation of plainsong, as in the tenors of the two motets for Ash Wednesday, ornaments the chant only slightly and at cadences. Harmonic and rhythmic repetition give a unity to these motets, and reiteration of melody and rhythm occurs throughout his music; the *Missa [quarti toni]*, for example, makes insistent use of a dotted three-note figure E–F–G. In the long Credo of the *Missa Rex virginum* he used variation of texture in accordance with a set scheme: one pair of voices, the other pair, then all four; the pattern is repeated six times and is clearly deliberate. Most triads are in root position; first inversions are almost always approached by step in the bass. Passages of parallel first-inversion chords are prominent in only one work, the three-voice *Magnificat* setting.

WORKS

SACRED

Missa [quarti toni], 4vv, *E-TZ*; ed. in MME, i (1941)
Missa Rex virginum, 4vv (Ky, Gl, Cr), *Bc*, *SE*, *TZ*; ed. in MME, i (1941)
Missa 'Ea iudios a enfardelar', 1492, lost, mentioned by Francisco de Salinas, *De musica libri septem* (1577)
Magnificat, 3vv, *SE*, *TZ*; ed. in Cohen
Magnificat, 4vv, *TZ* 2
Conditor alme siderum, 3vv, *SE*; ed. in Stevenson
Domine Jesu Christe qui hora in diei ultima, 4vv, *Sco*, *SE*, *TZ*, *Vp*, *P-Cug*; ed in Elústiza and Castrillo Hernández
Domine, ne memineris, 4vv, *E-SE*; ed. in Stevenson
Domine, non secundum peccata nostra, 3vv, *SE*; ed. in Cohen
Libera eme, Domine, 4vv, *TZ* 2
Salve regina, 4vv, *Bc*, *Sco*, *TZ*; ed. in Elústiza and Castrillo Hernández
Virgo et mater, 4vv, *Sco*, *SE*, *TZ*; ed. in Elústiza and Castrillo Hernández

O bone Jesu, 4vv, attrib. Anchieta in *SE*, is by Compère

SECULAR

Con amores, la mi madre, 4vv, ed. in MME, x (1951)
Donsella, madre de Dios, 3vv, ed. in MME, x (1951)
Dos ánades, 3vv, ed. in MME, v (1947)
En memoria d'Alixandre, 4vv, ed. in MME, v (1947)

BIBLIOGRAPHY

G. Fernández de Oviedo: *Libro de la camara real del prínçipe Don Juan* (Madrid, 1870), 182f
F. Asenjo Barbieri: Introduction to *Cancionero musical de los siglos XV y XVI* (Madrid, 1890)
A. Coster: 'Juan de Anchieta et la famille de Loyola', *Revue hispanique*, lxxix (1930), 1–332
J. B. de Elústiza and G. Castrillo Hernández: *Antología musical* (Barcelona, 1933)
A. Cohen: *The Vocal Polyphonic Style of Juan de Anchieta* (diss., New York U., 1953)
R. Stevenson: *Spanish Music in the Age of Columbus* (The Hague, 1960)

ROBERT STEVENSON

Ancient Concerts. Concert series given in London from 1776 to 1848 by the Concert of Ancient (Antient) Music; *see* LONDON, §VI, 4(i).

Ancina, (Giovanni) Giovenale (*b* Fossano, region of Cuneo, 19 Oct 1545; *d* Saluzzo, Cuneo, 31 Aug 1604). Italian music editor, composer and possibly writer on music. He was born into a leading aristocratic family of Melle, about 30 km from Fossano. He was educated at home and, from 1559, at Montpellier and then entered Turin University to study medicine, philosophy and rhetoric; he may also have studied music, since five of his 118 submissions for the doctorate were concerned with music. In 1566 he went to Pavia to continue his medical studies. On 29 January 1567 he graduated with outstanding results in arts and medicine from Turin University, and a few months later he was admitted to the university's college of doctors as a supernumerary lecturer. At the end of 1570 he left lecturing to become tutor and physician in the household of Count Madruzzi di Challant. When the count became an ambassador of the Duke of Savoy he accompanied him to Rome, where he arrived on 10 November 1574. Here he began to study theology and was strongly influenced by Filippo Neri, whom he met in the spring of 1576. He became keenly interested in Neri's work and ideas, and on 1 October 1580 he entered the Congregazione dei Preti dell'Oratorio founded by Neri; he was ordained on 9 June 1582. On 29 October 1586 Neri sent him to the newly established house of the Oratory at Naples, where besides undertaking pastoral and charitable work he wrote much devotional poetry. In the autumn of 1596

he was recalled to Rome, and in 1597 Pope Clement VIII offered him a vacant bishopric in northern Italy, which, after initial resistance, he accepted. On 26 August 1602 he was proclaimed bishop by the consistory of Saluzzo and enthroned on 1 September, but he was not officially permitted to enter his diocese until 6 March 1603. His death in the following year was apparently due to poisoning. He was beatified by Pope Leo XIII on 9 February 1890.

Ancina's significance in the history of music lies in his propagation and encouragement of sacred poetry and music as part of the religious renewal begun by Neri. Inspired by the Counter-Reformation, he collected the best and most popular pieces of music and supplied them with new sacred texts in place of the profane originals. The contrafacta written into a manuscript copy (in *I-Rv*) of *L'amorosa Ero* (*RISM* 1588[17]) are an early example of this technique. His most important enterprise was *Tempio armonico della beatissima vergine* (*RISM* 1599[6]), an anthology of three-part *laudi* by the foremost contemporary composers; at the back of the volume are some texts specifically intended for improvised setting by Giovanni Leonardo dell'Arpa. A second collection, for four and five voices, and a third, for six to nine and 12 voices, were planned but never published. Ancina was personally acquainted with almost all the leading Roman composers of his time, and among the manuscripts in his hand (now in *I-Rv*) is the only surviving source of Cavalieri's *Lamentationes* and a collection of spiritual canzonettas for five to eight voices, many of which are by Giovanni Animuccia. The same collection of manuscripts includes two treatises on music, *Regole del canto figurato e del contrapunto* and *Solfeggiamento e studi di musica*, which may be by Ancina. He also provided the texts of many *laudi* that appeared in Rome about 1600. As a composer he is less significant, though his five *laudi* in *Tempio armonico* are inventive, expressive, technically accomplished and not at all inferior to companion-pieces by more famous composers.

BIBLIOGRAPHY

C. Lombardo: *Della vita di Giovenale Ancina da Fossano* (Naples, 1656)
P. I. Bacci: *Vita del servo di Dio Giovenale Ancina* (Rome, 1671)
D. Alaleona: *Studi su la storia dell'oratorio musicale in Italia* (Turin, 1908, 2/1945 as *Storia dell'oratorio musicale in Italia*)
A. Einstein: *The Italian Madrigal* (Princeton, 1949/R1971), 848f
P. Damilano: *Giovenale Ancina, musicista filippino (1545–1604)* (Florence, 1956)
——: 'Ancina, Giovanni Giovenale', *DBI*
H. B. Lincoln: Introduction to *The Madrigal Collection 'L'amorosa Ero'* (Brescia, 1588) (Albany, NY, 1968)
H. E. Smither: 'Narrative and Dramatic Elements in the Laude Filippine, 1563–1600', *AcM*, xli (1969), 186

KLAUS FISCHER

Ancliffe, Charles (*b* Kildare, Ireland, 1880; *d* Richmond, Surrey, 20 Dec 1952). British composer and bandmaster. The son of a bandmaster, he graduated from the Royal Military School of Music, Kneller Hall, at the age of 20, having been awarded the gold baton for composition. For 18 years he was bandmaster of the 1st Battalion South Wales Borderers, and later held a similar position with the Scarborough Military Band. His best-known work is the waltz *Nights of Gladness* (1912), and the march *The Liberators* also retains its popularity. Besides waltzes and marches, he wrote suites, intermezzos and novelty items.

ANDREW LAMB

Ancona. Italian city in the Marches region. The earliest musical activity was in the Cathedral of S Ciriaco and in the city's convents and monasteries, where Augustinian and Franciscan monks acted as tutors in music theory and performance.

In the second half of the 16th century Eliseo Ghibellini (*b* *c*1520), *maestro di cappella* at the cathedral, instituted an active polyphonic school; his successor there from 1575 to 1586 was Giovanni Ferretti (*c*1540–*c*1610). *Maestri di cappella* of the early 17th century included Fabio Costantini (*b* *c*1575) at the Confraternita del S Rosario and Giacomo Finetti at the Chiesa del Ss Sacramento. Later in the century the Augustinian monk and teacher Scipione Lazzarini (*b* *c*1620) took an active part in training several Anconetan composers, including Anton Giuseppe Baroni, Anton Giuseppe Giamaglia, Filippo Giamaglia and Maria Francesca Nascimbeni (*b* 1658). The growing musical life encouraged Claudio Percimeneo to set up a music press and publish a collection of *Motetti* (1674) and *Salmi vespertini* (1675) by Lazzarini and a volume of *Canzoni e madrigali* by Nascimbeni (1674).

The earliest opera productions took place after the founding (7 January 1624) of the Accademia de' Caliginosi, which held its meetings at the Palazzo Comunale. One of the articles of its statutes provided for the performances of *drammi per musica* during Carnival. In March 1658 work was begun to convert part of the old arsenal into a public theatre fit for musical performances; it was inaugurated with a performance of Cavalli's *Giasone* (6 May 1665). Operas were given there every season until it burnt down on 20 November 1709. The new theatre, called La Fenice, was opened in 1711 and staged operas until 1818 when the building was declared unsafe; performances were temporarily accommodated at the Palazzo Acciaioli. In 1806 Marco Organari built a theatre in the city outskirts; it was amplified in 1821 but was found to be unsafe in 1845, and was soon officially closed.

On 2 May 1754 the city's nobility instituted a Casino Pubblico in one of the halls of the Palazzo Comunale. Their meetings, which took place on every feast day evening, were occasionally enhanced by performances of vocal or instrumental soloists. In April 1806 the society was renamed Casino Dorico; it continued throughout the 19th century.

Work on a new theatre, which was to be called the Teatro delle Muse, began in 1822, under the direction of Pietro Ghinelli, on the former site of the government prisons. The austere, Renaissance-style façade and the typical 19th-century interior both survive. The theatre opened on 28 April 1827 with Rossini's *Aureliano in Palmira*, a great success which ran for 18 performances. An administrative commission regulated the theatre's affairs and sanctioned two operatic seasons every year: a more ambitious one in April–May with at least 25 performances, and a more modest one devoted to comic operas during Carnival. In its first hundred years (1827–1927) 3299 works were staged during 163 seasons. Several improvements, which included lowering the orchestra pit and converting the highest tier into a new gallery, were made in 1927. It was severely damaged during the war (1943) and has never been wholly restored.

In 1888 the Società V. Bellini began to perform the choral repertory, and in April 1914 the society Amici della Musica was organized with the purpose of enhancing public concert life. The Istituto Musicale G. Pergolesi (founded 1920) is the city's conservatory.

BIBLIOGRAPHY

RicordiE

G. Saracini: *Notizie historiche della città d'Ancona* (Rome, 1675)

G. Mazzatinti: 'Ancona: Biblioteca comunale', *Inventari dei manoscritti delle biblioteche d'Italia*, vi (Forlì, 1896), 3

O. Morici: *Il Teatro delle Muse di Ancona nelle vicende e nelle tradizioni* (Rome, 1907)

G. Paleani: *Il Casino Dorico anconitano* (Ancona, 1921)

O. Morici: *I cento anni del Teatro delle Muse di Ancona MDCCXXVII–MCMXXVII* (Ancona, 1927)

A. Vitali: *La Società 'Amici della musica' di Ancona e i suoi primi cento concerti: notizie ed appunti* (Ancona, 1928)

P. Giangiacomi: *Guida spirituale di Ancona* (Ancona, 1932)

——: *La Biblioteca comunale e l'Archivio storico d'Ancona* (Ancona, 1932)

A. M. Bonisconti: 'Ancona', *ES*

A. Boni: *La Biblioteca comunale Luciano Benincasa di Ancona* (Ancona, 1956)

C. Posti: *Il duomo d'Ancona* (Iesi, 1958)

ELVIDIO SURIAN

Ancona, Mario (*b* Livorno, 28 Feb 1860; *d* Florence, 22 Feb 1931). Italian baritone. After study with Cenia, he made his début in 1889 at Trieste in Massenet's *Le roi de Lahore*. He first sang at La Scala, Milan, on 26 December 1890 in Massenet's *Le Cid* and at Covent Garden as Tonio in the first London performance of *Pagliacci* on 19 May 1893. Tonio was his début role at the Metropolitan, New York (11 December 1893), and he appeared as Sir Richard in Bellini's *I puritani* at the Manhattan Opera House on its opening night, 3 December 1906. His repertory included Mozart (Don Giovanni and Figaro), Verdi (Germont, Rigoletto, Amonasro, Iago and Don Carlo in *Ernani*), Wagner (Wolfram, Telramund and Sachs), Puccini (Lescaut and Marcello), Mascagni (Alfio and David in *L'amico Fritz*) and many French roles, Nevers in *Les Huguenots*, Escamillo in *Carmen* and Valentin in *Faust*. He retired in 1916.

BIBLIOGRAPHY

A. Bonaventura: *Musicisti livornesi* (Livorno, 1930)

H. Klein: 'Ancona, Mario', *Grove 5*

E. Gara: 'Ancona, Mario', *ES*

ELIZABETH FORBES

Ancot. South Netherlands family of musicians.

(1) **Jean Ancot (i)** (*b* Bruges, 22 Oct 1779; *d* Bruges, 12 July 1848). Composer and teacher. He was a choirboy at St Donatien and then went to Paris, where he studied the violin with Kreutzer and Baillot and harmony with Catel. He returned to Bruges in 1804 and established himself as a teacher of violin and piano. According to Fétis, he composed a great quantity of music (most of it never published and now lost), including military band music for political and nationalistic celebrations, two masses and other church music, four violin concertos, three string quartets etc.

(2) **Jean Ancot (ii)** (*b* Bruges, 6 July 1799; *d* Boulogne, 5 June 1829). Composer, violinist and pianist, son of (1) Jean Ancot (i). He studied with his father and appeared as a soloist on both the violin and the piano in 1811. His first concertos were composed about 1815; in 1817 he went to Paris to study at the Conservatoire. In 1823 he went to London and was appointed pianist to the Duchess of Kent, but returned two years later, settling eventually in Boulogne. He published over 200 works in Paris, London and Germany, including six overtures for orchestra, concertos for violin and for piano, piano sonatas and other pieces (of which *L'ouragan* was particularly popular),

many pieces for piano and violin, and several vocal works.

(3) **Louis Ancot** (*b* Bruges, 3 June 1803; *d* Bruges, Sept 1836). Pianist, teacher and composer, son of (1) Jean Ancot (i). He also studied with his father. After a continental tour he arrived in London and became pianist to the Duke of Sussex. Later he taught the piano in Boulogne and Tours before returning to Bruges. He published a number of works for piano.

JOHN LADE

Ancus (? from Gk. *agkos*: 'valley', or *agkōn*: 'neck'). A neume signifying three notes in descending order, the last of which is semi-vocalized. The *ancus* is the LIQUESCENT form of the CLIMACUS. Liquescence arises on certain diphthongs and consonants to provide for a semi-vocalized passing note to the next note (for illustration *see* NEUMATIC NOTATIONS, Table 1).

BIBLIOGRAPHY
H. Freistedt: *Die liqueszierenden Noten des gregorianischen Chorals: ein Beitrag zur Notationskunde* (Fribourg, 1929)
M. Huglo: 'Les noms des neumes et leur origine', *Etudes grégoriennes*, i (1954), 53

Anda, Géza (*b* Budapest, 19 Nov 1921; *d* Zurich, 14 June 1976). Swiss pianist and conductor of Hungarian birth. He studied at the Budapest Academy of Music, graduating from Dohnányi's master class, and made his début playing Brahms's Second Piano Concerto with the Budapest PO conducted by Mengelberg in 1939. He was also a soloist with the Berlin PO under Furtwängler but in 1943 fled to Switzerland where he settled; he took Swiss nationality in 1955. From 1947 he began to make an international reputation, at first in the virtuoso Romantic repertory, gradually specializing in Bartók, and then in Mozart whose concertos he conducted from the keyboard and recorded complete with, where necessary, his own cadenzas. He also conducted symphonic music. He regularly gave piano master classes, notably in Lucerne and Zurich.

It was Anda's command of a powerful, rich keyboard sonority, a thrilling dynamism, and a pungent cantabile which could soften to a whisper, that brought him to fame in Bartók's concertos and, for example, Brahms's Second Concerto or his F minor Sonata. His concentration on Mozart doubtless derived from a concern with refinement of phrasing and articulation, already evident in his readings of Beethoven, Chopin and Bartók, as well as late Brahms, though in the mid-1970s this specialization did not include the poise that characterizes the ideal Mozartian: there were signs of hurry, even of coarsening, unsuitable in high Viennese Classicism though acceptable in Beethoven and Bartók. His strength and leonine sensibility were useful correctives to preciosity in 18th-century music, and suggested that he could have excelled in Schumann and Liszt, indeed in some more 20th-century music. He published a book of cadenzas to Mozart concertos (Berlin and Wiesbaden, 1973).

BIBLIOGRAPHY
R. Offergeld: 'Stereo Review talks to Geza Anda', *Stereo Review* (1969), no.23, p.81
Obituary, *The Times* (16 June 1976)

WILLIAM S. MANN

Andamento (It.: 'walking'). A leisurely type of fugue subject of some length (ex.1), as opposed to the shorter 'attacco' and 'soggetto'. The term can also refer to a

Ex.1 Bach: '48', i, 2

short motif repeated at varying pitch levels (*see* SEQUENCE (ii)).

ROGER BULLIVANT

Andante (It.: 'easy-going', 'fluent', 'at a walking pace', 'uniform'; present participle of *andare*, to walk). A tempo (and mood) designation, often abbreviated to *and.e* and sometimes even *ad.e*, particularly in the 18th century. Though one of the most common tempo designations in the 19th century, its entry into musical scores was relatively late, and its use in the 17th and 18th centuries was often as an indication of performance manner rather than of tempo. For Brossard (1703) and Grassineau (1740) it referred primarily to bass lines and specifically to what are now (aptly) called 'walking' bass lines. One of the very few tempo or expression marks in J. S. Bach's keyboard music is *andante* for the B minor prelude in book 1 of the '48', which has just such a bass line. *Andante* there and in many other 18th-century sources is not a tempo designation but an instruction for clear performance of the running bass, and a warning not to play *inégale*. The anonymous *A Short Explication* (London, 1724) says: 'Andante, this word has respect chiefly to the thorough bass, and signifies, that in playing, the times must be kept very just and exact, and each note made very equal and distinct the one from the other'. And Brossard's definition included the comment 'cheminer à pas égaux' as though specifically to preclude *inégalité*. With this in mind, Walther's additional observation (1732) that it could also apply to upper parts is particularly interesting.

Andante was first unequivocally described as a tempo designation by Niedt (1706), who called it 'very slow' ('gantz langsam'), though Mattheson corrected this in the revised second edition to a more orthodox definition. But it does not appear, for instance, in the graduated list of tempo marks at the end of *A Short Explication* (1724), where the space between *largo* and *allegro* is occupied by VIVACE: *andante* is given only as a method of performance, as cited above. *Andante* seems to have been fully accepted as a tempo designation only with Leopold Mozart (1756). It was a gentle relaxed tempo for Haydn and for W. A. Mozart, who wrote to his sister on 9–12 June 1784: 'none of these concertos has an Adagio, but just andantes' ('sondern lauter andante seyn müssen'). This comment also exemplifies the common use of *andante* as a noun, describing a slow movement of only moderate solemnity.

Più andante and *molto andante*, found particularly in Brahms and Schubert, usually indicate something rather slower than *andante*, though many of the same ambiguities obtain as for ANDANTINO. Perhaps the most startling use of *molto andante* is in the finale to Act 2 of Mozart's *Le nozze di Figaro* at the moment when the Count has unlocked the closet door and revealed – to everybody's surprise and comic relief – not Cherubino but Susanna, who plays on the situation with biting sarcasm in a 3/8 section whose tempo designation *molto andante* is surely used to denote an extremely controlled and ironically measured tempo contrasting with the preceding *allegro*.

As one of the five main degrees of movement in music

named by Rousseau (1768) and later theorists, *andante* became ubiquitous in the 19th century and appeared with all kinds of qualifications from *andante sostenuto* and *andante con moto* to *andante religioso* (Liszt, final section of *Ce qu'on entend sur la montagne*) and even in macaronic forms such as *andante très expressif* (Debussy, opening of *Clair de lune*).

BIBLIOGRAPHY

I. Herrmann-Bengen: *Tempobezeichnungen*, Münchner Veröffentlichungen zur Musikgeschichte, i (Tutzing, 1959), 175ff

W. Gerstenberg: 'Andante', *GfMKB, Kassel 1962*, 156

For further bibliography *see* TEMPO AND EXPRESSION MARKS.

DAVID FALLOWS

Andantino (It., diminutive of *andante*, but current only in musical contexts). A tempo and mood designation for a slightly more lighthearted *andante*. Normally it is a little faster than *andante*; but Rousseau (1768), for instance, described it as an *andante* with 'a little less gaiety in the beat'. The ambiguity, which stems from whether *andante* is perceived as a fast or a slow tempo, troubled Beethoven, who wrote to George Thomson, his Edinburgh publisher, on 19 February 1813:

> In future, if there are any andantinos among the melodies you send me for setting, I would beg you to indicate whether that *andantino* is intended to be faster or slower than *andante*, because that word, like many others in music, is of such imprecise meaning that on one occasion *andantino* can be close to *allegro* and on another almost like *adagio*.

Zaslaw (1972) provided convincing evidence that for Mozart and his contemporaries *andantino* was normally slower than *andante*: Rousseau (1768), Wolf (1788), D. G. Türk (1789), Mason (c1801), Clementi (1801), Starke (1819) and Hummel (1828) all agreed on that; moreover Türk and Hummel went so far as to draw attention to it and to castigate those who thought otherwise.

In earlier editions of *Grove* Ebenezer Prout mentioned three movements in Mendelssohn's *Elijah*, the first of which, 'If with all your hearts', is marked *andante con moto*, the second, 'The Lord hath exalted thee', merely *andante* and the third, 'O rest in the Lord', *andantino*: all three have the same metronome mark, crotchet = 72. As Prout remarked, it illustrates the 'uncertainty which prevails in the use of those time-indications'; but it is also a consequence of the different texture and density of the music which in turn directly influence tempo, performed tempo and perceived tempo.

There seems little evidence for the commonly found assertion that *andantino* can refer to a somewhat shorter *andante* movement (see Herrmann-Bengen, 1959, p.181).

For bibliography *see* ANDANTE and TEMPO AND EXPRESSION MARKS.

DAVID FALLOWS

Anderberg, Carl-Olof (*b* Stockholm, 13 March 1914; *d* Malmö, 4 Jan 1972). Swedish composer, pianist and conductor. During the period 1936–8 he studied composition in Stockholm, Copenhagen, Paris and London, and later in Salzburg and Vienna. He was a piano pupil of Olof Wiberg in Stockholm and studied conducting with Paumgartner, Walter and Weingartner at the Salzburg Mozarteum. In 1934 he made his début as a pianist and composer in Malmö with the later discarded Concertino. He was conductor of the Hippodromen, the Malmö operetta theatre (1939–42, 1949–50), and in 1946 founded a chamber orchestra which he directed until its activities ceased in 1950. Thereafter he lived as a freelance composer in Malmö, latterly spending much time in Cologne and Vienna; he sometimes appeared as a pianist or conductor, particularly with the Malmö Ars Nova. His electronic works were composed in his own studio, FEM.

Anderberg's music of the 1930s and 1940s showed French influence, but later he went through a 12-note serial period, stimulated by his profound analyses of Schoenberg's piano music. In this way he integrated new techniques into an individual style, solidly craftsmanlike in the orchestral works and instrumentally brilliant in the chamber music. Many of his works were suggested by literature or by contemporary events, the latter particularly in later years: the piano concerto (1968) uses quotations from the *Internationale*, the *Horst Wessel Lied*, etc, to illustrate reactions to the Czech crisis. He has published *Hän mot en ny ljudkonst* ('Towards a new sound art'; Malmö, 1961) and many articles.

WORKS
(selective list)

Orch: Orkestermusik II, 1938; 3 estampier, op.27, 1953; Cyclus stellarum, str, I, 1949, II, op.37, 1957; Serenad, op.41, str, 1958; Teater, 1958; Transfers, op.60, sym. groups, 1960; Musik för stråkorkester, op.56a, 1965; 4 unabhängige Stücke, op.63, str, 1965, rev. 1968; Acroama I, op.57, 1965, II, op.58, 1966; '. . . för piano och orkester', op.66, 1968; Orkesterspel II, op.68, 1968; Konsert för en balett, op.70, pf, wind, perc, db, 1970; early concs. for pf (2), va, sax

Chamber: Tio etyder, op.24, vn, pf, 1950; Sonata, vc, pf, 1953; Fyra seriösa capricer, op.32, cl, pf, 1956; Lyriska sekvenser, op.52, vn, 1956; Str Qt no.2, 1956; Svenskt capriccio, op.38, vn, pf, 1957; Duo, fl, pf, 1958; Triad, op.46, vn, 1959; Exekution I, op.54, cl, perc, pf, 1963; Hexafoni, op.53, cl, tpt, trbn, pf, vn, db, 1963; Duo, vn, pf, I, 1965, II, op.62, 1968, III, op.64, n.d.

Pf: Klavierstück, op.61b, 1967; Klangskap för inriktat piano, op.64, 1968; 3 sonatas, Bewegungen

Vocal: Glaukos, op.25, T, orch, 1951; Fyra legeringar, op.43, S, 5 insts, 1958; Höstens Hökar, op.44, reciter, insts, 1959; Fossil inskrift, op.48, T, pf, 1960; Strändernas svall, op.55 (Eyvind Johnson: Odysseus Saga), S, Bar, reciter, insts, 1961; Di mi se mai, op.51, logofonia, S, reciter, orch, 1963; Ansiktets övre halva, op.67, chorus, 2 perc, 1969; Dubbelspel, op.69, S, Bar, cl, vc, pf, tape, 1971; 24 other songs

Elec: Övergångar, 1968; incidental music for theatre and cinema

Principal publisher: Suecia

HANS ÅSTRAND

Anders, Hendrik (*b* Oberweissbach, Thuringia, 1657; *d* Amsterdam, ?14 March 1714). Netherlands composer, organist, violinist and carillonneur of German origin. He settled at Amsterdam and became organist at the Lutheran church in 1683, but was dismissed for bad behaviour and drunkenness in 1694; he was carillonneur from 1696, and was also a violinist at the city theatre. The date of his death is usually given as 1714, but there are indications that he may have been musically active until 1719–20. He seems to have played an important part in the beginnings of opera in the Dutch language, along with Servaas de Konink (whose *Hollandsche minne- en drink-liedern* he edited) and others.

WORKS

VOCAL

Min- en wijn-strijd (opera, D. Buysero), The Hague, 1697, music lost

Venus en Adonis (opera, Buysero), c1697, music lost

Apollo en Dafne (opera, K. Sweerts), 1697, music lost

1 song, c1695[13]

INSTRUMENTAL

Trioos, allemande, courante, sarbande, gighe, etc (Amsterdam, 1696)

[12] Symphoniae introductoriae, 3–4 insts (Amsterdam, 1698)

BIBLIOGRAPHY

EitnerQ; FasquelleE; FétisB

D. F. Scheurleer: 'Het muziekleven', *Amsterdam in de zeventiende eeuw*, iii (The Hague, 1897–1904)

A. Jansen: 'Anders, Hendrik', *MGG*

PHILIPPE MERCIER

Anders, Peter (*b* Essen, 1 July 1908; *d* Hamburg, 10 Sept 1954). German tenor. He studied under

Grenzenbach and Mysz-Gmeiner in Berlin, making his début there in *La belle Hélène* (1931). In the following years he sang with the opera companies of Cologne, Hanover and Munich, returning to Berlin in 1936. He was then a lyric tenor, acclaimed in such roles as Tamino, which he also sang at the Salzburg Festival of 1943. His voice became stronger, and he added such heroic roles as Lohengrin and Florestan to his repertory, appearing at the Edinburgh Festival of 1950 as Bacchus in *Ariadne auf Naxos* and at Covent Garden (1951) as Walther in *Die Meistersinger*. He died after a car accident. Anders left many gramophone records, impressive for fine tone and technique as well as for the intelligence of his lieder singing.

BIBLIOGRAPHY

A. G. Ross: 'Peter Anders', *Record News*, iii/3 (Toronto, 1958) [with discography]

J. B. STEANE

Andersen, Anton Jörgen (*b* Kristiansand, 10 Oct 1845; *d* Stockholm, 9 Sept 1926). Swedish cellist and composer of Norwegian birth. He began his musical studies with the organist Rojahn. After playing the cello in the theatre orchestras of Trondheim (1864) and Oslo (1865), he moved to Sweden at the age of 21. There he studied composition with Johan Lindegren at the Stockholm Conservatory and was a cellist in the Hovkapellet from 1871 to 1905. From 1876 to 1911 he also taught the cello and the double bass at the conservatory, being appointed professor in 1912. He was elected to the Kungliga Musikaliska Akademien in 1882.

Like many of his Swedish contemporaries, Andersen as a composer was strongly influenced by the Austro-German tradition. His works, mostly unpublished, include five symphonies, one of which calls for 14 cello and three double bass parts, a string quartet, a sonata for cello and piano (Stockholm, 1876), other instrumental pieces scored largely or solely for cellos and double basses, as well as solo and choral songs.

BIBLIOGRAPHY

P. Vretblad: 'Andersen, Anton Jörgen', *SBL*

T. Norlind: 'Andersen, Anton Jörgen', *Allmänt musiklexikon*, ii (Stockholm, 1916, 2/1928)

B. Palm: 'Andersen, Anton Jörgen', *Sohlmans musiklexikon*, i (Stockholm, 1948)

ANDERS LÖNN

Andersen, Karl Joachim (*b* Copenhagen, 29 April 1847; *d* Copenhagen, 7 May 1909). Danish flautist. He and his younger brother Vigo (1852–95) were sons of the flautist Christian J. Andersen (*b* 1816); they were both grounded in the old-system flute by their father. Having started his orchestral career under Niels Gade, Karl Andersen entered the Copenhagen Royal Orchestra in 1869, remaining there until 1877. He then went to Russia, and later to Germany. Here in 1881 he became a founder-member of the Berlin PO, with which he stayed for ten years. A malady of the tongue terminated his playing career, and he returned to Copenhagen where he became conductor of the Palace Orchestra in 1894. He composed 48 flute studies as well as concert pieces for flute with orchestra. His brother, Vigo Andersen, emigrated to the USA where he was much esteemed as solo flautist in the Thomas Orchestra of Chicago.

PHILIP BATE

Anderson, Emily (*b* Galway, 17 March 1891; *d* London, 26 Oct 1962). Irish editor and translator. She was educated privately and at the universities of Berlin and Marburg, and in 1923, after a short period as lecturer in German at University College, Galway, entered the Foreign Office where she served until 1951, having been seconded to the War Office from 1940 to 1943 for intelligence work in the Middle East. She dedicated most of the scanty leisure of her working life and all her retirement to the successive tasks of editing and translating the letters of Mozart and his family and the letters of Beethoven. Her tireless, world-wide search for original sources of the text was complemented by scrupulous accuracy and thorough annotation. She developed a style of timeless English which she handled in as lively and readable a manner as was consistent with fidelity to the German. Despite an occasional lapse in musicological detail, the two editions were a fine achievement and likely to remain the standard English version for some time to come. Of the two, the Beethoven was perhaps the more remarkable because his illegible handwriting had produced so many inaccurate readings in earlier texts that Miss Anderson, besides mastering his orthography, had either to inspect personally all the extant autographs or else procure photographs. Of the 1750 Beethoven letters, she published 250 for the first time. In her will, she bequeathed to the Royal Philharmonic Society money to found an international prize for violin playing.

WRITINGS

ed. and trans.: *The Letters of Mozart and his Family* (London, 1938, 2/1966, ed. M. Carolan and A. H. King)

ed. and trans.: *The Letters of Beethoven* (London, 1961)

'Beethoven's Operatic Plans', *PRMA*, lxxxviii (1961–2), 61

BIBLIOGRAPHY

Obituary, *The Times* (29 Oct 1962)

ALEC HYATT KING

Anderson, Gordon A(thol) (*b* Melbourne, 1 May 1929). Australian musicologist. He studied at the University of Adelaide under John Bishop, J. B. Peters and Andrew McCredie (BMus 1958, BMus Hons 1969, MMus 1970, DMus 1977). From an early stage of his career he concentrated on the Notre Dame motet and particularly on identifying tenors of works where these were unknown. From 1970 to 1972 he was a research fellow at the Flinders University, Adelaide, and in 1973 he took up a lectureship in music at the University of New England, Armidale, New South Wales. Although he lives far from original sources, he is a prolific contributor to various scholarly journals. He has built up a collection of microfilms unique in Australia and played an important part in the establishment of an Australian Musicological Commission.

WRITINGS

'Mode and Change of Mode in Notre Dame Conductus', *AcM*, xl (1968), 92

'Notre Dame Bilingual Motets', *MMA*, iii (1968), 50–144

'A Small Collection of Notre Dame Motets ca 1215–1236', *JAMS*, xxii (1969), 157–96

'Newly Identified Clausula-motets in Las Huelgas Manuscript', *MQ*, lv (1969), 228

'Newly Identified Tenor Chants in the Notre Dame Repertory', *ML*, l (1969), 158

'Clausulae or Transcribed Motets in the Florence Manuscript?', *AcM*, xlii (1970), 109

'Notre Dame Latin Double Motets ca 1215–1250', *MD*, xxv (1971), 35–92

'Notre Dame and Related Conductus – a Catalogue Raisonné', *MMA*, vi (1972), 153–229

ed.: *The Latin Compositions in Fascicules VII and VIII of the Notre Dame Manuscript Wolfenbüttel Helmstadt 1099 (1206)* (New York, 1972) [transcr. in preparation]
'Thirteenth Century Conductus – Obiter Dicta', *MQ*, lviii (1972), 349
'Magister Lambertus and Nine Rhythmic Modes', *AcM*, xlv (1973), 57
'Motets of the Thirteenth-century Manuscript La Clayette', *MD*, xxvii (1973–) [transcr. in preparation]
'The Rhythm of *cum littera* Sections of Polyphonic Conductus in Mensural Sources', *JAMS*, xxvi (1973), 288
'A Unique Notre-Dame Tenor Relationship', *ML*, lv (1974), 398
'Johannes de Garlandia and the Simultaneous use of Mixed Rhythmic Modes', *MMA*, viii (1975), 11
'Notre Dame and Related Conductus', *MMA*, vii (1975), 1
'Three Variant Polyphonic Settings of a Notre Dame Conductus', *SMA*, ix (1975), 8
'Responsory Chants in the Tenors of some Fourteenth-century Continental Motets', *JAMS*, xxix (1976), 119
'The Rhythm of the Monophonic Conductus in the Florence Manuscript as indicated in Parallel Sources in Mensural Notation', *JAMS*, xxxi (1978), 480

EDITIONS

Motets of the Manuscript La Clayette, CMM, lxviii (1975)
Compositions of the Bamberg Manuscript, CMM, lxxv (1976)
Notre Dame and Related Conductus, Institute of Mediaeval Music, Collected Works (Brooklyn, 1976)

WERNER GALLUSSER

Anderson, Leroy (*b* Cambridge, Mass., 29 June 1908; *d* Woodbury, Conn., 18 May 1975). American composer, arranger and conductor. He studied with Spalding (theory), Ballantine (counterpoint), Heilman (fugue), and Enesco and Piston (composition) at Harvard (BA 1929, MA 1930), where from 1930 to 1934 he pursued studies in German and Scandinavian languages. During these latter years he became involved in numerous musical activities, serving as a tutor at Radcliffe College (1930–32), director of the Harvard University Band (1931–5), and organist, instrumentalist and conductor in Boston (1931–5). He then worked as an arranger and orchestrator in Boston and New York (1935–42) before war service in the US Army as a translator and interpreter in Iceland and the USA. A member of various organizations, he was chairman of the board of review of the American Society of Composers, Authors and Publishers, and a member of the boards of directors of the New Haven and Hartford (Connecticut) symphony orchestras. As a composer he specialized in light music for the standard orchestra, work which brought him renown in art- and popular-music circles. His works obtain their appeal by means of infectious melody, popular dance rhythms (*Belle of the Ball* and *Blue Tango*) and novel orchestral effects that often relate to the titles (e.g. pizzicato strings in *Plink, Plank, Plunk!*, percussion in *Sleigh Ride* and *The Syncopated Clock*, and unconventional instruments in *The Typewriter* and *Sandpaper Ballet*). He arranged his orchestral works for other instrumental combinations in order to make them accessible to amateur groups and soloists.

WORKS
(selective list)

Musical: Goldilocks (J. and W. Kerr), New York, 1958
Orch: Harvard Fantasy, 1936, rev. as A Harvard Festival, 1969; Promenade, 1945; The Syncopated Clock, 1945; Chicken Reel, 1946; Serenata, 1947; Irish Suite, 1947; Sleigh Ride, 1948; A Trumpeter's Lullaby, 1949; The Waltzing Cat, 1950; The Typewriter, 1950; Blue Tango, 1951; Belle of the Ball, 1951; The Penny-Whistle Song, 1951; Horse and Buggy, 1951; Forgotten Dreams, 1954; Sandpaper Ballet, 1954; Lady in Waiting, ballet, 1959; Arietta, 1962; Balladette, 1962; The Captains and the Kings, 1962; Home Stretch, 1962
Str orch: Jazz Pizzicato, 1938; Jazz Legato, 1938; Fiddle-Faddle, 1947; Plink, Plank, Plunk!, 1951; Suite of Carols, 1955

Principal publishers: Belwin-Mills, Woodbury Music

BIBLIOGRAPHY
'Leroy Anderson', *Pan Pipes*, xlv (1953), Jan, 38
L. W. Grant: 'Salute to a "Popular" Master', *Music Journal*, xii (1954), Nov, 25
'The "Syncopated Clock" Still Ticks', *Music Journal*, xxvi (1968), Sept, 30

DAVID E. CAMPBELL

Anderson [née Philpot], **Lucy** (*b* Bath, 12 Dec 1797; *d* London, 24 Dec 1878). English pianist. She was the daughter of John Philpot, a professor of music and music seller at Bath. About 1818 she went to London, where she soon became eminent in her profession and was the first woman pianist to play at the concerts of the Philharmonic Society. In July 1820 she was married to George Frederick Anderson (*d* 14 Dec 1876), a violinist who was from 1848 to 1870 Master of the Queen's Musick. In 1829 Mrs Anderson played at the Birmingham Festival. She taught the piano to Queen Victoria and her children. She retired in 1862.

BIBLIOGRAPHY
W. B. Squire: 'Anderson, Lucy', *DNB*

W. H. HUSK/R

Anderson, Marian (*b* Philadelphia, 17 Feb 1902). Black American contralto. She graduated from Southern High School, Philadelphia, and studied with Giuseppe Boghetti in New York, winning first prize in a competition of the New York PO. She went to Europe in 1930, giving a concert in London, making tours of Scandinavia and Germany, and winning from Toscanini the tribute: 'the voice that comes once in a hundred years.' By then a mature artist, she made a New York recital début in 1936 and undertook transcontinental and further European tours. At the invitation of Rudolf Bing, she made a belated début in opera at the Metropolitan on 7 January 1955, as Ulrica in *Un ballo in maschera*. Her voice was already in its decline, but, as the first black soloist there, she paved the way for others. Anderson's voice was of large volume and striking quality, not noted for evenness of scale though she could adapt it admirably to lieder. Artistic integrity was the hallmark of this pioneering artist, and in spirituals she was compelling.

BIBLIOGRAPHY
K. Vehanen: *Marian Anderson: a Portrait* (New York, 1941)
M. Anderson: *My Lord, what a Morning: an Autobiography* (New York, 1956)

MAX DE SCHAUENSEE

Anderson, Thomas Jefferson (*b* Coatesville, Penn., 17 Aug 1928). Black American composer. He was born into a musical family and studied the piano as a child. As a youth he toured with a jazz orchestra. He received degrees in music from West Virginia State College (BMus), Pennsylvania State University (MMusEd) and the University of Iowa (PhD). His career included teaching in public schools and several colleges before appointment in 1972 as chairman of the music department of Tufts University. His honours include appointment as the first black composer-in-residence of the Atlanta SO (1969–71), fellowship awards from foundations and numerous commissions. His music reflects the influence of both jazz and post-Webern styles. His predilection for rhythmic complexities and his imaginative use of instrumental colour are particularly noteworthy.

His principal works include five for orchestra, of which the best-known are *Squares* (1964), *Chamber Symphony* (1968) and *Intervals* (1971); he also wrote the cantata *Personals* (1966), seven chamber works, two works for band and pieces for piano, solo voice and male glee club. Much of his music is published by American Composers Alliance.

BIBLIOGRAPHY
E. Southern: *The Music of Black Americans: a History* (New York, 1971)
　　　　　　　　　　　　　　　　　　　EILEEN SOUTHERN

Anderson, W(illiam) H(enry) (*b* London, 21 April 1882; *d* Winnipeg, 12 April 1955). Canadian composer, choirmaster and tenor. After private training in England and vocal studies in Italy with Garcia and Battistini, he entered the Guildhall School of Music. In 1910 he moved to Winnipeg, where he became active as a singer, choral conductor, teacher, adjudicator and composer; he was largely responsible for developing the city's choral tradition. In later years he made a wider reputation through two regular CBC programmes in which he was involved as conductor, 'The Choristers' and 'Sunday Chorale'. His numerous compositions and arrangements, all vocal, show a complete understanding of medium and graceful melody and harmony.
　　　　　　　　　　　　　　　　　　　GODFREY RIDOUT

Anderson, W(illiam) R(obert) (*b* Blackburn, 7 Dec 1891; *d* Bournemouth, Jan 1979). English music critic and editor. He took the BMus at Durham University, trained as a piano teacher and then entered music journalism, first as editor of the *Music Teacher* (1921–5), then as a critic and contributor to many newspapers and periodicals, including *The Observer*, the *Evening News*, *Gramophone* (where his earliest reviews were signed 'K.K.'), the *Musical News*, the *Musical Times* and the *Music Teacher*. He was also very active as an adjudicator at music festivals, as a lecturer to evening classes and adult education classes, and as an examiner for Trinity College of Music (1949–61). His writings include studies of Brahms, Haydn, Rakhmaninov and Elgar, an introduction to music appreciation and a book on music in history.

WRITINGS
'Book I: the ABC of Music', *The Musical Companion*, ed. A. L. Bacharach (London, 1934, rev. 2/1957 as *The New Musical Companion*), 21–124
with H. D. McKinney: *Discovering Music: a Course in Music Appreciation* (New York, 1934, 3/1952)
Haydn (London, 1939)
Music as a Career (London, 1939)
with H. D. McKinney: *Music in History: the Evolution of an Art* (New York, 1940, 2/1957)
Rachmaninov and his Pianoforte Concertos (London, 1947)
Articles on Arne, J. S. Bach, Cherubini, Franck, Lalo, Bennett, Albéniz, Dvořák, Macdowell, Saint-Saëns, Barber, Bloch, Copland, Harris, Prokofiev, Rakhmaninov, Schumann and Stravinsky, *The Music Masters*, i–iv ed. A. L. Bacharach (London, 1948–54)
Introduction to the Music of Brahms (London, 1949)
Introduction to the Music of Elgar (London, 1949)
　　　　　　　　　　　　　　　　　　　MALCOLM TURNER

Andersson, Nils (*b* Hofterup, Malmöhus län, 29 July 1864; *d* Lund, 31 March 1921). Swedish jurist and collector of folk music. He took degrees in philosophy and law at the University of Lund, in which town he held a succession of legal and official appointments. His principal interest outside his professional work was folk music, and it was on his initiative that the Folk Music Commission was formed in 1908. He made a notable collection of some 12,000 melodies (songs, dances, wedding marches and herdsman's calls) which were later edited and published by Olof Andersson as Svenska Låtar (Stockholm, 1922–40).

WRITINGS
Teckningar och toner ur skånska allmogens lif (Lund, 1889)
Skånska melodier (Stockholm, 1895–1916)
BIBLIOGRAPHY
T. Norlind: 'Stadsnotarie Nils Andersson och den svenska folkmusiken', *Ur nutidens musikliv* (Stockholm, 1921), 91
O. Andersson: 'Melodisamlaren Nils Andersson: minner och anteckningar', *Budkavlen* (1940), 40–72
——: *Spel opp i spelemänner: Nils Andersson och den svenska spelmansrörelsen* (Stockholm, 1958)
——: *Hur svenska låtar kom till: en brevväxling mellan Nils och Olof Andersson* (Stockholm, 1963)
　　　　　　　　　　　　KATHLEEN DALE/MALCOLM TURNER

Andersson, Otto (Emanuel) (*b* Vårdö, 27 April 1879; *d* Turku, 27 Dec 1969). Finnish musicologist and folklorist. After qualifying as an organist and choirmaster (1900), he studied (1901–5) at the Helsinki Music Institute (later the Sibelius Academy) and Helsinki University (MA 1915), taking the doctorate there in 1923 with a dissertation on the bowed harp. In 1906 he was a co-founder of the Brage Society for the preservation of Swedish–Finnish culture and from its inception he was president of its music section and conductor of its choir. He taught music in Helsinki and then became a lecturer in Scandinavian music history at the university (1925) and professor of musicology and folk literature (1926–46) and rector (1929–36) at the Swedish University of Åbo (Turku). In 1926 he founded the latter's music history collection, which in 1950 became the basis of the Sibelius Museum. As a musicologist he made valuable contributions to the study of early music history in Finland; he also collected folk music and studied folk music instruments of Swedish-speaking regions in Finland.

WRITINGS
Inhemska musiksträfvanden (Helsinki, 1907)
Musik och musiker (Helsinki, 1917)
Martin Wegelius (Helsinki, 1919)
Johan Josef Pippingsköld och musiklivet i Åbo 1808–1827 (Helsinki, 1921)
Stråkharpan (diss., U. of Helsinki, 1923; Helsinki, 1923; Eng. trans., 1930 as *The Bowed Harp*)
Runeberg och musiken (Helsinki, 1925)
G. A. Petrelius (Turku, 1935)
Den unge Pacius och musiklivet i Helsingfors på 1830-talet (Helsinki, 1938)
Johanna von Schoultz (1813–1863) (Turku, 1939)
Musikaliska sällskapet i Åbo 1790–1808 (Helsinki, 1940)
'Oratoriet i Finland under det nittonde seklet', *Svenska oratorieföreningens festskrift* (Helsinki, 1945)
Conrad Greve (Helsinki, 1952)
'On Gaelic Folk Music from the Isle of Lewis', *Budkavlen 1952*, i/4 (Turku, 1953), 1–67
Jean Sibelius i Amerika (Turku, 1955)
Spel opp i spelemänner: Nils Andersson och den svenska spelmansrörelsen (Stockholm, 1958)
ed. A. Forslin: *Studier i musik och folklore* (Turku, 1964–9) [collected essays as 85th birthday tribute, with list of writings]
Finländsk folklore (Stockholm, 1967)

FOLKSONG EDITIONS
Finlandssvenska folkdiktning, v: *Folkvisor* (Helsinki, 1934); vi: *Folkdans*, A1, A3 (Helsinki, 1963–4)

BIBLIOGRAPHY
A. Forslin: 'Om insamling av folkmelodier i Svenskfinland under hundra år', *Suomen musiikin vuosikirja 1961–62* (Helsinki, 1962), 24
——: *Otto Andersson: bibliografi 1895–1964* (Turku, 1964)
P. Nisson: 'Otto Andersson och den finlandssvenska folkmusiken', *Suomen musiikin vuosikirja 1963–64* (Helsinki, 1964), 67
R. Jonsson: 'Otto Andersson – 27 December 1969', *STMf*, lii (1970), 5
　　　　　　　　　　　　　　　　　　ERKKI SALMENHAARA

Andersson, (Ernst Christian) Richard (*b* Stockholm, 22 Aug 1851; *d* Stockholm, 20 May 1918). Swedish pianist, teacher and composer. At the Stockholm Conservatory (1867–74) he studied the piano first with Jan van Boom and then with Ludwig Norman, harmony with Otto Winge, the organ with Gustaf Mankell and composition with Hermann Berens. After further piano study with Hilda Thegerström (1874–6), he went to the Berlin Hochschule für Musik where he became a pupil of Clara Schumann and Heinrich Barth and also studied composition with R. Würst and Friedrich Kiel. During this period he frequently deputized as a teacher for Barth, both at the Hochschule and privately. He returned to Stockholm in 1884 and two years later founded a piano school, where at first he was the only teacher of the instrument, with Emil Sjögren as teacher of harmony. The school gradually developed a more general curriculum, including courses in other instruments and in singing, and became the country's outstanding private music school. Noted Swedish musicians who studied at the school (Anderssons Musikskola) included Stenhammar, Astrid Berwald, Adolf Wiklund, Harald Fryklöf and Gustaf Heintze. Andersson was appointed professor of piano at the Stockholm Conservatory in 1904, but retired at his own wish in 1906; he was a member of the Swedish Royal Academy of Music from 1890. His compositions, mainly early and for the piano, show the influence of Chopin, Liszt and other virtuoso composers, as well as evidence of Andersson's own pianistic skill. They are often free in form and harmonically colourful. The collection *Skuggor och dagrar* ('Lights and shades') op.14 was awarded the *Svensk musiktidning* prize in 1885.

WORKS
(selective list; MSS in S-Skma)

Pf: Impromptu, op.2, 1869; 7 skisser (Berlin, 1878); Sonat, op.11, 1878 (Stockholm, 1889); Schwedische Tänze (Berlin, 1881); Skuggor och dagrar [Lights and shades], op.14 (Stockholm, 1886); 21 skisser, op.16 (Stockholm, 1889); 4 waltzes, op.17, 1901; works for 4 hands, incl. Bolero, op.7, Svenska nationaldanser (Stockholm, 1881)

Other works: Fantasiestück, vc, pf, op.13, 1881; songs; Pianospelets teknik, pf method (Stockholm, 1888–94)

BIBLIOGRAPHY
C. F. Hennerberg: 'Andersson, Ernst Christian Richard', *SBL*
S. Lizell: *Richard Andersson 1851–1918: minnesteckning* (Stockholm, 1919)
——: *Richard Anderssons musikskola 40 år* (Stockholm, 1925)
R. Almén: *Några minnen av professor Richard Andersson* (Uppsala, 1930)
                                                AXEL HELMER

Andrade, Mário (Raul) de (Morais) (*b* São Paulo, 9 Oct 1893; *d* São Paulo, 25 Feb 1945). Brazilian writer and musicologist. He was one of the founders of Brazilian ethnomusicology, and very influential in the assertion of musical nationalism in his country in the 1920s and 1930s. He studied at the São Paulo Conservatory where he later taught. He took an active part in the Semana de Arte Moderna (February 1922) whose basic goal was the reform of Brazilian art from academicism into 'modernismo'. Soon afterwards he began his lifelong investigations into Brazilian folk and popular music which produced a series of outstanding essays. His first monograph, *Ensaio sôbre a música brasileira* (1928), considers the relationship that ought to exist between art music and popular music, and analyses the rhythmic, melodic, harmonic, textural, instrumental and formal peculiarities of Brazilian music. Andrade was one of the chief organizers of the Congresso da Língua Nacional Cantada (1937) and from 1935 to 1938 was in charge of the Department of Culture; he founded the Discoteca Pública de São Paulo which still holds a splendid recorded collection of Brazilian folk music.

WRITINGS
Ensaio sôbre a música brasileira (São Paulo, 1928)
Pequena história da música (São Paulo, 1929, 6/1967)
Modinhas imperiais (São Paulo, 1930)
Música, doce música (São Paulo, 1934, 2/1957)
Cultura musical (São Paulo, 1936, 2/1965)
O samba rural paulista (São Paulo, 1937, 2/1965)
Os compositores e a língua nacional (São Paulo, 1938, 2/1965)
Evolução social da música no Brasil (Curitiba, 1941, 2/1965)
Música de feitiçaria no Brasil (São Paulo, 1941, 2/1963)
Danças dramáticas do Brasil (Rio de Janeiro, 1946, 2/1959)

BIBLIOGRAPHY
A. T. Luper: 'The Musical Thought of Mário de Andrade', *Yearbook of the Inter-American Institute for Musical Research*, i (1965), 41
                    NORMAN FRASER/GERARD BÉHAGUE

Andrae, Hieronymus. *See* FORMSCHNEIDER, HIERONYMUS.

André. German family of composers and music publishers, of French extraction.

(1) Johann [Jean] **André** (*b* Offenbach, 28 March 1741; *d* Offenbach, 18 June 1799). Composer and publisher. His peasant grandfather, a Huguenot, fled persecution in Languedoc and settled in 1688 in Frankfurt am Main, where he became a manufacturer of silks. When only ten years old Johann succeeded to the family firm, which was directed during his minority by his mother and an uncle. His early education in music, described by Gerber as 'notes, metre and some playing of chorales', came through a friend who took lessons in nearby Frankfurt; from 1756, while he learnt business management in the family firm, he had lessons in thoroughbass for several months from a transient musician – apparently the only regular instruction he ever received. Around 1758 he went to Mannheim to further his business training, and there he enthusiastically attended concerts, plays and operas, acquainting himself with the current repertory of serious and comic Italian opera as well as the modern instrumental style specific to Mannheim.

The decisive stimulus to André's artistic career occurred when he was a volunteer clerk in Frankfurt (1760–61), where during the French occupation a French troupe presented the *opéras comiques* of Philidor for the first time to a German public. It is noteworthy that André first approached this new, middle-class genre not as a musician but as a translator, preferring to transmit rather than imitate. The first of his translations, *Der Komödienfeind*, was published in 1765, and was followed two years later by his *Komische Versuche*. The removal of Theobald Marchand's renowned theatrical troupe to Frankfurt in 1770 made André's efforts particularly timely. Marchand, apparently drawn by the literary finesse of these translations, seems to have proposed André's close collaboration with the troupe; in any case André translated more than a dozen French plays and operettas in 1771–2, all of which appeared in Marchand's repertory. In addition Marchand cultivated German Singspiel, as represented by Georg Benda, Hiller, Neefe and others. André made adept use of the many-sided theatrical experiences and stimuli of these years in the libretto and score of his first work, *Der Töpfer* (1773), dedicated to Marchand. Goethe wrote at length in appreciation of this work (letter of 23 November 1773 to Johanna Fahlmer):

The piece exists for the sake of its music, bears witness to the good, gregarious soul of its creator, and fully meets our theatre's particular need that actors and audience be able to follow it. Now and then there are good conceits; yet its uniformity would not exist but for the music. This music is composed with understanding of the present capabilities of our theatres. The author has sought to combine correct declamation with light, flowing melody, and no further art is required to sing his ariettas than is demanded by the beloved compositions of Messrs Hiller and Wolf. So as not to leave the ear entirely empty, he has directed all his industry to the accompaniment, which he sought to render as full-voiced and harmonious as is possible without disadvantage to the sung parts. To this end he often used wind instruments, sometimes putting these in unison with the voice parts to make them strong and agreeable, as accomplished for instance by a single flute in the first duet. One cannot reproach him for copying or pilfering. And there is still more to be hoped from him.

Der Töpfer, first performed on 22 January 1773 at the Prince's Theatre in Hanau, was a success; and, as was characteristic of André's enterprise and practicality, he tried to turn this into a material success too. In that summer the score was published, 'at the author's expense'. The artistic and apparent financial success of *Der Töpfer* determined André's subsequent career and encouraged him to further undertakings both as a dilettante composer and as a music publisher. In 1774 he issued two collections of his songs; in the next year his setting of G. A. Bürgers's *Lenore* brought him widespread acclaim. Beyond these he had the satisfaction of being commissioned by Goethe to set the Singspiel *Erwin und Elmire*; the work had its première in Frankfurt in 1775 and appeared the next year in vocal score. (*Dichtung und Wahrheit*, iv/17, gives a vivid account of Goethe's relation to the Andrés in connection with his affair with Lili Schönemann.)

André withdrew from the family silk concern in 1774 (1773, according to Matthäus) to found his own 'Notenfabrique' and music publishing house. In 1776, perhaps through Marchand's intercession, he was appointed conductor at Theophil Doebbelin's theatre in Berlin, directing a troupe of 51 permanent, well-paid members, among them 16 orchestral musicians. There André disclosed his full talent as a composer in a period of extraordinary productivity, and at that time he also attempted to surmount his dilettantism by a serious study of Kirnberger's writings, particularly the *Grundsätze des Generalbasses als erste Linien zur Composition*. Of the 16 Singspiels of this period, most of them performed in Berlin, his settings of Goethe's *Claudine von Villa Bella*, C. F. Bretzner's *Die Entführung aus dem Serail* (shortly afterwards to be set by Mozart in a revised version by the younger Stephanie), and German versions of Palissot de Montenoy's *Le barbier de Baghdad* and Beaumarchais' *Le barbier de Séville* deserve special mention, as does his incidental music to Shakespeare's *Macbeth* and *King Lear*. He also continued to write songs.

André's mother died in 1784, and his publishing firm was faring poorly under the administration of his uncle J. B. Pfaltz. As the removal of the firm from Offenbach to Berlin was made impossible by J. J. Hummel's exclusive privilege in that city, André, by then bearing the honorary title of Kapellmeister to the Margrave Schwedt, accordingly chose to return to Offenbach, where he immediately took over the direction of his firm. Through good fortune and acumen he was able to establish relations with Pleyel, then (through Paul Wranitzky) with Joseph Haydn and later with Adalbert Gyrowetz. By virtue of its circumspect treatment of authors and many technical improvements in printing and production the firm flourished considerably, reaching its 1000th item in 1797. André apparently composed little after 1784, his Singspiel *Der Bräutigam in der Klemme* for the Frankfurt stage (1796) being a solitary late addition to his output. In 1798 he fell ill

while on a business journey to Bamberg, and he died the next year.

André was not a significant composer, and as a dilettante and 'original genius' he falls into no particular school. He had no high ambitions, and was content to use his talent for naive melody to meet the needs of his day. A sure theatrical instinct and a happy gift for folklike, vulgar humour allowed him to create entertainment in the best sense of the word, and in this he won the esteem of his contemporaries. His songs proved a more lasting part of his output: the ballad *Lenore* deeply impressed an entire generation, and many of his social songs continued to be sung with pleasure in the 19th century; the *Rheinwein-Lied*, to a text by Matthias Claudius, became almost excessively popular.

WORKS
Printed works published by André in Offenbach, unless otherwise stated.

STAGE
First performed in Berlin unless otherwise stated; for detailed list with MS sources see Stauder (1936).

Singspiels: Der Töpfer (J. André), Hanau, 1773, score (1773); Erwin und Elmire (Goethe), Frankfurt am Main, 1775, vocal score (1776); Der alte Freyer (André), 1776; Die Bezauberten (André), 1777; Die Schadenfreude (C. F. Weisse), 1778; Der Alchymist (Meissner), 1778; Laura Rosetti (D'Arien), 1778, vocal score (1778); Azakia (Schwan), 1778; Claudine von Villa Bella (Goethe), 1778, 2 arias in *Theater-Kalendar* (Gotha, 1778); Das tartarische Gesetz (F. W. Gotter), 1779; Alter schützt vor Thorheit nicht (F. L. W. Meyer), Mannheim, 1779; Kurze Thorheit ist die beste (Meyer), 1780; Das wüthende Heer oder Das Mädchen im Thurme (Bretzner), 1780; Die Entführung aus dem Serail (Bretzner), 1781; Elmine (Drais), 1782, song (Berlin, 1782); Eins wird doch helfen oder Die Werbung aus Liebe, 1782; Der Liebhaber als Automat oder Die redende Maschine (André), 1782; Der Barbier von Bagdad (André), 1783; Der Bräutigam in der Klemme (Meyer), Frankfurt, 1796, rondo (1799), aria (1800)

Other works: Herzog Michel (comedy); Der Barbier von Sevilien (comedy), 1776, arias (1777); Der Fürst im höchsten Glanze (prol), 1777; Die Grazien (prol), 1778; Harlekin Friseur (pantomime), 1778; incidental music to Macbeth and King Lear, 1778; Friedrichs glorreichster Sieg (prol), 1779; Die Friedensfeyer oder Die unvermuthete Wiederkunft (children's comedy), Leipzig, 1779; Das liebste Opfer Friedrichs (ballet), 1780; Mehr als Grossmuth (prol), 1781; music for Der Oberamtmann, 1781; Lanassa (tragedy), 1781; music for Der liebenswürdige Alte (comedy), 1782

OTHER WORKS
Lieder: Scherzhafte Lieder (C. F. Weisse) (1774); Auserlesene scherzhafte und zärtliche Lieder, i (1774); Lenore (G. A. Bürger) (1775), 4 subsequent edns., some with orch, 2 versions ed. in EDM, 1st ser., xlv (1970); Musikalischer Blumenstrauss (1776); Neue Sammlung von Liedern, i–ii (Berlin, 1784); Lieder, i–iii (1792–3), inst acc. to i–ii (1793)

Inst: 3 Sonaten, vn, vc, hpd obbl, op.1 (1776) [wrongly attrib. J. A. André]

Edns./arrs.: numerous collections of opera arias, works by Pleyel, Martín y Soler, inst arrs. etc

(2) Johann Anton André (*b* Offenbach, 6 Oct 1775; *d* Offenbach, 6 April 1842). Composer and music publisher, son of (1) Johann André. He showed an early gift for music, received instruction in the piano, the violin and later in singing, and began composing small pieces at the age of six. In 1787 he took violin lessons from his brother-in-law Ferdinand Fränzl, writing his first violin sonata at this time; two years later he went to Mannheim to pursue his studies under Ignaz Fränzl. After staying briefly in Offenbach, where he had to deputize for his father in the publishing firm, he studied composition in Mannheim with G. J. Vollweiler (1792–3). Thereupon he took a position in his father's firm, studying composition independently in his spare time. In 1796 he enrolled at Jena University as a student of fine arts, but soon had to abandon his studies when his father became ill. After his father's death he undertook an extended business journey in autumn 1799 through Germany to Vienna, accompanied by his friend, the pianist P. C. Hoffmann. It was to this journey that André owed (in his own words) 'the acquaintance of the foremost musicians of Germany' and the later, if only temporary, international importance of his firm. In Munich he acquired the rights to Senefelder's and Gleissner's lithographic process from its inventors, and engaged both of them for his Offenbach firm (in a contract of 28 September 1799). In Vienna he bought the so-called 'Mozart-Nachlass' from the composer's widow Constanze for 3150 gulden (by a contract of 8 November 1799), and immediately had Gleissner prepare a provisional manuscript catalogue, the so-called 'Gleissner-Verzeichnis' of 1800. The first print by the André firm to use Senefelder's lithographic method was a vocal score of André's own opera *Die Weiber von Weinsberg* (1800). The André brothers set up more or less short-lived lithographic plants in Paris (the 'Imprimerie lithographique' in Charenton from 1802) and in London (1801); a cousin in Offenbach, François Johannot, attempted at the same time to apply the process to works of art (1804).

It was however Mozart's estate that gave André his life's task. He viewed this purely in its editorial aspect, producing from 1800 a veritable plenitude of, for the most part, outstandingly reliable 'editions following the composer's original manuscript'; but above all he viewed his task as one of sorting and ordering the manuscripts. André's original plan, as arranged with Constanze and her husband Nissen as early as 1799–1800, called for a chronological catalogue of works and manuscripts to 1784, to be completed by appending Mozart's own autograph catalogue of 1784–91; but insurmountable difficulties prevented its realization. Over half a dozen manuscript sketches for a catalogue, in widely varying stages (of which only the 1833 catalogue is generally known), attest to André's continuing concern with the project, which occupied him intensively into the late 1830s. The results of André's groundwork was later gratefully excerpted and adopted by Otto Jahn and Ludwig von Köchel. Indeed André, if anyone, deserves to be called 'the father of Mozart research'. He entered the dispute over the authenticity of Mozart's Requiem, initiated by Gottfried Weber in 1825, with two editions of the work (1827 and 1829) accompanied by detailed commentary; even those who feel uneasy with the particulars of André's argument agree that at least the preface to the earlier edition is a brilliant showpiece of scholarly research. His edition in two colours of the score to *Die Zauberflöte* (1829), made 'in precise agreement with the composer's manuscript, as sketched, orchestrated and completed by him', established entirely new criteria for documentary editions of music. This and other accomplishments quickly placed André far ahead of his time, and even today have an unexpected immediacy.

As a composer André is difficult to evaluate, though he was perhaps among the most considerable of the many composers of his period who now stand in the shadow of Beethoven and Schubert. A self-appraisal, recorded by his pupil F. W. Rühl, runs as follows:

As a creative artist I did not become what I might have. While I was young I wrote well, but without planning or direction; after I had begun to think for myself and had learnt something, I was too old to recast my knowledge as fundamentally as only a child can.

The early works are mostly distinguished by an all but harmless, flaccid Classicism, deriving much more from Haydn than from Mozart. Occasionally there are surprising outbursts of genius, among which those in the string quartets op.14 (1801) even hint at Mendelssohn. Nor are the works lacking in eccentricities, as instanced by the contrapuntal development of a choral cantus firmus in the trio of the minuet in the Symphony op.11 no.2. André also had a striking tendency towards over-refinement, most apparent in the string quartets opp.22 and 54, nicknamed 'Poissons d'avril', where each instrument plays in a different metre; yet the highly complex whole rests on a disproportionately simple harmonic basis, and the piece fails to be convincing. His *Sprichwörter* op.32 had the distinction of being published (by Joseph Aibl in 1869) as a work of Haydn's (cf H XXV*c*:G2). Many of his didactic pieces, particularly those for piano duet (recently published in a complete edition), have pedagogical worth if no particular musical interest, and are still valued by teachers.

It is a great loss to music literature that André was unable to complete his *Lehrbuch der Tonsetzkunst*, grandly conceived in six volumes. Its torso breaks off with the treatise on fugue (vol.ii/3, posthumously edited by Heinrich Henkel), following the study of harmony (vol.i); only sketches remain for the further volumes, which were to deal directly with composition. What remains reveals a stimulating theorist and gifted teacher. His pupils included Aloys Schmitt, Wilhelm Speyer and Henkel.

André bore the title of court Kapellmeister to the grand dukes of Hesse from 1803 (he gave the later Grand Duke Ludwig I the autograph of Mozart's Serenade K361/370*a* in gratitude) and court councillor to the princes of Isenburg from 1813. In the wars of liberation he was plenipotentiary commander of the board of home reserves; later he was elected to the second peerage chamber of the Grand Duchy of Hesse, and in 1827 he received honorary citizenship from the city of Berne.

Of André's 15 children several sons (listed below) were musicians or publishers; a daughter Auguste (Elisabeth) André (1802–47) married Johann Baptist Streicher, a son of the noted Viennese maker of pianos, in 1823.

WORKS

(all printed works published by André, Offenbach)

Edition: *J. A. André: Originalkompositionen für Klavier zu 4 Händen*, ed. M. Streicher (Vienna, 1971); suppl. with opp.72–3 (Vienna, n.d.)

VOCAL

Stage: Rinaldo und Alcina (opera), ov. pubd as op.16 (1801); Die Weiber von Weinsberg (opera), vocal score (1800)

Choral: Der Friede Tuiskons, cantata, ov. pubd as op.9 (1800); Missa solemnis, op.43 (1819); Vater unser, 2 choirs, orch, op.50 (1827); Crucifixus über einen Basso Continuo von J. S. Bach, op.58 (*c*1830); Veni Creator Spiritus, op.59 (*c*1830); Te Deum, solo vv, chorus, orch, op.60 (1829)

Partsongs etc: Sprichwörter (Quartetto a canone), 4vv, pf, op.32 (*c*1808); Des Sängers Lied zu den Sternen, vv, pf, op.47 (*c*1825); Ruf der Freude, vv, pf, op.48 (1826); Ein alt Lied von Gott, vv, pf, op.49 (*c*1828); 6 Duette, S, A, op.51 (*c*1828); Kleine Kantate, 3 S, pf, op.55 (1829); Liederkranz, 4–5 male vv, op.57 (*c*1830); Liederkranz, male vv, op.61 (*c*1830); Deutsche Vaterlandslieder, op.67 (*c*1840); 6 Duette, S, A, op.69 (*c*1840); 24 Maurergesänge, male vv

Solo songs with pf: 48 Lieder und Gesänge, opp.38–40 (1819), excerpts pubd as op.62 (n.d.); Der 138. und 28. Psalm, op.63 (1840); other lieder

ORCHESTRAL

Syms.: C, op.4 (1795); F, op.5 (1795); C, op.6 (1795); D, 'zur Friedensfeier', op.7 (1797); 2 'd'une exécution facile', op.11 (1800); Grande sinfonie, op.13 (1801); Grosse Symphonie, Eb, op.25 (1804); Grande sinfonie, op.41 (1820)

Concs.: fl, G, op.3 (1795); ob, F, op.8 (1798); fl, op.10, 1796 (1800); hn, op.33 (*c*1808); vn, vc; 2 hn, collab. P. Dornaus

Ovs.: Ouverture militaire, op.24 (1804); Die Hussiten vor Naumburg, characteristic ov., op.36 (c1818); Concertante in Form einer Ouverture, op.37 (1819)
Numerous dances for orch and other works

CHAMBER
Trios, qts: 3 str qts, op.14, 1801 (1801), arr. fl, str trio, op.15 (1801); Sonata, pf, vn, vc, op.17 (1803); Str Qt 'Poissons d'avril' no.1, op.22, 1803 (1803); Trio, 3 fl, op.29 (1805); Str Qt 'Poissons d'avril' no.2, op.54 (c1828)
Sonatas etc, 2 insts: Sonata, C, vn, pf, ?op.1 (1789); Sonata, D, vn, pf, ?op.1 (1789); 3 sonatas, vn, pf, op.2 (1790); Sonata, vn, pf, op.21 (1803); 12 petits pièces, 2 hn, op.26 (1805); 2 grands duos, 2 vn, op.27, 1804 (1805); 12 duos d'une difficulté progressive, op.30 (1807); Instruktive Variationen, 2 fl, op.53 (1829)

KEYBOARD
Pf; 12 kleine Stücke zur Übung im Präludieren, op.23 (1804); Instruktive Variationen über 5 Tönen, op.31 (1807); 6 sonates progressives, op.34 (c1811); 6 pièces instructives, op.35 (c1814); 3 sonatinas, op.71 (c1840); variations
Pf 4 hands: Sonata, op.12 (1800); 12 divertissements, opp.18–20 (1803); 3 marches, op.28 (1805); Conversations musicales, op.42 (1819); 12 leichte Stücke, op.44 (c1820); 6 leichte Sonatinen, op.45 (c1820); 3 sonatas, op.46 (c1820); Leichte Sonate ('Constance'), op.56 (1829); 9 leichte Stücke, op.72 (c1863); Sonatine, op.73 (c1863)
Org: 25 Orgelstücke (Die 12 Dur- und 12 Molltonleitern und die chromatische Tonleiter für das Orgelpedal), op.64 (1840); 10 Orgelstücke, op.68 (c1840)

OTHER WORKS
Anleitung zum Violinspielen, op.30 (1805); Fuge, a 4, nebst deren Entwurf und den allgemeinen Regeln über die Fuge, op.52 (c1828)

Opp.65–6, 70 unknown

WRITINGS
Thematisches Verzeichnis sämtlicher Kompositionen von W. A. Mozart (Offenbach, 1805, 2/1828 as W. A. Mozarts thematischer Catalog) [edn. of Mozart's autograph catalogue of 1784–91]
Introductory essays to 2 edns. of W. A. Mozart: Requiem (Offenbach 1827, 1829); as 'Anzeige zu W. A. Mozarts Missa pro defunctis . . .', Caecilia, vi/93 (1827), 193 [the title Beiträge zur Geschichte des Requiems was devised by A. Fuchs for his personal copies]
Lehrbuch der Tonsetzkunst, i–ii (1832–42) [planned in 6 vols.; ii ed. H. Henkel]; abridged H. Henkel (1874–8)
Thematisches Verzeichnis W. A. Mozartscher Manuskripte, chronologisch geordnet von 1764–1784 (MS, 1833)
Thematisches Verzeichnis derjenigen Original-Handschriften von W. A. Mozart, welche Hofrath André in Offenbach besitzt, ed. H. Henkel (Offenbach, 1841)
Essay on the rudiments of music, inc. (n.d.)

(3) Carl August André (b Offenbach, 15 June 1806; d Frankfurt, 15 Feb 1887). Music dealer, son of (2) Johann Anton André. He directed the Frankfurt music shop founded by his father in 1828, and from 1839 also made pianos there, notably a series of 'Mozartflügel' from 1853. In 1855 he published a brochure Der Klavierbau und seine Geschichte.

(4) (Peter Friedrich) Julius André (b Offenbach, 4 June 1808; d Frankfurt, 17 April 1880). Pianist and organist, son of (2) Johann Anton André. From 1864 he was procurist in his brother's shop in Frankfurt. He wrote an organ method which was much used in its time, a school of pedal technique, a harmony textbook, and well-regarded vocal works and organ and piano pieces.

(5) Jean Baptiste (Andreas) André (b Offenbach, 7 March 1823; d Frankfurt, 9 Dec 1882). Pianist and composer, son of (2) Johann Anton André. Henkel regarded him as the most gifted of the sons. He made concert tours within and outside Germany, and later settled in Berlin, where he taught the Count Bolko von Hochberg, in particular overseeing the latter's operatic works. He was later court Kapellmeister to the Prince of Bernburg until the liquidation of the chapel on the prince's death. He composed numerous songs, choral works and salon pieces for piano, some of them published under the pseudonym 'de St Gilles', after the family's ancestral home in Languedoc.

The direction of the family's Offenbach concern passed in 1840 from (2) Johann Anton André to his son (Johann) August André (1817–87), who successfully staved off several financial crises by issuing cheap editions of the classics and attracting such composers as Franz Abt and Heinrich Marschner. Under his direction the Frankfurt and Offenbach branches merged; they later came under the joint direction of his sons Karl (1853–1914) and Adolf André (1855–1910) and, from 1910 to 1923, of their respective widows Elisabeth and Aurelie. Their successor Karl August Johann (Hans) André (1889–1951), Adolf's son, turned the firm's emphasis toward choral and teaching material, and rebuilt the house (without a music printing shop) after its almost complete destruction in 1944. The firm continues as Johann André Musikverlag, Offenbach, under the joint direction of Hans's widow Friederike (b 1901) and sister Elfriede (b 1904), and though not of importance for its new publications remains noteworthy for its archive, with rich holdings of composers' autographs, correspondence and the firm's own prints.

BIBLIOGRAPHY
GerberL; GerberNL
H. Henkel: 'Die Familie André', Didaskalia [suppl. of the Frankfurter Journal] (1 Sept 1887); Offenbacher Zeitung (1 Sept 1887)
H. Haupt, ed.: 'Johann Anton André', Hessische Biographien, i (Darmstadt, 1918)
C. B. Oldman: 'J. A. André on Mozart's Manuscripts', ML, v (1924), 169
O. Pretzsch: Johann André und seine Stellung in der Berliner Liederschule (diss., U. of Leipzig, 1924)
W. Stauder: Johann André: ein Beitrag zur Geschichte des deutschen Singspiels (diss., U. of Frankfurt am Main, 1936; extracts in AMw, i, 1936, pp.318–60)
O. E. Deutsch: 'Mozarts Verleger', MJb 1955, 49
E. Lebeau: 'Une succursale officieuse de Johann André à Paris, de 1802 à 1806', Kongressbericht: Wien Mozartjahr 1956, 324
A. H. André: Zur Geschichte der Familie André – Offenbach am Main (Offenbach, 1962)
——: Zur Geschichte der Familie André (Garmisch, 1963)
W. A. Bauer, O. E. Deutsch and J. Eibl, eds.: Mozart: Briefe und Aufzeichnungen, iv, vi (Kassel, 1963, 1971)
L. von Köchel: Chronologisch-thematisches Verzeichnis sämtlicher Tonwerke Wolfgang Amade Mozarts (Wiesbaden, 6/1964), pp.xxix ff
W. Matthäus: 'Das Werk Joseph Haydns im Spiegel der Geschichte des Verlages Jean André', Haydn Yearbook, iii (1965), 54–110
J. Eibl: 'Aus den Briefen Constance Mozarts an die Verleger Breitkopf & Härtel und Johann Anton André', Musik und Verlag: Festschrift Karl Vötterle (Kassel, 1968), 238
W. Plath: 'Mozartiana in Fulda und Frankfurt (Neues zu Heinrich Henkel und seinem Nachlass)', MJb 1968–70, 333–87
H. Unverricht: 'Vier Briefkopierbücher des Offenbacher Musikverlags André aus dem ersten Fünftel des 19. Jahrhunderts', Quellenstudien zur Musik: Festschrift Wolfgang Schmieder (Frankfurt, 1972), 161
W. Matthäus: Johann André Musikverlag zu Offenbach am Main: Verlagsgeschichte und Bibliographie 1772–1800 (Tutzing, 1973)
K. Hortschansky, H. Unverricht and others: Johann André Musikverlag (Offenbach, 1974)
W. Plath: 'Requiem-Briefe: aus der Korrespondenz Joh. Anton Andrés 1825–31', MJb 1976–7, 174–203
WOLFGANG PLATH

André, Charles-Louis-Joseph (b Ath, 23 Feb 1765; d Mechelen, 8 April 1839). South Netherlands composer. He is said to have been sent to Paris for his musical education at the expense of the Archbishop of Mechelen. For some time he was attached to Antwerp Cathedral and in 1788 was appointed organist to the Cathedral of St Rombout, Mechelen. In August of that year he went back to Paris and remained there until March 1789, when he returned again to Mechelen. On 18 December 1790 he was ordained priest, his salary being 200 florins; later that year he was made a canon. During the revolutionary troubles of 1797 he was deported to the island of Oléron and did not return to Mechelen until 1801, when he became organist at St Rombout and at Notre Dame. He also directed an orchestra.

WORKS

Le siège et bombardement de Valenciennes, pf/harp, vn acc., op.1

3 sonates, pf/harp, vn acc., op.2

3 pots-pourris, pf/hpd, harp, op.4

Ode sur l'arrivée et l'inauguration de S. M. l'Empereur et Roi François II, pf acc.

Pot-pourri, pf/harp; Le souvenir et air varié, pf sonata; Préludes, pf; church music with various inst acc.; all unpubd

ERIC BLOM/R

André, Franz (*b* Brussels, 10 June 1893; *d* Brussels, 20 Jan 1975). Belgian conductor. He studied the violin with César Thomson at the Brussels Conservatory until 1914, and composition and conducting with Weingartner at the Berlin Conservatory. From 1920 he taught at the Brussels Conservatory, resigning his directorship of the conducting class in 1944; he conducted the orchestra there, 1940–45. In 1935 he founded the Belgian Radio SO, of which he was conductor until 1958. From that year he became concerned with the administration of the Queen Elisabeth International Music Competition. A tireless interpreter of contemporary works, André was awarded the Schoenberg Medal in 1952 for his services to 20th-century music, especially Schoenberg's. He made orchestral transcriptions of works by Rameau, Lully, Grétry, Leclair and Bach and wrote incidental music for radio plays.

BIBLIOGRAPHY

C. Mertens: Obituary, *Vie musicale belge*, xiv/1 (1975), 7

André, Maurice (*b* Alès, nr. Cévennes, 21 May 1933). French trumpeter. At the age of 14 he became a miner like his father, from whom he learnt to play the trumpet (his father, also named Maurice, was an amateur trumpeter who played with great endurance). He studied under Sabarich at the Paris Conservatoire from 1951, receiving a *premier prix* for the cornet and for the trumpet after his first and second years of study. He played with the Lamoureux Orchestra (1953–60), the French Radio PO (1953–62) and the Opéra-Comique (1962–7). He won first prizes in the international contests in Geneva in 1955 and – brilliantly – in Munich in 1963. This was the start of an unprecedented international career as a soloist. In particular, he achieved great success through the use of the four-valved piccolo B♭/A trumpet, made under his supervision by Selmer. In 1967 he succeeded Sabarich at the Paris Conservatoire. He was consultant for Selmer until January 1973.

André combines the gifts of endurance, range and musicality with the magnetism of the true soloist. His recordings comprise the entire trumpet repertory. He has become increasingly interested in transcriptions of Baroque flute, oboe or violin works, even taking up the horn (in high B♭) in 1970. Many composers, including Jolivet, Tomasi and Blacher, have written for him. His brother Raymond (*b* 22 December 1941) is also a trumpeter and has toured with him; at one time trumpet professor at Poitiers, he then went to Nîmes.

EDWARD H. TARR

Andrea degli Organi. *See* ANDREAS DE FLORENTIA.

Andrea de' Servi. *See* ANDREAS DE FLORENTIA.

Andrea di Giovanni. *See* ANDREAS DE FLORENTIA.

Andreae, Carolus [Endres, Enders, Karl] (*d* ?Irsee, nr. Kaufbeuren, Swabia, 1627). German composer. He was a monk at the Benedictine abbey at Irsee and was its abbot from 1610 until his death. He helped, together with Johann Seytz and Gregor Stemmelius, to make the abbey a leading south German centre for the cultivation of liturgical music in the early 17th century, and a number of vocal works and transcriptions for organ by him survive in manuscript. Most are signed 'FCA' ('Frater Carolus Andreae') and must therefore date from before his appointment as abbot. A slightly later work, however, is the *Magnificat*, which he intended for the fine new organ which he had installed shortly after becoming abbot, probably in 1612. Some of his music, such as the eight-part *Te Deum*, is written in the Venetian polychoral style.

WORKS

Kyrie (Missa pro defunctis), 5vv, *D-As*

Te Deum laudamus, 8vv; 1st chorus, *Rp*; 2nd chorus, *As*

Facta est Judaea (Ps cxiii.2), 4vv, *As*

2 Magnificat; Vir vitae venerabilis, hymn; Domine ad adiuvandum: 6vv, *Rp*

Vesper antiphons, 6vv, *Rp*

8 falsi bordoni, 4vv, *Rp*

Organ arrs.: Magnificat, a 8, ?1612 (top and bottom parts only); 2 motets, 6vv, 1596, 1598; 1 hymn, 8vv: all *Mbs*

BIBLIOGRAPHY

U. Kornmüller: *Die Pflege der Musik im Benedictiner-Orden*, Wissenschaftliche Studien und Mitteilungen aus dem Benedictiner-Orden, ii/2 (Würzburg and Vienna, 1881)

FRIEDRICH BASER

Andreae, Volkmar (*b* Berne, 5 July 1879; *d* Zurich, 18 June 1962). Swiss conductor and composer. He spent his school years in Berne, studying the piano and composition with C. Munzinger, and was then a pupil of Wüllner in Cologne (1897–1900), where his first compositions were performed. There followed a one-year engagement as répétiteur at the Munich Hofoper, and in 1902 he settled in Zurich, where he was to dominate musical life for the next half-century. He was appointed director of the Zurich Gemischten Chor (1902), the Winterthur Stadtsängerverein (1902) and the Zurich Männerchor (1904); but his most important position was as conductor of the Tonhalle Orchestra (1906–49). In addition he directed the Zurich Conservatory (1914–41); and at the university (where he received an honorary doctorate in 1914) he held classes, served as musical director (1915) and conducted the Studentengesangverein (1914–16). In 1920 he was elected president of the Schweizerische Tonkünstlerverein, and was made first honorary president of the society on his retirement in 1925.

The extent of Andreae's international reputation is indicated by the fact that on Mahler's death he was offered the directorship of the New York PO, and by his activities as a guest conductor of leading European orchestras. In 1923 he made a tour of Italy with the Berlin PO, and subsequently he was permanent guest conductor of the Vienna PO, receiving the Nicolai Medal. The composers he particularly promoted in Zurich were Berlioz, Debussy, Ravel, Mahler, Strauss and Reger, and in later years he was an outstanding advocate of Bruckner's music; he also supported such contemporaries as Stravinsky, Hindemith, Honegger and Schoeck. As most of his compositions arose from his conducting associations, male choruses form a large part of his output. During his career he gradually reduced his creative work until he gave up composing altogether. Earlier works are rooted in the Romantic tradition, with Straussian orchestration, while the later music, still tonal, has a refined, transparent sound.

WORKS
(selective list)

STAGE AND VOCAL

Ratcliff, op.25 (opera, after Heine), Duisburg, 1914; Abenteuer des Casanova, op.34 (4 1-act operas, F. Lion), Dresden, 1924; La cité sur la montagne, op.41 (incidental music to Festspiel, G. de Reynold), Geneva, 1942

Choral orch: Das Göttliche, op.2 (Goethe), T, chorus, orch, perf. 1900; Charons Nachen, op.3 (J. V. Widmann), solo vv, chorus, orch, perf. 1901; Sinfonische Fantasie, op.7 (W. Schaedelin), T, T chorus, orch, org, perf. 1903; Vater unser, op.19, Mez/Bar, chorus, org; Magentalied, op.28, male vv, orch (1917)

Male choruses: Waldesfriede und Graf Isenburg, op.6 (M. Wetter); 4 Männerchöre, op.13 (M. Lienert); 3 Männerchöre, op.22 (Keller); Suite, op.38 (E. Zahn) perf. 1935; arrs.

Solo vocal: Der Spielmann, op.5 (Wetter), 4 Lieder (1903); 6 Gedichte, op.10 (Meyer) (1906); 4 Gedichte, op.23 (Hesse) (1913); Li-tai-pe, op.37 (Chin., trans. Klabund), 8 Lieder, T, orch perf. 1931

INSTRUMENTAL

Orch: Pf Conc., d, perf. 1898, unpubd; Sym., F, perf. 1899, unpubd; Konzertstück, b, pf, orch, perf. 1900, unpubd; Kleine Suite, op.27, perf. 1917; Notturno und Scherzo, op.30, perf. 1918; Sym., C, op.31, perf. 1919; Rhapsodie, op.32, vn, orch, perf. 1920; Musik für Orch, op.35, perf. 1929; Vn Conc., f, op.40, perf. 1936; Ob Concertino, op.42, perf. 1941 (1947); marches for band

Str Qt, Eb, perf. 1898, unpubd; Pf Trio no.1, f, op.1, perf. 1899; Sonata, D, op.4, vn, pf; Str Qt, B, op.9, perf. 1905; Pf Trio no.2, Eb, op.14, perf. 1908; 6 Klavierstücke, op.20 (1911); Str Trio, d, op.29, perf. 1917; Str Qt no.2, e, op.33 (1921); Divertimento, op.43, fl, str trio, perf. 1942

Principal publishers: Hug, Schott

BIBLIOGRAPHY

E. Tobler: 'Volkmar Andreae', *Wissen und Leben*, xvi (1923), 1007

F. Seiler: *Dr Volkmar Andreae, seit 1906 Leiter der Sinfoniekonzerte der Tonhallegesellschaft Zürich* (n.p., 1931)

Volkmar Andreae: Festgabe (Zurich, 1949)

Volkmar Andreae zum 70. Geburtstag (Zurich, 1949)

F. Giegling: *Volkmar Andreae*, Neujahrsblatt der Allgemeinen Musikgesellschaft Zürich, no.143 (Zurich, 1959)

W. Hess: 'Volkmar Andreaes Kompositionsunterricht', *SMz*, cii (1962), 236

PETER ROSS

Andreas, Magister Philipoctus (*fl* late 14th century). Theorist (?and composer). He may be identifiable with the trecento composer ANDREAS DE FLORENTIA, or with PHILIPPUS DE CASERTA, whose theoretical works date from the early 15th century. Andreas's treatise, *Regule de contrapuncto*, is known from *I-Fl* plut.XXIX.48 and *Ma* I.20.inf., and Coussemaker referred to *CH-E* 689 and an MS in Vienna (*CS*, iii, pp.xxii, 116–18). In the treatise he stated some 25 rules governing the construction of a second voice against a given voice. Each rule is illustrated by a series of short music examples showing brief phrases in void notation above which a note-against-note counterpoint is added by means of a mixed letter- and number-notation (o = octava, t = tertia, v = quinta, vi = sexta, etc).

ANDREW HUGHES

Andreas Contredit. *See* ANDRIEU CONTREDIT D'ARRAS.

Andreas de Florentia [Magister Frater Andreas de Florentia Horghanista de Florentia; Andrea degli Organi] Frate Andrea de' Servi; Fra Andrea di Giovanni] (*d* c1415). Italian composer and organist. A relatively large amount of information about Andreas's life is available, because of the important position he held in the Order of the Servi di Maria, which he entered in 1375. From 1380 until 1397, with interruptions, he was

prior of the monastery of the Ss Annunziata in Florence; in 1393 he was prior in Pistoia and from 1407 to 1410 he was the leader of the Tuscan Servites. Andreas was closely associated with Landini and worked with him on the construction of the organ at both the Annunziata and the Cathedral of Florence, in 1379 and in 1387. Moreover, the names 'Cosa' and 'Sandra', which occur in ballata texts that he himself set to music and in works by Landini (and Paolo da Firenze), point to the same social environment. Andreas was the teacher of the Florentine composer Bonaiuto Corsini who is known for several works. It is uncertain whether a Maestro Andrea who was commissioned in 1382 with the construction of a new organ in Rieti (to the northeast of Rome), is identical with the composer.

18 two-voice and 12 three-voice ballate, possibly a French ballade and perhaps a madrigal by Andreas have survived. The main source for his work is the Squarcialupi MS (*I-Fl* 87, containing 29 works). The MS includes a portrait of an organ player, presumed to be Andreas. The texts, some of which are probably

Portrait thought to be of Andreas de Florentia: detail of illuminated initial from the Squarcialupi MS (I-Fl 87, 184v)

written by Andreas himself, are either love songs or moralizing and sometimes polemic poems.

With his almost exclusive cultivation of the ballata, Andreas belongs among the representatives of the last Florentine generation. And yet in most of the two-voice pieces which have text supplied for both voices and in which there is simultaneous syllabic articulation, Andreas adheres to an older tradition. On the other hand, in the three-voice ballate all the techniques of textual underlay current at that time are to be found; in these – perhaps under French influence – the *piedi* sections in seven works have a double cadence (as opposed to three in the two-voice ballate), and in four works the cadences of *ripresa* and *piedi* are identical. The contratenor appears both as a secundus cantus (cf Landini) and as a true contratenor. The short imitations, usually restricted to single words, are a striking feature of Andreas's work. They give the pieces a lively, restless character which stands in contrast to the balanced style of Landini. Typical of Andreas's often original and versatile manner of writing are no.6, a ballata-caccia, and also no.3, with their pes-like tenors and with voice-exchange in the upper voices of the *ripresa*.

WORKS

Editions: *Der Squarcialupi-Codex Pal.87 der Biblioteca Medicea Laurenziana zu Florenz*, ed. J. Wolf (Lippstadt, 1955) [W]
    The Music of Fourteenth-Century Italy, ed. N. Pirrotta, CMM, viii/5 (1964) [P]
    Italian Secular Music, ed. W. T. Marrocco, PMFC, x (Monaco, 1974) [M]

BALLATE

1 Amor, già lungo tempo, 3vv, W 340, P 1, M no.1 (Senhal: 'Neincia')
2 Amor, i' mi lamento (M. Grifoni), 2vv, W 345, P 2, M no.2 (Senhal: 'Tadea')
3 Astio non morì mai, 3vv, W 343, P 3, M no.3
4 Checch'altra donna, 2vv, W 346, P 3, M no.4 (Senhal: 'Checa')
5 Cosa crudel m'ancide, 2vv, W 340, P 4, M no.5 (Senhal: 'Cosa', lauda 'El cor mi si divide')
6 Dal traditor non si può, 3vv, W 339, P 4, M no.6 (ballata-caccia)
7 Dè, che farò, signore?, 3vv, W 355, P 6, M no.7
8 Dè, quanto fa gran mal, 2vv, W 349, P 7, M no.8
9 Dolce sperança, 3vv, W 350, P 8, M no.9
10 Donna, bench'i mi parta, 3vv, W 335, P 8, M no.10
11 Donna, se per te moro, 2vv, W 351, P 10, M no.11 (Senhal: 'Checa')
12 Donna, s'e racçi, 2vv, W 338, P 11, M no.12
13 E più begli occhi, 3vv, W 342, P 12, M no.13 (text incipit from a canzona of C. da Pistoja; Senhal: 'Sandra')
14 Filippaion di fin or, 2vv, W 358, P 13, M no.14 (Senhal: 'Filippa')
15 Fugite Gianni Bacco, 2vv, W 348, P 14, M no.15
16 La divina giustizia, 2vv, W 336, P 14, M no.16 (Senhal: 'Giovanna')
17 Morrà la 'nvidia, 2vv, W 347, P 15, M no.17
18 Non già per mie fallir, 2vv, W 353, P 15, M no.18
19 Non ne speri mercede, 2vv, W 348, P 16, M no.19
20 Non più doglie ebbe, 3vv, W 356, P 17, M no.20
21 Perché languir mi fai, 2vv, W 345, P 19, M no.21
22 Perché veder non posso, 3vv, W 357, P 19, M no.22
23 Per fanciulla tènera, 3vv, W 359, P 21, M no.23
24 Per la ver'onestà, 2vv, W 352, P 21, M no.24
25 Pianto non partirà, 3vv, W 354, P 22, M no.25
26 Presunzion da ignorança, 3vv, W 337, P 24, M no.26
27 Questa legiadra luce, 3vv, W 350, P 25, M no.27
28 Sia quel ch'esser po', 2vv, P 26, M no.28 (wrongly called a madrigal in MS)
29 Sotto candido vel, 3vv, W 344, P 26, M no.29 (text inc.)
30 Voi, non voi loro, 3vv, W 346, P 28, M no.30

DOUBTFUL WORKS

— Dame sans per en qui, 2vv, P 45 (ballade; *I-MOe* α.M.5.24: Fr. A[ndrea] Ser[vorum])
— Girand'un bel falcon, 2vv (madrigal; *F-Pn* 568, see Günther, 1966, pp.84, 90)

BIBLIOGRAPHY

R. Taucci: 'Fra Andrea dei Servi', *Studi storici sull'ordine dei Servi di Maria*, ii (1935), 73
F. Ghisi: 'Un frammento musicale dell'ars nova italiana nell'archivio capitolare di Pistoja', *RMI*, xlii (1938), 162
A. Königslöw: *Die italienischen Madrigalisten des Trecento* (Würzburg-Aumühle, 1940), 34f
A. S. Sassetti: *La cappella musicale del duomo di Rieti* (Rome, 1941), 6
E. Li Gotti: *La poesia musicale italiana del sec. XIV* (Palermo, 1944), 96ff
K. von Fischer: *Studien zur italienischen Musik des Trecento und frühen Quattrocento* (Berne, 1956)
F. D'Accone: *A Documentary History of Music at the Florentine Cathedral and Baptistry during the Fifteenth Century* (diss., Harvard U., 1960), 65
N. Pirrotta: Introduction to CMM, viii/5 (1964)
U. Günther: 'Die "anonymen" Kompositionen des Manuskripts Paris, B.N. fonds it. 568 (Pit)', *AMw*, xxiii (1966), 73
N. Pirrotta: 'Andreas de Florentia', *MGG*
U. Günther: 'Das Manuskript Modena, Biblioteca Estense, α.M.5, 24 (olim lat.568 = Mod)', *MD*, xxiv (1970), 58
G. Corsi: *Poesie musicali del trecento* (Bologna, 1970), 289ff

For further bibliography *see* ITALY: BIBLIOGRAPHY OF MUSIC TO 1600.

KURT VON FISCHER

Andrée, Elfrida (*b* Visby, 19 Feb 1841; *d* Göteborg, 11 Jan 1929). Swedish organist and composer. Like her sister, the noted opera singer Fredricka Stenhammar,

she had her first instruction in music from her father. She studied composition with Ludwig Norman at the Royal Academy of Music, Stockholm, and later with Gade in Copenhagen. During the early 1860s she was active as an organist in Stockholm, moving to Göteborg in 1867 to become the cathedral organist. She was a keen supporter of the suffragette movement. Her style reflected the ideals of the Leipzig school and the Scandinavian nationalism of her day. She wrote two symphonies, a piano quintet, a string quartet and other chamber music. Her numerous organ works include two symphonies, one with wind instruments. Her opera *Fritiofs saga* was never performed, and her music has generally fallen into neglect.

WORKS
(MSS in S-Skma; complete catalogue in MS in S-Sm)

Fritiofs saga, opera (S. Lagerlöf), unperf.; lib (Göteborg, 1899)
Orch: sym. no.1, C, 1889; sym. no.2, a, 1893; ov., D, 1873
Chamber: pf qnt, e (Stockholm, 1865); pf qt, a, 1865; str qt, d, 1895; pf trio, g (Stockholm, 1877); vn sonata no.1, E♭; vn sonata no.2, B♭, 1872; 2 romanser, vn, pf (Stockholm, 1887)
Pf solo: Sonate, A, op.3 (Copenhagen, ?1873); Tonbilder, op.4 (Copenhagen, c1875); 5 smärre tonbilder, op.7 (Stockholm, 1880)
Numerous organ works, incl. Organ Symphony (London, n.d.); 2nd org sym., with wind insts, c1892 [arr. of vn sonata no.2]
Choral with orch: Snöfrid (V. Rydberg), vocal score (Stockholm, 1884); Svensk mässa nr.1 [Swedish mass], 1902, vocal score (Copenhagen, 1907)
Solo songs: 3 sånger med piano, op.8 (Oslo 1881); Skogsrået (Rydberg) (Göteborg, 1878); others, unpubd

BIBLIOGRAPHY

E. M. Stuart: *Elfrida Andrée* (Stockholm, 1925)
E. Stenhammar, ed.: *Fredrika Stenhammar: Brev* [Letters of Stenhammar] (Uppsala, 1958)

ROBERT LAYTON

Andreini, Giovanni [Giovan] **Battista** (*b* Florence, probably in 1579; *d* Reggio Emilia, 7 or 8 June 1654). Italian actor, dramatist and poet. His parents were among the foremost actors of their time; they were both good musicians, and his mother was also a poet. He appears to have been educated at the University of Bologna. In 1594, taking the stage name 'Lelio', he joined the Gelosi, the comic troupe to which his parents belonged, and in 1601 he married the actress and singer Virginia Ramponi ('La Florinda'). By the time the Gelosi disbanded in 1604 he had already formed his own company, the Comici Fedeli, which served the Dukes of Mantua, with brief interruptions, until about 1647–50, playing throughout northern and central Italy. During the celebrations at Mantua in 1608 to mark the wedding of Duke Francesco Gonzaga to Margherita of Savoy, Virginia sang in Monteverdi's *Ballo delle ingrate* and distinguished herself in the title role of his opera *L'Arianna*, which she undertoook at short notice following the death of Caterina Martinelli, for whom the part was intended. In 1613 Maria de' Medici invited the Fedeli to France. Their visit, which lasted from September 1613 to July 1614, was so successful that they performed there again from January 1621 to March 1622, December 1622 to March 1623 and December 1623 to June 1625. In 1627 they visited Prague and in 1628 Vienna. During this tour, or during the plague of 1630, Virginia died; soon after, Andreini married Virginia Rotari, an actress in his company for whom he had harboured an ill-concealed passion since about 1620. In 1643 the Fedeli returned to France, and in 1647, the year in which Luigi Rossi's *Orfeo* was performed in Paris, Andreini dedicated a presentation copy of his comedy *La Ferinda* to Cardinal Mazarin, evidently in the hope of having it set to music. He was the subject of eulogies and sonnets and belonged to the Accademia degli Spensierati of Florence.

Andreini was a prolific writer. About ten of his stage works straddle the borderline between spoken drama and opera. *La Ferinda* (Paris, 1622) is one of them. In writing it he tried to take account of the operas he had seen at Florence and Mantua. Although typical of the *commedia dell'arte* in its mixing of dialects and languages, it is entirely in verse, Andreini himself described it as a 'commedietta musicale', and much of it was sung. *La Centaura* (also Paris, 1622) marries comedy and pastoral with tragedy. It too included sections that were sung, as well as choruses at the end of each act, and most of the other comedies allowed for isolated pieces of music such as songs and dances. Andreini wrote two sacred dramas, both of which are in verse and in five acts, and well on the way to being operas. *L'Adamo* (Milan, 1613; ed. E. Allodoli, Lanciano, 1913), which inspired Milton's *Paradise Lost*, includes scenes with directions for music. Parts of *La Maddalena* (Mantua, 1617) were set to music by Monteverdi and others for a performance at Mantua in 1617; the music was published by Andreini as *Musiche de alcuni eccellentissimi musici . . . per La Maddalena* (Venice, 1617). Andreini based this 'sacra rappresentazione' on his poem of the same name (Venice, 1610), and a revised three-act version, *La Maddalena lasciva e penitente*, appeared at Milan in 1652. The interest of all these works is heightened by the fact that he combined personal experience of both the traditional *commedia dell'arte* and the practical and musical aspects of contemporary 'literary' drama. He helped to pave the way for Italian opera in France and for the *comédie-ballet* of Molière and Lully.

BIBLIOGRAPHY

G. M. Mazzuchelli: *Gli scrittori d'Italia*, i (Brescia, 1753), 708ff
F. Bartoli: *Notizie istoriche de' comici italiani* (Padua, 1782), i, 13ff
C. Magnin: 'Teatro celeste (Les comédiens en paradis): les commencements de la comédie italienne en France', *Revue des deux mondes*, iv (1847), 843
A. Baschet: *Les comédiens italiens à la cour de France* (Paris, 1882)
A. Ademollo: *La bell'Adriana ed altre virtuose del suo tempo alla corte di Mantova* (Città di Castello, 1888)
A. Bertolotti: *Musici alla corte dei Gonzaga in Mantova dal secolo XV al XVIII* (Milan, 1890/R1969), 77, 97
A. d'Ancona: *Lettere di comici italiani del secolo XVII* (Pisa, 1893)
A. Valeri (Carletta): 'Un palcoscenico del seicento: Lelio e Fritellino', *Nuova rassegna*, i (1893), 797
L. Rasi: *I comici italiani*, i (Florence, 1894 [dated 1897]), 117ff
E. Bevilacqua: 'Giambattista Andreini e la Compagnia dei Fedeli', *Giornale storico della letteratura italiana*, xxiii (1894), 76; xxiv (1895), 82
A. E. Picot: 'Gli ultimi anni di G. B. Andreini in Francia', *Rassegna bibliografica delle lettere italiane*, ix (1901), 61
A. Neri: 'Fra i comici dell'arte', *Rivista teatrale italiana*, xi (1906) xxxvi ff
H. Prunières: *L'opéra italien en France avant Lulli* (Paris, 1913), xxxvi ff
M. Ortiz: 'Filodrammatici e comici di professione in una commedia di Giovanni Battista Andreini', *Rivista teatrale italiana*, xvii (1917)
V. Mazzetti: *Un famoso comico e autore drammatico del seicento* (Reggio Emilia, 1915)
F. Neri: 'La commedia in commedia', *Mélanges d'histoire littéraire . . . offerts à Fernand Baldensperger* (Paris, 1930), ii, 130
A. Fiocco and C. E. Tanfani: 'Andreini, Giovan Battista', *ES*
N. Pirrotta: '*Commedia dell'Arte* and opera', *MQ*, xli (1955), 317
F. A. Frajese: 'Andreini', *DBI*

COLIN TIMMS

Andreis, Josip (*b* Split, 19 March 1909). Yugoslav musicologist. He studied Romance languages at the universities in Zagreb and Rome and graduated in 1931. Between 1931 and 1941 he was a schoolmaster in Šibenik, Hercegnovi, Zagreb and Split, where he also studied composition privately. In order to complete a formal university course in music, he then entered the Academy

of Music in Zagreb, although he had already written several articles and two books. In 1945 he became professor of the history of music at the Academy of Music and head of its musicology department; he occupied these positions until his retirement in 1972. In the year 1950–51 he was the editor of the musical periodical *Muzičke novine*, between 1958 and 1963 general editor of *Muzička enciklopedija*, the first publication of its kind in Yugoslavia; between 1965 and 1969 he edited the proceedings of the music section of the Yugoslav Academy of Arts and Sciences, and in 1969 founded and edited the first two volumes of the musicological annual *Arti musices*. He is a member of the Yugoslav Academy of Arts and Sciences.

Andreis's first significant contribution to Yugoslav musicology was a comprehensive history of music, completed before he entered the Academy of Music. Between 1951 and 1954 he produced a much bigger work on the same subject. Both were of pioneering significance in Yugoslavia; the latter book has established itself as the standard history of music in Serbo-Croat. His interests have always been divided between musical lexicography and general history of music on the one hand and, on the other, the history of music in Croatia, where his work has centred on the early Baroque and the 19th century. An erudite scholar, well versed in the literature and art of Italy and France, he has left an important mark on the development of musicology in Yugoslavia since World War II.

WRITINGS

Povijest glazbe [History of music] (Zagreb, 1942)
Uvod u glazbenu estetiku [Introduction to the aesthetics of music] (Zagreb, 1944)
Hector Berlioz (Zagreb, 1946)
Historija muzike (Zagreb, 1951–4, rev. 2/1966)
'Vatroslav Lisinski', *Zvuk*, no.1 (1955), 5
with S. Zlatić: *Yugoslav Music* (Belgrade, 1959)
'Razvoj muzičke umjetnosti u Hrvatskoj' [The development of the art of music in Croatia] in J. Andreis, D. Cvetko and S. Djurić-Klajn: *Historijski razvoj muzičke kulture u Jugoslaviji* (Zagreb, 1962)
'Rezultati i zadaci muzičke nauke u Hrvatskoj' [Results and tasks of musicology in Croatia], *Rad JAZU* no.336, p.5
'Pozabljeni nokturno Ferda Livadića' [A forgotten nocturne by Ferdo Livadić], *MZ*, iv (1968), 70
Vječni Orfej [Eternal Orpheus] (Zagreb, 1968)
'Umjetnički put Mila Cipre' [Artistic development of Milo Cipra], *Rad Jugoslavenske akademije znanosti i umjetnosti*, cccli (1969), 325
'Musicology in Croatia', *Arti musices*, special issue (1970), 7
Music in Croatia (Zagreb, 1974)
'Muzikologija u Hrvatskoj u razsoblju 1965–1973: ostvarenja i zasaci' [Musicology in Croatia 1965–73: results and future tasks], *Arti musices*, v (1974), 5–37

EDITIONS

I. Lukačić: *Šesnaest moteta iz zbirke 'Sacrae cantiones'* [Sixteen motets from the collection *Sacrae cantiones*] (Zagreb, 1970)

BIBLIOGRAPHY

K. Kovačević: 'Hrvatski muzikolog Josip Andreis' [Croatian musicologist Josip Andreis], *Arti musices*, iii (1972), 5 [includes a list of writings between 1940 and 1971]
I. Supičić: Doprinos Josipa Andreisa muzičkoj estetici u Hrvatskoj' [Josip Andreis's contribution to the aesthetics of music in Croatia], *Arti musices*, iii (1972), 19

BOJAN BUJIĆ

Andreoli. Italian family of musicians.

(1) Evangelista Andreoli (i) (*b* Disvetro, Modena, 27 June 1810; *d* Mirandola, Modena, 16 June 1875). Pianist and organist. He taught at the music school in Mirandola where he spent his entire life. Crippled in both legs, he constructed a device which enabled him to play the organ pedal-board. He should not be confused with the pianist Evangelista (ii), 1845–67.

(2) Guglielmo Andreoli (i) (*b* Mirandola, 22 April 1835; *d* Nice, 13 March 1860). Pianist and composer, son of (1) Evangelista Andreoli (i). A precocious music student, he studied first with his father and later with Antonio Angeleri at the Milan Conservatory (1847–53). From 1854 he was active as a concert pianist in Europe, principally in London, where he lived from 1856 to 1859. Subsequently he played in Italy, Paris and Nice. He was renowned for his taste, the delicacy of his touch and his virtuosity.

(3) Carlo Andreoli (*b* Mirandola, 8 Jan 1840; *d* Reggio Emilia, 22 Jan 1908). Pianist, composer and conductor, son of (1) Evangelista Andreoli (i), and the most celebrated member of the family. He studied with his father and with Angeleri at the Milan Conservatory (1852–8), where he received a piano diploma. In December 1858 he made his début as a concert artist in the Teatro S Radegonda in Milan. He made successful tours of Italy and gave concerts in England, France, Germany and Austria with such artists as Piatti, Bazzini, Bottesini, Alard, Borghi Mamo, Joachim and Sivori. From 1871 he taught the piano at the Milan Conservatory. He founded the Società dei Concerti Sinfonici Popolari (1877), which he and his younger brother (4) Guglielmo Andreoli (ii) directed for ten years, giving 96 concerts altogether. He became insane in 1891 and four years later was committed to an asylum in Reggio Emilia, where he died. A bust of him, with an epigraph by Boito, was placed in the Milan Conservatory in 1910.

As a pianist Andreoli had a precise technique and an exceptional singing tone. He was an outstanding representative of the Milanese piano school and he helped popularize German 18th- and 19th-century instrumental music in Italy, being among the first Italians to play Bach, Beethoven and the Romantics. His compositions show the influence of Chopin, Liszt, Mendelssohn and Schubert; his style is virtuoso and descriptive, rich in harmonic effects. Besides dances, military marches, nocturnes, songs without words, études and character pieces, he wrote a set of scenes – *Le stagioni* (1888). He also composed songs, cello sonatas, trios and other chamber works; he published a piano tutor (with Angeleri) and prepared editions of the keyboard music of Bach, Beethoven, Chopin and Clementi.

(4) Guglielmo Andreoli (ii) (*b* Mirandola, 9 Jan 1862; *d* Modena, 26 April 1932). Pianist, violinist, conductor and composer, son of (1) Evangelista Andreoli (i). He received his first musical instruction from his father, and from 1876 studied the organ with Fumagalli, the violin with G. Rampazzini and composition with Bazzini at the Milan Conservatory. He taught harmony, counterpoint and (from 1900) the piano at the conservatory, where his pupils included Victor De Sabata and Franco Vittadini. From 1878 to 1886 he took an active part in the Società dei Concerti Sinfonici Popolari and directed the Concerti della Società del Quartetto; he was a member of the Campanari Quartet for three years. His works include a *Fantasia sinfonica* and two overtures for orchestra, a requiem, a string quartet, short piano pieces, and songs. He also published *Manuale d'armonia* (with Edgardo Codazzi, Milan, 1898) and prepared editions of piano music of Beethoven, Chopin, Heller, Mendelssohn, Moscheles, Raff and Weber.

BIBLIOGRAPHY
L. A. Villanis: *L'arte del pianoforte in Italia* (Turin, 1907)
G. Tebaldini: *In memoria di Carlo Andreoli* (Milan and Mirandola, 1910)
——: 'Una famiglia di musicisti: gli Andreoli', *L'arte pianistica* (Naples, 20 Oct 1918)
G. Roncaglia: 'Una nidiata di musicisti: gli Andreoli di Mirandola', *Atti e memorie della R. Accademia di scienze, lettere e arti in Modena*, iv (1933–4), 33
F. Perrino: 'Figure della rinascita pianistica italiana: Carlo Andreoli', *Rassegna musicale Curci*, xviii/3 (1964), 21
S. Martinotti: *Poetiche e presenze nel pianismo italiano dell'ottocento*, Quaderni della rassegna musicale, iii (Turin, 1965)
——: *Ottocento strumentale italiano* (Bologna, 1973)
FRANCESCO BUSSI

Andreoni, Giovanni Battista (*b* Lucca; *d* Lucca, 23 April 1797). Italian mezzo-soprano castrato. On 22 March 1736 he was appointed first soprano to the Palatine Chapel at Lucca, with permission to spend two years at Bologna to improve his art. In 1738–9 he sang at Venice in operas by Pergolesi, Lampugnani, Hasse and Porpora. Lord Middlesex engaged him for his experimental opera season at London's New Haymarket Theatre in the winter of 1739–40; he appeared in three operas. He returned the two following years, singing in Handel's final unsuccessful opera season at Lincoln's Inn Fields in 1740–41 and as second man to Monticelli in Lord Middlesex's King's Theatre company in 1741–2. Early in 1741 he gave six concerts with Mrs Arne at Hickford's Room and sang in a 'New Eclogue' by Veracini at the New Haymarket on 9 March. Under Handel he created the parts of Tirinto in *Imeneo* and Ulysses in *Deidamia* and sang in revivals of *L'Allegro* (31 January 1741), *Acis and Galatea* (Acis), *Saul* (David) and probably *Il Parnasso in festa*. His roles in the English works were translated into Italian; Handel wrote a new recitative and aria for him in *L'Allegro*. At the King's he acted mostly in pasticcios. Burney called him 'a good singer of the second class'; his Handel parts indicate a capable technique and a voice and compass (*b* to *a''*) similar to Carestini's. He was immensely fat, and according to Horace Mann had no trill.

After leaving London Andreoni sang at Florence in 1742–3 and 1747–8 (Pergolesi's *Olimpiade* and Vivaldi's *Tamerlano*), and in Spain, where he was robbed by a servant. This is said to have so disgusted him with an artist's life that he went to Rome and was ordained priest. The Lucca Chapel pensioned him on 22 March 1785 at five scudi a month. Some arias attributed to Andreoni are in the library of the Gesellschaft der Musikfreunde, Vienna.

WINTON DEAN

Andreozzi, Gaetano (*b* Aversa, 22 May 1755; *d* Paris, 21 or 24 Dec 1826). Italian composer and singing teacher. He studied singing, harmony and counterpoint with Fedele Fenaroli and P. A. Gallo at the Conservatorio di S Maria di Loreto in Naples; his fellow pupils included Cimarosa, Zingarelli and Giordani. He was also a pupil of his maternal uncle, Niccolò Jommelli, from whom his nickname 'Jommellino' is derived. In 1779, shortly after completing his studies, he made his début in Rome with a sacred work, *Giefte*, which was the first of a series of theatrical successes in various Italian cities. He then visited Russia (probably in 1784), but the oratorio and two operas he had composed for the occasion were not produced. Returning to Italy in 1785, he visited Pisa, Naples and, in the following year, Florence, where he married his pupil, Anna de Santi. She had made her début in the same year at the Teatro S Benedetto in Venice, and he now made her the principal singer in his operas. They separated in 1799; de Santi died in a carriage accident three years later in Dresden.

Returning to Naples in 1801, Andreozzi remarried and continued his successful career, particularly in Rome and Naples, even attempting the role of impresario at the Teatro di San Carlo in Naples in 1806; but the arrival of the French troops frustrated the project, to the great advantage of Domenico Barbaja. From then on he devoted himself less to the theatre, and with decreasing success; instead, he made a name for himself as a singing teacher, becoming much sought after by the Neapolitan nobility and also at the court. But serious financial difficulties drove him to Paris in 1825, where his former pupil Maria Carolina, the Duchess of Berry and daughter of King Francesco I of Naples, gave him protection and, with the fees from his singing lessons, helped his family which had remained in Naples.

Andreozzi's compositions, the embodiment of empty virtuosity, show the most obvious features of the Neapolitan style; they are remarkable only for some striking instrumental effects and, according to Fétis and Florimo, a certain spontaneity and an agreeable melodic facility.

WORKS

OPERAS

L'equivoco, Florence, 1781; L'Arbace (G. Sertor), Livorno, 1781; I pazzi per disimpegno (A. Bagliacca), Venice, carn. 1782; L'Olimpiade (Metastasio), Pisa, 1782; Bajazet (A. Piovene), Florence, 1783; Medonte re d'Epiro (G. de Gamerra), Alessandria, 1783; La vergine del sole (F. Casoli), Genoa, 1783 or Palermo, aut. 1797; L'amore industrioso, Florence, 1783; Quello che può accadere, Venice, carn. 1784
Le tre fanatiche (G. Palomba), Naples, 1785; Didone abbandonata (Metastasio), Pisa, 1785; Partenope sul lido etrusco (C. Boccella), Lucca, 1785; Catone in Utica (Metastasio), Cremona, 1786; Virginia, Genoa, 1786; La pace tra Amore e Imeneo, Florence, 1787; Arminio, Venice, 7 May 1788; Agesilao re di Sparta (F. Ballani and others), Venice, 1788; Giovanna d'Arco ossia La Pulcella d'Orléans (A. Sografi), Vicenza, 27 June 1789; Artaserse (Metastasio), Livorno, 1789; La morte di Giulio Cesare, Rome, 1789; Teodolinda (G. Boggio), Turin, 1789; Sesostri (Zeno), Naples, 1789
Il finto cieco, Naples, 1791; Angelica e Medoro (Sertor), Venice, 1791; Amleto (G. Foppa), Padua, 1792; Gli amanti in Tempe (Gamerra), Florence, 1792; Sofronia ed Olindo (C. Sernicola), Naples, 1793; Giasone e Medea, Naples, 4 Nov 1793; Le nozze inaspettate, Naples, 1793; Ines de Castro (C. Giotti), Florence, 1793; La principessa filosofa ossia Il contraveleno (Sografi), Venice, aut. 1794
Il trionfo di Arsace (Ballani), Rome, 1795; Arsinoe (M. Rispoli), Naples, 13 Aug 1795; Argea (G. D. Boggio), Turin, 1799
Pamela nubile, Parma, carn. 1800; Armida e Rinaldo, Naples, 2 Sept 1802; Il ritorno dei numi (F. Villani), Naples, 1802; Il trionfo di Alessandro (A. Passaro), Naples, 1803; Piramo e Tisbe (G. Schmidt), Naples, 30 May 1803; Il trionfo di Claudia, Florence, 8 Sept 1803
Sedesclavo (M. Prunetti), Rome, 1805; Il trionfo di Tomiri (F. Cammarano), Naples, Lent 1807; Tutti i torti son dei mariti, Florence, 1814; Il trionfo di Alessandro Magno il Macedone, Rome, 1815

OTHER WORKS

Oratorios: Giefte, Rome, 1779; Isacco figura del Redentore, Jesi, 1785; La Passione di Gesù Cristo, Naples, 1789; Saulle, Naples, 1794; Assuero ossia La regina Ester, Palermo, 1798
Various shorter sacred choral and secular vocal works
3 qnts, fl, str (Venice, 1793); 3 qnts, ob, str; 6 str qts, op.1 (Florence, 1786)

BIBLIOGRAPHY

EitnerQ; FétisB; GerberNL
F. Florimo: La scuola musicale di Napoli e i suoi conservatorii (Naples, 1880–82)
F. Piovano: 'Notizie storico-bibliografiche sulle opere die P. C. Guglielmini con appendice su Pietro Guglielmi', RMI, xvi (1909), 263; xvii (1910), 866
A. Della Corte: L'opera comica italiana nel '700: studi ed appunti (Bari, 1923)
E. Zanetti: 'Andreozzi, Gaetano', ES
U. Prota-Giurleo: ' "Jommellino" e Signora', Nostro tempo, iv (Naples, 1955)

FRANCESCO BUSSI

Andrés, Juan [Andres, Giovanni] (*b* Planes, Alicante, 15 Feb 1740; *d* Rome, 12 Jan 1817). Spanish literary historian and music critic. He was professed in the Society of Jesus on 24 December 1754 and studied at Tarragona, Manresa, Gerona and Valencia from 1754 until 1763, when he was ordained a priest. Four years later, while teaching rhetoric and poetry at the University of Gandía, he was exiled with the rest of the Spanish Jesuits. He went first to Corsica, then to Italy, where he taught philosophy at Ferrara until 1773. After Clement XIV suppressed the Jesuits in 1773 Andrés devoted himself to letters and bibliography, living three years with the Bianchi at Mantua, and then travelling throughout Italy and in 1794 to Vienna. During his travels he maintained a correspondence with his brother Carlos, which was published from 1786 to 1794. The work contains much valuable material on music, particularly the third volume, which deals with Venetian conservatories, singers, opera and Greek-rite chant in 1788, and the fourth. In his magnum opus, the seven-volume universal history of literature published at Parma (1782–99, frequently re-edited and translated), he argued that Spanish–Arabic precedents determined the forms of medieval Catalan and Provençal poetry as well as music. He was also the first to claim Arabic influence in the cantigas of Alfonso X, a thesis later developed exhaustively by Julián Ribera.

WRITINGS
(*only those pertaining to music included*)

Dell'origine, progressi e stato attuale d'ogni letteratura (Parma, 1782–99, add vol., 1822, [8]/1838; Sp. trans., 1784–99; vol. i, Fr. trans., 1805)
Cartas familiares . . . á su hermano (Madrid, 1786–94)
'Lettera sopra la musica degli arabi', G. B. Toderini: Letteratura turchesca, i (Venice, 1787), 249ff
Carta . . . á su hermano . . . dandole noticia de la literatura de Viena, ed. C. Andrés (Madrid, 1794; Ger. trans., 1795; It. trans., 1795)

BIBLIOGRAPHY

G. Peignot: Répertoire bibliographique universel (Paris, 1812), 318ff
C. Sommervogel, ed.: Bibliothèque de la Compagnie de Jésus, i (Brussels and Paris, 1890), 341ff
J. F. Yela y Utrilla: Juan Andrés, culturalista español del siglo XVIII (Oviedo, 1940)
M. Batllori, ed.: E. Arteaga: I. Lettere . . . II. Del ritmo sonoro (Madrid, 1944), pp.xx–xxv
———: La cultura hispano-italiana de los jesuitas expulsos (Madrid, 1966), 531ff
A. V. Cervone: An Analysis of the Literary and Aesthetic Ideas in 'Dell'origine, dei progressi e dello stato attuale d'ogni letteratura' of Juan Andrés (diss., St Louis U., 1966)

ROBERT STEVENSON

Andrésen, Ivar (*b* Oslo, 27 July 1896; *d* Stockholm, 26 Nov 1940). Norwegian bass. He studied in Stockholm, where he made his début as the King in *Aida* in 1919. He joined the Dresden Staatsoper in 1925 and the Berlin Staatsoper in 1935. He sang regularly at Bayreuth (1927–36) as King Mark, Gurnemanz, Pogner, the Landgrave and Fasolt, and was made a German *Kammersänger*. His Covent Garden début was in 1928, and during the next four seasons he sang the leading Wagnerian bass parts in London, as well as Sarastro in Bruno Walter's 1931 *Zauberflöte*, a part he repeated at Glyndebourne in 1935, together with Osmin. He also sang at the Metropolitan, New York

(1930–32). He possessed a beautiful voice, noble in sound, and was an artist of the first rank.

HAROLD ROSENTHAL

Andreví y Castellar, Francisco (*b* Sanahuja, Lérida, 7 Nov 1786; *d* Barcelona, 23 Nov 1853). Spanish composer. He began his musical studies in the Urgel Cathedral, where he was a choirboy for nine years. Later he moved to Barcelona for advanced study with Juan Quintana (organ) and Francisco Queralt (composition). In 1808 he entered the competition for choirmaster of Tarragona Cathedral; although he was ranked first by the examining tribunal, the chapter of the cathedral did not grant him the position. On 1 June of the same year he won the post of choirmaster of Tafalla, but turned it down to take an identical position at Segorbe Cathedral, where he remained until 1814, when he was appointed choirmaster of S María del Mar in Barcelona. In 1819 he was named choirmaster of Valencia Cathedral and in 1830 advanced to the same post at Seville Cathedral. All of these appointments were obtained by competitions. In 1831 he won the highest possible post available to a contemporary Spanish musician, that of choirmaster of the royal chapel in Madrid. In 1836 he lost this appointment for political reasons and emigrated to France; in 1839 or 1840 he became *maître de chapelle* of Bordeaux Cathedral, where he remained until 1845. Later he seems to have lived for some time in Paris, and then returned to Barcelona, becoming choirmaster of the parish church of La Merced in 1850, a post he retained until his death.

Andreví's extraordinary merit was shown by his success in all of the competitions he entered for the position of choirmaster in various cathedrals, from the one at Tarragona at the age of 22, to those for the most coveted positions in Spain.

WORKS

Pubd: mass; 15 Lat. motets, incl. 3 Stabat mater; other Lat., Fr. and Sp. compositions; all (Paris, n.d.)

MSS: 5 masses, office and mass of the dead, Te Deum, Vespers, Compline, Christmas matins, 5 motets, 2 hymns, 2 litanies, Salve, Seq, 9 Lamentations, all in *E-Mn*; 4 masses, 12 psalms, Tantum ergo, exercises for competitions, all *Bc*; 2 masses, psalm, 2 motets, all *SC*; mass, motet, *PAL*

Oratorios: La dulzura de la virtud, Barcelona, before 1819; El juicio universal, Valencia, 1822

Pedagogical: *Tratado teórico práctico de armonía y composición*, 1835, autograph *E-Mn* (Barcelona, 1848; Fr. trans., 1848)

BIBLIOGRAPHY

LaborD [contains complete list of pubd works]

B. Saldoni: *Diccionario biográfico-bibliográfico de efemérides de músicos españoles*, iii (1880), 314f, 327

F. Pedrell: *Catàlech de la Biblioteca Musical de la Diputaciò de Barcelona* (Barcelona, 1908–9)

J. Subirá: 'Andrevi, Francisco', *MGG*

J. López-Calo: *Catálogo musical del archivo de la Santa Iglesia Catedral de Santiago* (Cuenca, 1972), 233ff [with extensive bibliography]

JOSÉ LÓPEZ-CALO

Andrew of Crete [Andrew Hierosolymites; Andrew of Jerusalem] (*b* Damascus, *c*660; *d* Mytilene, *c*740). Byzantine hymnographer. He was first a monk at Jerusalem, and later a deacon at Constantinople; in 711 or 712 he became Archbishop of Crete and from that time lived at Gortina.

His homilies (more than 50, of which half remain unpublished) and hymns can be assigned to the period when he was Archbishop of Crete. He was particularly famous as a writer of hymns, although the tradition that attributes to him the invention of the KANŌN has now been discredited, since his kanōnes (several dozen in number) show that the genre was already fully developed. His works in this form are remarkable for the originality of their metric and musical form and for their length. The most famous is the Great Kanōn, a penitential hymn of 250 stanzas, which is still sung during Lent. Andrew's hymns have been listed by Tomadakēs (206–9); some may be found in the Greek liturgical books (mēnaia, triōdion and pentekostarion).

BIBLIOGRAPHY

FACSIMILES, TRANSCRIPTIONS

E. Wellesz, ed.: *Die Hymnen des Sticherarium für September*, MMB, Transcripta, i (1936)

H. J. W. Tillyard, ed.: *The Hymns of the Sticherarium for November*, MMB, Transcripta, ii (1938), 149, 152, 158

——: *Twenty Canons from the Trinity Hirmologium*, MMB, Transcripta, iv (1952), 63ff, 106ff

A. Ayoutanti and others, ed: *The Hymns of the Hirmologium: I*, MMB, Transcripta, vi (1952), 87ff, 110ff, 172ff, 180ff, 187ff

——: *The Hymns of the Hirmologium: III/2*, MMB, Transcripta, viii (1956), 27ff

LITERATURE

PG, xcvii, 1305–1444

W. Christ and M. Paranikas, eds.: *Anthologia graeca carminum christianorum* (Leipzig, 1871), 97f, 147ff

E. Wellesz: *A History of Byzantine Music and Hymnography* (Oxford, 1949, 2/1962), 204f, 232ff

N. B. Tomadakēs: *Hē byzantinē hymnographia kai poiēsis* (Athens, 1965), 182ff

ENRICA FOLLIERI

Andrews, Ellen. The name under which JANET PATEY made her singing début.

Andrews, H(erbert) K(ennedy) (*b* Comber, Co. Down, 10 Aug 1904; *d* Oxford, 10 Oct 1965). Northern Irish music scholar, teacher, organist, composer and editor. He went to Bedford School, and studied at the RCM in London, Trinity College, Dublin, and New College, Oxford, gaining doctorates of music at both universities. In 1938, after four years as organist and choirmaster at Beverley Minster, he moved to a similar position at New College. Thereafter, he lived and worked in Oxford, where he was a university lecturer in music and a Fellow of New College, and later of Balliol. He also taught at the RCM.

Andrews's published work consists of three books, various articles (including contributions to *Grove 5*), reviews, and several motets, services and songs. *The Oxford Harmony*, vol.ii, traces the development of chromatic harmony through standard repertory works and relates this to techniques of composition. The opening chapters of *An Introduction to the Technique of Palestrina* and *The Techniques of Byrd's Vocal Polyphony* can be accepted as standard – and very lucid – expositions of the complex problems of modality and the mensural and proportional time systems. The latter book is particularly valuable as a comparative study of the development of polyphonic language during the 16th century.

WRITINGS

The Oxford Harmony, ii (London, 1950)

'Counterpoint'; 'Harmony'; 'Polyphony', *Grove 5*

with R. T. Dart: 'Fourteenth-Century Polyphony in a Fountains Abbey MS Book', *ML*, xxxix (1958), 1

An Introduction to the Technique of Palestrina (London, 1958)

'Transposition of Byrd's Vocal Polyphony', *ML*, xliii (1962), 25

'Printed Sources of William Byrd's "Psalmes, Sonets and Songs" ', *ML*, xliv (1963), 5

The Technique of Byrd's Vocal Polyphony (London, 1966)

PETER CLULOW

Andreyanova, Elena (1819–57). Russian dancer. *See* DANCE, §VI, 1(ii).

Andreyev, Vasily Vasil'yevich (*b* Bezhetsk, Tver govt., 15 Jan 1861; *d* Petrograd, 26 Dec 1918). Russian balalaika player. He was largely responsible for improving the design of the balalaika, domra and gusli, and at the end of 1886 founded in St Petersburg an orchestra of Russian folk instruments. With the orchestra he made successful tours of Russia, Germany, France, England, Canada and the USA, and he did much to awaken the interest of his contemporaries in Russian folk instruments: Rimsky-Korsakov, for example, used the gusli in his opera *Sadko* (1896). Under Andreyev's direction ensembles of folk instruments were established in schools and in the army. He made many arrangements of folksongs for his orchestra, and composed about 40 pieces, mostly waltzes, for the balalaika or balalaika ensemble. He wrote essays on Russian folk music and folk instruments, and a textbook on the balalaika.

WRITINGS

Shkola dlya balalayki s prilozheniyem pesen, aranzhirovannïkh dlya pyati balalayek [A balalaika tutor, with a supplement of songs arranged for five balalaikas] (St Petersburg, 1894)

K voprosu o russkoy narodnoy muzïke [The question of Russian folk music] (St Petersburg, 1899)

Les instruments nationaux en Russie, anciens et perfectionnés (St Petersburg, 1900)

Spravochnik ili kratkoye rukovodstvo dlya oborudovaniya velikorusskovo orkestra [A reference book or short guide to equipping a Russian orchestra] (Petrograd, 1916)

BIBLIOGRAPHY

ME

A. A. Novosel'sky: *Ocherki po istorii russkikh narodnïkh muzïkal'nïkh instrumentov* [Essays on the history of Russian folk instruments] (Moscow, 1931)

A. Chagadayev: *V. V. Andreyev* (Moscow, 1948, 2/1961)

V. Levashov and I. Gulyayev: 'Vecher pamyati V. Andreyeva, 1861–1918' [An evening in memory of Andreyev], *SovM* (1954), no.3, p.109

B. Granovsky: 'V. Andreyev i evo orkestr' [Andreyev and his orchestra], *SovM* (1959), no.7, p.125

P. Obolensky: 'Iz vospominanii o V. Andreyeve' [Reminiscences about Andreyev], *SovM* (1959), no.7, p.132

V. Andreyev: 'Iz vospominanii' [Reminiscences, written in 1917], *SovM* (1961), no.1, p.101

B. Granovsky: '100 let so dnya rozhdeniya V. Andreyeva' [The centenary of Andreyev's birth], *SovM* (1961), no.1, p.98

F. Sokolov: *V. V. Andreyev i evo orkestr* (Leningrad, 1962)

G. B. Bernandt and I. M. Yampol'sky: *Kto pisal o muzïke* [Writers on music], i (Moscow, 1971)

JENNIFER SPENCER

Andrez, Benoit (*b* Liège, 1714; *d* Liège, 12 Jan 1804). South Netherlands music engraver and publisher. His publications, only rarely dated, bear the address 'At Liège, behind St Thomas'. Some editions were engraved by Mlle J. Andrez, possibly his daughter, who continued the business until after 1820. He dealt primarily with instrumental music of the 'Belgian' composers of the period, publishing works by Renotte, J.-J. Robson, J.-N. Hamal, Delange, G. G. Kennis, F.-J. de Trazegnies, Regnier, Delhaise, Coppenneur and others. He also published music by Camerloher and Schwindl, as well as Boccherini's op.4 and Beethoven's op.46. For vocal music he produced the periodical *Echo ou journal de musique françoise, italienne* (1758–67), followed by the *Journal vocal composé d'airs, duos, trios* (or *Journal de musique vocale*). Besides these, Andrez published a comedy 'interspersed with songs', *La chercheuse d'esprit* by Du Boulay, and a choral work by d'Herbois, *Hymne au printemps*. He also ventured into music theory with his publication of *Ludus melothedicus* and Morel de Lescer's *Science de la musique vocale*. With the Liège musician Jean Joiris he obtained in 1752 a licence for the publication of a *Méthode pour dresser les nouvelles contredances françoises et angloises* and he was responsible for producing six volumes of the *Recueil de contredances angloises*.

BIBLIOGRAPHY

E. vander Straeten: *La musique aux Pays-Bas avant le XIXe siècle* (Paris, 1867–88/*R*1969), i, 109ff; v, 276ff

A. Goovaerts: *Histoire et bibliographie de la typographie musicale dans les anciens Pays-Bas* (Antwerp, 1880/*R*1963)

A. Auda: *La musique et les musiciens de l'ancien pays de Liège* (Brussels, 1930)

P. Deses: 'Opzoekingen naar de uitgaven van de XVIIIe eeuwse muziekdrukker Benoit Andrez', *Miscellanea musicologica Floris van der Mueren* (Ghent, 1950), 93

HENRI VANHULST

Andricu, Mihail G(heorghe) (*b* Bucharest, 22 Dec 1894; *d* Bucharest, 4 Feb 1974). Romanian composer, pianist and critic. At the Bucharest Conservatory (1903–9) he studied theory with Kiriac, harmony and composition with Castaldi, the violin with Klenck and chamber music with Dinicu; he returned there to teach chamber music (1926–48) and composition (1948–59). Andricu also spent some time studying in Paris with d'Indy and Fauré, and when he returned to Bucharest he promoted concerts of new Romanian and French chamber music. He wrote for numerous publications on subjects ranging from music aesthetics to jazz and folk music; he was made a member of the Société Française de Musicologie in 1937, and a corresponding member of the Romanian Academy in 1948. A composer of rare vitality and spontaneity, he quickly established an individual style within the Romanian tradition. The distinctive features of his music are melodies taken from folkdances or *colinde*, simple diatonic harmony sometimes coloured by modality and a preference for the woodwind in orchestral writing of great transparency. Sometimes he used folk instruments to render gypsy band sounds. He worked in all genres, but his temperament was not essentially dramatic, and he was at his best in music of serenity and moderation, although expressive contrasts are not excluded.

WORKS
(selective list)

STAGE AND ORCHESTRAL

Cenuşereasa [Cinderella], op.11 (musical fairytale, C. Halunga), 1929; Taina [The secret], op.17 (ballet, C. Sylva), 1933; Luceafărul [Hyperion], op.60 (ballet, A. Jar), 1951

7 suites, 1923–67; 3 chamber syms., 1927–65; 11 syms., 1944–73; 13 sinfoniettas, 1945–73; 2 ovs., 1947, 1950; 2 folksong suites, 1958

Poem, op.1, pf, orch, 1923; Serenadă, op.9, 1928; 3 capricii, op.24, 1937; Poem, op.33, vc, orch, 1944; Fantezie pe teme populare, op.61, 1951; Capriccio, op.63, folk orch, 1952; Vn Conc., op.93, 1960; Vc Conc., op.94, 1961; Poem, op.110, 1967

INSTRUMENTAL AND VOCAL

4 novelettes, op.4, pf, 1925; Octet, op.8, 3 wind, str qnt, 1928; 4 esquisses, op.19, pf, 1934; Sextet, op.20, wind qnt, pf, 1934; Pf Qnt, op.27, 1938; Sonată, op.32, vn, pf, 1944; Pf Sonata, op.55, 1949; 12 wind qnts, opp.77, 79, 1955–6; Wind Octet, op.90, 1960; Serenadă, op.99, 14 insts, 1961; 9 impresiuni, op.109, pf, 1965

3 lieduri, op.10 (Eminescu), 1v, pf, 1929; 4 coruri, 4 dansuri, op.49, 1949; Cântec de leagăn [Lullaby], op.57, 1v, chorus, orch, 1949; Prind visele aripi [Flying dreams], op.86, 1v, pf, 1959

Principal publishers: Editura muzicală (Bucharest), Hamelle, Salabert

WRITINGS

'Cîteva cuvinte despre jazz' [A couple of words on jazz], *Secolul XX*, iii (1965), 175

'Debussy', *Studii şi cercetări de istoria artei*, i (1969), 19

BIBLIOGRAPHY

A. Stroe: 'Probleme de concepţie şi stil în muzica lui Mihail Andricu', *Muzica*, iii (Bucharest, 1958), 1

Z. Vancea: *Creaţia muzicală românească: sec.XIX–XX* (Bucharest, 1968), 387ff

V. Cosma: *Muzicieni români* (Bucharest, 1970), 42ff

VIOREL COSMA

Andrien, Martin Joseph, *l'aîné. See* ADRIEN, MARTIN JOSEPH.

Andries, Jean (*b* Ghent, 25 April 1798; *d* Ghent, 21 Jan 1872). South Netherlands composer and teacher. He began his career in 1813 as a violinist in the orchestra of the Ghent theatre and from 1817 was its leader for more than 35 years. When the Ghent Conservatory was founded in 1835 Andries was appointed professor both of the violin and of instrumental ensemble. From 1851 until his retirement in 1859 he directed the conservatory and also taught harmony and composition. His music, all unpublished, includes a Concertino and *La tempête* for violin and *L'orpheline*, a three-act drama.

WRITINGS

Aperçu historique de tous les instruments de musique actuellement en usage (Ghent, n.d.)
Précis de l'histoire de la musique depuis les temps plus reculés, suivi de notices sur un grand nombre d'écrivains didactiques et théoriciens de l'art musical (Ghent, 1862)
Instruments à vent: la flûte (Ghent, 1866)
Remarques sur les cloches et carillons (Ghent, 1868)

JOHN LADE

Andriessen. Dutch family of musicians.

(1) **Hendrik Andriessen** (*b* Haarlem, 17 Sept 1892). Composer, organist and teacher. He studied the organ with J. P. de Pauw and composition with Bernard Zweers at the Amsterdam Conservatory, and in 1913 he succeeded to his father's appointment as organist in Haarlem. In 1926 Andriessen was appointed to teach composition and analysis at the Amsterdam Conservatory, concurrently teaching the organ at the Roman Catholic School for Church Music, Utrecht. He was made organist of Utrecht Cathedral in 1934 and, three years later, director of the conservatory in that city. In 1949 he was appointed director of the Royal Conservatory in The Hague, and in 1952 he became professor of music history at Nijmegen University, a post he held until his retirement in 1962.

Andriessen first received attention as a composer through a number of organ works and the *Missa in honorem Ss cordis* (1917). The outstanding feature of this piece was its novel treatment of the text: abandoning the conventional Romantic approach, Andriessen provided a meditative consideration of intimate, mystical simplicity. This style initiated a renewal of Dutch Catholic church music, and the large number of liturgical works that Andriessen subsequently composed are marked by the same manner of treating the text, and by a devout atmosphere of glorification. In settings of the Mass he has preferred cyclic forms, with all sections constructed from a single melodic idea.

During the 1930s Andriessen's orchestral works also began to attract notice. His Symphony no.1 (1930) has a form deviating widely from the conventional: a slow introduction precedes five short sections which merge into one another and are arranged symmetrically according to tempo and character. All of the thematic material develops from the introduction, and the orchestration is notable for surprising changes in colour and nuance. One of Andriessen's most successful orchestral pieces appeared in 1935: the Variations and Fugue on a Theme by Johann Kuhnau. This has entered the repertory of almost every Dutch orchestra and has also been performed frequently elsewhere. It is a particularly well-balanced composition, warm in sound and poetic in

atmosphere. The contemplative variation technique changes in nature with each new section; the first variation explores only the first notes of the theme; the second develops just four notes in a scherzo-like manner. In the third variation, the theme's inversion is the basis, and the fourth surrounds the theme with full, broad chords. After a fifth variant illuminating the harmonic possibilities of the idea, the work concludes in a lively double fugue that shows Andriessen's contrapuntal mastery.

In the same year, 1935, he wrote three Rimbaud songs, the *Trois pastorales*, which underline Andriessen's links with French culture and are among the finest Dutch songs of modern times. Two important liturgical works of the period are the *Magnificat* for chorus and organ, a work of apt exaltation and gladness, and the spacious six-part *Missa diatonica*, composed wholly in the Aeolian mode. The Second Symphony was written in 1937. Its first movement, Fantasia, freely uses elements of sonata form, the second is a polytonal pavane, and the third and last movement is a rondo. As a whole, the work shares those qualities of poetic expressiveness, inventive melodic treatment, transparent texture and organ-influenced changes of orchestration which were typical of the First. In 1939 Andriessen produced one of his major organ works, the Sinfonia, a piece that is characteristic of his music for the instrument in its frequent passages of polytonal harmony, its vigorous contrapuntal working and its modal melody. Aside from the solo pieces, he has written an Organ Concerto (1950) in two parts: a passacaglia and a toccata built on the Phrygian tetrachord of the passacaglia theme. Andriessen himself was one of the foremost organists of his generation, particularly renowned for skills in improvisation.

After 1945 he became more prolific in his production of sacred choral music, orchestral works and chamber pieces. During the war years he had composed little, although the few works from that period, such as the *Missa 'Christus Rex'*, give powerful expression to his faith in the victory of right. In 1946 the Symphony no.3 appeared. It shares with its predecessors the divergence from the classical pattern: an overture leads into a sonata-form first movement, in which all of the melodic ideas arise from a signal-like motif on the trumpet; this is followed by a sarabande and, finally, a large-scale double fugue. The orchestral Ricercare (1949) has been described by the composer as 'a summons of various themes which are apparently conflicting, but which form a symphonic whole precisely because of their contrapuntal dialogue'. Quite different in character is the *Symphonic Etude* (1952), four linked developments of an expressive, meditative melody which approaches a 12-note row, yet without serial technique being applied in the work. The Fourth Symphony (1954) may be seen as a development from the *Etude*, in that it employs a 12-note theme in a cyclic manner, with a distinct treatment of the material in each of the four movements. The first is a dramatic, impassioned Allegro, while the second is one of Andriessen's typical movements of contemplative lyricism, suggestive of the organist quietly improvising; there is great contrast between this and the capricious, rhythmically tense scherzo which follows.

The opera *Philomela*, completed in 1948, is based on an episode from Ovid's *Metamorphoses*, and is notable for the profound symphonic working of its leitmotifs.

The prelude has the character of a symphonic exposition, orchestral interludes constitute developments of the ideas and the ballet forms a scherzo. The finale, where the musical developments reach their climax, is also the culmination of the drama: the gods, in compassion for the people who destroy all in their unfettered passion, change them into birds, and so the conflicts are resolved in the triumph of eternal song. Broad, flowing melody, individual modal harmony and colourful orchestration make this one of Andriessen's most striking works. It was first performed at the 1950 Holland Festival; almost two decades passed before Andriessen composed the one-act opera *De spiegel van Venetie*, concerning an incident in the life of Sweelinck. Alongside his activities as a composer and organist, Andriessen has played an important part in Dutch musical life as a teacher; his pupils included Jan Mul, Herman Strategier, Albert de Klerk and his sons, (2) Jurriaan and (3) Louis.

WORKS

MASSES

Missa in honorem Ss cordis, 2vv, org, 1919; Missa in festo assumptionis, 3vv, org, 1925; Missa simplex, 3vv, 1928; Missa 'Sponsa Christi', 3vv, org, 1928; Missa 'Splendor veritatis', chorus, 1928; Requiem, 3vv, org, 1931; Missa diatonica, 6vv, 1935; Missa 'Lauda Sion', 6vv, org, 1945; Missa Sanctus Ludovicus, 3vv, org, 1947; Missa solemnis, 6vv, org, 1946; Missa Sanctus Gregorius Magnus, 1949; Missa 'Te Deum laudamus', 6vv, org, 1952; Missa 'Fiat voluntas tua', 2vv, org, 1958; Missa populi, 1v, org, 1959; Missa 'Cogitationes cordis', 4vv, org, 1960; Missa Sanctus Willibrordus, 1963

OTHER SACRED CHORAL

Veni Creator Spiritus, chorus, org, 1913; Salve regina, 3vv, org, 1920; Tantum ergo, chorus, 1919; De die aeternitatis, 1921; Tenuisti, chorus, 1922; Christus stervende, male chorus, 1922; De veertien stonden, chorus, str, 1928, unpubd; Te Joseph celebrant, 2vv, org, 1931, unpubd; Qui habitat, chorus, 1933; Magnificat, chorus, org, 1936; Te Deum laudamus, chorus, org, 1943; Septem Cantica Sacra, chorus, org, 1943; Laudes vespertinae, chorus, org, 1944
Psalm cxlviii, chorus, 1945; Pater noster, chorus, org, 1949; Offertorium Assumpta est Maria, chorus, org, 1952; Festum immaculati cordis, chorus, 3 tpt, 3 trbn, tuba, 1954; Psalm cl, chorus, org, 1958; Laudate Dominum, chorus, org, 1958; Veni Creator, chorus, orch, 1960; Psalm ix, chorus, orch, 1961; Psalm l, chorus, org, 1963; Lux iocunda, chorus, orch, 1968; Te Deum laudamus II, chorus, orch, 1968

SECULAR CHORAL

Sonnet de Pierre de Ronsard, chorus, 1917; Met kloeken arme, male chorus, 1918; Als 't licht wordt, chorus, 1920; September Blaas, male chorus, 1921; De stilte, chorus, 1922; Morgenzang, chorus, 1922; Driekoningenlied, chorus, 1922; Vrede, chorus, 1922; 2 madrigali, chorus, str, 1940; 3 liederen, chorus, 1951; Omaggio a Marenzio, chorus, 1965; Cantate, Bar, chorus, 7 brass, org, 1966, unpubd; Carmen saeculare, S, T, chorus, orch, 1968

VOCAL

(for 1v, pf unless otherwise stated)

Philomela, opera, 3, 1948; De spiegel van Venetie, opera, 1, 1964
Gebet an den Sonntag, 1913; Erwacht, 1913; Chanson, 1914; Abendgesang zur Geliebte, 1914; Das alte Lied, 1915; L'aube spirituelle, 1916; Crucem tuam, 1v, org, 1916; O sacrum convivium, 1v, org, 1916; Les larmes, 1916; Quand ton sourire me surprit, 1916; Harmonie du soir, 1917; L'invitation au voyage, 1v, str, 1918; Magna res est amor, S, org/orch, 1919; Loomheid is op uw hart, 1919; Fiat Domine, 1v, org/orch, 1920; Chaque heure, ou je songe, 1920; L'attente mystique, 1v, orch, 1920
Tractus 'Qui habitat', S, T, org, 1920; Sequentia Trinitatis, 1v, org, 1921, unpubd; Sequentia 'Audi tellus', 1v, org, 1921, unpubd; Cantique spirituel, 1v, org/orch, 1921; Le chemin de la croix, 1922; La sainte face, 1922, unpubd; Assumpta est Maria, 1v, org, 1922; Miroir de peine, 1v, org/str orch, 1923; A ces reines, 1923; Maria zart von edler Art, 1v, org/str orch, 1929; 3 pastorales, 1935, orchd M. Flothuis, 1971
Ballade van de merel, speaker, orch, 1936; Hymnus 'Frequentemus hodie', 1942; Cantilena della Madre, 1943; 3 sonnets spirituels, T, org, 1944; Dankbare Jubilate, 1945; De zee en het land, speaker, orch, 1953; Meditations on the Lord's wondrous mysteries, 1960; La Vierge à midi, 1v, chamber orch, 1966; Luci serene, 1966, unpubd; 3 romantische liederen, S, fl, ob, pf, 1969

ORCHESTRAL

Sym. no.1, 1930; Variations and fugue on a theme by Kuhnau, str, 1935; Sym. no.2, 1937; Capriccio, 1941; Variations on a theme by Couperin, fl, harp, str orch, 1944; Sym. no.3, 1946; Ballet suite, 1947; Ricercare, 1949; Wilhelmus Rhapsody, 1950; Org Conc., 1950; Sinfonic étude, 1952; Libertas venit, rhapsody, 1954; Sym. no.4, 1954; Sym. Concertante, vn, va, orch, 1962; Mascherata, 1962; Concertino, ob, str, 1969; Vn Conc., 1969; Concertino, vc, chamber orch, 1970; Chromatic Variations, str qt, str orch, 1970; Canzone, 1971; Chantecler, ov., 1972; Hymnus in Pentecostem, 1975–6

CHAMBER AND INSTRUMENTAL

Sonata no.1, vn, pf, 1914, unpubd; Pf Trio, 1915, unpubd; Sonata, vc, pf, 1926; Sonata no.2, vn, pf, 1932; Pf Sonata, 1934; 3 inventions, vn, vc, 1937; Pavane, pf, 1937; Pf Trio no.2, 1939; Pastorale, fl, vn, pf, 1942; Passepied, pf, 1942; Rigaudon, carillon, 1943, unpubd; Intermezzo, fl, harp, 1950; Suite, vn, pf, 1950; Wind Qnt, 1951; Suite, brass qt, 1951; Sonata, vc, 1951; Aubade, 2 tpt, hn, trbn, 1951; Ballade, ob, pf, 1952; Theme with Variations, fl, ob, pf, 1953
The Convex Looking Glass, pf, 1954; Quartetto in stile antico, str qt, 1957; Suite, fl/rec, pf, 1959; Il pensiero, str qt, 1961; Canzonetta, fl, harp, 1963, pubd; Canzonetta, kbd, 1963; Divertimento, fl, ob, str trio, pf, 1965; Canzone, fl, ob, pf, 1965; Petit concert spirituel, fl, ob, vn, vc, 1966; Pf Sonata no.2, 1966; 3 pezzi, fl, harp, 1967; Sonata, va, pf, 1967; Variations on a Theme by Haydn, ob, pf, 1968; L'indifférent, str qt, 1969; Serenade, fl, hn, pf, 1970; Sonata, cl, pf, 1971; Divertimento a cinque, fl, ob, str trio, 1972; Choral varié, 3 tpt, 3 trbn, 1973
Organ: Choral no.1, 1913; Choral no.2, 1916; Toccata, 1917; Fête Dieu, 1918; Choral no.3, 1920; Sonata da chiesa, 1927; Passacaglia, 1929; Zex choralen, 1929; Sinfonia, 1939; Intermezzi, 1943–6; Thema met variaties, 1949; Concerto, 1950; Choral no.4, 1952; 4 studi, 1953; Interlude, 1957; Advent to Whitsuntide, 1961; Offertorium, 1962; Pezzo festoso, 2 tpt, 2 trbn, org, 1962; Preghiera, 1965; Suite, 1968

Principal publishers: Donemus, van Rossum

WRITINGS

Over muziek (Utrecht, 1950)
Muziek en muzikaliteit (Utrecht, 1952)

BIBLIOGRAPHY

W. Paap: 'Hendrik Andriessen', *Contemporary Music from Holland* (Amsterdam, 1953)
T. J. Dox: *Hendrik Andriessen: his Life and Works* (diss., U. of Rochester, 1969)
J. Wouters: *Hendrik Andriessen* (Amsterdam, 1971)
J. H. Gottmer, ed.: *Hendrik Andriessen tachtig jaar* (Haarlem, 1972)

(2) Jurriaan Andriessen (*b* Haarlem, 15 Nov 1925). Dutch composer. Son of (1) Hendrik Andriessen, under whom he studied composition at the Utrecht Conservatory; he later studied instrumentation and conducting with Van Otterloo. After his final examinations in 1947 he spent several months in Paris with the particular aim of studying film music. On returning to the Netherlands he was commissioned to write the incidental music for the open-air play *Het monsterlijke uur* ('The strange clock'), performed in celebration of the 50th anniversary of Queen Wilhelmina's accession; this was his first score for the stage. From 1949 to 1951 he was in the USA on a Rockefeller Foundation Fellowship, and it was there that he wrote, to a commission from the Dutch government, the *Berkshire Symphonies* (1949), a work to which Balanchin and Robbins created the ballet *Jones Beach*, which was given in New York and in many European cities. Andriessen made several visits to Italy and Germany during the period 1951–3, and at this time he composed two ballet scores: *Das Goldfischglas* (1952) for the Deutsche Oper am Rhein and *De canapé* (1953) for the Netherlands Opera.

In 1954 he was appointed resident composer to the Hague Theatre Company; one of the first scores resulting from this appointment was that for *Mourning becomes Electra*, from which Andriessen made a widely performed orchestral suite. Much successful incidental music followed, and further derived concert pieces, including *Les bransles érotiques* from the score for

Rosencrantz and Guildenstern are Dead. Andriessen has also composed a quantity of film music in addition to his copious output of orchestral and chamber works and pieces for amateurs. His music exhibits sound professional skill in a style that draws on diverse recently developed techniques without being bound to any specific system. In 1964 he began work as a television producer.

WORKS
(*selective list*)

STAGE

Operas: Kalchas, monodrama, 1, 1959; Het zwarte blondje, S, Bar, hpd, pfs, 1964
Ballets: Das Goldfischglas, 1952; De canapé, 1953; Time Spirit, cl, 31 insts, 1970
Incidental music: Het monsterlijke uur [The strange clock], 1948; Eudipos (after Sophocles), 1955; Rouw past Elektra (after O'Neill), 1954; Richard III (after Shakespeare), 1961; A Taste of Honey (after S. Delaney), 1961; After the Fall (after Miller), 1964; Marat-Sade (after Weiss), 1965; Yerma (after Lorca), 1967; Rosencrantz and Guildenstern are Dead (after Stoppard), 1968; Much Ado about Nothing (after Shakespeare), 1969; Reigen, 1971; Maldoror II (after Lautréamont), 1971

ORCHESTRAL

Symphonietta concertante, 4 tpt, orch, 1947; Pf Conc., 1948; Berkshire Symphonies, 1949; Fl Conc., 1951; Cymbeline, ov., 1954; Rouw past Elektra, sym. suite, 1954; L'incontro di Cesare e Cleopatra, sym. suite, 1956; Inno della technica, 1957; Sym. no.2, wind, 1962; Pf Concertino, 1962; Sym. no.3, 1963; Sym. no.4 'Aves', chorus, orch, 1963; Concertino, bn, wind, 1963; Movimenti I, tpt, hn, trbn, str, perc, 1965; In pompa magna, 1966; Conc. Rotterdam, jazz group, orch, 1966; Intrada festiva, brass, perc, 1966; Sousaphone Concertino, 1967; Trelleborg Conc., hpd, 3 inst groups, 1967; Omaggio a Sweelinck, str, 1968; Antifona dell'Aja, 1969; Movimenti II, 1972; Animal-Qt, amateur orch, 1972; Een Prince van Oraengien, Wilhelmus-phantasy, chorus, orch, 1973; Midwinter Song, hns, orch, org, 1974; Movimenti III, str trio, 16 wind, perc, 1974; Sym. no.8 'La celebrazione', 1977

CHAMBER

Conc., 2 pf, 1945; Hommage à Milhaud, 11 insts, 1945; Sonata no.1, vn, pf, 1946; Octet, 1948; Etudes, pf, 1948; Hommage à Milhaud, fl, str qt, 1948; Trio, 1955; Sonata no.2, vn, pf, 1955; Trio no.4, 1957; Duo, 2 vns, 1958; Sonata da camera, fl, harp, 1959; Ballade, harp, 1961; Quattro madrigali, brass qt, 1963; Respiration Suite, wind ens, 1962; Sciardi spagnuola, wind qnt, 1963; Trio, cl, vc, pf, 1965; Antifona e fusione, wind qnt, brass qt, perc, 1966; Summer Dances, 7 perc, 1966; Elegia, hn, 1967; Dub, S/T, vc, 1967; Les bransles erotiques, 8 insts, 1967; Dolimah, fl, 1969; To Wet a Widow's Eye, A, T, 3 insts, 1970; Ars antiqua musicae, 7 insts, perc, 1971; 4 Tucholsky Chansons, S, fl, gui, vc, 1972; Les cloches des clochards, carillon, 1976; The Cave, vc, 12 wind, 4 kbd, elec, 1976

Principal publisher: Donemus

BIBLIOGRAPHY

W. Paap: 'Jurriaan Andriessen and Incidental Music', *Sonorum speculum*, xl (1969)

(3) **Louis Andriessen** (*b* Utrecht, 6 June 1939). Dutch composer. Son of (1) Hendrik Andriessen, he studied composition with his father at the Utrecht Conservatory and later became a pupil of Baaren at the Royal Conservatory in The Hague. He was awarded the conservatory's composition prize in 1962, and completed his studies with Berio in Milan and Berlin (1964–5). In *Nocturnes* (1959) he employed new compositional procedures together with conventional elements, and since 1965 he has often made use of collage and other avant-garde techniques. He participated with four colleagues in the composition of the opera *Reconstruction*, first performed at the 1970 Holland Festival.

WORKS
(*selective list*)

Piano Sonata, 1956; Series, 2 pf, 1958–64; Nocturnes, S, chamber orch, 1959; Registers, pf, 1963; Ittrospezione 2, orch, 1963; A Flower Song 2, 1964; A Flower Song 3, 1964; Ittrospezione 3,

concept 1, orch, 1964; Sweet, rec ens, 1964; Double, cl, pf, 1965; Ittrospezione 3, concept 2, orch, 1965; Anachrony, orch, 1967; Contra tempus, 22 insts, 1967–8; Anachrony 2, ob, orch, 1969; Spectacle, jazz ens, 1970; On Jimmy Yancey, jazz band, 1973; Il principe, chorus, 12 wind, pf, b gui, 1974; Symphonieën der Nederlanden, wind band, 1974; Workers Union, sym. movt, loud insts, 1975; De Staat, 4 female vv, 27 insts, 1972–6

Principal publisher: Donemus

JOS WOUTERS

Andrieu, F. (*fl* late 14th century). French composer. The only composition attributable to him with certainty is the four-part bitextual ballade *Armes, amours/O flour des flours* set to the text by Eustache Deschamps lamenting Machaut's death in 1377. Two three-part ballades by MAGISTER FRANCISCUS from the same MS (*F-CH* 564) suggest that the two composers may be the same person. One of these compositions borrows its first three bars from a similarly-titled piece by Machaut.

WORKS

Edition: *French Secular Compositions of the Fourteenth Century*, ed. W. Apel, CMM, liii/1 (1970)
1 Armes, amours/O flour des flours (ballade), 4vv
2 De Narcisus (ballade, 'Magister Franciscus'), 3vv
3 Phiton, Phiton, beste tres venimeuse (ballade, 'Magister Franciscus'), 3vv

BIBLIOGRAPHY

G. Reaney: 'The Manuscript Chantilly, Musée Condé 1047', *MD*, viii (1954), 66

For further bibliography see FRANCE, BIBLIOGRAPHY OF MUSIC TO 1600.

GILBERT REANEY

Andrieu Contredit d'Arras (*d* Arras, 1248). French trouvère. French royal accounts for 1239 mention Andreas Contredit, knight and minstrel, who had vowed to join the crusade led that year by Thibaut IV, Count of Champagne and Brie, King of Navarre. 'Contredit' is probably a sobriquet. It is possible that Andrieu was in the service of King Louis IX as a minstrel; *Au mois d'avril* is addressed to 'the king'. He was a member of the Arras Puy and addressed *Ja pour nul mal* to this group. The register that indicates his date of death mentions the death of his wife in 1225, suggesting that he may have been born in about 1200 or earlier. He participated in a jeu-parti with Guillaume li Vinier (R.1520) and addressed *Bone, bele et avenans* to 'Marote', probably the poet Maroie de Diergnau of Lille. He referred affectionately to his native city Arras in *L'autrier quant je chevauchoie*.

Andrieu named himself in 14 of his 20 works, which include a pastourelle, a lai, and a jeu-parti in addition to *chansons courtoises*. He lacked technical imagination. Except for the lai, all strophes are isometric, most are decasyllabic, four are heptasyllabic and three octosyllabic. 19 works begin with the customary *abab* rhyme pattern, and all but four continue *baab* (two continuing *bab* and two *ccbb*).

The melodies – all in bar form – show greater variety of construction. However, in some the repetition of the initial *pes* is strict, in others the second element is varied, and in three new material is introduced. In most the concluding section is non-repetitive, but motivic references and varied repetition of phrases are both found. In *Au mois d'avril*, the last two phrases (eighth and ninth) are variations of the fifth and sixth. Three melodies have a range of an 11th, combining plagal and authentic ranges, and the Noailles Chansonnier's version of *Quant voi partir* has the exceptional ambitus of a 13th (the last two phrases here may be written a 5th higher than was originally intended). In all but five melodies there is a strong sense of tonal centre. The rhythmic constructions range from the rather florid *Pré ne vert bois* to the simple *L'autrier quant je chevauchoie*. No readings are given in mensural notation, but the ligature disposition in phrases of *Au tens que je voi, Iriez, pensis chanterai* and *Mout m'est bel* suggests regular rhythmic patterning.

WORKS

Amours m'a si del tout a son voloir, R.1827
Au mois d'avril que l'on dit en Pascour, R.2004
Au tens que je voi averdir, R.1392
Bone, bele et avenans, R.262
Dame, pour vous m'esjoïs bonement, R.645
De bele Yzabel ferai, R.81 [text only]
[De] bone amour ki le set maintenir, R.754*a* (= 1425*bis*) [text only] (1st line of text lost)
Del guerredon ke j'atenc a avoir, R.1387*b* (= 1785*bis*) [text only] (1st line of text lost)
Guillaume le Viniers, amis (jeu-parti), R.1520 [text only]
Iriez, pensis chanterai, R.69
Ja pour nul mal ne pour nesun tourment, R.743
Ja pour nul mal ne pour nule pensee, R.545
Je ne me doi d'Amours de riens loer, R.870
L'autrier quant je chevauchoie, R.1699
Mout m'est bel quant voi repairier, R.1306
Pré ne vert bois, rose ne flour de lis, R.1561
Quant voi partir foille et flour et rosee, R.553
Tout tens est mes cuers en joie, R.1732
Tres haute Amours me semont que je chant, R.307
Vivre m'estuet en tristror, en pesance, R.235

BIBLIOGRAPHY

R. Schmidt: *Die Lieder des Andrieu Contredit d'Arras* (diss., U. of Halle, 1903)
A. Långfors, A. Jeanroy and L. Brandin: *Recueil général des jeux-partis français* (Paris, 1926)
R. Dragonetti: *La technique poétique des trouvères dans la chanson courtoise* (Bruges, 1960)
For further bibliography see TROUBADOURS, TROUVÈRES.

THEODORE KARP

Andronicus, Lucius Livius. See LIVIUS ANDRONICUS, LUCIUS.

Andropediacus, Lycosthenes Psellionoros [Spangenberg, Wolfhart] (*b* Mansfeld, probably before 1570; *d* Buchenbach, Baden-Württemberg, before Oct 1636). German theologian and writer. The first two names of his pseudonym are equivalents of Wolfhart Spangenberg, his original name, and Andropediacus derives from the name of his birthplace. He was the son of Cyriac and grandson of Johann Spangenberg (see SPANGENBERG family). His father having been obliged to leave his position as court preacher at Mansfeld in 1574 because he supported Matthias Flaccius's substantialist view of Original Sin, he spent his earliest years at, among other places, Strasbourg, from 1578, and Schlitz, near Fulda, from 1581 and came under his father's influence in theological and artistic matters. He matriculated at Tübingen University on 5 April 1586 and took the bachelor's degree in 1588 and master's degree in 1591. He too was an adherent of Flaccianism, which hindered his career as a theologian. In 1595 he followed his father to Strasbourg, where he gained citizenship and earned his living as a proofreader. In 1601 he joined the local guild of mastersingers (of which his father was already a member), and his plays and translations were a valuable contribution to the guild's theatrical performances; the texts of 20 mastersongs by him, mostly on biblical subjects, have survived, but he composed no melodies. In an ode celebrating the rebuilding of the organ of Strasbourg Cathedral in 1609 he recommended nature, and especially bird-song, as a source of sounds that could well be reproduced on the organ, and he also recounted some of the history of the cathedral organ. He became parish priest at Buchenbach in 1611 and remained there until his death, which must have occurred by October 1636, since after this date his successor was making the entries in the parish registers. Shortly after he moved to Buchenbach he revised his father's history of mastersongs, *Von der edlen und hochberümbten Kunst der Musica* (1598); he added new biographical data and incorporated the findings of more recent historical research. His comedy *Singschul* is a reworking in the form of a verse dialogue of material from the same work of his father's. Allegorical figures tell the farmer Simplicius about the life and work of the mastersingers from biblical times onwards, and, in accordance with the Christian and moral tendencies of the traditions of the mastersingers, secular songs and dance-songs are repudiated as a misuse of music.

WRITINGS
(only those on music)

Singschul: ein kurzer einfältiger Bericht vom ... Nutz und rechtem Gebrauch des alten löblichen teutschen Meister-Gesangs in Gestalt einer Comödi ... als ein Gespräch zwischen sechs Personen verfasset (Nuremberg, after 1613, ?1615); ed. in Vizkelety
Lobspruch auf die 1609 ... renovierte Orgel, in O. Schadaeus: *Summum Argentoratensium templum* (Strasbourg, 1617); ed. in *Jb für Geschichte, Sprache und Literatur Elsass-Lothringens*, xxx (Strasbourg, 1914)
Von der Musica, Singe-Kunst oder Meister-Gesang, so bei den Teutschen üblich und gebräuchlich gewesen, after 1614: D-HVl, PL-Wn, WRu [rev. edn of C. Spangenberg: *Von der edlen und hochberümbten Kunst der Musica*, 1598]

BIBLIOGRAPHY

H. Müller: 'Wolfhart Spangenberg', *Zeitschrift für deutsche Philologie*, lxxxi (1962), 129–68, 385; lxxxii (1963), 454 [incl. complete list of works and edns.]
A. Vizkelety: 'Wolfhart Spangenbergs Singschul', *Euphorion*, lviii (1964)
C. Kooznetzoff: 'Das Theaterspielen der Meistersinger', *Der deutsche Meistergesang*, ed. B. Nagel (Darmstadt, 1967), 442–97

LINI HÜBSCH-PFLEGER

Aneanes. The ENĒCHĒMA of the first plagal mode in the Byzantine modal system.

Aneimenos (Gk.: 'in a relaxed manner'). A term used in ancient Greece to describe a type of tuning or of modality; *see* ETHOS, §2.

Anémocorde (Fr.). *See* SOSTENENTE PIANO, §2.

Anenayki (Russ.). Elaborations of Russian chants in the 16th century; *see* RUSSIAN AND SLAVONIC CHURCH MUSIC, §2.

Aneotes, Michael. Composer of Byzantine chant; *see* GLYKYS, JOANNES.

Anerio, Felice (*b* Rome, *c*1560; *d* Rome, 26–7 Sept 1614). Italian composer, elder brother of Giovanni Francesco Anerio. He was one of the most important Roman composers of the late 16th and early 17th centuries.

1. LIFE. Anerio spent his entire life in Rome. From 23 December 1568 until December 1574 he was a choirboy at S Maria Maggiore, where from 1571 the music was directed by G. M. Nanino. He then sang as a soprano at the Cappella Giulia for a monthly salary of four scudi from 1 May 1575. From 1 January 1577 he

appears in the salary lists as an alto, first receiving two scudi a month and then, from August 1578 until he left on 1 April 1579, three. He was then a contralto at S Luigi dei Francesi, under Francesco Soriano, from 24 December 1579 to 16 May 1580. For the next four years there is no record of his movements, but the parish records of S Giordano show that he was living together with his brothers in his father's house. This was the period of his first known music: he wrote madrigals, choruses and solo songs for a *Passio di Nostro Signore in verso heroico*, an Italian Passion play by Curzio Faiani, which was performed in the church of the Servite fathers at Viterbo on 22 March 1582. In 1584–5 he was *maestro di cappella* of the Collegio degli Inglesi, and according to the dedication of the madrigal collection *Le gioie* (1589), which he edited, he then held a similar position in the 'Vertuosa Compagnia de i Musici di Roma', a society comprising the leading musicians in Rome founded in 1584. Like many Roman composers of the time, he was a member of the clergy. He first received the tonsure on 29 August 1584, and on 10 April 1607 he became deacon and shortly afterwards priest. In 1594, in accordance with the wishes of Pope Clement VIII and Cardinal Aldobrandini, he succeeded Palestrina as composer to the papal choir – testimony to his excellent reputation. During his time as papal composer he formed a close relationship with Duke Giovanni Angelo Altaemps, who maintained his own chapel and appointed him his musical director. In a papal brief of 6 March 1611 he was commissioned, together with Soriano, by Cardinal del Monte to reform the Roman Gradual, and the work was completed early in 1612; the reformed responsories are very similar to the versions in the *Editio medicea*.

2. WORKS. Most of Anerio's earlier works are secular, though some of the madrigals are of the spiritual variety. The four-part canzonettas (1586) are similar in melody and rhythm to villanella-like three-part canzonettas; their binary form, with repetition of both parts, is considerably disguised by numerous imitations and by regular interchanges of the two upper voices during the repetitions. In general they have little in common in words and music with popular canzonettas and are similar in approach to Marenzio's madrigals.

Anerio turned to sacred composition mainly after his appointment as papal composer. Although conservative in outlook, he did not slavishly follow Palestrina's style – except perhaps in the masses '*Or le tue forze adopra*' and '*Vestiva i colli*' – but enriched it with a number of personal, expressive elements. The motets of the *Sacri hymni et cantica* (1596–1602), many of which are for double choir, are still in the spirit of classical vocal polyphony. The basses of both choirs are generally flowing and linear and often participate in the imitation, and the two choirs frequently share thematic material through the close alternation of loosely homophonic textures. A few works include attempts at *passaggi* in the bass (e.g. *Regina caeli*) and also the more modern element of rapid homophonic declamation (as in *Veni, Sancte Spiritus* and *Tibi laus, tibi gloria*). The four-part Holy Week responsories (1606) are characterized by deeply felt religious sincerity and restrained personal expression, which are much enhanced by occasional chromaticism and the frequent infiltration of the ecclesiastical modes by 'foreign' notes. The essential simplicity of the pieces is enhanced too by frequently

changing textures, which include passages for two and three voices.

Anerio's attentive efforts to keep alive the above-mentioned forms are paralleled in his *alternatim* psalms (in *I-Rn*), which are among the most important of their kind about 1600. They include frequent word repetitions, usually to stress significant parts of the text but occasionally also to heighten devotional elements (as in the sixth verse of the psalm *Credidi*), and these pieces too are distinguished by subtle contrasts of texture. Several features bring them close to the genre of the *Magnificat*: runs in the bass part; the delaying and highlighting of individual entries that loosen predominantly homophonic passages; imitation that is occasionally extended to all four parts; and extensive polyphonic cadential sections. Anerio took a great interest in the reforming efforts of Filippo Neri and wrote several *laudi* for the Oratory. In his later years, during his service with Duke Altaemps, he wrote works for small forces possibly prompted by the example of Viadana, but the outwardly modern trappings do not conceal the fact that he remained rooted in the pervasive Palestrina tradition. For instance, the numerous solos and duets with organ in the *Collectio parva* of the Altaemps collection (the originals of which are lost) have conservative melodies, which in spite of frequent *passaggi* would not be out of place in old-fashioned polyphonic motets, while the organ bass mostly imitates the voice parts.

WORKS

SACRED VOCAL

Madrigali spirituali . . . libro primo, 5vv (Rome, 1585)
Madrigali spirituali . . . secondo libro, 5vv (Rome, 1585)
Sacri hymni, et cantica . . . liber primus, 8vv (Venice, 1596)
Sacri hymni et cantica . . . liber secundus, 5, 6, 8vv (Rome, 1602)
Responsoria ad lectiones divini officii feriae quartae, quintae, et sextae sanctae hebdomadae, 4vv (Rome, 1606)

13 spiritual canzonettas, 3, 4vv; 12 motets, some 8vv, bc; psalm, 8vv; litany, 8vv; 12 other works, some 8vv: 1586[2], 1586[3], 1588[2], 1591[13], 1592[2], 1592[5], 1599[2], 1599[6], 1600[2], 1607[2], 1613[2], 1614[3], 1615[1], 1616[1], 1616[2], 1616[6], 1618[3], 1620[1], 1621[1], 1621[2], 1622[1], 1624[7], 1628[3], 1634[1], 1639[2]

4 masses, 4, 8vv (1 doubtful); Benedictus, 4vv; responsories; 6 Marian antiphons; 2 other antiphons, 4vv; 2 Magnificat; psalms, 4vv; motets; hymns; laudi; spiritual madrigal; other works, 1, 2vv, bc: *I-Rn*, *Rv*, *Rvat*, Altaemps Collection (orig. MS lost, some works copied by K. Proske, in *D-Rp*); 6 psalms, 4vv, Magnificat, hymn, 6 Marian antiphons, 11 motets, 2, 3vv, ed. K. Proske, Musica divina, i/2–3 (1854–9)

Madrigals, choruses, solo songs for C. Faiani: *Passio de Nostro Signore in verso heroico* (Viterbo, 1604), perf. Viterbo, 22 March 1582, music lost

SECULAR VOCAL

Canzonette . . . libro primo, 4vv (Venice, 1586)
Il primo libro de madrigali, 5, 8vv (Venice, 1587)
Primo libro de madrigali, 6vv (Venice, 1590)
Madrigali, 3vv (Venice, 1598)
Madrigali, libro secondo, 6vv (Rome, 1602)
Madrigali, libro terzo, 5vv, lost, cited in Kast
ed.: Le gioie: madrigali di diversi eccellentissimi musici della compagnia di Roma, 5vv (Venice, 1589[7]) [incl. 3 madrigals by Anerio]

16 madrigals, 3, 5, 8vv; 12 canzonettas, 3, 4vv; 6 other works, 3, 5, 6vv: 1586[9], 1587[6], 1588[20], 1589[7], 1589[11], 1590[15], 1591[10], 1591[12], 1592[11], 1593[3], 1593[5], 1596[8], 1596[10], 1596[11], 1597[23], 1598[8], 1600[8], 1608[22], 1609[14], 1613[13]

BIBLIOGRAPHY

R. Molitor: *Die Nach-tridentinische Choral-Reform in Rom*, ii (Leipzig, 1902)
F. X. Haberl: 'Felice Anerio: Lebensgang und Werke nach archivalischen und bibliographischen Quellen', *KJb*, xviii (1903), 28
A. Cametti: 'Nuovi contributi alle biografie di Maurizio e Felice Anerio', *RMI*, xxii (1915), 122

R. Casimiri: ' "Disciplina musicae" e "mastri di cappella" dopo il Concilio di Trento nei maggiori istituti ecclesiastici di Roma: Seminario Romano – Collegio Germanico – Collegio Inglese (sec. XVI–XVII)', *NA*, xx (1943), 102

H.-W. Frey: 'Die Gesänge der Sixtinischen Kapelle an den Sonntagen und hohen Kirchenfesten des Jahres 1616', *Mélanges Eugène Tisserant* (Vatican City, 1964), 395–437

L. Pannella: 'Anerio, Felice', *DBI*

G. Dardo: 'Felice Anerio e la "Congregazione dell'Oratorio" ', *Chigiana*, xxi (1964), 3

J. M. Llorens: 'Felice Anerio, compositor pontificio, en los Códices Ottoboniani de la Biblioteca Vaticana', *AnM*, xix (1964), 95

P. Kast: 'Die Musikdrucke des Kataloges Giunta von 1604', *AnMc*, no. 2 (1965), 41

KLAUS FISCHER

Anerio, Giovanni Francesco (*b* Rome, *c*1567; *d* Graz, buried 12 June 1630). Italian composer and organist, younger brother of Felice Anerio. He was a prolific, comparatively forward-looking composer of the early 17th-century Roman school, particularly important in the early history of the vernacular oratorio.

1. LIFE. He spent much of his life in Rome. From letters of Ancina it appears that from at least 1583 he was closely connected with the Oratory of Filippo Neri. He decided at an early age to become a priest and received the tonsure on 17 December 1583; he became ostiary on 22 November 1584 and lector on 20 December 1586. He was ordained deacon on 17 July 1616 and became a priest seven days later. The first reference to his musical activities occurs in 1595, when he was organist for the Lenten performances of the Arciconfraternità del Ss Crocifisso at S Marcello. He was possibly *maestro di cappella* at St John Lateran, in succession to Francesco Soriano, from 1600 or 1601 until 1603. Certainly from at least January 1608 he was *maestro* at S Spirito in Sassia; how long he held this post cannot be determined, since records for 1606 and 1607 are missing, but as his predecessor, Vincenzo de Grandis (i), left on 29 November 1605 he may have taken it up shortly after that date. In November 1608 he was elected *maestro di cappella* of Verona Cathedral at a yearly salary of 180 gold scudi, and he arrived at Verona on 3 July 1609. After three months he resigned, but he remained at Verona at least until the end of 1610. He then went to Rome for a short period to attend to the publication of some of his works. He returned to Verona but finally left on 14 March 1611 and settled again in Rome. In 1611–12 he was music prefect at the Collegio Romano and from 1613 to 1620 *maestro di cappella* of S Maria dei Monti, after which he apparently continued to live in Rome. On 9 June 1624 he played the organ at the ceremonial robing of the novices at the convent of S Teonisto at Treviso. Shortly afterwards he became choirmaster to King Sigismund III of Poland at Warsaw – one of a long series of Italians to hold this position at the Polish court. He was succeeded in 1628 by his pupil Marco Scacchi, and he died two years later while on his way back to Rome.

2. WORKS. Anerio was a far more progressive composer than his brother. The balance in his output between a modified use of the Palestrina idiom and, especially in his secular music, a cautious adoption of more modern techniques is comparable to that found in the oeuvre of Antonio Cifra, another prolific Roman composer of the period. The *Selva armonica* (1617), containing works of various kinds for one to four voices, is particularly representative of him. The solo spiritual madrigals, which are among the most interesting Roman monodies,

have forms that are largely independent of the structure and rhyme patterns of the verses. The strophic, aria-like pieces include canzonettas that have in common with 16th-century canzonettas only their lively rhythms and the division into two parts, each repeated. Several of them have very expressive melodies, often tending to an almost folksong-like simplicity (as in *Sommo re delle stelle*). The motets are more conservative in style. The nature of their melodies and the treatment of the figured bass have much in common with similar works by Viadana. Formal unity is achieved by a skilful handling of repetition. This can be seen at its best in *Veni, sponsa Christi*, which falls into numerous sections and is in the expanding form $AA^1BB^1CC^1CC^1C^2$. The breaking up into several repeated sections, some of which are settings only of a single word, is characteristic of all the pieces in this collection. It can already be seen in the *Antiphonae* and *Sacri concentus* (both 1613), but the motets in these collections are less formally unified than the solo motets of the *Selva armonica*. The latter include numerous *passaggi*, which are never used merely for the sake of virtuosity but are organized through sequential sections into convincing melodic structures. *Ghirlanda di sacre rose* (1619) includes fewer melodic sequences, but they always enhance the musical expression, most persuasively in the three dialogue motets. The *Diporti musicali* (1617), which contains only madrigals, is similar in style to the *Selva armonica* and occasionally includes some even more striking monodic writing (e.g. in *Cruda Lilla, che fai*).

The *Teatro armonico spirituale* (1619), intended for the Oratory of Filippo Neri, is Anerio's foremost pioneering achievement, for it inaugurated the vernacular oratorio. Two works in it, the five-part *Dialogo del figliuol prodigo* and the six-part dialogue *La conversione di S Paolo* provide the first surviving examples of obbligato instrumental writing in Rome. The role of instruments in the latter work especially, playing introductions and sinfonias and imitating the vocal parts, served as a model of instrumental writing for vocal works by Paolo Tarditi and Quagliati.

Anerio's liturgical music is generally more conservative and was less influential. This is specially true of his masses, which in general follow the principles of the Palestrina style, with prominent use of imitation, including canon, and of parody technique (as in the *Missa 'Surge illuminare'*; he made a four-part arrangement of Palestrina's *Missa Papae Marcelli* (*RISM* 1619²). Cantus firmus technique is prominent only in the *Missa pro defunctis* (1614). The structure of the three *missae breves* is freer, and they include a few passages in which the text is set in an almost parlando manner. Parlando technique, and word-painting too, are specially characteristic of the four-part mass *La battaglia* (in *D-MÜs* dated 1608). The ideals of classical vocal polyphony still dominate Anerio's polychoral masses (e.g. *Missa Constantia* in *I-Bc*), as they do those of other prominent Roman composers of the period, such as his brother Felice and Soriano; each choir includes a succession of imitative sections, and the echoing between the choirs of whole sections of music is tantamount to the imitative treatment of individual vocal parts in non-polychoral works. In contrast to the comparatively uniform style of his masses, Anerio's psalms display a fairly wide range of styles. Most of the four-part psalms in the 1614 collection have basically homophonic textures but with a few imitative verses; several end with deviations from the specified psalm-tone cadences. The three-part works in the same volume bear witness to the stylistic changes occurring in early 17th-century Italy. The two upper parts (two sopranos or soprano and alto) often move in parallel 3rds or 6ths and have short subjects, often treated sequentially, and piquant rhythms – all of them features that were gradually transforming the Palestrina style – and there are occasional passages that would not be out of place in madrigals and canzonettas of the time; as in the antiphons of 1613, embellishments and chromaticism are introduced with restraint.

WORKS

(all printed works published in Rome unless otherwise stated)

SACRED VOCAL

Dialogo pastorale al presepio di nostro signore, 3vv (1600)
Motecta, 1–3vv, bc (org) (1609)
Motectorum, liber secundus, 1–6vv, bc (org) (1611)
Litaniae deiparae virginis, una cum quatuor illis antiphonis, quae pro varietate temporum post completorium cani solent, 7, 8vv (1611, 3/1626 as Litaniae deiparae virginis, maiores de ea antiphone temporales, & motecta, una cum aliis sacris cantionibus varie modulatis)
Motectorum, una cum litaniis beatae virginis, liber tertius, 1–6vv, bc (org) (1613)
Antiphonae, seu sacrae cantiones, quae in totius anni vesperarum ac completorii solemnitatibus decantari solent . . . prima, secunda, tertia pars, 2–4vv, bc (org) (1613)
Sacri concentus, liber primus, 4–6vv, bc (org) (1613⁴)
Responsoria Nativitatis Domini, una cum invitatorio, et psalmo Venite exultemus, ac Te Deum laudamus, 3, 4, 8vv, bc (org) (1614, 2/1629 as Responsorii della natività di nostro Signore Giesu Christo . . . con una messa, & motettini del Sig. Abundio Antonelli)
Psalmi vesperarum, qui in totius anni solemnitatibus decantari solent, nec non duo cantica beatae virginis, 3, 4vv, bc (1614)
Missarum, missa quoque pro defunctis una cum sequentia, et responsorium Libera me domine, liber primus, 4–6vv, bc (org) (1614); mass, 4vv, and responsory ed. A. G. Petti (London, 1966); masses ed. in Williams
Sacri concentus, liber quartus, 1–6vv, bc (org) (1617)
Selva armonica, dove si contengono motetti . . . arie, 1–4vv, bc (org) (1617)
Sacrarum cantionum, liber quintus, 1–5vv, bc (org) (1618)
Ghirlanda di sacre rose, 5vv (1619⁸)
Teatro armonico spirituale di madrigali, 5–8vv, bc (org) (1619)
Rime sacre concertate, 2–4vv, bc (org) (1620)
Missa Paumina Burghesia ad canones, 5vv (n.p., n.d.)

3 masses [1 arr. from Palestrina]; 83 motets, 1–4, 8vv, bc; 2 psalms, 8vv; 9 other sacred vocal works, some 3, 5, 8vv, bc: 1599⁶, 1604⁸, 1614³, 1615¹, 1616¹, 1618³, 1619², 1620¹, 1621¹, 1621³, 1623², 1624³, 1627¹, 1627², 1628², 1638⁵, 1646¹, F. Costantini: Salmi, himni et Magnificat concertati, 8vv, op.11 (Venice, 1630); masses ed. in Williams
Masses, 4–6, 8, 12vv, bc (2 dated, 1606, 1608); 2 Benedictus, 4, 5vv; 2 Miserere, 4vv; Te Deum, 4vv; 5 Magnificat, 4vv; 2 Marian antiphons, 4vv; 2 other antiphons; 27 responsories, 4vv; St Matthew Passion, 5vv; 2 other Passions, 4vv, 1596; hymns, 4vv; falsibordoni: D-MÜs, I-Bc, Rli, Rn, Rvat; masses ed. in Williams; 1 mass ed. in Musica divina, xi (1955)

SECULAR

Il primo libro de madrigali, 5vv (Venice, 1599)
Madrigali, libro secondo, 5, 6, 8vv (Venice, 1608)
Recreatione armonica: madrigali, 1, 2vv (Venice, 1611)
Diporti musicali, madrigali, 1–4vv (1617)
La bella clori armonica, arie, canzonetti, e madrigali, 1–3vv, bc (1619)
I lieti scherzi, cioe arie, villanelle, madrigali, 1–4vv (1621)
Gagliarde . . . intavolate per sonare sul cimbalo et sul liuto, libro primo (n.p., n.d.)
1 madrigal, 10 other secular vocal works, some 1v, bc, 5, 6vv, 1609¹⁷, 1616¹⁰, 1618¹³, 1621¹⁴, 1622¹⁰

BIBLIOGRAPHY

F. X. Haberl: 'Giovanni Francesco Anerio: Darstellung seines Lebensganges und Schaffens auf Grund bibliographischer Dokumente', *KJb*, i (1886), 51
D. Alaleona: *Studi su la storia dell'oratorio musicale in Italia* (Turin, 1908, 2/1945 as *Storia dell'oratorio musicale in Italia*)
R. Casimiri: 'Maurizio, Felice e Giovanni Francesco Anerio: nuovi documenti biografici', *RMI*, xvii (1920), 607
——: '"Disciplina musicae" e "mastri di cappella" dopo il Concilio di Trento nei maggiori istituti ecclesiastici di Roma: Seminario Romano – Collegio Germanico – Collegio Inglese (sec. XVI–XVII)', *NA*, xv (1938), 6
A. Allegra: 'La cappella musicale di S. Spirito in Saxia', *NA*, xvii (1940), 30
G. Liberali: 'Giovanni Francesco Anerio: un suo fugace soggiorno a Treviso', *NA*, xvii (1940), 171
H. Federhofer: 'Ein Beitrag zur Biographie von Giovanni Francesco Anerio', *Mf*, ii (1949), 210
——: 'Nochmals zur Biographie von Giovanni Francesco Anerio', *Mf*, vi (1953), 346
L. Pannella: 'Anerio, Giovanni Francesco', *DBI*
A. G. Petti: Introduction to edn. of *Missa pro defunctis* (London, 1966)
R. Münster: 'Seltene Musikdrucke des 17. Jahrhunderts im Stiftsarchiv Laufen an der Salzach', *Mf*, xx (1967), 284
H. E. Smither: 'The Latin Dramatic Dialogue and the Nascent Oratorio', *JAMS*, xx (1967), 403–33
W. C. Hobbs: *Giovanni Francesco Anerio's 'Teatro armonico spirituale di madrigali': a Contribution to the Early History of the Oratorio* (diss., Tulane U., 1971)
N. Z. Williams: *The Masses of Giovanni Francesco Anerio: a Historical and Analytical Study with a Supplementary Critical Edition* (diss., U. of North Carolina, 1971)
J. G. Kurtzman: *The Monteverdi Vespers of 1610 and their Relationship with Italian Sacred Music of the Early Seventeenth Century* (diss., U. of Illinois, 1972)
J. Armstrong: 'The "Antiphonae, seu Sacrae Cantiones" (1613) of Francesco Anerio: a Liturgical Study', *AnMc*, no.14 (1974), 89–150
H. E. Smither: *A History of the Oratorio*, i (Chapel Hill, 1977), 97ff, 110ff. 118ff

KLAUS FISCHER

Anet [Annet, Annette, Anette, Hanet], **Jean-Baptiste** (*b* Paris, 20 June 1650; *d* Paris, 26 or 28 April 1710). French violinist, father of Jean-Jacques-Baptiste Anet; the father and son are sometimes distinguished as Jean-Baptiste (i) and Jean-Baptiste (ii).

Jean-Baptiste (i) was the son of Claude Anet, an instrumentalist, and Claude Mouchet. In his youth he studied under Lully. By 1673, when he entered into the first of his three marriages, he was in the service of Louis XIV's brother, the Duke of Orleans. His first wife, Jeanne Vincent, was the mother of Jean-Baptiste (ii). Jean-Baptiste (i) remained in the service of the Duke of Orleans (and later that of the duke's son) but also served in the 24 Violons du Roy from 1699 until his death. On his deathbed, he sold his position in the 24 Violons to his colleague Joseph Francoeur for the latter's son Louis. He enjoyed a successful career, but nothing is known of his violin playing, and no music has been found to suggest that he was a composer. He is presumed to have been the first teacher of Jean-Jacques-Baptiste Anet.

NEAL ZASLAW

Anet, Jean-Jacques-Baptiste (*b* Paris, 2 Jan 1676; *d* Lunéville, 14 Aug 1755). French violinist and composer, son of Jean-Baptiste Anet, generally known as 'Baptiste'. About 1695–6 he travelled to Rome and studied under Corelli who, according to contemporary reports, was so pleased with Baptiste's performance of his music that he 'embraced him tenderly and made him a present of his bow', and subsequently regarded him as an adopted son. During 1699 and 1700 Baptiste travelled through Germany to Poland. On his return he entered the service of the Duke of Orleans, a position he abandoned after about a year to enter that of the Elector Maximilian Emanuel of Bavaria who, having lost his throne, was living in exile in France.

Baptiste's début at the French court on 23 October 1701 attracted the notice of the Parisian newspaper *Le Mercure galant*:

After his supper, the King heard in his study an exquisite concert of Italian airs, performed by Messrs Forqueray on the viol, Couperin at the harpsichord, and the young Baptiste (who is in the service of the Duke of Orleans) on the violin. The King appeared surprised at the excellence of the latter whom he had not yet heard.

During the first three decades of the 18th century Baptiste appeared frequently in and around Paris – at court, at the homes of the nobility and after 1725 at the Concert Spirituel. In 1715 Maximilian Emanuel regained his throne and returned to Bavaria; Baptiste left his service and soon entered that of Louis XIV. In 1724 he was granted a *privilège général* to publish 'several sonatas and other pieces of instrumental music'. Between 1724 and 1734 Baptiste published six volumes which represent his entire oeuvre. Two of them contain sonatas for violin and continuo, undoubtedly originally for his own use, while the others contain suites for the then popular musette (French bagpipes), and were dedicated to his friend, the musette virtuoso Colin Charpentier.

Baptiste's first appearance at the Concert Spirituel was as noteworthy an occasion as had been his first appearance at court. During Easter week 1725, reported *Le Mercure de France*, those attending the Concert Spirituel heard:

a species of duel between Messrs Baptiste, Frenchman, and [Jean-Pierre] Guignon, Piedmontese, who are regarded as the two best violinists in the world. They played by turns some instrumental pieces accompanied only by a bassoon and a bass viol, and they were both extraordinarily applauded. Mr Baptiste played without any accompaniment some preludes [i.e. improvisations] which were also extremely applauded.

The two violinists were heard together again in May and June of the same year. Abbé Pluche (1746) described Anet's playing:

Mr Baptiste . . . does not approve the ambition to devour all sorts of difficulties . . . He gives no advantage to a piece whose performance appears prodigious, and he gives his highest esteem to that which pleases the listener surely. He looks for, he often says, not what makes the musician perspire, not what dazzles the apprentice by swiftness or deafens him by noise, but what possesses the ability to touch him, to ravish him . . . This point of view requires that the instrumental sound be connected, sustained, mellow, impassioned, and conforming to the human voice, of which it is only the imitation and support . . . German, Italian, English – to him it is all the same. If he finds nobility and graciousness there, he plays it and gives its due by the purity of his intonation and the singular energy of his expressiveness. But he constantly refuses his ministrations to all that which has no other merit than to be difficult, bizarre or rough. The freedom and perseverance of his choice have often drawn him reproaches, sometimes as a too obstinate or even capricious man who yields to nothing, sometimes as a musician ignorant of frightening difficulties. He suffered a sort of persecution and exiled himself voluntarily before the honourable retreat which he enjoyed at the court of the King of Poland.

Baptiste left the 24 Violons du Roy in about 1735, undoubtedly for the reasons stated by Pluche but perhaps also due to his rivalry with Guignon, who only a year or so later also drove Leclair from the king's service. The self-exiled violinist remained in Paris until 1737 or 1738 when he became a violinist in the orchestra of Stanislaus Leszczynski, ex-king of Poland, at the court of Lorraine at Lunéville. Here he spent the rest of his days, playing the violin, hunting and fishing, and died poor after a lengthy illness, leaving no heirs.

The two major figures of the French violin school in the first quarter of the 18th century were Baptiste and Senaillé. Contemporary opinion held that the former was the superior performer, the latter the superior composer; this judgment appears to have been just. Baptiste was a moving performer, famed for his abilities as an improviser. He was the best French violinist before Leclair. His music is graceful and often interesting without being original: the first book of sonatas is strongly

influenced by Corelli, while the second book is more French in character. The compositions for musette clearly constitute an attempt to please the popular French taste of the time. By the 1730s his style was already old-fashioned, and this may have hastened the decline of his career.

WORKS
(*all published in Paris*)

Premier livre de sonates, vn, bc (1724)
Deuxième oeuvre de M. Baptiste, contenant deux suites de pieces à deux musettes, qui conviennent à 2 fl/ob/vn/vielle (1726)
[10] Sonates, vn, bc, op.3 (1729)
Premier oeuvre de musettes (before 1730)
Second oeuvre de musettes (1730)
IIIᵉ oeuvre de musettes, vns, fls, vielles (1734)

BIBLIOGRAPHY

J. L. Le Cerf de la Viéville: *Comparaison de la musique italienne et de la musique françoise* (Brussels, 1704/*R*1972)
N. A. Pluche: *Le spectacle de la nature* (Paris, 1732–)
L. de La Laurencie: *L'école française de violon de Lully à Viotti* (Paris, 1922–4/*R*1971)
M. Antoine: 'Naissance et mort de Jean-Baptiste Anet (1676–1755)', *RdM*, xli (1958), 99
——: 'Note sur les violinistes Anet', *RMFC*, ii (1961–2), 81
L. E. S. J. de Laborde: *Musiciens de Paris, 1535–1792*, ed. Y. de Brossard (Paris, 1965)

NEAL ZASLAW

Anfossi, Pasquale (*b* Taggia, 5 April 1727; *d* Rome, ? Feb 1797). Italian composer. According to the *Dizionario biografico degli italiani* (*DBI*), in 1744 he entered the Loreto Conservatory, Naples, where he specialized in the violin. After leaving the conservatory about 1752, he played in the orchestra of one of the small Neapolitan theatres, and after about ten years in that profession (Ginguené) decided to become a composer and took composition lessons from Sacchini and Piccinni. His first opera, *La serva spiritosa*, was produced at the Teatro Capranica, Rome, in Carnival 1763, but he only gradually established himself as a leading opera composer. According to Burney, he wrote some music for Sacchini's operas at the composer's request, while Ginguené and Grossi stated that Piccinni obtained opera commissions for him between 1771 and 1773 at the Teatro delle Dame, Rome, and that he achieved a success only with the third of these, *L'incognita perseguitata* (1773). Although certain details of this story do not agree with the known facts, there is no doubt of the success of *L'incognita*, which gained for Anfossi a degree of celebrity he had not previously enjoyed.

During the 1770s Rome and Venice were the main centres of Anfossi's activities. For part of this period he was *maestro di coro* at the Venetian girls' conservatory called the Derelitti or Ospedaletto, for which he wrote music between 1773 and 1777. It has not been possible, however, to determine from the surviving conservatory records (now in *I-Vas*) the exact dates of his appointment or resignation. It is said that he went to Paris in 1780, but if so, he composed no new operas there. The statement in *DBI* that he moved directly from Paris to London is dubious. His first opera for London, *Il trionfo della costanza*, was produced at the King's Theatre on 19 December 1782, and there is no evidence that he was in London much before then; the new operas that he had performed in Venice and Rome between 1780 and 1782 prove that he must have been working in Italy during this period. Off and on during the years 1782–6 he served as music director for the King's Theatre, where five new operas as well as several of his earlier works were produced. He also supervised the production of operas by other composers, including a version (first staged at the King's in May 1785) of Gluck's *Orfeo* with additional music by Handel and J. C. Bach. His last London opera, *L'inglese in Italia*, was unsuccessful, being performed only twice (20 and 27 May 1786); an extract from the *General Advertiser* for 22 May reads, 'The music evidently labours under a tedious monotony'.

By the following autumn Anfossi was back in Venice. At the start of 1787 he was in Rome for the production of his *Le pazzie de' gelosi*, a work which, according to Gerber, caused a fresh wave of enthusiasm for his music among the Romans. In 1790, however, his production of new operas, uninterrupted since the 1770s, came to an abrupt stop and he spent his last years in the service of the church. In August 1791 he was promised the post of *maestro di cappella* at St John Lateran, Rome, on G. B. Casali's resignation or death; he was appointed in July 1792 and held this position until his death.

The total of Anfossi's operas, both heroic and comic, has not been established, but is certainly over 60 and possibly 70 or more. He also composed a considerable amount of church music, including about 20 sacred oratorios in Latin (composed for female voices and orchestra and first performed in Venice) or Italian (composed for mixed voices and orchestra and first performed in Rome). Anfossi's early style is close to Piccinni's, a fact that supports the possibility that he had been Piccinni's pupil. His harmonies are diatonic and bland and his textures within any single number discreetly varied, though perhaps a little heavy at times because of constant note repetitions in the bass. His melodies, although not all equally inspired, contain moments of elegance and warmth. Several stylistic changes are noticeable in his later works: textures are lighter, and there is more effective use, both in accompaniments and melody, of pauses and rests; there are fewer embellishments and ornamental notes in the melodic parts; the orchestration is more colourful, partly because of a more imaginative use of wind instruments. Anfossi employed the old-fashioned da capo form in arias of his early heroic operas and oratorios, though not in those of his comic operas, where freer forms prevail; by the mid-1770s, however, he abandoned the form altogether in favour of freer structures. His operatic music has sometimes been criticized for not sufficiently enhancing characterization or creating dramatic impact. In these respects he was far inferior to Mozart, whose superiority as music dramatist can be seen from a comparison of Anfossi's *La finta giardiniera* of 1774 with Mozart's setting of the same libretto a year later.

WORKS

OPERAS

RA – *Rome, Teatro Argentina*
RD – *Rome, Teatro delle Dame*
RV – *Rome, Teatro alla Valle*
LK – *London, King's Theatre*
VB – *Venice, Teatro S Benedetto*
VM – *Venice, Teatro S Moisè*
VS – *Venice, Teatro S Samuele*

La serva spiritosa, ossia I ripieghi della medesima (farsetta, 2 pts.), Rome, Capranica, carn. 1763; ?*I-Gi(l)* [as La serva spiritata]
Lo sposo di tre e marito di nessuna (commedia per musica, 3, A. Palomba), Naples, Nuovo, aut. 1763, collab. P. A. Guglielmi; *A-Wn, I-Bc*
Il finto medico (commedia per musica, 3), Naples, Nuovo, wint. 1764
Fiammetta generosa (commedia per musica, 3), Naples, Fiorentini, carn. 1766; Act 1 by Piccinni

I matrimoni per dispetto (commedia per musica, 3), Naples, Nuovo, carn. 1767
La clemenza di Tito (dramma per musica, 3, Metastasio), RA, 1769, or Naples, S Carlo, 30 May 1772; *P-La* (2 copies)
Armida (dramma per musica, 3, ? J. Durandi), Turin, Regio, carn. 1770; *F-Pn, P-La*
Cajo Mario (dramma serio, 3, G. Roccaforte), VB, aut. 1770; *La* (2 copies)
Quinto Fabio (dramma per musica, 3, Zeno), RD, carn. 1771; *La*
Il barone di Rocca Antica (intermezzo, G. Petrosellini), RV, 1771, ? collab. C. Franchi; *F-Pn, I-Fc*
Nitteti (dramma per musica, 3, Metastasio), Naples, S Carlo, 13 Aug 1771; *Nc, P-La* (2 copies)
Alessandro nell'Indie (dramma per musica, 3, Metastasio), RA, carn. 1772; *F-Pn, I-Fc, P-La*
L'amante confuso (commedia per musica, 3, S. Zini), Naples, Fiorentini, aut. 1772; *GB-Lcm*
L'incognita perseguitata (dramma giocoso, 3, ? Petrosellini, after Goldoni), RD, carn. 1773; as Metilda ritrovata, Vienna, 1773; as La Giannetta, Bologna, 1773; as La Gianetta perseguitata, Dresden, 1774; in Fr. trans., Fontainebleau, 1776; Versailles, 1781 (Paris, 1781); *A-Wgm, Wn* [both as La Metilda ritrovata], *B-Bc,* ?*D-Dlb* [La Giannetta perseguitata], *GB-Cpl* (Act 1), *I-Bc, Fc, Mc* [La Giannetta], *Vnm, P-La, US-Bp, Wc*
Demofoonte (dramma per musica, 3, Metastasio), RA, carn. 1773
Antigono (dramma per musica, 3, Metastasio), VB, Ascension 1773; 15 arias, duet, arr. v, b (Venice, 1773)
La finta giardiniera (dramma giocoso, 3, ?Calzabigi), RD, carn. 1774; as La marchese giardiniera, London, 1775; as Die edle Gärtnerin, Frankfurt, 1782; *B-Bc, D-B, F-Pn, GB-Lbm* (Acts 1 and 2), *Lcm, I-Fc, P-La*
Lucio Silla (dramma per musica, 3, G. de Gamerra), VS, Ascension 1774; *F-Pn*
Il geloso in cimento (dramma giocoso, 3, G. Bertati), Vienna, Burg, 25 May 1774; as La vedova galante, Graz, 1779; as La vedova scaltra, Castelnuovo, 1785; as La vedova bizzarra, Naples, 1788; *A-K, Wn, D-B* [as Die Eifersucht auf der Probe], *F-Pn, Po, GB-Lbm, I-Fc, Gi(l), P-La* (2 copies), *S-Ssr* [in Ger.], *US-Wc*
Olimpiade (dramma per musica, 3, Metastasio), VB, 26 Dec 1774; *P-La*
La contadina incivilita (dramma giocoso, 3), VS, carn. 1775; as La contadina di corte, RD, 1775; ?*US-Wc* [as La contadina in corte]
Didone abbandonata (dramma per musica, 3, Metastasio), VM, Ascension 1775; *F-Pn, I-Nc, P-La*
L'avaro (dramma giocoso, 3, G. Bertati), VM, aut. 1775; as La fedeltà nelle angustie, Florence, 1777; as Il sordo e l'avaro, Brunswick, 1782; *D-B, GB-Lbm, I-Bc, Fc, P-La, US-Wc*; as Le tuteur avare, Paris, 1787 (Paris, c1787)
La vera costanza (dramma giocoso, 3, F. Puttini), RD, carn. 1776; as La pescatrice fedele, VM, 1776; as Il principe di Lago Nero, Florence, 1777; *A-Wgm, GB-Lbm, I-Fc, P-La, US-Bp, Wc* (2 copies, 1 as Il principe di Lago Nero)
Motezuma (dramma, 3, ? G. A. Cigna-Santi), Reggio, Pubblico, Fair 1776
Isabella e Rodrigo, o sia La costanza in amore (2, Bertati), VS, aut. 1776; *I-Fc, Mc* [as L'avventure di Donna Isabella e Don Rodrigo]
Il curioso indiscreto (dramma giocoso, 3 ?Bertati), RD, carn. 1777; in Fr., Paris, 1790; *F-Pn, Po, I-Nc* (Act 1), *US-Bp*
Gengis-Kan (dramma per musica, 3), Turin, Regio, carn. 1777; *P-La* (2 copies)
Adriano in Siria (dramma per musica, Metastasio), Padua, Nuovo, June 1777; *P-La*
Lo sposo disperato (dramma giocoso, 2, Bertati), VM, aut. 1777; as Il zotico incivilito, Bologna, 1777; *B-Bc, D-B, I-Fc, US-Bp*
Il controgenio, ovvero Le speranze deluse (intermezzo, 2 pts., ? G. Petrosellini), RV, carn. 1778
Ezio (dramma serio, 3, Metastasio), VM, Ascension 1778; *F-Pn*
La forza delle donne (dramma giocoso, 2, Bertati), VM, aut. 1778; as Il valore delle donne, Turin, aut. 1780; *F-Pn, I-Fc, S-Skma, US-Bp, Wc*
L'americana in Olanda (dramma giocoso, 2, N. Porta), VS, aut. 1778
Cleopatra (dramma serio, 3, M. Verazzi), Turin, Regio, carn. 1779; *F-Pn, P-La*
Il matrimonio per inganno (dramma giocoso, 2, ?Bertati), Florence, Cocomero, spr. 1779; *F-Pn, Po, US-Wc*
Azor re di Kibinga (dramma giocoso, 2, Bertati), VM, aut. 1779
Amor costante (intermezzo, 2 pts., ?Bertati), Rome, Capranica, carn. 1780
Tito nelle Gallie (dramma per musica, 3, ? P. Giovannini), RD, carn. 1780
La finta cingara per amore (farsa, 2), Venice, S Giovanni Grisostomo, carn. 1780; Act 1 by C. Franchi [? perf. Rome, 1774]
I viaggiatori felici (dramma giocoso, 2, F. Livigni), VS, aut. 1780; *A-Wn, D-B, F-Pn, I-Fc, US-Bf, Wc*); Favourite Songs (London, c1782)
Lo sposo per equivoco (intermezzo, 2 pts.), Rome, Capranica, carn. 1781
Il trionfo d'Arianna (dramma per musica, 2, G. Lanfranchi-Rossi), VM,

Ascension 1781; *I-Vc, P-La*
L'imbroglio delle tre spose (dramma giocoso, 2, ?Bertati), VM, aut. 1781; *I-Fc, P-La*
Gli amanti canuti (dramma giocoso, 2, Lanfranchi-Rossi), VM, aut. 1781; *?D-Dlb, US-Wc*
Zemira (dramma, 2, G. Sertor), VB, carn. 1782; *US-Wc*
Il disprezzo (azione drammatica giocosa, 1), VS, carn. 1782; perf. with Act 2 of Gli amanti canuti
Il trionfo della costanza (dramma giocoso, 2, C. F. Badini), LK, 19 Dec 1782; Favourite Songs (London, *c*1783)
I vecchi burlati (dramma giocoso, 2), LK, 27 March 1783
Le gelosie fortunate (dramma giocoso, 2, Livigni), Turin, Carignano, 1783, or VS, aut. 1786
Issipile (dramma per musica, 2, after Metastasio), LK, 8 May 1784; Favourite Songs (London, *c*1784)
Le due gemelle (dramma giocoso, 2, G. Tonioli), LK, 12 June 1784
L'inglese in Italia (dramma giocoso, 2, Badini), LK, 20 May 1786
Le pazzie de' gelosi (farsetta, 2 pts.), RV, carn. 1787
Creso (dramma, 3, G. Pizzi), RA, 1787
L'orfanella americana (commedia per musica, 4, Bertati), VM, aut. 1787
La maga Circe (farsetta, 1 pt.), RV, carn. 1788; *I-Gi(l), Rsc, US-Wc*
Artaserse (dramma per musica, 2, Metastasio), RD, carn. 1788; *F-Pn*
I matrimoni per fanatismo (dramma giocoso, 2,?C. Sernicola), Naples, Fondo, 1788
La gazzetta, o sia Il bagiano deluso (farsa, 2 pts., ?Petrosellini), RV, carn. 1789
Zenobia di Palmira (dramma, 3, Sertor), VB, 26 Dec 1789; *I-Bc, Fc*
Gli artigiani (dramma giocoso, 2, G. Foppa), VM, carn. 1794; as L'amor artigiano, Pavia, 1797; *D-MÜs, F-Pn, GB-Lbm, I-Gi(l), S-St, US-Wc*
Doubtful: Lucio Papirio, Rome, 1771; I visionari, Rome, 1771; La donna instabile, Vienna, 1776; La vaga Frascatana contrastata dagli amorosi umiliati, Ravenna, 1777; Orlando paladino, Vienna, 1778; Le gelosie villane, Casale Monferrato, 1779; La finta ammalata, Parma, carn. 1782–3; Chi cerca trova, Florence, 1783 or 1789; Gli sposi in commedie, Piacenza, 1784; Il cavaliere per amore, Berlin, 1784; La villanella di spirito, Rome, 1787; Erifile, Lucca, 1787; L'antiquario, Paris, 1789

ORATORIOS

La madre dei Maccabei (P. Barbieri), Rome, 1765; *GB-Lbm*; Noe sacrificium, Venice or Florence, 1769, *I-Pca, Vc*; Carmina sacra canenda in nosocomio pauperum derelictorum, Venice, 1773; Jerusalem eversa, Venice, 1774; David contra Philisthaeos, Venice, 1775; Giuseppe riconosciuto (Metastasio), Rome, 1776, *Bc, Mc, Rco*; Carmina sacra recinenda a piis virginibus, Venice, 1776; Samuelis umbra, Venice, 1777; Virginis assumptae triumphans, Venice, 1780; La nascita del Redentore (G. Terribilini), Rome, 1780, *Bc*; Esther, Venice, 1781, *Bc*; La Betulia liberata, ?1781, *Mc, US-Wc* (pt.1, dated 1781)
Sedecias, Venice, 1782, *I-Bc, Mc, Rco*; Il sacrificio di Noè uscita dall'arca, Rome, 1783 [? version of Noe sacrificium], *Bc, Rco, P-La*; Prodigus, Venice, ?1786, *I-Gi(l)*; S Elena al Calvario (Metastasio), 1st known perf. Rome, 1786; *GB-Lbm, I-Bc, Gi(l), Mc*; Ninive conversa, Venice, 1787, *GB-Lbm* (pt.1), *I-Mc*; Il figliuol prodigo (C. A. Femi), Rome, 1792, *Rco*; La morte di S Filippo Neri (Femi), Rome, 1796, *Rco*; Gerico distrutta, *Mc*; Il convito di Baldassare, mentioned in *LaMusicaD*; Per la nascita del N. S. Gesù Cristo, *Rco*

OTHER WORKS

Cantatas: I dioscuri (S. Mattei), Naples, S Carlo, 13 Aug 1771; L'armonia (M. Butturini), Venice, S Benedetto, 11 Jan 1790
Masses: 4vv, *I-Mc, Nc, PS*; 4vv, *Bc*; 4vv, org, *A-Wn*; 5vv, insts, *D-B*; 2, 8vv, *I-Rco*
Mass movts: 6 Kyrie–Gloria: *D-B, F-Pn, C, GB-Lbm*, 4vv, insts, *A-Wn, US-Wc*, 8vv, *D-MÜs*; Qui tollis, 4vv, *I-Rco*; Credos: 4vv, *A-Wn, I-Rco*, 2, *D-B*
Other sacred works: 5 Salve regina: S, SSA, insts, 1776, *GB-Lbm*, SS, str, bc, T, 5vv, *I-Mc*, S, str, org, *MOe*, A, insts, 1779, *Nc*; 6 motets, 1v, insts, 1775–8, *Vnm*; Motetti per l'Elevazione, 2vv, *Rco*; 2 O salutaris: 5vv, *Rco*, 3vv, *A-Wn*; Miserere, S, S, b, *I-Vc, Vnm*; Holy Week Responsories, T, T, b, *D-MÜs*; many psalms, H, *F-Pn, GB-Lbm, I-Bc, Mc, PS, Vc, Rco, US-Wc*; other motets, hymns etc, *D-Bds, MÜs, GB-Lbm, I-Mc, Vnm, Rco*
Orch: many sinfonie: D, *A-K*; B♭, *D-B*, 3 in D, *D-B*; 1 Dlb; B♭, DS; 5 *F-Pn*, 2, both 1771, *I-MAc*; 6 in D, 1 dated 1773, 2 dated 1775, *Mc*; B♭, *Mc*; 3, 2 dated 1773, 1775, *Nc*; 13 in D, *Rdp* [incl. 2 opera ovs.]; many ovs.: D, 1769, *GB-Lbm*; 9, *Lcm*; 3 in D, 1 dated 1773, *I-Mc*; D, *Nc*; 2 vc concs., 1 in G, Vn Conc., C, mentioned by Torchi
Chamber inst: minuets, 2 vn, vc, *Nc*; 5 qnts: D, F, fl, 2 vn, va, bc, C, F, C, ob, 2 vn, va, bc, all *MOe*

BIBLIOGRAPHY

BurneyH; GerberL; LaMusicaD
P. L. Ginguené: *Notice sur la vie et les ouvrages de Nicola Piccinni* (Paris, 1800)
G. B. G. Grossi: 'Pasquale Anfossi', *Biografia degli uomini illustri del regno di Napoli*, ed. D. Martuscelli, vi (Naples, 1819)

G. Baini: *Memorie storico-critiche della vita e delle opere di Giovanni Pierluigi da Palestrina*, i (Rome, 1828/*R*1966), 71
C. A. de Rosa, Marchese di Villarosa: *Memorie dei compositori di musica del regno di Napoli* (Naples, 1840)
L. Torchi: 'La musica strumentale in Italia nei secoli XVI, XVII, e XVIII', *RMI*, vi (1899), 724; pubd separately (Turin, 1901/*R*1969)
H. Kretzschmar: 'Mozart in der Geschichte der Oper', *Gesammelte Aufsätze über Musik*, ii (Leipzig, 1911), 257, esp.268
T. de Wyzewa and G. de Saint-Foix: *W. A. Mozart*, ii (Paris, 1936), 197
L. de Angelis: 'Musiche manoscritte inedite dei secoli xvi–xvii del' Archivio del Pio Sodalizio dei Piceni in Roma', *NA*, xvi (1939), 29
M. Pedemonte: 'Musicisti liguri: Pasquale Anfossi', *Genova*, xxii (1942), 32
W. Bollert: 'Anfossi, Pasquale', *MGG*
F. d'Amico: 'Anfossi, Pasquale', *ES*
G. Tintori: *L'opera napoletana* (Milan, 1958)
'Anfossi, Pasquale', *DBI*
F. Lippmann: 'Die Sinfonien-Manuskripte der Bibliothek Doria-Pamphilj', *AcM*, v (1968), 201

MICHAEL F. ROBINSON

Angeleri, Giuseppe Maria (*fl* 1678–91). Italian composer. He is known mainly for seven masses for small groups of voices and continuo, which he published in two volumes, three in the first, op.1 (Milan, 1678), and four in the second, op.2 (Milan, 1691). The first volume also contains a *Magnificat* and a *Tantum ergo* for solo voice. The second survives incomplete.

Angeli, Francesco Maria ['Il Rivotorto'] (*b* Rivotorto, nr. Assisi, 1632; *d* Assisi, 23 Dec 1697). Italian composer. He bore as a sobriquet the name of his birthplace. He first studied at the monastery there and later at Perugia, Assisi and, in 1655–6, Bologna. As a member of the Franciscan order he held a series of appointments as *maestro di cappella*, beginning at S Francesco, Bologna, in 1656. He then worked at Spoleto and Palermo and finally, until his death, at S Francesco, Assisi. Music at this basilica notably flourished under his direction, and he enjoyed a high reputation as a contrapuntist (he was called 'unequalled'); he wrote a short treatise on counterpoint, *Sommario del contrapunto* (MS, 1691, *I-Bc*). While at Assisi he was also superintendent of the Sacro Convento and wrote its history, which was published posthumously. All his compositions are sacred, and most are for two or more choirs. They are competently written, but they are sometimes marred by a too easy acceptance of superficial effects and massive sounds.

WORKS

Messa del secondo tono (Ky, Gl, Cr), 8vv, org, *I-Bc*
Missa 'Angelorum chori', 4 choirs, insts, org, 1677, *Ac*
Messa, 4vv, org, chorus, 1680, *Ac* (authenticity doubtful)
Many psalms, hymns, tracts, etc, 8vv, org, *Ac* (some holograph)

BIBLIOGRAPHY

S. Mattei: 'Serie dei maestri di cappella minori conventuali di San Francesco', *Miscellanea francescana*, xxi (1920), 46
D. M. Sparacio: 'Musicisti minori conventuali', *Miscellanea francescana*, xxv (1925), 13
R. Casimiri: 'Musicisti dell'ordine francescano dei minori conventuali dei sec. XVI–XVIII', *NA*, xvi (1939), 242
C. Sartori: *Assisi: la cappella della Basilica di San Francesco: catalogo del fondo musicale della Biblioteca comunale di Assisi* (Milan, 1962)

based on *MGG* (xv, 217–18) by permission of Bärenreiter

GIUSEPPE VECCHI

Angelica. See ANGÉLIQUE.

Angelieri, Giorgio (*fl* 1571–99). Italian printer, partner of CLAUDIO MERULO. He published independently Porta's *Litaniae deiparae Virginae Mariae* (1575) and a reprint of Rore's *Il primo libro de madrigali a quattro voci* (1573). He also worked as a printer for several other publishers.

Angelini, Giovanni Andrea. *See* BONTEMPI, GIOVANNI ANDREA.

Angelini, Orazio (*b* ?Gubbio; *fl* 1583–92). Italian composer. He may have been living in Gubbio when his first volume of madrigals, which is signed 'Horatio Angelini da Ugubbio', appeared in 1583. The remaining books are dedicated to his patron Cardinal Scipione Gonzaga. 32 of his 65 extant madrigals are settings of sonnets. Five others are settings of *ottava rima*, one has a villanella text, and the remainder are settings of free verse. Petrarch and Guarini are among the poets set.

WORKS
Primo libro de madrigali, 5vv (Venice, 1583)
Secondo libro de madrigali, 5vv (Venice, 1585)
Primo libro de madrigali, 6vv (Venice, 1592)

Works reprinted in 1585[19]; 1 piece intabulated lute in 1601[18]
W. RICHARD SHINDLE

Angélique (Fr. 'angel lute'; It. *angelica*). A double-necked lute with ten single strings on the lower head and six or seven on the upper (see illustration). Its characteristic feature, diatonic tuning, greatly restricts its compass, but the tone of the open strings is full and clear. An instrument of the lute family tuned in this way was depicted by Praetorius (1618), who said it was played

Damon with an angélique: engraving by Nicolas Bonnart

like a harp. (It is not a theorbo as the 23 strings run between a sloping bridge and a single pegbox angled to one side.) The name 'angel lute' or 'angélique' is found in the late 17th century and the 18th. The instrument can usually be distinguished from the theorbo by its having only ten pegs in the lower pegbox, most contemporary theorbos having 14. James Talbot (*c*1699) gave the tuning for the 16-course angel lute, running diatonically on 'white' notes from *D* to *e'*. He also said that the instru-

ment had nine frets. As he pointed out, the instrument is 'more proper for slow and grave lessons than for quick and brisk by reason of the continuance of sound when touched which may breed discord'.

BIBLIOGRAPHY
M. Praetorius: *Syntagma musicum*, ii–iii (Wolfenbüttel, 1618, 2/1619/*R*1958)
M. Prynne: 'James Talbot's Manuscript: IV: Plucked Strings–the Lute Family', *GSJ*, xiv (1961), 52
E. Pohlmann: *Laute, Theorbe, Chitarrone: die Instrumente, ihre Musik und Literatur von 1500 bis zur Gegenwart* (Bremen, 1968, rev. 4/1976)
IAN HARWOOD

Angelis, Angelo de. *See* DEANGELIS, ANGELO.

Angeloni, Carlo (*b* Lucca, 16 July 1834; *d* Lucca, 13 Jan 1901). Italian composer, teacher and bandmaster. He studied with Michele Puccini, father of Giacomo, and spent his life in Lucca except for a period in Florence (1855–62). Of his activities, the most important was his teaching at the Istituto Musicale Pacini. As the institute's director, and especially as teacher of singing, the organ, harmony and counterpoint (1864–95), he educated several generations of young musicians, among them Alfredo Catalani and Giacomo Puccini, who remained devoted to him. His works include eight operas, five of which were performed between 1854 and 1871 and the last after his death, in 1902, though all were given only in Lucca or other small towns. He produced a large number of sacred works distinguished by their originality, dignity of style and sound contrapuntal technique. Nevertheless, his entire output, which also includes songs, piano pieces, orchestral and band music, remains unpublished, despite posthumous attempts to make him better known.

BIBLIOGRAPHY
L. Landucci: *Carlo Angeloni: cronistoria* (Lucca, 1905)
EMILIA ZANETTI

Angelus Silesius, (Johann) [Scheffler, Johannes] (*b* Breslau [now Wrocław], Dec 1624; *d* Breslau, 9 July 1677). German poet. He received an excellent education and his first exposure to the budding vernacular literature at the Elisabeth Gymnasium, Breslau. He attended the universities of Strasbourg, Leiden and Padua, at the last of which he received the degrees of MD and PhD in 1648. Back in Silesia a clash with the Protestant censor led to his conversion to Catholicism on 12 June 1653, on which occasion he assumed the name of (Johann) Angelus Silesius. He defended his conversion in writing and soon became an outspoken and prolific agent and leading poet of the Counter-Reformation. He was ordained priest in 1661 and spent his later years – when his creative powers were in decline – mostly in religious activities and polemics.

Angelus Silesius's two principal poetic works are *Der cherubinische Wandersmann* (Breslau, 1657, 2/1674, 3/1675) and *Heilige Seelenlust* (Breslau, 1657, enlarged 2/1668). The former, a collection of 1679 poems mostly in rhymed Alexandrine couplets, is a product of his mystical disposition. Using the strict form of the epigram, a form given to antithesis and dialectic, he expressed the mystic's abnegation of will and his vision of the longed-for union with God. By employing such poetic devices as paradox, hyperbole, irrational circumlocution and contradictory statements he fulfilled the 'rationalistic' form of the epigram while conveying the ineffability of a basically irrational experience. In their daring expressiveness and mastery of form the epigrams represent a high point of German Baroque literature.

Heilige Seelenlust belongs to a tradition of religious pastoral in which Jesus is portrayed as the shepherd and the soul as his longing bride. Here Angelus Silesius often used the technique of the contrafactum, giving a secular poem or song religious content while retaining the original metre, rhyme and melody. He adopted a simple lyrical style and various common strophe forms in order to provide the Counter-Reformation with songs that could compete in popularity with the Protestant hymns. He furnished all the songs with melodies, for the most part composed by Georg Joseph.

These songs have lived on in the hymnals of both confessions but never with the original melodies. The Pietists in particular embraced his poems; 30 were included in the widely used *Geistreiches Gesangbuch* (1704), edited by J. A. Freylinghausen.

WRITINGS

ed. G. Ellinger: *Sämtliche poetische Werke und eine Auswahl aus seinen Streitschriften* (Berlin, 1923)
ed. H. L. Held: *Sämtliche poetische Werke* (Munich, 1922, rev. 3/1952)
trans. J. E. C. Flitch: *Selections from the Cherubinic Wanderer* (London, 1932)
trans. W. R. Trask: *The Cherubinic Wanderer: Selections* (New York, 1953)
ed. K. Isenberg: *Weihnachtslieder des Barock*, Geistliche Sololieder des Barock, iii (Kassel, 1962)

BIBLIOGRAPHY

C. von Winterfeld: *Der evangelische Kirchengesang*, ii (Leipzig, 1845/R1966), 505ff; iii (Leipzig, 1847/R1966), 21, exx.1–11
J. Zahn: *Die Melodien der deutschen evangelischen Kirchenlieder*, v (Gütersloh, 1892/R1963), 421 [lists 78 melodies of G. Joseph]
J. Sammons: *Angelus Silesius* (New York, 1967)

TRAUTE MAASS MARSHALL

Angerer, Paul (*b* Vienna, 16 May 1927). Austrian conductor, violist and composer. From 1941 to 1946 he studied theory, piano, violin and organ at the Vienna Academy of Music and the Vienna Conservatory. After playing the viola in the Vienna SO and winning a medal at the Geneva Music Competition in 1948, he was engaged by the Zurich Tonhalle Orchestra, and then by the Orchestre de la Suisse Romande (1949–52). From 1953 to 1956 he was principal viola player in the Vienna SO. He also won first prize for an organ composition in the competition in Haarlem in 1954.

Angerer's subsequent career as a conductor has extended from the post of director and chief conductor of the Vienna Chamber Orchestra (1956–63), and numerous tours as guest conductor, to an engagement as composer and conductor of the Vienna Burgtheater (1960–64). In this capacity he wrote and performed music for various plays. He was principal conductor of the opera house of Bonn (1964–6), musical director of the theatre in Ulm (1966–8) and musical director of the Salzburg Landestheater (1968–72). In these posts he also sometimes directed productions. From 1970 to 1971 he was artistic director of the Fest in Hellbrunn, a local offshoot of the Salzburg Festival, and in 1972 he became director of the South-west German Chamber Orchestra in Pforzheim.

Angerer has composed many instrumental works in a personal style which shows the influence of Hindemith. His gifts as conductor and composer may be heard in his gramophone records; he has edited Baroque and pre-Classical music, as well as works by Joseph Lanner.

BIBLIOGRAPHY

R. Klein: 'Paul Angerer', *ÖMz*, xi (1956), 191

RUDOLF KLEIN

Angermüller, Rudolph (*b* Gadderbaum, Bielefeld, 2 Sept 1940). German musicologist. He studied musicology in Mainz (1961–5), Münster (1965–7) and Salzburg (1967–70) with Schmitz, Massenkeil, Federhofer and Croll, as well as Romance languages with Lausberg and history with von Raumer. He received the doctorate at Salzburg University with a dissertation on Salieri in 1970 and was assistant lecturer at the musicology institute of Salzburg University under Gerhard Croll (1968–72). While continuing to teach at Salzburg University, in 1972 he became academic librarian of the Internationale Stiftung Mozarteum in Salzburg, a post in which he worked with Otto Schneider on the preparation of Mozart bibliography. In his Salieri studies, which have brought him international recognition, he has edited the opera *Tarare*. His work as one of the editors of the Neue Mozart-Ausgabe (editor-in-chief from 1973), including his own edition of *Bastien und Bastienne* (in 1974), has won him a reputation as a Mozart scholar.

WRITINGS

Antonio Salieri: sein Leben und seine weltlichen Werke (diss., U. of Salzburg, 1970; Munich, 1971–)
'Beaumarchais und Salieri', *GfMKB, Bonn 1970*, 325
with S. Dahms: 'Neue Brieffunde zu Mozart', *MJb 1968–70*, 211–41
'Bibliographie . . . Bernhard Paumgartner', *Bernhard Paumgartner*, ed. G. Croll (Salzburg and Munich, 1971), 38
'Nissens Kollektaneen für seine Mozartbiographie', *MJb 1971–2*, 217
'Opernreformen im Lichte der wirtschaftlichen Verhältnisse an der Académie Royale de Musique von 1775 bis 1780', *Mf*, xxv (1972), 267
'Eine französische Idomeneo-Bearbeitung aus dem Jahre 1822', *Mitteilungen der Internationalen Stiftung Mozarteum*, xxi/3–4 (1973), 1–43
'Sigismund Ritter von Neukomm (1778–1858) und seine Lehrer Michael und Joseph Haydn', *Haydn-Studien*, iii (1973), 29
'Zwei Selbstbiographien von Joseph Weigl', *DJbM*, xvii (1973), 46–85
'Johann Andreas Schachtners "Bastienne"–Libretto', *Mitteilungen der Internationalen Stiftung Mozarteum*, xxii/1–2 (1974), 5
'Die entpolitisierte Oper am Wiener und am Esterházyschen Hof', *Kongress: Oberschützen 1975*, 5
'Die Wiener Jahre Donizettis', *1° convegno internazionale di studi donizettiani: Bergamo 1975*
with O. Schneider: 'Mozart-Bibliographie', *MJb 1975*
'Mozart und Rousseau: zur Textgrundlage von "Bastien und Bastienne" ', *Mitteilungen der Internationalen Stiftung Mozarteum*, xxiii/1–2 (1975), 22
'Reformideen von Du Roullet und Beaumarchais als Opernlibrettisten', *AcM*, xlviii (1976), 227
'Salieris Gesellschaftsmusik', *AnMc*, no.17 (1976), 146
ed.: *Sigismund Ritter von Neukomm: Werkverzeichnis, Autobiographie* (Munich and Salzburg, 1976)
'Zigeuner und Zigeunerisches in der Oper des 19. Jahrhunderts', *Die "couleur locale" in der Oper des 19. Jahrhunderts*, ed. H. Becker (Regensburg, 1976), 131
'Wer war der Librettist von Mozarts *La finta giardiniera*', *MJb 1976–7*, 5
'Bemerkungen zu den französischen Bearbeitungen', *Così fan tutte: Beiträge zur Wirkungsgeschichte von Mozarts Oper*, ed. S. Vill (Bayreuth, 1978), 67
'Mozart und Metastasio', *Mitteilungen der Internationalen Stiftung Mozarteum*, xxvi/1–2 (1978), 12
Mozart und seiner Pariser Umwelt (in preparation)

EDITIONS

W. A. Mozart: *Bastien und Bastienne*, Neue Ausgabe sämtlicher Werke, II/5/3 (Kassel, 1964); *La finta giardiniera*, ibid, II/5/8 (Kassel, 1978) [with D. Berke]
A. Salieri: *Tarare* (Munich and Duisburg, 1978)

RUDOLF KLEIN

Angiolini, (Domenico Maria) Gaspero [Gasparo] [Gasparini, Domenico Maria Angiolo] (*b* Florence, 9 Feb 1731; *d* Milan, 6 Feb 1803). Italian choreographer, dancer and composer. He probably received his first music and dance lessons in Florence. From 1747 or 1748 he danced in north Italian cities and in 1752 worked in Rome as a choreographer. His real teacher and lifelong model was Franz Hilverding, ballet-master at the Viennese court. Angiolini probably first visited Vienna in the early 1750s and danced in Hilverding's ballets from about 1752. In 1754 he married his dancing partner, Maria Teresa Fogliazzi (1733–92), the daughter of a distinguished Parma family and prima ballerina in Vienna.

As a result of his success as a dancer in Vienna and on tour in Italy (Turin, 1756–7), Angiolini became Hilverding's successor when the latter went to St Petersburg in 1758. His first productions (1756–60) were on the lines of Hilverding's work, but 'alla mia maniera', as he wrote in his *Lettere . . . a Monsieur Noverre*, and were followed by his crowning success, the ballet-pantomime *Le festin de pierre* (*Don Juan*) (Burgtheater, 17 October 1761) with music by Gluck, which was soon performed in Paris, Italy and Germany. In 1762 he produced a ballet version of Gluck's *opéra comique La Cythère assiégée* (*Citera assediata*) and choreographed Gluck's *Orfeo ed Euridice*. In 1763 he also danced in Traetta's *Ifigenia in Tauride*, in 1764 staged his ballet *Le muse protette*, for which he also composed the music (score in *A-Wn*), and in 1765 collaborated with Gluck on the ballet-pantomimes *Semiramis*, which was a failure, and *Iphigénie en Aulide*. *Don Juan*, *La Cythère assiégée* and *Semiramis* were each accompanied by a *dissertazione*, or commentary, in which Angiolini set out his aims and principles.

After Durazzo's departure from Vienna in 1764 and the emperor's death in 1765, Angiolini gratefully seized the opportunity of becoming Hilverding's successor in St Petersburg. On 26 September 1766 he made his Russian début with his *ballet-héroïque Le départ d'Enée, ou Didon abandonnée*, a very successful ballet version of Metastasio's libretto (Angiolini's score was published in Venice in 1773). Between 1766 and 1772 he created at least eight more ballets for the Russian court, sometimes with music by others (Manfredini, Raupach, Springer), sometimes with his own, as well as numerous divertissements performed at the Winter Palace within the framework of Italian operas. In 1772 he went to Venice, where in 1773 he staged six ballets, including revivals and new works, performed between the acts of *opere serie*. He also published his *Lettere. . .a Monsieur Noverre* (Milan, 1773), in which he opposed Noverre's claim to be the inventor of the *ballet d'action*, asserting the priority of Hilverding. In this work, which initiated a long controversy, he also discussed the principles and problems of dance and choreography.

In spring 1774 Angiolini was back in Vienna as Noverre's successor. A strong faction of Noverre supporters greeted his first two ballets, *L'orphelin de la Chine* and *Le roi et le fermier*, with catcalls, managed by devious means to make a repeat performance of *Montezuma* impossible and demonstratively applauded a revival of Noverre's *Les Horaces* (10 September 1775). In 1776–9 Angiolini was once more at the Russian court, where his *Thésée et Ariane* was successfully performed in 1776 and *L'orphelin de la Chine* in 1777. From 1779 to 1782 he worked in Milan and Venice. During his last period in St Petersburg (1782–6) he produced choreography for many Italian operas and also staged some of his own works (*Le diable à quatre*, first performed in Milan in 1781). In the 1788–9 season he put on seven of his ballets in Milan, beginning with the *ballo tragico Fedra*, *Lorezzo* and *Divertimento campestre*, all first performed on 26 December 1788. *Amore e Psiche* (April 1789) was his last Milan production. In his last years his intervention as a convinced republican in theatrical political discussion resulted in his imprisonment and exile from Milan (1799–1801).

Angiolini's ambition of achieving unity of choreography and music was realized during his collaboration with Gluck. Later, in St Petersburg and in Italy, he tried to achieve this unity by writing his own music for his scenarios (besides *Le muse protette* and *Le depart d'Enée*, he is known to have composed that of *Les chinois en Europe* and *Divertissements des fêtes de Noël*, both performed at St Petersburg in 1767; *Le préjuge vaincu*, St Petersburg, 1768; *Sémira*, St Petersburg, 1772; *L'orphelin de la Chine* and *Le roi et le fermier*, both Vienna, 1774, and *L'amicizia alla prova*, Milan, 1782). As a dancer and choreographer he was passionately devoted to the goal of the 'azione completa pantomima', the *tragédie en ballet* with all the 'marvellous effects produced by the ancient pantomime'. After having begun, as a pupil of Hilverding, with national, historical and folkloristic ballets, he pursued this ideal uncompromisingly and believed that he had achieved it with *Semiramis* (1765), 'soggetto il più terribile'. After the complete failure of what Engländer called this 'extremist experiment', he proved willing to make concessions (as in the *lieto fine* of his *ballet tragique Iphigénie en Aulide*, 1765), while remaining essentially faithful to the principles of the *ballet d'action*. In comparison with Noverre, the enlightened rationalist and realist, Angiolini can be described as an idealist and uncompromising expressionist, and his work did not achieve the measure of public success that Noverre's did. Nor was he the victor in the infamous controversy, which also had nationalistic overtones. A man of great artistic seriousness and modesty, his attacks on Noverre were primarily the result of his advocacy of Hilverding as 'the true restorer of the art of pantomime'. His own achievements became involved in the dispute more from necessity than from quest for personal gain. There is no doubt that, as Engländer wrote, Angiolini and Noverre 'both developed the idea of the *ballet d'action* more or less simultaneously and independently'. However, Angiolini was clearly the first to put it into practice, since his *Don Juan* (1761), in which he performed the title part (unlike Noverre he was a superb dancer), preceded Noverre's Stuttgart masterpieces. Many 20th-century ballet reformers were influenced by Angiolini, in particular Isadora Duncan, Laban and Fokin.

BIBLIOGRAPHY

R. A. Mooser: *Annales de la musique et des musiciens en Russie*, ii (Geneva, 1951), 133

W. Toscanini: 'Gaspare Angiolini', *Metropolitan Opera News* (1955), April, 8

F. Mariani Borroni: 'Angiolini, Gasparo', *DBI*

R. Engländer: Preface to *C. W. Gluck: Don Juan, Semiramis*, Sämtliche Werke, ii/1 (Kassel, 1966)

L. Tozzi: *Il balletto pantomimo del settecento: Gaspare Angiolini* (L'Aquila, 1972) [with full bibliography and sources]

G. Gruber: 'I balli pantomimici viennesi di Gluck e lo stile drammatico della sua musica', *Chigiana*, xxix–xxx (1972–3), 501

A. Testa: 'Il binomia Gluck–Angiolini e la realizzazione del balletto "Don Juan" ', *Chigiana*, xxix–xxx (1972–3), 535

L. Tozzi: 'La poetica angioliniana del balletto pantomimo nei programmi viennesi', *Chigiana*, xxix–xxx (1972–3), 487

M. Viale Ferrero: 'Appunti di scenografia settecentesca, in margine a rappresentazioni di opere in musica di Gluck e balli di Angiolini', *Chigiana*, xxix–xxx (1972–3), 513

H. Winter: *The Preromantic Ballet* (London, 1975)

G. Croll: 'Glucks Don Juan freigesprochen', *ÖMz*, xxxi (1976), 12

GERHARD CROLL

Angiolini, Pietro (*b* ?Florence, ?1764; *d* after 1830). Italian dancer and choreographer, nephew of Gaspero Angiolini. He made his Venice début as a dancer in 1780, and his Milan début on 29 December 1781 in his uncle's ballet *Alzira, ossia Gli americani*, as leading dancer with the *primi ballerini seri*. In Milan he danced with Carolina Pitrot, whom he later married. He was in London with her in 1782, but then worked mainly in Italy. In 1789 he staged two ballets of his own in Venice, *Alessio ed Eloisa, o sia Il disertore* and *Le due rivali, o sia La prova del vero amore*. In Parma in 1802 he choreographed the ballets in the opera *La Giuletta*; in 1803 he choreographed his ballet *La morte di Attila* at La Fenice, Venice, and in autumn 1803 *Il trionfo di Vitellio Massimo* in Milan. From spring 1805 to autumn 1806 he again worked as a choreographer in Milan (by then he was no longer dancing), first with new productions of Noverre's *Adele di Ponthieu* and Gaspero Angiolini's *Solimano II*, then with two ballets of his own, *Upsaldo e Valwane* and *Achille in Sciro*. After leaving Milan he choreographed a production of *Il trionfo di Vitellio Massimo* in Venice, his *ballo mitologico Ercole ed Acheloo* in Padua in summer 1807 and *Il trionfo di Vitellio Massimo* in Vienna in 1808. After autumn 1810 he worked occasionally in Milan, his last known visit being for the première of his *La fedeltà combattuta* (7 October 1826). It is doubtful whether he was involved in the production of his *Hamlet* in Milan in 1833.

Pietro's brothers Niccolò [Nicola] (1765–1815) and Pasquale (1766–1817) were also dancers, in the grotesque genre, and choreographers. Giuseppa Angiolini, a prima ballerina of the Accademia dei Reali Teatri in Milan from 1815 to 1824, was probably a daughter of Pietro Angiolini, but the relationship to the family of Silcia [Silvia] Angiolini, a *ballerina di mezzo carattere* in Milan between 1830 and 1840, is unknown. The composer Giovanni Federigo Angiolini (*b* Siena, ?c1760; *d* ?Brunswick, after 1812), who worked in Germany from 1784 and was in St Petersburg about 1791, was probably not a member of this family.

GERHARD CROLL

Angklung. Onomatopoeic name of an Indonesian folk music instrument consisting of a set of three carved bamboo tubes, carefully tuned in octaves, rattled to and fro in a frame. An *angklung* player cannot handle more than one or two *angklung*, so in order to produce a melody an interlocking hocket method of playing is applied by a group of players.

See also INDONESIA, §V, 3(ii), §VI, 1(ii) and figs. 7*b*, 21, 24.

ERNST HEINS

Anglaise [anglois, angloise] (Fr.: 'English'). 18th-century term used on the Continent to refer to various types of English dance, primarily the ever-popular country dances, but occasionally also the hornpipe. Country dances were a recreational activity in the French court of Louis XIV as early as the 1680s, but they were soon altered to conform to French taste by the use of characteristic French steps such as the *pas de bourrée* and the *contretemps de gavotte*; the resulting hybrid was called CONTREDANSE. In 1699 Ballard published *Suite de danses . . . qui se joüent ordinairement aux bals chez le Roy* which contained 17 'contredanses anglaises'.

Pieces entitled 'anglaise' are generally in a style reminiscent of the music accompanying country dance: they may be in duple or triple metre or in 6/8, and they have an obvious accent on the first of the bar; the melodies are lively, often covering a wide range and with some disjunct motion. Examples of the stylized anglaise may be found in J. S. Bach's French Suite no.3, J. C. F. Fischer's *Musicalischer Parnassus* (where they are called 'balet anglois' or 'air angloise'), and Telemann's Ouverture in F♯ minor for strings and basso continuo (Musikalische Werke, x, Kassel and Basle, 1955). All of these pieces are in duple metre with no upbeat and in a bipartite form consisting of two strains, each of which is repeated.

German theorists who described the anglaise include J. Mattheson, who applied the term to English ballads and hornpipes as well as country dances (*Der vollkommene Capellmeister*, 1739), D. G. Türk (*Clavierschule*, 1789) and H. C. Koch (*Lexikon*, 1802). The anglaise was popular until the late 18th century; an example may be found in the third movement of the string quartet by E. B. J. Barrière, op.3 no.2, 1778.

BIBLIOGRAPHY
C. Sachs: *Eine Weltgeschichte des Tanzes* (Berlin, 1933; Eng. trans., 1938/*R*1963)
J.-M. Guilcher: *La contredanse et les renouvellements de la danse française* (Paris, 1969)

MEREDITH ELLIS LITTLE

Anglebert, Jean-Baptiste-Henri d'. French musician, son of JEAN-HENRI D'ANGLEBERT.

Anglebert, Jean-Henri d'. *See* D'ANGLEBERT, JEAN-HENRI.

Angleria, Camillo (*b* Cremona; *d* 1630). Italian theorist. He was a monk of the third order of Franciscans and studied composition with Claudio Merulo. According to Lucchini (p.19) he was *maestro di cappella* at the Florentine court in 1622, but this cannot have been so (Marco da Gagliano held the post at that time). He published *Regole del contrapunto, e della compositione* (Milan, 1622). In this treatise he was primarily concerned with strict counterpoint and appears as one of the closer adherents of Zarlino, together with Girolamo Diruta, Cerone, Artusi and Zacconi. He defended the *seconda prattica* as the outcome of the *prima prattica*, taking the mathematically established intervals from the speculative theory of harmony as the foundation of his theory of counterpoint. Like the majority of his contemporaries he did not follow up the ideas that the revelation of the dual nature of harmony suggested to Zarlino, and he did not free himself from the modality of the *prima prattica*. He discussed – with continual references to Merulo – intervals, keys, imitation and composition in two and more parts, including double counterpoint. The volume includes as practical illustrations two of his own ricercares and some canons and a ricercare by his friend Giovanni Paolo Cima.

BIBLIOGRAPHY
L. Lucchini: *Cenni storice sui più celebri musicisti cremonesi* (Casalmaggiore, 1887)
G. Gaspari: *Catalogo della Biblioteca del Liceo Musicale di Bologna*, i (Bologna, 1890/*R*1961)
R. Monterosso: *Musicisti cremonesi* (Cremona, 1951)
J. Hein: *Die Kontrapunktlehre bei den Musiktheoretikern im 17 Jahrhundert* (diss., U. of Cologne, 1954)
J.-H. Lederer: *Lorenzo Penna und seine Kontrapunkttheorie* (diss., U. of Graz, 1970)

JOSEF-HORST LEDERER

Anglès, Higini [Anglés, Higinio] (*b* Maspujols, nr. Tarragona, 1 Jan 1888; *d* Rome, 8 Dec 1969). Catalan priest and musicologist. From 1900 to 1912 he studied philosophy and theology at the Seminario de Tarragona and was ordained in 1912. In 1913 he settled in Barcelona, where he studied harmony with José Cogul, harmony, counterpoint, fugue and organ with Vicente de Gibert, composition and folksong with José Barberá, and musical history and musicology with Felipe Pedrell. In 1917 he was appointed director of the music section of the Biblioteca de Catalunya (now the Biblioteca Central) in Barcelona. From 1923 to 1924 he studied with Willibald Gurlitt in Freiburg and with Friedrich Ludwig in Göttingen. In 1927 he was appointed professor at the Conservatorio del Liceo in Barcelona, and in 1933 at the university. As a result of the Spanish Civil War he lived in Munich from 1936 to 1939. In 1941 he became a member of the Instituto d'Etudis Catalans in Barcelona and in 1943 the first director of the Instituto Español de Musicología. At the same time he was elected a member of the Real Academia de Bellas Artes de S Fernando in Madrid. In 1947 he moved to Rome to become president of the Pontificio Istituto di Musica Sacra. He was created Protonotario Apostolico by Pope Pius XII in 1958. Among the other honours he received were the Gran Cruz de Isabella Católica in 1958 and the Grosse Verdienstkreuz des Verdienstordens der Bundesrepublik Deutschland in 1960. He was a vice-president of the IMS from 1933 to 1958.

In his youth Anglès collected more than 3000 folksongs in the Pyrenees and other parts of Catalonia; but his career was devoted to the study and publication of music transmitted in writing. At the age of 33 he founded the Publicaciones del Departamento de Música de la Biblioteca de Catalunya, and followed this in 1941 by inaugurating the Monumentos de la Música Española, published from 1943 onwards by the Instituto Español de Musicología (the first volume was issued by the Instituto Diego de Velazquez). He not only directed both these series but himself contributed many of the volumes. The Catalan series is notable for his publication, in facsimile and transcription, of the 13th-century Las Huelgas Manuscript and for his edition, also in facsimile and transcription, of the cantigas of Alfonso el Sabio. In both cases detailed commentary was supplied. This was characteristic of all Anglès's publications: his commentaries were not confined to the music he was editing but ranged widely over the period as a whole. His meticulous care for detail and his encyclopedic knowledge of medieval music made him an ideal editor: it was choice, not a lack of experience, that made him confine his attention to the music of his own country. His interests extended also to the instrumental music of the 17th and 18th centuries. An important development of MME was the decision to include the complete works of Morales (beginning in 1952), Guerrero and Victoria. The editing of Morales and Victoria was undertaken by Anglès himself. Another of his activities was the publication of the *Anuario musical*, which first appeared in 1946.

Anglès enjoyed an international reputation as a scholar. His capacity for work was prodigious, and his readiness to contribute to Festschriften almost legendary. He was a familiar figure at international congresses, where his colleagues appreciated not only his scholarship but his natural simplicity and sense of humour. As director of the Pontificio Istituto in Rome

he believed strongly in the traditional Latin rite of the church and was firmly opposed to any change.

EDITIONS

Publicaciones del departamento de música de la Biblioteca de Catalunya (Barcelona):

i. *Els madrigals i la missa de difunts d'en Brudieu* (with F. Pedrell, 1921)
ii. *Catàleg dels manuscrits musicals de la Collecció Pedrell* (1921)
iii, vii. *J. Pujol: Opera omnia* (1927–32)
iv, viii, xiii, xvii. *J. Cabanilles: Opera omnia* (1927–56)
vi. *El códex musical de Las Huelgas* (1931/R1977)
ix. *A. Soler: Sis quintets per a instruments d'arc i orgue o clave obligat* (with R. Gerhard, 1933)
x. *La música a Catalunya fins al segle XIII* (1935)
xv, xviii, xix. *La música de las cantigas de Santa Maria del Rey Alfonso el Sabio* (1943–64)
xvi. *M. Flecha: Las ensaladas* (1955)

Monumentos de la música española:

i, v, x. *La música en la corte de los Reyes Católicos* (1941–51)
ii. *La música en la corte de Carlos V* (1944, 2/1965)
iv. *Recopilación de sonetos y villancicos a quatro y a cinco de Juan Vásquez* (1946)
xi, xiii, xv, xvii, xx, xxi, xxiv, xxxiii. *C. de Morales: Opera omnia* (1952–69)
xxv, xxvi, xxx, xxxi. *T. L. de Victoria: Opera omnia* (1965–9)
xxvii–xxix. *A. de Cabezón: Obras de música para tecla, arpa y vihuela* (1966)

Las canciones del Rey Teobaldo (Pamplona, 1973) [pubd posth.]

WRITINGS

Complete list of articles up to 1961 in *Miscelánea en homenaje a Monseñor Higinio Anglès* (Barcelona, 1958–61)

'La musique aux Xe et XIe siècles: l'école de Ripoll', *La Catalogne à l'époque romane* (Paris, 1932), 157
'Historia de la música española', in J. Wolf: *Historia de la música* (Sp. trans., Barcelona, 1934, 4/1957), 331–437
La música española desde la Edad Media hasta nuestros días (Barcelona, 1941)
with J. Subirá: *Catálogo musical de la Biblioteca nacional de Madrid* (Barcelona, 1946–51)
ed.: *Congresso internazionale di musica sacra: Roma 1950*
ed.: *Diccionario de la música Labor* (Barcelona, 1954)
'Latin Chant before St. Gregory', 'Gregorian Chant', *Ars Nova and the Renaissance*, NOHM, ii (1954), 58–127
L'opera di Morales e lo sviluppo della polifonia sacra spagnola nel 1500 (Rome, 1954)
Studia musicologica (Rome, 1959)
'Die Bedeutung der Plika in der mittelalterlichen Musik', *Festschrift Karl Gustav Fellerer* (Regensburg, 1962), 28
'Die Instrumentalmusik bis zum 16. Jahrhundert in Spanien', *Natalicia musicologica Knud Jeppesen* (Copenhagen, 1962), 143
'Mateo Flecha el Joven', *SM*, iii (1962), 45
'Musikalische Beziehungen zwischen Österreich und Spanien in der Zeit vom 14. bis 18. Jahrhundert', *SMw*, xxv (1962), 5
'Der sakrale Charakter der Kirchenmusik von Cristóbal de Morales', *Musicus–Magister: Festgabe für Theobald Schrems* (Regensburg, 1963), 110
'El canto religioso popular en los manuales litúrgicos de la Tarraconense', *AnM*, xviii (1963), 103
'Un tractat de cant plà d'autor anònim del segle XVI', *Joseph Vives zum goldenen Priesterjubiläum* (Münster, 1963), 277
'Alfonso V d'Aragona mecenate della música ed il suo ménestrel Jean Boisard', *Liber amicorum Charles van den Borren* (Antwerp, 1964), 6
'Problemas que plantea el canto gregoriano en su historia y en su valor oracional y artístico musical', *AnM*, xix (1964), 13
'Die volkstümlichen Melodien bei den Trouvères', *Zum 70. Geburtstag von Joseph Müller-Blattau* (Kassel, 1966), 11
'Early Spanish Musical Culture and Cardinal Cisneros's Hymnal of 1515', *Aspects of Medieval and Renaissance Music: a Birthday Offering to Gustave Reese* (New York, 1966), 3
'Relations épistolaires entre César Cui et Philippe Pedrell', *FAM*, xiii (1966), 15
'Sakraler Gesang und Musik in den Schriften Gregors des Grossen', *Essays Presented to Egon Wellesz* (Oxford, 1966), 33
'Der musikalische Austausch Österreich und Spanien im 16. Jahrhundert', *Festschrift 1817–1967 Akademie für Musik und darstellende Kunst in Wien* (Vienna, 1967), 15
'Die volkstümlichen Melodien in den mittelalterlichen Sequenzen', *Festschrift für Walter Wiora* (Kassel, 1967), 214
'Latin Church Music on the Continent – 3: Spain and Portugal', *The Age of Humanism 1540–1600*, NOHM, iv (1968), 372–418
'Problemas que presenta la nueva edición de las obras de Morales y de Victoria', *Renaissance-muziek 1400–1600: donum natalicium René Bernard Lenaerts* (Louvain, 1969), 21

'Eine Sequenzensammlung mit Mensuralnotation und volkstümlichen Melodien (Paris, B.N.Lat.1343)', *Speculum musicae artis: Festgabe für Heinrich Hausmann* (Munich, 1970), 9
'Die cantigas de Santa Maria König Alfons' des Weisen', *Gattungen der Musik in Einzeldarstellungen: Gedenkschrift für Leo Schrade*, i (Berne and Munich, 1973), 346

BIBLIOGRAPHY
70th birthday tributes: H. Hucke, *Musik und Altar*, x (1957–8), 97; C. van den Borren, *AcM*, xxx (1958), 1; H. Lemacher, *Musica sacra*, lxxviii (1958), 147
Miscelánea en homenaje a Monseñor Higinio Anglés (Barcelona, 1958–61) [with list of writings to 1961 and bibliography]
'Lettere "Jucunda laudatio" de S. S. Jean XXIII à Mgr. H. Anglés', *Etudes grégoriennes*, v (1962), 7
Obituary: *AcM*, xxiv (1969), 1 [with bibliography]; G. Bourligueux, *Bulletin hispanique*, lxxii (1970), 530; G. Bourligueux, *L'orgue*, no.136 (1970), 206; G. Bourligueux, *Musique sacrée*, no.130 (1971), 5; K. G. Fellerer, *Mf*, xxiii (1970), 125; R. Stevenson, *JAMS*, xxiii (1970), 541; R. Stevenson, *Revista musical chilena* (1970), no.112, p.6
J. López-Calo, ed.: *Scripta musicologica* (Rome, 1975–6) [vol.i incl. bibliography of writings]

JACK WESTRUP

Anglés, Rafael (*b* Rafalés, Aragon, 1730; *d* Valencia, 9 Feb 1816). Spanish organist and composer. While serving as *maestro de capilla* at the collegiate church of Alcañiz, near Saragossa, he competed in 1761 for the position of organist at Valencia Cathedral in succession to Vicente Rodríguez. He was narrowly defeated by Manuel Narro, though his playing was judged superior 'en el estilo moderno', but Narro remained only briefly and Anglés received the appointment 1 February 1762, retaining it until his death. Chapter records show that he also serviced and tuned the cathedral organ, served as professor (*catedrático*) of plainsong, and was active in adjudicating competitions for other musical posts in the cathedral; the choice of José Pons as *maestro de capilla* in 1793 seems to have been his.

Works credited by earlier authorities to Anglés (supposedly in the Barcelona Biblioteca Central and Orihuela Cathedral) apparently do not exist; the latter contains one eight-part villancico, *Brillantes luceros*. On the other hand, Valladolid Cathedral possesses an MS of his *pasos* and sonatas for organ or piano (see *AnM*, iii, 1948). Joaquín Nin published four pieces from an MS in the possession of José Iturbi in *Classiques espagnols du piano*, ii (Paris, 1928). On the evidence of these his music was dominated by Haydn's style; even the Fugatto is homophonic and pianistic in character, more scherzo than fugue. The intense Aria in D minor, however, with an embellished, spun-out melody over a steadily moving bass, suggests a late manifestation of the Baroque style. José Climent published an edition of two sonatas (Madrid, 1970).

BIBLIOGRAPHY
F. de Latassa y Ortín: *Biblioteca nueva de los escritores aragoneses* (Pamplona, 1798–1802), v, 315
F. Pedrell: *Diccionario biográfico-bibliográfico de músicos y escritores de música españoles* (Barcelona, 1897).
H. Anglés: 'El archivio musical de la Catedral de Valladolid', *AnM*, iii (1948), 59–108
J. Piedra and J. Climent: 'Organistas valencianos de los siglos XVII y XVIII', *AnM*, xvii (1962), 141–208

ALMONTE HOWELL

Anglesi, Domenico (*b* ? between *c*1610 and 1615; *d* after 28 Aug 1669). Italian composer and instrumentalist. He became an instrumentalist and composer to the Grand Duke of Tuscany at Florence on 16 March 1638. For several years he was also in the household (as *aiutante da camera*) of Cardinal Giovan Carlo de' Medici; a letter that the cardinal sent to Prince Mattias

de' Medici on 7 May 1647 (*I-Fas* Medicei, Prince Mattias 5438) shows that he had then entered the prince's service, perhaps only temporarily. He is mentioned by Atto Melani in two letters to Prince Mattias: in one of 7 September 1653 (ibid, 5414) he is named as one of the musicians who had slandered Melani on his recent arrival at the court at Innsbruck; in the other, dated 27 September 1654 (cited in Ademollo, 1884, p.70, n.1), Melani drew attention to his contrary opinion of Act 1 of Cavalli's *Ipermestra*. He is last heard of in Medici documents on 4 January 1666 and 28 August 1669. According to another letter to Prince Mattias, from Lorenzo Guicciardini on 3 September 1641 (ibid, 5407), he wrote the music for a cocchiata given at Florence a few evenings previously. The music is lost, as is that of three later dramatic works by him: *Alidoro il costante* (text by Antonio Malatesti, in *I-Fn* Magl.VII.359, pp.584ff), a dramatic cantata commissioned by Cardinal Giovan Carlo for performance on 8 August 1650; the comic opera *La serva nobile* (G. A. Moniglia; Florence, Teatro della Pergola, 1660, staged by the Accademia degli Immobili, whose patron was Cardinal Giovan Carlo); and *Il mondo festeggiante* (Florence, Palazzo Pitti, 1661), an equestrian ballet performed as part of the festivities celebrating the wedding of the future Grand Duke Cosimo III and Marguerite Louise d'Orléans.

Apart from two isolated pieces attributed to him – a keyboard piece (in *F-Pn*) and a solo song, *Occhi belli* (in *A-Wn* 17762) – no music by Anglesi survives except his *Arie* (Florence, 1635), for solo voice and continuo; this appears to be a matter for regret, since the book is one of the finest Italian song collections of its time. It consists mainly of 22 strophic arias; the other four items are two sectional songs midway between strophic arias and strophic variations, an extravagantly embellished sonnet setting similar in form and in the then rare key of E minor, and a long recitative with aria-like intrusions. Most of the songs are named after people prominent in Florentine society or arts. For example, the opening 'Aria detta La Salviata' no doubt refers to the volume's dedicatee, Duke Salviati; 'La Saracinella' probably denotes Ferdinando Saracinelli. 'La Niccolina' and 'Il Nero' (the recitative) possibly indicate connections with the dedicatee and compiler (or at least with members of their families) of an interesting Florentine song manuscript of the period (*I-Bc* Q49): certainly the style of many of the arias is reminiscent of those of Settimia Caccini, her husband Alessandro Ghivizzani and other composers represented in that manuscript and in a related one also of Florentine provenance (formerly at Roudnice, now in *CS-Pnm*; see Fortune, 1951). Anglesi's arias are notable for their spaciousness, long-breathed melodies and clearcut tonalities, which include such unusual keys as E major, for *Sott'aspetto ridente*, and F minor, for *E bella colei* ('La Saracinella'; in Racek, 249f, rather inaccurately). The latter is an admirable example of Anglesi's more pathetic vein, and the fine *La mia ninfa amore* ('La Salviata'; in Fortune, 1954, appx iv, 23ff) typifies his more forthright manner, though here too there are darker moments that anticipate so-called Neapolitan progressions in music of the next 100 years or so. Several songs include effective juxtapositions of duple and triple time and a close integration of vocal line and bass that gives them a strong momentum. *La mia ninfa* illustrates this last quality and also another important feature of Anglesi's songs – the expansive treatment of the last few lines of a verse as a refrain in a manner similar to that previously found in songs by G. P. Berti and only one or two other composers. Anglesi deserves to rank alongside Berti as one of the most progressive and rewarding Italian songwriters of the period.

BIBLIOGRAPHY

EitnerQ
Letters and other documents (*I-Fas* Guardaroba Mediceo 664; Prince Mattias 5407, 5414, 5438)
A. Ademollo: *I primi fasti della musica italiana a Parigi* (Milan, 1884), 70
——: *I primi fasti del Teatro di Via della Pergola in Firenze (1657–1661)* (Milan, 1885), 14
E. Vogel: 'Marco da Gagliano: zur Geschichte des florentiner Musiklebens von 1570–1650', *VMw*, v (1889), 544
R. Gandolfi: 'La cappella musicale della corte di Toscana (1539–1859)', *RMI*, xvi (1909), 511
N. Fortune: 'A Florentine Manuscript and its Place in Italian Song', *AcM*, xxiii (1951), 124
——: *Italian Secular Song from 1600 to 1635: the Origins and Development of Accompanied Monody* (diss., U. of Cambridge, 1954), 422ff; appx iv, 23ff
R. L. Weaver: *Florentine Comic Operas of the Seventeenth Century* (diss., U. of North Carolina, 1958), 62ff
J. Racek: *Stilprobleme der italienischen Monodie* (Prague, 1965), 12, 98, 189f, 205, 249f
R. L. Weaver: 'Opera in Florence: 1646–1731', *Studies in Musicology: Essays in Memory of Glen Haydon* (Chapel Hill, 1969), 69
F. Hammond: 'Musicians at the Medici Court in the Mid-seventeenth Century', *AnMc*, no.14 (1974), 158, 163

NIGEL FORTUNE

Anglia, Galfridus de. *See* GALFRIDUS DE ANGLIA.

Anglia, Robertus de. *See* ROBERTUS DE ANGLIA.

Anglican chant. Harmonized formulae used for the singing of psalms and canticles in the liturgy of the Church of England. A single chant (ex.1) comprises two sec-

Ex.1 Tallis

tions, paralleling the bipartite psalm or canticle verse to which it is sung; the initial chord in each half is the 'reciting' chord to which a substantial part of the verse section is freely sung. The first half of the chant is concluded by a progression of between three and five chords, the second half by a progression of between five and nine chords. These are invariably measured out in semibreve, minim and crotchet values, the first comprising three bars, the second, four. Double chants repeat the single chant formula once, and quadruple chants repeat it three times, being sung to two and four psalm or canticle verses respectively (triple chants are occasionally used). There are many ways of 'pointing' or fitting the words to these chants, and various systems of symbols are used to indicate how this may be done; in the following examples the barring is equivalent to the barring of the chant:

Oxford Psalter:
Glory / be. to the / Father: and to the Son, / and. to the / Ho-ly / Ghost;
As it was in the beginning,* is now, and / ever. shall / be:
World without / end, A / -/ men.

Revised Psalter:
Glory be to the Father, and / to the / Son: and / to the Holy / Ghost;
As it was in the beginning, is now and / ever / shall be: world without / end. / A- / men.

The pointed psalters that are most commonly used are the *Parish Psalter*, the *Oxford Psalter* and the *New Cathedral Psalter*. Congregational chanting is attempted in many churches from the unpointed texts of the *Book of Common Prayer*, but pointed psalters are essential if a satisfactory standard is to be achieved.

Anglican chant can be traced back to the pre-Reformation psalm-tone system and is obviously related to the continental FALSOBORDONE. The earliest sources of harmonized chant are Thomas Morley's *A Plaine and Easie Introduction* (1597), manuscript 34 from the first 'Caroline' set of partbooks at Peterhouse (*c*1635) and three early Restoration books: Edward Lowe's *A Short Direction for the Performance of Cathedral Service* (1661), James Clifford's *Divine Services and Anthems* (1664) and John Playford's *Introduction to the Skill of Music* (1673, many reprints to 1730). To these must be added various sets of *psalmi festivales* by some 20 composers dating from about 1550 to about 1640, published in John Barnard's *The First Book of Selected Church Musick* (1641).

In his *Booke of Common Praier Noted* (1550) Merbecke did no more than provide examples of the way in which the psalms and canticles could be sung to the Gregorian psalm tones: he used the 8th Gregorian tone, mostly without the intonation and with two variant endings, for seven psalms and canticles; the 5th tone occurs twice, while the 1st, 4th, 7th tones and *tonus peregrinus* are each used only once. The fact that Merbecke did not set out more fully and systematically the system of eight tones indicates that choirs were conversant with it and had no difficulties in adapting it to English use. Morley went one stage further in supplying simple harmonizations to the eight tones, though he gave no examples of how these might be fitted to words. The first evidence that choirs were actually singing the plainsongs in harmonized versions is to be found in the Caroline Peterhouse books, in which two voice parts from a set of chants that were probably for three or four voices are scribbled out on a single page; no words are supplied but the rhythms fit the opening verse of the *Venite*.

The three Restoration sources – Lowe, Clifford and Playford – provide a comprehensive guide to the use of the tones, as might be expected after a break in the tradition of some 15 years. All eight tones are printed, together with the Benedicite chant (described as 'from the Sarum Breviary'). What is more, harmonizations of four chants are provided: 'Adrian Batten's tune' (1st tone), 'Christ Church tune' (a different harmonization of the 1st tone), Dr Child's harmonization of the 8th, known as the 'Imperial tune', and a chant called 'Canterbury tune', which after the Restoration was commonly attributed to Byrd and attached to his third set of Preces.

In pre-Restoration times the psalms would normally have been sung at Matins and Evensong to Gregorian tones, either simply harmonized in the manner of Batten's tune, or monodically; but special settings of the psalms would have been sung on festal occasions. Many sets of pre-Restoration festal psalms are extant. The earliest are by Tallis for the Evensongs of 24, 25 and 26 December: those for Christmas Day (only the bass part of the others survives) are fairly simple harmonizations of the 1st and 7th, not far removed from the Batten tune in style but with the underlay of each verse carefully set out in measured notes. No doubt the simpler festal psalms of this kind provided the model for the later Anglican chant.

After the Restoration the Gregorian basis of chanting gradually disappeared and cantus firmus settings of the psalm tones were replaced by settings with the main melody in the top voice. It seems likely that during the late 17th and early 18th centuries each choir built up its own repertory of chants, much on the lines of those in Aldrich's collection (*GB-Och* 48). According to Rimbault the first printed collection of Anglican chants dates from about 1750: the *Fifty Double and Single Chants, being the Most Favourite, as performed at St. Paul's, Westminster and Most of the Cathedrals in England*. One of the first published collections to assign each psalm to a specific chant, and thus to show a particular interest in the expressive potential of the chant, was Dr Beckwith, whose *The First Verse of Every Psalm of David, with an Ancient or Modern Chant in Score* came out in 1808. Beckwith also called for a system of marking the psalm verses so that ordinary choirs would know which words were to be recited and which inflected. The first system of 'pointing' to appear in print, however, was that of Robert Janes, organist of Ely Cathedral, whose *The Psalter or Psalms of David* (1837) was

Carefully marked and Pointed to enable the Voices of a Choir to keep exactly together by singing the same Syllables to the same Note; and the accents as far as possible made to agree with the accents in the Chant; and also to remove the difficulty which individuals generally find who are not accustomed to the Chanting of the Psalms.

These publications marked the beginning of a flood of 19th-century chant books. Rimbault, deploring the tendency to increasingly 'pretentious' chants (like ex.2) edited a collection of cathedral chants (1844); the

Ex.2 J. S. Smith

earliest composers are Tallis, Byrd, Richard Farrant, Morley, John Farrant and Child, some of whose chants prove to be adaptations (and thus immense simplifications) of early festal psalm settings. Restoration composers are well represented, though without further research it is impossible to determine the extent to which their chants are original. Recently there has been a move towards simplicity again, and the Gregorian tones have been found to provide a refreshing alternative to the essentially 19th-century repertory of Anglican chants.

BIBLIOGRAPHY

T. G. Ackland: *Chanting Simplified* (London, 1843)

E. F. Rimbault: *Cathedral Chants of the XVI, XVII and XVIII Centuries* (London, 1844)

H. B. Briggs, ed.: *The Elements of Plainsong*, Plainsong and Mediaeval Music Society (London, 1895)

P. Scholes: 'Anglican Chant', *The Oxford Companion to Music* (London, 1938, 10/1970 by J. O. Ward)

J. E. Hunt, ed.: *Cranmer's First Litany and Merbecke's Book of Common Prayer Noted* (London, 1939)

K. L. Jennings: *English Festal Psalms of the 16th and 17th Centuries* (diss., U. of Illinois, 1966)

L. Ellinwood: 'From Plainsong to Anglican Chant', *Cantors at the Crossroads: Essays on Church Music in Honor of Walter E. Buszin* (St Louis, 1967), 21

P. G. le Huray: *Music and the Reformation in England, 1549–1660* (London, 1967)

L. Ellinwood: 'Anglican Chant', *Harvard Dictionary of Music*, ed. W. Apel (Cambridge, Mass., rev. 2/1969)

R. T. Daniel and P. G. le Huray: *The Sources of English Church Music, 1549–1660*, EECM, suppl.i (1972)

PETER LE HURAY

Angloise. See ANGLAISE.

Anglo-Soviet Press. Publishing firm run by ALFRED KALMUS.

Angola. State in southern Africa. It is one of few with available and detailed written data on music, ranging from the 16th century to the 20th. Numerous historical sources in Portuguese, Italian, Dutch, English and other languages contain material on Angolan music. The earliest refer to the kingdom of Kongo, which was situated in present-day northern Angola. A smaller state south of the kingdom of Kongo was formed by the (Ki-)Mbundu people. The Portuguese adopted the name of the (Ki-)Mbundu ruler, Ngola, and applied it to the territory which came under their influence and which is now called Angola (see map, fig.1). The earliest specific sources on music are de Pina and de Barros. De Pina reported that *trombetas de marfim* (ivory trumpets) were among the instruments played at the reception of a Portuguese delegation by the Kongo king in 1491. Lopes, who travelled to Luanda in 1578, described military music among the Kongo and (Ki-)Mbundu people. Da Roma, an Italian missionary, was the first author to describe xylophones in Angola in 1648 and also gave an interesting account of musical acculturation in the Kongo kingdom at that time. Cavazzi, a Capuchin monk who went as a missionary in 1654 from Genoa to Angola, described and illustrated Kongo music including musical practices and instruments such as the MARIMBA (xylophone) (*see* LAMELLAPHONE) and

1. *Map of Angola showing the distribution of its principal peoples*

the *nsambi* (pluriarc). Perhaps the most important among the early sources is Merolla, a Capuchin monk and missionary from Sorrento, who reached Luanda in 1683 and travelled widely in Angola. His book (1692) contains a beautiful illustration of instruments played in the Kongo/(Ki-)Mbundu region at that time (see fig.2) and also records their indigenous names. Hirschberg's translation (1969) of Merolla states:

One of the most common instruments is the *marimba*. Sixteen cala-bashes act as resonators and are supported lengthwise by two bars. Above the calabashes little boards of red wood, somewhat longer than a span, are placed, called *taculla*. The instrument is hung round the neck and the boards are beaten with small sticks. Mostly four *marimbas* are played together; if six want to play, the *cassuto* is added – a hollow piece of wood four spans long, with ridges in it. The bass of this orchestra is the *quilondo*, a roomy big-bellied instrument two and a half to three spans in height which looks like a bottle towards the end and is rubbed in the same way as the *cassuto*. When all the instruments are played together, a truly harmonic effect is produced from a distance . . . .

The *nsambi* is the name reported by Merolla for a five-string pluriarc, still an important instrument in the western half of Angola, which occurs throughout the area culturally influenced by the Kongo/(Ki-)Mbundu cluster. Among the Humbi and Handa in south-western Angola it usually has eight strings and is played by one musician with the string-bearers away from his body while another musician sings (fig.3). It has spread from south-western Angola further south as far as the Kalahari desert in Botswana. Some of the earliest reports on Angola described the double bell as a war instrument, and Merolla recorded the name *longa* in his

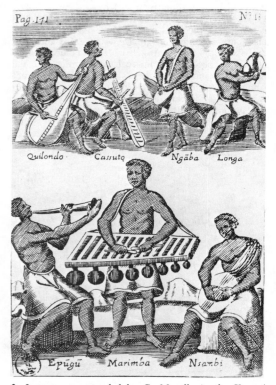

2. *Instruments recorded by G. Merolla in the Kongo/ (Ki-)Mbundu region of Angola between 1683 and 1688: woodcut from his 'Breve e succinta relatione del viaggio nel Regno di Congo nell'Africa Meridionale' (1692)*

illustration (see fig.2). With the 19th-century expansion of Portuguese influence from the coast towards the interior more historical reports became available, many of them dealing with the Lunda/Cokwe/Nkangala region in the east.

Angola can be divided into four main musical areas: the Kongo/Luanda coast, south-western Angola, eastern Angola and the Kung area. These areas are not always sharply delineated and are often separated by extensive buffer or transition zones. One such zone appears to be the country of the Ovi-Mbundu called Viye, or Bié, between the Kongo/Luanda coastal area and eastern Angola.

1. The Kongo/Luanda coast. 2. South-western Angola. 3. Eastern Angola. 4. The Kung area. 5. Influences and recent developments.

1. THE KONGO/LUANDA COAST. Music in this area is determined to a great extent by two historical circumstances: the influence of the Kongo and Ngola states on musical practice in the form of court and military music with iron bells and drums; and the impact of Portuguese cultural influence particularly in the 16th and 17th centuries. Da Roma reported in 1648 that musicians in the Kongo kingdom played military drums 'imported by the Portuguese' very skilfully. At about the same time side-blown ivory horns used in court ceremonial had been modified under Portuguese influence to become end-blown trumpets with wooden mouthpieces. These trumpets were played in church in the presence of the king. Musicians seem to have reverted to the side-blown variety, though end-blown horns do occur far from the old Kongo kingdom. Among the Mbwela and Nkangala of south-eastern Angola they are known as *vandumbu* and are regarded as secret instruments. They are associated with the dead kings, and the secrets of their manufacture and preservation are known only by those who have passed an initiation ceremony. Early Portuguese influence is also discernible in the presence of bowed violins with three strings along the Luanda coast. The Portuguese term is *viola*, and in Angola they are played in two- and three-part harmony by celebrated musicians who often sing with a head voice. In the Luanda region the *viola* is often accompanied by a long vertical scraper of the type known in Portugal as the *reque-reque*. Other instruments traditionally popular in this area are the slit-drum, various large skin drums, lamellaphones called *chisanje*, musical bows with gourd resonators, the pluriarc and the friction drum.

2. SOUTH-WESTERN ANGOLA. The music of the Nyaneka, the Ambo and the Herero in south-western Angola is distinguished stylistically from that of the rest of Angola, and sometimes shows a remarkable similarity to music in the areas of Rwanda, Burundi, south-western Uganda and central and western Tanzania, which are dominated by the Hima and the Tutsi. This is particularly evident in the music of the Herero, but it is also evident, for instance, in the Humbi men's dance known as the *chitita* and the Kuvale men's dance called the *lundongo*. A further characteristic of this area is the high degree of diversity in the music. Several types of partsinging co-exist in a single village; songs for the eight-string pluriarc, the *chihumba* (see fig.3), are usually hexatonic and sung in parallel 3rds, while dance-songs such as the *chitita* have a pentatonic structure; similarly many songs used in the boys' circumcision schools of the Handa are pentatonic with harmonies mainly in 4ths.

The musical instruments of this area are predominantly chordophones and membranophones. Besides the universally popular pluriarc, several types of musical bow occur: the *mbulumbumba*, with gourd resonator; the *sagaia*, a braced mouth bow with the string-bearer held between the teeth; and the *ohonji*, a braced mouth bow with the end of the string-bearer held in the mouth against the right inner cheek. Other important instruments are the drums *ng'oma*, *chikenjenjo*, and the *pwita*, a friction drum. Some of the principal dances in south-western Angola, accompanied by drums or by hand-clapping, are the *nkili*, the *mbanda*, the *vinjomba*, the *machikuma*, the *mbulunganga* and the *kaunjangera*.

3. EASTERN ANGOLA. The music of the Lunda, the Luvale, the Cokwe and the Nkangala in eastern Angola shares similar characteristics. There is also a close relationship between their languages: Nkangala, Mbwela, Luchazi, Lwimbi and (Ki-)Mbunda are in effect dialects of the same language, and the people share one cultural system. A large area of similar culture in which the people are genetically closely related, stretches from Serpa Pinto through eastern Angola and across the border into the North-western province of Zambia and the border areas of Zaïre. Music and dance in this area are characterized by a number of features. Initiation music and masked dancing are particularly important, the masks being attached to the *mukanda*, the traditional educational institution for male youths. Formal music and dance instruction play a great role in the *mukanda* and provide the young with the basis for all their musical activity in later life. Body movement is organized in relation to a 'time-line' pattern, which is usually struck with a stick on the body of the *chipwali*, a drum, or of the *likembe*, a lamellaphone. A time-line pattern much used by the Luvale (or Lwena) in the north-east is the *kachacha*, shown in ex.1, but it also occurs in Cokwe, Luchazi and Mbwela music.

All singing is in parts and usually three different voices combine in 3rds and 5ths. The musicians' concept is that several voices should sing together in harmony and that there are seven notes within the octave. In practice vocalists aim at producing what Westerners would call major triads even though this conflicts with

3. Humbi singer (left) and chihumba (pluriarc) player in Kalingiri, Dinde/Quilengues region, 1965

the equitonal nature of their heptatonic system. Minor triads are unknown even though full major harmony at all levels is impossible in a heptatonic scale. In performance, therefore, individual singers tend to neutralize some of the notes in certain contexts by slightly sharpened intonation, and in this way a fairly even distribution of approximately major sounds is maintained on all steps of the scale. Thus certain degrees of this near-equitonal heptatonic scale are intoned differently in different contexts. In ex.2, for instance, in which each line of the stave is used to represent a degree of the equitonal scale, the first note of voice *b* is exactly a 5th below the first note of voice *a*. But when voice *a* sings the same note at the end of the line, it is intoned more than a quarter-tone sharp in order to form an approximate major 3rd with voice *b* below it. This gives an elastic quality to the scale, which has often surprised Western observers to whom the same song may sound major on one occasion and minor on another. A further char-

Ex.1 *Kachacha* time-line pattern

⑯ | × • • × • × • × × • × • × • × × • • |

Ex.2 Equitonal partsinging from a *mukanda* school; rec. and transcr. G. Kubik

acteristic of this partsinging is the abundant use of oblique and contrary motion. This results when individual singers temporarily abandon their prescribed line, theoretically parallel to those of other singers, and intrude on a neighbour's line. This freedom is based on the convention that all melodic movement proceeds by step.

4. THE KUNG AREA. Small bands of Kung, a gathering and hunting people, are still found in south-eastern and south-western Angola. The near-genocide of all the Khoisan peoples of southern Angola was a result of pressure from Bantu-speaking groups who entered from the north in the 17th and 18th centuries, and from white Boer immigrants from the south. Though the Kung have established a symbiotic relationship with Bantu agriculturalists, which has also affected their musical culture, the south-eastern Kung, in the Cuando-Cubango district, seem to have retained much of their 'pre-Bantu' music.

Kung music is clearly differentiated from Bantu music, and is characterized by the use of hocket in polyphony; the absence of a solo and chorus division in singing; the prevalence of a tetratonic tonal system derived from the harmonics of musical bows, this system being often extended to a pentatonic one; the relationship of each type of Kung singing to particular scale patterns, a surprising result of recent research among Angolan Kung being that polyphonic singing is mainly tetratonic, while unison singing is usually pentatonic; a preference for melodic movement in disjunct intervals, with frequent leaps of 4ths, 5ths, 7ths and octaves; the importance of yodelling and bird-like sounds; a minimal use of words in songs, sometimes only syllables being used; dance characterized by shaking and shivering movements, and very few musical instruments. The most important instrument is the musical bow. A rarely seen women's instrument, the *bavugu*, is a percussion tube made from three fruit shells of the *Strychnos spinoza* plant stuck one on top of the other with a central hole running their length. It is stamped on the player's thigh.

5. INFLUENCES AND RECENT DEVELOPMENTS. Angolan instruments and dances were exported to Latin America with the deportation of black slaves mainly from south-west and central Angola. Ortiz reported the presence of the *mbulumbumba* musical bow in Cuba under the name *burumbumba*. The Handa *mbulumbumba* bow rhythm, the *chirumba*, is structurally very close to that of the modern Cuban *rumba*. The *pwita* friction drum occurs in Cuba, Brazil and other parts of Latin America and the *kasuto* (or *cassuto*, see fig.2) is found in Cuba. The *chisanje*, a lamellaphone, existed in Brazil in the 19th century under the Portuguese spelling *otchissage* but appears to be extinct.

Recent western musical influence is insignificant in Angola because of the absence of radios and record players in rural areas. There was some influence in the 1960s from Katanga guitar music and from jive from Zambia, this being limited to the north-east near the towns of Teixeira de Sousa on the Zaïrean border and Cazombo. Portuguese, Latin American and Congolese influence is found in Luanda, though to a very limited extent in comparison with other parts of Africa. Modern African music has as yet had little effect on Angola. Thus in south-eastern Angola, near Cuito-Cuanavale, the *likembe* appears to have been introduced only

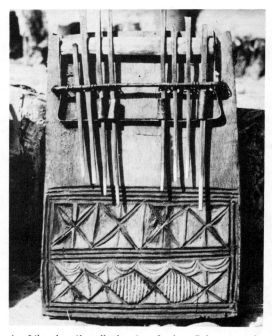

4. *Likembe (lamellaphone) of the Cokwe people, Chisende village, south-east Angola, 1965*

around 1950, whereas it appeared in most parts of Zaïre 50 to 60 years earlier. The *likembe* (see fig.4) in Angola could be called an instrument of the working class. In 1965 it was played mainly by migrant workers, aged between 14 and 25, who sought employment in eastern, south-eastern and central Angola, and at that time it was an instrument used exclusively by the eastern ethnic cluster, by people who spoke and sang in Luchazi, Mbwela, Nkangala, Cokwe or Luvale.

Recordings of Angolan music are held at Museu do Dundo, Companhia de Diamantes de Angola, Dundo, Angola; Instituto de Investigação Cientifica de Angola, Luanda; and the Phonogrammarchiv der Österreichischen Akademie der Wissenschaften, Vienna.

BIBLIOGRAPHY

D. Lopes: *Relatione del reame di Congo et delle circonvicine contrade* (Rome, 1591)
G. Francesco da Roma: *Breve relatione del successo della Missione de Frati Minori Cappucini . . . al regno del Congo* (Rome, 1648)
G. A. Cavazzi: *Istorica descrizione de tre regni Congo, Matamba et Angola* (Bologna, 1687)
G. Merolla: *Breve e succinta relatione del viaggio nel regno di Congo nell'Africa Meridionale* (Naples, 1692; partial Eng. trans. in Hirschberg, 1969)
R. de Pina: *Crónica de El-Rei D. João II* (Lisbon, 1792; Coimbra, 2/1950)
A. de Serpa Pinto: *How I crossed Africa* (London, 1881)
D. de Carvalho: *Expedição portugueza ao Muatiânvua* (Lisbon, 1890)
W. D. Hambly: *The Ovimbundu of Angola* (Chicago, 1934)
F. Ortiz: *Los instrumentos de la música afro-cubana* (Havana, 1952)
C. Estermann: *Etnografia do sudoeste de Angola* (Lisbon, 1957)
E. Veiga de Oliveira: *Instrumentos musicais populares portugueses* (Lisbon, 1966)
W. Hirschberg: 'Early Historical Illustrations of West and Central African Music', *African Music*, iv/3 (1969), 6 [partial trans. of Merolla (1692)]
G. Kubik: 'Masks of the Mbwela', *Geographica*, v/20 (1969), 2
J. Vansina: 'The Bells of Kings', *Journal of African History*, x (1969), 187

W. Hirschberg: 'Beitrag zur Geschichte der Doppelglocke im Kongoraum', *Mitteilungen der Anthropologischen Gesellschaft in Wien*, c (1970), 258

G. Kubik: *Música traditional e aculturada dos Kung de Angola* (Lisbon, 1970)

——: *Die Institution Mukanda und assoziierte Einrichtungen bei den Vambwela/Vankangela und verwandten Ethnien in Südostangola* (diss., U. of Vienna, 1971)

D. Thiermann: 'The Mbira in Brazil', *African Music*, v/l (1971), 90

G. Kubik: 'Oral Notation of some West and Central African Time-line Patterns', *Review of Ethnology*, iii (1972), 169

D. Schüller: *Beziehungen zwischen west- und westzentralafrikanischen Staaten von 1482 bis 1700* (diss., U. of Vienna, 1972)

GERHARD KUBIK

Anguilar, Antonia Maria. *See* GIRELLI, ANTONIA MARIA.

Angus, John (*fl* 1543–95). Scottish composer. Generally described as 'conventuall brether of the Abbay of Dunfermling', he is mentioned in a charter of 1543 dealing with the transaction of land at Carberry. In 1562, shortly after the Reformation, he was appointed to the vicarage of Crieff, but probably remained at Dunfermline. In general, after the Reformation in Scotland monks were not dislodged from an abbey, but after the death of the brethren suppression or secularization of the order took place.

Angus contributed some 12 canticles to THOMAS WOOD's anthology (*c*1566, *GB-Eu*, *Lbm*; some ed. in Elliot). All are settings in psalm tune style, ranging from those in a severe chordal idiom, such as *Our Father, which in Heaven art*, to those in a more gently decorative style, such as *Now suffer me, O Lord* (well illustrating Wood's affectionate description of the composer as 'gude Angus' or 'meike Angus') or *All my belief and confidence*. Here the composer's aim seems to have been to produce a polyphonic texture within the rather strict limits of a harmonic psalm tune setting. The result is admirable – animated but not fussy – and it is to be regretted that nothing has survived of Angus's work on a more ambitious scale. The editor of the 1635 Psalter states that Angus was one of several Scottish composers who wrote a 'set' of psalm tune harmonizations.

In the 1580s Angus received various pensions and benefices, and in 1595 he was presented to the parsonage of Crieff; by the following year he had died.

BIBLIOGRAPHY

J. Johnson: *The Scots Musical Museum*, i (Edinburgh, 1787, enlarged 3/1853)

H. Scott: *Fasti Ecclesiae Scoticanae*, v (Edinburgh, 1925)

K. Elliott and H. M. Shire, eds.: *Music of Scotland, 1500–1700*, MB, xv (1957, 2/1964)

K. Elliott, ed.: *Fourteen Psalm-settings of the Early Reformed Church in Scotland* (London, 1960)

KENNETH ELLIOTT

Anhalt, István (*b* Budapest, 12 April 1919). Canadian composer, teacher, conductor and pianist of Hungarian birth. He studied under Kodály at the Budapest Academy (1937–41). After a period of army service he became an assistant conductor at the Budapest Opera (1945). In 1946 he went to Paris for further studies in piano (Soulima Stravinsky), conducting (Fourestier) and composition (Boulanger), remaining there for three years. He moved to Canada in 1949 (he took Canadian nationality in 1955), and for three years he held a Lady Davis Fellowship and an appointment as assistant professor at McGill University. There he founded the electronic music studio and served for six years as chairman of the department of theoretical music. He has held grants for electronic music research from the Canada Council (1960–61) and the Columbia-Princeton Electronic Music Center (1961), and in 1969 he was Slee Visiting Professor in Composition at the State University of New York at Buffalo. In 1971 he left McGill to become head of the department of music at Queen's University in Kingston, Ontario.

The music Anhalt wrote in the 1950s is often characterized by bold abstraction and sustained intensity. Based on 'Classical' dodecaphonic procedures, his scores achieve large musical designs, avoid metrical redundancies and unfold in free, expressive lines, heavily underlined in cluster-like dissonances and/or unison doublings. A formal shape present in two works, the Piano Trio (1953) and the Piano Fantasia (1954), consists of an initial swift and violent plunge into a tense thematic complex, followed by the long and gradual relaxation of both musical meaning and feelings. The swift bold opening attack is again found in the Symphony (1958) and in some sections of *Foci* (1969). Counter-balancing the prevailing abstraction in earlier works, and possibly presaging later developments in Anhalt's output, is the three-movement suite *Comments* (1954), introduced by Maureen Forrester. The texts are clippings from the *Montreal Star*: the final section sets a weather report, elevating it into a simple but expressive 'found poem'. As a whole the suite exemplifies Anhalt's sense of colour, theatre and locally relevant sonority. The major work of this period, the Symphony, was dedicated 'to the 200th anniversary of Canadian Jewry' but is not programmatic. Written for a large orchestra, its single movement consists of 13 sections arranged in a deliberate pattern of changing (and irregularly cumulative) density. Anhalt 'thought of the various combinations of pitches, rhythms, dynamics, instrumental ensembles, tempi, as coalescing into what one could call degrees on a "density scale".' The Symphony, again highly abstract, is powerful and original in the way it relates density fluctuations to time and in its frequent reliance on a wave-like continuity, resembling perhaps the sea or human respiration.

Anhalt's work in electronic music resulted in four exclusively synthetic studies (1959–62) and a number of subsequent works in which a prepared tape is played simultaneously with live media. Of the former group, special interest lies in the third (sub-titled 'Birds and Bells', 1960) by reason of its minute and slow exploration of the various partials in a synthesized bell-like sonority. The length, seriousness and technical assurance of these studies gave a strong boost to the development of Canadian electronic music in the important formative period of the early 1960s. Though commissioned for the celebrations of the centenary of Canadian confederation (1967), the *Symphony of Modules*, for large orchestra and tape, has remained unperformed. Long and complex, it employs graphic notation in some sections. An offshoot of this centenary project was a smaller one – *Cento* ('Cantata urbana'), for 12 speaking voices accompanied by further vocal sounds on tape. The 100-word text was selected by the composer from the Canadian poet Eldon Grier's *An Ecstasy*, and it is often treated in a phonetically abstract way. However, the title refers neither to the text nor to the centenary occasion, but to the medieval concept of a mixture or patchwork composition. *Cento* introduced into Anhalt's work a new preoccupation with the musical properties of individual spoken and sung voices.

Foci (1969) fused this preoccupation with the trend towards mixed-media composition already foreseen in the *Symphony of Modules*, and fulfilled some of the theatrical potentialities glimpsed much earlier in *Comments*. Its forces include a live instrumental ensemble with soprano, a tape made up of utterances in nine different languages by many different voices, an accompaniment of slide projections in some sections, a lighting plan, and a simple scenario of exits and entrances for the performers. The work has a strongly ritualistic quality. Its sounds and sources range from a small mouth organ to an electronic organ, from words and phrases interjected live by the instrumentalists to voodoo chants on the tape, and from the soprano's long rising and falling dynamic waves to the formal offstage hammering which marks off the various sections. A mobile-like free assemblage of compositional components is employed in some of the nine movements (a feature also of the *Symphony of Modules*). The musical characteristics include imitations of familiar styles (such as the 'soft rock' canonic material at the flautist's first entrance) and the special Anhaltian intensity of heavy unison doublings. The theatrical and verbal images range wide, particularly in the fields of psychology and religion, and the combination of unfamiliar languages and intense feelings is one which may be specifically related to the Montreal environment. Anhalt's next major work, again to his own text, is *La tourangelle*, a long dramatic treatment of the career and writings of Marie de l'Incarnation, the 17th-century Ursuline from Tours who was one of the great pioneer figures of early Canada.

Anhalt's critical and analytical writings – on his own and other works – are informed, articulate and extraordinarily wide-ranging, often suggesting connections between the musical, literary, technological and empirical aspects of a given question. His influence as a teacher can be observed through the work of such younger composers as Allan Heard, John Hawkins, Hugh Hartwell, William Benjamin and Alexander Tilley.

WORKS

Dramatic: Arc en ciel, ballet, 2 pf, 1951, Montreal, 1952; Foci (Anhalt), S, 10 insts, tape, 1969, Buffalo, 1969; La tourangelle (Anhalt), 3S, 2 speakers, 15 insts, tape, 1974
Orch: Interludium, str, pf, timp, 1950; Sym., 1958; Sym. of Modules, orch, tape, 1967
Vocal: 6 Songs from Na Conxy Pan (S. Weöres), Bar, pf, 1941–7; Psalm xix, a Benediction (A. M. Klein), Bar, pf, 1951; 3 Songs of Love (de la Mare, anon., trad.), SSA, 1951; Journey of the Magi (Eliot), Bar, pf, 1952; 3 Songs of Death (Davenant, Herrick), SATB, 1954; Comments (newspapers), A, pf trio, 1954; Chanson d'aurore (A. Verdet), S, fl, pf, 1955; Cento (E. Grier), 12 speakers, tape, 1967
Inst: Funeral Music, 10 insts, 1951; Pf Sonata, 1951; Pf Trio, 1953; Sonata, vn, pf, 1954; Fantasia, pf, 1954
Tape: Elec Composition no.1 'Sine nomine I', 1959; Elec Composition no.2 'Sine nomine II', 1959; Elec Composition no.3 'Birds and Bells', 1960; Elec Composition no.4, 1962

Principal publisher: Berandol

WRITINGS

'The Making of *Cento*', *Canada Music Book* (1970), no.1, p.81
'About *Foci*', *Artscanada* (1971), no.28, p.57
'La musique électronique', *Musiques du Kébèk*, ed. R. Duguay (Montreal, 1971), 13
'Composing with Speech', *7th International Congress of Phonetic Sciences: Montreal 1971*, 447
'Luciano Berio's *Sequenza III*', *Canada Music Book* (1973), no.7, pp.23–60
Reviews in *Canadian Music Journal*, 1957–61

BIBLIOGRAPHY

J. Beckwith: 'Composers in Toronto and Montreal', *University of Toronto Quarterly*, xxvi/1 (1956), 47
——: 'Recent Orchestral Works by Champagne, Morel and Anhalt', *Canadian Music Journal*, iv/4 (1960), 44
R. Schallenberg: 'Anhalt's Symphony no.1', *Notes*, xxi (1964), 625
'István Anhalt: a Portrait', *Musicanada* (1968), no.15, p.8
Y. Rivard: 'L'enseignement de la composition à l'Université McGill', *Vie musicale* (1968), no.8, p.5
István Anhalt (Toronto, 1970) [BMI Canada publication]

JOHN BECKWITH

Anhemitonic. A term, meaning 'without semitones', used mainly in conjunction with 'pentatonic' to distinguish music in which the MODE or SCALE consists of combinations of major 2nds and minor 3rds.

Aniels, Arnaut d'. *See* DANIEL, ARNAUT.

Anievas, Agustin (*b* New York, 11 June 1934). American pianist of Spanish and Mexican descent. He was taught the piano by his mother from the age of four and later by Steuermann and Olga Samaroff. After some appearances as a child, he entered the Juilliard School of Music where he studied with Adele Marcus. In 1959 he made his début in New York as winner of the Concert Artists Guild Award. He won a number of other important competitions in Europe and the USA including the Mitropoulos Prize in 1961. Since then he has toured widely in the USA, South America, Europe, South Africa, Australia and the Far East. Anievas settled in Belgium for ten years but in 1974 returned to New York where he became a piano professor at Brooklyn College. His repertory is principally of 19th- and early 20th-century music and includes the concertos of Bartók and Prokofiev. He has recorded all Rakhmaninov's concertos and the complete waltzes, studies, ballades and impromptus of Chopin, as well as works by Liszt and Brahms.

RONALD KINLOCH ANDERSON

Anima (It.). SOUNDPOST.

Animando (It.). *See* ANIMATO.

Animato (It.: 'lively', 'enlivened'; past participle of *animare*, to enliven). A mark of tempo and expression which has never achieved particular prominence in any specific form but which appears in all kinds of shapes and forms in 18th- and 19th-century music. Brossard (1703) translated both *animato* and *anima* as meaning approximately the same as *allegro*; but his contemporary François Couperin used the French form *animé* (as well as its superlative *tres animé*) in his works. For musical purposes it is likely that the adjective *animoso* ('bold', 'spirited') and its adverbial form *animose* are to be understood in the same way. All are used in 18th-century scores either independently or as qualifications, particularly to *allegro*. *Animando* ('becoming more lively', 'getting faster'; the gerund of *animare*) belongs more to the 19th century. Verdi used it repeatedly, in the Dies irae of his Requiem, for instance, where he has *sempre animando, poco a poco animando*, etc, for the many increases of speed and excitement. Leonora's Act 1 cavatina in *Il trovatore* has *animando un poco* leading to *poco più animato*. In this context, and many others, *animato* may simply mean 'faster'.

For bibliography *see* TEMPO AND EXPRESSION MARKS.

DAVID FALLOWS

Animé (Fr.). *See* ANIMATO.

Animuccia, Giovanni (*b* Florence, *c*1500; *d* Rome, *c*20 March 1571). Italian composer.

1. LIFE. His birth and early training at Florence are attested to by the contemporary writer M. Poccianti. Einstein inferred from his first published compositions, the two volumes of madrigals (Venice, 1547–51), that Animuccia's early works were influenced by Francesco Corteccia, court composer to Duke Cosimo I de' Medici. Two *capitoli* by A. F. Grazzini (il Lasca) give evidence of his association with Florentine literary circles; one of these is addressed to 'M. Giovanni Animuccia' and the other mentions him. Although his later career and work were centred entirely at Rome, Animuccia was not a Roman composer in the same sense as Palestrina, but brought a Florentine background to his later musical activity. This helps to explain his later association with the Oratory of FILIPPO NERI, who was a fellow Florentine, and his composition of *laudi* for the oratory's use.

By 1550 he was at Rome in the service of Cardinal Guido Ascanio Sforza (1518–64). His friendship with Neri began as early as June 1551 when Animuccia became a member of the *Compagnia della pietà della nazione fiorentina*, which met at the church of S Giovanni dei Fiorentini. In January 1555 Animuccia became *magister cantorum* at the Cappella Giulia. In 1513 Pope Julius II had founded it to guarantee the newly rebuilt St Peter's Basilica a continuing body of singers for its daily services and to serve as a training establishment for Italian singers, in contrast to the foreign-dominated Cappella Sistina.

Animuccia remained there until his death. At the beginning of his tenure he succeeded Palestrina, and on its termination he was succeeded by him. Animuccia's period of employment coincided with a steady stream of publications of his music, consisting almost entirely of sacred works; they exceeded in number those of any Roman contemporary, including Palestrina himself, during the period 1550–70. His salary as head of the chapel of St Peter's was at first six scudi a month (the same amount that Palestrina had received in this post from 1551 to 1555); in 1569 it was raised to eight scudi. Animuccia's responsibilities included not only the supervision of the musical establishment but also the composition of works for its use and the copying of music for its growing archive; he also taught a group of boys attached to the chapel. Records published by Ducrot include a payment in December 1566 'for the composition of five masses [written] according to the requirements of the Council [of Trent]'; another payment of 20 September 1567 granted him 50 ducats as remuneration for their composition 'and to help him to have them published, since they will serve our chapel'. These were the masses for four to six voices of his *Liber primus missarum* (1567). The most revealing of these entries is a payment of 23 December 1568, in which he is paid 25 ducats 'for the trouble and expense that he has had in composing and copying and having copied the following hymns, motets and masses, which, again for our purposes, he has composed within the present year; they are needed for the chapel and are according to the requirements of the Council of Trent and of the new Office' (i.e. the revised breviary). The list includes 14 hymns, two masses *della madonna* and four motets, including three that are specified as being suitable for major festivals for use 'quando passa il papa'. A post-

humous payment of 9 September 1575 to his successor Palestrina is made for 'due conserti di mottetti dell'Animuccia et due conserte del Pelestrina' for the chapel's use.

2. WORKS. Animuccia's connection with the Oratory of Filippo Neri is one of the most interesting chapters in the development of sacred music in Rome during the period after the Council of Trent. Neri had begun his religious gatherings in 1554 at S Girolamo, giving sermons there to groups of participants. In 1558 he obtained the use of a space on the side of the church to serve as an 'oratorio' (prayer-room). Evidently from about this time the singing of devotional *laudi spirituali* was added to the sermons and prayers. In 1564, on becoming rector of S Giovanni dei Fiorentini, Neri seems to have moved his activities to that church; it is certain that what later became famous as the Congregazione dell'Oratorio in the Chiesa Nuova, was not constructed until 1575 on the site of the church of S Maria in Vallicella. Animuccia became *maestro di cappella* of the Oratory at S Girolamo in 1570, just one year before his death, but he had been associated with Neri for some 20 years before that. His first published volume of *laudi*, written for Neri's congregation, appeared in 1563, and a later and musically more elaborate set of *laudi* appeared in 1570. The general purpose of these collections was evident in their mingling of Latin and vernacular devotional texts, and their fundamentally simple, chordal style of composition. In the title of his first book, Animuccia made clear that they were intended 'for the consolation and needs of many spiritual and devout persons, religious and secular alike'; and in the preface to the second, he explained his purposes in more detail. While his aim in the earlier volume was a 'certain simplicity', in the second he wrote:

But the Oratory having increased, by the grace of God, with the coming together of prelates and of most important gentlemen, it seemed to me fitting in this second book to increase the harmony and the combination of parts, varying the music in diverse ways, now setting it to Latin words and now to the vernacular, sometimes with a greater number of voices and sometimes with fewer, with verses now of one kind and now of another, concerning myself as little as possible with imitations and complexities, in order not to obscure the understanding of the words.

Animuccia's *laudi* represent a deliberate departure from the contrapuntal style of his madrigals and other sacred compositions towards a simpler homophonic texture aimed at the musical participation of laymen in religious services. As a madrigalist Einstein singled him out as being the first Florentine composer to write extended cyclic madrigals in several sections, setting texts by Petrarch and Sanazzaro. His later three-voice madrigals of 1565 show signs of Counter-Reformation influence, including *madrigali spirituali* as well as a series of secular works on poems by G. B. Strozzi and a setting of a text from Giraldi Cintio's drama *Selene*. His masses of 1567 constitute one of the most important post-Tridentine collections in which a deliberate attempt is made, as in works by a few other composers of the period, to render the Mass text as intelligible as possible without loss of musical interest. Indicative of Counter-Reformation influence too is the avoidance of secular models and the use of plainsong melodies as the basis for paraphrase throughout. This type of mass had been cultivated in the early 16th century by Josquin Desprez (in his *Missa 'Ave maris stella'* and *Missa 'Pange lingua'*) but had lain fallow during the period from about 1520 to about 1560. Animuccia's skill in combining elaborate paraphrase with contrapuntal devices is notable; his approach to the problem of clarity is governed by a greater reluctance to abandon contrapuntal artifice than is visible in the more extreme contemporary works of this type (e.g. Vincenzo Ruffo's masses of 1570). Animuccia can be counted as Palestrina's most important Roman contemporary in the period 1550 to 1571.

WORKS

Il primo libro di madrigali, 4–6vv (Venice, 1547)
Il secondo libro de i madrigali, 5vv (Rome, 1551)
Il primo libro de i motetti, 5vv (Rome, 1552)
Madrigali, 5vv (Rome, 1554)
Il primo libro delle laudi . . . composte per consolatione et a requisitione di molte persone spirituali et devote, tanto religiosi, quanto secolari, 4vv (Rome, 1563)
Il primo libro de madrigali, 3vv . . . con alcuni motetti et madrigali spirituali (Rome, 1565)
Missarum liber primus, 4–6vv (Rome, 1567); Ky, Gl of Missa 'Conditor alme syderum', ed. in AMI, i (1897/R), 159
Canticum Beatae Mariae Virginis . . . ad omnes modos factum, 4vv (Rome, 1568); Magnificat quinti toni, AMI, i, 149
Il secondo libro delle laudi, dove si contengono motteti, salmi et altre diverse cose spirituali vulgari et latine, 2–8vv (Rome, 1570)
Magnificat, 8vv (Rome, n.d.) [fragmentary]
Works in 1574[4], 1582[6], 1587[5], 1599[6], A-Wn, I-Bc, Rn, Rv, Rvat C.S., C.G.

BIBLIOGRAPHY

M. Poccianti: Catalogus scriptorum florentinorum (Florence, 1589)
G. Baini: Memorie storico-critiche della vitta e delle opere di Giovanni Pierluigi da Palestrina (Rome, 1828/R1966)
D. Alaleona: Studi su la storia dell'oratorio musicale in Italia (Turin, 1908, 2/1945 as Storia . . . Italia)
A. Einstein: The Italian Madrigal, i (Princeton, 1949/R1971), 289ff
L. Cervelli: 'Le laude spirituali di Giovanni Animuccia e le origini dell'oratorio musicale a Roma', RaM, xx (1950), 116
L. Pannella: 'Animuccia, G.', DBI
A. Ducrot: 'Histoire de la Cappella Giulia au XVIᵉ siècle', École française de Rome, mélanges d'archéologie et d'histoire, lxxv (1963), 179–240, 467–559
H. W. Frey: 'Die Gesänge der Sixtinischen Kapelle an den Sonntagen und hohen Kirchenfesten des Jahres 1616', Mélanges Eugène Tisserant (Vatican City, 1964), 395–437
W. Osthoff: Theatergesang und Darstellende Musik in der Italienischen Renaissance, i (Tutzing, 1969), 111, 322f

LEWIS LOCKWOOD

Animuccia, Paolo (b ?Florence, c1500; d ?Urbino, c1570). Italian composer. Poccianti claimed that he was the brother of Giovanni Animuccia; although no other source confirms this relationship, there is no reason to doubt his authority. Paolo Animuccia must have spent his early years at Florence, but the first documented evidence of his musical activity is at Rome in 1550, when he is listed as maestro di cappella at St John Lateran, in succession to Rubino. He remained in this post until 1552, when he was succeeded by Bernardo Lupacchino. Although it is often asserted that Animuccia's tenure there coincided with the presence of the young Lassus, Boetticher's research indicates that the only secure date of Lassus's activity there is 21 May 1553, when he was given a surplice. As it was habitual to issue surplices to the cathedral singers a few weeks after their entry, it is likely that Lassus began his service in March or April 1553, after the period of Animuccia's formal tenure. That there was, however, some connection between them is strongly suggested by the inclusion of madrigals by Animuccia in two publications of madrigals by Lassus (RISM 1557[22] and 1563[11]).

After his period at St John Lateran, Animuccia's only known post is that of maestro di cappella at the court of Guidobaldo II della Rovere, Duke of Urbino from 1538 to 1574. This association may well go back to the late 1550s or earlier, since a motet by Animuccia dedicated to Guidobaldo had already appeared in Costanzo

Porta's Liber primus motectorum (1559). In Giornate dette le Soriane dell'imperiale di Pesaro (I-PESo 191), which narrates fictional events that are supposed to have taken place in the first ten days of August 1569, L. Agostini mentioned a performance of a madrigal by Animuccia, whom he referred to as maestro di cappella to the Duke of Urbino. Other references to him as maestro di cappella are found in Pietro Gaetano's De origine et dignitate musices (I-Vmc VI, 189), dedicated to Guidobaldo II. Although Poccianti gave Animuccia's date of death as 1563 he must have died after 1569 if Agostini's account can be believed.

Animuccia was a moderately productive composer of motets and madrigals, although he was clearly less successful and less gifted than his brother Giovanni.

WORKS

Responsoria Hebdomadae Sanctae ac natalis Domini, 4vv, liber I et II (Venice, n.d.)
3 other motets, 1559[6], 1563[4], H. Tartaglini: Motettorum (Rome, 1574); others I-MOe C313–4
9 madrigals, 1551[10], 1555[27], 1557[22], 1558[13], 1562[5], 1563[11], 1566[3], 1570[15], 1600[5]
Chanson, 1575[4]

BIBLIOGRAPHY

M. Poccianti: Catalogus scriptorum florentinorum (Florence, 1589)
G. Baini: Memorie storico-critiche della vita e delle opere di Giovanni Pierluigi da Palestrina (Rome, 1828/R1966)
V. Rossi: 'Appunti per la storia della musica alla corte di Francesco Maria I e di Guidobaldo della Rovere', Rassegna emiliana, i (1888), 453
A. Einstein: The Italian Madrigal, i (Princeton, 1949/R1971), 291f
A. Garbelotto: Il Padre Costanzo Porta da Cremona, O.F.M. Conv. (Rome, 1955), 158
W. Boetticher: Orlando di Lasso und seine Zeit (Kassel, 1958)
L. Pannella: 'Animuccia, Paolo', DBI

LEWIS LOCKWOOD

Anjos, Dionísio dos (b c1638; d Lisbon, 19 Jan 1709). Portuguese composer and harpist. On 6 January 1656 he professed as a Jeronymite monk at Belem Monastery, Lisbon, and he remained there until his death. His works, formerly in the monastery archive but now lost, included responsories for all important feasts, vesper psalms, masses, Magnificat settings, motets and vilhancicos.

BIBLIOGRAPHY

D. Barbosa Machado: Bibliotheca lusitana, i (Lisbon, 1741), 704f

ROBERT STEVENSON

Anjos de Gouvea, Simão dos (fl 1611). Portuguese composer. He studied with Manuel Mendes at the Évora Cathedral choir school. Around 1600, having already joined the order of S João Evangelista, he succeeded Pedro Thalesio as mestre de capela at the Hospital de Todos-os-Santos in Lisbon. In March 1611 he moved to Coimbra hoping to be elected to the chair of music at the university there, but after he had waited nine months, Thalesio was chosen. Sometime later until 22 December 1622, he held a royal appointment to head the music at the church of St John the Baptist, Tomar. Only three works have been identified as his: a four-voice motet, Pueri hebreorum vestimenta (in P-EVp), and a five-part hymn, O lingua mens sensus vigor, and a four-part alleluia (both in AR).

BIBLIOGRAPHY

E. Vieira: Diccionário biográfico de musicos portuguezes, i (Lisbon, 1900), 35
F. M. Sousa Viterbo: A Ordem de Christo e a música sagrada nas suas igrejas do continente (Coimbra, 1911), 8, 18f
J. Mazza: 'Dicionário biográfico de músicos portugueses', Ocidente, xxiv (1944), 156; xxvi (1945), 43

M. de Sampayo Ribeiro: *Sete 'Alleluias' inéditos* (*dum códice do Mosteiro de Arouca*) (Oporto, 1949)

ROBERT STEVENSON

Anna, Francesco d'. *See* ANA, FRANCESCO D'.

Anna Amalia [Amalie] **(i),** Princess of Prussia (*b* Berlin, 9 Nov 1723; *d* Berlin, 30 March 1787). Patron of music, amateur musician and composer. The youngest sister of Frederick the Great, she first studied music under Frederick himself and the Berlin cathedral organist Gottlieb Hayne. Though her talent was inferior to her brother's, she reached a high level of accomplishment as a keyboard player, and was fairly proficient as a violinist and flautist. The soirées in her royal apartments were attended by the artists and intelligentsia of Berlin and Europe, and her library, established in about 1735, reflected both a breadth of general education and a highly professional musical training.

She did not begin studying composition in earnest until her mid-30s. J. P. Kirnberger, Bach's pupil, became her Kapellmeister in 1758, and under his tutelage she was able to display a remarkable knowledge of counterpoint. She composed a setting of Ramler's *Der Tod Jesu* before C. H. Graun did, with such success that Kirnberger later published part of it in his *Kunst des reinen Satzes* as a model for professionals. She also produced a few sonatas, marches, chorales, arias and songs. The musical part of her library contains only one small bundle of works by her; it is unlikely that much more ever existed (a few attractive instrumental pieces were edited by G. Lenzewski, Berlin, 1927–8). Like Frederick, she allowed her musical taste to become reactionary; the instinct that made her such an apt student of counterpoint and of the old masters prevented her from seeing much virtue in newer styles. In a letter to Kirnberger about *Iphigénie en Tauride* she expressed a particularly unfavourable opinion of Gluck, whom she found greatly inferior to Graun and Hasse; however, she gave support to C. P. E. Bach and a few other progressive musicians.

Amalia's real significance in music lies in her music library, a collection of incalculable value. The Amalien-Bibliothek, as it has become known, is particularly rich in 18th-century music – that of J. S. Bach above all, including such works as the Brandenburg Concertos, the St Matthew Passion, the B minor Mass, a large collection of cantatas and most of the keyboard concertos. The Blechschmidt catalogue lists about 150 titles by Bach, mostly of autograph scores. There are rich holdings of C. P. E. Bach, the Grauns, Handel, Hasse, Kirnberger, Leo, Schaffrath, Stölzel, Telemann, Palestrina and Hassler. Kirnberger worked tirelessly not only in adding to the collection (the autograph of the Brandenburg Concertos was his personal copy), but also in making clear, precise copies in score. The Blechschmidt catalogue lists 680 musical items (separate volumes or bundles) altogether; more than 600 of these are compositions, mostly by German composers, and the remainder books or treatises on music. Sacred and secular music are in roughly equal balance.

Amalia willed her library to the Joachimsthalschen Gymnasium in Berlin. In 1914 the musical portion was transferred on permanent loan to the Royal Library in Berlin, remaining intact and under its own name there. Like other sections of the great Royal Library after World War II, one part of the Amalien-Bibliothek is in the library of the Stiftung Preussischer Kulturbesitz in West Berlin, and another in the Deutsche Staatsbibliothek in East Berlin. Between these two institutions most of the collection can be found; conspicuously missing (owing in part to the exigencies of wartime storage) are treatises and books on music.

The Amalien-Bibliothek was partially catalogued in the 18th century; Reichardt continued this project, as did Zelter (who added valuable items to its collection of Bachiana); but the first thorough catalogue was that of Eitner. The Blechschmidt catalogue, listing all musical items ever belonging to the library regardless of their present availability, is the most complete to date, but a fully satisfactory catalogue cannot be made until the Collection of the Royal Library is reassembled, or at least brought to a more permanent status.

BIBLIOGRAPHY

GerberL; GerberNL

C. Sachs: 'Prinzessin Amalie von Preussen als Musikerin', *Hohenzollern-Jb 1910*, 181

R. Eitner: *Katalog der Musikalien-Sammlung des Joachimsthalschen Gymnasium zu Berlin* (Berlin, 1884); repr. in *MMg*, xvi, suppl.

F. Bose: 'Anna Amalie von Preussen und Johann Philipp Kirnberger', *Mf*, x (1957), 129ff

P. Kast: *Die Bach-Handschriften der Berliner Staatsbibliothek* (Trossingen, 1958)

E. R. Blechschmidt: *Die Amalienbibliothek* (Berlin, 1965)

EUGENE HELM

Anna Amalia [Amalie] **(ii),** Duchess of Saxe-Weimar (*b* Wolfenbüttel, 24 Oct 1739; *d* Weimar, 10 April 1807). German amateur musician and patron. She was the daughter of Duke Karl I of Brunswick and a niece of Frederick the Great. As a child she was given a good musical education. At the age of 16 she married the 18-year-old Duke Ernst August Konstantin of Saxe-Weimar; after his death two years later until the accession of her eldest son Duke Karl August on 3 September 1775 she conducted the regency. Despite her heavy official responsibilities she cultivated intellectual interests, especially music. She continued to take lessons in composition and keyboard playing from the leading musician in Weimar at that time, Ernst Wilhelm Wolf (later the court Kapellmeister), and gathered round her a group of scholars, poets and musicians, professional and amateur, which was a lively centre of discussion and music-making. In this 'court of the muses', as Wilhelm Bode called it, whose members included Wieland, Herder and eventually Goethe, Anna Amalia herself played a significant part in bringing together the poetry of 'Weimar Classicism' and the music of the time. J. A. Hiller's most successful Singspiel, *Die Jagd* (the score of which is dedicated to the duchess), received its first performance in Weimar in 1770, and Weimar was also the scene of the notable première on 28 May 1773 of the 'first German opera', Wieland's *Alceste* in the setting by Anton Schweitzer. Further public performances were prevented by the destruction of the theatre by fire in 1774, but Anna Amalia continued the tradition of the Singspiel in later years with performances in the amateur court theatre of her own compositions to texts by Goethe. Free of the responsibilities of the regency, she devoted herself completely to her artistic interests. Between 1788 and 1790 she undertook a tour of Italy and was impressed by its visual arts as much as by its music. In an essay on music of 1799 (lost, but referred to by Bode) she particularly praised Italian singing. Her Singspiel *Erwin und Elmire*, without being eclectic in effect, reveals an intimate familiarity with the German Singspiel of Hiller and the contemporary Italian opera remarkable for an amateur, and shows thorough technical competence and spontaneous inventiveness. The majority of pieces, apart from occasional folklike songs, belong stylistically to the *Empfindsamkeit*, in the manner of Hiller and Schweitzer, combining features of song and of arioso. But Anna Amalia's main significance lies in her strong personality, which conveyed her artistic convictions and thus had a decisive influence on the character of her circle and thereby on German intellectual life at the period of its flowering in Weimar.

WORKS
(MSS in D-WRl)

Erwin und Elmire (Singspiel, Goethe), Weimar, 24 May 1776; vocal
  score, ed. M. Friedlaender (Leipzig, 1921)
Das Jahrmarktsfest zu Plundersweilern (Goethe), Weimar, 20 Oct 1778
Divertimento, pf, cl, va, vc (Weimar, n.d.)

Other works are of doubtful attribution

BIBLIOGRAPHY
W. Bode: *Amalie, Herzogin von Weimar* (Berlin, 1908)
H. Abert: *Goethe und die Musik* (Stuttgart, 1922)
A. Krille: *Beiträge zur Geschichte der Musikerziehung und Musikübung
  der deutschen Frau* (Berlin, 1938)
R. Münnich: 'Aus der Musiksammlung der Weimarer Landesbibliothek,
  besonders dem Nachlass der Anna Amalia', *Aus der Geschichte der
  Landesbibliothek zu Weimar und ihrer Sammlungen, Festschrift zur
  Feier ihres 250jährigen Bestehens* (Jena, 1941)
O. Heuschele: *Herzogin Anna Amalia* (Munich, 1947)
A. A. Abert: 'Anna Amalie', *MGG*
ANNA AMALIE ABERT

Ann Arbor. Town in Michigan, USA, site of the UNIVERSITY OF MICHIGAN SCHOOL OF MUSIC.

Annet [Annette], **Jean-Baptiste.** *See* ANET, JEAN-BAPTISTE.

Annibale Padovano. *See* PADOVANO, ANNIBALE.

Annibali, Domenico [Dominichino] (*b* Macerata, *c*1705; *d* ?Rome, 1779 or later). Italian alto castrato. His first known appearance was in Porpora's *Germanico* at Rome in 1725. He sang in one opera at Venice in 1727 and two in 1729, when he was engaged for the Saxon court at Dresden at a salary of 792 thaler. He sang there in Hasse's *Cleofide* (1731) and *Caio Fabricio* (July 1734), but was given frequent leave to take outside engagements: at Rome in 1730, 1732 (spring) and 1739 (Carnival, in Terradellas's *Astarto*), at Vienna in 1731, when his performance in Caldara's *Demetrio* won the approval of Metastasio, and from October 1736 to June 1737 as a member of Handel's company in London. He sang at a concert a few days after his arrival and made his stage début at Covent Garden in a revival of *Poro* on 8 December, when he introduced two arias by Ristori and one by Vinci – one of only two occasions on which Handel is known to have allowed this practice in one of his own operas. Annibali was in the first performances of Handel's *Arminio, Giustino* and *Berenice*, revivals of *Partenope* (Arsace) and *Esther* (Ahasuerus, in Italian), the pasticcio *Didone*, and probably the rewritten *Il trionfo del tempo*. Handel cast him as Barak in a revival of *Deborah* that never took place, and arranged the cantata *Carco sempre di gloria* for him; he may have sung it as an interlude in *Alexander's Feast*.

While Annibali was in London the Saxon envoy, perhaps fearing his defection, offered him an increased salary of 1500 thaler (raised to 2000 at the end of 1739), and he returned to Dresden. He is listed among the court and theatre musicians there until 1756, and left in 1764 with a pension of 1200 thaler and the title of *Kammermusikus*. He was living in his native town in 1776, and three years later moved to Rome. In Dresden

Annibali was particularly associated with the operas of Hasse, appearing in (besides the two already mentioned) *La clemenza di Tito, Demetrio, Lucio Papirio, Arminio, Semiramide, Demofoonte, Attilio Regolo* and *Adriano in Siria* between 1738 and 1752. He sang in Porpora's *Filandro* in 1747.

According to Burney 'his abilities during his stay in England seem to have made no deep impression, as I never remember him to have been mentioned by those who constantly attended the operas of those times, and were rapturists in speaking of the pleasure they had received from singers of the first class'. Mrs Pendarves however wrote, soon after Annibali's arrival in London, that he had 'the best part of Senesino's voice and Caristini's, with a prodigious fine taste and good action'. The parts Handel composed for him, *Arminio,*

Domenico Annibali: pastel portrait (1745) by Anton Raffael Mengs in the Gemäldegalerie, Dresden

Giustino and *Demetrio* in *Berenice*, confirm this as regards compass (*a* to *g''*). Other accounts emphasize his brilliant and flexible coloratura, though some found his acting wooden. The aria 'Fatto scorta' in *Arminio* with its many changes of register and even of clef gives some indication of his powers. Hasse made similar use of them, employing a slightly wider compass (*g* to *g''*), but in *Demofoonte* (1748) this had shrunk to *a* to *f''*. Raphael Mengs painted two portraits of Annibali (see illustration; the other is dated 1752).

WINTON DEAN

Annuerus. *See* AMERUS.

Annunciação, Gabriel da (*b* nr. Coimbra, *c*1526; *d* Landim, nr. Vila Nova de Fanalicão, 14 June 1603). Portuguese organist, copyist and composer. About 1550 he became an Augustinian canon at S Cruz monastery, Coimbra. During the 1550s he compiled an important anthology (*P-Cug* M.M.48) of 127 folios of organ transcriptions of motets and chansons by Josquin, Mouton, Verdelot, Richafort, Gombert, Crecquillon, Morales and others, together with all ten ricercares in Buus's *Recercari libro primo* (Venice, 1547) and a tiento by Francisco de Soto (from *RISM* 1557²). His own incomplete *Tento de meyo registo, outavo tom natural a 3* ('Tiento in three parts for divided keyboard, tone VIII untransposed') on f.66 is the earliest surviving organ work in a Peninsular manuscript specified for *medio registro*. In later life he held several high offices – counsellor, choirmaster, procurator and vicar – in the monastery at Landim, which was dependent on S Cruz, Coimbra.

BIBLIOGRAPHY

P. de Azevedo: 'Rol dos cónegos regrantes de Santo Agostinho, por Gabriel de S. Maria', *Boletim da segunda classe da Academia das sciencias de Lisboa*, xi (1916–17), 157

S. Kastner: 'Los Ms. 48 y 242, de la Biblioteca de la universidad de Coimbra', *AnM*, v (1950), 82

E. Gonçalves de Pinho: *Santa Cruz de Coimbra centro de atividade musical nos séculos XVI e XVII* (Coimbra, 1970), 137ff

ROBERT STEVENSON

Anoixantarion. A setting in Byzantine hymnody of Psalm ciii, beginning at verse 28*b*. The term is derived from the Greek word 'anoixantos' which begins this text.

Anonymous theoretical writings.

1. Introduction. 2. Plainchant. 3. Musica plana. 4. Organum. 5. Discant and contrapunctus. 6. Musica plana and musica mensurabilis. 7. Mensural music: late 13th and early 14th centuries. 8. Mensural music: *c*1350–1450. 9. Miscellaneous.

1. INTRODUCTION. Works whose authors are unknown are found in every art and craft, in every time and place. They are of particular importance in the body of medieval writing on music, partly because of the circumstances of publication of such works since the 18th century and partly because of the great significance attached to certain individual large-scale treatises, or to certain groups of shorter writings. References to such works in the secondary literature are often ambiguous, and an understanding of the manuscript sources and character of the works as a whole is not easily come by. This article is intended to alleviate such difficulties. The more important anonymous works (e.g. MUSICA ENCHIRIADIS) receive separate treatment, however, and much reference is made to the groups of lesser works under the appropriate subject matter heading (e.g. COUNTERPOINT). This article deals with musical writings of the Western Middle Ages which were explicitly published in modern times as anonymous and which have commonly been referred to as such. Consequently, writings on Greek music, either classical or Byzantine (e.g. the Bellerman Anonymous), are excluded, as are works written in the 16th century or after, and those widely known under an author's name, even if spurious (e.g. the *Dialogus* formerly attributed to Odo).

(*i*) *Reasons for anonymity*. Many medieval writings on music are anonymous through accident (loss of prefatory material, or of manuscripts close to the time and place of authorship), or through the uncertainty created by conflicting attributions. The modern scholarly principle that all sources be unequivocally identified by author, title and place and date of publication, does not hold to the same degree for the Middle Ages. Further uncertainty derives from medieval concepts of originality and the fact that the surviving manuscript

sources were sometimes not intended at the time for widespread distribution. It is nonetheless true that most of the influential works of large scope from the Middle Ages are securely attributed. It should however be said that the mere knowledge of an author's name often neither tells anything about the time or place of composition, nor leads to any further knowledge of his life. So while it is undoubtedly advantageous for conceptualization to know that a man named Johannes de Grocheo wrote an extensive and exceptionally important work on music, this is of no help (so far) in establishing the historical context of the work.

Works may be anonymous at first glance owing to deliberate concealment by the author of his name. The one major instance among medieval writers is that of Jacques de Liège who embedded his name as an acrostic in the initial letters of each of the seven books of his work. But since the author himself reveals the existence of the acrostic, the concealment is more apparent than real and could even be understood as a device to imprint his name more deeply on the reader's mind. There are a few related cases, in which a verse colophon encodes the author's name (see *CS*, iii, Anonymous VI, below).

The use of pseudonyms or *noms de plume* deliberately chosen by the author does not appear to be a factor with medieval anonymi. From the 16th century onwards their use grew, together with the fashion of the polemic public debate. As it became more common and acceptable to attack persons directly or so specifically that there could be no doubt as to identity, so it became necessary or a matter of propriety to hide behind an assumed name.

It has sometimes been asserted that a chief cause for the existence of a large body of anonymous medieval writings is an attitude of humility or deference to authority, understood as deriving from the monastic status of a writer, or from a more widespread and specifically medieval mentality. But there is much evidence to contradict such a view as a general principle, while not rejecting it as a possible cause in any specific case.

Finally, it may be that anonymity particularly flourished, almost as a matter of principle, in certain kinds of writing or subject matter. Glosses to pre-existing texts are, for example, frequently anonymous. They may represent comments made by a reader for his own use, or for teaching from an authoritative text. If such works are collected separately, or introduced into the original text by inadvertence without being designated as a formal commentary with indication of authorship, an anonymous work is generated. Many of the brief essays which clustered around such topics as monochord division, discant or mensural notation, seem rather like glosses, brief commentaries or supplements, or compendia, rather less than a work to which an author might be inclined to lay claim. Many treatises (or better, brief essays) on 14th-century French notation can only be regarded as satellites to the works of JEHAN DES MURS, a fact of which the writers – and readers, if any were intended – must have been well aware.

One should also consider the nebulous, but still no doubt considerable, category of lecture notes, either from professors or defenders of theses for their guidance in speaking, or from audiences. These would necessarily be more frequently encountered as the university system of education spreads, and as more and more copies of privately owned books (in which one's own unsigned contributions can easily become amalgamated with finished writings by known authors) survive in present-day libraries.

(*ii*) *Past and present scholarship in relation to anonymity.* The history of scholarship directed towards or founded upon medieval writings on music falls into four phases. The first is that of the anthologies of Abbot Martin Gerbert and C.-E.-H. de Coussemaker. Both men included, along with a majority of attributed works, a number of anonymi, usually, but not always, numbered according to the place they occupied in a given volume of the anthology. There was little logic in the positions these anonymi occupied, either of time, place, subject matter or manuscript origin. The concrete historical contexts were at best obscure. Since most historians of medieval music depended on these anthologies for their texts, the anonymi were subsequently cited in an excessively abstract and historically vague manner.

In the next phase, extending roughly to World War II, scholars, most of them German, published texts of individual anonymi who had dealt with subjects of particular interest to them. Often there was only one source to consider, but not always, and in any event the editing frequently did not meet a good philological standard, with incomplete or excerpted texts sometimes seeing the light of day.

Postwar publication, largely centring on the work of Joseph Smits van Waesberghe, took a different turn. The series Corpus Scriptorum de Musica – which in part responded to the need often expressed since the end of the 19th century for a new Gerbert and Coussemaker – although it did not at first publish anonymi, laid an important foundation for further study in the manuscript inventories included in its text editions. These inventories were the prototypes for the systematic cataloguing of all medieval theoretical manuscripts in the *RISM* project (series B/III, in progress). Many concordances between sources for well-established anonymi, as well as previously unknown brief treatises or fragments, were revealed through the detailed inventories of *RISM*.

Finally, there has recently been an increasing tendency for anonymous texts to be interpreted in the light of the subject matter concerned, or to be published in groups (see Gallo, 1966; Eggebrecht and Zaminer, 1970; Sachs, 1974). One may hope for an eventual comprehensive history of medieval music theory based on such work which would replace the old history by Hugo Riemann.

The two major postwar German reference works in music included articles on anonymi (Heinrich Hüschen in *MGG* and Hellmut Kühn in *RiemannL 12*) which, because of differing organization and emphases, may usefully be consulted along with this article. Reaney (1964) offered a brief but valuable introduction to some of the sources of difficulty in establishing authorship.

(*iii*) *False attributions.* There is more difficulty in contradicting mistaken or false attributions than in establishing authorship for a traditionally anonymous work. Not only are readers and writers of history generally happier with assertions of a positive character, but the conceptual manipulation of entities (in this case, individual writings on music) that do not have a memorable label or title is in practice extremely difficult. Numbers will not do, or if they are all we have, they are hypostatized. (Thus, there is room for only one Anonymous IV, that of *CS*, i.) From this point of view,

any name, even a fabricated one (music historians have not been so daring), is preferable to a number. Consequently, listings of medieval writers on music are littered with personal names with the 'Pseudo-' prefix, long after it has been established that their works are, by any reasonable standard of historical criticism, anonymous. Some major examples are (in every case, to be read with 'Pseudo-' prefixed): Alcuin, Hucbald, Regino, Odo, Guido, Berno, Franco, Jehan de Murs, Simon Tunstede, Johannes de Garlandia. Such cases are not listed here.

(*iv*) *Notes to the list.* Three categories of works that have traditionally escaped the bibliographer's net will be omitted here, not without regret: tonaries, which often have important prefatory essays (on these, consult Huglo, 1971); didactic poems; and sections on music included in more general works.

The listings of anonymous theoretical writings which follow are intended primarily to guide the reader to the editor, place of publication and manuscript source for a text and to give some notion of the subject matter. The latter is conveyed both in the brief explanatory comments and in the categories used to group texts similar in scope and subject – categories offered with the understanding that often the main attraction of a treatise for modern scholars has been matter secondary or accessory to its chief subject. The order of items within categories is alphabetical according to traditionally accepted labels, sometimes translated from German or slightly modified. Some bibliographical information is offered when it seems of particular merit in understanding the historical context or manuscript transmission of a work. References to general library catalogues have not been included. Dates appended to sources refer to the time of copying, but are not to be understood as authoritative. Place of copying or former ownership are sometimes mentioned when the evidence seems particularly strong. Most titles (immediately following the anonymous labels) are inauthentic constructions by modern editors.

GENERAL BIBLIOGRAPHY

M. Gerbert: *Scriptores ecclesiastici de musica* (St Blasien, 1784/*R*) [*GS*]

C.-E.-H. de Coussemaker: *Histoire de l'harmonie au moyen âge* (Paris, 1852/*R*) [*CH*]

——: *Scriptorum de musica medii aevi novam seriem* (Paris, 1864–76/*R*) [*CS*]

M. Schneider: *Geschichte der Mehrstimmigkeit* (Berlin, 1935)

H. Hüschen: 'Anonymi', *MGG*

J. Smits van Waesberghe, ed.: *Guidonis aretini Micrologus*, CSM, iv (1955)

——: *The Theory of Music from the Carolingian Era up to 1400*, i, RISM, B/III/1 (1961)

G. Reaney: 'The Question of Authorship in the Medieval Treatises on Music', *MD*, xviii (1964), 7

F. A. Gallo: *Mensurabilis musicae tractatuli*, AMI, Scriptores, i (1966)

H. Kühn: 'Anonymi', *RiemannL 12*

F. Reckow: *Der Musiktraktat des Anonymus 4* (Wiesbaden, 1967)

P. Fischer, ed.: *The Theory of Music from the Carolingian Era up to 1400*, ii: *Italy*, RISM, B/III/2 (1968)

J. Smits van Waesberghe: *Musikerziehung: Lehre und Theorie der Musik im Mittelalter* (Leipzig, 1969)

H. H. Eggebrecht and F. Zaminer: *Ad organum faciendum: Lehrschriften der Mehrstimmigkeit in nachguidonischer Zeit* (Mainz, 1970)

M. Huglo: *Les tonaires: inventaire, analyse, comparaison* (Paris, 1971)

K.-J. Sachs: *Der Contrapunctus im 14. und 15. Jahrhundert: Untersuchungen zum Terminus, zur Lehre und zu den Quellen* (Wiesbaden, 1974)

A. Seay, ed.: *Quatuor tractatuli italici de contrapuncto* (Colorado Springs, 1977)

2. PLAINCHANT. (Although this category is designed for works with an obvious practical slant it also includes

certain more theoretical works originating from before Guido's time.)

Becker anon. Incipit: Diatessaron alia constat ex tono et semitonio et tono. *D-EF8°*94, ff.80–84, 14th century. Ed. in A. Becker: 'Ein Erfurter Traktat über gregorianische Musik', *AMw*, i (1918–19), 145

This post-Guidonian but probably 11th-century work on plainchant seems poorly arranged and may well be incomplete. It includes a discussion of psalm tones and a table of neumes with their names (e.g. *gurtulus, epiphonus*).

Cistercian anon. Incipit: Cantum quem cisterciensis ordinis ecclesie cantare consueverant. *A-HE* 20, ff.1r–4r, 12th century; *GB-Cjc* 34, ff.109r–115v, Rievaulx, *c*1175; Ireland, Mount Melleray Abbey, unnumbered MS, ff.1–7, Switzerland, 12th century; *F-Pn* lat.16662, ff. 70v–77r, Sorbonne, 13th century. Ed. F. J. Guentner, CSM, xxiv. This edition gives further details on three minor 17th-century sources as well as several earlier printed editions.

Correction of plainchant with respect to text, modal assignment, B♭ and range. The work, dated by Guentner between 1142 and 1147, has a prefatory letter by Bernard of Clairvaux. It has sometimes been ascribed to Guido de Caroli loci or Guido Augensis. In any event it cites Guido of Arezzo in a number of instances.

CS, ii, Anon.I; Tractatus de musica plana cuiusdam Carthusiensis monachi. B-Gu 70(71) (olim 421), ff.124r–159v, Ghent, 1503–4. Ed. in *CS*, ii, 434–83

Coussemaker based his attribution to a Carthusian on the work which immediately precedes this in the MS, yet it is not clear even that the various sections he published truly belong together. The range of subjects covered is vast, including much on the ecclesiastical modes, psalm tones, the performance and composition of plainchant, the monochord (with reference to the vielle and citole), and something from the liberal arts tradition. While some of the contents must postdate the mid-14th century (e.g. references to the *Quatuor principalia*), some of it goes back to Guidonian times.

GS, i, Anon.I. Incipit: Duo semisphaeria, quas magadas vocant. From a 12th-century manuscript formerly in the library of the monastery of St Blasien but no longer extant; 18th-century MS copies of works contained in the destroyed St Blasien MSS are now in St Paul im Lavantthal, Stiftsbibliothek, MS 224[2] (formerly XXI, c.229) sometimes with annotations by Gerbert. This text is also in *A-Wn* cpv 51, ff.52v–55r, 12th century, ascribed to Abbot Berno. Ed. in *GS*, i, 330–38

Covers monochord mensuration, consonance, species of 4th, 5th and octave, modal finals and ambitus. Much can be traced back to Boethius and the general point of view seems to be that of the 10th century.

GS, i, Anon.II. Incipit: Quinque sunt consonantiae musicae. Same lost MS as for *GS*, i, Anon.I; further sources listed in Huglo (1971), 305. Ed. in *GS*, i, 338–42

Contents as for *GS*, i, Anon.I, with some words on the Greek Greater Perfect System and its pitch nomenclature. Huglo considered this an 11th-century south German recension of an introduction to a tonary which Gerbert chose not to print though it was in his source.

Mettenleiter anon. 3; Ratisbonensis cuiusdam ars musica. Incipit: [main text] Huius artis experienciam querere cupientibus. *D-Mbs* clm 5539, 13th century. Ed. in D. Mettenleiter: *Musikgeschichte der Stadt Regensburg* (Regensburg, 1866), 70ff

After a preface addressed to Bishop Heinrich of Regensburg (1277–96), an elementary treatment of standard topics (origins, etymologies, the hand, species of intervals, psalm formulae and *differentiae*), which serves to introduce a tonary.

Schneider anon.; British Museum anon. Incipit: Primum tractatum huius voluminis de symphonia. *GB-Lbm* Eg.2888, ff.27–39, Zeeland, 12th century. Ed. in Schneider (1935), ii, 106ff

Mostly on plainchant, particularly modality and composition, with a concluding section on discant; much is taken from Guido of Arezzo and Johannes Afflighemensis. The first part on traditional topics was not published by Schneider.

Vatican anon. Incipit: Quid est cantus? Peritia musice artis inflexio vocis . . .; tonus est sonus vocis armonie. *I-Rvat* Pal.lat.235, ff.38v–39r, 11th century. Ed. in P. Wagner: *Neumenkunde* (Freiburg, 1905), 214f [first pt.]; P. Wagner: 'Un piccolo trattato sul canto ecclesiastico in un manoscritto del secolo X–XI', *Rassegna gregoriana*, iii (1904), 480 [second pt.]. Facs. edn. in *KJb*, xix (1905), 70

Nomenclature and performance of plainchant neumes; enumeration of the 12 ecclesiastical modes, including four 'toni moesi' (mesoi); specific instances of modal ambiguity in antiphons. *RISM*, B/III/2, 106f

3. MUSICA PLANA. (Although strictly speaking this category should be reserved for works written according to the norm of the bipartite *musica plana–musica mensurabilis* type, it is used here for explanations of musical fundamentals (gamut, hexachords, intervals, monochord mensuration, theory of the ecclesiastical

modes) which do not have direct practical application to the singing of plainchant and which do not touch on mensural music.)

Adler anon. In Heb.; incipit of Fr. trans.: Juda fils du saint martyr rabbi Isaac a dit . . . La musique est la science des melodies. *F-Pn* héb.1037, ff.22v–27v, Italy, 15th or 16th century. Ed. in I. Adler: 'Le traité anonyme du manuscrit Hébreu 1037 de la Bibliothèque nationale de Paris', *Yuval*, i (Jerusalem, 1968), 1–47 [extensively annotated Heb. text with Fr. trans.]

Doubtless copied from Latin sources some time between the 12th century and the 14th. Topics are standard for *musica plana*: gamut, hexachords, Guidonian hand, mutations, intervals, a few remarks on notation and measurements of monochord, organ and bells.

CS, ii, Anon.II; Louvain treatise; Löwener Traktat; Tractatus de musica plana et organica. Incipit: Musica est ars recte canendi sono cantuque consistens. *B-LVu*, burnt in 1914, ff.186ff, St Jacobus in Insula, Liège, 13th century. Ed. in *CS*, ii, 484–98

Not actually designated anonymous by Coussemaker. Datable *c*1200. Treats standard topics of *musica plana* with some special features, chiefly references to Latin prosody and a group of discant rules much like those of Pseudo-Guido Caroli loci or *CH* Anon.IV.

De La Fage anon.; St Martial anon. Incipit: Discantus cantui debet esse contrarius. *I-Fn* II.I.406 Magl.XIX.19, ff.1–5, 15th century. Ed. in A. de La Fage: *Essais de dipthérographie musicale* (Paris, 1864), 355ff [only extracts of an already incomplete MS]. J. Handschin: 'Aus der alten Musiktheorie', *AcM*, xiv (1942), 23 [excerpts only]; A. Seay: 'An Anonymous Treatise from St. Martial', *AnnM*, v (1957), 7–42 [complete edn. based on collation with *I-PIu* IV.9, pt.2, pp.52–7, and *I-Vnm* VIII.85 (3570), ff.24–7; the work may perhaps also be found in *E-Bc* 833, ff.13v–15v; Seay's incipit: Incipit prologus in musicam planam Quoniam de canendi scienti doctrinam]

Unusual for its three-part structure: (i) *musica plana* with a notable section on composition; (ii) discant in three as well as two parts, the composition of organum; (iii) dialogue on church modes. Hüschen ('Anonymi', *MGG*, items 45–56) lists several de La Fage anonymi from both the *Essais de dipthérographie* and the extremely rare *Nicolai Capuani presbyteri Compendium musicale*, but without page or MS references. They are mostly extracts, and as the item above is the only one commonly called the 'de La Fage anon.' they have not been listed here.

Gümpel anon.1968a. Incipit: Devemos saber que en el arte del canto llano. *E-Bc* M.1327, ff.72v–89 [further sources listed in Gümpel]. Ed. in K.-W. Gümpel: 'Zur Frühgeschichte der vulgärsprachlichen spanischen und katalanischen Musiktheorie', *Spanische Forschungen der Görresgesellschaft*, 1st ser., xxiv (Münster, 1968), 257–336

Musical fundamentals, especially solmization (*deducçiones, mutanças, claves, tonos, dijuntas, conjuntas*). Gümpel suggested comparison with Seay anon. (CSM, ix) and close connection with *Quatuor principalia* (*CS*, iv, 200–98); and he believed the various versions went back to a vanished archetype.

Mettenleiter anon.1; Murrscher Anon. Incipit: Ex omni innumera varietate . . . Breviarium de musica. Compendiosum de musica breviarium collecturi et quasi quamdam introductionem. *D-Mbs* clm 14965b, ff.2v–33v, formerly owned by the abbey of St Emmeram, Regensburg, 12th century. Extracts ed. in D. Mettenleiter: *Musikgeschichte der Stadt Regensburg* (Regensburg, 1866), 13ff

Musical theory of the late 11th and early 12th centuries, with little application to practice unless it be construed as an introduction to the tonary on ff.34r–70.

Mettenleiter anon.2; Regulae de musica. Incipit: Prologus: Venerantissimis et in Christo plurimum diligendis. Extracts ed. in D. Mettenleiter: *Musikgeschichte der Stadt Regensburg* (Regensburg, 1866), 60ff

As the work was apparently composed by two monks from Hailsprunne in 1295 it seems perverse to list it among the anonymi. Two sections are very long, one on the ecclesiastical modes, the other a 'Commendatio omnium scientiarum et specialis musice'. There are also sections on the monochord, hexachords and consonance.

Wolf anon.1; Tractatus cuiusdam monachi de musica. Incipit: Quindecim chordae habentur in monochordo secundum Boetium. *D-Ds* Gr.8°1988, ff.182r–189v, once at the Benedictine monastery of St Jacques, Liège, late 11th century. Ed. in J. Wolf: 'Ein anonymer Musiktraktat des elften bis zwölften Jahrhunderts', *VMw*, ix (1893), 186–234

Standard topics of 11th-century music theory (e.g. tetrachords and species of intervals) with much borrowing from (or bearing on) Hermannus Contractus. Other writers quoted are Berno, *GS*, i, Anon.I, and Notker on the *litterae significativae*. The treatise was apparently known to the author of *Questiones in musica*.

Wolf anon.2; Basel Anon. First pt., 'Ars musice'. Incipit: Tractaturi de musica videndum est. Second pt., 'Ars musice armonia', incipit: Quoniam inter VII liberales artes. *CH-Bu* F.IX.54, ff.1r–8v, 13th–14th century.

Extracts ed. in J. Wolf: 'Anonymi cujusdam Codex Basiliensis', *VMw*, ix (1893), 408

Dated by Wolf in the 12th century, and also thought to be Germanic. The first part is primarily on the church modes with an interesting passage on their ethical character (illustrated by a diagram). There are connections with Johannes Afflighemensis and the *Questiones in musica*. The second part touches on hexachords, mutation, intervals and was thought by Wolf to be related to *CS*, ii, Anon.II.

4. ORGANUM.

CH, anon.I; Milan organum treatise; Ad organum faciendum. Incipit: Cunctipotens genitor (with alphabetical notation for two voices). *I-Ma* M.17 sup, ff.56v–61r, possibly from Laon, c1100. Ed. in *CH* no.1; Eggebrecht and Zaminer (1970), 44ff, 109ff, with Ger. trans. and facs.

Discusses note-against-note organum in two voices in both parallel and contrary motion. Eggebrecht and Zaminer deal in great detail with this work and other texts related to it. *RISM*, B/III/2, 59ff

Handschin anon.; Montpellier organum treatise. Incipit: Diaphonia duplex cantus est, cuius talis est diffinitio. *F-MO* H.384, ff.122–3, 12th century. Ed. in J. Handschin: 'Der Organumtraktat von Montpellier', *Festschrift für Guido Adler* (Vienna, 1930/R1971), 50; Eggebrecht and Zaminer (1970), 185ff

Written probably at the end of the 11th century; chiefly on cadence formation in two-voice note-against-note organum.

Müller anon.1; Cologne organum treatise. Incipit: De organo. Ed. in H. Müller: *Hucbalds echte und unechte Schriften über Musik* (Leipzig, 1884), 74

Probably from the 9th century and one of the earliest organum theorists.

Vatican anon.; Vatican organum treatise. Incipit: Organum est cantus subsequens precedentem. *I-Rvat* Ottob.3025, ff.46r–50v, 13th century. Ed. in F. Zaminer: *Der vatikanische Organum-traktat* (Tutzing, 1959), 185ff

Definitions and rules for organum originating in the 12th century, with a profusion of music examples. *RISM*, B/III/2, 106

5. DISCANT AND CONTRAPUNCTUS. (On discant rules in general see K.-J. Sachs: 'Zur Tradition der Klangschritt-Lehre', *AMw*, xxviii (1971), 233–70.)

CH anon.II. Incipit: Quiconques veut deschanter il doit premier savoir. *F-Pn* lat.15139 (formerly St Victor 813), ff.269r–270r in the margin, formerly in the possession of the abbey of St Victor, Paris, 13th century; also a fragment earlier in the same MS, f.263. Ed. in *CH*, no.2, 244–6 as 'Traité de déchant en langue romane'.

Discant rules closely related to a number of Latin versions, e.g. *E-Sco* 5.2.25, ff.81v–82v. *RISM*, B/III/1, 122

CH, anon.III; Discantus positio vulgaris. Incipit: Viso igitur quid sit discantus. *F-Pn* lat.16663, pp.129–30, Paris, 13th century. Ed. in *CH*, no.3; *CS*, i, 95–6; S. M. Cserba: *Hieronymus de Moravia*, Freiburger Studien zur Musikwissenschaft, 2nd ser., ii (Regensburg, 1935), 191f

Title coined by Coussemaker. In addition to discant rules the brief essay offers definitions of 'sonus', 'ligatura', 'consonantia' and some note forms. To Jerome of Moravia it was the oldest and most widely used work on discantus, thus probably from the early 13th century.

CH, anon.IV; Pseudo-Guido Caroli Loci (Gui de Chalis). Incipit: Ars probat artificem . . . si cantus ascendit duas voces. *F-Psg* 2284 (formerly 1611), ff.109v–110v, 13th century. Ed. in *CH* no.4; *CS*, ii, 191–2

Discant rules with no organic relation to the preceding work. *RISM*, B/III/1, 127; see also M. Bernard: *Répertoire de manuscrits médiévaux contenant des notations musicales*, i (Paris, 1965).

CH, anon.V; De arte discantandi. Incipit: Quando duae notae sunt in unisono et tertia ascendit. *F-Pn* lat.15139 (formerly St Victor 813), ff.270–75, in the margin, formerly in the possession of the abbey of St Victor, Paris, 13th century. Ed. in *CH*, no.5, pp.259–73

To the section on discant rules the MS joins one on mensural notation according to Franco, beginning: Gaudent brevitate moderni. Punctus quadratus.

CS, i, anon.V; De discantu. Incipit: Est autem unisonus. *GB-Lbm* Roy. 12.C.VI, f.50r–51v, Bury St Edmunds, 13th century; *Lbm* Add.4909, ff.94v–96v, 18th-century copy. Ed. in *CS*, i, 366–8

This brief treatment of intervals and consonance, along with a set of discant rules, seems exceptionally tolerant towards 3rds and 6ths; the notated examples use semibreves with tails both ascending and descending; the treatise is consequently a very late example of its type.

CS, iii, anon.VIII; Regulae de contrapuncto. Incipit: Consonantie contrapuncti demonstrativi ad oculum. *I-Fl* Plut.29/48, ff.72r–73r, Italy, 15th century. Ed. in *CS*, iii, 409–11

Contrapunctus rules. According to Sachs (1974) Coussemaker's edition comprises two distinct sets. *RISM*, B/III/2, 39

CS, iii, anon.XIII; Tractatus de discantu. Incipit: Qui veult savoir l'art de dechant. *F-Pn* lat.14741 (formerly St Victor 665), ff.viiiv–ixv. Ed. in *CS*, iii, 496–8

Brief but interesting treatment of discant, tolerant towards *musica ficta* and stern towards parallel 5ths and octaves. Datable possibly in the later 13th or early 14th century. The immediately preceding Latin work is drawn from Franco.

CS, iv [anon.I], Tractatus de musica figurata et de contrapuncto. Incipit: [hexachord diagram] Item notandum quod septem sunt reformationes. *F-Pn* lat.16664, ff.62v–85v. Ed. in *CS*, iv, 434–69

Doubtless from the latter half of the 15th century, this work on late mensural notation (with significant mention of proportions and diminution) also includes a section on contrapunctus devoting much attention to the contratenor. Following the treatise in the MS is an important collection of French polyphonic chansons with some pieces in Dutch, Italian and Latin. The work may be compared to *CS*, iii, anon. XII, in some respects.

6. MUSICA PLANA AND MUSICA MENSURABILIS.

CS, iii, anon.XI; Tractatus de musica plana et mensurabili. Incipit: Item diceres, quare musica studetur. *D-Rp* 98 Th.4°, ff.1–62, formerly owned by Abbey of St Maximinus, Trier, copied 1471; *GB-Lbm* Add.34200, ff.1–42, Germany, 15th century; other versions in *Ob* can.misc.177 and in a MS used by Bartha (see below) copied in 1490. Only the first of these MSS was used for Coussemaker's edn. in *CS*, iii, 416–75

A comprehensive work on *musica plana*, with noteworthy passages on *conjuncturae*, nomenclature of German neumes and detailed discussion of modality followed by counterpoint rules with special emphasis on the contratenor and treatment of signs of mensuration and proportion. A dating around the middle of the 15th century seems appropriate although there are substantial borrowings from Johannes Afflighemensis (11th century). It may be that *CS*, iii, anon. XII, which follows in the MS, belongs with this treatise. See Sachs (1974); D. Bartha: 'Studien zum musikalischen Schrifttum des 15. Jahrhunderts', *AMf*, i (1936), 59, 176

Michaelbeuern anon. Incipit: Musica est motus vocum rationabilium in arsim et a thesim. *A-MB* Cod.man.cart.95, ff.148r–153r, 15th century. Ed. in R. Federhofer-Königs: 'Ein anonymer Musiktraktat aus der 2. Hälfte des 14. Jahrhunderts in der Stiftsbibliothek Michaelbeuern/Salzburg', *KJb*, xlvi (1962), 43

Written in Prague, 1369 or possibly 1367. First part on *musica plana*, including ethical character of the ecclesiastical modes; second part (in hexameters) on 14th-century mensural notation and *musica ficta*. Generally highly derivative and possibly the work of a university student.

Seay anon. Incipit: Jesus: Libellus musicae adiscendae valde utilis et est dialogus . . . Discipulus: Modo quaeritur quid est musica? *I-Rvat* lat.5129, ff.145r–157r, 15th century. Ed. A. Seay, CSM, ix (1964)

Musica plana: gamut, hexachords, modal characteristics; with some counterpoint rules and a simple exposition of Ars Nova notation (termed 'regula organi'), thus possibly written early in the 14th century. *RISM*, B/III/2, 96f

7. MENSURAL MUSIC: LATE 13TH AND EARLY 14TH CENTURIES. (Many of these works contain sections on discantus.).

Anglès anon.1958; De cantu organico. Incipit: Ad evidentiam cantus organici est sciendum. *E-Bca* cuaderno de papel in 8°, Catalonia, slightly before 1350. Ed. in H. Anglès: 'De cantu organico: tratado de un autor catalán del siglo XIV', *AnM*, xiii (1958), 1

Mensural and Ars Nova notation with references to local Catalan practice. Interprets two semibreves in *tempus perfectum* with the first double the length of the second; enumerates seven rhythmic modes.

CH, anon.V; Ars musicae mensurabilis secundum Franconem. Incipit: Figura est representatio vocis in aliquo modorum ordinatae. *F-Pn* lat.15129 (formerly St Victor 1106), ff.1–3, 13th or 14th century. Ed. in *CH*, 274–94, as 'Quaedam de arte discantandi'; A. Gilles and G. Reaney, CSM, xv (1971) [inc.]

'Franconian' mensural notation, discant rules with elaborate examples in two and three voices. Gilles and Reaney also publish a similar work from *S-Uu* C.55, f.22r–v, 13th or 14th century.

CS, i, anon.II; Tractatus de discantu. Incipit: Gaudent brevitate moderni: quandocumque punctus quadratus. *F-SDI* 42, ff.34r–43r, Italy, 15th century. Ed. in *CS*, i, 303–19

After a first section on mensural notation clearly dependent on Franco (and found in several MSS of Italian provenance), there follow sections on the 13 species of intervals, discant rules, and 'falsa musica'. A chapter on musical proportions appears to have been planned but is not extant. The work is clearly related to *CH*, anon.VI, and for the first part to the *Abbreviatio magistri Franconis* by Johannes Balox (*CS*, i, 292–6).

CS, i, anon.III; De cantu mensurabili. Incipit: Gaudent brevitate moderni: Quandocunque nota quadrata . . . quicunque bene et secure. *F-SDI* 42, ff.53r–58v, Italy, 15th century. Ed. in *CS*, i, 319–27

First section on later 13th-century notation (with examples from motets); the second, comprising discant rules, is closely related to a number of other texts, especially the Faenza anon. See Sachs (1974).

CS, i, anon.IV; De mensuris et discantu. Incipit: Cognita modulatione melorum. *GB-Lbm* Roy. 12.C.VI, ff.59r–80v, Bury St Edmunds, 13th century; *Lbm* Cotton Tib.B.IX, ff.215r–224r, Bury St Edmunds, 14th century, burnt in 1731 but partly legible: *Lbm* Add.4909, ff.56v–93r, 18th-century copy of the latter. Ed. in *CS*, i, 327–65; F. Reckow: *Der Musiktraktat des Anonymus 4* (Wiesbaden, 1967); Eng. trans. by L. Dittmer: *Anonymous IV*, Music Theorists in Translation, i (Brooklyn, 1959)

The best known of all anonymi for having provided the key to understanding the Notre Dame school. It was evidently written by an Englishman, between 1270 and 1280. The treatise, heavily dependent on Johannes de Garlandia, follows after its verbose fashion a normal order of topics for treatises on mensural music: rhythmic modes, notation, consonance and dissonance, organum and discantus, with final less usual sections on genres of composition, books and modal irregularities. A final section ed. in Coussemaker, 'De sinemenis', is clearly not part of Anon.IV's work, but interesting in its own right in its treatment of *musica ficta*. All significant bibliography is listed in Reckow (1967).

CS, i, anon.VI; Tractatus de figuris sive de notis. Incipit: Cum in isto tractatu. *GB-Lbm* Roy. 12.C.VI, ff.54r–58r, Bury St Edmunds, 13th century; *Lbm* Add.4909, ff.98r–104v, 18th-century copy of *Lbm* Cotton Tib.B.IX which is thought to have contained this work before being heavily damaged by fire. Ed. in *CS*, i, 369–77; G. Reaney, CSM, xii (1966)

Early 14th century. Reaney suggested Torkesey as possible author, *c*1350. The treatise devotes its three chapters in turn to the *minima*, the *semibrevis* and the *brevis*, with mention of *longae*, *largae* and *largissimae*. There are a few citations of Aristotle, but the work seems conceptually earlier than Jehan des Murs.

CS, i, anon.VII; De musica libellus. Incipit: Modus in musica est debita mensuratio temporis. *F-Pn* lat.6286, ff.13r–14v, 14th century. Ed. in *CS*, i, 378–83

A brief treatment, apparently from the 13th century, of rhythmic modes, 'pre-Franconian' notation, species of intervals etc. The conclusion, on the finals of the church modes, seems to be out of order.

CS, iii, anon.I; De musica antiqua et nova. Incipit: Dictis aliquibus circa planum cantum. *GB-Lbm* Cotton Tib.B.IX, ff.205v–214r, probably Bury St Edmunds, 14th century; *Lbm* Add.4909, ff.31v–56r, 18th-century copy of *Lbm* Cotton Tib.B.IX. Ed. in *CS*, iii, 334–64

This mid-14th-century work is also found as the fourth book of the *Quatuor principalia* formerly attributed to Tunstede (*CS*, iv, 254–98), and covers in detail most of the topics of treatises on *musica mensurabilis*, including discant rules and some discussion of genres and performing practice. An English origin may be supposed in the absence of contradictory evidence. Coussemaker thought that the work immediately preceding it in the MSS belonged with it, but this seems questionable. On the MSS see Reckow (1967).

CS, iii, anon.II; De musica antiqua et nova. Incipit: Ad evidentiam valoris notularum. *F-Pn* lat.15128, ff.120r–122v, 14th century. Ed. in *CS*, iii, 364–70

This brief essay on notation appears, from its treatment of the *minima*, to antedate the systematic application of Ars Nova principles. It should probably be studied in the context of the works which accompany it in the MS: the *Abbreviatio magistri Franconis* by Johannes Balox (*CS*, i, 292–6), the extracts or reworking of Magister Lambertus's treatise (*CS*, i, 251–81) and *CS*, iii, anon.III and IV. *RISM*, B/III/1, 120f

CS, iii, anon.III; Compendiolum artis veteris ac novae. Incipit: Quoniam per ignorantiam artis musice. *F-Pn* lat.15128, ff.127r–129r. Ed in *CS*, iii, 370–75; A. Gilles: 'L'anonyme III de Coussemaker, *Scriptores* III', *MD*, xv (1961), 27

A brief treatment of mensural notation, not long after Philippe de Vitry to judge by the comment: 'De nova arte quam Philippus de Vitriaco nuper invenit, dicam'. Noteworthy references to minims, semiminims, the dragma (or *fuiscée*) and red notation.

CS, iii, anon.IV; Compendium artis mensurabilis tam veteris quam novae. Incipit: Si quis artem musice mensurabilis. *F-Pn* lat.15128, ff.129r–131v. Ed. in *CS*, iii, 376–9

A brief work with some interesting comparisons of old and new notational practice in the early 14th century. Red notation mentioned with two meanings (different modus or tempus from that shown by black notes; octave transposition). *RISM*, B/III/1, 121.

CS, iii, anon.IX; De musica mensurabili. Incipit: In der mensurabili musica so heissen die noten. *F-Sm* 222, burnt in 1870, though it is possible that other copies survive. Ed. in *CS*, iii, 411–13

On the ligatures of 13th-century mensural notation; only five modes enumerated; citation of motet triplum *O Maria virgo davitica*.

Faenza anon; Compendium musicae mensurabilis artis antiquae. Incipit: Gaudent brevitate moderni: quandocumque punctus quadratus vel nota quadrata. *I-FZc* 117, f.24/23r, 15th century. Ed. in F. A.

Gallo: *Petrus Picardus: Ars motettorum*, CSM, xv (1971), 61ff

This is one member of a far-flung family of brief treatises on late 13th-century notation in orbit around Franco. It cites Franco, Petrus de Cruce and some seven motets. *RISM*, B/IV/4, 898ff

OP anon. Incipit: Quod punctus per sui additionem . . . illud est causa alicuius. *GB-Ob* Bodley 77, ff.104a–105b, 15th century; *F-Pn* lat.14741, ff.5–6. Ed. in U. Michels: 'Der Musiktraktat des Anonymus OP', *AMw*, xxvi (1969), 49

The work, thought by Michels to have been written before 1321 (and consequently the first known document of Ars Nova theory), takes the form of a *disputatio* over five theses concerning imperfection and alternation in mensural notation.

Sowa anon.; St Emmeram anon. Incipit: Quoniam prosam artis musice mensurabilis. *D-Mbs* clm 14523 (formerly St Emmeram, Regensburg, F XXVI), ff.134v–159v. Ed. in H. Sowa: *Ein anonymer glossierter Mensuraltraktat 1279* (Kassel, 1930)

Prologue followed by sections on simple figures, composite figures, semibreves, mensural modes, hockets, motets, rests, consonances, discant, copula and organum. Arranged as a brief text in Leonine verse (410 lines) with extensive prose glosses, designed as an attack on the teachings of Magister Lambertus (*CS*, i, 251–81); mention and quotation of several motets from the Montpellier MS (*F-MO* H196).

Wolf anon.3; Compendium totius artis motetorum [authentic title]. Incipit: Primo punctus quadratus vel nota quadrata. *D-EF* 8°94, ff.68v–70r, 14th century. Ed. in J. Wolf: 'Ein anonymer Musiktraktat aus der ersten Zeit der "Ars Nova" ', *KJb*, xxi (1908), 33

Dated by Wolf *c*1340 (and thus of considerable import) this work deals with Ars Nova notation with particular mention of semiminims, *fusae* and coloration. There are many citations of motet titles, some attributed to Philippe de Vitry.

8. MENSURAL MUSIC: *c*1350–1450.

Anglès anon.1929. Incipit: [first pt.] Omni desideranti notitiam artis mensurabilis; [second pt.] Notandum primo quod quatuor sunt voces. *E-Sco* 5.2.25, ff.63r–66r, Verona, 15th century. Ed. in H. Anglès: 'Dos tractats medievals de música figurada', *Musikwissenschaftliche Beiträge: Festschrift für Johannes Wolf* (Berlin, 1929/R1973), 6

First part on mensural notation of later 14th century, comparable to the *Ars perfecta* (*CS*, iii, 28–35) wrongly attributed to Philippe de Vitry. Second part comprises three sections, thought by Sachs (1974, p.116) to be of separate authorship, the first dealing with discant rules by Nicola da Siena, the second with 'contrapunctus' and the last with rules for making ballades, rondeaux and virelais. On the MS see Sachs (1974) and F. A. Gallo: 'Alcuni fonti poco note di musica teorica e pratica', *L'ars nova italiana del trecento: convegni di studio 1961–1967* (Certaldo, 1968), 49–78.

Carapetyan anon.; Notitia del valore delle note del canto misurato. Incipit: Per avere alcuna notitia del valore delle note del canto misurato. *I-Fl* Redi 71, ff.13r–24r, early 15th century. Ed. A. Carapetyan, CSM, v (1957)

Thought by the editor to have served as a textbook for a Florentine convent of nuns *c*1400. It is embedded in a group of seven treatises, all in Tuscan. Treats of French notation of the later 14th century, handled in a relatively elementary manner, though with special attention to *maximodus*. The last section is very similar to the *Libellus cantus mensurabilis* of Pseudo-Jehan des Murs (*CS*, iii, 46–58).

CS, iii, anon.V; Ars cantus mensurabilis mensurata per modos iuris [authentic title]. Incipit: Cum multi antiqui modernique cantores. *F-Pn* lat.7369; *I-Fl* Plut.29/48, ff.73r–82v; *Fr* 734, ff.109v–122r, 15th century. Ed. in *CS*, iii, 379–98

An exceptionally interesting and detailed work on French notation of the later 14th century, with references to Italian practice. Particularly noted for its references to works of Machaut, Landini and the otherwise unknown Nicolaus de Aversa as well as for its discussion of color and talea. Coussemaker believed the author to be French, and it is clear that he was a disciple of Jehan des Murs. *RISM*, B/III/2, 39f, 51; see also U. Michels: *Die Musiktraktate des Johannes de Muris* (Wiesbaden, 1970), 30.

CS, iii, anon.VI; De musica mensurabili. Incipit: Cum dictum sit musicam in numero ternario. *US-Cn* 54.1, copied in 1391 by 'Frater G. de Anglia', in a Viennese private library when copied by F. Wolf for Coussemaker. Ed. in *CS*, iii, 398–403

Orthodox treatment (i.e. according to Jehan des Murs) of the numerical relationships of the basic note forms of French notation, from the minim unit to the *longissima* of 81 minims, with mention of larger values attributed to Philippus de Caserta and some curious practices in notating rests. The author of this essay, if one is to trust the verse colophon, was Frater Petrus. See K. von Fischer: 'Eine wiederaufgefundene Theoretikerhandschrift des späten 14. Jahrhunderts', *Schweizer Beiträge zur Musikwissenschaft*, 3rd ser., i (1972), 23.

CS, iii, anon.VII; De diversis manieribus in musica mensurabili. Incipit:

Sic formantur breves plicatae. *F-SDI* 42, ff.123*r*–127*v*. Ed. in *CS*, iii, 404–8 [seriously defective and does violence to the context of the MS]

Primarily on Italian 14th-century notation, this work, or fragment of a work, makes important references to Philippe de Vitry. K. von Fischer: 'Zur Entwicklung der italienischen Trecento-Notation', *AMw*, xvi (1959), 87, supersedes all previous discussions of the MS.

CS, iii, anon.X; De minimis notulis. Incipit: Item notandum quod notularum species quantum plures. *F-Sm* 222, burnt in 1870. Ed. in *CS*, iii, 413–15

On small note values (the minim or less) and on *diminutio*. References to compositions of Zeltenpferd and the work entitled *Molendinum de Paris* (*see* MOLINS, P. DES).

CS, iii, anon.XII; Tractatus de musica; Compendium cantus figurati; De discantu. Incipit: Quoniam per magis noti notitiam ad ignoti . . . Est diversorum cantuum. *D-Rp* 98 Th.4°, formerly owned by the abbey of St Maximinus, Trier, copied 1471. Ed. in *CS*, iii, 475–95

The longer first part is a rather advanced treatment of proportions, alteration, syncopation and coloration. The second is an elementary treatment of 14th-century French notation. A third section with citations of French polyphonic chansons was not published by Coussemaker.

Gallo anonymi 1966. A group of eight brief treatments of 14th-century notation, published in Gallo (1966). As none of them appears to have currency as an anonymous in its own right, see Gallo's edition for further details.

Kellner anon.; Kremsmünster anon.; Brieger anon. Incipit: Pra ficili informatione eorum, qui ad culmen artis musicae scientiae. *A-KR* 312, ff.210*v*–212*v*, possibly from Bohemia or Silesia, *c*1400. Ed. in P. A. Kellner: 'Ein Mensuraltraktat aus der Zeit um 1400', *Anzeiger der Österreichischen Akademie der Wissenschaften, philologisch-historische Klasse*, xciv (1957), 72

Mensural notation, particularly noteworthy for values smaller than the *minima*; symbols for modus, tempus and prolation; *transpositio* (= ?syncopation); *longa cardinalis*. See also *CS*, iii, anon.X, and other discussions of small note values, e.g. Philippus de Caserta, *CS*, iii, 118–24. Should possibly be read in conjunction with the table of mode and tempus found on ff.214*v*–215*r* of the MS and published in facs. by Kellner.

Melk anon.; Tractatulus de cantu mensurali seu figurativo musice artis. Incipit: Quoniam cantum mensuralem seu figuratum musice artis. *A-M* 950², ff.76(188)*v*–83(204)*v*, late 15th century. Ed. F. A. Gallo, CSM, xvi (1971)

On mensural notation of the mid to late 14th century, with some discussion of genres (e.g. the *trumpetum*). The many citations of compositions resemble those of Wolf anon.4. There are textual citations of Aristotle, Jehan des Murs and the Graz (Federhofer-Königs) anon., which is also found in the Melk MS.

Wolf anon.4; Breslau (Wrocław) anon. Incipit: Quoniam circa artem musicalis sciencie hodiernis. *PL-WRu* cart.IV.Qu.16, ff.144*v*–153*r*, 15th century. Ed. in J. Wolf: 'Ein Breslauer Mensuraltraktat des 15. Jahrhunderts', *AMw*, i (1918–19), 329

Treatise on notation *c*1400, with notable stress on lesser note values, e.g. various forms of *fusa*, and an important concluding section on *transpositio*. There are also many citations of specific works and genres; see Kellner anon.

9. MISCELLANEOUS. (This section includes works of the liberal arts or quadrivial tradition.)

Casimiri anon.; Ars et modus pulsandi organa. Incipit: C. D. E. F. . . . nota quod omnes voces totius organi. *I-Rvat* Barberini 307, f.37*v*/29*v*, Italy, *c*1400. Ed. in R. Casimiri: 'Un trattatello per organisti di anonimo del sec. XIV', *NA*, xix (1942), 98

Proposes a compass of three octaves and a 2nd, *c–d′′*, in which the lowest 6th is diatonic, but the rest from B♭ up is chromatic, for 35 keys in all. It states that *mi–fa* is possible anywhere, which would presumably require a non-Pythagorean tuning.

CS, i, anon.I; Tractatus de consonantiis musicalibus. Incipit: Tredecim consonantie [with annotated melody] . . . Harum consonantiarum. *B-Br* 10162/66, ff.1*r*–3*v*, St Laurence's Abbey, Liège, 15th century. Ed. in *CS*, i, 296–302

The initial didactic interval song is adapted from Hermannus Contractus. In addition to the discussion of intervals, and concord and discord, there are closing remarks on discantus. The work is thought to date back to the 13th century with some influence from Franco. *MD*, viii (1954), 6, ascribes it to the young Jacques de Liège. *RISM*, B/III/1, 58–62

Franciscan anon. of Bristol. J. Smits van Waesberghe's designation (*KJb*, 1 (1966), 15) for the author of *Quatuor principalia*; *see* TUNSTEDE, SIMON. See also Reaney (1964).

GS, i, anon.III; Fragmentum musices. Incipit: Ab omni superparticulari si continuam ei. From a 12th-century MS formerly in the library of the monastery of St Blasien but no longer extant (see note for *GS*, i, anon.I). Ed. in *GS*, i, 343–4

Comprises three lengthy glosses to Boethius, *Musica*, ii/10/21, and at the beginning is identical with the letter of Gerbertus Scholasticus (Pope Sylvester) to Constantinus. See N. Bubnov: *Gerberti . . . opera mathematica* (Berlin, 1899), 28.

GS, ii, anon.I; De mensura fistularum in organis; De mensura fistularum. Incipit: Fac tibi fistulam secundum aestimationem . . . primam fistulam quam longam . . . cognita omni consonantia. St Blasien, MS destroyed in 1768 but copied in part in the 18th-century *I-Bc* A 43; also in *US-R* ML92 1200 (formerly Admont 494), ff.74*v*–75*v*, 12th century. Ed. in *GS*, ii, 283–7; for the organ mensurations K.-J. Sachs: *Mensura fistularum* (Stuttgart, 1970), 99f, 115ff

Organ pipe mensurations and one for the *organistrum*; from 12th century or before.

Graz anon.; Federhofer-Königs anon. Incipit: Musica disciplina est que de numeris loquitur. The work appears to be incomplete. *A-Gu* 1201, ff.61*v*–63*v*, second half of 14th century. Ed. in R. Federhofer-Königs: 'Ein unvollständiger Musiktraktat des 14. Jahrhunderts im Ms. 1201 der Universitätsbibliothek Graz', *KJb*, xliv (1960), 14

Definitions, etymologies, correspondence of melodic intervals with planetary distances; consequently there are many concordances with treatises of the liberal arts tradition. Among the authorities cited by name are Maimonides, Plato, Aristotle and Alchabitio. See A. Kern: *Die Handschriften der Universitätsbibliothek Graz*, ii (Vienna, 1956), 256.

Gümpel anon.1968b. Incipit: Musica est una de septem artibus quas liberales appellamus. *E-Bc* M1327, ff.71–72*v*, 15th century. Ed. in K.-W. Gümpel: 'Zur Frühgeschichte der vulgärsprachlichen spanischen und katalanischen Musiktheorie', *Spanische Forschungen der Görresgesellschaft*, 1st ser., xxiv (Münster, 1968), 257–336

A collection of commonplaces (definitions, etymologies, utility of music) with many borrowings from Boethius and Johannes Afflighemensis.

Handschin anon. A brief text on 15th-century keyboard tuning; *see* TEMPERAMENTS.

Leibowitz anon. René Leibowitz's translation into French of a forgery by Hugo Riemann. Ed. in R. Leibowitz: *Un traité inconnu de la technique de la variation (XIVe siècle)* (Liège, 1950). See H. Besseler: 'M. Ugolini de Maltero Thuringi "De cantu fractabili": ein scherzhafter Traktat von Hugo Riemann', *AcM*, xli (1969), 107.

Smits van Waesberghe anonymi. 'Liber specierum'; 'Liber argumentorum'; 'Commentarius in Micrologum'; 'Metrologus'. *See* GUIDO OF AREZZO, to whose works they are directly related.

Steglich anon.; Quaestiones in musica. See RUDOLF OF ST TROND.

Vivell anon.; Commentarius in Micrologum. See GUIDO OF AREZZO, §2, vi.

See also THEORY, THEORISTS.   LAWRENCE GUSHEE

Anrooy, Peter van (*b* Zaltbommel, 13 Oct 1879; *d* The Hague, 31 Dec 1954). Dutch conductor and composer. He studied theory (under Johan Wagenaar) and the violin at the Utrecht Music School and in 1899 went to Moscow, where he learnt conducting with Willem Kes, and composition with Sergey Taneyev. After experience as an orchestral violinist in Glasgow and Zurich, he became conductor of symphony orchestras at Groningen (1905) and Arnhem (1910) before being appointed in 1917 to the Residentie-Orkest at The Hague. He remained there, winning a good reputation for the orchestra, until his retirement in 1935, and also succeeded Wagenaar as conductor of the Toonkunst Choir at The Hague (until 1940). His works, in neo-Romantic style, include an orchestral rhapsody *Piet Hein* (1901, his best-known work), a ballade for violin and orchestra, and a piano quintet.

BIBLIOGRAPHY
W. Paap: 'Dr Peter van Anrooy', *Mens en melodie*, x (1955), 1
J. de Geus: 'Dr Peter van Anrooy als leraar', *Mens en melodie*, x (1955), 2

ARTHUR JACOBS

Ansalone. *See* ANZALONE family.

Ansanus S [?Senese] (*fl* 1515). Italian composer. He probably lived in Siena; his compositions appear only in

Canzone sonetti strambotti et frottole, libro primo printed by Petrus Sambonettus in Siena in 1515. It contains probably 15 frottolas by Ansanus, but some of the ascriptions are open to doubt: the most complete form of his name, 'Ansanus S', is given before *Ingrata gelosia, ben sei cruda*, but *La virtù si è nostra stella* is ascribed only to 'S'. Ansanus set seven *barzellette* (of which three are carnival songs), three *ode*, two canzoni, one *capitolo* and one *strambotto*. The folio containing *Non domandar pietà*, ascribed to 'A' in the table of contents, is lacking from the sole surviving copy of the book. Particularly interesting are a political canzone, *Volge fortuna*, with its reference to the changing fortunes of Charles VIII of France and Pope Julius II, and three carnival songs, *Chi volessi Turchi siamo, Noi siamo galeotti* and *Logiamenti noi cerchiamo*, a part of the small repertory of non-Florentine mascheratas. Also important are three pieces that include texts in the altus as well as in the cantus, perhaps indicating that the lower parts were to be performed vocally. Three pieces are edited by R. Bartoli (*Composizioni vocali polifoniche*, Milan, 1917), Gallucci and Jeppesen.

BIBLIOGRAPHY

L. Cellesi: 'Ricerche intorno ai compositori dello "Zibaldoncino Musicale" marucelliano', *Bollettino senese di storia patria*, new ser., ii (1931), 307

F. Ghisi: *I canti carnascialeschi nelle fonti musicali del XV e XVI secolo* (Florence, 1937)

A. Einstein: *The Italian Madrigal*, i (Princeton, 1949/R1971)

J. Gallucci: *Festival Music in Florence, ca. 1480–ca. 1520* (diss., Harvard U., 1966)

K. Jeppesen: *La frottola* (Copenhagen, 1968)

WILLIAM F. PRIZER

Ansatz (Ger.). (1) In wind playing, EMBOUCHURE.

(2) In singing, the arrangement of the vocal apparatus or the attack of a note.

(3) In piano playing, touch.

Ansbach. Town in the southern Federal Republic of Germany, formerly the seat of the Hohenzollern margraves of Brandenburg-Ansbach. The margravate was established in the 14th century, but it was only after George 'the Pious' (ruled 1536–43) had recognized Lutheranism as his official creed that music began to assume considerable importance. After 1565, under the Kapellmeisters Jacob Meiland and Teodore Riccio, the music staff of the court included Flemings, Italians and Saxons, and the repertory became more cosmopolitan. Because the margraves also maintained a residence at Königsberg the staff was peripatetic; thus Johannes Eccard, Riccio's pupil and successor, encouraged by his employer, published his two sets of *Geistliche Lieder* (1597) at Königsberg.

In the later 17th century the Ansbach court began to develop towards its final Baroque splendour, and this was also a climactic period in the musical life of the court. In 1679 the opera *Die drey Töchter des Cecrops* by J. W. Franck, a court official and Kapellmeister from 1672 to 1679, was first performed, and his *Diocletianus* was produced in 1682 following its Hamburg première earlier that year. J. S. Kusser, fresh from his studies in Paris, was Kapellmeister in 1682–3; he was succeeded by J. G. Conradi (1683–6). The *Hochfürstliche Brandenburgisch Onolzbachischen Inventarium de Anno 1686* (Staatsarchiv, Nuremberg) suggests further French influence at this court; many Lully operas (including *Thésée, Cadmus, Isis, Psyché, Bellérophon, Proserpine, Roland, Alceste* and *Atys*) and the ballet *Le*

triomphe de l'amour, extant in both score and parts, may have been performed at Ansbach. C. L. Boxberg, already well known as an opera composer in Leipzig, was active at court in the late 1690s and his *Orion, Die verschwiegene Treue* and *Sardanapolus* were first performed at Ansbach in 1697–8. In 1697, when his first German commission, *Il Narciso*, was produced, F. A. M. Pistocchi became Kapellmeister and held the post until 1701; he was the first teacher of J. G. Pisendel, who was a chorister at Ansbach. Queen Caroline, consort of George II of England and a friend of Handel, and J. C. Smith, Handel's amanuensis, were born and brought up in Ansbach. Although the 18th century was musically less interesting, musical activity continued at the court. Important Kapellmeisters included J. C. Rau (1698–1717) and G. H. Bümler (1717–23 and 1726–45).

In 1831 a choral society was founded, and two years later a male-voice choir. Weber's nephew Anton Wilhelm was Kapellmeister for a time, and Johann Dürrner (1810–59) Kantor. A native of Ansbach, Dürrner was a pupil of Mendelssohn and in later life active in Edinburgh. He was a prolific composer, inflecting his partsongs with a Scottish idiom.

The biennial Ansbach Bach Festival, first held in 1948, was instigated partly because the Ansbachers J. M. Gesner and L. C. Mizler were Leipzig acquaintances of Bach and because J. G. Voigt, organist of St Gumbertus (1752–65), was his pupil. Two dedicated Ansbach musicians, Edmund Hohmann (1858–1955) and Herman Meyer (1902–45), had laid the foundations for a Baroque revival on which the first directors of the Bach Festival, Ferdinand Leitner and Fritz Rieger, were able to build. Performances take place in the traditional auditoriums of the town: St Johann, St Gumbertus (which has a fine neo-Baroque Steinmeyer organ, 1961), the state room of the palace and the orangery.

BIBLIOGRAPHY

C. Sachs: 'Die Ansbacher Hofkapelle unter Markgraf Johann Friedrich (1672–1686)', *SIMG*, xi (1909–10), 105–37

R. Oppel: 'Beiträge zur Geschichte der Ansbacher-Königsberger Hofkapelle unter Riccius', *SIMG*, xii (1910–11), 1

H. Mersmann: *Beiträge zur Ansbacher Musikgeschichte* (Ansbach, 1916)

F. W. Schwarzbeck: *Ansbacher Theatergeschichte bis zum Tode des Markgrafen Johann Friedrich (1686)* (Emsdetten, 1939)

G. Schmidt: *Die Musik am Hofe der Markgrafen von Brandenburg-Ansbach vom ausgehende Mittelalter bis 1806* (Kassel, 1956)

M. Ruhnke: *Beiträge zu einer Geschichte der deutschen Hofmusikkollegien im 16. Jahrhundert* (Berlin, 1963), 230ff

R. Brockpähler: *Handbuch zur Geschichte der Barockoper in Deutschland* (Emsdetten, 1964)

A. Lang: 'Das Werk des Thomaskantors lebt in Ansbach', *Ansbach* (Munich, 1965), 24

O. Meyer: 'Zur Geschichte der St. Gumbertus-Orgel', *Ansbacher Kulturspiegel mit Veranstaltungskalender*, xxi (1969)

Bachwoche Ansbach: offizieller Almanach (Ansbach, 1969, 1971, 1973, 1975)

PERCY M. YOUNG

Ansbach, Elizabeth, Margravine of. See ANSPACH, ELIZABETH.

Anschlag (Ger.). (1) A 'double appoggiatura', that is, an ornament consisting of two notes rising by a leap and falling back by a step to the principal note, described in more detail under ORNAMENTS.

(2) In piano playing, touch.

Anschlussmotiv (Ger.: 'annexed motif'). A term used by Hugo Riemann to denote a subsidiary phrase unit, usually two or three beats in length, placed immediately after the last strong beat of a main phrase unit. It occupies the relatively weaker beats that follow that strong beat, and serves to generate a second strong beat, equal in stress to the first, on one of those weaker beats. Thus it falls within the natural metrical structure of the main phrase; that is, it cannot itself give rise to an extension of the phrase's natural metrical pattern although it can occur within such an extension. In practice the *Anschlussmotiv* takes either of two forms: a reiteration of the strong beat itself, or an elaborate form of FEMININE ENDING. Ex.1 illustrates the former: not only the downbeat of bar 2 (similarly of bar 4) but also its preceding upbeat is rhythmically reiterated to form the

Ex.1

Anschlussmotiv, the pitch of the downbeat being restated. The *Anschlussmotiv* in this example thus occupies the second and third beats of bar 2 (and bar 4), and is 'annexed' to the first beat. In his 'phrase-structure editions' Riemann marked the device with a slur mark, open-ended at the left.

See also RHYTHM.

Anschütz, Georg (*b* Brunswick, 15 Nov 1886; *d* Hamburg, 25 Dec 1953). German psychologist. He studied psychology and aesthetics under Lipps (Munich), Külpe (Bonn), Binet (Paris) and Wundt (Leipzig), and from 1915 to 1919 was guest professor at the University of Istanbul. He was especially interested in the phenomenon of synaesthesia and between 1927 and 1936 he organized in Hamburg four congresses on the psychological relationship between colours and musical sounds. From 1931 to 1945 he was a professor (from 1942 director) of the Institute for Psychology, Hamburg.

WRITINGS

Die Intelligenz (Osterwieck, 1913)
Farbe-Ton-Forschungen (Leipzig, 1927–36)
Kurze Einführung in die Farbe-Ton-Forschung (Leipzig, 1927)
Das Farbe-Ton-Problem im psychologischen Gesamtbereich (Halle, 1929)
Abriss der Musikästhetik (Leipzig, 1930)
'Zur Frage der echten und unechten "audition colorée" ', *Zeitschrift für Psychologie*, cxvi (1930), 309–54
'Das Verhältnis der Musik zu den bildenden Künsten im Lichte stilistischer Betrachtung', *AMw*, iii (1938), 3
'Auftreten und Sinn subjektiver Tonempfindungen', *Zeitschrift für Psychologie*, cxxviii (1942)

BIBLIOGRAPHY

A. Wellek: 'In memoriam Georg Anschütz', *Mf*, vii (1954), 199

MALCOLM TURNER

Anseaume, Louis (*b* Paris, ?1721; *d* Paris, ?7 July 1784). French librettist. From the 1750s onwards he held various posts at the Opéra-Comique and the Théâtre-Italien; he wrote more than 30 librettos, mainly for those theatres. His earliest works were mostly parodies of Italian operas. Working closely with Laruette and Egidio Duni (he also wrote for F.-A. Philidor, Grétry and Gluck) he participated in the formation of the *comédie mêlée d'ariettes*; he particularly favoured the *opéra comique larmoyante*. Among his most popular works were *Les deux chasseurs et la laitière* (1763, for Duni) and *Le tableau parlant* (1769, for Grétry). Although Grimm praised his naturalism and lyric qualities, his comic scenes were generally considered weak and sometimes distasteful. Many of his texts appeared in the three-volume *Théâtre de M. Anseaume* (Paris, 1766).

BIBLIOGRAPHY

F. M. von Grimm, E. Diderot and others: *Correspondance littéraire, philosophique et critique* (Paris, 1812–14); ed. M. Tourneux (1877–82) [orig. censored]
P. Wechsler: *Louis Anseaume und das französische Singspiel* (Leipzig, 1909)
M. Prevost: 'Anseaume (Louis)', *DBF*
P. Letailleur: 'Jean-Louis Laruette: chanteur et compositeur', *RMFC*, viii (1968), 165; ix (1969), 150; x (1970), 78

Anselmi, Giorgio (*b* Parma, before 1386; *d* c1440–43). Italian scholar whose many works on astronomy, astrology and medicine also include a treatise *De musica*, notable for its influence on Franchinus Gaffurius. He studied as a youth in Pavia and in about 1428 practised medicine in Ferrara, each time returning to Parma, where he was a member of a distinguished family.

The only remaining copy of the treatise is Gaffurius's well-glossed mid-century copy (*I-Ma* H 233 Inf.). Written in April 1434, the work was purportedly the record of conversations between Anselmi and Pietro di Rossi which took place in September 1433 near Lucca at the baths of Corsenna. The treatise presents in dialogue form the topics of *harmonia celestis*, *harmonia instrumentalis* and *harmonia cantabilis*; each part represents one day's conversation. The influence of the medieval tripartite division is apparent, and although he did not disagree with the main ideas, Anselmi did not accept some of the lesser aspects of the Boethian doctrines (e.g. tonal division).

The first portion of the treatise presents a traditional understanding of the heavens in its discussion of music's reflection of the proportions of the universe. The second section, devoted entirely to a demonstration of the mathematical ratios of the intervals, utilizes the monochord as a vehicle. Anselmi's four-octave division includes a complete set of flat semitones. These speculative sections are followed by the final dialogue, which covers the more practical aspects of notation, solmization and the ecclesiastical modes. The final portion on the rules of counterpoint is preceded by a forward-looking section that attempts to clarify some of the problems of mensural notation by using specific shapes for the notes.

As one of many writers on music in the 14th-century Italian tradition, Anselmi was no more distinguished than many of his contemporaries, but his work is often more interesting for its presentation of inventive solutions to a number of current theoretical problems.

BIBLIOGRAPHY

J. Handschin: 'Anselmi's Treatise on Music annotated by Gafori', *MD*, ii (1948), 123
S. Clercx: 'Le traité *De musica* de Georges Anselme de Parme', *RBM*, xv (1961), 161
G. Massera: *Giorgio Anselmi Parmensis, De musica* (Florence, 1961) [see review by A. Seay in *JAMS*, xv (1962), 214]

CECIL ADKINS

Anselmi, Giuseppe (*b* Catania, 16 Nov 1876; *d* Zoagli, nr. Rapallo, 27 May 1929). Italian tenor, violinist and composer. He first appeared at the age of 13 as a violinist in his native city. After some experience in operetta he made his operatic début at Athens in 1896 as Turiddu, always one of his best roles. Serious studies with the conductor Mancinelli led to appearances in Italy, notably at the San Carlo, Naples, again as Turiddu, in January 1901. The same year he sang at Covent Garden in *Rigoletto*, *La bohème* (with Melba and *Cavalleria rusticana*; during subsequent London seasons (in 1904 and 1909) he was also seen in *Adriana Lecouvreur*, *Tosca*, *Il barbiere di Siviglia* and *Lucia*. His success was very great in Buenos Aires, Warsaw, Moscow and St Petersburg; but greatest of all in Spain, where he was decisively preferred to Caruso. He retired in 1917, making his final public appearance, once more as a violinist, at Rapallo in 1926. His compositions include songs, chamber music and a *Poema sinfonico* for orchestra. His warm, beautiful timbre and impassioned delivery were helped by vivid enunciation as well as by a romantic appearance. The elegance and individuality of his singing are clearly evident on the 100 or so Fonotipia records that he made between 1907 and about 1910. Although in Mozart's 'Il mio tesoro' his style now strikes one as almost comically wayward, no-one has surpassed his interpretations of Verdi's 'Quando le sere al placido' (*Luisa Miller*), of Giordano's 'Amor ti vieta' (*Fedora*) and of the Siciliana from *Cavalleria rusticana*.

BIBLIOGRAPHY

D. Shawe-Taylor: 'Giuseppe Anselmi', *Opera*, vii (1956), 146
R. Celletti: 'Anselmi, Giuseppe', *Le grandi voci* (Rome, 1964) [with opera discography by R. Vegeto]

DESMOND SHAWE-TAYLOR

Anselmo. *See* REULX, ANSELMO DE.

Ansermet, Ernest (*b* Vevey, 11 Nov 1883; *d* Geneva, 20 Feb 1969). Swiss conductor. He first followed his father's profession of mathematician, graduating from Lausanne University in 1903 and returning there as professor of mathematics, 1905–9. By then he had become more keenly interested in music, taking lessons in composition with Ernest Bloch and watching local conductors carefully. He decided to make music his

Ernest Ansermet

career, and after a year in Berlin (where he sought advice from Nikisch and Weingartner) he conducted his first concerts at Lausanne and Montreux in 1910. In the following year he took over the Kursaal concerts at Montreux from Francisco de Lacerda (whom he

acknowledged as the model for his mainly self-taught conducting technique), and in 1915 he became conductor of the Geneva SO.

During this time he formed friendships with several composers, including Debussy, Ravel and Stravinsky (then living in Switzerland). In 1915, on Stravinsky's recommendation, Ansermet became principal conductor for Dyagilev's Ballets Russes, with whom he made his North American début at New York in 1916, his South American début in 1917, and his London début in 1919. On the 1916 tour he made his first gramophone records with the orchestra of the Ballets Russes. His growing international reputation in this appointment was enhanced by his premières of such ballets as *El sombrero de tres picos* (Falla), *The Buffoon* (Prokofiev) and *Parade* (Satie), as well as various Stravinsky works including *The Soldier's Tale*, *Pulcinella* and *Renard*.

Ansermet formed L'Orchestre de la Suisse Romande at Geneva in 1918 and directed it continuously until his retirement in 1966. His performances were distinguished by his instinct for clarity of timbre and texture, and a scholar's concern for accuracy. He was a perceptive exponent of the classics but an even more persuasive advocate for the music of his contemporaries – notably the French school of Debussy, Ravel and Roussel, as well as Stravinsky. He championed his compatriots, Honegger and Frank Martin, and displayed a particular regard for Bartók and Britten, conducting the premières of the latter's *The Rape of Lucretia* at Glyndebourne and the *Cantata misericordium* at Geneva.

His earlier admiration for Stravinsky cooled with the composer's adoption of serial technique in the 1950s, and he published a strongly argued case against serial composition in a theoretical and philosophical treatise *Les fondements de la musique dans la conscience humaine*. Although he toured widely as a guest conductor, his sense of artistic responsibility kept him firmly linked to his own orchestra in Geneva ·in preference to tempting offers from elsewhere. With his Suisse Romande players he made numerous gramophone records which notably enriched the repertory and remain a testament to his musical character. His own compositions include *Feuilles au printemps* for orchestra, and settings of French verse.

See also ANALYSIS, §II, 8.

WRITINGS

La geste du chef d'orchestre (Lausanne, 1943)
Débat sur l'art contemporain (Neuchâtel, 1948)
Les fondements de la musique dans la conscience humaine (Neuchâtel, 1961)
with J.-C. Piguet: *Entretiens sur la musique* (Neuchâtel, 1963)
'The Crises of Contemporary Music – I. The Musical Problem', *Recorded Sound* (1964), no.13, p.165
'The Crises of Contemporary Music – II. The Stravinsky Case', *Recorded Sound* (1964), no.14, p.197
'After Twenty Years of Recording', *Gramophone*, xlv (1967), 145
ed. J.-C. Piguet: *Ecrits sur la musique* (Neuchâtel, 1971)

BIBLIOGRAPHY

R. Gelatt: *Music Makers* (New York, 1953, 2/1972)
F. F. Clough and G. J. Cuming: 'Ansermet Discography', *Gramophone Record Review*, new ser. (1958), no.50, p.228
B. Gavoty: *Ernest Ansermet* (Geneva, 1961) [with discography]
A. Blyth: 'Ernest Ansermet, 1883–1969', *Gramophone*, xlvi (1969), 1406
G. Larner: 'Ansermet – Radical or Revolutionary?', *Records and Recording*, xiv (1970), 42
J.-C. Piguet and J. Burdet: *Ernest Ansermet et Frank Martin: correspondance 1934–1968* (Neuchâtel, 1976)

NOËL GOODWIN

Ansetzen (Ger.). EMBOUCHURE.

Anson, H(ugo) V(ernon) (*b* Wellington, 18 Oct 1894; *d* London, 4 Aug 1958). New Zealand composer and teacher. He studied in England at the RCM (1912–13, 1920–21) and at Trinity College, Cambridge (1913–20 with a break for war service; MA, MusB 1921). After a period as music director at Alleyn's School (1922–5), he joined the staff of the RCM, where he was made a Fellow and registrar in 1939.

WORKS
(*selective list*)

Choral: Alkestis (incidental music, Euripides, trans. Murray), chorus, orch; Magnificat, Nunc dimittis, Te Deum, Benedictus, unison vv; 3 Partsongs (Blake), female/boys' vv; Saadabad (Flecker), Bar, chorus, orch; carols

Inst: Conc., 2 pf, str; Str Qt; Berceuse, vn, pf; Chorale, 2 vn, pf; 4 Character Sketches, vn, pf; Suite, fl, pf; Tranquillity, vn, pf; 2 Poems, vc, pf; 5 Pf Preludes; 11 Easy Pf Pieces; St Tropez Suite, 2 pf

Songs: 2 images; Full Moon (Sackville-West); Last Night (Darley); New Zealand, patriotic song; 2 Songs (Blake)

ERIC BLOM/R

Ansorge, Conrad (*b* Buchwald, Silesia, 15 Oct 1862; *d* Berlin, 13 Feb 1930). German pianist and composer. He studied at the Leipzig Conservatory and with Liszt in Weimar (1885–6). He toured in the USA and in 1893 returned to Weimar as professor of the piano. He taught at the Klindworth–Scharwenka Conservatory in Berlin from 1898 to 1903. In 1920 he became head of the piano master class at the German Academy in Prague. Ansorge ranked high as a pianist especially in the music of Beethoven. He also distinguished himself as a composer but none of his works has survived in the current repertory. They include orchestral and chamber music, a piano concerto and three sonatas and a Requiem for male-voice chorus and orchestra.

BIBLIOGRAPHY

R. M. Breithaupt: 'Conrad Ansorge', *Nord und Süd* (1908–9), 292

W. Niemann: *Meister des Klaviers* (Berlin, 1919), 21f

K. Schubert: 'Conrad Ansorge', *Berliner Musik Jb* (1926), 60

E. L. Schellenberg: 'Conrad Ansorge', *Die Musik*, xx/8 (1928), 578

R. M. Breithaupt: 'Conrad Ansorge zum Gedächtnis', *Die Musik*, xxii/7 (1930), 519

G. Howard: 'The Recorded Legacy of Liszt Pupils', *78 rpm* (1968), no.2, p.2 [with discography]

RONALD KINLOCH ANDERSON

Anspach [Ansbach], **Elizabeth,** Margravine of [Craven, Elizabeth] (*b* London, 17 Dec 1750; *d* Naples, 13 Jan 1828). English composer and playwright. She was the daughter of Augustus, 4th Earl of Berkeley, and at the age of 17 married William Craven (later 6th Earl of Craven), from whom she separated in 1780. After some years of extensive travels she settled at Anspach (now Ansbach) in Franconia, and 16 days after the death of her husband, on 13 October 1791, she married the Margrave Christian Frederick (1736–1808) at Lisbon. After the incorporation of the tiny Anspach principality into Prussia in 1792, the margrave and margravine went to England and lived at Brandenburgh House, Hammersmith. R. J. S. Stevens recorded a visit there, in 1794, in his memoirs (in *GB-Cpl*).

Under her first married name, Elizabeth Craven wrote a number of plays, in English and French, most of which were privately performed; some were also given in public, for example the comedy *The Miniature Picture* (London, Drury Lane Theatre, 24 May 1780), and the operas *The Silver Tankard* (Haymarket Theatre, 18 July 1781) and *The Princess of Georgia* (Covent Garden Theatre, 19 April 1794). For the last two she also provided part of the music, as she did for *The Arcadian Pastoral* (1782) and for some French plays performed at Anspach, 1788–90, such as *Nourjad et Fatmé*, *Le repentir des voeux* and *Le philosophe moderne*. None of her music is known to have survived, apart from a setting of Shakespeare's *O Mistress Mine* as a madrigal (London, *c*1856).

ALFRED LOEWENBERG/CHARLES CUDWORTH

Ansseau, Fernand (*b* Boussu-Bois, nr. Mons, 6 Nov or 6 March 1890; *d* Brussels, 1 May 1972). Belgian tenor. A pupil of Demest in Brussels, he made his début at Dijon in 1913 as Jean in Massenet's *Hérodiade*, and soon followed this successful start by singing leading French repertory roles at La Monnaie. The war delayed his international recognition, but in 1919 he sang Des Grieux at Covent Garden, where he established himself as a favourite guest in the 1920s. From 1920 he sang at the Opéra-Comique, where he was chosen in 1921 as the first tenor Orpheus since Nourrit and Duprez. Mary Garden engaged him for Chicago from 1923. The Paris Opéra selected him for *Alceste* (with Lubin) and Lohengrin. Later in his career he sang mostly at La Monnaie, undertaking the more taxing Tannhäuser and Alvaro. His extremely beautiful voice not only suited him for lyrical roles, but with its inner animal drive and dramatic verve he always gave vivid stage performances. After he retired in 1939 he taught at the Brussels Conservatory.

BIBLIOGRAPHY

A. De Cock: 'Fernand Ansseau', *Record Collector*, ix (1954), 5 [with discography]

R. Celletti: 'Ansseau, Fernand', *Le grandi voci* (Rome, 1964) [with opera discography by R. Vegeto]

ANDRÉ TUBEUF

Anstieg. A term used in Schenkerian analysis; *see* UNTERGREIFEN.

Answer (Ger. *Gefährte*; It. *risposta*; Lat. *comes*). An entry of a theme which 'answers' an immediately preceding entry of it. The most common use of the term refers to the EXPOSITION of a FUGUE. There the theme is first delivered by one part (this statement is called the SUBJECT) and then 'answered' by another, usually at the pitch interval of a 4th or 5th. From this usage it has become conventional to speak of further entries as 'answers', both in the exposition and later in the fugue, whenever they closely relate to a previous entry, being at the 4th or 5th to it (Bach, *Das wohltemperirte Clavier*, i, no.16, bar 13, where the bass is the answer to bar 12, alto).

The original concept of the answer was that it should preserve the tone–semitone relationships of the theme exactly in another position of the scale (Fux, *Gradus ad Parnassum*, 1725, p.143: 'Fuga est quarundam Notarum in parte praecedenti positarum, ab sequente repetitio, habita modi, ac plerumque toni, semitoniique ratione'). Fux also mentioned the later practice of defining the key by stressing the tonic and dominant notes. Alterations are sometimes made to the theme when it is 'answered', for one or both of the above purposes. By convention an altered answer is called 'tonal', an unaltered one 'real'. Although various changes may be needed to ensure that the answer remains securely in the tonic, the most obvious device involves substitution of the tonic note in the answer where the dominant note occurred in the subject (and vice versa), which usually results in melodic 5ths in the subject being 'answered' by melodic 4ths (e.g. Bach, *Das wohltemperirte Clavier*, ii, no.7; *see* TONAL ANSWER, ex.1). The need for such alterations was recognized in theoretical writing as early as Vicentino's *L'antica musica* (1555), and also by Fux in his model fugue in the A mode (*Gradus*, p.152).

From such alterations another use of the term 'answer' arose, to refer to any entry, whether or not answering a previous one, which is altered in accordance with answer principles (e.g. in Bach's Organ Fugue in E♭ BWV552, the final pedal entry). Yet another use of the term derives from the fact that the answer was commonly the second entry of the theme: the term may refer to the second entry as such even if it is not at the 4th or 5th to the first one; in more modern works, with initial entries at almost any interval, this is an obvious extension of the term. Less reasonable, perhaps, is the reference to a second entry at the octave, quite common in Baroque fugue and not unknown even in Classical fugue, as an 'octave answer': in such cases it is probably better to reserve the term 'answer' for the first entry that occurs at the 4th or 5th – commonly, in such instances, that of the third voice to enter (e.g. in Haydn's *The Seasons*, final chorus, fugue beginning last note of bar 76, with the answer at bar 81).

ROGER BULLIVANT

Antara. A species of Peruvian PANPIPES.

Antecedent and consequent. The names given to a pair of musical statements that complement one another by virtue of a rhythmic symmetry and, more important, a harmonic balance established by their juxtaposition (ex. 1). Antecedent and consequent phrases often begin with the same musical material, the first phrase ending with

Ex.1 Mozart: Quartet in B♭ K458, theme of finale

an imperfect cadence and the second with a perfect cadence or a completed modulation to a new key; these make up what is commonly referred to as a PERIOD. The terms are most applicable to music built in regular (two-, four- or eight-bar) phrases grouped by pairs (*see* RHYTHM, §II, 13), especially dance music and settings of verse organized in couplets or quatrains.

Antegnati. Italian family of organ builders, composers and instrumentalists. They were active continuously from the last decades of the 15th century to the second half of the 17th. The earliest member was Giovanni Antegnati, a lawyer and academic of Brescia where he was a citizen from 1436. His son Bartolomeo ('magister Bartolomeus de Lumesanis') was the first organ builder in the family. He may have been trained in Brescia, and he worked at S Maria, Brescia (1481), Milan Cathedral (c1490) and S Maria Maggiore, Bergamo (1496). Of his sons, Gian Battista Antegnati (*b* 1500) was highly regarded as an organist, while Gian Giacomo Antegnati (*b* 1501) and his son Benedetto Antegnati were organ builders. Gian Giacomo's organs included instruments at Brescia: S Maria delle Grazie (1533; nine stops),

Duomo Vecchio (1536; 12 stops) and S Faustino Maggiore (1538; nine stops); Milan: S Eustorgio (1540), Cathedral (1552; 12 stops), S Maurizio (1554) and S Maria della Passione (1558); Salò Cathedral (1548) and Vigevano Cathedral (1554). Benedetto was active at Parma: Cathedral (1559 and 1575), S Maria della Steccata (1573) and S Giovanni (1580); Duomo Vecchio, Brescia (1563); and Turin Cathedral (1567).

Gian Battista's son Graziadio Antegnati (i) (*b* 1525) is considered the most outstanding organ builder of the family. He built organs at Bergamo: S Maria Maggiore (1564–6) and S Spirito (1566–7; ten stops); S Barbara, Mantua (1565); Asola Cathedral (1575); S Giuseppe, Brescia (1581; 12 stops); and SS Pietro, Paolo e Stefano, Bellinzona (1584); of these, only S Giuseppe, Brescia, survives.

Graziadio's son Costanzo Antegnati (*b* Brescia, baptized 9 Dec 1549; *d* Brescia, 14 Nov 1624) is the best-known member of the family on account of his *L'arte organica* (Venice, 1608; ed. R. Lunelli, 1938, 2/1958). From 1570 he worked with his father and from 1584 to 1624 he was cathedral organist in his native city; he also composed music. A number of his works were published, including a book of four-voice madrigals (1571), two books of masses (1578, 1589), for six and eight voices, two books of four- and five-voice motets (1575, 1581), a book of psalms (1592), a collection of

Title-page, with a portrait of the composer, of Costanzo Antegnati's 'L'Antegnata, intavolatura de ricercari d'organo' (1608)

masses, motets and other works, for 12 voices (1603), and a number of ricercares for organ (published as op.16 with his *L'arte organica*; ed. in CEKM, ix, 1965). His music is typical of 16th-century Italian ensemble and keyboard works; in his ricercares he showed a fondness for free treatment unusual for his time, and often achieved thrilling effects and impressive climaxes. He built organs at S Giorgio, Bagolino (1590); S Maria della Steccata, Parma (1593); Gardone (1594); S Gaetano, Brescia (1596); the Carmelite church, Salò (beginning of 17th century); and S Agostino, Bergamo (1607).

Costanzo's grandson, Graziadio Antegnati (ii) (*b* 1609) is known to have worked on organs at Rovereto; S Marco and S Giorgio Maggiore, Venice; S Antonio, Padua; Vicenza Cathedral; and the Cathedral and S Maria delle Grazie at Brescia. He was cathedral organist at Padua for a time, but is not heard of after 1651, when many of his relations and partners died.

The typical Antegnati organ has a single manual and a pull-down pedal-board. The keyboard of the *organo mezzano* (38 keys) has a compass from *FGA* to *g″a″*, and that of the organo grosso (50 keys) from *F′G′A′* to *g″ a″* (*tastatura doppia*); instruments with keyboards starting at *C*, *G* or *c* are also known. The maximum number of pedals is 20, with a compass *FGA–d′*. Every organ has a Principale (8′; of which the longest pipe was 12′ at *F*). The *ripieno* was then built up on this Principale, and almost always consisted of single-rank stops, including an Ottava (4′), Quintadecima (2′), $1\frac{1}{3}'$, 1′ and $\frac{2}{3}'$; the $\frac{1}{2}'$, $\frac{1}{3}'$ and $\frac{1}{4}'$ can also be found (the Duodecima, or 12th, was only rarely included). In addition to the *ripieno* there was a 4′ Flauto and often another of 2′ (later one of $2\frac{2}{3}'$ was preferred); there are also examples of three flutes (4′, $2\frac{2}{3}'$, 2′ or 4′, 2′, 1′) in a single instrument. In some rare organs the pedal had its own Principale or a Principale grosso (based on 24′ *F′*), while after about 1550 the Fiffaro, a Principal (treble only) which is tuned slightly sharp or flat to create an acoustic tremulant, was fairly common. Also used was the Tremulante, which acted mechanically on the wind supply. In several of their contracts the Antegnatis promised to supply reed stops, but appear never to have built them. The drawstops for the Principale, the Ottava and the flutes were frequently divided into bass and descant; but on some instruments the two highest *ripieno* ranks were controlled by a common drawstop. The *ripieno* stops of Antegnati organs were narrow-scaled (the common belief that 'Italian Principals' were specially wide is fallacious).

The organ-tuning method described by Costanzo Antegnati is based on $\frac{1}{4}$-comma mean-tone temperament, in which the 3rds C–E, D–F♯, E♭–G, E–G♯, F–A, G–B, A–C♯ and B♭–D are absolutely pure, but the 5th G♯–E♭ is unusable; the Antegnati organ of S Giuseppe, Brescia, is tuned a good semitone higher than modern organs. The Antegnatis built their wind-chests according to the spring-chest system, widely used in Italy at that date. The wind pressure of the organ of S Giuseppe, Brescia, is lower than that of north European instruments. Of the registrations recommended by Costanzo in his *L'arte organica*, the ripieno and *mezzo-ripieno* correspond exactly to the *grand jeu* and *grand jeu doux* of Louis Gaudet, in his advice on registration (Bordeaux, 1510) and Antegnati's *cornetti* are similar to Gaudet's *cornet*. Otherwise Antegnati suggested only combinations of one, two or three stops of Principale

(8′), Ottava (4′) and flutes of 4′, $2\frac{2}{3}'$ and 2′, and suggested no uses of the *ripieno* stops of 2′ and higher, unlike the advice given by Gaudet (1510), Diruta (1609) and Monteverdi (1610).

In addition to the 144 instruments built under Costanzo's direction and enumerated by him in *L'arte organica*, the Antegnati family built about 250 organs. These represent the typical Italian organ of the Renaissance, the instruments for which Banchieri, the Cavazzonis, Frescobaldi, the Gabrielis, Mayone, Merulo, Trabaci and others composed. The characteristic sound of Antegnati organs was described as 'delicato' and 'dolce', and rather restrained and veiled.

BIBLIOGRAPHY

RicordiE

O. Rossi: *Elogi historici di bresciani illustri* (Brescia, 1620)
G. A. Serassi: *Lettere sugli organi* (Bergamo, 1816)
D. Muoni: *Gli Antegnati, organari insigni* (Milan, 1883)
A. Valentini: *I musicisti bresciani ed il Teatro grande* (Brescia, 1894)
P. Guerrini: *La bottega organaria degli Antegnati* (Brescia, 1930)
R. Lunelli: Preface to *C. Antegnati: L'arte organica* (Mainz, 1938, 2/1958)
K. Jeppesen: *Die italienische Orgelmusik am Anfang des Cinquecento* (Copenhagen, 1943, 2/1960)
R. Lunelli: *Der Orgelbau in Italien in seinen Meisterwerken vom 14. Jahrhundert bis zur Gegenwart* (Mainz, 1956)
L. F. Tagliavini: 'Il problema della salvaguardia e del restauro degli organi antichi', *Musica sacra*, lxxx (1956), 134
C. Sartori: 'L'archivio del duomo di Piacenza e il liber XIII di Costanzo Antegnati', *FAM*, iv (1957), 28
W. Apel: *Geschichte der Orgel- und Klaviermusik bis 1700* (Kassel, 1967; Eng. trans., rev., 1972)
M. A. Vente: 'Una polizza d'estimo di Graziadio Antegnati', *L'organo*, vi (1968), 231
J. Mertin: 'The Old Italian Organ', *ISO Information* (1969), no.2, p.157
D. Kämper: 'Studien zur instrumentalen Ensemblemusik des 16. Jahrhunderts', *AnMc*, no.10 (1970)
O. Mischiati: 'Il contratto di Graziadio Antegnati per l'organo di S Spirito a Bergamo (1566)', *L'organo*, x (1972), 223
H. Klotz: *Über die Orgelkunst der Gotik, der Renaissance und des Barock* (Kassel, 1975), 132ff

HANS KLOTZ

Antenoreo, Onofrio (*b* ?Padua; *fl* 1505–14). Italian composer. He is probably identifiable with the 'Honophrius Patavinus' of Petrucci's sixth and eleventh books of frottolas. His frottolas comprise nine *barzellette*, two *ode*, a ballata and a *strambotto*, the last, *Se un pone un fragil vetro*, a poem by Serafino dall'Aquila. *Sed libera nos a malo*, from Petrucci's sixth book (*RISM* 1506³), is one of a group of macaronic works in the frottola repertory that parody biblical or liturgical texts; it begins with a phrase of music and text from the *Pater noster*. His *Se io ti dico el mio gran danno* from Petrucci's eighth book (*RISM* 1507⁴) uses the popular melody *Si vivesse cento e un anno* in its *ripresa*, and *Crudel amore*, from the same source, is one of the earliest settings of a ballata in the frottola repertory. Antenoreo's works are notable for their stereotyped hemiola rhythm.

WORKS

13 frottolas, 1505³ (attrib. Antenoreo in repr. 1508²), 1506³, 1507⁴, 1514²; 6 ed. G. Cesari and others, *Le frottole nell'edizione principe di Ottaviano Petrucci*, IMa, I/1 (1954)

BIBLIOGRAPHY

A. Einstein: *The Italian Madrigal* (Princeton, 1949/*R*1971)
K. Jeppesen: *La frottola* (Århus and Copenhagen, 1968–70)

WILLIAM F. PRIZER

Antes, John [Johann] (*b* Frederick, nr. Bethlehem, Penn., 24 March 1740; *d* Bristol, 17 Dec 1811). American Moravian composer, minister and missionary. He was educated in the Moravian boys' school in Bethlehem; among his early teachers was Johann Christoph Pyrlaeus (1713–85). In 1764 he went to

Herrnhut, Saxony, for further training and to Neuwied for an apprenticeship in watchmaking. His musical talents and careful craftsmanship are shown in a violin, viola and cello which he made before leaving America (the violin and viola are in museums in Nazareth and Lititz, Pennsylvania). Ordained a Moravian minister in 1769, Antes accepted missionary service in Egypt from 1770 to 1781. In 1779 he was captured by the henchmen of Osman Bey, with the intent of extorting money from him, and received a severe beating which impaired his health for the rest of his stay. In 1781 he returned to Herrnhut and Neuwied, and two years later he became warder (business manager) of the Fulneck, England, Moravian community, a position he occupied for most of the rest of his life. He was an uncle of C. I. Latrobe, who named a son after him.

Antes's music consists of three trios for two violins and cello (op.3, London, c1790), 35 concerted anthems and solo songs, and 55 hymn tunes. Besides the trios, only one solo song and several hymn tunes appeared in print during his lifetime. Manuscripts of his anthems are in the archives of the Moravian Church in Bethlehem, Pennsylvania, and Winston-Salem, North Carolina, and in the Archiv der Brüder-Unität, Herrnhut, Germany. The London Moravian Archives have two manuscript books of hymn tunes. The music is close to Haydn's in technique and spirit. The three trios composed while Antes was in Egypt, the earliest known chamber music by a native American composer, show him as a composer of real talent with a good command of technique and a lively imagination. The anthems and solo songs are finely wrought works with instrumental accompaniment for strings and occasional winds: the solo and chorus *Go, Congregation, Go – Surely He Has Borne Our Griefs* is one of the most moving works in the Moravian repertory.

Antes was modest about his musical accomplishments, and referred to himself as a musical dilettante on several occasions. His long memoir, written shortly before his death, does not even mention his musical activities. He published a summary of his experiments for improving piano hammers, the violin tuning mechanism and violin bows (*AMZ*, viii, 1806, 657) and invented and patented a music stand with which a player could turn pages automatically.

BIBLIOGRAPHY

EitnerQ; *FétisB*
'Lebenslauf des Bruders John Antes', *Nachrichten aus der Brüder-Gemeine* (1845), no.2, p.249 [autobiography]
D. M. McCorkle: 'John Antes, "American Dilettante" ', *MQ*, xlii (1956), 486 [with list of works]
F. M. Blandford: 'John Antes – an American Hero', *The Moravian* (1962), April
KARL KROEGER

Antesignanus, Pierre. See DAVANTES, PIERRE.

Antheil, George [Georg] (**Johann Carl**) (*b* Trenton, NJ, 8 July 1900; *d* New York, 12 Feb 1959). American composer and pianist of German descent. He studied the piano from the age of six and from the age of 13 commuted to Philadelphia to take lessons in theory and composition with Constantin von Sternberg. In 1920 he studied composition privately with Bloch and wrote the Symphony no.1 'Zingareska', the last movement of which was one of the first symphonic pieces to incorporate jazz elements. His piano studies were continued in 1921 under George Boyle at the Curtis Settlement School. The First Symphony was first performed by the Berlin PO under von Dornberg in 1922, when Antheil

moved to Europe to pursue a career as a concert pianist. He soon decided to abandon this in favour of composition and, beginning with the *Airplane Sonata* (1922), he developed a consciously modern, machine-like style in reaction, by his own account, to the 'mountainous sentiment' of Strauss and the 'fluid diaphanous lechery' of the impressionists. Other pieces of the period, all for piano, were the *Sonata Sauvage*, the Sonatina 'Death of the Machines' and the *Jazz Sonata*, as well as several short pieces entitled *Mechanisms*. All are percussive, boisterous, dissonant and rhythmically violent.

Antheil moved from Berlin to Paris in June 1923. His playing of his piano pieces at the Champs Elysées on 4 October 1923 caused a riot which ensured his notoriety, and he was championed and befriended by Joyce, Yeats, Pound, Satie, Picasso and other artists. Pound wrote a book and numerous articles in praise of Antheil's music, and, together with Olga Rudge, he commissioned two violin sonatas which had their premières at the Salle Pleyel on 7 November 1923. These works were frequently played by Rudge and Antheil, with Pound turning the pages and performing the part for tenor and bass drums at the end of the second sonata.

In 1924 Antheil began working with Léger and with the film maker Dudley Murphy on the *Ballet mécanique*. Léger and Murphy created one of the first abstract films, which was to be accompanied by Antheil's music for 16 player pianos controlled from a switchboard. When synchronization of the pianos with one another and with the film was deemed impossible, the film and the music became autonomous works. The score, built around piano rolls specially cut by the Pleyela Company, was first performed in a version for eight pianos, one player piano, four xylophones, two electric bells, two propellers, tam-tam, four bass drums and siren. The Paris première on 19 June 1926 was quite successful, but the work was poorly received at Carnegie Hall on 10 April 1927, when it was given a carnival-like presentation by the over-eager promoter Donald Friede.

Several neo-classical works were composed in 1926, and then Antheil turned his attention to opera, returned to Germany and was appointed assistant musical director of the Berlin Stadttheater (1928–9). The opera *Transatlantic*, to his own text, was centred on an American presidential election and presented a wild caricature of life in the USA, including in the score jazz motifs. It was probably the first American opera to have a major production in a foreign country when it was staged at Frankfurt in 1930. From then until 1936 Antheil divided his time between Europe and the USA. Among several chamber works of the period, the most interesting is *La femme 100 têtes*, a set of 45 piano preludes after the book of etchings by Ernst. Antheil also wrote ballet scores for Balanchine and Graham, and the opera *Helen Retires*, which fails to sustain musical or dramatic interest.

In 1936 he travelled across the USA, gathering impressions which were synthesized in the *American Symphony*, neither version of which was performed. He settled in Los Angeles in the late summer of 1936, and there he orchestrated film scores, wrote for *Esquire*, invented (in collaboration with Hedy Lamarr) a torpedo, maintained a syndicated lonely hearts column and acted as a war analyst for the press and radio. In 1945 his unabashed autobiography *Bad Boy of Music* became a bestseller. He was also the author of *Death in the Dark* (London, 1930), a mystery published under the name of Stacey Bishop. Much of Antheil's music of the late 1940s is cast in classical forms, incorporating a very individual mixture of bitter-sweet lyricism, satirical paraphrases of military marches, American folktune quotations and rambunctious boogie-woogie rhythms, often tempered with the metallic dissonance of his early style. The best of these later works are the Serenade no.1 for strings, the Fourth Piano Sonata, the *Songs of Experience* and the *Eight Fragments from Shelley*.

WORKS

STAGE

Ballet mécanique, 1923–5, rev. 1952–3
Transatlantic (opera, Antheil), 1927–8; cond. Steinberg, Frankfurt, 25 May 1930
Oedipus, incidental music, 1928, lost
Fighting the Waves (incidental music, Yeats), Mez, unpitched chorus ad lib, 10 insts, 1929
Flight (ballet-opera, G. and B. Antheil), 1927–30
Helen Retires (opera, J. Erskine), 1930–32; New York, Juilliard School, 28 Feb 1934
Course, ballet, 5 insts, 1935, lost
Dreams, ballet, 1935
Volpone (opera, A. Perry, after Jonson), 1950–52; Los Angeles, 9 Jan 1953
Capital of the World, ballet, after Hemingway, 1953; television, 6 Dec 1953
The Brothers (opera, Antheil), 1954; Denver, 28 July 1954
Venus in Africa (opera, M. Dyne), 1954; Denver, 24 May 1957
The Wish (opera, Antheil), 1955; Louisville, 2 April 1955

ORCHESTRAL

Sym. no.1 'Zingareska', 1920–22, rev. 1923; A Jazz Sym., 22 insts, 1923–5, rev. orch 1955; Pf Conc., 1926; Suite, chamber orch, 1926; Sym. no.2, F, 1925–6; Crucifixion, after Miró, str, 1927; lost; Capriccio, 1930; Morceau, 1932, lost; Archipelago (Rhumba), 1935; Sym. no.3 'American', version 1, 1931–8, rev. 1943, withdrawn, version 2, 1936–9, rev. 1946; The Golden Spike, 1939; Sym. no.4 '1942', 1942–3; Decatur in Algiers, nocturne, 1943
Tragic Sym., 1943–5, rev. 1948; Over the Plains, 1945; Heroes of Today, 1945; Carnival of the Beautiful Dresses, 1946; Vn Conc., 1946; Spectre of the Rose Waltzes, 1946–7; Autumn Song, andante, 1947; Sym. no.5 'Joyous', 1947–8; Sym. no.6 'after Delacroix', 1947–8, rev. 1949–50; Hot-time Dance, 1948; McKonkey's Ferry Ov., 1948; Serenade no.1, str, 1948; Serenade no.2, chamber orch, 1948; Accordion Dance, 1951; Nocturne in Skyrockets, 1951

VOCAL

Choral: Election [from opera Transatlantic] (Antheil), 1927; 8 Fragments from Shelley, chorus, pf, 1951, 3 movts orchd 1951; Cabeza de Vaca (cantata, A. Dowling, after A. Nuñez), chorus, orch, 1955–6, orchd E. Gold 1959
Songs for 1v, pf: 5 Songs (A. Crapsey): November Night, Triad, Suzanna and the Elders, Fate Defied, The Warning, 1919–20; You are old Father William, 1924; Turtle Soup, 1924; Nightpiece (Joyce), 1932, pubd in *Joyce Book* (London, 1932); 6 Songs of Love: The Vision of Love (G. Russell), Down by the Salley Gardens (Yeats), The Sorrow of Love (Yeats), Lightning (D. H. Lawrence), I hear an army (Joyce), inc., An End Piece (F. M. Ford), 1933; Antheil's Frankie and Johnny, 1936; 9 Songs of Experience (Blake): The Garden of Love, A Poison Tree, The School Boy, The Sick Rose, The Little Vagabond, I told my love, I laid me down upon a bank, Infant Sorrow, The Tyger, 1948; 2 Odes of Keats: On a Grecian Urn, To a Nightingale, speaker, pf, 1949; Sighs and Grones (?Herbert), 1956

CHAMBER

Sym. for 5 Insts, fl, bn, tpt, trbn, va, 1923; Sonata no.1, vn, pf, 1923, pf part of movts 2–3 lost; Sonata no.2, vn, pf, ten drum, b drum, 1923; Str Qt no.1, 1924; Sonata no.3, vn, pf, 1924; Str Qt no.2, 1927; Concertino, fl, bn, pf, 1930; Sonatina, vn, vc, 1932; Chamber Conc., wind qnt, dbn, C-tpt, trbn, 1932; Dance in 4 Parts arr. from La femme 100 têtes, 1936, lost; Sonatina, vn, pf, 1945; Sonata no.4 (no.2), vn, pf, 1947–8; Str Qt no.3, 1948; Sonata, tpt, pf, c1951; Sonata, fl, pf, 1951

PIANO

4-hand Suite, 1922, rev. 1939; Fireworks and the Profane Waltzers, 1922; Airplane Sonata, 1922; Sonatina 'Death of the Machines', 1923; Sonata Sauvage, 1923; Jazz Sonata, 1923; Mechanisms, 1923–4, lost; Habañera, Tarantelle, Serenata, 2 pf, 1924; Tango [from opera Transatlantic], arr. A. Steinbrecher 1927; Sonatina für Radio, 1929; La femme 100 têtes, 45 preludes, 1932–3

La vie parisienne, suite, 1939; Suite, 1941; The Ben Hecht Valses, 1943; Musical Picture of a Friend, 1946; Sonata no.3, 1947; Sonata no.4, 1948; 2 Toccatas, 1948; Prelude, d, c1948; Valentine Waltzes, 1949; Sonata no.5, 1950; Waltzes from Volpone, 1955; Pf Pastels, 1956

FILM SCORES

Harlem Picture, 1934; Once in a Blue Moon, 1935; The Plainsman, 1936; Make Way for Tomorrow, 1938; Angels over Broadway, 1940; That Brennan Girl, 1946; The Plainsman and the Lady, 1946; Repeat Performance, 1946; Knock on any Door, 1948; Tokyo Joe, 1949; We were Strangers, 1949; Sirocco, 1949; Fighting Kentuckians, 1949; House by the River, 1949; In a Lonely Place, 1949–50

The Sniper, 1951; Actors and Sin, 1952; The Juggler, 1952; Dementia, 1953; Hunters of the Sea, 1954; Not as a Stranger, 1955; The Pride and the Passion, 1956; The Young Don't Cry, 1956; Woman without Shadow, 1957; Twentieth Century, 10 CBS TV documentaries, n.d.

Principal publishers: Weintraub, Schirmer, Universal, Boosey & Hawkes, Leeds

WRITINGS

'Abstraction and Time in Music', *Little Review* (1924–5), Autumn-Winter, 13
'My Ballet mécanique: what it Means', *Der Querschnitt* (1925), Sept
'The Negro on the Spiral (or A Method of Negro Music)', *Negro: an Anthology*, N. Cunard (London, 1934), 346
'Music in 1955', *Coronet* (1936), Dec, 83
The Shape of the War to Come (New York, 1940) [pubd anonymously]
Bad Boy of Music (Garden City, NY, 1945) [autobiography]
Numerous essays in *MM* (1930–39)

BIBLIOGRAPHY

M. Lee: 'George Antheil: Europe's American Composer', *The Reviewer* (1924), 267
E. Pound: 'George Antheil', *The Criterion*, ii (1924), 321
A. Copland: 'George Antheil', *MM*, i (1925), Jan
H. M. Stuckenschmidt: 'George Antheil', *Das Kunstblatt* (1925), Jan, 181
E. Walsh, ed.: Antheil supplement, *This Quarter* (Paris, 1925), no.2
E. Pound: *Antheil and the Treatise on Harmony* (Chicago, 1927, R1968)
M. Anderson: *My Thirty Years' War* (New York, 1930)
R. Thompson: 'George Antheil', *MM*, viii (1931), May–June
J. Cage: 'The Dreams and Dedications of George Antheil', *MM*, xxiii (1946), Winter, 78
D. Friede: *The Mechanical Angel* (New York, 1948), 44ff
M. D. Candee, ed.: 'George Antheil', *Current Biography 1954* (1954), 29
E. Malins: *Yeats and Music* (London and Dublin, 1968)

CHARLES AMIRKHANIAN

Anthem. A choral setting of a religious or moral text in English, generally designed for liturgical performance. *See also* NATIONAL ANTHEMS.

I. England. II. America.

I. England

1. Terminology. 2. History *c*1549–65. 3. History *c*1565–*c*1644. 4. History *c*1600–*c*1770. 5. History *c*1770–*c*1890. 6. History *c*1890 to the present.

1. TERMINOLOGY. The term was in use by the early 11th century, being derived from and largely synonymous with ANTIPHON (see Harrison). During the course of the 15th century it came to be applied to the votive antiphon, or 'Benedicamus substitute ex licencia' which was sung in 'prick-song' (polyphony) on festal occasions at the end of Lauds, Lady Mass and Vespers. The term was also used at times in connection with choral polyphony sung at extraordinary ecclesiastical and state ceremonies: on one occasion, for instance, when Henry VII visited St Paul's Cathedral in 1485 he was censed 'with the great Senser of Paules by an Angell commyng oute of the Roof, During which Tyme the Quere sange a solempne Antyme' (Harrison, p.99).

Under the terms of the First Act of Uniformity (January 1549) English replaced Latin as the principal language of the English Church. The new English services, published in *The Booke of the Common Prayer* (1549) were very obviously modelled on the old, but the rubrics did little to clarify the part that music was to have in these services; indeed, the rubrics for Matins and Evensong barely referred to music at all (see le Huray, 1967, pp.20ff). To judge, however, from the format and contents of the earliest extant source of music for the new rites (the Wanley Partbooks, *GB-Ob* Mus.Sch.E.420–22, *c*1546–8) the form of the Anglican choral service, as it is now known, was clearly discernible from the beginning. The contents of the Wanley Partbooks (le Huray, 1967, pp.173ff) comprise settings of the Ordinary of Communion, settings of the daily canticles, and settings of miscellaneous biblical and prayer book texts, all of which may broadly be described as anthems. The function of many of these pieces is clearly shown by such sub-headings as 'Offertory', 'Communion', 'Postcommunion', 'Weddings', 'At Burial' and 'For Ash Wednesday'. Others, however, are simply labelled 'antem', and some have no heading at all. The context in which such compositions as these would have been sung is not defined, but by analogy with pre-Reformation practices, they would doubtless have been sung, as votive antiphons often were, at the conclusion of Matins and Evensong.

The rubrics of the revised Edwardian prayer book and those of the first Elizabethan prayer book of 1559 contained even fewer references to music than did those of the 1549 prayer book, but a passage from the Elizabethan Injunctions of 1559 does make it clear that the anthem was by then a recognized component of the choral service, if at the same time an optional one:

for the comforting of such that delight in music, it may be permitted that in the beginning, or in the end of common prayers, either at morning or evening, there may be sung an Hymn, or such like song, to the praise of Almighty God, in the best sort of melody and music that may be conveniently devised, having respect that the sentence [sense] of the Hymn may be understood and perceived.

The wording of the Injunction suggests that the term 'anthem' was not then in very general use, and indeed, 'anthem' and 'prayer' were used synonymously in the first printed collection of service music – John Day's *Certaine Notes* (London, 1565; the partbooks are dated variously 1560 and 1565, but publication was in the latter year). By the beginning of the 17th century the term was well established, and it was widely used in both printed and MS collections to define a composition set to an English text of the composer's choosing deriving from the Bible, the prayer book or from a work of a religious or moral character.

During the early years of the 17th century there were no very clear divisions between the sacred and the secular. Many anthem-like compositions were published in books of a predominantly secular kind, and many others are to be found in MS anthologies, side by side with madrigals, lute songs and instrumental pieces. Many of the anthems in these secular sources are scored for combinations of voices and instruments that would have been unsuited to a cathedral or chapel choir, and it is therefore hardly surprising that they are not to be found in liturgical sources of the period. There remains, nevertheless, a considerable repertory of anthems sung both in church and in the home during the golden age of the English madrigal. From the time of the Restoration, however, the anthem was increasingly regarded as a composition appropriate only to a church service or religious ceremony. Although by 1600 the anthem had become one of the principal musical forms of the English choral service, the 1662 Book of Common Prayer was the first specifically to refer to it. In this, as in all subsequent prayer books, the anthem was formally acknowledged as an optional extra at the end of Matins and Evensong, for performance 'In quires and Places where they sing'.

2. HISTORY *c*1549–65. Knowledge of the early history of the English anthem derives from a handful of imperfect sources, of which the most important are the Wanley and Lumley Partbooks (*GB-Ob* Mus.Sch.E.420–22, *c*1546–8 and *Lbm* Roy.App.74–6, *c*1549) and John Day's *Certaine Notes* (London, 1565). The provenance of the Wanley and Lumley books is not known, but there are good reasons for believing that both may have been designed for small choirs, of the kind to be found in private chapels and parish churches. The preponderance of music for men's voices in the Wanley Partbooks and the absence of communion music in the Lumley books lend support to this supposition. Most of the anthems in the three sources are based on texts from the Bible, English primers, metrical psalters and from the Prayer Book. The composers are for the most part anonymous; the named composers include Caustun, Heath, Robert Johnson (i), Mundy, Okeland, Sheppard, Tallis, Tye and Whitbroke. Tallis's *Hear the voice and prayer*, Sheppard's *Submit yourselves*, Mundy's *He that hath my commandments* and the anonymous *Rejoice in the Lord* well represent the style of the early anthem (see le Huray, *The Treasury* and *Anthems*, 1965). The four-part textures are predominantly imitative or in a regular note-against-note counterpoint typical of the simpler Flemish motet of the early 16th century (see ex.1). Attempts at word-painting are few, the characteristic mood being of measured solemnity. The simplicity of these anthems is attributable in part to the concern, often expressed at that time, to develop an idiom that would ensure the maximum clarity of diction while at the same time allowing for some interesting variation in musical textures. Although the liturgical reformation undoubtedly acted as a catalyst in the process of change from luxuriant melisma to syllabic, note-against-note counterpoint, the new musical techniques came from abroad, and from countries that had not yet been touched by Protestant ideologies. It would be wrong, moreover, to draw conclusions as to the nature and extent of stylistic change during the early years of the Reformation from a study of the anthem alone. Comparatively elaborate settings of the canticles and of the Ordinary of the Communion service have survived from the period 1549–52, showing that in certain fields at least composers were allowed far greater freedom for the imaginative development of a new liturgical style than had once been believed.

3. HISTORY *c*1565–*c*1644. Easily the most significant development of the period was the creation of the 'verse' style, in which verses for solo voices and instrumental accompaniment (normally organ) alternated with passages for full choir. The basic principle may indeed have emerged in about 1550, for there is what appears to be an embryonic verse anthem in the Wanley Partbooks: an anonymous setting of *Now let the congregation*. The first verse of this metrical psalm seems to have been scored for a solo alto, the verse then being repeated in a harmonized version for all the voices. As Thomas Sternhold pointed out in the preface to his *Certayne Psalmes* (London, 1549; 19 psalms with no musical settings), metrical psalms were frequently sung at the time by a soloist, to a simple instrumental accompani-

Ex.1 William Mundy: *O Lord, the maker of all things*

Transposed up a minor 3rd

ment. The first substantial verse compositions, however, date from the 1560s and early 1570s. Two of the very earliest are John Farrant's *When as we sat in Babylon* (reconstructed in le Huray, 1967, p.221) and William Mundy's *Ah helpless wretch* (see le Huray, *The Treasury*, 1965, p.28). These, like nearly all pre-Restoration verse anthems, open with a brief introduction for organ, after which follows a verse for a solo voice or voices supported by a fully independent instrumental accompaniment. This leads into the first chorus where the instrumental part(s) do no more than double the voices. The full section comes to a close, and the anthem continues with as many verse/chorus pairs as the text demands. In some anthems the text of the verse is reworked in the succeeding chorus, and in certain anthems (notably those by Weelkes and Gibbons) musical ideas are repeated and developed. Most full and verse anthems, however, are through-composed.

The verse anthem has its roots not only in the early metrical psalm, but also in the Elizabethan CONSORT SONG, and in the Elizabethan choirboy play. Most consort songs dating from *c*1550–80 are scored for a solo boy with an accompaniment of three or four viols. Some were written for the choirboy plays performed with music which were fashionable at that time. The dramatic productions presented by the boys of the Chapel Royal were especially popular during Richard Farrant's term of office as Master of the Choristers, and it is perhaps significant that the earliest extant verse anthems are by composers closely associated with the Chapel Royal, including Farrant himself. Some of Byrd's consort songs suggest possible links between the consort song and the early verse anthem: *Lord, to thee I make my moan* has a short closing phrase of some three bars that is repeated; in at least one of the MS sources words have been added to the supporting instrumental lines at the repetition, to make a very elementary verse–chorus structure.

The advantages of the new style must soon have been obvious, for by the turn of the century (judging by the extant repertory) composers were writing rather more verse anthems than full anthems. The verse style obviously saved a good deal of rehearsal time; it was potentially a most colourful medium, and musicians found that words tended to be more audible (and more moving) when sung by solo voices against an instrumental background than when sung chorally.

Byrd's fine Easter anthem for two solo boys, five-part choir and viols, *Christ rising again*, well illustrates the new verse anthem at its best (*Songs of Sundrie Natures*, London, 1589). Compared with Tallis's setting of the same text its impact is subjectively dramatic; the words are 'presented' to the listener with admirable clarity and its moods are 'represented' with great originality and power (see ex.2). Byrd may not have been the first to develop the new verse style but he was certainly the first to reveal its very considerable potential. Well over a dozen of his verse anthems are still extant. His full anthems, which far outnumber them, also reveal a close concern for the spirit of the text. The most substantial of these are of considerable proportions. *Sing joyfully*, for six-part choir, is a particularly imaginative composition, being constructed on an embryonic tonal plan that heralds the Classical tonal system of the 18th century. Byrd published most of his anthems in his three great English anthologies (1588, 1589, 1611), and many of these, in the light of their unusual scoring, were obviously intended for the home rather than the church.

The most distinguished of Byrd's younger contemporaries was perhaps Thomas Morley, whose setting of *Out of the deep* (le Huray, *The Treasury*, 1965, p.114) for solo alto, five-part choir and organ, is one of the most moving verse anthems of the entire period. Morley indeed conceived it to be the musician's task 'to draw the hearer as it were in chains of gold by the ears to the consideration of holy things'. Of Morley's immediate contemporaries the most important were the Chapel Royal musicians Nathaniel Giles and Edmund Hooper, who both wrote much for the English rites, mostly in verse form. Other comparatively minor composers included John Mundy, the two John Hiltons, John Holmes, Matthew Jeffreys, John Milton (father of the poet) and William (?or Thomas) Wilkinson.

The next generation, of which Tomkins, Weelkes and Gibbons are the principal representatives, sought to give even greater dramatic impact to the anthem; they used more vivid contrasts of texture, developed a widening range of harmonic and melodic rhythms, and they began to seek out ways of integrating the total structure of an anthem by means of motivic recapitulation and redevelopment. Weelkes approached the anthem from a madrigalian standpoint, and it is no accident perhaps that his most effective anthems are in the full style (see MB, xxiii, 1966). The full anthems *Alleluia, I heard a voice*, *Gloria in excelsis Deo* and *Hosanna to the Son of*

Ex.2
(a) Byrd: *Christ rising again* (1589)

(b) Tallis: *Christ rising again* (1549—52)

David reach the highest levels of inspiration, and of the verse anthems, *Give ear, O God* is of the highest formal and musical interest. Gibbons, most of whose anthems are in the verse style, was equally forward-looking. He was particularly successful in conveying the declamatory shape of a text: *This is the record of John, Glorious and powerful God* and especially *See, see the word is incarnate* (EECM, iii) all owe much in this respect to Morley, and are some of the most remarkable verse anthems of the pre-Restoration period. Tomkins was a particularly prolific composer, with an unusually keen ear for vocal colour, and a feeling for imitative polyphony (see EECM, v, ix, xiv). In matters of structure and style, however, he was comparatively conser-

vative, although there are one or two exceptional anthems such as the chromatic *Know ye not*, written for Prince Henry's funeral in 1613 (see le Huray, 1967, pp.149f), and the very moving anthem or 'sacred madrigal', *When David heard*. A profusion of minor composers continued to work the established idioms of the full and verse anthem. Some, like Amner, Batten, Michael East, Nicholson, William Smith and Ward produced worthwhile music that still merits a hearing. Others, such as Cranford, Fido, Hinde, Thomas Holmes, the Lugges, Palmer, Portman, Stonard, Giles and John Tomkins, Warwick, Wilson and the Woodsons are now primarily of historical interest.

Although the decani/cantoris disposition of the

Ex.3 Purcell: *Let mine eyes run down with tears* (?1682)

Anglican choir was well suited to the exploitation of polychoral effects, English composers in the 16th and 17th centuries showed little interest in these possibilities. Even in so extensive a work as Tomkins's 12-part *O praise the Lord*, spatial considerations play very little part in the overall disposition of voices (not even Tallis's 40-part *Spem in alium nunquam habui* is so arranged). Nor indeed did English composers show a great interest in the innovations of the *stile nuovo*. One or two Chapel Royal composers did graft Italianate mannerisms on to a basically English idiom with some success, notably William Child, William and Henry Lawes and Walter Porter. Child's *Turn thou us* contains some very Italianate turns of phrase for the solo voices, and the harmonic idiom is unusually tonal, as are also the harmonies of the full anthems *O God, wherefore art thou absent* (*Treasury*, 1965, p.248) and *Bow down thine ear*. Porter, a pupil of Monteverdi, was the most obviously Italian composer in London before the Civil War, so much so that his many anthems failed to gain a foothold outside the Chapel Royal. If the verse anthem *Praise the Lord* (*Treasury*, 1965, p.232) is typical of his general style it is easy to see why this was so for the solo lines are full of melisma and ornament, and extremely difficult to sing. George Jeffreys's style is somewhat akin to Porter's. His church music dates from considerably later, however, and is unlikely to have influenced the mainstream development of the English anthem.

4. HISTORY *c*1660–*c*1770. After a break of some 15 years during the period of the Civil War and the Commonwealth, choral services were resumed in 1660. To judge from James Clifford's wordbook of anthems, *The Divine Services and Anthems* (1663, rev., enlarged 2/1664) a great deal of pre-Restoration music had been recovered and was forming the bulk of the daily repertory. At the Chapel Royal Henry Cooke and Matthew Locke were writing anthems in a wholly new style for performance at the Sunday and festal services, when the king was present (see MB, xxxix, 1974). Textures in their anthems are basically homophonic, the harmonic idiom is tonal rather than modal, and the structure is less an alternation of verses and choruses than a succession of contrasting verses, interspersed with an occasional chorus, often of a somewhat perfunctory kind. Both composers had been abroad during the Commonwealth, and the influence of French and Italian styles is very evident in their work.

A further step away from the pre-Restoration style was taken in 1662, when a string group was established to play symphonies and ritornellos between the verses of the anthem, a practice that continued regularly until 1688 and after that sporadically on occasions of an extraordinary and solemn kind. Locke's *Be thou exalted Lord* represents at once one of the earliest 'orchestral' anthems and one of the grandest, being scored for three four-part choirs, five-part string band, a consort of viols and various groups of soloists. Of Purcell's other elder contemporaries, Pelham Humfrey is of particular interest (see MB, xxxiv and xxxv, 1972). His orchestral anthems are much less angular than Locke's, the French influence being much in evidence. Blow had already written much when Purcell came of age, and was still active some ten years after Purcell's death. His style is most akin to Locke's, although it has a greater sense of harmonic direction, as for instance in the powerful orchestral anthem for the 1685 coronation, *God spake*

sometime in visions (see MB, vii, 1953, no.1). Of all Restoration composers, Blow was the most prolific.

The Restoration period is often spoken of as the 'Purcellian' period, however, for Purcell synthesized and developed all that was most successful in the work of his predecessors. His full anthem *Hear my prayer, O God* represents a moving continuation of the 16th-century polyphonic style: his early verse anthem, *Let mine eyes run down with tears* is richly harmonic in Blow's best manner (see ex.3); and the orchestral anthems, of which *Rejoice in the Lord, My heart is inditing* and *They that go down to the sea* (ex.4), are particularly effective examples, owe much to Locke and Humfrey.

Ex.4 Purcell: *They that go down to the sea* (after 1685)

At no time before or since the Restoration was the Chapel Royal so central to the history of English cathedral music, for every composer of standing was connected with it in some way or other. After the accession of James II (a Catholic) in 1685, however, the Chapel Royal steadily lost its pre-eminence, and musical standards everywhere declined. During the 18th century the opera house and the concert hall were of greater interest to the musical public. It was an age in which the soul was extinct and the stomach well alive; although a great deal of agreeable church music was composed little of it was of great spiritual depth.

Handel's Anglican music comprises a set of 11 anthems for the Duke of Chandos, the last and in many ways the grandest of the Restoration orchestral anthems (1716–18), and some ten other occasional anthems. Of Purcell's younger contemporaries, William Croft achieved some eminence. Other minor figures include Aldrich, Jeremiah Clarke, Robert Creighton, James Hawkins and Roseingrave. Of the many English composers of the early 18th century Greene and Boyce deserve some attention. Greene's indebtedness to Handel has perhaps been overstressed. His most effective full anthems look back to the time of Gibbons – his *O clap your hands* is akin to Gibbons's setting of the same text, in strength and dignity; his most original verse anthems, notably *Lord let me know mine end*, also have a personal stamp. Although no anthem by Boyce quite measures up to Greene's best work, verse anthems such as *O where shall wisdom be found* and *I have surely built thee an house* are creditable extensions of the Restoration tradition. Other minor figures include John Alcock, Thomas Kempton, Thomas Kelway, James Kent, James Nares and John Travers.

5. HISTORY *c*1770–*c*1890. The period from 1770 to 1817 was described by Foster as a 'trackless desert'. It was the period of adaptations and arrangements, in which some editors dismembered the compositions of English and foreign composers, replacing the original texts with incongruously chosen passages from the Bible. Nevertheless, Jonathan Battishill and Samuel Wesley will continue to be remembered for some effective anthems. Of Battishill's anthems, *O Lord, look down* has a contrapuntal and harmonic strength that places it in the highest class (see ex.5). Samuel Wesley was largely responsible for bringing the music of J. S. Bach before the English public, and the best of his own anthems and motets reflect the influence of Bach both in the scale of their design and in the strength of their melodic lines. In discussing the English renaissance of the late 19th century, Samuel Wesley should not be forgotten. The impressive motets *Exultate deo* and *In exitu Israel*, especially, foreshadow later developments, and are of considerable intrinsic musical interest. Among Wesley's contemporaries, Thomas Attwood, John Clarke-Whitfeld, Benjamin and Robert Cooke, William Crotch, Thomas Ebdon and Thomas Norris deserve mention.

The nadir of the English anthem, and of English cathedral music generally, was reached during the early years of the 19th century. The daily services were performed in a perfunctory and incompetent manner; the average repertory was small and representative of only the simplest 18th- and early 19th-century composition. As S. S. Wesley remarked (*A Few Words on Cathedral Music*, 1849), no cathedral in the country possessed 'a musical force competent to embody and give effect to the evident intentions of the Church with regard to music'. The foundations of the Victorian revival, however, were being laid at this time. Maria Hackett (1783–1874) and S. S. Wesley led vigorous campaigns, the former to improve working conditions and the latter to raise levels of musical competence in cathedral establishments. Scholars such as John Jebb, Frederick Oakley and Thomas Helmore sought to restore to the musical part of public worship the same propriety and dignity that was being sought in other fields by leaders of the Oxford Movement and the Cambridge Camden Society. Among composers active at the time were Sterndale Bennett, J. B. Dykes, G. T. Elvey, John Goss, F. A. G. Ouseley, R. L. Pearsall, Henry T. Smart, T. A. Walmisley and S. S. Wesley. Of these S. S. Wesley is unquestionably pre-eminent. Many of his best anthems (composed between 1830 and 1850) were published in a collected edition of 1853, and several are of considerable proportions, lasting between 15 and 20 minutes. *O Lord, thou art my God*, *Let us lift up our heart*, *Blessed be the God and Father* (ex.6) and *Ascribe unto the Lord* are particularly memorable. Like Mendelssohn's *Hear my prayer* (1844) these anthems clearly show the influence of contemporary oratorio: the organ accompaniments are conceived in more orchestral terms than had formerly been the case, a trend that was greatly assisted by the introduction of pedals and easily manipulated stop-change mechanisms. Wesley's use of clearly differentiated recitative and aria styles, and his imaginative harmonic vocabulary point to an awareness of developments well beyond the confines of the cathedral organ loft. None of his immediate contemporaries was in any way his equal, and many of the younger composers, including Joseph Barnby, G. M. Garrett and Sullivan, fell too easily under the saccharine influence of Spohr, Gounod and Mendelssohn himself.

6. HISTORY *c*1890 TO THE PRESENT. The two names most commonly associated with the English musical renaissance are those of Parry and Stanford. Stanford was particularly influential in the field of church music. He condemned the practice, common in his younger days, of adapting as anthems compositions that had been 'imported from sources, foreign in more senses than

Ex.5 Battishill: *O Lord look down from heav'n*

Ex.6 S. S. Wesley: *Blessed be the God and Father*

But as He which hath call-ed you is ho-ly, so be-

ye ho-ly in all man-ner of_ con-ver-sa-tion.

Pass the time of your so-journ-ing here in fear,_

in_ fear. _

Allegretto

Love one an-o-ther with a

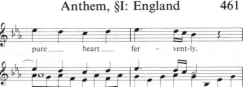

pure_ heart fer - vent-ly,

one, foreign to our buildings, to our services and to our tastes' ('Music in Cathedral and Church Choirs', *Paper Read before the Church Congress in London*, 1899). He was greatly concerned to further a 'genuinely English' school of composition, and paid a generous tribute to the Wesleys and to 'their influence upon the modern renaissance in England, of which they were as undoubtedly as they were unconsciously the forerunners'. While Stanford's own church music reflects his lively interest in contemporary music abroad, it is unmistakably English in style and structure. The anthem *The Lord is my shepherd* well illustrates the composer's concern to integrate large-scale forms by means of motivic development. It also contains many imaginative harmonic turns of phrase, as indeed do all his most memorable anthems, not least being the three splendid motets *Coelos ascendit hodie*, *Justorum animae* and *Beati quorum via* (ex.7), written for the choir of Trinity College, Cambridge.

Ex.7 Stanford: *Beati quorum via*

During this time of renaissance, a multitude of minor craftsmen, nearly all of them church musicians, produced well-wrought, if generally unremarkable, music for the Anglican rites, including Edward Bairstow (whose fine *Let all mortal flesh keep silence* will long be remembered), Ernest Bullock, Darke, Dyson, Harris, Basil Harwood, C. S. Lang, Moeran, Sydney Nicholson, Thiman, and Wood.

Few major English composers since the 1920s, however, have written much of significance for the Anglican rites; Vaughan Williams's greatest contribution in this field is his imposing Mass in G minor, which far outweighs the few incidental 'anthems' that he wrote. John Ireland's *Greater love hath no man* was his only essay in this form (see ex.8). Berkeley has written anthems of distinction for a number of special events. Isolated compositions of an anthem-like character suggest what might have been achieved had there been more effective communication between the organ loft and the outside world, notably Holst's setting of *The Evening Watch*, Bax's motets *This worldes joie* and *Mater ora filium*, Walton's *The Twelve* and Britten's *Rejoice in the Lamb*. None of these, however, is practicable for daily use, and as cathedral choirs are expected to sing so much music with little rehearsal, it is difficult to see how complex music of this kind can ever be fitted into the repertory.

Ex.8 John Ireland: *Greater love hath no man*

The work of 20th-century scholars in publishing editions of anthems by composers from the Reformation to the 18th century has added to the repertory so that choirmasters may now draw on the best Anglican music from all periods; the demand for new works in the form is therefore small. Howells has made a substantial and significant contribution to English church music, but his anthems, like Stanford's, form the least important part of his work. Leighton, too, has made a major contribution. There is still a need, however, for high-quality canticle settings, and since World War II several composers have used this form, in some cases adopting idioms from pop music.

See also SERVICE and MOTET.

II. America

The American anthem originated in the late 18th century. Its models were the English anthems which had begun to appear in American publications about the middle of the 18th century and in the collections of church music brought by immigrants or imported from England. The most important of those collections were William Tans'ur's *The Royal Melody Complete* (1735) and Aaron Williams's *The Universal Psalmodist* (1763). Two Americans, Josiah Flagg of Boston and Daniel Bayley of Newburyport, Massachusetts, were most influential in introducing the anthem into the New World. Flagg issued *A Collection of Tans'ur's and a Number of Other Anthems* in 1766, and Bayley was responsible for printing and distributing Tans'ur's collection as well as his own *New Universal Harmony* (1773), which contained 20 anthems by seven English composers including John Arnold, William Knapp, Joseph Stephenson and Aaron Williams. He also published John Stickney's *The Gentleman and Lady's Musical Companion* (1774), the largest collection of English anthems compiled in America during the 18th century. English composer–musicians such as William Tuckey and William Selby were also influential when

they immigrated to the Colonies and established themselves as leaders of the musical communities in New York and Boston.

Generally, these English anthems, composed for rural Anglican parishes or nonconformist congregations, were short unaccompanied works for four-part mixed chorus with occasional brief solos. Each line of the text, usually a paraphrase of verses from the *Psalms*, served as the basis of an independent section, most of which were chordal with only short insertions of imitative polyphony.

After independence was established, works by native composers quickly outnumbered the English models in American publications. The centre of anthem composition during the 18th century was New England, where the pioneer was William Billings. 47 of his anthems appeared in his several collections of church music beginning with *The New England Psalm Singer* (1770) and ending with *The Continental Harmony* (1794). Other leading composers of anthems in New England were Jacob French, Daniel Read, Jacob Kimball and Oliver Holden. While the earliest efforts of American anthem composers were understandably primitive, though not without a certain charm of naivety, those of the second generation were equal in musical technique to their English models, which, in turn, were predictably inferior to the products of the cathedral and collegiate composers trained in the polyphonic tradition.

Outside the mainstream were the Germanic immigrants, most notably the Moravians (*see* MORAVIANS, AMERICAN) who settled in Pennsylvania and North Carolina. Chief among them were Christian Gregor, Johannes Herbst, John Antes and J. F. Peter; their works, unlike the English models, featured combinations of voices and instruments. Their anthems appeared in several 19th-century American collections but, unfortunately, were generally confined to their isolated communities.

During the 19th century the nationalistic fervour of the late 18th century abated, and the English anthem remained the model for American composers. Immigrants such as George K. Jackson, Benjamin Carr and Edward Hodges continued to set the standard for the new generation of native composers, the most significant of whom was Lowell Mason. Beginning with *The Boston Handel and Haydn Society Collection of Church Music* (1882), Mason established the pattern adopted by many students, contemporaries and successors: publication of adaptations of European works, both vocal and instrumental, with English words. George Webb, Nathaniel Gould, Thomas Hastings, William Bradbury and Isaac Woodbury, among others, followed Mason's example in publishing collections of church music consisting of hymns and anthems, some original but mostly adaptations.

During the second half of the 19th century the European influence on American anthems was intensified because a large number of American composers spent time studying in Europe, especially in Germany. At the same time numerous anthems by local composers were published, either singly or in collections or magazines, simply because the form was functional and the market was great. Edmund Lorenz's *The Choir Leader* followed the pattern of Novello's *Musical Times* in issuing a monthly publication containing anthems suitable for a volunteer choir. Most of these works were as undistinguished and undemanding as many of their

English counterparts of the period, although some anthems by Americans trained in Europe were musically admirable and suitable primarily for the professional quartet choirs then popular.

Most influential among the European-trained Americans were Dudley Buck, who spent four years in Leipzig and Paris before returning to serve as organist and choirmaster in several American cities, and Horatio Parker, who served churches in New York and Boston before becoming a professor of music at Yale in 1894. The immense volume of American anthem publication begun in the 19th century has continued in the 20th. Some who have been the most prolific are most lacking in taste, originality and artistic merit. But such composers as Willan and Sowerby must be mentioned as the most influential. Those who were immigrants to Canada and the USA reinforced the pervasive influence of British models on the American anthem.

BIBLIOGRAPHY

J. Day, ed.: *Certaine Notes set Forth in Foure and Three Parts to be Sung at the Morning Communion and Evening Prayer* (London, 1565)
J. Barnard, ed.: *The First Book of Selected Church Musik* (London, 1641/*R*1973)
W. Boyce, ed.: *Cathedral Music* (London, 1760–73)
S. Arnold, ed.: *Boyce's Cathedral Music* (London, 1790)
J. Page, ed.: *Harmonia sacra* (London, 1800)
V. Novello, ed.: *A Collection of Sacred Music* (London, 1811, 2/1825)
F. A. G. Ouseley, ed.: *Cathedral Music, Services and Anthems* (London, ?1850)
T. A. Walmisley, ed.: *Cathedral Music* (London, 1857)
M. B. Foster: *Anthems and Anthem Composers* (London, 1901)
W. Davies, ed.: *The Church Anthem Book* (London, 1933)
E. H. Fellowes: *English Cathedral Music* (London, 1941, rev. 5/1969)
F. Ll. Harrison: *Music in Medieval Britain* (London, 1958, 2/1963)
J. J. McCloy: *The English Anthem of the 16th Century* (diss., U. of Belfast, 1958)
D. Stevens: *Tudor Church Music* (London, 1961)
P. le Huray, ed.: *The Treasury of English Church Music*, ii [1545–1650] (London, 1965)
C. Dearnley, ed.: *The Treasury of English Church Music*, iii [1650–1760] (London, 1965)
G. Guest, ed.: *The Treasury of English Church Music*, iv [1760–1900] (London, 1965)
D. Lumsden, ed.: *The Treasury of English Church Music*, v [1900–65] (London, 1965)
P. le Huray and others, eds.: *Anthems for Men's Voices* (London, 1965)
E. Routley: *Twentieth Century Church Music* (London, 1965, rev. 2/1966)
R. T. Daniel: *The Anthem in New England before 1800* (Evanston, Ill., 1966)
A. Hutchings: *Church Music in the Nineteenth Century* (London, 1967)
P. le Huray: *Music and the Reformation in England, 1549–1660* (London, 1967)
J. Morehen: *The Sources of English Cathedral Music, 1617–1644* (diss., U. of Cambridge, 1967)
A. Smith: *The Practice of Music in English Churches and Cathedrals, and at the Court, during the Reign of Elizabeth I* (diss., U. of Birmingham, 1967)
E. Routley: *The Musical Wesleys* (London, 1968)
G. H. Cummings: *Henry Purcell's Verse Anthems with Orchestra: Background and Structure* (diss., U. of Birmingham, 1970)
C. Dearnley: *English Church Music, 1650–1750* (London, 1970)
L. Ellinwood: *The History of American Church Music* (New York, 1970)
B. Rainbow: *The Choral Revival in the Anglican Church* (London, 1970)
E. A. Wienandt and R. H. Young: *The Anthem in England and America* (New York, 1970)
D. Wulstan, ed.: *An Anthology of English Church Music* (London, 1971)
J. H. Blezzard: *The Sacred Music of the Lumley Books* (*British Museum Mss. Roy. App.74–76*): an Edition and Critical Study* (diss., U. of Leeds, 1972)
R. T. Daniel and P. le Huray: *The Sources of English Church Music, 1549–1660*, EECM, suppl.i (1972)
A. J. Goodwin: *The Anthems of Maurice Greene* (diss., U. of Bangor, 1972)
K. R. Long: *Music of the English Church* (London, 1972)
J. Morehen: 'The English Consort and Verse Anthems', *Early Music*, vi (1978), 381
N. Temperley: *The Music of the English Parish Church* (Cambridge, 1979)

PETER LE HURAY (I), RALPH T. DANIEL (II)

Anthems, national. *See* NATIONAL ANTHEMS.

Anthimos. 15th- or 16th-century composer of Byzantine chant; *see* GREECE, §II.

Anthoin, Ferdinand d'. *See* ANTOINE, FERDINAND D'.

Anthologia [anthologion]. An alternative, later designation for AKOLOUTHIAI.

Anthology. A printed or manuscript collection of musical works selected from a particular repertory. Most anthologies contain works by more than one composer. Certain types of collection, which may be anthologies in the broadest sense – folksong collections, tune books, songsters, hymnals, psalters, pasticcios, ballad operas, organ and lute intabulations, and theory or performance manuals with music examples – are not considered in this article, which is confined to printed anthologies of music roughly contemporary with date of publication and containing works by different composers. For manuscript anthologies, *see* SOURCES, MS; for anthologies of earlier music, *see* EDITIONS, HISTORICAL.

The value of printed anthologies for the musical scholar goes beyond the individual musical items contained, for the entire make-up of each one reflects the judgment of a knowledgable contemporary, its compiler, of the interests, tastes and needs of the musical public of that time and place. Thus anthologies can suggest many aspects of social usage. Sometimes the very wording of an anthology title can offer a surprisingly vivid picture of the circumstances of its intended use, as in 'bey jetzigen langwerenden trawigen Kriegs Pressuren zu sonderlichen Recreation unterweilen in ehrlichen Zusammenkünfften practiciret' (*Fasciculus secundus geistlicher wolklingender Concerten*, 1637³); 'the words consistent with female delicacy' (*Apollonian Harmony: a Collection of . . . Glees, Catches, Madrigals, Rounds, & Canons . . . Sung at the Noblemen's Catch-Club*, London, c1790); or 'to which is added original charades for parlor performance' (*Parlor Gems: a Choice Selection of Music, Instrumental and Vocal*, edited by C. M. Cady, New York, 1875).

Throughout the 16th century, beginning with the earliest printed anthology (Petrucci's *Odhecaton*, 1501, which contains for the most part French polyphonic chansons), it is most common for anthology contents to be chosen from a specific and cohesive repertory, as in Petrucci's other early publications devoted entirely to masses, motets, frottolas or settings of the Lamentations of Jeremiah. Relatively few anthologies offer mixed contents, so that collections such as *Motetti novi e chanzoni franciose* (Venice, 1520³) remain exceptional, while collections of separate popular forms proliferate. Attaingnant alone published over 70 separate chanson collections between 1528 and 1552. Publication of madrigal collections began in 1530 (*Madrigali de diversi musici*, 1530²) and grew to dominate the secular music anthologies of the second half of the 16th century and the opening decades of the 17th. Instrumental anthologies, among which those for solo lute predominate, are far fewer than vocal ones, but it is not uncommon for titles to state that the vocal contents are also suitable for performance on instruments. Bicinia, especially instrumental ones, appeared frequently in the second half of the century, with one collection (1559[24], containing works by Bernardino Lupacchino, G. M. Tasso and anonymi) attaining an astounding publication record: 20 extant editions by 14 different publishers in six cities, appearing between 1559 and 1701.

In the later decades of the 16th century, and continuing well into the first half of the 17th, collections of religious but non-liturgical vocal music became more popular, such as the several books of *laude* printed by Gardane in Rome between 1583 and 1591. Many compilers assembled collections of favourite secular music which they supplied with new religious texts, one example of which is provided by the publishing history of the famous madrigal collection *Il trionfo di Dori* (1592[11]). Immediately popular, it was reprinted by its original publisher, Gardane of Venice, in 1599, and published in Antwerp by Phalèse in 1595, 1596, 1601, 1614 and 1628. It also served as model for the English madrigal collection *The Triumphes of Oriana* (1601[16]) in honour of Queen Elizabeth. In 1619 it appeared in Leipzig but with changed texts, entitled *Triumphi de Dorothea, non illâ italica-prophanâ; sed angelico-coelesti & immortali, id est: musica, sive laus musicae . . . mit gantz newen deutschen geistlichen Texten* (1619[16]). Several extensive liturgical collections were also produced in the first half of the 17th century, one of the best known being the *Promptuarii musici* which appeared between 1611 and 1627, edited by Abraham Schadaeus. It is in four volumes, arranged according to the liturgical year, and contains 436 compositions by 114 composers.

Anthology publications of the second half of the 17th century clearly reflect a growing market for music suitable for domestic music-making, and especially for performers of modest technical attainment. Music of this sort had by no means been neglected earlier, but from this period onwards it began to occupy an increasing proportion of anthology publications. Collections of simple music for few parts became prominent, such as the several multi-volume publications by the house of Ballard in Paris, of which one, *Airs de différents autheurs à deux parties*, ran to 37 volumes between 1658 and 1694. It is significant that the medium alone gained this popularity, for composers are not named. The increasing attention of publishers to amateur needs is also shown in the greater tendency to include both vocal and instrumental works in the same collection, and in the frequent addition of instructional material to assist beginners, a practice that has continued to the 20th century. Both tendencies are apparent in *A Musicall Banquet* (1651[6]), which contains lessons for the lyra viol, a collection of dances for treble and bass viol, catches and rounds for three and four voices, and 'some few rules and directions for such as learne to sing, or to play on the viol'.

In the closing years of the 17th century the demand for collections of new music was large enough to create a new type of publication: the periodical of music scores. The earliest was probably *Mercurius Musicus: or, the Monthly Collection of New Teaching Songs* (London, 1699–1702). Before this many successful publications had extended to cumulatively long series (such as the Ballard *Airs* cited above), but the continua-

tion had probably not been planned in the first place. An ambiguous case, perhaps the first yearbook of music, was another Ballard publication, *Airs sérieux et à boire*. Irregular previous publications of this title were succeeded in 1694 by a volume 'pour les mois d'octobre, novembre et decembre 1694', and in 1695 appeared a volume 'pour l'année 1695', to start an annual series which continued until 1724. Throughout the 18th century many dozens of periodical publications of music were initiated, catering for a wide variety of musical interests and performing media. Only a small number of these ambitious starts, however, continued beyond a few years, and many ceased publication within a year. One of the most durable was *Journal hebdomadaire ou recueil d'airs choisis dans les opéra-comiques* (Paris, 1764–83), which continued as *Journal hebdomadaire, composé d'airs d'opéra et opéra comiques* from 1784 until 1808.

Separate anthologies in the 18th century show the same emphasis on music for home performance, with greater numbers of collections offering arrangements as well as, or often instead of, original compositions for favourite instruments, such as the flute, harp, violin and guitar. Collections of piano music and solo songs are prominent in publications of the later decades of the century, becoming the most common sorts of anthology in the 19th and 20th centuries.

During the last part of the 18th century appeared the first anthologies devoted to music of the past, leading to numerous historical anthologies throughout the 19th century (*see* EDITIONS, HISTORICAL). Interest in this repertory had a gradual but increasing effect on anthology contents in the 19th century, which tended more and more to include music from earlier periods along with recent works. This can be seen clearly in an anthology from the end of the century, *The Music of the Modern World, Illustrated in the Lives and Works of the Greatest Modern Musicians*, ii (New York, 1895), edited by Anton Seidel. It included about 50 composers, of whom fewer than a third were alive at the time of publication and barely half could be considered fairly recent. The actual space filled by contemporary music is in even smaller proportion, the rest being devoted to songs, piano works and arrangements (often excerpts from larger works) by composers ranging back to Palestrina. This type of anthology emphasizing a wide chronological range has also dominated in 20th century publications, exclusively contemporary collections being found in far smaller numbers.

Music anthologies issued periodically remained a popular publication type in the 19th century, though individual examples were, as earlier, generally short-lived. By the early 20th century Krehbiel (*Grove 2*, iii, 687f) could refer to a large number of periodicals 'filled with music for choirs, brass bands, banjo and mandoline clubs, small dance orchestras and the like . . . Few are devoted to the art in its highest phases'. The later 20th century saw the virtual extinction of the periodical of music (although several music literature periodicals include music scores occasionally or regularly). Recent years have however seen some new ventures, for instance *Journal of Music Scores*, a publication of the American Society of Composers which began publication in 1973.

Throughout the centuries there have been many anthologies of special interest because of their selection of some particular focus for the contents. One type is the musical equivalent of the Festschrift or 'In memoriam' volume of essays. An early example is *Le septiesme livre contenant vingt et quatre chansons ... composées par feu de bonne memoire et tres excellent en musique Josquin des Pres, avecq troix epitaphes dudict Josquin* (1545[15]). Another is *In epitaphiis Gasparis Othmari* (1554[30]). *Choice Psalmes* (1648[4]) includes 'divers elegies, set in musick by sev'rall friends, upon the death of William Lawes'. This tradition has continued in the 20th century with such anthologies as *Hommage à Gabriel Fauré* (*Revue musicale*: supplement to Année iii, Oct 1922); *Kompositionen der jetzigen und früheren Schüler der Meisterschule Hans Pfitzners an der Preussischen Akademie der Künste zu Berlin: Festgabe zum 60. Geburtstage 5. Mai 1929* (Berlin, 1929); *Festgabe Joseph Haas: Beiträge von seien Schulern, Mitarbeitern und Freunden ... zum 60. Geburtstage am 19. März, 1939* (Mainz, 1939); *Homage to Paderewski* (New York and London, 1942); and *Words and Music: the Composer's View: a Medley of Problems and Solutions, Compiled in Honor of G. Wallace Woodworth by Sundry Hands* (Cambridge, Mass., 1972). There are also numerous examples of anthologies honouring non-musical figures, such as *The Triumphes of Oriana* (cited above), *Choral Songs by Various Writers and Composers, in Honour of Her Majesty Queen Victoria* (London, 1899) and *Garland for the Queen* (London, 1953).

Another class of anthology centres on a single event, such as the one commemorating five Protestant martyrs: *Suyte du premier livre des chansons spirituelles: contenant cinq chansons spirituelles composées par cinq escholiers detenus prisonniers à Lyon pour le tesmoignage de nostre Seigneur Iesus Christ, en l'an 1553, au moys de juing & qui depuis souffrirent mort cruelle soustenans constamment la querelle de l'Evangile* (1554[19]). There are many others whose entire contents are the music performed on a specified occasion, such as a funeral (e.g. *Exequiae saxonicae: christliche leichenpredigten Orationes funebres, Epicedia und Grabschrifften uber ... den Abgang des ... Herrn Iohansen Hertzogen zu Sachsen ... am 31 Octobris ... 1605*, 1606[14]); a wedding (e.g. *Musiche fatte nelle nozze dello illustrissimo Duca di Firenze il signor Cosimo de Medici et della illustrissima consorte sua mad. Leonora da Tolleto*, 1539[25]); or victory celebration (e.g. *Breve racconto della festa o ballo fattasi in Napoli per l'allegrezza della salute acquistara dalla Maestà Cattolica di Filippo III. d'Austria, rè della Spagne ... al I di marzo, 1620*, 1620[14]). Broader but still specialized coverage is offered by a large number of anthologies which purport to present the repertory of particular places, organizations or individual performers, such as: *Musica de' virtuosi della florida capella dell'illustrissimo et eccellentis. S. Duca di Baviera* (1569[19]) or *Farinelli's Celebrated Songs* (London, c1736–55).

Some vocal anthologies gain added literary interest by presenting a collection of texts by a single poet. Examples of such collections are *Odes d'Anacréon, traduites en français, avec le texte grec* (Paris, 1798); *Geminae undeviginti Odarum Horatii* (1551[17]); *Sei ode di Oratio tradotte in lingua italiana* (London, c1775); *Les Amours de P. de Ronsard Vandemoys* (1552[6]); *Filip Zesens dichterische Jugend-Flammen in etlichen Lob-Lust- und Liebes-Liedern* (1651[5]); *Herrn Professor Gellerts Oden und Liedern nebst einigen Fabeln* (Leipzig, 1759); *Songs from the Published Writings of Alfred Tennyson* (London, 1880); *Album-Rostand* (Paris, c1920); and *The Joyce Book* (London, 1933). A small category of anthologies, but one of particular interest, presents settings of the same text or topic by different composers, as in *L'amorosa Ero* (1588[17]); *Sdegnosi ardori* (1585[16]); *Rosetum Marianum* (1604[7]); *Angst der Hellen und Friede der Sellen, das ist: der CXVI Psalm* (1623[14]); and *Vierzehn Compositionen zu Schillers Ode an die Freude* (Hamburg, c1800).

BIBLIOGRAPHY
R. Eitner: *Bibliographie der Musik-Sammelwerke des XVI und XVII Jahrhunderts* (Berlin, 1877)
F. Lesure, ed.: *RISM*, B I/1: *Recueils imprimés XVIe–XVIIe siècles* (Munich, 1960)
——: *RISM*, B II: *Recueils imprimés XVIIIe siècle* (Munich, 1964); suppl. in *Notes*, xxviii (1972), 397
SYDNEY ROBINSON CHARLES

Anthonello de Caserta [Anthonellus, (An)tonelus, Antonellus Marot de Caserta, A. Marotus de Caserta abbas] (*b* ?Caserta, nr. Naples; *fl* ?northern Italy, ?Naples, late 14th and early 15th centuries). Italian composer.

1. Sources and chronology. 2. Works.

1. SOURCES AND CHRONOLOGY. It is possible to infer the period and locality of Anthonello's activity from the manuscripts in which his works survive. His eight French settings survive in the older fascicles of *I-MOe* α.M.524, which was compiled in 1410 or 1411 at Bologna from the largely French repertory of the courts of the schismatic popes Alexander V (elected Pisa, 1409) and his successor John XXIII. Two of them appear also in the Codex Reina (*F-Pn* 6771), copied in the region of Venice and Padua. The principal source for Anthonello's seven or eight Italian works is *I-La* 184 (the Mancini manuscript), in which his name appears in the forms 'Antonellus Marot de Caserta' and 'Antonellus Marot' above each of them. Since these ascriptions appear only in the upper margins, however, the ascription to Anthonello of *De mia farina*, noted on two staves below *Del glorioso titolo*, remains uncertain (and is doubtful on other grounds).

Because Anthonello's French and Italian settings survive separately, Wilkins has suggested that there were two composers of the same name. There is, however, a similar division of the works of Ciconia and of Magister Zacharias (*see* ZACAR); and in Anthonello's case two manuscript fragments relate to both traditions. One of these, *I-Pu* 1115, contains – besides a ballata by Anthonello – a French setting by Jacob de Senleches from *I-MOe* α.M.524 and *F-Pn* 6771; the other, *I-P Aas* Armadio B 75, no.52, contains the ballata *Piu chiar* ('A. Marotus de Caserta abbas') with a substitute contratenor by M[atteo] d[a] Per[ugia], the main composer in *I-MOe* α.M.524, who died before 1418 and evidently had close connections with Pope Alexander V. This provides the latest possible date for one of Anthonello's works.

Anthonello's only madrigal, *Del glorioso titolo*, contains references to the marriage of a lady, and predictions that her husband would enhance the glory of Italy as king. Pirrotta associated the text with Johanna II, Queen of Naples, who married Count Giacomo de la Marche in 1415 and Louis III, Duke of Anjou, in 1423; Clercx on the other hand connected it with Johanna I and her marriage to Louis, Duke of Taranto, in 1348. Neither the style nor the notation of the madrigal supports so early a date as the latter, however, and

Anthonello is absent from the main Florentine sources of 14th-century Italian music.

2. WORKS. In Anthonello's madrigal, *Del glorioso titolo*, the two voices are given independent texts, and the lines are connected with linking phrases in the tenor. The several changes of metre and the nervous, syncopated rhythms recall the style of Bartolino da Padova. Anthonello's ballate are simpler: the two voices largely declaim the texts simultaneously, and both the *piedi* end with the same cadence. Lively melismas occur at the beginning and end of all but one of them, the frottola-like *De mia farina*, whose attribution is doubtful. The notation is Italian throughout, although often without indication of the *divisiones*. The texts – like Anthonello's French texts – are all courtly love lyrics.

Anthonello's Italian works do not approach the complexity of his five ballades, two rondeaux and single virelai, which adhere exactly to the usual French forms. In rhythm these works exhibit the complexities of the ARS SUBTILIOR, i.e. chains of syncopations, conflicting rhythms and changes of metre, notated entirely in the French manner with *signa*, red notes, void notes and red void notes. *Amour m'a le cuer mis* contains what may be the earliest use of signs of proportions. *Dame d'onour en qui* combines voices written in augmentation, in diminution and in normal notation; prolation and time are indicated by numbers resembling fractions. *Tres nouble dame* employs units of two bars of perfect time in diminution against hemiola rhythm; a canon reveals that the special sign of a reversed C means that the note values are to be altered in the proportion 4 : 3 ('de modo epitrito'). In *Dame d'onour c'on ne puet*, three different time signatures are combined so that the smallest note values coincide and bars of different lengths result. In the second section of this rondeau, there is a fundamental change in the time relationships: the outer voices exchange time signatures (6/8 and 3/4) and the contratenor changes from 9/8 to 2/4. Despite their complexities, these pieces sound less dissonant than comparable works by French composers of the period.

In *Beauté parfaite*, Anthonello set a ballade text by Machaut; at the beginning of the refrain section of *Dame d'onour en qui*, he quoted a passage from Vaillant's virelai *Par maintes foys*.

WORKS

Editions: *French Secular Music of the Late Fourteenth Century*, ed. W. Apel (Cambridge, Mass., 1950) [M]
French Secular Compositions of the Fourteenth Century, ed. W. Apel, CMM, liii/1 (1970) [C]

BALLADES

Amour m'a le cuer mis, 3vv, M no.26, C no.3
Beauté parfaite, 3vv, M no.2, C no.4, facs. in Apel (1942), facs.85
Dame d'onour en qui, 3vv, M no.24, C no.5, facs. in Fano, xviii
Du val prilleus, 3vv [*F-Pn* 6771: Du ciel perileus] M no.25, C no.6, facs. in M, pl.ii
Notes pour moi ceste ballade, 3vv, M no.27, C no.7

RONDEAUX

Dame d'onour c'on ne puet esprixier, 3vv, M no.30, C no.9
Dame zentil en qui est ma sperance, 3vv, M no.29, C no.10, facs. in Apel (1942), facs.84

VIRELAI

Tres nouble dame souverayne, 3vv, M no.28, C no.8

BALLATE

(all in *I-La* 184; nos. from Pirrotta's inventory, 1949)

A pianger [piaçer] l'ochi, 2vv, no.36
Con dogliosi martire, 2vv, no.39
De', vogliateme oldire, 2vv, no.38
Madonna, io me ramento, 2vv, no.41
Or tolta pur me sey, 2vv, no.40
Piu chiar ch'el sol, 3vv, no.37 [contratenor frag. and without text; substitute contratenor by M[atteo] d[a] Per[ugia]]

De mia farina, 2vv, no.35 [doubtful authenticity; ed. in Disertori]

MADRIGAL

Del glorioso titolo d'esto duce, 2vv, no.34, facs. in Bonaccorsi

BIBLIOGRAPHY

G. Bertoni: 'Poesie musicali francese nel codice estense lat.568', *Archivum romanicum*, i (1917), 21 [edn. of the French texts set by Anthonello]
C. van den Borren: 'L'apport italien dans un manuscrit du XVe siècle perdu et partiellement retrouvé', *RMI*, xxxi (1924), 530
H. Besseler: 'Studien zur Musik des Mittelalters, I: neue Quellen des 14. und beginnenden 15. Jahrhunderts', *AMw*, vii (1925–6), 231
W. Apel: *The Notation of Polyphonic Music 900–1600* (Cambridge, Mass., 1942, 5/1953), 414ff
N. Pirrotta: 'Il codice estense lat.568 e la musica francese in Italia al principio del '400', *Atti della Reale Accademia di scienze, lettere e arti di Palermo*, 4th ser., v/2 (1944–5), 20, 35
F. Ghisi: 'Italian Ars-Nova Music', *JRBM*, i (1946), 184
A. Mancini: 'Frammanti di un nuovo codice dell'ars nova', *Rendicondi dell'Accademia nazionale dei Lincei*, 8th ser., ii (1947), 89
A. Bonaccorsi: 'Un nuovo codice dell'ars nova: il codice lucchese', *Atti della Accademia nazionale dei Lincei*, 8th ser., i (1948), 590
N. Pirrotta: 'Il codice di Lucca, I: Descrizione e inventario', *MD*, iii (1949), 136
E. Li Gotti: 'Il codice di Lucca, II: Testi letterari', *MD*, iv (1950), 111, 128 [edn. of the It. texts set by Anthonello, pp.111ff]
N. Pirrotta: 'Il codice di Lucca, III: Il repertorio musicale', *MD*, v (1951), 133
B. Disertori: *La frottola nella storia della musica* (Cremona, 1954) [incl. edn. of *De mia farina*]
F. Fano and G. Cesari: *La cappella musicale del duomo di Milano*, i: *Le origini e il primo maestro di cappella, Matteo da Perugia* (Milan, 1956), 64f, 117ff, 135, 139
K. von Fischer: *Studien zur italienischen Musik des Trecento und frühen Quattrocento* (Berne, 1956), 78, 85, 88
——: 'The Manuscript Paris, Bibl. nat., nouv. acq. frç. 6771 (Codex Reina, PR)', *MD*, xi (1957), 38
——: 'Trecentomusik – Trecentoprobleme', *AcM*, xxx (1958), 181, 188, 195, 198
S. Clercx: *Johannes Ciconia: un musicien liégeois et son temps* (Brussels, 1960), i, 66
U. Günther: 'Der Gebrauch des tempus perfectum diminutum in der Handschrift Chantilly 1047', *AMw*, xvii (1960), 295
N. Wilkins: 'Some Notes on Philipoctus de Caserta', *Nottingham Mediaeval Studies*, viii (1964), 84
W. Marggraf: 'Tonalität und Harmonik in der französischen Chanson zwischen Machaut und Dufay', *AMw*, xxiii (1966), 21
N. Wilkins: 'The post-Machaut Generation of Poet–Musicians', *Nottingham Mediaeval Studies*, xii (1968), 40–84
U. Günther: 'Das Manuskript Modena, Biblioteca Estense, α.M.5, 24 (*olim* lat.568 = Mod)', *AMw*, xxiv (1970), 24, 54
N. Wilkins, ed.: *La louange des dames by Guillaume de Machaut* (Edinburgh, 1972), 168ff [edn. of *Beauté parfaite*]
URSULA GÜNTHER

Anthony [Anthoni, Anthonus], **Cristofferus** (*fl* c1440–70). Composer. His name could be English, German or Italian. His Sanctus, in spite of its structure and 6-3 harmonies, seems un-English in rhythm and dissonance treatment; the fauxbourdon of his *Magnificat* cannot be paralleled in the work of any known English contemporary, nor is any composition of his copied in close proximity to a piece known to be English. Disertori suggested that he was a native of Trent.

WORKS

1 Sanctus, 3vv, *I-TR* 90 (no chant; inc. edn. in Disertori)
2 Magnificat primi toni, 3vv, *TR* 90, 93 (even verses only, based on chant; edn. in Disertori)
3 Ut queant laxis, 3vv, *TR* 90 (freely based on non-Guidonian chant; alternative text honouring S Vigilio; edn. in Lunelli (1934); inc. edn. in Disertori)

BIBLIOGRAPHY

R. Lunelli: 'I codici musicali tridentini del '400', *Trentino*, xii (1934), 163
——: 'I codici musicali trentini del quattrocento', *Trentino*, xix (1941), 184
B. Disertori: 'Un Magnificat del Quattrocento in stile di falsobordone', *Musica sacra*, 11th ser., ii (Milan, 1957), 45
F. Ll. Harrison: *Music in Medieval Britain* (London, 1958, 2/1963), 347f
B. L. Trowell: *Music under the later Plantagenets* (diss., U. of Cambridge, 1960), i, 76f, 79, 88; ii, 168
BRIAN TROWELL

Anthony, Jacob (*b* Germany, 1736; *d* Philadelphia, 29 Dec 1804). American woodwind instrument maker. Jacob Anthony was one of the earliest woodwind makers to bring his skills to the New World. He arrived in Philadelphia in about 1764 and continued in business as a turner and musical instrument maker until his death in 1804. Two of his instruments are in the Dayton C. Miller collection at the Library of Congress. One of these is an excellent ebony flute with three graduated upper joints, foot to *c'* and five silver keys. Although this instrument has a *c'* key there is no key for *c#'*. Anthony's business was continued by his son Jacob Anthony jr until 1811.

ROBERT E. ELIASON

Anthony, James R(aymond) (*b* Providence, Rhode Island, 18 Feb 1922). American musicologist. He attended Columbia University (BS 1946, MA 1948), the University of Paris (diploma 1951) and the University of Southern California, where he took his doctorate in 1964 with a dissertation on André Campra's operaballets. After serving on the faculty of the University of Montana (1948–50) he became a professor at the University of Arizona (1952). His particular area of study is French music of the 17th and 18th centuries, and he has concentrated on opera-ballet of the French Baroque in many of his writings. Although marred by typographical and factual errors, his book on French Baroque music is valuable as an introduction to a vast body of instrumental and vocal music which has not been thoroughly explored. He is also known as a harpsichordist.

WRITINGS

The Opera-ballets of André Campra: a Study of the First Period French Opera-ballet (diss., U. of Southern California, 1964)
'The French Opera-ballet in the Early 18th Century: Problems of Definition and Classification', *JAMS*, xviii (1965), 197
'Thematic Repetition in the Opera-ballets of André Campra', *MQ*, lii (1966), 209
Review of *Documents du minutier central concernant l'histoire de la musique (1600–1650)*, i, ed. M. Jurgens (Paris, 1968), *Notes*, xxvi (1969–70), 511
'Some Uses of the Dance in the French Opera-ballet', *RMFC*, ix (1969), 75
'Printed Editions of André Campra's *L'Europe galante*', *MQ*, lvi (1970), 54
Review of G. Seefrid: *Die Airs de danse in den Bühnenwerken von Jean-Philippe Rameau* (Wiesbaden, 1969), *Notes*, xxviii (1971–2), 697
French Baroque Music from Beaujoyeulx to Rameau (London, 1973, rev. 2/1978)
with N. Dufourcq: 'Church Music in France: (b) 1661–1750', *NOHM*, v (1975), 437–92
'French Music of the XVIIth and XVIIIth Centuries: a Checklist of Research in Progress', *RMFC*, xv (1975), 262
'Lully, Jean-Baptiste', 'Motet', §III (3), 'Paris', §III, 'Tragédie lyrique', *Grove 6*

EDITIONS

with D. Akmajian: *M. P. de Montéclair: Cantatas for One and Two Voices*, RRMBE, xxix–xxx (1978)

PAULA MORGAN

Antichi, Adam degli. *See* ANTIQUIS, A. DE.

Anticho, Andrea. *See* ANTICO, ANDREA.

Antichrist, plays of. One of the three medieval eschatological dramas appropriate to Advent (*see also* SPONSUS, PLAY OF; Last Judgment plays occur only in the vernacular and have no especial musical interest). The plays of Antichrist deal with the legend of 'the false Messiah, or adversary and complete opposite of Christ, who was expected to appear on earth to deceive and corrupt the faithful before the second coming of the

Redeemer and the Last Judgment' (Young). The most famous medieval play on this theme is from Tegernsee (south Germany) and dates from the 12th century; it is a wide-ranging, ambitious ecclesiastical Latin play, with political significance. The single source (*D-Mbs* lat.19411) contains no music, but there are at least 76 references to singing in the rubrics.

For further information and bibliography *see* MEDIEVAL DRAMA, §II, 2, esp. Young (1933) and Stäblein (1966).

JOHN STEVENS

Anticipation. In part-writing, an unaccented NON-HARMONIC NOTE that belongs to and is repeated in the harmony immediately following; an extra statement of an entire chord on a preceding weak beat is called 'rhythmic anticipation'.

Antico. *See* STILE ANTICO.

Antico [Anticho, Antigo, Antiquo, Antiquus], **Andrea** (*b* Montona, Istria, *c*1480; *d* after 1539). Italian engraver, publisher and composer. His birthplace is frequently appended to his name, as in his papal privilege of 1516: 'to our beloved son Andreas Antiquus de Montona, cleric of the diocese of Parenzo now living in Rome'. Active as an engraver and music publisher in Rome from 1510 to 1518, in Venice 1520–21 and again from 1533 to 1539, he was the first competitor of OTTAVIANO PETRUCCI, who had initiated the printing of volumes of polyphonic music at Venice in 1501. Antico was the first to publish such books in Rome.

Antico's method differed fundamentally from Petrucci's: Antico was an engraver of blocks that printed music and text in one impression, whereas Petrucci employed multiple impression from moveable type. Antico both engraved and published, usually with the help of partners, his Roman editions and those of his first two years in Venice. After 1533, however, he was mainly an engraver for the SCOTTO publishing firm in Venice, although he began the publication of the last of the many editions with which he was involved in 1539.

His career began with a collection of frottolas entitled *Canzoni nove* (9 October 1510), which he engraved and published in collaboration with Marcello Silber. Giovanbattista Columba, also mentioned in the colophon, was the graphic artist probably responsible for the title-page design. Although not named, he probably also designed illustrated title-pages for some of Antico's other Roman editions, including the *Liber quindecim missarum* (1516), *Frottole intabulate* and *Canzoni . . . libro quarto* (both 1517).

The *Canzoni nove* in oblong quarto is based on the design and content of Petrucci's frottola books, from which about half its pieces are drawn. Antico would have encountered no difficulty in this reprinting since Petrucci's privilege from the Venetian signory afforded no protection outside its territory. Antico's subsequent frottola books, however, show little or no dependence on Petrucci.

Before issuing a second book, Antico secured from Leo X the first privilege (dated 3 October 1513) to print music in the papal states; it provided a ten-year copyright for all the music to be published by Antico. Petrucci received a similar privilege on 22 October, as well as the exclusive right to print organ tablature.

Antico probably published the first edition of his *Canzoni . . . libro secondo* shortly thereafter. *Libro ter-*

tio, which includes two frottolas composed by Antico himself, contains a reprint of his papal privilege: *Libro quarto* was printed in association with Nicolò de Judici. The second and third books were reprinted in 1518 from the original plates (without crediting Antico) by Jacopo Mazzocchi and Jacopo Giunta in Rome.

Title-page of 'Liber quindecim missarum', engraved by Antico, and published by Scotto & Giunta (Rome, 1516)

On 15 January 1516 Leo X awarded Antico a new privilege for the exclusive printing of music 'in magno volumine' for ten years, specifically prohibiting Petrucci from printing such books. Antico issued only one large folio choirbook, his *Liber quindecim missarum*, dated 9 May 1516 and containing masses by Josquin, Brumel, Févin, Mouton and others. The engraved title-page depicts the pope receiving a music book from the publisher (see illustration; see also PRINTING AND PUBLISHING OF MUSIC, fig.2*b*). In a dedication addressed to Leo X, Antico stated:

Your generation seems to me to have reached the highest perfection. . . . From the works of these many excellent musicians I have collected fifteen masses that seem to me of high significance and quality, and for these I have engraved the notes on wooden plates (which no-one before me had done) and executed them with a new method of printing and with the aid of partners in meeting the expense; and moreover I have published them in royal volumes with great care and long labour; indeed, I have devoted nearly three years to this from its inception.

Contracts dealing with the printing and sale of the work show that Antico shared expenses with Ottaviano Scotto and that the printing was done by ANTONIO GIUNTA.

On 27 December 1516 the pope cancelled Petrucci's privilege for printing organ tablature because of his failure to issue such music and transferred it to Antico. Less than a month later Antico issued his *Frottole intabulate da sonare organi*, consisting of keyboard arrangements of pieces drawn mostly from his frottola collections, the majority by Bartolomeo Tromboncino. It was the first book of Italian keyboard music to be printed. The term 'organ' in its title must be understood to mean keyboard instruments in general as the illustration of a harpsichord on the title-page shows.

Between 1518 and 1520 Antico moved to Venice where his new partner was Luca Antonio Giunta, uncle of Jacopo Giunta of Rome and one of the most active printers in Venice. In addition to reprints of earlier books, they published music by Franco-Netherlanders and a new book of arrangements for voice and lute, *Frottole de Misser Bortolomio Tromboncino & de Misser Marcheto Carra*. Its contents in large part are drawn from Antico's fourth book of frottolas. It was probably modelled on Petrucci's two books of Bossinensis's intabulations (1509, 1511); Antico even included Petrucci's 'Regula' for reading the tablature, in somewhat simplified form. In 1521, together with Andrea Torresano, Antico published several volumes of sacred music including the important *Missarum diversorum authorum* (containing masses by Mouton, De Silva and Gascongne).

Antico's activities from 1522 to 1533 are unknown. Chapman has suggested that he may have been associated with another Istrian music printer, Jacques Moderne, at Lyons some time before 1530, but this hypothesis is unproven.

In 1533 he engraved a book of Verdelot's madrigals commissioned by Scotto and printed by the brothers Da Sabio. Antico seems to have been Scotto's employee rather than partner, engraving several publications for him in the 1530s. In addition he brought out *La couronne et fleur des chansons a troys* (printed by Anthoine dell'Abbate) in 1536. His last work is the *Mottetti di Adrian Willaert, libro secondo a quattro voci* (1539). In this, a companion volume to the first book printed by Scotto in the same year, Antico is credited with initiating its publication. An elegantly engraved book of motets by Venice's pre-eminent composer, it is the only print of Antico's last period to name him as publisher; typographically it is far superior to Scotto's first book and the new editions of both books by Gardane (1545). Thus Antico's final publication brought his long career as an editor and engraver to a fitting close.

Antico included two of his own frottolas in his *Canzoni . . . libro tertio* (1513): *S'il focho in chui sempre ardo* and *De chi potra piu mai*. Both are signed 'Andrea Anticho D. M.' ('de Montona' in the 1520 edition) and are in a simple, homophonic style. Many writers also assign to Antico the 17 pieces attributed to 'A. de Antiquis (Venetus)' in Petrucci's frottolas and *laude* collections (1505–9) and in Antico's own *Canzoni nove* (1510). However, since Antico never signed his name in this way, it is doubtful that A. DE ANTIQUIS is to be identified with him.

ENGRAVINGS
(*printer's name where known follows date of publication*)

ROME, 1510–18

Canzoni nove con alcune scelte de varii libri di canto (1510; M. Silber)
1 piece ed. IMi, iii, new ser. (1964), 133; Canzoni, sonetti, strambotti

et frottole, libro tertio (1513¹), ed. in SCMA, iv (1941); Canzoni libro secondo con cose nuove (1516), lost [probably a revised enlarged edn. of a book first pubd in 1513 before 1513¹]; Liber quindecim missarum (1516¹; O. Scotto & A. Giunta), 4 masses ed. MMRF, viii–ix (1894); Canzoni, sonetti, strambotti et frottole, libro quarto (1517²; N. de Judici); Frottole intabulate da sonare organi, libro primo (1517³/R1970), 7 pieces ed. IMi, iii, new ser. (1964), 271; Frottole, libro quinto (1518), lost, mentioned in the catalogue of Columbus's library; Motetti libro primo (1518), lost, mentioned in the catalogue of Columbus's library

VENICE, 1520–21

B. Tromboncino and M. Cara: Frottole . . . per cantar et sonar col lauto (c1520⁷; L. A. Giunta); Chansons, 3vv (1520⁶; L. A. Giunta); Motetti nove e chanzoni franciose a quatro sopra doi (1520³; L. A. Giunta); Motetti novi, libro secondo [–III] (1520¹⁻²; L. A. Giunta); Missarum diversorum authorum liber primus [–II] (1521¹⁻²; A. Torresano); Motetti, liber quartus (1521⁵; A. Torresano)

VENICE, 1533–40

P. Verdelot: Il primo libro de madrigali (1533²; G. A. Nicolini da Sabio); P. Verdelot: Il secondo libro de madrigali (1534¹⁶; O. Scotto); Libro secondo delle canzoni francese (1535⁹; O. Scotto); P. Verdelot, arr. A. Willaert: Intavolatura de li madrigali . . . da cantare et sonare nel lauto (1536, ?O. Scotto); La couronne et fleur des chansons, 3vv (1536¹; A. dell'Abbate); Madrigali, 5vv, libro primo (c1536–7; ?O. Scotto); J. Arcadelt: Il secondo libro de madrigali (c1537⁶; ?O. Scotto) [date of engraving, 1539]; P. Verdelot: Il terzo libro de madrigali (1537¹¹; O. Scotto); Madrigali, 3vv (1537⁷; O. Scotto); Dei madrigali di Verdeloto et di altri eccellentissime autori, 5vv, libro quarto (1538²¹, ?O. Scotto); A. Willaert: Motetti . . . libro secondo, 4vv (1539; B. & O. Scotto), ed. in CMM, iii/1–2 (1950)

DOUBTFUL

Motetti e canzone, libro primo (1521⁶); Motetti et carmina gallica (c1521⁷); Motetti, libro secondo, 4vv (1521⁴)

BIBLIOGRAPHY

D. P. Tomasin and G. Piber: Andrea Antico chierico di Montona nell'Istria, primo calcografo musicale (Trieste, 1880)

A. Zenatti: 'Andrea Antico da Montona', Archivio storico per Trieste, l'Istria e il Trentino, i (1881–2), 167–99; 'Nuovi appunti', iii (1884–6), 249–61

A. Gravisi: 'Andrea Antico istriano da Montona', Atti e memorie della Società istriana di archeologia e storia patria, i (Parenzo, 1885), 141

K. Jeppesen: Die italienische Orgelmusik am Anfang des Cinquecento (Copenhagen, 1943, 2/1960)

A. Einstein: 'Andrea Antico's Canzoni nove of 1510', MQ, xxxvii (1951), 330

A.-M. Bautier-Regnier: 'L'édition musicale italienne et les musiciens d'outremonts au XVIᵉ siècle (1501–1563)', La Renaissance dans les provinces du nord: CNRS Entretiens d'Arras 1954, 27

D. Plamenac: 'Excerpta Colombiniana: Items of Musical Interest in Fernando Colon's "Regestrum" ', Miscelánea en homenaje a Monseñor Higinio Anglés (Barcelona, 1958–61), 663

C. W. Chapman: 'Andrea Antico' (diss., Harvard U., 1964)

D. Plamenac: 'The Recently Discovered Complete Copy of A. Antico's Frottole Intabulate (1517)', Aspects of Medieval and Renaissance Music: a Birthday Offering to Gustave Reese (New York, 1966), 683

C. W. Chapman: 'Printed Collections of Polyphonic Music Owned by Ferdinand Columbus', JAMS, xxi (1968), 34–84

K. Jeppesen: La Frottola: Bemerkungen zur Bibliographie der ältesten weltlichen Notendrucke in Italien (Copenhagen, 1968)

E. E. Lowinsky: Introduction to MRM, iii (1968)

F. Luisi: 'Il secondo libro di frottole di Andrea Antico', NRMI, vii (1974), 491–535

M. Picker: 'The Motet Anthologies of Petrucci and Antico', Formen und Probleme der Überlieferung mehrstimmiger Musik im Zeitalter Josquins Desprez: Wolfenbüttel 1976

——: 'The Motet Anthologies of Andrea Antico', A Musical Offering: Essays in Honor of Martin Bernstein (New York, 1977)

MARTIN PICKER

Antient Concerts. Concert series given in London from 1776 to 1848 by the Concert of Ancient (Antient) Music; see LONDON, §VI, 4(i).

Antier, Marie (b Lyons, 1687; d Paris, 3 Dec 1747). French soprano. Trained as a singer and actress by Marthe le Rochois, she made her début at the Opéra in the 1711 revival of Michel de la Barre's La vénitienne (1705). For the next 30 years she sang major roles in up to five productions each season, and she retired with a generous pension at Easter 1741. After her début she was immediately given important roles in new productions beginning with Campra's Idoménée (1712) and Salomon's Médée et Jason (1713); 23 years later she sang the same role, Cléone, in a revival of the Salomon opera and was warmly praised by the Mercure (Dec 1736). Antier appeared in almost two dozen Lully revivals; at one performance of the 1713–14 revival of Armide (1686) she had the honour of presenting the victorious Marshal of Villars with a laurel crown. In 1720 she became première actrice of the Académie Royale de Musique and in the following year she was made a musicienne de la chambre du roi.

In the early 1720s Antier sang at the Château des Tuileries in private performances of opéras-ballets, in which Louis XV loved to dance, and later in the 'concerts chez la Reine'. She became maîtresse en titre to the Prince of Carignan and on her marriage in 1726 to Jean Duval, inspecteur du grenier à sel de Paris, she received lavish gifts from the royal family. An imprudent affair in 1727 with Le Riche de La Pouplinière caused La Pouplinière to be temporarily banished from Paris. Antier herself was installed for a time in the Convent of Chaillot while apparently continuing her career at the Opéra. Beginning in 1725, and continuing through this period, she frequently served as a soloist in motets by Destouches and Lalande performed at the Concert Spirituel; in 1727–9 she sang cantatas at the Concert Français. Her career had passed its zenith: major roles at the Opéra were increasingly given to her younger colleagues – Le Maure, Pélissier, Erremans and Petitpas. Destouches made disparaging remarks about the aging singer in a letter of 8 February 1728 (trans. from Tunley):

Mlle Antier has a most beautiful voice, of noble quality and fantastic flexibility; it is a pity that she does not possess an extra semitone at both ends of her range. She sings all styles – gracious, tender, expressive, and above all shines in cantatas. . . . As nothing is perfect in this world these fine qualities are balanced by faults. Sometimes she lacks intonation; her tendency to sing light music has somewhat diminished the beauty of her trills and takes away that intensity of tone so necessary when expressing terror.

Nevertheless, she sang in such new productions as Montéclair's Jephté (1732), Rameau's Hippolyte et Aricie (1733), Les Indes galantes (1735) and Castor et Pollux (1737). Her last appearances were in revivals of works in which she had sung earlier in her career. After maintaining a lavish residence at 47 rue d'Auteuil from 1715 until 1729, she spent her last years living rent-free in the Magasin de l'Opéra; she was survived by her husband (d 1755). Her younger sister sang in the chorus of the Opéra from 1719 until 1743. She was the mother of the soprano Mlle de Maiz.

BIBLIOGRAPHY

Mémoire pour servir à l'histoire de l'Académie royale de musique (MS, F-Po, Amelot), 284

J.-B. Durey de Noinville: Histoire du théâtre de l'Académie royale de musique en France (Paris, 2/1757/R1969), ii, 67f

J.-B. de La Borde: Essai sur la musique (Paris, 1780/R1972), iii, 491f

T. Lajarte: Bibliothèque musicale du Théâtre de l'Opéra (Paris, 1876)

A. Pougin: Pierre Jélyotte et les chanteurs de son temps (Paris, 1905), 45ff

G. Cucuel: La Pouplinière et la musique de chambre au XVIIIe siècle (Paris, 1913/R1971), 25ff

D. Tunley: The Eighteenth-century French Cantata (London, 1974), 9, 17, appx B

JULIE ANNE VERTREES

Antill, John (Henry) (*b* Sydney, 8 April 1904). Australian composer. After initial training as a chorister of St Andrew's Cathedral, Sydney, he studied at the NSW State Conservatorium under Alfred Hill. He had experience in amateur theatre and orchestras before taking a position, in 1934, with the Australian Broadcasting Commission as conductor and music presentation officer. On his retirement in 1971 as federal music editor, he was awarded the OBE for services to Australian music. The performance of his orchestral suite *Corroboree* conducted by Goossens in London in 1947 led to Antill's immediate recognition abroad, and he was hailed as the creator of a specifically Australian music. *Corroboree* introduced an instrumental and rhythmic language new to audiences in Australia when it was first performed there as a ballet by the National Theatre Ballet, Sydney (1950). The work may have been stimulated by Antill's first hearing of a native corroboree near Botany Bay in 1913; he conducted extensive research into aboriginal music during the period of more than a decade when he was working on the score. He later held an Australian government composer's fellowship to investigate the ethnic music of the South Pacific Islands (1972–3).

WORKS
(*selective list*)

Operas: Endymion, 1922; The Music Critic, 1953; The First Christmas, television opera, 1970
Ballets: The Sentimental Suite, 1955; Wakooka, 1957; Black Opal, 1961; Snowy, 1961; Paean to the Spirit of Man, 1968
Orch: Corroboree, *c*1935–?1946; Variations, 1953; Sym. of a City, 1959; Music for a Royal Pageant, 1962; Harmonica Conc., 1967; The Unknown Land, str, 1968
Vocal: 5 Australian Lyrics, Bar, pf/str, 1953; Song of Hagar, oratorio, 1958; Cantate Domino, chorus, 1970

Principal publishers: Boosey & Hawkes, Australasian Performing Right Association

BIBLIOGRAPHY
L. McCallum: 'John Antill', *Canon*, viii (1953), 353
R. Covell: *Australia's Music* (Melbourne, 1967), 154ff, 241
A. D. McCredie: *Musical Composition in Australia* (Canberra, 1969), 10f
J. Murdoch: *Australia's Contemporary Composers* (Melbourne and Sydney, 1972), 9ff

ELIZABETH WOOD

Antimasque. A comic or grotesque interlude in a MASQUE, normally preceding the terminal dances of the masquers. There were usually more than one and they consisted of a variety of spoken dialogue, pantomime, singing and dancing. Unlike the grand masquing dances, which were performed by a group of nobility from the floor of the hall, antimasques were usually danced by professional actors from the stage. In contrast to the serious matter of the main masque (allegory, mythology, *deus ex machina*) the themes of the antimasques concentrated on mundane humour and the bizarre: the low-class comedy of beggars, cripples and drunkards, housewives and shopkeepers, barmaids and chimney-sweeps, foreigners, criminals, soldiers and common labourers; the pantomimed antics of dancing birds, bears, cats, apes and baboons; and the fantastical capers of furies, witches, spirits, sprites, satyrs and other magical beings. The spoken burlesques often imitated folk characters and situations, as well as *commedia dell'arte* types. The music, in addition to partsongs and solo airs, ballads, catches and drinking-songs, included dances in fast duple or triple time (jigs, country dances, 'moriscos', 'corantos', galliards and 'almans') and also the slower measures for some comic situations. These antimasque dances can often be identified by such characteristics as

the reversed *alla breve* sign (₵), notes marked with fermatas indicating held choreographic gestures, lively repeated notes on one pitch or a series of disjunct intervals portraying a prancing or cavorting action, and the linking of several short strains in contrasting metres indicating quick changes in mood and character. Often these dance sequences were accompanied by violins or folk instruments and even by mock musical instruments.

Comedy had been an important element of the masque since the early 16th century, but the term 'antimasque' was probably not coined until 1609, when it was used by Ben Jonson in his introduction to the *Masque of Queens* (*see* MASQUE, §2). Before this, and even afterwards, the terms 'antick masque' and 'antemasque' are encountered; the latter probably arose due to its position before the main masque, whereas the former may have contributed to the term 'antimasque' as a portmanteau formed from 'antick' and 'masque'. Jonson's usage introduced the element of antithesis: the number of farcical characters balanced that of the noble grand masquers, the actors playing both types of role in elaborate contrasting disguises. Jonson attempted unsuccessfully to use this 'foil' technique to control the amount of comedy in the masque. After his quarrel with Inigo Jones, which resulted in his defeat, the number of antimasques rapidly increased, so that the norm of one, two or three in the Jacobean masque rose to as many as 20 'entries' in the last of the Caroline masques, thereby contributing to the transformation and demise of the court masque. Influences from the contemporary French *ballet à entrées* also played a prominent role in this dissolution.

The antimasques of the Caroline period were also used for purposes of satire and political propaganda, and by the time of James Shirley's *Cupid and Death* (1653) they had become a stock genre, integrated and dispersed throughout the work. Antimasque elements continued to exert strong influence on the masque interludes of Restoration and 18th-century drama, most notably in the operas and semi-operas of Dryden and Purcell. Many antimasque dances with their characteristic titles ('the beares dance', 'turkes dance', 'antick' etc) survive in manuscript (*GB-Lbm* Add.10444) and in such early publications as William Brade's *Newe ausserlesene liebliche Branden* (Hamburg, 1617²⁵), John Adson's *Courtly Masquing Ayres* (London, 1621), Thomas Simpson's *Taffel Consort* (Hamburg, 1621¹⁹), and John Playford's *Court-Ayres* (London, 1655⁵) and *Courtly Masquing Ayres* (London, 1662⁸).

BIBLIOGRAPHY
A. J. Sabol: *Songs and Dances for the Stuart Masque* (Providence, Rhode Island, 1959)
J. E. Knowlton: *Some Dances of the Stuart Masque Identified and Analyzed* (diss., Indiana U., 1966)
M. Lefkowitz: *Trois masques à la cour de Charles Ier d'Angleterre* (Paris, 1970)

MURRAY LEFKOWITZ

Antinello, Abundio. *See* ANTONELLI, ABUNDIO.

Antinori, Luigi (*fl* 1725–34). Italian tenor. A native of Bologna, he was engaged by the Royal Academy in London for the season of 1725–6, replacing Francesco Borosini. He sang Borosini's parts in revivals of *Elpidia* (by Vinci and Orlandini) and *Rodelinda* (Handel) in November and December 1725, and appeared in the unsuccessful pasticcio *Elisa* on 15 January 1726. Handel composed the parts of Lelio in *Scipione* and Leonato in *Alessandro* for him; the fact that he had three arias in the former but only one in the latter suggests no great confidence in his powers, though Fétis described him as a fine singer with an excellent method. The compass is *d* to *a′*, the tessitura fairly high. He sang Argenio in Porpora's *Imeneo in Atene* (on a libretto subsequently adapted for Handel) at Venice in 1726, and was engaged at Genoa in 1732 and Florence (in operas by Pergolesi and A. Scarlatti) in 1733–4.

WINTON DEAN

Antioch. Ancient city in Asia Minor (now Antakya, Turkey), an important centre of early Christian chant; *see* BYZANTINE RITE, MUSIC OF THE, §1; CHRISTIAN CHURCH, MUSIC OF THE EARLY, §4; PLAINCHANT, §I, 1; SEVERUS OF ANTIOCH.

Antiphon. In Latin Christian chant generally, a liturgical chant with a prose text, sung in association with a psalm. In Gregorian psalmody, for example, psalms and canticles are usually preceded and followed by a single antiphon, and the psalm tone used for the recitation of the psalm itself is often musically incomplete without the antiphon. Antiphons of this type may be regarded as 'normal' and are represented above all by the Gregorian antiphons to the psalms of Matins, Lauds and Vespers; there are however other categories, some of which may lack psalmody or have rhymed texts. The antiphon and responsory are the two musical genres with Latin prose texts which occur in all the Western liturgies.

The antiphon in early texts is frequently to be distinguished from 'antiphony' (i.e. antiphonal psalmody: *see* PSALMODY, §I) although the two are historically linked: when antiphonal psalmody replaced responsorial psalmody, the respond was replaced by the antiphon. The latter then became varied in its manner of performance, although its form remained clearly defined and it never lost its essential characteristics.

1. Early history and terminology. 2. Origins and composition of texts. 3. Origins and composition of melodies: (i) Adaptation (ii) Centonization. 4. The Gregorian antiphons to the psalms at Matins, Lauds and Vespers. 5. Other Gregorian antiphons: (i) Antiphons to the psalter (ii) Verse antiphons (iii) Antiphons to the *Benedictus* and *Magnificat* (iv) Mass antiphons: introits and communions (v) Marian antiphons (vi) Processional antiphons (vii) Rhymed antiphons.

1. EARLY HISTORY AND TERMINOLOGY. The Greek word 'antiphōna', derived from the classical Greek *antiphōnos* ('resonating with'), was adopted in Latin without translation. For Pseudo-Aristotle (*Problems*, xix, 39) the neuter adjective *antiphōnon* signified the interval of an octave; like other ancient Greek theorists he scarcely distinguished *antiphōnia*, the octave, from the unison (*Problems*, xix, 17). Even in the writings of the 14th-century Byzantine theorist Manuel Bryennius the term retained this meaning.

With the Jewish philosopher Philo of Alexandria (*d* AD *c*54), the term underwent an interesting change: to describe the practice of the Therapeutae sect, he used the word to mean chant alternating between a male and a female choir (*De vita contemplativa*, xi; even there, the term may retain a link with its original sense, since women's voices are pitched an octave above those of men). And in later Christian texts, the term 'antiphōnia' was used to mean 'antiphony', or psalmody sung by two choirs, perhaps to distinguish it from responsorial psalmody, performed by a soloist. Thus Theodore of Mopsuestia (*d* 428), theologian of the church of Antioch, wrote of 'that type of psalmody which we call *antiphōnia*'.

The term appeared first in the West in a description of the liturgy of the Middle East. The Gaulish pilgrim Egeria (also known as Aetheria or Silvia), in her *Itinerarium*, a late 4th-century description of the liturgy at Jerusalem, used the term 'antiphona' about 30 times, usually associating it with the psalms ('psalmi et antiphonae'). Here the term seems to mean a piece sung with the psalms, and not to refer to antiphonal psalmody. The ancient antiphonal psalmody of Jerusalem, indeed, did not survive: in the Byzantine rite it was replaced by troparia (*see* TROPARION) and kanones (*see* KANŌN). Vestiges of it did survive in the West, however: the Mozarabic antiphon *Introeunte te*, and others, are literal translations of Byzantine *stichēra* derived from the ancient antiphonal psalmody of Jerusalem.

The term 'antiphona' (taken as a neuter plural) appeared at an early date in Provence: for example, John Cassian (*d* 435), founder of the abbey of St Victor at Marseilles ('cum stantes antiphona tria concinuerint', *Institutiones*, iii, 8; cf ii, 2), and the Rule of Aurelian of Arles (*c*547), modelled on the usage at Lérins ('antiphona tria parvula').

The real origins of the antiphon in the West, as well as those of the Ambrosian antiphoner, are to be sought in the biography of St Ambrose (*d* 397) by Paulinus (*PL*, xiv, 31). When the bishop and his flock were besieged in the *basilica portiana* by Valentinian in 386, they sang antiphons and hymns, these being Ambrose's own compositions in iambics, described a little later in the Rule of St Benedict by the term 'ambrosianum'. These 'antiphons' were no longer psalms sung antiphonally but, like those of Egeria, chants repeated as a refrain after each verse of the psalms. This practice is explicitly stated to have been borrowed from the East in the *Confessions* of St Augustine, who had been converted to the faith by Ambrose ('hymni et psalmi ut canerentur secundum morem orientalium partium institutum est', ix, 7, 15). Augustine must have introduced antiphons into Africa when he became Bishop of Hippo, since he wrote himself that the new practice spread throughout the Christian world.

The Rule of St Benedict (*d* *c*547) uses the term for a separate chant sung with a psalm, the number of repetitions not, however, being specified. Chapters 8–18 of the Rule contain a developed Office; in the *Regula magistri*, the supposed model of the Rule, the term 'antiphon' appears only twice.

The encyclopedist Isidore of Seville (*d* 636) and Aurelian of Réôme (mid-9th century) returned to the original meaning of the term as a chant using two choirs in alternation ('antiphona vox reciproca duobus scilicet choris alternatis psallentibus', Isidore, *Etymologies*, vi, chap.19, 7). In Spanish and Gregorian antiphoners and fragments of the late 8th century, however, the abbreviations 'A', 'AN' or 'ANA' (i.e. *antiphona*) indicated a chant to be performed with a psalm.

Most of the antiphons for the Psalter are brief texts (not always grammatically self-contained) comprising a simple invocation or acclamation of a few words; they are quite similar to the responds (*responsae*) used in ancient responsorial psalmody. In the Psalter of St Germain-des-Prés (*F-Pn* lat.11947, written in 6th-century uncials), which may have been written in Italy, the *responsae* are indicated by the letter 'R' in gold. These responds are very brief: they include 'Praeceptum Domini lucidum' (f.30*v*) for Psalm xix, 'Beatus qui intelligit' (f.77*v*) for Psalm xli, etc; even the responds for the vesper psalms are equally brief, such as 'Juravit

Dominus nec penitebit eum' (f.225v) for Psalm cx. For Psalms cxlviii–cl, sung in most liturgies at Lauds (Ainoi), the respond is 'Alleluia' (written in gold at f.288v): this corresponds to the *alleluiaticum* of the old Gallican liturgy (*see* GALLICAN RITE, MUSIC OF THE, §10). These ancient responds, like later antiphons, are very short (between three and six words as a rule), and often comprise the first words of the psalm. The following examples of antiphons from the Roman Psalter will make this clear: 'Diligam te Domine virtus mea', antiphon to Psalm xviii, borrowed from the first words of the psalm; 'Benedictus Dominus in eternum', antiphon to Psalm lxxxix; 'Benedicite gentes Deum nostrum', antiphon to Psalm lxvi. Of the 95 antiphons to the Psalter, 50 comprise the opening words of the psalm. The suspicion must therefore arise that the antiphons to the Psalter were derived directly from the older responds.

In antiphoners of the late 8th century the number of repetitions of the antiphon in performance is never indicated. Descriptions of contemporary practice may, however, be found elsewhere. For the antiphons of the Mass (i.e. introits), the usage is described in the *Ordines romani* (*see* INTROIT (i), §2). For the antiphons of the Office, according to Amalar of Metz, in the 9th century the antiphon was repeated after each verse of the psalm ('antiphonis quas vicissim chori per singulos versus repetunt', *PL*, cv, 1251). This practice was maintained in the INVITATORY psalm (the *Venite*, Psalm xcv, sung every day at the beginning of Matins except at the end of Holy Week): in it the antiphon is sung in full (e.g. for Tuesday 'Jubilemus Deo salutari nostro') at the end of all the odd-numbered verses, and the second half of the antiphon (e.g. 'Salutari nostro') after all the even-numbered verses, including the doxology; besides this the antiphon is sung in full (as normal) before and after the invitatory psalm. It was impossible for musical reasons to separate the antiphon from the psalm and sing it merely at the beginning and the end, as was done elsewhere: the invitatory has eight special melodies, one in each mode except the 1st and 8th (none), and 4th (three). These potentially numerous and time-consuming repetitions of the antiphon (especially at Matins, with nine psalms in the secular rite and 12 in the monastic) were rapidly abandoned in subsequent centuries for other psalms (cf the texts collected by Stäblein in 'Antiphon', *MGG*).

In the various ancient Latin rites – Gregorian, Ambrosian, Gallican and Mozarabic – the term 'antiphona' generally precedes short chants, with texts averaging between ten and 25 words and simple melodies. These antiphons precede psalms and are also occasionally copied before the final melodic formulae of the psalms. Such indications were essential to the performance of the antiphons, which were conceived as integral parts of the psalm in the succession antiphon–psalm–antiphon. This form has several consequences. The antiphon ends with a clear cadence on the final note, which then determines the choice of the reciting note for the psalm (in Gregorian psalmody five reciting notes are possible; in Ambrosian chant, seven). The psalm tone ending (*differentia, diffinitio, varietas*) is chosen with the first notes of the antiphon in mind, so that a smooth progression may be achieved from the psalm to the repetition of the antiphon. Furthermore, composers of antiphons regularly adopted intonation formulae in the psalms designed to follow the final note of the antiphon melody.

In Offices written at the end of the 9th century and the beginning of the 10th, both by eastern Frankish composers (as in the Office of St Otmar composed at St Gall) or western Frankish composers (as in the Office *In plateis* by Hucbald and the Offices by Stephen of Liège), the numerical position of a chant in an Office determines the choice of its psalm tone. Thus the first antiphon corresponds to a psalm sung to the 1st psalm tone, and so on until the eighth antiphon; the ninth antiphon again corresponds to a psalm sung to the 1st psalm tone, and so on. Psalm tones continued to be chosen thus, according to their numerical order in the Office, until the end of the Middle Ages, especially in the 13th-century RHYMED OFFICE.

Several categories of antiphon developed without any link with psalmody, such as the great processional antiphons of the Gregorian processional (see §5(vi) below), various categories of antiphon in the Ambrosian rite (*antiphona in choro, antiphona dupla* etc) and the Gallican and Ambrosian antiphons with verses which resembled responsories in that the antiphons were repeated after the verse.

2. ORIGINS AND COMPOSITION OF TEXTS. The antiphons of the various Latin rites normally have biblical texts. Those of the normal Sunday and weekday Offices are drawn from the Psalter (see §5(i) below), the earliest source of Latin antiphon texts. Some Mozarabic antiphons retained textual variants originating in the African Psalter: this seems to indicate that at the revision of the Bible and liturgy attributed to Isidore of Seville no-one dared touch the oldest antiphons in the repertory, perhaps for the sake of their melodies. Similarly, certain Ambrosian antiphons display textual variants older than the Milanese psalter.

The antiphons of the Proper of the Time are biblical, often drawn from texts read during the Office or at the Mass of the day; a single biblical extract may often be used quite differently in the various western liturgies. The antiphons of the Proper of Saints have texts drawn from the *Acta martyrum* or from biographies of famous saints. The Gregorian antiphoners contain about 100 antiphon texts drawn from Christian poets or basilical inscriptions: these are in metrical or rhymed verse. Many of the prose texts too are assonanced and balanced quantitatively in the manner of verse. Finally, a few antiphon texts in Latin are known also in Greek, although the musical connections between the respective melodies are not always easy to analyse.

The origin of the antiphon texts had already exercised the minds of the copyists of the Mozarabic Léon antiphoner and the copyist of the Gregorian Petershausen antiphoner (*D-KA* Aug.LX). In the latter the scribe indicated the biblical sources of antiphons in the margins, and marked with the term 'cantor' those texts of ecclesiastical origin for which he had been unable to discover the source. Research on the sources has been undertaken by C. Marbach (*Carmina scripturarum*, Strasbourg, 1907), W. Lipphardt (*Der karolingische Tonar von Metz*, Liturgie wissenschaftliche Quellen und Forschungen, xliii, Münster, 1965) and Hesbert (*Corpus antiphonalium officii*, iii).

A textual comparison of antiphons with their sources in the various Western liturgies illustrates the independence of the respective authors, who aimed to create a balanced structure, with additions (such as the word 'Dominus' before 'Jesus', or one or two 'alleluias' at the end of a chant) or omissions (for example, of the enclitic 'autem', common in the Gospels) where necessary. In such ways the author generally produced two sub-divisions, each further subdivided into two clauses. (Other schemes are also found, some particularly with tripartite divisions; even more complex schemes were favoured, especially in the antiphons from Offices composed in the 10th and 11th centuries.) Thus composers of antiphon texts felt quite free to modify them according to the requirements of musical composition.

The composition of new antiphons seems to have ceased fairly soon in the Ambrosian and Mozarabic liturgies, but it continued in the churches of the Carolingian Empire even after the promulgation of the 'antiphoner of St Gregory' (*see* GREGORIAN AND OLD ROMAN CHANT and GREGORY THE GREAT). The composition of Proper chants for the Office, both antiphons and responsories, never ceased, particularly for the patron saints of dioceses and great abbeys; by contrast, however, very few new Proper chants for the Mass were introduced apart from alleluias. In the Proper of the Time, for example, the antiphon *O virgo virginum* was added to the series of seven Advent 'O' antiphons after the diffusion of the original Gregorian antiphoner (*see* O ANTIPHONS). The same is true of the antiphon *Rex pacificus* and others for first Vespers of Christmas, composed about AD 800 (see Hucke, 1953), the *Veterem hominem* antiphons for the octave of the Epiphany, with texts translated from the Greek and melodies related to the surviving Byzantine melodies (see Strunk, 1964) and, according to Amalar of Metz, the antiphons for the three Matins psalms of Easter and Pentecost.

3. ORIGINS AND COMPOSITION OF MELODIES. There is no evidence that the composers of the texts, even where known (e.g. St Ildefonsus of Toledo, *c*606–67, author of an alleluia and other chants for St Leocadia), were the composers of the melodies; experienced singers may seem as likely. The musical evidence – the manner in which melodies were adapted to texts, and the relationship between text and music – suggests that the composers of the music knew Latin at least as thoroughly as Carolingian scholars like Alcuin, Hrabanus Maurus and Loup de Ferrières. It suggests also a remarkable knowledge of musical theory, and in particular of the rules governing the relationships between words and music (see E. Cardine, *Etudes grégoriennes*, ii, 1957, p.27).

These composers did not, however, always place the textual accents according to the practice of classical Latin (the accents normally correspond to a note or melisma in the chant higher in pitch than those placed on neighbouring syllables). Thus 'mulierem', originally accented on the antepenultimate syllable, was turned into a paroxytone (i.e. a word accented on the penultimate syllable) in the antiphons *Inter natos mulierum* and *Mulieres*. Latin was still spoken by educated men, and had changed over the centuries; and the composers of Gregorian chant in the second half of the 8th century adopted current rather than Ciceronian usage in the

pronunciation and accentuation of Latin (see H. Gavel, *Etudes grégoriennes*, i, 1954, pp.83–148). Latin changed further in later medieval antiphons; and moves were made in the mid-16th century to correct the 'errors' (i.e. deviations from the Ciceronian standard). The melodic accentuation of words was usually 'corrected' by the placing of a single breve (lozenge-shaped note) on unstressed syllables, as in the normal cadence of the communion antiphon of the Epiphany (ex.1). These adjustments were retained by the composers of NEO-GALLICAN CHANT in the 17th century. The study of word accentuation has been revolutionized since the late 19th century, however, and the melodies accordingly reconstructed in reliable editions.

Ex.1
(a) Original version   (b) 'Corrected' version

...Do - mi - num   ...Do - mi - num

The composers of the antiphon melodies, like all composers of chant, borrowed the elements of their compositions from pre-existing models, and did not seek originality. The models themselves seem to have been fixed in the second half of the 8th century for Gregorian chant. Subsequently, new settings were created mainly by adapting prototype melodies to new texts or by CENTONIZATION. These principles are clearly visible at work in the antiphon repertory, owing to its size.

(*i*) *Adaptation*. In the process of adaptation, an old antiphon melody is adapted to a new text approximating to its old text in shape and structure, so that the melodic accentuation of the two corresponds. Such a melody is termed a 'prototype melody' and cited by one of its texts, most often the first in order in the antiphoner. This process is extremely common: sometimes two successive antiphons in the same Office may be sung to the same melody, e.g. the *Veterem hominem* antiphons for the octave of the Epiphany (see Hesbert, *Corpus antiphonalium officii*, i–ii, no.25) and three antiphons for Passion Sunday (no.66; see ex.2). The alleluiatic antiphons of Septuagesima, for the Office of 'farewells' to the alleluia, and of Paschaltide, which consist of numerous repetitions of the word 'alleluia', are other examples of the procedure: the oldest antiphoners, which lacked neumatic notation, explicitly gave the incipits of the prototype antiphons as indications of the melodies to be used (cf Hesbert, iii, nos.1327–37).

The number of prototype melodies is fairly limited: there are none in the modes on D, except among the 'O' antiphons sung to the *Magnificat* during Advent, and all the melodies in this mode are composed by centonization. Some of the prototypes had more texts adapted to them than others. One of the commonest prototypes of the antiphoner is in the 4th mode (ex.3, transposed up a 4th); this prototype was used for a number of texts comprising four clauses, and was adapted to them by *syneresis* (the contraction of occasional notes, indicated in the example with a horizontal bracket) or *dieresis* (the

Ex.2 Antiphons for Passion Sunday

3.   Ju - di - ca - sti   Do -   - mi - ne   cau - sam   a - ni - mae   me - ae...
5.   Num - quid   red -   -   - di   -   - tur   pro   bo - no   ma - lum...
4. Po - pu - le   me   -   - us,   quid   fe - ci   ti - bi...

Ex.3

expansion of formulae with extra notes, here placed in parentheses). It is found with about 90 different texts in an antiphoner copied about AD 1000, even though it is totally absent from the series of antiphons to the Psalter, and no similar melody occurs in the Ambrosian repertory. No doubt it was composed by the Gregorian composers when they needed to organize complete series quickly, such as the series of antiphons for the weekdays of Advent and Lent. Of the 50 antiphons for the weekdays of Advent, 21 (i.e. 42%) are set to this prototype; the proportion is less for the weekdays of Lent (seven out of 56, or 12·5%) but almost as great for the weekdays of the two Passion weeks (16 out of 40, or 40%).

This prototype presents difficulties from the modal point of view, and was often criticized (and even altered) by the theorists. Its modality is ambiguous, especially when it is adapted to short texts in which the note above the final does not occur at the end of the fourth phrase; the first two phrases lack a semitone; the third phrase has a semitone which creates a 1st-mode cadence (g–f–e–d–c–d); only in the fourth phrase is the mode clear, and even then only if the text is long enough to require the full number of notes. In the late 9th century, the *Commemoratio brevis* proposed the use of the 2nd psalm tone rather than the 4th with this antiphon – a solution entirely justified where the antiphon text has a short fourth phrase, as is the case in *Benedicta tu* and *Ex Aegypto* (see Huglo, 1971, pp.64f).

Another solution to this problem was proposed by Regino of Prüm and 12th-century Italian theorists and was adopted in 1134 by the Cistercians. These theorists noted that the first phrase of the antiphon is identical to certain intonations of the 7th psalm tone (ex.4). Since any chant must be modally unified, these theorists proposed that this chant should be modified so as to continue and conclude in the 7th mode. The Cistercians

even went beyond the obvious logical changes which these proposals required, to the complete reshaping of the melody, in the same way as they modified the antiphons using the *tonus peregrinus* to fit the 1st psalm tone.

Of the two prototype melodies in the F mode, that set to *Alleluia, Lapis revolutus est* is used for antiphons for Paschaltide. It may be of Gallican origin: similar chants framed by alleluias occur among Gallican fragments in certain antiphoners written in insular script, such as *Alleluia, Quem quaeris mulier* (Hesbert, iii, nno.1350) and *Alleluia, Noli flere Maria* (no.1348). At a later date further texts of similar structure were set to the same melody, such as the following, which occur in German antiphoners: *Alleluia, Resurrexit Dominus*; *Alleluia, Ego sum vitis vera*; *Alleluia, Quoniam in eternum*; *Alleluia, Nimis exaltatus es* (see respectively Hesbert, iii, nos.1352, 1342, 1351, 1347).

The second prototype melody in the F mode is used for about 20 antiphons for Paschaltide and for six from the Christmas cycle, and is associated with the 6th psalm tone. Its structure is exactly that of the lesser responsories of Paschaltide, and is characterized by repetition in its two phrases (ex.5, with the text *Ego sum vitis vera alleluia*; Hesbert, iii, no.2604).

There are three prototypes in the G mode for four-clause antiphons. That of the antiphon *Tu es Petrus* was adopted for some 60 antiphons, and uses the 7th psalm tone, whereas the other two use the 8th: the *Ecce ancilla* prototype occurs with about ten further texts (see E. Omlin: *Die Sankt-Gallischen Tonarbuchstaben*, Engelberg, 1934, p.316) and the *Omnes de Saba* prototype occurs with more than 20 further texts (comparative table in Ferretti, pp.112f).

(ii) Centonization. The second technique by which new antiphons could be created without original composition in the proper sense has often been termed CENTONIZATION. It occurs in the early liturgical repertories in which the material was transmitted orally, and can only be fully understood in this light: once a psalm tone had been chosen, together with a psalm tone ending, possible formulae for the intonation at once sprang into the mind of the 'composer'. If the 1st tone is chosen, for example,

Ex.4

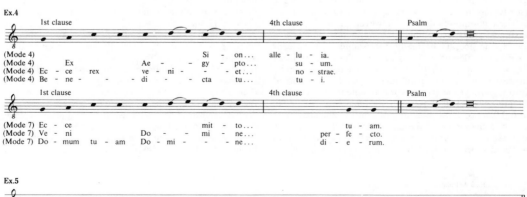

Ex.6

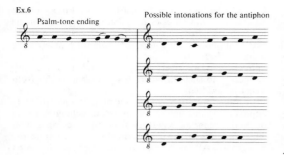

Psalm-tone ending | Possible intonations for the antiphon

and the ending whose cadence is on the 3rd above the final of the mode, a choice of intonation is possible (ex.6). After the intonation, the singer reaches an intermediate cadence (see Ferretti, pp.118f); the intermediate cadences given particular attention by theorists such as Pseudo-Odo (*see* ODO; *Dialogus de musica*, GS, i, 257f) or Wilhelm of Hirsau (*GS*, ii, 172) are those which fall on the final of the mode or a degree compatible with it

The final cadence is the most important of all, for it introduces the intonation of the psalm and also stands at the close of the chant, thus defining the mode. It must therefore fall on the final of the mode; nevertheless, the singer again has a choice of several possible formulae (ex.7 shows the possibilities in the D mode). Of the

Ex.7

formulae in ex.7, the last occurs only in later chants such as the antiphons *Montes Gelboe* (see Hesbert, iii, no.3807) and *Angeli archangeli* for All Saints. The same cadential formulae occur in introits and communions, together with others which are more ornate although they are merely elaborations of simple cadences (ex.8).

Ex.8
(a) Simple antiphon cadence

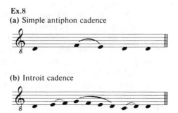

(b) Introit cadence

Many cadential and intonation formulae also appear in the same form in Byzantine chant (see Huglo, 1966, p.279).

It is possible, following Ferretti, to number the formulae which are used and then analyse chants by substituting numbers for the formulae (*Estetica gregoriana*, pp.118ff); all possibilities of combination could be analysed by computer if the formulae were to be replaced by a series of numbers for each mode, following a method outlined by N. Schiødt in Byzantine chant (*Studies in Eastern Chant*, ii, London, 1971, pp.129ff). Nevertheless, Gregorian composition was no matter of juggling with formulae: various factors, indeed, could modify the structure of a chant. In particular, important words tended to attract to them the melodies to which they were sung in other chants, despite the change of context: this practice is common in repertories whose transmission is oral. Thus the word 'ascendit' in *Assumpsit Jesus* (Hesbert, iii, no.1501) is sung to the same figure as 'ascendam' in *Vos ascendite* (no.5493). Even the opening melody of the antiphon may be affected by this practice (see ex.9, showing the antiphons *In velamento clamabant* and *In velamento clamavi*: Hesbert, iii, nos.3306–7; and the antiphons *Dixit autem paterfamilias*, *Dixit autem Pater* and *Dixit Jesus discipulis*, nos.2281, 2280 and 2296). Even a single

Ex.9
(a)

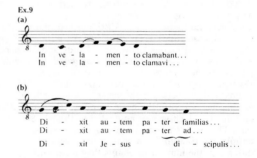

In ve - la - men - to clamabant...
In ve - la - men - to clamavi...

(b)

Di - xit au - tem pa - ter - familias...
Di - xit au - tem pa - ter ad...

Di - xit Je - sus di - scipulis...

syllable, regardless of sense, can attract the same melody, as occurs in the three antiphons *Pater manifestavi*, *Vadam* and *Pacem* (ex.10: Hesbert, iii, nos.4237, 5299 and 4205). Sometimes a similar melodic fragment

Ex.10

Vadam...pa - ter,   fac me
Pa - ter   manifestavi...
Pa - cem...

may appear in chants of different categories (ex.11, with the antiphon *O vos omnes*: Hesbert, iii, no.4095; and the responsory *O vos omnes*, no.7303), or in antiphons of both

Ex.11

Antiphon: O vos om - nes qui tran - si - tis   per viam...
Responsorium: O vos om - nes qui tran - si - tis...

Mass and Office (ex.12, with the antiphon *Spiritus Domini*: Hesbert, iii, no.4988; and the introit *Spiritus Domini*: Hesbert, *Antiphonale missarum sextuplex*, no.106; and with the phrases 'hoc autem' and 'hoc facite' from the antiphon *Solvite templum*: Hesbert, iii, no.4982;

Ex.12

(a)

Antiphon: Spi - ri - - - tus   Domini...
Introit: Spi - ri - - tus   Domini...

(b)

Antiphon: Solvite templum hoc   au - tem   di - xit...
Communion: Ultimo...   hoc   au - tem   di - xit...
Communion: Hoc corpus...   hoc   fa - ci - te...

and the communions *Ultimo* and *Hoc corpus*: Hesbert, *Antiphonale missarum sextuplex*, nos.105 and 67). These correspondences presuppose an amazing familiarity with the whole repertory, and they testify to the unified style of composition which governed the redaction of the Gregorian gradual and antiphoner.

Further details of the composing process adopted in the more elaborate antiphons of the original Gregorian corpus, and of the evolution in musical style which commenced in the 10th century and became more marked in the 13th, are given below (§5(iii) and (vi) in particular).

4. THE GREGORIAN ANTIPHONS TO THE PSALMS AT MATINS, LAUDS AND VESPERS. Seven categories of Gregorian antiphon may be distinguished, mainly following the categories of text set in them: antiphons from the Psalter, antiphons of Matins, Lauds and Vespers, antiphons to the *Benedictus* and *Magnificat*, Mass antiphons, Marian antiphons, processional antiphons and rhymed antiphons. Those of the psalms at Matins, Lauds and Vespers are the most characteristic of the antiphons, and form the basic corpus of the Gregorian antiphoner which was promulgated in the late 8th century. They were transmitted in two main branches of the antiphoner tradition – monastic and secular – which differed in the number of chants they included.

Secular antiphoners were used by the secular clergy, canons and the Dominican and Franciscan friars, and prescribed for Matins nine antiphons and psalms, together with lessons and responsories, distributed over three 'nocturns' each containing three psalms, lessons and responsories. The secular antiphoners prescribed five antiphons for Lauds, which are then repeated for Vespers (except at certain festivals such as Christmas, St Peter etc, where separate vesper antiphons are laid down). The monastic antiphoners, on the other hand, which were used by the regular (monastic) clergy (Benedictines, Cistercians and Carthusians), prescribed 13 antiphons for Matins, five for Lauds and only four for Vespers. The 13 Matins antiphons were also distributed over three nocturns (6 + 6 + 1).

In consequence of the difference in numbers, secular and monastic antiphoners agree in their series of antiphons only in that for Lauds, where both prescribe five antiphons. Here, indeed, there is fairly close agreement, especially for the festivals of the Proper of the Time and of the Saints, as may be seen from a comparison of the first two volumes of Hesbert's edition of the antiphoner (*Corpus antiphonalium officii*, i–ii).

For Matins, the monastic antiphoners adopted the nine antiphons of the secular antiphoners as their first nine, and then added a further four, borrowed from the Common of Saints for the feasts of the Proper of the Saints, and from series of interchangeable pieces for the feasts of the Proper of the Time. Occasionally these extra antiphons were composed foollowing pre-existing models. These brief comments will explain in part the differences existing between secular and monastic antiphoners – no such difference distinguishes secular from monastic graduals.

In modern editions of the chant it is unfortunately impossible to distinguish the antiphons belonging to the original Gregorian repertory from those composed in later centuries: at least 200 or 300 years separate the two groups. Although composition may have proceeded along broadly similar lines during that time, the resulting forms are sometimes very different, as can be seen by comparing the 13th-century antiphons for the feast of Corpus Christi, or those of contemporary rhymed Offices (e.g. of St Dominic or St Francis), with the old repertory of antiphons for the greater festivals of the Proper of the Time (Christmas, Easter and Pentecost) or of the Proper of Saints (24 and 29 June, 10 August etc). Study of the Gregorian antiphon must begin from the original repertory.

The texts of the antiphons of the original repertory comprise between one and four clauses. Some are very brief – between three and eight words – and are performed as a single phrase; some consist of two clauses separated by a caesura; some contain three clauses; and some, with four, seem to be modelled on the distich of Latin prosody. The following examples illustrate some of the possibilities:

Omnis plebs ut vidit/dedit laudem Deo (two clauses: Hesbert, iii, no.4149); Dixit angelus ad Petrum/Circumda tibi vestimentum tuum/et sequere me (three clauses: no.2268); Hic vir despiciens mundum/et terrena triumphans//divitias coelo/condidit ore, manu (four clauses: distich; no.3069); Solve jubente Deo/terrarum Petre catenas//qui facis ut pateant/coelestia regna beatis (four clauses: two hexameters; no.4981); In praesepio jacebat/et in coelis fulgebat//ad nos veniebat/et apud patrem manebat (four clauses: assonanced prose; no. 3272).

There is normally a greater number of clauses in the texts of the antiphons to the *Magnificat* and *Benedictus* (see §5(iii) below). Other longer antiphons also exist, in particular those composed in honour of the patron saints of dioceses and of monasteries from the late 9th century.

5. OTHER GREGORIAN ANTIPHONS.
(*i*) *Antiphons to the Psalter*. The Psalter is distributed over the Divine Office of each week, and most of the antiphons used during its recitation are rather simpler than those at Matins, Lauds and Vespers. Generally one antiphon is sung to each psalm, and its text is derived from that psalm, but some psalms are grouped in pairs (e.g. Psalms lxiii and lxvii in the Roman Office of Lauds) or in groups of three (e.g. Psalms cxlviii–cl, also at Lauds) under a single antiphon. In the Little Hours, on the other hand, Psalm cxix is subdivided into 22 sections each comprising eight verses, each section with its own antiphon. The invitatory (Psalm xcv) is a special case (see §1 above and *see* INVITATORY).

For the Offices of Sunday and the days of the week, the antiphon texts are drawn from the psalm; for the feasts of the Proper of the Time and of the Saints, the texts are of 'ecclesiastical composition' (i.e. non-biblical), but similar in spirit to Psalm xcv – in other words, an exhortation to praise.

Most of the Psalter antiphons are very short, and

Ex.13

Antiphon to Psalms lxiii–lxvii [lxii–lxvi]	In	ma - tu - ti - nis							(Corpus antiphonalium officii, iii, no. 3252)
		Do - mi - ne	me - di - ta - bor	in				te.	
Antiphon to Psalm cxx [cxix]	Cla - ma - vi		et	ex - au - di - vit				me.	(Corpus antiphonalium officii, iii, no. 1824)
Antiphon to Psalm cxxxi [cxxx]	Spe - ret		Is - ra - el	in	Do - mi -		no.		(Corpus antiphonalium officii, iii, no. 4990)
Antiphon to Psalm cxxxii [cxxxi]	Et	om - nis	man - su - e - tu - di - nis	e -	jus.				(Corpus antiphonalium officii, iii, no. 2713)
Antiphon to Psalm cxlvii	Lau - da	Je - ru - sa - lem	Do - mi -	num.					(Corpus antiphonalium officii, iii, no. 3582)
Antiphon to Canticle of Moses	Do - mi - no	Can - te - mus glo - ri -		o - se.					(Corpus antiphonalium officii, iii, no. 1765)

appear to be derived from the responds (*responsae*) of ancient responsorial psalmody (see §1 above). In early psalters, the antiphons were copied at the beginnings and ends of psalms; they also occur in antiphoners, for the post-Epiphany period, at the end or, less frequently, at the beginning. In noted breviaries, they occur together with the Psalter, usually at the beginning of the manuscript. The various invitatory melodies often occur at the ends of antiphoners sometimes together with the tonary, as was the custom in Cistercian antiphoners.

The melodies of the Psalter antiphons are almost entirely syllabic: the brevity of their texts prevents melodic development as extended as that of other antiphons, where the melody is able to rise to a climax and fall again over three or four phrases. These simple melodies often comprise a few notes around a central reciting note – sometimes the reciting note of the appropriate psalm tone – confined within a range of a 4th or 5th. The simplicity of the melodies makes their transmission unreliable: there are many variants in individual melodies, rendering investigation into the sources difficult. Some antiphons exist in totally different versions.

When, in the late 8th century, the eight Gregorian psalm tones were adopted for the singing of the weekday Offices, it was found difficult to fit them to the Psalter antiphons, which more closely resemble Ambrosian antiphons than classical Gregorian antiphons. In the Ambrosian rite, the antiphon style itself determines the psalmody; there the psalm tones had to be imposed on the antiphons indiscriminately, and they are at times at odds with them. As evidence for this assertion, statements may be cited of theorists such as Frutolfus of Michelsberg (ed. Vivell, *Akademie der Wissenschaften in Wien, phil.-hist. Klasse,* clxxxviii/2, 1919, pp.145f) concerning the difficulties of classifying Psalter anti-

phons according to the eight-mode system. The musical evidence of those antiphons described as 'of irregular tone' should also be considered (AM, Paris, 1934–7): although the tonaries and antiphoners prescribe the 4th psalm tone for these, Gajard in his edition prescribed a tone borrowed from Ambrosian psalmody, restricted in range to a 4th, and better suited to them despite its lack of authenticity (ex.13; see Huglo, 1971, pp.390 n.2, 444).

The celebrated *tonus peregrinus* ('wandering' or 'alien' tone: the name occurs in the 12th century in Germany) is another irregularity within the system, since it includes two different reciting notes and thus disobeys the rules of Gregorian psalmody. It is prescribed for six antiphons (ex.14). No doubt it was taken over into Gregorian psalmody from the Gallican rite, but it may be ultimately of Jewish origin (see Huglo, 1971, p.394 n.3). It was adopted in the tonary not as a part of the 8th tone (as is commonly believed) but originally as an appendix, quite separate from the tonary proper and added after the last psalm tone ending of the 8th tone. The *tonus peregrinus* then, omitted from the antiphoner but restored in the tonary, is further evidence of the conservative attitude of the organizers of Gregorian chant: in their unwillingness to touch the Psalter antiphons they even tolerated elements that disturbed the system.

Nevertheless, the *tonus peregrinus* antiphons were reshaped in various ways during the course of time in order to bring the final note into conformity with the intonation. The most far-reaching of these changes occurred about 1134, when the Cistercians modified the *tonus peregrinus* antiphons, in the interests of the modal unity which should prevail in any chant, so that they fitted the 1st psalm tone.

Ex.14

Antiphon to Psalm cxiv [cxiii]	Nos	qui	vi - vi - mus...			(Corpus antiphonalium officii, iii, no. 3960)
Antiphon to Canticle of the Three Young Men	An - ge - li	Do - mi - ni...				(Corpus antiphonalium officii, iii, no. 1399)
Antiphon to Canticle of the Three Young Men	Mar - ty - res	Do - mi - ni...				(Corpus antiphonalium officii, iii, no. 3717)
Antiphon to Canticle of the Three Young Men	San - cti	Do - mi - ni...				(Corpus antiphonalium officii, iii, no. 4727)
Antiphon to Canticle of the Three Young Men	Vir - gi - nes	Do - mi - ni...				(Corpus antiphonalium officii, iii, no. 5443)

Very few additions were made over the centuries to the Psalter antiphons. For the Sunday Offices of the year, however, a series of rhymed antiphons was composed, *Pro fidei meritis* (Hesbert, i, no.36; cf iii, no.4383), which may have been the work of King Robert the Pious (*d* 1031), to whom a number of chants has been falsely attributed (cf PalMus, 1st ser., x, 1909, p.25 n.4). The series has also been attributed to Drogo, Abbot of Bergues in Flanders and composer of the Office of St Winnoc; and it is also possible that the composer was from northern Italy, since the series appeared first in Italy in the Silos Antiphoner (see Hesbert, i, iii; Huglo, 1971, p.162).

(ii) *Verse antiphons.* Antiphons with verses occur in the Offices of three festivals of the Proper of the Saints: the two festivals of St Paul, 25 January (Hesbert, i, ii, no.47) and 30 June (ii, no.102), and that of St Lawrence, 10 August (i, ii, no.103). These antiphons are followed by verses recalling the *versus ad repetendum* of the introit. Such verses are also found in the antiphons of Gallican chant, especially the Maundy antiphons sung during the Washing of the Feet in the Maundy Thursday liturgy, and in those of Ambrosian chant. The verses were sung after the doxology at the end of the psalm and after the repetition of the antiphon to the same melody as the psalm; the antiphon itself was repeated a second time at the end (PalMus, ix, 1906, p.49). (*See also* GALLICAN RITE, MUSIC OF THE, §12.)

(iii) *Antiphons to the Benedictus and Magnificat.* The antiphons to the Gospel canticles of Lauds (the *Benedictus*) and Vespers (the *Magnificat*) are very similar to the other antiphons of Matins, Lauds and Vespers. Even though the Gospel canticles are sung to a more ornate psalm tone than the other psalms and canticles (attested in the late 9th-century *Commemoratio brevis* and in the tonaries), the musical style of the antiphons is not analogously ornate. They are distinguished, however, by their literary sources. The antiphons to the Gospel canticles are normally settings of texts drawn from, or summing up, the Gospel of the Mass of the day; this series of antiphons was probably intended originally to comprise two antiphons for each Sunday, but additions may quite soon have been made to it. The series of antiphons to the Gospel canticles for the Sundays in summer, whose texts are drawn from the Gospels of the Sundays after Pentecost, often provides more than two antiphons for each Sunday (cf Hesbert, i, ii, no.144). The absence of some of these antiphons from the original repertory is suggested also by the fact that some are polymelodic (i.e. they exist with different melodies in different regions): it is a fundamental rule of criticism that such pieces cannot have been present in a general original source. For example, *Scriptum est enim quia*, an antiphon with a verse (Hesbert, iii, no.4836), occurs in most manuscripts with an 8th-mode melody (AM, p.600), but in German antiphoners with a 1st-mode melody, and in Cluniac manuscripts and in the gradual-antiphoner of Brescia (*GB-Ob* misc.lit.366, f.260) with a 4th-mode one. Another reason for the proliferation of these antiphons lies in the fact that the series of Gospels of the day varied (especially towards its end) from one church to another (cf PalMus, 1st ser., xiv, 1931, pp.130ff).

Some antiphons to the Gospel canticles from the Sundays in summer contain melodic formulae which do not occur in the antiphons discussed in previous sections. The *Scriptum est enim quia* antiphon cited above, for example, contains a melisma on the first syllable of 'docens': this syllable is the fifth from the end of the chant – that which generally bears a melisma in prolix responsories. The same melisma occurs on the sixth syllable from the end of *Dixit Dominus ad Adam*, the *Magnificat* antiphon for Septuagesima; since this antiphon replaced an antiphon from the alleluiatic Office of 'farewell' to the alleluia, it is not an antiphon from the original corpus of the antiphoner.

Some of the antiphons in this group contain intermediate cadences on the note below the final (e.g. *d–e–f–c–c* in the 1st mode). These 'lowered' cadences are comparable with inverted cadences (e.g. *f–g* instead of *g–f*) and serve to avoid the monotony of several identical cadences in an extended chant. Examples occur on 'thronos' in *Qui coelorum* (Hesbert, iii, no.4460) and on 'altare' in *Si offers* (no.4903). These cadences are followed by the usual re-intonations, or by others, for example, *a–g–g–f–g–a* on 'et', 'ut' or 'ex-' in the antiphons *Exi cito, Vidi Dominum sedentem, Si offers* and *Qui coelorum* (respectively Hesbert, iii, nos.2785, 5404, 4903 and 4460).

Ex.15

...et qui   se   hu - mi - li - at...

In a few passages in antiphons in this group, it is also justified to speak of descriptive music: a descending melody is used to suggest the idea of descent or of humility, as in the antiphon *Descendit hic* (ex.15: Hesbert, iii, no.2158) and in the antiphon *Homo quidam*, where the melody descends at the words 'descendebat ab Jerusalem in Jericho' (no.3131).

The antiphons to the *Magnificat* for Saturdays in summer, unlike those for Sundays, are settings of texts from the Old Testament lessons from Matins of the following day; this is true of the feasts of the Proper of the Time and of many in the Proper of the Saints. In the latter however the antiphons to the Gospel canticles, like other chants in the Office, may have texts drawn from the martyrology, or the *Magnificat* antiphon at second Vespers may be a text summing up the significance of the festival, as in the *Hodie* antiphons (Hesbert, iii, nos. 3088–124). Their texts may have been suggested by Byzantine *stichēra* beginning with the word 'sēmeron' ('today'); and the word 'sēmeron' in the Byzantine *stichēra* has the same rising melody as is given to the word 'hodie' in the Latin antiphons (ex.16; see Huglo, 1966, p.273). This represents a further example of a key word attracting the same melody even in different contexts (see §3(ii) above). In other Latin chants, in honour of the Virgin, where the texts are translations of Byzantine chants (e.g. the *Benedictus* antiphon *Mirabile mysterium*: Hesbert, iii, no.3763, and the *Magnificat* antiphon *Nativitas tua*: no.3852), however, the melodies may not necessarily be dependent on Byzantine models (see Huglo, 1966, pp.271ff).

(iv) *Mass antiphons: introits and communions.* Responsorial psalmody was originally the sole form of psalmody at the Mass and survives, for example, in the gradual; but it was replaced by antiphonal psalmody at the entry of the celebrant and at the distribution of communion. The chant at the entry of the celebrant is termed the *antiphona ad introitum*, or introit; that at the communion is termed the *antiphona ad communionem*, or communion. In the introit, the psalm verses are sung to a more ornate psalm tone than is used for the psalm and canticles of the Office; the intermediate cadences are accentual (governed by the rules of Latin accentuation: *see* CURSUS). This type of psalmody also influenced the

separate from psalmody, the Marian antiphons and the processional antiphons. The Marian antiphons have been sung, since the 13th century, at the close of Compline, the last Office of the liturgical day; they occur in groups in antiphoners and processionals, usually together with the Proper of the Assumption (15 August). They comprise a group from the early repertory of antiphons (expecially those for Christmas), with a supplement of new chants in a novel musical style.

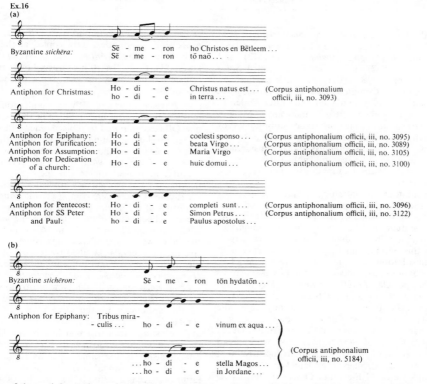

composition of the antiphons themselves, which at times bear traces of embellished psalmody (*see* INTROIT (i); for the connection of the offertory with antiphonal psalmody, *see* OFFERTORY).

Like the other categories of the Proper (except the alleluia) the introit repertory grew very little, except in south-west France and central and southern Italy. Troped introits occur from the 10th century, with the tropes either preceding the introit text (C. Blume, ed.: Analecta hymnica medii aevi, xlix, Leipzig, 1906, pp.24ff) or inserted into it.

The communion lost its psalmody between the 10th and 12th centuries, according to region (see Huglo, 1971, pp.401f); the series of Roman communions is related to the two series of Ambrosian communion chants (the confractoria, chanted at the fraction of the Host, and the transitoria, during communion). These chants are less unified than the introits, from a modal point of view, and they were less often subject to troping (*see* COMMUNION).

(v) *Marian antiphons.* Even though the antiphon is almost by definition a chant linked with a psalm, two series of antiphons in the Gregorian repertory are quite

Some of the early Marian antiphons have very ancient texts: *Sub tuum praesidium*, for example (Hesbert, iii, no.5041), was a part of the Ambrosian liturgy, and its original Greek text ('Hypo tēn sēn eusplanchnian') survives in a 3rd-century papyrus (*see* CHRISTIAN CHURCH, MUSIC OF THE EARLY, §3; cf Mercenier). The antiphon *Sancta Maria* (Hesbert, iii, no.4703) is derived from the prayer ending a sermon formerly attributed to St Augustine but now to Ambrose Autpert (*d* 781), abbot of St Vincent on the Volturno: its earliest possible date is the 9th century. A similar date may be assigned to *Ascendit Christus*, included at 15 August in Anglo-Norman manuscripts; it is not Gallican as Gastoué (*Le chant gallican*, Grenoble, 1939) suggested, since the text is from the letter of Pseudo-Jerome now attributed to Paschase Radbert (*d c*865), abbot of Corbie. These two antiphons occur, moreover, with different melodies in different regions, a fact which supports a late date for them. The same is true of a series of antiphons based on the *Song of Solomon*, and following the numerical order of the modes, which is included in the antiphoners at 15 August (Hesbert, ii, nos.106f) or 8 September.

The most important of the Marian antiphons are,

TABLE 1

	Senlis	Aix-en-Provence	La Chaise-Dieu	Sélestat
Sunday:	[?]	Alma Redemptoris mater	Quam dilecta	Ave regina
Monday:	Alma Redemptoris mater	Mater patris	Gaude virgo	Nigra sum
Tuesday:	Sub tuum	Ave regina	Ave regina	Ista est
Wednesday:	Haec est	Ave virgo sanctissima	Ave stella	Tota pulchra
Thursday:	Tota pulchra	Ave regina … mater	Gaude Dei genitrix	Descendi
Friday:	Ave regina coelorum	Ave virgo sanctissima	Speciosa	Alma Redemptoris mater
Saturday:	Salve regina	Salve regina (Regina coeli in Paschaltide)	Salve regina (Regina coeli in Paschaltide)	Salve regina

however, the large-scale antiphons: *Salve regina, Alma Redemptoris mater* (with a text in hexameters, Hesbert, iii, no.1356), *Ave regina coelorum* (no.1542) and *Regina coeli* (no.4597). The Cistercians chanted *Salve regina* daily from 1218; the Dominicans at Bologna chanted it daily at Compline after a miracle in 1230, and the custom was adopted by the entire Order in 1250. The chapter general of the Franciscans at Metz in 1249 prescribed all four of these antiphons for Compline, though not in the same way as in the Roman breviary of 1568; indeed, practice varied considerably in this matter, as may be seen in Table 1 (showing the distribution of the Marian antiphons in four churches in the 15th century).

The unanimous adoption of *Salve regina* for Saturdays shows that this antiphon was composed when the Saturday votive Mass of the Virgin was developing in the 11th century. The literary style and vocabulary of its text ('regina misericordiae', 'advocata', 'eia ergo') place it in this period; and its earliest occurrence is in 1010, in an addition to a manuscript (*D-KA* Aug.LV, f.42). Attributions to individual composers such as Peter of Compostela (*d* c1002), Aymar du Puy (*d* 1098) and Hermannus Contractus (*d* 1054) of either text or music cannot be taken seriously (in any case, the musical style of the 3rd-mode melody in certain German manuscripts is very different from that of Hermannus's Office of St Afra). A more widespread melody for this antiphon, in the 1st mode, occurred first in the pontifical of Aurillac (*F-Pn* lat.944); it resembles the musical style of 11th-century Offices in that use is made of the entire theoretical ambitus of the mode (here *A* to *d*), motifs are repeated from one clause to the next, and there is a noteworthy melisma near the end of 'O dulcis Maria'.

(*vi*) *Processional antiphons.* The second series of antiphons quite lacking psalmody is the processional antiphons. The earliest group of them is that chanted in the Major Litanies of 25 April, a procession at Rome which replaced a pagan procession on the same day (*see* LITANY and PROCESSIONAL). An antiphon from this series, *Deprecamur te*, was cited by Bede and in the biography of St Augustine of Canterbury: Augustine, sent to England by Gregory the Great (*d* 604), is said to have chanted this antiphon together with his companions as they entered Canterbury; and the whole series probably dates from this period (see Hesbert, *Antiphonale missarum sextuplex*, p.CXXI). Among the processional antiphons of Roman origin there are, however, some from the Gallican liturgy, such as the antiphon with verse *Collegerunt* (*Antiphonale missarum sextuplex*, no.213b) and the other Palm Sunday antiphons, whose musical and literary style is distinct from that of the rest of the repertory. The series awaits detailed analysis.

The processional antiphons for 25 April, and other processional antiphons, were copied at the end of the earliest graduals (*Antiphonale missarum sextuplex*, nos.200ff). From the 10th century, however, they were transferred to a new liturgical book of their own, the PROCESSIONAL.

(*vii*) *Rhymed antiphons.* Rhymed antiphons evolved a musical as well as a literary style of their own, because new Offices composed to replace older Offices were as a rule more elaborate and longer than those they replaced; an example is the Office of St Martin composed by Odo, abbot of Cluny (*d* 942; *see* ODO, §1). In the 13th century, moreover, the modal theory – by now fully developed – was particularly applied to these antiphons: the rhymed Offices were composed following the numerical order of the modes (see Huglo, 1971, pp.126ff), and the full theoretical ambitus of each mode, usually an octave, is explored in the chants. Also cultivated within the Office was a type of crescendo effect by the progressive use of intervals classified by Jerome of Moravia as 'beautiful', 'more beautiful' and 'most beautiful' (*pulcher, pulchrior, pulcherrimus*: *Tractatus de musica*, ed. Cserba, Regensburg, 1935). New intonation and cadential formulae were adopted; melismas occur at the close of the antiphons in the *Benedictus* and *Magnificat* similar to those in the final responsory of each nocturn at Matins; and from the first half of the 12th century, the antiphons to the Gospel canticles were extended by a final melisma in the same mode as the antiphon and borrowed from modal formulae in the tonaries. The latter practice is attested by cathedral ordinals, by liturgists such as John Beleth (*d* c1165), Siccardo of Cremona (*d* 1215) and Guillaume Durand of Mende (*d* 1296), and by the English priest Alfred (*Practica artis musice*, 1271); it was also very popular in the late Middle Ages. These *neumae* (melismas) occur as tenors in polyphonic works of the Notre Dame and Ars Nova periods, and in the 16th century the sung *neuma* was replaced by organ playing (see Huglo, 1971, pp.388ff).

Most of the rhymed Offices in which these antiphons occur were in honour of local saints, and were composed for dioceses or abbeys, on the occasion of the translation of relics or at a new dedication. Thus their area of diffusion was limited – they are often found in only one or two manuscripts – except where the saint was particularly popular, as in the case of the Office of St Nicholas composed by Regimbold of Eichstätt (966–91), and especially after the translation of the relics of the saint to Bari in 1087, or in the case of the Offices of St Thomas of Canterbury, who was canonized two years after his death in 1172. Most such Offices remained unknown outside their area of origin: examples are the Office of the Transfiguration by Peter the Venerable, abbot of Cluny (*d* 1156), in a unique manuscript from St Martin-des-Champs (*F-Pn* lat.17716), and the chants in honour of the Holy Cross composed by Nicholas de Montiéramey, secretary to St Bernard, between 1140 and 1160 (*GB-Lbm* Harl.3073, ff.108ff). They originated in the 9th century (*see also* RHYMED OFFICE).

BIBLIOGRAPHY

GENERAL
A. Gevaert: *La mélopée antique dans le chant de l'Eglise latine* (Ghent, 1895)

W. H. Frere, ed.: *Antiphonale sarisburiense* (London, 1901–24/ R1966)

P. Ferretti: *Estetica gregoriana* (Rome, 1934; Fr. trans., 1938)

B. Stäblein: 'Antiphon', *MGG*

B. Botte: 'Antiphona', *Sacris erudiri*, iv (1952), 239

H. Hucke: *Untersuchungen zum Begriff 'Antiphon' und zur Melodik der Offiziumsantiphonen* (diss., U. of Freiburg, 1952); see also *Römische Quartalschrift*, xlviii (1953), 147–94

——: 'Zur Formenlehre der Offiziumsantiphonen', *KJb*, xxxvii (1953), 7

R. J. Hesbert, ed.: *Corpus antiphonalium officii*, i: *Manuscripti 'cursus romani'*, Rerum ecclesiasticarum documenta, Fontes, vii (Rome, 1963)

——: *Corpus antiphonalium officii*, ii: *Manuscripti 'cursus monasticus'*, Rerum ecclesiasticarum documenta, Fontes, viii (Rome, 1965)

M. Huglo: 'Relations musicales entre Byzance et l'occident', *XIIIth International Congress of Byzantine Studies: Oxford 1966*, 267

R. J. Hesbert, ed.: *Corpus antiphonalium officii*, iii: *Invitatoria et antiphonae*, Rerum ecclesiasticarum documenta, Fontes, ix (Rome, 1968)

R. Bryden and D. G. Hughes: *An Index of Gregorian Chant* (Cambridge, Mass., 1969)

M. Huglo: *Les tonaires: inventaire, analyse, comparaison* (Paris, 1971)

MASS ANTIPHONS
R. J. Hesbert: *Antiphonale missarum sextuplex* (Brussels, 1935)

J. A. Jungmann: *Missarum solemnia: eine genetische Erklärung der römischen Messe* (Vienna, 1948, 5/1962; Eng. trans., 1951)

J. Froger: *Les chants de la messe aux VIII–IXe siècles* (Tournai, 1950)

M. Huglo: 'Antifone antiche per la "fractio panis" ', *Ambrosius*, xxxi (1955), 85

O. Strunk: 'The Latin Antiphons for the Octave of the Epiphany', *Mélanges Georges Ostrogorsky* (Belgrade, 1963–4), 417

SPECIAL STUDIES
A. Baumstark: 'Die Hodie-Antiphonen des römischen Breviers', *Die Kirchenmusik*, x (1909), 153

J. de Valois: *En marge d'une antienne, le Salve regina* (Paris, 1912)

F. Mercenier: 'La plus ancienne prière à la Vierge "Sub tuum praesidium" ', *Questions liturgiques et paroissiales*, xxv (1940), 33

A. A. R. Bastiaensen: 'Observations sur le vocabulaire liturgique dans l'Itinéraire d'Egérie', *Latinitas christianorum primaeva*, xvii (Utrecht, 1962)

J. M. Canal: *Salve regina misericordiae: historia y legendas*, Temi e testi, ix (Rome, 1963)

V. Fiala: 'Ein Sonderform der O-Antiphonen', *Archiv für Liturgiewissenschaft*, xii (1970), 261

S. Burstyn: 'Early 15th-century Polyphonic Settings of Song of Songs Antiphons', *AcM*, xlix (1977), 200

RHYMED ANTIPHONS
Fasquelle E (Offices rythmiques)

G. M. Dreves and C. Blume, eds.: *Analecta hymnica medii aevi*, v (Leipzig, 1889); xiii (1892); xvii–xviii (1894); xxiv (1896); xxv–xxvi (1897); xxviii (1898); xlia (1903); xlva (1904)

W. Irtenkauf: 'Reimoffizien', *MGG*   MICHEL HUGLO

Antiphona ad accedentes (Lat.). A mass chant in the Mozarabic rite, corresponding to the communion of the Roman rite; *see* MOZARABIC RITE, MUSIC OF THE, §4 (xiii).

Antiphona ad confractionem (Lat.). See CONFRACTORIUM.

Antiphona ad pacem (Lat.). A mass chant sung at the kiss of peace in the Mozarabic rite; *see* MOZARABIC RITE, MUSIC OF THE, §4(x).

Antiphona ad praelegendum (Lat.). A mass chant of the Gallican and Mozarabic rites, corresponding to the introit of the Roman rite or the ingressa of the Ambrosian rite; *see* GALLICAN RITE, MUSIC OF THE, §7, and MOZARABIC RITE, MUSIC OF THE, §4(i).

Antiphona ante evangelium (Lat.: 'antiphon before the Gospel'). A mass chant of the early Latin Christian rites; *see* GALLICAN RITE, MUSIC OF THE, §7, and GOSPEL, §1.

Antiphonal. (1) *See* ANTIPHONER.

(2) A term describing works in which an ensemble is divided into distinct groups, performing in alternation and together. See ANTIPHONAL PSALMODY; CHORUS (i), §3; CORI SPEZZATI.

Antiphonal psalmody. The chanting of a psalm by two choirs or half-choirs in alternation, commonly with an added refrain-like text called an ANTIPHON. Its parent term, 'antiphony' (*antiphōnia*) at first referred to the octave or double octave and hence to the alternation of men's voices with those of women and boys, but came in time to embrace any musical alternation.

There is no explicit reference in the Bible to this method of singing the psalms, but antiphonal singing was generally practised in the Near East, and by the Jews, in biblical times (see *1 Samuel* xviii.7; *Ezra* iii. 10–11; *Nehemiah* xii.31–42). Psalm texts often seem to have been intended for antiphonal performance; there are, for instance, psalms in dialogue form, and the effect of literary parallelism, so common in the psalms (*see* PSALM, §I) is obviously enhanced by alternate singing.

By joining antiphons to their antiphonal psalmody, the Christians of the 4th century gave it a more formal structure, though surviving antiphonal chants vary widely in form as well as in melodic character. Introits, offertories and communions were perhaps all sung antiphonally in the early Roman Mass, and may all at one time have been whole psalms with antiphons interspersed among the verses. But surviving examples, none earlier than the 9th century, are much shortened. The COMMUNION was truncated to an antiphon alone, without any psalm verses, while surviving offertories are more responsorial in form, melodically free and quite complex (*see* OFFERTORY). The introit remained strictly antiphonal (*see* INTROIT (i)); its antiphon was followed by the first verse of the psalm, the lesser doxology, and a later verse *ad repetendum*, all three being set to the same psalm tone. The psalms of the Office were also sung in strictly antiphonal fashion by opposite sides of the choir, again to a psalm tone, and with a modally appropriate antiphon before and after. The most complete surviving example of antiphonal psalmody is found in the INVITATORY psalm, Psalm xcv, sung at least since the time of St Benedict at the beginning of Matins. It has continued to be sung to more elaborate, but still rigidly formulaic, psalm tones, with the antiphon for the day sung not only before and after the psalm but between its verses as well. For the relationship between early antiphonal psalmody and responsorial psalmody, *see* ANTIPHON, §1.

See also PSALM, §II.   THOMAS H. CONNOLLY

Antiphona post evangelium (Lat.: 'antiphon after the Gospel'). A mass chant of the early Latin Christian rites; *see* GALLICAN RITE, MUSIC OF THE, §7, and OFFERTORY, §1.

Antiphonary. *See* ANTIPHONER.

Antiphonel. An automatic player attachment for harmoniums and organs, invented by Alexandre François Debain in 1846. *See* MECHANICAL INSTRUMENT.

Antiphoner [antiphonal, antiphonary] (from Lat. *anti-phona*; *antiphonarius* [*liber*], *antiphonarium*, *antiphonale*). Liturgical book of the Western Church containing the antiphons and other choir chants sung at the services of the DIVINE OFFICE and sometimes also the chants for the Mass (*see* ANTIPHON).

1. Origins of the Gregorian antiphoner. 2. Evolution of the Gregorian antiphoner. 3. Handlist of the main manuscript antiphoners: (i) Eastern group (ii) Transitional group (iii) Western group (iv) Manuscripts of religious orders. 4. Printed antiphoners.

1. ORIGINS OF THE GREGORIAN ANTIPHONER. The term *antiphonarius* first appeared at the end of the 8th century in Carolingian library catalogues, although the word *antiphona* had occurred in Latin five centuries earlier:

> Catalogue from St Wandrille de Fontenelle in Normandy, compiled between 787 and 806 ('antiphonarii romanae ecclesiae'; G. Becker: *Catalogi bibliothecarum antiqui*, Bonn, 1885, §4, no.21);
> Catalogue from St Riquier in Picardy, in 831 ('antiphonarii sex': ibid, §11, no.238);
> Catalogue from Cologne, in the 9th century (ibid, §16, nos.7, 18, 33);
> Catalogue from St Gall in the mid-9th century ('antiphonarii III et veteres II'; P. Lehmann: *Die Bistümer Konstanz und Chur*, Mittelalterliche Bibliothekskataloge Deutschlands und der Schweiz, i, Munich, 1918, p.77);
> Catalogue from Reichenau, at the end of the 8th century (ibid, i, p.236).

Another source is Amalar of Metz (*c*775–*c*850) who at Corbie consulted Roman antiphoners presented to Abbot Wala (822–35) and compiled at the time of Pope Adrian I (772–95). The antiphoner of Gregory the Great (*d* 604), indeed, is (less reliably) supposed to have been at Rome, according to the 9th-century evidence of the pope's biographer, John the Deacon (*Sancti Gregorii magni vita*, ii, §6: *PL*, lxxv, 90). There is further evidence of Roman antiphoners in a note made by the copyist of the Codex Blandiniensis (*B-Br* lat.10127–44) at the end of the 8th century: he noted that the Mass for the 7th Sunday after Pentecost was not in the Roman books ('ista ebdomada non est in antefonarios romanos'; see Hesbert, 1935, no.179). It is noteworthy that this copyist did not use the word *graduale* for his collection of Mass chants (*see* GRADUAL (ii)), but the word *antiphonarius*. At this period the antiphoner often contained both Mass and Office chants. The late 8th-century Lucca fragments (*I-Lc* 490), for example, contain chants (for Advent only) divided into two categories for each Sunday: first for the Office, then for the Mass.

According to Amalar in the prologue to his *Liber de ordine antiphonarii*, the antiphoner once contained the Office antiphons and also the antiphons of the Mass (i.e. introits and communions), whereas the Office responsories were collected in a different book, the responsorial. This unexpected statement is confirmed by a phrase in a letter of Pope Paul I in about 760: 'antiphonale et responsoriale ... necnon et horologium nocturnum' (*Epistolae Merowingici et Karolini aevi: I*, Monumenta Germaniae historica, *Epistolarum*, iii, Berlin, 1899, p.529). The division provides a clue about the process of transition from the earliest Roman system (a single book for all types of chant), found also in the Ambrosian (Milanese) and Spanish liturgies, to the subsequent Gregorian system, in which Mass chants were

collected in the gradual and separated from the Office chants (antiphons and responsories) in the antiphoner.

For the sake of clarity in modern writings, it is best to avoid using the word 'antiphonale' (antiphoner) to signify a book of Mass chants (as Pamelius, Hesbert and Gamber have done); the latter is more appropriately termed a gradual, particularly when the word *antiphonarius* is by contrast to be reserved for a book of Office chants (as it has been by Gamber).

The attribution of the antiphoner to St Gregory the Great, traditional since John the Deacon, has an echo in the verse prologue that preceded the antiphoners (found in *I-Lc* 490), and in miniatures representing St Gregory setting down liturgical melodies under the inspiration of the Holy Spirit, as in the antiphoner of Hartker of St Gall (see below, §3(i); for further details of the prologue, *see* GREGORY THE GREAT). The change in terminology at the end of the 8th century, when the terms *cantus gregorianus* and *cantus sancti Gregorii* progressively replaced *cantus romanus*, corresponds to a change in the chant itself, i.e. from the chant repertory called 'Old Roman' (Stäblein), 'basilical' (Andoyer) or 'divergent' (Jammers) to the Gregorian chant that survives today. (The question of this development is complicated and controversial: *see* GREGORIAN AND OLD ROMAN CHANT.) This change must have occurred in about 780 when the first tonaries appeared (*see* TONARY), in which the Office and Mass antiphons were classified according to the order of the eight psalm tones. The new attribution of the chant to St Gregory was necessary to give it authority – an essential factor in medieval liturgy as much as in canon law or theology to provide a certain juridical validity.

Most 9th-century antiphoners contain all the chants for the period from Advent to Eastertide grouped into Offices according to the liturgical calendar. In the sequence of Sundays after Pentecost, the responsories were copied separately from the antiphons in five groups according to the months from July to November, corresponding with the sapiential and prophetic books read on the Sundays of summer and autumn. The antiphons 'ex evangelio' to the Benedictus and *Magnificat* for the Sunday after Pentecost were grouped according to Sundays, corresponding with the Gospel readings. These 'Gospel antiphons' may not originally have been included in the book, as is suggested by a remark of Amalar (*Liber de ordine antiphonarii*, lxviii) and by their omission in some antiphoners as well as their inclusion as an isolated group in others (*F-CHR* 47: PalMus, xi, 1912, p.134; *Pn* lat.909, f.260*v*; *Pn* lat.1121, f.187) as a kind of supplement (*see* ANTIPHON, §4(iii)).

In these early antiphoners, the chants of the Proper of Saints were partly mingled with those of the movable feasts of the Proper of Time. The Common of Saints and the invitatory psalm of Matins were usually copied at the end. Occasionally these antiphoners ended with a brief tonary, in which the chants were grouped according to the eight psalm tones and, within each tone, by psalm endings (*differentiae*).

Antiphoners may be divided into two main classes, secular and monastic. The two are distinguished by the number of chants they contain for Matins, the Little Hours (Prime, Terce, Sext and None) and Vespers. Secular antiphoners were used by ordinary clergy, canons and friars of the 13th-century mendicant orders (Franciscans and Dominicans); they contain nine anti-

1. Opening of the Mass for St John's Day from the antiphoner of Mont-Renaud, written in the 1st half of the 10th century, with French neumes added later (private collection)

phons and nine responsories, in groups of three for each of the three nocturns of Matins, a short responsory for the Little Hours and five psalms for Vespers. Monastic antiphoners (i.e. those used in monasteries, e.g. of the Benedictines, Cistercians and Carthusians) contain 12 antiphons and 12 responsories in groups of four for Matins, as well as another antiphon for the Old Testament canticles in the third nocturn of Matins. They contain no short responsories for the Little Hours and only four psalms for Vespers.

2. EVOLUTION OF THE GREGORIAN ANTIPHONER. The Gregorian antiphoner was imposed upon the Carolingian empire at the end of the 8th century; it spread through the Christian West at the same time as the Gregorian sacramentary and lectionary. At this time antiphoners lacked musical notation: the melodies were memorized, a feat which took 10 years to achieve. Consequently (according to a letter from Helisachar to Nebridius of Narbonne) an experienced singer accompanied an antiphoner to a church in order to teach the singers the melodies.

In the second half of the 9th century neumatic notation was introduced; this saved the singers some, though not all, of the effort of memorization. Traditional practice was disrupted at this time: copyists had formerly written the texts of chants in continuous lines of script, and had now to set them down with wider spaces between the lines and to break up words in antiphons and responsories where the syllables carried melismas that were at all elaborate. To do this, the copyists needed to know the traditional melodies or to work in association with singers who did.

This transition in practice was made only gradually. The conventional manuscript text abbreviations had to be expanded and the amount of space needed for the melismas had to be found by trial and error. If the space was insufficient, the copyist of the music would be forced to crowd the neumes along the margin; this can be seen in the antiphoner of Mont-Renaud (PalMus, xvii, 1958), where the text was written in the ordinary unbroken manner, and neumatic notation (not originally

envisaged) was added to it some time later (fig. 1).

The notation, is, however, less important than another development: the division of the repertory into two main groups. Antiphoners fall into these groups – one ('eastern') for countries of Germanic language and one ('western') for countries of Romance language – according to details of textual and musical criticism: melodic variants and differing lists of verses in the Matins responsories and in the alleluias from the Mass. For different historical reasons northern Italian and English antiphoners hover between the two groups; there is also a transitional group, and antiphoners of the religious orders form a group of their own (see §3).

The division into two groups no doubt originated at the division of the Carolingian empire: as early as February 842 Charles the Bald swore the Oaths of Strasbourg in the Romance language, and Louis the German in the Germanic language; the empire was formally divided by the Treaty of Verdun in 843 and more completely by the Treaty of Mersen in 870. The same division is evident in the musical tradition, where east and west are distinct while sharing a common origin. Thus German chant manuscripts often have melodies differing from those of French or Aquitanian manuscripts.

In consequence, the study of a particular melody or group of melodies requires not only the evidence of the earliest manuscripts, but also that of the most important sources from each region. The most important manuscripts are, in practice, the best examples of each type of musical notation and the best examples of the particular chants of the different religious orders, especially those that revised their traditions.

3. HANDLIST OF THE MAIN MANUSCRIPT ANTIPHONERS. The earliest manuscript antiphoners contained the text alone, since they were written when the melodies were still memorized. The earliest of all is the Lucca fragment (*I-Lc* 490) mentioned above (§1), copied at the end of the 8th century. Its Mass chant texts have been edited by Hesbert (1935, p.xxvi with facs.) and its Office texts by Huglo (1951). The St Gall fragments (*CH-SGs* 1399)

contain a few texts for the Office of 2 February and of the 2nd Sunday in Lent, copied by Winithar in the second half of the 8th century (ed. A. Dold: 'Ein neues Winitharfragment mit liturgischen Texten', *Texte und Arbeiten*, xxxi, 1940, p.77). Finally, in *F-ROU* A 292 (catal.26), there are a few texts without notation for Advent and for 27 December, copied in the 9th century but later erased to accommodate other texts; these were texts of pieces added to adapt the Roman antiphoner to the monastic use of Jumièges, as Hesbert has shown (1954, p.28).

The only complete 9th-century antiphoner is the antiphoner of Compiègne (more accurately, the antiphoner of Charles the Bald: *F-Pn* lat.17436), which contains the Mass chants followed by those for the Office; this royal manuscript was copied in the Soissons district (see the comments by Brou, 1961, pp.20–23). An edition was made by the Benedictines of St Maur (1705, repr. in *PL*, lxxviii, 725–850) but it has been superseded by that of Hesbert (1963). (See also Barber, 1972.)

In addition to antiphoners with musical notation it is necessary to study breviaries, which are in effect antiphoners completed with lessons and prayers so that the Office may be read using a single book (*see* BREVIARY). According to their notation, textual and musical variants and repertory, manuscript antiphoners and breviaries with musical notation fall into four groups as detailed below.

(*i*) *Eastern group.* The earliest eastern antiphoner with neumes was written and notated by Hartker, a monk of St Gall (*c*980–1000) (facs. edn. in PalMus, 2nd ser., i, 1900; text ed. R.-J. Hesbert, 1965). It begins with a tonary and contains marginal letters indicating the psalm endings (*differentiae*) appropriate to the antiphons (see Huglo, 1971, p.233). *CH-SGs* 388 is a 12th-century copy of this antiphoner.

The St Gall group also contains the following, of which the first two are breviaries with neumatic notation: *CH-SGs* 414 (copied *c*1030); *SGs* 413 and 387 (copied between 1034 and 1047); *Zz* Rh.28 (the Rheinau antiphoner: ed. Hesbert, 1965, pp.ix–xi).

German antiphoners, properly speaking, include the following: *D-B* mus.40047 (the Quedlinburg antiphoner, copied *c*1018 with very delicate neumes: analysed by Lipphardt, 1954); *A-Gu* 211 (antiphoner with German neumes, copied at Stuhlweissenburg [now Székesfehérvár] in Hungary at the beginning of the 12th century: facs. edn., Z. Falvy and L. Mezey, 1963; text ed. with notes and index, C. Barber: *Codex Albensis*); *D-BAs* lit.23 (11th- or 12th-century antiphoner from Bamberg Cathedral with German neumes: text ed. Hesbert, 1965); *BAs* lit.24 (12th- or 13th-century antiphoner from Bamberg Cathedral with German neumes); *Mbs* Clm.23037 (11th- or 12th-century breviary with neumes from St Georg at Prüfening); *A-Wn* series nova 2700 (12th-century gradual and antiphoner of St Peter at Salzburg, in *Ssp* a.XIII.7 until 1937); *Wn* Cpv 1826 (11th-century breviary); *Wn* Cpv 14319 (12th-century).

The principal German antiphoners notated with lines are those from Aachen, particularly the one known as the antiphoner of Franco (*D-AAm* G.20), who was a canon of the chapter and who died in 1318 (see Gatzweiler, 1926, pp.109–25). Hesbert saw as alternatives the 12th-century manuscripts of the canons of Klosterneuburg (*A-KN* 1010, 1012 and 1013), in Lorraine notation on coloured lines, before he edited

D-BAs lit.23. The Petershausen antiphoner, from the library at Reichenau (*KA* Aug.LX), had very fine 12th-century notation on lines, which was erased and replaced by Gothic notation (see K. Hain: *Ein musikalischer Palimpsest*, Fribourg, 1925).

From Bohemia, the following two manuscripts may be mentioned: *CS-Pu* VI.E.4.C (12th-century antiphoner from St Jiří [George] at Prague); *Pu* XII.C.3 (12th-century Bohemian antiphoner of unknown provenance).

(*ii*) *Transitional group.* Two groups of manuscripts form a transition between the eastern and western groups of antiphoners, as a result of liturgical or musical borrowings from one or the other. The first such group comprises manuscripts from the diocese of Liège, resembling those of Aachen, but notated in French neumes (Liège changed its notation several times), such as *GB-DRc* B.III.11 (text ed. Hesbert, 1963; description of the manuscript, ibid, p.xix).

The second transitional group comprises manuscripts from the school of Metz. The 11th-century Metz antiphoner is known from Amalar's treatise; it has been reconstructed by J. M. Hanssens in his edition of the *Liber de ordine antiphonarii* (1950) and by W. Lipphardt, who used in addition the 9th-century tonary in *F-MZ* 351 (*Der karolingische Tonar von Metz*, Münster, 1965). Noted MSS include the following: *F-MZ* 83 (13th century, from St Arnould at Metz); *MZ* 461 (13th century); *D-B* Phillipps 1678 (12th-century noted breviary, which compensates for the loss of two Metz manuscripts, now surviving only in photographs, during World War II).

The transitional group also includes the following two Utrecht manuscripts in Messine notation: *D-Ngm* 4984 (13th century); *NL-Uu* 406 [3 J 7] (12th–13th century).

(*iii*) *Western group.* The earliest French antiphoners belong to the St Denis group. The most famous of these is the gradual-antiphoner of Mont-Renaud, transferred from that castle to Paris in 1914 after its discovery there by Professor J. Jeanneteau of Angers. It was first suggested (in PalMus, xvi, 1955) that it originated at Noyon but Beyssac (1957) showed later that St Denis was its place of origin. This manuscript, written in the first half of the 10th century, had French neumes added to it later, and a few pieces in Messine or Lorraine notation.

The 11th-century gradual of St Denis (*F-Pm* 384) is followed by an antiphoner index. Melodies on staves appear in an early 12th-century antiphoner (*F-Pn* lat.17296: text ed. Hesbert, 1965; description of the manuscript ibid, pp.xi–xv), and in the 12th-century noted breviary (MS 17C) in the Bibliotheque municipale, Vendôme.

The French group with notation on staves includes the following: *F-Pn* nouv.acq.lat.1535 (12th-century antiphoner from Sens); *Pn* nouv.acq.lat.1236 (12th-century antiphoner from Nevers); *Psg* 117 (13th-century antiphoner from St Michel de Beauvais: see M. Bernard: *Bibliothèque Sainte-Geneviève, Paris, Répertoire des manuscrits médiévaux contenant des notations musicales*, i, Paris, 1965, pp.61–3 and pl.xix–xx).

Within the French group the Lyons manuscripts represent a special tradition originating at the time of Bishop Agobard (*d* 840), the author of the *Epistola de*

2. *Vespers, first Sunday in Advent, from the Penwortham breviary (Sarum Use), English, early 14th century (GB-Lbm Add.52359, f.1r)*

3. *Palm Sunday Vespers from a monastic antiphoner and tonary of the Roman rite from Silos, with Visigothic neumes, 11th century (GB-Lbm Add. 30850, f.93r)*

correctione antiphonarii. They excluded all chants with texts of 'ecclesiastical composition' (i.e. not drawn from the Scriptures). Their musical tradition is seen in the following: *F-LYm* 537 (457) (11th or 12th century, with neumatic notation); *C* 43 (13th-century noted breviary); the Lyons antiphoner printed in 1738.

English manuscripts are most important, since their tradition was originally derived directly from Rome through St Augustine of Canterbury in the 6th century,

and later through Benedict Biscop in the 8th century (see PalMus, xii, 1922, preface). This old tradition was, however, obscured by practices and traditions adopted from the Continent (especially from Corbie and Fleury) which themselves became overlaid by Norman traditions from Rouen and Bayeux. The 11th-century Exeter breviary (*GB-Lbm* Harl.2961), and the Worcester antiphoner (PalMus, xii, 1922) notated on lines, are early examples of the English tradition.

In 1197 Richard Poore, later Bishop of Salisbury (1217–28), and Edmond Rich reformed the liturgy, including the gradual and the antiphoner. The resulting 'use of Sarum' (*see* SARUM RITE, MUSIC OF THE) was to spread throughout the British Isles, except York, and there are many surviving noted antiphoners following the Sarum use. A list of such antiphoners was compiled by Frere (in *Antiphonale Sarisburiense*, 76ff, a facsimile edition of *GB-Cu* Mm.II.9 completed from Salisbury, Chapter Library, 152). The British Museum has acquired a noted English breviary (*GB-Lbm* Add.52359; see fig.2 and D. H. Turner: 'The Penwortham Breviary', *British Museum Quarterly*, xxviii, 1964, p.85).

In western and south-western France, the musical notation was mixed, with a use of dots, either mainly on the accents (Breton notation) or even exclusively, written in vertical alignment (Aquitanian notation). No complete surviving manuscript is written in Breton notation, and only a few early fragments survive (*GB-Ob* Auct.F.4.26, 10th century; see J., J. F. R. and C. Stainer, eds.: *Dufay and his Contemporaries*, London, 1898/*R*1966, p.xxii and pl.ix). There are several antiphoners from south-western France and Spain using Aquitanian notation, including the following: *F-Pn* lat.1085, f.3v–110v (10th-century antiphoner index from St Martial); *E-Tc* 44.1 (antiphoner from a French church taken to Spain at the suppression of the Mozarabic rite); *Tc* 44.2 (12th-century; undoubtedly modelled on *E-Tc* 44.1). In Catalonia, where Catalan neumatic notation was employed, two antiphoners survive, one at S Feliù, Gerona, and one at Montserrat (*MO* 72). At Ripoll in Catalonia, Aquitanian notation was used after the reform of the abbey by St Victor of Marseilles (see J. Lemarié: *Le bréviaire de Ripoll: Paris B.N.lat.742*, Montserrat, 1965). At Silos, at the time of the suppression of the Mozarabic rite, the first Gregorian antiphoners were copied in Visigothic script and notation: *GB-Lbm* Add.30850 (11th century, see fig.3: text ed. Hesbert, 1965; description of manuscript, ibid, pp.xvii–xix); *Lbm* Add.30848 (11th-century noted breviary). Later at Silos a return was made to Aquitanian notation (*E-SI*, 12th-century antiphoner, from a dependent priory of Silos).

Italy was influenced both from the north (Switzerland and Germany) and the north-west (Provence) in notation as well as repertory. Italian manuscripts are in consequence not the most reliable for the reconstruction of the original Gregorian antiphoner. The most important of them are found in Tuscany: *I-IV* CVI (12th century: text ed. Hesbert, 1963; description of manuscript, ibid, p.xx); *IV* LXIV (12th century); *VCd* LXX (13th century); *MZ* C 12/75 (11th century: text ed. Hesbert, 1963; description of manuscript, ibid, p.xxi); *MZ* C 15/79 (late 11th century, from Pavia); *GB-Ob* Misc.lit.366 (11th-century noted gradual-breviary from Brescia); *I-VEcap* XCVIII (11th-century antiphoner from Verona: text ed. Hesbert, 1963; description of manuscript, ibid, p.xxii); *UD* f.20 (breviary from Pomposa, with neumatic notation); *Rvat* lat.7018 (11th-century missal-breviary from Emilia; see P. Salmon: 'Un bréviaire-missel du XIe siècle: le manuscrit vatican lat.7018', *Mélanges Eugène Tisserant*, in Studi e testi, ccxxxvii, 1964, pp.327–43); *PCsa* 65 (a great collection, begun in 1142, containing all the books of the liturgy notated and gathered in a single MS; see Huglo, 1971, p.174); *PCsa* 54 (containing the antiphoner

alone); *Tn* F.II.10 (antiphoner from Bobbio). Further south in Tuscany an early 12th-century antiphoner from the archiepiscopal archives at Florence has outstandingly beautiful notation (see Huglo, 1971, p.186 and pl.iii).

Finally, a transitional zone with its own notation is found between Tuscany and the Beneventan region (see PalMus, xv, 1953, p.96). From this region come the following manuscripts: *I-Rv* C 5 and C 13 (two 12th-century manuscripts from Norcia); *Rvat* S.Pietro B.79 and *GB-Lbm* Add.29988 (two Roman antiphoners with the Old Roman version of the melodies; see fig.4).

The manuscripts in Beneventan notation are the best diastematic sources (PalMus, xiv, 1931) and consequently received particular attention when the *Antiphonale monasticum* was being restored in 1933. They include the following: *I-BV* V.21 (12th century: text ed. Hesbert, 1965; description of the manuscript, ibid, pp.xx–xxiv); *BV* V.19 and V.20 (12th-century breviary-missal); *MC* 420 (11th-century noted breviary); *MC* 542 (12th century).

(*iv*) *Manuscripts of religious orders.* The Benedictines used the antiphoner of the dioceses in which they lived. Monasteries grouped in congregations, like the Cluniacs, however, had their own traditions. Several important noted Cluniac sources survive: *D-B* theol. lat.Qu.337; *F-Pn* lat.12044 and 12584 (from St Maur des Fossés); *AM* 115 (from Corbie after the introduction of the Cluniac reform); the breviary from Lewes Priory (now in *GB-Cfm*; see V. Leroquais: *Le bréviaire-missel du prieuré clunisien de Lewes*, Paris, 1935).

A Vallombrosan antiphoner survives (*I-Fl* Conv.soppressi 560: end of the 11th century), and two manuscripts reflecting the practice of the Camaldolese: *Lc* 601; *E-Tc* 48.14 (12th century).

The liturgy of the Premonstratensians was established only under the successor of their founder, St Norbert (*c*1080–1134); they had their own tradition, seen in the following antiphoners: *D-Mbs* Clm.17010 (12th century, from Schäftlarn; for this and the following six manuscripts, see P. Ruf: 'Die Handschriften des Klosters Schäftlarn', *1200 Jahre Kloster Schäftlarn*, Munich, 1962, pp.21–122); *D-Mbs* Clm.17004 (1331, from Schäftlarn); *Mbs* Clm.17003 (15th century, from Schäftlarn); *Mbs* Clm.17002 (1405, from Schäftlarn); *Mbs* Clm.17007 (1467, from Schäftlarn); *Mbs* Clm.17018 (1467, from Schäftlarn); *Mbs* Clm.17001 (1471, from Schäftlarn); *F-Pn* lat.9425 (13th century, from Auxerre).

The Augustinians also had a tradition of their own, which may be studied in their antiphoners, such as those of the Augustinian canons of Utrecht (*F-Pm* 385: *c*1400) or the Augustinians of Guisborough in Yorkshire (*GB-Lbm* Add.35285; the calendar has been analysed by F. Wormald in the *Yorkshire Archaeological Journal*, xxx, 1934, pp.5–35).

The Carthusians used only chants with scriptural texts, as was the practice at Lyons. Their tradition is seen in the Carthusian antiphoner *F-G* 91(867), written between 1282 and 1318, and in seven later manuscripts (*F-G* 92–8); besides these there are about 30 antiphoners in various European libraries, including *GB-Lbm* Add.17302.

The Cistercians initiated their own tradition only after the order had existed for 30 years. In 1185 and 1191 the official liturgy and chant were gathered together in a single collection (*F-Dm* 114) in which all

4. *Paschal alleluias peculiar to the Old Roman use, from an Old Roman antiphoner with Central Italian Beneventan neumes, mid-12th century (GB-Lbm Add.29988, f.74r)*

the liturgical books, with and without musical notation, were included. This collection served as a standard reference source for books copied for new foundations. Today it contains only the gradual and antiphoner; the latter was originally preceded by a prologue (*Cantum quem cisterciensis ordinis: PL*, clxxxii, 1121–32) drawn up according to the *regulae* of the Cistercian Guy d'Eu. This prologue set out principles underlying chant reform rather similar to those in the prologue of the Cistercian tonary (see Huglo, 1971, pp.357–67, with a table showing the psalm endings (*differentiae*) in the antiphons). About 75 Cistercian antiphoners survive; the earliest seems to be one in Gethsemane (USA) mentioned by Marosszeki (1952, p.142). Most large libraries have Cistercian antiphoners from the first period of the order (the 12th century); examples are the following: *B-Br* 142 [cat.661]; *Br* 268 [cat.662]; *F-Pn* lat.8882; *Pn* nouv.acq.lat.1410, 1411 and 1412 (from Morimundo). Examples from the beginning of the 13th century include *GB-Lbm* Egerton 2977 (from Columbo in the diocese of Piacenza) and a manuscript in *D-KA*. Some of the sources remain in Cistercian abbeys: *A-HE* 20 (12th century); *HE* 65 (13th century); Mount Melleray, Co. Waterford, Ireland (from Hauterive, diocese of Fribourg in Switzerland); Westmalle, Belgium (12th century).

The Dominicans' reform was based on that of the Cistercians, though not identical in every detail. They collated their chant books with a standard copy at the convent of St Jacques in Paris (now in *I-Rss*); this was drawn up a little before 1254. The vicar-general of the order checked the accuracy of performance in the chant with a small book which he took with him when he visited Dominican houses (*GB-Lbm* Add.23935). All the Dominican antiphoners in European libraries (especially at Brussels, Colmar, Freiburg, Karlsruhe and Rome) are thus identical. They did not all, however, contain the prologue setting out the rules of transcription for books with music (see M. Huglo: 'Règlement du XIIIe siècle pour la transcription des livres notés', *Festschrift Bruno Stäblein*, Kassel, 1967, p.121).

The Franciscans adopted the Roman curial breviary and antiphoner in 1223. In 1230 the chapter general sent copies of the new book to the provinces, and in 1254 an official prototype of the books of the order was drawn up, in which square notation replaced the central Italian notation of the earliest notated Franciscan breviaries, which are as follows: *I-Ac* 694; antiphoner in *D-Ma*; *I-Nn* VI.E.20; *Rvat* lat.8737 and Borgia 405 (227).

The Carmelites followed the tradition of the Roman antiphoner, except in a few details of ceremonial.

4. PRINTED ANTIPHONERS. The earliest printed antiphoners with musical notation were German: the antiphoner of Augsburg (1495; copies in *GB-Lbm* (IB 6753) and *Ob*), and the antiphoner of Würzburg (between 1496–9) using German Gothic notation. The earliest known antiphoners with square notation are the Hieronymite antiphoner (Seville, 1491; copy in *F-Pn* rés.vél.807) and, above all, the Roman antiphoner printed by Spira at Venice (1499; a copy at *GB-Lbm* (IC 24247)). Various churches began printing their own antiphoners, e.g. Salisbury in 1519–20.

At the end of the 19th century and the beginning of the 20th, in order to improve the performance of the chant, performing editions of the antiphoner and diurnal

were published, some for parish churches, others for religious orders, e.g. the *Liber antiphonarius pro diurnis horis* (Solesmes, 1891) by Dom Pothier, and the *Antiphonale monasticum* (Tournai, 1934) by Dom Gajard. The Vatican edition of the Roman antiphoner, for parish use, was published in 1912. In 1903 the Cistercian antiphoner was printed as two folio choirbooks at Westmalle in Belgium. The Dominican antiphoner printed at Mechelen in 1862 was replaced by a vesperal in 1900. The Carthusians printed their antiphoner in 1876 and 1878 and published an *Antiphonarium abbreviatum* in 1881. Finally, the Benedictines of the Swiss Congregation published the *Antiphonale monasticum secundum traditionem helveticae congregationis* in 1943. These editions, especially those of 1934 and 1943, must suffice until the publication of the critical edition by Hesbert, which is to give a composite version based on the best manuscript antiphoner sources.

BIBLIOGRAPHY

ANTIPHONERS IN MODERN OR FACSIMILE EDITIONS

G. M. Tomasi, ed.: *Responsorialia et antiphonaria romanae ecclesiae*, i–ccxv (Rome, 1686); also in A. F. Vezzosi, ed.: *G. M. Tomasi: Opera omnia*, iv (Rome, 1747–54), 1–170 [from *I-Rvat* S Pietro Basilicanus B 79]

Sancti Gregorii papae I: Opera omnia (Paris, 1705), 733–878; also in *PL*, lxxviii, 725–850 [Compiègne antiphoner: *F-Pn* lat.17436]

Antiphonale ambrosianum, PalMus, v–vi (1896) [*GB-Lbm* Add. 34209]

W. H. Frere, ed.: *Antiphonale Sarisburiense*, Plainsong and Mediaeval Music Society (London, 1901–25/*R*1967) [*GB-Cu* Mm.II.9]

Antiphonaire monastique: Codex 601 de la bibliothèque capitulaire de Lucques, PalMus, ix (1906)

Antiphonaire monastique: Codex F 160 de la bibliothèque de la cathédrale de Worcester, PalMus, xii (1922)

Antiphonarium mozarabicum de la catedral de León (Burgos, 1928)

R.-J. Hesbert, ed.: *Antiphonale missarum sextuplex* (Brussels, 1935) [*B-Br* lat.10127–44, *CH-Zz* Rh.30, *F-Pn* lat.17436, lat.12050, *Psg* lat.111, *I-MZ*]

L. Brou and J. Vives, eds.: *Antifonario visigótico-mozárabe de la catedral de León*, Monumenta hispaniae sacra, *liturgica*, v/2 (Madrid, 1953)

L'antiphonaire du Mont-Renaud, PalMus, xvi (1955)

Z. Falvy and L. Mezey, eds.: *Codex Albensis: ein Antiphonar aus dem 12. Jahrhundert*, Monumenta hungariae musica, i (Budapest, 1963) [*A-Gu* 211]

R.-J. Hesbert, ed.: *Manuscripti 'cursus romanus'*, Corpus antiphonalium officii, i (Rome, 1963) [*D-BAs* lit.23, *F-Pn* lat.17436, *GB-DRc* B.III.11, *I-IV* CVI, *MZ* c 12/75, *VEcap* XCVIII]

——: *Manuscripti 'cursus monasticus'*, Corpus antiphonalium officii, ii (Rome, 1965) [*CH-SGs* 390–91, *Zz* Rh.28, *F-Pn* lat.17296, lat.12584, *GB-Lbm* Add.30850, *I-BV* V.21]

C. C. Barber, ed.: *Codex Compendiensis* (diss., U. of Oxford, 1972) [*F-Pn* lat.17436]

——: *Codex Albensis* [*A-Gu* 211] (MS, *GB-AB*, *Lbm*, *Ob*)

R.-J. Hesbert, ed.: *Fontes earumque prima ordinatio*, Corpus antiphonalium officii, v (Rome, 1975) [collation of antiphoners and breviaries for a critical edition]

ANTIPHONERS ANALYSED IN CATALOGUES OF LITURGICAL MANUSCRIPTS

H. Ehrensberger: *Bibliotheca liturgica manuscripta* (Karlsruhe, 1889), *Antiphonaria*, nos.1–18

——: *Libri liturgici bibliothecae apostolicae Vaticanae manu scripti* (Freiburg, 1897), 37ff

W. H. Frere: *Biblioteca musico-liturgica* (London, 1894–1932/*R*1967)

——: *Antiphonale Sarisburiense*, i (London, 1901/*R*1967), 76ff

O. Gatzweiler: *Die liturgischen Handschriften des Aachener Münsterstifts*, Liturgiegeschichtliche Quellen und Forschungen, x (Münster, 1926), 109ff

B. Stäblein: 'Antiphonar', *MGG* [chronological handlist of antiphoners]

M. Huglo: 'Die Adventsgesänge nach den Fragmenten von Lucca', *KJb*, xxxv (1951), 10

S. Marosszeki: *Les origines du chant cistercien*, Analecta sacri ordinis cisterciensis, viii (1952), 142ff

R.-J. Hesbert: 'Un curieux antiphonaire palimpseste de l'office', *Revue bénédictine*, lxiv (1954), 28 [*F-ROU* A 292 (catal.26)]

W. Lipphardt: 'Ein Quedlinburger Antiphonale des XI. Jahrhunderts', *KJb*, xxxviii (1954), 13 [*D-B* Mus.40047]

F. Bussi: *L'antifonario-graduale della basilica di S. Antonino in Piacenza, sec.XII: saggio storico-critico*, Biblioteca storica piacentina, xxvii (Piacenza, 1956) [*I-PCsa* 65]

M. Huglo and E. Moneta Caglio: *Fonti e paleografia del canto ambrosiano*, Archivio ambrosiano, vii (Milan, 1956)

G. Beyssac: 'Le graduel-antiphonaire du Mont-Renaud', *RdM*, xl (1957), 131

L. Brou: 'L'antiphonaire de Compiègne', *Etudes grégoriennes*, iv (1961), 20 [*F-Pn* lat.17436]

K. Gamber: *Codices liturgici latini antiquiores*, Spicilegii friburgensis subsidia, i (Freiburg, 1963), 237 (nos.1301–8)

L. Eizenhöfer and H. Knaus: *Die liturgischen Handschriften der hessischen Landes- und Hochschulbibliothek Darmstadt*, ii (Wiesbaden, 1968), 155ff

P. Salmon: *Les manuscrits liturgiques latins de la bibliothèque Vaticane: I*, Studi e testi, ccli (Rome, 1968)

M. Huglo: *Les tonaires: inventaire, analyse, comparaison* (diss., U. of Paris, 1971), 22f, 349ff, 390ff

A. Renaudin: 'Deux antiphonaires de Saint-Maur: BN lat.12584 et 12044', *Etudes grégoriennes*, xiii (1972), 53–150

B. Lambres: 'L'antiphonaire des Chartreux', *Etudes grégoriennes*, xiv (1973), 213

STUDIES OF THE ANTIPHONER

Amalar of Metz: *Liber de ordine antiphonarii*, PL, cv, 1243–1316; also ed. J. M. Hanssens, Studi e testi, cxl (Rome, 1950)

Agobard: *Liber de correctione antiphonarii*, PL, civ, 329; also in Monumenta Germaniae historica, *Epistolae*, v, *Karolini aevi*, iii, 232

P. C. C. Bogaerts and E. Duval: *Etudes sur les livres choraux* (Mechelen, 1855)

C. Marbach: *Carmina scripturarum scilicet antiphonas et responsoria ex sacra scriptura fonte* (Strasbourg, 1907)

J. Baudot: *L'antiphonaire* (Paris, 1913)

A. Gastoué: *Musique et liturgie: le graduel et l'antiphonaire romains: histoire et description* (Lyons, 1913)

P. Alfonso: *L'antifonario dell'Ufficio romano: note sull'origine della composizione dei testi* (Subiaco, 1935)

H. Hucke: 'Die Entstehung der Überlieferung von einer musikalischen Tätigkeit Gregors des Grossen', *Mf*, viii (1955), 259

B. Stäblein: ' "Gregorius praesul": der Prolog zum römischen Antiphonale', *Musik und Verlag: Karl Vötterle zum 65. Geburtstag* (Kassel, 1968), 537

MICHEL HUGLO

Antiphonia (Gk.: 'returning a sound'). In Greek and Byzantine theory, it denotes the octave (or double octave) and singing in octaves, as opposed to 'symphonia' (the unison) and 'paraphonia' (the 4th or 5th).

See also ANTIPHONAL PSALMODY.

RICHARD SHERR

Antiphony. A term for music in which an ensemble is divided into distinct groups, used in opposition, often spatial, and using contrasts of volume, pitch, timbre etc. *See* ANTIPHONAL PSALMODY; CHORUS (i), §3; CORI SPEZZATI.

Antiquis, A(dam) de (*b* probably Venice; *fl* early 16th century). Italian composer of frottolas and *laude*. 17 compositions are attributed to 'A. de Antiquis' (sometimes abbreviated 'A. de A.') in the collections of Ottaviano Petrucci and Andrea Antico. Petrucci appended 'Venetus' to Antiquis's name in the *Frottole libro quinto* and once in the *Laude libro secondo* gave his name in full. Many scholars have attempted to identify Antiquis with ANDREA ANTICO, engraver, publisher and composer from Montona; however, Antico never signed himself 'Venetus' and it seems likely that different people are involved. Einstein cited Antiquis's setting of the sonnet *Io mi parto* as the first printed example of the polyphonic working out of an entire composition of the frottola type and an important precursor of the madrigal.

WORKS
(all for 4vv)

Editions: *Die mehrstimmige italienische Laude um 1500*, ed. K. Jeppesen (Leipzig and Copenhagen, 1935), 44f [incl. edns of both *laude*]

Sedamnaest frottola [17 frottolas], ed. L. Županović, Spomenici hrvatske glazbene prošlosti, iii (Zagreb, 1972) [incl. edns. of all frottolas]

Laude, 1508³: Senza te, sacra regina; Volgi gli occhi, o madre pia

Frottolas: A ti sola ho dato el core, 1505⁶; Io mi parto, 1509²; Io son quel doloroso e tristo amante, 1505⁶; La insupportabil pena, 1509²; Non tardar, o diva mia, 1509²; Ochi mei, mai non restai, 1507³; Poi che son si sfortunato, 1505⁴; Prendi l'arme, o fiero Amore, 1505⁶; Quel ch'el ciel ne da per sorte, 1507³; Questa amara aspra partita, 1505⁶; Questo tuo lento tornare, 1507³; Resta hor su madonna in pace, 1505⁶; Siegua pur chi vuol amore, 1505⁶; Vale, iniqua, vale hormai, 1505⁶; Voi che ascoltate, 1510¹

BIBLIOGRAPHY
A. Einstein: *The Italian Madrigal* (Princeton, 1949/*R*1971)
C. W. Chapman: *Andrea Antico* (diss., Harvard U., 1964)

MARTIN PICKER

Antiquis, Andrea de. *See* ANTICO, ANDREA.

Antiquis, Giovanni Jacopo de (*b* Bari; *fl* 1574–1606). Italian composer. Antiquis was choirmaster of the Schola Cantorum at the basilica of S Nicola, Bari, about 1574. In 1606 he was chaplain and singing teacher at S Maria a Colonna, the church of the Conservatorio dei Poveri di Gesù Cristo, Naples. His two anthologies of 1574 contain 13 of his own villanellas and 31 by various friends employed in Bari, among them P. Nenna, S. Felis, S. de Baldis and G. F. Capuano. Most of his villanellas begin in chordal style, short points of imitation being reserved for the refrain. Like G. L. Primavera he used parallel 5ths only in exclusively chordal pieces. His instrumental pieces are instructional bicinia.

WORKS

Editions: *Villanelle alla napoletana a tre voci di musicisti Baresi del secolo XVI*, ed. S. A. Luciani (Rome, 1941) [L]
Musica instrumentalis, iv, ed. H. Mönkemeyer (Zurich, 1960) [M]

Il primo libro delle villanelle alla napolitana, 3vv (1574⁵); 7 in L
Il secondo libro della villanelle alla napolitana, 3vv (1574⁶); 6 in L
Canzonette, 2vv (Venice, 1584); lost
Madrigali, 4vv (Venice, 1584); lost, cited in *FétisB*
2 bicinia in 1590¹⁹
2 ricercares in 1591²⁷; 1 in 1595¹⁴, ed. in M; 1 in 1600¹⁰, attrib. S. de Antiquis; 2 in 1609¹⁸
8 ricercares in 1686⁵, 2 of these from 1591²⁷, 2 from 1609¹⁸

BIBLIOGRAPHY
G. M. Monti: *Le villanelle alla napoletana e l'antico lirica dialettale a Napoli* (Città di Castello, 1925)
P. Sorrenti: *I musicisti di Puglia* (Bari, 1966)

DONNA G. CARDAMONE

Antiquo [Antiquus], Andrea. *See* ANTICO, ANDREA.

Antiquus episcopus Beneventinus. An unnamed Beneventan bishop credited in the 12th-century Calixtine MS (*E-SC*) with a polyphonic piece, *Jacobe sancte tuum repetito*. The attribution is probably fictitious, particularly since the Beneventan see was an archbishopric from 969.

SARAH FULLER

Antoine [Anthoin], Ferdinand d' (*fl* Bonn, 1780–92). German soldier, composer and aesthetician. According to Neefe he was a captain in the service of the Elector of Cologne and an amateur musician who had acquired his knowledge from the writings of Marpurg, Kirnberger and Riepel, and on a journey to Italy. Besides some symphonies and quartets 'in Haidnischer Manier und Laune' he composed a number of theatrical works for Bonn and probably some sacred works as well. He is also known for an essay 'Wie muss die Kirchenmusik beschaffen seyn, wenn sie zur Andacht erheben soll?' in the *Beiträge zur Ausbreitung nützlicher Kenntnisse* (Bonn, 1784–5). This work, based in the language and aesthetics of the *Affektenlehre* and *Empfindsamkeit*, prefigured the outlook on church music which came into general currency in the Romantic era, with the Cologne performance of Allegri's *Miserere* and Palestrina's *Stabat mater* (1810).

WORKS
(all lost)

Il mondo alla roversa (opera buffa, 3, C. Goldoni), c1780
Das tartarische Gesetz (Singspiel, W. F. Gotter, after C. Gozzi), Bonn, 9 Jan 1782
Prol to Goethe's Clavigo (C. F. Cramer), Bonn, 4 Dec 1782
Das Mädchen in Eichthale (Singspiel, after J. Burgoyne), Bonn, 2 Jan 1783
6 choruses in Lanassa (tragedy, C. M. Plümicke), 9 April 1783
Otto der Schütz (Singspiel), ?Bonn, 1792
Ende gut, alles gut (Singspiel, 2), Bonn, 9 May 1792
Der Fürst und sein Volk (Singspiel), ?1793

Syms., qts, mentioned in Cramer (1783); sacred works

BIBLIOGRAPHY
GerberL; GerberNL
C. G. Neefe: Nachricht, *Magazin der Musik*, i (1783), 366ff, 393
E. Forbes, ed.: *Thayer's Life of Beethoven* (Princeton, 1964, 2/1967)
K. G. Fellerer: 'Ferdinand d'Anthoins Ästhetik der Kirchenmusik 1784', *Colloquium amicorum: Joseph Schmidt-Görg zum 70. Geburtstag* (Bonn, 1967), 82
          ALFRED LOEWENBERG/KARL GUSTAV FELLERER

Anton (Clemens Theodor) of Saxony (*b* Dresden, 27 Dec 1755; *d* Dresden, 6 June 1836). German prince and amateur composer. The third son of Friedrich Christian of Saxony and Maria Antonia Walpurgis, a noted patroness and composer, he was originally intended for the Catholic priesthood, but in 1781 he married Maria Antonia of Sardinia, and after her death Maria Theresia of Austria (1787). Peter August was responsible for Anton's musical education, and he was later tutored by the court musician A. Schmiedel. He produced his first major composition, the cantata *Montagnes, ode di Fénélon* in 1772. Throughout most of his life he remained outside government, and instead pursued his favourite pastimes, musical composition and genealogy. On the death of his brother King Friedrich August I in 1827 he succeeded to the throne of Saxony. Religious controversies and his advancing age led to a co-regency with his nephew Friedrich August in 1830, and a constitutional monarchy in 1831.

Anton of Saxony was a typical skilful musical dilettante and one of the most prolific composers of the House of Wettin (his brothers Friedrich August and Maximilian and nieces Auguste and Amalie also composed). His works (which fill more than 50 manuscript volumes in *D-Dlb*) are mainly operas (including *Triumph der Treue*, 1779; *Tamas*, 1785; *Il poeto ridicolo*, 1786; *Il fosso incantato*) and cantatas (many to texts by his brother Maximilian), and were performed by other amateur musicians at Dresden and Pillnitz to celebrate court occasions. Anton also composed sacred music, instrumental works (dances for court balls, symphonies, variations, etc), chamber music, keyboard sonatas (many of them on operatic themes), and over 100 songs, ballads, duets, arias and chansons. Though Weber described the cantata *Il trionfo d'Imene* as being 'full of talent', Anton's wide-ranging compositions are rather monotonous with regard to harmony and motif. They belong to the *galant*, early Classical style, and hardly reflect the move towards early Romanticism which occurred specifically in Dresden.

BIBLIOGRAPHY
EitnerQ
H. Meynert: *Anton, König von Sachsen* (Leipzig, 1836)
W. Schäfer: *Anton der Gütige* (Dresden and Leipzig, 1836)
M. M. von Weber: *Carl Maria von Weber*, ii (Leipzig, 1864), 192ff
M. Fürstenau: *Die musikalischen Beschäftigungen der Prinzessin Amalie, Herzogin zu Sachsen* (Dresden, 1874)
O. Schmid: *Das sächsische Königshaus in selbstschöpferischer musikalischer Bethätigung* (Leipzig, 1900)
——, ed.: *Musik am sächsischen Hofe*, iii, v (Leipzig, 1900–03)
——: *Fürstliche Komponisten aus dem sächsischen Königshause* (Langensalza, 1910)
W. Steude: 'Anton Clemens Theodor von Sachsen', *MGG* [with list of works]

                              DIETER HÄRTWIG

Antonelli [Antonelli da Fabrica, Antonellio, Antinello], **Abundio** [Abbondio, Abondio, Abundii] (*b* Fabrica, nr. Viterbo; *d* probably at Rome, ? in or before 1629). Italian composer and teacher. According to Casimiri he must have taught music at the Seminario Romano, Rome, some time between 1602 and 1606. The first post he held that is specifically documented is that of *maestro di cappella* at St John Lateran, Rome, where he is recorded from 1 June 1611 to 20 July 1613 (there is no evidence to substantiate Pitoni's and Baini's statements that he was there by 1608); Tullio Cima was one of the boys who sang under him there. The title-pages and dedications of works that Antonelli published in 1614 and 1615 indicate that he was then *maestro di cappella* of Benevento Cathedral. That he had returned to Rome by February 1616 can be determined from the dedication of his print of that year. In 1619 he corresponded with ROMANO MICHELI regarding what he considered to be Micheli's excessive application of *obblighi* to a ten-part mass by him; Micheli printed the letter and his replies in two theoretical works of 1621. Antonelli probably remained in Rome for the rest of his life. Casimiri conjectured that he was no longer alive in 1629, since a volume (*RISM* 1629⁶) ostensibly by him (from the designation 'Liber quartus') but also containing four pieces by his brother Francesco and two by his brother Angelo was edited by Francesco (there are also three motets by Angelo Antonelli in Abundio's 1614 volume). The presence of works by an Antonelli in six anthologies of the 1640s led early biographers to assume that Abundio Antonelli was in fact Antonello Filitrani.

Antonelli was primarily a composer of sacred works, most with continuo, which are typical products of the early 17th-century Roman school. The masses and many of the motets tend to be conservative, with mainly contrapuntal – frequently canonic – textures. Greater textural, harmonic and melodic diversity is to be found in the three books of 1615–16. These include pieces in which strict counterpoint or freely imitative two-part writing predominates and others in which solo and choral passages alternate. Antonelli's most progressive and interesting music is to be found in the occasional works for three and four choirs written for St John Lateran, and the Latin dramatic dialogues such as *Adiuro vos* (in *RISM* 1616¹, a publication associated with the Arciconfraternità di S Marcello), *Gaude virgo gloriosa* (*D-Rp*: a concerted dialogue for four soloists, four-part chorus and continuo), and *Abraham, tolle filium tuum* (*D-Rp*), a cantata-like piece on subject matter from the Old Testament which is scored for soloists, eight-part chorus, violin, cornett, theorbo, lute and organ and is organized as follows: opening sinfonia for concerted instruments; bass solo accompanied by concerted instruments; instrumental interlude; tenor solo, with theorbo and organ; dialogue in recitative style accompanied by lute and organ; soprano solo accompanied by all instruments; and a concluding double chorus. Through the last two works Antonelli contributed to the early development of the oratorio.

WORKS

SACRED VOCAL

(all printed works except anthologies published in Rome)
Sacrarum cantionum, liber primus, 4–6vv, bc (org) (1614[4])
Liber primus diversarum modulationum, 2–7vv (1615)
Liber secundus diversarum modulationum, 2–5vv (1615)
Liber tertius diversarum modulationum, 2–5vv (1616)
Missa ac sacrarum cantionum. . .trino fratrum germanorum Abundii, Francisci et Angeli Antonelliorum. . .liber quartus, 2–4vv (1629[6]); mass ed. in Basilica, ii (Düsseldorf, 1953)

11 works, 1616[1], 1618[3], 1623[2], 1625[1], 1627[1], 1627[2], 1642[1]
Magnificat, 8vv, bc; antiphons, 12vv, chorus; psalm, 12vv; 2 motets, 3, 12vv; 18 other works, 2–6, 8, 12vv: *A-Wn, D-MÜp, Rp, I-Rsg*

SECULAR VOCAL

Madrigali, libro primo, 5vv, bc (org) (1614)
5 works, 1621[14], 1621[15], 1621[16], 1634[1]

BIBLIOGRAPHY

R. Micheli: *Certezza d'artificii musicali non più fatti, contenuti nelli dieci oblighi della Messa a dieci voci; con la risposta all'opposizione fatta dal Sig. Abundio Antonelli, musico in Roma, sopra la quantità di essi obblighi* (Venice, 1621)
——: *Copia di lettera con mano scritta, mandata dal Sig. Abundio Antonelli . . . a me Romano Micheli . . . con la risposta fattagli nella presente stampa, dove si contengono l'esperienze di diversi studi di musica* (Venice, 1621)
G. O. Pitoni: *Notitia de contrapuntisti e de compositori di musica* (MS, *I-Rvat* C.G.I/1–2, *c*1725)
G. Baini: *Memorie storico-critiche della vita e delle opere di Giovanni Pierluigi da Palestrina* (Rome, 1828/*R*1966), i, 71; ii, 316
D. Alaleona: *Studi su la storia dell'oratorio musicale in Italia* (Turin, 1908, 2/1945 as *Storia dell'oratorio musicale in Italia*), 169f
R. Casimiri: ' "Disciplina musicae" e "mastri di capella" dopo il Concilio di Trento nei maggiori istituti ecclesiastici di Roma: Seminario Romano – Collegio Germanico – Collegio Inglese (sec. XVI–XVII)', *NA*, xii (1935), 79; xv (1938), 50, 56
C. Winter: 'Studien zur Frühgeschichte des lateinischen Oratorios', *KJb*, xlii (1958), 65, 70, 76
H. E. Smither: 'The Latin Dramatic Dialogue and the Nascent Oratorio', *JAMS*, xx (1967), 408, 430
A. Ziino: 'Antonelli, Abondio', *MGG*

PATRICIA ANN MYERS

Antonelli, Angelo (*fl* 1614–?1629). Italian composer, brother of ABUNDIO ANTONELLI.

Antonelli, Francesco (*fl* 1629). Italian composer, brother of ABUNDIO ANTONELLI.

Antonelli, Giulio Cesare (*fl* Mantua, 1606–49). Italian composer. He was a canon. His known works survive in two manuscripts (in *I-Mc*, Fondo S Barbara), the first containing 12 madrigals dated from Luzzara, near Mantua, in 1606, the second a setting in six sections of Rinuccini's *Lamento d'Arianna* which is ascribed to him on the cover in a contemporary hand. The title-page of the 1606 manuscript describes him as *maestro di cappella* at S Andrea, Mantua, and a copy of his will dated 22 March 1649 and kept with the manuscript implies that he was still at S Andrea at this date. The madrigals are all settings of Guarini, more specifically texts that had already been set by Monteverdi, then also working at Mantua, most of them in his fifth book of madrigals (1605). Reliance on Monteverdi's example is also evident in the *Lamento*, which thus places Antonelli even more firmly among those composers working at Mantua during the first decade of the 17th century – for example Amante Franzoni – who were heavily indebted to Monteverdi for textual, formal and sometimes stylistic models. Monteverdian gestures are, however, rare in Antonelli's music, which is generally closer to the sonorous homophony of another leading Mantuan composer, Gastoldi.

BIBLIOGRAPHY

G. Barblan: 'Un ignoto "Lamento d'Arianna" mantovano', *RIM*, ii (1967), 217

Conservatorio di Musica 'Giuseppe Verdi' di Milano: Catalogo della Biblioteca. Fondi speciali, i: Musiche della cappella di Santa Barbara in Mantova (Florence, 1972), 5

IAIN FENLON

Antonellus Marot de Caserta. See ANTHONELLO DE CASERTA.

Antoni, Antonio d' (*b* Palermo, 25 June 1801; *d* Trieste, 18 Aug 1859). Italian composer and conductor. His grandfather and father, both composers and conductors, gave him his first instruction in music. He was a precocious pupil, and at the age of 12 conducted his own mass for St Cecilia's Day. In 1817 he made his début in Palermo, as both conductor and composer, with the opera *Un duello*. He subsequently travelled for a number of years, as a conductor and an impresario, in Italy, France and England. In Trieste he met Meyerbeer, who encouraged him to write *Amina ossia L'orfanella di Ginevra* (based on the same libretto as that of *La sonnambula*). The opera, performed in Trieste at the Teatro Comunale at carnival time 1825, was a great success, and was believed to be by Meyerbeer. Other operas soon followed, one of which, *Amazilda e Zamoro*, was performed in Florence at the Teatro della Pergola in the spring of 1826. In about 1828 d'Antoni settled in Trieste, having been appointed musical director of the newly-formed Società Filarmonico-Drammatica, for the official inauguration of which he wrote the cantata *Il genio di Trieste* (22 June 1829). He also composed the vaudeville *La festa dell'Archibugio* (1829) for the Società. He remained in Trieste until his death (by suicide), and contributed greatly to raising the musical standards of the city.

FRANCESCO BUSSI

Antoni, Pietro degli. See DEGLI ANTONI, PIETRO.

Antonicek, Theophil (*b* Vienna, 22 Nov 1937). Austrian musicologist. He studied with Schenk and Wessely at the University of Vienna, taking the doctorate there in 1962 with a dissertation on Ignaz von Mosel; in 1967 he spent a year of study with Remo Giazotto in Italy. In 1963 he was appointed research musicologist for the Music Research Commission of the Austrian Academy of Sciences; concurrently he has served as secretary of the Gesellschaft zur Herausgabe der Denkmäler der Tonkunst in Österreich (1963–75) and of the Österreichische Gesellschaft für Musikwissenschaft (appointed 1973), becoming editor of its *Mitteilungen* in November 1973. He is also editor (1976 with C. Harten) of the series Musicologica Austriaca. His chief areas of research have been Austrian (particularly Viennese) music history from the 17th century to the 19th, and relations between Italian and Austrian music of the same period; his publications include articles on Cavalieri, Cesti, Monteverdi and Beethoven.

WRITINGS

Ignaz von Mosel (1772–1844): Biographie und Beziehungen zu den Zeitgenossen (diss., U. of Vienna, 1962)
Zur Pflege Händelscher Musik in der 2. Hälfte des 18. Jahrhunderts (Vienna, 1966)
'Italienische Musikerlebnisse Ferdinands II. 1598', *Anzeiger der Österreichischen Akademie der Wissenschaften: philosophisch-historische Klasse*, civ (1967), 91
Das Musikarchiv der Pfarrkirche St. Karl Borromäus in Wien, i: *Die Drucke*; ii: *Die Handschriften A–H*; iii: *Die Handschriften I–Z, Anonymi* (Vienna, 1968–)

'Emilio de' Cavalieri und seine "Rappresentazione di anima et di corpo" ', *ÖMz*, xxiv (1969), 445
'Johann Rosenmüller und das Ospedale della Pietà in Venedig', *Mf*, xxii (1969), 460
'Zum 300. Todestag Antonio Cestis', *ÖMz*, xxiv (1969), 573
'Antonio Cesti alla corte di Vienna', *NRMI*, iv (1970), 307
'Beethoven und die Gluck-Tradition', *Beethoven-Studien*, ed. E. Schenk (Vienna, 1970), 195
'Das Salzburger Ordensdrama', *ÖMz*, xxv (1970), 370
'Claudio Monteverdi und Österreich', *ÖMz*, xxvi (1971), 266
Musik im Festsaal der Österreichischen Akademie der Wissenschaften (Vienna, 1972)
' "Vergangenheit muss unsere Zukunft bilden": die patriotische Musikbewegung in Wien und ihr Vorkämpfer Ignaz von Mosel', *RBM*, xxvi–xxvii (1972–3), 38
'Adalbert Stifters Beethoven-Bild', *ÖMz*, xxix (1974), 81
'Die Damira-Opern der beiden Ziani', *AnMc*, no.14 (1974), 176–207
with C. Harten: *Franz Schmidt, 1874–1939, Ausstellung zum 100. Geburtstag* (Vienna, 1974) [catalogue]
'Bruckners Universitätsschüler in den Nationalien der Philosophischen Fakultät: mit einem Verzeichnis der Hörer von Vorlesungen über musikalische Gegenstände vom Sommersemester 1875 bis zum Wintersemester 1896/97', *Bruckner-Studien*, ed. O. Wessely (Vienna, 1975), 433–87
ed. with R. Flotzinger and O. Wessely: *De ratione in musica: Festschrift Erich Schenk* (Kassel, 1975) [incl. 'Humanitätssymbolik im Eroica-Finale', 144]
'Vienna', §§1–3, *Grove 6*

Antonii, Giovanni Battista. See DEGLI ANTONI, GIOVANNI BATTISTA.

Antonio. See GUIDO, GIOVANNI ANTONIO.

Antonio da Lucca. Italian 15th-century music theorist. He was a servite friar and pupil of one Laurentius of Orvieto, a canon of S Maria Maggiore. His treatise *Ars cantus figurati* (*CS*, iv, 421–33) is a compilation on *musica mensurabilis* according to the theories of Jehan des Murs; it deals with ligatures, alterations, proportions and prolations, giving diagrams and music examples.

See also ITALY: BIBLIOGRAPHY OF MUSIC TO 1600 and THEORY, THEORISTS.

BEATRICE PESCERELLI

Antonio da Tempo (*fl* Padua, early 14th century). Italian poet and theorist. He was a judge in Padua between 1329 and 1337, and in 1332 wrote a treatise *Delle rime volgari* which he dedicated to Alberto della Scala, ruler of the city. This is a work on metrics which describes, with examples, the main poetic forms of the 14th century (sonnet, ballata, *cantio extensa*, *rotundellus*, *mandrialis*, *serventensius* and *motus confectus*). Although Antonio stated expressly that he was not a musician, there are references to music in the treatise, particularly concerning the madrigal, which is described as a composition preferably for two or more voices.

BIBLIOGRAPHY
G. Grion, ed.: *Delle rime volgari: trattato di Antonio da Tempo giudice padovano composto nel 1332* (Bologna, 1869/*R*1968)
For further bibliography *see* ITALY: BIBLIOGRAPHY OF MUSIC TO 1600.

F. ALBERTO GALLO

Antonio degli Organi [del Bessa, di Bartolomeo]. See SQUARCIALUPI, ANTONIO.

Antonio de Leno. See ANTONIUS DE LENO.

Antoniotto [Antoniotti], **Giorgio** (*b* ?Milan, *c*1692; *d* Milan, 1776). Italian theorist and composer. Apart from his 12 sonatas op.1, published by Le Cène at Amsterdam in the mid-1730s, none of his music has come to light. The collection consists of five cello son-atas and seven for two cellos or violas da gamba, all of which reveal an advanced knowledge of the cello and display skilful counterpoint. Antoniotto was living in Holland when this work appeared but then moved to London, where he stayed for more than two decades and wrote his treatise *L'arte armonica: or, A Treatise on the Composition of Musick* (1760). It was published in an anonymous English translation, which the *Monthly Review* found lacking in purity and elegance of style but intelligible and valuable for advanced students of music. In many respects it is an up-to-date and sophisticated presentation of theory, for instance in its use of Corelli's op.5 no.1 to illustrate the transformation of chord progressions into melodies and counterpoint. About 1770 Antoniotto returned to Milan, where he gave Giovenale Sacchi his scheme for creating dissonances by sustaining chords until all the notes of the scale sound together. Fétis, the most important source of information on Antoniotto, reported that he died in Milan in 1776.

BIBLIOGRAPHY
EitnerQ; *FétisB*; *GerberL*; *GerberNL*; *HawkinsH*
'L'arte armonica', *Monthly Review, or, Literary Journal*, xxiv (1761), 293 [review]
J. A. Serre: *Observations sur les principes de l'harmonie* (Geneva, 1763), 5
P. Lichtenthal: *Dizionario e bibliografia della musica*, iv (Milan, 1826), 345
B. Weigl: *Handbuch der Violoncell-Literatur* (Vienna, 3/1929), 55
W. S. Newman: *The Sonata in the Baroque Era* (Chapel Hill, 1959, rev. 2/1966/*R*1972), 188ff
L. F. Chenette: *Music Theory in the British Isles during the Enlightenment* (diss., Ohio State U., 1967)

SVEN HANSELL

Antoniou, Theodore (*b* Athens, 10 Feb 1935). Greek composer. He studied violin, singing and composition at the National Conservatory, Athens (1947–58); he also studied composition under Papaioannou at the Hellenic Conservatory, Athens (1956–61). His studies were continued with Günther Bialas at the Munich Musikhochschule, where he gained his first experience in electronic music. During 1966 he made a tour of the USA and a Ford Foundation grant enabled him to spend the year 1968 in Berlin. In 1967 he founded the Hellenic Group of Contemporary Music in Athens. He has taught composition and orchestration at the universities of Stanford (1969–70) – where he founded the 'Alea II' ensemble – and Utah (1970), at the Philadelphia Academy of Music since 1970 and at Tanglewood (1975). Awards made to him include the Richard Strauss Prize of the City of Munich (1964), the City of Stuttgart Prize (1966) for his Violin Concerto, the Steghi Grammaton Prize (1967) for his *Miniatures*, a prize from Spanish television for *Cassandra* in 1970 and a US National Endowment for the Arts Grant (1975). An enormously prolific composer, he has also received many commissions. His music hesitated at first between a somewhat naive atonality (Violin Sonatina, 1959) and an engaging Bartókian folklorism (Trio, 1961). Later he adapted serial procedures in writing pieces constructed in elegantly designed small forms. The influences of Christou, Zimmermann and Penderecki became evident in the large-scale works of the early 1970s.

WORKS
(*selective list*)
STAGE
Epirus (ballet), chamber chorus, orch, 1964; Noh-Musik (music-theatre), 4 performers, 1964; Rhinoceros (ballet, after Ionesco), 5

insts, tape, 1964; Clytaemnestra (sound-action, T. Roussos), actresses, dancers, orch, tape, 1967; Cassandra (sound-action for television), mixed media, 1969; Protest I, actors, tape, 1970; Protest II, mixed media, 1971; Aftosyngentrossi-peirama [Meditation-experiment], mixed media, 1972; Chorochronos I, mixed media, 1973

Incidental music for 24 plays (1960–76) and 6 films (1962–75)

ORCHESTRAL

Suite, chamber orch, 1959; Conc., cl, tpt, vn, orch, 1960; Ov., 1961; Antitheses, 1962; Pf Concertino, 1962; Jeux, vc, str, 1963; Mikrographies, 1964; Vn Conc., 1965; Kinesis ABCD, 2 str orch, 1966; Op Ov., orch, tape, 1966; Events I, vn, pf, orch, 1967–8, II, 1969, III, small orch, tape, slides, 1969; Threnos, wind, pf, perc, db, 1972; Fluxus I, 1974–5; Fluxus II, pf, chamber orch

VOCAL

Choral: Griechische Volkslieder, SATB, 1961; Epirus [after folksongs], 1962; Kontakion (Romanos the Melode), S, Mez, T, B, chorus, str, 1965; 10 School Songs, 1965–6; Nenikikamen [We are victorious], Mez, Bar, narrator, chorus, orch, 1971; Verleih uns Frieden [after Schütz], 3 choruses, 1971–2; Die weisse Rose (T. Tolia and others), Bar, 3 narrators, children's chorus, chorus, orch, 1974–5

Solo vocal: Melos (Sappho), Mez/Bar, orch, 1962; Epilogue (Odyssey), Mez, narrator, 6 insts, 1963; Klima apoussias [Climate of absence] (O. Elytis), Bar, chamber orch, 1968; Moirologia for Jani Christou, Mez/Bar, pf, 1970; Parodies (H. Ball), lv, pf, 1970; Chorochronos II, lv, orch, 1973; Chorochronos III, Bar, pf, perc, tape, 1975

INSTRUMENTAL AND TAPE

Large ens: Concertino, pf, 9 wind, perc, 1963; Katharsis, fl, ens, tape, lights, 1968; Cheironomiai [Gestures], at least 8 performers, 1971; Synthesis, ob, elec org, perc, db, 4 synth, 1971; Circle of Accusation, 16 insts, 1975

Small ens: Sonatina, vn, pf, 1959; Str Qt, 1960; Trio, fl, va, vc, 1961; Dialogues, fl, gui, 1962; Quartetto giocoso, ob, pf trio, 1965; Lyrics, vn, pf, 1967; Stychomythia, fl, gui, 1976

Solo inst: Aquarelles, pf, 1958; Pf Sonata, 1959; Vn Sonata, 1961; Music, harp, 1965; Sil-ben, pf, 1965; 6 likes, tuba, 1967; 5 likes, ob, 1969; 4 likes, vn, 1972; 3 likes, cl, 1973; 2 likes, db, 1976

Tape: Gravity, video, 1966; Heterophony, 1966; Telemusic, 1970

Principal publishers: Antoniou, Bärenreiter, Gerig, Modern, Orlando

GEORGE S. LEOTSAKOS

Antonius de Arena. *See* ARENA, ANTONIUS DE.

Antonius [Antonis] **de Civitate Austrie** [Cividal, Cividale, Civitato] (*b* ?Cividale in Friuli; *fl* 1420–25). Italian composer. He was a Dominican friar; in his motet *O felix flos Florencia/Gaude felix Dominice*, the patron saint of his order is invoked to protect Florence, and the motet *Inclita persplendens* (dated 1422) was composed in honour of St Katherine, the patron of the Dominican tertiary order for women. The isorhythmic motet *Strenua/Gaudeat*, dated 8 June 1423 and hitherto incorrectly regarded as a wedding motet, refers to the regency of the Ordelaffi house at Forlì: at Giorgio Ordelaffi's death in 1422, his wife Lucrezia took power on behalf of their son; she was taken prisoner, but escaped on 4 June 1423 (Pirrotta).

Three mass movements, five motets and a virelai survive in the northern Italian manuscripts *I-Bc* Q15, *Bu* 2216 and *GB-Ob* 213, dating from about 1430 or before. There are three rondeaux in the somewhat earlier manuscripts *I-La* 184 and *Fn* Panciatichi 26. In places the rondeaux are supplied with only a few words of text; the upper voices labelled 'triplum' often lack text altogether. The only Italian setting is *Io veggio* in the form of a French ballade. The paired Gloria and Credo (*Bc* Q15, nos.83–4) share the same mode, clefs and mensuration, and the use of brief points of imitation in their Amens. The repetition and sequential use of short figures characterize Antonius's style; frequent rests cause the melodic lines to be split up into short sections. There is some use of canonic writing in the upper voices of *Strenua/Gaudeat* and *Je suy si las*; the canonic

instruction in the latter work indicates that it is composed in perfect time with diminution. Isorhythm occurs in the ostinato of the tenor and contratenor of *Vous soyez*, in the repeated tenor of a single Gloria, and in the motets *Strenua/Gaudeat* and *Inclita persplendens*.

WORKS

Edition: *Early Fifteenth-century Music*, ed. G. Reaney, CMM, xi/5 (1975) [complete]

MASS MOVEMENTS

Gloria and Credo, 3vv
Gloria, 3vv
Gloria, 3vv

MOTETS

Inclita persplendens [frag.: only inc. top voice survives]
O felix flos Florencia/Gaude felix Dominice, 3vv
Pie pater Dominice/O Petre martir/O Thoma lux, 3vv
Sanctus itaque patriarcha, 4vv
Strenua/Gaudeat, 4vv

ITALIAN SONG

Io veggio, 3vv

RONDEAUX

Longtemps j'ay mis, 3vv
Merçi pour Dieu, 3vv
Vous soyez très bien venus, 4vv

VIRELAIS

Je suy si las, 3vv

FRAGMENTARY CONTRATENOR

A tendre, 'secunda pars contratenoris' ascribed, *I-La* 184

BIBLIOGRAPHY

G. de Van: 'An Inventory of the Manuscript Bologna, Liceo musicale, Q 15 (*olim* 37)', *MD*, ii (1948), 231

N. Pirrotta: 'Il codice di Lucca, I: Descrizione e inventario', *MD*, iii (1949), 119

E. Li Gotti: 'Il codice di Lucca, II: Testi letterari', *MD*, iv (1950), 111

N. Pirrotta: 'Il codice di Lucca, III: Il repertorio musicale', *MD*, v (1951), 115

H. Besseler: 'Antonius de Civitate', *MGG*

G. Reaney: 'The Manuscript Oxford, Bodleian Library, Canonici misc. 213', *MD*, ix (1955), 73–104

F. A. Gallo: *Il codice musicale 2216 della Biblioteca universitaria di Bologna* (Bologna, 1968–70)

HANS SCHOOP

Antonius de Leno (*b* ?Leno, nr. Brescia; *fl* 1st half of the 15th century). Italian ?theorist. An incomplete treatise on music, in Italian, found in a manuscript of the second half of the 15th century, contains musical examples attributed to 'Antonius de Leno musichus'; it is uncertain, however, whether the text of the treatise can safely be attributed to him. Three sections only survive: the first, on mutations, may have been the final part of a larger section on *musica plana*; next follows a discussion of counterpoint – note-against-note, and two and three notes against one; and finally there is a section on the application of elements of mensural music to counterpoint (the prolations, alteration, dots of division, proportions and rests). These latter two sections have been published under the title *Regulae de contrapunto* (*CS*, iii, 307–28). Originally they may have been followed by a section on instrumental music. The treatise, which is obviously practical in aim, offers valuable evidence of compositional techniques in Italy in the first half of the 15th century. Since Antonius was from the vicinity of Brescia, it seems significant that the notation described in the treatise is precisely that used in *I-Bu* 2216, thought to have been copied near Brescia about 1440. The treatise is edited by A. Seay (Colorado Springs, 1977).

BIBLIOGRAPHY

F. A. Gallo: *Il codice musicale 2216 della Biblioteca universitaria di Bologna*, ii (Bologna, 1970), 15

——: 'Teoria e cultura musicale nel quattrocento', *Storia della cultura veneta*, ed. G. Folena, ii (Venice, 1976)

For further bibliography *see* ITALY: BIBLIOGRAPHY OF MUSIC TO 1600.

F. ALBERTO GALLO

Antonius Romanus [Antonius de Roma] (*fl* 1400–32). Italian composer. The only secure facts of his life are that he was 'magister cantus' at St Mark's, Venice, in 1420 and was listed in a notarial act of 20 July 1425 as a 'cantor S Marci'. The text of his motet, *Aurea flammigera*, in honour of Gianfrancesco Gonzaga, was probably composed in 1432 as a part of a welcome for the return of that captain to Milan, thus suggesting that Antonius was at that date still serving at St Mark's.

Only seven works by him survive: three mass movements, three motets and one ballata. The sacred works (in *I-Bc* Q15) reflect the changes in style brought about by the impact of composers from the north. The Gloria–Credo pair has its uppermost voice or voices in sections alternately marked 'chorus' and 'unus'. There is also the implication that the choral portions are to be accompanied instrumentally, the solo sections without instruments. The earliest of the motets, *Ducalis sedes/Stirps Mocenigo*, probably dates from around 1415 and is in honour of the then doge, Tommaso Mocenigo. *Carminibus festos* is in honour of Francesco Foscari, who became doge in 1523; the second half of the work repeats the rhythmic pattern of the first, like a long talea without color. *Aurea flammigera*, in honour of Gianfrancesco Gonzaga, is built on a tenor whose sections are in part repeated exactly and which also contains isometric repetitions. The ballata *Deh s'i' t'amo con fede*, in *GB-Ob* Can. misc. 213, is incomplete, only the uppermost voice existing with all its music but not the full poetic text.

Antonius was, as his dates suggest, a composer between the Ars Nova and the generation of Dufay. His works contain reminders of earlier isorhythmic techniques as well as hints of the fuller sound of fauxbourdon; there are simple, almost homophonic, passages as well as complicated areas of syncopation recalling the 14th century. Antonius has an important place as a composer caught in a time of great changes, reflecting the influences of his day.

WORKS

Editions: *Antonii Romani opera*, ed. F. A. Gallo (Bologna, 1969) [G] [see review by P. Gülke, *Mf*, xxii (1969), 135]
        Early Fifteenth-century Music, ed. G. Reaney, CMM, xi/5 (1975)

Gloria, Credo, 4vv, G 20
Gloria, 4vv, G 36
Ducalis sedes/Stirps Mocenigo, 4vv, G 1
Carminibus festos/O requies populi, 4vv, G 7
Aurea flammigera, 4vv, G 13
Deh s'i' t'amo con fede, inc., G 42 (only 1v survives)

BIBLIOGRAPHY

W. Korte: *Studie zur Geschichte der Musik in Italien im ersten Viertel des 15. Jahrhunderts* (Kassel, 1933), 30ff, 47ff, 68f
M. Bukofzer: *Studies in Medieval and Renaissance Music* (New York, 1950), 52
K. von Fischer: 'On the Technique, Origin and Evolution of Italian Trecento Music', *MQ*, xlvii (1961), 52
F. A. Gallo: 'Musiche veneziane nel ms. 2216 della Biblioteca universitaria di Bologna', *Quadrivium*, vi (1964), 108
                                        ALBERT SEAY

Antonowycz [Antonowytsch], **Myrosław** (*b* Dolina, Ukraine, 1 March 1917). Dutch musicologist and choir conductor of Ukrainian birth. He studied at the University of Lwów with Chybiński (1936–40), at the University of Utrecht with Smijers (1940–50) and at Harvard University with Gombosi (1953). From 1939 to 1944 he was a professional singer. In 1948 when the Ukrainian seminary of priests (established after the war and first settled in south Germany) moved to Culemborg in the Netherlands, Antonowycz became lecturer in church music and conductor of the choir. He held this post until the seminary was closed in 1950. The next year he took his doctorate under Smijers at the University of Utrecht. Since 1951 he has been at the Institute of Musicology at the University of Utrecht, first as assistant lecturer and later as research-associate specializing in Renaissance music and the liturgical music of the Byzantine-Slavonic Rite. From the inception of the Utrecht Byzantine Choir in 1951 Antonowycz has been its conductor, helping to introduce Ukrainian choral repertory to many countries of Europe. In 1958 he was entrusted with the completion of Smijers's edition of Josquin, to which he has contributed several volumes.

WRITINGS

Die Motette Benedicta es von Josquin des Prez und die Messen super Benedicta von Willaert, Palestrina, de la Hêle und de Monte (diss., U. of Utrecht; Utrecht, 1951)
'Renaissance-Tendenzen in den Fortuna-desperata-Messen von Josquin und Obrecht', *Mf*, ix (1956), 1
'Die byzantinischen Elemente in den Antiphonen der ukrainischen Kirche', *KJb*, xliii (1959), 8
'The Present State of Josquin Research', *IMSCR*, viii *New York, 1961*, i, 53
'Ukrainische Hirmen im Lichte der byzantinischen Musiktheorie', *Musik des Ostens*, v (1969), 7
The Chants from Ukrainian Heirmologia (Bilthoven, 1974)

EDITIONS

Josquin Desprez Motetten, Werken, v/19–25, fascs.45–9, 51–2 (Leipzig, 1957–64); *Wereldlijke werken*, ibid, i/4, fascs. 53–4 (Leipzig, 1965) [with W. Elders]; *Supplement* (Leipzig, 1969) [with W. Elders]
                                        ELLINOR BIJVOET

Antunes, Jorge (*b* Rio de Janeiro, 23 April 1942). Brazilian composer. He studied the violin, conducting and composition at the Federal University of Rio de Janeiro under Morelembaum, Siqueira and de Carvalho (1960–68), also taking the BSc in physics (1965). In 1969–70 he was at the di Tella Institute in Buenos Aires, working in the electronic music studio and studying further with Ginastera, de Pablo and Gandini. He continued his electronic studies at the University of Utrecht in 1970, and in 1972–3 worked with the Groupe de Recherches Musicales in Paris. In 1973 he was appointed professor of composition and director of the electronic music studio at the University of Brasilia.

By the late 1960s Antunes had established himself as one of the leaders of avant-garde music in Brazil. He pioneered the use of electronic means there, beginning with apparatus he built himself, and from about 1965 he cultivated what he called 'integral art', using sounds, colours and even odours and flavours, as in *Ambiente I*. His *Tartinia MCMLXX*, performed at the 1971 ISCM Festival, established him as an international figure with its subtle and remarkable handling of difference tones in the solo violin part and its tense, imaginative orchestration.

WORKS
(*selective list*)

Chamber opera: Contato, 1966–8
Orch: Sarau no.1, 1962; Sarau no.2, 1963; Dissolução, chamber orch, perc, tape, 1966; 3 eventos da luz branca, chamber orch, tape, 1967; Cromoplastofonia, orch, tape, moving object, 1967–8; Acusmorfose (1968), 1968; Isomerism, chamber orch, 1970; Tartinia MCMLXX, vn, orch, 1970

Vocal: Acusmorfose (1969), 2 choruses, 2 orchs, 1969; Cromorfonética, chorus, 1969; Concertatio I, vocal ens, elec gui, elec db, orch, tape, 1969; Proudhonia, chorus, tape, 1973; Source, 1v, fl, va, vc, pf, synth, tape, 1974

Ens and inst: Pf Trio, 1963; Prelúdio boêmio, vn, pf, 1964; Trio, vn, pf, theremin, 1965; (1, 6–1, 6) × 10⁻¹⁹; Coulombs, fl, bn, pf, elec, 1967; Insubstituível segunda, vc, tape, 1967; Str Qt no.1, 1967–8; Invocação em defesa da máquina, perc ens, tape, 1968; 3 comportamentos, pf trio, 1969; Bartokollagia MCMLXX, str qt, 1970; Music for 8 Persons Playing Things, perc, 1970–71; Flautatual F, fl, 1972

Tape: 3 estudos cromofônicos, 1966; Fluxo luminoso para sons brancos I–III, 1966, 1966, 1966–7; Movimento browniano, 1968; Cinta cita, 1969; Historia de un pueblo por nacer o carta abierta a Vassili Vassilikos y a todos los pesimistas, 1970; Para nascer aquí, 1970–71

Integral art: Ambiente I, tape, 1965; Cromoplastofonia II–III, tape, 1966, 1968; 3 comportamentos, pf trio, lamps, projectors, 1969

Principal publishers: Instituut voor Sonologie (Utrecht), Serviço de Documentação Musical (Rio de Janeiro), Suvini Zerboni

BIBLIOGRAPHY

Composers of the Americas, xvi (Washington, DC, 1970), 13

GERARD BÉHAGUE

Antwerp (Flemish Antwerpen; Fr. Anvers). Belgian city. For centuries it has been an important musical centre and has played a leading role in the music of the Low Countries. Around 1410 the choir school of the Onze-Lieve-Vrouwekerk (later the cathedral) began to develop an active musical life. Up to the 17th century its choirmasters, organists and singers included such composers as Pullois, Ockeghem, Barbireau, Obrecht, Waelrant, Gérard de Turnhout, Séverin Cornet, Pevernage and John Bull; in addition Rore, Lassus and Monte all spent some time in the city. Secular music was promoted by the establishment of the town players (before 1430) and the formation of a musicians' guild (c1500). Music printing flourished after 1540 through the work of Cock, Susato, Waelrant & Laet, Phalèse & Bellère and Plantin. Musicians who either came from Antwerp or were active there outside the cathedral included the composers Faignient, Hèle, Canis, Verdonck, Luython and Messaus, and the lute virtuosos Adriaensen, Huet and Hove. The Antwerp harpsichord builders of the 17th and 18th centuries were famous: the Ruckers family, Jan Couchet and J. D. Dulcken. Following an economic crisis in the 17th century there was a decline in the city's musical life; in the 18th century, however, the musical life of the cathedral and of other churches flourished once more with composers such as Eve, Fesch, J.-H. Fiocco, Croes, A.-J. Blavier, Trazegnies and Raick.

The French Revolution put an end to the dominating position of the Church, and music education was thenceforth entrusted to civic foundations such as the Ecole de Musique de la Ville d'Anvers (1842). Musical taste was dictated by the Italian and French opera performed at the Théâtre Royal (1802–1933). Brought up in this atmosphere, Albert Grisar devoted himself to the genre of comic opera, with which he later scored an unrivalled triumph at Paris. Through the auspices of Peter Benoit, champion of Flemish nationalism, the Vlaamsche Muziekschool (1867) was raised in status in 1898, becoming the Koninklijk Vlaams Conservatorium. Benoit's Romantic oratorios and cantatas, to Flemish texts, were intended to rouse national consciousness, and with his enthusiastic support the Vlaamse Opera was founded in 1893 by the bass Hendrik Fontaine and the composer Edward Keurvels. Renamed the Koninklijke Vlaamse Opera in 1920 the company won international fame during the 1920s for its Wagner productions with the tenor Ernest van Dijck. Under its director Sylvain Deruwe, it has given Flemish operas and concert performances, as well as the standard repertory in Flemish translation. The children's choir of the opera (Kinderkoor Mia Vinck, 1966) also appears independently. One-act operas and works using smaller forces are given by the Vlaamse Kameropera (1958, director Ernest Maes).

The directors of the conservatory who followed Benoit, i.e. Blockx, Emiel Wambach (1857–1924), Mortelmans, Flor Alpaerts, Hoof, Vocht and Peeters, adhered to a nationalist style in their compositions, as did Karel Candael and Renaat Veremans (1894–1969). Contemporary composers of more modern outlook have included Jong, Baeyens, Karel Albert, Maes, Durme, Velden, Kersters, Glorieux and the avant-garde Goeyvaerts. In 1970 the structure of the Belgian royal conservatories was fundamentally altered, and they became restricted to the domain of higher education, providing professional tuition of a high standard; the conditions of entry became a certificate of higher secondary education and proof of maturity, in addition to proof of artistic capability. In 1975 this new structuring was adopted at the Antwerp Conservatory (director Eugène Traey). Beginners, amateurs and performers at the pre-professional stage are catered for in the Rijksmuziekacademie (director Gilbert de Greef), founded in 1970, which covers primary and secondary music education using the Kodály method. In 1972 the Kunsthumaniora, the music department of the Institute of Higher Secondary Artistic Education, was founded under the auspices of the conservatory. The Halewynstichting (founded 1951) sponsors a number of music schools for young people providing an elementary music education based on the methods of Orff and Kodály, directed towards the performance of music in the home and choral singing. The municipal music academies of the suburbs of Borgerhout (director Louis Cauberghs), Hoboken (Jan van Mol), Berchem (Marcel Mattheessen), Deurne (Irène van Poppel), Wilrijk (Herman Verschraegen), Merksem (Alfons de Mulder) and Mortsel (François Cuypers) provide primary and secondary music tuition and are held in high regard.

A number of concert organizations cater for an active and diverse concert season: symphony concerts with guest ensembles and soloists (the Cofena and Dierentuin concerts); early music at the Rubenshuis and Vleeshuis; recitals and chamber music at the conservatory and Protestant Church; and organ recitals and choral concerts at the cathedral and several churches. The Philharmonie (1955) gives subscription concerts with guest conductors and soloists; other performing ensembles are Consortium Antiquum, directed by J.-P. Biesemans (1964), Camerata Belgica (1967), Solisten van Antwerpen (1970), the Theo Mertens Brass Ensemble (1958) and the Panoramic Trio François Glorieux (1974). The Antwerp section of Jeunesses Musicales, Jeugd en Muziek (1948), holds its own series of concerts and also has a youth orchestra (1962) directed by François Cuypers. The regional station of Belgian Radio (BRT) organizes public concerts.

The tradition of fine sacred concerts with a large choir, soloists, organ and full orchestra in St Pauluskerk has existed since the 19th century. The Artiestenmis ('Artists' mass', 1943) in the St Carolus-Borromeuskerk, in which vocal and instrumental ensembles and soloists cooperate, was set up to benefit needy Antwerp artists. In the St Jozefskerk a monthly 'cantata service' was

Théâtre Royal, Antwerp: lithograph, c1834

started in 1973, consisting of an evening Mass with a Bach cantata given by the Antwerp Bach Choir and Collegium under the direction of Michael Scheck, continuing the work of Walter Weyler and his Halewynkoor (1951). Among the numerous church choirs, that of the cathedral, under the direction of Jan Schrooten, is noteworthy. The oldest surviving choral societies are the Lassallekring (1879) directed by Oscar van Hoof, and Arti Vocali (1910) directed by Jan Valach. The Nieuw Ceciliakoor (1968), directed by Frans Dubois, continues the tradition of the famous Koninklijke Chorale Caecilia (1915–68), which under its director Lodewijk de Vocht gave premières of contemporary vocal works. Other fine choirs are Audite Nova (1961, directed by Kamiel Cooremans), Singhet Saem (1952, Jeanne Lambrechts), the Philharmonisch Koor (1965, Jan Verbogt) and the Alma Musica of Borgerhout (1951, Peter Hermans). Antwerp is also the headquarters and documentation centre of the Algemeen Nederlands Zangverbond, a choral federation with the aim of stimulating folksong and choral music through festivals, including the annual Vlaams Nationaal Zangfeest in the Antwerp Sports Palace.

Other annual music festivals, most of them broadcast, include the Dagen van de Gitaar (1964), organized by the Gitaarcentrum (1962, Marcel Monden), the Antwerpse Bachdagen (1974) of the Antwerps Bachgenootschap (1974), and the Middelheim Jazzfestival (1969) of the Middelheim Promotors (1966). Beiaardconcerten (carillon concerts), given by the city carillonneur Jo Haazen and by guest carillon-

neurs, have become a tourist attraction. Because of its pure tone the city carillon, acquired in 1540, is held to be one of the best in the Netherlands. It has 47 bells, the oldest dating from 1459, and a four-octave compass, and chimes mechanically every quarter-hour. The main part, consisting of 36 bells, was made between 1655 and 1658 by the Hemony brothers. In 1971–2 it was restored by the firm of Eijsbouts of Asten. From 1480 to 1877 the cathedral also had a carillon.

The conservatory library contains one of the richest music collections in Belgium, while precious early music prints are also to be found in the Plantinmuseum and the Stadsbibliotheek. The notable music library of J. A. Stellfeld was sold by his heirs in 1952 to the University of Michigan. The Archief en Museum voor Vlaams Cultuurleven offers documentation on all aspects of the musical life of the city, in the form of press cuttings, letters, manuscripts, photographs etc. In addition Antwerp has three public record libraries. There is a collection of instruments in the Vleeshuis Museum, which is also the headquarters of the Ruckers Genootschap (1970). The Antwerpse Vereniging voor Muziekgeschiedenis was founded in 1931 and publishes the important series Monumenta Musicae Belgicae. The Peter Benoit Fund was set up in 1902 with the intention of disseminating and publishing the work of Benoit; Jef van Hoof's work is promoted by De Crans (1917), which also offers a biennial composition prize and publishes the music of other Flemish composers. The oldest and most important firm of music publishers in Antwerp, Metropolis, publishes mostly instrumental music of contemporary Belgian composers, but also tutors and books on musical history.

BIBLIOGRAPHY
AMe
F. Donnet: *Les cloches d'Anvers* (Antwerp, 1899)
L. de Burbure and L. Theunissens: 'La musique à Anvers aux XIVᵉ, XVᵉ et XVIᵉ siècles', *Annales de l'Académie royale d'archéologie de Belgique*, lviii (1906), 159–256
A. Monet: *Een halve eeuw Nederlandsch lyrisch tooneel en Vlaamsche opera te Antwerpen* (Antwerp, 1939)
J. A. Stellfeld: 'Bronnen tot de geschiedenis der Antwerpsche clavecimbel- en orgelbouwers in de XVIe en XVIIe eeuwen', *Vlaamsch jaarboek voor muziekgeschiedenis IV, 1942*, 3–110
A. M. Pols: *Vijftig jaar Vlaamsche opera* (Antwerp, 1943)
W. Dehennin: 'Het muziekleven', *Antwerpen in de XVIIIde eeuw* (Antwerp, 1952), 301
——: 'Het muziekleven in de XIXde eeuw', *Antwerpen in de XIXde eeuw* (Antwerp, 1964), 384
R. Verbruggen: *KVO Antwerpen: gedenk-klanken 1893–1963* (Antwerp, 1965)
J. van Brabant and others: *Muziekcultuur in de Onze-Lieve-Vrouw kathedraal van Antwerpen* (Antwerp, 1968)
G. Spiessens: 'Geschiedenis van de gilde van de Antwerpse speellieden', *RbM*, xxii (1968), 5–50; xxx (1976), 24
——: 'De Antwerpse stadsspeellieden', *Noordgouw*, x (1970), 1–53
Antwerpen in de XVIde eeuw (Antwerp, 1975) [incl. articles by G. Persoons, H. Slenk and G. Spiessens]
G. Spiessens: 'De torenwachters van de Antwerpse Onze-Lieve-Vrouwekerk', *Noordgouw*, xvi (1976), 15–68
GODELIEVE SPIESSENS

Anvers (Fr.). ANTWERP.

Anvil (Fr. *enclume*; Ger. *Amboss*; It. *incudine*). In the orchestra, a percussion instrument of indefinite pitch. It may consist of one or two metal bars mounted on a resonating frame, or, on occasion, an actual blacksmith's anvil. In each case, although definable notes are produced, they are not usually prescribed. Praetorius illustrated a blacksmith's anvil struck with a sledgehammer in his *Syntagma musicum* (2/1619). An earlier reference to the instrument occurs in Agricola's *Musica instrumentalis deutsch* (1528). In the Anvil Chorus of Verdi's *Il trovatore* two anvils (*incudini*) are required. Wagner scored for one anvil in the forging song in *Siegfried*, and for 18 in *Das Rheingold*. Other notable instances of the use of the anvil in orchestral scores include Auber's *Le maçon*; Gounod's *Philémon et Baucis*; Berlioz's *Benvenuto Cellini*; Bax's Third Symphony; Walton's *Belshazzar's Feast*; Varèse's *Ionisation*; and Britten's church opera *The Burning Fiery Furnace*.

JAMES BLADES

Anvilla, Adriano (*fl* 1566–8). Italian composer. He is known by compositions published in two of the collections edited by Giulio Bonagiunta: five four-voice madrigals (in *RISM* 1566²) and one five-voice piece (in 1568¹⁶).

Anzalone [Ansalone]. Italian family of musicians, teachers and composers. 14 members of this Neapolitan family over four generations were active in the later 16th century and up to the middle of the 17th, notably as wind players. Many of them were employed in the royal chapel at Naples, and several members of the third generation taught in the city's conservatories. The three members of this generation discussed below, of whom the first and third at least were cousins, were also composers; all three, together with at least one other member of the family, died as a result of the plague of 1656. Giacinto (*b* Naples, 13 March 1606; *d* Naples,

1656) was from 1630 until his death director of the Conservatorio della Pietà dei Turchini and also *maestro di cappella* of the Chiesa di Monte Oliveto. His only extant print is *Psalmi de vespere a quattro voci, con un Laudate pueri alla venetiana*, op.3 (Naples, 1635), and a *canzona francese* for keyboard survives in the so-called Cemino manuscript (*I-Nc* 73, olim 34.5.28; transcr. in Oncley). Francesco (*b* Naples, 7 Oct 1607; *d* Naples, 1656 or 1657) was a violinist in the royal chapel and is recorded as a violin teacher at two conservatories: at the Poveri di Gesù Cristo in 1633 and at the Pietà dei Turchini from 1641 until his death. There are several manuscript motets by him (in *I-Nf*). Andrea (*d* Naples, 1656) was a musician at Castelnuovo; four dances by him are extant (in *RISM* 1620¹⁴).

BIBLIOGRAPHY
RicordiE
S. Cerreto: *Della prattica musica vocale e strumentale* (Naples, 1605/R1969), 158
S. di Giacomo: *I quattro antichi conservatorii musicali di Napoli* (Milan, 1924–8), i, 35; ii, 297, 305, 311; iii, 68
U. Prota-Giurleo: 'La musica a Napoli nel seicento (dal Gesualdo allo Scarlatti)', *Samnium*, i/4 (1928), 84f
——: 'I musici di Castelnuovo', *Corriere di Napoli* (5 April 1940), 3
F. Strazzullo: 'Inediti per la storia della musica a Napoli', *Il Fuidoro*, ii (1955), 106; additions by U. Prota-Giurleo, 273
W. Apel: 'Die süditalienische Clavierschule des 17. Jahrhunderts', *AcM*, xxxiv (1962), 128
L. A. Oncley: *The Conservatorio di Musica San Pietro a Majella Manuscript No.34.5.28: Transcription and Commentary* (diss., Indiana U., 1966)
KEITH A. LARSON, ALEXANDER SILBIGER

Aoidos (Gk.: 'singer'). Term used by Homer to describe epic singers (e.g. Phemius and Demodocus in the *Odyssey*) who sang and accompanied themselves on the PHORMINX or kitharis. Their tradition, which must underlie the poetry of the *Iliad* and *Odyssey* themselves, was an oral one; recent studies have explored its similarities with traditions such as that of the modern Yugoslav heroic epic sung to the accompaniment of the *gusle*. From the 6th century BC the *aoidos* in the older sense was replaced by the rhapsode ('stitcher of songs', a term not found in Homer), or professional declaimer of epic, without musical accompaniment. The change may be due to the increased size of audiences at that time; but the precise relationship between the *aoidos* of the early oral tradition and the rhapsode is not clear.

BIBLIOGRAPHY
G. S. Kirk: *The Songs of Homer* (Cambridge, 1962)
GEOFFREY CHEW

Äolsharfe (Ger.). AEOLIAN HARP.

Apel, Matthäus. See LÖWENSTERN, MATTHÄUS APELLES VON.

Apel, Nikolas (*b* Königshofen, *c*1475; *d* Leipzig, 1537). German cleric and scholar. He is of importance to the music historian as the first owner of one of the major sources for German music of the last quarter of the 15th century (*D-LEu* 1494). He studied at Leipzig University (1492–7) and began teaching in 1497 simultaneously with beginning his theological studies. He held several important posts in the university: deacon in 1508–9 and 1514–15, rector in 1514 and procancellarius in 1518.

Apel's connection with the manuscript is established by a note inside the back cover that Nikolas Apel of Königshofen paid three groschen for its binding in 1504. Other notes inside the front cover, primarily references to the deaths of different individuals and copies of various texts, are in the same hand, which is not the same as that of the texts to the music. Thus it is unlikely that Apel copied the manuscript himself; whether he directed the making of the book, received the individual unbound gatherings as a gift, or took some other part in its origin is not known.

BIBLIOGRAPHY
R. Gerber and L. Finscher, eds.: *Der Mensuralkodex des Nikolas Apel*, EDM, 1st ser., xxxii–xxxiv (1956–75)

TOM R. WARD

Apel, Willi (*b* Konitz, Germany [now Chojnice, Poland], 10 Oct 1893). American musicologist of German birth. He studied mathematics at the universities of Bonn and Munich (1912–14) and, after war service, at the University of Berlin (1918–22). Active as a pianist and music teacher, his interests turned to musicology while he was at the Freie Schulgemeinde at Wickersdorf (1922–8), and he was largely self-taught as a musicologist. He took his doctorate in Berlin in 1936, the year of his immigration to the USA, with a dissertation on 15th- and 16th-century tonality. He was a lecturer at Harvard University (1938–42) and professor of musicology at Indiana University, Bloomington (1950–70); he was made professor emeritus in 1963, though he continued to teach until 1970, and was awarded an honorary doctorate in 1972.

When Apel arrived in the USA he was junior in the company of hundreds of German-speaking scholars and artists who immigrated there to the great fortune of American culture and education. He was just beginning his productive years and his career was thereafter essentially 'American'. His first large books in English, addressed to students in a newly expanding subject, were remarkable for their timeliness and durability. The *Notation of Polyphonic Music* has served since 1942 as an essential tool for young scholars. The *Harvard Dictionary of Music* was to many the key to an attitude of 'historical equality' in which earlier and exotic musics received as much attention as the familiar ground. The same attitude was reflected in the *Historical Anthology of Music*, a well-chosen and -edited selection of music from ancient times to the 18th century. These three contributions from Apel as generalist and teacher were major agents in changing the climate of higher music education in the USA.

Apel then turned to his favourite studies: the transcription of 14th-century music, Latin chant and the history of keyboard music. The first of these arose out of his interest in notation. The problems of transcribing late 14th-century music had received full and sympathetic attention in his *Notation of Polyphonic Music*, and a selection of 50 pieces had appeared, with some additional facsimiles, in *French Secular Music of the Late Fourteenth Century*. His work in this sphere culminated in the three-volume collection of 14th-century French music (1970–71) which, with the work of Schrade, Hoppin and Harder, practically completes the whole repertory in excellent modern editions. In his *Gregorian Chant* Apel provided, for the first time in English, a reliable guide to the entire field of plainsong. Though leaning heavily on Peter Wagner's *Einführung*, the work makes its own substantial contribution and in particular has done a service in ventilating the question of the period and place of origin of the main repertory. Finally in his *Geschichte der Orgel- und Klaviermusik*,

an English translation and revision of which appeared in 1972, Apel exhaustively reviewed the entire body of keyboard music to 1700 in what has become an indispensable reference work. He is also the general editor of the Corpus of Early Keyboard Music, to which he has contributed ten volumes and his pupils many more.

WRITINGS

Die Fuge (Berlin, 1932)
'Die Tabulatur des Adam Ileborgh', *ZMw*, xvi (1934), 193
'Early Spanish Music for Lute and Keyboard Instruments', *MQ*, xx (1934), 289
Accidentien und Tonalität in den Musikdenkmälern des 15. und 16. Jahrhunderts (diss., U. of Berlin, 1936; Strasbourg, 1937/R1972)
'Accidentals and the Modes in 15th- and 16th-century Sources', *BAMS*, ii (1937), 289
'The Importance of Notation in Solving Problems of Early Music', *PAMS 1938*, 51
'The Partial Signatures in the Sources up to 1450', *AcM*, x (1938), 1
'A Postscript to "The Partial Signatures in the Sources up to 1450"', *AcM*, xi (1939), 40
The Notation of Polyphonic Music: 900–1600 (Cambridge, Mass., 1942, rev. 5/1961; Ger. trans., rev., 1970)
'Anton Bruckner', *American–German Review*, x/4 (1943–4), 8
Harvard Dictionary of Music (Cambridge, Mass., 1944, enlarged 2/1969)
'A Remark about the Basse Danse', *JRBM*, i (1946), 139
'The Collection of Photographic Reproductions at the Isham Memorial Library, Harvard University', *JRBM*, i (1946), 68, 144, 235
'The French Secular Music of the Late Fourteenth Century', *AcM*, xviii–xix (1946–7), 17
Masters of the Keyboard (Cambridge, Mass., 1947)
'Early History of the Organ', *Speculum*, xxiii (1948), 191
'Die menschliche Stimme als Instrument', *Stimmen* (1949), no.15, p.404
'From St Martial to Notre Dame', *JAMS*, xi (1949), 145
'Imitation Canons on L'homme armé', *Speculum*, xxv (1950), 367
'Anent a Ritornello in Monteverdi's Orfeo', *MD*, v (1951), 213
'Rondeaux, Virelais and Ballades in French 13th-century Song', *JAMS*, vii (1954), 121
'Remarks about the Isorhythmic Motet', *L'ars nova: Wégimont II 1955*, 139
'The Central Problem of Gregorian Chant', *JAMS*, ix (1956), 118
'The Earliest Polyphonic Composition and its Theoretical Background', *MD*, x (1956), 129
'Imitation in the 13th and 14th Centuries', *Essays on Music in Honor of Archibald Thompson Davison* (Cambridge, Mass., 1957), 25
Review of L. Schrade, ed.: *Polyphonic Music of the Fourteenth Century*, *Speculum*, xxxii (1957), 863; xxxiii (1958), 433; *Notes*, xix (1961–2), 511
Gregorian Chant (Bloomington, Ind., 1958, 3/1966)
'The Birth of Polyphony'; 'The Notre-Dame School', *Music and Western Man*, ed. P. Garvie (London, 1958), 37; 43
'Bemerkungen zu den Organa von St Martial', *Miscelánea en homenaje a Monseñor Higinio Anglés* (Barcelona, 1958–61), 61
with R. T. Daniel: *The Harvard Brief Dictionary of Music* (Cambridge, Mass., 1960)
'Der Anfang des Präludiums in Deutschland und Polen', *Chopin Congress: Warszawa 1960*, 495
'Drei plus Drei plus Zwei = Vier plus Vier', *AcM*, xxxii (1960), 29
'Die handschriftliche Überlieferung der Klavierwerke Frescobaldis', *Festschrift Karl Gustav Fellerer* (Regensburg, 1962), 40
'Die Celler Orgeltabulatur von 1601', *Mf*, xix (1966), 142
Geschichte der Orgel- und Klaviermusik bis 1700 (Kassel, 1967; Eng. trans., rev., 1972)
'Probleme der Alternierung in der liturgischen Orgelmusik bis 1600', *Congresso internazionale sul tema Claudio Monteverdi e il suo tempo: Venezia, Mantova e Cremona 1968*, 171
'Solo Instrumental Music', *The Age of Humanism 1540–1630*, NOHM, iv (1968), 602–708
'Der deutsche Orgelchoral um 1600', *Musa-mens-musici: im Gedenken an Walther Vetter* (Leipzig, 1969), 67
'Bach erede della tradizione', *NRMI*, iii (1969), 3
'Music and Mathematics in the Middle-ages', *Musica e arte figurativa nei secoli X–XII: XIII convegno del Centro di studi sulla spiritualità medievale: Todi 1972*, 133–66
'La harpe de melodie', *Scritti in onore di Luigi Ronga* (Milan and Naples, 1973), 28
'Studien über die frühe Violinmusik', *AMw*, xxx (1973), 153; xxxi (1974), 185; xxxii (1975), 272; xxxiii (1976), 213
'Orgelmusik in Ost-Europa im 15. und 16. Jahrhundert', *Musica antiqua Europae orientalis IV: Bydgoszcz 1975*, 391
'Klaviermusik', §§I–VI, 'Orgelmusik', §B, I–III, *MGG*
Further articles and many reviews in *Speculum* and *JAMS*

EDITIONS

Musik aus früher Zeit für Klavier (Mainz, 1934)

Concord Classics for the Piano (Boston, 1938)

with A. T. Davison: *Historical Anthology of Music*, i (Cambridge, Mass., 1946, rev. 2/1950); ii (Cambridge, 1950)

French Secular Music of the Late Fourteenth Century (Cambridge, Mass., 1950)

Keyboard Music of the Fourteenth and Fifteenth Centuries, CEKM, i (1963)

M. Facoli: Collected Works, CEKM, ii (1963)

C. Antegnati: L'Antegnata intavolatura, CEKM, ix (1965)

The Tablature of Celle, c.1600, CEKM, xvii (1967)

A. Reincken: Collected Keyboard Works, CEKM, xvi (1967)

J. U. Steigleder: Compositions for Keyboard, CEKM, xiii (1968–9)

P. Cornet: Collected Keyboard Works, CEKM, xxvi (1969)

French Secular Compositions of the Fourteenth Century, CMM, liii (1970–71)

Spanish Organ Masters after Antonio de Cabezón, CEKM, xiv (1971)

D. Strungk and P. Mohrhardt: Original Compositions for Organ, CEKM, xxiii (1973)

J. Jimenez: Collected Organ compositions, CEKM, xxxi (1975)

BIBLIOGRAPHY

H. Tischler, ed.: *Essays in Musicology: a Birthday Offering for Willi Apel* (Bloomington, Ind., 1968) [incl. C. G. Rayner: 'Willi Apel: a Complete Bibliography', 185]

JOHN REEVES WHITE/JOHN CALDWELL

Apel Codex (*D-LEu* 1494). See SOURCES, MS, §IX, 6, and SOURCES OF INSTRUMENTAL ENSEMBLE MUSIC TO 1630, §4.

Apell [Capelli], **David August von** (*b* Kassel, 23 Feb 1754; *d* Kassel, 30 Jan 1832). German composer and author. The son of a tax official, Apell followed his father's profession and was employed in the treasury at Kassel; he also had some musical instruction from local court musicians. Once settled in his profession, Apell concentrated on both composition (public performances date from 1780) and conducting; he founded and directed a philharmonic society. He received many honours in the course of his career, including honorary membership of the Accademia Filarmonica in Bologna and the Stockholm Royal Academy of Music. For the mass composed in 1800 for Pope Pius VII he received the Order of the Golden Spur. From 1815 he was vice-president of the Kassel Academy of Fine Arts. In 1792 Count Wilhelm IX (later Elector Wilhelm I) made him Intendant of the court theatre, and he remained at Kassel throughout the wars with France. In 1822, however, possibly as the result of intrigues, he was relieved of all theatrical duties. He died alone and in poverty.

Apell's compositions were admired by his contemporaries, including Gerber, but he outlived their fame. His writings include *Galerie der vorzüglichsten Tonkünstler und merkwürdigsten Musik-Dilettanten in Cassel vom Anfang des XVI Jahrhunderts bis auf gegenwärtige Zeiten* (Kassel, 1806), an account of the musicians of Kassel from the 16th century; this work remains his principal achievement.

WORKS
(selective list)

SACRED

Mass, 4vv, insts, Kassel, 1799, *D-B*

Missa pontificale: Kyrie, Laudamus, Crucifixus, Benedictus, solo vv, 4vv, str, org, *US-Wc*; Crucifixus and Benedictus pubd separately (Erfurt, n.d.)

Mass, 4vv, insts, 1817; Magnificat, S, 4vv, insts, 1818: both *D-Dlb*

Te Deum, 4vv, insts (Mainz, 1815); Ave corpus, 4vv (Bologna and Milan, n.d.)

Psalm lxvi (n.p., n.d.); Vespers, 4vv, insts, *US-Wc*

Lasset unsere Lieder erschallen (cantata), 4vv, insts, 1795, *D-B*

SECULAR

11 theatrical works, all lost except: Euthyme und Lyris (ballet), Kassel, 1782, *D-DS*; Anakreon (Singspiel, 1), 1824, *DS*; Griselda (opera), 1 aria in *Bds*

Il trionfo della musica (cantata), 4vv, orch (Mainz, *c*1787)

La gelosia (cantata, Metastasio), 1786, *DS*; 5 other cantatas, lost

Basta così, S, orch, *WRgm*

Scena e duetto, S, A, orch (Offenbach, n.d.)

Duetto con recitativo, 2vv, kbd (Offenbach, n.d.)

[6] Canzonette di Metastasio (Kassel, 1784)

La partenza, 2vv, hpd (Erfurt, n.d.)

3 symphonies, 1783; 3 quartets, 1784; pieces for orch and for wind insts: all lost

BIBLIOGRAPHY

EitnerQ; FétisB; GerberNL

W. Lynker: *Geschichte des Theaters und der Musik in Kassel* (Kassel, 2/1886)

R. Lebe: *Ein deutsches Hoftheater* (Kassel, 1964)

JEFFRY MARK/DAVID CHARLTON

Apelles von Löwenstern, Matthäus. See LÖWENSTERN, MATTHÄUS APELLES VON.

Aperghis, Georges (*b* Athens, 23 Dec 1945). Greek composer. He studied serialism with Yannis Papaioannou in 1963 and that same year left for Paris, where he took lessons in conducting (with Dervaux) and percussion. However, he completed none of these courses; the determining influence on him came rather in 1964, when he met Xenakis. This is apparent in his first compositions, the *Antistixis* and *Anakroussis* series, which were played in Paris and in Athens in 1967. But within two years he had turned in the direction of Kagel, producing a large number of theatrical projects, often of an 'absurd' character. *Sports et rebondissements*, for example, took advantage of the location for which it was written (a sports hall) to propose some comparisons between instrumentalists and athletes. Even his later non-dramatic pieces, such as the Piece for percussionists, depend on visual effect. A day was devoted to his works at the 1974 La Rochelle Festival, the climax being *Parcours*, in which the visitor to a modest stately home found himself the spectator of situations not normally encountered in such surroundings.

WORKS
(selective list)

Antistixis, 12 str, 1967; Antistixis III, orch, 1967; Anakroussis I–II, 7 insts, 1967; Freak Map, 8 insts, 1968; Music for an Orange Girl, 21 insts, 1968; Contrepoint, 12 str, 1968; Plastic-piece, 2 orch, 1968; Bis (music-theatre, J. C. Moineau), 1968; Libretto, orch, 1969; Variations, 10 insts, 1969; Color Music, 19 insts, 1969; B–A–C–H, 40vv, orch, 1969; Eluding Game, 10 insts, 1970; Entretiens, tape, 1970; Awake, 6 ob/tpt, 1970; Musical Box, hpd, 1970; Qt, 4 db, 1970; Qt, 4 perc, 1970; Puzzles, 12 insts, 1970

Lecture (music-theatre), lv, pf, tape, 1970; Vesper, oratorio, S, Mez, Ct, T, Bar, ens, 1970; Symplexis, 22 jazz insts, orch, 1970; Simata, prepared pf/hpd, 1970; Kryptogramma, 6 perc, 1970; La tragique histoire du nécromancien Hiéronimo et de son miroir, lv, gui, vc, marionettes, 1971; Von Zeit zu Zeit, 16 insts, 1971; Oraison funèbre, Bar, actress, 6 insts, tape, 1971; Hommage à Jules Verne, 17 insts, 1972; Conc. grosso, 30 insts, 1972; Ascoltare stanca, 17 insts, 1972; Die Wände haben Ohren, orch, 1972; Ov., 2 musicians, 1972

Jacques le fataliste (opera, after Diderot), Lyons, 1974; Parcours (theatre piece for house), 1974; Piece, 8/14 perc, 1974; Sports et rebondissements (theatre piece for sports hall), 1974; De la nature de l'eau (music-theatre), 1974; Il gigante Golia, S, ens, 1975; Les lauriers sont coupés, S, Mez, fl, ob, eng hn, bn, trbn, va, 1975; Mouvement, cl, vn, va, vc, pf, 1975; Quartet, B/hn, vn, va, vc, 1975; Récitatif de concours, lv, fl, cl, vc, pf, 1975; Etudes d'harmoniques, 2 vn, vc, 1976; Histoires de loup, vv, ens, 1976

Principal publisher: Salabert

PAUL GRIFFITHS

Aperto (It.: 'open', 'clear', 'frank', 'bold', 'plain'). (1) A direction for horn players to return to normal after playing stopped notes (*chiuso*).

(2) A direction in string music to play on the open string.

(3) A direction in piano music to play with the damper pedal down.

(4) In medieval music, particularly in the ESTAMPIE, but also in the DUCTIA and in many song forms, *aperto* and *chiuso* are used in the same sense as the modern words 'prima volta' and 'seconda volta'. Normally the open ending (*aperto*) was on a less final pitch than the closed ending.

(5) A word used several times by Mozart in the tempo designation *allegro aperto*. Examples are the first movements of the Violin Concerto in A K219 and the Piano Concerto in B♭ K238, as well as two strikingly similar early arias: 'Per la gloria in questo seno' from *Ascanio in Alba* and 'D'ogni colpa la colpa maggiore' from *Betulia liberata*. Rudolf Steglich ('Mozarts Mailied: Allegro Aperto?', *MJb 1962–3*, 96) attempted to draw general conclusions about the meaning of *aperto*. The direction is found very rarely in the work of composers other than Mozart.

For bibliography *see* TEMPO AND EXPRESSION MARKS.

DAVID FALLOWS

Apeso. Sign paired with the *exo* in Greek EKPHONETIC NOTATION.

Apfel, Ernst (*b* Heidelberg, 6 May 1925). German musicologist. After studying Protestant church music at the Church Music Institute in Heidelberg (1945–51), he returned there to study music theory (with W. Fortner) and organ. From 1947 he also studied musicology with Georgiades, medieval Latin with W. Bulst and philosophy with K. Löwith at the University of Heidelberg; he took his doctorate in 1953 with a dissertation on discant in medieval music theory. From 1953 to 1956 he was research assistant and assistant lecturer in the musicology department of the University of Heidelberg; he then held a scholarship from the Deutsche Forschungsgemeinschaft and the Heidelberg Academy of Sciences (1956–61) before becoming assistant lecturer at the musicology institute of the University of Saarbrücken (1961–3). He completed his *Habilitation* in musicology at Saarbrücken with a dissertation on medieval English music in 1962. In 1963 he was made lecturer at Saarbrücken University, in 1969 *ausserplanmässiger Professor* and in 1972 professor for life. Apfel's main field of research has been in the field of the history of compositional techniques and the history and systematization of music theory.

WRITINGS

Der Diskant in der Musiktheorie des 12.–15 Jahrhunderts (diss., U. of Heidelberg, 1953)
'Der klangliche Satz und der freie Diskantsatz im 15. Jh.', *AMw*, xii (1955), 297
'Zur Entstehungsgeschichte des Palestrinasatzes', *AMw*, xiv (1957), 30
'England und der Kontinent in der Musik des späten Mittelalters', *Mf*, xiv (1961), 276
'Über einige Zusammenhänge zwischen Text und Musik im Mittelalter, besonders in England', *AcM*, xxxiii (1961), 47
'Die klangliche Struktur der spätmittelalterlichen Musik als Grundlage der Dur-Moll-Tonalität', *Mf*, xv (1962), 212
'Ostinato und Kompositionstechnik bei den englischen Virginalisten der elisabethanischen Zeit', *AMw*, xix–xx (1962–3), 29
Studien zur Satztechnik der mittelalterlichen englischen Musik (Habilitationsschrift, U. of Saarbrücken, 1962; Heidelberg, 1959)
'Wandlungen der Polyphonie von Palestrina zu Bach', *AMw*, xxi (1964), 60
Beiträge zu einer Geschichte der Satztechnik von der frühen Motette bis Bach (Munich, 1964–5)
'Probleme der theoretischen Harmonik aus geschichtlich-satztechnischer Sicht', *Festschrift für Walter Wiora* (Kassel, 1967), 140
'Volkskunst und Hochkunst in der Musik des Mittelalters', *AMw*, xxv (1968), 81
'Wandlungen des Gerüstsatzes vom 16. zum 17. Jh.', *AMw*, xxvi (1969), 81, 209
Anlage und Struktur der Motetten im Codex Montpellier (Heidelberg, 1970)
Zur Vor- und Frühgeschichte der Symphonie, Begriff, Wesen und Entwicklung vom Ensemble- zum Orchestersatz (Baden-Baden, 1972)
with C. Dahlhaus: *Studien zur Theorie und Geschichte der musikalischen Rhythmik und Metrik* (Munich, 1974)
Grundlagen einer Geschichte der Satztechnik (Saarbrücken, 1974–6)
'Rhythmisch-metrische und andere Beobachtungen an Ostinatobässen', *AMw*, xxxiii (1976), 48
Aufsätze und Vorträge zur Musikgeschichte und historischen Musiktheorie (Saarbrücken, 1977)

HANS HEINRICH EGGEBRECHT

Aphrem. See EPHREM SYRUS.

Ap Huw [ap Hugh], **Robert** (*b* Bodwigan, Llanddeusant, Anglesey, *c*1580; *d* Pen-y-Dentyr, Llandegfan, 1665). Welsh harpist and poet. He was the writer of the unusual manuscript of Welsh harp music, now *GB-Lbm* Add.14905. Compiled possibly about 1613, it contains the only extant contemporary copy of the harp music of his time, although there is another shorter manuscript (*Lbm* Add.14970) that was copied by Iolo Morgannwg in about 1800 from an earlier manuscript.

Robert ap Huw was virtually the last Welsh harpist to play and understand the ancient Welsh tradition, for there is no trace of this style in later harp music. According to 15th- and 16th-century Welsh treatises there was early contact between Welsh and Irish harpists. Some of the technical terms used in ap Huw's manuscript sound Irish, and the fact that these words had become corrupt by 1600 (Celtic scholars cannot now identify their etymology) confirms the likelihood of this Irish influence.

A poem by Huw Machno calls ap Huw King James I's musician, and from ap Huw's will we know that the King's arms (in silver) were on his harp. It is unlikely that he remained long at the royal court, for no records of payment to him have been discovered. He may have escaped with relief from the treachery and deceit of the Stuart court to the quiet of his country home in Anglesey; certainly he ended his days as a well-to-do gentleman farmer. He was an accomplished poet and copied in his manuscripts the poetry of his contemporaries (one such manuscript is *Lbm* Add.14918).

There were 30 strings on his harp, mostly gut; these he would play with the medieval nail-technique, similar to that of a lutenist.

None of the many interpretations of his manuscript has been satisfactory, for all transcribers have made assumptions about the Welsh 'keys', namely, the five principal ones: *cras gywair*, *lleddf gywair*, *gogywair*, *isgywair* and *bragod gywair*. Ap Huw's manuscript shows (on pp.108–9) the first two as pentatonic scales, and *gogywair*, in *Lbm* Add.15036, f.150v, is given as a minor scale. But the keynotes of the scales were variable; according to this manuscript 'whichever keynote the harpist selects, for *gogywair* he must flatten by a semitone the 3rd above the keynote'. Further, certain strings on ap Huw's harp would be re-tuned, in the manner of scordatura, by a semitone or a tone, as in *cras gywair*, giving a scale of *c′, d′, e′, e′, g′, a′, a′, c″*. It is not generally realized that his harp was chromatic, with hooks (*gwrachïod*) emerging from the soundboard; these were pressed on to the strings, raising their pitch by a semitone or a tone, and these strings were then termed 'oblique' (*tannau lleddf*). Indeed, sharp signs are found in music at the end of Iolo Morgannwg's manuscript.

In Welsh literary manuscripts of the 16th and 17th centuries hundreds of pieces of music – airs, divisions and laments – are named. It is sad that the only surviving contemporary manuscript so inadequately reveals the full nature of medieval Welsh music.

See also WALES, §I.

BIBLIOGRAPHY
Myfyrian Archaiology of Wales (Denbigh, 1801–7, 2/1870)
H. Lewis, ed.: *Musica neu Beroriaeth* (Cardiff, 1936) [facs.]
P. Crossley-Holland: 'Secular Homophonic Medieval Music in Wales', *ML*, xxiii (1942), 135
T. Dart: 'Robert ap Huw's Manuscript of Welsh Harp Music (c1613)', *GSJ*, xxi (1968), 52
J. Travis: *Miscellanea musica celtica* (Brooklyn, 1968)
O. Ellis: 'Welsh Music: History and Fancy', *Transactions of the Honourable Society of Cymmrodorion* (1973–4)
——: 'Ap Huw: Untying the Knot', *Soundings*, vi (1977), 67
OSIAN ELLIS

A piacere (It.: 'at pleasure'). An indication to the performer that he may use his discretion as to the manner of performance of a passage so marked, particularly in the matter of time. It is generally prefixed to a cadenza, or cadenza-like passage, in solo music, to indicate that the expressions and the alterations, whether of time or force, are left to the will of the individual performer. Liszt, who used the direction more than most, tended to use *giusto* to denote a return to regularity.

For bibliography *see* TEMPO AND EXPRESSION MARKS.
GEORGE GROVE/DAVID FALLOWS

Apiarius [Biener], **Mathias** (*b* Berching, nr. Eichstätt, Bavaria, *c*1500; *d* Berne, autumn 1554). German music printer and publisher. He settled in Basle, where he worked as a bookbinder and was given citizenship on 3 April 1527, having been admitted to the Saffran Guild on 10 December 1525. He seems to have been associated with the Reformation at an early stage; he attended the religious debates held in Berne in 1528, and it was possibly at this time that he met the Berne precentor Cosmas Alder. In 1536 he published three four-part songs by Alder, in a book of songs produced jointly with Peter Schöffer in Strasbourg; in 1553 he also published hymns by Alder. From the middle of 1533 to 1537 he printed numerous Reformation writings (e.g. by W. F. Capito and M. Bucer) in Strasbourg, and he and Schöffer jointly published works on music theory and practice; their association probably stemmed from Apiarus's thorough knowledge of music and his contact with composers. In 1539 he opened the first printing press in Berne, and on 19 January he became a citizen of Berne. Besides music he published historical, religious and literary works, and also many songsheets (usually without the melodies). Because of their political and religious content these song publications often led to disputes within the Swiss regions. For financial reasons Apiarius worked for many years as bookbinder to the Berne government. The works published jointly with Schöffer were double-printed, but those produced in Berne were simple type-prints, and were all of good quality (see Bloesch for a complete bibliography of Apiarius's output). His son Samuel (*c*1530–90) took over the printing press after his father's death, but apart from a considerable number of songsheets he did not publish any new music. Mathias's second son, Sigfried, also worked as a bookbinder in Berne, where he became a Stadtpfeifer in 1553. Wannenmacher's *Bicinia* (*RISM* 1553³¹) were dedicated to Sigfried and two other Stadtpfeifer (Michel Copp and Wendlin Schärer). This publication also contained two bicinia by Mathias (*Ach hulff mich leid* and *Es taget vor dem walde*).

BIBLIOGRAPHY
A. Thürlings: 'Der Musikdruck mit beweglichen Metalltypen im 16. Jahrhundert und die Musikdrucke des Mathias Apiarius in Strassburg und Bern', *VMw*, viii (1892), 389
A. Fluri: 'Mathias Apiarius, der erste Buchdrucker Berns (1537–1554)', *Neues Berner Taschenbuch* (1897), 196–253
——: 'Die Brüder Samuel und Sigfrid Apiarius, Buchdrucker in Bern (1554 bis 1565)', *Neues Berner Taschenbuch* (1898), 168–233
——: 'Mathias Apiarius, Berns erster Buchdrucker', *Schweizerisches Gutenbergmuseum*, xiv (1928), 105; xvi (1930), 6, 47, 120
W. Schuh: 'Anmerkungen zu den Berner Musikdrucken des Mathias Apiarius', *SMz*, lxix (1929), 282
A. Geering: *Die Vokalmusik in der Schweiz zur Zeit der Reformation* (Aarau, 1933)
H. Bloesch, ed.: *Dreissig Volkslieder aus den ersten Pressen der Apiarius, im Faksimiledruck herausgegeben mit einer Einleitung und Bibliographie* (Berne, 1937)
K. J. Lüthi: 'Die Einführung der Buchdruckerkunst in Bern 1537', *Schweizerisches Gutenbergmuseum*, xxiii (1937), 5–58 [with 16 facs.]
F. Ritter: *Histoire de l'imprimerie alsacienne au XVe et XVIe siècles* (Strasbourg, 1955)
J. Benzing: 'Peter Schöffer der jüngere, Musikdrucker zu Mainz, Worms, Strassburg und Venedig (tätig 1512–1542)', *Jb für Liturgik und Hymnologie*, iv (1958–9), 133
JÜRG STENZL

ApIvor, Denis (*b* Collinstown, 14 April 1916). Irish composer of Welsh origin. His early musical education was as a chorister, at Christ Church, Oxford, and at Hereford Cathedral. Since his parents were not in favour of a musical career he studied medicine at London University, remaining essentially self-taught as a composer until, from the age of 21, he had private lessons with Hadley and Rawsthorne. His earliest compositions are songs which reflect the influence of Warlock and van Dieren: the Chaucer Songs op.1 were dedicated to van Dieren's memory. ApIvor regarded the war as 'a severe set-back' in his development as a composer; he had reached a decisive stage only to find that almost all musical activity was impossible for six years. Nevertheless, in 1942 he began work on the libretto of his first opera *She Stoops to Conquer*. The basically light style of this and other early pieces is, in part, a reflection of Lambert's influence. Lambert helped to obtain a commission from Covent Garden for a ballet (*A Mirror for Witches* op.19) and he conducted the première of ApIvor's Eliot setting *The Hollow Men* in 1951.

She Stoops to Conquer can be regarded as completing the first phase of ApIvor's development. In the Piano Concerto op.13 (1948) there are the first signs of an interest in 12-note technique, and for the next ten years ApIvor explored a serial method which did not necessarily eliminate all tonal references. *Blood Wedding* (1953), a Royal Ballet commission based on the play by Lorca, was a success, and when the Sadler's Wells Trust commissioned an opera in 1955 he chose Lorca's tragedy *Yerma*. The work remained unstaged though a radio version was broadcast in 1961. After *Yerma*, ApIvor's style became more radical, the serialism atonal and athematic. Most of the works of this period exploit short forms, smaller instrumental groups and more polyphonic textures. ApIvor has shown no interest in either aleatory or electronic techniques, but from 1968 he favoured a freer serialism. The extent of his development – from post-Warlock to post-Webern – is obvious enough, and the fact that his music has been little played or published may be due in part to the stylistic distance which he has travelled.

WORKS

STAGE

She Stoops to Conquer, op.12 (opera, ApIvor, after Goldsmith), 1942–7; The Goodman of Paris, op.18, ballet, 1951; Suite concertante, op.18a, pf, small orch, 1951; A Mirror for Witches, op.19, ballet, 1951, sym. suite, op.19a, 1954; La belle dame sans merci, op.20 (television ballet), lost; Blood Wedding, op.23, ballet after Lorca, 1953; Saudades, op.27, ballet, 1954; Yerma, op.28 (opera, M. Slater, after Lorca), 1956; Ubu roi, op.40 (opera, ApIvor, after Jarry), 1966; Corporal Jan, op.42, ballet, 1967; Bouvard et Pécuchet, op.49 (opera, ApIvor, after Flaubert), 1971

CHORAL AND VOCAL

The Hollow Men, op.5 (Eliot), Bar, chorus, orch, 1939, rev. 1946; Estella Marina, op.10 (P. de Corban), small chorus, str, org, 1946; Thamar and Amnon, op.25 (Lorca, trans. ApIvor), solo vv, chorus, orch, 1954; Cantata, op.32 (Thomas: Altarwise by Owl Light), solo vv, speaker, chorus, 21 insts, 1960; Chorales, op.38 (H. Manning: The Secret Sea), Bar, chorus, orch, 1964–5; Triptych, op.59, 3 carols, SATB, org, 1975

Chaucer Songs, op.1, 1v, str qt, 1936; Alas Parting, op.2 (Elizabethan), 1v, str qt, 1937; Songs, op.3 (Wyatt, Beddoes, Dowson etc), 1v, pf, 1936–40; 7 Songs, op.6 (Scottish anon., Goldsmith, Corvo, Aldington), 1v, pf, 1936–40; 6 canciones de Federico Garcia Lorca, op.8, 1v, gui/pf, 1945; Here we go Round, op.11, children's songs, 1949; Landscapes, op.15, T, fl, cl, hn, str trio, 1950; 4 Songs, op.24 (Beddoes), 1v, pf, 1954; Fern Hill, op.56 (Thomas), T, 11 insts ad lib, 1973; Vox populi, op.58, 14 songs, 1v, pf ad lib, 1974–5

ORCHESTRAL

Fantasia on a Song of Diego Pisador, op.4, str, 1938; Pf Conc., op.13, 1948; Conc., op.16, vn, 15 insts, 1950; Bouvard et Pécuchet, op.17, ov., destroyed; Sym. no.1, op.22, 1952; Concertino, op.26, gui, orch, 1954; Overtones, op.33, 9 variations after Klee, 1961; Sym. no.2, op.36, 1963; Str Abstract, op.43, str trio, orch, 1967; Tarot, op.46, 22 insts, 1969; Neumes, op.47, 1969; The Tremulous Silence (El silencio ondulado), op.51, gui, chamber orch, 1972; Resonance of the Southern Flora, op.54, 1972; Vn Conc., op.61, 1975; Vn Conc., op.64, 1976–7

CHAMBER AND INSTRUMENTAL

Concertante, op.7, cl, pf, perc, 1945, arr. as op.7a, cl, orch, 1945; Sonata, op.9, vn, pf, 1946; 7 Pf Pieces, op.14, 1949; Aquarelles, op.21, pf, lost; Variations, op.29, gui, 1956; 7 Pf Pieces, op.30, 1960; Wind Qnt, op.31, 1960; Mutations, op.34, vc, pf, 1962; Animalcules, op.35, 12 pf pieces, 1962; Str Qt, op.37, 1964; Crystals, op.39, 6 insts, 1964

Harp, Piano, Piano-Harp, op.41, 1966; Ten String Design, op.44, vn, gui, 1968; The Lyre-playing Idol, op.45, 5 pf pieces, 1968; Discanti, op.48, gui, 1970; Orgelberg (Paul Klee Pieces II), op.50, org, 1972; Exotics Theatre (Klee Variations), op.52, 10 insts, 1972; Saeta, op.53, gui, 1972; Psycho-Pieces, op.55, cl, pf, 1973; Studies, op.57, solo wind insts, 1974; Cl Qnt, op.60, 1975; Liaison, op.62, gui, kbd, 1976; Str Qt no.2, op.63, 1976

Principal publishers: Bèrben, Oxford University Press, Schott

WRITINGS

'Bernard van Dieren', *Music Survey*, iii (1951), 270

'Setting The Hollow Men to Music', *T. S. Eliot: a Symposium for his 70th Birthday* (London, 1958), 89

'Three Ballets', *The Decca Book of Ballet*, ed. D. Drew (London, 1958), 35

BIBLIOGRAPHY

F. Routh: *Contemporary British Music* (London, 1972), 100ff

ARNOLD WHITTALL

Apodeipnon. The Byzantine office of Compline which completes the daily cycle of Orthodox services. Two forms exist, Great and Small, which comprise psalms, troparia and a doxology (*see* TROPARION).

Apollo. Ancient Greek god. The origins of Apollo remain uncertain. In myth he is the child of Leto and Zeus. His worship may have come into Greece from Macedonia; or possibly it travelled westward from Asia Minor. Often he was termed *Lykeios*: if the epithet means 'wolf-god', he may originally have been a god of shepherds. This hypothesis would explain an active concern with music. It leaves unexplained the fact that he is constantly shown in art and literature with the kithara or lyre rather than the shepherd's panpipes (*syrinx*) or the aulos, although several Greek writers do associate him with reed-blown instruments.

The Homeric evidence indicates that Apollo's nature was complex. In the early passages of *Iliad* i, as the avenging archer-god, he angrily sends shafts of pestilence upon the Greek host, while at its close (603–4) he appears as the lyre-god accompanying the Muses' song; and in the *Odyssey* (xv.410–11) his arrows represent the painless cause of natural death. For Hesiod (*Theogony*, ll.94–5; *Shield of Heracles*, ll.201–3, cf *Odyssey* viii.488), writing perhaps during the later 8th century, as for the unknown authors of the *Homeric Hymn to Apollo* (iii.131, 182–5 are typical) in the succeeding period, his instrument is always the lyre and his musical role that of accompanist, not singer. The *Homeric Hymn to Hermes* (iv.502) contains the first known reference to his singing; Aeschylus (frag.350) continues the tradition.

During the 5th century, Apollo came to be regarded as the most vivid and brilliant figure among the 12 Olympian gods. Pythagorean thought, which credited music with a cosmic significance, had already long embodied many attributes of his worship; there is evidence that these included catharsis and ecstasy. In general, however, the god's province was taken to be all that is serene, ordered and rational. PLATO's preference for 'the instruments of Apollo' (*Republic*, ll.399el–3) comes out of a belief that precisely such qualities characterized the music of the kithara. Here the contrast is with the aulete MARSYAS; far more commonly, during much of the Hellenic period, it involved DIONYSUS instead.

Vase paintings of the earlier 5th century show Apollo with the massive kithara. During succeeding decades he was represented as playing the smaller and lighter lyre now identified with his name. Traditions connecting him with music were particularly strong at his cult centre, Delphi, where the Pythian games honouring him began as exclusively musical competitions. The earliest form of the paean was apparently a hymn of supplication addressed to him as healer (as in *Iliad* i.473). Symbolic references to the lyre by poets and philosophers helped to establish his special place in Greek thought. Later, for the Romans, Apollo embodied the supreme values of music as a performing art and provided an ideal model of the professional musician.

BIBLIOGRAPHY

W. K. C. Guthrie: *The Greeks and Their Gods* (London and Boston, 1950, rev. 2/1954), 73ff, 183ff

J. Duchemin: *Hermès et Apollon*, La houlette et la lyre, i (Paris, 1960)

G. Wille: *Musica romana* (Amsterdam, 1967), 515ff, 533ff

For further bibliography *see* GREECE.

WARREN ANDERSON

Apollo Club. Choral society founded in CHICAGO in 1872.

Apolloni [Apollonio, Appolloni], **Giovanni Filippo** (*b* Arezzo, *c*1635; *d* Arezzo, ?15 May 1688). Italian librettist. The name Apollonio Apolloni is spurious and refers to Giovanni Filippo (see Pirrotta). On the recommendation of Cardinal Giovanni Carlo de' Medici, he entered the service of Archduke Ferdinand Karl of Austria about September 1653, perhaps at the instigation of Cesti (also a native of Arezzo). During his service at Innsbruck he wrote the librettos for *Mars und Adonis* and *L'Argia* (both 1655, the latter performed with music by Cesti in honour of the visit of Queen Christina of Sweden) and *La Dori* (1657). He returned to Italy by 1659, perhaps again in the company of Cesti, and entered the service of Cardinal Flavio Chigi at Rome in

May 1660, remaining in that post until his death; at some point he was given an abbotship. Like Cesti, who in 1666 tried without success to obtain service for him at the imperial court at Vienna, he belonged to the circle of Salvator Rosa and G. B. Ricciardi. He set to verse *L'empio punito* of FILIPPO ACCIAIUOLI, a friend of Chigi, for the Teatro Tordinona, Rome, in 1669; he may have done the same for Acciaiuoli's *Girello* (Rome, 1668), and in any case he supplied the prologue for it. His other works include *Amor per vendetta, ovvero L'Alcasta* (Rome, 1673, music by Bernardo Pasquini; it is not clear whether this is the libretto of Apolloni which Matteo Noris revised for Venice in 1677 as *Astiage*), the 'componimento drammatico rusticale' *Con la forza d'amor si vince amor* (Pratolino, near Florence, 1679; perhaps identical with *La forza d'amore*, 'cantata scenica a 3 voci', set to music by P. P. Cappellini and later by Pasquini), the 'operetta à tre' *La Circe* (Frascati, 1668, music by Stradella), the opera *Adelinda* (Ariccia, 1673, music by P. S. Agostini) and the oratorios *Jefte* (Mantua, 1689, music by G. B. Tomasi), *L'Assalone* (in *I-Rli*) and *Oratorio dell'Angelo*.

Crescimbeni recognized Apolloni as 'one of the best followers' of GIACINTO ANDREA CICOGNINI. The work that most clearly shows him in that tradition is *La Dori*, which, with music by Cesti, rivalled *Giasone* and *Orontea* as one of the most widely performed Italian operas of the 17th century. *La Dori* relies heavily on mistaken identity and misunderstanding in its concentrated love plot, which makes little use of historical or pseudo-historical superstructure; it has in common with Cicognini's dramas much rapid dialogue, direct and lively language, strong but traditional comic elements and a 'surprise' resolution of the plot.

BIBLIOGRAPHY

Apolloni poesie (MS, *I-Rn* Ebor.26) [incl. texts set by Carissimi, Cesti, Stradella]
Other texts by Apolloni in *I-Fn* and *Rvat*
Raccolta di componimenti per musica del Sig.r Abb. Gio: Filippo Apolloni Aretino (MS, *I-PAc*) [incl. texts of oratorios and other dramatic works]
Versi per musica di G. F. A. P[oeta] A[retino], parte seconda (MS, *I-Rvat* Chigi L.VI.193) [incl. texts of cantatas and other works]
G. M. Crescimbeni: *L'istoria della volgar poesia* (Rome, 2/1714)
L. Allacci: *Drammaturgia* (Venice, enw. 2/1755)
A. Cametti: *Il teatro di Tordinona poi di Apollo* (Tivoli, 1938)
A. de Rinaldis, ed.: *Lettere inedite di Salvator Rosa a G. B. Ricciardi* (Rome, 1939)
U. Limentani, ed.: *Poesie e lettere inedite di Salvator Rosa* (Florence, 1950)
N. Pirrotta: 'Tre capitoli su Cesti', *La scuola romana: G. Carissimi – A. Cesti – M. Marazzoli*, Chigiana, x (1953), 59
W. Senn: *Musik und Theater am Hof zu Innsbruck* (Innsbruck, 1954)
N. Burt: 'Opera in Arcadia', *MQ*, xli (1955), 145
F. Schlitzer: *Intorno alla 'Dori' di Antonio Cesti* (Florence, 1957)
R. Lefevre: 'Accademici del '600; gli "Sfaccendati"', *Studi romani*, viii (1960), 154, 288
G. Macchia: *Vita, avventure e morte di Don Giovanni* (Bari, 1966) [incl. edn. of *L'empio punito*]
C. Schmidt: *The Operas of Antonio Cesti* (diss., Harvard U., 1973)
——: 'Antonio Cesti's "La Dori": a Study of Sources, Performance Traditions and Musical Style', *RIM*, x (1975), 455–98
——: '"La Dori" di Antonio Cesti: sussidi bibliografici', *RIM*, xi (1976), 197–229
M. Murata: 'Il carnevale a Roma sotto Clemente IX Rospigliosi', *RIM*, xii (1977), 83

THOMAS WALKER

Apolloni [Appoloni, Appolini], **Salvatore** [Salvadore] (*b* Venice, *c*1704). Italian composer. According to Caffi, he was closely associated with Baldassare Galuppi. Like Galuppi's father, he was a barber by trade and a part-time violinist. He was a friend of Galuppi's from childhood and it is likely that they both received early musical training from the elder Galuppi. A libretto of 1727 names him as first violinist of the Teatro di S Samuele in Venice. Caffi said that Apolloni was one of Baldassare Galuppi's few students, and eventually Galuppi made a place for him in the orchestra of the ducal chapel of St Mark's.

Apolloni is reputed to have had a lively, cheerful disposition, a fact according well with the lighthearted subjects of his music (of which none is known to survive). He gained an early local reputation as a composer of songs in the style of the Venetian gondoliers (barcarolles), serenatas and other occasional works. As a theatrical composer, he worked almost exclusively for Giuseppe Imer's troupe of comedians (i.e. for non-professional singers), suggesting that his musical style must have been relatively simple. His theatrical works, intermezzos and parodies of *opera seria*, catered to a taste for musical satire which according to Dent was peculiarly Venetian. Such parodies are a curious mixture of the *opera seria* and *buffa* conventions then current in Venice: the characters are people of high social degree (but one of the kings speaks in Venetian dialect); da capo exit arias are regularly used, but so are ensemble finales and short arias to open scenes. The works are much shorter than normal operas, whether serious or comic, and they contain about half as many musical numbers. Although early historians spoke slightingly of Apolloni's talents as a composer, performance records attest to his popularity at home and even beyond the Alps.

His works, all for the Teatro di S Samuele, are: *La fama dell'onore* (M. Miani, May 1727; revived in Vienna, 1730); *Le metamorfosi odiamorose* (A. Gori, carn. 1732; revived in Dresden, 1747, as *La Contesa di Mestre e Malghera*); *La Pelerina* (Goldoni-Gori, carn. 1734); and possibly *Il pastor fido* (carn. 1739). It was probably G. Maccari, rather than Apolloni, as is sometimes stated, who set Goldoni's later intermezzos.

BIBLIOGRAPHY

J.-B. de La Borde: *Essai sur la musique ancienne et moderne* (Paris, 1780/*R*1972), iii, 165
F. Caffi: *Storia della musica nella già cappella ducale di San Marco in Venezia dal 1318 al 1797* (Venice, 1854–5/*R*1931), i, 402f; ii, 67f
T. Wiel: *I teatri musicale veneziani del settecento* (Venice, 1897), 132
E. J. Dent: 'Giuseppe Maria Buini', *SIMG*, xiii (1911–12), 331
G. Ortolani, ed.: *C. Goldoni: Tutte le opere* (Verona, 1935–56), i, 716 and passim on Imer's troupe; x, 1217, 1226, 1232, 1234
O. E. Deutsch: 'Das Repertoire der höfischen Oper, der Hof- und der Staatsoper', *ÖMz*, xxiv (1969), 388

JAMES L. JACKMAN

Apollonicon. A large chamber organ including both keyboards and barrels constructed by the English organ builders Flight & Robson between 1812 and 1817. This MECHANICAL INSTRUMENT was for many years publicly exhibited by them at their London showrooms in St Martin's Lane. With the Apollonicon they attempted to reproduce mechanically the entire orchestra. A similar but smaller instrument built for Viscount Kirkwall is described at length and illustrated in Abraham Rees: *The Cyclopaedia* (London, 1819), xxv: article 'Organ'.

Apollonius of Perga (*b* Perga, Pamphylia; *fl* 2nd half of the 3rd century BC). Greek mathematician, whose work in conics and theoretical astronomy was of basic importance. He studied at Alexandria with the disciples of Euclid. The invention of a musical automaton was attributed to him by a 9th-century Arabic source, apparently without foundation. The device consisted of an aulos-like pipe, the holes of which were opened and stopped by a revolving cylinder similar to that of the modern player-piano or musical box, while wind was supplied by hydraulic pumps like those activating the hydraulis.

BIBLIOGRAPHY

H. G. Farmer: *The Organ of the Ancients: from Eastern Sources, Hebrew, Syriac and Arabic* (London, 1931), 79ff

J. Perrot: *L'orgue de ses origines hellénistiques à la fin du XIIIe siècle* (Paris, 1965; Eng. trans., adapted, 1971), 203

JAMES W. MᶜKINNON

Apollo Society. London tavern music club founded in 1731 by Maurice Greene; *see* LONDON, §VI, 1.

Apolytikion. The dismissal hymn in Byzantine services. Each major feast has its own apolytikion which is chanted before the conclusion of Vespers as well as in ORTHROS and during the liturgy.

Apostel, Hans Erich (*b* Karlsruhe, 22 Jan 1901; *d* Vienna, 30 Nov 1972). Austrian composer of German birth. After studying at the conservatory in his home town, he was appointed co-répétiteur and conductor at the Landestheater there. In 1921 he moved to Vienna, worked as a freelance artist and took lessons with Schoenberg (1921–5) and Berg (1925–35). From 1922 he gave private tuition in piano, theory and later composition, devoting himself particularly to slow learners. During the period of Nazi rule, Apostel's music was not performed in public. He obtained work as a publisher's reader at the end of World War II, and he was often invited to lecture at congresses (e.g. Prague 1948 and Darmstadt 1951) or to adjudicate at competitions and festivals. From 1947 to 1950 he was president of the Austrian section of the ISCM. His many honours include the Emil Hertaka Prize (for *Requiem*, 1937), the Major Art Prize of the City of Vienna (1948), a prize in the competition for the Austrian State Prize (for the Haydn Variations, 1952), the Major Austrian State Prize (1957) and the Major Monaco Composition Prize (for the Chamber Symphony, 1968). Apostel received the title of professor in 1948; in 1960 he was made a member of the Austrian Arts Council and in 1962 he became a corresponding member of the Vienna Secession. He was nominated honorary director of the North Carolina Music Society in 1963.

Apostel belonged to the second generation of the 'Second Viennese School'. His work showed a 'progression from lyrical expression to controlled architecture' (Kaufman). In an interview published by Kaufman he described his development as passing through four phases: first, 'a tonal-romantic . . ., or to put it more critically, an epigonal-bourgeois period'; secondly, 'an egocentric phase in expressionistic and – as determined historically at this stage of my development – dissonant garb'; thirdly, 'a period of reflection, and of coming to grips for the first time with the problems of 12-note technique' and lastly 'the realization that architecturally based musical content must reckon today with the application of the 12 moderated notes of our scale'.

No music from the first period survives: Apostel either withdrew or re-wrote the works of this time. To the second period belong the piano pieces *Kubiniana*, op.13 and the Johst and Rilke songs. These songs gained Apostel a reputation as one of the most talented lyricists of Schoenberg's circle. The third phase was characterized by free dodecaphony, the use of 12-note sets

without fixed serial ordering, e.g. in his Haydn Variations op.17. The first work based on a single 12-note series was the *Rondo ritmico* op.27 (1957) which opened Apostel's final period. Major works of these last years include the *Epigramme* op.33 and the *Paralipomena dodekaphonika* op.44. At this time he adopted a classical aesthetic – consciously orientated to Hanslick – with a pronounced emphasis on formal and architectural considerations and a rigid observance of 12-note serial principles. He often worked in three-, five- or seven-part palindromic structures (*ABA*, *ABCBA* or *ABCDCBA*) and, although he sought to give individuality to his forms, he was not always successful and some of his work is rather stereotyped. Throughout his career Apostel retained thematic working as the basis of his formal development.

Apostel wrote a number of orchestral works and choruses (all of them to secular texts). His chamber and instrumental music often employs the piano, and he frequently used unusual combinations of instruments. The sonatinas for solo winds were intended partly as teaching works. In the songs, he showed a preference for low voices. Many of his works testify to Apostel's belief in the affinities between music and the visual arts: in his pre-dodecaphonic works he made several attempts to 'translate' pictures into musical forms, as in the Piano Variations op.1 after Kokoschka and later piano works (opp.13 and 13*a*) after Kubin. In addition, all of Apostel's later pieces began as graphic sketches which contained the seed for the complete development of a composition. Apostel numbered many visual artists, including Kubin and Wotruba, among his associates.

WORKS

ORCHESTRAL

op.
11 Adagio, large str orch, 1937
17 Variations on a Theme of Joseph Haydn, 1949
21 Ballade, 1955 [for ballet choreographed by composer]
23 Variations on 3 Folksongs, 1956
27 Rondo ritmico, 1957
30 Piano Concerto, 1958
—   5 Austrian Miniatures, 1959
—   Festliche Musik, wind orch, 1962
41 Chamber Symphony, 1968
43 Epitaph, str, 1969
44 Paralipomena dodekaphonika, 1970 [2nd part of Haydn Var.]
50 Concerto for Orchestra, 1972 [3 movts, only 2nd finished]

VOCAL

3   5 Songs (Hanns Johst), low v, pf/orch, 1930–31
4   Requiem (Rilke), 8vv, orch, 1933
6   4 Songs (Rilke), low v, pf, 1935
9   5 Songs (Hölderlin), low v, orch, 1939–40
10/1 O sage, wo du bist (Rückert), 6 female/boys' vv, 1942
10/3 Es waren zwei Königskinder (trad.), chorus, 1944
15   3 Songs (George), medium v, pf, 1948
16   Um Mitternacht (Mörike), 6vv, 1957
18   3 Songs (Trakl), A, 4 va, 2 vc, db, 1951
22   5 Songs (R. Felmayr), medium v, fl, cl, bn, 1953
28   Höhe des Jahres (J. Gunert), 4 male vv, 1958
36   Ode (Apostel), A, large orch, 1961–2
37   Triptychon (Felix Braun), 1–6 boys' vv, a fl, 1964
40   2 Songs (A. Mombert), medium v, pf, 1964
—   Couplet (Albert Drach), v, pf, perc, 1968

CHAMBER AND INSTRUMENTAL

1   Piano Variations [after a work by Kokoschka], 1928
2   Piano Sonata, 1929
5   Sonatina ritmica, pf, 1934
7   String Quartet no.1, 1935
8   Piano Piece, 1938
13   Kubiniana [10 pieces], pf, 1945–50
13a 60 Schemen, pf, 1948–9
14   Quartet, fl, cl, bn, hn, 1947–9
19   3 Sonatinas, 1951: 19/1 for fl, 19/2 for cl, 19/3 for bn
20   5 Bagatelles, fl, cl, bn, 1952
—   Fantasia ritmica, pf, 1951–2 [reworked as orch Ballade]

23   Intrade, 9 tpt, 3 trbn, 6 hn, 2 tubas, perc, 1954
24   Concise [suite of 7 pieces], pf, 1955
25   6 Musiken, gui, 1955
26   String Quartet no.2 [1 movt], 1956
29   Study, fl, va, gui, 1958 rev. 1964
31a   4 Little Piano Pieces, 1959
31b   Fantasie, pf, 1959
32   Alpbach Miniatures, hpd, 1960 [studies on a 12-note series]
33   6 Epigramme, str qt, 1962
34a   Little Passacaglia, pf, 1961
34b   Toccata, pf, 1961
35   Sonata, vc, pf, 1962
38   Little Chamber Concerto, fl, va, gui, 1964
39   2 Sonatinas, 1964: 39a for ob, 39b for hn
42   2 Sonatinas, 1970: 42a for tpt, 42b for trbn [inc.]
45   Fischerhaus Serenade, 4 ww, 3 brass, str qt, 1972

Publishers: Universal, Doblinger

BIBLIOGRAPHY
H. Kaufman: *Hans Erich Apostel*, Österreichische Komponisten des 20. Jahrhunderts, iv (Vienna, n.d.)
W. Szmolyan: 'Hans Erich Apostels Kammersymphonie', *ÖMz*, xxiii (1968), 266
——: 'Hans Erich Apostels letzte Werke', *ÖMz*, xxviii (1973), 29
REINHOLD BRINKMANN

Apostichon (Gk.). A STICHERON chanted at the end of Orthodox Vespers; *see also* HESPERINOS.

Apostles' Creed. *See* CREDO.

Apostolos (Gk.: 'apostle'). Lessons from the Epistles of St Paul in the music of the Byzantine rite and the MUSIC OF THE COPTIC RITE; *see also* EPISTLE.

Apostrophe [strophicus] (Gk.). In Western chant notations, a neume added as an auxiliary to another neume. It was distinguished from the simple PUNCTUM probably by the manner of its performance, although there is no agreement as to what this might have entailed. Because it was practically always used on F, B♭ and C, and because later manuscripts differed in the way they placed it on the staff, Wagner believed intervals of less than a semitone were implied; but the Dijon tonary (*F-MO* H159), which uses special signs possibly signifying quarter-tone steps, does not use them in contexts involving the *apostrophe*. For Cardine it signified a note performed lightly. Modern Vatican books do not distinguish the *apostrophe* from the *punctum*, but the *Antiphonale monasticum* (Tournai, 1934) uses a special shape (for illustration *see* NEUMATIC NOTATIONS, Table 1).

BIBLIOGRAPHY
P. Wagner: *Einführung in die gregorianischen Melodien*, ii: *Neumenkunde: Paläographie des liturgischen Gesanges* (Leipzig, 1905, rev., enlarged 2/1913/R1962)
H. M. Bannister: *Codices e vaticanis selecti, phototypice expressi*, Monumenti vaticani di paleografia musicale latina, xii (Leipzig, 1913/R1969)
G. M. Suñol: *Introducció a la paleografia musical gregoriana* (Montserrat, 1925; Fr. trans., rev., enlarged 2/1935)
M. Huglo: 'Les noms des neumes et leur origine', *Etudes grégoriennes*, i (1954), 53
E. Jammers: *Tafeln zur Neumenkunde* (Tutzing, 1965)
E. Cardine: 'Sémiologie grégorienne', *Etudes grégoriennes*, xi (1970), 1–158

Apostrophos (Gk.). Sign used in pairs in Greek EKPHONETIC NOTATION.

Apothéose (Fr.). A musical form current in Parisian society in about 1725 whose programmatic element usually honoured a dead musician. It is an offshoot of the habit of referring to the French king as an Apollo of the arts; in these *apothéoses* the favoured dead are welcomed by Apollo on to Parnassus. (The form's popular-ity was thus contemporary with Titon du Tillet's *Le Parnasse françois*, in which dead musicians and poets were honoured.)

Surviving *apothéoses* are few; the two finest examples are both trio sonatas published by François Couperin, which make strong musical reference to the dead composers' styles: *Le Parnasse ou L'Apothéose de Corelli: Grande sonade en Trio* (1724, as part of *Les goûts réünis*) and *Concert instrumental sous le titre d'Apothéose, composé à la mémoire immortelle de l'incomparable Monsieur de Lully* (1725). The latter, the more substantial work, depicts both Lully and Corelli in Elysium. Their decision to agree that French and Italian musical styles are equally good leads to an *Essai en forme d'ouverture*, combining elements of both national styles, closed by a section entitled 'La paix du Parnasse'.

There is nothing sombre about these memorial compositions. Couperin obviously intended to entertain his audience: references to stylistic polarities between Italian and French music had direct relevance for his faction-ridden audience, as did the 'rumeur souteraine, causée par les auteurs contemporains de Lulli' and the subsequent 'plainte des mêmes', a reference to the unpopular control exercised by Lully over royal music. Couperin's preface to the Lully *apothéose* also gives detailed instructions for playing these trios (and many others) as pieces for two harpsichords, with each player taking a melody line and both playing the bass. Corelli and Lully both appeared in another work in *apothéose* manner, also from 1725, *Le triomphe des Mélophilètes*, an 'idyll in music' with text by Pierre Bouret; it is not known who composed and arranged the music.

DAVITT MORONEY

Apotomē (Gk.: 'segment'). A chromatic semitone in the Pythagorean system of intervals, equal to the difference between seven pure 5ths and four pure octaves, amounting to 113·7 cents and with a theoretical ratio of 2187:2048. According to the definition of Gaudentius (ed. Jan, p.344), by subtracting the LIMMA from the whole tone, i.e. (9:8) − (256:244), the apotomē may be obtained. The difference between the two semitones – i.e. between the apotomē and limma – is equal to the difference between 12 pure 5ths and seven pure octaves, the Pythagorean comma.

Appalachian dulcimer [Kentucky dulcimer, mountain dulcimer]. A partly- or fully-fretted zither, derived from north-west European forms some time since the late 18th century in the Appalachian mountains. The most usual combination of an elongated '8'-shaped box, a fretboard (or, more accurately, fretbox) set centrally along its entire length, and three or four metal strings tuned from lateral pegs, was being made there in the late 19th century, concurrently with oblong and oval instruments which are now rare. Stopping and striking techniques were similar to those on the *scheitholt*, though a few players are known to have used a bow. A standard tuning is *g'* for the melody string (on which a major scale starts at the third of 13 or 14 frets) and *g'* and *c'* for the bourdons; one or more strings are differently tuned for other modes. Its original use appears to have been chiefly for dance music. The accompaniment of English-language ballads and dance-songs with which it is now primarily associated was a Kentucky practice, popularized since the 1950s by performers such as John Jacob Niles and Jean Ritchie. A fully-fretted form is

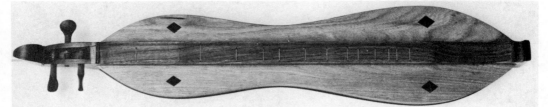

Appalachian dulcimer by Homer Ledford, Winchester, Kentucky, 1969 (private collection)

now made, stopped chordally with the left hand and plucked with finger plectra in the right hand.

See also UNITED STATES OF AMERICA, §II, 3(iii).

BIBLIOGRAPHY
C. Seeger: 'The Appalachian Dulcimer', *Journal of American Folklore*, lxxi (1958), 40
J. Putnam: *The Plucked Dulcimer* (Berea, Kentucky, 1961, rev. 2/1964)
J. Ritchie: *The Dulcimer Book* (New York, 1963)
M. Murphy: *The Appalachian Dulcimer Book* (St Clairsville, 1976)
JOAN RIMMER

Appassionato (It.: 'impassioned', 'passionate'). Although the title 'Sonata appassionata' for Beethoven's op.57 is not known any earlier than the 1838 four-hand arrangement published by Cranz of Hamburg, Beethoven did use the word several times. The slow movement of his Piano Sonata in A op.2 no.2 is marked *largo appassionato*; that of the String Quartet in F op.18 no.1 *adagio affettuoso ed appassionato*; that of the Piano Sonata in B♭ op.106 *adagio sostenuto: appassionato e con molto sentimento*; the main section of the first movement of his Piano Sonata in C minor op.111 is marked *allegro con brio ed appassionato*; and the finale of his String Quartet in A minor op.132 is marked *allegro appassionato*. It was defined in Koch's *Musikalisches Lexikon* of 1802, and many later composers used it, primarily as an expression mark: Schubert marked the opening of his posthumous trio movement (D897) *adagio* with *pp appassionato*.

For bibliography *see* TEMPO AND EXPRESSION MARKS.

DAVID FALLOWS

Appelmeyer, Franz. *See* ASPLMAYR, FRANZ.

Appelt, Matthäus. *See* LÖWENSTERN, MATTHÄUS APELLES VON.

Appenzeller, Benedictus (*b* c1480–88; *d* after 1558). ?Netherlands composer and singer. He was *maître de chapelle* to the regent of the Netherlands, Mary of Hungary, from 1537 until some time after 1551. All biographical facts relate him to the Netherlands, the earliest evidence being a three-voice chanson in a Netherlands manuscript of 1506 (*GB-Lbm* Add.35087). In 1517 he was a singer and later choirmaster at St Jacob, Bruges. After 1519, contemporary publications by Attaingnant and Moderne are the only source of evidence of his activity until 1536, when he became a singer in Mary of Hungary's chapel choir in Brussels. The following year he succeeded Jehan Goessins as master of the choirboys. Later, calling himself *maître de la chapelle*, he also assisted the select choir of the Marian Brotherhood at 's-Hertogenbosch. He was among the musicians who accompanied Mary to Germany in 1551 (not Spain, as some biographies have it; Mary went to Spain in 1556, when Appenzeller, then

an old man, remained in the Netherlands). The last contemporary evidence of him is a request for a pension from his patron in 1558, giving his age as over 70.

The simple attribution, 'Benedictus', found frequently in contemporary sources, has caused confusion with the contemporary composer Benedictus Ducis. Bartha's study of the styles of Appenzeller and Ducis showed that the evidence favours Appenzeller as the composer of most of the questionable works. Additional sources that have become available since Bartha's study require similar analysis. The most important source for Appenzeller's music is *Des chansons a quattre parties* (Antwerp, 1542), devoted exclusively to his chansons. Manuscripts and anthologies of Franco-Flemish and German origin contain an additional 24 chansons and dances as well as 31 motets, 12 *Magnificat* settings and seven masses, all of which seem to be by Appenzeller.

Appenzeller used both polyphonic and homophonic textures to produce sensitive interpretations of chanson texts. The continued influence of the lyric forms in his music is shown by refrains and other repetition patterns. There are no documents to support the common statement that he was a pupil of Josquin, but in two instances his style and choice of texts specifically allude to the older composer: the chanson *Cueurs desolez* for four voices, and the elegy for Josquin *Musae Jovis*. The melodic designs, phrase elisions and cadences of these two works are particularly reminiscent of Josquin.

WORKS

Des [23] chansons a quattre parties (Antwerp, 1542); ed. in Thompson
Chanson, 3vv, *GB-Lbm* Add.35087; ed. in Thompson
6 motets, 1554[8], 1555[9], 1557[3]

Other works probably by Appenzeller: 7 masses, 12 Magnificat, 31 motets, 24 chansons and dances: *B-Br* R.p.VI/18613/C; *D-Mbs* 156/5, 156/10; *E-MO* 765, 769, 771; *F-CA* 125–8 (formerly 124); *NL-Lml* 861, 864–6; canon, illustration in vander Straeten, vii, opposite p. 420

BIBLIOGRAPHY
E. vander Straeten: *La musique aux Pays-Bas avant le XIXe siècle* (1867–88/*R*1969), esp. iii, vii, viii
W. B. Squire: 'Who was Benedictus?', *SIMG*, xiii (1911–12), 264
D. Bartha: *Benedictus Ducis und Appenzeller* (Wolfenbüttel and Berlin, 1930)
A. Dunning: 'Een tombeau musical voor Erasmus', *Mens en melodie*, xxiv (1969), 368
G. G. Thompson: *Benedictus Appenzeller: Composer for Mary of Hungary* (diss., U. of North Carolina, 1975) [incl. thematic catalogue of works and further bibliography]
GLENDA GOSS THOMPSON

Appia, Adolphe (François) (*b* Geneva, 1 Sept 1862; *d* Nyon, 29 Feb 1928). Swiss theatrical theorist and stage designer. He studied in 1879–89 at Geneva, and at the conservatories of Leipzig and Dresden, at the same time acquainting himself with contemporary theatrical practice by attendance at theatres, as a visitor to the Bayreuth Festival (from 1882) and as a guest at the

Stage design by Adolphe Appia for Gluck's 'Orfeo ed Euridice' (1913) in the Institut für Theaterwissenschaft, University of Cologne

court opera houses of Dresden (1889) and Vienna (1890). After 1890 he pursued his interests as a writer and artist and led a secluded existence in the vicinity of Lake Geneva.

Like many contemporary artists Appia reacted against the economic and social conditions of his day with their alienating and obscuring effect, registering a Romantic protest by aspiring to a theatrical art independent of reality and determined solely by the creative imagination of the artist. Wagner's music dramas were the focal point of his ideas. Whereas Wagner's music and text as a product of the 'first and primordial idea of creation' was to his mind free from the conventions of the real world, its stage representation had been taken over by the 'conventional influence of the milieu'. For Appia, the solution followed on from the insight that in Wagner the music constituted not only the time element but also that of space, taking on 'bodily form' in the staging itself. However, this could come about only if there were a hierarchical order of the factors of presentation to guarantee that the music, as the prime revelation of the artist's soul, would determine all the relationships on the stage. Appia's hierarchical synthesis – a departure from the equal participation of the arts in Wagner's *Gesamtkunstwerk* — gives the central role to the actor trained in dance and rhythm. His actions, pre-formed by the score, transfer the music on to the stage, whose 'arrangement' must match its physical properties: a 'scenic construction set up in an ad hoc manner, with its surfaces and their various angles extending unconcealed in space'; electrical lighting takes on the function of articulating the stage area, while

painting and costumes are reduced to a colouring agent with the task of 'simplification'. His aesthetics, which appear to turn away from the conventions of the industrial era, are however subservient to them, because his stage art was not only dominated by the new technology of electricity, but (as a result of his negation of the producer's creativity) ultimately aimed at an automatic process, at an art of machines set in motion by the music. Under the influence of his friend Houston Stewart Chamberlain, his approach was also determined by his agnosticism, his mingling of intuitional and positivist theses, and his extreme Germanophilia. Appia had his first opportunity of trying out his theories at the theatre of the Contesse de Béarn in Paris in 1903 with scenes from Schumann's *Manfred* and Bizet's *Carmen*, using a new lighting system developed by Mariano Fortuny. A decisive influence on his later work was his encounter (1906) with Emile Jaques-Dalcroze, in whose rhythmical gymnastics he saw the realization of the synthesis of music with the living body that was essential to his theatrical ideas – reflected in his 'espaces rythmiques', from 1909 onwards. They demonstrated the principles of 'living space', not formulated until *L'oeuvre d'art vivant* (1921). In order to correspond to the form and movements of the living actors, this space consists of freely adaptable, purpose-built stage structures formed of a limited number of linear elements, on which each transformation or each fresh combination happens in full view of the audience. The concept was demonstrated in Jaques-Dalcroze's *Echo und Narzissus* (1912) and Gluck's *Orfeo ed Euridice* (1913; see illustration) in the Jaques-Dalcroze educational institute in Dresden.

Appia is the father of non-illusionist musical theatre. All anti-realistic tendencies of the moderns can more or less be traced back to him. Like EDWARD GORDON CRAIG, who was comparable to him in many respects, his influence found a more effective medium in his theoretical writings than in his practical activities. Only after his ideas were already widespread and to some extent even superseded was he recalled to the public stage: in 1923 he designed *Tristan und Isolde* for La Scala and in 1924 and 1925 *Das Rheingold* and *Die Walküre* for the Stadttheater at Basle. In Bayreuth, Cosima Wagner, to whom his reforming projects were primarily addressed, rejected them; it was only with the 'new' Bayreuth of Wieland and Wolfgang Wagner that his ideas made a deep mark on stage design at the Festspielhaus.

See also OPERA, §VIII, 6, and fig. 44.

WRITINGS
(selection)

La mise en scène du drame wagnérien (Paris, 1895)
Die Musik und die Inszenierung (Munich, 1899; Eng. trans. 1962)
L'oeuvre d'art vivant (Geneva, 1921; Eng. trans. 1960)
Art vivant ou nature morte? (Milan, 1923)
Album de reproductions, ed. O. L. Forel, E. Junod, and J. Mercier (Zurich, 1929)
'The Future of Production', *Theatre Arts Monthly*, xvi (1932), 649

BIBLIOGRAPHY
J. Mercier: 'Adolphe Appia: The Re-birth of Dramatic Art', *Theatre Arts Monthly*, xvi (1932), 615
L. Simonson: 'Appia's Contribution to the Modern Stage', *Theatre Arts Monthly*, xvi (1932), 631
E. Stadler: 'Adolphe Appia', *Maske und Kothurn*, v (1959), 144
F. Marotti: *La scena di Adolphe Appia* (Bologna, 1966)
D. Kreidt: *Kunsttheorie der Inszenierung: Zur Kritik der ästhetischen Konzeptionen Adolphe Appias und Edward Gordon Craigs* (diss., Free U. of Berlin, 1968)
W. R. Volbach: *Adolphe Appia: Prophet of the Modern Theatre* (Middletown, Conn., 1968)
E. Stadler: *Adolphe Appia: Victoria and Albert Museum* (London, 1970) [exhibition catalogue]
J. Fiebach: *Von Craig bis Brecht: Studien zu Künstlertheorien in der ersten Hälfte des 20. Jahrhunderts* (Berlin, 1975), 11, 51ff, 65ff
G. Giertz: *Kultus ohne Götter: Emile Jaques-Dalcroze und Adolphe Appia: Versuch einer Theaterreform auf der Grundlage der rhythmischen Gymnastik* (Munich, 1975)

MANFRED BOETZKES

Appia, Edmond (*b* Turin, 7 May 1894; *d* Geneva, 12 Feb 1961). Swiss conductor. He studied the violin under Marteau in Geneva, Rémy and Capet in Paris (1908–13) and César Thomson at the Brussels Conservatory (1920), gaining a *premier prix*. He became leader of the Geneva Opera House orchestra, and made his début as an international soloist. From 1928 to 1943 he held master classes at the conservatories of Lausanne and La Chaux-de-Fonds. While leader of the Orchestre de la Suisse Romande (1932–5) he also began, in 1935, to conduct. In 1938 Geneva radio engaged him as permanent conductor; in addition to contemporary music, he championed French and Italian music of the 17th and 18th centuries, particularly the operas of Lully and Rameau, of which he was considered a stylish and elegant interpreter. He also introduced the Jeunesses Musicales into Switzerland. In 1952 he was appointed Chevalier de la Légion d'honneur. His writings include a number of essays on French Classical music (mainly in *SMz*, 1949–52); the most important appeared in *De Palestrina à Bartók: études musicologiques* (Paris, 1965).

BIBLIOGRAPHY
SML
P. A. Gaillard: 'Edmond Appia', *SMz*, ci (1961), 120

Hommage à Edmond Appia (1894–1961): témoignages de ses amis (Geneva, 1961)

JÜRG STENZL

Applebaum, Louis (*b* Toronto, 3 April 1918). Canadian composer, conductor and administrator. After attending the University of Toronto (1936–40), he held scholarships enabling him to study in New York with Roy Harris and Bernard Wagenaar. On his return to Canada in 1941 he became staff composer and later music director of the National Film Board of Canada. Further film work followed in New York and Hollywood – including the score for *The Story of GI Joe*, nominated for an Academy Award in 1947. In 1953 he became musical director of the Shakespearean Festival at Stratford, Ontario. He inaugurated a music festival as part of this, and was responsible for the International Conference of Composers at Stratford in 1960. Between 1953 and 1972 he composed incidental scores for 28 productions, and conducted many festival opera and operetta presentations. After two years as music consultant to CBC television (1960–62) he became increasingly involved in administration, but without giving up composition. He has served such bodies as the Canada Council, the National Arts Centre and the Composers, Authors and Publishers Association of Canada. In 1971 he was appointed executive director of the Province of Ontario Council for the Arts. The greater part of his output is music for the stage, television, radio or film. He has prepared suites for concert performance from some of these scores, the most important being *Barbara Allen*, originally written for the National Ballet of Canada. His best-known works are the *Three Stratford Fanfares* (1953), a *Suite of Miniature Dances* (1958) and a *Concertante for Orchestra* (1967).

GILES BRYANT

Appleby, Thomas (*fl* c1535–63). English church musician and composer. He was apparently already a vicar-choral of Lincoln Cathedral when he was appointed acting organist there in 1536, and his formal appointment to the offices of organist and instructor of the choristers took place in April 1538. In July 1539, however, he moved to Oxford to become *Magister choristarum* at Magdalen College. Thomas Whythorne was then one of the choristers and, writing c1593, he loyally listed his three successive choirmasters – Appleby, Preston and John Sheppard – among the famous musicians of his time. Appleby stayed at Magdalen just over two years, and took up his former posts at Lincoln Cathedral in September 1541, remaining there until succeeded by William Byrd in February 1563.

His surviving compositions are both for the Latin rite. A five-part *Magnificat* setting, now lacking the tenor, is in *GB-Cu* Peterhouse 471–4; it is in melismatic style, sometimes, however, indistinguishable from mere note-spinning. A setting of the mass, described as 'for a mene' for four men's voices, is in *Lbm* Add.17802–5. It is in a more imitative style, and includes a Kyrie set for *alternatim* performance and a brief Alleluia, of which the tenor appears to be derived from the plainsong of the *Alleluia, Confitemini domino*.

ROGER BOWERS

Appleton, Thomas (*b* Boston, 26 Dec 1785; *d* Reading, Mass., 11 July 1872). American organ builder. Apprenticed as a young man to a Boston cabinetmaker, Appleton entered the workshop of WILLIAM GOODRICH in 1805. From 1810 to 1820 both men were associated with the Franklin Musical Warehouse, building church and chamber organs, pianos, and claviorgans. In 1821 Appleton became an independent builder, quickly gaining a reputation and securing important commissions. Between 1847 and 1850 Thomas D. Warren, son of the organ builder Samuel R. Warren (d 1882) and brother of the organist Samuel Prowse Warren (1841–1915), was his partner; in the latter year they moved their workshop from Boston to Reading, where he worked until his retirement in 1868. Appleton's most important work was carried out between 1825 and about 1845, and includes instruments made for the Bowdoin St Church (1831), where Lowell Mason was organist; one for the Handel & Haydn Society (1832) in Boston; for the Center Church, Hartford (1835) and for the Church of the Pilgrims, Brooklyn (1846). His work is characterized by its meticulous craftsmanship, refined tone and, during his most active period, strikingly handsome casework, often executed in mahogany in the Greek revival style.

BARBARA OWEN

Application (Ger. *Applicatur*; Lat. *applicatio*). In violin playing, a term used mainly in the 18th century for position playing or position fingering. '*Halb Applicatur*' (literally, 'half position') meant either 2nd position or, collectively, 2nd, 4th and 6th positions. '*Ganz Applicatur*' (literally, 'whole position') meant 3rd, 5th and 7th positions. '*Vermischte Applicatur*' (mixed position) was a term employed when 'now the whole, now the half position is used' (Leopold Mozart, 1756).

DAVID D. BOYDEN

Applicatur (Ger.). An 18th-century term equivalent to APPLICATION.

Applied dominant (secondary dominant] (Ger. *Zwischendominante*). The dominant of a degree other than the tonic, usually indicated by the symbol 'V/'. Thus in the key of C major, for instance, a D major triad may function as V/V, an E major triad as V/VI, an A major triad as V/II and a B major triad as V/III. Dominant 7th chords often function as applied dominants; again in C major, the chord C–E–G–B♭ may function as the dominant 7th of IV, and A♭–C–E♭–G♭ as the dominant 7th of ♭II, the 'Neapolitan 6th chord'. An American term for applied dominant is 'secondary dominant'. For an illustration of 'applied dominant' *see* CADENCE, ex.15.

Appoggiatura (It.; Fr. *appoggiature*; Ger. *Vorschlag*). A 'leaning-note'. As a melodic ornament, it usually implies a note one step above or below the 'main' note. It usually creates a dissonance with the prevailing harmony, and resolves by step on the following weak beat. It may be notated as an ornament or in normal notation. In the Baroque and Classical periods, and the early Romantic period, the appoggiatura, even when not notated, was taken for granted in certain contexts, particularly in recitative. *See* ORNAMENTS, §II, for a full discussion; *see also* IMPROVISATION, §I, 3(iii), and NON-HARMONIC NOTE.

Appolloni, Gioseffo (*b* Arezzo; *fl* 1591–c1600). Italian composer. The appearance of his earliest known work, *Raggio di pura luce*, in Orazio Tigrini's *Il secondo libro de madrigali a sei voci* (*RISM* 1591²⁴) suggests that he may have been a pupil of Tigrini, who was at that time *maestro di cappella* at Arezzo Cathedral. Appolloni's *Il primo libro de madrigali a quattro voci* (Venice, 1600), announced in its dedication as 'questi miei primi Madrigali', is dated from Arezzo on 22 November 1599. One sacred piece (in *RISM* 1612²) attributed to J. Appoloni is probably by Gioseffo Appolloni.

Appoloni [Appolini], **Salvatore.** *See* APOLLONI, SALVATORE.

Apprys, Philip. *See* RHYS, PHILIP AP.

Appunn, Anton (*b* Hanau, 20 June 1839; *d* Hanau, 13 Jan 1900). German acoustician, son of Georg Appunn. At the Leipzig Conservatory he continued the acoustical experiments of his father, especially the determination of vibration ratios of very high tones by optical means, and constructed fine acoustic apparatus. He devised a new shape for the glockenspiel, with right-angled metal rods in a circular arrangement and a metal half-sphere above as a resonator.

WRITINGS
'Akustische Versuche über Wahrnehmung tiefer Töne', *Berichte der Wetterauischen Gesellschaft für die gesammte Naturkunde zu Hanau* (Hanau, 1889), 37–68
'Ein natürliches Harmoniesystem', *Berichte der Wetterauischen Gesellschaft für die gesammte Naturkunde zu Hanau* (Hanau, 1893), 47–78
'Schwingungszahlenbestimmungen bei sehr höhen Tönen', *Annalen der Physik und Chemie*, lxiv (1898), 409; lxvii (1899), 217

MARK HOFFMAN

Appunn, Georg August Ignatius (*b* Hanau, 1 Sept 1816; *d* Hanau, 14 Jan 1888). German musical theorist and acoustician. He studied theory with Anton Andre and Schnyder von Wartensee, the piano with Suppus and Alois Schmitt, the organ with Rinck and the cello with Mangold. He became a well-rounded musician who could play almost every instrument. Until 1860 he was a popular teacher of singing, theory and instruments in Hanau and Frankfurt am Main. Later he worked exclusively on acoustical research (e.g. harmoniums tuned with 36 and 53 intervals to the octave). His research was acclaimed by such scholars as Helmholtz, Oettingen and Engel.

WRITINGS
'Über die Helmholtzsche Lehre von den Tonempfindungen', *Berichte der Wetterauischen Gesellschaft für die gesammte Naturkunde zu Hanau* (Hanau, 1868), 73

MARK HOFFMAN

Aprem. *See* EPHREM SYRUS.

Ap Rhys [Apryce], **Philip.** *See* RHYS, PHILIP AP.

Aprile, Giuseppe [Scirolino, Sciroletto] (*b* Martina Franca, Taranto, 28 Oct 1732; *d* Martina Franca, 11 Jan 1813). Italian singer and composer. He began music studies with his father Fortunato, a notary and church singer. The boy was gifted with a good voice and was evirated at the age of 11 at his father's wish. On 28 April 1751 he began to study singing in Naples at the private school of Gregorio Sciroli (hence his nicknames); on 23 September 1752 he was engaged as soprano in the royal chapel of Naples. He made his opera début the following season in a secondary role in Jommelli's *Ifigenia in Aulide*. After further operatic performances in Rome and Parma he gave up his place in the royal chapel and began a brilliant career, singing in the most important theatres of Italy. In 1756 he went to the court of Württemberg in Stuttgart, where Jommelli was Kapellmeister; there he performed in many of Jommelli's works and toured often in Italy and elsewhere. In the season 1765–6 he sang in Naples and Palermo, then returned to Stuttgart, at an annual salary of 6000 gulden, with his brother Raffaele, a violinist. He left the Württemberg court in 1769 with considerable debts against the treasury. In 1770 Burney heard him perform in Naples, and Mozart heard him there and in Milan and Bologna. He performed throughout Italy until 1783, when he succeeded Caffarelli as first sopranist in the royal chapel in Naples. Having retired from public performance in 1785, he became a successful singing teacher; among his pupils were Domenico Cimarosa and Lady Catherine Hamilton, and the exercises of his highly appreciated vocal method (1791) were frequently reprinted throughout France, Germany and Italy. He was pensioned by the royal chapel on 12 July 1798 and spent his remaining years in his native town.

Aprile was considered one of the greatest singers of his time, as much for his acting as for the quality of his voice and the diversity of expression he brought even to bravura passages. Schubart, who heard him in Stuttgart, particularly praised his manner of varying arias and spoke of his great importance to Jommelli.

WORKS

Six favorite Italian duos (London, c1780)
Five . . . Italian Duettos . . . and one by Signr. G. Sarti (London, c1780)
Twelve Favorite Canzonets, ed. P. Seybold with pf/harp acc., op.4 (Brighthelmstone, c1785)
Six Canzonets, harp/pf/hpd acc. (London, c1790)
Pieces in A Select Collection of the most admired Songs, Duetts & from Operas in the highest Esteem, iii (Edinburgh, c1788)
1 inst piece in Six Divertimentos, 2 vn, b (London, c1772)
Divertimenti, 2vv, hpd; Arie, 1–2vv, bc: both I-Nc

VOCAL EXERCISES

36 solfeggi per soprano col basso numerato (Naples, 1790)
Exercises pour la vocalisation à l'usage du Conservatoire de Naples (Paris and Leipzig, n.d.)
20 solfeggi per voce di contralto (Naples, n.d.)
20 solfeggi per voce di basso (Milan, n.d.)

THEORETICAL WORK

The Modern Italian Method of Singing, with a Variety of Progressive Examples and Thirtysix Solfeggi (London, 1791)

BIBLIOGRAPHY
G. Rutini: Letter to G. B. Martini, Livorno, 22 May 1764 (MS, I-Bc)
C. Burney: The Present State of Music in France and Italy (London, 1771/R1969), 328
F. Haböck: Die Kastraten und ihre Gesangskunst (Stuttgart, Berlin and Leipzig, 1927)
J. Sittard: Zur Geschichte der Musik und des Theaters am württembergischen Hofe, 1733–1793 (Stuttgart, 1891)
N. Vacca and S. Simonetti: 'Aprile', DBI
E. Anderson, ed.: The Letters of Mozart and his Family (London, 2/1966), i, 111, 123, 143

MARIANGELA DONÀ

Apthorp, William Foster (b Boston, Mass., 24 Oct 1848; d Vevey, 19 Feb 1913). American critic and writer on music. In 1869 he graduated from Harvard College, where he studied music theory under J. K. Paine. After brief service on the staff of other newspapers he became music critic of the Boston Transcript, in which capacity he exercised much influence. He retained this post until 1903, when he retired and went to live in Switzerland. From 1892 to 1901 he edited the programme books of the Boston SO, giving them a value and individual character that were afterwards maintained by Philip Hale. He published Musicians and Music Lovers (New York, 1894), By the

Way, being a Collection of Short Essays about Music and Art in General (Boston, 1898), The Opera, Past and Present (New York, 1901) and several translations. He was editor, with John Denison Champlin, of Scribner's Cyclopaedia of Music and Musicians (New York, 1888–90).

RICHARD ALDRICH

Apt Manuscript (F-APT 16bis). See SOURCES, MS, §VII, 3.

Aquanus [Loer, Luyr], **Adam** (b Aachen, c1492). Belgian composer. He came from the diocese of Liège and studied music under Thomas Tzamen of Aachen. On 23 November 1510 he entered the University of Cologne where he met Heinrich Glarean, who later published Aquanus's humanistic motet, Juppiter omnipotens for three voices, in the Dodecachordon. The superius part of another motet, Sub tuum praesidium for four voices, is found in Tschudi's Songbook (CH-SGs 463).

BIBLIOGRAPHY
H. Glarean: Dodecachordon (Basle, 1547); ed. and trans. C. A. Miller, MSD, vi (1965), 362

CLEMENT A. MILLER

Aquanus, Thomas. See TZAMEN, THOMAS.

Aquila, Marco dall'. See DALL'AQUILA, MARCO.

Aquileia. Northern Italian city. From early Christian times it was a patriarchate and an important city in the Friuli region. Bishop Valeriano (371–88) was surrounded by a body of clerics, known as the Chorus beatorum, a fact which is recorded in the contemporary chronicle of St Jerome. Valeriano's successor Cromatius is mentioned in an anonymous 7th-century tract on the origins of chant, and the pamphlet Ad virginem lapsam, possibly the work of Bishop Niceta (5th century), seems to confirm the importance of plainchant at early Aquileia. In view of the distinctive liturgy which it served it is probable that the music also developed some individual features. An 11th-century neumatic manuscript (I-Ma, T27 suppl.) records a preCarolingian baptismal rite, whose melodies, though notated in campo aperto, are clearly simpler than their Ambrosian and Gregorian counterparts (see NEUMATIC NOTATIONS).

The Carolingian reform, with its emphasis on the liturgical unity of the Holy Roman Empire, witnessed the introduction into Aquileia of both the Roman rite and Gregorian chant. Composition by local musicians continued, however, as is shown by a 12th-century troper and other manuscripts at Udine. A strong tradition of liturgical drama also grew up at the church. In 1245, 12 prebends were created for the singers, and before long Aquileia became one of the first churches in the region to appoint a cantor. An organ existed by 1328. For the next 100 years documentary evidence is scarce, but late 15th-century chapter acts, which record the hiring of extra singers for the major feasts, show that the musical establishment was still quite strong at that time. Cathedral archives of the 16th century reveal a similar state of affairs, but by about 1650 the choir had fallen into disorder, a situation remedied only by the suppression of the patriarchate in 1751.

BIBLIOGRAPHY
G. Vale: 'Vita musicale nella Chiesa Metropolitana di Aquileia', Note

d'archivio per la storia musicale, ix (1932), 201
P. L. Zovatto: 'Il Santo Sepolcro di Aquileia e il dramma medievale', *Atti e memorie dell'Accademia di Udine*, 6th ser., xiii (1954–7), 127
M. Huglo: 'Vestigio di un antico repertorio musicale dell'Alta Italia apparentato col canto ambrosiano', *Ambrosius*, xxxi (1955), 34
——: 'La liturgia e la musica sacra aquileiese', *Storia della cultura veneta*, ed. G. Folena (Vicenza, 1976–)

DAVID BRYANT

Aquilino, Jacomo. *See* ØRN, JACOB.

Aquinas, Thomas (*b* Roccasecca, late 1224 or early 1225; *d* Fossanova, 9 March 1274). Italian Dominican priest and theologian. He was described as 'Doctor Angelicus'. He led a life of intense study, lecturing and writing at Cologne, Paris and Naples. His works form the most profound, comprehensive and ordered scholastic synthesis of the scriptures, patristic teaching and philosophy; his philosophical work consists primarily of a judicious interpretation of Aristotle and his Greek and Arab commentators, integrated with an often neglected element of Platonist thought (mostly derived through St Augustine and neo-Platonist intermediaries). He was canonized in 1323.

Although Aquinas wrote no treatise specifically on music (the *Ars musica* is spurious) there are pericopes scattered throughout his works that have a musical aesthetic consistent with his whole system and isomorphic with his visual art aesthetic. This musical aesthetic is austere, not only because of its Aristotelian terms of expression, but also because Aquinas maintained (as did his age) that the sounds of instruments are modelled on the human voice (*In libros de anima*, ii, lesson 18). Aquinas's interpretation of the distinction Aristotle made between mathematical and acoustical harmony (*Analytica posteriora*, 79a 1–2) did not cause him, as Boethius's did, to pursue 'musica intelligibilis' as distinct from audible music, even though he believed that music must be studied within arithmetic, which is 'prior and more certain' (*In libros posteriorum analyticorum*, i, lesson 41), as part of the Quadrivium. His concern was not with the division between concrete sound and abstract pattern but with their factual union: music is concerned with 'numerical proportions applied to sound' (*In VIII libros physicorum*, ii, lesson 5). Following a number metaphysic from Aristotle, he insisted that a normative unit of sound (diesis) is as essential to melody as a normative unit of colour is to painting (*In XII libros metaphysicorum*, x, lesson 3).

As used by Aquinas the term 'harmony', with respect to physical things, includes the notion of 'absence of contrariety', and consequently being more easily destructible: 'stones and metals are more durable because there is less harmony in them' (*Quaestio disputata de anima*, article 8 ad 11), and the harmony of the human body is disturbed by violent stimuli (*Summa contra Gentiler*, ii, chap.82). It is in this equivocal and physical sense that music of the spheres should be understood (*In libros de coelo et mundo*, ii, lesson 14). He maintained that as beauty is found in 'integritas sive perfectio, debita proportio sive consonantia' and 'claritas' (*Summa theologica*, I, question xxxix, article 8), so music moves in distinct notes and with harmony which is *consonantia sonorum* (*In libros de anima*, i, lesson 9) and, in both its simultaneous and consecutive aspects, involves numerical ratios. Moreover the ordering of all things by God gives them their *consonantia* (*Expositio in Dionysium De divinis nominibus*, iv, 5), and that in God the three persons are 'per consonantiam unum' (*Commentum in IV*

libros sententiarum magistri Petri Lombardi, i, 31, question 3, article 2). Thus the divinity and all creation are seen together under a musical analogy according to which, at the highest level, all variety is gathered together in perfect unity of sound. It is not surprising that music so purely conceived should be the medium of worship: it is powerful in turning the affection of man to God (*In psalmos Davidis*, xxxii, 2) and for this purpose should be 'simplex' (ibid, 3); but Aquinas said that a nobler way to God than through music is 'through doctrine and preaching' (*Summa theologica*, II/ii, question 91, article 2 ad 3).

Aquinas deliberately rejected the Pythagorean–Platonic theory of the presence of numbers in the soul (*In libros de anima*, i, lesson 9) as having immediate connections with cosmic or purely intellectual and mathematical harmonies. For Aquinas musical education was not the awakening of dormant knowledge and capacities, but, as for Aristotle, the passing on of knowledge from someone competent in music, which he regarded more as a skill than as a fine art (*In XII libros metaphysicorum*, ix, lesson 7); nevertheless he maintained that subjective good taste is needed in order to find pleasure in music (*In X libros ethicorum*, x, lesson 4).

BIBLIOGRAPHY
G. M. Allodi, ed.: *Thomas Aquinas: Opera omnia* (Parma, 1852–73/R1948–50)
S. Bullough: 'St. Thomas and Music', *Dominican Studies*, iv (1951), 14
K. Foster, ed. and trans.: *The Life of Saint Thomas Aquinas: Biographical Documents* (London, 1959)
H. J. Burbach: *Studien zur Musikanschauung des Thomas von Aquin*, Kölner Beiträge zur Musikforschung, xxxiv (Regensburg, 1966)
R. Busa, ed.: *Index Thomisticus* (Stuttgart, 1974), esp. entries 'Consonantia', 'Harmonia', 'Musicus' and paronyms

EDWARD BOOTH

Aquisgranum (Lat.). AACHEN.

Aquitaine. Region of south-west France with an important and distinctive repertory of both monophonic and polyphonic music in the Middle Ages. *See* ANTIPHONER, §3(iii); GALLICAN RITE, MUSIC OF THE, esp. §§2, 4–5; GRADUAL (ii), §4(ii); MASS, §I, 5; NEUMATIC NOTATIONS, §IV, 5; ORGANUM, §7; PROCESSIONAL, §1; PSALM, §II, 2; REPROACHES; ST MARTIAL; SEQUENCE, §2; TONARY, esp. §§1–2, 6; TROPE.

Arabesque (Ger. *Arabeske*). A term, apparently introduced into Europe during the Moorish conquest of Spain, first applied to architecture and painting to describe an ornamental frieze or border, whose elaborations, foliate and curlicued, have their counterparts in music in ornamentation and complex figuration. (Arabian music itself is of this ornate, arabesque nature.) In music the term was implied in, if not applied to, three musical devices: (1) the contrapuntal decoration of a basic theme, e.g. the obbligato to the chorus 'Jesus bleibet meine Freude' in Bach's cantata *Herz und Mund und Tat und Leben* BWV147; (2) an elaboration by *gruppetti*, scale figures, etc, of the theme itself which was to lead to the variation techniques of the 19th century – an excellent example is Schubert's Andante in A D604; (3) a rapidly changing series of harmonies which decorate, without furthering, a point in the progress of a composition, such as we find in, for example, the nocturnes of Field and Chopin.

The term was also used for piano pieces by Stephen Heller (op.49) and Schumann, whose op.18 is in the form of a rondo with recurring episodes, which are in marked contrast to the main theme. Gade's op.27 is similarly entitled, but the most typical examples of the form are Debussy's *Deux arabesques* (1888), whose charm and delicacy reflect perfectly the conception of the arabesque as a piece in which the composer aims at a decorative rather than emotional effect.

MAURICE J. E. BROWN

Arabian Gulf. The Arabian (or Persian) Gulf has since prehistoric times been an important commercial link between the Near East and Mediterranean on one hand, and India and the Far East on the other. The Arabs of this area (living in what is now southern Iraq, Kuwait, the Hasā province of Saudi Arabia, Bahrain, Qatar and the United Arab Emirates) were until the 20th century nomads, pearl-divers or – to some extent – fishermen, shipbuilders and merchants. In addition many minority groups have since ancient times made their homes in the region. There are people with roots in East Africa, who are often (but not always) descendants of freed slaves. A fairly large Persian group lives in Bahrain and many Baluchi may be found in the United Arab Emirates. Indians and Pakistani are widely distributed, active as doctors, tailors and, most recently, bankers. Since World War II the wealth from the abundant oil sources has attracted many more foreigners to the area, mostly from other Arab countries. This demographic diversity is reflected in the variety of the music to be found in the Gulf area.

Classical Arab art music is a rarity, mostly performed by Egyptians, although classical *'ud* (lute) music is performed by Bahraini musicians and – to a lesser degree – by musicians from Abū Dhabi. Other art-music instruments like the *nāy* (flute) and the *qanūn* (zither) have no traditional connections with the area.

The war dances of the beduins are called *arda* or *ayala*. Like most beduin dances (e.g. *ashuri*, *khamāri*, *arubi*, *la'abuni* etc.) the war dances are associated with festive occasions, and are accompanied by a percussion ensemble consisting of one or two *ṭabl* (a double-headed barrel-shaped drum, worn on the shoulder and struck on one side with a stick, and on the other with the hand), several *ṭār* (frame-drums with small bells or iron rings inside the frame) and one pair of *ṭūs* (small cymbals). However, in contrast with the other festivity dances mentioned above, which are responsorial, the *arda* use a double chorus.

Some kinds of beduin songs (*rad'he*, *sameri*, *mader*, *ghazal* etc.) are found in the desert areas of the United Arab Emirates. They may be presented either by at least two alternating male soloists or by a single person; in the latter case the performer is a poet who provides his own accompaniment on a *rabābah* (a fiddle with one or two strings; see fig. 1). A popular type of song performed at wedding festivities by a double chorus without instrumental accompaniment is called *razfa* (plural *rezif*). Shepherds in the desert sometimes play a small double clarinet, widely known in the Arab world, called either *zummāra* or *jifti* (a Turkish-derived word).

The most refined music-making of the area is that of the pearl-divers. When leaving for the oyster banks, where they stay for a couple of months, the divers and the sailors are accompanied by one or two professional singers (*naham*). To every stage of the work correspond some special work songs, sung by the *nahami* while the chorus of divers and sailors produce a vocal drone in a

1. Salubbi singer with rabābah (fiddle), 1958

very low register – two octaves below the fundamental singing tone of the *naham*. Other songs (*fijīri*) are performed only at night; these are accompanied by percussion instruments, including one or two *ṭabl*, four or five *muruas* (a small double-headed cylindrical drum) and three *jahele* (a great earthen pot with no membrane). The rhythms of the *fijīri* are cyclic and of remarkable length: in some of the sub-genres (e.g. *bahri* and *adhāni*) each cycle covers 32 beats.

A special kind of traditional urban music in the Gulf area is found in the dance-songs *sawt* and *bastah*. They are heard quite often at informal parties in private houses or in one of the *dār* (a communal house belonging to a group of musicians). The traditional performance of a *sawt* requires a singer who can also perform on the *'ud* (lute), as well as four *muruas* players. The traditional performance of a *bastah* requires a singer playing the *'ud* and two drummers, one playing a *derbanka* or *dombok* (i.e. *darabukka*, a single-headed vase-shaped drum) and the other a *deff* (i.e. *daff*, a frame drum with cymbals inserted in the wooden frame). The *sawt* is probably Yemenite in origin, while the *bastah* is of Iraqi derivation. *Sawt* and *bastah* may also sometimes be played with *ṭabl* and *ṭār* and include choral singing. All the above-mentioned genres are differentiated according to their use of rhythmic patterns.

For the minority groups in the Arabian Gulf region music is important in preserving the social cohesion and identity of each group. But a wider social impact has been made by some of this music, particularly by some of the African-derived genres. The *leiwah*, a type of dance-song originally from Kenya and Tanzania (*see* TANZANIA, §1), is not only performed in the African quarters of large Gulf towns like Manāmah or Dubayy-

2. *Jirba (bagpipe) with tar (frame drums) and ṭabl (cylindrical drum) at Rifa'a as Sharki, Bahrain, 1962*

Dayrah, but may even appear as entertainment at an important Arab wedding festivity. It is performed by an ensemble consisting of shawm (called *surnāy* or *mizmār*), four or five percussion instruments and a chorus of dancer–singers. The music is a cycle of short strophic songs. Another kind of African music is played on the Sudanese lyre *tambūra*, a six-string instrument normally accompanied by two cylindrical drums played in unison and by a *manjur* (a belt with rattling goat hooves) worn by a dancer. The *tambūra* player is also a singer, and his solos alternate with choral sections sung by the assistants. His music is anhemitonic-pentatonic and is the only pentatonic music from this area; by contrast, Arab singing of the area uses smaller intervals within a much narrower range, being based on tetrachords or pentachords.

The *jirba* (bagpipe; see fig.2), a common instrument in Bahrain and on the Kuwaitian island of Faylakah, has no drone-pipe. Its chanter is a double clarinet of the *jifti* type. The *jirba* is in general accompanied by four or five cylindrical drums, whose rhythms are often very subtle and complicated. It is particularly popular with the Iranian minorities and could be called the 'Persian bagpipe'.

In the Gulf area, the Baluchi are considered good *surnāy* players. Here as in many other Islamic-influenced areas, the *surnāy* is mainly used at festive occasions, particularly at weddings (accompanied by two drums which provide the rhythmic pattern).

BIBLIOGRAPHY
P. R. Olsen: 'Enregistrements faits à Kuwait et à Bahrain', *Ethnomusicologie III: Wégimont V 1960*, 137–70
——: 'La musique africaine dans le Golfe persique', *JIFMC*, xix (1967), 28
——: 'Pêcheurs de perles et musiciens du Golfe persique', OCR 42 [disc notes]

POUL ROVSING OLSEN

Arab music.

I. Art music. II. Folk music.

I. Art music. Modern Arab art music may be related to a wider set of Middle Eastern traditions embracing also Persian and Turkish art music. Although now quite clearly distinct, their historical development has been marked by reciprocal influences to an unusual degree, and they still have much in common, not only in the domain of nomenclature and theory, but also, broadly, in such areas as performance practice, modal structure, and the types of instrument employed. Further, all three have suffered from the ambiguities and tensions resulting from the generally hostile attitude of Islam to art music and its practitioners.

Within Arab art music itself two major traditions may be distinguished, each with internal subdivisions: that of the eastern Arab world (principally Egypt, Lebanon, Syria and Iraq), and that of the western (Morocco, Algeria and Tunisia). Both may be said to derive ultimately from the court music that evolved during the Umayyad and early Abbāsid periods (7th to 9th centuries), when Persian influence had already made itself felt. But the north African tradition, although not completely isolated, was less exposed to the subsequent waves of Persian and, later, Turkish influence that had a significant impact in the east, and it is often considered to represent a survival of the Andalusian music of Moorish Spain.

1. Early history. 2. Theory. 3. Musical characteristics. 4. Instruments. 5. After 1900.

1. EARLY HISTORY.

(*i*) *The pre-Islamic period* (*before 622*). The sources for the early history of Arab music are for the most part no earlier than the 9th century, and often need to be treated with considerable caution. Thus although certain general features emerge with tolerable clarity, it is not possible to trace in any detail the formative stages in the development of art music during the first century of Islam, still less to speak with any certainty about the pre-Islamic Arab tradition that stands behind it.

In terms of their descriptive content, references to the earliest types of music are brief and unrevealing, and are of interest chiefly for the distinctions of genre they make. The most ancient genre, it is said, is the *ḥudā'* (caravan song), this and the *naṣb* being associated with male performers. The *naṣb*, of which no description is given, belongs to a wider category clearly differentiated from the *ḥudā'* (although according to one account deriving from it) and by implication considered to be more sophisticated – *ghinā'* ('song', later sometimes used generically for musical practice). The other sub-categories of *ghinā'* are the *sinād*, characterized as 'heavy' and ornate, and the 'light' and gay *hazaj* (the 'heavy–light' opposition, however, might be a projection back of a later stylistic distinction). It is probably mainly these two types of music that were performed by the *qayna* ('singing slave-girl'), with whom the emergence of entertainment music may be associated. In poetry the *qayna* is also portrayed as playing an instrument, most frequently a lute (*kirān, muwattar*), shawm (*mizmār*), or frame drum (*daff*). Also performed by women, although not by the *qayna*, was the *nawḥ* (lament): unfortunately there is again no description of this genre, nor is it defined in relation to the others – possibly it was perceived as subordinate to its ritual context.

(*ii*) *The first century of Islam.* The first century of Islam was a period of considerable upheaval and change. The sources point to the introduction of new elements resulting from more intense exposure to outside influences, mainly from Persia but also from former Byzantine provinces, and further emphasize the shifts taking place in attitudes to music and in the social role and identity of the musician. The main centre for these new developments was the Ḥijāz region (particularly the cities of Mecca and Medina) which, after the founding of the Umayyad caliphate (661–750) and the consequent shift of power to Syria, was marked by the tensions between continuing wealth and an increasing loss of political influence, and between the survival of pre-Islamic patterns of behaviour and the evolution of new Islamic norms. Entertainment music, previously the preserve of the *qayna*, gradually came to be dominated by male performers, being associated in the first stages of this transfer with the *mukhannathūn*, a group of effeminates who were as renowned for their immoral behaviour as for their artistic accomplishments. Thus music as a profession, given both its long-standing connection with the *qayna* and the inevitable hostility of the pious to the more recent activities of the *mukhannathūn*, could hardly become a respectable calling, and the important early male singers were generally non-Arabs of low social status. Further, the close association of entertainment music with attitudes and patterns of behaviour that were to become increasingly unacceptable led eventually to its being at least disapproved of, and sometimes condemned outright, by Muslim legists. Inevitably other types of musical activity also became suspect, and while grudging acceptance was normally accorded to the music that traditionally formed an integral part of im-

portant social ceremonies, the specifically religious use of music (e.g. in the cantillation of the Koran) could only be tolerated under the cover of a separate terminology.

Social change was paralleled by developments in the musical system itself: musicians of the first century of Islam are consistently portrayed as innovators. Two of the most famous early Umayyad musicians, for example, Ibn Misjaḥ and Ibn Muḥriz (both *d c*715), are described (if in suspiciously similar terms) as having travelled through former Byzantine and Persian territories, subsequently integrating into their own tradition the more readily acceptable features of the musics they encountered. Such accounts ring true at least in so far as they point to a period of transition during which the emerging art music idiom was characterized by considerable flexibility and the capacity to assimilate new elements, but without compromising the essential character of the Arab tradition on which it was ultimately based. It would also be reasonable to assume, as a result of increasing professionalism, a gradual distancing of art music from folk music, not just in terms of performance context, but more particularly in conscious artistry and technical proficiency, both vocally and instrumentally. It became more common for the singer to provide his own instrumental accompaniment, normally on a lute, and instrumental innovations included the introduction of the Persian wooden-bellied variety of short-necked lute ('ŪD) and, probably, a change in the accordatura, from a tuning with whole tones and a 4th to one all in 4ths, giving an increased range. A further feature of art music during this period was apparently the broad distinction, whether carried over from pre-Islamic practice or newly introduced, between a more serious and 'heavy' style (*thaqīl*) and a 'light' and gayer one (*khafīf*), the former commanding greater prestige, the latter greater popularity.

While Persian influences seem to have had a more significant impact on the development of musical practice in this period, the organization, or at least the classification, of the modal system of Umayyad art music may have been affected by Byzantine models. Some features of the system, which consisted of eight modes, are described by AL-MUNAJJIM (*d* 912), who discussed them in terms of the diatonic lute fretting to which their names relate (strictly a Pythagorean fretting producing scales of whole tones (204 cents) and limmas (90 cents), see IRAN, Table 1). The modes are divided into two sets (Arabic *majrā*, 'course') of four, distinguished by the occurrence in one set of the note produced by the middle-finger fret, and in the other of that produced by the annular fret, these two notes being mutually exclusive. The names of the modes (e.g. *muṭlaq fī majrā al-binṣir*: 'open string in the course of the annular') are a kind of descriptive shorthand, one term specifying the set, and the other presumably defining a prominent note of particular importance to the identity of the mode. Accounts of virtually extempore composition suggest that modal structure involved considerable use of melodic formulae, but the nature and precise degree of prescription remain unknown.

The final formulation of the nomenclature may, however, be post-Umayyad. It has been attributed to al-Munajjim's principal authority, ISḤĀQ AL-MAWṢILĪ (767–850), and certainly it is often the case that where Isḥāq is not the source for the technical description of a song, only the reference to the set is supplied. During the Umayyad period, therefore, it is possible that the internal differentiation between the members of each set may not have been very clear-cut or indeed considered particularly important. As a means of identification (or at least labelling), specifying the melodic mode of a song seems to have been less crucial than indicating the rhythmic cycle. The earliest extant definition of the rhythmic cycles, that of AL-KINDĪ (c801–73), is, unfortunately, imprecise and in some respects obscure (and in any case presumably relates to early Abbāsid rather than to Umayyad practice), but the presence in the names of some of the cycles of the terms 'heavy' and 'light' suggests not only that they may have been divided, like the melodic modes, into two sets, but also that the identity of the cycle may have been important in coding stylistic differences.

(iii) Early 'Abbāsid court music. The overthrow of the Umayyads by the 'Abbāsids in 750, with the resulting shift of the centre of power eastwards to Iraq, and the founding of a new imperial capital at Baghdad, exposed what was still a predominantly Arab art music tradition to a further wave of Persian influence. By the early 9th century, perhaps as part of a wider dispute between supporters and opponents of Arab cultural supremacy, most of the prominent musicians, now increasingly associated with the court, formed themselves loosely into two groups: one defending tradition, the other encouraging innovation. The latter had as its figurehead IBRĀHĪM IBN AL-MAHDĪ (779–839), famous for the quality and range of his voice, while the former was dominated by the chief upholder of the classical Arab heritage, Isḥāq al-Mawṣilī, the son of IBRĀHĪM AL-MAWṢILĪ (742–804), who had himself had an illustrious career at court and was also celebrated as a teacher and prolific composer. A man of wide general scholarship and a talented poet, Isḥāq was considered the most complete musician of his day, compensating by impeccable technique for the less than outstanding quality of his voice. Whether because of the almost legendary reputations acquired by such musicians, or because of the more informative nature – at least biographically and socially – of the sources, the early 'Abbāsid period has sometimes been termed the 'golden age' of Arab music: a rather misleading description, however, for there is no evidence to substantiate the implicit assumption of a subsequent decline in levels of artistic achievement. Particularly important as a source for any account of musical life during this and earlier periods is the monumental Kitāb al-aghānī ('Book of songs') of AL-IṢFAHĀNĪ (897–967) which, however, exhibits a marked bias in favour of Isḥāq al-Mawṣilī, so that it contains, for example, no account of the career of the latter's potential rival ZIRYĀB (d c850). Encouraged to seek his fortune elsewhere, Ziryāb eventually went to Spain, where the Umayyads had been able to re-establish themselves. There his fame equalled that of Isḥāq, and he was celebrated as both performer and teacher (as well as general arbiter of taste), and was credited on the instrumental side with improvements to the 'ūd (short-necked lute) including the addition of a fifth string. An earlier 'Abbāsid musician, the famous lutenist ZALZAL (d 791), is credited with a more radical innovation to the 'ūd: the introduction, alongside the frets producing the diatonic scale to which the early modal system related, of a new middle-finger fret producing approximately a neutral 3rd from the open string. But whatever their origin, the use of neutral intervals (chiefly the approximate three-quarter tone) is attested from the 10th century, and has remained a characteristic feature of Arab and Persian art music ever since. Also attributed to Zalzal is the introduction of an improved type of lute, and parallel to a number of such organological developments and innovations further refinements in playing technique probably took place during the early 'Abbāsid period. Specifically instrumental forms are mentioned, but instrumental music was to remain subservient to vocal, and references to particular formal features suggest the elaboration of fairly precise conventions governing the setting of verse.

2. THEORY.

(i) Early theorists. The 9th and 10th centuries were significant not only for the flowering of court music, but also for the development of a theoretical literature. Incorporating various ideas derived from Greek sources being translated at this time, the several short treatises of the philosopher al-Kindī, the first important theorist whose works are extant, prefigured two of the most significant areas of concern of this theoretical literature by the emphasis they placed on cosmology and on the analysis of intervals and scales. Most of the major theorists concentrated on the latter aspect, tending towards abstractions of a more purely mathematical order, while particular attention was paid to the former by the IKHWĀN AL-ṢAFĀ' ('Brethren of Purity', 10th century), and by a number of post-13th-century texts concerned with the cosmological affiliations of the modes. Al-Kindī's cosmological interest focussed rather on correlations of number sets (i.e. numerology): thus the four strings of the lute were related, among other things, to the zodiac, the elements, the seasons and the humours.

Although utilizing concepts derived from Greek theory, al-Kindī's treatment of scale, like that of later writers, was expressed in terms of a fretting on the 'ūd. Despite its basis in practice, the reference to lute frets quickly became in essence a purely theoretical method of demonstration, and al-Kindī's own fretting (Table 1),

TABLE 1: Fretting for the 'ūd (al-Kindī, 9th century)

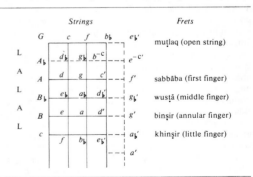

although still close to the one in terms of which the early modal system was discussed, already posited one hypothetical fret (and further included a notional fifth string to complete the second octave). It proceeds by steps of limma (L) and apotomē (A) being the difference between limma (90 cents) and whole tone (204 cents), i.e. 114 cents; the difference between limma and apotomē being a comma (C) of 24 cents). Al-Kindī

TABLE 2: Series of intervals for any string of the lute
(al-Fārābī, 10th century)

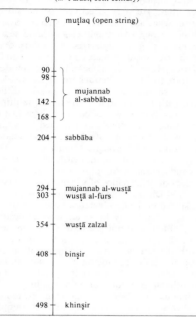

0	muṭlaq (open string)
90	
98	
142	mujannab al-sabbāba
168	
204	sabbāba
294	mujannab al-wusṭā
303	wusṭā al-furs
354	wusṭā zalzal
408	binṣir
498	khinṣir

also listed a number of variant tunings and these, in contrast to the highly artificial ones elaborated by some of his successors, clearly relate to practice: F–c–f–b♭; A–c–f–b♭; and B♭–c–f–b♭.

Al-Kindī's treatises demonstrate familiarity with the Greater Perfect system as an analytical framework, and a further aspect of the Greek heritage stressed by the other major philosophers who wrote extensively on music, AL-FĀRĀBĪ (d 950) and IBN SĪNĀ (Avicenna) (980–1037), is the codification of various tetrachord types and the numerical analysis of their constituent intervals. Since many of the tetrachords they list were not in current use, the amount of attention paid to them points to a new concentration on theory for its own sake – an extension of the purely speculative side of music viewed as one of the mathematical sciences (the Western medieval Quadrivium). Much of their work, however, notably the material on instruments in al-Fārābī's magisterial Kitāb al-mūsīqī al-kabīr ('Great book on music'), did relate to contemporary practice, even if obliquely. For example, if one takes the main set of interval values defined by al-Fārābī for the lute, the series shown in Table 2 occurs on each string (expressed in cents). The apparent complexity, at least in comparison to earlier frettings, results from the superimposition of different analytical strands. Thus the values 90, 204, 294, 408 and 498 are inherited from al-Kindī, while those at 98 and 303 may be viewed as variant definitions of the semitone and minor 3rd arrived at not by ratios but by an alternative (and less precise) empirical technique of halving the distance between other frets. Of the remainder, 142 and 168 are again alternatives, being approximations to a value one whole tone below the neutral 3rd at 354. The above set can thus be related to a situation in practice where neutral intervals have been added alongside the diatonic ones, so that on a single

lute string (tuned, for example, to G) the following functional pitch discriminations are made (ḇ represents a value roughly halfway between ♭ and ♮): G (A♭, A♭̮), A, B♭, B♭̮, B, c. The particular hesitation over the values to be assigned to A♭ and A♭̮ indicates that at this period the area between open string and first-finger fret was just beginning to be tentatively explored by practitioners.

The other main melody instruments are each described by al-Fārābī as having their own distinctive scales, although in most cases these can be reconciled with structures derivable from the lute scale norm. The scales that appear to differ most markedly from that of the 'ūd are associated with two varieties of ṭunbūr (long-necked lute). The ṭunbūr baghdādī is said originally to have had a scale proceeding by approximate quarter-tone steps over a range of little more than a minor 3rd, while the ṭunbūr khurāsānī scale, which may in reality have included neutral intervals, is analysed in terms of steps of limma and comma, a model that was taken up and extended in the 13th century.

Another major area of theoretical concern was the study of rhythm. Here the Greek concept of the chronos prōtos is sometimes encountered, but most analyses were conceived in terms relating to what was for the Arabs the sister science of prosody. The problematic nature of the earliest account of the rhythmic cycle, that of al-Kindī, has been mentioned above, and the version in Table 3, showing relative durations only, must be considered tentative. Ibn Sīnā and, particularly, al-Fārābī dealt with rhythm at great length, but in an extremely complicated and abstract way. A rather simpler treatment was provided by IBN ZAYLA (d 1048), a pupil of Ibn Sīnā, who, like al-Fārābī, emphasized the flexible nature of the internal structure of many cycles, and detailed the various patterns of beats that can occur.

TABLE 3: Rhythmic cycles (8th–9th centuries)

'heavy'/slow					'light'/fast				
thaqīl awwal	O O O	.			khafīf al-thaqīl	O O O	.		
thaqīl thānī	O O O	.	O		mākhūrī		O O	.	O .
ramal	O .	O O	.		khafīf al-ramal	O O O			
					khafīf al-khafīf	O O	.		
					hazaj	O O	.		.

O – sounded beat; . – unsounded beat

Of all the theorists of this period the most profound, and also the most wide ranging in scope, was undoubtedly al-Fārābī. Important aspects of his Kitāb al-mūsīqī al-kabīr include the general methodology of the introduction (which also contains speculations on the origins of music and the nature of musical talent), the discussion of the physics of sound, the survey of melodic types and the remarks on vocal technique. This last subject is also dealt with in a substantial treatise by AL-ḤASAN IBN AḤMAD (probably late 10th century), which discusses in addition aspects of instrumental technique and supplies certain details about post-Umayyad developments in the modal system. Further information about the modes is provided by Ibn Sīnā (early 11th century). Some of the modes he cited may in terms of scale be resolved into conjunct tetrachords, but overall there is no clear structural pattern. The prevailing impression is of a relatively unstable transitional stage (incorporating elements deriving from different sources) between the early diatonic system, of which parts still survived, and the rather complex, more varied, but highly regular system described by Arab and Persian theorists of the 13th and subsequent centuries.

(ii) *Persian–Arab synthesis.* Among the most noteworthy contributions to Near Eastern musical literature in the period between Ibn Zayla and ṢAFĪ AL-DĪN (d 1294), the first of the later theorists, are those made by the celebrated theologian AL-GHAZĀLĪ (d 1111) and his brother MAJD AL-DĪN AL-GHAZĀLĪ (d 1126). On the vexed question of the legal permissibility of music, they presented a defence based, if with slightly differing emphases, on a common Sufi standpoint. Thus rather as, in mystical literature, the language of profane love became a recognized vehicle for the expression of religious experiences and yearnings, so a distinction was drawn with regard to the listener's reactions to music (the erotic associations of which were well recognized) stressing in addition to a purely sensual response the possibility of a spiritual apprehension legitimizing music as an aid to progress on the Sufi path.

The period from 1050 to 1250 is, however, devoid of theoretical texts of major importance, and it is consequently not possible to trace developments in the musical system in any detail. But one major issue would in any case hardly have been dealt with by the theorists: the rate and extent of diffusion of a single broadly unified art music idiom embodying a synthesis of Arab and Persian elements. During the 9th and 10th centuries it appears that although the ʿAbbāsid court music tradition continued to absorb new features and, perhaps more importantly, constituted a model to be imitated, a reasonable degree of regional variation nevertheless persisted. But except in the domain of rhythm, where the distinction between Arab and non-Arab stubbornly persists, texts of the 13th to 15th centuries make no reference to differences between Arab and Persian practice.

Although a final integration of the two no doubt seems a logical outcome of earlier contacts and prolonged mutual influences, at first sight it would appear to accord less well with the general trend of political developments during the protracted decline of the ʿAbbāsid caliphate. Power had begun to slip from the ʿAbbāsid caliphs even before the death of al-Kindī (c873), and their authority, real or symbolic, was soon restricted to the central provinces, while elsewhere ambitious governors and army commanders were able to set up virtually independent local dynasties. But such fragmentation led to an increase in artistic activity and patronage, and in music to a decentralization that could well have promoted (parallel to the diffusion of the military band, valued as an emblem of authority) a wider adoption of the prestigious form of art music that had hitherto been cultivated primarily at the Baghdad court. In effect the available evidence suggests that with reference to the modes, forms and instruments, a virtually complete fusion of the Arab and Persian systems had taken place by the mid-13th century at the latest, resulting in the spread of a common art music idiom over most of the eastern Arab world (but not north Africa and Spain, which must be presumed to have already begun to develop along slightly different lines) and Persia, and penetrating in addition, perhaps, to some of the major Islamic cultural centres in Central Asia. The following account, rhythm excepted, may therefore be considered to be as valid for Persian art music of the 13th to 15th centuries as it is for Arab.

(iii) *The Systematist school.* The two treatises of Ṣafī al-Dīn (d 1294) supply the analytical framework which was used by nearly all the major writers of the following two centuries. He may effectively be considered the founder of what has come to be termed the Systematist school of theory. Although clearly indebted to al-Fārābī, his work generally evinces in its most developed aspect, the treatment of scale, a new rigour and analytical clarity. He took as his basis the division described by al-Fārābī for the first tetrachord of the *ṭunbūr khurāsānī* scale, so that the neutral intervals, difficult to reconcile with the traditional stress on the primacy of simple ratios, were now treated virtually as just intonation intervals. The octave was arranged in symmetrical layers: it was divided into two conjunct tetrachords and a whole tone, each tetrachord being made up of two whole tones and a limma, and each whole tone of two limmas and a comma. Adopting earlier ideas concerning the degrees of consonance of various interval types and sizes, Ṣafī al-Dīn elaborated a further theory of consonance designed in the first instance as a generative device producing all and only those tetrachords occurring in practice, but in addition deemed partly applicable to pentachords and to the octave scales which they combine with the tetrachords to produce. Ṣafī al-Dīn also relied on al-Fārābī for most of his basic definitions, but his exposition of rhythm was independent, employing the traditional prosodic terminology in a clear and unambiguous way. Beyond these main areas his range was rather restricted – instruments for example were not dealt with – but he did, for the first time, although using an alphabetic method already known to al-Kindī, supply a few fragments of notation.

A more extended example of notation – in fact of a song by Ṣafī al-Dīn – is provided by the next Systematist theorist, QUṬB AL-DĪN (1236–1311), whose work is also significant for its fuller and less doctrinaire account of the modes. Although new additions are recorded, most other writers tended to reproduce the corpus of modes recorded by Ṣafī al-Dīn, so that it was not until the end of the 15th century, with theorists such as AL-LĀDHIQĪ, that major developments within that corpus were revealed. Like earlier theorists of the Systematist school, al-Lādhiqī also gave a fairly full account of the rhythmic cycles employed in his time, so that it is possible to see the ways in which the system continued to evolve and expand, showing an increasing predilection for cycles with an extremely large number of time units.

After Ṣafī al-Dīn one generally finds on the more strictly theoretical side, true to the intellectual temper of the times, not original thought but rather the elaboration of existing ideas in commentaries and reworkings that are nevertheless by no means uncritical. Of particular importance in this respect are, firstly, the *Sharḥ Mawlānā Mubārak Shāh bar adwār* ('The Mubārak Shāh commentary on the *Kitāb al-adwār*', 1375), which is an extensive commentary on the first of Ṣafī al-Dīn's two treatises, the *Kitāb al-adwār* ('Book of cycles'), and which in its general coverage of theory perhaps stands second only to al-Fārābī's *Kitāb al-mūsīqī al-kabīr*, and, secondly, the influential works of ʿABD AL-QĀDIR (d 1435), which also deal in some detail with the major musical forms and with the classification and description of instruments, an aspect covered in the 14th-century *Kanz al-tuḥaf* ('Treasure of rarities') but ignored by most Systematist theorists.

The available evidence suggests that from the 13th

century to the 15th, the period dominated by theorists of the Systematist school, art music continued to evolve through the gradual introduction of new modes, rhythms, forms and instruments, and there is no reason to suppose that the process should have come to a halt during the Ottoman period (early 16th century to early 20th century). But this period, during which most of the Arab world formed part of the Turkish Ottoman empire, is extremely poor in Arabic texts relating to music, and it is therefore difficult to trace the development of Arab music as something separate from the increasingly dominant style of Turkish art music, which was itself based on the earlier composite Arab and Persian tradition. The history of Persian music after the 15th century is also poorly documented, but it probably began to develop along slightly different lines at the latest during the 16th century, a time of continuing hostility between Safavid Persia and the Ottomans.

3. MUSICAL CHARACTERISTICS.

(i) *Mode.* Wherever possible, Ṣafī al-Dīn described the modes in terms of his theoretical octave scale, distortions notwithstanding. He listed 20 modes in all, of which 12 form a set known as the *shudūd* and a further six a set termed *āwāzāt*. (The symbolic importance of these numbers was generally disregarded by Systematist writers, few of whom touched upon musical cosmology.) The great majority of the modes may be viewed as fixed combinations of tetrachord and pentachord species, the latter generally resolvable into tetrachord plus whole tone. From Quṭb al-Dīn's account it is also possible to see the importance within the system as a whole of certain non-tetrachordal species that rarely occurred in combinations expressible in terms of an octave scale abstract. The basic units from which the system was compounded in the latter part of the 13th century are shown in ex.1. These units were not juxtaposed at

Ex.1 Basic units of the modal system (13th century)

random: diatonic units, for example, were normally segregated from non-diatonic. But the most important factor was consonance: nearly all the combinations noted as occurring were characterized by complete or partial parallelism (normally at the 4th or, less frequently, the 5th) or, if at the same pitch level, by minimum differentiation.

Within this general framework more specific features contributed to modal identity. A few modes were characterized by particular melodic movements, while a more common convention concerned the identity of the initial or final note, or both, so that in some cases the order of occurrence of the constituent units was fixed. It was probably in terms of these units that the melody was

for the most part articulated: one unit would be explored, at least to the extent of establishing its identity, before passing on to the next in a sequence that could also modulate through units not intrinsic to the mode in question. In some modes one unit would be more prominent than another, and the important feature of prominence also frequently attached to the note linking the two units, for example the C in the case of *rāst* (ex.2).

Ex.2 The mode rāst (13th century)

Indeed, the pivotal importance of this note was such that it sometimes led to the emergence of a parallel derived mode, as in the case of *rāst* (ex.3).

Ex.3 Mode derived from rāst (13th century)

During the 14th and 15th centuries the system was gradually enlarged, partly as a result of such developments, partly because changes in its structural basis allowed slightly different patterns to develop. The type of unit combination exemplified by *rāst* was to become less normative, with relatively greater stress being laid on melodic matrices often relating to a single unit, and indeed at the end of the 15th century *rāst* was defined as precisely such an entity (ex.4). Thus the modern *maqām rāst* is probably not a direct continuation of the derived form given above, despite the apparent close similarity. In the history of this modal system continuity would seem to reside primarily in the basic units (although they are not immutable), while the way in which they combine is subject to constant change and development.

Ex.4 The mode rāst (15th century)

(ii) *Rhythm.* Following Ṣafī al-Dīn, Systematist theorists normally defined the rhythmic cycles in two ways. One was to divide a circle into the same number of sectors as there are time units and to add symbols indicating those normally sounded. The other was to employ, parallel to the methods used in the analysis of the poetic metres, the syllables *ta*, *na* (each equivalent to one time unit) and *tan*, *nan* (each equivalent to two time units), and to divide the rhythmic cycle into feet of two to four time units, *ta* and *tan* always being initial in a foot, *na* medial, and *nan* final. In these theoretical abstracts of the cycles it is assumed that the initial time unit in a foot is always sounded, the final one almost always not, with the sounding of medial ones being generally optional. The first version of each cycle listed in Safī al-Dīn's *Kitāb al-adwār* ('Book of cycles') is shown in Table 4. Except for the final one, these cycles are said to be used by the Arabs, but at least two were presumably also known to Persian musicians. According to a later author they called the *thaqīl* 'warshān', while Ṣafī al-Dīn himself states that the cycle they most commonly employed was the *thaqīl al-ramal*, which they termed *ḍarb al-aṣl* ('basic beat'), a designation otherwise used by theorists to indicate the two most important sounded time units in a cycle, which presumably were thought sufficient to identify it. The *fākhitī*, in which only the initial time unit in each foot is sounded, is said by Ṣafī al-Dīn tó be a less common cycle used by Persian musicians.

TABLE 4: Rhythmic cycles (Ṣafī al-Dīn, 13th century)

thaqīl awwal	Oo.Oo.Ooo.O.Ooo.	(3+3+4+2+4)
thaqīl thānī	Oo.Oo.O.Oo.Oo.O.	(3+3+2+3+3+2)
khafīf al-thaqīl	O.OxO.OxO.OxO.Ox	(2+2+2+2+2+2+2+2)
thaqīl al-ramal	Ooo.Ooo.O.O.O.O.O.O.Ooo.	(4+4+2+2+2+2+2+2+4)
ramal	O.O.O.O.O.O.	(2+2+2+2+2+2)
khafīf al-ramal	O.Oo.O.Oo.	(2+3+2+3)
hazaj	Ooo.Oo.Oo.O.	(4+3+3+2)
fākhitī	O...O.O...O...O.O...	(4+2+4+4+2+4)

O – initial time unit of foot (always sounded); o – medial time unit (optionally sounded); . – final time unit (not sounded); x – final time unit (sounded)

For several of the cycles the *Kitāb al-adwār* gives variant forms, and the versions in Ṣafī al-Dīn's other treatise, the *Risāla al-sharafiyya*, are sometimes different again, so that the cycles in Table 4 should perhaps best be considered not definitions but representative examples each belonging to a set of closely related forms. The relationship between members of a set is in certain cases obvious (for example another form of *ramal* is 2 + 2 + 2 + 2 + 4, and a variant of *thaqīl thānī* is 3 + 3 + 2), but in other cases suggests that there might have been a considerable degree of flexibility in the arrangement and identity of feet, involving re-ordering (for example 2 + 4 + 2 + 4 and 4 + 2 + 4 + 2 are both listed as variants of *ramal*); substitution (2 + 4 + 2 + 4 is also listed as a variant of *khafīf al-ramal*, given in Table 4 as 2 + 3 + 2 + 3); elision (a variant of *hazaj* is 4 + 2); and extension (*fākhitī* has a re-ordered variant with two extra feet: 2 + 4 + 4 + 4 + 2 + 4 + 4 + 4).

Later accounts were generally somewhat fuller. Quṭb al-Dīn added a further five cycles, including one called *turkī*. By the late 15th century the system had expanded to the extent that al-Lādhiqī was able to describe 18 cycles as being in common use, and to list a further nine rarer ones. Several are extremely complex, involving an exceptionally large number of time units: *thaqīl*, 48; *ḍarb al-fataḥ*, 88; *chahār ḍarb*, 96. The longer cycles are for the most part duple (compounds of feet of 2, 4 and 8 time units), while asymmetrical combinations of duple and triple occur mainly among the shorter cycles (for example *rawān* 2 + 3 + 4 and *samā'ī* 3 + 3 + 4).

(*iii*) *Form*. Early theorists discussed a number of formal features, and texts such as the 10th-century *Kitāb al-aghānī* exhibit several terms relating to song structure. The precise meaning of these, however, is not always clear, and in effect it is not until the early 14th century, in the works of Abd al-Qādir, that a fairly complete descriptive account of the main forms is found. The definitions he gave relate in part to the verbal or literary aspect, i.e. whether the form or section in question is with or without words, and, if the former, whether the language of the verse set is Arabic or Persian. The discussion of specifically musical structural features concerns such matters as the differences between the various types of section, the presence or absence of one or other of these in a given form, and whether or not a fixed rhythmic cycle is used. The notated example he gave (which is not assigned to any particular form) has a structure marked by an alternation of declamatory and florid passages of vocal writing, and this pattern may have been quite common.

One of the forms described by 'Abd al-Qādir is the *basīṭ*, a setting of Arabic verse with an instrumental prelude. Another is the *nashīd al-'arab*, again a setting of Arabic verse (although in this case there was also a Persian-language counterpart, *nashīd al-'ajam*), with sections in free rhythm alternating with others in a fixed rhythmic cycle. Although it is impossible to trace the history of these forms, a not unrelated use of the terms is found as early as the 10th century, *nashīd* designating an initial section extending over one or two lines of verse which is in free rhythm, in contrast to the remainder of the song, called *basīṭ*. Equally obscure are the stages in the development of the most complex form of all, the *nawba*, a suite of four movements which may have been the result of a gradual process of crystallization that shaped into a conventional sequence pieces in contrasting styles. The original impulse was perhaps provided by early 'Abbāsid etiquette, which sometimes prescribed a fixed order (or 'turn': *nawba*) for the appearance of performers at court. A rather similar process of development also appears to lie behind the separate north African *nawba* tradition, and the notion of establishing a particular sequence for different types of song has been ascribed to Ziryāb. Interestingly enough the terms used to designate the first two of these types are *nashīd* and *basīṭ*, and the progression of the sequence seems to have been from pieces in slow (or 'heavy') rhythms to pieces in faster (or 'light') rhythms.

As described by 'Abd al-Qādir the first movement of the *nawba*, called *qawl*, and the fourth, *furūdāsht*, are settings of Arabic poetry; the second, *ghazal*, is a setting of Persian poetry; and in the third, *tarāna*, the verse may be in either language. The *nawba* would normally be in one of three rhythmic cycles, *thaqīl awwal*, *thaqīl thānī* or *thaqīl al-ramal*, although the restriction was not absolute: 'Abd al-Qādir mentioned that he himself had used two other cycles. He also claimed to have added a fifth movement, *mustazād*, but it is not clear whether this innovation gained general acceptance.

Some of the other forms 'Abd al-Qādir discussed are of a technical complexity that could only be appreciated by an audience of some sophistication. They include the *ḍarbayn* ('two rhythms'), in which two rhythmic cycles were played simultaneously, and the *kull al-ḍurūb* ('all the rhythms'), in which all the rhythmic cycles were introduced successively. The latter could further be combined with the modal counterpart, the *kull al-nagham* ('all the notes'), of which there were two types: one in which all the modes were played in succession, and another in which various modes were introduced (at different relative pitch levels) so as to use all the notes of the theoretical gamut.

4. INSTRUMENTS. Apart from the *'ūd*, about which al-Kindī, for example, provided information regarding dimensions and construction, the instruments associated with the art music tradition were seldom discussed by the early theorists. The most significant exception is al-Fārābī, but even he was concerned less with the structure of the instruments than with the scales that were, or theoretically could be, produced on them. It is thus hardly surprising that, although percussion and concussion instruments are mentioned in the introduction of his *Kitāb al-mūsīqī al-kabīr*, none is described in the section on instruments. The categories exemplified there are plucked string instruments (e.g. *'ūd*), wind instruments (called generically *mazāmīr*) and bowed string instruments (*rabāb* being the one example), and a fur-

1. Bayād sings and plays the 'ūd (lute) for Riyād and her companions: miniature from a 13th-century MS, 'The Story of Bayād and Riyād', from Maghrib (I-Rvat Arab 368, f.10r)

ther classificatory distinction is maintained between instruments on which each note is produced by a separate open string (e.g. *jank*, 'harp'), and those on which the strings are stopped.

Ṣafī al-Dīn and, following him, many theorists of the Systematist school paid even less attention to instruments. The most important later texts in this respect are the anonymous *Kanz al-tuḥaf* and the treatises of 'Abd al-Qādir. The former lists only nine instruments (see fig.2), but describes them in more than usual detail, mentioning materials as well as proportions and construction. The latter list a far larger number of instruments, but although some indication of shape and relative dimensions is given, attention is concentrated more on defining the number of strings and the nature of the accordatura (aspects more closely related to the concerns of the theorist). 'Abd al-Qādir's classification, unlike al-Fārābī's, includes percussion, but the categories he illustrates are wind and strings, comprising some 40 instruments in all. He, too, subdivides the strings into open and stopped, and makes a parallel distinction for the wind instruments. Several of the instruments he describes, however, were never used in the context of art music, which seems to have continued to be performed only on a rather narrow (but not static) range of types of instrument, among which the *'ūd* retained its position of pre-eminence. In effect, it appears that 'Abd al-Qādir was

concerned to give a general survey of the various instruments known to him, however exotic: some were specifically stated to be Chinese, and one Indian, and he even included a description of the European organ. But if none of these was ever adopted by the Arabs or Persians as a vehicle for art music, 'Abd al-Qādir's awareness of and interest in them is symptomatic of the ease with which instruments (as distinct from the musical systems originally associated with them) can travel, and it is perhaps in this area that the musical debt of the surrounding cultures to the Islamic Middle East is greatest.

See also IRAN, §I.

5. AFTER 1900.

(*i*) *Theory.* At the beginning of the 19th century the Lebanese theorist Mikhā'īl Mashāqa, in his *Risāla al-shihabiyya fī al-ṣinā'a al-māūsīqiyya* ('Treatise on the art of music for the Emir Shihab'), introduced a new system for analysing scale, which is now accepted in much of the Near East. In this system an octave is divided into 24 intervals of approximately a quarter-tone (each about 50 cents). This type of scale division makes it possible to transpose modes containing the neutral 3rd to any scale degree. The computation of the exact sizes of those quarter-tones as they occur in practice is rather complicated, and several alternatives were presented at the Cairo Congress on Arab Music in 1932. Some of the

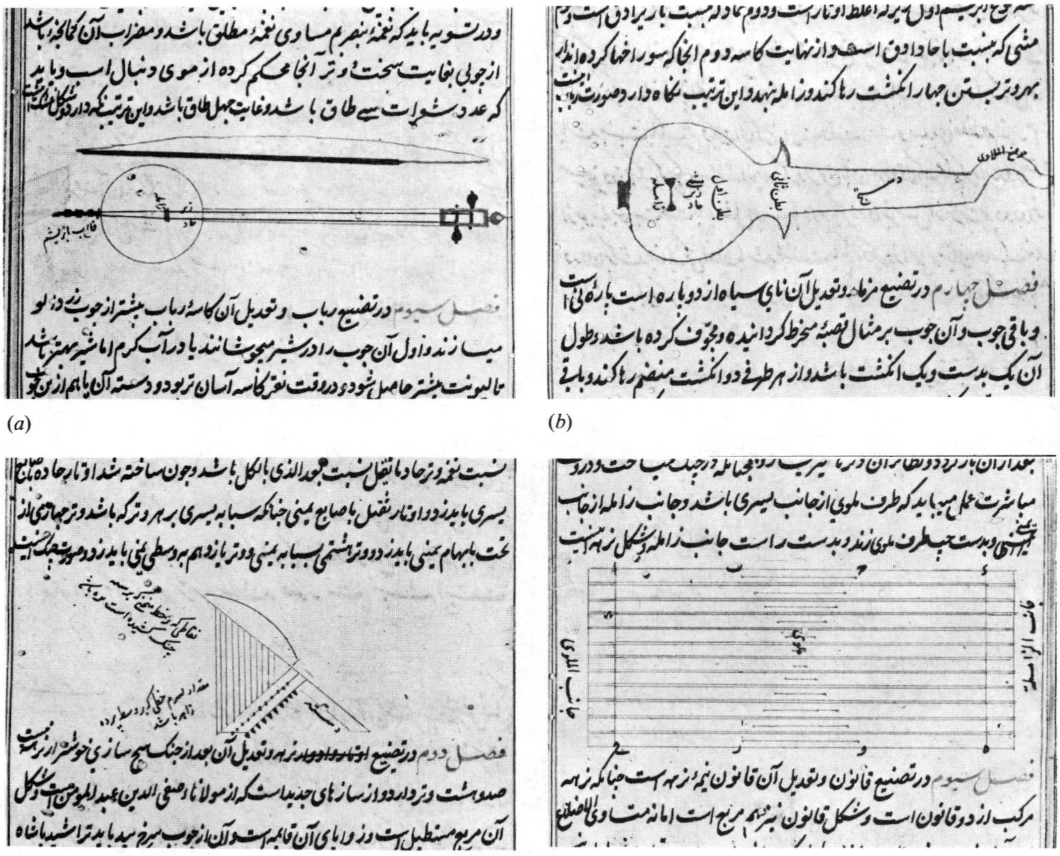

(a)

(b)

(c)

(d)

2. Drawings from Kanz al-tuḥaf (author unknown), a 14th-century treatise from Iran (GB-Lbm Oriental 2361, ff.262r, 262v, 263v, 264r): (a) ghizhak (spike fiddle) with hamān (horsehair bow); (b) rabāb (lute); (c) chang (angular harp); (d) nuzha (psaltery)

scale systems discussed at this meeting were obtained through mathematical computation and some were established experimentally. The most important systems were those presented by representatives of the Royal Institute of Arabian Music in Cairo, by Idris Rāġīb Bey and I. Shalfūn of Egypt, by Xavier Maurice Collangettes of the University of St Joseph in Beirut, the Turkish system of Ra'ūf Yektā Bey, and the system of Shaykh 'Alī al-Darwīsh. The differences between theorists and musicians, as well as modern research on the tonal structure of vocal and instrumental music (see, for example, Nettl, 1973), indicate that none of these systems provides an accurate description of actual musical practice. They are merely convenient tools for prescriptive and didactic purposes. The quarter-tone system is, however, still used in describing the tonal material of the modes. For notation of Arab art music the accepted Western five-line system has been augmented by additional signs indicating pitch deviation of one-quarter and three-quarters of a tone (Table 5).

At the 1932 congress an attempt was made to codify and classify the melodic modes (maqāmāt, plural of maqām) used in Arab countries. Each maqām was described in terms of scale (intervallic structure), ambitus, its division into tetrachords (or pentachords) and its tonics, the last being used as a criterion for classification. (The definition of maqām was later extended to include recognition of a hierarchy of pitches and melodic patterns.) Besides the starting pitch (mabdā') and the tonic (qarār) there are other important points of melodic emphasis in the maqām such as the ghammāz and zahīr, which are elaborated upon in a certain prescribed order. The ghammāz is the most prominent note of the climactic part of the melody and is often a 5th above the qarār, but it may also be a 3rd or 4th above it. The term zahīr is applied both to the note a step below the qarār, functioning like a leading note to the tonic, and to a cadential phrase leading from a lower pitch up to the qarār. The zahīr may be a semitone, a three-

TABLE 5: Accidentals used in Arab art music notation

♯	raises the pitch a quarter-tone
♯	" " " " semitone
♯	" " " " three-quarter tone
♭	lowers the pitch a quarter-tone
♭	" " " " semitone
♭	" " " " three-quarter tone

quarter tone or a whole tone below the *qarār*, its distance varying according to the structure of the *maqām*.

The scale of a particular *maqām* is divided into melodic units called *ajnās* (plural of *jins*, 'genre'), a concept similar to that of tetrachord or pentachord. There are 17 *ajnās* now in use, each with a different intervallic structure. Ex.5 gives a list, modelled on that of d'Erlanger, of the *ajnās* arranged in order from the

Ex.5 The 17 *ajnās* ('genres' or melodic units) used in the modern modal system

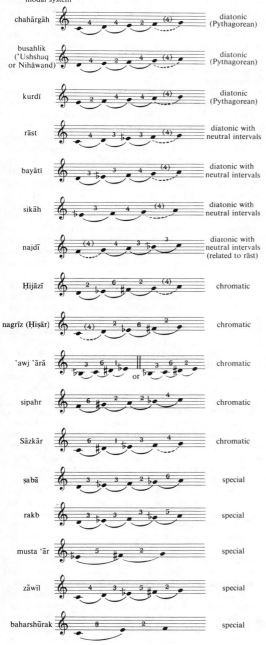

Pythagorean diatonic (i.e. using whole tones and semitones), the diatonic using neutral intervals, the chromatic (i.e. using augmented 2nds and two smaller intervals within the same tetrachord) to the special ones which fit into none of these categories (compare with those of the 13th century given in ex.1). The intervals between degrees are given in multiples of a quarter-tone; the intervals in parentheses are additional intervals in *ajnās* functioning as pentachords.

Maqāmāt can be composed either of *ajnās* of the same type or of ones of different types. Some *maqāmāt* reduplicate the same *jins* at different pitch levels. The majority, however, use different *ajnās*; some *maqāmāt* are characterized by the use of more than one *jins* at the same pitch level, a process known as *tarkib* ('mixing'). The sequence in which the *ajnās* occur is usually fixed for each *maqām* and is part of the definition of that mode.

There is no complete list of the *maqāmāt* of the Arab Near East. A number of lists have, however, been drawn up (beginning with that of the Cairo Congress) which exhibit within the broad Near Eastern tradition local or regional variations. The most comprehensive is that of d'Erlanger (1949), which names 119 *maqāmāt* in use in the eastern Arab countries. The *maqāmāt* of the western Arab countries (i.e. those of north Africa) are similar in broad structural principle to those of the eastern, but they form a separate tradition and their number is more restricted (d'Erlanger listed only 29 for Tunisia, for example). The names for the *maqāmāt* are not technical and do not usually indicate structure; they may indeed be used to indicate different modes in different regions. For example, the nomenclature used in north Africa overlaps with that used in eastern countries, but there are significant differences in the musical forms employed and in the ways in which the modes are used within them. (*See also* MODE, §V.)

The temporal aspect of modern Arab art music is organized in a system of rhythmic modes expressed in cycles. The cycle (*dawr* in Egypt, *ṭaqm* in Syria) is a determined succession of qualitatively differentiated beats or accents (*naqarāt*, plural of *naqara*), which is repeated throughout the entire piece or a section of it. Each cycle consists of principal beats (*naqarāt aṣliyya*) divided into *ajzā'* ('parts'), each of the *ajzā'* consisting of one to five smaller units. Among the different qualities of beat recognized by modern musicians are: *dum* (strong beat); *tak* (weak beat); *mah* (a beat stronger than *dum* and usually following it); *kā* (a beat weaker than *tak* and usually following it); *kah* or *ke* (a beat weaker than *tak*); and *ta* (a beat much weaker than *tak* and always appearing together with it). The cycles of a mode are often very long and can have intricate patterns of beats. One of the longest rhythmic modes now used is the Syrian *ḍarb al-fatḥ* with 176 beats. At least 111 rhythmic modes have been listed for the eastern part of the Arab world, but only a small proportion are commonly used. North African musicians seem to employ far fewer rhythmic modes than do those of the east (paralleling the situation with regard to melodic modes): for example, only five modes have been listed for Morocco.

(ii) *Forms*. The principal form of art music of the Arab Near East is the *nawba* or *waṣla*. It is a suite of movements performed as a unit (see §3 (iii) above for its early history and development). There are now two major types of *nawba*: the eastern *nawba*, performed principally in Egypt and Syria, and the Andalusian *nawba*, further differentiated into three types (Moroccan, Algerian and Tunisian) and believed to derive from the traditions of Muslim Spain.

(*a*) The eastern nawba. The eastern *nawba* consists of eight movements (pieces) centred around a single mode and ordered in a certain pattern or succession of rhythmic modes, the most complex rhythmic modes appearing at the beginning of the suite and the simpler ones towards the end. The *nawba* opens with a *taqsīm*, an improvised solo instrumental prelude. This is basically a virtuoso piece (which may also occur between movements) in which a soloist can demonstrate his technical skills. When it opens the *nawba*, however, the *taqsīm* serves to set the mode for the performer(s), and then its primary purpose is to prepare, explore and define the mode, to which virtuosic display is secondary. The performer improvises passages in which he realizes structurally important degrees of the chosen *maqām*, in an order peculiar to that mode. Rhythmically the *taqāsīm* can be either free or measured, although most are free.

The *taqsīm* is followed by the *bashraf*, an instrumental piece based on a relatively long and complex rhythmic mode. It consists of four or five sections (*khāna*), each containing the same number of rhythmic cycles and each ending with a coda (*taslīm*). In the first *khāna* the principal theme and the *maqām* are established, and the second *khāna* contains modulations to related *maqāmāt*. In the third section melodic activity centres in the upper register of the scale, and in the fourth *khāna* it returns to the principal theme in the lower register.

The third movement of a *nawba* is a *samā'i*. It too consists of four or five sections, the first three or four being based on the quintuple metre *samā'i thaqīl* (5/4 or 10/8), and the last section on a ternary metre, *dārij samā'i* (3/4 or 6/8 or 3/8) or *sanguīn samā'i* (6/4 or 12/8).

The fourth movement is a group of several *tawāshīḥ* (plural of *tawshīḥ*; composed vocal pieces with texts from the strophic poems of the same name, a genre developed in Andalusia but found throughout the Arab Near East). *Tawāshīḥ*, also called *mūwashshaḥāt*, are sung by the members of the ensemble. There are several kinds of *tawshīḥ*: *tawshīḥ ma'lūf* ('simple'), based on a single rhythmic mode; *tawshīḥ ḍarbayn*, based on two different rhythmic modes; and *tawshīḥ zanjīr*, in which each rhythmic phrase is composed of five or six cycles of different rhythmic modes.

The climax of the eastern *nawba* is the *qaṣīda* (plural *qaṣā'id*), an improvised solo vocal piece based on two, three, five or seven verses of the classical Arabic poems of the same name, and with the rhythmic scheme determined by the poetic metre of the text. It is composed of several segments loosely related thematically and unified by the common rhyme and poetic rhythm. The performer usually accompanies himself on the *'ūd* or is accompanied by another musician on some other instrument. The accompaniment consists only of short interludes between verses and supplies the pitch reference to the singer. The *qaṣīda* gradually came to include elements from various poetic genres such as hymns, elegy and satire.

The *qaṣīda* terminates the first, 'classical' section of the *nawba*. The second large section, of a lighter character, opens with the *taḥmīla*, an instrumental piece com-

posed of alternate sections played by the ensemble and solo instruments. The ensemble sections, a kind of ritornello, are pre-composed and are repeated without much variation. The solo sections are played in turn by the instrumentalists and are to a considerable extent improvised, using material from the ensemble ritornello. Following the *taḥmīla* is the *dawr*, a vocal folk form, primarily Egyptian, based on *zajal*, a genre of popular poetry. It has three parts: *madhhab*, in which the performers, chorus and orchestra present a principal musical piece in a slow tempo, usually in the *maṣmūdī kabīr* rhythmic mode; the *dawr* itself, in which the principal singer presents phrases, each preceded by the obligatory instrumental prelude, *lāzima*; and *qafla*, a coda performed in unison by singers and instrumentalists, and containing material related to *madhhab*. The *nawba* ends with the *dārij*, a series of *tawāshīḥ* in short and fast rhythmic modes.

The eastern *nawba* is now traditionally performed by an ensemble (*takht*) consisting of *'ūd* (lute), *qānūn* (a trapezoidal plucked zither), Western violin and *nāy* (end-blown flute), with the rhythmic part provided by the *darabukka* (goblet-shaped single-headed drum). *Nawbāt* are now rarely performed by themselves, but are given in concerts along with other pieces that were never part of the original nawba. Some of these added pieces include: *layālī* (solo vocal virtuoso improvisation on the words 'yā layl(ī) yā 'aynī' ('oh, night, oh, my eyes'): this is a vocal counterpart of a *taqsīm*); *mawwāl* (an unmeasured improvisatory form based on the popular poetic genre of the same name); *dūlāb* (short instrumental prelude played in unison by the ensemble); and *lunja* or *lunga* (an instrumental piece, probably of Turkish origin, with a structure somewhat similar to that of the *bashraf*).

(*b*) The western or Andalusian nawba. The Moroccan, Algerian and Tunisian *nawbāt* are part of the so-called Andalusian tradition, and are claimed by modern musicians to be a continuation of traditions developed in Spain during the Muslim rule between the 8th century and the 15th. At first court music of Spain followed the Damascus tradition. The development of a distinct Andalusian style is associated with the arrival in 822 of Ziryāb, the pupil of the Baghdadi musician Isḥāq al-Mawṣilī. The mystical and musico-therapeutical concepts which arose at this time became the philosophical basis of the 24 Andalusian *nawbāt*, each in a different mode, and the symbolic modal system *shajara al-ṭubū'* ('tree of temperaments'). These mystical concepts included cosmological associations with music which, while known at the time also in the eastern Arab world, have endured more strongly in the western areas.

The political decentralization and instability following the Umayyad rule in Spain (661–750) affected music. In the eastern Arab world music was the preserve of an élite and performed chiefly by solo virtuosos. In the western areas it spread from the courts to a larger audience and became more popular as well as more orchestral and choral in character. As new musical styles developed in Spain new poetic forms were created, mainly the *mūwashshaḥ* (court poetry) and *zajal* (popular poetry). Both these forms were strophic, the *mūwashshaḥ* being in literary Arabic and the *zajal* in the Andalusian dialect. *Mūwashshaḥāt* supplied the texts for most of the Andalusian *nawbāt*.

The gradual reconquest of Spain by the Christians caused massive migrations of Muslims to north Africa.

The earliest, in the 10th to 12th centuries, was from Seville to Tunis. There were later migrations in the 12th century from Córdoba to Tlemcen in Algeria and from Valencia to Fez in Morocco; finally in the 15th century the last refugees from Granada settled in Fez and Tetouan, both in modern Morocco. The musicians now living in these three countries claim their music is a continuation of the Andalusian tradition. There are now three different types of Andalusian *nawba*.

(*c*) The Moroccan nawba. After the fall of Granada in 1492 the immense repertory of 24 *nawbāt* was gradually forgotten, and only one new *nawba*, in the mode *istihlāl* ('the rising of the moon'), was composed in Fez by El Ḥāj 'Allāl al-Batta at the beginning of the 18th century. The mode of this composition was not part of the original 'tree of temperaments'.

In Morocco only 11 *nawbāt* are still remembered and performed; and some parts of one of them are said to be known only to one musician. The individual *nawbāt* are associated with particular times of the day most suitable for their performance: at dawn the *nawbāt 'ushshāq*, *'irāq al-'ajam*, *ḥijāzī al-msharqī*, *istihlāl* and *raṣd* are performed; at sunset *gharibat al-ḥusayn* and *māya*; in the evening *ḥijāzī al-kabīr* and *iṣbihān*; and at midnight *raṣd al-dhīl* and *ramal al-māya*. This last *nawba* has as its text *madīḥ* (religious poems) glorifying the Prophet, and can be performed at any time.

The Moroccan *nawba* is a suite of songs (*ṣanā'ī'*, plural of *ṣan'ā*). The songs are grouped in five sections (*miyāzen*, plural of *mizān*), each section based on a different rhythmic mode: *bsit*, corresponding to Western 6/4 or 3/2 metre; *qaim wa nusf*, corresponding to Western 16/4 metre; *btāyh-i*, corresponding to Western 16/8 metre (subdivided 3/4 + 6/8 + 2/4); *quddām*, corresponding to Western 6/8 metre; and *derj*, corresponding to Western 4/4 metre. Each *mizān* starts with the instrumental introduction *tushiya*. The *ṣanā'ī'* which follow, all metrical, are separated by orchestral interludes in which the orchestra repeats the theme of the *san'ā*. The unity of the *mizān* with its single melodic and rhythmic mode is balanced by the agogic elements which create variety. Each *mizān* follows a certain pattern of acceleration. It opens with a first *san'ā*, *ṭshdīra* in slow tempo, and after several songs reaches *qanṭra al-ūla* ('first bridge'), the songs in which the first gradual acceleration occurs. After several more songs there is a second bridge, *qanṭra al-thania*, with further acceleration followed by a group of fast songs, *inṣirāf*. The last song, *qfel*, acts as a coda.

The performance of the entire *nawba* lasts for several hours, but few complete *nawbāt* are performed now. The usual performance, for example at a wedding party, might consist of *tushiya* in one mode, followed by several *miyāzen* from different *nawbāt*, separated by an elaborate vocal *inshād*.

The orchestra is usually composed of one *rabāb* played by the leader of the group, one small European violin played on the knee, two or three violas, two *'ūd* (lutes), the *ṭār* (tambourine), sometimes also a *darabukka* (goblet-shaped drum) and *ṭbilāt* (a pair of ceramic kettledrums). All members of the orchestra perform the choral part. In addition there is a solo singer, *munshid*, who performs *inshād*. The singers chant in unison. The instrumentalists follow the composed melodic line, but each part is slightly different and determined by the idiom of the instrument and its function: the principal violinist improvises a more elaborate line

than those of the other performers. The resulting complex of heterophony contains elements of improvisation although the music is basically composed. The music is always transmitted orally, but the text is written down.

The Moroccan *nawba* belongs to the category *'āla* (instrumental, secular classical music). There is, however, a second category of classical music, *samā'*, a type of religious vocal music performed without instrumental accompaniment, whose texts are *madīḥ* (religious poems) glorifying the Prophet Mohammed. It is performed in *zāwiyya* (houses of Sufi fraternities), and is, as Chottin stated, a private expression of certain mystical ideas that border on the five religious obligations of Muslims, and yet is entirely secular in spirit.

The *grīh'a* is an offshoot of the classical music which was developed in Morocco during the Sa'dian dynasties: it is traditional popular music with texts based on the *qṣīda*, a type of long strophic poem. The *qṣīda*, however, is quite different in form from the classical *qaṣīda* and is a part of the poetic genre *milḥūn* ('incorrect' or 'sung'), in Moroccan dialect rather than in classical Arabic. The musical style resembles that of the classical *nawba*, but the melodic and rhythmic modes are simplified and some eastern Arab instruments are used in addition to the traditional instruments of the *nawba*. In the 1970s *milhūn* enjoyed tremendous popularity.

(*d*) The Algerian nawba. In Algeria, as in Morocco, musicians now know only a part of the old repertory of *nawbāt*. Only 12 *nawbāt* are still remembered and some of them are incomplete. Performances of them, as in Morocco, are traditionally associated with particular times of day. The *nawba sīka* is performed between 1 and 4 p.m.; *ramal* between 4 and 6 p.m.; *ramal māya* between 6 and 8 p.m.; *nawba 'arāq* (known in fragments), *ḥassīn*, *zīdān* and *ghrībt* between 8 p.m. and midnight; and at midnight the *nawba mejenba* is performed, followed by *nawba raṣd* and *mazmūm*. From 2 to 3 a.m. the *nawba ārbi* (which is not part of the old Andalusian tradition) is performed and, between 3 a.m. and noon, *nawbā dhīl*, *māya*, and *raṣd al-dhīl*.

The Algerian *nawba* is composed of nine movements or pieces: *dā'ira*, a short instrumental or vocal prelude in free rhythm, chanted using the syllables *yā lā lan* or *yā layl*; *mustakhbar al-san'ā*, a free-rhythm instrumental prelude performed in unison by the orchestra; *tū shiyya*, an instrumental overture in slow, binary rhythm; *muṣaddarāt* (plural of *muṣaddar*), a suite of *muwashshaḥāt* in a short metre; *baṭayhiyāt* (plural of *baṭayhi*), a suite of *mūwashshaḥāt* similar to *muṣaddarāt*; *drajjāt* (plural of *draj*), a suite of *mūwashshaḥāt* in fast ternary rhythm, usually preceded by the instrumental prelude, *kursī*; *tushiya al-inṣirāfāt*, a fast instrumental interlude; *inṣirāfāt*, a suite of fast, light songs in ternary metre; and *makhlaṣ*, a very rapid vocal piece, also with *mūwashshaḥ* text, in ternary metre and rich in vocal melismas.

In Algeria, besides the Andalusian *nawba* which is considered the most noble form, other genres are also performed, such as *neqlabāt* ('songs'; romances with poetic texts of lighter character than in Andalusian music). The repertory of some of the classical musicians also contains some *'arbī* pieces, the music of the Arabs of small towns and villages in the interior of Algeria. At various concerts and family celebrations as well as in coffee houses the popular music, *ḥawzī* (a short romance song), is performed as well as the *'arbī*. These songs are sung and accompanied mainly by male musicians. Female musicians have their own repertory, consisting chiefly of two genres: *qadriyāt ṣan'ā* and *qadriyāt zendānī*, the first related to classical music and the second to popular.

(*e*) The Tunisian nawba. The Tunisian *nawba* consists of ten movements: *istiftāḥ*, a free-rhythm instrumental prelude performed in unison by the orchestra (there are only a few of these, one in each mode); *mṣaddar*, a measured instrumental overture which is played by the orchestra and is the Tunisian equivalent of the eastern *bashraf*; *bayt*, a vocal piece based on a classical poem (this is the most refined part of Tunisian *nawba*, equivalent to the *qaṣīda* in the eastern *nawba*); *bṭayhiyāt*, slow *mūwashshaḥāt* in a 4/4 metre of the same name; *tushiya*, an instrumental piece in quadruple metre; *mshad*, an interlude played by lute and drum; *barwal*, a *mūwashshah* in 6/4 metre preceded by an instrumental prelude; *draj*, a *mūwashshah* in 6/4 metre preceded by an instrumental prelude; *khafīf*, a vocal piece of light character in ternary rhythm, in the rhythmic mode of the same name; *khatm*, the final vocal piece in fast ternary metre with rapid acceleration towards the end.

Since a full performance of the Tunisian *nawba* lasts for an hour and a half to two hours, the abbreviated form of *nawba*, *mḥat*, is often performed; this consists of several pieces, those in slower and longer rhythmical modes being performed at the beginning and those in shorter and faster ones towards the end. Besides the *nawba* other pieces of classical repertory are also performed, such as the *qaṣīda*, a solo vocal piece often performed between movements of *mḥat*; *bashrāf*, a measured instrumental overture of Turkish or Persian origin; *shambar*, a form similar to *bashrāf* based on the rhythm named *tshambar*; and *shghul*, a vocal piece of the *tawshīh* type.

(*iii*) *Westernized music*. The increasing contacts with the Western world since the late 19th century have had a profound influence on Near Eastern music. Western culture and technology have affected the traditional system of values. In the countries that have been most affected, such as Egypt and Lebanon, conservatories and music academies have been established where classical Arab and Western music are taught. The popularity of Arab classical music has diminished and composers are trying to find new methods of composition using elements and methods borrowed from Western music. Some musicians continue to perform traditional types of music, such as *taqsīm*, on traditional instruments but introduce some Western elements of melody and occasionally suggest simple harmony through triadic motion. Others are introducing Western instruments of fixed pitch, such as the piano, and are limiting the repertory of modes to those that can be played upon them.

New popular Westernized music to meet the changing needs of society has been created by such composers as Sayyid Darwīsh (1892–1923), Muḥammad 'Abd al-Wahhāb and Farīd al-Aṭrash, who have become popular far beyond their native Egypt. 'Abd al-Wahhāb's success was in part due to the principal performer of his works, Um Kalthum (1908–75), whose reputation as a singer spread throughout the Islamic world. The music of these composers, although rooted in tradition, borrows some features from Western music: elements of harmony are used and long rhythmical cycles are replaced by short binary or ternary metres. There is a tendency to enlarge the orchestra, both by increasing the numbers of traditional instruments and by introducing such Western instruments as accordion and electric guitar.

After World War II a new trend, the nationalist movement, developed in Egypt. Composers began to try to combine Arab and European traditions and to create an Egyptian art music, using Western forms and techniques of composition. These composers vary in the degree of their acquaintance with Western music. Some were trained in Egypt and others in the leading centres of music in Europe. The principal composers of the first generation were Yusef Greiss (1899–1961), whose most important works are a symphonic poem *Misr* ('Egypt') and Symphony no.2 'Folklorique', and Abū Bakr Khayrat (1910–63), whose main works are *Suite folklorique* for orchestra and *Poem pour piano* in F minor, op.18.

The second generation is more numerous and the most important composers are Muḥammad al-Shujā', 'Abd al-Ḥamīd, 'Abd al-Raḥmān, Ibrāhīm Ḥajjāj, 'Alī Ismā'īl, 'Azīz al-Shawān and Gamāl 'Abd al-Raḥīm. The works of this last composer, a violin sonata and a suite for orchestra, were performed abroad and achieved some success.

TREATISES

'Abd al-Qādir: *Jāmi' al-alḥān* [Compendium of melodies] (MS, *GB-Ob* Marsh 282)

Kanz al-tuḥaf [Treasury of rarities] (MS, *GB-Lbm* Oriental 2361)

Sharḥ Mawlānā Mubārak Shāh bar adwār [The Mubārak Shāh commentary on the Kitāb al-adwār] (MS, *GB-Lbm* Oriental 2361) [attrib. al-Jurjani; see,d'Erlanger, 1930–59]

al-Isfahānī: *Kitāb al-aghānī al-kabīr* [Great book of songs]; ed. N. al-Hūrinī (Cairo, 1868–9, suppl. Leiden, 1887, 2/1905–6, rev. 1927–); part Fr. trans. in E. M. Quatremère: 'Mémoire sur l'ouvrage intitulé Kitab al-agani, c'est-à-dire "Recueil de chansons"', *Journal asiatique*, 2nd ser., xvi (1835), 385–419, 497–545; 3rd ser., vi (1838), 465–526; see also Stigelbauer (1975)

al-Maqqarī: *Nafḥ al-ṭīb* [The history of the Mohammedan dynasties in Spain]; ed. in P. de Gayangos: *The History of the Mohammedan Dynasties in Spain* (London, 1840–43)

al-Mas'ūdī: *Murūj al-dhahab* [Meadows of gold]; ed. in C. Barbier de Meynard and P. de Courteille: *Les prairies d'or* (Paris, 1861–77)

Ikhwān al-Ṣafā': *Rasā'il* [The treatises] (MS, *GB-Ob* Hunt 296); ed. in F. Dieterici: *Die Propaedeutik der Araber im zehnten Jahrhundert* (Berlin and Leipzig, 1865), 100–53; ed. in A. Shiloah: 'L'épître sur la musique des Ikhwān al-Ṣafa', *Revue des études islamiques*, xxxii/1 (1964), 125–62; xxxiv (1966), 159–93

Ibn al-Nadīm: *Kitāb al-fihrist* [Index of books]; ed. R. Tajaddud (Tehran, 1971); Eng. trans., 1970, as *The Fihrist of al-Nadīm: a Tenth-century Survey of Muslim Culture*

M. Mushāqa [Mashāqa]: *Al-risāla al-shihābiyya fī l-ṣinā'a al-mūsīqiyya* [Treatise on the art of music for the Emir Shihab], ed. (Beirut, 1899)

al-Ghazālī: *Iḥya' 'ulūm al-dīn* [Revival of religious sciences]; ed. in D. B. Macdonald: 'Emotional Religion in Islam as Affected by Music and Singing: being a Translation of a Book of the Iḥyā' 'ulūm al-dīn of al-Ghazzali with Analysis, Annotation, and Appendices', *Journal of the Royal Asiatic Society* (1901), 195–252, 705–48; (1902), 1; ed. (Cairo, 1928–9)

al-Fārābī: *Kitāb al-mūsīqī al-kabīr* [Great book on music] (MS, *NL-Lu* Cod.651), ed. in d'Erlanger, 1930–59

——: 'Risāla fī l-mūsīqī' [Treatise about music], *Kitāb al-Najāt* (MS, *GB-Ob* Marsh 521); ed. in M. al-Ḥefnī: *Ibn Sina's Musiklehre*, hauptsächlich an seinem 'Naǧāt' erläutert: nebst Übersetzung und Herausgabe des Musikabschnittes des Naǧāt (diss., U. of Berlin, 1931); ed. in *Majmū rasā'il al-shaykh al-ra'īs* [Seven short treatises], ed. Uṣmani Encyclopedia Committee (Hyderabad, 1935)

Ibn Sīnā: *Kitāb al-shifā* [The cure] (MS, *GB-Lbm* Oriental 11190); ed. in d'Erlanger, 1930–59

Abū Bakr ibn Abī l-Dunyā: *Dhamm al-malāhī* [The censure of forbidden pleasures] (MS, *D-B* 5504), ed. in J. Robson: *Tracts on Listening to Music* (London, 1938)

Abū Ṭālib ibn Salama: *Kitāb al-'ūd wa-l-malāhī* [Book of the lute and other musical instruments] (MS, National Library, Cairo, f.j.533); ed. in J. Robson: *Ancient Arabian Musical Instruments* (Glasgow, 1938)

Majd al-Dīn: *Bawāriq al-ilmā'* [Flashes of enlightenment] (MS, *D-B*

5505); ed. in J. Robson: *Tracts on Listening to Music* (London, 1938)

Ṣafī al-Dīn: *Al-risāla al-sharafiyya fī l-nisab al-ta'līfiyya* [The Sharafian treatise on musical proportion] (MS, *GB-Ob* Marsh 521); ed. in d'Erlanger, 1930–59

——: *Kitāb al-adwār* [Book of cycles] (MS, *GB-Lbm* Oriental 136, *Ob* Marsh 521); ed. in d'Erlanger, 1930–59

al-Lādhiqī: *Al-risāla l-fatḥiyya fī al-mūsīqī* [The victory treatise concerning the theory of music] (MS, *GB-Lbm* Oriental 6629; National Library, Cairo, f.j.7); ed. in d'Erlanger, 1930–59

Muḥammad ibn Murād Treatise (MS, *GB-Lbm* Oriental 2361); ed. in d'Erlanger, 1930–59

Quṭb al-Dīn: *Durrat al-tāj* [Pearl of the crown] (MS, *GB-Lbm* Add.7694); ed. S. M. Mashkūt and N. A. Taqwā (Tehran, 1939–46)

'Alī ibn Yaḥyā al-Munajjim: *Risāla fī l-mūsīqī* [Treatise on music] (MS, *GB-Lbm* Oriental 2361); ed. M. Bahjah: Risāla fī l-mūsīqī, *Majallat al-Majma' al-'ilmī al-'irāqī*, i/l (1955), 113; ed. Z. Yūsuf (Cairo, 1964)

al-Jāḥiẓ: *Kitāb al-qiyān* [Treatise on the singing-girls] (MS, Dāmād Ibrahīm Pāshā Library, Stamboul, 949); ed. in C. Pellat: Les esclaves-chanteuses de Ğāḥiẓ', *Arabica*, x (1963), 121

Ibn Zayla: *Kitāb al-kāfī fī l-mūsīqī* [Book of sufficiency concerning music] (MS, *GB-Lbm* Oriental 2361); ed. Z. Yūsuf (Cairo, 1964)

Abd al-Qādir: *Maqāṣid al-alḥān* [Purports of melodies] (MS, *GB-Ob* Ouseley 264, 385); ed. T. Bīnish (Tehran, 1966)

al-Kindī: *Risāla fī khubr ṣinā'at al-ta'līf* [Treatise concerning knowledge of the art of composition] (MS, *GB-Lbm* Oriental 2361, fol. 165–8); ed. in C. Cowl: 'The Risāla fī ḥubr ta'līf al-'alhan of Ja'qūb ibn Isḥāq al-Kindī', *The Consort*, xxiii (1966), 129–66; ed. Y. Shawqī (Cairo, 1969)

al-Hasan ibn Aḥmad: *Kitāb kamāl adab al-ghinā'* [The perfection of musical knowledge], ed. in A. Shiloah, *La perfection des connaissances musicales* (Paris, 1972)

BIBLIOGRAPHY

G. A. Villoteau: 'De l'état actuel de l'art musical en Egypte', *Description de l'Egypte: état moderne*, i, ed. E. F. Jomard (Paris, 1809), 607–845

——: 'Description historique, technique et littéraire des instrumens de musique des orientaux', *Description de l'Egypte: état moderne*, i, ed. E. F. Jomard (Paris, 1809), 846–1016

E. W. Lane: *An Account of the Manners and Customs of the Modern Egyptians* (London, 1836, 5/1860/R1966)

R. G. Kiesewetter: *Die Musik der Araber* (Leipzig, 1842)

A. Christianowitsch: *Esquisse historique de la musique arabe aux temps anciens* (Cologne, 1863)

A. P. Caussin de Perceval: 'Notices anecdotiques sur les principaux musiciens arabes des trois premiers siècles de l'Islamisme', *Journal asiatique*, 7th ser., ii (1873), 546–92

J. P. N. Land: 'Recherches sur l'histoire de la gamme arabe', *VIe Congrès internationale des orientalistes: Leiden 1883*, ii, 35–168

——: 'Tonschriftversuche und Melodieproben aus dem muhammedanischen Mittelalter', *VMw*, ii (1886), 347

I. Bey Muṣṭafā: *La valeur des intervalles dans la musique arabe* (Cairo, 1888)

M. Collangettes: 'Étude sur la musique arabe', *Journal asiatique*, iv (1904), 365–422; viii (1906), 149–90

E. M. von Hornbostel: 'Phonographierte tunesische Melodien', *SIMG*, viii (1906–07), 1–43

M. T. Houtsma and others, eds.: *The Encyclopaedia of Islām* (Leiden and London, 1913–38, rev. 2/1960–) [incl. H. G. Farmer: Mūsīḳī]

A. Z. Idelsohn: 'Die Maqamen der arabischen Musik', *SIMG*, xv (1913–14), 1–63

A. Christensen: 'Some Notes on Persian Melody-names of the Sasanian Period', *The Dastur Hoshang Memorial Volume . . . in Honour of the Late Shams-ul-Ulama Sardar Dastur Hoshang Jamasp* (Bombay, 1918), 368

B. Bartók: 'Die Volksmusik der Araber von Biskra und Umgebung', *ZMw*, ii (1919–20), 489–522

J. Ribera: *La música de las cantigas* (Madrid, 1922; Eng. trans., 1929/R1970 as *Music in Ancient Arabia and Spain*)

J. Rouanet: 'La musique arabe', *EMDC*, I/v (1922), 2676–939

R. Yekta Bey: 'La musique turque', *EMDC*, I/v (1922), 2945–3064

H. G. Farmer: 'Arabic Musical Manuscripts in the Bodleian Library', *Journal of the Royal Asiatic Society* (1925), 639

——: 'Clues for the Arabian Influence on European Musical Theory', *Journal of the Royal Asiatic Society* (1925), 61 [pubd separately as *Influence on Musical Theory* (London, 1925)]

——: 'The Influence of Music: from Arabic Sources', *PMA*, lii (1925–6), 89–124

——: 'The Old Persian Musical Modes', *Journal of the Royal Asiatic Society* (1926), 93

J. Ribera: *Historia de la música árabe medieval y su influencia en la española* (Madrid, 1927)

H. G. Farmer: *A History of Arabian Music to the Thirteenth Century* (London, 1929/R1973)

A. Chottin: 'Les genres dans la musique marocaine', *Revue musicale du Maroc* (1930)

R. d'Erlanger: *La musique arabe* (Paris, 1930–59)

H. G. Farmer: 'Greek Theorists of Music in Arabic Translation', *Isis*, xiii (1930), 325

——: *Historical Facts for the Arabian Musical Influence* (London, 1930/R1970)

A. Chottin: *Corpus de musique marocaine* (Paris, 1931–3)

H. G. Farmer: *The Organ of the Ancients: from Eastern Sources, Hebrew, Syriac and Arabic* (London, 1931)

——: *Studies in Oriental Musical Instruments*, i (London, 1931); ii (Glasgow, 1939)

Congrès de musique arabe: Caire 1932 (Hég 1350) [incl. H. G. Farmer: 'Histoire abrégée de l'échelle de la musique arabe', 647]

——: *An Old Moorish Lute Tutor* (Glasgow, 1933) [four Arabic texts from unique manuscripts]

O. Rescher: *Abriss der arabischen Literaturgeschichte*, ii (Stuttgart, 1933)

H. G. Farmer: *Al-Farabi's Arabic-Latin Writings on Music* (Glasgow, 1934/R1965)

R. d'Erlanger: *Mélodies tunisiennes: hispano-arabes, arabo-berbères, juive, nègre* (Paris, 1937)

H. G. Farmer: 'The Lute Scale of Avicenna', *Journal of the Royal Asiatic Society* (1937), 245 [also in H. G. Farmer: *Studies in Oriental Musical Instruments*, ii (Glasgow, 1939), 45]

——: 'An Outline History of Music and Musical Theory', *A Survey of Persian Art*, ed. A. U. Pope, iii (London, 1938–9/R1964), 2783ff

A. Chottin: *Tableau de la musique marocaine* (Paris, 1939)

H. G. Farmer: *The Sources of Arabian Music: an Annotated Bibliography of Arabic Music Manuscripts* (Bearsden, 1940, rev. 2/1965)

——: *Sa'adyah Gaon on the Influence of Music* (London, 1943)

——: 'The Minstrels of the Golden Age of Islam', *Islamic Culture*, xvii (1943), 273; xviii (1944), 53

H. G. Farmer: *The Minstrelsy of 'The Arabian Nights': a Study of Music and Musicians in the Arabic 'Alf Laila wa Laila'* (Bearsden, 1945)

M. Schneider: 'A propósito del influjo árabe: ensayo de etnografía musical de la España medieval', *AnM*, i (1946), 31–141

A. Chottin and H. Hickmann: 'Arabische Musik', *MGG*

'A. al-Azzāwī: *Al-mūsīqā al-'irāqiyya fī 'ahd al-mughūl wa-l-turkumān* [Iraqi music in the period of the Mongols and Turkmen] (Baghdad, 1951)

H. Avenary: 'Abu'l-Ṣalt's Treatise on Music', *MD*, vi (1952), 27

A. A. Bulos: *Arabic Music* (Beirut, 1955)

Kh. al-Wahhābī: *Marāji tarājim al-udabā' al-'arab* [Source materials for the biographies of Arabian littérateurs] (Nejef, 1956–8)

H. G. Farmer: 'The Music of Islam', *NOHM*, i (1957), 421ff

N. Akel: *Studies in the Social History of the Umayyad Period as Revealed in the Kitāb al-Aghānī* (diss., U. of London, 1960)

M. Barkechli: 'La musique iranienne', *Encyclopédie de la Pléiade: histoire de la musique*, i (Paris, 1960), 453–525

A. Chottin: 'Nordafrikanische Musik', *MGG*

H. Husmann: *Grundlagen der antiken und orientalischen Musikkultur* (Berlin, 1961)

G. Oransay: *Die traditionelle türkische Kunstmusik* (Ankara, 1961)

H. G. Farmer: 'Persische Musik', *MGG*

A. Shiloah: *Caractéristiques de l'art vocal arabe au Moyen Age* (Tel-Aviv, 1963)

A. Taymūr: *Al-mūsīqā wa-l-ghinā' 'ind al-'arab* [Music and song among the Arabs] (Cairo, 1963)

'A. al-Alūchī: *Rā'id al-'mūsīqā al-'arabiyya* [Guide to Arab music] (Baghdad, 1964) [bibliography]

P. Collaer: 'La migration du style melismatique oriental vers l'Occident', *JIFMC*, xvi (1964), 70

A. Kāzim: *Al-iṣṭilāḥāt al-mūsīqiyya* [The terminology of oriental music] (Baghdad, 1964)

H. G. Farmer: 'The Old Arabian Melodic Modes', *Journal of the Royal Asiatic Society* (1965), 99

E. Neubauer: *Musiker am Hof der frühen 'Abbāsiden* (diss., U. of Frankfurt am Main, 1965)

F. Sezgin: *Geschichte des arabischen Schrifttums* (Leiden, 1967–75)

J. Porte, ed.: 'Musique musulmane', *Encyclopédie des musiques sacrées*, i (Paris, 1968), 388–466 [8 articles by different authors]

H. H. Touma: *Der Maqām Bayatī im arabischen Taqsīm* (diss., Free U. of Berlin, 1968)

T. Battisti: 'La musique traditionelle iranienne: aspects sociohistoriques', *Objets et mondes*, ix (1969), 317

L. Manik: *Das arabische Tonsystem im Mittelalter* (Leiden, 1969)

E. Neubauer: 'Musik zur Mongolenzeit in Iran und den angrenzenden Ländern', *Der Islam*, xlv (1969), 233

E. Gerson-Kiwi: 'On the Technique of Arab Taqsim Composition', *Musik als Gestalt und Erlebnis: Festschrift Walter Graf* (Vienna, 1970), 66

H. Hickmann: 'Die Musik des arabisch-islamischen Bereichs', in H. Hickmann and W. Stauder: *Orientalische Musik* (Leiden and Cologne, 1970), 1–134

H. Husmann: 'Arabische Maqamen in ostsyrischer Kirchenmusik', *Musik als Gestalt und Erlebnis: Festschrift Walter Graf* (Vienna, 1970), 102

S. M. A. Khavas: *Sovremennaya arabskaya narodnaya pesnya* [Modern Arab folksongs] (Moscow, 1970)

S. Jargy: *La musique arabe* (Paris, 1971)

E. Neubauer: 'Neuere Bücher zur arabischen Musik', *Der Islam*, xlviii (1971–2), 1

H. H. Touma: 'The *Maqam* Phenomenon: an Improvisation Technique in the Music of the Middle East', *EM*, xv (1971), 38

S. el Mahdi: *La musique arabe* (Paris, 1972)

A. Simon: *Studien zur ägyptischen Volksmusik* (Hamburg, 1972)

J. Elsner: *Der Begriff des Maqām in Ägypten in neuerer Zeit* (Leipzig, 1973)

H. Farhat: *The Traditional Music of Iran* (Tehran, 1973)

M. T. Massoudieh: 'Tradition und Wandel in der persischen Musik des 19. Jahrhunderts', *Musikkulturen Asiens, Afrikas und Ozeaniens im 19. Jahrhundert*, ed. R. Günther (Regensburg, 1973), 73

B. Nettl and R. Riddle: 'Taqsim Nahawand: a Study of Sixteen Performances by Jihad Racy', *YIFMC*, v (1973), 11–50

J. M. Pacholczyk: 'Vibrato as a Function of Modal Practice in the Qur'ān Chant of Shaikh 'Abdu'l-Bāsiṭ 'Abdu'ṣ-Ṣamad', *Selected Reports*, ii/1 (1973), 33

J. E. Bencheikh: 'Les musiciens et la poésie. Les écoles d'Isḥāq al-Mawṣilī (m. 235 H.) et d'Ibrāhīm Ibn al-Mahdī (m. 224 H.)', *Arabica*, xxii (1975)

J. Elsner: 'Zum Problem des Maqām', *AcM*, xlvii (1975), 208

L. I. al-Faruqi: Muwashshaḥ: a Vocal Form in Islamic Culture', *EM*, xix (1975), 1

M. Stigelbauer: *Die Sängerinnen am Abbasidenhof um die Zeit des Kalifen al-Muttawakkil* (Vienna, 1975)

H. H. Touma: *Die Musik der Araber* (Wilhelmshaven, 1975; Fr. trans., 1977)

O. Wright: *The Modal System of Arab and Persian Music, A.D. 1250–1300* (London, 1978)

L. I. al-Faruqi: *Annotated Glossary of Arabic–English Musical Terms* (Westport, Conn., 1979)

II. Folk music

1. Historical introduction. 2. General musical considerations. 3. Vocal music: (i) Texts (ii) Music (iii) Song types and their social functions (iv) Performers: the poet-musician. 4. Instrumental music.

1. HISTORICAL INTRODUCTION. After 622 (the date of the Flight of Mohammed and the official beginning of the Muslim calendar) a new musical art developed, associated with the court life of the caliphs; it was rapidly established in areas from Central Asia to the Atlantic. However, various folk traditions already existed in all these areas as well as in the Arabian peninsula, the conquerors' country of origin. In the nomads' encampments music emphasized every event in man's life, enhanced social gatherings, incited warriors, encouraged the desert traveller and exhorted pilgrims to come to the black stone of the Kaaba (Arabic: *ka'bah*) in Mecca, a holy shrine even in pre-Islamic times. That there was probably much interaction among all art and folk styles at that time in the Arabian peninsula is suggested by the frequent occurrence even now of certain common musical denominators in the region: the use of oral transmission; the predominance of vocal music and a predilection for varied types of vocal production and subtleties of intonation; a fondness for poetry; and improvisation. But, while art music has been described and its theory perpetuated in a multitude of scientific and literary writings, folk traditions have usually been ignored, except for scattered references. Some *ḥadīth* ('traditions of the Prophet': sayings and practices that had acquired the force of law) indicate that, although Mohammed banned music in general, he specifically allowed all folksongs and instruments which served a social function. Ikhwān al-Ṣafā' (a brotherhood which flourished in the second half of the 10th century) mentioned many forms of folksong in its *Al-risālah al-khamīsa fī al-mūsīqī* ('The fifth epistle on music') and showed its awareness of the differences of styles in the

ethnic repertories represented. The geographer Yāqūt al-Rūmi (1179–1229), in his dictionary *Mu'jam al-buldān*, described special trumpet tunes expressing the joy of the inhabitants of the island Nishtaru in Egypt at the arrival of the boat carrying their drinking water. In his travel memoirs Nāṣir-i-Khusraw (11th century) described a ceremony for the opening of a dyke on the Nile: an ensemble of long trumpets and drums, performing appropriate tunes, was followed by a long procession of 10,000 cavaliers and 10,000 other individuals. Ibn Khaldūn (*d* 1406), in the chapter on music in his *Prolegomenes*, defined the difference between art music and folk music: the former is based on well-established rules and conventions and consequently skill has to be acquired through long training, while the latter is simple and spontaneously created without special instruction. In the same chapter there is a detailed description of the robed-horse dance, in which dancers imitate mounted horsemen by using wooden frames draped in cloth. This type of reference suggests the diversity of folksong types and genres existing independently in the overwhelming shadow of art music, although scholars did not focus their attention on folk music in Islamic areas until the early 19th century. Villoteau devoted several pages of his works (1809) to folksongs and dances; and Lane (1836) provided an adequate survey of Egyptian folk tradition based on his powers of observation and insight. The Cairo Congress on Arab Music (1932), which gave special attention to folk music and attracted many distinguished scholars, finally initiated genuinely comprehensive and systematic investigation of ethnic music.

2. GENERAL MUSICAL CONSIDERATIONS. It is possible to speak of art music in the Arabic-speaking world as having a single large tradition, in spite of all the differences of local styles; but no such generalization can be made about the folk tradition. Despite a common mother tongue, geographical continuity and a long common history, the many ethnic groups living in the area of Arabic influence do not constitute one homogeneous cultural entity or even a family of related cultures (though some groups are culturally connected with each other). Among the present countries of the Near East, there is hardly one with a homogeneous folklore. In Libya, for example, Berbers, Sudanic peoples and Arabs live side by side; in the Arabian Gulf there are native Arabs, both nomadic and sedentary, Persians, Iraqis and Indians; in Iraq, in addition to the Arabs, there are gypsies and other minorities such as Jews and Christians who have particular repertories with special characteristics of style. In 1836 (p.27) Lane wrote of Egypt that 'In various parts of the country, there are families or small tribes, descended from Arab settlers who have generally disdained marrying women of less pure race than themselves and these are hardly, if at all, to be distinguished in their persons from the tribes in the Arabian deserts. . . . The country people are called *al-fallahin* (or "the agriculturalists")'. Despite many changes since Lane's day the basic cultural distinction between sedentary, beduin and 'agriculturalist' is still valid for the majority of the countries concerned and, almost everywhere, there is a marked distinction between the sedentary, beduin, agricultural and urban musical traditions.

The impressive variety of ethnic groups is reflected in the musical folklore: each group feels that its music has special stylistic characteristics, even though the differences between its music and that of neighbouring groups may be subtle and difficult for an untrained ear to distinguish. Indeed, these very nuances and barely perceptible variations are an important aspect of the creative process of the area.

The incessant internal migration of populations, particularly of the beduin peoples, has always been a strong factor in acculturation. Economic progress and wealth acquired from oil resources have strengthened urban influence, which now affects even the sheltered traditions of the nomadic beduins. The modern media of communication have had a significant impact. Observers have predicted the gradual disappearance of native musical styles, but in fact the original forms are becoming more complicated and being transmuted. To a lesser extent, this has always been the case: if changes did not violate the underlying spirit of the tradition they were accepted by the 'living body', but if they clashed radically with traditional principles they were rejected and vanished. Thus an investigation of all its forms of expression, whether 'new' or 'old', is necessary to an understanding of traditional music.

Although there is such diversity in folk tradition, neighbouring groups which intermingle have developed common traits, perhaps derived from the same sources. Poetry has great importance in social life and at all social levels among both the nomadic and the sedentary peoples of all Arab countries. This poetry is not primarily a mode of literary expression but rather an accompaniment to ceremonies and daily work. Its language varies from near-classical to completely colloquial, but the principles of prosody, the forms and the method of composition are consistent. The number of forms and genres of sung folk poetry is impressive and greater than that of classical art songs; and the folk poet-musician has a distinguished position as the narrator and translator of events and the spokesman for the moods and aspirations of his fellow men.

Folk groups of the Arab world show great similarities in the functions, occasions and topics of their songs and dances. The same metaphors and formulae, in both text and tune, are used by many groups for similar occasions or situations (e.g. epic songs and religious processional songs).

Responsorial forms are frequently used, implying the importance of audience participation. This is particularly evident in the collective and individual dances, many of which are accompanied by songs and hand-clapping or drumming. Even those accompanied by melodic instruments almost always include sung verses. Vocal production, including a guttural nasal timbre, special techniques such as vibrato and the use, by women, of ululation, are common throughout most of the area. In ensembles the combination of instruments, their shape and playing technique are similar, although their names differ from group to group. Thus for instance the double-reed pipe and drum always occur together, in open-air ceremonies, in processions, etc.

The beduins' music is probably the oldest part of the entire repertory, and their way of life helps to perpetuate many archaic features. The migration patterns of tribes indicate the origins of many stylistic elements and also their ramifications in the rural traditions. The oldest category of folk music is that of social and group songs, which are usually simple, without any embellishment. The other category, which includes the melismatic and formally varied music, is more recent; it predominates

in Egypt and areas to the north-east and may have been influenced by art music.

3. VOCAL MUSIC.
(i) *Texts*. Text and music are indissolubly linked in Arab folk music. There are many types of sung poetry which differ from each other in prosodic form, in mode of performance and in their social or musical functions.

(a) The qaṣīda. This is one of the most ancient and most sophisticated forms. Created by beduins in the Arabian desert, it is still used in artistic as well as popular poetry. The classical *qaṣīda* consists of many lines (sometimes over 100), each in two equal parts and subdivided into feet. Each *qaṣīda* has a single rhyme and a uniform metre, any one of 16 traditional metres. In its subject matter the *qaṣīda* follows a schematic development of themes and images. The basic compositional concept is that each line should be independent and contain a complete, self-sufficient idea. Hence the poet's originality is measured by his ability to reformulate conventional material and to invent additional lines. The sung *qaṣīda* follows, in general, the principles of sung poetry and, since it is considered a form of entertainment, the spirit of amusement is emphasized by the use of unusual words. Natural variants may occur through lapses of memory and the dependence on oral transmission, so the order of individual lines can seldom be established accurately. The poems are never sung twice in exactly the same way or sung in their entirety; the original words and often whole lines are changed. Even when it is set to a standard tune, with the text only slightly changed or with the lines rearranged, a *qaṣīda* is accepted as 'new' by singers and listeners. The *qaṣīda*, like most sung poetry, is always performed at gatherings which mark events in man's private and social life and improvisation is often extensive.

This classical *qaṣīda* form is still used by beduins as well as rural and urban poets, particularly for religious or sophisticated subjects. There is also a folk form of the *qaṣīda* (*qṣīda*), differing from the classical one both in its prosodic structure, which cannot be analysed quantitatively, and in its language, which varies from near-classical to colloquial. In the folk *qṣīda* the tune influences the construction of the text, even more than does the poetic metre. However, the classical *qaṣīda* and folk *qṣīda* have the same performing practice and social function.

(b) Strophic forms. Small strophic forms, particularly those with four-line stanzas, are prevalent in Arab folk music. The '*atāba*, found in Lebanon, Syria, Palestine and Jordan, is of this type, as is its counterpart in Iraq, '*ubudhiyya*. In this form the first three lines have the same rhyme (i.e. they end with homonyms). The last word of the fourth line must end with *āb* or *āba*, or *iyya* or *dhiyya* (the last syllable respectively of '*atāba* and '*ubudhiyya*). Here is an example of an '*atāba* stanza:

> Bani-l-Ḍabbah bid-deyr ḥamūlī
> Idha bindāq bi-l-hayja ḥamūlī
> Bnifsi fī mhabbatkum ḥumūlī
> Il-shruqi wa-l-m'anna wa-l-'atāb.
>
> (Sons of Dabbah, you form a clan in Dayr al-Asad.
> When I am in trouble in battle, they defend me.
> My load becomes lighter because of your love.
> [Let us sing] the *shruqi*, the *m'anna* and the '*atāb*.)

Here the last line names the genre and two other important forms. Both the '*atāba* and the '*ubudhiyya* are soloistic improvised song types, often performed antiphonally by two poet-musicians. In another strophic type each stanza usually consists of four eight-syllable lines with the rhyme scheme: *aaab, cccb, dddb* etc; this is the form of the *majruda* (Libya) and the *murabba'* (Lebanon, Syria, Palestine, Jordan). Songs of this type are very rhythmic and are always accompanied by hand-clapping; they include responsorial participation by the audience, which either repeats the final line of each stanza or sings a refrain not included in the sung poem. A related type, the *muthamman*, has stanzas of eight seven-syllable lines, with the rhyme scheme *ababābac* (refrain), *dedededc* (refrain), etc. The *murabba'* and the *muthamman* types are often used without refrain in disputation songs (similar to the medieval French *jeu-parti*) in which two protagonists argue with each other in verse.

A more complicated form, the *m'anna*, has four-line stanzas with the rhyme scheme *aaba* (refrain), *ccbc* (refrain), *dded* (refrain) etc. The audience sings a refrain consisting of the final line of each stanza set in a strict rhythm, which contrasts with the free and melis-matic character of the soloist's material.

In addition to these four-line stanza forms, there are also strophic types with five-line stanzas (e.g. the Egyptian *mawwāl*) in which lines 1, 2, 3 and 5 rhyme; with six-line stanzas (e.g. the short *zajal*); and with seven-line stanzas (e.g. the Baghdadi *mawwāl*), in which lines 1, 2, 3 and 7 have one rhyme and lines 4, 5 and 6 another. In these forms lines 1, 2 and 3 end with homonyms as in the *'atābā* and *'ubudhiyya*.

Characteristics of the small poetic forms, other than textual structure and prosody, which relate particularly to the musical structure and to performing practice, include the recurrence of certain vowel and consonant sounds, repetition of a line or a part of a line, the addition of meaningless syllables and the refrain. There are various types of refrain: one consists of the reitera-tion of the last line of each stanza and consequently varies from one stanza to the next; another uses a phrase or formula which has nothing to do with the text of the song to which it belongs, and is repeated exactly throughout the song. An example of the latter is the formulaic refrain 'Ḥalālī ya mālī' ('the girl or the money') which, although it may originally have belonged to one particular song, is now found in at least three types of song, among them the *muthamman*, in Lebanon, Syria and Israel. The formulaic refrain sometimes consists of meaningless words or vocables: in Ḥaḍramawt (Yemen), for instance, there is a category of songs called *dana dana* which include the refrain 'Dana dana ya dani/ya dani dana dana' sung by the audience after each of the soloist's improvised stanzas; sometimes this nonsense refrain is attached to a meaningful line such as 'After the heat of day, the breeze blows' (repeat). A performance of this type of song can last a whole night.

A third type of refrain is recognizably derived from a pre-existing source, sometimes from older non-strophic social or group songs. This kind of refrain usually oc-curs at the beginning of the song, either as an indepen-dent line, or as the opening line or two of the first stanza. In the latter case the refrain is a stock formula, identify-ing a well-defined song genre which takes its name from the formula used and whose songs always begin with the same words. The last line of each stanza in this type of song ends with the rhyme of the archetype (i.e. the song in which the formulaic refrain originated), the lines are the same length as those of the archetype, there are often

similar images and ideas and even related lines. The genres with this type of refrain are *'alā dal'ūnā, mijānā, rozānā* and to some extent *Barhum ya Barhum*, which is here taken as an example since it has been most studied. *Barhum ya Barhum* is well known in a wide area stretching from Egypt to Syria. There are dozens of versions, of which, since 1925, at least six have been published. They all begin with a refrain which includes 'Barhum ya Barhum' (diminutive of 'Abraham, oh Abraham'), followed in the Egypt and Sinai versions by 'Abu Zayd Hlal' (Abu Zayd al-Hilālī is an ancient epic hero) or in versions from further north by 'abu-l-jadīla' ('father of the curled locks'). These lines are also used in the refrain repeated after each verse. In all the versions the last two words of each verse are repeated, preceded by an exclamation such as 'Eh wallah' ('O in the name of God'), 'ya yumma' ('O my mother'), or 'ya weyli' ('woe is me'). Some also contain common metaphors. The song itself, which was created during the first two decades of the 20th century, rapidly became popular, incorporating in various versions a great variety of topics and current social concerns. Compared with these extreme fluctua-tions of text, the tune used has remained relatively un-changed: although stylistic differences exist, the basic structure is consistent (ex.6). This pattern of stable tune and widely varying text seems characteristic of all the genres whose refrains come from pre-existing sources.

Ex.6

(a) *Barhum ya Barhum*, beduins of Sinai: transcr. A. Shiloah

(b) *Barhum ya Barhum*, 'Akko, Israel; transcr. A. Shiloah

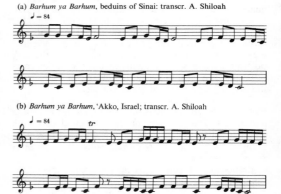

(*c*) Non-strophic forms. This category comprises a repertory of social group songs consisting of simple exhortatory or exclamatory formulae with separate lines which accompany dances. It is a type commonly used for weddings, work, processions etc, and includes many texts and few tunes. The *far'awiyya* and the *mḥorabe* are typical examples. They begin with a *ṭal'a*, a phrase (sometimes changed for another during performance), which is then repeated as a response after each solo verse. The solo verses are not related to each other or to the *ṭal'a*. Some *ṭal'a* have religious connotations: 'God is the greatest, O my land, glorify him'; or 'May your religion be strong, O Mohammed'. Other *ṭal'a* relate to a particular occasion or function: 'The fair one stepped out of the bath'; or 'Greet your guests, O Abu S'ud'.

These songs are usually accompanied by hand-clapping and sometimes by a kind of marching dance. In one such dance, the *razīḥ* of Sinai and Yemen, the *shallal* (precentor) recites the first half-verse and the other participants sing one of the hundreds of traditional and very ancient refrains, such as 'Praise to him who passeth not away,/and whose power never ceaseth'; or 'God give us good fortune'.

The same category includes the genres *tanṣūrah*, *hanhunnāt* and *zaghārīd*; songs of these types are sung by women during wedding festivals. They consist of improvised verses which start with the interjection 'ayha' or 'iyha' intoned at a high pitch, followed by verses sung in a fast parlando style and interrupted by the traditional *yuyu* (ululation or shrilling sounds). There are songs for the bridegroom (e.g. 'O our bridegroom, we are today your guests./Prepare the bed for us and leave your house for us'; or 'No one is like our bridegroom./The wedding is celebrated in his uncle's house') and others for the bride (e.g. 'Your anklet, O beautiful one, resounds and gives voice;/Your skirt, this one of pepper colour, has in it life and death'; or 'Walk gracefully, O beautiful one, O magnificent one;/O rose which has bloomed in the garden').

This category also includes the *hōsa* (an Iraqi beduin genre) and various religious processional songs, such as songs of pilgrimage to Mecca or to the tombs of saints and songs for the *mawlid* (birthday of the Prophet). For instance, in the procession held on the occasion of the *mawlid* in Libya the formula 'Pray O worshipper for the Magnificent (Prophet)' is continually repeated.

Epic songs also belong to this category. They are popular throughout the area and among all classes of people. They are associated with the *shā'ir* (bard or poet-musician), who sings them while accompanying himself on the *rabāb* (one-string fiddle) which he holds on his knee. The epics may relate the heroic events of his tribe or adventures of legendary heroes, and a performance may last all night. The *shā'ir* is respected for his skill, his memory and his dramatic talent. In beduin society he is important to his tribe or clan not only as its official entertainer, but also as its walking archive and as the interpreter of its memorable events, customs and manners.

There are also poet-musicians in villages and towns who function as entertainers, particularly during the evenings of religious festivals. They usually perform in coffee-houses, entertaining the patrons not only with the story, but also with their lively and dramatic manner of narration. Some poet-musicians specialize in particular epics: the 'Abū Zaydiyyah', for example, are singers of the *Abū Zayd* romance which relates the life and adventures of Abu Zayd al-Hilālī. This narrative song is supposed to be based on events which took place in the mid-3rd century of the Muslim calendar. During a single evening of Ramadan the same epic song, in various versions, can be heard in Libya, Yemen and Egypt. There are also epics about other famous heroes (such as Antar), which are sung in the same manner all over the Near East and which originated among beduins.

(*ii*) *Music*. (*a*) Melody. Apart from a very few poems recited in a style which is itself quasi-musical, poetic forms and genres are meant to be sung. For the folk-singer text and melody form an integral unit. Such cohesion implies that they are also conceived together and a folksinger often finds it impossible to recite the text separately from the melody. The length of the lines is often determined by the melodic or rhythmic texture, while in some instances the text may determine the nature of the melodic and rhythmic events. From syllabic recitative to highly ornamented melody, the changing modalities in the relation between text and tune, especially the role of poetic metre, cannot be understood fully without a knowledge of the music used. But the subject is still more complex, in that both text and tune undergo constant changes from performance to performance.

The song genres utilize various musical structures: some are solo, others are responsorial or mixed; some are syllabic with rigid rhythm, others are melismatic and consequently performed with a certain rhythmic freedom; some are accompanied, by hand-clapping, dances or percussion or melodic instruments, others are for voice alone.

By comparison with the constant addition of 'new' texts to the total repertory of song, the number of 'new' melodies is very limited. In a given genre one tune can be used for several texts, and various means are used to fit the text to the tune: contraction of syllables, elision of letters or addition of meaningless syllables. The links between the simpler tunes and particular social functions are very flexible: a certain number of simple tunes are used without differentiation both in work songs and in processional, religious and wedding songs. The function of this music is not necessarily to furnish a distinct setting for a distinct text; rather, since the text cannot stand alone, the melody is seen as its necessary vehicle. However, songs are musically differentiated according to whether they have social and group functions or individual and psychological functions.

The songs pertaining to groups are often older, simpler, less artistic and less varied in content than other kinds, in both their texts and tunes. In such songs associations of text, melody, rhythm and sonority are made from practice, without recourse to theoretical disciplines. As they belong to a somewhat self-enclosed tradition the songs have a limited number of such associations and there is thus a high incidence of common patterns. Perhaps because of their social function these songs use many types of responsorial form and the audience participates to a marked degree.

Some of these principles of relationship also apply to the solo strophic songs, although these, because of their more complex form, usually have more intricate relationships between text and tune, and more distinct styles. In syllabic songs the regular musical beats are adjusted to the scansion of the syllables and the musical and textual expression are coordinated, sometimes in the framework of a line and sometimes in the framework of a whole stanza. In both cases the end of each melodic phrase is distinctly marked by a cadential formula. In the free rhythmic and melismatic songs the melodic stresses are coordinated with the textual stresses, and fioritura and melismatic passages are placed so as not to disturb the meaning and general flow of the text. Cadences do not always coincide with the ends of textual lines, particularly in songs which are musically more elaborate and perhaps influenced by art music. When at the end of a line or a stanza the musical idea has not been completely exhausted, the singer adds meaningless syllables or vowel sounds before reaching his melodic cadential formula. A further characteristic connecting the more soloistic genres to art music is the use of elements of the *maqām* system by certain educated folk musicians. Although it is not yet very clear, it seems possible that there are links between folksong genres and *maqām*. There may also be associations of some genres with particular emotions or affections.

(*b*) Structure. There have been so few analyses of the ethnic musics of the region that an attempt to establish a system which would comprehend all the diverse musical components would involve serious difficulties, and would probably lead merely to useless generalizations. It seems preferable to limit discussion to verifiable observations and to defer far-reaching comparisons with other musical cultures until there have been more thorough studies.

In Arab vocal folk music there are three main types of melody: simple melodies with short repeated formulae; melodies which use repeated formulae, but are more complex; and soloistic, highly intricate melodies. The simplest melodies are usually performed antiphonally or responsorially. In some, formulae are exactly repeated throughout the song (exx.7, 8 and 9); in

Ex.7 Egyptian antiphonal song, transcr. A. Shiloah

others, the repeated formulae proceed according to the principle of open and closed phrases. Open phrases frequently end on the 2nd below the *finalis* (ex.10), or sometimes on the 2nd above the *finalis*. These simple

Ex.8 Persian Gulf Song I, transcr. P. Olsen (Olsen, 1960)

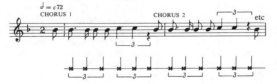

melodies have narrow ranges, rarely more than a 4th, and some are on one note. They are sung in a very plain manner, totally different from the ornamented style which characterizes the complicated melodies of the third category. However, even these simple melodies are often marked by various types of intonation and glissandos. Their melodic plainness contrasts with their varied rhythms, which have complicated formulae. These are frequently determined by the scansion of the

text, often resulting in certain asymmetrical rhythms, but simple, straightforward formulae also occur (see ex.9). The rhythmical richness is always emphasized and enhanced by hand-clapping, using the whole of both hands, fingers against fingers and palm against palm. The hand-clapping, often doubled by drumbeats, creates a polyrhythmic pattern with the melody (see ex.8). In the Egyptian song (ex.7) percussive accompaniment is relatively important, competing with the melody and creating independent cadences.

Ex.9 *Far'awiyya, maqām bayyātī*, transcr. A. Shiloah (Shiloah 1974)

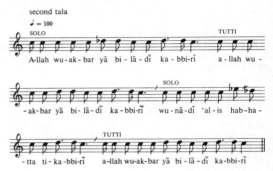

In addition to having complex rhythmic accompaniment, simple melodic songs (e.g. the *zaghārīd*) are frequently interrupted or marked by exhortatory shouts, or by *yuyu* (female shrilling sounds), as well as by body movements which give a spatial dimension to the rhythms and the hand-clapping. The body gestures of the participants, who form a long row, are augmented gradually by slight steps and movements which become a rudimentary form of dance. Thus, while continuing their singing and clapping, the participants make an unbroken transition to a kind of collective dance. In performing the *far'awiyya* dance, for example, the line starts moving to its right in very slow steps until it

Ex.10 Persian Gulf Song II, transcr. P. Olsen (Olsen, 1960)

forms a full circle. This is also done in the beduin *dahḥiyya* in Sinai and Iraq: at a given moment in the evening or festival the men get up and, while forming a row, repeat 'dahḥiyya, dahḥiyya' until they feel inspired. Then the poet-musician faces the line and starts singing verses which he sometimes improvises himself. Sometimes there are two soloists who sing the verses of the *dahḥiyya* antiphonally. The group only sings responses, accompanying them by uniform rhythmic clapping, while taking small steps backwards and forwards, keeping their feet close to the ground. This dance, which takes place in complete darkness, reaches its climax at the appearance of an unmarried woman, clad entirely in black, brandishing a sword in her right hand. She takes large steps and jumps while waving her sword, and the dancers alternately move towards her and retreat, repulsed by the sword's movement.

Although this young woman is supposedly anonymous, all the participants know who she is, but ignore her identity in order to protect her honour. The *marbū'a*, a variation of the *daḥḥiyya*, is musically almost identical but is sung at a higher pitch than the *daḥḥiyya* in order to attract young girls and women. Another form of dance-song, the *radīḥ*, occurs in Yemen and perhaps throughout the Arabian peninsula. The form is physically as well as musically antiphonal, for the line of participants divides into two sections while performing the verses. There are many other forms of dance-song, particularly in Yemen where both men and women show a strong predilection for dance.

In these responsorial songs melodic overlapping occurs when the soloist or chorus begin their phrase before the end of the previous one. Certain scholars consider this phenomenon a type of rudimentary folk polyphony. Songs of this first category use only one or two scales and are the songs most closely associated with man's basic physical and spiritual life; they are considered collective property to be preserved in as pure a state as possible.

Songs of the second melodic category are similar to those of the first in their frequent use of simple repeated formulae and their recourse to the same rhythmic patterns, accompanied by hand-clapping and drum-beating. However, their melodies are more complex in form, organization, range and tonality. Indeed, many of these melodies probably developed from tunes of the first category, but have since been influenced by urban music, either directly or through songs of the third category. Their melodic range is a 4th or a 5th and the series of notes which forms the scales appears to be distantly related to the *maqām* tradition, although the precise nature of the relationship between art and folk music, a more crucial problem in the third category, has not yet been clarified.

Ex.11 *Mūwashshaḥ, maqām segāh*; transcr. A. Shiloah (Shiloah, 1974)

Bin - qa - ddim ta - hā nī - na   li - 'a hi   nā
clapping   etc
wa - bu 'a li da - 'i - nan ga - nī qa - sid
TUTTI
ba - ddi___ tri - ddū 'a - la - yyab - far   hat Sa - 'īd
ba - d di - tri - ddū 'a - la - yyab - far hat Sa - 'īd

O Abu S'ud, at the rejoicing of the two (sons)
Let me sing and say 'Ya 'eyni' (oh, my eye)
The men of the village and the guests are brothers,
From the one-year-old to the ninety-year-old.

The *mūwashshaḥ* (ex.11) illustrates some of the characteristics of songs of the second category: the

simple repeated melody is fairly melismatic, the range is a diminished 5th and the mode is the *maqām segāh*. The refrain, musically identical with the soloist's part, is sung twice by the chorus, both at the beginning of the song and after each stanza. The Egyptian *Ramadan Lantern Song* (ex.12) shows another common pattern: the response, no longer identical with the soloist's part,

Ex.12 Ramadan Lantern Song, transcr. B. S. Rasheed (Rasheed, 1958)

response

progresses within the tetrachord below the *finalis* while the soloist's part undulates around the *finalis*. There is more complex organization in the *muthamman* (ex.13), which has a stanza of eight short lines, each divided textually into seven syllables but musically into a duple

Ex.13 *Muthamman, maqām bayyātī*; transcr. A. Shiloah (Shiloah, 1974)

SOLO
♩ = 96
Bin - ḥa - yyi kul - i - ḍḍu - yūf ha - llī ḥa - llū ḥaf - lit - nā
clapping
etc
min mi - yyāt wu min u - lūf fi - kum nir fa' rā - yit - nā
niḥ - fil nal - lei - le maw ṣūf wu'am bit - ga - nni le - lit - na wu
ha - nni ğa - mī' i - liḍ - yūf ya - lli ḥal - lū fī hal - ma -
SOLO
kān   Ha bad - di a' - riḍ ḥal - fi lim
TUTTI
Ḥa la li ya ma li___
wur - ğa - lī a - ḥa - yyi - ha etc

metre of four crotchets. The fourth crotchet in each of the first six lines, coinciding with the *finalis* reached from the 3rd above, allows the seven syllables to cover eight quaver beats. While the simple melodic motif is exactly repeated six times, the last two lines constitute a developed cadence followed by the choral response, the melody and text of which are unrelated to the main song.

The third melodic category includes fairly sophisticated songs which show more complexity, a broader range and a greater variety of pitches than songs of the other categories. They are marked by influences of art music and are essentially soloistic. The simplest have repeated melodic and rhythmic lines with slight variations, such as the Yemenite welcome song (ex.14) in

Ex.14 Welcome song, south Yemen, transcr. A. Shiloah

which there is a systematic descent from the 6th, reached from the 4th below it, to the *finalis*. This descent is characterized by an undulating progression and syncopated rhythm, ending on a cadence which occurs after the *finalis*. The melody is also enriched by inflecting the *e*. Most of the free rhythmical songs are of a more complicated type (e.g. the *'atābā*) and often begin with an introductory melismatic vocal improvisation on meaningless words and syllables (ex.15). By performing this improvisation the singer adjusts himself and his listeners to the mode of the song. Short improvised

Ex.15 *'Atābā, maqām bayyātī*, improvised introduction; transcr. A. Shiloah
(Shiloah, 1974)

passages of this kind sometimes also precede each stanza. Although the structure of the melodic phrases is in part determined by the poetic lines, their respective conclusions do not necessarily coincide. Indeed, although the poetic lines are equal in length and in number of syllables, the musical lines are not repeated exactly; the unit on which the musical structure is based is the stanza. As a result there are long musical periods which are highly melismatic and use frequently fluctuating intonations as an expressive device. The musical lines also have a wide range, often more than an octave. In this category improvisation and variability are much more evident in both music and text. Bartók described this phenomenon of variability as universal, but in Near Eastern music it seems particularly strongly marked.

(c) *Polyphony*. Although most Arab tunes are sung or performed monophonically, rudimentary polyphony, both vocal and instrumental, is common. An interesting

occurrence of vocal drone in the *nahami* genre was described by Poul Rovsing Olsen (1960) in his studies of the music of Kuwait and Bahrain (*see* ARABIAN GULF). The *naham* is a singer paid to travel on the boat to encourage and entertain the pearl fishers during their long periods at sea. While the *naham* is performing the fishermen intone an extremely low note two octaves below the level of his melody. This drone may be a fixed pitch or may attempt to follow the outline of the melody. This practice has similarities to the *ison* in Byzantine chant and also occurs in other Persian Gulf genres. Olsen mentioned an upper drone in some religious chant (*mawlid*) and in the beduins' night songs (*al-ahalla*), as well as a prolongation of the *finalis* at the end of a verse in certain songs of Iraqi origin. The striking style of singing at extremely low pitches also occurs in Egypt in the Laythi order's *zikr* (a type of religious ceremony): while the *munshid* (precentor) performs melismatic tunes, the worshippers intone at an extremely low pitch an ostinato with the repeated sentence 'There is no other god but God'.

Samaritans and Yemenite Jews still sing in various parallel intervals; and heterophony and overlapping are also common.

(iii) *Song types and their social functions*. Certain types predominate in the beduin repertory: caravan songs such as the *rakbānī* (Iraq), *hujaynī* (Egypt), *ḥidā'* (Yemen) and *barrakah* (Libya); songs of war; processional songs; epic and political songs; songs for the veneration of saints; panegyrics; mocking songs; laments; love-songs; dance-songs of the *daḥḥiyya* and *radīḥ* types; question-and-answer or disputation songs; and work songs relating to hunting, watering animals and fertilizing the date-palm. The repertory of villages and towns includes some of these types of song and, in addition, agricultural or other work songs, songs relating to food and drink and social injustice, and songs connected with the life-cycle. In this repertory there are also songs for public festivals and commemorations such as the *mawlid* (a festival commemorating the anniversary not only of the Prophet but also of venerated saints). The *fazzaziyya* are tunes performed during the nights of Ramadan and the *ḥusayniyyāt* are elegies sung in Iraq on 'Ashūrā, the tenth day of the month of *muḥarram*, on which the martyr Ḥusayn, the Prophet's grandson, was slain at the battle on the plain of Karbalā'. The religious ceremonies of diverse mystic orders are called *zikr*, a spoken form of the word *dhikr* ('remembrance'; *see* ISLAMIC RELIGIOUS MUSIC, §2 (i)); in these devotions music and dance are prominent.

Work songs are among the most important of the village song types. E. W. Lane, who lived in Egypt from 1825 to 1849 and whose account of the work songs there remains one of the most representative of the region, noted songs and chants of boatmen rowing, peasants raising water, porters carrying loads, sawyers, reapers and many other labourers. Most of these are still sung and also exist in other Near Eastern countries. Some types of labour specific to one area have given rise to appropriate repertories (e.g. that of the flooding of the fields and well-irrigation in Hadramawt, and the unique and beautiful repertory of the pearl fishers in the Arabian Gulf).

The *zār*, a song type of Egypt, Sudan and other places near the Red Sea, is connected with the practice of exorcism. It is part of a ceremony, intended to expel evil spirits and mysterious diseases from possessed individuals, in which specialized ensembles of singers, dancers and instrumentalists, particularly players of the *simsimiyya* (lyre), have a large part.

(iv) *Performers: the poet-musician.* The *shā'ir* or poet-musician has played a prominent role in the creation of many of the song genres described above as well as in their perpetuation. He embellishes all ceremonies, social gatherings and festivities, and is considered a gifted and inspired man, capable of improvising and reiterating verses and tunes in every traditional genre. He usually has a good or pleasing voice and an exceptional memory. However, his 'creativeness' is often mostly skill in adapting or rearranging existing material from the traditional store of motifs and formulae, although this is no reflection on his multiple and inseparable talents as poet, composer and performer. Since he improvises spontaneously and in doing so draws on memorized material, he often repeats certain verses in different contexts and in songs belonging to various genres. However, he always sets the repeated verses in a way that fits the particular content, form and tune. Often a second poet-musician takes part in the performance and alternates with the first: the resulting exchange of improvised verses and stanzas introduces an element of competition which stimulates their imagination, gives them time to rest and think, and greatly amuses the audience. Sometimes, when one has difficulty continuing, the second immediately intones a vocal improvisation followed by a new stanza. For the poet-musician the presence of a large audience is also a stimulus – indeed, it is a necessary condition for improvisation; when he is by himself he finds improvisation difficult and even pointless.

Poet-musicians who are invited to sing at ceremonies are considered professional, but their payment does not amount to a living wage. Some specialize in a particular genre such as epic songs; dirges are the province of female singers who excel as keeners. There is no formal teaching: a gifted individual with a natural predisposition for music listens to the recognized poet-musicians of his group, memorizes the songs he hears while working in the field or herding and starts occasionally creating songs based on these models. Having acquired a certain degree of confidence, he is invited as a novice to give an example of his ability. At a later stage he attends a small gathering to try to perform for a whole evening, and in return receives token payment. Finally, once he becomes recognized as an able singer, he is considered professional.

Although oral transmission has always been an essential feature of this tradition, educated poets now frequently write down their poems in notebooks and classify them according to genres, and some collections have been published. The poets use their notebooks as memory aids, and do not refer to them in performance.

The social status of the poet-musician and society's general attitude towards him are ambivalent: he is highly appreciated for his talent and as an indispensable entertainer, but in everyday life and human relationships he is treated with a certain distrust and even contempt, perhaps because he is unusual and is not integrated into the social structure: music and other creative activities have always tended to be considered superfluous oc-

cupations and the lowest of professions. In a sense the payments given to the poet-musicians are like alms given to begging street musicians and public entertainers.

4. INSTRUMENTAL MUSIC. Apart from some dances of rural origin and epic songs, almost all songs are performed without any accompanying melodic instruments. Independent instrumental musical forms are practically non-existent; the development of such instrumental forms as the *simsimiyya* (beduin lyre; fig.10 below) repertory was probably influenced by modern tendencies in art music (which formerly also lacked independent instrumental forms). Whereas melodic instruments play only a small role, percussion instruments, particularly membranophones, are relatively important. Though most instrumental music is monophonic, there are rudimentary polyphonic elements similar to those in vocal music. Ensembles of single- and double-reed instruments often play in simple forms of two-part polyphony, such as drone with melody or parallel octaves.

There are only a few types of idiophone. Two varieties of concussion idiophone are common: *kāsāt* (cymbals) are used mainly in religious processions, usually together with the cylindrical drum, and also in the course of the *zikr* rituals of certain dervish orders; tiny finger cymbals (*sunūj* or *sājāt*) attached to the thumb and middle finger of each hand are used by dancers. Percussion idiophones include the copper plate played by women in Yemen; oilcans (used as drums); the mortar which is pounded in lively rhythmic patterns while grinding coffee (according to Olsen each sheik has his own rhythms for grinding coffee); and empty jars which pearl fishers beat with their right hand.

3. Daff (frame drum) player, Iraq

Membranophones are by far the most varied in type and function. Frame drums in this region have usually been associated with women. The generic name *daff* refers to any frame drum (fig.3); the terms *dā'ira* and

4. Naqqārāt (kettledrum) player, Iraq

5. Beduin nāy (end-blown flute) player

7. Zamr mujwiz (double clarinet) player in Ma'ān, Jordan

6. Shabbābah (end-blown flute) player in Marrakesh, Morocco

8. Bagpipe player, Iraq

ṭār are reserved for the tambourine or frame drum with jingling discs. They are beaten with the fingers in the middle, near the edge or in the area in between. Cylindrical drums, known variously as *ṭabl*, *dawul*, *ṭabl baladī*, *hadjir* etc, are shallow wooden double-headed drums struck with flexible beaters. The player, who hangs the drum obliquely on his shoulder, can produce both muted and sharp sounds. In ensembles with cymbals or with a double-reed instrument, the cylindrical drum accompanies all kinds of processions and open-air ceremonies. Sometimes these drums play in ensemble, as in Iraq where the *dammāmāt*, a group of four or five players with cylindrical drums of various sizes, performs special rhythmic compositions on certain occasions. Another Iraqi ensemble, the *daqqāqāt* ('beaters'), is composed of four female drummers and a female singer.

Kettledrums are generally known as *ṭāsāt* or *naqqārāt* (which occur in different sizes; fig.4). An ensemble of two shallow kettledrums of unequal dimensions is connected with pilgrimages: the player, riding a camel, strikes them with two sticks. On the nights of Ramadan the *musaḥḥir* uses either a little *ṭabl* or a *bāz* (small kettledrum) to attract attention to his call marking the beginning of the fast. The widely known vase-shaped drum *darabukka* is played by men and women in villages and cities. Made of wood or clay, it is placed under the left hand or between the legs and beaten with both hands.

Among aerophones, the flutes known as *nāy* (fig.5) or *qaṣaba* ('reed') are usually 60–70 cm long with five or six finger-holes arranged in two groups. There is also a small type called *shabbābah* (fig.6). Although traditionally made of reed or cane, flutes are now often made of simple metal tubes or pieces of pipe. They are played by shepherdesses in beduin society; in the sedentary rural regions of Iraq, Syria, Lebanon, Palestine and Jordan such dances as the *dabkah* (a dynamic line-dance) are accompanied by a flute or by reed instruments. The *nāy* is also used in some dervish orders to accompany the chant of the *munshid*.

Because of their similar functions there has always been terminological confusion between the single-reed instruments (simple or double clarinet), and the double-reed instruments (simple or double oboe). In ancient literature *mizmār* occurs sometimes as a generic term for all wind instruments and sometimes as a designation for all reed instruments, or just for the oboe; this confusion still persists. The most common names for the double-reed instrument are *zurna*, *zamr*, *ghayṭa* and (rarely) *mizmār*. The wooden tube terminates in a bell; the player holds the entire double reed inside his mouth. The generic names for the single-reed instrument composed of two pipes are *mujwiz* or *mijwiz*, *maqrūna*, *muṭbiq* or *muṭabbiq*; it is called *zamr mujwiz*, *zummāra* or *jifti* when the two pipes are equal in length and have the same number of finger-holes (fig.7); and *arghūl* or *mashūra* when one of the pipes is much longer than the other and serves as the drone. The one-pipe clarinet is known as *'uffāta* and *'anfīta*. The bagpipe (fig.8), called *zummāra bi-soan*, *jirba* or *hibbān*, has a goatskin bag and two single-reed pipes.

All these instruments are played during open-air events such as processions, pilgrimages, military marches, dances at weddings and circumcisions, and during some types of labour such as that of the Nile boatmen and the pearl fishers. They are generally played in a small ensemble such as one oboe and one cylindrical drum – a widespread combination – or a larger ensemble such as *ṭabl baladī* which comprises three shawms (two large and one small), a pair of kettledrums and the cylindrical drum, *ṭabl baladī*, which gives the ensemble its name.

In some regions one particular type of reed instrument predominates, while in other regions different kinds co-exist. Iran, Turkey, Asia Minor, Central Asia, Kurdistan, parts of Iraq and Syria, North Africa and the neighbouring area are double-reed territory; while south Iraq, Syria, Lebanon, Palestine, Jordan and most of the Arabian peninsula are single-reed territory. The instruments are equally common in the Arabian Gulf and in Egypt, where all varieties of reed instrument co-exist. Though straight trumpets were formerly important in the Arab world they are now rare, except in North Africa; fishermen in Yemen, however, use conch shell trumpets.

Chordophones include the one-string fiddle, the *rabāb* (fig.9), common throughout much of the Arab-influenced world. It usually has a quadrilateral frame covered on the front and (usually) back with skin; its string is of horsehair. In the Near East this type is also known as *rabāb al-shā'ir* ('rabāb of the poet') because it is played by poet-musicians to accompany their epic songs. It doubles the voice at the unison and is used to play improvisatory interludes which are more subject to variation than the vocal part: in ex.16, for instance, the

Ex.16 *Shā'ir* song, *rabāb* accompaniment, beduin; transcr. A. Shiloah

player performs each interlude differently, though always within the range of a 5th. One variety of *rabāb*, with two strings, called *rabāb al-mughannī* ('rabāb of the singer') is played by poor street singers and beggars.

Another chordophone, the five-string lyre (*simsimiyya* or *tambūra*; fig.10), is found in the Red Sea

9. *Rabāb* (*one-string fiddle*) *player in Maʻān, Jordan*

area. Its body was formerly made of wood shaped like a box or bowl, covered with a skin stretched round it and sewn together with wire (the shape resembled that of the Ethiopian *krar*). The soundbox now consists of a small oilcan; the five strings pass over a small movable wooden bridge and then straight up in a fan shape to the yoke, where they are wound round five pegs. The instrument is held horizontally against the left hip, one of its arms resting on the player's leg. The player uses his right

10. *Simsimiyya* (*five-string lyre*), *Sinai desert, 1967*

hand to pluck the strings with a plectrum; the left-hand fingers rest on the strings, each finger being lifted only when the corresponding string is plucked. The playing is usually strongly rhythmical. The *simsimiyya* is used to accompany the songs and dances of fishermen in beduin encampments and coffee-houses, but is also connected with ceremonies of exorcism, in which it may be used for long preludes to *zār* songs (ex.17); it is also occasionally used for independent pieces and interludes. Its repertory forms a link between beduin music and that of sedentary

Ex.17 *Yamania, zār* exorcism song, introduction, Red Sea area, played on *simsimiyya*, transcr. A. Shiloah

rural and urban society, being open to diverse influences including popular songs from the radio; it thus reflects the processes of change, caused by urbanization and the impact of modern media of communication, which are affecting all the folk traditions of the Arab world.

See also BERBER MUSIC, NORTH AFRICA and entries on separate countries.

BIBLIOGRAPHY

G. A. Villoteau: 'Description historique, technique et littéraire des instrumens de musique des orientaux', *Description de l'Egypte: Etat moderne*, i, ed. E. F. Jomard (Paris, 1809), 846–1016

——: 'De l'état actuel de l'art musical en Egypte', *Description de l'Egypte: Etat moderne*, i, ed. E. F. Jomard (Paris, 1809), 607–845

E. W. Lane: *An Account of the Manners and Customs of the Modern Egyptians* (London, 1836, 5/1860/R1966)

M. Hartmann: 'Arabische Lieder aus Syrien', *Zeitschrift der deutschen morgenlandischen Gesellschaft*, li (1897), 177–214

——: 'Lieder der libyschen Wüste', *Abhandlung für die Kunde des Morgenlandes*, xi/3 (1899), 1–243

G. H. Dalmann: *Palästinischer Diwan* (Leipzig, 1901)

J. C. Ewald Falls: *Beduinen-Lieder der libyschen Wüste* (Cairo, 1908)

S. H. Stephan: 'Modern Palestinian Parallels to the Song of Songs', *Journal of the Palestine Oriental Society*, ii (1922), 202–78

A. Z. Idelsohn: *Thesaurus of Hebrew Oriental Melodies* (Leipzig and New York, 1922–3)

P. Toschi: 'Musica popolare tripolina', *Lares*, viii (1937), 136

A. Abdullah: 'Dancing East of Suez', *Dancing Times*, new ser., no.333 (1938), 274

M. Schneider: 'A propósito del influjo árabe', *AnM*, i (1946), 31–141

R. A. Waterman, W. Lichtenwanger, V. H. Herrmann, H. I. Poleman and C. Hobbs, eds.: 'Bibliography of Asiatic Musics', *Notes*, v (1947–8), 21, 178, 354, 549; vi (1948–9), 122, 281, 419, 570; vii (1949–50), 84, 265, 415, 613; viii (1950–51), 100, 322

R. B. Serjeant, ed.: 'The Haḍrami Song', *Prose and Poetry from Hadramawt* (London, 1951), 17–50

H. Hickmann: 'La daraboukkah', *Bulletin de l'Institut d'Egypte*, xxxiii (1952), 229

F. Meier: 'Der Derwischtanz, Versuch eines Überblicks', *Asiatische Studien*, viii (1954), 107

M. A. Murray: 'Ancient and Modern Ritual Dances in the Near East', *Folklore*, lxvi (1955), 401

B. S. Rasheed: *Egyptian Folk Songs* (New York and Cairo, 1958)

P. R. Olsen: 'Enregistrements faits à Kuwait et Bahrain', *Ethnomusicologie III: Wégimont V 1960*, 137–70

E. F. Wente: 'Egyptian "Make Merry" Songs Reconsidered', *Journal of Near Eastern Studies*, xxi (1962), 118

M. Molé: 'La danse extatique en Islam', *Les danses sacrées* (Paris, 1963), 147–280

M. Abdelkafi: *Les mariages en Tripolitaine* (Tripoli, Libya, 1964)

E. Gerson-Kiwi: 'Women's Songs from the Yemen: their Tonal Structure and Form', *The Commonwealth of Music, in Honor of Curt Sachs* (New York, 1965), 97

P. R. Olsen: 'Pêcheurs de perles et musiciens du Golfe Persique', OCR 42 [disc notes]

M. A. Havas: *The Contemporary Arab Folk Song* (*United Arab Republic*) (Moscow, 1970)

S. Jargy: *La poésie populaire traditionnelle chantée au Proche-Orient arabe*, i (Paris, 1970)

J. Kuckertz: 'Origin and Development of the Rabab', *Sangeet natak*, xv (1970), Jan–March, 16

I. J. Katz: *Judeo-Spanish Traditional Ballads from Jerusalem: an Ethnomusicological Study* (New York, 1972)

A. Shiloah: 'The Simsimiyya: a Stringed Instrument of the Red Sea Area', *Asian Music*, iv/1 (1972), 15

——: 'A Group of Arabic Wedding Songs from the Village of Deyr al-Asad', *Studies of the Folklore Research Center*, iv (1974), 267

——: 'Instruments à anches de types hautbois et clarinette double en Proche Orient: de leur diffusion, terminologie, fonction', *Makedonski folklor*, vii/13 (1974), 47

J. Elsner: 'Zum Problem des Maqām', *AcM*, xlvii (1975), 208

O. WRIGHT (I, 1–4), JOSEF PACHOLCZYK (I,5)
AMNON SHILOAH (II)

Aragall, Giacomo [Jaime] (*b* Barcelona, 6 June 1939). Spanish tenor. He studied in Barcelona with Francesco Puig and in Italy under Vladimiro Badiali. After winning the Busseto singing competition in 1963, he made his début in the title role of *L'amico Fritz* at La Scala during the 1963–4 season. His Covent Garden début was in 1966 as the Duke of Mantua, one of his most admired roles. He has a forwardly produced, keen-edged voice, which he uses with some sensitivity; he has been criticized for failing to pitch it truly, but praised for his idiomatic phrasing in the Italian repertory.

ALAN BLYTH

Aragonaise (Fr.: 'from Aragon'). A term used to describe an Aragonese dance, normally the jota.

Araia [Araja], **Francesco** (*b* Naples, 25 June 1709). Italian composer. No information is available on his musical education, so most scholars assume that he was taught by his father, Angelo, and his grandfather, Pietro, both professional musicians. His first important engagement was on 29 October 1723, when he directed the music at a religious function in honour of St Joseph at the Neapolitan church of S Maria la Nova. The *Avvisi di Napoli* for 2 November 1723, reporting the event, stated that the 14-year-old composer had performed 'to the amazement and acclamation of everybody'. According to some authorities he wrote a comic opera *Lo matremmonejo pe' vennetta* for Naples in 1729. This is the only comic opera that has been attributed to him. His first heroic opera, and the first that can be credited to him with certainty, was *Berenice* (Pratolino, 1730). In 1731 he composed two more operas as well as an oratorio, *S Andrea Corsini*, for performance in Rome. Another opera, *La forza dell'amore e dell'odio*, was presented in Milan in 1734, and yet another, *Lucio Vero*, in Venice early in 1735.

It is in the libretto of this last that Araia is called for the first time '*maestro di cappella* of Her Majesty, ruler of all the Russias'. The invitation to go to Russia was probably extended to him in Venice by the violinist Pietro Mira, who had come from St Petersburg with orders from the Empress Anne to collect an Italian opera troupe for her. Araia arrived in St Petersburg late in 1735 when he was confirmed in his post and awarded 1220 roubles a year, free board and other perquisites. He began his activities at the Russian court by presenting early in 1736 a new production of his *La forza dell'amore e dell'odio*. This was later followed by the composition and presentation of cantatas and two further operas, *Il finto Nino, overo La Semiramide riconosciuta* (1737) and *Artaserse* (1738). After Anne's death in autumn 1740 he returned on leave to Italy with the task of collecting new personnel for the opera troupe. By late 1742 he was back in St Petersburg with new performers and a new production team that included the librettist Giuseppe Bonecchi. The Empress Elizabeth had by this time established herself upon the Russian throne. Araia continued to write operas for the court until the end of 1755. Of these the most famous is undoubtedly *Cephalus and Procris* (1755), because it is the first opera known to have been sung in Russia in the vernacular and not in Italian. He wrote no operas after 1755, partly because of the arrival in St Petersburg in 1757 of a comic-opera troupe under the impresario Giovanni Battista Locatelli. The court's taste then seems to have swung in favour of comic opera and away from heroic opera, which was Araia's preferred genre. From this time he wrote only occasional pieces for the various royal residences in and around the capital. In autumn 1759 he obtained leave to retire to Italy permanently. However, when the new tsar, Peter III, succeeded to the throne at the start of 1762, Araia was recalled to write music for the coronation. For a short while he seems to have taken up his old position as court *maestro di cappella*. But following the deposition and then assassination of Peter by order of his wife, the Empress Catherine, in mid-1762, Araia finally withdrew from the court's service. He settled down to retirement in

Bologna, but it has not yet been established whether he died there.

Araia's works include at least 14 operas, a few short compositions for the stage, an oratorio, several cantatas and some keyboard capriccios. Only one aria of his is known to have been published in his lifetime, 'Felice ai dì sereni', in Walsh's Favourite Airs from Orfeo, a pasticcio performed in London in March 1736. Information on his music in MSS in Russia is given by Mooser. Two of his operas survive intact in western European libraries, La forza dell'amore (A-Wn) and Il finto Nino (D-B, GB-Lbm). Of his other surviving and unpublished works the most impressive is La Cimotoe (I-MC), a cantata for four voices and instruments composed in honour of the marriage (date not determined) of Francesco Caracciolo, Prince of Avellino, and Maria Antonia Carafa.

WORKS

OPERAS

?Lo matremmonejo pe' vennetta, ?Naples, 1729
Berenice (A. Salvi), Florence, Pratolino, 1730
Ciro riconosciuto (Metastasio), Rome, Delle Dame, carn. 1731
Il Cleomene (V. Cassani), Rome, Delle Dame, spring 1731
La forza dell'amore e dell'odio, Milan, Ducale, Jan 1734; A-Wn
Lucio Vero (Zeno), Venice, S Angelo, carn. 1735
Il finto Nino, overo La Semiramide riconosciuta (F. Silvani), St Petersburg, 9 Feb 1737; D-B, GB-Lbm
Artaserse (Metastasio), St Petersburg, 9 Feb 1738
Seleuco (G. Bonecchi), Moscow, 7 May 1744
Scipione (Bonecchi), St Petersburg, 4 or 5 Sept 1745
Mitridate (Bonecchi), St Petersburg, 7 May 1747
L'asilo della pace (festa teatrale, Bonecchi), St Petersburg, 7 May 1748
Bellerofonte (Bonecchi), St Petersburg, 9 Dec 1750
Eudossa incoronata, o sia Teodosio II (Bonecchi), St Petersburg, 9 May 1751
Cephalus and Procris (A. P. Sumarokoff), St Petersburg, 9 March 1755
Amor prigioniero (dialogo per musica, Metastasio), Oranienbaum, 1755
Alessandro nell'Indie (Metastasio), St Petersburg, 29 Dec 1755

OTHER WORKS

S Andrea Corsini, oratorio, Rome, 1731
La Cimotoe, cantata, 4vv, inst (for the marriage of Francesco Caracciolo, Prince of Avellino, and Maria Antonia Carafa), I-MC
Felice ai dì sereni, aria, in Favourite Airs from the Opera Call'd Orfeo (London, 1736)
Cantatas, short stage compositions, kbd capriccios, arias

BIBLIOGRAPHY

R. A. Mooser: 'Des origines à la mort de Pierre III (1762)', Annales de la musique et des musiciens en Russie au XVIIIe siècle, i (Geneva, 1948), 121
U. Prota-Giurleo: 'Araja, Francesco', DBI

MICHAEL F. ROBINSON

Araiz (Martínez), Andrés (b Saragossa, 30 Nov 1901). Spanish musicologist and composer. He studied in Saragossa with Ramón Borobia Cetina and Salvador Azara Serrano, and in Madrid with del Campo. In 1932 he was one of the founders of the Saragossa Conservatory, in 1947 he was appointed professor of aesthetics and history there and was its director from 1953 to 1957. In 1957 he moved to Mexico and became professor of music history at the Mexico Conservatory in 1960. He has been active as a musicologist, critic, lecturer and folklorist, and his compositions are deeply marked by the music of Aragon. An honorary member of the Spanish Musicology Institute, he was involved in the compilation of the Diccionario de la Música Labor (Barcelona, 1954). He has also published Historia de la música religiosa en España (Barcelona, 1942) and other studies, and is the editor of the series Reseña histórico-crítica acerca de la escritura musical española de los siglos XI y XII.

GUY BOURLIGUEUX

Arakishvili, Dimitri Ignat'yevich (b Vladikavkaz [now Ordzhonikidze], 23 Feb 1873; d Tbilisi, 13 Aug 1953). Georgian composer, ethnomusicologist and teacher. One of the founders of modern Georgian art music, he spent his childhood and youth in various towns in the northern Caucasus, receiving his first music lessons in church choirs. In 1890 he attended concerts given at Armavir by Lado Agniashvili's Georgian folk choir, and his acquaintance with this ensemble had a decisive influence on his choice of career. On moving to Ekaterinodar he took part in the activities of a circle of music lovers and in 1893 published his first composition under the pseudonym Satskalishvili ('son of a poor peasant'). His formal studies began in 1894 with his admission to the Music and Drama College of the Moscow Philharmonic Society, where until 1901 he studied with Il'yinsky (theory and composition) and Kes (conducting). During his years of study he began to contribute articles on Georgian folk music to the Georgian and Russian press, laying the foundations for his future research. He became a member of the music-ethnographical commission of the Imperial Society for Literature, Natural Science, Anthropology and Ethnography of Moscow University, organized expeditions and took part in four of them across Georgia (1901, 1902, 1904 and 1908). The material collected and classified, amounting to over 500 songs recorded by phonograph, was published in the first, second and fifth volumes of Trudï muzïkal'no-etnograficheskoy komissii Imperatorskovo obshchestva literaturï, estestvoznaniya, antropologii i etnografii pri Moskovskom Universitete. Arakishvili published the same material in three volumes of 1906–16 which aroused great interest, being among the first publications of and commentaries on Georgian folk choral polyphony, and he was awarded the gold medal of the International Congress for this work in 1916. The next year he completed his work at the Moscow Archaeological Institute.

While pursuing these intensive studies and increasing his mastery of composition, Arakishvili engaged in social and educational work during his years in Moscow. Among other activities, he established and was one of the first teachers at the Narodnaya Konservatoriya (People's Conservatory) in Moscow; he organized and was co-editor of Muzïka i zhizn' (1908–12), the leading music journal; and he founded the music section of the Moscow society Sodeystviye Vneshkol'nomu Obrazovaniyu (Aid for Out-of-school Education). At the same time he composed several of his best-known songs, the symphonic picture Gimn Ormuzdu ('Hymn to Ormuzd', the first example of the genre in Georgian music) and the opera Tkmuleba Shota Rustavelze ('The legend of Shota Rustaveli'). He moved permanently in 1918 to Tbilisi, where he worked intensively in many areas until the end of his life. At various times he was director of the Georgian Philharmonic Society, and he founded the Second Tbilisi Conservatory, where he was made professor in 1919. He lectured on historical–theoretical subjects and Georgian folk music, and for many years he was senior research worker of the Academy of Sciences of the Georgian SSR. In addition, he was chairman of the Georgian Composers' Union (1932–4) and a board member of the Composers' Union of the USSR (from 1948). Among the awards he received were the title People's Artist of the Georgian SSR (1929), the USSR

State Prize (1950), the Order of the Red Banner of Labour (twice) and the Badge of Honour.

Arakishvili's activities as composer, scholar, researcher and teacher exerted a strong influence on the whole development of music in Georgia. His output covers the entire period during which modern Georgian art music became established; *The Legend of Shota Rustaveli*, the chamber music and the songs (of which there are more than 80) were particularly important contributions. Though as an ethnomusicologist he was one of the first to focus attention on the variety of polyphony in Georgian folk music, in his compositions he drew most heavily on the intonational and stylistic features characteristic of the region's urban folklore, on the lyrical urban song and on the melismas marked by specific modal and intonational features, so that his music has an oriental colouring and often a monodic quality. Most of his works are lyrical, spontaneous in feeling, tuneful and romantic and elevated in their ideas.

WORKS
(selective list)

Operas: Tkmuleba Shota Rustavelze [The legend of Shota Rustaveli], 1914, Tbilisi, 1919; Sitsotskhle sikharulia [Life is a joy] (Dinara), 1926

Orch: Gimn Ormuzdu [Hymn to Ormuzd], sym. picture, 1911; 3 syms., 1932, 1942, 1947; Gimn novovo vostoka [Hymn of the new east], 1933

Other works, choruses, songs, film scores, folksong arrs.

Principal publishers: Muzfond Gruzii (Tbilisi), Muzgiz, Muzïka, Sovetskiy Kompozitor (Moscow and Leningrad)

WRITINGS

Kratkiy ocherk razvitiya Kartalino-Kakhetinskoy narodnoy muzïki [A brief outline of the development of Kartalino-Kakhetian folk music] (Moscow, 1906) [incl. 27 folksong transcriptions]

O narodnoy pesne zapadnoy Gruzii i muzïkal'nïkh instrumentov Moskvï i Tiflisa [On the folksong of western Georgia and musical instruments in Moscow and Tiflis] (Moscow, 1908) [incl. 83 folksong transcriptions]

Gruzinskoye narodnoye muzïkal'noye tvorchestvo [Georgian folk music] (Moscow, 1916) [incl. 225 folksong transcriptions]

Kartuli musika [Music manual] (Kutaisi, 1925, 2/1940; Russ. trans., 2/1940, as *Gruzinskaya muzïka* [Georgian music])

Opisaniye i obmer narodnïkh instrumentov [Description and measurement of folk instruments] (Tbilisi, 1940)

Obzor narodnïkh pesen vostochnoy Gruzii [Survey of the folksongs of eastern Georgia] (Tbilisi, 1948)

BIBLIOGRAPHY

G. Sakvarelidze: articles in *Teatri da tskhovreba* (Tbilisi, 1914), nos. 16, 24, 27, 30

A. Begidzhanov: *Dimitri Arakishvili* (Moscow, 1953)

D. Shostakovich: 'Yarkaya, krasivaya zhizn' ' [A bright, beautiful life], *Zarya vostoka* (Tbilisi, 31 May 1953)

A. Begidzhanov: *D. Arakishvili* (Tbilisi, 1955)

V. Donadze: 'Muzïkal'noye naslediye Gruzii' [Georgia's musical heritage], *Gruzinskaya muzïkal'naya kul'tura* (Moscow, 1957), 103

P. Khuchua: 'Sovetskaya opera i balet', *Gruzinskaya muzïkal'naya kul'tura* (Moscow, 1957), 177

A. Khachaturian: 'Truzhenik, tvorets' [Toiler, creator], *Zarya vostoka* (4 April 1965)

Kh. Arakelov: 'Obrabotki narodnïkh pesen D. Arakishvili' [Arakishvili's folksong arrangements], *Voprosï teorii muzïki* (Moscow, 1968), 35

P. Khuchua: 'D. Arakishvili', *Muzïkal'naya zhizn'* (1973), no.10, p.17

N. Kavtaradze and M. Dzhaparidze: *Mogonebebi sakhelovan kompozitorze* (Tbilisi, 1974)

Sh. Mshvelidze: 'Kartuli musikis didi moamage' [A great figure in Georgian music], *Sabchota khelovneba* (Tbilisi, 1974), no.3, p.7

EVGENY MACHAVARIANI

Arámbarri (y Gárate), Jesús (*b* Bilbao, 13 April 1902; *d* Madrid, 11 July 1960). Spanish conductor and composer. He studied singing, the piano, organ and composition at the Vizcaino Conservatory in Bilbao; a scholarship took him to Paris in 1929 for further study in composition with Paul Le Flem and at the Ecole Normale with Dukas, and in conducting with Vladimir Golschmann. He also worked with Weingartner at Basle

in 1932. On his return to Spain the next year he took charge of the part-time Bilbao SO, which he steadily developed and improved and which, in 1938, became the first civic orchestra in Spain on a regular basis. Arámbarri helped to organize musical activities in other parts of Spain and conducted frequent concerts in all the large Spanish cities. He was enthusiastically concerned to perform large-scale choral works involving the Basque choirs of northern Spain with their distinctive vocal tradition, and he introduced several works by Britten, Vaughan Williams and Walton to the Spanish concert repertory. In 1953 he was appointed a professor at the Madrid Conservatory, and became conductor of the Madrid SO and president of the Spanish conductors' association. His compositions include *Viento del sur*, a zarzuela in two acts (1952); *Castilla* for soprano, chorus and orchestra (1941; text by Manuel Machado); Eight Basque Songs, for soprano and orchestra (1932); *Gabon-zar sorginak*, for soprano and orchestra; a string quartet; and piano pieces.

BIBLIOGRAPHY

F. Sopeña: *Historia de la música española contemporanea* (Madrid, 1958)

M. Valls Gorena: *La música española después de Manuel de Falla* (Madrid, 1962)

NOËL GOODWIN

Aranaz y Vides, Pedro (*b* Tudela, Navarre, baptized 2 May 1740; *d* Cuenca, 24 Sept 1820). Spanish composer. After studying eight years with Luis Serra at El Pilar Cathedral in Saragossa, he competed for the music directorships of the cathedrals S Domingo de la Calzada (1763), El Pilar (1765) and Zamora (1768), but was each time rejected, probably because he was not yet in holy orders. In 1765 he went to Madrid, where he made his name as a composer of tuneful, folkloric *tonadillas*. On 11 September 1769 he was appointed *maestro de capilla* at Cuenca Cathedral, where despite offers from better-paying cathedrals he remained until his death, composing much staid ecclesiastical music. He was ordained a priest in 1773 and retired from conducting in 1797.

WORKS

16 tonadillas, *E-Mm*, incl. La maja limonera, 2vv, *c*1765, ed. in Subirá (1930); La satisfacción de los amantes, 2vv, 1765; Dos payos y dos soldados, 4vv, 1766; El Gallego, 1v, 1767; El remedo de los locos, 1v, 1769; El chasco del perro, 3vv, 1769; El chusco y la maja, 1772

*c*300 Lat. and Sp. sacred works in *CU*, *c*160 in *E*, incl. 14 masses, 4–8vv, with/without insts; *c*150 motets, 4–8vv, insts; 20 Salve; responsories; Lamentations; villancicos; Confitemini Domino, motet, 8vv, org obbl, ed. in Martínez Millán

BIBLIOGRAPHY

J. Subirá: *La tonadilla escénica*, iii (Madrid, 1930), 30ff

H. Anglès and J. Subirá: *Catálogo musical de la Biblioteca nacional de Madrid*, i (Barcelona, 1946), 239f

R. Navarro Gonzalo: *Catálogo musical del Archivo de la Santa Iglesia Catedral Basílica de Cuenca* (Cuenca, 1965)

M. Martínez Millán: 'D. Pedro Aranaz y Vides (1740–1820), maestro de capilla de Cuenca', *Tesoro sacro musical*, no.627 (1974), 3

ROBERT STEVENSON

Aranda, Matheo de (*b* ?Aranda de Duero, *c*1495; *d* Coimbra, ?15 Feb 1548). Spanish theorist. He studied music theory with Pedro Ciruelo at the University of Alcalá de Henares sometime before 1524; later he went to Italy for practical instruction. By 3 April 1528 he was *mestre de capela* at Évora Cathedral in Portugal, a post which he held until 26 July 1544, when he was appointed professor of music at Coimbra University. During most of this period the Portuguese court resided in Évora rather than in Lisbon, and Aranda earned praise from the administrator of the see, Cardinal Dom

Afonso. At Coimbra however, the native Portuguese professors proved so resentful towards the foreigner that according to a colleague, Juan Fernández, Aranda died of 'pure vexation'. His body was carried back to Évora for burial on 2 June 1549.

Aranda's two music treatises were the first to be printed in Portugal, although they are written in Spanish. In the *Tractado d'cāto llano* he agreed with Juan Espinosa and Martín de Rivafrecha in declaring the sung diatonic semitone (i.e. A to B♭) smaller than the chromatic (i.e. B♭ to B♮). He allowed the breaking of ligatures for the sake of 'correct' accentuation and like most contemporary Spanish theorists, preferred liberal use of ficta in plainsong. The examples of species counterpoint in his second treatise, the *Tractado de canto mēsurable* (Lisbon, 1535), were the first polyphony published in Portugal.

BIBLIOGRAPHY

M. de Aranda: *Tractado de cāto llano* (Lisbon, 1533/R1962) [with introduction and notes by J. A. Alegria]
R. Stevenson: *Spanish Music in the Age of Columbus* (The Hague, 1960), 96ff
A. Nobre de Gusmano: 'Cantores e músicos em Évora nos anos de 1542 a 1553', *Anais da Academia portuguesa da história*, 2nd ser., xiv (1964), 102

ROBERT STEVENSON

Arañés [Arañiés], **Juan** (*b* Catalonia; *d* ?Seo de Urgel, in or after 1649). Spanish composer briefly resident in Italy. He studied at Alcalá de Henares and became a priest. In 1623 he accompanied to Rome the newly appointed Spanish ambassador to the Holy See, Ruy Gómez de Silva y Mendoza, Duke of Pastrana, and in 1624, when dedicating a volume of music to the duke, he described himself as his chaplain and musical director. From 1627 to 1634 he was *mestre de canto* at Seo de Urgel Cathedral. In 1649 he was recalled to this post for one year only. He published *Libro segundo de tonos y villancicos*, for one to four voices and guitar (Rome, 1624; three three-part pieces and a four-part chacona ed. in MME, xxxii, 1970). It comprises 12 secular pieces, the concluding chacona being the first for voices by a Spanish composer to appear in print. The first book implied by this 'second book' is lost, but what are evidently six three-part pieces from it survive in the manuscript Cancionero Casanatense (in *I-Rc*). Arañés's fondness for sequences, overt dominant 7ths and fast dance rhythms and his obsession with triple time and use of guitar letter notation proclaim him a thoroughly up-to-date Baroque composer. Some anonymous three-part masses that he had tried to modernize with an added fourth voice were known (in *E-SU*) in 1921.

BIBLIOGRAPHY

R. Mitjana: 'La musique en Espagne', *EMDC*, I/iv (1920), 2016
F. Pedrell and H. Anglès, eds.: *Els madrigals i la Missa de Difunts d'En Brudieu*, Publicacions del Departament de Música de la Biblioteca de Catalunya, i (Barcelona, 1921), 144f, 147
M. Querol Gavaldá: Introduction to *Musica barroca española*, i, MME, xxxii (1970), 13f, 33

ROBERT STEVENSON

Arangi-Lombardi, Giannina (*b* Marigliano, nr. Naples, 20 June 1890; *d* Milan, 9 July 1951). Italian soprano. As a mezzo-soprano she studied with Beniamino Carelli at the Conservatory of S Pietro a Maiella, Naples, making her début at the Teatro Costanzi, Rome, in 1920 as Lola in *Cavalleria rusticana*. After encouragement from the soprano Emma Carelli (daughter of her teacher, and at that time artistic director of the Costanzi), she began a period of further study with Adelina Stehle in Milan,

during which she became a soprano. She made her début at La Scala as Helen of Troy in *Mefistofele* (26 December 1924), after which she appeared there regularly until 1930 as Santuzza, Aida, Gioconda, the Grand Vestal (*La vestale*), the *Trovatore* Leonora, and Donna Anna (which she also sang at Salzburg in 1935). She made guest appearances throughout Europe and at the Teatro Colón, Buenos Aires (where she made her début as Asteria in Boito's *Nerone*, 1926), and toured Australia with Melba's company in 1928. At Turin she took the title role of *Ariadne auf Naxos* in its first Italian performances in 1925; at the first Florence Festival in 1933 she played Donizetti's Lucrezia Borgia. After retiring from the stage in 1937 she taught singing, first in Milan and then (1947–51) in Ankara. Considered Giannina Russ's successor, she had a large, beautiful voice, pure in emission, used with excellent technique and impeccable musicianship; but her small stature and lack of dramatic ability were handicaps throughout her career.

BIBLIOGRAPHY

R. Celletti: 'Arangi-Lombardi, Giannina', *Le grandi voci* (Rome, 1964) [with opera discography by R. Vegeto]

HAROLD ROSENTHAL

Arányi, Jelly d' [Arányi de Hunyadvar, Jelly Eva] (*b* Budapest, 30 May 1895; *d* Florence, 30 March 1966). British violinist of Hungarian birth, younger sister of Adila Fachiri and great-niece of Joachim. She started to learn the piano, but in 1903 went to the Budapest Academy as a violinist, under Grunfeld and later Hubay. Her career began in 1908 in a series of joint recitals with her sister; the tour included Vienna. In 1909 they played in England and settled there four years later, becoming well known for their performance of Bach's Double Violin Concerto. Jelly was a vivid personality and a born violinist, with fine technique and a good measure of gypsy fire. The warmth and freedom of her playing found full scope in a concerto such as Brahms's; but her rhapsodic style suited also Bartók's two violin and piano sonatas and Ravel's *Tzigane*, which were written for and dedicated to her. Other works she inspired were a concerto by Röntgen, Ethel Smyth's Concerto for violin and horn, and Vaughan Williams's Concerto Accademico; the Double Concerto of Holst was composed for both sisters. In 1938, after much questionable publicity and despite Joachim's express wish, she gave the first British performance of Schumann's Concerto. She formed a piano trio with Suggia and Fanny Davies in 1914; she played later with Felix Salmond and with Myra Hess, who was also her duo partner for over 20 years.

BIBLIOGRAPHY

J. MacLeod: *The Sisters d'Aranyi* (London, 1969)
J. Creighton: *Discopaedia of the Violin, 1889–1971* (Toronto, 1974)

ROBERT ANDERSON

Arapov, Boris Alexandrovich (*b* St Petersburg, 12 Sept 1905). Russian composer and teacher. He studied music from earliest childhood in Poltava, first with his mother and then with the pianist Zaytseva-Zhukovich. At the age of nine or ten he began composing small piano pieces. He lived from 1921 in Petrograd, where he continued piano studies with Yudina and later with Savshinsky, but a disease of the hand forced him to abandon his career as a pianist, and in 1923 he entered the Petrograd Conservatory to study composition and theory with Shcherbachov and Chernov. Immediately after graduating in 1930 he was invited to join the teaching staff, and in 1940 he was appointed professor; he directed the orchestration department and also held a class in composition, his pupils including Sergey Slonimsky and many other composers from the USSR and abroad. He has taken an active part in the Composers' Union from its foundation in 1932, notably as head of the composers' section and as a board member of the union and of its Leningrad branch. An Honoured Art Worker of the RSFSR and the Uzbek SSR, he also holds the Order of the Red Banner of Labour.

Large-scale works predominate in Arapov's output, his compositions are programmatic in the broadest sense, and they abound in picturesque images, to which his highly coloured and resourceful orchestration makes an important contribution. A deep knowledge of various national musics (he spent considerable periods in field studies in Armenia, Georgia, Uzbekistan, China and Korea) and an ability to capture their spirit and style have enabled him to produce several important works on folk themes.

WORKS
(selective list)

STAGE AND ORCHESTRAL

Operas: Khodzha Nasreddin (V. Vitkovich, after Solov'yov: Disturber of the peace), 1944, unpubd; Fregat 'Pobeda' [The frigate 'Victory'] (V. Rozhdestvensky, A. Ivanovsky, after Pushkin: Peter the Great's negro), 1957, unpubd; Dozhd' [Rain] (T. Todorova, Arapov, after Maugham), 1967
Ballet: Portret Doriana Greya (G. Alexidze, after Wilde), 1971, unpubd
Orch: Fugato, 1927, unpubd; Tadzhikskaya syuita, 1938, unpubd; Sym. no.1, 1947, unpubd; Russkaya syuita, 1951, unpubd; Sym. no.2 'Svobodnïy Kitay' [Free China], 1959; Sym. no.3, 1962; Vn Conc., 1964; Conc. for Orch, 1969; Conc., pf, vn, perc, chamber orch, 1973

OTHER WORKS

Vocal orch: Vocal-sym. Cycle (Pushkin), 1937; Pokhodnaya pesnya geologov [Marching song of the geologists] (A. Prokof'yev), 1933; Pesni protesta [Songs of protest], B, jazz orch, 1940, unpubd; Dzhelal-Eddin (Atabayev), oratorio, 1944, collab. A. Kozlovsky, unpubd
Songs: Blok song cycle, 1947–67; Monolog (A. Voznesensky), Bar, tpt, perc, pf, 1969; folksong arrs.
Inst: Variations, pf, 1929, unpubd; Sonata, vn, 1930, unpubd; Yumoresk, pf, 1937; Trio, cl, vn, pf, 1943; 10 uzbekskikh pesen, pf, 1944, unpubd; 6 Pf Pieces, 1955; Etyud-skertso, pf, 1967; Pf Sonata, 1970; 3 Pf Pieces, 1970, unpubd
6 film scores, 1932–54

Principal publishers: Muzgiz, Muzïka, Sovetskiy kompozitor

WRITINGS

ed., with others: 55 sovetskikh simfoniy (Leningrad, 1961)
——: Sovetskaya simfoniya za 50 let [The Soviet symphony through 50 years] (Leningrad, 1967)
——: Leningradskaya ordena trudovovo krasnovo znameni filarmoniya [The Leningrad Order of the Red Banner Philharmonia] (Leningrad, 1972)
Articles in these and other collections, and in periodicals

BIBLIOGRAPHY

I. Smirnov: 'Svobodnïy Kitay', SovM (1959), no.11, p. 43
S. Slonimsky: B. Arapov: Simfoniya 'Svobodnïy Kitay' (Leningrad, 1962)
E. Bonch-Osmolovskaya: 'V zashchitu mira' [In defence of peace], SovM (1963), no.11, p. 39 [on the Sym. no.3]
A. Kenigsberg: Boris Alexandrovich Arapov (Moscow and Leningrad, 1965)
M. Byalik: 'V kamernom zhanre' [In a chamber genre], Stranitsï-muzïkal'noy leniniani (Leningrad, 1970) [on Monolog]
E. Finkel'shteyn: 'K voprosu o spetsifike zhanra' [On the question of the specifics of genre], Muzïka i zhizn', i (Leningrad and Moscow, 1972) [on the Conc. for Orch]
I. Vïzgo-Ivanova: 'Pod znamenem druzhbï' [Under the banner of friendship], Muzïka i zhizn', ii (Moscow and Leningrad, 1973) [on the Tadzhikskaya syuita]
L. Dan'ko: 'Na puti obnovleniya muzïkal'novo teatra' [On the way to a renewal of the musical theatre], Muzïka i zhizn', iii (Leningrad and Moscow, 1974) [on Dozhd' and Portret Doriana Greya]

A. KLIMOVITSKY

Arārāy. One of the three zēmā (genres) of Ethiopian chant; see ETHIOPIAN RITE, MUSIC OF THE.

Arascione, Giovanni (b Cairo Montenotte, nr. Savona, 18 Oct 1546; d in or after 1600). Italian music editor. Fétis stated incorrectly that he was born at Novara. He was probably educated at Mondovì, but he spent most of his life in Rome, where he was a member of the Congregazione dell'Oratorio (founded by Filippo Neri) and a friend and colleague of Giovenale Ancina. His only extant publication, Nuove laudi ariose della Beatissima Virgine scelte da diversi autori (Rome, 1600[5]), for four voices, contains 70 laudi by 26 composers, including Animuccia, Dentice, Giovannelli, Ingegneri, Lassus and Vecchi. All the works are contrafacta of secular pieces for which Arascione provided the sacred texts. According to the four dedicatory letters by Ancina and several sonnets prefacing the volume, it was intended as the second part of Ancina's Tempio armonico, published the year before (RISM 1599[6]). Like Ancina's volume it was designed for the use of the Congregazione; the pieces are firmly in the religious tradition of the Philippine laudi repertory (see Alaleona), and they have tuneful melodic lines and show distinct features of the new monodic style.

BIBLIOGRAPHY

EitnerQ; FétisB
D. Alaleona: Studi su la storia dell'oratorio musicale in Italia (Turin, 1908, 2/1945 as Storia dell'oratorio musicale in Italia), esp. 215
P. Damilano: Giovenale Ancina, musicista filippino (1545–1604) (Florence, 1956)
H. E. Smither: 'Narrative and Dramatic Elements in the Laude Filippine, 1563–1600', AcM, xli (1969), 186
P. Damilano: 'Arascione, Giovanni', MGG

Araujo, Francisco Correa de. See CORREA DE ARAUXO, FRANCISCO.

Araujo, Juan de (b Villafranca de los Barros, Extremadura, 1646; d La Plata [now Sucre], Bolivia, 1712). Composer of Spanish birth, resident in South America. He went to Lima at an early age with his father, a civil official, and there attended the University of S Marcos during the late 1660s. He may have been a pupil of Torrejón y Velasco. After being involved in student disruption he was banished from Lima by the viceroy of Peru, the Count of Lemos. There is documentary evidence that he moved to Panamá, where he worked as choirmaster, and by 1672, when he returned to Lima, he had been ordained a priest. He was then appointed choirmaster of Lima Cathedral and held the post until 1676. He is not heard of again until 1680: from then until his death he was choirmaster of the cathedral at La Plata, Bolivia. He may have spent some time at Cuzco, Peru, since several of his works survive in the library of the S Antonio Abad Seminary there, but there is no evidence to support this suggestion.

Araujo's career at La Plata coincided with the wealthiest period of the Audiencia de Charcas region, of which it was the capital. The number of his works copied there and their performing forces (from eight to ten voices) indicate that he must have had the benefit of a flourishing musical establishment. Stevenson (The Music of Peru, p.189) observed that his 'unusual success in training choirboys assured him throughout his career of an abundant stream of high tiples. This good supply could indeed be inferred from his compositions themselves. One of the choruses almost invariably calls for boys' voices supported by only a tenor'. He was a prolific composer; some 200 pieces by him are known, almost all of them polyphonic villancicos. While he followed the traditional form of the villancico, he was quite innovatory in his search for unusual effects, whether through word-painting or unexpected rhythmic drive by systematic crotchet and quaver syncopation in 6/8 time. Many of his settings are *jácaras* which exude vivid spirits and good humour.

WORKS

2 Magnificat, 10, 11vv, Seminario de S Antonio Abad, Cuzco, Peru
3 Lamentations, Sucre Cathedral archives, Bolivia
Pasionario en canto fygurado, 23vv, inc., Sucre
Dixit Dominus, 11vv, Cuzco
Ut queant laxis, 8vv, ed. in Stevenson, 1960, p.236
Los negritos, 6vv, ed. in Stevenson, 1960, p.228
106 or more villancicos, J. E. Fortún de Ponce private collection, La Paz, Bolivia; Sucre, Bolivia; Cuzco, Peru; Museo Histórico Nacional, Montevideo, Uruguay

For complete list of works see Stevenson, 1970

BIBLIOGRAPHY

J. E. Fortún de Ponce: *Antología de Navidad* (La Paz, 1956)
——: *La Navidad en Bolivia* (La Paz, 1957)
R. Stevenson: *The Music of Peru* (Washington, DC, 1960)
L. Ayestarán: 'El barroco musical hispano-americano: los manuscritos de la iglesia de San Felipe Neri (Sucre, Bolivia), existentes en el Museo Histórico Nacional del Uruguay', *Yearbook of the Inter-American Institute for Musical Research, Tulane University*, i (1965), 58, 61, 64f, 76f, 91
R. Stevenson: *Renaissance and Baroque Musical Sources in the Americas* (Washington, DC, 1970)
S. Claro: *Antologia de la música colonial en America del Sur* (Santiago, 1974)

GERARD BÉHAGUE

Araújo, (José) Mozart de (*b* Campo Grande, Ceará, 25 Jan 1904). Brazilian musicologist. He studied at the school of medicine in Rio de Janeiro (1928), but then returned to his early interest in music, in which he was mainly self-taught; from the 1930s to his retirement (1974) he established music associations of various kinds in Rio de Janeiro and served as director of the Radio MEC (Ministry of Education), vice-president of the OSB (Brazilian SO), president of the federal council of the Brazilian Musicians' Union, a founder of the National SO, and chief of the music division of the ministry of foreign relations. He is a member of the Brazilian Academy of Music and of the Art Music Council of the Museu da Imagem e do Som, and editor-in-chief of the *Revista brasileira de cultura*, published by the Federal Council of Culture. In his research he has concentrated on 18th- and 19th-century music in Brazil, and has discovered several historical documents concerning Brazilian art and folk music.

WRITINGS

'A aculturação musical no Brasil', *Revista do Instituto Brasil–Estados Unidos*, viii/17 (1950), 46
A modinha e o lundu no século XVIII: uma pesquisa histórica e bibliográfica (São Paulo, 1963)
'Sigismund Neukomm: um músico austríaco no Brasil', *Revista brasileira de cultura*, i/1 (1969), 61

BIBLIOGRAPHY

Quem é quem nas artes e nas letras do Brasil (Rio de Janeiro, 1966), 131

GERARD BÉHAGUE

Araújo [Arauxo, Arraujo], Pedro de (*fl* mid-17th century). Portuguese organist and composer. The principal theme of one of his tientos is identical with one in a work by Francisco Correa de Arauxo, but it is not known whether or not he was related to Francisco. A few MS keyboard pieces by him survive (edns. in *Cravistas portuguezes*, ii, ed. M. S. Kastner, Mainz, 1950 and PM, xi, ed. K. Speer, 1967).

KLAUS SPEER

Arauxo, Francisco Correa de. *See* CORREA DE ARAUXO, FRANCISCO.

Arba' an-naqūs (Arabic: 'strophes accompanied with cymbals'). A category of hymn in the MUSIC OF THE COPTIC RITE.

Arban, (Joseph) Jean-Baptiste (Laurent) (*b* Lyons, 28 Feb 1825; *d* Paris, 9 April 1889). French cornet player and conductor. He studied the trumpet with Dauverné at the Paris Conservatoire from 1841 to 1845. He acquired renown for conducting salon orchestras, an activity that he had taken up in 1856, and later conducted at the Opéra. In 1857 he became professor of saxhorn at the Ecole Militaire, and in 1869, after an unsuccessful attempt seven years earlier, established a cornet class at the Conservatoire. He and Cerclier, who taught the trumpet, both succeeded Dauverné, thus originating a separation of the trumpet class into sections for cornet and for trumpet, a practice that has continued. From 1873 on, he conducted annually in St Petersburg, the reason for which he resigned his Conservatoire post in 1874. When the position became vacant again in 1880 at the death of Maury, he forsook his international career to return to the Conservatoire, devoting the rest of his life to teaching.

Arban was the founder of the modern school of trumpet playing. He was the first complete technician on the cornet; his setting of *The Carnival of Venice*, with variations, was the cornettist's solo piece *par excellence* during his and the next two or three generations. His *Grande méthode complète pour cornet à pistons et de saxhorn* (Paris, 1864) is still the standard instruction work, though its success is due more to its thorough, systematic approach than to its musical inspiration.

BIBLIOGRAPHY

J.-P. Mathez: *Joseph Jean-Baptiste Laurent Arban (1825–1889)* (Moudon, 1977)

EDWARD H. TARR

Arbeau, Thoinot [Tabourot, Jehan] (*b* Dijon, 17 March 1520; *d* Langres, 23 July 1595). French cleric and author. The pen name Thoinot Arbeau is an anagram of his real name. He studied at Dijon and Poitiers and possibly also at Paris, receiving a Licentiate of Laws. A churchman, in 1542 he became treasurer of the chapter at Langres; in 1547 he became canon of the cathedral, and in 1565 he was canon-treasurer at Bar-sur-Aube. Succeeding appointments include that of *official* (ecclesiastical judge), *chantre scoliarque* (inspector of the diocesan schools), director of cathedral restoration after its damage by lightning in 1562, and finally vicar-general of his diocese. His most famous work is a dance manual, the only one published in France in the second half of the 16th century: *Orchésographie, et traicte en forme de dialogue, par lequel toutes personnes peuvent facilement apprendre & practiquer l'honneste exercice des dances* (Langres, 1588, 2/1589). It was reprinted with a new title-page as *Metode et teorie en forme de discours et tablature pour apprendre a dancer, battre le tambour en toute sorte & diversité de batteries, jouër du fifre & arigot, tirer des armes & escrimer, avec autres honnestes exercices fort convenable à la jeunesse* (Langres, 1596). In addition he is known to have published two other works: *Kalendrier des bergers* (Langres, 1582) and the more important *Compot et manuel kalendrier* (Paris, 1588).

Arbeau's positive attitude toward dancing, both for health and in the pleasurable search for a mate, references in the text to his own youthful skill in dancing, and his neo-Platonic view that earthly dance is harmonious with the dance of the universe, place him in the tradition of those robust Renaissance ecclesiastics so vividly portrayed by Rabelais. The significance of his work is manifold. His text, in the form of a dialogue, explains most of the basic social dance types of the period with the aid of an explicit dance tablature apparently devised by him. This correlates dance steps with music more precisely than any other source of the time, and is invaluable in modern reconstructions of the dances; it also provides important clues to the performance of that huge body of dance music – and dance-inspired music – from the period. Illustrations in the text, though seemingly crude, assist quite specifically in the interpretation of the step descriptions. Furthermore, Arbeau made it clearer than do other sources (e.g. Fabritio Caroso and Cesare Negri) that the manly arts included dancing as well as fencing, by 'recounting both . . . martial and recreative dances'. He framed the book with the warlike arts; a lengthy introduction justifies the importance of dancing for men and describes marching techniques while the final portion of the book is devoted to six passages of *Les bouffons* (also known as *matassins* or *mattachino*), a popular, athletic sword dance for four mentioned only in passing elsewhere (for illustration of Arbeau's tablature *see* MATACHIN). Arbeau amplified his instructions with some delightful reflections on the social *mores* of the times ('spit and blow your nose sparingly'; '[after dancing the dancers] are permitted to kiss their mistresses . . . to ascertain if they are shapely or emit an unpleasant odour as of bad meat').

Dances described by Arbeau in varying detail include the basse danse and its accompanying *tordion* (both 'out of date some 50 years', he claimed), the pavan, 15 galliard variations, 25 different types of branles, the courante, allemande, volte, a *morisque*, a canary and a *Pavane d'Espagne*, as well as *Les bouffons*. Some descriptions are so cursory as merely to pique the curiosity (e.g. the *morisque* and *Pavane d'Espagne*); others are obviously incomplete (e.g. the *Branle de guerre*, which lacks any warlike gestures); still others are in duple metre (courante and canary) instead of the usual triple metre, thus presenting unsolved riddles to modern performers. In general, Arbeau's dances are simpler than those in the books by Caroso and Negri; he also omitted the complicated ballettos and the large figure dances in those sources, as well as the complex and highly specific variations they give for the pavan, passamezzo or canary; nor can Arbeau's galliard variations compare with the extremely balletic types in Negri's book. Yet Arbeau gave the only extant descriptions of the vigorous volte and *matassins*, and he included the largest number of branles. Despite their differences, however, the correlation of the steps in these sources, and other internal evidence, support the view that there was a basic international step vocabulary at that time, with regional stylistic differences or preferences for different dance types.

Musical references and clues to the performance of dance music are found throughout the book. In connection with marching techniques, Arbeau gave many valuable examples of tabor rhythms (his coat-of-arms carries three military tabors), and two long examples of fife music. He also listed preferred or characteristic instruments for dance music, hinted at improvisational techniques ('those who play improvise to please themselves'), and gave important tempo variations between dance categories ('the *tordion* is danced close to the ground to a light, lively beat, and the galliard is danced higher off the ground to a slower, stronger beat'), or for one dance ('[the galliard] must be slower for a man of large stature than for a small man, inasmuch as the tall one takes longer to execute his steps'). Many musical concordances for the 44 dance tunes have been found (see Moe and Heartz), and indeed Arbeau himself referred to well-known music publishers (Attaingnant, Nicolas du Chemin), thus authenticating additional musical sources for his dances, and negating the hypothesis sometimes put forward that his was a purely provincial style.

WRITINGS

Kalendrier des bergers (Langres, 1582)
Compot et manuel kalendrier (Paris, 1588, 2/1589)
Orchésographie (Langres, 1588, 2/1589); repr. as *Metode et teorie en forme de discours et tablature pour apprendre a dancer* (Langres, 1596/R1972); ed. J. Sutton (New York, 1967); Eng. trans. by C. W. Beaumont, 1925/R, by M. S. Evans, 1948, 2/1967)

BIBLIOGRAPHY

A. Arena: *Ad suos compagnones* (Avignon, ?1519)
F. Caroso: *Il ballarino* (Venice, 1581/R1967)
——: *Nobiltà di dame* (Venice, 1600, 2/1605/R1970; 3/1630 as *Raccolta di varii balli*)
C. Negri: *Le gratie d'amore* (Venice, 1602/R1969; 2/1604/R as *Nuove inventioni di balli*)
M. Praetorius: *Terpsichore* (Wolfenbüttel, 1612)
F. de Lauze: *Apologie de la danse* (n.p., 1623, Eng. trans., 1952)
M. Mersenne: *Harmonie universelle* (Paris, 1636–7/R1963)
D. Heartz: *Sources and Forms of the French Instrumental Dance in the Sixteenth Century* (diss., Harvard U., 1956)
L. Moe: *Dance Music in Printed Italian Lute Tablatures from 1507 to 1611* (diss., Harvard U., 1956)
D. Heartz, ed.: *Preludes, Chansons and Dances for Lute Published by Pierre Attaingnant, Paris (1529–30)* (Neuilly-sur-Seine, 1964)

JULIA SUTTON

Arbós, Enrique Fernández (*b* Madrid, 24 Dec 1863; *d* San Sebastián, 2 June 1939). Spanish violinist, conductor and composer. He studied the violin with Jesús Monasterio at the Madrid Conservatory, with Vieuxtemps at the Brussels Conservatory and with Joachim in Berlin. He travelled extensively as a soloist and, after leading the orchestra in Glasgow for its short winter season (under Manns), appeared in London early in 1891, playing works for violin and piano with Albéniz, and Bach's Double Concerto with Joachim. He served with distinction as a professor of the violin and viola at the RCM from 1894 to 1915.

In 1904 Arbós was appointed conductor of the Madrid SO; he became a leading influence in Spanish musical life until retiring from the conductorship on the outbreak of the Civil War in 1936. A *Fanfare* by Falla for brass and percussion, saluting Arbós's 70th birthday (1933), was later made part of Falla's set of orchestral *Homenajes*. Works of which Arbós conducted the first performance included Falla's *Noches en los jardines de España* in 1916. In the 1930s he made a number of gramophone records of Spanish music with his Madrid orchestra. He was guest conductor with the Boston SO and other American orchestras during 1928–31 and conducted also in London, Paris, Rome, Prague, Budapest and elsewhere. Active in modern music, he gave the first performance in Spain of Stravinsky's *The Rite of Spring* (1932) and was president of the Spanish section of the ISCM. It was apparently under his influence that the 1936 festival was held in Barcelona.

During the festival his orchestral arrangement of *Triana* from Albéniz's *Iberia* was first heard.

The arrangement of *Triana* and of eight other numbers from *Iberia* (including *Navarra*, of which Albéniz's unfinished piano version had been completed by Séverac) won considerable success in the concert hall. Arbós had studied composition under Gevaert while at the Brussels Conservatory, but his own original compositions – including three piano trios and the opera *El centro de la tierra*, produced in Madrid in 1895 – have not remained in the repertory.

WRITINGS

Del violín, de su estilo y de su relación con la evolución de la música (Madrid, 1914)

BIBLIOGRAPHY

V. Espinós Molto: *El maestro Arbós* (Madrid, 1942)

ARTHUR JACOBS

Arcadelt [Archadelt], Jacques (*b* ?1505; *d* Paris, 1568). ?Flemish composer.

1. Life. 2. Output. 3. Sacred music. 4. The chanson. 5. The madrigal.

1. LIFE. Although it is often suggested that he was Flemish by birth, this hypothesis rests only on the assumption that he was the Jacobus Flandrus who was appointed to the Cappella Giulia in 1539, an assumption that has been shown to be unfounded. Clercx-Lejeune (*RicordiE*) suggested that he was probably French and, in the early part of his life, a member of the circle around Philippe Verdelot. A close connection between Verdelot and Arcadelt is clearly suggested by the appearance of works by both composers in composite collections, manuscript and printed, around 1530, a period when Verdelot's ties to the Medici pope, Clement VII, and Florence were quite close. On this basis it is probable that Arcadelt spent some time in Florence after 1532, when the Medici regained control in the city. He may have accompanied Verdelot to Lyons in the period immediately preceding this to escape the Florentine troubles. With the assassination of Alessandro de' Medici by Lorenzino in 1537, Arcadelt probably settled in Venice, coming into close contact there with the Venetian musical circles that included Adrian Willaert, then *maestro di cappella* at St Mark's. The publication of his first four books of madrigals by Gardane in 1539 strongly implies his presence there at that date. Certainly it is true that his reputation and fame were clearly recognized by then, for he is called the 'most excellent and divine' Arcadelt in the titles of these prints.

From 1540 Arcadelt was a member of the Roman papal establishment, receiving prebends in 1545 at St Barthélemy and St Pierre, Liège, from Pope Paul III. In 1551 he left papal service to go to France and, in 1544, he entered the service of Charles of Lorraine, who was eventually appointed Archbishop of Rheims; Arcadelt may also have been associated with the royal chapel of France for a time, for he is described as a musician of the king in an Attaingnant volume of 1557. He belonged to Charles' chapel until at least 1562, dying in retirement in Paris in 1568. At his death, he was a canon at St Germain l'Auxerrois, Notre Dame de Paris and Rheims.

2. OUTPUT. The earliest compositions by Arcadelt are almost certainly the six motets appearing in *I-Rv* S.Borr.E.II.55–60, a manuscript completed in 1531 and containing a purely Florentine repertory. It is likely that the two madrigals *Deh dimmi amor* and *Io dico che fra*

noi, both with texts by Michelangelo, and *Vero inferno è il mio petto*, a madrigal to a text by Lorenzino de Medici probably written as a compliment to the ruling family of Florence, are products of this period. Only a handful of other compositions can be dated with any degree of security, for, although it is certain that they must have circulated in manuscript form before publication, the only surviving sources are prints that, in some cases, must surely come long after the date of composition. As becomes increasingly the case for all composers throughout the 16th century, the primary sources for Arcadelt's works, particularly the secular ones, are not manuscripts, but are volumes from the presses of the ever growing music printing industry.

Like many of his contemporaries Arcadelt began his career with religious music, in particular with the motet. In addition to the six motets of the Vallicelliana manuscript three more were brought out in 1532 by Jacques Moderne in Lyons, and six more were printed there and in Ferrara in 1538 and 1539. During Arcadelt's employment at the Vatican nine others were copied into Sistine Chapel manuscripts. It cannot be certain that all of these were composed in that period; some may have been written earlier. Two of the three masses later printed by Le Roy & Ballard in 1557 may also have been written during this period. The *Magnificat* and Lamentation sections, printed by Le Roy & Ballard in 1557, were probably commissioned by the printers, who may also have demanded the six psalm settings brought out in 1559. Although religious composition was not Arcadelt's major concern, at least in terms of total output, it was the motets and not the secular works (printed and reprinted only in France or in Italy) that spread into Germany. In common with other composers' sacred music, these were taken over by many German publishers: Schöffer of Strasbourg, Petreius of Nuremberg, Kriesstein and Ulhart of Augsburg and others. Some pieces were reprinted as many as eight times in Arcadelt's lifetime and numerous manuscript copies were made for German churches. Not all of Arcadelt's religious music has survived, for a Le Roy & Ballard book of 1556 or 1557 has disappeared, together with all but a bassus part of a collection of six psalm settings printed in 1559; two of these were later reprinted in 1577, so the loss is not total.

Arcadelt's primary interest was obviously in secular music, for 126 chansons and over 200 madrigals survive (because of conflicting ascriptions, an exact figure cannot be given). Unlike the madrigals, whose appearance is concentrated between 1539 and 1544, the chansons show a steady rise in production from after 1537, when his first efforts in the form appeared. For the early part of his output, Moderne in Lyons and Attaingnant in Paris were his printers, including one or two in various collections from that date until 1547, when the exceptional number of six appeared in Attaingnant's *Vingtcinqiesme livre* (*RISM* 1547[12]). When Du Chemin and Le Roy & Ballard began printing in Paris in the middle of the century, Arcadelt's works became a staple in the chanson repertory, with new ones continuing to appear as well as many reprints of earlier ones. The importance of Arcadelt's name as an enticement to the purchaser is seen in the prominent mention of his name on title-pages after 1561. Some idea of the popularity of his work may also be noted in the two editions of *L'excellence des chansons* prepared by Claude Goùdimel and printed by de Tournes in Lyons; there 45 of Arcadelt's chansons were reprinted, 44 of them given religious contrafacta to make them usable by the more spiritual-minded. The first edition, now lost, probably came out after 1565, the second in 1586. As with the religious works, some of Arcadelt's chanson output has disappeared; four of the six chansons in a lost book of 1570 cannot be recovered.

Arcadelt's earliest published madrigal appears in a collection printed by Scotto in Venice in 1537 (*RISM* 1537[11]), which is primarily concerned with works by Verdelot. A second collection, similarly emphasizing Verdelot, appeared the following year, also in Venice but printed by Scotto's rival Gardane; this volume (*RISM* 1538[20]) contained five pieces by Arcadelt. There is evidence that in that year Gardane printed the first edition of the *Primo libro dei madrigali*. A pirated edition was issued in Milan by an unknown printer shortly afterwards. Copies of the first four of the numbered books of madrigals survive from the end of 1539. All four were popular in varying degree. The *Primo libro* was by far the most successful, for in one form or another, with Arcadelt's name always prominent, it went through over 45 known edtions from 1539 until 1654; its contents changed from time to time, its title never. The *Secondo libro* exists in five editions (the last in 1560), the *Terzo libro* in four (the last in 1556) and the *Quarto libro* in three (the last in 1545). The numbered series closed with the publishing of the *Quinto libro* in 1544, with a second edition in 1550. These five volumes constitute the bulk of Arcadelt's madrigal production; all works included in them are for four voices. Only 63 other madrigals appear in other collections, most of them published by Gardane, Arcadelt's seemingly preferred printer. A sign of the composer's increasing neglect of the category is the failure to see new madrigals printed between 1545 and 1549. Only seven were added in 1549 and there was another break until 1555. As far as can be determined, his last madrigal was published in 1557, 11 years before his death. Once he had returned to France he would have had no reason to continue to compose madrigals.

3. SACRED MUSIC. It seems almost certain that Arcadelt studied with Josquin Desprez in his youth although when or where is not known. The early motets of the Vallicelliana manuscript show a technical mastery in the use of imitation and the exploitation of motivic development that reflect the ideals of the earlier master. There is already an air of easy skill in the handling of problems of contrapuntal flow, whether in a work involving cantus firmus techniques or in one in which equality of voices by interweaving motifs is desired. Although Arcadelt appears never to have lost sight of Josquin's methods, he was evidently aware that techniques might be borrowed from other categories on occasion if they were compatible with his more normal style. For example, in *Domine Deus omnipotens*, published in 1538, there are strong influences from the chanson: clearly defined cadential points, short rhythmic motifs that recall chanson styles, and somewhat lengthy homophonic sections that provide contrasts in texture against contrapuntal ones. The same mixture can also be seen in *Hodie Beata Virgo Maria*, published a year later, where the number of long melismas is curtailed and the opposition of homophony and polyphony is put even more in balance. The Lamentations of 1557 show in their variety the final stages of complete mastery and ease in the handling of technical procedures, from the melismas governing the intonations of the Hebrew letters to the almost syllabic settings of individual verses. In all these cases techniques originally foreign to the motet have been assimilated without destroying the nature and individuality of the motet. To some extent the three masses printed in the same year show a little of this but are slightly more archaic. Their nearness to Josquin is much more apparent. Two are parody masses, the *Missa 'Noe Noe'* (on a motet by Mouton) and the *Missa 'Ave regina caelorum'* (on a motet by de Silva); the third, the *Missa de beata virgine*, uses paraphrase technique. Josquin's influence is obvious in the last work, particularly in the 'Amen' of the Gloria, a rhythmically complicated passage in much the same vein as the parallel passage of Josquin's mass on the same material. A comparison of the two works will show the depth of Arcadelt's debt to his teachers.

4. THE CHANSON. As with his religious output, Arcadelt began within the tradition of his time. The earliest chansons are filled with conventions: the opening motto of four syllables set to longer values, the almost simultaneous cadencing at the ends of poetic lines and the predominance of syllabic setting. There are a handful that reflect Arcadelt's familiarity with Josquin's music in their use of canon as a foundation (e.g. *Tout au rebours*, mentioned by Rabelais), or in comparatively elaborate passages that lead to a motet-like texture; nevertheless, Arcadelt did not write the motet-chanson seen in, for example, the work of Gombert.

Strictly speaking, Arcadelt stands well outside the Parisian circle of chanson composers (Sermisy and others) for, although he relied in part on Clément Marot for some of his texts, the older Mellin de Saint-Gelais is more important. In addition, Arcadelt composed nothing in what could be called the grivois style of licentious patter songs; his texts are normally sentimental and, even when they turn to the implied obscene as in *Margot, labourez les vignes* and others, the style uses the larger note values of the sentimental chanson. Although not a major characteristic of Arcadelt's approach to the chanson, the use of homophonic sections in triple metre for contrast with others in simple polyphony in duple comes quite early. In this, many of his chansons resemble those of Pierre Sandrin, with whom the manner became almost an obsession. There are a few chansons scattered throughout Arcadelt's output that restrict themselves entirely to triple rhythm. The reliance on a homophonic style in the late chansons is almost complete, with simultaneous pronunciation by all voices a major element. There is more than a hint of the principles of *musique mesurée* at work in certain of these late compositions, where the rhythmic drive so characteristic of the chanson in the first half of the century is no longer evident. Nevertheless there are flashes of the old skill at times, as though Arcadelt could never forget whence he started. Fashions may have changed during his lifetime and Arcadelt was obviously aware of the current novelties, but his goal was their assimilation into his own framework, one built on the precepts and example of Josquin.

5. THE MADRIGAL. In view of Arcadelt's background, it is no surprise that many of his early madrigals in some way resemble the early chanson. But even in these Arcadelt recognized the difference between the two categories. For one thing, the cadences are even clearer

and the care for correct pronunciation more marked. Contrapuntal intricacy is not so evident and the independence of voices is achieved with considerably fewer means. Some of the devices used in both his religious music and the chanson appear, for example the long-held note at the end in one voice, most often the cantus, with a coda-like extension in the others. In all of these works, Arcadelt seems to have started from the assumption that the rhythmic requirements of the pronunciation of the text are paramount: its other elements of purely musical interest were used only when the demands of declamation were not disturbed. Declamation is not however the sole way of meeting the demands of the text, for simple and rather obvious madrigalisms are often a part of the vocal fabric: the word 'sospiri' is often divided by rests, while references to sadness or death are underlined by homophonic treatment in longer note values, often even suggesting the motto technique of the chanson. Madrigalisms do not govern the course of the piece as they do in works by later composers; there is little or no reliance on tone-painting as a way of deriving motifs. Even the *note nere* madrigals, by comparison with those of other composers, are of less flamboyant character; in some the reduction in note values is the only technical characteristic, for the results to the ear are much the same as with those in the normal notation. The five-voice setting of *Chiare, fresch'e dolce acque*, with its variety of scoring and rhythmic treatment and various degrees of polyphony, is an early example of the later madrigal cycles which sought to expand the possibilities inherent in a single movement. It has long been obvious that Arcadelt, with Verdelot and Festa, is a major figure in the early history of the madrigal, if only in terms of madrigals composed and their popularity. Some of the works, such as *Il dolce e bianco cigno*, appear to have never lost their popularity throughout the period. Certainly this position has been gained by Arcadelt's ability to balance all the elements within the form, and to respect the needs of both words and music without completely subordinating the nature of the one to that of the other. The text may be the master, but its accompanying music is not thereby made a slave.

What is most important in the consideration of Arcadelt's position is the understanding of his reactions to the requirements of each of the three main categories in which he composed. In religious music the stylistic characteristics to be followed had already been set for some years. In the chanson a set of musical postulates had been made but not explored to their limits. In the madrigal the style was only beginning to emerge, for the frottola had to be elevated into a true art form. Arcadelt had the merit of seeing that the techniques and requirements of each category could help the other, yet realized that the autonomous nature of each had to be maintained. All three categories received from his hands equally considered treatment, based on material from his own vast storehouse of knowledge and insight, but each received that which retained and reinforced their separateness, not what would have reduced their individuality.

WORKS

Edition: *J. Arcadelt: Opera omnia*, ed. A. Seay, CMM, xxxi/1–10 (1965–71) [S]

MASSES, ETC

Missa tres (Paris, 1557): Missa 'Ave regina caelorum', 5vv, S i (on de Silva's motet); Missa de beata virgine, 4vv, S i; Missa 'Noe Noe', 6vv, S i (on Mouton's motet)

Magnificat primi toni, 6vv, S x
Lamentationes Jeremiae (i; Zain. Recordata est; Nun. Prophetae tui, Jerusalem), 5vv, 1557[7], S x
Lamentationes Jeremiae (ii; Caph. Defecerunt; Lamed. O vos omnes; Jerusalem), 5vv, 1557[7], S x
Lamentationes Jeremiae (iii; Res. Sordes eius; Zain. Vidisti Domine; Convertere), 4vv, 1557[7], S x

OTHER SACRED
(all ed. in S x)

Benedixit Deus Noe, 4vv, 1532[11]; Candida virginitas, 6vv, *I-Rvat*; Congregati sunt, 5vv, 1538[2]; Corona aurea, 5vv, *Rvat*; Domine Deus omnipotens, 4vv, 1538[5]; Domine exaltetur manus, 4vv, 1539[13]; Domine non secundum peccata nostra, 3–5vv, *Rvat*; Dum complerentur dies Pentecostes, 5vv, 1538[2]; Estote fortes in bello, 6vv, *Rv*; Filiae Jerusalem, 4vv, 1532[11]; Gaudent in caelis, 5vv, 1538[2]; Gloriosae virginis Mariae, 5vv, *Rvat*

Haec dies, 4vv, 1532[11]; Hodie Beata Virgo Maria, 4vv, 1539[10]; Istorum est enim, 1564[2], 7vv; Memento salutis auctor, 4vv, *Rvat*; Michael archangele, 5vv, 1538[2]; O gloriosa domina, 4vv, 1538[5]; O pulcherrima mulierum, 5vv, 1539[5]; O sacrum convivium, 4vv, 1539[7]; Pater noster, 1545[2], 8vv; Recordare Domine, 5vv, 1540[7]; Regina caeli, 5vv, *Rvat*; Salve regina, 5vv, *Rvat*

Dont vient l'esjouissance, 4vv, 1555[16]; Il faut que de tous mes esprits, 4vv, 1555[16]

CHANSONS

Most of the chansons in the volumes devoted mainly to Arcadelt, listed immediately below, had already appeared in earlier anthologies. The earliest source is cited in the list of individual pieces. All are for 4vv unless otherwise stated.

Tiers livres de chansons, 4vv (Paris, 1567[4])
Quatrième livre de chansons, 4vv (Paris, 1567[5])
Cinquième livre de chansons, 4vv (Paris, 1567[6])
Sisième livre de chansons, 4–5vv (Paris, 1569[13])
Neuvième livre de chansons, 4–6vv (Paris, 1569[14])
Quatorsiesme livre de chansons, 4–6vv (Paris, 1561[6])

Amour a pouvoir sur les dieux, 3vv, 1554[27], S viii; Amour en moy (i), 1557[15], S viii; Amour en moy (ii), 1559[10], S viii; Amour est un grand maistre, 1557[13], S viii; Amoureux suis mais, 1556[15], S viii; Amour me sçauriez vous apprendre, 1554[27], S viii; Amour se plaint de ton forfait, 1559[12], S ix; Amour, je le fais aussi, 1565[5], S ix; Après le fait la repentence vient, 1569[13], S ix; Au temps heureux que ma jeune, 1539[15], S viii; Avec les plus beaux yeulx, 1552[4], S viii; Ayant fuy pour aymer, 1561[4], S ix

Celle que j'estime tant, 1561[6], S ix; Celluy qui seullement a vaincu, 1564[11], S ix; Ce n'est bien ny plaisir, 3vv, 1554[27], S viii; Comme l'argentine face, 1554[27], S viii; Comment amour me veux tu, 1559[12], S ix; Comment mes yeux avés vous, 1561[4], S ix; Contentez vous, heureuses violettes, 1549[22], S viii; Dames, plorez-vous point, 1552[4], S viii; De ceux qui tant de mon bien, 1569[13], S ix; Dedans voz yeux, 1561[2], S ix; De mes ennuys prenés, 1561[3], S ix; D mille ennuis que je porte, 1559[14], S ix; De son cueur et du mien, 1559[14], S ix; De tant de peine endurer, 1561[2], S ix

Dieu des amants qui mon feu, 1542[14], S viii; Dieu inconstant pourquoy, 3vv, 1554[27], S viii; D'un extreme regret mortellement attainte, 1564[11], S ix; De temps que j'estois amoureux, 1561[6], S ix; Elle a voulu serviteur, 1561[3], S ix; En ce mois delicieux, 1565[8], S ix; En lieu du bien, 1561[4], S ix; Entendez vous point vostre amy, 1547[12], S viii; Est-il advis qu'on doibve, 1538[13], S viii; Est-il douleur cruelle, 1559[10], S ix; Extreme amour est entre moy et elle, 1567[6], S ix; Franc berger pour soulager, 1556[15], S viii; Hélas amy que ta longuue demeure, 1556[15], S viii; Hélas mes yeux pourquoy, 1553[23], S viii

Il est vray que vostre oeil, 1543[7], S viii; Il me prend fantasie de vous dire, 1547[12], S viii; J'ay acquis un serviteur, 1561[6], S ix; J'ay entrepris d'une dame de France, 1554[27], S viii; J'ay tant bon credit qu'on voudra, 3vv, 1557[13], S viii; Je me repute bien heureux, 1552[4], S viii; J'en ayme deux, 1561[2], S ix; Je ne me confesseray point, 3vv, 1553[22], S viii; Je ne me puis dissimule, 3vv, 1559[12], S ix; Je ne sçay que c'est qu'il me fault, 3vv, 1553[22], S viii; Je ne suis pas si sot berger, 1551[9], S viii; Je ne suis pas si sot berger, 5vv, 1569[13], S ix; Je ne veux plus à mon mal, 3vv, 1553[22], S viii; Je suis attaint je le confesse, 1561[6], S ix; Je t'ay donné tout pouvoir, 1559[10], S ix

La Diane que je serts ne court plus, 1560[a], S ix; L'affection si longtemps prisonnière, 1559[10], S ix; Laissés la verde couleur, 1561[2], S ix; La pastorella mia, 3vv, 1554, S viii; Las je sçay bien que je fais, 1542[14], S viii; Las pourquoy n'est il permis, 3vv, 1559[12], S ix; Le bien que j'ay, 1561[3], S ix; Le coeur qui n'est point amoureux, 1564[11], S ix; Le fainct serviteur eshonté, 1556[15], S viii; Les yeux qui me sceurent prendre, 1554[26], S viii; Le temps coulle et passe, 1564[11], S ix; Le triste cueur, que avec vous, 1538[16], S viii; L'hiver sera et l'été variable, 1553[23], S viii; Lors tout ravy pour ce que je pensay, 1547[12], S viii

Mais de quoy sert le désirer, 1559[10], S ix; Margot labourez les vignes, 1554[27], S viii; Me montre amour ou douceur, 1559[10], S ix; Mon amytié tousjours augmente, 1550[5], S viii; Mon coeur en moy plus, 3vv, 1554[27], S viii; Mon plaint soit entendu, 3vv, 1554[27], S viii; Non, je ne veux j'en jure, 1561[6], S viii; Nostre amytié est seulement, 1561[2], S ix; Nous boirons du vin clairet, 1556[16], S viii; Nous voyons que les hommes, 3vv, 1554[27], S viii; O le grand bien, 1559[15], S ix; Où se peult myeulx assoyr mon esperance, 1549[21], S viii; Pour bien aymer je reçois, 1561[2], S ix; Pour heur en amour demander, 1556[15], S viii; Puisque tu sens l'object de l'amoureuse, 1549[20], S viii; Puisque vivre en servitude, 1559[14], S ix (also attrib. Sandrin)

Quand je compasse la hauteur, 1557[15], S viii; Quand je me trouve (i), 1549[22], S viii; Quand je me trouve (ii), 1554[27], S viii; Quand je me trouve, 5vv, 1572[2], S ix; Quand je vous ayme ardentement, 1547[12], S viii; Quand viendra la clarté, 3vv, 1553[22], S viii; Que te sert amy d'estre ainsi, 3vv, 1573[15], S ix; Qui en terre desire voir le ciel, 1564[11], S ix; Qui n'a senti qu'une flamme, 1564[11], S ix; Qui pourra dire la douleur, 3vv, 1554[27], S viii; Qui veut du ciel et de nature, 1569[13], S ix; Robin par bois et campagnes, 1561[6], S ix; Rossignolet du bois qui chante, 1565[5], S ix

Sa grand beauté, 1561[6], S ix; Si ce n'est amour, qu'est-ce, 3vv, 1554[27], S viii; Si faux danger sçavoit, 1561[2], S ix; Si j'ay deux serviteurs, 1557[15], S viii; Si la beauté de ma dame, 5vv, 1547[12], S viii; Si le bien qui au plus grand bien, 1561[6], S ix; Si mon cueur a fait offence, 1561[6], S ix; Si sa vertu et grace à l'aymer, 1547[12], S viii; Si vous regardez ma dame, 1561[6], S ix; Si vous voulez estre aymée, 1561[4], S ix; S'on pouvoit acquerir ta grace, 1557[15], S viii; Souspirs ardens, parcelles de mon âme, 1557[15], S viii; Souvent amour ne sçay pourquoy, 1554[27], S viii

Tant que mon oeil, 1561[4], S ix; Ta privauté d'amour, 1561[4], S ix; Tousjours vous me semblates belle, 1569[13], S ix; Tout au rebours de mon affaire, 5vv, 1548[3], S viii; Tout le desir et le plaisir, 1557[15], S viii; Vielle plus vielle, 3vv, 1573[15], S ix; Vive sera et tousjours pardurable, 1553[23], S viii; Vostre doulx entretien, 1548[3], S viii; Voulant amour sans parler, 1537[4], S viii; Vous n'aurez plus mes yeux, 1553[23], S viii; Vous ne pouvez au moins, 1561[6], S ix; Vous perdez temps de me dire, 1538[17], S viii

MADRIGALS
(all for 4vv unless otherwise stated)

Il primo libro di madrigali, 4vv (Venice, 1539[22]) [S ii]
Il secundo libro di madrigali, 4vv (n.p., 1539) [S iii]
Terzo libro de i madrigali novissimi, 4vv (Venice, 1539[23]) [S iv]
Il quarto libro di madrigali, 4vv (Venic, 1539[24]) [S v]
Primo libro di madrigali, 3vv (Venice, 1542[18])
Il quinto libro di madrigali, 4vv (Venice, 1544[16]) [S vi]

Other madrigals in 1537[?], 1537[11], 1538[20], 1540[18], 1540[20], 1541[15], 1541[16], 1542[16], 1542[17], 1543[18], 1544[17], 1544[22], 1549[30], 1549[31], 1554[28], 1555[25], 1555[31], 1559[19]

Ahime, dov'è 'l bel viso, S ii; Ahi, se la donna mia, S ii; Alma mia luce pura, S iii; Alma perchè si trist', S ii; Altri che voi so ben, 5vv, 1538[20], S vii; Amanti, amanti, tutt'il bel, S iv; Amanti, o liet'amanti, 1540[19], S vii; Amor, a talla gioia, S vi; Amorosetto fiore, S vi; Amorosetto fiore, 6vv, 1544[22], S vii; Amorosi pensier che di dolore, S v; Amor quanto più lieto, S iv; Amor s'al primo sguardo, S iv; Amor tu sai pur far, S ii

Ancidetemi pur, grievi martiri, S ii; Angela assai via più, S iv; A pie d'un chiaro fonte, S vi; Apri 'l mio dolce carcer le porte, S v; Ardea tutt'a voi presso, 1540[20], S vii; Ardenti miei desiri, S v; Bella Fioretta, io vorrei pur lodar, S ii; Benedett'i martiri, S ii; Benedetto si'al dì che gli occhi miei, S iv; Bianch'e vermiglia rosa, S vi; Bramo morir per non patir, S iv; Carissima Isabella, S iii; Che cosa al monde far potea, S iv; Che poss'io più se'l cielo, 5vv, 1540[18], S vii; Che foc'al mio foco, S ii; Chiare, fresch'e dolce acque, 5vv, 1555[25], S vii; Chi potrà dir quanta dolcezza, S ii; Chi può fiso mirar, S iv

Col pensier mai non maculai, S v; Come, donna, poss'io, 3vv, 1542[18], S vii; Comme più amar potrei, 1549[31], S vii; Come potrò fidarmi di te giamai, S v; Come purpureo fior vinto dal cielo, 1549[30], S vii; Com'esser può ch'io viva, S iii; Com'esser puot'amore, 6vv, 1541[16], S vii; Con lachrim'e sospir, 1540[20], S vii; Con lei fuss'io, 1542[17], S vii; Cosi mi guid'amore, 1542[17], S vii; Crudel'acerb'inesorabil morte, 5vv, 1538[20], S vii

Da bei rami scendea, 1542[17], S vii; Dai dolci campi Elisi, S iv; Dal bel suave raggio, S v; Da si felice sorte, S iii; Deh come pur al fin lassa, S ii; Deh come trista dei, S vi; Deh dimm'amor se l'alma, S iv; Deh fuggite, o mortali, S iii; Deh fuss'il ver che quei bei santi rai, S v; Deh perchè non è in voi tanta pietade, 6vv, 1541[16], S vii; Deh perchè si ribella, S v; Deh quanto fu pietoso degli amanti, S iv; Deh sarà mai, spiriti miei, S iii; Deh se lo sdegn'altiero, S ii; Del più leggiadro viso, S iii; Desio perchè mi meni?, S iii

Dolcemente s'adirà, S v; Dolce nemica mia, S v; Dolci parole morte, S iii; Dolci rime leggiadre, S vi; Donna beata e bella, S iv; Donna fra più bei volti, S v; Donna grav'è le doglia, S v; Donna, i vostri belli occhi, S v; Donna per amarvi io più che me stesso, 5vv, 1540[18], S vii; Donna quando pietosa, S iii; Donna se'l mio servire, S iv; Donna, s'ogni beltade, S v; Doppoi, doppoi ch'io viddi, 1549[30], S vii; Dormendo un giorno a Baia, 3vv, 1542[18], S vii; Dov'ito son, 1540[19], S vii; Dunque credete ch'io, S ii

Ecco che pur doppo si lung'affanni, S iv; Ecco d'oro l'età pregiata, S vi; È morta la speranza, S iv; Fammi pur guerr'amor, S ii; Fatto son esca della donna mia, S vi; Felice me se di i bei lumi, S ii; Felici alme contrade, 1554[28], S vii; Felici amanti, voi che d'amor lieti, 1541[15], S vii; Fiamma gentil, entr'a cui chiari lampi, S iv; Folle è chi crede la prudenz', S iv; Fra più bei fiori, S ii; Fu tempo già, 1542[17], S vii; Fu pur fero destino acerbe e rio, 1549[30], S vii

Già desiai ch'ai bei vostr'occhi, 1554[28], S vii; Giovenetta regal pur innocente, S iv; Gite rime dolenti, 5vv, 1542[16], S vii; Gite sospir dolenti, 1541[15], S vii; Giurando l' dissi amore, S v; Gli prieghi miei tutti, S v; Gravi pene in amor, 3vv, 1542[18], S vii; Honorata mia donna, S vi; Hor che 'l ciel e la terra, S iv; Hor che pui far potete, S iii; Hor tregu'avranno i miei caldi sospiri, S vi; Hor ved'amor, che giovenetta donna (i), S v; Hor ved'amor, che giovenetta donna (ii), 1540[19], S vii; Hor vedete madonna, S iii

I coralli e le perle, 1543[18], S vii; Il bianco e dolce cigno, S ii; Il capo d'Hydra, 1542[17], S vii; Il ciel che rado virtù tanta mostra, S ii; Il vagh'e dolce sguardo, S ii; Iniustissim'amore che val l'unico servir (i), S v; Iniustissim'amore che val l'unico servir (ii), S v; Iniustissim'Amor, perchè si raro, 3vv, 1537[?], S vii; In me sol regna fede, S vi; In un boschetto adorno, S ii; In un boschetto adorno, S v

Io de di viver sciolto, 5vv, 1540[18], S vii; Io dico che fra noi, potenti dei, S ii; Io ho nel cor un gielo, S ii; Io mi pensai che spento fusse'l foco, S ii; Io mi rivolgo indietro, S iii; Io nol dissi giamai, S v; Io non ardisco di levar più gli occhi, 1541[15], S vii; Io no vo già per voi, S iii; Io potrei forsi dire, S iv; Io son tal volta donna per morire, S iv; Io vo piangendo, 1554[28], S vii; Io vorrei pur fuggir crudel'amore, S ii; Ite, tristi sospiri, S iii; I vaghi fiori e l'amorose fronde, 1549[30], S vii

L'aer gravat'e l'importuna nebbia, 1555[31], S vii; L'alma mia donn'e bella, 1554[28], S vii; Languir non mi fa amore, S iv; Lasciar il velo o per sol'o perombra, S ii; Lasso che giova poi, S v; Lasso che pur hormai, S iv; Lasso quand'io gli occhi alzo, S iv; Lieta e serena in vista, S iv; Lodar voi donn'ingrate, S ii; Luce creata in terra per dar luce, S iv

Madonna al volto mio pallido e smorto, S iv; Madonna mia gentile, se tropp'ardito fui, S ii; Madonna, oimè, ch'io ardo, S v; Madonna, oimè, ch'io ardo, 1540[19], S vii; Madonna, oimè, per qual cagion m'havete, S ii; Madonna per oltraggi o per martire, S v; Madonna, s'io credessi, S iv; Madonna, s'io v'offendo, S ii; Mentre gli ardenti rai, 1540[19], S vii

Ne' dolent'occhi e nell'aspett'appare, 1541[15], S vii; Non ch'io non voglio mai altro pensiero, S ii; Non mai sempre fortuna, 5vv, 1540[18], S vii; Non più chiance madonna, S ii; Non prima l'Aurora, S iii; Non sia chi pensa'al mio cocent'ardore, S iv; Non v'accorgete amanti che di costei, S ii; Nova donna m'apparve di beltà tale, S iv; Novo piacer che nelli uman'ingegni, 1542[17], S vii; Occhi miei lassi, mentre ch'io vi giro, S ii; O felic'occhi miei, S ii; O s'io potessi donna dir quel che nel mirar, S ii

Parole estreme, anzi ultimi sospiri, S vi; Perch'al viso d'amor portar'insegna, 5vv, 1538[20], S vii; Perchè la vita è breve, 1559[19], S vii; Perchè non date voi, donna crudele, S ii; Per folti boschi e per alpestre valle, 1543[18], S vii; Per non saperti ringraziar amore, S iv; Pietose rime, S vi; Più non sento 'l mio duol, S iii; Poi che 'l fiero destin, S iv; Poi ch'ogni spem'ho persa, 1541[15], S vii; Posando le mie membra in pover letto, S iv; Poss'io miror di mala morte, S ii; Pungente dardo che 'l mio cor consumi, S ii; Puro ciel, Phillid', è qualla tua fronte, S iii

Quai pomi mai, qual'oro, S ii; Qual Clitia sempre al maggior lum'intenta, S ii; Qual Clitia sempre al maggior lum'intenta, S iv; Qual'hor m'assal'Amore, 5vv, 1538[20], S vii; Qual'ingegn'o parole, S vi; Qual mai più vagh'e bella, 5vv, 1555[31], S vii; Qual paura ho quando mi torn'a mente, S iv; Qual senza mot'senza razz'e'l sole, S v; Quand'io pens'al martire, S iv; Quando col dolce suono, S ii; Quando i vostri belli occhi, S v; Quando talhor al mio unico sole, S iv; Quando tal volta fra perle e viole, S iii; Quanta beltà, quanta grazia e splendore, S ii; Quant'è madonna mia, S ii; Quanto dolce è 'l conforto, S iii; Quanto più di lasciar, S v; Quanti travaglie pene, S ii; Quel si grave dolor, 1542[17], S vii; Quest'è la fede amanti, S v

Ragion'è ben ch'alcuna volt'io canti, S ii; S'advien che la beltade, S vi; S'altrui d'amor sospira, S iv; S'amante fu fiamai di sperar privo, 1544[22], S vii; Sapete amanti perchè amore è cieco, S ii; Se contra vostra voglia, S iv; Se gli occhi non temprat'ov'entr'io ardo, S ii; Se i sguardi di costei, S iv; Se i vostri bei sembianti, S iv; Se 'l chiar'almo splendore, 5vv, 1542[16], S vii; Se la dura durezza in la mia donna, S ii; Se la durezza in voi fusse men dura, S iv; Se 'l foco in cui sempr'ardo,

S v; Se 'l foco in cui sempr'ardo, 5vv, 1538[20], S vii; Se 'l mio bel sol è spento, S iv; Se 'l pensier amoroso, S v; Se 'l superchio splendore, S iii; Se 'l tuo partir mi spiacque, S ii; Se 'l volto donna, S iii

Se nel mirarvi con dolce contento, 1541[15], S vii; Se non fosse nel volto di costei, S iv; Se per amar vostra beltà infinita, S iii; Se per colpa del vostro fiero sdegno, S ii; S'era forsi represo il pensier mio, S v; Se tanta grazia amor mi concedesse, S v; Se tolto m'è 'l veder, S v; Se tutto 'l bel in questa, S iv; Se vi piace signora, S ii; Si come dit'ogn'-hor bella vi paio, S iv; Si come d'ogni donna sei più bella, S iv; Si com'el sol da luce, S iii; Si grand è la pietà, S v; Si lieto alcun giamai, S iv; S'infinita bellezza, 5vv, 1544[17], S vii

S'io non lodo madonna il vostro volto, S v; S'io pensasse che morte, S iii; S'io vi potessi dire, 3vv, 1542[18], S vii; Solo e pensoso, 1540[19], S vii; Sostenette quei di fugaci e rei, S vi; Standomi un giorno solo alla fenestra, 1543[18], S vii; Tante son le mie pene, S vi; Tengan dunque ver me, S v; Tra freddi monti, 1549[31], S vii; Tronchi la Parca ogn'hora ch'io non amo, S v; Tutt'il di piango e poi la notte, S v

Un dì lieto giamai, 1540[19], S vii; Vaghi pensier che cosi passo, S iv; Ver'inferno è 'l mio petto, S ii; Viddi fra l'erbe verde, S v; Vivace amor, 1541[15], S vii; Viva nel pensiero vostro, S iii; Voi che prendete gioia, S iv; Voi la mia vita siete, S ii; Voi mi poneste in foco, 3vv, 1537[7], S vii; Voi non m'amat'ed io pur troppo v'amo, S iii; Voi sapete ch'io v'amo anzi, S ii; Voi ve n'andat'al cielo, S ii; Vostra fui e sarò, S ii; Vostra merce, madonna, 1542[17], S vii

OTHER SECULAR

At tredpida et coeptis, 4vv, 1556[15], S viii; Integer vitae scelerisque, 3vv, 1559[8], S ix; Montium custos nemorumque, 3vv, 1559[8], S ix; Poscimur, si quid vacui, 3vv, 1559[8], S ix; Vitam que faciunt beatiorem, 4vv, 1556[15], S viii

BIBLIOGRAPHY

RicordiE
T. Kroyer: *Die Anfänge der Chromatik im italienischen Madrigal des XVI. Jahrhunderts* (Leipzig, 1902)
W. Klefisch: *Arcadelt als Madrigalist* (Cologne, 1938)
E. Helm: *The Beginnings of the Italian Madrigal and the Works of Arcadelt* (diss., Harvard U., 1939)
——: *The Chansons of Arcadelt*, i (Northampton, Mass., 1942)
A. Einstein: *The Italian Madrigal* (Princeton, 1949/*R*1971)
E. E. Lowinsky: 'A Newly-discovered Sixteenth-century Motet Manuscript at the Biblioteca Vallicelliana in Rome', *JAMS*, iii (1950), 173–232
H.-W. Frey: 'Michelagniolo und die Komponisten seiner Madrigale', *AcM*, xxiv (1952), 147–97
F. Lesure: 'Arcadelt est mort en 1568', *RdM*, xlvii (1961), 195
J. Haar: 'The *Note Nere* Madrigal', *JAMS*, xviii (1965), 22
A. Seay: 'Arcadelt and Michelangelo', *RN*, xviii (1965), 299
R. van Haarlem: 'The *Missa de beata Virgine* by Josquin used as a model for the Mass of the Same name by Arcadelt', *TVNM*, xxv/2 (1975), 33

ALBERT SEAY

Arcangelo del Leuto [Arcangelo del Liuto]. *See* LORI, ARCANGELO.

Arc-en-terre (Fr.). GROUND HARP.

Arched viall. *See* SOSTENENTE PIANO, §1.

Archer, Frederick (*b* Oxford, 16 June 1838; *d* Pittsburgh, Penn., 22 Oct 1901). Anglo-American organist, conductor and composer. As a boy he was a chorister at All Saints', Margaret Street, London. He became organist of Merton College, Oxford, and in 1873 was appointed to Alexandra Palace in London. On the resignation of Weist-Hill he became conductor of Alexandra Palace, a post he held until 1880. He was also conductor (1878–80) of the Glasgow Select Choir and director of a provincial opera company.

In 1881 he went to the USA and became organist at the Rev. Henry Ward Beecher's church in Brooklyn, and later of the Church of the Incarnation, New York. He founded and edited the *Keynote* in 1883. In 1887 he became conductor of the Boston Oratorio Society, and he conducted the Pittsburgh Orchestra from 1895 to 1898. His connection with Pittsburgh began with the opening of the Carnegie Library and Music Hall on 7 November 1895, when he gave the first of his free organ recitals. These recitals on Saturday evenings and Sunday afternoons were continued until his death. He was also organist of the Church of the Ascension and music examiner of the University of Toronto.

Archer composed many works for the organ, piano pieces, songs, etc, as well as a cantata, *King Witlaf's Drinking-Horn*; he also wrote two books, *The Organ*, a theoretical and practical treatise, and *The College Organist*.

ALEXIS CHITTY/R

Archer, Violet (Balestreri) (*b* Montreal, 24 April 1913). Canadian composer, pianist and teacher. She studied composition with Douglas Clarke and Claude Champagne at the McGill Conservatorium (1932–6, BMus 1936), with Bartók in New York (1942) and with Hindemith at Yale University (MMus 1949). Her awards have included four scholarships at McGill, the Woods–Chandler composition prize at Yale (1949) and an honorary doctorate from McGill (1971). She has taught at McGill (1944–7), at North Texas State College, where she was also composer-in-residence (1950–53), at the University of Oklahoma (1953–61) and at the University of Alberta (from 1962), where she was appointed professor and chairman of the theory and composition department.

Archer's compositional activities began in 1938; like other Canadian composers at that time she suffered from lack of exposure, isolation and a certain amount of selfconsciousness. Her music is informed by some qualities which have become equated with the spacious Canadian country and its often rugged landscape. These are the use of dark sonorities (*Fantasy on a Ground*, 1946) and long, winding, somewhat austere lines set over agitated rhythms (Violin Concerto, 1959), characteristics associated with some of her compatriots such as Weinzweig and Somers. Archer's musical imagination has also been influenced to a great extent by Hindemith's, especially in its *Gebrauchsmusik* orientation. This would account for the anthems, organ voluntaries, piano and choral pieces which make up a considerable part of her output. She also uses Hindemith's system of progressive harmonic weights (e.g. *Fanfare and Passacaglia*, 1948–9).

Bartók, too, made a strong impression on her. It was perhaps his keen interest in folk music as a powerful source of creative material which instilled in her a preoccupation with Canada's folksongs and folklore. Among the many works that show this are the *'Habitant' Sketches* (1947), *Life in a Prairie Shack* (1966) and *Three Folk Songs from Old Manitoba* (1966). Since 1964 Archer has used expressionist techniques (*Prelude-Incantation*), and this has led her music away from the earlier more dignified style to a dramatic one, culminating in her first opera, *Sganarelle* (1973).

WORKS

(selective list)

STAGE AND ORCHESTRAL

Comic opera: Sganarelle, 1973
Orch: Timp Conc., 1939; Scherzo sinfonico, 1940; Poem, 1940; Britannia, ov., 1941; Fantasy, cl, str, 1942; Sym., 1946; Fantasy on a Ground, 1946, rev. 1956; Cl Concertino, 1946, rev. 1956; Fanfare and Passacaglia, 1948–9; Pf Conc. no.1, 1956; Divertimento, 1957; Vn Conc., 1959; 3 Sketches, 1961; Prelude-Incantation, 1964; Sinfonietta, 1968; Sinfonia, 1969

VOCAL

Choral: Choruses from 'The Bacchae' (Euripides), female vv, orch, 1938; Leaves of Grass (Whitman), vv, orch, 1940; The Bell (Donne), cantata, vv, orch, 1949; Landscapes (Eliot), SATB, 1950; Songs of Prayer and Praise (Donne), SATB, 1953; 3 French-Canadian Folk Songs, SATB, 1953; Apocalypse (Apocalypse), S, SATB, brass, timp, 1958; Paul Bunyan (A. S. Bourinot), legend poem, SATB, pf, 1966; I will lift up mine eyes, SATB, org, 1967; O sing unto the Lord, SA, 2 tpt, 1968; 18 other works

Solo: Moon Songs (V. Lindsay), B, pf, 1942–4; 3 Biblical Songs, Mez, pf, 1950; Life in a Prairie Shack (trad.), 1v, pf, 1966; 3 Folk Songs from Old Manitoba, 1v, vc, pf, 1966; Cantata sacra (late medieval), 5 solo vv, small orch, 1967

CHAMBER AND INSTRUMENTAL

6 Pieces, pf, timp, 1939; 4 works, str qt, 1940, 1942, 1948–9, 1949; 3 trios, wind, 1944, 1949, 1949; Qt, wind, 1945; 2 Pieces, fl, 1947; Fantasy in the Form of a Passacaglia, brass, 1952; 2 str trios, 1953, 1961; 2 pf trios, 1954, 1956–7; 2 vn sonatas, 1954, 1956; 3 Duets, 2 vn, 1955; 2 vc sonatas, 1956, 1970; Divertimento no.2, ob, vn, vc, 1957; Divertimento, brass qnt, 1963; Sonata, hn, pf, 1965; 3 Studies, vn, 1970; Suite, 4 vn, 1971; Sonata, a sax, pf, 1972; Fantasy, vn, pf

Pf: Sonata no.1, 1945, rev. 1957; 6 Preludes, 1946–7; 'Habitant' Sketches, 2 pf, 1947; many educational pieces

Org: 8 Chorale Preludes, 1940–48, 2 rev. 1960; Sonatina, 1944; Prelude and Allegro, 1955; Chorale Improvisation, 1967

Carillon: Variations on an Original Theme, 1958

Principal publishers: Berandol, Peer, Waterloo

BIBLIOGRAPHY

K. MacMillan and J. Beckwith, eds.: *Contemporary Canadian Composers* (Toronto, 1975)

DORITH R. COOPER

Archet (Fr.). BOW.

Archicantor [archicantator] (Lat.). The choirmaster in charge of the regular singers of the early Roman *schola cantorum*; see PLAINCHANT, §II, 4.

Archicembalo. See ARCICEMBALO.

Archilei, Antonio ['Antonio di S Fiora'] (*b* ?Rome, ?*c*1550; *d* probably at Florence, Nov 1612). Italian singer, lutenist and ?composer, husband of VITTORIA ARCHILEI. He was in the service in Rome of the Cardinal di S Fiora, who died on 16 May 1581, after which he entered the service of Cardinal Ferdinando de' Medici. The latter became Grand Duke of Tuscany in 1587, and Archilei, with his wife, followed him to Florence, where he became a musician at court, with a salary of 18 scudi a month from 1 September 1588; his salary was reduced to 11 scudi on 30 November 1589. He participated in the spectacular *intermedi* marking Ferdinando's wedding in 1589: he is known to have played one of two chitarroni accompanying his wife's singing of the florid solo song 'Dalle più alte sfere' (in Walker, 2ff; original text 'Dalle celesti sfere') at the beginning of the first *intermedio*. In the publication of the music (1591) he is named as the composer of this song, but the official description of the event by Bastiano de' Rossi (Florence, 1589, p.19) attributes it to Cavalieri. Archilei was paid up to and including August 1612. The Ferdinando Archilei who saw through the press Pomponio Nenna's eighth book of five-part madrigals (1618) was one of his sons.

BIBLIOGRAPHY

V. Giustiniani: *Discorso sopra la musica de' suoi tempi* (MS, *I-La*, 1628); ed. C. MacClintock, MSD, ix (1962), 70
A. Solerti: *Musica, ballo e drammatica alla corte medicea dal 1600 al 1637* (Florence, 1905/R1968 and 1969), 31, 39, 58f
R. Gandolfi: 'La cappella musicale della corte di Toscana (1539–1859)', *RMI*, xvi (1909), 508
F. Boyer: 'Les Orsini et les musiciens d'Italie au début du xviie siècle', *Mélanges de philologie, d'histoire et de littérature offerts à Henri Hauvette* (Paris, 1934), 301
E. Zanetti: 'Archilei, Vittoria', *ES*

C. V. Palisca: 'Musical Asides in the Diplomatic Correspondence of Emilio de' Cavalieri', *MQ*, xliv (1963), 346
D. P. Walker, ed.: *Musique des intermèdes de 'La Pellegrina'* (Paris, 1963)
F. Hammond: 'Musicians at the Medici Court in the Mid-seventeenth Century', *AnMc*, no.14 (1974), 168

NIGEL FORTUNE

Archilei [née Concarini], **Vittoria** ['La Romanina'] (*b* Rome, 1550; *d* 1620s or later). Italian soprano, lutenist and dancer, wife of Antonio Archilei. Probably a pupil of her husband, whom she married on 20 September 1578, she was a protégé of Emilio de' Cavalieri in Rome and was with him in the service of Cardinal Ferdinando de' Medici before he became Grand Duke of Tuscany in 1587. She participated in the festivities for the wedding of Eleonora de' Medici and Vincenzo Gonzaga in 1584. When Cavalieri was made artistic superintendent at the Medici court in 1588, she went with her husband to Florence, where she became one of the most famous singers of her time. Like him, she apparently remained in the service of the Medici until her death.

She had a major part, as soprano soloist and lutenist, in the spectacular 'intermedii et concerti' for the comedy *La pellegrina* during the celebration in 1589 of the marriage of Ferdinando de' Medici and Christine of Lorraine. The opening piece in the first *intermedio* ('Dalle più alte sfere'), composed by her husband or Cavalieri, was a solo for her to the accompaniment of her own 'leuto grosso' and two other chitarroni; it was published in 1591 (along with the other music of the *intermedi*) with the treble part in both its original form and a highly elaborated one, much as she must have sung it, suggesting her extraordinary virtuosity in improvisatory passage-work and ornamentation. Her performance in Cavalieri's *Disperazione di Fileno* (winter of 1590–91) was said, by the editor of his *Rappresentazione di Anima e di Corpo*, to have moved the audience to tears. She was in close touch with modern tendencies in Florentine music and obviously sympathetic to them; both Giulio Caccini and Jacopo Peri cited her, by way of buttressing their respective claims to primacy in the new monodic style, as having performed their music. Caccini (preface to *L'Euridice*, 1600) wrote that she had, 'long ago', adopted the new manner of passage-work 'invented' by him. Peri (preface to *L'Euridice*, 1600/01) called her the 'Euterpe of our time' and said that she adorned his music not only with brilliant *passaggi* but with graces too subtle to write out. Another, perhaps more impartial, musician, Sigismondo d'India, lauded her (preface to *Le musiche . . . da cantar solo . . .*, 1609) as being 'above any other' as an excellent singer, spoke of her as 'most intelligent' and emphasized the sweetness and tenderness of her voice.

After about 1610 she is mentioned in Medici court chronicles mainly as a singer of sacred music, usually together with Caccini's daughters, on special court occasions in Florence and Pisa. In 1629 Marino published a poem on 'La morte di Vittoria cantatrice famosa', which must refer to her; on the other hand, Medici account books seem to record payments to a Vittoria Archilei (possibly a younger relation) up to and including August 1642.

BIBLIOGRAPHY

A. Ademollo: *I teatri di Roma nel secolo XVIIº: memorie sincrome* (Rome, 1888)
——: *La bell'Adriana ed altre virtuose del suo tempo alla corte di Mantova* (Città di Castello, 1888)
A. Solerti: *Gli albori del melodramma* (Milan, 1904/R1969)

——: *Musica, ballo e drammatica alla corte medicea dal 1600 al 1637* (Florence, 1905/*R*1969)

F. Boyer: 'Les Orsini et les musiciens d'Italie au début du xviie siècle', *Mélanges de philologie, d'histoire et de littérature offerts à Henri Hauvette* (Paris, 1934), 301

E. Zanetti: 'Archilei, Vittoria', *ES*

D. P. Walker, ed.: *Musique des intermèdes de 'La Pellegrina'* (Paris, 1963)

F. Hammond: 'Musicians at the Medici Court in the Mid-seventeenth Century', *AnMc*, no.14 (1974), 151

H. WILEY HITCHCOCK

Archilochus (*fl* ?650 BC). Iambic and elegiac poet, native of the Ionian island of Paros. 'I am the squire of lord Ares', he sang, 'and skilled in the lovely gift of the Muses' (Edmonds, frag.1). More artist than military man, he expressed both the external world and his responses to it with a fiercely individual immediacy.

His surviving poems contain no certain references to string instruments. The first word (*tēnella*) of his victory hymn, however, supposedly imitates the twang of a lyre string (Scholiast on Pindar, *Olympian* ix.1–4); and one heavily restored fragment (Edmonds, frag.114, xiv) may refer to lyre playing accompanying the dance. He did clearly mention the aulos as a feature of religious or convivial occasions (frags.76; 32); possibly, though not certainly, he associated it with the performance of elegiac verse (frag.123) – a likely combination in this early period of elegy. According to a late source (Pseudo-Plutarch, *De musica*, xxviii), Archilochus abolished the strict rule which had ordained only one note for each syllable of text, and also introduced the practice of allowing the text to be spoken as well as sung. While the use of recitative relates most naturally to iambic verse (which he developed with particular skill), elegy may have been involved as well. He not infrequently combined different metrical patterns; his use of iambs and trochees, moreover, shows several kinds of substitution. Possibly his metrical subtlety was paralleled by a characteristic imputed to Archilochus, the refined handling of varied and intermingled musical rhythms.

WRITINGS

In *Elegy and Iambus*, ed. and trans. J. M. Edmonds (London and Cambridge, Mass., 1931, 4/1968)

In *Anthologia lyrica graeca*, ed. E. Diehl (Leipzig, 1925, 3/1940/*R*)

Archiloque: fragments, ed. F. Lasserre and A. Bonnard (Paris, 1958)

BIBLIOGRAPHY

M. Treu, ed.: *Archilochos* (Munich, 1959)

F. Will: *Archilochos* (New York, 1969)

M. L. West, ed.: *Iambi et elegi graeci*, i (Oxford, 1971), 1–108

G. M. Kirkwood: *Early Greek Monody: the History of a Poetic Type* (London and Ithaca, 1974), 20–52

D. L. Page, ed.: *Supplementa lyricis graecis* (Oxford, 1974), 151ff

For further bibliography *see* GREECE, §I.

WARREN ANDERSON

Archiluth (Fr.). ARCHLUTE.

Archipoeta [Archpoet] (*b* ?Cologne, *c*1130; *d* shortly after 1165). Goliard poet. His real name is unknown. He was a clerk of knightly birth who by 1161 had come under the patronage of Reinald of Dassel, Archbishop of Cologne and chancellor to Frederick Barbarossa. In this capacity he travelled throughout Germany and to Austria and Italy, where he was desperately ill in 1165. He must have written many Latin poems, but only ten survive; their technique follows that of his older contemporary Hugh Primas, but they are less spiteful and more witty in tone. The *Confessio*, written at Pavia, is his greatest achievement and illustrates his best characteristics: a keen knowledge of biblical and classical authors,

ingenious rhythm and supreme rhyming skill, great wit and genial humour, cunning word-play and melodious cadence. No melodies are known for his poems. His poetic style greatly influenced the writers of Notre Dame conductus texts.

BIBLIOGRAPHY

B. Schmeidler: *Die Gedichte des Archipoeta* (Leipzig, 1911)

——: 'Zum Archipoeta', *Historische Vierteljahrschrift*, xiv (1911), 367

M. Mantius: *Die Gedichte des Archipoeta* (Munich, 1913, 2/1929)

J. J. Frantzen: 'Die Gedichte des Archipoeta', *Neophilologus*, v (1920), 170

J. H. Hanford: 'The Progenitors of Golias', *Speculum*, i (1926), 38

W. Stapel: *Des Archipoeta erhaltene Gedichte* (Hamburg, 1927)

M. Manitius: *Geschichte der lateinischen Literatur des Mittelalters*, iii (Munich, 1931), 978

F. Gennrich: 'Archipoeta', *MGG*

F. J. E. Raby: *A History of Secular Latin Poetry in the Middle Ages*, ii (Oxford, rev. 2/1957), 180

H. Krefield: *Die Gedichte des Archipoeta* (Heidelberg, 1958)

various authors: [miscellany on Archipoeta], *Mittellateinisches Jb*, iv (1967–8), 145

For further bibliography *see* EARLY LATIN SECULAR SONG.

GORDON A. ANDERSON

Archiquier (Fr.). CHEKKER.

Archives and music. Archival documents contain accurate and detailed information of a sort relevant to many aspects of musical scholarship: to biography, chronology, history of institutions and societies, the place and function of musicians in society, and performing practice (in the fullest sense of that phrase). They yield the kind of information that purely musical manuscripts and printed sources cannot provide.

The term 'archive' is here used as defined under §2 below. It is also widely used in a second sense, to denote what would more exactly be called a 'collection' or even 'library' – for example, the Deutsches Musikgeschichtliches Archiv in Kassel, which is a library of photographic materials relating to sources of German music. Many collections fall halfway between an archive in the strict sense, being based on the surviving papers of a historical person, and a collection, having been amplified by subsequent collectors. Such a case is the collection in the Library of Congress known as the 'Rachmaninoff Archives'. *See also* LIBRARIES; COLLECTIONS, PRIVATE and SOUND ARCHIVES.

1. Types of archive. 2. Preservation; location. 3. Archival research. 4. Application to music history. 5. Skills; aids.

1. TYPES OF ARCHIVE. Archives are the totality of documents originated or received by a person or an organization in the course of its administrative activity and the transaction of its affairs. They are kept as an organized body of records in an authorized repository and are maintained in their original chronological order. Both the source of the documents and their method of classification thus differ from those of an ordinary collection or group of manuscripts in a library, where the documents are normally classified for the convenience of the user.

Archive collections differ greatly according to their institution of origin. Public archives are produced by the many and various organs of government, including both national and local government, the legislature and the judiciary. They comprise archives of national scope, including the records of all central government departments, of parliament, and of the higher courts of law, as well as archives of local governmental and judicial activity, at provincial, county and municipal level. Private archives arise from the activity of private businesses and organizations, institutions both ecclesiastical and lay, and individuals. They include the archives of all religious institutions, especially those of parish, collegiate, monastic and cathedral churches; the records of notarial and business organizations of all kinds; and archives accumulated by individuals, especially by landowners in the creation and administration of extensive households and landed estates. In free societies the principle that public archives should be accessible to the public is generally accepted. Private archives remain the property of their owners, and special permission must be sought before they can be consulted.

2. PRESERVATION; LOCATION. Since the late 18th century it has become acknowledged that the state is responsible for the preservation of its documentary heritage, and throughout Europe public archives are readily accessible in record offices maintained by the state. In general a central repository is provided for central government archives, and in the larger countries there are also provincial repositories. Since this movement began, with the establishment of the French Archives Nationales in 1789 and Archives Départementales in 1796, efforts have been made in every country to centralize dispersed materials and create a unified administration for national and local archives.

In western Europe there exist the following national public archives: the Archives Nationales in Paris, the Staatsarchiv in Vienna, the Archives Générales du Royaume in Brussels, the Public Record Office in London, the Bundesarchiv for the Federal Republic of Germany at Koblenz, the Bundesarchiv for Switzerland in Berne, and the Archivo Histórico Nacional for Spain in Madrid. Then come the archives of the provinces in Austria, Belgium and the Netherlands; of the départements in France; of the cantons in Switzerland; and of the counties in Britain. Next come the district, parish and municipal archives in these countries. In Italy there is no single central record office, but a repository in each of the former sovereign states, as is the case in the German Federal Republic. An exception are the archives of the Vatican, which are extraordinarily rich in history for almost every country, and which have a distinct and unique organization.

In the USA, because of its federal constitution, there are two levels of governmental administration and legal process. The federal archives are held in Washington, DC, by the National Archives and Records Services, a unit of the General Services Administration, or (in the case of material primarily of regional interest) in regional branch archives; state and municipal archives are held locally.

Obviously each national archive collection reflects the history of its country of origin. Where the state has been relatively recently centralized, as in Italy, it is necessary to search the archives of all the provinces that made up the nation; but where centralization was early, as in England and France, the archives have been grouped together in the capital from an early date. In many countries, administration of both national and local archives has been vexed by changes in national boundaries, particularly in Germany where a regrouping of the archives was begun in 1815. A national Reichsarchiv was established in Potsdam in 1919, but the partition of Germany in 1945–9 resulted in its division into an archive for the Federal Republic in

Koblenz and another at Potsdam for the Democratic Republic. As a result of transfers of territory, there have been several exchanges of archive collections between nations; for example, in 1861 France gave Italy the Piedmont archives, and in return received from Italy those of Savoy.

However, archive centralization has not always happened. For instance, archival material relating to certain provinces of northern Italy remains in Austria; indeed, it was only by virtue of a special clause in the Treaty of Versailles (1919) that the volumes of 15th-century music known as the Trent Codices were transferred to Italy at the same time as the city of Trent was ceded by Austria. Further, many archives have been destroyed, such as those of the city of Paris in 1870, and of the state of Naples in 1943. The archives of the Irish Free State (modern Eire) were severely damaged by fire in 1922, those of the city of Florence by flood in 1966, and those of the town of Boston (Lincolnshire) by the negligence of the town clerk in 1876.

European countries show great differences in the way they maintain certain classes of archive. In France, for example, ecclesiastical archives, of special value for the history of liturgical music, have been kept in the public repositories since the Revolution and its attendant separation of church from state. In most other Western countries they remain at their institution of origin. Similarly, it is usual in France and Italy for notaries' archives to be kept in official vaults, whereas elsewhere they remain in their place of origin.

Records of birth, death and marriage are of great importance in biographical work. For many centuries such records were produced and retained by the church, but in some countries a system of civil registration was introduced. Such registration began in England, for example, in 1837, and since 1858 all wills (previously proved in the church courts) have been proved in civil probate courts. As a result, the scholar can consult one central repository (Somerset House, London) for such information since those dates. And where earlier records survive they can often be found in local archival repositories like county record offices. With the growth of demography in the 19th century, many countries have taken population censuses; the results, with a wealth of personal information, are often available for consultation, as are registers of electors.

Since respect for historical material is relatively recent, there are numerous exceptions in the distinction between libraries and archive repositories. Occasionally, for example, whole music manuscripts are found in archive collections, not to mention the many fragments discovered bound in as fly-leaves to non-musical volumes. A few examples may be cited: there is a music manuscript dating from the end of the 15th century in the archives of the city of Heilbronn; an entire collection of printed 18th-century music in the departmental archives of Agen; and censored or forbidden operas and songs in the national archives of France. Conversely, many libraries hold important archival material. A whole series of account books of the French royal household, originating in dispersed collections and important for music history, is in the manuscript department of the Bibliothèque Nationale, as well as in stray ecclesiastical archives (notably the chapter registers of Parisian churches) and among the considerable quantity of scattered pieces gathered by private collectors and genealogists. Archives of defunct organizations may turn up in a variety of places; in Britain, for instance, extensive archive collections of extinct landed families and of religious houses dissolved in the 16th century are in the Public Record Office and the manuscript department of the British Library.

3. ARCHIVAL RESEARCH. In western Europe general appreciation of the importance of preserving archival records, for purely practical legal and administrative purposes, is of long standing; their use by historians, however, is much more recent. It was during the 19th century that the study and writing of history ceased to be merely a branch of literature, and evolved into an exact science with techniques for seeking accurate information. By supplying a wholly untapped reserve of data that appeared to be completely free of bias and subjective distortion, archives began to be appreciated as an important source of historical information. Before long, historians of the arts discovered that archival research could do much to illuminate the history of architecture, of painting, of the theatre, and in due course also of music.

Even before the centralization of national archives was far advanced, national series began to be published containing editions of important chronicles (Monumenta Germaniae Historica for Germany, The Rolls Series for England); and from the mid-19th century on, several countries issued transcripts and calendars of archival documents together with lists, indexes and catalogues. Local and regional history societies began similar publications, as did private organizations and societies. There is now a massive literature, diffuse and highly complex yet immensely rich. (See also MUSICOLOGY, §2 (iv).)

4. APPLICATION TO MUSIC HISTORY. Archival research can be profitable in many ways to a musicologist. It can produce biographical material about a composer or performer; the date of composition of a particular piece; the history of a musical institution (chapel royal, church school, liturgical choir, orchestra, conservatory); the music history of a town, a concert society or a lyric theatre; insight into the practices of instrument making and music publishing. In fact, it can produce information relating to all the external aspects of music-making. In broader terms, it can give insight into the place of the musician in society in past ages, and into the place of music among the aesthetic values of the time. Further, archival sources can be of value in the reconstruction of authentic performing practice in music of the pre-Classical era. In the case of liturgical music for choir, it is from the archives of the churches maintaining the choirs that details of performing method can best be obtained. The most valuable sources are codes of statutes; accounts and hall books; registers and volumes of chapter acts; indentures of choirmasters, singers and organists; inventories of music books; and visitation records. From these it is possible to reconstruct certain features of authentic performance: for instance, the number of singers, the number of voices to a part, the deployment of solo voices and chorus, the availability and participation of instruments, and by inference even such matters as approximate pitch of performance. Similarly the archives of royal and aristocratic households frequently reveal the exact composition of bands of household musicians and minstrels, and list the instruments available to them.

European scholars first felt the need to use the contents of archives during the 19th century. Italy (Baini, Caffi, Bertolotti, Valdrighi, Radiciotti, Solerti), France (de la Fage, Campardon, Jullien), England (Grattan Flood, Lafontaine) and Germany (Haberl) were the first countries to show an example. These pioneers were often amateurs, spurred on by the growth of learned societies. Succeeding generations were more predominantly made up of professional musicologists (La Laurencie, Ecorcheville, Michel Brenet, Prunières etc) and organ specialists (Dufourcq and many others), of whom the latter were the most active. However, few were willing to publish coherent and complete editions of the texts, with the intention of providing a base for future research. Exceptions were the Note d'archivio by Casimiri, and the publication by the Archives Nationales of the 17th-century archives of the notaries of Paris, and more recently the 'documentary biographies' of Schubert, Handel and Mozart by Deutsch. There remains a vast amount of editing (of accounts, archives of churches, chapels and schools, diplomatic correspondence, theatre archives, and particularly notaries' archives), for which the musicologist will have to acquire the skills of the administrative historian.

5. SKILLS; AIDS. Archival research can add a new dimension to the study of certain aspects of musical history; but to be successful the searcher must have mastered a number of skills not normally related to serious musical study. It is essential to be acquainted with the rigorous standards of scholarship set by professional historians for the acquisition, collation, evaluation and interpretation of archival information. A sound knowledge of palaeography (the decipherment of handwriting), and of at least the principles of diplomatic (the study of the forms of documents), is no less essential. The techniques of full diplomatic transcription (making clear exactly what is in the original document and what has been supplied by the transcriber), of calendaring (producing a summary of the essential information-giving section of a document) and abstracting (taking and tabulating the vital facts from a document, particularly a will) are essential. For this the scholar needs to understand how, administratively, the document concerned was produced. He should consult existing guides and inventories, printed and handwritten, and bear in mind the wide range of categories of archival material that may be relevant to his inquiry. Thus he might have to consult royal household accounts for a musician's career in courtly circles, university archives for his years of study, judicial archives in the case of a lawsuit, notary's and civil records for his private and family life, diplomatic correspondence for his journeys abroad, parish archives for references to his participation in some local event, his marriage and his death, possibly police records, copyright records for publication dates etc. For modern times, private archives still in the possession of those who produced them are sources that must not be overlooked, and that usually have no inventory; for instance, the archives of music and record publishers, radio stations, music schools etc.

BIBLIOGRAPHY

GENERAL

C. Samaran: Introduction to *Guide international des archives* (Paris, 1934)

R. H. Bautier: 'Bibliographie sélective des guides d'archives', *Journal of Documentation*, ix (1953), 1–41

A. Brennecke: *Archivkunde: ein Beitrag zur Theorie und Geschichte des europäischen Archivwesens* (Leipzig, 1953)

R. H. Bautier: *Annuaire international des archives* (Paris, 1955)

J. Favier: *Les archives* (Paris, 1965)

F. Lesure: 'Archival Research: Necessity and Opportunity', *Perspectives in Musicology* (New York, 1972), 56

SPECIFIC GUIDES

H. de Curzon: *Etat sommaire des pièces et documents concernant le théâtre et la musique aux archives nationales* (Besançon, 1899)

R. Piattoli: *Guida storica e bibliografica degli archivi e delle biblioteche d'Italia* (Rome, 1932–40)

H. Courteault, ed.: *Etat des inventaires des archives nationales, départementales, communales et hospitalières au 1er janvier 1937*, Direction des Archives de France (Paris, 1938)

Gli archivi di stato italiani, Ministero dell'Interno, Ufficio degli Archivi di Stato (Bologna, 1944)

H. Jenkinson: *Public Record Office: Guide to the Public Records* (London, 1949)

D. P. M. Graswinckel: *De Rijkarchieven in Nederland* (The Hague, 1953)

I. Andersson: *Libraries and Archives in Sweden* (Stockholm, 1954)

L. Sanchez: *Bibliografía de archivos espanoles y de archivística* (Madrid, 1963)

Guide du lecteur, Direction des Archives de France (Paris, 1966)

Guide to the National Archives of the United States (Washington, DC, 1974)

J. M. Kinney: *Directory of State and Provincial Archives 1975* (Austin, 1975)

FRANÇOIS LESURE, ROGER BOWERS

Archlute (Fr. *archiluth*; Ger. *Erzlaute*; It. *liuto attiorbato, arcileuto, arciliuto*). A lute with two pegboxes, the second of which houses unstopped diapasons (bass strings) about one-and-a-half times the length of the stopped strings, which run over the fingerboard to the first pegbox. In appearance the archlute resembles the THEORBO and the CHITARRONE, but differs from them in that its body is smaller and that the first and second courses are at lute pitch rather than an octave lower. This was possible because the stopped string length was shorter. Furthermore, the archlute's stopped strings were normally double-strung, while those of the theorbo were frequently single-strung. The archlute was used for both solo music and continuo from about 1600 to 1730. In Italy it inherited the role of the Renaissance solo lute (from about 1610 'liuto' often refers to the archlute) and retained the G tuning abandoned for solo music by the rest of Europe in the 1630s. The instrument had 13 or 14 courses, six to eight of which ran over the fingerboard, and was normally double-strung throughout – except possibly the first course and the diapasons. Many instruments conforming to this description were made by Matteo Sellas of Venice in the 1630s (see fig.1a) with a stopped string length of about 55 to 64 cm (whereas a continuo theorbo of the period could have a stopped string length of about 90 cm and normally would be tuned in A with the top two courses lowered an octave).

Alessandro Piccinini (*Intavolatura di liuto*, 1623) said that he had invented the *arciliuto* (which others mistakenly called 'liuto attiorbato', he said) at Padua in

(a)   (b)

1. (a) Archlute (or liuto attiorbato) by Matteo Sellas, Venice, 1638, with 7 stopped and 7 unstopped double courses of 58·8 and 84·3 cm; (b) archlute (or liuto attiorbato), anonymous, undated, with 7 stopped (13-string) and 5 unstopped (8-string) courses of 54·7 and 84 cm; the neck which carries the stopped strings has probably been cut down by approximately a quarter of its length (both Conservatoire de Musique, Paris)

1594. He gave full instructions for its playing technique, and both he and, later, S. L. Weiss (1723) mentioned using the right-hand fingernails. Praetorius in 1619 gave the following tuning, in which the first six courses, the

2. Archlute (or arciliuto) by Martinus Harz, Rome, 1665, with 6 stopped double courses and 8 unstopped single courses of 67 and 143·7 cm (Collection of Musical Instruments, Edinburgh University)

diapasons, are single-strung while the stopped courses are double-strung in unison: *F′–G′–A′–B′–C–D–E–F–G–c–f–a–d′–g′*. He said that the lute of his day normally had a long neck like that of a theorbo; his illustration (1620) of a *Laute mit Abzuegem oder Testudo theorbata* shows the strings passing through or over the bridge to

the capping strip, an arrangement one might expect for strings of metal rather than gut. An instrument of this type, with the soundboard 'bent' at the bridge to withstand the extra tension of metal strings, can be seen in the Paris Conservatoire Museum (no.E528.C229; fig.1*b*).

Solo music in tablature for archlute was printed by Saracini (1614), Melli (1614, 1616 and 1620), Piccinini (1623 and 1639) and Gianoncelli (1650). In the first half of the 17th century the *liuto* (i.e. *arciliuto*) was also

3. Archlute player: painting (c1720) by an artist of the north Italian school (private collection)

named in about a dozen songbooks as an alternative to the chitarrone or *tiorba* for playing continuo from the bass clef.

In the second half of the century the *arciliuto* was increasingly specified to provide continuo in preference to the *tiorba* and as an alternative to the violone in violin sonatas and trio sonatas (e.g. Veracini and Corelli). Italian archlutes surviving from that time are larger than those of Sellas, although the tuning was the same. An instrument by M. Harz of Rome (1665; see fig.2) has six double-stopped strings measuring 67 cm and eight single diapasons of 143·7 cm. This stopped string length does not seem long enough for a theorbo in that there is no need to lower the top courses an octave. Joseph Sauveur (*Principes d'acoustique*, Paris, 1701, see pl.3) confirmed the distinction between *theorbe* and *archiluth* and said that the latter has 14 courses tuned in G with the top courses at lute pitch. Handel included a fully written-out part for *arciliuto* in the aria 'Come la ron-dinella' from his cantata *Clori, Tirsi e Fileno*. An anony-mous Italian manuscript of about 1720 (privately owned in London) contains a *Sinfonia a solo di arciliuto* and two *Concertini per cammera con arciliuto obligato, violini e basso*. The archlute part, alternating between solo sections and figured bass, is written in staff notation on one staff transposed up an octave (as is guitar music today; see fig.4). (One of the concertinos includes also a figured bass part for organ.) This manuscript illustrates

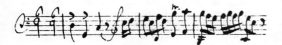

4. Archlute part, showing figured bass changing to solo line, from 'Concertini per cammera con arciliuto obligato, violini e basso' in an MS of c1720 (private collection)

the advantage of archlute over theorbo for continuo, in that solo sections are possible if the top strings are at lute pitch. The disadvantage would be the smaller volume of sound produced by the shorter stopped strings, but this would have been improved by the invention of covered strings (first mentioned in print in 1664). Indeed this invention, together with the increased range that late 17th-century composers such as Corelli gave to the bass line, may have led to a preference for the archlute over the theorbo.

In England the archlute came into prominence as an alternative to the theorbo at the very end of the 17th century. About 1700 James Talbot measured an arch-lute with one single and five double courses of 68·5 cm on the fingerboard and seven single diapasons of 152·7 cm. Between 1703 and 1708 Thomas Dean advertised London concerts in which he played the archlute to accompany in turn the violin, the German flute and the voice. John Blow scored for 'lute' (probably intending archlute) in an anthem to celebrate the Battle of Blenheim (1704). Walsh listed the archlute as a con-tinuo instrument in nine publications (1705–17). In 1715 John Shore, whose archlute Talbot had measured some years earlier, was appointed 'Lutanist' to the Chapel Royal. In the following year John Weldon specified the 'arch-lute' to provide continuo for his anthems in *Divine Harmony*. Handel wrote a figured bass part for 'archilute' in 'Gentle airs' from the oratorio *Athalia* (1733), but its style is indistinguishable from his 'teorbe' parts from the period 1724 to 1739.

See also LIUTO ATTIORBATO.

BIBLIOGRAPHY
R. Spencer: 'Chitarrone, Theorbo and Archlute', *Early Music*, iv (1976), 407

ROBERT SPENCER

Archpoet. *See* ARCHIPOETA.

Archytas (*fl* Tarentum [now Taranto], first half of 4th century BC). Greek mathematician and statesman. He was a distinguished member of the school of Pythagoras and was visited at Tarentum by Plato. He seems to have been one of the first to state that sound was produced

by pulsations of the air and that the more rapid were the pulsations, the higher was the note produced. The ratios which he worked out for the intervals of the enharmonic, chromatic and diatonic genera were recorded by Ptolemy and largely confirmed by other evidence.

See also GREECE, §I, 6.

R. P. WINNINGTON-INGRAM

Arcicembalo [archicembalo] (It.). A term used by NICOLA VICENTINO (*L'antica musica ridotta alla moderna prattica*, 1555) to designate a harpsichord equipped with many divided keys, or even a second manual, in order to permit playing in his reconstruc-tions of the diatonic, chromatic and enharmonic genera of the ancient Greeks. Later writers have also applied the term to harpsichords having many divided keys for the simpler purpose of playing in good intonation in remote tonalities. Vicentino also built an *arciorgano* for the same purpose (*Descrizione dell'arciorgano*, 1561).

See also ENHARMONIC KEYBOARD.

EDWIN M. RIPIN

Arciconfraternita del Gonfalone. Union of Roman religious fraternities, active in mounting sacred dramas in the Middle Ages; *see* ROME, §II, 1.

Arcileuto [arciliuto] (It.). ARCHLUTE.

Arciorgano. An organ with divided keys; *see* ARCICEM-BALO.

Arcipreste de Hita [Ruiz, Juan] (*b* ?Alcalá de Henares, *c*1283; *d c*1350). Spanish poet and ecclesiastic. His *Libro de buen amor* (1330, enlarged 1343), written during an unjust imprisonment of 13 years, gives him a place in medieval Spanish literature comparable to that of Chaucer in English literature. He mentioned at least 37 instruments in his long poem (6912 lines), often with characterizations: the *mandurria* (bandurría) is alluded to as silly and whining, the *rabé* (rebec) as sufficiently noisy for a traditional Arab tune such as *Calvi garabi* (*E-Mn* V*ª*-6-1, f.9), and the *tamborete* (side drum) as the indispensable time-beater for instrumental ensembles. According to Ruiz, the Moors preferred plucked instruments or percussion to the sweet sounds of the *vihuela de arco* (bowed fiddle); instrumental accompani-ments were given even to processional motets and *chanzo-netas* sung at compline in 14th-century Castile.

BIBLIOGRAPHY
H. B. Richardson: *An Etymological Vocabulary to the Libro de buen amor* (New Haven, 1930)
R. Stevenson: *Spanish Music in the Age of Columbus* (The Hague, 1960), 21, 44f
M. R. Lida de Malkiel: *Two Spanish Masterpieces* (Urbana, 1961), 1–50
M. Criado del Val and E. W. Naylor, eds.: *Libro de buen amor* (Madrid, 1965), 377ff
J. Corominas, ed.: *Libro de buen amor* (Madrid, 1967), 458ff

ROBERT STEVENSON

Arciviolatalira. *See* LIRONE.

Arc musical (Fr.). MUSICAL BOW.

Arco (It.: 'bow'). The term refers to the bow used in playing string instruments such as rebecs, fiddles, viols and members of the violin family. As a musical term in western music 'arco' is generally used after the word PIZZICATO to indicate to the player that he should resume playing with the bow.

Lanfranco, in *Scintille di musica* (1533), referred to 'violoni da tasti e da Arco' (fretted and bowed viols) and 'violette da arco senza tasti' (small bowed violas without frets). The term also appears in a number of Italian treatises on the art of bowing, the most famous being Tartini's *L'arte del arco*.

Perhaps the first use of 'arco' to indicate resumed playing with the bow occurs in Monteverdi's *Combattimento di Tancredi e Clorinda* (1624). His instructions are: 'here one puts aside the bow and plucks the strings with two fingers', followed by 'here one retakes the bow [l'arco]'. J. J. Walther at the beginning of the tenth Capriccio in *Hortulus musicus* (1688) wrote 'senza arco' to indicate that the piece should be plucked throughout. In his *Violinschule* (1756), Leopold Mozart wrote 'Col arco: means with the bow. . . . This is to remind you that the bow is to be used again'. From the time of Paganini to the present there are innumerable examples of the pizzicato–arco combination.

SONYA MONOSOFF

Arcoleo, Antonio (*b* Venice; *fl* 1685–90). Italian librettist. He lived at Candia (now Iraklion), Crete. He wrote three opera librettos which were used by Domenico Gabrielli and G. A. Perti and performed and printed in Venice between 1685 and 1690. They treat historical subjects in a heroi-comic manner; each, by concealing the true identity of a principal character, arrives at a happy ending. They contain many da capo arias and exit arias. There are sometimes ballets between the acts.

BIBLIOGRAPHY
R. S. Freeman: *Opera without Drama: Currents of Change in Italian Opera, 1675–1725, and the Roles Played therein by Zeno, Caldara, and Others* (diss., Princeton U., 1967)
K. Leich: *Girolamo Frigimelica Robertis Libretti (1694–1708): ein Beitrag insbesondere zur Geschichte des Opernlibrettos in Venedig* (Munich, 1972)
KARL LEICH

Arco musical (Sp.; It. *arco sonore*; Fr. *arc sonare*). MUSICAL BOW.

Arct, Michał (*b* Lublin, 31 Dec 1840; *d* Warsaw, 15 Feb 1916). Polish bookseller and music publisher. He served his apprenticeship in the bookshop of his uncle Stanisław Arct in Warsaw, then at Behr & Bock in Berlin. In 1862 he took over the management of Stanisław Arct's bookshop, becoming its proprietor in 1881. In 1900 he founded his own printing house, and devoted himself almost completely to publishing, especially dictionaries, encyclopedias, school and children's literature, and music. As a distinguished authority on music publishing he developed considerably the retailing of scores, as well as introducing a system of lending music for the students of the Warsaw Conservatory. He increased his number of publications to 100 titles yearly, mainly for teaching purposes. The publishing firm M. Arct existed until 1939 and, as the firm S. Arct, from 1946 to 1949.

Music series published by M. Arct include *Etudes et exercises*, *Sonates and sonatines*, *Musique moderne*, *Młody muzyk* ('Young musician'), *Przyjaciółki* ('The friends'; for four hands) and *Podręcznik dla miłośników oper* ('A manual for opera lovers'). Catalogues published include *Katalog książek i nut* (Warsaw, 1892),

Wydawnictwa muzyczne Księgarni i składu nut (1895), *Wydawnictwa pedagogiczno-muzyczne M. Arcta* (1916), *Katalog utworów muzycznych* (1929) and *Książki i nuty wydane od 1946 roku* (1949).

BIBLIOGRAPHY
J. Muszkowski: *Polski słownik biograficzny*, i (Kraków, 1936), 155
J. Kacprzak: *Słownik pracowników książki polskiej* (Warsaw, 1972), 14f
KORNEL MICHAŁOWSKI

Ardanaz, Pedro (*b* 1638; *d* Toledo, 11 Dec 1706). Spanish composer. He succeeded Juan de Padilla as *maestro de capilla* of Toledo Cathedral on 15 July 1674 and held the post for the 32 years up to his death – longer than any *maestro* there before or since. Between 1675 and 1702, 18 volumes of villancico texts were published at Toledo, and he was named as composer of the music for them. Rubio Piqueras confirmed that many of his settings survived (in *E-Tc*) but made no attempt to catalogue them. Ardanaz joined the Cofradía de S Acacio (a musicians' guild) on 23 June 1687 and on 24 July 1688 acted as the guild's agent in contracting for a new organ. The cathedral organist was José Solana, but Ardanaz's most notable musician was the harpist Diego Fernández de Huete, who arrived in 1682 and for whose *Compendio numeroso de zifras armonicas* (1702) he wrote a commendation. An Easter carol by Ardanaz, *Ven aurora ven*, for solo soprano and harp, and two sacrament villancicos, the three-part *Arroyeulo misterioso* (analysed by Francisco Valls in his *Mapa armónico*) and the four-part *Oigan al embozado* are extant (all are in *E-Bc*). The contrapuntal mastery, rhythmic vitality and harmonic chiaroscuro of his villancicos show that he is worthy to rank with Sebastián Durón, Cristóbal Galán and Juan del Vado.

BIBLIOGRAPHY
F. Rubio Piqueras: *Música y músicos toledanos* (Toledo, 1922), 23, 54, 100, 104
ROBERT STEVENSON

Ardel. *See* HARDEL family.

Ardemanio, Giulio Cesare (*b* *c*1580; *d* 1650). Italian composer. All that is known of his life is that he was organist at S Maria della Scala and S Fedele, Milan, and at the ducal court there. He is known to have composed only church music: two published volumes – of motets (1616) and *falsobordone* settings (1618) – are known about but have not survived; a third, *Musica a più voci* (Milan, 1628), which does survive, was, according to its title-page, connected with a particular dramatic pastoral presentation about the life of St Charles (possibly S Carlo Borromeo). Some motets, canzonas and a madrigal by Ardemanio appear in anthologies edited in Milan between 1608 and 1626 by Francesco Lucino (*RISM* 1605[6], 1608[13], 1610[1], 1612[9], 1617[2], 1626[5]). The comparative provincial obscurity of Ardemanio's musical activity may be due to the Spanish domination which somewhat isolated Milan from the mainstream developments which were centred on Venice.

JEROME ROCHE

Ardesi, Carlo (*b* Cremona, ?1550–60; *d* ?Prague, in or after 1612). Italian composer and instrumentalist resident in Bohemia. From 1582 until 1612 he served at the imperial court at Prague, where there were other instrumentalists with the same surname, of whom the older Alberto Ardesi may have been his father. He published *Il primo libro de madrigali* (Venice, 1597[19]), for four voices, which includes 13 pieces by him as well as four by Giovanni Paolo Ardesi (*b* Cremona, after ?1550–60; *d* ?Prague, in or after 1612), who served at the imperial court at Prague from 1580 until 1612 and was probably his brother. An ode by Carlo Ardesi is also extant (in *RISM* c1610[18]).

BIBLIOGRAPHY

L. von Köchel: *Die kaiserliche Hof-Musikkapelle in Wien von 1543–1867* (Vienna, 1869)

W. Pass: *Musik und Musiker am Hof Maximilians II.* (diss., U. of Vienna, 1973)

WALTER PASS

Ardesi, Giovanni Paolo. Italian composer, probably brother of CARLO ARDESI.

Ardespin [Ardespine], **Melchior d'** [Dardespin, Melchior] (*b* c1643; *d* Munich, 1717). German composer and instrumentalist, ? of French birth. On 9 October 1669 he was employed as a cornettist at the Bavarian electoral court at Munich with an annual salary of 250 florins, increased on 27 October 1670 to 400 florins. In a decree of 2 September 1683 he received the title of *Kammerdiener*, and thenceforth he received 600 florins annually. In 1687 he was appointed director of the court orchestra and in 1690 electoral councillor; he held both positions until his death. In 1688 his salary increased by 300 florins, to which certain payments in kind were added, and it reached an annual total of 1073 florins in 1699; this was, however, reduced to 400 florins on 20 March 1700 as a result of Austria's taking possession of Bavaria. His output, much of which is lost, consisted mainly of ballet music. Apart from a few isolated pieces and a ballet composed in 1690 for the Bishop of Freising, he wrote the ballet music for a number of operas by Steffani and G. A. Bernabei.

WORKS

STAGE

(all dance music for operas and cantatas)

G. A. Bernabei: Diana amante, opera, 1688; Gli dei festeggianti, cantata, 1688 (minuet, 1v, insts); Eraclio, opera, 1690 (13 pieces); Il segreto d'amore, opera, 1690 (11 pieces); Vaticinio di Apollo e Diana, cantata, 1690 (minuet, 1v, insts): *A-Wn*

A. Steffani: Servio Tullio, opera, 1686; Alarico, opera, 1687; Niobe, opera, 1688: *Wn* (libretto only)

INSTRUMENTAL

Minuet, *D-Mbs*

2 sonatas mentioned in Fellerer

BIBLIOGRAPHY

EitnerQ; *FétisB*

K. G. Fellerer: *Beiträge zur Musikgeschichte Freisings* (Freising, 1926)

A. Würz: 'd'Ardespin, Melchior', *MGG*

R. Münster: 'Die Musik am Hofe Max Emanuels', *Katalog der Max Emanuel-Ausstellung*, i (Munich, 1976)

GERHARD CROLL, ERNST HINTERMAIER

Ardévol, José (*b* Barcelona, 13 March 1911). Cuban composer and administrator of Spanish birth. He studied composition, conducting and the piano with his father, Fernando Ardévol, and began composing as a boy. In addition, he read arts at Barcelona University and studied conducting with Scherchen in 1930. Later that year he moved to Cuba, where he taught history and aesthetics at the Havana Municipal Conservatory (1936–41) and composition at the universities of Havana (1945–50) and Oriente (1949–51). He took an important part in the Revolution and was director of the underground National Music Committee (1958–9). On the establishment of Castro's government he became in large part responsible for the reorganization of musical life as conductor of the Ministry of Education radio orchestras (1959–65), editor of the music journal *Revolución* and national director of music. In 1965 he was appointed to teach composition at the Havana Conservatory, and in 1968 he took a similar post at the National School of Music, while continuing to occupy various government functions. His early music, that of the 1930s and 1940s, shows a typically Cuban nationalist neo-classic tendency. This gave way in the 1950s to a Webern-influenced style, and in 1967 he began to use aleatory techniques. He has published a volume of essays, *Música y revolución* (Havana, 1966), and a study, *La música* (Havana, 1969).

WORKS

(selective list)

Orch: 3 ricercari, str, 1936; Conc., 3 pf, orch, 1938; Sym. no.2 'Homenage a Falla', 1945; Sym. no.3, 1946; Suites cubanas nos.1–2, 1947, 1949; Sym. Variations, vc, orch, 1951; El son, vn, orch, 1952; Música, chamber orch, 1957; Música, gui, chamber orch, 1967; Movimientos sinfónicos nos.1–2, 1967, 1969

Vocal: Versos sencillos (Martí), 1v, orch, 1952; Cantos de la Revolución, chorus, 1962; Che comandante (Guillén), cantata, 3 solo vv, chorus, orch, 1968; Lenin (Lenin, F. P. Rodríguez), 6 solo vv, chorus, orch, 1970

Chamber and inst: Study in the Form of a Prelude and Fugue, perc, 1933; Suite, perc, 1934; Música da camera, 6 insts, 1936; Sonate a 3 nos.1–6, 1937, 1938, 1942, 1942, 1943, 1946; Pf Sonatas nos.1–3, 1944; Vc Sonata, 1948; Sonata, gui, 1948; Sonatina, vc, pf, 1950; Wind Qnt, 1957; Str Qt no.3, 1958; 3 Short Pieces, vn/ve, pf, 1965; Tensiones, pf left hand, 1968

Principal publishers: Empresa de Grabaciones y Ediciones Musicales, Music for Percussion (New York), Pan American Union, Southern

Arditi, Luigi (*b* Crescentino, Piedmont, 16 July 1822; *d* Hove, 1 May 1903). Italian conductor, composer and violinist. After studying the violin in his home town, where he led a small orchestra, he was educated at the Milan Conservatory from 1836, studying the violin and composition with Ferrara, Rolla and Vaccai. In 1841 he composed the first of three early operas, *I briganti*. After working in Milan from 1842 to 1846, he went with Bottesini, a lifelong friend, to Havana, where he worked at the Teatro Imperiale and produced a one-act opera, *Il corsaro*. In the summer months he conducted in the USA; his opera *La spia* was produced in New York in 1856.

After more European trips including an appointment in Constantinople and a visit to Russia, Arditi settled in London as conductor at Her Majesty's in 1858. He remained there for 11 years, conducting Italian operas and taking the company on provincial tours, especially to Dublin. He continued to compose, mostly occasional orchestral music, popular songs and ballads; the vocal waltz *Il bacio* was renowned. He made many tours to Europe out of the London season, chiefly with Italian opera companies. In 1869 he succeeded Costa at Covent Garden for one year, and followed this with winter seasons at the St Petersburg Italian Opera in 1871 and 1873, and several seasons at Vienna. From 1874 to 1877 he alternated seasons in Vienna with promenade concerts at Covent Garden, his own 1865 promenade season at Her Majesty's having previously proved popular.

Between 1878 and 1894 Arditi was largely concerned with Mapleson's annual opera tours of the USA. He worked at Her Majesty's in 1880, at Covent Garden in 1885 and 1889, at the Shaftesbury Theatre in 1891, and made a provincial tour with the Carl Rosa Company in 1894. Henry J. Wood, once his assistant, recalled that Arditi's knowledge of English was very limited and that the orchestra enjoyed wilfully misunderstanding him. But his considerable contribution to London musical life included the introduction of 27 important operas during the course of his career.

BIBLIOGRAPHY
L. Arditi: *My Reminiscences* (London, 1896)

KEITH HORNER

A re. The pitch *A* in the HEXACHORD system.

Arefece, Antonio. *See* OREFICE, ANTONIO.

Arel, Bülent (*b* Istanbul, 23 May 1919). American composer of Turkish birth. He studied composition under Akses and Zuckmayer at the Ankara Conservatory (1941–7) and sound engineering in Paris (1951). Active as a teacher and conductor, he held positions with Radio Ankara during the years 1951–9 and 1963–5. In 1959 he went to the USA (of which he became a citizen in 1973), where he worked as a technician at the Columbia–Princeton Electronic Music Center (1959–63) and taught at Yale University (1961–2, 1965–70). He was appointed professor of music at the State University of New York at Stony Brook in 1971.

WORKS
(selective list)
Music for Str Qt and Tape, 1957, rev. 1962; Elec Music no.1, tape, 1960; Stereo Elec Music no.1, tape, 1961; For Vn and Pf, 1966; Mimiana I–III, dance series, tape, 1968, 1969, 1973; Stereo Elec Music no.2, tape, 1970

Principal publisher: American Composers' Alliance

BRIAN FENNELLY

Arellano, Juan Salvador Bautista de (*b* Seville; *fl* 1628–33). Spanish writer. He was a Franciscan monk of the convent of Ss Trinidad, Seville. Between 1628 and 1633 he wrote several pseudo-historical works on local and religious topics as well as one pertaining to music: *El psalterio de David: exortación, y virtudes de la música, y canto, para todo género de gentes, en particular para los eclesiásticos, y obligación que tienen de cantar, o rezar las divinas alabanzas con toda atención, y devoción* (Jerez de la Frontera, 1632). This is a curious mixture of legend and history. The first part traces music from classical and biblical times up to and including the medieval period, the second treats of its various uses, not only religious but also military, social, educational and recreational. Arellano mingled ancient fable with contemporary anecdote and drew fanciful analogies between the realms of music and religion. His book is of particular interest as a compendium of the kind of material used in the traditional 'praise of music' (*loor de musica*) that prefaces so many Spanish treatises and music collections of the period.

BIBLIOGRAPHY
R. Mitjana y Gordón: 'La musique en Espagne', *EMDC*, I/iv (1920), 2107
H. Anglès and J. Subirá: *Catálogo musical de la Biblioteca nacional de Madrid*, iii (Barcelona, 1951)

ALMONTE HOWELL

Arena, Antonius de [Arènes, Antoine des; de la Sable; du Sablon] (*b* Solliès, Provence, late 15th century; *d* St Remy or Solliès, 1544 or a little later). French judge, man of letters and dance theorist. In 1519 he began to study law at the University of Avignon. After completing his studies he joined the French troops that invaded Italy. Late in 1528 he returned to Provence and spent several years in Aix until he was named *juge ordinaire* of St Remy in 1536.

The most widely read of Arena's writings is the dance instruction manual *Ad suos compagnones studiantes qui sunt de persona friantes bassas dansas de novo bragarditer*, a book that also includes an account of his experiences in the Italian campaign. Its 32 editions published between 1529 and 1770 testify to its popularity. The sections on dance date from his student days in Avignon; the main subject is the basse danse as it was practised in the south of France. 58 basses danses 'qui ne sont pas communes' are given with their choreography in the traditional French–Burgundian letter tablature, the only difference being that the letter 'b' (*branle*) of the older sources has been replaced by the letter 'c' (*congé*). The high-spirited, humorous text, intended to improve not only the dance technique but ballroom manners in general, contains much valuable information concerning measure, tempo and step sequences of the dances. Particularly important is Arena's full description of the *reverence*, a movement so common to the courtiers of 15th-century Burgundy and Italy that no earlier writer had thought it necessary to describe it in detail.

Arena is also well known for his *Meygra entrepriza* (Avignon, 1537; ed. N. Bonafous, Aix, 1860), in which he condemned the ravages afflicted on Provence by Charles V's armies. He wrote it in macaronic language, a mixture of classical Latin, French, Italian and Provençal. His verse is supple, his gifts of observation and characterization keen, and his humour irrepressible.

BIBLIOGRAPHY
A. Fabre: *Antonius Arena: notice historique et littéraire* (Marseilles, 1860)
F. Dollieule: 'Antonius Arena de bragardissima villa de Soleriis: sa vie et ses oeuvres', *Revue de Marseille et de Provence*, xxxi (1885), 481, 543; xxxii (1886), 129, 239 [incl. list of all edns. of Arena's treatise]
J. Plattard: 'Antonius de Arena et les danses au XVIᵉ siècle', *Revue des livres anciens*, i (Paris, 1913–14), 140
I. Brainard: *Die Choreographie der Hoftänze in Burgund, Frankreich und Italien im 15. Jahrhundert* (diss., U. of Göttingen, 1956)
D. Heartz: 'The Basse Danse: its Evolution circa 1450–1550', *AnnM*, vi (1958–63), 287–340

INGRID BRAINARD

Arena, Giuseppe (*b* Malta, 1713; *d* Naples, 6 Nov 1784). Italian organist and composer. In 1725 he entered the Conservatorio di Gesù Cristo in Naples where he remained for ten years; among his teachers were Gaetano Greco and Francesco Durante, and Pergolesi was a fellow student. Arena composed operas for Rome, Turin, Venice and Naples, and music by him was included in Galuppi's London pasticcio *Alessandro in Persia* (31 October 1741). According to the libretto of *Il vecchio deluso* (1746), Arena was in the service of the Prince of Bisignano; he is also reported to have been organist at the Chiesa dei Filippini in Naples. Arena's treatise *Principij di musica con intavolature di cembalo e partimenti* (autograph in *I-Nc*) is described by Fétis as 'un ouvrage élémentaire'.

WORKS
Stage (all inc.; for sources see Mondolfi): Achille in Sciro (opera seria, 3, Metastasio), Rome, delle Dame, 7 Jan 1738, 1 aria in *I-Nc*; La clemenza di Tito (opera seria, 3, Metastasio), Turin, Regio, 26 Dec 1738; Il vello d'oro, Rome, 1 May 1740; Artaserse (opera seria, 3, Metastasio), Turin, Regio, carn. 1741; Tigrane (opera seria, 3, F. Silvani, rev. G. Goldoni), Venice, S Giovanni Grisostomo, 18 Nov 1741; Farnace (opera seria, 3, A. M. Lucchini), Rome, Capranica, 23 Jan 1742, completed by G. Sellitto; Il vecchio deluso (opera comica, 3, G. Palomba), Naples, Nuovo, carn. 1746
Componimento per musica per la solennita del Corpus Domini, Naples, 1765, ?lost, lib in *I-Rsc*; Christus, 2S, bc, autograph *Nc*; Ave Maria, S, org, *LT*

BIBLIOGRAPHY
EitnerQ; *FétisB*; *LaMusicaD*; *RicordiE*
A. Mondolfi: 'Arena, Giuseppe', *MGG*
E. Zanetti: 'Arena, Giuseppe', *ES*

GORDANA LAZAREVICH

Arènes, Antoine de. *See* ARENA, ANTONIUS DE.

Arensky, Anton Stepanovich (*b* Novgorod, 12 July 1861; *d* Terioki, Finland, 25 Feb 1906). Russian composer, pianist and conductor. His father, a doctor, was a keen cellist, and his mother an excellent pianist who gave him his first music lessons. By the age of nine he had already composed some songs and piano pieces. When the family moved to St Petersburg, Arensky took lessons with Zikke before entering the St Petersburg Conservatory (1879), where he studied composition with Rimsky-Korsakov and counterpoint and fugue with Johannsen. He graduated with a gold medal in 1882. Even before this Rimsky-Korsakov had been sufficiently impressed by Arensky's talent to entrust him with a share in preparing the vocal score of *The Snowmaiden*. After graduating Arensky went straight to the Moscow Conservatory as a professor of harmony and counterpoint; among his pupils were to be Rakhmaninov, Skryabin and Glier. The move to Moscow brought him into close contact with Tchaikovsky and Taneyev. From 1888 to 1895 he directed the concerts of the Russian Choral Society and also appeared as a conductor at symphony concerts. In 1889 he was appointed to the council of the Synodal School of Church Music in Moscow, remaining until 1893. One of Arensky's greatest personal successes was with his opera *Son na Volge* ('A dream on the Volga'), based on the same Ostrovsky play as Tchaikovsky's opera *Voyevoda*, and produced in Moscow in 1891. Parts of the opera had been composed under Rimsky-Korsakov's supervision when Arensky was still a conservatory student.

In 1894 Balakirev recommended Arensky as his successor to the directorship of the imperial chapel in St Petersburg, and in 1895 Arensky moved to that city, resigning from his professorship at the Moscow Conservatory. A second opera, *Rafael'* ('Raphael'), composed in 1894 on the occasion of the First Congress of Russian Artists, was less successful than its predecessor. In 1901 Arensky left the imperial chapel with a pension of 6000 rubles. The rest of his life was devoted to composition and to very successful appearances both as pianist and conductor at concerts in Russia and abroad. From his early years he had been addicted to drinking and gambling and, according to Rimsky-Korsakov, his life became more disordered still in his last years. His health was quickly undermined, and he succumbed to tuberculosis.

Arensky was one of the most eclectic Russian composers of his generation. The early Piano Concerto (1882) reveals the overwhelming influence of Chopin in its first two movements, which are filled with delicately ornamented cantabile melodies often linked by sparkling passage-work after the fashion of Chopin's own two piano concertos. The finale shows a generalized Russianness, the most unusual feature of the piece being its five-beat bars; Arensky was to show a particular liking for such unusual metres (and was reproached for the habit by Tchaikovsky). In his best-known extended work, the Piano Trio no.1 in D minor, the presence of Mendelssohn (and especially of that composer's own D

minor piano trio) is clearly apparent. The trio is one of Arensky's most successful large-scale pieces, displaying his melodic facility and fluent compositional technique. It was composed in memory of the cellist Davïdov, and its commemorative purpose is particularly apparent in the third movement. Such an elegiac vein was characteristic of Arensky; it is significant that, despite being Rimsky-Korsakov's pupil, he seems to have responded far more to the influence of Tchaikovsky.

In general, Arensky's short works are his most satisfactory pieces. His ready flow of lyrical, often sentimental melody, and his easy command of keyboard textures equipped him splendidly to be a composer of songs in the *romance* manner that dominated Russian song in the 19th century. Similarly, he could produce beautifully turned keyboard miniatures. As in the finale of the Piano Concerto, his use of unusual rhythms is evident in his set of piano pieces *Essais sur les rythmes oubliés* op.28, based on the unorthodox metres of certain archaic poetic forms; the results are curious rather than convincing. While being in no way original, Arensky could produce distinctive music, and despite Rimsky-Korsakov's prediction that he would be 'soon forgotten', some of his pieces, notably the waltz from the first suite for two pianos and the variations for string orchestra on Tchaikovsky's famous *Legend*, have continued to occupy a corner of the modern repertory.

WORKS
(places and dates of publication unknown)

STAGE

op.
16 Son na Volge [A dream on the Volga] (opera, 4, Ostrovsky), completed 1888, Moscow, Bol'shoy, 2 Jan 1891
37 Rafael' [Raphael] (opera, 1, A. Kryukov), 1894, Moscow, Conservatory, 18 May 1894
50 Egipetskiye nochi [Egyptian nights] (ballet, 1, Fokin), 1900, St Petersburg, Mariïnsky, 21 March 1908
47 Nal' i Damayanti [Nal and Damayanti] (opera, 3, M. Tchaikovsky, after Zhukovsky), completed 1903, Moscow, Bol'shoy, 22 Jan 1904
75 The Tempest (incidental music, Shakespeare), solo vv, chorus, orch, 1905

CHORAL
(for unaccompanied chorus unless otherwise stated)

3   Lesnoy tsar' [The wood king] (Goethe, trans. Zhukovsky), cantata, 1v, chorus, orch, 1882
—   Gimn iskusstvu [Hymn to art] (Ostrovsky, after Schiller), solo vv, chorus, orch, 1884
14 Anchar (Pushkin), mixed vv
26 Kantata na 10-letiye koronovaniya [Cantata on the 10th anniversary of the coronation] (Kryukov), solo vv, chorus, orch, 1891
31 Two Choruses, male vv: Molitva [Prayer]; Noch' [Night]
39 Three choruses: Kolïbel'naya pesnya [Lullaby]; Zhemchug i lyubov' [The pearl and love]; Serenada [Serenade]
40 Four Sacred Choruses, from the Liturgy of St John Chrysostom: Kheruvimskaya pesn' [Cherubim's song]; Tebe poyom [We sing to thee]; Otche nash [Our Father]; Khvalite Gospoda [Praise the Lord]
46 Bakhchisarayskiy fontan [The fountain of Bakhchisaray] (after Pushkin), cantata, solo vv, chorus, orch, 1899
55 Two Quartets, SATB: Ustalo vsyo krugom [All around has grown weary]; Oni lyubili drug druga [They loved each other]
57 Three Quartets, vc acc.: Serenada [Serenade]; Ugasshim zvezdam [To the dying stars]; Goryachiy klyuch [The hot spring]
61 Kubok [The goblet] (Zhukovsky), cantata, 1v, chorus, orch
69 Tsvetnik [The bed of flowers], 8 pieces, 1v, female vv, pf

ORCHESTRAL

2   Piano Concerto, f, 1882
13 Intermezzo, g, str, 1882
4   Symphony no.1, b, 1883
7   Suite, g, 1885: Variations; Air de danse; Scherzo; Basso ostinato; March
9   Marguerite Gautier, fantasia, completed 1886
18 18 November 1889, ceremonial march for Anton Rubinstein's jubilee, 1889
22 Symphony no.2, A, 1889
54 Violin Concerto, a, 1891

35a Variations on a theme of Tchaikovsky, str, 1894 [based on Tchaikovsky's Legend op.54, no.5; arr. of slow movt of Arensky's Str Qt no.2, op.35]
48 Fantasia on a Russian folksong, pf, orch, 1899
50a Egipetskiye nochi [Egyptian nights], suite from the ballet
— Pamyati Suvorova [To the memory of Suvorov], march

CHAMBER

11 String Quartet no.1, G, 1888
12 Two Pieces, vc, pf: Petite ballade; Danse-capricieuse
30 Four Pieces, vn, pf: Prélude; Sérénade; Berceuse; Scherzo
32 Piano Trio no.1, d, 1894
35 String Quartet no.2, a, 1894 [slow movt arr. str orch, op.35a]
51 Piano Quintet, D, 1900
56 Four Pieces, vc, pf: Eastern melody; Romance; Sad song; Humoresque
72 Four Pieces, vn, pf
73 Piano Trio no.2, f, 1905

KEYBOARD
(for solo pf unless otherwise stated)

1 Six Canonic Pieces: Sympathy; Contradiction; March; Lightheartedness; Confession; Sadness
5 Six Pieces, 1884: Nocturne; Intermezzo; Romance; Valse; Basso ostinato; Etude
8 Scherzo, A
15 Suite no.1, F, 2 pf: Romance; Valse; Polonaise
19 Three Pieces: Etude; Prélude; Mazurka
20 Bigarrures, 3 pieces
23 Silhouettes [Suite no.2], 2 pf, 1892: The scholar; The coquette; The buffoon; The dreamer; The dancer
24 Trois esquisses
25 Four Pieces: Impromptu; Rêverie; Etude (on a Chinese theme); Scherzino
28 Essais sur les rythmes oubliés: Logaèdes; Péons; Ioniques; Sari; Strophe alcéenne; Strophe sapphique
33 Variations [Suite no.3], 2 pf: Dialogue; Valse; Marche solenelle; Minuet XVIIIéme siècle; Gavotte; Scherzo; Marche funèbre; Nocturne; Polonaise
34 Six Children's Pieces: Conte; Le coucou; Les larmes; Valse; Berceuse; Fugue sur un thème russe
36 Twenty-four Characteristic Pieces, 1894: Prélude; La toupie; Nocturne; Petite ballade; Consolation; Duo; Valse; In modo antico; Papillon; Ne m'oubliez pas; Barcarolle; Intermezzo; Etude; Scherzino; Le ruisseau dans la forêt; Elégie; Le rêve; Inquiétude; Rêverie du printemps; Mazurka; Marche; Tarantella; Andante con variazioni; Aux champs
41 Four Studies, 1896
— Improvisation, 1896
42 Three Pieces: Prélude; Romance; Etude
43 Six Caprices
52 Près de la mer: 6 esquisses
53 Six Pieces, 1901: Prélude; Scherzo; Elégie; Mazurka; Romance; Etude
62 Suite no.4, 2 pf: Prélude; Romance; Le rêve; Finale
63 Twelve Preludes
65 Children's suite, pf 4 hands: Praeludium; Aria; Scherzino; Gavotte; Elegia; Romance; Intermezzo; Alla polacca
66 Twelve Pieces, pf 4 hands: Prélude; Gavotte; Ballade; Menuetto; Elégie; Consolation; Valse; Marche; Romance; Scherzo; Berceuse; Polka
67 Arabesques
74 Twelve Studies, 1905
— Two Pieces: Fugue; Valse

VOCAL
(for 1v, pf unless otherwise stated)

6 Four Songs: Vstrechu l' ya yarkuyu v nebe zaryu? [Shall I meet a clear dawn in heaven?]; Ti ne sprashivay [Do not ask]; Kak dorozhu ya prekrasnïm mgnoven'yem [How I value the beautiful moment]; Ya ne skazal tebe [I did not tell you]
10 Six songs: Ya prishol k tebe s privetom [I came to you with a greeting] (A. Fet); V dïmke [In the mist]; Ya boyus' rasskazat' [I fear to tell] (N. Minsky); Kogda ya bïl lyubim [When I was beloved]; Zhelaniye [Desire] (A. Khemyakov); Na nivï zheltïye [In the yellow cornfields] (A. K. Tolstoy)
17 Four romances: Menestrel' [The minstrel] (A. Maykov); Vesnoy [In spring]; Snovideniye [The dream] (Pushkin, after Voltaire); Noch' [Night]
21 Two Romances: Razbitaya vaza [The broken vase] (A. Apukhtin); Ona bïla tvoya [She was yours] (Apukhtin)
27 Six Romances: Pesn' rïbki [Song of the fish] (Lermontov); Osen' [Autumn] (Fet); Pevets [The singer] (Khomyakov); Starïy rïtsar' [The old knight] (V. Zhukovsky); Dve pesni [Two songs] (Khomyakov); Ya videl smert' [I beheld death] (Pushkin)
29 Three Duets: Minutï schastya [Minutes of happiness]; Vcherashnyaya noch' [Last night]; Fialka [The violet]

38 Six romances: V tishi i mrake tainstvennoy nochi [In the quiet and gloom of the mysterious night] (Fet), pf, vc obbl; Landïsh [The lily of the valley] (P. Tchaikovsky); Ne zazhigay ognya [Do not kindle the fires] (O. Rathaus); Ne plach', moy drug [Do not cry, my friend] (Longfellow, trans.); O chom mechtayesh tï? [What are you dreaming about?] (Rathaus); Ya videl inogda [Sometimes I beheld] (Lermontov)
44 Six Romances (A. Golenishchev-Kutuzov) (1899): Oryol [The eagle]; Letnyaya noch' [Summer night]; Odin zvuk imeni [One sound of the name]; Den' otoshol [The day has gone]; Nad ozerom [Over the lake]; Est' v serdtse u menya [There is in my heart]
45 Two Duets: Tikho vsyo sred charuyushchey nochi [All is quiet in the bewitching night]; Dve rozï [Two roses]
49 Five Romances: Ugasnul den' [The day has died]; Poslushay, bït mozhet [Listen, perhaps] (Lermontov); Kogda poet skorbit [When the poet mourns] (S. Andreyevsky); V albome [In the album] (Lermontov); Davno-li pod volshebnïye zvuki [Long since beneath enchanted sounds] (Fet)
58 Volki [The wolves] (A. K. Tolstoy), ballad, B, orch
59 Six Children's Songs: Ptichka letayet [The bird flies]; Krugovaya poruka [Mutual responsibility]; Tam vdali, za rekoy [There in the distance, beyond the river]; Rasskazhi, motïlyok [Tell me, moth]; Spi, ditya moyo, usni [Sleep, my child]; Pod solntsem vyutsya zhavoronki [Beneath the sun the larks climb upwards]
60 Eight Romances: Znakomïye zvuki [Familiar sounds] (A. Pleshcheyev); Ya zhdal tebya [I waited for you] (Apukhtin); V polusne[Half-waking] (Munstein); Vchera uvenchala dushistïmi tsvetami [Yesterday I crowned with fragrant flowers] (Fet); Net, dazhe i togda [No, even then] (Fet); Stranitsï milïye [Dear pages] (Fet); Sad ves' v tsvetu [The garden is all in bloom] (Fet); Odna zvezda nad vsemi dïshit [One star breathes over all] (Fet)
64 Five Romances: Lebedinaya pesnya [Swan song] (Golenishchev-Kutuzov); V sadakh Italiy [In the gardens of Italy] (Golenishchev-Kutuzov); Gornïmi tikho letala dusha nebesami [Softly the spirit flew up to heaven] (A. K. Tolstoy); Ya ne lyublyu tebya [I do not love you] (Lermontov); Zmey [The serpent] (Fet)
68 Three Declamations (Turgenev), 1v, orch, 1903: Kak khoroshi, kak svezhi bïli rozï [How fine and fresh were the roses]; Lazurnoye tsarstvo [The azure kingdom]; Nimfï [The nymphs]
70 Five Songs (T. Shchepkina-Kupernik): Schast'ye [Happiness]; Osen' [Autumn]; Vsyo tikho vokrug [All around is quiet]; Nebosklon oslepitel'no siniy [The dazzlingly blue horizon]; Ya na tebya glyazhu s ulïbkoy [I look at you with a smile]
71 Vospominaniya [Memories] (Bal'mont, after Shelley), suite, 1v, pf: Iz divnïkh dney [From wonderful days]; Nad morem [Over the sea]; Drug s drugom sosnï obnyalis' [The pines embraced one another]; Kak tikho vsyo [How still all is]; I dolgo mï, sklonivshi vzor [And a long while we, having inclined our gaze]
— Five Romances: Poeziya [Poetry] (S. Nadson); Gnot zabveniya [The weight of oblivion] (Rathaus); Mne snilos vecherneye nebo [I dreamed of the evening sky] (Nadson); Ya lask tvoikh strashus [I fear your caresses] (Bal'mont, after Shelley); Zvezda blestyashchaya sorvalasya s nebes [The brilliant star shot from the heavens] (Rathaus)

WRITINGS

Kratkoye rukovodstvo k prakticheskomu izucheniyu garmonii [A short guide to the practical study of harmony] (Moscow, 1891, 5/1929)
Rukovodstvo k izucheniyu form instrumental'noy i vokal'noy muzïki [A guide to the study of form in instrumental and vocal music] (Moscow, 1893–4, 6/1930)
Sbornik zadach (1000) dlya prakticheskovo izucheniya garmonii [A collection of exercises for the practical study of harmony] (Moscow, 1897)

BIBLIOGRAPHY

E. Lyatsky: *Skazhitel' I. T. Ryabinin i evo bïlinï: muzïkal'naya zametka A. S. Arenskovo* [The story-teller I. T. Ryabinin and his epics: Arensky's musical note] (Moscow, 1894)
Obituary, *EIT 1907–8*, no.18, p.285
A. P. Lensky: 'Zametki A. P. Lenskovo o perepiske s nim A. S. Arenskovo po povodu *Buri* Shekspira' [Lensky's notes about the correspondence between him and Arensky regarding Shakespeare's *The Tempest*], *EIT 1909*, no.4, p.107
N. Rimsky-Korsakov: *Letopis' moyey muzïkal'noy zhizni* [Chronicle of my musical life] (St Petersburg, 1909, 7/1955; Eng. trans., 1923, enlarged 2/1942/*R1974*)
Yu. D. Engel: *V opere* [At the opera] (Moscow, 1911)
M. F. Gnesin: 'A. Arensky', *Rostovskya rech'* (1916), no.47
I. E. Grabar' and others, eds.: *B. V. Asaf'yev: izbrannïye trudï* [Selected works], ii (Moscow, 1954)
V. A. Zolotaryov: *Vospominaniya o moikh velikikh uchitelyakh i tovarishchakh* [Reminiscences about my great teachers and friends] (Moscow, 1957)
G. M. Tsïpin: *A. S. Arensky* (Moscow, 1966)

DAVID BROWN

Arenzana, Manuel (*fl* Puebla, 1791–1821). Mexican composer. His numerous dated compositions in Puebla Cathedral name him as *maestro de capilla* from 1792 to 1821 (one is labelled 1843, probably a copying date). He was recommended for this position in 1791 by Martín de Cruzealegui, organist and composer in Mexico City and colleague of Junipero Serra. His successor was probably José Manuel Plata (*fl* 1843–55). The splendour of musical performances in the cathedral may be gauged from Arenzana's compositions, all of which have orchestral accompaniment. His liturgical works are in large forms, usually with several movements and characterized by lyrical melodies, elaborate instrumental figurations, strong contrasts of tempo and dynamics and the figured continuo still normal in Spanish cathedral music. Two masses and three offices for matins, listed in a Mexico City Cathedral catalogue of 1875, have apparently disappeared.

Arenzana was also listed by the *Diario de México* among the 'outstanding composers' of musical *comedias* and zarzuelas produced for Mexico City's Coliseo Nuevo between 1800 and 1810. The 1805 season that produced Cimarosa's *El filósofo burlado*, for example, included Arenzana's two-act comedy *El extrangero* and his 'new duo' *Los dos ribales en amore*.

WORKS
(*MSS in Puebla Cathedral, Mexico*)

With large orch [2 fl, 2 cl, bn, 2 tpt, 2 hn, va, db, org]: 2 masses, 8vv; Missa pro defunctis, 8vv; Officium defunctorum, 8vv; Lamentation, 4vv; Lamentation, 8vv; Magnificat, 8vv; 4 psalms: Beatus vir, 8vv; Dixit Dominus, 4vv; Laudate Dominum, 8vv; Miserere mei Deus, 8vv

With small orch [2 fl, 2 hn, 2 vn, va, db, org]: 3 invitatories: for Holy Sacrament, 4vv; for San Juan Nepomuceno, 8vv; for San Pedro, 8vv; many pss, 4vv and 8vv

BIBLIOGRAPHY

H. Leicht: *Las calles de Puebla* (Puebla, 1934), 97ff, 340
R. Stevenson: *Music in Mexico* (New York, 1952), 173f
M. Merín and E. Castro Morales: *Puebla y su universidad* (Puebla, 1959), 11ff, 137ff
A. R. Catalyne: 'Music of the 16th through the 18th Centuries in the Cathedral of Puebla', *Yearbook, Inter-American Institute for Musical Research*, ii (1966), 75
L. B. Spiess and E. T. Stanford: *An Introduction to Certain Mexican Musical Archives* (Detroit, 1969)

ALICE RAY CATALYNE

Aresti, Floriano. *See* ARRESTI, FLORIANO.

Aretino, Paolo [Paolo Antonio del Bivi] (*b* Arezzo, baptized 1 March 1508; *d* Arezzo, 19 July 1584). Italian composer and priest. Although there is no evidence for the frequent assertion that he studied in Florence with Francesco Corteccia, his cordial relations with the Tuscan court (revealed in two extant letters and in the dedication to Francesco de' Medici of his 1558 madrigal book) suggest that he was acquainted with leading Florentine composers and aware of current developments in music there. He spent his life in the service of two churches in Arezzo: in 1530 he was appointed teacher of chant at S Maria della Pieve, a position he held until he became canon at the cathedral in 1533; from 1538 to 1544 he was teacher of chant and *maestro di cappella* there too. He returned to S Maria della Pieve as a canon in 1545 and remained there until his death.

Most of Aretino's sacred music is harmonically conservative and contrapuntally simple, yet often effective in its careful accentuation of the text and occasional heightening of descriptive passages with appropriate vocal ranges and harmonies. The *Passio Jesu Christi secundum Johannem* is set polyphonically throughout, and uses various combinations of voices to depict the words of individual characters and of the turba. Aretino introduced characterization by using the same chord at the beginning or end of each piece sung by the same character. His first madrigal book comprises four-voice madrigals in common time ('madrigali cromati'); the second contains settings of a carnival song, verse by Petrarch and courtly poetry, some of which refers to the nobility of Florence or Arezzo. Einstein characterized Aretino's madrigals as representing a provincial art, and in them found traces of the earlier style of Bernardo Pisano and the music of Corteccia.

WORKS
(*all printed works published in Venice unless otherwise stated*)

SACRED

Sacra responsoria, 4vv (1544)
Piae, ac devotissimae Lamentationes Hieremiae prophetae, 4vv (1563)
Responsorium . . . una cum Benedictus ac Te Deum laudamus, liber primus et secundus, 4vv (1564)
Musica super hymnos totius anni, 4–6vv (Milan, 1565), lost
Magnificat . . . liber primus, 5vv (1569)
Passio Jesu Christi secundum Johannem, solo vv, 2–7vv, *I-Fn*; ed. in Musica liturgica, i/6 (Cincinnati, 1958)

SECULAR

Libro primo delli madrigali cromati, 4vv (1549)
Li madrigali, 5–8vv (1558)

BIBLIOGRAPHY

R. Gandolfi: 'Lettere inedite scritte da musicisti e letterati', *RMI*, xx (1913), 527
F. Coradini: 'Paolo Aretino (1508–1584)', *NA*, i (1924), 143, 275
A. Einstein: *The Italian Madrigal* (Princeton, 1949/*R*1971), i, 293
K. von Fischer: 'Zur Geschichte der Passionskomposition des 16. Jahrhunderts in Italien', *AMw*, xi (1954), 189

FRANK A. D'ACCONE

Aretz (de Ramón y Rivera), Isabel (*b* Buenos Aires, 13 April 1913). Venezuelan ethnomusicologist, folklorist and composer, of Argentinian birth, wife of Luis Felipe Ramón y Rivera. She studied the piano under Rafael González (1923–31) and composition with Athos Palma (1928–33) at the Buenos Aires National Conservatory of Music, instrumentation with Villa-Lobos in Brazil (1937), anthropology (1938–40) and, with Carlos Vega, folklore and musicology (1938–44) at the Museo de Ciencias Naturales de Buenos Aires. She took her doctorate in musicology in 1967 at the Argentine Catholic University with a dissertation on Argentine folk music. She was an associate member of the Instituto Argentino de Musicología from 1938 to 1950. After working as the first professor of ethnomusicology at the Escuela Nacional de Danzas de Argentina (1950–52) she moved to Caracas, Venezuela, where she has held appointments as research fellow in folklore and ethnomusicology at the Instituto Nacional de Folklore de Venezuela (1953–65), head of the folklore department of the Instituto Nacional de Cultura y Bellas Artes (1965–70) and director of the Instituto Interamericano de Etnomusicología y Folklore (appointed 1970).

Isabel Aretz is a leading authority on South American folk music. With her husband she has travelled extensively throughout Hispanic America, collecting the folk music of Venezuela, Argentina, Chile, Bolivia, Peru, Uruguay, Paraguay, Colombia, Ecuador, Panama and Mexico, and has published numerous important analytical and descriptive accounts of their research. Her many awards and fellowships, for both scholarly work and composition, include a scholarship from the Argentine National Commission of Culture (1941–3), a Guggenheim Foundation fellowship (1966–7), the Polifonía prize of Buenos Aires (1952) and the first prize in Caracas (1972) for *Yekuana* (*Yanoama*), a work for orchestra, voices and tape. She is an active member of many national and international organizations, a board member and delegate of the International Folk Music Council and a council member of the Society for Ethnomusicology. As a composer Aretz has cultivated a highly personal nationalist style, based on a combination of indigenous or Afro-Hispanic folk traditions with avant-garde European elements, including electronic techniques.

WRITINGS

Música tradicional argentina: Tucumán, historia y folklore (Buenos Aires, 1946)
El folklore musical argentino (Buenos Aires, 1952)
'Musicas pentatonicas en Sudamerica', *Archivos venezolanos de folklore*, i (1952), 283
Costumbres tradicionales argentinas (Buenos Aires, 1953)
Manual de folklore venezolano (Caracas, 1957, rev. 2/1969, 3/1972)
with M. Cardona, L. F. Ramón y Rivera and G. L. Carrera: *Panorama del folklore venezolano* (Caracas, 1959)
with L. F. Ramón y Rivera: *Folklore tachirense* (Caracas, 1961–3)
Cantos navideños en el folklore venezolano (Caracas, 1962)
ed. with A. Lloyd: *Folk Songs of the Americas* (London, 1965)
'Raíces europeas de la música folklórica de Venezuela: el aporte indígena', *2nd Inter-American Conference on Ethnomusicology: Bloomington 1965* [*Music in the Americas*, ed. G. List and J. Orrego-Salas, The Hague, 1967], 7
Instrumentos musicales de Venezuela (Cumaná, 1967)
La artesania en Venezuela (Caracas, 1967)
Música tradicional argentina: La Rioja (diss., Catholic U., Buenos Aires, 1967)
'The Polyphonic Chant in South America', *JIFMC*, xix (1967), 49
'El folklore musical de Venezuela', *Revista musical chilena* (1968), nos.104–5, pp.53–82
'Cantos araucanos de mujeres', *Revista venezolana de folklore*, iii (1970), 73–104
El traje en Venezuela (Caracas, 1972)
El tamunangue (Barquisimeto, 1976)
with L. F. Ramón y Rivera: *Música indigena y folklórica de Latinoamerica* (in preparation)
Historia de la etnomusicología en America Latina (in preparation)
Articles on South American countries in *Grove 6* incl. 'Argentina', §II, 'Peru', §II, 'Latin America', §I
Further articles in *EM*, *Folklore americano*, *JIFMC*, *Revista musical chilena*, *Revista venezolana de folklore*

WORKS
(selective list)

Ballet: El llamado de la tierra, 1954; Ahónaya, 1958; Movimientos de percusión, 1960; Páramo, 1961
Orch: Puñenas, 1937; 2 acuarelas, str, 1939; Serie criolla, small orch, 1949
Vocal orch: Soneto de la fe en Cristo, S, str, 1956; Simiente (J. Liscano), cantata, narrator, S, Mez, T, B, orch, 1964; Yekuana (Yanoama) (D. Barandiaran), cantata, 8 solo vv, orch, tape, 1972
Chamber: Sonata a 3, vn, va, pf, 1966; Birimbao, timp, tape, 1969
Solo vocal: Primera serie criolla, 1v, pf, 1941; 3 cantos indios, 1v, pf, 1962; 5 fulías, 1v, pf, 1966
Kbd: Segunda serie criolla, pf, 1942; 3 preludios negros, pf, 1954; Sonata 1965, pf, 1965; Suite, hpd, 1967

Principal publishers: Ricordi Americana

BIBLIOGRAPHY
Composers of the Americas, xvii (Washington, DC, 1971), 27
GERARD BÉHAGUE

Arezzo, Guido of. *See* GUIDO OF AREZZO.

Argenta (Maza), Altaulfo (*b* Castro Urdiales, Santander, 19 Nov 1913; *d* Madrid, 21 Jan 1958). Spanish conductor. He studied the piano with distinction at the Madrid Conservatory and proceeded for further study to Belgium and to Germany, where he was a pupil for conducting of Carl Schuricht. He had obtained a conservatory teaching post at Kassel when the outbreak of war in 1939 obliged him to return to Spain, where among other duties he played the piano and celesta with the National Orchestra in Madrid. He made his conducting début with his country's radio orchestra, then in 1945 became conductor of the National Orchestra. He first appeared in Britain as José Iturbi's conductor (with the LSO) at the Harringay Arena, London, in 1948. His early death cut off what promised to be a highly successful career. Some of his recordings with the National Orchestra (including Granados's opera *Goyescas*) and with the Paris Conservatoire Orchestra (including the *Danzas fantásticas* of Turina) remained in the current catalogues into the 1970s.

BIBLIOGRAPHY
A. Fernández-Cid: *Ataulfo Argenta* (Madrid, 1958)
ARTHUR JACOBS

Argentil, Ciarles. *See* CHARLES D'ARGENTILLE.

Argentina. South American federal republic.

I. Art music. II. Folk music.

I. Art music

1. Colonial period. 2. 1800–1930. 3. After 1930.

1. COLONIAL PERIOD. There is little remaining evidence of musical life during this period. As in most Latin American countries the earliest efforts to establish a regular musical life were made by missionaries, especially the Jesuits whose missions covered the Paraná River area and the La Plata region (Paraguay and Argentina). Music was important in the catechization of the Indian population, but the absence of conventual historians and the disappearance of the music archives of the Jesuits (see Lange) restrict any assessment of music-making during the 16th and 17th centuries.

The first reference to an organ in the church of Santiago del Estero dates from 1585; the first school of music was founded by Father Pedro Comental (1595–1665). The music taught was mainly plainchant and polyphonic song, and Indians and Negro slaves soon became skilful musicians and instrument makers: there is documentary evidence of locally made European instruments before 1600. Among the best-known music teachers active in the missions were the Belgian Juan Vasseau, or Vaisseau (1584–1623), the Frenchman Luis Berger (1588–1639) and the Austrian Antonio Sepp (1655–1733). Berger's activities and influence extended to Paraguay and Chile; Sepp made the mission of Yapeyú one of the most flourishing music centres of the area. The repertory of the missions consisted mainly of sacred music, but secular music was not excluded.

The early 18th century was dominated by the presence of the distinguished Italian organist and composer Domenico Zipoli (1688–1726) who arrived in Argentina in 1717. He was assigned to Córdoba, then the country's most important cultural centre. None of his works presumably written in the New World has been found, with the exception of a mass for four voices and continuo, of which the manuscript was copied at Potosí (Bolivia) in 1784. With the expulsion of the Jesuits in 1767 musical activities in the area were much curtailed. Studies in the archives of various churches and convents (Humahuaca, Jujuy, Tucumán, Santiago del Estero, Rioja, Córdoba, Santa Fe, etc) have revealed very few manuscripts of original works.

There was substantial development of theatre pieces with music during the 18th century, partly because almost all official festivities in the viceroyalty required theatrical representations with music. Mission Indians are said to have performed an opera on the occasion of the proclamation of King Fernando VI (1746–7). The repertory of the Teatro de Operas y Comedias, in Buenos Aires (1757–61) consisted mainly of *tonadillas*, a genre currently fashionable in Spain. A regular orchestra (four violins, a bassoon, two oboes and two horns) was maintained at the Teatro de la Ranchería from 1783 to 1792. The Teatro Porteño (later Teatro Argentino), founded in 1804, presented *sainetes, tiranas* and similar forms of lyric theatre; Blas Parera (*d* 1817), composer of the Argentine national anthem, had several of his works performed there.

Buenos Aires became the capital of the Viceroyalty of the La Plata River in 1776, and, thereafter, the most important musical centre, activity being concentrated on the church and opera houses. Of the musicians associated with Buenos Aires Cathedral the *maestro de capilla* José Antonio Picasarri (1769–1843) was influential in the whole musical life of the city.

2. 1800–1930. The predominant forms of 19th-century Argentine music included opera (directly influenced by Italian models, beginning with Rossini and Bellini), *zarzuelas* and other stage genres, piano and salon music and, by the end of the century, symphonic music. Most of the native composers of this period were amateur musicians who had to compete with European professional immigrants, primarily Italians; the most distinguished Argentine composers were Alcorta, Juan Pedro Esnaola (1808–78) and Alberdi. Alcorta's works (piano pieces, solo songs and some church music) reveal the strong influence of Rossini. Esnaola studied at the Paris and Madrid conservatories, and his style was heterogeneous; he wrote church music and orchestral and piano pieces, many based on local dance forms.

A large number of salon pieces and operas appeared, mostly in Buenos Aires, during the latter part of the 19th century, the leading composers being Francisco A. Hargreaves (1849–1900) who had his opera *La Gata Blanca* produced in 1877, and Juan Gutiérrez (1840–1906) who founded the Conservatorio Nacional de Música (1880). Both professional and semi-professional musicians of the next generation had closer connections with European music centres. Opera, operetta, the symphonic poem, ballet and solo song were the preferred genres of such composers as Eduardo García Mansilla (1866–1930), who studied with Rimsky-Korsakov in St Petersburg, and Justino Clérice (1863–1908), who wrote successful comic operas for the Parisian theatres.

Concurrently nationalist feeling was apparent in the works of Alberto Williams, the most prolific and influential composer of his generation, and of Arturo Berutti, who treated Argentine national themes in his operas (*Pampa* and *Yupanki*). Although an academic composer, Williams tried to create a national style in many of his works, such as the album of *Aires de la Pampa* for piano, a stylization of gaucho traditional songs and dances. The champion of the native composer, he founded the Conservatory of Buenos Aires and edited an important anthology of Argentine composers. His immediate followers included Aguirre and Gilardi.

Most of the first half of the 20th century was dominated by the nationalist movement, with notable exceptions. Composers drew on various national folk traditions, and most of the considerable amount of music produced for all media at this time reveals varying degrees of national concern, from the direct use of folk and popular sources to a more subjective assimilation of folk material. Some composers, such as Juan Bautista Massa (1885–1938), active in the city of Rosario, and Carlos López Buchardo, used national sources directly. Ugarte, Ficher, the brothers Juan José, José María and Washington Castro, and Gianneo achieved a more cosmopolitan expression through the adoption of some contemporary European techniques but at the same time maintained a subjective Argentine character.

The inauguration of the Teatro Colón, Buenos Aires (capacity 2487), in 1908, provided a strong incentive for the continuation of opera production. Early 20th-century Argentine opera composers, who found in Italian *verismo* a suitable expression for their nationalist attitude, included Pascual de Rogatis, a student of Williams, Enrique M. Casella (1891–1948), active mainly in Tucumán, Arnaldo D'Espósito (1907–45) and Felipe Boero. Boero's opera *El Matrero* (1929) to a libretto based on the gaucho folk tradition utilizes some folksong themes and an effective *pericón*, a typical gaucho dance.

3. AFTER 1930. During the 1930s the nationalist movement waned. Juan Carlos Paz, a founder of the Grupo Renovación (1929) and the Agrupación Nueva Música (1937), denied musical nationalism any value and favoured expressionism instead; already during the 1930s he became a strong supporter and practitioner of dodecaphonic and serial techniques. Several of his works of the 1950s (e.g. *Continuidad*, 1953) are applications of total serialism. He wrote an important book *Introducción a la música de nuestro tiempo* (1954) which provides insight into Argentine music of the period; his influence as a composer and a theorist in Argentina has been considerable.

The stylistic development of Alberto Ginastera, one of the leading Latin American composers, has been exceptional. His style evolved from an obviously nationalist orientation in the 1930s and 1940s (in such works as *Impresiones de la Puna*, the ballets *Panambi* and *Estancia*, the series of *Pampeanas*) to a neo-classical idiom in the 1950s (Piano Sonata, *Variaciones concertantes*, etc). In the 1960s he turned to a highly personal manipulation of atonal and serial techniques, and developed a meticulous preoccupation with timbres (*Cantata para América mágica*, Piano Concerto, Violin Concerto, the operas *Don Rodrigo, Bomarzo* and *Beatrix Cenci*). In some works such as *Estudios sinfónicos* op.35 (1967) he combined serial and microtonal textures with fixed and aleatory structures. His activity as director of the Centre for Advanced Musical Studies at the Buenos Aires Institute Torcuato di Tella (1962–70) greatly benefited many young Latin American composers.

In opposition to the prevailing nationalist current a number of composers active in the 1940s and 1950s sought an abstract style through neo-classical and post-Webern serialist idioms, for example Roberto García Morillo (*b* 1911) and Roberto Caamaño. In such works by Morillo as *Tres pinturas de Paul Klee* (1943) or Music for Oboe and Chamber Orchestra (1965) there is no trace of nationalist implication. Caamaño, professor of Gregorian chant at the Institute of Sacred Music,

Buenos Aires, has cultivated a dissonant neo-classical style and a serialist style, in both instrumental and sacred choral works.

A group of talented avant-garde musicians, with varied aims and means, appeared during the 1960s. It included Tauriello, Alcides Lanza, Davidovsky (a resident of the USA), Kagel (a resident of Germany, particularly active in electronic and aleatory music), Armando Krieger and Gandini. In works of the 1960s such as *Música III* (1966) for piano and orchestra, Tauriello adhered to several procedures of new music, including electronics, aleatory and sonic collages. For several years he directed the permanent orchestra at the Teatro Colón and he has written two operas, one of which, *Les Guerres picrocholines*, to a libretto based on Rabelais' *Gargantua*, was commissioned for the Fifth Inter-American Music Festival, held in Washington DC in May 1971, though it was not produced then. Lanza has held many fellowships and awards since 1957 (he was Guggenheim fellow, 1965). He became interested in electronic music at the Princeton–Columbia Electronic Music Center, and has also been successful in dealing with contemporary orchestral and vocal techniques. Gandini, also a very accomplished pianist, has employed a post-Webern serialism, microtonalism and aleatory forms. His *Fantasie Impromptu* for piano and orchestra (1971), an 'imaginary portrait of Chopin', is a novel 'study of fragmentation and superimposition' based on Chopin's characteristic stylistic elements. Krieger, who has made a career as a pianist and conductor, has also cultivated a post-Webern serialist style, together with aleatory techniques. All these composers were at various times fellows of the Centre for Advanced Musical Studies in Buenos Aires and many of them have gained an international reputation.

Among the great Latin American capitals Buenos Aires now enjoys a musical life of unique importance by virtue of its many theatres, orchestras and choral associations, and its good educational institutions. In addition frequent contact with visiting foreign composers, musicologists or performers has afforded local musicians a comprehensive view of the contemporary musical world.

See also BUENOS AIRES.

BIBLIOGRAPHY

G. Fúrlong: *Músicos argentinos durante la dominación hispánica* (Buenos Aires, 1945)
A. T. Luper: *The Music of Argentina* (Washington, DC, 1953)
F. C. Lange: 'La música eclesiástica argentina en el período de la dominación hispánica: una investigación', *Revista de estudios musicales*, v (1954), 17–171
——: *La música eclesiástica en Córdoba durante la dominación hispánica* (Córdoba, 1956)
M. G. Acevedo: *La música argentina durante el periodo de la organización nacional* (Buenos Aires, 1961)
V. Gesualdo: *Historia de la música en la Argentina* (Buenos Aires, 1961)
G. Chase: *A Guide to the Music of Latin America* (Washington, DC, 1962)
H. Dianda: *Música en la Argentina de hoy* (Buenos Aires, 1966)
H. Otero: *Música y músicos de Mendoza* (Buenos Aires, 1970)
R. Arizaga: *Enciclopedia de la música argentina* (Buenos Aires, 1971)

II. Folk music

The folk music of Argentina has a rich and varied tradition and is extensively represented in scholarly and popular works. The music of the small indigenous population (about 30.000) can be classified by area: Tierra del Fuego in the extreme south (Yahgan and Alacaluf Indians); Patagonia (Ona, Tehuelche and Araucanian Indians); Chaco (various tribes, some of which are relatively acculturated); the north-west, particularly Jujuy province bordering on Bolivia (Quechua and Aymara), this region also including the more widely diffused Incaic-Hispanic music which extends as far as the Cuyo Provinces of San Juan and San Luis; and the Calchaquí valley (provinces of Tucumán and Salta). There is a rich creole music tradition found with regional variations throughout the country; it remains little affected by foreign commercial music.

1. Sources and collections. 2. Indigenous music. 3. Mestizo and creole music.

1. SOURCES AND COLLECTIONS. The earliest collection of folk music is that of V. R. Lynch, consisting of gaucho music from Buenos Aires province. The first transcriptions of indigenous music are those of Charles Wilkes. Recorded sources date back to 1905, when Lehmann-Nitsche recorded some Tehuelche and Chaco Indians on cylinders, followed in 1907–8 by Fúrlong's recordings among the Fuegians. Not until the 1930s were recordings accompanied by a scientific study: this was carried out by Carlos Vega and, after 1940, by Isabel Aretz and others. Copies of these recordings are in the Instituto Interamericano de Etnomusicología y Folklore (INIDEF), Venezuela. The studies themselves were sponsored by the Instituto Nacional de Musicología, Buenos Aires, which also holds a large sound archive and publishes recordings in collaboration with the Fondo Nacional de las Artes.

2. INDIGENOUS MUSIC. (*i*) *Fuegian and Patagonian music.* The collections made among the Fuegians by Fúrlong in 1907–8 (12 cylinders with 38 items from the Yahgan and the Selk'nam or Ona) and by Martin Gusinde in 1923–4 (44 phonograms, mostly of the Yámana) were deposited in the Museum für Völkerkunde in Berlin and transcribed and studied by Erich von Hornbostel. He wrote that 'The Selk'nam have the characteristic "emphatic" manner of delivery in common with all other Indians – including the Eskimo and certain Northern Asiatic tribes (Palaeoasiatics, Tungus) – while it is lacking in the Yámana and the Halakwulup'. Among these tribes, song is so much a part of magic that 'to sing' and 'to fall in a trance' are expressed by the same word: *yewin*. Fuegian songs are generally simple in structure, consisting of brief motifs repeated with few variations. Sometimes the music ranges over only two notes a tone apart, with emphasis on one for the first half of the stanza and on the other for the second half. The rhythm is constant, with much repetition, and the tempo moderate (ex.1).

Ex.1 *Yámana* song (Hornbostel, 1948)

Jorge Novatti recorded the music of some Ona who survive in Lago Fagnano reservation in Tierra del Fuego (*Folklore musical y música folklórica argentina*, vi, 1966–7). Of the three published songs, as analysed by Ramón y Rivera, the first is notably oscillating in pitch and the other two are tritonic.

Lehmann-Nitsche recorded music of the Tehuelche in 1905 as well as investigating their history and studying the musical bow which they played at that time. Erich Fischer transcribed 51 of these Tehuelche melodies and analysed their scales and range, concluding that the tonal system was 'problematic'. Nevertheless he noted three significant stylistic traits: rhythmic interruption of a single note, as if the musician were striking his mouth; the singing of stressed motifs in falsetto and with imprecise pitches; and the manner of breathing, which is regular and does not bear on the rhythm, and cannot be considered a true pause (p.945). A comparison of recordings made by Escalada in the 1940s of the Tehuelche of Rio Negro and by Aretz in 1941 of the Araucanians of Neuquén shows that the Tehuelche had largely adopted the style and instruments of the Araucanians. But they have probably also retained some of their own traditional melodies, such as the initiation song shown in ex.2. (For further discussion of Fuegian and Patagonian music *see* CHILE, §II.)

Ex.2 Tehuelche song, transcr. L. Ramón y Rivera

(ii) *Araucanian music*. The music of the Araucanians, as recorded in 1941 by Aretz, included songs connected with their principal ceremony, the Nguillatun, an annual collective prayer for health and well-being. The extensive ritual calls for singing at various points. This music shares certain characteristics with the songs which Aretz collected later in Chile, namely: a similar tuning; the free use of different scales; a preference for certain intervals such as falling augmented 4ths (with an intermediate degree: B–A–F), 2nds and 3rds: a great variety of glissandos (simple, double, rising and falling); rapid reiteration or separation of notes by means of breath pulses, mordents and appoggiaturas; dynamic effects including marked stresses, crescendos and decrescendos; and a particular manner of delivery which consists of filling the lungs with air and singing until out of breath, interrupting the phrase at any point to breathe in again. The rhythm may be free or regular, but the melodies always fall into phrases which are repeated, sometimes with notable variations, as in ex.3.

Araucanian instruments at that time included the *trutruka*, a large straight trumpet made from a *coligüe* stem cut lengthwise and hollowed, then threaded together with gut, and with a bell made of horn attached

at one end, and also the *pifülka*, a long whistle carved out of wood, which produced a single note and was blown in alternation with another *pifülka*, sometimes a tone apart, for long periods. Percussion music was provided by the *kultrun*, a drum made from a hollow basin in which pebbles were placed, with a single head secured with horsehair. The *kultrun* could be played by shaking – in which case the pebbles struck the head to produce the sound – but more generally it was struck with a drumstick by the shaman, a woman who stood holding the drum on her left arm, or sat with the drum on the ground before her, in the latter case using two sticks.

Ex.3 Araucanian song, coll. and transcr. I. Aretz (Neuquén, 1941)

(iii) *Chaco Indian music*. Three groups of descendants of the ancient Chaco, each with a different language, survive in Argentina: the Guaycuruan group (including the Pilagá, Toba and Mocoví tribes), hunters and gatherers of wild food inhabiting parts of the Chaco, Formosa or Salta provinces; the Matacoan group (including the Mataco, Chorotí and Chulupí), hunters and incipient cultivators who live mostly in Formosa but also in Salta; and the Tupí-Guaranian group, which includes the Guaraní, Cainguá, Chiriguano and Chané (these last under Arawak domination). They dwell in Salta and (the Cainguá only) in Misiones. These were originally agricultural peoples, who also hunted, fished and gathered wild food, but they are now becoming extinct.

Among the Guaycurú the maraca accompanies dances and songs. Rattles made from pig-hooves, tied in bunches around the wrists and ankles, are worn by young girls during their puberty ceremony. The cane pounding-stick is played by women, who strike it against the ground. Membranophones include the water-drum, made from a tree-trunk or clay pot, with a detachable head so that the water level can be adjusted. Aerophones include the small flute of cane or bone with three finger-holes described by Vega (1946). Novatti (*Folklore musical y música folklórica argentina*, vi, 1966–7) described similar flutes gathered from different tribes: these flutes had rectangular finger-holes placed irregularly regardless of any preconceived acoustical arrangement, which is why the scale produced resembled no known scale. Chordophones include the musical bow and one-string fiddle. The dances, music and texts of the Guaycurú are related to ceremonies of magic, prayer, the learning of sorcery etc. A Toba group was studied in 1909 by Lehmann-Nitsche, and in 1964 Carlos Vega recorded the music of a Chaco group in Resistencia (but Locatelli, in a trip to Resistencia in 1967, found no remaining traces of the music). Instruments included the *mbike* (a one-string fiddle), a product of early acculturation. Singing was characterized by strong, regular rhythm. The various scales – tritonic, tetratonic and pentatonic – included semitones and oscillating pitches. Like some other Chaco Indians, the Pilagá play the *naseré*, a flattened globular flute made from hardwood with two lateral holes: it is used for signalling or for individual recreation. Vega recorded melodies played by a young Macá who could obtain four different pitches from this instrument (ex.4).

Ex.4 Macá Indian instrumental piece (Vega, 1946)

The Mataco, who retain more of their traditional music, use bell rattles, the musical bow and an adopted instrument, the *birimbao* (jew's harp). They sing loudly, solo or in chorus, to accompany various types of dance: propitiatory dances, those that precede coupling and those connected with fertility, health or recreation. Ex.5 shows a Mataco choral song performed by a group of youths.

Ex.5 Mataco choral song, Formosa (Vega, 1946)

Guaraní music includes monotonic propitiatory songs, with rapid portamentos accompanied on the guitar; tritonic songs; and panpipe pieces, probably of Andean origin.

The Chiriguano are known for their *serere* (fipple flute) which is also found among other Chaco Indians: made of a rectangular piece of wood, it produces two pitches which, according to Vega, are approximately a minor 6th apart. They also play the notched flute. The Chané play the flute and have adopted the European violin, as observed by Aretz in 1938.

Locatelli carried out exhaustive research among these Chaco groups in the late 1960s: she collected 526 musical items, including vocal and instrumental solos, accompanied songs and choral pieces, from 26 communities of these groups whom she found in varying stages of acculturation. Her work documents a variety

of instruments including *quenas* (notched flutes), fipple flutes, panpipes, natural trumpets and guitars. Many of these instruments have been introduced in modern times.

(*iv*) *Incaic music*. The Indians who live in the Humahuaca valley and along the Bolivian frontier are often recent immigrants who have come in the annual influx of Bolivian workers hired for the sugar-cane harvest and who are descendants of Quechua and Aymara Indians. There is also an ancient musical tradition of Inca origin in this part of Jujuy province, extending to Santiago del Estero and La Rioja. Its most salient characteristic, the pentatonic scale, is widespread and is sometimes found even in Araucanian music, but the typical Incaic compositional process of weaving together a few brief motifs into a longer phrase (which is repeated at length) is less widely diffused. The melodies are either sung (with verses in Spanish or Quechua) or played on various instruments such as the *quena* or *sicus* (panpipes) which may be accompanied by the drum. The typical genres of this tradition are the *huayno* or *huaynito* dance, as in Bolivia and Peru, the *cacharpari* and the *carnavalito* (see ex.6; for further discussion of Inca music see INCA MUSIC and PERU, §II).

Ex.6 *Carnavalito*, Jujuy province; coll. and transcr. I. Aretz

(*v*) *Calchaquí valley Indian music*. This area in northwestern Argentina is peopled by descendants of the Atacameño, Homahuaca, Calchaquí and Diaguita. The *baguala* is typical of this region; it is also called *joijoi*, *vidala* or *vidalita* and is sometimes confused with creole genres of the same name. The *baguala* is a tritonic song characterized by *kencos* (portamentos and mordents) and sometimes by the use of falsetto (ex.7). The text

Ex.7 *Baguala*, La Rioja, (Aretz, 1967)

Refrain in italics

consists of verses, generally recited before each performance, interrupted at various points by refrains. The singer is accompanied by a *caja* (snare drum; see fig.1) with two heads tied to rattan rings attached to the wooden or tin body. One of the heads may have a snare.

The *baguala* is the typical song of Carnival, which is the most characteristic festival of north-western Argentina and is called *chaya* (*chayar*: to sing or make music at Carnival). Groups of people sing while making their way to the canvas tents where Carnival is celebrated; there they form a circle with much dancing, singing, drinking etc.

Tritonic music is also performed on two wind instruments: the *erkencho*, a clarinet made of horn with an attached reed (see fig.1); and the *erke*, a side-blown trumpet made from a long cane (two metres or more) ending in a bell made of horn or brass. The *erkencho* is generally accompanied by the snare drum. The *erke* may be played during religious feasts, when many *erkeros* may be seen marching and playing together. The *erke* is never played until after Carnival, since it is said to attract frosts.

3. MESTIZO AND CREOLE MUSIC. The creole song repertory is predominantly European in origin; it may be divided into three basic types, differentiated by function: Carnival songs, performed collectively; entertainment songs, performed by one or two singers for an audience; and songs forming part of popular religious ceremonies, performed solo or in chorus, or sometimes by a *rezandero* (chanter). Each of these categories includes various genres of song which in turn are subject to local variations. Dances, however, may take place on any occasion and in any place, but especially in the north-west during Carnival in the canvas tents or *carpas*. Mestizo music of Jujuy province, along the Bolivian border, shows a strong Inca influence, particularly in its use of the pentatonic scale and certain pre-Columbian instruments. These include the *quena*, accompanied by the *charango*, a small guitar of post-Conquest origin with five double strings (tuned as shown in ex.8), and a resonator made from a *tatu* or *quirquincho* (armadillo) shell. The *charango* may be plucked or strummed (*rasgueado*). The typical mestizo song form is the *yaraví* or *triste*, and the characteristic dance is the *bailecito*, of Bolivian origin.

Ex.8 *Charango* tuning.

The most characteristic types of Carnival song are the *vidala* (especially in Santiago del Estero and Tucumán) and the *vidalita* (once practised from San Juan to Catamarca). The *vidalita* is the more varied of the two in scale, and may be sung with or without doubling in parallel 3rds and in duple or triple time. This music uses the portamentos and mordents and some other characteristics of the *baguala*, and is accompanied on the snare drum. *Vidalas* are accompanied by drums and guitars, the latter providing harmonies centring on a major key and its relative minor, invariably cadencing in the minor. When the key is major, the fourth degree is generally sharpened in the upper voice of a duo singing in parallel 3rds. The phrases are generally short and the stanzaic texts include refrains,

1. Erkencho player accompanying himself on the caja (snare drum)

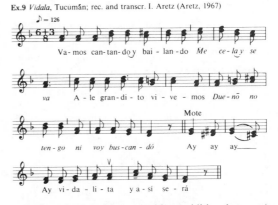

Ex.9 *Vidala*, Tucumán; rec. and transcr. I. Aretz (Aretz, 1967)

sometimes separated by *motes* (short additional stanzas) as in ex.9. Also in Santiago del Estero and Tucumán may be found certain related dances such as the *chacarera*, *zamba* and *gato*, the last being one of the most important rural Argentinian dances. In modern practice these dances are accompanied on the accordion and *bombo* (large drum; see fig.2), but originally they were played on the violin and, when at home, on the *arpa rústica* (harp without pedals), sometimes with strummed guitar accompaniment. Their musical affinity (as shown in ex.10) and their resemblance to the *vidalas* led Vega (1944) to group all these dances in a single category, which he called the *cancionero ternario colonial*.

In gatherings other than Carnival, *estilos* and *tonadas* are sung. The *estilo*, found throughout the country, derives from the Peruvian *triste*: the text is in *décima* form (stanzas of ten octosyllabic lines), the melodies often fluctuating between major and minor modes. Per-

Ex.10

(a) *Chacarera*

Cha-ca-re-ra me has pe-di-do__ To-ca-ré lo que yo pue-da__ sal-gan man-cos

(b) *Gato* from La Rioja

Del ar-bol de l'au-sen-cia trai-go un ga-ji-to

formance is free in expression, sometimes includes singing in parallel 3rds, and is accompanied on the guitar. Its structure is ternary: the first part is slow and in duple time; the second lively in triple time, announced by a *zamba* accompaniment which begins on the last note of the slow section; the last part is a repeat of the first section. The *tonada* resembles the *estilo* in text and music, although it generally remains in the major mode; if it does move into the minor mode the final cadence nevertheless returns to the major, as in ex.11.

The *cueca* – a dance which, like the *zamba*, derives from the *zambacueca* or *zamacueca* – is found in the Cuyo provinces (western Argentina) and in Chile. The *cueca* is more lively and varied in rhythm than the *zamba*; it is sung to guitar accompaniment, generally in a major key (ex.12). Intermediate between the *cueca* and *zamba* are the *chilena* and the *cueca del altiplano* (highland *cueca*), the latter showing Peruvian Indian influence.

The dying art of *payada* singing, an improvisatory contest between two or more poet-musicians, uses the genres *cifra* and *milonga*. The *cifra* (named after Spanish guitar tablature) generally consists of seven musical phrases which are repeated to a text of four, eight or ten octosyllabic lines. *Cifras* are always in a major key and duple time, and the range varies (an 11th, octave or 5th). Some phrases are freely recited, others are more melodic as in the *estilo*, with a preference for

descending scales. The guitar prelude is strummed forcefully, as are some interludes (others make use of arpeggiated chords). The guitar may sometimes play with the melody and some cadential phrases are marked by a tremolo. The sung *milonga* (the *milonga* dance-song is another type of later origin) may be in a major or minor key or may fluctuate between the two. The text may be a *romance* (traditional ballad) or, more often, a

Ex.11 *Tonada*, San Juan (Aretz, 1954)

Ex.12 *Cueca*, Catamarca; coll. and transcr. I. Aretz

De tus her-mo-sos o-jos no-ten-go que-ja e-llos quie-ren mi-rar__ me__ tu no los de-jas

Repeated with variations to strummed guitar accompaniment.

2. *Bombo (bass drum) and accordion players, La Rioja*

Ex.13 from *milonga*, La Rioja (Aretz, 1954)

Ex.14 *Padre Nuestro*, Tucúman (Aretz, 1946)

corrido (ballad, usually based on contemporary events). The rhythm is in duple time and based on short two-bar phrases, as shown in ex.13. The guitarist usually maintains this duple time but sometimes moves into 6/8 time to create a cross-rhythm against the melody.

Competitive alternation between solo dancers to guitar accompaniment is a feature of a genre called *malambo*, which was formerly popular among the gauchos. Other types of creole song accompanied by the guitar include romantic songs such as serenades and habaneras with texts by Colombian or Central American poets. The Argentinian TANGO derives from the habanera and *milonga*. It is not a true folk genre but an urban style developed primarily in Buenos Aires by known composers, and recreated by rural folk musicians. It is characteristically accompanied on the accordion, although a modern trend is the use of the *bandoneón* (large concertina).

Music in the littoral provinces resembles that of Paraguay and is therefore often described as 'Guaraní music' (although the only Guaraní element retained is the language, which is mixed with Spanish in texts of a romantic nature). The performers sing and play the guitar in triple time or sing in duplets over a strummed accompaniment in 6/8 time, with much syncopation. The various forms, such as the *polca*, the more modern *chamamé* and the *galopa*, may also be danced. Among modern popular songs the *guarania*, also performed in Paraguay, may become a permanent part of the folk repertory. (For further description of the *guarania*, *see* PARAGUAY.)

Among songs of direct Spanish descent are those which accompany domestic religious ceremonies such as the praise of saints, souls, angels or the child Jesus. This category also includes villancicos (carols), some of which are similar to the Argentine *arrullo* or lullaby, sung prayers such as the *Padre nuestro*, *Humilde*, or *Gloria*, saetas for Holy Week, *trisagios*, *rogativas*, and the special song for the *Niño Alcalde de la Rioja*, known as *Año nuevo pacari*. The music of these songs is of three types: in the first the melody is syllabic and measured, and the rhythm, whether binary or ternary, is simple; in the second the melodies are in free rhythm; and in the third the melodies are unmeasured and melismatic, as in ex.14.

Processionals for saints, in which heavy figures of saints are carried through the countryside, are accompanied by flutes (of bone or bamboo) and drum. Sometimes violins are also used, as well as *erkes* (in Jujuy) and the accordion (in central Argentina). The processional tune is sometimes a *polquita* (little polka)

in European diatonic melodies, but some pentatonic (or even, in the extreme north, tritonic) pieces may also be found sharing various characteristics with other pentatonic genres.

Children's play songs are frequently of European origin, as can be seen from the names of some popular examples of this repertory: *Arroz con leche*, *Hilito de oro*, *Hilito de plata*, *La farolera*, *Aserrín aserrán*, *Mambrú se fue a la guerra*, *Sobre el puente de Aviñón* and *La torre en guardia*.

BIBLIOGRAPHY

C. Wilkes: *Narrative of the United States Exploring Expedition During the Years 1838, 1839, 1840, 1841, 1842*, i (Philadelphia, 1845), 125f

V. R. Lynch: *Cancionero bonaerense* (Buenos Aires, 1883/*R*1925)

E. Fischer: 'Patagonische Musik', *Anthropos*, iii (1908), 941

R. Lehmann-Nitsche: 'Patagonische Gesänge und Musikbogen', *Anthropos*, iii (1908), 916

M. Gusinde: *Die Selk'nam*, i: *Die Feuerland-Indianer* (Mödling, 1931)

C. Vega: *Danzas y canciones argentinas* (Buenos Aires, 1936)

M. Gusinde: *Die Yamana*, ii: *Die Feuerland-Indianer* (Mödling, 1937)

——: *Anthropologie der Feuerland-Indianer*, iii: *Die Feuerland-Indianer* (Mödling, 1939)

C. Vega: *Panorama de la música popular argentina* (Buenos Aires, 1944)

I. Aretz: *Música tradicional argentina: Tucumán historia y folklore* (Buenos Aires, 1946)

C. Vega: *Los instrumentos aborigenes y criollos de la Argentina* (Buenos Aires, 1946)

E. M. von Hornbostel: 'The Music of the Fuegians', *Ethnos*, xiii (Stockholm, 1948), 61–102

E. Palavecino: 'Areas y capas culturales en el territorio argentino', *Gaea*, viii (1948), 447–523

I. Aretz: *El folklore musical argentino* (Buenos Aires, 1952)

——: *Costumbres tradicionales argentinas* (Buenos Aires, 1954)

J. H. Steward, ed.: *Handbook of South American Indians* (New York, 1963)

Folklore musical y música folklórica argentina, ed. Fondo Nacional de las Artes (Buenos Aires, 1966–7) [with 6 discs, 9F 3000–3005]

I. Aretz: *Música tradicional argentina: La Rioja* (diss., Catholic U., Buenos Aires, 1967)

B. C. Jacovella: 'Las canciones folklóricas de la Argentina', Instituto Nacional de Musicología SADAIC (Buenos Aires, 1969) [disc notes]

C. Alvarez and M. E. Grebe: 'La trifonía atacameña y sus perspectivas interculturales', *Revista musical chilena* (1974), nos.126–7, p.21

M. E. Grebe: 'Presencia del dualismo en la cultura y música mapuche', *Revista musical chilena* (1974), nos.126–7, p.47

——: 'La música alacalufe: aculturación y cambio estilístico', *Revista musical chilena* (1974), nos.126–7, p.80

C. Munizaga A.: 'Atacameños, araucanos y alacalufes: breve reseña de tres grupos étnicos chilenos', *Revista musical chilena* (1974), nos.126–7, p.7

GERARD BÉHAGUE (I), ISABEL ARETZ (II)

Argentina, L'. *See* FILIPPINI, STEFANO.

Argento, Dominick (*b* York, Penn., 27 Oct 1927). American composer. He studied at the Peabody Conservatory and at the Eastman School (PhD 1957), his principal teachers being Rogers and Hovhaness; private study with Weisgall directed his work to the theatre. A founder of the Minnesota Opera, he wrote two chamber operas for that company: *The Masque of Angels* (written for its début in 1964) and *Postcard from Morocco*. In 1959 he was appointed professor of composition at the University of Minnesota. He was awarded the Pulitzer Prize in 1975.

WORKS
(selective list)

Operas: The Boor, 1957; Colonel Jonathan the Saint, 1961; Christopher Sly, 1963; The Masque of Angels, 1964; Shoemakers' Holiday, 1967; Postcard from Morocco, 1971; A Waterbird Talk, 1974; The Voyage of Edgar Allan Poe, 1974–6
Other stage works: The Resurrection of Don Juan, ballet, 1955; Royal Invitation, ballet, 1964; Volpone, incidental music, 1964; The House of Atreus, incidental music, 1968
Choral: Revelations of St John the Divine, 1966; Jonathan and the Whale, 1973
Orch: The Mask of Night (Variations), 1965; Bravo Mozart, 1967; A Ring of Time, 1972
Solo vocal: 6 Elizabethan Songs, 1v, pf, 1958; Letters from Composers, T, gui, 1968; To be Sung upon the Water, T, cl, pf, 1972; From the Diary of Virginia Woolf, 1v, pf, 1974

Principal publisher: Boosey & Hawkes

MARY ANN FELDMAN

Argerich, Martha (*b* Buenos Aires, 5 June 1941). Argentinian pianist. She made her début in 1946 and gave recitals in Buenos Aires at the Astral (1949) and the Colón (1952). She has had many teachers, including Scaramuzza in Argentina, and, after her arrival in Europe in 1955, Friedrich Gulda, Nikita Magaloff and Michelangeli. In her 16th year she won the International Music Competition (Geneva) and the Busoni Competition (Bolzano). Before her London début in November 1964 she had toured western Europe and Poland, where she was to achieve great success, in March 1965, as winner of the Seventh Warsaw International Chopin Competition and the Polish Radio Prize for Chopin mazurkas and waltzes. Her technical skills, not always used with emotional discipline, are among the most formidable of her generation; at its best – in the more demanding works of Chopin, Liszt, Bartók and Prokofiev – her playing is notable for its uninhibited brilliance.

MAX LOPPERT

Arghūl. Double clarinet with a cylindrical bore, composed of melody pipe and drone pipe each with single-beating reeds; the drone is much longer than the melody pipe (*see* EGYPT, fig.9). The *arghūl* belongs to the family of idioglott clarinets, which includes the *zummāra*, *çifte* (Turkey), *launeddas* (Sardinia) etc; its similarity to the double *aulos* of ancient Greece suggests a pre-Christian origin. Etymologically the term *arghūl* is a metaplasm of *urgun*, the Arabic word frequently used to describe the organ. Villoteau (p.967) mentioned three different sizes of *arghūl*: the 'arghoul el-kebyr' (big), 'arghoul el-soghayr' (medium) and 'arghoul el-asghar' (small). Elsner listed a variety of names applied to various types of *arghūl* (without reference to relative size) including 'el-arġūl el-kebīr, el-arġūl el-ṣoġair, arġūl ġāb (ġāb means pipe, reed-pipe), ġāb, sibs ġāb, sibs, and miz-mār muzdawaġ (mizmār is a general term for wind instrument, muzdawaġ means double, in pairs)'.

The big *arghūl* is made in nine parts, each having a name, which may vary from region to region. It consists of a pair of mouthpieces which include the up-cut reeds; two short sections called *luqma* ('mouthful') as these

first four parts of the instrument are all played from inside the player's mouth; the melody pipe; and the principal drone pipe and its three extensions. Elsner gave a detailed description of the proportions for the big *arghūl*, which are traditionally measured in basic body units (fist, finger breadth etc). In the instrument he described, the entire melody pipe was 76·6 cm long and the entire drone pipe was 239·7 cm long. The *arghūl* is made from bamboo or some other suitable material and the two parts are bound together with string and tar or wax. The detachable sections of the drone are usually linked by lengths of cord to prevent them being lost.

The melody pipe is usually bored with five or six finger-holes, producing a diatonic scale. Either simple or cross fingering can be used when playing the instrument and by partially covering ('shading') the stops a wide range of pitches can be produced. The drone can be changed by varying the number of lengthening pieces; usually only three drone notes are used – that is, only the last two lengthening pieces are removed. Circular breathing is used.

The contemporary *arghūl* is essentially an Egyptian folk instrument and is used by a variety of people including Nile boatmen, shepherds and professional folk musicians. It is used to accompany folksongs, ballads and popular *mawwāl* songs, and can be heard at weddings, dances and other social gatherings.

BIBLIOGRAPHY
M. Villoteau: 'D'une espèce de flûte champêtre appelée en arabe arghoul', *Description de l'Egypte: état moderne*, ed. E. F. Jomard, I/i (Paris, 1809), 962ff
E. W. Lane: *Modern Egyptians* (London, 1860), 244, 367
J. Elsner: 'Remarks on the Big Arġūl', *YIFMC*, i (1969), 234
J. Jenkins and P. Rovsing Olsen: *Music and Musical Instruments in the World of Islam* (London, 1976), 58
WILLIAM J. CONNER, MILFIE HOWELL

Argilliano, Ruggiero [Roggerio] (*b* Castelnuovo di Garfagnana; *fl* 1612). Italian music editor and composer. He edited *Responsoria Hebdomadae Sanctae, psalmi, Benedictus, et Miserere, una cum missa ac vesperis Sabbati Sancti*, for eight voices and continuo (Venice, 1612; *RISM* 1612²). It includes pieces by 20 composers, among them Croce and Viadana, and two are anonymous; Argilliano himself, with 11 pieces, is the best-represented composer.

Argyll Rooms. London concert rooms; *see* LONDON, §VI, 5(iii).

Argyropoulos, Isaac (*fl* Florence, late 15th century). Italian organist and organ builder, probably a pupil of Antonio Squarcialupi; he has sometimes been confused with HEINRICH ISAAC.

Århus (Old Dan. Aarhus). Second-largest city in Denmark (population 245,000 in 1973). Early musical life revolved around the cathedral and its school. The most significant musical figure in the early history of the Århus Cathedral was the cantor Morten Börup (*c*1500). An important personality active there from 1760 to 1789 was the cantor H. E. Grossmann (1732–1811), whose cantatas are in the city library.

The growth of the middle classes in the 19th century brought with it a flowering of amateur-orientated secular music. From the 1830s singing groups and choirs have played a meaningful part in the city's musical life; the Århus Sangforening, founded in 1843, has remained active. Other groups include Århus

Byorkesters Koncertkor, Århus Studentersangere, Århus Studiekor, Da Camera, Jysk Akademisk Kor, Musikstuderendes Kammerkor and a number of choirs attached to particular societies and organizations. The Århus Musikforening, established in 1843, was for many years a dominant music society in the city. From its foundation in 1919 the Århus Philharmoniske Selskab has sponsored a series of orchestral concerts and solo recitals; the Århus Unge Tonekunstnere has given particular support to contemporary music. Jazz and rock concerts are sponsored privately.

The city's role in the musical life of the country has grown constantly from 1925 with the establishment of a resident orchestra, regular performances of opera, the founding of a conservatory and a programme of musicological study at the university. The Århus Byorkester was established in 1935 as the city's resident orchestra, giving regular concerts as well as serving as the opera orchestra. It was conducted from 1935 to 1957 by Thomas Jensen. Among the many amateur orchestras are Århus Privatorkester, Jysk Akademisk Orkester and Tonika.

The Jyske Opera, founded in 1947, performs two or three works each year, and tours to other cities. The Århus Theater performs operettas and musicals in addition to plays, and the opera group of the conservatory performs smaller operatic works. The Jutland Conservatory, founded in 1927 and later becoming a state institution, trains both performers and teachers; the Århus Folkemusikskole is also a strong force in local music education. A professorship in musicology was created at the university in 1946, and until 1957 was held by Knud Jeppesen.

The State Library in Århus, established in 1902, has a music collection of about 50,000 volumes, including rare 18th- and 19th-century prints and 18th-century copies of Telemann cantatas. The library's printed catalogue contains the most extensive list of works by Danish composers.

An annual festival, the Århus Festuge, has been held each September from 1965; it organizes a wide range of musical presentations and has enjoyed broad popularity.

JENS PETER JACOBSEN

Aria (It.: 'air'). A term normally signifying any closed lyrical piece for solo voice (exceptionally for more than one voice), either independent or forming part of an opera, oratorio, cantata or other large work. Strictly, its Italian sense may be rendered as 'style, manner or course', as of a melody. In Italian vocal music of the 16th and 17th centuries it was a closed form, usually strophic, for one or more voices, with or without instrumental accompaniment. In instrumental music 'aria' implies a subject suitable for variations, or a piece of light dance music, usually in duple time. See AIR and SONG.

1. Derivation and use to the early 17th century. 2. 17th-century vocal music. 3. Instrumental music. 4. 18th century. 5. 19th and 20th centuries.

1. DERIVATION AND USE TO THE EARLY 17TH CENTURY. The collateral forms *aer*, *aere* are derived directly from the Latin *aer* (accusative *aera*), 'air, atmosphere', which is a simple transliteration of the Greek. The expressions 'aere italico', 'aere gallico' used by an anonymous 14th-century Italian theorist (see Cesare) are probably equivalent to Marchetto da Padova's 'modus gallicus' and 'modus italicus', and thus imply 'way' or 'manner'.

A similar relationship between 'aiere' and 'maniera' occurs in the 15th-century dance treatises of Guglielmo Ebreo da Pesaro and Antonio Cornazano, and much the same thing is implied by a statement of Nicolò Sagudino (early 16th century) to the effect that certain English organists 'non eseguiscono la musica con troppo bono aiere'.

In the late 15th century Duke Sforza's chancellor proposed to ask for the music of two or three of the canzoni of the poet Leonardo Giustiniani, 'per intendere l'aere veneziano' ('in order to hear the Venetian type of melody'); a letter dated 1460 from a certain Nicolò Tedesco in Ferrara to the Marquis of Mantua recommended Giovanni Brith as singing master for his ability 'in cantare moderno massime arie alla veneziana' ('at singing in the modern way, and particularly Venetian-type songs'). Here 'aere' and 'aria' mean 'tune', but they also imply a strophic song or scheme for singing strophic poetry. In particular, 'aria veneziana' referred to the *giustiniana* and like forms (see Rubsamen). The sense of scheme or formula for poems of a given form applies to several pieces in the fourth book of Petrucci's collection of frottolas (*RISM* 1505⁵), which has the title *Strambotti, ode, frottole sonetti, et modo de cantar versi latini e capituli*. No.62 in this collection is a textless piece by Antonio Caprioli entitled 'Aer de versi latini' (in the index 'Aer de cantar versi latini'). Similarly no.91, an anonymous piece with words, is an 'Aer de Capituli' and no.19, 'Modo de cantar sonetti', has an analogous meaning. Baldassare Castiglione (*Il libro del cortegiano*, 1528) preferred singing to the viol because thus 'si nota e intende il bel modo e l'aria'.

By the 1530s 'aria' was commonly used to describe simple settings of light strophic poetry in such terms as 'aria napoletana' (*see* VILLANELLA); in a related vein, it was probably the homophonic melody-dominated character of certain madrigals printed in collections from 1555 onwards that earned them the name *madrigale arioso* (*see* MADRIGAL). Arias as melodies or schemes for singing fixed poetic types were printed throughout much of the 16th century in instrumental as well as vocal publications. Antonio di Becchi's *Libro primo d'intabulatura da leuto* (1568), G. C. Barbetta's *Intavolatura di liuto* (1585) and Marco Facoli's *Il secondo libro d'intavolatura di balli d'arpicordo* (1588) all contain arias meant as accompaniments to the singing of *terza rima* (*capitoli*) and other verse forms. They are mostly in triple metre and consist of two, three or four eight-bar phrases followed by a pair of cadential four-bar phrases, occasionally more highly figured, often marked 'riprese' and clearly meant as a ritornello between stanzas. Barbetta and Facoli applied the forms 'aere' and 'aria' to the same pieces, making their equivalence quite clear. 'Aere' is used in much the same sense as in Petrucci in the vocal collection *Aeri racolti ... dove si cantano sonetti stanze e terze rime* (*RISM* 1577⁸); and Galilei, in his unpublished essay *Dubbi intorno a quanto io ho detto dell'uso enharmonio* (1591), spoke of 'l'aria comune della terza rima'.

This use of 'aria' continued well into the 17th century. The most familiar of these melodic formulae or bass patterns, designed as settings for privileged poetic forms, were the *aria di Ruggiero* and the *aria di romanesca*, nearly always associated with the ottava (see Einstein, 1911–12). The former is found in this context as early as Galilei's *Libro d'intavolatura di liuto* (MS, 1584); other examples occur in Nicolò Borboni's

Musicali concenti (1618), Rafaello Rontani's *Le varie musiche* (six books, 1614–22) and, most prolifically, Antonio Cifra's *Li diversi scherzi* (five books, 1613–17). Kapsberger's *Libro secondo d'arie* (1623) includes an 'aria da cantar ottave'.

The 'arie della battaglia' of Andrea Gabrieli and Annibale Padovano (*Dialoghi musicali*, RISM 1590[11]) are probably so called because they are paraphrases of an existing model or groundplan; whereas 'manner' or 'style' is the key to such pieces as M. A. Ingegneri's 'arie di canzon francese per sonar' (*Il secondo libro de madrigali, . . . a quattro voci*, 1579), Viadana's 'aria di canzon francese' (*Canzonette . . . libro primo*, 1590) and Banchieri's 'sonata in aria francese' (*L'organo suonarino*, 1605). Something of the same sort was doubtless intended by the title of Montesardo's vocal collection *I lieti giorni di Napoli: concertini italiani in aria spagnuola* (1611).

From the last quarter of the 16th century, 'aria' is found in close association with the (at least in origin) poetically more specific term 'canzonetta', in strophic pieces mostly for three and four voices (e.g. Vecchi, *Selva di varia ricreatione*, 1590; Bargnani, *Canzonette, arie et madrigali*, 1599).

2. 17TH-CENTURY VOCAL MUSIC. Although around 1600 the term did not have a strong connotation of music for solo voice, 'aria' played a leading role in the early development of monody. Settings of such poetic forms as strophic quatrains (particularly in prologues), ottavas and *capitoli* abound in opera from Peri's and Corsi's setting of *Dafne* (Ottavio Rinuccini, *c*1594) onwards (see Porter). 'Possente spirto' from Monteverdi's *Orfeo* (Alessandro Striggio (ii); 1607) is a particularly elaborate example of an 'aria per cantar terza rima', though not so indicated.

The arias in Giulio Caccini's *Le nuove musiche* (1601/2), which also includes non-strophic madrigals, are characteristic in range and type for the first two decades of the 17th century. Caccini called these pieces 'canzonette à aria', suggesting a relationship between poetic and musical form. The poems, which are all strophic and set for solo voice with continuo accompaniment, reflect the metrical variety sought by Italian poets from the 1580s on and most notably by GABRIELLO CHIABRERA, whom Caccini acknowledged in his preface. The arias whose verse remains closest to the mainstream of tradition by using lines of seven and 11 syllables, are irregular in melodic and harmonic rhythm, have considerable ornamentation and differ from the madrigals only in that they have a strophic form. The verse types, such as lines of five or eight syllables, that most sharply depart from classical norms provoke the simplest tunes, the greatest regularity of rhythm and even, in some cases, triple metre.

One canzonetta is set without musical repetition, several are strophic variations in which the bass is substantially the same for each stanza (this kind of piece is closest to the tradition that includes the *aria di romanesca*) and the rest are simply strophic. The last piece is in effect an 'aria per capitoli sdruccioli' (a *verso sdrucciolo* is a line with antepenultimate accent) from *Il rapimento di Cefalo* (Chiabrera; 1600). Caccini's second book, *Nuove musiche e nuova maniera di scriverle* (1614), contains a larger proportion of straight strophic settings of five- and eight-syllable lines in triple metre. Such pieces are at least not inconsistent with

Praetorius's definition (*Syntagma musicum*, iii, 1618) of 'Aria vel Air' as 'eine hübsche Weise oder Melodey, welche einer aus seinem eignen Kopffe also singet' ('a pretty tune or melody which one sings by heart').

In general the only distinction between monodic madrigal and solo aria in the early 17th century is in the matter of repetitive – usually strophic – poetic form. A similar distinction between 'cantata' and 'aria' is apparent in the *Cantade et arie a voce sola* (four books, 1620–29) of Alessandro Grandi (i) and perhaps those of G. F. Sances (1633, 1636). Exceptionally, 'aria' is used in a more inclusive way, as in Kapsberger's *Libro primo di arie passeggiate* (1612). Frescobaldi, too, used the term in a general sense in the title of his *Primo libro d'arie musicali* (1630), since the collection includes pieces of other kinds; but in fact only the strophic songs for solo voice are called 'aria' in the body of the work. Sometimes settings of specific forms such as *sonetti*, ottavas and *capitoli* are set apart from arias, as in Borboni's *Musicali concenti*, the collection *Vezzosetti fiori* (1622[11]) and as late as Domenico Mazzocchi's *Musiche sacre, e morali* (1640).

Strophic variations are common throughout the first half of the 17th century, both in opera to early Cavalli and in printed books such as Vittori's *Arie a voce sola* (1649). Most are in recitative style, but some use more regular rhythms. These include pieces – often laments (*see* LAMENTO) – built on ostinatos, particularly frequent in the 1630s and 1640s; the practice may well have been borrowed from instrumental music. Monteverdi included two strophic arias with variations in his *Scherzi musicali, cioè aria, & madrigali in stil recitativo* (1632); both are in a regular metre, and one of them, *Chiome d'oro*, has an instrumental ritornello, which is also a strophic variation, before each verse.

Occasionally a series of strophes is distributed over two or more musical units, as in Fasolo's *Il carro di Madama Lucia* (1628); many ensemble finales to acts of operas, from Landi's *La morte d'Orfeo* (1619) to Vittori's *La Galatea* (1639), are constructed in this way. There is a specially curious instance, actually marked 'aria', sung by Amor towards the end of Act 2 of Monteverdi's *L'incoronazione di Poppea* (Busenello; 1642). There are four verses, separated by the same ritornello. The first and the fourth have the same music, although in different notation; the second and the third, though not identical, are closely allied. If one accepts the ritornello as part of the structure the form is *ACBCB'CA*. Variation forms, including those built on ostinatos, except for modulating ones, are rare after 1650.

'Recitative' and 'aria' are not musically exclusive terms in the early 17th century: the former refers to style, whereas the most reliable implication of the latter is a formal one: thus the designation 'aria recitativa di sei parti' (six-strophed aria in recitative style) in Mazzocchi's opera *La catena d'Adone* (1626), which also continues to indicate strophic ensemble pieces as arias. In this work Mazzocchi introduced the term 'mezz' aria' to refer to passages having the lyrical character expected of an aria but lacking its strophic form (for a slightly different view, see Reiner); in that category are probably the several non-strophic pieces, without ritornellos, for solo voice (called 'aria' in the score), mostly using a walking bass. Recitative intrusions into more regular movement occur in Cavalli's earlier operas, but went out of fashion in the early 1650s, as did recitative arias generally. The opposite phenomenon, a lyrical moment (arioso) in the setting of poetry meant for recitative, remained an essential ingredient of Italian opera throughout the 17th century.

In Venetian operas before 1660 (most surviving works are by Cavalli) the majority of arias are in triple time or a mixture of triple and duple; the same pattern occurs in many aria books from Pesenti's *Arie a voce sola* (1636) to P. P. Sabbatini's *Ariette spirituali* (1657) and in Michelangelo Rossi's opera *Erminia sul Giordano* (1637). Before 1630, however, duple time often held its own (Domenico Crivellati, *Cantate diverse*, and Orazio Tarditi, *Amorosa schiera*, both 1628). Many early arias have four or five strophes, or even more; after 1650, in opera at least, two rapidly became the standard number.

Most 17th-century opera arias have continuo accompaniment to the vocal line and ritornellos for three to five parts between the strophes. In this respect they differ from those of printed books, which mainly have no ritornello at all, a prescription for one (e.g. the 'riprese di ciaccona' of Crivellati's *Cantate diverse*) or a ritornello for continuo only. This difference is probably more apparent than real, since many manuscript collections of opera arias from late in the century give only the bass part or leave out altogether the ritornellos found in the full scores.

Arie concertate, those pieces in which an instrumental ensemble intervenes between vocal phrases within a strophe or accompanies the voice, first penetrated opera to any extent in the 1640s; early Cavalli works offer several examples. Although their number grows during the second half of the century, they remain a minority until the age of Metastasian *opera seria*. Their accompaniment nearly always consists of string orchestra and continuo, just as for ritornellos. The only wind instrument to gain currency before 1690 (except in such isolated court extravaganzas as Cesti's *Il pomo d'oro*, Vienna, 1667) was the trumpet, used in dialogue with the voice from about 1670, apparently first in Venice and Bologna. The texts of trumpet arias express bellicose sentiments, and the voice imitates the instrument's characteristic figures.

Although aria strophes exhibit great variety of form, the same procedure of composition underlies most of them: the text is set line by line, by and large syllabically despite isolated flourishes, and often with modest repetition of single words or phrases; the end of each line – or sometimes couplet – is marked by a cadence, with or without a rhythmic hiatus. Two formal schemes, each corresponding to a distinct poetic type, account for the bulk of arias in the later 17th century. In the so-called *ABB* (better *ABB'*) aria, the last line or group of lines is rendered twice to similar music, having a cadence on the tonic only the second time; the repeat may involve anything from simple transposition to complete reworking of material. The form at its most complete consists of two strophes and ritornellos, for example, *ABB'–R–ABB'–R*; some arias, however, have only a single strophe. The two poetic strophes often have parallel or identical final lines, with an epigrammatic or emphatic quality that justifies their musical repetition. In the other type of aria the first line or couplet is repeated as a refrain at the end of the same strophe; the music for the repeated text is often varied in pieces of the 1650s and 1660s (*ABA'*) but comes increasingly to be a literal restatement of the opening (*ABA*; or, giving the complete form, *ABA–R–ABA–R*). This is the source of the da capo aria.

An extension of the possibilities of prosody continued throughout the period 1640–80, yielding line lengths of nine, ten and 12 syllables and a range of internal rhythms, of which the anapest was particularly favoured. The object of this extension was to inspire variety of musical rhythm, just as Caccini had sought inspiration in the poetic licence of Chiabrera. The generation of P. A. Ziani, Antonio Sartorio, Legrenzi and Carlo Pallavicino had to hand poetry of this sort, which moreover often changed pattern in mid-strophe – a procedure not unknown to the early 17th century, but less assiduously applied. These changes usually produced a corresponding change of musical metre. In general the range of figure and type of movement greatly expanded during these years.

Most arias even of the later 17th century are short and simple, commensurate with their number (30 to 50 per opera is a fair average). Many have rhythmic patterns in which some writers have seen a relationship to contemporary dance music (see Wolff), but it remains uncertain to what extent the resemblance is a by-product of regular text accent in a syllabic setting. Perhaps the clearest evidence of a connection is in G. L. Gregori's *Arie in stil francese* (1698), which includes titled examples of vocal galliards, minuets and bourrées.

Passage-work, often associated with a conventionally placed text image, waxed during the 1670s. The aria with motto opening, or DEVISENARIE, in which a brief vocal proclamation is repeated by the accompaniment, then taken up again by the voice and given its continuation, came into vogue; a parallel development is the 'tag' ending, or repeated final short phrase. The works of Legrenzi and his contemporaries afford numerous examples of these, and of bass lines built on a single melodic or rhythmic idea, or on a modulating ostinato. The sections of many arias are marked off, as if for repetition.

By 1680 the da capo aria had gained a dominant position, though its dimensions remained small into the early 18th century. The trend seems first to have taken hold in Venice, still the principal market-place of opera. It certainly does not have the connection with Alessandro Scarlatti that many writers, mainly out of a limited knowledge of the repertory, have suggested. With the establishment of the hegemony of the da capo, and in any case by 1690, the second strophe disappeared.

The cantata, earlier used as a term of contrast to 'aria', in the second half of the 17th century includes arias among its components. Their form and style obey the laws of contemporary opera: thus the majority of labelled arias in G. B. Mazzaferrata's *Il primo libro delle cantate da camera* (1677) and Antonio del Ricco's *Urania armonica* (1686) are strophic pieces in a variety of forms, while G. B. Bassani's *Languidezze amorose* (1698) has mostly da capo arias of a single 'strophe'.

3. INSTRUMENTAL MUSIC. The use of 'aria' as a subject for variation in instrumental music has a history nearly coinciding with that of the vocal strophic variation. Antonio Brunelli's *Varii esercitii* (1614) contains an 'aria di Ruggiero per sonare', and Frescobaldi's first book of *Toccate e partite* (1615–16) has 'partite sopra l'aria della romanesca'. As late as 1664 Bernardo Storace's keyboard book, *Selva di varie compositioni*,

includes an 'aria sopra la Spagnoletta'. The aria in Bach's Goldberg Variations belongs to the same category. Mattheson, in *Der vollkommene Capellmeister* (1739), gave as a subordinate definition of aria 'a short, singable, simple melody, divided into two parts, which in most cases is so plainly drawn that one may turn it about, embellish it and vary it in countless ways'.

Pieces called 'aria' join company with 'sinfonie', 'sonate' and 'balletti' in Biagio Marini's *Affetti musicali* (1617), and are common in ensemble dance music of the second half of the century, particularly in the works of composers published at Bologna, such as Giuseppe Colombi (from 1668), Pietro Degli Antoni (from 1670), G. M. Bononcini (from 1666, Venice), O. Pollarolo (1673) and G. B. Viviani (from 1678). Most of these are brief binary forms with regular harmonic rhythm in crotchets or quavers and patches of short-breathed imitation. It has been argued that certain of them were meant as substitutes for the more formal allemande (see W. Klenz: *Giovanni Mario Bononcini of Modena: a Chapter in Baroque Instrumental Music*, Durham, North Carolina, 1962). In a similar vein, arias occur as movements of 'sinfonie' by Pietro Sanmartini (1688) and of sonatas by Corelli and B. G. Laurenti (1691). The earlier meaning of 'style' survives in G. F. Biumi's 'arie de correnti à 4' (*Partito delle canzoni alla francese*, 1627) and in Viviani's 'aria di gigha' (*Concertino per camera*, after 1687), similar to the sense of, for example, 'tempo di gavotta' in Corelli's op.2 and in many instrumental pieces of the 18th century.

4. 18TH CENTURY. The da capo form dominated the Italian aria by the beginning of the 18th century, but there was then still some fluidity in its relationship to the text. There is usually a binary construction of the setting of the first part of the text, although arias from this date tend to be so short that this binary structure often consists only of two periods with a half cadence, rather than a modulation, at the end of the first (and the second often repeated). The text of this, the *A* part of the *ABA* da capo structure, usually consisted of two to four lines of verse. If a couplet, it was nearly always repeated completely in the second part of the binary form, but this was not yet always the case with quatrains, in which sometimes only the second couplet was repeated. The middle or *B* section of the aria was often treated exactly like the *A* section, even occasionally using the so-called 'motto' beginning, which remained popular in the early years of the century. In many arias of this period the *A* and *B* sections of the aria are equal in length and musical weight, but in others the *A* is as much as twice as long as *B*, and when the text of *B* consists of a quatrain it is seldom repeated in full. The accompaniment of arias in this period also tended towards diversity. The continuo aria continued into the 1720s, but became increasingly rare. In the works of conservative composers at the beginning of the century one still occasionally finds independent ritornellos in several parts following a continuo aria; and arias in which the voice is accompanied only by continuo, but with instruments playing between the phrases, are quite common. More individual textures, such as the accompaniment of the voice in unison and octaves or with several instruments weaving contrapuntal parts above the voice as lowest sounding part, also had periods of vogue. A considerable variety of instruments in combination or solo were used.

By the 1720s longer arias were favoured, but not to an extent as to destroy the intimacy of the relationship between music and text. This might be called the 'classic' moment in the development of the da capo aria, especially as it was accompanied by the rise to prominence of a generation of composers – Vinci, Hasse, Pergolesi etc – who were to be regarded as the originators of the modern style of 18th-century music, as well as the appearance of a poet, Metastasio, who provided a body of aria poetry that was to be the main source for composers and the model for other poets until near the end of the century. The usual da capo format at this period consists of an instrumental introduction, or ritornello, varying in length but self-contained with a full cadence at the end, then a statement of the first stanza of the poem, with a cadence in the secondary key (the dominant, of course, if the aria is in the major), followed (or overlapped) by another, usually shorter, ritornello in that key, after which there is a second statement of the first stanza with a tonic cadence, confirmed by a concluding ritornello. The second stanza of the text is usually stated only once (with internal repetitions of parts of it, particularly the final line or couplet) and by this time is nearly always considerably shorter than the preceding part of the piece. It departs further from the central tonality, ending in a subsidiary key, usually the mediant, subdominant or submediant. The first part is then repeated. Cadenzas could be inserted at the ends of the statements of both stanzas, and the da capo was an opportunity for the singer to ornament. Coloratura often appeared in the final line of the first stanza.

A specific example, Vinci's setting of 'L'onda dal mar' from *Artaserse* (Metastasio; 1730), may illustrate the relationship between text and music:

> L'onda dal mar divisa
> Bagna le valle e'l monte,
> Va passeggiera in fiume,
> Va prigioniera in fonte,
> Mormora sempre e geme
> Fin che non torna al mar;
>
> Al mar dov'ella naque,
> Dove acquistò gli umori,
> Dove da' lunghi errori
> Spera di riposar.

A simple natural metaphor concerning the motion of water, these lines have to be spoken aloud in order to savour the poet's style. That they were made expressly for music is evident from their sounds (predominance of liquid consonants, the ideal sound of 'mar' at the end of the first stanza, where tradition dictated melismas) as well as from their sense: several opportunities for painting individual words, a motion of travelling and returning that allows parallels with the binary tonal scheme of the *A* section and then 'wandering' with hopes of repose to suggest the tonal function of the *B* section. The first line, set syllabically, receives three bars, the second is extended to five so that the depth of 'valle' can be contrasted with the height of 'monte'. The modulation to the dominant sets in with the third line (at a verb of motion), a three-bar phrase which is then repeated, and is confirmed by the setting of the fourth line, again three bars, to the accompaniment of gently agitated semiquavers in the strings in order to suggest perpetual murmuring and shuddering. The final line is extended to seven bars by repeating the two-bar melisma on 'mar', the whole then deftly extended by an interrupted cadence, allowing a final melodic peak and a graceful descent into the cadence.

Metastasio and many critics – particularly those who

held that the opera belonged to the tragic genre – compared the aria's function with that of the chorus in Greek tragedy. This accounts for the large number of aria texts in his works and those of his imitators that might, like 'L'onda dal mar', be said to trope the action sententiously or imagistically (as in the so-called 'simile' aria) rather than forming a direct part of it. Such a function for the aria helped justify it for critics of a primarily literary orientation, but it was seen as a grave defect by reformers later in the century, who began to form a concept of the opera in which music was to take a more central role in the drama. Dramatic arias, however, are by no means lacking in Metastasio's work as a whole.

As the da capo form itself was nearly universal, a dramatic effect could be won by playing on its very predictability. Thus the opening ritornello could be dropped if the dramatic situation suggested that the singer should begin impetuously without one; this happened a few times in nearly every opera. In some remarkable, and much rarer, cases the dramatic situation might cause the aria to be interrupted before its completion, as in Apollo's 'Mie piante correte' in Handel's early cantata *Apollo e Dafne*, where the second section has hardly begun before it breaks off into recitative, and there is no da capo; or Saul's aria 'A Serpent in my Bosom Warm'd' in *Saul* (1739), where the second section stops abruptly as Saul hurls his javelin. In Micah's aria 'Return, O God of Hosts' in *Samson* (1743) the return to the first section includes the chorus, while the second section of 'Why do the Nations' in *Messiah* (1742) is followed not by a return to the first section but by a chorus, 'Let us Break their Bonds Asunder'. A recitative could be interpolated between the second section and the return to the first, as in Cleopatra's 'V'adoro, pupille' in Handel's *Giulio Cesare* (1724) or Susanna's 'If Guiltless Blood' in *Susanna* (1749).

Within the da capo form itself a considerable variety of musical treatment was possible, for example in thematic and tonal relationships. The voice usually entered with the material heard at the beginning of the ritornello. As in instrumental binary forms, the second solo might begin with the same phrase transposed to the dominant, or a developmental transformation of it; if however the preceding ritornello itself stated this idea, it was likely to begin with different material, and examples can be found where the opening idea reappears only at the beginning of the middle section. Similarly, again as in instrumental binary forms, the tonal treatment of the second solo had many possibilities. It could begin in the tonic; it could return to the tonic almost immediately; or it could put off that return for some time. The variety in the treatment of the middle section was even greater. The accompaniment was often reduced, for a chiaroscuro effect, and at times there was a complete musical contrast, with different tempo and metre.

In the period that followed, the music of the main section of the da capo continued to expand in length. The text, however, did not; and that led to a weakening of the closeness of their previous union. The text had now to be much more repeated, in whole or in part, and this tended to dissolve it into the music. Perhaps partly for this reason, a chronological survey of Metastasio's arias reveals that while in his earlier work he had used a considerable variety of metres and stanza lengths, in his later ones arias in quatrains of *settenario* (seven-

syllable) verse predominate more and more. By the 1720s one occasionally finds that the first two solos each have a second statement of all or most of the text as a coda-like appendage to the main statement, with music that is an extension or reinforcement of the new key in the first or the return to the original one in the second. As time went on this became the standard format for the da capo, as a result of which the first stanza was heard eight times in a complete performance of an aria, the second usually only once; composers in this period often set the middle section in a contrasting tempo and metre (usually a moderate 3/8 if the main section was an Allegro in common time, as it usually was) as if to emphasize it and relieve the sameness. The aria and the *opera seria* in general underwent increasing criticism after the middle of the century, both from those who felt that musical expansion had got out of hand in the arias and that the old balance should be restored, and those, including Gluck and Calzabigi, who wanted an altogether new relationship. By the middle of the century, however, a tendency to retrenchment had set in with regard to aria form. At first this was entirely mechanical, replacing the da capo with the dal segno, that is, the indication of a return not to the beginning of the piece but to a point marked with a sign within it. The dal segno had been used much earlier to dispense with all or part of the repeat of the opening ritornello. Now composers wrote out the beginning of the first solo after the middle section (with or without an intervening orchestral passage) and then indicated by the sign a return to that point in the second solo where the music returned to the tonic key. This shortening was carried even further at times with the sign placed at the coda-like restatement of the text at the end of the second solo. When this happened the formal proportions of the aria were so radically altered that the middle section had the structural effect of an episode within the second part of a binary form.

Gradually, in the 1760s and 1770s, the dal segno aria gave way to an aria close in tonal plan to the contemporary symphony or sonata, with the first section ending in the dominant, the middle section functioning as development or contrast and the following statement of the first section as tonic recapitulation. This aria form came into use gradually with differing degrees and speeds of acceptance. In some cases it was first given to secondary characters. In some operas the arias in the third act, which was gradually withering away, were reduced in dimensions, regardless of who sang them. The rondeau, introduced into Italian opera in the 1760s, became very popular in the 1770s, along with arias that began in a slow tempo and concluded with an allegro (this vogue coincided with the dying out of the practice of setting the middle sections of dal segno arias in contrasting metre and tempo). By the end of the decade the two-tempo (slow–fast) rondo had become popular, largely replacing the simple, one-tempo French variety. Two-tempo rondos were originally showpieces for leading singers, and not more than one or two of them were to be found in an opera. With their increasing vogue, about which the more serious critics complained, they became more frequent, the prototype of the cantabile–cabaletta of the early 19th century (the term 'cabaletta' was in use by the late 1780s). The insertion of recitative into arias again begins to be found in the 1770s with increasing frequency; so too do *pertichini* (the name for other characters when they intrude into a solo number) from the 1780s, and from about that period the use of the chorus in solo numbers, in centres where a chorus was available, increased.

For well over 50 years, from the 1730s to the late 1780s, the majority of *opere serie* were written to Metastasio librettos, the most popular of which received dozens of settings by several generations of composers. In consequence, composers sometimes had difficulty in finding new musical approaches to well-known aria texts. According to Saverio Mattei, in his *Elogio di Jomelli* (1785), even the fertile Hasse was so awed by Gluck's setting of 'Se mai senti spirarti' in *La clemenza di Tito* that, after eight unsuccessful attempts to begin his own setting, he was able to proceed only by composing the second stanza first. In some cases, however, a strong tradition grew up round the music of certain famous arias, constituting not so much an inhibition to the composer as a model and foil for his own work. One of these was 'Se cerca, se dice' in *L'Olimpiade*, following the example of Pergolesi, who provided the classic setting. This is another aria in which Metastasio exploited the musical qualities of the Italian language to the full and created, besides, a dramatic stimulus to composition to the extent that he must be considered a truly equal partner with the composer. In form the text offered an exception to the da capo rule: its three stanzas, because of their rising tension, suggested an initial binary form concluded by a quicker, stretto finale, which is how most composers, following Pergolesi's example, set it.

> Se cerca, se dice
> 'L'amico dov'è?',
> L'amico infelice,
> Rispondi, 'mori'.
>
> Ah no! Si gran duolo
> Non darle per me:
> Rispondi, ma solo,
> 'Piangendo parti'.
>
> Che abisso di pene
> Lasciare il suo bene,
> Lasciare per sempre,
> Lasciarlo cosi!

G. J. Vogler commented at length on two settings of this aria in *Betrachtungen der Mannheimer Tonschule* (1778). Galuppi's setting (1747), he maintained, served to illustrate an earlier style. He commended the simple treatment of the first four words, the emphasis on 'amico' lent by the rise in the melody, the repeat of the question, the rising then sinking of the line at the thought of misfortune to its lowpoint at 'mori', followed by 'sobbing sighs' in the orchestra. The change of sense at 'Ah no!' he found appropriately painted by a powerful departure from the key. Another modulation and a sequential climbing of the vocal line conveyed the depth of sorrow, further intensified by a turn to the minor and the Phrygian cadence approached by an augmented 6th, deemed a happy choice for exclamations. Vogler continued his analysis in like detail throughout the entire aria with remarkable historical consciousness. In contrasting Anfossi's then recent (1778) setting with Galuppi's, Vogler did not point out certain obvious resemblances between them. He found Anfossi's beginning good in its syllabic simplicity, had doubts about the correctness of a connecting wind passage between phrases, 'although this is now the fashion', and took great exception to some pretty, quite 'Mozartian' 10ths between the violins, sounds that he found too sweet to be appropriate to the desperate dramatic situation of the

singer, and moreover falling into the *opera buffa* sphere by virtue of their repeated-note pattern (Anfossi probably intended to paint an anxiously beating heart). The entire aria, which is in the binary form (without stretto finale) characteristic of his generation, and well known from Mozart's operas, occupies 157 bars. Galuppi's occupied 136, but his Andantino–Presto must have taken considerably less time than Anfossi's Andantino. Even so, Anfossi's spacious proportions do not come close to the scope of some of the concerto-like arias in Mozart's Milanese operas of the same decade, pieces judged by Einstein to be overburdened with instrumental clatter. Vogler's conclusion is that the public of his day, spoiled to the point of forgetting dramatic situation and liking only music that tickled the ears, would find Galuppi's setting, which he rated far superior for its dramatic drive, relatively dry in comparison with Anfossi's.

Arias in comic operas were generally freer and more varied in form than in the *opera seria*. Few comic operas are extant from the first half of the 18th century, but the da capo aria appears to have been widely used in them as well. The *parti serie* sang much in the style as well as the form of the *opera seria*. It is in the arias of the most farcical characters that texts tend to become longer, and the development of a rapid patter style for such characters may have contributed to this. In the second half of the century the form in which the whole text is stated completely and then run through a second time became very common, as did multi-tempo arias, particularly those with a slow beginning and a conclusion in a 6/8 Allegro movement.

5. 19TH AND 20TH CENTURIES. The last decade of the 18th century and the opening years of the 19th were a period of considerable freedom and experimentation in aria form. In *opera seria* the sonata form aria was becoming old-fashioned and dying out, replaced by multi-tempo forms. The slow–fast succession (often called 'rondo' even when displaying no formal characteristics of the instrumental rondo) was highly favoured, although it had not yet achieved its later hegemony. Three- and four-tempo arias are also found, as are strophic romanzas and the like. By the 1820s the so-called cavatina–cabaletta (more correctly 'cantabile–cabaletta', as 'cavatina' was used in this period for entrance arias) had become standard, as had the four-part scene format, whose core they formed: an introductory recitative (scena), establishing the dramatic situation and culminating in (second) a slow or moderate aria (the cantabile or *primo tempo*); this was followed by (third) the *tempo di mezzo*, in recitative or *parlante*, often with choral or ensemble passages, and providing some dramatic turn to which there came, as reaction (fourth), the fast cabaletta (or *secondo tempo*), usually in two parts separated by a passage for the chorus, which may also join in a final coda or stretto. This pattern was much used by Bellini, Donizetti and their contemporaries.

19th-century operas in general show a continuing reduction in the number of arias and their increasing distance from the centre of musical–dramatic attention. This tendency was hastened by the move away from the older style of bel canto singing towards a more dramatic style from the 1830s. Before that, the chief agent of dramatic expression had been a style centred on lyricism, ornamentation and agility that lent itself to presentation in expansive, formal arias. Such arias were much less in keeping with the new vocal style and the changed relationship between music and drama that it implied. Composers strove to mould the forms of solo numbers to the action rather than the opposite, and standard forms tended to disappear. Verdi's development exemplified the move towards free and fluid constructions that can be extracted from their context with difficulty or not at all. In *Rigoletto*, for example, the tenor is given a conventional cantabile–cabaletta, 'Parmi veder le lagrime', while Rigoletto, a character conceived as an acting part, never sings an aria in a standard form and in the next scene has, in 'Cortigiani, vil razza', a solo individually shaped to the dramatic requirements of the scene, beginning 'agitato' as Rigoletto denounces the courtiers and turning to 'cantabile' as he pleads with them, thus almost reversing the old pattern. There are few detachable arias in *Aida* (1871) and none at all in *Otello* (1887) and *Falstaff* (1893). Iago's 'Credo' is not an aria in the traditional sense: an earlier age would have described it as a *recitativo stromentato*. Equally in Puccini an aria, if it may be called so, is part of the dramatic texture and cannot usually be extracted without producing an effect of fragmentation or mutilation. In Wagner's mature operas the same applies: the extended sections for a single voice are mostly of a narrative character.

19th- and even 20th-century composers did, however, carry on the tradition of introducing songs, ballads and romances as such into the opera, either as a reflection of mood or state of mind (as, most wonderfully, the Willow Song in *Otello*) or as a frankly undramatic divertissement, of which the tenor's song in *Der Rosenkavalier* (1911) is a late example. Wagner characteristically turned this practice to strongly dramatic ends in Senta's Ballad and even more in the trial and prize songs in *Die Meistersinger* (1867).

The Italian opera had a strong influence on most other contemporary operatic genres, including French grand opera, partly no doubt because Italian operas were presented in Paris in translation and partly because foreign composers, including Rossini, Meyerbeer and Verdi, wrote operas to French texts. But this influence is apparent also in *opéra comique* arias, for example Zampa's 'Toi dont la grâce séduisante' in Hérold's *Zampa* (1831) and Hero's 'Je vais le voir' in Berlioz's *Béatrice et Bénédict* (1862), both examples of the cavatina–cabaletta type. Berlioz came even closer to the Italian model by introducing coloratura and an elaborate cadenza. In the Slavonic countries, too, in spite of obvious folk elements, the aria was accepted as a natural form of expression, for instance Lyudmila's aria (with a cadenza) in Act 4 of Glinka's *Ruslan and Lyudmila* (1842), Lensky's aria in Act 2 of Tchaikovsky's *Eugene Onegin* (1879) and Přemysl's 'Již plane slunce' ('Already the sun burns') in Smetana's *Libuše* (1872), even if Smetana's serious operas owe more to Wagner than to Italian models. Wagner's influence on opera in general was so profound that by the 20th century the older traditions had been almost entirely discarded, though Hindemith in *Cardillac* (1926) and Schoenberg in *Von Heute auf Morgen* (1929) were among those who reverted to the old conception of an opera with separate 'numbers'. Stravinsky, in *The Rake's Progress* (1951), revived the form, but not the substance, of the 18th-century aria; the success of this work did not stimulate others to follow his example, for the revival was essentially in a neo-classical framework. More recent tendencies have been towards highly integrated forms of music-theatre from which the aria, as representing a formal or artificial element, has generally been excluded.

BIBLIOGRAPHY
A. Einstein: 'Die Aria di Ruggiero', *SIMG*, xiii (1911–12), 444
G. Cesare: 'Aria come termine musicale', *Enciclopedia italiana*, iv (Milan, 1929)
A. Einstein: 'Ancore sull'aria di Ruggiero', *RMI*, xli (1937), 163
H. C. Wolff: *Die venezianische Oper in der zweiter Hälfte des 17. Jahrhunderts* (Berlin, 1937)
E. Gerson-Kiwi: *Studien zur Geschichte des italienischen Liedmadrigals im XVI. Jahrhundert* (Würzburg, 1938)
N. Fortune: 'Italian Secular Monody from 1600 to 1635: an Introductory Survey', *MQ*, xxxix (1953), 171
W. Rubsamen: 'Frottola', *MGG*
E. Downes: *The Operas of Johann Christian Bach as a Reflection of the Dominant Trends in Opera Seria 1750–1780* (diss., Harvard U., 1958)
C. V. Palisca: 'Vincenzo Galilei and some Links between "Pseudo-Monody" and Monody', *MQ*, xlvi (1960), 344
M. Robinson: 'The Aria in Opera Seria, 1725–1780', *PRMA*, lxxxviii (1961–2), 31
H. S. Powers: 'Il *Serse* trasformato', *MQ*, xlvii (1961), 481; xlviii (1962), 73
B. Hjelmborg: 'Aspects of the Aria in the Early Operas of Francesco Cavalli', *Natalicia musicologica Knud Jeppesen* (Copenhagen, 1962), 173
N. Fortune: 'A Handlist of Printed Italian Secular Monody Books, 1602–1635', *RMARC*, iii (1963), 27
B. Hjelmborg: 'Om den venezianske arie indtil 1650', *DAM*, iv (1964–5), 91
W. V. Porter: 'Peri and Corsi's *Dafne*: some New Discoveries and Observations', *JAMS*, xviii (1965), 170
R. Freeman: *Opera without Drama: Currents of Change in Italian Opera, 1675 to 1725, and the Roles Played therein by Zeno, Caldara and Others* (diss., Princeton U., 1967)
R. Celletti: 'Il vocalismo italiano da Rossini a Donizetti', *AnMc*, no.5 (1968), 267; no.7 (1969), 214–47
N. Fortune: 'Solo Song and Cantata', *The Age of Humanism 1540–1630*, NOHM, iv (1968), 125–217
N. Pirrotta: 'Early Opera and Aria', *New Looks at Italian Opera: Essays in Honor of Donald J. Grout* (Ithaca, 1968), 39–107
S. Reiner: 'Vi sono molt'altre mezz'Arie', *Studies in Music History: Essays for Oliver Strunk* (Princeton, 1968), 241
S. Döhring: 'Die Arienformen in Mozarts Opern', *MJb 1968–70*, 66
F. Lippmann: 'Vincenzo Bellini und die italienische Opera seria seiner Zeit', *AnMc*, no.6 (1969), 1–104
R. Hudson: 'The Ripresa, the Ritornello, and the Passacaglia', *JAMS*, xxiv (1971), 364–94
H. W. Hitchcock: 'Caccini's "Other" *Nuove musiche*', *JAMS*, xxvii (1974), 438
R. Strohm: *Italienische Opernarien des frühen Settecento (1720–1730)*, *AnMc*, no.16 (1976)
JACK WESTRUP (1–3, with THOMAS WALKER; 4–5, with DANIEL HEARTZ, DENNIS LIBBY)

Aria napolitana. *See* VILLANELLA.

Aribo [Aribo Scholasticus] (*fl* ?Freising, *c*1068–78). Music theorist, author of a treatise *De musica*. There are only two pieces of substantial evidence relating to his life, both deriving from his treatise: the first is the dedication to Ellenhard, Bishop of Freising (*d* 1078); the second is a reference to Wilhelm as Abbot of Hirsau (1068–91). These place the date of the writing of the treatise between 1068 and 1078.

Aribo's association with Freising is supported by his knowledge of Wilhelm, who was previously a monk of St Emmeram at nearby Regensburg. A 12th-century anonymous author from Melk referred to Aribo as 'Cirinus' (*PL*, ccxiii, 981–2), an epithet given also to the 8th-century Bishop Aribo of Freising. Meichelbeck in 1724 referred to Aribo as 'Freisingensis' without documentation. Citing Aribo extensively, the 14th-century theorist Engelbert of Admont called him 'scholasticus Aurelianensis' (*GS*, ii, 289): this constitutes a unique reference to Orleans. Smits van Waesberghe in his *Muziekgeschiedenis* (1936, pp.23–

111) presented extensive evidence in favour of Aribo's connection with Liège, with a sojourn at some time in Rome (in his edition of *De musica* this argument was considerably shortened); his evidence, however, consists largely of records of the name 'Aribo' that cannot safely be identified with the theorist.

Of the manuscripts listed in Smits van Waesberghe's edition, one, used by Gerbert (*GS*, ii, 197–230) and now in Rochester, New York, is particularly corrupt.

Part of the treatise is devoted to two distinct commentaries on the difficult 15th chapter of Guido's *Micrologus*, which deals with plainsong rhythm, notation and textual metre. Aribo's main concern was, however, the establishment of a diagram showing the modal tetrachords superimposed on the gamut. This diagram, called the *caprea* ('goat') because of the speed by which music may be measured by it on the monochord (see Smits van Waesberghe, 1951, p.5), represents Aribo's improvement on earlier diagrams (called 'quadripartita figura modernorum') which he deemed unclear and incorrect (ibid, pp.2f). In the latter diagram (shown in fig.1) four gamuts are staggered so that the tetrachords of plagal modes and of the finals are vertically aligned. Aribo objected to this scheme partly because the modal tetrachords appear in it to be disjunct. His *caprea* (fig.2) avoids this fault. Aribo explained the derivation from the monochord of the intervals of the gamut and the manner in which the measurement of organ pipes is affected by their diameter.

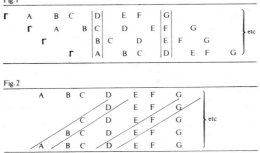

The succeeding section, concerning *musica naturalis* and *artificialis*, is an aggregate of passages from Cassiodorus, Boethius, Isidore and others; the treatise quotes Augustinian ideas to an unusual extent. Metrical patterns, for example, are likened to intervals (the pattern long–long–short is equivalent to the pattern tone–tone–semitone). Using a highly elaborate literary style, with numerous scriptural quotations, Aribo frequently made symbolical analogies. Plagal and authentic are likened to poor and rich, female and male; the tetrachords signify Christ's humility, Passion, Resurrection and Ascension. There are numerous plainsong examples, quoted either in staffless neumes or by their text alone.

BIBLIOGRAPHY

J. Smits van Waesberghe: *Muziekgeschiedenis der middeleeuwen*, i (Tilburg, 1936)
J. Kreps: 'Aribon de Liège: une légende', *RBM*, ii (1948), 138
J. Smits van Waesberghe, ed.: *Aribonis De musica*, CSM, ii (1951)
C. H. Rawski: 'Notes on Aribo Scholasticus', *Natalicia musicologica Knud Jeppesen* (Copenhagen, 1962), 19
F. J. León Tello: *Estudios de historia de la teoria musical* (Madrid, 1962)

ANDREW HUGHES

Arienzo, Nicola d' (*b* Naples, 24 Dec 1842; *d* Naples, 25 April 1915). Italian composer, writer on music and teacher. Because of paternal opposition he first studied music secretly, but when his father later relented he made rapid progress, aided by Mercadante. His first opera, *Monzù Gnazio*, a comic opera in Neapolitan dialect, was performed at the Teatro Nuovo in 1860. During the next 20 years he wrote seven more, all in the comic or semi-serious genres, of which *Il cuoco* (1873) was the most widely performed and *La figlia del diavolo* (1879) the most controversial, because of its *verismo* tendencies. After 1880 he had only one more opera performed, devoting himself mostly to instrumental and sacred music and to teaching and writing.

In 1872 he won the competition for the chair of harmony and counterpoint at the music school of the Real Albergo dei Poveri and in 1874 became director. In 1875 he moved to the conservatory where he taught harmony and, from 1877, counterpoint and composition; Leoncavallo was among his pupils. In 1878 he published the *Introduzione del sistema tetracordale nella musica moderna*, which attempts to formulate a new harmonic system based on a scale related to the Phrygian mode and which he linked historically to Neapolitan folk music with its flattened 'Neapolitan' 2nd. He claimed to have put this system into use in *La figlia del diavolo*. He later published a number of historical and critical studies, most notably on the old Neapolitan *opera buffa*. In 1904 he won the chair of music history at the conservatory. In 1909 he became director, but gave up the post in 1911 and retired from teaching in 1912. D'Arienzo's uncle, Marco d'Arienzo (1811–77), a government bureaucrat by profession, was a librettist by avocation. Between 1839 and 1877 he wrote about 30 librettos for Neapolitan theatres, collaborating with Mercadante, De Giosa, Lauro Rossi, Luigi Ricci, Petrella and others. Among the best known were Ricci's *La festa di Piedigrotta* (1852) and De Giosa's *Napoli di carnevale* (1876).

WORKS

OPERAS

(unless otherwise stated, comic and first performed in Naples)
Monzù Gnazio, o La fidanzata del parrucchiere, 1860; I due mariti, 1866, rev. 1871, vocal score (Milan, ?1876); Le rose, 1868; Il cacciatore delle Alpi, 1870; Il cuoco, 1873; I viaggi, Milan, 1875; La figlia del diavolo, 1879; I tre coscritti, 1880; La fiera, 1887
Not perf.: Rita di Lister, before 1875; Lesbo di Rodio; Capitan Fracassa

OTHER WORKS

Orch: A Roma, conc. sinfonico, 1871; Orlando, sym., D; Pensiero sinfonico, perf. 1871, arr. pf, 4 hands (Milan, n.d.); Piccolo [Vc] Conc., c, 1881, with pf acc. (Milan, 1885); Vn Conc., a, 1880, with pf acc. (Milan, 1912); Vn Conc.-fantasia, with pf acc. (Milan, 1912)
Chamber: Pf Trio, C, perf. Feb 1864; Vc Sonata, perf. 1884; Str Qt, 1888; Nonet, 1889; pf pieces; harp pieces, c100 songs
Sacred: Cristo sulla croce, oratorio, solo vv, vv, orch, before 1875; Miserere, 5vv; Stabat mater, 6 solo vv, vv, str orch

WRITINGS

Introduzione del sistema tetracordale nella musica moderna (Milan, 1878)
Dell'opera comica dalle origini a G. B. Pergolesi (1887)
'Origini dell'opera comica (delle origini della musica moderna)', *RMI* (1895), 597–628; iv (1897), 421–59; vi (1899), 473; vii (1900), 1–33; also pubd separately (Turin, 1900)
La musica in Napoli (Naples, 1900)

BIBLIOGRAPHY

FétisB; *SchmidlD*
F. Florimo: *La scuola musicale di Napoli*, iii (Naples, 1882/*R*1969), 139
M. Caputo: 'Nicola D'Arienzo', *Gazzetta musicale di Milano*, xlii (1887), 135
A. Della Corte: 'Un maestro: Nicola D'Arienzo', *RMI*, xxii (1915), 327

G. Napoli: 'Nicola D'Arienzo', *Arte pianistica*, ii (1915)

G. Pannain: 'Saggio su la musica a Napoli nel sec. XIX: da Mercadante a Martucci', *RMI*, xxxix (1932), 51; repr. in *Ottocento musicale italiano: saggi e note* (Milan, 1952), 150ff

F. Schlitzer: *Salvatore di Giacomo: ricerche e note bibliografiche* (Florence, 1966), 123ff

ANDREA LANZA

Arietta (It.: diminutive of 'aria'). A song in an opera or similar work, shorter and less elaborate than a fully developed aria. The distinction did not become valid until the aria outgrew its simple origins. In Landi's *San Alessio* (1632), where the term 'arietta' is used apparently for the first time, it does not seem to have any special significance. In later usage it came to have much the same meaning as 'cavatina'. Like other terms originally applied to vocal music it was also adopted for instrumental pieces of a similar character, e.g. the theme on which variations are based in the second movement of Beethoven's Piano Sonata in C minor op.111.

JACK WESTRUP

Ariette (Fr., from It. 'arietta'). Strictly speaking a short aria. In 18th-century French opera, however, it was used to mean a vivacious piece with orchestral accompaniment, modelled on the style of the Italian da capo aria, e.g. 'Brillez, astres nouveaux' in Rameau's *Castor et Pollux* (1737) and 'Accourez, jeunesse brillante' in his *Zoroastre* (1749). Arias of this kind sometimes had Italian words. In the latter half of the 18th century the term changed its meaning. A 'comédie mêlée d'ariettes' was a comic opera with dialogue, interspersed with songs which might be long or short, fast or slow. The word thus became virtually synonymous with 'song'. Rosine's song in Act 3 of Beaumarchais' *Le barbier de Séville* (1775), with two stanzas and a *petite reprise*, is described in a footnote as an 'ariette, dans le goût espagnol' and in the stage directions as an 'air'; and Bartholo, after she has sung it, thinks she ought to study more lively things than 'ces grandes aria'. In the 19th century Verlaine gave the title *Ariettes oubliées* to a sequence of poems, some of which, with other pieces by the same author, were included in a cycle by Debussy, published originally as *Ariettes, paysages belges et aquarelles* (1888) and reissued in 1903 with Verlaine's original title.

JACK WESTRUP

Arigoni, Giovanni Giacomo. *See* ARRIGONI, GIOVANNI GIACOMO.

Arimino, Abbas de. *See* VINCENZO DA RIMINI.

Arion (*b* Methymna [now Molyvos], Lesbos; *fl* 625–600 BC). Greek singer to the kithara and choral lyric poet, associated with the beginnings of the dithyramb. None of his works has survived. According to Herodotus he spent most of his life at the court of Periander, tyrant of Corinth (*c*625–585 BC); this account (i, chaps.23–4) consists almost entirely of a legend that a music-loving dolphin saved Arion from drowning, but nevertheless describes him as 'to our knowledge the first man who composed a dithyramb and gave it a name and produced it in Corinth'. The Byzantine *Suda* lexicon attributes to Arion the invention of the tragic mode or style (*tragikos tropos*) and the introduction of 'satyrs speaking verses', but without citing its authorities. Proclus (AD 412–85) in chapter 12 of his *Chrestomathy*, claimed that Pindar had said 'the

dithyramb was discovered in Corinth', and that Aristotle had spoken of Arion 'as having begun the song' ('*arxamenon tēs ōdēs*': see below on the compound *exarchein* in the *Poetics*). These are late sources, but a writer actually contemporary with Arion was cited very circumstantially by John the Deacon, whose date is unknown: 'the first performance [*drama*] of [?]tragedy was introduced by Arion of Methymna, as Solon stated in his *Elegies*' (text and translation in Pickard-Cambridge, pp.98, 294). John was familiar with several very early texts, and there is no adequate reason to reject his evidence.

It is therefore no longer possible to deny (with Crusius) Arion's historical existence. The evidence is confusing, but it seems that Arion may well have taken the free dithyrambic invocation, consisting of ritual cries hailing Dionysus (the rude form known to Archilochus and termed *dithyrambos* by him in frag.77, ed. Edmonds) and made it into an art form, both literary and musical. He may have composed narratives on heroic subjects (the 'naming' ascribed to him by Herodotus) and have given the chorus a genuine sung part, rather than a mere refrain, in their exchanges with the *exarchōn* ('leader'). Aristotle's declaration (*Poetics*, p.1449*a*, l.11) that tragedy originated with 'those who led off [*exarchontōn*, the verb used by Archilochus] the dithyramb' can now be seen, thanks to the explicit reference cited by Proclus, to include Arion.

Aristotle cast Arion as a singer. If, as seems probable, Arion altered the music of the early dithyramb, the nature of the changes remains unknown. The *tragikos tropos* which the *Suda* biographer mentioned can hardly have been a mode (it is a type of melodic composition in Aristides Quintilianus, p.30, ll.2–3, ed. Winnington-Ingram). Whatever term Solon employed (*tragōdia* would have been unmetrical), it cannot have referred to anything like the developed genre of tragedy. He may have been describing as 'goatlike' the fat men and hairy satyrs of the dithyrambic choruses, if *tragikos* was taken to derive from *tragos*, 'he-goat'. The abundant evidence of Corinthian vase paintings contemporary with Arion would support such a conclusion. In that case, the *Suda* reference to satyrs 'speaking' is confused and the satyr-play is not in question.

It would seem likely that Arion gave the dithyramb its initial shape as a force in Greek poetry and music. Minor Hellenistic commentators credited Lasus of Hermione with having done this, but Hellanicus and Dicaearchus (scholium on Aristophanes, *Birds*, l.1403) put the considerable weight of their opinion behind Arion, and were probably correct. It appears equally likely that among the Peloponnesian composer-poets he was the first to provide the early Attic tragedians with 'models of choral lyric poetry', set to 'music appropriate to serious themes' (Pickard-Cambridge, p.112). No more precise description of that music can be justified from the evidence; Arion remains a major figure, indistinctly perceived.

BIBLIOGRAPHY

O. Crusius: 'Arion', §5, *Paulys Realencyclopädie der classischen Alterthumswissenschaft*, ii/1 (Stuttgart, 1895), 836

J. M. Edmonds, ed. and trans.: *Lyra graeca*, i (London and Cambridge, Mass., 1922, rev. 2/1928/*R*1963), 136ff

A. W. Pickard-Cambridge: *Dithyramb Tragedy and Comedy* (Oxford, 1927, 2/1962 rev. T. B. L. Webster), esp. 97ff

C. M. Bowra: *Greek Lyric Poetry* (Oxford, 1936, rev. 2/1967), 82f

——: 'Arion and the Dolphin', *Museum helveticum*, xx (1963), 121

K. Preisendanz: 'Arion', *Der kleine Pauly*, i (Stuttgart, 1964), 548

WARREN ANDERSON

Arioso (It.: 'like an aria', 'melodious'). A singing, as opposed to a declamatory, style of performance; a short passage in a regular tempo in the middle or at the end of a recitative; a short aria not so connected; an instrumental movement in a similar style.

The introduction of arioso passages in recitative occurs first in Roman opera of the early 17th century, and they are frequent in Venetian opera. Domenico Mazzocchi, in the index to his opera *La catena d'Adone* (1626), wrote: 'Vi sono molt'altre mezz'Arie sparse per l'Opera, che rompono il tedio del recitativo' ('there are many other semi-arias scattered through the work which interrupt the tediousness of the recitative'). In Monteverdi's *Il ritorno d'Ulisse* (1641) there is an example of an arioso developing into an aria. When Minerva assures Ulysses in recitative that he will return disguised to find the suitors impudent and Penelope faithful, he twice exclaims in arioso: 'O fortunato Ulisse', which at the end of the following scene becomes the opening phrase of an aria.

Alessandro Scarlatti understood arioso to mean 'in a flowing melodic style'. He wrote in the dedication of his opera *Lucio Manlio* (1705): 'Dove è segnato grave, non intendo malenconico; dove andante, non presto, ma arioso' ('where the music is marked "grave" I do not mean "melancholy"; where it is marked "andante" not fast but "arioso"'). Bach used 'arioso' in various ways: (i) as a passage in recitative, as defined above: see ex.1, from the cantata *O Ewigkeit, du Donnerwort* BWV60. Such passages are sometimes merely marked 'Andante' or 'Adagio' and sometimes have no indication at all. (ii) As the main body of a movement, e.g. the setting of the chorale 'Er ist auf Erden kommen arm' in the first part of the *Christmas Oratorio*, where the verses of the chorale are separated by short recitatives. (iii) As the description of a short aria, e.g. 'Fürchte dich nicht' in the cantata *Schau, lieber Gott* BWV153. (iv) As the equivalent of *recitativo accompagnato*, e.g. 'Mein Herz!' in the *St John Passion*, where the vocal line, though unmistakably recitative, has to keep in time with the instruments. Bach normally described such movements simply as recitatives, even though in many cases the accompaniment is far more regular than it is in 'Mein Herz!' e.g. 'Am Abend, da es kühle war' in the *St Matthew Passion*. (v) As the title of the introductory movement, marked 'Adagio', of the *Capriccio sopra la lontananza del suo fratello dilettissimo* BWV992, with the inscription: 'Ist eine Schmeichelung der Freunde, um denselben von seiner Reise abzuhalten' ('his friends are trying by persuasion to stop him from travelling').

Handel used 'arioso' to mean a short aria, e.g. Dorinda's 'Quando spieghi i tormenti' in *Orlando* (1733) or Melissa's 'Io già sento l'alma in sen' in *Amadigi* (1715), where it is immediately preceded by a *recitativo accompagnato*. There are many solos of the same kind, both in the operas and in the English oratorios, which are ariosos in this sense without being so described. Later composers generally preferred to use the term 'cavatina' for a short aria. Arioso, however, is still found occasionally in the 19th century, e.g. 'I will sing of thy great mercies' in Mendelssohn's *St Paul* (1836) and 'Woe unto them who forsake him' in *Elijah* (1846), and several times in Tchaikovsky's *Eugene Onegin* (1878) and *The Queen of Spades* (1890). Its use in Hindemith's *Cardillac* (1926) and Stravinsky's *The Rake's Progress* (1951) is an artificial revival of 18th-century practice. In instrumental music the term is rare. Beethoven, in the

Ex.1

last movement of his Piano Sonata in A♭ op.110, wrote 'arioso dolente' over a short songlike melody in slow tempo (*Adagio, ma non troppo*). When the passage recurs later in the movement it is marked 'L'istesso tempo di Arioso'.

JACK WESTRUP

Ariosti, Attilio (Malachia [Clemente]) [Frate Ottavio] (*b* Bologna, 5 Nov 1666; *d* England, ?1729). Italian composer. He often substituted Clemente for his baptismal name Malachia. He belonged to an illegitimate branch of the noble Bolognese Ariosti family and was the brother of Giovanni Battista Ariosti. Nothing is known of his musical training, but he became a skilled singer and player of the organ, harpsichord, viola d'amore and cello, as well as a composer. On 21 June 1688 he entered the Bologna monastery of the Order of S Maria de' Servi as a probationer. His investiture, at which he took the name Frate Ottavio, was on 25 July 1688, his public profession on 28 July 1689 and he took minor orders on 13 September 1689. On 25 May 1692 he received his diaconate. His *La passione* (Modena, 1693), which in the preface to the libretto he called his first work, was followed by another oratorio at Bologna in 1694 and in 1695 by a published set of 12 divertimentos for violin and cello. On the divertimentos, as well as the libretto of *La passione*, he is referred to as organist in his order's church.

By spring 1696 Ariosti had left his cloister to enter the service of the Duke of Mantua. That autumn and the following Carnival he had operas performed at Venice (where the duke was accustomed to spend Carnival), but in 1697 he went to Berlin in response to a request from the music-loving electress, Sophie Charlotte, to the duke for a good musician. Court records, which first mention Ariosti in October 1697, do not show him to have held an official appointment; however, he was commonly referred to as Kapellmeister to the electress, with whom he was soon on a footing of close personal friendship, and he was paid large sums from her private purse. In a letter of December 1699 he mentioned some concertos about to be published in the Netherlands and a mass for the coming Christmas Eve, but no trace of these remains. In 1700, for the festivities accompanying a royal wedding, he composed in collaboration with K. F. Rieck *La festa del Himeneo*, an opera-ballet in the French style popular at court, and, by himself, *Atys*, a pastorale in a more Italianate vein. Another opera followed in 1701, as well as an Italian stage work known only from a mention in a French source, where it is called *Le fantôme amoureux*. He also wrote the libretto for G. B. Bononcini's opera *Polifemo*, performed in 1702.

Soon after his arrival in Berlin, Ariosti became the subject of a controversy: it centred on his presence as a Catholic monk at a Protestant court, and led to an extensive diplomatic and private correspondence involving a large number of important people all over Europe (much of which has been published, principally by Ebert). After resisting much pressure, in spring 1703 he received a recall to Italy from his order. Having delayed as long as possible (he was still in Berlin on 13 October), he went to Vienna, where on 15 November he had a musical *poemetto drammatico* performed for Leopold I's name day. The stay in Vienna had been announced as a brief stop on his way to Italy, but Ariosti, who must have been a skilful courtier, succeeded in attaching himself to the Austrian court. He seems never to have held an official musical post there, although in the following years he produced a series of occasional works, oratorios and an opera. For a visit he made to Italy in 1707–8 (including his native Bologna), he was named minister and agent from Joseph I to all the courts and princes of Italy. The duties of this appointment are not known, but he is said to have lived in Italy in considerable pomp and luxury. He returned to Vienna in 1708, but no new works by him are known to have been performed there after 1709. After Joseph I's death in 1711, the empress-regent is said to have banned Ariosti from the Austrian possessions and to have recommended to the pope his dismissal from his order, because of his worldly behaviour. Whether he was then still in Vienna is uncertain; he is said to have been defrocked, but there is no record of it. In 1711 he was in Novara for the conveyance of the relics of St Gaudentius.

Ariosti is next heard of on 12 July 1716, when he played the viola d'amore between the acts of Handel's *Amadigi* in London. According to Loewenberg (*Grove 5*), a manuscript score formerly in the Aylesford collection attributed to him the opera *Tito Manlio*, performed

on 4 April 1717. On 27 May 1717 he wrote to the Elector Palatine, asking to be made his agent in England. On 28 February 1719 the soprano Mrs Robinson sang his cantata *Diana on Mount Latmos* at her benefit concert at the King's Theatre, and in the next season she sang it several times at the theatre in Drury Lane as an afterpiece to Congreve's *The Old Bachelor*. In December 1719 Ariosti helped negotiate with singers for the Royal Academy of Music, which was then being formed; he was engaged there as a composer, along with Handel and Bononcini, though only from the 1722–3 season. He made his début with the very successful *Coriolano* (19 February 1723), followed the next season by *Vespasiano* (14 January 1724), also a success. Chrysander attributed to him *Aquilio Consolo*, given four times at the end of that season, but no composer is named on the libretto or the *Favourite Songs*.

Ariosti was now at the height of his London popularity, and he took advantage of it by publishing by subscription a collection of six cantatas and six lessons for the viola d'amore, dedicated to George I (brother of his former patroness Sophie Charlotte) and patronized by six other members of the royal family. From the subscription list, which includes the names of 41 dukes and duchesses, a large number of other nobles, foreign ambassadors, holders of high public office and many subscribers to the Royal Academy, Fétis's statement that Ariosti realized £1000 would not appear unreasonable; however, according to Hawkins, 'Attilio applied himself to such as he thought his friends, and, as well where he failed of a promise, as where he obtained one, he enrolled the name of the person applied to, in his list of subscribers'. (This publication, which is undated, has frequently been assigned the impossible date 1728, even though Chrysander placed it in 1724, correctly, as an analysis of the subscription list confirms.)

Ariosti's operas for the 1724–5 season, *Artaserse* and *Dario*, seem to have been successful, if not to the same degree as his earlier ones, but he did not produce another until *Lucio Vero* (7 January 1727). His last, *Teuzzone* (21 October 1727), was a failure, given only three times. Its libretto was dedicated by the composer to Prince Friedrich Wilhelm of Prussia, for which he no doubt hoped to receive some advantage. In his last years he is said to have been needy. Rolli, who mentions his death in a letter dated 3 September 1729, wrote a burlesque epitaph for him that plays on his practice of begging money from acquaintances.

Nearly every writer who has examined Ariosti's music has praised it highly, especially for its lyrical qualities. The instrumental works have received the most attention. The early divertimentos consist of 12 three-movement *balletti*, or dance suites. The 57 pieces for viola d'amore and continuo discovered in Stockholm by Weiss are believed by him to fall into 15 suites or sonatas; these are mostly in three or four movements, often in binary form, alternating slow and fast tempos and mixing abstract and dance elements in the manner of the hybrid sonata of the time. In all this they are similar to Ariosti's best-known works, the six lessons for viola d'amore and continuo, published in 1724 and, since the 19th century, republished in numerous practical editions, usually for the standard viola or for cello.

The early Passion was singled out by Schering for the dramatic realism of its one chorus. *La festa del Himeneo* contained a mad scene and a descriptive 'simphonie infernale' that greatly impressed its audience.

Ariosti's were the first Italian operas to be performed in Berlin, although they started no tradition. *Atys* is lost, but *La fede ne' tradimenti* is an impressive work of typical late 17th-century style and construction (it was set to an already existing libretto by Gigli, but with the number of characters pared to four by the omission of two servants): the recitative is highly wrought (by later standards), with occasional passage-work and triple-time sections; there is considerable variety in accompanimental techniques and textures, instrumentation and aria forms (the full da capo aria, with two complete statements of the first stanza, is used, but only as one of several formal possibilities). An *ombra* scene and a sleep scene show Ariosti's penchant for descriptive and atmospheric writing.

The works of the Vienna period have been discussed by Wellesz, who particularly emphasized the exquisite instrumental effects produced by a wide variety of solo combinations. The London operas are practically unknown – surprisingly for a major competitor of Handel – perhaps partly because none of them survives complete, although most of the formal numbers in *Coriolano* and *Vespasiano*, the first and most successful of them, were published. The arias are nearly all in the full da capo form (though varying in proportions), but Ariosti also shows old-fashioned traits: he tended to use the so-called 'motto' beginning and arias accompanied only by continuo much more often than Handel at that period, while the setting of the second stanza of the aria poem is sometimes as long as that of the first stanza. Most impressive in his slow arias in the cantabile, pathetic style, he sometimes weighted the distribution of arias heavily on that side: four of the first seven arias in *Coriolano*, for example, are marked 'Largo'. The prison scene in Act 3 of *Coriolano*, consisting of an elaborate accompanied recitative and aria, was perhaps Ariosti's most successful essay in both the atmospheric and the pathetic, making a dramatic impression on its audiences that was long remembered.

WORKS

STAGE
(music lost unless otherwise stated)

Tirsi (dramma pastorale, 5, Zeno), Venice, S Salvatore, aut. 1696, collab. Lotti and Caldara

Erifile (dramma per musica, 3, G. B. Neri), Venice, S Salvatore, carn. 1697

La festa del Himeneo (azione drammatica con ballo, O. Mauro), Berlin, Theater am Stallplatz, 1 June 1700, collab. K. F. Rieck, *D-Bds*

Atys, o L'inganno vinto della costanza (pastorale, 3, Mauro), Berlin, Lietzenburg, 6 June 1700

La fede ne' tradimenti (dramma per musica, 3, G. Gigli), Berlin, Lietzenburg, 12 July 1701, *GB-Lbm*

Le fantôme amoureux (It. opera, 1), Berlin, Lietzenburg, 1701

Mars und Irene (Singspiel, C. Reuter), Berlin, Lietzenburg, 12 July 1703

La più gloriosa fatica d'Ercole (poemetto drammatico, P. A. Bernardoni), Vienna, court, 15 Nov 1703, *A-Wn*

Il bene dal male (trattenimento carnavalesco), Vienna, court, carn. 1704, *Wn*

I gloriosi presagi di Scipione Africano (trattenimento musicale, D. Cupeda), Vienna, court, 19 March 1704, *Wn*

Marte placato (poemetto drammatico, Bernardoni), Vienna, court, 19 March 1707, *Wn*

Il Danubio consolato (poemetto drammatico, Bernardoni), Vienna, court, 19 March 1707

La gara delle antiche eroine ne' Campi Elisi (Stampiglia), Vienna, court, 21 April 1707, *Wn*

Amor tra nemici (dramma per musica, 3, Bernardoni), Vienna, court, 26 July 1708, *Wgm* (Act 3), *Wn*

La Placidia (poemetto drammatico, Bernardoni), Vienna, court, 15 July 1709, *Wn*

Tito Manlio (dramma per musica, ? M. Noris), London, 4 April 1717, formerly Earl of Aylesford's private collection: doubtful, see *Grove 5*

Coriolano (dramma per musica, 3, N. Haym), London, King's, 19 Feb 1723; ov. (bc only), duet, 25 arias, march (London, 1723)

Vespasiano (dramma per musica, ? Haym, after A. Morselli), London, King's, 14 Jan 1724; ov., 32 arias, 2 duets, final chorus (London, 1724)

Artaserse (dramma per musica, 3, after Zeno and Pariati), London, King's, 1 Dec 1724; Favourite Songs (London, 1724)

Dario (dramma per musica), London, King's, 10 April 1725; Favourite Songs (London, 1725)

Lucio Vero (dramma per musica, 3, Zeno), London, King's, 7 Jan 1727; Favourite Songs (London, 1727)

Teuzzone (dramma per musica, 3, Zeno), London, King's, 21 Oct 1727

Ov., duet, 12 arias, probably from a work of the Vienna period, *GB-Lbm*

ORATORIOS

La passione (C. Arnoaldi), 5 solo vv, chorus, orch, Modena, 1693, *I-MOe*; rev. Vienna, 1709, *A-Wn*

S Radegonda reina di Francia (G. B. Taroni), Bologna, 1694

La madre dei Maccabei, Vienna, 1704, *F-Pc*

Le profizie d'Eliseo nell'assedio di Samaria (G. B. Neri), Bologna, 1705, *A-Wn*

Nabucodonosor (R. M. Rossi or P. A. Bernardoni), Vienna, 1705 or 1706, *Wn*

CANTATAS

6 cantatas (London, 1724): La rosa, S, 2 vn, bc; L'amore onesto, S, bc; L'olmo, S, 2 vn, bc; Libertà acquistata in amore, S, bc; Naufragio vicino, S, 2 vn, bc; La gelosia, S, bc

Al voler del bene amato, 1v, bc, *A-Wn, D-Dlb*; Ardo, ne so per chi, S, bc, *GB-Lbm*; Augelletto garuletto, A, bc, *Lbm*; Belle stille, che grondate, 1v, bc, *A-Wn, ?D-Bds*; Che mi giova esser regina, 1v, bc, *A-Wn*; Che si può far, gia sono amante, 1v, bc, *Wn*; Cieco nume, alato arciero, 1v, bc, *Wn, ?D-Bds, Dlb*; Ciò che trova, mentioned by Gerber; Così tosto o mio bel sole, S, bc, *A-Wn, GB-Lbm*; Diana on Mount Latmos, London, 28 Feb 1719, 2 arias (London, ?1719); D'una rosa che mi punse, S, bc, *?D-Bds, Dlb*; E pur dolce a un cor legato, S, bc, *A-Wn*; Filli gentil, nel tuo bel fior degli anni, S, bc, *Wgm*

Genio, che amar volea, 1v, bc, *Wn*; Il più fiero dolor, *Wn*; Il ratto di Proserpine, 1v, bc, *I-Bc*; Insoffribile tormento, 1v, bc, *A-Wn*; Lontananza crudel, S, bc, *D-DS, GB-Lbm*; Lontananza (Senza te, dolce tiranno), 1v, bc, *A-Wn*; Mirate, occhi, mirate, S, bc, *GB-Lbm*; Nice quella severa amabil ninfa, S, bc, *A-Wgm*; Non han più gl'occhi, S, bc, formerly Singakademie, Berlin; Non v'è pena maggior del mio tormento, *A-Wn, D-Dlb*; Occhi belli ma troppo superbi, S, bc, *SWl*; O filli, o dolce, S, bc, formerly Singakademie, Berlin; O miseria d'amante core, 1v, bc, *A-Wn*

Or vantatevi, o pupille, S, bc, *GB-Lbm*; Per vincer il mio cor, *GB-T*; Pur alfin gentil viola, 1v, va d'amore, bc, *D-DS*, ed. van Waefelghein (Paris, n.d.); Quando Nice era fide, 1v, bc, *A-Wn*; Quanti sospiri, ?*D-Bds*; Quell'augel che sciolto nola, 1v, bc, *GB-Lbm*; Questo mar di vita, 1v, bc, *?D-Bds, GB-Lbm*; Qui dove il fato rio, 1v, str, ob, *J-Tn*; Risolvo ad adorarvi, S, bc, *?D-Bds*; Se lontan stà l'idol mio, ?*D-Bds*; Se t'offesi, o bella Irene, 1v, bc, *A-Wn*; Simbolo del mio, S, bc, mentioned by Gerber; Tante e tante del ciel, 1v, bc, *Wn*; Un barbaro rigor, 1v, bc, *Wn*

Others, *B-Bc, GB-Lgc*

OTHER WORKS

Sacred: Salve regina, 4vv, *I-Fa*; O quam suavis, cantata, T, str, ob, org, *D-Dkh*

Inst: [12] Divertimenti, vn, vc (Bologna, 1695); 6 lessons, va d'amore, bc (London, 1724); 57 pieces [? = 15 sonatas], va d'amore, bc, *S-Skma*, 6 sonatas ed. G. Weiss (Kassel, 1974), 2 sonatas (Mainz, n.d.)

BIBLIOGRAPHY

BurneyH; EitnerQ; FétisB; GerberNL; Grove 5; HawkinsH

F. Chrysander: *G. F. Händel*, ii (Leipzig, 1860), 95ff, 135ff

L. Torchi: 'La musica strumentale in Italia nei secoli XVI, XVII e XVIII', *RMI*, v (1898), esp. 310–11; pubd separately (Milan, 1901), 101f

A. Ebert: *Attilio Ariosti in Berlin* (Leipzig, 1905)

A. Einstein: 'Italienische Musiker am Hofe der Neuburger Wittelsbacher', *SIMG*, ix (1907–8), 336–424, esp. 416

A. Schering: *Geschichte des Oratoriums* (Leipzig, 1911/R1966), 90, 121f

E. Wellesz: *Die Opern und Oratorien in Wien von 1660–1708* (Vienna, 1913)

R. Casimiri and A. Vincentini: 'Attilio Ottavio Ariosti: nuovi documenti', *NA*, ix (1932), 1

D. Boyden: 'Ariosti's Lessons for Viola d'amore', *MQ*, xxxii (1946), 545

K. Gofferje: 'Ariostis "Lezioni" für die Viola d'amore', *DJbM*, vi (1961), 58

F. Bose: 'Ariosti und Bononcini am Berliner Hof', *AMw*, xxii (1965), 56

D. L. Dardo: '"La Passione" di Attilio Ariosti', *Chigiana*, xxiii (1966), 59

G. Weiss: '57 unbekannte Instrumentalstücke (15 Sonaten) von Attilio Ariosti in eine Abschrift von Johan Helmich Roman', *Mf*, xxiii (1970), 127

JAMES L. JACKMAN, DENNIS LIBBY

Ariosti, Giovanni Battista (*b* Bologna, 1668). Italian composer, brother of ATTILIO ARIOSTI. He was a member of the religious order 'dei Serviti' at Bologna in which, under the name Odoardo, he was music teacher. In his mother's will of 4 February 1716 he was named 'erede universale' of her estate. He is known only by a collection of 44 dance-tunes, *Modo facile di suonare il sistro nomato il timpano* (Bologna, 1686, 2/1695/ R1933), printed in a simple number notation; the 'timpano' or 'sistro' was a 12-bar glockenspiel played with wooden hammers. Brief instructions on how to play the instrument precede the tunes. The second and third, enlarged editions of the collection appeared as the work of Giuseppe Paradossi who, under the name of Troili, published another work for the instrument in 1705. While the musical significance of the publication is slight – the dance-tunes are of the common type well-known from contemporary manuscripts of guitar and violin tunes – it is one of a series of publications for the 'sistro' issued within two decades that point to the local popularity of the instrument around the turn of the century.

BIBLIOGRAPHY
R. Nielsen: 'Ariosti', *DBI*
A. Rosenthal: 'Two Unknown 17th-century Music Editions by Bolognese Composers', *CHM*, ii (1956), 375

ALBI ROSENTHAL

Ariosto, Ludovico (*b* Reggio Emilia, 8 Sept 1474; *d* Ferrara, 6 July 1533). Italian poet and playwright. After moving with his family to Ferrara in 1484, he spent some time studying law (1488–93); but his interests lay in the field of literature, especially that of Latin antiquity. Forced as the eldest son to support his family after his father's death in 1500, he entered the service of Cardinal Ippolito d'Este, to whom *Orlando furioso* is dedicated, in 1503. Combining the life of a courtier and civil servant with literary work, Ariosto wrote lyric poems and a series of comedies, the first of which, *La cassaria*, was performed in Ferrara in 1508; like several other plays of his, it was originally written in prose, later recast in verse. The plays were presented with *intermedii* containing music.

By 1505 Ariosto had begun work on *Orlando furioso*; in 1509 the first redaction of the poem, described as an 'addition' to Boiardo's *Orlando innamorato*, was substantially complete. On several occasions, including one in 1512, Ariosto read portions of his work to Isabella d'Este; in 1516 the first version of the poem was published. The next year Ariosto entered the service of Alfonso I, Duke of Ferrara; except for a difficult period when he served as Governor of Garfagnano (1522–5), he now led a more tranquil life, devoting much time to revising his great epic poem, new editions of which appeared in 1521 and 1532.

Einstein's long (but incomplete) list of printed madrigal settings of Ariosto's verse shows that *Orlando furioso* clearly was immensely popular with 16th-century musicians. Tromboncino's setting of 'Queste non son più lagrime' (xxiii.126), the earliest known piece, appeared in 1517, at a time when settings of *ottave rime* by *strambottisti* were still circulating in Petrucci's publications. During the decades 1540–70, a period of experiment and stylistic change in the madrigal, Ariosto's popularity among composers was at its highest peak. The practice of selecting continuous or nearly continuous groups of stanzas such as Bradamante's plaint beginning 'Dunque fia ver' (xxxii.18ff) became common, resulting in cyclic madrigals of half-narrative, half-expressive character. By combining a number of such cycles Jacquet de Berchem assembled in his *Capriccio ... con la musica da lui composta sopra le stanze del Furioso* (1561) over 90 stanzas arranged in narrative order, with summaries of the poem's action.

In the last quarter of the 16th century Tasso's *Gerusalemme liberata* rivalled and to some extent eclipsed Ariosto's popularity among madrigalists; but settings of favourite stanzas were made well into the 17th century. Among composers of the monodic, accompanied madrigal, Antonio Cifra (*d* 1629) was particularly fond of Ariosto's verse. In all over 200 stanzas (about one twentieth of the poem) were set. Of individual stanzas those of a pastoral, descriptive quality, such as 'La verginella è simile alla rosa' (i.42) were favoured. For cyclic groups impassioned laments such as those of Orlando (xxiii.126ff), Bradamante (xxxii.18ff, xliv.61ff), Olimpia (x.19ff) and Isabella (xxiv.77ff) were often chosen.

The first setting, by Ruffo, of the most famous single stanza among musicians, 'Ruggier, qual sempre fui tal esser voglio' (xliv.61) appeared in 1545. In Valderrábano's *Silva de sirenas* (1547) 'Ruggiero' has for a melody a simple pattern used by Corteccia and Hoste da Reggio (both in 1547) for other stanzas; and in 1553 a 'Ruggiero' appeared among the bass melodies of Ortiz's *Tratado*, starting a long period of use like that of the romanesca and passamezzo patterns. As early as the 1530s Ariosto's verse, particularly that of famous scenes, was parodied and rewritten either in serious style or as villanellas. From *Orlando furioso*'s first appearance, singers strumming their own accompaniment performed it to stereotyped melodies such as the one given by Valderrábano – a practice described by Zarlino, Montaigne (in his *Journal du voyage en Italie*) and G. B. Doni.

BIBLIOGRAPHY
G. Zarlino: *Istitutioni harmoniche* (Venice, 1558/R1966, 4/1593)
M. de Montaigne: *Journal du voyage en Italie* (MS, 1581)
G. B. Doni: *Trattato della musica scenica* (Florence, 1763)
A. Einstein: 'Die Aria di Ruggiero', *SIMG*, xiii (1911–12), 444
M. Catalano: *Vita di Ludovico Ariosto ricostruita su nuovi documenti* (Geneva, 1930–31)
G. Agnelli and G. Ravegnani: *Annali delle edizioni ariostee* (Bologna, 1933)
A. Einstein: 'Ancora sull'aria di Ruggiero', *RMI*, xli (1937), 163
——: 'Narrative Rhythm in the Madrigal', *MQ*, xxix (1943), 475
——: *The Italian Madrigal* (Princeton, 1949/R1971), 206ff, 564ff
——: '*Orlando furioso* and *La Gerusalemme liberata* as set to Music during the 16th and 17th Centuries', *Notes*, viii (1950–51), 623
N. Sapegno: 'Ariosto', *DBI*
J. Ward: 'Ruggiero', *MGG*

Aristides Quintilianus [Aristeidēs Koïntilianos] (*fl* AD *c*200). Author of a treatise *Peri mousikēs* ('On music') in three books. The conjecture that he was a son or freedman of the celebrated 1st-century rhetorician Quintilian is not generally accepted. His work on music is heavily derivative, with nothing by way of content or organization that can safely be attributed to Aristides himself. For certain of its doctrines, however, the source remains conjectural. Although the same doubt applies at times to the main sources, for the most part these seem clearly established.

Book 1, concerned with harmonic, rhythmic and metrical theory, derives in the first two instances from the *Harmonics* of Aristotle's pupil ARISTOXENUS, and in the third from the later metricians of Alexandria. Book 2, on the ethical and paideutic aspects of music, refers at several points to the authority of PLATO, always with the greatest deference. It has been thought to represent the doctrines of the Periclean theorist DAMON. Book 3 sets out the numerical and cosmological relationships in which music supposedly is involved. It echoes an extremely diverse assortment of neo-Pythagorean and neo-Platonic beliefs. The portions of the treatise are not of equal merit. Their effectiveness varies with the degree of personal concern felt by their author, and only in book 2 is this concern strikingly evident. Portions of the work are described and commented upon, with chapter numbers, in what follows.

Aristides began book 1 by speaking of music as having lifelong utility. It provides us, he believed, with modal beauty and with seemly (*euprepēs*) rhythms. He cited with approval the dictum of a Pythagorean philosopher that the true function of music is to bring the whole of nature into a fitting relationship (i). Here he revealed his chief concerns; the treatise obviously was not to be a mere technical handbook. His choice of an opening citation, important in that it sets the tone of the treatise, provides one reason for placing him more in the neo-Pythagorean tradition than the neo-Platonic. Later Aristides defined music as 'the knowledge of what is fitting [*prepon*] in sounds and bodily movements' (iv). The use here of *prepon*, like that of *euprepēs* above, may be Damonian; Plato associated these terms with Damon in the *Republic*, which Aristides cited especially often in book 2. After speaking of incomplete modal sequences from 'the most extremely ancient' period, he went on (ix) to set out diagrammatically the six modes discussed by Plato in *Republic* (398e1–399c4). The irregularities in his arguments (departures from known Aristoxenian precedent and lack of emphasis on tetrachordal scale-building) all suggest that he may be presenting a genuine tradition, possibly handed down in an incomplete form.

According to Aristides in book 2, there are two divisions of the subjects of learning: those which preserve the rational element of the soul and those which soothe the irrational element. They are presided over by philosophy and music respectively. The latter, acting upon us from childhood, shapes our character (*ēthē*, plural of *ēthos*) through modes, and orders our bodily movements through rhythms (iii). In limiting ethical power to the modes he shows a drastic departure from Platonic theory. Although Aristides held the Platonic view of music as a propaideutic to philosophy, this does not become explicit until the closing sentences of the treatise. Music is said to imitate character, emotion, speech and actions, operating by means of 'imitations and likenesses' (iv). *Mimēsis*, the first of these two terms, comes more probably from Platonic than from Damonian theory. The second, *homoiōsis*, may be a part of Damon's heritage; like the idea of fittingness, it is associated with him in the *Republic*.

'The ancients', we are further told, regarded pleasure, pain and *enthousiasmos* (the frenzy of inspiration by divine forces) as excesses of feeling in the portions of the soul representing the appetites, the spirit and reason,

respectively. For each of these there was a suitable type of musical therapy (v). The tripartite soul is the only Platonic element of this statement. Aristotle first spoke of *enthousiasmos* in a musical context; his pupil Theophrastus is known to have reduced music itself to the three qualities specified here. The emphasis on therapy, moreover, lacks any parallel in either Platonic or Aristotelian musical doctrine.

Aristides defended at some length the use of 'relaxed' melodies as well as paideutic ones. He referred several times to Plato, and specifically to the testing of virtue by such melodies in the *Republic* (vi). Yet his true position seems to be the very different one advocated by Aristotle in the *Politics*: namely that of pleasing the crowd rather than educating it. This he adopted with an added emphasis upon the individual that probably developed along with the great post-Hellenic ethical systems centred in ethical behaviour. In every political change music leads the way, Aristides continued. This is bolder than Damon's comparable statement (Plato, *Republic*, 425c5–6), and it is not reconciled with the later definition (vii) of music as a therapy of the soul. Aristides next imputed to the soul and to all things, inanimate as well as animate, a dyadic masculine–feminine nature (viii). On the basis of this unproved premise, he set forth a large number of fantastic dichotomies (xiii–xvi). One specific passage of considerable importance contains the claim that Damon and his school sought to show how, through similarity, the notes even of a conjunct melody create a new character (*ēthos*) or bring out a latent one. For proof, Aristides pointed out that in the *harmoniai* handed down by Damon the use of male or female 'variable' notes (those within the tetrachord) obviously differs according to what arrangement would benefit 'each soul' (xiv); the phrase is intended literally. The concept of similarity has already been noted as very possibly Damonian; nothing else here is necessarily more than Aristides' inference. The late tendency towards individualization again becomes evident.

In book 3 the reader is told that PYTHAGORAS on his death-bed advised his followers to use the monochord, declaring that the highest level of music should be grasped intellectually, by the use of number, rather than perceptually through the hearing (ii). After this sober beginning, Aristides proceeded to fill his text with extravagant analogies between the technical components of music and such numerical groupings as the five senses or the twelve houses of the zodiac. Nevertheless, the good sense of his concluding remark that music is the propaideutic to philosophy (xxvii) calls to mind the other profitable passages in his treatise, which has aptly been termed the musical encyclopaedia of antiquity.

BIBLIOGRAPHY

H. Abert: *Die Lehre vom Ethos in der griechischen Musik* (Leipzig, 1899/*R*1968), 24ff

R. Schäfke, trans.: *Aristeides Quintilianus: Von der Musik* (Berlin, 1937)

O. J. Gombosi: *Tonarten und Stimmung der antiken Musik* (Copenhagen, 1939, repr. 1950), 85f, 112f, 140f

R. P. Winnington-Ingram, ed.: *Aristidis Quintiliani De musica libri tres* (Leipzig, 1963)

R. Schäfke, ed. and trans.: *Des Aristeides Quintilianus Harmonik* (Tutzing, 1976)

For further bibliography *see* GREECE, §I.

WARREN ANDERSON

Ariotobulos Eutropius. *See* FEIND, BARTHOLD.

Aristophanes [Aristophanēs] (*b c*450 BC; *d c*385 BC). Greek dramatist. The chief poet of Athenian Old Comedy, he wrote over 40 plays; 11 have survived.

Of the works of his first period (427–421 BC), the revised *Clouds* (*Nephelai*) includes many references to music; the most noteworthy are the mockery of DAMON for his concern with technicalities of metre (ll.647ff) and a description (ll.961ff) of 'the old-fashioned education' (*hē archaia paideia*) provided by the *kitharistēs* (not merely a teacher of the kithara but more properly a schoolmaster). The *Knights* (*Hippēs*, also from the first period) similarly shows a special concern with music. A criticism of grotesque MIMESIS in drama leads to a parody of the Pythagorean theory of the soul as a *harmonia* (ll.521ff, 531ff). There are also passages on lyre tuning and modality (ll.989ff), and on the 'high-pitched' nome (*nomos orthios*, ll.1278ff).

The plays of Aristophanes' early period exemplified with particular aptness the structure of Old Comedy, especially in the use of *parodos* (entrance song) and *parabasis* a long passage in the middle of the play in which the chorus came forward (*parabainein*) and addressed the audience directly, sometimes as spokesmen for the poet. It is generally thought that during his middle period (415–405 BC), beginning with the *Birds* (*Ornithes*), a major change took place: choral songs and dances became less relevant to the action, as the stage direction *chorou* suggests (for another view, see Beare).

The *Frogs* (*Batrachoi*) is the only comedy from the middle period in which Aristophanes dealt particularly with music, the central action being a contest between Aeschylus and Euripides for the chair of poetry in Hades. Aristophanes considered that the ideals of *mousikē* which he upheld – poetry with music – were perfectly exemplified in Aeschylean tragedy (cf ll.1500ff). While admitting the brilliance of Euripides, he indicted him on many counts of musical malfeasance, such as making melismatic settings of individual syllables and deriving lyric choruses from unlikely and unsavoury sources, and introduced for a Euripidean lyric Muse, summoned to appear as pseudo-accompanist, a dancing girl rattling her krotala (clappers or 'bones'; ll.944, 1281f, 1301ff, 1314). Nor was Socrates spared: Aristophanes charged him with having advocated the destruction of the musical and literary traditions of tragedy (l.1493, *apobalonta mousikēn*).

During his final period (392–388 BC) Aristophanes continued to diminish the relevance of the chorus to the exposition; its presence in the revised *Plutus* actually constitutes a problem. Topical references also decrease steadily in the plays of both the middle and the later periods.

See also ETHOS and GREECE, §I.

BIBLIOGRAPHY

F. W. Hall and W. M. Geldart, eds.: *Aristophanis comoediae* (Oxford, 1906–7, 2/1945)

B. B. Rogers, ed. and trans.: *Aristophanes* (London and Cambridge, Mass., 1924, 6/1967–72)

W. Beare: *The Roman Stage* (London, 1950, 3/1964), 340ff

M. Hadas, ed., B. B. Rogers and others, trans.: *The Complete Plays of Aristophanes* (New York, 1962, 2/1968)

J. Taillardat: *Les images d'Aristophane* (Paris, 1962, rev. 2/1965), 456ff

E. Moutsopoulos: 'La philosophie de la musique et le théâtre d'Aristophane', *Mélanges Vourvéris* (Paris, 1964), 201ff

W. D. Anderson: *Ethos and Education in Greek Music* (Cambridge, Mass., 1966, 2/1968), 55ff

J. Defradas: 'Le chant des Grenouilles: Aristophane critique musical', *Revue des études antiques*, lxxi (1969), 23

WARREN ANDERSON

Aristotle [Aristotelēs] (*b* Stagirus, 384 BC; *d* Chalcis, 322 BC). Greek philosopher.

1. Theories of sense perception and ethical behaviour. 2. Symbolism, number, harmonic theory. 3. Paideia and ethos. 4. Relationship to Plato. 5. Modes. 6. General characteristics of Aristotelian thought. 7. Influence on his immediate successors. 8. Aristotelian influence since the late Middle Ages.

1. THEORIES OF SENSE PERCEPTION AND ETHICAL BEHAVIOUR. In order to consider Aristotle's views on music with adequate understanding, it is necessary to make some reference to the theories of sense perception and ethical behaviour on which they are based. The *De anima*, his treatise on the soul, defines perceiving as the process of acquiring the form, or mental image, of an object. Considered in subjective terms it is a developing of the potential into the actual, since a thing cannot become what it is not (§424a, ll.18–19; §425b, ll.23–4; §417b, ll.2–7). The attitudes which characterize an individual have thus always existed potentially within him; music can evoke them, but it cannot implant them.

According to the same treatise, every affection (*pathos*) of the soul involves a concurrent affection of the body (§403a, ll.16–19). Bodily affections, however, cannot cause movement in the soul, which is the unmoved mover. This definition of the soul occurs in the *De motu animalium*, which includes an account of how it initiates action. In matters of conduct the object of desire or of the intellect causes movement. Here the motive is at best a relative good; true beauty and goodness cannot be relative, hence the soul moves but is not moved (§700b, l.17,–701a, l.2). Nowhere in Aristotle is there a sufficiently full explanation of the complex relationship between soul and body, nor is active reason ever adequately accounted for, particularly as a factor in sensation and reaction. The main outlines of his doctrine, however, can be discerned in this broad area of theory.

Ethical attitudes, defined in the *Metaphysics* (§1022b, ll.4–14) as dispositions towards evil or good, are expressed through actions of a corresponding nature. Virtue and vice come under close examination in the second book of the *Nicomachean Ethics* (abbreviated below to *Ethics*) (§1103a, l.14,–1106a, l.24); certain statements may be taken as representative. Moral virtue (or 'excellence') is described as being a result of habituation. 'Like attitudes arise from like activities', and virtues are created and fostered by observing due measure rather than excess or deficiency, and by thus keeping to the principle of the mean. Aristotle held that an action is meaningful and may be termed unequivocally just only when it expresses the pre-existing inward nature of the agent.

Accordingly, an action undertaken by accident, or at the suggestion of another person, does not qualify; and yet this second possibility touches upon the central nature of *paideia*, a concept which for the Greeks included both their system of education and the entire pattern of their culture. The point has vital importance for music, which was accorded so prominent a role in elementary schooling that masters were universally known as *kitharistai*, 'teachers of the kithara'. Here the difficulty is only a seeming one: in the *Physics* (§247b, l.18,–248a, l.2) Aristotle showed his unwillingness to hold restless children accountable by adult standards such as those of the *Ethics*. In later life a man does become accountable; and by that time, both Plato and

Aristotle believed, his taste should have become properly formed.

The argument of the *Ethics* goes on to set forth the criteria of a just or wise act. Unlike a fine work of art, which is required merely to have its own self-contained excellence, such an act must satisfy the three further requirements of deliberate intent, disinterestedness and constancy of disposition. Virtues are therefore different from skills; and as one example of a skill Aristotle cited music, using a neuter plural form (*ta mousika*) for which the English term 'music' provides a close equivalent. This example of the way in which Aristotle attenuated the old concept of *mousikē*, in which music and literature were joined together, is unobtrusive but far from insignificant.

Aristotle thus prepared the ground for a definition of virtue in general. Together with the individual virtues, it must be an attitude of the soul rather than a capacity or feeling – specifically that attitude which causes a man to become good and to perform his special function well. At this point the relevant arguments of the *Ethics* conclude. It remains to note the definitive comments in the *Physics* on the nature of alteration (*alloiōsis*): neither acquired states nor the process of acquiring or losing them may properly be considered instances of alteration. These states are either examples of excellence, or defects; and 'excellence is a perfection . . . while a defect is a perishing of or departure from this condition', whether of body or of soul (§245*b*, 1.3,–247*a*, 1.8).

2. SYMBOLISM, NUMBER, HARMONIC THEORY. Unlike Plato, Aristotle avoided musical symbolism, chiefly because of his quite different attitude towards Pythagorean number theory. This theory, he said, had developed out of the discovery that the ratios of the *harmoniai* or modes could be expressed numerically. Unfortunately it had led to the claim that 'the whole heaven is a *harmonia* and a number' and to the charming but untrue notion of the harmony of the spheres. In its debased popular form as numerology, it produced such fantasies as the belief that the number of notes on the aulos, 24 in all, 'equals that of the whole choir of heaven'. All this, according to Aristotle, proceeds out of the mistaken fundamental idea that real things are numbers (*Metaphysics*, §985*b*, 1.32,–986*a*, 1.2; §1090*a*, ll.20–23; §1093*a*, 1.28,–*b*, 1.4; *De caelo*, §290*b*, ll.21–3).

The fact that harmonic relationships such as the 5th and octave can be expressed mathematically is quite another matter. Aristotle often referred to this, and he classified harmonics, the technical theory of music, as a physical science. Although the *harmonia* itself is usually presented as fact, there are noteworthy exceptions to this rule. In the *Politics* (§1254*a*, ll.32–3) it illustrates the idea of a ruling principle even in inanimate things, and according to the *Metaphysics* (§1018*b*, 1.29), in the lyre this principle is the note called *mesē* ('middle') – a statement which never has been satisfactorily explained. The Pseudo-Plutarchian treatise on music (chap.23 or §1139; Lasserre, p.121, ll.25–30) cites Aristotle as having called the *harmonia* 'celestial' because its nature is 'divine, noble and marvellously wrought', but also as adding that in operation it is quadripartite and embodies two kinds of mean, the arithmetic and the harmonic. These added comments show his characteristic position; it becomes unmistakably clear in the flat statement that the *harmonia*

consists of notes alone, and again in his equally flat denial that either of its main meanings ('arrangement', 'ratio') may properly be used to describe the soul (*Topics*, §139*b*, ll.37–8; *De anima*, §408*a*, ll.5–10).

When he discussed mode as such, Aristotle seems to have had in mind not the *harmoniai* of the 5th century but instead the complex of interchangeable sequences which, according to every probability, had by this time replaced them. He noted that the Dorian and Phrygian were considered by some to be the chief modal categories, subsuming the other modes (*Politics*, §1290*a*, ll.19–22). This happened in the case of the Aeolian and Iastian modes, renamed, during the process of systematization, Hypodorian and Hypophrygian respectively. It is also a familiar fact that the Lydian, with its related modes, was for a long time in disfavour. Two points seem noteworthy here: Aristotle relied on the opinions of others, as he often did when discussing modality; in this deference to authority, moreover, he was willing to grant the Phrygian a place of chief importance, even though he criticized Plato for having allowed it in the ideal city-state of the *Republic*.

3. PAIDEIA AND ETHOS. Like his great teacher, however, Aristotle often stressed the importance of the role of music in education, and he agreed with the Platonic definition of correct education as a training to experience pleasure and pain in the right way. His own definition (*Politics*, §1340*a*, 1.15) follows it closely. When he took up in the *Ethics* the question of the manner in which pleasure relates to goodness and happiness, he supported his answer with a parallel involving music. The case is the same, he said, with the man who is musical: such a person enjoys good melodies and is pained by bad ones (§1170*a*, ll. 6–11). Here the adjectives are not ethical but refer to technique (cf §1105*a*, ll.27–33). They express the trained responses of an expert – in modern terminology, a musicologist. The appearance of such a figure, like that of the polymath, foreshadows the beginning of the Hellenistic age. Yet Aristotle belonged to the Hellenic period, as its last great representative. Normally, therefore, he directed his attention not to the scholarship of music but to the much broader field of musical and literary training known as *mousikē*. Examining the role of music in education, he saw that it had a good or bad influence according to the attitude it fostered. The postulates of his system kept him from applying such terms to the actual hearing of music, for the latter is not an attitude of the soul but only an affection (*pathos*), something that one experiences.

The one extended examination of the paideutic aspects and values of music, unique not merely in the vast body of Aristotle's works but in the whole of surviving Hellenic literature, is to be found in the final chapters of the *Politics* (§1339*a*, 1.11,–1342*b*, 1.34). It is preceded by a brief attempt to determine why 'the ancients' made music a part of *paideia*. This ends with the explanation that it is 'useful for rational enjoyment [*diagōgē*] in leisure' (§1338*a*, ll.22–3). Nowhere is there a recognition of its liturgical use; one will look in vain for the devoutness of a Plato. In both respects the prelude evokes something of the tone which marks the central discussion of music. From that long and complex examination a limited number of arguments will be cited, normally in the order of the text.

Aristotle set out to determine whether the proper

paideutic end of music is amusement, moral betterment or the enriching of cultivated leisure and practical wisdom (*phronēsis*). He found all three possibilities promising but unequal in merit. At length he returned to the original question and shaped it in a slightly different form, omitting wisdom: education, amusement and cultivated leisure are now the possibilities; the paideutic function of music has become one of them. Its effectiveness, he concluded, presumably applies to all three. The proofs which he then added, however, touch only upon the second and third, and show the pleasure that music gives naturally and indiscriminately. Surmising that its essential nature might be more honourable than this incidental aspect would suggest, he raised the possibility that it somehow also reaches the character and the soul. Obviously it influences us in this way, he continued; and at this point an intricate series of statements and conjectures begins, concerned in every instance with aspects of ETHOS theory.

Especially challenging is the claim (reading §1340*a*, ll.12–14, as brilliantly emended by Susemihl) that purely instrumental music possesses ethical force through its rhythms and melodies. The mimetic aspect of his theory emerges in the claim that these contain 'likenesses' (*homoiōmata*) or imitations of all the emotions and ethical states. Proof is found in the varying effects of individual *harmoniai* and rhythms as propounded by certain experts; the latter are described but not named, and their identity remains uncertain. Children must therefore be educated in music, Aristotle concluded. It is naturally pleasurable, and we 'seem to have a certain affinity with modes and rhythms'. His presentation, taken as a whole, raises many questions. The attribution of ethos to instrumental music without a sung or recited text (a clear attempt to refute Plato) can be defended on several grounds. The proofs throughout are strikingly empirical, however, with very little theory of any kind as a balance; the evidence is derivative; and the reader is left with no explanation either of the 'likenesses' or of the affinity of the soul with mode and rhythm (asserted also in the *Poetics*, §1448*b*, ll.20–21). It is true that Aristotle's death cut short the task of completing the *Politics*, and that the treatise devoted to music remains tantalizingly among the lost works.

Passing to the consideration of music lessons and the choice of an instrument, Aristotle counselled that actual performance be limited to childhood. Maturity should bring ethical discretion, based upon this early training. His next point, the admission that some kinds of music may be vulgarizing, seems a digression. It is linked to what has preceded it, however, by strong though implicit reservations about the role of instruments, especially in solo performance. To play the aulos or kithara as a soloist required some degree of professionalism and virtuosity, qualities associated with the vulgar rather than the freeborn man. This had even influenced lyre study in the schools: Aristotle sought to abolish from the curriculum showpieces that demand 'marvellous and extraordinary' displays of technique. He also believed that the aulos must be banned, on the ground that it is distracting and exciting rather than morally beneficial. When he therefore described it as belonging to occasions which produce purgation (*katharsis*) rather than instruction, he was in a sense denying ethical effectiveness to tragedy as well. Although he raised the further point that learning to play the aulos has nothing to do with the intellect, he never said that the case was

different with other instruments used alone. It will be recalled that when the question of the purpose of music is reintroduced, the furthering of practical wisdom no longer appears among the possibilities. Aristotle's strong belief in the ethical power of purely instrumental music has also been noted. This, and the fact that he regularly spoke of music in connection with the ethical rather than the intellectual virtues (although he classified it as a skill), suggests his attitude concerning its relation to the active reason.

4. RELATIONSHIP TO PLATO. Several points which have been mentioned illustrate the ways in which Aristotle's approaches differed from those of Plato. Besides clashing deliberately with his teacher on the subject of the ethos of instrumental music, he went beyond him in seeking to ban the kithara from education. This may be a sign of an increase in professionalism, with its emphasis upon solo playing. The apparent denial of any ethical potential to tragedy furnishes another instance of disagreement. In every case, the difference may be ascribed to differing concepts of *paideia*.

For Plato it was a lifelong process. His consequent belief that audiences ought always to be exposed to an ethic higher than their own made him object to vulgar dramatic performances as well as vulgar music. Probably the same concern underlay his remark in the *Gorgias* that tragedy is primarily hedonistic; this description is certainly an ethical one (§502*b*, l.1,–*c*, l.1).

For Aristotle, however, *paideia* had its restricted sense of elementary schooling, valuable for mature life; and he no longer felt the unity of literary text and musical accompaniment that had been central to the idea of *mousikē*. It was possible for him, therefore, to look calmly at the reality of solo instrumental music performed in public. He could even say that such music should be no better than its audience. Where music and morals are concerned, this marks the extreme point of difference between the two philosophers.

5. MODES. The closing section of the *Politics* deals exclusively with the modes; a promised treatment of the rhythms is not found in the extant portion of the text. Leaving detailed analysis to the experts, Aristotle accepted their division of melodies into three categories and their assignment of individual modes to each category. The types are the 'ethical', productive of moral betterment; the 'practical', productive of action; and the 'enthusiastic' or 'passionate', productive of emotional excitement. Also, and for the fourth time, he listed the proper ends of music: education, purgation and the cultivation of leisure. Once again the possibility of wisdom has been passed over; and the inclusion of leisure on all four occasions is an unmistakable step towards the recognition of a distinctively aesthetic province of judgment.

A discriminating use of all the modes is proper, Aristotle concluded. The proposal that follows shows his pragmatism and his avoidance of Plato's moral criticism: he recommended that the most markedly 'ethical' types be used for education and the other two types for public performances by professionals. He advocated separate competitions and public spectacles for freeborn, educated men and for the common crowd, supporting his contention with the remark already noted. His added explanation that all men enjoy what is naturally suited to them further emphasizes his great divergence from Platonic ideals. Moreover, the triple division of melodies and modes allows much more freedom than Plato ever permitted. Probably an important purpose of this freedom is to provide for the range of moods in the aulos music used to accompany performances of tragedy. To be sure, the theory does not seem consistent with a recognition of only two modes and a corresponding view of the others as composite rearrangements of them (§1290a, ll.19–29, part of which has been discussed above); but the latter view is merely mentioned, not espoused.

The last 18 lines of the *Politics* may be passed over as probably the work of a late interpolator. There can be no other explanation, at any rate, for the praise of Lydian modality as particularly suitable for *paideia*. Immediately before these lines, Aristotle attacked Plato for allowing the use of the Phrygian in the *Republic*. He himself was, of course, willing to have Dorian used in the schools, together with whatever other modes the experts might recommend. Everyone agrees that Dorian is outstanding for its sedateness and manly ethos, he noted. Adding a comment of his own, he characterized its relation to the other modes as that of a mean between extremes. The reference here may be to the system of octave species, in which the Dorian does occupy such a position.

6. GENERAL CHARACTERISTICS OF ARISTOTELIAN THOUGHT. Broadly considered, Aristotle's comments on music create a mixed impression. As one would expect, the theoretical basis is difficult but impressive. Occasionally its principles lead to strange conclusions, as occurs when tragedy apparently proves to be both ethical and non-ethical: tragedy deals with problems of character, unquestionably, yet it is cathartic rather than paideutic, and it lacks the vital element of habituation. Apart from such exceptional instances, his theory provides a sound foundation.

The resulting structure has a number of valuable features. A sane and tolerant recognition of the value of music as a part of the good life – the life of cultured leisure – is certainly one of them; and they include many points of useful detail. Yet the whole is somehow less than the sum of the parts. It must be admitted that music makes no significant contribution to Aristotelian doctrine. When modality and rhythm come under discussion, much of the theoretical material proves to be derivative, and central questions such as the purpose of music receive shifting answers. Superstition and loose thinking are quite rightly demolished; whether any adequate system replaces them may be questioned. It is essentially as a supplement to the more committed and ethically sensitive thought of Plato that Aristotle's contribution to the history and analysis of Greek musical culture is significant.

7. INFLUENCE ON HIS IMMEDIATE SUCCESSORS. Although he had no comparable link with any successor, Aristotle established for the future not only general techniques of argument but also specific views on music. The Pseudo-Aristotelian *Problems*, a later collection concerned in part with music, reflects these views, together with the doctrines of his pupils, especially Theophrastus. Aristoxenus, the most outstanding music theorist trained by Aristotle, demonstrated that training by the use of categories for the analytical definition of musical concepts, and in particular by reliance upon the ear. Even his counterbalancing belief that serious students must also rely upon 'right judgment' probably draws upon the concept of 'right reason', familiar from the *Nicomachean Ethics*.

During the two centuries that followed, the Stoics turned to the Aristotelian corpus for an analysis of emotional response to music. They elaborated these beginnings into a highly detailed system which underlies the arguments employed by Diogenes of Seleuceia, a philosopher of the 2nd century BC whose views on music survive through his Epicurean contemporary and adversary, Philodemus. The emphasis that Diogenes placed upon the role of the listener may perpetuate a genuinely Aristotelian view, hinted at in the *Problems*.

8. ARISTOTELIAN INFLUENCE SINCE THE LATE MIDDLE AGES. By the late 9th century AD, the *Problems*, together with the (unquestionably authentic) *De anima* and *Historia animalium*, had become well-known to Muslim philosophers and music theorists through translations into Arabic and Syriac. In the West, however, Aristotle's ideas concerning music scarcely came to light again until the close of the 14th century, when Johannes de Grocheo systematically categorized varieties of music and dismissed the notion of a harmony of the spheres (the *musica mundana* of medieval terminology: *see* MUSIC OF THE SPHERES), first demolished in Aristotle's *De caelo*. It was at best an uncertain revival. The technical details – tempo and melodic contour, with no mention of pitch – and supposed ethical effects that Johannes cited seem to echo Plato as often as Aristotle; no consistent theoretical basis can be discerned. He nevertheless sided with the Aristotelians at times, and was critical of the hallowed tradition of authority that, according to medieval thinkers, originated with Pythagoras and Plato and was finally enshrined in Boethius's *De musica*.

The 15th-century theorist Johannes Tinctoris made more evident use of Aristotelian views in his *Complexus effectuum musices*. Besides dealing with the aesthetic effect produced by music, he defined its rightful role as one which relates to the concerns of men; and he insisted, against the neo-Pythagoreans, that it could not lie outside the capacities of the human senses. The medieval view of music as a propaideutic to philosophy, originally set forth by Boethius on Aristotle's authority, had become obsolete. This appears also in the work of Gaffurius (d 1522): in his early *Theoricum opus* (1480) he followed a Boethian view of music as based upon mathematics and geometry, but when he wrote the *Practica musicae* (first published 1496) he treated music as living experience. Gaffurius stands in clear contrast to the humanists of the first half of the 16th century, who clung to Pythagorean mysticism and showed almost no awareness of the significance of music as sounding reality. By the middle of the century it was possible to hold that musical performances should be heard and enjoyed as a gentlemanly pastime – a view neither more nor less, considered theoretically, than that of the *diagōgē* or 'rational enjoyment' recommended in the *Politics*.

This new view characterizes Gioseffe Zarlino's *Istitutioni armoniche* (1558). It was shortly to be superseded: some 20 years later his pupil Vincenzo Galilei constructed a theory of mimesis essentially Aristotelian in approach, despite obvious links with Plato. Its firm foundations in classical scholarship had been laid by his friend Girolamo Mei, a master of Greek musical theory. The heroic and self-effacing labours of this learned man made the *Poetics* truly accessible for the first time since antiquity. As a result, Aristotle's comments on poetry and music that belonged to the world of reality began to supplant the *Timaeus* of Plato, with its music of the spheres and its wholly theoretical scale-system. The change represented an abandonment of the former preoccupation with ideal beauty and harmoniousness of proportion, essentially the attitude taken by Zarlino, in favour of a concern with the mimetic and with human emotions. Correspondingly, music now came to be associated not with mathematics or cosmology as in the *Timaeus*, but with poetry and rhetoric, on which the definitive critical studies had been written by Aristotle.

The results of this new trend were not in every instance equally happy. Galilei cited approvingly Aristotle's willingness to tolerate public performances of a better and a worse type of music, mimetic of the natures of two kinds of audience. This double standard may also have influenced a comparable statement by Grétry, who held that all melodic types have associations either with cultivated persons or with the common people. Four centuries earlier, Johannes de Grocheo had made the same class distinction between audiences for works composed by rule and those for whom 'simple' music is appropriate.

According to Aristotle, mimetic activity involved the representation of human character. Although Galilei reaffirmed this belief, other Renaissance thinkers, among them Leonardo da Vinci, had already initiated a radical redefinition. Mimesis, they asserted, is concerned with nature rather than man. They took wholly out of context Aristotle's passing remark in the *Meteorologica* that 'art imitates [*mimeitai*] nature'. He was simply commenting on the way the boiling of water as a rudimentary human skill or 'art' [*technē*] represents its natural analogue, the process of digestion. Employed to justify the new interpretation, his words became at times the warrant for copying musical or even non-musical sounds.

This altered conception of the mimetic was vigorously restated two centuries later when Charles Batteux asserted that each one of the arts imitates nature. Another 18th-century theorist, the Englishman James Harris, suggested that mimesis involves not only such imitation but also the expression of feeling. His view combines the two main categories of the Renaissance definition, *imitatio naturae* in the crudest sense, and also the far more complex 'imitation of the word' that bears a recognizable relationship to the doctrines of 4th-century Greek philosophy. Harris's followers rejected his twofold approach and formulated instead the now familiar view that music, unlike painting or poetry, is fundamentally non-mimetic. In the 20th century, debates about Aristotelian mimesis and the *Poetics* have had a measure of importance outside the academic realms of classical philology and musicology, but only in connection with strictly literary problems. By contrast, the direct comments in the *Politics* concerning the various proper functions of music have occasionally prompted a less specialized response, as in Britain before World War I and in Germany after it.

Aristotle's teachings, which present music as a many-faceted experience, possess a power that is both continuing and ambivalent. Today they appear more nearly consonant with modern attitudes than the views of Plato; their presentation is more compact, less difficult to interpret; and if they lack comparable depth, they have perhaps a greater likelihood of remaining active on the surface of Western intellectual and cultural life.

BIBLIOGRAPHY

I. Bekker, ed.: *Aristoteles: Opera* (Oxford, 1831; 2/1960–61 ed. O. Gigon)

W. D. Ross, ed.: *The Works of Aristotle*, trans. J. J. Beare and others (Oxford, 1908–52)

R. H. Bradley: 'Aristotle's Views on Music, and their Relation to Modern Ideas', *Westminster Review*, clxxix (1913), 158

W. D. Ross: *Aristotle* (London, 1923, rev. and enlarged 6/1964)

H. G. Farmer: 'Greek Theorists of Music in Arabic Translation', *Isis*, xiii (1930), 325

W. Vetter: 'Die antike Musik in der Beleuchtung durch Aristoteles', *AMf*, i (1936), 2–41

D. J. Allan: *The Philosophy of Aristotle* (Oxford, 1937, rev. 2/1970)

D. P. Walker: 'Musical Humanism in the 16th and Early 17th Centuries', *MR*, ii (1941), 1, 111, 220, 288; iii (1942), 55

P. O. Kristeller: 'Music and Learning in the Early Italian Renaissance', *JRBM*, i (1946–7), 255

L. Richter: *Zur Wissenschaftslehre von der Musik bei Platon und Aristoteles* (Berlin, 1961)

J. H. Randall: *Aristotle* (New York, 1962)

W. D. Anderson: *Ethos and Education in Greek Music* (Cambridge, Mass., 1966), 111ff

I. Düring: *Aristoteles* (Heidelberg, 1966), 486ff

D. Zoltai: *A zene esztétika története*, i: *Ethosz és affektus* (Budapest, 1966; Ger. trans., 1970 as *Ethos und Affekt*)

E. Pöhlmann: 'Antikenverständnis und Antikenmissverständnis in der Operntheorie der Florentiner Camerata', *Mf*, xxii (1969), 5

E. Braun: *Aristoteles und die Paideia* (Leiden, 1974)

WARREN ANDERSON

Aristoxenus (*b* Tarentum (now Taranto), *c*375–60 BC; *d* ?Athens). Greek theorist. He was the pupil – and perhaps son – of a musician called Spintharus, and studied at Mantinea, a city in Arcadia which had a strong conservative musical tradition. Later he moved to Athens and became a pupil of Aristotle at the Lyceum, where his standing was such that he hoped, in vain, to succeed to the headship of the school.

A prolific output of 453 works was attributed to him, some of them no doubt spurious. His topics included education and political theory, Pythagorean doctrine, biographies, miscellanies and memoranda of various kinds, but his greatest fame was as a musical theorist. Considerable portions of three books on harmonics, or the theory of scales, have survived under the title of *Harmonic Elements*. It is generally agreed, however, that these are drawn from at least two separate treatises, and that the second and third books represent a later stage of his doctrine than the first. The loss of the remainder is compensated for in some degree by the treatises of later writers, particularly Cleonides, who reproduced his teaching, and who followed him so closely where his work is preserved that there is considerable probability that they did so elsewhere. His other writings on music are lost, including those on musical history, but much of the miscellaneous information in pseudo-Plutarch, *On Music*, and in other authors certainly or probably derives from him. Part of the second book of a treatise on *Elements of Rhythm* also survives, and there are two papyrus fragments, one on harmonics (*Oxyrhynchus papyri*, iv, 667), one on rhythm (ibid, xxxiv, 2687), which may be his.

For details of his theoretical system *see* GREECE, §I, 6–7. Some general comments will, however, be appropriate here. First, the prestige of Aristoxenus was such that the work of his predecessors was largely obliterated and it is not known how far the theoretical analysis of scales begun in the 5th century BC had been carried before his time. The only school he mentioned was that of the harmonikoi, to whose inadequacy he frequently referred. Pythagoras and his followers had concerned themselves with the mensuration of intervals, but it is not clear that they had produced a comprehensive theory of scales.

Second, there was a fundamental difference of attitude between Aristoxenus and the Pythagoreans which continued to dominate the history of Greek theory. The latter were aware that musical intervals could properly be measured and expressed only as mathematical ratios, e.g. of string-lengths or pipe-lengths; that the ratios of octave, 5th, 4th, tone, etc, were super-particular and incapable of exact division (by methods then available to mathematicians); and that 'semitone' (for example) was thus a misnomer. Aristoxenus, a native of Tarentum where the famous mathematician ARCHYTAS had held political power, must have been familiar with this doctrine but rejected it, asserting that the ear was the sole criterion of musical phenomena. He conceived the gamut of pitch as a continuous line which could be divided into simple fractions, so that the octave could be divided into six tones, the tone into semitones or quarter-tones, the 4th into two tones and a semitone, and so on. Which intervals were 'melodic', or capable of taking their places in a musical scale, could be decided only empirically by the trained ear.

Third, since Aristoxenus divided the octave into six equal tones and the tone into equal semitones, it has been held by some modern writers that he was deliberately propagating a system of equal temperament. This seems most unlikely, since the problem that equal temperament was designed to meet, the tuning of keyboard instruments so as to facilitate modulation between keys, did not present itself to ancient Greek musicians. Moreover, Aristoxenus always seemed to imply that his 5ths and 4ths were the true intervals grasped as such by the ear and his tone the true difference between them.

By clear definition and sub-division, Aristoxenus, who had profited from the teaching and methods of Aristotle, reduced the phenomena of Greek music to a coherent and orderly system; this may well reflect an actual process of regularization that had been taking place in practical music since the late 5th century. It is nevertheless likely that, in the interests of symmetry and logic, he sometimes falsified or over-simplified the musical facts. Although this cannot be established without the aid of contemporary melodies, there are indications – some of them provided by himself – that he did so; and his self-satisfied polemics detract from confidence in him. He is perhaps seen at his best in the fragment upon rhythm. He seems to have been the first to realize – or at least to state – that rhythm as an organized system of time-relations expressible in ratios could be abstracted from the words, melodies and dance-movements in which it was incorporated (*ta rhythmizomena*). Unfortunately, the details of his rhythmical doctrine cannot be recovered with any certainty.

BIBLIOGRAPHY

R. Westphal: *Aristoxenos von Tarent* (Leipzig, 1883–93/*R*1965)
H. S. Macran, ed. and trans.: *The Harmonics of Aristoxenus* (Oxford, 1902) [incl. notes, introduction and index of words]
L. Laloy: *Aristoxène de Tarente* (Paris, 1904)
F. Wehrli: *Die Schule des Aristoteles: Texte und Kommentar*, ii (Basle, 1945)
R. da Rios, ed.: *Aristoxeni Elementa harmonica* (Rome, 1954)

For further bibliography *see* GREECE, §I.
R. P. WINNINGTON-INGRAM

Arizaga, Rodolfo (*b* Buenos Aires, 11 July 1926). Argentinian composer and writer on music. He received his initial musical training at the National Conservatory in Buenos Aires, where his teachers were Alberto Williams, José Gil (harmony) and Luis Gianneo (composition). He also studied law at the National University and philosophy at the Free Institute of Higher Studies. In 1954 he settled in Paris, where he studied composition with Messiaen, Boulanger and Martinot. He later taught at the Higher Institute of Music of the National University in Rosario (1960–61) and at Buenos Aires University (1967–9). In his later compositions he has employed 12-note serial technique, modal writing and notation providing performers with an element of choice. An active journalist, he has served as critic for the daily *Clarín* (1946–64), has written articles and reviews for numerous Argentinian and foreign journals, and has published the monographs *Manuel de Falla* (Buenos Aires, 1961) and *Juan José Castro* (Buenos Aires, 1963). His *Enciclopedia de la música argentina* (Buenos Aires, 1971) surveys 20th-century Argentinian composers.

WORKS
(*selective list*)

Orch: Passacaglia, 1953; Delires, 1957; Pf Conc., 1963; Música para Cristóbal Colón, 1966; Hymnus, 1970
Chamber: Divertimento, 2 ob, cl, bn, 1945; Cantatas humanas, A, va, 1952, rev. 1961; Martirio de Santa Olalla, A, fl, cl, vn, vc, cel, hpd, 1950–52; 2 str qts, 1968, 1969
Pf: Suite, 1945; Sonata, 1946; Capricho, 1951; Serranillas del jaque, 1956; Piezas epigramáticas, 1961

Principal publisher: Editorial Argentina de Música

BIBLIOGRAPHY
Composers of the Americas, v (Washington, DC, 1959), 7ff
JOHN M. SCHECHTER

Arizmendi, Fermín de (*b* Puente La Reina, Navarra, baptized 11 June 1691; *d* Avila, 15 Dec 1733). Spanish composer. From 1705 to 1714 he was a *seise* in the choir of the church of the Primature of Toledo, where he was a pupil of Miguel de Ambiela (1666–1733). On 1 September 1714 he was appointed *maestro de capilla* of Avila Cathedral, succeeding Juan Cedazo (*d* 4 July 1714), and remained there for the rest of his life. He was succeeded by Juan Oliac y Serra (*d* 1780). A number of his religious works survive in manuscript (*E-Ac, E*).

BIBLIOGRAPHY
G. Bourligueux: 'Quelques aspects de la vie musicale à Avila: notes et documents (XVIIIe siècle)', *AnM*, xxv (1970), 173, 188, 196
GUY BOURLIGUEUX

Arizo [Arizu], Miguel de (*b* ?Arizu, nr. Pamplona, *c*1595; *d* ?Madrid, in or after 1642). Spanish composer. From 1604 to 1608 he was a choirboy and on 1 January 1614 was appointed a contralto in the Flemish royal chapel at Madrid, supported by House of Burgundy funds. At some time between 1616 and 1627 he was appointed to the Spanish royal chapel at Madrid, supported by House of Castile funds. On 1 March 1629 his name was again added to the Flemish chapel payroll. In 1642 he accepted an annual pension of 350 ducats, payable against Pamplona episcopal funds in exchange for his salaries from both the Spanish and Flemish chapels. His only extant works are a four-part canción, *Filis del alma mia*, and a *romance* for three voices, *Vistióse el prado galán*, both in the Sablonara cancionero of 1625 (in *D-Mbs*, ed. in Aroca; the canción also ed. in MME, xxxii, 1970), and a sacred villancico, *Por coronar a Maria las flores se deojaron* (in *US-NYhsa*). The canción has some tortured harmonies that would do

Gesualdo credit. The *romance*, for high voices, is completely Baroque in conception and veers after every three strophes into a fast, sequential triple-time *estrivo*.

BIBLIOGRAPHY

J. Aroca: *Cancionero musical y poético del siglo XVII recogido por Claudio de la Sablonara* (Madrid, 1916), 334

N. A. Solar-Quintes: 'Panorama musical desde Felipe III a Carlos II', *AnM*, xii (1957), 188

A. Rodriguez-Moñino and M. Brey Mariño: *Catálogo de los manuscritos poéticos castellanos existentes en la biblioteca of The Hispanic Society of America* (New York, 1965), 288

P. Becquart: *Musiciens néerlandais à la cour de Madrid: Philippe Rogier et son école (1560–1647)* (Brussels, 1967), 127f

R. A. Pelinski: *Die weltliche Vokalmusik Spaniens am Anfang des 17. Jahrhunderts* (Tutzing, 1971), 73f

ROBERT STEVENSON

Arkhangel'sky, Alexander Andreyevich (*b* Staroye Tezikovo, Penza, 23 Oct 1846; *d* Prague, 16 Nov 1924). Russian choral conductor and composer. He studied music theory while at the imperial chapel in St Petersburg, gaining also a wide knowledge of Russian church music. In 1880 he founded a mixed choir which soon won a reputation for high standards of performance. At first the choir comprised 20 voices but was later increased to 90; its repertory was extensive and included folksongs and pieces by Classical and contemporary composers. Arkhangel'sky took his choir on a tour of the major cities of Russia (1899–1900), and in 1907 and 1912 they went to western Europe, where their concerts of Russian church music were well received. He supported the movement to reform Russian church music, and his experiment of substituting women's for boys' voices in sacred music was widely adopted. He composed two masses, a requiem and many unaccompanied choral pieces. He also arranged folksongs for his choir and made transcriptions of Russian hymns and other liturgical pieces.

BIBLIOGRAPHY

D. Lokshin: *Vīdayushchiyesya russkiye khorī i ikh dirizhorī* [Distinguished Russian choirs and their conductors] (Moscow, 1953, rev. 2/1963 as *Zamechatel'nīye russkiye khorī i ikh dirizhorī: kratkiye ocherki* [Outstanding Russian choirs and their conductors: short essays])

D. Tkachov: *A. A. Arkhangel'sky: òcherk zhizni i tvorcheskoy deyatel'nosti* [Life and works] (Leningrad, 1972)

JENNIFER SPENCER

Arkhipova, Irina (Konstantinovna) (*b* Moscow, 2 Dec 1925). Soviet mezzo-soprano. She graduated in 1948 from the Moscow Institute of Architecture, where she learnt singing in N. Malīsheva's group, and in 1953 from L. Savransky's class at the Moscow Conservatory. She was a soloist at the Sverdlovsk Opera (1954–6) and in 1956 joined the Bol'shoy Opera, where she made her début as Carmen. Arkhipova is one of the leading Soviet opera singers. At her best her performances are thoughtful, polished and convincingly characterized. Her voice, of wide range, is remarkable for its emotional warmth and variety of tone-colour. Her roles include Lyubasha (*The Tsar's Bride*), Polina and Lyubov (*The Queen of Spades* and *Mazeppa*), Marina and Marfa, Azucena, Amneris and Eboli, and Massenet's Charlotte. Roles in operas by Soviet composers have a significant place in her repertory, and she has participated in many first performances at the Bol'shoy, including those of Khrennikov's *The Mother* (Nilovna, 1957), *War and Peace* (Hélène, 1959) and *The Story of a Real Man* (Klavdiya, 1960), Shchedrin's *Not Love Alone* (Varvara, 1961) and Kholminov's *An Optimistic Tragedy* (Commissar, 1965). She has appeared in opera and concert throughout eastern Europe, and in the USA, Japan, Austria and Scandinavia. After appearances in Naples in 1960, as Carmen, she sang Hélène with the Bol'shoy company at La Scala in 1964, returning in 1967 and 1971 as Marfa, and in 1968 as Marina. She scored a great success as Azucena (to Caballé's Leonora) at Orange in 1972, and this led to her début in the same role at Covent Garden in 1975; she was much praised for her intensely dramatic performance. In 1966 she was made People's Artist of the USSR.

BIBLIOGRAPHY

E. Grosheva: 'Muzīkant s umom i temperamentom' [A musician of intellect and temperament], *SovM* (1972), no.4

N. Tumanov: 'Tvorcheskoye otmechennoye poiskom' [In search of creative characteristics], *SovM* (1972), no.4

I. M. YAMPOL'SKY

Arkor, André d' (*b* Tilleur, nr. Liège, 23 Feb 1901; *d* Brussels, 19 Dec 1971). Belgian tenor. He studied at the Liège Conservatory and made his début at the Théâtre Royal there in 1925 in *Lakmé*. After three seasons in Ghent and one in Lyons, he joined the Brussels Théâtre de la Monnaie, making his début there on 2 August 1930 as Des Grieux in *Manon*. In 1931 he appeared at the Paris Opéra Comique, and during 1932–3 toured the USA. His was a light, smooth voice, in the French tradition of Léon David, Clément and Devriès. He remained the principal tenor in Brussels, gradually taking on heavier roles, until 1945, when he was appointed director of the Théâtre Royal in Liège until 1965. He then became artistic adviser to La Monnaie.

LEO RIEMENS

Arkwright, Godfrey Edward Pellew (*b* Norwich, 10 April 1864; *d* Highclere, Hants., 16 Aug 1944). English music scholar. He studied at Eton and Oxford, where he was subsequently editor of the *Musical Antiquary* (1909–13/*R*1968). He edited a large body of English vocal music of the 16th, 17th and 18th centuries – madrigals and songs by Weelkes, Ferrabosco and Blow, and sacred works by Tye and Milton – published in 25 volumes in the Old English Edition (London and Oxford, 1889–1902/*R*1969). For the Purcell Society he edited *Three Odes for St Cecilia's Day* (London, 1899) and *Birthday Odes for Queen Mary*, i (London, 1902). He also compiled a *Catalogue of Music in the Library of Christ Church, Oxford* (London, 1915).

Arkwright's sister, Marian (Ursula) Arkwright (*b* Norwich, 25 Jan 1863; *d* Highclere, 23 March 1922) composed the children's operetta *The Water Babies* (after Kingsley), *Winds of the World* (a symphonic suite for string orchestra, 1907) and a requiem (1915), in addition to choral, orchestral and chamber music and songs.

BIBLIOGRAPHY

Collection of Old and Rare Music and Books on Music, the Property of G. E. P. Arkwright (London, 1939) [auction catalogue, 13 Feb 1939]

E. VAN DER STRAETEN/R

Arlen, Harold [Arluck, Hyman] (*b* Buffalo, 15 Feb 1905). American songwriter. The son of a Jewish cantor, he studied the piano, performed in ragtime bands and in cinemas, and from about 1920 arranged songs and performed with jazz dance bands, notably the Buffalodians. He took the name Harold Arlen and in New York from 1925 he made some arrangements for Fletcher Henderson, and worked as a pianist and singer on radio, in theatres and with dance bands. In 1929 he became a composer for the Piantadosi publishing firm, and began writing songs for revues. With the lyricist Ted Koehler he wrote most of the songs for eight revues at the Cotton Club in Harlem (1930–34). After 1934 Arlen increasingly turned to composing for musicals and films, with lyrics chiefly by E. Y. Harburg, Johnny Mercer and Ira Gershwin. His brother Jerry Arlen (Julius Arluck) (*b* Buffalo, 11 Nov 1912) was a theatre conductor from 1937.

A capable performer of his own songs, Arlen made several recordings. His chief importance however is as a composer of songs that reflected the American mood during the depression of the 1930s and during the war (e.g. *Get Happy*, *It's only a Paper Moon* and *Over the Rainbow*) that blended the idioms of Tin Pan Alley and Afro-American music and helped provide a mass commercial market for black performers. Such songs as *I Gotta Right to Sing the Blues* (1932) and *Stormy Weather* (1933) use mild blues inflections within a basic American popular song style. *Blues in the Night* (1941) is a more radical departure with a prominent train whistle motif, short repeated phrases and a text (by Mercer) using black speech idioms. Arlen wrote two musicals with all-black casts, *St Louis Woman* (1946, revised as a blues opera, *Free and Easy*, 1959) and *Jamaica* (1957), and several of his stage shows are about slavery and freedom. Many of his tunes have become standard subjects for jazz treatment, notably *That Old Black Magic* (1942) and *Come Rain or Come Shine* (1946), both of which have melodies consisting almost entirely of repeated notes. Many of Arlen's films are musical plays, with less spectacle and fewer dance numbers than in musical comedies. *The Wizard of Oz* is one of the most enduringly popular of all film musicals, and one of the first in which the music is integral to the story and character development. Arlen has written a number of concert works, mostly in a blues-like idiom.

WORKS

STAGE
(*revues, dates of first New York performance unless otherwise stated*)
Earl Carroll Vanities (T. Koehler), collab. J. Gorney, 1 July 1930; You said it (J. Yellen), 19 Jan 1931; Rhythmania (Koehler), 1931; Cotton Club Parade (Koehler), 23 Oct 1932, 6 April 1933, 23 March 1934; Life Begins at 8:40 (I. Gershwin and E. Y. Harburg), 27 Aug 1934; Hooray for What? (Harburg), 1 Dec 1937; Bloomer Girl (musical, book F. Saidy and S. Herzig; lyrics Harburg), 5 Oct 1944; St Louis Woman (musical, book A. Bontemps and C. Cullen; lyrics J. Mercer), 30 March 1946, rev. as Free and Easy (blues opera, Mercer and Koehler), Amsterdam, 17 Dec 1959; House of Flowers (musical, book T. Capote; lyrics Capote and Arlen), 30 Dec 1954; Jamaica (musical, book Harburg and Saidy; lyrics Harburg), 31 Oct 1957; Saratoga (musical, book M. DaCosta; lyrics Mercer), collab. Mercer, 7 Dec 1959

FILMS
Let's Fall in Love (Koehler), 1934; Strike me Pink (L. Brown), 1936; The Singing Kid (Harburg), 1936; Stage Struck (Harburg) 1936; Gold Diggers of 1937 (Harburg), 1936; The Wizard of Oz (Harburg), orchd H. Stothart, 1939; At the Circus (Harburg), 1939; Blues in the Night (Mercer), 1941; Star Spangled Rhythm (Mercer), 1942; The Sky's the Limit (Mercer), 1943
Up in Arms (Koehler), 1944; Kismet (Harburg), 1944; Here come the Waves (Mercer), 1944; Casbah (L. Robin), 1948; My Blue Heaven (R. Blane and Arlen), 1950; The Petty Girl (Mercer), 1950; Mr Imperium (D. Fields), 1951; Down among the Sheltering Palms (Blane and Arlen), 1953; The Farmer takes a Wife (Fields), 1953; A Star is Born (Gershwin), 1954; The Country Girl (Gershwin), 1954; Gay Purr-ee (Harburg), 1962; I Could Go on Singing (Harburg), 1963

SONGS
(*selective list*)
The Album of my Dreams (L. Davis), 1929; Get Happy (T. Koehler), 1930; I Gotta Right to Sing the Blues (Koehler), 1932; It's only a Paper Moon (B. Rose and Harburg), 1932; Last night when we were young (Harburg), 1935; Happiness is a thing called Joe, for Cabin in the Sky (film, Harburg), 1943

INSTRUMENTAL
(*selective list*)
Minor Gaff (blues fantasy), pf, collab. D. George, 1926; Rhythmic Moments, pf, 1928; Mood in Six Minutes, orchd R. R. Bennett, 1935; American Minuet, orch, 1939; Americanegro Suite (Koehler), vv, pf, 1940

BIBLIOGRAPHY
E. Jablonski: *Harold Arlen: Happy with the Blues* (Garden City, NY, 1961) [incl. list of works]

DEANE L. ROOT

Arlen, Stephen (Walter) (*b* Birmingham, 19 Oct 1913; *d* London, 19 Jan 1972). English administrator. He began his theatrical life in 1929 as an actor, but soon turned to stage management. After World War II he became general manager of the Old Vic and in 1951 was appointed general manager of Sadler's Wells, and then administrative director. In 1959 he advised Maurice Huisman on the reorganization of the Théâtre Royal de La Monnaie, Brussels. In 1966 he was appointed managing director of Sadler's Wells and in 1968 responsible for the company's move from Rosebery Avenue, Islington, to the London Coliseum. He was awarded the CBE in 1968 and was married to the soprano Iris Kells.

BIBLIOGRAPHY
E. Tracey: 'Stephen Arlen, 1913–72', *Opera*, xxiii (1972), 219

HAROLD ROSENTHAL

Arles. French city. Originally a Greek settlement, it became a Roman colony in 46 BC. A theatre, amphitheatre, circus and arenas were built within the city, which with its docks and important naval yards was a centre for marketing, commerce and industry. In the 4th century Arles became a centre for Gallican chant and at the beginning of the 5th century Constantine established the imperial residence there; his church of St Etienne became the primacy of Gaul. Caesarius, who came from the Abbey of Lérins and was bishop from 502, made a collection of popular hymns. In 796 a choir school was founded to cultivate the Gregorian repertory. Two rich antiphoners, a missal and a choir loft indicate the lively practice of religious music in the 12th and 13th centuries. From the same period secular songs survive by the Arles troubadours Guillem de l'Olivier, Ramonz Bistortz and Jaime Mote. The romance of St Trophime, in honour of the first Bishop of Arles, dates from the 14th century. Organs were installed in the cathedral, thenceforward known as St Trophime, in 1470.

During the whole of the 16th and 17th centuries the choir school, which had few members, even including instrumentalists, went through difficult times both financially and musically. The directors, none of whom remained there long, included Sauveur Intermet (1590–99), Annibal Gantez (1638–40, 1644–57), Nicolas Saboly (1642–3), Guillaume Poitevin, born in Arles and a former St Trophime scholar (1664–7), André Campra (1681–3) and François Estienne (1694–6). However, Arles prospered in the 17th century and the St Trophime organs were continually improved. An academy, affiliated to the Académie Française in 1666, occasionally organized spectacles with music, and in November 1696 Gautier de Marseille's opera troupe gave a number of successful performances, despite some religious objections. In the 18th century the St Trophime choir school still had difficulty in retaining its directors, even though towards 1759, for example, it consisted of 11 singers and seven to eight instrumentalists. In 1715 an academy of music was established, but the plague of 1720–21 destroyed it. For several years Jean Clavis attempted to enliven Arles' musical life; he became *maître de chapelle* at St Trophime in 1724, directed a new academy of music and conducted a musical ensemble of *bons vivants*, the Chambre Noire. Documents from the library of the Marquis de St Andéol show that, in the second part of the 18th century, chamber music of the Mannheim School was played in Arles and that operas by Dauvergne, Philidor and Gluck, among others, were well known.

The inauguration of the Marseilles to Arles railway in 1848 marked the end of Arles' importance as a port; the town's cultural vitality also waned, and it now has very little formal musical life. The summer St Trophime Cloister Concerts, a festival with famous soloists, are essentially for tourists.

BIBLIOGRAPHY

Le théâtre et les oeuvres de M. de Moran, iii (Paris, 1751) [on the Arles Academy of Music]

L. Pic: 'Mémoires sur tous les plus considérables évènements de la ville d'Arles depuis l'année 1694 jusqu'à l'année 1712', *Le musée: revue arlésienne historique et littéraire*, v (1873)

A.-J. Rancé: *L'Académie d'Arles au XVIe siècle*, ii-iii (Paris, 1887–90)

P. Masson: *Encyclopédie des Bouches du Rhône* (Marseilles, 1937)

F. Raugel: 'La maîtrise et les orgues de la primatiale St-Trophime d'Arles', *RMFC*, ii (1962), 99

H.-A. Durand: 'Arles', *MGG*

MARCEL FRÉMIOT

Arlt, Wulf (Friedrich) (*b* Breslau, 5 March 1938). German musicologist. He studied musicology at the universities of Cologne (1958–60), and Basle (under Schrade), where he obtained the doctorate in 1966 with a dissertation on the Beauvais Office for the Feast of the Circumcision. As an assistant he maintained and expanded the Basle microfilm archives, and became editor of *Paläographie der Musik*, prepared by Schrade. In 1965 he was appointed lecturer at Basle University, where he completed his *Habilitation* in musicology in 1970 with a work on the theory and practice of Ars Subtilior; he was appointed professor in 1972. Since 1971 he has also been director of the Schola Cantorum Basiliensis, the teaching and research institute for early music in Basle.

In his research Arlt has concentrated on music of the Middle Ages. His detailed study of the Beauvais Office combines precision in source work and an integration of theological, liturgical and literary history, and reveals a view of medieval music history (moulded by Schrade and W. von den Steinen) in which music is seen as an integrating cultural factor. In his work with the Schola Cantorum Basiliensis, he has successfully fused new findings in musicology with new standards of performance, assisted by international specialists in early music.

WRITINGS

'Die Neuordnung der Kölner Dom-Musik in den Jahren 1825–6', *Studien zur Musikgeschichte des Rheinlandes*, ii, ed. H. Drux, K. W. Niemöller and W. Thoene (Cologne, 1962), 1–30

'Zum Repertoire der Kölner Dom-Kapelle im ausgehenden achtzehnten Jahrhundert', *KJb*, xlvii (1963), 125

'Zur Deutung der Barock-Oper "Il Trionfo dell'Amicicia e dell'Amore" (Wien, 1711)', *Musik und Geschichte: Leo Schrade zum sechzigsten Geburtstag* (Cologne, 1963), 69

Ein Festoffizium des Mittelalters aus Beauvais in seiner liturgischen und musikalischen Bedeutung (diss., U. of Basle, 1966; Cologne, 1970)

Praxis und Lehre der 'Ars subtilior': Studien zur Geschichte der Notation im Spätmittelalter (Habilitationsschrift, U. of Basle, 1970)

'Musikwissenschaft und musikalische Praxis: Gedanken aus der Arbeit der Schola Cantorum Basiliensis', *Jahresbericht der Musikakademie der Stadt Basel*, civ (1970–71), 51; Eng. trans. in *CMc* (1972), no.14, p.88

'Der *Tractatus figurarum*: ein Beitrag zur Musiklehre der "Ars subtilior" ', *Schweizer Beiträge zur Musikwissenschaft*, i (1972), 35

'Aspekte des Gattungsbegriffs in der Musikgeschichtsschreibung', *Gattungen der Musik in Einzeldarstellungen: Gedenkschrift Leo Schrade*, i (Berne and Munich, 1973), 11–93

'Der Beitrag des 18. Jahrhunderts zum Verständnis der Tonschrift', *Festschrift Arno Volk* (Cologne, 1974), 47–90

'Die mehrstimmigen Sätze der Handschrift Madrid, Biblioteca Nacional, Ms.19421, insbesondere des Crucifixum in carne', *GfMKB, Berlin 1974*

'Peripherie und Zentrum: vier Studien zur ein- und mehrstimmigen Musik des hohen Mittelalters, I', *Forum musicologicum*, i (1974)

'Natur und Geschichte der Musik in der Anschauung des 18. Jahrhunderts: J.-J. Rousseau und J. N. Forkel', *Melos/NZM*, ii (1976), 301

'Einstimmige Lieder des 12. Jahrhunderts und Mehrstimmiges in französischen Handschriften des 16. Jahrhunderts aus Le Puy', *Schweizer Beiträge zur Musikwissenschaft*, iii (1977), 7–47

'Zur Idee und Geschichte eines "Lehr- und Forschungsinstituts für alte Musik": Paul Sacher als Gründer und Direktor der Schola Cantorum Basiliensis', *Alte und Neue Musik: 50 Jahre Basler Kammerorchester* (Zurich, 1977), 37–93

'Zur Interpretation zweier Lieder: *A madre de Deus* und *Reis glorios*', *Basler Jb für historische Musikpraxis*, i (1977), 117

JÜRG STENZL

Arma, Paul [Weisshaus, Imre] (*b* Budapest, 22 Oct 1905). French composer, pianist and ethnomusicologist of Hungarian birth. He studied the piano at the Budapest Academy of Music with Bartók (1921–4), whose advice on composition he often sought in later years and who kindled his love for folksong and collection. (In a lecture given at Harvard in 1943, Bartók spoke of Arma's textless song for solo voice on one pitch with variations of vowel sound, dynamic and rhythm.) Arma began his career as a member of the Budapest Piano Trio (1925–6). Between 1924 and 1930 he gave many recitals in Europe and the USA and lectured on contemporary music at American universities. He settled in Germany in 1931, and for a time he led the musical activities at the Dessau Bauhaus, lecturing on modern music and experimenting with electronic music produced on gramophone records. Later he lived in Berlin and Leipzig, where he conducted several smaller choirs and orchestras. The advent of the Nazi regime in Germany forced his move to Paris, where he made his permanent home. At first he was associated with the RTF, notably as founder-director of the Loisirs Musicaux de la Jeunesse (1936–40). He was a member of the Commission Interministrielle des Loisirs de l'Enfance (1936–8), he lectured at the Phonothèque Nationale and at the University of Paris (1949), and from the 1950s he was associated with the RTF *musique concrète* group. In 1962 he was made a Chevalier de l'Ordre des Arts et des Lettres and a life member of the Institut International des Arts et des Lettres. He has been active in the collection of French folksongs, French Resistance songs (his material includes some 1600 such) and black American spirituals. As a composer he is known chiefly for his experimental work, though he has also published didactic pieces and folksong arrangements.

WORKS
(selective list)

Orch: Pf Conc., 1939; Suite de danses, fl, str, 1940; Conc., str qt, str, 1949; Sym., 1950; 31 instantanés, ww, perc, cel, pf, xyl, 1951; Polydiaphonie, 1962; Structures variées, 1964; Divertimenti de concert, solo insts (fl/vn, cl/va, etc), orch; Résonances, sets of 6, 7, 8

Vocal: Chant indien, chorus 4vv, gui, tambourine, 1937; Cantate du gai travail (A. Gerard), children's chorus 3vv, speaking chorus, orch, 1937; Gerbe hongroise, 7 folksong arrs., 1v, pf, 1943; Chants du silence, 11 songs, 1v, pf, 1942–4; Cantate de la terre, folksong arrs., 4 solo vv, chorus, 1952; Conc., Mez, T, chorus, 1954; Cantata da camera (J. Cassou), Bar, chorus, str, 1957; other songs, cantatas, choruses

Chamber: Recitativo nos.1–2, vn, 1925; 3 danses populaires russes, vn, pf, 1938; La fête au village, str qt for young people, 1938; Divertimenti, fl/vn, pf; cl/va, pf; vc, pf; 2 fl; 2 ob; 2 hn; 2 tpt; etc; Résonances, bn; 2 fl; Sonatas, vn; va; Sonatinas, solo insts (fl, ob, cl, bn, etc), str qt/str orch; Transparences, pf; 2 pf; fl, va; fl, cl; 2 cl; str qt; str, xyl, perc; etc

Pf: Accelerando, 1925; 2 Pf Pieces, 1926–7; Images paysannes [arr. Fr. folksongs], 1939; Sonata da ballo [arr. Fr. folksongs], 1939; 5 esquisses [arr. Hung. folksongs], 1946; Le tour du monde en vingt minutes, 1951

Elec: Improvisation précédée et suivie de ses variations, orch, tape, 1954; Quand la mesure est pleine (M. Seuphor), cantata on tape, 1962; Convergence de mondes arrachés (Arp, Cendrars, Ionesco, Perse, Tzara), speaker and orch on tape, 1968

Principal publishers: Billaudot, Editions Ouvrières, Editions Transatlantiques, Heugel, Lemoine, ORTF, Salabert, Schott, Universal

BIBLIOGRAPHY
B. Bartók: 'Revolution and Evolution in Art', Tempo (1972), no.103, p.4
'Propos impromptu: Paul Arma', Courrier musical (1974), no.45, p.4
VERA LAMPERT

Armaganian, Lucine. See AMARA, LUCINE.

Armandine. A gut-strung kind of harp-psaltery, without a keyboard, invented by PASCAL TASKIN.

Armbruster, Reimundo. See BALLESTRA, REIMUNDO.

Armenia. Area in the Caucasus, now a constituent republic of the USSR; see UNION OF SOVIET SOCIALIST REPUBLICS, §I.

Armenian rite, music of the. A tradition of monophonic liturgical music in use in the Armenian Christian Church.

1. History. 2. Hymnody, theory, style. 3. Notation.

1. HISTORY. In AD 301 St Gregory the Illuminator converted King Tiridates (Trdat) III to Christianity; Armenia thus became the first Christian state. In the following year Gregory became Catholicos of the Armenian church. A descendant of Gregory, Catholicos Sahak I (or Isaac, 387–439), in 404 helped the monk Mesrop-Mashtots to devise an Armenian alphabet. Subsequent literary activity was influenced by Syria and Byzantium. After the Council of Chalcedon (451) the Armenian Church held national councils at Dvin (506–7 and 552), and later lent its support to pre-Chalcedonian doctrines. The council of 552 marked the beginning of the autonomy of the Armenian Church.

The Catholicos see has been moved more than once and is now at Edjmiadsin. There are a number of Armenian centres outside Armenia under different ecclesiastical hierarchies, which possess different musical traditions: Edjmiadsin and Jerusalem maintain the chant in the reformed notation of Limondjian (see §3 below), and there are independent traditions in Iran and India (see Abgar). The Mekhitarists of Venice have another (see §3 below), and those of Vienna have since 1787 used melodies mainly from Constantinople to Western harmony (Ekmalyan), often accompanied by the organ (ex.1.).

2. HYMNODY, THEORY, STYLE. 1166 canonical hymns

Ex.1 from *Surb Pataragi ergets 'oghut 'yunner (Polsakan eghanakner)*

[Kyrie eleison]

(*sharakan*) are sung in the Divine Office. These are collected in a book known as the *Sharaknots*, where they are divided into eight groups named after biblical canticles. This division is reminiscent of that of the Byzantine kanōn, except that the latter is based on nine canticles and sung entirely at Orthros. The present form of the *Sharaknots* was reached between the 13th and 15th centuries; its earlier history is unknown although some early manuscripts exist and national tradition claims the Catholicos Sahak I (387–439), Mesrop-Mashtots (d 440) and the 5th-century Catholicos Hovhannes Mandakuni as the earliest hymnographers. A famous list of redactors precedes the *Sharaknots*, including the name of the Catholicos Nerses IV Klayetsi (1112–73), nicknamed Shnorhali ('Gracious'). He considerably enlarged the *Sharaknots*, and introduced popular elements: his poems and melodies were praised even by the Byzantine Emperor Manuel I Comnenus (1143–80), who wrote to the Catholicos Gregory IV that the chants of the Armenian Church had brought him consolation. Other Armenian hymns include the *gandz*, *erg*, *tagh* and *meghedi*, collected in books such as the *gandzaran*, *ergaran*, *tagharan* and *manrusmun*. The first composer and poet of the *gandz* was Gregory of Narek (950–1003), who fixed the basic content of the *gandzaran*. The most celebrated *tagh* is *Khorhurd khorin* ('Deep mystery'), attributed to Abbot Khachatur of Taron (1100–84), which is still sung at the beginning of the Armenian Eucharist.

Since no medieval Armenian musical treatise survives, information on the theory of Armenian chant must come from the hymns themselves. It is generally claimed that transcriptions of *sharakan* since the 19th century represent the older tradition in substance. Like Byzantine and Syrian chant, Armenian chant is based on a theory of eight modes (*dzayn*); the Armenian modes correspond to an eightfold division of the psalter and to prototype melodies and intonations. The prototype melodies were classified according to the eight modes by Step'annos Siunetsi (fl 8th century). Four of the modes are authentic, four plagal (*koghm*); there are also ambiguous modes (*dardzvadsk'*) comparable to the Byzantine *mesoi*. The scale of each mode is characterized by a dominant and a final note. Ex.2 shows the intonation of the 1st mode (authentic and plagal).

Like Byzantine hymns, Armenian hymns can be sung in either a simple or a florid style. Monasteries and choir schools in Great Armenia, Cilicia and elsewhere had developed variant melodic traditions as early as the Middle Ages, partly because the *khaz* notation (see below, §3) allowed free variation within a prescribed modal structure. Medieval Armenian chant may have been purely diatonic, although analysis of the reformed notation of Limondjian (see §3 below) by Tntesian, and modern transcriptions by Dayan, suggest the use of intervals other than those in European music.

Khaz notation in a 'Sharaknots' of 1312 (Vienna, Library of the Armenian Mekhitarist Monastery 202, ff.88v–89r)

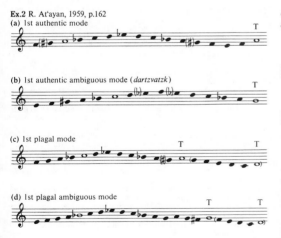

Ex.2 R. At'ayan, 1959, p.162

(a) 1st authentic mode

(b) 1st authentic ambiguous mode (*dartzvatzk*)

(c) 1st plagal mode

(d) 1st plagal ambiguous mode

depending on its place in a sentence (ex.3). (For further details of this system *see* EKPHONETIC NOTATION.)

Ex.3 R. At'ayan, 1959, p.34

A second notational system, the so-called *khaz* notation (see illustration, from a *Sharaknots* of 1312), also appears in 9th-century manuscripts. This is not a diastematic notation; it comprises only indications of the rising or falling direction of the melody, of standard melodic motifs, and rhythmic and expressive details of the manner of performance. It is thus analogous to palaeo-Byzantine notation. Besides approximately 25 neumes, it uses 12 of the Armenian consonants; the latter do not specify the pitch of notes (as the Russian *kinovarnïye pometï* do) but their precise function is unknown. This *khaz* notation permits free variation in performance within prescribed limits according to the modal system.

The origin of the *khaz* system is unknown, as are its relationships with comparable systems such as the Byzantine and Georgian: the similarities between specific Armenian and Georgian signs may be explained without suggesting a direct relationship between the two systems. The 13th-century historian Kirakos of

3. NOTATION. The Armenian 5th-century historian P'awstos Biuzand claimed that Sahak I was 'perfectly versed in singers' letters'. Armenian musical notation dates, however, only from the 9th century, when a lectionary (ekphonetic) notation was introduced for the liturgical reading of the Bible. This system, like Byzantine lectionary notation, developed from prosodic accents. In present-day use a single sign (e.g. *verdjaket*, a sign for a cadence) may carry several meanings,

Gandzak attributed the invention of the *khaz* system to Abbot Khachatur of Taron (*History of Armenia*, chap. 14); but he was its first reformer, and from his time black ink was substituted for red. It is more likely that the *khaz* notation was introduced by Step'annos Siunetsi when the prototype melodies were classified according to the modal system.

From the 16th century, the *khaz* notation became progressively more complicated (in the same way as the Byzantine notation from the 15th century), and it eventually became unintelligible to church musicians. In about 1813 the system was reformed by Baba Hambardzum Limondjian (1768–1839): some of the *khaz* neumes were retained, but with new meanings (cf the comparable reform of Byzantine notation by CHRYSANTHOS OF MADYTOS). Limondjian's system was introduced at Vagharshapat (now Edjmiadsin) by N. T'ashchyan (1841–85); liturgical books using it were printed at Vagharshapat under the Catholicos George IV, and it is still in use. The Armenian Mekhitarist monastery at S Lazzaro, Venice (founded by Abbot

Ex.4

(a)

E - a - kic' ba - nəd Hor____ ew Ho -

- gwoyn____ or i jer____ i yerk - nic'

i____ p'ər ku t'iwn az__ gi mard - kan

As - tə - wac har - c'ən me - roc'

(b)

E - a - kic'____ ba - nəd Hor__

ew__ Ho - gwoyn__ or i jer____ i__ yerk

nic' i____ p'ər ku - t'iwn az__ gi mard__ kan

As - tə - wac__ har__ c'ən me - roc'

Mekhitar of Sebasta in 1717), however, has never adopted the reformed notation and is unique in retaining the use of the *khaz* notation according to the 17th-century Vagharshapat tradition. (For a neume table according to the Mekhitarist system, see *Kargavorut'iwn hasarakats' aghotits Hayastaneayts' ekeghets'woy*, Venice, 1898, pp. xxxi–xxxiv.)

In the reformed notation, each of the seven notes of the octave is indicated with a sign borrowed from the

old *khaz* notation, and additional dashes are used to distinguish the octaves and to add supplementary rhythmic and chromatic indications. The system is thus fully diastematic. Ex.4 shows a *harts* (hymn) from the *Sharaknots*, for the Common of Apostles, according to Limondjian's notation and according to the Mekhitarist tradition of Venice. Attempts to transcribe the *khaz* notation in modern times began with Komitas (1869–1935) (see T'ahmizyan, 1969).

BIBLIOGRAPHY

F. Nève: 'L'hymnologie arménienne', *Muséon*, iv (1885), 359
A. Abgar: *Melodies of the Holy Apostolic Church of Armenia* (Calcutta, 1896, enlarged 2/1920)
F. E. Brightman: *Liturgies Eastern and Western*, i (Oxford, 1896)
M. Ekmalean: *Gesänge der heiligen Messe der armenisch-apostolischen Kirche* (Leipzig and Vienna, 1896)
Komitas: 'Die armenische Kirchenmusik, i: Das Interpunktionssystem der Armenier', *SIMG*, i (1899–1900), 54
P. Aubry: 'Le système musical de l'église arménienne', *Tribune de Saint-Gervais*, vii (1901), 325; viii (1902), 23, 72, 110, 320; ix (1903), 136, 287
N. Ter-Mikaëlian: *Das armenische Hymnarium: Studien zu seiner geschichtlichen Entwicklung* (Leipzig, 1905)
E. Tntesian: *Sharakan dzaynagreal* (Istanbul, 1934)
L. D. Dayan: *Les hymnes de l'église arménienne* (Venice, 1954)
A. Patmagrian: *L'utilisation des éléments folkloriques dans le chant liturgique arménien au XIIe siècle* (Paris, 1955)
Kh. Tetean: *Ěnt'ats'k' Hay ekeghets'akan erazhshtut'ean* [Course of Armenian church music] (Venice, 1957–8)
Kh. Kushnaryev: *Voprosi istorii i teorii armyanskoy monodicheskoy muziki* [Questions on the history and theory of Armenian monody] (Leningrad, 1958)
R. At'ayan: *Haykakar khazayin notagrut'yuně (usumnasirut'yan ev verdsanut'yan harts'er)* [Armenian *khaz* notation: questions of study and transcription] (Erevan, 1959)
A. K. K'och'aryan: 'Erazhshtakan gortsik'neře hayastanum' [Musical instruments in Armenia], *Patma-banasirakan handes* (1963), no.22, p.163
R. Atajan: 'Armenische Chasen', *BMw*, x (1968), 65
M. P. Minasyan: 'Pier Obrin ev hay erazhshtut'yně' [Pierre Aubry and Armenian music], *Patma-banasirakan handes* (1968), no.43, p.193
N. T'ahmizyan: 'Haykakan khazagrut'yan himnakan nshanneri erku ts'uts'akneri masin' [The two lists of basic signs in the Armenian system of neumes], *Patma-banasirakan handes* (1968), no.40, p.67
——: 'Komitasé ev haykakan khazeri verdsanut'yan khndiré' [Komitas and the problem of deciphering the Armenian neumes], *Patma-banasirakan handes* (1969), no.47, p.30
R. Atajan: 'Die armenische professionelle Liederkunst des Mittelalters', *Revue des études arméniennes*, new ser., vii (1970), 241
N. T'ahmizyan: 'Les anciens manuscrits musicaux arméniens et les questions relatives à leur déchiffrement', *Revue des études arméniennes*, new ser., vii (1970), 267
A. K'yoshkeryan: 'Grigor Narekats'u gandzern u gandzaranneri skzbnavorum' [The *gandz* of Gregory of Narek and the origin of the *gandzaran*], *Banber Matenadarani*, x (1971), 55
N. T'ahmizyan: 'Himnakan druyt'ner khazagrut'yan arvesti veraberyal' [Fundamental principles of *khaz* notation], *Banber Matenadarani*, x (1971), 129
——: 'Parzaguyn khazagrut'yunneri verdsanut'yan p'ordz' [An attempt to decipher the simplest neumes], *Patma-banasirakar handes* (1971), no.53, p.145
N. Aroyan: *O teorii srednevekovoj nevmennoj notacii po osnove armjanskich chazov (predvaritel'noe soobshtsenie)* [The theory of medieval neumatic notation on the basis of the Armenian *khaz* (preliminary report)] (Erevan, 1972)
R. At'ayan: 'Nerses Shnorhali "Vardanants' Norahrashě" Ekmalyaniev Komitasi mshakmamb' [Nerses Shnorhali's *Norahrash* as arranged by Ekmalyan and Komitas], *Patma-banasirakan handes* (1972), no.59, p.87
H. Husmann: 'Die Gesänge der armenischen Liturgie', *Geschichte der katholischen Kirchenmusik*, ed. K. G. Fellerer, i (Kassel, 1972), 99
N. Aroyan: *Rasshifrovka nevmennoj notacii na osnove armjanskich chazov* [The deciphering of neumatic notation on the basis of the Armenian *khaz*] (Erevan, 1973)
A. L. Hovhannisyan: 'Muzïka v drevney Armenii' [Music in ancient Armenia], *Patma-banasirakan handes* (1973), no.61, p.61
B. Outtier: 'Recherches sur la genèse de l'octoéchos arménien', *Etudes grégoriennes*, xiv (1973), 127–211
N. T'ahmizyan: 'Grigor Gapasak'alyani 'Hamarotut'iwn erazhshtakanigitut'ean" antip ashkhatut'yune' [The unpublished *Manual of Musical Science* by G. Gapasakalian], *Banber Matenadarani*, xi (1973), 291–334

——: *Nerses Shnorhalin ergahan ev erazhisht* [Nerses Shnorhali, composer and musician] (Erevan, 1973)

CHRISTIAN HANNICK

Armenreich, Bernhard. *See* AMENREICH, BERNHARD.

Armes, Philip (*b* Norwich, 15 Aug 1836; *d* Durham, 10 Feb 1908). English cathedral organist, teacher and composer. After training as a chorister at Norwich Cathedral (1846–8) and at Rochester Cathedral (1848–50) Armes became pupil-assistant to J. L. Hopkins at Rochester (1850–56). He was subsequently organist of Trinity Church, Gravesend (1855–7), St Andrew's, Wells Street, London (1857–61), Chichester Cathedral (1861–2) and Durham Cathedral (1862–1907). He took the Oxford BMus in 1858 and DMus in 1864. He was resident examiner in music at Durham from 1890, professor from 1897 and examiner at Oxford from 1894. During the 1880s Armes collated and indexed the four sets of MS partbooks surviving at Durham. These contained the service music together with separate organ parts of a wide repertory from Tallis to Purcell, formerly used in the cathedral. He composed three oratorios, various anthems, services and other church music.

BERNARR RAINBOW

Armingaud, Jules (*b* Bayonne, 3 May 1820; *d* Paris, 27 Feb 1900). French violinist and composer. He attempted to enter the Paris Conservatoire in 1839 but was refused admission, according to Fétis, because of his advanced and individualistic talent. He played in the Paris Opéra orchestra and in 1855 formed, with Edouard Lalo, Mas and Léon Jacquard, a string quartet in which he played first violin. The quartet enjoyed a great reputation, particularly for the Beethoven quartets, many of which had seldom been performed before; it was later transformed, by the addition of wind instruments, into the Société Classique. Armingaud was praised for his graceful but solid playing and his beautiful tone. His compositions, which run to at least op.53, are primarily light works for violin and piano, described by Van der Straeten as 'florid [and] showy'. He also published two books, *Consonances et dissonances* (Paris, 1882) and *Modulations* (Paris, 1895), which contain musical and philosophical observations.

BIBLIOGRAPHY

FétisB
A. P[?ougin].: Obituary, *Le ménestrel*, lxvi (1900), 72
E. van der Straeten: *The History of the Violin* (London, 1933)

Armitage, Reginald Moxon. *See* GAY, NOEL.

Armonica. A sophisticated form of MUSICAL GLASSES, invented by Benjamin Franklin in 1761, in which a row of glass bowls are nested within one another concentrically on a horizontal axle, which is turned with a pedal.

Armonica a bocca (It.). HARMONICA.

Armonica a manticino (It.). ACCORDION.

Armonioso (It.: 'harmonious'). An expression mark particularly favoured by Liszt who used it in his piano music for long sections to be played under the sustaining pedal.

Armonipiano. *See* SOSTENENTE PIANO, §4.

Armsdorff, Andreas (*b* Mühlberg, nr. Gotha, 9 Sept 1670; *d* Erfurt, 31 Dec 1699). German composer and organist. He studied law as well as music. He held organ posts at Erfurt, successively at the Reglerkirche, Andreaskirche and Kaufmannskirche. Although he wrote little because of his early death, his chorale-preludes were very popular in his day, judging from the numbers of manuscript copies of them circulating in Germany. *Allein Gott in der Höh' sei Ehr* is a charming trio, with the modified tune in the discant in canon with the real tune in the pedals, while *Allein zu dir, Herr Jesu Christ* exemplifies the ornamental discant chorale. Such pieces bear out Jakob Adlung's view in the following century that Armsdorff wrote music grateful to the ear.

WORKS

Editions: *Elf Orgelchoräle des 17. Jahrhunderts*, ed. F. Dietrich (Kassel, 1932) [D]
    Achtzig Choralvorspiele deutscher Meister des 17. und 18. Jahrhunderts, ed. H. Keller (Leipzig, 1937) [K]
    Orgelchoräle um J. S. Bach, ed. G. Frotscher, EDM, 1st ser., ix (1937) [F]

Ach, was soll ich Sünder machen, *D-B*
Allein Gott in der Höh' sei Ehr, F
Allein zu dir, Herr Jesu Christ, F
Aus tiefer Not schrei ich zu dir, F
Es spricht der Unweisen Mund wohl, *D-B*
Herr Jesu Christ, dich zu uns wend, D, *USSR-KAu*
Komm, heiliger Geist, K
Kommt her zu mir, spricht Gottes Sohn, *KAu*
Wenn dich Unglück tut greifen an, F
Wer nur den lieben Gott lässt wolten, *KAu*
Wo soll ich fliehen hin, *D-B*
Wie schön leuchtet der Morgenstern, Bds, *LEm*

Ach Gott und Herr; Der Herr ist mein getreuer Hirt; Erbarm dich, mein, o Herre Gott; Gleich wie sich fein; Gott hat das Evangelium; Herr Jesu Christ dich zu uns wend (2 versions); Herr Jesu Christ du höchstes Gut; Herr Jesu Christ ich weiss gar wohl; Jesu meines Lebens Leben; Liebster Jesu wir sind hier (2 versions); Mitten wir im Leben sind; Nun danket alle Gott; Wie's Gott gefällt: lost (see Seiffert)
Fugue, lost, formerly Fürstliche Stolbergsche Bibliothek, Wernigerode
Other keyboard works, lost (see Ritter)

BIBLIOGRAPHY

RiemannL 12
J. Adlung: *Anleitung zu der musikalischen Gelahrtheit* (Erfurt, 1758/ R1953, 2/1783)
A. G. Ritter: *Zur Geschichte des Orgelspiels, vornehmlich des deutschen, im 14. bis zum Anfange des 18. Jahrhunderts*, i (Leipzig, 1884), 173ff
M. Seiffert: 'Das Plauener Orgelbuch von 1708', *AMw*, ii (1920), 371
F. Dietrich: *Geschichte des deutschen Orgelchorals im 17. Jahrhundert* (Kassel, 1932) [with musical supplement]
W. Apel: *Geschichte der Orgel- und Klaviermusik bis 1700* (Kassel, 1967; Eng. trans., rev. 1972)

G. B. SHARP

Armstrong, (Daniel) Louis ['Satchmo'; 'Satchelmouth'; 'Pops'] (*b* New Orleans, 4 July 1900; *d* New York, 6 July 1971). Black American jazz trumpeter, singer and band-leader.

1. LIFE. Armstrong's parents separated when he was five, and the family lived in poverty in New Orleans, near the saloons and dance halls whose music, along with what he heard and sang in church, was his first musical influence. He worked at odd jobs and began performing on the streets with a vocal quartet. In 1912, while out with his quartet, he fired a pistol and was arrested and sent to the Colored Waifs' Home in New Orleans, where he received his first formal musical tuition from Peter Davis, a member of the staff. After his release at the age of about 14 he again held various jobs and lived with his mother. He was befriended, taught and given his first cornet by his lifelong idol, the jazz cornettist Joe 'King' Oliver. He began to play professionally, working with many New Orleans jazz musicians who later moved to the north, and in 1919 he joined Kid Ory's band, replacing Oliver himself, who

had left for Chicago. At this time he also began working in Fate Marable's riverboat bands on excursions from New Orleans and St Louis.

In 1922 Oliver sent for Armstrong to join his successful Creole Jazz Band at Lincoln Gardens, Chicago. This offer was crucial for Armstrong, who maintained that he would have left New Orleans for no-one else; he now played with the finest and most influential New Orleans group in the north. He was recorded for the first time in Oliver's noteworthy 1923–4 series; the discipline and sensitivity of his improvised second cornet parts to Oliver's lead are specially apparent on the third strain, first statement, of *Mabel's Dream*. While with Oliver's group Armstrong married the band's pianist, Lillian Hardin (they were divorced in 1938). Her influence and his own growing discontent with the band's restricting style led him reluctantly to accept Fletcher Henderson's invitation in 1924 to join his big band in New York. As a section player in a larger group Armstrong made his ensemble playing conform to the stiff rhythms then favoured by Henderson; but his sophisticated, flowing solos introduced a novel style into the city's jazz and dance music and exerted a wide influence on New York musicians, among them the band's arranger, Don Redman, who soon found orchestral counterparts for many of Armstrong's devices. While in New York Armstrong made several records with other groups, including the striking *I ain't gonna play no second fiddle* (1925) with Perry Bradford's Jazz Phools and noteworthy series with Clarence Williams's groups and as an accompanist to Bessie Smith and other blues singers.

In 1925 Armstrong returned to Chicago, where he played with his wife's group, Carroll Dickerson's, Erskine Tate's and, for most of 1927, his own group. In 1925 he also began a series of records under his own name. His originality and range as an improviser and the power and beauty of his ideas, as revealed in these remarkable early recordings, established his international reputation as the greatest and most creative jazz musician. The series also traces the search for an accompaniment appropriate to his increasingly virtuoso solo manner. The earliest of these – the Hot Five and Hot Seven recordings with his wife, the Dodds brothers, Kid Ory and Johnny St Cyr – were modelled on New Orleans ensembles, leading to such masterpieces of the later New Orleans style as *Butter and Egg Man* (1926), *Potato Head Blues* (1927) and *Struttin' with some Barbecue* (1927). Then in 1928 he turned to a more modern small band, which included the pianist Earl Hines, and made greater use of arranged material, as in *West End Blues*, *Beau Koo Jack* and the remarkable *Weatherbird Rag*, a duet with Hines. Finally, in mid-1929 he adopted the format he was to use until 1947 – a big band as a neutral accompaniment to his playing and singing, which by now was dominated by large-scale, virtuoso conceptions. At the same time he began to concentrate on a popular repertory. There is controversy about Armstrong's big-band period. Although his technical innovations had ceased, his performing still had artistic merit, and he made records of great power, beauty and maturity such as *Body and Soul* (1930), *Star Dust* (1931), *Sweethearts on Parade* (1932) and *I gotta right to sing the blues* (1933). He toured and recorded with large groups, particularly Luis Russell's (1935–44), in the USA and Europe (1932–5). He made film appearances, the first in *Pennies from Heaven* with

Bing Crosby (1936), and hundreds of records with his own and other groups, becoming increasingly influential as a singer of popular music and reaching a wider audience. The serious jazz content of his playing diminished, and he was criticized for the low quality of his bands, his repertory and his failure to live up to the promise of his earlier achievements.

After successful appearances with small groups in 1947, including one in the film *New Orleans*, Armstrong formed his All-Stars, a sextet on the New Orleans model with which he worked until his death. Its personnel, but not its instrumentation, varied, and at times included the clarinettists Barney Bigard and Ed Hall, the trombonists Jack Teagarden and Trummy Young, Armstrong's earlier associate Hines and the drummers Sid Catlett and Cozy Cole. With this group Armstrong again showed his superlative quality as a jazz musician, playing less elaborately than he had for some time and making many excellent records. At the same time he continued to make popular recordings, such as *Mack the Knife*, *Hello Dolly* and *What a Wonderful World*. The All-Stars toured with great success in the USA, Australia, the Far East, Europe and South America. In 1960 they toured Africa twice, and their international travelling in the 1960s earned Armstrong the nickname 'Ambassador Satch'. Illness incapacitated him several times in the late 1960s and took its toll on his playing. In public appearances from mid-1969 to September 1970 he was able only to sing; he resumed playing, but he suffered a heart attack in March 1971. (*See* JAZZ, figs.2, 4 and 6.)

2. WORK. Armstrong's importance in the history of jazz is inestimable. The testimony of contemporary jazz musicians shows that his playing greatly impressed all who heard him. Much of his power lay in the grace, sensitivity and poise of his work, features not susceptible to imitation; but his concepts of tone and range, or rhythm and phrasing (both to some extent initially influenced by Oliver), and his sophisticated pitch choice were imitated. Almost all aspects of jazz technique and style, whether played or sung, were influenced directly by Armstrong's innovations of the 1920s.

Armstrong acquired a basic beauty and strength of sound early in his career, and it is apparent even in his work with Oliver and Henderson. His studies with Oliver and his New Orleans background had made him familiar with the expressive possibilities of timbre; but he developed still more expressive ways of attacking and sustaining notes, often, for example, increasing ambitus of vibrato after an attack to give an accumulating energy and a kind of interior rhythm to individual notes and an additional propulsion to entire phrases. Even in the relatively early *Potato Head Blues* (1927) he showed a repertory of devices for varying timbre, including alternative fingerings for the same note (ex.1, bars 9–10). This was coupled with a dramatic expansion of his instrument's range: he had cultivated a solid low register as auxiliary cornettist with Oliver and Henderson and he now gradually extended his range upwards to encompass an unprecedented three octaves, throughout which he could play with equal fluency and fullness of tone. His rhythms drew on the flowing New Orleans style and again on Oliver's example; but he was able to free his playing still further from the rhythmic predictability of early jazz by using short spans and later whole phrases that seemed at first to contradict the underlying pulse only to merge with it again. This was a basic element in his lyricism that for a long time set him apart. Further, Armstrong was able to link phrases without the characteristic problem in early jazz of vacant or formulaic cadences. He had acquired from Oliver a dynamic ability to imply harmony through line and pitch, yet to this basic technique he added a harmonic awareness far in advance of his contemporaries, for example the augmented passing harmonies in bars 6 and 22 of ex.1 and the implicit II^7–V^7 in bar 20. Further, although Armstrong did not introduce 9ths, 13ths and chromaticisms into jazz harmony, he used them so systematically and with such effective placing that his choice of pitch sounded completely fresh. The cogency of his technical innovations, each solving a particular problem faced by the jazz soloist, and his untiring wealth of lyric improvisation, enabled him to extend his solos for several choruses and to structure entire performances, another aspect of his originality.

Armstrong was equally noteworthy for his singing, particularly for his 'scat' performances, some of which are among the earliest recorded examples. His unique 'gravelly' voice, a mid-tenor but with an enlarged range,

was a natural extension of his instrument: he elaborated a given melody or improvised new lines on the principles found in his trumpet playing. When applied to his singing his rhythmic subtleties were all the more striking, and he introduced a freedom and jazz sensibility that continue to be an important influence in popular singing.

Armstrong's publications for trumpet include *Fifty Hot Choruses* and *125 Hot Breaks* (both 1927), *Louis Satchmo Armstrong's Dixieland Trumpet Solos* (1947) and *Trumpet Method* (1961).

BIBLIOGRAPHY
L. Armstrong: *Swing that Music* (New York, 1936)
W. Russell: 'Louis Armstrong', *Jazzmen*, ed. F. Ramsey jr and C. Smith (New York, 1939), 119
A. McCarthy: *The Trumpet in Jazz* (London, 1946)
R. Goffin: *Louis Armstrong: le roi du jazz* (Paris, 1947; Eng. trans., 1947/R1977 as *Horn of Plenty*)
H. Panassié: *Louis Armstrong* (Paris, 1947)
L. Malson: *Les maîtres du jazz* (Paris, 1952), 36ff
J. Slawe: *Louis Armstrong: zehn monographische Studien* (Basle, 1953)
L. Armstrong: *Satchmo* (New York, 1954)
A. Hodeir: *Hommes et problèmes du jazz* (Paris, 1954; Eng. trans., 1956/R as *Jazz: its Evolution and Essence*)
M. Edey: 'Louis Armstrong', *Jazz Review*, ii (1959), Aug, 28
A. McCarthy: *Louis Armstrong* (London, 1960)
R. Hadlock: *Jazz Masters of the 20s* (New York, 1965), 13–49
M. Harrison: 'Armstrong at Symphony Hall', *Jazz Monthly*, x (1965), Jan, 22
B. Rust: *Jazz Records: 1897–1942* (London, 1965, rev. 2/1969)
W. Austin: *Music in the 20th Century* (New York, 1966)
J. Grunnet Jepsen: *Jazz Records: 1942–1965*, i (Holte, 1966)
M. Williams: *Jazz Masters of New Orleans* (New York, 1967), 162ff
G. Schuller: *Early Jazz* (New York, 1968), 89–133
M. Williams: *The Jazz Tradition* (New York, 1970), 47ff
L. Armstrong: *A Self-portrait* (New York, 1971)
M. Jones and J. Chilton: *Louis: the Louis Armstrong Story* (London, 1971)
L. Feather: *From Satchmo to Miles* (New York, 1972), 13ff
H. Caffey: 'The Musical Style of Louis Armstrong', *Journal of Jazz Studies*, iii (1975), Aug, 72
                                                    JAMES DAPOGNY

Armstrong, Sheila (Ann) (*b* Ashington, Northumberland, 13 Aug 1942). English soprano. She studied at the Royal Academy of Music, winning, in 1965, a Kathleen Ferrier Memorial Scholarship and the Mozart Prize; that year she made her professional operatic début at Sadler's Wells, as Despina. The following year she sang Belinda in *Dido and Aeneas* at Glyndebourne, where she later undertook Pamina, Zerlina, and Fiorilla in *Il turco in Italia*. She made her Covent Garden début as Marzelline in May 1973. A singer whose voice is warm, flexible and richly coloured (even when slightly insecure under pressure in its upper register), and whose lively artistry is enhanced by her charm of appearance, she also appears frequently on the concert platform. Her New York début was at a Philharmonic concert in April 1973. She was the first performer of John McCabe's *Notturni ed alba* (dedicated to her) at the 1970 Three Choirs Festival.   MAX LOPPERT

Armstrong, Sir Thomas (Henry Wait) (*b* Peterborough, 15 June 1898). English organist, conductor, adjudicator and educationist. He was trained as an articled pupil to Haydn Keeton, organist of Peterborough Cathedral. After being assistant organist there from 1915 to 1916 he won music awards at the Royal College of Music and then at Keble College, Oxford, where his studies were interrupted by service in France in World War I. He later resumed them and then became successively assistant organist of Manchester Cathedral (1921–2) and organist of St Peter's, Eaton Square, London (1922–8); during the latter period he studied at the RCM with

Ex.1 (rhythm section plays only on first beat of odd-numbered bars)

Holst and Vaughan Williams. He took the Oxford DMus in 1929. From 1928 to 1933 he was organist of Exeter Cathedral. When William Harris was appointed to St George's Chapel, Windsor, in 1933 he succeeded him as organist of Christ Church, Oxford, and remained there until he was appointed principal of the Royal Academy of Music in 1955, a post from which he retired in 1968. He was knighted in 1958. He was also made an honorary DMus of Edinburgh University. While organist of Exeter Cathedral he was also director of music to the University College of the Southwest and this experience stood him in good stead in his appointment at Oxford, where he achieved success as a tutor and lecturer and – in succession to Hugh Allen – as conductor of the Bach Choir and the Orchestral Society.

Armstrong's enviable fluency as a speaker, coupled with his meticulous choice of words and imagery, made him one of the most sought-after adjudicators in the country and qualified him ideally to succeed Walford Davies in 1936 in a series of excellent music broadcasts to schools. Through these two activities he reached a very wide public and was an obvious choice as a judge at international music competitions. In his earlier days he was influenced by Hamilton Harty, for whom he worked while in Manchester, and by his teachers Vaughan Williams and Holst but probably above all by Allen, director of the RCM and then professor of music at Oxford, who became an intimate friend. When he was principal of the RAM he travelled abroad extensively, meeting foreign musicians in their own environment and gathering ideas that would broaden the basis of the RAM and encourage an outward-looking attitude among its students. An extremely competent and versatile musician, he has published two short books and a few articles and is an able composer in the smaller choral forms; much of his church music, as well as other pieces for small choral ensembles, has been published.

WRITINGS
' "The Messiah" Accompaniments', *ML*, ix (1928), 18
Mendelssohn's Elijah (London, 1931)
Strauss's Tone-poems (London, 1931)
'The Influence of Organists upon English Music', *ML*, lxii (1931), 1
'Bach and the English Choralist', *MT*, lxxxxi (1950), 261
'The Organist in the Community', *MT*, lxxxxiv (1953), 163
'The Frankfort Group', *PRMA*, lxxxv (1958–9), 1
'Cyril Scott: a Pioneer', *MT*, c (1959), 453
'A National Policy for Music: the Young Musician', *MT*, ci (1960), 291
Other articles in *MT*

BIBLIOGRAPHY
T. Armstrong: 'My First Year', *RAM Magazine* (1956), no.164, p.30
R. Golding: *RAM Magazine* (1968), no.195, p.2
BERNARD ROSE

Arnaud, François (*b* Aubignan, Carpentras, 27 July 1721; *d* Paris, 2 Dec 1784). French man of letters. He came to Paris from Provence in 1752 as attaché to Prince Louis of Württemburg. He was Abbé de Grandchamp (1768), librarian to the Comte de Provence and historiographer to the order of St Lazare, and in 1771 became a member of the Académie Française. He was a classical scholar and accomplished linguist and translator, and collaborated with his close friend J. B. A. Suard (whose wife was said to be his mistress) on the *Journal étranger*, *Gazette littéraire de l'Europe*, *Variétés littéraires* and other writings. His humour, historical knowledge and vigorous polemical style make him stand out among the many literary writers on music of the second half of the 18th century. Arnaud was a member of the Encyclopedist generation and deeply influenced by its ideas, but he did not share Marmontel's or Rousseau's exclusive admiration for Italian music. The *Lettre sur la musique* of 1754 sketches an unrealized plan for a major historical work; La Borde included it in his *Essai sur la musique*. Arnaud was particularly interested in prosody, arguing that every language should have its own melody or 'déclamation lyrique'; his ideas had considerable influence on Grétry. Arnaud had long advocated operatic reform, and his fervent admiration for Gluck, who seemed to revive antique tragedy, led to his being nicknamed the Gluckists' High Priest. He engaged in a duel of wits with Marmontel, in whose *Polymnie* he figures as Trigaut. He saw Gluck's synthesis of French and Italian elements as the logical outcome of Encyclopedist ideas, especially those of d'Alembert, and attacked the superficiality of Italian opera in his 'Profession de foi en musique' (*Journal de Paris*, 1777). The pamphlet *La soirée perdue à l'Opéra* is attributed to him in his posthumous *Oeuvres*, in the *Mémoires pour servir à l'histoire de la révolution opérée dans la musique par M. le Chevalier Gluck*, and by Bricqueville, but it may be the work of Pascal Boyer. When he died Arnaud was beginning work on the musical part of Pancoucke's *Encyclopédie méthodique*.

WRITINGS
(only those on music)
Lettre sur la musique à M. le comte de Caylus (Paris, 1754)
Réflexions sur la musique en général, et sur la musique française en particulier (Paris, 1754)
'Lettre sur un ouvrage italien intitulé Il Teatro alla Moda', *Oeuvres complètes*, ed. L. Boudon (Paris, 1808), i
'Essai sur le mélodrame ou drame lyrique', *Oeuvres complètes*, ii

The following are in *Oeuvres complètes*, ii, and in G. M. le Blond, ed.: *Mémoires pour servir à l'histoire de la révolution opérée dans la musique par M. le Chevalier Gluck* (Naples, 1781):
'Lettre à Mme D'[Augny] et à la comtesse de B . . . sur l'Iphigénie de Gluck' (1774)
'La soirée perdue à l'opéra' (1776)
'Le souper des enthousiastes' (1776)
'Lettre au P. Martini' (1776)
'Lettre à l'ermite de la forêt de Sénart' (1777)
'Profession de foi en musique, d'un amateur des beaux-arts, à M. de la Harpe' (1777)
'Lettre sur l'Iphigénie en Tauride de M. le Chevalier Gluck' (1779)

BIBLIOGRAPHY
L. G. Michaud: *Biographie universelle* (Paris, 1842–65)
E. de Bricqueville: *L'Abbé Arnaud et la réforme de l'opéra au XVIIIᵉ siècle* (Avignon, 1881)
——: *Un critique musical au siècle dernier* (Paris, 1883)
——: *Deux abbés d'opéra au siècle dernier: J. Pellegrin, F. Arnaud* (Avignon, 1889)
JULIAN RUSHTON

Arnaud, (Germaine) Yvonne (*b* Bordeaux, 20 Dec 1890; *d* London, 20 Sept 1958). British actress and pianist of French birth. She entered the Paris Conservatoire at the age of nine, and when she was 12 won a *premier prix* for the piano. Early in her career she toured extensively in Europe, playing under such conductors as Nikisch, Mengelberg and Mahler. After settling in London she appeared in *The Quaker Girl* at the Adelphi Theatre in 1911, and thereafter her career was primarily that of a popular actress, though she still from time to time took part in concerts and broadcasts as a fluent and lively pianist. After her death a memorial LP record was issued of her performing as pianist, actress and singer, and in 1965 a new repertory theatre at Guildford (where she lived) was named after her.

BIBLIOGRAPHY
O. Malet [pseud. of Lady Auriel Rosemary Malet Vaughan]: *Marraine: a Portrait of my Godmother* (London, 1961)
FRANK DAWES

Arnaut de Mareuil [Maroill] (*fl c*1170–1200). Provençal troubadour. He was apparently born at Mareuil-sur-Belle in the diocese of Périgord. According to his romanticized biography, he was by profession a scribe and notary, but abandoned his poorly paid duties in favour of a more enjoyable existence as troubadour; in the latter capacity he was first at the court of Roger II, Viscount of Béziers, and his wife Adelaide, and afterwards at the court of William VIII, Count of Montpellier. Of the 26 chansons attributed to him, six survive with music; 13 more works are ascribed to him in various sources, but are apparently not his. In addition, he wrote both *saluts d'amours* – poetic love-letters, five of which survive – and an *ensenhamen*, a didactic, moralizing poem commenting on contemporary customs. He was among the first to cultivate the latter two genres. Arnaut's poetry was much appreciated by Petrarch. Among the surviving melodies, only that for *La grans beutatz* is cast in bar form, the second *pes* recurring in varied form in the cauda and set off by new material. The remaining melodies do not repeat entire phrases, although characteristic motifs may recur in irregular fashion. *Si.m destreignetz* has a range of an 11th, but all other melodies remain within a 9th. There is no strong evidence for regularity of rhythmic organization.

See also TROUBADOURS, TROUVÈRES.

WORKS

Edition: *Der musikalische Nachlass der Troubadours*, ed. F. Gennrich, Summa musicae medii aevi, iii–iv, xv (Darmstadt, 1958–65) [G]

PC[no.] Number of chanson in A. Pillet and H. Carstens: *Bibliographie der Troubadours*, Schriften der Königsberger Gelehrten Gesellschaft, Sonderreihe, iii (Halle, 1933)

Aissi com cel qu'am'e non es amatz, PC 30.3, G iii, 57
La franca captenensa, PC 30.15, G iii,58; iv, 143
La grans beutatz e.l. pretz fis enseignamens, PC 30.16, G iii, 58; iv, 143
L'ensignamens e.l. pretz e la valors, PC 30.17, G iii, 59; iv, 144
Mout eron dous mei consir, PC 30.19, G iii, 60
Si.m destreignetz, domna, vos et amors, PC 30.23, G iii,61; iv, 144

BIBLIOGRAPHY

H. J. Chaytor: *The Troubadours* (Cambridge, 1912)
R. C. Johnston: *Les poésies lyriques du troubadour Arnaut de Mareuil* (Paris, 1935)

For further bibliography *see* TROUBADOURS, TROUVÈRES.

THEODORE KARP

Arnaut de Zwolle, Henri (*b* Zwolle, late 14th or early 15th century; *d* Paris, 6 Sept 1466). Netherlands doctor of medicine, astrologer, astronomer and author of a treatise on musical instruments. He was probably educated at the University of Paris, since he called himself a student of Jean Fusoris, a professor there and a doctor and astronomer like his student. After receiving his medical degree, Arnaut entered the service of Philip the Good, Duke of Burgundy. He is listed in a court record of 1432 as 'professeur en médecine et astronomier'. Probably between 1454 and 1461 he left the Burgundian court in Dijon and entered the service of the French kings, firstly Charles VII and later Louis XI, where he remained until he died of the plague in 1466.

Arnaut's descriptions of musical instruments appear in a manuscript (*F-Pn* lat.7295) that also contains various scientific and particularly astronomical treatises and diagrams, many of them copied out by Arnaut himself (for his diagrams of the *dulce melos* and harpsichord, *see* DULCE MELOS; HARPSICHORD, fig.2). It was probably written in Dijon about 1440. The musical section includes a treatise by Jehan des Murs and later 15th-century additions dealing with musical intervals and matters relating to the organ, for example formulae for scales, the specifications of several instruments, and notes on the construction of bellows and the composition of pipe metal. Arnaut himself furnished detailed technical information on the design and construction of the lute, the harp and various keyboard instruments – the harpsichord, clavichord, *dulce melos* and organ. Unfortunately his Latin is not always clear and some of his instructions therefore remain ambiguous.

Arnaut's work is important, for it gives the earliest technical description of most of these instruments and hence is an invaluable source for their history. His account of the harpsichord is particularly interesting since he explains that any one of four actions can be used, and none is quite like any that later became standard. One of these is a form of primitive hammer action not unlike that on a pianoforte. Arnaut's name for the harpsichord, *clavisimbalum* (derived from *clavis* and *cimbalum*), i.e. keyed dulcimer, suggests that the hammer action was the earliest and that plucking was only later found to be preferable, a value judgment that Arnaut himself made. He stated that metal plectra were used in the harpsichord, but he also mentioned quill, the substance most often used in succeeding centuries. The hammer action appears also on Arnaut's *dulce melos* that F. W. Galpin identified as the echiquier or CHEKKER, but Ripin (1975) challenged Galpin's assumption and suggested that 'chekker' is a synonym for 'clavichord'.

BIBLIOGRAPHY

G. le Cerf and E. R. Labande: *Instruments de musique du XVIe siècle: les traités d'Henri-Arnaut de Zwolle et de divers anonymes* (Paris, 1932) [incl. facs., transcr. and trans.]
C. Clutton: 'Arnault's MS', *GSJ*, v (1952), 3
I. Harwood: 'A Fifteenth Century Lute Design', *LSJ*, ii (1960), 3
E. M. Ripin: 'The Early Clavichord', *MQ*, liii (1967), 518
——: 'Towards an Identification of the Chekker', *GSJ*, xxviii (1975), 11

HOWARD MAYER BROWN

Arndt, Günther (*b* Charlottenburg, Berlin, 1 April 1907; *d* Berlin, 25 Dec 1976). German choral conductor and radio producer. He studied at the Academy for School and Church Music at Berlin, 1925–30, and musicology at the university there. A choirmaster and lecturer in music at the Berlin Volkshochschule (1932–40), he also taught music at a secondary school (1932–4), and was co-founder and conductor of the Berlin Heinrich Schütz Chorale. With the resumption of post-war musical life in Berlin he was appointed head of Berlin radio's chamber music department and from 1949 was a specialist adviser on symphonic music for Rundfunk im Amerikanischen Sektor Berlins. He founded the Berlin Motet Choir in 1950 and was its conductor to 1960, and he was also conductor of the RIAS Chamber Choir, 1955–72. From 1964 until his retirement in 1972 he was deputy head of music for RIAS, and he was also music director at Berlin's Freie und Technische Hochschule. Arndt gave the RIAS Chamber Choir an international reputation through numerous broadcasts and concert tours; he has done much to promote contemporary music, giving many first performances including works by Bialas, Henze, Krenek, Schoenberg, Genzmer, Milhaud, Reimann and Sakać. Arndt was awarded the Grosse Verdienstkreuz der Bundesrepublik Deutschland in 1971.

RUDOLF LÜCK

Arndt-Ober, Margarethe (*b* Berlin, 15 April 1885; *d* Bad Sachsa, Harz, 24 March 1971). German contralto.

She studied with Benno Stolzenberg and her future husband Arthur Arndt in Berlin, and made her début in 1906 in Frankfurt an der Oder as Azucena in *Il trovatore*. She joined the Berlin Court Opera in 1907 and remained a prominent member of it until 1945. From 1913 to 1917 she was at the Metropolitan: she was its first Octavian, and took part in the première of de Koven's *Canterbury Pilgrims*. She sang at the Zoppot Woods Festival (1922–42), and as a guest in Spain, Holland and Norway. She had a dark but very supple voice, a fine figure (which made her a splendid Octavian) and remarkable ability as an actress. After retiring she lived in the Harz mountains.

LEO RIEMENS

Arne, Cecilia. English soprano, wife of Thomas Augustine Arne; *see* YOUNG family.

Arne, Michael (*b* c1740; *d* Lambeth, 14 Jan 1786). English composer. According to Burney's unsubstantiated statement, Michael was Thomas Arne's 'natural son'. His aunt, Mrs Cibber, was responsible for his upbringing. Under her guidance he is said to have made his stage début as the Page in Otway's tragedy *The Orphan*. He ·first appeared as a singer in Manfredini's concert on 20 February 1750, but his career as actor and vocalist was brief. Burney comments that 'his father tried to make him a singer, but he was naturally idle and not very quick. However, he acquired a powerful hand on the harpsichord'. He showed an early gift as a composer. *The Floweret*, his first collection of songs (1750), contains 'The Highland Laddie', a song in the Scottish style which became popular and as late as 1775 was adapted by Linley in *The Duenna*.

On 5 February 1751, he first played one of his father's organ concertos, of which he was the principal exponent for 30 years. Thereafter he found his true vocation as keyboard player and composer to the theatres and pleasure gardens. From 1756 onwards he contributed songs to various dramatic productions and in 1764 collaborated with Battishill in setting Rolt's *Almena*, which enjoyed a limited success. His most famous song, *The Lass with the Delicate Air*, first appeared in 1762. On 5 November 1766, he married Elizabeth Wright, a young singer whom he had heard at Ranelagh in 1763. His wife sang the leading roles in many Drury Lane productions, including Arne's setting of Garrick's *Cymon* in 1767; this was his biggest success. In the same year he is reputed to have built a laboratory at Chelsea in order to study alchemy, which led him to a debtors' prison. When Mrs Arne died, on 1 May 1769, Burney bluntly placed the blame for her early death on the overwork to which her husband had subjected her.

In 1771–2 he toured Germany with a pupil, Ann Venables, and conducted the first public performance in Germany of Handel's *Messiah* on 21 May 1772 at Hamburg (preceded by a private performance on 15 April). On his return to England he married Miss Venables. In December 1776 he was engaged by Thomas Ryder to produce *Cymon* in Dublin, where his second wife was a popular attraction. But the lure of alchemy again prevailed; he took a house at Clontarf to resume the search for the philosopher's stone, which again drove him into debt. While confined to a Dublin

spongeing-house, he was assisted by Michael Kelly's father, who provided him with a piano in return for young Kelly's daily lesson. Returning to London, he was engaged as composer at Covent Garden for several seasons. One unusual engagement was to provide a harpsichord accompaniment for a display of moving pictures, *Eidophusikon*, in 1781. In 1784–5 he directed the Lenten Oratorios at the Haymarket. After his father's death he retained many of his unpublished MSS, including the organ concertos, and in 1784 announced his intention of publishing them. But he died, leaving his second wife destitute, without having done so. The concertos were preserved and published in 1787 by John Groombridge.

His daughter, Jemima, who had nursed him in his last illness, was a leading singer at Drury Lane from 1795 to 1800.

WORKS

DRAMATIC

CG – Covent Garden   DL – Drury Lane

Florizel and Perdita, or The Winter's Tale (Garrick, after Shakespeare)	DL, 21 Jan 1756	by Boyce; 1 song by Arne
The Humorous Lieutenant (Beaumont, Fletcher)	CG, 10 Dec 1756	
Harlequin Sorcerer (L. Theobald)	CG, 1757	by T. A. Arne; 1 song by M. Arne
Harlequin's Invasion (Garrick)	DL, 31 Dec 1759	by Boyce, Aylward and Arne
The Heiress or the Antigallican (Mozeen)	DL, 21 May 1759	
Edgar and Emmeline (John Hawkesworth)	DL, 31 Jan 1761	
A Midsummer Night's Dream: later renamed The Fairy Tale (Garrick, Colman, after Shakespeare)	DL, 23 Nov 1763	by Burney; 3 songs by Arne
Hymen (Allen)	DL, 23 Jan 1764	
Almena (Richard Rolt)	DL, 2 Nov 1764	with Battishill
Cymon (Garrick)	DL, 2 Jan 1767	revival, 17 Jan 1778, new ov., songs
Linco's Travels (Garrick)	DL, 6 April 1767	with J. Vernon
Tom Jones (Garrick)	CG, 14 Jan 1769	1 song
The Maid of the Vale (Holcroft, after Goldoni)	Smock Alley, 15 Feb 1775	
Emperor of the Moon (after Aphra Behn)	Patagonian, 22 March 1777	
The Fairy Tale (2-act version of A Midsummer Night's Dream)	Haymarket, 18 July 1777	5 numbers
The Fathers, or the Good-natured Man (Fielding)	CG, 30 Nov 1778	1 song
Love in a Village (Bickerstaffe), revival	CG, 13 Feb 1779	songs
All alive at Jersey, pasticcio	Sadler's Wells, 22 May 1779	songs
The Conscious Lovers (Steele), revival	CG, 27 Sept 1779	1 song
The Belle's Stratagem (Hannah Cowley)	CG, 22 Feb 1780	1 song, minuet
The Artifice (W. A. Miles)	DL, 14 April 1780	
The Choice of Harlequin, or the Indian Chief (Messink)	CG, 26 Dec 1781	
Vertumnus and Pomona (Matthew Feilde)	CG, 21 Feb 1782	
The Positive Man (J. O'Keefe)	CG, 16 March 1782	by S. Arnold, Arne
The Maid of the Mill (J. O'Keefe), revival	CG, 25 Sept 1782	songs
The Capricious Lady (Beaumont, Fletcher, W. Cooke)	CG, 17 Jan 1783	1 glee
Tristram Shandy (L. McNally, after Sterne)	CG, 26 April 1783	2 songs

SONG COLLECTIONS

The Floweret (London, 1750); The Violet (London, 1756); A Favourite Collection of English Songs (London, 1757); New Songs and Ballads

(London, 1765); New Songs sung by Miss Wright at Vauxhall (London, c1765); A Collection of Favourite Songs sung by Mrs. Arne (London, 1773); Ranelagh Songs (London, 1780); c50 single songs for Vauxhall and Ranelagh

INSTRUMENTAL

Lesson, hpd (London, 1761)

BIBLIOGRAPHY

C. Burney: 'M. Arne', Rees's Cyclopaedia (London, 1802–19)
M. Kelly: Reminiscences (London, 1826, 2/1826/R1968)
W. H. Cummings: Dr. Arne and Rule Britannia (London, 1912)
M. Sands: Invitation to Ranelagh (London, 1946)
J. A. Parkinson: Index to the Vocal Works of Thomas and Michael Arne (Detroit, 1972)
T. J. Walsh: Opera in Dublin 1705–1797 (Dublin, 1973)

JOHN A. PARKINSON

Arne, Thomas Augustine (b London, baptized 28 May 1710; d London, 5 March 1778). English composer and violinist, the leading figure in English theatrical music in the mid-18th century. His birthdate is generally given as 12 March 1710.

1. LIFE. Arne's grandfather and father, both named Thomas, were upholsterers, and both held office in the city Company of Upholders. The grandfather, soon after being elected master of the company, became bankrupt and died in a debtors' prison. His son, Arne's father, was apparently prosperous at the time, and not only rented a large house in King Street, Covent Garden, where he carried on his business, but could also afford to send his own son to Eton College and planned afterwards to apprentice him to an attorney. Arne's love of music, however, had shown itself at an early age; Burney (who was later apprenticed to him) tells of the young composer smuggling a spinet into his room and muffling the strings with a handkerchief so that he could practice while the family was asleep. He also borrowed a servant's livery to gain admission to the gallery of the Italian Opera, and it was there that he probably met Michael Festing, a member of the orchestra and an ex-pupil of Geminiani.

Festing, roughly 30 years Arne's senior, taught him the violin and was probably a great influence on his career. Together they went to St George's, Hanover Square, to hear Roseingrave compete for the post of organist and in 1733 they went to Oxford for the Music Act, where Handel's Athalia was performed and where Handel gave one of his famous organ improvisations. It was probably Festing who persuaded Arne's father of his son's talent for music, and this would fit in with Burney's account of the elder Arne's accidentally discovering his son leading a group of players at a friend's musical evening. The outcome was that the father agreed to his son's turning his talent for music to account.

Arne at once set about teaching his sister Susanna Maria (later Mrs Cibber) and his younger brother Richard to sing, and the three young Arnes, with their father as impresario, gave a performance of Handel's Acis and Galatea at the Haymarket Theatre in April 1732, an act of musical piracy which, as Burney wrote 'seems to have been the origin of Handel's oratorios in still life'. They soon became associated with a group of musicians, including Henry Carey and J. F. Lampe, who aimed at establishing an English opera 'after the Italian manner'. Susanna sang the title role in Lampe's Amelia, and a year later both she and Richard took part in Arne's setting of Addison's Rosamond. Richard also played Tom Thumb in Lampe's burlesque Opera of

Operas, or Tom Thumb the Great, but the group split up and in the autumn of 1733 Arne produced his rival setting of the Opera of Operas at the Haymarket, which eclipsed Lampe's version at Drury Lane.

In 1734 Arne's masque Dido and Aeneas was performed at the Haymarket for nearly two months, and led to the Arnes' engagement at Drury Lane. Arne's first composition there was the masque Love and Glory, in which his sister and brother sang Venus and Mercury. It was intended to celebrate the marriage of Princess Anne and the Prince of Orange, but Handel preceded Arne's masque by a week with the serenata Il Parnasso in festa, the first performance of which was attended by the royal family. Drury Lane's offering was ignored, but two years later the Prince and Princess of Wales commanded a performance of Arne's successful masque The Fall of Phaeton.

Meanwhile Arne's sister Susanna Maria had married Theophilus Cibber, whose father Colley Cibber taught her to act so that she could obtain more status in the theatre. Her first appearance as an actress was in Aaron Hill's tragedy Zara for which Arne wrote incidental music, including a march which was encored every night. In the following year Arne married Cecilia Young, who had sung in Lampe's opera Britannia. The marriage, it seems, was made largely for professional reasons, and against the wishes of Cecilia's father since Arne was a Roman Catholic. However, the marriage began brilliantly with Arne's setting of Milton's Comus, adapted for the stage by John Dalton.

Comus, produced at Drury Lane on 4 March 1738, was an immediate and lasting success and two years later Arne clinched his reputation with the masque of Alfred, given by command of the Prince of Wales in the gardens of his Thames-side residence, Cliefden (Cliveden) House. Later that year Arne composed songs for the Drury Lane productions of Shakespeare's The Tempest and As You Like It, and in 1741 for Twelfth Night and The Merchant of Venice.

Mrs Cibber's marriage had now broken down, and to avoid scandal she left London for the Dublin stage. Handel was there, giving oratorio performances, including Messiah in April 1742. Three months later Arne and his wife arrived in Dublin, and after a benefit concert for Mrs Arne, at which Mrs Cibber also sang, plans were laid for the next two Dublin seasons. In these concerts and dramatic entertainments Arne introduced both his own and Handel's music, and included in 1744 the production of his oratorio The Death of Abel.

On his return to London Arne resumed his engagements at Drury Lane, and in September 1745 his setting of 'God Save the King' was sung 'by the Gentlemen of that House' every night until the danger of the Young Pretender's rebellion had passed. At Vauxhall Gardens his dialogue Colin and Phoebe was encored throughout the season and established him for the next 20 years or more as the leading composer at Vauxhall, Ranelagh and Marylebone. During this period he published yearly song collections with such titles as Lyric Harmony, Vocal Melody and The Agreeable Musical Choice.

In 1750 Mrs Cibber quarrelled with Garrick about her salary and for three seasons was engaged at Covent Garden. Arne followed her and a battle ensued between the two theatres, each giving rival productions of Romeo and Juliet, Arne composing a dirge for the Funeral

Procession at Covent Garden. Garrick put on a new version of *Alfred*, using only 'Rule, Britannia' and another song from Arne's score. Arne's reply was to give *Alfred* two years later 'in the Manner of an Oratorio' with music 'newly composed'. But the theatrical battle was soon over, and Mrs Cibber returned to Drury Lane to play Juliet to Garrick's Romeo.

1. Thomas Augustine Arne: etching after Bartolozzi

In 1755 Arne and his wife paid another visit to Ireland to introduce his pupil Charlotte Brent and his wife's young niece Polly Young to the Dublin public. Relations between Arne and his wife had for some years been strained. According to the composer the cause was her frequent indispositions, which he declared were the result of her 'passions, equal to raving madness'. Certainly in 1754 the production of *Eliza* was postponed from February to May on account of her illness. Similar postponements were made in Dublin, and when *Eliza* was eventually given there Mrs Arne 'had the Misfortune of a violent hoarseness'. The marriage had reached breaking-point, and after their benefit night at the end of the season Arne returned to London with Miss Brent while his wife remained in Dublin with Polly Young, Arne having legally contracted to provide her with an allowance of £40 a year.

In London Arne concentrated mainly on the publication of his music, the Eight Sets of Lessons for the Harpsichord, the Seven Sonatas for Two Violins and a Bass, the music in *Alfred* and *Eliza* and collections of his songs sung at the public gardens. In 1759 Arne was admitted to the degree of Doctor in Music at Oxford. Deciding that Miss Brent was ready for the London stage, he approached Garrick, who would not agree to the terms proposed; he then offered his pupil to Covent Garden, the management of which was virtually in the hands of the tenor, John Beard, who not only agreed to Arne's proposal but staged a revival of *The Beggar's Opera* with Miss Brent as Polly and himself as Macheath. This had a continuous run of nearly two months and was followed by *The Jovial Crew* with new music by Arne and the miniature English *opera buffa*, *Thomas and Sally*.

In Lent 1761 Arne produced his oratorio *Judith* at Drury Lane, and the following Lent announced performances of his own oratorios together with Handel's *Alexander's Feast*. This provoked an immediate response from John Stanley and John Christopher Smith, who had taken on the performance of Handel's oratorios since his death: they gave an oratorio season at Covent Garden on the same nights as Arne's at Drury Lane. Arne did not again attempt a similar venture. Meanwhile he had achieved the greatest success of his career with the production of *Artaxerxes* at Covent Garden in February 1762.

Artaxerxes was the first and only English opera 'after the Italian manner' to hold its place on the stage until the 19th century. It provided Miss Brent with a coloratura part the like of which had never before been heard in the English theatre, and her final air, 'The Soldier tir'd of War's Alarms' became a touchstone of vocal agility. Almost equally successful was the pasticcio *Love in a Village* (see fig.3) partly composed by Arne but also containing favourite songs from the pleasure gardens and airs by such Italian composers as Geminiani and Galuppi. Arne was at the summit of his career, and in January 1764 his masque *The Arcadian Nuptials*, celebrating the marriage of the Prince of Brunswick to Princess Augusta, was given at Covent Garden.

In December Arne's comic opera *The Guardian Outwitted*, composed to his own libretto, survived only six nights at Covent Garden, and the following April his sole Italian opera, *L'olimpiade*, written for the male soprano Manzuoli, was given only twice at the Italian opera. In 1766 his sister Mrs Cibber died and Miss Brent married the violinist Pinto. Two years later Covent Garden's production of *Artaxerxes* with Mrs Pinto as Mandane rivalled and outshone the revival directed by Arne at Drury Lane, and for the next few years he found little employment at either theatre.

Arne had, however, found a new, congenial and profitable activity. He had become a member of both the Noblemen and Gentlemen's Catch Club and the Madrigal Society, and in May 1767 he gave at Ranelagh House a concert of catches and glees which he claimed 'the first entertainment of the kind exhibited in this, or any other kingdom'. The enterprise was so successful that almost every year Arne gave similar concerts, in which he introduced short dramatic pieces to display the abilities of his singing pupils. But the lack of regular theatrical employment put him in financial difficulties, and in 1770 his wife's solicitor threatened legal proceedings for his being £10 in arrear with his maintenance payments.

Despite his financial troubles the last decade of Arne's life saw the production of many of his best works. Of these the most important were the *Shakespeare Ode* (1769), the masque *The Fairy Prince* (1771), the afterpiece *May Day* (1775) and the music to *Caractacus* (now lost). In October 1777 Arne and his wife were reconciled. Two months later he became seriously ill and died on 5 March 1778. In his will he left all his possessions, including his musical scores, to 'my beloved wife Cecilia and my only son Michael'.

2. WORKS. Nearly all of Arne's MS scores are either lost or destroyed, possibly on account of fires at Covent Garden, Drury Lane and the Sardinian Chapel, where Arne was organist for a time, and for which he wrote two masses and a Requiem. The lost works include his first oratorio *The Death of Abel*, of which a single printed song survives, the Italian opera *L'olimpiade* and the incidental music to *Caractacus*, which Samuel Arnold described as 'containing some of the brightest and most vigorous emanations of our English *Amphion*'. However, a considerable amount of his music for the theatre, instrumental music and songs was published. A few of his more important works were printed in full score, but even in these the recitatives and choruses were usually omitted, as was the custom in his day. This is particularly unfortunate in the case of *Alfred*, given originally as a Masque and later performed 'in the Manner of an Oratorio'. Several different editions of the songs were published, and it is difficult to assess Arne's actual achievement in this work, of which the composer himself evidently had a high opinion.

Burney described Arne's musical idiom as 'an agreeable mixture of Italian, English and Scots', but there is little doubt of its essentially English character. Wagner's remark about the first eight notes of 'Rule, Britannia' may seem an overstatement, unless it is remembered that Arne's Shakespeare settings have become part of England's musical heritage, despite their typically 18th-century response to Shakespeare's verse. In a composing life of some 45 years Arne's output of songs was prolific. The best of these songs have an elegance and melodiousness that rise above the tide of musical fashion. Their scope is admittedly limited, and the success of *Colin and Phoebe* gave rise to a succession of pastoral dialogues, just as 'Now Phoebus sinketh in the West' from *Comus* inspired the numerous bacchanalian songs that included the popular catch 'Which is the properest day to drink?'

Arne's genius was essentially lyrical. Of his Vauxhall songs 'The fond appeal' from *Lyric Harmony*, i, is typical, and a similar mood can be found in such melodies as 'Thou soft flowing Avon' from *Shakespeare Ode* and 'Sleep, gentle cherub' from *Judith*. *Judith*, indeed, is the only work in which Arne aspired to the epic heights of Handel, but despite such fine choruses as 'Who may Jehovah's wrath abide?' he was far from reaching Handelian grandeur of inspiration.

Of Arne's theatre music, *Comus* (1738) is his most individual and successful work. It owes not a little to Handel's *Acis and Galatea*, which Arne and his father had pirated in 1732. Its pastoral airs are limpid and expressive and the bacchanalian songs and choruses have sprightliness and vigour. There is an almost complete absence of da capo airs, and the recitative is always

melodious and natural. Apart from *The Judgment of Paris* Arne rarely achieved later such exuberant tunefulness.

His next important work, the masque of *Alfred* (1740), was originally a heroic drama with musical scenes of the type created by Dryden and Purcell. But in spite of the popularity of 'Rule, Britannia' and some of

2. A rare example of T. A. Arne's autograph MS: the opening of the Adagio from his Violin Sonata in E, recently discovered and identified (GB-Lbm Add.39957, f.34); see Parkinson, 1976

the solo songs, it never succeeded on the stage, and for some 15 years Arne added further music to his score so that it could be performed 'in the Manner of an Oratorio'. Choruses and recitatives are now lost, so that the work is difficult to judge (or perform) in its incomplete state. Evidently a more ambitious work than *Comus*, its dramatic framework is so slender that even in its final form as a secular oratorio it is in many ways unsatisfactory.

As Burney wrote, 'None of this ingenious and pleasing composer's capital productions had full and unequivocal success but *Comus* and *Artaxerxes*, at the distance of 24 years from each other.' *Artaxerxes*, an English *opera seria* based on Arne's translation of Metastasio, succeeded in its day because English theatre audiences were introduced for the first time to the florid style of operatic singing of the Italians Tenducci and

3. A scene from Arne's pasticcio 'Love in a Village' with Edward Shuter as Justice Woodcock (left), John Beard as Hawthorne (centre) and John Dunstall as Hodge: painting by Johann Zoffany (1734/5–1810) at the National Theatre, London

Peretti and the coloratura of Arne's pupil Charlotte Brent. But Arne was careful also to write for his English theatre singers, Beard, Mattocks and Miss Thomas, airs of the kind to which both they and their audiences were accustomed. Among his more traditionally English-style operas, *Thomas and Sally* is wholly delightful; and of the later works *May Day* is an excellent example of Arne's final musical style.

Arne, according to Burney, was an excellent violinist until rheumatism crippled his bowing arm. He published trio sonatas and two sets of overtures or symphonies, and these little-known works show his easy yet unambitious command of instrumental writing. Of his Lessons for the Harpsichord Parry wrote in the first edition of *Grove* 'though not rich in treatment, nor impressive in character, [they] have genuine traits of musical expression and clearness of workmanship'. This evaluation applies equally to the whole of Arne's instrumental music, including the organ or harpsichord concertos which he wrote for his son Michael to play.

It was indeed Arne's unique gift of melody that made him the most significant English composer of his century. As a 19th-century writer put it:

There was in Arne's compositions a natural ease and elegance, a flow of melody which stole upon the senses, and a fullness and variety in the harmony which satisfied, without surprising the auditor by any new, affected, or extraneous modulation. He had neither the vigour of Purcell, nor the grandeur, simplicity and magnificence of Handel; he apparently aimed at pleasing, and he has fully succeeded.

WORKS
(all printed works published in London)

CG – *Covent Garden*	HM – *Little or New Theatre, Haymarket*	MG – *Marylebone Gardens*
CL – *Cliveden House*	KT – *King's Theatre, Haymarket*	SA – *Smock Alley Theatre, Dublin*
DL – *Drury Lane*	LF – *Lincoln's Inn Fields*	SW – *Sadler's Wells*

DRAMATIC

Title	Librettist	First performance	Sources and revivals
Rosamond	J. Addison	LF, 7 March 1733	2 songs (1734, 1762); 9 songs, *GB-Lbm*
The Opera of Operas, or Tom Thumb the Great	E. Haywood, W. Hatchett, after H. Fielding	HM, 29 Oct 1733	1 song (1734), lib lists 17 others
Dido and Aeneas	B. Booth	HM, 12 Jan 1734	2 songs in The British Musical Miscellany (1734)

Title	Librettist	First performance	Sources and revivals
Love and Glory	T. Phillips	DL, 21 March 1734	Lib lists 14 numbers, lost
Harlequin Orpheus, or The Magical Pipe	—	DL, 3 March 1735	Lost
The Twin Rivals	Farquhar	HM, 21 Aug 1735	Medley ov., act tunes (1736)
Harlequin Restor'd, or The Country Revels	—	DL, 18 Oct 1735	Medley ov., comic tunes (1736)
Greenwich Park		DL, 10 Nov 1735	Act tunes, ?from The Twin Rivals
The Miser	Fielding, after Molière	DL, 13 Nov 1735	Act tunes, ?from The Twin Rivals
Zara	A. Hill, after Voltaire	DL, 12 Jan 1736	March (c1746)
The Fall of Phaeton	Pritchard	DL, 28 Feb 1736	1 song in The Songs in As You Like It (1741), lib lists 5 others
The Rival Queens, or The Death of Alexander the Great	N. Lee	DL, 22 Nov 1736	1 duet in The Songs in As You Like It (1741)
The King and the Miller of Mansfield	R. Dodsley	DL, 29 Jan 1737	1 song in The Musical Entertainer, i (1737)
Comus	J. Dalton, after Milton	DL, 4 March 1738	Score (1740); recits, choruses, Lbm; ed. in MB, iii (1951)
The Tender Husband	R. Steele	DL, 25 Nov 1738	1 song in The Songs in As You Like It (1741)
An Hospital for Fools	J. Miller	DL, 15 Nov 1739	4 songs pubd in lib
Don John, or The Libertine Destroy'd	T. Shadwell	DL, 13 Feb 1740	Songs, Dance of Shepherds, Dance of Furies, lost
Alfred	J. Thomson, D. Mallett	CL, 1 Aug 1740	Expanded, DL, 20 March 1745; revived as Alfred the Great, CG, 12 May 1753; score (1756)
The Judgment of Paris	Congreve	CL, 1 Aug 1740	London, DL, 12 March 1742 (but see Fiske 1966); revived with adds, CG, 3 April 1759; score (c1745); final chorus, Lbm
Oedipus, King of Thebes	Dryden, Lee	DL, 19 Nov 1740	Song, sacrificial scene, lost
The Tempest	Shakespeare	DL, 28 Nov 1740	Revived DL, 31 Jan 1746, with masque Neptune and Amphitrite; 1 song (1746), others Lbm; revived with adds CG, 27 Dec 1776
As You Like It	Shakespeare	DL, 20 Dec 1740	3 songs, incl. When daisies pied, from Love's Labour's Lost (1741)
Twelfth Night	Shakespeare	DL, 15 Jan 1741	Songs, incl. Tell me where, from The Merchant of Venice (1741); score with 2nd setting of Come away, death (c1785)
The Merchant of Venice	Shakespeare	DL, 14 Feb 1741	2 interpolated songs (1742): My bliss too long, To keep my gentle Jessy
The Blind Beggar of Bethnal Green	R. Dodsley	DL, 3 April 1741	6 songs, 1 duet (c1742)
The Rehearsal	G. Villiers	DL, 21 Nov 1741	Battle Duet, Lcm
Miss Lucy in Town	Fielding	DL, 6 May 1742	Lib lists 10 songs, lost; revived as The Country Madcap in London, DL, 10 June 1770
Theodosius, or The Force of Love	N. Lee	SA, 26 April 1744	5 numbers, Lbm
The Temple of Dullness	after interludes in L. Theobald: The Happy Captives	DL, 17 Jan 1745	Lib lists 16 songs, incl. 3 from Miss Lucy in Town, lost; revived as Capochio and Dorinna, MG, 28 July 1768, music lost
The Picture, or The Cuckold in Conceit	J. Miller, after Molière	DL, 11 Feb 1745	Lib lists 5 numbers, lost
King Pepin's Campaign	Shirley	DL, 15 April 1745	Lib lists 19 numbers, lost
Neptune and Amphitrite	—	DL, 31 Jan 1746	Masque added to The Tempest, lost
Harlequin Incendiary, or Columbine Cameron	—	DL, 3 March 1746	Lib lists 14 numbers, lost
The She-gallants	G. Granville	DL, 13 March 1746	1 song in Lyric Harmony, ii (1746)
The Wild-goose Chase	Beaumont, Fletcher	DL, 7 March 1747	Lib lists 1 song, lost
The Foundling	E. Moore	DL, 13 Feb 1748	1 song in Amaryllis, i (1746)
The Provok'd Wife	Vanbrugh	DL, 21 March 1748	1 song in Vocal Melody, i (1749); dialogue lost
Much Ado about Nothing	Shakespeare	DL, 14 Nov 1748	1 song in Vocal Melody, i (1749)
Lethe, or Aesop in the Shades	D. Garrick	DL, 18 Jan 1749	1 song in The Agreeable Musical Choice, vi (c1752), other music by Boyce
The Triumph of Peace	Dodsley	DL, 21 Feb 1748	1 song in A Favourite Collection of English Songs (1757), lib lists 6 other numbers
The Muses' Looking Glass	T. Randolph	CG, 9 March 1749	Masque: War, Peace and Plenty, lost
Henry and Emma, or The Nut-brown Maid (1st setting)	M. Prior	CG, 31 March 1749	Lib lists 14 numbers; ov. as no.3 of Eight Overtures (1751)
Don Saverio	Arne	DL, 15 Feb 1750	Lib lists 18 numbers; 1 song in London Magazine (1752)
The Sacrifice of Iphigenia	—	SW, 16 April 1750	1 song in London Magazine (1751)
Romeo and Juliet	Shakespeare	CG, 28 Sept 1750	Solemn Dirge (c1765)
The Country Lasses, or The Custom of the Manor	C. Johnson	CG, 14 Dec 1751	Sheep-shearing Song in Vocal Melody, iv (1752)
Harlequin Sorcerer	after Theobald	CG, 11 Feb 1752	Comic tunes, 4 songs in Vocal Melody, iv (1752)
The Oracle	S. Cibber, after Saint-Foix	CG, 17 March 1752	Song, chorus in Vocal Melody, iv (1752)
The Drummer, or The Haunted House	Addison	CG, 8 Dec 1752	Dialogue Damon and Florella in Vocal Melody, iv (1752), later added to Harlequin Sorcerer; other music lost
The Sheep-shearing, or Florizel and Perdita	after Shakespeare: The Winter's Tale	CG, 25 March 1754	Revived CG, 22 Dec 1760 with added song, Come let us all be blithe and gay, in The Winter's Amusement, xiii (1761); other music lost
Eliza	R. Rolt	HM, 29 May 1754	Score (1758)

Title	Librettist	First performance	Sources and revivals
Britannia	Mallett	DL, 9 May 1755	Score (1755)
Injured Honour, or The Earl of Westmoreland	H. Brooke	SA, 8 March 1756	Anthem, dirge, triumphal hymn, lost
The Pincushion	J. Gay	SA, 20 March 1756	Songs, duet, lost
Mercury Harlequin	H. Woodward	DL, 27 Dec 1756	1 song (1757)
The Fair Penitent	N. Rowe	CG, 22 April 1757	1 song, lost
Isabella, or The Fatal Marriage	Garrick, after T. Southerne	DL, 2 Dec 1757	4 songs in The Agreeable Musical Choice, viii (1757)
The Prophetess, or The History of Dioclesian	Betterton, after Beaumont, Fletcher	CG, 1 Feb 1758	1 song in A Collection of Songs, ix (c1760)
The Sultan, or Solyman and Zayde		CG, 23 Nov 1758	Masque for The Prophetess; duet in A Choice Collection of Songs, xii (1761)
The Ambitious Stepmother	Rowe	DL, 5 Feb 1759	Hymn to the Sun, lost
The Beggar's Opera	Gay	CG, 10 Oct 1759	Hornpipe, country dance; vocal score (1769); revived 17 Oct 1777, with new finale by Arne
The Desert Island	A. Murphy, after Metastasio	DL, 24 Jan 1760	1 song in The Monthly Melody (1760)
The Way to Keep Him	Murphy	DL, 10 Jan 1761	2 songs (1760, 1763)
The Jovial Crew	E. Roome, after R. Brome	CG, 14 Feb 1760	7 songs in A Collection of Songs, ix (c1760); revived as The Ladies' Frolic, 1770
Thomas and Sally, or The Sailor's Return	I. Bickerstaffe	CG, 28 Nov 1760	Score (1761)
The Provoked Husband	C. Cibber	CG, 7 April 1761	2 songs in The Winter's Amusement, xiii (1761)
Artaxerxes	Arne, after Metastasio	CG, 2 Feb 1762	Score (1762) add recit, air (1777)
Love in a Village	Bickerstaffe	CG, 8 Dec 1762	Pasticcio, incl. 19 songs by Arne
The Arcadian Nuptials	—	CG, 19 Jan 1764	Pastoral dialogue (1764)
The Guardian Outwitted	Arne	CG, 12 Dec 1764	Score (1764)
L'olimpiade	Bottarelli, after Metastasio	KT, 27 April 1765	Only lib survives
Miss in her Teens	Garrick	DL, 25 April 1766	1 song in Thalia (1767)
King Arthur, or The British Worthy	Garrick, after Dryden	DL, 13 Dec 1770	Ov., numbers for Purcell's opera, score (c1770)
The Fairy Prince	G. Colman, after B. Jonson: Oberon	CG, 12 Nov 1771	Score (1771)
Squire Badger	Arne, after Fielding: Don Quixote in England	HM, 16 March 1772	Lib lists 15 songs, only The Dusky Night survives; revived as The Sot, KT, 16 Feb 1775
The Cooper	Arne, after Audinot, Quétant	HM, 10 June 1772	Score (1772)
Elfrida	Colman, after W. Mason	CG, 21 Nov 1772	Score (1772)
The Rose	?Arne	DL, 2 Dec 1772	Lib lists 19 songs, lost; ov. later used with A Trip to Portsmouth
Alzuma	Murphy	CG, 23 Feb 1773	Procession of virgins, Ode to the Sun, lost
Achilles in Petticoats	Colman, after Gay	CG, 16 Dec 1773	Score (1774)
Henry and Emma (2nd setting)	H. Bate, after Prior	CG, 13 April 1774	Lib lists 4 songs, lost
May-day, or The Little Gipsy	Garrick	DL, 28 Oct 1775	Score (1776)
Phoebe at Court	Arne, after R. Lloyd: Capricious Lovers	KT, 22 Feb 1776	Lost
Caractacus	W. Mason	CG, 6 Dec 1776	Lib lists 21 numbers, lost
Cymbeline	Shakespeare	—	To fair Fidele's grassy tomb, dirge (W. Collins) in Lyric Harmony, ii (1746); Fear no more, in The Winter's Amusement, xiii (1761)
The Nunnery Expedition	—	—	Advertised for DL, 20 April 1748, not perf.
Trick upon Trick	R. Fabian	—	2 songs (1761)
The Birth of Hercules	Shirley	—	Rehearsed 1763, not perf.; lib (1765), lists 19 numbers, lost

DRAMATIC WITH CONTRIBUTIONS BY ARNE

Title	Librettist	First performance	Composer and Arne's contribution
The Temple of Peace	—	SA, 1749	Pasticcio by Pasquali, lost
The Summer's Tale	R. Cumberland	CG, 6 Dec 1765	By Abel; 2 new, 2 adapted songs
Lionel and Clarissa, or A School for Fathers	Bickerstaffe	CG, 25 Feb 1768	By Dibdin; 1 new song
Tom Jones	J. Reed, after Fielding	CG, 14 Jan 1769	8 songs
The Pigmy Revels	J. Messink	CG, 26 Dec 1772	Songs by Dibdin; country dance by Arne
The Amorous Alderman		SA, 25 Jan 1773	Arne's contribution uncertain
The Golden Pippin	K. O'Hara	CG, 6 Feb 1773	3 songs
A Trip to Portsmouth	G. A. Stevens	HM, 11 Aug 1773	Songs by Dibdin; ov., dance tunes by Arne
The Seraglio	Dibdin, E. Thompson	CG, 25 Nov 1776	Obbligato song, lost
The Prodigal Son	Hull	CG, 28 Feb 1777	Oratorio by Arnold; 1 new song, in The Syren (1777)
Love Finds the Way	Hull, after Murphy: School for Guardians	CG, 18 Nov 1777	Music by Arne, Sacchini, Fisher, etc, individual contributions not identified
Poor Vulcan	Dibdin, after Motteux: Loves of Mars and Venus	CG, 4 Feb 1778	By Dibdin; 1 song
All Alive at Jersey	—	SW, 25 May 1779	Music by Arne, M. Arne, Howard
Summer Amusement	—	KT, 1 July 1779	By Arnold; 3 songs
Tom Thumb	K. O'Hara	CG, 3 Oct 1780	By Markordt; 1 song
The Castle of Andalusia	—	CG, 2 Nov 1782	By Arnold; 1 song
The Knight of Malta	Beaumont, Fletcher	CG, 23 April 1783	Ceremonial music
Fontainbleau	J. O'Keefe	CG, 16 Nov 1784	By Shield; 1 song
The Battle of Hexham	G. Colman jr	HM, 11 May 1789	By Arnold; 1 round
The Crusade	F. Reynolds	CG, 6 May 1790	By Shield; 1 song

SACRED

The Death of Abel (oratorio, Arne, after Metastasio), SA, 18 Feb 1744; revived DL, 5 March 1762 as The Sacrifice, or Death of Abel; only Hymn of Eve (1756) extant
Judith (oratorio, Bickerstaffe), DL, 27 Feb 1761; score (1764); recits, choruses, *Lbm*
Mass in F, 3vv, lost
Mass in G, 4vv, in A Collection of Modern Church Music (1791)
Libera me, dirge; O salutaris hostia, motet: both *Lbm*

ODES AND CANTATAS

A Grand Epithalamium, DL, 7 April 1736, lost
God bless our noble King, arr. 3/3vv, 2 hn, va, DL, 1745, *Lbm*
Ode to Chearfulness, HM, 3 April 1750, lost
Cymon and Iphigenia (1753)
Six English Cantatas (1755): The School of Anacreon; Lydia; Frolick and free; Bacchus and Ariadne; The Morning; Delia
4 odes in Del canzionero d'Orazio (1757)
Beauty and Virtue, DL, 26 Feb 1762, lost
An Ode upon dedicating a Building to Shakespeare (1769)
Love and Resolution, KT, 10 Dec 1770, music lost
Reffley Spring, cantata (1772)
Whittington's Feast (1776)

SONG COLLECTIONS

Lyric Harmony (1745–6)
Vocal Melody, i–iv (1749–52); v–viii: The Agreeable Musical Choice (1753–8); ix: A Collection of Songs (1760); x: Britannia (1760); xi: British Melody (1760); xii: A Choice Collection of Songs (1761); xiii: The Winter's Amusement (1761); xiv: A Favourite Collection of Songs (1764)
A Favourite Collection of English Songs (1757–8)
The Monthly Melody (1760); reissued as British Amusement (1762)
The New Songs sung at Vauxhall (1765)
Summer Amusement (1766)
New Favourite Songs (1768)
The Vocal Grove (1774)
The Syren (1777)

CATCHES, CANONS AND GLEES

29 in A [1st–32nd] Collection of Catches, Canons and Glees (1763–94)
8 in A Collection of Vocal Harmony (c1775)
10 in *Lbm*

INSTRUMENTAL

The Peasant's Triumph on the Death of the Wild Boar, ballet music, in The Comic Tunes . . . to the Celebrated Dances, i (1744)
Eight overtures in 8 parts (1751): no.3: Henry and Emma; no.7: Comus; no.8: The Judgment of Paris
VIII Sonatas or Lessons, hpd (1756)
VII sonatas, 2 vn, bc (1757)
Four New Overtures or Symphonies in 8 and 10 parts (1767)
Six Favourite concertos, org/hpd/pf (1787)
A Medley Overture, G, in Six Medley or Comic Overtures (1763)
2 overtures in Abel, Arne and Smith's Six Favourite Overtures (c1760)
Solo, E, vn, bc, *GB-Lbm* Add.39957

MISATTRIBUTED

The Most Celebrated Aires in the Opera of Tom Thumb (London, 1733) by J. F. Lampe
Bonnel Thornton's Ode upon St. Cecilia's Day, lost, by C. Burney
Caractacus: the vocal score (c1795)
Epithalamium, At Cana's Feast, *US-Wc*, attrib. doubtful
Mass in D, *I-Rsc, GB-Lbm*, by A. d'Eve, see Grove 5

BIBLIOGRAPHY

BurneyH; DNB; HawkinsH
B. Victor: *History of the Theatres of London and Dublin* (London, 1761–7)
T. Davies: *Memoirs of the Life of David Garrick* (London, 1780)
C. Dibdin: *The Musical Tour of Mr Dibdin* (Sheffield, 1788)
C. Burney: 'Arne', *Rees's Cyclopaedia* (London, 1802–20)
C. Dibdin: *The Professional Life of Mr. Dibdin* (London, 1803)
C. Butler: *Historical Memoirs* (London, 1819–21)
T. Busby: *Concert-room Anecdotes* (London, 1825)
W. T. Parke: *Musical Memoirs* (London, 1830)
F. D'Arblay: *Memoirs of Dr Burney* (London, 1832)
J. Genest: *Some Account of the English Stage* (London, 1832)
G. Hogarth: *Memoirs of the Musical Drama* (London, 1838)
Mrs Delany: *Autobiography and Correspondence*, ed. Lady Llanover (London, 1861)
B. H. Horner: *Life and Works of Dr. Arne* (London, 1893)
W. H. G. Flood: *History of Irish Music* (Dublin, 1905)
H. Saxe Wyndham: *Annals of Covent Garden Theatre* (London, 1906)
W. H. G. Flood: 'Dr Arne's Visits to Dublin', *MA*, i (1909–10), 215
F. Kidson: 'T. A. Arne: a Bicentenary Appreciation', *MT*, li (1910), 153
W. B. Squire: 'Dr Arne's Masses', *MT*, li (1910), 361
W. H. Cummings: *Dr Arne and Rule Britannia* (London, 1912)
R. Griffin: 'An Arne Portrait', *PMA*, xli (1914–15)
O. G. Sonneck: 'Caractacus not Arne's Caractacus', *Miscellaneous Studies in the History of Music* (New York, 1921)
H. A. Scott: 'Sidelights on Thomas Arne', *MQ*, xxi (1935), 301
H. Langley: *Dr Arne* (Cambridge, 1938)
E. R. Dibdin: 'The Bicentenary of Rule Britannia', *ML*, xxi (1940), 275
P. C. Roscoe: 'Arne and "The Guardian Outwitted" ', *ML*, xxiv (1943), 237
M. Sands: *Invitation to Ranelagh* (London, 1946)
P. A. Scholes: *The Great Dr Burney* (London, 1948)
J. Herbage: 'The Vocal Style of T. A. Arne', *PRMA*, lxxviii (1951–2), 83
A. E. F. Dickinson: 'Arne and the Keyboard Sonata', *MMR*, lxxxv (1955), 88
J. Herbage: 'The Opera of Operas', *MMR*, lxxxix (1959), 83
——: 'Young Master Arne', *MMR*, xc (1960), 14
C. L. Cudworth: 'Boyce and Arne', *ML*, xli (1960), 136
W. Shaw: 'A Projected Arne Commemoration in 1802', *MMR*, xc (1960), 90
J. Herbage: 'T. A. Arne', *MT*, ci (1960), 623
——: 'Arne, his Character and Environment', *PRMA*, lxxxvii (1960–61), 15
S. Sadie: 'The Chamber Music of Boyce and Arne', *MQ*, xlvi (1960), 425
The London Stage, 1660–1800 (Carbondale, Ill., 1960–68)
C. Farncombe: 'Arne and Artaxerxes', *Opera*, xiii (1962), 159
J. Herbage: 'Artaxerxes', *Opera*, xiii (1962), 333
S. T. Farish: 'The Vauxhall Songs of T. A. Arne', *Dissertation Abstracts*, xxiii (1963)
C. L. Cudworth: 'Two Georgian Classics, Arne and Stevens', *ML*, xlv (1964), 146
P. Lord: 'The English-Italian Opera Companies 1732–3', *ML*, xlv (1964), 239
C. Deelman: *The Great Shakespeare Jubilee* (London, 1964)
J. M. Stochholm: *Garrick's Folly* (London, 1964)
P. Hartnoll, ed.: *Shakespeare in Music* (London, 1964)
R. Lonsdale: *Dr. Burney* (Oxford, 1965)
R. Fiske: 'A Cliveden Setting', *ML*, xlvii (1966), 126
J. A. Parkinson: 'Garrick's Folly, or the Great Shakespeare Jubilee', *MT*, cx (1969), 922
J. Herbage: 'A Page from Arne's Draft Will', *MT*, cxii (1971), 126
J. A. Parkinson: *An Index to the Vocal Works of Thomas Augustine Arne and Michael Arne* (Detroit, 1972)
R. Fiske: *English Theatre Music in the Eighteenth Century* (London, 1973)
T. J. Walsh: *Opera in Dublin 1705–1797* (Dublin, 1973)
A. Scott: 'Arne's "Alfred"', *ML*, lv (1974), 385
J. A. Parkinson: 'An Unknown Violin Solo by Arne', *MT*, cxvii (1976), 902

JULIAN HERBAGE (text)
JOHN A. PARKINSON (works, bibliography)

Arneiro, José Augusto da Ferreira Veiga, Visconde de. *See* FERREIRA VEIGA, JOSÉ AUGUSTO DA.

Arnell, Richard (Anthony Sayer) (*b* London, 15 Sept 1917). English composer. He studied at the RCM (1936–9) with Ireland (composition) and Dykes Bower (piano). From 1943 to 1945 he was music consultant to the BBC Northern American service, and in 1948 he began teaching composition, theory and orchestration at Trinity College of Music. He was Fulbright Exchange Professor at Bowdoin College, Maine (1969–70), and visiting professor at Hofstra University (1970–72). In 1972 he was appointed music consultant to the London Film School.

Arnell's early reputation was gained principally in the USA: Beecham conducted the première of the *Sinfonia quasi variazioni* at Carnegie Hall in 1942, and in 1947 he provided an important score, *Punch and the Child*, for the New York City Ballet. He has composed prolifically for almost every medium and in a variety of styles; works with a programmatic basis (notably *Punch and* the symphonic portrait *Lord Byron*) have tended to outlive those without, revealing a special flair for characterization within a basically Romantic idiom. However, he has refused to allow himself to stagnate, and many later works avail themselves quite freely of new techniques.

WORKS
(selective list)

Opera: Moon Flowers, op.83 (Arnell), 1958
Ballets: Punch and the Child, op.49, 1947; Harlequin in April, op.63, 1951; The Angels, op.81, 1957
Orch: Classical Variations, op.1, str, 1939; Divertimento no.2, op.7, chamber orch, 1940; Vn Conc., op.9, 1940; Sinfonia quasi variazioni, op.13, 1941; Sonata, op.18, chamber orch, 1942; Sym. no.1, op.31, 1943; Pf Conc., op.44, 1946; Abstract Forms, op.50, str, 1947; Sym. no.4, op.52, 1948; Lord Byron, op.67, sym. portrait, 1952; Conc. capriccioso, op.71, vn, orch, 1954; Sym. no.5, op.77, 1956–7; Landscape and Figures, op.78, 1956; Robert Flaherty Impression, op.87, 1960; Food of Love, op.112, ov., 1968
Choral: The War God, op.36, cantata, chorus, orch, 1944; Ode to the West Wind, op.59, chorus, orch, 1949; Town Crier, op.118, speaker, chorus, orch, 1970
Wind ens: Cassation, op.45, wind qnt, 1946; Serenade, op.57, wind, db, 1949; Brass Qnt, op.93, 1961; My Lady Greensleeves, op.119, band, 1965
Str qts: no.2, op.14, 1941; no.3, op.41, 1945; no.4, op.62, 1951; no.5, op.99, 1961
Inst: Org Sonata no.2, op.21, 1942; 22 Variations, op.24, pf, 1943; Partita, op.30, va, 1943; Pf Sonata, op.32, 1946; Sonata no.2, op.55, vn, pf, 1949; Suite, d, op.73, 2 pf, 1955; Fox Variations, op.75, pf, 1956; Chorale Variations on 'Ein' fest' Burg', op.89, org, 1960
Songs, song cycles, film scores, mixed-media compositions

Principal publishers: Associated, Gray, Hinrichsen, Lorien, Mills, Peer, Robbins, Schott, Southern

CHRISTOPHER PALMER

Arnestad, Finn (Oluf Bjerke) (*b* Christiania, 23 Sept 1915). Norwegian composer. He had violin lessons from E. Gunstrøm (1930–34) and studied at the Oslo Conservatory with Bogsrud, Fjeldstad, Dirdal, Eken and Gjerstrøm. Later he took work as a conductor of various choirs and orchestras. In his music he quickly began to work with the principle of 'interference tonality' that became the foundation for his work; during the 1960s this became combined with dodecaphonic procedures.

WORKS
(selective list)

Orch: Meditation, 1947; Constellation, 1948; Conversation, pf, orch, 1949; Vn Conc., 1956
Choral: INRI, 1954; Missa brevis, 1958; other pieces
Inst: Qt, fl, str, 1942; Berceuse, pf, 1946; Legend, vn, pf, 1946; Str Qt, 1947

NIKOLAI PAULSEN

Arnič, Blaž (*b* Luče, Slovenia, 31 Jan 1901; *d* Ljubljana, 1 Feb 1970). Yugoslav composer. After studies at the Ljubljana Conservatory he was a pupil of Nilius in Vienna (1930–32) and then studied composition further in Warsaw (1938) and Paris (1939–40). He taught music at Bol on the island of Brač (1934–5) and at the Intermediate Music School of the Ljubljana Academy (1940–43) before his appointment in 1945 as composition teacher at the Ljubljana Academy. At first under the influence of Bruckner and the Russian 'Five', he developed a neo-Romantic style, deeply attached to the landscape and people of Slovenia. His music is essentially symphonic with a powerful dramatic touch.

WORKS
(selective list)

Orch: 9 syms., 1932, 1933, 1934, 1937, 1941, 1949, 1949, 1951, 1960; Ples čarovnic [Witches' dance], sym. poem, 1936; Zapeljivec

[The seducer], sym. poem, 1937; Pesem planin [Song of the mountains], sym. poem, 1940; Gozdovi pojo [The forest sings], sym. poem, 1945; 3 vn concs., 1953, 1954, 1966; Vc Conc., 1960; Cl Conc., 1963
2 pf trios, 1929, 1942; Conc., org, perc, 1931; Str Qt, 1933; songs, choruses, piano pieces, film scores

Principal publisher: Edicije DSS

ANDREJ RIJAVEC

Arnim, Bettina [Elisabeth] von. *See* BRENTANO, BETTINA.

Arnold, Denis (Midgley) (*b* Sheffield, 15 Dec 1926). English musicologist. He studied music with F. H. Shera at Sheffield University from 1944 to 1948 (BMus 1948). He was awarded the MA for a dissertation on Weelkes in 1950 and was appointed a lecturer at Queen's University, Belfast, in 1951. He became reader in music in 1960, and in 1964 went to Hull University as senior lecturer. In 1969 he became professor of music at Nottingham University, where he instituted a postgraduate course on the editing and interpretation of Renaissance and Baroque music, and in 1975 Heather Professor of Music at Oxford University. In 1976 he became joint editor of *Music and Letters*, and in 1978 was named president of the Royal Musical Association. As a writer of criticism, he has contributed regularly to *The Listener* and *The Gramophone*.

Arnold is among the most prolific English writers on music, with a wider range of interests than his list of publications indicates. His research has predominantly been concerned with Italian (most of all Venetian) music from the mid-16th century to the mid-17th, an interest which developed from his early work on the English madrigal. His archival studies have cast light on performing styles and on educational methods at the Italian conservatories, while his critical work (exemplified by his Master Musicians study of Monteverdi and his volume on Marenzio in the Oxford Studies of Composers series, as well as his articles) has helped establish historical perspective in the study of style changes at the beginning of the Baroque period.

WRITINGS

'Thomas Weelkes and the Madrigal', *ML*, xxi (1950), 1
'Giovanni Croce and the Concertato Style', *MQ*, xxxix (1953), 37
'Croce and the English Madrigal', *ML*, xxxv (1954), 309
'Notes on Two Movements of the Monteverdi "Vespers" ', *MMR*, lxxxiv (1954), 59
'Instruments in Church: some Facts and Figures', *MMR*, lxxxv (1955), 32
'Ceremonial Music in Venice at the Time of the Gabrielis', *PRMA*, lxxxii (1955–6), 47
'Gastoldi and the English Ballett', *MMR*, lxxxvi (1956), 44
'Alessandro Grandi, a Disciple of Monteverdi', *MQ*, xliii (1957), 171
'Seconda Pratica: a Background to Monteverdi's Madrigals', *ML*, xxxviii (1957), 341
'Brass Instruments in Italian Church Music of the Sixteenth and Early Seventeenth Centuries', *Brass Quarterly*, i (1957–8), 81
'Monteverdi's Church Music: some Venetian Traits', *MMR*, lxxxviii (1958), 83
'The Influence of Ornamentation in the Structure of Early 17th-century Church Music', *IMSCR*, vii *Cologne 1958*, 57
'Con ogni sorte di stromenti: some Practical Suggestions', *Brass Quarterly*, ii (1958–9), 99
'Andrea Gabrieli und die Entwicklung der "cori-spezzati"-Technik', *Mf*, xii (1959), 258
'Music at the Scuola di San Rocco', *ML*, xl (1959), 229
'The Significance of "Cori spezzati" ', *ML*, xl (1959), 4
'The Monteverdian Succession at St Mark's', *ML*, xliii (1961), 205
'Towards a Biography of Giovanni Gabrieli', *MD*, xv (1961), 200
'Orphans and Ladies: the Venetian Conservatoires (1690–1797)', *PRMA*, lxxxix (1962–3), 31
'At the Courts of Italy and France', *Choral Music*, ed. A. Jacobs (Harmondsworth, 1963), 90

'L'incoronazione di Poppea and its Orchestral Requirements', *MT*, civ (1963), 176
Monteverdi (London, 1963)
'The Monteverdi Vespers: a Postscript', *MT*, civ (1963), 24
'Francesco Cavalli: some Recently Discovered Documents', *ML*, xlvi (1965), 50
'Il ritorno d'Ulisse and the Chamber Duet', *MT*, cvi (1965), 183
'Instruments and Instrumental Teaching at the Early Italian Conservatoires', *GSJ*, xviii (1965), 72
Marenzio (London, 1965)
'Music at a Venetian Confraternity in the Renaissance', *AcM*, xxxvii (1965), 62
Monteverdi Madrigals (London, 1967)
'Charity Music in Eighteenth-century Dublin', *GSJ*, xxi (1968), 162
'Formal Design in Monteverdi's Church Music', *Congresso internazionale sul tema Claudio Monteverdi e il suo tempo: Venezia, Mantova e Cremona 1968*, 187–216
ed., with N. Fortune: *The Monteverdi Companion* (London, 1968) [incl. with N. Fortune: 'The Man as Seen through his Letters', 19–90; 'The Musical Environment', 91–132]
God, Caesar and Mammon: a Study of Patronage in Venice, 1550–1750 (Nottingham, 1970) [inaugural lecture]
'Gli allievi di Giovanni Gabrieli', *NRMI*, v (1971), 943–72
ed., with N. Fortune: *The Beethoven Companion* (London, 1971) [incl. with E. Arnold: 'The View of Posterity: an Anthology', 493–530]
'Schütz's "Venetian" Psalms', *MT*, cxiii (1972), 1071
'A Background Note to Monteverdi's Hymn Settings', *Scritti in onore di Luigi Ronga* (Milan and Naples, 1973), 33
'Vivaldi's Church Music: an Introduction', *Early Music*, ii (1973), 66
Giovanni Gabrieli (London, 1974)
'Cavalli at St Mark's', *Early Music*, iv (1976), 266
'Con ogni sorte di stromenti', *Early Music*, iv (1976), 167
Giovanni Gabrieli (London, 1978)
'Gabrieli, Andrea', 'Gabrieli, Giovanni', 'Mass' §III, 1–4, 'Monteverdi, Claudio', 'Venice', *Grove 6*

EDITIONS

G. Gabrieli: Opera omnia, CMM, xii– (1956–)
Vier Madrigale von Mantuaner Komponisten zu 5 und 8 Stimmen, Cw, lxxx (1962)
A. Gabrieli: Drei Motetten zu 8 Stimmen, Cw, xcvi (1965)
O. di Lasso: Ten Madrigals (London, 1977)

DAVID SCOTT

Arnold, F(rank) T(homas) (*b* Rugby, 6 Sept 1861; *d* Bath, 24 Sept 1940). English musical scholar. He was educated at Rugby and Trinity College, Cambridge, and in 1886 became a lecturer in German at the University College of South Wales and Monmouthshire (Cardiff), a post he held for 40 years until his retirement. His lifelong interest in music, particularly as an amateur cellist, led him to make an exhaustive study of the tradition of writing and playing from a figured bass, which culminated in his comprehensive treatise on *The Art of Accompaniment from a Thorough-bass*. He studied an enormous number of sources, both practical and theoretical, and produced his findings authoritatively in this book, which was declared by Newman to be 'the greatest work of musicography ever produced in this country' and is still of value today. Arnold's fine collection of first editions of contemporary treatises on the theory and practice of the figured bass was bequeathed to Cambridge University library.

WRITINGS

'A Corelli Forgery', *PMA*, xlvii (1920–21), 93
'Mixed Rhythms in Bach', *MT*, lxi (1920), 836
'Did Viadana Use Figures?', *MT*, lxiii (1922), 505, 648
'Die Viola Pomposa', *ZMw*, xiii (1930–31), 141
The Art of Accompaniment from a Thorough-bass as Practised in the 17th and 18th Centuries (London, 1931/*R*1965)
'J. S. Bach and Consecutives in Accompaniment', *ML*, xiv (1933), 318

BIBLIOGRAPHY

W. G. Whittaker: 'The Art of Accompaniment from a Thorough-bass', *MT*, lxxiii (1932), 32, 123 [review]; 255 [Arnold's reply]
D. R. Wakeling: 'An Interesting Music Collection', *ML*, xxvi (1945), 159
Cambridge University Reporter (6 Feb 1945) [short-title catalogue of Arnold's collection]
M. Campbell: *Dolmetsch: the Man and His Work* (London, 1975)

MS catalogue of Arnold's collection in *GB-Cu* [incl. bibliographical details]

H. C. COLLES/MALCOLM TURNER

Arnold, Georg (*b* Feldsberg, Lower Austria [now Valtice, Czechoslovakia]; *d* Bamberg, 16 Jan 1676). Austrian composer and organist resident in Germany. After the end of the Thirty Years War, on 14 September 1649, he was appointed court organist at Bamberg through the influence of Prince-Bishop Melchior Otto Voit of Salzburg, who also began the Baroque restyling of the interior of Bamberg Cathedral and called on him to provide a new repertory of masses, vespers and motets for use there throughout the year. Arnold's collection of 1651, for example, was intended for the great procession of the four Bamberg collegiate churches to the Johanneskapelle, next to the church of St Stephan, the nave of which had just been completed. As an organ expert he was connected with Spiridion and Matthias Tretzscher and helped with the reconstruction of the organs in Bamberg that had been destroyed in the war. He became Hofkapellmeister at Bamberg in 1667. A painting of 1675 by his son Georg Adam shows the interior of the restored cathedral with the splendid Baroque organ on the left wall; Arnold is seen standing next to it in court dress and wig.

There was a long tradition of polyphonic music in Bamberg, to which Arnold added in much of his output the Venetian polychoral style, possibly to some extent inspired by the layout of the cathedral, with apses at either end of the nave. The use of the term 'sacrae cantiones' in the titles of his 1651 volume and op.4 is indeed reminiscent of Giovanni Gabrieli and Schütz; intended as open-air music, their contents are well suited to the forces at his disposal. In his masses of opp.2 and 6 he added the darker sound of viols as a contrast, and the closely woven lines in the parody masses of 1672–5 produce a notably rich texture. The marked antiphonal style of the psalms of 1662–3 owes something to Monteverdi and Viadana, in contrast to the more seamless polyphony of op.3, most of whose 47 pieces are canzonas. The 13 motets of 1672 are in the form of the sacred concerto. Arnold's varied output shows that he was an impressive representative of early Baroque music in Bamberg.

WORKS

Liber primus [22] sacrarum cantionum ... 2–5vv/insts, bc (Nuremberg, 1651)
Liber I, missarum, psalmorum et Magnificat, 5vv, 2 vn, va; 4vv, trbns/viols ad lib, bc (org), op.2 (Innsbruck, 1656)
[47] Canzoni, ariae et sonatae, 1–4 viols, bc (org), op.3 (Innsbruck, 1659)
Liber secundus [28] sacrarum cantionum de tempore et sanctis, 4–7vv/insts, bc, op.4 (Innsbruck, 1661)
Psalmi de BMV cum Salve regina, Ave regina, Alma Redemptoris mater, et Regina coeli, 5, 6vv/3vv, 2 vn, va ad lib, op.2 (Innsbruck, 1662)
[15] Psalmi vespertini, 4vv/2vv, 2 vn; other insts, ad lib, bc (org) (Bamberg, 1663[2])
3 missae pro defunctis et alia missa laudativa, 4, 5, 7vv; 3/4 violas ad lib, bc (org) op.6 (Bamberg, 1665)
Prima pars, 4 missae, 4vv, 2 vn; 3 va ad lib (Bamberg, 1672–5)
Motettae tredecim selectissime de nomine Jesu, ejusque Ss Virgine Matre Maria ... 1v, 2/4 insts ad lib (Kempten, 1672)
19 concerted motets, 1–5vv, insts, 1663–5, *S-Uu* [9 repr. from Liber I, II, 1651, 1661]
Canon, 2vv, holograph entry of 18 Feb 1660 in J. G. Fabricius: *Liber amicorum*, *D-B*

BIBLIOGRAPHY

R. Mitjana y Gordón: *Catalogue critique et descriptif des imprimés de musique des 16ᵉ et 17ᵉ siècles conservés à la Bibliothèque de l'Université royale d'Upsala, i* (Uppsala, 1911)

Å. Davidsson: *Catalogue critique et descriptif des imprimés de musique des 16ᵉ et 17ᵉ siècles conservés dans les bibliothèques suédoises* (Uppsala, 1952)

HANNS DENNERLEIN

Arnold, Gustav (*b* Altdorf, canton of Uri, 1 Sept 1831; *d* Lucerne, 28 Sept 1900). Swiss conductor, organist and composer. After instruction in singing (with Aloys Zwyssig) and piano, Arnold studied music in Engelberg (1842–4) and in Lucerne (1844–7), where he was active as a choral singer, organist and pianist and began to compose. In 1850 he went to England, where he was appointed organist and choirmaster at the Roman Catholic church in Lancaster and taught the piano and languages. Moving to Salford in 1854, he became organist and choral director at the cathedral. He studied with Charles Hallé, who greatly influenced him, and had singing lessons with M. Garcia. From 1856 he took positions in Manchester, first at St Augustine's and subsequently at St Wilfried's church.

Arnold returned to Switzerland permanently in 1865 to become musical director of Lucerne. His duties included conducting various choirs and an amateur orchestra for the performance of masses (at the cathedral), operas and oratorios. He founded an orchestra of professional musicians in 1875. Although he retired in 1883 he continued to adjudicate at singing festivals, worked to improve church music and became a music critic. He received honours from Lucerne and was elected president of the Schweizerischer Tonkünstlerverein in 1900.

Arnold's earliest publications include solo songs and piano music; later he wrote much sacred and secular music for male and mixed choruses, a mass, cantatas and incidental music for the theatre. He was best known for his works for male chorus, of which his cantatas *Siegesfeier der Freiheit* and *Der Rütlischwur* are particularly noteworthy.

BIBLIOGRAPHY

A. Portmann: 'Gustav Arnold, Musikdirektor', *Katholische Schweizerblätter*, new ser., xvi (1900), 504

A. Niggli: Obituary, *Biographisches Jb und Deutscher Nekrolog*, xxii (1907), 39

E. Refardt: 'Gustav Arnold', *SMz*, xc (1950), 473; repr. in E. Refardt: *Musik in der Schweiz* (Berne, 1952), 33 [with list of works]

GAYNOR G. JONES

Arnold, György (*b* Paks, 1781; *d* Szabadka [now Šubotica, Yugoslavia], 25 Oct 1848). Hungarian composer and church musician. He studied music with his father József Arnold (1751–96), cantor of the Catholic church in Hajós, and Pál Pöhm, cathedral choirmaster in Kalocsa. In 1800 he was appointed music director of the town and *regens chori* of St Theresa's church in Szabadka, posts which he held until his death. In order to enlarge his establishment, which in 1803 consisted of only five musicians, he gave free musical tuition to 12 boys from 1805 to 1814. His first known compositions are offertories based on themes from fashionable operas (Grétry's *Richard Coeur de Lion*, *Don Giovanni* and Weigl's *Die Schweizerfamilie*). In 1815, on the return of Pope Pius VII from captivity in France, he composed an offertory for which he received a letter of thanks from the pope, and in 1826 he was given a gold medal for an offertory composed for the coronation of Pope Leo XII; another papal breve (1831) thanked him for his offertory for the coronation of Gregory XVI. From 1836 he was an honorary member of the music society in Pressburg.

As well as church works, which were influenced by the Viennese Classical tradition, Arnold also composed secular music including stage works and dance music. As a stage composer experimenting with Hungarian themes, he was one of the pioneers of this art form in his country and is thus a predecessor of Ferenc Erkel. In his Hungarian dances, which were published in the largest collection of Hungarian dance music in the first three decades of the 19th century, *Magyar táncok Veszprém vármegyéből* ('Hungarian dances from County Veszprém'), Arnold expressed himself in the national musical idiom of the *verbunkos*. His other works include *Pismenik iliti skupljenje pisamâ razlicsitih za nadiljne, svetacsne i ostale dneve priko godine podobnih, za vechu slavu boxju i kriposli duhovne naroda Ilirickoju* (Eszék, 1819), a collection of religious songs in the Illyrian language, and an unpublished four-volume German dictionary of composers (1826).

WORKS

SINGSPIELS

Kemény Simon (after K. Kisfaludy), Szabadka, 1826

Mátyás királynak választása [The election of Matthew as king] (after L. Szentjóbi Szabó), Kassa, 1830, collab. J. Heinisch

A gotthardhegyi boszorkány [The witch of Mt Gotthard] (after A. Schuster), Debrecen, 1837

OTHER WORKS

Sacred choral: 13 offertories, 11 hymns, 3 Libera me, 2 Tantum ergo, Te Deum, 3 masses (incl. Ger. mass, Hung. requiem), Regina coeli, Et incarnatus; religious songs to Illyrian texts

Inst.: 4 ovs., orch; numerous Hung. dances, pf

BIBLIOGRAPHY

ZL

K. Isoz: *Arnold Györgў* (Budapest, 1908)

F. Brodszky: *A. Veszprémmegyei zenetársaság 1823–1832* [The music society in County Veszprém 1823–32] (Veszprém, 1941)

FERENC BÓNIS

Arnold, J(ohn) H(enry) (*b* London, 29 May 1887; *d* Stanmore, Middlesex, 19 June 1956). English organist and scholar. He studied music with Martin Shaw and Harvey Grace. In 1914 he became organist at the church of St Alphege, Southwark, and later at Christ Church, Streatham Hill; from 1920 to 1932 he was organist at the church of St Mary the Virgin, Primrose Hill, as assistant to Geoffrey Shaw. His scholarly activities were chiefly connected with the Plainsong and Medieval Music Society, the Alcuin Club and the Church Music Society; he was a council member of all three bodies. In addition to the works listed below he contributed plainsong accompaniments to *Songs of Praise*, *A Plainsong Hymnbook* and the second edition of *The English Hymnal*, and wrote reviews for the *Manchester Guardian*.

WRITINGS

Plainsong Accompaniment (London, 1927, 2/1964)

The Music of the Holy Communion (London, 1933, 1946)

The Approach to Plainsong Through the Office Hymn (London, 1936)

ed.: *Anglican Liturgies* (London, 1939)

ed., with E. G. P. Wyatt: *Walter Howard Frere: a Collection of his Papers on Liturgical and Historical Subjects* (London, 1940)

ed.: *A Manual of Plainsong* (London, 1951)

ed. and trans.: *The Eucharistic Liturgy of Taizé* (London, 1962)

BIBLIOGRAPHY

Obituary, *MT*, xcvii (1956), 440

A. Hughes: *Septuagesima* (London, 1959)

H. C. COLLES/MALCOLM TURNER

Arnold, Johann Gottfried (*b* Niedernhall, Württemberg, 1 Feb 1773; *d* Frankfurt am Main, 26 July 1806). German cellist. The son of a schoolmaster, who gave him preliminary musical training, he made local appearances with the cello when he was eight; in 1785 he was apprenticed to the town musician at Künzelsau, where he spent five years, followed by a period with his uncle, who held a similar position at Wertheim. But his predilection for the cello was hampered by the absence of training until, after a few abortive attempts to start a soloist's career, he went first to Regensburg for a few months' study with Maximilian Willmann, and then to Hamburg. There, in 1796, he heard and studied with Romberg, who helped him to develop great technical ability and recommended his engagement, a year later, as solo cellist of the Frankfurt Opera. Arnold is said to have been described by his contemporaries as a great virtuoso, with a 'consistently enchanting' tone. He died of a lung infection at the age of 33 and was greatly mourned by the people of Frankfurt. His compositions include five cello concertos (1802–8), which became favourite items of Dotzauer's repertory; the third was republished by Karl Schröder (ii) in 1880. He also wrote a *Symphonie concertante* for two flutes and orchestra, and various works for piano, cello, guitar and chamber ensembles.

Arnold's son, Carl (*b* Neukirchen, nr. Mergentheim, 6 May 1794; *d* Christiania, 11 Nov 1877) studied the piano first at Frankfurt with C. A. Hoffmann and Aloys Schmitt, and then, after his father's death, at Offenbach with J. A. André and J. G. Vollweiler. After concert tours in Germany, Poland and Russia (where in 1820 he married the singer Henriette Kisting), he settled in Berlin in 1824. He spent 16 years composing but gave up after the failure of his opera *Irene* in 1832. In 1835 he became music director at Münster, and in 1847, director of the Philharmonic Society at Oslo, where in 1857 he also became organist of Holy Trinity Church. His own son, Karl (*b* Berlin, 8 June 1824; *d* Oslo, 9 Aug 1867), studied the cello with Max Bohrer and became cellist of the royal chapel at Stockholm.

BIBLIOGRAPHY

W. Matthäus: 'Arnold, Johann Gottfried', *MGG*

LYNDA LLOYD REES

Arnold, John (*b* ?Essex, *c*1715; *d* Great Warley, Essex, March 1792). English psalmodist. He was a singing teacher, parish clerk and (at least in 1790) organist at Great Warley, Essex, and compiled several publications designed for country parish churches. The most important was *The Compleat Psalmodist* (seven editions, 1741–79) which was in general modelled on earlier books of the same kind, containing a didactic introduction, psalm tunes, hymns and anthems of the parochial kind. But it was unusually ambitious in including also a number of chants for the prose canticles and a complete setting of Morning and Evening Prayer (*see* ROBERT BARBER (i)). Many of the tunes and anthems were his own; others were supplied by members of his choir at Great Warley; the rest were taken from earlier collections.

Arnold published four other books of similar purpose and scope, and also *The Essex Harmony* (three editions, 1767–86) which contained songs, catches and glees from various sources. His prefaces give a colourful and informative picture of the musical life of an 18th-century village. The most expansive of these are in the fifth edition of *The Compleat Psalmodist* (1761) and in *Church Music Reformed* (1765).

BIBLIOGRAPHY

Bury and Norwich Post (14 March 1792)

R. Daniel: *The Anthem in New England before 1800* (Evanston, 1966), 75f

A. H. Mann: *Essex Musical Events and Musicians* (MS, *GB-NW* 448), 91ff

N. Temperley: *The Music of the English Parish Church* (Cambridge, 1978)

NICHOLAS TEMPERLEY

Arnold, Jurig (Karlovich) von. *See* ARNOLD, YURY.

Arnold, Malcolm (Henry) (*b* Northampton, 21 Oct 1921). English composer. He won an open scholarship in 1938 to the RCM, where he studied composition with Jacob and the trumpet with Ernest Hall. In 1941 he won the Cobbett Prize and joined the LPO, becoming first trumpet in 1942. After two years war service (1944–5) and one season with the BBC SO, he returned to the LPO in 1946. In 1948 he won the Mendelssohn Scholarship and left the orchestra to spend a year in Italy; since then he has devoted himself to composition and conducting. He was made an honorary DMus of Exeter University in 1969 and a CBE in 1970.

Arnold's early orchestral experience has enabled him to write for the conventional symphony orchestra with special understanding and absolute certainty. His scoring is clear and luminous, showing a liking for unmixed timbres, and striking in its use of simple but often unexpected instrumental combinations. Ideas and developments arise out of the instrumental context, so that it is often difficult to separate the substance from the manner of presentation, the character of the music from that of the instruments involved.

His music is basically diatonic and key-orientated. In smaller-scale works the main attraction often lies in the catchy tunes, the apt orchestration and (in the case of chamber works) the pleasure which the music gives to performers. In his larger works Arnold shows himself to be a melodist rather than a developer of themes: his tunes tend to change into new tunes rather than to break down into smaller constituents, they are often subtly and highly organized and events succeed each other with an ease and apparent spontaneity that often hides the skill of underlying processes. Much of the material in his most varied movements derives from a few basic intervals. His use of literal repetition (the opening passage of an extended movement will often be repeated three times) can be read as a sign of his expressed intention to make the listener's task easy rather than to demonstrate his intellectual superiority.

The forms and textures of Arnold's earlier works owe something to Sibelius (the use of sustained ostinatos as a background in development sections and of contrasting pairs of woodwind in 3rds or 6ths in the Second Symphony provide obvious examples). His use of canonic imitation, sometimes leading to curious though transient harmonic complexities, is reminiscent of Bartók (as in the slow movement of the Third Symphony and the outer movements of the Concerto for Two Violins). But Arnold has stated that the greatest musical influence on his life has been that of Berlioz, to whom he stands close in his mastery of expressive orchestration and melody, and in his frequent resort to shock tactics in harmony or in changes of mood and texture.

Arnold is a fluent and versatile composer, who has written more than 80 film scores (the 45-minute score of *The Bridge on the River Kwai*, which won him an Oscar, was composed in ten days) and much occasional music, designedly popular in tone and content. The first two symphonies were genial and high-spirited; since then the combination of simple tunes, often in popular idioms, with material that is dramatic, emotional and often violent in mood has created symphonic movements of greater ambiguity and tension. At other times the conflict of commonplace and disruptive elements may be stressed, as in the *Peterloo* overture, with its Ives-like meeting of opposing forces. Arnold's deliberate use of what he himself describes as 'emotional clichés', such as the sweet and sentimental tune in the slow movement of the Fifth Symphony, later brought back to cap the finale, has disconcerted many critics. He himself has little sympathy wth many contemporary trends, standing almost alone in his ability to move freely between many worlds of music, and in refusing to accept categorization in any one of them.

WORKS
(selective list)

ORCHESTRAL AND BAND

Syms.: Sym. for Str, op.13, 1946; Sym. no.1, op.22, 1949; Sym. no.2, op.40, 1953; Toy Sym., op.62, 1957; Sym. no.3, op.63, 1957; Sym. no.4, op.71, 1960; Sym. no.5, op.74, 1961; Sym. no.6, op.95, 1967; Sym. no.7, op.113, 1973

Concs.: Cl Conc. no.1, op.20, cl, str, 1948; Conc., op.32, pf 4 hands, str, 1951; Conc., op.39, ob, str, 1952; Fl Conc. no.1, op.45, fl, str, 1954; Harmonica Conc., op.46, 1954; Conc., op.47, org, D-tpt, B♭-tpt, str, 1954; Serenade, op.50, gui, str, 1955; Hn Conc., op.58, 1956; Gui Conc., op.67, 1959; Conc., op.77, 2 vn, str, 1962; Conc., op.104, 2 pf (3 hands), orch, 1969; Conc. for 28 Players, op.105, 1970; Va Conc., op.108, va, chamber orch, 1971; Fl Conc. no.2, op.111, fl, chamber orch, 1972; Cl Conc. no.2, op.115, cl, chamber orch, 1974; Fantasy on a theme of John Field, op.116, pf, orch, 1975; Philharmonic Conc., op.120, 1976

Other orch works: Divertimento no.1, op.1, 1942; Beckus the Dandipratt, op.5, comedy ov., 1943; The Smoke, op.21, ov., 1948; Serenade, op.26, small orch, 1950; English Dances, 2 sets, op.27, 1950, op.33, 1951; A Sussex Ov., op.31, 1951; Sinfonietta no.1, op.48, small orch, 1954; Tam o'Shanter, op.51, ov., 1955; Little Suite no.1, op.53, 1956; A Grand Grand Ov., op.57, 1956; 4 Scottish Dances, op.59, 1957; Sinfonietta no.2, op.65, 1958; Little Suite no.2, op.78, 1962; Sinfonietta no.3, op.81, 1964; Water Music, op.82, 1964; 4 Cornish Dances, op.91, 1966; Peterloo, op.97, ov., 1968; The Fair Field, op.110, ov., 1971

Brass band: 2 little suites, op.80, 1963, op.93, 1966; The Padstow Lifeboat, op.94, march, 1967; Fantasy, op.113a, 1974

Military band: HRH The Duke of Cambridge, op.60, march, 1957

DRAMATIC AND VOCAL

Operas: The Dancing Master, op.34, 1, 1951; The Open Window, op.56, 1, 1956

Ballets: Homage to the Queen, op.42, 1953; Rinaldo and Armida, op.49, 1954; Solitaire [after English Dances], opp.27, 33, 1956; Sweeney Todd, op.68, 1959; Electra, op.79, 1963

Film scores: more than 80, incl. The Bridge on the River Kwai, The Inn of the Sixth Happiness

Vocal: Psalm cl, op.25, chorus, org, 1950; 2 Ceremonial Psalms, op.35, SSA, 1952; John Clare Cantata, op.52, chorus, pf 4 hands, 1955; 5 William Blake Songs, op.66, A, str, 1959; Song of Simeon, op.69, mimes, solo vv, chamber orch, 1959; The Return of Odysseus (P. Dickinson), op.119, SATB, orch, 1976–7

CHAMBER AND INSTRUMENTAL

For 3 or more insts: 3 Shanties, op.4, wind qnt, 1943; Trio, op.6, fl, bn, va, 1943; Qnt, op.7, fl, bn, hn, vn, va, 1944; Str Qt, op.23, 1949; Divertimento, op.37, fl, ob, cl, 1952; Pf Trio, op.54, 1956; Ob Qt, op.61, 1957; Qnt, op.73, 2 tpt, hn, trbn, tuba, 1960; Trevelyan Suite, op.96, 3 fl, 2 ob, 2 cl, 2 hn, 2 bn, 1967; Str Qt no.2, op.118, 1975

For 1–2 insts: Variations on a Ukrainian Folksong, op.9, pf, 1944; 2 sonatas, vn, pf, op.15, 1947, op.43, 1953; Children's Suite, op.16, pf, 1947; Sonata, op.17, va, pf, 1947; Sonatina, op.19, fl, pf, 1948; Sonatina, op.28, ob, pf, 1951; Sonatina, op.29, cl, pf, 1951; Sonatina, op.41, rec, pf, 1953; 6 Pieces, op.84, vn, pf, 1965; Fantasies for solo fl, ob, cl, bn, hn, tpt, trbn, tuba, 1965–7; Fantasy, op.107, gui, 1970; Fantasy, op.117, harp, 1975; Sonata, op.121, fl, pf, 1977

Principal publishers: Faber, Lengnick, Paterson

BIBLIOGRAPHY

S. Goddard: 'A Young British Symphonist', *The Listener*, li (1954), 237

D. Mitchell: Review of Symphony no.2, *MT*, xcv (1954), 382

——: 'Malcolm Arnold', *MT*, xcvi (1955), 410

M. Arnold: 'I Think of Music in Terms of Sound', *Music and Musicians*, vi/11 (1956), 9

M. Schafer: *British Composers in Interview* (London, 1963), 147ff

C. Ford: 'Malcolm Arnold', *The Guardian* (17 April 1971)

HUGO COLE

Arnold, Samuel (*b* London, 10 Aug 1740; *d* London, 22 Oct 1802). English composer, organist and editor. He learnt music as a boy in the Chapel Royal, under Bernard Gates and (after 1757) James Nares. In autumn 1764 he was engaged by John Beard as Covent Garden's harpsichordist; his duties included rehearsing the singers and composing such new music as might be required. He compiled three pastiche operas at this time, of which *The Summer's Tale* most closely resembled the prototype, *Love in a Village* (1762), but *The Maid of the Mill* was by far the most successful. There were productions in such unlikely places as St Petersburg and Jamaica, and frequent revivals all over Britain, including one in 1814 that had some new music by Bishop. Bickerstaffe's libretto was a bowdlerized version of Richardson's *Pamela*, and the music broke new ground by borrowing not only from recent Italian operas but also from operas produced in Paris by Monsigny, Philidor and Duni. The small quantity of new music included an overture by the Earl of Kelly, a song by J. C. Bach and four items by Arnold himself which are the most interesting music in the score. His two finales are the first English examples in the new Italian style as exemplified in Galuppi's *Il filosofo di campagna* (London, 1761). In his later years Arnold seldom fulfilled the promise he showed here.

As a result of marrying Mary Ann Napier, an heiress, Arnold was able to leave Covent Garden and buy Marylebone Gardens from Thomas Lowe in time for the 1769 season. The gardens were open only during the summer, and specialized in fireworks as well as concerts and refreshments. The concerts seem always to have included a short, all-sung comic opera, and much the most popular was a version of Pergolesi's *La serva padrona*. Arnold introduced a number of new examples both by himself and by his bandleader, Barthélemon, but none of them was published. The criminal activities of an employee lost Arnold most of his money in this venture, and in 1776 the gardens were sold to a building speculator.

By this time Arnold had already composed four short oratorios, all of which were quite frequently revived. This makes it the more surprising that none of them was published. *The Prodigal Son* was performed in Oxford at the installation of Lord North as chancellor of the university; there does not seem to have been any implication in the choice of subject. On the strength of this oratorio, Arnold was made a Doctor of Music on 5 July 1773; it is said that Oxford's Heather Professor, William Hayes, felt it unnecessary to look at the exercise he had brought with him, a setting of John Hughes's ode *The Power of Music*. In his doctoral robes Arnold had his portrait painted by Thomas Hardy, but only the engraving is known to survive.

Arnold may have hoped to return to his job at Covent Garden; when Dibdin fled abroad deep in debt, Arnold completed for him *The Seraglio* (14 November 1776) and *Poor Vulcan* (4 February 1778). Dibdin even sent him a libretto, *The Gipsies*, which Arnold set out of compassion. But by this time he had thrown in his lot with George Colman the elder, who in 1777 had taken over the Little Theatre in the Haymarket from Samuel Foote; Colman and Arnold had collaborated when both were on the Covent Garden staff in the 1760s, and they were always close friends. Arnold composed for the Little Theatre for a quarter of a century; latterly George Colman the younger was manager. Like Marylebone

Gardens, the Little Theatre was open only in the summer (apart from seasons in the early 1790s when the King's Theatre and Drury Lane were being rebuilt), and that allowed Arnold time to pursue an astonishing number of other activities. In 1783 he succeeded Nares as organist and composer to the Chapel Royal. In 1787 he established the Glee Club with J. W. Callcott, who later helped him compile a large volume of psalm settings. In 1789 he became official conductor of the Academy of Ancient Music, and in 1790 founded the Graduates Meeting, a society of academic musicians which

Samuel Arnold: pencil portrait (1795) by George Dance in the National Portrait Gallery, London

included Haydn among its associates. Arnold's generous spirit is reflected in his continuous support for those in reduced circumstances, especially musicians; he established a Choral Fund in 1791, was for 40 years an active member of the Royal Society of Musicians and also conducted the annual performance at St Paul's for the benefit of the Sons of the Clergy. In 1793 he succeeded Cooke as organist at Westminster Abbey. Arnold also managed to edit for publication a vast quantity of music by others. Long before he had finished a four-volume revision of Boyce's *Cathedral Music*, he had issued proposals for a complete edition of Handel's works, and between 1787 and 1797 he published 180 parts; one major work comprised four or five of these, and it was for the subscriber to bind them as he thought best. Arnold intended many more parts (only five of Handel's operas appeared), but the project was very remarkable for its day, and Arnold deserves every credit for achieving as much as he did (*see also* EDITIONS, HISTORICAL). Throughout this period his theatre music showed no diminution in quantity; his industry was phenomenal.

Arnold's first job at the Little Theatre was to arrange the music for John Gay's ballad opera *Polly*, which had not been performed before and to which he contributed

some new songs. In 1778 he composed eight orchestral pieces for a production of *Macbeth*; five of them were based on Scottish song tunes (these entr'actes and background pieces supplemented Leveridge's short masques, which were always then used for the witch scenes). Apart from one or two isolated songs, this is the only theatre music by Arnold that survives in orchestral score. Judging by the orchestral cues given in so many of the published vocal scores, he often scored with variety and originality; wind cues abound, and there is some interesting writing for harps in *Cambro-Britons* (1798). The musical content of his operas is often abysmal, yet he could write well when he took trouble. The overtures to *The Spanish Barber*, *The Castle of Andalusia* and *Turk and No Turk* are outstanding. The first of these, one of the very few in a single movement, is based on the fandango theme Mozart used in *Le nozze di Figaro*, and the opera itself is an interesting version of Beaumarchais' *Le barbier de Séville*. Of the other operas the most popular were *The Agreeable Surprise*, *Inkle and Yarico* and *The Children in the Wood*, though they were not mainly liked for their music. Edwin's seedy ex-schoolmaster in *The Agreeable Surprise* and Jack Bannister's likable coward in *The Children in the Wood* were among the most admired dramatic performances of their time, while *Inkle and Yarico* had a thought-provoking story about slavery in the West Indies (which had just become the subject of parliamentary agitation by Wilberforce).

The most interesting feature of Arnold's operas is his frequent use of folktunes, in particular of English folktunes. Very few had been published and his source is not known. *The Castle of Andalusia* has a version of the folksong Cecil Sharp called 'The Keeper', and *The Children in the Wood* of the carol tune Vaughan Williams called 'The Truth from Above'. *Two to One* has several otherwise unrecorded examples, including what was probably the first publication of 'Yankee Doodle' (to new words).

In autumn 1798 Arnold fell off his library steps and was confined to bed for several months. In 1799 he wrote only the short oratorio *Elisha*, performed in 1801, but the following year he returned to theatre music, although he was never again fully mobile. Because of pantomime developments and also innovations in London by Noverre, Covent Garden had been making occasional experiments in ballet with a story throughout the 1790s. The first real success in this line was *Blackbeard* (1798) at the Royal Circus Theatre; the music was by Sanderson and the story was about pirates off Madagascar. In imitation of *Blackbeard* the younger Colman accepted from the actor Fawcett a scheme for an exciting ballet about voodoo and kidnapping in Jamaica, and Arnold's *Obi, or Three-fingered Jack* proved the most successful of his three ballets. The story was mimed mainly by actors, the dancing being mostly incidental; there were a few songs for variety. It was already usual for ballet composers to borrow freely from others; Arnold borrowed unexpectedly from Haydn's 'Surprise' Symphony (the slow movement) and from two Mozart string quartets (K421/417b and 575). His own contribution is of much more interest than anything in his own operas of the time.

According to Busby, Arnold's 'general habits were not the most abstemious', yet almost to the day of his death his energy never flagged. One of his last works was another short oratorio, *The Hymn of Adam and*

Eve, a setting of *Paradise Lost* (v,ll.153–208). Arnold was buried in Westminster Abbey. His son, Samuel James Arnold, author of some poor opera librettos that Arnold set, later became the first manager of the Lyceum Theatre.

WORKS

CG – *Covent Garden*
DL – *Drury Lane*
KT – *King's Theatre*
LT – *Little Theatre in the Haymarket*
MG – *Marylebone Gardens*
ap – *afterpiece*
a-s – *all-sung*

Vocal scores and librettos published in London soon after first performance, unless otherwise stated; all printed works published in London.

OPERAS

(*all dialogue operas unless otherwise stated*)

op.

— The Maid of the Mill (pasticcio, I. Bickerstaffe, after Richardson), CG, 31 Jan 1765, 4 nos. by Arnold
— Daphne and Amintor (ap, pasticcio, Bickerstaffe, after Saint-Foix and Mrs Cibber), DL, 8 Oct 1765, music selected by author, collab. Arnold
— The Summer's Tale (pasticcio, R. Cumberland), CG, 6 Dec 1765, 6 nos. by Arnold; rev. as Amelia, DL, 14 Dec 1771, music not pubd
— Rosamond (ap, a-s, Addison rev.), CG, 21 April 1767, music not pubd
— The Royal Garland (ap, a-s, Bickerstaffe), CG, 10 Oct 1768, music not pubd
— Tom Jones (pasticcio, J. Reed and Poinsinet, after Fielding), CG, 14 Jan 1769, 6 nos. by Arnold
— Amintas (ap, pasticcio, Tenducci, after Rolt and Metastasio), CG, 15 Dec 1769, new music by Arnold and others
— The Servant Mistress (ap, a-s, anon. trans. of La serva padrona), MG, 16 June 1770, Pergolesi's music arr. and airs added by Arnold, not pubd
— The Madman (ap, pasticcio, a-s), MG, 28 Aug 1770, music not pubd
— The Portrait (ap, a-s, G. Colman, after Anseaume: Le tableau parlant), CG, 22 Nov 1770, vocal score lacks recits
— The Magnet (ap, a-s, D. Dubois), MG, 27 June 1771, music not pubd
— Don Quixote (ap, a-s, D. G. Piguenit, after Cervantes), MG, 30 June 1774, music not pubd
— The Weathcock (ap, pasticcio, T. Forrest), CG, 17 Oct 1775; ov. by Arnold, music not pubd
— The Seraglio (ap, C. Dibdin and E. Thompson), CG, 14 Nov 1776, music by Dibdin with 4 airs by Arnold
— Lilliput (ap, D. Garrick after Swift), LT, 15 May 1777, revival, new music by Arnold, not pubd
— Polly (ballad opera, Gay, rev. Colman), LT, 19 June 1777, score, US-CA (with Arnold's addns)
— A Fairy Tale (ap, pasticcio, Garrick, after Shakespeare, rev. Colman), LT, 18 July 1777, music by J. C. Smith and M. Arne with epilogue song by Arnold, not pubd
— The Sheep Shearing (ap, pasticcio, Colman, after Shakespeare), LT, 18 July 1777, music not pubd
— April Day (ap, a-s, K. O'Hara), LT, 22 Aug 1777, music not pubd
17 The Spanish Barber (Colman, after Beaumarchais), LT, 30 Aug 1777, music and song words pubd
— Poor Vulcan! (ap, a-s, Dibdin, after Motteux), CG, 4 Feb 1778, music by Dibdin with 1 song by Arnold
— The Gipsies (ap, Dibdin, after Favart: La Bohémienne), LT, 3 Aug 1778, music not pubd
— Summer Amusement or An Adventure at Margate (part pasticcio, M. P. Andrews and W. A. Miles), LT, 1 July 1779
14 The Son in Law (ap, J. O'Keeffe), LT, 14 Aug 1779, only pirated lib extant
— Fire and Water (ap, Andrews), LT, 8 July 1780, 1 song and lib pubd
— The Wedding Night (ap, J. Cobb), LT, 12 Aug 1780, music and lib not pubd
— The Dead Alive (ap, O'Keeffe, after Arabian Nights, LT, 16 June 1781, 1 song pubd, only pirated lib extant
— Baron Kinkvervankotsdorsprakingatchdern (ap, Andrews, after Lady Craven), LT, 9 July 1781, music not pubd
— The Silver Tankard (ap, Lady Craven), LT, 18 July 1781, music and lib not pubd
16 The Agreeable Surprise (ap, O'Keeffe), LT, 4 Sept 1781, only pirated lib extant

— The Banditti (part pasticcio, O'Keeffe), CG, 28 Nov 1781, song words pubd; rev. as The Castle of Andalusia, op.20, CG, 2 Nov 1782
— None so blind as those who won't see (ap, Dibdin, after Dorvigny), LT, 2 July 1782, music and lib not pubd
21 The Birthday or The Prince of Arragon (ap, O'Keeffe), LT, 12 Aug 1783
22 Gretna Green (ap, C. Stuart and O'Keeffe), LT, 28 Aug 1783
24 Two to One (G. Colman jr), LT, 19 June 1784
26 Hunt the Slipper (ap, H. Knapp), LT, 21 Aug 1784, only pirated lib extant (1792)
25 Peeping Tom (ap, O'Keeffe), LT, 6 Sept 1784, only pirated lib extant
28 Turk and No Turk (Colman jr), LT, 9 July 1785, music and song words pubd
29 The Siege of Curzola (O'Keeffe), LT, 12 Aug 1786, music and song words pubd
30 Inkle and Yarico (Colman jr), LT, 4 Aug 1787
31 Ut Pictora Poesis! or The Enraged Musician (ap, a-s, Colman, based on Hogarth), LT, 18 May 1789
32 The Battle of Hexham (Colman jr), LT, 11 Aug 1789
33 New Spain or Love in Mexico (ap, J. Scawen), LT, 16 July 1790
— The Basket Maker (ap, O'Keeffe), LT, 4 Sept 1790, music not pubd
33 The Surrender of Calais (ap, Colman jr), LT, 30 July 1791
35 The Enchanted Wood (ap, Francis'), LT, 25 July 1792
34 The Mountaineers (Colman jr, after Cervantes), LT, 3 Aug 1793
35 The Children in the Wood (ap, T. Morton), LT, 1 Oct 1793
— Thomas and Sally (ap, a-s, Bickerstaffe), LT, 24 Feb 1794, music by T. Arne with new finale by Arnold, music not pubd
36 Auld Robin Gray (ap, part pasticcio, S. J. Arnold), LT, 26 July 1794
— How to be happy (ap, G. Brewer), LT, 9 Aug 1794, 1 song pubd, lib not pubd
— Rule Britannia (ap, pasticcio, J. Roberts), LT, 18 Aug 1794, music not pubd
— Britain's Glory (ap, part pasticcio, R. Benson), LT, 20 Aug 1794, 1 song pubd
— The Death of Captain Faulkner (ap, part pasticcio, ? W. Pearce), CG, 6 May 1795, ov. by Arnold, music not pubd
37 Zorinski (Mofton, after Brooke: Gustavus Vasa), LT, 20 June 1795
— Who pays the Reckoning? (ap, S. J. Arnold), LT, 16 July 1795, music not pubd, song words pubd
38 Love and Money (ap, part pasticcio, Benson), LT, 29 Aug 1795
— Love and Madness! (ap, F. Waldron, after Shakespeare and Fletcher: Two Noble Kinsmen), LT, 21 Sept 1795, music not pubd, song words pubd
39 Bannian Day (ap, Brewer, after Cross: The Apparition), LT, 11 June 1796
40 The Shipwreck (ap, S. J. Arnold), DL, 10 Dec 1796
— The Hovel (ap), DL, 23 May 1797, music and lib not pubd
— The Irish Legacy (ap, S. J. Arnold), LT, 26 June 1797, music and lib not pubd
43 The Italian Monk (J. Boaden, after A. Radcliffe), LT, 15 Aug 1797, incl. only 4 songs
— Throw Physic to the Dogs! (ap, H. Lee), LT, 8 July 1798, music not pubd, song words pubd
45 Cambro-Britons (Boaden, after Lewis), LT, 21 July 1798
46 False and True (ap, G. Moultrie), LT, 11 Aug 1798
52 The Review (ap, Colman jr, after Lee and Dibdin), LT, 1 Sept 1800
50 The Veteran Tar (ap, S. J. Arnold, after Le petit matelot), DL, 29 Jan 1801
— The Sixty-third Letter (ap, W. C. Oulton), LT, 18 July 1802

OTHER STAGE

— Harlequin Dr Faustus (pantomime, Woodward and others), CG, 18 Nov 1766, music and song words pubd
— Mother Shipton (pantomime, Colman), 26 Dec 1770
27 The Genius of Nonsense (pantomime, Colman), LT, 2 Sept 1780, music and song words pubd
19 Harlequin Teague (pantomime, part pasticcio, Colman and O'Keeffe), LT, 17 Aug 1782
— Here and There and Everywhere (pantomime, Delpini), LT, 31 Aug 1785, music and lib not pubd
— The Gnome (pantomime, Wewitzer and others), LT, 5 Aug 1788, 1 song pubd, song words pubd
— Harlequin Peasant (pantomime), LT, 26 Dec 1793, music and lib not pubd
48 Obi, or Three-fingered Jack (ballet, Fawcett, after Moseley), LT, 2 July 1800
51 The Corsair (ballet, C. Farley), LT, 29 July 1801
53 Fairies' Revels (ballet, Fawcett, after Little: The Ring), LT, 14 Aug 1802
— 8 entr'actes for Macbeth, LT, 7 Sept 1778, score (1778)
— The Tobacco Box (interlude, a-s), LT, 13 Aug 1782, Fr. air, arr. Arnold

Dramas including selections from Arnold's works: Harlequins Museum (pasticcio, compiled Goodwin and Shield), CG, 20 Dec 1792; Wives in Plenty! (pasticcio, after Molloy: The Coquet), LT, 23 Nov 1793; The Red Cross Knights (pasticcio, compiled J. Holman and Attwood), LT, 21 Aug 1799; Foul Deeds Will Rise (compiled S. J. Arnold and J. Smart), LT, 18 July 1804

Dramas incl. only 1 song: Fatal Curiosity (ap, Lillo, rev. Colman), LT, 29 Aug 1782; A Beggar on Horseback (ap, O'Keeffe), LT, 16 June 1785; The Wedding Day (ap, E. Inchbald), DL, 1 Nov 1794

ORATORIOS
(not published unless otherwise stated)

The Cure of Saul (Dr. J. Brown), pasticcio, KT, 23 Jan 1767
Abimelech, LT, 16 March 1768
The Resurrection, CG, 9 March 1770
The Prodigal Son (T. Hull), LT, 5 March 1773
Omnipotence (Arnold and E. Toms), LT, 25 Feb 1774, *GB-Lbm* [arr. from works by Handel]
Redemption (?W. Coxe), DL, 10 March 1786 (*c*1814) [arr. from works by Handel]
The Triumph of Truth, pasticcio, DL, 27 Feb 1789
Elisha or The Woman of Shunem (Hull), LT, Lent 1801
The Hymn of Adam and Eve (Milton), ?not perf., *Lcm* (dated 28 Jan 1802)

OTHER SACRED

Psalms and Hymns for the Chapel of the Asylum, ed. W. Riley (1767); collab. Battishill, Nares and others
The Psalms of David, ed. Arnold and J. W. Callcott (1791)
Arnold's New Set of Hymn Tunes, 4vv (*c*1791)
A Collection of Hymn Tunes, 3–4vv (*c*1797); collab. G. Breillat and W. Dixon
6 Services: 5 for Morning, Communion and Evening, B♭ (*c*1840), C, D, F, G; 1 for Communion and Evening, A (*c*1860) [continuation of Boyce: Morning Service]
Anthems (4vv unless otherwise stated; MSS, *c*1783–1800):
O be joyful unto the Lord (1783) [adaptation of Arne: Artaxerxes ov.]
Who is this that cometh from Edom?, 3vv (1800) [for Palm Sunday]
Our Lord is risen from the dead (1805) [for Easter]
God in the great assembly, holograph frag., *T*
Have mercy upon me, holograph, 1783, *Ob*
Hear O thou Shepherd . . . My song shall be of mercy, 1v; *Ob*
I will magnify Thee . . . O praise the Lord . . . Hallelujah Chorus, *Y*
My song shall be always, *Ckc*, *Lwa*, *T*, *Y*
Shepherds rejoice . . . Who is the King of Glory?, double chorus, orch, *US-BETm*
Wherewithal shall a young man, 2vv, *GB-Lbm*
Hallelujah Salvation and Glory, frag., *Lwa* [for Thanksgiving]

SECULAR VOCAL

A Collection of the Favourite Songs sung at Vaux-Hall, i–ii (1767–8)
Ode to the Haymakers (C. Smart), 1769
Ode to Shakespeare (Scott), 1769
The New Songs sung at Marylebone (*c*1770)
A Collection of the Favourite Airs in Score sung at Haberdashers Hall (*c*1770)
Ode: The Power of Music (J. Hughes), 1773
A Third Collection of Songs sung at Vaux-Hall . . . with the Favourite Cantata call'd the Milk Maid, op.9 (1774)
6 Canzonets, pf/harp acc., op.12 (1778)
Elegy on the Death of Mr Shenstone (1778), *US-Wc* [Arne's glee scored by Arnold]
The Favourite Cantata and Songs sung this Season at Vaux-Hall (*c*1778)
From Earth to Heaven, 4vv (1784)
Ode for the Anniversary of the London Hospital (1785)
Anacreontic Songs, 1–4vv (1785)
The Prince of Arcadia, pastoral elegy (1788)
Alcanzor: a Moorish Tale, 3vv (*c*1797)
Ode to Charity (1798), *GB-T* [for the Choral Fund]
Songs with orch: If 'tis joy too wound a lover (*c*1770); Come hope thou queen of endless smiles (*c*1779); No sport to the chace can compare (*c*1780); The Royal British Tar (1783); Jockey was a braw young lad (*c*1785); The Je ne sais quois (1786); Simplicity, thou fav'rite child (1789); What citadel so proud can see (1789); The Princess Elizabeth (*c*1790); Little Bess (*c*1794); Poor little Gypsey (1798)
Catches, canons and glees incl. in: anthologies ed. Warren (1776–7), Clementi (*c*1790) and Sale (*c*1800); Amusement for the Ladies (*c*1785–93, *c*1800); Social Harmony (1818); *Lcm* 115 (partly autograph); *Ckc* 199, 404

INSTRUMENTAL

A Favourite Lesson, hpd/pf (1768)
6 Sonatas, hpd/pf (*c* 1770); collab. Galuppi and F. Mazzinghi
8 Lessons, hpd/pf, op.7 (*c*1770)
14 Lessons, hpd/pf, *c*1770–75, private collection, Dublin
Sonata, B♭, hpd/pf, *c*1773, *GB-Lbm*
6 Overtures in 8 parts, op.8 (*c*1775) [also for hpd/pf]

8 Lessons, 2nd set, hpd/pf, op.10 (1775; 2/Paris, n.d.)
8 Sonatas, 3rd set, hpd/pf, vn acc., op.11 (*c*1775)
12 Minuets, hpd, vn/fl (*c*1775)
A Set of Progressive Lessons I–II, hpd/pf, op.12 (*c*1777–9)
Lesson, D, hpd/pf, *c*1777, *Ckc*
3 concs., hpd/pf, org, str, op.15 (1782)
3 Grande Sonatas, hpd/pf, op.23 (1783)
Largo and Allegro, D, org, *c*1783, *Lbm*
12 duets, 2 fl (1784); incl. works by Handel, Arne and others
Duettos on Scots songs, hpd, vn (*c*1785); collab. Barthélemon, Carter, Shield
New Instructions for the German Flute . . . with . . . a Variety of Favourite Tunes and other Easy Lessons (1787)
La Chasse or The Hunter's Medley, hpd/pf (*c*1790) [with words]
The New British Tar, medley sonata, hpd/pf (*c*1790) [with words]
Ally Croaker, with variations, hpd/pf (*c*1790)
The Princess of Wales; a Scots Minuet, hpd/pf, 1795, *Lbm*

EDITIONS AND ARRANGEMENTS

The New Musical Magazine or Compleat Library of Vocal and Instrumental Music . . . with an Universal Dictionary . . . and General History of Music [by T. Busby] (1783–6) [compiled by Arnold]
Convivial Harmony, ed. Arnold (*c*1785)
The Songs of Handel (1786–7) [Harrison's edn. corrected by Arnold]
12 English Ballads, pf acc. (*c*1788) [adapted to music by Haydn]
The Works of Handel, 180 nos., ed. Arnold (1787–97)
Cathedral Music, 4 vols., ed. and rev. Arnold (1790) [orig. by Boyce]

Writings by Arnold incl.: *Lesson on Thorough-bass* (MS, 1798, *GB-Lbm*)[?pt. of treatise]; *Exercise Book for Realization of Figured basses, Exercises and Examples for Teaching Purposes* (MSS, 1790s, *US-Wc*); chapter on music in D. Fenning: *The Young Man's Book of Knowledge* (1786)

BIBLIOGRAPHY

Letters of S. J. Arnold (MS, *US-Lu*)
W. C. Oulton: *A History of the Theatre in London, 1771–95* (London, 1796)
C. Dibdin: *The Professional Life of Mr. Dibdin Written by Himself* (London, 1803, enlarged 2/1809)
W. Bingley: *Musical Biography or Memoirs of Eminent Musicians*, ii (London, 1814)
T. Busby: *Concert Room and Orchestra Anecdotes*, iii (London, 1825), 148ff
J. O'Keeffe: *Recollections of his Life*, ii (London, 1826)
G. Colman jr: *Random Records*, i (London, 1830)
'Memoir of Samuel Arnold, Mus. Doc.', *Harmonicon*, viii (1830), 137 [probably by William Ayrton, Arnold's son-in-law]
W. S. Ayrton: *Memoir* [1876] *and Correspondence of Marianne Ayrton, c1793–1834* (MS, *US-Wc*)
J. M. Coopersmith: 'The First Gesamtausgabe: Arnold's Edition of Handel's Works', *Notes* (1947), iv, 277, 439
P. Hirsch: 'Dr Arnold's Handel Edition', *MR*, viii (1947), 102
C. Cudworth: 'English Symphonists of the Eighteenth Century', *PRMA*, lxxviii (1951–2), 31
R. Fiske: *English Theatre Music in the Eighteenth Century* (London, 1973)

ROGER FISKE (text),
ROBERT HOSKINS (work-list, bibliography)

Arnold, Yury (Karlovich) [Jurig von] (*b* St Petersburg, 13 Nov 1811; *d* Karakesh, nr. Simferopol, Crimea, 20 July 1898). Russian writer on music and composer. His father was a councillor of state. After studying political economy at the German University of Dorpat in Estonia, he served in the army during the Polish campaign (1831–8). On resigning his commission he decided to make a career in music and studied composition with Fuchs and Hunke. In 1839 his cantata *Svetlana*, to words by Zhukovsky, was awarded a Philharmonic Society prize and performed in St Petersburg. He was a friend of the leading Russian musicians of his day, and his three volumes of memoirs *Lyubov muzikal'novo uchitelya* ('The love of a music teacher'), published in 1892–3, are a valuable record of 60 years of Russian musical life. From 1840 he contributed criticisms and reviews to a number of journals (the St Petersburg *Vedomosti*, *Biblioteka dlya chteniya*, *Literaturnaya gazeta*, *Severnaya pchela*, *Panteon* and others) under a variety of pseudonyms, including Meloman, Karl Karlovich, A. Yu., Harmonin and Karl Smelïy.

During the 1860s Arnold was in Leipzig. He wrote for the journal *Signal*, edited the *Neue Zeitschrift für Musik* (1863–70) and founded the *Neue allgemeine Zeitschrift für Theater und Musik*. It is reasonably certain that at this time he was employed as an espionage agent by the tsarist secret service, and it has also been suggested, by V. Kozlovsky in a pamphlet published in Moscow in 1917, that the articles which appeared above his name were in fact written by a certain Peshenin who was handsomely rewarded for his silence. He published several useful monographs on the history of Russian church music, and travelled extensively to collect material for his studies of folk music. His views on the origins of Russian folksong are now generally discredited. From 1870 to 1894 he taught music in Moscow, for a short time in 1870 as a professor at the conservatory. He lectured in music history at the conservatory in 1888 and was invited to speak on Russian music in Leipzig the next year. From 1894 to his death he taught singing in St Petersburg.

Arnold's compositions provide little evidence of real inspiration and are of academic interest only. They include the operas *Invalid* (Moscow, 1852), *Noch pod Ivana Kupala* ('St John the Baptist's night', Moscow, 1853), *Tsïganka* ('Gypsy girl', 1853), *Posledniy den Pompei* ('The last day of Pompeii') and a vaudeville; an overture to *Boris Godunov* (1861); sacred choral music; and over 50 songs to words by Koltsov, Mey and others.

WRITINGS

Betrachtungen über die Kunst der Darstellung in Musikdrama (Leipzig, 1867)

Der Einfluss des Zeitgeistes auf die Entwicklung der Tonkunst (Leipzig, 1867)

Die Tonkunst in Russland bis zur Einführung des abendländischen Musik- und Notensystems (Leipzig, 1867)

Über Schulen für dramatische und musikalische Kunst (Leipzig, 1867)

24 auserlesene Opern-Charaktere im Berug auf deren musikalisch-declamatorische, wie dramatisch-mimische Darstellung, analysirt und beleuchtet, i–xii (Leipzig, 1867)

Über Franz Liszt's oratorium 'Die Heilige Elisabeth' (Leipzig, 1868)

Nauka o muzïke na osnovanii esteticheskikh i fiziologicheskikh zakonov [A study of music on the basis of aesthetic and physiological laws] (Moscow, 1875)

Die alten Kirchenmelodie, historisch und akustisch entwickelt (Leipzig, ?1878)

Teoriya drevnerusskovo tserkovnovo i narodnovo peniya na osnovanii avtenticheskikh traktatov i akusticheskovo analiza [The theory of old Russian church and folk singing on the basis of authentic treatises and acoustic analysis], i (Moscow, 1880)

Garmonizatsiya drevnerusskovo tserkovo peniya po ellinskoy i vizantiy-skoy teorii i akusticheskomu analizu [The harmonization of old Russian church singing based on ancient Greek and Byzantine theory and acoustic analysis] (Moscow, 1886)

Teoriya postanovki golosa po metodu staroy ital'yanskoy shkolï i primeneniye teorii k prakticheskomu obucheniyu krasivomu obrazovaniyu pevcheskikh zvukov [The theory of voice training based on the old Italian school method and its practical application for good voice production], i–iii (St Petersburg, 1898)

BIBLIOGRAPHY

'Yury Arnold', *Vsemirnaya illyustratsiya* (1886), no.37, p.186

G. B. Bernandt and I. M. Yampol'sky: *Kto pisal o muzïke* [Writers on music], i (Moscow, 1971) [incl. list of writings]

JENNIFER SPENCER

Arnold de Lantins. *See* LANTINS, DE.

Arnoldo Fiamengo [Arnoldus Flandrus]. *See* FLANDRUS, ARNOLDUS.

Arnold von Bruck. *See* BRUCK, ARNOLD VON.

Arnone [Arnoni], **Guglielmo** (*b* Milan, *c*1570; *d* Milan, 1630). Italian composer and organist. We know from the dedication of his *Partitura del 2° libro delli motetti* (1599) that he was Milanese and a pupil of Claudio Merulo, with whom he probably studied between 1584 and 1586 in Mantua. On 12 December 1591 he was appointed organist of the Duomo of Milan at a salary of 400 imperial lire, and he kept this post until his death. The influence of Merulo is recognizable in his works 'in the clarity of the counterpoint and the nature of the invention' (to quote his own words). Banchieri numbered him among the most celebrated organists of his time.

WORKS

Partitura del 2° libro delli motetti, 5–8vv (Milan, 1599)

Il 1° libro de madrigali, 6vv (Venice, 1600); 4 repr. in 1613[10]

Sacrarum modulationum, 6vv, liber tertius (Venice, 1602), lost

Missa una, motecta, Magnificat, Litaniae B. Maria Virginis, falsis bordonis et Gloria Patri, 8vv, bc (org), op.6 (Venice, 1625)

Motets in 1608[13], 1610[1], 1611[1], 1612[3], 1615[13], 1617[1], 1619[4], 1622[5], 1626[6]

Pieces in 1605[6], 1610[10]; 2 pieces in L. Beretta's I° libro delle canzoni (Milan, 1604)

Pater noster, 5vv, *I-Mcap*(*d*), also in 1619[4]

BIBLIOGRAPHY

A. Banchieri: *Conclusioni nel suono dell'organo* (Bologna, 1609), 12

P. Morigia: *La nobiltà di Milano* (Milan, 1619), 303

F. Mompellio: 'La musica a Milano nell'età moderna', *Storia di Milano*, xvi (1962), 518

MARIANGELA DONÀ

Arnould [Arnoult], **(Magdeleine)** [Madeleine] **Sophie** (*b* Paris, 13 Feb 1740; *d* Paris, 22 Oct 1802). French soprano. A precocious child, she studied Latin and Italian and received a solid general education. She first attracted attention as a soloist in a convent choir and

Sophie Arnould: portrait by Jean-Baptiste Greuze (1725–1805) in the Wallace Collection, London

soon sang before the queen and later Mme de Pompadour; shortly thereafter the king appointed her to the Opéra. She studied acting with Hippolyte Clairon and singing with Marie Fel. From her début in Mouret's

Les amours des dieux in 1757 she was the leading female singer at the Opéra until 1778, taking part in over 30 works. Her greatest role was probably in Rameau's *Castor et Pollux*; she also sang Iphise in his *Dardanus*, created the title role in Monsigny's *Aline, reine de Golconde* (1766) and performed in revivals of Rousseau's *Le devin du village*, Lully's *Amadis de Gaule* (as Oriane), *Thésée* (as Eglé) and *Proserpine*. She adapted with difficulty to the demands of Gluck, but with such success that her Iphigenia in *Iphigénie en Aulide* was a triumph. Less impressive as Eurydice in *Orphée*, she was mortified by the choice, attributed to favouritism, of Rosalie Levasseur for Alcestis in 1776; Arnould's voice, however, had begun to deteriorate and this massive role was probably beyond her. She retired into private life and comparative indigence, for she had never been careful with money.

Arnould was the last great singer in the French style preceding Gluck. Her voice was sweet and expressive rather than powerful, and she particularly emphasized good diction; her acting ability was praised by Garrick. She was equally known for her biting wit, which caused considerable trouble with her social and political superiors and with fellow artists. Her career was further jeopardized by her love affair with the Count of Lauraguais, by whom she had three children. Nevertheless her personality and intelligence attracted the company of such figures as Voltaire, Rousseau, Beaumarchais, Diderot and Benjamin Franklin, and inspired several biographies, two comedies and an opera by Gabriel Pierné (*Sophie Arnould*, 1927). J.-B. Greuze painted two portraits of her (in the Wallace Collection, London, reproduced here, and a collection of Lord Normanton, Somerly, Hants.) and J. A. Houdon made a bust of her, which is in the Louvre.

BIBLIOGRAPHY

C. Y. Cousin d'Avalon: *Grimmiana* (Paris, 1813)
[A. Deville:] *Arnoldiana, ou Sophie Arnould et ses contemporaines* (Paris, 1813)
F. Fayolle: *L'esprit de Sophie Arnould* (Paris, 1813)
E.-L. Lamothe-Langon, ed.: *Mémoires de mademoiselle Sophie Arnoult* (Paris, 1837)
E. and J. de Goncourt: *Sophie Arnould d'après sa correspondance et ses mémoires inédits* (Paris, 1857/*R*1973, 2/1859)
H. Sutherland Edwards: *Idols of the French Stage* (London, 1889)
R. Douglas: *Sophie Arnould: Actress and Wit* (Paris, 1898)
F. Rogers: 'Sophie Arnould', *MQ*, vi (1920), 57
B. Dussanc: *Sophie Arnould: la plus spirituelle des bacchantes* (Paris, 1938)
E. Zanetti: 'Arnould, Magdeline Sophie', *ES*

JULIAN RUSHTON

Arno Volk. *See* VOLK.

Arnschwanger, Johann Christoph (*b* Nuremberg, 28 Dec 1625; *d* Nuremberg, 10 Dec 1696). German poet and theologian. He spent virtually his entire life at Nuremberg. He was educated at the St Egidien Gymnasium (whose director from 1642 was J. M. Dilherr), and from 1644 at Altdorf University. He gained the master's degree at Jena in 1647. In 1648 he went to Leipzig and then travelled to Hamburg but arrived completely destitute after risking his life in an escape from marauding soldiers. During 1649 he participated in a disputation at Helmstedt on Original Sin chaired by the controversial syncretist G. C. Calixtus. In 1650 he returned to Nuremberg and in 1651 was appointed curate, and in 1652 deacon, of St Egidien. He officiated as Monday preacher at St Salvator and, after being ordained at Altdorf on 14 May 1653, was from 1654

morning preacher at St Walpurg auf der Vesten. In 1659 he became deacon of St Lorenz, the leading church in Nuremberg, where in 1679 he was promoted to senior rank and in 1690 to chief minister.

From 1675 until its dissolution in 1680, Arnschwanger was a member of the Fruchtbringende Gesellschaft, the oldest language society in Germany. He published two collections of sacred poems, with melodies, and included others in his various theological writings. The two collections are: *Neue geistliche Lieder* (Nuremberg, 1659) and *Heilige Palmen, und christliche Psalmen, das ist: Unterschiedliche neue geistliche Lieder ·und Gesänge* (Nuremberg, 1,680[1]) (32 poems from both volumes in Fischer and Tümpel, nine melodies in Zahn). It may be noted that the second collection coincided with the dissolution of the Fruchtbringende Gesellschaft, that its title refers to the society's emblem, a palm tree, and that Arnschwanger signed it with his name in the society, 'Der Unschuldige' ('The Innocent'). In the preface to the 1659 volume he stated that its artistry 'does not aspire to individual treatment of the words nor to the exceedingly high standard of contemporary German poetry' but that 'music lovers are amply compensated for shortcomings in the texts by the beautifully worked settings of Nuremberg's leading organists and directors of music'. The poems in both volumes in fact were written to familiar melodies and newly set to music for solo voice and continuo by Nuremberg musicians. The composers of the 1659 collection are Paul Hainlein, A. M. Lundsdörffer, David Schedlich, Heinrich Schwemmer and G. C. Wecker. Johann Löhner replaced Schedlich in the 1680 volume, which also includes a melody by an otherwise unknown musician, A. C. Hültz, the only one Arnschwanger did not mention in his preface. Unlike the poets of another leading Nuremberg literary society, the Pegnesische Blumenorden, he used popular diction in his verses. The musical settings offer a good cross-section of German continuo song of the period. 23 items were taken into the *Nürnberger Gesangbuch* (1690), though divorced from their new settings, and only the chorale *Merk, Seele, was du dir hast vorgenommen* (1680) appears with its new melody (by Wecker) among the 42 texts reappearing in J. B. König's *Harmonischer Lieder-Schatz* (Frankfurt am Main, 1738).

BIBLIOGRAPHY

G. A. Will: *Nürnbergisches Gelehrtenlexikon*, i (Nuremberg, 1755), 42ff
C. von Winterfeld: *Der evangelische Kirchengesang und sein Verhältnis zur Kunst des Tonsatzes*, ii (Leipzig, 1845/*R*1966), 456ff
E. E. Koch: *Geschichte des Kirchenlieds und Kirchengesangs*, iii (Stuttgart, 3/1867/*R*1973), 517ff
J. Zahn: *Die Melodien der deutschen evangelischen Kirchenlieder* (Gütersloh, 1889–93/*R*1963)
A. Fischer and W. Tümpel: *Das deutsche evangelische Kirchenlied des 17. Jahrhunderts*, v (Gütersloh, 1911/*R*1964)

LINI HÜBSCH-PFLEGER

Arnstadt. Town in the German Democratic Republic, in Thuringia. It is rich in associations with the Bach family. It has a long tradition of hymn writers and was for a time the home of the Scwarzburg-Rudolstadt princes. Its buildings include Schloss Neidecksburg, where the Bachs served as instrumentalists, the Stadtmuseum's 'Mon Plaisir' portrait gallery, which is of musical interest, a Bach church, a Bach house, and archives rich in documentary material. Dominated by the middle-class guild tradition, music in Arnstadt flourished in the period preceding J. S. Bach's time as organist of the Bonifaciuskirche (1703–7).

Arnstadt's leading composers included the city wait Caspar Bach (c1600), Heinrich Bach (organist from 1641 to 1692), J. M. Bach (b Arnstadt, 1648 and organist at nearby Gehren from 1673), J. C. Bach (b Arnstadt, 1642 and organist of the Schlosskapelle from 1663 to 1665), Adam Drese (Kapellmeister, 1678–1701), the lutenist Paul Gleitsmann (c1700), J. N. Tischer, who studied in Arnstadt in 1731, J. P. Treiber (b Arnstadt, 1675, and a pupil of Drese), and the 17th- and 18th-century organ builders Weisse, Wender, Häner and Schmalz. After World War II Arnstadt became part of the Erfurt administrative area, and it is a lively musical centre. Organ recitals are given in the Bonifaciuskirche, and the Bach tradition is promoted through chamber music concerts, congresses of the Neue Bach-Gesellschaft, publications and research. There are choirs, instrumental groups and a music school. The Bach house has a collection of instruments, and in neighbouring Dornheim is the church where Johann Sebastian and Maria Barbara Bach were married.

BIBLIOGRAPHY
G. Kraft: Die thüringische Musikkultur um 1600, i (Würzburg, 1941)
F. Wiegand: Johann Sebastian Bach und seine Verwandten in Arnstadt (Arnstadt, 1950)
G. KRAFT

Arnt von Aich. See AICH, ARNT VON.

Arnulph of St Gilles. ?14th-century French theorist. His treatise, De differenciis et generibus cantorum (GS, iii, 316–18), categorizes in highly florid language four kinds of musician. There are those who do not understand the principles of music and perform it barbarously. Next, certain laymen and some clerics are expertes, performing on instruments difficult melodies scarcely possible for the voice. The third category comprises those (clerics) who know the science of music, and also sing well. Most prized of all are those, compared to larks, who direct their singing 'modo, mensura, numero et colore'. Apparently rising even above this category are women singers (discussed at length) who divide the indivisible semitone and delight the ears like the Sirens; they are to be compared with angels rather than humans.

BIBLIOGRAPHY
H. Riemann: Geschichte der Musiktheorie (Berlin, 1920; Eng. trans., 1962), 184
ANDREW HUGHES

Aroca y Ortega, Jesús (b Algete, Oct 1877; d Madrid, 30 Oct 1935). Spanish composer and musicologist. He studied the piano and composition at Madrid Conservatory, where he taught harmony from 1933; he was also a pianist and conductor, and president of the National Association of Spanish Conductors. Though Aroca belonged to a generation of Spanish musicians who were untrained for the musicological investigations they undertook, his work has considerable merit and has too often been dismissed as insignificant. His two most important publications are his transcription of Claudio de Sablonara's Cancionero musical y poético del siglo XVIII (Madrid, 1916) with biographies of its composers, and the Reseña histórica de la tonada (Madrid, 1913), with transcriptions of early music. His thorough and important research on Spanish folklore formed the basis for some of his compositions (e.g. Arrabales castellanos); he also composed zarzuelas and symphonic works.

BIBLIOGRAPHY
R. Mitjana: 'Comentarios y apostillas al Cancionero poético y musical del siglo XVII, recogido por Claudio de la Sablonara y publicado por D. Jesús Aroca', Revista de filología española, vi (1919), 24–56, 233–67
L. Pfandl: Über einige spanische Handschriften der Münchener Staatsbibliothek', Homenaje ofrecido a Menendez Pidal, ii (Madrid, 1925), 531
JOSÉ LÓPEZ-CALO

Aron, Pietro. See AARON, PIETRO.

Aronowitz, Cecil (b King William's Town, South Africa, 4 March 1916; d Ipswich, 7 Sept 1978). British viola player of Russian–Lithuanian parentage. He studied the violin with Achille Rivarde at the RCM, London, and played in the major London orchestras until the war, after which he changed to the viola. He became principal viola with the Goldsbrough Orchestra (later the English Chamber Orchestra) in 1949 and with the London Mozart Players from 1952 to 1964. In the English Opera Group Orchestra he played in the early performances of Britten's church parables. However, it was chiefly in chamber music that he achieved distinction; he was a founder-member of Musica da Camera (1946), the Melos Ensemble (1950) and the Pro Arte Piano Quartet (1965). He had a particularly polished technique and an easy manner of integration, qualities very evident when he played as extra viola with the Amadeus String Quartet in quintets, blending with those players to produce performances of outstanding merit. He married the pianist Nicola Grunberg, with whom he formed a duo ensemble. He was professor of the viola and chamber music at the RCM from 1948, and director of studies in strings at Snape Maltings from 1977.
WATSON FORBES

Arpa [Mollica], Giovanni Leonardo [Giovan, Gian, Gianleonardo] dell' [dall'] (b Naples, c1525; d Naples, Jan 1602). Italian harpist, composer and actor. He was generally known as 'dell'Arpa' because of his outstanding playing of the double harp. He was praised by several Neapolitan writers, among them G. B. del Tufo (Ritratto delle grandezze, delizie e meraviglie della nobilissima città di Napoli, 1588) and G. C. Cortese (Viaggio di Parnaso, c1610). As a musician-actor he played the role of an old man in a comedy given at the Palazzo Sanseverino in 1545, and he took part in Piccolomini's Alessandro in 1558. He was a favourite entertainer in aristocratic circles and served the Neapolitan branch of the Colonna family, particularly Giovanna d'Aragona (see Luigi Dentice: Duo dialoghi della musica, 1552). His reputation spread beyond Naples, and he was invited to Ferrara in 1584, although it is not known if he went there. G. P. Lomazzo mentioned him as a celebrated harpist in Trattato dell'arte (1584), and Giovenale Ancina compared him to King David in the dedication to his Il tempio armonico (1599). In 1594 Count Alfonso Fontanelli from Ferrara heard him play at the home of Ettore Gesualdo in Naples and found 'his technique marvellous but his manner of improvisation old-fashioned'. He published 22 napolitane in various collections between 1565 and 1570. Like those of Giovanni Leonardo Primavera (with whom he has often been confused), these pieces are among the simplest and most compact in the repertory. Repeated-note recitation, frequent parallel 5ths and chordal textures are characteristic. Most of the poems, consisting of rhymed couplets, are set in the balanced form *AABCC*. The first strophe of his *Villanelle crudel* is quoted by G. B. Cini in the comedy *La vedova* (1569).

WORKS

6 canzoni in 1565[17]; 6 in 1566[9]
3 villanelle in 1567[22], 1 of these attrib. S. Lando in 1566[10]
7 napolitane in 1570[18]
5 pieces intabulated for lute in 1570[33]; another in 1571[8]

BIBLIOGRAPHY

G. Monti: *Le villanelle alla napoletana e l'antico dialetti a Napoli* (Città di Castello, 1925)
A. Einstein: *The Italian Madrigal* (Princeton, 1949/*R*1971)
B. Galanti: *Le villanelle alla napoletana* (Florence, 1954)
U. Proto-Giurleo: *Gian Leonardo dell'Arpa nella storia della musica* (Naples, 1964)
E. Barassi: 'Costume e pratica musicale in Napoli al tempo di G. Basile', *RIM*, ii (1967), 74
——: 'La villanella napoletana nella testimonianza di un letterato', *NRMI*, vi (1968), 1064
A. Newcomb: 'Carlo Gesualdo and a Musical Correspondence of 1594', *MQ*, liv (1968), 409
D. Cardamone: *The 'Canzone villanesca alla napolitana' and Related Italian Vocal Part Music: 1537 to 1570* (diss., Harvard U., 1972)

DONNA G. CARDAMONE

Arpa, Orazio dell'. *See* MICHI, ORAZIO.

Arpa, Rinaldo dall'. *See* RINALDO DALL'ARPA.

Arpa-citara (Sp.). ARPANETTA.

Arpa d'eolo [arpa eolia] (It.). AEOLIAN HARP.

Arpanetta (It.; Ger. *Spitzharfe*, *Harfenett*; Sp. *arpaneta*, *arpa-citara*). An upright double psaltery, with each main side of the trapezial box acting as a soundboard (see fig., p.624). As shown in Renaissance and Baroque paintings, the instrument was placed on a table or on the seated player's lap, with the shortest strings at closest reach. Those associated with the right-hand soundboard (see fig.1*a*) were of case-hardened iron and were used for the melody; those at the left (fig.1*b*) were of brass (or some similar copper alloy heavier than iron) and, with their curved bridge quite near to the upper edge of the box, provided a bass accompaniment. A height of some 90 cm was common, but instruments between perhaps 60 and 150 cm tall were also made. The total range might vary between two-and-a-half and four octaves; Eisel gave a range from *f* to *d'''*, chromatic except for the lowest 5th. The seven diatonic notes in each octave were each supplied with double courses while the five chromatic notes were single-strung.

Surviving instruments date from 1621 to about 1730. The arpanetta's first appearance in the West may have been in Italy, but it had its greatest popularity in Germany and the Netherlands after 1650. J. G. Walther's *Musicalisches Lexicon* of 1732 refers to three types of *Harfe*, the first of which was the 'common one, known everywhere, strung with wire and called *harpanetta*'.

BIBLIOGRAPHY

A. Furetière: *Dictionnaire universel* (Paris, 1690)
J. P. Eisel: *Musicus autodidactus* (Erfurt, 1738)
A. Buchner: *Hudební automaty* (Prague, 1959; Eng. trans., 1959 as *Mechanical Musical Instruments*)
S. Marcuse: *A Survey of Musical Instruments* (Newton Abbot and London, 1975)

Arpeggiation (Ger. *Brechung*). In Schenkerian analysis (*see* ANALYSIS, §III) the fundamental progression of the bass from the tonic to the dominant and back again, or a method of PROLONGATION by which any part or voice is elaborated in the form of a broken chord; in both instances a vertical configuration, namely a chord, is made linear or, as it is sometimes said, 'horizontalized' (Ger. *horizontalisiert*). In tonal music harmonic interest is maintained over an entire piece or movement by establishing the tonic key, moving away from it (usually to another key or keys), and returning to it through a dominant preparation. The arpeggiation of the bass I–V–I, which is specifically referred to in German as *Bassbrechung*, represents the establishment of the tonic key, the dominant preparation and the return of the tonic, thus forming the harmonic element of the two-part contrapuntal unit (called the URSATZ) that encapsulates all the melodic and harmonic motion of a tonal piece. Without the bass arpeggiation the harmony would be essentially 'fixed' to the tonic and true modulation would be impossible.

As a method of prolongation an arpeggiation can be applied to the melodic line (ex.1) or the bass line (the arpeggiation I–VI–IV before the dominant is common, as in ex.2); or it can join the melody to the bass (ex.3). Sometimes it occurs in conjunction with another

Ex.1 Mozart: String Quartet in D minor K421/417*b*, Menuetto

Ex.2 Mozart: String Quartet in B♭ K458, Menuetto

Ex.3 Chopin: Study in A minor op. 25 no. 11

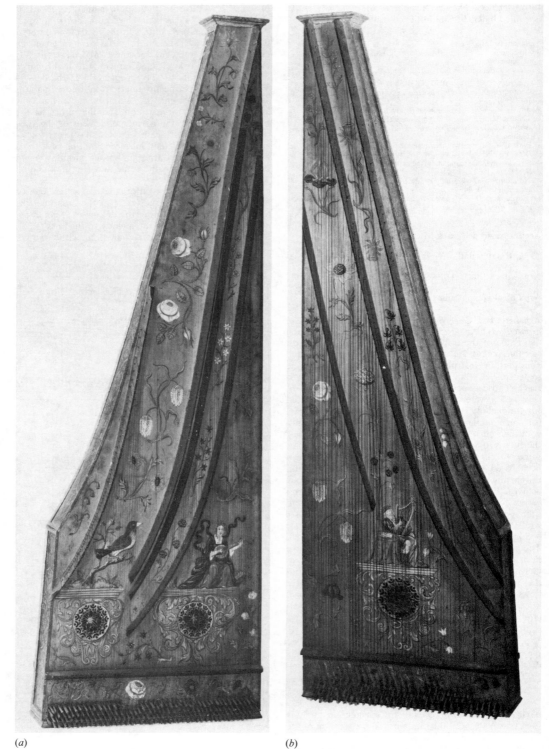

(a)   (b)

1. Right-hand (a) and left-hand (b) views of an arpanetta, ?Flemish, c1700 (Royal College of Music, London)

method of prolongation; an ascending arpeggiation is often combined with a series of *Übergreifzüge* (ex.4; *see also* ÜBERGREIFEN, ex.2). The arpeggiated chord need

Ex.4 Beethoven: Piano Sonata in A♭ op.110, 2nd movt

not be a triad; 7th chords are frequently arpeggiated, and in chromatic music there are arpeggiations of altered chords (the melody of the first bars of *Tristan und Isolde* actually arpeggiates the 'Tristan' chord, as outlined in ex.5). It is also possible for the arpeggiated

Ex.5 Wagner: *Tristan und Isolde*, outline of beginning of Prelude

chord to be a mixture of the major and minor triads; in Schenker's analysis of Schubert's *Auf dem Flusse* from *Winterreise* as given in *Der freie Satz*, fig.40/2, the basic melodic motion is an elaboration of the arpeggiation $e'-g\sharp'-b'-e''-g\natural''$.

WILLIAM DRABKIN

Arpeggio (It. from *arpeggiare*: 'to play the harp'). The sounding of the notes of a chord in succession rather than simultaneously; also, especially in keyboard music, the breaking or spreading of a chord. The ability to play (or sing) arpeggio figuration fluently has traditionally been counted an important part of instrumental (or vocal) technique.

The use of arpeggio patterns as an accompaniment in keyboard music dates from the mid-18th century (*see* ALBERTI BASS). Such passages are normally written out in full, but even earlier than this the term 'arpeggio' ('arpeggiato', 'arpeggiando') may be found to indicate that a player is to interpret a series of chords by playing them in arpeggiated fashion, as shown in ex.1;

Ex.1 J. S. Bach: Violin Sonata in A BWV1015

sometimes the arpeggiation of the first chord in such a sequence is written out in full to indicate the required manner of performance for the entire passage.

The arpeggiation of a single chord (*see also* ORNAMENTS, §IV, 5) may be notated in a number of ways. The commonest method in present-day notation is

Ex.2

shown in ex.2*a*; ex.2*b* shows the notation generally used by Mozart, Hummel and others of the late 18th and early 19th centuries. Ex.2*c* and *d* show Türk's notation for upwards and downwards arpeggios respectively (*Clavierschule*, 1789). Ex.3 shows notations used when

Ex.3

certain of the arpeggiated notes are not to be held for the full duration of the main note, and ex.4 shows notations

Ex.4

and interpretations of arpeggiated chords with acciaccaturas or appoggiaturas. A distinction should properly be made between arpeggiation in the two hands separately and the two together (ex.5).

Ex.5

FRANKLIN TAYLOR/R

Arpeggione. A string instrument, also called 'guitar violoncello', played with a bow, which had a very brief life in the early 19th century, and is recorded only because Schubert wrote a fine sonata for it which was played by Vincenz Schuster. It was invented and made by J. G. Staufer of Vienna in 1824 and was, in essentials, a bass viol with a guitar tuning (see illustration).

The body was coarser in structure and the frets (24 in number) were, guitar fashion, metal strips fixed in the neck; it was bowed like a cello. The body was smooth-waisted, though this was done in imitation of the guitar and not as a revival of the early viol form. The six strings were tuned *E–A–d–g–b–e'*.

Arpeggione by Johann Georg Staufer, Vienna, 1824 (Musikinstrumenten-Museum, Karl-Marx-Universität, Leipzig)

Schuster, who was virtually its only professional exponent, wrote a tutor for it, which Diabelli published.

GERALD HAYES/R

Arpichordum. (1) A device most commonly found on Flemish virginals of the centre-plucking (MUSELAR) type, but also mentioned in connection with German harpsichords, in which a sliding batten brings a series of metal hooks or wires close to the strings at one end. When the strings are plucked, they jar against the hooks or wires, producing a buzzing sound. On muselars, the arpichordum is normally provided only for the two and a half octaves of strings passing over the straight portion of the right-hand bridge, i.e. from C/E to f'.

(2) According to Praetorius (*Syntagma musicum*, ii, 1618, 2/1619/R1958), a virginal equipped with a

device of the kind described above, which gave it 'a harp-like sound'.

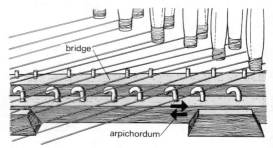

Section of an arpichordum

BIBLIOGRAPHY
A. Nevin: 'L'arpicordo', *AcM*, xlii (1970), 230
G. Leonhardt: 'In Praise of Flemish Virginals of the Seventeenth Century', *Keyboard Instruments*, ed. E. M. Ripin (Edinburgh, 1971), 43

EDWIN M. RIPIN

Arpicordo. A term used in the first half of the 16th century to designate a gut-strung virginal or harpsichord apparently made for imitating the sound of a harp, and sometimes equipped with metal pins against which the strings buzzed when they were plucked (*see* ARPICHORDUM). Subsequently the term seems also to have been applied to ordinary wire-strung instruments.

BIBLIOGRAPHY
A. Neven: 'L'arpicordo', *AcM*, xlii (1970), 230
J. H. Van der Meer: 'Das Arpicordo-Problem nochmals erörtert', *AcM*, xlix (1977), 275

EDWIN M. RIPIN

Arquimbau, Domingo (*b* c1758; *d* Seville, 26 Jan 1829). Spanish composer. On 1 November 1790, after having been *maestro de capilla* at Gerona Cathedral, he became substitute *maestro de capilla* at Seville Cathedral with the right of succession. When Ripa died he took the post on 6 November 1795, occupying it until his death. In 1815, on submitting as a test piece his Maundy Thursday *Lamentación primera* for chorus, soloists and full orchestra, he was admitted to the Accademia Filarmonica at Bologna and on 23 November given the title *dottore*. Of his many sacred works in Seville listed by Rosa y López (1904), Anglès in 1928 encountered only the three *Magnificat* settings, three hymns, a *Pange lingua* and a four-voice mass concordant with another at Santiago, Chile. Though always brilliant and competently written, his church works lack the piquant Spanish flavour characteristic of Ripa, bearing instead a closer resemblance to Paisiello's.

WORKS

13 masses with orch, 4 masses a cappella, 38 motets, 11 Lamentations, 11 hymns, 2 Te Deum, 3 Salve, 22 vesper psalms, 3 Magnificat, 2 Miserere with orch, 8 Miserere a cappella, 4 villancicos: all *E-Sc* (see Rosa y López)
2 masses, Santiago Cathedral, Chile; mass, with orch, 1807, Sucre Cathedral, Bolivia; Dixit Dominus, 8vv, *E-E*
Que ynstante dichoso, villancico, 4vv, orch, Archivo Arzobispal, Lima, Peru
La tigre ircana, rondo, 1v, wind insts, bc, *E-Bc*

BIBLIOGRAPHY
S. de la Rosa y López: *Los seises de la Catedral de Sevilla* (Seville, 1904), 328ff
H. Anglès: 'La música conservada en la Biblioteca Colombina y en la Catedral de Sevilla', *AnM*, ii (1947), 34

R. Stevenson: *Renaissance and Baroque Musical Sources in the Americas* (Washington, DC, 1970), 117, 235, 320
J. E. Ayarra Jarne: *La música en la catedral de Sevilla* (Seville, 1976), 65

ROBERT STEVENSON

Arrangement (Ger. *Bearbeitung*). The reworking of a musical composition, usually for a different medium from that of the original.

1. Definition and scope. 2. History to 1600. 3. 1600–1800. 4. 19th and 20th centuries. 5. Conclusion.

1. DEFINITION AND SCOPE. In its broadest possible sense the word 'arrangement' might be applied to all Western music from Hucbald to Hindemith, since each composition involves the rearrangement of the basic and unchanging melodic and harmonic components of music, whether these be understood as belonging to the harmonic series or the chromatic scale. In a narrower but still fairly comprehensive sense the term might be used for any piece of music based on or incorporating pre-existing material. Thus variation form, the contrafactum, the parody mass, the pasticcio, and liturgical works based on a cantus firmus all involve some measure of arrangement. In the sense in which it is commonly used among musicians, however, the word may be taken to mean either the transference of a composition from one medium to another or the elaboration (or simplification) of a piece, with or without a change of medium. In either case some degree of recomposition is usually involved, and the result may vary from a straightforward, almost literal, transcription to a paraphrase which is more the work of the arranger than of the original composer. It should be added, though, that the distinction implicit here between an arrangement and a TRANSCRIPTION is by no means universally accepted (cf the article 'Arrangement' in *Grove 5* and the title-pages of Liszt's piano 'transcriptions').

Arrangements exist in very large numbers from all periods of musical history, and though external factors have influenced their character the reasons for their existence cut across stylistic and historical boundaries. Commercial interest has played an important part, especially since the invention of music printing. Opportunist publishers from Petrucci onwards have looked for financial reward either from arrangements of established works or from the simultaneous publication of music in different forms. English madrigals were advertised as being 'apt for voices as for viols'; Dowland's songs were published in a form which allowed for performance either as a solo with lute accompaniment or as a part-song; in the 18th century the English market was flooded with arrangements of vocal and other music for the popular and ubiquitous flute; and ever since the early composition popular 'classics' such as Rakhmaninov's C♯ minor Prelude and Rimsky-Korsakov's *Flight of the Bumble Bee* have been arranged for almost every conceivable instrument and instrumental combination. Practical considerations of a different kind govern the preparation of vocal scores of operas and choral works, in which the orchestral part is reduced and printed, usually on two staves, in a form more or less playable at the keyboard. Such arrangements require little more than technical competence on the part of the arranger, though creative artists of the first rank have occasionally undertaken the task, often in a spirit of homage to the composer. Bülow prepared the vocal scores of some of Wagner's music dramas, and Berg did a similar service

for Schoenberg's *Gurrelieder*. Several composers have arranged the music of others with the aim of perfecting themselves in a particular form, technique or medium. Bach and Mozart, for example, both approached the composition of concertos through arrangements of other composers' music.

A large number of arrangements originate because performers want to extend the repertory of those instruments which, for one reason or another, have not been favoured with a large or rewarding corpus of original solo compositions. Until such players as Segovia and Tertis improved the status of their instruments, guitarists and viola players had to rely to a considerable extent on arrangements, and this is still the case with brass bands and (in so far as they exist) salon orchestras. Arrangements of this kind necessarily involve a transference from one instrumental medium to another, but there are also numerous examples of arrangements which alter the layout but not the instrumentation of the original. Virtuoso piano pieces have often been published in arrangements which place them within the scope of the amateur; others have been made even more difficult as a challenge to professional keyboard technique. Orchestral works have sometimes been re-orchestrated, either to take advantage of improvements in the design of instruments (the brass parts of Beethoven's Third Symphony, for example, are rarely heard as the composer wrote them) or because the original is considered to be in some respect deficient. Mahler's reorchestration of Schumann's symphonies and Rimsky-Korsakov's of Musorgsky's operas come into this category. There is also a relatively small group of arrangements made to accommodate a player's physical disability, for example those for the one-handed pianist Paul Wittgenstein, and those for the three-handed piano duo, Cyril Smith and Phyllis Sellick.

In considering all these and other categories of arrangements, any attempt to equate the motives of the arranger with the artistic merits of the result would be misleading. It is, however, possible to distinguish between the purely practical arrangement, in which there is little or no artistic involvement on the arranger's part, and the more creative arrangement, in which the original composition is, as it were, filtered through the musical imagination of the arranger. Arrangements by creative musicians are clearly the more important kind, both on account of their intrinsic merits and because they often serve to illuminate the musical personality of the composer-arranger; it is therefore towards this second type of arrangement that attention will be mainly directed in the historical conspectus that follows.

2. HISTORY TO 1600. Some element of arrangement is present in the medieval trope and clausula, as well as in those early motets where a vocal part is replaced by an instrumental one (or vice versa), but the most important type of arrangement in the period up to 1600 is the keyboard or lute intabulation of vocal polyphony. The earliest examples of such keyboard arrangements (indeed the earliest extant keyboard pieces of any kind) are in the early 14th-century Robertsbridge Manuscript (*GB-Lbm* Add.28550), whose contents include intabulations of two motets from the musical appendix to the contemporary *Roman de Fauvel* (*F-Pn* fr.146). Far from being simple transcriptions of the vocal originals, these intabulations feature a florid elaboration of the upper part which is unmistakably instrumental in con-

Ex.1

ception, and this is something which remains characteristic of all later keyboard intabulations. Ex.1a shows the beginning of the motet *Adesta–Firmissime–Alleluya Benedictus*, and ex.1b the keyboard version of the same passage. Also from the 14th century are some of the

organisandi (*D-B* 40613) (1452). Where the original vocal source is a monody, this is often made to serve as a cantus firmus in the left hand, supporting what is presumably a free and often very florid part in the right. The technique had been applied in the Faenza Manuscript to plainsong Kyries and Glorias, but is here used for secular melodies also. Ex.2 shows the opening of the song *Ellend du hast*: (a) from the Lochamer Liederbuch (*D-B* 40613) (c1450); (b) from Paumann's *Fundamentum*, with the melody in the left hand; and (c) from one of the six versions in the Buxheimer Orgelbuch (no.50). Clearly such pieces as these, and similar ones based on basse danse melodies, should be regarded as variations rather than as arrangements.

With the introduction of music printing and the wider dissemination of instruments in the 16th century, intabulations proliferated not only in Germany but in Italy, Spain and France as well (see *BrownI* for a list of all printed arrangements with their sources). To those for

Ex.2

keyboard arrangements in the important Faenza Manuscript 117 (*I-FZc*), which includes intabulations of vocal music by Jacopo da Bologna, Machaut, Landini and others. The principles governing these arrangements are similar to those of the Robertsbridge Manuscript, but the finger technique required of the performer is more advanced.

Intabulations are also to be found in the Buxheimer Orgelbuch (*D-Mbs* Cim.352b), which dates from about 1470, as well as examples of a rather different type of arrangement (if it can be called that) which occurs also in several other German organ books of the 15th century, including Conrad Paumann's *Fundamentum*

keyboard must be added a vast literature of similar pieces for lute and vihuela, beginning with Francesco Spinacino's first book of *Intabulatura de lauto*, published by Petrucci in 1507. Lute intabulations have a particular interest for the scholar since the tablature does not directly indicate pitch but tells the player which fret to use for each note; consequently lute arrangements can assist in determining the application of *musica ficta* to 16th-century vocal polyphony. Among the most famous examples is the arrangement for vihuela by Luys de Narváez of Josquin's motet *Mille regretz* as *Cancion del Emperador*. Here melodic elaboration is not confined to the top part (see ex.3). The

Ex.3

lute's function as an accompanying instrument is exemplified in numerous arrangements of polyphonic music in which all voice parts but the top one are transcribed for the instrument, resulting in a solo song with lute accompaniment. Such arrangements were important in preparing for the new monodic style that emerged towards the end of the 16th century.

3. 1600–1800. The practice of transferring vocal music to instruments continued during the next two centuries and beyond. Among the many keyboard arrangements of vocal pieces in the Fitzwilliam Virginal Book (*GB-Cfm*) is one by Peter Philips of Caccini's well-known song *Amarilli mia bella*. Philips repeated the first part of the song as printed in Caccini's *Le nuove musiche* (Florence, 1601–2) and gave a different version each time, so that the result is both an arrangement and a variation of the original (see ex.4). Arrangements of this

century and early 18th) which saw the rise and dissemination of the concerto. Francesco Geminiani, as well as arranging his own music for the harpsichord, adapted Corelli's op.3 and op.5 violin sonatas as concerti grossi. At Weimar the German theorist and composer J. G. Walther adapted concertos by Albinoni, Torelli, Telemann and others for the organ, and probably stimulated his distant relative, J. S. Bach, to similar treatment of some of Vivaldi's concertos. Bach left altogether 16 concertos for solo harpsichord (without orchestra) and six for organ, based mainly on works from Vivaldi's opp. 3, 4 and 7, but also on concertos by Telemann, Alessandro Marcello, and Walther's pupil, Prince Johann Ernst of Weimar. In many cases Bach made an almost literal transcription of the original, but often he subtly altered the harmony or filled out the texture with new counterpoints. In ex.5*b*, from the slow movement of BWV975 (arranged from Vivaldi's op.4

kind are to be found throughout the Baroque period; the six 'Schübler' chorale-preludes of Bach (BWV645–50) – transcriptions for organ of movements from the cantatas – are much later examples in the same tradition.

However, the surge of interest in instrumental music of all kinds that characterizes the Baroque period brought with it a new type of arrangement in which vocal music was for the first time not involved. Transcriptions from one instrumental medium to another were particularly cultivated in the period (late 17th

no.6) he elaborated Vivaldi's straightforward violin melody (ex.5*a*) and enriched the harmony with a totally chromatic bass line, while replacing the original bass suspensions with others in the middle of the harmony. Bach's other arrangements include one of Vivaldi's Concerto for four violins and strings op.3 no.10 as a concerto for four harpsichords (BWV1065), and most of his other keyboard concertos with accompaniment are similarly arrangements of earlier works by himself or others.

Another aspect of Bach as arranger is his practice of re-using material from earlier, and sometimes quite different, works; the Mass in B minor furnishes several familiar examples. This was a practice fairly widespread in a period when themes were largely fashioned on prototypes and when originality was measured as much in terms of craftsmanship as of melodic invention. Schütz incorporated music by Andrea Gabrieli, Alessandro Grandi and Monteverdi into his own compositions, and Francesco Durante transformed recitatives from Alessandro Scarlatti's secular cantatas into chamber duets; Handel's habit of re-using old music of his own, as well as appropriating such music by other composers as suited his needs, is well known. The practice was justified by the extent to which the 'borrowed' material was refashioned. In the case of Handel this amounted often to a complete recomposition which entirely transformed the original.

Haydn's three different versions of *Die sieben letzten Worte unserers Erlosers am Kreuze* (as an orchestral piece, 1785; for string quartet, 1787; and as an oratorio, *c*1796) provide a locus classicus in the history of arrangement. But the key figure of the late 18th century is Mozart. Mozart is important less for the number than for the nature of his arrangements. His piano concertos K37, 39–41 and 107, based on movements from sonatas by Raupach, Honauer, J. C. Bach and others are not without interest, but of more far-reaching importance is the rescoring for string trio and quartet of fugues by J. S. Bach (including some from *Das wohltemperirte Klavier*) and the reorchestration of Handel's *Acis and Galatea, Messiah, Alexander's Feast* and Ode for St Cecilia's Day. These arrangements, all done for Baron van Swieten, an enthusiast for Baroque music, are significant in representing the attitudes of their time to earlier music and because they stand at the head of a long line of Bach transcriptions and Handel reorchestrations which continued throughout the 19th and early 20th centuries, only to be discredited afterwards.

4. 19TH AND 20TH CENTURIES. The nature of arrangements during the 19th century was largely determined by two important developments. One was a new interest (already evident to some extent in the late 18th century) in instrumental colour for its own sake; the other was the rise of the piano as both concert and domestic instrument *par excellence*. The first of these developments brought with it the concept of the composer's creation as an inviolable entity, so that while the 19th-century arranger would happily reorchestrate the music of the past the 19th-century composer would go to considerable trouble to ensure that his own music was played only on those instruments for which it was conceived. It is difficult to find a Romantic counterpart to the Corelli–Geminiani or Bach–Vivaldi concerto. One result of this was that most creative arrangements of contemporary instrumental music were made by the original composer himself. Examples include Beethoven's arrangements of the Violin Concerto as a piano concerto and of the Second Symphony as a piano trio, and the various versions of Brahms's Piano Quintet and First Piano Concerto.

The exception to most of these remarks is the piano arrangement, probably the most interesting and the most widely cultivated type of arrangement in the 19th century. Innumerable transcriptions brought the orchestral and chamber repertory into the homes of the domestic pianist (or piano-duettist), but more interesting are those with which the travelling virtuoso dazzled and delighted his audiences. Pre-eminent are those of Liszt, whose operatic arrangements range from straightforward transcriptions (the Prelude to Wagner's *Tristan und Isolde*, for instance, presents fewer problems to the pianist than does Bülow's version in the vocal score) to elaborate paraphrases of enormous technical difficulty, such as those based on Mozart's *Don Giovanni*, Verdi's *Rigoletto* and several of Wagner's music dramas. Liszt's voluminous arrangements also include many Schubert songs, all the Beethoven symphonies and Berlioz's *Symphonie fantastique*; further, he was the first important Romantic pianist–composer to reflect the spirit of the Bach revival in arrangements of the organ music (six fugues), a tradition continued later in the century by Tausig, Busoni and others.

Arrangements of piano music for orchestra have usually been either by the composer himself, or by others working after his death. An example of the former is Brahms's orchestration of his Variations for two pianos on a theme of Haydn (1873); an almost equally famous (if less often played) example of the latter is Joachim's orchestral version of Schubert's Sonata in C for piano duet D812 (Grand Duo). Similar orchestral arrangements exist in great numbers in the 20th century. In most cases some attempt is made to match the orchestration to the style of the music (provided this is later than Bach and Handel), but that is less often the case when the arranger was himself a real composer. In Ravel's orchestral version (1922) of *Pictures at an Exhibition*, for example, the black-and-white originals of Musorgsky are filled out with colours which are very much Ravel's own. It is interesting to observe how later composer–arrangers have crossed the stylistic divide between their own work and that of the past. Schoenberg's arrangement of Brahms's G minor Piano Quartet, op.25 (1937), even more than his earlier ones of pieces by Monn, Bach and Handel, seems to constitute a conscious act of identification with (perhaps even nostalgia for) the past. Schoenberg uses a slightly expanded Brahmsian orchestra in a more or less Brahmsian way. Webern's orchestral version of the six-part ricercare from Bach's *Musical Offering* (1935), on the other hand, sets out with the opposite intention of adapting the past to the language of the present (ex.6). It is instructive to compare it with the version by Igor Markevich (published 1952), who aimed (but failed) 'to delve into and absorb as faithfully as possible Bach's own sonorities'. The parodic element in Webern's fragmented instrumentation is pursued to the point of distortion in the several arrangements and 'realizations' of Peter Maxwell Davies.

A number of external factors have affected 20th-century practice in the making of arrangements. The implementation of copyright agreements has made it illegal to adapt and arrange musical works which are the property of a copyright holder without prior permission. Radio and the gramophone have largely replaced the piano transcription as a disseminator of the chamber, orchestral and operatic repertory, and the Lisztian paraphrase now exists only in isolated examples such as Ronald Stevenson's Fantasy on themes from Britten's *Peter Grimes*. The harmonic crisis of the 1920s led many composers to delve into the past for the seeds of a new musical language, which they did by collecting and

Ex.6

arranging earlier music. J. C. Bach, Haydn and Beethoven had responded to a vogue for folksong arrangements in Britain during the late 18th and early 19th centuries, but the folksong arrangements of Bartók and Vaughan Williams were directed towards quite different ends. They were a means by which both composers achieved a musical style which was at the same time nationalistic and intensely individual. Similarly, Stravinsky's move in an opposite direction (away from a recognizably Russian style and towards neo-classicism) was effected with *Pulcinella* (1920), a ballet based on music by Pergolesi and others. Stravinsky's lasting obsession with the past is evident in his arrangements of composers as diverse as Gesualdo, Bach, Beethoven, Grieg and Tchaikovsky.

The concern for authenticity in the performance of older music, which has characterized the period since about 1950, has profoundly influenced attitudes towards arrangements. The inflated orchestral versions of Bach and Handel by Elgar, Beecham, Harty and Stokowski are now discredited. The 'edition' has replaced the 'arrangement', in critical esteem at least. Usually the distinction between one and the other is quite clear, but this is dependent to some extent on interpretation of the historical evidence. Raymond Leppard's versions of 17th-century Venetian opera, for example, purport to be editions, though many musicologists would class them as arrangements.

5. CONCLUSION. Few areas of musical activity involve the aesthetic (and even the moral) judgment of the musician as much as does the practice of arrangement. This involvement is at its most intense in the case of those arrangements which set out to 'popularize' an acknowledged masterpiece, either by adapting it for the stage or film (or, worse still, for the television advertisement), or by 'jazzing up' its rhythms and instrumentation. In either case the arrangement will often earn the musician's disapproval, and even his resentment. However, it is clearly inconsistent to deplore solely on aesthetic grounds the arrangements of Borodin's music in the musical *Kismet*, or the Bach arrangements made for the Swingle Singers, while using lack of 'historical authenticity' as the only stick to beat other, more seriously intentioned arrangements. Every arrangement creates its own historical authenticity, and Mozart's version of

Handel's *Messiah* has already been accorded the distinction of two scholarly editions and a complete, carefully prepared recording. Perhaps one day there will be 'historically accurate' performances of Ebenezer Prout's version (1902), with ornamentation restricted to frequent use of the portamento.

It would be unrealistic to propose that arrangements should be judged without reference to the original, but it is perhaps only by regarding both the arrangement and the original as two different versions of the same piece that a solution to the aesthetic and moral dilemma they so often create will be found.

BIBLIOGRAPHY
R. Franz: *Offener Brief an E. Hanslick, über Bearbeitung älterer Tonwerke* (Leipzig, 1871)
P. G. Waldersee: 'Antonio Vivaldi's Violinconcerte unter besonderer Berücksichtigung der von Johann Sebastian Bach bearbeiteten', *VMw*, i (1885), 356
W. Voigt: 'Über die Originalgestalt von J. S. Bach's Konzert für zwei Klavieren in C moll (Nr. 1)', *VMw*, ii (1886), 482
S. Taylor: *The Indebtedness of Handel to Works by other Composers* (Cambridge, 1906)
K. Grunsky: *Die Technik des Klavierauszuges, entwickelt am dritten Akt von Wagners 'Tristan'* (Leipzig, 1911)
——: 'Bachs Bearbeitung und Umarbeitungen eigener und fremder Werke', *BJb*, ix (1912), 61
A. Aber: 'Studien zu Bachs Klavier-Konzerten', *BJb*, x (1913), 5
W. Altmann: 'Beethovens Umarbeitung seines Streichtrios op. 3 zu einem Klaviertrio', *ZMw*, iii (1920–21), 129
A. Orel: 'Beethovens Oktett op. 103 und seine Bearbeitung als Quintett op. 4', *ZMw*, iii (1920–21), 159
E. Friedländer: *Wagner-Liszt und die Kunst der Klavierarbeitung* (Detmold, 1922)
K. Grunsky: 'Zur Frage der Auszüge', *NZM* (1922)
M. Broesike-Schoen: 'Der moderne Klavierauszug: eine Rundfrage', *Die Musik*, xvi (1923), 81
M. Seiffert: 'G. Ph. Telemanns *Musique de table* als Quelle für Händel', *Bulletin de la Société 'Union musicologique'*, iv (1924), 1
J. Mathel: *Bearbeitung und freie Benutzung im Tonwerkrecht* (diss., U. of Leipzig, 1928)
O. Baumann: *Das deutsche Lied und seine Bearbeitung in den frühen Orgeltabulaturen* (diss., U. of Berlin, 1934)
F. Lederer: *Beethovens Bearbeitung schottischer und anderer Volkslieder* (diss., U. of Bonn, 1934)
A. Mantelli: 'Compositore e trascrittore', *RaM*, vii (1934), 97
E. Howard-Jones: 'Arrangements and Transcriptions', *ML*, xvi (1935), 305
F. Munter: 'Beethovens Bearbeitung eigener Werke', *NBJb*, vi (1935), 159
F. Ballo: 'Interpretazione e trascrizione', *RaM*, ix (1936), 190
V. Gui: 'Sull'uso di trascrivere per orchestra', *RaM*, ix (1940), 353
G. Tagliapietra: 'Ferruccio Busoni trascrittore e revisore', *RaM*, xiii (1940), 12
G. Troeger: *Mussorgskij und Rimskij-Korsakoff* (Breslau, 1941)

H. Boettcher: 'Bachs Kunst der Bearbeitung, dargestellt am Tripelkonzert a moll', *Von Deutscher Tonkunst*, ed. P. Raabe (Leipzig, 1942)

E. T. A. Armbruster: *Erstdruckfassung oder Originalfassung?* (Leipzig, 1946)

H. Engel: 'Bearbeitung in alter und neuer Zeit', *Das Musikleben*, i (1948), 39

R. Caporali: 'Le trascrizioni pianistiche delle opere di Bach', *RaM*, xx (1950), 239

V. Terenzio: 'La trascrizione musicale come arte', *RaM*, xxi (1951), 130

W. Kolneder: 'Vivaldi als Bearbeiter eigener Werke', *AcM*, xxiv (1952), 45

P. Mies: 'Kritik an Bearbeitung', *Deutsche Sangerbundeszeitung*, xli (1952)

M. F. Bukofzer: 'Interrelations between Conductus and Clausula', *AnnM*, i (1953), 65–103

W. Hess: 'Eine Bach-Bearbeitung Beethovens', *SMz*, xciii (1953), 401

A. Briskier: 'Piano Transcriptions of J. S. Bach', *MR*, xv (1954), 191

W. Hess: 'Eine Bach- und Handel-Bearbeitung Beethovens', *SMz*, xciv (1954), 142

G. Feder: *Bachs Werke in die Bearbeitung 1750–1950. I. Die Vokalwerke* (diss., U. of Kiel, 1955)

C. Marinelli: 'La trascrizione come opera d'arte', *RaM*, xxvi (1956), 40

B. Vondenhoff: 'Die beiden Fassungen der d-moll Symphonie R. Schumanns', *NZM*, cxvii (1956), 407

R. Craft: 'Strawinsky komponiert Bach', *Melos*, xxiv (1957), 35

H. L. Schilling: 'I. Strawinskys Erweiterung and Instrumentation der Canonischen Orgelvariationen *Vom Himmel hoch, da komm ich her* von J. S. Bach', *Musik und Kirche*, xxvii (1957)

U. Siegele: *Kompositionsweise und Bearbeitungstechnik in der Instrumentalmusik J. S. Bachs* (diss., U. of Tübingen, 1957)

F. Giegling: 'Geminiani's Harpsichord Transcriptions', *ML*, xl (1959), 350

E. J. Simon: 'Sonata into Concerto', *AcM*, xxxi (1959), 170

A. Holschneider: *Händel's 'Messiah' in Mozarts Bearbeitung* (diss., U. of Tübingen, 1960)

H. J. Marx: 'Zu Arnold Schönbergs Bach-Instrumentation', *NZM*, cxxii (1961), 41

F. Kaiser: 'Die authentischen Fassungen des D-dur-Konzertes op. 61 von Ludwig van Beethoven', *GfMKB Kassel, 1962*, 196

B. Disertori: *Le frottole per canto e liuto intabulate da Franciscus Bossinensis* (Milan, 1964)

S. Scionti: 'Trascrizioni (Sono le trascrizioni un'offesa all'arte?)', *Rassegna musicale Curci*, (1965)

G. Dardo: 'Trascrizione', *LaMusicaE*

W. Apel: *Geschichte der Orgel- und Klaviermusik* (Kassel, 1967; Eng. trans., rev. 1972)

N. Carrell: *Bach the Borrower* (London, 1967)

J. T. Igoe: *J. S. Bach's Transcriptions for Solo Keyboard* (diss., U. of North Carolina, 1967)

W. Mohr: 'Händel als Bearbeiter eigener Werke: Dargestellt an fünf Orgelkonzerten', *HJb 1967–8*, 83

K. Morawska: 'Kompozycje Orlando di Lasso w repertuarze instrumentalnym', *Muzyka*, xiii (1968), 3

H. Keller: 'Arrangement For or Against?', *MT*, cx (1969), 22

L. F. Tagliavini: 'J. G. Walther, trascrittore', *AnMc*, no.7 (1969), 112

T. Göllner: 'J. S. Bach and the Tradition of Keyboard Transcriptions', *Studies in Eighteenth-century Music: a Tribute to Karl Geiringer* (London, 1970), 253

E. Markowska: 'Faktura tanecznej muzyki lutniowej', *Muzyka*, xv (1970), 31

S. Wollenberg: 'Handel and Gottlieb Muffat', *MT*, cxiii (1972), 448

H. M. Brown: 'Embellishments in early Sixteenth-century Intabulations', *PRMA*, c (1973–4), 49

MALCOLM BOYD

Arras. City in northern France, capital of the modern département of Pas-de-Calais, formerly the province of Artois. From the 12th century Arras was an important commercial centre and, increasingly in the 13th century, a bastion of the urban middle class. Much of its activity as a literary and musical centre originated with the Confrérie des Jongleurs et des Bourgeois d'Arras, a lay religious guild whose existence is documented from the last decade of the 12th century to about the mid-14th. During a plague in Arras (according to local legend) the Virgin Mary appeared separately to two *jongleurs*, Pierre Normand and Itier of Brabant, telling them to go to Arras and there reconcile their differences before Bishop Lambert. When they did this in the church of Notre-Dame in Arras the Virgin appeared again and gave them a candle (the *sainte chandelle*); its wax was poured into the water used to treat the wounds of the plague-stricken, and they were miraculously healed. This prompted the Confrérie; and although written accounts of the miracle in both Latin and French place it at the beginning of the 12th century, the Confrérie was more probably founded in about 1200.

The *Nécrologe* which records the deaths of the members extends from 1194 to 1361, and while the number of trouvère poets and composers it includes is considerably smaller than the figure of 180 found in many reference works, it nonetheless shows a considerable group to have come from or been active in Arras during the 13th century. A conservative list of these follows, many of them recorded in the *Nécrologe*: Adam de Givenchi, Adam de la Halle, Andrieu Contredit, Andrieu Douchet, Andrieu de Paris, Audefroi le Bastart, Gautier de Dargies, Gille li Vinier, Gillebert de Berneville, Henri d'Amion, Hue, chastellain d'Arras, Jaques le Vinier, Jehan Bretel, Jehan Bodel, Jehan le Cuvelier, Jehan Erart, Jehan Fontainnes, Jehan de Grieviler, Jehan de Neuville, Lambert Ferri, Moniot d'Arras, Oede de la Couroierie, Robert de Castel, Robert de le Piere, Sauvage d'Arras, Sauvale Cosset, Simon d'Authie, Villain d'Arras. As the names indicate many of these trouvères were probably tradesmen, and most were of the middle class. The two outstanding names are Jehan Bretel (*d* 1272), a prolific poet and the principal exponent of the *jeu-parti*, a genre cultivated extensively in Arras, and Adam de la Halle (*d* 1285–8), the only trouvère known to have composed polyphonic music and the author of the *Jeu de Robin et de Marion*.

With the decline of secular monophony in the 14th century musical activity was concentrated in the churches, and Arras became an important centre for the training of singers until the 17th century. During the late 15th and 16th centuries Arras produced a number of composers, the best known of whom were (probably born there) Antoine de Févin, Philippe Rogier and Valérian Gonet. Musicians and composers from the area were to be found all over Europe during this period, and the Sainte-Chapelle in Paris regularly sought singers in Arras.

With the incorporation of Artois into France in 1659 Arras lost most of its former importance as a musical centre. Despite municipal subsidies for visiting opera and operetta troupes Arras remained a musical backwater throughout the 18th century. In the 19th century musical activity centred on a number of amateur societies and a municipal music school.

BIBLIOGRAPHY

E. vander Straeten: *La musique aux Pays-Bas avant le XIXᵉ siècle* (Brussels, 1867–88/R1969)

A. Guesnon: *La Confrérie des jongleurs d'Arras et le tombeau de l'évêque Lambert* (Arras, 1913)

A. Jeanroy, ed.: *Le chansonnier d'Arras* (Paris, 1925)

A. Langfors, ed.: *Recueil général des jeux-partis*, i (Paris, 1926)

L. Petitot: *La musique à Arras au XIXᵉ siècle* (Arras, 1942)

F. Lesure: 'Arras', *MGG*

R. Berger: *Le nécrologe de la Confrérie des jongleurs et des bourgeois d'Arras* (Arras, 1963–70)

ROBERT FALCK

Arras, Chansonnier d' (*F-AS* 657). *See* SOURCES, MS, §III, 4.

Arras, Jean d' (*b* Arras; *d* ?Madrid, 1584). Flemish organist active in Italy and Spain. On 1 January 1566 he was engaged at the ducal chapel of Parma. In 1580 he was organist in the chapel of Philip II of Spain, as is shown by a receipt that he signed for wages. His tenure there continued until his death.

A madrigal by him, *Due rose* (*secunda pars*: 'Non vide un simil') is found in Josquino Persoens's first book of madrigals (Parma, 1570). A chanson by him was published by Phalèse in 1575.

Jean d'Arras should not be confused with a younger man of the same name who was listed in 1596 as a *mozo de capilla* ('youth in the chapel') to Philip II, and to whom further references occur in listings of chapel personnel in 1598, 1599 and 1608.

BIBLIOGRAPHY

P. Becquart: *Musiciens néerlandais à la cour de Madrid: Philippe Rogier et son école* (Brussels, 1967), 32

LAVERN J. WAGNER

Arrau, Claudio (*b* Chillán, 6 Feb 1903). Chilean pianist. A child prodigy, he gave his first public recital at the age of five in Santiago. After studying with Paoli for two years, he was sent, with the support of the Chilean government, to study at Stern's Conservatory in Berlin, where he was a pupil of Martin Krause from 1912 to 1918. He never went to another teacher. During this period he won many awards including the Ibach Prize and the Gustav Holländer Medal. He gave his first recital in Berlin in 1914, followed by extensive tours of

Claudio Arrau in 1961

Germany and Scandinavia, and a European tour in 1918. At this time he played with many of the leading orchestras of Europe under conductors including Nikisch, Muck, Mengelberg and Furtwängler. In 1921 he returned for the first time to South America, where he gave successful concerts in Argentina and Chile. He first played in London in 1922, in a concert shared with Melba and Huberman, and this was followed a year later by a tour of the USA.

In 1924 Arrau joined the staff of Stern's Conservatory, where he taught until 1940, and in 1927 he further enhanced his international reputation by winning the Grand Prix International des Pianistes in Geneva. Notable among his European concerts before World War II was a series of 12 recitals in Berlin in 1935, in which he played the entire keyboard works of Bach. However, he gave up playing Bach in public, after deciding that his music could not be performed satisfactorily on the piano. In 1940 he left Berlin, returning to Chile to found a piano school in Santiago. A year later, after a further tour of the USA (which was greeted with the highest critical acclaim), he and his family settled in New York. Highlights of his subsequent international career have included complete performances of Beethoven's piano sonatas in London, New York and elsewhere, including a broadcast of the cycle by the BBC in 1952.

Arrau has acquired a special reputation for his interpretations of Brahms, Schumann, Liszt, Chopin and, above all, Beethoven, a reputation which is reflected by his many recordings. He has the technique of a virtuoso, but is one of the least ostentatious of pianists. His tempos are sometimes unusually slow, and even when they are not he gives the impression of having considered deeply the character and shape of each phrase. He can give a performance that is so thorough in its consideration of detail that it seems lacking in spontaneity and momentum. But at its best his rich-toned and thoughtful playing conveys exceptional intellectual power and depth of feeling.

BIBLIOGRAPHY

N. Boyle: 'Claudio Arrau', *Gramophone Record Review* (1960),no.76, p.195 [with discography by F. F. Clough and G. J. Cuming]
J. Kaiser: *Grosse Pianisten in unserer Zeit* (Munich, 1965; Eng. trans., 1971, with enlarged discography), 86ff
C. Arrau: 'A Performer looks at Psychoanalysis', *High Fidelity*, xvii/2 (1967), 50
R. Osborne: 'Keyboard Oracle: Claudio Arrau in Conversation', *Records & Recording*, xvi/1 (1972), 26

ROBERT PHILIP

Arraujo, Pedro de. *See* ARAÚJO, PEDRO DE.

Arregui, José Maria (*b* Villardo, *c*1875; *d* 1955). Spanish composer. At the age of ten he entered the Franciscan college at Aranzazu, Guipuzcoa; he became a Franciscan in 1895 and then continued his music studies. After a missionary journey to Peru, he returned to Spain in 1912, completing his music education with Goberna and Borges. In addition to touring as a pianist, he became in 1918 conductor at the Capilla del Santuario, Aranzazu, which he reorganized. He also founded the Orfeon Caspolina in Caspe, Aragon, and conducted the Orquesta Seráfica Antoniana of Barcelona. His compositions, most of them sacred choral pieces, remain very largely unpublished.

WORKS
(*selective list*)

Missa 'Sanctus Franciscus', 4vv; Ave Maria, 8vv; Benedicta, 6–7vv; Miserere, 8vv; Tota pulchra, 6–8vv; psalms, motets, responsories
Folksong arrs. for chorus

ANTONIO RUIZ-PIPÓ

Arregui Garay, Vicente (*b* Madrid, 3 July 1871; *d* Madrid, 2 Dec 1925). Spanish composer. He studied at the Madrid Conservatory, where he won first prizes in piano and composition and the Spanish Rome Prize (1899). In 1910 he received the National Music Prize for the orchestral *Historia de una madre*. With the exception of the *Sinfonia vasca* his works do not reflect the nationalist trends of the time; he was, rather, a complete independent. For many years up to his death he was music critic for the Madrid daily paper *El debate*.

WORKS
(*selective list*)

Operas: La maja, 2; Yolanda, 1, Madrid 1933
Operettas: La sombra del rey galan o El alcalde cantarranas; Colón

Zarzuelas: Los ojos garzos; La madona; La sombra del molino; La duquesita y el cuento de barba azul
Orch: Sinfonia vasca; Historia de una madre, sym. poem, after Andersen
Choral: San Francisco, oratorio; El lobo ciego, cantata, 1916; Mass, 3vv, org; motets
Inst: Str Qt; Pf Sonata

Principal publisher: Unión Musical Española

ANTONIO RUIZ-PIPÓ

Arresti [Aresti], Floriano (b Bologna, ?c1660; d Bologna, 1719). Italian organist and composer. He was the son of Giulio Cesare Arresti, and studied keyboard and composition in Rome with Bernardo Pasquini. By 1684 he had returned to Bologna, and on 16 April he became a member of the Accademia Filarmonica there; his musical attainments were sufficiently distinguished for him to serve the Accademia as its *principe* in 1714. In 1692 he succeeded his father as second organist at the church of S Petronio (Gerber's statement that he was *maestro di cappella* in Venice seems to be incorrect); by 1717 he was named in librettos as 'Organista della Metropolitana'. He composed a quantity of music for both the church and the stage, but all his major works are lost.

WORKS
ORATORIOS
Zoe e Nicostrato convertiti da S Sebastiano martire; Bologna, 1708
Lo zelo trionfante di S Filippo; Bologna, Oratorio of the Madonna di Galliera, 1710
La Giuditta; Bologna, church of S Maria della Morte, 1717, perhaps also at Teatro Marsigli-Rossi
Jezabele, with G. C. Predieri; Bologna, Oratorio of the Madonna di Galliera, 1719

OPERAS
L'enigma disciolta (trattenimento pastorale, G. Neri); Bologna, Formagliari, carn. 1710
Crisippo (opera seria, G. Braccioli); Ferrara, Bonacosi, May 1710; perf. with puppets, Bologna, (?)Barbellini, 1710
L'inganno vince l'inganno; perf. with puppets, Bologna, Dec 1710
La costanza in cimento con la crudeltà (opera seria, G. Braccioli); Venice, Sant'Angelo, carn. 1712; as La costanza in cimento, ossia Il Radamisto, Bologna, Marsigli-Rossi, 1715
Il trionfo di Pallade in Arcadia; Bologna, Marsigli-Rossi, 1716

MISCELLANEOUS
2 cantatas: Cieli! che cara pena; Sdegno ed amor in me, I-Bc, Pca
3 arias, GB-Lbm
Kyrie e Gloria, GB-Lbm; Kyrie e Gloria, F-Pn
Sonata (?by G. C. Arresti) in XVII sonate da organo o cimbalo . . . (Amsterdam, n.d.)
Elevazione, org, c, I-Bc, pubd in AMI, iii (Milan, 1899/R)

BIBLIOGRAPHY
J.-B. de La Borde: *Essai sur la musique ancienne et moderne* (Paris, 1780/R1972), iii, 165
F. X. Haberl: 'Beiträge zur italienischen Litteratur des Oratoriums im 17. und 18. Jahrhundert', *KJb*, xxvi (1901), 52, 55, 60, 62
N. Morini: *La Reale accademia filarmonica di Bologna* (Bologna, 1930), 92, 95

JAMES L. JACKMAN

Arresti, Giulio Cesare (b Bologna, 1625; d Bologna, 1704 or later). Italian composer and organist. Some sources give his date of birth as 1617. He spent his entire life at Bologna. He was second organist of S Petronio from 1649 to 1659 and first organist from then until 1661 and from 1671 to 1699. For a time between his two spells as first organist – certainly in 1668 – he was *maestro di cappella* of S Salvatore, and he held a similar appointment at S Domenico from 1674 to 1704. He was one of the founders, in 1666, of the Accademia Filarmonica, Bologna, and was its president in 1671, 1686 and 1694. He had previously been a member of the Accademia dei Filomusi.

In 1659 he circulated an attack on MAURIZIO CAZ-ZATI, *maestro di cappella* of S Petronio, entitled *Dialogo*

fatto tra un maestro ed un discepolo desideroso d'approfittare nel contrappunto. In it he heaped scathing abuse upon Cazzati, who responded with a skilful defence, which was published in 1663. The dispute raged for more than ten years, and eventually, in 1671, Cazzati felt compelled to resign his post. Arresti composed principally sacred vocal works and instrumental music. Among the latter are the 12 sonatas of his op.4, which are of moderate interest and whose textures parallel the concertato writing of, for instance, the masses of his op.2. He was the leading Bolognese composer of organ music of his day. His anthology of organ sonatas by various composers, compiled possibly in the 1680s and published several years later, is of some historical significance because part of its contents, including two of his own pieces, depart from the mainstream of Italian organ music, in a forward-looking way; one of Arresti's pieces shows the influence of violin music.

WORKS
Messa e Vespro della beata virgine con l'inno, reali composte di 3 figure cantandosi senza battuta, 8vv, org ad lib, op.1 (Venice, 1663)
Messe, 3vv, bc (org), con sinfonie e ripieni ad lib [2 vn], . . . motetti, e concerti, op.2 (Venice, 1663; 2/1664 as Gare musicali, i)
[12] Sonate a 2, 3, vc ad lib, bc, op.4 (Venice, 1665)
Partitura di modulationi precettive sopra gl'hinni del canto fermo gregoriano con le riposte intavolate in 7 righe, org, op.7 (Bologna, after 1665; probably after 1685, according to Apel)
1 cantata, 1685¹; 3 sonatas, org, 1697⁸; ed. A. G. Ritter, *Geschichte des Orgelspiels* (Berlin, 1884)

Oratorios: L'orto di Getsemani, Bologna, 1661; Licenza di Gesù da Maria, Bologna, 1661; Lo sposalizio di Rebecca, Bologna, 1675; La decollazione di S Giovanni, Bologna, 1708: all lost

WRITINGS
Dialogo fatto tra un maestro ed un discepolo desideroso d'approfittare nel contrappunto (MS, 1659, I-Bc C.55)

BIBLIOGRAPHY
A. Schering: *Geschichte des Oratoriums* (Leipzig, 1911/R1966)
G. Frotscher: *Geschichte des Orgel-Spiels und der Orgel-Komposition* (Berlin, 1935–6, enlarged 3/1966)
K. G. Fellerer: 'Zur italienische Orgelmusik des 17./18. Jahrhunderts', *JbMP 1937*, 70
W. S. Newman: *The Sonata in the Baroque Era* (Chapel Hill, 1959, rev. 2/1966/R1972)
W. Apel: *Geschichte der Orgel- und Klaviermusik bis 1700* (Kassel, 1967; Eng. trans., rev. 1972)
A. Schnoebelen: 'Cazzati vs. Bologna: 1657–1671', *MQ*, lvii (1971), 26

NONA PYRON

Arriaga (y Balzola), Juan Crisóstomo (Jacobo Antonio) (b Bilbao, 27 Jan 1806; d Paris, 17 Jan 1826). Spanish composer. He played the violin and composed from an early age. In Bilbao before he was 15 he composed his only opera, *Los esclavos felices*, which was performed there, an overture and some instrumental chamber works. In October 1821 he entered the Paris Conservatoire, studying the violin under Baillot and harmony and counterpoint under Fétis, to whose brief biographical account of him very little information has since been added. According to Fétis, 'he learnt the first principles of his art almost without a teacher, guided by his genius'. Although he may have had little formal training in Bilbao, the music that he wrote there shows that he had a practical understanding of composition, and Fétis's assertion that at the Conservatoire 'only three months were necessary to give him a perfect knowledge of harmony' must be viewed in that light. (Fétis's information must have derived from Arriaga himself or his sponsors, who may have exaggerated the boy's ignorance in order to make his talent appear greater; his belief that Arriaga was two years younger than he actually was may have had the same source.)

After two years Arriaga had mastered counterpoint and fugue, winning *second prix* in these in 1823, and had made rapid progress on the violin. In 1824 he was appointed répétiteur in a *classe de répétition* in harmony and counterpoint and issued the only work he published, the three string quartets on which his reputation as a composer mainly rests. In the short period remaining before his death he applied himself intensively to composition (Fétis said that 'the need to create [produire] tormented him, as it torments every man of genius'), producing a symphony, overture, mass, *Stabat mater*, cantatas and songs.

Of Arriaga's early music, the larger works imitate the lightly textured Italian style of the day, while the chamber music mostly places a virtuoso violin part, probably designed to show off its composer, against a simple accompaniment. In the later Paris pieces like the quartets and symphony, the effects of his Conservatoire training are clearly evident in the easy mastery and proliferation of contrapuntal devices, and in the neoclassical correctness and elegance of the writing and the forms used, qualities of primary importance in the traditionalist view of Fétis and the Conservatoire. The strength of Arriaga's talent is revealed in his ability to maintain an element of individual expression unstifled by the stringent requirements of musical orthodoxy to which he had submitted. His death was thus a great loss to the traditionalists and lamented as such by Fétis.

For several decades Arriaga was largely forgotten, but with the rise of Spanish musical nationalism towards the end of the century, and on the Romantic basis of his promise more than his actual achievement, he was metamorphosed into a kind of cult figure and compared with Mozart and other victims and beneficiaries of an early death. In his native Bilbao, the centre of this, the theatre was named after him and a monument erected. Much was published on his life and work, but mostly in a rhapsodic vein, and he still remains little touched by serious critical and scholarly investigation.

WORKS

VOCAL

Los esclavos felices (opera semiseria, 2, Comella y Comella), Bilbao, 1820; ov. (Bilbao, *c*1950)
Agar (scène biblique-dramatique), S, orch; 1 romance, S, pf (Barcelona, ?1920), finale, S, orch (Madrid, ?1920)
Erminia (scène lyrique-dramatique, after Tasso), S, orch (Madrid, ?1923)
Où vais-je malheureux, recit., Hélas d'une si pure flamme, aria (N. F. Guillard: Oedipe à Colone), T, pf (Madrid, ?1924)
Hymen, viens dissiper (aria of Médée), S, pf (Barcelona, ?1920)
All'aurora, duet, B, T, orch; romances, 1v, pf
Sacred: O salutaris, 3vv, str qnt (?Madrid, n.d.); Stabat mater, 3vv, small orch (Madrid, before 1924); Mass, 4vv, lost; Salve regina, lost; Et vitam venturi, fugue, 8vv, lost

INSTRUMENTAL

Orch: 2 ovs., 1 in f, small orch, op.1, 1818 (Bilbao, n.d.); Sym., D (Bilbao, *c*1950)
Chamber: Nada y mucho: ensayo en octeto, F, 2 vn, va, vc, db, tpt, gui, pf, 1817 (Bilbao, 1929); Tema variado en cuarteto, F, str qt, op.17, 1820 (Bilbao, 1928); La Húngara, variations, D, str qt, op.23, 1822, arr. vn. pf (Bilbao, 1925); 3 Str Qts, d, A, E♭ (Paris, 1824); 3 estudios de carácter, pf (Bilbao, n.d.)

BIBLIOGRAPHY

FétisB

F. J. Fétis: Obituary, *Revue musicale*, ii/4 (1829), 199
E. de Uriarte: 'El Mozart español', *La ciudad de Dios: revista agustiniana*, vii/15 (1888), 258
J. de Eresalde: *Los esclavos felices, opera de J. C. Arriaga: antecedentes, comentarios, argumento y algunas noticias bio-bibliográficas* (Bilbao, 1935)
C. A. Figuerido: *El arte y la mente del músico J. C. de Arriaga* (Bilbao, 1948)

DENNIS LIBBY

Arrieta y Corera, Don **Pascual Juan Emilio** (*b* Puente la Reina, Navarra, 21 Oct 1823; *d* Madrid, 11 Feb 1894). Spanish composer. He studied with Vaccai at the Milan Conservatory from 1839 to 1845, and his first opera, *Ildegonda*, was produced there in 1845. He returned to Spain in 1846. In Madrid he first held the post of singing teacher to Queen Isabel II and in 1857 he became professor of composition at the Madrid Conservatory. From 1868 to his death he was director of the conservatory.

Arrieta's works were nearly all for the stage. They include the Italian operas *Ildegonda* (Milan, 1845; Madrid, 1849), and *La conquista de Granada* (1850; rev. as *Isabel la Católica*, 1855), with librettos by Solera, Verdi's collaborator; also more than 50 *zarzuelas* (comic operettas), the first and best of which were *El domino azul, El grumete* and *La estrella di Madrid* (all 1853). The most popular, however, was *Marina* (1855), which after a cool initial reception was performed all over Spain and South America. It was given by a Spanish company in New York in 1916 and was revived at Barcelona as late as 1938. Arrieta wrote recitatives and added a third act for its production at the Teatro Real, Madrid (16 March 1871).

His works show an Italian influence and make use of the folk elements; they were the first to be sung at the Madrid court in Spanish (see lists in *MGG* and *ES*).

BIBLIOGRAPHY

A. Peña y Goñi: *La opera española y la musica drammatica en España* (Madrid, 1885), 473f
M. Muñoz: *Historia de la zarzuela y el geuero chico* (Madrid, 1946)
J. Subirá: *Historia y anecdotario del Teatro real* (Madrid, 1949)
——: 'Arrieta, Emilio', *MGG*
——: *El Teatro del Real palacio* (Madrid, 1950)

ALFRED LOEWENBERG/R

Arrieu, Claude (*b* Paris, 30 Nov 1903). French composer. She studied at the Paris Conservatoire with Caussade, Long, Roger-Ducasse and Dukas, taking a *premier prix* for composition in 1932. Her subsequent career has been in teaching and in work of various kinds for French radio, which she joined in 1946. A prolific composer, she has retained in her music the ease of flow and elegance of structure that typified Parisian neoclassicism, while avoiding the often concomitant frivolity. Within that general style she has developed an individual harmonic manner, and she has taken a discriminating interest in later innovations: she was, for example, among the first to work with Schaeffer, though she has not used electronic means in any concert work. Her radio score *Frédéric Général* won an Italia Prize in 1949.

WORKS

(selective list)

DRAMATIC

Operas: Noé (imagerie musicale, 3, A. Obey), 1932–4, Strasbourg, 1949; Cadet-Roussel (opéra bouffe, 5, A. de la Tourrasse, J. Limozin), 1938–9, Marseilles, 1953; Les deux rendez-vous (opéra comique, 1, P. Bertin, after Nerval), 1948, RTF, 1951; Le chapeau à musique (opéra enfantine, 2, Tourrasse, P. Dumaine), 1953; La princesse de Babylone (opéra bouffe, 3, P. Dominique, after Voltaire), 1953–5, Rheims, 1960; La cabine téléphonique (opéra bouffe, 1, M. Vaucaire), 1958, RTF, 1959; Cymbeline (2, J. Tournier, M. Jacquemont, after Shakespeare), 1958–63; Balthazar ou Le mort vivant (opéra bouffe, 1, Dominique), 1966; Un clavier pour un autre (opéra bouffe, J. Tardieu), 1969–70, Avignon, 1971; Barberius (3, after Musset), 1972
Ballets: Fête galante (Kochno), 1947, Berne, 1947; Commedia umana (after Boccaccio), 1960, Nervi, 1960; La statue (J. Provins), 1968
Adaptation of *J.-P. Rameau: Zoroastre*, 1964, Bordeaux, 1964
Many scores for the theatre, cinema and broadcasting

Vocal orch: Cantate des sept poèmes d'amour en guerre (Eluard), S, Bar, orch, 1946; Mystère de Noël (L. Masson), oratorio, 1951

Orch: concs. for pf, 1932, vn, 1938, 2 pf, 1938, fl, 1946, vn, 1949, tpt, 1965; many other pieces, most of them short

Chamber: Trio, ob, cl, bn, 1936; Sonatine, fl, pf, 1943; Histoires de Paris, str qt, db, perc, 1947; Sonata, vn, pf, 1948; Wind Qnt, 1955; Pf Trio, 1957; many duos with pf and other pieces

Songs: Chansons bas (Mallarmé), 1933; many others

Pf compositions, unacc. choral works

Principal publishers: Amphion, Billaudot, Editions Françaises de Musique, Heugel, Leduc, Ricordi

PAUL GRIFFITHS

Arrigo [Henricus]. Italian 14th-century composer. He is known only by a ballata for two voices, *Il capo biondo*, which appears in *F-Pn* 568 (no.138) under the name Arrigo and in *F-Pn* 6771 (no.49) under Henricus. This combines elements of style both conservative and new for Italian music for the second half of the 14th century. Since from the musical style he was evidently Italian, no identification is possible with other known composers named Henricus.

BIBLIOGRAPHY
J. Wolf: *Geschichte der Mensuralnotation von 1250–1460* (Leipzig, 1904/*R*1965), ii/iii, no.57a/b
W. T. Marrocco, ed.: *Italian Secular Music*, PMFC, x (in preparation)
For further bibliography *see* ITALY, BIBLIOGRAPHY OF MUSIC TO 1600 and SOURCES, MS.
KURT VON FISCHER

Arrigo, Girolamo (*b* Palermo, 2 April 1930). Italian composer. He studied under Belfiore and others at the Palermo Conservatory, receiving diplomas in horn playing and composition, and then with Deutsch in Paris, where he lived from 1954 to 1964 and where he settled in 1968. He spent periods in New York (1964–5) and Berlin (1967) under grants from the Koussevitzky and Ford foundations and the Deutscher Akademischer Austauschdienst. Placed second in the third ISCM composition competition (1963), he has won several other prizes, among them the Pour que l'Esprit Vive Award (1957) and a Paris Biennale prize (1965).

Arrigo's first important works – the String Trio (1958–9), *Quarta occasione* (1960) and *Fluxus* (1961) – were seemingly influenced by Boulez's music of the late 1950s. The furthest development that, during the next few years, these early experiences opened up was a modified adaptation of current 'informal' tendencies, as, for example, in *Shadows* and *Infrarosso* (1966 and 1967), whose structures are generated by kaleidoscopic mutations of basic 'micro-forms'. In 1969 Arrigo's views on composition changed radically. *Petit requiem* is still equally far from any extreme, either rational or irrational, but in *Orden*, a theatrical piece, Arrigo decisively accepted the theory of socially committed music. Its impassioned denunciation of Spanish fascism – staged, following contemporary music-theatre experiments, with a close interdependence between scenic and musical elements – anchored Arrigo's invention to a highly stimulating functionalism. Both the ideologically charged contents that, in *La cantata Hurbinek* and *Ciascuno salutò nell'altro la vita*, pushed music to the boundary of action, and the political satire musically expressed in the stage work *Addio Garibaldi* through a review of the usually iconoclastic technique of quotation, can be taken not only as indications of a new poetics, but also of a creative participation in the problems of the new music.

Stage: Orden (opera, P. Bourgeade), Avignon, 1969, concert excerpts: Adios recuerdos, 6vv, 4 trbn; Dalla nebbia verso la nebbia, 6vc, 6db, Eclatements/Funérailles, 6 hn, 6 trbn; E venne la notte, S, 2 Mez, Bar; Addio Garibaldi (musical epic, 2 parts, Arrigo), Paris, 1972, excerpt: Sonata delle vocazioni; Rorogigasos (ballet), 1973, Palermo, 26 Feb 1977; L'o schiavo (Michelangelo), dancer, T, hn, Venice, 1975

Vocal: 3 occasioni (Montale), S, orch, 1958; Quarta occasioni (Montale), T, 7 solo vv, 5 insts, 1960; Serenata, gui, 1962; Epitaffi (Michelangelo), chorus, orch, 1963; Episodi (Gk. verse), S, fl, 1966; La cantata Hurbinek (P. Levi), chorus, insts, 1970; Ciascuno salutò nell'altro la vita (Levi), 1v, 1972; 3 madrigali (Michelangelo), 5 solo vv, 1973; Organum Jeronimus (textless), book 1, 8 solo vv, 14 insts (1973); ... Chi d'amor s'arma ... (Michelangelo), 3 solo vv, 1974 Crudele, acerbo e dispietato core (Michelangelo), 3 solo vv, 1974; Tardi conosco (Michelangelo), 12vv, 1975

Inst: Str Trio, 1958–9; Fluxus, 9 insts, 1961; Thumos, wind, perc, 1965; Shadows, orch, 1966; Infrarosso, 16 insts, 1967; Petit requiem pour une troisième possibilité, 9 players, 1969; Par un jour d'automne, b cl, 1971

Principal publishers: Bruzzichelli, Heugel, Ricordi

BIBLIOGRAPHY
M. Cadieu: 'Orden', *Les lettres françaises* (1969), no.1296, p.17
——: 'Entretien avec Girolamo Arrigo', *Les lettres françaises* (1972), no.1454, p.12
CLAUDIO ANNIBALDI

Arrigo d'Ugo. *See* ISAAC, HEINRICH.

Arrigo il Tedesco. *See* ISAAC, HEINRICH.

Arrigoni, Carlo (*b* Florence, 5 Dec 1697; *d* Florence, 19 Aug 1744). Italian lutenist, theorbo player and composer. Although he may have directed music for the Prince of Carignan in his early years, Arrigoni's name is principally associated with Florence. By at least 1718 he was a member of the musicians' company there. He is listed as theorbo player at an oratorio performance on 31 March 1720 and as a violinist at a private concert on 30 July 1724, both in Florence. By 1722 Arrigoni had been elected a member of the Accademia Filarmonica of Bologna, as the title-page of an oratorio of his performed in Florence in that year shows. His presence in London in 1732–6 coincided with the life-span of the Opera of the Nobility, rival to Handel's company, which presented four performances of his *Fernando* beginning on 5 February 1734. In the 1732–3 season he was to have directed concerts at Hickford's Rooms in London, together with Giuseppe Sammartini, according to a newspaper announcement quoted by Burney. Other announcements mention his participation in London concerts on 20 April and 7 May 1733, 27 March and 11 April 1735, and 21 January, 5 March and 8 March 1736, either at Hickford's Rooms or Lincoln's Inn Fields. Arrigoni also sang and played his own music in Dublin on 20 October 1733, and sang the tenor part in the cantata *Cecilia volgi* and played the lute in concerto op.4 no.6, both at original performances of Handel's *Alexander's Feast* at Covent Garden in February and March 1736 (see Dean). Later in 1736 Arrigoni was made *aiutante di camera* by Grand Duke Giovanni Gastone of Tuscany, and in 1737 the new Grand Duke, Franz II, named him chamber composer. Performances of Arrigoni's music in Vienna in 1737 and 1738 reflect the fact that the new Tuscan grand duke was the husband of Maria Theresia, and do not necessarily place the composer in that city. After 1740 Arrigoni played his theorbo several times in Lucca at the festivals of the Holy Cross (13–14 September). In a letter of 12 August 1742, Horace Mann mentioned Arrigoni as an arranger of private concerts in Florence. A fellow lutenist at the court, Nicolò Susier, reported that Arrigoni was survived by a wife and four sons, one of whom may be the 'signor Arrigoni' mentioned in connection with performances in England, Scotland and Ireland in 1756–63.

In his surviving music Arrigoni is revealed as a composer of modest ability. His instrumental music is saturated with conventional figuration and organized into shortwinded periods of sequences, voice-exchanges, frequent cadences and literal repetitions of small units. His arias often seem to be constructed of brief, unrelated phrases which awkwardly return to a few pitches and thus lack directional flow. Perhaps his relative success as a composer was due to his mastery of fashionable stylistic conventions rather than to the real worth of his music.

WORKS

OPERAS
La vedova, Foligno, 1722; lib pubd
Fernando (G. Gigli, P. Rolli), London, Lincoln's Inn Fields, 5 Feb 1734; 8 arias, *GB-Lbm*
Scipione nella Spagne, Florence, carn. 1739; lib pubd
Sirbace, Florence, carn. 1739; lib pubd

ORATORIOS
L'innocenza di S Eugenia scoperta nel tradimento, Florence, 1719
Il pentimento d'Acabbo doppo il rimprovero della strage di Nabot (G. G. Arrigoni), Florence, 1722; lib pubd (Brussels, 1728)
Ester (Metastasio), Vienna, 1738; *A-Wgm*

OTHER WORKS
[10] Cantate da camera, S, b (London, 1732)
3 arias in Rigacci's Raccolta di varie canzoni (Florence, 1739, 1740)
Cantatas for the name days of the emperor and empress, 1737, *A-Wn*
Cantatas, *A-Wn, Wgm; D-DÜl; GB-Lbm*; aria, *B-Bc*
3 sonatas, concerto, mand, *US-Wc*; minuet, *US-NYp*

BIBLIOGRAPHY
The London Stage, 1660–1800 (Carbondale, Ill., 1960–68)
W. Dean: 'An Unknown Handel Singer: Carlo Arrigoni', *MT*, cxviii (1977), 556

JOHN WALTER HILL

Arrigoni [Arigoni], Giovanni Giacomo (*b* Milan; *d* after 1663). Italian composer and organist. There is no evidence that he was related to Carlo Arrigoni. From January to October 1637 he is recorded as an organist in the Hofkapelle, Vienna; he was already in Vienna by 1 December 1635, since he signed from there the dedication of the volume that he published in that year. He probably remained in Vienna until at least 1640 but then appears to have returned to Italy. He did not, however, sever his relationship with the Viennese court, since he composed his opera *Gli amori d'Alessandro Magno e di Rossane* for it. According to Gerber he was a member of the Accademia Fileleutera in Venice, with the academic name of 'L'Affettuoso', although that need not signify that he lived there. He may also have had connections with the court of Duke Carlo II of Mantua, since he dedicated his volume of 1663 to him. His three surviving collections show that he was an adherent of the concertato style. Their contents include independent instrumental parts, and the 1635 book contains four sonatas, two in six parts and two in eight. The vocal works in this book embrace a wide variety of forms – chamber duet, madrigal, dialogue and chaconne among them – and show that Arrigoni was a fluent, competent composer. His opera is also very varied in its forms and textures and includes comic scenes.

WORKS

Madrigals, 2, 3vv (Venice, 1623); lost, cited in Walther
Sacrae cantiones . . . liber secundus, 2–5vv, bc (org) (Venice, 1632)
Concerti di camera, 2–9vv, insts, bc (Venice, 1635)
[8] Salmi concertate ed alquanti con li ripieni, 3vv . . . con 1 Magnificat, 5vv, 2 vn, op.9 (Venice, 1663)
Works in 1624³, 1624¹¹, 1625², 1641³, 1649⁶

Gli amori d'Alessandro Magno e di Rossane (G. A. Cicognini), opera, Vienna, spr. 1657, *A-Wn* (prol, Act 1 and Ger. trans. of lib)

BIBLIOGRAPHY
GerberL; WaltherML
L. von Köchel: *Die kaiserliche Hof-Musikkapelle in Wien von 1543–1867* (Vienna, 1869)
G. Savioli: *Bibliografia universale del teatro drammatico italiano*, i (Venice, 1903), 260
R. Haas: *Die Musik des Barocks* (Potsdam, 1928), 175f
A. Bauer: *Opern und Operetten in Wien* (Graz and Cologne, 1955), 5

JOSEF-HORST LEDERER

Arro, Elmar (*b* Riga, 2 July 1899). Estonian musicologist. He studied musicology in Vienna, where he took the doctorate in 1928 with a dissertation on music in Estonia in the 19th century. In 1933 he was appointed to a chair of musicology and also taught Slavonic studies at the German Luther Academy in Dorpat (now Tartu), Estonia. He moved to Germany in 1939 and in 1955 was teaching at Heidelberg. From 1959 he was involved in establishing the Ost-Europa Institut, first at Freiburg and later in Kiel, where it was renamed J. G. Herder Forschungsstelle für Musikgeschichte. Subsequently he moved to Vienna where he founded the periodical *Musica slavica*. Arro is one of the finest and most erudite scholars of Russian music history and musical life. Before he moved to Germany he published a number of studies on the history of music in the Baltic countries; while in Kiel, he established a superb collection of publications dealing with the history of music in eastern Europe, particularly the history of Russian chant. He was the founder and editor of the first four volumes of *Musik des Ostens* (until 1967).

WRITINGS

Über das Musikleben in Estland im 19. Jahrhundert (diss., U. of Vienna, 1928)
'Zum Problem der Kannel', *Sitzungsberichte der Gelehrten Estnischen Gesellschaft* (1929), 158–90
'Baltische Choralbücher und ihre Verfasser', *AcM*, iii (1931), 112, 166
'Die "Dorpater Stadt-Musici, 1587–1809", *Sitzungsberichte der Gelehrten Estnischen Gesellschaft* (1931)
Geschichte der estnischen Musik, i (Dorpat, 1933)
'Das estnische Musikschaffen der Gegenwart', *Baltische Revue* (1935)
'F. David und das Liphart-Quartet in Dorpat', *Baltische Revue* (1935)
ed., with others: *Muzïka sovetskoy Estonii* (Tallinn, 1956)
'Hauptprobleme der osteuropäischen Musikgeschichte', *Musik des Ostens*, i (1962), 9–48
'Über einige neuere deutsche Publikationen zur russischen Musikgeschichte', *Musik des Ostens*, i (1962), 122
'Das Ost-West-Schisma in der Kirchenmusik: über die Wesensverschiedenheit der Grundlagen kultischer Musik in Ost und West', *Musik des Ostens*, ii (1963), 7–83
'Die deutschbaltische Liedschule: Versuch einer nachträglichen musikhistorischen Rekonstruktion', *Musik des Ostens*, iii (1965), 175–239
'Richard Wagners Rigaer Wanderjahre: über einige baltische Züge im Schaffen Wagners', *Musik des Ostens*, iii (1965), 123–68
'Die russische Literatur-Oper, eine musikslawistische Studie', *ÖMz*, xxvi (1971), 538–77
'Die Frage der Existenz einer lokalen Dialekt: Variante des gregorianischen Chorals im Baltikum des 13.–15. Jahrhunderts', *Musica antiqua Europae orientalis IV: Bydgoszcz 1975*, 7–44

MILOŠ VELIMIROVIĆ

Arroio, João Marcelino (*b* Oporto, 4 Oct 1861; *d* Colares, 18 May 1930). Portuguese composer. A politician and a member of the Coimbra University law faculty, he was an amateur musician. His most important work, the opera *Amor de perdição* (Italian text after the novel by Camilo Castelo Branco), was introduced in 1907 at the São Carlos Opera House, Lisbon, and performed at Hamburg in 1910. Of another opera, *Leonor Teles*, only the second act survives; the work was an attempt at introducing a Wagnerian style into

Portuguese music. Arroio's other compositions include the symphonic poem *Amor*, piano pieces and songs.

JOSÉ CARLOS PICOTO

Arróspide de la Flor, César (*b* Lima, 3 Jan 1900). Peruvian músicologist, music teacher and critic. He was primarily self-taught in music and studied law at San Marcos University (qualified 1925), where he took a doctorate in letters, philosophy and history in 1929. In the course of his career he was a professor of music history at the National Music Academy in Lima (1927–51), a lecturer in art and music history at the Peruvian Catholic University (1932–53), music critic of the leading Lima newspaper *La prensa* (1934–45), dean of the department of philosophy and letters of the Peruvian Catholic University (1945–7) and professor of music history at San Marcos University (1949–71). He also contributed to Lima's musical life as director of artistic education in the Ministry of Public Education (1947–8), president of the Lima Philharmonic Society (1956–8), delegate of the executive branch to the National Council of Culture (1963–6) and director of the extramural activities of San Marcos University (1964–9). His musicological research has dealt primarily with Peruvian colonial music and aesthetic issues involving indigenous music and art.

WRITINGS

'Significación del carácter monódico y vocal de la música antigua', *Boletín latino-americano de música*, ii (1936), 61

'Valoración de la música como expresión cultural en el imperio de los Incas', *Revista de la Universidad católica del Perú*, xviii/2–3 (1940), 124

'Valor cultural del arte indígena', *Mercurio peruano* (1941), no.175, p.541

'La expresión americana en el arte virreinal del Perú', *Mercurio peruano* (1946), no.229, p.171

with R. Vargas Ugarte and R. Holzmann: *Folklore musical del siglo XVIII* (Lima, 1946)

with R. Holzmann: 'Catálogo de los manuscritos de música existentes en el Archivo Arzobispal de Lima', *Cuaderno de estudio*, iii/2 (1949), 36

'La música de teatro en el virreinato de Lima', *Revista musical chilena* (1971), nos.115–16, p.39

BIBLIOGRAPHY

C. Raygada: 'Guía musical del Perú', *Fénix* (1956–7), no.12, p.51

GERARD BÉHAGUE

Arrow Music Company. The name of the COS-COB PRESS for three years from 1938.

Arroyo, Martina (*b* New York, 2 Feb 1937). Black American soprano. She studied at Hunter College, New York, and (with Grace Bumbry) won the 1958 Metropolitan Opera Auditions. That year she sang in the American première of Pizzetti's *L'assassinio nella cattedrale* at Carnegie Hall. After taking minor roles at the Metropolitan, she went to Europe, for major roles at Vienna, Düsseldorf, Berlin, Frankfurt and Zurich (where she was under contract from 1963 to 1968). In 1965 she was a substitute Aida for Birgit Nilsson at the Metropolitan; she has played there all the major Verdi parts that form the basis of her repertory, as well as Donna Anna, Cio-cio-san, Liù, Santuzza, Gioconda and Elsa. She sang first in Britain, as Valentine at a London concert performance of *Les Huguenots*, in 1968 – the year of her first Covent Garden appearance, as Aida. She first performed at the Paris Opéra in 1973. Her rich, powerfully projected voice, heard to greatest advantage in the Verdi *spinto* roles, is yet flexible enough for Mozart; her stage presence is dignified, if somewhat undramatic. In the USA she has often sung in oratorio and recital – she was the first performer of Barber's concert scena, *Andromache's Farewell* (April 1963). Her many recordings, ranging from Handel and Mozart to Rossini and Verdi, include the 1965 version of Stockhausen's *Momente*, whose first vocalist she had been at the 1965 Donaueschingen Festival.

BIBLIOGRAPHY

J. B. Steane: *The Grand Tradition* (London, 1974), 413ff

ALAN BLYTH

Ars Antiqua [Ars Veterum, Ars Vetus] (Lat.: 'ancient art'). A term used by writers of the Parisian circle in the early 14th century to distinguish the polyphony of the immediate past from that of a new art (Ars Nova, Ars Modernorum) exemplified in the compositions and writings of Jehan des Murs (*Notitia artis musicae*, 1321) and Philippe de Vitry (*Ars nova*, c1322). (The word 'art' in this context translates the Greek word *technē* – a 'technique' or 'craft', and its meaning excludes all modern aesthetic associations of the word.)

The staunchest champion of the Ars Antiqua was Jacques de Liège, who in his encyclopedic *Speculum musicae* (c1323–5) upheld the authority of Franco of Cologne, Magister Lambertus (Aristoteles) and Petrus de Cruce, and while criticizing the moderns defined the main virtues of the ancient art: (1) modern composers wrote only motets and cantilenas, neglecting other important forms such as organa, conductus and hockets (*CS*, ii, 428f); (2) modern composers used a multiplicity of imperfect mensuration in their works, whereas the ancient art, the art of Franco, adhered strictly to the proper use of perfection (*CS*, ii, 427); (3) the moderns divided semibreves into perfect and imperfect groups of minims and semiminims, whereas the ancients divided breves into semibreves in perfect mensuration, holding that these were indivisible (*CS*, ii, 400ff, 409); (4) melodically, the moderns indulged too much in broken rhythms and capricious movement, *musica lasciva*, but the ancients kept within the confines of a restrained *musica modesta* (*CSM*, iii/1, p.60; *CS*, ii, 394). From this, the most authoritative source, it follows that the Ars Antiqua is that period which includes the three theorists cited above, and in which were practised the five musical forms mentioned by Jacques, with the retention of the 'modest' art in perfect mensuration, namely, the polyphony of northern France from about 1260 to 1320.

There is, however, ample justification for extending the use of the term 'Ars Antiqua' to include the music of the whole Notre Dame period, particularly that of its two most renowned composers Léonin and Pérotin, as general usage has now clearly sanctioned. The forms that Jacques praised and the notation of definite rhythmic values implicit in his discussion developed from this earlier time; and indeed, the forms organum and conductus had already developed to their fullest extent and were beginning to decline by the time of Franco. The Ars Antiqua, therefore, includes two main divisions: French music of the Notre Dame school from about 1160 to 1260 (the early Gothic; see Husmann); and the period from about 1260 to 1320, specifically referred to by Jacques, when the Ars Nova or high Gothic begins. These two divisions and the Ars Nova may be further characterized by the quickening of tempo of motets about the beginning of each period.

The principal theorists for the extended Ars Antiqua are Johannes de Garlandia, Franco of Cologne,

Magister Lambertus, St Emmeram Anonymous (ed. Sowa), Petrus de Cruce, Hieronymus de Moravia, Johannes de Grocheo, Anonymous IV (*CS*, i) and Jacques de Liège; the musical forms are organum, clausula, conductus, motet, hocket and cantilena, excluding the secular and vernacular songs and instrumental music which flourished concurrently; and the main sources are the four great Notre Dame manuscripts (*D-W* 628, 1099, *I-Fl* Plut.29.1, *E-Mn* 20486) and the manuscripts La Clayette (*F-Pn* n.a.fr.13521), Montpellier (*F-MO* H196), Bamberg (*D-BAs* lit.115), Turin (*I-Tr* Vari 42), Las Huelgas (*E-BUlh*) and Fauvel (*F-Pn* fr.146).

See also THEORY, THEORISTS and SOURCES, MS, §§IV, V, VII.

BIBLIOGRAPHY
H. Besseler: 'Ars antiqua', *MGG*
R. Bragard: *Jacobi Leodiensis Speculum musicae*, CSM, iii (1955)
H. Husmann: 'Notre-Dame-Epoche', *MGG*
F. J. Smith: *Iacobi Leodiensis Speculum musicae: a Commentary* (Brooklyn, 1966–71)

For further bibliography see FRANCE: BIBLIOGRAPHY OF MUSIC TO 1600.

GORDON A. ANDERSON

Arsenal, Chansonnier de l' (*F-Pa* 5198). *See* SOURCES, MS, §III, 4.

Arshawsky, Arthur. *See* SHAW, ARTIE.

Arsis, thesis (from Gk.: 'raising', 'lowering'). In measured music, the terms used respectively for unstressed and stressed beats or other equidistant subdivisions of the bar. Originally they referred to raising and lowering the foot in ancient Greek dance. Later they were applied to the unaccented and accented parts of a poetic foot, and hence acquired their association with weak and strong beats. For music since the 17th century they mean much the same as UPBEAT (or OFF-BEAT) and DOWNBEAT; the directions 'up' and 'down' remain associated with them by their respective functions in conducting.

The terms have a number of meanings in the expression 'per arsin et thesin'. Zarlino and Morley used this phrase for the INVERSION of a theme; for Walther (*Lexicon*, 1732), 'canon per arsin et thesin' meant canon by inversion. But Marpurg (*Abhandlung von der Fuge*, 1753–4) defined it in the way it is normally understood today, namely, for the entrance of a theme (usually a fugue subject) with displaced accents, former strong beats becoming weak and vice versa; an example of this occurs in fugue no.17 in book ii of Bach's *Das wohltemperirte Clavier* (entry of the bass in bar 37). Entries in STRETTO may well be 'per arsin et thesin', but are not usually referred to as such because the 'strong' and 'weak' beats of the subject are superimposed. Displacement of the subject by half a bar in long 4/4 bars, common in Baroque fugue (e.g. Bach, i, no.1, bars 1–2), does not constitute an example of the device.

Ars Nova (Lat.: 'new art'). In the most general terms Ars Nova is used as a synonym for '14th-century polyphony' just as Ars Antiqua stands for '13th-century polyphony'. The concept of Ars Nova is based on the enormous new range of musical expression made possible by the notational techniques explained in Philippe de Vitry's treatise *Ars nova* (*c*1322). The term was first used as a historical slogan by Johannes Wolf in his *Geschichte der Mensural-Notation* (Leipzig, 1904) in which the treatise was seen as one of the major turn-ing-points in the history of notation; and it was perhaps the chapter titles rather than the specific content of Wolf's work that brought about the use of 'Ars Nova' to include all 14th-century French music in the work of subsequent scholars.

Several 14th-century theorists referred to the idea of an Ars Antiqua, represented primarily by Franco, and an Ars Nova instituted by Philippe de Vitry (see, for instance, *CS*, iii, 371, 408); but in historical terms the usefulness of the idea is supported more by the treatise *Ars novae musicae* of Jehan des Murs, the 1324–5 bull of Pope John XXII decrying the musicians who were 'novellae scholae discipuli' and the reference in Jacques de Liège's *Speculum musicae* to 'moderni cantores' and to 'aliqui nunc novi'. That there was some awareness of a change in musical techniques and outlook in the years around 1320 is suggested also by the earliest music to exemplify the notation described in Philippe de Vitry's treatise, the motets for the ROMAN DE FAUVEL copied into manuscript *F-Pn* fr.146 in 1316, some of them extensive works several times longer than the motets of the previous generation and displaying a range of notational values far greater than it was possible to notate with the previous Franconian and post-Franconian techniques.

Relatively few French musical sources survive from the years immediately following the *Roman de Fauvel* manuscript, and those few are fragments whose dating and provenance are subject to substantial disagreement, so there remain very few sources in the purest Ars Nova notation as described by PHILIPPE DE VITRY. The term was therefore almost inevitably applied (by Wolf and many later scholars) to the work of Machaut and, since several Machaut manuscripts are from the early 15th century, to all French 14th-century music in spite of Schrade's insistence that after 1330 the style was no longer new. Indeed, so convenient was the label that it came to stand for all music between the *Roman de Fauvel* and the Renaissance: thus volume iii of the New Oxford History of Music is entitled *Ars Nova and the Renaissance, 1300–1540* (London, 1960) and the major historical surveys in *MGG* follow the sequence 'Ars Antiqua', 'Ars Nova', 'Renaissance'. In such surveys Ars Nova can include music from all parts of Europe and stretch to about 1430 (*see* MEDIEVAL).

Italian music of the 14th century is now more often separated off with the name 'trecento'; but there is a reasonable (and strong) school of opinion that since the surviving repertory stretches from about 1325 to 1425 it is historically misleading to call it by a name that implies a division at the year 1400, and geographically separatist to use such an exclusively Italian name. Major considerations in support of excluding Italy from the idea of Ars Nova are: that Italian music until about 1370 was stylistically and notationally entirely different from French music; and that Italian notation evolved more gradually and a precise demarcation point between an Ars Antiqua and an Ars Nova in Italy cannot be established in any historically useful sense (see Clercx).

A further narrowing down of the terminology has recently been effected by Günther who formulated the term ARS SUBTILIOR to designate music of the post-Machaut generation of composers, those musicians of an International Gothic who fused the styles of France and Italy paving the way for the simpler styles of the 15th century. In a sense this terminology is again an attempt to transfer a description of a notational style (called by Apel 'manneristic notation') to denote a musical style. But since this distinction has been generally accepted and has led to the French Ars Nova being considered to end about 1370, at a time when French and Italian styles were still clearly separated, there has been subsequently less force of opinion to support any references to an Italian Ars Nova.

It is therefore customary to use 'Ars Nova' to refer to French music from the *Roman de Fauvel* to the death of Machaut, for though this is not historically the most precise way of using the term, it is historiographically the most useful. At the same time it is worth observing that 'Ars Nova', like 'Renaissance', is a term found at many times in the course of history (see Schrade). Perhaps the most famous use outside the 14th century is that of Tinctoris (*CS*, iv, 154) who described Dunstable (*d* 1453) as 'ut ita dicam, novae artis fons et origo'.

BIBLIOGRAPHY
H. Besseler: 'Ars nova', *MGG*
C. van den Borren: 'L'ars nova', *L'ars nova: Wégimont II 1955*, 17
E. Perroy: 'Le point de vue de l'historien', *L'ars nova: Wégimont II 1955*, 261
N. Pirrotta: 'Cronologia e denominazione dell'Ars nova italiana', *L'ars nova: Wégimont II 1955*, 93
L. Schrade: 'The Chronology of the Ars Nova in France', *L'ars nova: Wégimont II 1955*, 37
S. Clercx: 'Propos sur l'ars nova', *RBM*, x (1956), 154
G. Reaney: 'The *Ars Nova* of Philippe de Vitry', *MD*, x (1956), 5
F. Fano: 'Punti di vista su l'Ars-nova', *L'ars nova italiana del trecento I: Certaldo 1959*, 105
G. Fellerer: 'La "Constituto docta sanctorum patrum" di Giovanni XXII e la musica nuova del suo tempo', *L'ars nova italiana del trecento I: Certaldo 1959*, 9
U. Günther: 'Das Ende der Ars Nova', *Mf*, xvi (1963), 105
F. J. Smith: 'Ars Nova – a Re-definition?', *MD*, xviii (1964), 19; xix (1965), 83
N. Pirrotta: 'Ars nova', *LaMusicaE*

DAVID FALLOWS

Ars Subtilior. The highly refined musical style of the late 14th century, centred primarily on the secular courts of southern France, Aragon and Cyprus. The term was introduced to musicological vocabulary by Ursula Günther (1963) and derives from references in (?)Philippus de Caserta's *Tractatus de diversis figuris* to composers moving away from the style of the ARS NOVA motets 'post modum subtiliorem comparantes' and developing an 'artem magis subtiliter' as exemplified in the motet *Apta caro* (*CS*, iii, 118); similarly Egidius de Murino referred to composition 'per viam subtilitatis' in his *Tractatus cantus mensurabilis* (*CS*, iii, 127). The development of the idiom (chiefly encountered in *grandes ballades*) may be traced in successive, roughly chronological stages. Of these, the post-Machaut generation – De Landes, Franciscus, Grimace, Pierre de Molins, Solage, Suzoy (*A l'arbre sec*) and Vaillant – was largely engaged in developing the classical ballade style of Machaut.

There is a more florid extension in the works of Matheus de Sancto Johanne, Goscalch, Hasprois and Olivier. Aside from the growing contrapuntal independence of the contratenor, their works are notable for an admirable tonal and motivic cohesion. That Hasprois' *Ma doulce amour* is found in *GB-Ob* Can.misc.213 (after 1428) illustrates the underlying link between the early Ars Subtilior and the subsequent 15th-century chanson. The final disruption of the traditional Machaut style occurs in the compositions of Cuvelier, Egidius, Johannes de Alte Curie, Philippus de Caserta and Trebor. Their music is permeated with lavish minim displacements and Italianate sequential patterns. Yet

more advanced was a final group of composers (Jacob de Senleches, Rodericus and Zacharia), who used elaborate rhythmic subdivisions, displacements (split colorations) and proportional, motet-like devices. On occasion, even the less radical composers (such as Solage and Galiot in *S'aincy estoit* and *Le sault perilleux*) adopted this style, which ultimately spread to the French cultural outpost of Cyprus (anonymous ballade *Sur toute fleur*, *c*1410).

BIBLIOGRAPHY
U. Günther: 'Das Ende der Ars Nova', *Mf*, xvi (1963), 105
N. Josephson: 'Vier Beispiele der Ars subtilior', *AMw*, xxvii (1970), 41
J. Hirshberg: *The Music of the Late Fourteenth Century: a Study in Musical Style* (diss., U. of Pennsylvania, 1971)
N. Josephson: 'Rodericus, *Angelorum psalat*', *MD*, xxv (1971), 113
U. Günther: 'Zitate in französischen Liedsätzen der Ars nova und Ars subtilior', *MD*, xxvi (1972), 85

NORS S. JOSEPHSON

Ars Veterum. *See* ARS ANTIQUA.

Ars Viva. German firm of music publishers. It was founded in 1950 by Hermann Scherchen to publish music by postwar avant-garde composers. The future of the Ars Viva catalogue was assured when in 1953 it was incorporated into the catalogue of B. Schott's Söhne, Mainz (*see* SCHOTT). Since then the Ars Viva list has gradually increased, the majority of its scores being by contemporary German or Swiss composers including Heinz Holliger, Klaus Huber, Giselher Klebe, Rolf Liebermann and Aribert Reimann, as well as important compositions by Luigi Dallapiccola and Niccolò Castiglioni and most of the early works of Luigi Nono. In addition, the firm published a few relatively unknown works by earlier composers, including Beethoven, Cavalieri and Pergolesi, some in editions by Hermann Scherchen himself.

ALAN POPE

Artaria. Austrian firm of music publishers. It was founded in Mainz in 1765 and in 1766 moved to Vienna, where it became the first important music publishing firm in the city.

1. History of the family and firm. 2. Publishing history.

1. HISTORY OF THE FAMILY AND FIRM. The Artaria family originated in Blevio on Lake Como, Italy. On 15 January 1759 the brothers Cesare Timoteo (1706–85), Domenico (i) (1715–84) and Giovanni Casimiro Artaria (1725–97) obtained passes to visit the fairs in Frankfurt am Main, Leipzig and Würzburg; Carlo (1747–1808), son of Cesare, and Francesco (1744–1808), son of Domenico (i), accompanied them as *giovini* (commercial assistants). Cesare and Domenico (i) returned to their own country; Carlo and Francesco founded with their uncle Giovanni Casimiro the firm Giovanni Artaria & Co. in Mainz in 1765. In 1766 the brothers left Mainz and travelled to Vienna, where they at first carried on business without their own premises. According to the *Wiener Diarium* of 25 July 1770, Carlo owned a shop in the Kleine Dorotheergasse until that date, but there is no further evidence to support this. On 31 October 1770 the shop known as 'Zum König von Dänemark' was opened. The firm was called Cugini Artaria, becoming Artaria & Comp. in 1771; the licence granted to Carlo Artaria on 23 February covered only dealings in copper engravings. In 1774 connections with the firm in Mainz were re-established. The businesses developed so favourably that on 28 January 1775 the Vienna firm was able to open a shop

in the Kohlmarkt, which also bore the name 'Zum König von Dänemark'.

Giovanni Casimiro's son Pasquale (1755–85) entered the business as his father's successor and from 19 October 1776 (*Wiener Diarium*, no.84) trade in printed music began with the import of prints from London, Amsterdam and particularly Paris (no first stock catalogue is extant). With the new dealing in printed music, plans for a music publishing business were also developed; the rise of the Viennese Classical period provided an encouraging context. The Paris music publisher ANTON HUBERTY offered a stimulus to the business side of the undertaking. He had been selling his publications on the Viennese market since 1770 through various booksellers; at the beginning of 1777 he moved to Vienna with his family and established himself very successfully with a music engraving and printing shop, but his undertaking was short-lived owing to his advanced age. The Artarias seized the opportunity to issue their first publication, six trios by Bonaga, on 12 August 1778 (the plate numbers 1 and 2 of these insignificant works were later reassigned to Pleyel's quartets op.1). Huberty was an engraver for Artaria until his death on 13 January 1791.

In 1780 Ignazio Artaria (1757–1820), brother of Francesco, entered the business. He was granted a ten-year printing licence on 28 January 1782 by Emperor Joseph II: published pieces from this time bear the mark C.P.S.C.M. ('cum privilegio Suae Caesareae Majestatis'). After the death of Pasquale Artaria in 1785, his brother Domenico (ii) (1765–1823) joined the business, and in the same year the firm set up its own music engraving workshop, using at first pewter plates. Another publisher, Christoph Torricella, a competitor in the Viennese market since 31 January 1781, and now 71 years old, was soon outstripped: on 12 August 1786 Artaria bought 980 of his engraving plates at a public auction, together with all his publishing rights.

In 1789 the flourishing business was transferred to the house 'Zum englischen Gruss', in the Kohlmarkt. Domenico (ii), who with his brother Giovanni Maria (1771–1835) had carried on the Mainz branch of the firm, resigned in 1793, bringing about the final division of the firm, until then known as 'Artaria & Comp., Wien und Mainz'. The Mainz branch moved to Mannheim and combined with the firm of Fontaine to form an art bookshop and publishing business which existed until 1867.

Giovanni CAPPI (whose sister, Maria, Carlo Artaria subsequently married) became an apprentice in the firm in 1773, then an employee, and finally a partner in 1792. Another employee, TRANQUILLO MOLLO (1767–1837), from Bellinzona, also became a partner, in 1793. Finally PIETRO CAPPI, a nephew of Giovanni, was employed in the firm. During these years an increasing number of music publications were transferred from the publisher FRANZ ANTON HOFFMEISTER to Artaria. Between 1793 and 1798 the Artaria firm had five partners: Carlo, Francesco and Ignazio Artaria, as well as Cappi and Mollo. The war years and disagreements within the firm brought about a crisis which lasted until 1804 and had an extremely detrimental effect on the business. The contracts with Ignazio and Mollo expired in 1798; the former returned to Italy while Mollo established his own arts shop (his assets were paid over to him in publications). A further division was agreed on 16 May 1801: Francesco obtained a new licence and

transferred it to his son Domenico (iii) (1775–1842), who was in partnership with Mollo, but operating from the Artaria premises; Carlo, who had continued as sole owner of the original firm, sold it to Mollo in October 1802. After the parting with Mollo in 1804 Domenico (iii) took over the sole direction of the firm at the Kohlmarkt. From 1805 to 1816 Pietro Cappi was a partner in the firm, and from 1807 until 1824 Carlo Boldrini was a third partner. In 1818 a share in the music publishing house was bought by Johann Traeg and in 1832 another by Thaddäus Weigl. In about 1830 the firm opened an auction room. After the death of Domenico (iii) on 5 June 1842, his son August (1807–93), who had entered the firm in 1833, became sole owner. The music publications of the house became fewer; new publishers were appearing and capturing the market, in particular Haslinger, Diabelli and Mechetti. In February 1858 the *Wiener Zeitung* carried the last announcement of an Artaria music publication (although the Denkmäler der Tonkunst in Österreich was published by Artaria between 1894 and 1918). August's sons Karl August (1855–1919) and Dominik (1859–1936) entered the firm in 1881 and 1890 respectively, and after their father's death in 1893 became sole owners.

Mathias Artaria (1793–1835), son of Domenico (ii), was involved in music publishing independently of the family firm. He took over Daniel Sprenger's arts shop in 1818; his firm (which issued some Schubert first editions) was continued after his death (in 1835) by his widow (*see* MAISCH, LUDWIG).

2. PUBLISHING HISTORY. The Artaria firm's activities

Title-page of the first edition of Haydn's Six Quartets op.33, published by Artaria in 1782

began in the art trade and expanded into geography and iconography. In these areas it achieved world-wide importance, and the art and map publishing business was carried on as an integral branch of the firm into the 20th century. The arts shop offered paintings, foreign art journals, engravings, lithographs, contemporary portraits of famous men (from its own press) and numerous pictorial views; the house of Artaria gained international recognition and established itself as a cultural focus of the Viennese upper middle classes.

It was in music publishing however that the firm revealed a particularly felicitous touch (although its first owners apparently had no musical education). As early as 1779 they established contact with Joseph Haydn and on 12 April 1780 they published a set of his piano sonatas (HXVI: 20, 35–9) with plate no.7; this inaugurated a series of over 300 editions of Haydn's compositions. Composer and publisher enjoyed a warm relationship, reflected in their lively correspondence. On 8 December 1781, a set of piano and violin sonatas by Mozart appeared; Artaria subsequently published 83 first editions and 36 early editions of Mozart in addition to publications taken over from Hoffmeister, and thus were Mozart's chief publisher during his lifetime. The young Beethoven, on arriving in Vienna, was also quickly drawn to Artaria; his first published work, a set of piano variations, appeared on 31 July 1793, followed by first editions of his works up to op.8. Despite subsequent disagreements, the firm continued to receive new works from Beethoven, and by 1858 editions of his works – including arrangements and reprints – numbered over 100. The numerous catalogues remaining from this early period reveal many other well-known names, including Boccherini, Clementi, Gluck, Kozeluch, Pleyel, Salieri and Vanhal.

A unique business relationship developed between Artaria and the composer and music publisher F. A. Hoffmeister, who until the turn of the century several times simply surrendered portions of his publishing business to Artaria. In 1802 production had reached publication no.906, almost entirely works of fine quality. Then came the interregnum of co-production with T. Mollo & Co., which embraces publication nos.907–1000 as well as 1501–1692 and which ended by 25 August 1804. Nos.1001–1500 are found in the firm's main ledger reserved for a series with the title Raccolta d'arie, but in fact were used for the publication of piano reductions from current operas and of individual arias (the pieces appeared between 1787 and 1804 with the special 'Raccolta' number, as distinguished from the plate number, on the bottom left margin). While they at first used several independent music engravers, Artaria later employed its own engravers and also established its own press. Ferdinand Kauer is known to have been employed as a publisher's reader, and according to his own records carried out his duties for 17 years. Beyond its encouragement of Classical composers, the firm was committed to a demanding publishing programme; an impressive list of other composers, represented by numerous works, included Cramer, Hummel, Moscheles, Rossini, Sarti and Sterkel (Schubert, however, published only three works with Artaria).

Towards the middle of the 19th century publishing activities waned and works of poor quality began to be accepted; in 1858, under August Artaria, the music

publishing house closed down. It has not been established whether he was unable to keep up with the times, or simply lost interest and gave way to younger men. Towards the end of the century the remaining assets went to the Viennese music publisher Josef Weinberger. The important collection of autographs which the family had accumulated over the years, partly through publishing activities and partly through subsequent independent purchases by Domenico Artaria (iii), was later transferred to the Preussische Staatsbibliothek.

BIBLIOGRAPHY

L. von Köchel: Chronologisch-thematisches Verzeichnis sämtlicher Tonwerke Wolfgang Amade Mozarts (Leipzig, 1862, rev. 6/1964)

G. Adler: Verzeichnis der musikalischen Autographen von Ludwig van Beethoven . . . im Besitze von Artaria in Wien (Vienna, 1890)

F. Artaria and H. Botstiber: Joseph Haydn und das Verlagshaus Artaria (Vienna, 1909)

K. E. Blümml and G. Gugitz: Von Leuten und Zeiten im alten Wien (Vienna and Leipzig, 1922)

J. P. Larsen: Die Haydn-Überlieferung (Copenhagen, 1939)

A. Weinmann: Vollständiges Verlagsverzeichnis Artaria & Comp. (Vienna, 1952)

G. Kinsky and H. Halm: Thematisch-bibliographisches Verzeichnis aller vollendeten Kompositionen Ludwig van Beethovens (Munich and Duisburg, 1955)

A. van Hoboken: Thematisch-bibliographisches Werkverzeichnis Joseph Haydns (Mainz, 1957–71)

A. Weinmann: Verlagsverzeichnis Tranquillo Mollo (Vienna, 1964)

——: Verlagsverzeichnis Giovanni Cappi bis A. O. Witzendorf (Vienna, 1967)

Geschichte der Firmen Artaria & Compagnie und Freytag–Berndt und Artaria (Vienna, 1970)

R. Hilmar: Der Musikverlag Artaria & Comp.: Geschichte und Probleme der Druckproduktion (Tutzing, 1977)

ALEXANDER WEINMANN

Arteaga, Esteban de [Arteaga, Stefano] (b Moraleja de Coca, nr. Segovia, 26 Dec 1747; d Paris, 30 Oct 1799). Spanish aesthetician and opera historian. After entering the Society of Jesus on 23 September 1763 he studied for four years at Madrid, which led him to call himself a native of that city. With the expulsion of the Jesuits in 1767, he went with them first to Corsica, then to Italy. In the vain hope of regaining the favour of Charles III, he abandoned the Society of Jesus on 21 June 1769 without having been ordained a priest.

While attending Bologna University (1773–8), he enjoyed access to Martini's library, and there prepared for publication a three-volume opera history (1783–5). The immediate success of this work caused his pension from the Spanish crown to be doubled. Seeking a better printer he moved to Venice. In January 1787 he moved to Rome where he prepared a treatise on ideal beauty (1789). About 1796 he wrote a letter to a librarian at the Madrid Royal Library on the meaning of Aristotle's musical terminology, and five dissertations on ancient and modern rhythm. His last years were disrupted by the Napoleonic invasion, which forced him to travel about with his chief patron José Nicolás de Azara, the Spanish ambassador to the papal see.

In his Rivoluzioni Arteaga argued that opera was more than the sum of its parts, and that neither the music nor the text could be criticized separately. Nonetheless, he eulogized Metastasio in a separate chapter devoted solely to librettos. In the second and third volumes, which were less favourably received than the first, he decried contemporary opera, arguing that the 'modern' librettist Calzabigi was saved only by Gluck's music. Calzabigi countered these remarks in a sarcastic Risposta (Venice, 1790).

WRITINGS

(*only those relating to music*)

Le rivoluzioni del teatro musicale italiano dalla sua origine fino al presente (Bologna, 1783–8, rev. 2/1785; Ger. trans., 1789 as *Geschichte der italiänischen Oper*; Fr. trans., 1802)

Investigaciones filosoficas sobre la belleza ideal, considerada como objeto de todas las artes de imitacion (Madrid, 1789)

Della influenza degli arabi sull'origine della poesia moderna in Europa (Rome, 1791)

Del ritmo sonoro e del ritmo muto nella musica degli antichi (MS, c1796, *E-Mah*) [ed. in Batllori]

Lettere musico-filologiche (MS, c1796, *Mah*) [ed. in Batllori]

BIBLIOGRAPHY

V. Manfredini: *Difesa della musica moderna, e de' suoi celebri esecutori* (Bologna, 1788)

C. Sommervogel: *Bibliothèque de la Compagnie de Jésus* (Brussels and Paris, 1890), i, 589ff

M. Batllori: 'Estudio preliminar', *E. de Arteaga: I. Lettere . . . II. Del ritmo sonoro* (Madrid, 1944)

R. Allorto: 'Stefano Arteaga e "Le rivoluzioni del teatro musicale italiano" ', *RMI*, lii/2 (1950), 124

E. M. K. Rudat: *The Aesthetic Ideas of Esteban de Arteaga: Origin, Meaning and Current Value* (diss., U. of California, Los Angeles, 1969), 17–74, 467ff

ROBERT STEVENSON

Arteaga, Manuel Gaytán y. *See* GAYTÁN Y ARTEAGA, MANUEL.

Arthopius [Artocopus, Artopaeus], Balthasar (*b* end of the 15th century; *d* Speyer, late July 1534). German organist and composer. There is no evidence to support Jauernig's assumption that he was the Balthasar Pistorius from Besike who matriculated at Heidelberg University on 12 April 1498. Arthopius was organist in Weissenburg, Alsace, around 1527. In 1527 he applied for the post of organist at Speyer Cathedral, but was not appointed because the cathedral chapter at Speyer wanted to fill the vacant organist's post with a cleric. At the end of July 1530 he again offered his services to the chapter, and after some negotiation he was installed as cathedral organist on 17 August 1530 for a period of four years. His yearly wage was one fuder of wine, 18 malters of corn and 52 guilders. The humanist Theodor Reyssmann visited Speyer in 1531 and praised Arthopius's organ playing, comparing it with the ability of his predecessor, Conrad Bruman, a pupil of Hofhaimer. The chapter archives report that Arthopius composed some pieces for Christmas 1533 and that for them he received a gift of four guilders. After Arthopius's death, the Heidelberg professor and humanist Jacob Micyllus dedicated an epitaph to him which was set to music by Johannes Heugel (*D-KL* Mus 4°118).

Arthopius used the elements of the later Netherlands style in his sacred compositions; his technical skill, however, lacks the perfection of a master. For him the tenor settings of Netherlands choral polyphony were compulsory but he treated the cantus firmus in a fairly original manner. Imitation and the use of motifs are found throughout the pieces, and their rhythmic and harmonic flexibility is characteristic. Arthopius's German secular songs show clearly the tendency towards simplification and conciseness. He made frequent use of imitation but subordinated it to harmonic considerations. As a rule the melody is in the tenor part, from which the other parts usually derive their melodic substance. The canonic setting of the melody in the tenor and alto of *Es fiel ein Baur* is unusual. The texts of the songs are often satirical and blunt.

WORKS

SACRED

Beatus qui intelligit, 5vv, *D-Z* 4; Cogniscimus Domine, 4vv, 1537[1]; Jubilate Deo omnis terra, 5vv, *Z* 4; Nisi Dominus aedificaverit domum, 4vv, 1542[4]

SECULAR

Die Brinlein, 4vv, 1535[10]; Es fiel ein Baur, 5vv, 1536[8]; Frawe, liebste Frawe, 5vv, 1536[8]; Wer Hoffart treibt, 4vv, 1536[8], ed. in *MMg*, xxvi (1894), 35

BIBLIOGRAPHY

R. Jauernig: 'Berichtigungen und Ergänzungen zu Eitners Quellen-lexikon für Musiker und Musikgelehrte des 16. Jahrhunderts', *Mf*, vi (1953), 39

G. Pietzsch: 'Orgelbauer, Organisten und Orgelspiel in Deutschland bis zum Ende des 16. Jahrhunderts', *Mf*, xi (1958), 311

MANFRED SCHULER

Artia. The name of the imprint under which SUPRAPHON exports.

Articulation. The manner in which successive notes are joined to one another by a performer. In the simplest terms, opposite kinds of articulation are staccato (detached, prominent articulation) and legato (smooth, 'invisible' articulation). In reality articulation involves myriad aspects of the voice or instrument that determine how the beginning and end of each note are to sound. Articulation is a principal component (together with nuances in dynamics, tempo, timbre and intonation) of phrasing. Control of articulation is also an important means by which performers achieve precise qualities of texture.

Resources of articulation differ with the performing medium and acoustical surroundings. To achieve clarity in a hall with abundant reverberation generally requires energetic articulation, as well as a relatively slow tempo. The articulative characteristics of various instruments are an important element in their musical capacities. Apart from vibrato the main differences in timbre of the violin, trumpet and oboe, for instance, are due to their different means of articulation: their recorded sound becomes virtually identical if the initial and terminal articulation of each note is excised from a recording. A distinct feature of bagpipe music is the use of grace notes, mordents and other ornamental devices to compensate for the unavailability of silence as an articulative resource. Ornaments are also a characteristic means of articulating notes on the organ or harpsichord when they might otherwise remain unduly submerged in the flow of the texture. Techniques of articulation in most wind instruments include various patterns of TONGUING; equivalent aspects of technique for instruments of the violin family involve the handling of the BOW (and the occasional use of pizzicato). In vocal music the resources of articulation, apart from grace notes and the like, portamentos, and such slivers of silence between notes as are available to most performers, are the consonants and the glottal or smooth beginning and ending of vowel sounds. Most keyboard instruments can achieve an almost perfect melodic legato, even in a small room, by producing the terminal articulation of one note after the initial articulation of the succeeding one.

As fig.1 suggests, the attack (initial articulation) of a note will most often occupy between 0·01 and 0·1 seconds. Bass notes are relatively slow in articulation, however, partly because more time is required to perceive waveforms of slower frequency and partly because more time is required to put into regular motion the larger bodies of air, string etc that are likely to be involved in producing bass notes. Hence the trombone, bassoon and string bass are generally less incisive than the trumpet, oboe and violin.

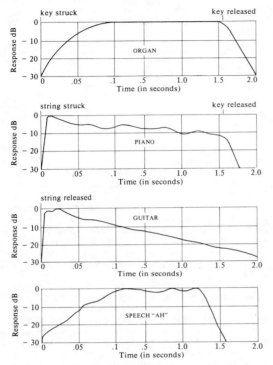

1. Growth and decay in the articulation of notes on an organ, piano, guitar and the voice; after H. F. Olson, 'Musical Engineering' (New York, Toronto and London, 1952, p.257)

Incisive articulation (as well as bright tone) assists the ear in sensing the location of an instrument. In this regard a Romantic inclination to diffuseness might be seen in such 19th-century trends as the increased orchestral prominence of horns and trombones, the use of ever more heavily padded hammers on the piano, the elimination of 'chiff' in the pipe organ and the popularity of the harmonium.

Technological developments since World War II have enabled the transient acoustical phenomena of articulation to be studied in some detail. In electronic music, the concept of articulation – like that of 'notes' – can readily be stretched to its logical limits. For example, if a note has a physical attack time of less than two milliseconds (0·002 second) the ear perceives a click that is not present in the recording. Some electronic music of the 1950s, for instance Stockhausen's *Studie I* and *Studie II*, was remarkably crude in its handling of articulation; by the mid 1960s, however, commercially available synthesizers could govern not only the duration of an attack or decay but also certain aspects of its internal shape. But the variety of transient waveforms in 'natural' articulation as wielded intuitively by vocal and instrumental artists has remained greater than that of synthetic music in general.

Such intricacies would be extremely difficult to notate. An exceptionally elaborate method of specifying qualities of articulation can be found in the *chien-tzu* notation of the Chinese zither (*see* CHINA, §V, 2, iii), wherein (Chou, 1969):

a combination symbol for both hands would usually specify how a certain right-hand finger is to pluck the string, inward or outward, with the flesh or the nail, or how two or more right-hand fingers are to be used simultaneously or in succession, how a left-hand finger stops the string, or how a left-hand finger is to tap the string or to pluck it, upward or sideways, how the pitch is altered or inflected by means of glissando or portamento after the excitation of the string, and how the timbre is varied by the addition of a certain type of vibrato or by changing from one type of vibrato to another during the decay.

In Western music, just as tempo and expression marks entered scores at a relatively late stage in the history of notation, so also articulation marks are scarcely to be found before the 17th century and did not become a normal constituent of the average musical score until well into the 18th. But whereas extreme contrasts of dynamic or tempo almost certainly did not occur in the earlier written music where they were not written in, it seems likely that manifold shades of articulation have always been an integral part of any sensitive musical performance. The earliest unmistakable notated articulation points are ornaments, and particularly mordents, in 15th-century keyboard music. Articulation signs other than ornaments remained relatively rare through the Baroque era. Even in the late 18th century, when articulation signs of the modern, more abstract type became common, the distinction between staccato and staccatissimo was notated differently by different composers and interpreted unpredictably by their publishers or printers. Of the three standard signs of articulation, the dot always had several meanings, the bow or slur was often ambiguous and changed meanings from one generation to the next, and only the tenuto dash was relatively consistent and predictable over the years and across Europe.

Ex.1

Some late 19th- and early 20th-century music is so laden with these and related articulation signs that a heroic effort would be required to interpret them all precisely. The opening of one of Verdi's most popular arias (see ex.1) gives some idea of the ways in which a composer might try to control his musicians. (The second stanza has different marks of articulation but the same notes.) But articulation is so often a mixture of the idiom and individual style of the performer that too much marking of this sort can be either superfluous or cramping. Human agents profit from a shrewd balance of explicitness and leeway.

BIBLIOGRAPHY

A. Dolmetsch: *The Interpretation of the Music of the 17th and 18th Centuries* (London, 1915, 2/1946/*R*1969)
K. Speer: 'Die Artikulation in den Orgelwerken J. S. Bachs', *BJb*, xli (1954), 66
H. Keller: *Phrasierung und Artikulation* (Kassel, 1955; Eng. trans., 1965)
H. Albrecht, ed.: *Die Bedeutung der Zeichen Keil, Strich und Punkt bei Mozart* (Kassel, 1957) [see also P. Mies, *Mf*, xi (1958), 428]
H. Unverricht: *Die Eigenschriften und die Originalausgaben von Werken Beethovens in ihrer Bedeutung fur die moderne Textkritik* (Kassel, 1960)
W. Thoene: 'Zur Frage der Artikulation im Cembalo- und Clavichordspiel', *Festschrift Karl Gustav Fellerer* (Regensburg, 1962), 55
R. Donington: *The Interpretation of Early Music* (London, 1963, rev. 3/1974)
C. A. Taylor: *The Physics of Musical Sounds* (London, 1965)
Chou Wen-chung: 'East and West, Old and New', *Asian Music*, i (1969), 19
DAVID FALLOWS, MARK LINDLEY, MAURICE WRIGHT

Artifices (Lat.). TECHNITAI.

Artificial intelligence. *See* PSYCHOLOGY OF MUSIC, §I, 5 (iii).

Artistichesky Kruzhok (Russ.: 'Artistic Circle'). Moscow society active from 1865 to 1883; *see* MOSCOW, §3.

Artocopus, Balthasar. *See* ARTHOPIUS, BALTHASAR.

Artomius [Artomiusz, Artotomius, Krzesichleb, Artomius Grodicensis], **Piotr** (*b* Grodzisk, nr. Poznań, 26 July 1552; *d* Toruń, 2 Aug 1609). Polish clergyman, hymnologist and ?composer. He first studied at Grodzisk, was then, from 1573, a private tutor at Ostrofóg and in 1577–8 attended the University of Wittenberg. An outstanding Protestant divine, he spent his whole career as a preacher – in Warsaw from 1578, at Wegrów from 1581, at Kryłów (in the Małopolska district) from 1584 and at Toruń from 1586 until his death. He was the editor of the most popular Polish Protestant hymnbook, *Cantional: Albo pieśni duchowne* (Toruń, 1587, or ?1578). It was enlarged and reprinted many times as *Cantional, to iest: Pieśni krześcijańskie* at Toruń in 1596, 1601, 1620, 1638, 1648, 1672 and 1697, at Gdańsk in 1640 and 1646 and at Leipzig as late as 1728. The biggest edition, that of 1601, contains 333 songs, 106 of which were set by Adam Freytag for three to five voices (the number of these settings was reduced in later editions). The melodies were taken from traditional Catholic sources and Czech and German hymnals, and some were native Polish tunes; some of the texts were adapted, presumably by Artomius himself, to fit the traditional melodies.

BIBLIOGRAPHY

M. Sipayłłówna: 'Artomius, Piotr', *PSB*
R. Pollak, ed.: *Bibliografia literatury Polskiej 'Nowy Korbut': Piśmiennictwo staropolskie* [Bibliography of Polish literature: early Polish writing], ii (Warsaw, 1964)
G. Kratzel: 'Die altpolnischen protestantischen Kantionalfrühdrucke', *Mf*, xviii (1965), 253
M. Przywecka-Samecka: *Drukarstwo muzyczne w Polsce do konca XVIII wieku* [Music printing in Poland up to the end of the 18th century] (Kraków, 1969)
ZYGMUNT M. SZWEYKOWSKI

Artopaeus, Balthasar. *See* ARTHOPIUS, BALTHASAR.

Artôt, Alexandre [Montagney, Joseph] (*b* Brussels, 25 Jan 1815; *d* Ville d'Avray, nr. Paris, 20 July 1845). Belgian violinist. He was the son of Maurice Artôt (1772–1829), first horn player at the Théâtre de la Monnaie, and Theresa Eva Ries, cousin of Ferdinand Ries. Maurice Artôt's real name was Montagney. At the age of five Alexandre began studying the violin with his father and within 18 months played a Viotti concerto at the theatre. He received further instruction from Snel, principal first violin at the theatre, who advised him to study in Paris. There he was admitted as a page at the Chapel Royal and continued his studies at the Conservatoire first with Rodolphe and later with Auguste Kreutzer, gaining the second and first prizes in 1827 and 1828. According to Fétis, Artôt then performed successfully in Brussels and London and toured Belgium, Holland, Italy, Germany and other European countries. At the Philharmonic on 3 June 1839 Artôt played a fantasy of his own for violin and orchestra; this was well received because of the delicacy of his playing and his remarkable execution rather than his tone, which, according to the *Athenaeum* (8 June 1839), was small.

In 1843 Artôt went on a concert tour of America and Cuba with the soprano Cinti-Damoreau. He was one of the first violin virtuosos to visit America, the others being Vieuxtemps and Ole Bull; they vied with each other for the admiration of the American public, the French elements preferring Artôt's Parisian elegance to the awkward but modest stage presence of Ole Bull. While in America Artôt showed the first symptoms of the lung disease from which he died. His compositions include a Concerto in A minor, fantasies and airs with variations and, in MS, string quartets and a Quintet for strings and piano.

ALEXIS CHITTY/MANOUG PARIKIAN

Artôt, (Marguerite-Joséphine) Désirée (Montagney) (*b* Paris, 21 July 1835; *d* Berlin, 3 April 1907). Belgian mezzo-soprano, later soprano. She was the daughter of Jean Désiré Montagney Artôt, horn player and professor at the Brussels Conservatory. She studied with Pauline Viardot in London and Paris, making her first concert appearances in Brussels (1857) and in the same year at a state concert in England before Queen Victoria. On Meyerbeer's recommendation she was engaged for the Paris Opéra in 1858, making her début as Fidès in *Le prophète*. In spite of the praise lavished on her by many critics, including Berlioz in the *Journal des débats* of 17 February, intrigues led her to ask to be released from her contract and, deciding to concentrate on the Italian repertory, she toured the south of France and Belgium as Rosina and Leonora in *Il trovatore*. Her vocal range had extended itself in both directions, allowing her to add soprano roles to her repertory. In 1859 she sang in Italy, and at the end of the year in Berlin, with Lorini's Italian company at the opening of the Victoria-Theater, where she won great acclaim as Rosina, Angelina (*La Cenerentola*), Leonora (*Il trovatore*) and even as Maddalena (*Rigoletto*). Thereafter the greater part of her career was spent in Germany, both in Italian and German opera.

During the 1859–60 season she appeared with great success in concerts in London, and in 1863 she sang with the Royal Italian Opera at Her Majesty's Theatre as Maria in *La figlia del reggimento*. In the same year she sang Adalgisa to the Norma of Tietjens and Violetta. In spite of the great impression she invariably made in London, her appearances at Covent Garden in 1864 and 1866 were her last in England. In 1868 she went to Russia where, after a brief friendship, Tchaikovsky proposed marriage to her. Without a word of explanation, however, she married the Spanish baritone Mariano Padilla y Ramos (1842–1906) at Sèvres in September 1869; she sang with him in Italian opera in Germany, Austria and Russia until her retirement. On 22 March 1887 they appeared together in a scene from *Don Giovanni*, performed for the kaiser's birthday at the Imperial Palace in Berlin. She taught singing in that city until 1889, when she and her husband went to live in Paris.

Their daughter, Lola Artôt de Padilla (*b* Sèvres, 5 Oct 1876; *d* Berlin, 12 April 1933), was a pupil of Artôt. She made her début in Paris in 1904 and subsequently sang in Berlin at the Komische Oper (1905–8) and at the Königliche Oper (1909–27), where in 1911 she was Berlin's first Octavian. Her other successful roles included Zerlina, the Countess and Cherubino, Amelia and Oscar and Micaëla. In 1913 she was awarded the title *Kammersängerin*.

BIBLIOGRAPHY

La Mara [pseud. of M. Lipsius]: *Musikalische Studienköpfe*, v (Leipzig, 1882)

B. Horowicz: 'Artôt, Désirée', *ES*

HAROLD ROSENTHAL

Arts Council of Australia. Promotional organization founded in SYDNEY in 1944.

Arts Council of Great Britain. An organization incorporated by royal charter in 1948 to take the place of the wartime Council for the Encouragement of Music and the Arts and to administer the subsidies granted by the state to artistic enterprises. The Arts Council has up to 20 members working with the minister responsible for the arts; a Scottish Arts Council and a Welsh Arts Council work in close cooperation with the national organization, and there is a separate Arts Council for Northern Ireland.

The Arts Council works through panels, musical, literary, dramatic etc, independently of the government, though the government supplies its funds. It is not intended to represent an 'establishment' view of the arts and their place in society, and aims for 'patronage without control'. Regional arts associations working under its aegis and partly supported by the council, are free to form their own policies. The council's care for music extends beyond professional orchestras and opera companies to amateur groups. London organizations (especially the Royal Opera House) take the greatest share of subsidies, but the policy in the 1960s and 1970s has been to foster the arts in the regions by its support of small touring companies.

HENRY RAYNOR

Arts Council of Ireland. Organization founded in 1951 in Dublin; *see* DUBLIN, §11.

Art song. A song of serious artistic purpose written by a professional composer, as opposed to a folksong. The term is more often applied to solo than to polyphonic songs and embraces the 19th-century lied and *mélodie*.

Artufel, Dámaso (*b* southern France; *fl* 1609–14). Spanish liturgist of French birth. A Dominican friar, educated at the monastery at St Maximin, Provence, he served as *cantor* in a number of houses of his order in France, Aragon and Castile, including S Pablo at Valladolid and finally Atocha in Madrid. He was commissioned to prepare a new simplified processional for the Spanish Dominicans, *Processionarium secundum morem almi ordinis Praedicatorum S. P. N. Dominici* (Madrid, 1609), which contains information on past chant manuals of the order, and the rubrics and music for the special services involving processions. Its music was badly garbled by the printer. Artufel's second work, *Modo de rezar las horas canónicas conforme al rezo de los Frayles Predicadores . . . con un Arte de canto llano y con la entonación de los hymnos y sus rúbricas* (Valladolid, 1614), is in three parts with separate paginations. The first, a ceremonial for the Office, is chiefly an extract in translation from the Dominican ordinary but with some interesting added material on the use of the organ; the second part contains the hymn intonations; the third is a manual on chant consisting of 23 chapters on the rudiments of music (notation, solmization, intervals, modes) and a collection of examples. The bulk of the technical material is taken verbatim from the *Arte de tañer fantasía* (Valladolid, 1565) of Artufel's great predecessor at S Pablo, Tomás de Santa María.

BIBLIOGRAPHY

H. Anglés and J. Subirá: *Catálogo musical de la Biblioteca nacional de Madrid*, ii (Barcelona, 1949)

ALMONTE HOWELL

Artusi, Giovanni Maria (*b* *c*1540; *d* Bologna, 18 Aug 1613). Italian theorist, polemicist and composer. He was one of the leading Italian theorists in the years around 1600, specially notable for his criticisms from a traditional viewpoint of certain modern tendencies in the music of his day.

1. Life and polemics. 2. Principal theoretical works.

1. LIFE AND POLEMICS. Except for becoming embroiled in several musical polemics, Artusi led a quiet, studious life as a canon regular in the Congregation of S Salvatore at Bologna, where there was an important and sumptuous library of Greek and Latin manuscripts and books. He entered the order on 14 February 1562 and professed on 21 February 1563. He studied for a time in Venice with Zarlino, to whom he always remained devoted, honouring him during his lifetime with a compendium of *Le istitutioni harmoniche* and after his death with a learned eulogy by way of an explication of his teacher's emblem or device, *Impresa del molto rev. Gioseffo Zarlino* (1604). It was as a defender of Zarlino's theories that he entered two famous controversies.

Some years after Vincenzo Galilei had published *Dialogo della musica antica et della moderna* (1581), much of which is directed against the teachings of Zarlino, Artusi rose to the latter's defence in several pamphlets known only through quotations in Ercole Bottrigari's *Aletelogia di Leonardo Gallucio*. In *Lettera apologetica* (1588) he urged composers to imitate the works of Willaert, Rore, Merulo and Costanzo Porta rather than the 'bagatelles of certain modern composers'. After Zarlino's *Sopplimenti* (1588) and Galilei's *Discorso* (1589) in reply to it, Artusi issued a

Trattato apologetico (1590). Galilei's final reply to Artusi and Zarlino remains in manuscript (*I-Fn* Gal.5).

The controversy that developed between Artusi and Bottrigari is not unrelated to that between Zarlino and Galilei. In *Il Desiderio* (1594) Bottrigari drew attention to some of the imperfections that arose in performance when instruments tuned to different standards were mixed in ensembles (*concerti*). The dialogue appeared under the name of one of the interlocutors, Alemanno Benelli; this is an anagram of Annibale Melone, a prominent Bolognese musician and teacher whom Bottrigari chose to honour. Melone greatly admired Bottrigari and used to spend hours each day studying theory with him and copying his works. When Melone died in April 1598, his widow Luccia handed over to Artusi at his request all of Melone's manuscripts, or so states an affidavit signed by her two years later when Bottrigari thought he recognized in Artusi's book, *L'Artusi*, published in December 1600, material from his own unfinished dialogue *Il Trimerone*. Artusi allowed his quarters to be searched, but nothing was found; then Bottrigari collected witnesses for the authorship of his own unpublished works (10 December 1600 to 15 July 1601, in *I-Bc* B.44 and B.46). Actually, although Artusi covered some of the same ground as Bottrigari and was probably stimulated by *Il Trimerone*, there is no evidence of plagiarism. Rather, Bottrigari's jealousy may have been aroused by Artusi's superior scholarship and theoretical acumen and by the understanding and detachment with which he dealt with the history of Greek theory on the basis of careful reading of Aristoxenus, Ptolemy and other ancient writers.

Meanwhile in 1599 Bottrigari had issued a new edition of *Il Desiderio* under his own name. This prompted Artusi to have it reprinted in Milan in 1601 under Melone's name, with a dedication to the senate of Bologna and a letter to the reader in which Artusi claimed that Bottrigari had stolen Melone's work. Bottrigari reacted with understandable indignation in *Lettera di Federico Verdicelli* (1602). Annoyed also by the fact that Artusi criticized his *Desiderio* without naming the author, Bottrigari answered in a dialogue, *Ant-Artusi*, which has not survived. To this Artusi replied in *Considerationi musicali*, printed in *Seconda parte dell'Artusi* (1603), mockingly dedicated to Bottrigari. It is devoted in large part to a refutation of *Il Patricio* (1593), in which Bottrigari had taken friendly issue with his old mentor, the philosopher Francesco Patrizi, on some points regarding the ancient Greek tuning systems. Bottrigari replied with *Aletelogia di Leonardo Gallucio* (1604), which apparently terminated the exchange.

2. PRINCIPAL THEORETICAL WORKS. Artusi's first book, *L'arte del contraponto ridotta in tavole* (1586), mainly outlines in tabular form Zarlino's *Le istitutioni harmoniche* (1558), including some of books 1, 2 and 4, but the core of it is a simplification of book 3, on counterpoint. Although these tables show remarkable synthetic powers and an occasional flash of original thought, it is only with the *Seconda parte dell'arte del contraponto* (1589) that Artusi emerged as an independent theorist of the first rank. It is the first published book devoted entirely to the use of dissonances. (Galilei completed in 1588 a draft of a book on dissonances, which was never published; Artusi knew of it but did not see it.) He noted that there are more dissonances in counterpoint than

consonances and that they are particularly useful for setting words expressing sorrow, tears and pain. Artusi made a primary contribution to the understanding of the suspension when he distinguished the note that moves to cause the dissonance as the *agente* and the note that is held over from the previous beat as the *paziente*. He stated the rule that the *paziente* must descend a step to a perfect or imperfect consonance or occasionally to a dissonance. The *agente*, on the other hand, is free to move anywhere (Zarlino obliged it to remain still by requiring the dissonant interval to be followed by the consonance closest to it). Artusi permitted the 4th to be resolved by a diminished 5th and the 2nd by a unison (p.29): see ex.1. He also recognized that certain dissonances arise from diminution, as in the occurrence in ex.2 of parallel 2nds, which otherwise would not be permissible.

Ex.1

Ex.2

L'arte del contraponto (1598) united the two previous books while replacing much of the material deriving from Zarlino with a broader-based theory to bring it into line with contemporary composition. He urged composers not to imitate those who obstinately remained within the strictures of their rules and forced fugues and clever subtleties into their counterpoint, missing opportunities for more pleasing passages. Rather he would have them imitate works by Andrea Gabrieli, Palestrina and Clemens non Papa, 'who, having avoided obstinacy, have given so much pleasure to all' (p. 38).

Artusi is rightfully famous, though unjustly maligned, for criticizing in his books of 1600 and 1603 certain contrapuntal licences taken by an unnamed composer (later identified as Monteverdi) in four madrigals not published until 1603 and 1605. This stimulated Monteverdi's famous reply in *Il quinto libro de' madrigali* (1605) and a gloss on this letter by his brother Giulio Cesare in *Scherzi musicali* (1607). The debate is important because it brought into focus the ideals of the new style, the *seconda prattica*, as Monteverdi called it. Through the interlocutor Vario in the 1600 dialogue Artusi accused the composer of improprieties in the use of dissonances and accidentals, in the coordination of parts and in mixing modes. Meanwhile through the interlocutor Luca, who defended Monteverdi, we learn that some of the free dissonances could be justified as arising from *accenti* (ornamental figures) and diminutions, others as written examples of improvised counterpoint and still others as modelled on the freer part movement used in instrumental performance. Through the defence of Monteverdi by an unidentified composer who wrote under the academic name of L'Ottuso quoted in Artusi's 1603 book, we learn of some of the precedents and pretexts for the expressive use of harmonic and melodic dissonances that were recognized in the works of Rore, Wert and

Marenzio, and also about the metaphoric use of dissonances as 'suppositions' or 'substitutions' for consonances. Artusi replied to Monteverdi's letter under the pseudonym 'Antonio Brassino da Todi' in a discourse of 1605 which is not extant and to Giulio Cesare's *Dichiaratione* through a second discourse under that name in 1608. In the latter he answered point for point the letters of the Monteverdi brothers and added to his other criticisms the allegation that Monteverdi did not use time signatures correctly. His most interesting retort is that it is not the text that should be mistress of the harmony and rhythm, as Monteverdi, following Plato, believed, but that rhythm ought to be the master of the other two.

Although the quarrel with Monteverdi has attracted the most attention, in both *L'Artusi* volumes it is almost a side issue. Central to the first is the subject of the imperfection of modern *concerti*, which he had first broached in chapter 16 of the counterpoint treatise of 1589 and which received a long commentary by Bottrigari in *Il Desiderio*. Now he showed that the criteria for a good ensemble are more complex than the question of tuning raised by Bottrigari. He also rejected Bottrigari's classification of instruments as 'altogether stable' in tuning, 'altogether alterable' and 'stable-alterable' and proposed instead the following 3 categories: with equal tones and unequal semitones; completely flexible; with both equal tones and equal semitones. The main conclusion of Artusi's dialogue was that a major imperfection of modern music stemmed from the fact that musicians had not yet calculated a way to tune instruments so that they could all play together and that any melody could be transposed to any key. Denouncing the syntonic diatonic of Ptolemy supported by Zarlino and Bottrigari as opening the way to a flood of difficulties, the interlocutors agreed that only the equal tones and equal semitones of Aristoxenus could satisfy the needs of modern music (f.34r).

WORKS
Canzonette, 4vv, libro I (Venice, 1598)
Cantate Domino, 8vv, in 1599[2]

WRITINGS
L'arte del contraponto ridotta in tavole (Venice, 1586)
Lettera apologetica del Burla academico Burlesco al R. D. Vincentio Spada da Faenza, 14 Jan 1588; lost, except for excerpts in Bottrigari
Seconda parte dell'arte del contraponto, nella quale si tratta dell'utile et uso delle dissonanze (Venice, 1589)
Trattato apologetico in difesa dell'opere del ... Zarlino da Chioggia, giuditio musicale del S. Cabalao Nobile di Pocceia, academico Infarinato intorno alle differenze note frà il Dottissimo Zarlino, et ... Vincenzo Galilej nobile Fiorentino, 8 April 1590; lost, except for excerpts in Bottrigari
L'arte del contraponto (Venice, 1598)
L'Artusi, overo Delle imperfettioni della moderna musica ragionamenti dui (Venice, 1600/R1969)
Letter of dedication and preface to E. Bottrigari: *Il desiderio, dialogo di Annibale Melone* (Milan, 1601)
Seconda parte dell'Artusi overo Delle imperfettioni della moderna musica (Venice, 1603/R1969) [with appendix: *Considerationi musicali*]
Impresa del molto rev. Gioseffo Zarlino da Chioggia ... dichiarata (Bologna, 1604)
Discorso secondo musicale di Antonio Braccino da Todi per la dichiaratione della lettera posta ne' Scherzi musicali del sig. Claudio Monteverdi (Venice, 1608)

BIBLIOGRAPHY
E. Bottrigari: *Lettera di Federico Verdicelli ... in difesa del Sig. Cav. Hercole Bottrigaro, contro quanto ... di lui ha scritto un certo Artusi* (Milan, 1601; MS copy, *I-Bc* I.68)
Aletelogia di Leonardo Gallucio ... per la difesa del M.I. sig. Cav. Hercole Bottrigaro, contra a quanto ha scritto lo autore delle

Inconsiderationi musicali (26 Feb 1604; MSS, *I-Bc* B.43, *Bu* 345 Busta III no.4)
G. C. Trombelli: *Memorie istoriche concernenti le due canoniche di S. Maria di Reno et di S. Salvatore* (Bologna, 1752)
G. Gaspari: 'Dei musicisti bolognesi al XVI secolo', *Atti e memorie della R. deputazione di storia patria per la provincia di Romagna*, ii (1876), 55
D. Arnold: '"Seconda Pratica": a Background to Monteverdi's Madrigals', *ML*, xxxviii (1957), 341
C. Dahlhaus: 'Zur Theorie des klassischen Kontrapunkts', *KJb*, xlv (1961), 47
D. Arnold: *Monteverdi* (London, 1963)
A. Damerini: 'G. M. Artusi e alcune sue opere teoriche', *Le celebrazioni del 1963 e alcune nuove indagini sulla musica italiana del XIII e XIX secolo*, Chigiana, xx (1963), 9
C. V. Palisca: 'The Artusi–Monteverdi Controversy', *The Monteverdi Companion*, ed. D. Arnold and N. Fortune (London 1968), 133–66
CLAUDE V. PALISCA

Artusini, Antonio (*b* Ravenna, baptized 2 Oct 1554; *d* Ravenna, before 6 May 1604). Italian composer, lawyer, poet and orator. His only known musical work is *Il primo libro de madrigali a cinque voci* (Venice, 1598) which contains 23 madrigals, including a setting of Guarini's popular *Ah dolente partita*. His poetic writings include a canzonetta on the death of Cristina Racchi Lunardi.

BIBLIOGRAPHY
S. Pasolini: *Huomini illustri di Ravenna antica* (Bologna, 1703), 99
P. P. Ginanni, ed.: *Rime scelte de' poeti ravennati antichi, e moderni defunti* (Ravenna, 1739), 61f, 413
P. P. Ginanni: *Memorie storico-critiche degli scrittori ravennati*, i (Faenza, 1769), 58f
PIER PAOLO SCATTOLIN

Arundell [Arundel], **Dennis (Drew)** (*b* Finchley, London, 22 July 1898). English opera producer, writer and composer. He studied the piano under his mother (both his parents were musicians) from the age of six, and was educated at Tonbridge School (1912–17) and St John's College, Cambridge (1919–29), where he read classics and music and became a Fellow. His musical studies were under C. B. Rootham, Henry Moule and Stanford. He made appearances as an actor, and singer, from 1926, and from 1929 was a professional actor and producer, for radio and later television as well as the musical and non-musical stage. An influential figure in English musical–theatrical life for many years, his opera and masque productions cover a remarkably wide historical range: from Locke (*Cupid and Death*, London, 1929), Purcell (*Fairy Queen*, in Hyde Park, London, 1927, which he conducted; also Cambridge, 1931), John Eccles (*Judgment of Paris*, Cambridge, 1923) and Handel (*Semele*, stage première, Cambridge, 1925) to Delius (*Irmelin*, première, Oxford, 1953), Janáček (*Kat'á Kabanová*, British première, London, 1950), Britten (*Peter Grimes*, Helsinki, 1949), Honegger (*Le roi David*, British première, Cambridge, 1929) and Stravinsky (*Soldier's Tale*, British première, Cambridge, 1928); he has also produced many works in the standard repertory, including several Mozart operas, as well as Balfe's *Bohemian Girl* at Covent Garden under Sir Thomas Beecham, with whom he several times worked. His productions are noted for their sense of style, their dramatic vigour and their stage mastery.

Arundell has written many articles, mostly on matters concerning musical drama, as well as several books. He has been a prolific composer of theatre music, including operas (*Ghost of Abel* and *A Midsummer Night's Dream*) and incidental music for plays, films, radio and television, mostly unpublished. He was appointed to the staff of the Royal College of Music Opera School in 1956, and was Crees lecturer at the college in 1971; he was made FRCM in that year. In 1974 he was appointed opera producer and coach at the Royal Northern College of Music, Manchester, and in 1975–6 he produced *Hänsel und Gretel* and *Don Pasquale* in Melbourne.

WRITINGS

Henry Purcell (London, 1927)
The Critic at the Opera (London, 1957)
The Story of Sadler's Wells (London, 1965)
Introduction to Le nozze di Figaro and Così fan tutte (London, 1971)

ERIC BLOM/R

Arutyunyan, Alexander Grigori. *See* HARUT'UNYAN, ALEXANDER GRIGORI.

As (Ger.). A♭; *see* PITCH NAMES.

Asaf'yev, Boris Vladimirovich [Glebov, Igor] (*b* St Petersburg, 29 June 1884; *d* Moscow, 27 Jan 1949). Soviet musicologist and composer. He received his general musical education at the Gymnasium in Kronstadt, and in 1908 graduated in history and philology from St Petersburg University. He studied orchestration with Rimsky-Korsakov and composition with Lyadov at the St Petersburg Conservatory (1904–10), and from 1910 was répétiteur at the Mariinsky Theatre. After the 1917 revolution, he organized, with the help of Lyapunov and Bulich, the music department of the Petrograd Institute for the History of the Arts (now the Leningrad Institute of Theatre, Music and Cinematography), and from 1920 was director of its music history department. From 1925 to 1943 he was professor of history, theory and composition at the Leningrad Conservatory, where he also founded the musicology department. Also in the 1920s he was an active member of the Leningrad branch of the Association for Contemporary Music, arranging concerts of contemporary Western music and contributing articles on aspects of modern music to a number of journals. In 1943 he moved to Moscow to become professor and director of the research section of the Moscow Conservatory, a senior research fellow at the Institute for the History of the Arts, and a consultant to the Bol'shoy Theatre; he was also chairman of the Union of Soviet Composers (1948–9).

Asaf'yev began his career as a musicologist in the 1920s with various writings on 19th-century Russian music, and produced the first Russian book on Stravinsky, *Kniga o Stravinskom* (Leningrad, 1929). During the 1930s he was occupied primarily with composition, writing several operas, symphonies, songs and piano works, and incidental music to a number of plays. He returned to academic work in the 1940s with further writings on Russian music and the second volume of his important theoretical work *Muzïkal'naya forma kak protsess* ('Musical form as a process', Moscow, 1947), in which he expounded his influential theories of music 'intonation', a term which, in Russian, has broader implications than in English, embracing the diverse expressive aspects of musical form. On the basis of this theory, he produced several analyses of the Russian classics, including Tchaikovsky's *Eugene Onegin* and *The Sorceress*. As a scholar of 19th-century Russian music, Asaf'yev was also responsible, with Pavel Lamm, for important studies of Musorgsky's manuscripts.

WORKS
(selective list)

STAGE

Operas: Zolushka [Cinderella] (2, L. A. Levandovskaya), 1906; Snezhnaya koroleva [The snow queen] (4, S. M. and V. M. Martïnov), 1907; Minin i Pozharsky (4, M. A. Bulgakov), 1936; Mednïy vsadnik [The bronze horseman] (sym.-monodrama, 8 episodes, after Pushkin), 1940; 7 others

Ballets: Belaya liliya [The white lily] (3 scenes, N. M. Leont'yev), 1910; Dar fei (3 scenes, I. N. Kusov), 1910; Ledyanaya deva [The ice maiden] (Sol'veyg) (3, B. G. Romanov) [after Grieg], 1918; Plamya Parizha [The flame of Paris] (4, N. D. Volkov, V. V. Dmitriyev), 1932; Bakhchisarayskiy fontan [The fountain of Bakhchisaray] (4, Volkov, after Pushkin), 1933; Utrachennïye illyuzii [Lost illusions] (3, Dmitriyev, after Balzac), 1935; Kavkazskiy plennik [The prisoner of the Caucasus] (3, Volkov, after Pushkin), 1936; Krasavitsa Radda [Radda the beauty] (3, Volkov, after Gor'ky), 1937; Barïshnya-krest'yanka [The peasant princess] (6 scenes, Volkov, after Pushkin), 1945; Vesennyaya skazka [A spring fairy tale] (3, Yu. O. Slonimsky, after trad.) [after Tchaikovsky], 1946; 18 others

OTHER WORKS

Orch: Sym. no.1 'Pamyati Lermontova' [In memory of Lermontov], b, 1938; Sym. no.2 'Iz epokhi krest'yanskikh vosstaniy' [From the age of the peasant uprisings], f♯, 1938; Sym. no.3 'Rodina' [Homeland], C, 1938–42; Sym. no.4 'Privetstvennaya' [Welcome], B♭, 1938–42; Sym. no.5 'Vremena goda' [The seasons], 1942, inc.; 3 works, wind orch; Suite, folk orch

Chamber music, pf pieces, songs etc

For complete list see *Akademik B. V. Asaf'yev: izbrannïye trudï*, v (Moscow, 1957), 374

WRITINGS

Items marked with an asterisk written under the name Asaf'yev; all others written under the pseudonym Igor Glebov

Russkaya poeziya v russkoy muzïke [Russian poetry in Russian music] (Petrograd, 1921, rev., enlarged 2/1922)

Skryabin: opït kharakeristiki [A descriptive essay] (Petrograd, 1921, 2/1923)

Frants List: opït kharakeristiki (Petrograd, 1922)

Instrumental'noye tvorchestvo Chaykovskovo [Tchaikovsky's instrumental works] (Petrograd, 1922)

Pyotr Il'ich Chaykovsky: evo zhizn' i tvorchestvo [Life and works] (Petrograd, 1922)

Shopen: opït kharakeristiki (Petrograd, 1922)

Simfonicheskiye etyudï [Symphonic studies] (Petrograd, 1922, 2/1968) [collection of articles on Russian music]

Musorgsky: opït kharakeristiki (Moscow, 1923)

Glazunov: opït kharakeristiki (Leningrad, 1924)

'O politonal'nosti' [Polytonality], *Sovremennaya muzïka* (1925), no.7, p.9

'Stroitel'stvo sovremennoy simfonii' [The structure of the contemporary symphony], *Sovremennaya muzïka* (1925), no.8, p.29

Anton Grigor'yevich Rubinshteyn v evo muzïkal'noy deyatel'nosti i otzïvakh sovremennikov [Rubinstein's musical activities and opinions of his contemporaries] (Moscow, 1929)

Kniga o Stravinskom [A book about Stravinsky] (Leningrad, 1929)

*Muzïkal'naya forma kak protsess [Musical form as a process], i (Moscow, 1930–47, 2/1963 ed. E. M. Orlova, 3/1971; Cz. trans., 1965; Ger. trans., 1976)

*Russkaya muzïka ot nachala XIX stoletiya [Russian music from the beginning of the 19th century] (Moscow, 1930, 2/1968 ed. E. M. Orlova as *Russkaya muzïka: XIX i nachala XX veka* [Russian music: the 19th and early 20th centuries])

*M. I. Glinka: k 100-letiyu so dnya pervovo predstavleniya operï Ruslan i Lyudmila [Glinka: on the centenary of the first performance of *Ruslan and Lyudmila*] (Leningrad, 1942)

'Cherez proshloye k budush chemu' [Through the past to the future], *SovM: sbornik* (1943), no.1, p.7; (1944), no.2, p.3

*Evgeny Onegin, liricheskiye stseni P. I. Chaykovskovo: opït intonatsionnovo analiza stilya i muzïkal'noy dramaturgii [Eugene Onegin, Tchaikovsky's lyric scenes: an attempt at intonation analysis of style and musical dramaturgy] (Moscow and Leningrad, 1944; Ger. trans., 1949)

*Nikolay Andreyevich Rimsky-Korsakov (1844–1944): k 100-letiyu so dnya rozhdeniya [Rimsky-Korsakov: on the centenary of his birth] (Moscow and Leningrad, 1944)

*Kompozitorï pervoy polovinï XIX veka: russkaya klassicheskaya muzïka [Composers of the first half of the 19th century: Russian classical music] (Moscow, 1945)

S. V. Rakhmaninov (Moscow, 1945)

'Sovetskaya muzïka i muzïkal'naya kul'tura: opït vïvedeniya osnovnïkh printsipov' [Soviet music and musical culture: an attempt to find its basic principles], *SovM: sbornik* (1946), no.5, p.3

Charodeyka, opera P. I. Chaykovskovo: opït raskrïtiya intonatsionnovo soderzhaniya [Tchaikovsky's opera *The Sorceress*: an attempt to reveal its tonal content] (Moscow and Leningrad, 1947)
Glinka (Moscow, 1947, 2/1950)
Grig (1843–1907): issledovaniye [Grieg: research] (Moscow and Leningrad, 1948)
'Pushkin v russkoy muzïke', *SovM* (1949), no.6, p.7
Izbrannïye stat'i o russkoy muzïke [Selected articles on Russian music], i, ed. N. Braudo (Moscow, 1952)
Izbrannïye trudï [Selected works], ed. T. N. Livanova and others (Moscow, 1952–7) [vol.v contains complete list of works]
'Mïsli o sovetskoy muzïke' [Thoughts on Soviet music], *SovM* (1952), no.11, p.12
Izbrannïye stat'i o muzïkal'nom obrazovanii i prosveshchenii [Selected articles on musical training and education], ed. E. M. Orlova (Leningrad, 1965)
Kriticheskiye stat'i, ocherki i retsenzii [Critical articles, essays and reviews], ed. I. V. Beletsky (Moscow, 1967)
Ob opere: izbranniye stat'i (Leningrad, 1976) [collected opera criticism]

BIBLIOGRAPHY
B. V. Asaf'yev: 'Moy put'' [Autobiography], *SovM* (1934), no.8, p.47
V. Bogdanov-Berezovsky: *B. V. Asaf'yev* (Moscow and Leningrad, 1937)
A. V. Ossovsky: *B. V. Asaf'yev: sovetskaya muzïka* (Moscow, 1945)
B. V. Asaf'yev: 'Moya tvorcheskaya rabota v Leningrade v pervïye godï Velikoy Otechestvennoy voynï' [My creative work in Leningrad during the early years of World War II], *SovM* (1946), no.10, p.90
D. B. Kabalevsky, ed.: *Pamyati akademika Borisa Vladimirovicha Asaf'yeva* [In memory of academician Asaf'yev] (Moscow, 1951)
D. B. Kabalevsky: *B. V. Asaf'yev – Igor Glebov* (Moscow, 1954)
E. M. Orlova: 'Rabotï B. V. Asaf'yeva o A. G. Rubinshteyne, A. K. Glazunove, A. K. Lyadove, S. I. Taneyeve, S. V. Rakhmaninove i drugikh russkikh kompozitorakh-klassikakh' [Asaf'yev's works on Rubinstein, Glazunov, Lyadov, Taneyev, Rakhmaninov and other classical Russian composers], *B. V. Asaf'yev: izbrannïye trudï*, ii, ed. E. M. Orlova and V. V. Protopopov (Moscow, 1954), 193
——: 'Rabotï B. V. Asaf'yeva o Musorgskom, Rimskom-Korsokove, Borodine, Balakireve i Stasove', *B. V. Asaf'yev: izbrannïye trudï*, iii, ed. E. M. Orlova (Moscow, 1954), 3
V. V. Protopopov: 'Rabotï B. V. Asaf'yeva o haykovskom', *B. V. Asaf'yev: izbrannïye trudï*, ii, ed. E. M. Orlova and V. V. Protopopov (Moscow, 1954), 5
T. N. Livanova and V. A. Vasina-Grossman: 'Rabotï B. V. Asaf'yeva o zarubezhnoy muzïke' [Asaf'yev's works on foreign music], *B. V. Asaf'yev: izbrannïye trudï*, iv, ed. T. N. Livanova and V. A. Vasina-Grossman (Moscow, 1955), 193
V. A. Vasina-Grossman: 'Russkaya muzïkal'naya kul'tura v rabotakh B. V. Asaf'yeva' [Russian musical culture in the works of Asaf'yev], *B. V. Asaf'yev: izbrannïye trudï*, iv, ed. T. N. Livanova and V. A. Vasina-Grossman (Moscow, 1955), 5
A. D. Alexeyev and V. A. Vasina-Grossman, eds.: *Istoriya russkoy muzïki* (Moscow, 1956–9)
M. A. Rïbnikova: *Baletï Asaf'yeva* [Asaf'yev's ballets] (Moscow, 1956)
D. B. Kabalevsky: 'Sovetskaya muzïke v rabotakh B. V. Asaf'yeva' [Soviet music in Asaf'yev's works], *B. V. Asaf'yev: izbrannïye trudï*, v, ed. D. B. Kabalevsky and others (Moscow, 1957), 5
L. A. Mazel: 'O muzïkal'no-teoreticheskoy kontseptsii B. Asaf'yeva' [Asaf'yev's concepts of music theory], *SovM* (1957), no.3, p.73
M. Montagu-Nathan: 'The Strange Case of Professor Assafiev', *ML*, xxxviii (1957), 335
E. M. Orlova: 'Issledovaniye B. V. Asaf'yeva Intonatsiya' [Asaf'yev's study *Intonation*], *B. V. Asaf'yev: izbrannïye trudï*, v, ed. D. B. Kabalevsky and others (Moscow, 1957), 153
V. Kučera: 'Vývoj a obsah Asaf'jevovy intonacni teorie' [Development and content of Asaf'yev's intonation theory], *HV, 1961*, no.4, p.7
M. A. Rïbnikova: 'Baletï B. V. Asaf'yeva Plamya Parizha i Bakhchisarayskiy fontan' [Asaf'yev's ballets *The Flame of Paris* and *The Fountain of Bakhchisaray*], *Muzïka sovetskovo baleta*, ed. L. N. Raaben and others (Moscow, 1962), 163–99
E. M. Orlova: *B. V. Asaf'yev: put' issledovatel'ya i publitsista* [Asaf'yev's development as a researcher and writer] (Leningrad, 1964)
J. Jiránek: *Asafajevova teorie intonace: jeji geneze a vyznam* [Asaf'yev's intonation theory: its origins and significance] (Prague, 1967)
——: 'Nové asafjevovské publikace v SSSR' [New publications on Asaf'yev in the USSR], *HV*, iv (1967), 589
G. B. Bernandt and I. M. Yampol'sky: *Kto pisal o muzïke* [Writers on music], i (Moscow, 1971) [incl. list of writings]
J. Jiránek: 'Statistika jako pomocný nástroj intonacní analýzy' [Statistics as an auxiliary means to intonation analysis], *HV*, vii (1971), 165
——: 'Assafjews Intonationslehre und ihre Perspektiven', *De musica disputationes pragensis*, i (1972), 13–45

GEOFFREY NORRIS

Asas (Ger.). A♭♭; *see* PITCH NAMES.

ASCAP. American Society of Composers, Authors and Publishers; *see* COPYRIGHT COLLECTING SOCIETIES, §IV.

Aschenbrenner, Christian Heinrich (*b* Stettin, 29 Dec 1654; *d* Jena, 13 Dec 1732). German composer and violinist. He was taught the violin by his father, a Stettin town musician, and in 1668 he received composition lessons from Johann Theile. He studied with J. H. Schmeltzer in Vienna in 1676 and 1677 and in the latter year became a violinist in the Hofkapelle at Zeitz, where he remained until the Kapelle was disbanded in 1682. In the following year he became Konzertmeister in the Hofkapelle at Merseburg. There he enjoyed friendly relations with the Hofkapellmeister, David Pohle, whom he had known when he held a similar position at Zeitz from 1680 to 1682. In 1695 Aschenbrenner returned to Zeitz, where he was director of music until, in 1713, he went back to Merseburg as Hofkapellmeister. He still, however, retained an honorary title from Zeitz as 'Kapellmeister von Haus aus', though this cannot have continued beyond 1718, when the death of the reigning duke at Zeitz put an end to musical life at the court there. He retired from Merseburg in 1719 and from then until his death lived at Jena on a small pension provided by Duke Moritz Wilhelm of Merseburg. He twice went to Vienna as a performer – in 1692, when he dedicated six violin sonatas to the Emperor Leopold I, and in 1703. His compositions, of which only two sacred vocal pieces survive, were known throughout Saxony and Thuringia, as is evident from their inclusion in inventories and catalogues of the time.

WORKS
(all printed works lost)

Gast- und Hochzeit-Freude, bestehend in Sonaten, Präludien, Allemanden, Curanten, Balletten, Arien, Sarabanten, 3–6vv, bc (Leipzig, 1673)
Sonaten, Praeludien . . . etc, 3–6vv, bc (Leipzig, 1675)
Die Seele Christi heilige mich, 4vv, 4 insts, *S-Uu*
O Jesu süss, wer dein gedenkt, 3vv, 3 insts, bc, *D-Bds*

2 masses, 10vv, lost
14 motets, 1–16vv, 1–8 insts, lost
5 secular songs, 1–3vv, 1, 2 insts, lost
6 sonatas for Viennese court, 1692, lost
18 sonatas, insts, lost
1 sonata, va da gamba, lost, mentioned in Rudolstadt inventory (see Baselt)

BIBLIOGRAPHY
EitnerQ; *Fétis B*; *Gerber NL*; *Walther ML*
A. Göhler: *Verzeichnis der in den Frankfurter und Leipziger Messkatalogen der Jahre 1564–1759 angezeigten Musikalien* (Leipzig, 1902/R1965)
M. Seiffert: 'Die Chorbibliothek der St. Michaelisschule in Lüneburg zu Seb. Bachs Zeit', *SIMG*, ix (1907–8), 593
A. Werner: *Städtische und fürstliche Musikpflege in Zeitz bis zum Anfange des 19. Jahrhunderts* (Bückeburg and Leipzig, 1922)
O. Dörfer: 'Chr. H. Aschenbrenner. Gestorben 1732 in Jena. – Wo sind seine Notenhandschriften?', *Das Thüringer Fähnlein*, v (1936)
E. Wennig: 'Von den Anfängen bis zum Jahre 1750', *Chronik des musikalischen Lebens der Stadt Jena* (Jena, 1937)
W. Serauky: *Musikgeschichte der Stadt Halle*, ii/1 (Halle and Berlin, 1939/R1970)
B. Baselt: 'Die Musikaliensammlung der Schwarzburg-Rudolstädtischen Hofkapelle unter Philipp Heinrich Erlebach', *Traditionen und Aufgaben der hallischen Musikwissenschaft: Wissenschaftliche Zeitschrift der Universität Halle*, suppl. (1963), 105–34
F. Krummacher: *Die Überlieferung der Choralbearbeitungen in der frühen evangelischen Kantate* (Berlin, 1965)
H. Engel: *Musik in Thüringen* (Cologne and Graz, 1966), 198
A. Schmiedecke: 'Aufführungen von Opern, Operetten, Serenaden und Kantaten am Zeitzer Herzogshof', *Mf*, xxv (1972), 169

KARL-ERNST BERGUNDER

Ascherberg, Hopwood & Crew. English music publishers. The firm was the outcome of an amalgamation in 1906 of Eugene Ascherberg & Co. (founded 1878) and Hopwood & Crew (founded 1860), together with their subsidiaries, the music publishers Duncan Davison & Co., John Blockley, Orsborn & Co. and Howard & Co. Their substantial catalogue covered music of every description, but was based mainly on light music including the waltzes of Waldteufel, Archibald Joyce and Charles Ancliffe. Among their successful stage works were the operettas *The Geisha* and *The Belle of New York*, and later musical comedies such as *The Maid of the Mountains* and *The Last Waltz*. The firm also held the British copyrights for Mascagni's *Cavalleria rusticana* and Leoncavallo's *Pagliacci*. Its many instrumental and choral series included works by Elgar, Reger and Coleridge-Taylor. In 1970 the firm was taken over by CHAPPELL.

BIBLIOGRAPHY
'The Music Publisher of Tradition: Ascherberg and his Amalgamations', *MO*, lxiv (1940–41), 508
J. A. FULLER MAITLAND/PETER WARD JONES

Aschpellmayr, Franz. *See* ASPLMAYR, FRANZ.

Asciolla, Dino [Edoardo] (*b* Rome, 9 June 1920). Italian violist and violinist. He studied the violin and viola at the Rome Conservatory and later attended master classes at the Accademia di S Cecilia, Rome, and at the Accademia Chigiana, Siena. He began his career as a violinist and won the 1950 Vivaldi Competition at Venice. For a time he was leader of the Scarlatti Orchestra and the Salzburg Mozarteum Orchestra, but he later concentrated on the viola and became one of its best-known exponents. Firmino Sifonia, Ennio Morricone, Domenico Guaccero and Manuel De Sica are among the composers who have written works for him. He has an international reputation as a soloist and chamber player, having toured widely with various ensembles such as the Virtuosi di Roma, I Musici, the Boccherini Quintet, Chigi Quintet and Rome Quartet. He plays a Maggini viola, a rare instrument from the 17th-century Brescia school. His recordings include Paganini's Sonata for viola and orchestra, in which his performance is distinguished by richness of tone and flexibility of technique. He teaches at the Aquila Conservatory.

PIERO RATTALINO

Ascone, Vicente (*b* Siderno, Calabria, 16 Aug 1897). Uruguayan composer of Italian birth. Early in life he moved with his family to Montevideo, where he studied harmony and composition with Luis Sambucetti, and the trumpet with Aquiles Gubitosi. He was for several years first trumpet and soloist with the Montevideo Radio SO, which he conducted occasionally, and from 1940 to 1954 he directed the municipal band of Montevideo. He has also taught harmony at the Montevideo Verdi Institute, and wind and percussion instruments at the Municipal School of Music, where he was later appointed director and professor of harmony. In 1938 the Venezuelan government asked him to establish a course for teaching choral music at the experimental music schools in Caracas; during his stay he composed *Venezuela*, a book of school songs. A prolific composer whose music has a nationalist character, he has received various national awards and his works have been favourably received outside Uruguay. Among his later compositions, the Trumpet Concerto (1969) places strongly rhythmic outer movements, in unstable harmonies and with reminiscences of military music, against a tonal, lyrical second movement consisting primarily of an extended melody by the trumpet soloist.

WORKS
(selective list)
Stage: Paraná Guazú (opera, 4), 1930; Santos Vega (incidental music), 1953
Orch: Suite uruguaya, 1926; Preludio y marcha de los bramines, 1926; 3 syms., 1948, 1955, 1964; Politonal, pf, orch, 1967; Tpt Conc., 1969; Vn Conc., 1970
Principal publishers: Andebu (Montevideo), Ricordi Americana

BIBLIOGRAPHY
Composers of the Americas, xvi (Washington, DC, 1970), 23ff
JOHN M. SCHECHTER

Ascot, Rosa García. Pianist and composer, wife of JESÚS BAL Y GAY.

Asenjo Barbieri, Francisco. *See* BARBIERI, FRANCISCO ASENJO.

Ásgeirsson, Jón (*b* Ísafjördur, 11 Oct 1928). Icelandic critic, composer and teacher. He studied at the Reykjavík College of Music with Urbancic and Kristjánsson, and in England (1957–8, 1965). A former president of the Icelandic Composers' Society, he teaches at the conservatory and the Icelandic Teachers' University in Reykjavík, and is music critic of the *Morgenbladid*. His works are mainly traditional in style, though he has written a few serial compositions. He is particularly interested in reviving Icelandic folksongs and dances and has set related folk poetry found without music; he has also served as music director for productions of the ancient dances by the National Dance Company.

WORKS
(selective list)
Opera: Thrymskvida (5, after Elder edda), Reykjavík, National, 1974
Orch: Sjöstrengjaljod [A poem of 7 strings], str, 1968; Lilja, sym. poem, 1971
Vocal: Time and Water (S. Steinarr), 7 songs, 1971; Oljo (J. úr Kötlum), children's chorus, 1974
Chamber: Wind Qnt, 1971

BIBLIOGRAPHY
A. Burt: *Iceland's Twentieth-century Composers and a Listing of their Works* (Fairfax, Virginia, in preparation)
AMANDA M. BURT

Ashanti music. The Ashanti are a dominant and culturally important ethnic group in Ghana. They number about 1,500,000 and are grouped politically in large territorial units; each unit is headed by a paramount chief under whom are district chiefs of different ranks. The constitutional head of Ashanti is the Asantehene, to whom all paramount chiefs owe allegiance. In the precolonial period the Ashanti sphere of influence spread over many parts of Ghana and extended westwards to the borders of the Ivory Coast and eastwards across the Volta.

1. Musical organization. 2. Musical instruments. 3. Vocal music.

1. MUSICAL ORGANIZATION. The traditional political organization of the Ashanti is reflected in their music. Thus the music of the court is separate from that of the community, while the hierarchical ordering of chiefs under the Asantehene is reflected in the number and

types of instruments and ensembles that each royal court may have. Court music is performed on state occasions and festivals, whereas community music is performed on all other social occasions. The music of the community is organized according to its social groups, so that the community's musical repertory is much larger than that of the court. Although there is no idiomatic differentiation between court music and community music, the music of the court tends to be more sophisticated or elaborate in organization, and more complex in structure. Because of this the training and recruitment of court musicians is institutionalized.

2. MUSICAL INSTRUMENTS. In Ashanti music there is a greater emphasis on the use of idiophones and membranophones than on other instrumental types. Idiophones include *dawuro* and *nnawuta* (single and double clapperless bells); *firikyiwa* (iron vessel clappers or castanets); *torowa* (vessel rattles); *astratoa* (concussion rattles); *mmaa* (stick clappers); *sraka* (scraped idiophones); and *prempensua* (large lamellaphones used as substitutes for drums). The flat board lamellaphone with five wooden lamellae is no longer widely used.

Ashanti membranophones are generally single-headed and open-ended. They fall into three groups: *twenesin* (signal drums), *akukuadwo* and *atumpan* which are the principal talking drums of the court, and those drums played in ensembles either as basic supporting drums, or as master drums. A few closed or double-headed membranophones such as the *donno* (hourglass drum) and *gyamadudu* (large cylindrical drum) as well as some frame drums are also used.

Aerophones include two varieties of flute: the *atenteben* (bamboo flute) and the *odurugya* (cane flute) played at the court of the Asantehene. Court trumpets are made from animal horns or elephant tusks and are played hocket fashion in ensembles of five or seven instruments. Chordophones are rare, and only the *benta* (mouth-resonated bow) and the *seperewa* (harp-lute) are found.

3. VOCAL MUSIC. With the exception of the *kwadwom* historical chant and the song preludes of *kete* drum music and dance, the music of the court is almost entirely instrumental, while that of the community emphasizes vocal music. Ashanti songs are based on a diatonic scale with a descending tendency in the mèlodic line. Melodic movement within the phrase is limited to 2nds, 3rds and 4ths and may be stepwise, interlocking or pendular. The singing of simultaneous melodies in parallel 3rds and the use of solo–chorus forms in alternating or overlapping sections are dominant characteristics of Ashanti vocal style. As Asante is a tone language, the melodic contour follows the intonation contour of speech. The rhythm of songs similarly follows speech rhythm closely. Hence spoken verse, declamations and other styles which treat song as an extension of speech are particularly prominent in Ashanti music.

BIBLIOGRAPHY
J. H. Nketia: *African Music in Ghana* (London, 1962)
——: *Drumming in Akan Communities of Ghana* (London, 1963)
——: *Folk Songs of Ghana* (London, 1963)
J. H. NKETIA

Ashbrook, William (Sinclair) (*b* Philadelphia, 28 Jan 1922). American scholar and musicologist. He received a BA from the University of Pennsylvania in 1946 and an MA from Harvard University in 1947. Since 1955 he has been a member of the humanities department at Indiana State University; he was appointed professor of English and humanities in 1963 and chairman of the humanities department in 1972. Although trained as a teacher of English literature, Ashbrook also has a lively interest in Italian opera and has contributed numerous articles on the subject for *Opera News*. His books on Donizetti and Puccini are particularly valuable for the careful presentation of biographical material, the discussion of the literary and dramatic aspects of the operas and the description of the various revisions.

WRITINGS
'Anna Bolena', *MT*, cvi (1965), 432
Donizetti (London, 1965)
The Operas of Puccini (New York, 1968)
PAULA MORGAN

Ashdown, Edwin (*b* 1826; *d* 1912). English music publisher. He and Henry John Parry were employed by Wessel & Co. and took over the business on the retirement of CHRISTIAN RUDOLPH WESSEL in 1860; the firm then became known as Ashdown & Parry. Parry retired in 1882 and the firm's name changed to Edwin Ashdown, becoming a limited company in 1891. The firm's publications included much new English music and the short-lived periodical *Hanover Square* (1867–9), edited by the pianist Lindsay Sloper, which consisted largely of new music. Composers in their catalogue included G. A. Macfarren, Sullivan, Elgar and Vaughan Williams, and for many years the firm was also the English agent for BOTE & BOCK of Berlin. Piano and choral music and solo songs came to form the core of their publishing activities. Ashdown also took over the music publishing firms of Hatzfeld & Co. (1903), Enoch & Co. (1927) and J. H. Larway (1929).

BIBLIOGRAPHY
'Mr. Edwin Ashdown', *Musical Herald* (1903), 99
'The House of Ashdown', *The Windmill*, i/13 (1958), 9
PETER WARD JONES

Ashe, Andrew (*b* Lisburn, Co. Antrim, *c*1759; *d* Dublin, 1838). Irish flautist. When 12 he was adopted by Baron Bentinck and travelled widely with him in Europe. At 16 his dissatisfaction with the contemporary one-keyed flute led him for a time to abandon that instrument. He met the flautist Vanhall at The Hague in 1774 and obtained from him a six-keyed flute. By 1778 he had become the first flute at the Brussels Opera, but returned to Ireland four years later and was engaged by Saloman in 1791 for his Haydn concerts in London, where he made a solo début the next year. He succeeded Monzani at the King's Theatre *c*1800, and in 1810 became director of the Bath concerts on the death of Rauzzini, whose pupil, Miss Comer, he had married in 1799. He was made professor at the RAM (1822) but in the same year returned finally to Dublin. Ashe's ability and wide travels made him an influential advocate of the flute with 'the extra keys' when this was still much opposed by older players.

PHILIP BATE

Ashewell, Thomas. *See* ASHWELL, THOMAS.

Ashkenazy [Ashkenazi], Vladimir (Davidovich) (*b* Gorky, 6 July 1937). Soviet pianist. He began piano lessons at the age of six, and made his Moscow début two years later, in 1945. For ten years his teacher at the Moscòw Central School of Music was Anaida Sumbatyan. In 1955 he entered Lev Oborin's class at the Moscow Conservatory. That year he gained second prize in the Fifth Warsaw International Chopin Competition; the following year, in another competition – the Queen Elisabeth International in Brussels – he won the gold medal. Before graduating from the conservatory in 1960 he had already toured the USA in 1958. In May 1962 he shared first prize with John Ogdon in the Second Tchaikovsky Competition in Moscow. A year later (7 March) he made his London début in a Festival Hall orchestral concert. Its success, and that of a subsequent Festival Hall recital, was triumphant.

Ashkenazy is generally considered the finest of the younger Russian pianists. His playing combines intellectual probity with warm and sincere feeling, and is marked by exceptional sensitivity to tone colour and delicacy of fingerwork. He has displayed considerable insight into the music of Mozart, and is a renowned interpreter of Skryabin, Rakhmaninov and Prokofiev. His repertory, as soloist and chamber pianist, includes the masterworks of Beethoven, Schubert, Schumann, Brahms, Chopin and Liszt. He has made many recordings. From 1963 to 1968 he lived in England and after that in Iceland, where in 1971 he was awarded the Order of the Falcon. He took Icelandic nationality in 1972.

MAX LOPPERT

Ashley. English family of musicians active in London and the provinces c1780–1830.

(1) John Ashley (b ?London, 1734; d London, 14 March 1805). Bassoonist and conductor. He was first bassoon at Covent Garden Theatre, and became more widely known after his success as assistant conductor to Joah Bates at the 1784 Commemoration of Handel in Westminster Abbey. Charles Burney (*An Account of the Musical Performances...in Commemoration of Handel*; London, 1785) records that the 'unwearied zeal and diligence' of 'Mr John Ashly of the Guards ... were constantly employed with such intelligence and success, as greatly facilitated the advancement of the plan'. According to Burney he was also the 'Mr Ashley' who played the then novel double bassoon at these celebrations. Secondary evidence supports this identification although Barclay Squire (*DNB*) and Edward F. Rimbault (*Grove 1*) suggest Ashley's brother Jane (b ?London, 1740; d London, 9 April 1809) as the instrumentalist. Ashley's four sons (see below) also took part in the commemoration and later in 1784 the whole family first appeared in the provinces at the Hereford meeting of the Three Choirs; they took part in subsequent Handel commemorations and from 1789 were regularly billed at Ranelagh Gardens.

On this experience, and sometimes working in conjunction with a local musician, Ashley promoted some 13 two-, three- and four-day 'Grand Musical Festivals' in provincial towns from Portsmouth to Newcastle upon Tyne in the summers between 1788 and 1793. His sons led various sections of the orchestra and he engaged professional singers from the London theatres together with leading chorus singers from the Antient Concerts and boys from the Chapel Royal. Local rank-and-file singers and instrumentalists augmented the touring troupe. His interest in such ventures waned when he became director of the Lenten Oratorios at Covent Garden in 1795, a position he held until his death, although in 1801 he arranged an impressive five-town festival tour through East Anglia.

Ashley's enterprises have been doubly criticized.

Rimbault's suggestion that unscrupulous profiteering lay behind the festival schemes cannot be substantiated. Ashley, and later his sons, consistently featured eminent performers of the day at places otherwise bereft of metropolitan talent and the programmes always provided substantial, and at times novel, musical fare, such as performances of *The Creation* at Hull in 1801, Norwich in 1802 and Stamford in 1803. Ashley has also been condemned for changing the character of the Lenten Oratorios by replacing performances of complete works with miscellaneous selections of sacred and secular music. In fact complete performances did not entirely disappear, and the innovations made must be seen as a response to a public taste nurtured on the miscellaneous concerts in vogue at all important festivals. Ashley's particular achievements at the Oratorios are too frequently overlooked: the first performances in England of *The Creation* (28 March 1800, a month before Salomon) and Mozart's *Requiem* (27 February 1801), for which Ashley prepared a special biographical note.

Ashley was also briefly a publisher, bringing out a second edition of Boyce's *Cathedral Music* in 1788. From 1765 he was a member of the Royal Society of Musicians (of which all his sons were also members) and he was Master of the Worshipful Company of Musicians, 1803–4.

(2) Charles Ashley ['the General'] (b London, 1770; d London, 21 Aug 1818). Violinist, son of (1) John Ashley. He studied the violin with Felice Giardini and F. H. Barthélemon and gained a considerable reputation especially in the performance of 'ancient and sacred music'. A second-violin player at the 1784 Handel Commemoration, he led the orchestra at his father's musical festivals and the Covent Garden Oratorios and appeared as soloist, probably in his own concertos, at Ranelagh. After his father's death he jointly managed the oratorios with (4) Charles Jane Ashley and produced the first performance in England of *Messiah* with Mozart's additional accompaniments, on 29 March 1805. These two brothers were also the mainstays of the festivals the family continued to promote in the provinces between 1807 and 1815.

(3) John James Ashley (b London, 1772; d London, 5 Jan 1815). Son of (1) John Ashley. He and his two younger brothers were trebles in the chorus at the 1784 Handel Commemoration. Although noted as both organist (at Covent Garden Theatre) and pianist, being a pupil of the celebrated J. S. Schroeter, he was even more famed as a singing teacher. His pupils included Mrs Salmon, Mrs Vaughan (Miss Tennant), Master (James) Elliot and Charles Smith, and it was through him that so many eminent vocalists were heard in the family's festivals. He was also a composer; his known works are three sonatas for piano and violin, op.1 (London, c1790) and three vocal canzonets, op.5 (London, c1795).

(4) Charles Jane Ashley (b London, 1773; d Margate, 29 Aug 1843). Cellist, son of (1) John Ashley. He appeared as soloist at Ranelagh, Covent Garden, in his father's festivals and at major music meetings throughout the country; he was often considered second only to Lindley among cellists of the time. He was one of the founders of the Glee Club (1793), secretary of the

Royal Society of Musicians (from 1811) and an original member of the Philharmonic Society (1813). Besides managing the Covent Garden Oratorios, he continued promoting festivals in the provinces after the deaths of his elder brothers, running a particularly extensive series late in 1818. He later became manager of the Tivoli Gardens, Margate.

(5) **Richard G. Ashley** (*b* London, 1775; *d* London, 11 Oct 1836). Viola player, son of (1) John Ashley. He appeared in all his father's and brothers' undertakings and assisted in managing the 1818 festival series. He was in demand at major festivals, being listed as principal viola at the Three Choirs Festival of 1811 and leader of the section at the York Musical Festival, 1823, and was principal viola in the orchestra at the King's Theatre, London. Samuel Wesley thought him 'a most capital Performer . . . laudable for his rigid observance of Time: moreover his Tone was universally steady, full and rich' (*GB-Lbm* Add.27593, 105f).

BIBLIOGRAPHY

J. Sainsbury, ed.: *A Dictionary of Musicians* (London, 2/1825/*R*1966)

H. Saxe Wyndham: *The Annals of Covent Garden Theatre* (London, 1906)

B. W. Pritchard: 'The Provincial Festivals of the Ashley Family', *GSJ*, xxii (1969), 58

BRIAN W. PRITCHARD

Ashley, John (*b* Bath; *d* Bath, after 1834). English singer, composer and bassoonist. He was called John Ashley of Bath to distinguish him from his London namesake. He received his musical training from his elder brother Josiah, who was a well-known flautist and oboist. From about 1780 to 1830 he was active in Bath both as a bassoonist and singer. He wrote words and music to a number of songs and ballads, many of which acquired considerable popularity. He also published two pamphlets on *God save the King*, in which he refuted the since disproved theories of Richard Clark.

WRITINGS

Reminiscences and Observations respecting the Origin of God Save the King (Bath, 1827)

A Letter to the Rev. W. L. Bowles, supplementary to the 'Observations' (Bath, 1828)

WILLIAM WATERHOUSE

Ashley, Robert (*b* Ann Arbor, 28 March 1930). American composer and performer of electronic music. He studied at the University of Michigan (1948–52, 1957–60) and at the Manhattan School of Music (1952–4), his teachers including Riegger, Bassett and Gerhard. However, his development was more decisively influenced by his association with Mumma and by the ideas and compositions of Cage. Ashley and Mumma collaborated with the visual artist Milton Cohen on 'Space Theater' productions (1957–64) involving light projections, dance, sculpture and electronic sound improvisation. The two musicians also co-founded the Cooperative Studio for Electronic Music (1958–66) in Ann Arbor, where, with other composers, artists and architects, they established the ONCE Festival (1961–8). Ashley directed the ONCE Group touring ensemble in large-scale electronic music-theatre pieces (1965–9), and in 1966 he formed with Behrman, Lucier and Mumma the Sonic Arts Union to perform live electronic music on specially designed circuits and instruments. In 1969 Ashley was appointed co-director of the Center for Contemporary Music at Mills College, Oakland, California.

WORKS
(*selective list*)

Pf Sonata, 1959; The 4th of July, tape, 1960; Maneuvers for Small Hands, pf, 1961; Public Opinion Descends Upon the Demonstrators, elec music-theatre, 1961; Something for Cl, Pfs and Tape, 1961; Details for 2 Pianists, pf duet, 1962; Complete with Heat, orch, tape, 1962; Detroit Divided, tape, 1962–72; In memoriam Esteban Gomez (quartet), 4 players, 1963; In memoriam John Smith (concerto), 3 players, assistants, 1963; In memoriam Crazy Horse (symphony), 20 or more sustaining insts, 1963; In memoriam Kit Carson (opera), 8 players, 1963

Trios (White on White), various insts, 1963; Kittyhawk, an Antigravity Piece, elec music-theatre, 1964; The Wolfman, amp 1v, tape, 1964; Quartet, any insts, 1965; The Entrance, org, 1965–70; Unmarked Interchange, dance theatre, 1965; She Was a Visitor, chorus, 1967; The Trial of Anne Opie Wehrer and Unknown Accomplices for Crimes Against Humanity, elec music-theatre, 1968; Illusion Models, hypothetical computer tasks, 1970; In Sara, Menken, Christ and Beethoven There Were Men and Women (elec music-theatre, J. B. Wolgamot), 1972; String Quartet Describing the Motions of Real Bodies, str qt, elec, 1972

Principal publisher: Composer–Performer

WRITINGS

'The ONCE Group', *Arts in Society*, v (1968), 86

'The ONCE Group', *Source* (1968), no.3, p.19

BIBLIOGRAPHY

H. W. Hitchcock: 'Current Chronicle', *MQ*, xlviii (1962), 244

U. Kasemets: 'Current Chronicle', *MQ*, l (1964), 515

G. Mumma: 'The ONCE Festival and how it Happened', *Arts in Society*, iv (1967), 381

GERALD WARFIELD

Ashton, Algernon (Bennet Langton) (*b* Durham, 9 Dec 1859; *d* London, 10 April 1937). English composer and teacher. His father, who made a reputation as a tenor, was a lay clerk of Durham Cathedral; on his death in 1863 his widow and son went to live in Leipzig. Ashton studied music under Franz Heinig and Iwan Knorr, and subsequently at the Leipzig Conservatory, where he studied theory and composition with Jadassohn, Richter and Reinecke, and the piano with Papperitz and Coccius. In 1879, having won the Helbig composition prize, he left the conservatory and returned to England. He later became a pupil of Raff for six months in the winter of 1880–81. At the age of 22 Ashton settled in London, and by 1885 was appointed to teach the piano at the RCM, where he remained for 25 years.

Ashton's compositions cover most conventional forms except for opera, but he was best known for his piano and chamber works; they include a series of 24 string quartets, and 24 piano sonatas in all the major and minor keys. His published music exceeds 160 works. In 1898 Hofbauer issued a catalogue of the first 100 opus numbers (published by a variety of German and British publishers) and they are indicative of his early and typical style: they include works for solo piano, piano trio, quartet and quintet, songs, short choral works and songs. Ashton's orchestral music, which includes at least five symphonies written early in the 20th century, three overtures, an orchestral suite, a Turkish March, a scena for voice and orchestra, a cantata and violin and piano concertos, made no impression. None of these works was published, and all attempts to trace the manuscripts have failed.

The surviving piano works are largely in the style to be expected of a minor 19th-century composer heavily influenced by his German contemporaries, especially Raff, Brahms and Schumann. However, the sonatas show considerable personality and are well worth investigation, the early ones in particular being memorable in invention and vigorous in execution.

Late in his life Ashton became something of a musical reactionary, which in no way decreased a natural pomposity evinced particularly in the hobby that has largely obscured his real merits as a teacher and composer, his passion for writing letters to the newspapers. His hobbyhorses included the neglect of the graves of famous men, and he was a vehement opponent of cremation and an ardent Baconian; his subjects were often musical, and the letters include a number of useful scraps of information. He published them in two collections: *Truth, Wit and Wisdom* (London, 1905) and *More Truth, Wit and Wisdom* (London, 1908).

BIBLIOGRAPHY
Obituary, *MT*, lxxviii (1937), 464
H. Truscott: 'Algernon Ashton, 1859–1937', *MMR*, lxxxix (1959), 142
LEWIS FOREMAN

Ashton, Sir Frederick (William Malandaine) (*b* 1904). English dancer and choreographer; *see* DANCE, §VII, 1 (ii).

Ashton, Hugh. *See* ASTON, HUGH.

Ashwell [Ashewell, Asshwell, Aswell, Hashewell], **Thomas** (*b* c1478; *d* after 1513). English composer. He was admitted as a chorister to St George's Chapel, Windsor, on 29 October 1491 and remained there until 14 January 1493. The roll of accounts of the stewards of Tattershall College, Lincolnshire, for Michaelmas 1502 to Michaelmas 1503 lists him as one of the singing clerks (*clerici conducticii*). An entry dated 29 January 1508 in the chapter acts of Lincoln Cathedral shows that at that time he was *Informator choristarum* there but the date of his appointment is unknown. In 1513 he was cantor at Durham Cathedral. The inclusion of his song *She may be callyd a sovrant lady* in a collection printed in 1530 cannot be taken as evidence that he was still alive then for Fayrfax (*d* 1521) and Cornysh (*d* 1523) are also represented. Ashwell is one of the English authorities listed by Morley at the end of his *Plaine and Easie Introduction to Practicall Musicke* (1597).

The recently discovered information about his admission as a chorister at St George's Chapel in 1491 (see Bergsagel, 1976) suggests he was born about 1478, which would dispose of the unsubstantiated claim by Flood that Ashwell had composed an anthem *God Save King Harry* for the wedding of King Henry VII and Elizabeth of York on 17 January 1487. This assertion was apparently based on a curious statement by Strickland (*Lives of the Queens of England*, London, 1840–48) referring to the chance discovery of the piece in an old church chest and its recognition as a precursor of the British national anthem. There may have been some confusion with the Mass *'God Save King Harry'* by Ashwell, two vocal parts of which have survived in Cambridge libraries.

Ashwell's presence at Tattershall College is particularly interesting for its support of a suspected teacher–pupil relationship between him and Taverner, who is supposed to have been a chorister at Tattershall at about this time. The only two works by Ashwell surviving complete are the six-voice *Missa 'Ave Maria'* and *Missa Jesu Christe* in the Forrest–Heyther Partbooks copied by or for Taverner when he assumed his duties as choirmaster at the new Cardinal College, Oxford, in 1526. According to the indenture of Ashwell's appointment at Durham Cathedral (printed in Harrison, 1958) he was expected to teach 'planesong, priknott, faburden, dischant, swarenote et countre', to play the organ, to

sing and to compose each year a four- or five-voice mass or equivalent work to the glory of God, the Blessed Virgin Mary, or St Cuthbert. A mass by Ashwell to each of these dedications has survived, and though it is reasonable to suppose that his mass to St Cuthbert was composed for Durham it cannot be automatically assumed that the other two were also written after his appointment there in 1513.

One vocal part survives of a *Te matrem Dei laudamus* in *GB-Lbm* Harl.1709; this piece is the same as the *Te Deum* attributed to Hugh Aston in *Ob* Mus.Sch.E.1–5 (ed. in TCM, x, 1929). John Baldwin copied two sections of this work into *Lbm* Roy.24.d.2 attributing it to Taverner (ed. in TCM, iii, 1924) but on the grounds of the relationship of the piece to Aston's *Missa 'Te Deum'* it is probably by Aston.

WORKS
Missa 'Ave Maria', 6vv, *GB-Ob*; ed. in EECM, i (1963)
Mass 'God Save King Harry', inc., *Cjc* 234 (B), *Cu* Dd.13.27 (Ct)
Missa Jesu Christe, 6vv, *Ob*, ed. in EECM, xvi (1976), facs. of T in *MD*, xvi, 1962, pls.iv–vi; *Eu* (T only)
Missa Sancte Cuthberte, *Lbm* Add.30520 (frag.)
Sancta Maria, *Lbm* Add.34191 (B only)
Stabat mater, *Lbm* Harl.1709 (mean only)
She may be callyd a sovrant lady, inc., 1530⁶ (B); facs. in R. Steele, *The Earliest English Music Printing* (London, 1903), pl.vi

BIBLIOGRAPHY
W. H. G. Flood: *Early Tudor Composers* (London, 1925)
F. Ll. Harrison: *Music in Medieval Britain* (London, 1958, 2/1963)
——: 'English Polyphony (c. 1470–1540)', *NOHM*, iii (1960), 303–45
J. Bergsagel: Introduction to EECM, i (1963)
——: 'The Date and Provenance of the Forrest–Heyther Collection of Tudor Masses', *ML*, xliv (1963), 240
——: Introduction to EECM, xvi (1976)
JOHN BERGSAGEL

Asia. For discussions of Asian music *see* CENTRAL ASIA; EAST ASIA; INDIA, SUBCONTINENT OF; SOUTHEAST ASIA. The coverage of the music of western Asia is discussed under the heading NEAR EAST. For information on the secular and ecclesiastical music of individual countries, see under the names of the countries and the rites concerned.

Asian Music Forum. Congress instituted in 1969 by the INTERNATIONAL MUSIC COUNCIL.

Asioli, Bonifazio (*b* Correggio, nr. Reggio Emilia, 30 Aug 1769; *d* Correggio, 18 May 1832). Italian composer, theorist and pianist. Born into a family of musicians, he was essentially self-taught. At the age of eight he had already written complex sacred pieces and chamber music. He studied in Parma under Angelo Morigi (1780) and in 1782 stayed for a time in Vicenza, Bologna and Venice, where he had great success as a harpsichordist and improviser. Having returned to Correggio, at the age of 14 he taught the harpsichord, flute and cello at the Collegio Civico and in 1786 was appointed *maestro di cappella*. *La volubile*, performed in Correggio in 1785 with the intermezzo *Il ratto di Proserpina*, marked the beginning of his career as an opera composer. In the retinue of the Marchese Gherardini, he moved to Turin (1787), then to Venice (1796–9) and finally to Milan, where his opera *Cinna* had already been staged at La Scala (1793). In 1805 he was appointed *maestro di cappella* and music director at the court of the viceroy, Eugène Beauharnais; the appointment involved the composition of both sacred and secular music, for the *accademie* held at the royal palace. In 1808, at the suggestion of Mayr, who had refused the post, he became the first director of the newly founded Milan Conservatory, and held the chair of composition. The second part of his life was devoted to teaching by the production of a series of theoretical works. He was responsible for the first performance in Italy, by his pupils, of Haydn's *Creation* and *Seasons*. During his Milanese period he was in touch with Weigl, Clementi and Haydn, who, in a letter in 1806, recommended Karl Mozart to him as a pupil. Apart from a journey to Paris in Beauharnais' retinue in 1810, he remained in Milan until 1814, when he was compelled to leave the conservatory as a 'foreigner' after the fall of the Kingdom of Italy. Because of his exceptional merits he was allowed to retain his post at court but in October he was again in Correggio, where he remained, universally respected until his death.

In his house in Correggio he established a music school, in which he was joined by his brother Giovanni Asioli (1767–1831), who, during a life spent entirely in Correggio, was municipal *maestro di cappella* (from 1755), organist at the basilica, a pianist and composer. In this final period of his life, Bonifazio composed mostly sacred music and continued his theoretical writings. In 1826 he supplied the statutes for the Reggio music school, of which, having refused the directorship, he was made honorary president.

Asioli's music is now forgotten, although the brilliance of his talent was widely acknowledged by his contemporaries. His idiom, pleasant and at times sentimental, is at its best in his vocal chamber music, which in style recalls Haydn and Mozart, without showing many traces of the stylistic crisis undergone by music at the beginning of the 19th century. His didactic work survived longer, and it is to him that the Milan Conservatory owes the foundation of its library.

His brother Luigi Asioli (1778–1815) was a tenor, pianist and composer. A pupil of his brother Giovanni Asioli, he worked first in Naples and Palermo, and from 1804 in London, where he became a fashionable singing teacher. He composed a large amount of music in all forms, much of which, particularly vocal and instrumental chamber pieces, was published in London.

WORKS

VOCAL

Operas: 6 comic operas and intermezzi, 1785–6; Cinna (dramma serio), Milan, 1793, autograph *I-Mr*; Pigmalione (azione teatrale), 1796, vocal score (London, ?1800); Gustava al Malabar (dramma serio), Turin, 1802; numerous insertion nos.

Oratorios: Giuseppe in Galaad, 1785

Sacred: 10 masses, 1 pubd: TTB, orch, 1820 (Milan, ?1827); mass movts; Vesper service, 3vv, orch (Milan, ?1829); 5 Magnificat; 4 Te Deum; 7 Tantum ergo, incl. 1 for B, vv, orch (Milan, ?1827); numerous ps, hymns, motets; others

Vocal chamber: numerous cantatas, incl. Il ciclope, autograph *Mr*; Il nome (Metastasio) (London, ?1795); 3 cantate (?London, 1808): Il consiglio, La scusa, La primavera; scene liriche; duets; trios; qts; qnts; nocturnes, 2–5vv; arias; canzonettas; sonnets; canons; cavatinas; stanzas; divertimentos; odes; dialogues

INSTRUMENTAL

Orch: 8 sinfonie, incl. Sinfonia campestre, arr. pf (Milan, c1815); Hpd Conc., *MOe*; 2 fl concs.; Vn Conc.; Act 5 of La Galzenna, ballet; ovs.; divertimenti

Band: Suonate; Marcia funebre

Chamber: serenatas; Sextet, cl, 2 vn, vc, hn, bn, 1817; Sextet, cl, va, vc, 2 hn, bn, 1817 (Milan, c1820); 16 qts in 16 keys, cl, vc, 2 hn, bn, 1817; Qt, vn, fl, hn, b, 1782; Str Qt, 1785; Trio, mand, vn, b; divertimentos; Sonata, pf, vc acc., c1801 (Milan, c1817); Harp Sonata, 1800; Vn Sonata, ?1783; db pieces; others

Pf: numerous sonatas, incl. 3 Sonatas op.8 (London, 1803), Sonata (Milan, c1816); sonatinas; sinfonie; variations; studies; divertimentos

THEORETICAL WRITINGS AND METHODS

Primi elementi di canto (Milan, 1809)
Principj elementari di musica (Milan, 1809)

Trattato d'armonia e d'accompagnamento (Milan, 1813)
Corso di modulazioni classificate a 4 e più parti (Milan, ?1814)
Dialoghi sul Trattato d'armonia (Milan, 1814)
Osservazioni sul temperamento proprio degl'istromenti stabili: dirette agli accordatori di pianoforte ed organo (Milan, 1816)
I. Scale e salti per il solfeggio, II. Preparazione al canto ed ariette (Milan, 1816)
L'allievo al clavicembalo (Milan, 1819)
Elementi di contrabasso con una nuova maniera di digitare (Milan, 1823)
Il maestro di composizione, ossia Seguito al Trattato d'armonia (Milan, 1832)
Disinganno sulle osservazioni fatte sul temperamento proprio degli istromenti stabili (Milan, 1833)
Elementi di contrappunto (Florence, 1836)

BIBLIOGRAPHY

EitnerQ
'Verzeichniss sämmtlicher Compositionen nebst einer kurzen Biographie des Herrn Bonifacio Asioli', *AMZ*, xxii (1820), col.667
A. Coli: *Vita di Bonifazio Asioli da Correggio* (Milan, 1834) [incl. detailed list of works]
I. Saccozzi: 'Di Bonifazio Asioli', *Notizie biografiche e letterarie in continuazione della Biblioteca Modenese del Cavalier Abate G° Tiraboschi*, ii (Reggio Emilia, 1834) [incl. letters and Asioli's *Riflessioni sopra l'opera del Signor di Momigni intitolata 'La sola e vera teorica della musica'*]
O. S. Ancarani: *Sopra alcune parole di Carlo Botta intorno al metodo musicale di Bonifazio Asioli* (1836)
A. Amadei: 'Intorno allo stile della moderna musica di chiesa', *Giornale ecclesiastico di Bologna*, i/5 (1841) [also in extract]
G. Vitali: *Della necessità di riformare i 'Principi elementari di musica' di Bonifazio Asioli* (Milan, 1850)
L. Melzi: *Cenni storici sul R. Conservatorio di musica in Milano* (Milan, 1873), 18
G. C. Marchi Castellini: *Luigi Asioli: vita e lavori* (Correggio, 1880)
L. Corio: *Ricerche storiche sul R. Conservatorio di musica di Milano* (Milan, 1908)
R. Finzi: *Asoliana: catalogo di quante opere di Bonifazio Asioli sono esistenti nella Civica biblioteca di Correggio preceduto dalla biografia del maestro* (Correggio, 1930)
F. Mompellio: *Il R. Conservatorio di musica 'Giuseppe Verdi' di Milano* (Florence, 1941)
G. Roncaglia: 'Bonifazio Asioli', *Atti e memorie della Deputazioni di storia patria per le antiche provincie modenesi*, 8th ser., ix (1956), 202
R. Nielson: 'Asioli, Bonifacio', *DBI*
——: 'Asioli, Luigi', *DBI*
R. Finzi: *Celebrazione del musicista Bonifazio Asioli (1769–1832) nel secondo centenario della nascita* (Reggio Emilia, 1969)
A. Zecca Laterza: 'Bonifacio Asioli maestro e direttore della real musica', *Chigiana*, xxvi–xxvii (1971), 61 [with chronological list of church works perf. in Milan 1805–13 and sources]

SERGIO LATTES

Asioli, Francesco (*b* probably in Reggio Emilia, ?1645–50; *d* in or after 1676). Italian composer, guitarist and guitar teacher, ancestor of Bonifazio Asioli. He is known by two collections of guitar music, *Primi scherzi di chitarra* (Bologna, 1674) and *Concerti armonici per la chitarra spagnuola* op.3 (Bologna, 1676; two ballettos and a capriccio in Chilesotti, 1886, the capriccio also in Chilesotti, 1921); from the latter it appears that he was then guitar teacher at the Collegio dei Nobili, Parma. The pieces in both books are typical of conventional guitar music of the period. The first book comprises 28 dances, most of them allemands, correntes and gigues. The second is more varied and apart from dances includes arias, preludes, capriccios and a sonata with fugue.

BIBLIOGRAPHY

O. Chilesotti: 'Fasolo-Asioli', *Gazzetta musicale di Milano*, xli (28 Nov 1886), 349f, 354
——: 'Notes sur les tablatures de luth et de guitare, XVIe et XVIIe siècles', *EMDC*, I/i (1921), 679
G. Dardo: 'Asioli, Francesco', *MGG* [incl. fuller bibliography]

NIGEL FORTUNE

Askenase, Stefan (*b* Lwów, 10 July 1896). Belgian pianist of Polish birth. He studied in Lwów under Theodor Pollak and at the Vienna Academy of Music under Emil von Sauer. After serving in the Austrian army during World War I he resumed his studies with Sauer and also studied composition with Joseph Marx. He made his début in Vienna in 1919 and his first appearance with the Warsaw PO in 1920. He taught at a private conservatory in Cairo, 1922–5, and at the Rotterdam Conservatory, 1937–40. In 1950 he became a Belgian citizen and from 1954 to 1961 was a professor at the Brussels Conservatory. He has given master classes at the Hochschulen für Musik in Hamburg and Cologne and at the Jerusalem Academy. Askenase has made many appearances throughout Europe in recital and with orchestra, and has toured the Far East, Israel and South America. He is generally regarded as a Chopin specialist, in a style more expressive than brilliant; his repertory also includes the classics.

RONALD KINLOCH ANDERSON

Askew [Askue], **R.** (*fl c*1595). Nothing is known of his identity. His extant compositions for lute are mostly in the University Library of Cambridge: they comprise a Jigg (Dd.ii.11, f.100 and Dd.v.78, f.32*v*); Askewes Galliarde (Dd.ii.11, f.80); R. Askue (one part of a duet; Dd.ix.33, f.88*v*); and (in *GB-Gu*) Robin hoode (R.d.43, f.46*v*). One piece for cittern – a Conceipte – is in *Cu* Dd.iv.23, f.6*v*.

DIANA POULTON

Asmatikon (Gk., from *asma*: 'song'). A choirbook of the Constantinopolitan Greek rite, containing florid Proper chants; *see* BYZANTINE RITE, MUSIC OF THE, §§3, 7, 11–12, 15; KONTAKION; LITURGY AND LITURGICAL BOOKS, §III, 4.

Asola [Asula, Asulae], **Giammateo** [Giovanni Matteo] (*b* Verona, ?1532 or earlier; *d* Venice, 1 Oct 1609). Italian composer. On 7 May 1546 he entered the congregation of secular canons of S Giorgio in Alga. After this he probably studied with Vincenzo Ruffo in Verona. From 1566 until his death he held benefices at S Stefano, Verona. After 1569, not wishing to take monastic vows, he left the congregation, became a secular priest and on 1 June 1571 went to work in the parish of S Maria in Organo, Verona. In 1577 he was appointed *maestro di cappella* at Treviso Cathedral but after a year accepted a better position at Vincenza Cathedral. In 1582 he probably went to Venice and in 1588 was appointed one of four chaplains at S Severo, a church under the jurisdiction of the monks of S Lorenzo. In 1590–91 he was again in Verona but otherwise probably remained at S Severo until his death. His most notable pupils were Leone Leoni and Amedeo Freddi.

Asola's large body of sacred music is close in style to that exemplified by the late works of Palestrina, whom, in a dedication, he called the greatest musician of the period. Like Palestrina's his music is based essentially on the polyphonic combination of flowing, balanced melodic lines. There are no chromaticisms, disjunct dissonant intervals or extreme contrasts. Homophonic and canonic passages appear, but most of his music is in a freely imitative contrapuntal style balanced occasionally by brief sections of non-imitative texture. Some of the less spectacular innovations of the Venetian school, particularly in the treatment of *cori spezzati*, can be found in the eight-part works and to a lesser extent in those for six voices. Too much has been made of the in

fact doubtful assertion that Asola was one of the first composers to write an independent continuo part.

WORKS

Editions: Musica divina, ed. K. Proske, i/1–2, ii (Regensburg, 1853–4)
 Composizioni sacre e profane a più voci secolo XVI, ed. L. Torchi, AMI, ii (1897/*R*)
 Iohannes Mathaei Asulae opera omnia, ed. G. Vecchi, AntMI, 6th ser., *Monumenta veronensia*, ii (1963–) [only vol. of madrigals has appeared]
 G. Asola: Sixteen Liturgical Works, ed. D. M. Fouse, RRMR, i (1964)

(all published in Venice unless otherwise noted)

MASSES

Missae tres, 5vv, quorum nomina sunt dum complerentur, Reveillez. Standomi un giorno, liber I (1570)
Missae tres, 6vv, quorum nomina sunt. Primi toni. Andreas Christi famulus. Escoutez . . . liber II (1570)
Le messe, 4vv pari . . . sofra li 8 toni . . . insieme con dui altre, l'una de S Maria a voce piena, l'altra pro defunctis . . . libro primo (1574); Il secondo libro della messa, 4vv pari . . . sopra li toni rimanenti al primo libro insieme con una messa pro defunctis accomodata per cantar à 2 chori (si placet) (1580)
Messa pro defunctis, 4vv pari (1576)
Secundus liber in quo reliquae missae, 4vv, compositae [5–8] tonis . . . ad facilitatem, brevitatem, mentemque sanctorum Tridentini concilij patrum accommodatae (1581)
Missae octonis compositae [1–4] tonis . . . continentur, facilitati, brevitati mentique sanctorum concilii Tridentini patrum accomodatae . . . 4vv (1586)
Missae tres, 8vv . . . liber I (1588); Liber II missas tres, duasque sacras cantiones continens, 8vv (1588)
Missae quatuor, 5vv (1588)
Missae duo decemque sacrae laudes, 3vv (2/1588; 3/with bc (org), 1620)
Missae tres totidemque sacrae laudes, 5vv . . . liber II (1591)
Missae tres sacraque ex canticis canticorum cantio, 6vv (1591)
Missa defunctorum, 3vv (?1600)

OTHER SACRED

Completorium per totum annum quatuorque illae beatae virginis antiphonae . . . 6vv (1573)
Psalmodia ad vespertinas . . . 8vv, canticaque duo BVM (1574)
Falsi bordoni per cantar salmi in 4 ordini divisi, sopra gli 8 tuoni . . . del . . . Asola et alcuni di M. Vincenzo Ruffo. Et anco per cantar gli hymni secondo il suo canto fermo, 4vv (1575¹); enlarged 3rd edn.: Falsi bordoni . . . aggiontovi ancora il modo di cantar letanie communi, e della beata vergine, et Lauda Sion Salvatorem . . . con alcuni versi a choro spezzato, 4vv (1584)
Vespertina majorum solennitatum psalmodia, 6vv (1576)
Vespertina omnium solennitatum psalmodia, juxta decretum sacrosancti Tridentini concilii, duoque beatae virginis cantica primi toni . . . 8vv (1578); Secundus chorus vespertinae omnium solennitatum psalmodiae . . . 4vv (1578)
Duplex completorium romanum . . . quibus etiam adjunximus quatuor illas antiphonas . . . chorus primus, 4vv (1583); Secundus chorus duplicis completorii romani (1587)
In passionibus quatuor evangelistarum Christi locutio, 3vv (1583)
Introitus, missarum omnium solemnitatum . . . et alleluia ac musica super cantu plano . . . psalmi immutatis . . . 4vv (Brescia, 1583)
Prima pars musices continens officium Hebdomadae Sanctae, videlicet benedictionem palmarum et alia missarum solemnis . . . 4vv (1583); Secunda pars continens officium Hebdomadae Sanctae, idest lamentationes, responsoria . . . 4vv (1584)
Sacrae cantiones in totius anni solennitatibus . . . 4vv (1584)
Secundi chori quibusdam, respondens cantilenis, quae in secunda parte musicis maioris Hebdomadae . . . cantico Benedictus . . . et psalma Miserere mei Deus, atque versiculis Heu heu domine . . . 4vv (1584)
Completorium romanum duae beatae virginis antiphonae, scilicet Salve regina et Regina coeli quatuorque alia motetta . . . 8vv (1585)
Hymni ad vespertinas omnium solennitatum horas decantandi. Ad breviarii cantique plani formam restituti. Pars prima . . . 4vv (1585); Secunda pars hymnorum vespertinis omnium solennitatum horis deservientium . . . 4vv (1585)
Officium defunctorum, 4vv (1586)
Psalmi ad tertiam . . . cum hymno Te Deum laudamus. Chorus primus, 4vv . . . chorus secundus ad 4vv pares (1586)
Nova vespertina omnium solennitatum psalmodia, cum cantico beatae virginis, 8vv (1587)
Lamentationes improperia et aliae sacrae laudes, 3vv (1588)
Officium defunctorum, 4vv (1588)
Vespertina omnium solennitatum psalmodia, canticum beata virginis duplici modulatione, primi videlicet, et 8 toni. Salve regina, missa, et 5 divinae laudes, 12vv, ternis variata choris, ac omni instrumentorum genere modulanda (1590)

Sacra omnium solemnitatum psalmodia vespertina cum cantico beatae
virginis . . . 5vv (1592)
Officium defunctorum addito cantico Zachariae, 4vv (1593)
Sacra omnium solemnitatum vespertina psalmodia cum beatae virginis
cantico . . . 6vv (1593)
Officium maioris Hebdomadae, videlicet benedictio palmarum atque
missarum solemnia; et que in 4 evangelistarum passiones concinun-
tur, 4vv, et in eisdem passionibus . . . 3vv (1595)
Vespertina omnium solemnitatum psalmodia, 4vv pares (1597)
Completorium romanum primus et secundus chorus, Alma
Redemptoris mater, Ave regina coelorum, 3vv (1598)
In omnibus totius anni solemnitatibus introitus et alleluia ad Missalis
romani formam ordinati, musica super cantu planu restituto, 4vv
(1598)
Introitus in dominicis diebus totius anni, et ad aspersionem aque ben-
edicte . . . musica super cantu plano restituto, 4vv (1598)
Nova omnium solemnitatum vespertina psalmodia, 6vv (1599)
Divinae Dei laudes, 2vv (1600)
Sacro sanctae Dei laudes, 8vv (1600³)
Hymnodia vespertina in maioribus anni solemnitatibus, 8vv, org (1602)
Lamentationes Jeremiae prophetae . . . nec non et Zachariae canticum,
BVM planctus, 6vv (1602)
Psalmi ad vespertinas omnium solemnitatum horas. Una cum cantico
beatae virginis, Salve regina, et Regina coeli, 3vv (1602); Secundi
chori vespertinae omnium solemnitatum psalmodiae, 3vv (1599)
Various works in 1586¹, 1588⁶, 1590⁷, 1591¹, 1592³, 1598⁶, 1599¹,
1606⁶, 1612¹³, 1613², D-As

SECULAR

Le vergini, 3vv . . . libro I (1571)
Madrigali, 2vv, accomodati da cantar in fuga (1584, 2/1587)
[Le] Vergini, 3vv . . . libro II (1587)
Madrigali, 6vv (1605)
Madrigali spirituali, 5vv (n.d.), lost; cited in Gardano's *Indice* of 1591
Various works in 1584⁴, 1587⁶, 1588¹⁹, 1588²⁰, 1590¹⁹, 1591²⁶,
1592¹¹, 1613¹⁰

Canto fermo sopra messe, hinni, et altre cose ecclesiastiche appartenenti
à sonatori d'organo per giustamente rispondere al choro (1592), is a
publication of chant in mensural notation edited by Asola, not a work
of his own.

BIBLIOGRAPHY

F. Caffi: *Della vita e delle opere di Giammateo Asola* (Padua, 1862)
G. d'Alessi: *La cappella musicale del duomo di Treviso* (Vedelago,
1954), 127ff, 146, 182, 186 [includes one of 3 motets]
D. Fouse: *The Sacred Music of Giammateo Asola* (diss., U. of North
Carolina, 1960)
E. Paganuzzi: 'Notizie biografiche sul primo periodo veronese di
Giovan Matteo Asola', *Vita veronese*, xxi (1968), 91
DONALD FOUSE

'Asor (Heb.). Ancient Jewish instrument, possibly a
lyre; *see* JEWISH MUSIC, §I, 4(iv).

Aspen Music Festival. An annual festival and music
school in Aspen, Colorado, a major mountain skiing
resort during the winter. The summer programme,
which developed from the 1949 Goethe Bicentennial
Convocation and Music Festival, has since 1950
included lectures, discussions and concerts of vocal,
chamber and orchestral music performed by visiting
artists and students. The festival and music school
provide courses in performance, theory, music literature, music criticism and choral, contemporary and
electronic music.

RITA H. MEAD

Asplmayr [Aspelmayr, Aspelmeier, Asplmeyr, Aschpellmayr, Appelmeyer etc], **Franz** (*b* Linz, baptized 2
April 1728; *d* Vienna, 29 July 1786). Austrian composer and violinist. He studied the violin with his father,
but had no good composition teaching; this is reflected
in certain technical weaknesses in his compositions. He
was a member of the imperial Hofkapelle in Vienna. His
first position was as *Secretarius* to Count Morzin
(1759–61; Haydn was in Morzin's service at the same
time). In 1760 he married Elisabeth Reiss, and the
next year he took a position as composer at the
Kärntnertortheater, holding it probably until 1763. He

was later among the collaborators of the choreographer
and dancer Noverre, who first went to Vienna in 1767
and settled there in 1771; Noverre's principal composers
were Josef Starzer and Asplmayr, who is known to have
composed at least five ballets for him at this period. In
1774 Asplmayr wrote a ballet, *L'espiègle du village*, for
Angiolini. After that time he worked principally on
music for the theatre, and played the violin at aristocratic gatherings. He was second violinist in a concert of
Haydn quartets on 25 December 1781, with Tomasini
(first violin), Weibl and Huber; each performer received
a lavish gift, and Haydn a gold box with diamonds
(*Wiener Zeitung*, 9 January 1782). When in 1771
Gassmann founded the Tonkünstler-Sozietät for the
benefit of musicians' widows and orphans, Asplmayr
was elected to the Seniores and was assessor until 1776.
He later had to resign, and his last years were financially
stringent. He was acquainted with Leopold and W. A.
Mozart (see Leopold's letter of 21 February 1785).

Asplmayr's works were known throughout Europe.
His ballets for Noverre coincided with the latter's significant reforms of the genre. His *Pygmalion* was the
first melodrama to be performed in German-speaking
lands – indeed its first performance may have been the
earliest public one of a work in this newly invented
genre. As a composer of Singspiels he ranks with
Starzer and early Haydn.

Asplmayr also wrote orchestral pieces and numerous
chamber works which (along with those of Leopold
Hoffmann and Vanhal) contributed significantly to the
early Viennese instrumental style. The chamber works
mix elements of the Baroque and Classical styles and
trace the gradual independence of chamber music from
continuo practice. Asplmayr's symphonies were performed by the Tonkünstler-Sozietät, and much of his
instrumental music was distributed in print by French
publishers. Though conventional in melodic development and harmonic progression, it is consistently pleasant and charming.

WORKS

Principal MS sources: *A-LA, Wgm; B-Bc; CS-Pnm, RAJ; D-Bds,*
Ehreshoven, *FS, Rtt, SI; H-Gc*

Br. cat. – *listed in Breitkopf catalogue(s)*

STAGE

(*first performed in Vienna*)

Flora (ballet), 1766, doubtful
Les petits riens (ballet), 1768, doubtful, lost
Agamemnon vengé (Der gerächte Agamemnon) (ballet), 1771, rev.
1772
La lavandara di Citere (ballet), 1771, lost
Leben und Tod des Königs Makbeth (Makbeth der Hexenkönig)
(pantomime, Moll, after Shakespeare), 1771, lost
Ifigenie (Iphigénie en Tauride) (ballet), 1772
Acis et Galathée (ballet), 1773
Alexandre et Campaspe de Larisse (Apelles et Campaspe; Le tri-
omphe d'Alexandre sur soi-même) (ballet), 1773
L'espiègle du village (Der Dorfeulenspiegel) (ballet), 1774
I mori espagnuoli (ballet), 1770s, lost
Pygmalion (melodrama, 1, J.-J. Rousseau, trans. J. G. von Laudes),
1776, frag.
Die Kinder der Natur (Singspiel, 2, L. A. Hoffmann), 1778, lost
Frühling und Liebe (Singspiel), 1778, lost
Der Sturm (incidental music, J. J. Schink, after Shakespeare),
1779–80, lost
Orpheus und Euridice (melodrama, Bursay, trans. von Laudes),
1779–80, lost
Montgolfier, oder die Luftkugel, lost

INSTRUMENTAL

Orch: Symphonie périodique (Paris, c1767), lost; 7 syms., Br. cat.
(1766–9); 2 syms., D, F, *A-LA*; Sym., C, *Wgm*

Chamber: 31 partitas (Prague, c1810); Partita, *LA*; Serenades, wind insts, str, 6 as op.1 (Lyons, c1777), 6 in Br. cat. (1778); Str qts, 6 as op.2 (Paris, 1769), no.2 ed. in Collegium musicum, xl (Leipzig, 1906), 6 as op.6 (Paris, 1765), 13 in Br. cat.; 12 divertimentos (trios), 2 vn/2 va, b, ed. in Henrotte (1967); 6 trio modernes, 2 vn/2 tr viols, b, op.1 (Paris, 1761), no.4 ed. in Hausmusik, clxii (Vienna, 1970), no.455; 6 trios, 2 vn, b, op.5 (Paris, 1765), no.1 ed. in Collegium musicum, xxxix (Leipzig, 1906); 6 sonate o sia dilettamenti, 2 vn, vc, op.7 (Paris, 1774); 6 trios, Br. cat. (1767); 6 duos, 2 vn/2 tr viols, op.2 (Paris, c1768); 6 duos, vn, vc, op.3 (Paris, c1770)

BIBLIOGRAPHY

EitnerQ; *GerberL*

A. Sandberger: 'Zur Geschichte des Haydnischen Streichquartetts', *Bayerische Monatsblätter* (1900); repr. in *Ausgewählte Aufsätze zur Musikgeschichte*, i (Munich, 1921/R1970)

G. H. Neurath: 'Das Violinkonzert in der Wiener klassischen Schule', *SMw*, xiv (1927), 125

E. Valentin: 'Aspelmayr, Franz', *MGG*

H. Riessberger: *Franz Aspelmayer* (diss., U. of Innsbruck, 1954)

G. A. Henrotte: *The Ensemble Divertimento in Pre-Classic Vienna* (diss., U. of North Carolina, 1967)

F. Stieger: *Opernlexikon* (Tutzing, 1975–)

GAYLE A. HENROTTE

Asproys, Jehan Simon [Johannes Symonis]. *See* HASPROIS, JOHANNES SYMONIS.

Aspull, George (*b* Manchester, June 1813; *d* Leamington, 19 Aug 1832). English pianist and composer. He was the ninth of ten sons of Thomas Aspull, another of whom, William (1798–1875), was organist of St Mary's Church, Nottingham, in 1830–35. After performing in Paris in April 1825, where he was praised by Rossini, George undertook a number of concert tours throughout Great Britain and Ireland. In spite of his death (from tuberculosis) at the age of 19, he was extraordinarily famous. He is credited with having given the first performance in England of Weber's *Konzertstück*, in 1824.

Aspull left several MS compositions for the piano, which were subsequently edited by his father and published under the title *George Aspull's Posthumous Works for the Pianoforte* (London, 1837), with a portrait and a prefatory memoir.

BIBLIOGRAPHY

'Musical Phenomenon', *The Harmonicon*, ii (1824), 42

E. Taylor: 'Aspull, George', *Biographical Dictionary of the Society for the Diffusion of Useful Knowledge* (London, 1842)

[J. E. Cox]: *Musical Recollections of the Last Half-century* (London, 1872), i, 206f

W. B. Squire: 'Aspull, George', *DNB*

M. Silburn: 'The Most Extraordinary Creature in Europe', *ML*, iii (1922), 200

J. A. FULLER MAITLAND/BRUCE CARR

Asriel, Andre (*b* Vienna, 22 Feb 1922). German composer of Austrian-Turkish origin. He studied the piano with Hinterhofer and theory with Stohr at the Vienna Academy, took lessons with Merrick at the RCM, London (1939–40) and was later a pupil of E. H. Meyer for composition and F. Osborn for the piano. After his studies in England he moved to Germany in 1947 and attended the West Berlin Hochschule für Musik for a short time, later studying with Eisler at the German Arts Academy, East Berlin. He then taught at the Eisler Musikhochschule, East Berlin, as lecturer in theory (1950–67) and professor of composition (from 1967). One of the most gifted of Eisler's pupils, he wrote mainly political songs and marches between 1949 and 1955. At that time he began to concentrate on songs and film music, and has taken an interest in North American popular music, publishing a study, *Jazz: Analysen und Aspekte* (Berlin, 1966, 2/1977).

WORKS
(*selective list*)

Orch: 4 Inventionen, tpt, trbn, orch, 1963; Volksliedersuite, 1964; Metamorphosen, 1968

Vocal: 3 Kommentare zu 'Moro lasso' von Gesualdo, chamber chorus, 6 insts, 1971; 6 Fabeln nach Äsop, chorus, 1973; other choral pieces, songs

Inst: Pf Sonata, 1953; Serenade, 9 insts, 1969

Incidental music: Der Frieden (Hacks, after Aristophanes), 1962; Polly (Hacks, after Gay), 1965; Faust I, 1968

Film scores

Principal publishers: Deutscher Verlag für Musik, Lied der Zeit, Peters (Leipzig), Verlag für Neue Musik

HORST SEEGER

Assai (It.: 'very'). A word often used in tempo designations (like the approximately equivalent adjective *molto*) to indicate the superlative. *Allegro assai* ('very fast') is its commonest use, and is found particularly in 19th-century scores. *Allegro assai moderato*, 'a very moderate *allegro*', appears characteristically at the opening of Act 2 of Verdi's *Otello*. The Marcia funebre of Beethoven's Third Symphony is marked *adagio assai*.

But the meaning of the word for Beethoven may not have been consistent. Brossard in his *Dictionaire* (1703) gave the usual meaning and added that *assai* could also mean 'rather' or 'moderately'; and although Rousseau roundly chastised him for his ignorant interpretation of the word in terms of the cognate (*assez*) in his mother tongue there is considerable evidence that most early uses of the word should be taken in that sense. The anonymous *A Short Explication* (London, 1724) gives only the meaning 'moderately'; J. G. Walther (1732) translated *allegro assai* as *ziemlich geschwind* ('fairly fast'); and late in the 19th century Stainer and Barrett's *Dictionary* translated *allegro assai* as '(lit.) Fast enough. A quicker motion than simple *allegro*'. Herrmann-Bengen (*Tempobezeichnungen*, 1959) drew attention to works by R. I. Mayr (1677) and Gottlieb Muffat (1735–9) which may well use *assai* in this moderate sense; and Brossard himself is witness that he used it thus in his own first book of motets (1695). Stewart Deas ('Beethoven's "Allegro assai"', *ML*, xxxi, 1950, p.333) argued plausibly that Beethoven also sometimes understood *assai* to mean 'moderately': of his copious evidence perhaps the most striking concerns the main theme in the finale of the Ninth Symphony, marked *moderato* in a late sketch but *allegro assai* in the finished product.

For bibliography *see* TEMPO AND EXPRESSION MARKS.

DAVID FALLOWS

Assandra [Alessandra], **Caterina** (*b* Pavia; *fl* 1609). Italian composer. A nun at the Convent of S Agata at Lomello, near Milan, she was one of a number of north Italian composers who published motets for a few voices and organ continuo in the new concertato style. Her *Motetti* op.2 (Milan, 1609) consists of two- and three-part motets with continuo following the model of Viadana's *Cento concerti ecclesiastici* of 1602; vocal lines are melismatic, there is much imitation between the voices in duets, and where one voice is a bass it has a more ornate part than the continuo bass. The sequential approach to harmony, apparent for example in the works of Viadana and in Monteverdi's madrigals, can also be seen in Assandra's motets. Her op.1 has not survived, but anthologies of the period include three of her motets (*RISM* 1616², 1622²).

BIBLIOGRAPHY
J. L. A. Roche: *North Italian Liturgical Music in the Early 17th Century* (diss., U. of Cambridge, 1968)

                                JEROME ROCHE

Assessment. See PSYCHOLOGY OF MUSIC, §IV.

Asseton [Assheton], Hugo. See ASTON, HUGH.

Assez (Fr.). See ASSAI.

Asshwell, Thomas. See ASHWELL, THOMAS.

Assisi. Italian city in the Umbria region. The earliest evidence of a flourishing musical activity in Assisi is given by a Franciscan breviary and two fragments with neumatic notation from the 13th century (*I-Ac* 683, 694 and 696). Another source from the same century (*Ac* 695), including nine compositions in early polyphonic style and probably originating at Rheims, provides a link between Assisi's musical life and the prevailing polyphonic practice of the time. Giuliano da Spira (*d* *c*1250) was at Assisi (1227–30) after having served at the court of Louis VIII in Paris; he was delegated to compose the first rhythmical Office of the Franciscan Order. Troubadour songs were cultivated by several secular societies (the most famous being the Del Monte) and were heard on 1 May each year when the town's districts competed in a musical contest called the Calendimaggio.

The community of the Friars Minor, founded by St Francis (*c*1181–1226) at Assisi, promoted the singing of *laude* during sermons and religious services. In the 13th and 14th centuries the singing of *laude* was also practised in Assisi by 12 religious confraternities. The statutes of the Confraternita di S Stefano, compiled in 1327, report that meetings were held at least twice weekly, when *laude* were sung to stir the hearts of the brothers to lamentation and tears.

From its construction in the last quarter of the 13th century the Basilica di S Francesco was the centre of the city's musical activities. In 1363 a new organ was installed by Francesco di Santa Colomba of Rimini. The most noted *maestro di cappella* in the 15th century was Lorenzo Panconi of Arezzo (1489–94). Venanzio da Alessandria filled the post in 1503, probably preceded by Ruffino Bartolucci, who subsequently returned there (1534–9) and who organized the installation of a new organ in the lower church in 1537. Among the composers who held posts at the basilica in the 16th century were Ludovico Balbi (a pupil of Costanzo Porta), Lorenzo da Porciano (1563), Nicolò d'Assisi (1587) and Silvestro d'Assisi (*c*1599).

In the Cathedral of S Rufino a *cappella musicale* was officially instituted in 1525 and organized on the model of the Roman papal chapel, after a new organ had been constructed in 1516 by Maestro Andrea da Firenze. The cathedral's *Atti capitolari* cite the appointments as organists and *maestri di cappella* of Ambrogino da Spello (1551), Matteo Rocchichiola (1561), Camillo da Frascati (1562), Gaetano Gabrat (1570), Francesc-antonio Contolini (1571), Camillo Lameto (1573), Giuseppe da Gubbio (1577), the Flemish Giovanni Tollio (1584) and Camillo Mattlem (1592).

In the 17th century *maestri di cappella* at S Francesco were Targhetti da Brescia (intermittently from 1614 to 1641), Claudio Cocchi (1632), Giovanni Battistini (1642), Antonio Cossando (1639–53). From 1649 at least 40 singers were employed, and the *cappella* reached its greatest splendour under the direction of Francesco Maria Angeli in the second half of the century.

The theorist and singer Giovanni Battista Bovicelli (*d* *c*1627) was active in Assisi from 1592 to 1627, singing at S Rufino from 1622 to 1627. Giacomo Carissimi also served the cathedral from 1628 to 1630, and Giuseppe O. Pitoni from 1674 to 1676. Outside the churches, music was promoted by the Accademia dei Disiosi (founded 1554) which later (1656) changed its name to Accademia degli Eccitati. In 1657 the academy presented a *dramma per musica*, *Dafne*, with players and singers from the basilica.

Maestri di cappella at S Francesco during the 18th century were the Bohemian Bohuslav Černohorsky (1712–15), Francesco Benedetti (intermittently from 1716 to 1746), Francesco Zuccari (intermittently from 1725 to 1788), Clemente Mattei (1781–3) and Luigi Vantaggi (1798–1800), while the cathedral was served by Pietro Sabbatini (intermittently from 1705 to 1743), Pietro Serafini (1745–55) and Giovanni Ricci in the second half of the century.

In 1750 the Accademia degli Eccitati was renamed Accademia dei Rinati and, in 1754, Accademia Properziana. Under its sponsorship, the architect Lorenzo Carpinelli began in 1836 the construction of the Teatro Metastasio, which was inaugurated in autumn 1840 with S. Mercadante's *Emma d'Antiochia*.

From 1858 to his death in 1896 Alessandro Borroni, a pupil of Rossini, directed the *cappella* at S Francesco. During this period, the cathedral frequently drew on the basilica for its singers and directors. During the first half of the 20th century Domenico Stella reorganized and catalogued the musical archives at the basilica and directed its *cappella* (1919–56); L. Perosi directed the première of his *Transitus animae Sancti Patris Nostri Francisci* there on 4 October 1937.

In 1927 the Accademia Properziana began to revive the tradition of the Calendimaggio, and each September since 1946 some of the musical productions of the Sagra Musicale Umbra have also taken place at Assisi. The Cantori di Assisi, directed by Evangelista Nicolini, was founded in 1960 and performs early music and folk music.

BIBLIOGRAPHY
RicordiE
Notizie relative al Teatro Metastasio di Assisi (Assisi, 1881)
G. Fratini: *Storia della Basilica e del Convento di S. Francesco d'Assisi* (Prato, 1882)
G. Mazzatinti and L. Alessandri: 'Assisi: Biblioteca del Convento di S. Francesco', *Inventari dei manoscritti delle biblioteche d'Italia*, iv (Forlì, 1894), 21–141
D. Stella: 'Serie dei maestri di cappella minori conv. di S. Francesco: compilata dal P. Stanislao Mattei [1800]', *Miscellanea francescana di storia, di lettere, di arti*, xxi (1920), 42; xxii (1921), 44, 134; xxiii (1922), 122
F. Pennacchi: 'Città di Assisi: Biblioteca comunale', *Bollettino dell'Associazione dei musicologi italiani: catalogo generale*, xi (Parma, 1921)
E. Bruning: 'Giuliano da Spira e l'Officio ritmico di S. Francesco', *NA*, iv (1927), 129–202
A. Fortini: 'La tradizione musicale della Basilica di Assisi', *Perusia: rassegna del Comune di Perugia*, ix (1937), 14
V. de Bartholomaeis: *Laude drammatiche e rappresentazioni sacre*, i (Florence, 1943), 315ff
A. Seay: 'Le Manuscrit 695 de la Bibliothèque communale d'Assise', *RdM*, xxxix (1957), 10
F. Noske: 'J. Tollius, ein niederländische Meister des Frühbarock', *IMSCR*, vii *Cologne 1958*, 203
G. Abate: 'Il primitivo Breviario Francescano (1224–1227)', *Miscellanea francescana*, lx (1960), 47–240

A. Fortini: *La lauda in Assisi e le origini del teatro italiano* (Assisi, 1961)
C. Sartori: *Assisi: la Capella della Basilica di S. Francesco*, i: *Catalogo del fondo musicale nella Biblioteca comunale di Assisi* (Milan, 1962)
G. Zaccaria: 'Il principale fondo musicale della Cappella di S. Francesco', *Miscellanea francescana di storia, di lettere, di arti*, lxii (1962), 155
A. Varotti: *La cappella musicale di San Rufino in Assisi: contributo per una storia* (Assisi, 1967)
G. Zaccaria: 'Ricordi di Saverio Mercadante in Assisi', *Altamura: bollettino dell'Archivio-Biblioteca-Museo Civico*, xiii (1971), 133
S. Martinotti: 'Assisi', *MGG*

ELVIDIO SURIAN

Assisi, Ruffino d'. *See* RUFFINO D'ASSISI.

Associated Board of the Royal Schools of Music. An institution established in 1889 which organizes local examinations on behalf of the RAM, the RCM, the Royal Northern College of Music and the Royal Scottish Academy of Music and Drama. It conducts grade examinations in a wide variety of practical and theoretical subjects, in Britain and abroad, and includes a licentiate award overseas (LRSM); its publishing department at its headquarters in London issues the music for these examinations and editions of the classical repertory, principally for piano.

Associated Music Publishers. American firm of music publishers. It was founded in 1927 by Paul Heinicke, originally as a sole American agency for leading European music publishing houses, including Bote & Bock, Breitkopf & Härtel, Doblinger, Eschig, Schott, Simrock, Union Musical Español and Universal Edition. The firm began publishing in its own right and has built up an important catalogue of contemporary American composers including Carter, Cowell, Harris, Piston and Riegger. About 1970 it was acquired by G. Schirmer, but it has retained an independent publishing programme.

ALAN PAGE

Association Artistique des Concerts du Châtelet. Parisian concert association active from 1874; *see* PARIS, §VII, 1.

Association Internationale des Bibliothèques Musicales (Fr.). INTERNATIONAL ASSOCIATION OF MUSIC LIBRARIES.

Assoucy, Charles d'. *See* DASSOUCY, CHARLES.

Assyria. *See* MESOPOTAMIA.

Assyrian rite, music of the. *See* SYRIAN CHURCH MUSIC.

Ast, Dietmar von. *See* DIETMAR VON AIST.

Astarita [Astaritta], **Gennaro** (*b* ?Naples, *c*1745–9; *d* after 1803). Italian composer. He has been called a Neapolitan, but his surname is very common on the Sorrento peninsula. He is first heard of in summer 1765, when he contributed some music to Piccinni's comic opera *L'orfana insidiata* at the Teatro dei Fiorentini, Naples. This has led to the suggestion that he may have been Piccinni's pupil. He left Naples after producing two operas at the Fiorentini (1765–6); in 1768 an *azione drammatica* by him was performed in Palermo, and in 1770–71 he had two comic operas performed in Turin. From Carnival 1772 to autumn

1779 he produced a series of operas in Venice and other northern and central Italian cities, including Florence (1773) and Bologna (1778). In 1779 he completed his friend Traetta's last opera and in 1780 was at Pressburg (now Bratislava) where he produced three operas. After a long gap in his output he went to Moscow as music director of the Petrovsky Theatre (1784), producing a ballet there in January 1785; he then moved to St Petersburg (1786), where he may have had an opera performed in 1787 (the evidence is a score with that date in Leningrad). He evidently spent the rest of his life working in Italy and Russia: several new operas were performed in Venice, Milan and Florence between 1789 and 1793; and in 1794 he was sent by the director of the imperial theatres to engage an Italian opera company. He returned to St Petersburg in 1795 as its *maestro compositore*, and in 1796 he composed for it a comic opera, *Rinaldo d'Asti*; in 1799 the company was taken into the imperial service. In July 1803 he announced his departure from Russia.

Astarita wrote over 40 operas, almost all of which are comic. La Borde called him a 'very pleasant modern composer' who appealed more to the general public than to great connoisseurs; he singled out the rondò 'Come lasciar poss'io l'anima mia che adoro' as one of the best known.

WORKS

Operas: more than 40, incl. Il re alla caccia, Turin, 1770, ov. *D-Bds* (autograph); La contessa di Bimbimpoli (Il divertimento in campagna), Venice, 1772, *Dlb*; I visionari, Venice, 1772, *I-Mr*, *P-La* (as I filosofi immaginari), *USSR-Lit*; L'isola disabitata, Florence, 1773, *A-Wn* (as perf. Pressburg, 1780); Le finezze d'amore, o sia La farsa non si fa, ma si prova, Venice, 1773, rev. Milan, 1791, *I-Mr* (as Non si fa ma si prova); Il principe ipocondriaco, Venice, 1774, *P-La* (without Act 3); Armida, Venice, 1777, *I-Fc*, *P-La* (as Rinaldo)
L'isola del Bengodi, Venice, 1777, *I-Fc* (autograph); Il francese bizzarro, Venice, 1779, *D-Dlb*, *F-Pc*; Nicoletto bellavita, ?Naples, ?1779, *I-Mr*; La Didone abbandonata, Pressburg, 1780, *A-Wn* (autograph); Il trionfo della pietà, Pressburg, 1780, *Wn* (autograph); I capricci in amore, ?1787, *USSR-Lit* (autograph); Il curioso accidente, Venice, 1789, *I-Fc*; Il medico parigino, Venice, 1792, *USSR-Lit*; Rinaldo d'Asti, St Petersburg, 1796, *Lit*; Gl'intrighi per amore, *Lit*
Other works incl.: Cantata, S, b, *D-Dlb*; Alma redemptoris mater, T, orch, *A-Wgm*; Laudate pueri, B, insts, 1784, *I-Gi(l)*; Tantum ergo, S, insts, *Nc*; Salve tu Domine, S, orch, *E-Mp*

BIBLIOGRAPHY

EitnerQ
J.-B. de La Borde: *Essai sur la musique ancienne et moderne* (Paris, 1780/R1972)
S. di Giacomo: 'Paisiello e i suoi contemporanei', *Musica e musicisti*, lx (1905), 762; repr. in *Napoli: figure e paesi* (Naples, 1909) and *Opere*, ii (Milan, 1945), 535
R. A. Mooser: *Annales de la musique et musiciens en Russie au XVIIIème siècle* (Geneva, 1949–51)
U. Prota-Giurleo: 'Astarita, Gennaro', *DBI*
DENNIS LIBBY (text), JAMES L. JACKMAN (work-list)

Aste, Dietmar von. *See* DIETMAR VON AIST.

Aston [Asseton, Assheton, Ashton, Haston], **Hugh** [Hugo] (*b c*1485; *d* ? Nov 1558). English composer. On 20 November 1510, having spent eight years in the study of music, he supplicated at Oxford University for the degree of BMus, submitting as his exercise a mass and an antiphon. Harrison noted that Aston's *Te Deum* (which may originally have had the text 'Te matrem Dei laudamus') has its opening few bars in common with three of the four movements of his *Missa 'Te Deum'*, comprising a musical pair which may have been the works submitted. Aston was formerly identified with the canon of St Stephen's, Westminster, and archdeacon of York Minster, but he is now believed to have been *magister choristarum* at St Mary Newarke Hospital and

College in Leicester from about 1525 until its dissolution in 1548. He was presumably the master of the choristers whom Bishop Longland proposed to send from Newarke College to Wolsey's new Cardinal College, Oxford, in 1526, but Taverner accepted the appointment instead and Aston remained in Newarke. His pension was paid up to 17 Nov 1558.

Although only four pieces of church music by Aston have survived intact, his keyboard music occupies a special place in music history. His 'Hornepype' shows a grasp of idiomatic keyboard writing in advance of continental practice of the time. On stylistic grounds *My Lady Careys Dompe* and *The Short Mesure off my Lady Wynkfelds Rownde* have been attributed to Aston but there is no manuscript evidence for this. There can be little doubt that this keyboard music was associated with Henry VIII's court and this leads to the supposition that Aston was in London during the period 1510–25. *Hugh Ashton's Maske* (*Och* 979–83; lacking the bass) may be by William Whytbroke, whose name occurs against one of the parts; the same ground was used by Byrd.

WORKS

Editions: *H. Aston, J. Merbecke, O. Parsley*, ed. P. C. Buck and others, TCM, x (1929) [contains all the vocal music]
      Schott's Anthology of Early Keyboard Music, ed. F. Dawes, i (London, 1951) [S]

VOCAL

Missa 'Te Deum', 5vv, *GB-Ob* Mus.Sch. E. 376–81; inc. in *Cjc* 234, *Cu* Dd.13.27, *Cu* Peterhouse 471–4 (471 contains beginning of another copy with heading 'Te matrem')
Missa 'Videte manus meas', 6vv, *Ob* Mus.Sch. E. 376–81
Gaude mater matris Christe, 5vv, *Ob* Mus.Sch. E. 1–5; inc. in *Cu* Peterhouse 471–4, *Lbm* Harl.1709, Add.34191 as Gaude virgo mater Christi
Te Deum laudamus, 5vv, *Ob* Mus.Sch. E. 1–5; inc. in *Cjc* 234, *Cu* Dd.13.27, *Lbm* Harl.1709 (attrib. T. Ashwell) as Te matrem dei laudamus; two passages for 3vv 'Tu ad liberandum' and 'Tu angelorum domina' in *Lbm* Roy.App.24.D.2 (attrib. J. Taverner)
Ave domina, inc. *Lbm* Harl.7578 (triplex)
Ave Maria ancilla, inc. *Cu* Peterhouse 472–4
Ave Maria divae matris, inc. *Cu* Peterhouse 471–4
O baptista, inc. *Cu* Peterhouse 472–4

KEYBOARD

A Hornepype, *Lbm* Roy.App.58, ed. in S
Attributed to Aston on stylistic grounds (but possibly not by him): My Lady Careys Dompe, *Lbm* Roy.App.58; The Short Mesure off my Lady Wynkfelds Rownde, *Lbm* Roy.App.58; both ed. in S

BIBLIOGRAPHY

F. Ll. Harrison: *Music in Medieval Britain* (London, 1958, 2/1963)
N. Sandon: 'The Henrician Partbooks at Peterhouse, Cambridge', *PRMA*, ciii (1976–7), 106

JOHN BERGSAGEL

Aston, Peter (George) (*b* Birmingham, 5 Oct 1938). English composer and teacher. He studied at the Birmingham School of Music, at the University of York as a postgraduate, and privately with Mellers for composition. He was appointed lecturer in music at York in 1964 and became professor of music at the University of East Anglia in 1974. While pursuing his academic career he has directed the Tudor Consort (which he founded), the English Baroque Ensemble, the York University Choir and Chamber Choir and, from 1975, the Aldeburgh Festival Singers.

As a composer Aston has written almost exclusively for voices, with or without instrumental accompaniment. This reflects his activities as a conductor, the inspiration he finds in setting religious texts, and his particular interest in the music of the Italian and English Baroque. His first acknowledged work, *Five Songs of Crazy Jane* (1960), is a folklike monody for solo soprano. But there are few traces of folk idiom in his later and more characteristic work, which is derived

rather from the European church music tradition. The stimulus comes mainly from the Baroque, most fruitfully in his most important work, *Haec dies*, but also from the Renaissance and the Middle Ages. Monteverdi and George Jeffreys are acknowledged influences; he has edited the latter's collected works (London, 1977–) The consequent antique flavour of his music, modified by his personal melodic voice, some influence from Messiaen and his own fresh rhythmic imagination, makes Aston among the most distinctive of contemporary British composers of church music.

WORKS

Sacred: 3 Hymns to the Virgin, SATB, 1962; There is no Rose, S, SATB, org, 1965; Balulalow, SATB, org, 1966; Lullay, my Child, SA, 1966; Psalm lxvii, SSATB, org, 1967; Alleluya psallat I, 6 solo vv, 1967; And I saw a new heaven, S, SATB, org, 1969; For I went with the multitude, SATB, org, 1970; Divine Image, SATB, 1970; Psalm cl, SSAATTBB, brass, 1970; Alleluya psallat II, SATB, 1971; Magnificat and Nunc dimittis, SSAATTBB, org, 1972; Communion Service, F, 1973; Make we Joye, 4 carols, SATB, 1973; Hosanna to the Son of David, SATB, org, 1974; Hodie, Christus natus est, SATB, org, 1974; 14 Short Introits, SATB, org, 1974
Secular choral: Chamber Cantata, A, Bar, chorus, small orch, 1960; 3 Shakespeare Songs, S, SSA, 1964; There was a Boy, SATB, 1964; 2 Choruses (Raine), SATB, 1965; Love Song, SATB, 1966; Illuminatio, cantata, SATB, wind qnt, 1969; Haec dies, dialogues and sonatas, SATB, org, 1971; Carmen lumenis, chorus, wind, 1974; Paean, SATB, org, 1976; The True Glory, chorus, str orch, 1976
Solo voice: 5 Songs of Crazy Jane, S, 1960; A Northumbrian Sequence, Mez, pf, 1964; My Dancing Day, cantata, S, T, fl, cl, str qt, 1966
Inst: Nocturne, fl, perc, 1965; 3 Pieces, ob, 1968
Children's opera: Sacrapane the Sorcerer, 1970

WRITINGS

'George Jeffreys', *MT*, cx (1969), 772
with J. Paynter: *Sound and Silence* (London, 1970)
The Music of York Minster (London, 1972)
'Tradition and Experiment in the Devotional Music of George Jeffreys', *PRMA*, xcix (1972–3), 105

GERALD LARNER

Astor & Co. Anglo-American firm of musical instrument makers of German origin. The two founders were the sons of Jacob Astor, a merchant of Mannheim. George [Georg] Astor (*b* Waldorf, nr. Heidelberg, *c*1760) went to England as a young man in about 1778, and, getting employment with a flute maker, asked his younger brother John [Johann] Jacob Astor (*b* Waldorf, 1763; *d* ?New York, 1848) to join him in London. Together they started business as flute makers. In 1783 John Jacob went to the USA with a small consignment of flutes, visiting another brother who was settled at Baltimore. The value of his stock of flutes is said to have been only about £5, but on advice given him by a fellow voyager he invested the proceeds of his sales in furs and by selling these in England made a handsome profit. He went again to the USA and quickly profited by fur trading and by the sale of musical instruments sent to him from England. He appears to have settled permanently in New York before 1795. A New York newspaper of 10 January 1798 shows his advertisement:

J. Jacob Astor, at No. 81 Queen Street. . . . Has for Sale an Assortment of Pianofortes of the Newest Construction, Made by the best Makers in London. . . . He gives cash For All Kinds of Furs. . . .

Some of the instruments which he had taken to America when visiting Baltimore in 1783 are claimed as having been purchased by Samuel W. Hildebrandt of 19 North Liberty Street, Baltimore, the oldest maker of brass instruments in the USA. They are still owned by this firm and include a flute and a bass clarinet. This latter, according to the *Musical Courier* (USA) of 9 August 1899, bears the inscription '1748, Astor & Co., 79 Cornhill, London'. As the firm was not at this address until about 1796, and as it is also doubtful if a bass clarinet with an upturned bell existed so early, the date may be a misprint for 1798.

In 1809 John Jacob established a fur-trading company, and by this and the purchase of land in The Bowery laid the foundations of the Astor wealth. The family has maintained its active interest in music. The 2nd Viscount Astor served as Master of the Worshipful Company of Musicians in 1934–5, of which company the original George Astor had become a member on 28 December 1796. The Hon. John Jacob Astor, brother of Lord Astor, became a member of the council of the RCM and founder there of a fund for the benefit of students starting their professional careers.

The elder brother, George, who remained in London, occupied a small shop in Wych Street, Drury Lane, making flutes and other musical instruments. Before the end of 1796 he moved to 79 Cornhill, and he was also at 27 Tottenham Street near Fitzroy Square. Before 1800 he was making pianos and publishing sheet music and minor books, such as flute instructors. In 1801 he was in partnership, and the firm styled itself 'organ builders'.

In 1815 the firm was Astor & Harwood, at 79 Cornhill and 76 Bishopsgate Street. It made some very dainty pianos of satinwood, and before 1824 Christopher Gerock became senior partner. (He had been a manufacturer of pianos at 76 Bishopsgate Street Within before 1805.) In 1831 the Astor firm seems to have been merged into that of Gerock & Wolf, at the old Cornhill address. George Astor and his successors published yearly books of country dances, those for 1805 and 1818 being in the British Museum.

FRANK KIDSON/H. G. FARMER/R

Astorga, Emanuele (Gioacchino Cesare Rincón) d', Baron (*b* Augusta, Sicily, 20 March 1680; *d* ?Madrid, ?1757). Italian composer. Before Volkmann's research his biography (as given, for example, by Fétis) was largely a tissue of colourful legend. He came of a family of Spanish descent that acquired a Sicilian barony in the early 17th century. After an earthquake in 1693 the family moved from Augusta to Palermo. Soon after, his father attempted to murder his mother and was banished from Palermo with loss of civil and political rights, the title passing to Emanuele's elder brother. In 1702 his father was reinstated in his rights and title and in 1706 became a senator of Palermo. After quarrelling with him, Emanuele left home, by early 1708 at the latest, and for several years lived on his wits. He had shown signs of great musical talent at an early age, and in 1698 an opera of his, *La moglie nemica*, had been performed privately in Palermo by aristocratic amateurs, with himself and his brother in the leading female parts. In later years he gave salon performances of his own cantatas, which make up the bulk of his compositions and are mostly for solo voice and continuo.

Going to Rome, Astorga became part of the circle of the Duke of Osseda, Spain's papal ambassador; there he made friends with the Neapolitan poet Sebastiano Biancardi, who provided the texts for some of his cantatas. The 1732 Venice edition of Biancardi's poems is prefaced by an account of his life which is an important source of information about Astorga at this period. They went to Genoa, where they were robbed by their servant, and to raise money Astorga wrote an opera, *Dafni*, performed there on 21 April 1709. Under the assumed names Giuseppe del Chiaro and Domenico Lalli, they then visited Tortona, Mantua and Venice.

Probably late in 1709 or early in 1710 Astorga went to Barcelona at the summons of Charles III, the Hasburg claimant to the Spanish throne, who had been impressed by *Dafni* when it was performed at Barcelona in summer 1709. In 1711 Charles III became emperor as Charles VI and returned to Vienna. Astorga may have accompanied him there or may have gone earlier, as he was granted a large pension by Emperor Joseph I, later confirmed by Charles VI. On 9 May 1712 he stood, in the place of his friend the Dutch ambassador Bruyninx, godfather to a daughter of Antonio Caldara. He may have composed the anonymous one-act opera, *Zenobia*, produced in Vienna a few weeks later.

Astorga left Vienna (and a number of debts) in spring 1714, returning to Palermo the following year. Probably because he had sided with the Austrians during the War of the Spanish Succession, the estates he would normally have inherited (along with the title, his brother having also died) on his father's death in 1712 had been confiscated. They were reclaimed by his mother and sister and made over to him on his return. In October 1717 he married the 15-year-old Emanuela Guzzardi, who bore him three daughters. From May 1717 to June 1718 he was a senator of Palermo and from 1718 to 1720 a governor of the hospital for incurables there. In 1721, however, he restored his wife's dowry and made over to her the income from his estates in return for an annuity; he then left Sicily and apparently never returned. Manuscript cantatas (in *GB-Lcm*) are dated Lisbon, 1721 and 1722. Two villancicos by him in honour of St Vincent were sung at the cathedral there on 21 June 1723, and in 1726 he published there a volume of 12 chamber cantatas, *Cantadas humanas a solo*, with Spanish and Italian words, his only works to be printed in his lifetime.

Hawkins relates that Astorga 'was at Lisbon some time, and after that at Leghorn, where being exceedingly caressed by the English merchants there he was induced to visit England, and passed a winter or two in London, from where he went to Bohemia'. The London visit is not supported by documentary evidence, but Hawkins's details (for example that Astorga was very shortsighted) suggest that his information came from someone who had known the composer. Nothing certain is known about the latter part of Astorga's life. The latest manuscript date is 1731. His Sicilian estates were sold in 1744 by his deserted wife and sister, who were heavily in debt. The date and place given for his death are highly doubtful, being known only from a notation on a manuscript in the Santini collection (*D-MÜs*).

The opera *Dafni* was revived at Parma in 1715 and Breslau in 1726. Only the first act is extant (in *A-Wn* and *D-Dlb*); the overture and some arias were published by Carreras y Bulbena in 1902. In his own day Astorga was best known for his chamber cantatas, which exist in numerous manuscripts. Volkmann found 162 (and 15 that he considered doubtful); Tiby claimed to have found about 20 more without giving details. These very fluently written and agreeable works, several of which have been published in modern editions, move within the same general formal and stylistic bounds as Scarlatti's cantatas without attaining the degree of musical invention or sensitivity towards the joining of words and music displayed by Scarlatti at his best. Astorga's only sacred work known to be extant, the *Stabat mater* in C minor for solo voices, mixed chorus, strings and continuo, was dated about 1707 by

Volkmann on purely stylistic, and rather debatable, grounds. No performances of it are known before the middle of the century, but from about 1760 to 1840 it enjoyed great popularity and was published several times in the 19th century.

BIBLIOGRAPHY

FétisB; HawkinsH
S. Biancardi: *Rime* (Venice, 1732)
J. R. Carreras y Bulbena: *Carlos d'Austria y Elisabeth de Brunswick Wolfenbüttel a Barcelona y Gerona* (Barcelona, 1902)
H. Volkmann: *Emanuel d'Astorga* (Leipzig, 1911–19) [incl. list of works]
L. Genuardi: 'Emmanuele Rincon d'Astorga, musicista siciliano del secolo XVIII', *Archivio storico siciliano*, new ser., xxxvi (1912), 488
G. Sorge: *I teatri di Palermo* (Palermo, 1926), 207ff, 383
F. Walker: 'Emanuele d'Astorga and a Neapolitan Librettist', *MMR*, lxxxi (1951), 90
O. Tiby: 'Emanuele d'Astorga: aggiunte e correzioni da apportare alle richerche del Prof. Hans Volkmann', *IMSCR, v Utrecht 1952*, 398
    ALFRED LOEWENBERG, FRANK WALKER/R

Astorga, Jean Oliver. *See* OLIVER Y ASTORGA, JUAN.

Astor Place Opera House. New York theatre opened in 1847; *see* NEW YORK, §2.

Åstrand, (Karl) Hans (Vilhelm) (*b* Bredaryd, 5 Feb 1925). Swedish musician and lexicographer. He studied the double bass, cello, organ and music theory privately and romance languages at Lund University (graduated 1958). He was appointed to teach French and Spanish at the Malmö Gymnasium (1959), and has continued to pursue various musical activities, including posts as music critic of the Malmö newspaper *Kvällsposten* (from 1950), founder and leader of Chamber Choir '53 (1953–62), founder (1960) and director (1965–71) of the Ars Nova society for new music, programme director of Sal. Smith Chamber Music Society (from 1966) and (from 1976) music critic of the Stockholm weekly *Veckojournalen*. He has also taught music history at the Malmö National School of Drama (1963–71), and served as a board member of the Malmö High School of Music (from 1964) and the Stockholm Royal Academy of Music (from 1966; secretary from 1973). In 1972 he was appointed editor-in-chief of the second edition of *Sohlmans musik-lexikon* (Stockholm, 1975–). Apart from his work for this, Åstrand has written mostly about the musical life of Skåne, the south-western province of Sweden, in which he himself has played a particularly active role; he has contributed several chapters to *Musik i Skåne* (Malmö, 1971) and to *Svenska musikperspektiv* (Stockholm, 1971).

JOHN BERGSAGEL

Asuar, José Vicente (*b* Santiago, 20 July 1933). Chilean composer and acoustic engineer. He studied composition with Urrutia-Blondel at the Santiago National Conservatory (1947–56), with Blacher at the Berlin Hochschule für Musik (1959–60) and with Wildberger at the Baden Hochschule für Musik. In addition, he studied engineering at the Catholic University of Chile (1953–9) and at the Technical University in Berlin (1959–60); while in Berlin he had lessons with Winckel and Meyer-Eppler. He also attended the Darmstadt summer courses of 1960–62. From 1958 to 1959 he directed the electronic music studio at the Catholic University of Chile, where he composed the *Variaciones espectrales*, and he organized a studio at Karlsruhe (1960–62). He gave a seminar in electronic music at Salvador, Brazil (1962) and served as professor of

acoustics and contemporary music at the Santiago National Conservatory (1963–5). At the invitation of the Institute of Culture and Fine Arts, he moved to Caracas to establish and direct the first electronic music studio in Venezuela (1965–8). He then prepared and directed a course in sound technology at the University of Chile (1968–72). In 1970 he received a Fulbright Grant to study computer music with Hiller at Buffalo, New York.

WORKS
(*selective list*)

Inst: Encadenamientos, fl, bn, vn, vc, 1957; 3 ejercicios, str qt, 1960; Heterofonias, orch, 1964; Octet, 4 fl, 4 perc, 1966; Guararia repano, Venezuelan Indian insts, tape, 1968; Formas I–II, computer scores, orch, 1970, 1972
Vocal: Imagen de Caracas, vv, insts, tape, 1968
Tape: Variaciones espectrales, 1959; Preludio a la noche, 1961; Estudio aleatorio, 1962; Serenata para mi voz, 1962; La noche II, 1966; Catedral, 1967; Kaleidoscopio, 1967; Divertimento, 1968; Buffalo 71, 1971

WRITINGS
Generación mecanica y electronica del sonido musical (diss., Catholic U. of Chile, 1957)
Articles in *Revista musical chilena*

JUAN A. ORREGO-SALAS

Asula [Asulae]**, Giammateo.** *See* ASOLA, GIAMMATEO.

Aswell, Thomas. *See* ASHWELL, THOMAS.

Atehortúa, Blas Emilio (*b* Medellin, 3 Oct 1933). Colombian composer. He studied with Roots, Pardo Tovar and González-Zuleta at the Conservatory of the National University of Colombia (1960–63). In 1963–4 and again in 1966–8 he studied in Buenos Aires with Ginastera, Xenakis, Nono and others at the Torcuato Di Tella Institute. He was an invited contributor to the Second Panamerican Music Festival (Mexico City, 1963), the First Symposium of American Composers (New Orleans, 1965) and the Fourth Interamerican Music Festival (Washington, DC, 1968). The 1965 première at the Bogotá Conservatory of his *Cántico delle creature* gained him the reputation of a member of the avant garde. From that year he has frequently conducted in Argentina, Bolivia, Colombia and Peru, usually including one of his own works in his programmes. He was appointed professor at the Universidad Pedagógica y Tecnológica in Tunja (1969) and head of the Bogotá Conservatory (1973). His orchestral compositions are moderately astringent, tightly constructed, usually quite shapely and rhythmically pungent.

WORKS
(*selective list*)

Cántico delle creature (St Francis), B, 2 chamber choruses, wind, perc, dbs, tape, 1965; Concertante, timp, chamber orch, 1968; Estudios sinfónicos, orch, 1968; 5 piezas breves, fl, va, harp, 1969; Ww Qnt, 1969; Conc., str orch, 1970; Divertimento, str orch, 1970; Diagramas, orch, 1971; Partita 72, str, 1972

ROBERT STEVENSON

Atempause (Ger.: 'breath-break'). Usually a breathing-pause indicated by a superscript comma; *see* LUFT-PAUSE.

A tempo (It.: 'in time'). An instruction to return to the previous tempo after a deliberate deviation.

Ath, Andreas d' (*fl* 1622–30). South Netherlands composer and organist. The title-page of his first publication shows that in 1622 he was chaplain and organist of the collegiate church of St Paul, Liège. From 17 October

1623 he held a benefice at Liège Cathedral. On the title-page of his volume of 1626 he is described as chaplain of the cathedral, and he is mentioned in documents in the cathedral archives dated 4 August 1628 and 20 April 1630. He was replaced as beneficiary before 1639. As a composer he is known by two books of motets, *Prolusiones musicae*, for two to five voices and continuo (Douai, 1622, incomplete), and *Tomus secundus Prolusionum musicarum*, for three to six voices and continuo (Douai, 1626). They are similar on all counts. Ath was brought up in the polyphonic tradition, but he included continuo parts and made each voice equally important. The motets begin with strict imitation and continue with freer imitative textures. The motifs are generally short, and there are some roulades, often in dotted rhythm. As a disciple of the Jesuits he took special care over the correct accentuation of the words. His works most probably influenced those of Hodemont and the young Du Mont.

BIBLIOGRAPHY
E. vander Straeten: *La musique aux Pays-Bas avant le XIXe siècle*, viii (Brussels, 1888/*R*1969)
A. Auda: *La musique et les musiciens de l'ancien pays de Liège* (Liège, 1930)
JOSÉ QUITIN

Athanasian Creed. See CREDO.

Athanassov, Georgi (*b* Plovdiv, 6 May 1882; *d* Lake Garda, 17 Nov 1931). Bulgarian composer and conductor. Orphaned at an early age, he taught himself to play several instruments and was sent by his uncle to study the trombone and the piano at the Bucharest Conservatory. He played the trombone at the Bucharest Opera, and then returned to Bulgaria for a short while before travelling to Italy in 1901; there he studied composition with Mascagni at the Pesaro Conservatory. Returning to Bulgaria again, he served as a military bandmaster in various towns (1903–14). Later he conducted more than 90 orchestral concerts in Sofia over a period of many years; these were the first regular symphony concerts in Bulgaria since the liberation of 1878. He died while undergoing medical treatment in Italy.

WORKS
(*selective list*)
Stage: Borislav (opera, after I. Wasov), perf. 1911; Moralisti, operetta, 1916; Gergana (opera, after P. Slaweikov: Iswora na belonogata), perf. 1917; Sapustjalata wodeniza (The abandoned mill, opera, A. Morfov), perf. 1923; Zveta (opera, Tschernodrinski), perf. 1925; Kossara (opera, B. Danovski), perf. 1929; Alzek (opera, P. Karapetrov), perf. 1930
Many military marches, 25 children's songs, 10 songs, pf pieces

BIBLIOGRAPHY
L. Sagaev: *Maestro Georgi Athanassov* (Sofia, 1961)
LADA BRASHOVANOVA

Athenaeus (*b* Naucratis, Egypt; *fl* AD *c*200). Greek grammarian and encyclopedist. He settled in Rome at the beginning of the 3rd century AD. None of his works has survived except the *Deipnosophistae*, a vast compendium in 15 extant books. Its generic form is that of the literary symposium; as a species, it deals with antiquarian lore rather than such 'higher themes' as philosophy. Its main topic is food; the mock-academic title, often mistranslated as 'The doctors at dinner' or the like, properly describes specialists whose learning centres tirelessly upon the joys of the kitchen. The work is not, however, a cookery book.

Many characters engage in this marathon after-dinner conversation; they include representatives of every profession thought to be consequential, among them musicians, both professional and amateur. It has been rightly noted that the diverse themes are related to the banquet itself with but indifferent success. The unified structure of Plato's *Symposium*, like its wit, has no parallel in the quite miscellaneous learning of Athenaeus. When his speakers turn their attention to music, they are no whit less pedantic or arbitrary than usual. Nevertheless, what they say has frequent, and sometimes unique, value for the Greek music historian. (Except for a handful of scattered references, the work ignores Roman music.)

Almost at the outset (14*b–d*), Athenaeus interpreted the function of bards in Homer, wrongly, as didactic: for him they were.sober teachers of morality, not entertainers. A long section on instruments (174*a*–185*a*) proves more reliable: after a description of the hydraulis or water-organ (174*a–e*), the author went on to consider the varieties of aulos and its popularity among the Greeks 'of the olden time' (176*f*–182*e*, 184*d–f*). He discussed the aulos further in a much later passage (616*e*–618*c*) which contains especially valuable literary quotations. Unfortunately, the evidence seems to have been wrongly construed at least twice here. There follows an extensive and highly important section on the ethical and educational aspects of music (623*f*–638*e*). It embodies long passages (624*c*–625*e*) taken from the writings of an anonymous Academic theoretician from Heraclea in Pontus, a figure of the 4th century BC usually given the meaningless name 'Heraclides Ponticus'. Most notably, he held that there were only three modes, corresponding to the broad national characteristics of the Dorians, Aeolians and Ionians. The claim at the end of this section that 'a mode must have a specific character (*ēthos*) or feeling (*pathos*)' sounds like a distorted version of Aristotle's comment in the opening passages of the *Poetics* (1447*a*, l.28), perhaps including also the favourite *ethos–pathos* distinction made by later rhetoricians. A notable reference follows (628*c*) to the Damonian theory of singing and dancing as consequences of the soul's motion. He also mentioned Pythagoras's belief in music as the binding principle of the cosmos (632*b–c*).

Athenaeus's claim to literary eminence is that of the colporteur. He salvaged from oblivion more than 10,000 lines of Greek verse, including some of the finest surviving fragments of the lyrics of Sappho and Alcaeus. The great number of citations and comments concerning Hellenic and Hellenistic music has secured for him an unquestioned place among the valued later sources.

BIBLIOGRAPHY
G. Kaibel, ed.: *Deipnosophistarum libri xv* (Leipzig, 1887–90/*R*1961)
C. B. Gulick, ed. and trans.: *Athenaeus: the Deipnosophists* (London, 1927–41, 2/1957–63)
A. M. Desrousseaux, ed. and trans.: *Athénée de Naucratis: Les deipnosophistes* (Paris, 1956)
G. Turturro, ed. and trans.: *I deipnosofisti* (Bari, 1961)
WARREN ANDERSON

Athens (Gk. Athínai). For discussion of Athenian musical life *see* GREECE.

Atherton, David (*b* Blackpool, 3 Jan 1941). English conductor. After reading music at Cambridge University, where he conducted the university operatic society, he attended the répétiteurs' course at the London Opera Centre. In 1967 he joined Covent Garden's staff and in 1968 became the youngest conductor ever to appear at that house (in *Il trovatore*) as well as the youngest to conduct at a Henry Wood Promenade Concert – in a single item, John Tavener's *In alium*. In the same year he conducted at the Aldeburgh Festival the first performances of Harrison Birtwistle's opera, *Punch and Judy*.

Atherton's committed sympathy for modern music, and his special role as a midwife to British works in 'advanced' styles, were conspicuously shown in his work with the London Sinfonietta, of which he was musical director from its début at the Queen Elizabeth Hall in 1968 until he retired on completing a Schoenberg–Gerhard series in 1973. The first concert included the première of Tavener's *The Whale*, which he afterwards recorded with the Sinfonietta. Other works of which he directed first performances with the Sinfonietta included Birtwistle's *Verses for Ensembles* (1969) and Iain Hamilton's *Voyage* (with Barry Tuckwell, horn, 1971). At Covent Garden, he has conducted *Carmen*, *Don Giovanni*, *Eugene Onegin*, *King Priam* and other works. He has also conducted the Welsh National Opera Company and various British symphony orchestras. His recordings, apart from those with the London Sinfonietta, include a series of modern Welsh orchestral works for the Welsh Arts Council. In January 1970 he gave a series of concerts in various Dutch cities with the Netherlands Chamber Orchestra, and he has since conducted in Italy, the USSR, Japan, Canada and elsewhere. He occasionally appears as a pianist, and at the Brighton Festival of 1973 partnered Tuckwell and Menuhin in Berkeley's Horn Trio.

ARTHUR JACOBS

Athesinus, Leonardus. *See* LECHNER, LEONHARD.

Athos, Mount. Semi-autonomous monastic 'republic' comprising numerous Greek and other Christian monastic communities, on a peninsula of the same name, east of Thessaloniki in northern Greece; the peninsula is also known as the 'Holy Mountain' (*Hagion oros*) or the 'Garden of the All-Holy Virgin'. Since the Middle Ages, and especially since the fall of Constantinople, Athos has been an important centre of the music of the Byzantine rite. A number of important musicians and composers worked there, including Joannes Koukouzelēs, who lived near Lavra in the 14th century. Many important manuscripts were written there, and the Athonite monasteries are now unusual in their adherence to the regular recitation of the Byzantine Offices.

1. History. 2. Organization. 3. Manuscripts.

1. HISTORY. Owing to its isolation and semi-desert nature, Athos is an ideal monastic site, and monasteries were established there in the 9th century (earlier references to monasteries seem to be legendary). The oldest continuously inhabited monastery, however, is the Great Lavra (Laura), founded in 963 by St Athanasius of Athos with the support of the Byzantine Emperor Nicephorus Phocas. The number of subsequent foundations grew rapidly; there are references, perhaps exaggerated, to some 180 monastic settlements in the 11th century and close to 300 by the early 13th century. Later, however, the number of monasteries diminished. In the early 13th century crusaders conquered Constantinople and many monasteries lost their property and suffered economic decline. In the early 14th century Athos was ravaged by Catalan soldiers; for over 20 years in the middle of that century it was a part of the Serbian Empire. The monks were sharply divided during the 14th century by the theological controversy over the views of Gregory Palamas. At that period, too, the 'idiorhythmic' system of monastic organization was introduced (see §2 below).

From about 1430 Athos submitted to the Turks, who granted the area internal autonomy but taxed it heavily. By the end of the 16th century, the number of 'ruling' monasteries had been established as 20 (see §2 below). In 1783 Athos obtained its sixth constitution which, with some minor modifications, is still in effect. With the disintegration of the Ottoman Empire in the 1912 Balkan War, Greece assumed the responsibility for maintaining the traditions of Mount Athos.

A Greek Academy (school for monks) had been established under the Turks in about 1749 but abolished after barely ten years. An abortive attempt was made to reopen it in 1930, but it was finally reopened in 1953. Besides the monks, orphans are educated there, who, it is hoped, may later choose to become monks themselves. In the last 300 years it is believed that the number of monks at its maximum exceeded 12,000; in 1905 there were more than 7500 (nearly half of them Russians, with slightly fewer Greeks and a small number of Bulgarians, Romanians and Serbs). In 1968, however, there were fewer than 1300 (excluding servants); the average age of monks is 55–60. The monks at Athos have never been exclusively Greek: at one time there was a Latin monastery of Amalfitans; the monastery of Iviron (Ibērōn) was founded by Georgians from the Caucasus; and there are Russian, Bulgarian, Serbian and Romanian monks.

2. ORGANIZATION. Athos resembles a confederation: each monastery sends a delegate to the 'Holy Community' (*hiera koinotēs*), the highest ruling body, which acts like a parliament. Daily affairs are administered by an executive 'Holy Epistasia' (*hiera epistasia*) of four members; each monastery is represented in the Epistasia one year in five, and the *protepistat* or head of the Epistasia must come from one of the five 'great' monasteries, Lavra, Vatopedi (Batopediou), Iviron, Chilandari(ou) and Dionysiou.

Besides these five monasteries, the 'ruling' monasteries are, in order of rank rather than age, Koutloumousi(ou), Pantocrator (Pantokratōr or Pantokratōros), Xiropotamou (Xēropotamou), Zografou (Zōgraphou), Dochiariou (Docheiariou), Karakalou, Philotheou, Simonos Petras, Agiou Pavlou (Hagiou Paulou, St Paul), Stavronikita (Staurōnikēta), Xenofontou (Xenophōntos), Grigoriou (Grēgoriou), Esfigmenou (Esphigmenou), Agiou Panteleimonos (Hagiou Panteleēmonos, Panteleimonos, Rossikon) and Ko(n)stamonitou. These monasteries comprise at least a *katholikon* (main church), additional chapels and quarters for monks and servants. Besides the ruling monasteries there are communities termed *skiti* (*skētē*) and *kelia*, and also solitary hermitages. A *skiti*, juridically a dependency of a monastery, lacks the rank of the latter but is for practical purposes identical to it; it may, indeed, be more populated than the monastery to which it 'belongs'. A *kelia* (cell) is a small settlement with a chapel or chapels. Some monasteries have a cenobitic organization, where no monk has personal property and meals are taken communally; others are idiorhythmic, where monks may even receive salaries and mostly eat in their own quarters.

The Offices are recited in full: an Athonite monk spends eight hours daily in their recitation, eight hours at work and eight hours at rest. In this and other ways Mount Athos represents a relic of the Middle Ages. Time is reckoned in the ancient way: the day begins at sunset, with midnight reckoned as the sixth hour of the day; all the monasteries except Vatopedi adhere to the Julian ('old style') calendar, rejecting the Gregorian calendar as an innovation of Rome. The custom, attested since the 10th century, of refusing any female (even female animals) access to Athos is maintained.

3. MANUSCRIPTS. Approximately 12,000 manuscripts survive in the Athonite monasteries. Work in monastic libraries and catalogues of them suggest that 15–20% of these (approximately 2000) are music manuscripts. Most (perhaps 90%) of them date from the 16th century and later, but the rest (about 200) are from the period between the 10th century and the 15th, and constitute an important source of documentation for the evolution of Byzantine musical style and notation as well as that of the liturgy. Only some 20% of these have so far been studied. The present manuscript holdings do not represent the entire corpus of those written at Mount Athos, however, and it cannot be assumed that the location of a manuscript represents its original provenance. There have been losses: the library of Simonos Petras was completely destroyed by fire in 1891, and that of the *skiti* of St Andrew in 1958 (the fire of 1966 at Vatopedi spared the library). 50 manuscripts originally from Lavra are now in the Biblioteca Laurenziana, Florence, and 70 others in the *fonds Coislin* of the Bibliothèque Nationale, Paris. Maxim the Greek took many Athonite manuscripts to Russia; in 1654 A. Sukhanov, a Russian merchant, bought 504 manuscripts on Athos, and of these some 400 came into the possession of the Synodal Library in Moscow (148 of them from Iviron). Further Athonite manuscripts are now in the British Library, London, and among the manuscripts of the Bibliothèque Nationale, Paris (suppl.gr.). The Russian archimandrite Porphyry Uspensky (later Metropolitan of Kiev) not only stole complete manuscripts but also cut initials and miniatures from others.

The largest library is that of Lavra, with approximately 2000 manuscripts, of which about 600 were written before 1500. They include some of the earliest Byzantine music manuscripts, the well-known heirmologion B32, and two triōdia, Γ12 and Γ67, all of which date from the 10th century. 11th-century manuscripts include Γ72 and Γ74, and a partly notated fragment from the euchologion, Δ11. There is a late 13th-century heirmologion, Δ35, and a large group of akolouthiai anthologies of the 14th and 15th centuries, of which the most complete and sumptuous is E173, written in the 1430s by Raidestinos. Most of these manuscripts appear to have been written on Athos. A few sheets from Γ67, one bearing a 10th-century list of neumes, were torn off and taken to Chartres in 1840 (see Strunk, 1955). Two folios from the heirmologion B32 are in Leningrad (Thibaut, no.371).

The triōdion 1488 of Vatopedi is published in facsimile in the Monumenta Musicae Byzantinae series. Vatopedi has several beautiful and well-notated 13th-century stichēraria and at least three interesting heirmologia (1531, 1532 and 1529), as well as an unknown number of akolouthiai. A late 12th-century heir-mologion from Iviron (470), was the first of its type to be published in facsimile in the Monumenta Musicae Byzantinae series, in 1938. Other heirmologia from Iviron include 1101 and 1259; there are numerous stichēraria and akolouthiai (as in nearly every other library) awaiting investigation. Of the akolouthiai at Iviron, the most interesting is perhaps the voluminous autograph of Manuel Chrysaphes (1120) dating from 1458. Esfigmenou has an 11th-century heirmologion (54) and an 11th-century triōdion (53). Pantocrator has several deserving study (208, 214 etc). Dionysiou has at least one curious heirmologion (95); the Serbian monastery of Chilandari has two early Slavic manuscripts (307 and 308; facsimile in MMB). The collections in Philotheou, Karakalou and Koutloumousi are known only in part.

Manuscripts outside Athos of Athonite provenance include the collection of Uspensky, described by Thibaut, and the *fonds Coislin*, briefly described by Gastoué. In the latter collection the 12th-century heirmologion Coislin 220 is well known.

BIBLIOGRAPHY
A. Gastoué: *Introduction à la paléographie musicale byzantine* (Paris, 1907)
J. B. Thibaut: *Monuments de la notation ekphonétique et hagiopolite de l'église grecque* (St Petersburg, 1913)
C. Korolevskij: 'Athos', *Dictionnaire d'histoire et de géographie ecclésiastique*, v (1931), 54–124
P. de Meester: 'Monte Athos', *Enciclopedia cattolica*, ii (Rome, 1949), 300
O. Strunk: 'The Notation of the Chartres Fragment', *AnnM*, iii (1955), 7
P. Sherrard: *Athos: the Mountain of Silence* (London, 1960)
P. Davos: 'Athos', *Thriskeftiki ke ithiki enkyklopedia*, i (Athens, 1962), 855
I. Doens: 'Bibliographie de la sainte montagne de l'Athos', *Millénaire du mont Athos*, ii (Chevetogne and Venice, 1965), 337–495 [comprehensive bibliography for Athos and individual monasteries and libraries]
O. Strunk: *Specimina notationum antiquiorum*, MMB, main ser., vii (1966), pls.1–28
G. A. Maloney: 'Mount Athos', *New Catholic Encyclopedia*, i (New York, 1967), 1008
E. A. de Mendieta: *Mount Athos: the Garden of the Panaghia*, Berliner byzantinische Arbeiten, xli (Berlin and Amsterdam, 1972)
MILOŠ VELIMIROVIĆ

Atienza y Pineda, Francisco de (*b* ?c1657; *d* Puebla, Mexico, March 1726). Mexican composer, probably of Spanish birth. He became a priest, and by 1695 ranked among the leading musicians at Mexico City Cathedral. In 1710 he officially protested against the selection of Zumaya as substitute for the ailing choirmaster Salazar, noting that he himself was considerably older than Zumaya, and indeed had substituted for Salazar in 1703. He departed soon after for Puebla, where he won the post of *maestro de capilla* on 15 January 1712 and served until his death. The Biblioteca Palafoxiana there contains texts of 12 sets of villancicos printed between 1715 and 1722 (and an undated one) and sung at Puebla Cathedral with music composed by Atienza. His surviving liturgical compositions reveal a skilled composer with a fluent command of polyphonic techniques. He adhered to the Spanish tradition in generally employing the *prima prattica*.

WORKS
Missa, 5vv, Archivo del Colegio de Santa Rosa, Morelia, Mexico
Missa, 4vv, vns, Archivo del Colegio de Santa Rosa, Morelia
Missa quinto tono, 5vv, Colección Jesús Sánchez Garza, Instituto Nacional de Bellas Artes, Mexico City
2 vesper psalms, 6, 7vv; 4 motets, 4–7vv (incl. 1 dated 'año de 706'); 2 hymns, for Feast of St Joseph, 4, 5vv: Cathedral archive, Puebla
Villancico, Colección Jesús Sánchez Garza, Instituto Nacional de Bellas Artes, Mexico City

BIBLIOGRAPHY

J. T. Medina: *La imprenta en la Puebla de los Angeles 1640–1821* (Santiago de Chile, 1908/*R*1964)

M. Bernal Jiménez: *El archivo musical del Colegio de Santa Rosa de Santa María de Valladolid, siglo XVIII* (Mexico City, 1939)

R. Stevenson: 'Mexico City Cathedral Music: 1600–1750', *The Americas*, xxi (1964), 111

A. R. Catalyne: 'Music of the Sixteenth through the Eighteenth Centuries in the Cathedral of Puebla', *Yearbook, Inter-American Institute for Musical Research*, ii (1966), 75

R. Stevenson: *Renaissance and Baroque Musical Sources in the Americas* (Washington, DC, 1970)

——: *Christmas Music from Baroque Mexico* (Berkeley and Los Angeles, 1974)

ALICE RAY CATALYNE

Atis. See ATYS.

Atkins, Sir Ivor (Algernon) (*b* Llandaff, 29 Nov 1869; *d* Worcester, 26 Nov 1953). English organist, composer and editor. After instruction from his father and C. Lee Williams, Atkins became a pupil and assistant of G. R. Sinclair at Truro and Hereford, and was appointed organist of Ludlow parish church in 1893. In 1897 he became organist of Worcester Cathedral, retiring in 1950, having directed the Worcester Three Choirs Festivals from 1898 to 1948. He revived the festivals after World War I and was knighted in 1921. Though he was not a gifted conductor, the programmes of the Worcester Festivals under him showed considerable breadth of taste, and it was at his insistence that Elgar's *The Dream of Gerontius* was performed in 1902. His own *Hymn of Faith* was given in 1905.

Atkins produced (with Elgar) an English-language edition of Bach's *St Matthew Passion*, and (alone) of Bach's *St John Passion*, Brahms's *German Requiem* and Debussy's *La demoiselle élue*. Though not escaping subsequent criticism, the treatment of Bach's recitative in relation to the English Bible marked an important stage in the appreciation of Bach's Passion settings in England. Atkins also edited Bach's *Orgelbüchlein* and Mendelssohn's organ sonatas. He took the Oxford DMus in 1920, was elected a Fellow of the Society of Antiquaries in 1921 and was Worcester Cathedral librarian from 1933 to 1953.

WRITINGS

The Early Occupants of the Office of Organist and Master of the Choristers of the Cathedral Church of … Worcester, Worcester Historical Society, (1918)

with N. R. Ker: *Catalogus Librorum Manuscriptorum Bibliothecae Wigorniensis, 1622–23* (Cambridge, 1944)

BIBLIOGRAPHY

DNB

W. Shaw: *The Three Choirs Festival, 1713–1953* (Worcester and London, 1954)

WATKINS SHAW

Atkins [Atkinson], John (*d* London, 1671). English violinist and composer. He entered the royal band in 1660 and served up to the beginning of the year of his death. John Playford did not print any of his songs, but several (mostly drinking-songs) survive in the following MSS: *GB-Lbm* Add.29396, *F-Pn* Rés.2489 and *US-NYp* Drexel 4275 and particularly 4041, which, since it is an important source of pre-Commonwealth play songs, could indicate that the composer was a theatre musician. Indeed, it is possible that Atkins compiled this collection. His setting of Davenant's *This lady ripe, and calm, and fresh* may have been made for the original production of *The Just Italian* in 1629. Four of his songs are printed in *English Songs, 1625–1660*, MB, xxxiii (1971).

IAN SPINK

Atlanta. Capital city of Georgia, USA. First known in the early 19th century as Terminus because of a decision to build a railway centre there, and later for a short while as Marthasville, Atlanta enjoyed a sporadic musical life in the aftermath of the American Civil War (1861–5). Most music-making was of local origin, although famous artists such as Victor Herbert, Walter Damrosch, Sousa, Pachmann and Melba visited later in the century. The Cotton State and International Exposition of 1895 was the scene of many such performances. Probably the city's earliest first-rate musical event was a recital by Paderewski on 22 February 1900.

In 1909 the Atlanta Music Festival Association arranged a series of five concerts over a three-day period, featuring famous opera singers such as Caruso (who was, however, indisposed), Geraldine Farrar, Fremstad and Scotti. The concerts included performances by the Dresden PO (with Albert Spalding as violin soloist) and were enormously successful. Special excursions from neighbouring cities were provided by the railways, indicating the degree of interest generated. The venture whetted Atlanta's appetite for opera and, as a result, the New York Metropolitan Opera was engaged in 1910 for six performances, with spectacular success. This marked the beginning of regular spring visits by the company, interrupted only during the two world wars. The 'Opera Week', comprising seven performances in six days, has become a social highlight of the season.

The Atlanta Music Club was formed in 1915 for the purpose of enriching the city's musical life through engaging famous artists as well as supporting local endeavour. Primarily a women's organization, the club continues its role of providing vital musical stimulus to the community. It was instrumental in creating the Atlanta SO, the Choral Guild of Atlanta (1940) and the amateur Atlanta Community Orchestra (1958), as well as other musical organizations that have not survived. The club also sponsors a broad and effective music scholarship programme for talented young musicians.

Earlier attempts to establish an enduring symphony orchestra for Atlanta had met with little success, but in 1944 the Atlanta Music Club founded the Atlanta Youth SO by the amalgamation of two school orchestras. The Chicago conductor Henry Sopkin was engaged as musical director, a post he held through the transformation of the group three years later into the Atlanta SO until his retirement in 1966. Sopkin was responsible for building the orchestra into a reasonably proficient body of semi-professional players.

An air crash in Paris on 3 June 1962 took the lives of more than 100 Atlanta art patrons on a chartered European tour, an event which sent a powerful wave of feeling, first of grief and then of determination to honour the victims, through the community. Funds were raised to build the Memorial Arts Center, with four performances halls, the largest of which is Symphony Hall (capacity 1762), the orchestra's first permanent home; the complex, which also houses an art school and an art museum, opened in 1968. The decision was also made to upgrade the orchestra to full professional status and engage a musical director of international repute to succeed Sopkin. Robert Shaw, then serving as associate conductor to Szell in Cleveland, was appointed in 1967. Shaw has brought the orchestra close to becoming one of the nation's finest. From the two concerts of the 1944–5 season the orchestra has progressed to some 200 performances in Atlanta and on tour for the 1975–6 season; in 1976 the tours extended as far as Washington and New York.

In 1974 the Atlanta Symphony Youth Orchestra was created. Section leaders of the main orchestra coach young Atlanta musicians in weekly rehearsals; the orchestra gives several concerts a year and has maintained a high standard.

Atlanta boasts a wealth of churches, predominantly Protestant, in which the sacred music repertory is continually performed; many have fine organs, affording ample opportunity for outstanding recitals. Virtually all the universities, colleges and junior colleges in the area offer some musical instruction. The most important is Georgia State University (19,000 students), with a music teaching staff numbering 33 (in 1976) and offering music degrees in a number of specialized areas. Emory University also contributes to the musical life of the city, chiefly through a series of fine concerts sponsored by endowment funds. Two predominantly black colleges, Spelman and Morehouse, provide advanced music training programmes, Spelman being the only school in Atlanta other than Georgia State nationally accredited to offer music degrees. The Georgia Academy of Music, a private endeavour, has demonstrated noteworthy success in stimulating interest in music study for children of all ages.

Other prominent features of local musical life include the Atlanta Boy Choir, the Pro-Mozart Society of Atlanta, the Atlanta SO Chorus, a number of amateur performing groups and recitals presented by the many excellent artists resident in Atlanta. One setback was the failure of Atlanta's most important attempt (1968) to establish local opera as part of the move to commemorate the 1962 tragedy. Mismanagement and unrealistic planning brought the project to financial collapse in its second month of operation, following a series of performances of Purcell's *King Arthur* and of a highly controversial version of Puccini's *La bohème*, set in the Paris of the 1920s.

JOHN SCHNEIDER

Atlantov, Vladimir (Andreyevich) (*b* Leningrad, 19 Feb 1939). Soviet tenor. The son of an opera singer, he graduated from Bolotina's class at the Leningrad Conservatory in 1963, and had further training (1963–5) in Milan at La Scala opera school. He won the 1966 Tchaikovsky and the 1967 Sofia international competitions. In 1963 he was engaged as a soloist by the Kirov Theatre, and in 1967 by the Bol'shoy. His voice is full and ample, but capable of great beauty and delicacy; he has a strong temperament and a gift for character portrayal. His roles include Hermann, Vladimir (*Prince Igor*), Alfredo and Don José. He sings also in concerts, has toured in Europe, Canada and Japan, and was made People's Artist of the RSFSR in 1972.

I. M. YAMPOL'SKY

Atnaḥ. Sign marking the end of a half-verse in Hebrew EKPHONETIC NOTATION.

Ato [Hatto] **episcopus Trecensis.** Bishop of Troyes from 1123 to 1145. He is credited with the composition of six polyphonic pieces for two voices in the Codex Calixtinus (*E-SC*; *see* SOURCES, MS, §IV), probably apocryphally. They are a versus *Nostra phalanx plaudat leta*, the soloists' portions of four responsories from the Matins and 2nd Vespers of St James's Day and Trans-

lation (with a *prosa* for its *neuma* or melisma), and the soloists' portions of the gradual from Mass on that day.

DAVID HILEY

Atonality. A term which may be used in three senses: first, to describe all music which is not tonal; second, to describe all music which is neither tonal nor serial; and third, to describe specifically the post-tonal and pre-12-note music of Berg, Webern and Schoenberg. (While serial music is, by the first definition, atonal, it differs in essential respects from other atonal music and is discussed in the articles SERIALISM and TWELVE-NOTE COMPOSITION; it is, therefore, not considered here.)

1. Relations between tonality and atonality. 2. Differences between tonality and atonality. 3. The atonality of Schoenberg, Berg and Webern. 4. Conclusion.

1. RELATIONS BETWEEN TONALITY AND ATONALITY. An important aspect of tonality is the way in which pitches are contextually defined so that each particular definition of a given pitch yields a different tonal function. A G which is the root of a G major triad, for example, has a different function or meaning from that of a G which is the 3rd of an E♭ major triad. Such a definition is, in turn, further refined by larger musical contexts, and the roles of rhythm, register, dynamics and timbre in tonal music are closely related to, and interactive with, the definition of tonal functions.

Atonality may be seen roughly to delimit two kinds of music: 1. That in which there is no such contextual definition with reference to triads, diatonic scales or keys, but in which there are, nonetheless, hierarchical distinctions among pitches. This category would include some of the works of Schoenberg, Stravinsky and Hindemith. The inadequacy of theories of tonality in dealing with this music lends support to such a classification.

2. That in which such hierarchical distinctions are not so explicit, though sometimes present. This includes some of the pre-serial music of Webern, Schoenberg and, to a lesser extent, Berg.

The usual attitudes concerning atonality and its development are vague and misleading. It is often said that tonality developed to a point of complexity where it was no longer possible to determine contextual definition as described, and tonal functions were therefore abandoned. This attitude has a basis in reality but is a simplification which obscures essential issues. Two compositions near either side of the imagined border between tonality and atonality, Liszt's *Sonetto 104 del Petrarca* from the second book of *Années de pèlerinage*, and Skryabin's Prelude op.74 no.3, shed light on this question.

It is not difficult to determine tonal contextual definition in the opening measures of the *Sonetto* (ex.1). The F♯ dominant 7th chord at the downbeats of bars 1, 4 and 5 serves as a dominant to the B dominant 7th in bar 5, which is in turn the dominant of E in bar 7. In the opening bars of this composition, however, the diminished 7th chord plays a fundamental role as a referential collection through the use of different interpretations of that chord. The chords at the upbeats to bars 1, 2, 3, 4 and 5, and at the fourth quaver beats of bars 3 and 4, are all enharmonically equivalent forms of the initial diminished 7th collection B♯, D♯, F♯, A, which is transformed into the dominant 7th chord C♯, E, F♯, A♯ on the downbeat of bar 1. In that bar the F♯ octave moves to G as an upper neighbour, at which point another

Ex.1

bars 2–3 also emphasizes the unfolding of a diminished 7th collection.

In response to the above attitude concerning the development of atonality, it would seem safe to say, rather, that tonality developed new ideas, which then lost some of their association with older concepts, and in doing so gained more independent status as compositional determinants. The diminished 7th chord in the music of Mozart, for example, most often acts as a tonicizing agent, with the two tritones resolving in contrary motion to a major or minor triad, but in the Liszt piece this is not so clearly the case, in that the chord seems to have some significance as a referential collection, and in the Skryabin it certainly functions in a completely different way.

In as much as notation reflects compositional thinking, it is interesting to observe the expanded denoting of key signatures in the late 19th and early 20th centuries as a kind of musical barometer. The point of a key signature in the music of Debussy, for example, is often only to delimit a pitch-class collection – usually the whole or part of a diatonic scale – rather than to prescribe a diatonic scale with the implied functional associations of tonic and dominant triads, consonance and dissonance, etc, as in the notation and music of Liszt. On the other hand, the key signature of four sharps in Schoenberg's Chamber Symphony op.9 serves more to indicate that an E major triad will function in some hierarchically significant way than to delimit a scale. The first pages of the composition are, in fact, so full of symmetrical collections, such as the whole tone scale, the augmented triad, etc, that the key signature serves virtually no practical purpose. In the fourth movement of Schoenberg's Second Quartet op.10 the convention of a key signature is abandoned. Schoenberg commented upon this work as follows (as quoted by W. Reich in *Schoenberg* (London, 1971), 31):

there are many sections in which the individual parts proceed regardless of whether or not their meeting results in codified harmonies. . . . The

diminished collection is implied: C♯, E, G, (B♭). The sequence is repeated at successive minor 3rd transpositions until in bar 4 an octave transposition of the F♯ dominant 7th chord of bar 1 is reached. All pitches in bars 1–4 are thus enharmonically equivalent members of one of two diminished 7th collections. While it is useful to observe that these measures prolong the dominant of the dominant of E major, the actual method of prolongation is most easily understood in relation to the enharmonically undefined diminished 7th collections 0, 3, 6, 9 and 1, 4, 7, 10 (with 0 denoting C or B♯, 1 denoting C♯ or D♭, etc). The absence of a key signature further emphasizes the non-diatonic nature of the passage.

The opening of Skryabin's Prelude op.74 no.3 provides an interesting counter-example (ex.2). The music is not tonal in the senses described above or in the sense of the Liszt composition. It is not clear that any note is defined as a member of a major or minor triad, or that the passage is using notes of some major or minor scale. There is a 'dominant 7th chord' embedded in bar 2, but this does not seem to function as a dominant of D major or minor. On the other hand a special aspect of this passage is that all notes except G♯ in bar 1 and D in bar 3 belong to one of the diminished 7th collections A♯, C♯, E, G and B♯, D♯, F♯, A; and Skryabin's spelling is consistent with this view. The 'dominant 7th chord' in bar 2 is thus understood as a conjunction of members of these two collections. In bar 3 the tritone transposition of the right hand of bar 1, against the untransposed bass, results in the appearance of the same collection as in bar 1 since the diminished 7th collection is invariant under transposition by a tritone. The G–A♯ succession in the middle register in

Ex.2

key is presented distinctly at all the main dividing points of the formal organization. Yet the overwhelming multitude of dissonances cannot be balanced any longer by occasional returns to such triads as represent a key.

The concept of atonality thus evolved as various components of tonality lost the high degree of interdependence they had formerly possessed.

An important aspect of late-19th-century music lies in a set of relatively abstract ideas about what music is and can be: a referential sonority (the triad) as the basis of a musical language; a motif as a compositional tool; the progress and unfolding of a musical composition as something defined by the transformation and development of motivic, contrapuntal and harmonic ideas; the concept of closure; significant relations between discrete parts of a musical composition; and the hierarchic superiority of certain specific pitches or configurations of pitches in a given composition. The first composers whose music might be defined as atonal were trained in the traditions of 19th-century tonality, and their music reveals, in one way or another, the profound influence of these concepts, as may be exemplified by the opening of the second of Schoenberg's Five Orchestral Pieces op.16 (ex.3 is taken from Webern's two-piano reduction).

Ex.3

A succession of simultaneities between the two right hands unfolds transpositions and inversions (of interval content) of the same referential sonority: in bar 1, (A, D, G♯), (F, C, G♭); in bar 2, (A♭, D♭, G), (G, C, G♭), (E, B, F). The significance of the D–A dyad is emphasized by its role in the first movement, where the trichord D, A, C♯ is sustained as a pedal for most of the movement, and by the octave doubling in bar 1 of ex.3 and the retention of the D–A dyad for the first three bars. An important motivic idea here is a three-note melodic cell consisting of some kind of 2nd and some kind of 3rd. (In the opening of the first movement the cellos play the line (E, F, A, G♯, A, C♯) which consists of several interlocking versions of this cell.) The first

three bars form a phrase unit defined by the new rhythmic and registral placement of the descending minor 3rd (G♯–F in bar 1; A♭–F in bar 3), and the rest on the first beat of bar 4. The concept of a musical language as inferred from tonality thus extends deeply into atonality and forms a significant basis for the development of new ideas.

2. DIFFERENCES BETWEEN TONALITY AND ATONALITY. Although an attempt has been made to indicate the ways in which tonality developed into atonality and the similarities between the two, there are also significant differences. As has been noted, one of the remarkable aspects of tonality is the high degree of interdependence between the various dimensions of a composition, such as pitch, rhythm, dynamics, timbre and form. In atonality the functional relations between these dimensions are not clearly defined. The concept of a suspension in tonality, for example, embodies a conjunction of rhythmic and harmonic ideas, but the body of atonal works offers no similar operation as a general procedure. Comparisons of this sort have given rise to a second prevalent attitude concerning atonality: that its processes do not extend beyond the boundaries of a given composition. Again, this attitude is not entirely without basis but is highly oversimplified. As understanding of tonality is aided by the existence of a relatively highly developed theory, while no such assistance exists for atonality, the former is perceived as a more highly unified musical language than the latter. Atonal works do, however, have properties in common, but the manifestations of these properties are very different. Examples may be taken from two compositions in which, as in exx.1 and 3, the diminished 7th collection has some structural significance: the first movement of Bartók's Music for Strings, Percussion and Celesta, and the opening of Varèse's Density 21.5 for solo flute.

Ex.4 is the theme of the 'fugue' that opens the Bartók work. The voices of the fugue make their entries at successive perfect 5ths alternately above and

Ex.4

below the original entry until, in bars 26 and 27, F♯ and C are reached, a major 13th above and below the original entry. The F♯ and C are members of the same diminished 7th collection as the initial A. They are doubled at the octave to emphasize their structural significance, and they initiate a more complex process of development which culminates in bar 56 where an E♭ (the pitch class at which the two diverging cycles of 5ths meet, and the remaining member of the diminished 7th collection A, C, E♭, F♯) is reached. The linear structure of the theme is relevant to the large-scale structure of the movement. The first two phrases span A–E♭, an interval of the diminished 7th collection; the third and fourth phrases span B–E and B♭–E♭, respectively. Thus a tritone, an interval which figures in the large-scale structure, is outlined by the first and second phrases, and also by the third and fourth phrases together. The span of the entire theme is a perfect 5th, anticipating the second statement on E. At bar 65, after E♭ is stated in several octaves, the literal inversion of the theme is introduced, and at the end of the movement (ex.5) a simultaneous

Ex.5

statement of the second phrase of the theme and of its inversion, both beginning on A, telescopes structural aspects of the movement in the unison A and octave E♭, and in the statement of all 12 pitch classes, a totality implied by the succession of fugal transpositional levels, and created by any two adjacent fugal entries.

Ex.6 contains the first large phrase of Varèse's *Density 21.5*. The number 0, 1, or 2, inserted below

Ex.6

each note, shows the diminished 7th collection to which that note belongs: 0 denotes the collection on C, 1 that on C♯ and 2 that on D. Except for the Fs in bars 1 and 3, all notes in bars 1–10 belong to the 0 and 1 collections. These bars seem, in addition, to prolong the 1 collection since the 0 collection appears less frequently and with less rhythmic emphasis. The opening F–E–F♯ motif is special in that it contains one member of each collection. Bar 9 represents an important structural point: it is the loudest moment in the piece so far; the initial rhythmic figure returns, but with new and more emphatic articulation; an octave has been spanned from the lowest note so far and, since the 1 collection is now represented on the first semiquaver of this figure, a kind of 'modulation' occurs. The repetition of D♭–C in bars 9 and 10 delays the arrival of D (dynamically emphasized) until the downbeat of bar 11, thus prolonging a transposition of the initial motif. In bars 11–13 there are successive prolongations of the 2 and 0 collections, and a final return to the initial 1 collection. The B♭–E dyad in bars 13–14 contains the remaining members of the 1 collection as it appeared in its first salient statement in bar 2.

In both the Bartók and the Varèse works a governing structural principle is the symmetrical partition of the octave through the diminished 7th collection. But the compositional procedures are very different and the respective results could hardly be more dissimilar.

3. THE ATONALITY OF SCHOENBERG, BERG AND WEBERN. Many of the atonal compositions of Berg, Webern and Schoenberg use procedures and concepts such as those discussed in relation to Schoenberg's op.16 no.2. Just as tonality yielded concepts which were reinterpreted for use in atonality, so the interactions between the various aspects of the atonality of Berg, Webern and Schoenberg yielded new concepts which eventually became relevant to serialism. A fundamental development was the elimination of hierarchical pitch-class distinctions, typified in tonality by entities such as the major scale. This led to the use of all 12 pitch classes within smaller time spans. Webern's Bagatelles for string quartet, for example, emphasize the unfolding of 12-note collections through a reduction of pitch and pitch-class repetition, and by very careful and precise attention to the articulation and orchestration of individual pitch classes (ex.7). The extreme brevity of each of the Bagatelles is a consequence of this approach.

Ex.7

The sense of octave relations as manifested in tonality undergoes a radical transformation in a composition such as the Bagatelles. Clearly defined octave relations would shift the focus away from an unfolding of the 12 pitch classes. This thinking strongly influenced the development of the 12-note system where the collection of 12 pitch classes plays a fundamental role. (The meaning of an octave relation in this music differs profoundly from that in the Bartók and Varèse examples quoted above. In the latter compositions the octave has significance as a boundary, framing its symmetrical divisions – the whole tone scale, the diminished 7th collection, the augmented triad, the tritone and the cycles of 5ths and semitones – and octave intervals may thus signify the culmination of a process of development or a common feature of different subdivisions.) In this sense one motivic idea of the Bagatelles is a tendency towards the unfolding of 12-note collections. In general the concept of a motif in this music merges into a much broader background encompassing the rhythmic and instrumental textures.

The atonal works of Berg, Webern and Schoenberg employ a wide variety of procedures and techniques for securing musical coherence. It is only necessary to compare Schoenberg's *Erwartung* with his Six Little Piano Pieces op.19, for example, to see, on the one hand, a large-scale unfolding of complex and varied pitch relations, and on the other, a small, detailed and precise expression of specific and simple musical ideas. The evolution to the 12-note system and serialism was guided mainly by a tendency to subdue traditional hierarchical pitch distinctions and to emphasize the use of ordered, or partially ordered, collections of pitch classes, or motifs, to generate chords and lines. Eventually the former tendency, in its encouragement of the use of 12-note collections, merged with the latter to become Schoenberg's 12-note system.

4. CONCLUSION. Atonality thus roughly delimits a wide range of compositional practices whose only features are the absence of the normative and interrelated procedures of tonality and of the basic concept of serialism. It remains to be seen to what extent atonality is a useful or relevant musical category. The tendency of historical criticism to construct systems of classification which attempt to index individual entries as neatly and unambiguously as possible has certainly been frustrated so far by musical thought in the 20th century. The individuality of the contributions of Schoenberg, Stravinsky, Bartók, Webern, Berg and others ultimately transcends and trivializes such attempts, if it does not contradict them.

BIBLIOGRAPHY

A. Schoenberg: 'Problems of Harmony', *MM*, xxi (1934), 167 [repr. in *Style and Idea* (London, 1975), 268ff]
A. Berg: 'Was ist atonal?', *23: eine wiener Musikzeitschrift* (1936), no.26–7; Eng. trans., in N. Slonimsky: *Music Since 1900* (New York, 1938, rev. 4/1971), 1311ff
E. Křenek: *Music Here and Now* (New York, 1939)
H. Pousseur: 'Anton Webern's Organic Chromaticism', *Die Reihe* (1955), no.2; Eng. trans., in *Die Reihe* (1958), no.2, p.51
W. and A. Goehr: 'Arnold Schoenberg's Development towards the Twelve-note System', *European Music in the Twentieth Century*, ed. H. Hartog (London, 1957)
M. Wilkinson: 'An Introduction to the Music of Edgard Varèse', *Score* (1957), no.19, p.5
R. Reti: *Tonality, Atonality, Pantonality: a Study of Some Trends in Twentieth Century Music* (London, 1958)
G. Perle: *Serial Composition and Atonality* (Berkeley, 1962, rev. 4/1977)
E. Carter: 'Expressionism and American Music', *PNM*, iv/1 (1965), 1
M. DeVote: 'Some Notes on the Unknown *Altenberg Lieder*', *PNM*, v/1 (1966), 37–74
A. Elston and others: 'Some Views of Webern's Op.6, No.1', *PNM*, vi/1 (1967), 63
G. Perle: 'The Musical Language of *Wozzeck*', *Music Forum*, i (1967), 204–59
R. Craft: 'Schoenberg's Five Pieces for Orchestra', *Perspectives on Schoenberg and Stravinsky*, ed. B. Boretz and E. T. Cone (Princeton, 1968, rev. 2/1972), 3
A. Schoenberg: 'Analysis of the Four Orchestral Songs Opus 22', *Perspectives on Schoenberg and Stravinsky*, ed. B. Boretz and E. T. Cone (Princeton, 1968, rev. 2/1972), 25
J. Maegaard: *Studien zur Entwicklung des Dodekaphonen Satzes bei Arnold Schönberg* (Copenhagen, 1972) [review in *MQ*, lxiii (1977)]
A. Forte: *The Structure of Atonal Music* (New Haven, 1973)
P. Lansky: 'Pitch-class Consciousness', *PNM*, xiii/2 (1975), 30
E. Lendvai: 'Modality: Atonality: Function', *Soundings*, vi (1977), 1–41
G. Perle: 'Berg's Master Array of the Interval Cycles', *MQ*, lxiii (1977), 1–30

PAUL LANSKY, GEORGE PERLE

Atrash [El Atrash], **Farid** (*b* Syria, ?1915; *d* Cairo, 26 Dec 1974). Egyptian composer and singer of Syrian origin. Born into a Druz family, he was brought up in Cairo as a political refugee. He studied the lute with El Sonbaty at the Arabic Music Club (now the Institute of Arabic Music), and made a reputation as a fine player of that instrument. Having begun his career as a singer of modern sentimental songs, including those by the Lebanese F. Ghosn, he soon began to compose his own melodies. His Syrian pronunciation (later discarded) and his voice quickly won him wide popularity, and he was regarded as a strong competitor to Abdel-Wahab. He played and sang in many musical films, sometimes with his sister, the singer Asmahan; all his film music was of his own composition, including the final 'oper-etta' in *Intissar al shabab* ('Triumph of youth'). Of his hundreds of recorded songs, all of them monodic, some of the most popular are in the microtonal modes such as *bayati*, one of his favourites and a mode very popular in Egypt.

SAMHA EL KHOLY

Atrio, Hermannus de. *See* HERMANNUS DE ATRIO.

Attacca (It.: 'attack', 'begin'; imperative of *attacare*). When placed at the end of a movement – as in the scherzo of Beethoven's C minor Symphony – this direction signifies that no pause is to be made, but that the next movement is to be joined immediately to the preceding. It also appears in the form *attacca subito*, 'begin immediately'. In Baroque music a movement without a normal cadence on the tonic at the end implied an *attacca*.

GEORGE GROVE/R

Attacco (It.: 'attack'). A fugue subject consisting only of a single short figure (ex.1), as opposed to the longer

Ex.1 Purcell: Fantasia for viols no.7, final section

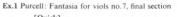

'andamento' and ricercare-like 'soggetto'. Some apparent instances of the attacco are in fact longer subjects whose first appearance is in STRETTO exposition (e.g. Bach, *Das wohltemperirte Clavier*, ii, no.3; ex.2).

Ex.2 Bach: '48', ii, 3

ROGER BULLIVANT

Attaingnant, Pierre (*b* probably in or nr. Douai, *c*1494; *d* Paris, late 1551 or 1552). French music printer, publisher, bookseller, punchcutter and typecaster.

1. LIFE. He is probably the 'Pierotin Attaingnant', a minor, named as residuary legatee in the 1503 will of Canon Simon Attaingnant of Douai. By a document notarized 13 January 1513/14 Attaingnant, described as a 'bookseller, living in Paris', leased a press to Jean de la Roche, reserving the right to print ecclesiastical pardons and the like, should he receive commissions. He may have gone to Paris originally with a chorister's scholarship for the Collège de Dainville, which was subject to the cathedral chapters of Arras and Noyon. This institution leased the part of its buildings on the rue de la Harpe to Philippe Pigouchet (*fl* 1490–1514), the printer-engraver famous for his Hours and the master to whom Attaingnant was probably apprenticed. Marriage to one of Pigouchet's daughters, Claude, made Attaingnant his heir. Another of Pigouchet's daughters,

1. The French court at Mass: woodcut by Oronce Fine from 'Primus liber tres missas' printed by Attaingnant (1532)

Germaine, was married to Poncet le Preux (1481–1559), one of the four 'grands libraires jurés' of the university, Master of the Printers' Guild and a prolific publisher of scholarly texts.

The earliest surviving book to bear Attaingnant's name is a Noyon breviary of 1525, the only book that he is known to have published in conjunction with Le Preux. Attaingnant continued to publish liturgical books for Noyon throughout his life as well as syllabuses for schoolboys. After experimenting with music types for several years he brought out the *Chansons nouvelles*, dated 4 April 1527/8. Within a year they were followed by at least 7 other books in the same format. At this time he sought and obtained royal protection in the form of a privilege preventing others from copying the contents of his books for three years after printing. It specifically mentioned books 'tant en musique, jeux de Lutz, Orgues, et semblables instruments' which he had printed or at least planned. (These intentions were realized with the lute tablatures of 1529 and 1530 and the keyboard scores of 1531.)

When the protection covering his earliest music books began to run out in spring 1531, he sought a wider, six-year privilege covering 'messes, motetz, hymnes, chansons que desditz jeux de Lutz, Flustes et Orgues, en grans et petitz volumes'. The royal decree of 18 June 1531 granting this is printed in the first volume of folio masses (1532). Also in this volume is Attaingnant's dedicatory address to the Cardinal of Tournon, who was praised in a Latin poem, written by Nicolas Bourbon for the occasion. Each of the seven

mass volumes was illustrated with a woodcut of the court hearing Mass by Oronce Fine, royal mathematician and cosmographer (see fig.1). Further royal preferment was natural after the achievement represented by the folio masses – Tournon was a powerful statesman as well as titular head of the royal chapel. Hopes mentioned in the second privilege were also realized by the imposing 13-volume set of motets in quarto brought out in 1534 and 1535. A 14th volume devoted to Manchicourt appeared in 1539 (see fig.2).

In 1537, in addition to a renewal of his privilege, Attaingnant received the unprecedented distinction of 'imprimeur et libraire du Roy en musique'. The other royal printers were men of learning such as Robert Estienne. About the time of Attaingnant's nomination, he began to abandon the older text types for the italics and romans more in keeping with humanist tastes. In 1538 he took a partner, Herbert Jullet, husband of his daughter Germaine, with whom he jointly signed a portion of the firm's output from then until Jullet's death in 1545. After his wife's death in 1543, an inventory of the firm's extensive stock and equipment was made. Two years later Attaingnant married Marie Lescallopier. He witnessed a contract as late as 3 October 1551 but died before the end of 1552. His widow printed a few music books between 1553 and 1557, then restricted her publications almost exclusively to the scholarly commentaries of Léger du Chesne, the last of which appeared in 1567. In the general tax of 1571 she was levied 6 livres on the considerable fortune of 300,000 livres.

2. WORKS. Attaingnant invented and introduced a new

method of printing music in which the staff-segments and notes were combined, so that both could be printed in a single impression (see fig.2). It soon swept all Europe, replacing the double- or triple-impression techniques required to produce Petrucci's expensive quartos and becoming the first international method of music printing. The reason was primarily economic, for it allowed the time and cost of production to be reduced by half, or more. The role formerly ascribed to PIERRE HAULTIN in this invention has been traced to the fictitious account of Pierre Fournier *le jeune*, writing in 1765. A similar but more primitive method produced the music types used by JOHN RASTELL in his *Interlude*, which may even antedate the *Chansons nouvelles*. But Rastell's workmen were probably French and may have had some knowledge of experimental stages in the Attaingnant shop before the perfection of the new technique. An altogether different method that it gradually displaced was the printing of music from engraved woodblocks, of which Andrea Antico was the foremost craftsman. Attaingnant at first followed the small octavo format made popular by Antico in the 1520s, but by the mid-1530s oblong quarto became the norm for all his music publications.

The commercial success of the new method coincided with the flowering of the Parisian chanson. The leading chanson composers, Claudin de Sermisy, Clément Janequin and Pierre Certon, all in royal service of one kind or another, are very well represented in Attaingnant's collections, which diffused their works widely. The tastes and liberality of Francis I were decisive: his patronage effectively made Attaingnant the official printer of the king's music. With this development a major step was taken towards the highly centralized establishment that has characterized French musical life ever since. In compiling his extensive catalogue of sacred and secular publications Attaingnant opened the way, showing others not only how to print, but also what to print; for example, his 1546 publication of settings by Certon and Mornable of the psalms in Marot's translations, the first books of their kind, were harbingers of a wave of similar settings.

Attaingnant was the first music publisher to achieve a true mass-production. The numbered series of chansons from his later years, for instance, ran to 36 volumes and many of these went through two or three editions. With press-runs conservatively estimated at 1000 copies, the total number of chansons put on the market by Attaingnant alone reached a staggering figure. To sell in such volume required outlets on an international level. These were facilitated through the publishing business of Le Preux, who had dealings with some of the large German syndicates and maintained depots in various centres. He is known to have held stocks of Attaingnant's music books and may have been responsible for their foreign distribution.

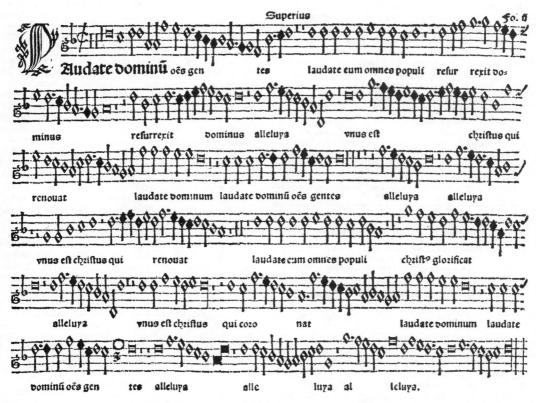

2. *The superius voice of 'Laudate Dominum' by Manchicourt from 'Liber decimus quartus XIX musicus cantiones' printed from type by single impression by Attaingnant (1539)*

As far as is known, Attaingnant was not a composer; yet he must have been skilled enough to do his own editing. At least, no house editor was named until the very last years, when CLAUDE GERVAISE was given credit for revising and correcting some books of ensemble dances. PIERRE BLONDEAU may have had a hand in editing the two early lute tablatures, in which some pieces bear his initials. The accuracy of edition was generally high, with the exception of the earliest prints and some from 1550. Verbal corrigenda were sometimes used to point out errors, but more frequently cancel slips were pasted over the original to correct passages or even single notes. Concern for utility and practical convenience are evident in the listing of voice combinations in the index for the six- and eight-voice motets, and the instrumentation indications for flutes or recorders or both in two chanson books of 1553.

For the most part, Attaingnant offered the public new and original works of French composers. The music of the generation before Francis I found scant place in his books; the same is true for composers outside France, with the exception of certain Franco-Netherlands masters working in the Low Countries (such as Gombert, Lupi and Richafort) or in Italy (Arcadelt, Verdelot and Willaert). Although he pirated Antico's canonic duets of 1520 and borrowed occasionally from Moderne, later from Susato and even from Du Chemin, he was by contemporary standards quite scrupulous. Certainly he was more imitated by other printers than imitative of them. He was chiefly responsible for starting the vogue for printing two- and three-voice arrangements of four-voice chansons – one of the clearest examples of a vast repertory created at the behest of the publishing business.

With the accession of Henry II in 1547, Attaingnant's special position soon vanished. Several other printers also received royal privileges, a fact which may explain Attaingnant's frenetic burst of activity at the end, with its concomitant lowering of standards in printing and proofreading. After Attaingnant's death, the title of 'King's Music Printers' was acquired by Le Roy & Ballard, who gradually re-established the near monopoly first held by Attaingnant.

BIBLIOGRAPHY
F. Lesure: 'Pierre Attaingnant: notes et documents', MD, iii (1949), 34
D. Heartz: 'La chronologie des recueils imprimés par Pierre Attaingnant: la période gothique', RdM, xliv (1959), 176
——: 'A New Attaingnant Book and the Beginnings of French Music Printing', JAMS, xiv (1961), 9
P. Renouard: Imprimeurs et libraires parisiens du XVIᵉ siècle, i (Paris 1964) [incl. chronological list of all publications, including the non-musical ones of Attaingnant's widow]
D. Heartz: Pierre Attaingnant, Royal Printer of Music: a Historical Study and Bibliographical Catalogue (Berkeley and Los Angeles, 1969) [lists contents of all music books, with citation of modern edns.]
——: 'Au pres de vous' – Claudin's Chanson and the Commerce of Publishers' Arrangements', JAMS, xxiv (1971), 193–225
A. H. King: 'The Significance of John Rastell in Early Music Printing', The Library, 5th ser., xxvi (1971), 197
DANIEL HEARTZ

Attenhofer, Carl (b Wettingen, canton of Aargau, 5 May 1837; d Zurich, 22 May 1914). Swiss choral conductor and composer. He was a pupil of D. Elster and studied at the Leipzig Conservatory (1857–8) where E. F. Richter was among his teachers. After holding several minor teaching posts at Muri (1859), in 1863 he became director of music at Rapperswil, where his excellence as a choral conductor during a national singing festival in 1866 soon made his name known throughout the country. In the same year he moved to Zurich and fulfilled a number of important choral conducting engagements. In 1870 he was appointed director of music at the university, and in 1896 became second director, with Friedrich Hegar, of the conservatory. Together with the painter Arnold Böcklin and Hegar, he was given an honorary doctorate by the university in 1889. In addition to his various conducting duties he was an active composer; he wrote a great deal of church and chamber music, but excelled primarily in vocal music. His best works are, perhaps, his accompanied and a cappella compositions for male voices which have been printed in numerous collections and are still popular in Switzerland.

BIBLIOGRAPHY
SML
A. Glück: Karl Attenhofer (Zurich, 1888)
E. Isler: 'Karl Attenhofer', 103. Neujahrsblatt der Allgemeine Musikgeschichte (Zurich, 1915)
E. Refardt: 'Attenhofer, Karl', Historisch-biographisches Musikerlexikon der Schweiz (Leipzig and Zurich, 1928)
F. R. BOSONNET

Atterberg, Kurt (Magnus) (b Göteborg, 12 Dec 1887; d Stockholm, 15 Feb 1974). Swedish composer, administrator, conductor and critic. He studied the cello at school in Göteborg and then entered the Stockholm College of Technology. Having passed the examination in civil engineering in 1911, he spent his working life (1912–68) in the patent office. He was largely self-taught although he studied composition and instrumentation with Andreas Hallén at the Stockholm Conservatory (1910–11), and partly used the state composer's scholarships he received between 1911 and 1915 to study in Germany (1911 and 1913). He made his début as a conductor at Göteborg in 1912, when the programme included his First Symphony; thereafter (particularly during the 1920s) he often conducted his own music and that of contemporaries, both at home and abroad (where he promoted Swedish music). From 1916 to 1922 he was kapellmästare at the Royal Dramatic Theatre, Stockholm; he also worked enthusiastically as co-founder and president (1924–47) of the Swedish Composers' Society, and as co-founder, president (1924–43) and vice-president (1943–62) of the Swedish Performing Rights Society (STIM). He was secretary to the Swedish Royal Academy of Music from 1940 to 1953 (he had been made a member in 1926), and was music critic of the Stockholms-tidningen from 1919 to 1957, gradually tending to dislike younger composers and new techniques.

Atterberg's manifold activities have diluted appreciation of his music, and in later years he met with less response than at the beginning of his career. Nevertheless, with Rangström, he was one of the leading Swedish composers in the generation after Peterson-Berger, Stenhammar and Alfvén, producing his best work in symphonies and stage music. The point of departure for his first two symphonies was German and Scandinavian Romanticism (Brahms and Alfvén), though he inclined less to detailed thematic working than to a kind of al fresco technique, with melodic lines – often cantilenas in an assimilated folk style – set off against colourful backgrounds. Having added an impressionist touch in the Third Symphony and realistic effects in the symphonic poem Älven ('The river', 1929), he completed his repertory of symphonic procedures with polytonal elements, which he used in varying degrees up to his last symphony, the Ninth (1955–6). His Sixth Symphony won the prize awarded by the Columbia Graphophone Company for the Schubert centenary (1928). Some of his five operas and his two best ballets had many performances in Europe during the 1920s and 1930s, particularly in Germany. Best known of these was the ballet *De fåvitska jungfrurna* ('The foolish virgins', 1920), written for the Ballets Suédois of Paris. *Bäckahästen* ('The white horse', 1923–4), with its naive folkloristic tone and Singspiel character, also met with success, and *Fanal* (1929–32) is an effective, ballad-style drama of freedom in 16th-century Germany. All Atterberg's stage works rely on decorative effect rather than psychological profundity. His music for Maeterlinck's *Soeur Béatrice* is typical in its lyrical-elegiac, slightly impressionist treatment of sentiment; the suite drawn from it is one of his most frequently performed works.

WORKS
(selective list)

STAGE

op.
— Jefta (incidental music, Didring), 1913; used in Suite no.1
9 Per Svinaherde (ballet), 1914–15; Stockholm, 1921
— Mats och Petter (incidental music, J. Bauer), 1915; used in Suite no.2
12 Härvard harpolekare [Härvard the harpist] (opera), 1916–18, Stockholm, 1919; rev. 1934–5; rev. 1952 as Härvards hemkomst [Härvard's homecoming], Stockholm, 1954
— Syster Beatrice (incidental music, Maeterlinck), 1917; used in Suite no.3
13 Perseus och vidundret (incidental music, T. Hedberg), 1918
— Balettskizzer, 1919; Stockholm, 1920
17 De fåvitska jungfrurna [The foolish virgins] (ballet), 1920; Paris, 1920
— Turandot (incidental music, Gozzi), 1920; used in Suite no.4
18 Stormen (incidental music, Shakespeare), 1921; orch suite
— De tre mostrarna (incidental music, G. Holmgren), 1923
— En vintersaga (incidental music, Shakespeare), 1923; used in Suite no.5
24 Bäckahästen [The white horse] (opera), 1923–4; Stockholm, 1925
— Hassan (incidental music, Flecker), 1925; used in Suite no.6
— Antonius och Kleopatra (incidental music, Shakespeare), 1926
35 Fanal (opera), 1929–32; Stockholm, 1934
43 Aladdin (opera), 1936–41; Stockholm, 1941; ov., op.44, 1941
49 Stormen (opera), 1946–7; Stockholm, 1948

ORCHESTRAL

Syms.: no.1, b, op.3, 1909–11; no.2, F, op.6, 1911–13; no.3 (Västkustbilder), op.10, 1914–16; no.4 (Sinfonia piccola), g, op.14, 1918; no.5 (Sinfonia funebre), d, op.20, 1919–22; no.6, C, op.31, 1927–8; no.7 (Sinfonia romantica), op.45, 1942; no.8, e, op.48, 1944; no.9 (Sinfonia visionaria), op.54 (Voluspa), solo vv, chorus, orch, 1955–6
Concertante works: Rhapsody, op.1, pf, orch, 1909; Vn Conc., e, op.7, 1913; Vc Conc., c, op.21, 1922; Hn Conc., A, op.28, 1926; Pf Conc., b♭, op.37, 1935; Double Conc., g–C, vn, vc/va, str, 1959–60
Suites: no.1 (Orientalisk svit), 1913; no.2, 1915; no.3, op.19 no.1, vn, va, str, 1917; Stormen, op.18, 1921; no.4 'Turandot', op.19 no.2, 1920; no.5 (Suite barocco), op.23, 1923; no.6 (Orientalisk legend), op.30, 1925; no.7, op.29, str/str qnt, 1926; no.8 (Suite pastorale in modo antico), op.34, 1931; no.9 (Suite drammatica), op.47, 1944
Other works: Concert Ov., a, op.4, 1910; Rondeau rétrospectif, op.26, 1925; Älven [The river], op.33, sym. poem, 1929; Ballad och passacaglia, op.38, 1935; Concert Ov., op.41, 1940; Rondeau caractéristique, op.42, 1940; Indian Tunes, op.51, sym. movt, 1950; Svensk sommarfest, 1957

VOCAL

Requiem, op.8, solo vv, chorus, orch, 1914; Järnbäraland, op.16, solo vv, chorus, orch, 1919; Sången, op.25, solo vv, chorus ad lib, orch, 1925; Sångens land, op.32, solo vv, chorus ad lib, orch, 1928

CHAMBER AND INSTRUMENTAL

Str Qt no.1, D, op.2, 1909; Str Qt no.2, op.11, 1918; 2 Höstballader, op.15, pf, 1918; Sonata, b, op.27, vc, pf, 1925; Pf Qnt, op.31 bis [arr. of Sym. no.6]; Str Qt no.3, D, op.39, 1937; Variations and Fugue, op.46, str qt, 1944

Principal publishers: Breitkopf & Härtel, Eulenburg, Leuckart, Musikaliska Konstföreningen

WRITINGS
ed.: *Föreningen svenska tonsättare 25 år* (Stockholm, 1943)
Med notpenna och taktpinne: ett och annat om partiturskrivning och taktslagning (Stockholm, 1946)
'Ut- och inländska musikminnen från tidigt 1900–tal', *Musikrevy* (1967)

BIBLIOGRAPHY
E. M. Stuart: *Kurt Atterberg* (Stockholm, 1925)
G. Bergendal: 'Atterberg, vad vill du mig?', *Musikrevy*, xxii (1967)
I. Liljefors: 'Femtio år med Atterberg', *Musikrevy*, xxii (1967), 327
G. Percy: 'Kurt Atterberg 85 år', *Musikrevy*, xxviii (1973), [incl. list of works]

HANS ÅSTRAND, BO WALLNER

Atterbury, Luffmann (*b* c1740; *d* London, 11 June 1796). English glee composer. He was apparently a builder or carpenter by trade, but later became a musician-in-ordinary to George III. He sang in the Handel Commemoration of 1784. He composed about 50 glees and catches, the great majority for male voices. Many of them first appeared in Warren's *Collection of Catches Canons and Glees* (London, 1763–94) and in Atterbury's three collections of his own music (1777, c1790, c1797). The glee *Come let us all a-maying* and the catch *Hot cross buns* long remained popular. He also composed an oratorio *Goliath*, performed at the Haymarket Theatre on 5 May 1773, and provided airs for a pasticcio, *Mago and Dago* (1794).

NICHOLAS TEMPERLEY

Attey, John (*fl* 1622; *d* Ross, Herefordshire, 1640). English lutenist and composer. In his book of ayres Attey described himself as 'Gentleman and Practitioner in Musicke', while in the dedication to the Earl and Countess of Bridgwater he wrote that his songs were for 'the best part composed under your roofe while I had the happiness to attend the service of those worthy and incomparable young Ladies your daughters'. John Egerton (1579–1649), Earl of Bridgwater and his wife Frances, daughter of Ferdinando, Earl of Derby, lived at Ashridge, in the parish of Little Gaddesden, Hertfordshire. Fellowes gave his death date as above (*English Madrigal Composers*) but the source for his statement is not known.

Attey's only publication, *The First Booke of Ayres* for four voices and lute (London, 1622/*R*1967; ed. in ESLS, 2nd ser., ix, 1967), was the last of its kind to be printed in England. All the songs are set for four voices as well as for solo voice, and the song *In a Grove of Trees of Mirtle* is the only four-part ayre in all the songbooks to have a purely instrumental prelude. In his works the lute parts are not such close intabulations of the three lower voices as is generally found in the earlier books of ayres. Attey had a pleasant talent for melody, but his songs have, as Warlock wrote, 'no outstanding qualities save for the last song in the book, *Sweet was the song the Virgin sung*, a flawless work of serene beauty which forms a fitting conclusion to this golden period of English song'.

BIBLIOGRAPHY
E. H. Fellowes: *The English Madrigal Composers* (Oxford, 1921, 2/1948/*R*1975), 324
P. Warlock: *The English Ayre* (London, 1926)
E. H. Fellowes: *English Madrigal Verse* (Oxford, 1929, 3/1967)
E. Doughtie: *Lyrics from English Airs 1596–1622* (Cambridge, Mass., 1970)

DIANA POULTON

Attwood, Thomas (*b* London, baptized 23 Nov 1765; *d* London, 24 March 1838). English composer and organist. His father was a coal merchant, and also a viola player and trumpeter in the King's Band. Throughout his life Attwood benefited from royal patronage. At the age of nine he became a chorister in the Chapel Royal. When he left the choir in 1781 he became one of the Pages of the Presence to the Prince of Wales, who was so impressed by his musical ability that he sent him abroad to study. From 1783 to 1785 he lived in Naples, studying with Felipe Cinque and Gaetano Latilla. He then travelled to Vienna, where he lived from August 1785 until February 1787, still apparently supported by the Prince of Wales, and taking lessons in composition from Mozart. His exercises, with Mozart's corrections, are extant and have been printed. In Oldman's words, they 'are valuable not only for the light they throw on the prentice years of a notable English composer, but as evidence that Mozart, given an apt and congenial pupil, took his duties as a teacher with the utmost seriousness'. Mozart became much attached to Attwood: according to Kelly (who is not always reliable) Mozart said of him, 'He partakes more of my style than any scholar I ever had; and I predict, that he will prove a sound musician'.

Attwood returned to his court position in England, and began to publish some of his instrumental compositions. In December 1791 he was appointed music teacher to the Duchess of York, and in April 1795 to the Princess of Wales. More important appointments followed in 1796, when he was made organist of St Paul's Cathedral and, later in the year, composer to the Chapel Royal. Meanwhile he had become a successful composer for the stage. Beginning with *The Prisoner* (1792), for the next ten years he provided music in whole or in part for well over 30 productions. The great majority of these were afterpieces of slight musical substance, and many were pasticcios; but in Attwood's original contributions it is easy to see the polish and grace that distinguish him from such contemporaries as Arnold and Kelly, and which evidently derive from Mozart's teaching. In many of these pieces, particularly the earlier ones, he adapted Mozart's own music to the English texts.

After 1801 there were only five more dramatic pieces, spread over the next quarter of a century, as Attwood was increasingly occupied with other kinds of music. He was one of the 30 original members of the Philharmonic Society on its foundation in 1813, one of its directors in 1816–20 and 1824–32 and he conducted one concert almost every year, usually including one of Mozart's symphonies. He was also concerned with several vocal societies, for which he composed a number of glees. In 1821 he composed an anthem *I was glad* for the coronation of his former patron, now George IV, and shortly afterwards was appointed organist of the king's newly built private chapel at Brighton, a sinecure position. He was one of the professors of the RAM on its foundation in 1823. He succeeded his father as musician-in-ordinary to the king in 1825; finally, in 1836, he was appointed organist of the Chapel Royal in succession to Stafford Smith. During all this time the emphasis in his composition moved steadily in the direction of church and organ music. In 1831 he was again called upon for a coronation anthem, this time for the 65-year-old William IV (*O Lord, grant the king a long life*), and on his death he is said to have left behind a third which had been commissioned for the coronation of Victoria.

Attwood was a man of kind and genial disposition, and had many friends in the musical world. In his later years he had the pleasure of a close friendship with

Mendelssohn, who stayed with him at his house on Beulah Hill, Norwood, on several occasions: the Fantasia op.16 no.2 was composed there in 1829. Mendelssohn dedicated to him his Three Preludes and Fugues op.37, and the autograph of a *Kyrie eleison* in A minor is inscribed 'For Mr. Attwood, Berlin, 24th March 1833'. Attwood was a great admirer of Mendelssohn's brilliant performances on the organ of St Paul's Cathedral, and was converted by them to a tardy recognition of the genius of Bach. He was not himself a great executant on the organ.

Thomas Attwood: portrait by an unknown artist in the Royal College of Music, London

Attwood's compositions, whether for the stage, the church or the home, were profoundly affected by his intense experience as Mozart's pupil. But the influence did not take the form of direct imitation except in some of the earliest stage pieces; it is found rather in the feeling for melodic shape and the beautifully tasteful organization of harmony that distinguish him from his English contemporaries. His style is recognizably English, as much as it is Mozartian, and he had a particularly sensitive feeling for verbal accent: this is noticeable in the songs, including *The cold wave my love lies under*, in glees like *The Curfew*, and in the many treble solos in his longer anthems. The dramatic works are collections of songs and choruses in the manner of their time, offering little opportunity for imitation of Mozart's operatic methods. The early instrumental trios, like Mozart's but unlike most English 'accompanied sonatas' of the time, treat the string instruments on equal terms with the piano. Attwood's most ambitious music is in his great coronation anthems with orchestral accompaniment, containing elaborate counterpoint (but also unfortunately introducing patriotic airs), and in the Service in F, with its *Gloria Patri* in strict canon. However his slender reputation now rests not on these large-scale works, but on intimate, exquisitely polished pieces such as *Turn thy face from my sins* and the hymn *Come, Holy Ghost*. They are in direct line from the Mozart of *Ave verum corpus* and the Andante section of the Fantasia K608. To him they owe their balance and serenity, their melodic grace, and the sweetness of their full four-part harmony.

In 1793 Attwood married Mary Denton, who bore him five sons and a daughter. Some of his most distinguished pupils were Thomas Attwood Walmisley (who was also his godson), John Goss, George Bridgetower and Cipriani Potter. Walmisley inherited or acquired many of his manuscript compositions; he published a selection of the church music in 1852, but many other compositions, including most of the organ music, passed from the Walmisley family to Frederick Fertel, organist of Bromley, and were dispersed after his death.

WORKS
(all printed works published in London)

THEATRICAL

See detailed list in Oldman, 1965. All first produced in London and published (vocal score) in same year unless otherwise indicated; MSS of most librettos at *US-SM*.

CG – *Covent Garden*; DL – *Drury Lane*; HY – *Haymarket*
* – *partly adapted*

*The Prisoner (musical romance, 3, J. Rose, after J. M. Boutet de Monvel), HY, 18 Oct 1792
*Ozmyn and Daraxa (musical romance, 2, J. Boaden), HY, 7 March 1793, not pubd
*The Mariners (musical entertainment, 2, S. Birch), HY, 10 May 1793
*Caernarvon Castle, or The Birth of the Prince of Wales (entertainment, 2, Rose), HY, 12 Aug 1793
The Packet Boat, or A Peep behind the Veil (musical farce, 2, S. Birch), CG, 13 May 1794, not pubd
*The Adopted Child (musical farce, 2, Birch), DL, 1 May 1795
The Poor Sailor, or Little Ben and Little Bob (musical drama, 2, J. Bernard), CG, 29 May 1795
*The Smugglers (musical drama, 2, Birch), DL, 13 April 1796
The Fairy Festival (masque, 1, Rose), DL, 13 May 1797, 4 songs pubd
*The Irish Tar, or Which is the Girl? (musical piece, 1, W. C. Oulton), HY, 24 Aug 1797, not pubd
Fast Asleep (farce, 2, Birch, after Powell), DL, 28 Oct 1797, 2 songs pubd
Britain's Brave Tars!! or All for St Paul's (musical farce, 1, J. O'Keeffe), CG, 19 Dec 1797, 1 song pubd
The Devil of a Lover (musical farce, 2, G. Moultrie), CG, 17 March 1798, not pubd
Reform'd in Time (comic opera, 2, H. Heartwell), CG, 23 May 1798, not pubd
A Day at Rome (musical farce, 2, C. Smith), CG, 17 Oct 1798, not pubd
*The Mouth of the Nile, or The Glorious First of August (musical entertainment, 1, T. Dibdin), GC, 25 Oct 1798
*Albert and Adelaide, or The Victim of Constancy (musical drama, 3, Birch, after Marsollier, Boutet de Monvel), 11 Dec 1798, not pubd; collab. Steibelt
*The Magic Oak, or Harlequin Woodcutter (pantomime, 2, T. Dibdin), CG, 29 Jan 1799
The Old Clothesman (comic opera, 3, T. Holcroft), CG, 2 April 1799, ov. by M. Parke
*The Castle of Sorrento (comic opera, 2, Heartwell, G. Colman, after Duval: Le prisonnier), HY, 13 July 1799
*The Red Cross Knights (play, 5, J. G. Holman, after Schiller), HY, 21 Aug 1799
True Friends (musical farce, 2, T. Dibdin), CG, 19 Feb 1800
*St David's Day (musical piece, 2, T. Dibdin), CG, 25 March 1800; incl. Welsh airs
*The Hermione, or Valour's Triumph (musical piece, 1, T. Dibdin), CG, 5 April 1800, not pubd
*Il Bondocani, or The Caliph Robber (serio-comic musical drama, 3, T. Dibdin), CG, 15 Nov 1800; collab. J. Moorehead
Harlequin's Tour, or The Dominion of Fancy (pantomime, T. Dibdin), CG, 22 Dec 1800; collab. J. Moorehead
*The Sea-side Story (operatic drama, 2, W. Dimond), CG, 12 May 1801, not pubd
*The Escapes, or The Water-carrier (musical entertainment, 2, T. Holcroft, after Bouilly: Les deux journées), CG, 14 Oct 1801, incl. music of Cherubini

Songs and glees contributed to 6 works: Adrian and Orilla, or A Mother's Vengeance (play, 5, W. Dimond), CG, 15 Nov 1801; The Curfew (play, 5, J. Tobin), DL, 19 Feb 1807; Guy Mannering, or The Gipsey's Prophecy (musical play, 3, D. Terry, after Scott), CG, 12 March 1816; Elphi Bey, or The Arab's Faith (musical drama, 3, R. Hamilton), DL, 17 April 1817; David Rizzio (serious opera, Hamilton), DL, 17 June 1820; The Hebrew Family or A Traveller's Adventures (play, 3), CG, 8 April 1825

VOCAL

Edition: *Services and Anthems Composed by Thomas Attwood*, ed. T. A. Walmisley (London, 1852) [W]

4 morning and evening services, W: F, 1796; A, 1825; D, orch, 1831; C, 1832
Morning and Evening Service, B♭ (c1837)
4 Kyrie and Sanctus: C (1828), E (1818), F (c1817), G (c1833)
18 anthems, all pubd: Be thou my judge, 1800; Blessed is he that considereth, 1804; Bow down thine ear, c1833; Enter not into judgment, 1834; Grant, we beseech thee, 1814, W; I was glad, orch, 1821; Let the words of my mouth, 1835, W; Let thy hand be strengthened, 1821; My soul truly waiteth, 1823; O God, who by the leading of a star, 1814, W; O Lord, grant the king a long life, orch, 1831; O Lord, we beseech thee, 1814, W; Teach me, O Lord, 1796, W; Teach me thy way, 1817, W; They that go down to the sea, 1837, W; Turn thee again, O Lord, 1817; Turn thy face from my sins, 1835, W; Withdraw not thou thy mercy, 1827, W
Kyrie, Gloria (Lat.), Naples, 1784
Come, Holy Ghost, hymn, 1831 (1851)
God, that madest earth and heaven, vesper hymn (1835)
Psalm tunes, chants, responses, 9 sacred songs, 2 duets, some in *GB-Lbm*
Secular: 9 Glees, 3–6 vv (1828); songs, c50 other glees pubd separately

INSTRUMENTAL

Chamber: 3 Pf Trios, op.1 (?1787); Pf Trio, in Storace's Collection of Original Harpsichord Music (1789); 3 Pf Sonatas, ad lib vn, vc, op.2 (1791); Marches, pf
Wind insts: Royal Exchange March, 2 cl, 2 fl, hn, tpt, bn, serpent (?1803), pf score (?1803); Piece, 3 cl, 2 hn, bn, *Lbm*; Divertimento, 2 basset hn, 2 ob, 2 hn, 2 bn, serpent, collab. Pleyel, Storace, *Lbm*
Org: March, Piece (1797); Dirge, d (1805); Cathedral Fugue, E♭
Pedagogical: Easy Progressive Lessons for Young Beginners, pf/hpd (c1795); A Short Introduction to the Pianoforte (?1805)
Arrs. of works by Beethoven, Hummel, Mayseder, Meyerbeer, Mozart, Spontini, Weber, Winter, mostly pf, other insts

EXERCISES

Thomas Attwoods Theorie- und Kompositionsstudien bei Mozart, ed. E. Hertzmann, C. B. Oldman, D. Heartz and A. Mann, W. A. Mozart: Neue Ausgabe sämtlicher Werke, x/30/1 (Kassel, 1965)

BIBLIOGRAPHY

M. Kelly: *Reminiscences*, ed. T. Hook (London, 1825), i, 225
Musical World, viii (1838), 220f, 227f
D. Baptie: *Sketches of the English Glee Composers* (London, 1895), 58ff
F. G. Edwards: 'Thomas Attwood (1765–1838)', *MT*, xli (1900), 788 [with letters between Attwood and Mendelssohn]
E. Hertzmann: 'Mozart and Attwood', *JAMS*, xii (1959), 178
C. B. Oldman: 'Thomas Attwood, 1765–1838', *MT*, cvi (1965), 844
——: 'Attwood's Dramatic Works', *MT*, cvii (1966), 23
D. Heartz: 'Thomas Attwood's Lessons in Composition with Mozart', *PRMA*, c (1973–4), 175

NICHOLAS TEMPERLEY

Atys [Atis; first name unknown] (*b* St Domingue [now Haiti], 18 April 1715; *d* Paris, 8 Aug 1784). French creole flautist, composer and teacher. His skill as a flute virtuoso and teacher made him renowned in Paris and Vienna, but his concert career was cut short by a chin wound received in a pistol duel. He was among the first flautists to use crescendo and diminuendo instead of simple echo contrasts. His compositions, all published in Paris, are primarily intended for amateur flautists: they include duos 'en forme de conversation' op.1 (1754), sonatas 'dans le goût italien' op.2 (1756, lost), further duos and quartets, and a *Feste concertante* (1775, lost) and minuets for orchestra. He also published two flute methods.

BIBLIOGRAPHY

FétisB
J.-B. de La Borde: *Essai sur la musique ancienne et moderne*, iii (Paris, 1780/*R*1972), 493

ROGER COTTE

Atzmon [Groszberger], **Moshe** (*b* Budapest, 30 July 1931). Israeli conductor. His family settled in British-mandated Palestine in 1944 and he has followed Israeli custom in changing his original surname to the present Hebrew form. Having studied the piano and horn, he graduated from the Tel-Aviv Academy of Music in composition and conducting and was encouraged by Antal Dorati to pursue a conducting career. In London, where he studied at the Guildhall School of Music, he won the school's conducting prize in 1963, followed in 1964 by the first prize at the international conducting competition sponsored by the Royal Liverpool PO. In 1967 he conducted the Vienna PO at the Salzburg Festival. From 1969 to 1971 he was chief conductor of the Sydney SO, and in 1972 he became chief conductor of the North German (Hamburg) Radio SO and of the Basle SO. His operatic début was in October 1969 with Rossini's *La Cenerentola* at the Deutsche Oper, Berlin, and he first appeared on record conducting the New Philharmonia Orchestra in 1968, having already brought a skilled baton technique and a lively personality to concerts in Britain, the USA and Israel.

ARTHUR JACOBS

Aubade (Fr.: 'dawn song'). A term originally applied to music intended for performance in the morning. It has now become simply a generic title. In the 17th and 18th centuries, aubades were played at court by military bands in honour of French sovereigns, and in provincial towns to celebrate the election of municipal officials. The ALBA of the troubadours is a distant antecedent. In the 19th and 20th centuries the term and its Spanish equivalent, ALBORADA, came into use as the title of a characteristic piece, for example the *Aubade* for piano by Bizet and the *Aubade et allegretto* for strings and wind by Lalo (1872). Poulenc used it as the title of a more extended work, his 'choreographic concerto' for piano and 18 instruments (1929).

Aube (Old Fr.). ALBA.

Auber, Daniel-François-Esprit (*b* Caen, 29 Jan 1782; *d* Paris, 12 or 13 May 1871). French composer, principally of *opéras comiques*, and the foremost representative of this genre in 19th-century France.

The son of a royal huntsman (later a dealer in art materials), Auber showed an early talent for the piano. He studied under Ignaz Anton Ladurner, and between 1793 and 1800 wrote several romances, a piano sonata, at least one string quartet and two Italianate concert arias. In 1802, during the cessation of hostilities between France and England, Auber came to London to study commerce, but returned to Paris the following year to devote himself to music. His one-act 'comédie melée d'ariettes', *L'erreur d'un moment* (1805), attracted the attention of Cherubini, who accepted him as his pupil. The fruits of this period of study include cello concertos (appearing under the name of the cellist Jacques-Michel de Lamare), a violin concerto and other chamber and vocal works, culminating in the mass for three voices of 1812.

Auber's first attempt as a composer of *opéras comiques* for the Paris public was unsuccessful, and he temporarily abandoned composition. In 1819 the bankruptcy of his father, who had hitherto been able to support him in relative idleness, spurred Auber to return to composition; Cherubini procured for him

three librettos by François-Antoine-Eugène de Planard, a bureaucrat and amateur librettist. Though the first work, *Le testament*, failed, Auber achieved success with the second, *La bergère châtelaine* (1820), and with *Emma* (1821). Soon after, Auber met the librettist Augustin-Eugène Scribe and began a collaboration that endured until Scribe's death in 1861.

In 1823 Auber fell under the influence of Rossini's music and his next three operas, especially in the vocal writing, are virtual imitations of Rossini's musical mannerisms. However, he returned to the French style in 1824 with *Léocadie*, which he subtitled 'opéra français',

Daniel-François-Esprit Auber: caricature by André Gill from the cover of 'L'éclipse' (1 March 1868)

and in the following year with *Le maçon*, one of the works which inaugurated the golden age of French *opéra comique*. The synthesis of the French style of *opéra comique* with Rossini's spirited writing is best seen in Auber's major light *opéras comiques* from *Fiorella* (1826) to *La sirène* (1844), especially in his most famous work in this genre and the only one in the permanent repertory, *Fra Diavolo* (1830). These *opéras comiques* are characterized by the alternation of sentimental romances or witty couplets with deft ensembles, often marked by orchestral melodies supported by syllabic vocal declamation, and with vocal *fioritura* generally restricted to the first soprano and first tenor.

The successes of Auber and Scribe soon led to their being commissioned to write *La muette de Portici* for the Académie Royale de Musique. Its first performance in 1828 inaugurated the epoch of French grand opera through such elements as the use of local colour in the ballets, the portrayal of crowds, a revolutionary topic from modern history (the Neapolitan insurrection under Masaniello in 1647), the skilful orchestration and the wide variety of musical and dramatic effects. Its Brussels première in 1830 is said to have sparked off the Belgian revolt against the Dutch. Auber continued to write for the Opéra until 1851, but he was able to equal the daring spirit of *La muette de Portici* only in occasional passages in *Gustave III* (1833) and the *opéra comique*, *Lestocq* (1834).

Auber began to change his style after 1840 towards a more serious and lyrical type of *opéra comique*; *La part du diable* (1843), *Haydée* (1847) and *Manon Lescaut* (1856), the best works in this new style, strongly influenced the development of *opéra lyrique*. He continued to compose until his death but his only significant late work is *Le premier jour de bonheur* (1868).

Auber's early *opéras comiques* show the transition from the simple style of Isouard and the young Boieldieu to a sparkling, lively style characterized by triadic melodies (diatonic with occasional chromatic seasonings), four-bar phrases, piquant dotted or dance-like rhythms (especially those of the waltz, polka, schottische and quadrille), skilful orchestration with a light sonority, conservative harmonic practice and an overwhelmingly homophonic texture: in his words, 'counterpoint makes the symphony live but it kills the opera'. In his works after 1840, his harmony became richer, with more chromaticism and altered chords and a wider range of modulation, which added to the expressive quality of his music. The role of the baritone was also expanded; Jean-Baptiste Faure was the first interpreter of many of these parts.

Auber's non-operatic works deserve only brief mention. The first two movements of his C major string quartet (1799) are harmonically imaginative and well written, more Romantic in spirit than his piano sonata or concertos. The church music composed in his late years consists of motets, hymns and mass sections (no complete masses); its style is prevailingly operatic, with execrable Latin declamation and generally commonplace thematic material. His best sacred work is the simple and dignified *Litanies de la sainte vierge*.

In person, Auber was diminutive, and so shy that he could not conduct his music or even endure hearing it performed. He never married, though as a young man he had a romantic liaison with Pauline Duchambge, a Martiniquaise composer of romances who was 20 years his senior. He was famed for his mordant wit and epigrams; he was also a keen horseman. As director of the Paris Conservatoire from 1842 to 1870 he engaged Halévy to teach composition, strengthened the departments of piano and orchestral instruments, and conscientiously discharged his administrative duties until the Conservatoire was converted into a hospital during the siege of 1870.

Nearly all the successive governments of France honoured him. Under Charles X he was made a member of the Légion d'honneur in 1825 and elected to the Institute (Académie) in 1829; Louis Philippe appointed him Cherubini's successor as director of the Paris Conservatoire; Napoleon III made him musical director of the imperial chapel in 1852. Most of Auber's mature non-operatic works were governmental commissions. Particularly warm tributes to him were paid by Rossini ('*piccola musica, ma grande musicista*') and Wagner.

WORKS

Unless otherwise indicated, all printed works were published in Paris, and works without publication dates are in MS at *F-Pn*.

STAGE

Unless otherwise indicated, works were written to Scribe librettos, first performed in Paris, at the Théâtre de l'Opéra-Comique, and published in year of first performance.

L'erreur d'un moment (J.-M. Boutet de Monvel), Salle Doyen, 1805, by amateurs; rev. as Julie, Belgium, Château de Chimay, 1811, not pubd

Jean de Couvin (N. Lemercier), Belgium, Château de Chimay, Sept 1812, not pubd

Le séjour militaire (J.-N. Bouilly, E. Mercier-Dupaty), 27 Feb 1813

Le testament et les billets-doux (F.-A.-E. de Planard), 18 Sept 1819

Le bergère châtelaine (Planard), 27 Jan 1820

Emma, ou La promesse imprudente (Planard), 7 July 1821

Leicester, ou Le château de Kenilworth (Scribe, Mélesville, after Scott), 25 Jan 1823

La neige, ou Le nouvel Éginard (Scribe, G. Delavigne), 8 Oct 1823

Vendôme en Espagne (A.-J.-S. d'Empis, E. Mennechet), Opéra, 5 Dec 1823, not pubd; collab. Hérold

Les trois genres (Scribe, Dupaty, M. Pichat), Odéon, 27 April 1824; collab. Boieldieu

Le concert à la cour, ou La débutante (Scribe, Mélesville), 3 June 1824

Léocadie (Scribe, Mélesville, after Cervantes: La fuerça del sangre), 4 Nov 1824

Le maçon (Scribe, Delavigne), 3 May 1825

Le timide, ou Le nouveau séducteur (Scribe, X.-B. Saintine), 30 May 1826

Fiorella, 28 Nov 1826

La muette de Portici [Masaniello] (Scribe, Delavigne), Opéra, 29 Feb 1828

La fiancée, 10 Jan 1829

Fra Diavolo, ou L'hôtellerie de Terracine, 28 Jan 1830

Le dieu et la bayadère, ou La courtisane amoureuse (opera-ballet), Opéra, 13 Oct 1830

Le philtre, Opéra, 20 June 1831

La Marquise de Brinvilliers (Scribe, Castil-Blaze), Opéra, 31 Oct 1831; collab. Batton, Berton, Blangini, Boieldieu, Carafa, Cherubini, Hérold, Paer

Le serment, ou Les faux-monnayeurs (Scribe, E.-J.-E. Mazères), Opéra, 1 Oct 1832

Gustave III, ou Le bal masqué, Opéra, 27 Feb 1833

Lestocq, ou L'intrigue et l'amour, 24 May 1834

Le cheval de bronze, 23 March 1835; rev. as an opera-ballet, Opéra, 21 Sept 1857

Actéon, 23 Jan 1836

Les chaperons blancs, 9 April 1836

L' ambassadrice, 21 Dec 1836

Le domino noir, 2 Dec 1837

Le lac des fées (Scribe, Mélesville), Opéra, 1 April 1839

Zanetta, ou Jouer avec le feu (Scribe, J.-H. Vernoy de Saint-Georges), 18 May 1840

Les diamants de la couronne (Scribe, Vernoy de Saint-Georges), 6 March 1841

Le Duc d'Olonne (Scribe, Saintine), 4 Feb 1842

La part du diable, 16 Jan 1843

La sirène, 26 March 1844

La barcarolle, ou L'amour et la musique, 22 April 1845

Les premiers pas (A. Royer, G. Vaëz), Opéra national, 15 Nov 1847; collab. Adam, Carafa, Halévy

Haydée, ou Le secret (Scribe, after Mérimée: Six et quatre), 28 Dec 1847

L'enfant prodigue, Opéra, 6 Dec 1850

Zerline, ou La corbeille d'oranges, Opéra, 16 May 1851

Marco Spada (Scribe, Delavigne), 21 Dec 1852; rev. as Marco Spada, ou La fille du bandit (ballet, choreographed by Mazilier), Opéra, 1 April 1857

Jenny Bell, 2 June 1855

Manon Lescaut (Scribe, after Prévost), 23 Feb 1856

La circassienne, 2 Feb 1861

La fiancée du Roi de Garbe (Scribe, Vernoy de Saint-Georges), 11 Jan 1864

Le premier jour de bonheur (A.-P. d'Ennery, E. Cormon), 15 Feb 1868

Rêve d'amour (D'Ennery, Cormon), 20 Dec 1869

SACRED

Mass, 3vv, orch, 1812; Ag later used in La muette de Portici, Act 3, 1828

Domine salvum fac rempublicam, 4vv, orch, c1848–51

Litanies de la Sainte Vierge, 4vv, orch, after 1852

Noël; Hymne à S Cécile: both c1852

Sub tuum presidium, 4vv, org, 1852–4

O Dieu puissant, 4vv, org

O Salutaris, Bb, S, 4vv, orch, 1852–4

7 Agnus Dei, from 1854: ab, 4vv, small orch; c, 4vv, orch; d, 4vv, orch; bb, S, Bar, 4vv, orch; eb, 6vv orch (also in c, 3vv, orch); bb, 4vv, org, harp; d [rev. of Ag from 1812 mass], 4vv, orch, or 4vv, org, harp

Gloria, Bb, 4vv, orch, 1854

3 Credo, inc., 1854

4 Benedictus, 1854: Eb, 4vv, small orch; Eb, S, small orch; Bb, S, small orch; Ab, S, small orch

O salutaris, Eb, 4vv, orch, 1854; ed in B. Jouvin, Auber (Paris, 1868)

O salutaris, F, 4vv, orch/org, 1854

4 Kyrie, 4vv, orch/org, 1854: g, g, F, f
O crux ave, 4vv, pf, harp, 1854 (also as Vexilla regis, 4vv, org, harp, 1855)
Parce Domine, 4vv, org, 1854
Kyrie, f, 4vv, orch/org, 1855
O salutaris, B♭, 4vv, ob, orch/org, c1855 [based on L'enfant prodigue, 1850]
O salutaris, B♭, 4vv, ob, orch/org, c1855 (also as Ave Maria)
Gloria, B♭, 4vv, org, harp, c1855
Benedictus, D, S, orch, c1855
Credo, B♭, 4vv, orch, 1859
Benedictus, C, Bar, cl, orch, 1859
3 O salutaris, 1859: B♭, T, ob, org, harp; B♭, S, hn, org, harp; F, S, T, org, harp
Ecce panis angelorum, 4vv, org, c1860
2 Kyrie, c1860: d, 4vv, org, harp; g, 4vv, orch
O salutaris, G, S, vn, org, harp, 1860
Pie Jesu, S, org, 1861
Benedictus, A♭, 2 S, org, 1862
Gloria, B♭, 4vv, orch, 1863
2 O salutaris, c1863: B♭, 2 S, org/orch; E, 3vv, org, rev. in E♭, 3vv, harmonium, org, harp
Kyrie, a, 4vv, org, 1865, later used in Le premier jour de bonheur, 1868
Ave Maria, 4vv, org, 1865
Kyrie, C, 4vv, org, 1865
Veni Creator, 4vv, orch/org, 1865
Kyrie, f, 4vv, org, 1870

SECULAR VOCAL

Non s'è più barbaro, T, orch, 1798
Rendi mi il figlio mio, T, orch, 1799
Procris, S, str orch, c1800
Trio, 3vv, fl, vn, va, c1812
La parisienne, marche national, 4vv, orch, 1830
Chant des polonais, solo vv, 4vv, orch, 1832
Folyfo, choeur chinois, c1834
Cantata for the dinner offered to the king by the city of Paris, 1837
Je suis cette cousine, S, orch
Je suis alsacienne, 3 equal vv
La belle bourbonnaise, 1v, orch
Entrée du Roi Henri, Pau, 1843
Sauve, ô mon Dieu, le roi/God Save the Queen, c1843; later used in Jenny Bell, 1855
La parisienne républicaine, c1848 [after music in La parisienne, 1830]
Chant des normands, Caen, 1851
5 cantatas: for the marriage of Napoleon III, 1853; for the baptism of the Prince Imperial, 1854; for the capture of Sebastopol, 1855; for the festival of arts and industry, 1855; for the distribution of the prize of the Société des Gens de Lettres, 1856
Magenta, 1857
28 romances and chansonettes, c1783–1869: 22 listed in Malherbe (1911), also Au coin de ta bouche; Loin de lui; Chasseur, qui parcourez, c1800; Ecoutez l'histoire, c1800; Les yeux, Hamburg, 1820s; La sibille, 1833

ORCHESTRAL

4 cello concertos, 1806–8, 1 lost: B♭; D, solo part only; a, ed. F. Grützmacher (Leipzig, 1902), also ed. J. Salmon (Paris, 1921)
Air varié, vc, orch/pf, 1807, lost
Violin concerto, D, 1808, ed. S. Beck (New York, 1938)
Pièce symphonique, C
Pièce symphonique or overture, A, c1825
Marche militaire, 1836
Divertissement de Versailles, 1837
Pas de Diane, for Mlle Taglioni, 1837
Fête venetienne, 1837
Music for Molière's Le bourgeois gentilhomme, 1838
La gitana; Cachuca; El taleo; Pas styrien: all c1838
Pas à deux faces; Pas des hussars; Pas pour Mlle Taglioni; Pas de deux pour Mlle Augusta: all c1840
Air de danse, for Gluck's Iphigénie
Grand overture for inauguration of universal exposition, London, 1862 (Paris, c1865)
Orchestrations and arrangements of Handel's Alleluia and the Variations from hpd suite in E; Pergolesi's Sicilienne; Gluck's Orfeo, Act 2; Grétry's La caravane du Caire and L'épreuve villageoise; the Bishop of Nancy's O salutaris; E. Troupenas' La caravane

OTHER INSTRUMENTAL

Str Qt, C, 1799
Sonata, C, pf, 1800
Str Qt, 1800, lost
Trio, D, pf, vn, vc, op.1 (Paris, c1806)
8 pieces, 2 vc, c1808
Pf Qt, e, c1808
Fugue on a theme from Cherubini's Faniska, 1808
Nouvelle marche parisienne, pf (Copenhagen, c1818)
5 variations on a theme by Handel, pf, c1835

4 variations on a theme by Handel, pf, c1835
Numerous short albumleaves, pf
Pieces for str qt, 1871, lost

THEORETICAL WORKS

Règles de contrepoint, 1808
Quelques sujets de fugue
Fugues et contrepoints, sujets de fugues pour les concours, datés de 1833 à 1870, esquisses et réalisations
Leçons de solfège à changements de clef, 1842–69
Leçons pour la lecture à première vue, 1844–70
Observations . . . sur la méthode de musique de M. le docteur Emile Chevé (Paris, 1860)
Recueil des leçons de solfège à changements de clef, 1842–69 (Paris, 1886)

BIBLIOGRAPHY

X. Eyma and A. de Lucy: *Auber* (Paris, 1841)
L. de Loménie: *Auber* (Paris, 1842)
E. de Mirécourt: *Auber* (Paris, 1857)
B. Jouvin: *Auber* (Paris, 1868)
E. Hanslick: 'Ein Besuch bei Auber', *Geschichte des Concertwesens in Wien* (Vienna, 1869), ii, 479, 530
Anon.: 'Auber', *MMR*, i (1871), 75
A. Pougin: 'Les derniers jours d'Auber', *Le charivari* (6 Feb 1872)
——: *Auber: ses commencements, les origines de sa carrière* (Paris, 1873)
V. Massé: *Notice sur la vie et les travaux de D. F. E. Auber* (Paris, 1873)
J. Carlez: *L'oeuvre d'Auber* (Caen, 1874)
——: *Auber* (Caen, 1875)
H. Blaze de Bury: 'Scribe et Auber', *Revue des deux mondes*, xxxv (1879), 43
E. Hanslick: 'Von Gounod, Thomas und Auber', *Musikalische Stationen* (Berlin, 1880), 115
A. Kohut: *Auber* (Leipzig, 1895)
L. Douriac: *La psychologie dans l'opéra français* (Paris, 1896)
R. Wagner: 'Reminiscences of Auber', *Richard Wagner's Prose Works*, trans. W. Ellis (London, 1893–1900), v, 35
E. Hanslick: 'Auber', *Die moderne Oper* (Berlin, 1900), 123
J. Chantavoine: 'Quelques lettres inédites d'Auber', *RHCM*, iii (1903), 161
E. Prout: 'Auber's *Le philtre* and Donizetti's *L'elisire d'amore*', *MMR*, xxx (1900), 25, 49, 73
C. Malherbe: *Auber* (Paris, 1911) [includes nearly complete list of works]
H. Grierson: 'My Visit to Auber', *English Review*, xviii (1914), 173
J. Tiersot: 'Auber', *ReM*, xiv (1933), 265
R. Longyear: *D. F. E. Auber: a Chapter in French Opéra Comique 1800–1870* (diss., Cornell U., 1957)
——: 'La muette de Portici', *MR*, xix (1958), 37
——: 'Le livret bien fait', *Southern Quarterly*, i (1963), 169
K. Pendle: 'Scribe, Auber and the Count of Monte Cristo', *MR*, xxxiv (1973), 210

R. M. LONGYEAR

Aubert. French family of violinists and composers active in Paris during the 18th century.

(1) Jacques Aubert [*le vieux, le père*] (*b* Paris, 30 Sept 1689; *d* Belleville, nr. Paris, 17 or 18 May 1753). Violinist and composer. He was probably a son of Jean Aubert, a member of the Vingt-quatre Violons du Roy until his death in 1710. By 1717 Jacques Aubert was known as a dancing-master and violin player in the cabarets, and had written the music for at least five ballets and comedies. In 1719, the year in which he married Marie Louise Lecat and published his first book of violin sonatas, Aubert was appointed to the service of Louis-Henri, Duke of Bourbon and Prince of Condé. In this capacity he composed a *Fête royale* and a *Ballet des XXIV heures* for the duke's entertainment when the young Louis XV passed through Chantilly to Rheims in 1722; Aubert played the violin in the role of Orpheus in the latter work.

In 1727 Aubert succeeded Noël Converset in the Vingt-quatre Violons, remaining a member until 1746, and in the next year he accepted a position with the Académie Royale de Musique and was named first violinist of the Opéra orchestra, with which he performed for the next 24 years. He made his début at the

Concert Spirituel in 1729, and often played there until 1740.

Like many of his contemporaries, Aubert was greatly influenced by the Italian style. At the Concert Spirituel, he must have heard and possibly played concertos and sonatas by Vivaldi and Corelli. Jean-Baptiste Senaillé, Aubert's teacher (with whom he played a sonata for two violins at the Concert Spirituel in 1730), may have stimulated his growing interest in Italian music, and he was encouraged too by Madame de Prie, a friend of Aubert's patron, the Duke of Bourbon, and an adherent of the Italian style.

Aubert's large output as a composer includes sonatas for violin and continuo, concertos, ballet and dance music, and what he called 'concerts de simphonie' (pieces in suite form for trio, to which different sonorities could be added). He wrote the first violin concertos to be printed in France; whether they are the first concertos by a Frenchman is questionable (see Paillard and Brofsky).

Aubert was more than a composer of salon music or an imitator of the Italian style. While he accepted the basic concerto and sonata form from the Italian school, and their belief that the violin should be more than an instrument *pour faire dancer*, he retained many French elements in his music, the most characteristic being the use of the gavotte, menuet, or other dance form as the slow middle movement and the fully written-out melodic embellishment of the solo pieces.

WORKS

All printed works published in Paris; op. nos from Nouvelle edition, op.1 (1794)

STAGE

La paix triomphante (ballet), 1713, lost
Arlequin gentilhomme malgré lui ou L'amant supposé (comic opera, 3, A.-R. LeSage and d'Orneval), Paris, Foire St Germain, 3 Feb/27 March 1716; Act 3 perfd as Les arrêts de l'amour (comic opera, 1), Paris, Foire St Germain, 17 July 1716, music in Théâtre de la Foire, ii (1721)
Arlequin Hulla ou La femme répudiée (comic opera, 1, LeSage and d'Orneval), Paris, Foire St Laurent, 24 July 1716, music in Théâtre de la Foire, ii (1721)
La fête champêtre et guérrière (ballet), 1716; as op.30 (c1746)
Les animaux raisonnables (comic opera, 1, L. Fuzelier and M.-A. LeGrand), Paris, Foire St Germain, 25/27 Feb 1718; collab. Gilliers; music in Théâtre de la Foire, iii (1721)
Diane (divertissement, A. Danchet), Chantilly, 8 Sept 1721; sym. only; vocal music by L.T. Bourgeois pubd (1721)
Le regiment de la calotte (comic opera, 1, Fuzelier, LeSage and d'Orneval), Paris, Foire St Laurent, 1 Sept 1721; collab. Gilliers; music in Théâtre de la Foire, v (1724)
Fête Royale (divertissement), Chantilly, 4–8 Nov 1722; pubd (1722), see La Laurencie, i (1922), 203
Le ballet de 24 heures (comedy, prol, 4, LeGrand), Chantilly, 5 Nov 1722; as op.6 (1723); music possibly known as Le ballet de Chantilly (1723)
La reine des Péris (comedy, prol, 5, Fuzelier), Paris, Académie Royale de Musique, 10 April 1725; as op.5 (1725)
La reine des Péris (parody and vaudeville, 1, LeSage and d'Orneval), n.d.; parody of the above, F-Pn
La triple Hécate (ballet, 2 scenes, C.-J.-F. Hénault), n.d., lib in Oeuvres inédites (1806)
Numerous airs and dances pubd in 18th-century anthologies

INSTRUMENTAL

Premier (–IVᵉ) livre de [10] sonates, vn, bc: op.1 (1719); op.2 (1721); op.3 (1723); op.4 (1731); Vᵉ livre de [6] sonates, vn, bc, op.25 (c1738)
Pièces, 2 fl/vn, première suite (1723)
Concert de simphonies, suite première (–XIIᵉ), vns/fls/obs, bc: op.8 (1730); opp.9–12 (1731); op.13, also for viols/musettes (1733); opp.18–23 (1735–7)
Les amuzettes, vielles/musettes/vns/fls/obs, op.14 (c1733)
Pièces, 2 vn/fl, op.15 (c1734)
Les petits concerts, musettes/vielles/vns/fls/obs, op.16 (1734)
[6] Concerto, 4 vn, vc, bc, op.17 (1734)
Sonates, 2 vn, op.24 (1738)
[4] Concerto, 4 vn, vc, bc, op.26 (1739); no.4 as Le carillon (n.d.)

Les jolis airs, 2 vn, premier (–VIᵉ) livre: opp.27–9 (c1740–5); op.31 (1749); opp.32–3 (c1750)
Menuets nouveaux avec la basse (n. d.)
Various pieces pubd in 18th-century anthologies

(2) **Louis Aubert** [*le jeune, le fils*] (*b* Paris, 15 May 1720; *d* after 1783). Violinist and composer, eldest and most famous child of (1) Jacques Aubert. Taught by his father and hailed as a child prodigy, he was a back-desk violinist at the Opéra by the time he was 11 and perhaps even when he was only eight. In 1732 Joseph Francoeur nominated him to the Vingt-quatre Violons du Roy, although he was not officially appointed until 1746. By 1756 he was first violinist and one of the principal conductors of the Opéra orchestra. He retired from these duties in 1774 with a pension and special gratuities 'in consideration of 43 years of service'; his name can be found on lists of patrons as late as 1783. Considering that he was active at a later time, Louis was a more conservative composer than his father; his sonatas, each of which is really a series of dances, reflect the French early 18th-century style. He is remembered more for his *simphonies*, which have been mentioned among the precursors of the French symphony; but his works seem to look backward rather than forward. In four of the six *simphonies*, for example, all the movements are in the same key, and in orchestrating them he used three violins and bass without a viola as intermediate voice, the combination that his father had used in the concertos of the 1730s.

An Etienne-Louis Aubert, presumably distinct from Louis (and probably a younger brother), took (1) Jacques Aubert's place in the Vingt-quatre Violons in 1746 and was relieved of his position on Jacques' death in 1753; no compositions survive in his name.

WORKS
(*all published in Paris*)

[6] Sonates, vn, bc, op.1 (1750); some for fl
6 simphonies à quatre, 3 vn, bc, op.2 (1755)
6 trio, 2 vn, vc (n.d.)

(3) **Jean-Louis Aubert** (*b* Paris, 15 Dec 1732; *d* c1810). Writer, dramatist and abbé, son of (1) Jacques Aubert. He may have composed some of the music to his own plays (*Jephté ou le voeu*, 1765; and *La mort d'Abel*, 1765), but he is remembered more for his essays on music, the most famous being his reply to J.-J. Rousseau's controversial *Lettre sur la musique françoise*. In his *Refutation suivie et détaillée des principes de M. Rousseau de Genève touchant la musique françoise* (1754) (taking up arms in the Querelle des Bouffons) Aubert met Rousseau on his own ground and, in language often sarcastic and witty, stressed the genius of French composers such as Rameau, Leclair and Mondonville.

BIBLIOGRAPHY
L. de La Laurencie: 'Jacques Aubert et les premiers concertos français de violon', *BSIM*, ii/1 (1906), 441
L. de La Laurencie and G. de Saint-Foix: 'La symphonie française vers 1750', *Année musicale* (1911), 1–123
L. de La Laurencie: *L'école française de violon de Lully à Viotti* (Paris, 1922–4/R1971)
C. D. Brenner: *A Bibliographical List of Plays in the French Language, 1700–1789* (Berkeley, 1948)
J.-F. Paillard: 'Les premiers concertos français pour instruments à vent', *ReM* (1955), no.226, p.144
B. S. Brook: *La symphonie française dans la seconde moitié du XVIIIᵉ siècle* (Paris, 1962)
L. E. S. J. de Laborde: *Musiciens de Paris, 1535–1792*, ed. Y. de Brossard (Paris, 1965)
H. Brofsky: 'Notes on the Early French Concerto', *JAMS*, xix (1966), 87
M. Benoit: *Musiques de cour: chapelle, chambre, écurie, 1661–1733* (Paris, 1971)

———: *Versailles et les musiciens du roi, 1661–1733* (Paris, 1971)
D. Launay: *La querelle des bouffons* (Geneva, 1973)
ELIZABETH KEITEL

Aubert, (Pierre-François-)Olivier (*b* Amiens, 1763; *d* Paris, *c*1830). French cellist and guitarist. He studied music at the *maîtrise* of his home town but was self-taught at his principal instrument, the cello. In 1787 he was established as a cello teacher in Paris, and he played for 25 years in the orchestra of the Opéra-Comique. Aubert also took up the guitar after Ferdinando Carulli's famous appearance in Paris in 1808, and later taught the guitar in the rue du Faubourg Montmartre, where he also published music. He wrote important methods for the cello and the guitar, and one book of solfège. His published compositions, which show him to have been a cellist of considerable ability and to have enjoyed favour in Vienna, Zurich and Milan as well as Paris, begin with three sets of string quartets opp.1, 2 and 4, but consist mainly of duets for two cellos of which one, op.13, is based on Paris street cries: *Les marchandes de plaisirs d'artichauds, de pommes de terre et de gateaux de Nanterre*. There are five books of potpourris for guitar and some sets of guitar duets. In 1827 Aubert published his 44-page *Histoire abrégée de la musique ancienne et moderne, ou Réflexions sur ce qu'il y a de plus probable dans les écrits qui ont traité ce sujet*, the fruit of 25 years' reflection – a long time, as Fétis observed, devoted to very little.

BIBLIOGRAPHY
FétisB
K. Stephenson: 'Aubert, Pierre François', *MGG* [incl. list of works]
HUGH MACDONALD

Aubéry du Boulley, Prudent-Louis (*b* Verneuil, 9 Dec 1796; *d* Verneuil, 28 Jan 1870). French composer and teacher. His later achievements in the encouragement of amateur music-making in the provinces were fore-shadowed in his youth when, at the age of 11, he wrote some marches for the local wind band at Verneuil. He played the flute and the horn, and in 1808 went to Paris to study composition under Momigny and later under Méhul and Cherubini at the Conservatoire. He returned to Verneuil in 1815 and divided his life between music and the management of his estate in the village of Grosbois nearby. He composed an opera *Les amants querelleurs*, accepted by the Opéra-Comique but played at the Théâtre du Gymnase in 1824. He was prolific in the popular genres of the time and devoted much attention to the guitar, for which he wrote a tutor. Many of his chamber works combine the guitar with strings or wind. He also supplied several books of wind music for the newly reorganized National Guard. In 1830 he published his *Grammaire musicale*, an introduction to musical theory, presented in dialogue form, which ran to three editions. Thereafter his main preoccupation was the coordination of music in his local region, especially music for wind band. In 1835 he formed a society of wind bands drawn from Evreux, Nonancourt, Dreux, Vernon, Alençon, Chartres and other towns of the area west of Paris, which came together twice a year to form a massed band of several hundred players. Despite ill-health du Boulley travelled from village to village providing instruments and instruction and recruiting players. His own village had a band of over 20. He published an account of the society in 1839 with a list of his own works. His opus numbers exceed 170 and

include, besides much music for brass and wind band and guitar, a symphony for full orchestra (1847).

WORKS
Les amants querelleurs (opéra comique, 1), Paris, Gymnase, 1824
Sym., orch, 1847
Works for military band: Marche funèbre; Collection of military music, 1830–32; Collection of fanfares, 1835–6; Cantata in honour of St Cecilia, 3vv, band, 1836; Collection of music for brass, 1858–9; Collection of syms., ovs., fantasias; Les échos des rives de l'Eure, op.152
Chamber and inst (most mentioned by Fétis): Septet, fl, cl, hn, gui, vn, vc, b; Qnt, fl, pf, vn, vc, gui; 7 qts, pf, vn, fl, gui; many trios and duos; Contredanses and waltzes, op.2, 2 gui; 3 sonates faciles, pf, op.1; La bataille de Montmirail, pf, 1814; romances, quadrilles, waltzes, polkas, gui; others
Méthode complète et simplifiée pour la guitare, op.42 (Paris, n.d.)

WRITINGS
Grammaire musicale (Paris, 1830, 3/after 1834)
Des associations musicales en France et de la Société philharmonique de l'Eure, de l'Orne et d'Eure-et-Loir (Verneuil, 1839)

BIBLIOGRAPHY
H. Berlioz: 'Des progrès de l'enseignement musical en France', *Journal des débats* (18 Sept 1836)
———: 'De l'art dans les provinces', *Revue et gazette musicale*, iv (1837), 206–7
De Jémonville: 'Aubéry de Boulley', *Revue des sciences, des lettres et des arts* (15 Dec 1858)
F.-J. Fétis: *La Société philharmonique de l'Eure, de l'Orne et d'Eure-et-Loir* (Laigle, 1859, 2/1866)
J. de l'Avre: *Notice sur Aubéry du Boulley* (Verneuil, 1895)
HUGH MACDONALD

Aubin, Tony (Louis Alexandre) (*b* Paris, 8 Dec 1907). French composer, teacher and conductor. He studied at the Paris Conservatoire (1925–30) with Samuel-Rousseau (harmony), Noël Gallon (counterpoint) and Dukas (composition), winning the Prix de Rome in 1930 with *Actéon*. Having studied conducting with Gaubert (1934–5) he took up the artistic direction of the RTF station Paris Mondial (1937–44) and then served as a conductor for French radio (1945–60), for whom his work included a recording of *Ariane et Barbe-Bleue*. In 1945 he was appointed professor of composition at the Conservatoire, and in 1969 he was elected to the Institut. His compositions pursue the more harmonically rich and colourful aspects of the music of Ravel and Dukas.

WORKS
(selective list)
Opera: La jeunesse de Goya (4, R. Escholier), 1968–70, unpubd
Ballets: Fourberies [after Rossini] (after Molière), 1950; Variations [after Schubert], Paris, 1953; Grand pas [after Brahms], Paris, 1953; Périls, 1958; Au fil de l'eau, c1970
Orch: Symphonie romantique, 1937; Le chevalier Pécopin, after Hugo, 1942; Suite danoise, 1945; Sym. no.2, F, 1951; Suite éolienne, fl, cl, str, 1958; Concertino delle scoiattolo, ob, pf, str, 1970
Vocal orch: Actéon (P. Arosa), cantata, S, T, B, orch, 1930; Cressida (A. Suarès), speaker, S, T, chorus, orch, 1935; Jeanne d'Arc à Orléans, 1943
Chamber: Prélude, recitatif et final, pf, 1930; Str Qt, 1930; Pf Sonata, 1933; Cantilène variée, vc, pf, 1937, orchd 1944; Concertinetto dell'amicizia, fl, pf, 1964; Concertinetto, vn, pf, 1964; Brughiera, bn, pf, 1966; Divertimento dell'incertezza, cl, pf/str orch, 1967; Toccatrotta, hpd 1972; Divertimento dell'incertezza, cl, pf, 1973; Hidalgoyas, gui, 1975; Concertino della brughiera, bn, pf, 1975
Songs: 6 poèmes de Verlaine, 1v, pf, 1932
Incidental music, incl. Athalie (Racine), 1943; film scores

Principal publishers: Editions Françaises de Musique, Leduc

BIBLIOGRAPHY
'Propos impromptu: Tony Aubin', *Courrier musical* (1968), no.23
PAUL GRIFFITHS

Aubry, Pierre (*b* Paris, 14 Feb 1874; *d* Dieppe, 31 Aug 1910). French musicologist and philologist, known particularly for his work on the sources of troubadour and trouvère song. He graduated in philology (1892) and law (1894), and subsequently became archiviste paléographe at the Ecole des Chartes in Paris (1898). He took a diploma in Armenian (1900), and after travelling in Central Asia published articles on Armenian church music and on music of the Tadzhiks and Sarts in Turkestan. He later taught in Paris at the Institut Catholique, the Ecole des Hautes Etudes Sociales and at the Schola Cantorum, through whose Bureau d'Edition he issued his early articles.

Aubry brought to bear on musical problems the skills of the philologist (comparing concordant sources and establishing the best reading for a text) and of the palaeographer. In this he resembled his contemporary Friedrich Ludwig and others of the senior generation of 20th-century music scholars. He continued the work of Coussemaker and Riemann in the field of 13th-century French music, making texts available in edition and facsimile: his name is closely associated with three major sources, the Roman de Fauvel, the chansonnier de l'Arsenal and the Bamberg MS. He produced much textual criticism in article form, and two series of larger studies, many of them in collaboration with literary scholars.

Aubry's rhythmic interpretations of monophonic song were largely based on the application of Franconian rules to the ligatures of the notation. In 1907 (with 'La rhythmique musicale' and the recast form of *Iter hispanicum*) he adopted the modal interpretation (*see* RHYTHMIC MODES) evidently developed by Ludwig and J.-B. Beck. A dispute arose between Aubry and Beck in 1909 as to which of them was the originator of modal theory; the result was Aubry's death from a foil wound, apparently while preparing for a duel.

WRITINGS

Huit chants héroïques de l'ancienne France, XIIe – XVIIIe siècle: poèmes et musique (Paris, 1896, 2/1896) [music in 2nd edn. only]
'L'idée religieuse dans la poésie lyrique et la musique française au moyen âge', *Tribune de Saint-Gervais*, iii (1897), 37, 52, 84; iv (1898), 150, 202, 248, 286; also pubd separately (Paris, 1897)
'L'inspiration religieuse dans la poésie musicale en France', *Tribune de Saint-Gervais*, v (1899), 16, 40; also pubd separately (Paris, 1899)
Mélanges de musicologie critique: i *La musicologie médiévale: histoire et méthodes* (Paris, 1900); ii *Les proses d'Adam de Saint-Victor* (Paris, 1901) [with E. Misset]; iii *Lais et descorts français du XIIIe siècle* (Paris, 1901) [with A. Jeanroy and L. Brandin]; iv *Les plus anciens monuments de la musique française* (Paris, 1905)
with A. Jeanroy: 'Une chanson provençale à la Vierge', *Annales du midi*, xii (1900), 67
'Le système musical de l'église arménienne', *Tribune de Saint-Gervais*, vii (1901), 325; viii (1902), 23, 72, 110, 320; ix (1903), 136, 287
Souvenir d'une mission d'études musicales en Arménie (Paris, 1902)
Essais de musicologie comparée: i *Le rhythme tonique dans la poésie liturgique et dans le chant des églises chrétiennes au moyen-âge* (Paris, 1903); ii *Esquisse d'une bibliographie de la chanson populaire en Europe* (Paris, 1905)
with R. Meyer and J. Bédier: 'La chanson de Bele Aelis par le trouvère Baude de la Quarière', *Tribune de Saint-Gervais*, x (1904), 151; also pubd separately (Paris, 1904)
'La chanson populaire dans les textes musicaux du moyen âge', *RHCM*, iv (1904), 594; also pubd separately (Paris, 1905)
'La musique de danse au moyen âge', *RHCM*, iv (1904); also pubd separately (Paris, 1904)
with A. Jeanroy and Dr Dejeanne: 'Quatre poésies de Marcabru, troubadour gascon du XIIe siècle', *Tribune de Saint-Gervais*, x (1904), 107; also pubd separately (Paris, 1904)
'Un coin pittoresque de la vie artistique au XIIIe siècle', *RHCM*, iv (1904), 484; also pubd separately (Paris, 1904)
'Une "estampida" de Rambaut de Vaqueiras', *RHCM*, iv (1904), 305; also pubd separately (Paris, 1904)
'Au Turkestan: note sur quelques habitudes musicales chez les Tadjiks et les Sartes', *BSIM*, i (1905), 97; also pubd separately (Paris, 1905)
Cent motets du XIIIe siècle, publiés d'après le manuscrit Ed.IV.6 de Bamberg (Paris, 1905/R1964)
'Esquisse d'une bibliographie de la chanson populaire hors de France', *RHCM*, v (1905), 131; also pubd separately (Paris, 1905)

with E. Dacier: *Les caractères de la danse: histoire d'un divertissement pendant la première moitié du XVIIIe siècle* (Paris, 1905)
'Estampies et danses royales: les plus anciens textes de musique instrumentale au moyen-âge', *BSIM*, ii (1906), 169–201; also pubd separately (Paris, 1907)
'Iter hispanicum: notices et extraits de manuscrits de musique ancienne conservés dans les bibliothèques d'Espagne', *SIMG*, viii (1906–7), 337, 517; ix (1907–8), 32; x (1908–9), 157, 175; also pubd separately (Paris, 1908)
'La musique et les musiciens d'église en Normandie au XIIIe siècle d'après le "Journal des visites pastorales" d'Odon Rigaud', *BSIM*, ii (1906), 337, 455, 505, 556; also pubd separately (Paris, 1906)
'Un "explicit" en musique du roman de Fauvel', *BSIM*, ii (1906); also pubd separately (Paris, 1906)
'La rhythmique musicale des troubadours et des trouvères', *RHCM*, vii (1907), 317, 347, 369; also pubd separately (Paris, 1907)
Le roman de Fauvel: reproduction photographique du manuscrit français 146 de la Bibliothèque Nationale de Paris, avec un index des interpolations lyriques (Paris, 1907)
'L'oeuvre mélodique des troubadours et des trouvères', *RHCM*, vii (1907), 317, 347, 359
Recherches sur les "tenors" français dans les motets du XIIIe siècle (Paris, 1907)
with A. Gastoué: 'Recherches sur les "tenors" latins dans les motets du XIIIe siècle d'après le manuscrit de Montpellier', *Tribune de Saint-Gervais*, xiii (1907), 145, 169; also pubd separately (Paris, 1907)
with A. Jeanroy: 'Huit chansons de Bérenger de Palazol', *Anuari de l'institut d'estudis Catalans*, i (1908), 520
'La danse au moyen-âge', *RHCM*, ix (1909), 109
with A. Jeanroy: *Le chansonnier de l'Arsenal* (Paris, 1909) [incomplete]
with J. Bédier: *Les chansons de croisade* (Paris, 1909)
'Refrains et rondeaux du XIIIe siècle', *Riemann-Festschrift* (Leipzig, 1909), 213
Trouvères et troubadours (Paris, 1909, 2/1910; Eng. trans., 1914)
'Lettre ouverte à M. Maurice Emmanuel sur la rhythmique musicale des trouvères', *RHCM*, x (1910), 261

BIBLIOGRAPHY

J.-B. Beck: 'Die modale Interpretation der mittelalterlichen Melodien, besonders der troubadours und trouvères', *Caecilia*, xxiv (1907), 97
F. Ludwig: *Repertorium organorum recentioris et motetorum vetustissimi stili*, I/1 (Halle, 1910/R1964), 56
J.-B. Beck: 'Zur Aufstellung der modalen Interpretation der troubadours-melodien', *SIMG*, xii (1910–11), 316 [contains full text of judicial tribunal; also a response by J. Wolf]
Obituaries in *Bibliothèque de l'école des chartes*, lxxi (1910), 701 (E. Dacier); *ZIMG*, xii (1910–11), 13 (J. Wolf); *BSIM*, vii (1911), 41 (J. Écorcheville)
'Bibliographie des ouvrages de Pierre Aubry', *BSIM*, vii (1911), 45
H. Anglès: 'Les melodies del trobador Guiraut Riquier', *Estudis Universitaris Catalans*, xi (1926), 10; also pubd separately (Barcelona, 1926), 11
J. Chailley: 'Quel est l'auteur de la théorie modale?', *AMw*, x (1953), 213
F. Gennrich: 'Wer ist der Initiator der "Modaltheorie"?', *Miscelánea en homenaje a Monseñor Higinio Anglés*, i (Barcelona, 1958–61), 315

IAN D. BENT

Aucassin et Nicolette. A French 13th-century *chantefable*, the only surviving example of the genre; its sole source is *F-Pn* fr.2168. It tells, in prose, the romantic story of the love of a count's son for a foreign girl-captive. Interspersed in the narrative are verse sections (laisses) written in lines with equal numbers of syllables, all sung to the same double phrase of melody (a relic of narrative singing; *see* CHANSON DE GESTE), concluding with a single four-syllable line, which forms a musical coda. The melody is published in the standard edition by Roques and in the translation by Matarasso.

For bibliography *see* MEDIEVAL DRAMA.

JOHN STEVENS

Auda, Antoine (*b* St-Julien-en-Loiret, 28 Oct 1879; *d* Brussels, 19 Aug 1964). French musicologist. He was a choirboy in the Maîtrise de St Joseph, Marseilles, where he experienced a large repertory of plainsong and 16th-century polyphony, under the direction of J.-B. Grosso. He became a lay brother of the Salesian order, and (after a year in Paris) taught in Liège from 1905 to 1925. Following a year in Tournai he settled in Brussels, where he lived until his death. Among his many interests was a far-sighted fascination with colour photography; he also first demonstrated the use of microfilms as aids to scholarship at a congress of archaeology at Mons in 1928.

Auda's chief work centred on plainsong, the music of Liège, scales and modes and the concept of *tactus* in music before 1650. In his *tactus* work, he gave pride of place to A. Tirabassi, whose doctoral dissertation (1925) prepared much of the ground that the two men were later to explore with a zeal and devotion fostered partly by the general opposition which met their conclusions. This resistance led Auda into several protracted scholarly disputes (carried out in articles and published letters) notably with Casimiri and van den Borren. His last publication (finished a month before he died) was a complete survey of musical examples and theory clarifying the concept of *tactus*. This volume is an impressive testament to his logical scholarship; however, as it was privately printed, delayed by his death, and very difficult to obtain, it has been generally neglected. Apart from his major researches, Auda published studies of two neglected musicians with whom he felt a personal connection: the 19th-century Belgian organist and composer P.-L.-B. Thielemans, born at Woluwé-Saint-Pierre (the part of Brussels in which Auda lived), and the 16th-century adolescent prodigy Barthélemy Beaulaigue, poet and composer from Marseilles (the town where Auda himself had spent his adolescence singing polyphony). Auda dedicated this second study to the memory of his former teacher J.-B. Grosso.

WRITINGS

'L'école musicale liégeoise au XIIe siècle: l'office de Saint Trudon', *La tribune de Saint-Gervais: revue musicologique de la Schola cantorum*, xvi (1910), 273; xvii (1911), 11, 33, 63, 88, 147

Manuel de chant à l'usage des paroisses et des maisons d'éducation (Liège, c1924)

L'école musicale liégeoise au Xe siècle: Etienne de Liège (Brussels, 1926)

La musique et les musiciens de l'ancien pays de Liège … jusqu'à … 1800 (Brussels, 1930)

Les modes et les tons de la musique et spécialement de la musique médiévale (Brussels, 1930)

Contribution à l'histoire de l'origine des modes et des tons grégoriens (Grenoble, 1932)

'Le tactus ou théorie de la transcription de la musique proportionnelle', *Musica sacra*, xl (1933), 147

'La mesure dans la messe "L'homme armé" de Palestrina', *AcM*, xiii (1941), 39

'Le "tactus" dans la messe "L'homme armé" de Palestrina', *AcM*, xiv (1942), 27–73

'Pierre-Léon-Benoît Thielemans, organiste et compositeur, 1825–1898', *Hommage à Charles Van den Borren: mélanges* (Antwerp, 1945), 54

'La transcription en notation moderne du "Liber missarum" de Pierre de La Rue', *Scriptorium*, i (1946–7), 119

Les gammes musicales: essai historique sur les modes et sur les tons (Woluwé-Saint-Pierre, Brussels, 1947) [printed privately]

'La prolation dans l'édition princeps de la messe "L'homme armé" de Palestrina et sa résolution dans l'édition de 1559', *Scriptorium*, ii (1948), 85

'Le tactus, clef de la paléographie musicale des XVe et XVIe siècles', *Scriptorium*, ii (1948), 257

'Le tactus, principe générateur de l'interprétation de la musique polyphonique classique' *Scriptorium*, iv (1950), 44

Les 'Motets Wallons' du manuscrit de Turin: Vari 42 (Woluwé-Saint-Pierre, Brussels, 1953) [printed privately]

'La théorie du tactus explique tous les faits paléographiques de la notation musicale des XVe et XVIe siècles', *Scriptorium*, x (1956), 65

Barthélemy Beaulaigue, poète et musicien prodige (Woluwé-Saint-Pierre, Brussels, 1957) [printed privately]

Théorie et pratique du Tactus: transcription et exécution de la musique antérieure aux environs de 1650 (Woluwé-Saint-Lambert, Brussels, 1965) [printed privately]

BIBLIOGRAPHY

[A. Gillet]: *Notice biographique*, A. Auda: *Théorie et pratique du Tactus* (Brussels, 1965)

B. Huys: 'Bibliographie van de werken van Antoine Auda (1879–1964)', *Archives et Bibliothèques de Belgique*, xxxviii (1967), 197

DAVITT MORONEY

Audefroi le Bastart (*fl* 1190–1230). French trouvère. The dedication of two chansons (*Amours, de cui j'esmuef* and *Pour travail*) to Jehan de Nesle, castellan of Bruges, suggests their having been written before 1200, when Jehan joined the fourth crusade with Conon de Béthune. The interpolation of the first strophe of *Destrois, pensis* into Gerbert de Montreuil's *Roman de la violette* (1225 or slightly later) indicates that Audefroi belonged to one of the earlier generations of trouvères. He was probably a native of Picardy, perhaps of the area near the Artois border. He may have been associated with the Pui d'Arras; the *Registre* records the death of his wife in 1259.

Although the creator of ten *chansons courtoises*, Audefroi did not achieve the recognition that such early trouvères as Gace Brulé or the Chastelain de Couci achieved. His works are to be found chiefly in the Noailles Chansonnier and the Manuscrit du Roi (*F-Pn* 12615 and 844), and appear only rarely in as many as four sources. His six romances (*Bele Emmelos*; *Bele Idoine*; *Bele Ysabiaus*; *En chambre a or*; *En l'ombre*; *En nouvel tens*), however, are an important contribution to the genre, elaborating on the older, popular tradition of the *chanson de toile*. The freshness of these works, their use of monologue and dialogue, and their expansive length (9–25 strophes) are distinguishing traits. Half of them open with a series of dodecasyllabic lines on a single rhyme, closing with octosyllabic refrains. The use of the hexasyllabic line as the main or sole structural unit of one romance and two *chansons courtoises* is also distinctive, and *Com esbahis* is one of a group of only 14 works in the repertory that open with a four-syllable line.

All of the romances except *En l'ombre* open with the characteristic repeat of the first phrase (two of them employing a varied repeat). Half employ no further repetition, but the rest exhibit either motivic quotation or varied repetition of some kind. The *chansons courtoises* employ bar form, except for *Pour travail*, which is non-repetitive. Several melodies are characterized by a comparatively small range. *Bele Emmelos* – with nine strophes – spans only a 5th, including a whole step below the final; two other works remain within the compass of a 6th. Of the two melodies that range widely, one involves a probable error of clef, whereas the other is a late setting. Most melodies are at least moderately florid. None survives in mensural notation, although there are brief suggestions of regular patterns of rhythmic organization in *Destrois, pensis*, *Fine amour* and *Onques ne seu chanter*.

WORKS

(V) etc   MS (using Schwan sigla – see SOURCES, MS) in which a late setting of a poem occurs. When the letter appears in italics, the original setting connot be identified with certainty.

Amours, de cui j'esmuef mon chant, R.311

Bele Emmelos es prés desous l'arbroie, R.1688, Schläger, (V)

Bele Idoine se siet desous la verde olive, R.1654, Gérold (1936), 297

Bele Ysabiaus, pucele bien aprise, R.1616, Gennrich, 30

Bien doi faire mon chant öir, R.1436 (R)

Com esbahis, R.1534a (= 729) (*M, T*)

Destrois, pensis, en esmai, R.77
En chambre a or se siet la bele Beatris, R.1525, Gérold (1931), 196
En l'ombre d'un vergier, R.1320
En nouvel tens Pascour que florist l'aubespine, R.1378
Fine amour et esperance, R.223, Van der Werf, 119
Na sai mès en quel guise, R.1628 (R)
Onques ne seu chanter, R.831
Pour travail ne pour paine, R.139
Quant voi le tens verdir et blanchoier, R.1260
Tant ai esté pensis ireement, R.688

BIBLIOGRAPHY

G. Schläger: 'Über Musik und Strophenbau der französischen Romanzen', Forschung zur romanischen Philologie: Festgabe für Hermann Suchier (Halle, 1900), 115–60

A. Cullman: Die Lieder und Romanzen des Audefroi le Bastard (Halle, 1914)

T. Gérold: La musique au moyen âge (Paris, 1931)

——: Histoire de la musique (Paris, 1936)

F. Gennrich: Troubadours, Trouvères, Minne- und Meistergesang, Mw, ii (1951; Eng. trans., 1960)

H. Van der Werf: The Chansons of the Troubadours and Trouvères (Utrecht, 1972)

For further bibliography see TROUBADOURS, TROUVÈRES.

THEODORE KARP

Auden, W(ystan) H(ugh) (b York, 21 Feb 1907; d Vienna, 29 Sept 1973). English poet, later naturalized American. The third part of his Collected Poems (New York, 1945) consists of 38 'songs and other musical pieces', including the five lyrics set in Britten's cycle On this Island (1938), his Song for St Cecilia's Day (1941) and arias from his 'choral operetta' Paul Bunyan (1941); and of all the mid-century poets, Auden was the most actively concerned with music. With Britten he collaborated on films (Coal Face, 1935; Night Mail, 1936), broadcasts (Hadrian's Wall, 1937; The Dark Valley, 1940), plays (The Ascent of F.6, 1937; On the Frontier, 1938), on the 'symphonic cycle' Our Hunting Fathers (1936) and on cabaret songs for Hedli Anderson (1938). Two quotations from the St Cecilia poem show how well Auden wrote words for music. The opening lines:

> In a garden shady this holy lady
> With reverent cadence and subtle psalm,
> Like a black swan as death came on
> Poured forth her song in perfect calm

demonstrate his command of cantabile, of rhythm and of vowel pattern, while the subsequent scherzo section is prompted by the lilt of:

> I cannot grow;
> I have no shadow
> To run away from,
> I only play.

Then, in 1948, Auden declared himself an 'opera addict'; his friend CHESTER KALLMAN 'was the person who was responsible for arousing my interest in opera, about which previously, as you can see from Paul Bunyan, I knew little or nothing'. In that year Kallman and Auden collaborated on the libretto for Stravinsky's The Rake's Progress. In 1953 they published Delia, a delicate masque, written for Stravinsky, but unset. Thereafter for Henze they produced two librettos, Elegy for Young Lovers and The Bassarids, and for Nabokov adapted Love's Labour's Lost. About half of The Rake's Progress and, by Auden, 'about 75%' of Elegy has been credited to Kallman – though, in a joint essay, the collaborators described themselves as a 'corporate personality'. Auden's theories about opera (among them: 'a good libretto plot is a melodrama in both the strict and the conventional sense of the word; it offers as many opportunities as possible for the characters to be swept off their feet by placing them in situations which are too tragic or too fantastic for "words" ') were set out in several essays; his practice produced the most elegantly wrought librettos of the day. Elegy, for example, opens with full-voiced pentameters, linked by patterns of alliteration and internal rhyme:

> At dawn by the window in the wan light of today
> My bridegroom of the night, nude as the sun, with a brave
> Open sweep of his wonderful Samson-like hand

and, among its variety of carefully planned forms, includes simple songs:

> On yonder lofty mountain
> a lofty castle stands
> where dwell three lovely maidens,
> the fairest in the land

and scherzo patter:

> Blood-pressure drops,
> Invention stops;
> Upset tum,
> No images come,

conversational exchanges for recitative, conventional declarations of love, and a chorale. The 'opera-mad' poet with so much experience of the play of music upon his own words was, despite his preference for opera in the original, also drawn to fit words to existing scores, and with Kallman he made several opera translations. These are mellifluous, elegant, and better poetry than anything else of the kind, but on occasion they stray far from the original – quite deliberately so, since 'a too-literal translation of the original text may sometimes prove to be a falsification' – and on occasion they can be over-ingenious and easier for the eye than the ear to follow. For example, Donna Anna's

> Non mi dir, bell'idol mio,
> Che son io crudel con te

is rendered as

> Let yonder moon, chaste eye of heaven
> Cool desire and calm your soul.

The sense and the sentiment are altered, and, moreover, the listener who hears 'cool' and 'calm' as adjectives may well miss the third line while he struggles with the syntax of the second.

Many composers have been attracted to set Auden's poetry, among them Berio (Nones), Berkeley (Night covers up the rigid land and Five Poems), Marvin David Levy (For the Time Being), and Maw (in his Nocturne). (See Bloomfield and Mendelson for a complete list up to 1969.) Later poems written specifically for musical setting include two translations in Barber's Hermit Songs (1953), Stravinsky's Elegy for J. F. K. (1964) and Walton's The Twelve (1965). Auden and Kallman were the text editors of An Elizabethan Song Book (Garden City, NY, 1955), whose music editor was Noah Greenberg, and in 1957 Auden wrote the narratives for Greenberg's performing edition of The Play of Daniel.

WRITINGS

LIBRETTOS

B. Britten: Paul Bunyan, New York, 1941

with C. Kallman: I. Stravinsky: The Rake's Progress, Venice, 1951

——: Delia or A Masque of Night (1, after Peele: The Old Wives' Tale), Botteghe oscure, xii (1953), 164–210

——: H. W. Henze: Elegy for Young Lovers, Schwetzingen, 1961 [Ger. trans.], Glyndebourne, 1961 [orig.]

——: H. W. Henze: The Bassarids, Salzburg, 1966 [Ger. trans.], Santa Fe, 1968 [orig.]

H. W. Henze: Moralities, Cincinnati, 1969

with C. Kallman: N. Nabokov: Love's Labour's Lost, Brussels, 1973

LIBRETTO TRANSLATIONS
(all with Kallman)

W. A. Mozart: *The Magic Flute*, NBC, 1956 (New York, 1956)

K. Weill: *The Seven Deadly Sins of the Lower Middle Class*, New York, 1959

W. A. Mozart: *Don Giovanni*, NBC, 1960 (New York, 1961)

K. Weill: *The Rise and Fall of the City of Mahagonny*, 1960, unperf. (Boston, 1976); scenes 18–20 in *Delos*, iv (1970), 29

C. D. von Dittersdorf: *Arcifanfano*, New York, 1965

ESSAYS

'Opera on an American Legend: Problems of Putting the Story of Paul Bunyan on the Stage', *New York Times* (4 May 1941), section 9, p.7

Introduction to *An Elizabethan Song Book* (Garden City, NY, 1955)

'A Public Art', *Opera*, xii (1961), 12

with C. Kallman: 'Genesis of a Libretto', *Elegy for Young Lovers* (Mainz, 1961)

The Dyer's Hand (New York, 1962), 463–527 [essays 'Notes on Music and Opera', 'Cav & Pag', 'Translating Opera Libretti' (with Kallman) and 'Music in Shakespeare']

'The World of Opera', *Secondary Worlds* (London, 1969)

Forewords and Afterwords (New York, 1973), 244ff, 256ff, 345ff, 432ff [essays on Gutman's *Wagner*, Verdi's letters and the Strauss-Hofmannsthal correspondence, and 'A Tribute' (to Stravinsky)]

BIBLIOGRAPHY

J. Kerman: 'Opera à la mode', *Hudson Review*, vi (1954), 560; rev. in *Opera as Drama* (New York, 1956), 234ff

J. W. Beach: *The Making of the Auden Canon* (Minneapolis, 1957), 190ff

J. Kerman: 'Auden's Magic Flute', *Hudson Review*, x (1957), 309

I. Stravinsky and R. Craft: *Memories and Commentaries* (New York, 1960), 144ff

M. K. Spears: *The Poetry of W. H. Auden: the Disenchanted Island* (New York, 1963), 105ff, 262ff

I. Stravinsky and R. Craft: *Dialogues and a Diary* (New York, 1963)

B. Wright: 'Britten and Documentary', *MT*, civ (1963), 779

H. W. Henze: *Essays* (Mainz, 1964), 95ff

J. C. Blair: *The Poetic Art of W. H. Auden* (Princeton, 1965), 163ff

U. W[einstein]: 'Sarastro's Brave New World, or "Die Zauberflöte" Transmogrified', *Your Musical Cue*, ii (Bloomington, Ind., 1965–6), 3

I. Stravinsky and R. Craft: *Themes and Episodes* (New York, 1966), 56ff

E. W. White: *Stravinsky: the Composer and his Works* (London, 2/1966), 412ff

P. H. Salus: 'Auden and Opera', *Quest*, ii (New York, 1967), 7

I. Stravinsky and R. Craft: *Retrospectives and Conclusions* (New York, 1969), 145ff, 160ff, 173ff

E. W. White: *Benjamin Britten* (London, 2/1970), 22ff, 95ff

U. Weisstein: 'Reflections on a Golden Style: W. H. Auden's Theory of Opera', *Comparative Literature*, xxii (1970), 108

B. C. Bloomfield and E. Mendelson: *W. H. Auden: a Bibliography* (Charlottesville, 2/1972)

ANDREW PORTER

Audiffren, Jean (*b* Barjols, Provence, baptized 24 Sept 1680; *d* Marseilles, 8 Aug 1762). French composer and priest. The son of Jean-Baptiste Audiffren and Marguerite Fabre, he presumably received his initial musical training as a choirboy at Barjols church; in 1694 he entered the service of the chapter of La Major Cathedral in Marseilles, where he was taught by the precentor, Melchior Barrachin. In 1696 he received the tonsure, and about the turn of the century began to show his talents. In 1702 he became deputy precentor at Marseilles Cathedral; from 1716 to 1720 he was precentor of the primate's church of St Trophime at Arles and subsequently held the same office at Marseilles Cathedral until his retirement in August 1758. His masses, although of unequal merit, contain some fine movements, and attest to the existence in southern France at this period of a concertante style of *missa brevis* with instruments or continuo.

His nephew, Joseph-Lazare Audiffren (*b* Marseilles, 21 Oct 1736; *d* Marseilles, 17 June 1804), was organist at the royal abbey of St Victor in Marseilles from 1771 to 1786, and at La Major Cathedral until 1790, when the chapter was dispersed in accordance with the decree of the Civil Constitution of the Clergy. His only known work is the *Premier recueil d'ariettes* with keyboard and violin accompaniment (Paris, 1773).

WORKS

Mass, C, 4vv, 2 vn, bc; 3 masses, a, d, g, 4vv, bc; Requiem, F, 4vv, bc: all *F-C*

Magnificat, d, 4vv, bc, *C*

2 Magnificat, Bb, lost

BIBLIOGRAPHY

F. Raugel: 'La maîtrise et les orgues de la primatiale Saint-Trophime d'Arles', *RMFC*, ii (1961–2), 99, esp. 107

H. A. Durand: 'Audiffren, Jean', *MGG*

GUY BOURLIGUEUX

Audinot, Nicolas-Médard (*b* Bourmont-en-Bassigny, Haute-Marne, 1732; *d* Paris, 21 May 1801). French bass, librettist, composer and impresario. He acted in the provinces and at the Paris Comédie-Italienne before 1762, was in the service of the Prince of Conti (1762–4) and sang lead roles at the Comédie-Italienne (1764–7), leaving after a dispute with other actors. In 1769 he founded at the Foire St Germain a marionette theatre in which actors from the Comédie-Italienne were imitated maliciously; its success led to the establishment of the Théâtre de l'Ambigu Comique, first as a marionette theatre and later as a full-scale one, active until 1795 (except for 1784–6). There Audinot directed, sang and wrote librettos for pantomimes and *opéras comiques* set by various undistinguished composers. His satirical theatrical productions, and scandalous personal life, often led to considerable trouble.

In 1761 Audinot wrote the libretto and, he claimed, the music for *Le tonnelier*, an early *opéra comique*. Maurice stated that the music was written by several composers, each of whom Audinot had invited to dinner individually, asking them to set some verses as an 'after-dinner amusement'; after several dinners, *Le tonnelier* was presented as Audinot's composition. Weckerlin wrote on the manuscript score (*F-Pc*) that its composers included F.-A. Philidor, Gossec, Schobert and J.-C. Trial.

BIBLIOGRAPHY

C. Maurice: *Histoire anecdotique du théâtre*, i (Paris, 1856), 373

M. Prévost: 'Audinot (Nicolas-Médard)', *DBF*

R. Averini and E. Zanetti: 'Audinot, Nicholas-Médard', *ES*

Audran, Edmond (*b* Lyons, 12 April 1840; *d* Tierceville, nr. Gisors, Oise, 17 Aug 1901). French composer. Son of Marius-Pierre Audran (1816–87), at one time tenor at the Opéra-Comique, Audran studied under Duprato at the Ecole Niedermeyer, where he won the composition prize in 1859. In 1861 he moved with his family to Marseilles, where his father became a singing teacher and later director of the conservatory. He himself became organist at the church of St Joseph, for which he wrote religious music including a mass (1873) which was also performed at the church of St Eustache in Paris. His other compositions included a funeral march on the death of Meyerbeer, some songs in Provençal dialect and early attempts at *opéra bouffe*, beginning with *L'ours et le Pacha* (1862) and *La chercheuse d'esprit* (1864). *Le grand mogol* (Marseilles, 1877) brought an invitation from Cantin, director of the Bouffes-Parisiens and himself a native of Marseilles, and with *Les noces d'Olivette* (1879) and *La mascotte* (1880) Audran established himself in Paris as a rival to Lecocq and also gained international fame. With *La cigale et la fourmi* (1886) and others he was the most successful French operetta composer of the 1880s, but apart from *La poupée* (1896) his later works were less successful. During his last years he suffered a mental and physical breakdown which caused his withdrawal from Paris society and eventually led to his death. Audran's music displays no great technical accomplishment, but has great melodic appeal and rhythmic variety.

WORKS
OPERETTAS

All first performed in Paris unless otherwise stated; vocal scores pubd shortly after first performances

Le grand mogol (3; Henri Chivot, Alfred Duru), Marseilles, Gymnase, 24 Feb 1877; rev. in 4 acts, Gaîté, 19 Sept 1884
Les noces d'Olivette (3; Chivot, Duru), Bouffes-Parisiens, 13 Nov 1879
La mascotte (3; Chivot, Duru), Bouffes-Parisiens, 29 Dec 1880
Gillette de Narbonne (3; Chivot, Duru), Bouffes-Parisiens, 11 Nov 1882
Les pommes d'or (3; Chivot, Duru, Blondeau, Monréal), Menus-Plaisirs, 12 Feb 1883
La dormeuse éveillée (3; Chivot, Duru), Bouffes-Parisiens, 27 Dec 1883
Serment d'amour (3; Maurice Ordonneau), Nouveautés, 19 Feb 1886
La cigale et la fourmi (3; Chivot, Duru), Gaîté, 30 Oct 1886
Miss Helyett (3; Maxime Boucheron), Bouffes-Parisiens, 12 Nov 1890
L'enlèvement de la Toledad (3; F. Carré), Bouffes-Parisiens, 17 Oct 1894
La poupée (4; Ordonneau), Gaîté, 21 Oct 1896
Over 20 other operettas

MISCELLANEOUS

Sacred music, incl. Mass, 1873; La sulamite, oratorio, 1876; Adoro te, motet (Paris, 1882)
Songs, incl. La cour d'amour (in Provençal dialect) (Marseilles, 1881)
Funeral march on the death of Meyerbeer, salon pieces, dances etc

For bibliography see OPERETTA.

ANDREW LAMB

Aue, Hartmann von. *See* HARTMANN VON AUE.

Auer, Leopold (von) (*b* Veszprém, 7 June 1845; *d* Loschwitz, nr. Dresden, 15 July 1930). Hungarian violinist and teacher. He began his studies at the age of eight at the Budapest Conservatory with Ridley Kohne, continued them at the Vienna Conservatory with Jacob Dont (1857–8), and, after concert tours in the provinces, completed them with Joachim in Hanover (1863–4). After a successful début at the Leipzig Gewandhaus, he was engaged as orchestral leader at Düsseldorf (1864–6) and then at Hamburg where he also led a string quartet. Visiting London in 1868, he played Beethoven's Trio op.97 at the Musical Union with Anton Rubinstein and Piatti. On Rubinstein's recommendation, Auer was appointed to succeed Wieniawski as violin professor at the St Petersburg Conservatory in 1868; he remained there until 1917. He also taught outside Russia: in London during the summers of 1906–11 and in Loschwitz (Dresden) in 1912–14. In June 1917 he left strife-torn Russia for Norway, ostensibly on a holiday, and sailed for New York in February 1918. Despite his age, Auer still gave concerts and taught, both in New York and at the Curtis Institute in Philadelphia.

Auer spent half a century in St Petersburg, during which time he exerted a decisive influence on the Russian violin school. As court violinist, one of his functions was to play the solos at the Imperial Ballet. Traditionally, these were entrusted to famous violinists (among Auer's predecessors were Vieuxtemps and Wieniawski), which stimulated Tchaikovsky and other composers to write attractive solos for them. From 1868 to 1906 Auer led the string quartet of the Russian Musical Society; he also conducted the society's orchestra in 1883 and from 1887 to 1892.

Auer's technique lacked a certain virtuoso flair – perhaps because of the poor physical structure of his hand – and in the early years some Russian critics compared him unfavourably to Wieniawski; yet his noble and fine-grained interpretations of the great concertos succeeded in convincing the sceptics. Tchaikovsky (*Sérénade mélancolique*), Glazunov, Arensky and Taneyev all dedicated works to him. Yet he declined the dedication of Tchaikovsky's Violin Concerto, declaring it technically awkward and too long. Tchaikovsky rededicated it to Adolph Brodsky who gave the première in 1881. Auer later made some revisions in the violin part and played the concerto in 1893, shortly before the composer's death.

Auer's influence as a teacher grew slowly. His first students to arouse world-wide attention were Elman in 1905 and Zimbalist in 1907, followed by Heifetz, Poliakin and many others. Most of his students came to him as finished technicians so that he could develop their taste and interpretative powers. His approach was geared to the temperament of each. It is more appropriate to speak of an Auer style than of a school: virtuosity controlled by fine taste, classical purity without dryness, intensity without sentimentality. The so-called 'Russian' bow grip (ascribed to Auer by Flesch in his *Kunst des Violin-Spiels*) consists of pressing the bow stick with the centre joint of the index finger; the result is a richer tone, though at the expense of some flexibility. The heritage of the Auer style can still be felt in today's Russian school.

Auer's transcriptions and arrangements are tasteful but largely forgotten. His editions of the Classics are still useful, as are his *Violin Playing as I Teach it* (New York, 1921) and *Violin Masterworks and their Interpretation* (New York, 1925). He also published *My Long Life in Music* (New York, 1923).

BIBLIOGRAPHY

L. Raaben: *Leopold Semenovich Auer* (Leningrad, 1962)
J. Hartnack: *Grosse Geiger unserer Zeit* (Gütersloh, 1968)
BORIS SCHWARZ

Auerhan, Chrétien. *See* URHAN, CHRÉTIEN.

Auernhammer [Aurnhammer], Josepha Barbara von (*b* Vienna, 25 Sept 1758; *d* Vienna, 30 Jan 1820). Austrian pianist and composer. She was a student of Georg Friedrich Richter or Joseph Richter, Leopold Anton Kozeluch and, from 1781, W. A. Mozart. Mozart, whom she apparently wanted to marry, wrote about her on 27 June 1781: 'This young lady is a fright, but plays enchantingly, though in cantabile playing she has not got the real delicate singing style. She clips everything'. He dedicated to her the violin sonatas K296 and K376–80, which were published by Artaria in Vienna at the end of November 1781; she also proof-read many of Mozart's sonatas and *ariettes* for this publisher, and her performances with Mozart drew high praise from the Abbé Stadler. The death of her father in 1782 left her in difficult financial circumstances, but with Mozart's intervention she was able to take up free board and lodging with the Baroness Waldstätten from that autumn. In 1786 she married Johann Bessenig, who subsequently became a magistrate, but she retained her maiden name as a concert pianist in Vienna and as a composer (her most notable work being six variations on 'Der Vogelfänger bin ich ja' from Mozart's *Die Zauberflöte*). She retired from public performance in 1813. Her daughter Marianna was active in Vienna under the name of Auenheim as a singer, singing teacher and composer.

WORKS
(published in Vienna unless otherwise stated)

Kbd variations: 6 on Nel cor piu non mi sento [G. Paisiello: La Molinara] (Speyer, 1791); 6 on Der Vogelfänger bin ich ja [Mozart: Die Zauberflöte] (1792; Offenbach, 1793); 8 on contredanse [S. Viganò: La figlia mal custodita] (1794); 6 variazioni per il forte piano (1801); 10 on La stessa [A. Salieri] (1803); 6 on march [L. Cherubini: Les deux journées] (1803); Variations pour le piano-forte (1810); 6 variations sur un thême hongrois (c1810); 10 on theme from Les folies amoureuses (n.d.), lost
Other works incl. German lieder, 1790, vn sonata, sonatas and minuets for kbd, lost

BIBLIOGRAPHY
O. E. Deutsch: 'Ein Fräulein will Mozart heiraten', *National-Zeitung Basel: Sonntagsbeilage*, xix (1 May 1938); suppl. (4 July 1938)
R. Haas: 'Abt Stadlers vergessene Selbstbiographie', *MJb 1957*, 57
O. E. Deutsch: 'Das Fräulein von Auernhamer', *MJb 1958*, 12
O. E. Deutsch, ed.: *Mozart: die Dokumente seines Lebens* (Kassel, 1961; Eng. trans. 1965, 2/1966, as *Mozart: a Documentary Biography*)
W. Bauer and O. E. Deutsch: *Mozart: Briefe und Aufzeichnungen* (Kassel, 1962–75)

RUDOLPH ANGERMÜLLER

Auffmann [Aufmann], **Joseph Anton** (*b* c1720; *d* after 1773). German composer. Shortly before 1750 he succeeded F. X. Richter as Kapellmeister to the Prince-Abbot of Kempten-Allgäu, holding the post until 1756. He published *Triplex concentus organicus, seu III. concerti organici a octo instrumentis* as his op.1 (Augsburg, 1754). On leaving Kempten he worked for a time in Straubing, where he composed the incidental music for two plays, *Hirlanda* (1756) and *Pompejus Magnus* (only text material is extant, *D-MT*). The survival of several works – an organ concerto in F, organ preludes and a concerto in D – at Donaueschingen (*D-DO*) suggests that he held a post at the court there. In 1773, when Auffmann was organist and composer to the Bishop of Pruntrut, Switzerland, he dedicated two symphonies to the Zurich Musiksaalgesellschaft.

BIBLIOGRAPHY
E. Refardt: *Historisch-biographisches Musikerlexikon der Schweiz* (Leipzig and Zurich, 1928), 15
A. Layer: *Musikgeschichte der Fürstabtei Kempten* (Kempten, 1975), 50

ADOLF LAYER

Aufheben [absetzen] (Ger.: 'to lift up'). In string playing, an 18th-century term for a 'lifted', off-string bowstroke, a controlled stroke executed mainly by the fingers and wrist. It is limited in speed by the ability of the wrist and fingers to produce it. At faster tempos, the bow remains on the string or bounces of its own accord (i.e. SAUTILLÉ or SPICCATO). *Aufheben* produces a separation of one note from another; in this general sense it denotes a type of STACCATO in the 18th-century meaning of separation which 'staccato' in general conveys. (Staccato may also mean a detached, but not 'lifted', bowstroke.)

See also ABGESTOSSEN.

DAVID D. BOYDEN

Aufklärung (Ger.). ENLIGHTENMENT.

Auflösungszeichen (Ger.). NATURAL.

Aufschnaiter [Aufschneider, Auffschnaidter], **Benedict Anton** (*b* Kitzbühel, baptized 21 Feb 1665; *d* Passau, buried 24 Jan 1742). Austrian composer. His main appointment was in Passau, where he succeeded Georg Muffat as court Kapellmeister in 1705. He spent his early years in Vienna, where he may have been a pupil of Johannes Ebner (a member of the well-known family of organ players and son of Wolfgang Ebner) whom he declared his model. Apparently he came into contact with members of the Viennese nobility, and he may have been employed at a court. In a letter of 1724 to Prince-Bishop Lamberg, while complaining about the quality of the violinists in Passau, Aufschnaiter claimed to have had in Vienna, where he spent many years, '16–18 excellent musicians' at his disposal. His op.1 (of which no copy is extant) was dedicated to Count Ferdinand Ernst von Trautmannsdorf, who may have been his employer. In 1695 his op.2 appeared in Nuremberg with a dedication to Archduke Joseph (later Emperor Joseph I). Under the title *Concors discordia* it contains six orchestral suites which show Italian concerto grosso structure but also an apparent French influence; they probably followed the example of Georg Muffat. All that is known of op.3 is that it was dedicated to Emperor Leopold I; no copy is extant. Op.4 consists of eight church sonatas published under the title *Dulcis fidium harmonia symphoniis ecclesiasticis concinnata*, which appeared in 1703 and were dedicated to the four early fathers of the church and the four evangelists. These are orchestral sonatas for two solo violins (which have complicated double stops), two violins ad libitum, viola, violone and organ; they may have been inspired by Heinrich Biber's works. From 1705, when he became Kapellmeister at Passau, Aufschnaiter was active as a composer of church music (although he was not officially appointed cathedral Kapellmeister as Muffat had been). His opp.5 and 8 comprise vespers for four voices, strings and continuo instruments (1709, 1728), his op.6 five masses (1712) and his op.7 offertories with two solo violas (1719). In all his church works Aufschnaiter favours a more traditional style similar to the Roman cantata style; there are fewer demanding violin passages and double stops than in his earlier works, and he prefers to please with melodic charm. In his theoretical writings he emphasizes the difference between church, chamber and theatre music.

WORKS
Concors discordia, 2 vn, 2 va, vc, op.2 (Nuremberg, 1695)
Dulcis fidium harmonia symphoniis ecclesiasticis concinnata, 2 vn solo, 2 vn, va, vle, org, op.4 (Augsburg, 1703)
Memnon sacer ab oriente animatus, seu Vesperae solemnissimae, 4vv, str, 2 bc, op.5 (Augsburg, 1709)
Alaudae V ad aram purpurati honoris victimae sive Sacra V [5 masses], 4vv, vn, 2 va, 3 tpt, 3 trbn, ?org, op.6 (1712)
Aquila clangens, exaltata supra domum Domini, sive 12 offertoria, 4vv, 2 vn, 2 va solo, 2 bc, 2 trbn ad lib, op.7 (Passau, 1719)
Cymbalum Davidis vespertinum seu Vesperae pro festivitatibus, 4vv, 2 vn, 2 va, 2 bc, op.8 (Passau, 1728), 2 with 2 tpt and 2 ob ad lib
Miserere pro tempore quadragesimae, op.9, c1724, unpubd, ?lost Opp.1 and 3 lost

6 Miserere, *A-KR* [4 also in *D-OB*], ?orig. intended as part of op.9
Numerous other works, incl. masses, requiems, responses for Holy Week, graduals and offertories in the following libraries: *A-KR*, Berlin Singakademie, *Dkh*, Munich Domarchiv, *OB*, *Po*, *Rp*, *S-Uu*
Praeludien, Fugen à 4, formerly *A-GÖ*, lost

WRITINGS
Regulae compositionis fundamentales Musurgiae (MS, *D-Po*)
Anweisung oder Fundamentalregeln um eine gute Musik zu componieren (MS, *D-Po*)

BIBLIOGRAPHY
F. Lehrndorfer: *B. A. Aufschnaiter, Domkomponist in Passau* (diss., U. of Munich, 1920; *Die ostbairischen Grenzmarken*, Jg.19, xi–xii (1930)
W. M. Schmid: 'Zur Passauer Musikgeschichte', *ZMw*, xiii (1931), 303
E. F. Schmid: 'Aufschnaiter, Benedict Anton', *MGG*

EVA BADURA-SKODA

Aufstrich (Ger.). Up-bow, when playing bowed string instruments.

Augener. English music publishers. The firm originated in 1853, when Charles Louis Graue set up as a foreign music importer in London with the assistance of George Augener (*b* Fechenheim, Hesse, 1830; *d* London, 25 Aug 1915), who had come to England in 1852 from employment in the firm of André in Offenbach. Graue was succeeded by Gustav Scheuermann in 1854, and in the following year Augener left the business to set up on his own as Augener & Co. In 1858 he bought the Scheuermann business at public auction and took over its premises. In November 1898 the firm acquired the trade name and goodwill of ROBERT COCKS, and the two businesses were fully amalgamated as Augener Ltd in 1904. With George Augener's retirement in 1910, Willy Strecker purchased full control of the concern; through him they reverted to B. Schotts Söhne of Mainz in 1913, though with the outset of the war Schott forfeited its ownership. About 1960 Augener acquired the firm of Joseph Weekes, and in 1961 that of JOSEPH WILLIAMS. In May 1962 the firm, together with its various concert and wholesale concerns, was purchased by Galaxy Music Corporation (New York) and made part of GALLIARD LTD; this firm was subsequently absorbed by Stainer & Bell, in whose catalogue the Augener titles now appear.

The firm began mainly as importers of foreign music, and from 1873 to 1937 held the sole agency for Peters Edition. As publishers they were notable for the early adoption of lithographic methods, and were active from 1867 in producing cheap editions of the classics as well as modern works in their extensive Augener Edition. In 1878, under the direction of William Augener (*b* ?1854–5; *d* Tunbridge Wells, 19 June 1904), George's eldest son, they began printing their own publications, achieving a high standard of production; from 1871 to 1960 they published the *Monthly Musical Record*, with Ebenezer Prout (whose theoretical works they published) as its first editor, followed by J. S. Shedlock, Richard Capell, J. A. Westrup and Gerald Abraham. The firm was particularly identified with educational music, especially piano works, and published many volumes of music for examining bodies.

BIBLIOGRAPHY
'Mr. George Augener', *Musical Herald* (1900), no.631, p.291
'The Music Publisher of Tradition: George Augener and the Augener Edition', *MO*, lxiv (1940–41), 428
PETER WARD JONES

Augenmusik (Ger.). EYE MUSIC.

Auget [Auger], **Paul** (*b* Pontoise, *c*1592; *d* Paris, 22 March 1660). French composer. The son of a wine merchant, Auget had the money and social connections to obtain quickly a musical position worthy of his talents. He found favour with Jean-François de Goudy, Abbé of St-Autin, and through him began his career at court. He served as master of the abbé's music and at various times as singer and master to the queen, the queen mother and the king. On 13 January 1625 he became *Surintendant de la musique de la chambre du roi*, and he still held this position in 1654 when he participated in the coronation of Louis XIV. Contrary to statements by Prunières and others his daughter did not marry Jean de Cambefort, his successor as *surintendant* – it was one of his nieces who did so.

Only 14 compositions by Auget, all songs, survive, and it is likely that he wrote them for his own perform-

ance. Most were originally sung in *ballets de cour*: *Ballet de la folie* (1618), *Ballet royal du grand bal de Douairiere de Billebahaut* (1626) and *Ballet du sérieux et de grotesque* (1627). All but two were published twice in versions for voice alone and for voice accompanied by lute. They are typical *airs de cour*: strophic, in binary or bar forms, syllabic, simple in harmony and rhythm and restricted in tessitura. The lute part in *Les charmants attraits de vos yeux* is slightly more interesting than in most accompanied *airs* in that it is rhythmically independent of the voice and introduces the song with a motif derived from the opening vocal phrase.

WORKS
Edition: *Airs de cour pour voix et luth (1603–1643)*, ed. A. Verchaly (Paris, 1961) [includes 1 *air* by Auget]
Airs de cour, lv, ii (Paris, 1617⁹), nos. 38–43. iii (Paris, 1619¹⁰), nos.52–5, and viii (Paris, 1628⁹), nos.4–5
Airs de différents autheurs, mis en tablature, 1v, lute, vii (Paris, 1617⁸), nos.38–43, viii (Paris, 1618⁹), nos.50–53, xiii (Paris, 1626¹²), no.9, and xiv (Paris, 1628¹¹), nos.8–9
Airs de différents autheurs, lv (Paris, 1621¹³), no.3 [wrongly listed in some bibliographies as Airs de cour, iii]

BIBLIOGRAPHY
M. Jurgens: *Documents du minutier central concernant l'histoire de la musique (1600–1650)* (Paris, 1967)
M. le Moël: 'Paul Auget, Surintendant de la musique du roi (1592–1660)', *RMFC*, viii (1968)
JOHN H. BARON

Augmentation. (1) In proportional notation, the process whereby note shapes acquire additional value in a simple mathematical ratio. The process is the opposite of diminution, and was normally used in Renaissance polyphony to restore to note shapes their original value after a period of diminution (*see* PROPORTIONS).

(2) In a related sense, the term augmentation describes the restatement of a cantus firmus in note values longer than when it was first sounded in a composition, an extremely common device in the motets of the late Middle Ages and masses and motets in the Renaissance (*see* MOTET). From its application to the cantus firmus, augmentation passed into the repertory of technical devices of early ricercares and fantasias, by such composers as Sweelinck and Frescobaldi (e.g. Sweelinck: *Fantasia chromatica*, bars 71–8, alto), and of contrapuntal, canonic and fugal technique generally (*see* FUGUE), though to a lesser extent in the later Baroque period and subsequently. Since augmentation makes the theme longer in time and more noticeable, it is effective as a climax device, particularly when its first appearance is delayed until near the end of the fugue. A well-known example is Bach's C major organ fugue BWV 547 where the entry of the pedals is delayed: they eventually enter at bar 49 with the subject heard for the first time in augmentation (this point also represents a prominent return to the tonic key prepared by minor-key harmonies).

In non-fugal music augmentation is also occasionally used. In Beethoven's Pastoral Symphony the hymn-like figure at bars 146–50 of the 'Storm' movement originates from augmentation of the initial motif of bar 3; and the recapitulation of the first movement of Brahms's Fourth Symphony augments the opening figure of the first subject (compare bars 1–4, violins, with 246–58, wind).

See also AUGMENTED INTERVAL.

ROGER BULLIVANT

Augmented interval. A perfect or major INTERVAL that has been increased by a chromatic semitone. The perfect 4th C–F is made into an augmented 4th by raising F or lowering C (i.e. C–F♯ or C♭–F). A doubly augmented interval has been increased by two chromatic semitones: for example, C–D𝄪, C♭–D♯ and C♭♭–D are all doubly augmented 2nds derived from the major 2nd C–D.

Augmented sixth chord. A chord built on the flattened submediant and containing the note an augmented 6th above (i.e. the raised subdominant): in C major, A♭–F♯. The normal resolution of this interval is outwards to the octave; thus an augmented 6th chord characteristically resolves to the chord of the dominant or to a I6-4 chord. The character of an augmented 6th chord is largely determined by the other notes it contains. The simplest type, commonly (but arbitrarily) called the Italian 6th chord, has a major 3rd above the flattened submediant and resolves more easily to the dominant (ex.1a). The so-called French 6th chord has both a major 3rd and an augmented 4th and therefore also resolves more easily to the dominant (ex.1b); it also contains more of the flavour of the whole-tone scale.

Ex.1 Augmented 6th chords and their resolutions

The so-called German 6th chord has a major 3rd and a doubly augmented 4th or a perfect 5th and naturally resolves to I6-4 or V, being spelt accordingly (ex.1c–d); the latter resolution creates a type of consecutive 5ths called 'Mozart' 5ths (see CONSECUTIVE FIFTHS, CONSECUTIVE OCTAVES). In equal temperament the German 6th sounds like a dominant 7th chord, and therefore it can resolve 'deceptively' on to the chord of the flattened supertonic, or 'Neapolitan' chord (see NEAPOLITAN SIXTH CHORD).

See also HARMONY.

WILLIAM DRABKIN

Augmented triad. A chord built of two successive major 3rds, e.g. C–E–G♯, D–F♯–A♯.

Augsburg. City in the Federal Republic of Germany on the River Lech in Bavaria. It was founded by Augustus in 14 BC and was the seat of a bishopric from the Middle Ages. Throughout its long history the city had several periods of economic expansion which generally led to a flowering of cultural activities, particularly music. A conspicuous rivalry developed from the 13th century between the prince-bishop, who ruled the city, and the increasingly independent imperial city, which led to denominational schisms at the time of the Reformation.

1. To 1600. 2. 17th and 18th centuries. 3. 19th and 20th centuries. 4. Printing and instrument making.

1. TO 1600. In the high and late Middle Ages the principal centres of sacred music in Augsburg were the cathedral and the Benedictine abbey of St Ulrich and St Afra. These two churches cultivated liturgical music, particularly Gregorian chant, and contained the city's first organs. Hermannus Contractus (d 1054), the author of several treatises on music and a composer of hymns, studied at the cathedral school, and the poet and composer Abbot Udalscalcus of Maisach (d 1151) lived at the abbey. The cathedral received a bequest from the bishop in 1313 to promote choral singing. In the 14th

century a middle-class musical culture arose, fostered by trumpeters, minstrels, lied composers and, somewhat later, the Meistersinger, and quite distinct from the courtly art of the Minnesinger. Musicians with municipal salaries were incorporated into the Stadtpfeiferei, and lutenists, representatives of the so-called 'stille Musik' (quiet music), also flourished in the city. Several ornate manuscripts attest to the rich musical life of Augsburg's middle class during the late Middle Ages: the Augsburger Liederbuch (1454), containing love songs and student songs, the Liederbuch of Clara Hätzerlin (1470–71), and an anthology of lieder found among the possessions of the patrician family Hörwart (1458–1513).

During the Renaissance Augsburg became a leading centre of music in Europe. The city owed much of its importance to the presence of Maximilian I, whose Kapelle included Isaac, Senfl and Hofhaimer. In the 16th century many prominent musicians, such as Virdung and Luscinius in 1510, gathered at the Augsburg Imperial Diet. Johannes Frosch, the prior of the Carmelite convent of St Anna and a close friend of Luther, helped to establish the practice of Lutheran sacred music in the city. After the Peace of Augsburg (1555) Catholics and Protestants competed to increase the role of music in their services, and the schools of St Anna (Lutheran) and St Salvator (Jesuit) vied to improve the quality of their musical education.

Soon after its founding in 1561 the cathedral Kapelle went through its first period of brilliance, performing polychoral music in Venetian style. Among the most notable members of the Kapelle about 1600 were the organists Kerle and Christian Erbach, the Kapellmeister Klingenstein (a pupil of Johannes de Cleve), and the chorvicar Aichinger. Lassus and Giovanni Gabrieli were on friendly terms with the abbey of St Ulrich and St Afra, where music was reorganized by F. A. Dreer after the Counter-Reformation. The leading Lutheran composer and teacher about 1600 was Gumpelzhaimer.

The FUGGER family, wealthy Augsburg merchants, endowed organs at St Anna, St Ulrich, St Moritz and the church of the Dominicans, paid part of the organists' salaries, established valuable music libraries and instrument collections, and engaged such prominent musicians as Melchior Neusidler, Eccard and Hans Leo Hassler. The Kollegium der Stadtpfeifer, which had a fine reputation during the 16th and 17th centuries, employed not only members of Augsburg's established families of musicians such as Hurlacher and Rauh, but also newly-arrived virtuosos such as Jakob Baumann and Philipp Zindelin. Many Renaissance musicians born in Augsburg achieved fame abroad as composers: the Kugelmann brothers in Innsbruck and Königsberg, Sixt Dietrich in Constance, Brayssing in Paris, Jakob Paix in Lauingen and Neuberg-an-der-Donau, and Zängel in Hechingen and Sigmaringen.

2. 17TH AND 18TH CENTURIES. In the Thirty Years War (1618–48) Augsburg lost two thirds of its population, and its cultural life suffered for decades. Musical activity first revived at the cathedral, where the Kapellmeisters Baudrexel and Gletle restored the concertato style introduced by Aichinger. These Kapellmeisters and their successors (Johann Michael Caesar, J. M. Galley and others) were expected to be able to compose, but few of their compositions appeared in print and most of the manuscripts used by the cath-

Interior of Augsburg Cathedral: painting (1616) by Tobias Maurer in Augsburg Cathedral; the organist is believed to be Christian Erbach, and the Kapellmeister (in front of the trombonist, wearing a white surplice) is possibly Bernhard Klingenstein

edral Kapelle have been destroyed. Several of the cathedral organists were also composers, including Speth, Nauss and J. M. Demmler. Most young Catholic musicians received basic schooling at the cathedral choir school and at the Seminary of St Joseph. In addition to the cathedral, Catholic sacred music was outstanding at St Ulrich, the Augustine monastery of the Holy Cross, the collegiate chapter of St Moritz and the Jesuit church of St Salvator. Two provosts of the Holy Cross were composers – Vitalis Mozart (a student of Christian Erbach) and Ludwig Zöschinger – and the monastery also employed the composers P. L. Hözl and P. O. Panzau.

A succession of composers began at the Lutheran Kantorei of St Anna with Tobias Kriegsdorfer and his pupils Schmezer and Merck. Their successors, P. D. Kräuter, Johann Caspar Seyfert and F. H. Graf, because of their educational or hereditary backgrounds, modelled their works on the compositions of north German composers, including Bach and Telemann. The choir of the Barfüsserkirche was directed by Jakob Scheiffelhut, a master of the instrumental suite; this popular form was also cultivated by Johann Fischer, son of a Stadtpfeifer and a pupil of Lully, and by Schmierer, director of the Fuggersche Stiftung. The *Gesellschaftslied* and quodlibet, favourite forms of Baroque light music, were cultivated by such notable composers as the cathedral Kapellmeisters Gletle and Caesar, the government official Matthias Kelz (ii) (who also wrote sonatas and dance pieces) and, later, Rathgeber.

Middle-class amateurs met regularly in the collegium musicum. Talented young composers were able to compose for the frequent theatrical productions at the schools of St Salvator and St Anna, and occasionally at those of St Ulrich, the Holy Cross and the Carmelites. Music at the court of the prince-bishop reached a peak between 1740 and 1770; during this period the Kapelle included J. A. Meichelbeck, J. M. Schmid and P. P. Sales as Kapellmeisters and J. G. Lang, J. B. Baumgartner and Joseph Almerigi as resident virtuosos who were also capable composers. Several musicians born in Augsburg in the 17th and 18th centuries achieved prominence elsewhere: Wolfgang and Markus Ebner in Vienna, T. Eisenhut in Kempten, Johann Fischer at northern German and Scandinavian courts, Motz in Tilsit and Leopold Mozart in Salzburg. The Mozart family had been associated with Augsburg for several centuries, and W. A. Mozart visited the city several times.

3. 19TH AND 20TH CENTURIES. The secularization of the religious chapters and the decline of the imperial city at first brought a decrease of musical activity in Augsburg. However, it was revived through the efforts of a few amateurs, who established concert series and founded such organizations as the Harmoniegesellschaft (1816), the Musikliebhaberverein (1839), the male-voice choirs Liederkranz (c1830) and Liedertafel (1843), the Oratorienverein (1866), a school of singing (founded by Donat Müller) and a music school (1873). The tradition of the church musician–composer was revived shortly after 1800, with Drexel (d 1801) at the cathedral, Matthäus Fischer and Anton Schmid at Augsburg's other Catholic churches and lesser figures at St Anna. Augsburg's industrial expansion in the 19th century led to the growth of civic cultural institutions, including the Städtisches Orchester (1865) and the Stadttheater, devoted primarily to operatic productions (1867, re-

built 1944 and 1956). Past musical directors of these organizations include Sawallisch and Kertesz; Hans Pfitzner, Richard Strauss and Werner Egk (who grew up in Augsburg) have appeared as guest directors. The summer home of the opera has been the open-air stage at Das Rote Tor from 1929. The Leopold Mozart Konservatorium (1925), the Albert Greiner Singschule (1905) and the Deutsche Seminar für Singschullehrer und Chorleiter have been the city's main institutions for musical education. Among their instructors and directors H. K. Schmid and Otto Jochum have achieved prominence as composers. In the 20th century Augsburg has become, with Salzburg and Vienna, a centre of Mozart research and publication. It is one of the headquarters of the Neue Mozart Ausgabe (1955–), and since 1969 *Acta mozartiana* has been published there. An annual festival held in June and July is devoted to Mozart's works.

4. PRINTING AND INSTRUMENT MAKING. The achievements of Augsburg's music scribes, engravers, printers and publishers are among the finest in southern Germany. Outstanding music calligraphers, including Leonhard Wagner, wrote splendid manuscripts at the abbey of St Ulrich and St Afra during the 15th and 16th centuries, and at approximately the same time early German music printing culminated in the magnificent choral incunabula of Ratdolt. Music printing with movable type was introduced to Germany by Oeglin, who printed the earliest odes of the German Humanists; Johann Miller, Sigmund Grimm and Marx Wirsung similarly served the Humanist movement. In the mid-16th century Melchior Kriesstein and Philipp Ulhart printed anthologies edited by Salminger. The first large retail stock of printed music in southern Germany was established in Augsburg (with affiliated branches in Vienna and Tübingen) by Georg Willer, who published his first catalogue for the Frankfurt Fair of 1564. The printing houses established by Valentin Schönig and Johannes Praetorius were continued after the Thirty Years War by Andreas Erfurt, J. J. Schönig, J. C. Wagner, Jakob Koppmayer and Andreas Maschenbauer. The booksellers Goebel, Kroniger, Schlüter and Happach and printers Simon Utzschneider, J. M. Labhart, August Sturm and J. K. Bencard further contributed to Augsburg's active trade in music selling. In the 18th century the Lotter firm assumed a leading role in music publishing as did the music engravers J. F. and J. C. Leopold and the publishers Matthäus Rieger and J. K. Gombart. In 1803 the *Stadtmusikant* Andreas Böhm founded the music publishing house Anton Böhm & Sohn, which is still active. The publishing house of Bärenreiter, established by Karl Vötterle of Augsburg, set up business there in 1924.

Augsburg was an important centre of instrument building during the 17th and 18th centuries. About 1600 the Bildermann family and others worked on the development of early mechanical instruments, while many lute, violin, organ and piano manufacturers were also active there, most notably J. A. Stein in the late 18th century, whose pianos were highly regarded by Mozart.

BIBLIOGRAPHY

E. F. Schmid: 'Hans Leo Hassler und seine Brüder', *Zeitschrift des Historischen Vereins für Schwaben*, liv (1941), 60–212
H. F. Deininger, ed.: *Augsburger Mozartbuch* (Augsburg, 1942–3)
E. F. Schmid: *Ein schwäbisches Mozartbuch* (Stuttgart, 1948)
——: 'Augsburg', *MGG*
——: *Das goldene Zeitalter der Musik in Augsburg, Augusta 955–1955* (Munich, 1955)

A. Layer: *Musik und Musiker der Fuggerzeit: Begleitheft zur Ausstellung der Stadt Augsburg* (Augsburg, 1959)

H. F. Deininger, ed.: *Neues Augsburger Mozartbuch* (Augsburg, 1962)

A. Layer: 'Augsburger Musikdrucker der frühen Renaissancezeit', *Gutenberg-Jb* (Mainz, 1965), 124

L. Wegele, ed.: *Musik in der Reichsstadt Augsburg* (Augsburg, 1965)

L. E. Cuyler: 'Musical Activity in Augsburg and its *Annakirche*, ca. 1470–1630', *Cantors at the Crossroads: Essays on Church Music in Honor of Walter E. Buszin* (St Louis, 1967), 33

A. Layer: 'Augsburger Musik im Barock', *Augsburger Barock* (Augsburg, 1968), 453

——: 'Augsburger Notendrucker und Musikverleger der Barockzeit', *Gutenberg-Jb* (Mainz, 1969), 150

——: 'Musikpflege am Hofe der Fürstbischöfe von Augsburg in der Renaissancezeit', *Jahrbuch des Vereins für Augsburger Bistumsgeschichte*, x (1976), 199

For further bibliography *see* FUGGER.

ADOLF LAYER

August, Peter (*b* ?Warsaw, 1726; *d* Dresden, 16 Feb 1787). German harpsichordist, organist and composer. He received a thorough musical grounding before becoming chamber musician and organist at the Dresden court in 1745. In the early 1750s he became first organist at the Catholic court chapel, a position he held until his death. He was responsible for the musical education of the elector's children, including the electoral prince. When the latter ascended to the throne in 1763 as Friedrich August III, August remained his musical adviser, 'directeur des plaisirs' and librarian, with the task of procuring church and chamber music for the court. As a harpsichordist he alternated with C. S. Binder at Dresden public concerts, and also took part in opera performances.

August's extant works, all in manuscript (*D-Dlb*), comprise eight harpsichord concertos with orchestra, six more concertos, one divertimento each for one and two harpsichords, and 48 keyboard sonatas. All reflect their origins as pieces for the entertainment or instruction of the royal family. Many of the movements approach sonata form, but their texture is that of the *galant* style, with clear periodization and transparent accompaniment.

BIBLIOGRAPHY

EitnerQ

O. Schmid: 'Peter August', *Die Musik-Woche*, xxv (1901), 196

——, ed.: *Musik am sächsischen Hofe*, iv (Leipzig, 1903)

H. Fleischer: *Christlieb Siegmund Binder (1723–1789)* (Regensburg, 1941)

R. Engländer: 'Die Dresdner Instrumentalmusik in der Zeit der Wiener Klassik', *Uppsala universitets årsskrift 1956*, no.5, pp.1–160

J. Gress: 'August, Peter', *MGG*

DIETER HÄRTWIG

Augustine of Hippo [Aurelius Augustinus] (*b* Thagaste, 13 Nov 354; *d* Hippo, 28 Aug 430). Saint and the most profound of the Fathers of the Church. His neo-Platonic tendency prompted him to make numerous remarks about music and to compose a treatise on the subject.

Born some 75 km south of Hippo (Annama, formerly Bône, in Algeria), he was the son of a pagan father, Patricius, and a Christian mother, Monica. At the age of 18 he went to Carthage to complete his education. He was drawn to philosophy and also became an ardent devotee of Manicheism. His primary studies, however, were in grammar and rhetoric, and he later became a teacher of these arts.

In search of better pupils than he could find at the Carthaginian university, Augustine went to Rome (382) and was subsequently appointed Public Orator in Milan, at that time the capital of the Western Empire. There he came upon neo-Platonic works including some of the *Enneads* of Plotinus, and was impressed by the sermons of Ambrose, Bishop of the Milanese church. In the summer of 386, he resolved to embrace Christianity. Before doing so, he retired to the country; there he meditated and began his writings, including the first portions of his treatise on music.

After his baptism by St Ambrose in 387, Augustine returned to Africa and, on reaching Thagaste, set up a religious community; he stayed until 391 when he was called to Hippo to assist the bishop, Valerius. In 395 he succeeded to the bishopric, and remained in Hippo until his death. His energies during these years were devoted to the strengthening of the church and the extermination of the Donatist and Pelagian heresies, efforts which prompted hundreds of letters and many of his most extensive works.

Augustine was evidently drawn to music, but frequently felt that his delight in it was excessive. 'The lust of the ear had caught me in its mesh and made a slave of me', he wrote in his *Confessions*. 'Even now, I confess that I do not fear to surrender myself to the delights of sound, if they are uttered by a pleasant and well-trained voice, so long as Thy word gives life to them'. At Milan, where St AMBROSE had instituted antiphonal singing and had begun to write hymns in the form which still bears his name, Augustine was overwhelmed by the music he heard in the church. He introduced several Ambrosian hymns (*Deus Creator omnium, Eterne rerum conditor, Jam surgit hora tertia, Veni Redemptor gentium*) into the services at Hippo, and quite probably also the Milanese antiphonal manner of singing. In psalm singing, however, the apparent tunefulness and sensuous quality of many of the melodies caused him to suggest (again in his *Confessions*, ix, p.6) that a simple type should be preferred.

Nevertheless, in his ministry, Augustine was much concerned with psalm and hymn singing, and his commentaries on the psalms (*Enarrationes in psalmos*) give valuable information about contemporary practice. The congregation evidently joined in the songs, since Augustine in citing verses of the psalms frequently said 'as we [or you] have just sung'. It may be that he was here referring to responsorial singing where the congregation sang the refrain, for elsewhere (Psalm xlvi, introduction) he referred to the 'psalm which we heard sung, to which we responded singing'. In Psalm lxxxvii he defined the praecentor as one who leads in singing, whereas the succentor subsequently responds in song (v.1). In his commentary on Psalms xxxii, xcvii, cxlix he mentioned the ALLELUIA and made much of its wordless exultation.

Augustine, however, did not confine his interest in music to its practical aspects. In 387 he began a treatise on music, *De musica libri sex*, which he intended as part of a series devoted to the liberal arts. He mentioned that he finished one book on grammar and began others on dialectic, rhetoric, geometry, arithmetic and philosophy (*Retractiones*, i, p.6). None of these survives, except the book on music, and this is incomplete; we learn from a letter to Memorius: 'I have written six books solely about rhythm and, I confess, I was disposed to write perhaps another six concerning melody when I had future leisure' (*Epistola*, ci).

Augustine had apparently changed the original purpose of the treatise when he completed it in 391, for the detailed presentation of rhythm in the first five books gives way in the sixth to a discussion of the philosophical and theological implications of the study of music. The numbers and proportions found in music are the sounding symbols of those with which the Creator framed the universe. Thus the study of the theory of music is justified for it leads one into contemplation of the divine. This conception of a musical cosmology is obviously the fruit of Augustine's acquaintance with the neo-Platonists, and it brings to mind the world created of musical numbers of which Plato wrote in his *Timaeus*.

In the second chapter of book 1 Augustine gave his famous definition of music, calling it 'the art of measuring well' ('bene modulandi scientia'). It measures movement of all kinds, and in musical sounds it is the measurement of time and intervals. To be 'well measured' the movement must be in harmonious proportions, and the true science of music rests in knowing these mathematical ratios which rule musical art. Augustine then discussed in minute detail the orderly movements that prevail in rhythm.

The intention of the first five books has frequently been misinterpreted, for Augustine chose to discuss rhythm in terms of poetry. This has led many to regard the book as a bad treatise on metrics. But Augustine makes it clear that he chose to present his doctrines in terms of words rather than in terms of any other art governed by rhythm, because 'it is easier to discern in words whatever numbers prevail in all motions of things' (*Epistola*, ci).

The rhythmic system expounded by Augustine is based on two temporal units, short and long, the latter having twice the value of the smaller. These are, of course, the values of short and long syllables in quantitative metrics. These two quantities are combined in feet of two, three or four syllables. Each foot is assumed to be divisible into two proportional parts; the proportion of the trochee (long, short) is 2:1, while that of the iamb (short, long) is the opposite, 1:2. Musical rhythm is created in metrical terms when feet of similar proportion are joined together to form a verse or phrase. Because of their identical proportions, 1:1, spondees (two longs), dactyls (a long and two shorts) and anapests (two shorts and a long) may follow one another in any desired combination. Similarly, any other of the 28 feet recognized by Augustine can be joined to another as long as the two halves are in the same proportion. Incompatible proportions such as those of the trochee and iamb cannot be combined.

This theoretically infinite series of like modules which constitutes rhythmic movement will in practice be articulated in more readily comprehended phrases. To articulate these phrases they must be given definite endings. Each must be brought to a close, which in turn will make the continuation sound like a new beginning. The measurement of such a phrase is called metre (*metrum*); each metre must have at least two feet, for rhythm is formed only when the chosen temporal module is repeated. To bring a phrase to an end, a silence, or rest must be introduced; this is effected by replacing the second half of the final foot with a rest. The importance of the exact measurement of the rest is the most distinctive feature of the Augustinian treatise, and in order to apply this theory to existing literature the author was frequently constrained to scan the poetic lines in a far from traditional manner.

The *De musica* was widely disseminated in the Middle Ages. The sixth chapter was drawn upon by many writers for their aesthetic statements, and it is generally acknowledged that most speculations on the nature of beauty were Augustinian in inspiration. It has been proposed by the author of this article that this treatise may also have been the source of the system of modal rhythm formulated in the 12th century at Notre Dame in Paris by Léonin and Pérotin. (*See also* CHRISTIAN CHURCH, MUSIC OF THE EARLY; ROME, §I; RHYTHMIC MODES.)

WRITINGS

'De musica', *PL*, xxxii (1841), 1081–1194
G. Finnaert and F. J. Thonnard, ed. and trans.: *La musique: De musica libri sex*, Oeuvres de Saint Augustin, 1st ser.: Opuscules, vii: Dialogues philosophiques, iv (Paris, 1947)
R. C. Taliaferro, ed. and trans.: 'On Music: De musica', *The Fathers of the Church, a New Translation: Writings of Saint Augustine*, ii (New York, 1947), 153–379
W. F. J. Knight: *De musica, a Synopsis* (London, ?1949)

BIBLIOGRAPHY

A. J. H. Vincent: *Analyse du traité de métrique et de rhythmique de Saint Augustine intitulé 'De musica'* (Paris, 1849)
H. Abert: *Die Musikanschauung des Mittelalters und ihre Grundlagen* (Halle, 1905)
W. Scherer: 'Des heilige Augustinus sechs Bücher "De musica" ', *KJb*, xxii (1909), 63
J. Hure: *Saint Augustin musicien* (Paris, 1924)
F. Amerio: *Il 'De musica' di San Agostino* (Turin, 1929)
H. Edelstein: *Die Musikanschauung Augustins* (diss., U. of Freiburg, 1929)
W. Roetzer: *Des heilige Augustin Schriften als liturgiegeschichtliche Studien* (diss., U. of Freiburg, 1930)
G. Borghezio: *La musica in San Agostino* (Rome, 1931)
T. Gérold: *Les pères de l'église et la musique* (Paris, 1931)
W. Hoffmann: *Philosophische Interpretation des Augustinus-Schrift 'De arte musica'* (diss., U. of Freiburg, 1932)
G. Pietzsch: *Die Musik in Erziehungs- und Bildungsideal des ausgehenden Altertums und frühen Mittelalters* (Halle, 1932)
H. Davenson: *Traité de la musique selon l'esprit de Saint Augustin* (Neuchâtel, 1944)
E. de Bruyne: *Etudes d'esthétique médiévale* (Bruges, 1946)
F. van der Meer: *Augustinus de zielzorger: een studie over de praktijk van een kerkvader* (Utrecht, 1947; Eng. trans., 1961)
H. Hüschen: 'Augustinus, Aurelius', *MGG*
W. G. Waite: *The Rhythm of Twelfth-century Polyphony* (New Haven, 1954)
G. Bonner: *St. Augustine of Hippo: Life and Controversies* (Philadelphia, 1963)
M. Oberleitner and F. Römer: 'Die handschriftliche Überlieferung der Werke des heiligen Augustinus', *Sitzungsberichte der Österreichische Akademie der Wissenschaften: Philosophisch-historische Klasse*, cclxiii (1969), 1–407; cclxvii (1970), 1–384; cclxxvi (1972), 1–340; cclxxxi (1972), 1–394
A. Nowak: 'Die "numeri judicales" des Augustinus', *AMw*, xxxii (1975), 196

For further bibliography *see* CHRISTIAN CHURCH, MUSIC OF THE EARLY

WILLIAM G. WAITE

Augustini, Pietro Simone. *See* AGOSTINI, PIETRO SIMONE.

Augustinian canons. Augustinian canons, also known as Austin canons, or canons regular of St Augustine, are an order of priests living the full common life, as distinct from secular canons supported by prebends. The ideal of the canons regular was to imitate the 'apostolic life' of the first Christians. The most celebrated early attempt to follow this ideal was the community life established by St Augustine of Hippo and his clergy.

It was not until the mid-11th century that the order emerged as an organized body, its rapid expansion being intimately connected with the Gregorian reform. Officially recognized by the Lateran Synods of 1059 and 1063, the revitalized order spread quickly over the whole of western Europe. In England it increased rapidly under the patronage of Henry I (1100–35). A century later it was the most numerous order in England, counting some 228 houses. Most were small priories, but the order also possessed some famous abbeys, including Waltham and Osney.

The tautological title 'Canonici Regulares' was in common use by the early 12th century, by which time most houses of the order had adopted the Rule of St Augustine. This rule's complex historical and textual problems are being gradually elucidated. Existing in two versions, one for men and one for women, it is built up of several elements, notably St Augustine's Letter 211 to his sister. The rule's characteristic qualities are its fundamental sanity, flexibility and insistence on brotherly love, making it suitable for widely differing forms of apostolic or contemplative life. Besides their normal pastoral duties, the canons have undertaken the care of travellers (Great St Bernard) and of the sick (St Bartholomew's and St Thomas's Hospitals in London) and the promotion of learning (Abbey of St Victor, Paris). The celebrated Hugh of St Victor contributed his *Didascalion* to the study of music in his day.

A fully developed liturgical life characterizes the order. St Chrodogang strove to introduce the Roman chant and liturgy. Some independent congregations (Victorines, Premonstratensians) had their own Use. Augustinian canons have also contributed to the development of the liturgy, one of the most celebrated sequence writers being the poet Adam of St Victor. After a lapse of centuries, the Consilium ad Exsequendam Constitutionem de Sacra Liturgia has recently recommended the adoption into the Roman Breviary of five poems ascribed to him, among them the famous *Salve mater Salvatoris*.

Some houses appear to have had a strong tradition of polyphonic music. St Andrew's Priory, in Scotland, possessed the rich collection of 13th-century music now in *D-W* 677. It includes a large proportion of the Notre Dame repertory but none of the motets. The Abbey of St Victor owned the equally famous collection *F-Pn* lat.15139 and the anonymous French *Tractatus de discantu*. We know from archival documents that the choir of Notre Dame in later centuries paid regular annual visits to the abbey and that polyphony was sung.

Although Wolsey's Statutes of 1519 forbade the use of polyphony and excluded secular singers from conventual choirs, polyphony was undoubtedly practised in English houses of the order. Wolsey himself made provision for polyphony and organ playing by seculars during the Lady Mass and the Mass of the Name of Jesus. Thomas Tallis probably took charge of the 12 'singing-men' and five choristers employed by Waltham Abbey. Finally, at least three Augustinian canons were themselves composers of polyphony: T. Preston and W. Charite of St Mary de Pratis, Leicester, and Robert Carver of Scone Abbey in Scotland.

BIBLIOGRAPHY

C. Dereine: 'Vie commune, règle de St-Augustin et chanoines réguliers au xie siècle', *Revue d'histoire ecclésiastique*, xli (1946)
J. C. Dickinson: *The Origins of the Austin Canons and their Introduction into England* (London, 1950)
'Augustinian Canons', *Oxford Dictionary of the Christian Church* (London, 1957/R1963)
F. Ll. Harrison: *Music in Medieval Britain* (London, 1958, 2/1963)
P. Brown: *Augustine of Hippo: a Biography* (London, 1967)
L. Verheijen: *La règle de Saint-Augustin* (Paris, 1967)
Hymni instaurandi Breviarii Romani (Rome, 1968)
L. Verheijen: 'Eléments d'un commentaire de la règle de Saint Augustin', *Augustiniana*, xxi (Louvain, 1971), 5, 357–404 [to be completed]
MARY BERRY

Aulen, J. (*fl* late 15th century). German composer. A three-voice mass by him exists in several sources (*D-Bds*

40021, *LEm* 1494, *Mbs* Mus.3154, *Rp* B216–19; *E-SE* ascribed to Agricola; *PL-WRu* Mf2016; ed. in Cw, xxxi, 1934/*R*); although the earliest source dates from the end of the century it appears to have been composed some decades earlier. It is written in a relatively homophonic, treble-dominated manner, showing the influence of the Netherlands chanson style, and each movement has a head-motif. A four-voice motet, *Salve virgo virginum*, attributed to 'Joannes Aulen' in one of Petrucci's collections (*RISM* 1502²), is probably not by the same composer. The motet is in a later style, more typical of the works of Josquin's generation.

BIBLIOGRAPHY
H. Besseler: *Bourdon und Fauxbourdon* (Leipzig, 1950, rev. 2/1974)
STANLEY BOORMAN

Aulete (Gk. *aulētēs*; Lat. *tibicen*). In antiquity, a performer on the aulos or tibia. A singer to aulos accompaniment was termed an 'aulode' (*aulōdos*).

Auletta, Domenico (*b* Naples, 1723; *d* Naples, 1753). Italian composer and organist, son of PIETRO AULETTA. He was active in Naples as a composer of sacred music, but nothing is known of any appointments he may have held. His three sons were also musicians: Raffaele (*b* Naples, 1742; *d* Naples, 18 Feb 1768), composer of a motet *Alto Olimpo triumfate* (*GB-Lbm*), of whose life nothing is known; Ferdinando, a singer, who studied at the Conservatorio della Pietà dei Turchini, 1759–69, with Fago and Cafaro; and the younger Domenico (*d* Naples, 16 Nov 1796), who was appointed in November 1779, with Cimarosa, 'supernumerary' organist without salary in the royal chapel in Naples and in 1796 second organist (Cimarosa having been promoted to first). The homonymy between father and son poses problems of attribution, especially as regards undated works.

WORKS

Ammiro quel volto, aria (G), S, bc, *I-Mc*
Psalms, vv, insts: 5 salmi brevij (Dixit, Laudate pueri, Laetatus sum, Nisi Dominus, Magnificat), SATB, 2 vn, org; 3 Salve regina, 5vv, str, org; 2 De profundis, S, 2 hn, str, org; Dixit Dominus, SATB, 2 vn, 2 ob, 2 tpt, org; Requiem aeternam, S, 2 hn, str, org: all *GB-Lbm* Add.14162
3 concertos, hpd, vns, bc, *I-Nc*

BIBLIOGRAPHY
H. B. Dietz: 'A Chronology of Maestri and Organisti at the Cappella Reale in Naples 1745–1800', *JAMS*, xxv (1972), 396, 403
RENATO BOSSA

Auletta, Pietro (*b* S Angelo, Avellino, *c*1698; *d* Naples, Sept 1771). Italian composer. He completed his musical training at the Neapolitan conservatory S Onofrio. Sometime before 1724 (according to Prota-Giurleo) he was appointed *maestro di cappella* of the important Neapolitan church S Maria la Nova. In 1725 he composed his first comic opera, *Il trionfo dell'amore, ovvero Le nozze tra amici*, for production at the Teatro Nuovo in Naples. His second comic opera, *Carlotta*, appeared in Naples in 1726, and his first heroic opera, *Ezio*, in Rome in 1728. After eight years, in Carnival 1737, he re-emerged as a dramatic composer with the first production in Naples of his highly successful comic opera, *Orazio*. This work, which was extremely popular, had a long subsequent history, being continually modified as it was performed in city after city and quickly turned into a pasticcio. In this form the opera was sometimes ascribed to Auletta and sometimes to other composers. One famous production, a much-shortened version of the original *Orazio*, took place in

Paris in 1752 under the title *Il maestro di musica*. The score printed in Paris in 1753 attributed the music to Pergolesi, but in fact it was by several composers including Auletta, represented by four items from his original opera. As a pasticcio it was also known as *Le maître de musique*, *La scolara alla moda*, and perhaps *El maestro di capilla*. Of the two extant MS scores, that of *Orazio* (*I-Fc*) does not, according to Walker, correspond to any known production of the opera or pasticcio. An anonymous *Impresario abbandonato* (*D-Dlb*) is identified in the library catalogue as a revised version of *Orazio*, probably performed in Munich in 1749 and 1758.

For a few years after the first production of *Orazio* Auletta was much in favour among the Neapolitans. Between 1738 and 1740 he wrote no fewer than five comic operas for Naples as well as an intermezzo for the marriage of the Infante Filippo in Madrid. After 1740, for a reason as yet unknown, his operatic output fell sharply. It is noteworthy that, in the librettos of certain of his operas, including *Il trionfo dell'amore* (1725), *Carlotta* (1726), *Ezio* (1728), *Il Marchese Sgrana* (1738), and *L'impostore* (1740), Auletta is called *maestro di cappella* to the Prince of Belvedere.

The small amount of Auletta's surviving music contains much that is of high quality. The two arias of his earliest surviving composition, the cantata *Sulla nascente herbetta* (1718), may be criticized for some awkward harmonies; their melodies, however, are most attractive. The melodic styles are surprisingly modern for a Neapolitan composition of 1718, exhibiting the lilting, buoyant qualities commonly associated with Neapolitan music of the late 1720s and 1730s; ex.1, from the vocal line of the second aria, typifies the style.

Ex.1

Of Auletta's extant operas the short, two-act *La locandiera* is probably the most appealing. Written in 1738 to celebrate the marriage of Queen Maria Amalia to King Charles III of Naples that year, it rivals Pergolesi's comic operas of the same period in its subtle musical characterization, its grotesque humour (especially in the parts for the elderly characters), its portrayal of the playful yet tender feelings of youth – all achieved with the utmost economy of technical means. Once again, Auletta's melodies are attractive and a crucial factor in the success of the work. His accompaniments are discreet and his orchestration never overbearing.

WORKS

STAGE
(music lost unless otherwise stated)

Il trionfo dell'amore, ovvero Le nozze tra amici (comic opera, C. de Palma), Naples, Nuovo, aut. 1725, *D-MÜs*
La Carlotta (comic opera, B. Saddumene), Naples, Fiorentini, spr. 1726
Ezio (heroic opera, Metastasio), Rome, Delle Dame, 26 Dec 1728

Orazio (comic opera, A. Palomba), Naples, Nuovo, carn. 1737, ?lost; as pasticcio Il maestro di musica, Paris, 1752 (Paris, 1753); Impresario abbandonato, ?Munich, *D-Dlb*; Orazio, *I-Fc*; for other perfs. see Loewenberg
Il Marchese Sgrana (comic opera, A. Palomba), Naples, Nuovo, spr. 1738
La locandiera (scherzo comico per musica, G. Federico), Naples, S Carlo, 10 July 1738, *I-Nc*
Don Chichibio (comic opera), Naples, Nuovo, carn. 1739
L'amor costante (comic opera), Naples, Fiorentini, 1739
Intermezzo for the marriage of the Infante Filippo, Madrid, 1739
L'impostore (comic opera, C. Fabozzi), Naples, Fiorentini, aut. 1740
Caio Fabricio (heroic opera, Zeno), Turin, Reggio, carn. 1743
Il Marchese di Spartivento, ovvero Il cabalista ne sa'men del caso (farsetta), Rome, Valle, carn. 1747, adds B. Micheli
Il conte immaginario (intermezzo), Venice, S Cassiano, aut. 1748
?2 arias in Il giocatore (intermezzo), Paris, Opéra-Comique, 22 Aug 1752 (Paris, 1752), arr. of Orlandini's Il marito giogatore e la moglie Bacchettona, adds ?Pergolesi; G. M. Biuni
Didone (heroic opera, Metastasio), Florence, Pergola, aut. 1759, *I-Fc*

OTHER WORKS

Ave maris stella, 5vv, insts, *GB-Lbm*; Christus factus est, vv, ob, 2 vn, va, bc; De profundis, S, 2 vn, ob, bc, *D-MÜs*
Duetto . . . ad laudem et honorem B. Mariae, 2vv, 2 vn, 2 ob, 2 hn, bc, *I-Nc*
Sulla nascente herbetta, secular cantata, 1718, *GB-Lcm*

1 aria in Venetian Ballads (London, c1742)

BIBLIOGRAPHY
A. Loewenberg: *Annals of Opera, 1594–1940* (Cambridge, 1943, rev. 2/1955/*R*1970)
F. Walker: 'Two Centuries of Pergolesi Forgeries and Misattributions', *ML*, xxx (1949), 297
——: 'Orazio: the History of a Pasticcio', *MQ*, xxxviii (1952), 369
U. Prota-Giurleo: 'Auletta, Pietro', *DBI*
M. F. Robinson: *Naples and Neapolitan Opera* (Oxford, 1972)
MICHAEL F. ROBINSON

Aulí, Juan (*b* Felanitx, Mallorca, 1797; *d* Felanitx, 10 Jan 1869). Spanish organist and composer. He had a precocious musical talent and was already an organist when he entered the Dominican order. On the dissolution of the Spanish monasteries in 1823 he wandered over Spain, playing the organ for a time at the church of Our Lady of Atocha in Madrid. He returned to Mallorca but, expelled again in 1835, abandoned his orders and became an organist at Gibraltar. The climate drove him back to the Balearic Isles, where he spent the rest of his life in farming, serving occasionally as an organist. His works are severe in style and frankly monastic in feeling; a *Misa de coro*, with organ accompaniment, was published by Noguera. His two zarzuelas, *Norma* and *La doncella de Misolongi*, have never been performed.

J. B. TREND/R

Aulin, Laura Valborg (*b* Gävle, 9 Jan 1860; *d* Örebro, 11 Jan 1928). Swedish pianist and composer, elder sister of Tor Aulin. After studying at the Stockholm Conservatory (1877–82) she was awarded a Jenny Lind stipend (1885), which enabled her to study composition for a short time with Gade in Copenhagen and then to spend two years in Paris studying with Massenet and Godard. She was admired as a pianist and became sought after as a piano teacher. In 1903 she settled in Örebro where she remained until her death. Her works include *Herr Olof*, a ballad for baritone, chorus and orchestra; a Christmas hymn for chorus and organ; *Procul este* for solo voice, chorus and orchestra; part-songs with and without accompaniment; a suite for orchestra; two string quartets and a piano sonata as well as other keyboard pieces. Three of her partsongs for women's voices were awarded a prize in Copenhagen in 1895.

BIBLIOGRAPHY
O. Morales: 'Aulin, Laura Valborg', *SBL*
ROBERT LAYTON

Aulin, Tor (Bernhard Vilhelm) (*b* Stockholm, 10 Sept 1866; *d* Saltsjöbaden, 1 March 1914). Swedish violinist, composer and conductor. He studied from 1877 to 1883 with J. Lindberg (violin) and C. Nordqvist (theory) at the Stockholm Conservatory and in Berlin from 1884 to 1886 with E. Sauret (violin) and P. Scharwenka (composition). He was active as an orchestral musician in the early years of his career and served as leader of the Swedish Hovkapellet from 1889 to 1902. In 1887 he founded the first continuously active Swedish string quartet. The Aulin Quartet made annual tours of Sweden and other northern European countries until 1912; it specialized not only in the Classical repertory, particularly Beethoven, but in a wide-ranging representation of the works of Scandinavian composers, above all Berwald, Grieg, E. Sjögren and W. Stenhammar. From 1890 on Aulin worked closely with Stenhammar, who also took part in most of the Aulin Quartet's tours as pianist. His circle of friends also included Grieg and Sjögren.

From 1900 Aulin devoted his time increasingly to conducting: until 1902 he directed the Svenska Musikerförbundets Orkester, from 1902 to 1909 the Stockholm Konsertföreningen (founded largely through his initiative) and from 1909 to 1912 the Göteborg Orkesterförening. He conducted the first performance of Berwald's *Sinfonie singulière*, which he subsequently edited for publication.

As a composer Aulin was stylistically as close to German Romanticism as to the Scandinavians. He is best remembered for the last of his three violin concertos, op.14 in C minor, a highly accomplished work reflecting the influence of Bruch and Schumann as well as that of Grieg. He also composed numerous songs and chamber works, wrote incidental music to the play *Mäster Olof* by his friend Strindberg, and made transcriptions for violin and piano of some of Sjögren's songs.

WORKS
ORCHESTRAL
3 vn concs., incl. no.3, c, op.14 (Leipzig, n.d.)
Mäster Olof, suite (incidental music for Strindberg's play), op.22 (Leipzig, n.d.)
3 göttlandische Tänze, op.28 (Leipzig, n.d.); arr. vn, pf, op.23 (Leipzig, n.d.)
4 schwedische Tänze, op.32 (Leipzig, n.d.); arr. vn, pf, op.30 (Leipzig, n.d.)

OTHER WORKS
Str qt, op.1
Numerous works for vn, pf, incl. Sonata, d, op.12; 4 Stücke in Form einer Suite, op.15 (Leipzig, 1914); 4 Stücke, op.16 (Leipzig, n.d.); Midsommar-dans, op.18 (Leipzig, n.d.); Albumblatt, op.20 (Leipzig, n.d.); Lyrische Gedicht, op.21 (Leipzig, 1908); Fyra violinstycken, op.27 (Stockholm, 1912); 4 Kinderstücke, op.33 (Leipzig, n.d.); 2 karakterstycken (Stockholm, 1892); Minnesblad [Albumleaf] (Stockholm, 1898); Fyra akvareller [Four watercolours] (Stockholm, 1899)
Songs, 1v, pf, incl. Tre dikter af Tor Hedberg, op.24 (Copenhagen and Leipzig, n.d.); Två dikter af August Strindberg, op.31 (Stockholm, 1913); Trenne sånger (Stockholm, 1899); Vier serbische Volkslieder nach J. Runeberg (Strasbourg, 1903); Drei Lieder aus Tannhäuser von Julius Wolff, Bar, orch (Leipzig, n.d.)
Works for pf, incl. Tre albumblade, op.5 (Copenhagen, n.d.); Kleine Suite (Strasbourg, 1903); Valse caprice, pf 4 hands (Stockholm, 1887)
Studies for violin, incl. Violinskola (Stockholm, 1903)
Cadenzas for Mozart: Vn Conc. no.5, A, op.17 (Leipzig, n.d.); Vn Conc. no.3, G, op.29 (Leipzig, n.d.)
Arrs., incl. Lyriska dikter (E. Sjögren), vn, pf (Stockholm, 1903); Etüden für Violine (H. E. Kayser) (Stockholm, 1902)
For complete list see *SBL*

BIBLIOGRAPHY
O. Morales: 'Aulin, Tor Bernard Vilhelm', *SBL*
A. Aulin: 'En fyrväppling av svenska tonsättare', *Musikmänniskor*, ed. F. H. Törnblom (Uppsala, 1943)
M. Pergament: 'August Strindberg och Tor Aulin' *Svenska tonsättare* (Stockholm, 1943)
T. Rangström: 'De tystlatna – och en stridsman!', *Musikmänniskor*, ed. F. H. Törnblom (Uppsala, 1943)
G. Törnbom: 'Aulin, Tor', *Sohlmans musiklexikon*, i (Stockholm, 1948)
B. Wallner, ed.: 'Edvard Griegs brev till Tor Aulin', *Ord och bild*, lxi (1952)
B. Wallner: 'Wilhelm Stenhammar och kammarmusiken', *STMf*, xxxiv (1952), 28; xxxv (1953), 5
——, ed.: 'Tor Aulins brev till Edvard Grieg', *Ord och bild*, lxiv (1955)
ROBERT LAYTON

Aulode. *See* AULETE.

Aulos (Gk.). A Greek reed instrument. It was the most important ancient Greek instrument; the name is often mistranslated 'flute' in modern sources.

1. Description. 2. History.

1. DESCRIPTION. The aulos, appearing usually in identical pairs as in figs.1 and 2, consists of a cylindrical or slightly conical tube (*bombyx*) of greatly variable length but generally about 50 cm. Primitive examples were of reed or even bone, but eventually wood and ivory became common. These materials are reflected in the instrument's many Greek and Latin names, for example *kalamos* ('reed pipe'), *lotos* ('wood', from the Lybian lotus tree) and *tibia* ('shinbone'). At the player's end of the *bombyx* is the *holmos*, a bulb of lathed wood or ivory,

1. Aulos player wearing a phorbeia, or halter: detail from a Greek amphora (c480 BC), Attic red-figure style (British Museum, London)

which serves as a staple for the *glōttai*, or reeds; frequently there are two bulbs, the one intervening between the *bombyx* and *holmos* being termed the *hypholmion*.

Whether the instrument had single or double reeds has occasioned much controversy. Becker, whose work on the aulos (1966) renders obsolete much earlier research, has argued effectively (pp.51–62) that Theophrastus unequivocally described the preparation of single idioglot reeds, but he has allowed for the less frequent use of double reeds. Picken (p.362) indicated convincing iconographic evidence for at least the occasional appearance of double reeds, referring to the illustration in Fleischhauer (pl.47). On balance it seems that the single idioglot reed was probably the norm, but that the double reed was not entirely uncommon.

Throughout the Greek period only three to five holes appear on each pipe, but the number increased substantially in Roman times. The additional holes were stopped by a device clearly seen on surviving fragments from Pompeii and Meroë (see Schlesinger, pl.12, and Bodley, pls.iii and v). Metal bands covering the holes could be revolved with the aid of a small knob (*keras*) to allow a hole in the band to correspond to a hole in the pipe. Probably these were pre-set (thus determining the intonation or tonality of the instrument) rather than worked during performance in the manner of a modern key mechanism. The knobs (*kerata*) appear on some Roman representations (see fig.3), but possibly the long irregular protrusions of instruments such as those held by Euterpe on the Monus mosaic (Becker, pl.53) were simple plugs for stopping the holes.

The aulos is typically pictured being played in pairs: the two instruments project from the player's mouth to form an acute angle, one held in each hand with the thumb supporting it from below and with the fingers (except for the fifth in many cases) above to stop the holes. There is no structure joining the two auloi; players at rest are pictured holding two separate and integral instruments. Often the player wears a kind of halter called in Greek *phorbeia* or, less frequently, *peristomion*, and in Latin *capistrum*; it encircles the back of the neck, with a supporting strap on the top of the head, and covers the cheeks and the lips with small openings for the insertion of the mouthpieces (see fig.1). The device is pictured only with men players, not with boys, maidens or *hetairai* (courtesans), and its function

remains conjectural. The purpose most frequently cited in classical sources, the cosmetic one of preventing an unsightly bulge of the cheeks, is refuted by the fact that women did not use it. A common modern speculation is that it helped the cheeks to maintain air pressure and the lips to remain closed (the latter point, in fact, is cited in a classical source, the scholion on Aristophanes' *Birds*, 861). Becker (p.125ff) reasoned that it was unnecessary when playing the easily activated single reed, but helpful when playing the double reed, especially when instead of being held by the lips (as with the modern oboe) the reed vibrated freely within the mouth. In this manner of playing the cheeks necessarily expand, and the instrument is pressed against the lips. Picken (p.507) countered that the pirouette of the Turkish *zurna*, which both he and Becker thought analogous in function to the *phorbeia*, actually served to protect the player from injury by the sharp reeds in the hurly-burly of dance and athletic competition.

A subject that has often excited the imagination of modern scholars is the musical potential of the double pipes. Most have stopped short of claiming genuine polyphony, but many have argued that one pipe served as an accompanying drone while the other played the melody. Plausible as this might be, there is much to be said against it. Becker (pp.102ff) pointed out that throughout most of the history of the aulos the pipes have an equal length and number of holes, and are shown fingered identically with the hands occupying the same relative position on each pipe. This suggests a quasi-unison or, at most, a narrow parallelism in playing, a phenomenon not uncommon in multiple pipe playing among contemporary folk cultures.

Roman art no longer shows the two aulos pipes always identical; there are occasional differences in length, bore and mouthpiece, and there is a crooked end on one pipe of the Phrygian aulos (see fig.3). Whatever musical possibilities these developments may have entailed, there is no compelling reason to suggest that one of the pipes was normally a drone. Both the literary and the iconographic sources contradict the simplistically symmetrical interpretation of later Latin terms maintained in many modern sources: that the Phrygian aulos is identical with the *tibiae impares*, the straight pipe being identical with the *tibia dextra* and the crooked one with the *tibia sinistra*, or the straight pipe identical with the *tibia incentiva* and the crooked one with the *tibia succentiva* (Becker, pp.144ff).

2. HISTORY. Aulos-like instruments are quite often encountered in most cultures of the Mediterranean basin and the Near East, although they enjoyed their greatest prominence in Greece and Rome. Homer occasionally mentioned the aulos, creating the impression that it was an instrument of the countryside and common people, whereas the kithara (*see* PHORMINX) was of primary importance in the aristocratic warrior society that he celebrated. The aulos, however, achieved comparable status to the kithara in being used to accompany the poetry of the Ionian lyricists. There was, however, a basic distinction between the two: the kithara was used to assist the solo singer whereas the aulos's role was in choral poetry. Thus the aulos was used in the later developing choral genres such as the dithyramb and the chorus of Athenian tragedy. Both of these (in a manner still obscure) originated in the cult of Dionysus, where the aulos was regularly used, together with percussion

2. Dionysus, with a satyr playing an aulos: detail from a Greek amphora (c540 BC), painted in Amasys (Antikenmuseum, Basle)

instruments such as the tympanum and cymbalum, as a stimulant of ecstasy in orgiastic dancing. At the same time its more ancient and widespread usages outside Athens continued, in Spartan military manoeuvres, Theban folk music and as accompaniment to athletic contests.

In the 5th and 4th centuries BC there developed in Athens a certain animus against the instrument, which found its most famous expression in the desire of both Plato and Aristotle to ban it from their ideal states. Modern literature tends both to take these strictures out of context, applying them to a wider span of Greco-Roman civilization than the sources warrant, and to attribute to them a motivation more in tune with 19th-century German classicism than with ancient Greek thought, suggesting that the aulos was banned as the instrument of Dionysian barbarism and frenzy and that the LYRE was favoured as the instrument of Apollonian Hellenism and calm.

Aristotle offered no more than a hint of this romantic conception when he wrote: 'The aulos is not an instrument which expresses moral character; it is too exciting'. Moreover he had stated only a few sentences earlier that the aulos songs of Olympus 'inspire enthusiasm, and enthusiasm is an ethical part of the soul'. Possibly a stronger suggestion of the romantic conception is contained in Plato's expressed preference for 'the instruments of Apollo to those of Marsyas'. This is a reference to the myth in which the lyre-playing Apollo defeated and subsequently flayed the aulos-playing satyr Marsyas. The goat-like satyr is prominent among the votaries of Dionysus, and one might be tempted to interpret the passage as applying equally to a preference for 'the instruments of Apollo to those of Dionysus' were it not for the fact that both Plato and Aristotle in many passages made provision in their ideal states for the exciting cult music of Dionysus.

Such passages not only force one to dissociate the prohibition of the aulos from Dionysian frenzy but seem even to have been reinstating the instrument's usage. Yet there remain the unambiguous statements of Plato in the *Republic* and Aristotle in the *Politics* excluding it from the ideal state. The contradiction is best resolved by understanding the ban within the confines of Plato's and Aristotle's conservative views on education. The simple lyre can be learnt more easily by Athenian youth and its steady intonation (*eutonos*) is more suited to preserving the traditional melodic types (*harmoniai*). On the other hand the fluttering aulos (*aiolos*) is the major vehicle of a musical revolution carried out by foreign virtuosos like Timotheus and Philoxenus. With as many as 15 borings which could be closed by sliding metal rings, the aulos moved from one *harmonia* to the next within a single composition, destroyed the distinctions between traditional genres such as the dithyramb and the kithar-oedic nome and upset the balance between voice and instrument in favour of the latter. To sober Athenian intellectuals this was musical demagoguery and wist-fully they envisioned the musical education of youth as a haven from it. Dionysian frenzy had little to do with it and indeed Pratinas referred to these innovations, taking place as they did within the dithyramb and the drama, as an outrage against Dionysus.

In succeeding centuries the aulos continued as an indispensable element in musical practice and recovered its respectability in literature as well. There were only occasional echoes of the bans of Plato and Aristotle. The

3. Phrygian aulos (or Berecyntian tibiae) with kerata: detail of a relief from a marble sarcophagus (middle of the 3rd century AD) (Catacombe di Pretestato, Rome)

4th-century Neo-Pythagorean Aristides Quintilianus, however, quoted the 3rd-century Neo-Platonist Iamblicus as having counselled his students 'to avoid hearing the sound of the aulos as something staining the spirit, whereas the lyre chases away the irrational desires of the soul'. Apollo and Dionysus are not mentioned, but this is possibly the earliest extant expression of that puritan psychological dualism which, while foreign to the earlier Greek mentality, was a basic element of the 19th-century conception.

See also ETHOS; GREECE, §I.

BIBLIOGRAPHY

A. Howard: 'The *Aulos* or *Tibia*', *Harvard Studies in Classical Philology*, iv (1893), 1–60
H. Abert: *Die Lehre vom Ethos* (Leipzig, 1899/*R*1968)
H. Huchzermeyer: *Aulos und Kithara in der griechischen Musik bis zum Ausgang der klassischen Zeit* (Emsdetten, 1931)
K. Schlesinger: *The Greek Aulos* (London, 1939)
C. Sachs: *The History of Musical Instruments* (New York, 1940)
N. B. Bodley: 'The Auloi of Meroë', *American Journal of Archaeology*, 1 (1946), 217
I. Henderson: 'Ancient Greek Music', *NOHM*, i (1957), 336–403
M. Wegner: *Griechenland*, Musikgeschichte in Bildern, ii/4 (Leipzig, 1963)
G. Fleischhauer: *Etrurien und Rom*, Musikgeschichte in Bildern, ii/5 (Leipzig, 1964)
W. Anderson: *Ethos and Education in Greek Music* (Cambridge, Mass., 1966)
H. Becker: *Zur Entwicklungsgeschichte der antiken und mittalterlichen Rohrblattinstrument* (Hamburg, 1966)
J. Mountford and R. P. Winnington-Ingram: 'Music', *The Oxford Classical Dictionary* (Oxford, 2/1970), 705

L. Picken: *Folk Musical Instruments of Turkey* (Oxford, 1975), 362, 498, 507, 586

JAMES W. McKINNON

Aumann [Aumonn, Aumon, Auman], **Franz Josef** [Franz-Seraph, Johann, Leopold] (*b* Traismauer, 24 Feb 1728; *d* St Florian, 30 March 1797). Austrian composer. He was a choirboy in the Vienna Jesuit hostel, where he befriended Michael Haydn and J. G. Albrechtsberger. In 1753 he entered the Augustinian monastery of St Florian; in the following year he took vows there, in 1757 was ordained a priest and from 1755 until his death served as *regens chori*. His works, circulated only in manuscript, show the influence of the Neapolitan and Venetian schools, although the local traditions of Vienna and Salzburg as well as the particular performance requirements of his monastery also affected his style. His early masses and Requiem settings are in a strong, cantata-like idiom with many sectional divisions, although the later through-composed *Missa brevis* shows a preference for simpler settings (two *missae brevissimae* are accompanied only by continuo). He wrote two secular Singspiels which contributed to the development of the Austrian dialect farce. His contemporaries commented particularly on his command of counterpoint, and his colourful harmony and delight in formal experimentation impressed the young Bruckner. A *Missa profana*, sub-titled 'a mass to satirize stuttering, bad singing and the onerous office of a schoolmaster', is attributed to Mozart and to Florian Gassmann in two Viennese copies, but a manuscript of the work in Göttweig and a notice in the Vienna Nationalbibliothek show it to be Aumann's.

WORKS

Lat. sacred: 37 masses with orch, 4 lost; 12 requiems, 1 lost; Gradual; 22 offertories, 3 lost; 7 Vespers; 29 psalms; 25 Magnificat; 10 litanies; 4 Te Deum; 8 responsories; In exequiis; hymns; sequences; duet cantatas

Ger. sacred: Missa germanica (Wir werfen uns darnieder); 4 Passion oratorios, 2 lost; arias and songs with orch

Secular vocal: 2 Singspiels; Missa profana (Missa parodica, Faschingsmesse); couplets, lieder, canons

Inst: 3 syms., 2 doubtful; 9 divertimentos; 9 cassations; 7 parthias; Serenata, str, wind insts

MSS mainly in *A-GÖ, H, LA, M, SF, SEI, Wn*

BIBLIOGRAPHY

EitnerQ

F. Kurz: 'Bericht über die Musikverhältnisse des oberennsischen Stiftes St. Florian', *Allgemeine musikalische Zeitung*, i (Vienna, 1817), 128

G. Huemer: *Die Pflege der Musik im Stift Kremsmünster bis 1877* (Wels, 1877)

B. O. Cernik: *Die Schriftsteller der noch bestehenden Augustiner-Chorherrnstifte von 1600 bis auf den heutigen Tag* (Vienna, 1905)

J. Hollnsteiner: *Das Chorherrnstift St. Florian: Bilder zur Kultur- und Kunstgeschichte* (Steyr, 1923)

A. Kellner: *Musikgeschichte des Stiftes Kremsmünster* (Kassel, 1956)

P. Dormann: *Josef Aumann: Leben und Werk* (diss., U. of Mainz, in preparation) [incl. list of works]

PETER DORMANN

Aura (from Lat. *aura*: 'breath'). (1) A plucked idiophone invented in 1816 by Heinrich Scheibler, a German dealer in musical instruments in the town of Krefeld. The aura consists of two identical metal, star-shaped frames, connected in the centre by a handle with a screw. Mounted into the frames are two groups of five jew's harps. They are arranged radially and held in place by the screw of the handle, so that their steel reeds may conveniently be placed to the mouth and plucked by the thumb. The first five harps are tuned *f-g-a-b-c′-d′*, and are played by the right hand, while the second five are tuned *c′-d′-d′-e′-f′* and are played by the left hand. To make the tuning easier Scheibler provided the tips of the steel reeds with balls of sealing wax. According to the melody performed it was possible to change the jew's harps by simply revolving the frame. It was also possible to extend the compass of the aura, and thus the pitch, by adding harps of different tuning. All jew's harps in the frame played by the left hand were marked with red dots, while those for the right hand were marked by Scheibler with strokes or the note-names. In the music published by the inventor for the aura the corresponding jew's harps are always marked in this fashion.

(2) A mouth-organ invented in 1821 by Friedrich Buschmann in Berlin.

See also JEW'S HARP.

BIBLIOGRAPHY

H. Scheibler: 'Die Aura', *AMZ*, xviii (1816), 505

C. Sachs: *Real-Lexikon der Musikinstrumente* (Berlin, 1913/*R*1962), 24

——: *Musikinstrumentenkunde* (Leipzig, 1920), 387

ALEXANDR BUCHNER

Aureli, Aurelio (*b* Murano, Venice; *fl* 1652–1708). Italian librettist. His literary production consists almost entirely of opera librettos: he wrote some 50, including a few adaptations, over more than half a century. Until 1687 he seems to have lived in Venice, except for a brief sojourn in 1659 at the Viennese court, for which he wrote *La virtù guerriera*. He supplied dramas to an impressive list of opera composers, including Cavalli (a single but particularly successful collaboration, *L'Erismena*, 1655), both Zianis, Boretti, G. and A. Sartorio, Freschi and Pallavicino. From 1688 to 1694 he was employed by the Duke of Parma. During this period he produced at least ten dramatic works for Parma, Piacenza and in one case Turin, all set to music by the court composer Bernardo Sabadini. Most of his subsequent librettos were written for Venice and other cities of the Venetian republic. His works are whimsical and at times bizarre transformations of the most disparate historical and mythological source material. They reflect the evolution of Venetian taste (to which he admittedly pandered) from the libretto's first point of stability to the era of Arcadian reform.

BIBLIOGRAPHY

A. Sandberger: 'Zur venetianischen Oper, II', *JbMP 1924*, 53

H. C. Wolff: *Die venezianische Oper in der zweiten Hälfte des 17. Jahrhunderts* (Berlin, 1937)

A. A. Abert: 'Aureli, Aurelio', *MGG*

U. Rolandi: 'Aureli, Aurelio', *ES*

C. Mutini: 'Aureli, Aurelio', *DBI*

THOMAS WALKER

Aurelian of Réôme [Aurelianus Reomensis] (*fl* AD 840–50). Latin writer on music, chiefly plainsong, and at least for a time a member of the community of the Benedictine abbey of St Jean de Réôme, in what is today the village of Moutiers-St-Jean (Côte-d'Or). His only known work, *Musica disciplina*, written in all likelihood between AD 840 and 850, provides the only clues to his life. We learn therein of some connection between Aurelian and the dedicatee of the treatise, Abbot Bernard of St Jean de Réôme, and perhaps later Bishop of Autun. In disgrace for an unspecified offence, Aurelian stated that he wrote *Musica disciplina* at the behest of colleagues anxious to learn about 'certain rules of melody they call *toni* or *tenores*', and, more particularly, to regain the favour of Bernard. Aurelian did not actually call himself a monk, but his intimate knowledge of plainsong argues for this. It has been suggested that Aurelian the author might be the Aurelian who was

Archbishop of Lyons from 876 to 895, but this conjecture is based only on Archbishop Aurelian's having been at one time archdeacon of an area contiguous with the territory of St Jean de Réôme.

The importance of Aurelian's work stems naturally enough from its priority: it is the first medieval treatise on music which has come down to us – unless the brief compilations of Cassiodorus and Isidore be reckoned medieval – and the first work to deal in detailed fashion with the antiphonal chant of the Christian liturgy. Such priority may well be factitious, a result of the disappearance of all writings of the 7th and 8th centuries. Large sections of such works may, however, be preserved in *Musica disciplina*, and consequently Aurelian's discursive and literary approach to church music may be the tail-end of a venerable tradition of writing on church music. Aurelian's historical position depends on interpretations of the relationships between the various MS versions of the text, interpretations which have been made only during the 1960s and which ought to be regarded as provisional.

In the case of the first part of Aurelian's chapter 8, 'De octo tonis', published by Gerbert in a slightly varying version as a work of Alcuin, there are strong reasons for suspecting that it was copied or borrowed from a work of the early 9th century. At the same time, the attribution to Alcuin, frequently encountered in scholarly writing since Gerbert's publication, has only one rather dubious 13th-century MS to speak for it and ought to be rejected.

Musica disciplina falls naturally enough into five sections of varying length and character, prefaced by a dedicatory poem and epistle to Abbot Bernard. Section 1, comprising chapters 1–8, is a kind of non-technical liberal-arts introduction to music covering the music of the spheres, the ethical effects of music, its discoverers (Pythagoras, Jubal, etc), its genera, fundamental definitions, elementary numerical proportions and the comparison of *musicus* and *cantor*. Authorities quoted at length in this section are Boethius (*De institutione arithmetica* as well as *De institutione musica*), Cassiodorus and Isidore of Seville, and there is only one brief reference to plainchant. Since neither notation (alphabetic, neumatic or any other type) nor the monochord are introduced, no foundation is laid for a discussion of melody in terms of definite pitch. This is particularly frustrating to any modern reader, who is naturally inclined to equate knowledge of a melody with knowledge of its component pitches.

The second section is formed by chapters 8 and 9, which serve in part as a prologue to the core of the work. Although no authorities are cited here (and none has yet been identified) it seems likely that these chapters were drawn from at least three separate sources. In the first subsection, 'De octo tonis' (see above), the eight *toni* (or, as we would call them, church modes) are not so much defined as interpreted through etymology. After a curious passage rambling through the other areas of the Quadrivium, there comes yet a third component bridging the end of chapter 8 and the beginning of 9. Here Aurelian spoke about the melodic signatures or mottoes of the various modes, which employ the made-up words 'nonannoeane', 'noeane', 'noioeane', 'noeagis', etc, and included a fascinating anecdote about the four extra modes ordained by Charlemagne.

Section 3 (chapters 10–17) is a detailed exposition, with one chapter for each of the eight modes, of how to manage the junction between the psalm–verse recitation formula and the antiphon in the various types of chant presenting this feature at or around Aurelian's time, namely the introit, communion, offertory (although there are special problems connected with this category), invitatory, responsory and antiphonal psalmody itself. This section cites concrete examples for every point under discussion; well over 100 individual chants are mentioned. Their primary classification into the various modes appears to be taken for granted, and is certainly not justified by reference to intervallic structure, octave species and the like. It is not known whether Aurelian simply followed the tonaries which may have been available to him. He was sometimes quite explicit in stating adherence to a tradition – albeit of uncertain age – in the face of modern innovation; and most of his modal assignments agree with tonaries, treatises and service books of the centuries to come.

Aurelian's main concern was with the *differentiae* (*varietates*, etc), those variable terminations to the psalm–verse recitation formulae which are necessitated by the varying beginnings of the antiphons that follow them. Here too Aurelian was perhaps following established practice in his classifications. Be that as it may, the criteria brought to bear are of a predominantly aesthetic rather than rational character, although in so saying we may be misled by Aurelian's metaphorical vocabulary for describing pitch relationships. Not only did he totally avoid the old Greek or Latin monochord notations, or the nomenclature of the Greater Perfect System which would have been readily available in the writings of Boethius; he also avoided for the most part the simple interval names which he used (from Boethius and Cassiodorus) in his own sixth chapter.

In general, there is nothing in these chapters to make us think Aurelian was describing a chant much different from the standard reconstructed version we know today. Where there are discrepancies, there is often a difficulty with the main tradition as well. Although Aurelian's chief interest lies in pitch relationships within the context of the *differentiae*, he alluded from time to time to nuances of tempo, and insisted in the next section that singers be aware of the length of syllables. He cannot be said, however, to provide fuel for the fires of controversy concerning the rhythmic performance of medieval plainsong.

Chapter 18 is a kind of tabular résumé of the numbers of *differentiae* within the categories of mode and type of chant cited in chapters 10–17. Although it belongs logically with these earlier chapters, there are arithmetical discrepancies which point to an independent origin.

Section 4 is formed by chapter 19 alone, and is an independent essay on the verse recitation formulae themselves, in introits (grouped with communions), responsories and canticles (or perhaps psalms in general). One salient fact indicates that this is an independent section: musical notation is absolutely essential to the discussion, is explicitly referred to throughout, and is in fact found at four points in this chapter in the oldest MS. The notation is adiastematic, and related to 'palaeo-Frankish' notation. Some scholars (among them Willi Apel and Joseph Ponte) have attempted to reconstruct the mid-9th-century recitation formulae from Aurelian's verbal description, but this cannot reliably be done from the few scraps of notation that the chapter includes.

Chapter 20 counts as the fifth and final section, and

may be from yet another source. It is a compendium of definitions of plainsong categories. The definitions are culled from a wide variety of authors, not represented in earlier sections, together with two anecdotes which recount the hearing of angel choirs on earth. In two MSS of the main tradition, the treatise concludes in the florid epistolary manner of the preface.

Only a few later medieval writers, notably Berno of Reichenau, cited Aurelian, and there is little evidence that he was much read in the later Middle Ages. However, the present distribution and provenance of the extant MSS argues for some popularity up to c1100. After that time the currency of staff notation and sophisticated theory applied to plainsong (e.g. the theory of the tetrachords and of the species) may have rendered *Musica disciplina* obsolete. Thenceforth, Aurelian was merely a name in various lists of illustrious ecclesiastical authors, until the publication of his work in a rather good text by Gerbert in 1784 (*GS*, i).

BIBLIOGRAPHY

J. Ponte, trans.: *The Discipline of Music (ca. 843) by Aurelian of Réôme*, Colorado College Music Press Translations, iii (1968)

L. Gushee, ed.: *Aurelianus Reomensis: Musica disciplina*, CSM, xxi (1975)

LAWRENCE GUSHEE

Aurelius Augustinus. *See* AUGUSTINE OF HIPPO.

Auriacombe, Louis (*b* Pau, 22 Feb 1917). French conductor. He attended the Toulouse Conservatory, where he won first prizes for violin (1931), singing, recitation (1937) and harmony (1939). He studied conducting under Markevich at the International Conductors' Course at Salzburg between 1951 and 1956. It was with the orchestra of the Salzburg Summer Academy that he made his first appearance as a conductor (Linz, 1956). Later he assisted Markevich in his conducting courses in Salzburg and Mexico (1957), Santiago de Compostela (1966), Madrid (1967) and Monte Carlo (1968). In 1953 he founded the National Chamber Orchestra of Toulouse, an ensemble of 12 strings and harpsichord, which specializes in Baroque music but has also played many contemporary works. These include the first performance of *Ombres* by Boucourechliev (Toulouse, 1970) and the American première of *Ramifications* by Ligeti (Washington, DC, 1970). As head of this orchestra, which rapidly acquired an international reputation, Auriacombe made several recordings, some of which have won the Grand Prix du Disque. Although his experience has been principally with chamber orchestras, he has also conducted larger bodies, including l'Orchestre du Théâtre du Capitole, the orchestras of Toulouse and Paris radio, and the Paris Conservatoire Orchestra. He is an elegant conductor, with a thorough understanding of string playing.

CHRISTIANE SPIETH-WEISSENBACHER

Auric, Georges (*b* Lodève, 15 Feb 1899). French composer. His early musical studies were at the Montpellier Conservatory; later he studied counterpoint and fugue with G. Caussade at the Paris Conservatoire (1913) and composition with d'Indy at the Schola Cantorum (1914–16). It was during these years that he became acquainted with Satie, Milhaud and Honegger, then with the other future members of Les Six and with Cocteau, who dedicated *Le coq et l'arlequin* (partly based on their conversations) to him. Auric made his début as a composer at the age of 15, first with a series of songs (accompanied by Casella), then when his *Trois interludes*, settings of poems by Chalupt for voice and piano, were heard at the Société Nationale, and in 1919 he contributed the Prélude to the *Album des six* which marked the foundation of the group (for photograph *see* LES SIX). During the 1920s he frequented the circle of the Ballets Russes and Dyagilev, for whom he wrote several works, and he also had much contact with Stravinsky – Auric was one of the pianists at the première of *The Wedding*. Until World War II he combined his activities as a composer with work as a music critic, contributing to *Paris-soir*, *Marianne* and the *Nouvelles littéraires*. In 1954 he was elected president of the SACEM; in 1962 he was made a member of the Institut and was appointed director of the Paris Opéra and the Opéra-Comique, in which post he helped to revivify French operatic life. He was re-elected president of the SACEM but resigned his other official positions in 1968 to devote his time to composition.

Auric's musical development may be considered in three phases, the first being the period of Les Six. Although the group lacked a common aesthetic standpoint, they may be said to have shared some general principles: a reaction against Wagner and against both expressionism and impressionism, and a return to clarity of melody, texture and form, with a certain amount of humour. These principles were clearly evident in Auric's ballets *Les fâcheux* (1923), *Les matelots* (1924) and *Pastorale* (1925), and in the songs of the period. A more turbulent and deliberately modernistic phase began with the Piano Sonata in F (1930–31), an abrupt disavowal of straightforward harmony and, indeed, of tonality. The harmonic style is influenced by early Berg and late Skryabin, and, with the exception of the final chord, the piece is not in F at all. Melody is of prime importance, together with complex contrapuntal developments quite new to Auric's music. This freedom of harmony and polyphony is held in check by the rhythm, always a major factor in his work. The Piano Sonata was poorly received and Auric was discouraged from continuing along these lines. Of the many instrumental pieces which followed, the Sonata in G for violin and piano (1936) occupies a position apart, in that it explores a 'popular' language, not without political overtones (this was the period of the socialist 'Popular Front' in France). But Auric was equally involved with music for the theatre and, in particular, the cinema. Among his finest scores for the former are those for *Le mariage de monsieur le Trouhadec* by J. Romains (1925), *Volpone* (1927) and *The Birds* (1928). In his film work, the visual image provided Auric, a naturally discreet artist, with protection rather than restriction, and his music for Cocteau's *Le sang d'un poète* (1930) and *L'éternel retour* (1943) and for Clair's *A nous la liberté* (1931) contributed greatly to the development of music in the cinema.

With the ballets *Le peintre et son modèle* (1948) and *Phèdre* (1949), Auric recaptured the spirit of the Piano Sonata. While *Phèdre* is a more expansive work, the characteristic modesty of expression is still apparent, and this very restraint contributes to the power of the tragedy. Both ballets combine finesse and violence; both are marked by eloquent melody, extremely vigorous rhythm and a Straussian brilliance of orchestration. The style of the third period began to take shape in a further ballet, *Chemin de lumière* (1951), which brings together tonality and atonality, with experiments in serial writing in some sections; the new manner was definitively affirmed in the Partita for two pianos (1953–5). In this major work Auric achieved an individual synthesis of the diatonic and the chromatic – the second movement, built from a theme in semitones, is a typical example of the ambiguity of this synthesis, henceforth typical of Auric's music. The Partita retains throughout a sense of tonal polarity (assisted by its rhythmic strength), and at the very end there is a reversion to straightforward tonality.

After a period of creative silence, corresponding with his time at the Opéra, Auric continued the musical development indicated by the Partita. In the series *Imaginées* and *Double-jeux*, he adopted some of the techniques of the youngest generation of composers, while preserving his individuality. The combination of chromatic and diatonic elements became more subtle and tenuous in music that was decidedly atonal. Auric used the series as a source of cells to be treated as principal motifs, and so he did not abandon thematic writing, although his conception of the interdependence of the various musical parameters indicates his sympathy with the work of his junior contemporaries.

WORKS

DRAMATIC

Sous le masque (opera, Laloy), 1927
Ballets: Les mariés de la tour Eiffel, after Cocteau, 1920, collab. 'Les Six'; Les fâcheux, 1923; Les matelots, 1924; Pastorale, 1925; Les enchantements de la fée Alcine, 1928; Rondeau, for L'éventail de Jeanne, 1928; La concurrence, 1931; Les imaginaires, 1933; Quadrille, 1946; La fontaine de jouvence, 1946; Le peintre et son modèle, 1948; Phèdre, 1949; Chemin de lumière, 1951; La chambre, 1954; Le bal des voleurs, after Anouilh, 1960
Incidental music: Les fâcheux (Molière), 1922; Marlborough s'en va-t-en guerre (M. Achard), 1924; La femme silencieuse (after Jonson), 1925; Le dompteur (Savoir, Tery), 1925; Le mariage de monsieur le Trouhadec (J. Romains), 1925; Volpone (after Jonson), 1927; Les oiseaux (after Aristophanes), 1928, rev. 1966; Le quatorze juillet (Rolland), 1931; Margot (E. Bourdet), 1935
Film scores incl. Le sang d'un poète (Cocteau), 1930; A nous la liberté, dir. Clair, 1931; Lac-aux-dames, dir. Allegret, 1934; L'enfer du jeu, dir. J. Delannoy, 1939; L'éternel retour (Cocteau), 1943; La symphonie pastorale, dir. Delannoy, 1946; La belle et la bête (Cocteau), 1946; Hue and Cry, dir. C. Crichton, 1947; L'aigle à deux têtes (Cocteau), 1947; Orphée (Cocteau), 1949; Lola Montès, dir. M. Ophuls, 1955

INSTRUMENTAL

Orch: La Seine au matin, 1937; Ouverture, 1938; Phèdre, ballet suite, 1949; Chemin de lumière, ballet suite, 1951; Ecossaise, for La guirlande de Campra, 1952; Hommage à Marguerite Long, 1956
Chamber: Suite [from Marlborough s'en va-t-en guerre], 6 insts, 1924; Sonata, G, vn, pf, 1936; Trio, D, ob, cl, bn, 1938; Impromptu, ob, pf, 1946; Imaginées, I, fl, pf, 1968; Imaginées II, vc, pf, 1969; Imaginées III, cl, pf, 1971; Imaginées IV, va, pf, 1973
Piano: L'après-midi dans un parc, 1914; Prélude, for Album des six, 1919; 3 pastorales, 1920; Adieu New-York, 1921; Sonatine, G, 1922; 5 Bagatelles [from La femme silencieuse and Le dompteur], duet, 1925; Petite suite, 1927; Sonata, F, 1930–31; 2 Impromptus, 1935, 1938; 3 Impromptus, 1940; Danse française, 1946; Impromptu, d, 1946; 9 Short Pieces, 1947; Valse, 2 pf, 1949; Partita, 2 pf, 1953–5; Double-jeux I–III, 2 pf, 1970–71

VOCAL

5 chansons françaises, chorus, 1940
Songs: 3 interludes (R. Chalupt), 1914; 8 poèmes (Cocteau), 1919; Les joues en feu (Radiguet), 1920; Alphabet (Radiguet), 1922; 5 poèmes (Nerval), 1925; Vocalise, 1926; 2 romances (M. Desbordes-Valmore), 1926; 3 caprices (Banville), 1927; 4 poèmes (G. Gabory), 1927; 5 chansons (L. Hirts), 1929; Printemps de Ronsard [from Margot], 1935; 6 poèmes (Eluard), 1941; 3 poèmes (Fargue), 1940; 3 poèmes (L. de Vilmorin), 1940; 4 chants de la France malheureuse (Aragon, Eluard, Supervielle), 1943; 3 poèmes (Jacob), 1946; 2 poèmes (Montherlant), 1965

Principal publishers: Chant du monde, Durand, Eschig, Heugel, Leduc, Noël, Salabert, Schott

BIBLIOGRAPHY

J. Cocteau: *Le coq et l'arlequin* (Paris, 1918)
A. Schaeffner: *Georges Auric* (Paris, 1928)
A. Goléa: *Georges Auric* (Paris, 1958)
C. Samuel: *Panorama de l'art musical contemporain* (Paris, 1962)
P. Collaer: *La musique moderne* (Brussels, 1963)

ANDRÉ BOUCOURECHLIEV

Aurisicchio [Euresicchio, Eurisechio, Orisicchio], **Antonio** (*b* Naples, *c*1710; *d* Rome, 3 or 4 Sept 1781). Italian composer. He studied in Rome, according to Giazotto (*Enciclopedia dello spettacolo*), and supported himself by playing the organ in various Roman churches. Then, like so many southern Italian composers of his generation, he made his professional début in Naples with a comic opera in the Teatro dei Fiorentini, in 1734. To judge from his operatic production he was back in Rome again by the early 1740s, where the librettos of his works call him *maestro di cappella napoletano* – a conventional honorific which may or may not be taken at face value. By 1751 he was working as assistant to Francesco Ciampi, *maestro di cappella* of the church of S Giacomo degli Spagnuoli and, after Ciampi's death, succeeded him as chief director on 30 November 1756, a position he held until at least 1766.

A libretto of 1754 names Aurisicchio as 'Virtuoso di Camera' of Cardinal Domenico Orsini d'Aragona. From 1776 to 1779 he was one of the directors of the *maestri* at the Accademia di S Cecilia, where he taught, among other students, the singing teacher and composer Domenico Corri, the composer Bartolomeo Lustrini, and the castrato Luca Fabris. Aurisicchio's death in September 1781 was of sufficient public interest for his funeral service in the church of S Maria in Via to be reported in the Roman news journals. The legend that Aurisicchio died young, reported by earlier historians, seems to have been started by Burney who, having visited Rome in 1770, ought to have known better.

A hint about Aurisicchio's personality may be found in an account written to Padre Martini in 1755 by Prospero Marmiroli of a social gathering in Rome at which Aurisicchio boasted of the praise he had had from Martini for his own works; Marmiroli dismissed him as a knave and a fool ('gran birbo è quell'Asino Regnicolo'). However, it should be remembered that Padre Martini had in fact earlier found Aurisicchio's music worth serious technical consideration, as the letter dated 12 August 1747 from another Roman correspondent, Girolamo Chiti, shows. Whether or not Aurisicchio was a braggart, he was capable of generosity: in 1778 he warmly and successfully recommended the young composer Giuseppe Pedota – not, apparently, one of his own students – for the position of *maestro di cappella* at the cathedral in Orvieto. Both Grétry, after studying in Rome in 1760, and Burney, after his visit there ten years later, expressed admiration for Aurisicchio's work and attested to his popularity with the Roman musical public.

Aurisicchio's reputation now must rest, as it did during his own time, on his church music. Although he obviously did not disdain the quick income brought by an occasional opera commission, it should be observed that many of these commissions were for a species of operatic hack work: for intermezzos (or 'farsette', as they had come to be called in Rome, where the genre maintained a vigorous life long after going out of fashion elsewhere in Italy, transformed in style and shape into miniature *opere buffe*) or for the revision of works by other composers. Though an aria by Aurisicchio was sufficiently admired to be included in the pasticcio *Attalo* for London in 1758 (and subsequently printed by Walsh in his Favourite Songs edition), it was, Burney said, his 'only air that was ever sung on our stage'. Again in Burney's account, so high did Aurisicchio rank among Roman composers for the church, that 'upon any festival wherever he is *Maestro di Capella*, and has composed a mass, there is sure to be a very great crowd'.

In Ziino's opinion Aurisicchio demonstrated his talents most impressively in large-scale polyphonic sacred pieces, where skilful fugues contrast with sections in highly decorated solo style. Otherwise, his aria and instrumental styles are characteristic of the period, exhibiting simply constructed but appealing melodic surfaces over essentially tonic–dominant harmonic foundations.

WORKS
SACRED
Surviving church music includes: 2 masses, 3 short masses (Kyrie, Gloria), several mass sections; at least 26 motets; 3 Lezioni for different days; Magnificat; cantatas, incl. La morte di Giesù, Già sento fremere le fauci orribili, Dunque fia vera; Te Deum; Dixit Dominus, 5 settings; Beatus vir, 4 settings; sacred songs, hymns, psalm settings, miscellaneous liturgical pieces; Oratio Jeremie prophete; Studj sopra il canto fermo del Benedicamus solenne. MSS mainly in *D-B*, *MÜd*, *MÜu*; Archivio della Chiesa Nazionale Spagnuola, Rome; Archivio Capitolare, Rieti; also *B-Bc*; *D-Bds*; *F-Pn*; *GB-Cfm*; *I-Rsc*, *Rvat*

STAGE
Chi dell'altrui si veste presto si spoglia (commedia, T. Mariani); Naples, dei Fiorentini, wint. 1734
L'inganno deluso (intermezzo a 4); Rome, Argentina, carn. 1743
Il cicisbeo consolato (farsetta a 4, C. Mazzarelli); Rome, della Pace, carn. 1748
Chi la fà l'aspetta (intermezzo a 3); Rome, della Pace, carn. 1752
Andromaca (opera seria, A. Salvi/A. G. Pampani); Rome, Argentina, carn. 1753; 6 arias, *GB-Lbm*
Eumene (opera seria, G. Pizzi); Rome, Argentina, carn. 1754; *P-La*
Lo sposalizio all'usanza (farsetta a 3); Rome, Valle, carn. 1757
Additional arias for Didone abbandonata (after Metastasio); Fano, della Fortuna, July 1745

MISCELLANEOUS
Componimento drammatico . . . per solennizare gli augustissimi nomi . . . di Francesco I . . . e di Maria Teresa, 1747
3 other componimenti, Rome, 1747; Rome, 1760; Florence, 1762
Betulia liberata; Rome, S Girolamo della Carità, 1756
Il furo Camillo, cantata; Rome, Collegio Calasanzio delle Scuole Pie, 1760
Giunone placata (componimento drammatico, for the marriage of Filippo Bernualdo Orsini and Teresa Caracciolo); Rome, carn. 1762
Ester, oratorio
Symphony, 3 movts, *I-Rdp*
Numerous scattered arias, *B-Bc*; *D-B*, *Dlb* (but the 88 arias, *EitnerQ*, were lost during World War II), *SWl*; *GB-Lbm*; *I-Gi(l)*; *P-La*

BIBLIOGRAPHY
BurneyH
C. Burney: *The Present State of Music in France and Italy* (London, 1771) [see P. A. Scholes: *Dr Burney's Musical Tours in Europe* (London, 1959), i, 293]
Diario ordinario, no.689 (Rome, 8 Sept 1781), 9
C. Goldoni: *Mémoires* (Paris, 1787); ed. G. Ortolani in *Tutte le opere* (Verona, 1935–56), i, 404f
M. Grétry: *Mémoires ou essai sur la musique* (Paris, 1789), 85f
D. Corri: foreword, 'Life of Domenico Corri', *The Singers Preceptor* (London, after 1794)
Catalogo dei Maestri dei Professori di musica e dei Socii di onore della Congregazione e Accademia di S. Cecilia di Roma residente nel Collegio di S. Carlo a Catinari (Rome, 1845), 99
F. Parisini, ed.: *Carteggio inedito del P. Giambattista Martini coi più celebri musicisti del suo tempo*, i (Bologna, 1888/*R*1969), 293, 398
U. Rolandi: 'Giuseppe Pedota, musicista altamurano (1754–1831)', *NA*, xiv (1937), 228
A. Ziino: 'Aurisicchio, Antonio', *MGG* [with detailed lists of surviving works and archival references on biographical information]
JAMES L. JACKMAN

Ausdrucksvoll (Ger.: 'with expression'). A direction for expressive playing found particularly in German music

of the generations after Beethoven. Brahms marked the opening of his *German Requiem 'ziemlich langsam und mit Ausdruck'* ('quite slow and with expression').
See also TEMPO AND EXPRESSION MARKS.

Ausfaltung (Ger.: 'folding out'). In Schenkerian analysis (*see* ANALYSIS, §III) a technique of PROLONGATION that

Ex.1 Beethoven: Cello Sonata in A op.69, last movt

consists in the breaking up of a two-part contrapuntal idea in such a way that its parts are presented as a single melodic line, as in ex.1.
WILLIAM DRABKIN

Ausführung (Ger.). A term used in Schenkerian analysis; *see* LAYER.

Auskomponierung (Ger.: 'composing out'). In Schenkerian analysis (*see* ANALYSIS, §III) the general term used for the articulation of the structural support for a piece or movement, namely the tonic triad; a piece may thus be said to be the final result of the *Auskomponierung* of its tonic triad. *Auskomponierung* is applied both to the ARPEGGIATION of the bass and the PROLONGATION of the fundamental melodic line (the tonic triad filled in with passing notes to make a descent by step). The first stage of *Auskomponierung* results in an URSATZ, which consists of an URLINIE (from the 3rd, 5th or octave above to the tonic note) and a supporting bass arpeggiation I–V–I.
WILLIAM DRABKIN

Auslösung (Ger.). ESCAPEMENT.

Ausm Thal, Alexander. *See* UTENDAL, ALEXANDER.

Aussensatz (Ger.: 'outer part'). A term used to describe the outer parts of a polyphonic structure (*see* PART).

Austin, Frederic (*b* London, 30 March 1872; *d* London, 10 April 1952). English baritone and composer. Born into a musical family, he had his first lessons from his mother and his uncle. He began his career as a church organist and then joined the staff of the Liverpool College of Music, where he remained until 1906. At the same time he was studying singing under Charles Lunn, making his London début in 1902. Thereafter he took leading parts at the long-established festivals (his performance in *Elijah* was much admired), and his intelligent sympathy with new music caused him to be in demand for premières, among them the first English performances of Delius's *Sea Drift*. He sang Gunther in the Covent Garden 1908 *Ring*, was a leading bass-baritone in the Beecham Opera Company, and took an active part in Boughton's Glastonbury festivals. In 1920 he sang Peachum in *The Beggar's Opera*, which he had arranged for the revival (his arrangement of *Polly* was staged two years later), and in 1924 he was appointed artistic director of the British National Opera Company. Success in these various directions overshadowed his work as a composer, but he had some success with orchestral pieces. The choral *Pervigilium veneris* was written for the 1931 Leeds Festival, and he also composed incidental music.

His brother Ernest Austin (*b* London, 31 Dec 1874;

d Wallington, Surrey, 24 July 1947) was a largely self-taught composer. He often based works on old English tunes, his best-known orchestral work being the Variations on 'The Vicar of Bray' op.35 for strings, performed at a 1910 Promenade Concert. Other works include chamber pieces, piano compositions, songs and *Pilgrim's Progress* for organ, a 12-part 'narrative tone-poem' after Bunyan.

H. C. COLLES/R

Austin, John (*b* Craigton, nr. Glasgow, 17 April 1752; *d* early 19th century). Scottish manufacturer, noted for his invention of steam-powered looms and other improvements in weaving machinery. He was apprenticed to William and Walter Tait, merchants in Glasgow, and became a burgess and guild brother on 18 January 1776. About 1790, Austin issued two one-sheet folio prospectuses, announcing a new invention, described in *A System of Stenographic Music* (Glasgow, *c*1802), whereby he reduced notation to one line and six characters. He divided a circle into eight equal parts; each of the six characters proceeded from the centre of the circle at angles of 45° from one another. By reversing and inverting the characters in the four positions in which they stood in the circle, Austin attempted to account for all necessary requisites of musical notation. Included in his *System* was an analysis of tone, called the 'Tonometer', and some songs printed in the new notation. According to a review in the *Scots Magazine*, lxv (1803), p.165, the *System* was taught for a time in several Edinburgh boarding schools and in Herriot and Watson's Hospital.

BIBLIOGRAPHY

H. Paton, ed.: *A Series of Original Portraits and Character Etchings, by the late John Kay* (Edinburgh, 1842)
H. T. Wood: *A History of the Royal Society of Arts* (London, 1913)
JAMIE CROY KASSLER

Austin, John Turnell (*b* Podington, Bedfordshire, 16 May 1869; *d* Hartford, Conn., 17 Sept 1948). American organ builder. The son of a gentleman farmer, Austin emigrated to America in 1889. He first worked for Farrand & Votey of Detroit, rapidly advancing to become their foreman. Here he first conceived the idea of a radically different system of organ construction. This system, called the 'universal wind-chest' system, consisted of an individual-valve chest, the lower portion of which was a walk-in air chamber with regulator. Pipe valves were operated by a thin wooden trace attached to a motor bellows for each note. Stop action was first achieved by sliders; later a pivoting fulcrum affecting the valves was used. Although Farrand & Votey allowed Austin to experiment, they showed no interest in his ideas, and in 1893 he left them for Clough & Warren of Detroit, who in the same year built their first small organ based on Austin's system. In 1898 Clough & Warren had a fire and closed; Austin moved to Boston. A year later he was persuaded by some Hartford businessmen to move to their city, and with their backing he opened a factory there. In 1913 the Austin all-electric console was patented, and in 1914 a unique self-player mechanism. Austin's mechanical ingenuity was not limited to organ mechanisms; he also designed many labour-saving machines for his factory. In 1937 he retired, and the firm reorganized under the name of Austin Organs Inc., with his nephew, Frederic B. Austin, as president. Richard J. Piper, vice-president and tonal director, joined the company in 1949. Donald

Austin became president in 1973. Austin and his company built organs for the City Hall Auditorium, Portland, Maine (1912), University of Pennsylvania (1926), and St Joseph's Cathedral (1962), and Trinity College (1972), both in Hartford.

BARBARA OWEN

Austin, Larry (Don) (*b* Duncan, Oklahoma, 12 Sept 1930). American composer. He obtained a BM in 1951 and MM in 1952, both from North Texas State University. His teachers were Andrew Imbrie, Darius Milhaud and Seymour Shifrin. He taught at the University of California, Davis, from 1958 to 1972 and was then appointed to the faculty of the department of music, University of South Florida. He was appointed Creative Associate at the Center of the Creative and Performing Arts of the State University of New York at Buffalo in autumn 1968 and received a Distinguished Alumnus Award from North Texas State University in 1968. He played a leading role in founding *Source*, a journal of avant-garde music, which he has edited since its inception in 1967. *Improvisations for Orchestra and Jazz Soloists* (1961) was the first of his compositions to gain wide recognition through performance by the New York Philharmonic over national television and on commercial recording. Subsequent experiments with group improvisation led to a series of works in 'open style', in which the performers are given areas of improvisational choice while overall control is maintained by means of analogue notation. Later works (e.g. *Walter*) reflect Austin's interest in electronic and theatrical media as compositional resources.

WORKS
(selective list)

Piano Variations, 1960; Chicago, 12 Jan 1962
Improvisations for Orch and Jazz Soloists, 1961; Washington, 31 May 1962
A Broken Consort, fl, cl, hn, db, pf, perc, 1962; New York, 14 March 1963
Piano Set in Open Style, 1964; Naples, 2 Dec 1964
Open Style for Orch and Piano Soloist, 1965; Buffalo, 29 Sept 1968
Bass: a Theatre Piece in Open Style for String Bass, Player, Tape and Film, 1966; Davis, Calif., 27 Jan 1967
Transmission One: Video/Audio Electronic Composition for Colour TV, 1969; San Francisco (Station KQED), Oct 1969
Walter: a Film Composition and Theatre Piece for Va, Va d'amore, Tape and Two Films, 1970; New York, 21 Nov 1970
Also 7 improvisation ensembles, 15 electronic pieces, 4 band pieces, 6 theatre pieces, 5 chamber works, 2 sacred works

Some works published in *Source*

JEROME ROSEN

Austin, Richard (*b* Birkenhead, 26 Dec 1903). English conductor, son of Frederic Austin. He was educated at the RCM and in Munich, conducted for the Carl Rosa Opera, 1929–31, and from 1934 to 1940 was conductor of the Bournemouth Municipal Orchestra, succeeding Sir Dan Godfrey. After World War II he made occasional guest appearances as conductor for Sadler's Wells Opera, and also conducted in South Africa and elsewhere. But his chief energies went into the New Era Concert Society (1948–58) which he founded. The society's concerts included the first performances in Britain of Martinů's Violin Concerto (1950), the first movement of Mahler's uncompleted Tenth Symphony (1955), and Hindemith's Sinfonietta in E (1951). In 1946 he joined the staff of the RCM; he conducted the first orchestra and in 1955 became director of opera. In 1957 he conducted there the first performance in Britain of Granados's opera *Goyescas*.

ARTHUR JACOBS

Austin, William W(eaver) (*b* Lawton, Oklahoma, 18 Jan 1920). American musicologist. He was educated at Harvard University, where he received the BA in 1939, the MA in 1940 and the PhD in 1951; his professors included Walter Piston, Archibald T. Davison and A. Tillman Merritt. Austin has taught at Cornell University since 1947 and in 1969 he was appointed Goldwin Smith Professor of Musicology and elected a Fellow of the American Academy of Arts and Sciences. He was a visiting professor at Princeton University during the academic year 1957–8. In 1970 he became a member of the Gesellschaft für Musikforschung.

Austin specializes in the music of Russia and the USA in the 19th century, and in the history of 20th-century music. With *Music in the 20th Century* he contributed a broad yet comprehensive survey of music from 1900 to 1950. The book deals with stylistic and technical developments, aesthetic trends and music as a facet of cultural history. The author's evaluations may be debated: Debussy is the subject of a lengthy chapter and the discussion of Schoenberg has been criticized by reviewers. But Austin avoided the use of 'isms' and similar labelling often used by writers attempting to come to grips with the musical developments of the past 75 years, and his scholarship produced a valuable body of factual material for the student of 20th-century music.

WRITINGS

Harmonic Rhythm in Twentieth-century Music (diss., Harvard U., 1951)
'Bartók's *Concerto for Orchestra*', *MR*, xviii (1957), 21
'Satie Before and After Cocteau', *MQ*, xlviii (1962), 216
'Quelques connaissances et opinions de Schoenberg et Webern sur Debussy', *Debussy et l'évolution de la musique au XXᵉ siècle: CNRS Paris 1962*, 319
Music in the 20th Century (New York, 1966)
Review of W. Mellers: *Caliban Reborn* (New York, 1967), *Notes*, xxiv (1966–7), 259
ed.: *New Looks at Italian Opera: Essays in Honor of Donald J. Grout* (Ithaca, NY, 1968)
'Music in Paris around 1920', *IMSCR, x Ljubljana, 1967*, 216
Review of I. Stravinsky: *Le sacre du printemps: Sketches, 1911–1913* (London, 1969), *Notes*, xxvi (1969–70), 502
'Ives and Histories', *GfMKB, Bonn 1970*
'Neue Musik', *Epochen der Musik in Einzeldarstellungen* (Kassel, 1974)
'Susanna', 'Jeanie', and 'The Old Folks at Home': the Songs of Stephen C. Foster from His Time to Ours* (New York, 1975)
'Copland, Aaron', *Grove 6*

PAULA MORGAN

Austral [Fawaz, Wilson], **Florence** (*b* Melbourne, 26 April 1894; *d* Newcastle, NSW, 16 May 1968). Australian soprano; her real name was Wilson, but until she adopted her familiar professional name she was generally known by that of her stepfather, Fawaz. Having studied at Melbourne Conservatory and with Sibella in New York, she is said to have been offered a contract with the Metropolitan Opera, but preferred to accept an invitation to appear in the Grand Opera Syndicate season at Covent Garden in 1921. When that season had to be abandoned, she made her début at Covent Garden with the British National Opera Company on 16 May 1922, as Brünnhilde in *Die Walküre*, with immediate success; by the end of the season she had appeared in the complete *Ring* in this role, which was to remain her most famous. She added Isolde and Aida to her repertory in later British National Opera Company seasons both in London and in the provinces, and was also frequently heard in oratorio and concert. Less forceful and more lyrical than many Wagnerian dramatic sopranos, she maintained a consistent beauty and evenness of tone through these arduous parts, which she occasionally sang also in the international Covent Garden seasons of 1924 and later. Together with her husband, the flautist John Amadio, she toured widely in Australia and America, interspersing many recitals with some operatic appearances. Her many admirable recordings for HMV include the pioneer late-acoustic English-language series of excerpts from the *Ring*; in the early-electric German-language series, as at Covent Garden, she shared the role with Frida Leider.

BIBLIOGRAPHY

D. White: 'Florence Austral', *Record Collector*, xiv (n.d.), 5 [with discography by W. Hogarth and D. White]

DESMOND SHAWE-TAYLOR

Australia.

I. Art music. II. Folk music.

I. Art music

1. Before 1945. 2. After 1945.

1. BEFORE 1945. The history of art music in Australia reflects the country's transition from the brutal frontier cultures of the early penal settlements to a modern, technologically sophisticated and highly urbanized society. The foundation of the Australian colonies in the late 18th century did not coincide with an epoch of illustrious musical culture in the mother country from which they might have drawn initial stimulation. Moreover, the establishment, settlement and federation of the Australian colonies occurred too late to permit the development of national traditions capable of withstanding the impact of modern communications in the second half of the 19th century.

Organized musical life in the early penal settlements (1788–*c*1840) was initially provided by the regimental bands stationed in the colony. Their unofficial activities included the provision of music for church services, soirées, balls and theatrical activities (among them the productions at Robert Sidaway's Sydney Theatre, 1803); supporting the Sydney Amateur Concert Society (reported in *The Australian*, 27 May 1826); or performances in a convict-built theatre at Emu Plains (1827). Thus the earliest music produced in Australia included quadrilles and bandmaster Kavanagh's *Original Australian Music* (1826). Such sets comprised newly composed music and melodies adapted from popular light operatic airs of the period. Other interesting early titles included 'A Song of the Women of the Menero Tribe in the Australian Alps, arranged with the assistance of several musical gentlemen for voice and pianoforte, most humbly inscribed as the first specimen of Australian Music' (Sydney, 1834), published by a Polish-born explorer–adventurer, Dr John Lhotsky.

In 1836 Thomas Stubbs's *The Minstrel Waltz*, announced by its Sydney engraver as the first work of an Australian-born composer, was harbinger of the later profusion of salon music in the collections periodically advertised as Henry Marsh's *Colonial Music Publications*. After 1830 the steady inflow of free settlers after the Napoleonic wars created a public for private musical academies and virtuoso and chamber concerts organized by itinerant or immigrant musicians such as Vincent Wallace (1812–65), John Phillip Deane (1796–1849) and Isaac Nathan (1790–1864). The programmes, presented in hotels, salons or theatres, included Deane's String Trio and virtuoso pieces by Wallace. Nathan's earlier professional experience in London as a composer of light operas, choirmaster and conductor enabled him to make a versatile contribution through productions of oratorios at St Mary's Cathedral, Sydney, composition of occasional and choral pieces, Australian anthologies (*The Southern Euphrosyne*, 1848) and two operas, *The Merry Freaks in Troublous Times* (1843) and *Don John of Austria* produced at the Victoria Theatre, Sydney, in 1847.

After 1850, with newer colonies for free settlers already established in Melbourne and Adelaide, the mass migrations and accelerated affluence stimulated by the gold rushes introduced the first patterns of urbanization and traditional middle-class culture; this provided a market for the commercial theatrical impresario, importation of pianos and a flourishing sheet-music industry, stimulating local composition of salon music often bearing titles of local or topical interest. This middle-class culture, already active in the foundation of mechanics' institutes and the universities of Sydney and Melbourne, also promoted the development of philharmonic societies (e.g. the Royal Melbourne Philharmonic Society, 1853, actually had its origins within the Mechanics' Institute), choral traditions and the *Liedertafel* movement. These societies sometimes fostered local composition by commissioning oratorios, occasional cantatas, patriotic masques and odes, often in conjunction with civic or colonial ceremonies, or through organization of competitions for composers. In keeping with the transplanted traditions, composers of such works were usually cathedral organists or conductors attached to a theatrical management. Occasionally these works were settings of texts by recognized Australian poets, such as Charles E. Horsley's setting of Henry Kendall's *Euterpe* (1870). Choral music was popular and there was widespread support for the opera seasons of William Saurin Lyster (1861–80) and other managements in Sydney, Melbourne, Brisbane and Adelaide. Public interest may have also encouraged composers in the production of a number of operas, a few of which were produced by commercial managements, for instance Stephen Hale Marsh's *The Man in Black* (1861).

An increased musical awareness became evident in the late 19th century. Leon Caron's *Australian National Cantata* and John A. Delany's *Captain Cook* were commissioned for the Melbourne Centennial Exhibition of 1888, and chairs of music were established at the universities of Adelaide (1884) and Melbourne (1891, through an endowment of Francis Ormond), soon followed by associated conservatories.

In 1888 the first professional symphony orchestra was assembled for the duration of the Melbourne Centennial Exhibition under Frederick Cowen. Orchestral and chamber music concerts (such as the Marshall Hall Concerts in Melbourne) assumed an increasingly important role during the quarter-century before 1914; the earliest significant string quartets written in Australia (by Leon Caron, Marshall Hall, Alfred Hill, Ernest Truman) also date from this period.

Alfred Hill (1870–1960), Ernest Hutcheson (1871–1951) and Ernest Truman (1870–1948), with their North and South American contemporaries at the Leipzig Conservatory, directed by Carl Reinecke, cultivated post-Mendelssohnian and mildly 'new German' idioms at a time when Strauss and Mahler were already emergent forces in German music. Hill, active in Australia from 1897 as a conductor, composer, teacher and polemicist, imparted these traditions as professor of

harmony and composition (1916–34) to several generations of students at the newly established New South Wales State Conservatorium of Music (1916). His operas, orchestral programmes and chamber music were influenced by Maori and Australian aborigine musical folklore and legend. He vigorously championed Australia's latent musical nationalism by supporting such schemes as the Australian Opera League, which presented two seasons of Australian opera in 1914.

In the 1920s and 1930s there was a new search for a national identity in Australian music. Percy Grainger (1882–1961), in a series of lectures and broadcasts (1933–5), proposed the revival of medieval styles, theories of beatless music and (prophetic of developments in Australian composition a generation later) an acculturation of the timbral and formal resources of East Asian music. Henry Tate's (1873–1926) pamphlets *Australian Musical Resources* (1917) and *Australian Musical Possibilities* (1924) put forward the use of deflected scales based on the intervallic pattern of Australian birdcalls in a series of aesthetic concepts expounded in chapters headed 'Bush Melody', 'Bush Rhythm', 'Bush Harmony' and 'Bush Orchestration'.

The years 1914–39 saw the decline of commercially managed opera seasons in the face of economic pressures of the Depression and competition of the mass media of radio and cinema. In 1935 a revival of a legitimate music theatre was undertaken with the foundation in Melbourne of the first of a series of National Theatre movements. After the spectacular achievements of the short-lived New South Wales State Orchestra (1916–22), orchestral concerts, tenuously maintained during the 1920s through the initiative of conservatories and subscribers' committees, were established with a more stable economic foundation through the intervention of the newly established Australian Broadcasting Commission (ABC), which in 1932 set up its first studio ensembles in Sydney and Melbourne. In 1934, and again in 1936, on the recommendation of Bernard Heinze, the commission enlarged its existing studio orchestras in Sydney and Melbourne and in 1936 created four smaller ensembles in Adelaide, Brisbane, Perth and Hobart. When the ABC orchestras in these cities were augmented for celebrity concerts and schools concerts they assumed the titles Sydney (Melbourne etc) Symphony Orchestra.

The generation of composers that emerged during the inter-war period (mainly born between 1890 and 1915) drew more freely than their predecessors on the cosmopolitan currents of their period, and their styles reflect English pastoralism, post-impressionism, neoclassicism and the orchestral virtuosity of Rimsky-Korsakov, Strauss and Ravel. Aspects of aboriginal lore and legend found their way into a number of composers' works, notably those of Clive Douglas (1903–77) and John Antill (*b* 1904). It was however significant that none of these composers, save Margaret Sutherland (*b* 1897) and Dorian Le Gallienne (1915–63) in isolated chamber works, ventured into the then more forward-looking innovations of Schoenberg, Bartók or Hindemith during the 1920s. Other exponents of this group include Fritz Hart (1874–1949), Frank Hutchens (1892–1965), Roy Agnew (1893–1944), George English (*b* 1912), Robert Hughes (*b* 1912), Raymond Hanson (1913–76), Miriam Hyde (*b* 1913), Felix Gethen (*b* 1916) and James Penberthy (*b* 1917), whose works since 1965 have adopted increasingly radical idioms.

Each generation of Australian musicians has produced several composers whose recognition and achievements overseas have caused them to take up residence outside Australia. To this group belong Arthur Benjamin (1893–1960), Peggy Glanville-Hicks (*b* 1912) and Malcolm Williamson (*b* 1931), all mainly successful in the musical theatre.

2. AFTER 1945. The decades after 1945 represent perhaps the most decisive watershed in the sociological, institutional and creative foundations of Australian musical life. Public interest in music during the war years increased, and the migration of European refugees not only constituted a substantial section of a rapidly enlarged musical public but elevated and enriched local standards through transplantation of their own traditions and cultural sophistication. The first of the major institutional changes was the creation through state and municipal subsidies of permanent symphony orchestras in Sydney (Sydney SO, 1946), Brisbane (Queensland SO, 1947), Hobart (Tasmanian SO, 1948), Adelaide (South Australian SO, Adelaide SO from 1975), Melbourne (Victorian SO, 1949, Melbourne SO from 1965) and Perth (West Australian SO, 1950) from the original, smaller broadcasting orchestras maintained by the ABC. In 1967 the commission created its own National Training Orchestra, while the Australian Elizabethan Theatre Trust established its own opera orchestras in Sydney (1967) and Melbourne (1969).

The foundation in 1945 of the society Musica Viva provided an institution capable of organizing chamber concerts nationwide, initially through maintaining its own instrumental ensemble (1946–51), and from 1955 through management of tours by visiting chamber music ensembles and through festivals. The society also sponsors Australian chamber music ensembles on overseas tours. Other societies with more specialized objectives or devoted to the music of specific composers include the Australian branch of the ISCM (Sydney, 1956), the Australian Society for Keyboard Music, and Mozart, Schubert and Bartók societies. In music theatre the sole remaining commercial entrepreneur J. C. Williamson Theatres Ltd, after arranging two postwar tours by Italian companies (1949 and 1955) and the Joan Sutherland Company (1965), ultimately gave way to the emerging national opera companies in Melbourne and Sydney (1947–54), and the Australian Opera, a touring company formed in 1956 by the Elizabethan Theatre Trust. After 1968 the activities of the Australian Opera were supplemented by smaller regional groups such as Young Opera (Sydney), Victoria State Opera, State Opera of South Australia, Western Australian and Queensland opera companies, and by the universities. To accommodate this rapid increase in the performing arts multi-purpose theatres or concert houses were erected in Canberra (1965), Perth (1973), Sydney (1973) and Adelaide (1973–4) and others are planned for Melbourne and Brisbane. Festivals for the performing arts are staged annually in Perth and Mittagong, biennially in Adelaide and Canberra, and a City of Sydney Festival was planned to begin in 1977. The annual Melbourne Moomba Festival includes music.

Music education developed through the foundation of new conservatories (Brisbane 1956, Canberra 1964, Melbourne 1973), the founding of new music departments in the universities (Sydney 1948, Western Australia 1953, Monash University Melbourne 1965,

Queensland, lectureship from 1933, chair 1965, New South Wales 1966, Flinders University 1966, New England 1971, La Trobe University Melbourne 1974; in Adelaide the Elder Conservatorium was founded in 1897 within the faculty of music, and a separate state music school founded in 1970), and the introduction of music courses into colleges of advanced education or institutes of technology. In 1977 musicological workshops, conferences and seminars were instituted at the Humanities Research Centre of the Australian National University in Canberra. In 1965 the increasing importance of music education and musicology was recognized through the establishment of an Australian Society for Music Education, musicological societies in Sydney, Adelaide, Perth and Melbourne, and the convocation (1970) of the Australian Musicological Commission; in 1975 musicology was admitted as a member discipline of the Australian Academy of the Humanities. Musicological research has embraced historical studies and ethno-musicological investigations of Australian aboriginal, Polynesian and east Asian musics. Musicological yearbooks and other occasional publications (including editions) have been produced by the Musicological Society of Australia (Sydney) and by the universities of Adelaide and Western Australia. The establishment of the Commonwealth Assistance to Australian Composers and the Australian Council for the Arts (1967; their roles were taken over in 1973 by the Music Board of the Australia Council) and the Australia Music Centre (1976) shows the interest of the government in supporting and coordinating the work of creative and performing musicians. An Australasian section of the International Association of Music Libraries was convened at Adelaide in 1970.

In contrast to the conservatism or tempered reserve of earlier generations there emerged a generation of composers prepared to confront and absorb the major 20th-century compositional techniques. Those techniques were sometimes synthesized with an interest in the vernacular of 'third stream' and pop styles, and a particularly fruitful fascination with formal and timbral resources of east Asian music (especially Japanese traditional court music and Javanese–Balinese gamelan styles). Several of the major figures (e.g. David Lumsdaine, Don Banks and Keith Humble) were active in such centres as London, Florence and Paris; four composers of European extraction – Eric Gross (Austrian, *b* 1922), the Germans Felix Werder (*b* 1922) and George Dreyfus (*b* 1928), and Larry Sitsky (*b* 1934, of Russian parents, in China) – were largely educated in Australia; and Australian-born composers include Bruce Clarke (*b* 1925), Peter Sculthorpe (*b* 1929), Richard Meale (*b* 1932), Colin Brumby (*b* 1933), George Tibbits (*b* 1933), Donald Hollier (*b* 1934), Nigel Butterley (*b* 1935) and Helen Gifford (*b* 1935). Sculthorpe and Meale, the most frequently performed outside their own country, have been the most consistent and articulate in their attempts to synthesize east Asian traditional styles with advanced Western techniques. Whereas Sculthorpe's synthesis (notably in the *Sun Music* series for orchestra) appears as a facet of his conscious search for an 'Australian' identity, Meale's is rather that of an eclectic 'dormant programme' suggesting affinities with his own extensive literary and philosophical interests. Those composers also active as lecturers in universities and conservatories have been mainly responsible for the education of a young group of composers including Ian Farr (*b* 1941), Ian Bonighton (1942–75), Barry Conyngham (*b* 1944), Peter Brideoake (*b* 1945), David Ahern (*b* 1947), Ross Edwards (*b* 1943), Ian Cugley (*b* 1945), Anne Boyd (*b* 1946), Alison Bauld (*b* 1944), Jennifer Fowler (*b* 1939), Martin Wesley-Smith (*b* 1945), Moya Henderson (*b* 1947) and Vincent Plush (*b* 1950). Theirs is a range of reference extending from a reactivation of medieval techniques to a reconciliation with modern technology, including computer techniques.

See also ADELAIDE; BRISBANE; MELBOURNE; PERTH; SYDNEY.

BIBLIOGRAPHY

F. C. Brewer: *The Drama and Music in New South Wales* (Sydney, 1893)
H. Tate: *Australian Musical Resources* (Melbourne, 1917)
E. H. Davies: 'Music in the Early Days of South Australia', *MT*, lxxvii (1936), 1078
J. Hall: 'History of Music in Australia', *Canon*, iv (1951)
A. Orchard: *Music in Australia* (Melbourne, 1952)
E. Keane: *Music for a Hundred Years: the Story of the House of Paling* (Sydney, 1954)
W. A. Carne: *A Century of Harmony: the Official History of the Royal Melbourne Philharmonic Society* (Melbourne, 1954)
G. Nadel: *Australia's Colonial Culture* (Melbourne, 1957)
A. K. Wentzel: *The First Hundred Years of Music in Australia: 1788–1888* (diss., U. of Sydney, 1963)
P. Richardson: 'Military Music in the Colony of NSW: 1788–1850', *Musicology*, i (1964), 5
L. Sitsky: 'Emergence of the New Music in Australia', *PNM*, iv/1 (1965), 176
F. Callaway: 'Some Aspects of Music in Australia', *Composer* (1966), no.19, p.78
W. Gallusser: 'Professor John Bishop: a Bibliography', *MMA*, i (1966), 8
D. R. Peart: 'Some Recent Developments in Australian Composition', *Composer* (1966), no.19, p.73
M. Williamson: 'A Composer's Heritage', *Composer* (1966), no.19, p.69
R. Covell: *Australia's Music: Themes of a New Society* (Melbourne, 1967)
B. and F. Mackenzie: *Singers of Australia: from Melba to Sutherland* (Melbourne, 1967)
D. R. Peart: 'The Australian Avant garde', *PRMA*, xciii (1966–7), 1
G. Bartle: *Music in Australian Schools* (Melbourne, 1968)
A. D. McCredie: 'Alfred Hill (1870–1960): Some Backgrounds and Perspectives for an Historical Edition', *MMA*, iii (1968), 181–257
H. Hort: 'An Aspect of Nationalism in the Music of Early Australia', *SMA*, iii (1969), 74
A. D. McCredie: *Musical Composition in Australia: Catalogue of 46 Australian Composers and Selected Works* (Canberra, 1969)
T. Radic: 'Aspects of Organized Amateur Music in Melbourne: 1836–1890', *MMA*, iv (1969), 147
A. K. Wentzel: 'The Rapid Development of Music in Australia (1851–1861)', *Musicology*, iii (1969), 69
D. M. Bridges: *The Role of Universities in the Development of Music Education in Australia* (diss., U. of Sydney, 1970)
W. Gallusser: 'Development of Musical Resources and Services in the Libraries of Australia and New Zealand since 1960', *MMA*, v (1970), 58
E. L. Scarlett: 'Music Making in Early Sydney', *MMA*, v (1970), 26–57
J. M. Thomson: 'The Role of the Pioneer Composer: Some Reflections on Alfred Hill', *SMA*, iv (1970), 52
The State of the Art of Electronic Music in Australia: Melbourne 1971
E. Irvin: 'Australia's First Public Concerts', *SMA*, v (1971), 77
D. E. Tunley: 'A Decade of Musical Composition in Australia: 1960–1970', *SMA*, v (1971), 66
The Contemporary Australian Composer and Society: Perth 1971
J. Murdoch: *Australia's Contemporary Composers* (Melbourne and Sydney, 1972)

II. Folk Music

1. General: (i) Historical background (ii) Aboriginal music (iii) British and Irish influences (iv) Other migrations (v) Jazz and popular music. 2. Aboriginal music and dance in northern Australia: (i) Historical introduction (ii) Visual arts (iii) Religion (iv) Instruments (v) Songs (vi) Dance. 3. Aboriginal music and dance in southern Australia: (i) Tribal music (ii) Common structural elements in the music of central Australia and the Western Desert (iii) Songs for ages and stages (iv) Regional differentiation of song styles (v) Transition (vi) Europeanized songs.

1. GENERAL. The only music indigenous and unique to Australia is the traditional music of the Australian abor-

igines. Nevertheless, as a country now populated by some 12 million non-aboriginal people, compared with 100,000 of aboriginal descent, its derived and adapted forms of European folk music are worthy of some attention.

(*i*) *Historical background.* After its 'discovery' by James Cook in 1770 and the arrival of the First Fleet under Arthur Phillip in 1788, the penal colony of New South Wales in eastern Australia saw the arrival of large numbers of convicts transported from England (especially metropolitan London), Ireland and, to a lesser extent, Scotland. Thus the earliest known 'folksongs' found in Australia were largely treasonable versions of songs sung in the lands of these convicts' origin, and protest songs were prominent. With the establishment of further penal colonies, such as those at Moreton Bay (Queensland) and Van Diemen's Land (now Tasmania), and the gradual exploration and free settlement of the country, British and Irish folk music continued to be the dominant influences on the music of the ordinary people. Irish traditions mainly affected convict and bush-ranger (bandit) songs, while English folk and street ballads predominated in the typical outback or rural workers' songs, such as those of stockmen, drovers, overlanders, sheep-shearers and 'bullockies' (bullock drivers).

With the discovery in 1851 of gold in Victoria, and later in New South Wales, Queensland and Western Australia, the ensuing gold-rushes brought an influx of people from many places, including Californian goldminers with their own versions of songs originally from the British Isles, together with a host of professional entertainers who gave wide currency to parodies and ballads of the day. Adaptations of these popular songs, frequently of known authorship, caused an interaction between 'folk' and 'popular' cultures, and it is convenient to reject the term 'folksong' in considering this music in favour of a twofold classification: 'traditional songs', with no known authorship; and 'bush ballads', whose authorship is known. Both types survived almost entirely through oral transmission and their texts, and hence their melody and rhythm, were constantly adapted to Australian experiences.

Increasing industrialization and urbanization led to a gradual decline of both types until after World War II, when serious attempts were at last made to collect and preserve what was left of this oral tradition, and many new or further adapted 'folksongs' began to be created. It is worth noting, however, that Australia was settled by whites at the beginning of the Industrial Revolution, and that consequent advances in transport, communication and compulsory education meant that it was too late for any great development of really individual regional folk music to take place.

(*ii*) *Aboriginal music.* Except for occasional references by settlers, travellers and, later, anthropologists, Australian aboriginal music was almost totally neglected or misunderstood by white Australians for 150 years, during which time many traditional ceremonies completely disappeared. The first to accord serious musical attention to it was E. Harold Davies, who studied some central and southern Australian desert singing. In 1949, 1952 and 1953 the anthropologist A. P. Elkin mounted major expeditions to record aboriginal music in Arnhem Land (Northern Territory) and the analysis of these recordings by Trevor Jones resulted in the first systematic studies to be published. Alice Moyle has since continued and deepened the study of northern Australian aboriginal music and Catherine Ellis that of the southern regions (see §§2 and 3 below). A major development in aboriginal research was the establishment by the Australian government in 1964 of the Australian Institute of Aboriginal Studies in Canberra, which has since sponsored work in all aspects of traditional aboriginal life, including music, and is the repository of large collections of recorded material.

Despite the late start to collection and research and the great amount of work still to be done, it is clear that this music is without parallels or obvious connections with any other cultures in the world. Though some broad differences are found between the styles of northern and southern music, and many sub-styles are identifiable, especially in the north, all are easily recognizable as Australian aboriginal, just as are the 200 or more surviving aboriginal languages. Because of the extreme antiquity (possibly 40,000 years) and almost changeless continuity of aboriginal life in Australia, as well as of its unique features, the discovery, study and preservation of its music is now considered to be of the greatest importance.

In aboriginal song performances the dividing lines between different kinds of vocalization are frequently blurred. Non-verbal sounds, such as hissing, high-pitched falsetto ululating, growling, grunting, shouting, shrieking and wailing may pass over into speaking, monotonal or bitonal syllabic chanting, partly melismatic singing of texts and wordless vocalizing of completely melismatic melodies ranging over more than an octave. Vocal qualities range from a husky, 'inward' style to powerfully extrovert dynamism, but an 'elided', gliding technique predominates. Polyvocality, in which a singer may produce more than one pitch simultaneously and may even sing in consecutive 5ths with himself, and multi-vocality, in which several markedly different vocal qualities may be used successively in different songs by the one singer, are sometimes found. In some styles vibrato and 'continuous' singing, in which intake of breath does not interrupt the sound, are practised.

Aboriginal melodies nearly always consist of a series of descents from a loud, high note to a soft, sustained (or repeated) lower note, with energetic leaps to the highest pitch or to a higher or intermediate pitch for subsequent descents, the overall compass ranging from a 2nd to a 12th or more. Constant and elaborate ornamentation frequently blurs the various pitches of the descent with slides and microtonal trills. Polyphony occurs in some areas, and may take the form of a drone, parallel octaves, 3rds, 4ths and 5ths, canon or singing in two independent parts.

Metre and rhythm are often very intricate. Both divisive and additive metres occur, the latter involving repeated groupings of five, seven, ten and even 13 beats. Polymetre (the simultaneous use of two or more different metres) and multi-metre (the successive use of different metres) are found, as well as non-metric or free-rhythm structures. Isorhythm, polyrhythm and elaborate syncopation are frequent and characteristic features. While many of these stylistic attributes are common to much traditional aboriginal music, individual styles combining or omitting some of them make for considerable regional differentiation. The DIDJERIDU is especially important in northern areas.

One peripheral area calls for special mention: the Torres Strait Islands, lying between the northern tip of Cape York Peninsula in Queensland and Papua New Guinea, are mainly populated by about 10,000 Melanesians, but the aborigines, Papuans and islanders who live there constitute a part of the Australian population. In addition to 'modern' music, which is an amalgam of indigenous, Anglo-Australian and Polynesian styles, and 'imported' music such as South Pacific hymns and chants, 'traditional' music is still performed by some of the older residents. From the few samples recorded it is clear that they are far more closely related to southern Papuan than to Australian aboriginal music. They are sung in a resonant, open-throated manner without vibrato or ornamentation, are commonly pentatonic and triadic in melodic structure, generate frequent sustained harmonies and are usually accompanied by a skin drum of Papuan origin. In earlier times there were ritual songs, sacred and secular dances, magic spell chants, serenades, laments and play songs and, in addition to the skin drum, the jew's harp, pan-pipes and notched flutes were used.

Although Australian aboriginal traditional culture was for a long time in danger of extinction, belated efforts are being made to conserve what is left and to encourage the aborigines to take a pride in their traditional way of life.

(iii) British and Irish influences. Because the scholarly investigation of Australian traditional songs and bush ballads did not gain any momentum until the 1950s a great deal of material has been lost, making it difficult to compile an adequate history of the subject. As early collectors of this folk music were usually either literary men, interested primarily in the texts of these songs as social documents, or musicians trained in European artistic traditions and almost totally lacking in an objective approach to what they found, such examples as are available are primarily of literary interest and have probably suffered considerable modification to accord with the collector's musical prejudices.

Though many tunes are of 18th- or early 19th-century origin, they have reached us in late 19th-century form. Few of them are modal; most appear in major tonalities and show a Victorian attitude to modulation and cadence. They also have a 'flattened-out' quality, with the curves and leaps of their original melodies reduced to repeated notes, foursquare rhythms and phrases and a marked monotony of shape (which some may attribute to the influence of the landscape and climate of much of outback Australia). Nevertheless, the work of such collectors as Percy Jones, John Manifold, Edgar Waters and John Meredith has produced several hundred tunes of British and Irish origin, including some that are now rare in their countries of origin. The application of Australian texts or variants has often forced interesting variations on the presumed originals, and connections have been found with their Canadian and American versions. Most were probably sung unaccompanied, but later such popular instruments as the banjo, concertina, button-key accordion, mouth-organ, fiddle, tin whistle, jew's harp and folded gum-leaf were introduced. These were used especially for dance-tunes; the dances took the form of solo step-dancing, usually based on Irish jigs and reels, and 19th-century ballroom dances such as the Lancers and quadrilles.

In a land of very few women, love-songs were rare by comparison with the British Isles, but the predominantly occupational men's songs emphasized boasting, drinking, gambling and the hardship and loneliness of their daily lot. Many early convicts' songs told of Irish rebellion; songs about bush-rangers frequently treated their subject as a folk hero and victim of police persecution. In later stages of Australian folksong-making 'popular' urban songs were significant as the basis for the tunes and the 'literary ballad' as the basis for the style and structure of the texts. The later ubiquitous influence of radio and recordings brought about the development and widespread popularity of guitar-accompanied 'hillbilly' songs based on the American pattern, which have replaced the earlier stage and music-hall influences from England. There are a few examples of children's play songs and sea shanties in local adaptations.

In general almost no regional styles have been observed other than those resulting from the obvious dichotomy between city and country ways of life, which is itself fast disappearing; this lack of regional typology is paralleled by the virtual absence of regional dialects in Australian speech. In summary, Australian folk music of British and Irish origin is primarily of literary interest, as a chronicle of the sufferings, longings and bravado of its traditional performers. Among the best-known Australian traditional songs and bush ballads are *Waltzing Matilda* (which has, for most Australians, the status of unofficial national anthem), *The Wild Colonial Boy*, *Botany Bay*, *Van Diemen's Land*, *Moreton Bay*, *Bold Jack Donahue*, *The Banks of the Condamine*, *Wild Rover No More*, *The Queensland Drover*, *The Old Bark Hut*, *The Dying Stockman*, *The Overlander*, *Click Go the Shears* and *Bound for South Australia*, to which today must surely be added the Rolf Harris composition *Tie Me Kangaroo Down Sport*, which has clearly passed into the category of a nationally sung bush ballad.

(*iv*) *Other migrations*. Since the gold-rushes in the second half of the 19th century successive migrations of non-British people, including substantial numbers from China, Italy, Greece and various Jewish communities, have increased Australia's population. The policy of assisted migration adopted by the Australian government since World War II in an attempt to populate the country as rapidly as possible has brought migrants from the British Isles and southern, central and eastern Europe, particularly to the larger cities. Many have come from rural areas and have brought their own folk cultures with them, and it is likely that aspects of these folk cultures which have atrophied or disappeared in their homelands will be maintained in Australia. So far, however, there is little evidence of any musical interpenetration between these folk cultures and the established Australian folk cultures already described.

(*v*) *Jazz and popular music*. Since the 1940s 'traditional' jazz deriving from the American New Orleans and Dixieland styles has flourished in Australia, notable band-leaders being Graeme Bell, Len Barnard, Frank Traynor and Ray Price, and some distinctively local idioms have at times appeared. 'Progressive' and 'mainstream' jazz have also produced some skilled and creative practitioners, in particular Don Burrows, John Sangster and Judy Bailey.

Australian popular music, in contrast, was until the 1960s almost stifled in its development by the all-pervasive influence of American and English groups propagated by radio, television, films and records. During the 1960s and early 1970s, however, Australian groups appeared and are now enjoying considerable national and international success, backed by a flourishing local record industry that has encouraged the creation of original Australian popular compositions. As a result, typically Australian subject matter, colloquialisms and pronunciation, formerly thought to be too provincial to succeed in the face of imported idioms, are now encouraged in popular music.

Throughout the history of Australian folk and popular music there has been virtually no interaction between indigenous aboriginal music, folk music and popular music, except for the influence of hillbilly 'country-style' music on detribalized aborigines. Since 1960, however, a remarkable fusion of all three has taken place, principally in the music of the internationally known Australian entertainer and songwriter Rolf Harris, whose best creative work shows both an instinctive response to each style and an ability to popularize the synthetic result.

BIBLIOGRAPHY
E. H. Davies: 'Aboriginal Songs', *Transcriptions and Proceedings of the Royal Society of South Australia*, li (1927), 81
——: 'Palaeolithic Music', *MT*, lxviii (1927), 691
——: 'Aboriginal Songs of Central and Southern Australia', *Oceania*, ii (1932), 454
——: 'Music in Primitive Society', *Occasional Publications of the Anthropological Society of South Australia*, ii (1947)
T. A. Jones: 'Arnhem Land Music: a Musical Survey', *Oceania*, xxvi (1956), 252–339; xxviii (1957), 1–30
D. Stewart and N. Keesing: *Old Bush Songs* (Sydney, 1957)
A. P. Elkin and T. A. Jones: *Arnhem Land Music, North Australia* (Sydney, 1958)
T. A. Jones: 'The Nature of Australian Aboriginal Music', *Hemisphere*, vi/1 (1962), 2; repr. in *Australian Journal of Music Education*, ii (1968), 9
J. Manifold: *The Penguin Australian Song Book* (Melbourne, 1964)
T. A. Jones: 'Australian Aboriginal Music: the Elkin Collection's Contribution toward an Overall Picture', *Aboriginal Man in Australia*, ed. R. M. and C. H. Berndt (Sydney, 1965), 283–374
R. Covell: *Australia's Music: Themes of a New Society* (Melbourne, 1967)
J. Beckett and T. A. Jones: 'Traditional Music of Torres Strait', AIAS/11 [disc notes]
R. L. Hausman: *Australia: Traditional Music in its History* (North Quincy, Mass., 1975)

2. ABORIGINAL MUSIC AND DANCE IN NORTHERN AUSTRALIA. The social organization of aboriginal groups living in isolated parts of northern Australia is still traditionally based. To a greater degree than elsewhere in Australia, indigenous socio-religious beliefs continue to determine the behaviour of members of northern communities and to find expression in ritual, song and dance. In some localities in Arnhem Land these performing arts remain closely integrated with the visual arts of painting and decoration. In the eastern states, where the history of European settlement is longest, remaining forms of art are to be found principally in paintings and engravings in caves.

(*i*) *Historical introduction*. From recent datings of carbon and ochre found at sites showing signs of human habitation, it has been inferred that Man has lived in Australia for at least 40,000 years. At the time of the last glaciation the shores of the northern part of the continent were continuous with those of the island of New Guinea. There is little doubt that the first Australians followed a route through south-east Asia, although the point – or points – of their entry into the Australian continent have not been determined with any certainty. For thousands of years semi-nomadic hunters and gatherers have roamed widely over the central arid regions of Australia, congregating in small groups near

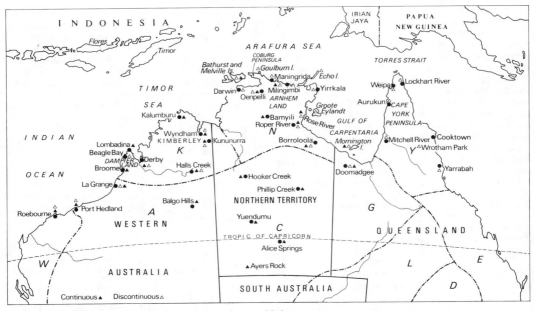

1. Map of northern Australia, showing the areas discussed below.

waterholes and soaks during periods of drought. In northern coastal regions, where monsoon rains alternate with dry seasons, other groups have remained within smaller and more abundant hunting and fishing territories, guarding themselves against periodic excess of water rather than a lack of it.

The dugout canoe has replaced the bark canoe in many coastal regions, a change attributed to knowledge gained by the Australian aborigines from Macassans from the Celebes, who made annual visits to northern Australia to fish for trepang, or bêche-de-mer. These Indonesian contacts were well established long before the spread into the north of European settlements, which started in the early decades of the 19th century with several short-lived attempts to establish a military garrison on Coburg Peninsula. Some of the older aboriginal men in Arnhem Land, an area which the former Indonesian visitors referred to as 'marega', still remember Macassan songs. Before the departure of a prau (or proa: a fast Malay sailing-vessel) the mast was raised then fixed securely to the deck; Warner noted that in north-eastern Arnhem Land the idea of an Indonesian ship's departure had been transferred to the idea of the departure of the soul of the dead, for aborigines of this region had incorporated the raising of a mast or flagpole into part of their burial ceremonies.

Trading observed in historical times between Cape York aborigines, Torres Strait islanders and Papuans is thought to have been part of another long tradition. In some of the myths of the aborigines of Cape York and Torres Strait there appear to be cultural links. Songs and dances performed by Cape York aborigines in 'the island way' represent comparatively recent contacts made through the Torres Strait islanders with contemporary Pacific islanders.

In the 200 or more identifiable Australian languages varying degrees of genetic relationship have been recognized; greater linguistic divergence is apparent in Arnhem Land in the Northern Territory than anywhere else. It has been estimated that about one-eighth of the continent, in an area north of the Tropic of Capricorn and west of the Gulf of Carpentaria, is occupied by all but one of 29 major language families. The accompanying map (fig.1) shows the main northern regions mentioned below.

(ii) Visual arts. Like their music and dance, the visual arts of Australian aborigines are principally manifestations of religious beliefs. In any one cave or rock gallery there are admixtures of styles and many paintings are superimposed on others. There are marked regional differences in the subjects portrayed, especially in regard to the anthropomorphic and 'sorcery' figures. Some of the rock paintings and engravings appear to have no social relevance to aboriginal culture as it is known and understood at present; on the other hand a number of rock sites are still visited by small parties of aboriginal men and the paintings retouched as part of a traditional rite. Singing usually accompanies this act of repainting. Aborigines in north Kimberley (area *K*) say that during the restoration of cave paintings of the *wandjina* (large mouthless figures) numbers of men used to congregate at the site for related ceremonies, many of which were associated with rain-making. Singing at such a time was performed to the accompaniment of a stick beaten against a bailer (or baler) shell. In another shell, containing water, was placed a clay model of a *wandjina* figure which disintegrated as the singing continued (see Crawford, 1968). The words of one of the songs in the rain-making series, recorded in Derby in 1968, have been translated as follows: 'I have done it – painted the *wandjina* – upper arm, hands, fingers, joints and nails'. When a light shower of rain fell after the conclusion of the series, it was taken as a natural and expected sequel to the singing.

Paintings on bark, which may resemble significant

rock paintings in the region, are still used as a means of instruction among more traditionally orientated groups in Arnhem Land. Schematic designs, drawn with ochre, pipeclay and charcoal, are visual reminders of the exploits of mythical beings and other related creatures, and are also used for decorating men and women before their participation in rites and ceremonies. These representations of 'dreamings', or of special links between individuals and the spiritual world, are also painted on the bodies of initiates about to be circumcised and again before burial.

(*iii*) *Religion*. The following three areas of religious beliefs and practices have been distinguished: the northwestern (areas *K* and west *N*), where the religious stimulus is seen as coming from the direction of the desert; Arnhem Land (north *N*), where a complex of fertility cults is centred on female as well as male 'ancestral' beings; and the eastern (area *Y*), where the emphasis is (or was) on the mythical dwelling places of numerous 'ancestral' creatures (e.g. birds, fish or reptiles). Except among groups in the extreme north-west (including Bathurst and Melville Islands) and north-east of the continent, initiatory practices include circumcision.

North Australian religious cults are centred on ancestral beings who came from the sea or rose from the ground and made long journeys on the Australian mainland, meeting others of their kind. Initiated men qualify for roles in the 'age-grading' rites. By watching performances of mimetic acts, seeing for the first time secret symbolic objects, and listening to songs and related stories, they learn from older, more knowledgeable men of the exploits of beings who mark their 'dreaming' sites and those of others in their lineage. Such performances are believed to assist in the procreation of all living species and to guide and instruct individuals morally in their passage from birth to death. In this sense male rituals are more important to the community as a whole than - exclusively female rites, which in northern Australia today consist only of singing and dancing for 'love-magic' purposes. In open ceremonies (those with no restrictions placed on attendance) women participate to a greater or lesser degree (see §(vi) below). Women also contribute the formal wailing ('crying') at times of death or during initiation, when a young boy ritually 'dies' before being reborn a man.

In the dual organization of Australian aboriginal society, songs, dances and the mythical beings to whom they are attributed are assigned to either of two moieties (halves or 'sides'). During large ceremonies the general management and work of preparing the ground, decorating the dancers, making head-dresses, etc, is under the control of one moiety, whereas the performance as such is carried out by the owners or chief custodians of the songs and other ceremonial acts. Dreaming sites, ritual objects, birds, fish, winds or stars, and members of clans

2. Aborigines using didjeridu and clapsticks to accompany dance in Arnhem Land, Northern Territory; for a further illustration, see DIDJERIDU

or lineages, are divided between the two moieties, as are the name-words and subjects of songs. Marriage is between members of opposite moieties but there are no special ceremonies to mark this event. Objects resulting from alien contacts such as dugout canoes, matches, tobacco and flags belong to the same moiety, which is *yiritja* (*jiridja*) in north-eastern Arnhem Land languages and *mandaridja* in the Nunggubuyu language (east *N*). On Groote Eylandt, *bara* ('west wind') songs belong to one moiety, *mamariga* ('north-east wind') songs to the other.

(*iv*) *Instruments*. Of 30 or more different types of instruments more than half have been reported at places north of the Tropic of Capricorn. 14 are confined to a small region bounded by Broome, in the south-western corner of the Kimberley regions, and Ingham, in south-east Cape York Peninsula. Materials used are wood (mainly), bark, bamboo, seed pods and the skin of fish or

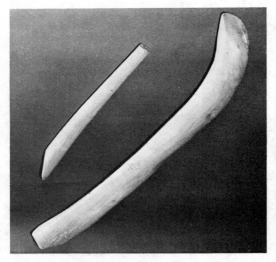

3. Rasp and scraper used to accompany tabi (dyabi) songs, West Kimberley, Western Australia, 1968

reptiles; technology amounts to little more than smoothing and carving, especially the pieces of wood which are struck together as paired concussion sticks and as boomerang clapsticks.

Australian instruments may be classified according to the sounds they produce, sustained or detached. Many of the former kind belong only to northern regions. The DIDJERIDU, however, is the only aerophone now in use (fig.2), is capable of producing both types of sound. It is made from the branch of a tree; the search for a suitable length of branch hollowed by termites may take longer than its transformation into an instrument. Bamboo didjeridus, which are rare, require only the burning out of nodes with a firestick and the fixing of gum or cloth to the mouth end. Some wooden didjeridus have a length of narrower bore inserted in the mouth end; others exhibit tool marks made during supplementary hollowing of the cone at the other. In the west of Arnhem Land, song accompaniments on the didjeridu consist of a rhythmic droning with sustained voiced as well as aerophonic notes; in the east, an additional overblown note, re-

latively short and sounded usually a 10th or 11th above, is incorporated into the rhythmic interplay between vocal and instrumental parts. Didjeridu accompaniments associated with clan songs of north-eastern Arnhem Land end with this upper note although the song may continue for unaccompanied voice.

Sustained rattling sounds are produced by bunches of seed pods held in the hand and shaken by male dancers in Cape York (area *Y*). Rattling effects, often heard in song endings, are also produced by rapid, alternating contact of the tapered ends of boomerang clapsticks (areas *N*, *K* and *C*).

Sustained sounds of a different kind are produced by a rasp which accompanies *tabi* (*dyabi*) songs, known only to singers in north-western regions (areas *W*, *A* and *K*). The rasp is a notched stick (fig.3), usually a spearthrower (*miro*, *mirru*), scraped with a smaller stick. Rasps of the latter kind are mentioned in Daisy Bates's unpublished manuscript *Corroborees, Games etc.* (National Library of Australia, Canberra, n.d.), and by Brandenstein.

Instruments producing detached sounds prevail in central and desert regions and, with the exception of large sticks beaten on the ground, are also widely used in song accompaniments further north. In Arnhem Land paired concussion sticks of ironwood (*Erythrophleum chlorostachys*) produce ringing sounds which carry for long distances (see fig.4). In Kimberley districts, in corroboree performances, male singing to paired sticks may be supported or followed (literally, 'tracked') by female singing, the women providing an accompaniment by slapping their laps with one hand held at the wrist by the other. Detached sounds are produced on Bathurst and Melville Islands by men slapping their buttocks as they chant on a monotone and dance. Additional handclapping is a feature of song accompaniment on these islands, as in parts of north-western Arnhem Land and in Cape York. A single-headed drum beaten with one hand is confined to Cape York and is believed to have come from Papua, via Torres Strait; in former times the head was of fish- or lizard-skin. At the conclusion of a song, the drum may be struck more rapidly, in a hand-executed 'roll'. In song and dance performances described by Cape York aborigines as being in the 'island way', the drummer stands up to play, holding the drum in the curve of one arm, and also sings. But for the mainland shake-a-leg dances in Cape York the drummer does not sing and is even occasionally seated (fig.5); the accompanying role is shared by a singer who beats two sticks. (These dances are performed in northern areas and finish with jumping steps and quivering limbs.)

Some instruments are sounded during rites connected with various cults, and only in the presence of initiated men. Women and the uninitiated are told these are the voices of spirits or cult beings. The bullroarer is sounded during *djungguwan* (*djunggawon*), a religious ceremonial complex, or succession of rituals including circumcision, performed by groups in Arnhem Land. It is likewise sounded during *kunapipi* (*gunabibi*), a fertility cult also known as 'old woman' and performed by groups in Arnhem Land and north-western regions of the Northern Territory and Western Australia; and during the associated *gadjari* (*katjiri*) rites performed by north central groups. It was formerly heard during the initiation of girls and boys in Cape York. The didjeridu, often exceptionally large, is sounded in *djungguwan* in northern Arnhem Land. In south-eastern Arnhem Land two heavy pieces of wood ('gongs'), one supported on the shoulder, are clashed together during *yabuduruwa* (*jabudura*), a cult allied to central and north central rituals. A stick is beaten against a hollow log (*banagaga*, *balnuknuk* or *purakakka*) in the rituals that form part of the fertility cult *ubar* (western Arnhem Land and Goulburn Island, called *uwar* or *ngurlmag* in north-eastern Arnhem Land). A bark bundle is struck on the ground during *narra* (*nara*) rites associated with the *djungkao* (*djunggawul*) myth in north-eastern Arnhem Land.

Aboriginal names for instruments, and techniques for sounding them, differ throughout northern Australia according to language. A collection of such names can reveal possible patterns of their diffusion. At the end of the 19th century a wooden trumpet (*yiki yiki*) was reported in regions near Cooktown, north Queensland. Names for the didjeridu in several northern languages include *a:ra:wi* (Maung, north-west *N*); *djalupu* (Ranjbarngu, south central Arnhem Land); *djalupun* (Worora, area *K*); *djubinj* (Njigina, area *K*); *ganbag* or *gamalag* (Djawan, south-western Arnhem Land); *ma:gu* (Gunwinggu, north-west *N*); *maluk* (Murinbata, west of *N*); *lhambilbilg* (Nunggubuyu, eastern Arnhem Land); *yiraki* (Ngandi, east central Arnhem Land, and also in languages in the north-east); and *yiraga* (Enindilyaugwa, Groote Eylandt). South of the Broome–Ingham line the didjeridu is still a novelty and players are usually young men from the north. A map showing the distribution of aboriginal sound instruments is in the *New Australian Encyclopaedia*.

Recordings of musical sounds did not begin until early in the 20th century. Nearly 40 years later tone qualities were reproduced with reasonable fidelity on wire, tape and disc; and in 1949, 1952 and 1953 during expeditions to places south and west of the Arnhem Land Reserve, the Australian anthropologist A. P. Elkin collected the recordings which form the basis of the first comprehensive description of northern Australian aboriginal music (see Elkin and Jones, 1958).

(*v*) *Songs.* Australian aboriginal music is primarily and essentially vocal. Most of the songs are believed to have been propagated by spirits, and there are few whose words do not have some 'sacred' connotation. Probably the only 'secular' songs, as seen from the aboriginal viewpoint, are those described in Kimberley regions as being 'like cowboy songs' and 'made with the brain'. According to their makers, these songs belong to a totally different category from those 'found in dream'.

From the point of view of ownership, north Australian songs have been classed as cult, clan and individually owned, although there are difficulties in separating some of the cult-owned songs from those that are owned by a clan (i.e. a local descent group). To the cult songs might be added a sub-category of magical songs, which include rain-making, rain-stopping, love-magic songs and secret incantations performed either to heal or to harm.

The term 'corroboree songs' has been used in a superficial sense to denote aboriginal dance-songs performed for camp entertainment (*see* CORROBOREE). But many such songs in the north are also heard during mortuary and mourning ceremonies. A more useful distinction can be made between dance-songs and a smaller repertory of songs normally sung without dancing. Some of the songs associated with ritual, and those

4. *Aborigine with concussion sticks, Blyth River, Arnhem Land, Northern Territory*

reserved for the painting of the dancers' skins, belong to the latter category. Among the numerous types of song referring to topical or personal matters there are some which singers say are not for dancing. These include: the *tabi* songs with rasp accompaniment of south-west Kimberley and the Pilbara district, Western Australia (see §(iv) above); *lildjin* or *ludin* songs of Dampier Land (area *K*); and the *pitale* (*bidala*) songs known only in Cape York. In some corroborees there are sections for singing only: in dance-songs of north-western regions, these sections are known as *lirrga*; in the corroborees of

5. *Aborigine with single-headed hourglass drum used to accompany shake-a-leg dance, Cape York Peninsula, Queensland, 1966*

the Yawur, Nyigina and Gadjari people (areas *A* and south-west *K*) they are *barubaru*.

Djatpangarri (*djedbangari*) songs, or *wagal* ('fun') songs, are performed in north-eastern Arnhem Land by young, single men of either moiety to the accompaniment of paired concussion sticks and didjeridu. In a region in which songs are short (30 seconds or less), they are distinguished by their longer duration and bipartite form. Associated dances are mimetic and always evoke amusement.

Methods of learning and transmitting songs and dances depend largely on their category or type. Corroborees performed openly and regularly in camp are readily absorbed by children who imitate them in play and invent similar models of their own. In eastern Arnhem Land, during the performance of clan songs and dances, children have been seen following their fathers on the dance ground. South-west of the Gulf of Carpentaria at Borroloola (area *N*) mothers with babies on their shoulders have been seen dancing in the individually-owned *galwangara* corroboree. A small boy, recognizing some of the words of the *galwangara*, sang them loudly at brief intervals in company with the song leader (and owner) of the series. In the north central desert region, a young Walpiri (Walbiri) girl of about nine was heard singing in play a *yawalyu* (women's love-magic) song. Further to the north-west a young girl was teased for singing *guluwada* ('sweetheart') songs.

During the period of their initiation, young boys are encouraged to adopt a more serious attitude towards learning songs and they begin to memorize the cult songs in seclusion, under the guidance of older men. The simultaneous sounding of an associated instrument by the singer needs skill and practice. Walpiri men are said to learn the *gadjari* (*katjiri*) cult songs 'from the boomerangs'. On Groote Eylandt young didjeridu players of 14 or 15 have been practising accompaniments to clan songs with leading male singers; they learn 'mouth sounds', or patterns of consonants and syllables, as a means of remembering and communicating – usually from singer to accompanist – the didjeridu rhythms appropriate to each song.

The trading of songs and dances in the north was reported frequently by earlier observers. In north-western regions similar processes of song and dance transmission are still taking place; such a process is called *djambar* (Yawur language, area *K*), a word meaning 'people who do not know how to sing and dance a *nurlu*' (an individually owned corroboree). On three consecutive nights the learners sit in rows watching the performance in silence, after which they are permitted to talk and join in the singing if they wish. Should a second group of learners arrive, the first group will be ready to take their places in the corroboree in company with the relinquishing owners.

There are no work songs sung by the aboriginal Australians who, traditionally, do not plant and harvest. It would seem that these hunters, gatherers and fishermen have always believed in the power of their songs and rituals to maintain subsistence.

Performances of aboriginal music in northern parts of the continent consist of chains (series or cycles) of songs with or without instrumental accompaniment. During a long and relatively continuous series of songs, whether cult, clan or individually owned, a number of factors may cause a marked change in melodic mode or contour. In a series of cult songs, a melodic change in the performance may represent another section of a related myth which, in the tropical north, would not be correlated with a particular local descent group as it is in north central desert regions. In a series of clan songs, melodic changes are more likely to result from changes in the male singers taking part, for particular tunes are associated over a period of time with particular lineages. If the songs are dance-songs, and individually owned, marked melodic changes may occur, particularly in north-western regions (area *N*). In a series of *gunborg* (dance) songs a melodic change, together with corresponding changes in stick-beating and didjeridu patterns, marks the conclusion of the dance. The last item in such a series has been called *manbadjan* ('mother') to distinguish it from the preceding *manjawu* ('little ones') and is an older, better-known tune 'found in dream' by the owner of the song.

Successions of descending leaps, some spanning an octave or more, distinguish the melodic contours of individually-owned dance-songs from the north-west, including *wongga*, *gurula* and *nurlu* (*nulu*) and also of some of the songs not connected with dancing, such as *lildjin* (*ludin*) and *tabi* songs. *Ubar* cult singing, accompanied by sticks, didjeridu and the stick-beaten hollow log, is also wide in compass. In contrast to these are most of the clan or individually owned dance-songs from Cape York, many of them sung or intoned on notes approximately the same in pitch, and the clan songs of north-eastern and eastern Arnhem Land including Groote Eylandt, with their short melodic motifs and relatively narrow spans of pitch (see ex.1, in which an attempt has been made to show the characteristic use of the 'shaky' voice).

Electronic notations (melograms) of songs recorded in north Australia have revealed an abundance of microtonal intervals in the vocal part; also clearly marked are certain pitches which recur more consistently in any one song sequence than do the microtonal intervals. 'Scales' derived from aural notations have been described as 'diatonic' (conjunct), 'chasmatonic' (disjunct), 'hemitonal' and 'anhemitonal'. Ex.2 shows pitch 'inventories' compiled from aural notations of

Ex.1 from *Yinunggura* or *Bara* ('West wind'), clan song, Groote Eylandt; rec. and transcr. A. Moyle

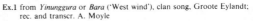

ρ = glottal tremor.

Ex.2 Pitch inventories of notations of songs, (a) north central desert regions, (b) east coast of Arnhem Land; rec. and transcr. A. Moyle (Berndt and Phillips, eds., 1973)

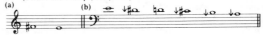

songs sung by young aborigines in north central desert regions (ex.2a) and on the eastern coast of Arnhem Land (ex.2b).

Tied notes and melismas characterize didjeridu-accompanied dance-songs in the north-west (ex.3). Similar features have been noted in *maraiin*, or higher clan songs, accompanied by heavy paired sticks and sung by men of the *yiritja* (north-eastern Arnhem Land) or *mandaridja* (eastern Arnhem Land) moiety. The word 'maraiin' (*maraian, mareiin, maḏayin*) denotes certain rites performed in Arnhem Land, but is also used to mean 'sacred' or 'taboo'.

Polyphony occurs during mortuary, or mourning, ceremonies in eastern Arnhem Land when the independent voices of two or more clan song leaders ('songmen') may combine canonically. In *djawala* (mortuary) singing, as performed by Lardil men on Mornington Island (south-east of the Gulf of Carpentaria), male voices combine in 3rds, producing isometric polyphony in a chordal style. Partsongs, composed in aboriginal languages by men in Cape York, are sung mainly in 3rds and 5ths.

Closely allied to the number and length of repeated strings of sung syllables are the metrical patterns of the vocal part, in which terminal long notes are preceded by short and ultra-short notes. In some songs from south-eastern Arnhem Land (ex.4, *maraiin, duwa* moiety) and in songs from Cape York the long notes are longer than in songs nearer to the centre (area *C*) and further to the west (area *K*). *Wongga* songs and many songs in Cape York often begin with relatively long notes (ex.3).

Sachs wrote: 'in Australia, rhythmically free and independent singing is often accompanied by the rigid,

Ex.4 from *Nardili* ('Black cockatoo'), higher clan song, Milingimbi; rec. and transcr. A. Moyle

 = glottal tremor.

Ex.3 from individually owned song, Oenpelli; rec. and transcr. A. Moyle

♪ = a 'voiced' didjeridu tone.

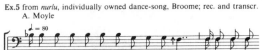

Ex.5 from *nurlu*, individually owned dance-song, Broome; rec. and transcr. A. Moyle

Ex.6 from *Walukulangu* dance-song series, Yuendumu; rec. and transcr. A. Moyle

♬ = indefinite pitch

uniform clatter of boomerangs struck against one another' (*Rhythm and Tempo*, 1953, p.43); Moyle's observations in north Australia, however, suggest that the 'detached' instrumental sounds provided by the singers themselves are controlled and related to their singing, which cannot therefore be entirely 'free and independent'. According to aural notations made of a *nurlu* (dance-song) recorded at Beagle Bay (area *K*) in 1968 (ex.5), and a *pulapa* (open dance-song) recorded at Yuendumu (area *C*) in 1967 (ex.6), the rhythmic relationship between the boomerang clapstick beating and each repeated string of syllables in the vocal part is strictly maintained. Such examples are the rule rather than the exception.

As seen in the accompanying map (see fig.1), an attempt has been made to plot the distribution of two classes of song called 'continuous' and 'discontinuous'. Continuous songs are characterized by repetitions of strings of similar syllables and divisions usually marked by descents in pitch; discontinuous songs contain either dissimilar strings of syllables, or similar strings of syllables interrupted by breaks in continuity, such as shouts and imitations of birdcalls, which are recognizably integrated with the structure of the song as a whole. It has been found that song series containing continuous items are more common nearer to the Tropic of Capricorn than in coastal regions further north. As defined, there are no continuous items in the Cape York Peninsula (area *Y*); in Arnhem Land (area *N*), songs so classed are cult songs. It would seem that continuous songs found in northern parts of Australia originated further south in desert regions.

The words of aboriginal songs, utterances normally inseparable from their song contexts, can present the collector with problems of recognition and translation. Some words are used only in songs or have dropped out of current speech; some name-words and words used as symbols cannot be understood without an appreciation of the song's context, mythical or mundane. Words used in normal speech may become distorted in singing through the omission and addition of syllables, vowel change and the alteration of normal patterns of emphasis. Sometimes song words have to be distinguished from 'sung talk', or from the singer's interpolations on the same pitch, which may serve as a running commentary on the song, expressions of personal discomfort, requests to bystanders ('get me a drink of water'), etc. The refrain of a play song from Yirrkala, north-eastern Arnhem Land, made by children about a favourite dog, consists of syllables imitating 'mouth sounds' practised by didjeridu players in the region: 'Ga-thirri dipthirri'. Occasionally, in individually owned songs and some clan songs, garbled English words appear requiring elucidation, for example *gabadima* ('cup of tea'), *brandala* ('verandah'), *wulmanili* ('old man') and *bribela* ('propeller').

As the expression of a deep attachment to the singer's own country the words of clan songs can reveal a variety of poetic forms and the vivid use of metaphor and imagery.

(*vi*) *Dance*. The diversity of the dance movements and the remarkable talents of some male dancers have attracted many film teams to northern parts of Australia, mainly to places in Arnhem Land. But spontaneous flashes of brilliance during long successions of dance items are difficult to capture on film. Eye-witness accounts have been given by Colin Simpson (*Adam in Ochre: Inside Aboriginal Australia*, Sydney, 1951) and by Beth Dean and Victor Carell. Male dancers, some now deceased, singled out for special mention by these writers include: Mosek (Wagatj people) of Delissaville (north-west *N*); Gilligan (Wagatj, related to Mosek) of Manbulloo (south-west *N*); and Ali (Tiwi) of Bathurst Island. To these should be added the names of Jolly Laiwonga (Ngalgbon) of Bamyili (central *N*) and Arrama and Malayu (Nunggubuyu) of Rose River (east *N*).

In his description of dancing filmed on Bathurst Island, Spencer referred to men with bodies bent forward, stamping furiously on the ground and at the same time striking their buttocks with open hands. In marked contrast are the springing leaps and flexible movements of *wongga* and *djanba* dancing by Wagatj, Garama and Djamingdjang men on the adjacent mainland (west *N*). Slow-stepping *balganya* dancers in west Kimberley, carrying large dancing boards of different kinds, suddenly 'freeze' with the periodic cessation of the singer's stick beats. Similar freezing in the movements of dancers and in the percussive song accompaniment has been observed in *galwangara* performances at Borroloola (south-east *N*). Field investigators reporting on dancing by both men and women include Catherine Berndt (1950), who drew attention to *kirdjir*, stylized movements that women in north-eastern Arnhem Land must learn before they can take part in *bunggul* (open clan dances) of this region; F. D. McCarthy (1964), who described dances filmed at Aurukun, Cape York; Jane Goodale, who discussed Tiwi dancing on Melville Island in its relation to song words and ceremonial context; Nancy Munn, who analysed *yawalyu* designs drawn in the sand or painted on the shoulders and chests of female participants in the *yawalyu* ceremony performed at Yuendumu (area *C*); and Elphine Allen (in Berndt and Phillips, 1973) who compared a range of movements executed by men of eastern and south-western Arnhem Land. Similarities have been noted in the stamping actions of Wagatj and Majali (Maeilli) groups (southwest), and a relationship has been seen between dancing on Groote Eylandt and in western Cape York, especially in the sliding step made with feet apart, knees bent and shaken. Body propulsion of this kind occurs in many types of aboriginal dancing, and may be recognized in cave drawings (see fig.6).

In general, female dancing is restricted in range. In some of the larger cult ceremonies women perform concurrently with men, though not always in the same part of the ground. The encircling of fires by women waving flaming torches is a notable feature in the *yabuduruwa* cult ceremony (south-east *N*). The exception to the general rule is on Bathurst and Melville Islands and in parts of the Kimberleys (area *K*) where women are as active on the dancing-ground as men. In *nurlu* (corroborees) in west Kimberley, they contribute to the special *ngarlbu*, or expiratory sounds, that begin and end the performance. In *wongga* and *gunborg* performances (west and north *N*) in which the chief participants are men, women dancers remain stationary in the background yet gracefully move their limbs and sway. Films were made by an expedition from Monash University in 1969 of Nunggubuyu and Warnindilyaugwa clan dancing (east *N* and Groote Eylandt) for the purpose of notating both music and movement, the latter according to the Benesh system. In its association with dance-song and ceremony, however, the study of Australian aboriginal dance has scarcely begun.

BIBLIOGRAPHY

W. B. Spencer: *Native Tribes of the Northern Territory of Australia* (London, 1914)

H. Basedow: 'Music and Dance', *The Australian Aboriginal* (Adelaide, 1925), 371

W. L. Warner: *A Black Civilization: a Social Study of an Australian Tribe* (New York and London, 1937) [incl. appx on 'Murngin Artifacts' and 'Mortuary Ceremony among the Western Clans of the Dua Moiety']

A. P. Elkin: 'Art and Ritual', 'Music and Dance', *The Australian Aborigines: How to Understand them* (Sydney and London, 1938, 4/1964), 222–66

C. H. Berndt: 'Expressions of Grief among Aboriginal Women', *Oceania*, xx (1950), 286–332

A. P. Elkin: 'Arnhem Land Music', *Oceania*, xxiv (1953), 81; xxv (1954–5), 74–121, 292–342; xxvi (1955–6), 59–152, 214

B. Dean and V. Carell: *Dust for the Dancers* (Sydney, 1955) [on initiation ceremonies of Australian aborigines]

R. A. Waterman: 'Music in Australian Aboriginal Culture: some Sociological and Psychological Implications', *Journal of Music Therapy*, v (1955), 40

T. A. Jones: 'Arnhem Land Music: a Musical Survey', *Oceania*, xxvi (1956), 252–339; xxviii (1957), 1–30

C. P. Mountford: *Records of the American–Australian Scientific Expedition to Arnhem Land*, i: *Art, Myth and Symbolism* (Melbourne, 1956)

A. P. Elkin: 'Australia and New Guinea Musical Records', *Oceania*, xxvii (1957), 313

E. A. Worms: 'The Poetry of the Yaoro and the Bad, Northwestern Australia', *Annali lateranensi*, xxi (1957), 213

A. H. Chisholm and others, eds.: 'Aborigines', *The Australian Encyclopedia*, i (Sydney, 1958)

A. P. Elkin and T. A. Jones: *Arnhem Land Music, North Australia* (Sydney, 1958) [incl. reprs. of *Oceania* articles]

A. M. Moyle: 'Sir Baldwin Spencer's Recordings of Australian Aboriginal Singing', *Memoirs of the National Museum of Victoria*, xxiv (1959), 7

F. D. McCarthy: 'The Cave Paintings of Groote Eylandt and Chasm Island', *Records of the American–Australian Scientific Expedition to Arnhem Land*, ii: *Anthropology and Nutrition* (Melbourne, 1960), 297–414

R. M. Berndt, ed.: *Australian Aboriginal Art* (Sydney, New York and London, 1964)

R. M. and C. H. Berndt: 'Art and Aesthetic Expression', *The World of the First Australians* (London and Sydney, 1964), 306–85

F. D. McCarthy: 'The Dancers of Aurukun', *Australian Natural History*, xiv (1964), 296

A. M. Moyle: 'Bara and Mamariga Songs on Groote Eylandt', *Musicology*, i (1964), 15

G. N. and A. O'Grady: 'Songs of Aboriginal Australia and Torres Strait', FE 4102 [disc notes]

T. A. Jones: 'Australian Aboriginal Music: the Elkin Collection's Contribution toward an Overall Picture', *Aboriginal Man in Australia*, ed. R. M. and C. H. Berndt (Sydney, 1965), 285–374

L. and B. Hiatt: 'Songs of Arnhem Land', AIAS/6 [disc notes]

A. M. Moyle: *A Handlist of Field Collections of Recorded Music in Australia and Torres Strait* (Canberra, 1966)

6. *Dancing figures in a cave painting at Inagurdurwil, near Oenpelli*

T. A. Jones: 'The Didjeridu', *SMA*, i (1967), 23–55

A. M. Moyle: 'Songs from the Northern Territory', IASM/001–005 [disc notes]

R. A. Waterman: 'Aboriginal Songs from Groote Eylandt, Australia', *Centennial Workshop on Ethnomusicology: Vancouver 1967*, 102

Australian Institute of Aboriginal Studies: *Catalogues of Tape Archive* (Canberra, 1967–72)

I. M. Crawford: *The Art of the Wandjina: Aboriginal Cave Paintings in Kimberley, Western Australia* (Melbourne and London, 1968)

A. M. Moyle: 'Aboriginal Music on Cape York', *Musicology*, iii (1968–9), 3

C. G. von Brandenstein: 'Tabi Songs of the Aborigines', *Hemisphere*, xiii (1969), 28

A. M. Moyle: 'Songs from Yarrabah', AIAS/7 [disc notes]

J. C. Goodale: *Tiwi Wives: a Study of the Women of Melville Island, North Australia* (Seattle and London, 1971)

A. M. Moyle: 'Source Materials: Aboriginal Music of Australia and New Guinea', *EM*, xv (1971), 81

D. J. Mulvaney and J. Golson, eds.: *Aboriginal Man and Environment in Australia* (Canberra, 1971)

J. Beckett and T. A. Jones: 'Traditional Music of Torres Strait', AIAS/11 [disc notes]

A. M. Moyle: 'Sound Films for Combined Notation: the Groote Eylandt Field Project, 1969', *YIFMC*, iv (1972), 104

R. M. Berndt and E. S. Phillips, eds.: *The Australian Aboriginal Heritage* (Sydney, 1973) [with 2 discs and colour slides]

E. J. Brandl: *Australian Aboriginal Paintings in Western and Central Arnhem Land* (Canberra, 1973)

R. Edwards and P. J. Ucko: 'Rock Art in Australia', *Nature* (1973), no.246, p.274

H. M. Groger-Wurm: *Australian Aboriginal Bark Paintings and their Mythological Interpretation* (Canberra, 1973)

N. D. Munn: *Walbiri Iconography: Graphic Representation and Cultural Symbolism in a Central Australian Society* (London, 1973)

R. M. Berndt: *Australian Aboriginal Religion*, i–iv (Leiden, 1974)

A. M. Moyle: *North Australian Music: a Taxonomic Approach to the Study of Aboriginal Song Performances* (diss., Monash U., 1974) [incl. detailed set of maps and lists of aboriginal words connected with instruments]

——: 'Pitch and Loudness Ambits in some North Australian Songs', *Selected Reports*, ii (1974), 17

T. A. Jones: 'The Traditional Music of the Australian Aborigines', *Music of Many Cultures: an Introduction*, ed. E. May (Berkeley, 1977)

3. ABORIGINAL MUSIC AND DANCE IN SOUTHERN AUSTRALIA. This section covers performances of music and, where possible, aspects of the associated dance, design and ceremonies of aboriginal people living south of the Tropic of Capricorn, that is in southern parts of Queensland, Northern Territory and Western Australia, and in the whole of New South Wales, Victoria, South Australia and Tasmania. In this vast area there are two main extant language and music groups: central Australian or Aranda-speaking; and Western Desert or Pitjantjara-speaking. These can be subdivided into approximately 40 Pitjantjara dialects and five Aranda ones. There are over 200 dialects in the remaining area covered in this survey. In the regions studied intensively, the distribution of differences in musical structures coincides with the linguistic boundaries; but very little recorded music is available for many of the known linguistic regions, a gap in knowledge which cannot now be filled because of the death of all indigenous speakers and performers.

As well as having many different tribal origins, aboriginal music now shows many different stages of acculturation. There are numbers of performers living in the sparsely populated desert areas and perpetuating their traditional music almost unchanged since before contact with white people. There are performers living on the outskirts of country towns who are basically tribal in musical orientation, but who introduce many non-traditional aspects. There are also aboriginal people living in cities, making and transmitting songs which, like their lives, are Europeanized in outward appearance, though not in actual content.

(i) *Tribal music*. There are certain elements of tribal music that remain constant throughout this large area. The music is basically vocal; in most places singing is syllabic, but in some lesser-known styles it is melismatic. Instruments are used almost exclusively for percussion effect (often related to the associated dance). The types of percussive accompaniment differ from one place to another but include paired sticks beaten together, a single stick, a stone or a shield beaten on a mound of earth, paired boomerangs beaten together, rasps, hand-clapping, foot-stamping, thigh-slapping, and a skin bundle beaten by hand. These last two are exclusively female forms of rhythmic accompaniment. Of the few instruments that are not percussive, both the bullroarer and the *ulbura* (*ilpirra*, 'trumpet') have supernatural rather than musical functions in performance: the bullroarer, for example, may be regarded as the voice of the sacred ancestor. The *ulbura*, used in central Australian aboriginal performances, is a hollow log about 60 cm long and 5 cm in diameter, usually decorated with special designs, and replaces the bullroarer in some sacred ceremonies. The sound is produced by singing through the instrument. Little is known of the traditional use or distribution of the folded-leaf whistle or the blown-reed pipe, both noted but not recorded in sound by observers along the River Murray in south-eastern Australia. The didjeridu, essentially a rhythmic instrument, is not found at all in southern Australia.

In all areas song is understood to be a powerful agent in influencing non-musical events; its use for such purposes as rain charms, love-magic and increase rites indicates this. There is evidence that among many Australian groups song is believed to enable performers to draw on supernatural powers left within the soil in ancient times by the sacred ancestral people. It is only by the correct presentation, simultaneously, of all the technical features of the song that this power becomes accessible to the performers. Because the power may be used for either good or evil, strict control is maintained over the teaching of these potent songs; a system of exclusion operates which results in only the oldest and wisest people knowing them.

Song is important for social control. In all localities the wrongdoer is likely to have his misdemeanours publicized in song. The talented (particularly the hunters) may also be given such public attention. Songs are important for educating children in both musical and social matters. More advanced education is primarily through songs which perpetuate the laws and moral codes of each community.

Myths about the 'beginning of time', when sky and earth alone existed and were without feature, differ from place to place but are essentially the same throughout Australia. Ancestral beings emerged from the earth and during their life created the landscape of their particular area and populated it. The Kangaroo ancestor created both the animals of his species and the humans belonging to the Kangaroo totem who consider themselves to be directly related to this animal. The original ancestor is portrayed in the songs sometimes as a human being, sometimes in his animal form, and the actual song is said to have been made by each ancestor and taught by him to his human offspring. Such a song contains a full account of the ancestor's life and therefore of the beginning of present human life and is called by some peoples a 'history' song. It is tied to successive geographic sites and often crosses boundaries between tribal groups. When correctly performed it contains all the latent power that enables the present population to draw on the inseminating forces left at particular sites by the ancestor, though such potent sections of the song are secret and are omitted in open performances of the history.

There are many different song styles in southern Australia, the main extant ones being the central Australian (Aranda, Arunta) and Western Desert (Pitjantjara or Pitjantjatjara, and Bidjandjara or Bidjandjadjara) styles, on which the discussion of tribal music will centre. These are closely related, but have minor differences which are emphasized by performers.

(ii) Common structural elements in the music of central Australia and the Western Desert. Most available information on technical musical terms is from Pitjantjara-speaking peoples and helps to explain their attitude to music.

'Inma' means music, but not the sound alone; it includes behavioural responses and mythical associations. It is used in conjunction with other words to differentiate important aspects such as 'proper' (traditional) songs as opposed to newly composed ones. Beating likewise involves a series of terms: one for the correct accompaniment of a ceremonial event such as the quivering of the dancers; another for describing the beating technique; yet another for the speed.

The word 'mayu' may be translated as either 'flavour' or 'sound'. When used in association with the songs transmitting the 'history' of a totemic ancestor, 'inma mayu' literally means the total sound linked with a specific ancestor, but is generally used to refer to the melodic shape which is a permanent record of the 'flavour' or personality of the ancestor. (The term used by Aranda people for the same concept has the general meaning 'scent'.) Associated with melodic terms are those for vocal register, particularly one which indicates a change of register without influencing the 'flavour' of a melody (i.e. is analogous to transposition).

There is a series of terms for dancing: dancing with song accompaniment; dancing with beating; stamping to produce percussive effect. Many describe the position of the dancer: 'head on one side'; 'rolling hips'. Others relate to the design painted on the dancer, important being the reference to 'painting the song' (i.e. putting into visual form the essence of *inma*). There is no specific word for rhythm; *mayu* can be used for rhythm, but unless so indicated is kept for melody. The only words which hint at rhythmic structure concern syncopation and accentuation.

The series of words associated with singing includes reference to singing in unison; divided parts (rare); wailing; singing on an intake of breath (necessary in secret songs to maintain the continuous connection with the supernatural power source); and two groups singing simultaneously, the one presenting the 'history' verses, the other singing the appropriate verses for 'painting the song'.

These words give some idea of the aboriginal musician's attitude to technical aspects of performing, but for a clearer picture of particular musical structures they must be correlated with analytical material available from research, which often reveals techniques for which no indigenous terms can be found.

Melody. There are three separate, closely related aspects of melody: melodic shape in general, particular melodies, and the intervallic structure on which these are based. Melodic shape in both the central Australian and Western Desert styles is one of continuous descent, with a slight rise followed by further descent – terraced melodies. Within this broad framework there are many ways in which the various descents can occur. The essential feature which distinguishes the 'flavour' of a particular totemic ancestor is the pitch distance between main pivot points and the length of time spent within the ambit of these tonal pivots; the individual decorations that occur in the descent from upper to lower extremes of each section are variable. The processes of melodic movement appear to differ slightly in men's and women's songs. In the former, the time spent at any one tonal point is not fixed, but is determined by a certain number of groups of notes arising from the poetic metre (see fig.7). In women's songs the shift of melodic position is governed by actual duration: either equal time is spent in two different pitch ranges, or a quarter of the total time required for a long rhythmic pattern falls within one tonal area, with the remaining three-quarters in the other tonal area (or vice versa). This division can be measured in a recorded performance by using a stopwatch; presumably it is determined during performance by the number of regular pulses present in each pitch range.

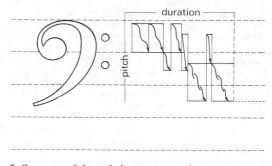

7. Structure of the melodic movement of a men's song as shown on an enlarged bass staff

It is the broad definition of the melodic movement towards firmly established pitch frequencies that constitutes the 'flavour' of the ancestor. This melodic pattern crosses tribal and language barriers tracing the ancestor's mythical travels. The skilled performer gains some information on the finer melodic requirements from the metre of the opening solo of a verse, always performed by the song leader. He knows then the type of melodic movement appropriate within the various melodic regions, for instance, on which metres it is usual to repeat notes, on which to place melismas. As a result the group, knowing the ancestor being commemorated and the opening of the song text as presented by the song leader, are equipped through many years of training to join in the performance, and agree remarkably with one another in an apparently spontaneous rendering which allows flexibility.

As a basis of all melodic movement, there is the accepted generative interval or intervals forming the series from which the various melodic steps are made. While Jones and Moyle assumed Europeanized interval structure in the areas of their work, Ellis (1965, 1967) suggested that this structure does not apply in central Australia or in the Western Desert, although it may in the south-east of Australia, where extant recordings are of too poor a quality to measure accurately. The structures analysed by Ellis indicate that the basic interval from which all others are derived is one of a small but constant difference in the number of cycles per second between the pitch frequencies of successive steps in the series. This constant difference generates a series of equidistant frequencies, some of which are selected for the principal notes. This work is controversial, for it implies that simple ratio intervals are not the only basis for the perception of two sounds; hence different physiological explanations from those normally accepted may be required to account for pitch perception if these research findings are valid.

The patterning taking place in relation to melody may be summarized as follows: from the basic series of culturally accepted intervals is formed a melodic framework which is characteristic of a particular sacred being. Its elaboration depends on separate rules which can be gleaned from the song leader's opening solo. The selection of the melody itself conforms with the overall characteristic of the central and Western Desert descending melodic line.

Rhythm. The rhythm of the melody is governed by the structure of the song text with which it is linked. There may be several different rhythmic settings for the one text, one a standard form and others classified by performers as variants which may sometimes be used. The most conspicuous feature of rhythmic construction is the beating accompaniment. This may proceed in regularly spaced beats which are separated by three units of the basic pulse; that is, if the basic smallest division is a quaver, then the beating proceeds in dotted crotchets. There are several variants of this, including the 'slower' form (shown in ex.7).

Ex.7 Types of beating accompaniment; rec. and transcr. C. and A. Ellis

(a) Usual beating (irrespective of rhythm of song-line)

(b) 'Slower' beating

(c) Form often used in children's songs

Strehlow noted the existence of 'songless sacred performances' in central Australia. These occasionally occur in men's secret ritual, singers participating in the total act only by beating a stone or shield on the ground. Beating is here shown to have an individual role; it may not be right, therefore, to consider it subordinate in the structure of a sung performance. The accentuation of the song line does not necessarily coincide with the occurrence of a beat in the rhythmic accompaniment. There is some evidence to suggest that these two are deliberately opposed to one another, and that it is only at key points in the cycle that the two will coincide. Polyrhythm therefore exists between the beating accompaniment and the accentuation of the singing.

The text of a song is given a rhythmic shape different from the spoken form, which always places the accent on the first syllable of each word. Some vowels are also altered. An example of the spoken form of a song text is shown underneath the sung form in ex.8. The sung form need not start at the beginning of the text in any particular performance. The masking of verbal information is more deliberate in secret songs, but follows the same principles as in this children's song.

Ex.8 Typical text with rhythmic setting; rec. and transcr. C. and A. Ellis

[Sung] tji - tji tju-ku-tju - ku   pi-lu - ka-ku ya - nai
[Spoken] tjitji   tjukutjuku   pilukaku   yanu

tji - tji tju-ku-tju - ku   pi-lu - ka-ku ya - nai

The bullocks move away from the small children,
leaving many tracks by the water's edge as they go.

The rhythmic pattern established in this way is structurally important, and the text may not be shifted in relation to it. It is constantly repeated in a verse until the melodic line has reached its closing point. Successive verses in the one long series are interrelated and developed through reference to several primary rhythmic patterns: thus songs with many hundreds of verses, of which most will have individual rhythmic patterns, can be divided into large sections by relating patterns which have taken either rhythmic cells or larger rhythmic phrases from one or another of the primary rhythmic patterns. Those verses drawing together rhythmic material from two primary patterns often function as bridges between sections. The interplay of rhythmic patterns developed from the primary forms is emphasized throughout the performance. The form, then, could be said to develop from the primary rhythmic patterns: either those presented at the outset of a performance, or those that find their most concise statement in the verses that are the most important from a non-musical viewpoint – usually those occurring as the climax of a section or entire series.

The text itself is always related to the extra-musical significance of the events being recounted in the myth. Information from some performers indicates that where a language boundary has been crossed in the myth (and therefore in the song) the performers may decode the specific information in the song text by reference to its rhythm. In the long, history songs there are some verses concerned with one place only. These must be sung by residents of that locality, usually in their own dialect. There are others known as 'travelling' verses, which seem to have well-known and repeatable rhythmic patterns understood to describe, for example, sandhill country. The rhythm, but not the text, crosses language boundaries. Verses 'naming' a particular sacred site are very powerful and each has a separate rhythmic pattern known only by the trusted.

Interpretation of texts. A song text itself, although it would appear to be the least ambiguous aspect of *inma*, carries several different possible interpretations. Translation and explanation of aboriginal song texts always lead to considerable confusion. The explanation of any text may not be obvious from its actual translation; where a translation is sought from a person not present at the performance from which a recording has been made, it is often necessary to explain to the translator where the song was performed, and under what circumstances. There are a number of reasons for this. A song text may be a general description, for example, of a dry riverbed (usually called a 'creek'); it takes on specific meaning in the history songs only when the sequence within the total performance is known, since events in the lives of the ancestors are re-created in the order in which they were supposed originally to have occurred. However, during the total life of the ancestor, re-created in an extended song cycle, the parts of which are performed at many different sites, many creekbeds similar to the original may require description. In such cases exactly the same 'travelling' verse may be used, but the significance may be quite different on each occasion. The actual translation remains a very brief description of a creekbed, but provided that all the necessary information on place of performance, stage of proceedings and performers themselves is known, the explanation may be quite long and complex. It conveys its actual significance only by presupposing an intimate knowledge of the total history.

For any one ceremonial verse there can be different levels of meaning, and the level offered as explanation of the translated text depends on the degree of knowledge, age and social status of both the translator and the person to whom the explanation is given. In one example the text refers to two emus travelling along a creekbed. The first level of meaning is the exoteric one; it merely describes the scene. The second level of meaning is erotic, and will usually be known only by one sex; it presupposes that the women in this performance knew that the two emus were in fact Emu Women, and that they were attempting to attract a man. The third level is esoteric and is known only to the most knowledgeable of the group: in this case, the singers were 'holding the song at Indulkana', that is, they understood that, by the performance of this verse at this point in the ceremony, they were 'naming' and drawing on the power of the sacred site to which the two ancestral Emu Women belonged.

The texts themselves are at times deliberately ambiguous. Not only are the syllables misplaced so as to be unintelligible to those not familiar with the method of encoding, but once decoded they sometimes yield grammatical structures which give rise to double meanings. These factors make direct verbal understanding difficult and show the importance of knowing the process of encoding information in musical forms.

Form. Rhythm and melody operate together in the music of the Western Desert and central Australia by a clearly understood overlay of patterns. There is the isorhythmic pattern, either identical in length to the verbal song text or, through several repetitions, encompassing the entire song text without overlap. This rhythmic pattern is regularly repeated for the duration of the melodic contour, itself built (as described earlier) from a combination of culturally defined characteristics. Underneath this, as a binding agent, is the regularly recurring beating pattern. In combination there is the added dimension of polyrhythm. Directly associated with these overlaid patterns are the designs, dances and other ceremonial paraphernalia forming part of the concept of *inma*.

In the complete performance there is an immense overlap of information which is at times quite incomprehensible to the uninitiated. In one performance recorded in the field and subsequently analysed in detail, those dances with designs to represent specific meaning occurred in conjunction with rhythmic patterns and song texts that referred to quite different incidents in the story. Those verses used for accompanying the painting of body designs contained rhythmic references to events in the story other than the events to be presented in the dance for which the design was being prepared, whereas the song text itself merely referred to women dancing. There was constant simultaneous cross-reference; at any one point the rhythmic construction might refer to one segment of the story, design to another, portrayal in dance to yet another. Multi-dimensional description of a performance (Ellis, 1970) shows the intricacy of overlay of design, song text, melodic structures and rhythmic patterns which can only be suggested in fig.8 (p.726).

(*iii*) *Songs for ages and stages.* Songs for each age group within the community have their own structures and functions, all basically covered by the above description.

Songs associated with birth are those used when the life of either mother or child is in danger, or to induce labour. These are not performed for researchers because of their inherent power. The texts of lullabies often stress fear; some simply reiterate, through the repeated rhythmic pattern, a simple phrase such as 'do not cry'.

Songs that children make themselves and pass on to one another may have disappeared because of the contact with European education. Only a few have been recorded. They all have short rhythmic patterns with only two main accents; most consist of two widely separated notes (an interval of approximately a 5th, or even an octave). Melodically they are different from children's songs created by adults, which are diminutive forms of adult songs and are made for training boys and girls, both in musical techniques and in the expected behaviour and extra-musical effects of songs; they differentiate between the sexes, even though some may be heard by both.

Songs of adults encompass almost the entire field of music-making. The more powerful the song, the more intricate is the overlay of patterning, to the point where variation is impossible without disruption of the interlocking process. In general, women's songs have a narrower melodic range and less rhythmic complexity than men's songs, a difference already apparent in the separate songs taught to girls and to boys. Men's secret songs often deliberately superimpose selected sections from two separate series.

Songs for death are directed to the soul of the departed; they concern his totemic affiliation and seek to allow the soul to return to its rightful spiritual home and thus become available for future reincarnation. Other songs performed at the death of a close relative may include, as well as the stylized mourning wailing, songs intended to identify the 'murderer'.

(*iv*) *Regional differentiation of song styles.* In all the song styles in Australia south of the Tropic of Capricorn, the quality of voice used by performers is the foremost means of distinguishing songs from different areas, both for performers and for outside observers. Strehlow quoted his northern Aranda informants as commenting:

Our western friends . . . always squeal like babies . . . when they are singing their chants; and in the same way they enjoy the whistling of tiny bullroarers during their ceremonies. We are different. We sing like

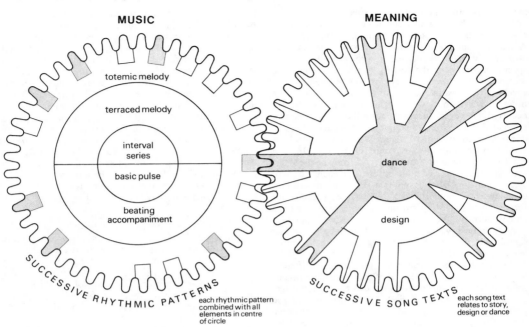

MUSIC

totemic melody

terraced melody

interval
series

basic pulse

beating
accompaniment

SUCCESSIVE RHYTHMIC PATTERNS

each rhythmic pattern
combined with all
elements in centre
of circle

MEANING

dance

design

SUCCESSIVE SONG TEXTS

each song text
relates to story,
design or dance

8. Interlocking of structures

grown men, with strong throats; and all our bullroarers are large and hum low during our ceremonies. We don't like men squeaking and wailing like infants.

In some places the voice is deliberately distorted, either by plucking the thumbs on the chin or beating the chest while singing, or by using a rasping quality to distort its production. In other places the range of voice differs as well as the quality of production, which may be 'nasal' or 'open throated'.

Styles of rhythmic accompaniment (e.g. sticks beaten together or one stick beaten on the ground) are another means of distinguishing regional differences, and as such have been mapped by Moyle (1966). There are marked territorial differences in structure, ranging from the free rhythm and undulating melodic line (often associated with melismatic setting of the text) found in most coastal areas and along the Murray Valley, to the rigid structures of the central Australian and Western Desert musics described earlier. Ornamentation also differs, more elaborate decoration of the basic melodic shape occurring in the regions with undulating melodies rather than in those with the terraced melodies. These changes in style are not gradual, but are contained within clearly marked geographical boundaries.

The distribution of different styles in South Australia has been mapped (Ellis, 1966): there are five regional differences shown in this restricted area. That from the Western Desert fully described earlier is characterized by a descending melodic line, with a range usually greater than an octave and a definite tonic (defined both by its position at the end of each melody and by the fact that it is the most frequently used note) at the lower extreme of the range; isorhythm and frequent syncopation; ornamentation in the form of exaggerated emphasis or rapid alternation of two notes; and a mostly low and sonorous vocal quality. The western peripheral song

style is characterized by greater use of the upper notes of the range, not necessarily at the start of the verse and often approached from the lower notes, but still with a definite tonic as the lowest main note; both isorhythmic and free rhythms; and light tenor voice. The Lakes song style has as its dominant characteristics some form of voice distortion; a descending melodic line usually of very narrow range, with a definite tonic on the lowest main note; both isorhythmic and free rhythm and an impression of slow tempos; an unusual ornament, consisting of the note itself, the note below and the note approximately a minor 3rd above; and a low and sonorous vocal quality (when not distorted). The north-eastern song style has only one additional characteristic to that of western peripheral songs, a husky quality in the voice. Presumably these two were originally one large musical region which was split by the infiltration of a later song form. The south-eastern song style is characterized by a highly ornamented upper note which never occurs at the start of the song, but at a central or final climax; no clear tonic; free rhythm, with some changes of tempo; many ornaments, particularly on upper notes; and a clear tenor voice.

It is possible that central Australian song types, which in South Australia divide to form the Western Desert and the Lakes styles and which in their oldest form are found in many isolated regions in Australia (including Tasmania), were introduced into Australia from a culture different from those of the south-eastern song types (found throughout south-eastern South Australia, Victoria, southern New South Wales and possibly Tasmania). It is also possible that the western peripheral and north-eastern styles are a hybrid form resulting from the fusion of the central Australian song type with the south-eastern one, and that their previous distribution has been disturbed by infiltration of a newer form of central Australian song.

Moyle (1966) covered the whole of Australia in her survey. Part of six regions listed by her fall south of the Tropic of Capricorn, and two others – those covering Victoria and Tasmania – wholly within it. She noted that much of the information from the latter two areas remains speculative; it is even doubtful whether or not Tasmania is a separate musical region from the extant recorded material. For the central and western-central areas she gave as principal characteristics the correspondence between verbal units and rhythmic formulae; regular verbal repetition, which exceeds melodic repetition; song accompaniment with sticks, boomerangs or, in the west coastal region, rasp or friction instruments. In her work on Tasmanian music, Moyle categorized two styles from the very old recordings available (made in 1889 and 1903); 'legato' and 'corroboree' styles. The former seems to have little similarity with mainland music, whereas the latter has many features reminiscent of Western Desert music.

Of the areas covered by Jones (1965), six are within the scope of this survey. General features noted include five- or four-note scales; exceptions are in central Murchison in Western Australia and in Woodenbong in New South Wales, which have respectively six- and seven-note scales predominating. Western Australian examples are also conspicuous for unusually large compass. Scales are chasmatonic (disjunct) except in the New South Wales examples, which are mainly diatonic hemitonal. Idiophones are used in all areas. Jones considered vocal quality and techniques to be similar throughout Australia, with the exception of 'extreme gutteralness and overwrought dynamism' in some central Australian singing. Singing in parallel octaves occurred, in the examples he studied, in central Murchison and central Australia.

To sum up, tribal music has broad similarities throughout a region where there are many differentiations of style. It is possible to examine in depth the music of central Australia and the Western Desert since these areas, having been subject to the least alien influence, have maintained unaltered large segments of their traditional performances, and display a complicated overlay of patterning and economy of form that requires great length and depth of learning from the performer. The ages and stages of this learning and its structural development, as well as its behavioural implications for the individual as he proceeds from birth to old age and death, can be observed. Throughout his time in the physical world the individual turns to music as the most powerful force for dealing with all the vicissitudes of life which cannot be met by practical measures; it is the link with his eternal self.

(v) *Transition.* Strangely, researchers have often failed to collect modified tribal materials which would assist examination of the changes of structure in an evolving process; rather they have preferred 'authentic' forms. In analysing transitional forms, not only the degree of acculturation but also the original tribal source of the music are important.

The first step in transition occurs with the production of new songs in the traditional idioms. Composition was rare in central Australia and the Western Desert, since all 'proper' songs were believed to be originally the work of the ancestral beings. The present new songs are said to come to their maker in a dream and he must

attempt, once awake, to realize them and teach them to others. There are recorded examples of both children's and women's songs produced in this way. These new songs are probably being made to fill gaps that have occurred through loss of the traditional forms.

Songs not far removed from the tribal idiom are rarely accompanied, other than by the traditional beating. The main change in central Australian and Western Desert songs seems to be that the overlay of patterns is becoming less intricate. Sometimes the interval structure is recognizably more European than the tribal form. In songs evolving from other tribal forms, the general shape of the melody and ornamentation are preserved, but melodic movement, interval usage and rhythm are Europeanized.

The textual content of the songs can be an interesting indication of previous experiences. A number of researchers have found themselves the subject of newly created songs. In one case, a 20-year interval elapsed between the visit of researchers collecting urine specimens in jam tins and the recognition of the source of the resultant song series and ceremonial which centred on jam tins. Many of the transitional songs mention aeroplanes, bicycles, motor cars, mail trucks and trains, occasionally attempting to reproduce some relevant sounds.

There are often descriptions of events not witnessed by performers themselves, but transmitted from another person. One, sung in Wemba-wemba, a River Murray language, tells of the principal character's escape from state policy by crossing the Victoria–New South Wales border (the River Murray). The details were known to the singer because his grandfather, the composer, had taught the song to him. Similarly, a recording from the Flinders Ranges in South Australia, sung in Wailpi, recounts the delay of the mail train coming from Adelaide in the early days. The particular event, captured in song, was then passed on through a new tradition, the singer having learnt it from the songmaker. Transitional songs are affected both by the original tribal source and by the type of culture contact. Often the new form itself becomes traditional and is passed from one generation to the next.

(vi) *Europeanized songs.* Many older aboriginal performers who have no tribal affiliation and speak only English have had close musical contact with white folksingers. Often these aboriginal singers know local folksongs forgotten by most white Australians, including songs referring to the country of emigration as well as to local events. Frequently the singer, who normally sings without accompaniment, has parodied the original text.

One form which occurs among aboriginal but not white folksingers is the 'coon song', presumably transmitted from other dark-skinned peoples outside Australia. This form is usually superficially lighthearted about race relations, but underneath there is a strong element of protest:

> Although it's not my colour, I'm feeling mighty blue;
> I've got a lot of trouble, and I'll tell it all to you.
> I'm certainly disgusted with life, and that's a fact,
> Because me 'air is woolly and because my skin is black.
> CHORUS:
> Then it's coon, coon, coon, I wish my colour would fade;
> Coon, coon, coon, I'd like a different shade.
> Coon, coon, coon, morning, night or noon.
> I wish I was a white man, instead of a coon, coon, coon.

New songs, influenced greatly by the modern cowboy idiom and invariably accompanied by guitar, are found mainly among city aboriginal people. Generally they are of two types. The one, regretting the passing of the old ways, can be summed up in the opening words of such a song: 'Who am I? What am I? And what will happen until I die?'. The other, the direct protest song, constantly refers to ill-treatment by police and poor living conditions. The main interest of Europeanized aboriginal songs lies in their texts, although social and cultural deductions can also be made from the musical structures used.

BIBLIOGRAPHY

A. M. Moyle: 'Two Native Song-styles Recorded in Tasmania', *Papers and Proceedings of the Royal Society of Tasmania*, xciv (1960), 73

C. J. Ellis: 'Pre-instrumental Scales', *EM*, ix (1965), 126 [with technical appx by B. Seymour]

T. A. Jones: 'Australian Aboriginal Music: the Elkin Collection's Contribution toward an Overall Picture', *Aboriginal Man in Australia*, ed. R. M. and C. H. Berndt (Sydney, 1965), 285–374

C. J. Ellis: 'Aboriginal Songs of South Australia', *MMA*, i (1966), 137–90

A. M. Moyle: *A Handlist of Field Collections of Recorded Music in Australia and Torres Strait* (Canberra, 1966)

C. J. Ellis: 'The Pitjantjara Kangaroo Song from Karlga', *MMA*, ii (1967), 171–265

——: 'The Role of the Ethnomusicologist in the Study of Andagarinja Women's Ceremonies', *MMA*, v (1970), 76–206

T. G. H. Strehlow: *Songs of Central Australia* (Sydney, 1971)

ANDREW D. McCREDIE (1), TREVOR A. JONES (II, 1)
ALICE M. MOYLE (II, 2), CATHERINE I. ELLIS (II, 3)

Austral Islands. See POLYNESIA, §4 (ii), and PACIFIC ISLANDS.

Austral String Quartet. Australian quartet. It was formed in 1958 by principals of the Sydney SO: Donald Hazelwood, Ronald Ryder, Ronald Cragg and Gregory Elmaloglou; when Ryder died in 1974 Peter Ashley succeeded him. It was disbanded in 1977. The quartet was foremost among Australian chamber groups and compared favourably with European and American ensembles in performances of the standard repertory. It gave authoritative performances of works by Australian composers, including Sculthorpe, Werder, Butterley and Banks, of which it made several valuable recordings. As well as touring extensively in Australia the quartet appeared in Britain in 1965, North America, Europe, Israel and India in 1972, and Japan, the USA and Europe in 1975.

ANN CARR-BOYD

Austria (Ger. Österreich).

I. Art music. II. Folk music.

I. Art music. This article deals with the area of the Republic of Austria, comprising the federated provinces (*Länder*) of Lower Austria, Upper Austria, Burgenland, Carinthia, Salzburg, Styria, Tyrol, Vienna and Vorarlberg. For the remaining successor states to the Danube monarchy, *see* CZECHOSLOVAKIA, HUNGARY and YUGOSLAVIA; *see also* GERMANY for the period up to 1806.

Prehistoric signal pipes, musical instruments and iconographical representations of musical activities from the Hallstatt Period (1000–500 BC) and the Roman occupation testify to the antiquity of Austrian civilization. The development of a musical culture from the beginning of the Middle Ages has essentially been determined by Austria's geographical position in the centre of Europe, its Alpine terrain, the coming of Christianity and the settlement by Germanic tribes. External influences, especially of the races at its borders – the Latin peoples, the Slavs and the

Magyars – further affected the area's cultural evolution. Although each province has a place in Austria's cultural history, the musical centres have always been the cities of Salzburg and Vienna.

1. The early period. 2. Humanism and the Renaissance. 3. The Baroque era. 4. Pre-Classicism and Classicism. 5. Romanticism. 6. The 20th century.

1. THE EARLY PERIOD. Christianity brought plainsong to the country and a *cantor moderatus* is recorded in the 5th century. After the turbulent period of migration St Rupert built the monastery of St Peter in Salzburg shortly before 700, and Bishop Virgil, a Scot who maintained contact with his homeland throughout his episcopacy, founded the cathedral in 774. Both institutions were at the centre of chant development in Salzburg when it was elevated to an archbishopric in 798 and given the task of converting the *Ostmark* ('Eastern March': Europe east of Austria and Germany). The *cantus romanus*, in the form prescribed by the Carolingian reforms, was disseminated from Salzburg under Archbishop Arno (785–821), a friend of Alcuin, while associations with St Gall and Metz resulted in the introduction of the types of neumes used there. The monastery of Kremsmünster was settled in 777 from Mondsee, the oldest Benedictine house in Upper Austria (748), itself a daughter house of Monte Cassino. Numerous other monastic establishments were responsible for the knowledge and dissemination of the chant repertory from the 11th century onwards. Manuscripts using neumes from Austrian monasteries date from the 9th and 10th centuries. Those of importance to liturgical history in the Alpine region include a plenary missal of 1136 from the monastery of St Paul in Carinthia (*D-Sl*, Cod.bibl.fol.20), copied from a Kremsmünster original, and a 12th-century gradual with Metz neumes from the monastery of Seckau in Styria (*A-Gu* 807), which shows the adaptation of the original Roman version to the German chant tradition. A 13th-century breviary from St Lambrecht (*Gu* 134) contains the oldest version of the Corpus Christi hymn *Pange lingua* with neumes and tonary note names. The ancient *Christ ist erstanden* is the outstanding example of vernacular sacred song; the earliest complete version of the text with neumes dates from 1325 (*KN* 1213). Paraliturgical music includes sacred dramas, such as the Klosterneuburg Easter play and the six Easter plays from Erlau in Carinthia, the sixth of which shows remarkable similarities to the Donaueschingen *Marienklage*, as well as rhymed Offices and hymns. In addition to the fact that there was practical musical instruction, a number of music treatises of Austrian provenance indicate that *musica theoretica* appeared in the quadrivium in monastic, cathedral and parish schools, and eventually at the University of Vienna (founded 1365). There is, nevertheless, only one well-known medieval Austrian music theorist, Engelbert of Admont.

Minnesang was established principally at the courts of the Babenbergs in Vienna, of Archbishop Eberhard II in Salzburg and of Duke Bernhard von Sponheim in St Veit, Carinthia. Numerous Minnesinger are known by name, the most important of whom are Walther von der Vogelweide, who claimed that he learnt to sing and write poetry in Austria, and the 'courtly village poet' Neidhart von Reuenthal, who integrated indigenous and popular elements into Minnesang. Only the names and some of the poems survive of most Austrian Minnesinger, for

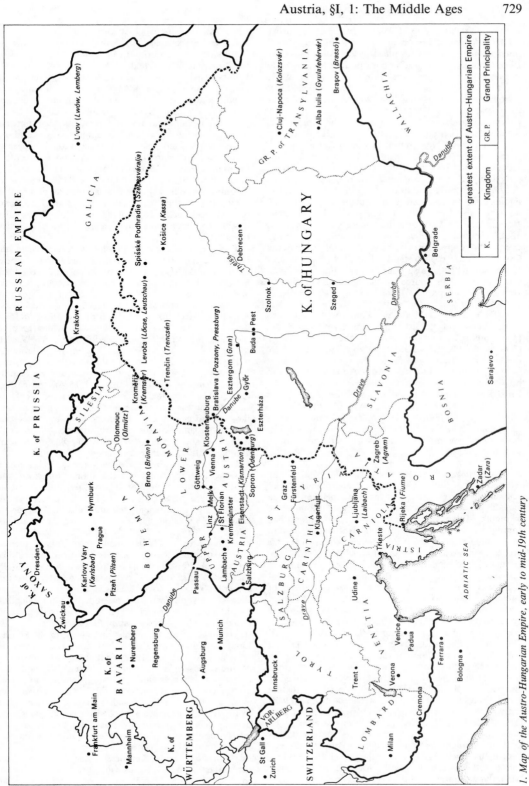

1. Map of the Austro-Hungarian Empire, early to mid-19th century

example Ulrich von Liechtenstein. Hugo von Montfort, a late exponent of Minnesang in the Vorarlberg, wrote poems which were set to music by his court musician, Bürk Mangolt. The last important figures in secular medieval monody were the Monk of Salzburg at the court of Archbishop Pilgrim II (1365–96) and the Tyrolean knight, Oswald von Wolkenstein. Both are also responsible for a small body of mensural polyphony and thereby stand at the threshold of an independent German polyphonic style. Traces of Ars Antiqua and Ars Nova music survive in German manuscripts of the time and seem to have been a strong influence on the growth of indigenous German polyphony: Perotin's organum *Sederunt* appears in an outdated and mixed notation (*Gu* 756 from the Seckau monastery), motets and a conductus in Franconian notation, also three French chansons (Stiftsbibliothek, Vorau, MSS 23, 380) and the ballade *Fies de moy* (*M* 486). Several French and Italian Ars Nova compositions appear as contrafacta among the works of Oswald von Wolkenstein. The 'Mondsee-Wiener Liederhandschrift', also known as the 'Spörlsches Liederbuch', is the source for various forms of secular vernacular polyphony from about 1400 and in particular for that of the Monk of Salzburg. Only when King Friedrich III (later Emperor) summoned Netherlands and English musicians to his court did polyphony begin to develop rapidly: the 'Trent Codices' (*I-TRmn* 87–92, *TRmd* 93) from the South Tyrol are the most important evidence for the rapid development of polyphony in mid-15th-century Austria. The oldest polyphonic arrangement of *Christ ist erstanden* is by Friedrich's *cantor principalis*, Johannes Brassart, a member of the Kapelle of Friedrich's predecessor, Albrecht II (*d* 1439), the first of an unbroken line of Germanic HABSBURG kings and emperors. The development of music in Austria is inseparably linked with this dynasty.

2. HUMANISM AND THE RENAISSANCE. Polyphony reached its first peak under Emperor Maximilian I, who ordered the reorganization of the Hofkapelle at Vienna in 1498, under the direction of Georg Slatkonia. The members of the Kapelle included such distinguished composers as Isaac, Senfl and Hofhaimer, whom Maximilian retained from the Innsbruck Kapelle of his predecessor, Archduke Sigismund of the Tyrol. The German Gesellschaftslied, which these composers cultivated alongside their other works, is the earliest significant German contribution to the history of polyphony, and soon became popular outside court circles. A collection of German polyphonic songs and quodlibets was published in Vienna in 1544 by Wolfgang Schmeltzl, schoolmaster at the Schottenstift. The work of Conradus Celtis led to Vienna becoming a centre of humanism; one of the results in music was to increase the importance of the text in polyphonic song, such as in the homophonic humanist odes performed in imitation of classical style with regard to the textual metre. The earliest example is a chorus form Celtis's festival play *Ludus Dianae* (1501), performed in Linz for Maximilian I; this genre was developed by composers in the circle known as the Sodalitas Litteraria Danubiana (which included Petrus Tritonius, Benedictus Ducis, Wolfgang Grefinger, Hofhaimer and Senfl), and was diffused in the form of school songs. Netherlands musicians became increasingly prominent

when Arnold von Bruck succeeded Heinrich Finck in 1527 as Kapellmeister at the Viennese court of Ferdinand I, a grandson of Maximilian I and the first of the Austrian line of Habsburgs. Other Netherlanders who later held the post included Maessens, Vaet, Monte and Lambert de Sayve; numerous singers, teachers and organists at the imperial court, such as Buus and Luython, also came from the Netherlands.

The contemporaneous flowering of instrumental music for domestic use resulted in intabulations and lute pieces of the kind written by Hans Judenkünig, who spent his last years in Vienna. A mid-16th-century German organ tablature has survived (Landesarchiv, Klagenfurt, Sign.4/3), containing works by Senfl, Josquin, Verdelot and La Rue as well as anonymous pieces. It probably originated in one of the Carinthian monasteries which was dissolved under Joseph II's edict; it is in a neat alphabetic notation and may be the earliest of its kind.

The Flemish influence greatly increased when the Habsburg territories were further divided among the heirs of Ferdinand I (*d* 1564). Thus Innsbruck and Graz again became Habsburg residences, each with its own Kapelle, and developed into cultural centres of the greatest influence and importance. Outstanding members of the Kapelle of Archduke Ferdinand of the Tyrol (*d* 1595) were Hollander, Regnart and Utendal, while the most distinguished musicians employed by Archduke Karl II in Graz were de Sayve and Cleve, who wrote 20 polyphonic settings of chorale tunes, including some of Protestant origins; they were published in Andre Gigler's *Gesang Postille* (1569 and 1574), the earliest music volume printed in Styria. The sacred works of such composers spread beyond court circles and into the monasteries, as demonstrated by surviving choirbooks and inventories. Archduchess Magdalena's Kapelle at the convent at Hall, Tyrol, was directed by another Netherlander, Franz Sales.

The Graz court, because of its geographical location, was the first to experience the Italian influence that gradually eclipsed that of the Netherlands. Annibale Padovano, an organist from St Mark's, Venice, went to Graz in 1565 as principal instrumentalist and succeeded Cleve as Kapellmeister in 1570. On the death of Archduke Karl II in 1590 the Graz Kapelle, then directed by Gatto, was largely made up of Italians, including the organist Rovigo and the singer Zacconi. The process of Italianization continued under Karl II's successor, Archduke Ferdinand of Styria (later emperor), who employed such well-known musicians as Bianco, Giovanni Priuli, Stivori and Giovanni Valentini. Ferdinand sent Alessandro Tadei, later court organist at Graz, to study under Giovanni Gabrieli; thus the only surviving Gabrieli autographs came to be in the Styrian Landesarchiv in Graz. Later Netherlands musicians in Austria also felt the Italian influence, as shown by Monte's madrigals, Regnart's villanellas and the polyphonic sacred works of de Sayve, who wrote exclusively in a Venetian style. The Netherlands musicians were usually trained as singers, whereas most of the Italians were accomplished instrumentalists. The development of polyphony was not confined to the courts, and even before the Reformation sacred and secular music in towns was in the hands of schoolmasters and Kantors, assisted by *Türmer* (watchmen) and town musicians. At a celebration of Mass in 1485 at St Daniel, the oldest church in the Gail

Valley (Carinthia), the best singers and instrumentalists took part. The humanist Vadian studied music in Villach, and he taught at the town's thriving Lateinschule between 1506 and 1508. The earliest known guild of musicians in German-speaking lands was the Nicolai-Bruderschaft in Vienna, which was founded in 1288 and survived until 1782 when Joseph II disbanded all such brotherhoods. In some places the post of *Spielgraf* (which also appears to date from the 13th century) was created; for example, in 1464 an imperial court trumpeter, Wolfgang Wetter, held the post for Styria, Carinthia and Carniola (now part of Yugoslavia). Musicians and bellfounders were already established in Salzburg in the 12th and 13th centuries, and can be traced from the first half of the 15th century in the Carinthian towns of Friesach, Völkermarkt, Klagenfurt, Wolfsberg and St Veit. Noteworthy Austrian and foreign organ builders appeared from the 15th century onwards, including Heinrich Traxdorfer from Mainz, who built an organ at St Peter's, Salzburg in 1444, and Hofhaimer, who was associated with Jan Behaim of Dubraw.

From the 15th and 16th centuries sacred and secular instrumental music in towns was often made the responsibility of a *Türmer*, a municipal appointment, while the *Landschaftstrompeter* and *Heerpauker*, who can be traced in Styria from 1527 to 1861, were typically employed by the nobility merely to swell their state; but in the late 16th century some of these musicians also performed polyphony at the Protestant abbey in Graz. The art of Meistergesang left few traces in Austria: *Singschulen* existed in, among other towns, Schwaz (Tyrol) from before 1532, Steyr (Upper Austria) from 1542 and from about 1549 in Wels (Upper Austria), where Hans Sachs had spent a short time in 1513. Music printing was introduced in Vienna in the early 16th century; music theorists were active chiefly in Vienna (e.g. Simon de Quercu, Venceslaus Philomathes and Stefan Monetarius) and in Salzburg (Johannes Stomius, an associate of Hofhaimer).

In the 16th and early 17th centuries many peeople became Protestants. Preachers, schoolmasters and organists arrived from countries with an older Protestant tradition, bringing with them the Lutheran chorale. Better-known Protestant composers included Brassicanus, Hitzler (who transmitted the local hymn repertory and was also a prominent theorist) and Rosthius in Linz; Peuerl in Horn and Steyr (both Upper Austria); Lagkhner in Loosdorf (Lower Austria); Widmann in Graz and Eisenerz (Styria); Fritzius in Kapfenberg (Styria); Johannes Herold and Posch in Klagenfurt; Haslmayr in the Tyrol; and Rauch in Hernals and Inzersdorf (both near Vienna). However, the most important composer born in the Tyrol, Lechner, a Protestant convert, worked chiefly in Nuremberg. The Counter-Reformation gradually brought an end to the Protestant music tradition in Austria, which began to decline as early as 1600 and died out after the Battle of the White Mountain in 1620. But the religious schism did not impair cultural development; works of Catholic composers such as Lassus were often used in Protestant services, while organists such as Perini in Graz moved freely between employment in Catholic ducal courts and Protestant churches.

3. THE BAROQUE ERA. When Emperor Matthias died in 1619 his Netherlands-dominated Hofkapelle was replaced by the Italianized establishment brought from Graz by his heir Archduke Ferdinand of Inner Austria (Ferdinand II), an event which marked the beginning of a Baroque musical style in Vienna and, in spite of the Thirty Years War and the Turkish invasions, the most brilliant period of the imperial Hofkapelle. During the 17th century and the first half of the 18th, the Habsburg emperors, among whom Ferdinand III, Leopold I and Joseph I were themselves reputable composers, brought a large number of notable Italian musicians to the Viennese court: Bertali, Sances, Draghi, Ziani, Bononcini, Caldara, Conti, Porsile, Badia, Palotta and Bonno. Opera was first produced at the court in about 1630 and was firmly established there by the reign of Leopold I. It became a regular part of festive occasions such as namedays, birthdays, births and weddings in the imperial family, princely visits and coronations. A great theatrical event of the 17th century was the performance for Leopold I's wedding in Vienna (1668) of *Il pomo d'oro* by Cesti, who was Kapellmeister in Innsbruck from 1652 and, after the Tyrolean Habsburg line died out, assistant Kapellmeister in Vienna from 1666. Opera became established even earlier in Salzburg, under Archbishop Marcus Sitticus (1612–18), with a performance of an *Orfeo* setting in 1614, followed by an *Andromeda* in 1616. Francesco Rasi, who had links with the Camerata in Florence, presented Archbishop Sitticus with a manuscript collection of his sacred and secular monodies in 1612. Bartolomeo Mutis, Count of Cesana, whose presence at the court of Graz can be traced from 1604, was the first Italian composer working north of the Alps to have secular monodies printed (*Musiche*, Venice, 1613); he moved to Vienna with Ferdinand II. G. B. Bonometti, court tenor in Graz and later in Vienna, dedicated *Parnassus musicus Ferdinandaeus* (Venice, 1615) to the emperor; this comprehensive anthology of motets for one to five voices with figured bass contains chiefly works by well-known contemporaries, at least nine of them from the Graz court, and it shows the impact of the early Baroque style on sacred music in Austria. Another example is the *Harmonia concertans* (Nuremberg, 1623) by Posch, who was active in Carinthia and Carniola and acknowledged the influence of Viadana.

Instrumental music developed rapidly during the 17th century. G. M. Radino, later organist in Padua, and his son Giulio, whose concertos were published in Venice in 1607, served the Khevenhüllers, a powerful Carinthian noble family. In 1618–19 polyphonic canzonas and sonatas by the Graz Hofkapellmeister Priuli were printed in Venice; motets by Bernardi appeared in Salzburg (1634) and sacred works by Valentini in Vienna (1621). Early variation suites were composed by Peuerl in Steyr and, a little later, by Posch. It was as instrumentalists that Austrians first replaced foreign musicians. Hofhaimer (who was born in Radstadt) was the most important 16th-century organist. Two musicians at the Graz court were outstanding cornett players: Georg Poss, Kapellmeister to the Bishop of Breslau after 1618, and Giovanni Sansoni, who had connections with Schütz. In 17th-century Vienna, the outstanding keyboard composers were Froberger and Kerll, and, on a lower plane, Ebner and Poglietti. The foundations of the Viennese violin school were laid by Italians such as Buonamente and Bertali. The long succession of Italian imperial Hofkapellmeister was finally broken in 1679–80 by the appointment of J. H. Schmelzer, an Austrian violinist and composer of international reputation. It was principally as a ballet and song composer that he introduced an indigenous element into the Venetian-dominated court music. Biber, a key figure in the development of violin music, was Hofkapellmeister in Salzburg. Muffat was his organist before becoming Kapellmeister at Passau in 1690; he studied in Paris (with Lully) and in Rome (with Corelli) and his conscious fusion of the Italian, French and German musical languages typifies the so-called *vermischter Stil*. The rise of instrumental music encouraged instrument making. Jacob Stainer of Absam founded the Tyrolean school of violin-making, and notable organ builders included the families of Egedacher in Salzburg, Schwarz in Graz, and Römer in Vienna, as well as Henke and Sonnholz in Vienna, Gabler (who died during the construction of the organ in the Bregenz parish church in 1771) and Chrismann, who built the organ of St Florian that later was associated with Bruckner.

Austrian taste in church music and opera was conservative; once Italian innovations were adopted, they were retained tenaciously. The Venetian polychoral style in Austria is exemplified by Valentini's *Messa, Magnificat et Jubilate Deo* (Vienna, 1621) for seven choirs, and the anonymous 53-part festival mass with continuo performed in Salzburg Cathedral, probably in 1682; it was still cultivated for its impressive effect in the time of Fux (e.g. his *Missa Ss Trinitatis*). The church music of Johann Stadlmayr (*d* 1648), the best-known Innsbruck composer of the time, is also conservative. A type of oratorio, the *sepolcro*, was created by Viennese opera composers for worshipping the Holy Sepulchre during Holy Week. Baroque music in Austria reached its high point under the musically discerning Emperor Charles VI (1711–40), during whose reign the Turks were finally driven from Austrian territory. The Styrian composer and theorist Fux was imperial Hofkapellmeister from 1715 until his death in 1741. Fux's sacred works, his most significant achievement, became widely known outside the court, especially in other parts of the empire. His music reflects a typical Baroque balance between older and more modern stylistic elements. The operas, oratorios and *sepolcri* of Fux and of his vice-Hofkapellmeister Caldara reflect for the last time the splendour of the imperial court.

In the second half of the 17th century, the influence of the composition teaching of Christoph Bernhard (a pupil of Schütz) is evident in treatises by Poglietti, Kerll, Prinner and Samber. Andreas Hofer and Georg Muffat (whose 1699 manuscript treatise contains important elucidation of thoroughbass practice) were teachers of Samber, a Salzburg composer who published a *Manuductio ad organum* and *Continuatio ad manuductionem organicum* (Salzburg, 1704, 1707), treatises which were succeeded by the frequently reprinted *Fundamenta partiturae* (Salzburg, 1719) of Samber's pupil, Matthäus Gugl. But it was Fux who became the first Austrian music theorist to achieve a European reputation, with his textbook on strict counterpoint, *Gradus ad Parnassum* (Vienna, 1725).

After the Counter-Reformation monastic culture revived, predominantly under the Jesuits and Benedictines, and continued to flourish until the reforms of Joseph II (reigned 1765–90) struck its death-blow. The close connections between the church and schools gave music education a broad base. The works of numerous church and monastic composers such as J. G. Zechner became widely known.

An official report made in Klagenfurt in 1742 reveals the organization of musical life in towns. For centuries the schoolmaster both directed the church choir and sang bass, with the assistance of an organist, two descant singers (boys), an alto, a tenor and the *Türmer* with his associates, who played the string instruments. These were the usual forces in town churches, where surviving music from Leoben (Styria), Gmünd (Carinthia) and elsewhere indicate that polyphony was common in services. In the mid-17th century the parish musicians of Graz joined with the *Türmer* and town violinists to form a musicians' guild. A charter granted by Ferdinand III in 1650 assured them a privileged position in the city's musical life, but also imposed on them the obligation to provide music in the parish churches. Similar conditions, laid down by charters and privileges, also obtained elsewhere until the time of Joseph II.

4. PRE-CLASSICISM AND CLASSICISM. The adoption of popular elements into art music, which were already a feature of the 16th-century German Gesellschaftslied, reached court circles, as exemplified by Prinner's thoroughbass songs for Archduchess Maria Antonia, German vocal music by Leopold I and even by the ländler rhythms in Fux's music. In instrumental works of the transition period from Baroque to Classicism composers placed increasing emphasis on easily assimilable melody. This can be seen in the works of Gottlieb Muffat (Georg's son and a pupil of Fux), J. G. Reutter, Monn and Wagenseil in Vienna; Eberlin, Adlgasser (whose best music is found in his *Schuldramen* and sacred works) and Leopold Mozart (who was most important as a teacher) in Salzburg; Steinbacher and Sgatberoni in Styria; and Haindl and Madlseder in the Tyrol. The divertimento and the string quartet gradually replaced the suite; the south German keyboard concerto took hold, owing much to the Italian violin concerto but independent of the north German keyboard concerto; the symphony became independent of the opera overture; and the *sonata da camera* ultimately led to the modern piano sonata and the genres for chamber ensemble with piano, such as the violin sonata, piano trio and piano quartet.

From the first half of the 18th century, performances outside the court theatres made opera accessible to the general public, in Vienna's Kärntnertortheater (from 1728) and by Italian itinerant troupes such as Pietro and Angelo Mingotti's company. *Opera buffa* rapidly became popular: Mingotti produced Pergolesi's *La serva padrona* in Graz as early as 1739. Soon after the middle of the century, Vienna saw the first example of Gluck's operatic reforms; in this process of renewal numerous minor masters also played their part. The combination of French and Italian stylistic features with German ones created the basis of Viennese Classicism, whose greatest representatives were Haydn, Mozart and Beethoven. This culture, enjoyed by the bourgeoisie as well as by the aristocracy, established Austrian musical pre-eminence.

After the deaths of Charles VI (1740) and Fux (1741), the imperial Hofkapelle forfeited its leading role in musical life. Its later directors included such respectable but historically unimportant composers as Predieri, J. G. Reutter, Gassmann (who instigated the founding of the Vienna Tonkünstler-Sozietät in 1771), Bonno and Salieri. The many aristocratic Kapellen, of all sizes, were more progressive, especially that of the Esterházys, associated with Haydn. Aristocratic and middle-class amateurs vied with each other in private and public concerts, spreading musical culture and encouraging music publishing, in which Austria had previously lagged behind Italy, England, the Netherlands, France and Germany. Music printing developed rapidly in Vienna from the end of the 18th century, with the establishment of the houses of Artaria, F. A. Hoffmeister, S. A. Steiner, Tobias Haslinger, Anton Diabelli, C. A. Spina and others. Through the reforms of Joseph II, astute at least in their social application, Austria was spared the fate of France at the end of the 18th century. Although Italians continued to play important roles in Austrian musical life well into the 19th century, they had already passed the height of their influence by the 1750s.

The Viennese Singspiel evolved after 1760, influenced by *opera buffa* and *opéra comique*, but with its roots in popular comedy with musical interludes, such as the *Teutsche Comödien-Arien* (c1750) attributed to Haydn. Mozart's *Bastien und Bastienne*, possibly written for performance at Dr Johann Anton Mesmer's house in Vienna, belongs to the new genre, which Joseph II encouraged by establishing a national Singspiel company in the Burgtheater. It opened in 1778 with Ignaz Umlauf's *Die Bergknappen*, and reached its zenith with Mozart's *Die Entführung aus dem Serail* (1782). Italian opera provided strong competition and the German opera house was soon closed (which is why Mozart went back to Italian texts); but popular Singspiels by Dittersdorf, J. B. Schenk, J. B. Weigl, Haibel (Mozart's brother-in-law), Wenzel Müller and others had numerous performances at non-court theatres and became widely known outside Vienna. The crown of the genre was Mozart's *Die Zauberflöte*, first performed in Vienna in 1791, which had a profound influence on the development of German romantic opera in the 19th century.

If German opera owed its classic form to Mozart, German oratorio was moulded by Haydn, whose *The Creation* (1798) and *The Seasons* (1801) had their first performances in Prince Schwarzenberg's Vienna palace. Church music too owed its classic profile to Mozart and Haydn, while the latter's brother Michael in Salzburg, Weber's teacher, made a specially large and pervasive contribution to the 19th-century liturgical repertory throughout the empire. The musical heritage of Mozart and Haydn passed to Beethoven, who made Vienna his home. Rejecting the ties of a permanent post which his deafness would have made impossible, he composed independently, though with the support of various noble patrons, notably his talented pupil Archduke Rudolph. Beethoven embodied the ideals of the middle class, which had newly come of age. Through Beethoven, who was no longer writing to commission, absolute music underwent an extraordinary expansion of its expressive potential and its forms, and an imposing legacy was created for future generations of composers.

5. ROMANTICISM. Beethoven's contemporaries and near-contemporaries in Austria include such respected composers as Albrechtsberger (an eminent theorist, with whom Beethoven studied), Eberl, E. A. Förster, Gyrowetz, J. N. Hummel, Leopold Kozeluch, Wölfl,

Paul and Anton Wranitzky; and Czerny (a pupil of Beethoven) attracted numerous piano pupils, the most celebrated being Liszt. Ignaz Schuppanzigh established the Viennese tradition of public quartet recitals; the most prominent violin teachers and performers were Joseph Mayseder and Joseph Böhm (the teacher of Ernst), Joseph Joachim (born, like Liszt, in the then Hungarian Burgenland) and the elder Georg Hellmesberger. Schubert, a generation younger than Beethoven, reinforced Austria's musical supremacy and established the importance of the lied. Like Beethoven, he wrote many of his works in Vienna or the immediate vicinity, but in 1827 ventured further afield, to Graz, where his old friend and fellow pupil of Salieri, Anselm Hüttenbrenner, the best-known Styrian composer between Fux and Hugo Wolf, came into possession of the 'Unfinished' Symphony. In 1865 he gave it to the Viennese Hofkapellmeister, Johann von Herbeck, for performance, and it finally became the property of the Gesellschaft der Musikfreunde in Vienna. This association of music lovers, led by Josef von Sonnleithner, was formed in 1814 in succession to the Gesellschaft Adeliger Frauen, founded in 1812, and soon became one of the foremost institutions of Viennese concert life and a model for music societies founded by both noble and middle-class amateurs in Innsbruck, Graz (1815), Radkersburg (Styria, 1820), Linz, Klagenfurt (1828), Fürstenfeld (1832) and other towns. In Salzburg public musical life suffered a setback as a result of extreme political instability (it changed rulers four times between 1803 and 1816, when it fell to the Habsburgs) but revived with the foundation in 1841 of the Dommusikverein und Mozarteum, through the initiative of Franz von Hilleprandt. The first Mozart festival took place in 1842, under the direction of Neukomm and with Mozart's two sons participating, on the occasion of the unveiling of the statue by Schwanthaler. In the meantime, Vienna was consolidating its position as a musical capital. Rossini celebrated one triumph after another there, beginning with *Tancredi* in 1816, and Donizetti and Bellini followed soon afterwards. Paganini and Liszt were outstanding among the instrumentalists who dominated public concerts during the first half of the century. The declining standards of the opera and concerts drew sharp criticism from Schumann, who failed to establish himself in Vienna in 1838 but discovered the 'Great' C major Symphony in Schubert's legacy. Orchestras normally consisted of amateurs, reinforced by professional players only on special occasions; standards rose only after the institution of the Philharmonic concerts by Nicolai and his colleagues in 1842; from 1860 they became the centre of Viennese concert life.

The Viennese waltz developed during the Biedermeier era in the hands of Joseph Lanner and Johann Strauss (i), its origins lying in the Upper Austrian ländler, the *Steirer* (from Styria) and the *Deutscher* ('German dances'), which Mozart, Haydn and Schubert admired and composed. Culminating with the composer and conductor Johann Strauss (ii), the waltz conquered the concert halls and ballrooms of the world. *An der schönen blauen Donau* became the most famous Viennese waltz and *Die Fledermaus* (first performed in 1874) marked the high point of the dance-inspired Viennese classical operetta, a genre owing much to Wenzel Müller's earthy and popular incidental music for the plays of Raimund

2. *A performance of Beethoven's Choral Fantasia: detail from the painting 'The Symphony' (1852) by Moritz von Schwind in the Bayerische Staatsgemäldesammlungen, Munich*

and Nestroy, as well as to Offenbach's tumultuously acclaimed operettas. Josef and Eduard Strauss were also conductors and prolific composers, who helped their brother to sweep the world with Strauss dances. Franz von Suppé and Carl Millöcker did the same for operetta, with remarkable interpreters like Marie Geistinger and Alexander Girardi contributing to their success.

A widespread awareness of folk music, previously transmitted only orally, arose during the Romantic era and led to systematic collections and catalogues. Concert performances, which adapted folk music to the conventions of art music, were given by the 'Alpensänger' on successful tours abroad. Folk-influenced song also became immensely popular; for example, both *Stille Nacht, heilige Nacht*, written in 1818 in Arnsdorf in the province of Salzburg, with words by a village priest and music by the schoolmaster and organist F. X. Gruber, and the sentimental song in Carinthian folk style, *Verlassen bin i*, by Thomas Koschat, were translated into many languages. Other forms of popular music which have retained their appeal are the songs associated with the inns in the vineyards of the Viennese suburbs (*Wirtshaus-* and *Heurigenlieder*), *Schrammelmusik*, named after the brothers Johann and Joseph Schrammel, and military marches, evolved from bugle calls as well as from folksongs and soldiers' songs and mostly composed by regimental bandmasters and bandsmen, notably C. M. Ziehrer.

Male-voice choral singing, harking back to Michael Haydn, received considerable impetus from the 1848 Revolution. Choral societies were founded in many cities and towns around the middle of the century, including a Männergesangverein in Vienna (1843), in Salzburg (1844) and in Graz (1846), of which one of the first chorus masters was Conradin Kreutzer.

Austrian supremacy in instrumental music and song in the second half of the 19th century was maintained by Brahms, Bruckner and Wolf. The development of opera was determined by Wagner, who, despite critical hostility, found rapid public favour, especially in Vienna and Graz, where *Tannhäuser* was performed in 1854 before its Viennese première. Wagner visited Vienna ten times between 1832 and 1876. Joseph Hellmesberger (i), Hanslick and Julius Epstein introduced Brahms to musical Vienna, which became a second home for him, the heir of the Viennese Classical composers, as it had been for Beethoven. Other Austrian towns associated with Brahms include Bad Ischl, Pörtschach on the Wörthersee (Carinthia) and Mürzzuschlag (Styria), where he spent summers. Bruckner lived more than half his life in Upper Austria and is the province's outstanding composer. He was an organist and conductor in St Florian and Linz until 1868, when he became a teacher of theory and the organ at the Vienna Conservatory. Despite Wagner's influence, the organ remained the determining factor for his conception of orchestral sound. The dispute between the supporters of Brahms and Bruckner was aggravated by the influential critic Hanslick and his championship of Brahms. Nevertheless the co-existence of diverse artistic personalities remained a characteristic of Austrian musical culture. Hugo Wolf first studied the piano at Johann Buwa's music school in Graz, one of the most important music academies in Styria. Wolf then studied with the Styrian Robert Fuchs in Vienna, where he spent the rest of his life. There his supporters, including Bruckner's pupil Joseph Schalk, enthusiastically promoted his songs. Noteworthy achievements in popular opera were made by Brüll and Kienzl. Graz was outstanding among the provincial cities in the second half of the 19th century; its opera, where conductors like Karl Muck, Schuch, Schalk and, in the early 20th century, Krauss, Oswald Kabasta and Böhm acquainted the public with contemporary as well as Classical works, was for performers a springboard to the most famous theatres. The music theorist W. A. Rémy (1831–98), who came to Graz from Prague, taught Busoni, Reznicek, Kienzl, Weingartner and Heuberger. At the same time the Carinthian-born Friedrich von Hausegger worked in Graz as a critic and aesthetician, advocating Wagner's ideas. In Salzburg in 1880 the Internationale Mozart-Stiftung, founded by Carl von Sterneck in 1869–70, united with the Mozarteum (which had severed its links with the Dommusik-verein) to form the Internationale Stiftung Mozarteum.

6. THE 20TH CENTURY. Gustav Mahler infused the Romantic symphony with the inner tension of his time; the tendencies to dissolution in his work have been interpreted by Adorno as a seismographic signal of sharpening social antagonisms and the political cata-strophes which were soon to tear Austria apart. As artistic director of the Vienna Hofoper from 1897 to 1907, the penultimate decade of the Danube monarchy, Mahler created an era of brilliant achievements, with the designer Alfred Roller as his collaborator. Before and immediately after Mahler's death, the Bavarian Richard Strauss was the most prominent musical personality. The first Austrian performance of *Salome* (Graz, 1906) was conducted by the composer and was supported by Ernst Decsey, the leading Graz music critic at the turn of the century. Of supreme importance in Strauss's career as an opera composer were his associations with Austrian writers, particularly that with Hofmannsthal, who wrote the librettos for several of Strauss's masterpieces (including *Der Rosenkavalier* and *Arabella*, which consciously cultivate Viennese local colour). Strauss, with Schalk, directed the Vienna Staatsoper from 1919 to 1924, and subsequently appeared there as guest conductor. His long association with the Vienna Philharmonic from 1906 had a significant positive influence on Viennese concert standards and strengthened Strauss's ties with Austria; he adopted Austrian citizenship in 1947. The successful operas of Julius Bittner, E. W. Korngold, Franz Schmidt and Franz Schreker and the late Romantic and impressionist songs of Joseph Marx also won international reputations for their composers. Schmidt, who was rector (1927–31) of the Akademie für Musik und Darstellende Kunst in Vienna, enriched the repertories of both the oratorio and symphony. The outstanding Viennese operetta composer after Johann Strauss was Lehár, who began his career as a military bandmaster; other late operetta composers were Oscar Straus, Eysler, Fall, Nedbal, Emmerich Kálmán and Robert Stolz.

Atonality and serial composition, the musical 'revolu-tion' originating in Vienna in the first decades of the century and regarded by Schoenberg, Berg and Webern as a direct continuation of the Classical–Romantic tradition, spread rapidly from the late 1920s. The circle of composers known as the Second Viennese School also included Wellesz, Apostel, Jelinek and, in a looser sense, Schreker's versatile pupil, Krenek, whose jazz-influenced opera *Jonny spielt auf* caused a sensation in the late 1920s. Berg's *Wozzeck*, which belongs to his pre-serial period, was influenced by Schreker, but also by

Alpine folk music, which he got to know in Trahütten (Styria) where he had a country house. Webern came from a South Tyrolean noble family and received his early musical education in Klagenfurt before he became, like Berg, a pupil of Schoenberg in Vienna. J. M. Hauer from Lower Austria, who developed a 12-note system at much the same time as Schoenberg, has had little influence. The teaching and theoretical writings of Heinrich Schenker became increasingly influential in Austria and abroad.

Under the Nazi regime (1938–45) Austria lost its independence and during World War II musical activity ceased. After 1945 it was reorganized in a new social environment. Even after World War I, the nobility and middle class had largely forfeited their former leading roles in upholding the arts. Former private initiative was gradually replaced by public patronage from the state, the provincial authorities, local authorities and the media. The most successful composer of operas active in Austria after World War II is Gottfried von Einem. The avant garde, represented by Cerha, Ligeti and Haubenstock-Ramati, is fostered by special occasions, such as the Musikprotokoll instituted by Austrian Radio as part of the Steirischer Herbst festival, founded in 1969 and supported by public subsidy.

After Vienna, institutes for musicology were estab-lished by the universities of Innsbruck, Graz (1940) and Salzburg (1966). Austria participates in an edition of musical monuments (Denkmäler der Tonkunst in Österreich) as well as in complete scholarly editions of the works of Bruckner, Fux, Mozart, Johann Strauss (ii) and Hugo Wolf. There are important music academies in Graz and Salzburg, as well as in Vienna. Comprehensive collections of early music are found primarily in Vienna (*Wn, Wgm, Wst*), in Salzburg (*Sd, Ssp, Sm*), in Graz (*Gd*) and in Innsbruck (*Imf*). Among the numerous monasteries, those at Göttweig and Kremsmünster have the most valuable music libraries; the Vienna Kunsthistorisches Museum has the largest collection of musical instruments, whose nucleus is the collection of Archduke Ferdinand II of the Tyrol.

See also GÖTTWEIG; GRAZ; INNSBRUCK; KLOSTERNEUBURG; KREMS-MÜNSTER; LAMBACH; LINZ; MELK; ST FLORIAN; SALZBURG; VIENNA.

BIBLIOGRAPHY

C. Burney: *The Present State of Music in Germany*, i (London, 1773, 2/1775)

M. von Millenkovich-Morold: *Die österreichische Tonkunst* (Vienna and Leipzig, 1918)

G. Adler: 'Musik in Österreich', *SMw*, xvi (1929), 3

A. Orel: 'Österreichisches Wesen in österreichischer Musik', *Öster-reichische Rundschau*, 2nd ser., i (1935)

L. Nowak: 'Die Musik in Österreich', *Österreich: Erbe und Sendung im deutschen Raum*, ed. J. Nadler and H. von Sbrik (Salzburg and Leipzig, 1936)

J. Jernek: *Der österreichische Männerchorgesang im 19. Jahrhundert* (diss., U. of Vienna, 1937)

R. Lach: 'Das Österreichertum in der Musik', *AMz*, lxv (1938), 529

E. Schenk: *Musik in Kärnten* (Vienna, 1941)

——: *950 Jahre Musik in Österreich* (Vienna, 1946)

L. Nowak: 'Vom Werden österreichischer Musik', *Österreichische Furche*, iii (1947), 89

R. F. Brauner: *Österreichs neue Musik* (Vienna, 1948)

J. Gregor: *Geschichte des österreichischen Theaters* (Vienna, 1948)

O. Wessely: *Musik in Oberösterreich* (Linz, 1951)

H. J. Moser: 'Melodien des österreichischen Meistergesang', *ÖMz*, vii (1952), 147

O. Wessely: 'Die Entwicklung der Musikerziehung in Österreich', *Musikerziehung*, vi (1952–3), 325

R. Quoika: *Die altösterreichischen Orgeln der späten Gotik, der Renaissance und des Barock* (Kassel, 1953)

O. Wessely: 'Alte Musiklehrbücher aus Österreich', *Musikerziehung*, vii (1953–4), 128

H. J. Moser: *Die Musik im frühevangelischen Österreich* (Kassel, 1954)

F. Zagiba: *Die ältesten musikalischen Denkmäler zu Ehren des hl. Leopold, Herzog und Patron von Österreich: ein Beitrag zur Choralpflege in Österreich am Ausgange des Mittelalters* (Zurich, Leipzig and Vienna, 1954)

O. Eberstaller: *Orgeln und Orgelbauer in Österreich* (Graz and Cologne, 1955)

H. Federhofer: 'Die Niederländer an den Habsburgerhöfen in Österreich', *Anzeiger der Österreichischen Akademie der Wissenschaften, Philosophisch-historische Klasse*, xciii (1956), 102

——: 'Monodie und musica reservata', *DJbM*, ii (1957), 30

O. Wessely: 'Die österreichische Musikforschung nach dem 2. Weltkrieg', *AcM*, xxix (1957), 111

H. Federhofer: 'Der Musikerstand in Österreich von circa 1200 bis 1520', *DJbM*, iii (1958), 92

——: 'Zur handschriftlichen Überliefung der Musiktheorie in Österreich in der zweiten Hälfte des 17. Jahrhundert', *Mf*, xi (1958), 264

O. Seewald: 'Die Lyrendarstellung der ostalpinen Hallstattkultur', *Festschrift Alfred Orel* (Vienna and Wiesbaden, 1960), 159

——: 'Hallstattzeitliche Flöteninstrumente in Österreich', *Oberösterreichische Heimatblätter*, xiv (1960), 181

E. Tittel: *Österreichische Kirchenmusik* (Vienna, 1961)

H. Anglès: 'Musikalische Beziehungen zwischen Österreich und Spanien in der Zeit vom 14. bis zum 18. Jahrhundert', *SMw*, xxv (1962)

W. Suppan: *Steirisches Musiklexikon* (Graz, 1962–6)

Theater in Österreich (Vienna, 1965) [*Notring Jb 1965*]

H. Goertz: *Österreichisches Musikhandbuch* (Vienna and Munich, 1971)

Musik in Österreich (Vienna, 1971) [*Notring Jb 1971*]

W. Pass: *Musik und Musiker am Hof Maximilians II* (diss., U. of Vienna, 1973)

R. Schollum: *Das oesterreichische Lied des 20. Jahrhunderts* (Tutzing, 1977)

R. Flotzinger and G. Gruber, eds.: *Musikgeschichte Österreichs* (Graz, 1977–9)

II. Folk music. Since Austrian folk music became the object of collection and research only comparatively recently, knowledge of it depends substantially on evidence which dates back to the end of the 18th century: earlier information is scarce and cannot be accepted as definitive. Until World War II a variety of songs and dances formed an integral part of rural customs and seasonal rites. They have survived as important artistic achievements even though many of the customs which gave rise to them have been forgotten. Two musical forms characterize Austrian vocal and instrumental folk music, the *Jodler* (yodel) and the LÄNDLER. The yodel is cast in the diatonic major key and employs a variety of techniques for developing the vocal line. Ex.1 illustrates its typical homophonic (three-part) form, with a falsetto upper part and a bass part, and the wordless yodelled refrain. For further discussion of the Alpine yodel *see* SWITZERLAND, §II, 2, and YODEL.

Ex.1 Yodel song

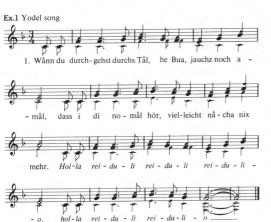

In spite of general similarities, however, the folk music of each region of Austria has distinctive characteristics which reflect the differing geography and ethnic make-up of the regions. They are therefore discussed individually.

Salzkammergut, a cultural and geographical area made up of the provinces of Salzburg, Upper Austria and Styria, has a very distinctive folk culture. The *Almlied* (mountain pasture song) and the *Ludler* (yodel), both usually in three or four parts, are the main forms of vocal music. Only the *Almschroa* (*Almschrei*: 'dairymaids' yodelling song') is monophonic: it served partly as a means of conveying messages over considerable distances. Ex.2 shows its typical wide-ranging yodelled leaps. Instrumental dance music is played by small ensembles typically consisting of two violins, a diatonic button-key accordion and a string bass (see fig.3). This type of accordion is also used as a solo instrument. A drum and two *Seitlpfeifn* (wooden transverse flutes with six finger-holes) usually provide the music for shooting gatherings. Favourite dances include the *Steirische*, the *Landla* (ländler; performed in duple time), the *Boarische* and the *Schleunige* (ex.3).

Ex.2 *Almschrei* from Ausseer-Land (Gielge, 1935)

Ex.3 *Schleunige* dance

3. Schleunige, accompanied by an ensemble of two violins, diatonic button-key accordion and string bass at a wedding in Bad Goisern, Salzkammergut, 1977

Whereas the dialects of all the other Austrian regions are based on the Bavarian tongue, the dialect of Vorarlberg, the most western region, belongs to the Alemannic group, and this difference is noticeable in its folk music. Today Vorarlberg has only a tenuous link with tradition, but some characteristic elements of its distinctive older folk music have survived into the present, particularly in Montafontal and the Bregenzer Wald. The older dance music ensembles comprise small groups of wind instruments led by clarinets and flugelhorns (valved bugles), while the newer ones consist of trios of zithers, guitars and accordions. Folk music in Vorarlberg has developed into a new, more broadly based indigenous music, with a variety of vocal and instrumental groups and choirs performing new arrangements of traditional melodies.

The Tyrol is a mountainous region where many authentic forms of traditional music survive. Its carols of the shepherds and the crib are widely known and are performed in two or more parts making up simple, semi-improvised harmony, as in ex.4. Hunters' and gamekeepers' songs, historical ballads and yodelling songs are also typical of this region. The harp is still the favourite instrument, used on its own for accompanying songs and as the main harmony instrument in every dance band. A xylophone-playing tradition survives: the instrument is known as the *Hölzernes Glachter*. In the Zillertal area string ensemble music (for two violins, harp and bass) is a relic of a rich Tyrolean string-playing tradition.

At the turn of the 19th century the 'Tiroler Nationalsänger' began the popularization of a commercially based type of song known as *Heimatlieder* (homeland songs). These continue to circulate, growing in number and variety with each successive generation: they are characterized by artistic yodelling.

The important musical history of the city of Salzburg has had a wide influence on the culture of the surrounding region. Apart from many song types linked to local customs, narrative songs are most popular at social gatherings. Christmas and Easter carols are also noteworthy: these are commonly performed in three-part harmony.

After World War II the musician Tobi Reiser and his circle were responsible for initiating and spreading the

Ex.4 Shepherd's carol

Frisch auf___ und frisch nie - der, ihr Hir - te-lein er -

- wacht!   Seids   ös   so fau - le   Brüa - der und

schlafts die gan - ze Nacht!   Glo - ri, Glo - ri -

- a,   Glo - ri,   Glo - ri - a.

Ex.5 *Bauernpolka* from Salzburg

custom of 'advent singing' and for significant innovations in instrumental music-making, including the invention of the chromatic dulcimer and the development of an ensemble comprising dulcimer, zither, guitar, harp and double bass. This combination is now typical of domestic music-making in the Alpine region. Ex.5 illustrates the use of such instruments for dance-tunes.

The heterogeneous character of Upper Austria results in a great variety of musical forms and idiosyncratic styles. Although songs associated with seasonal customs are rapidly disappearing, their basic form is preserved in newer music. The polyphonic yodel and the solo *Vierzeiler* (four-line song) are two distinct and contrasting forms. The *Landla* is the dominant instrumental form and at gatherings it develops into a magnificent dance, a compound of music, song, movement and rhythmic clapping. In performance the *Landlageiger* (ländler fiddler) changes the notated 3/4 rhythm into an irregular duple time, as in ex.6. In the region of the River Inn wind instruments are used with the fiddles, whereas around the River Traun the latter are nowadays accompanied by a button-key accordion.

Styria (Steiermark) has a name which is historically

Ex.6 *Landla*, as performed in the Inn 'viertel'

(usually in D or E♭)

closely associated with Alpine folk music. The *Steirische* is stylistically the most typically Alpine of all forms of ländler, being a short cyclical form based on a single motif usually complemented by an introduction and coda: it is performed in three or more parts, consisting of melody, *Überschlagstimme* (falsetto upper part often progressing in similar motion to the melody, as in ex.7) and figured bass.

The Styrian Ziehharmonika is an older type of diatonic button-key accordion on which the *Steirische* can be performed with particular ease: this may well account for its other name, the 'Steirische'. The diatonic dulcimer is also termed 'Steirisch': it was used in an ensemble which, although it was known throughout Austria, persisted longest in Styria and consisted of two fiddles, dulcimer and string bass. A traditional Styrian trio consisted of Styrian accordion, Styrian dulcimer and double bass. Apart from these very distinctive instrumental features, a special feature of Styrian vocal music is the yodel.

Ex.7 *Steirische* dance

Many of the folksongs of Carinthia lend themselves to a very individual style of interpretation. The love-song in particular is usually referred to as a *Kärntnerlied* and is characterized by the strict relationship between parts, whereby the leading voice – a middle part – is heard against almost stationary close harmony, as shown in ex.8. Since 1930 exclusively male group singing has given way to mixed group singing as part of a song revival, and after 1945 the composition of new *Kärntnerlieder* gave added impetus to a great singing movement throughout the region. Instrumental music is relatively unimportant in Carinthia, although here and there small ensembles, particularly wind groups, display some originality. In this region minority Slovenian groups have a rich repertory of songs linked to their customs and performed in the same polyphonic manner as the *Kärntnerlied*.

Lower Austria is historically the centre of Austria, where varied terrains have given rise to varying musical traditions. Traditional secular songs and dance music survive in southern Lower Austria, the Alpine foothills and the fruit-growing regions, where they are sung by solo singers and small groups in two or three parts, mainly in close harmony. In the woodland and wine-growing country religious singing is more common: the

Ex.8 Five-part *Kärntnerlied*

two-part hymns generally require a large congregation led by two soloists, except funeral hymns, which are sung only on more intimate occasions. In the area around Schneeberg the *Dudler* (slow yodel) and the *Almlied* (Alpine pasture song) are common. The former, sung in close harmony, is in ternary form and has become a model for the whole region (see ex.9). Among the most striking examples of Lower Austrian folk music are the songs and instrumental music performed at weddings. Here the band consists of two higher instruments (clarinets or flugelhorns or one of each), button-key accordion and bass flugelhorn; the ländler and the French polka are popular dances.

Ex.9 *Dudler* (slow yodel).

Burgenland still has many unbroken musical traditions which are outside the mainstream of Austrian folk music. The music is almost exclusively vocal (unison and two-part): narrative songs, religious songs, dance-songs and various types linked to local customs are prominent in the repertory, which is still performed chiefly at weddings, funerals and pilgrimages. Songs once used in religious folk dramas for different events in the church calendar are dying out, but have strongly influenced the general content of religious songs. Purely instrumental music survives only in central and southern Burgenland where, as in Lower Austria, the French polka and the ländler are found. The Croatian minority in Burgenland has introduced a new folk trend with its many *Tamburizza-Kapellen* (*tamburica* bands; the *tam-*

burica is a long-necked fretted lute). The music of the Hungarian minority has little influence on Austrian folk music; however, its repertory includes spinning songs, love-songs, soldiers' songs and music for the *Scheitholzzither* (log-zither), an instrument known to Praetorius.

While Vienna, the federal capital, is recognized for its leading historical role in Western art music (see §I above) it also has its own characteristic folk music, including the *Wiener-Tanz*, the *Wiener Walzer* (see §I, 5) and the *Wienerlied*. The *Wienerlied* provides both a musical and poetic framework for the citizens' view of themselves and an escape from their present surroundings into the idealized 'good old days'. In the Viennese dance stylistic features of Alpine music have been developed, through the use of chromaticism and richer harmonic variation, into a distinctive instrumental concert piece (*see* WALTZ).

BIBLIOGRAPHY

GENERAL

A. Schlossar: *Österreichische Cultur- und Literaturbilder* (Vienna, 1879)

J. Pommer: 'Über das älplerische Volkslied und wie man es findet', *Zeitschrift des deutschen und österreichischen Alpenvereins*, xxvii (1896), 89–131

Das deutsche Volkslied (1899–1947; cont. as *Volkslied, Volkstanz, Volksmusik*, 1947–9; index, 1947)

E. K. Blümml, ed.: *Quellen und Forschungen zur deutschen Volkskunde* (Vienna, 1908–12)

F. F. Kohl: *Die tiroler Bauernhochzeit* (Vienna, 1908)

A. Halberstadt: *Eine originelle Bauernwelt* (Vienna, 1912)

C. Rotter: *Der Schnaderhüpfl-Rhythmus* (Berlin, 1912)

E. Hamza: 'Folkloristische Studien aus dem niederösterreichischen Wechselgebiete', *Zeitschrift des deutschen und österreichischen Alpenvereins*, xliv (1913), 6–127

J. F. Knaffl: *Die Knaffl-Handschrift: eine obersteirische Volkskunde aus dem Jahre 1813*, Quellen zur deutschen Volkskunde, ed. V. von Geramb und L. Mackenson, ii (Berlin, 1928)

R. Lach: 'Die Tonkunst in den Alpen', in H. Leitmeier: *Die österreichischen Alpen* (Vienna, 1928), 332–80

D. Hummel: 'Bibliographie des weltlichen Volksliedes in Niederösterreich', *Jb für Landeskunde von Niederösterreich*, xxiv (1931), 124–258

J. Koller: *Das Wiener Volkssängertum in alter und neuer Zeit* (Vienna, 1931)

R. Preitensteiner: *Das geistliche Volkslied in Niederösterreich* (diss., U. of Vienna, 1931)

R. Wolfram: 'Die Frühform des Ländlers', *Zeitschrift für Volkskunde*, xlii/2 (1933)

A. Kollitsch: *Geschichte des Kärntnerlieds* (Klagenfurt, 1935–6)

L. Schmidt: 'Der Volksliedbegriff in der Volkskunde', *Das deutsche Volkslied*, xxxviii (1936), 73ff

——: 'Volksliedlandschaft Niederösterreich', *Südostdeutsche Forschungen*, ii (1937), 258–307

——: 'Niederösterreichische Flugblattlieder', *Jb für Volksliedforschung*, iv (1938), 104

H. Commenda: 'Die Gebrauchshandschriften der alten Landlageiger', *Zeitschrift für Volkskunde*, xlviii (1939)

K. Horak: *Burgenländische Volksschauspiele* (Vienna and Leipzig, 1940)

K. Liebleitner: *Das Volkslied in Niederdonau* (Vienna, 1941)

R. Holzer: *Wiener Volks-Humor* (Vienna, 1943–7)

R. A. Moissl: *Die Schrammel-Dynastie* (St Pölten, 1943)

L. Schmidt: *Das Volkslied im alten Wien* (Vienna, 1947)

R. Sieczynski: *Wienerlied, Wiener Wein, Wiener Sprache* (Vienna, 1947)

L. Schmidt: 'Die kulturgeschichtlichen Grundlagen des Volksgesanges in Österreich', *Schweizerisches Archiv für Volkskunde*, xlv (1948)

F. Hurdes: *Die niederösterreichische Bauernhochzeit* (Vienna, 1949)

W. Kolneder: *Die vokale Mehrstimmigkeit in der Volksmusik der österreichischen Alpenländer* (diss., U. of Innsbruck, 1949)

K. M. Klier: *Das Neujahrssingen im Burgenland* (Eisenstadt, 1950)

R. Zoder: *Volkslied, Volkstanz, Volksbrauch in Österreich* (Vienna, 1950)

L. Kretzenbacher: *Lebendiges Volksschauspiel in Steiermark* (Vienna, 1951)

R. Wolfram: *Die Volkstänze in Österreich und verwandte Tänze in Europa* (Salzburg, 1951)

I. Peter: 'Volkstanz in Theorie und Praxis', *Österreichischen Volkskunde*, ed. A. Mais (Vienna, 1952), 341ff
G. Gugitz: *Lieder der Strasse: die Bänkelsänger im josephinischen Wien* (Vienna, 1954)
F. Kirnbauer: 'Über Art und Wesen des Bergmanns-Volksliedes', *Jb des österreichischen Volksliedwerkes*, iii (1954), 53
K. M. Klier: *Das Totenwacht-Singen im Burgenland* (Eisenstadt, 1956)
——: *Volkstümliche Musikinstrumente in den Alpen* (Kassel and Basle, 1956)
O. Moser: *Die kärntner Sternsingbräuche: Beiträge zur Erforschung ihrer Vergangenheit und Gegenwart* (Klagenfurt, 1956)
E. Hamza: *Der Ländler* (Vienna, 1957)
A. Riedl and K. M. Klier: *Lieder, Reime und Spiele der Kinder im Burgenland* (Eisenstadt, 1957)
——: *Lied-Flugblattdrucke aus dem Burgenland* (Eisenstadt, 1958)
A. Koch: *Die Tiroler Schützenschwegel* (Innsbruck, 1959)
F. Koschier: *Lebendiger Volkstanz* (Klagenfurt, 1959)
L. Schmidt: 'Verbreitungskarten von Volkslied, Volkstanz und Volksschauspiel für Niederösterreich', *Jb des österreichischen Volksliedwerkes*, viii (1959), 124
F. Wild, W. Graf and E. Hermann: *Katalog des Phonogrammarchivs der österreichischen Akademie der Wissenschaften* (Vienna, 1960)
K. Horak: 'Tiroler Volksmusik: Überlieferung und Fortleben', *Jb des österreichischen Volksliedwerkes*, xi (1962), 181
F. Schunko: 'Vom Ratschen in Niederösterreich', *Jb des österreichischen Volksliedwerkes*, xii (1963), 29
K. M. Klier and J. Bitsche, eds.: *Bibliographie des Volksliedes in Vorarlberg* (Montfort, 1964)
K. M. Klier: *Allgemeine Bibliographie des Burgenlandes, v: Volkskunde* (Eisenstadt, 1965)
K. Gaál, ed.: *Spinnstubenlieder: Lieder der Frauengemeinschaften in den magyrischen Sprachinseln im Burgenland* (Munich and Zurich, 1966)
F. Stradner: 'Das Hackbrett: ein Beitrag zu seiner Entwicklungsgeschichte', *Jb des österreichischen Volksliedwerkes*, xv (1966), 134
J. Bitsche: 'Über das Volkslied in Vorarlberg', *Jb des österreichischen Volksliedwerkes*, xvi (1967), 38
L. Schmidt: 'Geschichte der österreichischen Volksliedsammlung im 19. und 20. Jahrhundert', *Beiträge zur österreichischen Volksliedkunde*, i (Graz, 1967), 59
W. Suppan: 'Volksmusik im Bezirk Weiz', *Handel, Wandel, Lied und Wort: Beiträge zur Volkskunde Wirtschafts- und Kulturgeschichte* (Weiz, 1967), 19–59
F. Eibner 'Die musikalischen Grundlagen des volkstümlichen österreichischen Musikgutes', *Jb des österreichischen Volksliedwerkes*, xvii (1968), 1
K. Horak: 'Das Liedgut der mittwinterlichen Umzugsbräuche in Tirol', *Jb des österreichischen Volksliedwerkes*, xvii (1968), 58; xviii (1969), 29; xix (1970), 1; xx (1971), 1–34
N. Wallner: 'Rhythmische Formen des alpenländischen Liedes', *Jb des österreichischen Volksliedwerkes*, xvii (1968), 22
J. Bitsche: *Der Liederschatz der Vorarlberger* (Lustenau, 1969)
W. Deutsch and G. Hofer: *Die Volksmusiksammlung der Gesellschaft der Musikfreunde in Wien* (Vienna, 1969)
Jb des österreichischen Volksliedwerkes: Register zu den Bänden 1–15, 1952–66 (1969)
L. Schmidt: *Volksgesang und Volkslied: Proben und Probleme* (Berlin, 1970)
G. Antesberger: 'Die Volksmusik in Kärnten', *Karntnarisch gsungan* (Klagenfurt, 1972), 17ff

COLLECTIONS

N. Beuttner: *Catholisch Gesang-Bůch* (Graz, 1602/R1968)
F. Ziska and J. M. Schottky: *Österreichische Volkslieder mit ihren Singweisen* (Pest, 1819, 3/1906/R1969)
J. Gabler: *Katholisches Wallfahrtbuch* (Neuhaus, 1854)
M. V. Süss: *Salzburger Volkslieder* (Salzburg, 1865)
R. Sztachovics: *Braut-Sprüche und Braut-Lieder auf dem Heideboden* (Vienna, 1867)
W. Pailler: *Weihnachtslieder und Krippenspiele aus Oberösterreich und Tirol* (Innsbruck, 1881–3)
A. Schlossar: *Deutsche Volkslieder aus Steiermark* (Innsbruck, 1881)
V. Zack: *Heiderich und Peterstamm: 25 steirische Volkslieder* (Graz, 1885)
H. Schrammel: *Alte österreichische Volksmelodien* (Vienna, 1888)
J. Gabler: *Geistliche Volkslieder, gesammelt in der Diözese St. Pölten* (Regensburg and Linz, 1890)
H. Neckheim and J. Pommer: *222 echte Kärntnerlieder* (Vienna, 1891–3)
J. Pommer: *252 Jodler und Juchezer* (Vienna, 1893)
F. F. Kohl: *Echte Tiroler-Lieder* (Vienna, 1899, rev. and enlarged 1913–15)
J. Pommer: *444 Jodler und Juchezer aus Steiermark* (Vienna, 1902)
E. K. Blümml: *Erotische Volkslieder aus Deutsch-Österreich* (Vienna, 1906)

E. Kremser: *Wiener Lieder und Tänze* (Vienna and Leipzig, 1912–25)
K. Mautner: *Alte Lieder und Weisen aus dem steiermärkischen Salzkammergute* (Vienna, 1919, 2/1925)
R. Wolkan: *Wiener Volkslieder aus fünf Jahrhunderten* (Vienna, 1920)
R. Zoder: *Altösterreichische Volkstänze* (Vienna, 1922–8)
H. Zoder: *Kinderlied und Kinderspiel aus Wien und Niederösterreich* (Vienna, 1923)
A. Angenetter and E. K. Blümml: *Lieder der Einserschützen* (Vienna, 1924)
H. Commenda: *Von der Eisenstrasse* (Vienna, 1926)
H. Pommer: *Volkslieder und Jodler aus Vorarlberg* (Vienna, 1926)
V. Zack: *Volkslieder und Jodler aus dem obersteirischen Murgebiet* (Vienna, 1927)
R. Zoder and K. M. Klier: *Echte Volkslieder aus dem Burgenland* (Vienna, 1927–31)
K. Kronfuss, A. and F. Pöschl: *Niederösterreichische Volkslieder und Jodler aus dem Schneeberggebiet* (Vienna, 1930)
R. Zoder: *Dorfmusik* (Kassel, 1931–7)
R. Zoder and K. M. Klier: *Volkslieder aus Niederösterreich* (Vienna, 1932–4)
O. Eberhard and C. Rotter: *Salzburgische Bauernlieder* (Vienna and Leipzig, 1933)
H. Commenda: *Burschentänze* (Kassel, 1934)
H. Derschmidt: *Unsere Jodler* (Carlsbad, 1934, 2/1958)
H. Gielge: *Rund um Aussee* (Vienna, 1935)
A. Asenbauer: *Kärntens Liederschatz* (Klagenfurt, 1937)
K. M. Klier: *Schatz österreichischer Weihnachtslieder* (Klosterneuburg, 1937–8)
V. Korda and K. M. Klier: *Volksmusik aus Niederösterreich* (Vienna, 1937)
F. Koschier and R. Maier: *Kärntner Heimattänze* (Klagenfurt, 1938)
G. Kotek: *Volkslieder und Jodler um den Schneeberg und Semmering* (Vienna, 1938, 2/1943)
K. M. Klier: *Volkslieder aus dem Waldviertel* (Vienna, 1942)
H. Lager: *Unsere Tänze* (Vienna, 1943)
C. Bresgen: *Fein sein, beinander bleiben: Lieder aus Bayern, Salzburg und Tirol* (Cologne, 1947)
I. Peter: *Tänze aus Österreich* (Vienna, 1947)
G. Kotek and R. Zoder: *Ein österreichisches Volksliederbuch* (Vienna, 1948–50)
A. Novak: *Steirische Tänze: Volkstänze und Bauernspiele aus Steiermark* (Graz, 1949)
R. Maier: *Kärntner Fasten- und Osterlieder* (Klagenfurt, 1953)
A. Anderluh: *Kärntens Volksliedschatz* (Klagenfurt, 1960–72)
A. Quellmalz: *Südtiroler Volkslieder* (Kassel, 1968–72)
N. Wallner: *Deutsche Marienlieder der Enneberger Ladiner, Südtirol* (Vienna, 1970)
K. Horak: *Tiroler Volkstänze aus alter Überlieferung* (Schwaz, 1971)
    HELLMUT FEDERHOFER (I), WALTER DEUTSCH (II)

Auszug (from *ausziehen*: 'to draw out', 'to extract'). (1) A term used to designate a vocal score of an opera or similar work.

(2) A slide (*Zug*) of a trombone or slide trumpet.

Authentic cadence. A perfect cadence, that is, a CADENCE made up of a dominant chord followed by a tonic chord (V–I), both normally in root position; the term is contrasted with 'plagal cadence', whose penultimate chord is a subdominant. The term is used mainly in American writings, which sometimes state that the uppermost note in the final chord should be the tonic.

Authentic mode (from Gk. *authentos*, Lat. *authenticus* or *authentus*). Any of the church modes whose AMBITUS, or range, includes the octave lying immediately above the FINAL of the mode. The term is thus applied to the four odd-numbered modes of Gregorian chant (1, 3, 5 and 7), whose Greek-derived names are DORIAN, PHRYGIAN, LYDIAN and MIXOLYDIAN; the ambitus of each of these modes is about a 4th higher than that of its corresponding even-numbered PLAGAL MODE, the term with which 'authentic mode' is contrasted.

The earliest definition of the term is given in Hucbald's *De musica* (?*c*880; *GS*, i, 116): 'Every authentic tone [i.e. mode] rises from its final up to the 9th [above]. It descends, moreover, to [the tone] next to it, and sometimes to the semitone or to the [minor] 3rd'. Later, the lower limit of the ambitus of an authentic mode was restricted in theory to the SUBFINAL, which lies a tone below the final in the modes where it is available (1st, 3rd and 7th). The contrast between authentic and plagal was extended to the IONIAN and AEOLIAN modes when these (and their corresponding plagals) were added to the original eight church modes in Glarean's *Dodecachordon* (1547).

The word 'authenticus', notwithstanding its Greek derivation, is not reflected in the early Byzantine modal terminology, unlike its counterpart *plagalis*; an 'authentic' Byzantine mode was simply designated *echos* (the later *kyrios* seems to be a back-translation from the Latin system).

HAROLD S. POWERS

Auto (Sp.: 'act'). A spanish dramatic composition originally of religious or allegorical character; the term was later also applied to other *representaciones*, such as Juan del Encina's *Auto del Repelón*, which deals with student life at Salamanca. The *auto* developed from medieval liturgical drama and attained its typically Spanish form in the 16th-century *autos sacramentales* performed in the streets during the feast of Corpus Christi. A 15th-century antecedent, Gómez Manrique's *Representación del nacimiento de Nuestro Señor*, includes a cradle song, various pastoral choruses and a closing villancico; this combination of music and drama was amplified in the *autos* of Encina and his contemporary Gil Vicente. The *auto* engaged the talents of the great Spanish poets, including Lope de Vega and Calderón, and of composers such as Cristóbal Galán, Manuel de León Marchante, Gregorio de la Rosa and Juan Romero.

Autos sacramentales generally consisted of one act with a *loa* (prologue) or other introduction and a finale in praise of the Sacrament. Although spoken verse predominated, the main characters often expressed their emotions in song, and an off-stage chorus commented on the action. There were frequent interruptions for *intermedios*, which often included *bailes* or *danzas*. In the 18th century these interpolations grew to large proportions, incorporating popular songs, *seguidillas*, *entremeses* and *tonadillas* (e.g. Luis Misón's *Los jardineros*, a *tonadilla*, was composed for *De lo que va ó El hombre de Dios*, an *auto sacramentale* presented in Madrid in 1761). The performances moved from the streets to the theatre and employed professional actors and musicians. This complete secularization of the *auto sacramentale* led to its prohibition by royal decree in 1765 (a decision not totally supported by the church), but it continued to be performed in small cities and villages for a considerable time afterwards.

Music drama derived from the Spanish *auto* survives in the south-western USA. There are two types, one based on the Old Testament (e.g. *Comedia de Adán y Eva*, based on an *auto* first presented in Mexico City in 1532) and the more popular cycle based on the New Testament, of which the best known is *Los pastores*, a re-enactment of the Nativity story.

BIBLIOGRAPHY

LaborD; *RiemannL 12*
M. Latorre y Badillo: 'Representación de los autos sacramentales en el periodo de su mayor florecimiento (1620–81)', *Revista de archivos, bibliotécas y museos*, xxv (1911), 189; xxvi (1912), 236
M. N. Hamilton: *Music in Eighteenth Century Spain* (Urbana, 1937/R1973)
M. Salazar: 'Music in the Primitive Spanish Theatre before Lope de Vega', *PAMS 1938*, 94
G. Chase: 'Origins of the Lyric Theater in Spain', *MQ*, xxv (1939), 292
M. Bataillon: 'Essai de l'explication de l'auto', *Bulletin hispanique*, xlii (1940), 193
A. A. Parker: *The Allegorical Drama of Calderón* (London and Oxford, 1943)
J. Sage: 'Calderón y la música teatral', *Bulletin hispanique*, lviii (1956), 275
N. D. Shergold and J. E. Varey: *Los autos sacramentales en Madrid en la época de Calderón, 1637–81: estudios y documentos* (Madrid, 1961)

Autograph. A manuscript written in the hand of a particular person; in normal musical parlance, the manuscript of a work in the hand of its composer. It is thus generally distinguished from 'copy', a manuscript in the hand of another person. 'Autograph' may be used adjectivally, for example in referring to 'a copy of the "Eroica" Symphony with Beethoven's autograph corrections'. The term 'holograph' is sometimes used to distinguish a manuscript wholly in the hand of its author or composer.

Composers' autographs from earlier than the 16th century are not known to survive, though there has been conjecture as to the possibility of certain earlier sources (e.g. the Old Hall Manuscript) containing autograph material. Autographs survive in increasing profusion from later periods. Several collections of musical autographs have been published in facsimile. For a fuller discussion, and a list of such collections, *see* SOURCES, MS, §I.

Autoharp (Fr. *cithare d'amateur*; Ger. *Akkordzither*). A chord zither invented in the last quarter of the 19th century. Simple chords can be played on it by strumming the strings with fingers, pick or plectrum, while damper bars controlled by buttons damp all the

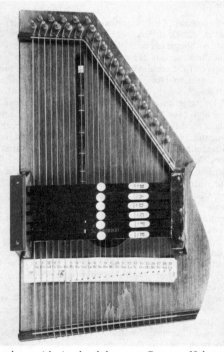

Autoharp with six chord dampers, German, 19th century (Stearns Collection, University of Michigan, Ann Arbor)

strings except those required for the chord (see illustration). According to Sachs, the autoharp was invented by C. A. Gütter of Markneukirchen. An American patent was granted in 1881 to C. F. Zimmermann, a German émigré, who began production in 1885 and sold 50,000 instruments within three years (see Moore). ALFRED DOLGE purchased controlling interest in the Zimmermann firm, and by the mid-1890s was producing 3000 autoharps a week which were sold by door-to-door salesmen and through the catalogues of Sears Roebuck and Montgomery Ward as well as by local music shops. Dolge's disastrous financial ventures soon obliged him to close his factories at Dolgeville, New York. The autoharp survived the impact of the gramophone and came to be widely used in schools in the USA and Germany for teaching rudimentary harmony. Meanwhile an Appalachian folk style of playing was developed by Ernest 'Pop' Stoneman, who made his first recording in 1924, and after World War II by Maybelle Carter.

BIBLIOGRAPHY

C. Sachs: *Real-Lexicon der Musikinstrumente, zugleich ein Polyglossar für das gesamte Instrumentengebiet* (Berlin, 1913/*R*1962)
P. Seeger: 'The Autoharp, played Stoneman Style', *Sing Out!*, xi/5 (1961–2), 16
A. D. Moore: 'The Autoharp: its Origin and Development from a Popular to a Folk Instrument', *New York Folklore Quarterly*, xix (1963)
M. Peterson: *Many Ways to Play the Autoharp* (Union, NJ, 1966)
E. Brown: 'The Autoharp', *Come all Ye: Journal of the Vancouver Folk Song Society*, iii (1974), 2

DAVID KETTLEWELL

Automelon. An IDIOMELON that serves as the musical model for various contrafacta. *See* PROSOMOION.

Autumnus, Johann Andreas. *See* HERBST, JOHANN ANDREAS.

Aux-Cousteaux [Hautcousteaux], **Artus** [Arthur] (*b* ?Amiens, *c*1590; *d* Paris, *c*1654). French composer and singer. Although his birthplace is not known, there were families bearing this name in Amiens; a member of one, a relative of the composer, served as mayor of the town. Aux-Cousteaux studied under Jean de Bournonville at the choir school of St Quentin Cathedral. From 1613 to 1627 he sang *haute-contre* in Louis XIII's chapel. A period at Noyon followed about which little is known. He succeeded Bournonville as *maître de musique* both at St Quentin (1631) and Amiens (*c*1632–4). On 24 June 1634 he relinquished this more lucrative post for that of a 'clerk' *haute-contre* at the Sainte-Chapelle in Paris. In spite of a recalcitrant and quarrelsome nature ('scandalous, insolent and disrespectful acts committed daily during the Office'), Aux-Cousteaux advanced rapidly and by 1643 was *maître de musique* secure in the protection of no less a personage than Mathieu Molé, first president of Parlement. He left the Sainte-Chapelle about 1651 and received a canonry at the church of St Jacques de l'Hôpital, where he remained until his death.

Although esteemed by Gantez (*L'entretien*) for his ability to write both 'agréable' and 'grave' music, Aux-Cousteaux was characterized by Brossard as a 'rank pedant' who 'never wished to hear of adding *Basses-continues* to his works' (*Catalogue*). In its use of conservative polyphony, Aux-Cousteaux's religious music perpetuates the 'learned' tradition of Du Caurroy and Jean de Bournonville. His chansons are models of clear textual declamation but in general lack the melodic grace of Antoine Boësset or Etienne Moulinié. They are closer in

spirit to the Le Jeune of the 1612 *Meslanges* than they are to the more progressive *airs de cour*.

WORKS

SACRED

Missa, 4vv, . . . secundi toni (Paris, 1726)
Missa quinti toni, 5vv, in J.-B. de La Borde: *Essai sur la musique* (Paris, 1726)
Missa, 5vv, ad imitationem moduli 'Quelle beauté ô mortels' (Paris, 1651)
5 masses are lost

[21] Psalmi, 4–6vv (Paris, 1631)
Octo cantica Divae Mariae Virginis, 4vv (Paris, 1641)
Noëls et cantiques spirituels, 2vv (Paris, 1644)
Second livre de nöels et cantiques spirituels, 2vv (Paris, 1644)
Canticum Virginis Deiparae (Paris, 1655)
Paraphrase des Psaumes de David, lv, bc (Paris, 1656)

SECULAR

Les quatrains de Mr. Mathieu, 3vv (Paris, 1643)
Meslanges de chansons, 3–6vv (Paris, 1644), 32 chansons, 2 madrigals, 1 villageoise, 1 voix de ville
Suite de la première partie des quatrains de Mr. Mathieu, 3vv (Paris, 1652)

BIBLIOGRAPHY

A. Gantez: *L'entretien des musiciens* (Auxerre, 1643); ed. with commentary by E. Thoinan (Paris, 1878/*R*1971)
M. Brenet: *Les musiciens de la Sainte-Chapelle du Palais* (Paris, 1910)
J.-G. Prod'homme, ed.: *Ecrits de musiciens* (*XVᵉ–XVIIIᵉ siècles*) (Paris, 1912) [includes dedications and *avertissement* from *Quatrains de Mr. Mathieu*]
T. Gérold: *L'art du chant en France au XVIIᵉ siècle* (Strasbourg, 1921/*R*1971)
R. Rebourd: 'Messire Arthus Aux Cousteaux, maître de musique de la Sainte-Chapelle du Palais', *Bulletin de la Société d'étude du XVIIᵉ siècle*, xxi–xxii (1954), 403
A. Bloch-Michel: 'Les messes d'Aux-Cousteaux', *RMFC*, ii (1961–2), 31
——: 'Les meslanges d'Aux-Cousteaux', *RMFC*, iii (1963), 11

JAMES R. ANTHONY

Auxiliary note [neighbor note] (Fr. *broderie*; Ger. *Hilfsnote*). In part-writing an unaccented NON-HARMONIC NOTE that lies a half step or whole step away from a 'main' note, which it ornaments by being approached from and returning to the main note directly (e.g. *e–f–e* and *b–a–b* over an E minor chord; *f* and *a* are the auxiliary notes).

Auza(-León), Atiliano (*b* Sucre, 5 Oct 1928). Bolivian composer and violinist. He was a choirboy at Sucre Cathedral and in 1950 graduated as a music teacher from the Escuela Normal in that city, working thereafter as a teacher and choir director. Then, at the La Paz Conservatory, he studied counterpoint with Eisner and the violin with Maldonado, and he joined the National SO as a violinist. On returning to Sucre he studied composition with Hochmann and the piano with Thorrez. He won Luz Mila Patiño Awards for the *Trío breve* (1964) and the choral *Madrigal y cueca* (1965) and received a scholarship to the Di Tella Institute in Buenos Aires (1965), where his teachers included Ginastera, Sessions, Le Roux and Davidovsky. Works following this period of study include *Anfiblástula*, 2 *epigramas griegos* (on texts by Franz Tamayo). *Tránsito* (to a poem by O. Campero Echazú) and the *Preludio, Invención, Passacaglia y Postludio* on a 12-note series of Dallapiccola; some of his music has been published by Ricordi Americana. He wrote *Dinámica musical en Bolivia* (La Paz, 1967).

CARLOS SEOANE

Avant garde (Fr.: 'vanguard'). A term used in its noun form as a collective description of artists who adopt techniques or expressive aims radically different from those hallowed by tradition, with the implication that their work makes advances which will subsequently be widely accepted and adopted. In the West there have always been such venturers: the Ars Nova revolution, for example, could be ascribed to an avant garde whose innovations met with disapproval in the highest quarters but whose work made a lasting contribution to musical thought. However, the notion of the avant-garde artist as an enlightened opponent to convention probably dates from the time of Baudelaire.

One may suppose that such composers as Wagner (and others of the New German School) and Debussy saw themselves to some extent in this light, and were so regarded by their contemporaries, but the term 'avant garde' entered common musical usage only with Stockhausen, Boulez and others in the years immediately after World War II. It was at that time, too, that it became possible to speak of 'avant-garde techniques', embracing total serialism, electronic means, new vocal and instrumental resources, aleatory composition and so on. The clearest statements of avant-garde aesthetics are to be found in the writings of Boulez, whose manifesto for the Institut de Recherche et Coordination Acoustique/Musique (1974) insists that 'we can no longer elude the essential trial; that of becoming an absolute part of the present, of forsaking all memory to forge a perception without precedent, of renouncing the legacies of the past, to discover yet undreamed-of territories'.

However, the avant garde of Boulez and others is something very different from that of the 'poètes maudits' in that their work, even if it does not receive popular acclaim, is supported by international festivals, broadcasting authorities and record companies. Some writers have attempted to distinguish therefore between the avant garde, who are officially recognized, and other anti-conventional artists who are not, often invoking the term 'experimental' to describe the latter group. Thus Stockhausen and Birtwistle might be called 'avant-garde' composers, Cage and LaMonte Young 'experimental' musicians. But even if one accepts this distinction, the term 'avant garde' remains more a slogan than a definition.

PAUL GRIFFITHS

Avanzolini, Girolamo (*b* Rimini, *c*1600; *d* Rimini, *c*1678). Italian composer and author. He was a priest and *maestro di cappella* of Rimini Cathedral and from 1649 was librarian of the Biblioteca Gambalunghiana, Rimini. He wrote literary and historical works; all his music dates from his early years. He had some connection with the pseudonymous composer Accademico Bizzarro Capriccioso, to each of whose opp.1 and 2 (1620–21) he contributed a madrigal, one for two voices, the other for three. As a composer he is known mainly for three volumes of sacred music written mostly in a simple style suited to the needs of a provincial choirmaster: 14 eight-part psalms with organ continuo, op.1, a book of four- and five-part concertato masses, op.2 (incomplete), and four masses and two motets with organ continuo, op.3 (all Venice, 1623). The description 'a tre voci variate' of op.3 refers to an unusual arrangement of partbooks – one each for the highest, middle and lowest voices.

ELEANOR SELFRIDGE-FIELD

Avars. Nomadic tribe of Asiatic origin who succeeded the Huns as inhabitants of the Hungarian steppe in the second half of the 6th century. They were in turn displaced by the Magyars, by at least 800. According to recent research, there were two distinct 'Avar' periods; in the second of these, the Magyars may already have begun to occupy the country (László). Accordingly, any theories advanced about Avar music may prove unreliable.

The early 7th-century Byzantine chronicler Theophylactus noted that Avar songs were well known, and differed from Germanic and Slavonic songs. Archaeological discoveries, dated in the period between 600 and 750, include a number of double auloi, found near Jánoshida (in 1933), near Felgyő and elsewhere. József Bige has shown that the Jánoshida pipe (which dates from the earlier Avar period) produces a major hexachord: Bartha's theories of a chromatic and microtonal scale were based on faulty premises, since the pipe was played with an unsuitable mouthpiece. The Felgyő pipe, dating from the later Avar period, produces a minor hexachord.

See also NOMADIC PEOPLES OF EUROPE AND ASIA (ANCIENT).

BIBLIOGRAPHY
D. Bartha: *Die avarische Doppelschalmei von Jánoshida* (Budapest, 1934)
W. Niemeyer: 'Awarische Musik', *MGG*
G. László: 'Kérdések és Feltevések a magyar hongfoglalásról' [Questions and hypotheses on the Hungarian conquest], *Valóság* (1970), 48

PÉTER P. VÁRNAI

Avdeyeva, Larisa (Ivanovna) (*b* Moscow, 21 June 1925). Soviet mezzo-soprano. She studied at the Stanislavsky Opera Studio (1945–6) with L. Ya. Shor-Plotnikova (singing) and N. S. Golovanov and M. I. Kedrov (dramatic art). From 1947 she was a soloist at the Stanislavsky Music Theatre, Moscow, where her roles were Suzuki, La Périchole, Kosova and Varvara (Khrennikov's *Into the Storm* and Frol Skobeyev) and Mistress of the Copper Mountain (Molchanov's *The Stone Flower*). In 1952 she moved to the Bol'shoy Theatre, where she has sung the leading Rimsky-Korsakov and Musorgsky mezzo roles, Tchaikovsky's Sorceress, Borodin's Konchakovna, Akhrosimova (*War and Peace*) and the Komissar (Kholminov's *The Optimistic Tragedy*). She married Evgeny Svetlanov. In the concert hall she has sung Mahler, Prokofiev and Skryabin, and she has toured widely, to the USA, Canada, Japan and Europe. She was made People's Artist of the RSFSR in 1964.

I. M. YAMPOL'SKY

Avella, Giovanni d' (*fl* 1657). Italian theorist and ?composer. His treatise *Regole di musica, divise in cinque trattati* (Rome, 1657) indicates that in that year he was preacher in the Minori Osservanti – an order of strict Franciscans – in the province of Terra Lavoro. In some reference works he is mentioned as a composer of lute music, but there are no known compositions. The *Regole di musica* is not only about music but ranges over many other matters, from astronomy to astrology. However, Avella's theories and views failed to impress his contemporaries and fellow theorists: GIOVANNI FRANCESCO BECCATELLI, for instance, in his *Annotazioni* (MS, *I-Bc*) on the *Regole* rightly accused him of ignorance of musical history in attributing the Guidonian Hand not only to Boethius but also to Plato and

Aristotle, and in making Guido d'Arezzo a contemporary of Pope Gregory I.

JOSEF-HORST LEDERER

Ave Maria (Lat.: 'Hail Mary'). A prayer of the Roman rite. It consists of the words of the Archangel Gabriel (*Luke* i.28), the words of Elizabeth (*Luke* i.42) and a formula of petition appended in the 15th century; the present wording was adopted in the 16th century for general liturgical use (*LU*, p.1861). The first segment of the text is used as an antiphon for the Feast of the Annunciation with a 10th-century melody (*LU*, p.1416). Moreover, as an Offertory antiphon it occurs once with the above-mentioned text and a modern melody (*LU*, p.1318) and once with both biblical portions of the text and a medieval melody (*LU*, p.355). A considerable number of polyphonic settings, often with textual variants and only loosely based on the chant melody, survive by Renaissance composers, including De Orto, Josquin, Willaert and Victoria, and there are *Ave Maria* masses by Pierre de La Rue, Morales and Palestrina. Giacomo Fogliano set the complete text as a simple four-voice *lauda* (HAM, i, 97). The title is used for Schubert's song after Scott's *Lady of the Lake*. Gounod's celebrated *Ave Maria* consists of a melody superimposed on the C major prelude from the first book of Bach's *Das wohltemperirte Clavier*.

See also ANTIPHON and MOTET, §II.

BIBLIOGRAPHY
R. Steiner: 'Ave Maria [Antiphon]', *New Catholic Encyclopedia* (New York, 1967)

Avena (Lat.: 'oaten straw'). A term used in Latin antiquity and the Middle Ages to mean, by metonymy, a reed pipe; *see* THEOCRITUS and VIRGIL.

Avenarius [Habermann], **Philipp** (*b* Lichtenstein, nr. Zwickau, *c*1553; *d* in or after 1610). German composer and organist. He is first heard of as an organist at Amorbach, Odenwald, in 1570 and until February 1571. The dedication of his *Cantiones sacrae* (1572) was written from Falkenau, Bohemia, where his father was working. According to Gerber he was later an organist at Altenburg and then, until 1610, at St Michael, Zeitz. He was one of a number of minor composers working in Saxony and Thuringia in the latter half of the 16th century. His output was less varied than, for example, that of Johann Steuerlein, but the pieces in his *Cantiones sacrae* were highly regarded by his contemporaries, as is shown by the praise accorded them by Christoph Schultze. The style of his motets is conservative, as was his preference for Latin texts.

WORKS
Cantiones sacrae, 5vv (Nuremberg, 1572)
Devota acclamatio novis honoribus, 6vv (Jena, 1608)
20 other sacred works *D-Bds, Rp, Z, PL-WRu*

BIBLIOGRAPHY
GerberNL
E. Bohn: *Die musikalischen Handschriften des XVI. und XVII. Jahrhunderts in der Stadtbibliothek Breslau* (Breslau, 1890)
A. Werner: *Städtische und fürstliche Musikpflege in Zeitz bis zum Anfang des 19. Jahrhunderts* (Bückeburg and Leipzig, 1922)
E. F. Schmid: *Die Orgeln der Abtei Amorbach* (Buchen, 1938)
R. Quoika: 'Christoph Harant von Polschitz und seine Zeit', *Mf*, vii (1954), 419
——: *Die Musik der Deutschen in Böhmen und Mähren* (Berlin, 1956)
G. Pietzsch: 'Orgelbauer, Orgeln und Orgelspiel in Deutschland bis zum Ende des 16. Jahrhunderts', *Mf*, xi (1958), 311

AUGUST SCHARNAGL

Avenary, Hanoch [Loewenstein, Herbert] (*b* Danzig [now Gdańsk], 25 May 1908). Israeli musicologist. He studied musicology, literature and art history at the universities of Leipzig, Munich, Frankfurt am Main and Königsberg (Kaliningrad), where he took the doctorate under Wilhelm Warringer in 1931 with a dissertation on Minnesang. He was prevented from pursuing an academic career in Germany, and turned to publishing Jewish art in Berlin (1932–6). In 1936 he settled as a publisher in Palestine, where research in musicology had barely begun, and he had to carry on his musicological work independently, publishing articles mostly in foreign periodicals. Urged to adapt himself to the demands of a country under war conditions, he developed a chemical production process and worked as technical manager in industry (1941–8) before joining the Israel Air Force research department. He left the service with the rank of major to take up a research fellowship in musicology at the Hebrew University, Jerusalem (1965–72); in 1966 he became a lecturer, and in 1972 assistant professor in the musicology department of Tel-Aviv University. He is co-editor of *Orbis musicae* and co-founder of the *Hebrew Quarterly for Music*. A regular contributor to several periodicals and encyclopedias, he also plays an active role in international congresses and Israeli professional organizations; he was appointed president of the Israel Musicological Society in 1971. His speciality is sacred music, particularly Jewish music and that of the ancient Near East.

WRITINGS
'Eine pentatonische Bibelweise in der deutschen Synagoge', *ZMw*, xii (1929–30), 513
Wort und Ton bei Oswald von Wolkenstein (diss., U. of Königsberg, 1931; Königsberg, 1932)
'Munachei hamusika bassafrut ha' Ivrit shel yemei habenayim' [Musical terms in Hebrew medieval literature], *Leshonenu*, xiii (1945), 140
'The Mixture Principle in the Medieval Organ', *MD*, iv (1950), 51
'Abu'l-Salt's Treatise on Music', *MD*, vi (1952), 27
'Formal Structure of Psalms and Canticles in Early Jewish and Christian Chant', *MD*, vii (1953)
'Magic, Symbolism and Allegory of Old-Hebrew Sound-instruments', *CHM*, ii (1957), 21
'Jüdische Musik', *MGG*
'Etudes sur le cancionero judéo-espagnol', *Sefarad*, xx (Madrid, 1960), 377
'Hieronymus' Epistel über die Musikinstrumente und ihre altöstlichen Quellen', *AnM*, xvi (1961), 55
'Pseudo-Jerome Writings and Qumrân Tradition', *Revue de Qumrân*, xiii (1963), 15
Studies in the Hebrew, Syrian and Greek Liturgical Recitative (Tel-Aviv, 1963)
'Geniza Fragments of Hebrew Hymns and Prayers Set to Music: Early 12th Century', *Journal of Jewish Studies*, xvi (1966), 87
'A Geniza Find of Saadya's Psalm-preface and its Musical Aspects', *Hebrew Union College Annual*, xxxix (1968), 145
'The Cantorial Fantasia of the 18th and 19th Centuries', *Yuval*, i (1968), 65
'Cantos españoles antiguos mencionadas en la literatura hebraea', *AnM*, xxv (1970), 67
'Flutes for a Bride or a Dead Man: the Symbolism of the Flute', *Orbis musicae*, i (1971), 11
Hebrew Hymn Tunes: the Rise and Development of a Musical Tradition (Tel-Aviv, 1971)
'Jewish Music: Post-biblical History', *Encyclopaedia Judaica* (Jerusalem, 1971), 566–671
'The Concept of Mode in European Synagogue Chant', *Yuval*, ii (1971), 11
'Die Diskrepanz der ikonographischen und literarischen Darstellungen altöstlicher Musikinstrumente', *IMSCR, xi Copenhagen 1972*, 141; Eng. trans. in *Orbis musicae*, ii (Tel-Aviv, 1973–4), 121
'Ebraica, musica', *Enciclopedia della musica* (Milan, 1973)
'The Hebrew Version of Abū l-Salt's Treatise on Music', *Yuval*, iii (1974), 7–82 [edn., trans. and commentary]
'Der Einfluss der judischen Mystik auf den Synagogengesang', *Kairos*, new ser., xvi (Salzburg, 1974), 79
'The Earliest Notation of Ashkenazi Bible Chant', *Journal of Jewish Studies*, xxvi (1975), 132

The Ashkenazi Tradition of Biblical Chant between 1500 and 1900 (Tel-Aviv, 1976)

'The Northern and Southern Idioms of Early European Music: a New Approach to an Old Problem', *AcM*, xlix (1977)

EDITIONS

S. Rossi: Il primo libro delle canzonette (1589) (Tel-Aviv, 1975)

WILLIAM Y. ELIAS

Avenpace. *See* IBN BĀJJA.

Aventinus, Johannes [Turmair, Johann; Thurnmaier, John; Thurnmayer, Jean; Thurinomarus] (*b* Abensberg, 4 July 1477; *d* Regensburg, 9 Jan 1534). German historian and music theorist. He studied at Ingolstadt University with Conradus Celtis, at Kraków University, and at Paris University with Jacobus Faber Stapulensis. After the death of Albrecht IV, Aventinus was appointed tutor to the young Dukes of Bavaria in 1508, and in·1517 became court historian. In this capacity he produced two of the most important and influential historical works of his time: *Annales ducum boiariae* and *Bayrischer Chronicon*.

Aventinus was the author of *Musicae rudimenta* (Augsburg, 1516; ed. in Keahey) sometimes incorrectly ascribed to Nicolaus Faber (ii). The treatise, in ten chapters, was written for the instruction of the youngest of the three dukes. In keeping with the traditional approach to music as a part of the Quadrivium, the work deals with speculation about the origins and uses of music, solmization and the mutation of Guidonian hexachords, and the Pythagorean division of the monochord. Problems of current musical practice are only lightly touched on. Aventinus cited many musical authorities, including Plato, Aristotle, Aristoxenus, Cleonides, Boethius, Guido of Arezzo, Ugolino of Orvieto, Jehan des Murs and Gaffurius. He gave a number of terms and phrases in German as well as in Latin.

BIBLIOGRAPHY

A. von Dommer: 'Nikolaus Faber', *MMg*, i (1869), 19

C. von Halm, ed.: *J. Turmairs sämmtliche Werke* (Munich, 1880–86)

K. W. Niemöller: 'Ist Nicolaus Faber oder Johannes Aventin der Verfasser der "Musicae Rudimenta" (Augsburg, 1516)?', *Mf*, xiv (1961), 184

T. H. Keahey, ed.: *Johann Turmair – Johannes Aventinus: Musicae Rudimenta, Augsburg, 1516* (New York, 1971)

T. HERMAN KEAHEY

Ave regina caelorum (Lat.: 'Hail Queen of Heaven'). One of the four Marian antiphons. It is now sung at the end of Compline from the Purification (2 February) until Wednesday in Holy Week, but its original role in the liturgy appears to have been to precede and follow the chanting of a psalm. Of the two melodies in the *Liber usualis* the more elaborate (p.274) is apparently the older. Dufay's four-voice setting, which he requested be sung at his deathbed, uses the chant melody as a cantus firmus in the tenor, with sections of the chant paraphrased in the upper two voices; the traditional text is troped with a personal supplication for mercy: 'Miserere tui labentis Dufay'. Several other settings by Dufay survive, including a *Missa 'Ave regina caelorum'*. Settings by 16th-century composers include four by Palestrina, an eight-part setting with organ and a mass by Victoria, and a five-voice setting by Gesualdo.

See also ANTIPHON and MOTET, §II.

BIBLIOGRAPHY

P. Wagner: *Einführung in die gregorianischen Melodien*, i (Fribourg, 1895, 3/1911/R1962; Eng. trans., 1907)

W. Apel: *Gregorian Chant* (Bloomington, 1958, 3/1966)

R. Steiner: 'Ave regina caelorum', *New Catholic Encyclopedia* (New York, 1967)

Averie. *See* AVERY.

Averroes. *See* IBN RUSHD.

Aversi (Lat.). A term used in the 15th century to describe mass settings in which the number of voices varies from one section to the next. Although the word itself is found in only one manuscript (*GB-Ob* Can.misc.213), where it is used in the index to describe mass movements by Binchois, Guillaume Legrant and Bartolomeo da Bologna, it is an appropriate word for describing an important series of works from the first half of the 15th century in which sections marked 'duo' (or 'soli') and 'chorus' alternate. The sources for these works are the earliest surviving evidence of choral polyphony. (*See also* CURSIVA and VIRILAS.)

BIBLIOGRAPHY

M. F. Bukofzer: 'The Beginnings of Choral Polyphony', *Studies in Medieval and Renaissance Music* (New York, 1950), 176

H. Schoop: *Entstehung und Verwendung der Handschrift Oxford Bodleian Library, Canonici misc. 213*, Publikationen der Schweizerischen musikforschenden Gesellschaft, 2nd ser., xxiv (Berne, 1971), 49ff

Avery [Burton, Avery] (*b* ?c1470; *d* ?c1543). English composer. Among the English authorities to whom Thomas Morley referred in preparing his *A Plaine and Easie Introduction to Practicall Musicke* (1597) is one listed simply as 'Averie'. This is undoubtedly the 'Master Averie' who composed an organ *Te Deum* (in *GB-Lbm* Add.29996; ed. in EECM, vi, 1966) and a *Missa 'Ut re mi fa sol la'* (in *Ob* Mus.Sch.E.376–80). In the latter, however, a later hand has added the surname 'Burton' in the bass partbook, and on the strength of this Flood ventured to identify the composer of the two pieces with a number of references to musicians of similar names which he found in his search of the state papers. If these all refer to the same man the following slender biography can be constructed.

On 29 November 1494 Henry VII made a payment 'To Burton for making a Mass, 20s.'. In November 1509 a David Burton was appointed a Gentleman of the Chapel Royal and on 22 February 1511 Davy Burton was issued with livery for the funeral of Prince Henry, the infant son of Henry VIII. The Chapel Royal accompanied the king to France On 20 June 1513 where on 17 September at Tournai a *Te Deum*, attributed without justification to Burton, was performed after Mass. In June 1520 he was again in France with the Chapel Royal attending King Henry's meeting with François I at the field of the Cloth of Gold, and in July 1527 'Master Avery' was among the Gentlemen of the Chapel who accompanied Cardinal Wolsey to France. In a list of salaries for the year 1526 Avery Burnett, Gentleman of the Chapel, is scheduled to receive 7½d. a day. During the next 15 years the names Burton and Burnet occur in connection with various payments and grants of leases of land (listed by Flood) in the last of which, dated 25 October 1542, he is described as David Burton, Gentleman of the King's Chapel.

If the composer and the Gentleman of the Chapel Royal are the same person it remains unexplained why both manuscripts should use only the name 'Avery'; though it is perhaps because they do that Avery alone of all the Englishmen listed by Morley is familiarly addressed by his first name. On the other hand, Morley did not use the title 'Master', nor is it clear what that title's significance is. In support of Flood's identification an annotation, presumably by Thomas Tomkins himself in his copy of Morley's treatise, describes a group of names which includes Averie as 'All these of the King's Chapel'.

Avery's *Missa 'Ut re mi fa sol la'*, the only piece of English vocal music on the hexachord, is incomplete, apparently lacking a second bass part, in spite of the fact that it occurs in a complete set of six partbooks. The mass was originally described in the *Tabula* as of 'vi parts' but this was later changed to 'v parts' and it seems quite certain that the sixth part was never copied into Mus.Sch.E.381.

BIBLIOGRAPHY
W. H. G. Flood: *Early Tudor Composers* (London, 1925)
J. Pulver: *Biographical Dictionary of Old English Music* (London, 1927)
L. D. Brothers: 'Avery Burton and his Hexachord Mass', *MD*, xxviii (1974), 153
JOHN BERGSAGEL

Avery, John (baptized Avening, nr. Stroud, Gloucs., 3 Jan 1738; *d* London, 1808). English organ builder. His premises in London were in St Margaret's Church Yard, Westminster. At the time of his death the organ that he had built for Carlisle Cathedral was being installed. Despite his reputation as an excellent organ builder, he appears to have suffered from financial difficulties. Organs he built or worked on include those at: St Stephen's, Coleman Street, London (1775); Westminster Abbey, London (1793; addition of 13 large-scale wood Open diapason pipes, *G'* to *G*, to be played by pedals, probably by Avery); St Andrew, Northborough, Northamptonshire (1783; chamber organ: 8', 8', 4', 4', 2', Sesquialtera bass, Cornet treble); St Michael's Mount, Cornwall (1786; case enlarged, some pipework remains); Royal Foundation of St Katherine in Ratcliff, London (1790; chamber organ); Croydon parish church (1794; burnt 1866); Leominster Priory, Herefordshire (1797; some pipework survives); Stroud parish church (1797–8; facsimile of contract with specification in Rigby); St Nicholas, Sevenoaks (1798; opened by Samuel Wesley; dated case remains); Winchester Cathedral (1799; three manuals and pedals); Christ Church, Bath (1800); Salem, Massachusetts (1800); St Margaret's, Westminster (1804); King's College Chapel, Cambridge (1804); Carlisle Cathedral (1808).

BIBLIOGRAPHY
J. Sutton: *A Short Account of Organs* (London, 1847), 86f
E. J. Hopkins and E. F. Rimbault: *The Organ: its History and Construction* (London, 1855, 3/1887), 149
E. Rigby: 'John Avery and Stroud Parish Church', *The Organ*, xlii (1962–3), 125
M. Wilson: *The English Chamber Organ* (Oxford, 1968)
GUY OLDHAM

Avery Fisher Hall. New York concert hall opened in 1962; it was known as the Philharmonic Hall until 1973 and is part of the Lincoln Center. *See* NEW YORK, §3, §5.

Avia, Jacob. Possibly the pseudonym of JAKOB BANWART.

Avianus, Johannes [Johann] (*b* Tonnedorf, nr. Erfurt; *d* Eisenberg, nr. Gera, 22 Jan 1617). German writer on music, composer and schoolmaster. In 1579 he was teaching at the Lateinschule at Ronneburg, near Gera, and in 1591 he was Rektor of the Lateinschule at Gera. Later he was a preacher at Bernsdorf, near Torgau, at Munich and at Krossen, near Gera, and from 1614 until his death he was superintendent at Eisenberg. He published *Isagoge in libros musicae poeticae* (Erfurt, 1581), which is typical of the many writings on *musica poetica* of the later 16th century. Another theoretical work survives in manuscript. His only known music is a four-part occasional work, *Delphica & vera pennae literatae nobilitas* (Erfurt, 1595).

Avicenna. *See* IBN SĪNĀ.

Avidom [Mahler-Kalkstein], **Menahem** (*b* Stanislav, 6 Jan 1908). Israeli composer of Russian birth. He studied at the Paris Conservatoire with Rabaud, but considered himself self-taught; in 1925 he emigrated to Palestine. His first compositions were dodecaphonic but, while studying arts and sciences at the American University (Beirut) and during a four-year stay in Egypt, he was deeply impressed by Mediterranean and oriental folk music. The Jewish national renaissance in Palestine was then at its height and Avidom, together with other composers who had settled in the country, began to search for a means to express this patriotic spirit. They arrived at the 'Mediterranean' style, combining modality, and melodic patterns typical of the indigenous music of the area, with a moderately dissonant harmony and impressionist orchestration. Avidom applied these principles for the first time in the Symphony no.1 (1945); his Symphony no.3 'Yam tichonit' (The Mediterranean) is an even more striking exposition of the new style. Both works are in a lighter vein, whereas the Second Symphony 'David', based on the life of the Jewish king, is more profound and has remained one of Avidom's major achievements. His Symphony no.5 'Shirat Eilat' (The song of Eilat) is an interesting combination of song cycle and conventional symphonic form. Among the several awards Avidom received at this period was the 1961 Israel State Prize for the historical opera *Alexandra ha' Hashmonait*.

The early 1960s witnessed a general reorientation of Israeli music away from regionalism towards international styles and techniques. Influenced by these trends, yet remaining essentially a melodist with his roots in oriental music, Avidom returned to 12-note procedures in the tragic Seventh Symphony (1961) and the Second String Quartet (1960). However, many of the works written after 1961 lack the freshness and originality of the earlier compositions. Notable exceptions are *Enigma* (1962) for seven instruments, a piece that displays his interest in sound patterns, imitating electronic effects, rather than melodic shapes, and also the radio opera *Ha' preida* ('The farewell') (1971), a work of strangely unreal atmosphere and a convincing expression of complex psychological situations. Apart from his creative work, Avidom has been very active in Israeli musical life as secretary general of the Israel PO, music critic, chairman of the Israel Composers' League and, from 1955, director general of Acum, the Israeli performing rights society.

WORKS
(selective list)

Operas: Alexandra ha' Hashmonait, 1953; B'chol dor va'dor [In every generation], ballad opera, solo vv, 10 insts, 1955; Ha'ramai [The crook], chamber opera, 1967; Ha' preida [The farewell], radio opera, 1971

Orch: Conc., fl, str, 1944; Sym. no.1 (Ha'amamit [A Folk Sym.]), 1945; Sym. no.2 'David', 1949; Sym. no.3 'Yam tichonit' [The Mediterranean], 1952; Sym. no.4, 1956; Sym. no.5 'Shirat Eilat' [The song of Eilat], Mez, orch, 1957; Sym. no.6, 1958; Triptyque symphonique, 1960; Sym. no.7 'The Philharmonic', 1961; Sym. no.8 (Sinfonietta l'moed [A festival sinfonietta]), c1965; Sym. no.9 (Symphonie variée), chamber orch, 1968; Spring, ov., 1973

Chamber: Concertino, vn, pf, 1949, orchd 1967; 2 str qts, 1954, 1961; Enigma, 5 wind, perc, pf, 1962; Brass Qt, 1969; BACH Suite, ww, str, pf, perc, n.d.; pf pieces

Kantatat t'hilim [Psalm cantata], chorus, 1955

Principal publishers: Israel Music Institute, Israeli Music Publications MSS in *IL-J*

BENJAMIN BAR-AM

Avignon. French city, capital of the Vaucluse département. Roman chant was introduced to Avignon at the end of the 7th century by the monks of Lérins, who were summoned there by Bishop Agricol. Of the troubadours, only two songs have survived, one by Bertran Folco d'Avigno and one by Raimon d'Avigno. A university was founded in 1303. In 1309 Avignon became the seat of Pope Clement V and the centre of Western Christianity, and also a European trading centre. The 14th century was the richest period in Avignon's musical history. The papal court comprised up to 1000 people employed in up to 500 different capacities. The town became over-populated and phenomenally rich, while the court enjoyed extreme luxury. 'From this impious Babylon from whence all shame has fled, I too have fled to save my life', wrote Petrarch. There were many opulent religious services, and also festivities and secular entertainments to mark official receptions. The writing of music for the services became an excuse to try out the latest methods of composition. Pope JOHN XXII (1316–34) issued a decretal ('Docta sanctorum') on the subject in 1325 which, however, is not the condemnation of polyphony it is sometimes said to be. Moreover, in addition to the *grande chapelle* of 30 or 40 members, Benedict XII, at the beginning of his pontificate in 1334, also established a private chapel, St Stephen's, with 12 singers. In Avignon itself no trace remains of the Ordinary repertory, which was most of the time largely improvised on the *super librum*. But two manuscripts, from Ivrea (written after 1350) and from Apt (*see* SOURCES, MS) give an idea of the type of music which was fashionable: polyphonic mass fragments for three voices, using Ars Nova techniques; motets, ballades, rondeaux and virelais occasionally written in *ars subtilior* style, which flourished from 1380; and hymns, in which the liturgical melody, in decorated form, appears in the upper voice of the polyphony, anticipating the 15th-century style. Jehan des Murs wrote a motet in honour of John XXII, and Philippe de Vitry stayed in Avignon several times on missions from the French king, and composed an isorhythmic motet in honour of Pope Clement VI (1342–52). The Apt manuscript, on the other hand, contains a Gloria by Baude Cordier which is quite different in feeling and much nearer to 15th-century style. The papal court was receptive to musical novelties, and composers in the service of Clement VII (antipope, 1378–94), and of Benedict XIII (antipope, 1394–1424) included Bosco, Matheus de Sancto Johanne, Hasprois, Haucourt and Philippus de Caserta. In 1372 an organ, one of the first in France, was installed in the Franciscan Monastery at Avignon. Jewish music also flourished under the Avignon popes since Clement V protected the Jews from the expulsion orders of King Philip the Fair (1306) and the musical traditions of the synagogue were thus preserved in the

four communities of Avignon, Carpentras, Cavaillon and L'Isle sur Sorgue.

The deposition of Benedict XIII at the Synod of Pisa (1409) led to the decline of the chapel choir, but the departure of the popes did not mean the end of all Avignon musical life; in 1449 organs were installed at the cathedral and in 1454 at St Agricol (restored 1489–93). At the end of the 15th century there were two organ makers in Avignon, Barthélémy Prévot and Ramon Vitus. In 1481 Archbishop Giulio della Rovere founded a cathedral choir school for the study of plainsong, and the post of *maître de chant* was created at the university in 1497. The first of many festivities with processions, allegories, music and dancing, characteristic of the Renaissance and clearly influenced by Italy, seems to have been in 1473 for the reception of Cardinal Charles de Bourbon. An early printing industry was briefly established: Etienne Briard, a type founder, cast new characters for music printing, and Jean de Channey published (1533–5) settings of the Mass, Lamentations, *Magnificat* and hymns by Carpentras, who died in Avignon in 1548. But the Avignon printers soon lost their importance to rivals in Lyons. In 1547 Claude Noguyer taught 'letters and musical instruments' to young children. Victor de Montbuisson, an Avignon lutenist at the end of the century, pursued his career in Kassel and The Hague: three of his galliards were included in J.-B. Besard's *Thesaurus harmonicus* (*RISM* 1603[15]). The late 16th century saw the first substantial collection of Provençal noëls, 130 carols from Notre Dame des Doms (1570–1610). The modern treatment of music in the town's religious ceremonies and secular festivities gave a livelihood to several violin bands, which sometimes included woodwind. A description of the festivities at a reception for Queen Marie de Médicis in November 1600 is in the *Labyrinthe royal de l'Hercule gaulois* (Avignon, 1601); the music for this occasion, by the cathedral organist Antoine Esquirol, was in the Venetian style. In 1622, for the visit of Louis XIII, an exceptional orchestra, 120 strong, was conducted by Sauveur Intermet (*d* 1657), canon and *maître de chapelle* at St Agricol, at that time the main musical centre. Its choir school was reputed to be one of the best in the kingdom and Intermet's reputation spread as far as Paris. When a dramatic performance was mounted in the Jesuit college, Intermet's airs so pleased the king that he asked for a copy of them and next day requested that motets by the canon should be sung during Mass. In 1660, for Louis XIV's visit, another *maître de chapelle*, Béraud (*d* 1687), composed a special motet. The 17th century was the heyday of the Provençal carol; one of the finest collections was of the 57 *Noëls nouveaux* published in seven volumes by Nicolas Saboly between 1669 and 1674. He was responsible for their texts but the music consists of traditional Provençal and French tunes. J.-J. Mouret, the future 'musicien des Grâces', was born in Avignon in 1682 and received his musical education there, in the cathedral choir school. During the last years of the century, Pierre Gautier's Marseilles Opera Company enjoyed great success at Avignon; in 1688 he even staged *Bellérophon* for two private performances in the home of the Marquis de Blauvac. Italian singers and composers were equally successful in Avignon; the repertory of the chapel included works by Carissimi and others.

Nicolas Ranc directed a permanent opera company from 1705, and music lovers remained numerous in the

18th century. Two guilds were formed in the mid-18th century, St Gregory and St Cecilia, for 'singing musicians' and 'symphonic musicians' respectively; they acquired a monopoly for giving public concerts, and were able to perform such large-scale choral works as settings of the Psalms by Blanchard and Lalande. But musicians with creative talents tended to leave Avignon to try their luck in Paris. Rameau directed the cathedral choir school, but only from January 1702 to May 1703; three or four years later Mouret left, and Jean-Claude Trial (*b* 1732), a choirboy in the cathedral choir school, became co-director with Berton of the Paris Opéra from 1767, and Antoine Trial (*b* 1737), who had the same background, went on to a glorious career as an opera singer in the Théâtre des Italiens in Paris. Pierre Ligon (*b* 1749, known as the abbé Ligon) witnessed the success of his comic opera *Les deux aveugles de Franconville* in Paris; his nephew and pupil, Joseph Agricol Moulet (*b* 1766), after leaving Avignon became a famous harpist. At this point strong regional feeling made itself felt in Provence and Languedoc. At the beginning of the 18th century Mallet, *maître de chapelle* at St Peter's, had composed *Cantates patoises* and an *Impromptu de Nismes*. In the following century Aubanel undertook the reprinting (1803 and 1807) of early regional works, including the carols. The hymn of the *félibres* (modern Provençal writers) 'la coupo santo' was based on a carol by Brother Sérapion, an Avignon monk of the mid-17th century. About 1850 J. S. and M. Crémieu collected together *Chants hébraïques suivant le rite des communautés israélites de l'ancien Comtat Vénaissin*. The lawyer J. V. Avy, at about the same time, became interested in the Apt manuscript. This interest matched that of certain Romantics in the works of the Renaissance and then of the Baroque period. F. J. Séguin, who edited Saboly's carols with piano accompaniment (1856), put on performances of works by Palestrina, Bach and Handel, and composed some *Préludes dans la tonalité grégorienne*. There was also a renewed interest in chamber and symphonic music: for example, Fuzet Imbert composed a quartet and a *Poème symphonique* and in 1897 the Société Avignonaise de Concerts Symphoniques was formed.

The 20th-century summer festival (Festival d'Avignon and Rencontres Internationales de Danse Contemporaine) has become a sort of fairground of musical and especially theatrical spectacle. The city has a national conservatory directed by Guy Lajouanie, an orchestral conductor; the wind instrument classes have a particularly high reputation, hence the city's famous wind quintet. A good opera company, directed by Albert Leduc, performs the traditional repertory and gives occasional first performances. Avignon also has the largest chamber music society in France (1500 members), with high artistic standards. The holdings of the Bibliothèque Municipale include music autographs and various records of the city's musical activities.

BIBLIOGRAPHY

A. Gastoué: 'F. J. Séguin, musicien avignonais', *Tribune de St Gervais*, (1901), no.3, p.77
——: 'Les anciens chants liturgiques des églises d'Apt et d'Avignon', *Revue du chant grégorien*, x (1902), 166
——: 'La musique à Avignon et dans le Comtat du XIVe au XVIIIe siècle', *RMI*, xi (1904), 265
J. G. Prod'homme: 'La société Ste Cécile d'Avignon au XVIIIe siècle', *SIMG*, vi (1904–5), 423
L. Duhamel: 'Le théâtre d'Avignon aux XVIIe et XVIIIe siècles', *Annuaire du Vaucluse*, xxii (1909)
J.-B. Ripert: *Musique et musiciens d'Avignon* (Avignon, 1916)
P. Pansier: *Histoire du livre et de l'imprimerie à Avignon du XIVe au XVIe siècle* (Avignon, 1922)
J. Clamon et P. Pansier: *Les noëls provençaux de Notre-Dame des Doms (1570–1610)* (Avignon, 1925)
R. Brun: *Avignon au temps des papes* (Paris, 1928)
N. Dufourcq: *Documents inédits relatifs à l'orgue français* (Paris, 1934)
Le manuscrit de musique polyphonique de trésor d'Apt, Monuments de la musique ancienne, x, ed. Société française de musicologie (Paris, 1936)
N. Pirrotta: 'Il codice "Estense lat." 568 e la musica francese in Italia al principio del '400', *Atti della Reale academia di scienze, lettere e arti di Palermo*, 4th ser., v/2 (1946), 101–54
F. Lesure: 'Two Documents from Avignon', *GSJ*, vi (1953), 105
U. Günther: 'Zur Biographie einiger Komponisten der Ars subtilior', *AMw*, xxi (1964), 172
J. Robert: 'Une famille de joueurs de violon au XVIIe siècle: les De la Pierre', *RMFC*, iv (1964), 54
——: 'Les Ranc d'Avignon, propagateurs de l'opéra à la fin du XVIIe siècle', *RMFC*, vi (1966), 95
U. Günther: 'Das Manuskript Modena, Biblioteca Estense α.M.5,24 (olim Lat 568 = Mod)', *MD*, xxiv (1970), 17–68
MARCEL FREMIOT

Avignone, Bertrand di. *See* FERAGUT, BELTRAME.

Avilez [Avilés, Avilés Lusitano], **Manuel Leitão** [Leitam, Leitán] **de** (*b* Portalegre; *d* Granada, between 13 Sept and 25 Oct 1630). Portuguese composer. He was a choirboy at Portalegre Cathedral, where according to Barbosa Machado he studied with António Ferro. By 1601 he was *maestro de capilla* at Úbeda. Early that year he tried for a similar post at the royal chapel at nearby Granada but did not secure it until two years later; he was inducted on 28 August 1603. He composed copious vernacular festive music (which is now lost), beginning in 1606; on 24 November of that year the royal chapel authorities granted him special leave to compose Christmas *chanzonetas*. The library of John IV of Portugal contained two of his polychoral masses, one, *Salva Theodosium*, in 12 parts, possibly written in 1603, the other the eight-part *Ave Virgo sanctissima*. His surviving music (in *E-GRcr*) includes four penitential motets (*Domine non secundum peccata nostra*, *In jejunio et fletu* and *Adjuva nos* for four voices and *Adjuva nos* for three), two four-part Passions – one for Palm Sunday (St Matthew), the other for Good Friday (St John) – and two incomplete Lamentations verses, *Quomodo sedet sola civitas* and *Non est inventus similis illi*, both for four voices.

BIBLIOGRAPHY

Primeira parte do index da livraria de musica do muyto alto, e poderoso Rey Dom João o IV. nosso senhor (Lisbon, 1649/R1967); ed. J. de Vasconcellos (Oporto, 1874–6)
D. Barbosa Machado: *Bibliotheca Lusitana* (Lisbon, 1752), iii, 194
J. López Calo: 'El Archivo de Música de la Capilla Real de Granada', *AnM*, xiii (1958), 106, 114
ROBERT STEVENSON

Avison, Charles (*b* Newcastle upon Tyne, baptized 16 Feb 1709; *d* Newcastle upon Tyne, 9 or 10 May 1770). English composer, conductor, writer on music and organist; he was the most important English concerto composer of the 18th century and an original and influential writer on music.

1. Life. 2. Writings. 3. Compositions.

1. LIFE. He was the fifth of nine children born to Richard and Ann Avison. Since his father, a Newcastle town wait, was a practising musician, his musical training probably began at home. Later, while in the service of Ralph Jenison, a patron of the arts and MP for Northumberland from 1724 to 1741, he had opportunity for further study. He had additional support in his

musical development from Colonel John Blathwayt (or Blaithwaite), formerly a director of the Royal Academy of Music, the operatic organization in London. There is no evidence that, as has been claimed, Avison went to Italy, but William Hayes and Charles Burney wrote that he studied with Geminiani in London.

The earliest known reference to Avison's musical activities is an announcement of a benefit concert on 20 March 1734 in Hickford's Room, London. On 13 October 1735 he was appointed organist of St John's Church, Newcastle, an appointment which took effect only in June 1736 when a new organ had been installed. Four months later, on 20 October, on the death of Thomas Powell, he was appointed to a similar post at St Nicholas (now the cathedral) at a yearly salary of £20; St Nicholas was the fourth largest parish church in England and had an organ larger than the one at Durham Cathedral.

In October 1735 a series of subscription concerts was organized in Newcastle, along the lines of those held in London, Edinburgh and elsewhere, under Avison's direction. In July 1738 Avison was formally appointed musical director, beginning with the fourth season; he retained the directorship of the Newcastle Musical Society, as well as the organist's post at St Nicholas, until his death. He also took part in other musical activities in Newcastle, including concerts at the pleasure gardens and benefit concerts.

Avison's musical activities were not limited to Newcastle. He collaborated with John Garth in promoting a similar series of subscription concerts in Durham; the Durham concerts were held on Tuesdays, theatre productions in Newcastle and Durham on Wednesdays, the Newcastle concerts on Thursdays, and on Sunday evenings from about 1761 informal concerts were given in a room added for the purpose to the St Nicholas vicarage. Mondays and Fridays were reserved for Avison's private pupils on the harpsichord, violin and flute. Some of the performers in the Avison–Garth concerts included Felice Giardini, William Herschel (who became a celebrated astronomer), William Shield, and Avison's sons Edward and Charles. Geminiani is believed to have visited Avison in 1760 while travelling between Edinburgh and London, but there is no record of his playing in any concerts. Although Avison was criticized for the anti-Handelian remarks in his writings, Handel's music was well represented in the Newcastle and Durham concerts. In the 1750s Avison and Garth organized a Marcello Society in Newcastle devoted to the performance of choral music and in particular to the edition of Benedetto Marcello's *First Fifty Psalms* which the two men were preparing for publication.

Avison's reputation was not confined to Newcastle. A letter signed 'Marcellinus' appearing in the *Newcastle Journal* of 17 March 1759 summarizes some of the opportunities he refused elsewhere: before he was established in Newcastle he had a favourable prospect of establishing himself in London; he was offered the organist's post at York Minster in 1734 (accepted by James Nares), two organists' posts in Dublin on Geminiani's recommendation between 1733 and 1740, a teaching post in Edinburgh with participation in the Musical Society there, and the succession to Pepusch as organist at the Charterhouse, London, in 1753. Burney wrote that Avison was 'an ingenious and polished man, esteemed and respected by all who knew him; and an elegant writer upon his art'.

Avison married Catherine Reynolds on 15 January 1737. Three of their nine children lived to adulthood: Jane (1744–73), Edward and Charles. Edward (1747–76) succeeded his father as organist of St Nicholas and musical director of the Newcastle Musical Society, and was a friend of John Wesley; Charles (1751–95), who held various appointments as organist in Newcastle, including that at St Nicholas from 1789 (succeeding Mathias Hawdon), composed several works and published a hymn collection. The Avison family is buried in the churchyard of St Andrew's, Newgate Street, Newcastle. Robert Browning had a lifelong interest in Avison; his poem *Parleying with Certain People of Importance in their Day: with Charles Avison* was supposedly inspired by a march by Avison in his father's possession.

2. WRITINGS. Avison's creative output can be divided between writings and musical compositions. Whether he was the author of numerous book reviews and music articles signed 'C.A.' in the local newspapers and magazines during his mature years is conjectural. He often included dedications and substantial, informative and sometimes controversial prefaces ('advertisements') with his published music. When his op.3 appeared in 1751 it included a lengthy preface discussing performing practice in concertos, which he incorporated the next year into his most important literary work, *An Essay on Musical Expression* (which Burney thought to be the first of its kind on musical criticism in England). The *Essay* is in three parts. Part i contains a brief discussion of the effect of music upon the emotions and character, and a section on the analogies between music and painting. Part ii is a systematic critique of some composers and their styles. Part iii is devoted to remarks on instrumental performance, especially of concertos. The *Essay* was highly controversial, especially in its critical judgments, for example Avison's view that Geminiani and Marcello were superior composers to Handel. William Hayes, Heather Professor of Music at Oxford, published (anonymously) a critical review in January 1753 called *Remarks on Mr Avison's Essay*. His criticism, although limited to the first and second parts of the *Essay*, was longer than the total original work, and included several interesting digressions. Avison published *A Reply to the Author of Remarks on the Essay on Musical Expression* on 22 February 1753, and later that year he published the second edition of the *Essay*, which included his *Reply* and also *A Letter to the Author, concerning the Music of the Ancients* by Dr John Jortin. The *Essay* was not all Avison's own work, but, on his own admission, that of a 'junto', never mentioned by name. It could have included Dr John Brown, who along with Avison and several others was a member of a literary club in Newcastle, the poets Thomas Gray of Cambridge and the Rev. William Mason of York (who is known to have contributed some material), Dr John Jortin of London, Joseph Barber, the engraver and printer in Newcastle, and Robert Shaftoe, a brother-in-law of Ralph Jenison. Avison's bias towards certain composers may have come partly from his musical training with Geminiani. While reviewers felt Hayes was correct in much of his criticism, they also praised Avison's own judicious observations. The third edition of the *Essay* (1775) consisted of a reprinting of the second edition; in the same year a German translation of the first edition was published in Leipzig.

Charles Avison: portrait by ?F. Lindo (active 1750–75) in St Nicholas's Cathedral, Newcastle upon Tyne

3. COMPOSITIONS. As a composer Avison is best known for his concerti grossi for strings, which total 60 works, including some in revised and renumbered versions (but excluding the 12 works arranged from harpsichord sonatas by Domenico Scarlatti). His op.2 (six concertos) was revised twice: first, when Walsh published it (along with two additional concertos) as organ concertos in the style made popular by Handel, second when Avison reworked all eight concertos into his op.6 (12 concertos). In 1742 he published two concertos without opus number (one for strings and one for organ), followed by his op.3 (six concertos) and op.4 (eight). In 1758, the year that op.6 appeared, he also issued his opp.3, 4 and 6 as *Twenty Six Concertos . . . in Score for the Use of Performers on the Harpsichord*. The idea of a full score came from the publication of Corelli's concertos and sonatas edited by Pepusch (dedicated to Ralph Jenison) about 1740 and of Geminiani's opp.2 and 3 in 1755. (In each case John Johnson was the publisher.) Avison did not always adhere to his original texts in the later full-score versions; there are many revisions as well as movements transposed or substituted without explanation. His op.9 (12 concertos) was a versatile and popular work, advertised as being playable several ways: by full string orchestra, as quartets, for harpsichord or organ with accompaniments, or as harpsichord 'sonatas'. His publishing activity ceased with op.10 (six concertos).

In general, Avison's concertos are modelled on Geminiani's; stylistically there is little difference between the early works and the late ones. If somewhat lightweight in texture and content, Avison's concertos are unusually tuneful; he was a firm believer in the value of 'air' or melody. His op.4 no.4 was very popular in the Concert of Antient Music, where it was much played

between 1785 and 1812 along with concertos by Corelli, Geminiani, Sammartini and Handel. During the 19th century the Andante cantabile from op.9 no.5 was set to several religious texts, with numerous arrangements for hymnals and vocal ensembles and transcriptions for various instruments.

The other important area of Avison's original composition is chamber music. His op.1 consists of six trio sonatas in a typical Baroque style. However, after he introduced Rameau's *Pièces de clavecin en concerts* (1741) at the Newcastle concerts in the early 1750s, Avison modelled his later sonatas on Rameau's, which are essentially keyboard pieces with accompaniments for other instruments. His opp.5, 7 and 8 (each of six sonatas) were the earliest of their kind to be composed in England. Earlier publications of accompanied keyboard sonatas usually had an accompaniment of a single violin or flute, but Avison's accompaniments were for two violins and cello, with the harpsichord part (in a complex style, closely akin to Geminiani's in his *Pièces de clavecin*) written out with great care and completeness, independent of the string parts, which do little more than provide supporting harmony. These sonatas clearly arose from Avison's objections to the Handelian type of keyboard concerto and the repetitiveness of its ritornello form. In contrast to the relatively conservative concertos, there is evidence here of stylistic change. These works were imitated by a number of composers in north England and the Midlands, most notably John Garth.

Avison's surviving original sacred works are limited to a verse anthem, a hymn and a chant. In collaboration with Giardini he composed a section of an oratorio, *Ruth*, which was first performed at the Lock Hospital, London, on 13 February 1765; it was repeated on 25 May 1768, wholly set by Giardini.

WORKS

All printed works published in London unless otherwise stated; for complete thematic index, known library holdings and listing of editions and arrangements, see Stephens.

ORCHESTRAL

op.
2 Six Concertos in 7 parts (g, B♭, e, D, B♭, D), 4 vn, va, vc, hpd (Newcastle and London, 1740); rev. with 2 new concs. (D, G), as 8 concertos, org/hpd (1747) [see op.6]
— Two Concertos, no.1 (C) in 8 parts, org/hpd, ?str [kbd part only extant]; no.2, vns in 7 parts, lost (Newcastle, 1742)
3 Six Concertos in 7 parts with General Rules for playing Instrumental Compositions (D, e, g, B♭, D, G), 4 vn, va, vc, hpd (1751); also incl. in 26 Concertos (London, Edinburgh and Newcastle, 1758)
4 Eight Concertos in 7 parts (d, A, D, g, B♭, G, D, c), 4 vn, va, vc, hpd (1755)
6 Twelve Concertos in 7 parts (g, B♭, e, D, B♭, D, G, e, D, C, D, A), 4 vn, va, vc, hpd (London and Newcastle, 1758) [incl. rev. of 8 Concertos (1747) plus 4 new concertos]
9 Twelve Concertos in 4 parts, set 1 (G, D, A, g/G, C, e), set 2 (E♭, B♭, c, F, A, D), 2 vn, va, vc (1766); also for org/hpd, or 2 vn, va, vc, org/hpd (1766)
10 Six Concertos in 7 parts (d, F, c, C, E♭, d), 4 vn, va, vc, hpd (1769)

CHAMBER

op.
1 VI Sonatas (chromatic dorian, g, g, dorian, e, D), 2 vn, b (c1737)
5 Six Sonatas (G, C, B♭, E♭, A), hpd, 2 vn, vc (1756)
7 Six Sonatas (G, g, B♭, d, a, A), hpd, 2 vn, vc (London, Edinburgh and Newcastle, 1760)
8 Six Sonatas (A, C, D, B♭, g, G), hpd, 2 vn, vc (London and Edinburgh, 1764)

OTHER WORKS

Glory to God [Christmas Hymn/Sanctus] (?c1760)
Ps. cvii, chant, in *Cantico ecclesiastica*, ed. T. Ions (1849)
Hast thou not forsaken us, verse anthem, c1741, *GB-DRc*
Ruth (oratorio), London, Lock Hospital, 13 Feb 1765, collab. Giardini, ?lost

EDITIONS AND ARRANGEMENTS

1 Concerto in 7 parts . . . done from the Lessons for the hpd composed by Sig. Domenico Scarlatti, 4 vn, va, vc, hpd (c1743), later incl. as part of conc. no.6 in 12 Concertos (1744)

12 Concertos in 7 parts . . . done from 2 books of Lessons for the hpd composed by Sig. Domenico Scarlatti, 4 vn, va, vc, hpd (1744)

The First 50 Psalms Set to Music by Benedetto Marcello . . . and adapted to the English version, 8 vols (1757) [edn. of Marcello's Estro Poetico-Armonico], collab. J. Garth

A Collection of Psalm Tunes (Newcastle, c1760)

Sae merry as we twa ha' been, a favourite Scotch Tune with variations, arr. pf/hpd (c1785)

12 [24] Canticles taken from the Compositions of Sig. Carlo Clari and adapted to English words selected from the Psalms, 1769, Newcastle Public Library

Another set of 24 Canticles, dated 1769, arr. from works by Clari, Ouf

WRITINGS

An Essay on Musical Expression (London, 1752, rev.2/1753/R1967, 3/1775)

A Reply to the Author of Remarks on the Essay on Musical Expression (London, 1753)

ATTRIBUTIONS

Flores musicae, 12 sonatinas, 2 vn, vc . . . taken from the Works of the best English and Italian authors by C. A. Esq (London, c1755)

March, D, 2 vn, b (Edinburgh, 1761)

Grand March, C, in The Complete and Dramatic Works of Robert Browning (Boston, 1895)

She's gone, the sweetest flower of May, dirge, S, str, Burghley House, Stamford, Lincs.

Untitled MS, c1745, Newcastle Public Library

BIBLIOGRAPHY

BurneyH; HawkinsH

R. Newton: 'The English Cult of Domenico Scarlatti', ML, xx (1939), 138

W. S. Newman: 'Concerning the Accompanied Clavier Sonata', MQ, xxxiii (1947), 327

H. M. Schueller: 'Imitation and Expression in British Music Criticism in the Eighteenth Century', MQ, xxxiv (1948), 544

M. Kingdon-Ward: 'Charles Avison', MT, xcii (1951), 398

C. L. Cudworth: 'The English Symphonists of the Eighteenth Century', PRMA, lxxviii (1951–2), 31

——: 'The English Organ Concerto', The Score (1953), no.8, p.51

A. F. Milner: 'Charles Avison', MT, xcv (1954), 16, 73

F. Howes: 'The Foundations of Musical Aesthetics', PRMA, lxxxiii (1956–7), 75

F. H. Teahan: English Literary Criticism of Music in England, 1660–1789 (diss., Trinity College, Dublin, 1957)

S. Sadie: British Chamber Music, 1720–1790 (diss., U. of Cambridge, 1958)

——: 'Concert Life in Eighteenth-century England', PRMA, lxxxv (1958–9), 17

J. B. Brocklehurst: Charles Avison and his Essay on Musical Expression (diss., U. of Sheffield, 1959)

K. H. Darenberg: Studien zur englischen Musikaesthetik des 18. Jahrhunderts: Britannica et America (Hamburg, 1960)

J. L. Cassingham: The Twelve Scarlatti–Avison Concertos of 1744 (diss., U. of Missouri, 1968)

N. L. Stephens: Charles Avison: an Eighteenth-century English Composer, Musician and Writer (diss., U. of Pittsburgh, 1968)

C. L. Cudworth: 'Avison of Newcastle, 1709–1770', MT, cxi (1970), 480

R. R. Kidd: 'The Emergence of Chamber Music with Obligato Keyboard in England', AcM, xliv (1972), 122

O. Edwards: 'Charles Avison, English Concerto-writer Extraordinary', MQ, lix (1973), 399

P. M. Horsley: 'Charles Avison: the Man and his Milieu', ML, lv (1974), 5

NORRIS L. STEPHENS

Avison, John (Henry Patrick) (b Vancouver, 25 April 1917). Canadian conductor, broadcaster and accompanist. He studied music at the Universities of Washington, British Columbia and Southern California, the Juilliard School of Music and Yale University. He became conductor of the CBC Vancouver Chamber Orchestra on its formation in 1952, and specializes in introducing contemporary compositions. His work on behalf of modern Canadian composers earned him a citation of merit from the Composers, Authors and Publishers Association of Canada. In 1959 he was awarded a Canada Council travelling fellowship to study and perform in Europe, and he has appeared as a guest conductor with numerous orchestras in North America, England and Europe. He is also known as a lecturer (at the University of British Columbia) and as a pianist.

MAX WYMAN

Avison Edition. Collection of music issued by the SOCIETY OF BRITISH COMPOSERS.

Avni, Tzvi (b Saarbrücken, 2 Sept 1927). Israeli composer of German origin. He studied in Israel with Ehrlich, Ben-Haim and Seter (composition) and with Pelleg (piano), graduating from the Tel-Aviv Academy of Music in 1958. In 1961 he was appointed director of the AMLI Central Music Library. His studies were continued in the USA from 1962 to 1964: he attended courses given by Copland and Foss at Tanglewood (1963), and his great interest in new musical developments led him to study electronic music with Ussachevsky at Columbia University (1963–4) and with Schafer at the University of Toronto (1964). Editor-in-chief of Guitite, the bimonthly publication of the Israeli Jeunesses Musicales, he regularly contributes its leading article. He has also worked as music adviser to the Bat Dor Dance Company (from 1968), and as composition teacher and director of the electronic music studio at the Rubin Academy, Jerusalem (from 1971, professor from 1976). In addition he has given numerous lectures and broadcasts on contemporary and Israeli music. He received the Engel Prize in 1973 for Dimuyim l'yom chag ('Holiday metaphors').

Avni's early works, influenced by Ben-Haim, absorbed eastern folk elements in an impressionist manner; this style is best represented by the Pastorale and Dance for clarinet and piano (1957), the Piano Sonata (1961) and T'fila ('Prayer') for strings (1961). His first string quartet, Kashtot kayits ('Summer strings', 1962), was written under the influence of Seter, whose teaching had a powerful effect on his music. At the same time he made about 100 orchestral arrangements of folksongs from the various Jewish communities in Israel. A new period was initiated by Vocalise for vocal and electronic sounds (1964), and from this work onwards Avni's compositional approach has been more radical. The major pieces that followed – Hirhurim al drama ('Meditations on a drama'), which in 1966 received a prize from the Israeli Association of Composers, Authors and Music Publishers, and the Five Pantomimes – introduced certain new features into his work: serialism, limited aleatoricism, clusters and noise effects. But oriental motifs have continued to be present, sometimes forming the basis of a series, as in Al naharot Bavel ('By the rivers of Babylon'), whose series is constructed from a Babylonian Jewish hymn. Two large-scale works were commissioned in 1968 by the Jerusalem First Testimonium: the 'dramatic vision' Churban habayit ('The destruction of the temple') and the 'allegoric fantasy' Yerushalayim shel ma'ala ('Jerusalem of the heavens').

In the early 1970s Avni came to make more use of electronic means, sometimes including recordings of the human voice, animal cries or instruments. Gilgulim ('Reincarnations'), for speaker and tape, sets a text on the premonition of death written by Avni's wife, the poet P'nina, who died young in 1973; Collage is an attempt at a more communicative music; *Requiem for Sounds* combines instrumental and animal sounds; and *Of Elephants and Mosquitoes* is a study for synthesizer, and so uses only electronic material. These tape compositions are tied to Avni's music for conventional forces, in that they contain similar melodic, rhythmic and harmonic characteristics.

WORKS
(*selective list*)

ORCHESTRAL AND VOCAL

Orch: T'fila [Prayer], str, 1961; Hirhurim al drama [Meditations on a drama], chamber orch, 1966; Dimuyim l'yom chag [Holiday metaphors], 1970; Al naharot Bavel [By the rivers of Babylon], orch/chamber orch, 1971; Al kaf yam mavet ze [On this cape of death], chamber orch, 1974; Genesis Reconsidered, ballet, 1978

Vocal: Collage (Y. Amihai), 1v, fl, perc, tape, 1967; Mizmorei tehilim [Psalm canticles], chorus, 1967; Churban habayit [The destruction of the temple] (Baruch), chorus, orch, 1968; Yerushalayim shel ma'ala [Jerusalem of the heavens] (Kabbalah), chorus, orch, 1968; Akeda [The binding], narrator, va, 4 inst groups, 1969; Kochav nafal [A star fell down] (M. Katz), Mez, pf, 1969; Gilgulim [Reincarnations] (P. Avni), speaker, tape, 1974

INSTRUMENTAL AND TAPE

Inst: Pastorale and Dance, cl, pf, 1957; Ww Qnt, 1959; Pf Sonata, 1961; Chaconne, harp, 1962; Kashtot kayits [Summer strings], str qt, 1962; 2 Pieces, 4 cl, 1965; Elegy, vc, 1967; 5 Pantomimes, 8 insts, 1968; Mima'amakim [De profundis], str qt/str orch, 1969; 4 Simple Pieces, fl, pf, 1970; Shadows from the Past, cl, 1970; Lyric Episodes, ballet, ob, tape, 1972

Tape: Vocalise, 1964; Requiem for Sounds, ballet; Ein dor, ballet, 1970; Of Elephants and Mosquitoes, 1971

Principal publishers: Culture and Education Centre of the Histadrut, Israel Music Institute, Mills

BIBLIOGRAPHY

W. Y. Elias: *Tzvi Avni* (Tel-Aviv, 1971)
Y. W. Cohen: *Werden und Entwicklung der Musik in Israel.*(Kassel, 1976) [pt.ii rev. edn. of M. Brod: *Die Musik Israels*]
W. Y. Elias: *The Music of Israel* (in preparation) [bibliography]

WILLIAM Y. ELIAS

Avoglio [Avolio], Christina Maria (*fl* 1729–46). Italian soprano. She was probably the 'Madame Avogli' who sang Cleopatra in Handel's *Giulio Cesare* at Hamburg on 24 October 1729. Otherwise she is first mentioned in Handel's letter of 29 December 1741 to Jennens from Dublin: 'Sig^ra Avolio, which I brought with me from London pleases extraordinary'. She was his leading soprano throughout the Dublin season, and sang the principal soprano part at the first performance of *Messiah* on 13 April 1742; the *Dublin Journal* mentioned her among those who 'performed their Parts to Admiration'. Her other Dublin roles included Galatea, Esther, Rosmene in *Imeneo* and Michal in *Saul*, and the soprano parts in *L'Allegro* and the two Dryden odes. She had two benefit concerts in the Dublin Music Hall, on 5 April and 23 June 1742, and was a member of Handel's company in the Covent Garden seasons of 1743 and 1744. At the first performance of *Samson* (18 February 1743) she shared the solos of the Philistine and Israelite Women with Miss Edwards, singing the airs 'Ye men of Gaza', 'With plaintive notes' (as an Attendant on Dalila) and 'Let the bright Seraphims'. She was in the earliest London performances of *Messiah* (March 1743), played Iris in the first production of *Semele* (10 February 1744), and appeared in revivals of *L'Allegro* (1743) and *Saul* (1744, probably as Merab). Handel marked some of Josabeth's music for her in a cancelled 1743 revival of *Athalia*. On 1 February 1744 Avoglio created the part of Hecate in Samuel Howard's pantomime *The Amorous Goddess* at Drury Lane, repeating it in the revival of 17 October, and in June that year was heard in three performances of Handel's *Alexander's Feast* at Ruckholt House, Essex. She sang

Italian and English songs at a benefit concert for herself and two local musicians at the Salisbury Assembly Room on 23 June 1746. Her Handel parts in 1742–3 require a moderate compass (*d'* to *a''*) but considerable flexibility.

WINTON DEAN

Avondano, Pedro [Pietro] **Antonio** (*b* Lisbon, baptized 16 April 1714; *d* Lisbon, 1782). Portuguese composer of Italian ancestry. His father, Pietro Giorgio Avondano, was a Genoese instrument maker and violinist who settled in Lisbon at the age of 19. Following his father's profession Pedro became a court violinist (1763). On his own premises in the Rua da Cruz he opened a popular dancing academy that catered mainly for foreigners; many of his minuets for balls of the English colony in Lisbon were printed in London. In 1764 his cantata *Le difese d'amore* was sung at the Ajuda Palace for the wedding of the Count of Oeiras, and in the following year his comic opera *Il mondo della luna* was presented at the Salvatierra theatre. He played an important role in the St Cecilia Society, Lisbon's most important musical association; at its reorganization in 1765 he was elected secretary and the inaugural meeting was held at his residence. On 15 June 1767 he purchased a knighthood in the Order of Christ. Two sacred dramas by him were performed at the Ajuda Palace (1771–2), and several oratorios have survived in German sources.

Other members of the Avondano family, all active in the Real Câmara in Lisbon, include António José (*d* 1783), João Francisco (*d* 1794), João Baptista André, who published a set of *Quattro sonate e due duetti* for two cellos (Paris and Lyons, by 1784), and a second João Baptista André (*d* after 1823). A Joaquim e Pedro Avondano (*d* 1804) is listed in the registers of the St Cecilia Society.

WORKS

VOCAL

Le difese d'amore, cantata, Lisbon, Ajuda, carn. 1764
Il mondo della luna (opera buffa, 3, C. Goldoni), Lisbon, Salvatierra, carn. 1765; score, *P-La*
Il voto di Jefte (dramma sacro, 2, G. Tonioli), Lisbon, Ajuda, aut. only lib extant
Adamo ed Eva (dramma sacro, 2), Lisbon, Ajuda, spr. 1772; only lib extant
Gioas, Re di Giuda (oratorio, Metastasio); score of pt.1, *D-B*
La morte d'Abel (oratorio, Metastasio); score, *B*
Die Aufopferung Isaacs (oratorio, after Metastasio); score, *SWl*
Arias for Lisbon productions of Perez's Dido, 1765, *B*, Majo's Antigono, 1772, *P-Ln*, Galuppi's Il filosofo di campagna, *B-Bc*

Magnificat, 4 vv, 2 vn, 2 hn, org; Psalms cxxi and cxlvii, 4 vv, 2 vn, 2 hn, bc; Ladainha lauretana, 4 vv, 2 vn, org; Tantum ergo, 4 vv, 2 vn, org: *P-EVc* (see Alegria)

INSTRUMENTAL

A Second Sett of 22 Lisbon Minuets, 2 vn, b (London, 1761)
18 entire new Lisbon Minuets, 2 vn, b (London by 1766)
A Collection of [6] Lisbon Minuets, 2 vn fl, b (London, 1766)
A Favourite Lesson, hpd (London, 1770)
2 syms., *B-Bc*; 3 vc concs., *D-B*; other inst works, incl. some from printed collections, *F-Pn*; ? 2 sonatas, vc, b, *D-Bds*

BIBLIOGRAPHY

DBP
F. M. Sousa Viterbo: 'Subsídios para a história da música em *Portugal*', *O Instituto* (Coimbra), lxxiii (1926), 388, 494
M. A. Machado Santos: [*Biblioteca da Ajuda:*] *Catálogo de música manuscrita* (Lisbon, 1958–68), i, 38; ix, p.xliii
C. Schröder-Auerbach: 'Avondano', *MGG*
J. A. Alegria: *Arquivo das músicas da Sé de Évora* (Lisbon, 1973), 29, 57, 68

ROBERT STEVENSON

Avos [Avosso], Girolamo. *See* ABOS, GIROLAMO.

Avosani, Orfeo (*b* Viadana, nr. Mantua; *fl* 1641–5). Italian composer and organist. The title-page of his *Compieta concertata a cinque voci* op.1 (Venice, 1641) describes him as organist of S Nicola, Viadana, and he was still there when he published his only other known music, *Messa e salmi a tre voci* op.2 (Venice, 1645). Both publications include continuo parts.

COLIN TIMMS

Avossa [d'Avossa; Avosa; Avos; d'Anossa], **Giuseppe** (*b* Paolo, Cosenza, 1708; *d* Naples, 9 Jan 1796). Italian composer, often confused with his contemporary Girolamo Abos, several of whose *opere serie* are sometimes attributed to him. The family is reputed to have been of Spanish origin. His father was in the service of Spinelli, Duke of Fuscaldo and (according to Mondolfi, *MGG*) the duke used his influence to place the young musician in the Conservatorio dei Poveri di Gesù Cristo in Naples. There he studied with Gaetano Greco and Francesco Durante. He subsequently became *maestro di cappella* at S Maria Verticelli; according to Schmidl he also taught singing in various Neapolitan monasteries and churches. By 1753 Avossa was working in north Italy as *maestro di cappella* in Pesaro and conductor of the municipal theatre orchestra there. He married a Rosa Travi in Naples in 1758.

Although Avossa's principal fame today derives from his highly popular comic opera *La pupilla*, he probably wrote mainly church music. Surviving works have concertato textures of chorus and solo voices, contrapuntal facility, a certain adventurousness in tonal thinking and, in some cases, an essentially symphonic conception of a whole movement.

WORKS

COMIC OPERAS

Don Saverio (A. Palomba), Venice, Teatro S Moise, aut. 1744
?Lo scolaro alla moda, Reggio Emilia, Teatro di Cittadella, 1748
I tutori, Naples, Teatro Nuovo, wint. 1757
La pupilla (Palomba), Naples, Teatro dei Fiorentini, carn. 1763; in *A-Wn* as Il ciarlone

CHURCH MUSIC

3 masses, several mass sections, *I-Nc*
2 Magnificat, *Nc, A-Wn*
2 motets, *GB-Lbm, I-Fc*

BIBLIOGRAPHY

SchmidlDS
C. A. de Rosa, Marchese di Villarosa: *Memorie dei compositori di musica, del regno di Napoli* (Naples, 1840), 8f [Abos and Avossa are confused]
M. Scherillo: *L'opera buffa napoletana durante il settecento: storia letteraria* (Naples, 1883, 2/1917), 280, 282
C. Cinelli: 'Memorie cronistoriche del Teatro di Pesaro (1637–1897)', *La cronaca musicale* (Pesaro, 1897), ii, 431f
A. Loewenberg: *The Annals of Opera, 1597–1940* (Cambridge, 1943, rev. 2/1955), i, 268f
U. Prota-Giurleo: *Ricordi digiacomiani* (Naples, 1956), 10
——: 'Avossa, Giuseppe', *DBI*

JAMES L. JACKMAN

Avramov Quartet. Bulgarian string quartet. It was formed in 1938 as the Bulgarian Quartet and took the name Avramov Quartet in 1948. The original members, all from the Sofia National Opera Orchestra, were Vladimir Avramov (*b* Sofia, 16 Dec 1909), Stoyan Sertev (*b* Nova Zagora, 14 Feb 1906; *d* Sofia, 21 Oct 1974), Stefan Magnev (*b* Veliko Tarnovo, 13 Nov 1906) and Konstantin Kugiisky (*b* Sofia, 11 March 1905; *d* Sofia, 25 April 1975). Kugiisky resigned in 1973 because of ill-health and his place was taken by Zdravko Yordanov (*b* Sofia, 5 April 1931). The quartet, the first such Bulgarian ensemble to gain a national and international reputation, has given numerous concerts and broadcasts; it has a repertory of over 500 works, including more than 50 quartets by Bulgarian composers, many of them commissioned for the ensemble. Its example has led to the formation of several other quartets in Bulgaria and has played a large part in making chamber music popular there.

LADA BRASHOVANOVA

Avshalomov, Jacob (*b* Tsingtao, China, 28 March 1919). American composer and conductor. Son of the composer Aaron Avshalomov, he was educated in China and came to the USA in 1937, becoming a naturalized citizen in 1944. He received an MA in 1942 from the Eastman School of Music, where he was a pupil of Bernard Rogers. He taught at Columbia University from 1946 to 1954. Since 1954 he has been conductor of the Portland (Oregon) Junior SO. He received a Guggenheim Fellowship in 1951, the New York Critics Award in 1953 for his *Tom O'Bedlam*, and the Naumburg Recording Award in 1956 for his Sinfonietta. In February 1968 President Johnson appointed him to the National Council on the Humanities. His large orchestral works include *Inscriptions at the City of Brass* (1957) and *Symphony: the Oregon* (1962). His music encompasses a broad spectrum from an exotic Chinese style to a colourful American folk idiom.

JAMES G. ROY JR

Awshīya. Prose prayers of the Coptic Church, sung in free rhythm; *see* COPTIC RITE, MUSIC OF THE.

Axamenta (Lat.). In ancient Rome, hymns with texts in Saturnian measure sung in ritual by the SALII.

Axman, Emil (*b* Rataje u Kroměříže, 3 June 1887; *d* Prague, 25 Jan 1949). Czech composer, musicologist and archivist. He studied at Prague University under Nejedlý and Hostinský, receiving the PhD in 1912 for a dissertation on Moravian opera in the 18th century. He studied composition under Novák (1908–10) and counterpoint under Ostrčil (1920), and he devoted himself to composition while head of the musical archive at the National Museum in Prague. His music was much influenced by the folk music of his native Moravia, but the political and social problems of the World War I period also had a deep effect on him. Passing from late-Romanticism through a transitional period marked by influences from contemporary developments, his music attained a broad lyricism with particularly strong traces of folksong and dance. Most of his works are cast in extended forms. It was in the field of vocal music that he was most successful: there are a number of valuable choral works (principally pieces for male chorus) and his song-cycles and folksong arrangements are notable.

WORKS
(selective list)

Cantatas: Balada o očich topičových [Ballad of the miner's eyes] (Wolker), 1927; Ilonka Beniačova (J. V. Rosůlek), 1929; Sobotecký hřbitov [Sobotece graveyard] (F. Šrámek), 1932
Male choruses: Z vojny [From the army], 1916; Měsíčné noci [Moonlit nights], 1920; Hlas země [Voice of the earth], 1926; Noc [Night] (K. H. Mácha), 1926; Věčný voják [The eternal soldier] (Šrámek), 1933
Mixed choruses: Nenarozenému [To the unborn child], 1921; Vánoce chudých [Christmas of the poor], 1922
Song cycles: Vzpomínání [Reminiscence], 1919; Duha [Rainbow], 1921; Noc [Night], 1928; U plamene [At the flame], 1930
Syms.: 'Tragická', 1926; 'Giocosa slovácká', 1927; 'Jarní' [Spring], 1928; Heroická, 1932; Dithyrambická, n.d.; Vlastenecká [Patriotic], 1942
Concs. for vn, 1936, pf, 1939, vc, 1942, vn, vc, 1944
Inst: Sonata, vn, pf, 1923; 4 str qts, 1924, 1925, 1930, 1946; pf sonatas

WRITINGS

Moravské opery ve století 18. [18th century Moravian operas] (diss., U. of Prague, 1912) [pubd in *Časopis moravského musea* (1912)]

Morava v české hudbě 19. století [Moravian and Czech music of the 19th century] (Prague, 1920)

'22 světských nápěvů ze 16. století' [22 16th-century secular songs], *Hudební výchova* (1920)

BIBLIOGRAPHY

L. Hovorka: *Sborová tvorba Axmanova* (Prague, 1940)

F. Pala: *E. Axman* (Prague, 1951)

JAN TROJAN

Ayala Pérez, Daniel (*b* Abalá, Yucatán, 21 July 1906; *d* Veracruz, 20 June 1975). Mexican conductor and composer. He studied at the Mexico City Conservatory (1929–32), where he was a pupil of Revueltas and where he allied himself with Contreras, Galindo Dimas and Moncayo in the 'Group of Four'. From 1931 to 1937 he played second violin in the Mexico SO, and he then directed a chorus in Morelia for two years. Returning to Yucatán in 1940, he quickly took a leading part in all aspects of musical life. He was director of the newly reorganized Mérida SO (inaugural concert 15 November 1944), of the Típica Yukalpetén, of the official state band, of the Yucatán Conservatory (from 1944) and of the Veracruz School of Music (1955–); later he also worked for the Veracruz Institute of Fine Arts. He composed little after 1944, but his bright picture-postcard pentatonic evocations, usually short danceable pieces with Maya titles or texts, had already established his reputation in Mexico and the USA. *U kayil chaac* was widely broadcast in a CBS concert conducted by Chávez (24 January 1936).

WORKS
(selective list)

Ballets: El hombre Maya, 1939; La gruta diabólica, 1940

Orch: Tribu, sym. poem, 1934; Paisaje, suite, 1935; Panoramas de Mexico, suite, 1936; Mi viaje a Norte América, suite, 1947; Pf Concertino, 1974

Vocal: Uchben x' coholte, S, chamber orch, 1931; El grillo (D. Castañeda), S, cl, vn, pf, rattle, 1933; U kayil chaac (Maya), S, chamber orch, indigenous perc, 1934

Chamber and inst: Radiogramma, pf, 1931; Str Qt, 1933; Vidrios rotos, ob, cl, bn, pf, 1938

BIBLIOGRAPHY

Enciclopedia yucatense, iv (Mexico City, 1944), 738, 816ff

Diccionario enciclopédico UTEHA: apéndice, i (Mexico City, 1964), 272

ROBERT STEVENSON

Ayestarán, Lauro (*b* Montevideo, 9 July 1913; *d* Montevideo, 22 July 1966). Uruguayan musicologist and ethnomusicologist. He studied in Montevideo at the Larrimbe Conservatory and at the school of law and social sciences of the university. In 1937 he was appointed professor of choral music and music history at the teachers' training institute; subsequently he became director of the division of musical research of the Instituto de Estudios Superiores, professor of musicology at the University of Montevideo (1946) and head of the musicology section of the National Historical Museum of Uruguay. He was also active as a music critic for several newspapers and as artistic director of the state broadcasting system, SODRE. Ayestarán was equally interested in music history and ethnomusicology. His first study of Hispano-American Baroque music (1941) dealt with the activities in Argentina of the Italian composer Domenico Zipoli. During the 1940s he did field work for the National Historical Museum, making some 4000 recordings of Uruguayan folk music and publishing his studies of them. He received (among several prizes) the national award Pablo Blanco Acevedo for the first volume of his major work, *La música en el Uruguay*. He was a corresponding member of several music organizations, including IFMC, the Brazilian Academy of Music, the Argentine Academy of Fine Arts and ISM, and served as vice-president of the Inter-American Music Council (CIDEM).

WRITINGS

Domenico Zipoli, el gran compositor y organista romano del 1700 en el Río de la Plata (Montevideo, 1941)

Crónica de uma temporada musical en el Montevideo de 1830 (Montevideo, 1943)

Fuentes para el estudio de la música colonial uruguaya (Montevideo, 1947)

'La música escénica en el Uruguay', *Revista musical chilena* (1947), no.19 p.17

Le música indígena en el Uruguay (Montevideo, 1949)

Un antecedente colonial de la poesía tradicional uruguaya (Montevideo, 1949)

El Minué montonero (Montevideo, 1950)

La primitiva poesía gauchesca en el Uruguay (Montevideo, 1950)

La Misa para Día de Difuntos de Fray Manuel Ubeda, 1802: comentario y reconstrucción (Montevideo, 1952)

La música en el Uruguay, i (Montevideo, 1953)

Virgilio Scarabelli (Montevideo, 1953)

Luis Sambucetti: vida y obra (Montevideo, 1956)

La primera edición del Fausto de Estanislao del Campo (Montevideo, 1959)

Domenico Zipoli: vida y obra (Montevideo, 1962)

'Domenico Zipoli y el barroco musical sudamericano', *Revista musical chilena* (1962), nos.81–2, p.94

'Fétis, un precursor del criterio etnomusicológico en 1869', *1st Inter-American Conference on Ethnomusicology: Cartagena de Indias 1963*, 13

'El barroco musical Hispanoamericano: los manuscritos de la iglesia San Felipe Neri (Sucre, Bolivia) existentes en el Museo Histórico Nacional del Uruguay', *Yearbook, Inter-American Institute for Musical Research*, i (1965), 55; rev. in *Revista histórica* (1968), nos.115–17, pp.1–43

with F. de M. Rodríguez de Ayestarán: *El tamboril, la llamada y la comparsa* (in preparation)

Articles in O. M. Serra: *Música y músicos de Latinoamérica* (Mexico, 1947), *LaborD, Folklore de las Américas*, ed. F. Coluccio (Buenos Aires, 1948), *Cancionero popular americano* (Washington, DC, 1950), *Revista musical chilena* and *Yearbook, Inter-American Institute for Musical Research*

BIBLIOGRAPHY

G. Chase: 'In memoriam Lauro Ayestarán', *Yearbook, Inter-American Institute for Musical Research*, ii (1966), 161

A. Soriano: 'Lauro Ayestarán, 1913–1966', *Revista musical chilena* (1967), no.101, p.26

GERARD BÉHAGUE

Ayler, Albert (*b* Cleveland, 13 July 1936; *d* New York, Dec 1970). Black American jazz saxophonist. At the age of ten he played the alto saxophone at funerals as a member of his father's band. Later he performed at a music hall, and at 16 toured with a rhythm-and-blues band. In 1956 the tenor saxophone became his main instrument. After moving to New York he became closely associated with the avant-garde pianist Cecil Taylor. In 1962 he played in Scandinavia, making his first recordings in Stockholm with two local musicians. Returning to New York, he worked with Gary Peacock, Sonny Murray and others, and in 1964 returned to Europe for engagements with them and the trumpeter Don Cherry in Denmark, Sweden and the Netherlands. From then until his death he intermittently led his own bands, which generally included his brother, the trumpeter Don Ayler.

Ayler was a major figure in avant-garde jazz of the 1960s. Rejecting jazz harmony even more completely than Ornette Coleman, he instead based his improvisations on the simplest possible material – bugle calls, brass band music or even New Orleans funeral dirges. Such fundamentalism meant, despite the fleeting influence of Sonny Rollins on his earliest recordings,

Albert Ayler

that the intermediate stages of jazz cast no shadow over his mature work. The four versions of *Ghosts* (1964) show what different results Ayler could obtain from the same thematic motifs, but these brief ideas always acquired greater significance as his improvisations unfolded with a real if unfamiliar musical logic and exact instrumental control. His improvisation involved sonority as well as line, with a fierce vocalization of tone and use of registral extremes, but it was chiefly Ayler's rich melodic invention that allowed so concise an expression of varied emotions as he achieved in *Holy Holy* (1964).

BIBLIOGRAPHY
M. Harrison: 'Albert Ayler', *Jazz on Record*, ed. A. McCarthy (London, 1968), 9
E. Raben: *A Discography of Free Jazz* (Copenhagen, 1969)
M. Williams: *Jazz Masters in Transition* (New York, 1970), 193ff
J. Cooke: 'Albert Ayler', *Modern Jazz: the Essential Records*, ed. M. Harrison (London, 1975), 118
E. Jost: *Free Jazz* (Maine, 1975), chap.7
                                                    MICHAEL JAMES

Ayleward, Richard (*b* Winchester, 1626; *d* Norwich, 15 Oct 1669). English organist and composer. He was a chorister at Winchester Cathedral under Christopher Gibbons from June 1638 to November 1639, his father Richard being a minor canon there. At the Restoration he became Organist and Master of the Choristers at Norwich Cathedral from 12 March 1661 to mid-1664 and again from 5 December 1666 until his death. During at least part of his absence, for some unknown reason Ayleward was at the Assizes. He was buried in the cathedral on 18 October 1669, and the inscription on his monument read:

> Here lyeth interred the body of Richard Yleward, Organist of this place, who was born at Winchester, and died here the 15th of October, An. Dom. 1669

> Here lyes a perfect Harmonie
> Of Faith, & Truth, & Loyaltie;
> And whatsoever Virtues can

> Be reckon'd up, was in this Man.
> His sacred Ashes here abide,
> Who in God's Service Liv'd and Dy'd;
> But now by Death advanced higher,
> To serve in the Celestial Quire.
> God Save the King.

Ayleward's output consists mainly of church music, of which the only known sources are a set of eight part-books and organbook (this latter may be autograph), and a score compiled from these by Dr John Beckwith, organist of the cathedral 1808-9. They are now in *GB-Ckc*, having formerly belonged to A. H. Mann, at one time a chorister at Norwich and organist of King's. 'I have in my library [Mann wrote] – a complete service – also 12 Anthems and one incomplete ... Also – a set of vocal parts – nearly complete – and Organ copy, all written by Mr. Aylward ... I bought them in an old book shop in Norwich.'

The partbooks contain a full Service in D, two verse settings of the *Magnificat* and *Nunc dimittis*, and 20 verse anthems. The Service in D is in the 'short' style of Gibbons, and was probably influenced by music Ayleward sang at Winchester. The verse anthems range from short pieces with one solo and four chorus parts, e.g. *Have pity upon me*, to the elaborate setting of *I was glad*. In several anthems, decani and cantoris (usually alto and tenor voices) divide in some sections of choruses which are otherwise in four parts. The style of the anthems tends towards that of Blow and Locke; *Holy, holy, Lord God*, one of the longer pieces, is a good example in the new idiom. *I charge you* is an interesting and dramatic setting, using antiphonal passages to illustrate the text; *O that I were* has chromatic word-painting of a madrigalian character at the phrase 'my harp is turn'd'. Many of the anthems have penitential texts and are in the minor mode.

Some of the keyboard pieces by Richard Ayleward in the MSS listed below may be by an earlier composer, possibly his father. Mann wrote of 'Airs, dance-tunes and suites' and also a song by 'Mr Aylward' (in *Lbm*), but this is by the later Theodore Aylward.

WORKS
SACRED
(*all in GB-Ckc*)
Service in D (Te D, Bs, Re, Preces, Re, Mag, Nunc), 4vv
Evening Service in d, 8/4vv
Triple Evening Service in F, 8/4vv
20 verse anthems

INSTRUMENTAL
Organ pieces, MS of W. H. Cummings (lost)
Virginal pieces, *Llp*
Pieces, lute/hpd, *Lcm*

BIBLIOGRAPHY
F. Blomefield: *History of Norfolk* (London, 1805–10)
N. Boston: *The Musical History of Norwich Cathedral* (Norwich, 1963)
A. H. Mann: *Norwich Cathedral Musicians* (MS, *GB-NWr*)
——: *Old Norwich Cathedral Musicians* (MS of lecture, *GB-Ckc*)
                                                    P. R. GRANGER

Ayliff [Aliff, Alyff, Ayloff, Ayloffe], Mrs (*fl* 1692–6). English soprano. Mrs Ayliff (whose first name is unknown) sang in Purcell's *The Fairy Queen* (1692) and became for a few years his leading stage soprano. Well over a dozen of Purcell's songs and dialogues were published as sung by her, and she was a soloist in his *Hail, bright Cecilia* (1692) and in his 1693 birthday ode for Queen Mary, *Celebrate this festival*. The *Gentleman's Journal* for August 1692 refers to her performance of his Italianate 'Ah mee! to many deaths decreed' in Crowne's *Regulus* as 'divinely sung'. In 1695 she left Purcell's company with a breakaway group under Betterton, and with them she also acted a little. She was the original Miss Prue in Congreve's *Love for Love*.

OLIVE BALDWIN, THELMA WILSON

Aylward, Theodore (*b* *c*1730; *d* London, 27 Feb 1801). English organist and composer. Nothing is known of his origins or upbringing. His successive appointments were as organist of Oxford Chapel, London, about 1760; St Lawrence, Jewry, 1762; St Michael's, Cornhill, 1768; and St George's Chapel, Windsor, 1788 until his death. Meanwhile, from 1771 he was also Gresham Professor of Music, and at the Handel Commemoration of 1784 he was one of the assistant directors. He took the Oxford degree of DMus in 1791. Most of his compositions were secular, and he won a Catch Club medal in 1769. Nevertheless, Edward Taylor, one of his successors at Gresham College, said that Aylward, 'though a musician by trade was not a musician by spirit' (*Lcm* 2145). But W. H. Husk (in *Grove 1*) on the authority of W. L. Bowles, credited him with 'considerable literary attainments'.

WORKS
(all printed works published in London unless otherwise stated)

VOCAL

Welcome sun and southern show'rs; a New Song (*c*1750)
Ode on the Dawn of Peace (*c*1763)
6 Songs in Harlequin's Invasion, Cymbeline, and Midsummer Night's Dream, 1v, hpd (1765)
Come nymphs and fauns, glee, 3vv (*c*1769)
Oft have I seen at early morn: a Favourite Sonnet (*c*1785)
8 canzonets, 2vv (*c*1790)
Elegies and Glees, op.2 (*c*1790)
Songs pubd in 18th-century anthologies
Morning Services, D, E♭; 5 anthems: St George's Chapel, Windsor

INSTRUMENTAL

6 Lessons, hpd/org/pf, op.1 (*c*1784)
6 Quartettos, 2 vn, va, vc, op.4 (*c*1795)

WATKINS SHAW

Ayne van Ghizeghem. *See* HAYNE VAN GHIZEGHEM.

Ayo, Felix (*b* Sestao, 1 July 1933). Italian violinist of Spanish birth. When he was 14 he graduated from the Bilbao Conservatory and played Beethoven's concerto with a local orchestra. He then moved to Rome and studied under Principe at the S Cecilia Conservatory, becoming leader of the chamber orchestra I Musici, with which he first performed in 1952, the year of its formation. He went on many international tours with I Musici until 1968 and with them made numerous records, several of which received international awards. In 1968 he formed a piano quartet with Cino Ghedin, viola, Vincenzo Altobelli, cello (both from I Musici), and Marcello Abbado, piano; after Carlo Bruno succeeded Abbado as pianist in 1970 the group was named Quartetto Beethoven and has since toured in many countries. Ayo was appointed to teach at the Rome Conservatory in 1972.

PIERO RATTALINO

Ayre. *See* AIR.

Ayres (Johnson), Frederic (*b* Binghamton, NY, 17 March 1876; *d* Colorado Springs, 23 Nov 1926). American composer. After a year at Cornell University studying engineering (1892–3) he worked designing electric motors. He studied composition with Edgar Stillman Kelley (1897–1901) and Arthur Foote (summer 1899) 'to perfect ... what I believed to be my proper work'. Because of ill-health he moved to Las Cruces, New Mexico (1901), and then to Colorado Springs (1902), where he lived for the rest of his life composing and teaching theory privately. His output was mainly vocal (45 songs) but included nine piano pieces, one orchestral work (the overture *From the Plains* op.14), a string quartet, and sonatas and trios for strings and piano. Occasionally these draw on thematic material evocative of the music of the American Indian, but the late works (the Trio in D minor, the Violin Sonata in B minor) move beyond influence into an open, sturdy and more abstract lyricism. Some of his songs were published by G. Schirmer; there is a manuscript collection in the Library of Congress.

BIBLIOGRAPHY

A. G. Farwell: 'Frederic Ayres', *The Wa-Wan Press Monthly*, vi (1907), April; *R*1970
W. T. Upton: 'Frederic Ayres', *MQ*, xviii (1932), 39

BARNEY CHILDS

Ayrton, Edmund (*b* Ripon, baptized 19 Nov 1734; *d* Westminster, London, 22 May 1808), English organist and composer. He was the younger brother of William Ayrton (*b* Ripon, baptized 18 Dec 1726; *d* Ripon, 2 Feb 1799), who was organist of Ripon Cathedral from 7 June 1748 until his death. Their father was Edward Ayrton (1698–1774), a barber-surgeon in Ripon, mayor there in 1760; the family can be traced back to Edward Airton (or Aerton), one of the minor clergy of Ripon Collegiate Church (now the cathedral) in the late 17th century. He was appointed organist, *rector chori* and 'singing-man' (with the additional post of auditor, perhaps merely as an augmentation of stipend) of Southwell Collegiate Church, or Minster (now the cathedral), on 23 October 1755, and in April 1756 he was granted leave of absence to study under James Nares for three months. He moved to London on his appointment as Gentleman of the Chapel Royal in 1764. He also became a vicar-choral of St Paul's Cathedral (1767), lay vicar of Westminster Abbey and Master of the Children of the Chapel Royal (1780), holding all these posts simultaneously. He resigned as Master of the Children in 1805, having earlier successfully rebutted charges that he starved the boys. In 1784 he took the Cambridge degree of MusD, and he is stated to have proceeded *ad eundem* at Oxford in 1788, which, despite absence of official record, is not impossible. Samuel Wesley is on record as regarding him as 'one of the most egregious blockheads', but that is not the judgment of a well-balanced figure.

Edmund Ayrton composed two services, one in E♭ (*GB-Lbm* Add.34609) and another in C which is lost. He also wrote a small amount of unimportant anthems and secular vocal music. His chief work is *An Anthem for Voices and Instruments in Score ... an Exercise Previous ... to the Degree of Doctor in Music* (London, [1788]), with the text *Begin unto my God*, a large-scale work for four soloists and chorus with accompaniments for oboes, bassoons, trumpets, drums and strings. This was sung in St Paul's Cathedral at the thanksgiving service for the end of the War of American Independence in 1784. It is a very competent piece in the English tradition of Greene with strong Handelian influences. It goes outside the normal pattern of such anthems by including slightly colourful passages of accompanied recitative.

Edmund Ayrton had many sons, among whom WIL-LIAM AYRTON was a musician. His brother William had sons William Francis Morrall Ayrton (*b* Ripon, baptized 28 July 1778; *d* Chester, 8 Nov 1850) and Nicholas Thomas Dall Ayrton (*b* Ripon, baptized 15 Jan 1782; *d* Ripon, 24 Oct 1822); the former succeeded his father as organist of Ripon Cathedral in 1799, and the latter followed him in 1802 or 1805, retaining the post until his death.

WORKS

(all printed works published in London)

The Prize Carnation (song, C. Smart) (1780)

Begin unto my God with timbrels, anthem of thanksgiving for end of American War of Independence, S, A, T, B, chorus a 4, 2 ob, 2 bn, 2 tpt, timp, str, London, St Paul's Cathedral, 29 June 1784; pubd as An Anthem for Voices and Instruments in Score (1788)

Glory be to the Father, double canon (1790)

Ode to Harmony: When music with th'inspiring bowl (glee), 4vv (1799)

Thy righteousness, anthem, S, A, T, B, org, 1778, *GB-Lbm*

Short Service, E♭, 29 July 1796, *Lbm*

Service in C, other anthems, canons, catches, glees, songs etc: all lost

BIBLIOGRAPHY

J. S. Bumpus: *A History of English Cathedral Music* (London, 1908), ii, 568

J. T. Lightwood: *Samuel Wesley, Musician* (London, 1937)

WATKINS SHAW

Ayrton, William (*b* London, 24 Feb 1777; *d* Westminster, London, 8 March 1858). English composer, writer and impresario, youngest son of EDMUND AYRTON. In 1803 he married Marianne, daughter of Samuel Arnold. He was one of the founders of the [Royal] Philharmonic Society, and an original member of the Royal Institution and the Athenaeum Club. In 1807 he was elected a Fellow of the Society of Antiquaries and became a Fellow of the Royal Society in 1837. He is of some importance in the history of Italian opera in London, though the statement, added in 1927 to the article on him written for *Grove 1*, to the effect that it was he who in 1811 first introduced *Così fan tutte* and *Die Zauberflöte* to England, has not been traced to its source. However, in 1817 and again in 1821, he was what was termed 'manager' or 'director' of the Italian opera at the King's Theatre in Haymarket – he was not responsible for directing the orchestra, but engaged the cast and had charge of the singing. A notable season was that of 1817 in which for the first time Cimarosa's *Penelope*, Mozart's *Don Giovanni* and Paer's *Agnese de Fitz-Henry* were given in England. *Don Giovanni*, against all predictions, was an enthusiastic success in 23 performances. Before this season he had gone to Paris to engage singers, and, wishing to avoid the pride and jealousies of established favourites, had the prescience to select some who, though not yet known, afterwards became celebrated, including Camporese, Pasta and Crevelli. On his death some 40 years later it was recalled that Ayrton 'very greatly reformed the Italian Opera in the country, and in so doing indirectly raised the public taste'. Unfortunately differences arose at the end of the 1817 season between him and the lessee of the theatre, Waters, whom Ayrton sued for £1200 remuneration. Attwood and Sir George Smart testified that they considered £1000 hardly enough; the jury awarded £700. The testimony of the musical profession was that the success of the season was due to Ayrton. The question whether he translated *Don Giovanni*, or merely caused it to be translated, into English was discussed; but it is difficult to see why, for a production in Italian, such a translation was necessary. His 1821 season introduced Rossini's *La gazza ladra* for the first time in London.

Ayrton contributed musical and literary criticism to the *Morning Chronicle* between 1813 and 1826 and to the *Examiner* between 1837 and 1851, besides writing the articles on music in the *Penny Cyclopaedia* and explanations of music references in the *Pictorial Shakespeare*. The *Harmonicon* (London, 1823–33), a monthly periodical which he edited and to which he contributed, set an admirable standard of musical journalism and still retains much value. *The Sacred Minstrelsy* (London, 1834), a wide-ranging anthology for domestic use, has the interesting feature of giving metronome marks for the Chapel Royal performances of such extracts from English cathedral music as it includes. Ayrton also edited *The Musical Library* (London, 1834–7) and *The Madrigalian Feast* (London, 1838). His commonplace-book (*GB-Lcm* 1163) includes numerous contemporary newspaper cuttings of interest.

BIBLIOGRAPHY

The Times (12 Jan 1818)

E. Waters: *A Statement of Matters relating to the King's Theatre* (London, 1818) [review in *The Quarterly Musical Magazine and Review*, i (1818), 239]

J. Ebers: *Seven Years of the King's Theatre* (London, 1828)

W. T. Parke: *Musical Memoirs* (London, 1830)

The Annual Register (1858)

A. H. King: *Some British Collectors of Music* (Cambridge, 1963)

WATKINS SHAW

Ayton, Fanny (*b* Macclesfield, 1806). English soprano. She studied singing with Manielli at Florence and first appeared in Italy, so successfully that Ebers engaged her for the season of 1827 at the King's Theatre in London at a salary of £500. She appeared there as Ninetta in Rossini's *La gazza ladra* (23 February) and also sang the principal roles in *Il turco in Italia* and Pacini's *La schiava in Bagdad*. In the same year she sang at Drury Lane in an English version of *Il turco* (Rophino Lacy's *The Turkish Lovers*) and as Rosetta in *Love in a Village*. In 1829 she sang at the Birmingham Festival and in opera, with Malibran, under Michael Costa. In 1831 she sang again at the King's Theatre for the season, as Creusa in Simone Mayr's *Medea*, and she played Isabel in a mutilated version of Meyerbeer's *Robert le diable* (*The Daemon, or The Mystic Branch*) at Drury Lane, 20 February 1832. Nothing is known of her later life.

BIBLIOGRAPHY

J. Ebers: *Seven Years of the King's Theatre* (London, 1828), 333

H. F. Chorley: *Thirty Years' Musical Recollections* (London, 1862), i, 240

ALEXIS CHITTY/R

Azaïs, Hyacinthe (*b* Ladern-sur-Lauquet, nr. Carcassonne, 4 April 1741; *d* Toulouse, *c*1795). French composer. He began his musical career as a choirboy at Carcassonne Cathedral where he obtained his musical education. He spent most of his life in the south of France. At the age of 15 he became *sous-maître de musique* in the church at Auch; in 1765 he was appointed *maître de musique* at the college in Sorèze (Languedoc). He married Marie Lépine, daughter of the organ builder J.-F. Lépine of Toulouse. After his wife's death, Azaïs spent a year (1770–71) in Paris, where he met Gossec and François Giroust, and had some of his works performed at the Concert Spirituel. His friendship with Abbé Roussier may have helped him obtain the position of *maître de musique* of the Concert de Marseille which he assumed in 1771. In 1772 he returned to the college in Sorèze (renamed Ecole Royale Militaire). In 1782 or 1783 Azaïs left Sorèze for Toulouse, where he established himself as a composer and teacher. At the beginning of the Revolution he fled to Bagnères-de-Bigorre in the Pyrenees; he returned to Toulouse in 1794.

Azaïs was proud of the success he had achieved with the performances of two of his motets, *Cantate Domino* and *Dominus regnavit*, during his stay in Paris. The *Mercure de France* (September 1770) praised his *Cantate Domino*: 'Sa composition a paru d'un bon style, d'une expression juste & d'un effet picquant'. Azaïs described *Dominus regnavit* in the *Méthode de musique* (p.150) as follows: 'j'ai fait entendre ce motet (avec succès) au Concert Spirituel, et plusieurs fois au Concert de Marseille ... tout les habiles gens qui frequentent ces Académies, ont été frappés (par l'emploie de l'accord sensible avec fausse quinte, Si, Re♯, Fa, La...une harmonie toute nouvelle)'. Azaïs indicated that the *Mercure de France* had failed to mention his name as the composer, and that he wished it to be known.

Azaïs's six symphonies exemplify the light Italo-French symphonic style of his time fused with some influences from the Mannheim school evident especially in the dynamics of the Symphony no.1. Usually, however, lyricism prevails (particularly in the Romance of no.1 and in the Andante of no.5); also notable are his use of minor tonalities and the presence of a slow introduction in no.6. The instrumentation comprises first and second violins, viola, bass (figured in nos. 1–3), two flutes (replaced by oboes in the slow movements of nos.1–2), and two horns (not used in no.4). All his symphonies have four movements except no.3 which has no minuet. The chamber music is unpretentious and seems to have been designed for amateurs. A rather unusual instrumentation is found in the *Six trios*: violin, cello and horn or clarinet.

Azaïs's fame rested primarily on his role as a teacher. His *Méthode de musique*, a large textbook designed for young performers, was praised by many influential musicians at the time of its publication, and later by La Borde (iii, p.567ff) and Gerber.

Azaïs's son, Pierre-Hyacinthe Azaïs (*b* Sorèze, Tarn, 1 March 1766; *d* Paris, 22 Jan 1845), was a philosopher, active in his early years as an organist. According to Fétis, he published a series of letters under the title 'Acoustique fondamentale' in the *Revue musicale*.

WORKS
(printed works published in Paris)

Choral: Cantate Domino, motet, perf. 1770, lost; Dominus regnavit, exultet terra, motet, perf. 1771, lost

Other vocal: Le désir de plaire, ariette (1771); Le beau jour, ariette, 'haute contre', 2 vn, b, and Le douceurs de la vie champêtre, ariette, 2vv, 2 vn, b, in Méthode de musique

6 symphonies, orch (1782) [orig. 1770 edn. lost]

Chamber, 6 trio and 4 parties, vn, vc, hn/cl (1776); 12 sonates, vc, bc (1777); 6 duo, 2 vc (*c*1778); 6 trios, 2 vn, b in Méthode de musique; Menuet d'Exaudet varié, vc (n.d.); pieces in Recueil de menuets ... par différent auteurs, 2 vn, pubd Jolivet (*c*1771–9); Pièce en rondeau and 5 sonata movts (from pubd sonatas) pubd in Le violoncelle classique, ed. J. Brizard and H. Classens (Paris, 1963–5)

Pedagogical: Méthode de musique sur un nouveau plan (1776) [incl. Traité abrégé d'harmonie, Dictionnaire de musique, vocal, chamber pieces]; Méthode de basse contenant des leçons élémentaires (n.d.) [incl. 12 sonates and 6 duos listed above]; Méthode de violoncelle (n.d.), lost [cited by Lichtenthal, ? = Méthode de basse]

BIBLIOGRAPHY
FétisB; *GerberL*

J.-B. de La Borde: *Essai sur la musique ancienne et moderne* (Paris, 1780/*R*1972)

A. Choron and F. Fayolle: *Dictionnaire historique des musiciens* (Paris, 1810–11/*R*1971)

P. Lichtenthal: *Dizionario e bibliografia della musica* (Milan, 1826)

M. Brenet: *Les concerts en France sous l'ancien régime* (Paris, 1900/*R*1969)

B. S. Brook: *La symphonie française dans la seconde moitié du XVIIIe siècle* (Paris, 1962)

B. S. Brook and J. Gribenski: 'Azaïs, Hyacinthe', *MGG*
BARRY S. BROOK, CARL MOSKOVIC

Azanchevsky, Mikhail Pavlovich (von) (*b* Moscow, 5 April 1839; *d* Moscow, 24 Jan 1881). Russian composer and scholar. In 1858 he resigned from the civil service and went to Leipzig, where he studied music theory with Richter and Hauptmann. Later he took lessons from Liszt in Rome. While in Paris in 1886, he bought the extensive collection of music which had belonged to G. E. Anders. On his return to Russia in 1870 he was appointed honorary librarian to the St Petersburg Conservatory, and in the following year succeeded Zaremba as its director. Before ill-health forced him to resign in 1876, he saw both the St Petersburg and Moscow conservatories become institutions of the first rank, with the right to award diplomas. Azanchevsky's compositions, which include chamber music, piano pieces, and songs with Russian and German texts, are pleasing rather than profound. He donated his valuable library to the St Petersburg Conservatory.

BIBLIOGRAPHY
Yu. A. Kremlyov: *Leningradskaya gosudarstvennaya konservatoriya* (Moscow, 1938)

P. A. Vul'fius, ed.: *Iz istorii Leningradskoy konservatorii: materialï i dokumentï (1862–1917)* [The history of the Leningrad Conservatory: materials and documents 1862–1917] (Leningrad, 1964)
JENNIFER SPENCER

Azavedo, Francisco Correa de. See CORREA DE ARAUXO, FRANCISCO.

Azbuki (Russ.: 'alphabets'). Lists of neumes in Russian chant, attested from the second half of the 15th century; *see* RUSSIAN AND SLAVONIC CHURCH MUSIC, §2.

Azerbaijan. Area in central Asia, now a constituent republic of the USSR. *See* UNION OF SOVIET SOCIALIST REPUBLICS, §II.

Azevedo, Luiz Heitor Corrêa de [Heitor, Luiz] (*b* Rio de Janeiro, 13 Dec 1905). Brazilian musicologist. At the Instituto Nacional de Música he studied the piano with Alfredo Bevilacqua (1924–5) and Charley Lachmund (1926–7) and harmony, counterpoint and fugue with Paulo Silva; initially he was a composer, but by the late 1920s had turned to musicology and music criticism. He became librarian of the Instituto Nacional de Música (1932) and in 1934 founded the *Revista brasileira de música*, which was under his editorship until 1941 and performed a valuable service to nascent Brazilian musicology. While professor of music at the conservatory (1937–47) he held the post of titular professor at the Escola (formerly Instituto) Nacional de Música; he developed there the ethnomusicology curriculum and founded the Centro de Pesquisas Folclóricas, which produced important publications based on fieldwork throughout Brazil. He served as a consultant to the Organization of American States in Washington, DC, for its newly established Music Division (1941–2) and subsequently moved to Paris (1947), where until his retirement (1965) he was the UNESCO music programme specialist and a professor of the Institut des Hautes Etudes de l'Amérique Latine of the University of Paris (1954–68). Besides general studies on Latin American music and history, Azevedo has published definitive works on Brazilian 19th- and 20th-century music and musicians and on folk and popular music. He is a founder-member of the Brazilian Academy of Music.

WRITINGS

'Luciano Gallet', *Revista da Associação brasileira de música*, ii/4 (1933), 2

'José Maurício Nunes Garcia', *Boletin latino-americano de música*, i/1 (1935), 133

'As primeiras óperas: "A Noite do Castelo" (1861); "Joanna de Flandres" (1863)', *Revista brasileira de música*, iii (1936), 201–45

'Carlos Gomes e Francisco Manuel: correspondência inédita (1864–1865)', *Revista brasileira de música*, iii (1936), 323

'Carlos Gomes folclorista', *Revista brasileira de música*, iii (1936), 177

'Carlos Gomes: sua verdadeira posição no quadro da ópera italiana no séc. XIX e na evolução da música brasileira', *Boletin latino-americano de música*, iii (1937), 83

Escala, rítmo e melodia na música dos indios brasileiros (Rio de Janeiro, 1938)

Relação das óperas de autores brasileiros (Rio de Janeiro, 1938)

'Introdução ao curso de folclore nacional da Escola nacional de música da Universidade do Brasil', *Revista brasileira de musica*, vi (1939), 1

'La musique au Brésil', *ReM* (1940), no.196, p.74

'Tupynambá melodies in Jean de Léry's "Histoire d'un voyage fait en la terre du Brésil" ', *PAMS 1941*, 85

'Mário de Andrade e o folclore', *Revista brasileira de música*, ix (1943), 11

'O Padre José Maurício', *Brasil musical*, i/6 (1945), 5, 48

'La música en el Brasil', *Cuadernos americanos* (1947), no.33, p.250

A música brasileira e seus fundamentos (Washington, DC, 1948)

Música e músicos do Brasil (Rio de Janeiro, 1950)

with C. Person de Matos and M. de Moura Reis: *Bibliografia musical brasileira (1820–1950)* (Rio de Janeiro, 1952)

La musique en Amérique latine (Rio de Janeiro, 1954)

150 anos de música no Brasil, 1800–1950 (Rio de Janeiro, 1956)

'Música y cultura en el siglo XVIII', *Revista musical chilena* (1962), nos.81–2, p.135

'Le chant de la liberté: compositeurs de l'Amérique latine à l'époque des luttes pour l'Indépendance, hymnographie patriotique', *Mélanges à la mémoire de Jean Sarrailh* (Paris, 1966), 64

'Vissungos: Negro Work Songs of the Diamond District in Minas Gerais, Brazil', *Music in the Americas*, ed. G. List and J. Orrego-Salas (Bloomington, Ind., 1967), 64

'Latin American Music', *Latin America and the Caribbean: a Handbook*, ed. C. B. Veliz (London, 1968), 814

'Music and Society in Imperial Brazil, 1822–1889', *Portugal and Brazil in Transition*, ed. R. S. Sayers (Minneapolis, 1968), 303

'La musique à la cour portugaise de Rio de Janeiro, 1808–1821', *Arquivos do Centro cultural português*, i (Paris, 1969), 335

'Arthur Napoléon 1843–1925: un pianiste portugais au Brésil', *Arquivos do Centro cultural português*, iii (Paris, 1971), 572–602

'The Present State and Potential of Music Research in Latin America', *Perspectives in Musicology*, ed. B. S. Brook (New York, 1972), 249

GERARD BÉHAGUE

Azevedo da Silva, Conde Fernando de (*d* Lisbon, 1923). Portuguese composer. He completed his education in Paris, where he met many of the leading intellectual and musical figures; in particular, he was markedly influenced by d'Indy's theories. He wrote several operas, among them *Flavia*, *Viviana*, *Rosario* and *Morte de Orfeu*; this last, his most important work, was first performed at Antwerp in 1907. Excerpts from his operas were heard at the Lamoureux Concerts, and he himself was a founder of the Circée Concerts. He translated the *Lusiads* into French and spent most of his life abroad in the diplomatic service.

MARIA HELENA DE FREITAS

Azione sacra. One of several terms commonly used for *sepolcri* in the Italian language composed for the Habsburg court in Vienna in the second half of the 17th century. Many of the *sepolcri* composed by Antonio Draghi to librettos by Nicolò Minato, for instance, bear the sub-title *azione sacra*; other terms applied to the same genre were *azione sepolcrale* and *rappresentazione*

sacra, as well as *sepolcro*. In 18th-century Vienna *azione sacra* was commonly used for oratorios in Italian; all the oratorio librettos by Zeno and some by Metastasio follow this usage. From Vienna the term spread to Italy as a synonym for ORATORIO, and to other countries where Italian oratorios were performed. Italian librettists and composers of the late 18th and 19th centuries used *azione sacra* and related terms for 'staged oratorios' (sacred operas) as well. Rossini, for example, called the earliest version of his opera *Mosè in Egitto* (1818) an *azione tragico-sacra*.

HOWARD E. SMITHER

Azione teatrale (It.). A genre of music theatre that enjoyed a brief vogue during the middle of the 18th century, particularly at the courts of Vienna and its environs (Schlosshof, Laxenburg, Schönbrunn etc). *Azioni teatrali* are almost invariably in a single act, with a cast of three to five characters. Because they were intended for performance in private theatres, they are scored for a comparatively small orchestra, especially as regards the wind section. The term is found most often in the writings of PIETRO METASTASIO, who may well have invented it. For all practical purposes it is identical with such terms as *azione scenica*, *festa teatrale* or *componimento da camera*. *Azioni teatrali* often formed one part of an evening's larger entertainment. A painting by Johann Franz Greippel in the Hofburg, Vienna, depicts a performance in 1765 of the *azione teatrale* entitled *Il Parnasso confuso* (text by Metastasio, music by Gluck) in the theatre at Schönbrunn, with an audience of about 150, an orchestra of 13 players, members of the imperial family in the cast and the Archduke Leopold conducting from the harpsichord. One of the last examples of this short-lived genre is Mozart's *Il sogno di Scipione* (1772), to a libretto by Metastasio.

OWEN JANDER

Azkue (Aberasturi), Resurrección María de (*b* Lequeitio, Biscay, 5 Aug 1864; *d* Bilbao, 9 Nov 1951). Spanish composer, ethnomusicologist and philologist. He studied at the seminaries of Vitoria and Salamanca, was ordained priest (1888) and took a doctorate in theology. In addition he studied music with Sáinz Basabe and then at the Paris Schola Cantorum, in Brussels and at the Cologne Conservatory. He was subsequently professor of Basque language at the Instituto de Bilbao for 30 years. In Bilbao he founded a Basque school, the Basque review *Euskalzale* and a Basque opera house, for which he composed works to be performed by pupils of his school. He was a great folklorist: he collected some 2000 folksongs of his native region and published around 1000 of them; he gave numerous lectures and he helped to compile the *Diccionario de la música Labor* (Barcelona, 1954). From 1918 he was president of the Basque Language Academy, and he was a member of the Russian Academy of Sciences and the Real Academia Española de la Lengua.

WORKS

(selective list)

Stage: Eguzkia nora, zarzuela, 2 (1896); Sasi-eskola, zarzuela (1898); Pasa de Chimbos, zarzuela, 2 (1898); Ortzuri, opera, 3, Bilbao, 1911; Urlo, opera, 3, Bilbao, 1913; Aitaren bildur, sainete lírico vasco (1917); Colonia inglesa, zarzuela, 2; Vizcaytik Bizkaira, zarzuela, 3

Oratorios: Andra Urraka, Daniel, Lemindano

Church music: Te Deum, 3vv (1933); many other works

EDITIONS

Cancionero popular vasco: canciones selectas harmonizadas (Barcelona, ?1919)

Cancionero popular vasco: edición manual, sin acompañamiento (Barcelona, 1923)

Las mil y una canciones populares vascas (Barcelona, ?1923)

WRITINGS

Música popular baskongada (Bilbao, 1901)

'La música', *Los baskos en la nación argentina* (Buenos Aires, 1916), 99

Música popular vasca: su existencia (Bilbao, 1919)

Aeskera edo Petiribero-inguruetako mintzaera (Bilbao, 1928)

GUY BOURLIGUEUX

Azpilcueta, Martín de [Navarrus, Martinus] (*b* Barasoain, *c*1491; *d* Rome, 1586). Spanish churchman and jurisconsult. He taught in Salamanca and Coimbra and spent his last 19 years in Rome, revered for his learning and piety. His numerous Latin writings were published throughout Europe in the 16th and early 17th centuries. Forkel, Fétis and others credited him with a musical treatise, *De musica et cantus figurato*, but no such work apparently exists; reports of it may stem from a misunderstanding of Walther's *Musicalisches Lexicon*. Azpilcueta's known writings on church music occur in *Commentarius de oratione horis canonicis atque aliis divinis officiis* (Coimbra, 1561) and the brief *Commentarius de silentio in divinis officiis* (Rome, 1580; Spanish and Italian translations soon afterwards). He justified music not for God's benefit but man's, as it contributed to man's ability to worship; all excesses and abuses worked against this end. Well-executed plainsong was much to be preferred, but neither polyphonic music nor instruments were inherently improper if they enhanced the attitude of reverence and did not obscure the text. His discussion of specific abuses in the liturgy of his time is of particular interest.

BIBLIOGRAPHY

FétisB; *WaltherML*

F. J. León Tello: *Estudios de historia de la teoría musical* (Madrid, 1962)

ALMONTE HOWELL

Aztec music. The Aztecs, a Náhuatl-speaking tribe, were one of the most important Indian groups in pre-Conquest America. According to their own tradition, the Aztecs came into central Mexico from the northern region of Aztlan in the 12th century. Based on a league of three cities, Mexico, Texcoco and Tlacopan, the Aztec empire by the time of the Spanish Conquest (1521) extended as far as present-day Central America. Approximately one million people in Mexico still speak Náhua. (For Mexican Indian music *see* MEXICO, §II, 3.)

Among the pre-Conquest Aztecs, music had no independent life apart from religious and cult observances. As did the Levitical guild in ancient Israel, so also among the Aztecs a professionalized caste controlled public musical manifestations. Training of an extremely rigid kind was prerequisite to a career in music. Since music was always thought of as a necessary adjunct to ritual, absolutely flawless performances, such as only the most highly trained singers and players could give, were demanded. Imperfectly executed rituals were thought to offend rather than to appease the deities, so that errors in the performances of ritual music, such as missed drumbeats, carried the death penalty. Singers and players, because of the important role music played in Aztec life, enjoyed considerable social prestige and in certain cases exemption from tribute payments. Despite this prestige, however, the names of musicians were not handed down to posterity; neither were the names of

poets, unless the poet belonged to royalty such as King Nezahualcóyotl (1402–72) of Texcoco.

Music was regarded as essentially a means of communal rather than individual expression, and therefore concerted rather than solo music was the norm. Instrumental performance and singing were always inseparable, as were dance and music, insofar as can be judged from the descriptions of Aztec musical performances bequeathed by Spanish 16th-century chroniclers. Certain instruments were thought to be of divine origin, and the *teponaztli* (slit-drum with two tongues played with mallets) and *huehuetl* (single-headed upright cylindrical drum open at the bottom, played with bare hands) were held to be gods temporarily forced to endure earthly exile. The *teponaztli* (into which the blood of sacrificed victims was poured at royal accessions) and the *huehuetl* were therefore often treated as idols as well as musical instruments. Not only were certain instruments thought to have mana (mysterious supernatural powers) but they were also held to represent symbolically such emotional states as joy, delight or sensual pleasure.

Aztec music communicated states of feeling that apparently even the Spaniards could grasp and appreciate, whereas much of the Indian tribal music north of Mexico meant nothing to European ears. In many instances Aztec music seems to have communicated the same emotion to Indian and European listener alike. Thus a lament, as composed by an Aztec priest-musician, was sad not only in the opinion of the Indians who heard and understood it, but also in the opinion of Spaniards unfamiliar with the Náhuatl language. Every piece of music was composed for a certain time, place and occasion, so that a musician needed a wide repertory if he was to satisfy the demands of the different days in the 260-day religious calendar.

Although the *calmécac* (priest's dwelling) at the Aztec capital served as a national conservatory, and by 1450 was (according to Diego Durán, *Historia de las Indias de Nueva-España*, Mexico, 1867–80) the model for similar training institutes in surrounding municipalities, the Aztecs themselves lacked any system of music notation; if they had one, it was kept a secret from Europeans. Any reconstructions of Mexican pre-Conquest music are therefore largely conjectural, based on the possibilities of surviving instruments in museums, verbal descriptions by Spanish 16th-century chroniclers and the contemporary sounds of Indian tribal music recorded in outlying areas.

Aztec musicians needed prodigious memories. Musicians not only learnt early traditional songs, but composed new ones. Creative ability was prized, especially in the households of those powerful *caciques* who were able to employ singers to compose ballads telling of their exploits. Court music, at least in the Aztec and Tarascan neighbouring kingdoms, differed as much from the music of the *maceualli* (peasant classes) as did court speech from the rude Náhuatl and Purépecha spoken by the common people of those kingdoms.

Although Aztec music was predominantly percussive (string instruments were a European importation), the Aztecs had acute pitch sense and tuned with considerable care their various idiophones: *ayacachtli*, *áyotl*, *cacalachtli*, *chichuaztli*, *chililitli* (*caililiztli*), *coyolli*, *omichicahuaztli*, *tecomapiloa*, *teponaztli*, *tetzilácatl*; aerophones: *atecocoli* (*atecuculli*), *chichtli*, *çoçoloctli*, *huilacapitztli*, *quiquiztli*, *tecciztli* (*tecziztli*, *tezizcatli*), *tepuzquiquiztli*, *tlapitzalli*; or membranophones: *huehuetl*, *tlapanhuehuetl*. (For descriptions of these instruments, see Stevenson, pp.30–85.) Bold, assertive qualities such as loudness, clarity and high pitch were preferred by players and singers alike. This crying aloud to their gods served their purpose even when the common people danced (as is still done by indigenous peoples of Mexico) to do penance.

Aztec huehuetl from Malinalco in the Museo de Arqueología, Toluca

The pre-Conquest Aztecs frequently inscribed their instruments with carvings that tell symbolically the purposes served by their instruments. For instance, the various carvings on the Malinalco *huehuetl* (see illustration), an upright drum about 90 cm tall, in the Toluca Museum show a group of captured warriors being forced to dance to music of their own making just before having their hearts torn out and waved aloft as offerings to the war god Huitzilopochtli. The Aztecs, who burst into the Valley of Mexico to found Tenochtitlan (Mexico City) about 1325, borrowed heavily from the organo-

graphy of earlier cultures in the extensive territories stretching south to present-day El Salvador, which they conquered during the next two centuries. To the European conquerors, the instruments used by Aztecs, Tarascans, Otomís, Zapotecs, Mixtecs and Mayas greatly resembled each other, only the names differing in the respective aboriginal languages. In none of these languages do 16th-century lexicographers record a single generic term for music, coming nearest to it in Alonso de Molina's *Arte de la lengua Mexicana* (Mexico, 1571) with *cuica tlamatiliztli* ('knowledge of singing'). Neither did Náhuatl have any single term for 'musician' or 'player' but numerous nouns meaning 'player on the *huehuetl*', 'player on the *teponaztli*', 'flute player' and 'trumpet player'. The Aztec language also included numerous verbs with such varied specific meanings as 'to sing in praise of someone', 'to sing derisive songs', 'to sing tenderly', or 'to sing in a high voice' (*see also* MEXIO §II, 1).

BIBLIOGRAPHY

F. W. Galpin: 'Aztec Influence on American Indian Instruments', *SIMG*, iv (1903–4), 661

L. M. Spell: 'Music and Instruments of the Aztecs: the Beginning of Musical Education in North America', *MTNA Proceedings* (1926), 98

F. H. Martens: 'Music in the Life of the Aztecs', *MQ*, xiv (1928), 413

R. Lach: 'Die musikalischen Konstruktionsprinzipien der altmexikanischen Tempelgesänge', *Musikwissenschaftliche Beiträge: Festschrift für Johannes Wolf* (Berlin, 1929), 88

D. Castañeda and V. T. Mendoza: 'Los teponaztlis en las civilizaciones precortesianas'; 'Los percutores precortesianos'; 'Los huehuetls en las civilizaciones precortesianas', *Anales del Museo nacional de arqueología, historia y etnología, cuarta época*, viii/1 (1933), 5–80; viii/2 (1933), 275, 287

V. T. Mendoza: 'Supervivencia de la cultura azteca: la canción y el baile del Xochipzahua', *Revista mexicana de sociología*, iv/4 (1942), 87

G. Chase: *A Guide to the Music of Latin America* (Washington, DC, 1945, 2/1962), 287ff, 304

S. Martí: *Instrumentos musicales precortesianos* (Mexico City, 1955, 2/1968)

L. S. Jena: *Alt-Aztekische Gesänge* (Stuttgart, 1957)

S. Martí: *Canto, danza y música precortesianos* (Mexico City, 1961)

G. P. Kurath and S. Martí: *Dances of Anáhuac: the Choreography and Music of Precortesian Dances* (New York, 1964)

R. Stevenson: *Music in Aztec & Inca Territory* (Berkeley, Los Angeles and London, 1968)

S. Martí: *Alt-Amerika: Musik der Indianer in präkolumbischer Zeit* (Leipzig, 1970), 5, 32–111

——: *La música precortesiana/Music before Cortés* (Mexico City, 1971)

ROBERT STEVENSON

Azza Gëra, (*fl* 16th century). Inventor with Azza Ragwel, according to Ethiopian national tradition, of the notational signs now in use for the Ethiopian chant; *see* ETHIOPIAN RITE, MUSIC OF THE.

Azzaiolo, Filippo (*b* Bologna; *fl* 1557–69). Italian composer. He is believed to have been a singer in one of the Bolognese churches, though probably not S Petronio since he is not mentioned in the account books; he may have been connected with members of the Bolognese singing academies as described by Giustiniani. His first two books of villottas were published anonymously and he acknowledged all three only in the third book, after the first two had been sufficiently successful to be reprinted. The value of these collections lies in their preservation of popular texts and melodies arranged in simple four-part homophonic settings, in which the top voice usually carries the melody. The first book contains 20 villottas, together with a 'todesca' by Girardo da Panico and madrigals by Caldarino, Spontone, Ruffo and 'P.H.', whom Vatielli believed to be Pietro de Hostia. Among the more well-known items are *Da* *l'horto se ne vien la vilanella*, incorporating two 15th-century songs of which the second, *Torèla mo' vilano*, was set by Verdelot, and *Chi passa per 'sta strada*; *Ti parti cuor mio* is found in a three-voice setting in Striggio's *Cicalamento delle donne al bucato* (1569) and *Poi che volse de la mia stella* occurs in Petrucci's collection (*RISM* 1504⁴) where it is ascribed to Tromboncino.

In the second book there are eight compositions by Azzaiolo, including *Girometta, senza te*, which was arranged for 'tromboni, cornetti et cornamuse' and performed in the main square of Bologna, and was also popular among 17th-century composers including Frescobaldi. The third book contains seven pieces by Azzaiolo, of which the most interesting is *E me levai d'una bella mattina*, an eight-voice version of the canzona of the same name from the first book.

WORKS

Il primo libro de villotte alla padoana con alcune napolitane, 4vv (Venice, 1557¹⁸); 13 ed. F. Vatielli: *Villotte del fiore* (Bologna, 1921)

Il secondo libro de villotte del fiore alla padoana con alcune napolitanae e madrigali, 4vv (Venice, 1559¹⁹); ed. in Maestri bolognesi, ii (Bologna, 1953)

Il terzo libro delle villotte del fiore alla padoana con alcune napolitanae e bergamasche, 4vv (Venice, 1569²⁴)

BIBLIOGRAPHY

C. Spontoni: *Il Bottrigaro* (Venice, 1583)

V. Giustiniani: *Discorso sopra la musica de' suoi tempi* (1628; repr. in A. Solerti: *Le origini del melodramma*, Turin, 1903/*R*1969; and Eng. trans. C. MacClintock, MSD, ix, 1962)

G. Gaspari: *Musicisti bolognesi del XVI secolo* (Imola, 1875), 14ff

F. Vatielli: *Arte e vita musicale a Bologna*, i (Bologna, 1927/*R*1969), 43ff

A. Einstein: *The Italian Madrigal* (Princeton, 1949/*R*1971), i, 348, 351, 375, 380; ii, 750

A. Calcaterra: *Poesie e canto* (Bologna, 1951)

R. Nielsen: 'Azzaiolo, Filippo', *DBI*

W. Kirkendale: 'Franceschina, Girometta, and their Companions in a Madrigal "a diversi linguaggi" by Luca Marenzio and Orazio Vecchi', *AcM*, xliv (1972), 181–235

E. Apfel: *Aufsätze und Vorträge zur Musikgeschichte und historischen Musiktheorie* (Saarbrücken, 1977)

ANNE SCHNOEBELEN

B

B. *See* PITCH NAMES.

Baaren, Kees van (*b* Enschede, 22 Oct 1906; *d* 2 Sept 1970). Dutch composer and teacher. He received his musical training in Berlin (1924–9), studying piano with Rudolf Breithaupt and composition at the Hochschule für Musik with Friedrich Koch. A meeting in Berlin with Pijper brought him back to the Netherlands in order to complete his studies with Pijper. He destroyed the works he wrote before 1930, and was the only one of Pijper's pupils to have used serial procedures consistently. After a few years in the eastern Netherlands, for the most part working with amateur ensembles, he became director of the Amsterdam Music Lyceum in 1948. In 1953 he was appointed director of the Utrecht Conservatory and became director of the Royal Conservatory in The Hague in 1958. Van Baaren was looked upon as the mentor of a large group of younger composers, whom he brought into close contact with new developments in composition. Amongst his most outstanding pupils were van Vlijmen, Schat, Mischa Mengelberg, Louis Andriessen and Porcelijn.

The first of his works to be performed publicly were the Piano Concertino (1934) and a Trio for winds (1936), in which van Baaren sought to provide characteristic melodic material for one of the instruments in each movement (1st movement, bassoon; 2nd movement, clarinet; 3rd movement, flute), combining this with canonic and fugal writing. The Concertino, on the other hand, shows the influence of Pijper in its germ-cell technique, a short motif forming the basis for the melodic organization of the whole work. After these pieces van Baaren wrote nothing until 1947, and in 1948 he wrote his first major work, the cantata *The Hollow Men*. The starting-point was here a melodic element of six notes, employed as a series, although a tonal centre remains present, if not always clearly so. His first 12-note work, still using Pijper's germ-cell principle, was the Settetto (1952), and after this piece he continued to employ 12-note serialism. Even if in his Sinfonia (1956) he dealt less strictly with the 12-note technique than in the piano piece *Muzikaal zelfportret* (1954), his Variazioni per orchestra (1959) display the powerful musical and technical possibilities within dodecaphony. The work is based on a bilaterally symmetrical all-interval series, and each of the five variations stresses a particular facet of 12-note technique. Thus the second variation explores different vertical groupings, and the third is concerned with various segments of the series.

After this important and successful work van Baaren wrote a few chamber works, which further developed 12-note serial writing in ingenious forms. There followed the Piano Concerto (1964), a fascinating and colourful work, and the Musica per orchestra (1966). The third and last movement of this work employs a collage of disparate materials. There was perceptible in these last works a strong tendency towards an increasing simplification, and an exploitation of combinatoriality. Van Baaren always used symmetrical all-interval series, and showed a preference for asymmetrical rhythmic and melodic patterns.

WORKS

Concertino, pf, orch, 1934; Trio, fl, cl, bn, 1936; Recueillement (Baudelaire), 1v, pf, 1947; 3 Poems by Emily Dickinson, female chorus, 1947; Sonatina in memoriam Willem Pijper, pf, 1948; The Hollow Men (Eliot), solo vv, chorus, orch, 1948, rev. 1955–6; 2 Songs, male chorus, 1952; Settetto, vn, wind qnt, db, 1952; Muzikaal zelfportret, pf, 1954; Sinfonia, orch, 1956
Variazioni per orchestra, 1959; Canzonetta triste, vn, pf, 1960; Partita, symphonic band, 1961; Quartetto per archi (Sovraposizioni I), 1962; Quintetto a fiato (Sovraposizioni II), 1963; Musica per campane, 1964; Concerto, pf, orch, 1964; Musica per flauto solo, 1965; Musica per orchestra, 1966

Principal publisher: Donemus

BIBLIOGRAPHY

J. Geraedts: 'Kees van Baaren: Variazioni per orchestra', *Sonorum speculum*, vi (1961)
J. Wouters: 'Kees van Baaren: his Place in Dutch Music', *Sonorum speculum*, xxxiv (1968)
J. Hill: *The Music of Kees van Baaren* (diss., U. of North Carolina, 1970)
J. Wouters: 'Kees van Baaren', *Dutch Composers' Gallery* (Amsterdam, 1971)

JOS WOUTERS

Baarpijp (Dutch). An ORGAN STOP.

Babadjanyan, Arno Harutyuni (*b* Erevan, 22 Jan 1921). Armenian composer and pianist. He graduated from Talyan's composition class at the Erevan Conservatory in 1947, and in 1948 from Igumnov's piano class at the Moscow Conservatory; his composition studies were continued under Litinsky at the House of Armenian Culture in Moscow (1946–8). He taught the piano at the Erevan Conservatory (1950–56) and is himself a brilliant pianist. In 1971 he was made a People's Artist of the USSR. His music draws on Khachaturian and Rakhmaninov, but is unmistakably individual, particularly in its scoring. The piano works are in a virtuoso style, liberal in its use of touch, texture, rhythm and register, and with expressive leading parts. This style was formed in the 1940s; later he introduced Prokofiev-like chromaticism, Bartókian rhythm and

763

Schoenbergian dodecaphony into his music, achieving his best work in the Violin Sonata, the Cello Concerto and the *Shest' kartin* ('Six pictures') for piano. Babadjanyan's variation technique, an important feature of his music, springs from folk ornamentation, and peasant music is also the source of his irregular rhythms.

WORKS
(*selective list*)

Orch: Pf Conc., 1944; Vn Conc., 1949; Herosakan ballad, pf, orch, 1950; Poema-rapsodiya, orch, 1954; Vc Conc., 1962

Chamber: 2 str qts, 1943, 1947; Pf Trio, 1952; Sonata, vn, pf, 1959

Pf: Polifonicheskaya sonata, 1947; Haykakan rapsodia, 2 pf, 1950; Vagharshapati par, 1954; 6 kartin [6 pictures], 1965; Poema, 1966; other pieces

Film scores

BIBLIOGRAPHY

A. Grigoryan: *Arno Babadjanyan* (Moscow, 1961)

S. T'ashchian: *Arno Babadjanyan* (Erevan, 1961)

Sh. Apoyan: *Fortepiannaya muzïka sovetskoy Armenii* (Erevan, 1968), 150ff, 201ff

SVETLANA SARKISIAN

Babán, Gracián (*b* ?Aragon, *c*1620; *d* Valencia, 2 Feb 1675). Spanish composer. In September 1649 he competed unsuccessfully for the post of *maestro de capilla* of La Seo, one of the two cathedrals at Saragossa. In 1653 he was chosen *maestro de capilla* of Huesca Cathedral with an annual salary of 120 escudos, which was raised to 160 escudos on 29 August that year in the expectation that he would be ordained priest. He asked for more money on 1 July 1655 but was offered only another 10 or 20 escudos a year for his composition of music for Christmas and Corpus Christi. On 27 April 1657 he accepted the post of *maestro de capilla* of Valencia Cathedral. He was one of the most prolific and respected Spanish composers of his age. He wrote the *Te Deum* and two villancicos performed at Valencia Cathedral on 20 May 1659 to celebrate the canonization of St Thomas of Villanueva, the music commemorating an indult granted by Pope Alexander VII in 1665 and five villancicos sung at S Domingo, Valencia, on 8 September 1674 in honour of the canonization of S Luis Beltrán. His music, which includes many polychoral pieces, circulated widely and survives in Latin America as well as in Spain. A painting showing Babán and his singers protected from the plague by the Virgin Mary was formerly in the Capilla de Nuestra Señora contra la Peste at Valencia Cathedral.

WORKS

2 masses, 8vv, 12vv, *E-SEG*

16 masses, 6–14vv, *VAc*

Requiem, 8vv, *SEG*

4 Lamentations, *SEG*

Motet (for the Adoration of the Cross), 4vv, *MA*

3 Passion motets, *SEG*

Psalms, 4, 8vv, *H, MA, SEG, VAc*; 1 ed. in Lira sacro-hispana, i/1 (Madrid, 1869)

Many other vocal works, incl. motets, psalms, hymns, sequences and villancicos: *CO-B, D-Mbs, E-Bc, E, MA, SEG, VAc*, Guatemala Cathedral archives; Puebla Cathedral, Mexico; 2 motets ed. in Lira sacro-hispana, i/1 (Madrid, 1869)

BIBLIOGRAPHY

M. A. Ortí: *Solemnidad festiva con que en la insigne, leal, noble y coronada ciudad de Valencia se celebro la feliz nueva de la canonizacion de su milagroso Arcobispo Santo Tomas de Villanueva* (Valencia, 1659), 47

F. de la Torre y Sebdil: *Luces de la aurora, dias del sol, en fiestas de la que es sol de los dias y aurora de las luces Maria santissima* (Valencia, 1665), 56

J. Alenda y Mira: *Relaciones de solemnidades y fiestas públicas de España* (Madrid, 1903), 344f, 382, 393

J. Ruiz de Lihory: *La música en Valencia: diccionario biográfico y crítico* (Valencia, 1903)

J. Sanchiz y Sivera: *La catedral de Valencia* (1909), 456

V. Ripollès Pérez: introduction to *El villancico i la cantata del segle XVIII a València* (Barcelona, 1935), p.vii

A. Durán Gudiol: 'Los maestros de capilla de la catedral de Huesca', *Argensola*, x/2 (1959), 127

J. Climent: 'La música en Valencia durante el siglo XVII', *AnM*, xxi (1966), 233, 238

R. Stevenson: *Renaissance and Baroque Musical Sources in the Americas* (Washington, DC, 1970), 6, 168

ROBERT STEVENSON

Babbi. Italian family of musicians.

(1) Gregorio (Lorenzo) Babbi (i) (*b* Cesena, 16 Nov 1708; *d* Cesena, 2 Jan 1768). Italian tenor. His first post was as virtuoso to the Grand Duke of Tuscany, Gian Gastone de' Medici. He made his début in Florence in 1730 and for the next 20 years sang in the leading theatres of Italy. He became a member of the Bologna Accademia Filarmonica on 5 January 1741 and shortly thereafter entered the service of Charles III, King of Naples. In 1748 both Babbi and his wife, Giovanna Guaetta [Guaetti], were engaged at the Teatro S Carlo, Naples. He remained in Naples until 1755, when he went to Lisbon to perform Mazzoni's *Antigono*. By spring 1756 he had returned to Italy and sang in Naples until 1759, when he received a pension and returned to Cesena. It has been said, but without reliable evidence, that Babbi sang in London, Vienna and Madrid. Being a tenor, he sang only secondary parts for much of his career, but because of his reputation as one of the best exponents of the expressive style, he commanded salaries comparable with those of the leading castratos. De Brosses, who heard him in his prime in 1741, described him as the 'loveliest high tenor [haut-taille]' and a good actor, and compared him with the French tenor Jélyotte. Burney called him a 'dignified, splendid and powerful performer', with the 'sweetest, most flexible, and most powerful voice of its kind, that his country could boast at the time'. According to Lalande his range was two octaves, c–c'', in full voice and even higher in falsetto, a 5th higher than most Italian tenors of the time and equal to Jélyotte's and Amorevoli's ranges. Babbi is not known to have composed; the pieces attributed to him by Schmidl are by his grandson, (3) Gregorio Babbi (ii).

BIBLIOGRAPHY

FétisB; GerberNL; SchmidlD

P. L. Ghezzi: *Il mondo nuovo del Cavalier Pier Leone Ghezzi* (MS, I-Rvat Cod. Lat. Ottoboniensis 3117), f.161 [caricature of Babbi]

J. J. de Lalande: *Voyage d'un françois en Italie, fait dans les années 1765 et 1766* (Venice and Paris, 1769, rev. and enlarged 2/1786), vii, 205ff

S. Goudar: *Remarques sur la musique et la danse, ou Lettres de Mr. G ... à Milord Pembroke* (Venice, 1773; It. trans., n.d.), 26ff

C. de Brosses: *Lettres historiques et critiques sur l'Italie* (Paris, 1799; ed. Y. Bezard as *Lettres familières sur l'Italie*, ii (Paris, 1931), 344

C. Burney: 'Gregorio Babbi', *Rees's Cyclopaedia* (London, 1879)

C. Ricci: *I teatri di Bologna nei secoli XVII e XVIII* (Bologna, 1888/R1965), 155, 555

B. Croce: *I teatri di Napoli, secole XV–XVIII* (Naples, 1891/R1968), ii, 341f, 350ff, 360ff, 402ff

N. Trovanelli: 'Due celebri cantanti cesenati del secolo scorso', *Il cittadino: giornale della Domenica*, v/30 (Cesena, 25 July 1897)

E. Zanetti: 'Babbi, Gregorio', *ES*

A. Zapperi: 'Babbi, Gregorio', *DBI*

H.-B. Dietz: 'A Chronology of Maestri and Organisti at the Cappella Reale in Naples, 1745–1800', *JAMS*, xxv (1972), 379, esp. 390

R. L. and N. Weaver: *A Chronology of Music in the Florentine Theater, 1590–1750* (Detroit, 1976)

M. McClymonds: *Niccolò Jommelli: the Last Years* (diss., U. of California, Berkeley, 1978)

(2) (Pietro Giovanni) Cristoforo (Bartolomeo Gasparre) Babbi (*b* Cesena, 6 May 1745; *d* Dresden, 19 Nov 1814). Italian violinist and composer, son of (1) Gregorio Babbi. He spent his childhood (1748–59) in

Naples, where his parents were employed in the Teatro S Carlo and in the royal chapel. After his return to Cesena in 1759 he was sent to Faenza (about 1763 or 1764) to study the violin with Tartini's disciple Paolo Alberghi, who also taught him counterpoint and composition. In Faenza he was *primo violino* for the *festa* of 8 December 1766 and again in 1769, 1770 and 1772. In Rimini he was a violinist in the orchestra for the 1773 opera season. He became a member of the Bologna Accademia Filarmonica on 4 February 1774. From 1775 to 1778 he served as *maestro di cappella* in the Teatro Comunale, Bologna, and as *primo violino* and *direttore d'orchestra* in Forlì in spring 1779.

On 3 March 1781, Babbi was engaged as provisional Konzertmeister in Dresden; after the first year his contract was formalized and extended. Under his direction the Dresden Kapelle was completely reorganized, and the orchestra acquired international renown for its accuracy, precision, discipline and brilliant, full sound. Babbi took part in the selection of musicians (with the elector); although he was officially only in charge of the violins, he actually directed the entire orchestra, and was in effect equal in importance to J. G. Naumann, the Kapellmeister. His administrative skills and leadership affected even the soloists and vocal ensembles, raising the level of musicianship in the church and opera choirs and generally improving the discipline and organization. Babbi's musicianship was greatly admired by the Dresden court and especially by the elector. He is described as playing with 'fire' and 'exquisite taste' in the Italian style of Hasse that was then in favour at the court (Engländer, 1921–2). 'When he played, his tone was as full and rich as that of a cello and although he could not sustain this tone in passages requiring great agility, yet when he played an Adagio, not an eye was dry' (Steinmann, 1863).

Babbi served as Konzertmeister until shortly before his death, when he retired with a pension. His compositions included symphonies for the church, the theatre and the Hofkapelle (after 1786), theatre pieces (1786), and entr'acte music performed during spoken dramas (1792–3) and operas (1796), sonatinas (1802–3), concertos and chamber music for the Hofkapelle, and arrangements of concertos and symphonies by other Italian composers. Of these, only one work is extant (piano score in *D-Dlb*), the introductory sinfonia to the cantata *Augusta* by C. E. Weinlig, written in honour of the Princess Maria Augusta, and given on 21 August 1786. This sinfonia is in the three-movement cantabile style of contemporary Italian opera overtures and is remarkable for its explicit tempo and dynamic indications: sudden contrasts between *f* and *pp* or *ppp*, crescendos and diminuendos, and even *pianissimo* ritardandos ('mancando poco a poco').

BIBLIOGRAPHY

EitnerQ; GerberNL
Indice de' spettacoli teatrali . . . 1779–1780 (Milan, 1780), 11
H. F. Steinmann [H. Mannstein]: *Denkwürdigkeiten der Churfürstlichen u. Königlichen Hofmusik zu Dresden im 18. u. 19. Jahrhundert* (Leipzig, 1863), 45f
R. Proelss: *Geschichte des Hoftheaters zu Dresden von seinen Anfängen bis zum Jahre 1862* (Dresden, 1878), 234, 239, 246, 379
C. Ricci: *I teatri di Bologna nei secoli XVII e XVIII* (Bologna, 1888/R1965), 654
R. Engländer: 'Zur Musikgeschichte Dresdens gegen 1800', *ZMw*, iv (1921–2), 199–241
——: *J. G. Naumann als Opernkomponist (1741–1801)* (Leipzig, 1922), 99f, 105ff, 112ff, 118f
H. Schnoor: *Dresden: vierhundert Jahre deutsche Musikkultur* (Dresden, 1948), 130f

R. Engländer: *Die Dresdener Instrumentalmusik in der Zeit der wiener Klassik* (Uppsala, 1956), 28f, 34, 121, 124ff
A. Zapperi: 'Babbi, Cristoforo', *DBI*
L. Malusi: *Musicisti e cantanti di Romagna* (MS dated 1972, *I-CEc*), 21f
L. Righetti: *Vita musicale e teatri a Rimini nel settecento* (diss., U. of Bologna, 1973), 219

(3) **Gregorio Babbi (ii)** (*b* ?Bologna, *c*1770–75; *d* ?Bologna, *c*1815). Italian bass, violinist, composer and organist, son of (2) Cristoforo Babbi. In 1788 he was a provisional supernumerary violinist, and in 1790 a bass singer in the Dresden Hofkirche. He was granted leave of absence in 1790 and sang in Forlì in 1791. He had returned to Dresden by 1794 and continued in his dual position as bass and violinist in the Hofkirche. He seems to have been a better singer than a violinist, however, and is reputed to have had a beautiful voice. In 1803 he was officially engaged as one of the two solo basses employed in the Hofkirche, although he also retained his former salary as violinist. He became Musikmeister (as assistant to the Kapellmeister) in 1805, replacing Frederick Gestewitz. In 1807 he received a pension and returned to Italy, where he served as *primo violino* and orchestra director in Bologna, first at the Teatro Comunale (1807–8) and then at the Teatro Marsigili-Rossi. His last years were spent in Bologna, where he served as organist in one of the churches.

Babbi's only extant compositions (all in *I-Bc*) were originally written for the Dresden Hofkapelle. The sinfonias (1804) are the most ambitious of the four works and contain several solo passages, probably a concession to the many virtuosos in the Dresden orchestra; he also wrote an orchestral pastorale (1798). Babbi's harmonic vocabulary is extremely limited; his melodies are rather unimaginative scale or triad figures, and there is virtually no thematic development. His polacca (1797) is a concert aria in rondo form and was evidently designed to display the vocal agility of its dedicatee, his sister Giovanna Babbi (*b* ?Bologna, *c*1780), an alto who, after making opera débuts in Trieste and Venice (1796–7) and scoring a striking success in Dresden during Carnival 1798–9 (reported in *AMZ*, i, 1799, cols.331–4), permanently damaged her voice in attempting to become a soprano; she left the stage in 1800. Another sister Teresa Babbi (*fl* 1800–1810) was a soprano in the Dresden Hofkapelle from about 1800 to 1806, and received the dedication of Paër's aria *Ti riposa in questo seno*.

BIBLIOGRAPHY

LaMusicaD
R. Proelss: *Geschichte des Hoftheaters zu Dresden von seinen Anfängen bis zum Jahre 1862* (Dresden, 1878), 245f
R. Engländer: 'Zur Musikgeschichte Dresdens gegen 1800', *ZMw*, iv (1921–2), 199–241, esp. 204, 213
A. Mambelli: *Musica e teatro in Forlì nel secolo XVIIIo* (Forlì, 1933), 205f

GLORIA EIVE-FELDMAN

Babbitt, Milton (Byron) (*b* Philadelphia, 10 May 1916) American composer. Brought up in Jackson, Mississippi, he started playing the violin at the age of four and several years later also studied the clarinet and saxophone. He graduated from high school in 1931, having already demonstrated considerable skills in jazz ensemble performance and 'pop song' composition. His father's professional involvement with mathematics (as an actuary) was influential in shaping Babbitt's intellectual environment. In 1931 Babbitt entered the University of Pennsylvania with the intention of becoming a mathematician, but he soon transferred to New

York University, concentrating on music under Marion Bauer and Philip James. In 1935 he received the BA in music. His early attraction to the music of Varèse and Stravinsky soon gave way to an absorption in that of Schoenberg, Berg and Webern – particularly significant at a time when 12-note music was unknown to many and viewed with scepticism by others.

After graduation he studied privately with Sessions, wrote criticism for the *Musical Leader* and then enrolled for graduate work at Princeton University where he continued his association with Sessions. In 1938 he joined the Princeton music faculty and in 1942 received one of Princeton's first MFAs in music. His *Composition for Orchestra*, a straightforward 12-note work, was completed in 1941.

During World War II he divided his time between Washington, DC, where he was engaged in mathematical research, and Princeton, as a member of the mathematics faculty (1943–5). Musically, these were years of thought and discovery, rather than of actual composition; they resulted in 1946 in a paper, *The Function of Set Structure in the Twelve-tone System*, which was the first formal and systematic investigation of Schoenberg's compositional method. In 1946–8, shuttling between Jackson and New York, he wrote some film scores and an unsuccessful Broadway musical, once again directing his energies to composition.

In 1948 he rejoined the music faculty at Princeton, eventually to become Conant Professor of Music (1960). He has also been on the faculty of the Salzburg Seminar in American Studies, the Berkshire Music Center, the Darmstadt summer courses, the New England Conservatory of Music and the Juilliard School of Music. He has won the Joseph Bearns Prize (for *Music for the Mass I* in 1942), New York Music Critics Circle citations (for *Composition for Four Instruments* in 1949 and for *Philomel* in 1964), a National Institute of Arts and Letters Award (1959) for demonstrating a 'penetrating grasp of musical order that has influenced younger composers', a Guggenheim Fellowship (1960–61), membership of the National Institute (1965) and a Brandeis University Gold Medal (1970). He has always been actively involved in contemporary music organizations, including the ISCM (he was president of the US section, 1951–2), the American Music Center, *Perspectives of New Music* (as a member of its editorial board), and the Columbia–Princeton Electronic Music Center (as a director since 1959). Articles, reviews and interviews by him have appeared in many serious music publications; he has travelled widely, speaking on issues of current musical thought. Babbitt is a remarkably successful lecturer; perceptive and adept at logical extemporization, he continually stimulates and provokes his audiences. He is also an inveterate follower of popular sports, a raconteur and punster, and an omnivorous reader.

Babbitt's early fascination with 12-note practice, particularly in its formal aspects, developed into a total reconsideration of musical relations. Throughout his compositional career he has been occupied with the extension of Schoenberg's (and Webern's) 'combinatorial' sets; with the invention of sets that have great flexibility and potential for long-range association; and with an exploration of the structuring of non-pitch components 'determined by the operations of the [12-note]

system and uniquely analogous to the specific structuring of the pitch components of the individual work, and thus, utterly nonseparable' (Babbitt, 1955). He has been a pioneer in his ways of talking and thinking about music, in invoking terms from other disciplines such as philosophy, linguistics, mathematics and the physical sciences. For example, 'pitch class', 'combinatoriality', and 'source set', terms derived from mathematics, were first introduced into contemporary musical discourse by Babbitt. His emphasis on the relation between practice and theory, his insistence on the composer's assumption of responsibility for every musical event in a work, and his reinterpretation of the constituent elements of the western musical tradition have had a vital influence in the thinking and music of numerous younger composers.

An example of Babbitt's approach may be seen in his *Three Compositions for Piano* (1947), one of his first consistent attempts to extend Schoenbergian 12-note procedures. A Schoenberg-like surface is apparent in the long, registrally dispersed lines in alternation with thickly clustered chordal attacks (and a quasi-ternary textural framework), yet the absence of expressive indications and the reliance on metronomic markings would seem to reveal a Stravinskian concern for a clear, undistracted projection of the temporal domain. The innovatory aspects of the work reside in the conjunction of the structuring of pitch and of other domains – the first instance of a 'totally serialized' music. The articulative phrasing of lines, the number of consecutive attacks and the number of pitches per attack are all precisely determined by a durational set (whose prime form is 5:1:4:2). There is also a correspondence between dynamics and pitch-set forms.

His *Composition for Four Instruments* and *Composition for Twelve Instruments* (both of which were written in 1948) go a step further towards a structuring of rhythm isomorphic with 12-note pitch structuring. In the 12-instrument work a set of 12 durations emerges and operates throughout. Each instrument unfolds its own set over different time spans, their completions determining the sections and the form of the work. Beginning with sparsely textured single events (which can be considered an extension of Webern's sound world) and slowly becoming more compact, the work concludes with thicker textures and sustained sonorities, within which singly attacked notes resound in newly shaped but familiar environments.

Although structure is a primary concern of his, lyricism and expressiveness are by no means absent from Babbitt's work, especially in his music for the voice. In *Du* (1951), a song cycle for soprano and piano (which represented the USA at the 1953 ISCM Festival), there is continual interplay between the text, the vocal and the piano lines. Phoneme, syllable, word and line have been considerably contoured, subtly and imaginatively set to music: the pitch, durational, dynamic and registral schema, themselves transformed from poem to poem, are in alliance with all verbal elements and indeed help to project the many delicate nuances of each poem. These lyrical, imagist tendencies were most fully realized in *Philomel* (1964). A variant instance of this inclination is evident in *All Set* (1957), for small jazz ensemble, with its conjunction of 12-note structure (based on an all-combinatorial set) and 'jazz-like properties . . . the use of percussion, the Chicago jazz-like juxtapositions of solos and ensembles recalling certain characteristics of group improvisation'.

Another continuing concern of Babbitt's has been electronic sound synthesis. At the time of the first hand-written film soundtrack, in the late 1930s, he had already recognized the enormous compositional potential of such synthesis. Two decades later, in the mid-1950s, when he was invited by RCA to be a composer-consultant, he became the first composer to work with its newly improved and developed synthesizer, the unique Mark II. *Composition for Synthesizer* (1961)

Milton Babbitt programming the Mark II RCA synthesizer (built early 1950s) at the Columbia-Princeton Electronic Music Center, New York

was Babbitt's first totally synthesized work. It was followed soon after by *Vision and Prayer* for soprano and synthesizer (1961) and *Ensembles for Synthesizer* (1962–4). His basic compositional attitudes and approaches underwent little change with the new resource; rather, with the availability and flexibility of the synthesizer's programming control they were now realizable to a degree of precision previously unattainable in live performances of his music.

Babbitt's interests in synthesis were not with the invention of new sounds per se, but with the control of all events, particularly in the timing and rate of changes of timbre, texture and intensity. (The notations in his Woodwind Quartet (1953) and String Quartet no.2 (1954) had already given some indication of the desired rapidity of changes of dynamics, both on single and consecutive pitches.) Due to the 'fineness of quantization available' with a synthesizer, the achievement of accurate 'rhythmic' changes in all domains was possible, such as a further conjunction of pitch and duration in which

duration is considered 'a measure of distance between pitch points [of a 12-note set, thus] we begin by interpreting interval as duration' (Babbitt, 1962–3). Such a set of intervals or 'time-points' could then be programmed (and thus 'performed') with any desired precision. His work with an electronic medium also gave rise to a number of speculations involving 'auditory effects ... acoustical specification, [and] perceptual limitations'.

Though the lucidity of his conceptual world finally became manifest under the ideal performance conditions provided by sound synthesis, Babbitt nerverless retained his interest in live performance. Perhaps the most appealing work combining live performance with tape is *Philomel*, written in conjunction with the poet John Hollander for the soprano Bethany Beardslee. It is based on Ovid's interpretation of the Greek legend of Philomela, the ravished, speechless maiden who is transformed into a nightingale. New ways of conjoining musical and verbal expressiveness were devised by composer and poet: music is as articulate as language; language (Philomel's thoughts) is transformed into music (the nightingale's song). The work is an almost inexhaustible repertory of speech-song similitudes and differentiations, and resonant word–music puns (inconceivable and unrealizable without the resources of the synthesizer), and it displays a mellowness which was to affect the quality of Babbitt's later 'live' music.

A new way of conceiving the available sonic resources of a large orchestra is noticeable in *Relata I* (1965). Here timbral 'families' are correlated with set structure and thus articulated as part of the overall relational network, with woodwind instruments as four trios, brass as three quartets and string instruments as two sextets (one bowed, the other plucked). The work is insistently polyphonic (with as many as 48 instrumental lines), framed at both ends by massive sonorities, and filled with constantly changing and recombined textures and colours. While parts of the work are analogous to other parts, there is no simple repetition: all aspects undergo reinterpretation, rearrangement and 'resurfacing'.

In the more timbrally homogeneous works of the late 1960s (*Sextets*, *Post-Partitions*, parts of *Correspondences*, String Quartets nos.3 and 4), the language seems even more refined. Sonorously embodied successions of relations are projected in ever-varying contexts, producing changes of 'atmosphere' from the most rarefied to the most dense, with every conceivable gradation.

The world which Babbitt's music evokes is not simple. He has said 'I want a piece of music to be literally as much as possible'. While some critics have felt that such an attitude has resulted in a body of inaccessible music, others have praised a rationalist approach – admittedly demanding a greater involvement on the listener's part – towards the presentation of a highly ordered, multiplex sound universe.

WORKS

INSTRUMENTAL

Orch: Generatrix, 1935; Composition for Orchestra, 1941; Into the Good Ground, film score, 1949; Relata I, 1965; Relata II, 1968
Chamber: Str Trio, 1939; Composition for 4 Insts, fl, cl, vn, vc, 1948; Composition for 12 Insts, wind qnt, tpt, harp, cel, str trio, db, 1948; Str Qt no.1, 1948; Composition for Va and Pf, 1950; Ww Qt, 1953; Str Qt no.2, 1954; All Set, a sax, t sax, tpt, trbn, db, drums, vib, pf, 1957; Sextets, vn, pf, 1966; Str Qt no.3, 1969; Str Qt no.4, 1970; Arie da capo, fl, cl/b cl, pf, vn, vc, 1973–4

Pf: 3 Compositions, 1947; Duet, 1956; Semisimple Variations, 1956; Partitions, 1957; Post-Partitions, 1966; Tableaux, 1973

VOCAL

Dramatic: Fabulous Voyage (musical, R. Childs, R. Koch, Babbitt), 1946; Kräfte (opera, A. Stramm), 2 S, T, Bar, elec, 1975
Choral: Music for the Mass I, chorus, 1941; Music for the Mass II, chorus, 1942; 4 Canons [after Schoenberg], female chorus, 1969
Solo: The Widow's Lament in Springtime (W. C. Williams), S, pf, 1950; Du (Stramm), S, pf, 1951; 2 Sonnets (Hopkins), Bar, cl, va, vc, 1955; Sounds and Words (Babbitt), S, pf, 1960; Composition for T and 6 Insts (Babbitt), T, fl, ob, str trio, hpd, 1960; Phonemena (Babbitt), S, pf, 1970; A Solo Requiem (Shakespeare, Hopkins, G. Meredith, Stramm, Dryden), S, 2 pf, 1976–7

WORKS WITH TAPE

Composition for Synth, 4-track tape, 1961; Vision and Prayer (D. Thomas), S, 4-track tape, 1961; Philomel (J. Hollander), S, 4-track tape, 1964; Ensembles for Synth, 4-track tape, 1962–4; Correspondences, str orch, tape, 1967; Occasional Variations, 4-track tape, 1971; Concerti, vn, small orch, tape, 1974; Phonemena, S, tape, 1974; Reflections, pf, tape, 1974

Principal publishers: Associated, Boelke-Bomart, Peters (NY)

WRITINGS

The Function of Set Structure in the Twelve-tone System, 1946 (unpubd)
'The String Quartets of Bartók', *MQ*, xxxv (1949), 377
'Some Aspects of Twelve-tone Composition', *The Score and IMA Magazine*, xii (1955), 53
'Who Cares if you Listen?', *High Fidelity Magazine*, viii (1958), 38; repr. in *The American Composer Speaks*, ed. G. Chase (Baton Rouge, 1966), 234
'Electronic Music: the Revolution in Sound', *Columbia University Magazine* (1960), spr., 4
'Twelve-tone Invariants as Compositional Determinants', *MQ*, xlvi (1960), 246
'Past and Present Concepts of the Nature and Limits of Music', *IMSCR, viii New York 1961*, i, 398
'Set Structure as a Compositional Determinant', *JMT*, v (1961), 72
'Twelve-tone Rhythmic Structure and the Electronic Medium', *PNM*, i/1 (1962), 49–79
'Remarks on the Recent Stravinsky', *PNM*, ii/2 (1964), 35
'An Introduction to the R.C.A. Synthesizer', *JMT*, viii (1963–4), 251
'The Synthesis, Perception, and Specification of Musical Time', *JIFMC*, xvi (1964), 92
'The Use of Computers in Musicological Research', *PNM*, iii/2 (1965), 74
'The Structure and Functions of Music Theory', *College Music Symposium*, v (1965), 49
'Edgard Varèse: a Few Observations of his Music', *PNM*, iv/2 (1966), 14
'Relata I', *The Orchestral Composer's Point of View*, ed. R. H. Hines (Norman, 1970); repr. as 'On Relata I', *PNM*, ix/1 (1970), 1
'Contemporary Music Composition and Music Theory as Contemporary Intellectual History', *Perspectives in Musicology*, ed. B. S. Brook, E. O. D. Downes and S. J. van Solkema (New York, 1971)
'Three Essays on Schoenberg', *Perspectives on Schoenberg and Stravinsky*, ed. B. Boretz and E. T. Cone (New York, 1972), 47
'Present Musical Theory and Future Practice', *IRCAM Conference: Abbaye de Senanque 1973*, 1
'Since Schoenberg', *PNM*, xii/1 (1973), 33

BIBLIOGRAPHY

E. Barkin: 'A Simple Approach to Milton Babbitt's "Semi-simple Variations"', *MR*, xxviii (1967), 316
R. Kostelanetz: 'The Two Extremes of Avant-garde Music', *New York Times Magazine* (Jan 1967)
E. Salzman: 'Babbitt and Serialism', *Twentieth Century Music: an Introduction* (Englewood Cliffs, NJ, 1967)
G. Perle: *Serial Composition and Atonality* (Berkeley, 1968)
D. Ewen: 'Milton Babbitt', *Composers of Tomorrow's Music* (New York, 1972)
B. Boretz: 'Milton Babbitt', *Dictionary of Contemporary Music*, ed. J. Vinton (New York, 1974)
P. Lieberson, E. Lundborg and J. Peel: 'Conversation with Milton Babbitt', *Contemporary Music Newsletter*, viii (1974), 2
PNM, xiv/2–xv/1 (1976) [special issue, incl. list of works and writings]

ELAINE BARKIN

Babcock, Alpheus (*b* Dorchester, Mass., 11 Sept 1785; *d* Boston, Mass., 3 April 1842). American piano maker. His most significant contribution to the evolution of the piano was his patent for a single-cast metal frame including hitchpin plate (17 December 1825). This patent is regarded as the basis for subsequent piano

frame development. His patents for 'cross-stringing' (24 May 1830), improved action (31 December 1833) and improvement in the jack or 'grasshopper' (31 October 1839) are not of lasting importance. Many historians erroneously credit Babcock with having invented or advocated the overstrung scale. This conclusion undoubtedly results from the equation of overstringing with cross-stringing. Babcock's 'cross-stringing' patent concerns itself with unison double-strung piano strings (formed from a single wire which crosses over itself when looped over either hitchpin or hook), not with bass strings running diagonally above the others.

Babcock began his career as an apprentice to Benjamin Crehore. He worked for or was a partner in the following firms: Babcock, Appleton & Babcock (Boston); Hayts, Babcock & Appleton (Boston); J. A. Dickson (Boston); John and G. D. Mackay (Boston); J. G. Klemm (Philadelphia); William Swift (Philadelphia); and Chickering & Co. (Boston). Babcock's instruments, acclaimed for their superb craftsmanship, are generally of the square variety, patterned after the double-action pianos of Broadwood, and with either one or two pedals and a range of either five and a half or six octaves (F' to c'''' or F' to f''''). Representative instruments are in the Smithsonian Institution, Washington, DC, and Yale University, New Haven, Connecticut.

BIBLIOGRAPHY

K. Grafing: *Alpheus Babcock, American Pianoforte Maker (1785–1842): his Life, Instruments, and Patents* (diss., U. of Missouri, Kansas City, 1972)
——: 'Alpheus Babcock's Cast-iron Piano Frames', *GSJ*, xxvii (1974), 118

KEITH G. GRAFING

Babcock, Edward Chester. See VAN HEUSEN, JIMMY.

Babell, William (*b* ?London, *c*1690; *d* Islington, London, 23 Sept 1723). English harpsichordist, organist, violinist, composer and arranger. He received his early musical instruction from his father, a bassoonist in the Drury Lane Theatre orchestra until he was 80, later from Pepusch and possibly Handel (according to Mattheson, but denied by Hawkins). Babell led an active professional life in London. He was said to have played in the private band of George I and, from 1711, his name frequently appears in London concert notices, usually in conjunction with those of Corbett, Paisible and (later) Dubourg. He was organist of All Hallows, Bread Street, for a number of years until his death (at the age of about 33) when he was buried in the church; he was succeeded at All Hallows by John Stanley.

Babell acquired an international reputation as a harpsichordist largely through his virtuoso arrangements of fashionable operatic arias, especially those of Handel. Burney criticized these arrangements:

Babel . . . seems to have been the first, in this country at least, who thinned, simplified, and divested the Music of keyed-instruments of the crowded and complicated harmony, with which, from the convenience of the clavier, and a passion for full and elaborate Music, it had been embarrassed from its earliest cultivation. This author acquired great celebrity by wire-drawing the favourite songs of the opera of Rinaldo, and others of the same period, into *showy* and brilliant lessons, which by mere rapidity of finger in playing single sounds, without the assistance of taste, expression, harmony or modulation, enabled the performer to astonish ignorance, and acquire the reputation of a great player at a small expence . . . Mr Babel . . . at once gratifies idleness and vanity.

Hawkins, on the other hand, considered that Babell deserved his success; he remarked that Babell's arrangement of favourite arias from Handel's *Rinaldo* 'succeeded so well . . . as to make from it a book of lessons which few could play but himself, and which has long been deservedly celebrated'. Babell's reputation reached France, the Netherlands and Germany, where some of his works were published; Mattheson reported that he was said to have surpassed even Handel as an organist.

Babell's harpsichord works give valuable insight into early 18th-century practices of ornamentation and extemporization; his solo sonatas too, in which the slow movements were printed 'With proper Graces adapted to each Adagio, by ye Author', represent the practice of melodic embellishment (ex.1). His keyboard style was undoubtedly influenced by his close acquaintance with Handel's performance on the harpsichord. Also of interest are Babell's concertos for violins and small flute (or 'sixth' flute), which owe more to Italian masters than to Handel.

Ex.1 Sonata no. 2, 3rd movement (12 solos for a violin, hoboy or German flute, part 2)

WORKS

(*printed works published in London unless otherwise stated*)

The 3rd Book of the Ladys Entertainment or Banquet of Musick, being a Choice Collection of . . . Aires and Duets in the Opera's of Pyrrhus and Clotilda, hpd/spinet (1709)
Suits of . . . Lessons, collected from the most Celebrated Masters Works, hpd/spinet (*c*1715)
The 4th Book of the Ladys Entertainment . . . Aires and Duets in the Opera's of Hydaspes and Almahide, hpd/spinet (1716)
Suits of the most Celebrated Lessons, hpd/spinet (1717)
The Harpsichord Master Improved . . . with a Choice Collection of Newest and most Air'y Lessons (1718)
Trios de diefferents autheurs, livre le [–2e] (Amsterdam, *c*1720)
Would you I the thing discover, A song . . . in the 3rd act of the play called Tis well if it takes (*c*1720)
Chamber Music: XII solos . . . with Proper Graces adapted to each Adagio, vn/ob, hpd, bk 1 (*c*1725)
XII Solos . . . with Proper Graces adapted to Each Adagio, vn/ob/fl, hpd, bk 2 (*c*1725)
Babell's Concertos in 7 Parts, vns, 1/2 fl, op.3 (1730)
Pièces de clavecin de Mr Händel . . . adjustées avec des variations, op.8 (Paris, *c*1745)
The Celebrated Grand Lesson, as adapted . . . from a Favourite Air [Vò far guerra] out of the opera Rinaldo [by Handel], hpd/pf (*c*1775)
Dance movts, *GB-Lbm*
Music for St Cecilia's Day, 1718, ?lost
Conc., formerly ?*D-Hs*, destroyed

BIBLIOGRAPHY

BurneyH; HawkinsH
J. Mattheson: *Der vollkommene Capellmeister* (Hamburg, 1739/ R1954)
C. W. Pearce: 'Vanished City of London Churches and their Organs', *Organ*, vii (1927–8), 177
S. Sadie: *British Chamber Music, 1720–1790* (diss., U. of Cambridge, 1958), 161f
A. J. B. Hutchings: *The Baroque Concerto* (London, 1961, rev. 3/1973)
P. M. Young: *A History of British Music* (London, 1967)

GERALD GIFFORD

Babin, Victor (*b* Moscow, 13 Dec 1908; *d* Cleveland, 1 March 1972). American pianist and composer of

Russian birth. He studied at Riga, in 1928 moving to Berlin for composition with Franz Schreker and the piano with Schnabel at the Hochschule für Musik. In 1933 he married another of Schnabel's pupils, Vitya (Victoria) Vronsky (*b* Evpatoria, Crimea, 22 Aug 1909), and his career as a player thereafter was almost exclusively that of a duo-pianist with his wife. Vronsky and Babin quickly established themselves in Europe, then moved to the USA in 1937. Babin taught at the Aspen School of Music (where he was director, 1951–4), at the Berkshire Music Center, Tanglewood, at the Cleveland Institute of Music (where he was director from 1961 until his death), and at Case Western Reserve University, also in Cleveland. His compositions, in a conservative, post-Romantic language, include two concertos for two pianos and orchestra, other compositions for one and two pianos, chamber music, and many songs, including a cycle, *Beloved Stranger*, on texts by Witter Bynner.

MICHAEL STEINBERG

Babitz, Sol (*b* Brooklyn, New York, 11 Oct 1911). American musicologist and violinist. He has been largely self-taught since leaving high school. His violin teachers included Carl Flesch and Marcel Chailley; his interest in performing practice was aroused by the writings of Arnold Dolmetsch and encouraged by Igor Stravinsky, whose string parts Babitz edited for many years. From 1933 to 1937 he was a violinist with the Los Angeles Philharmonic, then, until 1952, he played with Hollywood studio orchestras. From 1941 to 1962 he was an editor for *International Musician*. In 1948 he was a co-founder of the Early Music Laboratory, an organization which promotes historical accuracy in performance through the publication of bulletins and demonstration tape recordings. Babitz is concerned with a number of aspects of performance which he believes contribute to an accurate 17th- and 18th-century style. These aspects include clear articulation, use of metric accents, rhythmic freedom within the beat and a lighter tone. He has also worked for the modernization of violin fingering to facilitate the performance of works by such contemporary composers as Schoenberg and Stravinsky.

WRITINGS

Dance Writing; Preliminary Outline of a Practical System of Movement Notation (Los Angeles, 1939)
Principles of Extensions in Violin Fingering (Philadelphia, 1947)
'A Problem of Rhythm in Baroque Music', *MQ*, xxxviii (1952), 533
'Differences between 18th-century and Modern Violin Bowing', *Score*, xix (1957), 34
ed. and trans.: *G. Tartini: Treatise on the Ornaments of Music* (New York, 1959)
The Violin: Views and Reviews (Urbana, Ill., 1959)
'On Using J. S. Bach's Keyboard Fingerings', *ML*, xliii (1962), 123
'Identifying the Renaissance, Baroque and Transition Violins', *The Strad*, xv (1965), 2
'Notes Inégales: a Communication', *JAMS*, xx (1967), 473
'Modern Errors in Mozart Performance', *MJb 1967*, 62
'Concerning the Length of Time that every Note must be Held', *MR*, xxviii (1967), 21
'On Using Early Keyboard Fingering', *Diapason*, lx (1969), no.3, p.15; no.4, p.21; no.5, p.21
The Great Baroque Hoax: a Guide to Baroque Performance for Musicians and Connoisseurs (Los Angeles, 1970)
Commentary on EML Tape-recording 2 (Los Angeles, 1971)
with G. Pont: *Vocal De-Wagnerization and Other Matters* (Los Angeles, 1973)

PAULA MORGAN

Babou, Jean-François-Pascal. French musician, son of THOMAS BABOU.

Babou, Thomas (*b* Liège, 12 Feb 1656; *d* Liège, *c*1740). French organist and composer. He was organist of the collegiate church of St Jean l'Evangéliste in Liège at least from 1687 to 1704 (the registers preceding and following these dates are missing); from 1703 he was assisted by a young organist, Jean Buston (*d* 1731). The Babou recorded as organist in the accounts from 1726 to 1767 is his son Jean-François-Pascal (*b* Liège, 10 April 1700; *d* Liège, 13 May 1767), who was a notary from 1726 and secretary to the chapter of St Jean from 1742; he was probably the copyist of a *Livre d'orgue* at the Liège Conservatory containing several pieces attributed to 'Mr. Babou', dated 1709 and 1710, which must be by his father. The pieces (ed. P. Froidebise, Schola Cantorum, Paris, 1959) are in a lively and brilliant Italianate manner with little counterpoint, and show the introduction of a secular style into church music.

BIBLIOGRAPHY
A. Auda: *La musique et les musiciens de l'ancien Pays de Liège* (Liège, 1930)
G. Hansotte: 'Le personnel musical de la collégiale Saint-Jean l'Evangéliste', *Leodium*, xxxvi/7–12 (1949)
J. Quitin: 'Jean Buston et les Babou, organistes de Saint-Jean l'Evangéliste, a Liège', *Bulletin de la Société liégeoise de musicologie*, ii (1973), Jan
JOSÉ QUITIN

Babylonia. See MESOPOTAMIA.

Bacarisse, Salvador (*b* Madrid, 12 Sept 1898; *d* Paris, 5 Aug 1963). Spanish composer. He studied in Madrid at the university arts faculty and with Manuel Fernández Alberdi (piano) and Conrado del Campo (composition). In 1923 he won the Premio Nacional de Música for *La nave de Ulises*, again in 1931 for the *Música sinfónica* and in 1934 for the *Tres movimientos concertantes*. He was one of the leaders of the Grupo de los Ocho formed in Madrid in emulation of Les Six to combat conservatism, and as director of Unión Radio until 1936 he was able to pursue with particular success the difficult task of promoting new music. During the Civil War he held an administrative post in the Consejo Central de la Música, which enabled him to initiate a series of music publications, the journal *Música* and the National Orchestra. From 1939 until his death he worked in Paris as a Spanish language broadcaster.

The first performances of Bacarisse's works brought violent reaction from a very conservative public unable to accept the harsh dissonance and polytonality of such pieces as *Heraldos* (1923). In other compositions Bacarisse inclined towards impressionism, and in still others towards Falla-like, though quite individual, nationalism. Works such as *Cantarcillos* or the *Canciones medievales* show his taste for old Spanish traditions, which he distilled through his own stylistic approach. He used texts from classical and contemporary Spanish writers in vocal and stage works of a direct impact, though in some cases, perhaps swayed by the aesthetic of Les Six, he preferred a humorous, amiable, witty manner, as in the opera *Charlot*.

A certain neo-Romantic tendency, noticeable in some youthful works (e.g. the song *La rueca*), developed in much of his Parisian output, particularly in his last piano concertos (1957–8). In 1958 he won a French radio competition with the opera *El tesoro de Boabdil*, and he repeated that success with *Font aux cabres*, a radio version of *Fuenteovejuna* broadcast in 1962. On other occasions he worked a more fluent, personal Spanish vein, as in the Guitar Concertino (1957), the *Fantasía andaluza* for harp and orchestra, and the Harpsichord Concerto (1962), his last important orchestral work. A notable feature of his music is its brilliant orchestration, and the dramatic temperament with which he was endowed is often perceptible.

WORKS
(selective list)

Stage: Corrida de feria (ballet), 1930; Charlot (opera, G. de la Serna), 1933; El tesoro de Boabdil (opera, A. Camp, F. Puig), 1958; Fuenteovejuna (opera, Lope de Vega), 1962, radio version Font aux cabres, 1962
Vocal orch: Heraldos (R. Darío), 1923; La nave de Ulises, chorus, orch, 1923; La tragedia de Doña Ajada (M. Abril), 1929
Orch: Pf Concertino, 1929; Música sinfónica, 1931; Pf Conc., C, 1933; 3 movimientos concertantes, 1934; Vc Conc., a, 1935; Balada, pf, orch, 1936; Fantasía, D, vn, orch, 1937; Pf Conc., b, 1957; Gui Concertino, 1957; Pf Conc., D, 1958; Fantasía andaluza, harp, orch; Hpd Conc., 1962
Chamber: 3 str qts, 1930, 1932, 1936; Sonata en trío, 1932
Pf: 24 preludios, 1960; Variaciones, Toccata, Berceuse
Songs and choral pieces

Principal publishers: Armónico, Leduc, Salabert, Sociedad General de Autores de España, Unión Musical Español
ENRIQUE FRANCO

Baccaloni, Salvatore (*b* Rome, 14 April 1900; *d* New York, 31 Dec 1969). Italian bass. He was trained at the choristers' school of the Sistine Chapel. At 15 he entered the Academy of Fine Arts in Rome to study architecture, and graduated after his army service. In 1921 he was heard by the baritone Giuseppe Kaschmann, who accepted him as his pupil. Baccaloni made his début at the Teatro Adriano, Rome, in 1922 as Bartolo in *Il barbiere di Siviglia*. Toscanini heard him at Bologna in 1925 and engaged him for La Scala where he sang regularly from 1926 to 1940, first in serious roles and then, on Toscanini's advice, specializing in *buffo* characters such as Dulcamara in *L'elisir d'amore*, the two Bartolos, Don Pasquale and those in the Wolf-Ferrari operas. He appeared at Covent Garden (1928–9) and at Glyndebourne (1936–9), where his Leporello, Bartolo and Don Pasquale set a standard. He sang at the Colón, Buenos Aires (1931–41, 1947). His North American début was in Chicago in 1930. In 1940 he joined the Metropolitan Opera, and sang there regularly until 1962, mostly in the Italian *buffo* repertory. He also made numerous tours of the USA.

Portly in build and good-humoured, he was regarded by many as the greatest comic bass since Lablache. He had a communicative dramatic gift for comedy and was noted for his musicianship and the careful study of his roles. In his earlier years at the Metropolitan he displayed a vocal quality rarely met in *buffo* singing.

BIBLIOGRAPHY
R. Celletti: 'Baccaloni, Salvatore', *Le grandi voci* (Rome, 1964) [with opera discography by R. Vegeto]
FRANCIS D. PERKINS/HAROLD ROSENTHAL

Baccelli, Giovanna (*fl* 1774–1801). Italian dancer; *see* DANCE, §V, 1.

Baccelli, Matteo Pantaleone [Papia Leone] (*b* Lucca, 1690; *d* Lucca, *c*1760). Italian composer. He was a priest, and although he was probably *maestro di cappella* at the Seminary of S Giovanni e Riparata in Lucca by 1712, the first certain notice of him there is in 1725, when he was directing some of the most ambitious music in the city. Between 1717 and 1759 the Lucca confraternity of S Cecilia performed Baccelli's music (for first and second Vespers and Mass, with orchestral accompaniment) on nine different celebrations of the saint's feast; and each year he directed the Requiem Mass for dead members. He was further honoured by election to the society's governing committee (together with Giacomo Puccini) in 1754. In 1756 his oratorio *La concezione* was presented by the Congregazione degli Angeli Custodi, Lucca. The opera *La donna girandola* has been ascribed to him, but that is unlikely, for it appears from a libretto (in Bologna) that its composer was married to one of the singers. Baccelli's sacred music, to judge from his one extant work, the *Domine, e Dixit*, makes great, and able, use of the *stile concertante*: brilliant, rapid sections alternate with andante, lyrical writing; choruses alternate with solos; counterpoint with homophony; strings, trumpets and occasionally horns combine with continuo to provide rich four- or six-part accompaniment.

WORKS

Domine ad adiuvandum me, and Dixit Dominus, S, A, T, B, SATB, 2 tpt, 2 hn, 2 vn, va, bc, 1753, *I-Lc*
La concezione (oratorio), Lucca, 1756, lost
Several vesper settings and masses, all lost

BIBLIOGRAPHY
EitnerQ
L. Nerici: *Storia della musica in Lucca* (Lucca, 1879/*R*1969)
CAROLYN M. GIANTURCO

Bacchae. See MAENADS.

Bacchetta (It.). A drumstick, or the stick of a BOW.

Bacchini, Girolamo M. [Fra Teodoro del Carmine] (*fl* 1588–1605). Italian singer, composer and theorist. While at the Mantuan court, he wrote a treatise, *De musica*, now lost. In 1588 he published a madrigal, *Più che Diana*, in Alfonso Preti's *L'amoroso caccia* (Venice, 1588), a collection consisting of compositions by Mantuan musicians primarily associated with the church. He also published a book of masses, *Missarum quinque et sex vocum, liber primus* (Venice, 1589), written for the court chapel of S Barbara. In a letter dated 26 November 1594 to the vicar-general of the Carmelite order, Duke Vincenzo Gonzaga requested that Bacchini, a 'musico castrato', be exempt from wearing his monk's habit while singing in the court chamber. In 1594 he accompanied the duke for the *Reichstag* in Regensburg and in the following year, along with Monteverdi, G. B. Marinone and Serafino Terzi, he took part in the duke's military expedition to southern Hungary. The account books of the Mantuan court mention him in 1595, 1598 and 1605.

BIBLIOGRAPHY
P. Canal: *Della musica in Mantova* (Venice, 1881)
A. Bertolotti: *Musici alla corte dei Gonzaga in Mantova dal secolo XV al XVIII* (Milan, 1890/*R*1969)
PIERRE M. TAGMANN

Bacchius [Bakcheios Gerōn] (*fl* late 3rd – early 4th century AD). Greek music theorist of the age of Constantine (AD 274–337). He is known only for his *Introduction to the Art of Music* (*Eisagōgē technēs mousikēs*) in the form of a catechism; it is an eclectic production, though mostly following the school of Aristoxenus. The short treatise not in dialogue form, published under his name by F. Bellermann in 1841, is by Dionysius, his contemporary.

EDITIONS
C. von Jan, ed.: *Musici scriptores graeci* (Leipzig, 1895/*R*1962), 283–316
C. E. Ruelle, trans.: *Alypius et Gaudence, Bacchius l'ancien*, Collection des auteurs grecs relatifs à la musique, v (Paris, 1895)

See also GREECE, §I.
R. P. WINNINGTON-INGRAM

Bacchius [Bacchus, Bachus, Bachi, Bachy], **Johannes de** (*d* before 29 Jan 1557). Composer, described by Eitner as French. He became an alto in the Viennese Hofkapelle in March 1554. An Adrianus de Bachy, listed as a singer in the boys' choir of the court, may have been his son. Bacchius's works are typical polyphonic compositions of his time. The motets, most of which appeared in the large anthologies of Berg and Neuber, are in the full-voiced imitative style much favoured in Vienna. The two chansons have their roots in the Parisian style of the earlier part of the century, although they, too, have a higher level of imitative writing.

WORKS
Christus surrexit, 4vv, 1564⁵; Considerate dilectissimi, 5vv, 1559¹; Da Pater omnipotens pacem, 5vv, 1564⁴; Domine Deus caeli, 8vv, 1564¹; Domine Deus qui conteris, 8vv, 1564³; Dum transisset Sabbatum, 5vv, 1564⁴; Ecce Maria genuit, 4vv, 1564⁵; Ego flos campi et lilium, 5vv, 1564⁴
Factum est silentium, 5vv, *D-Bds* Z39, Z 74.1; Fuit homo missus a Deo, 6vv, 1564³; Oculi mei semper ad Dominum, 4vv, *Sl* 30; Si quis diligit me, 8vv, Brieg Gymnasiumsbibliothek 1 (now in *PL-WRu*), *WRu* 1, 3, 5, 18; Surge illuminare Jerusalem, 5vv, 1564⁴; Visitabo in virga, 5vv, 1559¹

Quant je voy son ceur estre mien, 6vv, 1553²⁵; Susanna ung jour, 4vv, 1556¹⁸
MS copies of printed motets in *D-Mbs*, *Rp*

BIBLIOGRAPHY
L. von Köchel: *Die kaiserliche Hof-Musikkapelle in Wien von 1543 bis 1867* (Vienna, 1869)
O. Wessely: *Arnold von Bruck: Leben und Umwelt* (Habilitationsschrift, U. of Vienna, 1958), 418ff
VICTOR H. MATTFELD

Baccholian Singers. English ensemble. A five- or six-part consort of tenors, baritones and basses, its members are Rogers Covey-Crump, Paul Elliott, Ian Humphris, Michael George and Brian Etheridge (director); former members and guest performers include Ian Partridge, John Elwes, Wynford Evans and Neil Jenkins. It was formed in 1961 while the singers were still students at Cambridge University to give concerts in aid of spastics. Since their professional début (Wigmore Hall, London, 1963) their aim has been to explore the vocal sonorities peculiar to a male-voice ensemble without countertenor, and to perform the extensive but rarely heard repertory ranging from Renaissance motets to partsongs of the Romantic era and into the 20th century. The consort has commissioned new works from composers such as Kenneth Leighton, Sebastian Forbes, Martin Dalby, Peter Wishart, Thomas Wilson and Michael Finnissy. Their 1975 recording of Holst's male-voice music was much praised.

ELISABETH AGATE

Bacchus. See DIONYSUS.

Bacchylides [Bakchylidēs] (*b* Iulis [now Tzia], Keos; *fl* c470 BC). Greek lyric poet. He was a nephew of Simonides and contemporary of Píndar; there are many indications of intense rivalry between the two as composers of victory odes. Unlike Píndar, Bacchylides had little to say of the power of music; his references are correct but conventional, rendered distinctive only by colourful adjectives. Thus in one of the many victory odes the champion has returned home to the triumphal accompaniment of auloi 'that delight mortals' and revel-songs 'sweetly breathing' (frag.40, ed. Edmonds, ll.72–3). In another, the sound of the phorminx and 'clear-ringing' choruses are alien to war (frag.41, ed. Edmonds, ll.12–15; *ligyklanggēs* is one of many Bacchylidean coinages). Two poems begin with references to the *barbitos*, 'lyre with many strings' (frags.70, 71, ed. Edmonds); here the term appears to be used with precision.

BIBLIOGRAPHY

O. Crusius: 'Bakchylides', §§2–3, *Paulys Realencylcopädie der klassischen Altertumswissenschaft*, ii A (Stuttgart, 1898), 2793
R. C. Jebb, ed. and trans.: *Bacchylides: The Poems and Fragments* (Cambridge, 1905)
J. M. Edmonds, ed. and trans.: *Lyra graeca*, iii (London and Cambridge, Mass., 1927, 5/1967), 80–223
A. Severyns: *Bacchylide* (Liège, 1933)
B. Snell, ed.: *Bacchylides: Carmina cum fragmentis* (Leipzig, 1949, rev. 10/1970 by H. Machler)
R. Fagles, trans.: *Bacchylides: The Complete Poems* (New Haven, 1961)
K. Preisendanz: 'Bakchylides', *Der kleine Pauly*, i (Stuttgart, 1964), 810
D. A. Campbell, ed.: *Greek Lyric Poetry* (London and New York, 1967), 106ff, 413–45

WARREN ANDERSON

Bacciccia. See RICCIOTTI, CARLO.

Baccio Fiorentino. See BARTOLOMEO DEGLI ORGANI.

Baccusi, Ippolito [Baccusii, Hippolyti] (*b* Mantua, *c*1550; *d* Verona, 1609). Italian composer. Although he was a prolific composer of madrigals and sacred music, the course of his career is not well documented. His earliest position appears to have been that of assistant choir director at St Mark's, Venice. That he must have held the post for only a short time can be established from a letter (in *I-MAc*) dated from Ravenna on 22 April 1570 in which he requested permission to remain another year in Ravenna, since he would be able to complete his degree by the end of a third year of study: he must therefore have left Venice for Ravenna by 1568. On the title-page of his second book of six-part madrigals (1572) he is described as director of music to the 'illustri signori di Spilimbergo', a musical society in Verona. The book is dedicated to the Accademia Filarmonica in Verona, and in the preface Baccusi indicated that he was employed as *maestro di cappella* at yet another institution there, the church of S Eufemia. The next document concerning his career occurs in the *Prattica di musica seconda parte* (Venice, 1622/*R*1967) of Lodovico Zacconi, which states that he went to Mantua in 1583 to study *contrappunto alla mente* with him and that he was a *maestro di cappella* there; Zacconi wrote as if Baccusi had held the post for some time, but the exact date of his appointment is not known. In the preface to his fourth book of masses (1593) Baccusi indicated that he was offered the choir director-ship at Verona Cathedral in 1592; he accepted and remained in the post until his death.

Stylistically Baccusi belongs to the Venetian school of composers; he early came under the influence of Willaert, Rore and Andrea Gabrieli. In 1573 he even contributed to the collaborative setting of the poetic cycle celebrating the Venetian victory over the Turks at Lepanto, *Canzona nella gran vittoria contra i Turchi*. The subject was a favourite one with Venetian composers, and Baccusi had published a similar cycle, *Fuor, fuori o muse*, in the preceding year. Other works of particular interest are the settings of Petrarch's 11-stanza canzone *Vergine bella* (1605) and of one of the cycles in Francesco Bozza's quaternion *I diporti della*

villa in ogni stagione (*RISM* 1601[7]). Among his contemporaries Baccusi had the reputation of being a fine contrapuntist and a master of improvisation: his works certainly illustrate the first quality. Baccusi was also one of the first composers to acknowledge and recommend the practice of instrumental doubling of vocal parts (see the title-pages of his masses of 1596 and psalms of 1597).

WORKS

(*all published in Venice unless otherwise noted*)

MASSES

[2] Missarum, 5, 6vv, liber I (1570)
[4] Missarum, 5, 6, 8vv, liber II (1585)
Il primo libro delle [5] messe, 4vv (1588)
Missarum, 5, 6vv, liber III (1589)
[4] Missarum, 5, 9vv, liber IV (1593)
Misse tres tum viva voce, tum omni instrumentorum genere cantatu commodissime, 8vv (1596)

OTHER SACRED

[25] Motectorum, 5, 6, 8vv, liber I (1579)
Psalmi omnes qui in vesperis a romana ecclesia decantantur cum cantico beatae virginis, 4vv (1588)
Psalmorum qui a santa romana ecclesia, ut plurimum in vesperis decantantur, triplici distinctorum ordine, cum cantico beatae virginis, 4vv, liber III (Verona, 1594)
Sacrae cantiones psalmi videlicet et omnia quae ad completorium pertinent, 5vv (1596)
Psalmi omnes qui a sancta romana ecclesia in solemnitatibus ad Vesperas decantari solent, cum 2 Magnificat, tum viva voce, tum omni instrumentorum genere, cantatu commodissimi, 8vv (1597)
Psalmi qui diebus festivis a sancta romana ecclesia in Vesperis decantari solent, 5vv (1602)
Single sacred works in 1583[2], 1592[3], 1596[1]

MADRIGALS

Il primo libro de [27] madrigali, 5, 6vv, 1 for 7vv, 1 for 8vv (1570)
Il secondo libro de [18] madrigali, 5vv (1572)
Il secondo libro de [18] madrigali, 6vv, con una canzone nella gran vittoria contra i Turchi (1572)
[21] Madrigali . . . libro III, 6vv (1579)
Il quarto libro de [21] madrigali, 6vv (1587)
Il primo libro de [19] madrigali, 3vv (1594)
Le vergini . . . [11] madrigali, 3vv, libro II (1605)
Secular works in 1583[14], 1584[15], 1585[16], 1585[19], 1588[14], 1588[18], 1588[19], 1588[20], 1590[11], 1590[17], 1591[10], 1591[23], 1592[11], 1592[13], 1593[3], 1594[6], 1596[10], 1597[6], 1597[13], 1598[6], 1600[5a], 1600[8], 1601[5], 1601[7] (ed. Siro Cisilino, Collana di Musiche Veneziane Inedite o Rare, i, 1962, p.61), 1601[18], 1604[13], 1605[9], 1606[6], 1609[14], 1609[15], 1612[13], 1619[16], 1624[16]

Various works in MS: *A-Wgm*, *D-B*, *Mbs*, *Z*, *I-Bc*, *PL-WRu*, *Wu*

BIBLIOGRAPHY

A Bertolotti: *Musici alla corte dei Gonzaga in Mantova dal secolo XV al XVIII* (Milan, 1890/*R*1969)
F. Chrysander: 'Lodovico Zacconi als Lehrer des Kunstgesangs', *VMw* (1894), 531–67
P. M. Tagmann: *Archivalische Studien zur Musikpflege am Dom von Mantua (1500–1627)* (Berne, 1967)

PATRICIA ANN MYERS

Bacewicz, Grażyna (*b* Łódź, 5 Feb 1909; *d* Warsaw, 17 Jan 1969). Polish composer and violinist. After violin, piano and theory studies at Kijeńska's private conservatory in Łódź, she attended the Warsaw Conservatory, where her teachers were Sikorski (composition), Jarzębski (violin) and Turczyński (piano). In 1932 she received diplomas in the violin and composition. She continued her training in Paris with Boulanger (composition), and with Touret and Flesch (violin). Setting out on a double career as composer and violinist, she quickly achieved success in both fields: her compositions won prizes in Paris and Warsaw in the mid-1930s, and she was awarded a first-class distinction in the first Wieniawski Competition (Warsaw, 1935). Before and after the war she toured as a violinist through most of Europe; a notable performance was that of Szymanowski's First Concerto under Kletzki in Paris in 1946. She gave public performances of her own works – not only those for the violin, but also her piano pieces, including the Second Sonata. During the 1950s she abandoned her career as a concert performer to give her attention to composition. She also worked occasionally as a teacher: she lectured in harmony, counterpoint and solfège and took a violin class at the Łódź Conservatory (1934–5, 1945–6), and from 1966 until her death she taught composition at the Warsaw Conservatory. In addition, she was active in music administration and as an adjudicator. She left several novels and stories in manuscript, published a small volume, *Znak szczególny* ('Outstanding feature'; Warsaw, 1970, 2/1974), and wrote a humorous dramatic sketch, *Jerzyki albo nie jestem ptakiem* ('Swifts, or I am not a bird'), presented on Polish television on 26 November 1968. Among the awards she received for her music were the first prize at the International Composers' Competition in Liège (1951 for the Fourth Quartet), the State Prize Second Class (1952), the Minister of Culture's Prize (1952), the highest award in the orchestral section at the International Rostrum of Composers (1958 for *Muzyka*) and the gold medal at the Queen Elisabeth Competition (1965 for the Violin Concerto no.7).

Bacewicz's output may be divided into four periods, of which the first three were unanimously designated by Polish critics as neo-classical. The first (from the Wind Quintet of 1933 up to 1945) saw her development of neo-classical forms; the music of the second (1945–54) is permeated by neo-classical counterpoint; and in the third (1955–60) the emphasis shifted to the neo-Baroque, though not in a Hindemithian sense – her work was now becoming more individual. Bacewicz argued against the 'neo-classical' label, stressing the universal character of the style she had evolved. Nevertheless, as a pupil of Sikorski and Boulanger, she had inherited techniques – formal, motivic and contrapuntal – commonly associated with neo-classicism. In the fourth and last phase of her work she sought to approach new procedures, though without inducing the profound stylistic renewal that accompanied this effort in the music of her fellow student Lutosławski; instead she remained faithful to the principles of her student days, which she held up only with great difficulty and no less ambition.

Though she showed no innovatory tendency and though she often had to struggle with her material (she was unable, for example, to find an individual harmonic style, and readily lapsed into a free, not to say impassive, manner), Bacewicz was, with Spisak, one of the few important Polish neo-classicists. Her early string quartets look back most directly to the Classical period, her violin sonatas and some of her symphonies to the Baroque, other symphonies to the Romantic. The themes are often folklike, occasionally, as in the Fourth Violin Sonata, direct quotations from folk music. A few works of this type established a great deal in pre-1958 Polish music, and during the 1950s Bacewicz was regarded as perhaps the leading contemporary Polish composer; the Symphony no.3, the Violin Concerto no.4, the String Quartet no.4 and the String Quartet no.5 were particularly well regarded. The prolific achievement of these years can be accounted for by an unusual concentration of skill, but also by a definitive ease, which implies the danger of shallowness. But while stressing Bacewicz's somewhat traditionalist (particularly by comparison with her later evolution) and unchanging attitude, it is important to note the stylistic

attainments of the first three periods. Among these were a development in formal technique – the works of the 1950s are distinguished by a widening of scale over those of the 1930s, often embodied in a dramatic, narrative manner – and a transition from classical restraint to powerful emotion, revealing new areas of temperament and sensitivity. In her third period Bacewicz effectively strove for this new spontaneous and expressive style, and also, on the other hand, for a certain monumentalism. This latter feature was expressed in an exposition of obsessively classical but highly dramatic 'great' themes, in extended formal development (as in the Fourth Symphony) and in a tendency to manipulate massive sounds.

The fourth stage of Bacewicz's work, from the *Pensieri notturni* for chamber orchestra (1961) to the unfinished ballet *Pożądanie* ('Desire'), was distinguished by her experiments in relating the sounds and colours of avant-garde music to her neo-classical style. The *Pensieri notturni* were to be, in a sense, a reply to the new tendencies in Polish music. A characteristically short piece, lasting for eight minutes, it abandons classical themes, but retains so many of her previous characteristics that the predicted turning-point did not immediately ensue. In the Cello Concerto no.2 and the Double Piano Concerto she returned to her well-tried methods, but without regaining the recognition she had enjoyed in the previous decade. Finally, in 1965, she relinquished neo-classicism. A new attitude is evident in the titles of these late works – *Inkrustacje*, *Contradizione*, *In una parte* – which demonstrate a discord, understandable enough in her situation, between a craftsmanship which had not transcended the standards of inter-war Paris and new techniques which could not be acquired mechanically or imitated. With these last compositions her position was alone and independent.

Throughout her career Bacewicz displayed a fine feeling for instruments. She was an outstanding violinist and an equally distinguished pianist, and she composed most intensively in instrumental genres. She was widely considered the most gifted woman composer of her time.

WORKS
(selective list)

DRAMATIC

Z chłopa król [The peasant king] (ballet, A. M. Swinarski, after P. Baryka), 1953–4; Poznań, 1954

Przygoda króla Artura [The adventure of King Arthur] (comic opera for radio, E. Fischer), 1959; Polish radio, 1959; televised 1960

Esik w Ostendzie [Esik in Ostend] (comic ballet, L. Terpilowski, after T. Boy-Żeleński), 1964; Poznań, 1964

Pożądanie [Desire] (ballet, 2, M. Bibrowski, after Picasso: Désir attrapé par la queue), 1968–9, inc.; Warsaw, 1973

ORCHESTRAL

Syms.: Sym., 1933, lost; Sym. no.1, 1945; Sym., str, 1946; Sym. no.2, 1951; Sym. no.3, 1952; Sym. no.4, 1953

Concs.: 7 vn concs., 1937, 1946, 1948, 1951, 1954, 1957, 1965; Conc., str, 1948; Pf Conc., 1949; 2 vc concs., 1951, 1963; Conc. for Orch, 1962; 2 Pf Conc., 1966; Va Conc., 1968

Other concert works: Sinfonietta, str, 1929; 3 karykatury, 1932; Pochód radości [Procession of joy], 1933; Sinfonietta, str, 1935; Ov., 1943; Introdukcja i kaprys, 1947; Rapsodia polska, vn, orch, 1949; Uwertura polska, 1954; Partita [arr. Partita, vn, pf], 1955; Wariacje symfoniczne, 1957; Muzyka, tpts, str, perc, 1958; Pensieri notturni, chamber orch, 1961; Divertimento, str, 1965; Inkrustacje, hn, insts, 1965; Musica sinfonica, 1965; Contradizione, chamber orch, 1966; In una parte, 1967

Pieces for radio: Mazur [Mazurka], 1944; Pod strzechą [Under the thatch], 1945; Suite, 1946; Ze starej muzyki [From old music], 1946; Szkice ludowe [Folk sketches], 1948; Groteska, 1949; Oberek, 1949; Waltz, 1949; Krakowiak, 1950; Serenada, 1950; Suita tańców polskich, 1950; Taniec mazowiecki, 1951; others

CHAMBER

Wind Qnt, 1933; Sonata, ob, pf, 1936; 7 str qts, 1938, 1942, 1947, 1950, 1955, 1960, 1965; Łatwe utwory [Easy pieces], cl, pf, 1948; Trio, ob, cl, bn, 1948; Oberek no.1, cl, pf, 1949; Qt, 4 vn, 1949; Wiwat, cl qnt, 1950; Kaprysy polskie, cl, 1952; 2 pf qnts, 1952, 1965; Qt, 4 vc, 1965; Trio, ob, harp, perc, 1965

VIOLIN

For vn, pf: Partita, 1930; Kaprys no.1, 1932; Witraż [Stained glass], 1932; Andante i allegro, 1934; Kaprys no.2, 1934; Pieśń litewska [Lithuanian song], 1934; Theme and Variations, 1934; Legenda, 1945; Sonata no.1 'da camera', 1945, 4th movt (Andante sostenuto) arr. vn/vc, org, 1945; Kaprys, 1946; Sonatas nos.2–5, 1946, 1947, 1949, 1951; Taniec polski, 1948; Melodia, 1949; Oberek no.1, 1949; Taniec antyczny [Antique dance], 1950; Taniec mazowiecki, 1951; Kołysanka [Lullaby], 1952; Oberek no.2, 1952; Taniec słowiański, 1952; Humoresque, 1953; Partita [no.2], 1955
For vn: Sonata, 1929; Sonata no.1, 1941; Kaprys polski, 1949; Kaprys no.2, 1952; Sonata no.2, 1958; 4 kaprysy, 1968
For 2 vn: Suite, 1943; Łatwe duety [Easy duets], 1945
Easy pieces for vn, pf: Concertino, 1945; Łatwe utwory, 1946, 1949

KEYBOARD

Pf: Theme with Variations, 1924; Preludium, 1928; Allegro, 1929; Sonata, 1930; Toccata, 1932; 3 pièces caracteristiques, 1932; Sonatina, 1933; Suita dziecięca [Children's suite], 1933; Scherzo, 1934; Sonata (Sonata 1935), 1935; 3 groteski, 1935; 3 preludia, 1941; Krakowiak koncertowy, 1949; Sonata no.1, 1949; Etiuda tercjowa [Study in 3rds], 1952; Sonata no.2, 1953; Sonatina no.2, 1955; 10 etiud koncertowych, 1957; Mały tryptyk [Little triptych], 1965
Org: Esquisse, 1966

VOCAL

With orch: De profundis, solo vv, chorus, orch, 1932; 3 Songs (10th-century Arabic, trans. Staff), T, orch, 1938; Kantata olimpijska (Pindar), chorus, orch, 1948; Kantata na 600-lecie Uniwersytetu Jagiellońskiego (S. Wyspiański: Akropolis), chorus, orch, 1964
Songs for 1v, pf: Trzy róe [Three roses] (Arabic, trans. Staff), 1934; Mów do mnie, miły [Speak to me, dear] (Tagore, trans. J. Kasprowicz), 1936; 3 Songs (10th-century Arabic, trans. Staff), 1938; Oto jest noc [Here is the night] (K. I. Gałczyński), 1947; Smuga cienia [Trail of shadow] (W. Broniewski), 1948; Rozstanie [Parting] (Tagore, trans. Kasprowicz), 1949; Usta i pełnia [Lips and fullness] (Gałczyński), 1949; Boli mnie głowa [My head aches] (Bacewicz), 1955; Dzwon i dzwonki [Bells and little bells] (A. Mickiewicz), 1955; Nad wodą wielką i czystą [Over the wide, clear water] (Mickiewicz), 1955; Sroczka [Little magpie] (trad.), 1956

Principal publisher: Polskie Wydawnictwo Muzyczne

BIBLIOGRAPHY

A. Malawski: 'Uwertura Bacewiczówny', Ruch muzyczny (1947), no.17, p.19
H. Swolkień: 'III koncert skrzypcowy Grażyny Bacewicz', Ruch muzyczny (1949), nos.11–12
S. Łobaczewska: 'IV sonata na fortepian i skrzypce Grażyny Bacewicz', Muzyka (1952), no.11
J. M. Chomiński: 'Koncert na orkiestrę smyczkową Grażyny Bacewicz', Studia muzykologiczne, v (1956), 385
F. Derewecka-Falkowska: 'Opery radiowe Grażyna Bacewicz: Przygoda króla Artura)', Ruch muzyczny (1960), no.21
T. A. Zieliński: 'VI kwartet Grażyny Bacewicz', Ruch muzyczny (1960), no.18
M. Gorczycka: ' "Pensieri notturni" ', Ruch muzyczny (1961), no.21, p.9
T. A. Zieliński: 'Walor szlachetnego rzemiosła (o twórczości G. Bacewicz)' [The value of noble craftsmanship (on Bacewicz's work)], Ruch muzyczny (1961), no.8, p.1
J. Kański: 'II koncert wiolonczelowy G. Bacewicz', Ruch muzyczny (1963), no.22
S. Kisielewski: Grażyna Bacewicz i jej czasy [Bacewicz and her times] (Kraków, 1964)
H. Schiller: 'Ze studiów nad muzyką Grażyny Bacewicz', Muzyka (1964), nos.3–4, p.3
T. Marek: 'Grażyna Bacewicz', Polish Music (1969), no.1
Ruch muzyczny (1969), no.7 [Bacewicz issue]
T. A. Zieliński: 'Ostatnie utwory Grażyny Bacewicz' [Bacewicz's late works], Ruch muzyczny (1972), no.12, p.3
B. Cisowska: ' "Pożądanie" – ostatnie dzieło G. Bacewicz', Ruch muzyczny (1973), no.13, p.3

BOGUSŁAW SCHÄFFER

Bach. German family of musicians. From the 16th century to the early 19th it produced musicians of every kind in number beyond parallel: from fiddlers and town musicians to organists, Kantors, court musicians and Kapellmeisters. The greatest among them was of course Johann Sebastian Bach, although there were distinguished musicians in earlier, contemporary and later generations of the family.

The following pages give, first, a list of musician members of the family, in alphabetical order, with brief biographical notes on those not considered more fully later in §III; second, a general history of the family; and third, individual articles on the family's most important members. The italic numeral in parentheses following the name of each member is taken from the family genealogy (or Ursprung; see Bach-Dokumente, i, no.184) drawn up in 1735, as far as no.53; numbers thereafter are assigned on a continuation of the same principle (the inadvertent fusion in 1735 into one nameless individual of Caspar (b c1570) and Lips (b c1552), both with the number 3, which was also allotted to their descendants, has been corrected, but the 3 is shown along with the new number to facilitate comparisons). The arabic numeral preceding the names of family members refers to their individual entries in §III below. Non-musician members of the family are not included in the list, but some musicians of the family who are apparently not members of the main, Wechmar line are included (without numbering).

I. List of the musicians. II. Family history. III. Individual members.

I. List of the musicians

Carl Philipp Emanuel Bach (46) (b Weimar, 8 March 1714; d Hamburg, 14 Dec 1788). Son of Johann Sebastian (24); see §III (9) below.

Caspar Bach (3/56) (b c1570; d Arnstadt, after 1640). Possibly a son of Hans (54). He was Stadtpfeifer in Gotha in 1619, and court and town musician (bassoonist) in Arnstadt, 1620–33.

Caspar Bach (3/58) (b c1600). Son of Caspar (3/56). He was educated as a musician (violinist) at the courts of Bayreuth (1621–3) and Dresden (1623), at the expense of the Count of Schwarzburg-Arnstadt; he probably went to Italy, and nothing further is known of him.

Christoph Bach (5) (b Wechmar, 19 April 1613; d Arnstadt, 12 Sept 1661). Son of Johann (2). He was a court musician in Weimar, then from 1642 a town musician in Erfurt and from 1654 court and town musician in Arnstadt. A musical entry by him in the album of Georg F. Reimann, Kantor in Saalfeld, survives (see BJb, xxv, 1928, p.175).

Ernst Carl Gottfried Bach (81) (b Ohrdruf, 12 Jan 1738; d Ohrdruf, 21 July 1801). Son of Johann Christoph (42). He was Kantor in Wechmar, 1765–72, then at St Michael's, Ohrdruf.

Ernst Christian Bach (82) (b Ohrdruf, 28 Sept 1747; d Wechmar, 29 Sept 1822). Son of Johann Christoph (42). He was Kantor in Wechmar, 1773–1819.

Georg Christoph Bach (10) (b Erfurt, baptized 8 Sept 1642; d Schweinfurt, 24 April 1697). Son of Christoph (5). He was Kantor in Themar from 1668 and in Schweinfurt from 1684. One composition by him is extant, the vocal concerto Siehe, wie fein und lieblich ist es (1689) for two tenors, bass and instruments (EDM, 1st ser., ii, 1935, p.22). See F. Müller: 'Georg Christoph Bach', Die Musik, xxxiv (1942), 361.

Georg Friedrich Bach (b Tann, 17 March 1793; d Iserlohn, 2 Oct 1860). Not a member of the Wechmar line, he was a son of Johann Michael (see §III (13) below). A flautist, he deserted from Napoleon's army and went to Sweden, where he became music teacher to the crown prince (later Oscar I). He returned to Germany and became music director in Elberfeld and Iserlohn. Manuscripts of works and a harmony textbook by him survive (*D-EIb*).

Georg Michael Bach (*74*) (*b* Ruhla, baptized 27 Sept 1703; *d* Halle, 18 Feb 1771). Son of Johann Jacob (*68*). He was Kantor at St Ulrich's, Halle, from 1747.

Gottfried Heinrich Bach (*48*) (*b* Leipzig, 26 Feb 1724; *d* Naumburg, buried 12 Feb 1761). Eldest son of Johann Sebastian (*24*) and Anna Magdalena Bach. Although he became feeble-minded at an early age, he played the keyboard well and, according to C. P. E. Bach, he showed 'a great genius, which however failed to develop'. From 1750 he lived with his brother-in-law J. C. Altnikol.

Gottlieb Friedrich Bach (*76*) (*b* Meiningen, 10 Sept 1714; *d* Meiningen, 25 Feb 1785). Son of Johann Ludwig (*3/72*). He was court organist and painter (*Kabinettsmaler*) in Meiningen.

Hans Bach: see under Johann Bach below (unnumbered, *2* and *4*).

Heinrich Bach (*3/62*) (*d* Arnstadt, 1635). Son of Caspar (*3/56*). He is listed in the death register as the blind son of Caspar, and is thus probably the 'blind Jonas' mentioned in the *Ursprung*. He was musically educated in Italy and may have received the nickname (an allusion to the biblical figure) as a result of his adventures. See M. Schneider: 'Thematisches Verzeichnis der musikalischen Werke der Familie Bach', *BJb*, iv (1907), 105.

Heinrich Bach (*6*) (*b* Wechmar, 16 Sept 1615; *d* Arnstadt, 10 July 1692). Son of Johann (*2*). He was town musician in Schweinfurt from 1629 and in Erfurt from 1635, and in 1641 became town musician and organist of the Liebfrauenkirche in Arnstadt. His funeral sermon (*MMg*, vii, 1875, p.178) calls him an experienced composer of chorales, motets, concertos, preludes and fugues. A vocal concerto *Ich danke dir, Gott* (1681) for five voices, strings and continuo (EDM, 1st ser., ii, 1935, p.3) and three organ chorales (*Orgelwerke der Familie Bach*, 1967, p.1) are extant.

Johann [Hans] Bach (*b* Andelsbuch, Vorarlberg, *c*1555; *d* Nürtingen, 1 Dec 1615). Not a member of the Wechmar line; see §III (1) below.

Johann(es) [Hans] Bach (*2*) (*b* *c*1550; *d* Wechmar, 1626). Son of Veit (*1*). He was a baker and carpentmaker, and, in that he was also a *Spielmann* (minstrel, fiddler), the earliest professional musician among the Wechmar Bachs. He received his instruction as a Stadtpfeifer before 1567 at Schloss Grimmenstein in Gotha from Matz Zisecke and his predecessor (not, as has repeatedly been stated, from a person by the name of Bach). By 1577 he owned a house in Wechmar and from there, according to the *Ursprung*, he travelled widely as a musician to various Thuringian towns, including Gotha, Arnstadt, Erfurt, Eisenach, Schmalkalden and Suhl. The Wechmar death register notes him as 'Hanss Bach ein Spielmann'.

Johann(es) Bach (*3/59*) (*b* 1602; *d* Arnstadt, 1632). Son of Caspar (*3/56*). He was a Stadtpfeifer in Arnstadt.

Johann(es) [Hans] Bach (*4*) (*b* Wechmar, 26 Nov 1604; *d* Erfurt, buried 13 May 1673). Son of Johann (*2*). He had a seven-year apprenticeship and journeyman period with the Stadtpfeifer Christoph Hoffmann in Suhl, after which he became a town musician in Erfurt;

from 1636 he was organist of the Predigerkirche there. Two motets by him are extant: *Unser Leben ist ein Schatten* (six parts with a three-part echo choir; ed. G. Graulich, Stuttgart, 1968) and *Sei nun wieder zufrieden* (eight voices), as well as an aria *Weint nicht um meinen Tod* for four voices and continuo (EDM, 1st ser., i, 1935, p.3). See S. Orth: 'Neues über der Stammvater der "Erfurter" Bache, Johann Bach', *Mf*, ix (1956), 447; S. Orth: 'Johann Bach, der Stammvater der Erfurter Bache', *BJb*, cix (1973), 79.

Johann Bach (*67*) (*b* Themar, 1621; *d* Lehnstedt, 12 Sept 1686). Son of the alderman Andreas (*64*) (*b* 1587; *d* Suhl, 21 April 1637). He was Kantor in Ilmenau and from 1668 deacon there; in 1680 he was appointed vicar of Lehnstedt.

Johann Aegidius Bach (*8*) (*b* Erfurt, baptized 11 Feb 1645; *d* Erfurt, buried 22 Nov 1716). Son of Johann (*4*). In 1671 he was a violinist in the Erfurt town music, becoming its director in 1682; from 1690 he also held the position of organist at St Michael's, in succession to Pachelbel.

Johann Aegidius Bach (*36*) (*b* Erfurt, baptized 4 Aug 1709; *d* Gross-Monra, nr. Kötteda, 17 May 1746). Son of Johann Christoph (*19*). He was Kantor of Gross-Monra.

Johann Ambrosius Bach (*11*) (*b* Erfurt, 22 Feb 1645; *d* Eisenach, 20 Feb 1695). Son of Christoph (*5*) and twin brother of Johann Christoph (*12*). On 8 April 1668 he married Maria Elisabeth Lämmerhirt (*b* Erfurt, 24 Feb 1644; *d* Eisenach, buried 3 May 1694). He was Stadtpfeifer in Arnstadt and from 1667 violinist in the Erfurt town music. From 1671 he was a court trumpeter and director of the town music in Eisenach. He must have been an outstanding and versatile musician: the Eisenach town chronicler noted that 'In 1672 the new Hausmann [director of town music] made music at Easter with organ, violins, voices, trumpets and kettledrums, something never before known in the history of Eisenach'. When in 1684 he was offered the important position of director of the town band in Erfurt, the Duke of Eisenach was unwilling to allow him to go and he was compelled to decline the offer. A portrait of him, painted after 1671, is extant (*D-Bds*). See F. Rollberg: 'Johann Ambrosius Bach, Stadtpfeifer zu Eisenach von 1671–1695', *BJb*, xxiv (1927), 133; C. Freyse: 'Das Porträt Ambrosius Bach', *BJb*, xlvi (1959), 149.

Johann Andreas Bach (*44*) (*b* Ohrdruf, 7 Sept 1713; *d* Ohrdruf, 25 Oct 1779). Son of Johann Christoph (*22*). In 1733 he was an oboist in the military band in Gotha; from 1738 he was organist of the Trinity Church in Ohrdruf and from 1743 of St Michael's in the same town. He owned the so-called *Johann Andreas Bach Buch* (*D-LEm*, Sammlung Becker III.8.4), one of the principal sources of the early keyboard works of Johann Sebastian (*24*).

Johann Balthasar Bach (*71*) (*b* Eisenach, 4 March 1673; *d* Eisenach, 11 June 1691). Son of Johann Ambrosius (*11*). He was Stadtpfeifer apprentice to his father.

Johann Bernhard Bach (*18*) (*b* Erfurt, baptized 25 Nov 1676; *d* Eisenach, 11 June 1749). Son of Johann Aegidius (*8*); see §III (5) below.

Johann Bernhard Bach (*41*) (*b* Ohrdruf, 24 Nov 1700; *d* Ohrdruf, 12 June 1743). Son of Johann Christoph (*22*). From 1715 to 1719 he studied with Johann Sebastian Bach in Weimar and Cöthen and from 1721 he was organist of St Michael's, Ohrdruf. A suite

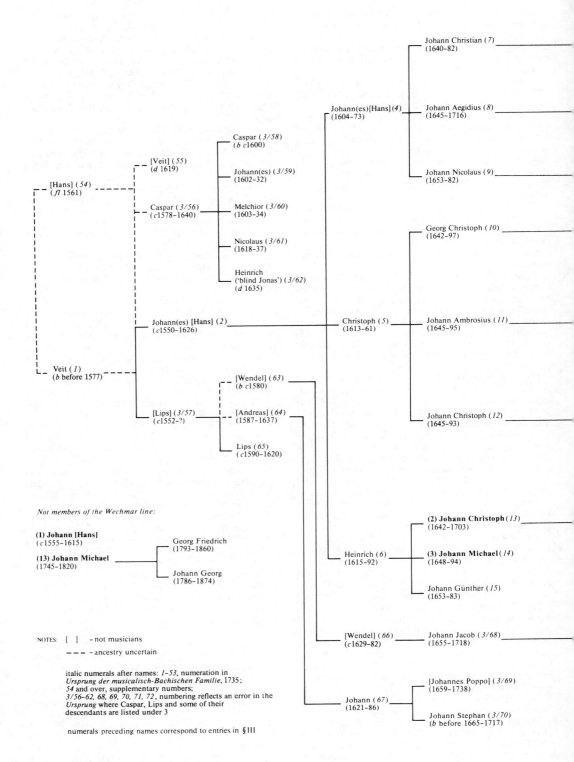

Not members of the Wechmar line:

(1) Johann [Hans]
(c1555–1615)

(13) Johann Michael
(1745–1820)

Georg Friedrich
(1793–1860)

Johann Georg
(1786–1874)

NOTES: [   ]   – not musicians

            – – – – ancestry uncertain

italic numerals after names: *1–53*, numeration in
Ursprung der musicalisch-Bachischen Familie, 1735;
54 and over, supplementary numbers;
3/56–62, 68, 69, 70, 71, 72, numbering reflects an error in the
Ursprung where Caspar, Lips and some of their
descendants are listed under 3

numerals preceding names correspond to entries in §III

1. The Bach family tree

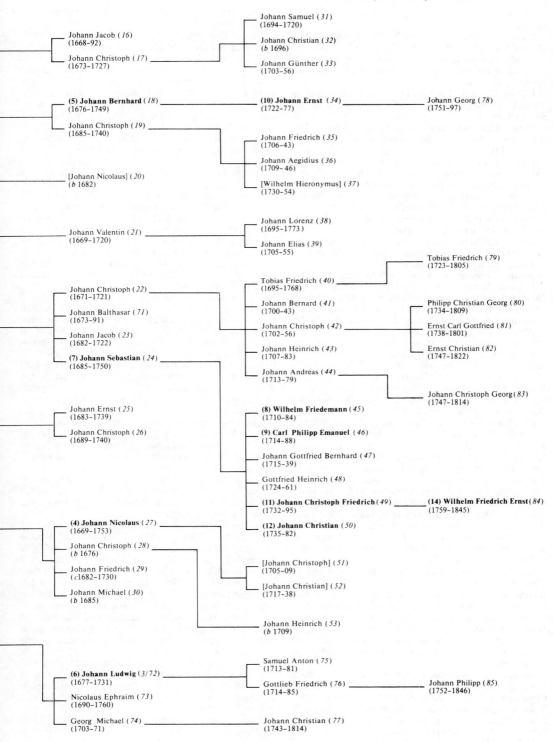

in E♭ and a sonata in B♭, both for keyboard, were cited by Spitta.

Johann Christian Bach (7) (b Erfurt, baptized 17 Aug 1640; d Erfurt, buried 1 July 1682). Son of Johann (4). He was a violinist in the Erfurt town music, then town musician in Eisenach; in 1667 he became director of the Erfurt town music.

Johann Christian Bach (32) (b Erfurt, 1696). Son of Johann Christoph (17). He was a musician in Sondershausen.

Johann Christian Bach (50) (b Leipzig, 5 Sept 1735; d London, 1 Jan 1782). Son of Johann Sebastian (24); see §III (12) below.

Johann Christian Bach (77) (b Halle, 1743; d Halle, 1814). Son of Georg Michael (74). He studied with Wilhelm Friedemann Bach in Halle and received from him the autograph of Johann Sebastian Bach's *Clavierbüchlein für Wilhelm Friedemann*. He was a teacher at the Pedagogium (preparatory school) in Halle and is known as the 'Clavier-Bach'.

Johann Christoph Bach (13) (b Arnstadt, baptized 8 Dec 1642; d Eisenach, buried 2 April 1703). Son of Heinrich (6); see §III (2) below.

Johann Christoph Bach (12) (b Erfurt, 22 Feb 1645; d Arnstadt, buried 28 Aug 1693). Son of Christoph (5). In 1666 he was a town musician in Erfurt, and from 1671 court and town musician (violinist) in Arnstadt.

Johann Christoph Bach (22) (b Erfurt, 16 June 1671; d Ohrdruf, 22 Feb 1721). Son of Johann Ambrosius (11). He studied in Erfurt with Pachelbel from 1685 to 1688, when he became organist of St Thomas's in Erfurt; from 1690 he was organist of St Michael's, Ohrdruf. From 1695 to 1700 he gave instruction to his brother Johann Sebastian (24), who lived in his house after their parents' death. See C. Freyse: *Die Ohrdrufer Bache in der Silhouette: J. S. Bachs ältester Bruder Johann Christoph und seine Nachkommen* (Eisenach, 1957).

Johann Christoph Bach (17) (b Erfurt, baptized 13 Jan 1673; d Gehren, buried 30 July 1727). Son of Johann Christian (7). He was Kantor in Erfurt from 1695 and Kantor and organist in Gehren from 1698.

Johann Christoph Bach (28) (b Eisenach, baptized 29 Aug 1676). Son of Johann Christoph (13). He was a harpsichordist in Erfurt, and travelled to England via Hamburg (where evidence of him is dated 1708–9) and Rotterdam (1717–20); it seems that he never returned to his home country. See C. Oefner: 'Neues zur Biographie von Johann Christoph Bach (geb.1676)', *DJbM*, xiv (1969), 121.

Johann Christoph Bach (19) (b Erfurt, baptized 17 Aug 1685; d Erfurt, buried 15 May 1740). Son of Johann Aegidius (8). He was a member of the Erfurt town music from 1705 and became its director in 1716.

Johann Christoph Bach (26) (b Arnstadt, 12 Sept 1689; d Blankenhain, buried 28 Feb 1740). Son of Johann Christoph (12). In 1714 he was organist in Keula and from 1729 organist, teacher and merchant in Blankenhain.

Johann Christoph Bach (42) (b Ohrdruf, 12 Nov 1702; d Ohrdruf, 2 Nov 1756). Son of Johann Christoph (22). He was Kantor in Ohrdruf from 1728.

Johann Christoph Friedrich Bach (49) (b Leipzig, 21 June 1732; d Bückeburg, 26 Jan 1795). Son of Johann Sebastian (24); see §III (11) below.

Johann Christoph Georg Bach (83) (b Ohrdruf, 8 May 1747; d Ohrdruf, 30 Dec 1814). Son of Johann

Andreas (44). He was organist of St Michael's in Ohrdruf from 1779.

Johann Elias Bach (39) (b Schweinfurt, 12 Feb 1705; d Schweinfurt, 30 Nov 1755). Son of Johann Valentin (21). He studied theology at Jena from 1728 and at Leipzig from 1738. He lived with Johann Sebastian (24) as his private secretary, pupil and tutor of his younger children until 1742. In 1743 he became Kantor of St John's in Schweinfurt and inspector of the church boarding-school. See K. Pottgiesser: 'Die Briefentwürfe des Johann Elias Bach', *Die Musik*, xii (1912–13), 3; F. Beyschlag: 'Ein Schweinfurter Ableger der thüringischen Musikerfamilie Bach', *Schweinfurter Heimatblätter*, xi (1925).

Johann Ernst Bach (25) (b Arnstadt, 5 Aug 1683; d Arnstadt, 21 March 1739). Son of Johann Christoph (12). He studied in Hamburg and Frankfurt and in 1707 became organist of the Neukirche at Arnstadt, succeeding Johann Sebastian (24). During winter 1705–6 he had deputized for Johann Sebastian during the latter's journey to Lübeck to visit Buxtehude. From 1728 he was organist of the Liebfrauenkirche, Arnstadt.

Johann Ernst Bach (34) (b Eisenach, baptized 30 Jan 1722; d Eisenach, 1 Sept 1777). Son of Johann Bernhard (18); see §III (10) below.

Johann Friedrich Bach (29) (b Eisenach, c1682; d Mühlhausen, buried 8 Feb 1730). Son of Johann Christoph (13). After attending the University of Jena, he succeeded Johann Sebastian (24) as organist of St Blasius's church in Mühlhausen in 1708. An organ fugue in G minor by him is extant (*D-Bds*).

Johann Friedrich Bach (35) (b Erfurt, baptized 22 Oct 1706; d Andisleben, nr. Erfurt, 30 May 1743). Son of Johann Christoph (19). He was organist in Quedlinburg and by 1735 a schoolmaster in Andisleben.

Johann Georg Bach (78) (b Eisenach, baptized 2 Oct 1751; d Eisenach, 1797). Son of Johann Ernst (34). In 1777 he succeeded his father as court and town organist, titular Kapellmeister, notary and town treasurer in Eisenach.

Johann Georg Bach (b Güstrow, c1786; d Elberfeld, 6 Dec 1874). Not a member of the Wechmar line, he was a son of Johann Michael (see §III (13) below) and a music teacher in Elberfeld.

Johann Gottfried Bernhard Bach (47) (b Weimar, 11 May 1715; d Jena, 27 May 1739). Son of Johann Sebastian (24). He was a pupil of his father; in 1735 he became organist of St Mary's in Mühlhausen and in 1737 of the Jakobikirche in Sangerhausen (a post his father had applied for in 1702). By spring 1738 he had left that position. In a letter of 26 May 1738 Johann Sebastian complained bitterly about his 'undutiful son', who displayed an unstable character and had incurred debts. He enrolled as a law student at the University of Jena on 28 January 1739 but died soon afterwards; the cause is unknown.

Johann Günther Bach (15) (b Arnstadt, baptized 17 July 1653; d Arnstadt, buried 10 April 1683). Son of Heinrich (6). He was assistant organist to his father in Arnstadt from 1682 and was also active as a keyboard and violin maker.

Johann Günther Bach (33) (b Gehren, 4 April 1703; d Erfurt, buried 24 Oct 1756). Son of Johann Christoph (17). He was a town musician (tenor and viola player) and a teacher in Erfurt by 1735.

Johann Heinrich Bach (*43*) (*b* Ohrdruf, 4 Aug 1707; *d* Oehringen, 20 May 1783). Son of Johann Christoph (*22*). He was a pupil of Johann Sebastian (*24*) at the Leipzig Thomasschule, 1724–8. He then became assistant organist to his father in Ohrdruf and in 1735 was appointed Kantor at Oehringen.

Johann Heinrich Bach (*53*) (*b* Hamburg, baptized 4 Nov 1709). Son of Johann Christoph (*28*). According to the *Ursprung* he was 'a good keyboard player'.

Johann Jacob Bach (*3/68*) (*b* Wolfsbehringen, 12 Sept 1655; *d* Ruhla, 11 Dec 1718). Son of Wendel (*66*) (*b* Wechmar, 1629 or 1631; *d* Wolfsbehringen, 18 Dec 1682), a farmer 'who could also sing well', and grandson of Wendel (*63*) (*b* c1580). Johann Jacob went to school in Eisenach, and was later organist in Thal, Kantor in Steinbach, Kantor in Wasungen (1690–94) and thereafter in Ruhla.

Johann Jacob Bach (*16*) (*b* Erfurt, baptized 14 Aug 1668; *d* Eisenach, buried 29 April 1692). Son of Johann Christian (*7*). He served his Stadtpfeifer apprenticeship and journeyman period under Johann Ambrosius Bach (*11*) in Eisenach.

Johann Jacob Bach (*23*) (*b* Eisenach, baptized 11 Feb 1682; *d* Stockholm, 16 April 1722). Son of Johann Ambrosius (*11*). He received instruction as a Stadtpfeifer in Eisenach with Johann Heinrich Halle, his father's successor, and in 1704 became an oboist with the Swedish guard. He went with the Swedish army under Charles XII to Turkey and took flute lessons in Constantinople with P. G. Buffardin. From 1713 he was a chamber musician at the Stockholm court. About 1704 Johann Sebastian (*24*) wrote a Capriccio (BWV992) on Johann Jacob's departure from his home country. See A. Protz: 'Johann Sebastian Bachs Capriccio sopra la lontananza del suo fratello dilettissimo', *Mf*, x (1957), 405.

Johann Lorenz Bach (*38*) (*b* Schweinfurt, 10 Sept 1695; *d* Lahm im Itzgrund, 14 Dec 1773). Son of Johann Valentin (*21*): He was a pupil of Johann Sebastian (*24*) in Weimar, 1715–17, and from 1718 was organist and Kantor in Lahm. An organ fugue in D by him is extant (*Orgelwerke der Familie Bach*, 1967, p.31); the manuscript of the prelude belonging to it (incipit in *BJb*, xxxvii, 1949–50, p.108) was lost in World War II. See O. Kaul: *Zur Musikgeschichte der ehemaligen Reichstadt Schweinfurt* (Würzburg, 1935).

Johann Ludwig Bach (*3/72*) (*b* Thal, nr. Eisenach, 4 Feb 1677; *d* Meiningen, buried 1 March 1731). Son of Johann Jacob (*3/68*); see §III (6) below.

Johann Michael Bach (*14*) (*b* Arnstadt, baptized 9 Aug 1648; *d* Gehren, 17 May 1694). Son of Heinrich (*6*); see §III (3) below.

Johann Michael Bach (*30*) (*b* Eisenach, baptized 1 Aug 1685). Son of Johann Christoph (*13*), He left Eisenach in 1703; nothing is certainly known of his later life except that he was active in Stockholm as an organ builder.

Johann Michael Bach (*b* Struth, nr. Schmalkalden, 9 Nov 1745; *d* Elberfeld, 1820). Not a member of the Wechmar line but from a Hessian branch of the family; see §III (13) below.

Johann Nicolaus Bach (*9*) (*b* Erfurt, baptized 5 Feb 1653; *d* Erfurt, buried 30 July 1682). Son of Johann (*4*). From 1673 he was an Erfurt town musician (viol).

Johann Nicolaus Bach (*27*) (*b* Eisenach, 10 Oct 1669; *d* Jena, 4 Nov 1753). Son of Johann Christoph (*13*); see §III (4) below.

Johann Philipp Bach (*85*) (*b* Meiningen, 5 Aug 1752; *d* Meiningen, 2 Nov 1846). Son of Gottlieb Friedrich (*76*). From 1790 he was court organist and painter (*Kabinettsmaler*) in Meiningen.

Johann Samuel Bach (*31*) (*b* Niederzimmern, 4 June 1694; *d* Gundersleben, 1 July 1720). Son of Johann Christoph (*17*). He was a musician and teacher in Sondershausen and Gundersleben.

Johann Sebastian Bach (*24*) (*b* Eisenach, 21 March 1685; *d* Leipzig, 28 July 1750). Son of Johann Ambrosius (*11*); see §III (7) below.

Johann Stephan Bach (*3/70*) (*b* Ilmenau, before 1665; *d* Brunswick, 10 Jan 1717). Son of Johann (*67*). He was Kantor at the Cathedral of St Blasius in Brunswick from 1690; he also wrote sonnets.

Johann Valentin Bach (*21*) (*b* Themar, 6 Jan 1669; *d* Schweinfurt, 12 Aug 1720). Son of Georg Christoph (*10*). He was town musician and head tower watchman (*Obertürmer*) in Schweinfurt from 1694.

Lips [Philippus] Bach (*65*) (*b* Wechmar, c1590; *d* Wechmar, 10 Oct 1620). Son of the carpetmaker Lips (*3/57*) (*b* c1552) who was a son of Veit (*1*); see §II (2) below. The younger Lips was a musician.

Melchior Bach (*3/60*) (*b* 1603; *d* Arnstadt, 7 Sept 1634). Son of Caspar (*3/56*). He was a Stadtpfeifer in Arnstadt.

Nicolaus Bach (*3/61*) (*b* Arnstadt, 1618; *d* Arnstadt, 1 Oct 1637). Son of Caspar (*3/56*). He was a Stadtpfeifer in Arnstadt.

Nicolaus Ephraim Bach (*73*) (*b* Wasungen, baptized 26 Nov 1690; *d* Gandersheim, 1760). Son of Johann Jacob (*3/68*). In 1708 he was appointed musician and in 1719 organist at the Meiningen court. In 1724 he became organist in Gandersheim.

Philipp Christian Georg Bach (*80*) (*b* Ohrdruf, 5 April 1734; *d* Wernigshausen, 18 Aug 1809). Son of Johann Christoph (*42*). He was Kantor of St Michael's, Ohrdruf, 1759–72, and thereafter a vicar in Wernigshausen.

Samuel Anton Bach (*75*) (*b* Meiningen, 26 April 1713; *d* Meiningen, 1781). Son of Johann Ludwig (*3/72*). He studied with Johann Sebastian (*24*) in Leipzig around 1732; later he was court organist in Meiningen and for a time also court painter.

Tobias Friedrich Bach (*40*) (*b* Ohrdruf, 21 July 1695; *d* Udestedt, 1 July 1768). Son of Johann Christoph (*22*). He was organist of the Trinity Church in Ohrdruf from 1714 until 1717, when he became court Kantor in Gandersheim. In 1720 he became Kantor in Pferdingsleben and the next year in Udestedt.

Tobias Friedrich Bach (*79*) (*b* Udestedt, 22 Sept 1723; *d* Erfurt, 18 Jan 1805). Son of Tobias Friedrich (*40*). In 1747 he became Kantor of the Reglerkirche in Erfurt and in 1762 of the Franciscan Church there.

Veit Bach (*1*) (*b* ?Pressburg [now Bratislava]; *d* Wechmar, before 1577). A baker by trade, he was the earliest member of the family to show musical proclivities and head of the Wechmar line; see §II (2) below.

Wilhelm Friedemann Bach (*45*) (*b* Weimar, 22 Nov 1710; *d* Berlin, 1 July 1784). Son of Johann Sebastian (*24*); see §III (8) below.

Wilhelm Friedrich Ernst Bach (*84*) (*b* Bückeburg, baptized 24 May 1759; *d* Berlin, 25 Dec 1845). Son of Johann Christoph Friedrich (*49*); see §III (14) below.

II. Family history

1. The family tradition and its context. 2. Origins and development.

1. THE FAMILY TRADITION AND ITS CONTEXT. The Bach family lived and worked in the central region of Germany, primarily in Thuringia, with the duchies and principalities of Saxe-Eisenach, Saxe-Gotha, Saxe-Meiningen, Saxe-Weimar, the county of Schwarzburg-Arnstadt and the town of Erfurt, belonging to the Mainz electorate. The region, bitterly split politically though unified denominationally, had its own cultural traditions and, despite the turmoils of war and other vicissitudes, enjoyed a varied and firmly based economic life. In these conditions a lively musical atmosphere flourished, encouraged by the ambitious displays of magnificence of the small courts, by the individual towns' need for prestige, and by the consciousness of a strong musical tradition and post-Reformation zeal in the church in this the home country of Lutheranism. The growth and decline of the Bach family, like that of other families of musicians (for example the Hasses), is closely linked with these social conditions: initially with the rapid expansion of musical practice in courts, towns and churches towards the end of the 16th century, then with the decline in importance of the leading musical institutions such as court orchestras, Stadtpfeifer bands and church choirs in the face of the increasingly popular bourgeois music culture of the later 18th century.

The musical life of Thuringia was small in scale but varied. The region – perhaps in the aftermath of the Thirty Years War – had no important centre, such as a city or court with a large opera company, and hence held no particular attraction for musicians of standing. A sound, ordinary ability served to accord members of the Bach family a pre-eminent position in local musical life; only a few achieved anything extraordinary, and most of those drifted away from their original environment.

The unusual concentration of musical talent within a single family and territory has long interested scholars concerned with genealogy, heredity and talent. The continual reappearance of musical talent during several generations (the singular culmination being Johann Sebastian Bach) within an increasingly large and then sharply declining number of prominent family members remains a unique phenomenon. The prerequisite for the development of such a dynasty of musicians was a general emphasis on craftsmanship in practical musical activities, so that from early childhood a musical career was virtually prescribed for the male members of the family. Musical training was given for the most part within the family group – by fathers, brothers, uncles, cousins or more distant relations. This is typical even of the later generations: for instance, Johann Sebastian taught six of his relatives (Johann Lorenz (38), Johann Bernhard (41), Johann Elias (39), Johann Heinrich (43), Samuel Anton (75), Johann Ernst (34)) as well as his own sons; Carl Philipp Emanuel (46) took his youngest brother Johann Christian (50) into his care, and Wilhelm Friedemann (45) taught his relative Johann Christian (77). Studies outside the region or educational journeys were certainly unusual, though Caspar's sons (3/58–62), Johann Nicolaus (27) and finally Johann Christian (50) went to Italy. In these circumstances, even Johann Sebastian's journey to study with Buxtehude in Lübeck must be considered out of the ordinary.

In a milieu so self-sufficient and so governed by guild thinking and professional regulations, intermarriage between families of musicians was frequent. This was certainly the case in Thuringia in, for example, the Wilcke, Lämmerhirt, Hoffmann and Bach families. Precisely these families were, in fact, mutually associated. The first wife of Johann (4), like that of his brother Heinrich (6), was a Hoffmann, and his second was a Lämmerhirt. Johann Sebastian too was typical: his mother was a Lämmerhirt (as, incidentally, was J. G. Walther's), his first wife was a Bach and his second a Wilcke. Common social standing, professional interdependence and musical interests created a close unity within the family, and their social status as 'outsiders' (during the 17th century musicians of lower rank were not normally permitted citizenship) was a significant factor in the family's solidarity. Strict religious attitudes also had an important role, and some members of the family even showed a tendency to sectarian religious behaviour. To deepen the manifold connections, there were regular family gatherings, which must have resembled small music festivals; Forkel wrote:

Since the company consisted of none but Kantors, organists and town musicians, all of whom had to do with the church . . . first of all, when all were assembled, a chorale was sung. From this devotional opening they proceeded to jesting, often in strong contrast to it. For now they would sing folksongs, the contents of which were partly comic and partly indelicate, all together and extempore, but in such a way that the several improvised parts made up a kind of harmony, although the text was different for each voice. They called this kind of extempore harmonizing [Zusammenstimmung] a quodlibet . . . and enjoyed a hearty laugh at it.

Johann Sebastian's early Quodlibet (BWV524), only partly extant, provides a characteristic example of this family speciality.

The family was keenly aware of its position as bearers of a musical tradition. It was with that consciousness that Johann Sebastian, in a letter to G. Erdmann (28 October 1730), described his children as 'born musici'; and as early as 1732 J. G. Walther's Musicalisches Lexicon, in which the first brief biography of Johann Sebastian appeared, referred expressly to the great master's roots in an unusual family of musicians. His obituary notice of 1754 made the point more fully. And it was Johann Sebastian himself who systematically investigated the family's history and musical heritage. His genealogy of the family, written down in 1735, is still the most reliable documentary evidence of the family history, above all in respect to the early generations. (The original manuscript of the Ursprung, written for Forkel, is lost, but several copies are extant, among them a particularly important one of 1774–5 by Anna Carolina Philippina Bach, with additions by her father, Carl Philipp Emanuel.) Further, Johann Sebastian's estate contained a manuscript collection of compositions by the most important earlier members of the family, under the title 'Alt-Bachisches Archiv' (when acquired by the Berlin Singakademie in the 19th century it contained 20 works; that collection was lost in World War II, but other manuscripts originally in the 'Archiv' survived individually – ed. in EDM, 1st ser., i–ii, 1935). A number of entries are in the hand of Johann Ambrosius (11), suggesting that it was he who initiated the collection; Johann Sebastian later reordered it, adding some new title-pages, and put it to practical use (he prepared some instrumental parts).

2. ORIGINS AND DEVELOPMENT. The Ursprung traces the family tree without a break back to Veit (1) in the middle of the 16th century. Up to the generation of

Veit's grandsons, however, much remains unclear, and the lack of available archival documents in church records and elsewhere makes it impossible to clarify this period in the family's history. The supposition, found in some Bach literature, that Veit was a son of Hans (*54*) is untenable; this Hans, who can be traced in Wechmar in 1561, must have been a brother, cousin or other relative. Nothing is known of his profession. Although Hans is the earliest bearer of the name of Bach to be found in Wechmar, no further conclusion can be drawn from that. By this time the name of Bach (also often spelt 'Baach', hinting at the phonetic value of a long 'a', as in 'father'; see *Bach-Dokumente*, ii, nos.1 and 6) was widespread in the Thuringian region, and it can be traced back to the 14th century, though there is no evidence that any of these earlier members of the family were involved in musical activity. The *Ursprung* says of Veit, who was a baker by trade, that his hobby was playing the 'cythringen' (a small cittern). There is an explicit additional sentence – 'this was, as it were, the beginning of music in his descendants' – which probably indicates that none of Veit's ancestors was a professional musician. Neither was Veit himself. He had most likely been driven from Moravia or Slovakia about 1545 as a result of the expulsion of Protestants in the Counter-Reformation, at the time of the Schmalkaldian War (1545–7). The reference to 'Hungary' in the *Ursprung* is not to be taken literally and in accordance with the terminology of the time must signify in general terms the central lands of the Habsburg Empire (including present-day Austria and Czechoslovakia). Veit took up residence in Wechmar and must have died by 1577 as for that year his sons Johann (*2*) and Lips (*3/57*) are recorded as house-owners in Wechmar. Contrary to current opinion (which is based on the assumption that Hans was Veit's father), Veit did not migrate from Wechmar or Thuringia but (according to Korabinsky, 1784) was born in Moravia or Slovakia, as the son of an earlier migrant, possibly in or near Pressburg (now Bratislava). There, and elsewhere in the Habsburg lands, various people by the name of Bach can be traced in the 16th and 17th centuries, among them musicians such as the *Spielmann* (violinist) and jester Johann or Hans Bach (see §III (1) below).

Another Veit Bach (*55*) died in Wechmar in 1619; nothing further is known of him. He should not be confused with Veit (*1*), the head of the Wechmar line of the Bach family; he may have been a son of Veit or Hans. In the 16th and early 17th centuries there were in Thuringia branches of the family which may have been connected either directly or indirectly with the Wechmar line and in which musicians are occasionally found (for example Eberhard Heinrich Bach, son of a Heinrich Bach, a trumpeter from Rohrborn near Erfurt who went to the Netherlands and emigrated to Indonesia about 1598). However, the *Ursprung* wisely limits itself to the smaller circle which can strictly be considered the musical family of Bachs.

Johann Bach (*2*), Veit's son, was the first member of the family to receive a thorough musical training and to pursue a musical career, even though he also pursued other activities. His sons were the first to follow music exclusively. By accepting salaried positions they became sedentary and distinct from non-organized musicians (or 'beer-fiddlers'), thereby taking the first step towards citizenship and breaking with the tradition of the *Spielmann* – although in their varied occupations as instrumentalists their background continued to have its effect.

Genealogical difficulties arise over a series of family members who were in some way connected with the main Wechmar line but whose precise extraction remains unclear. Indeed, the *Ursprung* has a lacuna concerning the brother of Johann (*2*). His name is not given, but his trade (carpetmaker) is mentioned and his sons are briefly described. This has led to a confusion between two family members, Caspar (*3/56*) and Lips (*3/57*). According to the *Ursprung*, the sons of Johann's brother visited Italy; that can refer only to Caspar's sons who, it has been established, were encouraged to go there by the Count of Schwarzburg-Arnstadt. Further, Caspar had a blind son Heinrich (*3/62*), who must surely be the 'blind Jonas' mentioned in the *Ursprung*; and the ancestors of Johann Ludwig (*3/72*), connected with Johann's brother, can be related only to Lips. Thus either Johann had two brothers, or Caspar and Lips must at least have been so closely related that family tradition could plausibly merge them into one. It appears that Lips's descendants were farmers. The connection between Andreas (*64*) and Lips remains unclear: Andreas was an alderman in Themar, and his son Johann (*67*) was Kantor and later vicar, as were several of his descendants. In the *Ursprung* Johannes Poppo (*3/69*), brother of Johann Stephan (*3/70*), is listed as a priest, and the presence of Georg Michael (*74*) at his funeral in 1738 implies that they came from closely related branches of the family. Most probably the two lines had a common origin in Lips.

Almost all the Bachs were first and foremost instrumentalists; they were mainly keyboard players, but virtually all other instruments were represented, and in the true Stadtpfeifer tradition most of them learnt to play several instruments. Several of them were also active in instrument manufacture, for example Johann Michael (*14*), Johann Günther (*15*), Johann Nicolaus (*27*) and Johann Michael (*30*). This interest in the quality and functioning of instruments, alongside his skill as a performer, is marked in Johann Sebastian, who was a considerable expert on the organ, stimulated the development of the viola pomposa and the Lautenklavier, and offered constructive criticism of Silbermann's early pianoforte. Most of the earlier Bachs concentrated on learning and playing instruments; composition ordinarily remained in the background, and was reserved for those who had the necessary training and from whom a supply of music was expected. Almost without exception among the 17th-century Bachs, that meant the organists; so it is hardly surprising that no compositions by even such eminent family members as Johann Ambrosius (*11*) were handed down. At all events, composing must have been a peripheral activity for the court trumpeter, if indeed he composed at all, whereas his two cousins, the organists Johann Christoph (*13*) and Johann Michael (*14*), were avid composers. Their vocal works were not primarily for liturgical use – the supply of music for the liturgy was the Kantors' responsibility – so they wrote mostly funeral motets, doubtless a well-paid side activity.

By the turn of the 17th century the musical family was so widespread in the Thuringian region that the name 'Bach' had come to be regarded as synonymous with 'musician'. In many places, particularly Erfurt and Arnstadt, they held the principal positions, and it was typical that the successor to a position vacated by a

Bach would be another Bach. When Johann Christoph (*13*) left Arnstadt, his younger brother Johann Michael (*14*) replaced him; Johann Sebastian's position in Mühlhausen went to his cousin Johan Ernst (*25*); and the post held by Johann Christoph (*22*) was even passed down through two generations (*41*, *79*). Carl Philipp Emanuel's application for his father's post as Kantor of the Thomaskirche in 1750 may be seen as in the same tradition. This almost automatic succession of musical positions, however, grew ever more difficult: the institutions which had given rise to a musician class organized by guilds – and thus the very means of existence to a family like the Bachs – began to crumble.

Having risen from simple *Spielmann* beginnings, the Bachs had gradually reached every level of the musical hierarchy, in the three spheres of contemporary musical activity (court, town, church): court musician, court Konzertmeister or Kapellmeister; Stadtpfeifer or director of the town music; organist or Kantor. By the middle of the 18th century, social change had affected the structure of each of these areas, and broke the patterns that for so long had governed the lives of the Bach family. Further, the sons of the thenceforth middle-class Bachs had quite different professional opportunities because of their new educational prospects (almost all the members of the generation of J. S. Bach's sons attended university); formerly they had had little alternative but to become musicians. It is natural that fewer took up music as a profession. Several members of the family turned to another artistic field, painting: the descendants of Johann Ludwig (*3/72*) were court painters, and Johann Sebastian (1748–78), the son of Carl Philipp Emanuel, studied with Goethe's friend Adam F. Oeser and was a highly respected landscape painter (he went to Italy and died in Rome at the age of 30: for his works see *BJb*, xxxvii, 1940–48, p.163ff). Considering the proliferation of musical gifts over more than six generations of the Bach family it may appear surprising, though understandable in the light of historical developments, that in 1843, at the ceremonial unveiling in front of the Thomaskirche of the Leipzig Bach monument, donated by Mendelssohn, Wilhelm Friedrich Ernst (*84*) was the solitary representative of a musical family with a tradition of more than 250 years.

BIBLIOGRAPHY

CATALOGUES, BIBLIOGRAPHIES

M. Schneider: 'Thematisches Verzeichnis der musikalischen Werke der Familie Bach (I. Teil)', *BJb*, iv (1907), 103–77 [continuations never appeared]
W. Schmieder, ed.: 'Das Bachschrifttum 1945–1952', *BJb*, xl (1953), 119–68; for 1953–7, *BJb*, xlv (1958), 127; for 1958–62, ed. E. Francke, *BJb*, liii (1967), 121–69; for 1963–7, ed. R. Nestle, *BJb*, lix (1973), 91–150; for 1968–72, ed. R. Nestle, *BJb*, lxii (1976)
K. Geiringer: *The Bach Family: Seven Generations of Creative Genius* (London, 1954; Ger. trans., enlarged, 1958) [bibliography, 490ff; Ger. edn., 542ff]
P. Kast: *Die Bach-Handschriften der Berliner Staatsbibliothek*, Tübinger Bach-Studien, ii–iii (Trossingen, 1958)
J. F. Richter: 'Johann Sebastian Bach und seine Familie in Thüringen', *Bach-Festbuch Weimar 1964*, 50

SOURCES

[J. S. Bach]: *Ursprung der musicalisch-Bachischen Familie*, 1735 [original MS lost]
M. Korabinsky: *Beschreibung der königlichen ungarischen Haupt- Frey und Krönungsstadt Pressburg*, i (Pressburg, 1784), 110ff
M. Schneider: *Bach-Urkunden: Ursprung der musikalisch-Bachischen Familie* (Leipzig, 1917) [facs. of copy by C. P. E. and A. C. P. Bach]
C. S. Terry: *The Origin of the Family of Bach Musicians* (London, 1929)
J. Müller-Blattau: *Genealogie der musikalisch-Bachischen Familie* (Kassel, 1950)

W. Neumann and H.-J. Schulze, eds.: *Bach-Dokumente*, i (Kassel, 1963), no.184 [critical edn.]

MONOGRAPHS

RiemannL 12
C. F. M.: 'Bemerkungen zu dem Stammbaum der Bachischen Familie', *AMZ*, xxv (1823), 187
Kawaczynsky: 'Über die Familie Bach: eine genealogische Mitteilung', *AMZ*, xlv (1843), 537
P. Spitta: *Johann Sebastian Bach*, i (Leipzig, 1873–80, 5/1962; Eng. trans., 1884–99/R1951)
A. Lorenz: 'Ein alter Bach-Stammbaum', *NZM*, lxxxii (1915), 281
G. Thiele: 'Die Familie Bach in Mühlhausen', *Mühlhäuser Geschichtsblätter*, xxi (1920–21), 62
H. Lämmerhirt: 'Bachs Mutter und ihre Sippe', *BJb*, xxii (1925), 101–37
C. S. Terry: *Bach: a Biography* (London, 1928/R1962)
E. Borkowsky: *Die Musikerfamilie Bach* (Jena, 1930)
H. Helmbold: 'Die Söhne von Johann Christoph und Johann Ambrosius Bach auf der Eisenacher Schule', *BJb*, xxvii (1930), 49
C. S. Terry: 'Has Bach Surviving Descendants?', *MT*, lxxi (1930), 511
E. Lux: 'Der Familienstamm Bach in Gräfenroda', *BJb*, xxviii (1931), 107
H. Miesner: 'Urkundliche Nachrichten über die Familie Bach in Berlin', *BJb*, xxix (1932), 157
H. Lämmerhirt: 'Ein hessischer Bach-Stamm', *BJb*, xxxiii (1936), 53–89
L. Bach: 'Ergänzungen und Berichtigungen zu dem Beitrag "Ein hessischer Bach-Stamm" von Hugo Lämmerhirt', *BJb*, xxxiv (1937), 118
K. Fischer: 'Das Freundschaftsbuch des Apothekers Friedrich Thomas Bach: eine Quelle zur Geschichte der Musikerfamilie Bach', *BJb*, xxxv (1938), 95
C. U. von Ulmenstein: 'Die Nachkommen des Bückeburger Bach', *AMf*, iv (1939), 12
W. G. Whittaker: 'The Bachs and Eisenach', *Collected Essays* (London, 1940)
H. Löffler: ' "Bache" bei Bach', *BJb*, xxxviii (1949–50), 106
R. Benecke: 'Bach, Familie', *MGG*
Bach in Thüringen: Gabe der Thüringer Kirche an das Thüringer Volk zum Bach-Gedenkjahr 1950 (Berlin, 1950)
H. Besseler and G. Kraft, eds.: *Johann Sebastian Bach in Thüringen: Festgabe zum Gedenkjahr 1950*, Quellenkundliche Studien thüringischer Musikforscher (Weimar, 1950)
K. Geiringer: 'Artistic Interrelations of the Bachs', *MQ*, xxxvi (1950), 363
W. Rauschenberger: 'Die Familien Bach', *Genealogie und Heraldik*, ii (1950), 1
E. Wölfer: 'Naumburg und die Musikerfamilie Bach', *Programmheft zu den Bach-Tagen Naumburg 1950*, 9
C. Schubart: 'Anna Magdalena Bach: neue Beiträge zu ihrer Herkunft und ihren Jugendjahren', *BJb*, xl (1953), 29
K. Geiringer: *The Bach Family: Seven Generations of Creative Genius* (London, 1954; Ger. trans., enlarged, 1958; enlarged, 2/1977)
C. Freyse: 'Wieviel Geschwister hatte J. S. Bach?', *BJb*, xlii (1955), 103
G. Kraft: 'Zur Enstehungsgeschichte des "Hochzeitsquodlibet" (BWV 524)', *BJb*, xliii (1956), 140
G. von Dadelsen: *Bemerkungen zur Handschrift Johann Sebastian Bachs, seiner Familie und seines Kreises*, Tübinger Bach-Studien, i (Trossingen, 1957)
K. Müller and F. Wiegand: *Arnstädter Bachbuch: J. S. Bach und seine Verwandten in Arnstadt* (Arnstadt, 1957)
K. Geiringer: 'Unbekannte Werke von Nachkommen J. S. Bachs in amerikanischen Sammlungen', *IMSCR*, vii *Cologne 1958*, 110
G. Kraft: 'Neue Beiträge zur Bach-Genealogie', *BMw*, i (1959), 29–61
A. Schmiedecke: 'Johann Sebastian Bachs Verwandte in Weissenfels', *Mf*, xiv (1961), 195
H.-J. Schulze: 'Marginalien zu einigen Bach-Dokumenten', *BJb*, xlviii (1961), 79
G. Kraft: *Entstehung und Ausbreitung des musikalischen Bach-Geschlechtes in Thüringen: mit besonderer Berücksichtigung des Wechmarer Stammes* (Habilitationsschrift, U. of Halle, 1964)
F. Wiegand: 'Die mütterlichen Verwandten Johann Sebastian Bachs in Erfurt – Ergänzungen und Berichtigungen zur Bachforschung', *BJb*, liii (1967), 5
E. Zavarský: 'Zur angeblichen Pressburger Herkunft der Familie Bach', *BJb*, liii (1967), 21
G. Kraft: 'Das mittelthüringische Siedlungszentrum der Familien Bach und Wölcken', *Musa–mens–musici: im Gedenken an Walther Vetter* (Leipzig, 1969), 153
P. M. Young: *The Bachs: 1500–1800* (London, 1970)

III. Individual members

(1) Johann [Hans] Bach (*b* Andelsbuch, Vorarlberg, *c*1555; *d* Nürtingen, 1 Dec 1615). He became a *Spielmann* (violinist) and jester at the Stuttgart court of Duke Ludwig of Württemberg about 1585, and in 1593 he followed the widowed Duchess Ursula to the court of Nürtingen, where he remained until his death. He apparently often travelled, both alone and in the court entourage. Of his work all that survives is the text of a narrative song of 1614 describing a visit to the town of Weil (*Hanss Baachens Lobspruch zur Weil der Statt*: 'Es ist nun über zwantzig Jahr'); its manner is reminiscent of the late medieval style of Oswald von Wolkenstein. There are two extant portraits of him, an etching of about 1605 and an engraving of 1617 (fig.2). The etching bears the inscription:

Hie siehst du geigen/Hansen Bachen
Wenn du es hörst/so mustu lachen
Er geigt gleichwol/nach seiner Art
Und tregt ein hipschen/Hans Bachen Bart.

2. Johann Bach: engraving (1617)

Nothing is known of his extraction; he was probably related in some way (perhaps nephew) to Veit Bach of the Wechmar line – Johann was Protestant (no matter of course in the Catholic south) and like Veit he came from Habsburg lands. C. P. E. Bach's ownership of the 1617 portrait of him suggests that he was traditionally considered a member of the family, although the fact that C. P. E. Bach's *Nachlassverzeichnis* of 1790 incorrectly cited him as 'Bach (Hans) a Gotha musician', perhaps confusing him with Johann (2), may imply that his true identity was unknown to C. P. E. Bach.

BIBLIOGRAPHY
W. Wolffheim: 'Hans Bach', *BJb*, vii (1910), 70
W. Irtenkauf and H. Maier: 'Gehört der Spielmann Hans Bach zur Musikerfamilie Bach?', *Mf*, ix (1956), 450

(2) Johann Christoph Bach (*13*) (*b* Arnstadt, baptized 8 Dec 1642; *d* Eisenach, buried 2 April 1703). Son of Heinrich Bach (*6*), and probably the most important member of the family before (7) Johann Sebastian (*24*). He received a thorough musical grounding under his father, and on 20 November 1663 was appointed organist of the Arnstadt castle chapel. Two years later he was

invited by the Eisenach town council to apply for the post of town organist, at St George's (where the Kantor was Andreas Christian Dedekind); after an audition on 10 December 1665 he was appointed to that position and also to the post of organist and harpsichordist in the court Kapelle of the Duke of Eisenach. He retained both positions until his death.

Little is known of his work in the court Kapelle. For some years the Kapellmeister was Daniel Eberlin, the father-in-law of Telemann, who was later to conduct the Kapelle on occasion, and for a short while Pachelbel was a member of the Kapelle. During most of his time there, Johann Christoph was a colleague of his cousin, the trumpeter Johann Ambrosius (*11*); Ambrosius often served as his copyist, and their relationship was doubtless a close one. The young Johann Sebastian must have received his first impressions of the organ from his uncle. While Johann Christoph's court position was one of high standing, his tenure of the civic one was marred by a succession of quarrels between him and the town council, for which he was not entirely blameless. These mostly involved matters of salary and the council's refusal to provide an official residence for him, a deficiency eventually made good by the court. For many years he also battled with the council over the restoration (or reconstruction) of the organ at St George's; he was successful only in 1696, and then did not live to see the completion (by J. C. Stertzing) of the famous instrument in 1707 (his copious, expert notes on the organ's reconstruction are extant; see Freyse). He died in 1703, just ten days after the death of his wife; her illnesses and those of their children, as well as other family difficulties, had plagued him throughout his Eisenach years.

Within the family Johann Christoph was highly respected as a composer (a 'profound' one according to the *Ursprung*). In Johann Sebastian's obituary notice of 1754 he is mentioned expressly as one who 'was as good at inventing beautiful thoughts as he was at expressing words. He composed, to the extent that current taste permitted, in a *galant* and *cantabile* style, uncommonly full-textured ... On the organ and the keyboard [he] never played with fewer than five independent parts'. Johann Sebastian performed some of his motets and vocal concertos (including the 22-part *Es erhub sich ein Streit*) in Leipzig (as did C. P. E. Bach later in Hamburg), and he added a final chorale (BWV Anh.159) to the motet *Ich lasse dich nicht*. Although Johann Christoph was primarily an organist and harpsichordist, his extant keyboard works are few, but they show him as a capable composer, stylistically akin to Pachelbel though in general less pedantic. The Eb prelude and fugue is a significant work, and his organ chorales (probably in effect written-down improvisations) demonstrate his mastery of the small form. His vocal works, in particular the motets and concertos, are notable for the variety of their settings. The concertos are characterized by their full instrumental writing, with unusually interesting inner part-writing. While the vocal writing is for the most part technically undemanding (bearing in mind the needs of elementary choirs), the instrumental parts are usually highly elaborate. There is much solo–tutti alternation. Basically the motets follow the central German type of the aria motet and the chorale motet, which indeed culminated in the works of Johann Christoph and his brother (3) Johann Michael (*14*). The older style of writing, with alternating chordal and imitative sections, still predominated; but the newer style, with its livelier lines (including melismatic semiquaver passages) and looser, more concertante writing, is found in *Sei getreu bis in den Tod* and *Der Mensch, vom Weibe geboren*, obviously later works. The lack of documentation and the small number of the surviving works preclude the establishment of a clear chronology of Johann Christoph's music.

WORKS

VOCAL

Arias: Es ist nun aus, 4vv, bc; Mit Weinen hebt sichs an, 1691, 4vv, bc: ed. in EDM, 1st ser., i (1935)

Motets: Der Gerechte, ob er gleich zu zeitlich stirbt, 1676, 5vv, ed. in EDM, 1st ser., i (1935); Der Mensch, vom Weibe geboren, 5vv, ed. in EDM, 1st ser., i (1935); Fürchte dich nicht, 5vv, ed. V. Junk (Leipzig, 1922); Herr, nun lässest du deinen Diener, 8vv, ed. V. Junk (Leipzig, 1922); Ich lasse dich nicht, 8vv, ed. in Johann Sebastian Bachs Werke, xxxix (Leipzig, 1892); Lieber Herr Gott, 8vv, 1672, ed. V. Junk (Leipzig, 1922); Sei getreu bis in den Tod, 5vv, ed. in EDM, 1st ser., i (1935); Unsers Herzens Freude, 8vv, ed. K. Straube (Leipzig, 1924), ed. P. Steinitz (London, 1968)

Konzerte: Die Furcht des Herrn, 5vv, 2 vn, 2 va, bc, ed. in EDM, 1st ser., ii (1935); Es erhub sich ein Streit, 10vv, 4 tpt, timp, 2 vn, 4 va, bc, ed. W. Krüger (Stuttgart, 1960); Lamentatio: Ach, dass ich Wassers genug hätte, A, vn, 3 va, bc, D-B; Lamentatio: Wie bist du denn, O Gott, ed. in DTB, x, Jg.vi/1 (1905), attrib. J. P. Krieger; Dialogue, Herr, wende dich, 4vv, 2 vn, 2 va, bc, D-B; Dialogue, Meine Freundin, du bist schön (wedding piece), 4vv, 4 vn, 3 va, bc, ed. in EDM, 1st ser., ii (1935)

INSTRUMENTAL

Aria Eberliniana [15 variations], hpd, ed. C. Freyse, Veröffentlichungen der Neuen Bachgesellschaft, Jg.xxxix/2 (1940)

Sarabande, G [12 variations], hpd, ed. H. Riemann (Leipzig, n.d.)

Aria, a [15 variations], hpd, lost

Praeludium und Fuge, Eb, org, ed. D. Hellmann, *Orgelwerke der Familie Bach* (Leipzig, 1967)

44 chorales with preludes, org, ed. M. Fischer (Kassel, 1936)

BIBLIOGRAPHY

M. Schneider: 'Thematisches Verzeichnis der musikalischen Werke der Familie Bach', *BJb*, iv (1907), 132–77

M. Fischer: *Die organistische Improvisation bei Johann Christoph Bach* (Kassel, 1928)

F. Rollberg: 'Johann Christoph Bach: Organist zu Eisenach 1665–1703', *ZMw*, xi (1929), 945

C. Freyse: 'Johann Christoph Bach', *BJb*, xliii (1956), 36

R. Benecke: 'Bach, Johann Christoph', *MGG*

(3) Johann Michael Bach (*14*) (*b* Arnstadt, baptized 9 Aug 1648; *d* Gehren, 17 May 1694). Son of Heinrich Bach (*6*). He received a solid music training from his father and the Arnstadt Kantor Jonas de Fletin; the latter's influence may account for his early interest in vocal music. In 1665 he succeeded his brother (2) Johann Christoph (*13*) as organist of the Arnstadt castle chapel. After an audition on 5 October 1673 he succeeded J. Effler (who later preceded Johann Sebastian as castle organist in Weimar) as town organist in Gehren. He was also active as an instrument maker there and held the important administrative post of town clerk. On 17 October 1707 his youngest daughter, Maria Barbara (*b* Gehren, 20 Oct 1684), married her distant cousin (7) Johann Sebastian (*24*).

A pamphlet issued by the Gehren council refers to Johann Michael as a 'quiet, withdrawn and artistically well-versed subject'; within the family he was considered a 'capable composer' (*Ursprung*). As a composer, in fact, he is on almost the same level as his brother Johann Christoph. Especially in the chorale motet, the vocal form to which he almost exclusively devoted himself, he composed works of real significance. His convincing treatment of spoken declamation is particularly notable. As in his brother's music, the older, strongly homophonic style predominates; but in such works as *Sei lieber Tag willkommen* he turned to the new, freer style with melismatic passages. His works for

double chorus stand firmly in the tradition of Schütz, Scheidt and Praetorius. His vocal concertos are less extended than those of his brother, but he too favoured full-textured orchestration. His arias with obbligato instruments are particularly charming; here, as in the concertos, his use of a virtuoso solo violin part is noteworthy. His organ chorales are typical of the central German tradition of practical settings in smooth counterpoint.

WORKS

VOCAL

Arias: Ach, wie sehnlich wart ich der Zeit, S, vn, 3 va da gamba, bc; Auf, lasst uns den Herrn loben, A, vn, 3 va da gamba, bc: ed. in EDM, 1st ser., ii (1935)

Motets: Das Blut Jesu Christi, 5vv; Dem Menschen ist gesetzt einmal zu sterben, 8vv; Fürchtet euch nicht, 8vv; Halt, was du hast, 8vv; Herr, du lässest mich erfahren, 8vv; Herr, ich warte auf dein Heil, 8vv; Herr, wenn ich nur dich habe, 5vv; Ich weiss, dass mein Erlöser lebt, 5vv; Nun hab ich überwunden, 8vv; Sei lieber Tag willkommen, 6vv; Unser Leben währet siebenzig Jahr, 5vv: all ed. in EDM, 1st ser., i (1935); Ehre sei Gott in der Höhe, 8vv, ed. in DDT, xlix–l (1915); Sei nun wieder zufrieden, 8vv; Unser Leben ist ein Schatten, 9vv: both ed. F. Naue (Leipzig, n.d.)

Konzerte: Ach bleib bei uns, Herr Jesu Christ, 4vv, 2 vn, 3 va, bc; Es ist ein grosser Gewinn, S, 4 vn, bc: both ed. in EDM, 1st ser., ii (1935); see also under (4) Johann Nicolaus (*27*)

Dialogue: Liebster Jesu, hör mein Flehen, 5vv, 2 vn, 2 va, bc, ed. in EDM, 1st ser., ii (1935)

Benedictus, 5vv, *A-Wgm*, cited by Eitner

INSTRUMENTAL

72 org chorales, cited in *GerberL*, incl. Partita, Wenn wir in höchsten Nöten sein; Dies sind die heilgen zehn Gebot; Wenn mein Stündlein vorhanden ist: all ed. D. Hellmann, *Orgelwerke der Familie Bach* (Leipzig, 1967); Wo Gott, der Herr, nicht bei uns hält, D-B; Wenn wir in höchsten Nöten sein, D-B; In dich hab ich gehoffet, Herr, ed. in EDM, 1st ser., ix (1937); Nun freut euch lieben Christen gmein, D-B; Von Gott will ich nicht lassen, D-B

Ensemble sonatas, further kbd works cited in *GerberL*

BIBLIOGRAPHY

M. Schneider: 'Thematisches Verzeichnis der musikalischen Werke der Familie Bach', *BJb*, iv (1907), 109

(4) Johann Nicolaus Bach (*27*) (*b* Eisenach, 10 Oct 1669; *d* Jena, 4 Nov 1753). Son of (2) Johann Christoph Bach (*13*). After his early musical training at home, he entered the University of Jena in 1690, pursuing his musical studies with J. N. Knüpfer (son of S. Knüpfer, Kantor of the Leipzig Thomaskirche). After a journey to Italy, the purpose and duration of which is not known, he succeeded Knüpfer in 1694 as organist of the town church at Jena. The university authorities were however reluctant to allow him to act in addition as organist at the Kollegienkirche, as Knüpfer had done, and it was not until 1719 that he finally took on the double post of town and university organist. In 1703 he had refused an appointment to Eisenach as successor to his father, primarily, no doubt, because of the better salary in Jena, where he lived in modest prosperity. Possibly he was in contact with his relative Johann Georg Bernhard (*47*) during the latter's spell in Jena, 1738–9. From 1745, in consideration of his age, he was provided with an assistant. In the *Ursprung* Johann Sebastian called him 'present senior of all the Bachs still living'.

Johann Nicolaus was a skilful composer; but the small number of his extant works hardly permits a characterization of his style. There are, however, no noticeable Italianate aspects such as might have resulted from his stay in Italy. Apart from being an organist, the leader of the university's collegium musicum and a composer, he was also an instrument maker, particularly of harpsichords. Adlung called him the inventor of the Lautenklavier. As an expert on organs he supervised the reconstruction of an instrument with three manuals and 44 stops in the Kollegienkirche, 1704–6. Among his pupils was F. E. Niedt, writer of the well-known thoroughbass method.

WORKS

Mass, sopra cantilena Allein Gott in der Höh, e, 1716 [Ky–Gl], ed. V. Junk (Leipzig, 1920) [begining of Gl by J. S. Bach]
Der Jenaische Wein- und Bierrufer (student music), ed. F. Stein (Leipzig, 1921)
Konzert, Herr, wie sind deine Werke, D-B, also attrib. (3) Johann Michael (*14*)
Org chorale, Nun freut euch lieben Christen gmein, *D-Bds*
Kbd suites, cited in J. Adlung, *Anleitung zu der musikalischen Gelahrtheit* (Erfurt, 1758/*R*1953, 2/1783)

BIBLIOGRAPHY
H. Koch: 'Johann Nicolaus, der "Jenaer" Bach', *Mf*, xxi (1968), 290

(5) Johann Bernhard Bach (*18*) (*b* Erfurt, baptized 25 Nov 1676; *d* Eisenach, 11 June 1749). Son of Johann Aegidius Bach (*8*). He studied with his father and about 1695 took up his first post, as organist at the Kaufmannskirche in Erfurt; he then went to Magdeburg, and in 1703 he replaced his uncle (2) Johann Christoph (*13*) as town organist and court harpsichordist in Eisenach, where he occasionally worked under Telemann. Repeated rises in salary show the esteem in which he was held, particularly at court. His pupils included J. G. Walther.

His only extant works are instrumental; some of the organ works are in copies by Walther. Johann Sebastian Bach evidently valued his orchestral suites, for he had four of them copied (he himself was involved in some of the copying) for his collegium musicum in Leipzig. The obituary notice of 1754 says that Johann Bernhard 'composed many beautiful overtures in the manner of Telemann', no doubt particularly referring to his use, in the French tradition, of programmatic movement titles.

WORKS

4 ovs., orch: g, ed. A. Fareanu (Leipzig, 1920); G; e; D, ed. K. Geiringer, *Music of the Bach Family* (Cambridge, Mass., 1955): all *D-Bds*
Org works: fugue, F, ed. H. Riemann (Leipzig, n.d.); fugue, D, ed. A. G. Ritter, *Zur Geschichte des Orgelspiels*, ii (Leipzig, 1884) [ed. G. Frotscher as *Geschichte des Orgel-Spiels und der Orgel-Komposition* (Berlin, 1935–6, enlarged 3/1966)]; Chaconne, B♭
Org chorales: Du Friedefürst, Herr Jesu Christ; Vom Himmel hoch: both ed. D. Hellmann, *Orgelwerke der Familie Bach* (Leipzig, 1967); Christ lag in Todesbanden; Nun freut euch lieben Christen: both ed. in EDM, 1st ser., ix (1937); Wir glauben all an einen Gott [3 versions]; Jesus, Jesus, nichts als Jesus

BIBLIOGRAPHY
H. Kühn: 'Vier Organisten Eisenachs aus Bachischem Geschlecht', *Bach in Thüringen: Gabe der Thüringer Kirche* (Berlin, 1950)
S. Orth: 'Zu den Erfurter Jahren Johann Bernard Bachs (1676–1749)', *BJb*, lvii (1971), 106

(6) Johann Ludwig Bach (*3/72*) (*b* Thal, nr. Eisenach, 4 Feb 1677; *d* Meiningen, buried 1 March 1731). Son of Johann Jacob Bach (*3/68*). Nothing is known of his musical training, although he may have received some early instruction from his father; he attended the Gotha Gymnasium, 1688–93, and then began to study theology. From 1699 he was a court musician at Meiningen, from 1703 Kantor and from 1711 court Kapellmeister. In 1706 he had unsuccessfully applied to succeed A. C. Dedekind as Kantor of St George's, Eisenach, although he had been interested only in the musical and not the teaching duties of the post. His lifelong patron Duke Ernst Ludwig died in 1724 and Johann Ludwig wrote the music for his funeral.

Johann Ludwig wrote an imposing number of vocal works. Although orchestral music was probably his principal activity from 1711 onwards, hardly any material is extant. The preservation of the cantatas is due entirely to Johann Sebastian, who performed 18 of them, as well as the two masses, in Leipzig in 1726; some were given again between 1735 and 1750. *Denn du wirst meine Seele* was long considered an early work by Johann Sebastian (BWV15). The cantatas constitute the most significant part of Johann Ludwig's work; in contrast with the main corpus of Johann Sebastian's cantatas, they represent the older type of mixed cantata, before Neumeister, which consists essentially of biblical text and chorale, in the following scheme: text from the Old Testament; recitative; aria; text from the New Testament; aria; recitative; chorus; chorale. The standard scoring is for four-part choir, strings and (usually) two oboes; in one cantata two horns are required, but there are no solo woodwind. These works had at least some small influence on Johann Sebastian, for example in his use of strings to the words of Jesus.

WORKS

19 cantatas, all *D-B*: Gott ist unser Zuversicht; Der Gottlosen Arbeit wird fehlen; Darum will ich auch erwählen; Darum säet euch Gerechtigkeit; Ja, nun hast du Arbeit gemacht; Wie lieblich sind auf den Bergen; Ich will meinen Geist in auch geben; Die mit Tränen säen, ed. H. Hornung and M. G. Schneider (Stuttgart, 1976); Mache dich auf, werde Licht; Es ist aus der Angst und Gericht; Er machet uns lebendig; Und ich will ihnen einen einigen Hirten erwecken; Der Herr wird ein neues im Land erschaffen; Die Weisheit kommt nicht in eine boshafte Seele; Durch sein Erkenntnis; Ich aber ging für dir über; Siehe ich will meinen Engel senden; Denn du wirst meine Seele nicht in der Hölle lassen, BWV15, ed. in Johann Sebastian Bachs Werke, ii (Leipzig, 1851); Klingt vergnügt (secular cantata)
7 motets: Die richtig für sich gewandelt haben, 10vv; Gedenke meiner, mein Gott, 8vv; Gott sei mir gnädig, 9vv; Ich will auf den Herrn schauen, 8vv; Sei nun wieder zufrieden, 8vv, ed. in Cw, xcix (1964); Uns ist ein Kind geboren, 8vv (Leipzig, 1930); Unser Trübsal, 6vv, ed. in Cw, xcix (1964)
Magnificat, 8vv
Mass, g [Ky–Gl], BWVAnh.166, ed. V. Junk (Leipzig, n.d.); Mass, c [Ky–Gl; Christe by J. S. Bach, BWV242], BWV Anh.26, *D-Bds*
Funeral music, Ich suche nur das Himmelleben, 1724, ed. K. Geiringer, *Music of the Bach Family* (Cambridge, Mass., 1955)
Funeral music, O Herr, ich bin, *Bds*
Passion: cantata cycle for 1713: lost, cited in S. Kümmerle, *Encyklopädie der evangelischen Kirchenmusik*, i (Gütersloh, 1888/*R*1974), 67
Ov., orch, G, 1715 (Vienna, 1939)

BIBLIOGRAPHY
A. Dörffel: 'Verzeichnis der Kirchenkompositionen des Johann Ludwig Bach in Meiningen', *Johann Sebastian Bachs Werke*, xli (1894), 275
A. M. Jaffé: *The Cantatas of Johann Ludwig Bach* (diss., Boston U., 1957)
W. H. Scheide: 'Johann Sebastian Bachs Sammlung von Kantaten seines Vetters Johann Ludwig Bach', *BJb*, xlvi (1959), 52–94; xlviii (1961), 5; xlix (1962), 5

(7) Johann Sebastian Bach (*24*) (*b* Eisenach, 21 March 1685; *d* Leipzig, 28 July 1750). The most important member of the family. His genius combined outstanding performing musicianship with supreme creative powers in which forceful original inventiveness and intellectual control are perfectly balanced. While it was in the former capacity, as a virtuoso, that in his lifetime he acquired an almost legendary fame, it is the latter virtues and accomplishments, as a composer, that have earned him a unique historical position. His art was of an encyclopedic nature, drawing together and surmounting the techniques, the styles and the general achievements of his own and earlier generations and leading on to new perspectives which later ages have received and understood in a great variety of ways.

The first authentic posthumous account of his life, with a summary catalogue of his works, was put together by his son Carl Philipp Emanuel and his pupil J. F. Agricola before March 1751 (published as *Nekrolog*, 1754). J. N. Forkel planned a detailed Bach biography in the early 1770s and carefully collected first-hand information on Bach, chiefly from his two eldest sons; the book appeared in 1802, by when the BACH REVIVAL had begun and various projected collected editions of Bach's works were under way; it continues to serve, together with the 1754 obituary and the other 18th-century documents, as the foundation of Bach biography.

1. Childhood. 2. Lüneburg. 3. Arnstadt. 4. Mühlhausen. 5. Weimar. 6. Cöthen. 7. Leipzig: 1723–9. 8. Leipzig: 1729–39. 9. Leipzig: 1739–50. 10. Iconography. 11. Sources, repertory. 12. Background, style, influences. 13. Cantatas. 14. Oratorios, Passions, Latin works. 15. Motets, chorales, songs. 16. Organ music. 17. Harpsichord and lute music. 18. Orchestral music. 19. Chamber music. 20. Canons, 'Musical Offering', 'Art of Fugue'. 21. Methods of composition.

1. CHILDHOOD. Johann Sebastian's parents were Johann Ambrosius Bach (*11*) and Maria Elisabeth Lämmerhirt (1644–94), daughter of a furrier and respected citizen of Erfurt, Valentin Lämmerhirt (*d* 1665). Another Lämmerhirt daughter became the mother of Bach's cousin J. G. Walther, suggesting that Lämmerhirt blood was perhaps not unimportant for the musical talents of the Bach family's greatest son. Ambrosius and Elisabeth were married on 8 April 1668, and had eight children. Sebastian, the last, was one of the four (three sons, nos.*22*, *71* and *23*, and one daughter, Maria Salome) who did not die young. The date of his birth was carefully recorded by Walther in his *Lexicon*, by Sebastian himself in the family genealogy, and by his son as the co-author of the obituary. It is supported by the date of baptism (23 March; these dates are old style) in the register of the Georgenkirche. His godfathers were Johann Georg Koch, a forestry official, and Sebastian Nagel, a Gotha Stadtpfeifer. The house of his birth no longer stands; it is not the handsome old structure (Frauenplan 21) acquired by the Neue Bachgesellschaft in 1907 as the 'Bachhaus' and established as a Bach Museum.

Like Luther, also an Eisenach boy, Sebastian attended the Lateinschule, which offered a sound humanistic and theological education. He probably entered in spring 1692. At Easter 1693 he was 47th in the fifth class, having been absent 96 hours; in 1694 he lost 59 hours, but rose to 14th and was promoted; at Easter 1695 he was 23rd in the fourth class, in spite of having lost 103 hours (perhaps owing to the deaths of his parents as much as to illness). He stood one or two places above his brother Jacob, who was three years older and less frequently absent. Nothing more is known about his Eisenach career; but he is said to have been an unusually good treble and probably sang under Kantor A. C. Dedekind at the Georgenkirche, where his father made instrumental music before and after the sermon and where his relation (2) Johann Christoph Bach (*13*) was organist. His musical education is matter for conjecture; presumably his father taught him the rudiments of string playing, but (according to Emanuel) he did not study keyboard instruments until he went to Ohrdruf. He later described Johann Christoph as 'a profound composer'; no doubt he was impressed by the latter's organ playing as well as by his compositions.

Elisabeth Bach was buried on 3 May 1694, and on 27 November Ambrosius married Barbara Margaretha, née Keul (daughter of a former mayor of Arnstadt, and already twice widowed). He died, however, on 20 February 1695. On 4 March the widow appealed to the town council for help; but she received only her legal due, and the household broke up. Sebastian and Jacob were taken in by their elder brother Johann Christoph (*22*), organist at Ohrdruf.

Both were sent to the Lyceum. Jacob left at the age of 14 to be apprenticed to his father's successor at Eisenach; Sebastian stayed on until 1700, when he was nearly 15, and thus came under the influence of an exceptionally enlightened curriculum. Inspired by the educationist Comenius, it embraced religion, reading, writing, arithmetic, singing, history and natural science. Sebastian entered the fourth class probably about March 1695, and was promoted to the third in July: on 20 July 1696 he was first among the seven new boys and fourth in the class; on 19 July 1697 he was first, and was promoted to the second class; on 13 July 1698 he was fifth; on 24 July 1699 second, and promoted to the first class, in which he was fourth when he left for Lüneburg on 15 March 1700. It has been claimed that he was always a year or so younger than the average for his class; but the register nowhere gives his age correctly, and may be equally untrustworthy over the others, so this remains uncertain.

In the obituary, Emanuel stated that his father had his first keyboard lessons from Christoph, at Ohrdruf; in 1775, replying to Forkel, he said that Christoph might have trained him 'simply as an organist', and that Sebastian became 'a pure and strong fuguist' through his own efforts. That is likely enough; Christoph is not known to have been a composer. Several biographers have told the story of how Christoph would not allow his brother to use a certain manuscript; how Sebastian copied it by moonlight; how Christoph took the copy away from him; and how he did not recover it until Christoph died. Emanuel and Forkel assumed that Christoph died in 1700, and that Sebastian, left homeless, went to Lüneburg in desperation. Later authors, knowing that Christoph lived on until 1721, and that the brothers had been on good terms, have tended to reject the story – perhaps unnecessarily, for it may illustrate contemporary attitudes to discipline and restraint. In fact, the story fits in well with the little that is known of the Ohrdruf years, and with the idea that Sebastian taught himself composition by copying. Most probably he recovered his copy when he went to Lüneburg. As for its contents, Forkel implied that it contained works by seven named composers, three of them northerners. He probably misunderstood Emanuel's reply to one of his questions; according to the obituary, the manuscript was exclusively southern (Froberger, Kerll, Pachelbel) – as one would expect, since Johann Christoph had been a Pachelbel pupil. The larger of the two organs at Ohrdruf was in almost unplayable condition in 1697, and Sebastian no doubt picked up some of his expert knowledge of organ building while helping his brother with repairs.

2. LÜNEBURG. According to the school register, he left 'ob defectum hospitiorum'. This has been taken to mean 'for lack of a free place', but it is simpler to suppose that Christoph no longer had room for his brother. Since the latter's arrival, he had had two children; by March 1700 a third was expected; and (if local tradition can be trusted) his house, now destroyed, was a mere cottage. The brothers' problem seems to have been solved by Elias Herda, Kantor and a master at the Lyceum. He had been educated at Lüneburg, and no doubt it was he who arranged for Sebastian to go north; probably he similarly helped Georg Erdmann, a fellow pupil of

Sebastian's, three years older, who left the school just before Bach (for the same reason) and who may have been his travelling companion – both were at Lüneburg on 3 April 1700.

The Michaeliskirche, Lüneburg, had two schools associated with it: a Ritteracademie for young noblemen, and the Michaelisschule for commoners. There were also two choirs: the 'chorus symphoniacus' of about 25 voices was led by the Mettenchor (Matins choir), which numbered about 15, and was limited to poor boys with good voices. Members of the Mettenchor, which Bach and Erdmann joined, received free schooling at the Michaelisschule, up to one thaler per month according to seniority, their keep, and a share in fees for weddings and other occasions (Bach's share in 1700 has been put at 14 marks). From the arrangement of the pay-sheets it has been deduced that they were both trebles. Bach was welcomed for his unusually fine voice; but it soon broke, and for eight days he spoke and sang in octaves. After that he may or may not have sung, but no doubt he made himself useful as an accompanist or string player. As the last extant pay-sheet is that for 29 May 1700, no details are known; but it is clear that the school was short of instrumentalists at just this time.

At school, Bach's studies embraced orthodox Lutheranism, Latin, arithmetic, history, geography, genealogy, heraldry, German poetry and physics. The Kantor was August Braun, whose compositions have disappeared; the organist, F. C. Morhard, was a nonentity. The organ was repaired in 1701 by J. B. Held, who had worked at Hamburg and Lübeck; he lodged in the school, and may have helped Bach to study organ building. There was a fine music library, which had been carefully kept up to date; but whether choirboys were allowed to consult it is uncertain. If Braun made good use of it, Bach must have learnt a good deal from the music he had to perform; but his chief interests probably lay outside the school. At the Nikolaikirche was J. J. Löwe (1629–1703), distinguished but elderly. The Johanniskirche was another matter, for there the organist was Georg Böhm (1661–1733), who is generally agreed to have influenced Bach. It has been argued that the organist of the Johanniskirche would not have been accessible to a scholar of the Michaelisschule, since the two choirs were not on good terms, and that Bach's knowledge of Böhm's music must have come later, through J. G. Walther. But Emanuel Bach stated in writing that his father had studied Böhm's music; and a correction shows that his first thought was to say that Böhm had been his father's teacher. This hint is supported by the fact that in 1727 Bach named Böhm as his northern agent for the sale of Partitas nos.2 and 3. That seems to imply that the two were on friendly terms; it is likelier that they became so between 1700 and 1702 than at any later date.

Bach went more than once to Hamburg, some 50 km away; probably he visited his cousin Johann Ernst (25), who is said to have been studying there about this time. The suggestion that he went to hear Vincent Lübeck cannot be taken seriously, for Lübeck did not go to Hamburg until August 1702, by which time Bach had almost certainly left the area. He may have visited the Hamburg Opera, then directed by Reinhard Keiser, whose St Mark Passion he performed during the early Weimar years and again in 1726; but there is no solid evidence that he was interested in anything but the organ and organist of the Catharinenkirche. Marpurg's

familiar anecdote makes the point neatly: how Bach, returning almost penniless to Lüneburg, once rested outside an inn; how someone threw two herring heads out on the rubbish heap; how Bach – a Thuringian, to whom fish were a delicacy – picked them up to see if any portion were edible; how he found that they contained two Danish ducats, and was thus able not only to have a meal, but also 'to undertake another and a more comfortable pilgrimage to Herr Reincken'.

J. A. Reincken (1623–1722), a pupil of Sweelinck and organist of the Catharinenkirche since 1663, was a father figure of the north German school. Böhm may have advised Bach to hear him; and his showy playing, exploiting all the resources of the organ, must have been a revelation to one brought up in the reticent tradition of the south. As for the organ itself, Bach never forgot it; in later years he described it as excellent in every way, said that the 32′ Principal was the best he had ever heard, and never tired of praising the 16′ reeds. Whether he actually met Reincken before 1720 is uncertain. If he did, Reincken might have given him a copy of his sonatas; Bach's reworkings of them (the keyboard pieces BWV954, 965 and 966) are more likely to have been made soon after 1700 than 20 years later, when Bach no longer needed to teach himself composition. Some 80 km south of Lüneburg lay Celle, seat of a duke who had acquired a Parisian veneer and maintained an orchestra consisting largely of Frenchmen. Bach had access to this household, but how, and in what capacity, is not known. He must have had a friend at court, and that friend could have been Thomas de la Selle, who was a member of the orchestra and also dancing-master at the Ritteracademie, next door to Bach's school in Lüneburg. Emanuel Bach knew only that his father had 'heard' this French music; but perhaps de la Selle took him to Celle as a performer.

The date of Bach's departure from Lüneburg is not recorded, and the reason for it is not known; but that reason must have been urgent, for he left without hearing Buxtehude, and took extraordinary pains to do so in winter 1705–6. All that is definitely known is that the organist of the Jakobikirche, Sangerhausen, was buried on 9 July 1702, and that Bach competed successfully for the post, but the Duke of Weissenfels intervened and had J. A. Kobelius, an older man, appointed in November. Bach is next heard of on 4 March 1703 at Weimar, when he was paid as a lackey; in the Ursprung he described himself as a court musician. This was at the minor Weimar court, that of Duke Johann Ernst, younger brother of the Duke Wilhelm Ernst whom Bach served from 1708 to 1717. Possibly the Duke of Weissenfels, having refused to accept Bach at Sangerhausen, found work for him at Weimar; also possible is that Bach owed his appointment to his distant relation David Hoffmann, another lackey–musician.

Of the musicians with whom Bach now became associated, three are worth mentioning. G. C. Strattner (c1644–1704), a tenor, became vice-Kapellmeister in 1695, and composed in a post-Schütz style. J. P. von Westhoff (1656–1705) was a fine violinist and had travelled widely, apparently as a diplomat, and is said to have been the first to compose a suite for unaccompanied violin (1683). J. Effler (c1640–1711) was the court organist: he had held posts at Gehren and Erfurt (where Pachelbel was his successor) before coming in 1678 to Weimar, where about 1690 he moved to the court. He may have been willing to hand over some of his duties to Bach, and probably did something of the kind, for a document of 13 July 1703 at Arnstadt, where Bach next moved, describes Bach as court organist at Weimar – a post that was not officially his until 1708.

3. ARNSTADT. The Bonifaciuskirche at Arnstadt had been burnt out in 1581, and rebuilt in 1676–83; it then became known as the Neukirche, and so remained until 1935, when it was renamed after Bach. In 1699 J. F. Wender contracted to build an organ, which by the end of 1701 had become usable; on 1 January 1702 Andreas Börner was formally appointed organist. The organ was complete by June 1703, and was examined before 3 July; there were more examiners than one, but only Bach was named and paid, and it was he who 'played the organ for the first time'. The result was that on 9 August Bach was offered the post over Börner's head; at the same time, 'to prevent any such "collisions" as are to be feared', Börner was given other work. Bach accepted the post 'by handshake' on 14 August 1703. The exact date of his removal to Arnstadt is not known, nor is his address. As his last board and lodging allowance was paid to Feldhaus, he probably spent at least that year in either the Golden Crown or the Steinhaus, both of which belonged to Feldhaus. Considering his age, and local standards, he was well paid; and his duties, as specified in his contract, were light. Normally, he was required at the church only for two hours on Sunday morning, for a service on Monday, and for two hours on Thursday morning; and he had only to accompany hymns. He thus had plenty of time for composition and organ playing, and he took as his models Bruhns, Reincken, Buxtehude (all northerners) and certain good French organists. There is no evidence as to whether he took part in the theatrical and musical entertainments of the court or the town.

The *Capriccio sopra la lontananza del suo fratello dilettissimo* was presumably written when Bach's brother Jacob went to Poland, to be an oboist in the army of Charles XII of Sweden. It has been suggested that this was in 1706, when the army came nearest to Thuringia; but the date given in the *Ursprung* is 1704, and that seems to have Bach's authority. 1703 is perhaps more likely still. When making biographical notes, about 1735, Bach may have remembered only that his brother left in the year when he himself went to Arnstadt; he dated his own appointment 1704 and may also have been wrong about his brother's departure.

Bach was in no position to put on elaborate music at Arnstadt. The Neukirche, like the other churches, drew performers from two groups of schoolboys and senior students. Only one of these groups was capable of singing cantatas; it was supposed to go to the Neukirche monthly in the summer, but there does not appear to have been a duty roster. The performers naturally tended to go to the churches that had an established tradition and friendly organists; and Bach had no authority to prevent this, for he was not a schoolmaster and was younger than many of the students. Further, he never had much patience with the semi-competent, and was apt to alienate them by making offensive remarks. One result was his scuffle with J. H. Geyersbach (*b* 1682). On 4 August 1704 he and his cousin Barbara, elder sister (aged 26) to his future wife, fell in with six students who had been to a christening feast; one of these was Geyersbach, who asked why Bach had

insulted him (or his bassoon), and struck him in the face with a stick. Bach drew his sword, but another student separated them. Bach complained to the consistory that it would be unsafe for him to go about the streets if Geyersbach were not punished, and an inquiry was held. The consistory told Bach that he ought not to have insulted Geyersbach and should try to live peaceably with the students; further, he was not (as he claimed) responsible only for the chorales but was expected to help with all kinds of music. Bach replied that if a musical director were appointed, he would be willing enough.

Bach, unimpressed, asked for four weeks' leave, and set off for Lübeck – 'what is more, on foot', says the obituary, adding that he had an overwhelming desire to hear Buxtehude. Dates and distance cast some doubts on his straightforwardness. He left Arnstadt about 18 October, and was therefore due to be back, or well on his way back, by about 15 November; he would thus have been unable to hear even the first of Buxtehude's special services, which were given on various dates from 15 November to 20 December. Perhaps, like Mattheson and Handel before him, he went primarily to see if there was any chance of succeeding Buxtehude, and was put off by the prospect of marrying Buxtehude's daughter, aged 30; in any case, by 1705 there was a rival in the field. However that may be, he stayed almost three months at Lübeck, and was absent altogether for about 16 weeks, not returning to Arnstadt until shortly before 7 February 1706, when he communicated.

On 21 February the consistory asked Bach why he had been away for so long; his replies were unsatisfactory and barely civil. They next complained that his accompaniments to chorales were too elaborate for congregational singing, and that he still refused to collaborate with the students in producing cantatas; further, they could not provide a Kapellmeister for him, and if he continued to refuse they would have to find someone more amenable. Bach repeated his demand for a musical director, and was ordered to declare himself within eight days. From the next case that the consistory heard that day it seems that there had been actual 'disordres' in the church between Bach and the students. There is no evidence that Bach declared himself, and the consistory dropped the matter for eight months. They brought it up again on 11 November, and Bach undertook to answer them in writing. They also accused him of inviting a 'stranger maiden' to make music in the church, but for this he had obtained the parson's permission; presumably the girl was his cousin and future wife, and she had simply sung to his accompaniment for practice.

Neither Bach nor the consistory took further action; no doubt they saw that the problem would soon solve itself. Probably Bach had come back from Lübeck with exalted ideas about church music, requiring facilities that Arnstadt could not provide. His ability was becoming known; on 28 November he helped to examine an organ at Langewiesen. Forkel said that various posts were offered to him; and with the death of J. G. Ahle, on 2 December, a sufficiently attractive vacancy seemed to have arisen.

4. MÜHLHAUSEN. Ahle had been something of a composer, a city councillor of Mühlhausen and organist of the church of St Blasius. Standards had fallen during his tenure of office, but the post was a respectable one and various candidates gave trial performances. One was to

have been J. G. Walther, the future lexicographer; he sent in two compositions for 27 February 1707 (Sexagesima), but withdrew after being told privately that he had no hope. Bach played at Easter (24 April) and may have produced Cantata no.4. At the city council meeting on 24 May no other name was considered, and on 14 June Bach was interviewed. He asked for the same salary that he was receiving at Arnstadt (some 20 gulden more than Ahle's); the councillors agreed, and an agreement was signed on 15 May. At Arnstadt, his success became known; his cousin Johann Ernst (25) and his predecessor Börner applied for the Neukirche on 22 and 23 June. He resigned formally on 29 June, and presumably moved to Mühlhausen within a few days. It was perhaps in July that he wrote Cantata no.131; this was clearly intended for a penitential service, perhaps connected with a disastrous fire of 30 May. It was not Bach's own Pastor Frohne who commissioned this cantata, but Pastor Eilmar of St Mary's; a fact whose possible significance will be seen later.

On 10 August Tobias Lämmerhirt, Bach's maternal uncle, died at Erfurt; it is reasonable to suppose that Cantata no.106 was performed at his funeral on 14 August. Tobias left Bach 50 gulden, more than half his salary, and thus facilitated his marriage to Maria Barbara (b 20 Oct 1684), daughter of (3) Johann Michael Bach (14) and Catharina Wedemann. The wedding took place on 17 October at Dornheim, a village near Arnstadt; the pastor, J. L. Stauber (1660–1723), was a friend of the family and himself married Regina Wedemann on 5 June 1708.

Pupils began to come to Bach at about this time, or perhaps even earlier. J. M. Schubart (1690–1721) is said to have been with him from 1707 to 1717, and J. C. Vogler (1696–1763) to have arrived at the age of ten (at Arnstadt), to have left for a time, and to have returned from about 1710 until 1715. These two were his immediate successors at Weimar; from their time onwards he was never without pupils.

On 4 February 1708 the annual change of council took place, and Cantata no.71 was performed. It must have made an impression, for the council printed not only the libretto, as was usual, but also the music. Bach next drew up a plan for repairing and enlarging the St Blasius organ; the council considered this on 21 February, and decided to act on it. Cantata no.196 may have been written for Stauber's wedding on 5 June. At about this time Bach played before the reigning Duke of Weimar, Wilhelm Ernst, who offered him a post at his court. On 25 June Bach wrote to the council asking them to accept his resignation.

No doubt the larger salary at Weimar was an attraction, particularly as Bach's wife was pregnant. But it is clear, even from his tactful letter to these councillors who had treated him well, that there were other reasons for leaving. He said that he had encouraged 'well-regulated church music' not only in his own church, but also in the surrounding villages, where the harmony was often 'better-fashioned' (Spitta found a fragment, BWV223, at nearby Langula). He had also gone to some expense to collect 'the choicest sacred music'. But in all this members of his own congregation had opposed him, and were not likely to stop. Some people no doubt disliked the type of music that he was trying to introduce. Further, Pastor Frohne may have distrusted his organist; an active Pietist, he was at daggers drawn with the orthodox Pastor Eilmar of St Mary's – Bach

had begun his Mühlhausen career by working with Eilmar, and they had become intimate enough for Eilmar and his daughter to be godparents to Bach's first two children.

The council considered his letter on 26 June and reluctantly let him go, asking him only to supervise the organ building at St Blasius. However badly Bach may have got on with his congregation, he was evidently on good terms with the council. They paid him to come and perform a cantata at the council service in 1709, and possibly also in 1710 (all trace of these works is lost). In 1735 he negotiated on friendly terms with the new council on behalf of his son Johann Gottfried Bernhard (47). He is not known to have been paid for supervising or opening the St Blasius organ, but he may have done so.

5. WEIMAR. When resigning from Mühlhausen, Bach said that he had been appointed to the Duke of Weimar's 'Capelle und Kammermusik'; and it was long thought that he did not become organist at once. In fact, Weimar documents show that on 14 July 1708, when his 'reception money' was paid over, he was called 'the newly appointed court organist', and that he was almost always so called until March 1714, when he became Konzertmeister as well. Effler, it seems, was pensioned off on full salary (130 florins); on 24 December 1709 he received a small gift as 'an old sick servant', and he died at Jena on 4 April 1711.

It is said that Bach wrote most of his organ works at Weimar, and that the duke took pleasure in his playing. His salary was from the outset larger than Effler's (150 florins, plus some allowances); it was increased to 200 from Michaelmas 1711, 215 from June 1713, and 250 on his promotion in 1714. On 20 March 1715 it was ordered that his share of casual fees was to be the same as the Kapellmeister's. Moreover, he seems to have had a fair amount of spare time, in which, for instance, to cultivate the acquaintance of Telemann while the latter was at Eisenach (1708–12).

Six of Bach's children were born at Weimar: Catharina (baptized 29 Dec 1708; d 14 Jan 1774); (8) Wilhelm Friedemann (45) (b 22 Nov 1710); twins (b 23 Feb 1713; both died in a few days); (9) Carl Philipp Emanuel (46) (b 8 March 1714); and Johann Gottfried Bernhard (47) (b 11 May 1715). The various godparents show that Bach and his wife kept in touch with relations and friends from Ohrdruf, Arnstadt and Mühlhausen, besides making fresh contacts at Weimar; it is noteworthy that Telemann was godfather to Emanuel.

On 13 March 1709 Bach, his wife, and one of her sisters (probably the eldest, Friedelena, who died at Leipzig in 1729) were living with Adam Immanuel Weldig, a falsettist and Master of the Pages. They probably stayed there until August 1713, when Weldig gave up his house, having secured a similar post at Weissenfels. Weldig was godfather to Emanuel; Bach (by proxy) to a son of Weldig's in 1714. Weldig's house was destroyed in 1944; where Bach lived before and after the given dates is not known.

Since 29 July 1707, J. G. Walther (the lexicographer) had been organist of the Stadtkirche; he was related to Bach through his mother, a Lämmerhirt, and the two became friendly. On 27 September 1712 Bach stood godfather to Walther's son. Forkel told a story of how Walther played a trick on Bach, to cure him of boasting that there was nothing he could not read at sight. Their relations did not deteriorate, as Spitta supposed; in 1735 Bach negotiated on Walther's behalf with the Leipzig publisher J. G. Krügner, and Walther's references to Bach in his letters to Bokemeyer carry no suggestion of any coolness. From one such letter it seems that during his nine years at Weimar Bach gave Walther some 200 pieces of music, some by Buxtehude, others compositions of his own.

Of Bach's pupils, Schubart and Vogler have already been mentioned. The pupil for whom Bach was paid by Ernst August's account in 1711–12 was not Duke Ernst August himself but a page called Jagemann. J. G. Ziegler (1688–1747) matriculated at the University of Halle on 12 October 1712, but before that he had studied with Bach for a year or so, and had been taught to play chorales 'not just superficially, but according to the sense of the words'; Bach's wife stood godmother to his daughter in 1718, and in 1727 Bach employed him as agent, in Halle, for Partitas nos.2 and 3. P. D. Kräuter of Augsburg (1690–1741) set out for Weimar in March 1712, and stayed until about September 1713. Johann Lorenz Bach (38) probably arrived in autumn 1713; he may have left Weimar by July 1717. Johann Tobias Krebs (1690–1762) studied with Walther from 1710, with Bach from about 1714 until 1717. Johann Bernhard Bach (41) worked with his uncle from about 1715 until March 1719, alongside Samuel Gmelin (1695–1752), who appears to have left in 1717. C. H. Dretzel of Nuremberg (1697–1775) may have been briefly with Bach. In 1731, when applying for a post, T. C. Gerlach (1694–1768) implied that Bach had been teaching him by correspondence for 14 years, but his confused phraseology should not be taken literally.

The specification of the organ in the castle chapel, published in 1737, has not always been reprinted correctly; in any case, it does not represent the organ that Bach left in 1717. Extensive alterations were made in 1719–30. Still less does the specification represent the organ that Bach was faced with in 1708, for he himself had made even more extensive alterations in 1713–14. The organ is said to have been built by Compenius in 1657–8. It was overhauled in 1707–8, and a sub-bass added, by J. C. Weishaupt, who carried out further maintenance work in 1712. A contract for alterations had however been signed on 29 June 1712 with H. N. Trebs (1678–1748), who had moved from Mühlhausen to Weimar in 1709. Bach and he had worked together on a new organ at Taubach in 1709–10, opened by Bach on 26 October 1710; in 1711 he gave Trebs a handsome testimonial, and in 1713 he and Walther became godfathers to Trebs's son. Bach and Trebs collaborated again about 1742, over an organ at Bad Berka. Trebs's new organ was usable during 1714; he had done 14 days' tuning in 19 May, and was paid off on 15 September. Of this rebuild nothing is known, except that either Bach or the duke was determined that the instrument include a glockenspiel; great trouble was taken over obtaining bells from dealers in Nuremberg and Leipzig, and it seems that the original set of 29 (a number hard to account for) had to be replaced because of difficulties over blend and pitch. In 1737 the organ had a glockenspiel on the *Oberwerk*, but alterations had been made in 1719–20 and it does not follow that the glockenspiel of 1714 was on a manual.

In December 1709 and February 1710 Bach was paid for repairing harpsichords in the household of the junior dukes, Ernst August and Johann Ernst. On 17 January 1711 he became godfather to a daughter of J. C. Becker, a local burgher. In February 1711 Duke Johann Ernst went to the University of Utrecht. From 21 February 1713 Bach was lodged in the castle at Weissenfels. Duke Christian's birthday fell on 23 February, and it is now thought that Cantata no.208 was performed in this year, not in 1716. The earlier date is stylistically suitable; moreover, it is compatible both with the watermark of the autograph score, and with the fact that in this score Bach contradicted sharps by flats rather than by naturals – an old-fashioned habit that he gave up progressively during 1714.

About May 1713 the young duke returned from Utrecht, apparently with a good deal of music, for in the year from 1 June there were bills for binding, copying and shelving (some of the music came from Halle). In February 1713 he had been in Amsterdam, and may have met the blind organist J. J. de Graff who was in the habit of playing recent Italian concertos as keyboard solos. This may have given rise to the numerous concerto arrangements made by Walther and Bach.

On 7 September 1713 Bach was probably at Ohrdruf, standing godfather to a nephew; and on 6 November he took part in the dedication of the new Jakobikirche at Weimar (there is no evidence that he composed any of the music). On 27 November he was at Weimar, as godfather to Trebs's son. At about this time he seems to have gone to Halle, perhaps to buy music, and to have become accidentally involved with the authorities of the Liebfrauenkirche. The organist there (Zachow, Handel's teacher) had died in 1712, and the organ was being enlarged to a three-manual of 65 stops. The story has to be pieced together from hints in an incomplete correspondence; but it looks as if the pastor, J. M. Heineccius, pressed Bach to apply for the vacant post. Bach composed and performed a cantata, attended a meeting on 13 December 1713, was offered the post, and let the committee suppose that he had accepted it, although he had not had time to find out what his casual fees would amount to. On 14 December they sent him a formal contract. Bach replied on 14 January 1714, saying cautiously that he had not been released from Weimar, was uneasy about his salary and duties, and would write again within the week. Whether he did so is not known; but on February the committee resolved to tell him that his salary was not likely to be increased. Thus at Halle he could expect a slightly smaller salary than he was already getting; the attraction was the organ, more than twice as large. Bach must then have approached the duke, for on 2 March, 'at his most humble request', he became Konzertmeister (ranking after the vice-Kapellmeister), with a basic salary of 250 florins from 25 February. In finally refusing the Halle post, he probably mentioned that figure, for the committee accused him of having used their offer as a lever to extract more money from the duke. This he denied on 19 March, in a letter so reasonable and so obviously honest that he remained on good terms with Halle and was employed there as an organ examiner in 1716. Gottfried Kirchhoff had meanwhile been appointed organist on 30 July 1714.

Few cantatas (apart from the secular no.208) can be ascribed to these early Weimar years. No.150 may date from 1708–9, the New Year Cantata no.143 from perhaps as late as 1714; both dates, especially the latter, are dubious. No.18 may be as early as 1713, or it may have been performed at Sexagesima in 1714, to show the duke what his organist could do. The work performed at Halle in December 1713 was formerly thought to be no.21, in an early version; but no.63 now seems just as likely. We know it as a Christmas work, but the music has no Christmas features, and the original words may have been different. As Bach seems to have spent the first half of December 1713 at Halle, he may possibly have written this work for 10 December, the second Sunday in Advent.

On 23 March 1714 it was ordered that cantatas should in future be rehearsed in the chapel, not at home or in lodgings; and on Palm Sunday, 25 March, Bach performed no.182. This was the fourth Sunday after his appointment as Konzertmeister, when he had become responsible for writing a cantata every four weeks. As he evidently hoped to complete an annual cycle in four years, he did not keep strictly to this rule; having written a cantata for Advent Sunday in 1714, he wrote for the last Sunday after Trinity in 1715, and for the second Sunday in Advent in 1716 (in 1717 he was in prison). Apart from such intentional irregularities, there are gaps in the series, and the strange thing is that these gaps became suddenly more numerous after the end of 1715. From 1717 there are no cantatas at all. A tentative explanation will be suggested for this; but it is hard to see why Bach's usual allowance of paper was paid for on 16 May 1716 when he is not known to have performed any church cantatas between 19 January and 6 December.

The young Duke Johann Ernst died at Frankfurt on 1 August 1715, and on 12 August Bach received an allowance for mourning garments (not for illness); court mourning may explain why there are no cantatas for 11 August or 8 September.

On 4 April 1716 Bach, like the librettist Salomo Franck and 'the book-printer', was paid for 'Carmina', bound in green taffeta, that had been 'presented' on some unspecified occasion; perhaps on 24 January, when Duke Ernst August had married Eleonore, sister of the Prince of Cöthen. Ernst's birthday was celebrated in April; two horn players from Weissenfels came to Weimar, possibly brought over for a repeat performance of Cantata no.208.

Meanwhile, the new organ at Halle had been making progress, and on 17 April the council resolved that Bach, Kuhnau of Leipzig and Rolle of Quedlinburg should be invited to examine it on 29 April. They all accepted; each was to receive 16 thalers, plus food and travelling expenses. The examination began at 7 a.m., and lasted three days – until some time on 1 May, when the experts wrote their report, a sermon was preached and fine music was performed. On 2 May the organist and the three examiners met the builder to discuss details. The council, who behaved liberally, gave a tremendous banquet, whose date is usually given as 3 May (1 May seems more likely).

On 31 July 1716 Bach and an Arnstadt organ builder signed a testimonial for J. G. Schröter, who had built an organ at Erfurt. In 1717 Bach was mentioned in print for the first time: in the preface to Mattheson's *Das beschützte Orchestre*, dated 21 February, Mattheson referred to Bach as 'the famous Weimar organist' saying that his works, both for the church and for keyboard, led one to rate him highly, and asked for biographical information.

It is against this background that Bach's departure from Weimar has to be considered. In 1703 he had been employed by Duke Johann Ernst; since his return in 1708, by Duke Wilhelm, Johann's elder brother. The brothers had been on bad terms, and when Johann Ernst died in 1707 and his son Ernst came of age in 1709, things became no better. For some time the ducal disagreements do not seem to have affected Bach; perhaps they were kept within bounds by Superintendent Lairitz, and Ernst's younger brother (Johann, the composer) may have had some influence. But the latter died in 1715, Lairitz on 4 April 1716, and the new superintendent certainly failed to cope with the 'court difficulties'; like the rest of Wilhelm's household, he was forbidden to associate with Ernst. The musicians, though paid by both households, were threatened with fines of ten thalers if they served Ernst in any way.

No extant Bach cantata can be securely dated between 19 January and 6 December 1716; it may seem unlikely that this long, continuous gap was due to casual losses. It is tempting to suppose that Bach found his position embarrassing (owing to his early connection with the junior court) and expressed disapproval of Duke Wilhelm's behaviour by evading his own responsibilities. In fact, Bach does not seem to have disapproved of the duke's behaviour until he discovered that a new Kapellmeister was being sought elsewhere. Drese senior died on 1 December 1716; his son, the vice-Kapellmeister, was by all accounts a nonentity. Bach produced Cantatas nos.70a, 186a and 147a on 6, 13 and 20 December (three successive weeks, not months), but there were no more, as far as is known. By Christmas, Bach may have found out that the duke was angling for Telemann. Negotiations with Telemann came to nothing; but apparently Bach now set about looking for a post as Kapellmeister. He was offered one by Prince Leopold of Cöthen, brother-in-law to Duke Ernst (Bach and the prince had probably met at Ernst's wedding in January 1716) and the appointment was confirmed on 5 August 1717. No doubt Bach then asked Duke Wilhelm's permission to leave, and no doubt he was refused – the duke being annoyed because his nephew had obviously had a hand in finding Bach a job that carried more prestige and, at 400 thalers, was better paid.

The duke and Bach must nevertheless have remained on speaking terms for the time being, for at some date hardly earlier than the end of September Bach was in Dresden and free to challenge the French keyboard virtuoso Louis Marchand. Versions of this affair differ, but according to Birnbaum (who wrote in 1739, probably under Bach's supervision), Bach 'found himself' at Dresden, and was not sent for by 'special coach'. Once there, some court official persuaded him to challenge Marchand to a contest at the harpsichord; the idea that they were to compete at the organ seems to have crept in later. Whatever may be the truth about these and other details, it is universally agreed that Marchand ran away.

On his birthday, 30 October 1717, Duke Wilhelm set up an endowment for his court musicians; and the second centenary of the Reformation was celebrated from 31 October to 2 November. Presumably Bach took part in these ceremonies, though there is no evidence that he set any of the librettos that Franck had provided. Emboldened, perhaps, by the Marchand affair, he then demanded his release in such terms that the duke had him imprisoned from 6 November until his dismissal in disgrace on 2 December. Terry's attractive idea that the *Orgel-Büchlein* was planned and partly written in prison is unfortunately untenable.

The Cöthen court had paid Bach 50 thalers on 7 August. Some have supposed that this was for travelling expenses, and that Bach had his wife and family moved to Cöthen soon after; but it seems unlikely that the duke would have allowed them to move until he had agreed to let Bach go. The younger Drese became Kapellmeister in his father's place and Bach's pupil J. M. Schubart became court organist. The post of Konzertmeister disappeared.

6. CÖTHEN. Except during the last months at Weimar, Bach had been on good terms with Duke Wilhelm; but his relations with that martinet must always have been official. At Cöthen, until the end of 1721, things were different; Prince Leopold was a young man who, as Bach himself said, loved and understood music. He was born in 1694, of a Calvinist father and a Lutheran mother. The father died in 1704, the mother ruled until Leopold came of age on 10 December 1715. There was no court orchestra until October 1707, when Leopold persuaded his mother to take on three musicians. While studying in Berlin in 1708, he met A. R. Stricker; from the end of 1710 to 1713 he was on the usual Grand Tour, during which he studied with J. D. Heinichen at Rome. He returned capable of singing bass, and of playing the violin, viola da gamba and harpsichord. The Berlin court orchestra had broken up in 1713, and from July 1714 he employed Stricker as Kapellmeister and his wife as soprano and lutenist; by 1716 he had 18 musicians. In August 1717 Stricker and his wife seem to have resigned, leaving the prince free to appoint Bach.

At Cöthen the Jakobikirche organ was in poor condition. The court chapel was Calvinist; it had an organist, but no elaborate music was performed there, and the two-manual organ had only 13 or 14 stops, though it may have had a complete chromatic compass to pedal *e'* and manual *e'''*. The Lutheran Agnuskirche had a two-manual organ of 27 stops, again with an exceptional pedal compass. There is not the slightest reason to suppose that Bach wrote any particular work to exploit these pedal compasses, but no doubt he used one or both of the organs for teaching and private practice. He communicated at the Agnuskirche, and took part in the baptisms at the court chapel, but had no official duties in either. He may, however, have been involved in the affair of May 1719, when a cantata was put on for the dedication festival of the Agnuskirche, and 150 copies of (presumably) the libretto were printed. The printer's bill for one thaler and eight groschen was endorsed by the pastor: 'The churchwardens can give him 16 groschen; if he wants more, he must go to those who gave the order'.

Bach's basic salary, 400 thalers, was twice Stricker's, and extra allowances made it up to about 450. Only one court official was paid more, and there is other evidence that Bach was held in high esteem. On 17 November 1718 the last of his children by his first wife (a short-lived son) was named after the prince, who himself was a godfather. Bach's residence in Cöthen is not definitely known, but it seems likely that he began as a tenant in Stiftstrasse 11; in 1721, when that house was bought by the prince's mother for the use of the Lutheran pastor, he moved to Holzmarkt 12. The orchestra needed a room for their weekly rehearsals; the prince supplied it by paying rent to Bach (12 thalers a year from 10 December 1717 to 1722). Presumably there was a suitable room in Bach's first house. Whether he continued to use that room after his move in 1721, and why he was not paid rent after 1722, is not clear.

The date of the first rent payments suggest that Bach and his household moved to Cöthen a day or two after he was released from prison (2 December); and that, after hasty rehearsals, he helped to celebrate the prince's birthday on 10 December. That would normally have been his duty. The court accounts suggest that something connected with the birthday was either printed or bound in 1717, as also in 1719 and 1720 (Anh.7); Bach certainly wrote a cantata in 1722, and Cantatas nos.66a and Anh.5 in 1718 (the latter was performed in church). In 1721 there may have been no birthday celebrations, for the prince was married, at Bernburg, the next day. Cantata no.173a was undoubtedly a birthday work, but Bach probably wrote it after he had left Cöthen; 36a, an arrangement of 36c (1725), was put on at Cöthen on 30 November 1726, for the birthday of the prince's second wife.

New Year cantatas also were expected. No.134a dates from 1719, Anh.6 from 1720, Anh.8 from 1723. There is no evidence for 1718, 1721 or 1722; printers' and binders' bills paid on 5 January 1722 may have been for music performed in December 1721. Bach may well have been unable to put on a wedding cantata, but there seems no reason why he should not have offered something for the prince's birthday. Nos.184 and 194 (Leipzig, 1724, and Störmthal, 1723) seem to be arrangements of Cöthen works, and so perhaps are parts of no.120. Whether or not Bach performed a cantata at Cöthen on 10 December 1717, he was at Leipzig on 16 December examining the organ at the university church (St Paul's). The work had been done by Johann Scheibe, with whose son Bach was later in dispute. Bach is not known to have done any other work of this kind while at Cöthen.

On 9 May 1718 the prince went to drink the waters at Carlsbad for about five weeks, taking with him his harpsichord, Bach and five other musicians. Early in 1719 Bach was in Berlin, negotiating for a new harpsichord. About this time he seems to have been busy composing or buying music, for between July 1719 and May 1720 some 26 thalers were spent on binding. During 1719 Handel visited his mother at Halle, only some 30 km away; it is said that Bach tried, but failed, to make contact with him. Bach also disregarded a renewed request from Mattheson for biographical material.

W. F. Bach was nine in 1719; the title-page of his *Clavier-Büchlein* is dated 22 January 1720. In May Bach again went to Carlsbad with the prince. The date of their return does not seem to have been recorded; but apparently it was after 7 July, for that was the date of Maria Barbara's funeral, and there is no reason to doubt Emanuel's story that his father returned to find her dead and already buried.

His wife had been nearly 36. Her death may well have unsettled Bach, and even led him to think of returning to the service of the church; but there was a more practical reason for his taking an interest in the Jakobikirche at Hamburg. The organist there, H. Friese, died on 12 September 1720; Bach had known Hamburg in his youth, and must have been attracted by the organ, a four-manual Schnitger with 60 stops. There is no evidence that Bach was actually invited to apply for the post; but he may well have made inquiries of his own.

At all events, his name was one of eight being considered on 21 November, and he was in Hamburg at about that time. A competition was arranged for 28 November, but Bach had had to leave for Cöthen five days before. Three candidates did not appear, and the judges were not satisfied with the other four. An approach was made to Bach, and the committee met on 12 December; as Bach's reply had not arrived, they met again a week later, when they found that Bach had refused. Perhaps he was unable, or unwilling, to contribute 4000 marks to the church funds, as the successful candidate actually did.

From the way in which the committee kept the post open for Bach, one may suppose that they had heard his recital at the Catharinenkirche. Exactly how this performance was arranged, no-one knows; but the obituary (Emanuel) states that Bach played before Reincken (aged 97), the magistracy and other notables; that he played for more than two hours in all; and that he extemporized in different styles on the chorale *An Wasserflüssen Babylon* for almost half an hour, just as the better Hamburg organists had been accustomed to doing at Saturday Vespers. As a fantasia on this chorale was one of Reincken's major works, this may seem a tactless choice; but the obituary makes it clear that the chorale was chosen by 'those present' and not by Bach himself. Reincken is reported to have said, 'I thought this art was dead, but I see it still lives in you', and showed Bach much courtesy. A later remark of Mattheson's has been taken to imply that Bach also played the G minor Fugue BWV542, but there are good reasons to doubt it.

During 1720 Bach made fair copies of the works for unaccompanied violin, and must have been preparing the Brandenburg Concertos, whose autograph full score was dedicated on 24 March 1721 to the Margrave Christian Ludwig, before whom Bach had played in Berlin while negotiating for the new Cöthen harpsichord, between June 1718 and March 1719. What he played is not known; but he was invited to send in some compositions. As he himself said, he took 'a couple of years' over this commission, and then submitted six works written to exploit the resources of Cöthen. Such resources do not seem to have been available to the Margrave of Brandenburg, and it is not really surprising that he did not thank Bach, send a fee or use the score.

One of Bach's friends at Cöthen was the goldsmith C. H. Bähr; Bach stood godfather to one of Bähr's sons in 1721, and deputized for a godfather to another in 1723. About the beginning of August 1721 he gave a performance of some unspecified kind for Count Heinrich XI Reuss, of Schleiz; this may have been arranged by J. S. Koch, Kantor there, who had held a post at Mühlhausen, though possibly not in Bach's time there.

On 15 June 1721 Bach was the 65th communicant at the Agnuskirche; one 'Mar. Magd. Wilken' was the 14th. This may well have been Bach's future wife – the mistake in the first name is an easy one – but Anna Magdalena makes no formal appearance until 25 September, when Bach and she were the first two among the five godparents of a child called Hahn. This baptism is recorded in three registers. In two of them Anna is described as 'court singer', in the third, simply as 'chamber musician' (*Musicantin*). In September Anna was again a godmother, to a child called Palmarius; again the registers differ in describing her occupation. Her name does not appear in court accounts until summer 1722, when she is referred to as the Kapellmeister's wife; her salary (half Bach's) is noted as paid for May and June 1722.

Practically nothing is known of her early years. She was born on 22 September 1701 at Zeitz. Her father, Johann Caspar Wilcke, was a court trumpeter; he worked at Zeitz until about February 1718, when he moved to Weissenfels where he died on 30 November 1731. The surname was variously spelt. Anna's mother (Margaretha Elisabeth Liebe, *d* 7 March 1746) was daughter of an organist and sister of J. S. Liebe who, besides being a trumpeter, was organist of two churches at Zeitz from 1694 until his death in 1742. As a trumpeter's daughter, Anna may well have met the Bachs socially. The stories that she was a public figure, having sung at Cöthen and the other local courts since the age of 15, have been discredited; they are said to have arisen through confusion with her elder brother, a trumpeter. However, she was paid for singing, with her father, in the chapel at Zerbst on some occasion between Easter and midsummer 1721. By September 1721, aged just 20, she was at Cöthen, well acquainted with Bach (aged 36), and ready to marry him on 3 December. The prince saved Bach ten thalers by giving him permission to be married in his own lodgings. At about this time Bach paid two visits to the city cellars, where he bought first one firkin of Rhine wine, and later two firkins, all at a cut price, 27 instead of 32 groschen per gallon.

On 11 December 1721 the prince married his cousin Friderica, Princess of Anhalt-Bernburg. The marriage, which took place at Bernburg, was followed by five weeks of illuminations and other entertainments at Cöthen. This was not however an auspicious event for Bach: he was to leave Cöthen partly because the princess was 'not interested in the Muses' and broke up the happy relationship between Bach and her husband. Perhaps her unfortunate influence had made itself felt even before she was married.

A legacy from Tobias Lämmerhirt (Bach's maternal uncle) had facilitated Bach's first marriage; Tobias's widow was buried at Erfurt on 12 September 1721, and Bach received something under her will too, though not in time for his second marriage. On 24 January 1722 Bach's sister Maria, together with one of the Lämmerhirts, challenged the will, saying that Bach and his brothers Jacob (in Sweden) and Christoph (at Ohrdruf) agreed with them (Christoph had died in 1721). Bach heard of this only by accident; and on 15 March he wrote to the Erfurt council on behalf of Jacob as well as himself. He objected to his sister's action, and said that he and his absent brother desired no more than was due to them under the will. On 16 April Jacob died; and the matter seems to have been settled on these lines towards the end of the year. Bach's legacy must have amounted to rather more than a year's pay.

In summer 1722 there was no Kapellmeister at the court of Anhalt-Zerbst, and Bach was commissioned to write a birthday cantata for the prince; for this he was paid ten thalers in April and May. The birthday was in August, and payments made during that month presumably refer to the performance. If so, the work, which seems to have disappeared, was scored for two oboes d'amore and 'other instruments'.

Several didactic works for keyboard belong to the Cöthen period. One is the *Clavierbüchlein* for Anna Magdalena Bach. 25 leaves are extant, about a third of the original manuscript; there is a kind of title-page, on which Anna Magdalena (probably) wrote the title and the date and Bach (certainly) noted the titles of three theological books. Despite the sceptics, it remains reasonable to suppose that Bach gave the book to his wife early in 1722. It seems to have been filled by 1725. The autograph of *Das wohltemperirte Clavier* (book 1 of the '48') is dated 1722 on the title-page but 1732 at the end. The writing is uniform in style, and for various reasons it is incredible that he did not finish the manuscript until 1732. This handsome fair copy was preceded by drafts, like those in W. F. Bach's *Clavier-Büchlein* (begun in 1720); and some of the movements look earlier than that. Presumably they were brought together for convenience, partly to serve as the last step in Bach's keyboard course, partly to exhibit the advantages of equal temperament. As in book 2, no doubt Bach transposed some of the pieces, to fill gaps in his key scheme; the odd pairing of the prelude in six flats with the fugue in six sharps suggests that the former was originally in E minor, the latter in D minor.

The title-page was almost certainly the only part of the *Orgel-Büchlein* that Bach wrote while at Cöthen, but as another educational work it is best mentioned here. It was meant to be a collection of chorale-preludes, not only for the ordinary church seasons but also for occasions when such subjects as the Lord's Prayer, or Penitence, were being emphasized. The paper is of a kind that Bach used, as far as is known, only in 1714. A few items date from about 1740; in the rest, the writing resembles that of the cantatas of 1715–16. Of the 164 preludes Bach allowed for, he completed fewer than 50. Last in this group of works come the Inventions and Sinfonias, whose autograph fair copy is dated 'Cöthen, 1723'. Its contents had already appeared, in earlier versions and under different titles, in W. F. Bach's *Clavier-Büchlein* of 1720.

The story of Bach's move to Leipzig begins with the death of Kuhnau, Kantor of the Thomasschule there, on 5 June 1722. Six men applied for the post, among them Telemann, who was still remembered for the good work he had done at Leipzig 20 years before. He had been doing a similar job at Hamburg for about a year, and was probably the most famous of German musicians actually living in Germany. One of the Kantor's duties was to teach Latin. Telemann refused to do that; nevertheless, he was appointed on 13 August. But the Hamburg authorities would not release him, and offered to increase his pay; by 22 November he had declined the Leipzig post. On that day Councillor Platz said that Telemann was no loss; what they needed was a Kantor to teach other subjects besides music. Of the remaining five candidates, three were invited to give trial performances; two dropped out, one because he would not teach Latin. By 21 December two Kapellmeisters had applied, Bach and Graupner. The other candidates were Kauffmann of Merseburg, Schott of the Leipzig Neukirche, and Rolle of Magdeburg. Of the five candidates, Graupner was preferred; he was a reputable musician, and had studied at the Thomasschule. He successfully performed his test (two cantatas) on 17 January 1723. But on 23 March he too withdrew,

having been offered more pay at Darmstadt. Meanwhile, Bach had performed his test pieces (Cantatas nos.22 and 23) on 7 February 1723. Rolle and Schott had also been heard, and possibly Kauffmann too. The Princess of Cöthen died on 4 April, too late to affect Bach's decision. On 9 April the council considered Bach, Kauffmann and Schott. Like Telemann, none of them wished to teach Latin. Councillor Platz said that as the best men could not be got, they must make do with the mediocre. The council evidently resolved to approach Bach, for on 13 April he obtained written permission to leave Cöthen. On 19 April he signed a curious document that reads as if he were not yet free from Cöthen, but could be free within a month; he also said he was willing to pay a deputy to teach Latin. On 22 April the council agreed on Bach, one of them hoping that his music would not be theatrical. On 5 May he came in person to sign an agreement; on 8 and 13 May he was interviewed and sworn in by the ecclesiastical authority; on 15 May the first instalment of his salary was paid; and on 16 May he 'took up his duties' at the university church, possibly with Cantata no.59. With family and furniture, he moved in on 22 May, and performed Cantata no.75 at the Nikolaikirche on 30 May. On 1 June, at 8.30 a.m., he was formally presented to the school.

This story has been told in some detail, because it throws light on the circumstances in which Bach worked at Leipzig. To him, the Kantorate was a step downwards in the social scale, and he had little respect for his employers. To the council, Bach was a third-rater, a mediocrity, who would not do what they expected a Kantor to do – teach Latin, as well as organize the city church music. The stage was set for trouble, and in due course trouble came. Councillor Platz on Telemann is curiously echoed by Councillor Stieglitz, ten days after Bach's death: 'The school needs a Kantor, not a Kapellmeister; though certainly he ought to understand music'.

7. LEIPZIG: 1723–9. The position of Kantor at the Thomaskirche, conjoined with that of civic director of music, had been associated with a wealth of tradition since the 16th century. It was one of the most notable positions in German musical life both in this and in the esteem it commanded; and there can be little doubt that the general attractiveness of the position in itself played a decisive part in Bach's decision to move from Cöthen to Leipzig. His subsequent remark about the social step down from Kapellmeister to Kantor must be seen in the context of his later disagreements with the Leipzig authorities, as indeed the letter in question (to Erdmann, a friend of his youth, on 28 October 1730) makes unequivocally clear. In any event, Bach was not the only Kapellmeister to apply for the post, and it seems that the Leipzig councillors were less interested in a common Kantor than in a reputable Kapellmeister to take charge of and upgrade the city's musical affairs. For Bach the duties attaching to the Leipzig position were incomparably more varied and demanding than those in Cöthen, Weimar, Mühlhausen or Arnstadt, and more or less corresponded to those undertaken by Telemann in Hamburg – it cannot have been mere chance that he wanted to tackle a range of duties comparable with those of his friend. There was also the greater economic security of a flourishing commercial town, the advantages of a relatively stable civic magistracy as an employer com-

pared with a less dependable private patron, and the superior schooling facilities for his growing sons.

The 'Cantor zu St. Thomae et Director Musices Lipsiensis' was the most important musician in the town; as such, he was primarily responsible for the music of the four principal Leipzig churches – St Thomas's (the Thomaskirche), St Nicolas's (the Nicolaikirche), St Matthew's (the Matthaeikirche or Neukirche) and St Peter's (the Petrikirche) – as well as for any other aspects of the town's musical life controlled by the town council. In carrying out his tasks he could call above all on the pupils of the boarding-school attached to St Thomas's, the Thomasschule, whose musical training was his responsibility, as well as the town's professional musicians. Normally the pupils, about 50 to 60 in number, were split up into four choir classes (*Kantoreien*) for the four churches. The requirements would vary from class to class: polyphonic music was required for St Thomas's, St Nicholas's (the civic church) and St Matthew's, with figural music only in the first two; at St Peter's only monodic chants were sung. The first choir class, with the best 12 to 16 singers, was directed by the Kantor himself, and sang alternately in the two principal churches; the other classes were in the charge of prefects appointed by Bach, who would be older and therefore more experienced pupils of St Thomas's.

Musical aptitude was a decisive factor in the selection of pupils for the Thomasschule, and it was the Kantor's responsibility to examine them and later to train them. This was furthered by the daily singing lessons, mostly given by the Kantor. There was also instrumental instruction for the ablest pupils, which Bach had to provide free of charge: he could thus help to make good any shortage of instrumentalists for his performances. Indeed, the number of professional musicians employed by the town (four Stadtpfeifer, three fiddlers and one apprentice) was held throughout his period of office at the same level as had obtained during the 17th century. For further instrumentalists Bach drew on the university students. In general the age of the Thomasschule pupils ranged between 12 and 23. Remembering that voices then broke at the age of 17 or 18, it is clear that Bach could count on solo trebles and altos who already had some ten years' practical experience – an ideal situation, impossible in boys' choirs today.

As far as church music was concerned, Bach's duties centred on the principal services on Sundays and church feasts, as well as some of the more important subsidiary services. In addition, he could be asked for music for weddings and funerals, for which he would receive a special fee. Such additional income was important to Bach, as his salary as Kantor of the Thomaskirche and director of music came to only 87 thalers and 12 groschen (besides allowances for wood and candles, and payments in kind, such as corn and wine). Including payments from endowments and bequests as well as additional income, Bach received annually more than 700 thalers. Further, he had the use of a spacious official residence in the south wing of the Thomasschule, which had been renovated at a cost of more than 100 thalers before he moved in in 1723. Inside the Kantor's residence was the so-called 'Komponirstube' ('composing room'), his professional office containing his personal music library and the school's. The buildings of the old Thomasschule were, scandalously, demolished in 1903 to make room for what is now the senior minister's quarters; it was also then that the west façade of the Thomaskirche was rebuilt in the neo-Gothic style.

During his early Leipzig years, Bach involved himself in church music with particular thoroughness and extreme energy. This activity centred on the 'Hauptmusic' composed for Sundays and church feasts, a cantata, whose text generally related to the Gospel – a tradition inherited from previous Kantors. Even so, Bach engaged on a musical enterprise without parallel in Leipzig's musical history: in a relatively short time he composed five complete cycles of cantatas for the church year, with about 60 cantatas in each, making a repertory of roughly 300 sacred cantatas. The first two cycles were prepared immediately, for 1723–4 and 1724–5; the third took rather longer, being composed between 1725 and 1727. The fourth, to texts by Picander, appears to date from 1728–9, while the fifth once again must have occupied a longer period, possibly extending into the 1740s. The newly established chronology of Bach's vocal works makes it clear that the main body of the cantatas was in existence by 1729, and that Bach's development of the cantata was effectively complete by 1735. The existence of the fourth and fifth cycles has been questioned, because of their fragmentary survival compared with the almost complete survival of the first, second and third; but until a positive argument for their non-existence can be put forward the number of five cycles, laid down in the necrology of 1754, must stand. Compared with the high proportion of Bach's works of other kinds that are lost (orchestral and chamber music, for instance), the disappearance of about 100 cantatas would not be exceptional. (The preservation of Bach's works is discussed below, §11; see §15 for the correspondence of excess chorales in the Breitkopf collection to the number of lost cantatas.)

The first cycle begins on the first Sunday after Trinity 1723 with Cantata no.75, which was performed 'mit gutem applausu' at the Nicolaikirche, followed by no.76, for the second Sunday after Trinity, performed at the Thomaskirche (see the calendar of cantata performances, *BJb*, xliv, 1957). The two largest churches in Leipzig are both Gothic in style, and in Bach's time they contained stone and wooden galleries. The choir lofts were on the west wall of the nave above the council gallery. The organs too were in the choir lofts (the 'Schüler-Chor'): the Nicolaikirche and the Thomaskirche each had a three-manual organ with 36 and 35 stops respectively (*Oberwerk, Brustwerk, Rückpositiv, Pedal*). The Thomaskirche had a second organ, fitted to the east wall as a 'swallow's nest', with 21 stops (*Oberwerk, Brustwerk, Rückpositiv, Pedal*); this fell into dilapidation and was demolished in 1740. The organs were always played before cantata performances, during which they would provide continuo accompaniment; they were played by the respective organists at each church – Bach himself, who had not held a regular appointment as an organist since his time in Weimar, directed the choir and the orchestra, and would not normally be playing an instrument.

The cantata was an integral part of the Leipzig Lutheran liturgy. It followed immediately on the reading from the Gospel, preceding the Creed and the sermon (the second part of a two-part cantata would follow the sermon, 'sub communione'). Besides organ playing and the congregational singing of hymns, selected by the Kantor, the other musical constituent of the liturgy was the introit motet, which would be taken from the

Florilegium portense (1603) by Erhard Bodenschatz, a collection mainly drawn from the 16th century (Lassus, Handl etc), and was performed *a cappella* with harpsichord continuo. Services began at about 7 a.m. and lasted three hours; this allowed a mere half-hour for the cantata, and Bach rarely overstepped this duration. The normal performing forces consisted of some 16 singers and 18 instrumentalists; it was rare for the total number of singers and players to fall below 25 or to exceed about 40 (the figure required on exceptional occasions, like the *St Matthew Passion*).

In the first weeks of Bach's holding office in Leipzig there was a funeral service for the postmaster's widow, Johanna Maria Keese (18 July 1723); it was probably for this occasion that he wrote the motet *Jesu meine Freude* BWV227. By 9 August (though possibly as early as 16 May, with the performance of Cantata no.59 in the university church, St Paul's) Bach had taken up his duties as musical director to the university, an office traditionally held by the Thomaskantor: on this occasion he performed the Latin Ode BWV Anh.20 (now lost) at festivities on the birthday of Duke Friedrich II of Saxe-Gotha. On 30 August he introduced Cantata no.119, as part of the celebrations for the change of town council in Leipzig. The enormous scope of Bach's new responsibilities, as well as his vast work-load, may be gauged from the fact that the day before (14th Sunday after Trinity) Cantata no.25 was heard for the first time, and the first performance of no.138 (for the 15th Sunday) was soon to follow.

September 1723 saw the start of Bach's protracted wrangle over the responsibility for services at the university. In a written request for payment, he laid claim to the traditional right of the Thomaskantor to be responsible for the so-called 'old' services (special feast days and academic ceremonies) and the 'new' services (normal Sundays and feast days); the 'new' services, however, together with the designation 'director of music', had in April 1723 been entrusted by the university to J. G. Görner, organist of the Nicolaikirche. On 28 September Bach's request was turned down, and he was paid only half the fee. He would not give in, and turned to the Elector of Saxony in Dresden with three petitions. The intervention of the Dresden court was apparently to little avail: the university left Görner in charge of the 'new' services and awarded Bach the 'old', with payment as before. After this, Bach seems to have withdrawn from the 'old' services too by 1726 and to have limited his activities at the university to festive occasions.

About 2 November 1723 Bach inaugurated a new organ in Störmthal, outside Leipzig (which he had previously appraised) with Cantata no.194. Then, from the second Sunday in Advent to the fourth, came his first break in the weekly routine of composing and performing cantatas; in Leipzig, unlike Weimar, this period was a 'tempus clausum', as was Lent up to and including Palm Sunday. On Christmas Day figural music returned, in a particularly splendid manner, with Cantata no.63, the *Magnificat* BWV243a (E♭ version) and probably the D major Sanctus BWV238. In Leipzig it was usual to have Latin mass settings on church feast days.

At the end of the next 'tempus clausum', Lent 1724, Bach produced his first large-scale choral work for Leipzig, the *St John Passion* BWV245. In its original version, it had its first performance at Vespers at the Nicolaikirche on Good Friday (7 April). Performances of Passion oratorios had been introduced to Leipzig by Kuhnau in 1721, and immediately became established as a tradition, alternating annually between the two main churches. There is no documentary evidence of a Passion performance under Bach's direction on Good Friday 1723, from which the older dating of the *St John Passion* derives. The work had several further performances, including three in revised versions: 1725, about 1730 and 1746–9.

With the first Sunday after Trinity 1724 (11 June) Bach began his second cycle; these were chorale cantatas. On 25 June he was in Gera for the dedication of the organ at the Salvatorkirche. In July he went to Cöthen with Anna Magdalena for a guest appearance as a performer; he had retained the title of Court Kapellmeister there, and it lapsed only on the death of Prince Leopold in 1728. There is evidence of further visits to Cöthen, with Bach performing alongside his wife (who sang as a soprano), in December 1725 and January 1728. During 1725 Bach started to prepare a second *Clavierbüchlein* for Anna Magdalena. On 23 February 1725 he performed Cantata no.249a at the Weissenfels court for the birthday of Duke Christian; this was the original version of the *Easter Oratorio* BWV249, first given at Leipzig the following 1 April. No.249a represents the beginning of a long-standing collaboration with the fluent Leipzig poet Christian Friedrich Henrici (Picander), the chief supplier of texts for Bach's later Leipzig vocal works.

Bach produced congratulatory cantatas for two Leipzig University professors in May and August (nos.36c and 205). On 19–20 September he played on the Silbermann organ at the Dresden Sophienkirche before the local court musicians, thus continuing his practice of giving virtuoso organ performances on concert tours (as he undoubtedly did in Leipzig, too, although he held no post as an organist). Early in 1726 – during the third cycle, which had started in June 1725 – there was an interruption of Bach's production of cantatas, for reasons that remain obscure: between February and September 1726 he performed 18 cantatas by his cousin (6) Johann Ludwig Bach (*3/72*). In particular, between Purification and the fourth Sunday after Easter, he performed none of his own music at the main Sunday services; even on Good Friday he used a work by another composer, Reinhard Keiser's *St Mark Passion*. Difficulties with performers may have been partly responsible; the instrumental forces required in J. L. Bach's cantatas are more modest than those Bach himself normally used. Even apart from this, however, the pattern of Bach's cantata production – as far as can be judged from the available material – changed during the third cycle; there are considerable gaps as early as the period after Trinity Sunday 1725, and it seems that the third cycle extended over two years. In the gaps, cantatas by other composers and further performances of Bach's own works were given.

Michaelmas 1726 saw the appearance in print of Partita no.1: with this Bach began his activity, later to increase in scope, as a publisher of keyboard music. Partita no.1, published singly, was followed by nos.2 and 3 (1727), no.4 (1728), no.5 (1730) and no.6 (1730 or 1731; no copy is known). According to an advertisement of 1 May 1730 the series was to have comprised seven partitas. There are early versions of nos.3 and 6 in the second book for Anna Magdalena of 1725. Bach sent no.1, with a dedicatory poem, to the Cöthen court as a form of congratulation on the birth of an heir, Prince Emanuel Ludwig (born 12 September 1726).

In December 1726, on the installation of Dr Gottlieb Kortte as university professor, Bach produced a more sizable occasional work, the *dramma per musica*, Cantata no.207. It is probable that the first performance of the *St Matthew Passion* took place on Good Friday of the following year: this would be in an earlier version, which it would now be impossible to reconstruct. Recent scholarship has produced evidence (the dating of Picander's text, the repairing of the second organ at the Thomaskirche, etc) which calls into question the traditional belief that the first performance was on Good Friday 1729. The *St Matthew Passion* would then come at the beginning of the cycle of cantatas planned by Bach and Picander for 1728–9. Bach had composed his first setting of a Picander Sunday cantata text for Septuagesima 1727 (no.84), and it seems that this was subsequently included in the later cycle. The texts for all the cantatas have survived, in the third volume of Picander's poems, but the music is extant of only nine pieces and a fragment (nos.84, 149, 188, 197a, 171, 156, 159, 145, 174). It is scarcely open to doubt, however, that Bach – named in Picander's foreword to his *Cantaten auf die Sonn- und Festtage durch das gantze Jahr* (1728) as the composer of the music of the cycle – set at least a large proportion of the texts, and indeed he probably did so in the weekly sequence that he followed in the first two cycles.

An important work composed by Bach in October 1727 was the *Trauer Ode*, Cantata no.198. The university planned a memorial ceremony on the death of Electress Christiane Eberhardine, the wife of August the Strong of Saxony, and commissioned Bach to set a text by the Leipzig professor of poetry, Johann Christoph Gottsched. This became a somewhat controversial affair, as the university director of music, Görner, felt he had been slighted. Bach however retained the commission and performed the two parts of his work, 'composed in the Italian manner', directing it from the harpsichord, in the university church, on 17 October. Between 7 September 1727 and 6 January 1728 there was a period of national mourning, with no other musical performances.

In September 1728 a brief dispute with the church authorities flared up. The sub-deacon, Gaudlitz, demanded that he himself should choose the songs to be sung before and after the sermon at Vespers; as it was usual for the Kantor to select these songs, Bach felt that his rights had been encroached upon. The dispute was settled in the sub-deacon's favour. Bach must have seen this as a setback, for once again his grievances had not been met; but his relations with the ecclesiastical authorities were on the whole good throughout his time at Leipzig. His relations with the town council and the head teachers of the Thomasschule went less smoothly, and were to become even more difficult in the 1730s. Documents dealing with the various disputes show Bach to have been a stubborn defender of the prerogatives of his office who frequently reacted with excessive violence and was often to blame if there was a negative outcome. It would be wrong, however, to draw hasty inferences about Bach's personality and his relations with the world about him. It is unfortunate that about a half of Bach's surviving correspondence is concerned with generally trivial but often protracted disputes over rights. This material is extant in public archives, while utter-

ances of kinds not appropriate to archival preservation, which might have complemented this rather austere view of his personality, have survived in only small quantity. From Bach's behaviour during these disputes it can be seen that, under pressure, he would defy bureaucratic regulations in order to preserve his independence and to clear himself an artistic breathing-space. His taking over of the collegium musicum in 1729, to be directed under his own management, must be seen in this context, as it represents something more than an incidental biographical fact.

Early in 1729 Bach spent some time at the Weissenfels court in connection with the birthday celebrations in February of Duke Christian, with whom he had long been associated. On this occasion the title of court Kapellmeister of Saxe-Weissenfels was conferred on him (his Cöthen title had lately expired); he retained the title until 1736. At the end of March he went to Cöthen to perform the funeral music for his former employer. On 15 April (Good Friday) the *St Matthew Passion* was performed at the Thomaskirche. On the second day of Whit week (6 June), what was probably the last cantata of the Picander cycle was performed, no.174. The manuscript, uniquely for Bach, is dated ('1729'); perhaps this represents some sort of final gesture after a heavy, six-year involvement in cantata composition. During this time instrumental music remained in the background. Besides the few harpsichord works already mentioned, his only instrumental productions were, it seems, a few organ pieces connected with his activities as a recital organist.

In June 1729 an invitation to visit Leipzig was delivered to Handel, then in Halle, by Wilhelm Friedemann, in place of his father, who was ill at the time; but nothing came of it. Thus Bach's second and last attempt to establish contact with his highly esteemed London colleague met with failure.

8. LEIPZIG: 1729–39. With his taking over of the collegium musicum, decisive changes came about in Bach's activities in Leipzig; and at the same time new possibilities were opened up. The collegium had been founded by Telemann in 1704 and had most recently been directed by G. B. Schott (who left to become Kantor at Gotha in March 1729); it was a voluntary association of professional musicians and university students that gave regular weekly (and during the fair season even more frequent) public concerts. Such societies played an important part in the flowering of bourgeois musical culture in the 18th century, and with his highly reputed ensemble Bach made his own contribution to this in the commercial metropolis of Leipzig. He took over the direction before the third Sunday after Easter – in other words, by April 1729 – and retained it in the first place until 1737. Bach must have had strong reasons for wanting to take on this fresh area of work in addition to his other duties. To some extent it is possible to guess those reasons. For six years he had immersed himself in the production of sacred music, and he had created a stock of works sufficient to supply the requirements of his remaining time in office. In his efforts to provide sacred music that was at once fastidious and comprehensive he had met with little appreciation from the authorities, and no additional facilities (for example, much needed professional instrumentalists) had been placed at his disposal: it would be understandable if he now felt resigned to the situation. Further, as a former

Kapellmeister, he must have been attracted by the prospect of working with a good instrumental ensemble. He must have felt that, as director of the collegium, he would be able to establish an area of musical activities where he would be completely independent and free to pursue his own ideas. This new position may also have involved some additional income.

Nothing, unfortunately, is known about the programmes of the 'ordinaire' weekly concerts. But it is generally acknowledged that Bach must have given performances of many of his Cöthen instrumental works, some of them in revised versions, as the surviving performing parts for the orchestral suites BWV1066–9 and the flute sonatas BWV1030 and 1039 testify. And there can be no doubt that the seven harpsichord concertos BWV1052–8, gathered together in a Leipzig manuscript collection, belong with these works. No evidence survives as to the extent to which Bach composed new music specially for collegium performances. But he often performed works by other composers, including orchestral suites by his cousin Johann Ludwig. Further, Bach's many musical acquaintances from other places must have made frequent appearances, including his colleagues in the Dresden court orchestra (there is evidence of visits from J. A. Hasse, Georg Benda, S. L. Weiss, C. H. Graun and J. D. Zelenka). C. P. E. Bach's remark that 'it was seldom that a musical master passed through [Leipzig] without getting to know my father and playing for him' must refer to performances of the collegium musicum, which took place on Wednesdays between 4 and 6 p.m. in the coffee-garden 'before the Grimmisches Thor' in the summer and on Fridays between 8 and 10 p.m. in Zimmermann's coffee-house in the winter. In addition, there were 'extraordinaire' concerts, to mark such events as visits of the Dresden court; on these occasions, during the 1730s, Bach performed his large-scale secular cantatas. His activities with the collegium must have made heavy demands on him, and the reduction in his production of sacred music is easy to understand.

This does not, however, mean that his interest in sacred music was diminished (as has been claimed, with undue emphasis in the light of the revised dating of his works). Such a view is contradicted not only by the major ecclesiastical works written after 1730 but also by the simple fact that, throughout his period of office, Bach provided performances of his cantatas, a repertory largely completed before 1729, every Sunday at the two main Leipzig churches. His reference in 1739 to the 'onus' of such undertakings, in connection with a projected performance of the Passion, might just as well have been made in the 1720s. Admittedly, his difficulties became particularly acute around 1730, as his important memorandum of 23 August 1730, dealing with the state of church music in Leipzig and outlining his remedies, testifies. His letter of 28 October that year, to his old friend Erdmann in Danzig, may be read in the same sense; sheer frustration that the memorandum had proved ineffectual drove him to consider leaving Leipzig. It would seem that his work with the collegium musicum had not yet brought about the intended equilibrium in his activities.

The situation had been aggravated by other, external factors. The old headmaster Johann Heinrich Ernesti had died in 1729 (Bach had performed a motet BWV226 at his funeral in October). During the subsequent interim in the Thomasschule's direction the organization

of school life was disturbed. Problems of space appear to have arisen too. It was in this context that complaints were made about Bach's neglect of his school duties (the dropping of singing lessons, absence on journeys without leave); in September 1730 there was even a question of reducing his salary 'because the Kantor is incorrigible'. It would appear that things were put right by J. M. Gesner, who took over the headship of the school in the summer, and who seems soon to have established friendly and familiar relations with Bach.

On Good Friday 1730 Bach apparently performed a *St Luke Passion*, not of his own composition. From 25 to 27 June the jubilee of the Confession of Augsburg was celebrated across Lutheran Germany, and Bach wrote three cantatas for the event (nos.190a, 120b, Anh.4a: all were parody cantatas). They are not untypical of his church compositions of this period, most of which were put together as parodies; and that is also true of the major vocal works like the *St Mark Passion*, the B minor Mass, the small masses and the *Christmas Oratorio*. Bach's only sacred cantatas composed as completely original works after 1729 seem to be nos.117 (1728–31), 192 (1730), 51 (c1730), 29, 112 and 140 (1731), 177 (1732), 97 (1734), 9 and 100 (1732–5), 14 (1735), 195 (after 1737), 197 (c1742) and 200 (fragment, c1742).

In 1731 a collected edition of the six partitas appeared as op.1, as the first part of the *Clavier-Übung*. From the wording of the title it is clear that Bach planned a series of 'keyboard exercises', which he now proceeded to produce. His new and continuing interest in publishing his own compositions is a clear indication of his change of attitude over an independent and freely creative activity of his own. The first performance of the *St Mark Passion*, predominantly a parody work, took place on Good Friday of that year. At the end of June 1731 Bach and his family had to move to temporary quarters while rebuilding and extension work were being carried out on the Thomasschule. His residence must have become increasingly cramped, for his family was growing. At the beginning of Bach's period in Leipzig Anna Magdalena had borne a child every year, to whom members of leading local families (noblemen, merchants, professors, theologians) had stood as godparents. But few of the children survived infancy:

Christiana Sophia Henrietta (b spring 1723; d 29 June 1726)
Gottfried Heinrich (48)
Christian Gottlieb (baptized 14 April 1725; d 21 Sept 1728)
Elisabeth Juliane Friederica (baptized 5 April 1726; d Naumburg, 24 Aug 1781)
Ernestus Andreas (baptized 30 Oct 1727; d 1 Nov 1727)
Regina Johanna (baptized 10 Oct 1728; d 25 April 1733)
Christiana Benedicta (baptized 1 Jan 1730; d 4 Jan 1730)
Christiana Dorothea (baptized 18 March 1731; d 31 Aug 1732)
Johann August Abraham (baptized 5 Nov 1733; d 6 Nov 1733)
Johann Christoph Friedrich (49)
Johann Christian (50)
Johanna Carolina (baptized 30 Oct 1737; d Leipzig, 18 Aug 1781)
Regina Susanna (baptized 22 Feb 1742; d Leipzig, 14 Dec 1809)

Joy and sorrow were everyday matters. But Bach's family life must have been harmonious in more than one sense; in 1730 he reported, as a proud paterfamilias, that with his family he could form a vocal and instrumental concert ensemble. The family moved into the new residence the next April. The school was reconsecrated on 5 June 1732 with a cantata, BWV Anh.18. In September 1731 Bach had been to Dresden for the first performance of Hasse's opera *Cleofide* and to give concerts at the Sophienkirche and at court (there were enthusiastic reports in the newspapers). In September 1732 he went with his wife to Kassel for the examination and inauguration of the organ of St Martin's, where he probably played the 'Dorian' Toccata and Fugue in D minor BWV538.

With the death of Elector Friedrich August I of Saxony on 1 February 1733 a five-month period of national mourning began. The collegium musicum obtained permission to restart its performances in the middle of June, when a new harpsichord was introduced (possibly in harpsichord concertos). During the mourning period Bach worked on the Kyrie and the Gloria of the B minor Mass, which, in the hope of obtaining a title at the court Kapelle, he presented to the new Elector Friedrich August II in Dresden, with a note dated 27 July 1733, as a *Missa* in a set of parts. Recent investigations suggested that the *Missa* was performed at this time, perhaps at the Sophienkirche in Dresden, where W. F. Bach had been working as an organist since June 1733. Bach may have stayed in Dresden from the middle of July to organize such a performance. Not until November 1736, however, was the title 'Hofkomponist' conferred on Bach, and even then only through the intervention of his patron Count Keyserlingk after a further letter of application. As a gesture of thanks, Bach paid his respects to the Dresden royal household and an enthusiastic public with a two-hour organ recital on the new Silbermann instrument at the Frauenkirche on 1 December 1736.

After the dedication of the *Missa* in July 1733, Bach kept the Saxon royal family's interests in mind with his 'extraordinaire' concerts of the collegium musicum. On 3 August, the name day of the new elector, Bach began his remarkable series of secular cantatas of congratulation and homage with BWV Anh.12 (music lost), followed by Cantata no.213 (5 September, for the heir to the electorate), no.214 (8 December, for the electress), no.205a (19 February 1734, for the coronation of the elector as King of Poland; music lost), an unknown work (24 August, again for the elector), and no.215 (5 October, also for the elector, who was at the performance). In these and similar later works Bach came closest to opera, not just in terms of the dramatic nature of some of the librettos but also stylistically. They indicate that he was not only thoroughly familiar with current operatic style, since his frequent visits to the Dresden opera house, but actually indebted to opera as a musical stimulus, as his own remark on 'the lovely Dresden ditties' ('die schönen Dresdner Liederchen', reported by Forkel) suggests. Much of the festive music was performed in the open air with splendid illuminations, and according to newspaper reports the music benefited from a resounding echo. (On the day after the performance of no.215 Bach's virtuoso trumpeter and the leader of the Leipzig Stadtpfeifer, Gottfried Reiche, died as a result of the exertions of his office.) During the following Christmas season Bach gave the people of Leipzig a chance to hear much of the music from his secular festive cantatas in modified form, as the *Christmas Oratorio*, which was heard in six sections between Christmas Day 1734 and Epiphany 1735 (and consisted predominantly of parodies of Cantatas nos.213–15).

On 21 November 1734 the new headmaster of the Thomasschule, Johann August Ernesti, was greeted with a cantata, BWV Anh.19 (Gesner had moved to the University of Göttingen). Bach's dealings with the directors of the school had been untroubled for four years, thanks to his friendly relations with Gesner; but with Ernesti he experienced the most violent of all his controversies. A dispute over prefects flared up in August 1736 over the authority to nominate choral prefects, in which the interests of the Kantor and the headmaster were diametrically opposed. With his neo-humanist educational ideals, whereby he set great store by the academic quality of training in school, Ernesti showed little appreciation of the musical traditions. In line with prevailing trends during the Enlightenment, the tendency at the Thomasschule, at least from the start of Bach's period of office, had been to restrict musical activities or at any rate to reduce their proportions; Bach, on the other hand, demanded the best-qualified pupils to assist him, and certainly he often made excessive demands (for music copying, rehearsals and so on). Against what were to some extent unfair arguments on the headmaster's part, his struggles were doomed to failure. The grievances over prefects were taken before the courts in Dresden; the affair, which led to Bach's having disciplinary difficulties with his pupils, was settled early in 1738 (the precise outcome is not recorded).

Among the more important events of 1735 was the appearance of the second part of the *Clavier-Übung* at Easter. In the context of Bach's activities as a publisher it should also be mentioned that by 1729 he was also involved in the distribution of musical publications by other authors and kept a stock, including Heinichen's book on figured bass, Walther's *Lexicon* and keyboard works by Hurlebusch, Krebs and his own sons. On 19 May the *Ascension Oratorio* (Cantata no.11) was first performed; probably the *Easter Oratorio* was heard on the preceding Easter Sunday. In June he travelled to the town where he had spent his youth, Mühlhausen, to appraise the rebuilt organ in the Marienkirche, where his son Johann Gottfried Bernhard (47) had just been appointed organist. During Advent 1735, when no music was performed, and Lent 1736 Bach was probably engaged on the revision of the *St Matthew Passion* and in making a carefully laid-out fair copy of the new version. In this form, characterized by its writing for double chorus (with two continuo parts), the work was performed in the Thomaskirche on 30 March 1736, with the cantus firmus parts in the opening and closing choruses of part 1 played on the 'swallow's nest' organ. Also at Easter the Schemelli Hymnbook, on whose tunes and figured basses Bach had collaborated, was published.

In summer 1737 Bach resigned the direction of the collegium musicum. For the last large-scale 'extraordinaire' concert on 7 October 1736 he had written the congratulatory Cantata no.206 on the birthday of the elector. Only two further works of homage are known from 1737–8 (BWV30a and Anh.13). He now turned to keyboard music, working on the second part of *Das wohltemperirte Clavier*, and on the third part of the *Clavier-Übung*, the largest of his keyboard works. This collection of organ pieces, freely based on chorales, with large-scale works for the church organ and small-scale ones for domestic instruments, appeared at Michaelmas 1739. Probably he also devoted himself more particularly about this time to private music teaching. Around this time J. F. Agricola (his pupil 1738–41) and J. P. Kirnberger (up to 1741) – his most important pupils apart from his own sons – were in Leipzig. Over

3. Bach's autograph letter (24 August 1735) of recommendation for his pupil Johann Ludwig Krebs (Zwickau, Stadtarchiv III Z.40.7, f.36r)

the years Bach had something like 80 private pupils; among them were C. F. Abel (c1743), J. C. Altnikol (1744–8), J. F. Doles (1739–44), G. F. Einicke (1732–7), H. N. Gerber (1724–7), J. C. G. Gerlach (1723–9), J. G. Goldberg (from 1737), G. A. Homilius (1735–42), J. C. Kittel (1748–50), J. L. Krebs (1726–35), L. C. Mizler (?–1734), J. G. Müthel (1750), J. C. Nichelmann (1730–33), J. G. Schübler (after 1740), G. G. Wagner (1723–6) and C. G. Wecker (1723–8).

In October 1737 Bach's nephew Johann Elias (39) came to live with the family, as private secretary and tutor for the younger children; he remained until 1742. The surviving drafts of letters he prepared give a lively picture of Bach's correspondence in these few years. At this period Bach gave close attention to the study of works by other composers. He was a subscriber to Telemann's Parisian flute quartets of May 1738; but more typical is his preoccupation with Latin polyphonic liturgical compositions. The *stile antico* tradition seems to have held a particular fascination for him. In the first place he owed his knowledge of this repertory, to which he marginally contributed by making transcriptions (works by Palestrina, Caldara, Bassani etc), to his connections at Dresden. His knowledge of Pergolesi's *Stabat mater* of 1736, which he reworked during the 1740s as a psalm setting, *Tilge, Höchster, meine Sünden* (not in BWV), is also surprising; the earliest trace of Pergolesi's work north of the Alps thus leads to Bach –

a sign of the latter's remarkable knowledge of the repertory. His interest in Latin liturgical music relates not only to his plans for and completion of the B minor Mass, but also, in the late 1730s, to the composition of the small masses in A and G (BWV234, 236). These may have been written for the Protestant court services in Dresden, but that would not exclude performances in Leipzig.

On 14 May 1737 J. A. Scheibe, in his journal *Der critische Musikus*, published a weighty criticism of Bach's manner of composition. This seems to have come as a severe blow to Bach. The Leipzig lecturer in rhetoric Johann Abraham Birnbaum responded with a defence, printed in January 1738, which Bach distributed among his friends and acquaintances. The affair developed into a public controversy which was pursued in 1739 with further polemical writings by Scheibe and Birnbaum, and by Mizler's Correspondirende Societät der Musicalischen Wissenschaften (who supported Bach), and was concluded by Scheibe in 1745 with a conciliatory review of the Italian Concerto. Scheibe acknowledged Bach's extraordinary skill as a performer on the organ and the harpsichord, but sharply criticized his compositions, claiming that Bach 'by his bombastic and intricate procedures deprived them of naturalness and obscured their beauty by an excess of art'. Birnbaum's not particularly skilful replies fail to recognize the true problem, which lies in a clash of irreconcilable stylistic ideals. His factual definition of what is natural and what artificial in Bach's style (in which he drew a historical parallel with Lotti and Palestrina – of whose works Bach possessed transcripts – as precedents) could not, ultimately, counter Scheibe's criticisms.

9. LEIPZIG: 1739–50. In October 1739 Bach resumed the direction of the collegium musicum, which had in the meantime been in the charge of C. G. Gerlach (organist at the Neukirche and a pupil of Bach). At the beginning of this period, in fact, there came a composition for the birthday of the elector (7 October; the music is lost), but it seems that Bach's ambitions and activities in connection with the 'ordinaire' and 'extraordinaire' concerts were considerably diminished. There were few performances of congratulatory cantatas, and these were probably repeats of earlier works. Nor is there evidence of any chamber music being produced during this period. Bach withdrew from the collegium musicum again in 1741. With the death of the coffee-house owner Gottfried Zimmermann (30 May 1741) the collegium had lost its landlord and organizer, and without him it could not long continue. In 1744 its 40 years as an important institution came to an end (possibly Bach still gave occasional performances up to that date). Civic musical life in Leipzig found a new focal point in the Grosse Concert, founded in 1743 and sponsored by a growing circle of musical dilettantes and hence less professional than the collegium.

In August 1741 Bach went to Berlin, probably to visit Carl Philipp Emanuel who in 1738 had been appointed court harpsichord player to Crown Prince Frederick of Prussia (later Frederick the Great). In the two previous years Bach had made brief journeys to Halle (early 1740) and Altenburg (September 1739; he gave an organ recital in the castle church). In November 1741 there was a further journey, this time to Dresden, where he visited Count von Keyserlingk. The 'Aria with 30 Variations', the so-called Goldberg Variations, appeared in 1741–2 as the fourth part of the *Clavier-Übung* (published by Schmidt of Nuremberg). Bach's visit to Dresden may lie behind the anecdote related by Forkel, according to which the variations were written as a commission for the count. But the lack of any formal dedication in the original edition suggests that the work was not composed to a commission. It is however known that Bach presented the count with a copy, apparently for the use of his young resident harpsichord player Johann Gottlieb Goldberg, who was a pupil of both J. S. and W. F. Bach. In a copy of the variations which came to light in 1975, Bach added a series of 14 enigmatically notated canons on the bass of the Aria (BWV1087); these appear at the outset of a period of intensive involvement in canonic writing.

On 30 August 1742, on the Kleinzschocher estate near Leipzig, a 'Cantata burlesque' (known as the Peasant Cantata, no.212) was performed in homage to the new lord of the manor, Carl Heinrich von Dieskau; this work is unique in Bach's output for its folklike manner. The thoroughly up-to-date characteristics of parts of the work show that Bach was not only intimately acquainted with the musical fashions of the times but also knew how to adapt elements of the younger generation's style for his own purposes (as he also did in the lute piece BWV998 and the third movement of the trio sonata from the *Musical Offering*).

Alongside this work, apparently his last secular cantata, only isolated sacred cantatas were composed or arranged during the 1740s: 197, 200 and possibly 195. Instead Bach gave regular repeat performances of his cantata revisions besides retouchings of earlier, larger works, such as the *St Matthew* and *St John Passions*, and also turned to performances of works by other composers: Telemann's *St Luke Passion*, Handel's *Brockes Passion*, a Passion Oratorio by Graun, and Passion pasticcios by Keiser and Handel, Graun and Telemann, and Kuhnau and Altnikol. The only new composition of any considerable scope was the 'Symbolum Nicenum' of the B minor Mass, in which Bach's preoccupation of the late 1730s with Latin polyphonic music is again seen. The occasion for its composition and performance is unknown, so it cannot be firmly dated (it was probably some time between 1742 and 1745). Recent research has however managed to establish that the work was written out only during Bach's last years, perhaps about 1748. The so-called 'B minor Mass' as an exemplary collection of the standard sections of the mass was completed with a Sanctus (composed in 1724) and the closing movements, from the 'Osanna' onwards (all parodies).

Instrumental music, however, once again came to the fore during the 1740s. Before 1745 Bach began to sift through his older organ chorales. Some of the Weimar pieces were extensively reworked and gathered into a new manuscript collection (the '18', BWV651–68). These revisions may have been undertaken with a view to the subsequent appearance of the chorales in print, as happened with the six chorales on movements from the cantatas (the 'Schübler Chorales') about 1748. Apparently Bach was still engaged on his work on the chorales in the last months of his life. The copying from dictation of the chorale *Vor deinen Thron* BWV668, later the subject of legend, was in fact probably confined to an improvement of an existing work (the chorale BWV641 from the Weimar *Orgel-Büchlein*).

Bach retained his interest in organ building. In 1746 there were two important examinations and inaugurations of organs: on 7 August in Zschortau and on 26–9 September at St Wenceslas, Naumburg. The Naumburg appraisal was one of Bach's most important; Bach subjected the instrument to the most searching possible examination of its technical reliability and its sound quality. He took a critical interest in Gottfried Silbermann's building of pianofortes, proposing alterations in the mechanism, which Silbermann adopted. Bach publicly praised Silbermann's later pianos and helped to sell them (a receipt for one sold to Poland, dated 6 May 1749, survives). On his visit to Potsdam Bach played on a series of Silbermann pianos.

The visit to the court of Frederick the Great in May 1747 is one of the most notable biographical events in Bach's unspectacular life. The invitation probably came about through Count Keyserlingk, the royal envoy in Dresden, who was then in Berlin. Bach's encounter with Frederick began on 7 May at the palace of Potsdam with an exercise in fugal improvisation; Bach's execution on the piano of an improvisation on a theme supplied by the king met with general applause. The next day Bach gave an organ recital in the Heiliggeist Church in Potsdam, and during chamber music that evening he improvised a six-part fugue on a theme of his own. He also visited the new Berlin opera house, and possibly went to look at organs in Potsdam and Berlin. On his

4. Johann Sebastian Bach: replica (1748) by Elias Gottlob Haussmann of his portrait (1746) showing the composer holding a copy of his six-part canon BWV1076 (*William H. Scheide Library, Princeton*)

return, probably in the middle of May, he worked industriously on an 'elaboration of the King of Prussia's fugue theme', beginning with writing down the fugue he had improvised (three-part ricercare), which, while in Potsdam, he had announced that he would print. But he now decided on a larger project and under the title *Musikalisches Opfer* ('Musical Offering') he prepared a work in several movements dedicated to Frederick the Great; this work was printed in its entirety by the end of September (Michaelmas) 1747. The royal theme serves

as the basis for all the movements (two ricercares, in three and six parts, for keyboard; a trio sonata for flute, violin and continuo; and various canons for flute, violin and continuo with harpsichord obbligato).

In June 1747, after some hesitation, Bach joined the Correspondirende Societät der Musicalischen Wissenschaften founded by Lorenz Mizler. It was probably in 1747 that he submitted, as a 'scientific' piece of work, his canonic composition on *Vom Himmel hoch* BWV769. At the same time he sent the members an offprint of the six-part canon from the series on the bass of the Goldberg Variations. He seems, however, to have taken no further interest in the society's affairs as (according to C. P. E. Bach) he thought nothing of the 'dry, mathematical matters' that Mizler wanted to discuss. Besides his long acquaintance with his pupil Mizler, Bach's most likely reason for joining the society was that prominent colleagues such as Telemann and Graun were fellow members.

The beginnings of his work on *Die Kunst der Fuge* ('The Art of Fugue') also belong to the mid-1740s. A complete version, earlier than the published one, survives in Bach's autograph. During his last years Bach worked at a revision of the work, which he intended to have printed – a process he himself still supervised to a large extent. The printing was probably largely complete by about the end of 1749 (in other words, before his son Johann Christoph Friedrich, who had contributed to this task, left to join the court at Bückeburg in January 1750). But Bach was not to see the entire work in print; his sons, probably C. P. E. in particular, took charge of the publication and the work appeared posthumously in autumn 1751. The organ chorale BWV668 (*Vor deinen Thron*) served as a supplement to mitigate the work's incompleteness.

In his last years Bach suffered from eye trouble, specifically cataract; and ultimately he was totally blind. It may date back to the early or middle 1740s. By the beginning of 1749 he was apparently incapable of work; otherwise the Leipzig town council would surely not have been so tactless as to allow J. G. Harrer, a protégé of the Dresden prime minister Count Brühl, to take the examination for the post of Kantor on 8 June 1749. Out of consideration for Bach the cantata performance was in a concert hall rather than one of the churches. The town chronicle reported that the authorities were counting on Bach's death. After the beginning of 1749 Bach composed only on the most exceptional occasions. The last known examples of his handwriting, which give an impression of increasing irregularity, clumsiness and cramping, date from May 1749. On the baptism of his grandson Johann Sebastian Altnikol (his pupil Johann Christoph Altnikol had married Elisabeth Juliane Friederica Bach) on 6 October 1749 Bach was unable to be present as godfather.

During his last year, Bach's state of health and his ability to work must have fluctuated. But he was not entirely inactive. From May 1749 to June 1750 he was engaged in a controversial correspondence about the Freiberg headmaster Biedermann. In May 1749 Biedermann had violently attacked the cultivation of music in schools; Bach immediately felt himself called into battle, and among other things he gave a repeat performance of the satirical cantata about the controversy between Phoebus and Pan, no.201. His involvement is understandable, for he must have seen parallels with the state of affairs at the Thomasschule. Bach solicited a rejoinder on the part of C. G. Schröter, a member of Mizler's society, and even Mattheson joined in, from Hamburg. Once again, the affair throws characteristic light on the increasingly unfavourable conditions surrounding the traditional role of music in schools during the Enlightenment.

At the end of March Bach underwent an eye operation, performed by the English eye specialist John Taylor (who was later to perform a similar operation on Handel). It was only partly successful, however, and had to be repeated during the second week of April. The second operation too was ultimately unsuccessful, and indeed Bach's physique was considerably weakened. Yet as late as the beginning of May 1750 Johann Gottfried Müthel could go to Leipzig, stay at Bach's house and become his last pupil. To what extent regular instruction was possible under these circumstances remains uncertain. In the next two months Bach's health had so deteriorated that, on 22 July, he had to take his last Communion at home. He died only six days later, on the evening of 28 July, after a stroke. He was buried two or three days later at St John's cemetery.

His wife, Anna Magdalena, who in addition to her domestic tasks was a loyal and industrious collaborator, participating in performances and copying out music, survived him by ten years. She died in abject poverty in 1760. On his death Bach had left a modest estate consisting of securities, cash, silver vessels, instruments – including eight harpsichords, two lute-harpsichords, ten string instruments (among them a valuable Stainer violin), a lute and spinet – and other goods, officially valued at 1122 thalers and 22 groschen; this had to be divided between the widow and the nine surviving children of both marriages.

10. ICONOGRAPHY. The coffin containing Bach's remains was exhumed in 1894: the identity of the bones was confirmed by a detailed anatomical investigation by Professor Wilhelm His, who showed that Bach was of medium build. From an impression taken of the skull Carl Seffner, in 1898, modelled a bust, which shows an undoubted similarity with the only likeness of Bach that can be guaranteed as authentic, that of the Leipzig portraitist Elias Gottlob Haussmann. That portrait exists in two versions, one dating from 1746 (Historisches Museum der Stadt Leipzig) and one of 1748 (William H. Scheide Library, Princeton; see fig.4). The earlier, signed 'E. G. Haussmann pinxit 1746', passed from the estate of a later Thomaskantor, August Eberhard Müller, into the possession of the Thomasschule in 1809; it is not known whence Müller had obtained the painting. It seems improbable that the portrait had been presented to Mizler's society; probably none was ever presented, and this one was painted for his own family. The Thomasschule picture had been severely damaged and repeatedly painted over. In 1912–13 it was restored, but it remains inferior to the excellently preserved replica of 1748, which came from C. P. E. Bach's estate and was long owned by the Jenke family, in Silesia and then in England, before being identified by Hans Raupach in 1950.

All the other portraits allegedly of Bach are at best doubtful. That is perhaps least so of the oil painting by Johann Jacob Ihle, dating from about 1720, which purports to show him as Kapellmeister in Cöthen; yet, coming from the palace at Bayreuth (and identified as a 'picture of Bach' only in 1897), the portrait gives no concrete indication of whom it represents, and its provenance is uncertain. Portraits of probable authenticity that no longer survive were once in the possession of J. C. Kittel (from the estate of the Countess of Weissenfels) and of J. N. Forkel. A pastel, again from C. P. E. Bach's collection, has not survived. There must have been at least one further replica of Haussmann's portrait, according to early Bach literature (from the estate of W. F. Bach), but all trace of it has been lost – unless what was taken to be a copy dating from 1848 (possibly painted by G. A. Friedrich) should turn out to be a genuine Haussmann (formerly in the possession of the Burckhardt family of Leipzig; now in that of Baron H. O. R. Tuyll van Serooskerken, Alabama, USA).

During the 18th and 19th centuries many copies were made of the Haussmann portraits, both in oils and by printing processes. Of these, the engraving (1774) by Samuel Gottlieb Kütner, an art student at Leipzig with C. P. E. Bach's son, Johann Sebastian Bach (1748–78), is of particular value; C. P. E. Bach described it to Forkel as 'a fair likeness'. In addition, numerous apocryphal 'pictures of Bach' exist (including the so-called Erfurt portrait and the Volbach picture); most are of the 'old-man-with-a-wig' type and have nothing to do with Bach. The nearest we can nowadays get to his true physiognomy is probably in the 1748 version of Haussmann's portrait, wherein, as a man in his early 60s, Bach is represented as a learned musician, with a copy of the enigmatic six-part canon BWV1076 in his hand to demonstrate his status.

11. SOURCES, REPERTORY. The earliest catalogue of Bach's works – admittedly a very rough and ready one – is in the necrology drawn up by C. P. E. Bach and J. F. Agricola. It scarcely provides an adequate idea of the extent of Bach's works. But most of the works printed in Bach's lifetime (Cantata no.71 and its lost Mühlhausen counterpart; the four parts of the *Clavier-Übung*; the Schemelli Hymnbook; the *Musical Offering*; the Canonic Variations BWV769; the Schübler chorales; the *Art of Fugue*; the canon BWV1076) and a great deal of the works surviving only in manuscript are included. Palpable losses appear to have occurred among the cantatas (more than 100 works: nearly two cycles of church cantatas and several secular occasional works) and among the orchestral and chamber music (the extent of these losses is unknown, but must be considerable); beyond these, there are isolated known losses of works in every genre.

Bach's works, speaking generally, were kept together in their essentials during his lifetime, and the losses occurred only on the division of his legacy in 1750, when the manuscripts, especially of the vocal works, were divided between the eldest sons and Bach's widow; according to Forkel, most of them went to Wilhelm Friedemann. He, unfortunately, was compelled for financial reasons to sell them off item by item, and the material is not simply scattered but for the most part lost. Only a few of the items owned by Johann Christian, including a printed copy of the *Musical Offering* and the autograph score of the organ Prelude and Fugue in B minor BWV544 (signed with his nickname 'Christel'), can be traced; and nothing is known of any material that may have passed to five of his brothers and sisters. C. P. E. Bach's and Anna Magdalena's shares were better preserved. Bach's widow gave her portion (the parts of the cycle of chorale cantatas) to the Thomasschule while most of C. P. E. Bach's estate passed through Georg Poelchau's collection into the Berlin Königliche Bibliothek (later the Preussische Staatsbibliothek, now divided between the Staatsbibliothek, West Berlin, and the Deutsche Staatsbibliothek, East Berlin). This collection forms the basis of the most important collection of Bach archives. During the 19th century this library acquired further, smaller Bach collections, notably those from the Singakademie and the estates of Forkel, Franz Hauser and Count Voss-Buch (in some of which fragments from W. F. Bach's inheritance appear).

Besides the original manuscripts – the autograph scores, and parts prepared for performances under Bach's direction – which, in their essentials, Bach kept by him, many copies were made in the circle of his pupils, particularly of organ and harpsichord music. As many of the autograph scores of the keyboard works are lost, this strand is specially significant for the preservation of Bach's works. For example, important copies have come down through Bach's pupils Krebs and Kittel. After Bach's death Breitkopf in Leipzig became a centre for the dissemination of his music (again, primarily the keyboard music). In Berlin a notable Bach collection was made for Princess Anna Amalia of Prussia, under the direction of Kirnberger, in which all facets of Bach's creative output were represented. These secondary sources often have to serve when autograph material is not available – relatively often with the instrumental works, more rarely with the vocal ones.

Research into source materials, notably in conjunction with the Neue Bach-Ausgabe, has proved fruitful. Most of the copyists who worked for Bach have been catalogued and some have been identified (e.g. Johann Andreas Kuhnau, 1703–?; Christian Gottlob Meissner, 1707–60); papers, inks and binding have been analysed; and examinations of Bach's handwriting have revealed its various stages of development. A far-reaching revision of the chronology of Bach's works (only some 40 of the originals are dated) has been made possible. For the vocal works this new dating is now basically complete; sometimes it is precise to the actual day. With the instrumental works the situation is more complicated, because the original manuscripts are often lost; in consequence, results have been less precise since the history of the secondary sources permits of only vague conclusions about composition dates (for example, copies originating from the circle around Krebs and J. G. Walther point to a date in the Weimar period); this makes it unlikely that any complete and exact chronology will be established for the instrumental works, though a relative one is largely achieved. Investigations of source material have also led to the solution of crucial questions of authenticity, particularly in connection with the early works. For example, Cantata no.15, hitherto regarded as Bach's earliest cantata, has now been identified as by Johann Ludwig Bach; similarly, Cantatas nos.53, 189 and 142 have been excised from the list of his works. Several instrumental works too have gone, such as BWV553–60, 834–5, 838–9, 964, 990, 1031, 1036 and 1070.

12. BACKGROUND, STYLE, INFLUENCES. Bach's output as a whole seems unparalleled in its encyclopedic character, and embraces practically every musical genre of his time besides opera. The accepted genres were significantly added to by Bach (notably with the harpsichord concerto and chamber music with obbligato keyboard); further, he opened up new dimensions in virtually every department of creative work to which he turned, in format, density and musical quality, and also in technical demands (a work like the *St Matthew Passion* is unique in music up to and including the 18th century). At the same time Bach's creative production was inextricably bound up with the external factors of his places of work and his employers, as was normal in his time. The composition dates of the various repertories thus reflect Bach's preoccupations in his various official

capacities. Thus most of the organ works were composed while he was active as an organist at Arnstadt, Mühlhausen and Weimar; most of his output of chamber music comes from the period when he was Kapellmeister at Cöthen; and the main vocal works belong to the period of his Kantorate at Leipzig. But Bach's production was by no means wholly dependent on the duties attaching to his office at the time. Thus during his Leipzig period he found time to produce a body of keyboard music to meet his requirements for concerts, for advertisement, for teaching and other purposes. And his career may be seen as a steady and logical process of development: from organist to Konzertmeister, then to Kapellmeister, and finally to Kantor and director of music – a continual expansion of the scope of his work and responsibilities. This is no matter of chance. Bach chose his appointments, and chose the moment to make each move. If he was unable to accomplish what he required (as was often the case in Leipzig), he was capable of turning his attention elsewhere in pursuit of his creative aims. Bach was a surprisingly emancipated and self-confident artist for his time.

The uncertainty about the dating of Bach's early works makes it difficult to reconstruct and assess the beginnings of his work as a composer. The Capriccio BWV992 of 1703–4 is the earliest of his works that can be dated within two or three years; and it is doubtful whether he had composed much music before then. He took no formal lessons with an established composer, like Handel with Zachow; but it would be mistaken to call him self-taught as a composer, for the significance of his belonging to a long-standing family of professional musicians should not be underestimated. Composing was probably overshadowed by instrumental playing in Ambrosius Bach's family; this must certainly have applied to the young Johann Sebastian, and probably he devoted more attention to his training as an instrumentalist, especially as an organist, than to composition studies. But the art of improvisation – in those days inseparably bound up with practice on the instrument – would at worst prepare the ground for his work as a composer. This reciprocity between performing and composing is reflected in the unruly virtuoso and improvisatory elements in Bach's early works.

As composers who influenced the young Bach, C. P. E. Bach cited (to Forkel) Froberger, Kerll, Pachelbel, Frescobaldi, Fischer, Strungk, certain French composers, Bruhns, Buxtehude, Reincken and Böhm – almost exclusively keyboard composers; C. P. E. Bach also said that Bach formed his style through his own efforts and developed his fugal technique basically through private study and reflection. In his letter of resignation from Mühlhausen Bach himself wrote of having procured a 'grossen Apparat' ('large supply') of vocal compositions, suggesting that in vocal music too he was decisively stimulated by the study of other composers' music. Bach came into personal contact with the last three of the composers named by C. P. E.; there was no question of any teacher–pupil relationship. As later influences, C. P. E. Bach named Fux, Caldara, Handel, Keiser, Hasse, the two Grauns, Telemann, Zelenka and Benda. This list, though certainly less representative than the earlier one, suggests that Bach's main interests still lay in his great contemporaries, whose music he not only heard but also studied in transcripts. His one-sided attention to earlier masters of organ music had disappeared, but his interest in the retrospective style

represented by Fux and Caldara, complemented by his enthusiasm (mentioned by Birnbaum, 1737) for Palestrina and Lotti, is notable, and is borne out by tendencies in his music from the mid-1730s. Clearly he also became interested in, and ready to follow, more recent stylistic trends, particularly after the time of his contact with the Dresden court (for example in the 'Christe eleison' of what was to become the B minor Mass); also in such works as the Peasant Cantata, the Goldberg Variations and the *Musical Offering*. Mizler, in an article of 1739 on Bach's cantata style, referring to the Scheibe–Birnbaum controversy, mentioned a work (BWV Anh.13, lost) composed 'perfectly in accordance with the newest taste' ('vollkommen nach dem neuesten Geschmack eingerichtet').

The literary sources, surprisingly, nowhere mention Vivaldi and other contemporary Italian composers. Yet it was Vivaldi who exercised what was probably the most lasting and distinctive influence on Bach from about 1712–13, when a wide range of the Italian repertory became available to the Weimar court orchestra. Bach drew from Vivaldi his clear melodic contours, the sharp outlines of his outer parts, his motoric and rhythmic conciseness, his unified motivic treatment and his clearly articulated modulation schemes. His confrontation with Vivaldi's music in 1713–14 provoked what was certainly the strongest single development towards Bach's personal style, and that style's unmistakable identity came about through his coupling of Italianisms with complex counterpoint, marked by busy interweavings of the inner voices as well as harmonic refinement. It is impossible to describe Bach's personal style by means of simple formulae; but the process of adaptation and mutation that can be felt throughout his output seems to have taken a particularly characteristic turn at that point in 1713–14 whose principal landmarks are the *Orgel-Büchlein* and the first Weimar series of cantatas. His adaptation and integration of various contemporary and retrospective styles represent his systematic attempt at shaping and perfecting his personal musical language and expanding its structural possibilities and its expressive powers.

An essential component of Bach's style can be seen in his combination of solid compositional craftsmanship with instrumental and vocal virtuosity. The technical demands made by his music reflect his own prowess as an instrumentalist. Bach's own versatility – his early involvement in singing (it is not known whether he was later active as a singer), and his experience as a keyboard player, violinist and violist – was partly responsible for the fact that demanding technical standards became the norm for every type of composition he wrote. This led to Scheibe's famous criticism: 'Since he judges according to his own fingers, his pieces are extremely difficult to play; for he demands that singers and instrumentalists should be able to do with their throats and instruments whatever he can play on the keyboard. But this is impossible'. It makes no essential difference at what level these demands are made (for instance between the Inventions and the Goldberg Variations, the four-part chorale and the choral fugue); everywhere Bach's requirements are the antithesis of conventional simplicity. Yet technical virtuosity never predominates; it becomes a functional element within the composition as a whole. Bach's impulse towards integration is also manifested in the typically instrumental idiom in which he cast his vocal parts. He thus produced in his music for voices and instruments a homogeneous language of considerable density. For all that, he differentiated between instrumentally and (less often) vocally dominated types of writing; but even in such vocally dominated pieces as the Credo of the B minor Mass he maintained both the density and the uncompromising, yet appropriate technical standard. It is of course significant, both as regards matters of technique and the quality of his music in general that, as far as we know, he wrote almost exclusively for himself, his own performing groups of his pupils, and never for a broader public (let alone a non-professional one). This partly explains why his music – unlike, say, Telemann's or Handel's – was disseminated within unusually narrow confines.

13. CANTATAS. About two-fifths of Bach's sacred cantatas must be considered lost; of the secular cantatas, more are lost than survive. The possibility of saying anything with absolute certainty about the cantata's evolution in Bach's hands is thus limited, even though the surviving repertory is considerable and roughly corresponds in its proportions to Bach's production of cantatas at the various places where he worked.

The earliest surviving cantatas, and probably Bach's first, date from the Mühlhausen period and include nos.131 and 106 (c1707). The only others from this time are nos.71 and 196 (1708) and nos.4 and 150

(c1708 or a little later). These are not cantatas of the type established by Neumeister in 1700 but rely closely on central German tradition. The texts were mostly taken from the Bible or the chorale repertory; more rarely they were freely conceived poetry. Musically they are marked by their varied sequence of sections representing different kinds of composition: concerto, motet, (strophic) aria and chorale, thus attaining a particularly high degree of interdependence and correspondence between text (even individual words and phrases) and music, in line with the Lutheran ideal of 'proclamation of the word'. His cantatas were put together from combinations of these formal sections adapted from the late 17th-century motet and the vocal concerto tradition, even the unique chorale cantata *per omnes versus* no.4. Bach did not call these works cantatas: generally he reserved that term for the solo cantata of the Italian type (like nos.211 and 212), calling his sacred cantatas 'Concerto', and in earlier works 'Motetto', sometimes 'Dialogus' (depending on the text) or simply 'Music'.

Bach's early cantatas are distinguished from their central German precursors by his tendency to give each movement a unified structure, assuring its artistic independence, and his development of a broad formal scheme. Further, he found the means to unify movements that are not self-contained by the use of motivic material, in solo movements, and, in choral

5. *Autograph MS of Bach's Serenata 'Durchlauchtster Leopold'* BWV173a, *composed ?c1722, with the text of the sacred cantata 'Erhöhtes Fleisch und Blut'* BWV173 *added 1724 (D-Bds Mus.ms.Bach P 42, f.1r)*

ones, with the 'permutational fugue', his earliest type of choral fugue, in which the subject and its counterpoints are retained and continually interchanged. Reacting against the use of a haphazard sequential form, with its danger of formal dissolution and small-scale, motet-like articulation, he began to use strictly symmetrical sequences of movements: for example, chorus–solos–chorus–solos–chorus (no.106).

During his early Weimar years, organ music must have dominated his output; at any rate, no vocal works have survived from then. His first secular cantata, the *Jagd-Kantate* no.208, written to a commission from the Weissenfels court, probably dates from 1713. Newly acquainted with the Italian style, he here began to take up the recitative and the modern kind of aria (for preference the da capo aria), a step which had a decisive effect on the subsequent sacred cantatas. The first of these seems to have been no.21, probably written in connection with his application for the position in Halle in December 1713. Then, with his nomination as court Konzertmeister in March 1714, he began his first cantata series with a view to producing an entire cycle over four years. The principle of cycles is closely bound up with the history of the cantata from Neumeister on; the texts too were for the most part collected and published in cycles. Bach, however, never adhered strictly to a single poet (except in the lost Picander cycle of 1728–9). In Weimar he turned for the first time to librettos by Neumeister (nos.18 and 61) and used texts by G. C. Lehms (1684–1717; nos.199 and 54), but evidently preferred texts by the Weimar court poet Salomo Franck (1659–1725), the author of extremely original and profoundly felt sacred and secular poetic texts, among the best Bach set. The sequence of the Weimar cantatas is: 1714 – nos.182, 12, 172, 54, 199, 61, 152, (?)18; 1715 – 80a, 31, 165, 185, 161, 162, 163, 132; 1716 – 155, 70a, 186a, 147a (?unfinished). No.21 may precede 1714.

Musically the works are of particular importance for the development they show in Bach's personal style of writing for voices and instruments. There is a wide variety of treatments. Bach gradually established a number of types of setting, which remain basically unchanged even in the later Leipzig cantatas. Solo movements prevail, especially arias, which become longer and vocally (as well as instrumentally) more virtuoso, and are generally in da capo form. For the first time Bach used recitative, usually with syllabic declamation. At first he also used extended, arioso-like passages, corresponding with the relatively reserved, speech-song manner of the recitative 'senza battuta' (as in no.182). The contrast between the more melodious arioso, often marked by characteristic motifs, and the free, harmonically more daring recitative is later much stronger. The choruses too follow a multiplicity of principles of construction, among them fugue and canon (no.182), passacaglia (12), concerto (172), motet (21) or French overture (61). They fall into two general categories (from which numerous mixed forms derive): concertante style in the manner of the aria and sectionalized polyphony in the manner of the motet. Bach also interspersed instrumental and vocal formal schemes, inserted choral sections into solo movements and used instrumental elaborations of chorale melodies. The instrumentation is sometimes extraordinarily colourful; within the smallest of performing ensembles Bach tried out a great variety of combinations. Following the

Italian ideal, his orchestral writing moved away from the French practice of five-part writing, with two violas, which predominates in the early cantatas towards a more flexible four-part style. Instead of the harmonic weight of the middle voices in five-part writing Bach provided a rhythmically and melodically active viola part that is particularly characteristic.

In Cöthen, corresponding to Bach's official responsibilities, only secular cantatas were composed (with the single exception of BWV Anh.5) and those were mostly written for New Year celebrations or the prince's birthday. Bach's librettist was C. F. Hunold ('Menantes', 1681–1721). Among the Cöthen cantatas, many survive only as verbal texts or are lost altogether. These pieces mostly exemplify the 'serenata' type of work, with succinct operatic treatment in dialogues between allegorical figures. It is not surprising that they reflect Bach's contemporary contact with the instrumental concerto or that dance characteristics appear, notably in the solo movements.

At Leipzig the performance of sacred cantatas on Sundays and feast days (some 60 a year) was one of Bach's chief tasks, and he produced a large number of new works. His vast work-load meant that within the first cycle he not only had to rely on repeat performances of earlier sacred cantatas (often revised) but also had to resort to parodies on secular cantatas written at Cöthen. Nevertheless, his first cycle (1723–4) contains the following new compositions: nos.75, 76, 24, 167, 136, 105, 46, 179, 69a, 77, 25, 119, 138, 95, 148, 48, 109, 89, 194, 60, 90, 40, 64, 190, 153, 65, possibly 154, 73, 81, 83, 144, possibly 181, 67, 104, 166, 86, 37 and 44; to these must be added his test works (nos.22 and 23, for Quinquagesima 1723). Apart from no.24 (Neumeister) the poet or poets are unknown.

In these works Bach used a large variety of different forms, free from any schematicism. Three favourite groundplans may be cited: biblical text–recitative–aria–recitative–aria–chorale (nos.46, 105, 136 etc); chorale–aria–recitative–aria–chorale (nos.40, 48, 64 etc); biblical text–aria–chorale–recitative–aria–chorale (nos.86, 144, 166 etc). A constant feature, characteristic of the Leipzig cantatas as a whole, is the framework, comprising an introductory choral movement in the grand style (solo pieces appear rarely at the start) and closing four-part chorales, simple but expressive. Compared with the Weimar cantatas, the instrumentation is more refined though in some ways less colourful. The orchestral forces are larger. From no.75 onwards the brass (mainly trumpets and horns) are more strongly deployed, the flute is brought into play increasingly after 1724, and the oboe d'amore (from no.75) and the oboe da caccia (from no.167) are introduced as new instruments. Instrumental virtuosity is heightened, and the melismatic quality of the vocal writing is further developed. The 'prelude and fugue' type of movement is frequently used for the introductory chorus (as in no.46).

With the second cycle, dating from 1724–5, Bach turned to the concept of a cantata cycle based on a unifying theme. It consists mainly of a series of freshly composed chorale cantatas: nos.20, 2, 7, 135, 10, 93, 107, 178, 94, 101, 113, 33, 78, 99, 8, 130, 114, 96, 5, 180, 38, 115, 139, 26, 116, 62, 91, 121, 133, 122, 41, 123, 124, 3, 111, 92, 125, 126, 127 and 1. From Easter 1725, this series was continued with cantatas in the usual form, *Easter Oratorio*, nos.6, 42 and 85, and then with nine cantatas to texts by Marianne von Ziegler (1695–1760): 103, 108, 87, 128, 183, 74, 68, 175 and 176. 1724–5 was not only the most productive year for cantatas; it also, with the chorale cantata, saw the beginnings of a type that perhaps represents Bach's most important contribution to the history of the genre. What is particularly striking is his endeavour to lay out the introductory movements as large-scale cantus firmus compositions, using a great variety of structural principle. Cohesion between the cantata's movements is guaranteed, at least from the textual point of view, by their relationship to the fundamental chorale (with chorale paraphrases for the solo pieces, as opposed to the procedure in no.4); often it is further emphasized by references to the cantus firmus and by the use of various ways of intermingling cantus firmus and free material. The author of the texts for the chorale cantatas is not known – Pastor Weiss of Leipzig is a possibility, but not Bach himself, as has been supposed. The way in which Ziegler's texts are set is not essentially different from the manner of the first cycle.

With the third cycle, from 1725–7, the continuous production of cantatas ends, or so the sources indicate. The forms include solo and dialogue cantatas, and large-scale works in two parts. Bach showed a wide variety of approaches. He continued the cycle of chorale cantatas with further words of that type (no.137), reverted to texts by Neumeister (28), Franck (72) or Lehms (110, 57, 151, 16, 32, 13, 170, 35), and experimented with forms using two different texts from the Bible – one from the Old Testament and one from the New (the former in the introductory movement, the latter in a central one). The third cycle, and also the fourth, make extensive use of pre-existing concerto material, perhaps from Cöthen, as instrumental sinfonias at the beginning of a number of cantatas (nos.110, 156, 174, 120a). From late 1726 obbligato organ parts appear (nos.35, 146, 169, 49, 188). The third cycle was followed by the 1728–9 cycle on texts by Picander, which has disappeared – all that remains are nine pieces and a fraction of a tenth. A chief feature of the Picander texts appears to be the interpolation of chorale and free poetry in arias and choruses, giving opportunities for various sorts of combinatorial technique (see the second movements of nos.156 and 159; also the first movement of the St Matthew Passion. The cantatas written after 1729 contribute nothing essentially new. It is interesting to find modifications of the chorale cantata type among later works in the genre (nos.117, 192, 112, 177, 97, 100); at the same time, Bach abandoned freely composed texts, although the central movements (unlike those in no.4) are constructed in the manner of recitatives and arias. His increasing receptiveness towards new stylistic trends should be noted in several arias in the later cantatas.

Besides the cantatas composed in connection with the church year, Bach also wrote sacred cantatas for other occasions, like changes of town council, weddings, funerals, the jubilee celebrations of the Confession of Augsburg (1730) and inaugurations of organs; in style these are essentially indistinguishable from the other works. The body of cantatas, for all its variety, has an unusually self-contained character, maintained above all by its constant high musical quality and its unfailing expressive profundity. Bach's expressive urge, as seen in individual arias and choruses, was not confined to single words as the primary bearers of expression, but from

the outset was geared to movements and formal sections as a whole, in keeping with Baroque formal models (like the *ABA* of the da capo aria). Only within the context of a movement's structural and expressive unity did he regard the special treatment of single words as possible or logical. Among the tools of Bach's craft the traditions of *musica poetica* and musical rhetoric (the theory of musical figures) must certainly be reckoned. They were deeply rooted in him. Yet to reduce Bach's intentions to their rhetorical and figural components, or even to emphasize those components, would be to diminish their true breadth. Over and above this objective of expressive unity, Bach was always primarily concerned with the contrapuntal organization of melodic–rhythmic and harmonic textures to establish coherence. That is a principal reason why his cantata movements lend themselves so readily to parody. The technical prerequisites for producing a parody work – which Bach did so often – are metrical similarity and expressive affinity; a further essential requirement is self-sufficiency of the musical substance, and its flexibility leaves considerable scope for the musical interpretation of a new text.

During his early Leipzig years Bach wrote only isolated secular cantatas. These were produced for various occasions: university ceremonies (nos.36b, 198, 205, 207), celebrations at the Thomasschule (BWV Anh.18, Anh.19, 36c), festivities in the houses of noblemen and prominent citizens (216, 210, 249b, 30a, 210a, 212) and commissions from court (249a, 36a). Most of his large-scale congratulatory and homage cantatas written for the electoral house of Saxony were produced at the collegium musicum. A favourite format was the operatic *dramma per musica*, with a simple plot suited to the nature of the festivities, with characters from mythology, shepherds or allegorical characters (nos.213, 206, 214, 207a, 215). The more lyrical cantatas such as no.204, or the two Italian works, nos.203 and 209, would certainly have been performed at the collegium musicum. The Coffee and Peasant Cantatas (nos.211 and 212), to some extent tinged with folk style, are distinguished by their lifelike and humorous characterization. The librettist of most of the works of 1725–42 was the versatile Picander, the only other important poet for Bach's cantatas during this period being J. C. Gottsched (1700–66), the influential Leipzig professor of rhetoric (no.198, *Auf süss entzückende Gewalt* (not in BWV) and Anh. 13).

14. ORATORIOS, PASSIONS, LATIN WORKS. The three works by Bach designated 'oratorios' fall within a very short period: the *Christmas Oratorio* of 1734–5, the *Easter Oratorio* and *Ascension Oratorio* of 1735. The librettists are not known for certain. The place of the oratorio in the Lutheran liturgy is the same as that for the cantata; the oratorio can be distinguished from the cantata only in that it has a self-contained plot. In this Bach's use of the term differs from its usual application. In the *Christmas Oratorio* the normal character of a single self-contained work is contradicted by its being split into sections for six different services between Christmas Day and Epiphany, and this is further emphasized by Bach in his use of different performing forces for the sections (although these are based on an underlying general scheme, and are grouped round six scenes from the Bible, with certain divergences from the allocation of lessons to be read at the various services). All three works are essentially based on parodies of

secular cantatas whose music, initially associated with a particular occasion, could reasonably be re-used in this way (the *Christmas Oratorio* from nos.213, 214 and 215 among other works; the *Easter Oratorio* by a re-working of parts of BWV249a; the *Ascension Oratorio* above all from BWV Anh.18). However, there is so much that is new and individual in the *Christmas Oratorio*, especially in the biblical choruses and the chorales and in the *Ascension Oratorio*, that the works are in no sense subordinate to their originals. The pervasive use of texts from the Gospels, moreover, gives the works a special status, linking them with the Protestant *historia* and thus ultimately with the Passion.

Of the five Passions mentioned in the necrology two survive (*St Matthew* and *St John*), for one the text survives (*St Mark*; the only known copy was destroyed in World War II, although some of the music survives in its original form in Cantatas nos.54 and 198, and one movement was revised for the *Christmas Oratorio*) and the other two are lost. The unauthentic *St Luke Passion* was probably included among Bach's works in error because the score, dating from about 1730, was copied in Bach's hand and contained additions by him. This means that only one Passion remains to be accounted for. Recent research on the *St John* and *St Matthew* has shown that some of their movements must have originated in a Passion setting dating from Bach's pre-Leipzig days, probably from his Weimar period, notably the chorus 'O Mensch bewein' (used in both works) as well as the three arias 'Himmel, reisse', 'Zerschmettert mich' and 'Ach windet euch nicht so' (*St John*). Hilgenfeldt (1850) mentioned a Passion by Bach dating from 1717, giving no indication of the source of his information. In Weimar, before 1714, Bach made a transcript of Keiser's *St Mark Passion*, so his interest in the genre is established for this period; the missing fifth Passion may thus well be a lost Weimar work.

The three known works represent the same type of Passion oratorio, in the tradition of the *historia*, in which the biblical text is retained as a whole (for the soloists – Evangelist, Jesus, Pilate etc – and the turba choruses), and is interrupted by contemplative, so-called 'madrigal' pieces set to freely composed verse, as well as by chorales. A special feature of Bach's Passions is the unusual frequency of the chorales, which are set in extremely expressive four-part writing. From the textual point of view the *St John Passion* of 1724 lacks unity. The freely composed parts of the text rely mainly on the

6. *Autograph MS of the opening Sinfonia (arranged from the Prelude of the Partita for violin in E BWV1006) from Bach's cantata 'Wir danken dir, Gott, wir danken dir' BWV29, composed 1731 (D-Bds Mus.ms.Bach P 166, f.1r)*

famous Passion poem by B. H. Brockes (*Der für die Sünde der Welt gemarterte und sterbende Jesus*, 1712) and the *St John Passion* libretto by C. H. Postel (*c*1700). Besides this, the Evangelist's part contains interpolations from *St Matthew*. Musically, various allusions to the Postel *St John Passion* long attributed to Handel, now generally ascribed to Böhm, can be enumerated. Bach made countless alterations in the work for its various performances. In 1725 the opening and closing choruses were interchanged and arias were added; the new additions may well be from the lost Weimar Passion. In a third version, dating from around 1730, the interpolations from *St Matthew* were deleted and replaced by a (lost) sinfonia. In a fourth and final version, dating from Bach's last years (1746–9), the original sequence of movements was largely re-established, and the performing forces were augmented.

The history of the *St Matthew Passion*, with its double chorus, is less complicated, though not entirely straightforward. Here again the date of the first performance is open to question (1727 or 1729); and because of lacunae in the source material it is not clear which items (apart from 'O Mensch bewein', which was incorporated in 1736 from the second version of the *St John Passion*) originated with an earlier Passion or Passion cantata of 1725 on a text by Picander – if indeed Bach set that text. The *St Matthew Passion*, however, right from its foundations in Picander's libretto, was essentially conceived as a unity; and its increased scope for arias and 'madrigal' pieces in general (the coupling of arioso with aria being especially typical) allowed for a greater breadth of design. A special feature, following an older tradition, is the inclusion of the strings to provide an accompanying halo in Jesus's recitatives. Clearly it was planned as a unity in a sense that the *St John Passion* was not: witness the relationships between the chorales, the distribution of tonalities, the couplings of movements; the *St John*, by comparison, lacks a structural centre (see Smend, 1926). The *St Matthew Passion* had at least two subsequent performances: in 1736, with the continuo part strictly divided between the two choruses, a simple chorale replaced by 'O Mensch bewein' at the end of part I, and the viola da gamba replacing the lute in 'Komm süsses Kreuz'; and in the 1740s, with some changes in the manner of performance and certain minor revisions.

In its main sections, that is in the 'madrigal' pieces, the *St Mark Passion* of 1731 is a parody work whose main sources are the *Trauer Ode* (Cantata no.198) and the Funeral Music for Leopold (BWV244a). Although only the text survives, the music can in part be reconstructed from these works; the possibility of adding movements from Cantatas nos.54 and 7, the *Christmas Oratorio* and some chorales has been suggested by Smend (1940–48) in particular.

In Bach's time Latin polyphonic music was still often used in ordinary Lutheran Sunday worship, and particularly at important church feasts. Further, the concerted *Magnificat* continued to hold its place in Vespers, notably at Christmas and Easter. Bach had been interested in Latin polyphonic music at least by his Weimar period, as his copies of pieces by other composers demonstrate (Peranda, Johann Ludwig and Johann Nicolaus Bach, Pez, Wilderer, Bassani, Caldara, Lotti, Palestrina etc; catalogue in Wolff, 1968). He also wrote insertions in this style for other composers' works, and made some arrangements (Sanctus BWV241; Credo

intonation for a mass by Bassani; 'Suscepit Israel' for a *Magnificat* by Caldara). His earliest surviving work of this type is probably the Kyrie BWV233a on the cantus firmus 'Christe, du Lamm Gottes'. Then in his first year at Leipzig came the *Magnificat*, first the E♭ version, with four inserted Christmas pieces (BWV243a), revised in D major in 1728–31, without the Christmas pieces, for use on any major feast day (BWV243). Among the various Sanctus settings attributed to Bach probably only BWV238 is an original composition (1723–4); BWV241 has been identified as an arrangement after J. C. Kerll's *Missa superba*. The two short masses in F and G minor (BWV233 and 235) probably date from the mid-1720s; like their later companion-pieces in A and G (BWV234 and 236) of 1735–40 they are for the most part parody works based on cantata movements (nos.11, 102, 40, Anh.18; 102, 72, 187; 67, 179, 79, 136; 179, 79, 138, 17). The Latin Christmas music Cantata no.191 comes from the Gloria of BWV232.

Bach's masterpiece in this genre is of course the work known – though not conceived as a unity – as the B minor Mass. Its genesis stretched over more than two decades. Bach's aim seems to have been to bring together a collection of large-scale mass movements to serve as models rather than to create a single, multi-movement work on an unprecedented scale. The oldest section is the Sanctus of 1724. The Kyrie and Gloria come from the 1733 *Missa* dedicated to the Dresden court, while the Credo or 'Symbolum Nicenum' was composed only during Bach's last years. In many respects these two main sections represent Bach's ideals of Latin polyphonic music: in their stylistic many-sidedness, with deliberately archaic styles contrasted with modern ones; in their abandonment of the da capo aria and the recitative; and in their formal autonomy. The Credo is a particularly good example of Bach's self-contained, symmetrical layout (Table 1). The *Missa* and

TABLE 1

the Credo have a series of parody originals (Cantatas nos.29, 46; 171, 12, 120); in the latter only the 'Credo' and the 'Confiteor' seem to be original compositions. Further, the last four pieces are parody movements that Bach added in 1748–9 ('Osanna', BWV Anh.11; 'Benedictus', an unknown aria; Agnus, Cantata no.11; 'Dona' from the *Missa*), alongside the old Sanctus, to complete the collection.

15. MOTETS, CHORALES, SONGS. In Bach's time motets were sung as introits for services and on certain special occasions. The Leipzig tradition was to select introit motets from the *Florilegium portense* (1603), a classical repertory from the 16th century compiled by Erhard Bodenschatz. For this reason, in Leipzig – no Weimar compositions of this kind are known – Bach wrote motets only for special occasions, probably only for burial services, although in only one case, *Der Geist hilft*, is there documentary evidence of this. Bach's

motet texts, following the tradition, are based on biblical quotations and chorales; freely composed poetry is used in only one case, and even this is songbook poetry (*Komm, Jesu, komm*, Paul Thymich). On the occasions for which the motets were composed, Bach normally had more than the school choristers at his disposal; he was thus able to use between five- and eight-part writing, as he did in five pieces (BWV225–9). It was a rule in the performance of motets at Leipzig, including those from *Florilegium portense*, that a continuo part should be included – to be precise, a harpsichord and string bass. The performing parts that have survived for *Der Geist hilft*, with strings (first chorus) and reed instruments (second chorus) doubling the voices, cannot necessarily be taken as applicable to the other motets; a similar special case, with partly obbligato instruments, is BWV118, *O Jesu Christ* (often referred to as a cantata, but in fact a motet).

Bach's use of double chorus and his exposition of forms of chorale treatment links the motets with the central German tradition. Among the movements closest to that tradition are the closing section of *Fürchte dich nicht*, in its combination of cantus firmus ('Warum sollt ich mich denn grämen') and freely imitative writing, and the opening section of *Komm, Jesu, komm*, with its chordal writing for double chorus. As a whole, the style of BWV118 too is retrospective, with its archaic instrumentation and its homophonic choral writing. By contrast, most movements in the motets have a markedly polyphonic vocal manner, dominated by instrumental style and showing unifying motivic work. Another characteristic is the clear formal articulation, with multi-movement works demonstrating different kinds of treatment. Thus *Jesu, meine Freude*, the longest work of this kind, in 11 movements, is the most strictly (that is, symmetrically) conceived: the opening and closing movements are identical, the second and the tenth use the same material, and the third to fifth largely correspond with the seventh to ninth; the central sixth is a fugue. *Der Geist hilft* begins with a concerto-like movement, followed by a double fugue and a simple chorale setting (apparently taken from the lost cantata of the preceding Whit Sunday, in the Picander cycle). The form of the instrumental concerto (fast–slow–fast) is used in *Singet dem Herrn*. For a repeat performance in the 1740s, *O Jesu Christ*, originally composed about 1736–7, was revised in its instrumentation, with strings, oboes, bassoons and horns; the original had only two *litui*, cornett and three trombones. The authenticity of *Lobet den Herrn* has been questioned (Geck, *BJb*, liii, 1967); the paucity of comparative material makes conclusions difficult. Bach's arrangement of Pergolesi's *Stabat mater* with the psalm text 'Tilge, Höchster, meine Sünden', dating from 1741–6, should be counted among the motets.

Bach's composition of chorales is most closely associated with his production of cantatas. Four-part chorale style, or *stylus simplex* (but generally with elaborate bass parts and contrapuntally active middle voices), was normal for his closing movements, particularly in the Leipzig cantatas; it also often occurred at the ends of subsections in large-scale works, notably the Passions. Bach's chorale writing is characterized by the 'speaking' quality of the part-writing and the harmonies – meaning that they aim to be a direct interpretation of the text. The posthumously published collections (Birnstiel, 2 vols., 1765, 1769; Breitkopf, 4

vols., 1784–7) contain almost 200 of the chorales known from Bach's vocal works, some under different titles; about 50 known chorales are lacking. The Breitkopf edition, prepared by C. P. E. Bach and Kirnberger, contains 371 chorales, among them more than 100 not found in the extant vocal works. This provides an important pointer to the lost vocal music, and though extremely difficult to follow up it has borne some fruits, as in the reconstruction of the *St Mark Passion* or the Picander cycle. It is worth remarking that the number of excess chorales more or less corresponds to the number to be expected from the lost cantata cycles and oratorio-type compositions.

Only three of the chorales are known to have been written for special occasions – BWV250–52, intended for weddings. The repertory of 348 known from the Breitkopf edition (23 of the 371 are duplicates) was already available before the printed edition in more or less complete manuscript collections circulating among Bach's pupils. As a teacher of composition Bach laid particular emphasis on chorale writing, and a specially didactic character may be ascribed to the chorale collections. According to C. P. E. Bach, his father treated chorale writing as the final stage of instruction in figured bass: he asked his pupils to write middle parts between a given melody and bass, or, at a more advanced level, required them to add a bass to a given melody. This procedure recalls his own approach to composition (outer parts first, then inner parts) and also his approach in adapting chorales from other sources (like Vopelius's *Neu Leipziger Gesangbuch*, 1682), where he would take over the outer parts and write new inner ones.

Under the generic heading of 'sacred songs' come the 69 melodies with figured bass in G. C. Schemelli's *Musicalisches Gesang-Buch* (1736). According to the foreword, Bach edited the figured basses of all the pieces; but only three melodies (BWV452, 478, 505) are demonstrably his. He seems to have been only peripherally occupied with the composition of songs and strophic arias, as the limited surviving repertory, for which the only source is the second *Clavier-Büchlein* for Anna Magdalena Bach (1725), indicates (BWV508–17).

Unique among his vocal works is a multi-sectional Quodlibet for four voices and continuo (BWV524) which has survived only in fragmentary form. It was probably composed for a wedding in 1707, and is evidently connected with the playing, in contrapuntal combinations of folktunes with comic and even obscene texts, as was customary in the Bach family circle.

16. ORGAN MUSIC. Unlike the vocal music and the chamber and orchestral works, Bach's output for keyboard instruments stretches from the very beginnings of his activities as a composer up to his last months in a relatively unbroken succession. There are certainly spells of heightened activity for example of organ music during the Weimar and pre-Weimar years or of harpsichord music in the Cöthen period and around 1730. As a whole, however, Bach seems to have cultivated the two genres alongside each other. It is thus the more surprising that, right from the beginning, in full awareness of the consequences, and in defiance of inherited 17th-century tradition, he abandoned under Buxtehude's influence the conventional community of repertory between organ and harpsichord, choosing to write specifically for the one or the other. The uncompromising use of obbligato pedals, in particular, is a distinguishing

7. *Autograph MS of the end of Bach's organ chorale 'Der Tag, der ist so freudenreich' (completed in new German organ tablature) from the 'Orgel-Büchlein', composed c1713–17 (D-Bds Mus.ms.Bach P 283, f.9r)*

mark of Bach's organ style. Only exceptionally (for example in the chorale partitas and the small chorale arrangements from the third part of the *Clavier-Übung*) do the performing possibilities coincide so that organ and harpsichord become truly interchangeable.

Since most of Bach's keyboard works from the pre-Leipzig years survive in copies (generally made in the circle of Bach's pupils) rather than in autograph scores, it is not possible to establish a precise chronology. Even a relative one is possible only in general terms, with considerations of style and authenticity holding the balance. In the earliest works the influence of Bach's model is pronounced. These include the chorale partitas BWV766–8, wrought in the manner of Böhm (BWV768 was expanded during Bach's Weimar period); but it is difficult to judge whether these pieces date back to the Lüneburg years. The Canzona BWV588, the *Allabreve* BWV589 and the Pastorale BWV590 show late 17th-century south German and Italian characteristics, while the Fantasia in G BWV572 looks to the French style. With its sectional layout and other north German features, the Prelude and Fugue in E BWV566 must have been written under Buxtehude's immediate influence, suggesting a date around 1706; its G minor counterpart BWV535a, datable before 1708 from the autograph (the earliest surviving keyboard one), shows a marked movement away from Buxtehude in its more sharply defined prelude-and-fugue structure.

The extraordinary harmonic boldness and the richness of fermata embellishment in the pieces BWV715, 722 and 732, intended to accompany chorales, imply that they belong to the Arnstadt period where Bach's treatment of chorales caused confusion among the congregation. The fugues after Legrenzi and Corelli, BWV574 and 579, should probably be placed among the early works; and to these must be added a further series of organ pieces, both based on chorales and freely composed, all markedly indebted to his brother's teacher Pachelbel and owing their impression of personal style basically to unusual harmonies and distinct virtuosity while following traditional models in form and in many other respects. Bach's early interest in pedal virtuosity is attested by the *Exercitium* BWV598.

The models recede in importance from the Mühlhausen period, at the latest, and Bach's individuality begins to pervade every note of his compositions. This applies particularly to the many extended organ chorale settings probably dating from between 1709 and 1712–13 (BWV651, etc). In his freely composed organ works

(toccatas, preludes, fantasias and fugues) Bach tightened up the formal scheme, preparing the way for the two-movement prelude and fugue through an intermediate type in which the fugue was a long, self-contained complex but the prelude was not yet a unified section (such as BWV532). Probably the most important work of these years is the Passacaglia in C minor BWV582. In about 1713–14 a decisive stylistic change came about, stimulated by Vivaldi's concerto form. Bach's encounter with Vivaldi's music found immediate expression in the concertos after Vivaldi's opp.3 and 7 (BWV593, etc). Features adapted from Vivaldi include the unifying use of motivic work, the motoric rhythmic character, the modulation schemes and the principle of solo–tutti contrast as means of formal articulation; the influence may be seen in the Toccata in C BWV564. Apparently Bach experimented for a short while with a free, concerto-like organ form in three movements (fast–slow–fast) but finally turned to the two-movement form, as in BWV534 and 536. Of comparable importance to the introduction of the concerto element is his tendency towards condensed motivic work, as in the *Orgel-Büchlein*. Bach's conception of this new type of miniature organ chorale, combining rhetorical and expressive musical language with refined counterpoint, probably dates back to 1713–14; among the earliest examples are BWV601, 608, 627 and 630, and around 1715–16 Bach added BWV615, 623, 640 and 644 (to cite some typical examples). By the end of the Weimar period the *Orgel-Büchlein* was complete in all essentials; only the fragment *O Traurigkeit* and BWV614 (added in about 1740) are later. The number of pieces, fewer than 50, is considerably below the 164 originally projected by Bach; evidently he lost interest in this most original form.

Among the few organ pieces composed at Cöthen are the C major Fantasia BWV573 of about 1722 and apparently at least the earlier version of BWV653 (*An Wasserflüssen*) and a revision of the Fantasia and Fugue in G minor BWV542, these last two probably prepared for Bach's Hamburg candidature in 1720. Then, in Leipzig, there came about 1727 the trio sonatas, a new genre of organ composition in three-part contrapuntal writing (the six works are at least in part based on chamber works); these were followed by a series of preludes and fugues, now always in two sections with the preludes as important as the fugues – surely a consequence of the '48'. There is a final flourish of virtuosity in works like the E minor Prelude and Fugue BWV548, though always in a clearcut form (BWV548 provides a rare example of a da capo fugue).

The organ music from this time on must be seen in conjunction with Bach's extensive activities as a recitalist. In 1739, as the third part of the *Clavier-Übung*, he published a comprehensive and very varied group of organ works. Framed by a Prelude and Fugue in E♭ (BWV552), there are nine chorale arrangements for Mass and 12 for the catechism followed by four duets. Bach's encyclopedic intentions can be seen in the form of the work – that of a collection of specimen organ pieces for large church instruments and smaller domestic ones (including the harpsichord), symbolized in his invariable coupling of a large piece with a small; they can equally be seen in the variety of his contrapuntal methods, whereby he constantly produced fresh kinds of cantus firmus treatment. At the very end of Bach's output for the organ are such disparate works as the 'Schübler' chorales (arrangements after solo movements from cantatas) and the canonic variations on *Vom Himmel hoch* BWV769. The latter, written for Mizler's society in 1747, survives in two original versions, printed and autograph, whose different sequence of movements shows Bach experimenting with symmetrical form and the placing of climaxes.

17. HARPSICHORD AND LUTE MUSIC. Bach's early compositions for harpsichord – to be taken as including those for clavichord, appropriate in music of a more intimate type – are in a similar situation to the corresponding organ works as regards dating and evaluation. Apart from the *Capriccio* BWV992, there are no compositions to which a date can be ascribed, but before 1712–13 there were countless individual pieces like toccatas, preludes and fugues (these last mainly using a 'repercussive' thematic technique, like the early organ fugues); variation form is represented by the *Aria variata* BWV989. In the toccatas (BWV910, etc), Italian, north German and French influences conjoin in equal importance (BWV912 is an interesting counterpart to the organ work BWV532); Bach's penchant for the French style is particularly evident in his abundant use of the *style brisé*. After 1712 the particular influence of Vivaldi's concertos can be seen in Bach's numerous concerto arrangements (BWV972, etc). The so-called English Suites BWV806–11 of the late Weimar years are mature examples of Bach's masterly integration of the Italian and French styles in his keyboard music.

To the early years in Cöthen belong several single works, such as the Chromatic Fantasia and Fugue BWV903, and also the *Clavier-Büchlein* for Wilhelm Friedemann, of 1720, which is predominantly didactic in layout. It is however less important for its instruction in playing technique (the *Applicatio* BWV994 gives fingering and tables of ornaments after d'Anglebert) than as a book of instruction in composition. For Bach himself, the two could not be dissociated: and the *Clavier-Büchlein* contains the beginnings of the '48' as well as early versions of the Inventions and Sinfonias, under such titles as 'preambulum' and 'fantasia'. To some extent the 1722 *Clavierbüchlein* for Anna Magdalena is a companion work, though differently laid out.

Then followed, also in 1722, *Das wohltemperirte Clavier* (book 1 of the '48'), with its 24 preludes and fugues in all the major and minor keys, surpassing, in logic, in format and in musical quality, all earlier endeavours of the same kind by other masters, like J. C. F. Fischer's *Ariadne musica*. The work shows a perfectly balanced contrast between free and strict styles, each represented by several different types of prelude and fugue. Bach's writing in book 1 of the '48' in the most varied fugues – from two- to five-part, in styles from the traditional slow ricercare to a brilliant Italianate manner, and using a wide range of technical device – represents the culmination of a 20-year process of maturation and stands unparalleled in the history of music. The final version of the two- and three-part Inventions and Sinfonias, also arranged by key, but representing a different method of composition whose object (according to Bach's foreword) was 'to teach clear playing in two and three obbligato parts, good inventions [i.e. compositional ideas] and a cantabile manner of playing', dates from 1723.

The first traces of the subsequent great works of the Leipzig period are to be found in the 1725 *Clavierbüchlein* for Anna Magdalena, which in fact anticipates the so-called French Suites BWV812–17 and the Partitas BWV825–30, respectively small-scale and large-scale suite types. The Partitas in particular represent a further culmination in Bach's output for the harpsichord; whereas the '48' shows the prelude and fugue type developed to its most consummate maturity, these present similarly matured specimens of the most popular harpsichord genre of the time, the partita, comprising a suite of dance movements and 'galanteries'. These – the burlesca, capriccio, and the like – do not appear in the English or French Suites; as in the English Suites, each of which begins with a prelude, usually in concerto style, each partita begins with a large-scale movement, each differently titled and each in a different style, among them pieces in the manner of an invention (no.3) and a French overture (no.4). Later, with the collected publication of all six in 1731, Bach inaugurated his series of published works under the general title *Clavier-Übung* (the title was borrowed from a publication by Kuhnau, his predecessor in office). In 1735 appeared the second part, whose contents were intended to be representative of the most prominent and fashionable kinds of style: the Concerto in the Italian Style BWV971 embodies the ultimate stage in the process of transcribing instrumental concertos for the harpsichord, and stands in contrast to an Overture in the French Manner BWV831 which, more markedly than the partitas, represents what was specifically French in harmony, rhythm, ornamentation and melodic invention. 1741–2 eventually saw the end of the *Clavier-Übung* series with the aria and 30 variations known as the Goldberg Variations. Apparently Bach had not cultivated the variation form since his youth, so that the contrast between the Goldberg Variations and the early works (chorale partitas, the *Aria variata*) is the more marked. This work outshines all others as far as performing technique is concerned. The large-scale sequential layout (based on a grouping of 10 × 3 movements, incorporating a series of nine canons, one at every chord variation, arranged in order of ascending intervals to move towards a climax, with a final quodlibet) is without precedent. The basis of the composition is a ground bass of 32 bars, developed from the Ruggiero and related bass patterns, first presented in the aria and then subjected to free and canonic elaboration in a wide variety of ways. In their monothematic and emphatically contrapuntal conception, the Goldberg Variations set the scene for Bach's last keyboard works – the *Musical*

8. *Autograph MS of Bach's Prelude and Fugue no.11 in F from 'Das wohltemperirte Clavier', ii*, BWV880, *composed c1740 (GB-Lbm Add.35021, ff.8r, and 8v, opposite); the final bars of the fugue are at the foot of f.8r*

Offering, Vom Himmel hoch variations and *Art of Fugue*.

Besides the harpsichord works published in the 1730s and 1740s, the only other major work is the second part of *Das wohltemperirte Clavier* (not so titled – the complete autograph does not survive). This companion-piece is less unified than book 1 and was partly assembled from existing preludes and fugues, some of them transposed. The freshly composed pieces probably date chiefly from the late 1730s; some of the preludes, particularly, show elements of the *galant* style. The work was complete by 1742.

The dates of composition of the seven surviving works for lute – apparently his total output for the instrument – cover at least 30 years. The earliest work is the Suite in E minor BWV996, which dates from the middle of the Weimar period; it already shows a surprisingly balanced construction. The Prelude in C minor BWV999 shows an affinity with the '48', and may thus belong to the Cöthen or early Leipzig period. All the other lute works were composed in Leipzig, starting with the Fugue in G minor BWV1000, an expanded polyphonic development from the violin fugue (in BWV1001), which is in a tablature copied by Bach's friend, the Leipzig lawyer and lutenist Christian Weyrauch. The Suite in G minor BWV995 (after 1011,

for cello) dates from the period 1727–31 and is dedicated to an unidentifiable 'Monsieur Schouster'. The Suite in E (BWV1006a, after 1006 for violin) survives in autograph form and is a much less demanding arrangement of its model as compared with BWV1000 and 995, and dates from the second half of the 1730s. Bach must have composed the Suite in C minor BWV997 before 1741; this is an original lute composition and is laid out in a similar virtuoso fashion to the Prelude, Fugue and Allegro in E♭ BWV998 which can be ascribed to the 1740s. The late works, with their markedly *galant* flavour, may have been written for the Dresden lutenists S. L. Weiss and J. Kropffgans, and in any case were probably played by them. There is evidence that Weiss and Kropfgans performed at Bach's house at least once, in 1739. Bach's contributions to the repertory of the lute, long past its heyday but enjoying a final flowering in the German-speaking countries, represent, along with the works of Weiss, the culmination of the instrument's 18th-century repertory. They require a 14-string instrument, but in Bach's day were at least occasionally played on the lute-harpsichord, an instrument in whose construction Bach had assisted. The indistinct line between lute and harpsichord music is illustrated by the autograph of BWV998, marked 'pour La Luth ò Cembal'.

18. ORCHESTRAL MUSIC. A considerable quantity of Bach's orchestral compositions must be reckoned as lost. The surviving repertory can in any case give only an incomplete idea of his output for larger instrumental ensembles, for he must have written many further works during his years at Cöthen and while he was working with the collegium musicum in Leipzig. Traces of lost concerto movements may be found in numerous cantatas, such as no.42, and other large-scale vocal works; and various of the surviving harpsichord concertos, in particular, invite inferences about lost originals. In the score bearing the dedication to Margrave Christian Ludwig of Brandenburg, the so-called Brandenburg Concertos are dated 24 March 1721. This is merely a *terminus ante quem*, for the concertos themselves must have been written over a considerable period before being assembled in 1721 as a collection of 'Concerts avec plusieurs instruments' (not as a single work in several parts). It cannot be proved that Bach composed instrumental music in his capacity as Konzertmeister in Weimar; but his position there and his preoccupation with the Italian concerto style during those years make it seem probable that he did. Of the Brandenburg Concertos, three (nos.1, 3 and 6) point to the Weimar period, and not only because of their particular structural and motivic indebtedness to the Italian type of concerto. The sinfonia version of no.1 (BWV1046a) appar-

ently served as instrumental introduction to Cantata no.208 of February 1713. The homogeneous string instrumentation of nos.3 and 6 also suggests an early date; the unusual combination of low strings in no.6 otherwise appears only in Weimar cantatas. Other concertos may also belong to the Weimar period, for example the violin version of BWV1052 with its markedly Vivaldian features; but no firm conclusions should be drawn about a Weimar orchestral repertory.

The special significance of the Brandenburg Concertos resides in the fact that, as a group, they abandon the standard type of concerto grosso and use a variety of solo combinations. The originality of Bach's solutions extends far beyond Vivaldi's, as do the density of the compositional texture and the level of professional virtuosity. The devising of concise head-motifs, particularly in the first movements, shows a strong Italian influence. Most of Bach's instrumentations are unprecedented. They feature all kinds of combinations, from homogeneous string sound (no.3, with its unusual three-way symmetries deriving from the use of three each of violins, violas and cellos with continuo; and no.6, with its violas in close canon and gambas providing the inner texture) to the heterogeneous mixing of brass, woodwind, string and keyboard instruments. Just as unusual is Bach's conflation of the group concerto with the solo concerto in nos.1, 4 and 5; no.4, for example, is both a solo violin concerto and a concerto grosso with a solo group of violin and two recorders. No.5 probably represents the latest stage in composition of the set and includes Bach's first use of the transverse flute. Possibly it was written for the inauguration of the harpsichord he brought back from Berlin early in 1719 (an earlier version survives from about this date). At the same time it marks the beginnings of the harpsichord concerto as a form.

The Orchestral Suites nos.1 and 4, with their leaning towards French style, can be dated in the Cöthen period. The only solo concertos to survive in their original form from this time are the violin concertos in A minor and in E and the two-violin concerto in D minor. Further concertos can be fairly accurately reconstructed, however, from their later arrangements as harpsichord concertos – for violin (after those in D minor and F minor, BWV1052 and 1056), oboe d'amore (A major, 1055), oboe and violin (C minor, 1060) and for three violins (C major, 1064) – and there are additionally several concerto movements, less readily reconstructed from their later transcriptions in cantatas and concertos (BWV35, 49, 169, 1053, 1059 and 1063). All these probably belong to the period spent at Weimar and Cöthen. Reconstructions of specific originals arranged by Bach are possible only up to a point, as in his transcriptions Bach never proceeded in a mechanical way; rather, he strove to give the arrangement an identity of its own by subjecting the model to further development and exhausting its potential. This often involved the addition of fresh contrapuntal parts, the alteration of detail and structural modification. Of special interest are Bach's adaptations of instrumental works into vocal ones, like the derivation of the first chorus of Cantata no.110 from BWV1069; also of note is the wresting of the other movements of an ensemble concerto (BWV1044) out of the Prelude and Fugue in A minor for harpsichord (BWV894).

Probably only a few works are demonstrably of Leipzig origins, written for the collegium musicum concerts; these include such works as Suites nos.2 and 3, the Triple Concerto in A minor BWV1044 (using the same instrumental forces as Brandenburg Concerto no.5), the eight harpsichord concertos BWV1052–9 and the concertos for two or more harpsichords BWV1060–65, which, like the Triple Concerto, are all reworkings of older works (the four-harpsichord concerto is an arrangement of Vivaldi's Concerto in B minor for four violins, op.3 no.10). BWV1061 appears to have been written originally for two harpsichords without accompaniment (c1732–5). In fact, Bach's alterations and restructurings are sufficiently important – especially the deployment of the left hand of the harpsichord part and the invention of idiomatic harpsichord figuration – for works of this rank to be considered compositions in their own right. They owe their special historical importance to their occurrence (simultaneously with Handel's inauguration of the organ concerto in England) at the beginning of the history of the keyboard concerto, a form which was to be taken up above all by Bach's sons so that in Germany, until about 1750, it remained the exclusive preserve of the Bach family. A stimulus for the composition of the harpsichord concertos may have been the new instrument introduced at a concert on 17 June 1733 ('a new harpsichord, the like of which no-one here has ever yet heard'), which may be the 'fournirt Clavecin' Bach left at his death (to remain in his family's possession).

19. CHAMBER MUSIC. As with the orchestral music, it is likely that a particularly large number of works in this category must be lost. Most of the surviving works were composed at Cöthen, although the trio BWV1040 dates back to early 1713. He was early familiar with the *sonata da chiesa* repertory, as his arrangements BWV574 after Legrenzi and BWV579 after Corelli's op.3 testify, and he used the four-movement Italian sonata model for most of his trio and solo sonatas. The unusual flexibility with which he manipulated the conventional genres is analogous with his handling of the orchestral forms. Particularly important is his emancipation of the harpsichord from its role as continuo instrument and its deployment as a true partner in the sonatas for harpsichord with viola da gamba (BWV1027–9), violin (1014–19) and flute (1030, 1032). The influence of the trio sonata with continuo still remains; but it progressively disappeared in favour of a more integrated three-part style. The development of this new type of trio writing from the trio sonata is illustrated by Bach's arrangement of BWV1027 after the Trio Sonata BWV1039 for two flutes and continuo. A similar procedure stood behind his development of the organ trio sonata, as his arrangement of the first movement of BWV528 from a trio sonata movement for oboe d'amore, viola da gamba and continuo in Cantata no.76 shows. The latter movement represents a trace of some trio sonatas of the Cöthen period which have apparently survived only in partial form.

The list of surviving duo sonatas is not much longer, with the violin sonatas BWV1021 and 1023 and the flute sonatas BWV1034–5. Among the duo and trio sonatas credited to Bach, a fairly sizable proportion are unauthentic or doubtful. This also applies to some of the sonatas with obbligato harpsichord, for example those in G minor with violin (BWV1020) and E♭ with flute (1031).

Bach's creative powers appear in a special light in the sonatas and partitas for solo violin (BWV1001–6), dating from 1720, the suites for solo cello (1007–12), which stylistically precede the violin works, and the sonata for solo flute (1013). They not only demonstrate Bach's intimate knowledge of the typical idioms and performing techniques of each instrument, but also show his ability to bring into effective play, without even an accompanying bass part, dense counterpoint and refined harmony coupled with distinctive rhythms. In this he far surpassed all his predecessors, both in the solo violin works (for example Westhoff, Biber and J. J. Walther) and the solo cello pieces (for example the solo gamba works of Schenck; there are no known works for solo cello before Bach). Bach's experience in writing lute music must have stimulated the composition of the solo string works.

Of his chamber works composed during his period with the collegium musicum at Leipzig probably only the sonatas for obbligato harpsichord and flute have survived; no doubt a larger repertory once existed, and a relic of it may well be found in the trio sonata of the *Musical Offering* – Bach's most artful, elaborate, complex and technically demanding chamber trio.

20. CANONS, 'MUSICAL OFFERING', 'ART OF FUGUE'. Bach's preoccupation with the canon as the strictest form of counterpoint can be traced back to the Weimar period. In his organ chorales and particularly in the *Orgel-Büchlein* the canonic principle plays a major role.

Canonic elements are also in several of the early vocal works, particularly in cantus firmus composition. Here however it is a matter of canonic technique cropping up in a context of complex contrapuntal construction; as a genre in its own right, the canon, in Bach's day, would appear almost exclusively as a theoretical example in composition teaching. It was in this sense that it was often favoured – generally in the form of a circular canon – by musicians for entries in students' albums: such entries were normally notated in enigmatic fashion, setting the would-be solver an intellectual exercise. Bach wrote such canons in albums more than once; for the most part they are probably lost. Except for BWV1076–7 and 1087, all the surviving individual canons (1072–5, 1078, 1086) were probably dedicatory works of this kind; 1077 was re-used for this purpose. What is probably the earliest of them is dated 2 August 1713 (BWV1073, dedicatee uncertain); the latest is dated 1 March 1749 (BWV1078; dedicatee Benjamin Faber).

A new kind of theoretical canon came into being in connection with the Goldberg Variations, in which the canonic principle played a special part. In his personal copy of the Goldberg Variations Bach wrote after 1742 a series of 14 perpetual canons on the first eight bass notes of the aria ground (BWV1087), exploring the most varied canonic possibilities of the subject, subsequently arranging the individual perpetual canons in a progressive order, organized according to their increasing contrapuntal complexity. The types included range from simple, double and triple canons and retrograde canons to a quadruple proportion canon by augmentation and diminution. Nos.11 and 13 of this series are early versions of BWV1077 (from the Fulde album) and 1076 (depicted on Haussmann's Bach portrait of 1746). With this first systematically organized series of canons Bach added a new facet to his work – that of theoretical reflection, which was to play a decisive role in the concept of his contrapuntal late works.

Closely related to these are the *Vom Himmel hoch* variations, where Bach first used a strictly canonic scheme for a monothematic work in several movements of progressive difficulty. Still more important is the *Musical Offering*. Here, for a theme incomparably more complex than that of BWV1087, he devised ten canons of differing structural types, notated as puzzle canons in the original printed edition of 1747. The series of canons on the 'royal theme' includes a canonic fugue, providing a bridge between the canons, which are primarily theoretical in conception though also intended for performance, and the two keyboard fugues or ricercares in three and six parts. Not even the Ricercar *a 6*, or the canonic movements, requires instrumentation exceeding the limits of the ensemble mentioned by Bach in the original edition. A further constituent part of the *Musical Offering* is a trio sonata for flute, violin and continuo, also based on the royal theme. In its second slow movement Bach introduced echoes of the fashionable style practised at the Prussian court. The *Musical Offering*, in effect a compendium in three sections, shows Bach elaborating on the theme supplied to him by Frederick the Great in every imaginable way for an ensemble of up to three instruments.

The *Art of Fugue* constitutes the final contribution to this group of monothematically conceived works intended as representative examples of a specific principle. As a didactic keyboard work, the *Art of Fugue* in some ways forms a counterpart to the two books of the

'48', with the difference that here it is exclusively the fugue that is in question, and, what is more, the fugues are developed from a single theme. Bach's work on the *Art of Fugue* was accomplished in two stages – from about the mid-1740s to about 1748, and then (in connection with preparing the work for publication) in about 1748–9 or even 1750. The extant autograph score represents the conclusion of the first stage in which the conception of the work already appears clearly: beginning with simple fugues (Bach avoided this term, speaking of 'contrapunctus'), progressing through 'counter-fugues', double fugues and triple fugues, with interpolated canons, and culminating in a mirror fugue. For the printed version the number of movements was slightly increased, by (among other things) two canons, a fourth simple fugue and most notably a closing quadruple fugue; their order was to some extent rearranged so as to expound more logically the 'chapter of instruction on fugues'. When Bach died the work may have been more 'complete' than it is in the form in which it has survived. In particular the quadruple fugue had surely been completed in all essentials, since the composition of its combinatorial section must necessarily be an early stage in the composition of a quadruple fugue. Only the three opening sections of the exposition, however, are extant, and these – further abbreviated by the editors, give the *Art of Fugue* the appearance of being a mighty torso.

21. METHODS OF COMPOSITION. Bach's methods of composition can be outlined only roughly since musical and literary sources present no more than a fragmentary picture. 'Methods' here refers to Bach's general procedures when composing individual works and groups of works, as far as these can objectively and systematically be described without venturing into assumptions about creative psychology, and as far as they can be related to certain essential impulses and particularly characteristic approaches.

Bach's vast knowledge of the musical repertory was a decisive factor behind his art. He had an intimate knowledge of the types and styles of composition of his time and in particular of the work of his most important contemporaries; moreover, he had a sound idea of the music of the past, extending back as far as Frescobaldi and Palestrina. The study of works by other masters went hand in hand with experimentation in his own. It is thus characteristic that his acquaintance with the works of Buxtehude and Böhm, with Vivaldi's concertos, with the Passions of Keiser and Handel and with the masses of Lotti and Palestrina should have left an immediate imprint on his compositions in the same genres. It was less a matter of imitation of a model than of an awareness of the possibilities, an expansion of his own manner of writing and a stimulation of his musical ideas. This is confirmed in a contemporary report by T. L. Pitschel on his manner of improvisation, according to which, before beginning his own fantasia, Bach as a rule played from music a work by another master (or perhaps one of his own) which would ignite his imagination. Further, C. P. E. Bach wrote that, in accompanying a trio, his father liked to extemporize a fourth part. This tendency to take compositions by others as a starting-point is paralleled in his late adaptations: in his arrangement of Pergolesi's *Stabat mater* an obbligato viola part is added, replacing the one following the continuo in the original; and his version of the 'Suscepit

Israel' from Caldara's *Magnificat* in C expands it from a five-part into a seven-part piece. An important aspect of Bach's procedure of composition is its systematic and encyclopedic nature. He habitually wrote works of one particular type within a relatively limited period: for example the *Orgel-Büchlein*, the '48', the solo violin sonatas and partitas, the canons, the chorale cantatas etc. He was concerned to try out, to develop, and to exhaust specific principles of composition. There are practically no completely isolated compositions. Relationships, correspondences and connections with other works can constantly be found. This approach to the procedure of composition is at once deep and yet of great natural simplicity; and it never results in mere repetition. Certainly there is repetition, of a kind, in the case of parodies or transcriptions of existing works. Yet even here it is inappropriate to speak of repetition, since in the process of parodying and transcribing, Bach always modified so that the end-product represents a fresh stage in the development of the original composition.

C. P. E. Bach related that his father did not actually compose at the keyboard – apart from some keyboard works whose material originated in improvisations – but that he often tried out his music on the keyboard afterwards. This procedure may be seen in the few instrumental works of which Bach's autograph draft survives, for example the early versions of the Inventions in the *Clavier-Büchlein* for Wilhelm Friedemann, where an abundance of inserted corrections are to be found. In the vocal music, where a wealth of source material is available, the main stages of composition can often be reconstructed. In thematically and motivically self-contained movements, like arias and choruses, Bach normally began with the development and formulation of a motif, a phrase or a theme, which would be guided by the prosody of the text; he then added the contrapuntal voices, and continued in the same way, sometimes using 'continuation sketches' to plan the music's progress in advance (see the critical edition of the sketches, Marshall, 1972). In choral fugues he generally began by outlining the thematic entries, and wrote in the accompanying parts afterwards. The decisive step was the embarkation on the writing of a movement, for progress was in its essentials determined by established models (harmonic–tonal groundplan, modulation patterns, aria schemes) and

governed by the principle of unified continuation ('style d'une teneur' and 'Affekteinheitlichkeit' – ensured by a unified motivic organization and interchange, permutation and transposition of component sections). The invention of the central idea was for Bach the critical moment in the process of composition, as the title-page of the Inventions specifies: 'gute inventiones zu bekommen' ('how to achieve good inventions'); and this is borne out by C. P. E. Bach's report that his first requirement of his composition pupils was the invention of ideas. With this the die was cast, down to a work's emotional content. Outlines and sketches relating to this operation can sometimes be found in the original manuscripts; typically, however, Bach hardly required more than one or two attempts before arriving at the definitive form of his principal idea. The further elaboration of the idea – the *dispositio*, *elaboratio* and *decoratio* – required mastery of his craft rather than inspiration.

In composing multi-movement vocal works, Bach, understandably, began as a rule with the self-contained movements and only afterwards worked at the recitatives and chorales. In the recitatives he normally first wrote out the text and then added the melody and bass, section by section. In the chorales the bass was added to the melody and the middle parts were inserted later. Then all the movements were revised in detail, and sometimes corrections were made. The appearance of Bach's working drafts is thus unusually clear and neat as a whole, although it is mainly in his fair copies that the particular quality of his handwriting, a quality comparable to that of his music, is expressed.

Ultimately, for Bach, the process of composition was an unending one. Dynamic markings and indications of articulation would be inserted as he looked through the parts; he would revise and improve a work when he was copying it out, and when giving further performances would make fresh alterations and improvements. He also inserted corrections in works already in print. Throughout his life Bach was his own severest critic. Even in works which went through two or three different versions, like the chorale prelude *An Wasserflüssen Babylon* bwv653, the 'final' version does not represent a definitive one but merely a further state in the search for perfection – the central and ultimate concern of Bach's method of composition.

WORKS

Editions: *J. S. Bach: Werke*, ed. Bach-Gesellschaft, i–xlvii (Leipzig, 1851–99/*R*1947) [BG]
    Neue Bach-Ausgabe, ed. Johann-Sebastian-Bach-Institut, Göttingen, and Bach-Archiv, Leipzig, ser. I VIII (Kassel and Basle, 1954–) [vols. in square brackets are in preparation] [NBA; CC = Critical Commentary]

Catalogue: W. Schmieder: *Thematisch-systematisches Verzeichnis der musikalischen Werke Johann Sebastian Bach: Bach-Werke-Verzeichnis* (Leipzig, 1950, 3/1966, rev. and enlarged 4th edn. in preparation) [BWV; A = Anhang]

* – *another version*

CHURCH CANTATAS

Advent I = 1st Sunday in Advent; Trinity/Easter I = 1st Sunday after Trinity/Easter, etc; most texts are compilations including at least one chorale; only single text sources given

BWV	Title (text/librettist)	Occasion; 1st perf.	Scoring	BG	NBA
1	Wie schön leuchtet der Morgenstern, chorale	Annunciation; 25 March 1725	S, T, B, 4vv, 2 hn, 2 ob da caccia, 2 vn, str, bc	i, 1	[I/xxviii]
2	Ach Gott, vom Himmel sieh darein, chorale	Trinity II; 18 June 1724	A, T, B, 4vv, 4 trbn, 2 ob, str, bc	i, 55	[I/xvi]
3	Ach Gott, wie manches Herzeleid, chorale	Epiphany II; 14 Jan 1725	S, A, T, B, 4vv, hn, trbn, 2 ob d'amore, str, bc	i, 75	I/v, 191
4	Christ lag in Todes Banden, chorale	Easter; ?1707–8	S, A, T, B, 4vv, cornett, 3 trbn, str, bc	i, 97	[I/ix]
5	Wo soll ich fliehen hin, chorale	Trinity XIX; 15 Oct 1724	S, A, T, B, 4vv, tpt, 2 ob, str, bc	i, 127	[I/xxiv]
6	Bleib bei uns, denn es will Abend werden	Easter Monday; 2 April 1725	S, A, T, B, 4vv, 2 ob, ob da caccia, vc piccolo, str, bc	i, 153	I/x, 45

BWV	Title (text/librettist)	Occasion; 1st perf.	Scoring	BG	NBA
7	Christ unser Herr zum Jordan kam, chorale	St John; 24 June 1724	A, T, B, 4vv, 2 ob d'amore, str, bc	i, 179	[I/xxix]
8	Liebster Gott, wann werd ich sterben?, chorale	Trinity XVI; 24 Sept 1724	S, A, T, B, 4vv, hn, fl, 2 ob d'amore, str, bc	i, 213	[I/xxiii]
9	Es ist das Heil uns kommen her, chorale	Trinity VI; c1732–5	S, A, T, B, 4vv, fl, ob d'amore, str, bc	i, 245	[I/xvii]
10	Meine Seel erhebt den Herren (Luke i.46–55)	Visitation; 2 July 1724	S, A, T, B, 4vv, tpt, 2 ob, str, bc	i, 277	[I/xxviii]
11	Lobet Gott in seinen Reichen (Ascension Oratorio)	Ascension; 19 May 1735	S, A, T, B, 4vv, 3 tpt, timp, 2 fl, 2 ob, str, bc	ii, 1	[II/vii]
12	Weinen, Klagen, Sorgen, Zagen (S. Franck)	Easter III; 22 April 1714	A, T, B, 4vv, tpt, ob, str, bc	ii, 61	[I/xi]
13	Meine Seufzer, meine Tränen (G. C. Lehms)	Epiphany II; 20 Jan 1726	S, A, T, B, 4vv, 2 rec, ob, ob da caccia, str, bc	ii, 81	I/v, 231
14	Wär Gott nicht mit uns diese Zeit, chorale	Epiphany IV; 30 Jan 1735	S, T, B, 4vv, hn, 2 ob, str, bc	ii, 101	[I/vi]
16	Herr Gott, dich loben wir (Lehms)	New Year; 1 Jan 1726	A, T, B, 4vv, hn, 2 ob, ob da caccia, str, bc	ii, 175	I/iv, 105
17	Wer Dank opfert, der preiset mich	Trinity XIV; 22 Sept 1726	S, A, T, B, 4vv, 2 ob d'amore, str, bc	ii, 201	I/xxi, 149
18	Gleichwie der Regen und Schnee vom Himmel fällt (E. Neumeister)	Sexagesima; c1714	S, T, B, 4vv, 4 va, vc, bn, bc [2 rec added 1724]	ii, 229	I/vii, 109
19	Es erhub sich ein Streit (after Picander)	St Michael; 29 Sept 1726	S, T, B, 4vv, 3 tpt, timp, 2 ob, 2 ob d'amore, ob da caccia, str, bc	ii, 255	I/xxx, 57
20	O Ewigkeit, du Donnerwort, chorale	Trinity I; 11 June 1724	A, T, B, 4vv, tpt, 3 ob, str, bc	ii, 293	I/xv, 135
21	Ich hatte viel Bekümmernis (?Franck)	Trinity III ['per ogni tempo']; ?before 1714	S, T, B, 4vv, 3 tpt, timp, 4 trbn, ob, bn, str, bc	v/1, 1	[I/xvi]
22	Jesus nahm zu sich die Zwölfe	Quinquagesima; 7 Feb 1723	A, T, B, 4vv, ob, str, bc	v/1, 67	[I/viii]
23	Du wahrer Gott und Davids Sohn	Quinquagesima; 7 Feb 1723	S, A, T, 4vv, 2 ob d'amore, cornett, 3 trbn, str, bc; *c1730: 2 ob, str, bc	v/1, 95	[I/viii]
24	Ein ungefärbt Gemüte (Neumeister)	Trinity IV; 20 June 1723	A, T, B, 4vv, tpt, 2 ob, 2 ob d'amore, str, bc	v/1, 127	[I/xvii]
25	Es ist nicht Gesundes an meinem Leibe	Trinity XIV; 29 Aug 1723	S, T, B, 4vv, cornett, 3 trbn, 3 rec, 2 ob, str, bc	v/1, 155	I/xxi, 81
26	Ach wie flüchtig, ach wie nichtig, chorale	Trinity XXIV; 19 Nov 1724	S, A, T, B, 4vv, hn, fl, 3 ob, str, bc	v/1, 191	I/xxvii, 31
27	Wer weiss, wie nahe mir mein Ende!, chorales	Trinity XVI; 6 Oct 1726	S, A, T, B, 4vv, hn, 2 ob, ob da caccia, org obbl, str, bc	v/1, 219	[I/xxiii]
28	Gottlob! nun geht das Jahr zu Ende (Neumeister)	Christmas I; 30 Dec 1725	S, A, T, B, 4vv, cornett, 4 trbn, 2 ob, ob da caccia, str, bc	v/1, 247	[I/iii]
29	Wir danken dir, Gott, wir danken dir	inauguration of town council; 27 Aug 1731	S, A, T, B, 4vv, 3 tpt, 2 ob, org obbl, str, bc	v/1, 275	[I/xxxii]
30	Freue dich, erlöste Schar (adapted ?Picander from 30a)	St John; 1738 or later	S, A, T, B, 4vv, 2 fl, 2 ob, ob d'amore, str, bc	v/1, 323	[I/xxix]
31	Der Himmel lacht! die Erde jubilieret (Franck)	Easter; 21 April 1715	S, T, B, 5vv, 3 tpt, timp, 3 ob, ob da caccia, str, bc	vii, 3	[I/xix]
32	Liebster Jesu, mein Verlangen, dialogue (Lehms)	Epiphany I; 13 Jan 1726	S, B, 4vv, ob, str, bc	vii, 55	I/v, 145
33	Allein zu dir, Herr Jesu Christ, chorale	Trinity XIII; 3 Sept 1724	A, T, B, 4vv, 2 ob, str, bc	vii, 83	I/xxi, 25
34	O ewiges Feuer, O Ursprung der Liebe (adapted from 34a)	Whit Sunday; early 1740s	A, T, B, 4vv, 3 tpt, timp, 2 fl, 2 ob, str, bc	vii, 117	I/xiii, 131
34a	O ewiges Feuer, O Ursprung der Liebe [partly lost]	wedding; 1726	S, A, T, B, 4vv, 3 tpt, timp, 2 fl, 2 ob, str, bc	xli, 117	I/xxxiii, 29
35	Geist und Seele wird verwirret (Lehms) [partly adapted from lost ob conc., cf 1059]	Trinity XII; 8 Sept 1726	A, 2 ob, ob da caccia, org obbl, str, bc	vii, 173	[I/xx]
36	Schwingt freudig euch empor (adapted ?Picander from 36c)	Advent I; 2 Dec 1731	S, A, T, B, 4vv, 2 ob d'amore, str, bc	vii, 223	I/i, 19, 43
37	Wer da gläubet und getauft wird	Ascension; 18 May 1724	S, A, T, B, 4vv, 2 ob d'amore, str, bc	vii, 261	I/xii, 81
38	Aus tiefer Not schrei ich zu dir, chorale	Trinity XXI; 29 Oct 1724	S, A, T, B, 4vv, 4 trbn, 2 ob, str, bc	vii, 285	[I/xxiv]
39	Brich dem Hungrigen dein Brot	Trinity I; 23 June 1726	S, A, B, 4vv, 2 rec, 2 ob, str, bc	vii, 303	I/xv, 181
40	Dazu ist erschienen der Sohn Gottes	2nd day of Christmas; 26 Dec 1723	A, T, B, 4vv, 2 hn, 2 ob, str, bc	vii, 351	[I/iii]
41	Jesu, nun sei gepreiset, chorale	New Year; 1 Jan 1725	S, A, T, B, 4vv, 3 tpt, timp, 3 ob, vc piccolo, str, bc	x, 3	I/iv, 39
42	Am Abend aber desselbigen Sabbats	Easter I; 8 April 1725	S, A, T, B, 4vv, 2 ob, bn, str, bc	x, 65	[I/xi]
43	Gott fähret auf mit Jauchzen	Ascension; 30 May 1726	S, A, T, B, 4vv, 3 tpt, timp, 2 ob, str, bc	x, 95	I/xii, 135
44	Sie werden euch in die Bann tun	Ascension I; 21 May 1724	S, A, T, B, 4vv, 2 ob, str, bc	x, 129	I/xii, 167
45	Es ist dir gesagt, Mensch, was gut ist	Trinity VIII; 11 Aug 1726	A, T, B, 4vv, 2 fl, 2 ob, str, bc	x, 153	I/xviii, 199
46	Schauet doch und sehet	Trinity X; 1 Aug 1723	A, T, B, 4vv, tpt, 2 rec, 2 ob da caccia, str, bc	x, 189	[I/xix]
47	Wer sich selbst erhöhet (J. F. Helbig)	Trinity XVII; 13 Oct 1726	S, B, 4vv, 2 ob, org obbl, str, bc	x, 241	[I/xxiii]
48	Ich elender Mensch, wer wird mich erlösen	Trinity XIX; 3 Oct 1723	A, T, 4vv, tpt, 2 ob, str, bc	x, 277	[I/xxiv]
49	Ich geh und suche mit Verlangen, dialogue [sinfonia adapted from lost conc. 1053]	Trinity XX; 3 Nov 1726	S, B, ob d'amore, org obbl, vc piccolo, str, bc	x, 301	[I/xxv]
50	Nun ist das Heil und die Kraft (Revelation xii.10)	St Michael	8vv, 3 tpt, timp, 3 ob, str, bc	x, 343	I/xxx, 143
51	Jauchzet Gott in allen Landen!	Trinity XV ['et in ogni tempo'] ?17 Sept 1730	S, tpt, str, bc	xii/2, 3	[I/xxii]
52	Falsche Welt, dir trau ich nicht	Trinity XXIII; 24 Nov 1726	S, 4vv, 2 hn, 3 ob, str, bc	xii/2, 27	[I/xxvi]

BWV	Title (text/librettist)	Occasion; 1st perf.	Scoring	BG	NBA
54	Widerstehe doch der Sünde (Lehms)	?Trinity VII; ?15 July 1714	A, str, bc	xii/2, 61	I/xviii, 3
55	Ich armer Mensch, ich Sündenknecht	Trinity XXII; 17 Nov 1726	T, 4vv, fl, ob d'amore, str, bc	xii/2, 75	[I/xxvi]
56	Ich will den Kreuzstab gerne tragen	Trinity XIX; 27 Oct 1726	B, 4vv, 2 ob, ob da caccia, str, bc	xii/2, 89	[I/xxiv]
57	Selig ist der Mann, dialogue (Lehms)	2nd day of Christmas; 26 Dec 1725	S, B, 4vv, 2 ob, ob da caccia, str, bc	xii/2, 107	[I/iii]
58	Ach Gott, wie manches Herzeleid, dialogue	New Year I; 5 Jan 1727	S, B, 2 ob, ob da caccia, str, bc	xii/2, 135	I/iv, 219
59	Wer mich liebet, der wird mein Wort halten (Neumeister)	Whit Sunday; 1723–4	S, B, 4vv, 2 tpt, timp, str, bc	xii/2, 153	I/xiii, 67
60	O Ewigkeit, du Donnerwort, dialogue	Trinity XXIV; 7 Nov 1723	A, T, B, 4vv, hn, 2 ob d'amore, str, bc	xii/2, 171	I/xxvii, 3
61	Nun komm, der Heiden Heiland (Neumeister)	Advent I; 1714	S, T, B, 4vv, str, bc	xvi, 3	I/i, 3
62	Nun komm, der Heiden Heiland, chorale	Advent I; 3 Dec 1724	S, A, T, B, 4vv, hn, 2 ob, str, bc	xvi, 21	I/i, 77
63	Christen, ätzet diesen Tag (?N. Heineccius)	Christmas; before 1716	S, A, T, B, 4vv, timp, 3 ob, str, bc [org obbl]	xvi, 53	I/ii, 3
64	Sehet, welch eine Liebe	3rd day of Christmas; 27 Dec 1723	S, A, B, 4vv, cornett, 3 trbn, ob d'amore, str, bc	xvi, 113	[I/iii]
65	Sie werden aus Saba alle kommen	Epiphany; 6 Jan 1724	T, B, 4vv, 2 hn, 2 rec, 2 ob da caccia, str, bc	xvi, 135	I/v, 3
66	Erfreut euch, ihr Herzen, dialogue [adapted from 66a]	Easter Monday; ?10 April 1724	A, T, B, 4vv, tpt, 2 ob, bn, str, bc	xvi, 169	I/x, 3
67	Halt im Gedächtnis Jesum Christ	Easter I; 16 April 1724	A, T, B, 4vv, hn, fl, 2 ob d'amore, str, bc	xvi, 217	[I/xi]
68	Also hat Gott die Welt geliebt (M. von Ziegler)	Whit Monday; 21 May 1725	S, B, 4vv, hn, cornett, 3 trbn, 2 ob, ob da caccia, vc piccolo, str, bc	xvi, 249	I/xiv, 33
69	Lobe den Herrn, meine Seele [adapted from 69a]	inauguration of town council; 1740s	S, A, T, B, 4vv, 3 tpt, timp, 3 ob, ob d'amore, str, bc	xvi, 283	[I/xxxii]
69a	Lobe den Herrn, meine Seele	Trinity XII; 15 Aug 1723	S, A, T, B, 4vv, 3 tpt, timp, rec, 3 ob, ob da caccia, str, bc	xvi, 379	[I/xx]
70	Wachet! betet! betet! wachet! (partly Franck) [adapted from 70a]	Trinity XXVI; 21 Nov 1723	S, A, T, B, 4vv, tpt, ob, str, bc	xvi, 329	I/xxvii, 109
70a	Wachet! betet! betet! wachet! (Franck) [music lost]	Advent II; 6 Dec 1716	—	—	I/xxvii, CC
71	Gott ist mein König	inauguration of Mühlhausen town council; 4 Feb 1708	S, A, T, B, 4vv; 3 tpt, timp; 2 rec, vc; 2 ob, bn; str, bc [org obbl]	xviii, 3	[I/xxxii]
72	Alles nur nach Gottes Willen (Franck)	Epiphany III; 27 Jan 1726	S, A, B, 4vv, 2 ob, str, bc	xviii, 57	[I/vi]
73	Herr, wie du willt, so schicks mit mir	Epiphany III; 23 Jan 1724	S, T, B, 4vv, hn/org obbl, 2 ob, str, bc	xviii, 87	[I/vi]
74	Wer mich liebet, der wird mein Wort halten (Ziegler) [partly adapted from 59]	Whit Sunday; 20 May 1725	S, A, T, B, 4vv, 3 tpt, timp, 2 ob, ob da caccia, str, bc	xviii, 107	I/xiii, 85
75	Die Elenden sollen essen	Trinity I; 30 May 1723	S, A, T, B, 4vv, tpt, 2 ob, ob d'amore, str, bc	xviii, 149	I/xv, 87
76	Die Himmel erzählen die Ehre Gottes	Trinity II; 6 June 1723	S, A, T, B, 4vv, tpt, 2 ob, ob d'amore, va da gamba, str, bc	xviii, 191	[I/xvi]
77	Du sollt Gott, deinen Herren, lieben	Trinity XIII; 22 Aug 1723	S, A, T, B, 4vv, tpt, 2 ob, str, bc	xviii, 235	I/xxi, 3
78	Jesu, der du meine Seele, chorale	Trinity XIV; 10 Sept 1724	S, A, T, B, 4vv, hn, fl, 2 ob, str, bc	xviii, 257	I/xxi, 117
79	Gott der Herr ist Sonn und Schild	Reformation Festival; 31 Oct 1725	S, A, B, 4vv, 2 hn, timp, 2 fl, 2 ob, str, bc	xviii, 289	[I/xxxi]
80	Ein feste Burg ist unser Gott (Franck) [adapted from 80a]	Reformation Festival; ?31 Oct 1724	S, A, T, B, 4vv, 2 ob, ob da caccia, str, bc [3 tpt, timp added by ?W. F. Bach]	xviii, 319, 381	[I/xxxi]
80a	Alles, was von Gott geboren (Franck) [music lost]	Lent III; 1715	—	—	[I/viii, CC]
80b	Ein feste Burg ist unser Gott (Franck)	31 Oct 1723	autograph frag., movts 1–2	—	—
81	Jesus schläft, was soll ich hoffen?	Epiphany IV; 30 Jan 1724	A, T, B, 4vv, 2 rec, 2 ob d'amore, str, bc	xx/1, 3	[I/vi]
82	Ich habe genug	Purification; 2 Feb 1727	B, ob, str, bc; other versions for S/A with altered ww	xx/1, 27	[I/xxviii]
83	Erfreute Zeit im neuen Bunde	Purification; 2 Feb 1724	A, T, B, 4vv, 2 hn, 2 ob, str, bc	xx/1, 53	[I/xxviii]
84	Ich bin vergnügt mit meinem Glücke (Picander)	Septuagesima; 9 Feb 1727	S, 4vv, ob, str, bc	xx/1, 79	I/vii, 23
85	Ich bin ein guter Hirt	Easter II; 15 April 1725	S, A, T, B, 4vv, 2 ob, vc piccolo, str, bc	xx/1, 101	[I/xi]
86	Wahrlich, wahrlich, ich sage euch	Easter V; 14 May 1724	S, A, T, B, 4vv, 2 ob d'amore, str, bc	xx/1, 121	I/xii, 47
87	Bisher habt ihr nichts gebeten (Ziegler)	Easter V; 6 May 1725	A, T, B, 4vv, 2 ob, 2 ob da caccia, str, bc	xx/1, 137	I/xii, 63
88	Siehe, ich will viel Fischer aussenden	Trinity V; 21 July 1726	S, A, T, B, 4vv, 2 hn, 2 ob d'amore, ob da caccia, str, bc	xx/1, 155	[I/xvii]
89	Was soll ich aus dir machen, Ephraim?	Trinity XXII; 24 Oct 1723	S, A, B, 4vv, hn, 2 ob, str, bc	xx/1, 181	[I/xxvi]
90	Es reisset euch ein schrecklich Ende	Trinity XXV; 14 Nov 1723	A, T, B, 4vv, tpt, str, bc	xx/1, 197	I/xxvii, 61
91	Gelobet seist du, Jesu Christ, chorale	Christmas; 25 Dec 1724	S, A, T, B, 4vv, 2 hn, timp, 3 ob, str, bc	xxii, 3	I/ii, 133
92	Ich hab in Gottes Herz und Sinn, chorale	Septuagesima; 28 Jan 1725	S, A, T, B, 4vv, 2 ob d'amore, str, bc	xxii, 35	I/vii, 43
93	Wer nur den lieben Gott lässt walten, chorale	Trinity V; 9 July 1724	S, A, T, B, 4vv, 2 ob, str, bc	xxii, 71	[I/xvii]
94	Was frag ich nach der Welt, chorale	Trinity IX; 6 Aug 1724	S, A, T, B, 4vv, fl, 2 ob, ob d'amore, str, bc	xxii, 97	[I/xix]
95	Christus, der ist mein Leben, chorale	Trinity XVI; 12 Sept 1723	S, T, B, 4vv, hn, 2 ob, 2 ob d'amore, str, bc	xxii, 131	[I/xxiii]

BWV	Title (text/librettist)	Occasion; 1st perf.	Scoring	BG	NBA
96	Herr Christ, der einge Gottessohn, chorale	Trinity XVIII; 8 Oct 1724	S, A, T, B, 4vv, hn, trbn, fl, rec, 2 ob, vn piccolo, str, bc	xxii, 157	[I/xxiv]
97	In allen meinen Taten, chorale	1734	S, A, T, B, 4vv, 2 ob, str, bc	xxii, 187	[I/xxxiv]
98	Was Gott tut, das ist wohlgetan	Trinity XXI; 10 Nov 1726	S, A, T, B, 2 ob, ob da caccia, str, bc	xxii, 233	[I/xxv]
99	Was Gott tut, das ist wohlgetan, chorale	Trinity XV; 17 Sept 1724	S, A, T, B, 4vv, hn, fl, ob d'amore, str, bc	xxii, 253	[I/xxii]
100	Was Gott tut, das ist wohlgetan, chorale	c1732–5	S, A, T, B, 4vv, 2 hn, timp, fl, ob d'amore, str, bc	xxii, 279	[I/xxii]
101	Nimm von uns, Herr, du treuer Gott, chorale	Trinity X; 13 Aug 1724	S, A, T, B, 4vv, cornett, 3 trbn, fl, 2 ob, ob da caccia, str, bc	xxiii, 3	[I/xix]
102	Herr, deine Augen sehen nach dem Glauben	Trinity X; 25 Aug 1726	A, T, B, 4vv, fl, 2 ob, str, bc	xxiii, 35	[I/xix]
103	Ihr werdet weinen und heulen (Ziegler)	Easter III; 22 April 1725	A, T, 4vv, tpt, rec, 2 ob d'amore, str, bc	xxiii, 69	[I/xi]
104	Du Hirte Israel, höre	Easter II; 23 April 1724	T, B, 4vv, 2 ob, ob da caccia, 2 ob d'amore, str, bc	xxiii, 97	[I/xi]
105	Herr, gehe nicht ins Gericht	Trinity IX; 25 July 1723	S, A, T, B, 4vv, hn, 2 ob, str, bc	xxiii, 119	[I/xix]
106	Gottes Zeit ist die allerbeste Zeit (Actus tragicus)	funeral; ?1707	S, A, T, B, 4vv, 2 rec, 2 va da gamba, bc	xxiii, 149	[I/xxxiv]
107	Was willst du dich betrüben, chorale	Trinity VII; 23 July 1724	S, T, B, 4vv, hn, 2 fl, 2 ob d'amore, str, bc	xxiii, 181	I/xviii, 57
108	Es ist euch gut, dass ich hingehe (Ziegler)	Easter IV; 29 April 1725	A, T, B, 4vv, 2 ob d'amore, str, bc	xxiii, 205	I/xii, 19
109	Ich glaube, lieber Herr, hilf meinem Unglauben!	Trinity XXI; 17 Oct 1723	A, T, 4vv, hn, 2 ob, str, bc	xxiii, 233	[I/xxv]
110	Unser Mund sei voll Lachens [cf 1069] (Lehms)	Christmas; 25 Dec 1725	S, A, T, B, 4vv, 3 tpt, timp, 2 fl, 3 ob, ob d'amore, ob da caccia, str, bc	xxiii, 265	I/ii, 73
111	Was mein Gott will, das g'scheh allzeit, chorale	Epiphany III; 21 Jan 1725	S, A, T, B, 4vv, 2 ob, str, bc	xxiv, 3	[I/vi]
112	Der Herr ist mein getreuer Hirt, chorale	Easter II; 8 April 1731	S, A, T, B, 4vv, 2 hn, 2 ob d'amore, str, bc	xxiv, 31	[I/xi]
113	Herr Jesu Christ, du höchstes Gut, chorale	Trinity XI; 20 Aug 1724	S, A, T, B, 4vv, fl, 2 ob d'amore, str, bc	xxiv, 51	[I/xx]
114	Ach, lieben Christen, seid getrost, chorale	Trinity XVII; 1 Oct 1724	S, A, T, B, 4vv, hn, fl, 2 ob, str, bc	xxiv, 83	[I/xxiii]
115	Mache dich, mein Geist, bereit, chorale	Trinity XXII; 5 Nov 1724	S, A, T, B, 4vv, hn, fl, ob d'amore, vc piccolo, str, bc	xxiv, 111	[I/xxvi]
116	Du Friedefürst, Herr Jesu Christ, chorale	Trinity XXV; 26 Nov 1724	S, A, T, B, 4vv, hn, 2 ob d'amore, str, bc	xxiv, 135	I/xxvii, 81
117	Sei Lob und Ehr dem höchsten Gut, chorale	c1728–31	A, T, B, 4vv, 2 fl, 2 ob, 2 ob d'amore, str, bc	xxiv, 161	[I/xxxiv]
119	Preise, Jerusalem, den Herrn	inauguration of town council; 30 Aug 1723	S, A, T, B, 4vv, 4 tpt, timp, 2 rec, 3 ob, 2 ob da caccia, str, bc	xxiv, 195	[I/xxxii]
120	Gott, man lobet dich in der Stille	inauguration of town council; 1728–9	S, A, T, B, 4vv, 3 tpt, timp, 2 ob d'amore, str, bc	xxiv, 249	[I/xxxii]
120a	Herr Gott, Beherrscher aller Dinge [adapted from 120, partly lost]	wedding; ?1729	S, A, T, B, 4vv, 3 tpt, timp, 2 ob, 2 ob d'amore, org obbl, str, bc	xli, 149	I/xxxiii, 77
120b	Gott, man lobet dich in der Stille (Picander) [adapted from 120, music lost]	200th anniversary of Augsburg Confession, 1730	—	—	—
121	Christum wir sollen loben schon, chorale	2nd day of Christmas; 26 Dec 1724	S, A, T, B, 4vv, cornett, 3 trbn, ob d'amore, str, bc	xxvi, 3	[I/iii]
122	Das neugeborne Kindelein, chorale	Christmas I; 31 Dec 1724	S, A, T, B, 4vv, 3 rec, 2 ob, ob da caccia, str, bc	xxvi, 23	[I/iii]
123	Liebster Immanuel, Herzog der Frommen, chorale	Epiphany; 6 Jan 1725	A, T, B, 4vv, 2 fl, 2 ob d'amore, str, bc	xxvi, 43	I/v, 49
124	Meinen Jesum lass ich nicht, chorale	Epiphany I; 7 Jan 1725	S, A, T, B, 4vv, hn, ob d'amore, str, bc	xxvi, 63	I/v, 117
125	Mit Fried und Freud ich fahr dahin, chorale	Purification; 2 Feb 1725	A, T, B, 4vv, hn, fl, ob, ob d'amore, str, bc	xxvi, 85	[I/xxviii]
126	Erhalt uns, Herr, bei deinem Wort, chorale	Sexagesima; 4 Feb 1725	A, T, B, 4vv, tpt, 2 ob, str, bc	xxvi, 113	I/vii, 157
127	Herr Jesu Christ, wahr' Mensch und Gott, chorale	Quinquagesima; 11 Feb 1725	S, T, B, 4vv, tpt, 2 rec, 2 ob, str, bc	xxvi, 135	[I/viii]
128	Auf Christi Himmelfahrt allein (Ziegler)	Ascension; 10 May 1725	A, T, B, 4vv, tpt, 2 hn, 2 ob d'amore, ob da caccia, str, bc	xxvi, 163	I/xii, 103
129	Gelobet sei der Herr, mein Gott, chorale	Trinity; 1726–7	S, A, B, 4vv, 3 tpt, timp, fl, 2 ob, ob d'amore, str, bc	xxvi, 187	I/xv, 39
130	Herr Gott, dich loben alle wir, chorale	St Michael; 29 Sept 1724	S, A, T, B, 4vv, 3 tpt, timp, fl, 3 ob, str, bc	xxvi, 233	I/xxx, 3
131	Aus der Tiefen rufe ich, Herr, zu dir	1707	S, A, T, B, 4vv, ob, bn, vn, 2 va, bc	xxviii, 3	[I/xxxiv]
132	Bereitet die Wege, bereitet die Bahn! (Franck)	Advent IV; 1715	S, A, T, B, 4vv, ob, str, bc	xxviii, 35	I/i, 101
133	Ich freue mich in dir, chorale	3rd day of Christmas; 27 Dec 1724	S, A, T, B, 4vv, cornett, 2 ob d'amore, str, bc	xxviii, 53	[I/iii]
134	Ein Herz, das seinen Jesum lebend weiss [adapted from 134a]	Easter Tuesday; 11 April 1724	A, T, 4vv, 2 ob, str, bc	xxviii, 83, 287	I/x, 71
135	Ach Herr, mich armen Sünder, chorale	Trinity III; 25 June 1724	A, T, B, 4vv, cornett, trbn, 2 ob, str, bc	xxviii, 121	[I/xvi]
136	Erforsche mich, Gott, und erfahre mein Herz	Trinity VIII; 18 July 1723	A, T, B, 4vv, hn, 2 ob d'amore, str, bc	xxviii, 139	I/xviii, 131
137	Lobe den Herren, den mächtigen König der Ehren, chorale	Trinity XII; 19 Aug 1725	S, A, T, B, 4vv, 3 tpt, timp, 2 ob, str, bc	xxviii, 167	[I/xx]

BWV	Title (text/librettist)	Occasion; 1st perf.	Scoring	BG	NBA
138	Warum betrübst du dich, mein Herz?, chorale	Trinity XV; 5 Sept 1723	S, A, T, B, 4vv, 2 ob d'amore, str, bc	xxviii, 199	[I/xxii]
139	Wohl dem, der sich auf seinen Gott, chorale	Trinity XXIII; 12 Nov 1724	S, A, T, B, 4vv, 2 ob d'amore, str, bc	xxviii, 225	[I/xxvi]
140	Wachet auf, ruft uns die Stimme, chorale	Trinity XXVII; 25 Nov 1731	S, T, B, 4vv, hn, 2 ob, ob da caccia, vn piccolo, str, bc	xxviii, 251	I/xxvii, 151
144	Nimm, was dein ist, und gehe hin	Septuagesima; 6 Feb 1724	S, A, T, 4vv, 2 ob, ob d'amore, str, bc	xxx, 77	I/vii, 3
145	Ich lebe, mein Herze, zu deinem Ergötzen (Picander)	Easter Tuesday; ?1729	S, T, B, 4vv, tpt, fl, 2 ob d'amore, str, bc	xxx, 95	I/x, 113
146	Wir müssen durch viel Trübsal [partly adapted from lost vn conc. 1052]	Easter III; c1726–8	S, A, T, B, 4vv, fl, 2 ob, ob da caccia, 2 ob d'amore, org obbl, str, bc	xxx, 125	[I/xi]
147	Herz und Mund und Tat und Leben (partly Franck) [adapted from 147a]	Visitation; 2 July 1723	S, A, T, B, 4vv, tpt, 2 ob, ob d'amore, 2 ob da caccia, str, bc	xxx, 193	[I/xxviii]
147a	Herz und Mund und Tat und Leben (Franck) [lost]	Advent IV; 20 Dec 1716	—	—	I/i, CC
148	Bringet dem Herrn Ehre seines Namens (after Picander)	Trinity XVII; ?19 Sept 1723	A, T, 4vv, tpt, 3 ob, str, bc	xxx, 237	[I/xxiii]
149	Man singet mit Freuden vom Sieg (Picander)	St Michael; 1728–9	S, A, T, B, 4vv, 3 tpt, timp, 3 ob, bn, str, bc	xxx, 263	I/xxx, 99
150	Nach dir, Herr, verlanget mich	c1708–9	S, A, T, B, 4vv, bn, 2 vn, bc	xxx, 303	[I/xli]
151	Süsser Trost, mein Jesus kömmt (Lehms)	3rd day of Christmas; 27 Dec 1725	S, A, T, B, 4vv, fl, ob d'amore, str, bc	xxxii, 3	[I/iii]
152	Tritt auf die Glaubensbahn (Franck)	Christmas I; 30 Dec 1714	S, B, rec, ob, va d'amore, va da gamba, bc	xxxii, 19	[I/iii]
153	Schau, lieber Gott, wie meine Feind	New Year I; 2 Jan 1724	A, T, B, 4vv, str, bc	xxxii, 43	I/iv, 201
154	Mein liebster Jesus ist verloren	Epiphany I; 9 Jan 1724	A, T, B, 4vv, 2 ob d'amore, str, bc	xxxii, 61	I/v, 91
155	Mein Gott, wie lang, ach lange (Franck)	Epiphany II; 19 Jan 1716	S, A, T, B, 4vv, bn, str, bc	xxxiii, 85	I/v, 175
156	Ich steh mit einem Fuss im Grabe (Picander) [sinfonia adapted from lost ob conc.; cf 1056]	Epiphany III; ?23 Jan 1729	A, T, B, 4vv, ob, str, bc	xxxii, 99	[I/vi]
157	Ich lasse dich nicht, du segnest mich denn (Picander)	funeral, Purification; 6 Feb 1727	T, B, 4vv, fl, ob d'amore, str, bc	xxxii, 117	[I/xxxiv]
158	Der Friede sei mit dir	Easter Tuesday, Purification	B, 4vv, ob, vn, bc	xxxiii, 143	I/x, 131
159	Sehet, wir gehn hinauf gen Jerusalem (Picander)	Quinquagesima; ?27 Feb 1729	A, T, B, 4vv, ob, str, bc	xxxii, 157	[I/viii]
161	Komm, du süsse Todesstunde (Franck)	Trinity XVI, Purification; 6 Oct 1715	A, T, 4vv, 2 rec, org obbl, str, bc	xxxiii,3	[I/xxiii]
162	Ach! ich sehe, jetzt, da ich zur Hochzeit gehe (Franck)	Trinity XX; 3 Nov 1715	S, A, T, B, 4vv, hn, str, bc	xxxiii, 31	[I/xxv]
163	Nur jedem das Seine (Franck)	Trinity XXIII; 24 Nov 1715	S, A, T, B, 4vv, str, bc	xxxiii, 49	[I/xxvi]
164	Ihr, die ihr euch von Christo nennet (Franck)	Trinity XIII; 26 Aug 1725	S, A, T, B, 4vv, 2 fl, 2 ob, str, bc	xxxiii, 67	I/xxi, 59
165	O heilges Geist- und Wasserbad (Franck)	Trinity; 16 June 1715	S, A, T, B, 4vv, str, bc	xxxiii, 91	I/xv, 3
166	Wo gehest du hin?	Easter IV; 7 May 1724	A, T, B, 4vv, ob, str, bc	xxxiii, 107	I/xii, 3
167	Ihr Menschen, rühmet Gottes Liebe	St John; 24 June 1723	S, A, T, B, 4vv, tpt, ob, ob da caccia, str, bc	xxxiii, 125	[I/xxix]
168	Tue Rechnung! Donnerwort (Franck)	Trinity IX; 29 July 1725	S, A, T, B, 4vv, 2 ob d'amore, str, bc	xxxiii, 149	[I/xix]
169	Gott soll allein mein Herze haben [partly adapted from lost conc.; cf 1053]	Trinity XVIII; 20 Oct 1726	A, 4vv, 2 ob d'amore, ob da caccia, org obbl, str, bc	xxxiii, 169	[I/xxiv]
170	Vergnügte Ruh', beliebte Seelenlust (Lehms)	Trinity VI; 28 July 1726	A, ob d'amore, org obbl, str, bc	xxxiii, 195	[I/xvii]
171	Gott, wie dein Name, so ist auch dein Ruhm (Picander)	New Year; ?1729	S, A, T, B, 4vv, 3 tpt, timp, 2 ob, str, bc	xxxv, 3	I/iv, 133
172	Erschallet, ihr Lieder (?Franck)	Whit Sunday; 20 May 1714	S, A, T, B, 4vv, 3 tpt, timp, ob, str, bc	xxxv, 37	I/xiii, 3
173	Erhöhtes Fleisch und Blut [adapted from 173a]	Whit Monday; ?29 May 1724	S, A, T, B, 4vv, 2 fl, str, bc	xxxv, 73	I/xiv, 3
174	Ich liebe den Höchsten von ganzem Gemüte (Picander)	Whit Monday; 6 June 1729	A, T, B, 4vv, 2 hn, 2 ob, ob da caccia, str, bc	xxxv, 105	I/xiv, 65
175	Er rufet seinen Schafen mit Namen (Ziegler)	Whit Tuesday; 22 May 1725	A, T, B, 4vv, 2 tpt, 3 rec, vc piccolo, str, bc	xxxv, 161	I/xiv, 149
176	Es ist ein trotzig, und verzagt Ding (Ziegler)	Trinity; 27 May 1725	S, A, B, 4vv, 2 ob, ob da caccia, str, bc	xxxv, 181	I/xv, 19
177	Ich ruf zu dir, Herr Jesu Christ, chorale	Trinity IV; 6 July 1732	S, A, T, 4vv, 2 ob, ob da caccia, bn, str, bc	xxxv, 201	[I/xvii]
178	Wo Gott der Herr nicht bei uns hält, chorale	Trinity VIII; 30 July 1724	A, T, B, 4vv, hn, 2 ob, 2 ob d'amore, str, bc	xxxv, 237	I/xviii, 161
179	Siehe zu, dass deine Gottesfurcht	Trinity XI; 8 Aug 1723	S, T, B, 4vv, 2 ob, 2 ob da caccia, str, bc	xxxv, 275	[I/xx]
180	Schmücke dich, o liebe Seele, chorale	Trinity XX; 22 Oct 1724	S, A, T, B, 4vv, 2 rec, fl, ob, ob da caccia, vc piccolo, str, bc	xxxv, 295	[I/xxv]
181	Leichtgesinnte Flattergeister	Sexagesima; 13 Feb 1724	S, A, T, B, 4vv, tpt, fl, ob, str, bc	xxxvii, 3	I/vii, 135
182	Himmelskönig, sei willkommen (?Franck)	Palm Sunday, Annunciation; 1714	A, T, B, 4vv, rec, str, bc	xxxvii, 23	[I/viii]
183	Sie werden euch in den Bann tun (Ziegler)	Ascension I; 13 May 1725	S, A, T, B, 4vv, 2 ob d'amore, 2 ob da caccia, vc piccolo, str, bc	xxxvii, 61	I/xii, 189
184	Erwünschtes Freudenlicht [adapted from 184a]	Whit Tuesday; 30 May 1724	S, A, T, 4vv, 2 fl, str, bc	xxxvii, 77	I/xiv, 121

BWV	Title (text/librettist)	Occasion; 1st perf.	Scoring	BG	NBA
185	Barmherziges Herze der ewigen Liebe (Franck)	Trinity IV; 14 July 1715	S, A, T, B, 4vv, ob, str, bc	xxxvii, 103	[I/xvii]
186	Ärgre dich, o Seele, nicht (partly Franck) [adapted from 186a]	Trinity VII; 11 July 1723	S, A, T, B, 4vv, 2 ob, ob da caccia, str, bc	xxxvii, 121	I/xviii, 17
186a	Ärgre dich, o Seele, nicht (Franck) [lost]	Advent III; 13 Dec 1716	—	—	I/i, CC
187	Es wartet alles auf dich	Trinity VII; 4 Aug 1726	S, A, B, 4vv, 2 ob, str, bc	xxxvii, 157	I/xviii, 93
188	Ich habe meine Zuversicht (Picander) [sinfonia adapted from lost vn conc.; cf 1052]	Trinity XXI; c1728	S, A, T, B, 4vv, 2 ob, ob da caccia, org obbl, str, bc	xxxvii, 195	[I/xxv]
190	Singet dem Herrn ein neues Lied! [partly lost]	New Year; 1 Jan 1724	A, T, B, 4vv, 3 tpt, timp, 3 ob, ob d'amore, bn, str, bc	xxxvii, 229	I/iv, 3
190a	Singet dem Herrn ein neues Lied! [adapted from 190, lost]	200th anniversary of Augsburg Confession, 1730	—	—	—
191	Gloria in excelsis Deo [adapted from mass 232]	Christmas; after 1740	S, T, 5vv, 3 tpt, timp, 2 fl, 2 ob, str, bc	xli, 3	I/ii, 173
192	Nun danket alle Gott, chorale [partly lost]	1730	S, B, 4vv, 2 fl, 2 ob, str, bc	xli, 67	[I/xxxiv]
193	Ihr Tore zu Zion	inauguration of town council; c1727	S, A, 4vv, 2 ob, str, bc	xli, 93	[I/xxxii]
194	Höchsterwünschtes Freudenfest [adapted from 194a]	consecration of Störmthal church and org, Trinity; 2 Nov 1723	S, T, B, 4vv, 3 ob, str, bc	xxix, 101	I/xv, CC
195	Dem Gerechten muss das Licht	wedding; after 1737	S, B, 4vv, 3 tpt, timp, 2 hn, 2 fl, 2 ob, 2 ob d'amore, str, bc	xiii/1, 3	I/xxxiii, 17
196	Der Herr denket an uns (Ps cxv)	wedding; ?1708	S, T, B, 4vv, str, bc	xiii/1, 73	I/xxxiii, 3
197	Gott ist unsre Zuversicht [partly based on 197a]	wedding; c1742	S, A, B, 4vv, 3 tpt, timp, 2 ob, 2 ob d'amore, bn, str, bc	xiii/1, 97	I/xxxiii, 119
197a	Ehre sei Gott in der Höhe (Picander) [partly lost]	Christmas; c1728	A, B, 4vv, 2 fl, ob d'amore, vc/bn, str, bc	xli, 109	I/ii, 65
199	Mein Herze schwimmt im Blut (Lehms)	Trinity XI; 12 Aug 1714	S, ob, str, bc	—	[I/xx]
200	Bekennen will ich seinen Namen [frag. of lost cantata]	Purification; ?c1742	A, 2 vn, bc	—	[I/xxviii]

Lost or incomplete

BWV	Title (librettist)	Occasion; 1st perf.	Remarks	BG	NBA, CC
223	Meine Seele soll Gott loben	—	lost	—	I/iv
244a	Klagt, Kinder, klagt es aller Welt (Picander)	funeral of Prince Leopold of Anhalt-Cöthen; 24 March 1729	music lost, largely from St Matthew Passion (244), and Trauer Ode (198)	—	[I/xxxiv]
A1	Gesegnet ist die Zuversicht (?Neumeister)	Trinity VII	cited in Breitkopf catalogue, 1770; lost	—	I/xviii
A2	[untexted frag.]	Trinity XIX; 1729	6-bar frag. in autograph of 226	—	—
A3	Gott, gib dein Gerichte dem Könige (Picander)	change of town council; 1730	only text extant	—	[I/xxxii]
A4	Wünschet Jerusalem Glück (Picander)	change of town council; ?1727	only text extant	—	[I/xxxii]
A4a	Wünschet Jerusalem Glück (Picander)	200th anniversary of Augsburg Confession, 1730	only text extant	—	—
A5	Lobet den Herrn, alle seine Heerscharen (C. F. Hunold)	birthday of Prince Leopold of Anhalt-Cöthen; 10 Dec 1718	only text extant	—	I/xxxv
A14	Sein Segen fliesst daher wie ein Strom	wedding; 12 Feb 1725	only text extant	—	I/xxxiii
A15	Siehe, der Hüter Israel	degree ceremony; ?27 April 1724	cited in Breitkopf catalogue, 1761; lost	—	[I/xxxiv]
A17	Mein Gott, nimm die gerechte Seele	funeral	cited in Breitkopf catalogue, 1761; lost	—	[I/xxxiv]
—	Herrscher des Himmels, König der Ehren	change of town council; 29 Aug 1740	last chorus adapted from 208, otherwise lost	—	[I/xxxii]
—	Ich bin ein Pilgrim auf der Welt (Picander)	Easter Monday; ?18 April 1729	only frag. of 4th movt extant	—	I/xxxiii
—	Ihr wallenden Wolken	New Year	cited in Forkel: Nachlassverzeichnis, 1819; lost	—	I/iv
—	Leb ich oder leb ich nicht (Franck)	Easter IV; 19 May 1715	music lost	—	—
—	Sie werden euch in den Bann tun	Ascension I	6-bar sketch in autograph score of 79	—	—
—	[title unknown]	change of Mühlhausen town council; 1709	lost	—	[I/xxxii]
—	[title unknown]	Trinity VI	autograph title: 'Concerto à 4 Voci e 4 stromenti'; in MS of music by C. P. E. Bach	—	—
—	[title unknown]	St Michael	14-bar sketch for opening of cantata autograph score of 201	—	—
—	[title unknown]	Easter I	7-bar sketch in autograph score of 103	—	—
1045	[title unknown]	c1742	autograph frag.: 'Concerto à 4 voci'	—	—

Doubtful and spurious

15	Denn du wirst meine Seele	Easter	by J. L. Bach	ii, 135	—
53	Schlage doch, gewünschte Stunde (?Franck)	funeral	by G. M. Hoffmann	xii/2, 53	—

BWV	Title (librettist)	Occasion; 1st perf.	Remarks	BG	NBA, CC
141	Das ist je gewisslich wahr (Helbig)	Advent III	by G. P. Telemann	xxx, 3	—
142	Uns ist ein Kind geboren (Neumeister)	Christmas	?by J. Kuhnau	xxx, 19	—
143	Lobe den Herrn, meine Seele	New Year; ?c1708–14	S, T, B, 4vv, 3 hn, timp, bn, str, bc	xxx, 45	I/iv, 167
160	Ich weiss, dass mein Erlöser lebt (Neumeister)	Easter	by Telemann	xxxii, 171	—
189	Meine Seele rühmt und preist	?Visitation	probably by Hoffmann	xxxvii, 215	—
217	Gedenke, Herr, wie es uns gehet	Epiphany I	spurious	xli, 207	—
218	Gott der Hoffnung erfülle euch (Neumeister)	Whit Sunday	by Telemann	xli, 223	—
219	Siehe, es hat überwunden der Löwe	St Michael	by Telemann	xli, 239	—
220	Lobt ihn mit Herz und Munde	St John	spurious	xli, 259	—
221	Wer sucht die Pracht, wer wünscht den Glanz		spurious	—	—
222	Mein Odem ist schwach		by J. E. Bach	—	—
A16	Schliesset die Gruft! ihr Trauerglocken (B. Hoffmann)	funeral; 9 Nov 1735	lost, doubtful	—	—
—	Siehe, eine Jungfrau ist schwanger	Annunciation; 25 March 1724	text, 1724	—	—

SECULAR CANTATAS

BWV	Title (librettist)	Occasion; date	Scoring	BG	NBA
30a	Angenehmes Wiederau, freue dich (Picander)	for J. C. von Hennicke; 28 Sept 1737	S, A, T, B, 4vv, 3 tpt, timp, 2 fl, 2 ob, ob d'amore, str, bc	v/1, 399; xxxiv, 325	I/xxxix, 53
36a	Steigt freudig in die Luft (Picander) [music lost; arr. from 36c]	birthday of wife of Prince Leopold of Anhalt-Cöthen; 30 Nov 1726	—	—	I/i, CC; I/xxxv, CC
36b	Die Freude reget sich (?Picander)	for member of Rivinus family; ?1735	S, A, T, 4vv, fl, ob d'amore, str, bc	xxxiv, 41	I/xxxviii, 257
36c	Schwingt freudig euch empor (?Picander)	birthday; 1725	S, T, B, 4vv, ob d'amore, va d'amore, str, bc	xxxiv, 41	I/xxxix, 3
66a	Der Himmel dacht auf Anhalts Ruhm und Glück (C. F. Hunold), serenata [music lost]	birthday of Prince Leopold of Anhalt-Cöthen; 10 Dec 1718	—	—	I/xxxv, CC
134a	Die Zeit, die Tag und Jahre macht (Hunold)	New Year; 1 Jan 1719	A, T, 4vv, 2 ob, str, bc	xxix, 209	I/xxxv, 51
173a	Durchlauchtster Leopold, serenata	birthday of Prince Leopold of Anhalt-Cöthen; ?c1722	S, B, 2 fl, bn, str, bc	xxxiv, 3	I/xxxv, 97
184a	[music and text lost, ?=A8]	?New Year; ?1722–3	—	—	I/xiv, CC; I/xxxv, CC
193a	Ihr Häuser des Himmels, ihr scheinenden Lichter (Picander), dramma per musica [music lost]	name day of August II; 3 Aug 1727	—	—	I/xxxvi, CC
194a	[music and text lost]	for court of Anhalt-Cöthen; before 1723	—	—	I/xxxv, CC
198	Trauer Ode: Lass, Fürstin, lass noch einen Strahl (J. C. Gottsched)	funeral of Electress Christiane Eberhardine; 17 Oct 1727	S, A, T, B, 4vv, 2 fl, 2 ob d'amore, 2 va da gamba, 2 lutes, str, bc	xiii/3, 3	I/xxxviii, 181
201	Der Streit zwischen Phoebus und Pan: Geschwinde, ihr wirbeln den Winde (Picander), dramma per musica	?1729	S, A, T, B, B, 5vv, 3 tpt, timp, 2 fl, 2 ob, ob d'amore, str, bc	xi/2, 3	I/xl, 119
202	Weichet nur, betrübte Schatten	wedding; ?1718–23	S, ob, str, bc	xi/2, 75	I/xl, 3
203	Amore traditore [not fully authenticated]	—	B, hpd obbl	xi/2, 93	[I/xlii]
204	Ich bin in mir vergnügt (Hunold)	1726–7	S, fl, 2 ob, str, bc	xi/2, 105	I/xl, 81
205	Der zufriedengestellte Äolus: Zerreisset, zerspringet, zertrümmert die Gruft (Picander), dramma per musica	name day of Professor A. F. Müller; 3 Aug 1725	S, A, T, B, 4vv, 3 tpt, timp, 2 hn, 2 fl, 2 ob, ob d'amore, va d'amore, va da gamba, str, bc	xi/2, 139	I/xxxviii, 3
205a	Blast Lärmen, ihr Feinde! [adapted from 205; music lost]	coronation of August III; 19 Feb 1734	—	—	I/xxxvii, CC
206	Schleicht, spielende Wellen, dramma per musica	birthday and name day of August III; ?7 Oct 1736	S, A, T, B, 4vv, 3 tpt, timp, 3 fl, 2 ob, 2 ob d'amore, str, bc	xx/2, 3	I/xxxvi, 159
207	Vereinigte Zwietracht der wechselnden Saiten, dramma per musica	installation of Professor Gottlieb Kortte; 11 Dec 1726	S, A, T, B, 4vv, 3 tpt, timp, 2 fl, 2 ob d'amore, ob da caccia, str, bc	xx/2, 73	I/xxxviii, 99
207a	Auf, schmetternde Töne, dramma per musica	name day of August III; ?3 Aug 1735	S, A, T, B, 4vv, 3 tpt, timp, 2 fl, 2 ob d'amore, ob da caccia, str, bc	xx/2, 141; xxxiv, 345	I/xxxvii, 3
208	Was mir behagt, ist nur die muntre Jagd! (Franck)	birthday of Duke Christian of Saxe-Weissenfels; ?1713	S, S, T, B, 2 hn, 2 rec, 2 ob, ob da caccia, bn, str, bc	xxix, 3	I/xxxv, 3
208a	Was mir behagt, ist nur die muntre Jagd! (after Franck) [music lost]	name day of August III; 1740–42	—	—	I/xxxvii, CC
209	Non sa che sia dolore	departure of scholar (?J. M. Gesner); ?1734	S, fl, str, bc	xxix, 45	[I/xli]
210	O holder Tag, erwünschte Zeit	wedding; after 1740	S, fl, ob d'amore, str, bc	xxix, 69	I/xl, 37

BWV	Title (librettist)	Occasion; date	Scoring	BG	NBA
210a	O angenehme Melodei! [music lost, mostly = 210]	for Joachim Friedrich, Graf von Flemming; ?1738–40	S, fl, ob d'amore, str, bc	xxix, 245	I/xxxix, 143
211	Schweigt stille, plaudert nicht (Coffee Cantata) (Picander)	c1734–5	S, T, B, fl, str, bc	xxix, 141	I/xl, 195
212	Mer hahn en neue Oberkeet (Peasant Cantata) (Picander)	for C. H. von Dieskau; 30 Aug 1742	S, B, hn, fl, str, bc	xxix, 175	I/xxxix, 155
213	Hercules auf dem Scheidewege: Lasst uns sorgen, lasst uns wachen (Picander), dramma per musica	birthday of Prince Friedrich Christian; 5 Sept 1733	S, A, T, B, 4vv, 2 hn, 2 ob, ob d'amore, str, bc	xxxiv, 121	I/xxxvi, 3
214	Tönet, ihr Pauken! Erschallet, Trompeten!, dramma per musica	birthday of Electress Maria Josepha; 8 Dec 1733	S, A, T, B, 4vv, 3 tpt, timp, 2 fl, 2 ob, ob d'amore, str, bc	xxxiv, 177	I/xxxvi, 91
215	Preise dein Glücke, gesegnetes Sachsen (J. C. Clauder), dramma per musica	anniversary of election of August III as King of Poland; 5 Oct 1734	S, T, B, 8vv, 3 tpt, timp, 2 fl, 2 ob, 2 ob d'amore, str, bc	xxxiv, 245	I/xxxvii, 87
216	Vergnügte Pleissenstadt (Picander) [only vv extant]	wedding; 5 Feb 1728	S, A, fl, str, bc	—	I/xl, 23
216a	Erwählte Pleissenstadt [music lost]	for Leipzig city council; after 1728	—	—	[I/xxxix, CC]
249a	Entfliehet, verschwindet, entweichet, ihr Sorgen (Picander) [music lost, but some in 249]	birthday of Duke Christian of Saxe-Weissenfels; 23 Feb 1725	S, A, T, B, 3 tpt, timp, 2 rec, fl, 2 ob, ob d'amore, str, bc	—	I/xxxv, CC
249b	Die Feier des Genius: Verjaget, zerstreuet, zerrüttet, ihr Sterne (Picander), dramma per musica [music lost]	birthday of Joachim Friedrich, Graf von Flemming; 25 Aug 1726	—	—	[I/xxxix, CC]

Lost

BWV	Title (librettist)	Occasion; 1st perf.	Remarks	BG	NBA (CC)
A6	Dich loben die lieblichen Strahlen (Hunold)	New Year; 1 Jan 1720	only text extant	—	I/xxxv
A7	Heut ist gewiss ein guter Tag (Hunold)	birthday of Prince Leopold of Anhalt-Cöthen; ?10 Dec 1720	only text extant	—	I/xxxv
A8	[title unknown]	New Year; 1 Jan 1723	lost; ? = 184a	—	I/xxxv
A9	Entfernet euch, ihr heitern Sterne (C. F. Haupt)	birthday of August II; 12 May 1727	only text extant	—	I/xxxvi
A10	So kämpfet nur, ihr muntern Töne (Picander)	birthday of Johann Friedrich, Graf von Flemming; 25 Aug 1731	only text extant	—	[I/xxxix]
A11	Es lebe der König, der Vater im Lande (Picander)	name day of August II; 3 Aug 1732	only text extant	—	I/xxxvi
A12	Frohes Volk, vergnügte Sachsen (Picander) [adapted from A18]	name day of August III; 3 Aug 1733	only text extant	—	I/xxxvi
A13	Willkommen! Ihr herrschenden Götter (Gottsched)	king's visit and marriage of Princess Maria Amalia; 28 April 1738	only text extant	—	I/xxxvii
A18	Froher Tag, verlangte Stunden (J. H. Winckler)	opening of Thomasschule after renovation; 5 June 1732	only text extant	—	[I/xxxix]
A19	Thomana sass annoch betrübt (J. A. Landvoigt)	in honour of new Rektor of Thomasschule J. A. Ernesti; 21 Nov 1734	only text extant	—	[I/xxxix]
A20	Latin ode [title unknown]	birthday of Duke Friedrich II of Saxe-Gotha; 9 Aug 1723	lost	—	I/xxxviii
—	Auf! süss entzückende Gewalt (Gottsched)	wedding; 27 Nov 1725	only text extant	—	I/xl

MASSES, MAGNIFICAT SETTINGS, ETC

BWV	Title	Remarks	Scoring	BG	NBA
232	[Mass in B minor]:	assembled c1747–9		vi	II/i
	Missa (Kyrie, Gloria)	ded. new Elector of Saxony, Friedrich August II, 1733; Gratias agimus from 29, 1731; Qui tollis from 46, 1723	2 S, A, T, B, 5vv, 3 tpt, timp, hn, 2 fl, 2 ob, 2 ob d'amore, 2 bn, str, bc		
	Symbolum Nicenum (Credo)	added to autograph score c1747–9; Patrem omnipotentem from 171, ?1729; Crucifixus from 12, 1714; Et expecto from 120, 1728–9	S, A, B, 5vv, 3 tpt, timp, 2 fl, 2 ob, 2 ob d'amore, str, bc		
	Sanctus	1st perf. Christmas Day 1724; added to autograph score c1747–9	6vv, 3 tpt, timp, 3 ob, str, bc		
	Osanna, Benedictus, Agnus Dei et Dona nobis pacem	added to autograph score c1747–9; Osanna from A11, 1732; Agnus Dei from 11, 1735	A, T, 8vv, 3 tpt, timp, 2 fl, 2 ob, str, bc		

BWV	Title	Remarks	Scoring	BG	NBA
	4 missae breves:	probably late 1730s; mostly adaptations of cantata movts			
233	F	from 11, 40, 102, ʌ18	S, A, B, 4vv, 2 hn, 2 ob, 2 bn, str, bc	viii, 3	[II/ii]
233a	Kyrie, F	orig. Kyrie of 233	5vv, bc	—	[II/ii]
234	A	from 67, 79, 136, 179	S, A, B, 4vv, 2 fl, str, bc	viii, 53	[II/ii]
235	g	from 72, 102, 187	A, T, B, 4vv, 2 ob, str, bc	viii, 101	[II/ii]
236	G	from 17, 79, 138, 179	S, A, T, B, 4vv, 2 ob, str, bc	viii, 157	[II/ii]
	5 settings of Sanctus:	except 238, all probably arrs. of music by other composers			
237	C	perf. 1723	4vv, 3 tpt, timp, 2 ob, str, bc	xi/1, 69	[II/viii–ix]
238	D	perf. ?Christmas Day 1723	4vv, cornett, str, bc	xi/1, 81	[II/ii]
239	d	perf. 1735–46	4vv, str, bc	xi/1, 89	[II/viii–ix]
240	G	perf. 1735–46	4vv, 2 ob, str, bc	xi/1, 95	[II/viii–ix]
241	D	arr. from piece by J. C. Kerll	8vv, 2 ob d'amore, bn, 2 str, bc	xli, 177	[II/viii–ix]
242	Christe eleison	inserted in Mass, c, by ?J. L. Krebs	S, A, bc	xli, 197	[II/ii]
1083	Credo	perf. c1740; inserted in Mass, F, by G. B. Bassani	4vv, bc	—	[II/8]
243a	Magnificat, E♭	perf. Christmas Day 1723; incl. 4 Christmas texts: Vom Himmel hoch; Freut euch und jubiliert; Gloria in excelsis; Virga Jesse floruit	2 S, A, T, B, 5vv, 3 tpt, timp, 2 rec, 2 ob, str, bc	—	II/iii, 3
243	Magnificat, D	rev. of above, c1728–31; without Christmas texts	2 S, A, T, B, 5vv, 3 tpt, timp, 2 fl, 2 ob, 2 ob d'amore, str, bc	xi/1, 3	II/iii, 67

PASSIONS, ORATORIOS

BWV	Title	Remarks	Scoring	BG	NBA
244	Passio secundum Matthaeum (St Matthew Passion) (Picander)	perf. Good Friday, 11 April 1727 and/or 15 April 1729; perf. 30 March 1736 with revs., incl. 2 org	S in ripieno; chorus I: S, A, T, B, 4vv, 2 rec, 2 fl, 2 ob, 2 ob d'amore, 2 ob da caccia, va da gamba, str, bc; chorus II: S, A, T, B, 4vv, 2 fl, 2 ob, 2 ob d'amore, va da gamba, str, bc	iv/1	II/v, v a (facs. of MS)
245	Passio secundum Joannem (St John Passion) (arr. Bach; free texts: B. H. Brockes and others)	perf. Good Friday, 7 April 1724; 30 March 1725 with 5 nos. replaced (see NBA II/iv, suppl. ii); c1730 and late 1740s with further revs.	S, A, T, B, 4vv, 2 fl, 2 ob, 2 ob d'amore, 2 ob da caccia, 2 va d'amore, va da gamba, lute/org/hpd, str, bc	xii/3	II/iv
247	Passio secundum Marcum (St Mark Passion) (Picander)	perf. Good Friday, 23 March 1731; lost except for 1 movt rev. in 248 and 7 movts in orig. form in 198 and 54; see NBA II/v, CC	—	—	—
248	Oratorium tempore Nativitatis Christi (Christmas Oratorio) (free texts: ?Picander):	6 cantatas for Christmas to Epiphany 1734–5; pts. of nos.1–5 adapted from secular cantatas 213–15, most of no.6 from lost church cantata 248a		v/2	II/vi
	Jauchzet, frohlocket, auf preiset die Tage	perf. Christmas Day 1734	A, T, B, 4vv, 3 tpt, timp, 2 fl, 2 ob, 2 ob d'amore, str, bc		
	Und es waren Hirten in derselben Gegend	perf. 26 Dec 1734	A, T, B, 4vv, 2 fl, 2 ob d'amore, 2 ob da caccia, str, bc		
	Herrscher des Himmels, erhöre das Lallen	perf. 27 Dec 1734	S, A, T, B, 4vv, 3 tpt, timp, 2 fl, 2 ob, 2 ob d'amore, str, bc		
	Fallt mit Danken, fallt mit Loben	perf. 1 Jan 1735	S, T, B, 4vv, 2 hn, 2 ob, str, bc		
	Ehre sei dir, Gott, gesungen	perf. 2 Jan 1735	S, A, T, B, 4vv, 2 ob d'amore, str, bc		
	Herr, wenn die stolzen Feinde schnauben	perf. Epiphany, 6 Jan 1735	S, A, T, B, 4vv, 3 tpt, timp, 2 ob, 2 ob d'amore, str, bc		
249	Kommt, eilet und laufet (Easter Oratorio) (?Picander)	perf. Easter, 1 April 1725 as cantata; rev. as oratorio 1732–5	S, A, T, B, 4vv, 3 tpt, timp, 2 rec, fl, 2 ob d'amore, str, bc	xxi/3	II/vii
246	Passio secundum Lucam (St Luke Passion)	spurious	—	xlv/2	—

MOTETS

Texts of 225–8 are compilations, incl. chorale; other texts and librettist given in parentheses

BWV	Title	Occasion; date	Scoring	BG	NBA
225	Singet dem Herrn ein neues Lied	?birthday of Friedrich August, King of Poland and Elector of Saxony; ?12 May 1727	8vv	xxxix, 5	III/i, 3
226	Der Geist hilft unser Schwachheit auf	funeral of J. H. Ernesti; 24 Oct 1729	8vv, 2 ob da caccia, bn, str, bc	xxxix, 41	III/i, 39
227	Jesu, meine Freude	?memorial service for Johanna Maria Kees; ?18 July 1723	5vv	xxxix, 61	III/i, 77
228	Fürchte dich nicht	?memorial service for Frau Stadthauptmann Winckler; ?4 Feb 1726	8vv	xxxix, 87	III/i, 107
229	Komm, Jesu, komm! (P. Thymich)	?memorial service for Maria Elisabeth Schelle; 26 March 1730	8vv	xxxix, 109	III/i, 127

BWV	Title	Occasion; date	Scoring	BG	NBA
230	Lobet den Herrn alle Heiden (Ps cxvii)	—	4vv, org	xxxix, 129	III/i, 149
118	O Jesu Christ, mein Lebens Licht (2 versions), chorale	burial or memorial service; 1736–7	4vv, 2 hn, cornett, 3 trbn; *4vv, 2 hn, str, bc; 2 ob, ob da caccia and bn, ad lib	xxiv, 185	III/i, 163, 171
—	Tilge, Höchster, mein Sünden, psalm [arr. from Pergolesi: Stabat mater]	1741–6	S, A, str, bc	—	[II/8]

CHORALES, SACRED SONGS, ARIAS

BWV	

	Wedding chorales, 3 for 4vv, 2 hn, ob, ob d'amore, str, bc; BG xiii/1, 147; NBA [III/ii]:
250	Was Gott tut das ist wohlgetan
251	Sei Lob und Ehr' dem höchsten Gut
252	Nun danket alle Gott
	Chorales, 4vv, from Joh. Seb. Bachs vierstimmige Choralgesänge, ed. J. P. Kirnberger and C. P. E. Bach, i–iv (Leipzig, 1784–7) [excluding those within larger works]; BG xxxix, 177; NBA [3/ii]:
253	Ach bleib bei uns, Herr Jesu Christ
254	Ach Gott, erhör' mein Seufzen
255	Ach Gott und Herr
256	Ach lieben Christen, seid getrost
259	Ach, was soll ich Sünder machen
260	Allein Gott in der Höh' sei Ehr'
261	Allein zu dir, Herr Jesu Christ
262	Alle Menschen müssen sterben
263	Alles ist an Gottes Segen
264	Als der gütige Gott
265	Als Jesus Christus in der Nacht
266	Als vierzig Tag nach Ostern
267	An Wasserflüssen Babylon
268	Auf, auf, mein Herz, und du mein ganzer Sinn
269	Aus meines Herzens Grunde
270	Befiehl du deine Wege
271	Befiehl du deine Wege
272	Befiehl du deine Wege
273	Christ, der du bist der heile Tag
274	Christe, der du bist Tag und Licht
275	Christe, du Beistand deiner Kreuzgemeinde
276	Christ ist erstanden
277	Christ lag in Todesbanden
278	Christ lag in Todesbanden
279	Christ lag in Todesbanden
280	Christ, unser Herr, zum Jordan kam
281	Christus, der ist mein Leben
282	Christus, der ist mein Leben
283	Christus, der uns selig macht
284	Christus ist erstanden, hat überwunden
285	Da der Herr Christ zu Tische sass
286	Danket dem Herren
287	Dank sei Gott in der Höhe
288	Das alte Jahr vergangen ist
289	Das alte Jahr vergangen ist
290	Das walt' Gott Vater und Gott Sohn
291	Das walt' mein Gott, Vater, Sohn und heiliger Geist
292	Den Vater dort oben
293	Der du bist drei in Einigkeit
294	Der Tag, der ist so freudenreich
295	Des heil'gen Geistes reiche Gnad'
296	Die Nacht ist kommen
297	Die Sonn' hat sich mit ihrem Glanz
298	Dies sind die heil'gen zehn Gebot'
299	Dir, dir, Jehova, will ich singen
300	Du grosser Schmerzensmann
301	Du, o schönes Weltgebäude
302	Ein' feste Burg ist unser Gott
303	Ein' feste Burg ist unser Gott
304	Eins ist Not! ach Herr, dies Eine
305	Erbarm' dich mein, o Herre Gott
306	Erstanden ist der heil'ge Christ
307	Es ist gewisslich an der Zeit
308	Es spricht der Unweisen Mund wohl
309	Es stehn vor Gottes Throne
310	Es wird schier der letzte Tag herkommen
311	Es woll' uns Gott genädig sein
312	Es woll' uns Gott genädig sein
327	Für deinen Thron tret' ich hiermit
313	Für Freuden lasst uns springen
314	Gelobet seist du, Jesu Christ
315	Gib dich zufrieden und sei stille

BWV	
316	Gott, der du selber bist das Licht
317	Gott, der Vater, wohn' uns bei
318	Gottes Sohn ist kommen
319	Gott hat das Evangelium
320	Gott lebet noch
321	Gottlob, es geht nunmehr zu Ende
322	Gott sei gelobet und gebenedeiet
323	Gott sei uns gnädig
325	Heilig, heilig
326	Herr Gott, dich loben alle wir
328	Herr, Gott, dich loben wir
329	Herr, ich denk' an jene Zeit
330	Herr, ich habe missgehandelt
331	Herr, ich habe missgehandelt
332	Herr Jesu Christ, dich zu uns wend'
333	Herr Jesu Christ, du hast bereit't
334	Herr Jesu Christ, du höchstes Gut
335	Herr Jesu Christ, mein's Lebens Licht
336	Herr Jesu Christ, wahr'r Mensch und Gott
337	Herr, nun lass in Frieden
338	Herr, straf mich nicht in deinem Zorn
339	Herr, wie du willst, so schick's mit mir
340	Herzlich lieb hab ich dich, o Herr
341	Heut' ist, o Mensch, ein grosser Trauertag
342	Heut' triumphieret Gottes Sohn
343	Hilf, Gott, dass mir's gelinge
344	Hilf, Herr Jesu, lass gelingen
345	Ich bin ja, Herr, in deiner Macht
346	Ich dank' dir, Gott, für all' Wohltat
347	Ich dank' dir, lieber Herre
348	Ich dank' dir, lieber Herre
349	Ich dank' dir schon durch deinen Sohn
350	Ich danke dir, o Gott, in deinem Throne
351	Ich hab' mein' Sach' Gott heimgestellt
352	Jesu, der du meine Seele
353	Jesu, der du meine Seele
354	Jesu, der du meine Seele
355	Jesu, der du selbsten wohl
356	Jesu, du mein liebstes Leben
357	Jesu, Jesu, du bist mein
358	Jesu, meine Freude
359	Jesu meiner Seelen Wonne
360	Jesu meiner Seelen Wonne
361	Jesu, meines Herzens Freud'
362	Jesu, nun sei gepreiset
363	Jesus Christus, unser Heiland
364	Jesus Christus, unser Heiland
365	Jesus, meine Zuversicht
366	Ihr Gestirn', ihr hohlen Lüfte
367	In allen meinen Taten
368	In dulci jubilo
369	Keinen hat Gott verlassen
370	Komm, Gott Schöpfer, heiliger Geist
371	Kyrie, Gott Vater in Ewigkeit
372	Lass, o Herr, dein Ohr sich neigen
373	Liebster Jesu, wir sind hier
374	Lobet den Herren, denn er ist freundlich
375	Lobt Gott, ihr Christen, allzugleich
376	Lobt Gott, ihr Christen, allzugleich
377	Mach's mit mir, Gott, nach deiner Güt'
378	Meine Augen schliess' ich jetzt
379	Meinen Jesum lass' ich nicht, Jesus
380	Meinen Jesum lass' ich nicht, weil
322	Meine Seele erhebet den Herrn
381	Meines Lebens letzte Zeit
382	Mit Fried' und Freud' ich fahr' dahin
383	Mitten wir im Leben sind
384	Nicht so traurig, nicht so sehr
385	Nun bitten wir den heiligen Geist
386	Nun danket alle Gott
387	Nun freut euch, Gottes Kinder all'
388	Nun freut euch, lieben Christen, g'mein

389   Nun lob', mein' Seel', den Herren
390   Nun lob', mein' Seel', den Herren
391   Nun preiset alle Gottes Barmherzigkeit
392   Nun ruhen alle Wälder
396   Nun sich der Tag geendet hat
397   O Ewigkeit, du Donnerwort
398   O Gott, du frommer Gott
399   O Gott, du frommer Gott
400   O Herzensangst, o Bangigkeit
401   O Lamm Gottes, unschuldig
402   O Mensch, bewein' dein' Sünde gross
403   O Mensch, schau Jesum Christum an
404   O Traurigkeit, o Herzeleid
393   O Welt, sieh hier dein Leben
394   O Welt, sieh hier dein Leben
395   O Welt, sieh hier dein Leben
405   O wie selig seid ihr doch, ihr Frommen
406   O wie selig seid ihr doch, ihr Frommen
407   O wir armen Sünder
408   Schaut, ihr Sünder
409   Seelen-Bräutigam
410   Sei gegrüsset, Jesu gütig
411   Singet dem Herrn ein neues Lied
412   So gibst du nun, mein Jesu, gute Nacht
413   Sollt' ich meinem Gott nicht singen
414   Uns ist ein Kindlein heut' gebor'n
415   Valet will ich dir geben
416   Vater unser im Himmelreich
417   Von Gott will ich nicht lassen
418   Von Gott will ich nicht lassen
419   Von Gott will ich nicht lassen
257   Wär' Gott nicht mit uns diese Zeit
420   Warum betrübst du dich, mein Herz
421   Warum betrübst du dich, mein Herz
422   Warum sollt' ich mich denn grämen
423   Was betrübst du dich, mein Herze
424   Was bist du doch, o Seele, so betrübet
425   Was willst du dich, o meine Seele
426   Weltlich Ehr' und zeitlich Gut
427   Wenn ich in Angst und Not
428   Wenn mein Stündlein vorhanden ist
429   Wenn mein Stündlein vorhanden ist
430   Wenn mein Stündlein vorhanden ist
431   Wenn wir in höchsten Nöten sein
432   Wenn wir in höchsten Nöten sein
433   Wer Gott vertraut, hat wohl gebaut
434   Wer nur den lieben Gott lässt walten
435   Wie bist du, Seele, in mir so gar betrübt
436   Wie schön leuchtet der Morgenstern
437   Wir glauben all' an einen Gott
258   Wo Gott der Herr nicht bei uns hält
438   Wo Gott zum Haus nicht gibt sein' Gunst

Sacred songs, 1v, bc, in G. C. Schemelli: Musicalisches Gesang-Buch (Leipzig, 1736) [only bc by Bach unless otherwise stated]; BG xxxix, 279; NBA [III/ii]:

439   Ach, dass nicht die letzte Stunde
440   Auf, auf! die rechte Zeit ist hier
441   Auf, auf! mein Herz, mit Freuden
442   Beglückter Stand getreuer Seelen
443   Beschränkt, ihr Weisen dieser Welt
444   Brich entzwei, mein armes Herze
445   Brunnquell aller Güter
446   Der lieben Sonnen Licht und Pracht
447   Der Tag ist hin, die Sonne gehet nieder
448   Der Tag mit seinem Lichte
449   Dich bet'ich an, mein höchster Gott
450   Die bittre Leidenszeit beginnet abermal
451   Die goldne Sonne, voll Freud' und Wonne
452   Dir, dir Jehovah, will ich singen [melody by Bach]
453   Eins ist Not! ach Herr, dies Eine
454   Ermuntre dich, mein schwacher Geist
455   Erwürgtes Lamm, das die verwahrten Siegel
456   Es glänzet der Christen
457   Es ist nun aus mit meinem Leben
458   Es ist vollbracht! vergiss ja nicht
459   Es kostet viel, ein Christ zu sein

460   Gieb dich zufrieden und sei stille
461   Gott lebet noch; Seele, was verzagst du doch?
462   Gott, wie gross ist deine Güte
463   Herr, nicht schicke deine Rache
464   Ich bin ja, Herr, in deiner Macht
465   Ich freue mich in der
466   Ich halte treulich still und liebe
467   Ich lass' dich nicht
468   Ich liebe Jesum alle Stund'
469   Ich steh' an deiner Krippen hier
476   Ihr Gestirn', ihr hohen Lüfte
471   Jesu, deine Liebeswunden
470   Jesu, Jesu, du bist mein
472   Jesu, meines Glaubens Zier
473   Jesu, meines Herzens Freud'
474   Jesus ist das schönste Licht
475   Jesus, unser Trost und Leben
477   Kein Stündlein geht dahin
478   Komm, süsser Tod, komm, sel'ge Ruh'! [melody by Bach]
479   Kommt, Seelen, dieser Tag
480   Kommt wieder aus der finstern Gruft
481   Lasset uns mit Jesu ziehen
482   Liebes Herz, bedenke doch
483   Liebster Gott, wann werd' ich sterben?
484   Liebster Herr Jesu! wo bleibest du so lange?
485   Liebster Immanuel, Herzog der Frommen
488   Meines Lebens letzte Zeit
486   Mein Jesu, dem die Seraphinen
487   Mein Jesu! was für Seelenweh
489   Nicht so traurig, nicht so sehr
490   Nur mein Jesus ist mein Leben
491   O du Liebe meine Liebe
492   O finstre Nacht
493   O Jesulein süss, o Jesulein mild
494   O liebe Seele, zieh' die Sinnen
495   O wie selig seid ihr doch, ihr Frommen
496   Seelen-Bräutigam, Jesu, Gottes Lamm!
497   Seelenweide, meine Freude
499   Sei gegrüsset, Jesu gütig
498   Selig, wer an Jesum denkt
500   So gehst du nun, mein Jesu, hin
501   So giebst du nun, mein Jesu, gute Nacht
502   So wünsch' ich mir zu guter Letzt
503   Steh' ich bei meinem Gott
504   Vergiss mein nicht, dass ich dein nicht
505   Vergiss mein nicht, vergiss mein nicht [melody by Bach]
506   Was bist du doch, o Seele, so betrübet
507   Wo ist mein Schäflein, das ich liebe

Pieces in Clavierbüchlein, ii, for Anna Magdalena Bach; BG xxxix, 289; NBA V/iv, 91:

511   Gib dich zufrieden, chorale, g [* 512]
512   Gib dich zufrieden, chorale, e (arr. of 511)
513   O Ewigkeit, du Donnerwort, chorale [from 397]
515[b] So oft ich meine Tobackspfeife, aria, g (bass by Bach)
518   Willst du dein Herz mir schenken, aria ('Aria di Giovanni')

524   Quodlibet, SATB, bc, frag., for wedding, Mühlhausen, 1707

Doubtful and spurious
Pieces in Clavierbüchlein, ii, for Anna Magdalena Bach; BG xxxix, 309; NBA V/iv, 102:

508   Bist du bei mir, aria (?by G. H. Stözel)
509   Gedenke doch, mein Geist, aria (anon.)
510   Gib dich zufrieden, chorale, F (anon. bass added)
514   Schaffs mit mir, Gott, chorale (anon.)
515[a] So oft ich meine Tobackspfeife, aria, d (anon., ?by Gottfried Heinrich Bach)
516   Warum betrübst du dich, aria (anon.)
517   Wie wohl ist mir, o Freund der Seelen (anon.)

Sacred songs, 5 for 1v, bc (probably spurious); NBA [3/iii]:

519   Hier lieg' ich nun
520   Das walt' mein Gott
521   Gott mein Herz dir Dank
522   Meine Seele, lass es gehen
523   Ich gnüge mich an meinem Stande

ORGAN

(independent of chorales)

BWV	Title	Remarks	BG	NBA
525–30	6 trio sonatas (E♭, c, d, e, C, G)	Leipzig, c1727; no.3: cf 1044; no.4 arr. from 76	xv, 3–66	[IV/vii]
531	Prelude and fugue, C	?before 1707	xv, 81	IV/v, 3
532	Prelude and fugue, D	?Weimar, 1708–17; *fugue, 532a	xv, 88	IV/v, 58; IV/vi, 95
533	Prelude and fugue, e	?pre-Weimar, before 1708; *533a	xv, 100	IV/v, 90; IV/vi, 106
534	Prelude and fugue, f	?Weimar, 1708–17	xv, 104	IV/v, 130
535	Prelude and fugue, g	?Weimar, 1708–17; 535a, before 1707, frag.	xv, 112	IV/v, 157; IV/vi, 109
536	Prelude and fugue, A	?Weimar, 1708–17; *536a, before 1708	xv, 120	IV/v, 180; IV/vi, 114
537	Fantasia and fugue, c	?Weimar, 1708–17	xv, 129	IV/v, 47
538	Toccata and fugue, 'Dorian', d	Weimar, 1708–17	xv, 136	IV/v, 76
539	Prelude and fugue, d	after 1720; fugue adapted from vn sonata, 1001	xv, 148	IV/v, 70
540	Toccata and fugue, F	?Weimar, 1708–17	xv, 154	IV/v, 112
541	Prelude and fugue, G	?Weimar, 1708–17; rev. after 1742	xv, 169	IV/v, 146
542	Fantasia and fugue, g	fugue: Weimar, 1708–17; fantasia: Cöthen, 1717–23	xv, 177	IV/v, 167
543	Prelude and fugue, a	?Weimar, 1708–17; *543a; fugue: cf 944	xv, 189	IV/v, 186; IV/vi, 121
544	Prelude and fugue, b	Leipzig, 1727–31	xv, 199	IV/v, 198
545	Prelude and fugue, C	Weimar, 1708–17; *545a, ?before 1708	xv, 212	IV/v, 10; IV/vi, 77
546	Prelude and fugue, c	fugue: ?Weimar, 1708–17; prelude, ?Leipzig, after 1723	xv, 218	IV/v, 35
547	Prelude and fugue, C	?Leipzig, after 1723	xv, 228	IV/v, 20
548	Prelude and fugue, e	Leipzig, 1727–31	xv, 236	IV/v, 94
549	Prelude and fugue, c	?Weimar, 1708–17; *549a, before 1707	xxxviii, 3	IV/v, 30; IV/vi, 101
550	Prelude and fugue, G	?pre-Weimar, before 1708	xxxviii, 9	IV/v, 138
551	Prelude and fugue, a	?pre-Weimar, before 1708	xxxviii, 17	IV/vi, 63
552	Prelude and fugue, 'St Anne', E♭	in Clavier-Übung, iii (Leipzig, 1739), see 669–89	iii, 173, 254	IV/iv, 2
562	Fantasia and fugue, c	fantasia: ?Weimar, 1708–17; fugue: Leipzig, c1745, inc.	xxxviii, 64, 209	IV/v, 54, 105
563	Fantasia, b	before 1707	xxxviii, 59	IV/vi, 68
564	Toccata, adagio and fugue, C	Weimar, 1708–17	xv, 253	IV/v, 3
565	Toccata and fugue, d	?pre-Weimar, before 1708	xv, 267	IV/vi, 31
566	Prelude and fugue, E	?pre-Weimar, before 1708	xv, 276	IV/iv, 40
568	Prelude, G	?pre-Weimar, before 1708	xxxviii, 85	IV/vi, 51
569	Prelude, a	?pre-Weimar, before 1708	xxxviii, 89	IV/vi, 59
570	Fantasia, C	?before 1707	xxxviii, 62	IV/vi, 16
572	Fantasia, G	before 1708	xxxviii, 75	[IV/vii]
573	Fantasia, C	Cöthen, c1722; frag. in Clavierbüchlein, i, for Anna Magdalena Bach	xxxviii, 209	IV/vi, 18
574	Fugue on theme by Legrenzi, c	?pre-Weimar; *574a–b	xxxviii, 94, 205	IV/vi, 19, 82, 88
575	Fugue, c	?Weimar, 1708–17	xxxviii, 101	IV/vi, 26
578	Fugue, g	?before 1707	xxxviii, 116	IV/vi, 55
579	Fugue on theme by Corelli, b	?pre-Weimar	xxxviii, 121	IV/vi, 71
582	Passacaglia, c	?pre-Weimar	xv, 289	[IV/vii]
583	Trio, d		xxxviii, 143	[IV/vii]
586	Trio, G	by Telemann, transcr. org by Bach	—	[IV/viii]
587	Aria, F	transcr. from Couperin: Les nations	xxxviii, 222	[IV/viii]
588	Canzona, d	Weimar, c1715	xxxviii, 126	[IV/vii]
590	Pastorale, F	Weimar, c1710	xxxviii, 135	[IV/vii]
	6 concertos:	Weimar, 1708–17; arrs. of works by other composers		
592	G	arr. of conc. by Duke Johann Ernst of Saxe-Weimar; *592a	xxxviii, 149; xlii, 282	[IV/viii]
593	a	arr. of Vivaldi op.3 no.8 = RV522	xxxviii, 158	[IV/viii]
594	C	arr. of Vivaldi op.7 no.5 = RV285a	xxxviii, 171	[IV/viii]
595	C	arr. of conc. by Duke Johann Ernst of Saxe-Weimar	xxxviii, 196	[IV/viii]
596	d	arr. of Vivaldi op.3 no.11 = RV565	—	[IV/viii]
597	E♭	arr. of conc. by unknown composer	—	[IV/viii]
598	Pedal-Exercitium	?pre-Weimar; ?Bach's improvisations recorded by C. P. E. Bach	xxxviii, 210	[IV/vii]
802–5	4 duettos (e, F, G, a)	inventions a 2 in Clavier-Übung, iii (Leipzig, 1739); see also 552, 669–89	iii, 242–51	IV/iv, 92–102
1027a	Trio, G	transcr. from last movt of va da gamba sonata, 1027	—	—

Doubtful and spurious

131a	Fugue, g	spurious adaptation from cantata, 131	xxxviii, 217	—
	[8 short preludes and fugues] (C, d, e, F, G, g, a, B♭)	probably spurious; ?by J. T. Krebs	xxxviii, 23	[IV/ix]
561	Fantasia and fugue, a	spurious	xxxviii, 48	—
567	Prelude, C	spurious	xxxviii, 84	—
571	Fantasia, G	spurious	xxxviii, 67	—
576	Fugue, G	spurious	xxxviii, 106	—
577	Fugue, G	spurious	xxxviii, 111	—
580	Fugue, D	spurious	xxxviii, 215	—

BWV	Title	Remarks	BG	NBA
581	Fugue, G	spurious	—	—
584	Trio, g	probably spurious	—	—
585	Trio, c	by J. F. Fasch	xxxviii, 219	—
589	Allabreve, D	doubtful	xxxviii, 131	[IV/vii]
591	Kleines harmonisches Labyrinth	probably spurious; ?by J. D. Heinichen	xxxviii, 225	[IV/ix]
		(based on chorales)		
	Das Orgel-Büchlein:	Weimar, c1713–17, unless otherwise stated		
599	Nun komm' der Heiden Heiland		xxv/2, 3	[IV/i]
600	Gott, durch deine Güte		xxv/2, 4	[IV/i]
601	Herr Christ, der ein'ge Gottes-Sohn		xxv/2, 5	[IV/i]
602	Lob sei dem allmächtigen Gott		xxv/2, 6	[IV/i]
603	Puer natus in Bethlehem		xxv/2, 6	[IV/i]
604	Gelobet seist du, Jesu Christ		xxv/2, 7	[IV/i]
605	Der Tag, der ist so freudenreich		xxv/2, 8	[IV/i]
606	Vom Himmel hoch, da komm' ich her		xxv/2, 9	[IV/i]
607	Vom Himmel kam der Engel Schar		xxv/2, 10	[IV/i]
608	In dulci jubilo		xxv/2, 12	[IV/i]
609	Lobt Gott, ihr Christen, allzugleich		xxv/2, 13	[IV/i]
610	Jesu, meine Freude		xxv/2, 14	[IV/i]
611	Christum wir sollen loben schon		xxv/2, 15	[IV/i]
612	Wir Christenleut'		xxv/2, 16	[IV/i]
613	Helft mir Gottes Güte preisen		xxv/2, 18	[IV/i]
614	Das alte Jahr vergangen ist	?Leipzig, after 1740	xxv/2, 19	[IV/i]
615	In dir ist Freude		xxv/2, 20	[IV/i]
616	Mit Fried' und Freud' ich fahr dahin		xxv/2, 24	[IV/i]
617	Herr Gott, nun schleuss den Himmel auf		xxv/2, 26	[IV/i]
618	O Lamm Gottes unschuldig		xxv/2, 28	[IV/i]
619	Christe, du Lamm Gottes		xxv/2, 30	[IV/i]
620	Christus, der uns selig macht	*620a of earlier date	xxv/2, 30, 149	[IV/i]
621	Da Jesus an dem Kreuze stund'		xxv/2, 32	[IV/i]
622	O Mensch, bewein' dein' Sünde gross		xxv/2, 33	[IV/i]
623	Wir danken dir, Herr Jesu Christ		xxv/2, 35	[IV/i]
624	Hilf Gott, dass mir's gelinge		xxv/2, 36	[IV/i]
625	Christ lag in Todesbanden		xxv/2, 38	[IV/i]
626	Jesus Christus, unser Heiland		xxv/2, 39	[IV/i]
627	Christ ist erstanden		xxv/2, 40	[IV/i]
628	Erstanden ist der heil'ge Christ		xxv/2, 44	[IV/i]
629	Erschienen ist der herrliche Tag		xxv/2, 45	[IV/i]
630	Heut' triumphieret Gottes Sohn		xxv/2, 46	[IV/i]
631	Komm, Gott Schöpfer, heiliger Geist	*631a of earlier date	xxv/2, 47, 150	[IV/i]
632	Herr Jesu Christ, dich zu uns wend'		xxv/2, 48	[IV/i]
633	Liebster Jesu, wir sind hier	*634	xxv/2, 49, 50	[IV/i]
635	Dies sind die heil'gen zehn Gebot'		xxv/2, 50	[IV/i]
636	Vater unser im Himmelreich		xxv/2, 52	[IV/i]
637	Durch Adam's Fall ist ganz verderbt		xxv/2, 53	[IV/i]
638	Es ist das Heil uns kommen her		xxv/2, 54	[IV/i]
639	Ich ruf' zu dir, Herr Jesu Christ		xxv/2, 55	[IV/i]
640	In dich hab' ich gehoffet, Herr		xxv/2, 56	[IV/i]
641	Wenn wir in höchsten Nöten sein		xxv/2, 57	[IV/i]
642	Wer nur den lieben Gott lässt walten		xxv/2, 58	[IV/i]
643	Alle Menschen müssen sterben		xxv/2, 59	[IV/i]
644	Ach wie nichtig, ach wie flüchtig		xxv/2, 60	[IV/i]
	Sechs Choräle ['Schübler' chorales]:	(Zella, c1748–9), transcrs. of cantata movts pubd by Schübler		
645	Wachet auf, ruft uns die Stimme	from 140, movt 4	xxv/2, 63	
646	Wo soll ich fliehen hin	source unknown	xxv/2, 66	
647	Wer nur den lieben Gott lässt walten	from 93, movt 4	xxv/2, 68	
648	Meine Seele erhebet den Herren	from 10, movt 5	xxv/2, 70	
649	Ach bleib' bei uns, Herr Jesu Christ	from 6, movt 3	xxv/2, 71	
650	Kommst du nun, Jesu, vom Himmel herunter	from 137, movt 2	xxv/2, 74	
	[17 (18) chorales]:	mostly Weimar, 1708–17 [early versions in NBA]; rev. as collection, Leipzig, ?1744–7, D-B P271; for 2 kbd, pedal; see also 668		
651	Fantasia super Komm, Heiliger Geist	organo pleno; c.f. in pedal	xxv/2, 79	IV/ii, 3
652	Komm, Heiliger Geist	alio modo	xxv/2, 86	IV/ii, 13
653	An Wasserflüssen Babylon		xxv/2, 92	IV/ii, 22
654	Schmücke, dich, o liebe Seele		xxv/2, 95	IV/ii, 26
655	Trio super Herr Jesu Christ, dich zu uns wend		xxv/2, 98	IV/ii, 31
656	O Lamm Gottes, unschuldig		xxv/2, 102	IV/ii, 38
657	Nun danket alle Gott	c.f. in soprano	xxv/2, 108	IV/ii, 46
658	Von Gott will ich nicht lassen	c.f. in pedal	xxv/2, 112	IV/ii, 51
659	Nun komm, der Heiden Heiland		xxv/2, 114	IV/ii, 55
660	Trio super Nun komm, der Heiden Heiland		xxv/2, 116	IV/ii, 59
661	Nun komm, der Heiden Heiland	organo pleno; c.f. in pedal	xxv/2, 118	IV/ii, 62
662	Allein Gott in der Höh sei Ehr	c.f. in soprano	xxv/2, 122	IV/ii, 68
663	Allein Gott in der Höh sei Ehr	c.f. in tenor	xxv/2, 125	IV/ii, 72
664	Trio super Allein Gott in der Höh sei Ehr		xxv/2, 130	IV/ii, 79
665	Jesus Christus, unser Heiland		xxv/2, 136	IV/ii, 87
666	Jesus Christus, unser Heiland	alio modo	xxv/2, 140	IV/ii, 91
667	Komm, Gott, Schöpfer, Heiliger Geist	organo pleno	xxv/2, 142	IV/ii, 94

BWV	Title	Remarks	BG	NBA
668	Wenn wir in hoechsten Noeten sein (Vor deinen Thron tret ich)	probably Leipzig, c1744–7, pubd in 1080; late addn to *D-B* P271 as Vor deinen Thron	xxv/2, 145	IV/ii, 113, 212
	Chorale preludes in Clavier-Übung, iii, bestehend in verschiedenen Vorspielen über die Cathechismus- und andere Gesaenge	(Leipzig, 1739); framed by 552; for 2 kbd, pedal unless otherwise stated		
669	Kyrie, Gott Vater in Ewigkeit	c.f. in soprano	iii, 184	IV/iv, 16
670	Christe, aller Welt Trost	c.f. in tenor	iii, 186	IV/iv, 18
671	Kyrie, Gott heiliger Geist	a 5, organo pleno; c.f. in bass	iii, 190	IV/iv, 22
672	Kyrie, Gott Vater in Ewigkeit	alio modo, manuals only	iii, 194	IV/iv, 27
673	Christe, aller Welt Trost	manuals only	iii, 194	IV/iv, 28
674	Kyrie, Gott heiliger Geist	manuals only	iii, 196	IV/iv, 29
675	Allein Gott in der Höh sei Ehr	a 3; c.f. in alto; manuals only	iii, 197	IV/iv, 33
676	Allein Gott in der Höh sei Ehr		iii, 199	IV/iv, 33
677	Fughetta super Allein Gott in der Höh sei Ehr	manuals only	iii, 205	IV/iv, 41
678	Dies sind die heilgen zehen Gebot	c.f. in canon	iii, 206	IV/iv, 42
679	Fughetta super Dies sind die heiligen zehen Gebot	manuals only	iii, 210	IV/iv, 49
680	Wir gläuben all an einen Gott	organo pleno	iii, 212	IV/iv, 52
681	Fughetta super Wir gläuben all an einen Gott	manuals only	iii, 216	IV/iv, 57
682	Vater unser im Himmelreich	c.f. in canon	iii, 217	IV/iv, 58
683	Vater unser im Himmelreich	alio modo, manuals only	iii, 223	IV/iv, 66
684	Christ, unser Herr, zum Jordan kam	c.f. in pedal	iii, 224	IV/iv, 68
685	Christ, unser Herr, zum Jordan kam	alio modo, manuals only	iii, 228	IV/iv, 73
686	Aus tiefer Not schrei ich zu dir	a 6, organo pleno, pedal doppio	iii, 229	IV/iv, 74
687	Aus tiefer Not schrei ich zu dir	a 4, alio modo, manuals only	iii, 232	IV/iv, 78
688	Jesus Christus, unser Heiland, der von uns den Zorn Gottes wandt	c.f. in pedal	iii, 234	IV/iv, 81
689	Fuga super Jesus Christus unser Heiland	a 4, manuals only	iii, 239	IV/iv, 89
690	Wer nur den lieben Gott lässt walten	manuals only; ?Weimar, 1708–17	xl, 3	IV/iii, 98
691	Wer nur den lieben Gott lässt walten	manuals only; autograph in Clavier-Büchlein for W. F. Bach; cf 691	xl, 4	IV/iii, 98
694	Wo soll ich fliehen hin	2 kbd, pedal; before 1708; source for 646	xl, 6	IV/iii, 103
695	Fantasia super Christ lag in Todes Banden	manuals only; ?Weimar, 1708–17; cf 695a	xl, 10	IV/iii, 20
696	Christum wir sollen loben schon	fughetta, manuals only	xl, 13	IV/iii, 23
697	Gelobet seist du, Jesu Christ	fughetta, manuals only; ?Weimar, 1708–17	xl, 14	IV/iii, 32
698	Herr Christ, der einig Gottes Sohn	fughetta, manuals only; ?Weimar, 1708–17	xl, 15	IV/iii, 35
699	Nun komm, der Heiden Heiland	fughetta, manuals only; ?Weimar, 1708–17	xl, 16	IV/iii, 73
700	Vom Himmel hoch, da komm ich her	before 1708, rev. 1740s	xl, 17	IV/iii, 92
701	Vom Himmel hoch, da komm ich her	fughetta, manuals only; ?Weimar, 1708–17	xl, 19	IV/iii, 96
703	Gottes Sohn ist kommen	fughetta, manuals only; ?Weimar, 1708–17	xl, 21	IV/iii, 34
704	Lob sei dem allmächtigen Gott	fughetta, manuals only; ?Weimar, 1708–17	xl, 22	IV/iii, 62
706	Liebster Jesu, wir sind hier	Weimar, 1708–17	xl, 25	IV/iii, 59
709	Herr Jesu Christ, dich zu uns wend	2 kbd, pedal; ?Weimar, 1708–17	xl, 30	IV/iii, 43
710	Wir Christenleut habn jetzund Freud	2 kbd, pedal; ?Weimar, 1708–17	xl, 32	IV/iii, 100
711	Allein Gott in der Höh sei Ehr	bicinium; ?Weimar, 1708–17; rev. 1740s	xl, 34	IV/iii, 11
712	In dich hab ich gehoffet, Herr	manuals only; ?Weimar, 1708–17	xl, 36	IV/iii, 48
713	Fantasia super Jesu, meine Freude	manuals only; ?Weimar, 1708–17; cf 713a	xl, 38	IV/iii, 54
714	Ach Gott und Herr	per canonem; ?Weimar, 1708–17	xl, 43	IV/iii, 3
715	Allein Gott in der Höh sei Ehr	Arnstadt, 1703–8, or Weimar, 1708–17	xl, 44	IV/iii, 14
717	Allein Gott in der Höh sei Ehr	manuals only; ?Weimar, 1708–17	xl, 47	IV/iii, 8
718	Christ lag in Todes Banden	2 kbd, pedal; before 1708	xl, 52	IV/iii, 16
720	Ein feste Burg ist unser Gott	3 kbd, pedal; Weimar, 1709	xl, 57	IV/iii, 24
721	Erbarm dich mein, o Herre Gott	manuals only; ?Weimar, 1708–17	xl, 60	IV/iii, 28
722	Gelobet seist du, Jesu Christ	Arnstadt, 1703–8, or Weimar, 1708–17; sketch, 722a	xl, 62, 158	IV/iii, 30–1
724	Gott, durch deine Güte (Gottes Sohn ist kommen)	before 1708; alternative title in BWV, BG	xl, 65	IV/iii, 33
725	Herr Gott, dich loben wir	a 5; ?Weimar, 1708–17	xl, 66	IV/iii, 36
726	Herr Jesu Christ, dich zu uns wend	?Weimar, 1708–17	xl, 72	IV/iii, 45
727	Herzlich tut mich verlangen	2 kbd, pedal; ?Weimar, 1708–17	xl, 73	IV/iii, 46
728	Jesus, meine Zuversicht	manuals only; autograph in Clavierbüchlein, i, for Anna Magdalena Bach	xl, 74	IV/iii, 58
729	In dulci jubilo	?Weimar, 1708–17; sketch, 729a	xl, 74, 158	IV/iii, 52, 50
730	Liebster Jesu, wir sind hier	?Weimar, 1708–17	xl, 76	IV/iii, 60
731	Liebster Jesu, wir sind hier	2 kbd, pedal; ?Weimar, 1708–17	xl, 77	IV/iii, 61
732	Lobt Gott, ihr Christen, allzugleich	Arnstadt, 1703–8, or Weimar, 1708–17; sketch, 732a	xl, 78, 159	IV/iii, 63–4
733	Meine Seele erhebt den Herren (Fuge über das Magnificat)	organo pleno; ?Weimar, 1708–17	xl, 79	IV/iii, 65
734a	Nun freut euch, lieben Christen gmein	manuals only; cf in tenor; ?Weimar, 1708–17; cf 734	xl, 160	IV/iii, 70
—	O Lamm Gottes, unschuldig	manuals only; ?Weimar, 1708–17	—	IV/iii, 74
735	Fantasia super Valet will ich dir geben	with pedal obbl; Leipzig, after 1723; *735a, Weimar, 1708–17	xl, 86, 161	IV/iii, 77, 81
736	Valet will ich dir geben	c.f. in pedal; ?Weimar, 1708–17	xl, 90	IV/iii, 84
737	Vater unser im Himmelreich	manuals only; ?Weimar, 1708–17	xl, 96	IV/iii, 90
738	Vom Himmel hoch, da komm ich her	?Weimar, 1708–17; sketch, 738a	xl, 97, 159	IV/iii, 94
739	Wie schön leucht't uns der Morgenstern	?Weimar, 1708–17	xl, 99	—
741	Ach Gott vom Himmel sieh darein	organo pleno; before 1708, rev. 1740s	xl, 167	IV/iii, 4
753	Jesu, meine Freude	frag.; autograph in Clavier-Büchlein for W. F. Bach	xl, 163	V/v
764	Wie schön leuchtet uns der Morgenstern	?Weimar, 1708–17	xl, 164	—
	Partite diverse:	chorale variations, ?Lüneburg, c1700		
766	Christ, der du bist der helle Tag		xl, 107	[IV/i]

BWV	Title	Remarks	BG	NBA
767	O Gott, du frommer Gott		xl, 114	[IV/i]
768	Sei gegrüsset, Jesu gütig	much rev. later	xl, 122	[IV/i]

Doubtful and spurious

BWV	Title	Remarks	BG	NBA
691a	Wer nur den lieben Gott lässt walten	*691; doubtful	xl, 151	[IV/ix]
692	Ach Gott und Herr	by J. G. Walther; *692a	xl, 4, 152	—
693	Ach Gott und Herr	by J. G. Walther	xl, 5	—
695a	Fantasia super Christ lag in Todes Banden	c.f. in pedal; *695; doubtful	xl, 153	—
702	Das Jesulein soll doch mein Trost	fughetta; doubtful	xl, 20	[IV/ix]
705	Durch Adam's Fall ist ganz verderbt	doubtful	xl, 23	[IV/ix]
707	Ich hab' mein' Sach' Gott heimgestellt	doubtful	xl, 26	[IV/ix]
708	Ich hab' mein' Sach' Gott heimgestellt	doubtful; *708a, doubtful	xl, 30, 152	[IV/ix]
713a	Fantasia super Jesu, meine Freude	c.f. in pedal; *713; doubtful	xl, 155	—
716	Fuga super Allein Gott in der Höh sei Ehr	doubtful	xl, 45	[IV/ix]
719	Der Tag, der ist so freudenreich	doubtful	xl, 55	[IV/ix]
723	Gelobet seist du, Jesu Christ	doubtful	xl, 63	[IV/ix]
734	Nun freut euch, lieben Christen gmein	c.f. in pedal; *734a; doubtful	xl, 84	—
740	Wir glauben all' an einen Gott, Vater	doubtful	xl, 103	[IV/ix]
742	Ach Herr, mich armen Sünder	spurious	—	—
743	Ach, was ist doch unser Leben	spurious	—	—
744	Auf meinen lieben Gott	?by J. L. Krebs	xl, 170	—
745	Aus der Tiefe rufe ich	?by (2) Johann Christoph Bach	xl, 171	—
746	Christ ist erstanden	?by J. C. F. Fischer	xl, 173	—
747	Christus, der uns selig macht	spurious	—	—
748	Gott der Vater wohn' uns bei	?by (2) J. C. Bach or J. G. Walther; *748a	xl, 177	—
749	Herr Jesu Christ, dich zu uns wend'	spurious	—	—
750	Herr Jesu Christ, mein's Lebens Licht	spurious	—	—
751	In dulci jubilo	spurious	—	—
752	Jesu, der du meine Seele	spurious	—	—
754	Liebster Jesu, wir sind hier	spurious	—	—
755	Nun freut euch, lieben Christen	spurious	—	—
756	Nun ruhen alle Wälder	spurious	—	—
757	O Herre Gott, din göttlich's Wort	spurious	—	—
758	O Vater, allmächtiger Gott	doubtful	xl, 179	—
759	Schmücke dich, o liebe Seele	by G. A. Homilius	xl, 181	—
760	Vater unser im Himmelreich	?by (2) J. C. Bach or G. Böhm	xl, 183	—
761	Vater unser im Himmelreich	?by (2) J. C. Bach or Böhm	xl, 184	—
762	Vater unser im Himmelreich	spurious	—	—
763	Wie schön leuchtet der Morgenstern	spurious	—	—
765	Wir glauben all' an einen Gott	spurious	—	—
770	Ach, was soll ich Sünder machen?	chorale variations; doubtful	xl, 189	—
771	Allein Gott in der Höh sei Ehr'	chorale variations; nos.3, 8 (?all) by A. N. Vetter	xl, 195	—

OTHER KEYBOARD

BWV	Title	Remarks	BG	NBA
772–86	15 Inventions (C, c, D, d, Eb, E, e, F, f, G, g, A, a, Bb, b)	Cöthen, 1723; *Clavier-Büchlein for W. F. Bach; 772: *772a	iii, 1	V/iii
787–801	15 Sinfonias (C, c, D, d, Eb, E, e, F, f, G, g, A, a, Bb, b)	Cöthen, 1723; *Clavier-Büchlein for W. F. Bach	iii	V/iii
806–11	6 [English] Suites (A, a, g, F, e, d)	Weimar, c1715	xlv/1, 3	[V/viii]
812–17	6 [French] Suites (d, c, b, Eb, G, E)	nos. 1–5: orig. versions in Clavierbüchlein, i, for Anna Magdalena Bach	xlv/1, 89	[V/viii]
	Clavier-Übung [i] bestehend in Präludien, Allemanden, Couranten, Sarabanden, Giguen, Menuetten, und anderen Galanterien:	partitas pubd singly (Leipzig, 1726–31) and as op. 1 (Leipzig, 1731); nos.3, 6; *Clavierbüchlein, ii, for Anna Magdalena Bach	iii, 46	V/i
825–30	6 Partitas (Bb, c, a, D, G, e)			
831	Ouvertüre [Partita] nach französischer Art, b	in Clavier-Übung, ii (Leipzig, 1735); see also 971; *831a, Leipzig, by 1733	iii, 154	V/ii
846–69	Das wohltemperirte Clavier, oder Praeludia, und Fugen durch alle Tone und Semitonia [i] [The Well-tempered Clavier]: 24 Preludes and fugues (C, c, C#, c#, D, d, Eb, eb/d#, E, e, F, f, F#, f#, G, g, Ab, g#, A, a, Bb, bb, B, b)	Cöthen, 1722; some preludes: *Clavier-Büchlein for W. F. Bach	xiv	[V/vi]
870–93	[Das wohltemperirte Clavier, ii]: 24 Preludes and fugues (C, c, C#, c#, D, d, Eb, eb/d#, E, e, F, f, F#, f#, G, g, Ab, g#, A, a, Bb, bb, B, b)	Leipzig, 1738–42; some pieces earlier	xiv	[V/vii]
971	Concerto nach italiänischen Gusto [Italian Concerto]	in Clavier-Übung, ii (Leipzig, 1735)	iii, 139	V/ii
988	Aria mit [30] verschiedenen Veraenderungen [Goldberg Variations]	Clavier-Übung, iv (Nuremberg, 1741–2)	iii, 263	V/ii
	Miscellaneous suites and suite movts:			
818	Suite, a	Cöthen, c1722	xxxvi, 3	[V/viii]
819	Suite, Eb	Cöthen, c1722	xxxvi, 8	[V/xiii]
820	Ouverture, F	Weimar, 1708–14	xxxvi, 14	[V/x]
821	Suite, Bb	Weimar, 1708–14; probably authentic	xlii, 213	[V/x]
822	Suite, g	?arr. of work by another composer	—	[V/x]
823	Suite, f	frag.; Weimar, 1708–14	xxxvi, 229	[V/xiii]
832	Partie, A	Weimar, 1708–14	xlii, 255	[V/xii]
833	Prelude and partita, F	Weimar, 1708–14	—	[V/xii]

BWV	Title	Remarks	BG	NBA
836–7	2 allemandes, g (1 inc.)	from Clavier-Büchlein for W. F. Bach; ?by W. F. Bach assisted by J. S. Bach	xlv/1, 214–15	V/v, 8–10
841–3	3 minuets, G, g, G	from Clavier-Büchlein for W. F. Bach	xxxvi, 209–10	V/v, 16–18
	Miscellaneous preludes, fugues, fantasias, toccatas:			
894	Prelude and fugue, a	Weimar, 1708–17; cf 1044	xxxvi, 91	[V/ix]
896	Prelude and fugue, A	Weimar, c1709; fugue only in edn.; prelude ed. in *BJb*, ix (1912), suppl.	xxxvi, 157	[V/ix]
900	Prelude and fughetta, e	Cöthen, c1720	xxxvi, 108	[V/ix]
901	Prelude and fughetta, F	fughetta = early version of 886	xxxvi, 112	[V/ix]
902	Prelude and fughetta, G	fughetta = early version of 884; alternative prelude, 902a	xxxvi, 114, 220	[V/ix]
903	Chromatic fantasia and fugue, d	Cöthen, c1720; rev. Leipzig, c1730; *903a of earlier date	xxxvi, 71, 219	[V/ix]
904	Fantasia and fugue, a	Leipzig, c1725	xxxvi, 81	[VI/ix]
906	Fantasia and fugue, c	Leipzig, c1738; fugue inc.	xxxvi, 145, 238	[V/ix]
910	Toccata, f♯	c1717	iii, 311	[V/ix]
911	Toccata, c	c1717	iii, 322	[V/ix]
912	Toccata, D	Weimar, c1710	xxxvi, 26	[V/ix]
913	Toccata, d	before 1708	xxxvi, 36	[V/ix]
914	Toccata, e	before 1708	xxxvi, 47	[V/ix]
915	Toccata, g	before 1708	xxxvi, 54	[V/ix]
916	Toccata, G	Weimar, c1719	xxxvi, 63	[V/ix]
944	Fugue, a	early version of org fugue 543	iii, 334	[V/ix]
946	Fugue, C	c1708	xxxvi, 159	[V/ix]
950	Fugue on theme by Albinoni, A	Weimar, c1710	xxxvi, 173	[V/ix]
951	Fugue on theme by Albinoni, b	Weimar, c1710; *951a of earlier date	xxxvi, 178, 221	[V/ix]
953	Fugue, C	c1723; from Clavier-Büchlein for W. F. Bach	xxxvi, 186	V/v, 46
954	Fugue, B♭	arr. of fugue from J. A. Reincken: Hortus musicus	xlii, 50	[V/xi]
955	Fugue, B♭	arr. of org fugue, G, by J. C. Erselius	xlii, 55	[V/xi]
958	Fugue, a	Weimar, c1710	xlii, 205	[V/ix]
959	Fugue, a	Weimar, c1710	xlii, 208	[V/ix]
	Pieces from Clavier-Büchlein for W. F. Bach:	Cöthen, 1720–; incl. also 836–7, 841–3, 924a–5, 931–2, 953, 994; see 691, 753, 772ff, 846ff	xxxvi, 118	V/v
924	Praeambulum, C	cf 924a		
926	Prelude, d			
927	Praeambulum, F			
928	Prelude, F			
929	Trio, g	inserted in Partita, g, by G. H. Stölzel		
930	Praeambulum, g			
	Clavierbüchlein, i, for Anna Magdalena Bach	Cöthen, 1722–5; see 573, 728, 812–16, 841, 991	xliii/2, 3	V/iv, 3
	Clavierbüchlein, ii, for Anna Magdalena Bach	Leipzig, 1725; incl. 82 (recit, aria), 299, 508–18, 691, 812–13, 827, 830, 846 (prelude), 988 (aria); see A113–32, A183	xliii/2, 6	V/iv, 47
933–8	[6 little preludes] (C, c, d, D, E, e)		xxxvi, 128	[V/ix]
939–43	5 Preludes (C, d, e, a, C)		xxxvi, 119	[VI/ix]
	Sonatas, variations, capriccios, etc:			
963	Sonata, D	c1704	xxxvi, 19	V/x
965	Sonata, a	arr. of sonata from J. A. Reincken: Hortus musicus	xlii, 29	[V/xi]
966	Sonata, C	arr. of part of sonata from Reincken: Hortus musicus	xlii, 42	[V/xi]
967	Sonata, a	arr. of 1st movt of anon. chamber sonata	xlv/1, 168	[V/xi]
989	Aria variata, a	Weimar, before 1714; incl. 10 variations	xxxvi, 203	V/x
991	Air with variations, c	frag.; in Clavierbüchlein, i, for Anna Magdalena Bach	xliii/2, 4	V/iv, 40
992	Capriccio sopra la lontananza del suo fratello dilettissimo [Capriccio on the Departure of his Most Beloved Brother], B♭	?1703, 1704 or 1706	xxxvi, 190	V/x
993	Capriccio, E	c1704	xxxvi, 197	V/x
994	Applicatio, C	1st entry in Clavier-Büchlein for W. F. Bach	xxxvi, 237	V/v, 4
	16 Concertos:	Weimar, 1708–17; arrs. of works by other composers		
972	D	from Vivaldi op.3 no.9 = RV230	xlii, 59	[V/xi]
973	G	from Vivaldi op.8/ii no.2 = RV332	xlii, 66	[V/xi]
974	d	from ob conc. by A. Marcello	xlii, 73	[V/xi]
975	g	from Vivaldi op.4 no.6 = RV316a	xlii, 80	[V/xi]
976	C	from Vivaldi op.3 no.12 = RV265	xlii, 87	[V/xi]
977	C	source unknown	xlii, 96	[V/xi]
978	F	from Vivaldi op.3 no.3 = RV310	xlii, 101	[V/xi]
979	b	source unknown	xlii, 108	[V/xi]
980	G	from Vivaldi op.4 no.1 = RV383a	xlii, 119	[V/xi]
981	c	source unknown	xlii, 127	[V/xi]
982	B♭	from conc. by Duke Johann Ernst of Saxe-Weimar	xlii, 135	[V/xi]
983	g	source unknown	xlii, 142	[V/xi]
984	C	from conc. by Duke Johann Ernst of Saxe-Weimar	xlii, 148	[V/xi]
985	g	from vn conc. by Telemann	xlii, 155	[V/xi]
986	G	source unknown	xlii, 161	[V/xi]
987	d	from conc. by Duke Johann Ernst of Saxe-Weimar	xlii, 165	[V/xi]
Doubtful and spurious				
824	Suite, A	frag.; by Telemann	xxxvi, 231	—
834	Allemande, c	spurious	xlii, 259	[V/xii]
835	Allemande, a	by Kirnberger	xlii, 267	—

BWV	Title	Remarks	BG	NBA
838	Allemande and courante, A	by C. Graupner	xlii, 265	[V/xii]
839	Sarabande, g	spurious	—	V/x
840	Courante, G	by Telemann		—
844	Scherzo, d	by W. F. Bach; arr., 844a	xlii, 220, 281	—
845	Gigue, f	spurious	xlii, 263	
895	Prelude and fugue, a	doubtful	xxxvi, 104	[V/xii]
897	Prelude and fugue, a	prelude, at least, by C. H. Dretzel	xlii, 173	[V/xii]
898	Prelude and fugue, B♭	doubtful		[V/xii]
899	Prelude and fughetta, d	doubtful	—	[V/xii]
905	Fantasia and fugue, d	probably spurious	xlii, 179	[V/xii]
907	Fantasia and fughetta, B♭	doubtful	xlii, 268	[V/xii]
908	Fantasia and fughetta, D	doubtful	xlii, 272	[V/xii]
909	Concerto and fugue, c	doubtful	xlii, 190	[V/xii]
917	Fantasia, g	doubtful	xxxvi, 143	[V/xii]
918	Fantasia on a rondo, c	doubtful	xxxvi, 148	[V/xii]
919	Fantasia, c	doubtful	xxxvi, 152	[V/xii]
920	Fantasia, g	doubtful	xlii, 183	[V/xii]
921	Prelude [Fantasia], c	doubtful	xxxvi, 136	[V/xii]
922	Prelude [Fantasia], a	doubtful	xxxvi, 138	[V/xii]
923	Prelude, b	also attrib. W. H. Pachelbel; spurious arr., 923a	xlii, 211	[V/xii]
945	Fugue, e	spurious	xxxvi, 155	[V/xii]
947	Fugue, a	doubtful	xxxvi, 161	[V/xii]
948	Fugue, d	doubtful	xxxvi, 164	[V/xii]
949	Fugue, A	doubtful	xxxvi, 169	[V/xii]
952	Fugue, C	doubtful	xxxvi, 184	[V/xii]
956	Fugue, e	doubtful	xlii, 200	[V/xii]
957	Fugue, G	doubtful	xlii, 203	[V/xii]
960	Fugue, e	inc.; spurious	xlii, 276	[V/xii]
961	Fughetta, c	doubtful	xxxvi, 154	[V/xii]
962	Fugato, e	by Albrechtsberger	xlii, 198	—
	Pieces from Clavier-Büchlein for W. F. Bach:	Cöthen, 1720–		
924a	Prelude, C	1725/6; reworking of 924; ? by W. F. Bach	xxxvi, 221	V/v, 41
925	Prelude, D	1725/6; ? by W. F. Bach	xxxvi, 121	V/v, 42
931	Prelude, a	spurious	xxxvi, 237	V/v, 45
932	Prelude, e	1725/6; ? by W. F. Bach	xxxvi, 238	V/v, 44
964	Sonata, d	arr. of vn sonata 1003; ? by W. F. Bach	xlii, 3	V/x
968	Adagio, G	arr. of vn sonata 1005, movt 1; ? by W. F. Bach	xlii, 27	V/x
969	Andante, g	spurious	xlii, 218	[V/xii]
970	Presto, d	by W. F. Bach		[V/xii]
990	Sarabande con partite, C	spurious	xlii, 221	[V/xii]
	Clavierbüchlein, ii, for Anna Magdalena Bach [only anon. pieces listed]:	Leipzig, 1725; also incl. 5 pieces by C. P. E. Bach (A122–5, 129), 1 by F. Couperin (A183), 1 by G. Böhm (without no.); remainder anon., ? by J. S. Bach and/or Bach's sons	xliii/2, 25	V/iv, 47
	Minuet, F (A113); Minuet, G (A114); Minuet, g (A115); Minuet, G (A116); Polonaise, F (A117a, 117b); Minuet, B♭ (A118); Polonaise, g (A119); Minuet, a (A120); Minuet, c (A121); Musette, D (A126); March, E♭ (A127); [Polonaise], d (A128); Polonaise, G (A130); [untitled], F (A131); Minuet, d (A132)			

LUTE

BWV	Title	Remarks	BG	NBA
995	Suite, g	Leipzig, 1727–31; arr. of vc suite 1011	—	V/x
996	Suite, e	Weimar, c1708–17 (or earlier)	xlv/1, 149	V/x
997	Partita, c	Leipzig, 1737–41	xlv/1, 156	V/x
998	Prelude, fugue and allegro, E♭	Leipzig, early to mid-1740s	xlv/1, 141	V/x
999	Prelude, c	Cöthen, c1720	xxxvi, 119	V/x
1000	Fugue, g	?Leipzig, c1725; arr. of fugue from vn sonata 1001	—	V/x
1006a	Partita, E: see 1006			

CHAMBER

BWV	Title, scoring	Remarks	BG	NBA
1001–6	Sonatas and partitas, solo vn:	Cöthen, 1720; 1006 arr. lute = 1006a (BG xlii, 16)	xxvii/1, 3	VI/i, 3
	Sonata no.1, g; Partita no.1, b; Sonata no.2, a; Partita no.2, d; Sonata no.3, C; Partita no.3, E			
1014–19	6 sonatas, vn, hpd:	Cöthen, 1717–23; earlier version of no.5 (Adagio only) = 1018a (BG ix, 250; NBA VI/i, 195); earlier version of no.6 = 1019a (BG ix, 252; NBA VI/i, 197)	ix, 69	VI/i, 83
	no.1, b; no.2, A; no.3, E; no.4, c; no.5, f; no.6, G			

BWV	Title, scoring	Remarks	BG	NBA
	Miscellaneous vn pieces:			
1021	Sonata, G, vn, bc	?Cöthen, before 1720	—	VI/i, 65
1023	Sonata, e, vn, bc	Weimar, 1714–17	xliii/1, 31	VI/i, 73
1007–12	6 suites, solo vc (G, d, C, E♭, c, D)	Cöthen, c1720	xxvii/1, 59	[VI/ii]
1027–9	3 sonatas, hpd, va da gamba (G, D, g)	Cöthen, c1720: no.1 = rev. of 1039	ix, 175	[VI/ii]
	Miscellaneous fl pieces:			
1013	Partita, a, fl	early 1720s	—	VI/iii, 3
1030	Sonata, b, fl, hpd	?Leipzig, mid-1730s; orig. version, g, Cöthen, 1717–23	ix, 3	VI/iii, 33, 89
1032	Sonata, A, fl, hpd	Cöthen, 1717–23; 1st movt inc.	ix, 245, 32	VI/iii, 54
1034	Sonata, e, fl, bc	?Cöthen, 1717–20	xliii/1, 9	VI/iii, 11
1035	Sonata, E, fl, bc	?Cöthen, 1717–20	xliii/1, 21	VI/iii, 23
	Trio sonatas:			
1039	Sonata, G, 2 fl, bc	Cöthen, c1720; cf 1027	ix, 260	VI/iii, 71
1040	Trio, F, vn, ob, bc	early 1713; movt based on material from Cantata 208, ?perf. with cantata; later used in Cantata 68	xxix, 250	I/xxxv, 47
Doubtful and spurious				
1020	Sonata, g, vn, hpd	doubtful	ix, 274	[VI/iv]
1022	Sonata, F, vn, hpd	arr. of 1038; ?by one of Bach's sons or pupils	—	[VI/iv]
1024	Sonata, c, vn, bc	doubtful	—	[VI/iv]
1025	Suite, A, vn, hpd	doubtful	ix, 43	[VI/iv]
1026	Fugue, g, vn, hpd	doubtful	xliii/1, 39	[VI/iv]
1037	Sonata, C, 2 vn, hpd	?by J. G. Goldberg	ix, 231	[VI/iv]
1031	Sonata, E♭, fl, hpd	doubtful	ix, 22	[VI/iv]
1033	Sonata, C, fl, bc	doubtful	xliii/1, 3	[VI/iv]
1036	Sonata, d, 2 vn, hpd	probably spurious		[VI/iv]
1038	Sonata, G, fl, vn, bc	constructed on bass of 1021; probably by one of Bach's sons or pupils; cf 1022	ix, 221	[VI/iv]

ORCHESTRAL
(where applicable, scoring given as concertino/solo; ripieno)

BWV	Title, key	Scoring	Remarks	BG	NBA
1041	Concerto, a	vn; str, bc	Cöthen, 1717–23; cf 1058	xxi/1, 3	[VII/iii]
1042	Concerto, E	vn; str, bc	Cöthen, 1717–23; cf 1054	xxi/1, 21	[VII/iii]
1043	Concerto, d	2 vn; str, bc	Cöthen, 1717–23; cf 1062	xxi/1, 41	[VII/iii]
1044	Concerto, a	fl, vn, hpd; str, bc	Leipzig, ?after 1730; movts adapted from prelude and fugue 894 and trio sonata 527	xvii, 223	[VII/iii]
1045	Concerto movt, D	vn; 3 tpt, timp, 2 ob, str, bc	frag.; intended as opening sinfonia for church cantata	xxi/1, 65	—
	Brandenburg Concertos:		Weimar, Cöthen, 1711–20; autograph MS ded. Christian Ludwig, Margrave of Brandenburg, 24 March 1721		
1046	no.1, F	2 hn, ob, vn piccolo; 2 ob, bn, str, bc	?Cöthen, 1717	xix, 3	VII/ii, 3
1046a	Sinfonia, F	2 hn, 3 ob, bn, str, bc	?Weimar, 1713; early version of 1046; formerly 1071; also used in 52	xxxi/1, 96	VII/ii, 225
1047	no.2, F	tpt, rec, ob, vn; str, bc	?Cöthen, 1717–18	xix, 33	VII/ii, 43
1048	no.3, G	3 vn, 3 va, 3 vc, bc	?Weimar, 1711–13	xix, 59	VII/ii, 73
1049	no.4, G	vn, 2 rec; str, bc	?Cöthen, c1720; cf 1057	xix, 85	VII/ii, 99
1050	no.5, D	fl, vn, hpd; str, bc	? Cöthen, 1720–21; 1050a = early version, ?c1719	xix, 127	VII/ii, 145, appx
1051	no.6, B♭	2 va, 2 va da gamba, vc, bc	?Weimar, 1708–10	xix, 167	VII/ii, 197
	Harpsichord concertos:		Leipzig, 1735–40; mostly transcrs. of vn concs.; some orig./transcrs. also used in church cantatas		
1052	d	hpd; str, bc	from lost vn conc. reconstructed in NBA VII/vii	xvii, 3	[VII/iv]
1053	E	hpd; str, bc	from lost ?ob conc.; see NBA VII/vii, CC	xvii, 45	[VII/iv]
1054	D	hpd; str, bc	from 1042	xvii, 81	[VII/iv]
1055	A	hpd; str, bc	from lost ob d'amore conc. reconstructed in NBA VII/vii	xvii, 109	[VII/iv]
1056	f	hpd; str, bc	outer movts from lost ob conc. in g reconstructed in NBA VII/vii	xvii, 135	[VII/iv]
1057	F	hpd, 2 rec; str, bc	from 1049	xvii, 153	[VII/iv]
1058	g	hpd; str, bc	from 1041	xvii, 199	[VII/iv]
1059	d	hpd, ob; str, bc	inc.; from lost ob conc., see NBA VII/vii, CC	xvii, p.xx	[VII/iv]
1060	c	2 hpd; str, bc	from lost ob and vn conc. reconstructed in NBA VII/vii	xxi/2, 3	[VII/v]
1061	C	2 hpd; str, bc	orig. hpd conc.	xxi/2, 39	[VII/v]
1062	c	2 hpd; str, bc	from 1043	xxi/2, 83	[VII/v]
1063	d	3 hpd; str, bc	source unknown, see NBA VII/vii, CC	xxxi/3, 3	[VII/vi]
1064	C	3 hpd; str, bc	from lost 3 vn conc. in D reconstructed in NBA VII/vii	xxxi/3, 53	[VII/vi]
1065	a	4 hpd; str, bc	from Vivaldi op.3 no.10 = RV580	xliii/1, 71	VII/vi
	4 orchestral suites:				
1066	C	2 ob, bn, str, bc	Cöthen, c1717–23	xxxi/1, 3	VII/i, 3

BWV	Title, key	Scoring	Remarks	BG	NBA
1067	b	fl; str, bc	Leipzig, late 1730s	xxxi/1, 24	VII/i, 27
1068	D	3 tpt, timp, 2 ob, str, bc	Leipzig, c1729–31	xxxi/1, 40	VII/i, 49, 119
1069	D	3 tpt, timp, 3 ob, bn, str, bc	Cöthen, c1717–23; movt 1 adapted as opening chorus of cantata 110	xxxi/1, 66	VII/i, 81
1070	Overture, g	str, bc	probably spurious	xlv/1, 190	—
1071	Sinfonia: see 1046a				

STUDIES IN COUNTERPOINT, CANONS ETC

BWV	Title, scoring	Remarks	BG	NBA
769	Einige [5] canonische Veränderungen über das Weynacht Lied, Vom Himmel hoch da komm ich her, org	written on becoming member of Mizler's Societät der Musicalischen Wissenschaften, June 1747 (Nuremberg, 1748); autograph version 769a, chronology of versions uncertain	xl, 137	IV/ii, 197, 98
1079	Musikalisches Opfer [fl, 2 vn, bc, kbd]	May–July 1747 (Leipzig, 1747); 2 Ricercars, a 3, a 6; 10 canons; sonata, fl, vn, bc; insts not fully specified; for order see Wolff (1971)	xxxi/2	VIII/i, 12
1080	Die Kunst der Fuge [kbd]	Leipzig, c1745–50, autograph, D-B P200; rev. and enlarged (Leipzig, 1751, 2/1752); series of fugues (contrapuncti), mostly a 4, on same theme; for contents see Wolff (1975)	xxv/1	[VIII/ii]
1072	Canon trias harmonica	a 8, in contrary motion; in F. W. Marpurg: Abhandlung von der Fuge, ii (Berlin, 1754)	xlv, 131	VIII/i, 3, 6
1073	Canon a 4 perpetuus	Weimar, 2 Aug 1713	xlv, 132	VIII/i, 3, 6
1074	Canon a 4	Leipzig, 1727; completely invertible; ded. L. F. Hudemann, in J. Mattheson: Der vollkommene Capellmeister (Hamburg, 1739/R1954)	xlv, 134	VIII/i, 3, 7
1075	Canon a 2 perpetuus	Leipzig, 10 Jan 1734; ded. J. M. Gesner	—	VIII/i, 3, 7
1076	Canon triplex a 6	3 simultaneous canons a 2, each in contrary motion; written for Haussmann portrait and Mizler's Societät der Musicalischen Wissenschaften; 1087 incl. earlier version	xlv, 138	VIII/i, 3, 8
1077	Canone doppio sopr'il soggetto	2 simultaneous canons a 2, each in contrary motion; Leipzig, 15 Oct 1747; ded. J. G. Fulde; 1087 incl. earlier version	—	VIII/i, 4, 8
1078	Canon super fa mi a 7 post tempus musicum	Leipzig, 1 March 1749; ded. 'Schmidt' (alias Benjamin Faber)	xlv, 136	VIII/i, 4, 9
1086	Canon concordia discors	a 2, in contrary motion	—	VIII/i, 4, 10
1087	[14] Verschiedene Canones	14 canons on first 8 notes of aria ground of 988; autograph, 1742–6, in Bach's copy of 988; incl. earlier versions of 1076–7	—	V/ii

BIBLIOGRAPHY

CATALOGUES, BIBLIOGRAPHIES, TEXTUAL CRITICISM ETC

Prefaces to *J. S. Bach: Werke*, ed. Bach-Gesellschaft (Leipzig, 1851–99/*R*1947) [BG]

A. Dörffel: *Thematisches Verzeichnis der Instrumentalwerke von Joh. Seb. Bach* (Leipzig, 1867, 2/1882)

H. Kretzschmar: *Johann Sebastian Bachs Handschrift in zeitlich geordneten Nachbildungen*, BG, xliv (1895)

——: *Verzeichnis sämtlicher Werke und der einzelnen Sätze aus Werken Johann Sebastian Bachs*, BG, xlvi (1899)

M. Seiffert: 'Neue Bach-Funde', *JbMP 1904*, 15

Bach-Jahrbuch (*BJb*) (1904–)

M. Schneider: 'Verzeichnis der bisher erschienenen Literatur über Johann Sebastian Bach', *BJb*, ii (1905), 76–110

——: 'Verzeichnis der bis zum Jahre 1851 gedruckten (und der geschrieben im Handel gewesenen) Werke von Johann Sebastian Bach', *BJb*, iii (1906), 84–113

M. Seiffert: 'Zur Kritik der Gesamtausgabe von Bachs Werken', *BJb*, iii (1906), 79

M. Schneider: 'Neues Material zum Verzeichnis der bisher erschienenen Literatur über Johann Sebastian Bach', *BJb*, vii (1910), 133

J. Schreyer: *Beiträge zur Bach-Kritik*, i (Dresden, 1910); ii (Leipzig, 1912)

G. Frotscher: 'Übersicht über die wichtigsten im Zeitschriften erschienenen Aufsätze über Seb. Bach aus den Jahren 1915–1918', *BJb*, xv (1918), 151

R. Schwartz: 'Die Bach-Handschriften der Musikbibliothek Peters', *JbMP 1919*, 56

H. Tessmer: 'Joh. Sebastian Bach im öffentlichen Schrifttum seiner Zeit', *Neue Musik-Zeitung*, xl (1919), 127–215

A. Landau: 'Übersicht über die Bach-Literatur in Zeitschriften vom 1. Januar 1928 bis zum 30. Juni 1930', *BJb*, xxvii (1930), 132

——: 'Übersicht über die Bach-Literatur in Zeitschriften vom 1. Juli 1930 bis zum 1. Juli 1931', *BJb*, xxix (1932), 146

G. Kinsky: *Die Originalausgaben der Werke Johann Sebastian Bachs* (Vienna, 1937/*R*1968)

H. Miesner: 'Philipp Emanuel Bachs musikalischer Nachlass: vollständ-

iger, dem Original entsprechender Neudruck des Nachlassverzeichnisses von 1790', *BJb*, xxxv (1938), 103; xxxvi (1939), 81; xxxvii (1940–48), 161

L. R. Picken: 'Bach Quotations from the Eighteenth Century', *MR*, v (1944), 83

W. Schmieder: 'Die Handschriften Johann Sebastian Bachs', *Bach-Gedenkschrift 1950*, ed. K. Matthaei (Zurich, 1950), 190

——: *Thematisch-systematisches Verzeichnis der musikalischen Werke Johann Sebastian Bachs: Bach-Werke-Verzeichnis* (Leipzig, 1950, 3/1966, rev., enlarged 4/in preparation)

Die wissenschaftliche Bachtagung der Gesellschaft für Musikforschung: Leipzig 1950

W. Schmieder: 'Das Bachschrifttum 1953–1957', *BJb*, xl (1953), 119–68

Critical Commentaries to *Johann Sebastian Bach: Neue Ausgabe sämtlicher Werke* (*Neue Bach-Ausgabe*), ed. Johann-Sebastian-Bach-Institut, Göttingen, and Bach-Archiv, Leipzig (Kassel and Basle, 1954–)

P. Kast: *Die Bach-Handschriften der Berliner Staatsbibliothek*, Tübinger Bach-Studien, ii–iii (Trossingen, 1958)

W. Schmieder: 'Das Bachschrifttum 1953–1957', *BJb*, xlv (1958), 127

S. W. Kenney, ed.: *Catalog of the Emilie and Karl Riemenschneider Memorial Bach Library* (New York and London, 1960)

G. von Dadelsen: 'Originale Daten auf den Handschriften J. S. Bachs', *Hans Albrecht in memoriam* (Kassel, 1962), 116

M. McAll, ed.: *Melodic Index to the Works of Johann Sebastian Bach* (New York, 1962)

P. Krause, ed.: *Handschriften der Werke Johann Sebastian Bachs in der Musikbibliothek der Stadt Leipzig* (Leipzig, 1964)

W. Blankenburg: 'Zwölf Jahre Bachforschung', *AMw*, xxxvi (1965), 95–158

F. Blume: 'Der gegenwärtige Stand der Bachforschung', *NRMI*, iii (1969), 381

M. Geck, ed.: *Bach-Interpretationen* (Göttingen, 1969)

H. Zietz: *Quellenkritische Untersuchungen an den Bach-Handschriften P 801, P 802 und P 803 aus dem Krebsschen*

Nachlass unter Berücksichtigung der Choralbearbeitungen des jungen Bach (Hamburg, 1969)

P. Krause, ed.: *Originalausgaben und ältere Drucke der Werke Johann Sebastian Bachs in der Musikbibliothek der Stadt Leipzig* (Leipzig, 1970)

Y. Kobayashi: 'Zu einem neu entdeckten Autograph Bachs: Choral Aus der Tiefen', *BJb*, lvii (1971), 5

W. Hobohm: 'Neue "Texte zur Leipziger Kirchen-Music" ', *BJb*, lix (1973), 5

Y. Kobayashi: *Franz Hauser und seine Bach-Handschriftensammlung* (diss., U. of Göttingen, 1973)

R. Nestle: 'Das Bachschrifttum 1963–1967', *BJb*, lix (1973), 91

I. S. Duyzenkunst and K. Vellekoop, eds.: *Bachboek* (Utrecht, 1975)

Wissenschaftliche Bach-Konferenz: Leipzig 1975

R. Nestle: 'Das Bachschrifttum 1968–1972', *BJb*, lxii (1976), 95

SOURCE MATERIAL: DOCUMENTS, LETTERS ETC

Ursprung der musikalisch-Bachischen Familie, genealogy, first draft, 1735, by J. S. Bach, in *Bach-Urkunden*, Veröffentlichungen der Neuer Bach-Gesellschaft, xvii/3, ed. M. Schneider (Leipzig, 1917), and in C. S. Terry: *The Origin of the Family of Bach Musicians* (London, 1929)

L. C. Mizler: *Neu eröffnete musikalische Bibliothek* (Leipzig, 1736–54)

J. A. Scheibe: *Der critische Musikus* (Leipzig, 1745/R1970)

J. F. Agricola and C. P. E. Bach: Obituary in L. Mizler: *Neu eröffnete musikalische Bibliothek*, iv/1 (Leipzig, 1754); repr. in *BJb*, xvii (1920), 11

E. Müller von Asow: *Johann Sebastian Bach: gesammelte Briefe* (Regensburg, 1938, 2/1950)

H. T. David and A. Mendel: *The Bach Reader: a Life of Johann Sebastian Bach in Letters and Documents* (New York, 1945, rev. 2/1966)

W. Neumann, ed.: *Facsimile-Reihe Bachser Werke und Schriftstücke* (Leipzig, 1954–)

H. Besch: 'Eine Auktions-Quittung J. S. Bachs', *Festschrift für Friedrich Smend* (Berlin, 1963), 74

W. Neumann and H.-J. Schulze, eds.: *Schriftstücke von der Hand Johann Sebastian Bachs*, Bach-Dokumente, i (Leipzig, 1963; Fr. trans., 1976)

H.-J. Schulze: 'Beiträge zur Bach-Quellenforschung', *GfMKB, Leipzig 1966*, 269

——: *Fremdschriftliche und gedruckte Dokumente zur Lebensgeschichte Johann Sebastian Bachs 1685–1750*, Bach-Dokumente, ii (Leipzig, 1969)

A. Dürr: 'Zur Chronologie der Handschrift Johann Christoph Altnickols und Johann Friedrich Agricolas', *BJb*, lvi (1970), 44

H.-J. Schulze, ed.: *Dokumente zum Nachwirken Johann Sebastian Bachs 1750–1800*, Bach-Dokumente, iii (Leipzig, 1972)

'Johann Sebastian Bach: Studies of the Sources', *Studies in Renaissance and Baroque Music in Honor of Arthur Mendel* (Kassel and Hackensack, 1974), 231–300 [contributions by P. Brainard, A. Dürr, G. Herz, E. May and C. Wolff]

H.-J. Schulze: 'Wie enstand die Bach-Sammlung Mempell-Preller?', *BJb*, lx (1974), 104

K.-H. Köhler: 'Die Bach-Sammlung der Deutschen Staatsbibliothek – Überlieferung und Bedeutung', *Bach-Studien*, v (1975), 139

W. Neumann, ed.: *Bilddokumente zur Lebensgeschichte Johann Sebastian Bachs*, Bach-Dokumente, iv (Leipzig, 1978)

ICONOGRAPHY

E. Vogel: 'Bach-Porträts', *JbMP 1896*, 11

M. Schneider: 'Verzeichnis von Bildnissen Bachs', *BJb*, ii (1905), 109

A. Kurzwelly: 'Neues über das Bachbildnis der Thomasschule und andere Bildnisse Johann Sebastian Bachs', *BJb*, xi (1914), 1–37

J. Müller: 'Bach Portraits', *MQ*, xxi (1935), 155

G. Herz: 'A "New" Bach Portrait', *MQ*, xxix (1943), 225

K. Geiringer: *The Lost Portrait of J. S. Bach* (New York, 1950)

H. Raupach: *Das wahre Bildnis J. S. Bachs* (Wolfenbüttel, 1950)

F. Smend: *J. S. Bach bei seinem Namen gerufen* (Kassel, 1950)

H. Besseler: *Fünf echte Bildnisse Johann Sebastian Bachs* (Kassel, 1956)

H. O. R. van Tuyll van Serooskerken: *Probleme des Bachporträts* (Bilthoven, 1956)

C. Freyse: *Bachs Antlitz* (Eisenach, 1964)

BIOGRAPHY, LIFE AND WORKS

J. N. Forkel: *Über Johann Sebastian Bachs Leben, Kunst und Kunstwerke* (Leipzig, 1802/R1966; Eng. trans., 1820/R in *The Bach Reader: a Life of Johann Sebastian Bach in Letters and Documents*, ed. H. T. David and A. Mendel (New York, 1945, rev. 2/1966); also R1974)

C. L. Hilgenfeldt: *Johann Sebastian Bach's Leben, Wirken und Werke: ein Beitrag zur Kunstgeschichte des achtzehnten Jahrhunderts* (Leipzig, 1850/R1965)

C. H. Bitter: *Johann Sebastian Bach* (Berlin, 1865, enlarged 2/1881)

P. Spitta: *Johann Sebastian Bach* (Leipzig, 1873–80/R1964, 5/1962; Eng. trans., 1884–99/R1951)

A. Schweitzer: *J. S. Bach, le musicien-poète* (Paris, 1905; Eng. trans., 1911/R1967)

A. Pirro: *Johann-Sebastian Bach* (Paris, 1906; Eng. trans., 1958)

P. Wolfrum: *Johann Sebastian Bach*, i (Berlin, 1906, 2/1910); ii (Leipzig, 1910)

C. H. H. Parry: *Johann Sebastian Bach* (London, 1909, 2/1930/R1968)

J. Tiersot: *J.-S. Bach* (Paris, 1912, 2/1934)

C. S. Terry: *Bach: a Biography* (London, 1928; Ger. trans., rev., 1929)

H. J. Moser: *J. S. Bach* (Berlin, 1935, 2/1943)

J. Müller-Blattau: *Johann Sebastian Bach* (Leipzig, 1935)

W. Gurlitt: *Johann Sebastian Bach: der Meister und sein Werk* (Berlin, 1936, rev., enlarged 2/1947; Eng. trans., 1957)

W. Cart: *J. S. Bach: 1685–1750* (Lausanne, 1946)

A. E. Cherbuliez: *Johann Sebastian Bach: sein Leben und sein Werk* (Olten, 1946, 2/1947)

E. M. and S. Grew: *Bach* (London, 1947/R1965)

H. Engel: *Johann Sebastian Bach* (Berlin, 1950)

W. Neumann: *Auf den Lebenswegen Johann Sebastian Bachs* (Berlin, 1953)

——: *Bach: eine Bildbiographie* (Munich, 1960; Eng. trans., 1961)

E. Buchet, ed.: *Jean-Sebastien Bach: l'oeuvre et la vie* (Paris, 1963)

K. Geiringer: *Johann Sebastian Bach: the Culmination of an Era* (London, 1966)

E. Buchet: *Jean-Sébastien Bach, après deux siècles d'études et de témoignages* (Paris, 1968)

B. Schwendowius and W. Dömling, eds.: *Johann Sebastian Bach: Zeit, Leben, Wirken* (Kassel, 1976; Eng. trans., 1978)

BIOGRAPHY: SPECIAL STUDIES

C. Scherer: 'Joh. Seb. Bachs Aufenthalt in Kassel', *MMg*, xxv (1893), 129

B. F. Richter: 'Stadtpfeifer und Alumnen der Thomasschule in Leipzig zu Bachs Zeit', *BJb*, iv (1907), 32–78

K. Pottgiesser: 'Die Briefentwürfe des Johann Elias Bach', *Die Musik*, xii/2 (1912–13), 3

B. F. Richter: 'Johann Sebastian Bach im Gottesdienst der Thomaner', *BJb*, xii (1915), 1–38

C. Freyse: *Eisenacher Dokumente um Sebastian Bach* (Leipzig, 1933)

——: 'Das Bach-Haus zu Eisenach', *BJb*, xxxvi (1939), 66; xxxvii (1940–48), 152

G. Herz: 'Bach's Religion', *JRBM*, i (1946), 124

G. Fock: *Der junge Bach in Lüneburg* (Hamburg, 1950)

F. Wiegand: *J. S. Bach und seine Verwandten in Arnstadt* (Arnstadt, 1950)

F. Smend: *Bach in Köthen* (Berlin, 1951)

H. Löffler: 'Die Schüler Joh. Seb. Bachs', *BJb*, xl (1953), 5

K. Geiringer: *The Bach Family: Seven Generations of Creative Genius* (New York, 1954)

W. Neumann: 'Das "Bachische Collegium Musicum" ', *BJb*, xlvii (1960), 5

F. Blume: 'Outlines of a New Picture of Bach', *ML*, xliv (1963), 214

P. M. Young: *The Bachs, 1500–1850* (London, 1970)

I. Ahlgrimm: 'Von Reisen, Kirchererbsen und Fischbeinröcken', *Bach-Studien*, v (1975), 155

R. Eller: 'Gedanken über Bachs Leipziger Schaffensjahre', *Bach-Studien*, v (1975), 7

W. Schrammek: 'Johann Sebastian Bach, Gottfried Silbermann und die französische Orgelkunst', *Bach-Studien*, v (1975), 93

H.-J. Schulze: 'Johann Sebastian Bach und Georg Gottfried Wagner – neue Dokumente', *Bach-Studien*, v (1975), 147

E. Zavarský: 'J. S. Bachs Entwurf für den Umbau der Orgel in der Kirche Divi Blasii und das Klangideal der Zeit', *Bach-Studien*, v (1975), 83

WORKS: GENERAL

A. Pirro: *L'esthétique de Jean-Sébastien Bach* (Paris, 1907)

R. Oppel: 'Beziehungen Bachs zu Vorgängern und Nachfolgern', *BJb*, xxii (1925), 11

F. Jöde: *Die Kunst Bachs* (Wolfenbüttel, 1926)

F. Rochlitz: *Wege zu Bach* (Augsburg, 1926)

C. S. Terry: *The Music of Bach: an Introduction* (London, 1933)

A. E. F. Dickinson: *The Art of J. S. Bach* (London, 1935, rev., enlarged 2/1950)

G. Herz: *Joh. Seb. Bach im Zeitalter des Rationalismus und der Frühromantik* (Kassel, 1935)

G. Frotscher: *J. S. Bach und die Musik des 17. Jahrhunderts* (Wädenswil, 1939)

A. Schering: *Johan Sebastian Bach und das Musikleben Leipzigs im 18. Jahrhundert* (Leipzig, 1941)

W. Blankenburg: *Die innere Einheit von Bachs Werk* (diss., U. of Göttingen, 1942)

L. Schrade: 'Bach: the Conflict between the Sacred and the Secular', *Journal of the History of Ideas*, vii (1946), 151–94

F. Blume: *Johann Sebastian Bach im Wandel der Geschichte* (Kassel, 1947; Eng. trans., 1950)

M. Dehnert: *Das Weltbild J. S. Bachs* (Leipzig, 1948, 2/1949)

W. Blankenburg: 'Bach geistlich und weltlich', *Musik und Kirche*, xx (1950)

K. Geiringer: 'Artistic Interrelations of the Bachs', *MQ*, xxxvi (1950), 363

R. Petzoldt and L. Weinhold: *Johann Sebastian Bach: das Schaffen des Meisters in Spiegel einer Stadt* (Leipzig, 1950)

R. Steglich: *Wege zu Bach* (Regensburg, 1950)

W. Vetter: *Der Kapellmeister Bach: Versuch einer Deutung* (Potsdam, 1950)

H. Besseler: 'Bach und das Mittelalter', *Die wissenschaftliche Bachtagung der Gesellschaft für Musikforschung: Leipzig 1950*, 108

A. T. Davison: *Bach and Handel: the Consummation of the Baroque in Music* (Cambridge, Mass., 1951)

F. Hamel: *J. S. Bach: geistige Welt* (Göttingen, 1951)

A. Salazar: *Juan Sebastian Bach: un esayo* (Mexico City, 1951)

P. Hindemith: *Johann Sebastian Bach: Heritage and Obligation* (New Haven, 1952)

H. Besseler: 'Bach als Wegbereiter', *AMw*, xii (1955), 1–39

F. Blume: 'Bach in the Romantic Era', *MQ*, l (1964), 290

WORKS: SPECIAL STUDIES

E. Dannreuther: 'Die Verzierungen in den Werken von J. S. Bach', *BJb*, vi (1909), 41–101

K. Grunsky: 'Bachs Bearbeitungen und Umarbeitungen eigener und fremder Werke', *BJb*, ix (1912), 61

M. Schneider: 'Der Generalbass Joh. Seb. Bachs', *JbMP 1914–15*

E. Kurth: *Grundlagen des linearen Kontrapunkts: Einführung in Stil und Technik von Bachs melodischer Polyphonie* (Berne, 1917, 4/1946)

R. Oppel: 'Zur Fugentechnik Bachs', *BJb*, xviii (1921), 9–48

A. Schering: 'Über Bachs Parodieverfahren', *BJb*, xviii (1921), 49–95

J. Müller: 'Motivsprache und Stilart des jungen Bach', *BJb*, xix (1922), 38–70

A. Schering: 'Bach und das Symbol, insbesondere die Symbolik seines Kanons', *BJb*, xxii (1925), 40

M.-A. Souchay: 'Das Thema in der Fuge Bachs', *BJb*, xxiv (1927), 1–102; xxvii (1930), 1–48

A. Schering: 'Bach und das Symbol, ii: Das "Figürliche" und "Metaphorische" ', *BJb*, xxv (1928), 119

W. Danckert: *Beiträge zur Bachkritik* (Kassel, 1934)

G. Schünemann: 'Bachs Verbesserungen und Entwürft', *BJb*, xxxii (1935), 1–32

A. Schering: 'Bach und das Symbol, iii: Psychologische Grundlegung des Symbolbegriffs aus Christian Wolffs "Psychologia empirica" ', *BJb*, xxxiv (1937), 83

W. Emery: 'Bach's Symbolic Language', *ML*, xxx (1949), 345

——: *Bach's Ornaments* (London, 1953)

F. Rothschild: *The Lost Tradition in Music: Rhythm and Tempo in J. S. Bach's Time* (London, 1953)

K. Geiringer: *Symbolism in the Music of Bach* (Washington, DC, 1955)

A. Mendel: 'On the Pitches in Use in Bach's Time', *MQ*, xli (1955), 332, 466

A. Dürr: 'Gedanken zu J. S. Bachs Umarbeitungen eigener Werke', *BJb*, xliii (1956), 93

B. Paumgartner: 'Johann Sebastian Bach, Mozart und die Wiener Klassik', *BJb*, xliii (1956), 5

G. von Dadelsen: *Bemerkungen zur Handschrift Johann Sebastian Bachs, seiner Familie und seines Kreises*, Tübinger Bach-Studien, i (Trossingen, 1957)

——: *Beiträge zur Chronologie der Werke Johann Sebastian Bach*, Tübinger Bach-Studien, iv–v (Trossingen, 1958)

A. Mendel: 'Recent Developments in Bach Chronology', *MQ*, xlvi (1960), 283

R. Steglich: 'Johann Sebastian Bach über sich selbst und im Urteil der Mit- und Nachwelt', *Festschrift Hans Engel* (Kassel, 1964), 393

W. Blankenburg: 'Zwölf Jahre Bachforschung', *AcM*, xxxvii (1965), 95ff

F. Neumann: 'A New Look at Bach's Ornamentation', *ML*, xlvi (1965), 4, 126

N. Carrell: *Bach the Borrower* (London, 1967)

A. Dürr: 'Neues über Bachs Pergolesi-Bearbeitung', *BJb*, liv (1968), 89

C. Wolff: *Der stile antico in der Musik Johann Sebastian Bachs* (Wiesbaden, 1968)

D. Gojowy: 'Wie entstand Hans Georg Nägelis Bach-Sammlung? Dokumente zur Bach-Renaissance im 19. Jahrhundert', *BJb*, lvi (1970), 66

R. L. Marshall: 'How J. S. Bach Composed Four-part Chorales', *MQ*, lvi (1970), 198

W. Emery: 'Is your Bach Playing Authentic?', *MT*, cxii (1971), 483, 697, 796

M. Geck: 'Bachs Probestück', *Quellenstudien zur Musik: Wolfgang Schmieder zum 70. Geburtstag* (Frankfurt am Main, 1972), 55

R. Stephan: 'J. S. Bach und das Problem des musikalischen Zyklus', *BJb*, lix (1973), 39

'Johann Sebastian Bach: Approaches to Analysis and Interpretation',

Studies in Renaissance and Baroque Music in Honor of Arthur Mendel (Kassel and Hackensack, 1974), 139–230 [contributions by W. Blankenburg, E. T. Cone, W. Emery, R. L. Marshall, F. Neumann, N. Rubin and W. H. Scheide]

W. Emery: 'A Note on Bach's Use of Triplets', *Bach-Studien*, v (1975), 109

H. Eppstein: 'Zum Formproblem bei J. S. Bach', *Bach-Studien*, v (1975), 29

H. Grüss: 'Tempofragen der Bachzeit', *Bach-Studien*, v (1975), 73

R. L. Marshall: 'Bach the Progressive: Observations on his Later Works', *MQ*, lxii (1976), 313

VOCAL WORKS

R. Rolland: *Bachs Matthäuspassion* (1905)

B. F. Richter: 'Über die Schicksale der der Thomasschule zu Leipzig angehörenden Kantaten Joh. Seb. Bachs', *BJb*, iii (1906), 43–73

——: 'Über Seb. Bachs Kantaten mit obligater Orgel', *BJb*, v (1908), 49

W. Voigt: 'Zu Bachs Weihnachtsoratorium, Teil 1 bis 3', *BJb*, v (1908), 1–48

A. Heuss: *Bachs Matthäuspassion* (Leipzig, 1909)

R. Wustmann: 'Bachs Matthäuspassion, erster Theil', *BJb*, vi (1909), 129

——: 'Sebastian Bachs Kirchenkantatentexte', *BJb*, vii (1910), 45

B. F. Richter: 'Über die Motetten Seb. Bachs', *BJb*, ix (1912), 1–32

L. Wolff: *J. Sebastian Bachs Kirchenkantaten* (Leipzig, 1913)

R. Wustmann: *Joh. Seb. Bachs Kantatentexte* (Leipzig, 1913, 2/1967)

C. S. Terry: *Bach's Chorales* (Cambridge, 1915–21)

W. Voigt: *Die Kirchenkantaten Johann Sebastian Bachs* (Stuttgart, 1918, 2/1928)

W. Werker: *Die Matthäuspassion* (Leipzig, 1923)

C. S. Terry: *Bach's B minor Mass* (Oxford, 1924)

H. J. Moser: 'Aus Joh. Seb. Bachs Kantatenwelt', *Die Musik*, xvii (1924–5), 721

F. W. Franke: *Bachs Kirchen-Kantaten* (Leipzig, 1925)

C. S. Terry: *Bach: the Cantatas and Oratorios* (London, 1925/R1972)

W. G. Whittaker: *Fugitive Notes on certain Cantatas and the Motets of J. S. Bach* (Oxford, 1925)

F. Smend: 'Die Johannes-Passion von Bach', *BJb*, xxiii (1926), 105

C. S. Terry: *Johann Sebastian Bach: Cantata Texts, Sacred and Secular* (London, 1926/R1964)

F. Smend: 'Bachs Matthäus-Passion', *BJb*, xxv (1928), 1–95

C. S. Terry: *Bach: the Passions* (London, 1928)

H. Abert: *Bachs Matthäuspassion* (Halle, 1929)

F. Atkins: *Bach's Passions* (London, 1929)

K. Ziebler: *Das Symbol in der Kirchenmusik Bachs* (Kassel, 1930)

F. Blume: *Die evangelische Kirchenmusik*, HMw, x (1931, rev. 2/1965 as *Geschichte der evangelischen Kirchenmusik*; Eng. trans., enlarged, 1974, as *Protestant Church Music: a History*)

H. Sirp: 'Die Thematik der Kirchenkantaten J. S. Bachs in ihren Beziehungen zum protestantischen Kirchenlied', *BJb*, xxviii (1931), 1–50; xxix (1932), 51–118

R. Gerber: 'Über Geist und Weisen von Bachs h-moll-Messe', *BJb*, xxix (1932), 119

W. Lütge: 'Bachs Motette, Jesu meine Freude', *Musik und Kirche*, iv (1932), 97

C. S. Terry: 'The Spurious Bach "Lukas-Passion" ', *ML*, xiv (1932), 207

K. Ziebler: 'Aufbau und Gliederung der Matthäuspassion von Johann Sebastian Bach', *Musik und Kirche*, iv (1932), 145

A. Schering: 'Kleine Bachstudien', *BJb*, xxx (1933), 30–70

C. O. Dreger: 'Die Vokalthematic Johann Sebastian Bachs: dargestellt an den Arien der Kirchenkantaten', *BJb*, xxxi (1934), 1–62

W. Lütge: 'Das architektonische Prinzip der Matthäuspassion J. S. Bachs', *Zeitschrift für Ästhetik und allgemeine Kunstwissenschaft*, xxx (1936), 65

A. Schering: *Johann Sebastian Bachs Leipziger Kirchenmusik* (Leipzig, 1936, 2/1954)

——: 'Die Hohe Messe in h-moll', *BJb*, xxxiii (1936), 1–30

E. Thiele: *Die Chorfugen J. S. Bachs* (Berne, 1936)

M. Jansen: 'Bachs Zahlensymbolik, an seinen Passionen untersucht', *BJb*, xxxiv (1937), 96

F. Smend: 'Bachsh-moll-Messe: Entstehung, Überlieferung, Bedeutung', *BJb*, xxxiv (1937), 1–58

W. Neumann: *J. S. Bach's Chorfuge* (Leipzig, 1938)

A. Schering: 'Zur Markus-Passion und zur "vierten" Passion', *BJb*, xxxvi (1939), 1–32

F. Smend: 'Bachs Markus-Passion', *BJb*, xxxvii (1940–48), 1–35

A. Schering: *Über Kantaten Johann Sebastian Bachs* (Leipzig, 1942, 3/1950)

F. Smend: 'Neue Bach-Funde', *AMf*, vii (1942), 1

H. S. Drinker: *Texts of Choral Works of J. S. Bach in English Translation* (New York, 1942–3)

W. Neumann: *Handbuch der Kantaten Johann Sebastian Bachs* (Leipzig, 1947, rev. 3/1967, 4/1971)

F. Smend: *Joh. Seb. Bach: Kirchen-Kantaten* (Berlin, 1947–9, 3/1966)

A. Dürr: 'Zu den verschollenen Passionen Bachs', *BJb*, xxxviii (1949–50), 81

W. Blankenburg: *Einführung in Bachs h-moll Messe* (Kassel, 1950, rev. 3/1973)

A. Dürr: 'Zur Aufführungspraxis der vor-Leipziger Kirchenkantaten J. S. Bachs', *Musik und Kirche*, xx (1950)

——: 'Über Kantatenformen in den geistlichen Dichtungen Salomon Francks', *Mf*, iii (1950), 18

I. F. Finlay: *J. S. Bachs weltliche Kantaten* (Göttingen, 1950)

——: 'Bach's Secular Cantata Texts', *ML*, xxxi (1950), 189

R. Gerber: 'Über Formstrukturen in Bachs Motetten', *Mf*, iii (1950), 177

A. Mendel: 'On the Keyboard Accompaniments to Bach's Leipzig Church Music', *MQ*, xxxvi (1950), 339

A. Schmitz: *Die Bildlichkeit der wortgebundenen Musik J. S. Bachs* (Mainz, 1950)

F. Smend: 'Bachs Himmelfahrts-Oratorium', *Bach-Gedenkschrift 1950*, ed. K. Matthaei (Zurich, 1950), 42

A. Dürr: *Studien über die frühen Kantaten J. S. Bachs* (Leipzig, 1951, rev. 2/1977)

——: 'Zur Echtheit einiger Bach zugeschriebener Kantaten', *BJb*, xxxix (1951–2), 30

W. H. Scheide: *J. S. Bach as a Biblical Interpreter* (Princeton, 1952)

W. Serauky: 'Die "Johannes-Passion" von Joh. Seb. Bach und ihr Vorbild', *BJb*, xli (1954), 29

F. Hudson and A. Dürr: 'An Investigation into the Authenticity of Bach's "Kleine Magnificat" ', *ML*, xxxvi (1955), 233

W. Neumann, ed.: *Johann Sebastian Bach: sämtliche Kantatentexte* (Leipzig, 1956, 2/1967)

L. F. Tagliavini: *Studi sui testi delle cantate sacre di J. S. Bach* (Padua, 1956)

A. Dürr: 'Zur Chronologie der Leipziger Vokalwerke J. S. Bachs', *BJb*, xliv (1957), 5–162; pubd separately, rev. (Kassel, 1976)

B. Smallman: *The Background of Passion Music: J. S. Bach and his Predecessors* (London, 1957, rev., enlarged, 2/1970)

H. Melchert: *Das Rezitativ der Kirchenkantaten J. S. Bach* (diss., U. of Frankfurt am Main, 1958; extract in *BJb*, xlv (1958), 5–83)

W. H. Scheide: 'Johann Sebastian Bachs Sammlung von Kantatenseines Vetters Johann Ludwig Bach', *BJb*, xlvi (1959), 52–94; xlviii (1961), 5; xlix (1962), 5

W. G. Whittaker: *The Cantatas of Johann Sebastian Bach* (London, 1959, 2/1964)

P. Mies: *Die geistlichen Kantaten Johann Sebastian Bachs und der Hörer von heute* (Wiesbaden, 1959–64)

K. Ameln: 'Zur Entstehungsgeschichte der Motette "Singet dem Herrn ein neues Lied" von J. S. Bach (BWV 225)', *BJb*, xlviii (1961), 25

J. C. F. Day: *The Literary Background to Bach's Cantatas* (London, 1961)

U. Siegele: 'Bemerkungen zu Bachs Motetten', *BJb*, xlix (1962), 33

J. Chailley: *Les Passions de J.-S. Bach* (Paris, 1963)

A. Mendel: 'Traces of the Pre-history of Bach's St John and St Matthew Passions', *Festschrift Otto Erich Deutsch* (Kassel, 1963), 31

A. Dürr: 'Beobachtungen am Autograph der Matthäus-Passion', *BJb*, l (1963–4), 47

D. Gojowy: 'Zur Frage der Köthener Trauermusik und der Matthäuspassion', *BJb*, li (1965), 87–134

W. Neumann: 'Über Ausmass und Wesen des Bachschen Parodieverfahrens', *BJb*, li (1965), 63

R. Bullivant: 'Zum Problem der Begleitung der Bachschen Motetten', *BJb*, lii (1966), 59

F. Smend: 'Zu den ältesten Sammlungen der vierstimmigen Choräle J. S. Bachs', *BJb*, lii (1966), 5

J. A. Westrup: *Bach Cantatas* (London, 1966)

F. Zander: *Die Dichter der Kantatentexte Johann Sebastian Bachs: Untersuchungen zu ihrer Bestimmung* (diss., U. of Cologne, 1966; extract in *BJb*, liv (1968), 9–64)

P. Mies: *Die weltlichen Kantaten Johann Sebastian Bachs und der Hörer von heute* (Wiesbaden, 1966–7)

M. Geck: 'Zur Echtheit der Bach-Motette "Lobet den Herrn, alle Heiden" ', *BJb*, liii (1967), 57

——: *Die Wiederentdeckung der Matthäuspassion im 19. Jahrhundert* (Regensburg, 1967)

P. Brainard: 'Bach's Parody Procedure and the St Matthew Passion', *JAMS*, xxii (1969), 241

G. Herz: 'BWV131: Bach's First Cantata', *Studies in Eighteenth-century Music: a Tribute to Karl Geiringer* (New York and London, 1970), 272

H. Schmalfuss: 'Johann Sebastian Bachs "Actus tragicus" (BWV106): ein Beitrag zu seiner Entstehungsgeschichte', *BJb*, lvi (1970), 36

A. Dürr: *Die Kantaten von Johann Sebastian Bach* (Kassel, 1971)

R. Leavis: 'Bach's Setting of Psalm CXLII (BWV230)', *ML*, lii (1971), 19

R. L. Marshall: *The Compositional Process of J. S. Bach: a Study of the Autograph Scores of the Vocal Works* (Princeton, 1972)

W. Neumann: 'Johann Sebastian Bachs "Rittergutskantaten" BWV30a und 212', *BJb*, lviii (1972), 76

A. Robertson: *The Church Cantatas of J. S. Bach* (London, 1972)

R. Gerlach: 'Besetzung und Instrumentation der Kirchenkantaten J. S. Bach und ihre Bedingungen', *BJb*, lix (1973), 53

G. Herz: 'Der lombardische Rhythmus im "Domine Deus" der h-Moll-Messe J. S. Bachs', *BJb*, lx (1974), 90

F. Krummacher: 'Textauslegung und Satzstruktur in J. S. Bachs Motetten', *BJb*, lx (1974), 5–43

A. Dürr: 'Bachs Kantatentexte: Probleme und Aufgaben der Forschung', *Bach-Studien*, v (1975), 49

M. Geck: 'Zur Datierung, Verwendung und Aufführungspraxis von Bachs Motetten', *Bach-Studien*, v (1975), 63

A. Glöckner: 'Bach and the Passion Music of his Contemporaries', *MT*, cxvi (1975), 613

D. Gojowy: 'Ein Zwölftonfeld bei J. S. Bach? Beobachtungen am Rezitativ BWV 167, Satz 2, Takte 13–19', *Bach-Studien*, v (1975), 43

K. Häfner: 'Der Picander Jahrgang', *BJb*, lxi (1975), 70

A. Mendel: 'Meliora ac Melioranda in the Two Versions of BWV 245/1', *Bach-Studien*, v (1975), 113

E. Platen: 'Zur Echtheit einiger Choralsätze Johann Sebastian Bachs', *BJb*, lxi (1975), 50

J. Rifkin: 'The Chronology of Bach's Saint Matthew Passion', *MQ*, lxi (1975), 360

W. H. Scheide: 'The "Concertato" Violin in BWV139', *Bach-Studien*, v (1975), 123

W. Schrammek: 'Fragen des Orgelgebrauchs in Bachs Aufführungen der Matthäus-Passion', *BJb*, lxi (1975), 114

H. E. Smither: *A History of the Oratorio*, ii (Chapel Hill, 1977), 154ff

G. J. Buelow: 'Symbol and Structure in the "Kyrie" of Bach's B minor Mass', *Essays on Bach and Other Matters: a Tribute to Gerhard Herz* (in preparation)

A. Mann: 'Bach's A major Mass: a *messa natale*?', ibid

W. Morgan: 'J. S. Bach's Motets: another Speculation', ibid

INSTRUMENTAL WORKS

H. Riemann: *Katechismus der Fugenkomposition*, iii (Leipzig, 1894, 2/1906)

A. Pirro: *L'orgue de Jean-Sébastien Bach* (Paris, 1895; Eng. trans., 1902/*R*1978)

M. Seiffert: *Geschichte der Klaviermusik* (Leipzig, 1899)

A. Schering: *Geschichte des Instrumentalkonzerts* (Leipzig, 1905, 2/1927/*R*1965)

R. Oppel: 'Die neuen deutschen Ausgaben der zwei- und dreistimmigen Inventionen', *BJb*, iv (1907), 89

R. Buchmayer: 'Cembalo oder Pianoforte?', *BJb*, v (1908), 64–93

A. Aber: 'Studien zu J. S. Bachs Klavierkonzerten', *BJb*, x (1913), 5

J. A. Fuller Maitland: 'The Toccatas of Bach', *SIMG*, xiv (1915), 578

H. Luedtke: 'Seb. Bachs Choralvorspiele', *BJb*, v (1918), 1–96

A. Halm: 'Über J. S. Bachs Konzertform', *BJb*, xvi (1919), 1–44

H. Luedtke: 'Zur Entstehung des Orgelbüchleins (1717)', *BJb*, xvi (1919), 62

A. Moser: 'Zu Joh. Seb. Bachs Sonaten und Partiten für Violine allein', *BJb*, xvii (1920), 30–65

H. Grace: *The Organ Works of Bach* (London, 1922)

W. Werker: *Studien über die Symmetrie im Bau der Fugen und die motivische Zusammengehörigkeit der Präludien und Fugen des Wohltemperierten Klaviers von J. S. Bach* (Leipzig, 1922)

W. Fischer: 'Zur Chronologie der Klaviersuiten J. S. Bachs', *Kongressbericht: Basel 1924*

W. Graeser: 'Bachs "Kunst der Fuge" ', *BJb*, xxi (1924), 1–104

J. A. Fuller Maitland: *The '48': Bach's Wohltemperirtes Clavier* (London, 1925)

——: *The Keyboard Suites of J. S. Bach* (London, 1925)

H. David: 'Die Gestalt von Bachs Chromatischer Fantasie', *BJb*, xxiii (1926), 23–67

R. Rietsch: 'Zur "Kunst der Fuge" von J. S. Bach', *BJb*, xxiii (1926), 1

K. A. Rosenthal: 'Über Sonatenformen in den Instrumental-werken Joh. Seb. Bachs', *BJb*, xxiii (1926), 68

F. Blume: 'Eine unbekannte Violinsonate von J. S. Bach', *BJb*, xxv (1928), 96

G. Oberst: 'J. S. Bachs englische und französische Suiten', *Gedenkschrift für Hermann Abert* (Halle, 1928)

P. Wackernagel: *Bachs Brandenburgische Konzerte* (Berlin, 1928)

F. Dietrich: 'J. S. Bachs Orgelchoral und seine geschichtlichen Wurzeln', *BJb*, xxvi (1929), 1–89

J. A. Fuller Maitland: *Bach's 'Brandenburg' Concertos* (London, 1929, 2/1945)

K. Hasse: 'Die Instrumentation J. S. Bachs', *BJb*, xxvi (1929), 90–141

A. E. Hull: *Bach's Organ Works* (London, 1929)

R. Sietz: *Die Orgelkompositionen des Schülerkreises um Bach* (diss., U. of Göttingen, 1930)

F. Dietrich: 'Analogieformen in Bachs Tokkaten und Präludien für die Orgel', *BJb*, xxviii (1931), 51

H. Neemann: 'J. S. Bachs Lautenkompositionen', *BJb*, xxviii (1931), 72

E. Schwebsch: *J. S. Bach und die Kunst der Fuge* (Stuttgart, 1931, 2/1955)

D. F. Tovey: *A Companion to the Art of Fugue* (London, 1931)

W. Krüger: 'Das Concerto grosso Joh. Seb. Bachs', *BJb*, xxix (1932), 1–50

C. S. Terry: *Bach's Orchestra* (London, 1932, 2/1958)

W. Ehmann: 'Der 3. Teil der Klavier-Übung', *Musik und Kirche*, v (1933)

L. Landshoff: *Revisionsbericht zur Urtextausgabe von J. S. Bachs Inventionen und Sinfonien* (Leipzig, 1933)

F. Smend: 'Bachs Kanonwerk über "Vom Himmel hoch da komm ich her" ', *BJb*, xxx (1933), 1–30

H. Klotz: *Über die Orgelkunst der Gotik, der Renaissance und des Barock* (Kassel, 1934)

W. Menke: *History of the Trumpet of Bach and Handel* (London, 1934)

H. E. Huggler: *J. S. Bachs Orgelbüchlein* (diss., U. of Berne, 1935)

G. Frotscher: *Geschichte des Orgel-Spiels und der Orgel-Komposition* (Berlin, 1935–6, enlarged 3/1966)

H. Keller: 'Unechte Orgelwerke Bachs', *BJb*, xxxiv (1937), 59

C. Gray: *The 48 Preludes and Fugues of J. S. Bach* (London, 1938)

H. Husmann: 'Die "Kunst der Fuge" als Klavierwerk: Besetzung und Anordnung', *BJb*, xxv (1938), 1–61

H. J. Moser: 'J. S. Bachs sechs Sonaten für Cembalo und Violine', *ZfM*, cv (1938), 1220

B. Martin: 'Praktische Anwendung der im Studium der *Kunst der Fuge* von J. S. Bach gewonnenen Erkenntnisse vom perspektivischen (dreidimensionalen) Raum auf die Komposition einer Fuge', *BJb*, xxxvii (1940–48), 56

——: 'Zwei Durchformungsmodi der Tripelfuge zum Fragment aus der *Kunst der Fuge* von Johann Sebastian Bach', *BJb*, xxxvii (1940–48), 36

——: *Untersuchungen zur Struktur der Kunst der Fuge* (Regensburg, 1941)

S. Taylor: *The Chorale Preludes of J. S. Bach* (London, 1942)

H. T. David: *J. S. Bach's Musical Offering: History, Interpretation and Analysis* (New York, 1945/R1972)

W. Apel: *Masters of the Keyboard* (Cambridge, Mass., 1947)

J. M. Barbour: 'Bach and "The Art of Temperament" ', *MQ*, xxxiii (1947), 64

F. Florand: *Jean-Sébastien Bach: l'oeuvre d'orgue* (Paris, 1947)

N. Dufourcq: *J. S. Bach, le maître de l'orgue* (Paris, 1948)

H. Keller: *Die Orgelwerke Bachs: ein Beitrag zu ihrer Geschichte, Form, Deutung und Wiedergabe* (Leipzig, 1948; Eng. trans., 1967)

N. Dufourcq: *Le clavecin* (Paris, 1949)

F. Germani: *Guida illustrativa alle composizioni per organo di J. S. Bach* (Rome, 1949)

K. Ehricht: 'Die zyklische Gestalt und die Aufführungsmöglichkeit des III. Teiles der Klavierübung von Johann Sebastian Bach', *BJb*, xxxviii (1949–50), 40

H. Keller: *Die Klavierwerke Bachs* (Leipzig, 1950)

H. Klotz: 'Bachs Orgeln und seine Orgelmusik', *Mf*, iii (1950), 200

K. Matthaei: 'Johann Sebastian Bachs Orgel', *Bach-Gedenkschrift 1950*, ed. K. Matthaei (Zurich, 1950), 118–149

A. Riemenschneider: *The Use of the Flutes in the Works of J. S. Bach* (Washington, DC, 1950)

H. Shanet: 'Why did J. S. Bach Transpose his Arrangements?', *MQ*, xxxvi (1950), 180

P. Aldrich: *Ornamentation in J. S. Bach's Organ Works* (New York, 1951)

W. David: *Johann Sebastian Bachs Orgeln* (Berlin, 1951)

W. Kaegi: *Die simultane Denkweise in J. S. Bachs Inventionen, Sinfonien und Fugen* (Basle, 1951)

W. Emery: 'The London Autograph of the "Forty-eight" ', *ML*, xxxiv (1953), 106

——: *Notes on Bach's Organ Works: a Companion to the Revised Edition* (London, 1953–7)

W. Schrammek: 'Die musikgeschichtliche Stellung der Orgeltriosonaten von Joh. Seb. Bach', *BJb*, xli (1954), 7

A. E. F. Dickinson: *Bach's Fugal Works* (London, 1956)

L. Czaczkes: *Analyse des Wohltemperierten Klaviers* (Vienna, 1956–65)

J. N. David: *Die zweistimmigen Inventionen von Johann Sebastian Bach* (Göttingen, 1957)

G. Hausswald: 'Zur Stilistik von J. S. Bachs Sonaten und Partiten für Violine allein', *AMw*, xiv (1957), 304

K.-H. Köhler: 'Zur Problematik der Violinsonaten mit obligatem Cembalo', *BJb*, xlv (1958), 114

J. N. David: *Die dreistimmigen Inventionen von Johann Sebastian Bach* (Göttingen, 1959)

E. Bodky: *The Interpretation of Bach's Keyboard Works* (Cambridge, Mass., 1960)

R. Donington: *Tempo and Rhythm in Bach's Organ Music* (London, 1960)

C. Dahlhaus: 'Bach und der "lineare Kontrapunkt" ', *BJb*, xlix (1962), 58

J. N. David: *Das wohltemperierte Klavier* (Göttingen, 1962)

N. Carrell: *Bach's Brandenburg Concertos* (London, 1963)

G. von Dadelsen: 'Zur Entstehung des Bachschen Orgelbüchleins', *Festschrift Friedrich Blume* (Kassel, 1963), 74

G. Friedemann: *Bach zeichnet das Kreuz* (Pinneberg, 1963)

P. F. Williams: 'J. S. Bach and English Organ Music', *ML*, xliv (1963), 140

H. Eppstein: 'Zur Problematik von J. S. Bachs Sonate für Violine und Cembalo G dur (BWV 1019)', *AMw*, xxi (1964), 217

H. Keller: *Das Wohltemperierte Klavier von Johann Sebastian Bach: Werk und Wiedergabe* (Kassel, 1965)

E. Arfken: 'Zur Entstehungsgeschichte des Orgelbüchleins', *BJb*, lii (1966), 41

H. Eppstein: 'Studien über J. S. Bach's Sonaten für ein Melodieinstrument und obligates Cembalo', *Acta Universitatis uppsalensis*, new ser., ii (1966)

E. Franke: 'Themenmodelle in Bachs Klaviersuiten', *BJb*, lii (1966), 72

H. Ferguson: 'Bach's "Lauten Werck" ', *ML*, xlviii (1967), 259

H.-J. Schulze: 'Johann Sebastian Bachs Kanonwidmungen', *BJb*, liii (1967), 82

C. Wolff: 'Der Terminus "Ricercar" in Bachs Musikalischem Opfer', *BJb*, liii (1967), 70

C. Albrecht: 'J. S. Bachs "Clavier Übung dritter Theil": Versuch einer Deutung', *BJb*, lv (1969), 46

F.-P. Constantini: 'Zur Typusgeschichte von J. S. Bachs Wohltemperiertem Klavier', *BJb*, lv (1969), 31

H. Eppstein: 'Grundzüge in J. S. Bachs Sonatenschaffen', *BJb*, lv (1969), 5

C. Wolff: 'Ordnungsprinzipien in den Originaldrucken Bachscher Werke', *Bach-Interpretationen*, ed. M. Geck (Göttingen, 1969)

T. Göllner: 'J. S. Bach and the Tradition of Keyboard Transcriptions', *Studies in Eighteenth-century Music: a Tribute to Karl Geiringer* (New York and London, 1970), 253

C. Wolff: 'New Research on Bach's Musical Offering', *MQ*, lvii (1971), 379–408

J. Chailley: *L'Art de la fugue de J.-S. Bach* (Paris, 1971–2)

L. Hoffmann-Erbrecht: 'Johann Sebastian Bach als Schöpfer des Klavier Konzerts', *Quellenstudien zur Musik: Wolfgang Schmieder zum 70. Geburtstag* (Frankfurt am Main, 1972), 69

P. Schmiede: 'Zum Gebrauch des Cembalos und des Klaviers bei der heutigen Interpretation Bachscher Werke', *BJb*, lviii (1972), 95

S. Vogelsänger: 'Zur Herkunft der kontrapunktischen Motive in J. S. Bachs "Orgelbüchlein" (BWV599–644)', *BJb*, lviii (1972), 118

C. Wolff: 'Überlegungen zum "Thema Regium" ', *BJb*, lix (1973), 33

H.-J. Schulze: 'Johann Sebastian Bachs Konzertbearbeitungen nach Vivaldi und anderen – Studien- oder Auftragswerke?', *DJbM*, xviii (1973–7), 80

H. Hering: 'Spielerische Elemente in J. S. Bachs Klaviermusik', *BJb*, lx (1974), 44

E. May: 'Eine neue Quelle für J. S. Bachs einzeln überlieferte Orgelchoräle', *BJb*, lx (1974), 98

U. Meyer: 'Zur Einordnung von J. S. Bachs einzeln überlieferten Orgelchorälen', *BJb*, lx (1974), 75

W. Breig: 'Bachs Goldberg-Variationen als zyklisches Werk', *AMw*, xxxii (1975), 243

A. Dürr: 'Zur Entstehungsgeschichte des 5. Brandenburgischen Konzerts', *BJb*, lxi (1975), 63

H. Eichberg: 'Unechtes unter Johann Sebastian Bachs Klavierwerken', *BJb*, lxi (1975), 7–49

C. Wolff and others: 'Bach's "Art of Fugue": an Examination of the Sources', *CMc* (1975), no.19, p.47

W. Breig: 'Bachs Violinkonzert d-Moll: Studien zu seiner Gestalt und Entstehungsgeschichte', *BJb*, lxii (1976), 7

H. Eppstein: 'Chronologieprobleme in Johann Sebastian Bachs Suiten für Soloinstrument', *BJb*, lxii (1976), 35

N. Kenyon: 'A Newly Discovered Group of Canons by Bach', *MT*, cxvii (1976), 391

H. Schmidt: 'Bach's C major Orchestral Suite: a New Look at Possible Origins', *ML*, lvii (1976), 152

H.-J. Schulze: 'Melodiezitate und Mehrtextigkeit in der Bauernkantate und in den Goldberg-Variationen', *BJb*, lxii (1976), 58

C. Wolff: 'Bach's *Handexemplar* of the Goldberg Variations: a New Source', *JAMS*, xxix (1976), 224

W. Kolneder: *Die Kunst der Fuge: Mythen des 20. Jahrhunderts* (Wilhelmshaven, 1977)

T. Harmon: *The Registration of J. S. Bach's Organ Works* (Buren, 1978)

P. Williams: 'The Musical Aims of J. S. Bach's "Clavierübung III" ', *Source Materials and the Interpretation of Music: a Memorial Volume to Thurston Dart* (in preparation)

(8) Wilhelm Friedemann Bach (*45*) (*b* Weimar, 22 Nov 1710; *d* Berlin, 1 July 1784). The 'Halle Bach', eldest son of (7) Johann Sebastian (*24*) and Maria Barbara Bach. A greatly gifted composer, who did not fully set aside his background of contrapuntal training in favour of the new styles of the mid-18th century, he led an unstable life and never quite developed his full creative potential.

1. LIFE. His first academic studies were at the Latein-schule in Cöthen. In early 1720 Sebastian began a 'Clavier-Büchlein vor Wilhelm Friedemann Bach' that was to be used for Bach's other children and pupils as well. The 'Clavier-Büchlein' abandons the beginner's realm in its first few pages and becomes a compendium of preludes, inventions, dances and similar works, including a foretaste of *Das wohltemperirte Clavier*; its contents no doubt reflect young Friedemann's rapid progress as a keyboard player. The year 1720 also brought the death of Maria Barbara; that unhappy event, followed a year and a half later by Sebastian's marriage to Anna Magdalena, may have had a bearing on Friedemann's later difficulties in life.

When the family moved to Leipzig in 1723, the 13-year-old Friedemann (like the nine-year-old Emanuel) was enrolled in the Thomasschule; and for the first Christmas in their new home Sebastian presented to his beloved 'Friede' a certificate showing his registration for eventual matriculation at the university. Friedemann's academic success was not allowed to interfere with his musical education, which must have been uniquely thorough and systematic: book 1 of the '48', for instance, was composed with the 12-year-old Friedemann in mind. Nor did Sebastian permit too much keyboard specialization; in 1726 Friedemann was sent to Merseburg to study the violin with J. G. Graun for almost a year. It is plain that Friedemann was Sebastian's favourite child.

In 1729 Friedemann graduated from the Thomas-schule, and his outstanding career as a scholar continued for four more years at the University of Leipzig, where he studied mathematics, philosophy and law. It was also during 1729 that he visited Handel in Halle with an invitation to the Bach home in Leipzig, which Handel was unable to accept. By that time Friedemann, like Emanuel, was regularly working as Sebastian's assistant in such tasks as private instruction (one of his pupils was Christoph Nichelmann), the conducting of rehearsals and music copying; when the opportunity to become organist at the Dresden Sophienkirche presented itself in 1733, he was able, as a finished musician, to win the trials for the post easily, earning the warmest commendation from Pantaleon Hebenstreit, vice-Kapellmeister at the Dresden court. Friedemann had been present at Sebastian's recital on the Silbermann organ in the Sophienkirche two years earlier, and had visited Dresden with Sebastian on other occasions. Sebastian's reputation obviously helped his candidature.

The new position was a part-time one and his pay was modest, but Friedemann did have time to pursue other interests in Dresden: composition, further study in mathematics, the operas and ballets presented at the brilliant Dresden court, the friendship of such musicians as Hebenstreit, Sylvius Weiss, J. G. Goldberg (his pupil), J. A. Hasse, Faustina Bordoni Hasse and P. G. Buffardin. Entrée to the music of the court was made possible to him through Count Kayserlingk, Sebastian's

9. *Wilhelm Friedemann Bach: portrait (2nd half of the 18th century) by Wilhelm Weitsch in the Staatliche Galerie Moritzburg, Halle*

patron. His opulent surroundings in Dresden, the prodigality and luxuriousness of the court, must have contrasted sharply with the austerity of the Bach home and St Thomas's; it must also have been disturbing for him to realize that the combined salary of the Hasses was more than 16 times that paid to his father. As a Protestant organist, moreover, he gradually came to realize that in this Catholic city where opera reigned supreme, both his religion and his music would always make him something of an outsider. In 1742 the organist's position at the Liebfrauenkirche in Dresden (considerably more important in Protestant circles than his part-time appointment at the Sophienkirche) became vacant; it constituted a natural step up for him. But he failed to secure it, and the post went to G. A. Homilius. In 1746 he had better luck, thanks to Sebastian's influence: his application for the important position of organist at the Liebfrauenkirche in Halle (for which Sebastian himself had unsuccessfully competed 33 years earlier) was enough to give him the post without even a trial performance.

In his new occupation, as a successor in the Liebfrauenkirche of such eminent figures as Scheidt and Zachow, Friedemann might well have made a distinguished career. By this time he was widely regarded as the best organist in Germany, and the last survivor of the Baroque organ tradition – though this recognition came primarily through his improvisations, not through his performances of works composed by or in the style of his father. In addition to his duties as organist he was in charge of the productions of music, involving orchestra, in the three principal churches of Halle. He began his stay there with a performance of his first cantata, *Wer mich liebet*. But Halle was under the rule of Pietism in its most doctrinaire form, and Friedemann, coming from 13 years in liberal Dresden, was incapable of being an earnest and sober Pietist. To make matters worse, his free-thinking tendencies were abetted by the presence of Christian Wolff in Halle University. Wolff, once banished from Halle for his reputation as a philosopher–mathematician of the Enlightenment, had now been restored by Frederick the Great; and Friedemann's young mind, like many others of his time, was irresistibly attracted to Wolff's rationalistic system. It was hardly an appropriate mode of thought for a Lutheran church organist, least of all a son of J. S. Bach. After Friedemann accompanied Sebastian on his famous visit to Frederick's court in 1747 (the visit that produced the *Musical Offering*), at the height of that enlightened despot's brilliant patronage of a music far removed from his own, his surroundings in Halle no doubt seemed drab by comparison. A second trip to Berlin took place in 1750, after Sebastian's death, when he delivered young Johann Christian to Emanuel's care; that time he overstayed his leave and earned a reprimand from his Halle employers.

Without Sebastian's steadying influence, and in spite of marriage at the age of 41 (only one of his children, a daughter, survived infancy), Friedemann was unable to settle down happily in Halle. He repeatedly left town to apply for other posts, to the displeasure of his superiors, who were none too tolerant to begin with. When the Seven Years War began, in 1756, Halle became an open city, subject to exploitation and outrageous taxation by occupying troops of one side or another. Friedemann and his family suffered like all Halle residents, and in 1761 he did not hesitate to ask the church elders to produce, from their exhausted treasury, a rise in salary for him. The elders' refusal was vituperative, even threatening.

In 1762 a change of fortune seemed imminent: the court of Darmstadt offered him the post of Kapellmeister, an important and well-salaried position which had fallen vacant on the death of Christoph Graupner. He accepted; yet, incredibly, through circumstances that are obscure, the position slipped through his fingers. He delayed moving his belongings, even though moving expenses were offered. The official decree naming him as Kapellmeister awaited him in Darmstadt, yet he insisted that it be sent to him in Halle. The details are unknown, but evidently his behaviour in general was inappropriate. Eventually the Darmstadt court gave him only the title, without the position. He went back to his uncomfortable relation with his Halle superiors, and finally, on 12 May 1764, he unceremoniously walked away from his job without notice. There were no prospects of further employment, and this was indeed the last formal post he would occupy.

Friedemann remained in Halle until 1770, earning his living mainly as a teacher; his distant relative Johann Christian Bach (77) (1743–1814), F. W. Rust and J. S. Petri were among his pupils. In 1770 his wife's property in Halle was sold, and the family moved to Brunswick. There he began those occupational vacillations that were to be the point of departure for the characterizations of him (especially the grossly inaccurate and unfair accounts by Marpurg, Reichardt and Rochlitz) as an eccentric, giving organ recitals, composing, applying here and there in vain for permanent employment. He also received some money from the sale of manuscripts of his father's music, especially autographs, of which he was the chief owner. Friedemann was a shockingly poor custodian of this treasure, much of which has never been found; even Forkel, who befriended him around this

time, was unable to account for the loss.

By 1774 he found himself in Berlin, where his prospects looked better. His power as an organ virtuoso was especially appreciated, and he was strongly favoured by Princess Anna Amalia, sister of Frederick the Great. Among his Berlin pupils was Sara Levy, Mendelssohn's great-aunt. J. P. Kirnberger, Anna Amalia's court composer and a former pupil of Sebastian, offered his friendship to Friedemann, who reciprocated by trying to discredit Kirnberger at court so that Kirnberger's position might be offered to him. His plan backfired, and he had to look elsewhere in Berlin for favour.

Hardened now in his aloofness, his unwillingness to see through the eyes of others, and his inability to pursue a task to its end, the aging composer remained in Berlin for ten years, in poverty and ill-health, gradually retreating from reality. An opera, *Lausus und Lydie*, was begun but left unfinished. He was reduced to claiming some music by Sebastian as his own, and on at least one occasion he signed his father's name to his own work. He died of a pulmonary disease, leaving his widow and daughter in dire poverty. Proceeds from a Berlin performance of Handel's *Messiah* in 1785 were donated to them.

2. WORKS. In spite of such aids as the Falck thematic list and the Kast study on Bach family manuscripts, many of Wilhelm Friedemann's compositions cannot yet be either positively identified or dated. But the general outline is clear enough: while living at home (before 1733) he wrote only a few pieces, mainly for keyboard; at Dresden (1733–46) he largely concentrated on instrumental works; at Halle (1746–70), while continuing to compose in instrumental genres, he produced some two dozen church cantatas, which are almost the whole body of his vocal compositions; and at Brunswick and Berlin (1771–84), aside from the abortive attempt at an opera, what little he composed was primarily for keyboard or chamber groups.

Of the four Bach sons who became well known as composers, Friedemann, the oldest, seems to have been the one least interested in reconciling his training under Sebastian with the new styles. Rather than forging the old and new into a unique blend, as Emanuel did, or turning wholeheartedly to the new, like Johann Christian, Friedemann shifted back and forth throughout his career between old and new, from work to work and even within single works.

It is often a very attractive vacillation. In the brilliant *Concerto à duoi cembali concertati* for two unaccompanied harpsichords (F10), composed early in the Dresden period, the last movement follows the ritornello procedure characteristic of Baroque concertos, with the 'orchestral' and 'solo' parts carried on by the two harpsichords; yet the first movement, not concerto-like at all, is actually a sonata movement in clear sonata form. Similarly, the important Sinfonia in F (F67), also from the Dresden years, straddles two eras by managing to be both a sinfonia and an orchestral suite. The double-dotted French overture that is its first movement is repeatedly shattered by sudden harmonic and metrical shifts in *empfindsamer Stil*; if initially disturbing, these surprising changes of *Affekt* soon seem charming, and even well integrated. The second movement is an Andante, beautiful but indistinguishable in style from hundreds of other Baroque andantes. The third movement, an Italianate Allegro in duple time, presents Classical-sounding antecedent and consequent phrases in a clear though truncated sonata form. That is not the end of the so-called 'Sinfonia': the final movement is made up of a pair of *abwechselnde Menuetten* whose serene cantilena is quite specifically Handelian. Four superb flute duets composed in Dresden (F54, 55, 57, 59) are quite conservative, especially in their adherence to imitative polyphony. The 12 equally superb keyboard polonaises (F12), composed in the Halle period and particularly esteemed in the 19th century, are paramount among the intensely expressive works that cause some scholars to classify Friedemann Bach as a proto-Romantic composer. And by the end of his career Friedemann was hardly closer to the dominant musical language of the Classical era than he had been while still under his father's tutelage. During the Berlin years he dedicated excellent works in sharply opposed styles to Princess Amalia: on the one hand, a keyboard sonata in D (F4) with a 'Mozartian' first movement; on the other, a set of eight keyboard fugues (F31).

This mixture of old and new was not always so successful, of course. The cantatas, sublime moments notwithstanding, follow too slavishly in Sebastian's footsteps, too often consist of parodies and borrowings from earlier works rather than original composition, and too seldom adopt the new homophonic textures. The keyboard sonatas sometimes present nearly insoluble problems of performance in their sudden changes of tempo or texture in the *empfindsamer Stil*. Some important forms, such as rondo and variation, are neglected. He composed not a single known lied. There are evidences of indolence or expediency even in Friedemann's prime years, and of failing inspiration towards the end of his career.

Yet Friedemann's great gifts remain evident in an outpouring of rich melody, a harmonic palette more varied and more daring than that of most of his contemporaries, a consistent deepening of homophonic texture by means of effortless counterpoint and, above all, a highly personal style of emotional expression. 'The cultivated musician who chooses the esoteric, precious music of Friedemann in place of the lighter, more popular, standardized music of Christian is akin to the literate who chooses Sterne's *Sentimental Journey* or one of Klopstock's followers in place of the more pedestrian writings of a C. F. Nicolai' (Newman).

WORKS

Principal MS sources are *D-B*, *Bds*; there is a catalogue in Falck [F], with corrections in Blume and Kast.
Edition: *W. F. Bach: Complete Works for Organ*, ed. E. P. Biggs and G. Weston (New York, 1947) [CW]

KEYBOARD
(for hpd unless otherwise stated)

F
1   Sonata (C), c1745, 2 versions; 1 ed. E. Pauer, Alte Meister, xxiv (Leipzig, 1875), 1 ed. in NM, clvi (1941)
2   Sonata (C), c1778 [movts 2–3 rev. in F15];·ed. in NM, clvi (1941)
3   Sonata I (D), as Sei sonate (Dresden, 1745) [according to Falck, F5–9 were intended to form remainder of set]; ed. in NM, lxxviii (1930)
4   Sonata (D), c1778; ed. in NM, lxxviii (1930)
5   Sonate pour le clavecin (Eb) (Dresden, 1748); ed. in NM, lxxviii (1930)
6–9 Sonatas (F, G, A, Bb), ? all complete by 1745, F6 in 3 versions; F6 ed. in NM, clvi (1941), F7–9 ed. in NM, lxiii (1930)
10 Concerto â duoi cembali concertati (F), 2 hpd, c1773; ed. J. Brahms as Sonate für 2 Klavier (Leipzig, 1864/R1966), ed. in *Johann Sebastian Bachs Werke*, xliii (Leipzig, 1894) [attrib. J. S. Bach], ed. H. Brandts Buys (London, 1953)

11 Sonata (D), 2 kbd, lost
—   6 sonatas, *D-Bds*, cited by Kast
12 12 polonaises (C, c, D, d, Eb, eb, E, e, F, f, G, g), c1765; ed. in Le trésor des pianistes, x (Paris, c1865), ed. W. Niemann (Leipzig, 1914), ed. F. Wührer (Vienna, 1949), 6 ed. in Hausmusik, xcviii (Vienna, 1951)
13 Polonaise (C), c1765
—   28 polonaises, *Bds*, cited by Kast
14–23 10 fantasias (C, c, c, D, d, d, e, e, G, a), F20 from 1770, F15–16 from 1784 [see F2], some others from Dresden, 1733–46; F14 ed. L. Hoffmann-Erbrecht (Lippstadt, 1963)
—   Fantasia (c), *Bds*, cited by Kast
24 Suite (g); ed. H. Riemann (Leipzig, 1893)
25–30 Various short pieces, most ? before 1733; selections ed. H. Riemann (Leipzig, c1890), and as Leichte Spielstücke (Zurich, 1971)
—   2 minuets, *Bds*, cited by Kast
31 VIII Fugen (C, c, D, d, Eb, e, Bb, f) (Berlin, 1778); ed. in Le trésor des pianistes, x (Paris, c1865), ed. as Huit fugues (Paris, 1959)
32–4 3 fugues (C, F, Bb), all ? before 1735 [F34 arr. of fugue in ov. to Handel's Esther]
35–7 3 fugues (C, F, g), org, F35 frag., F36 a triple fugue composed in Halle; ed. in CW, ed. T. Fedtke, *W. F. Bach: Orgelwerke* (Frankfurt am Main, 1968)
—   3 fugues, *Bds*, cited by Kast
38/1 7 chorale-preludes, org; ed. in CW, ed. T. Fedtke, *W. F. Bach: Orgelwerke* (Frankfurt am Main, 1968)
38/2 Trio on 'Allein Gott in der Höh', org, lost
39 Canons and studies, org
40 Concerto (G), ? before 1735 [see F97]; ed. L. Hoffmann-Erbrecht (Lippstadt, 1960)
—   Praeludium (c), cited by Blume
—   March (Eb), cited by Blume

Doubtful: sonatas (C, Eb [although autograph], F, G [1 movt]); fugue (c), ed. in CW
Spurious: sonatas (c, D, Eb, e); polonaises (F, G); divertimento (a); fantasia (F); sonata (A), 2 kbd, after Couperin

CONCERTOS
(for hpd and orch unless otherwise stated)

41 Conc. (D), ? Dresden, 1733–46; ed. H. Riemann (Leipzig, 1897)
42 Conc. (Eb), inc., 1750s [rev. as introduction to F88]
43 Conc. (e), ? before 1767; ed. H. Riemann (Leipzig, c1880), ed. W. Upmeyer (Berlin, 1931)
44 Conc. (F), Dresden, 1733–46; ed. H. Riemann (Leipzig, 1894)
45 Conc. (a), date controversial [see Geiringer, 326]; ed. H. Riemann (Leipzig, 1897)
46 Conc. (Eb), 2 hpd; ed. H. Riemann (Leipzig, 1894)
—   Conc. (f), cited by Kast; ed. W. Smigelski (Hamburg, 1959)

Doubtful: Conc. (g)
Spurious: Conc. (c) [? by Kirnberger]; Conc. (d), org [arr. by J. S. Bach of Vivaldi's Vn Conc., op.3 no.11]

CHAMBER AND ORCHESTRAL

47–9 4 trio sonatas (D, D, a [frag.], Bb), 2 fl, bc, ? before 1762; ed. L. Schittler (Munich, 1910/Rc1960)
50 Trio sonata (Bb), 2 vn, bc
51–3 3 sonatas (F, a, D), fl, bc, cited in Breitkopf catalogues 1761, 1763, lost
54–9 6 duets (e, Eb, B, F, f, G), 2 fl, F54–5, 57, 59 composed in Dresden, 1733–46, F56, 58 after 1770; ed. K. Walter (Wiesbaden, 1969)
60–62 3 duets (C, G, g), 2 va, after 1770; ed. K. Haas (London, 1953)
63 Sinfonia (C), 1733–46
64 Sinfonia (D), 1746–64 [used as introduction to F85]; ed. W. Lebermann (Mainz, 1971)
65 Sinfonia (d), 2 fl, str; ed. L. Schittler (Munich, 1910), ed. W. Lebermann (Mainz, 1971)
66 Sinfonia ['Ricercata'] (d) [anon. arr. c1800 of 2 of W. F. Bach's choral fugues incl. as add to MS containing fugues F31/8, 31/5, 37]
67–71 Sinfonias (F, G, G, A, Bb), 1733–46; F67 ed. M. Schneider (Leipzig, 1954)
—   Sinfonia (a), 1758, cited by Blume

Doubtful: Trio (B), vn, hpd, ed. L. Schittler (Munich, 1910/Rc1960); trio (c), va, hpd, ed. Y. Pessl (London, 1947)
Spurious: Sonata (G), 2 fl, va; sonata (C), 2 fl,·bc; sonata (F), (vn/fl. hpd)/(vn, fl, bc)

CHURCH CANTATAS
(for 4vv, insts, 1746–64)

72 Wer mich liebet, 1746

73   Der Herr zu deiner Rechten, 1747
74   Wir sind Gottes Werke, 1748
75   Gott fähret auf, 1748
76   Wohl dem, der den Herrn fürchtet
77   Vergnügte Ruh [partly parody of J. S. Bach's cantatas BWV170, 147]
78   Heilig, heilig ist Gott; ed. A. Schering (Leipzig, 1922)
80   Lasset uns ablegen, 1749
81   Der Herr wird mit Gerechtigkeit, before 1756
82   Wie schön leucht uns [partly parody]
83   Erzittert und fallet
84   Dienet dem Herrn, 1755, 'W.F.' changed to 'J.S.' Bach on MS, but by Friedemann
85   Dies ist der Tag, da Jesu Leidenskraft [see F64]; ed. L. Nowak (Leipzig, 1937)
86   Der Höchste erhöret, 1756 [partly parody]
87   Verhängnis, dein Wüten, after 1756 [partly parody]
88   Ertönet, ihr seligen Völker [partly parody; see F42]
89   Es ist eine Stimme eines Predigers
91   Wo geht die Lebensreise hin
92   O Wunder, wer kann dieses fassen
93   Ach, dass dir den Himmel zerreissest
96   Heraus, verblendeter Hochmut, ? composed at Brunswick [partly parody]
101–5 only printed texts extant: Wertes Zion, sei getrost, 1756 [? by J. S. Bach]; Blast Lärmen, ihr Feinde, 1756 [? borrowed from J. S. Bach's cantata BWV205a; Blast Lärmen, 1757 [mostly a parody of the preceding]; Ja, ja, es hat mein Gott, 1757; Halleluja, wohl diesem Volk, 1757; Viele sind berufen, 1757; Lobe den Herrn in seinem Heiligtum, 1762; Gott, ist unsere Zuversicht und Stärke, 1762
—   Man singet mit Freuden, 1756 [parody of J. S. Bach's cantata BWV149], cited by Blume
—   Es ist das Heil uns kommen her [parody of J. S. Bach's cantata BWV9], cited by Blume
—   Gaudete omnes populi [partly parody of J. S. Bach's cantata BWV80], cited by Blume
—   Nimm von uns, Herr [parody of J. S. Bach's cantata BWV101], cited by Blume
—   Church cantata for Easter 1747

Spurious: Jesu, deine Passion, D-Bds

OTHER SACRED

98   Deutsche Messe [partly parody]
99   Amen–Alleluja [parody]
100   Kyrie, 'W.F.' changed to 'J.S.' on MS, authorship uncertain

SECULAR CANTATAS

90   O Himmel, schöne, for birthday of Frederick the Great, 1758 [partly parody]; sinfonia ed. E. Prieger (Cologne, c1910)
95   Auf, Christen, posaunt, for celebration of end of Seven Years War, 1763 [partly parody]

OTHER VOCAL

79   . . . Gnade finden, aria, frag.
94   Zerbrecht, zerreist, aria, S, hn, obbligato [? cantata frag.]; ed. L. Schittler (Munich, 1910)
97   Herz, mein Herz, sei ruhig, 'Cantilena nuptiarum consolatoria', 1774–84 [parody of Andante from F40]
106   Lausus und Lydie (opera, C. M. Plümicke, after Marmontel), inc., 1778–9, lost

Spurious: Kein Hälmlein wächst auf Erden (lied, E. Brachvogel), 19th-century falsification, music by Brachvogel and Emil Bach

WRITING

Abhandlung vom harmonischen Dreiklang, begun c1754, advertised in Leipzig newspapers in 1758 for Easter fair 1759, unpubd, lost

BIBLIOGRAPHY

F. Chrysander: 'Johann Sebastian Bach und sein Sohn Friedemann Bach in Halle', *Jb für musikalische Wissenschaft*, ii (Leipzig, 1863–7), 235
C. H. Bitter: *Carl Philipp Emanuel und Wilhelm Friedemann Bach und deren Brüder* (Berlin, 1868)
W. Nagel: 'W. Fr. Bachs Berufung nach Darmstadt', *SIMG*, i (1900), 290
K. Zehler: 'W. Fr. Bach und seine hallische Wirksamkeit', *BJb*, vii (1910), 103–32
M. Falck: *Wilhelm Friedemann Bach* (Leipzig, 1913, 2/1919)
H. Miesner: 'Portraits aus dem Kreise Ph. E. und W. Fr. Bachs', *Musik und Bild: Festschrift Max Seiffert* (Kassel, 1938), 101
F. Blume: 'Bach, Wilhelm Friedemann', *MGG*
W. S. Newman: *The Sonata in the Classic Era* (Chapel Hill, 1963, rev. 2/1972)
W. Braun: 'Material zu Wilhelm Friedemann Bachs Kantatenaufführungen in Halle (1746–1764)', *Mf*, xviii (1965), 267
H.-J. Schulze: 'Eine "Drama per Musica" als Kirchenmusik: zu Wilhelm Friedemann Bachs Aufführungen der Huldigungskantate BWV205a', *BJb*, lxi (1975), 133

(9) Carl Philipp Emanuel Bach (*46*) (*b* Weimar, 8 March 1714; *d* Hamburg, 14 Dec 1788). The second surviving son of (7) Johann Sebastian Bach (*24*) and his first wife, Maria Barbara. The most famous and most prolific of the Bach sons, he held positions of great influence in Berlin and Hamburg, was widely esteemed as a keyboard player and theorist, and stands as the chief representative of the north German *empfindsamer Stil*.

1. The early years. 2. Berlin. 3. Hamburg. 4. Keyboard music. 5. Orchestral and chamber music. 6. Vocal music. 7. The Essay.

1. THE EARLY YEARS. He was descended from musicians – and Bachs – on both sides of his family. His godfathers were Telemann and the Weissenfels court musician A. E. Weldig. Emanuel was three years old (Wilhelm Friedemann was seven) when the family moved to Cöthen, seven when Sebastian married Anna Magdalena after Maria Barbara's premature death, nine when Sebastian became Kantor of the Leipzig Thomasschule. In Cöthen, Sebastian sent the children to the Lutheran seminary rather than to the better-equipped Calvinist school; in Leipzig, Emanuel and Friedemann were of course among the 'Scholaren' at the Thomasschule that Sebastian had to oversee.

Emanuel makes it clear in his little autobiographical sketch that he never had any music teacher besides his father. There is no evidence that he seriously studied any instrument except the keyboard; by the age of 11, according to Schubarth, he could play Sebastian's keyboard pieces at sight. Throughout his career he was hardly to travel at all in an age when travel, especially to Italy, was considered an important part of a young German musician's training. All this might have resulted in a certain narrowness of musical outlook, even in a man whose teacher was the author of such pedagogical works as the Inventions, the *Orgelbüch!ein*, the *Clavier-Übung* and *Das wohltemperirte Clavier*; but quite the opposite was the case: Sebastian's penetrating and lifelong study of Italian and French music, the frequent visits to the Bach home of distinguished musicians from various parts of Europe, and the performance of many styles, genres and nationalities of music, instrumental and vocal, sacred and secular, undoubtedly gave the young Emanuel a rare breadth of musical experience. The only major genre of music relatively closed to him as a boy was opera (though he no doubt had some slight experience of opera, probably mainly Hasse's, in nearby Dresden).

Emanuel also received a sound general education at the Thomasschule, in spite of its decline under J. H. Ernesti; whatever its faults, and whatever Sebastian's difficulties in it, the school was to remain important enough, thanks in part to its proximity to and its connections with the great University of Leipzig, to attract such outstanding rector–scholars as J. M. Gesner and J. A. Ernesti. From the Thomasschule to the University of Leipzig was a predictable step for a superior student. Emanuel matriculated at the university on 1 October 1731 to study law, though still living with his parents, still acting as a most important musical assistant to Sebastian, and even applying unsuccessfully in 1733 for a position as organist at Naumburg. Not so predictable was his move to the University of Frankfurt an der Oder, again as a law student, where he matriculated on 9 September 1734 and remained, according to the autobiographical sketch, until the end of the academic year in 1738, supporting himself in this musically arid town mostly by giving keyboard lessons and by composing for or directing public concerts and ceremonies such as the dedication of a church renovation, the production by students of congratulatory cantatas for visiting royalty etc.

The years 1731–8 also mark the real beginning of his composing career. In 1731, under Sebastian's supervision, he engraved with his own hands a little one-page minuet 'with hand-crossings' (W111; H1), his earliest known work. By 1734, as further products of his apprenticeship with his father, he completed five keyboard sonatas, seven trios, solos for oboe and flute, a keyboard suite, two harpsichord concertos and six keyboard sonatinas; by 1738, now on his own as a composer, he added about a dozen more such instrumental works to this list.

Thus the objective evidence is that until his 24th year Emanuel Bach energetically pursued both an unusually extensive university training, lasting almost seven years, and a thoroughly professional career in music. Whether he intended his lifetime career to be legal or musical is a question that has been much discussed by scholars; but his actions seem to indicate that he simply wanted to keep his options open as long as possible, and that he was guided and encouraged in that by Sebastian. Regarding his study of law, it should be understood that a 'law' curriculum in European universities was one of the most ordinary approaches to a university (meaning liberal, not vocational) education, and did not necessarily lead to the practice of law. Handel, Mattheson, J. F. Agricola, Schütz, Kuhnau and many other German musicians studied law. Some, like J. D. Heinichen (a product of the University of Leipzig), actually practised law in an incidental fashion while concentrating on music; others, like C. G. Krause (a product of the University of Frankfurt an der Oder), had distinguished legal careers while also making significant achievements in music.

Sebastian Bach was determined that, if possible, his sons would have the university education he lacked; he wanted them to be able to rise above the petty indignities that he had to suffer throughout his career. Friedemann, then Emanuel, and then Johann Christoph Friedrich were enrolled by Sebastian at the University of Leipzig, all as students of law (Friedemann also studied mathematics and philosophy). Of these three, Emanuel was the one who perceived most clearly the value of a liberal education as a defence against 18th-century society's evaluation of ordinary musicians as ignorant servants, an evaluation richly articulated by his father's superiors, especially J. A. Ernesti, for all the Bach family to hear. For the rest of his life Emanuel generally preferred the company of literati to that of musicians; he would be able to show his literacy and intellectual discipline in an epoch-making *Essay*; and in financial matters he would become quite lawyer-like, keeping scrupulous account books and unapologetically billing his patrons for services rendered. If this sounds rather dull (and dullness is indeed his chief characteristic in letter after letter dealing primarily with money), it should be balanced against his considerable breadth of interest, his keen enjoyment of good company, and his reputation as a ready wit, especially as a punster, from boyhood until old age.

'When I finished my academic year in 1738 and went to Berlin', he said in the autobiographical sketch, 'I was given a very advantageous opportunity to guide a young gentleman in foreign travel; an unexpected and gracious summons to Ruppin from the then crown prince of Prussia, now king, caused me to break off plans for my journey'. The 'young gentleman' whom Emanuel was about to accompany as tutor on the traditional grand tour (in this case to Austria, Italy, France and England) was Heinrich Christian Graf von Keyserlingk, son of the Russian ambassador to Dresden, Reichsgraf Hermann von Keyserlingk, for whom Sebastian had composed the Goldberg Variations. The Reichsgraf had been a friend of Sebastian for some years. Here was a chance for foreign travel, of the kind that Emanuel would later regret not having experienced; but an offer from the 26-year-old crown prince, the future Frederick II of Prussia, represented an opportunity not to be refused – even though Frederick, in these last two years at Ruppin and Rheinsberg before he became king, would pursue music as he pursued literature and philosophy: rather clandestinely, on borrowed money, under the disapproval of his father.

Some 17 musicians, devoted primarily to chamber music in which Frederick took a leading part as flautist, were already in Frederick's employ when Emanuel was engaged, including J. J. Quantz, C. H. and J. G. Graun, and Franz and Johann Benda. Several interesting anecdotes notwithstanding, it is not known exactly why Frederick chose Emanuel to be his harpsichordist; it seems likely that the royal flautist must have heard of him through Quantz or the Grauns, all of whom came from Saxony and knew the Bachs (Wilhelm Friedemann, at the age of 15, had been under J. G. Graun's tutelage for almost a year). Frederick might also have been favourably impressed by Emanuel's production, by 1738, of no less than ten chamber works involving the flute. It is even possible that Emanuel laid the groundwork for his new position while still in Frankfurt: among the Prussian royalty musically honoured there in 1737 was Margrave Friedrich Wilhelm, then a student at the university; perhaps Friedrich Wilhelm had brought favourable word of Emanuel back to Berlin (presuming Emanuel was involved in this little congratulatory cantata, of which only the text survives). Whatever prompted Frederick's interest in Emanuel, the unofficial nature of the musical establishment at Ruppin and Rheinsberg prevented the regularization of the appointment until after Frederick's accession to the throne in 1740. Emanuel's salary was among the lowest paid to the musicians: a budget-list of 1744–5 in Frederick's hand shows it to be 300 thalers, as against 2000 each for Quantz and C. H. Graun, 1200 for J. G. Graun and 800 for Franz Benda. In the same season, the leading castrato received 3000 thalers.

2. BERLIN. Emanuel served Frederick the Great for nearly 30 years. He writes proudly in the autobiographical sketch that in 1740 he 'had the honour of accompanying in Charlottenburg, alone at the harpsichord, the first flute solo played by Frederick as king'. His basic role at court, as accompanist in the royal chamber music, did not change. It is charmingly illustrated in Menzel's famous and historically meticulous painting, now in the Neue Nationalgalerie, Berlin, of a candlelit musical evening in the splendid rococo music room of Sans Souci (see fig.10): Frederick is soloist; C. H. Graun, as director of the Opera, stands to one side as an observer, amid members of the royal family, cabinet ministers and visiting intellectuals; Emanuel and a few other musicians provide the accompaniment; and

10. Flute concert at Sans Souci: painting (1852) by Adolf Menzel in the Neue Nationalgalerie, Berlin; Frederick the Great plays the flute, Carl Philipp Emanuel Bach is at the keyboard, and Quantz stands on the extreme right

Quantz stands by to supervise the performance. What the painting could not show is that at various times the 'accompanist' had to fulfil the roles of soloist, teacher, coach, transposer, Kapellmeister, composer and arranger. These chamber-music evenings usually took place at least three times a week; Emanuel alternated every four weeks with a second harpsichordist (from 1741, C. F. Schale; 1744–56, J. S. Bach's pupil Christoph Nichelmann; from 1756, C. F. C. Fasch).

Being in close company with Frederick the Great – a monarch whose quite good if not completely professional flute playing was his way of resting from the prosecution of unprecedented social reforms and international warfare – and working daily with musicians of considerable distinction must have been immensely stimulating at first to the young Emanuel. The sections on accompaniment in his *Versuch über die wahre Art das Clavier zu spielen*, or *Essay on the True Art of Playing Keyboard Instruments*, among the most important such writings ever published, were largely an outgrowth of his work as Frederick's accompanist. He was on hand at precisely the right time to witness Frederick's personal establishment of the great Berlin Opera, which opened its doors in 1742. As the Italian singers, French dancers, extra instrumentalists and all the other ingredients of *opera seria* poured into Berlin, as Emanuel heard the operas of Hasse and C. H. Graun, in many cases for the first time, the dramatic style crept into his compositions. He never composed an opera – Johann Christian was the only Bach son young enough to escape totally the Protestant-organist syndrome so antithetic to that genre – but instead he channelled his

dramatic impulse into instrumental works, beginning with the Prussian Sonatas dedicated to Frederick in 1743 and the Württemberg Sonatas dedicated to his pupil the Duke Carl Eugen of Württemberg in 1744. This dramatic impulse, which was to take many forms, continued to influence his style.

Yet the flowering of music under Frederick the Great was not without its disadvantages, the most discouraging of which was Frederick's arch-conservative musical taste. Almost no operas but those of Graun and Hasse were heard at the opera house. It became apparent that staple fare at the chamber-music soirées would be the flute concertos of Quantz, played in rotation or interspersed with compositions by Frederick himself, with Frederick as soloist. Quantz, the only member of the ensemble privileged to compliment the king with an occasional, judicious 'bravo', received bonuses for making new flutes and writing new compositions to supplement his salary (already enormous for an instrumental musician); he eventually composed about 300 flute concertos for Frederick's exclusive use. Another important member of the chamber group, Franz Benda, writing his autobiography in 1763, stated proudly that by that date he had accompanied 'our truly great Frederick' in flute concertos 'at least ten thousand times'. That kind of statistic held little appeal for Emanuel. Emanuel's works were seldom heard; his true importance was never understood by the king; and his independence of mind offended a monarch who was accustomed to obedience in artistic matters as in civil and political ones. The other accompanists could readily accommodate themselves to Frederick's free rhythms, his occasional missed notes, his narrow musical outlook; for Emanuel it was not so easy, and Frederick knew it.

Emanuel's application for a Kantorate in Zittau in 1753 attests to his dissatisfaction with his Berlin position. In 1755 his salary was still 300 thalers, while that paid to J. F. Agricola and Christoph Nichelmann, both his pupils, was raised above his own; only after he threatened to resign was his pay increased to 500 thalers. In the same year he applied unsuccessfully for the post of Thomaskantor in Leipzig, just vacated by Gottlob Harrer, his father's successor. From 1756 to 1763 the Seven Years War caused the curtailment of all music in Berlin. In 1758 a Russian attack on the city made it necessary for Emanuel and his family to move for some months to Zerbst. During the war all court employees were paid in paper money whose severe depreciation more than offset Emanuel's increase in salary. At the end of the war, in 1762–3, his salary was still 500 thalers. Frederick, fighting for Prussia's existence, rapidly lost interest in his musical establishment, and in the postwar years this interest returned only in the most attenuated form.

Berlin offered compensations to a court musician. Emanuel had time for a substantial amount of teaching, both within the court and privately. His most important pupil was his own young half-brother, Johann Christian, who lived in Emanuel's home from Sebastian's death in 1750 to 1754. Other notable pupils were J. A. P. Schulz and F. W. Rust. There was also time for composing and writing on a very large scale, as the list of works below testifies. His most influential compositions in the Berlin years were the solo keyboard pieces making up w48 and 49 (H24–9 and H30–34, 36; the Prussian and Württemberg sonatas), w50 (H126, 136–40, 'Sonatas with Varied Repeats'), parts of w62 and 65, w63 (H70–75, the 'sample pieces' published with the *Essay*), w67 (H300) and the *Essay* itself. The first part of the *Essay* appeared in 1753, a year after Quantz's book on playing the flute. It established Emanuel's reputation as the leading keyboard teacher of his time. The main causes of its inception were Emanuel's desire for a creative outlet outside court circles, and the theorizing–explaining atmosphere of mid-18th-century Berlin, the city that Frederick had made into a centre of Enlightenment thought. Quantz, Marpurg, Kirnberger, Sulzer, Agricola, Krause and other treatise-writing members of the rather pedantic 'Berlin School' exercised a not altogether wholesome influence on Emanuel; but in his great *Essay* he produced the best kind of treatise, permanently valuable not only for its broad and practical approach but also in the clarity of its language and organization.

Although he undoubtedly respected his fellow Berlin musicians, Emanuel's best friends were from literary and commercial circles: the poets Lessing, Ramler and Gleim; the banking family of Itzig, including Sara Levy, Mendelssohn's great-aunt, whose assiduously collected library of Bach family music became a major source of Bachiana; and the hard-working burghers and officials among whom he could escape from court protocol at the Berlin Monday Club, and whose wives he honoured in little Frenchified musical portraits for the keyboard.

In 1744 he married Johanna Maria Danneman, daughter of a wine merchant. Of their two sons and one daughter, none was a musician. Johann August [?Adam] (1745–89) became a lawyer. The second son,

born in 1748, was named Johann Sebastian after his grandfather; he was a painter of some accomplishment, a pupil of A. F. Oeser, but his promising career was cut short by his death in Rome in 1778 after a prolonged illness. His medical expenses were high during more than five months of intense suffering and, as Emanuel described it, 'three of the most frightful life-and-death operations'. A letter from Emanuel to Forkel, in which as much sorrow seems to be expressed over the expense as over the suffering, has often been cited as an example of Emanuel's miserliness; but a reading of the entire letter shows that Emanuel is asking Forkel's assistance towards the quick publication of a new set of sonatas as a means of dealing with a real financial crisis. The daughter, Anna Carolina Philippina (1747–1804), never married and, as neither of the sons had children, Emanuel's branch of the family died out in 1804.

In his household Emanuel continued the tradition of hospitality that he had known in his parents' home. Baldassare Galuppi was one of his visitors; Schulz and Fasch were among the young musicians for whom his house became a haven while they established themselves in Berlin. Sebastian visited him in 1741; a second visit in 1747, during which he met Frederick the Great, was the occasion of his composition of the *Musical Offering*.

On Sebastian's death in 1750, Emanuel came into possession of about a third of Sebastian's musical estate, along with the 'Alt-Bachischen Archiv' of music, portraits and documents from earlier generations of Bachs. Emanuel has often been criticized for offering for sale in September 1756, after the outbreak of the Seven Years War, one of the most valuable parts of this legacy, the copper engraving plates of the *Art of Fugue*, from which only 30 copies had been printed; but, without attempting to excuse any mercenary attitude on his part, it should be understood that his aim was further publication of the work, and that the 60-odd plates were a heavy mass to move should evacuation of Berlin become necessary. Emanuel was, in fact, an honourable and effective guardian of Sebastian's music and other Bach family treasures important to Bach research; most of the Bachiana now extant were owned by him. Less defensible is his treatment of his stepmother after Sebastian's death: for nearly ten years, until her own 'almswoman's' funeral in 1760, Anna Magdalena subsisted mainly on charity. Geographic separation and the difficulty of communication in wartime are reasons that do not go far in justifying this behaviour on the part of the Bach sons, especially Emanuel, who was in the best position to help her. In any case, Sebastian's sons were sadly distant from one another, and not only geographically (except for a little friendly business communication between Emanuel and Johann Christoph Friedrich, his half-brother in Bückeburg).

When the Seven Years War ended in 1763 and it became apparent that Frederick was not going to compensate his musicians for their losses, Emanuel made his resentment known and intensified his search for new career opportunities. For many years Emanuel had engaged in a correspondence of almost a filial character with his godfather, Telemann, in Hamburg, exchanging music, discussing aspects of Emanuel's duties at court and Telemann's position as Kantor and music director in Hamburg. Telemann's death in June 1767 opened up

11. Carl Philipp Emanuel Bach (centre), Pastor Sturm (right) and the artist Andreas Stöttrup: pen and ink drawing with wash (1784) by Andreas Stöttrup in the Kunsthalle, Hamburg

a possible avenue of escape. Emanuel's competitors for the vacated post were well-known musicians – his brother J. C. F. Bach, H. F. Raupach and J. H. Rolle; but after five months of deliberation Emanuel was chosen. Telemann, before his death, had probably suggested Emanuel as his replacement, and Emanuel's candidature was helped by the recommendation of G. M. Telemann, grandson of the deceased. Procuring his

release from the king, who was displeased with his attitude, proved difficult; only after repeated requests and a trumped-up plea of ill-health was it granted. After all those years, and in spite of the antipathy between the two men, Frederick obviously continued to value his harpsichordist. Emanuel's health was probably satisfactory throughout his long life, except for severe attacks of gout and a tremor of the hands, both of which appeared fairly early in life. On his departure the king's sister Anna Amalia, who had been his friend (though not closely associated with him) and to whom in 1760 he had dedicated his first collection of 'Sonatas with Varied Repeats' W50 (H126, 136–40), named him her Kapellmeister *von Haus aus*. In March 1768, at the age of 54, the most famous keyboard player and teacher in Europe assumed his new position in Hamburg, being formally installed on 19 April with an elaborate ceremony, according to the local custom, during which he delivered an inaugural speech, 'de nobilissimo artis musicae fine'.

3. HAMBURG. Emanuel's duties in the new post were similar to Sebastian's in Leipzig: to act as Kantor of the Johanneum (the Lateinschule) and director of music in the five principal churches. According to church and city regulations more than a century old at the time of his arrival in Hamburg, the position required that the Kantor teach both musical and non-musical subjects in the Johanneum; but Telemann had been permitted to relinquish the teaching of non-musical subjects, and Emanuel was allowed the additional privilege of paying a helper to teach music in the school. Still, the workload was enormous: to provide about 200 musical performances (including 10 Passions within 13 days) yearly among the five churches, as well as sacred music in the school, funeral music, cantatas for the inaugurations of an endless procession of new pastors, congratulatory cantatas or musical celebrations for various new city officials, music for school plays and even for public examinations at the school, birthday cantatas for prominent citizens, music for visiting royalty, etc. Like his predecessor Telemann, he naturally sought suitable music wherever he could find it to supplement his own compositions, often manufacturing an 'inaugural music' here or a Passion there out of bits and pieces of his own and others' works. After 20 years of such demands on Emanuel and the students and town musicians under his directorship in Hamburg, it is no wonder that after his death the 'Report concerning the New Arrangement of Church Music' of 1789–90 recommended halving the yearly number of performances of concerted music in the five churches, both to improve the quality of the performances and to spare the performers who, according to the report, were often overwhelmed with work.

The bright side was that Emanuel throve on all this activity. Although his basic salary was a fairly modest 600 Hamburg marks (a rector was paid 1000), there were extra fees attached to most of his duties outside the school and churches, and he found himself rather well off financially. The many administrative tasks required by his position – recruitment and payment of performers and copyists, keeping expense accounts etc – were handled by him with easy competence. Life in the free Hanseatic city-state of Hamburg, completely under the influence of commercial enterprises, was informal, busy and cheerful, a welcome change from court life. Emanuel found himself very much at home, even though Hamburg could not compare with Berlin in musical sophistication. As in Berlin, his closest friends were not musicians but poets, writers, professors, burghers and intellectuals who, like him, had been attracted by the freedom and openness of Hamburg; he was particularly close to Professor J. G. Büsch, the famous writer on mercantile topics. In his attractive home, decorated with

portraits of more than 150 well-known musicians, Bach entertained Lessing (now living in Hamburg), Klopstock, J. H. Voss, Gerstenberg and the preacher–teacher Sturm, all poets whose verses he set to music; the historian C. D. Ebeling, one of the translators of Burney's *Present State of Music in Germany* into German; the publisher J. J. C. Bode; and the philosopher J. A. H. Reimarus.

A visit to Emanuel's home in 1773 was the source of Burney's famous description, in his *Present State of Music*, of Emanuel's rapturous improvisation at the clavichord:

After dinner, which was elegantly served, and chearfully eaten, I prevailed upon him to sit down again to a clavichord, and he played, with little intermission, till near eleven o'clock at night. During this time, he grew so animated and possessed, that he not only played, but looked like one inspired. His eyes were fixed, his under lip fell, and drops of effervescence distilled from his countenance. He said, if he were to be set to work frequently, in this manner, he should grow young again.

Among other musical visitors were J. F. Reichardt and Antonio Lotti. Gottfried van Swieten, while Austrian ambassador to the Prussian court, went from Berlin to Hamburg expressly to meet Emanuel, who wrote the six symphonies of W182 (H657–62) for him, and dedicated to him the third collection of keyboard pieces 'für Kenner und Liebhaber' ('for connoisseurs and amateurs'). Van Swieten's presentation in his Viennese concerts of music by Emanuel and especially Sebastian Bach was a source of inspiration to Mozart. Through repute and correspondence, Emanuel's circle of influence steadily widened. Diderot, seeking music for his harpsichord-playing daughter, wrote to him with a request for manuscripts of keyboard sonatas. Haydn had discovered one or two sets of his keyboard music (probably the Prussian and Württemberg sonatas) years earlier, and later testified that he was unable to leave the keyboard until he had played through them all. C. G. Neefe, Beethoven's teacher in Bonn, was one of the most dedicated and voluble admirers of Emanuel's music and his *Essay*, both of which were basic to his teaching of Beethoven. Emanuel's communication with Klopstock, Claudius and Gerstenberg, dealing with the aesthetic boundary between word and note (a popular concern of the 'Sturm und Drang' generation of poets), casts light on the *empfindsamer Stil* in his instrumental works, as does his learned and detailed announcement, in the *Hamburger unpartheiischer Correspondent*, of the first volume of Forkel's history of music.

As the only musician of major stature in a city built on free enterprise, Emanuel found many opportunities to exercise his entrepreneurial talents. Only a few weeks after his inauguration ceremony he announced in the *Hamburger unpartheiischer Correspondent*, 'with the permission of high authority', a concert series 'at which, along with a variety of vocal pieces and other musical things, he will be heard in harpsichord concertos. The start will be at five-thirty. Price of tickets, two marks'. In some of these concerts he directed performances of choral and dramatic works by such composers as C. H. Graun, Hasse, Telemann, Jommelli, Haydn, Handel, Gluck and J. S. Bach, as well as his own music. After a few seasons he discontinued such productions because of too much competition from (as one journalist put it) 'clubs, assemblies, lotteries, picnics, balls and banquets'. Other ventures were more successful: his teaching (F. J. Hérold, Niels Schiörring, Baron von Grotthus, Dussek and N. J. Hüllmandel were among his Hamburg pupils);

his *Musikalisches Vielerley* of 1770, which was a serially issued compilation designed for the popular market and consisting of keyboard pieces, arias and songs with keyboard accompaniment, and chamber music, mostly by such former Berlin colleagues as J. G. Graun, C. F. C. Fasch and Kirnberger, in addition to pieces of his own; his personal management of the sale of the librettos of his church music, in the matter-of-fact mixing of commerce and religion that was characteristic of Hamburg; and his actions as his own publisher and advertiser. The announcement in the *Correspondent* for 20 October 1773 of his forthcoming settings of the Cramer Psalms W196 (H733) is typical in giving the names of his selling agents in a far-flung, and alphabetically arranged, list of cities: Berlin, Brunswick, Bückeburg, Celle, Copenhagen, Dresden, Eisenach, Göttingen, Gotha, Hamburg (not himself, but no less than three other persons), Hanover, Leipzig, Ludwigslust, Parchim, (St) Petersburg, Riga, Schleswig, Stettin and Weimar. Later this kind of list would be extended to include such capitals as Moscow, Vienna, Warsaw, London, Prague and Stockholm. The market for the bulk of his published works, both popular ('für Liebhaber') and serious ('für Kenner'), was always reasonably satisfying.

In the Hamburg period, the last 20 years of his life, Emanuel was required to represent himself as a composer of church music; in all his Berlin years his only important church work was the excellent *Magnificat* of 1749. As a result of the demand for sheer quantity, his church music generally is the poorest part of his output. Much of it is pasticcio; every one of the 21 Passions so impressively listed in the *Verzeichniss des musikalischen Nachlasses*, for instance, is a mixture of original work and portions of works by such composers as Sebastian Bach, (2) Johann Christoph Bach and Telemann, often with new instrumental parts added to the borrowed sections. The church compositions written for publication, on the other hand, are superior creations from a church-music era hardly noted for superiority, and many non-liturgical choruses, songs, arias and cantatas composed by Emanuel in this period were works of high reputation. But the habit of casting his finest thoughts in instrumental terms was too firmly established. Above everything else in importance are the six keyboard collections of sonatas, rondos and fantasias 'für Kenner und Liebhaber' (W55–9, 61), begun in Berlin and continuing to appear almost up to the end of his life, written to please himself in spite of criticism over their difficulty and declining numbers of subscribers. Nearly as important are ten symphonies (W182–3; H657–66), 12 keyboard concertos (W41–7; H410, 469–79) and certain chamber works (W79, 89–91, 93–5; H522–35, 537–9).

Throughout his career it seems that it was necessary for Emanuel to observe two standards in his compositions, his own and those of his present patron or public; even the titles of his compositions reflect this duality. Articulate and idealistic, he nevertheless liked the practical more than the theoretical (e.g. in his *Essay*), making music more than discussing it. Nothing illustrates his practical turn of mind better than the list of works below: its most striking characteristic is the number of arrangements, alternative versions, revisions and variants it contains. If a piece did not suit it was retailored.

His criticisms of shallow music critics seem strikingly modern, and in his insistence on craftsmanship along with originality even in the most 'popular' composition he rose above the weaknesses of the post-Baroque age. In his edition (with Kirnberger) of Sebastian's chorales, in his long correspondence with Forkel as preparation for Forkel's essay on Sebastian, and in the detailed and telling comparison of Sebastian's music with Handel's that he sent anonymously in 1788 to the editor of the *Allgemeine deutsche Bibliothek*, he showed himself increasingly aware of his father's greatness. He was far from being the counterpoint-hater Burney opportunely described him to be.

Emanuel died of an acute 'chest ailment'. In 1795, when Haydn, returning to Vienna from London via Hamburg, stopped at the Bach household hoping to meet Emanuel, he found only the daughter surviving. The family, except for the son who died in Rome, are buried in the vault of St Michael's Church in Hamburg (the grave was discovered by Heinrich Miesner in 1925). Emanuel's wife and daughter were apparently well enough provided for after his death, and were able to derive income from the sale of his works along with his rich collection of other Bachiana, all listed with considerable thoroughness (though in some parts misleadingly) in the *Verzeichniss des musikalischen Nachlasses des verstorbenen Capellmeisters Carl Philipp Emanuel Bach*, published under the guidance of his widow in Hamburg in 1790. Although the collection of portraits of musicians was scattered, most of the music was acquired by Georg Pölchau, later librarian of the Berlin Singakademie. The bulk of the Pölchau collection, together with several other Berlin collections rich in autographs and manuscript copies of Emanuel's music, is now in the two divisions of the Berlin Staatsbibliothek (see Kast). Another extensive, but curiously unrelated, collection of Emanuel's music, in clear manuscript copies (with very few autographs), was made by a remarkably assiduous admirer, the Schwerin court organist J. J. H. Westphal (apparently unrelated to the Hamburg publisher J. C. Westphal). This collection was assembled almost under Emanuel's supervision – that is, in a correspondence with Westphal during the last few years of Emanuel's life. It was acquired virtually intact, along with Westphal's meticulous thematic catalogue of it, by F. J. Fétis, and purchased from the Fétis estate in 1871 by the Belgian government. It is now divided between the Conservatory and the Royal Library in Brussels, and has been augmented through the purchase of important items from the libraries of other admirers of Emanuel Bach, such as the 19th-century physician Richard Wagener.

The *Thematisches Verzeichnis* of 1905, made by Alfred Wotquenne of the Brussels Conservatory, is essentially little more than a copy of the Westphal catalogue. It provides incipits of first movements only, and does not describe or give locations of sources. Titles in the Wotquenne catalogue are frequently Westphal's rather than the composer's, attached as part of the categorizing process.

4. KEYBOARD MUSIC. Music for solo keyboard instrument was central to C. P. E. Bach's long career, and remained so even when he was most pressed to fulfil commitments involving other media. The clavichord – specifically, the large instrument built to his exacting requirements – remained his most personal mode of expression, although he composed more and

more for the piano in the last two decades of his life. His advocacy of the clavichord persisted in spite of the fact that the instrument had never been widely accepted outside Germany and was being speedily forgotten even there, just as he brought it to the artistic peak of its existence. Any study of the *empfindsamer* ('highly sensitive') *Stil*, of which he was the chief exponent, must begin with an understanding (or better, a reconstruction) of the best traditions of 18th-century clavichord playing, and by extension, of 18th-century piano playing. The fantasias above all, but also most of the rondos and about a third of the sonatas, often demand alternations of mood so abrupt as to be difficult to perform on the relatively impersonal modern piano (especially in a large hall), and nearly unperformable altogether on the harpsichord: sudden remote modulations, startling departures from supposedly cursive statements, melodies shaped like the pitch patterns of emotional speech, painstakingly exact dynamic indications depicting an orator's emphases, rhythms imitating an actor's hesitations and changes of pace. The source of these features was the French-created atmosphere of rapprochement between music and literature then penetrating northern Europe, especially among 'Sturm und Drang' poets, many of whom were Emanuel's friends. Emanuel's own part in this rapprochement took place, not in the seemingly more suitable genres of song or opera, but in the realm of pure instrumental music; and his goal, conscious or unconscious, was to speak emotively without words.

Played properly on the clavichord or early piano, or even on the modern piano in relatively intimate surroundings, such passages can be made to sound not only original and forceful, but also coherent; for these are not the meanderings of a dilettante. Even in the most *empfindsam* work there is never a moment when the hand of the consummate craftsman is not in evidence. Emanuel's famous complaints about the shallowness and faddishness of other composers, especially composers in the *galant* style, have to be taken seriously today, just as they were, because of his formidable reputation, in his own. The fantasias, even when they are so 'free' as to be partly or wholly without bar-lines, are usually in clear tripartite or rondo-like forms, and their harmonic progressions, daring in microcosm, fall obediently under the rule in the *Essay* that the principal tonality be impressed upon the memory of the listener.

Most of his keyboard works are in a more conservative idiom, however, and many of these, such as the 'Easy Keyboard Sonatas' w53 (H164–5, 180–83) and the sonatas 'for ladies' w54 (H184–5, 204–7), are frankly written for the popular market. Before 1740 Emanuel showed his heavy indebtedness to Sebastian in this genre, and throughout his career he perpetuated the brilliant harpsichord idiom of Domenico Scarlatti. His keyboard sonatas are usually in three movements, quick–slow–quick. Slow movements are generally through-composed, and outer movements are in binary form with a recapitulation in the second half, marking him as one of the scores of composers already using sonata form. That is only an incidental aspect of his style.

The keyboard works show that his gradual (though never total) abandonment of contrapuntal and continuous-expansion techniques was not matched by a corresponding adoption of the regular phraseology and slow harmonic rhythm of the Classical style. Instead, he

pursued the *empfindsam* mode on the one hand, and on the other created a kind of motivic variation that must be considered a cornerstone of his style. This technique appears in many different guises. In his sonata-form recapitulations the opening theme is usually given a new twist as soon as it reappears. In the rondos of the 'Kenner und Liebhaber' series the rondo theme is subjected to every imaginable reshaping; in any restatement literal repetition seems to be abhorrent, and is endured only briefly, for establishing formal signposts. Emanuel's many revisions of sonatas nearly always involve reshapings of motif or melody, but not alteration of form. On the other hand, the urge for varied restatement sometimes has formal consequences, as in the varied repetitions of entire movements in the sonatinas for harpsichord and orchestra, or in the first movement of a sonata of 1758 or later (w65/32; H135), which consists of six statements of one musical sentence, the last five being variants of the first. The idea of varied restatement is raised to a formal principle in the 'Amalian' sonatas 'with altered repeats' w50 (H126, 136–40; 1760) as well as in the single-movement 'Short and Easy Keyboard Pieces' w113–14 (H193–203, 1766; H228–38, 1768), where the repeats of binary form are a point of departure for written-out varied repetitions in place of the traditional improvisation of varied repetitions. Curiously, none of those procedures resulted in important development sections in his sonata forms; his kind of 'development' is present in nearly all parts of the movement. Having satisfied his desire for variation in this all-pervading way, he wrote only a few traditional sets of variations, and these, along with his numerous minuets, polonaises, *solfeggi* and other single-movement keyboard pieces, were designed primarily to fill pages in the popular collections of the time.

5. ORCHESTRAL AND CHAMBER MUSIC. If the relatively inaccessible medium of the clavichord still impedes our understanding of Emanuel's solo keyboard works, no such impediment exists for the keyboard concertos. There he is seen as a harpsichord virtuoso, not improvising rapturously at home for a Burney or a Reichardt, but performing brilliant, fiery compositions on the concert stage for a large audience. Emanuel and Johann Christian form perhaps the chief link between the harpsichord concertos of their father (who virtually created the genre) and the piano concertos of Mozart. Not surprisingly, Emanuel's concertos are a blend of the Bach–Vivaldi type of ritornello procedure with the principles of sonata form, yet they should be regarded not as leading to Mozart but as the finished and sophisticated apex of the north German concerto style. Their standard movement plan is quick–slow–quick. They show a fine balance between soloist and orchestra, with each having opportunity to sound assertive. These more public works are painted with a broader brush than are the compositions for keyboard alone. They are much more homophonic and slower in harmonic rhythm, often with long stretches of repeated notes in the bass. Whereas sequences are fairly rare in the music for keyboard alone, here they are too frequent; they seem to be the standard mode of transition from one key to another, usually via a circle-of-5ths progression, with arrival at the desired key often being announced by a harmonic side-slip. Yet the tutti and solo themes are delightfully flamboyant, the opportunities for virtuoso display are

12. Autograph MS of the opening of C. P. E. Bach's 'Clavier-Fantasie mit Begleitung einer Violine, C. P. E. Bachs Empfindungen' in F♯ minor, composed 1787 (D-B Mus.ms.Bach P 361)

abundant, and the slow movements are elegiac poems of considerable beauty. As the list of works below shows, the ten concertos for non-keyboard solo instruments are all alternative versions of keyboard concertos; these are in no way inferior to their keyboard counterparts, and the adaptation ensures that each is eminently idiomatic to its solo instrument.

Apparently alone among north German composers of his time, Emanuel wrote 'sonatinas' for a solo harpsichord (two require two solo harpsichords) with orchestra. Because of the concertato and often quite virtuoso nature of their harpsichord parts, they are categorized in the list below as 'miniature concertos', for want of a better term and in spite of their often inflated proportions. Clearly experimental works, they resemble not only the concerto but also the suite, in their general adherence to a single key throughout, with fluctuations between major and minor modes; the Viennese divertimento, in having two to ten sections or movements, and in the lightness or even triviality of their musical content; and the sonata in their use of diminutive binary and sonata forms (hence the term 'sonatina'). Of the 12 such sonatinas that are indisputably genuine, not counting versions with altered instrumentation, four are played through without pause, and six are stretched out by repetitions of previous sections or movements, with the repetitions usually consisting of 'varied repeats'. The most extreme use of this technique is in W97 (H450), whose plan can be expressed as $ABA^1B^1A^2CDC^1EC^2$. This is music for light entertainment only.

Emanuel's chamber music reliably depicts his conservative side from the very beginning to the very end of his career, and it may be taken as illustrative of the whole development of north German chamber music between the late Baroque and high Classical eras: he gradually learnt to prefer written-out keyboard accompaniments to the continuo, he helped preside over the disappearance (by about 1756 in his own works) of the trio sonata, he adopted the clarinet and the piano, and in his best chamber works he slowly abandoned Baroque contrapuntal–canonic texture in favour not of galant simplicity but of equal importance among non-imitative parts.

It is important to single out his chamber works that have a leading or concertante, rather than accompanying, keyboard part, as (following Sebastian's lead) he was among the first to make keyboard players leaders rather than followers in all kinds of instrumental ensembles. Still, his chamber music remains comparatively conservative, no doubt largely because of the reactionary taste of his royal patron in Berlin. He returned again and again to canonic entries at the beginnings of movements or sections. The solo sonata with continuo accompaniment was never completely given up. The genre of the string quartet was ignored. The movement plans of the ensemble sonatas show no clear preference for the quick–slow–quick pattern. Except for an abortive experiment with programme music in a trio sonata of 1749 (W161/1; H579) and an accompanied version (W80; H536) of his 'Empfindungen' fantasia W67 (H300), there is little evidence of the empfindsamer Stil. In chamber music, as elsewhere, this keen businessman turned out a steady stream of readily marketable, but nevertheless delightful, single-movement trifles for small instrumental ensembles: minuets, polonaises, marches, 'little pieces', 'little sonatas', even pieces for mechanical instruments. Not until the

accompanied sonatas of 1775–7 (W89–91; H522–34) and the quartets (not trios) of 1788 (W93–5; H537–9) is there a clear turn to the Classical style; in the former, the accompanying instruments – essential, not optional – are insistently independent, and in the latter the Beethovenian piano quartet is adumbrated.

In considering the symphonies the empfindsamer Stil is met again. Except perhaps the first four, these are not 'easy pre-Classical symphonies'. They bear little resemblance to the galant and sometimes watery symphonies of Johann Christian Bach and his stylistic contemporaries except in their quick–slow–quick movement plan. Not one of them begins with a triad in three hammer-strokes. Most are based on the idea that the day of the Italian opera sinfonia is past, and that a symphony, in order to stand alone, must sound arresting and audacious in its first movement, meditatively beautiful in its second and cheerful or innocent in its third. Most of the audacities are tonal. The first movement of W182/3 (H659) begins with five bars of diatonic broken triads in C, which come to rest on a unison A♭; the 'recapitulation' consists only of those same five bars, stopping this time on a B♭, which begins (without pause) the Adagio second movement, whose key is E. The first movement of W183/1 (H663) so successfully avoids perfect cadences that it is not solidly in any key at all until bar 115, shortly before the recapitulation begins. The themes in all movements of the symphonies, but especially the first movements, are wide-ranging and compelling, one theme being derived from another in a modification of Baroque continuous-expansion technique; there is seldom a feeling of real thematic contrast. The texture is homophonic except for the tossing of motifs back and forth. Emanuel's handling of the orchestral instruments is remarkably sensitive and individual, especially in the profoundly poetical slow movements; the woodwind are handled with great mastery, and solo passages and chamber-music combinations are woven into the orchestral fabric with a sophistication hardly surpassed in the 18th century. Some formal and expressive devices almost become trademarks: sudden interruptions of forward movement and changes in tempo or dynamics; the connection of movements without pause, often by a transition whose modulatory purpose is perhaps too obvious; the truncated or aborted recapitulation; the statement of intact themes on so many tonal levels that the perception of principal and subsidiary key areas is blurred; and the comparative conservatism of third movements, which often sound a bit anti-climactic. It needs to be emphasized, even when notions about evolution in musical form are suffering the disrepute they deserve, that Emanuel's use of formal patterns must be assessed in its own terms rather than in the terms of later musical eras: truncated recapitulations and the blurring of key areas, for instance, may well be cause for admiration in the contexts where they occur.

6. VOCAL MUSIC. Emanuel wrote about 300 songs (lieder, Oden, Gesänge, Psalmen) with keyboard accompaniment. All but a few are miniatures in comparison to the standard song repertory, and are strophic, with all strophes (sometimes over two dozen) sung to the same music (on average about 20 bars in length) and simple in musical design and texture. Comparing them with 19th-century lieder on a qualitative basis would be illogical since, like most of the songs of Emanuel's

contemporaries, they were intended to heighten awareness of the poem rather than to draw attention to the music for its own sake. Goethe's complaint about the too-sensitive, and hence smothering, musical expression of every line of a poem in through-composed songs could never have been levelled against Emanuel's songs as a group.

Once the genre is understood, it is seen at its highest level in Emanuel's works. The typical texture is three parts, fully written out, with the voice line doubling the upper part. The harmony is often so thin that one is tempted to fill it out, especially on short acquaintance with a work (modern editors have too frequently succumbed to this temptation). The restraint and dignity of the settings – especially of the sacred poems, which make up about two-thirds of the total – are Classical in the best sense rather than merely simple; Emanuel generally escaped the dryness characteristic of the 'ode manufacturers' of his time, notably through sensitive portrayal of general emotional atmosphere and carefully wrought melodic interchanges (subtle effects which many modern editors have obscured by being too heavy-handed with additions to the harmony). The sacred texts, most of which are by Gellert, Cramer or Sturm, are universal in their appeal, expressing hope, thanks, joy and reassurance, frequently a bit tedious (especially after a dozen verses) but seldom doctrinaire or in bad taste. The secular songs celebrate nature, mythology, romantic love, fellowship, the drinking of good German wine and the rewards of virtue.

The huge demand for choral music during Emanuel's Hamburg years affected him in several striking ways. It came just when the long and tragic decline of Lutheran church music was beginning and when constant novelty was more highly valued than quality and tradition; small wonder that as an enemy of superficiality he found such a demand uninspiring. And it was surely obvious to Emanuel that the height of that fading tradition had been most fully embodied in the church music of his father. Thus, on the one hand, he satisfied the undiscriminating appetites of his congregations and audiences by more or less anonymously pasting together great quantities of choral music from various quickly composed or prefabricated materials; on the other, he preserved his integrity – in the choral works actually issued under his name – by successfully coming to grips with a problem that defeated many lesser choral composers of his time, doing so not so much through the aid of his family inheritance as in spite of it. The problem may be simply described as the necessity of building one's own structure in the presence of a venerable and imposing edifice. For Emanuel, solving the problem was primarily a matter of rejection, substitution and modification.

The technique most often rejected was counterpoint. Even the *Magnificat* of 1749, which shows Sebastian's influence on nearly every page, contains only one contrapuntal movement, the 'Sicut erat in principio' (a fugue whose theme has often been compared with that of the Kyrie in the Mozart Requiem); in the other movements counterpoint appears only in briefly canonic treatments of new lines of text. Among substitutes for contrapuntal interest are chromaticism, as in the first movement of the totally homophonic oratorio *Die Israeliten in der Wüste* of 1769, or in the continual reharmonizations of a single motif that comprise the *Zwey Litaneyen* of 1786 in their entirety; remarkably colourful orchestration, as in the accompanied recitatives

of the *Auferstehung und Himmelfahrt Jesu* (1777–80); and minute attention to dynamic levels, as in a 'Halleluja' duet celebrating dawn in the *Morgengesang am Schöpfungsfeste* (1783), where continually rising groups of three quavers – miniature sunrises – are individually marked 'piano–crescendo'. Modification of his artistic inheritance takes place in such procedures as simplification of ritornello procedure, where the orchestra presents a systematically returning statement that serves both as ritornello and as accompaniment to broad chordal statements by the chorus (e.g. the opening of the *Magnificat*); returning in homophonic garb to the ancient practice of writing for antiphonally opposed choirs of voices and instruments (the *Heilig* of 1778); following his famous inclination towards written-out varied repeats, as in the dramatic aria 'Donnre nur ein Wort der Macht' of *Die letzten Leiden des Erlösers* (1770), where the normal plan of the da capo aria is expanded to $ABA^1B^1A^2$; featuring a distinctive and uninterrupted instrumental figure or countermelody that runs like a single, bright thread through the fabric of an entire movement, sometimes for the sake of musical unity alone (as in the opening movement of the *Magnificat*) and sometimes for the most unmistakable and non-mystical kind of tone-painting (as in the chorus of thanks in the *Israeliten*, where a constantly flowing violin figure represents the water coming out of the rock that Moses struck). The texts and the music of the choral works generally stop short of the sentimentality then rife in Lutheran church music. At its best, and especially in *Morgengesang*, *Israeliten*, *Heilig* and *Auferstehung*, this music has a power and a universal appeal that point clearly towards Beethoven.

7. THE ESSAY. Emanuel's *Essay on the True Art of Playing Keyboard Instruments* is probably the most important practical treatise on music written in the 18th century. More widely owned and studied today than any of his compositions, it is a standard guide to 18th-century keyboard fingering, ornamentation, aesthetic outlook, continuo playing and improvisation. It led the way towards the acceptance of the modern standards of keyboard fingering (especially the use of the thumb) that had been inaugurated by his father and was to form a basis of 19th-century keyboard virtuosity. It stated the rules of embellishment in a clear and authoritative way at a time when scores of other treatises were compounding the confusion. (If, for instance, performers of today dutifully begin trills on the upper auxiliary note and give appoggiaturas the right duration – yet start both before the beat – it is their fault, not Emanuel's; if they take every word he wrote as unalterable gospel, on the other hand, it might well be Emanuel's fault for writing so clearly and convincingly.) While requiring technical mastery of the performer in no uncertain terms, Emanuel warned against empty virtuosity. Unlike the many inept discussions of continuo playing then being published (and which should probably never be resurrected), the *Essay* leads the reader steadily and clearly through mountains of detail on harmony at the keyboard. In the chapter on accompaniment it shows how, for the sake of spontaneity, the accompanist's written music may be considered only as an outline to be filled in or even changed during performance. And in the remarkable chapter on improvisation Emanuel demonstrated that, in his own time at least, inspiration had to be harnessed to the intellect and the improviser had to

know exactly where he was going, even when, as in his own case, 'his eyes were fixed, his under lip fell, and drops of effervesence distilled from his countenance'.

WORKS

Catalogues: *Verzeichniss des musikalischen Nachlasses . . . Carl Philipp Emanuel Bach* (Hamburg, 1790) [NV]

A. Wotquenne: *Thematisches Verzeichnis der Werke von Carl Philipp Emanuel Bach (1714–1788)* (Leipzig, 1905/R1964) [W]

E. Helm: *A New Thematic Catalog of the Works of Carl Philipp Emanuel Bach* (in preparation) [H]

Principal MS sources are *A-Wgm, B-Bc, Br, D-B, Bds, F-Pc, GB-Lbm* (for full information see H); individual MSS listed below contain versions different from the better-known form of a work. Nos. quoted refer to H unless otherwise indicated.

* – *alternative version*   † – *partial alternative version*

SOLO KEYBOARD

Editions: Le trésor de pianistes (Paris, 1861–72) [T]

Die Sechs Sammlungen von Sonaten, freien Fantasien und Rondos für Kenner und Liebhaber, ed. C. Krebs (Leipzig, 1895, rev. 2/1953 by L. Hoffmann-Erbrecht) [K]

Klavierwerke, ed. H. Schenker (Vienna, 1902) [S]

Ausgewählte Kompositionen, ed. H. Riemann (Leipzig, n.d.) [R]

Kleine Stücke für Klavier, ed. O. Vrieslander (Hanover, 1930) [VK]

Vier leichte Sonaten, ed. O. Vrieslander (Hanover, 1932) [VL]

Sonaten und Stücke, ed. K. Herrman (Leipzig, 1938) [HS]

Klavierstücke, ed. V. Luithlen and H. Kraus (Vienna, 1938) [LK]

Leichte Tänze und Stücke für Klavier, ed. K. Herrman (Hamburg, 1949) [HL]

Six Sonatas for Keyboard, ed. P. Friedheim (New York, 1967) [F]

Sei sonate . . . che all'augusta maesta di Federico II ré di Prussia (Nuremberg, 1742 or 1743) [1742]

Sei sonate . . . dedicate all'altezza serenissima di Carlo Eugenio duca di Wirtemberg (Nuremberg, 1744) [1744]

Sechs Sonaten . . . mit veränderten Reprisen (Berlin, 1760), ded. to Princess Amalia of Prussia [1760]

Fortsetzung von Sechs Sonaten (Berlin, 1761) [1761¹]

Musikalisches Allerley (Berlin, 1761) [1761²]

Musikalisches Mancherley (Berlin, 1762–3) [1762]

Zweyte Fortsetzung von sechs Sonaten (Berlin, 1763) [1763]

Clavierstücke verschiedener Art (Berlin, 1765) [1765]

Kurze und leichte Clavierstücke mit veränderten Reprisen und bey-gefügter Fingersetzung für Anfänger (Berlin, 1766) [1766¹]

Sechs leichte Clavier-Sonaten (Leipzig, 1766) [1766²]

Six sonates, op.1 (Paris, before 1768) [1768¹]

Kurze und leichte Clavierstücke mit veränderten Reprisen und bey-gefügter Fingersetzung, ii (Berlin, 1768) [1768²]

Six sonates . . . à l'usage des dames (Amsterdam, 1770) [1770¹]

Musikalisches Vielerley, ed. C. P. E. Bach (Hamburg, 1770) [1770²]

Sechs Clavier-Sonaten für Kenner und Liebhaber, i (Leipzig, 1779) [1779]

Clavier-Sonaten nebst einigen Rondos . . . für Kenner und Liebhaber, ii (Leipzig, 1780) [1780]

Clavier-Sonaten nebst einigen Rondos . . . für Kenner und Liebhaber, iii (Leipzig, 1781) [1781]

Clavier-Sonaten und freye Fantasien nebst einigen Rondos . . . für Kenner und Liebhaber, iv (Leipzig, 1783) [1783]

Clavier-Sonaten und freye Fantasien nebst einigen Rondos . . . für Kenner und Liebhaber, v (Leipzig, 1785) [1785]

Clavier-Sonaten und freye Fantasien nebst einigen Rondos . . . für Kenner und Liebhaber, vi (Leipzig, 1787) [1787]

Preludio e 6 sonate, org (Berlin, 1790) [1790]

Trois rondeaux (Vienna, c1791) [1791]

Trois sonates (Berlin, 1792) [1792]

Six fugues (Bonn and Cologne, n.d.) [n.d.]

H	W	
1	111	Menuet, C, 1731 (Leipzig, 1731)
2	62/1	Sonata, B♭, 1731, rev. 1744 (1761²); ed. in T
3–6	65/1–4	4 sonatas, F, a, d, e, 1731–3, rev. 1744; 5 ed. in T
7–12	64/1–6	6 sonatinas, F, G, a, e, D, E♭, 1734, rev. 1744; 7 rev., *D-Kll*; ed. K. Johnen (Frankfurt, 1952)
13	65/5	Sonata, e, 1735, rev. 1743
14	118/7 [269]	Minuet (by Locatelli) with variations, G, 1735 (Vienna, 1803)
15–19	65/6–10	5 sonatas, G, E♭, C, B♭, A, 1736–8, rev. 1743–4; 18 (1768¹); ed. in F
20	62/2	Sonata, G, 1739, in Nebenstunden der berlinischen Musen, i (Berlin, 1762)
21	65/11 [266]	Sonata, g, 1739 (1792); ed. in VL, T
22	62/3	Sonata, D, 1740, in F. W. Marpurg: Clavierstücke mit einem practischen Unterricht (Berlin, 1762–3)
23	65/12	Sonata, G, 1740, variant in *US-Wc*
24–9	48	6 sonatas, F, B♭, E, c, C, A, 1740–2 (1742); 28 pubd as by J. S. Bach (Hamburg, n.d.); ed. in T
30–34	49/1–2, 4, 3, 5	5 sonatas, a, A♭, B♭, e, E♭, 1742–3 (1744); ed. in T
35	65/13	Sonata, b, 1743; ed. in T
36	49/6	Sonata, b, 1744 (1744); ed. in T
37	52/4	Sonata, f♯, 1744 (1763); variant in W; ed. in R
38–41	62/4–7	4 sonatas, d, E, f, C, 1744, 38–9 in Oeuvres mêlées (Nuremberg, 1760–63), 40 (1761²), 41 in Collection récréative (Nuremberg, 1760–61); ed. in T
42	65/14	Sonata, D, 1744; ed. in VL
43	65/15	Sonata, G, 1745
	118/3	Minuetto con V variationi, C, 1745
45	122/1	Sinfonia, G, 1745 [*648]
46–9	65/16–19	4 sonatas, C, g, F, F, 1746, 48 (1768¹); 46 ed. in F, 47 ed. in T
50	52/1	Sonata, E♭, 1747 (1763); 2nd movt with 119, *D-GOl*
51–2	65/20 [268]; 65/21	2 sonatas, B♭, F, 1747, 51 as Grande sonate (Vienna and Leipzig, c1802); 51 ed. in T, R
53	69	Sonata 'a due tastature', d, 1747 (1790); variant, *D-GOl*; ed. J. Langlais (Chicago, 1957)
54	118/4	Arioso con VII variationi, F, 1747 (1768); ed. in VK
55–7	62/8; 65/22–3	3 sonatas, F, G, d, 1748, 55 (1768) and in Tonstücke . . . vom Herrn C. P. E. Bach und andern classischen Musikern (Berlin, 1762, 2/1774 as C. P. E. Bachs, Nichelmanns und Handels Sonaten und Fugen), 56 (1768); variants of 57, *D-B*, *US-Wc*; 55 ed. in T, 56 ed. in VL, 57 ed. in F
58–61	62/9–10; 65/24–5	4 sonatas, F, C, d, C, 1749, 58 in Oeuvres mêlées (Nuremberg, 1760–63), 59 (1762); 58–60 ed. in T
62	51/6	Sonata, G, 1750 (1761¹)
63	62/11	Sonata, G, 1750 (1761²); variant, *D-B*
64	65/26	Sonata, G, 1750
65	118/5	Allegretto con VI variationi, C, 1750; ed. in HL
66	62/12	Sonata, e, 1751 (1761²); ed. in T, LK (inc.)
67–8	62/13; 65/27	2 sonatas, D, g, 1752, 67 in Raccolta delle più nuove composizioni (Leipzig, 1756) and (1768¹); 68 ed. in T
69	118/1	24 Veränderungen über das Lied: Ich schlief, da träumte mir, F, 1752, variations 1–17 (1761²), variations 18–24 (1770²); also as Canzonetta with [15] variations (London, n.d.); as Was helfen mir tausend Ducaten, with 15 variations, *DS*
70–75	63/1–6; 202/M without text	18 Probestücke in 6 Sonaten, C, d, A, b, E♭, f, 1753; bound with exx. for *Versuch*, i [see 869]; nos.2–6 ed. in T, no.6 ed. in R
76	119/1	Duo in contrap. ad 8, 11 & 12 mit Anmerkungen, a, by 1754, in F. W. Marpurg: Abhandlung von der Fuge (Berlin, 1754), 'Anmerkungen' [? by Marpurg]
77–8	62/14; 65/28	2 sonatas, G, E♭, 1754, 77 (1762); 78 ed. in T
79	117/17	La Borchward, polonoise, G, 1754
80	117/18	La Pott, minuet, C, 1754, in Raccolta delle più nuove composizioni (Leipzig, 1756) [cf 480]; ed. in LK
81	117/26	La Boehmer, D, 1754; as Murqui, *A-Wgm*
82	117/37	La Gause, F, 1754 [cf 480]
83	65/29	Sonata, E, 1755, *D-B*
84–7	70/3–6	4 org sonatas, F, a, D, g, 1755 (1790)
88	112/19	Fuga a 3, g, 1755 (1765)
89–90	117/19–20	La Gleim, rondeau, a; La Bergius, B♭:

H	W	
		1755, in Raccolta delle più nuove composizioni (Leipzig, 1756); ed. in R
91	117/21	La Prinzette, F, 1755, in Raccolta delle più nuove composizioni (Leipzig, 1757); ed. in HL
92–5	117/23–5, 27	L'Herrmann, g; La Buchholz, d; La Stahl, d; L'Aly Rupalich, C: 1755 (1762); 92 ed. in HL, 94–5 ed. in R, 94 ed. in HS
96–8	117/34–5, 39	La Philippine, A: La Gabriel, C; La Caroline, a: 1755; ed. in HL
99	119/2	Fuga a, 2, d, 1755, in F. W. Marpurg: Fugen-Sammlung, i (Berlin, 1758) and (n.d.); ed. in Barford
100	119/3	Fuga a 3, F, 1755, in Tonstücke . . . vom Herrn C. P. E. Bach und andern classischen Musikern (Berlin, 1762, 2/1774 as C. P. E. Bachs, Nichelmanns and Handels Sonaten und Fugen) and (n.d.)
101–2	119/4, 6	Fuga a 3 mit Anmerkungen, A; Fuga a 4, org, mit Anmerkungen, E♭: 1755, 101 in Raccolta delle più nuove composizioni (Leipzig, 1757), both in F. W. Marpurg: Clavierstücke mit einem practischen Unterricht (Berlin, 1762–3); ed. in Barford
103	119/7	Fantasia e fuga a 4, c, 1755; Fuga (n.d.)
104	122/2	Sinfonia, F, ?1755 or later, in F. W. Marpurg: Raccolta delle migliore sinfonie (Leipzig, 1761–2) [*650]
105–6	62/15; 65/30	2 sonatas, d, e, 1756, 105 in Raccolta delle più nuove composizioni (Leipzig, 1757); 105 ed. in T
107	70/7	Preludio, org, D, 1756 (1790)
108	116/18	Andantino, F, 1756, in F. W. Marpurg: Kritische Briefe über die Tonkunst (Berlin, 1760)
109	117/28	La complaisante, B♭, 1756 (1761²) [*456]
110–13	117/30–33	Les langueurs tendres, c; L'irrésoluë, G; La journalière, c; La capricieuse, e: 1756 (1761²); 110 also as La memoire raisonée; 110, 113 ed. in LK
114	117/36	La Louise, D, 1756 [*507, 585]
115	122/3	Sinfonia, e, ?1756 or later, lost [*652, *653]
116–20	62/16–19; 62/20 [266]	5 sonatas, B♭, E, g, G, C, 1757, 116–17 in Oeuvres mêlées (Nuremberg, 1760–63), 118–20 (1762), 120 (1792); 119, cf 50; 116–19 ed. in T, 119 ed. in F
121	65/31 [266]	Sonata, c, 1757 (1792); ed. in T
122	117/22	L'Auguste, polonoise, F, 1757, in Raccolta delle più nuove composizioni (Leipzig, 1757); ed. in LK, HL
123	117/29	La Xénophon–La Sybille, C♯, 1757 (1761²) [*455]; ed. in LK
124–5	117/38, 40	L'Ernestine, D; La Sophie, aria, B♭: 1757 [*685]
126	50/5	Sonata, B♭, 1758 (1760); ed. in HS
127–9	51/3–4; 52/6	3 sonatas, c, d, e, 1758, 127–8 (1761¹), 129 (1763); 127 ed. in HS
130	55/2	Sonata, F, 1758 (1779); ed. in T, K, S
131–2	62/21–2	2 sonatas, a, b, 1758, 131 in Oeuvres mêlées (Nuremberg, 1760–63), 132 in Collection récréative (Nuremberg, 1760–61); ed. in T
133–4	70/1–2	2 sonatas, A, B♭, org, 1758, 134 (1790) and in III sonates . . . par Mrs. C. P. E. Bach, C. S. Binder e C. Fasch (Nuremberg, n.d.); cf 135
135	65/32	Sonata, A, 1758 or later [rev. of 133]; orig. version, D-B
136–40	50/1–4, 6	5 sonatas, F, G, a, d, c, 1759 (1760); 136 ed. in H. Fischer, Die Sonate (Berlin, 1937)
141–2	51/5; 52/2	2 sonatas, F, d, 1759, 141 (1761¹), 142 (1763); 142 ed. in F
143	65/33	Sonata, a, 1759, KNu; ed. in VL
144–9	112/2, 4, 8, 10, 15, 18 [117/8, 5, 9, 6, 10, 7]	Fantasia, D; Solfeggio, G; Fantasia, B♭; Solfeggio, C; Fantasia, E; Solfeggio, G: 1759 (1765); 144, 146, 148–9 ed. in VK, 145, 147 ed. in HL
150–52	51/1–2; 65/34	3 sonatas, C, B♭, B♭, 1760, 150–51 (1761¹) [cf 156–7]
153	116/21	Allegro, C, 1760; ed. in HS
154	116/22	Polonoise, g, 1760 [*170]
155	118/2	Clavierstück mit [22] Veränderungen, A, 1760 [? only variations 13–14, 17–22 by Bach, others by [J. A.] Steffan, C. Fasch]; theme and variations 1–17 (1761²), theme and variations 18–22 (1770)
156–7	65/35–6	2 sonatas, C, 1760 or later; revs. of 150
158	52/3	Sonata, g, 1761 (1763); ed. in HS
159–60	116/1–2	Minuet, Polonoise, E♭, by 1762 (1762)
161	116/15	Minuet, C, by ?1762 [*601]
162	117/14	Fantasia, D, by 1762, pubd in Versuch, ii [cf 871]
163–5	52/5; 53/1, 5	3 sonatas, E, C, C, 1762, 163 (1763), 164–5 (1766²)
166	68	Veränderungen und Auszierungen über einige meiner Sonaten, completed 1762 or later autograph D-Bds
167–72	112/3, 5, 9, 11, 16–17 [116/9–14]	Minuet, D; Alla polacca, a; Minuet, D; Alla polacca, g; Minuet, A; Alla polacca, D: 1762–5 (1765) [*154, *602–5]; 167, 171 ed. in HL, 168, 170, 172 ed. in VK, 171 ed. in LK
173	57/6	Sonata, f, 1763 (1781) and (Berlin, n.d.); ed. in K, S, T, R
174–8	65/37–41	5 sonatas, A, B♭, e, D, C, 1763; 174, 176–8 ed. in T
179	112/7	Sonata, d, 1763 (1765); ed. in T
180–83	53/2–4, 6	4 sonatas, B♭, a, b, F, 1764 (1766²); 181 ed. in F
184–5	54/3, 5	2 sonatas, d, D, 1765 (1770¹); ed. K. Johnen (Frankfurt am Main, 1950)
186–7	55/4, 6	2 sonatas, A, F, 1765 (1779); ed. in K, T, S
188–9	58/4; 65/42	2 sonatas, e, E♭, 1765, 188 (1783); 188 ed. in K, S (inc.); 189 ed. in T
190	112/1	Concerto, hpd solo, C, 1765 (1765)
191	112/13 [122/4]	Sinfonia, hpd solo, G, 1765 (1765) [*657]
192	65/43	Sonata, A, 1765–6
193–203	113/1–11 [113/3 = 117/15]	Allegro, G; Arioso, a; Fantasia, d; Minuet, F; Alla polacca, C; Allegretto, a; Alla polacca, D; Allegretto, A; Andante e sostenuto, g; Presto, B♭; Allegro, d, 1765–6 (1766¹); ed. O. Vrieslander, Kurze und leichte Klavierstücke (Vienna, 1914), O. Jonas (Vienna, 1962)
204–7	54/1–2, 4, 6	4 sonatas, F, C, B♭, A, 1766 (1770¹); ed. K. Johnen (Frankfurt am Main, 1950)
208	57/4	Sonata, d, 1766 (1781); ed. in K, T, S
209	60	Sonata, e, 1766 (Leipzig, 1785)
210–13	62/23; 65/44–6	4 sonatas, g, g, B♭, E, 1766, 210 (1770²); ? orig. version of 213 autograph, D-B; 211–13 ed. in T
214–19	116/3–8	Minuet, D; Alla polacca, C; Minuet, C; Alla polacca, D; Minuet, F; Alla polacca, G: 1766 (1770²) [*606–9]; 214–16, 218 ed. in VK, 214, 219 ed. in LK
220–22	117/2 [271]; 117/3–4	3 solfeggios, c, E♭, A, 1766 (1770²), 220 (Stockholm, n.d.; Berlin, n.d.); ed. in VK, 220 ed. in R, 221 ed. in LK
223–5	117/11–13	3 fantasias, G, d, g, 1766 (1770²); 223–4 ed. in VK, 224 ed. in LK
226	118/6	Romance, avec XII variations, G, 1766
227	122/5	Sinfonia, hpd solo, F, 1766 (1770²) [*656]
228–38	114/1–11 [114/7 = 117/16]	Allegro di molto, d; Andantino e grazioso, B♭; Presto, c; Minuet, G; Alla polacca, D; Alla polacca, E♭; Fantasia, d; Allegro, E; Allegretto, A; Andante, C; Poco allegro, e: 1767 (1768²); ed. O. Vrieslander, Kurze und leichte Klavierstücke (Vienna, 1914), O. Jonas (Vienna, 1962), 234 ed. in R
239	—	Polonoise, G, 1768 or later
240	62/24	Clavier-Sonate mit veränderten Reprisen, F, 1769 (1770²)
241	117/1	Clavierstück für die rechte oder linke Hand allein, A, by 1770 (1770²); ed. in VK, LK
242		Concerto, hpd solo, 1770, autograph, D-B [*470]
243–7	55/5, 1, 3; 56/2; 57/2	5 sonatas, F, C, b, G, a, 1772–4, 243–5 (1770), 246 (1780), 247 (1781); ed. in K, HS, S [245 inc.], 244, 246–7 ed. in T
248	65/47	Sechs leichte Clavier-Stückgen, C, F, D, G, B♭, D, 1775, B (autograph), B-Bc, intended as a set [518, 521, 534, 610–11,

H	W	
		613–14, 618, 620, 635: all *; 255–6, variants]; cf 259
255–8	—	Allegro, D; Allegro, F; Allegretto, D; Minuet, F: ?1775, autograph, *D-B* [*625, *635; 252, 254, 306, variants]
259	118/10	Variationes mit veränderten Reprisen, C, 1777 or later; on theme of 534, which is a set of variations on 249; cf 492
260–62	56/1, 3, 5	3 rondos, C, D, a, 1778 (1780); ed. in K
263	118/9 [270]	12 Variationes über die Folie d'Espagne, d, 1778 (Vienna, 1803); ed. in HS
264	120	[75] Cadenzen, 1778 or later, *B-Bc*, written for his own concs. and sonatas
265–8	57/1, 5; 58/5; 59/2	4 rondos, E, F, B♭, G, 1779, 265–6 (1781); 267 (1783), 268 (1785); ed. in K, 265 ed. in R, 267 ed. in T, 268 ed. in S
269–71	56/4, 6; 57/3	2 sonatas, F, A; Rondo, G: 1780, 269–70 (1780), 271 (1781); ed. in K, 269 ed. in T
272	66	Abschied von meinem Silbermannischen Claviere, in einem Rondo, e, 1781
273–4	58/2–3	Sonata, G; Rondo, E: 1781 (1783); ed. in K, 274 ed. in T
275	118/8	Canzonetta der Herzogin von Gotha, mit 6 Veränderungen, F, 1781, pubd as Canzonette fürs Clavier von einer Liebhaberin der Musik (Gotha, 1781), incl. variations by G. Benda, C. F. Cramer, Golde, Scheidler, Scherlitz, A. Schweitzer
276–9	58/1, 6–7; 59/5	Rondo, A; 3 fantasias, E♭, A, F: 1782, 276–8 (1783), 279 (1785); ed. in K, 276 ed. in T
280	65/48	Sonata fürs Bogen-Clavier, G, 1783, *A-Wn, B-Bc, D-B*; ed. for standard kbd in HS, T
281–4	59/1, 3–4, 6	2 sonatas, e, B♭; Rondo, c; Fantasia, C: 1784 (1785), 283 (1791); ed. in K, 282 ed. inc. in S, 282–3 ed. in T
285	—	Fughetta on the name 'C. Filippo E. Bach' [C–F–E–B–A–C–H], F, 1784; pubd in Bitter, ii, 303–4; cf 868
286–91	61/2, 5, 1, 3, 4, 6	2 sonatas, D, G; Rondo, E♭; Fantasia, B♭; Rondo, d; Fantasia, C: 1785–6 (1787), 288, 290 (1791); ed. in K, 288 ed. in HS, 291 ed. in R
292–7	63/7–12	VI sonatine nuove, G, E, D, B♭, F, d, 1786, pubd in 869 (2/1787), also pubd as 2 sonatas of 3 movts (Leipzig, 1786); ed. in VK, ed. L. Hoffmann-Erbrecht (Leipzig, 1957)
298–9	65/49–50	2 sonatas, E♭, G, 1786 [*517, *633]; 298 ed. in T
300	67	Freie Fantasie fürs Clavier, f♯, 1787 [*536]; ed. A. Kreutz (Mainz, 1950)
301–9	116/19–20, 29–35	Allegretto, F; Allegro, D; Minuet, G, Minuet, G; Minuet, G; Minuet, F; Minuet, D; Polonoise, A; Minuet, D: *622–7, *635, *638; cf 258
310–14	116/36–40	Allegro di molto, A; Allegro, E; Allegro, B♭; Presto, a; Minuet, D: *635; 310 ed. in HL, 311 ed. in HS
315–18	116/41–4	4 polonoises, F, A, B♭, E♭ [*635]
319–22	116/45–8	2 marches, F, D; 2 minuets, C, G *635, *637; 320 ed. in HL
323–31	116/49–57	Polonoise, D; Langsam und traurig, a; Allegro, C; Allegro ma non troppo, E♭; Allegro, C; Allegro, G; Allegro, E♭; Allegro, D; Allegretto grazioso, C: *612, *615, *617–19, *632, *634–5; 325 ed. in HL
332	—	Sonata, D
333	—	La Juliane, F
334	—	Variations, C, ? late work
335	—	Adagio per il organo a 2 claviere e pedal, d, *B*
336	—	5 Choräle mit ausgesetzten Mittelstimmen, kbd, no text: O Gott du frommer Gott, Ich bin ja Herr in deiner Macht, Jesus meine Zuversicht, Wer nur den Lieben Gott, Komm heiliger Geist; cited in NV 64, 2 in *D-B*; see W, p.96
337	—	Chorale: Wo Gott zum Haus nicht gibt, a 4, bc, *Bds*

H	W	
338	116/16–17	2 unattrib. single movts ['Allegro'], A, G, ?1755, in F. W. Marpurg: *Anleitung zum Clavierspielen* (Berlin, 1755); in *B-Bc* as by C. P. E. Bach; ? same as Zwey Allegro in NV 11; ed. in HS
339	—	Fantasia, E♭, *c*1755 or later; in *D-Bds* unattrib.
340	—	Garten-Sonata, D, by 1762; unattrib. in (1762); attrib. C. P. E. Bach in *GOI*
341	—	Sonata, e, by 1762; unattrib. in (1762); attrib. C. P. E. Bach in *B*
342	—	Sinfonia per il clavicembalo, B♭, ?1786, *LEm*
343–5	—	3 sonatas, C, c, F, *A-Wn, D-B*
346	—	Sonata, D, n.d., *B, Bds, USSR-KAu*
347	—	Sonata, E♭, *D-B*
348	—	Solo, F, *B*
349–51	—	3 sonatas, c, B♭, B♭, *GOI*
352	—	Sonata [Suite], B♭, *KII*
353–8	—	6 sonatas, F, F, G, G, a, B♭, *USSR-KAu*
359	—	Fantasia e fuga, d, *B-Bc*
360	—	Fuga, C, ? by 1767, *D-B*
361	—	Arioso con variazioni, A, *GOI, KII*
362–4	—	Alla pol[acca] con variatio, G; Giga con variazioni, F; Minuetto, D: *US-Wc*
365–9	—	1 untitled, a frag.; Menueten zum Tantzen, D, frag.; Polonoise, D; Polonoise, D; Polonoise, A; Larghetto, G
370	—	La Walhauer, A, *GOI*

doubtful or spurious

H	W	
371	—	Chorale: Ach Gott und Herr, kbd, *c*1732, autograph, *B* [chorale from cantata bwv48]
372	—	VI Sonaten, B♭, G, d, F, G, D, by 1757, *GOI* [G. Benda: 6 Sonate (Berlin, 1757)]
373	—	Sonata, F, by 1763, *B*, kbd arr. [? by C. P. E. Bach] of sonata by J. C. Bach
374	—	Fugue, B♭, *B*, not in NV
375	—	Polonoise, E♭, *c*1765, *GOI* [by W. F. Bach]
376	—	Clavier-Sonate, C, by 1770, *B* (1770²) [described by C. P. E. Bach in the print as by J. C. F. Bach, cf DDT, lvi (1917), xiii]
377	—	5., 4., 6. Sonate, E, D, e, *c*1770, *GOI* [no.4 same as 73, nos.5–6 by J. C. Bach]
378	—	Sonata: Concerto, A, *c*1771, *GOI* [anon. kbd arr. of conc. probably by J. C. Bach; *389]
379	—	A Favourite Concerto, A, kbd, *c*1771 [probably by J. C. Bach (London, *c*1775)]
380	—	Due sonate . . . del Sigl. Daniele Turk, La troisi – La quartiem Mons. P. E. Bach, B♭, D, by 1776, *GOI* [nos.3–4 also by Türk]
381	272	La Bataille de Bergen, F, *c*1778 (Worms, n.d.), also as La Bataille de Rosbach; in *S-Skma, US-Wc* attrib. J. C. Bach and Graun; cf Jacobi (1790)
382	—	A Favourite Overture of Sig. Bach of Berlin, *c*1785 (London, *c*1785) [pf arr. of sym. by J. C. Bach]
383	—	Sonata, e, *USSR-KAu*; 1 movt uncertainly attrib. W. F. Bach in *D-B*
384	—	Parthia, C, *B*
385–90	—	VI petites pièces arrangées pour le piano forte: Le Travagant, G; Le Caressant – Le Contente, C; Le petit maître, F; Le Flegmatique – En Colère, B♭; Le Moribant, d; Il est vive, D: *B*
391	—	And.te ed Allegro, *B*
392	—	Fuga, C, ?1764; not in NV [*F-Pc* attrib. C. P. E. Bach, *D-B* attrib. J. S. Bach (cf bwv suppl. 90)]
393	—	Fuga, c, in bwv575 as by J. S. Bach
394	—	Fuga [Sopra il nome di Bach], C, *A-Wgm, Wn* [in bwv suppl.108 as doubtful work of J. S. Bach]
395–6	—	2 chorales: Allein Gott in der Höh, Vater unser im Himmelreich, kbd, *D-B*
397	—	Allegro, c, *B*
398	—	Menuetto mit V Variationen, E♭, *KII*
399–401	—	Tempo di men[uetto]-variation, A; 2 works in 1 movt: *D-B*

CONCERTOS AND SONATINAS

Concertos, hpd/org, vns, insts (London, c1753) [1753]
A Second Sett of Three Concertos, org/hpd, insts (London, c1760) [1760]

H	W	
402	—	1 untitled, a, frag.
403	1	Conc., a, hpd, str, 1733, lost, rev. 1744; in D-B, misattrib. J. S. Bach
404	2	Conc., E♭, hpd, str, 1734, lost, rev. 1743 as op.2 (Paris, n.d.)
405	3	Conc., G, hpd, str, 1737, lost, rev. 1745
406	4	Conc., G, hpd, str, 1738
407	5	Conc., c, hpd, str, 1739, lost, rev. 1762
408–9	6–7	2 concs., g, A, hpd, str, 1740
410	46	Conc. doppio, F, 2 hpd, 2 hn, str, 1740; 2nd version, B, with hns ad lib
411–13	8–10	3 concs., A, G, B♭, hpd, str, 1741–2
414	11	Conc., D, hpd, str, 1743 (Nuremberg, 1745), and (1753) also with added 2 tpt, timp ad lib, B-Bc
415–17	12–14	3 concs., F, D, E, hpd, str, 1744, 417 (1753) and (Berlin, 1760); for fl conc. version of 417 see Newman (1965); 417 also with added 2 hn
418–21	15–18	4 concs., e, G, d, D, hpd, str, 1745, 421 (1760); another version of 419, ?1738, US-BE
422–5	19–22	4 concs., A, C, a, d, hpd, str, 1746–7, 425 rev. 1775
426	—	Conc., fl, str, ?1747, ? orig. version of 425, D-B, Bds
427	23	Conc., d, hpd, str, 1748; ed. in DDT, xxix-xxx (1906/R)
428	24	Conc., e, hpd, str, 1748 (1760); ? earlier version, US-BE
429	25	Conc., B♭, hpd, str, 1749 (Nuremberg, 1752) and (1753); arr. 2 hpd, D-Dlb
430–32	26; 166; 170	Conc., a, hpd, str, 1750; versions for fl, str, ?1750, and for vc, str, ?1750; 432 orig. version, autograph, B
433	27	Conc., D, hpd, str, with 2 ob, 2 tpt/hn, 2 fl ad lib, timp ad lib, 1750; 2nd version, NV 31, for str, 2 hn
434–6	28; 167; 171	Conc., B♭, hpd, str, 1751; versions for fl, str, 1751 and for vc, str, ?1751; cf Newman (1965)
437–9	29; 168; 172	Conc., A, hpd, str, 1753; versions for fl, str, ?1753, and for vc, str, ?1753
440–43	30–33	4 concs., b, c, g, F, hpd, 2 vn, b, 1753–5, 441, autograph, B; 442 with opt. 2 fl
444–5	34; 169	Conc., G, org/hpd, str, 1755 (1760); version for fl, str, ?1755 or later; cf NV 32
446	35	Conc., E♭, org/hpd, 2 hn, str, 1759; ? orig. for org. cf NV 33; also without hns
447–8	36–7	Conc., B♭, hpd, str, 1762; conc., c, hpd, 2 hn, str, 1762; 448, Bds with added 2 hn
449–52	96–9	4 sonatinas, D, G, G, F, hpd, 2 fl, 2 hn, str, 1762; 2nd version of 449, LEm; †602/1, 4, 11
453	109	Sonatina . . . con 18 stromenti, D, 2 hpd, 2 fl, 2 ob, bn, 2 hn, 3 tpt, timp, 2 vn, va, vc, vle, 1762; variant, B
454	38	Conc., F, hpd, str, 2 fl ad lib, 1763
455–7	100; 102–3	3 sonatinas, E, D, C, hpd, 2 fl, 2 hn, str, 1763; †109, †123, *600/7
458	106	Sonatina I, C, hpd, 2 fl, str, 1763 (Berlin, 1764); cf 460
459	110	Sonatina, B♭, 2 hpd, 2 fl, 2 hn, str, 1763; also for pf, hpd, SWl, and for 1 kbd, LEm
460	101	Sonatina, C, hpd, 2 fl, 2 hn, str, 1763 or later; rev. of 458
461–4	107–8; 104–5	Sonatinas II, III, F, E♭; 2 sonatinas, F, E♭; hpd, 2 fl, str, 1764–5, 463–4 [revs. of 461–2] also 2 hn, 461 (Berlin, 1764) [see Newman, (1965)], 462 (Berlin, 1766)
465–8	39; 164; 40; 165	Conc., B♭, hpd, str, 1765, version for ob, str, ?1765; Conc., E♭, hpd, str, 1765, version for ob, str, ?1765; ob concs., ? orig. versions, see autographs, Bds
469	41	Conc., G, hpd, 2 fl, 2 hn, str, 1769
470	42	Conc., F, hpd, 2 hn, str, 1770 [*242]
471–6	43/1–6	Sei concerti, F, D, E♭, c, G, C, hpd, str, with 2 hn, 2 fl ad lib, 1771 (Hamburg, 1772)

H	W	
477–8	44–5	2 concs., G, D, hpd, 2 hn, vn, va, b, 1778
479	47	Conc. doppio, E♭, hpd, pf, 2 fl, 2 hn, str, 1788

probably authentic

480	—	Sonatina III, D, hpd, 2 fl, str, 1758 or later, LEm; combination of 80, 82, 600/9 and 12
481	—	Sonatina, D, hpd, 2 fl, str, c1762, D-B, alternative version of 453
482	—	11 fl concs., ? before 1768; formerly Berlin, Singakademie, now lost
483	—	Conc., B♭, hpd, str, B
484–5	—	2 concs., g, e, US-Wc

doubtful or spurious

486	—	Concert, f, hpd, insts, ?c1753, D-B [by J. C. Bach, rev. C. P. E. Bach]; attrib. C. P. E. Bach, ed. W. Szarvady (Leipzig, c1900)
487	—	Conc., d, hpd, insts, c1759, B [by C. Nichelmann]
488–9	—	2 concs., B♭, G, hpd, insts, by 1763, CS-Bm [by J. C. Bach]
490	—	Sonatina, C, glass harmonica, 2 vn, vc, 1775 or later, Pnm; combination of movts from 522, 524
491	—	Conc., C, hpd, insts, by 1777, Bm [by J. C. Bach]
492	—	Sonatina, C, glass harmonica, str, by 1777, Pnm; arr. of variations selected from 259
493–4	—	2 concs., E♭, B♭, hpd, insts, by 1780, 493, D-GOl, 494, WRtl [both by J. C. Bach]
495	—	Conc., E♭, hpd, str, B
496	—	Conc., f, hpd, insts, GOl [by G. Benda]
497	—	Conc., B♭, hpd, insts, B [by C. Nichelmann]
498–500	—	3 concs., C, b, F, hpd, insts, CS-Bm, D-DS [? by J. C. Bach]
501	—	Conc., D, vn/va/4 viols, pf/orch; [? by member of the Casadesus family, c1905]

CHAMBER MUSIC WITH OBBLIGATO KEYBOARD

502	71	Sonata, D, hpd, vn, 1731, rev. 1746
503	72	Duetto, d, hpd, vn, 1731, rev. 1747; also as sonata, fl, vn, bc, US-Wc
504	73	Duetto, C, hpd, vn, ?1745 or later [*573]
505	83	Sonata, D, hpd, fl, ?1747 or later [*575]
506	84	Duetto, E, hpd, fl, ?1749 or later [*580]
507	74	Sonata o vero sinfonia, D, hpd, vn, 1754 [*585; †114]; attrib. J. S. Bach in 1 MS
508–9	85–6	2 sonatas, G, hpd, fl, 1754–5 [*580, *582, *585]
510	88	Sonata, g, hpd, va da gamba, 1759
511–14	75–8	4 sonatas, F, b, B♭, c, hpd, vn, 1763
515	87	Sonata, C, hpd, fl, 1766
516–21	92	Sechs kleine Sonaten, E♭, E♭, E♭, B♭, E♭, B♭, hpd, cl, bn, after 1767 [*251, *254, *299, *610, *613–14, *629–31, *633, *635]
522–4	90	[3] Claviersonaten, i, a, G, C, hpd, vn, vc, 1775 (Leipzig, 1776); [†490]
525–30	89	Six Sonatas, B♭, C, A, E♭, e, D, hpd/pf, vn, vc, 1775–6 (London, 1776)
531–4	91	[4] Claviersonaten, i, e, D, F, C, hpd, vn, vc, 1777 (Leipzig, 1777); 534 variations on 249 [cf 259]
535	79	Arioso con variazioni, A, hpd, vn, 1781
536	80	Clavier-Fantasie mit Begleitung (C. P. E. Bachs Empfindungen), f♯, hpd, vn, 1787 [*300]; sketches in 868
537–9	93–5	3 quartets, a, D, G, hpd, fl, va, [vc], 1788; listed as qts in NV 51, 537–8 also entitled Trio; kbd part incl. indications for vc in 1 MS [cf Schmid, 139]
540	—	[Sonata], e, kbd, melody inst, B-Bc, frag.
541	—	[Sonata], G, kbd, va [modern copy listed in Katalog der bedeutenden Musiksammlung . . . Erich Prieger . . . Versteigerung, iii (Cologne, 1924), no.186; ? in private collection]

probably authentic

542	—	Sonata, A, hpd, vn, ?1731 or 1747, D-B [*570]
543	—	Trio, B♭, hpd, vn, ?1755, US-Wc [*587–9]
544	—	Sonata, E, hpd, vn, D-DS

H	W	
		doubtful or spurious
545	—	Sonata, g, hpd, vn, by ?1763, *A-Wgm*; attrib. C. P. E. Bach in Breitkopf Catalogue, 1763, but ? disowned by him [cf Bitter, i, 338]; listed in bwv1020 as doubtful work by J. S. Bach
546–7	—	2 sonatas, C, G, kbd, vn, *c*1775, *D-RH, DO* [by J. C. Bach]

SOLO SONATAS FOR WIND AND STRINGS

H	W	
548	134	Sonata, G, fl, bc, by ?1735
549	135	Solo, g, ob, bc, by ?1735
550–56	123–9	7 sonatas, G, e, B♭, D, G, a, D, fl, bc, 1735–40; ed. K. Walther (Kassel and Frankfurt, 1936–58)
557	138	Solo, g, vc, bc, 1740, rev. 1769, lost
558–9	136–7	2 solos, C, D, va da gamba, bc, 1745–6
560–61	130–31	2 sonatas, B♭, D, fl, bc, 1746–7
562	132	Sonata, a, fl, 1747 (Berlin, 1763) and in Musikalisches Mancherley (Berlin, 1762–3)
563	139	Solo, G, harp, 1762
564	133	Sonata, G, fl, bc, 1786
		probably authentic
565	—	2 sonatas, G, b, fl, bc, by 1763, collab. C. Schaffrath [listed in *Katalog der bedeutenden Musiksammlung . . . Erich Prieger . . . Versteigerung*, iii (Cologne, 1924), no.353; ? in private collection]

TRIO SONATAS

H	W	
566	—	Trio . . . mit Johann Sebastian Bach gemeinschaftlich verfertigt, vn, va, bc, by ?1731, lost; title in NV 65 [cf Bitter, ii, 307]
567–71	143–7	5 sonatas, b, e, d, A, C, fl, vn, bc, 1731, rev. 1747; 569 similar to trio sonata listed as doubtful work of J. S. Bach (bwv1036), ? composed jointly by J. S. and C. P. E. Bach
572–5	148–51	4 sonatas, a, C, G, D, fl, vn, bc, 572 1735, rev. 1747, 573–5, 1745–7 [*504–5]
576–7	154–5	2 sonatas, F, e, 2 vn, bc, 1747; 576 incl. in doubtful works of J. S. Bach (bwv suppl.186)
	161/2, 4	Sonata, B♭, fl and vn/fl/vn, bc, 1748; Sonata, E♭, 2 vn/vn, bc, 1749: pubd as Zwey Trio (Nuremberg, 1751) ·
580–81	162; 152	Trio, E, 2 fl, bc, 1749; trio, G, fl, vn, bc, 1754 [*506, *508, *583]
582	156	Sinfonia, a, 2 vn, bc, 1754
583–4	157–8	2 sonatas, G, B♭, 2 vn, bc, 1754, 584 (Berlin, 1763), also in Musikalisches Mancherley (Berlin, 1762–3) [*508, *581]
585	—	Sinfonia a 3 voce, D, 2 vn, bc, ? 1754, *D-B, US-Wc* [for autograph, cf M. Pincherle, *Cent raretes musicales* (Paris, 1966)] [*507]
586	153	Sonata, G, f., vn, bc, 1755 [*509]
587–9	159; 163–4	Sonata, B♭, 2 vn, bc, 1755; versions as trio, F, va, b rec, hpd, 1755, and trio, bn, b rec, hpd, ?1755 [*543]; 587 listed as doubtful work of J. S. Bach
590	160	Sonata, F, 2 vn, bc, 1756, variant in Musikalisches Mancherley (Berlin, 1762–3)
		probably authentic
591	—	Sonata, E, 2 vn, bc, ? before 1768, *US-Wc*
592	—	Sonata, c, fl/vn, vn, bc, *D-HVs*
593–4	—	2 sonatas, E♭, F, fl, vn, bc, formerly Berlin, Singakademie, now lost
		doubtful or spurious
595	—	Sonata, G, fl, vn, 1735 [listed in Bitter, 27, but not found]
596	—	Sonata, F, ?1747, *US-Wc* [*503]
597	—	Trio, F, fl, vn, hpd, ? before 1768, attrib. C. P. E. Bach *US-Wc, D-Bds*, Berlin, Singakademie; also attrib. J. C. Bach, doubtfully attrib. W. F. Bach; ed. H. Brandts-Buys, attrib. W. F. Bach (Amsterdam, n.d.), ed. K. Maguerre, attrib. J. C. Bach (Celle, 1960)

OTHER CHAMBER

H	W	
598	140	Duett, e, fl, vn, 1748, in Musikalisches Vielerley (Hamburg, 1770); ed. W. Stephan (Kassel, 1928), J. Marx (New York, 1948)
599	141	Duetto, d, 2 vn, 1752, lost
600	81	Zwölf kleine Stücke mit 2 und 3 Stimmen, fl/vn, hpd, 1758 (Berlin, 1758) [*450, *456, *480]; ed. F. Oberdörffer (Berlin, 1934), K. Walther (Frankfurt am Main, 1971)
601	192	Zwey Menuetten, C, 2 fl, 2 bn, 3 tpt, timp, 2 vn, bc, by 1762, in Musikalisches Mancherley (Berlin, 1762–3) [*161]
602–3	189/1–2	2 minuets, D, 2 fl, 2 cl, 2 vn, bc, ?c1765 [*167, *169]
604–5	190/1, 3	Polonoise, D, 2 cl, 2 vn, bc; Polonoise, a, 2 vn, bc: ?c1765 [*168, *172]
606–9	189/8; 190/2, 4–5	Minuet, D, 2 fl, 2 cl, 2 hn, 2 vn, bc; Polonoise, G, 2 vn, bc; Polonoise, D, 2 cl, 2 hn, 2 vn, bc; Polonoise, C, 2 vn, bc: ?c1766 [*214–15, *217, *219]
610–13	115/1–4	4 kleine Duetten, B♭, F, a, E♭, 2 hpd, ? after 1767 [*251, *324, *518, *614, *620, *635]
614–19	185/1–6	VI Märsche, D, C, F, G, E♭, D, 2 ob, 2 cl, bn, 2 hn, after 1767; [*252, *254, *327–330, *518, *613]
620	186	2 kleine Stücke, C, F, 2 cl, bn, 2 hn, after 1767, lost [*250, *324, *611–12, *635]; with 2 ob in NV 52
621	188	Marcia . . . für die Arche, C, 3 tpt, timp, after 1767
622	189/3	Minuet, G, 2 fl, bn, 2 hn, 2 vn, bc, ? before 1768 [*303]
623–6	189/4–7	4 minuets, G, G, F, D, 2 fl, 2 hn, 2 vn, bc, ? before 1768 [*258, *304–7, *635]
627	190/6	Polonoise, A, 2 vn, bc, ? before 1768 [*308]
628	82	Zwölf 2- und 3-stimmige kleine Stücke, fl/vn, hpd, 1769 (Hamburg, 1770)
629–34	184/1–6	VI sonate, D, F, G, E♭, A, C, 2 fl, 2 cl, bn, 2 hn, 1775 [*299, *326, *331, *516–17, *519–20]; ed. J. Lorenz (Milan, 1939), K. Janetzky (London, 1958)
635	193	[29] Stücke für Spieluhren, auch Dreh-Orgeln, no.2 1775 or later [*251, *257–8, *305–6, *310–25, *521, *610, *612, *620, *624–5, *636–7]
636	142	Duett, 2 cl [*635/26–7]
637	187	2 Märsche, F, D, 2 ob, bn, 2 hn; [*319–20, *635]
638	191	Zwo abwechselnde Menuetten, D, 2 fl, 2 ob, 2 hn, 3 tpt, timp, str, bc [*309]
		probably authentic
639		Fantasia sopra Jesu meines Lebens Leben, ob, 3 insts, ? before 1735, *D-B*
		doubtful or spurious
640	—	Sonata, C, harmonica, vc, 1753 or later, *CS-Pnm* [*74–5]
641	—	3 trios, d, E♭, G, 2 vn, va, *c*1765, *A-M* [by J. C. Bach]
642	—	Quintette, C, fl, ob, vn, va, vc, *c*1772, *CS-Bm* [by J. C. Bach]
643	—	III sonate, D, G, C, fl, vn, *A-Wn* [? by J. C. Bach]
644–5	—	2 divertimentos, D, G, fl, vn, va, vc, *PL-WRu*
646	—	Frühlings Erwachen, 2 vn, pf, ? 19th century
647	—	Adagio, str, ? 1904

SYMPHONIES

H	W	
648	173	Sinfonie, G, str, 1741 [*45]
649	174	Sinfonia, C, 2 fl, 2 hn, str, 1755, also without hns/fls
650	175	Sinfonia, F, 2 fl, 2 bn, 2 hn, str, 1755 [*104]; wind pts. opt.
651	176	Sinfonia, D, 2 fl, 2 ob, 2 hn, 3 tpt, timp, str, 1755; wind and timp pts. opt.
652	177	Sinfonia, e, str, 1756 (Nuremberg, 1759) [*115, *653], ed. K. Geiringer, *Music of the Bach Family: an Anthology* (Cambridge, Mass., 1955)

H	W	
653	178	Sinfonia, e, 2 fl, 2 ob, 2 hn, str, ? 1756 [*115, *652]
654–6	179–81	3 sinfonias, E♭, G, F, 2 ob, 2 hn, str, 1757–62 [*191, *227]; wind pts. opt.
657–62	182	Sei sinfonie, G, B♭, C, A, b, E, str, 1773; for G. van Swieten
663–6	183	[4] Orchester-Sinfonien mit 12 obligaten Stimmen, D, E♭, F, G, 2 fl, 2 ob, bn, 2 hn, 2 vn, va, vc, db, 1775–6 (Leipzig, 1780); ed. in EDM, 1st ser., xviii (1942/R)
667	—	Sinfonia, G, str, ?1750–51, D-B; probably collab. Prince Ferdinand Philipp von Lobkowitz [cf NV 65 and Suchalla, 128ff]

doubtful or spurious

| 668 | — | Numerous further syms., divertimentos attrib. C. P. E. Bach ('Bach', 'Baach', 'Pach' etc), A-M, Gd, B-Bc, CH-E, CS-Bm, D-LEm, Rtt, PL-Wn; none is authentic, mostly by J. C. Bach |

WORKS FOR SOLO VOICE

(with kbd acc. unless otherwise stated)

Editions: *Geistliche Lieder*, ed. K. H. Bitter (Berlin, 1867) [B]
Fünfundzwanzig ausgewählte geistliche Lieder, ed. J. Dittberner (Leipzig, 1917) [D]

Oden mit Melodien (Berlin, 1762/R1774) [1762]
Neue Lieder-Melodien nebst einer Kantate zum singen beym Klavier (Lübeck, 1789) [1789]

H	W	
669	211	3 arias: Edle Freiheit, Götterglück; Himmels Tochter, Ruh der Seelen; Reiche bis zum Wolkensitze: T, str, bc, ? by 1738
670–72	199/2, 10, 12	3 songs: Schäferlied (M. von Ziegler), 1741; Der Zufrieden (Stahl), 1743; Die verliebte Verzweifelung (Steinhauer), 1743: (1762) and in Sammlung verschiedener und auserlesener Oden (Halle, 1737–43)
673–5	199/4–5, 11	3 songs: Die Küsse (N. D. Giseke); Trinklied (J. W. L. Gleim); Amint (E. von Kleist): 1750–53 (1762) and in Oden mit Melodien, i (Berlin, 1753), 673–5 in Lieder der Deutschen mit Melodien (Berlin, 1767–8)
676	199/14	Die märkische Helene (G. E. Lessing), 1754 (1762) and in F. W. Marpurg: *Historisch-kritische Beyträge*, i/1 (1754)
677–8	199/1, 7	2 songs: Die sächsische Helene (Gleim); Dorinde (Gleim): 1754 or 1755 (1762) and in Oden mit Melodien, ii (Berlin, 1755) and Lieder der Deutschen mit Melodien (Berlin, 1767–8)
679–80	199/3, 6	2 songs: Lied eines jungen Mägdchens (Fräulein von H [?Lessing]); Der Morgen (F. von Hagedorn): 1756 (1762), 679 in Berlinische Oden und Lieder (Leipzig, 1756), 680 in F. W. Marpurg: Neue Lieder zum singen beym Claviere (1756)
681–4	199/9, 13, 8, 15	4 songs: Die Biene (Lessing); Die Küsse (Lessing); Der Stoiker; Serin: 1756–7 (1762) and in Berlinische Oden und Lieder (Leipzig, 1756)
685	—	La Sophie, aria, 1757, autograph, D-B [125 with added text]
686	194	[55] Geistliche Oden und Lieder mit Melodien (C. F. Gellert), 1757 (Berlin, 1758/R1973) [*790, *794, *800, *826, *836]; 5 nos. in Lieder und Arien aus Sophiens Reise (Leipzig, 1779), 9 nos. in Fünfzig und sechs neue Melodien (Memmingen, 1780), no.1 in Musikalische Blumenlese (Zurich, 1786); various songs ed. in B, D
687	199/20	Herausforderungslied vor der Schlacht bey Rosbach (Gleim), 1758 (1762)
688	202/A	Freude, du Lust der Götter und Menschen (C. M. Wieland), 1760, in Drey verschiedene Versuche eines einfachen Gesanges für den Hexameter (Berlin, 1760) [*723]
689–92	199/16–19	4 songs: Auf den Namenstag der Mademoiselle S.; Der Traum; Die Tugend (A. von Haller); Doris (von Haller): 1761–2 (1762)

H	W	
693–5	202/B/1–3 [112/6, 12, 14]	3 songs: Das Privilegium (N. D. Giseke); Die Landschaft; Belinde (K. W. Müller): 1762–5 (1762) in Clavierstücke verschiedener Art, i (Berlin, 1765)
696	195	Zwölf geistliche Oden und Lieder als ein Anhang zu Gellerts geistliche Oden und Liedern mit Melodien (no.4: L. F. F. Lehr, nos.8, 10–11: A. L. Karschin), 1764 (Berlin, 1764/R1973) [*830]; various songs ed. in D
697	232	Phillis und Thirsis, cantata, 2 S, 2 fl, bc, 1765 (Berlin, 1766)
698	202/D	Bachus und Venus (H. W. von Gerstenberg), 1766, in Musikalisches Vielerley (Hamburg, 1770)
699	201 [264]	Der Wirth und die Gäste (Bleim), 4 solo vv, kbd, 1766 (Berlin, 1766, rev. 2/1790) and in Notenbuch zu des akademischen Liederbuches ersten Bändchen (Dessau and Leipzig, 1783); also in D-B for 4 solo vv, insts
700–01	200/10, 20	Belise und Thrysis; An eine kleine Schöne (Lessing): before 1767 (1789); 700 also as Allgutiger! gewohnt Gebet zu hören, autograph, B
702–8	200/6, 8, 11–12, 15, 17, 19	7 songs (J. H. Röding, J. H. Lütkens, C. D. Ebeling, J. C. Unzer), after 1767 (1789)
709–11	202/C/1–3	3 songs: Der Unbeständige ('W.'); Phillis (von Kleist); An die Liebe (von Hagedorn): c1768, in Unterhaltungen (Hamburg, 1768–70)
712–17	202/C/4–9	6 songs (some by D. Schiebeler), 1769, in Unterhaltungen (Hamburg, 1768–70)
718–21	202/C/10–13	4 songs (Schiebeler, Karschin, von Gerstenberg, D. P. Scriba), 1770, in Unterhaltungen (Hamburg, 1768–70)
722–3	236–7	2 cantatas: Selma (J. H. Voss), S, 2 fl, str, bc, ?1770; Der Frühling (Wieland), T, str, bc, 1770–72: [*688, *739]
724–9	202/E/1–6	6 songs (D. B. Münter), 1772–3, in D. B. Münters erste Sammlung geistlicher Lieder mit Melodien (Leipzig, 1773) [*797]
730–32	202/O/2; 202/F/1–2	3 songs: Klagelied eines Baueren (Miller); Vaterlandslied (F. G. Klopstock); Der Bauer (Miller): c1773, 1773–2 in Göttinger Musen-Almanach . . . 1774 (Göttingen, 1774); 732 autograph, Mbs, with 736–9
733	196	[42] Übersetzte Psalmen mit Melodien (J. A. Cramer), 1773–4 (Leipzig, 1774) [*774, *796, *798, *831–2]; selections ed. in B, D
734–5	200/9, 22	Der Frühling (Miller), ?1773–82; Die Grazien, cantata (von Gerstenberg), 1774: (1789)
736–7	200/G/1–2	Die Schlummernde (Voss); Lyda (Klopstock): 1774, in Göttinger Musen-Almanach . . . 1775 (Göttingen and Gotha, 1775) [cf 732]
738–9	202/I/1–2	Trinklied für Freye (Voss); Selma (Voss): 1775, in Musen-Almanach, ed. J. H. Voss (Hamburg, 1776) [cf 732; *722]
740–43	200/13, 21; 202/O/1, 4	4 songs: Trinklied (L. C. H. Hölty), 1775–82; An Doris (von Haller), 1775–6; Auf den Flügeln des Morgenroths (C.F. Cramer), ?1775–6; Da schlägt des Abschieds Stunde (Metastasio, trans. J. J. Eschenburg), ?1775–6: 740–41 (1789)
744–5	202/H; 200/1	An den Schlaf, 1776; Todtengräberlied (Hölty), 1776–82: 744 in Die Muse, i (Leipzig, 1776), 745 (1789)
746	202/J	Selma (Voss), 1777, in Musen-Almanach, ed. J. H. Voss (Hamburg, 1778) [not same as 739 or 722]
747–8	200/14, 5	Aus einer Ode zum neuen Jahr; An die Grazien und Musen (Gleim): ?1777–82 (1789)
749	197	[30] Geistliche Gesänge (C. C. Sturm) (Hamburg, 1780) [*795, *798–9, *833–4]; selections ed. in B, D
750–51	202/K/1–2	Fischerlied (C. A. Overbeck); Tischlied (Voss): 1780, in Musen-Almanach, ed. J. H. Voss (Hamburg, 1781)

H	W	
752	198	[30] Geistliche Gesänge, ii (Sturm) (Hamburg, 1781) [*795–7, *807, *826]; selections ed. in B, D, and ed. H. Roth (Leipzig, 1922)
753–4	202/L/1–2	Lied (F. L. von Stolberg); Das Milchmädchen (Voss): 1781, in Musen-Almanach, ed. J. H. Voss (Hamburg, 1782)
755–60	200/2–4, 7, 16, 18	6 songs: Lied der Schnitterinnen (Gleim); Nonnelied; Das mitleidige Mädchen (Miller); Bevelise und Lysidor (J. A. Schlegel); Mittel, freundlich zu werden (Gleim); Ich hoff auch Gott mit festem Muth (E. von der Recke): 755–7 by ?1782, 762 1785, all (1789)
761–2	214; 231	Fürsten sind am Lebensziele, aria, S, str, bc, lost; Freudenlied (auf die Wiederkunft des Herrn Dr. C. aus dem Bade), 2 S, bc, 1785
763	—	[Die Alster] (von Hagedorn), and Harvestehude (von Hagedorn), ?c1788 [cf Busch, 211ff]
764	202/N/1–12	12 Masonic songs, 1788, in Freymaurer-Lieder mit ganz neuen Melodien von den Herren Capellmeister Bach, Naumann und Schulz (Copenhagen and Leipzig, 1788), also in Allgemeines Liederbuch für Freymaurer, iii (Copenhagen, 1788) [misattrib. W. F. E. Bach in Miesner, cf Busch, 181ff]
765–6	202/O/3, 5	Kommt, lasst uns seine Huld besingen (J. A. Cramer); Die schönste soll bey Sonnenschein
767	213	D'amor per te languisco, arietta, S, 2 fl, bc, F-Pc; in NV 64 with added pts. for 3 vn

probably authentic

768	—	An der Mond: Sophiens Reise auf der See [Ich sah durch Tränenbache], D-B
769	—	Weil Gott uns das Gesicht verlieh, aria, B
770	—	Se amore per lei t'accende, cancionetta, B
771	—	Nachahmung einiger Stellen des anderen Psalms, von Kohler [Der Herr ist meines Lebens Kraft] (?Kohler), B

CHORAL

All those formerly at the main source, Berlin, Singakademie, are lost (further information in Miesner); 774–826 are for solo vv, chorus, orch, 827–40 are mostly for chorus, orch; the Passions, incl. much material by J. S. Bach and Telemann, are lost, unless otherwise indicated.

772	215	Magnificat, S, A, T, B, SATB, 2 fl, 2 ob, 2 hn, 3 tpt, timp, str, bc, 1749, ed. G. J. D. Pölchau (Bonn, 1829–30); tpt, timp and most of hn parts added later [† 776, †782, †807, †817]; alternative version of 'Et misericordia', D-B, 1780–82; ed. G. Darvas (Budapest, 1971), ed. G. Graulich and P. Horn (Neuhausen, nr. Stuttgart, 1971)
773–4	205–6	Der Zweyte Psalm, SATB; Der Vierte Psalm, S, A, bc: by 1761, in Musikalisches Allerley (Berlin, 1761) [*733]
775	238	Die Israeliten in der Wüste (D. Schiebeler), oratorio, solo vv, SATB, 2 fl, 2 ob, bn, 2 hn, 3 tpt, timp, str, bc, 1769 (Hamburg, 1775): ed. G. Darvas (Budapest, c1970)
776	233	Die letzten Leiden des Erlösers (L. Karsch), Passion cantata, solo vv, SATB, 2 fl, 2 ob, 2 bn, 3 hn, timp, str, bc, 1770, A-Wgm, DK-Kk
777	240	Auferstehung und Himmelfahrt Jesu (C. W. Ramler), oratorio, S, T, B, SATB, 2 fl, 2 ob, bn, 2 hn, 3 tpt, timp, str, bc, 1777–80 (Leipzig, 1787); ed. G. Darvas (Budapest, 1974)
778	217	Heilig, SATB, SATB, 2 ob, bn, 3 tpt, timp, str, bc, 1778 (Hamburg, 1779); used in 2 cantatas from 823 and 824 [cf 805–6, 813–14]
779	239	Morgengesang am Schöpfungsfeste (Klopstock), ode, solo vv, SSTB, 2 vn, 2 va, vc, bc, 1783 (Leipzig, 1784)
780	204	Zwey Litaneyen aus dem Schleswig-Holsteinischen Gesangbuche, SATB,

H	W	
		SATB, bc, 1786 (Copenhagen, 1786) [cf 871; *802]
781	203	[14] Neue Melodien zu einigen Liedern des neuen Hamburgischen Gesangbuchs, 1v, bc, 1787 (Hamburg, 1787) [see Busch, 178f]
782	—	St Matthew Passion, by 1768–9 [†772]
783–5	—	3 Passions: St Mark, by 1769–70; St Luke, by 1770–71; St John, by 1771–2
786	—	St Matthew Passion, by 1772–3
787–9	—	3 Passions: St Mark, by 1773–4; St Luke, by ?1774–5; St John, by 1775–6
790	—	St Matthew Passion, by 1776–7 [†686/14]
791	—	3 Passions: St Mark, by 1777–8; St Luke, by 1778–9; St John, by 1779–80
794	—	St Matthew Passion, by 1780–81, sketches, B [†686/23]
795	—	St Mark Passion, by 1781–2 [†749, †752/6, 26, 29]
796	—	St Luke Passion, by 1782–3, incl. recit and aria, autograph, B [†733, †752, †794]
797	—	St John Passion, by 1783–4, incl. 2 arias, recit, B [†752, †724]
798	—	St Matthew Passion, by 1784–5 [†733, †749]
799	—	St Mark Passion, by 1785–6 [†749, †826/4]
800	234	St Luke Passion, by 1786–7, D-Bds [incl. indication of borrowed material, inc. autograph and †686/21]
801	—	St John Passion, by 1787–8
802	235	St Matthew Passion, by 1788, ? composer's last work [†780/1]; inc. autograph, D-Bds [incl. indication of borrowed material], copy A-Wgm
803	244	Oster-Musik (Cochius), cantata, 1756
804–5	242; 241	Oster-Musik, cantata, by 1778, Oster-Musik, cantata, 1778 or later; 804 partly borrowed from J. S. Bach; 805 incl. 778
806	—	Oster-Musik, cantata, by 1780, sources inc.; incl. 778, 831, pts. of 804, 805
807	243	Oster-Musik, cantata, by 1784 [†752/14, †772, †inc. cantata from 824]; pt. ii lost
808	—	MSS of Oster-Musik for 1768–9, 1771, 1775, 1781–2, 1787, lost, mostly borrowed from other works
809–11	248; 245	3 Michaelis-Musik, cantatas, c1769–c1772; 809 sources inc.; 811 lost
812	247, 212	Michaelis-Musik, cantata, c1775, incl. w212, aria
813	—	Michaelis-Musik, cantata, c1778, D-B, collab. J. C. F. Bach [incl. 778]
814	246	Michaelis-Musik, cantata, by 1785 [incl. 778]
815	249	Weihnachts-Musik, cantata, 1775
816	—	At least 4 lost MSS of Weihnachts-Musik
817	—	Herr, lehr' uns thun, cantata, 1769, in NV 65, collab. G. A. Homilius [†772]
818	—	Der Gerechte, ob er gleich, cantata, 1774, D-B, Bds, after (2) Johann Christoph Bach
819	—	Meine Seele erhebt den Herrn, cantata, in NV 65, collab. 'Hoffmann', lost
820	—	At least 4 lost MSS of Sonntagsmusik
821–4	250–53; —	c50 congratulatory cantatas, variously entitled Einführungsmusik, Jubelmusik, Serenata, Oratorio, Musik am Dankfest, Trauungs-Cantate, Dank-Hymne, Geburtstags-Cantate, 1768–87, in NV 56–9, occasional works for Hamburg, A-Wgm, D-B, Hs; often incl. 856 and much borrowed material [cf 772, 778/7, 809, 814]
825	207	Veni, Sancte Spiritus, after 1767
826	208	4 Motteten, nos.1–3 after 1767, no.4 c1781 [*686/30, 53, 9; *752/3; *799]; no.3 (Bonn, c1823)
827–8	218–19	Einchöriges Heilig; Sanctus: after 1767; 827 *chorus from J. S. Bach: Magnificat
829	216	Spiega, Ammonia fortunata, occasional work, 1770
830	221	Mein Heiland, meine Zuversicht, ?Sonntagsmusik, 1771 [*696/12; ? part of cantata listed in NV 65]
831	222	Wer ist so würdig als du, 1774 [*733/4]
832	223	Zeige du mir deine Wege, 1777 [*733/9]; ? part of Sonntagsmusik, 1777

H	W	
833	225	Gott, dem ich lebe, 1780 [*749/9]; attached to 857
834–5	226–7	Amen, Amen, Lob und Preis; Leite mich nach deinem Willen: 1783 [*749/4] ? part of Sonntagsmusik 1783; 836 ed. G. Pölchau (Vienna, c1818)
836–7	228–9	Meine Lebenszeit verstreicht, 1783; Meinen Leib wird man begraben, ?1788: funeral music [*686/37]
838	—	Merkt und seht, *D-B*, inc.; ? from Passion
839–40	209–10	Antiphonia, 4vv; Amen, 4vv: lost
841	—	Wirf dein Anliegen auf, in NV 65, arr. of anon. motet, lost
842	p.96n	10 Choräle (Grafen von Wernigerode), 4vv, by 1767, autograph, *PL-WRu*
843	—	Naglet til et Kors paa Jorden, chorale, by 1781, in Kirke-Melodierne til den 1778 udgangne Psalmebog (Copenhagen, 1778); ed. in Busch, suppl.
844	—	3 chorales, by 1785, in Vollständige Sammlung der Melodien . . . des neuen allgemeinen Schleswig-Holsteinischen Gesangbuchs (Leipzig, 1785); ed. in Busch, suppl.
845	—	Chorale, by 1786, in Vierstimmige alte und neue Choralgesänge (Berlin, 1786) [cf Busch, 176–7]
846	p.96n	4 Choräle, 4vv, 3 tpt, timp, str, bc, in NV 64, lost
847	—	Tpt and timp pts. added to C. H. Graun: Te Deum, after 1756, in NV 66, lost
848	—	Inst parts to (2) Johann Christoph Bach chorus Die Gerechte, 1676, *D-B*
849	—	Inst introduction to Credo of J. S. Bach: B minor Mass, 1768 or later; *D-B*
850	—	2 recits, in NV 89, for 2 cantatas by C. F. C. Fasch, lost
851	—	Christ, sey Gefühl – Die Unschuld, autograph, *B*, recit and unacc. aria from choral work
852	—	Muster der Geduld und Liebe, 2vv, *B*, from choral work
853	—	Sey mir gesegnet, *Bds*, aria from choral work
854	—	Various acc. recits added to works by other composers, listed in NV 66, lost

doubtful or spurious

H	W	
855	—	Hilf dass ich folge, 4vv, c1725, *B* [transposition with new text of Was mein Gott will from Cantata bwv144]
856	220	Veni, Sancte Spiritus, 1760 [by Telemann; cf 821–4]
857	—	Selig sind die Todten, cantata, ? before 1781, *A-Wn*, used with 833 as funeral music, by 1781 [? by Telemann]
858	—	Missa, *Wgm*
859	—	Die Pilgrime auf Golgatha, oratorio, *D-Mbs* [? by Telemann]
860	—	Passion cantata [St Mark Passion], *KNu* (as St Matthew Passion) [? by Telemann]
861	—	Esto mihi, cantata [misattrib. C. P. E. Bach in *EitnerQ*; by J. E. Bach]
862–3	—	Ecce cui iniquitatibus; Miserere mei, frag.: *B*
864	—	Kommt, lasst uns anbeten, motet, *PL-Wu*
865	—	11 motets, *D-ARk* [? by J. E. Bach]
866	—	Der Todt Jesu, aria, *RH* [from larger work]

THEORETICAL WORKS

H	W	
867	121	*Miscellanea musica*, *B-Bc*; technical exercises collected by Westphal, incl. 285 and various sketches, some for 536
868	254	*Versuch über die wahre Art das Clavier zu spielen, mit Exempeln und achtzehn Probe-Stücken in sechs Sonaten erläutert*, 1 (Berlin, 1753/R1957, reissues 1759, 1780, rev. 2/1787) [for Probe-Stücken, see 70–75, 2nd edn., incl. 292–7; cf 873]; Eng. trans., ed. W. J. Mitchell, as *Essay on the True Art of Playing Keyboard Instruments* (New York, 1949) [incl. printed revs. by C. P. E. Bach]
869	257	'Einfall, einen doppelten Contrapunct in der Octave von 6 Tacten zu machen, ohne

die Regeln davon zu wissen', c1757, in F. W. Marpurg: *Historisch-kritische Beyträge zur Aufnahme der Musik*, iii (Berlin, 1757/R1970) [a permutational scheme of composition]; trans. in E. Helm: 'Six Random Measures of C. P. E. Bach', *JMT*, x (1966), 139

H	W	
870	255	*Versuch über die wahre Art das Clavier zu spielen . . . in welchen die Lehre von dem Accompagnement und der freyen Fantasie abgehandelt wird*, ii (Berlin, 1762/R1957, reissues 1780, 1787, rev. 2/1797); Eng. trans., ed. W. J. Mitchell, as *Essay on the True Art of Playing Keyboard Instruments* (New York, 1949) [incl. printed revs. by C. P. E. Bach]
871	204	Zwey Litaneyen aus dem Schleswig-Holsteinischen Gesangbuche, SATB, SATB, bc, 1786 (Copenhagen, 1786) [contains nearly 100 different harmonizations of 1 motif; cf 780]

doubtful or spurious

H	W	
872	—	*Gedanken eines Liebhabers der Tonkunst über Herrn Nichelmanns Tractat von der Melodie* (Nordhausen, 1755) [pamphlet ? by G. Leopold in response to C. Nichelmann: *Die Melodie nach ihrem Wesen sowohl, als nach ihren Eigenschaften* (Danzig, 1755)]
873	256	*Von der Fingersetzung*, *B-Br* [Westphal's copy of exx. accompanying 868]
874	258	*Kurze Anweisung zum General-Bass*, *B-Br* [in Westphal's hand]
875	—	*Anleitung, so viel Walzer man will mit Würfeln zu componieren* (Berlin, n.d.) [adaptation of J. P. Kirnberger: *Allzeit fertige Menuetten- und Polonoisenkomponist* (Berlin, 1757); see O. E. Deutsch: 'Mit Würfeln komponieren', *ZMw*, xii (1929–30), 595]

BIBLIOGRAPHY

BurneyH
C. Burney: *The Present State of Music in Germany, the Netherlands, and United Provinces* (London, 1773, 2/1775); ed. P. Scholes as *Dr. Burney's Musical Tours* (London, 1959)

C. P. E. Bach: Autobiographical sketch, in C. D. Ebeling's trans. of the above as *Carl Burney's der Musik Doctors Tagebuch seiner musikalischen Reisen*, ii, iii (Hamburg, 1773); trans. W. S. Newman as 'Emanuel Bach's Autobiography', *MQ*, li (1965), 363 [source of the autobiographical quotations above]

[J. M. Bach, C. P. E. Bach's widow]: *Verzeichnis des musikalischen Nachlasses des verstorbenen Capellmeisters Carl Philipp Emanuel Bach* (Hamburg, 1790) [based on earlier lists by C. P. E. Bach and Johanna Maria]; repr. with notes by H. Miesner as 'Philipp Emanuel Bachs musikalischer Nachlass', *BJb*, xxxv–xxxvii (1938, 1939, 1940–48)

C. H. Bitter: *Carl Philipp Emanuel und Wilhelm Friedemann Bach und deren Brüder* (Berlin, 1868)

[F. Chrysander, ed.]: 'Briefe von K. Ph. E. Bach und G. M. Telemann', *Leipziger allgemeine musikalische Zeitung*, iv (1869), 176

A. Wotquenne: *Thematisches Verzeichnis der Werke von Carl Philipp Emanuel Bach (1714–1788)* (Leipzig, 1905/R1964)

H. Schenker: *Ein Beitrag zur Ornamentik* (Vienna, 1908)

H. von Hase: 'Carl Philipp Emanuel Bach und Joh. Gottl. Im. Breitkopf', *BJb*, viii (1911), 86

R. Steglich: 'Karl Philipp Emanuel Bach und der Dresdner Kreuzkantor Gottfried August Homilius im Musikleben ihrer Zeit', *BJb*, xii (1915), 39–145

O. Vrieslander: *Carl Philipp Emanuel Bach* (Munich, 1923)

H. Uldall: *Das Klavierkonzert der Berliner Schule* (Leipzig, 1928)

H. Miesner: *Philipp Emanuel Bach in Hamburg* (Heide, 1929/R1969)

E. F. Schmid: *Carl Philipp Emanuel Bach und seine Kammermusik* (Kassel, 1931)

A. Schering: 'C. Ph. E. Bach und das redende Prinzip in der Musik', *JbMP 1938*, 13

A. E. Cherbuliez: *Carl Philipp Emanuel Bach 1714–1788* (Zurich and Leipzig, 1940)

D. Plamenac: 'New Light on the Last Years of Carl Philipp Emanuel Bach', *MQ*, xxxv (1949), 565

K. von Fischer: 'C. Ph. E. Bachs Variationenwerke', *RBM*, vi (1952), 190

E. Beurmann: *Die Klaviersonaten Carl Philipp Emanuel Bachs* (diss., U. of Göttingen, 1952)

C. R. Haag: *The Keyboard Concertos of Karl Philipp Emanuel Bach* (diss., U. of California, Los Angeles, 1956)

G. Busch: *C. Ph. E. Bach und seine Lieder* (Regensburg, 1957)

W. S. Newman: *The Sonata in the Classic Era* (Chapel Hill, 1963, rev. 2/1972)

——: 'Emanuel Bach's Autogiobraphy', *MQ*, li (1965), 363

P. Barford: *The Keyboard Music of C. P. E. Bach* (London, 1965)

E. Suchalla: *Die Orchestersinfonien Carl Philipp Emanuel Bachs nebst einem thematischen Verzeichnis seiner Orchesterwerke* (Augsburg, 1968)

M. Terry: 'C. P. E. Bach and J. J. H. Westphal – a Clarification', *JAMS*, xxii (1969), 106

E. R. Jacobi: 'Five hitherto unknown Letters from C. P. E. Bach to J. J. H. Westphal', *JAMS*, xxiii (1970), 119

E. Helm: 'The "Hamlet" Fantasy and the Literary Element in C. P. E. Bach's Music', *MQ*, lviii (1972), 277

E. R. Jacobi: 'Three Additional Letters from C. P. E. Bach to J. J. H. Westphal', *JAMS*, xxvii (1974), 119

R. Angermüller: Complete edn. of C. P. E. Bach's correspondence (in preparation)

See also bibliography to §II.

(10) Johann Ernst Bach (*34*) (*b* Eisenach, baptized 30 Jan 1722; *d* Eisenach, 1 Sept 1777). Son of (5) Johann Bernhard Bach (*18*). On 16 January 1737 he entered the Thomasschule in Leipzig and became a pupil of his uncle (7) Johann Sebastian (*24*). After studying law at the university he returned to Eisenach in 1742 and deputized, without pay, for his ailing father. In 1748 he became his father's official assistant and the next year his successor. He continued to practise as a lawyer as well, and in 1756 he was appointed Hofkapellmeister 'in view of his well-known skill and musical knowledge'. He wrote the foreword to Adlung's *Anleitung zu der musikalischen Gelahrtheit* (Erfurt, 1758). Because of the fusion of the courts, he travelled between Weimar, Gotha and Eisenach and worked with Georg Benda on the reorganization of the Hofkapelle. When it was dissolved in 1758, after the death of Duke Ernst August, he retained his title and undertook duties in the administration of the ducal finances.

As a composer, Johann Ernst was abreast of the stylistic innovations of his time although, like Johann Sebastian's sons, he did not exclude contrapuntal writing. His vocal works are often highly dramatic and full of effects. His songs depend on the older tradition of Görner, Gräfe and Mizler; he wrote *galant* melodies full of expressive word-painting with lively basses and often elaborate accompaniments. His Passion oratorio is modelled on C. H. Graun's well-known *Der Tod Jesu*.

WORKS

VOCAL

O Seele, deren Sehnen (Passion oratorio), 1764, ed. in DDT, xlviii (1914)

Cantatas: Straf mich nicht in deinem Zorn; Alles was Odem hat, *D-Bds*; Der Meer ist nahe, *B*; Die Liebe Gottes ist ausgezogen, *B*; Kein Stündlein geht dahin, *B*

Magnificat, *B*; Herzlich lieb hab ich dich (Ps xviii), *B*; Mass [Ky–Gl] on Es wolle Gott uns gnädig sein, *Bds*

Sammlung auserlesener Fabeln, i (Nuremberg, 1749) [pt.ii lost], ed. in DDT, xlii (1910)

INSTRUMENTAL

3 Sonaten, vn, bc, pt.1 (Eisenach, 1770)

3 Sonaten, vn, bc, pt.2 (Eisenach, 1772)

2 fantasias and fugues, F, d, ed. D. Hellmann, *Orgelwerke der Familie Bach* (Leipzig, 1967)

Sonatas, kbd: A, *D-B*; D. ed. in NM, ii (1927); f, ed. K. Geiringer, *Music of the Bach Family* (Cambridge, Mass., 1955); G. in J. U. Haffner, Oeuvres melées, vi (Nuremberg, *c*1760)

10 org chorales

BIBLIOGRAPHY

H. Kühn: 'Vier Organisten Eisenachs aus Bachischem Geschlecht', *Bach in Thüringen* (Berlin, 1950)

G. Kraft: 'Bach, Johann Ernst', *MGG*

(11) Johann Christoph Friedrich Bach (*49*) (*b* Leipzig, 21 June 1732; *d* Bückeburg, 26 Jan 1795). The 'Bückeburg Bach', eldest surviving son of (7) Johann Sebastian (*24*) and Anna Magdalena Bach, and third of the four Bach sons who reached musical eminence. Taught music by his father, and well tutored in other subjects as well as music by his distant cousin (39) Johann Elias Bach, Friedrich matriculated at the University of Leipzig to study law, probably in late 1749; but by early 1750 Sebastian was seriously ill, and Friedrich gave up his student career to accept a position as chamber musician to Count Wilhelm of Schaumburg-Lippe in Bückeburg, at a salary of 200 thalers. He remained in the service of that court until his death.

The Bückeburg court, though small, was among the most genuinely cultured in Germany, thanks to Count Wilhelm. Its predominantly Italian music was led by Angelo Colonna as 'Concert-Meister' and Giovanni Battista Serini as composer; Friedrich was at first only a member of the orchestra. When the Seven Years War broke out in 1756 the Italians departed, and their duties fell to Friedrich. The count, involved in the war as an outstanding commander, was not able to transfer the title of 'Concert-Meister' officially to Friedrich until 1759, when he took the occasion of his promotion to raise Friedrich's salary to 400 thalers and to stand godfather to his first son, Wilhelm Friedrich Ernst. Friedrich had married the singer Lucia Elisabeth Münchhausen (1728–1803), daughter of a court musician, in 1755.

When the war ended the count was able to encourage the blossoming of music and intellectual life in Bückeburg. Friedrich gave performances twice a week from a repertory that included oratorios, cantatas, symphonies, operas and chamber music, mainly in the Italian style – by Tartini, Jommelli, Pergolesi, Hasse etc – but also by composers such as the Stamitzes, Haydn, Rolle, Holzbauer and Gluck. His own works, however, seem to have been received with indifference by the count, and he was not always content with the provinciality of little Bückeburg and his conditions of employment there. In 1771 Friedrich's creative life took a decided turn for the better with the arrival of Johann Gottfried Herder as court pastor and consistorial counsellor. The two became close friends, and Herder provided a series of texts for oratorios, cantatas and dramatic works that Friedrich set to music in careful collaboration with the poet. Another consolation to him during this time was the warm admiration of the count's new wife. But in 1776 Herder, responding to an invitation from Goethe, abandoned the limited horizons of Bückeburg and moved to Weimar. His departure was made more depressing for Friedrich by the death of the countess; the count himself died a year later.

By this time young Wilhelm Friedrich Ernst, 18 years old, had made good progress as a musician and needed the stimulation of other surroundings. The circumstances seemed appropriate for Friedrich to take a leave of absence, so in April 1778 he and Wilhelm travelled to England to visit Johann Christian. They went by way of Hamburg and visited Emanuel. Arriving in London at the height of the musical season, they took full advantage of the city, hearing, among other attractions, Johann Christian's new opera *La clemenza di Scipione* and the Bach–Abel concerts in Hanover Square. Friedrich bought a pianoforte for himself, along with much new music, and became a confirmed admirer of Mozart. After some weeks in London he returned to Bückeburg, leaving Wilhelm in Christian's care.

In his last years at Bückeburg, under Count Philipp Ernst and the regent Countess Juliane, Friedrich was able to maintain a high standard of performance. He enjoyed the friendship of K. G. Horstig, who had succeeded Herder at the court. Horstig's obituary–biography of Friedrich, which refers to his 'uprightness, magnanimity, obliging nature and courtesy', is the most valuable primary source of information about the composer's life. Friedrich died at the age of 62 of an 'acute chest fever'.

When J. C. F. Bach arrived at the Bückeburg court at the age of 18, he had been imbued with the contrapuntal style of his father, and with the north German seriousness of expressive purpose exemplified by Emanuel; yet at Bückeburg he found himself in Italianate musical surroundings: lyrical melody, with homophonic textures and slow harmonic rhythms. It is therefore no surprise that his first solid body of work is a compromise – or, in successive works, an alternation – between northern and southern stylistic ideals. Towards the end of his career his style became increasingly Classical, partly because of the influence of Johann Christian. His attraction to Mozart and Gluck was illustrated after his return from London by his Bückeburg productions of *Die Entführung aus dem Serail* and *Iphigénie en Tauride*.

Friedrich was an outstanding virtuoso of the keyboard, yet the sonatas and short keyboard pieces he chose to have published are mainly lightweight, verging on the *galant* style (though some show the influence of C. P. E. Bach's expressive style). Also rather superficial is his chamber music, in spite of the remarkably forward-looking independence of its individual parts. His keyboard concertos and symphonies, especially his last symphony (1794), show him in the progressive last stage of his career: not an innovator, but certainly under the influence of Haydn and Mozart. Hardly a single genre of vocal music was neglected by him. In his sacred and secular songs he did not altogether escape the aridity of the *Odenfabrikanten* who filled the popular collections of his time; but where there was a chance for dramatic expression, as in the accompanied recitatives of his 'monodramas' (solo cantatas), he showed real imagination. The choral compositions, especially the oratorios on texts by Herder, are essentially conservative and lyrical in style but laid out with real dramatic understanding.

WORKS

Catalogue: H. Wohlfarth: 'Neues Verzeichnis der Werke von Johann Christoph Friedrich Bach', *Mf*, xiii (1960), 404; repr. in *Johann Christoph Friedrich Bach* (Berne, 1971) [HW]

Edition: *J. C. F. Bach: Ausgewählte Werke*, ed. G. Schünemann, Fürstliches Institut für Musikwissenschaftliche Forschung, ser.3 (Bückeburg, 1920–22) [AW]

Sources: principal MSS in *D-B*, *Bds*; most lost MSS not recovered after World War II; for full information see HW

C. P. E. Bach, ed.: *Musikalisches Vielerley* (Hamburg, 1770), contains HW VII/1, VIII/2, X/3, XI/1–2, XII/3–7, XIX/1

J. C. F. Bach, ed.: *Musikalische Nebenstunden*, i–iv (Rinteln, 1787–8), contains HW I/5, IX/2–3, XI/4–7, XII/13, XVIII/3 and 6, XIX/2

ORCHESTRAL

HW	
I/1–20	20 syms., nos.7–9, 11–19 MSS lost; nos.6, 10, 20 facs. edn. ed. H. Wohlfarth (Bückeburg, 1966)
II/1–5	5 concs., kbd, orch, no.3 lost
III	Concerto, kbd, ob, orch, lost

CHAMBER

IV	Septet, 2 hn, ob, 2 cl, 2 bn, lost
V	Sextet, pf, 2 hn, ob, vn, vc, MS lost; ed. in AW, vii/3 (1920) [also attrib. to (12) J. C. Bach]
VI	Sei quartetti, fl, vn, va, b (Hamburg, ?1768); no.1 ed. H. Ruf (Kassel, 1958); no.3 ed. K. Geiringer,

	Music of the Bach Family (Cambridge, Mass., 1955)
VII/1–7	7 trios: 1, fl, vn, bc, ed. G. Frotscher (Hamburg, 1956); 2, 2 vn, bc; 3, 2 vn, bc; 4, hpd, fl/vn, vc, ed. in AW, vii/4 (1920), also ed. in NM, cxcii (1957); 5, hpd/pf, vn, va, ed. in AW, vii/1 (1920); 6, hpd/pf, vn, va; 7, hpd/pf, fl, vn, ed. in AW, vii/2 (1920)
VIII/1–2	8 sonatas, kbd, fl/vn; no.1 ed. W. Hinnenthal (Leipzig, 1937)
VIII/3	Sechs Sonaten, kbd, fl/vn (Riga, 1777); ed. H. Ruf (Mainz, 1967)
IX/1–3	3 sonates, vn, kbd, no.1 lost
X/1–3	3 sonatas, vc, bc, no.2 lost
X/4	Sonata, vc, kbd, MS lost; transposed and ed. J. Smith (Brunswick, 1905)

KEYBOARD
(all for harpsichord or piano)

XI/1–2, 4–7, 9	7 sonatas; no.1 ed K. Schubert (Stuttgart and Berlin, 1928); no.9 lost
XI/3	Sechs leichte Sonaten (Leipzig, 1785); ed. H. Ruf and H. Bemmann (Mainz, 1968); 2 ed. in AW, v/1–2 (1920)
XI/8	Drey leichte Sonaten (Rinteln, 1789); 1 ed. in AW, v/3 (1920)
XII/1–12	13 small pieces: variations, minuets, polaccas; no.1 lost; no.2 ed. H. Riemann (Leipzig, n.d.); no.3 ed. K. Herrmann (Frankfurt am Main, n.d.); nos.5 and 11 ed. K. Soldan (Frankfurt am Main, n.d.)
XII/13	69 small pieces: variations, minuets, polaccas, marches, character-pieces etc, in *Musikalische Nebenstunden* [see above]; some ed. K. Soldan (Frankfurt am Main, n.d.); some ed. K. Geiringer (Vienna, 1936), and in *Music of the Bach Family* (Cambridge, Mass., 1955)
XII/14	Fughetta on the name H(ans)-C(hristoph)-F(Friedrich)-B(ückeburger)-B-A-C-H
XIII/1–2	2 sonatas for 4 hands; no.1 ed. H. Riemann (Leipzig, n.d.); no.2 ed. in AW, v/4 (1920)

ORATORIOS AND SACRED CANTATAS
(all those extant are for solo voices, chorus and orchestra)

XIV/1	Der Tod Jesu (cantata, C. W. Ramler); ed. H. Salzwedel (Bückeburg, 1964)
XIV/2	Die Kindheit Jesu (oratorio, J. G. Herder); ed. in DDT, lvi (1917/R)
XIV/3	Die Auferweckung Lazarus (oratorio, Herder); ed. in DDT, lvi (1917/R)
XIV/4	Pfingstkantate (Herder), music lost
XIV/5	Michaels Sieg (cantata, Herder)
XIV/6	Michaelis-Kantate (Herder)
XIV/7	Der Fremdling auf Golgotha (oratorio, Herder), music lost
XIV/8	Himmelfahrts-Musik (cantata, Herder)
XIV/9	Die Hirten bey der Krippe Jesu (oratorio, Ramler), music lost
XIV/10	Die Auferstehung und Himmelfahrt Jesu (oratorio, Ramler), music frag.
XIV/11	Singet dem Herrn ein neues Lied (cantata), music frag.
XIV/12	Gott wird deinen Fuss nicht gleiten lassen (cantata)

OTHER SACRED VOCAL

XV/1–2	2 motets, SATB, ed. in AW, i/1–2 (1921)
XV/3–4	2 partsongs, SATB
XXI/1–3	3 arrs. of C. P. E. Bach solo songs for SATB
XVI/1	5 solo songs in D. Balthasar Münters Erste Sammlung geistlicher Lieder (Leipzig, 1773)
XVI/2	50 solo songs in J. Balthasar Münters ... Zweyte Sammlung geistlicher Lieder (Leipzig, 1774)

DRAMATIC

XVII/1	Brutus (Drama zur Musik, Herder), music lost
XVII/2	Philoktetes (Scenen mit Gesang, Herder), music lost
XVII/3	Mosis Mutter und ihre Tochter (Duodrama, H. S. C. Stille), S, S, insts, music frag.

SOLO CANTATAS, DUETS, ARIAS AND SONGS

XVIII/1	Cassandra (cantata), A, insts; ed. K. Geiringer, Music of the Bach Family (Cambridge, Mass., 1955)
XXVIII/2	L'inciampo (cantata), S, bc
XVIII/3	Die Amerikanerin (lyrisches Gemählde, H. W. von Gerstenberg), S, insts (Riga, 1776); ed. G. A. Walter (Berlin, 1919)
XVIII/4	Ino (cantata, Ramler), S, insts, vocal score (Leipzig, 1780)

XVIII/5	Pygmalion (cantata, Ramler), A/B, insts
XVIII/6	Prokris und Cephalus (cantata), S, S, ?bc [known only in vocal score in *Musikalische Nebenstunden*]
XVIII/7	O, wir bringen gerne dir (duet), S, S, bc
XVIII/8	Luci amate a non piangete (aria), S, insts
XIX/1	5 solo songs in *Musikalisches Vielerley*
XIX/2	24 solo songs in *Musikalische Nebenstunden*

BIBLIOGRAPHY

K. G. Horstig: 'Nekrolog auf den Tod Johann Christoph Friedrich Bachs', *Nekrolog der Deutschen auf das Jahr 1795*, ed. A. H. F. von Schlichtegroll (Gotha, 1797)

G. Schünemann: 'Johann Christoph Friedrich Bach', *BJb*, xi (1914), 45–165

——: 'Friedrich Bachs Briefwechsel mit Gerstenberg und Breitkopf', *BJb*, xiii (1916), 20

——: *Thematisches Verzeichnis der Werke von Johann Christoph Friedrich Bach*, DDT, lvi (1917) [with monograph on the composer]

G. Hey: 'Zur Biographie Johann Friedrich Bachs und seiner Familie', *BJb*, xxx (1933), 77

U. Wolfhorst: 'Ein Orgelgutachten von Johann Christoph Friedrich Bach', *Mf*, xiii (1960), 55

W. S. Newman: *The Sonata in the Classic Era* (Chapel Hill, 1963, rev. 2/1972)

H.-J. Schulze: 'Frühe Schriftzeugnisse der beiden jüngsten Bach-Söhne', *BJb*, l (1963–4), 61

H. Wohlfarth: *Johann Christoph Friedrich Bach* (Berne, 1971) [incl. list of works]

(12) Johann [John] **Christian Bach** (*50*) (*b* Leipzig, 5 Sept 1735; *d* London, 1 Jan 1782). Son of (7) Johann Sebastian Bach (*24*). He was one of the most versatile composers of the second half of the 18th century. His style, which was largely derived from Italian opera, was the most important single influence on Mozart, and rested on a foundation of excellent craftsmanship, graceful melody and a fine sense of form, texture and colour. With C. F. Abel, he played an important part in the establishment of regular public concerts in London.

1. Germany and Italy. 2. London, 1762–72. 3. Mannheim and London, 1772–8. 4. The last years. 5. Church music and oratorio. 6. Operas. 7. Orchestral music. 8. Keyboard and chamber music. 9. Reputation.

1. GERMANY AND ITALY. Johann Christian was the youngest son and the tenth of the 12 children of Johann Sebastian Bach and his second wife, Anna Magdalena. Nothing is known of his schooling, but his second cousin Johann Elias (*39*), who lived with the family from 1738 to 1743, may have assisted with his education. Probably, in accordance with family tradition, he began lessons in keyboard playing and theory with his father in 1743 or 1744.

After his father's death in 1750, Johann Christian (who had inherited a generous share of the estate, including three harpsichords) left Leipzig to live with his brother Carl Philipp Emanuel in Berlin; under him he studied composition and keyboard playing. His performances, according to Gerber, were much admired in Berlin; his compositions of this period include keyboard pieces and concertos.

In 1754 (according to a note in C. P. E. Bach's *Ursprung*, supported by Gerber), Johann Christian went to Italy; possibly he travelled with an Italian lady singer. No details are known of his early years there, but probably he spent some time in Bologna, studying under Padre Martini; his correspondence with Martini, written in tones of affection and respect, starts with a letter from Naples in 1757 and continues with others from Milan in the following years (in *I-Bc*). He also acquired a patron, Count Agostino Litta, of Milan. Martini's tuition and Litta's influence directed Bach towards a safe career as a church musician. By 1757 he had been received into the Roman Catholic faith, and in June 1760 he was appointed one of the two organists at Milan Cathedral. As organist Bach was not required to

compose; most of his liturgical works were in fact written before his appointment.

Bach was not, however, as attentive to his cathedral duties as Count Litta wished, and was absent from Milan during much of 1761. His career was already moving in another direction. He had received an invitation to compose a work for the Teatro Regio in Turin and his first opera, *Artaserse*, was given there on 26 December 1760; the libretto, like several that Bach was to set, was by Metastasio. He was next commissioned to write an opera for Naples, to celebrate the name day of Charles III of Spain: this was *Catone in Utica*, performed at the Teatro S Carlo on 4 November 1761 and revived there in 1764. It was a great success, and proved to be Bach's most widely performed opera, with other revivals in Milan (1762), Pavia, Perugia and Parma (1763), and Brunswick (1768). While in Naples Bach was apparently specially attentive to a ballet dancer, Colomba Beccari, whom he had first met in Turin. The success of *Catone* and Hasse's inability to gain leave of absence from Vienna to fulfil a commission led to Bach's writing a second opera for Naples, *Alessandro nell'Indie*, which, preceded by a cantata (also by Bach), was given on 20 January 1762 in celebration of the King of Spain's birthday. The reception of this opera, although less enthusiastic than that for *Catone*, was sufficiently warm for the S Carlo administration to seek permission to re-engage Bach for the following season. But by then he had received offers from Venice and London, and in May 1762 he petitioned the cathedral authorities in Milan for a year's leave of absence to compose two operas for the King's Theatre in London.

2. LONDON, 1762–72. Unlike the court theatres of the European mainland, the London opera houses were run on commercial lines. It was doubtless because of the need for economy that, for the first three months of the 1762–3 season, Bach was engaged in the presentation only of pasticcios (they included items of his own composition). Burney suggested that the delay in producing his own operas may have been occasioned by lack of faith in the available singers. The first of his contracted operas, *Orione*, was given on 19 February 1763, with considerable acclaim ('every judge of Music perceived the emanations of genius' – Burney) and the second, *Zanaida*, on 7 May. At the end of the season the management of the King's Theatre changed hands and, as one of the new directors was the composer Giardini, who was unfavourably disposed towards potential rivals, particularly non-Italians, Bach was not re-engaged. He was invited to return to Naples for the 1763–4 season, but preferred to remain in London. His activities had not been confined to the King's Theatre. The dedication of his op.1 concertos to Queen Charlotte, who was of German birth, shows that by March 1763 he enjoyed royal favour and patronage, and within a year he was able to advertise himself as the queen's music master. On 15 December 1763 he obtained a privilege for the publication of his works.

During his first year in London Bach lodged with the director of the King's Theatre, Colomba Mattei. On her return to Italy, he moved to new lodgings in Meard's Street, Soho, which he shared with his compatriot, Carl Friedrich Abel, the composer and viola da gamba player who had lived in London since 1758. This friendship, which may have dated back to their boyhood days in Leipzig, was to have a major impact on London's concert life. Their first joint concert, which included an unidentified serenata in two acts by Bach, was at the Great Room in Spring Gardens on 29 February 1764. Two months later the eight-year-old Mozart arrived in London for a stay that was to last until July 1765; during that time he not only established a warm personal relationship with Bach but also fell under his influence as a composer. They are known to have improvised jointly at least once. No formal master–pupil relationship seems to have existed, but the charm of Bach's personality and the quality of his music clearly attracted the young Mozart.

In 1764 the management of the King's Theatre changed hands, and Bach's services were again called upon. He contributed to the two pasticcios that opened the season, and on 26 January 1765 his new opera *Adriano in Siria* had the first of its seven performances. Perhaps Bach's popularity had raised the expectations of the public too high and 'the opera failed. Every one seemed to come out of the theatre disappointed' (Burney); but the songs published separately enjoyed considerable success.

Three days earlier Bach, assisted by Abel, had directed the first concert in the subscription series organized by Teresa Cornelys at Carlisle House, Soho Square. They gave ten concerts that year; in 1766 the number was increased to 15 and it remained at that level until 1781, when only 12 concerts were given. The concerts took place on Wednesdays from January to May except in Holy Week. Bach and Abel alternated as director, and much of the music performed was of their own composition, including Bach's cantatas, his op.3 symphonies (published in 1765) and later his op.18 symphonies. The concerts remained at Carlisle House for three seasons; in January 1768, when Bach and Abel took over the management, they moved to Almack's Assembly Rooms in King Street, St James's, where the Bach–Abel Concerts (as they became known) remained until 1774.

January 1765 also saw the first performance of the ballad opera *The Maid of the Mill* at the Theatre Royal, Covent Garden; Bach's contributions, a song and a duet, brought his art to a wider audience than those that frequented the King's Theatre or the fashionable concerts of the nobility and gentry. In 1766 he reached a still wider public with the songs he composed for Mrs Weichsell to sing in Vauxhall Gardens; altogether he published three collections of Vauxhall songs.

In autumn 1766 the soprano Cecilia Grassi, later to become Bach's wife, came to London for a season as prima donna for the serious operas at the King's Theatre. Poor health prevented her from taking part in Bach's new opera, *Carattaco*, first performed on 14 February 1767. The work was only a limited success; the public was more interested in Piccinni's comic operas. Bach apparently also supplied the music for an operetta, *The Fairy Favour*, presented at Covent Garden on 31 January when the four-year-old Prince of Wales, making his first visit to a theatre.

Since his arrival in England Bach had always been ready to help his professional colleagues by taking part in their benefit concerts (his 'expressive and masterly', but not brilliant, keyboard style is interestingly discussed by Burney, ii, p.866). On 2 June 1768 at a concert at the Thatched House Tavern in St James's Street in aid of the oboist J. C. Fischer, he played a 'Solo on the Piano Forte', using an instrument by Johannes Zumpe: appar-

ently this was the first time that the piano was publicly used as a solo instrument in London. Bach's op.5 sonatas were published, in 1766, as 'pour le clavecin ou le piano forte'.

In autumn 1769 Cecilia Grassi returned to London, having sung in Palermo and Naples since her departure in 1767. Bach too returned to the King's Theatre. He contributed not only to the two pasticcios that began the season but also joined with Guglielmi in arranging the London première of Gluck's *Orfeo ed Euridice*, supplementing the music so that it would be 'of a necessary length for an evening's entertainment'. Although their additions, inserted between the scenes of Gluck's opera, ran counter to Gluck's 'reform' principles (Burney remarked on the damage done to the 'unity, simplicity, and dramatic excellence of this opera'), the arrangement enjoyed a considerable public success. There were 13 performances in 1770, six in 1771 and three in 1773, and on 4 November 1774 this version was given at the S Carlo theatre in Naples.

In 1770 Bach presented a series of oratorio performances at the King's Theatre on Thursdays in Lent and in Easter week, competing with the well-established series on Wednesdays and Fridays at Drury Lane and Covent Garden. The repertory consisted of a Passion by Jommelli, Pergolesi's *Stabat mater* and Bach's own oratorio *Gioas, rè di Giuda*. Cecilia Grassi was prevented by illness from taking part in the first of the three performances, on 22 March. The oratorio venture was not a commerical success, and Bach, who at the 'express command' of the queen played a concerto on the organ between the acts, suffered a public humiliation when his style of organ playing – markedly different from the Handelian tradition – was hissed by the audience and laughed at by the boys in the chorus. *Gioas* was revived in January 1771, but after two more oratorio evenings in Lent Bach abandoned the form.

The following spring Johann Baptist Wendling, first flautist in the electoral orchestra at Mannheim and husband of Dorothea Wendling, the prima donna of the Mannheim Opera, visited London; he, with Bach, Abel and the cellist J.-P. Dupont, held a concert in May 1771. Wendling lodged with Bach and Abel in King's Square Court during the first part of his stay in London and moved with Bach to his new home in Queen Street, Golden Square, before April 1772. On 6 April 1772 Wendling and Cecilia Grassi took part in the first performance of Bach's cantata *Endimione* at the King's Theatre.

3. MANNHEIM AND LONDON, 1772–8. It may have been Bach's collaboration with Wendling that led to his receiving a commission to compose an opera for the name day celebrations of Elector Carl Theodor in Mannheim in autumn 1772. He accepted, and arrived in Mannheim in August or September (possibly having visited Italy during the summer), where he almost certainly enjoyed the hospitality of the Wendlings; according to Mozart's mother, Bach fell in love with their daughter, Augusta (*b* 1756). The first performance of the opera, *Temistocle*, was given on 4 or 5 November, before a distinguished audience and with an excellent cast; it was so successful that it was revived in November 1773, and Bach was invited to return to write a new opera for 1774. This was *Lucio Silla*, also first performed on 4 November. The libretto was the one written by Giovanni de Gamerra for Mozart in

13. *Johann Christian Bach: portrait by Thomas Gainsborough (1727–88) in the Civico Museo Bibliografico Musicale, Bologna*

1772 and adapted, as was Metastasio's for *Temistocle*, to the Mannheim taste by the court poet Mattia Verazi. *Lucio Silla* was less successful; but Mozart examined the score in 1777, and his letter of 13 November makes clear his high opinion of it. Other works from Bach's periods at Mannheim include the cantatas *Amor vincitore* and *La tempesta*.

Between his visits to Mannheim Bach maintained his usual busy round of activities in London. His duties at court included giving music lessons to the queen and her growing family, directing the Queen's Band, accompanying the king's flute playing, and contributing both as composer and performer to chamber music for the queen's entertainment in the evenings.

In summer 1773 Bach and Cecilia Grassi visited the west of England: they performed in Blandford on 14 July and in early October appeared at the Salisbury Musical Festival, where Bach 'favoured the company with an elegant performance on the harpsichord'. He revisited Blandford in 1776. His marriage to Cecilia may have taken place shortly after the 1773 journey; by January 1774 he had moved to 80 Newman Street and Abel elsewhere. In that month the Bach–Abel concerts returned to Carlisle House, Soho, now vacated by the bankrupt Mrs Cornelys and a cheaper venue than Almack's. This was to be their home for only one season. On 28 June 1774 Bach, Abel and Giovanni Andrea Gallini acquired a property on the corner of Hanover Street and Hanover Square, Bach and Abel each providing a quarter of the capital of £5000, and had a new concert hall built in the garden. On 1 February 1775 it was inaugurated by the first concert of the new season of Bach–Abel concerts. The move was not a financial success; Bach had overreached himself, and was not helped by a fall in the receipts for the concerts, which suffered from the competition of the new Monday series at the Pantheon. On 12 November 1776 the syndicate was dissolved; the Bach–Abel concerts remained at the Hanover Square Rooms, but declined rapidly in popularity, as the sharp drop in receipts after 1774 shows. It has been suggested that they were able to continue only because of support from the Earl of Abingdon, Gallini's father-in-law.

Bach continued to take part in benefit concerts for his colleagues. The first performance of his cantata *Cefalo e Procri* was given at Hanover Square on 26 April 1776 for the 'Benefit of Signora Salis'; it was performed twice in May 1777 (it also formed part of Tenducci's Bach Commemoration on 17 May 1786). In that month Bach appeared on the London concert platform on no fewer than ten occasions, and *Orione* was revived on 24 May. The following season he presented a new opera, *La clemenza di Scipione*, which began a run of eight performances on 4 April 1778; between the sixth and seventh Bach presented a new cantata, *Rinaldo ed Armida*, at the Hanover Square Rooms.

In 1776 Padre Martini had asked Bach for a portrait for his private collection; according to Bach it was finished in May 1776, but it was not until July 1778 that he despatched it to Bologna, in the care of the castrato Francesco Roncaglia. The artist was his friend Thomas Gainsborough, who also executed a second portrait of him; one is still in Bologna (see fig.13), the other in the Earl of Hillingdon's collection. A bust of Johann Christian almost certainly dates from this time too; Johann Christoph Friedrich Bach, who formerly owned it, visited his brother in London in summer 1778

(leaving his son Wilhelm Friedrich Ernst in London with his uncle).

4. THE LAST YEARS. Bach's music had been played and published in Paris for more than a decade, and in 1778 he received a commission to write an opera for the Académie Royale de Musique. He visited Paris in August 1778 to hear the singers who were to take part; Mozart, then in Paris, wrote to his father of Bach's and his mutual delight in meeting, commenting on his affection for Bach and his pleasure in Bach's friendly praise of him. Bach wrote his new opera in London and returned to Paris in August 1779; the first performance of *Amadis de Gaule* was given on 14 December, before Queen Marie Antoinette. The opera was much criticized, partly because of the revisions that had been made to Quinault's 1684 libretto, partly because, given at the height of the Gluck–Piccinni controversies, it pleased neither side. It was withdrawn for revision after three performances, returning to the stage for four more a month later. However, Bach's first attempt at a French opera was a disaster neither for the Opéra nor for him: according to Brenet, he was engaged on a new commission at the time of his death.

Back in London, Bach's name appeared on the list of composers for the coming season in the King's Theatre advertisements in autumn 1779, 1780 and 1781; but he never again composed for that theatre. The Bach–Abel concerts continued their decline in popularity, although Bach and his music still figured prominently in public concerts. On 17 May 1779 at the Hanover Square Rooms Tenducci considered it to his advantage to include several works by Bach – a symphony for two orchestras (in the op.18 set, *c*1781), a Scotch Air, a quintet and *Amor vincitore* – in his benefit concert.

Bach's declining fortunes suffered another blow when, as the result of a rumour that he was about to give up his house in Richmond, the local tradesmen pressed for the settlement of their accounts; it was found that Bach's housekeeper had forged receipts for over £1000 and absconded with the money. He was in serious financial straits; his music was no longer in demand at the opera house, where the dominant figure was Sacchini, and his position as a leading teacher had been undermined by the advent of J. S. Schroeter, a pianist and composer to whom Bach had earlier given generous help and advice 'and assisted . . . as a friend, for his heart was too good to know the littleness of envy' (that comment of Mrs Papendiek is one of many in her memoirs referring to Bach and his activities in court circles, in which, as in London's artistic community and particularly its German-biassed part, he was treated with admiration and affection).

His health began to decline in 1781, and he moved to Paddington for a change of air. In November he made his will, leaving everything to his wife; he died on 1 January 1782, and was buried on 6 January in St Pancras Churchyard. His debts, amounting to some £4000, were never fully repaid. Neither the Bach–Abel concerts, which his widow continued for one season with Abel, nor the benefit performance at the King's Theatre on 27 May 1782 contributed significantly to their reduction. The queen helped to meet immediate expenses and enabled Cecilia Bach to return to her native Italy in summer 1782.

Bach's death – noted by Mozart as 'a loss to the musical world' – went almost unnoticed by the London public, whose appetite for novelty was no longer satisfied by the music of a man who had lived and worked among them for nearly 20 years. Mrs Papendiek noted that 'this man of ability in his profession, of liberal kindness in it, of general attention to friends, and of worthy character, was forgotten almost before he was called to the doom of us all, and every recollection of him seems buried in oblivion'.

5. CHURCH MUSIC AND ORATORIO. Bach composed almost all his Latin church music before he left Italy in 1762. Except for two solo cantatas, all the works are settings of liturgical texts with orchestral accompaniment, and demonstrate the range of styles used by composers of church music in Italy at the time. The most conservative feature is the writing for chorus. Movements in the so-called Palestrina style or 'strict style' are to be found in three works of 1757. In the Requiem (or *Ingresso*) and Kyrie in F, a plainsong cantus firmus appears in long notes in the bass in two movements ('Requiem' and 'Te decet'), 'scartato e mutato' (i.e. used freely), according to a letter from Bach to Padre Martini; this type of composition was required of all applicants for membership of the Accademia Filarmonica of Bologna, with which Martini was closely associated. (There is no record of Bach's having applied.) In the responsorial portions of the *Invitatorio* ('Regem cui omnia vivunt'), the cantus firmus appears in the upper voices but never in the bass; in the responses of the three *Lezioni* imitative counterpoint without cantus firmus is used. The influence of the Roman school is also evident in the Kyrie double fugues of 1757. Elsewhere Bach's choral fugues follow the traditional 18th-century ecclesiastical style of Fux and Martini; they appear mainly in the concluding movements of lengthy works. Double fugues are used in the earliest works; single fugues predominate from 1758. All are relatively short and lack extended episodic development, though the double fugue for eight-part chorus concluding the *Dies irae* is quite substantial. In Bach's other, homophonic choral movements the chief musical interest is often found in the accompanying figuration, but there is also often antiphonal writing, notably in the double-choir music of the *Dies irae*.

In the standard style for Catholic church music of the time, all Bach's sacred works except the shortest are divided into series of movements; sometimes they occupy unusual key relationships, moving progressively around the circle of 5ths. He often followed the contemporary practice of relating the first and last movements thematically, for example in the *Laudate pueri* in G (1760), and the *Dixit Dominus* (1758), where the favourite device of bringing back the opening material at 'sicut erat in principio' ('as it was in the beginning') is strengthened by a fugal coda on the word 'Amen'. Where soloists are used, movements employing them predominate. A considerable number of these are for two or three solo voices. Those from works written in 1757–8 are in the comparatively simple chamber duet style, but the duets and trios in the two *Gloria* settings of 1759 are highly sophisticated and original. The *Dies irae* contains the only movement for a quartet of soloists. Most of the solo movements, however, are for a single voice, and are in the expressive manner favoured in Italian church music: they show the young Bach at his most inventive, and responding to the mood of the text. Most are in standard aria form, without da capo; a

few, where the text allows, adopt a fully written-out three-part plan with contrasting middle section. One such, 'Cor mundum' from the *Miserere*, sets the central impassioned prayer ('Ne projicias me in facie tua') as an *allegro moderato* in C minor against calmer outer sections in F major ('Cor mundum crea in me, Deus' and 'Redde mihi laetitiam salutaris tui'), which use Bach's favourite Lombardic rhythm. The arias show a wide range of expression, from the *aria cantabile* to the *aria di bravura*, and cadenzas are common.

Obbligato instrumental accompaniments appear in many of Bach's church compositions. They may include short passages for a pair of flutes or a solo organ, a full-scale violin solo (*Gloria* in D), a concertante aria with two violins and cello (*Gloria* in G) and, in the aria 'Intellectus bonus' from the *Confitebor*, a chamber accompaniment of six instruments.

Bach's solitary oratorio, *Gioas, rè di Giuda*, was an attempt to adapt the Italian oratorio to the Handel-dominated English tradition. The solo numbers are in the operatic manner traditional to Italian oratorio; the choral items, most of them to texts added to Metastasio's libretto, lean heavily on the style of the church music, and indeed three of them contain reworkings of music from the *Miserere*, the *Dies irae* and the *Gloria* in D.

6. OPERAS. As a composer of Italian opera Bach was a traditionalist, preferring to follow current fashions, rather than an innovator. All ten of his Italian operas conform in essentials at least to the Metastasian type of *opera seria*. The operas he composed in Italy are all settings of revised versions of Metastasio's most popular librettos. The first, *Artaserse* (Turin, 1760), shows the most revisions: the dialogue is considerably shortened, and some of Metastasio's elegant but impersonal aria texts are replaced by others, more subjective in tone if less polished in diction. Like earlier settings of the opera, Bach's has a large number of arias, but the aria forms show a move away from the da capo types. It may be that the larger proportion of arias in da capo form found in the two operas for Naples reflect that city's greater conservatism. Bach's early success derived less from his musico-dramatic skill and the perfection of his musical forms than from the quality of his melodic invention, of which notable examples are to be found in the exquisite melancholy of 'Confusa, smarrita' (*Catone in Utica*) and the restrained grace and dignity of 'Non sò d'onde viene' (*Alessandro nell'Indie*; Mozart later commented on the beauty of Bach's setting).

In his first opera written to meet the taste of London audiences, *Orione* (1762), Bach turned away from the more orthodox *opera seria*. The subject involved the stage depiction of ritual, and gave him the opportunity to supply important parts for the chorus. The orchestra too assumed a larger role, with richer figuration, a greater prominence given to wind instruments, and the novel use of english horns and clarinets (Burney remarked on 'the richness of the harmony, the ingenious texture of the parts, and, above all, the new and happy use he had made of wind-instruments'). There are few da capo arias and, while the Metastasian ideal of elegant objectivity is observed in most solo items, the depiction of Retrea's grief in 'Più madre non sono' shows an interesting move towards the closer identification of the characters with their predicament. In the revised version (1777) this trend is taken further when Orion is allowed to die on stage. *Carattaco* (1777), with its large choral scenes, has much in common with *Orione*.

Temistocle (1772) is the most sumptuous of Bach's Italian operas. He clearly revelled in the opportunities afforded by the virtuosity of the Mannheim singers and orchestra and produced vocal numbers of extreme difficulty with accompaniments of unprecedented richness. The aria for Themistocles at the end of Act 1 is an extreme example, being virtually a double concerto for tenor, bassoon and orchestra lasting more than 12 minutes. In a number of ways, however, *Temistocle* shows a return to the purer Metastasian opera that he had begun to put behind him in his London operas *Orione* and *Carattaco*: almost all the arias are in da capo form and the chorus has an insignificant role. But the revisions by the Mannheim court poet of the ends of Acts 2 and 3 enabled Bach for the first and only time to compose extended finales. *Lucio Silla* (1774), with its very few da capo arias and more important role for the chorus, is musically on a smaller scale, and that may account for its lack of success. Both these operas have parts for the rare *clarinetto d'amore*.

La clemenza di Scipione (1778), too, with no da capo arias, shows the Metastasian *opera seria* at a late stage (and again possibly reflecting the taste of London audiences): the action is simplified, the dialogue reduced, the chorus has a dramatic function and the arias are almost all short. Arsinda's great second-act scena and aria with flute, oboe, violin and cello obbligato is a glorious exception to this general move towards more directness and economy in expression (the resemblance between this and 'Martern aller Arten' in Mozart's *Die Entführung aus dem Serail*, 1782, may be noted). The thematic link between the overture, the first scene of Act 1 and the final chorus represents an attempt to provide a special unity to the work.

Like Gluck's *Armide*, Bach's *Amadis de Gaule* (1779) was a setting of a libretto written for Lully. Its original five acts were compressed into three, and in the traditional French style there are divertissements at the end of each. The recitative is all orchestrally accompanied. The orchestra is imaginatively used; Bach seized upon every opportunity to exploit instrumental colour, particularly in the delightful ballet music. The choral writing too is impressive in quality and extent. Yet the compromise between the French conception and Italianate detail is often uneasy, and Bach clearly was handicapped by the absence of set-piece arias in the Italian style in the opera's scheme.

7. ORCHESTRAL MUSIC. At the beginning of Bach's career as an orchestral composer, there was little difference between the operatic overture and the orchestral symphony. Both were usually in three movements in a fast–slow–fast pattern; Bach never really adopted the four-movement Mannheim–Viennese pattern. His first set of six overtures (published by Walsh soon after his arrival in England), some dating from his Italian years, some from his early London years, shows brilliant invention, formal mastery and melodic charm, and was immediately successful with English audiences. However, the six symphonies op.3 make it clear that by 1765 Bach was beginning to recognize the concert symphony as a different genre from the opera overture. The two share a brisk Allegro, an Andante and a quick finale in 2/4 or 3/8 time; but in detail the first movements at least are rather different. The triadic themes and insistent

forte of the beginnings of the operatic overtures give way to a greater thematic variety in op.3, and the melody-and-bass texture of the overtures is succeeded by a fuller texture and greater use of thematic development in the symphonies. Full sonata-form recapitulations appear in some of the first movements; previously Bach had favoured a binary structure in which the recapitulation had begun only with second-subject material.

All the symphonies of the two sets published in Amsterdam as opp.6 and 8 appear to date from before 1769. They are generally on a larger scale and more serious in tone than op.3. Op.6 no.6 is the most serious of all, with its fiery, energetic outer movements and its sombre Andante, and is unique in Bach's orchestral output in using minor keys in all three movements. It is one of the most significant of the remarkable series of G minor symphonies written about this time by (for example) Haydn, Mozart, Rosetti and Vanhal.

Bach published a number of miscellaneous orchestral works, sometimes called symphonies, sometimes overtures. Thus about 1769 came the overture to *Carattaco*, a piece of great vigour, which appears in various versions, one of them serving as the overture to *Temistocle*. A set of three overtures or symphonies, appearing as op.9 (and later as op.21) is of great distinction, the little Bb symphony–overture to *Zanaida* (1763) being of particularly vivacious charm, while no.2 in Eb is a work of true symphonic dimensions, opening with a spacious Mannheim-style crescendo (an earlier example may be found in op.3 no.5) and ending with an extended minuet. Other works of a similar calibre, published both in England and on the Continent, show Bach's growing mastery of orchestral effect and formal neatness.

The peak of Bach's purely orchestral output, however, is to be found in the late op.18 collection of Six Grand Overtures published in London. Late in publication, that is; individual works date from 1769 onwards, up to at least 1779. No.2, written for *Lucio Silla* (1774), is Bach's finest operatic overture, with its sophisticated phrase structure, melodic distinction and richness of colour. No.4 in D is a taut and vigorous work, and no.6 incorporates material from *Amadis de Gaule*. No less distinguished among the set are the three grandiose Mannheim-influenced overtures for double orchestra, which exploit all possible contrasts of space and time between the two differently constituted orchestras: one of strings, oboes, bassoon and horns, one of strings and flutes (the latter often used for echo effects). Bach's use of the same music in the overtures to different operas, and his habit of rearranging works with different combinations of movements, as well as his publishers' tendency to reissue works under different numbers, has complicated the study of his symphonic output; the existence of many dubiously attributed works in manuscript (as by simply 'Bach', 'Pach' or 'Back' etc) confuses the matter further.

Bach's feeling for orchestral colour attracted him to the sinfonia concertante in the 1770s. As early as 16 April 1773 one of his compositions in this genre, much associated with Mannheim and Paris, was performed at the Concert Spirituel, and he composed many more. The number of solo instruments varies from two to nine and the orchestra always includes at least two pairs of wind instruments. Most of these works are in three movements; about a third are in the *galant* two-movement form. Many were written for leading London soloists, inluding J. C. Fischer and others of Bach's circle. Their style is apt to be leisurely. The most successful of them are the most Italianate, with no more than four solo instruments; larger solo groups created problems that Bach appeared reluctant to attempt to solve, resorting to cliché or the pedantic making of points of imitation. Yet their melodic invention and orchestral writing is highly attractive. Bach's attitude to the solo group was never rigid and it was his regular procedure to supplement it with an instrument or two from the tutti if it suited his purpose.

Apart from one concerto for flute and two each for oboe and bassoon, all apparently early works, Bach wrote solo concertos only for keyboard. Those of his Berlin period and the doubtful two published in Riga (which have also been ascribed to J. C. F. and C. P. E. Bach) exhibit the serious, somewhat angular style of the north German concerto of the time, and have little in common with his London concertos. Some of the concertos of his op.1 set, published in London in 1763 as a kind of preliminary flourish to justify his appointment as music master to the queen, may have been composed in Italy. As a whole, the set sent the English concerto off on a new path, quite different from the traditional one of Handel's concertos or of the composers of the London school.

The fourth and sixth, the only works in this set with three movements, are entitled 'Concerto o Sinfonia', and have first movements in ritornello form. However the first movements of the other four concertos establish the form of Bach's own later concertos, and may have influenced that of Mozart. The plan of the Classical concerto sonata form, with its orchestral and solo expositions and flexible attitude to motivic development and repetition, is already present in all its essentials. The opening allegros of opp.7 and 13 pursue the same pattern, now broadened and deepened, and the introduction of new thematic material to start the dominant section of the solo exposition is an innovation in some of the op.7 concertos. The op.7 no.2 concerto is almost certainly the one Bach wrote to play on the organ in the oratorio *Gioas*. Bach's most dramatic and developed concertos are nos.2 and 4 of the op.13 set, three-movement Classical concertos in miniature, with dramatic and highly developed first movements; in accordance with the growing interest in national song Bach incorporated sets of variations on popular Scottish songs in both these works.

8. KEYBOARD AND CHAMBER MUSIC. Throughout his professional life Bach was a player and teacher of keyboard instruments; and that is reflected in his output of instrumental music. Much of his published work was designed to meet the needs of his pupils and other amateur performers, and his accompanied sonatas in particular (keyboard with violin or flute, sometimes with cello), though always well written, are decidedly modest in scale and scope. (Some of the works in this genre published after Bach's death must be regarded as highly suspect.) It was no doubt Bach's accompanied sonatas that Leopold Mozart had in mind when he urged his son to write in Bach's manner, praising his 'natural, easy and flowing style' and 'sound composition'.

Bach's two sets of solo keyboard sonatas, opp.5 and 17, each open with an easy piece, presumably designed to encourage amateur performers of limited technique to purchase the publications. Both sets are described as

'for harpsichord or pianoforte', but the C minor Sonata op.5 no.6, with its prelude, fugue and gavotte structure, would seem to have been conceived for the harpsichord – unless composed to meet the conservative English taste for fugues, it may belong to the 1750s. Most of the sonatas are in two movements and in the lyrical vein of that favourite *galant* form. The three-movement works are more demanding both musically and technically, and the C minor Sonata op.17 no.2 is a particularly powerful work. The young Mozart arranged three of the op.5 sonatas as concertos, probably in about 1771 (K107).

Bach's output includes a set of six trios for two violins and viola or continuo, published in Paris by 1764 and later in London and Amsterdam. While owing something to the Baroque trio sonata, they are each in the *galant* two-movement form (a slow movement followed by a minuet); they have stylistic resemblances to the notturnos of G. B. Sammartini. Virtually all Bach's quartets involve one or two flutes and strings. Those of the op.8 set, possibly composed for J. B. Wendling, are elegant, unpretentious works in two movements, as are the three quartets originally published in 1776 along with works by Abel and Giardini. The four posthumously published quartets op.19, in three movements, are rather more substantial, doubtless reflecting the sophisticated taste of Lord Abingdon, for whose private concerts they were written, and perhaps also Haydn's influence.

Outstanding among Bach's chamber works, however, are the six quintets op.11, for flute, oboe, violin, viola and continuo, dedicated to that famous connoisseur the Elector Palatine Carl Theodor. One (no.4 in E♭) was composed, according to Mrs Papendiek, for a chamber music evening with the Queen's Band; others may also have been. There is no discernible Mannheim influence on these pieces, whose scoring is unique for their time. They are in Bach's most warm and graceful style, of exceptional melodic charm and formal elegance, and are scored with much sensitivity, ingeniously exploiting (with thematic material specially apt to the purpose) the various available combinations of instrumental colour, often in dialogue patterns. Half of them are in two movements, half in three. Two further quintets, published posthumously as op.22, are also highly characteristic works, and represent early examples of obbligato keyboard parts in concerted chamber music; associated with them, in other publications, are a piano quartet and a sextet with keyboard, violin, cello, oboe and two horns, an attractive work that has often been ascribed to Bach's brother J. C. F. Bach. In most of these works the cello is not always tied to the bass line. Besides his true chamber music, Bach contributed to the repertory of the wind (or military) band, with a number of marches and two sets of works: a collection of 'symphonies' (including music arranged from Gluck and other composers) issued in 1780 and one of 'Military Pieces' or quintets published posthumously.

9. REPUTATION. J. C. Bach enjoyed a high reputation, particularly as a composer of instrumental music, in his lifetime; his slow movements especially were regarded as music for the connoisseur. After his death his music faded from public notice, as Haydn (and later Mozart) came to be seen as the chief representatives of the later 18th century. As his own father's music came into the repertory writers lamented that Johann Sebastian's youngest son should have composed works lacking the

high seriousness of his father's as well as the originality of those of his brother, Carl Philipp Emanuel; they came to be regarded as facile and decadent. A succeeding view acknowledged that Johann Christian, being of a later generation and having been exposed to, and amenable to, a greater measure of operatic influence than any other of the Bachs, could legitimately have written music in a different style; but the same view regarded him merely as an interesting minor figure of the lower foothills of the mountainous achievement of the mature style of Mozart. In a broader historical perspective he can be seen as a highly significant figure of his time, the chief master of the *galant* style, who produced music of elegance, formality and aptness for its social purpose, and was able to infuse it with both vigour and refined sensibility.

WORKS
(printed works published in London unless otherwise stated)

Catalogue: C. S. Terry: *John Christian Bach* (London, rev. 2/1967 by H. C. R. Landon) [T] [τ numbers – page no./no. of incipit on page, not Terry's numbering; only first incipit of group given; roman numerals denote corrigenda pages]

Sources: principal MS sources are listed; items listed in T as in *D-BNu* and autographs in *D-Hs* were destroyed in World War II, and *D-SWl* 824–9 and *WRl* 349 are missing; contrary to Landon, items cited in T as in *D-W* are still there but differently numbered. Items in T not listed here are duplicated or misattributed.

* – autograph

SACRED VOCAL

T	(aria arrangements given only if not in T)
199/4	Attendite mortales, motet, T, orch, c1770, *D-Bds*, 1st aria arr. from Carattaco
200/6	Beatus vir (F), S, A, T, B, SATB, orch, 1758, *CH-E*; movt 6 = τ202/5, Dispersit; movt 7 = τ204/4, Gloria Patri
202/1	Confitebor tibi Domine (Eb), S, A, T, B, SATB, orch, 1759, *CH-E, D-Mbs, F-Pn*
202/3	Credo (C), SATB, orch, *CH-E, I-BGc* Sam E.2.10 (with Gloria, τ204/1 and Kyrie, τ204/8, headed 'Messa')
202/4	Dies irae (c), S, A, T, B, SSAATTBB, orch, 1757, *I-Bc* DD97, ?*GB-T, copies *CH-E, D-Dlb, Mbs*; ed. J. Bastian (Mainz, 1972); movt 9 with new text = τ201/4, Confitebor
202/6	Dixit Dominus (D), S, A, T, B, SATB, orch, 1758, *CH-E, I-Bc, Gi(l)*; ed. S. van Marion (Hilversum, 1973)
203/3	Domine ad adiuvandum (D), 1758, lost
203/2	Domine ad adiuvandum (G), S, A, SATB, orch, 1760, *CH-E*
204/3	Gloria in excelsis (D), S, A, T, B, SATB, orch, 1759, *CH-E, I-Gi(l)* (inc.); ed. in Vos (1969), ii, 77; movt 2 = τ205/5, Laudamus te
204/1	Gloria in excelsis (G), S, A, T, B, SATB, orch, *CH-B* (inc.), *D-B, BNms, DS, LEm, F-Pn, I-BGc*, Sala E.2.10 [see Credo, τ202/3], ?*USSR-KAu*; movt 4 = τ203/4, Domine Deus
204/8	Kyrie (D), S, T, SATB, orch, 1758, *CH-E, I-BGc* Sala E.2.10 [see Credo, τ202/3], *Gi(l)*
205/2	Larvae tremendae (A), motet, S, orch, *CH-E* [MS dated 1782]
206/3	Laudate pueri (E), S, orch, Milan, 12 Aug 1758, lost
206/1	Laudate pueri (G), S, T, orch, 1760, *E, D-B, DS*
—	Laudate pueri (Bb), S, orch, *I-Gi(l)*
199/1	Let the solemn organs blow (W. Dodd), anthem for Magdalen Chapel, c1764, in *The Christian's Magazine*, vi (1765), 140
206/4	[3] Lezioni del officio per gli morti: Parce mihi, Domine (Bb), S, A, SATB, orch, 1757; Taedet animam meam (F), S, A, T, B, SATB, orch, 1757; Manus tuae (C), S, A, T, SATB, orch, 1757 [movt 5 of no.3 = τ204/5, Gratias agimus, *CH-E*]: all *E*
207/1	Magnificat (C), SATB, SATB, orch, 1758, **GB-Lbm, Lcm*
207/2	Magnificat (C), SATB, SATB, orch, c1758, *Lbm (inc.)
207/3	Magnificat (C), S, A, T, B, SATB, orch, 1760, **Lbm, Lcm, CH-E*; ed. F. van Amelsvoort (Hilversum, 1960); ed. W. Ehret (New York, 1973)
207/5	Miserere (Bb), S, A, T, B, SATB, orch, 1757, *E, D-Mbs*; movt 2 = τ203/5, Et secundum; movt 5 = τ202/2, Cor mundum; movt 7 = τ206/7 Libera me de sanguinibus
—	Pater noster, 1757, sent to Padre Martini 6 Sept 1757, lost
208/4	Regem cui omnia vivunt (F), invitatorio, S, A, T, B, SATB, orch, 1757, *CH-E*; movt 2 with new text = τ199/2. Ad coenam agni; movt 4 with new text = τ199/3. Ad coenam agni; movt 6 = τ208/3, O lux beata Trinitatis; movt 8 = τ203/6, Exultet coelum; movt 10 = τ207/6, Nisi Dominus
208/5	Requiem, Te decet hymnus and Kyrie [Messa de' morti] (F), SSAATTBB, orch, c1757, ?*GB-T 388, copies *CH-E, D-Mbs*

209/3	Salve regina (Eb), S, orch, c1758, *GB-Lbm*
209/1	Salve regina (F), S, orch, *A-Wn*
209/5	Si nocte tenebrosa (F), motet, S/T, orch, *D-B, GB-Lbm*
210/2	Tantum ergo (F), S, orch, 1757, *CH-E*
209/7	Tantum ergo (G), S, SATB, orch, 1759, *E*
210/3	Te Deum (D), SATB, SATB, orch, 1758, *GB-Lbm (inc.)
210/5	Te Deum (D), S, A, T, B, SATB, orch, 1762, *Lbm, CH-E, D-Mbs*; ed. A. M. Müller (Augsburg, 1968)
	(spurious)
202/7	Domine ad adiuvandum (C), SATB, str, *GB-Lbm*
204/6	Mesa a più voci (Ky–Gl) (G), SATB, orch, *Lbm* [MS dated 1741]
204/7	Messa in pastorale (Ky–Gl) (D), SATB, orch, *LBm* [MS dated 1740]
208/6	Salve regina (D), S, S, A, T, B, SSATB, orch, *Lbm* [MS dated 1740]

DRAMATIC

(3-act operas unless otherwise stated)

KT – *London, King's Theatre*   CG – *London, Covent Garden Theatre*
SC – *Naples, Teatro S Carlo*   HAY – *London, New Theatre in the Haymarket*

† – *favourite songs published shortly after first performance*

217; xl	Artaserse (after Metastasio), Turin, Regio, 26 Dec 1760, *GB-Lbm (inc. *P-La, I-Nc* (1 aria), ?*Tf; ov. in Six Favourite Overtures (1763)
222; xlii	Catone in Utica (after Metastasio), SC, 4 Nov 1761, *D-Ws, F-Pc, I-Nc* (2 copies: 1761 version without recits; 1764 version with recits, Acts 1 and 2 only), *P-La*; original ov. = τ277/10
212; xxxii	Alessandro nell'Indie (after Metastasio), SC, 20 Jan 1762, *F-Pc, I-Mc, Nc, P-La*; ov. in Six Favourite Overtures (1763)
237; xlvii	Orione, ossia Diana vendicata (G. G. Bottarelli), KT, 19 Feb 1763, †, *GB-Lbm, T, US-Wc* (all inc.); ov. arr. in Six Favourite Overtures (1763)
241; xlix	Zanaida (Bottarelli), KT, 7 May 1763, †; ov. = τ269/1
211; xxxi	Adriano in Siria (after Metastasio), KT, 26 Jan 1765, †, *P-La*
—	The Fairy Favour (masque, T. Hull), CG, 31 Jan 1767, perf. by children as afterpiece, music lost
221; xli	Carattaco (?Bottarelli), KT, 14 Feb 1767, †, **B-Bc, GB-Lbm* (both inc.): ov. (n.d.)
226; xliv	Gioas, rè di Giuda (oratorio, 2, after Metastasio), KT, 22 March 1770, †, *Lcm (inc.), *A-Wgm, Wn*
238; xlviii	Temistocle (M. Verazi, after Metastasio), Mannheim, Hoftheater, 4 or 5 Nov 1772, *GB-Cfm 23.J.11–12 (Acts 1, 3), *D-B, Dlb, DS, F-Pc* (Act 1), *US-NH*; ov., *D-DS* = τ278/3; vocal score ed. E. Downes, H. C. R. Landon (Vienna, 1965), ov. ed. F. Stein, EDM, 1st ser., xxx (1956)
232; xlv	Lucio Silla (Verazi, after G. de Gamerra), Mannheim, Hoftheater, 4 Nov 1774, *DS* 60.1–3; ov. in Six Grand Overtures, op.18 (c1781); ov. ed. F. Stein (Leipzig, 1925) and G. Beechey (London, 1971)
229; xliv	La clemenza di Scipione, KT, 4 April 1778, op.14 (1778/R1972); ov. as no.1 of Deux sinfonies à grande orchestre, op.18 (Amsterdam, n.d.); ov. ed. in Diletto musicale, xcvi (1968); scene 'Arsinda', ed. R. Meylan (Frankfurt am Main, 1971)
215; xxxiii	Amadis de Gaule (de Vismes, after Quinault), Paris, Académie Royale de Musique, 14 Dec 1779 (Paris, c1780/R1972), *F-Po* (Acts 1–2, rev., ballet music; some material from cantata Cefalo e Procri, 1776)
	Material inserted in operas and pasticcios
252/2	[Ferradini: Demofoonte, Milan, 26 Dec 1758]: Misero pargoletto, aria, *A-Wgm* Q2685, *D-SWl* 832
250/5	[Cafaro: Ipermestra, Naples, 1761]: Abbiamo penato, aria, *I-Mc* Noseda B36 3
273/2	[Il tutore e la pupilla (pasticcio, Bottarelli), KT, 13 Nov 1762]: ov., from Cantata a 3 voci per festiggiare, with new 2nd movt, *GB-Lbm*, incl. in Six Favourite Overtures (1763)
273/5	[La cascina (pasticcio, Bottarelli), KT, 8 Jan 1763]; ov. in Six Favourite Overtures (1763)
273/81	[Astarto, rè di Tiro (pasticcio, Bottarelli), KT, 4 Dec 1762]: ov., from Alessandro nell'Indie, *D-B* and elsewhere, incl. in Six Favourite Overtures (1763); Deh, torna in te stesso, qt, based on τ224/7 from Catone in Utica; Io so ben, duet, lost; Per quel gentil affetto, aria, Deh, seconda, duet, lost
272/5	[Galuppi: La calamità de' cuori, KT, 3 Feb 1763]: ov., in Six Favourite Overtures (1763); Pupilla vezzosa, aria, *GB-Lbm* Add.31717
1	[Issipile (opera, Metastasio), Naples, 26 Dec 1763]: Per il bosco, aria, ? music lost; Caro se vuoi così, aria, *I-Nc*
244/1	[Menalcas (pastoral, J. Harris), Salisbury, 22 or 24 Aug 1764]: Relentless Death, aria; Muse divine, aria; See him falling, chorus; Cease, cease your tragic measures, aria; Swaynes be gay, chorus: *D-LEb* GO.S.42; arias based on τ237/2, 237/6 from Orione, 241/3 from Zanaida
225/1; xlii	[Ezio (pasticcio, after Metastasio), KT, 24 Nov 1764, †]: Non

sò d'onde viene, aria; Se il ciel mi divide, aria: from Alessandro nell'Indie

245/3 [The Maid of the Mill (pasticcio, compiled by S. Arnold, I. Bickerstaffe), CG, 31 Jan 1765]: Trust me, aria, based on τ236/1 from Orione: My life, my joy, duet

li [Zophilette (pasticcio, Marmontel), Paris, 1765]; music ?lost

219/3; xli [Berenice (pasticcio), KT, 5 Jan 1765, †]: Confusa, smarrita, aria, τ224/5 from Catone in Utica

246; li [The Summer's Tale (pasticcio, R. Cumberland), CG, 6 Dec 1765, †]: So profound an impression, aria; Yes, 'tis plain, duet, based on τ213/8 from Alessandro nell'Indie; Nature, when she gave us pleasure, aria, based on τ241/3 from Zanaida, pubd as 'See the kind indulgent gales' (c1780)

238/1 xxlviii [Sifare (pasticcio), KT, 5 March 1767, †]: Fiumicel che s'ode appena, aria, τ233/2 from Catone in Utica; Se è ver, aria τ214/4 from Alessandro nell'Indie; Per quel lo stesso labro, aria; Dovea svenarlo allora, aria, τ224/1 from Catone in Utica

li [Tom Jones (pasticcio, J. Reed, after H. Fielding), CG, 14 Jan 1769, †]: Thirst of wealth, aria; Blest with thee, aria, τ220/4 from Carattaco; When I'm in nuptial union join'd, aria

231/2 [Piccinni: Le contadine bizzarre, KT, 7 Nov 1769, †]: Sono in mar, aria, based on τ223/3 from Catone in Utica

231/3 [L'olimpiade (pasticcio, after Metastasio), KT, 11 Nov 1769, †]: Quel labbro adorato, aria

234; xlvi [Gl·ck: Orfeo ed Euridice (Bottarelli), KT, 7 April 1770, †; also SC, 4 Nov 1774, I-Nc]: Non è ver, il dir talora, aria; Chiari fonti, aria; Accorda amico, aria; Più non turbo, aria based on τ213/3 from Alessandro nell'Indie; Sulle sponde del torbido Lete, aria; Non temer, amor lo guida, aria; Obliar l'amato sposo, aria; La sventura del figlio, scena with chorus, τ251/5, *D-B (inc.), probably intended as opening of pasticcio

li [Amelia (pasticcio, R. Cumberland: The Summer's Tale), London, 14 Dec 1771]: music lost

245/2 [The Flitch of Bacon (pasticcio, compiled by W. Shield, H. Bate), HAY, 17 Aug 1778]: No, 'twas neither shape nor feature, aria, based on τ250/4, J. C. Bach's transcription of Mortellari: Io ti lascio, τ250/4

(doubtful)

[Ifigenia o le barbare furie]: Arrestatevi olà barbare furie, scena with chorus, D-B P1004

253/4 [Cleonice ?(pasticcio), KT, 26 Nov 1763]: Tu parti, mio ben, duet, D-B, Bds, GB-Lbm, by F. Bertoni

— [Demofoonte (Metastasio)]: Non dura una sventura, aria, US-AA M1505.B12.D4. ?for M. Vento: Demofoonte, KT, 2 March 1765 [according to London Stage, all music by Vento]

253/2 [?L'Olimpiade]: Quel labbro adorato, D-LÜh, different from τ231/3

CANTATAS AND SERENATAS

(cantatas unless otherwise stated)

244/6 Ode on the Auspicious Arrival and Nuptials of . . . Queen Charlotte [Thanks be to God who rules the deep] (J. Lockman), S/T, SAB, vn, bc, ?*GB-Lbm* [Charlotte arrived 8 Sept 1761, when Bach was in Italy; no perf. date known]

— Cantata a 3 voci per festiggiare il felicissimo giorno natalizio di sua Maestà cattolica (?Passeri), 2 S, T, chorus, orch, Naples, 20 Jan 1762, P-La [see ov. to Il tutore, τ273/2]; La pace all'alma mia, aria, I-Nc

— Gli orti esperidi (?Passeri, after Metastasio), Naples, S Carlo, 1765, lost, cited in F. de Filippis and R. Arnese: Cronache del Teatro di S Carlo: 1737–1960, i (Naples, 1964), 37

248/3 Endimione (serenata, after Metastasio), 3 S, T, orch, London, King's Theatre, 6 April 1772; ?rev. Mannheim, Hoftheater, 1774; *of pt.1 without ov. but with added duet [not in τ]. GB-Cfm 23.J.13, copy D-DS; ov. in Six Grand Overtures, op.18 (c1781)

247/2 Amor vincitore (?Verazi), 2 S, SATB, orch, Schwetzingen, ? Aug 1774, A-Wgm, Ds-DS, F-Pc

247/1; li Cefalo e Procri (?Bottarelli), 2 S, A, orch, London, Hanover Square Rooms, 26 April 1776, *US-Wc; ed. E. S. Derr (Ann Arbor, 1970); Già Febo, recit, Vo cercando, aria, pubd as Aurora: a Favorite Cantata (c1819), ? from MS, GB-Lbm; material from Scorsa 'o tutta la solva, acc. recit, Già Febo and Vo cercando, aria, used in Amadis de Gaule; Sconsolata, andai vagando, aria, rev. as 'Comfortless is ev'ry thought' in Orpheus and Eurydice (pasticcio assembled by William Reeve), CG, 1792, Lcm

— La tempesta (Metastasio), S, orch, Mannheim, c1776, A-Wgm Q3700, D-Bim Bach, J.C. 1; in G. J. Vogler: Betrachtungen der Mannheimer Tonschule (1778), July, pls.x–xvi, Aug, pls.vii–xvi

250/2 Rinaldo ed Armida, 3vv, orch, London, Hanover Square Rooms, 20 May 1778; lost except Serba, o caro, aria, B-Bc

3707; incl. Ebben si vada . . . Io ti lascio [see 'Transcriptions']

243/1 Happy morn, auspicious rise, 2 S, T, chorus, *GB-Lbm; ov. in oratorio Gioas, rè di Guida

(doubtful)

249/7 L'Olimpe, SATB, 2 hn, 2 cl, str, D-B (2 MSS, late 18th century)

OTHER VOCAL

Chamber duets

— [9] Duetti, 2 S, bc, ?c1760, I-Gi(l), Nc 170 (nos.1–4), F-Pc D9638(3) (not no.8): 1 Chi mai di questo core; 2 Che ciascun per te sospiri; 3 Trova un sol; 4 Io lo sò; 5 Ascoltami, oh Clori; 6 Eccomi alfin; 7 Parlami pur; 8 Lascia chi'io posso; 9 Ah che nel dirti addio [nos.5, 8 rev. as op.4 nos.6, 1; others different from op.4, 6]

259/1 Sei canzonette a due, 2 S, bc, op.4 (1765): 1 Già la notte; 2 Ah rammenta oh bella Irene; 3 Pur nel sonno almen talora; 4 T'intendo si mio cor; 5 Che ciascun per te sospiri; 6 Ascoltami, oh Clori; ed. E. Reichert (Wiesbaden, 1958)

260/2 Sei canzonette a due, 2 S, bc, op.6 (1767): 1 Torna in quel l'onda; 2 Io lo sò; 3 E pur fra le tempeste; 4 Trova un sol; 5 Chi mai di questo core; 6 S'infida tu mi chiami

Miscellaneous arias

250/6 Accender mi sento, GB-Lbm

— Ah che gli stessi numi . . . Cara ti lascio, A, orch (c1785), Lbm

— A quei sensi di gloria, I-Nc

251/2 Cato mio bene, A-Wn

247/1 Infelice . . . Là nei regni, Mez, kbd 4 hands, pubd as A Favourite Scene and Rondo on the Duke of Nirvenois Air (c1783), [? red. of orch score]

252/3 O Venere vezzosa (Horace, trans. Bottarelli), in Sei ode di Oratio . . . da Signori Bach . . . Holzbauer (c1775)

256/3 When an angry woman's breast [Neptune] (London, c1775)

(doubtful or spurious)

— Amiche solitudine . . . Verdi prati, I-Gi (l)

lii A! si barbaro colpo . . . Morte vieni, A-Wgm Q2683, US-AA M1613.B13 M6 17 – –

— Fosca Nube, che in alto s'aggira, A-Wgm Q2688

251/3 Hvad fasligt qval mitt hjerta plågar, S-Skma

251/4 La sorte spietata, in B. Mengozzi: Methode de chant du Conservatoire (Paris, 1803), 204

252/1 Misera, misera, S-Skma

— Nel cammin di nostra vita, S, orch, I-MAav

— Non temer, bell'idol mio, S, ob, orch, GB-Er W13

252/6 Parto, ma se tu m'ami, D-B

252/7 Principe non temer . . . Con si bel nome, D-B

— Se quel folle . . . Figlia, oh dio!, S, orch, I-MAav

— [9] Solfeggi . . . del Sig. Giovanni Bach in Genova 1781, S, bc, Gi(l) SS.A2.7 (G8)

— Questa date l'ho impregata, A-Wgm Q2687

253/3 Sospiri del mio cor, D-LÜh

253/5 Una semplice agnelletta, B

— Sventurata in van mi lagno, S, 2 hn obbl, orch, B P1155 [after 1773]

— Vieni, dell'amorosa Glicera . . . Di gioventù desia, A-Wgm Q3700, pp.96–128

— Vo solcando, S, orch, I-Nc

— Vò cercando, attrib. Bach, D-MÜu Bach 14; by Piccinni: La buona figliuola maritata

Vauxhall songs

254/1 A Collection of [4] Favourite Songs sung at Vaux Hall by Mrs. Weichsell (1766): 1 By my sighs; 2 Cruel Strephon; 3 Come, Colin; 4 Ah, why shou'd love

254/5 A Second Collection of [4] Favourite Songs sung at Vaux Hall by Mrs. Pinto and Mrs. Weichsel (1767): 1 In this shady blest retreat; 2 Smiling Venus; 3 Tender virgins shun deceivers (rev. of Non è ver, τ220/4 from Carattaco, later pubd as 'Blest with thee' (c1769), τ254/6 from Tom Jones (pasticcio); 4 Lovely yet ungrateful swain

255/2 A Third Collection of [4] Favorite Songs, sung at Vaux-Hall by Miss Cooper (1771): 1 Midst silent shades; 2 Ah seek to know; 3 Would you a female heart inspire; 4 Cease awhile, ye winds, to blow [pubd separately (c1800)]

256/2 Farewell, ye soft scenes: a Celebrated Air by Mr Bach (? 1790). Eng. rev. of τ231/3 from L'Olimpiade

257/2 See the kind indulgent gales: a Favourite Song sung by Mrs Weichsell at Vaux Hall Gardens (c1780), Eng. rev. of τ241/3 from Zanaida

Folksong settings

— The Braes of Ballenden [Beneath a green shade] (T. Blacklock), A, ob, vn, va, vc, pf (1779); ed. R. Fiske (London, 1969)

257/– The Broom of Cowdenknows [How blyth was I each morn] ('S.R.'), A, 2 fl, 2 vn, bc (c1784); ed. R. Fiske (London, 1969)

—	I'll never leave thee (R Crawford), A, 2 fl, 2 vn, bc (c1784); ed. R. Fiske (London, 1969)
256/-	Lochaber [Farewell to Lochaber] (A. Ramsay), A, 2 fl, 2 vn, bc (c1785); ed. R. Fiske (London, 1969)
	The Yellow-hair'd Laddie, lost; attrib. Bach in Storace: Gli equivoci, 1786, *A-Wn*

Transcriptions

250/2	Ebben si vada . . . Io ti lascio, acc. recit and rondo, Mez, ob, pf, orch, *A-Wn, B-Bc, US-NYp*, formerly *D-BNu, F-Pc, GB-Lbm*, pubd as The Favourite Rondeau [sung] by Mr Tenducci (c1778); ? from cantata Rinaldo ed Armida; expanded version of Ombra felice . . . Io ti lascio from M. Mortellari; Arsace, ¶775, cf T245/2 Flitch of Bacon; rondo also as First Favourite Rondo [Venus, Queen of tender passion], Mez, ob, hpd (?c1785)
251/7	Mi scordo i torti miei . . . Dolci aurette, acc. recit and rondo, Mez, orch, *D-Bds, WRtl*, pubd as The Favourite Rondeau (before c1785), lost; rondo from G. Gazzaniga: Perseo e Andromeda; in Six Favourite Italian Songs . . . Mr Tenducci (1778) without Bach's concluding allegro
251/1	Al mio bène (after G. Roccaforte: Antigona), rondo, Mez, pf, orch, as Rondeau . . . sung by Mr Tenducci at Messrs Bach and Abels Concert . . . 1779 (1779); vocal score in A Select Collection of the Most Admired Songs, i (Edinburgh and London, c1785); original by V. Ciampi or F. Bertoni; see Oldman (1961)
253/6	Wenn nach der Stürme Toben, aria, S, kbd, in J. A. Hiller: Deutsche Arien und Duette (Leipzig, 1785); transcr. of Allor che il vincitore, T229/4 from La clemenza di Scipione

SYMPHONIES AND OVERTURES

277/4	Ov. (D), 2 ob, 2 hn, str, no.1 in The Periodical Overture in 8 Parts (1763)
272/2	Six Favourite Overtures (1763): ovs. from the operas 1 Orione, 2 La calamità, 3 Artaserse, 4 Il tutore, 5 La cascina, 6 Astarto (= Alessandro nell'Indie)
276/3	Sym. (C), 2 ob, 2 hn, str, in Sinfonie a più stromenti, composte da vari autori, op.12 (Paris, ?1763); *CH-E* with different finale
262/1	Six simphonies (C, D, Eb, Bb, F, G), 2 ob, 2 hn, str, op.3 (1765), ed. in Diletto musicale, ccclxxix–ccclxxxiv (1975); also arr. hpd as Six Overtures Composed and Addapted for the Harpsichord (before 1769) = T347/2
275/3	An Overture in 8 Parts (D), 2 ob, 2 hn, str (1766); corrected version of Periodical Overture no.xv (1766) [pubd by Bremner]
264/1	Six simphonies (G, D, Eb, Bb, Eb, g), 2 ob, 2 hn, str, op.6 (Amsterdam, 1770), in Breitkopf suppl. 1770; nos.4, 5 in Breitkopf suppl. 1766; no.3 in Breitkopf suppl. 1767; no.6 ed. in EDM, 1st ser., xxx (1956) and ed. R. Platt (London, 1974); also with T273/2 (ov., Il tutore) as no.3 and T266/1 as no.4 (Paris, 1769), in Breitkopf suppl. 1769
266/1	Sym. (Eb), 2 ob, 2 hn, str, *D-WER*, no.4 in edn. of op.6 (Paris, by 1769)
266/4	Six symphonies périodiques (Eb, G, D, F, Bb, Eb), 2 ob, 2 hn, str, op.8 (Amsterdam, by 1770); nos.1, 5, 6 = op.6 nos.3–5; nos.4–6 in Breitkopf suppl. 1766; nos.1–3 in Breitkopf suppl. 1767
268/3	Trois simphonies (Bb, Eb, Bb), 2 fl/ob, 2 hn ad lib, str, op.9 (The Hague, 1773) [also as op.21]; no.2 = ov., Zanaida, also in Trois simphonies . . . par Mrs. Gossec, Haydn et Bach (Paris, ?1777) with different finale; no.1 ed. in EDM, 1st ser., xxx (1956)
274/4	Sym. (Eb), 2 fl/ob, 2 hn, str (Paris, ?1773), cited in Breitkopf suppl. 1773; also as Symphonie périodique, no.xxviii (Amsterdam, 1774), Periodical Overture, no.xliv (1775)
283/6	Sym. no.2 (D), 2 fl, 2 ob, 2 hn, str, in Trois symphonies . . . composées par J. C. Bach e Leduc l'aîné (Paris, ?1781)
269/4	Six Grand Overtures (Eb, Bb, D, E, D), 2 fl, 2 ob, 2 cl, 2 bn, 2 hn, 2 tpt, timp, str, op.18 (c1781); no.1 *I-Gi(l)* [MS dated 1779]; nos.1, 3, 5, for double orch (2 ob, bn, 2 hn, str; 2fl,str); no.2 = ov., Lucio Silla, no.3 = ov., Endimione, pt. of no.6 from Amadis de Gaule; no.4 = no.2 of T271/6, Deux sinfonies, op.18; nos.1–3 ed. F. Stein (Leipzig, 1925–32); nos.5–6 ed. in EDM. 1st ser., xxx (1956), no.2 ed. G. Beechey (London, 1971); no.4 ed. A. Einstein (London, 1934)
271/6	Deux sinfonies (D, D), 2 fl, 2 ob, 2 bn, 2 hn, str, op.18 (Amsterdam, c1785): no.1 = ov., La clemenza di Scipione, no.2 = no.4 of T269/4, Six Grand Overtures, op.18
279/4	Sym. (F), 2 ob, 2 hn, str, *CH-E, D-Rtt*
279/7	Sym. (F), 2 ob, 2 tpt, str, *CH-Bu, E, I-MAav*
282/5	Sym. (Bb), 2 ob, 2 hn, str, *CH-E, I-Mc, S-Skma*
282/7	Sym. (Eb), 2 hn, 2 tpt, str, *CH-E*
282/10	Sym. (Eb), 2 ob, 2 hn, str, *D-B*
—	Sym. (Eb), *I-MAav*

361/7	Two Minuets, orch with hns [contrary to T], in short score in Entratas and Minuets for the Balls at Court, i, *GB-Lbm*

(doubtful)

276/6	Sym. (C), 2 ob, 2 tpt, str, attrib. J. C. Bach, *CH-Bu*; many other attribs. incl. Holzbauer, DTB, iv, Jg.iii/1 (1902), xliv, and Hofmann
277/7	Sym. (D), str, attrib. 'Sign. Back', *S-Uu*
278/9	Sym. (D), 2 ob, 2 hn, str, attrib. 'Sigre Giuseppe Pach', *A-Wgm*; attrib. J. J. Lang in Breitkopf suppl. 1767
279/1	Sym. (D), 2 ob, 2 hn, str, attrib. 'Sigre Giuseppe Baach', *Wgm*; attrib. Lang in Breitkopf suppl. 1767
—	Sym. (D), 2 ob, 2 hn, str, *I-Gi(l)*, *MAav*
—	Sym. (D), 2 ob, 2 hn, str, *Gi(l)*
—	Sym. (D), 2 hn, str, *MAav*
—	Sym. (D), incipit in Breitkopf suppl. 1766
280/3	Sym. (F), 2 fl, 2 hn, str, attrib. 'Sigre Giuseppe Bach', *A-Wgm*; attrib. Lang in Breitkopf suppl. 1767
—	Sym. (Bb), incipit in Breitkopf suppl. 1767
280/7	Sym. (Bb), 2 ob, 2 hn, str, *D-Dlb*
280/10	Sym. (Bb), 2 ob, 2 hn, str, *A-Wgm, B-Bc, CH-E, D-B, RH, SWl, I-MAav* [attrib. Filtz in Breitkopf suppl. 1767; attrib. Jommelli, *D-SWl*]
281/3	Sym. (Bb), 2 ob, 2 hn, str, attrib. 'Sigre Giuseppe Baach', *A-Wgm*; attrib. Lang in Breitkopf suppl. 1767
—	Sym. (Eb), incipit in Breitkopf suppl. 1767
281/6	Sym. (Eb), 2 ob, 2 tpt, str, *S-Skma*
281/9	Sym. (Eb), 2 ob, 2 hn, str, *Skma*; attrib. J. Stamitz, DTB, iv, Jg.iii/1 (1902), xl
282/3	Sym. (Eb), 2 ob, 2 hn, str, *Skma*
283/3	Sym. (Eb), 2 tpt [?or cl], hns, bns, str, *D-W*

CONCERTED SYMPHONIES

(instruments listed as concertante; ripieno)

284/1	Simfonie concertante (G), 2 vn, vc; 2 ob, 2 hn, 2 vn, 2 va, b (Paris, by 1775); ed. J. A. White (Tallahassee, 1963)
284/4	Simphonie concertante (A), vn, vc; 2 ob, str (Paris, 1773); ed. A. Einstein (London, 1934)
284/6	Concert ou symphonie (Eb), 2 vn/ob; 2 fl, 2 hn, str (Amsterdam, 1774); ed. F. Stein (London, 1935); also as pf conc. T290/1 and 300/8
286/1	Conc. sym. (C), 2 vn, vc; 2 ob, 2 hn, str, *D-Bds, GB-Lbm* (inc., with added solos T290/8)
286/4	Conc. sym. (G), ob, vn, va, vc; 2 fl, 2 hn, str, *D-Bds*
286/6	Conc. sym. (E), 2 vn, vc; 2 fl, 2 ob, 2 hn, str, *Bds, GB-Lbm* (inc., with added ob, vc solos, fl obbl T290/6a)
287/2	Conc. sym. (F), ob, vc; ob, 2 hn, str, *D-Bds, GB-Lbm* (with added ob solos T289/2); ed. F. Dawes (London, 1973)
287/7	Conc. sym. (Bb), vn, vc; 2 cl, 2 bn, str, *D-Bds*; see White, i, 318
288/4	Conc. sym. (Eb), 2 vn; 2 ob, 2 hn, str, *Bds*; also as bn conc. in Breitkopf suppl. 1782–4
288/7	Conc. sym. (Eb), 2 ob, 2 hn, 2 vn, 2 va, vc; orch, **A-Wn*; other versions (Eb), *GB-Lbm* R.M.21.a.8 and (F), *Lbm* R.M.21.a.5–7(10); 1st movt = T290/7; ed. J. A. White (Tallahassee, 1963)
289/4	Conc. sym. (C), fl, ob, vn, vc; 2 fl, 2 cl, 2 bn, 2 hn, str, *Lbm*; ed. R. Maunder (London, 1961)
289/7	Conc. sym. (Bb), ob, vn, vc, kbd; 2 fl, 2 hn, str, *Lbm* (inc.)
290/2	Conc. sym. (D), 2 fl, 2 vn, va, vc; 2 fl, 2 hn, str, *Lbm*
290/4	Conc. sym (Eb), fl, bn; 2 ob, 2 hn, str, *Lbm*
290/9	Conc. sym. (Eb), 2 cl, bn; 2 ob, 2 hn, str, *Lbm*; ed. J. A. White (Tallahassee, 1963)

(doubtful)

—	Sinfonia concertante (Bb), 2 vn, vc; 2 hn, str, *I-MAav*
—	Sinfonia concertante (D), 2 vn; 2 fl, 2 hn, str, *MAav*
—	Sinfonia concertante (Eb), 2 vn; 2 ob, 2 hn, str, *MAav*
—	Sinfonia concertante (G), 2 fl, 2 hn, str, *MAav*

CONCERTOS

292/1	Six Concertos (Bb, A, F, G, C, D), hpd, 2 vn, vc, op.1 (1763)
286/7	Conc. (D), fl, 2 hn, str, **D-B* (dated 1768; inc.), ?**Tu* (inc.), ? **F-Pn* (inc.); ed. R. Meylan (Vienna, 1958)
293/4	Sei concerti (C, F, D, Bb, Eb, G), hpd/pf, 2 vn, vc, op.7 (1770); nos.5–6 ed. in Antiqua (1927, 1954)
295/1	A Third Sett of Six Concertos (C, D, F, Bb, G, Eb), hpd/pf, 2 vn, vc (2 ob, 2 hn, ad lib), op.13 (1777); nos.2, 4, ed. L. Landshoff (Frankfurt, 1931–3)
298/1	5 concs. (Bb, f, d, E, G), hpd, str, part **D-B*; no.2 ed. in NM, clxx (1954)
300/8	Conc. (Eb), pf, 2 fl, 2 hn, 2 cl, str, *B, GB-Lbm* (inc.) = T290/1; version of conc. sym. T284/6
301/1	Conc. (Eb), kbd, str, hns ad lib, *D-Dlb*; ?as 1er concerto (Eb), hpd, str, op.14 (Paris, n.d.) [cited in RISM as op.13 no.6], in Breitkopf suppl. 1781
288/1	Conc. (Bb), bn, 2 ob, str, *B, SWl*, in Breitkopf suppl. 1782–4; ed. J. Wojciechowski (Hamburg, 1953)

288/4	Conc. (E♭), bn, orch, *B*, *Bds*; ed. J. Wojciechowski (Hamburg, 1953); also as conc. sym.
290/7	Conc. (F), ob, 2 hn, str, *GB-Lbm*; not = conc. sym. т288/7; ed. R. Maunder (London, 1963)
	(*doubtful*)
287/4	Conc. (F), ob, 2 hn, str, *D-HR*
297/1	[2] Concerto [i–ii] (E♭, A), hpd, str (Riga, *c*1776); attrib. 'I. C. Bach' in Breitkopf suppl. 1776–7, following 'I. C. F. Bach' entry; also attrib. C. P. E. Bach; attrib. J. C. F. Bach in J. N. Forkel, *Musikalischer Almanach für Deutschland* (Leipzig, 1784/*R*1974); no.2 also pubd (*c*1775) as 'by Signor Bach of Berlin'; no.1 ed. E. Praetorius (London, 1937), no.2 ed. in Antiqua (1935)
300/1	Conc. (A), hpd, str, *B* St487 [? by C. P. E. Bach]; ed. A. Hoffmann (Wolfenbüttel, 1963)
300/4	Kbd Conc. (E), *Dlb*
301/4	Conc. (f), hpd, str, *B*, 'riveduto dal Sigr. C. F. E. Bach', attrib. C. P. E. Bach in Breitkopf catalogue, 1763
—	Kbd Conc. (D), *DS* Mus.Ms.56

WIND MUSIC

(*see Sadie for discussion of borrowed material and transcriptions*)

285/3	Sei sinfonie (E♭, B♭, E♭, E♭, B♭, E♭, B♭), 2 cl, 2 hn, [2] bn (1782); ed. F. Stein (Leipzig, 1957–8)
—	Military Piece's [Quintettos] (E♭, E♭, B♭, B♭), 2 cl, 2 hn, bn (Dublin, *c*1794), ed. S. Sadie (London, 1957)
359/3	3 military marches: March du Régiment de Prince Ernst; Marche du Regiment de Braun; Marche du Regiment de Wurmb: all in E♭, 2 ob/fl, 2 hn, bn, *D-SWl*; variants of nos.2–3 [see marches, т361/1]; ed. J. Wojciechowski (Hamburg, 1956)
360/1	2 marches (E♭), 2 ob, 2 cl, 2 hn, 2 bn, *Bds*; no.2 also attrib. C. F. Abel, к218, in *GB-Lbm* R.M.24.k.15
360/3	Due marce . . . Prince Wallis (F), 2 cl, 2 hn, bn, *D-Bds*; also attrib. C. F. Abel, к220–21, in *GB-Lbm* R.M.24.k.15
360/5	Due marce . . . della Maestà (F), 2 hn, 2 ob, 2 cl, bn, *D-Bds*; variants [see marches, т361/1]
361/1	8 marches, *GB-Lbm* R.M.24.k.15 [nos.1–2 not cited in т]; no.1 = variant of т359/4; no.2 = variant of т360/6; т361/3 = variant of т360/5; т361/4 = variant of т359/5

CHAMBER MUSIC

302/1	Sestetto (C), ob, 2 hn, vn, vc, hpd/pf, op.3 (Offenbach, 1783); ed. S. Sadie (London, 1968): issued in 2 edns. by J. C. Luther: (1) orig. parts; (2) arr. hpd, vn, in Three Favorite Quartetts and One Quintett (1785) = т311/3, often misattrib. J. C. F. Bach
305/1	Quintet (B♭), 2 vn/ob, va, vc/bn, bc (Paris, 1770); 1st movt similar to qt, op.8 no.6, т307/2
303/1	Six quintettos (C, G, F, E♭, A, D), fl, ob, vn, va, bc, op.11 (1774); ed. in EDM, 1st ser., iii (1935), nos.4, 6, ed. in NM, cxxiii–cxxiv (1935–6); nos.1–3, 5, ed. S. Sadie (London, 1962)
304/6	Deux quintettes (D, F), op.22 (Berlin, 1785); 1, fl, ob, vn, vc, hpd/pf, ed. in HM, xlii (1944); 2, ob, vn, va, da gamba, vc, hpd/pf; both issued in 2 edns. by J. C. Luther: (1) orig. parts; (2) arr. hpd, vn, in Three Favorite Quartetts and One Quintett (1785) = т311/2–4
306/1	Six quartettos (C, D, E♭, F, G, B♭), fl, vn, va, vc,op.8 (1772); no.1 ed. H. von Dameck (Wiesbaden, n.d.), no.2 ed. S. Sadie (London, 1970), no.3 ed. F. Nagel (Mainz, 1970), no.4 ed. in NM, cxxvii (1936), nos.5–6 ed. F. Nagel (Wolfenbüttel, 1969); nos.2, 5, 6 (Mannheim, *c*1780), 1 ed. in NM, cxxvii (1936)
309	3 quartets (D, C, A), fl/vn, vn, va, bc, nos.1, 3, 5, in Six Quartettos . . . by Messrs Bach, Abel and Giardini (1776), ed. S. Sadie (London, 1962)
	Sei quartetti, 2 vn, va, bc, op.17 (Paris, by 1779), transcrs. (? by Bach) of vn sonatas op.10, т322–3, *US-AA*
310/9	Quartetto (G), vn, vc, kbd (Offenbach, 1783); ed. in Antiqua (1951); issued in 2 edns. by J. C. Luther: (1) orig. parts; (2) arr. hpd, vn, in Three Favorite Quartetts and One Quintett (1785) = т311/5
307/4	Four quartettos (C, D, G, C), op.19 (1784): 2 for 2 fl, va, vc, 1 for 2 fl, vn, vc, 1 for fl, ob/fl, va, vc; ed. in Organum, iii/63–4, 66, 68 (1962), no.2 ed. in HM, cxix (1954), nos.2–3 ed. S. Sadie (London, 1961)
311/6	Sonata (B♭), vn, vc, no.1 in Six Sonatas . . . by Messrs Bach, Abel and Kammel (1777) [no.2 ? also by J. C. Bach; see Breitkopf suppl. 1778]
330/5	Sonata (B♭), harp, (vn, vc)/hpd, no.6 in Musical Remains: or The Compositions of Handel, Bach, Abel, Giuliani, &c (?1796); 1st movt version of sestetto т302/1
317/2	Trio (C), fl, fl/vn, vn, vc, no.1 in Two Trios . . . Selected by T. Monzani (*c*1800)
314/5	Six trio (B♭, A, E♭, G, D, C), 2 vn, va/bc, op.2 (Paris, by 1764), also as op.4 (Amsterdam, 1767), in Breitkopf suppl.

	1766 as first 6 of set of 12 (see also т317/5); ed. W. Höckner (Locarno, 1963), nos.2, 4, 6, ed. in HM, xxxvii (1949)
317/5	6 trio sonatas (G, D, E, F, B♭, B♭), 2 vn, bc, *I-Mc*; nos.3–4, *Gi(l)*; in Breitkopf suppl. 1766 as second 6 of set of 12 (see also т314/5)
317/7	Trio sonata (G), 2 fl, b, *Mc*, *Gi(l)* (2 vn, b)
318/8	Trio sonata (F), 2 va, bc, formerly Singakademie, Berlin, destroyed
313/1	Six sonates (F, G, D, C, D, E♭), hpd, vn/fl, vc, op.2 (1764); ed. in Diletto musicale, dlxxi–dlxxvi (in preparation), no.3 ed. in Collegium musicum, xix (New York, 2/1955), 1 ed in NM, cxcii (1957)
322/1	Six Sonatas (B♭, C, G, E, F, D), hpd/pf, vn, op.10 (1773) [for transcrs. see Sei quartetti, op.17]; nos.1–5 ed. L. Landshoff (London, 1939)
335/1	Six Duetts (D, G, B♭, B♭, A, C), 2 vn (by 1775), also as op.13 (Paris, *c*1775); ed. in NM, cxxvi, cxl (1937–8), attrib. G. Kennis in Breitkopf suppl. 1768
323/2	Sonatas (C, A, D, B♭), hpd/pf, vn, vc, nos.1–4 in Four Sonatas and Two Duetts, op.15 (1778); 2 ed. in Diletto musicale, ccclxxvii–ccclxxviii (in preparation), no.4 ed. in Collegium musicum, xix (Leipzig, n.d.)
325/1	Six Sonatas (D, G, C, A, D, F), hpd/pf, vn/fl, op.16 (1779/*R*1961); 2 ed. in NM, i (1927), 1 ed. in NM, ciii (1933)
326/3	Sonatas (C, D, E♭, G), hpd/pf, vn/fl, nos.1–4 in Four Sonatas and Two Duetts, op.18 (1781)
336/6	4 canzonettes (F, E♭, G, B♭), 2 vn, *GB-Lbm*, arrs. of Sei canzonette op.6 [see т260/2, nos.1, 4, 3, 2]
331/2	Sonata (D), hpd, vn, *D-B*; ed. in Mekota (1969), 243; also as Trio (D) hpd, vn, vc, *B* (dated 1771)
332/4	[7] Sonate (F, D, G, A, G, D, F), hpd, vn, *I-Mc*; no.1 ed. in Mekota (1969), 264
—	Quartetto, hpd, 2 vn, vc, *Fc*; = hpd conc., op.1 no.2, see т291/2
—	Sonata (A), hpd, vn, *Mc*; 2nd movt = т333/5
—	Sonata con cembalo o spinetta (F), probably vn, bc, *Mc*
	(*doubtful or spurious*)
—	Sonata (F), ob, vn, va, vc, *Gi(l)*
—	Sonata (D), 2 vn, va, vc, *Gi(l)*
—	Sonata (E♭), eng hn, vn, va, vc, *Gi(l)*
—	4 trio sonatas (C, F, A, E♭), 2 vn, vc, *Gi(l)*
—	3 sonatas (D, F, c), hpd, vn, vc, *Gi(l)*
—	2 sonatas (B♭, G), hpd, vn, *Vc*; = J. S. Schroeter's op.2 nos.4, 2
—	6 sonatas (C, G, F, B♭, E♭, D), hpd, vn, *PEsp*
279/10	Trio sonata (F), 2 vn, bc, *S-Uu*, attrib. 'Sign. Back' [not sym. as in т]
319/4	Trio sonata (B♭), 2 vn, bc, *GB-Lbm*, by C. P. E. Bach (w158, н585)
319/7	Trio sonata (B♭), 2 vn, bc, *D-Mbs*
319/9	Divertimento (B♭), 2 vn, bc, *A-Wgm*, as J. S. Schroeter's op.2 no.4 in Breitkopf suppl. 1772
320/1	Trio sonata (B♭), 2 vn, bc, *D-Mbs*
320/4	Trio sonata (E♭), 2 vn, bc, *S-Skma*
320/4	Trio sonata (E♭), 2 vn, bc, *Skma*
320/6	Trio sonata (B♭), 2 vn, bc, formerly in Socznik collection, Gdańsk, ? lost; attrib. Wagenseil in Breitkopf catalogue 1762
320/9	Trio sonata (B♭), fl, vn, b, *D-KA*; ed. H. Kölbel (Zurich, 1968)
321/1	Trio sonata (E♭), hpd, 2 vn, *Mbs*
—	Sonata, gui, vn (*c*1770)
327/5	Six Sonatas (D, G, D, A, E♭, B♭), hpd/pf, vn/fl, op.19 (1783)
329/1	Three [=6] Sonatas [i–ii] (C, D, F, G, A, B♭), hpd/pf, vn, op.20 (*c*1785)
332/1	Sonata (F), hpd, fl, *B*, also attrib. C. P. E. Bach and W. F. Bach; ed. K. Maguerre (Celle, 1960)
331/5	Sonata (D), vn, bc, *D-Bds*, ?lost
337/1	3 sonatas (D, G, C), fl, vn, *A-Wn*
344/2	Trois sonates (E♭, B♭, D), hpd/pf, vn, op.21 (Paris, after 1785)

KEYBOARD

345/7	5 opera ovs. (Orione, Zanaida, Artaserse, La Cascina, Astarto [= Alessandro nell'Indie]), arr. hpd/org in Six Favourite Opera Overtures (London, *c*1765)
338/1	Six Sonatas (B♭, D, G, E♭, E, c), op.5 (1766/*R*1976)
	Minuet (F), in Minuets for the Harpsichord, Violin, German Flute or Hoboy as they were Performed at the Ball at Court for 1767 (1767)
340/5	2 duets (G, C): 1, 2 kbd; 2, kbd 4 hands; in Four Sonatas and Two Duetts, op.15 (1778); no.1 ed. in NM, iv (1938); no.2 ed. W. Weissmann (New York, 1941)
341/1	Six Sonatas (G, c, E♭, G, A, B♭), hpd, op.17 (*c*1779/*R*1976); previously pubd as op.12 (Paris, *c*1774)
343/3	2 duets (A, F), kbd 4 hands, in Four Sonatas and Two Duetts, op.18 (1781); 1 ed. in NM, cxv (1935), both ed. W. Weissmann (New York, 1941)
352/2	Sonata (C), The Feast of Apollo (*c*1789)

355/8   Sonata (F), 1768, *I-Mc*
—   Arioso con variazioni (A), *D-Mbs* Mus.Ms.1797
—   6 minuets (c, C, d, g, C, C), 2 polonaises (B♭, E♭), aria (a), *B* P672, attrib. 'J. C. Bach'; also attrib. J. C. Bach in *Verzeichniss des musikalischen Nachlasses ... Carl Philipp Emanuel Bach* (Hamburg, 1790), see *BJb*, xxxv–xxxvii (1938, 1939, 1940–48), *I-Bc*

Sonata (B♭), *I-Bc*

             (doubtful or spurious)

—   Canzonette with Variations (?c1765), also attrib. C. P. E. Bach (w118) and Kirnberger
—   Andante (c), in J. A. Hiller: Sammlung kleiner Clavier- und Singstücke (Leipzig, 1774)
—   Ov. (C), in Periodical Overtures for the Harpsichord, Pianoforte (c1775)
—   Five Sonatas and One Duett (D, F, B♭, C, E♭, C) ... by Mr Bach (c1780); 1st movt = T356/5; probably by W. F. E. Bach
350/8   Four Progressive Lessons ... and Two Duetts (C, F, D, G, D, G) (c1782); no.4 uses theme from rondo T250/4, by Mortellari, transcr. Bach
—   Menuetto (F), in Sammlung vermischter Clavierstücke von verschiedenen Tonkünstlern auf das Jahr 1782, i (Nuremberg, 1782)
—   Minuetto (D), in Journal de clavecin par les meilleurs maîtres, i (Paris, 1782)
343/7   Sonata ... qui represente la bataille de Rosbach (F) (c1782), also attrib. C. P. E. Bach (w272, h381) and Graun; probably by C. P. E. Bach
349/1   Six Progressive Lessons (1783); by C. P. E. Bach: Probestücke (w63, h70) incl. in *Versuch* (w254, h869)
—   Méthode ou recueil ... pour le forte-piano ou clavecin ... composé ... par J. C. Bach et F. P. Ricci (Paris, c1786/R1974); unlikely J. C. Bach had anything to do with text or exx.; pieces in pt.i unattrib.; pieces in pt.ii = C. P. E. Bach's Probestücke for *Versuch*; J. C. Bach's name taken from T349/1
—   Sonata (F), no.1 in Six Sonatas ... by Bach, Benda, Graun, Wagenseil, Hasse and Kirmberger (1799)
348/4   Fugue (c), on B–A–C–H (Leipzig, c1809), *D-Dlb*
352/5   Alla polacca (G), *Bds*; by J. C. F. Bach
352/6   Variationen (C), *Dlb* 3374–T–10
353/1   Rondeau ... con [12] variationi (C), *Dlb* 3374–T–11 [attrib. J. C. Bach], (c1770) [attrib. Joseph Dietz]; (on theme from J. C. Fischer's Ob Conc., no.1)
356/2   Allegro vivace (C), *CH-E*
356/3   Sonata (C), *E*
356/4   Andante (f), *E*; ed. in Mekota (1969)
356/5   Sonata (E♭), *E* 66–12, only menuetto in T
356/6   XI Variationen über eine bekannte Ariette von J. C. Bach (C), *D-B* P706
356/7   Ballo Montezuma, *A-Wgm*
358/4   Solo (a), *D-Bds*
—   Sonata (A♭), *I-Bc*
—   Toccata (b♭), *Bc*
—   Variazioni (F), kbd 4 hands, *PEsp*
353/2   Six sonates (E♭, G, B♭, D, C, F), kbd 4 hands, c1764, formerly *B-Bc* (lost)

BIBLIOGRAPHY

BurneyH; EitnerQ; FétisB; GerberNL
The Lyric Muse Revived in Europe (London, 1768)
G. Vogler, ed.: *Betrachtungen der Mannheimer Tonschule* (Mannheim, 1778–81/R1974)
ABCDario Musico (Bath, 1780)
C. Cramer, ed.: *Magazin der Musik* (Hamburg, 1783–6/R1971–4)
H. Angelo: *The Reminiscences of Harry Angelo* (London, 1828–30)
Earl of Mount Edgcumbe: *Musical Reminiscences* (London, 4/1834)
MacKinlay: *Mrs. Cornely's Entertainments at Carlisle House, Soho Square* (London, c1840)
J. Jesse: *Memoirs of the Life and Reign of King George III* (London, 1867)
C. F. Pohl: *Mozart und Haydn in London* (Vienna, 1867/R1970)
C. Papendiek: *Court and Private Life in the Time of Queen Charlotte* (London, 1887)
A. Paglicci Brozzi: *Il regio ducal teatro di Milano nel secolo XVIII* (Milan, 1894)
M. Schwarz: *J. Christian Bach: sein Leben und seine Werke* (Leipzig, 1901)
——: 'Johann Christian Bach', *SIMG*, ii (1900–01), 401–54
M. Brenet: 'Un fils du grand Bach à Paris en 1778–1779', *Guide musical*, xlviii (1902), 551, 571
H. Saxe-Wyndham: *The Annals of Covent Garden Theatre from 1732 to 1897* (London, 1906)
C. von Mannlich: *Lebenserinnerungen* (Berlin, 1913)
H. Abert: 'Joh. Christian Bachs italienische Opern und ihr Einfluss auf Mozart', *ZMw*, i (1919), 313

A. Einstein: 'Mitteilungen der deutsche Musikgesellschaft, Ortsgruppen München', *ZMw*, iv (1921–2), 121 [précis of lecture by L. Landshoff on Bach's secular vocal music]
G. de Saint-Foix: 'A propos de Jean-Chrétien Bach', *RdM*, x (1926), 83
H. Schökel: *J. Christian Bach und die Instrumentalmusik seiner Zeit* (Wolfenbüttel, 1926)
F. Tutenberg: *Die Sinfonik Johann Christian Bachs* (Wolfenbüttel, 1928)
C. Terry: *John Christian Bach* (London, 1929 [review by H. Miesner in *ZMw*, xvi (1934), 182]; rev. 2/1967 by H. C. R. Landon [review by S. Sadie in *MT*, cviii (1967), 330])
A. Wenk: *Beiträge zur Kenntnis des Opernschaffens von J. Christian Bach* (diss., U. of Frankfurt am Main, 1932)
E. Reeser: *De zonen van Bach* (Amsterdam, 1941; Eng. trans., 1949)
H. Wirth: 'Bach, Johann Christian', *MGG*
——: 'Johann Christian (Jean Chrétien) Bach', *Revue internationale de musique*, new ser. (1950), no.8, p.133
H. Blomstedt: 'Till kännedomen om J. C. Bachs symfonier', *STMf*, xxxiii (1951), 53
S. Sadie: 'The Wind Music of J. C. Bach', *ML*, xxxvii (1956), 107
R. Seebandt: *Arientypen Johann Christian Bachs* (diss., Humboldt U., Berlin, 1956)
F. van Amelsvoort: 'Johann Christian Bach en zijn oratorium Gioas', *Mens en melodie*, xii (1957), 300
E. O. D. Downes: *The Operas of Johann Christian Bach as a Reflection of the Dominant Trends in Opera Seria 1750–1780* (diss., Harvard U., 1958)
J. A. White jr: *The Concerted Symphonies of John Christian Bach* (diss., U. of Michigan., 1958) [incl. edns. of 3 concerted syms.]
E. J. Simon: 'A Royal Manuscript: Ensemble Concertos by J. C. Bach', *JAMS*, xii (1959), 161
The London Stage 1660–1800 (Carbondale, Ill., 1960–68)
C. B. Oldman: 'Mozart's Scena for Tenducci', *ML*, xlii (1961), 44
W. Haacke: *Die Söhne Bachs* (Königstein im Taunus, 1962)
P. M. Young: 'Johann Christian Bach and his English Environment', *GfMKB, Kassel 1962*, 32
H.-J. Schulze: 'Frühe Schriftzeugnisse der beiden jüngsten Bach-Söhne', *BJb*, l (1963–4), 61
S. Kunze: 'Die Vertonungen der Arie "Non sò d'onde viene" von J. Chr. Bach und W. A. Mozart', *AnMc*, no.2 (1965), 85
E. Warburton: 'J. C. Bach's Operas', *PRMA*, xcii (1965–6), 95
B. S. Brook, ed.: *The Breitkopf Thematic Catalogues, 1762–1787* (New York, 1966)
B. Matthews: 'J. C. Bach in the West Country', *MT*, cviii (1967), 702
E. S. Derr: *J. C. Bach: Cefalo e Procri (London, 1776): a Critical Edition* (diss., U. of Illinois, 1968)
N. J. Fujisawa: *Johann Christian Bach: London ni okeru kareno katsudo to ongaku* [Life and works in his London years] (diss., Tokyo U. of Arts, 1968)
B. A. Mekota: *The Solo and Ensemble Keyboard Works of Johann Christian Bach* (diss., U. of Michigan, 1969) [incl. corrections and additions to Terry's catalogue]
M. A. H. Vos: *The Liturgical Choral Works of Johann Christian Bach* (diss., Washington U., 1969)
E. Warburton: *A Study of Johann Christian Bach's Operas* (diss., U. of Oxford, 1969)
P. M. Young: 'Johann Christian, der Englischer Bach', *Musa–mensmusici: im Gedenken an Walther Vetter* (Leipzig, 1969), 189
——: *The Bachs: 1500–1850* (London, 1970)
N. Krabbe: 'J. C. Bach's Symphonies and the Breitkopf Thematic Catalogue', *Festskrift Jens Peter Larsen* (Copenhagen, 1972), 233
R. Fiske: *English Theatre Music in the Eighteenth Century* (London, 1973)
I. S. Baierle: *Die Klavierwerke von Johann Christian Bach* (diss., U. of Graz, 1974)
B. Matthews: 'The Davies Sisters, J. C. Bach and the Glass Harmonica', *ML*, lvi (1975), 150
H. Brofsky: 'J. C. Bach, G. B. Sammartini, and Padre Martini: a Concorso in Milan in 1762', *A Musical Offering: Essays in Honor of Martin Bernstein* (New York, 1977)
M. R. Charters: *The Bach–Abel Concerts* (diss., U. of London, 1978)
S. W. Roe: *The Keyboard Music of J. C. Bach* (diss., U. of Oxford, in preparation)

(13) Johann Michael Bach (*b* Struth, nr. Schmalkalden, 9 Nov 1745; *d* Elberfeld, 1820). He was the descendant of a Hessian line of Bachs, traceable back to Caspar Bach (*d* Struth, 1640). Geiringer's description of Johann Michael as a son of Johann Elias Bach (*39*) is incorrect; there was probably some connection with the Wechmar Bachs, although none has been proved. Johann Michael began travelling at an early age, visiting the Netherlands (in about 1767, where he had some contact with the music publisher Hummel), England and America. On his return he studied law at the University of Göttingen, where he came into contact with Forkel. He practised law in Güstrow (Mecklenburg), evidently also working as a composer, and by 1793 he was Kantor and organist in Tann; his *Kurze und systematische Anleitung zum General-Bass und der Tonkunst überhaupt* was published at Kassel in 1780. It is not known where he went to Elberfeld, where he was a professor (probably music teacher at the Gymnasium) until his death. As a composer and theorist Johann Michael represents in a derivative way a style similar to that of (11) Johann Christoph Friedrich Bach (*49*). He had two sons who were musicians, Johann Georg and Georg Friedrich (see §I above).

WORKS

6 Klavierkonzerte, C, G, D, F, D, B, op.1 (Amsterdam, 1767)
Concerto, kbd, B♭, *D-Bds* [with final fugue on B–A–C–H]
2 cantatas: Gott fähret auf mit Jauchzen; Jehova, Vater der Weisen: *Bds*

BIBLIOGRAPHY
H. Lämmerhirt: 'Ein hessischer Bach-Stamm', *BJb*, xxxiii (1936), 78

(14) Wilhelm Friedrich Ernst Bach (*84*) (*b* Bückeburg, baptized 24 May 1759; *d* Berlin, 25 Dec 1845). Son of (11) Johann Christoph Friedrich Bach (*49*). He was the only one of Johann Sebastian's grandsons of any musical importance. He studied under his father in Bückeburg and in 1778, after a brief stay with C. P. E. Bach in Hamburg, went to live with (12) Johann Christian Bach (*50*) in London, working there as a piano virtuoso and teacher. After his uncle's death at the beginning of 1782 he began a long concert tour which took him in particular through the Netherlands and to Paris. In 1787 he became music director in Minden, near his home town. On Friedrich Wilhelm II's visit to that city in 1788 he composed the cantata *Westphalens Freude*, which made such an impression on the king that he appointed Bach Kapellmeister and harpsichordist at the court of Queen Friedrike of Prussia in Berlin; in 1797 he assumed a similar post at the court of Queen Luise (in 1795 he had applied unsuccessfully for the professionally more attractive position of Hofkapellmeister at Bückeburg). He was chiefly responsible for the music training of the Prussian princes until 1811, after which he lived in retirement in Berlin on a pension of 300 thalers. As the last musically significant descendant of Johann Sebastian he attended the dedication of the Bach monument in Leipzig on 23 April 1843.

Many of his numerous compositions, most of them written in London and Minden, were circulated in print (as well as manuscript copies) in his lifetime. In Berlin he also played an influential role in the musical life of the city. His compositions are not without conventional features, notably in their use of strict contrapuntal writing; his style is generally vapid and does not approach the originality of his two famous uncles and mentors, Johann Christian and Carl Philipp Emanuel.

WORKS

VOCAL

Trauer-Cantate, on the death of Frederick the Great (Minden, 1787)
Westphalens Freude (Die Nymphen der Weser), for Friedrich Wilhelm II of Prussia, 1788 (Rinteln, 1791)
Columbus oder die Entdeckung von America, T, B, chorus, orch, 1798, *GB-Lbm*
Concerto buffo, B, toy insts, orch, *Lbm*
L'amour est un bien suprême; Ninfe se liete, S, orch, *Lbm*
Vater unser, T, B, choir, orch, *Lbm*
Lieder: Auswahl deutscher und französischer Lieder und Arietten (Berlin, n.d.); Rheinweinlied (Berlin, n.d.); Wiegenlied einer Mutter, ed. K. Geiringer, *Music of the Bach Family* (Cambridge, Mass.,

1955); 12 Freymaurer-Lieder (Copenhagen and Leipzig, 1788) [wrongly attrib. C. P. E. Bach as w202]; others, *Lbm*

INSTRUMENTAL

Orch: 2 sinfonias, C, G, *GB-Lbm*; 2 suites, E♭, B♭, *Lbm*; ballet-pantomime, *Lbm*; 3 pf concs., Conc. for 2 pf, all formerly *D-B*
Chamber: Sextet, E♭, 2 hn, cl, vn, va, vc, ed. K. Janetzky (Halle, 1951); 6 Sonatas, hpd/pf, vn, vc, op.1 (London, 1785); 3 sonates, hpd/pf, vn, op.2 (Berlin and Amsterdam, n.d.); Trio, G, 2 fl, va, ed. in HM, lvii (1951); Sinfonia, C, vn, pf, *GB-Lbm*
Kbd: 5 Sonatas and 1 Duett (London, n.d.); XII grandes variations sur un air allemand populaire (Berlin, n.d.); Andante, a, kbd 4 hands, ed. A. Kreutz (Mainz, n.d.); Das Dreyblatt, C, pf 6 hands, ed. K. Geiringer, *Music of the Bach Family* (Cambridge, Mass., 1955); Grand sonata, E♭, 1778; Variations on 'God save Frederick our King'; A Favourite Overture, and Divertimento, kbd 4 hands, both *Lbm*; other small pieces, *Lbm*

BIBLIOGRAPHY
G. Hey: 'Zur Biographie Johann Friedrich Bachs und seiner Familie', *BJb*, xxx (1933), 77
H. Wohlfarth: 'Wilhelm Friedrich Ernst Bach: Werkverzeichnis', *Schaumburg-Lippische Heimatblätter*, xi/5 (1960), 1
——: 'Wilhelm Friedrich Ernst Bach', *Schaumburg-Lippische Mitteilungen*, xvi (1964), 27

I and II: CHRISTOPH WOLFF
III, 1–6, 10, 13–14: CHRISTOPH WOLFF
III, 7: WALTER EMERY (1–6),
CHRISTOPH WOLFF (7–21),
RICHARD JONES (work-list, bibliography)
III, 8–9, 11: EUGENE HELM
III, 12: ERNEST WARBURTON (text, work-list),
ELLWOOD S. DERR (work-list, bibliography)

B–A–C–H. In German nomenclature, the letters of Bach's name provide a motif (ex.1) which is frequently found as a germinal idea in musical compositions. It was first used by Bach himself in the unfinished Contrapunctus XIV of *Die Kunst der Fuge* (1750), though its possibilities were earlier mentioned in Walther's *Musicalisches Lexikon* (1732). Probably because of the context in which Bach used it, later composers have mostly regarded this rather intractable motif as a challenge to their contrapuntal skill. Bach's son, Johann Christian, and his pupil, J. L. Krebs, both wrote organ fugues on it, but its wider popularity follows the 19th-century Bach revival and the development of a harmonic vocabulary which could more easily accommodate its tonal ambiguities. Schumann, whose interest in letter–pitch equations is well known, wrote six fugues on B–A–C–H (op.60) for organ or pedal piano, and Liszt, Reger and Busoni also used the motif to raise imposing contrapuntal monuments to its originator. Others have used it, including Rimsky-Korsakov and d'Indy.

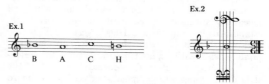

Ex.2

Ex.1

B   A   C   H

The B–A–C–H motif is easily incorporated into a totally chromatic idiom and has been widely used by members and disciples of the Second Viennese School, e.g. by Schoenberg as an incidental theme in his Variations op.31 for orchestra and Third String Quartet, by Webern as the basic set of his String Quartet, and by Humphrey Searle as a motto in his First Symphony. More recently it has been heard in Zsolt Durkó's *Episodi* (1963) and Reginald Smith Brindle's *Variants* for guitar (1970). A list of B–A–C–H-inspired works is in the German edition of Young's *The Bachs*. The name B–A–C–H has also been expressed as a single note (ex.2).

BIBLIOGRAPHY

M. Hinrichsen: 'Compositions based on the Motive B–A–C–H', *HMYB*, vii (1950), 379

A. Benkö: 'Motivul B–A–C–H in muzica secolului XX', *LM*, iv (1968), 137

P. M. Young: *The Bachs, 1500–1850* (London, 1970; Ger. trans., rev. 1974)

MALCOLM BOYD

Bach, August Wilhelm (*b* Berlin, 4 Oct 1796; *d* Berlin, 15 April 1869). German organist, teacher and composer. He was not a descendant of J. S. Bach. He received his earliest musical training from his father Gottfried, organist at Berlin's Dreifaltigkeitskirche, and accompanied services there while still a boy. After completing his secondary education he took a teaching position in a noble household outside Berlin. On his father's death in 1814 he returned to seek the post of organist at the Dreifaltigkeitskirche, but received instead an appointment at the Gertraudenkirche. During his two-year term there he studied counterpoint and fugue with Zelter and the piano with Ludwig Berger. He joined the Berlin Singakademie in 1815 and was appointed organist and music director at the Marienkirche in 1816; at this time he studied the violin with C. W. Henning, and broadened his general education through travel and the study of languages. In 1819, Bach was one of the first members of Berger's 'jüngere Liedertafel'; the next year he became music director and teacher in Stettin. In 1822 he was engaged to teach the organ, harmony and chorale setting at Zelter's new Institute for Church Music and in 1826 he received a commission to oversee organ building estimates in Prussia; this gave him not only a wide influence on organ building, but also the opportunity of travelling throughout Europe. When Zelter died in 1832 Bach succeeded him as director of the Institute for Church Music. He was elected to the senate of the Royal Academy of the Arts in 1833, and taught theory and composition there. In 1845 he was awarded the medal of the Order of the Red Eagle, and in 1858 was granted the title of Royal Professor.

As organist Bach not only played for services, but also gave important chamber and concert performances; of his organ students Mendelssohn is the most famous, though many others won local prominence in the mid-19th century. His organ method, *Der praktische Organist* (*c*1840), and his *Choralbuch für das Gesangbuch zum gottesdienstlichen Gebrauch für evangelische Gemeinden*, first published in 1830 and repeatedly abridged for use until well after his death, established his reputation. His largest work is the oratorio *Bonifaz, der deutsche Apostel*, not inappropriately described by a contemporary critic as 'a hotchpotch of opera and church' (*NZM*, xiv (1841), 61). The style of his compositions, mostly sacred and keyboard music, shows his attempt to accommodate the academic tendencies inherent in his studies and his profession as a teacher to the lyricism and saccharine harmonies popular in his time.

BIBLIOGRAPHY

G. Schilling, ed.: *Encyclopädie der gesammten musikalischen Wissenschaften oder Universal-Lexicon der Tonkunst* (Stuttgart, 1835–42/*R*1973)

C. von Ledebur: *Tonkünstler-Lexicon Berlin's* (Berlin, 1861/*R*1965)

A. Schering: *Die Geschichte des Oratoriums* (Leipzig, 1911/*R*1966), 427, 457

G. Frotscher: *Geschichte des Orgel-Spiels und der Orgel-Komposition*, ii (Berlin, 1936, enlarged 3/1966)

D. Siebenkäs: *Ludwig Berger* (Berlin, 1963), 25f, 244

F. Blume: *Geschichte der evangelischen Kirchenmusik* (Kassel, rev. 2/1965; Eng. trans., enlarged, 1974, as *Protestant Church Music: a History*)

A. Meyer-Hanno: *Georg Abraham Schneider* (Berlin, 1965), 139, 141, 160ff

T.-M. Langner: 'Bach, August Wilhelm', *MGG*

DOUGLASS SEATON

Bach, Cecilia. *See* GRASSI, CECILIA.

Bach, Charles Ernest. *See* BAGGE, CHARLES ERNEST.

Bach, Vincent (*b* Baden, nr. Vienna, 24 March 1890; *d* New York, 8 Jan 1976). American brass instrument maker of Austrian birth. At the age of six he started to play the violin and the bugle. When he was 12 he began trumpet instruction with Josef Weiss, first trumpeter in the Vienna Volksoper; at 16, he studied with Georg Stellwagen, first trumpeter with the Tonkünstler-Orchester. At the same time, he pursued a complete course in mechanical engineering, a training which was later to stand him in good stead. In 1910 he earned a degree (*Matura*) from the Maschinenbauschule in Wiener Neustadt. In 1912 he studied the solo trumpet literature in Wiesbaden with Fritz Werner, and then toured until 1914 as a cornet virtuoso – playing an Alexander cornet – through Germany, Denmark, Sweden, Russia, Poland, England and the USA. There he was invited to play first trumpet with the Boston SO (1914), with which he remained for a year. He then spent one and a half years as first trumpeter with the Dyagilev Ballet Orchestra at the Metropolitan Opera House. During World War I he was bandmaster of the 306th US Field Artillery Regiment. He became an American citizen in 1923.

On 1 April 1919 Bach set up a shop at 204 East 85th Street in New York, mainly for the purpose of making mouthpieces for his own use. In 1922 he moved to 241 East 41st Street, where he had ten employees; the manufacture of cornets and trumpets was started there in 1924. From 1928 to 1952 he was at 621 East 216th Street, with 50 employees, and began the manufacture of tenor and bass trombones. In 1952 he built a factory at 52 McQuesten Parkway, Mount Vernon, New York. He sold his business to the H. & A. Selmer Co. in 1962; two years later the firm moved to Elkhart, Indiana.

In combining his musical proficiency with his engineering training, Bach succeeded in establishing the most exacting standards of brass instrument design and construction. His point of departure, as with Elden Benge, was the French Besson B♭ trumpet; unlike Benge, however, who desired more flexible intonation, Bach strove to give his instruments a secure 'feel' for each note in the scale. Bach was also the first to set up a system for duplicating mouthpieces exactly. His instruments, especially trumpets, are employed more widely than any others. They are prized for their full and yet compact tone, with a solid core.

EDWARD H. TARR

Bach-Abel Concerts. London concert series organized between 1765 and 1781 by J. C. Bach and C. F. Abel; *see* LONDON, §VI, 4(i).

Bachauer, Gina (*b* Athens, 21 May 1913; *d* Athens, 22 Aug 1976). British pianist of Greek and Austrian descent. At parental insistence her early piano studies at the Athens Conservatory under Woldemar Freeman were combined with legal training at Athens University, but eventually she was allowed to enter the Ecole Normale in Paris for lessons with Cortot, and later she worked with Rakhmaninov. She made her début under Mitropoulos in Athens in 1935, then made several European tours, but her career was interrupted by World War II during which, stranded in Egypt, she gave over 600 concerts for allied troops. Her London début was at the Albert Hall in 1947, her New York début at Carnegie Hall in 1950. After that she spent half of each year in coast-to-coast tours of the USA. She gave the first solo recital, as Founding Artist, in the Kennedy Centre, Washington. A general practitioner rather than a specialist, she was however at her best in the 19th- and early 20th-century repertory, impressing with the strength and breadth of her keyboard command and essentially balanced musicianship. She was the wife of the former conductor Alec Sherman.

JOAN CHISSELL

Bach Cantata Club. London club founded in 1926; *see* LONDON, §VI, 3(ii).

Bach Choir. London amateur choir founded in 1875; *see* LONDON, §VI, 3 (i).

Bache. English family of musicians.

(1) **Francis Edward Bache** (*b* Birmingham, 14 Sept 1833; *d* Birmingham, 24 Aug 1858). Composer and pianist. He was the eldest of the seven children of Samuel Bache (1804–76), a well-known Unitarian minister who officiated at the New Meeting, Birmingham (1832–59), and his wife Emily Higginson (*d* 1855), from whom Francis inherited his musical gifts. He was educated at his father's school and studied with James Stimpson, city organist of Birmingham, and with Alfred Mellon. He played the violin in the 1846 Birmingham Festival, and in 1849 went to London as a private pupil of Sterndale Bennett, with whom he studied composition for more than three years. In October 1850 he became organist of All Saints, Gordon Square. In this period he composed concertos, overtures, two dramatic pieces, a string quartet and a piano trio, as well as many piano pieces. His first appearance as a concert performer was at Keighley, Yorkshire, on 21 January 1851. When he played the Allegro of an unpublished piano concerto of his own in June 1852, Henry Chorley was moved to remark: 'We have met with no Englishman more likely to give us the English composer for whom we have so long been waiting than Mr Bache'. In November 1851 he went to live with Mellon, by then resident in London, and in 1852 was given a contract by Addison, Hollier and Lucas to write light piano pieces, which he turned out in considerable numbers. Of one of these he wrote, 'I must say that I would *sooner* have written my *Galop di Bravura* than many a Sonata which is only printed to lie on the shelf a dead weight on account of deficiency of anything like idea'.

In October 1853, on Bennett's recommendation, Bache went to Leipzig, where he studied with Moritz Hauptmann, and acquired the conventional prejudices against the music of Berlioz, Liszt and Wagner. He visited Dresden, and returned to England by way of Paris in February 1855. He attended the 1855 Birmingham Festival, writing some of the reviews for the local newspapers, but was then attacked by a severe recurrence of the tuberculosis which had troubled him for several years. Early in 1856 he went to Algiers on medical advice, where he gave a concert on 28 March.

He travelled by way of Paris to Leipzig (June 1856), and then, through Dresden and Vienna, to Rome (December 1856). His health again deteriorated and he returned home in June 1857, spending the next winter in Torquay, where he succeeded in giving a concert in February 1858. On his return to Birmingham he gradually declined, and after a farewell concert of his music on 5 August, he died less than three weeks later, at the age of 24.

Bache's piano music has many qualities of his master, Sterndale Bennett, with a pleasant freshness and vitality to compensate for a certain lack of solidity and substance. More remarkable are the Six Songs op.16, which come near to establishing an English analogue of the lied; and the Piano Trio in D minor op.25, which, in spite of obvious gleanings from Mozart, Beethoven, Mendelssohn and Bennett, has a vigour found in few English instrumental compositions of its period (it was revived at a concert given by the Victorian Society at Leighton House on 26 September 1964). Bache's early death deprived Victorian music of one of its most promising talents.

WORKS
Selective list; printed works published in London unless otherwise indicated
Which is Which? (opera, A. Mellon), 1851, not perf.
Rubezahl (opera, J. Palgrave Simpson), *c*1852, not perf.
Orch: 3 pf conc., 1, E, perf. June 1852; Fl Conc., 1852; Jessie Gray, ov., Adelphi Theatre, Nov 1850; Ov., E, March 1851, *GB-Lam*; Polonaise, pf, orch, op.9, pf score (1854)
Chamber: Str Qt, I, *Lcm*; Pf Trio, d, op.25 (1852); 2 romances, pf, vn/vc, op.21 (1859), op.posth.
48 pubd pf pieces, incl. 3 Impromptus, op.1 (1851); 5 Characteristic Pieces, op.15 (1855–8); [8] Souvenirs d'Italie, op.19 (1857); [5] Souvenirs de Torquay, op.26 (1859)
Introduction and Allegro, 2 short voluntaries, org, in Stimpson's Organist's Standard Library (London, n.d.), xxi, xxii, xxiv
17 songs, incl. 6 Songs (Uhland, Goethe, Heine), op.16 (*c*1850); 4 songs, n.d.

(2) **Walter Bache** (*b* Birmingham, 19 June 1842; *d* London, 26 March 1888). Pianist and conductor, brother of (1) Francis Edward Bache. Like his elder brother he attended his father's school and studied with Stimpson. In August 1858 he too went to Leipzig, but after a short stay at Milan and Florence he arrived at Rome in the summer of 1862, where for three years he received regular lessons from Liszt; this experience gave his life a different direction. In 1865 he returned to London, and soon began his lifelong crusade to establish his master's reputation there: he played a two-piano arrangement of *Les préludes* with Edward Dannreuther on 4 July 1865. In the summer of 1867 he and Dannreuther formed a small association for the promotion of the music of Wagner and Liszt in England, dubbing themselves 'The Working Men's Society', with Karl Klindworth as a kind of elder statesman. At first they had to be content with piano arrangements, but in 1871 Bache began annual orchestral concerts at which more and more works by Liszt and other controversial composers were introduced to the London public. In the course of these concerts (1871–86) Bache introduced five of Liszt's symphonic poems, the *Faust* and *Dante* symphonies, *Jeanne d'Arc au bûcher*, the *Legend of St Elizabeth*, and other major works. In this enterprise he had to face an almost continuous barrage of opposition and scorn from other musicians and critics. Joseph Bennett wrote of him: 'I was content to remain on my own side of the great gulf which circumstances had fixed between us'. But, largely through Bache's indomitable perseverance, a section of the public was gradually

brought round. On Liszt's visit to England in the spring of 1886 Bache gave a memorable reception at the Grosvenor Gallery on 8 April, followed by a series of concerts in which he and his master appeared together. Bache was a professor of piano at the RAM, and was instrumental in founding the Liszt Scholarship there.

(3) **Constance Bache** (*b* Birmingham, 11 March 1846; *d* Montreux, 28 June 1903). Writer on music, sister of (1) Francis Edward Bache. She prepared the English version of Humperdinck's *Hänsel und Gretel* and also translated La Mara's edition of *Letters of Franz Liszt* (London, 1894) and *The Early Correspondence of Hans von Bülow* (London, 1896).

BIBLIOGRAPHY
F. E. Bache: Letters to his parents, 1840–53 (MS, *GB-Lbm* Add.54193)
C. Bache: *Brother Musicians* (London, 1901) [with list of F. E. Bache's works]
G. Langley: 'The Pianoforte Works of Francis Edward Bache', *MMR*, xxxv (1905), 83
J. Bennett: *Forty Years of Music 1865–1905* (London, 1908)
                                    NICHOLAS TEMPERLEY

Bachelbel, Johann. *See* PACHELBEL, JOHANN.

Bacheler [Bachelar, Bachiler, Batchelar, Batchiler], **Daniel** (*b* ?c1574; *d* after 1610). English composer. The only two printed sources of his music are the two volumes selected and edited by Robert Dowland in 1610. In the *Varietie of Lute-lessons* he is described as 'one of the Groomes of her Majesties Privie Chamber'. It is likely that it was the composer who was granted a coat-of-arms in February 1607, since the document refers to 'Daniell Bacheler of Aston Clinton in com. Barkeshire [actually Buckinghamshire] and of the privey Chamber' (*GB-Lbm* Harl.6095, f.6v, Harl.1422 f.12v). In Thomas Lant's pictorial record of the funeral of Sir Philip Sidney, *Sequitur celebritas et pomposa funeris* (London, 1587), a page on horseback, so small that his feet can hardly reach the stirrups, is labelled 'Daniell Batchiler', and it seems likely that this was the composer when aged about 12 or 13. In 1599 a Danyell Batchiler was commissioned to carry letters to Ireland, and in 1604 Queen Anne granted William Gomeldon and Daniel Bacheler a chest of arrows 'cast up by a wreck within her manor of Portland'.

The scarcity of Bacheler's works in the earliiest of the Cambridge lute manuscripts and the number in later sources place his main productive period as about 1600 to 1610. But one piece of consort music in the Walsingham Partbooks is dated as early as 1588, which might suggest the existence of another composer with the same name, perhaps a relative. The titles of the consort pieces suggest that their composer was connected with the Sidney and Walsingham families; since it was Sir Francis Walsingham who organized Sidney's funeral it might be that the Daniel Bacheler in Lant's funeral procession was the son of the composer responsible for the consort music (although it is not impossible on stylistic grounds for the same composer to have written both the lute music and the consort music: only the early date of one piece would suggest a very precocious talent on the part of the lutenist composer).

The earlier lute music shows Bacheler's style to be firmly rooted in the English tradition: the paired pavan and galliard, a fairly thick contrapuntal structure and frequent imitation are notable features. No ballad settings – an important source of inspiration in the previous generation – are found in his surviving works.

Those pieces unique to Lord Herbert of Cherbury's Lutebook show a distinct move towards a later style, with thinner textures and a more chordal basis. In this manuscript his pieces are sometimes attributed to 'Mr Daniel' or 'Sr Danielli' but it is considered unlikely that this is an indication that the music is by John Danyel. By far his most popular work seems to have been the galliard related to his song *To plead my faith*; it appears in nine manuscripts and was printed in Fuhrmann's *Testudo gallo-germanica* (Nuremberg, 1615). Although two sources attribute it to John Dowland there is no reason to suppose it is not Bacheler's work.

WORKS

LUTE SOLO

(for numbering and full source information see edn.)
Edition: D. Bacheler: *Selected Works for Lute*, ed. M. Long (London, 1972) [L]

1   Fantasia, *GB-Cfm* 689; L no.14
2   Pavan, *Cfm* 689
3   Pavan, *Cu* Nn.vi.36
4   [Pavan], *Cu* Nn.vi.36
5   [Pavan], *Cu* Nn.vi.36
6   [Pavan], *Cu* Nn.vi.36; L no.13
7   [Pavan], *Cu* Nn.vi.36
8   Pavan, *Cfm* 689 [on grounds of style attrib. may be erroneous]
9   [Pavan], *Cu* Nn.vi.36
10   Pavan, *Cfm* 689, *Cu* Dd.ix.33, Add.3056; L no.4
11   [Pavan], *Cu* Dd.v.78.3
12   Pavan, *Cu* Nn.vi.36
13a Pavan, 1615²⁴; L no.5
13b Galliard [to no.13a, *Cu* Dd.v.78.3, Add.3056
14   [Pavan], *Cu* Dd.v.78.3, Dd.ix.33, Nn.vi.36
15   [Pavan], *Cu* Dd.v.78.3
16   Pavan, 1610²³
17   Pavan, *Cfm* 689, *Cu* Nn.vi.36
18   Pavan, 1615²⁴; L no.6
19   Pavan, *Cu* Nn.vi.36
20   [Galliard], *Cu* Dd.ii.11, Dd.v.78.3, Dd.ix.33; L no.2
21   [Galliard], *Cu* Dd.v.78.3
22   [Galliard], *Cu* Nn.vi.36
23   [Galliard], *Cu* Nn.vi.36; L no.3
24   [Galliard], *Cu* Dd.v.78.3
25   Galliard [related to song To plead my faith], 1603¹⁵ [attrib. J. Dowland]; L no.1
26   [Galliard], *Cu* Nn.vi.36
27   [Galliard], *Cu* Dd.v.78.3
28   [Galliard], *Cu* Dd.ix.33
29   [Galliard], *Cu* Nn.vi.36 [another version of 13b: 2nd strain and all divisions different]
30   Galliard, *Cu* Nn.vi.36, *Lbm* Eg.2046
31   [Galliard], *Cu* Nn.vi.36 [inc.]
32   [Galliard], *Cu* Dd.v.78.3
33   [Galliard], *Cu* Dd.v.78.3
34   [Galliard], *Cu* Nn.vi.36
35   Almain, *Cfm* 689; L no.7
36   Courante, *Cfm* 689; L no.8
37   [Courante], *Cfm* 689
38   Volta [Courante], *Cfm* 689, *Cu* Nn.vi.36
39   Courante, *Cfm* 689, *Cu* Dd.iv.22; L no.11
40a Mounsiers Almain (i), 1610²³
40b Mounsiers Almain (ii), *Cu* Add.3056 ff.15v [attrib. J. Danyell], 44v
41   La jeune fillette, *Cfm* 689, *Lbm* Eg.2046; L no.10
42   [?fantasia], *Cu* Nn.vi.36
43   [?G]round, *Ctc* 0.16.2, *Cu* 3056; L no.9
44   Prelude, *Cfm* 689
45   Prelude, *Cfm* 689
46   Prelude, *Cfm* 689; L no.12
47   Prelude, *Cfm* 689
48   Prelude, *Cfm* 689
49   Prelude, *Cfm* 689
Galliard, *Cfm* 689, *Cu* Add.3056 f.48 [unattrib.; setting of J. Dowland's Earl of Essex Galliard]
Galliard [setting of a galliard by J. Harding], *Cu* Dd.v.78.3 f.25, Weld MS, owned by Lord Forester, f.9v (doubtful)

CONSORT MUSIC

All in the Walsingham Consort Books: for sources and their location see Edwards, 1974
Sr Frances Walsinghams Goodnight
Sr Frances Walsinghams Good morowe
The Lady Fra: Sidneys Goodnight
The Lady Fra: Sidneys Felicitye

The Lady Walsinghams Conceites
Daniells Triall 1588
Daniells Almayne
The Widowes Mite

SONG
To plead my faith [words attrib. Robert Devereux, Earl of Essex], 1610[20]

BIBLIOGRAPHY
D. Lumsden: *The Sources of English Lute Music, 1540–1620* (diss., U. of Cambridge, 1957)
E. Doughtie: 'Sidney, Tessier, Bachelar and *A Musicall Banquet*: Two Notes', *RN*, xviii (1965), 123
W. Edwards: 'The Walsingham Consort Books', *ML*, lv (1974), 209
———: *The Sources of Elizabethan Consort Music* (diss., U. of Cambridge, 1974)
                                    DIANA POULTON

Bachfarrt, Valentin. *See* BAKFARK, BÁLINT.

Bach-Gesellschaft. A society founded on the centenary of Bach's death (1850) to publish a complete critical edition of his works. By that time all the important keyboard and organ works had been printed, but it was obvious that a non-commercial scheme was needed for the vocal works. Schumann had raised the question in 1837, and again in 1843, when the English Handel Society was founded; the final stimulus probably came from his friend Sterndale Bennett, who organized an English Bach Society on 27 October 1849. Besides Schumann, Otto Jahn, C. F. Becker and Moritz Hauptmann were influential in founding the society. With Breitkopf & Härtel, they issued a preliminary announcement on 3 July 1850, and by 28 July had gained the support of Liszt, Spohr and others; they founded the society on 15 December. Their first volume (the first ten cantatas) appeared in December 1851.

Handsome and expensive, the edition long enjoyed an exaggerated reputation for scholarship. In fact its quality varied from editor to editor, but was never outstanding. For instance, the differences between Bach's writing and his wife's were not discovered (this was left to Philipp Spitta in 1873). Sources were inadequately described, and no serious attempt was made to determine their relationship on Lachmannian principles. Further, in their desire to publish the final versions of works that Bach was known to have revised, some of the editors neglected the early versions.

It is only fair to add that the society was always short of money, and that its plans were disorganized at the outset by Hermann Nägeli, who for several years refused the editors access to his autograph score of the B minor Mass, on the extraordinary grounds that the English Handel Society was doing German music quite enough honour. For its period the edition was a considerable achievement: it was essentially free from editorial additions, it was very nearly complete and it provided some form of critical apparatus. It made a tolerable foundation for aesthetic studies and served as a model for all subsequent editions of its kind.

The 46th volume of the edition was presented to the committee on 27 January 1900, and with it the society was thought to have finished its work. It was dissolved, but immediately reconstituted as the Neue Bach-Gesellschaft, whose object was to popularize the music and promote discussion. The NBG has held Bach festivals, annually as far as possible, from 1901. It acquired the house in which Bach was supposed to have been born, and opened a museum there in 1907. Its popular albums of selected arias are now of no importance, but some of its publications have been of permanent value, including the newly discovered Cantata no.

199 (1913) and the facsimile and transcription of the Bach Genealogy (1917). Its journal, the *Bach-Jahrbuch*, has appeared in almost every year since 1904, and continues to be required reading for anyone who is seriously interested in Bach.

See also BACH REVIVAL.

BIBLIOGRAPHY
J. N. Forkel: *Über Johann Sebastian Bachs Leben, Kunst und Kunstwerke* (Leipzig, 1802, rev. 3/1932)
H. Kretzschmar: 'Die Bach-Gesellschaft: Bericht über ihre Thätigkeit', *BJb*, xlvi (1900), p.xv
A. Schweitzer: *Johann Sebastian Bach* (Leipzig, 1908/*R*1960; Eng. trans., 1911/*R*1958)
F. Blume: *Johann Sebastian Bach im Wandel der Geschichte* (Kassel, 1947; Eng. trans., 1950)
                                    WALTER EMERY

Bachiler, Daniel. *See* BACHELER, DANIEL.

Bachmann, Carl Ludwig (*b* Berlin, 1743; *d* Berlin, 26 May 1809). German violist and instrument maker. He was an outstanding violist in the royal chapel from 1765, and in the following year, together with J. F. Benda, he established the Berlin Liebhaber-Konzerte. With Benda's death in 1785 Bachmann succeeded him as director of the concerts; in the same year he married the noted singer and pianist Charlotte Wilhelmine Caroline Stöwe. Throughout this period he also made instruments in the shop of his father, the violin maker and court violinist Anton Bachmann (1716–1800), and may have been responsible for several innovations, including the introduction of screw-tuning mechanisms for cellos and double basses. He continued alone in his father's business from 1791, at about which time he passed the directorship of the Liebhaber-Konzerte to his younger brother, the court violinist Friedrich Wilhelm Bachmann (1749–1825). Rellstab, though agreeing with the generally held low opinion of Bachmann's musical abilities, found his instruments excellent, a judgment which has been borne out by Henley alone among later commentators.

BIBLIOGRAPHY
J. C. F. Rellstab: *Über die Bemerkungen eines Reisenden* (Berlin, 1789)
C. von Ledebur: *Tonkünstler-Lexicon Berlin's* (Berlin, 1861/*R*1965)
W. Henley: *Universal Dictionary of Violin and Bow Makers* (Brighton, 1959–65)
C. Schröder-Auerbach: 'Bachmann', *MGG*
                                    EUGENE HELM

Bachmann [née Stöwe], **Charlotte Wilhelmine Caroline** (*b* Berlin, 2 Nov 1757; *d* Berlin, 19 Aug 1817). German singer. The daughter of a musician, she received early training in singing and keyboard playing, and at the age of nine sang in the Berlin Liebhaber-Konzerte, whose performances she was later to dominate. In 1785 she married the Berlin violist and instrument maker Carl Ludwig Bachmann (1743–1809). She was one of the original 20 members of the Berlin Singakademie (founded in 1791), and was essential in establishing its annual performances of C. H. Graun's *Der Tod Jesu* between 1797 and 1806, the beginning of the cult of that work. Her singing was highly regarded in her native Berlin, though the *Bermerkungen eines Reisenden* (1788) found her voice lacking in natural qualities, and declared her excellent keyboard playing to be her finest attainment. She also composed a few songs, of which one appeared in Rellstab's *Clavier-Magazin* (1787).

BIBLIOGRAPHY
A. Hartung and K. W. Klipfel: *Zur Erinnerung an Charlotte Wilhelmine Karoline Bachmann* (Berlin, 1818)
C. Schröder-Auerbach: 'Bachmann', *MGG*
                                    EUGENE HELM

Bachmann, Sixt [Joseph Siegmund Eugen] (*b* Kettershausen, nr. Illertissen, 18 July 1754; *d* Reutlingendorf, nr. Ehingen an der Donau, 18 Oct 1825). German composer, keyboard player and theologian. A child prodigy, he probably received his earliest instruction in music from his grandfather Franz Joseph Schmöger, choral director and organist in Markt Biberbach. It was there on 5 or 6 November 1766 that the famous organ contest between Bachmann and the ten-year-old Mozart took place, from which both emerged with credit. In 1771 he entered the Premonstratensian monastery in Ober Marchthal where he took his vows in 1773 and was ordained to the priesthood in 1778. There he met the writer Sebastian Sailer (*d* 1777) whose *Schriften im schwäbischen Dialekte* he later edited (Buchau, 1819). In Ober Marchthal he taught music and directed choirs, and was professor of theology (from 1800). He was also responsible for the monastery parish of Reutlingendorf (1779, 1789, 1796–9); he then became pastor in Seedorf but returned to Reutlingendorf in 1800. In 1803 the monastery in Ober Marchthal was dissolved and he settled in Reutlingendorf.

Bachmann obtained his grounding in composition principally from the study of theoretical works, especially G. J. Vogler's. His output includes piano sonatas characterized by contrapuntal technique and monothematic movements; he also wrote organ works and ecclesiastical music combining (according to Wilss) the new homophonic style with the traditional contrapuntal language of church music. Gerber stated that after one of his sonatas had been arbitrarily altered by the Viennese publisher Hoffmeister, Bachmann allowed only a few of his works to be printed.

WORKS

Pf: 2 sonatas, both (Vienna, 1786); Sonate, op.1 bk 1 (Munich, 1800); pieces in Clavier-Magazin für Kenner und Liebhaber (Berlin, 1787), Sammlung kleiner Clavier Stücke, i (Vienna, *c*1787) and Notenblätter zur musikalischen Korrespondenz (Speyer, 1792); Sonatine, 4 hands, *D-Rp*; 6 sonatas, 2 fantasias, variations, further single works in Musikalische Aufsätze, i–ii, 1803–*c*1820, *Rp* [Allegrino from vol.ii ed. U. Siegele, *Musik des oberschwäbischen Barock* (Berlin and Darmstadt, 1952), 18f]

Other works, incl. masses, cantatas, syms., org fugues, str qts, pf sonatas and songs, many cited in Gerber, Christmann and Schilling, lost

BIBLIOGRAPHY

GerberNL
J. F. Christmann: 'Brief', *Musikalische Korrespondenz* (Speyer, 1790), 103, 163
L. Wilss: *Zur Geschichte der Musik an den oberschwäbischen Klöstern im 18. Jahrhundert* (Stuttgart, 1925)
E. F. Schmid: *Ein schwäbisches Mozartbuch* (Lorch and Stuttgart, 1948)
W. Siegele: 'Musik des oberschwäbischen Barock', *Der Barock: seine Orgeln und seine Musik in Oberschwaben*, ed. W. Supper (Berlin and Darmstadt, 1952), 40
U. Siegele: 'Bachmann, Sixt', *MGG*

EBERHARD STIEFEL

Bachmann, Werner (*b* Frohburg, 13 Oct 1923). German musicologist. He studied in Halle at the Hochschule für Musik and with Max Schneider and Reuter at the university (1947–52), and at the musicological institute, where he also did some lecturing (1952–5); he took the doctorate in 1959 with a dissertation on the origins and early development of bowed instruments (later published in German and English). In 1955 he became an editor and in 1959 a senior editor at the Deutscher Verlag für Musik, Leipzig, and is editor-in-chief of the ambitious and successful series Musikgeschichte in Bildern, founded by Besseler and Schneider. His research has been concerned with medieval instruments, folksong and iconography.

WRITINGS

'Samuel Scheidt und das Volkslied', *Samuel Scheidt: eine Gedenkschrift zu seinem 300. Todestag* (Leipzig, 1954), 28
'Die Verbreitung des Quintierens im europäischen Volksgesang des späten Mittelalters', *Festschrift Max Schneider* (Leipzig, 1955), 25
'Bilddarstellungen der Musik im Rahmen der artes liberales', *GfMKB, Hamburg 1956*, 46
'Der Zupfgeigenhansl: zur Entstehung eines musikalischen Volksbuches', *Tradition und Gegenwart: Festschrift ... Friedrich Hofmeister* (Leipzig, 1957), 68
Die Anfänge des Streichinstrumentenspiels (diss., U. of Halle, 1959; Leipzig, 1964, /1966; Eng. trans., 1969 as *The Origins of Bowing and the Development of Bowed Instruments up to the 13th Century*)
'Das byzantinische Musikinstrumentarium', *Anfänge der slavischen Musik: Symposia I: Bratislava 1964*, 125

HORST SEEGER

Bachofen, Johann Caspar [Hans Kaspar] (*b* Zurich, 26 Dec 1695; *d* Zurich, 23 June 1755). Swiss composer and music pedagogue. The year of his birth has been given incorrectly in some sources as 1697. His father Joseph, originally a tailor and from 1692 a schoolteacher, planned a theological training for Johann Caspar, who was his second son. After study at the cathedral school, the Collegium Humanitatis, and (from 1715) the theology class, Bachofen gained the title V.D.M. (*verbi divini minister*) in 1720. In 1711 he joined the collegium musicum at the chapter house, and in 1715 he became a member of one that met at the German School. In 1720 he became a singing teacher at the lower grammar school. His small income compelled him to seek a secondary source of income, from trading in violin strings. Despite disputes with officials and colleagues, he was appointed, after J. K. Albertin's death in 1742, to the important position of Kantor at the Grossmünster, the most important cathedral in Zurich; at the same time he became director of the chapter house collegium musicum. In 1739 he had also assumed the role of Kapellmeister at the German School, thus combining several of the most important musical posts in Zurich. By 1748, however, he had become ill, and bad health hindered the execution of his duties and overshadowed his final years.

Bachofen's significance in the history of Swiss music lies primarily in the exceptional popularity of some of his works. His music was criticized, even by his contemporaries, for deficiencies of construction, harmonic language and melodic development; but his most important collection of sacred songs, *Musicalisches Hallelujah*, appeared in no less than 11 editions between 1727 and 1803, and became one of the favourite songbooks for popular music-making in the home. In the St Gall district the term 'bachofele' was used well into the 19th century for a gathering of singers for rehearsal. Three of Bachofen's arrangements of sacred songs were reprinted by Goldschmid (1942), and he is represented today in the hymnbook of the Swiss Reformed Church by the hymn *Auf, auf ihr Reichsgenossen*.

As the preface of the *Musicalisches Hallelujah* makes clear, Bachofen's works were specifically intended for domestic use. He broke away from the tradition of four-part writing (in the manner of Goudimel's psalms), and most of his settings are in three voices. The continuo part, presumably to be played on the home organ, also constitutes the vocal bass, and there are two soprano parts which frequently cross. Solo songs with organ are inserted to fill gaps on the printed pages resulting from publication in separate parts, with each three-part song beginning a new page.

Bachofen is also important for his pedagogical work,

in particular his expansion of the collegia musica, the centres of the day for German Swiss music and the predecessors of the future concert institutions. He also published a *Musicalisches Noten-Büchlein* (Zurich, n.d.), designed to provide the beginning student with a 'theoretical conception of the art of music and song in a short time'.

WORKS
(all printed works published in Zurich)

Musicalisches Hallelujah: Oder [206] schöne und geistreiche Gesänge, 1–3vv, bc (1727, rev. and enlarged 2/1733 with 570 Gesänge; rev. 3/1739; rev. 4/1743; rev. 5/1750 with 581 Gesänge; rev. and abridged 6/1754 with 380 Gesänge; rev. 11/1803 with 570 Gesänge), examples in A. Nef, Goldschmid (1917, 1942), and Geering

Psalmen Davids, 3vv, bc (1734, rev. 2/1759)

[12] Musicalisch-monatliche Aussgaaben, bestehend in teutschen, geistlichen Arien, 2–3vv, bc (?1729, 2/1732)

Herrn B. H. Brockes ... Irdisches Vergnügen in Gott, bestehend in physicalisch und moralischen Gedichten, 1v, bc (1740)

Musicalisch-wöchentliche Aussgaaben, 2vv, bc (1748–50)

Musicalische Ergezungen, bestehende in [17] angenehmen Arien, 1–2vv, bc, vn ad lib (1755)

Der für die Sünden der Welt gemarterte und sterbende Jesus (B. H. Brockes) (1759), with appendix containing short solos

New Year's cantatas for the Musikgesellschaft zur deutscher Schule, 1733–5, 1741

Kantate zum 50. Jubiläum der Musikgesellschaft zur deutschen Schule, 1729; Sonett, dem Obmann Hans Jacob Lavater gewidmet (J. H. Köchli), 1735; Kantate, dem neuen Obmann des Musikkollegiums 'auf dem Musiksaal', J. H. Köchli, gewidmet, 1739; Huldigungstück an den Obmann Junker Landvogt Escher, 1750; Konzert zur Einweihung des neuen Saales der Musikgesellschaft Bischofszell, 14 Nov 1745; all lost

BIBLIOGRAPHY

M. Friedländer: *Das deutsche Lied im 18. Jahrhundert* (Stuttgart, 1902, 2/1962)

A. Nef: *Das Lied in der deutschen Schweiz* (Zurich, 1909)

T. Goldschmid: *Schweizerische Gesangbücher früherer Zeiten* (Zurich, 1917)

M. Fehr: 'Kantor Joh. Kaspar Bachofen', *Zürcher Wochen-Chronik* (Zurich, 1917), 397, 405, 413

——: 'Das alte Musikkollegium Bischofszell', *SMz*, lviii (1918), 185, 194, 202

E. M. Fallet: 'Johann Kaspar Bachofen', *SMz*, lxvi (1926), 363, 379

E. Refardt: *Historisch-biographisches Musikerlexikon der Schweiz* (Leipzig and Zurich, 1928)

K. Nef: 'Schweizerische Passionsmusiken', *Schweizerisches Jb für Musikwissenschaft*, v (1931), 113

A. E. Cherbuliez: *Die Schweiz in der deutschen Musikgeschichte* (Frauenfeld, 1932)

A. Geering: 'Von der Reformation bis zur Romantik', *Schweizer Musikbuch*, i (Zurich, 1939), 54–130

T. Goldschmid: *Geistliche Sologesänge und Duette ... aus alten schweizerischen Gesangbüchern*, ii (Zurich, 1942)

B. D. Arnold: *The Life and Works of J. C. Bachofen* (diss., U. of Southern California, 1956)

PETER ROSS

Bach Revival. The rediscovery during the first half of the 19th century of Johann Sebastian Bach's music marked the first time that a great composer, after a period of neglect, was accorded his rightful place by a later generation. Palestrina, Lully, Purcell and Handel had never been quite forgotten by the musical public, but Bach was known only to a small circle of pupils and devotees until the Romantic movement stimulated a growing interest in his art. The Bach Revival was an early example of a new historicism which eventually opened all periods of Western music to discovery and performance, and which now constitutes the dominant factor in the musical taste of advanced Western societies. It began at about the same time in Germany, where most of Bach's descendants and pupils, and most of his surviving music, were to be found; and in England, where musical historicism was already well advanced by the end of the 18th century.

1. Germany and Austria. 2. England.

1. GERMANY AND AUSTRIA. Bach was always a conservative composer, and in the latter part of his career his style had become outmoded, failing to win for him any reputation as a composer in the fashionable world. His music was attacked by Scheibe in 1737 for 'excess of art' and for its 'turgid and confused style'. In the works of his last few years – the completed Mass in B minor, *Das musicalische Opfer*, *Die Kunst der Fuge* and others – he virtually turned his back on what remained of his public, writing for himself and, perhaps, for posterity. At his death public knowledge of his music was at a low ebb. Even at the Leipzig Thomaskirche, his successors only occasionally used his cantatas; the organ works, too, were rarely heard, unless they were played by one of his sons or pupils. For the rest of the century he was remembered, if at all, as a master of organ playing and of learned counterpoint. The first extended biographical notice of Bach, by J. A. Hiller, his third successor at the Thomaskirche, gave only a superficial and condescending account of his compositions (1784); while Reichardt remarked in 1782: 'Had Bach possessed the high integrity and the deep expressive feeling that inspired Handel, he would have been much greater even than Handel; but as it is he was only more painstaking and technically skilful'.

The rejection, by musicians of the succeeding generation, of the artistic principles that Bach stood for went beyond the normal changes in style that are found at other periods. His own sons played a part in it, though Philip Emanuel's feelings were ambivalent, and at the last he published a passionate though anonymous defence of his father's art. It was indeed at Berlin, where Emanuel was employed until 1767, that the strongest group of Bach disciples was concentrated, including Kirnberger, Marpurg, Agricola and Princess Amalia, sister of Frederick the Great. It was this group that preserved and passed on most of the original manuscripts of Bach's works that have survived. From the Berlin group of Bach disciples, too, Baron van Swieten carried the tradition to Vienna, where in the 1780s meetings were held at his house at which the works of Bach and others were performed. There Mozart came to know Bach's music, and to be influenced by it, as to a lesser extent was Haydn.

A more general appreciation of Bach came only as a result of the Romantic cult of the past. Arising in England, this movement was immensely strengthened in its German phase by patriotic and religious motives. The military and political humiliations of the Napoleonic period generated a desire to recover older German traditions, while a religious revival prompted the search for what was truly and distinctively religious in the cultural heritage. In this Bach was to become the archetypal figure. A leader in the nationalistic cult of Bach was J. N. Forkel, whose pioneering biography (1802) was inscribed 'for patriotic admirers of true musical art', and was dedicated to Swieten. 'This great man', Forkel wrote, 'was a German. Be proud of him, German fatherland, but be worthy of him too.... His works are an invaluable national patrimony with which no other nation has anything to be compared'.

Forkel was joined by Rochlitz in the Leipzig *Allgemeine musikalische Zeitung*, whose first volume (1798) contained a portrait of Bach. Rochlitz was inclined to paint a romantic, saintly picture of the master, comparing him aesthetically and morally with

Dürer, Rubens, Newton and Michelangelo. The religious aspect of Bach's art was important to another early convert, C. F. Zelter, the founder of the Berlin Singakademie (1791), one of the earliest German institutions to organize historical concerts. He had inherited an extensive collection of Bach's music from Kirnberger and Agricola, and he drew from it in his pioneering revivals of Bach's motets and other sacred works. He rehearsed the Mass in B minor in 1811 and the *St Matthew Passion* in 1815, but did not think it practical to perform them. Through Rochlitz and Zelter, Goethe in his old age came to a profound appreciation of Bach. E. T. A. Hoffmann, another influential literary figure, developed the idealized Romantic conception that Rochlitz had begun to build.

The mounting enthusiasm for Bach culminated in the performance of the *St Matthew Passion* by the Singakademie in 1829, with Mendelssohn conducting. This was the decisive turning-point in Bach's reputation, for it swiftly transformed the revival from a cult of intellectuals into a popular movement. Zelter had allowed a copy of the autograph to be made in 1823; with commendable self-effacement he turned over the honour of conducting the performance to his pupil. Mendelssohn, though at first hesitant, eventually agreed to attempt the formidable task. He made his own arrangement of the music from Zelter's copy; cuts, changes and additions were made. After nearly two years of rehearsals, the performance took place on 11 March 1829, and was far more successful than the first performance exactly a century earlier. The audience was

A page of Mendelssohn's performing edition of Bach's 'St Matthew Passion', showing the end of no.4, with Mendelssohn's tempo, dynamic and phrasing marks in pencil (GB-Ob MS M. Deneke Mendl. 46, p.44)

deeply moved; Hegel, who was present, later wrote of 'Bach's grand, truly Protestant, robust and erudite genius which we have only recently learnt again to appreciate at its full value'. Two more performances followed, the last conducted by Zelter. Mosevius, who also heard the work at Berlin, conducted it in 1830 at Breslau, an important centre of the Protestant religious revival and the home of Winterfeld. Königsberg was the next city to hear the Passion; it was not performed at Leipzig until 1841. Meanwhile the Berlin Singakademie produced the *St John Passion* in 1833, and a truncated version of the Mass in B minor in 1835 (the Credo had been revived by Schelbe at Frankfurt in 1828). A growing number of the cantatas were added to the choral repertory at this period.

Publication of Bach's music had also been accelerating. After Emanuel Bach's collected edition of the chorales (1784–7), the next landmark was the publication of *Das wohltemperirte Clavier* (the '48') by three firms almost simultaneously, in 1801 (Simrock, Nägeli and Hoffmeister). Hoffmeister and Kühnel continued to publish the keyboard works in a collection entitled 'Oeuvres complettes' (1801–17). The motets appeared in 1802–3, the sonatas for violin and keyboard in 1804–17, the *Magnificat* in 1811, the solo violin sonatas in 1817–28, the solo cello suites in 1828. Peters's edition of the organ works appeared in 1845–7. Other works were published, in editions of varying quality, so that by the middle of the century the bulk of Bach's organ and keyboard music was already available, but only a meagre proportion of the choral and chamber music. The most glaring deficiency was that the Mass in B minor and the bulk of the cantatas were still unpublished.

The idea of an edition in score of all Bach's works had been proposed by Forkel in 1802 and warmly advocated by Schumann in 1837; and its practicality had been proved by the success of the London Handel Society editions, beginning in 1843. At last, in 1850, the centenary of the composer's death, the Bachgesellschaft was formed, and during the next 50 years completed its monumental task. The volumes, though they varied in scholarly precision, were a remarkable achievement, and established the basic principles for scholarly musical editions that have been followed ever since. They completed the Bach Revival, and made it possible for Bach to take his place in public esteem beside or above other great composers whose music did not need reviving.

2. ENGLAND. England lacked the group of pupils and descendants who formed the nucleus of the German Bach Revival; but historicism and antiquarianism were more advanced than in Germany. The music of Handel, Corelli, Domenico Scarlatti and other late Baroque composers continued to be popular throughout the 18th century, while such bodies as the Academy of Ancient Music (1710–92), the Madrigal Society (founded 1741) and the Concert of Antient Music ('Antient Concerts', 1776–1848) cultivated a taste for the music of the remoter past. Burney and Hawkins, though they failed to appreciate Bach's importance, gave him due mention in their histories of music – books of a kind that did not yet exist on the Continent.

There is evidence that a good deal of Bach's music was circulating in manuscript in England during the last three decades of the 18th century. Johann Christian

Bach probably had little interest in his father's music, but he may have possessed some copies. Burney received a copy of book 1 of the '48' from Emanuel Bach in 1772, while Clementi possessed a partly autograph copy of book 2. Queen Charlotte owned a manuscript volume dated 1788, containing the '48', *Clavierübung*, iii, and the Credo from the Mass in B minor. This music may have reached the queen through either of two German musicians recently arrived in London: K. F. Horn (1762–1832), her music teacher from 1782, or A. F. C. Kollmann (1756–1829), organist at the German chapel in the court of St James's from 1784.

Clementi, Horn and Kollmann are the most important early figures in the English Bach Revival. Clementi is said to have practised Bach for hours on end during his time at Peter Beckford's house in the early 1770s. His own music shows early traces of Bach's influence which become much stronger in the late sonatas and the *Gradus ad Parnassum*. He incorporated several of the keyboard pieces in his didactic works. He must have passed on his love of Bach to his two most famous pupils, J. B. Cramer, whose studies of 1804 and 1810 show an obvious influence of the '48', and Field, who astonished audiences with his playing of Bach during his European tour of 1802–3 and who taught Bach's music to his Russian pupils. Kollmann consistently stressed the importance of Bach in his theoretical works in English, beginning with the *Essay on Musical Harmony* (1796), which offered a detailed analysis of the F minor fugue from book 2 of the '48'. In 1799 he advertised a plan to issue an analytical edition of the entire '48', but the scheme was anticipated by the three continental editions of 1801, two of which were reissued in London. He published the Chromatic Fantasia in 1806, with 'additions' by himself, analysed 12 Bach fugues in his *Quarterly Musical Register* (1812), and translated Forkel's life of Bach into English (1820). Horn arranged 12 organ fugues for string quartet – with figured bass – and published them in 1807, and later collaborated with Wesley in the first English edition of the '48'. His son, C. E. Horn, another Bach enthusiast, included part of a fugue from the '48' in the overture to his comic opera *Rich and Poor* (1812).

The movement quickly spread to native English musicians. William Shield's *Introduction to Harmony* (1800) gave due place to Bach, and incorporated the D minor prelude from book 1 of the '48'. George Pinto, a close friend of Field's, tried to imitate Bach in his C minor Fantasia and Fugue (published posthumously, c1808), and it was he who first introduced Samuel Wesley to Bach's preludes and fugues, according to Wesley's memoirs. Wesley took up the cause with feverish intensity, shown in his well-known letters to Benjamin Jacob, another English Bach enthusiast. He edited, with Horn, the six organ trios, published (for the first time anywhere) in 1809–10 in instalments, and a 'new and correct edition' of the '48' in 1810–13. In 1808 he began a series of concerts of Bach's music at Surrey Chapel, with Jacob, who was organist there; and soon afterwards he began a similar series at the Portuguese Embassy chapel, where his friend Vincent Novello was organist and soon became a Bach convert. Because of the lack of pedals on most English organs, Wesley often played Bach's organ music as duets with Jacob or Novello assisting him on a second manual (in some cases Dragonetti played the pedal parts on his double bass). He also played fugues from the '48', which he regarded as organ music.

Wesley saw Bach as a superhuman genius, even though there is a touch of whimsy in the nicknames he used for him – 'Saint Sebastian', 'The Man', 'Our Apollo' and so on. He felt that militant propaganda was needed to persuade the English that any musician could be superior to Handel. He found that his brother Charles was an unrepentant Handelian. But he won many converts, including even the aged Burney who at last recanted his earlier criticism of Bach. William Crotch was recruited to the cause, and was the first to play the 'St Anne's' fugue in public (on the piano). Both Wesley and Crotch gave prominence to Bach in lectures on the history of music. In later life Wesley's enthusiasm was unabated, and he converted Henry Gauntlett and his own son S. S. Wesley, who played the 'St Anne's' fugue as an organ duet at St Stephen's, Coleman Street, in 1827.

As well as the keyboard works, Wesley endeavoured to promote other music of Bach. The motet *Jesu, meine Freude* was sung at his concert in the Hanover Square Rooms on 3 June 1809, and the following year he presented to the Madrigal Society a score of the same work (with text translated into Latin). He played the sonatas for violin and keyboard many times with Jacob, and on 6 June 1814 he played one with Salomon at the latter's benefit. Nevertheless, for many years Bach was known in England more by reputation than by experience. John Sainsbury's *Dictionary of Musicians* (1824) gave twice as much space to J. S. Bach as to all his sons and relatives put together – in itself a surprising fact; yet as late as 1849, at the opening of the Bach Society, he was still called 'this great and comparatively unknown master'. After Wesley's early efforts there was a period when little new progress was made. Mendelssohn's visits of 1829 and 1832 were a fresh stimulus, and his performances of organ works at St Paul's Cathedral, with pedals, and played with a degree of confidence and understanding that no English musician could equal, were undoubtedly a revelation to English audiences. Moscheles also played his part: he performed the D minor keyboard concerto (with additional orchestral parts of his own) at the King's Theatre on 13 May 1836, and the following year included preludes and fugues from the '48' at several concerts. Monck Mason announced Bach's Passion oratorios for the 1832 season of oratorio concerts at the King's Theatre, but nothing came of this. Parts of the *St Matthew Passion*, B minor Mass and *Magnificat* were given at the Birmingham Festival (1837) and at the Antient Concerts. Prince Albert, after his marriage to Victoria in 1840, introduced music by Bach into concerts at Buckingham Palace and Windsor Castle and at aristocratic musical societies in which he was concerned. Sterndale Bennett was another champion of Bach, performing keyboard and chamber works at many of his concerts and editing some of the music, including the *St Matthew Passion*, for publication. At Cambridge in the 1840s T. A. Walmisley lectured on Bach and taught his students to revere him above all other composers.

The English Bach Revival culminated in the formation of the Bach Society, founded by Sterndale Bennett. The first meeting, on 27 October 1849, at Bennett's house in Russell Place, formulated the objects of the society, which included the collection and promotion, but not publication, of the works of the master (though the society did publish a volume of the motets, with English text added, in 1851). A number of concerts were given, and at last the *St Matthew Passion* had its first English performance (with English words) at the Hanover Square Rooms on 6 April 1854, Bennett conducting. Several other important works were revived before the society disbanded in 1870. The popularization of Bach was completed when his choral masterpieces were accepted alongside Handel's and Mendelssohn's. The *St Matthew Passion* was introduced at the Three Choirs Festival in 1871, and the London Bach Choir undertook the regular performance of the larger choral works, beginning with the Mass in B minor in 1876.

BIBLIOGRAPHY

J. F. Reichardt: 'Johann Sebastian Bach', *Musikalisches Kunstmagazin*, iv (1782), 196; repr. in Schulze, 357ff
J. A. Hiller: 'Bach (Johann Sebastian)', *Lebensbeschreibungen berühmter Musikgelehrten und Tonkünstler neuerer Zeit* (Leipzig, 1784), i, 9; repr. in Schulze, 395ff
[C. P. E. Bach]: comparison between Bach and Handel, *Allgemeine deutsche Bibliothek*, lxxxi (1788), 295; repr. in Schulze, 437ff
J. N. Forkel: *Über Johann Sebastian Bachs Leben, Kunst, und Kunstwerke* (Leipzig, 1802; Eng. trans. in David and Mendel)
A. F. C. Kollman: 'Of John Sebastian Bach and his Works', *Quarterly Musical Register*, ii (1812), 105
M. Mason: announcement of plans for opera season, *Harmonicon*, x (1832), 29
E. Wesley, ed.: *Letters of Samuel Wesley to Mr. Jacobs* (London, 1875)
M. Schneider: 'Verzeichnis der bis zum Jahre 1851 gedruckten (und der geschrieben im Handel gewesenen) Werke von Johann Sebastian Bach', *BJb*, iii (1906), 84–113
J. R. Sterndale Bennett: *The Life of Sterndale Bennett* (Cambridge, 1907), 202ff, 232ff
L. E. R. Picken: 'Bach Quotations from the 18th Century', *MR*, v (1944), 83
F. Blume: *Johann Sebastian Bach im Wandel der Geschichte* (Kassel, 1947; Eng. trans., 1950, as *Two Centuries of Bach*)
H. Redlich: 'The Bach Revival in England (1750–1850)', *HMYB*, vii (1952), 274, 287
W. Emery: 'The London Autograph of "The Forty-eight" ', *ML*, xxxiv (1953), 114
H. T. David and A. Mendel: *The Bach Reader* (New York, rev. 2/1966)
S. Grossman-Vendrey: *Felix-Mendelssohn-Bartholdy und die Musik der Vergangenheit* (Regensburg, 1969)
W. Wiora, ed.: *Die Ausbreitung des Historismus über die Musik* (Regensburg, 1969)
L. Plantinga: 'Clementi, Virtuosity, and the "German Manner" ', *JAMS*, xxv (1972), 303
H.-J. Schulze, ed.: *Bach-Dokumente*, iii: *Dokumente zum Nachwirken Johann Sebastian Bachs 1750–1800* (Kassel, 1972)
NICHOLAS TEMPERLEY

Bachschmidt [Bachschmid], **(Johann) Anton (Adam)** (*b* Melk, Lower Austria, 11 Feb 1728; *d* Eichstätt, 29 Dec 1797). German composer and violin virtuoso of Austrian birth. He came from a long line of musicians who immigrated to Melk late in the 17th century from Traunstein, Bavaria. While still a young man he was appointed *Thurnermeister* (director of instrumental music) in Melk, a post which he held from July 1751 to May 1753. He left his native town for travels as a virtuoso and may have been employed briefly at Würzburg (or Wurzbach) before settling in Eichstätt. There he established himself as a versatile musician in the court orchestra of Prince-Bishop Johann Anton II, rising steadily in rank from violinist (September 1753) to Konzertmeister (March 1768) and finally to court Kapellmeister (July 1773). Although he developed a reputation primarily as a church composer, Bachschmidt wrote a number of dramatic works for Eichstätt's theatres. His turn from Latin school drama to Italian opera reflects the closing of the Jesuit theatre in Eichstätt in 1773.

WORKS

(*MSS mainly in CH-E, D-BB, EB, Es, Ew, Mbm, OB, Rtt, WEY, WS*)

Operas: Erstickter Neid und Eifersucht, 1762, lost; Die Liebe zum Vaterland, 1766, lost; Il re pastore (Metastasio), 1774; L'eroe cinese (Metastasio), 1775, lost; La clemenza di Tito (Metastasio), 1776; Demetrio (Metastasio), 1777, lost; Antigono (Metastasio), 1778; Ezio (A. Raimund), 1780, lost

Lat. school dramas, music lost: Constantinus ultimus orientis Caesar, 1761; Jactura fidei, 1764; Pietas in parentem, 1765; S Richardus rex, 1766; Sol ex eclipsi, 1768

Church music: 21 masses, incl. Missa pastoritia, *A-M*; 1 Requiem; 3 Domine; 10 hymns; 29 litanies; 34 offertories; 2 processional songs for Corpus Christi; 9 psalms; 2 Stabat mater; 6 Te Deum; 12 vespers

Inst: 1 orch suite; 1 ov.; 3 vn concs.; Bn Conc.; 24 syms. listed in catalogue of *D-Rtt*; 6 str qts listed in Breitkopf catalogue (1773), lost; Ob Conc., listed in *Gerber L*, lost

BIBLIOGRAPHY

EitnerQ
F. J. Lipowsky: *Baierisches Musik-Lexikon* (Munich, 1811)
R. Schlecht: *Musikgeschichte der Stadt Eichstätt* (MS, *D-Es*, 1883) [with thematic catalogue]
J. Sax: 'Musik und Theater in der fürstbischöflichen Residenzstadt Eichstätt bis zum Jahre 1802', *Jahresbericht des historischen Vereins für Mittelfranken*, xlvi (Ansbach, 1898), 6
J. Gmelch: *Die Musikgeschichte Eichstätts* (Eichstätt, 1914)
H. Dennerlein: 'Musik des 18. Jahrhunderts in Franken: die Inventare der Funde von Ebrach, Burgwindheim, Maria Limbach und Iphofen', *Bericht des historischen Vereins . . . Bamberg*, xcii (1952–3), 273–321
B. S. Brook, ed.: *The Breitkopf Thematic Catalogue, 1762–1787* (New York, 1966)
R. Münster and R. Machold: *Thematischer Katalog der Musikhandschriften der ehemaligen Klosterkirchen Weyarn, Tegernsee und Benediktbeuern* (Munich, 1971)
R. N. Freeman: *The Practice of Music at Melk Monastery in the Eighteenth Century* (diss., U. of California, Los Angeles, 1971)
ROBERT N. FREEMAN

Bach Society. *See* BACH REVIVAL.

Bach trumpet (Ger. *Bachtrompete*). A misnomer still prevalent in German-speaking countries for any high TRUMPET used in modern performances of Baroque music. Originally, the term was applied to a straight trumpet in A (a 5th higher than the Baroque trumpet in D and a semitone lower than the modern B♭ trumpet) with two valves, and such an instrument was first employed by the Berlin trumpeter Julius Kosleck in September 1884 in Eisenach. He also played it on 21 March 1885 in a historic performance of Bach's Mass in B minor in London's Albert Hall, with Walter Morrow and John Solomon playing the second and third parts on normal instruments. Kosleck's trumpet was described as being in B♭/A and possessing a posthorn (conical) bore. Its mouthpiece was also deeply conical. Morrow and Solomon immediately had such instruments made by Silvani (later Silvani & Smith, London), although theirs had a standard cylindro-conical trumpet bore and were played with a normal trumpet mouthpiece. Morrow first employed it in the 1886 Leeds Festival; Solomon's instrument still survives.

The public was misled by journalists to believe that the 'Bach trumpet' was a replica of the valveless trumpet of Bach's day, even though W. F. H. Blandford, with Morrow's support, published an article thoroughly exploding the fallacy. The straight 'Bach trumpet' in B♭/A was, furthermore, discarded as soon as still shorter trumpets in D were made, also in the straight form but with three valves. The first was manufactured by Mahillon in 1892. (Even before this, in 1885, Besson of Paris had made a high G trumpet for the Parisian Teste for a performance of Bach's *Magnificat*.) The shorter instruments, with correspondingly greater distance between the notes of the harmonic series in any given register, considerably simplified the problem of accuracy in the high register. Curiously, the term 'Bach trumpet' was used to refer both to the shorter instruments as well as to Kosleck's original model.

BIBLIOGRAPHY

W. Menke: *History of the Trumpet of Bach and Handel* (London, 1934/*R*1972), 228

W. F. H. Blandford: 'The "Bach Trumpet" ', *MMR*, lxv (1935), 49, 73, 97

P. Bate: *The Trumpet and Trombone* (London, 1966), 174ff

E. Tarr: 'The Baroque Trumpet, the High Trumpet and the So-called Bach Trumpet', *Brass Bulletin* (1972), no.2, pp.25, 40; no.3, pp.44. 54

EDWARD H. TARR

Bachus, Johannes de. *See* BACCHIUS, JOHANNES DE.

Bacilieri, Giovanni (*fl* 1607–19). Italian composer. All that is known of his life is that for a time he was a priest at Ferrara. His three published collections are of church music intended for particular liturgical rites: some double-choir psalms and two rather more unusual compilations, for Holy Week and the Office of the Dead, neither of which was commonly set to measured music at this period. The pompous Latin titles and the five-part scoring suggest a rather conservative style for Ferrara, which on the whole had a progressive musical outlook at this time.

WORKS

(all published in Venice)

Lamentationes, Benedictus et Evangelia, quae publice in ecclesiis diebus Dominicis Palmarum, et Feriae Sextae leguntur, ad novum musicae concentum, 5vv, redacta, op.1 (1607)

Vesperae 8vv, una cum parte organica concinendae, op.2 (1610)

Totum defunctorum officium ex Pauli V Pont. Max. rituali recentiori modulatione, 5vv, musice redditum, op.3 (1619)

JEROME ROCHE

Bacilly [Basilly, Bassilly], **Bénigne de** (*b* ?Normandy, ?c1625; *d* Paris, 27 Sept 1690). French singing teacher and composer. He may have been a priest. He lived for most of his life in Paris. Although he was important as a composer and teacher, Bacilly's most valuable legacy is the vocal treatise *Remarques curieuses sur l'art de bien chanter*, which has for long been recognized as one of the most detailed sources of information on French 17th-century vocal practice. However, until the recent publication of an English translation with the examples included, the application of its precepts to vocal performance had been virtually impossible since the examples Bacilly used to illustrate his teachings were not included in the text (he simply referred instead to specific passages in published volumes of *airs de cour*). The importance of the *Remarques* lies in two main areas: it is one of the earliest volumes to give specific descriptions and applications of the expressive melodic figures (*agréments*) that had been adopted into the musical language of all Europe by the 18th century; and fully half the treatise is devoted to an exhaustive discussion of the meaning, structure, pronunciation and rhythm of French poetry, with detailed instructions as to its amp-

lification through musical ornamentation – ample evidence of the master–servant relationship between poetry and ornamentation. Bacilly took his examples from *airs* whose short, delicate couplets are matched by tender, unobtrusive melodies. In the anthologies of *airs* of Bacilly's time it was the composer's custom to print the melody of the second verse as an elaborate variation of the first. Bacilly referred to those diminutions as written-down improvisations of the singer-composer and analysed their relationship to the poetry. He was himself active as a composer in this genre.

WORKS

(all printed works pubd in Paris)

EDITIONS

Recueil des plus beaux vers . . . mis en chant. 3me partie (1661)

Recueil des plus beaux vers . . . Seconde et novelle partie dans laquelle sont compris les airs de Versailles (1668)

Recueil de tous les plus beaux airs bachiques, avec les noms des autheurs du chant et des paroles (1671)

SACRED

Les airs spirituels . . . sur les stances chrestiennes de M l'Abbé Testu . . . avec basse continue, et les seconds couplets en diminution (1672)

Les airs spirituels . . . avec la basse continue, les chifres pour l'accompagnement, et les seconds couplets en diminution, seconde partie (1677)

Les airs spirituels . . . dans un plus grand nombre et une plus grande perfection que dans les précédents éditions, deux parties (1688) [revision of the two collections above; further edns. in 1692 and 1693]

SECULAR

Nouveau livre d'airs (1661) [probably by Bacilly, but also attrib. M. Lambert: see Prunières]

XXII livre de chansons pour danser et pour boire à deux parties (1663)

Second livre de chansons pour danser et pour boire à deux parties (1664)

Second livre d'airs à deux parties . . . dédié à son Altesse Mademoiselle de Nemours (1664)

III. livre de chansons pour danser et pour boire (1665)

IIII. livre de chansons pour danser et pour boire (1666)

V. livre de chansons pour danser et pour boire (1667)

Capilotade bachique à deux parties contenant 4 alphabets de fragmens choisis des meilleures chansons à boire (1667)

Les trois livres d'airs à deux parties . . . augmentez de plusieurs airs nouveaux, de chiffres pour le théorbe et d'ornemens pour la méthode de chanter, première partie (1668)

Meslanges d'airs à deux parties, d'airs à boire et autres chansons (1671)

II. livre des meslanges, de chansons, airs sérieux et à boire, à 2 et 3 parties (1674)

Second livre d'airs bachiques . . . contenant plusieurs récits de basses et autres airs à deux et à trois parties avec une seconde édition du premier recueil corrigée et augmentée (1677)

Songs, sacred and secular, in Airs et brunettes à 2 et 3 dessus pour les flûtes traversières tirez des meilleurs autheurs (n.d.); Nouvelles poésies spirituelles et morales (1737); Airs notez des cantiques sur les points les plus importans de la religion et de la morale chrétienne (1738); Mercure Galant (1678–90); MSS in *F-Pn*

WRITINGS

Remarques curieuses sur l'art de bien chanter (Paris, 1668/*R*1971, 4/1681; Eng. trans., 1678)

BIBLIOGRAPHY

T. Gérold: *L'art du chant en France au XVIIe siècle* (Strasbourg, 1921/*R*1971)

H. Prunières: 'Un maître de chant au XVIIe siècle: Bénigne de Bacilly', *RdM*, iv (1923), 156

A. B. Caswell: *The Development of Seventeenth-Century French Vocal Ornamentation and its Influence upon Late Baroque Ornamentation Practice* (diss., U. of Minnesota, 1964)

AUSTIN B. CASWELL

Illustration Acknowledgments

We are grateful to those listed below for permission to reproduce copyright illustrative material, and those contributors who supplied or helped us obtain it. Every effort has been made to contact copyright holders; we apologize to anyone who may have been omitted. Brian and Constance Dear prepared the maps and technical diagrams, and Oxford Illustrators the typographic diagrams (except where otherwise stated). Photographs acknowledged to the following sources are Crown copyright: Her Majesty the Queen, the Victoria and Albert Museum (including the Theatre Museum), the Science Museum and the National Monuments Record. The following forms of acknowledgment are used where the copyright of an illustration is held by a contributor:

photo John Smith – John Smith is contributor and photographer
John Smith – John Smith is contributor and copyright holder
photo John Smith, London – John Smith is a contributor (not of the article concerned) and photographer
John Smith, London – John Smith is a contributor (not of the article concerned) and copyright holder.

Where illustrations are taken from books out of copyright, the full title and place and date of publication are given, unless in the caption.

Abel Henry E. Huntington Library and Art Gallery, San Marino, California

Accordion after M. Hohner Ltd, London

Acoustics *1, 2a–b, 3, 4, 5, 6a, 7a–c, 10* after R. Lewcock; *2c, 11* Faber & Faber Ltd, London: after P. H. Parkin and H. R. Humphreys, *Acoustics, Noise and Buildings* (3/1969); *6b, 9, 28* John Wiley & Sons Inc., New York: after L. L. Beranek, *Music, Acoustics and Architecture* (1962); *6c–d, 12, 13, 20, 21, 29* Methuen & Co. Ltd, London: after H. Bagenal and A. Wood, *Planning for Good Acoustics* (1931); *14, 15* Oxford University Press: after J. G. Landels, 'Assisted Resonance in Ancient Theatres', *Greece and Rome*, 2nd ser., xiv (April 1967); *16* from G. M. Hills, 'Earthenware Pots (Built into Churches) which have been called Acoustic Vases', *Transactions of the Royal Institute of British Architects* (London, 1882); *17* after G. M. Hills; *18* Institute of Physics, London: after P. V. Brüel, 'Panel Absorbents of the Helmholtz type', *First Summer Symposium of the Acoustics Group, 1947: Papers and Discussions on Resonant Absorbers and Reverberations* (Physical Society, London, 1949); *19* Longman Group Ltd, London and Longman Inc., New York: after C. Stewart, *Early Christian Byzantine and Romanesque Architecture* (1954); *22* Harvard Theatre Collection, Cambridge, Massachusetts; *25* photo Surveyor to the University, Oxford; *27* British Library, London; *30* Boston Symphony Orchestra; *31* Städtisches Verkehrsamt, Bonn; *32* Arup Associates, London / John Donat Photography; *33, 40* W. H. Freeman & Co., San Francisco: after C. M. Hutchins, 'The Physics of Violins', *Scientific American*, ccvii (Nov 1962); *34, 39* after C. M. Hutchins; *35–8* W. H. Freeman & Co., San Francisco: after J. C. Schelleng, 'The Physics of the Bowed String', *Scientific American*, ccxxx (Jan 1974); *41, 42* Oxford University Press Inc., New York: after A. H. Benade, *Fundamentals of Musical Acoustics* (1976); W. H. Freeman & Co., San Francisco: after A. H. Benade, 'The Physics of Brasses', *Scientific American*, ccxxix (July 1973); *44* after A. H. Benade; *45–7, 49* after J. Sundberg; *48* American Institute of Physics, New York

Adam de la Halle Bibliothèque Nationale, Paris

Aeolian harp *1, 2* E. R. Mickleburgh Collection, Bristol / photo Stephen Bonner; *3* Historisches Museum, Basle

Afghanistan *1, 2, 3, 5* International Institute for Comparative Music Studies and Documentation, Berlin / photo Alain Daniélou; *4* photo Mark Slobin

Africa International Folk Music Council, Kingston, Ontario: from D. Rycroft, 'Nguni Vocal Polyphony', *JIFMC*, xix (1967)

Albani, Emma Stuart-Liff Collection, Tunbridge Wells

Albania *1, 2* Erich Stockmann; *3* Musée de l'Homme, Paris / photo Albturizem

Albéniz, Isaac Editions d'Art Lucien Mazenod, Paris: from J. Lacroix, *Les Musiciens célèbres* (1948)

Alberti, Gasparo Accademia Carrara di Belle Arti, Bergamo

Albinoni, Tomaso Giovanni Sächsische Landesbibliothek, Dresden

Alboni, Marietta Harold Rosenthal, London

Albrechtsberger, Johann Georg Gesellschaft der Musikfreunde, Vienna

Aldeburgh Festival Arup Associates, London / John Donat Photography

Aleatory *1* Universal Edition (London) Ltd (1972); *2, 3* Universal Edition (Alfred A. Kalmus Ltd), Vienna (1973, 1974); *4* Henmar Press Inc., New York (1960)

Algaita photo Anthony King

Alkan, Valentin Dora Ray, Paris

Allemande Bibliothèque Nationale, Paris

Allen, Henry 'Red' photo Marc Sharratt

Alphorn Swiss National Tourist Office, London

Alta Ente Provinciale per il Turismo, Florence

Althorn Royal Pavilion, Art Gallery and Museums, Brighton

Amadeus Quartet Deutsche Grammophon, London / photo Reinhart Wolf

Amadino, Ricciardo British Library, London

Amati *1, 2* Ashmolean Museum, Oxford

Amato, Pasquale Mander and Mitchenson, London

Ammerbach, Elias Nikolaus British Library, London

Amsterdam *1* Brook Collection, Research Center for Music Iconography, New York; *2* photo Kors van Bennekom, Amsterdam

Analysis *1–8, 11, 12, 14–17* British Library, London; *18* Schott & Co. Ltd, London; *19* Faber & Faber Ltd, London and Belmont Music Publishers, Los Angeles; *20* Universal Edition (Alfred A. Kalmus Ltd) Vienna; *21, 22* Dover Publications Inc., New York; *23–6* Faber & Faber Ltd, London, and Macmillan Publishing Co. Inc., New York; *27* from H. Riemann, *Präludien und Studien: gesammelte Aufsätze zur Ästhetik, Theorie und Geschichte der Musik*, i (Frankfurt am Main, 1895); *28, 29* from H. Riemann (with C. Fuchs), *Katechismus der Phrasierung* (Leipzig, 8/1912 as *Handbuch der Phrasierung*); *30* Cornell University Press, Ithaca, NY; *31* Société Belge de Musicologie, Brussels; *32–4* Union Générale d'Editions, Paris; *35* Edition Wilhelm Hansen, Copenhagen

Anatolia *1* photo James Mellaart, London; *2* Wilhelm Stauder, Buchschlag, W. Germany; *3, 6, 8* Trustees of the British Museum, London; *7* photo Maurice Chuzeville, Malakoff, France; *9* Ankara Turizmi

Ančerl, Karel Artia Publishing House, Prague

Andreas de Florentia Biblioteca Medicea Laurenziana, Florence

Angélique Bibliothèque Nationale, Paris

Angola *2* Akademische Druck- und Verlagsanstalt, Graz: from *Monumenta Ethnographica*, i (1962); *3, 4* photo Gerhard Kubik

Annibali, Domenico Staatliche Kunstsammlungen, Dresden / Deutsche Fotothek Dresden

Ansermet, Ernest Decca Record Co. Ltd, London

Antegnati British Library, London

Antico, Andrea British Library, London

Antiphoner *1* Verlag Peter Lang AG, Berne: from *Paléographie Musicale*, 1st ser., xvi (1955); *2–4* British Library, London

Antwerp Stadsarchief, Antwerp

Appalachian dulcimer Joan Rimmer / photo Frank Harrison, Utrecht

Appia, Adolphe Institut für Theaterwissenschaft, University of Cologne

Arabian Gulf *1, 2* photo Poul Rovsing Olsen

Arab music *1* Biblioteca Apostolica Vaticana, Rome; *2* British Library, London; *3, 4* International Institute for Comparative Music Studies and Documentation, Berlin / photo H. H. Touma; *5* photo Amnon Shiloah; *6, 8* Popperfoto, London; *7, 9* photo Jean Jenkins, London; *10* National Archive, Hebrew University of Jerusalem

Archlute *1* Conservatoire National Supérieur de Musique, Paris; *2* Tony Bingham, London

Argentina *1* Alexandr Buchner, Prague; *2* photo Isabel Aretz

Armenian rite, music of the Library of the Armenian Mekhitarist Monastery, Vienna

Arne, Thomas Augustine *1* National Portrait Gallery, London; *2* British Library, London; *3* photo Victoria and Albert Museum, London

Arnold, Samuel National Portrait Gallery, London

Arnould, Sophie Trustees of the Wallace Collection, London

Arpanetta Royal College of Music, London

Arpeggione Musikinstrumenten-Museum, Karl-Marx-Universität, Leipzig

Arrau, Claudio photo Erich Auerbach, London

Artaria Österreichische Nationalbibliothek, Vienna

Articulation McGraw-Hill Book Company, New York

Attaingnant, Pierre *1* Library of the Boston Athenaeum, Boston; *2* Österreichische Nationalbibliothek, Vienna

Attwood, Thomas Royal College of Music, London

Auber, Daniel-François-Esprit Bibliothèque Nationale, Paris

Augsburg Stadtbildstelle, Augsburg

Aulos *1* Trustees of the British Museum, London; *2* Antikenmuseum und Skulpturhalle, Basle; *3* photo Deutsches Archäologisches Institut, Rome

Australia *1* after A. M. Moyle; *2, 4* photo Axel Poignant, London; *3, 5* photo Alice M. Moyle; *6* Melbourne University Press: from C. P. Mountford, *Records of the American–Australian Scientific Expedition to Arnhem Land, i: Art, Myth and Symbolism* (1956); *7, 8* after C. J. Ellis

Austria *2* Bayerische Staatsgemäldesammlungen, Munich; *3* Institut für Volksmusikforschung, Vienna

Autoharp Stearns Collection of Musical Instruments, University of Michigan, Ann Arbor

Avison, Charles Decca Record Co. Ltd, London

Ayler, Albert photo Hans Harzheim, Düsseldorf

Aztec music John Hillelson Agency Ltd, London / photo Gisèle Freund, Paris

Babbitt, Milton Camera Press Ltd, London / photo Vytas Valaitis

Bach *2* Bibliothèque Nationale, Paris; *3* Stadtarchiv, Zwickau; *4* William H. Scheide, Princeton, New Jersey / photo Willard Starks; *5–7* Deutsche Staatsbibliothek, Berlin; *8* British Library, London; *9* Staatliche Galerie Moritzburg, Halle; *10* Staatliche Museen Preussischer Kulturbesitz, Berlin; *11* Kunsthalle, Hamburg; *12* Staatsbibliothek Preussischer Kulturbesitz, Musikabteilung, Berlin; *13* Mansell Collection, London, and Alinari, Florence

Bach Revival Bodleian Library, Oxford